## Format for Bank Reconciliation:

| | | | |
|---|---|---|---|
| Cash balance according to bank statement | | | $XXX |
| Add: Additions by company not on bank statement | | $XXX | |
| Bank errors | | XXX | XXX |
| | | | $XXX |
| Deduct: Deductions by company not on bank statement | | $XXX | |
| Bank errors | | XXX | XXX |
| Adjusted balance | | | $XXX |
| | | | |
| Cash balance according to company's records | | | $XXX |
| Add: Additions by bank not recorded by company | | $XXX | |
| Company errors | | XXX | XXX |
| | | | $XXX |
| Deduct: Deductions by bank not recorded by company | | $XXX | |
| Company errors | | XXX | XXX |
| Adjusted balance | | | $XXX |

## Inventory Costing Methods:

- First-in, First-out (FIFO)
- Last-in, First-out (LIFO)
- Average Cost

## Interest Computations:

$$\text{Interest} = \text{Face Amount (or Principal)} \times \text{Rate} \times \text{Time}$$

## Methods of Determining Annual Depreciation:

**Straight-Line:** $\dfrac{\text{Cost} - \text{Estimated Residual Value}}{\text{Estimated Life}}$

**Double-Declining-Balance:** Rate* × Book Value at Beginning of Period

*Rate is commonly twice the straight-line rate (1 ÷ Estimated Life).

## Adjustments to Net Income (Loss) Using the Indirect Method:

| | Increase (Decrease) |
|---|---|
| Net income (loss) | $ XXX |
| Adjustments to reconcile net income to net cash flow from operating activities: | |
| Depreciation of fixed assets | XXX |
| Amortization of intangible assets | XXX |
| Losses on disposal of assets | XXX |
| Gains on disposal of assets | (XXX) |
| Changes in current operating assets and liabilities: | |
| Increases in noncash current operating assets | (XXX) |
| Decreases in noncash current operating assets | XXX |
| Increases in current operating liabilities | XXX |
| Decreases in current operating liabilities | (XXX) |
| Net cash flow from operating activities | $ XXX |
| | or |
| | $(XXX) |

**Contribution Margin Ratio** $= \dfrac{\text{Sales} - \text{Variable Costs}}{\text{Sales}}$

**Break-Even Sales (Units)** $= \dfrac{\text{Fixed Costs}}{\text{Unit Contribution Margin}}$

**Sales (Units)** $= \dfrac{\text{Fixed Costs} + \text{Target Profit}}{\text{Unit Contribution Margin}}$

**Margin of Safety** $= \dfrac{\text{Sales} - \text{Sales at Break-Even Point}}{\text{Sales}}$

**Operating Leverage** $= \dfrac{\text{Contribution Margin}}{\text{Income from Operations}}$

## Variances:

$$\begin{array}{l}\text{Direct Materials} \\ \text{Price Variance}\end{array} = \left(\begin{array}{l}\text{Actual Price} - \\ \text{Standard Price}\end{array}\right) \times \text{Actual Quantity}$$

$$\begin{array}{l}\text{Direct Materials} \\ \text{Quantity Variance}\end{array} = \left(\begin{array}{l}\text{Actual Quantity} - \\ \text{Standard Quantity}\end{array}\right) \times \begin{array}{l}\text{Standard} \\ \text{Price}\end{array}$$

$$\begin{array}{l}\text{Direct Labor} \\ \text{Rate Variance}\end{array} = \left(\begin{array}{l}\text{Actual Rate per Hour} - \\ \text{Standard Rate per Hour}\end{array}\right) \times \text{Actual Hours}$$

$$\begin{array}{l}\text{Direct Labor} \\ \text{Time Variance}\end{array} = \left(\begin{array}{l}\text{Actual Direct Labor Hours} - \\ \text{Standard Direct Labor Hours}\end{array}\right) \times \begin{array}{l}\text{Standard Rate} \\ \text{per Hour}\end{array}$$

$$\begin{array}{l}\text{Variable Factory} \\ \text{Overhead Controllable} \\ \text{Variance}\end{array} = \begin{array}{l}\text{Actual Variable} \\ \text{Factory} \\ \text{Overhead}\end{array} - \begin{array}{l}\text{Budgeted Variable} \\ \text{Factory Overhead}\end{array}$$

$$\begin{array}{l}\text{Fixed Factory} \\ \text{Overhead} \\ \text{Volume} \\ \text{Variance}\end{array} = \left(\begin{array}{l}\text{Standard Hours for} \\ \text{100\% of Normal} \\ \text{Capacity}\end{array} - \begin{array}{l}\text{Standard} \\ \text{Hours for} \\ \text{Actual Units} \\ \text{Produced}\end{array}\right) \times \begin{array}{l}\text{Fixed Factory} \\ \text{Overhead} \\ \text{Rate}\end{array}$$

**Rate of Return on Investment (ROI)** $= \dfrac{\text{Income from Operations}}{\text{Invested Assets}}$

Alternative ROI Computation:

$$\text{ROI} = \dfrac{\text{Income from Operations}}{\text{Sales}} \times \dfrac{\text{Sales}}{\text{Invested Assets}}$$

## Capital Investment Analysis Methods:

Methods That Ignore Present Values:

- Average Rate of Return Method
- Cash Payback Method

Methods That Use Present Values:

- Net Present Value Method
- Internal Rate of Return Method

**Average Rate of Return** $= \dfrac{\text{Estimated Average Annual Income}}{\text{Average Investment}}$

**Present Value Index** $= \dfrac{\text{Total Present Value of Net Cash Flow}}{\text{Amount to Be Invested}}$

**Present Value Factor for an Annuity of $1** $= \dfrac{\text{Amount to Be Invested}}{\text{Equal Annual Net Cash Flows}}$

# Have the tools you need **to be successful**

A variety of tools are available in CengageNOW, all combined in one easy-to-use resource designed to improve your grades. Some resources get you prepared for class and help you succeed on homework, and others show you specific areas where you can work to improve.

## Stay ahead of the course requirements

CengageNOW shows you the path through your course—from first day through finals. Once you know what's expected, it's easier to complete your assignments.

## Gain understanding that stays with you

Do well on tests as well as the assignments! Bridge the gap between homework and tests by using CengageNOW to truly understand the material. Self-study and review materials keep you on the right track, to make sure your understanding goes beyond memorization.

## Set yourself up for better grades

Why wonder where you stand? CengageNOW includes trackable assignments and grades. It tells you what to do to improve your grade, and gives you the tools to accomplish it!

> I love the check your work option. Really, when you're having a hard time figuring out an answer, sometimes working backwards is the best way to understand conceptually what you're doing wrong.
>
> **Brad Duncan**
> University of Utah

### CengageNOW Helps Students Learn

93%
CengageNOW helped me understand course materials better

93%
Using CengageNOW allowed me to better track my progress in this course

78%
The feedback and explanations provided in CengageNOW helped me learn the material

78%
CengageNOW helped me to better understand the expectations of my instructor

> I liked the videos because they were short enough to teach me and because they were short, I was able to find time to watch them again and again if I did not understand the first time.
>
> **Jennifer Wright**
> Northeast Wisconsin Technical College

## Ask your instructor about CengageNOW for this course.

Engaged with you.
www.cengage.com

CENGAGE Learning

# ACCOUNTING

## 26e

**Carl S. Warren**
Professor Emeritus of Accounting
University of Georgia, Athens

**James M. Reeve**
Professor Emeritus of Accounting
University of Tennessee, Knoxville

**Jonathan E. Duchac**
Professor of Accounting
Wake Forest University

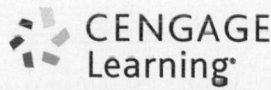
CENGAGE
Learning·

Australia • Brazil • Japan • Korea • Mexico • Singapore • Spain • United Kingdom • United States

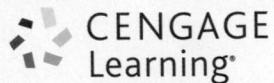
**CENGAGE**
Learning·

**Accounting, 26e**

**Carl S. Warren**
**James M. Reeve**
**Jonathan E. Duchac**

Vice President, General Manager, Science, Math, and
   Quantitative Business: Balraj Kalsi

Product Director: Mike Schenk

Sr. Product Manager: Matt Filimonov

Product Development Manager: Krista Kellman

Sr. Marketing Manager: Robin LeFevre

Sr. Marketing Coordinator: Eileen Corcoran

Managing Content Developer (Media): Scott Fidler

Content Developer (Media): Jessica Robbe

Software Development Manager: Phil Bower

Digital Content Designer: Peggy Hussey

Sr. Content Project Manager: Tim Bailey

Production Service: Cenveo Publisher Service

Manufacturing Planner: Doug Wilke

Sr. Art Director: Stacy Jenkins Shirley

Cover and Internal Designer: Red Hangar Design

Cover Image: © Design Pics Inc/Alamy

Intellectual Property:
   Analyst: Christina Ciaramella
   Project Manager: Betsy Hathaway

Library of Congress Control Number: 2014952910

ISBN-13: 978-1-285-74361-5
ISBN-10: 1-285-74361-X

**Cengage Learning**
20 Channel Center Street
Boston, MA 02210
USA

Cengage Learning is a leading provider of customized learning
solutions with office locations around the globe, including Singapore,
the United Kingdom, Australia, Mexico, Brazil, and Japan. Locate your
local office at: **www.cengage.com/global**

Cengage Learning products are represented in Canada by
Nelson Education, Ltd.

To learn more about Cengage Learning Solutions, visit
**www.cengage.com**

Purchase any of our products at your local college store or at our
preferred online store **www.cengagebrain.com**

Printed in the United States of America
Print Number: 01     Print Year: 2014

# Warren/Reeve/Duchac Accounting & CengageNOWv2

## An Integrated Learning System to Keep Students on Track and Progressing!

**Example Exercise 3-3  Adjustment for Prepaid Expense** OBJ. 2

The prepaid insurance account had a beginning balance of $6,400 and was debited for $3,600 of premiums paid during the year. Journalize the adjusting entry required at the end of the year, assuming the amount of unexpired insurance related to future periods is $3,250.

**Follow My Example 3-3**

Insurance Expense .......................................................... 6,750
    Prepaid Insurance ....................................................     6,750
      Insurance expired ($6,400 + $3,600 − $3,250).

Practice Exercises: PE 3-3A, PE 3-3B

**Example Exercises (EE)** throughout the chapter show students how to solve problems by reinforcing fundamental concepts. Students can follow these examples when completing Practice Exercises.

**EE 3-3** p.112  **PE 3-3A  Adjustment for prepaid expense** OBJ. 2

The supplies account had a beginning balance of $3,375 and was debited for $6,450 for supplies purchased during the year. Journalize the adjusting entry required at the end of the year, assuming the amount of supplies on hand is $2,980.

**Practice Exercises (PE)** are homework problems that refer back to the Example Exercises (EE) in the chapter. These exercises encourage students to practice key concepts and procedures.

**Adjusting Entry for Prepaid Insurance**

The balance in the prepaid insurance account, before adjustment at the end of the year, is $21,700. Journalize the adjusting entry required under each of the following alternatives for determining the amount of the adjustment: (a) the amount of insurance expired during the year is $16,450 (b) the amount of unexpired insurance applicable to future periods is $5,250.

| | Journal | | | | |
| Date | Description | Post. Ref. | Debit | Credit |
|---|---|---|---|---|
| Dec. 31 | Insurance Expense | | 16,450 | |
| |   Prepaid Insurance | | | 16,450 |
| |     Insurance expired | | | |

| Assets | = | Liabilities | + | Owner's Equity (Expense) |
|---|---|---|---|---|
| **Prepaid Insurance** | | | | **Insurance Expense** |
| Bal. 21,700 | Dec. 31 16,450 | | | Dec. 31 16,450 |

CENGAGE**NOW**v2

**Show Me How** problem demonstrations, linked to exercises in CengageNOWv2, mirror the structure of exercises and problems found in the textbook and include teaching tips and warnings to help students learn and avoid common mistakes.

**Adjustment for Prepaid Expense**

Instructions   Chart of Accounts   Journal

Instructions

The supplies account had a beginning balance of $3,375 and was debited for $6,450 for supplies purchased during the year.

Journalize the adjusting entry required at the end of the year (December 31), assuming the amount of supplies on hand is $2,980.

Journal

Journalize the adjusting entry on December 31.

PAGE 10

| | GENERAL JOURNAL | | | |
| DATE | ACCOUNT TITLE | POST. REF. | DEBIT | CREDIT |
|---|---|---|---|---|
| 1 | Adjusting Entries | | | |
| 2 | | | | |
| 3 | | | | |

**Practice Exercises** are assignable in CengageNOWv2, which allows students to access helpful resources such as Check My Work and Show Me How problem demonstrations.

# Set Course Expectations and Guide Students to Success!

Motivate students by reshaping their misconceptions about the introductory accounting course. Students are often surprised by both the approach to learning accounting and the necessary amount of time they need to spend outside of class working through homework assignments.

## CengageNOWv2 Start-Up Center  *NEW!*

The CengageNOWv2 **Start-Up Center** will help students identify what they need to do and where they need to focus in order to be successful with a variety of brand new resources.

*NEW* **Success Strategies Module** includes **Student Advice Videos** and a **Success Strategies Tip Sheet** to ensure that students understand course expectations (and how they may differ from other courses) and how to best plan and prepare so as to be successful in the introductory accounting course.

The **Student Advice Videos** feature real introductory accounting students giving guidance to students who are just starting the course about what it takes to be successful in introductory accounting.

*NEW* **Math Review Module**, designed to help students get up to speed with necessary math skills, includes **math review assignments** and **Show Me How** math review videos to ensure that students have an understanding of basic math skills, including:

- Whole number operations
- Decimal operations and rounding
- Percentage operations and conversion
- Fraction operations
- Converting numbers expressed in one form to a different form
- Positive and negative numbers
- Ratios and averages

*NEW* **How to Use CengageNOWv2 Module** allows students to focus on learning accounting, not on a particular software system. Quickly familiarize your students with CengageNOWv2 and direct them to all of its built-in student resources.

# Expose Students to Concepts Before Class Begins!

With all the outside obligations accounting students have, finding time to read the textbook before class can be a struggle. Point students to the key concepts they need to know before they attend class.

## Video: Animated Activities

Animated Activities are engaging animated scenarios that visually guide students through selected core topics in introductory accounting. Each activity uses a realistic company example to illustrate how the concepts relate to the everyday activities of a business. These activities include multiple-choice questions that gauge student understanding of the overarching chapter concepts.

*Animated Activities are assignable/gradable in CengageNOWv2 and available for self-study and review.*

## Prepaid Insurance

- The debit balance of $2,400 in NetSolutions' prepaid insurance account represents the December 1 prepayment of insurance for 12 months.

| Dec. | 31 | Insurance Expense | 55 | 200 | |
| | | Prepaid Insurance | 15 | | 200 |
| | | Insurance expired ($2,400 ÷ 12). | | | |

### Accounting Equation Impact

Assets    =    Liabilities    +    Owner's Equity (Expense)

| Prepaid Insurance | 15 | | | increase | Insurance Expense | 55 |
| Bal. | 2,400 | Dec. 31 | 200 | | Dec. 31 | 200 |
| Adj. Bal. | 2,200 | | | | | |

decrease

©2018 Cengage Learning. All Rights Reserved. May not be scanned, copied or duplicated, or posted to a publicly accessible website, in whole or in part.

## Video: Tell Me More  NEW!

Tell Me More lecture activities explain the core concepts of the chapter through an engaging auditory and visual presentation that is ideal for all class formats—flipped model, online, hybrid, face-to-face.

*Tell Me More lecture activities for every Learning Objective are assignable/gradable in CengageNOWv2 and available for self-study and review.*

# Expose Students to Concepts Before Class Begins!

Students don't want to waste time going over concepts that they have already mastered. With the NEW Adaptive Study Plan, they can focus on learning new topics and fully understanding difficult concepts.

## Adaptive Study Plan *NEW!*

The Adaptive Study Plan in CengageNOWv2 is an assignable/gradable study center that adapts to each student's unique needs and provides a remediation pathway to keep students progressing.

*The Adaptive Study Plan is assignable/gradable in CengageNOWv2 and available for self-study and review.*

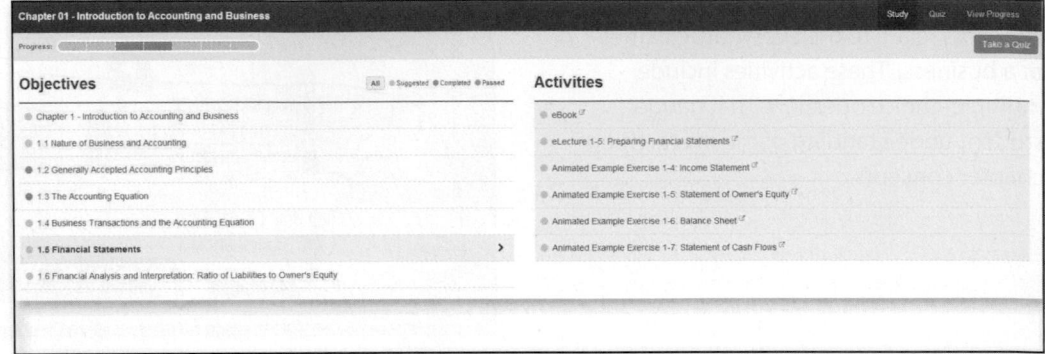

## *How does it work?*

**Step 1:** Students take a chapter-level quiz consisting of randomized questions that cover both conceptual and procedural aspects of the chapter.

**Step 2:** Feedback is provided for each answer option explaining why the answer is right or wrong.

**Step 3:** Based on the quiz results, students are provided a remediation path that includes media assets and algorithmic practice problems to help them improve their understanding of the course material.

Instructors may use prerequisites that require students to achieve mastery in the Adaptive Study Plan before moving on to new material.

> *The new Adaptive Study Plan offers the benefit of customization coupled with remediation.*
>
> *— Jennifer Schneider, professor at University of North Georgia*

# Make Content Relatable!

Show students how the material they are learning matters in real life and help them connect accounting concepts to the world around them.

*Experience Managerial Accounting Videos are assignable/gradable in CengageNOWv2 and available for self-study and review.*

## Video: Experience Managerial Accounting

Experience Managerial Accounting Videos, available in CengageNOWv2, show students how progressive companies such as Cold Stone Creamery, Second City, and Hard Rock Café incorporate managerial accounting to fuel better business performance.

## Pathways Commission "THIS is accounting!" NEW!

Pathways Commission "THIS is accounting!" illustrates what students should understand as a result of their first exposure to accounting. Incorporated into Chapter 1, this graphic gives students a big picture view of how accounting can lead to a prosperous society.

## Service Focus NEW!

Service Focus features highlight the differences between manufacturing companies and service companies and illustrate how managerial accounting concepts apply to service companies such as The Walt Disney Company and Sierra Nevada.

Source: *Charting a National Strategy for the Next Generation of Accountants,* The Pathways Commission, July 2012.

---

### Service ⏾ Focus

**PROFIT, LOSS, AND BREAK-EVEN IN MAJOR LEAGUE BASEBALL**

Major League Baseball is a tough game and a tough business. Ticket prices (unit selling price), player salaries (variable costs), stadium fees (fixed costs), and attendance (volume) converge to make it difficult for teams to make a profit, or at least break even. So, which major league baseball team was the most profitable in 2013? Well, it wasn't the World Champion Boston Red Sox. Nor was it the star-studded New York Yankees. Then, it had to be the recently turned around Los Angeles Angels, right? Not even close. It was actually the worst team in baseball—the Houston Astros.

Just how profitable were the Astros? They earned $99 million in 2013, which was more than the combined 2013 profits of the six most recent World Series champions. How could the team with the worst record in baseball since 2005

have one of the most profitable years in baseball history? By paying careful attention to costs and volume. Between 2011 and 2013, the Astros cut their player payroll from $56 million to less than $13 million. That's right, all of the players on the Houston Astros baseball team combined, made less in 2013 than Alex Rodriguez (New York Yankees), Cliff Lee (Philadelphia Phillies), Prince Fielder (Detroit Tigers), and Tim Lincecum (San Francisco Giants) made individually. While attendance at Astros games has dropped by around 20% since 2011, the cost reductions from reduced player salaries have far outpaced the drop in attendance, making the 2013 Astros the most profitable team in baseball history. While no one likes losing baseball games, the Houston Astros have shown that focusing on the relationship between cost and volume can yield a hefty profit, even when they aren't winning.

Source: D. Alexander, "2013 Houston Astros: Baseball's Worst Team Is The Most Profitable In History," *Forbes,* August 26, 2013.

MOTIVATION

# Close the Gap Between Homework and Exam Performance!

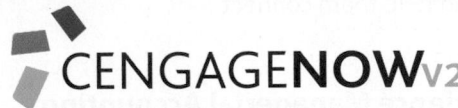

> *Good tool to make students understand concepts without overly relying on technology's help.*
>
> **– Ramesh Narasimhan, professor at Montclair State University**

> *I like it because it appears to bridge the gap between the homework and my exam.*
>
> **– Lawrence Chui, professor at University of St. Thomas**

> *This will minimize students' complaints about how the exam looks different from the homework format.*
>
> **– Rama Ramamurthy, professor at Georgetown University**

Many students perform well on homework but struggle when it comes to exams. Now, with the new Blank Sheet of Paper Experience, students must problem-solve on their own, just as they would if taking a test on a blank sheet of paper.

## Blank Sheet of Paper Experience

A less-leading Blank Sheet of Paper Experience discourages overreliance on the system.

- The use of drop down menus and Smart Entry (type-ahead) has been eliminated.
- Students must refer to the Chart of Accounts and decide for themselves what account is impacted.
- The number of accounts in each transactions is not given away.
- Whether the account should be debited or credited is not given away.
- Transactions may be entered in any order (as long as the entries are correct).
- Check My Work feedback only reports on what students have actually attempted, which prevents students from "guessing" their way through the assignment.

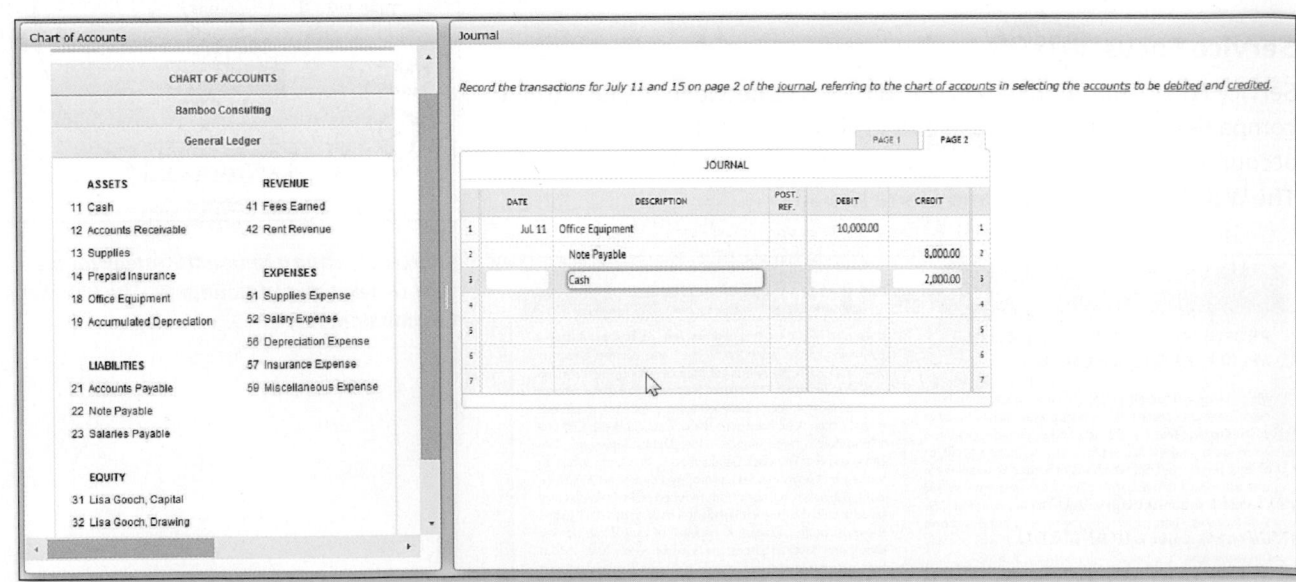

*Check it out!* Visit **cnowv2demo.cengage.com** for an interactive demo.

# Help Students Make Connections and See the Big Picture!

Homework software should not get in the way of learning. One of the biggest complaints students have about online homework is the scrolling, which prevents students from seeing the big picture and understanding the accounting system. The new Multi-Panel View addresses this issue and enhances student learning.

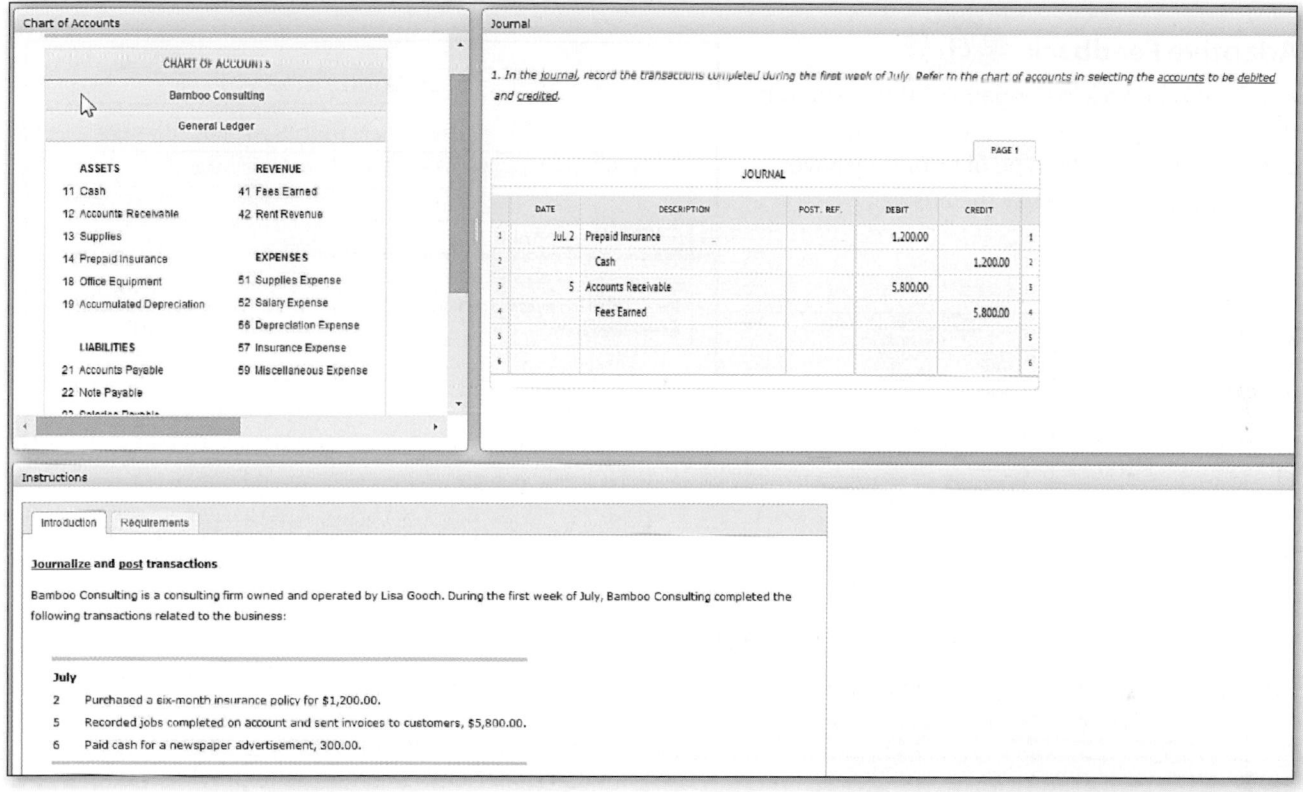

## Multi-Panel View NEW!

The NEW Multi-Panel View in CengageNOWv2 enables students to see all the elements of a problem on one screen.

- Students make connections and see the tasks as connected components in the accounting process.
- Dramatically reduced scrolling eliminates student frustration.

With the ability to move and resize journals, ledgers, forms, and financial statements, it is easier to navigate the problem and understand the accounting system.

*This is just a lot better and less confusing than scrolling up and down. . . . Having it like that would make it much easier —not so much scrolling and it wouldn't be so confusing.*

**– Tyler Mason, student at Northern Essex Community College**

*Multi-Panel View makes it much easier for students to see how each piece of the accounting cycle impacts the other pieces. Having it all in one view reduces student frustration and gives them a clearer picture of the complete accounting cycle.*

**– Kristen Quinn, professor at Northern Essex Community College**

Students often complete homework at odd times. And when they use CengageNOWv2, they get help right when they need it.

## Adaptive Feedback  *NEW!*

Adaptive Feedback in CengageNOWv2 responds to students based upon their unique answers and alerts them to the type of error they have made without giving away the answer.

| | DATE | DESCRIPTION | POST. REF. | DEBIT | CREDIT | |
|---|---|---|---|---|---|---|
| 1 | Jul. 11 | Office Equipment | ✓ | 10,000.00 | | 1 |
| 2 | | Cash | ✓ | | 8,000.00 | 2 |
| 3 | | Note Payaable | | | 2,000.00 | 3 |

JOURNAL — Score: 33/138 — PAGE 1 | PAGE 2

There is a minor spelling error in the account title. You will be graded as if you had entered "Note Payable."

**Line**
- The amount for this account is incorrect, although you've entered the amount in the correct column. [-2]

---

JOURNAL — PAGE 1 | PAGE 2 — Score: 33/138

| | DATE | DESCRIPTION | POST. REF. | DEBIT | CREDIT | |
|---|---|---|---|---|---|---|
| 1 | Jul. 11 | Office Equipment | | 10,000.00 | | 1 |
| 2 | | Cash | | | 8,000.00 | 2 |
| 3 | | Note Payaable | | | 2,000.00 | 3 |
| 4 | | | | | | 4 |
| 5 | | | | | | 5 |
| 6 | | | | | | 6 |
| 7 | | | | | | 7 |
| 8 | | | | | | 8 |
| 9 | | | | | | 9 |
| 10 | | | | | | 10 |
| 11 | | | | | | 11 |

Points: ▬ 0.24 / 1

**Feedback**

▼ Check My Work

Identify which accounts are affected in each transaction. Keep in mind that every transaction involves at least two accounts. Determine whether the account increases or decreases and record each increase or decrease following the rules of debit and credit. Use the Posting Reference column to enter the corresponding account number from the general ledger account. Remember total debits should equal total credits in your entries.

Learning Objective 1
Learning Objective 2
Learning Objective 3

*I like the adaptive feedback. It will reduce a number of errors that cause students to give up.*

**— Kevin Jones, professor at Drexel University**

*Excellent! Often learning from feedback is more powerful than learning from the instructor, text, etc.*

**— Lisa Brown, professor at Indiana Institute of Technology**

In addition to groundbreaking, adaptive feedback, CengageNOWv2 continues to provide multiple layers of guidance to keep students on track and progressing.

- **Check My Work Feedback** provides general guidance and hints as students work through homework assignments.

- *NEW* **Check My Work Feedback** in CengageNOWv2 now only reports on what students have actually attempted, which prevents them from "guessing" their way through assignments.

- **Explanations** are available after the assignment has been submitted and provide a detailed description of how to arrive at the solution.

*Check it out!* Visit **cnowv2demo.cengage.com** for an interactive demo.

# Help Students Make Connections and See the Big Picture!

The best way to learn accounting is through practice, but students often get stuck when attempting homework assignments on their own.

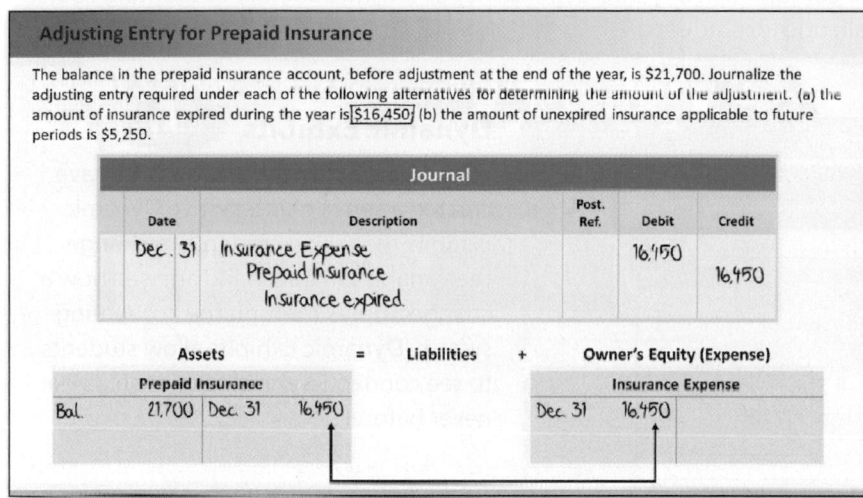

*Identified by an icon in the text margins, Show Me How videos are linked to assignments in CengageNOWv2 and available for self-study and review.*

## Video: Show Me How **NEW!**

Created for the most frequently assigned end-of-chapter Items, hundreds of NEW Show Me How problem demonstration videos provide a step-by-step model of a similar problem. Embedded tips and warnings help students avoid common mistakes and pitfalls.

## Blueprint Problems

Blueprint Problems are teaching problems that walk students through a single accounting topic. These problems cover the primary learning objectives and are designed to help students understand foundational content and the associated building blocks versus memorizing the formulas or journal entries.

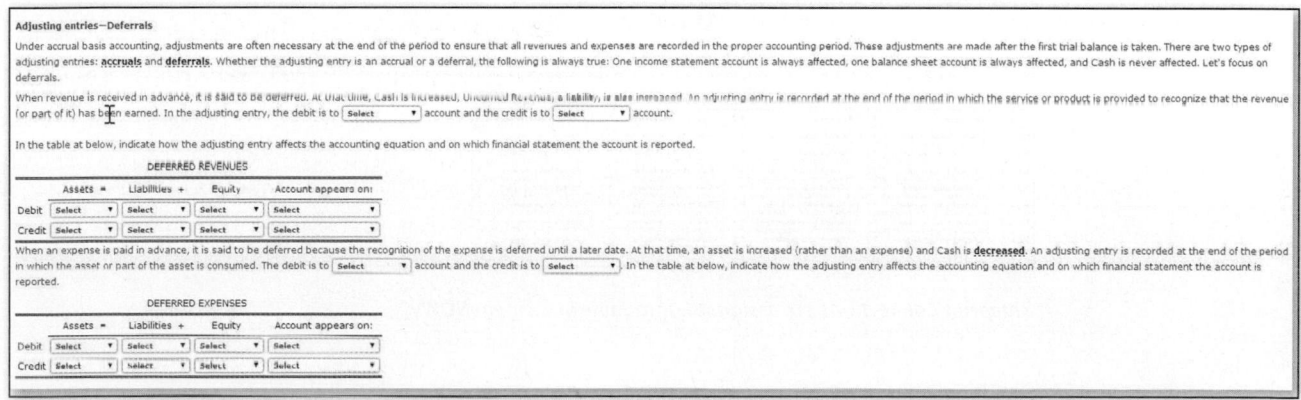

*Blueprint Problems are assignable/gradable in CengageNOWv2.*

## NetSolutions Continuing Case Study

Students follow a fictitious company, **NetSolutions**, which demonstrates a rich variety of transactions. The continuity of presentation helps students master difficult concepts such as the accounting cycle.

# Help Students Go Beyond Memorization to True Understanding!

Students often struggle to understand how concepts relate to one another. For most students, an introductory accounting course is their first exposure to both *business transactions* and the *accounting system*. While these concepts are already difficult to master individually, their combination and interdependency in the introductory accounting course often pose a challenge for students.

### Dynamic Exhibits

To overcome this gap, the authors have created a series of interactive Dynamic Exhibits that allow students to change the variables in a scenario and see how a change ripples through the accounting system. Dynamic Exhibits allow students to see connections and relationships like never before!

*Identified by an icon in the text, Dynamic Exhibits are embedded within the MindTap eReader in CengageNOWv2. They are assignable/gradable in CengageNOWv2 and available for self-study and review.*

## Blueprint Connections

Blueprint Connections are scenario-based teaching problems that solidify concepts and demonstrate their interrelationships, as well as promote critical thinking. Blueprint Connections combine multiple topics, allowing students to explore a larger concept more fully, and strengthen analytical skills.

*Blueprint Connections are assignable/gradable in CengageNOWv2.*

# Help Students Build Critical Thinking Skills!

Students often resort to memorization as a way to pass the course, but such surface learning does little to develop the critical thinking skills and deep understanding that are necessary for success in future business courses.

## Activation Exercises

To overcome these challenges, the authors have created Activation Exercises to provide a learning system that focuses on developing a better understanding of:

- Key terms and definitions
- Economics of business transactions
- How transactions are recorded in the accounting system
- How transactions are ultimately reflected in the financial statements

These "what if" exercises help students understand relationships using interactive tools.

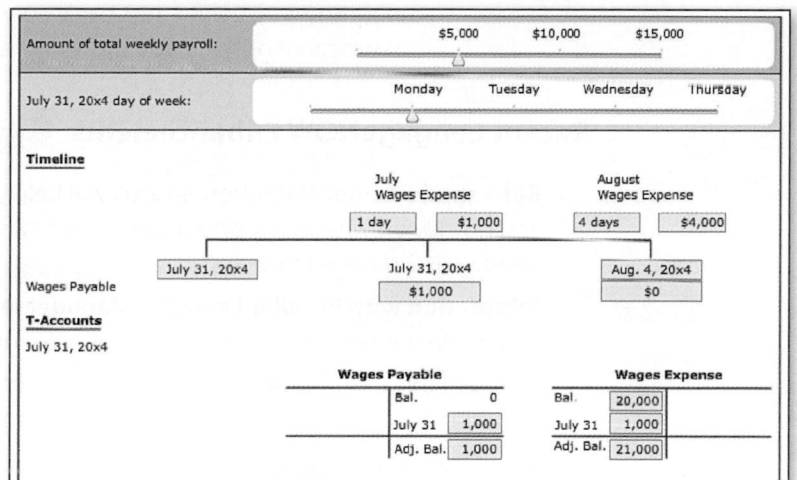

*The Activation Exercises are assignable/gradable in CengageNOWv2.*

*These exercises are interactive and actually allow students to experiment with the data, visually viewing the impact when data is altered. The exercises show not only how a transaction looks in the journal and ledger accounts, but also the impact it ultimately has on financial statements. Finally, students are challenged to analyze the overall impact of a transaction by answering questions related to the topic. This is an excellent learning tool.*

**— Rita Mintz, professor at Calhoun Community College**

The Activation Exercises structure builds the critical thinking skills that are necessary for students to succeed in both introductory accounting and future accounting courses. Reviewers have enthusiastically praised the authors' online activities and indicated that they would be both ideal for pre-class activities and after-class assignments.

 ## Financial Statement Analysis and Interpretation

The Financial Statement Analysis and Interpretation sections, at the end of financial accounting chapters, help students understand key ratios and how stakeholders interpret financial reports. These sections encourage students to go deeper into the material to analyze accounting information and improve critical thinking skills.

# Online Solutions

CengageNOWv2 is a powerful course management and online homework resource that provides control and customization to optimize the student learning experience. Included are many proven resources including algorithmic activities, test bank, course management tools, reporting and assessment options, and much more.

## Recent CengageNOW Enhancements

- **Refreshed Design:** This refreshed look will help you and your students focus easily and quickly on what is important, while maintaining the same functionality that CengageNOW users know and love.

- **Integration with Popular Learning Management Systems:** Single login, deep linking, and grade return! (Check with your local Learning Consultant for more details!)

- **Upload Files Capability:** You can now upload files in CengageNOW for student use—including videos, Excel files, Word files, and more.

- **Email Instructor Feature**: Students can now send you a screenshot of the question they are working on directly through CengageNOW and ask specific questions about where they are stuck.

- **Better Date Management**: When modifying assignment due dates for a whole course, the system will now automatically adjust due dates based on a new start date, making it easier to reuse a course from one term to the next and adjust for snow days.

- **Streamlined Assignment Creation Process:** A simplified and streamlined Assignment Creation process allows instructors to quickly set up and manage assignments from a single page!

- **New Report Options:** New reporting options allow you to get better reports on your students' progress.

- **New Student Registration Process:** When you create a course, a URL will be generated that will automatically take students right into the instructor's course without them having to enter the course key!

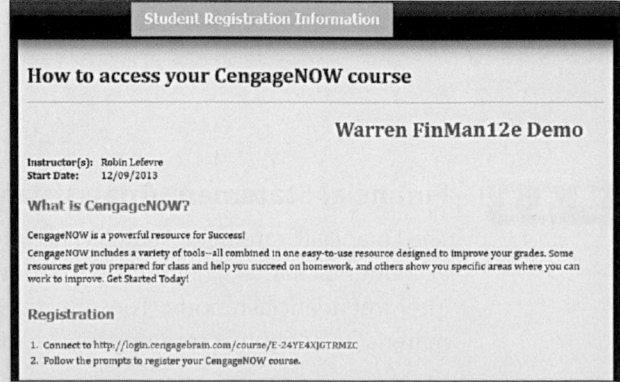

## MindTap eReader

The MindTap eReader for Warren/Reeve/Duchac's *Accounting* is the most robust digital reading experience available. Hallmark features include:

- Fully optimized for the iPad.
- Note taking, highlighting, and more.
- Embedded digital media such as Dynamic Exhibits.

The MindTap eReader also features ReadSpeaker®, an online text-to-speech application that vocalizes, or "speech-enables," online educational content. This feature is ideally suited for both instructors and learners who would like to listen to content instead of (or in addition to) reading it.

## Cengage Learning General Ledger Software (CLGL)

CLGL exposes students to computerized accounting software without teaching the specifics of a certain software system—preparing students for *any* software program they might encounter in the real world.

- Now available in CengageNOWv2, CLGL allows students to work through end-of-chapter assignments and practice sets in a format that emulates commercial general ledger software, but in a manner that is more forgiving of errors.
- Assignments are automatically graded online.
- Selected problems that can be solved using CLGL are designated by an icon in the textbook and are listed in the assignment preparation grid in the Instructor's Manual.

# New to This Edition

In addition to the many new digital assets created for this edition of *Accounting*, the textbook content itself has also been revised. The most significant changes for this edition involve the inclusion of the new revenue recognition standard and a greater emphasis on service companies in the managerial accounting chapters.

In all chapters, the following improvements have been made:

- Updated dates and real company information for currency
- Added headers and sub-headers to help students navigate through the chapter and easily reference sections when completing homework assignments
- Set unlabeled graphics as numbered exhibits for easier student reference
- Used more bulleted lists to call students' attention to specific information
- Refreshed end-of-chapter assignments with different numerical values and updated information

The new revenue recognition standard required the following changes:

- Revised the definitions of revenue and revenue recognition in Chapters 1–3, including the glossary. These revisions are consistent with the new revenue recognition standard, **Revenue from Contracts with Customers (Topic 606)**, FASB, May 2014.
- Revised Chapter 6, *Accounting for Merchandising Businesses*, to be consistent with the preceding standard. These revisions include using the net method for all purchase and sales discounts. In addition, the accounting for customer returns and allowances, including cash refunds, has been updated. As a result, sales discounts and sales return and allowances accounts are no longer used.
- Added new Appendix E, *Revenue Recognition*, which describes and illustrates the new Five-Step process for recognizing revenue. The illustration includes the accounting for a bundled product with different performance obligations.

## Chapter 1
- New Business Connection includes The Pathways Commission definition of *accounting*

## Chapter 2
- New Business Connection on Microsoft's unearned revenue

## Chapter 3
- New chapter opener on Pandora
- Revised introduction to revenue recognition
- New Business Connection on Microsoft dealing with unearned revenue for support services

## Chapter 4
- New chapter opener on Zynga
- Updated exposition of Appendix 1 showing end-of-period spreadsheet usage

## Chapter 6
- Updated the Sales Discounts and Sales Returns and Allowances discussion for accuracy with the new revenue recognition standard

## Chapter 10
- New chapter opener on McDonald's

## Chapter 11
- New chapter opener on Starbucks
- Updated Exhibit 3 to reflect current wage withholding rates

## Chapter 12
- New chapter opener on the Boston Celtics

## Chapter 14
- Updated learning objective 1 to more clearly explain alternatives in financing corporations

## Chapter 15
- New chapter opener on The Coca-Cola Company
- Significantly streamlined learning objective 5
- New Business Connection on cash and investments in the pharmaceutical industry

## Chapter 16
- New chapter opener on National Beverage Co.
- Updated Exhibit 1 to more clearly detail specific examples of sources and uses of cash

## Chapter 18
- New exhibit with income statements for merchandising and manufacturing businesses

## Chapter 19
- New Service Focus on job order costing in a law firm

## Chapter 21
- New chapter opener on Ford Motor Company

## Chapter 22
- New chapter opener on Hendrick Motorsport
- New Service Focus on film budgeting
- Updated two learning objectives to reflect the differences between operating and financial budgets
- New Exhibit 7 on the master budget for a manufacturing company

## Chapter 23
- New Business Connection on standard costing for breweries
- New Service Focus on standard costing in the restaurant industry

## Chapter 24
- New Service Focus on Charles Schwab

## Chapter 26
- New chapter opener on Vail Resorts, Inc.
- New Service Focus on network business models

# Instructor Resources

## Solutions Manual

Author-written and carefully verified multiple times to ensure accuracy and consistency with the text, the Solutions Manual contains answers to the Discussion Questions, Practice Exercises, Exercises, Problems (Series A and Series B), Cases, and Continuing Problems that appear in the text. These solutions help you easily plan, assign, and efficiently grade assignments.

## Test Bank *NEW!*

NEW for this edition, Test Bank content is now delivered in an online platform. Cengage Learning Testing Powered by Cognero is a flexible, online system that allows you to:

- Author, edit, and manage test bank content from multiple Cengage Learning solutions
- Create multiple test versions in an instant
- Deliver tests from your LMS, your classroom, or wherever you want

Also *NEW* for this edition, 100 new Test Bank questions have been added (in addition to revising numeric values for approximately 20% of the existing questions).

## Companion Website

This robust companion website provides immediate access to a rich array of teaching and learning resources–including the Instructor's Manual, PowerPoint slides, and Excel Template Solutions. Easily download the instructor resources you need from the password-protected, instructor only section of the site.

**Instructor's Manual** Discover new ways to engage your students by utilizing the Instructor's Manual ideas for class discussion, group learning activities, writing exercises, and Internet activities. Moreover, simplify class preparation by reviewing a brief summary of each chapter, a detailed chapter synopsis (*NEW* for this edition), teaching tips regarding a suggested approach to the material, questions students frequently ask in the classroom, lecture aids, and demonstration problems in the Instructor's Manual. Transparency Masters and

Handouts (with solutions) are also included. Quickly identify the assignments that best align with your course with the assignment preparation grid that includes information about learning objective coverage, difficulty level and Bloom's taxonomy categorization, time estimates, and accrediting standard alignment for business programs, AICPA, ACBSP, and IMA.

**PowerPoint Slides** Bring your lectures to life with slides designed to clarify difficult concepts for your students. The lecture PowerPoints include key terms and definitions, equations, examples, exhibits, and all Example Exercises (with solutions) from the textbook.

- *NEW* for this edition, descriptions for all graphics in the PowerPoints have been added to enhance PowerPoint usability for students with disabilities.
- Two separate PowerPoint decks that include just the Example Exercises (and solutions) and just the Exhibits from the textbook are ideal for instructors that create their own PowerPoint decks and just want to refresh them.

**Excel Template Solutions** Excel Templates are provided for selected long or complicated end-of-chapter exercises and problems to assist the student as they set up and work the problem. Certain cells are coded to display a red asterisk when an incorrect answer is entered, which helps students stay on track. Selected problems that can be solved using these templates are designated by an icon in the textbook and are listed in the assignment preparation grid in the Instructor's Manual. The Excel Template Solutions provide answers to these templates. *NEW* for this edition, 10 more Excel Templates have been added.

**Practice Set Solutions** Establish a fundamental understanding of the accounting cycle for your students with Practice Sets, which require students to complete one month of transactions for a fictional company. Brief descriptions of each Practice Set are provided in the Table of Contents. The Practice Set Solutions provide answers to these practice sets.

## Study Guide

Now available free in CengageNOWv2, the Study Guide allows students to easily assess what they know with a "Do You Know" checklist covering the key points in each chapter. To further test their comprehension, students can work through Practice Exercises, which include a "strategy" hint and solution so they can continue to practice applying key accounting concepts.

## Working Papers

Now available free in CengageNOWv2, students will find the tools they need to help work through end-of-chapter assignments with these working papers. The preformatted templates provide a starting point by giving students a basic structure for problems and journal entries. Working Papers are also available in a printed format as a bundle option.

## Practice Sets

For more in-depth application of accounting practices, instructors may choose from among six different Practice Sets for long-term assignments. Each Practice Set requires students to complete one month of transactions for a fictional company. Practice Sets can be solved manually or with the Cengage Learning General Ledger software.

## Website

Designed specifically for your students' accounting needs, this website features student PowerPoint slides, Excel Templates, learning games, and flashcards.

- **PowerPoint Slides:** Students can easily take notes or review difficult concepts with the student version of this edition's PowerPoint slides.

- **Excel Templates:** These Excel Templates help students stay on track. If students enter an incorrect answer in certain cells, a red asterisk will appear to let them know something is wrong. Problems that can be solved using these templates are designated by an icon.

- **Crossword Puzzles:** Students can focus on learning the key terms and definitions for each chapter in a different way by completing these crossword puzzles.

- **Flashcards:** Students can prepare with these flashcards, which cover the key terms and definitions they need to know for each chapter.

# Acknowledgements

The many enhancements to this edition of *Accounting* are the direct result of one-on-one interviews, surveys, reviews, WebExes, and focus groups with over 300 instructors and students at institutions across the country over the past two years. We would like to take this opportunity to thank those who helped us better understand the challenges of the principles of accounting course and provided valuable feedback on our content and digital assets.

## Instructors:

Aaron Pennington, York College of Pennsylvania

Adam Myers, Texas A&M University

Aileen Huang, Santa Monica College

Ajay Maindiratta, New York University

Alex Gialanella, Manhattanville College

Andrea Murowski, Brookdale Community College

Angelo Luciano, Columbia College, Chicago

Ann Gervais, Springfield Technical Comm College

Ann Gregory, South Plains College

Anna Boulware, St. Charles Community College

Anne Marie Anderson, Raritan Valley Community College

April Poe, University of the Incarnate Word

Barbara Kren, Marquette University

Bea Chiang, The College of New Jersey

Becky Hancock, El Paso Community College

Brenda McVey, Green River Community College

Bruce England, Massasoit Community College

Bruce L. Darling, University of Oregon

Bruce Leung, City College of San Francisco

Carol Dickerson, Chaffey College

Carol Graham, The University of San Francisco

Cassandra H. Catlett, Carson Newman University

Cecile Roberti, Community College of Rhode Island

Charles J.F. Leflar, University of Arkansas

Charles Lewis, Houston Community College

Chris Kinney, Mount Wachusett Community College

Chris McNamara, Finger Lakes Community College

Christopher Ashley, Everest College

Christopher Demaline, Central Arizona College

Cindy Bleasdal, Hilbert College

Colleen Chung, Miami Dade College

Cynthia Bolt, The Citadel

Cynthia J. Miller, University of Kentucky

Cynthia Johnson, University of Arkansas at Little Rock

Darlene Schnuck, Waukesha County Technical College

Dave Alldredge, Salt Lake Community College

David Centers, Grand Valley State University

David E. Laurel, South Texas College

Dawn Lopez, Johnson & Wales University

Dawn Peters, Southwestern Illinois College

Dawn W. Stevens, Northwest Mississippi Community College

Debbie Adkins, Remington College Online

Debbie Luna, El Paso Community College

Debbie Rose, Northeast Wisconsin Technical College

Debora Constable, Georgia Perimeter College

Denise Teixeira, Chemeketa Community College

Don Curfman, McHenry County College

Dori Danko, Grand Valley State University

Dorothy Davis, University of Louisiana, Monroe

Edwin Pagan, Passaic County Community College

Elizabeth Ammann, Lindenwood University

Emmanuel Danso, Palm Beach State College

Ercan Sinmaz, Houston Community College

Eric Blazer, Millersville University

Erik Lindquist, Lansing Community College

Esther S. Bunn, Stephen F Austin State University

Felicia R. Baldwin, Richard J. Daley College

Gary Bower, Community College of Rhode Island

Geoffrey D. Bartlett, Drake University

Gerald Smith, University of Northern Iowa

Glenn (Mel) McQueary, Houston Community College

Gloria Grayless, Sam Houston State University

Greg Lauer, North Iowa Area Community College

Gregory Brookins, Santa Monica College

Harold Little, Western Kentucky University

Jacqueline Burke, Hofstra University

James Lock, Northern Virginia Community College

James M. Emig, Villanova University

James Webb, University of the Pacific

Jamie O'Brien, South Dakota State University

Jan Barton, Emory University

Jana Hosmer, Blue Ridge Community College

Janice Akeo, Butler Community College

Jeanette Milius, Iowa Western Community College

Jeff Varblow, College of Lake County

Jeffrey T. Kunz, Carroll University

Jennifer LeSure, Ivy Tech Community College

Jennifer Mack, Lindenwood University

Jennifer Schneider, University of North Georgia

Jennifer Spring Sneed, Arkansas State University-Newport

Jenny Resnick, Santa Monica College

Jill Mitchell, Northern Virginia Community College

Jim Shelton, Harding University

Joel Strong, St. Cloud State University

John G. Ahmad, Northern Virginia Community College

John Babich, Kankakee Community College

John Nader, Davenport University

John Seilo, Irvine Valley College

John Verani, White Mountains Community College

Johnna Murray, University of Missouri-St. Louis

Joseph M. Nicassio, Westmoreland County Community College

Judith A. Toland, Bucks County Community College

Judith Zander, Grossmont College

Judy Patrick, Minnesota State Community and Technical College

Judy Smith, Parkland College

Julia M. Camp, Providence College

Julie Dawson, Carthage College

Julie Miller Millmann, Chippewa Valley Technical College

Karen C. Elsom, Fayetteville Technical Community College

Katherine Sue Hewitrt, Klamath Community College

Katy Long, Hill College

Keith Hallmark, Calhoun Community College

Kevin McNelis, New Mexico State University

Kimberly Franklin, St. Louis Community College

Kirk Canzano, Long Beach City College

Kristen Quinn, Northern Essex Community College

La Vonda Ramey, Schoolcraft College

Lana Tuss, Chemeketa Community College

Larry G. Stephens, Austin Community College

Lawrence A. Roman, Cuyahoga Community College

Lawrence Chui, University of St. Thomas

Leah Arrington, Northwest Mississippi Community College

Leah Russell, Holyoke Community College

Lee Smart, Southwest Tennessee Community College

Len Heritage, Tacoma Community College

Leonard Cronin, University Center Rochester

Linda Christiansen, Indiana University Southeast

Linda H. Tarrago, Hillsborough Community College

Linda Miller, Northeast Community College

Linda Muren, Cuyahoga Community College

Linda Tarrago, Hillsborough Community College

Lisa Busto, William Rainey Harper College

Lisa Novak, Mott Community College

Lori A. Grady, Bucks County Community College

Lori Johnson, Minnesota State University Moorhead

Louann Hofheins Cummings, The University of Findlay

Lucile Faurel, University of California Irvine

Lynn Almond, Virginia Tech

Lynn K. Saubert, Radford University

Lynn Krausse, Bakersfield College

Machiavelli W. Chao, University of California, Irvine

Magan Calhoun, Austin Peay State University

Marcela Raphael, Chippewa Valley Technical College

Marci Butterfield, University of Utah

Marianne James, California State University, Los Angeles

Marie Saunders, Dakota County Technical College

Marilyn Stansbury, Calvin College

Marina Grau, Houston Community College

Martin Hart, Manchester Comm College

Mary Zenner, College of Lake County

Meg Costello Lambert, Oakland Community College

Merrily Hoffman, San Jacinto College

Michael G. Schaefer, Blinn College

Michael Goeken, Northwest Vista College

Michael Gurevitz, Montgomery College

Michael J. Gallagher, DeSales University

Michael Lawrence, Mt. Hood Community College

Michael P. Dole, Marquette University

Michael P. Prockton, Finger Lakes Community College

Michele Martinez, Hillsborough Community College

Michelle Moshier, University at Albany

Ming Lu, Santa Monica College

Mon Sellers, Lone Star College-North Harris

Nancy Emerson, North Dakota State University

Nancy L. Snow, University of Toledo

Nino Gonzalez, El Paso Community College

Noel McKeon, Florida State College at Jacksonville

Odessa Jordan, Calhoun Community College

Pam Meyer, University of Louisiana at Lafayette

Pamela Knight, Columbus Technical College

Patricia Doherty, Boston University School of Management

Patricia Walczak, Lansing Community College

Patricia Worsham, Norco College

Patrick Rogan, Cosumnes River College

Perry Sellers, Lone Star College System

Rachel Pernia, Essex County College

Rebecca Grava Davis, East Mississippi Community College

Rebecca Hancock, El Paso Community College

Richard Lau, California State University, Los Angeles

Richard Mandau, Piedmont Technical College

Rick Andrews, Sinclair Community College

Rick Rinetti, Los Angeles City College

Rita Mintz, Calhoun Community College

Robert A. Pacheco, Massasoit Community College

Robert Almon, South Texas College

Robert E. (Reb) Beatty, Anne Arundel Community College

Robert Foster, Los Angeles Pierce College

Robert Urell, Irvine Valley College

Robin D'Agati, Palm Beach State College

Ron O'Brien, Fayetteville Technical Community College

Roy Carson, Anne Arundel Community College

Ryan Smith, Columbia College

Sandra Cohen, Columbia College Chicago

Sara Barritt, Northeast Community College

Saturnino (Nino) Gonzalez, El Paso Community College

Shani N. Robinson, Sam Houston State University

Sharif Soussi, Charter Oak State College

Sharon Agee, Rollins College

Sheila Ammons, Austin Community College

Sheila Guillot, Lamar State College-Port Arthur

Sol. Ahiarah, SUNY Buffalo State

Stacy Kline, Drexel University

Stani Kantcheva, Cincinnati State Technical and Community College

Steven J. LaFave, Augsburg College

Sue Cunningham, Rowan Cabarrus Community College

Suneel Maheshwari, Marshall University

Susan Cordes, Johnson County Community College

Suzanne Laudadio, Durham Technical Community College

Sy Pearlman, California State University, Long Beach

Tara Laken, Joliet Junior College

Taylor Klett, Sam Houston State University

Teresa Thompson, Chaffey Community College

Terri Walsh, Seminole State College

Thane Butt, Champlain College

Thomas Branton, Alvin Community College

Tim Green, North Georgia Technical College

Timothy Griffin, Hillsborough Community College

Timothy J. Moran, Aurora University

Timothy Swenson, Sullivan University

Tony Cioffi, Lorain County Community College

W. Jeff Knight, Flagler College

Wanda Wong, Chabot College

**Students:**

Allison Seaman, University of Findlay

Amber Bostick, Joliet Junior College

Amelia Lupis, Community College of Rhode Island

Andrew Buckley, Community College of Rhode Island

Andrew Mancini, Valparaiso University

Anita Jordan, Henry Ford Community College

Billie Ma, Middlesex County College

Blair Ericksen, The University of Findlay

Bonnie Eme, Ivy Tech Community College

Bradley "The Snowman" Koepke, Valparaiso University

Briana E Garrity, Community College of Rhode Island

Brittany Smothers, Ivy Tech Community College

Carly Butler, Sinclair Community College

Carmen Macvicar, Henry Ford Community College

Cassie Skal, University of Findlay

Charlene Resch, Ivy Tech Community College

Chcila Soares, Community College of Rhode Island

Christopher W. Gregory, Fayetteville Technical Community College

Colby Zachary, Austin Community College

Courtney Murphy, Sinclair Community College

Daniel Hart, Ivy Tech Community College

David Camargo, Fayetteville Technical Community College

Debborah Gideon, Ivy Tech Community College

Diana Contreras, Joliet Junior College

Dolores Velasquez, Ivy Tech Community College

Eleticia Feliciano, Henry Ford Community College

Eli Coulton, Sinclair Community College

Emilie Ferdelman, Sinclair Community College

Geoffrey Hlavach, Joliet Junior College

Jayme Thornley, Community College of Rhode Island

Jessie Laberge, Community College of Rhode Island

Joel Mondragon, Austin Community College

Jonathan Balsavich, Joliet Junior College

Jose Nieto, Austin Community College

J. Stoll, The University of Findlay

Karolina Tovpenec, The University of Findlay

Kathryn Shaw, Ivy Tech Community College

Kaylene Slayton, The University of Findlay

Kevin McMaster, Community College of Rhode island

Khadija Brikatc, Erie Community College

Kimberlee Serrano, Middlesex County College

Kimberly Arruda, Community College of Rhode Island

Krista Jalette, Community College of Rhode Island

Leslie Bryant, Henry Ford Community College

Luke Fleming, Ivy Tech Community College

Malorie Masek, Valparaiso University

Marah Jammal, Henry Ford Community College

Marshall Miller, Valparaiso University

Matthew Vizzaccaro, Henry Ford Community College

Mayra Vargas, Austin Community College

Meghan Traster, Ivy Tech Community College

M. Lallier, Community College of Rhode Island

Michael L. Bardey, Sinclair Community College

Min Dou, Valparaiso University

Nicholas Johnson, Ivy Tech Community College

Nick L., Holyoke Community College

Nicholas Oliveira, Community College of Rhode island

Rachel Brown, Sinclair Community College

Ramona Hawkins, Ivy Tech Community College

Ryan Dvorak, Joliet Junior College

Ryan Truschke, Grand Valley State University

S.J. Cross, Ivy Tech Community College

Scott Nicol, Joliet Junior College

Sean Bingham, The University of Findlay

Sheila Diodonet, Holyoke Community College

Stephanie Theresa Plante, Community College of Rhode Island

Tasha Finley, Ivy Tech Community College

Trang Thi Vu, The University of Findlay

Tyler Philbin, Community College of Rhode Island

William Carter, The University of Findlay

# About the Authors

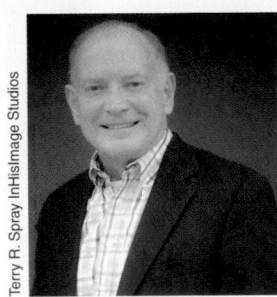

Terry R. Spray InHisImage Studios

## Carl S. Warren

Dr. Carl S. Warren is Professor Emeritus of Accounting at the University of Georgia, Athens. Dr. Warren has taught classes at the University of Georgia, University of Iowa, Michigan State University, and University of Chicago. Professor Warren focused his teaching efforts on principles of accounting and auditing. He received his Ph.D. from Michigan State University and his B.B.A. and M.A. from the University of Iowa. During his career, Dr. Warren published numerous articles in professional journals, including *The Accounting Review, Journal of Accounting Research, Journal of Accountancy, The CPA Journal,* and *Auditing: A Journal of Practice & Theory.* Dr. Warren has served on numerous committees of the American Accounting Association, the American Institute of Certified Public Accountants, and the Institute of Internal Auditors. He has also consulted with numerous companies and public accounting firms. Professor Warren is an avid handball player and has played in the World Handball Championships in Portland, Oregon, and Dublin, Ireland. He enjoys backpacking and recently took an eleven-day, ten-night trip in the Thorofare area of Yellowstone National Park. He has rafted the Grand Canyon and backpacked rim-to-rim. Professor Warren also enjoys fly fishing, skiing, golfing, and motorcycling.

Charles J. Garvey III / Garvey Photography

## James M. Reeve

Dr. James M. Reeve is Professor Emeritus of Accounting and Information Management at the University of Tennessee. Professor Reeve taught on the accounting faculty for 25 years, after graduating with his Ph.D. from Oklahoma State University. His teaching efforts focused on undergraduate accounting principles and graduate education in the Master of Accountancy and Senior Executive MBA programs. Beyond this, Professor Reeve is also very active in the Supply Chain Certification program, which is a major executive education and research effort of the College. His research interests are varied and include work in managerial accounting, supply chain management, lean manufacturing, and information management. He has published over 40 articles in academic and professional journals, including the *Journal of Cost Management, Journal of Management Accounting Research, Accounting Review, Management Accounting Quarterly, Supply Chain Management Review,* and *Accounting Horizons.* He has consulted or provided training around the world for a wide variety of organizations, including Boeing, Procter & Gamble, Norfolk Southern, Hershey Foods, Coca-Cola, and Sony. When not writing books, Professor Reeve plays golf and is involved in faith-based activities.

© Ken Bennett

## Jonathan Duchac

Dr. Jonathan Duchac is the Merrill Lynch and Co. Professor of Accounting and Director of International Programs at Wake Forest University. He holds a joint appointment at the Vienna University of Business and Economics in Vienna, Austria. Dr. Duchac currently teaches introductory and advanced courses in financial accounting and has received a number of awards during his career, including the Wake Forest University Outstanding Graduate Professor Award, the T.B. Rose Award for Instructional Innovation, and the University of Georgia Outstanding Teaching Assistant Award. In addition to his teaching responsibilities, Dr. Duchac has served as Accounting Advisor to Merrill Lynch Equity Research, where he worked with research analysts in reviewing and evaluating the financial reporting practices of public companies. He has testified before the U.S. House of Representatives, the Financial Accounting Standards Board, and the Securities and Exchange Commission and has worked with a number of major public companies on financial reporting and accounting policy issues. In addition to his professional interests, Dr. Duchac has served on the Board of Directors of The Special Children's School of Winston-Salem, a private, nonprofit developmental day school serving children with special needs. Dr. Duchac is an avid long-distance runner, mountain biker, and snow skier. His recent events include the Grandfather Mountain Marathon, the Black Mountain Marathon, the Shut-In Ridge Trail run, and NO MAAM (Nocturnal Overnight Mountain Bike Assault on Mount Mitchell).

# Brief Contents

# Contents

## Chapter 11 Current Liabilities and Payroll 503

## Chapter 12 Accounting for Partnerships and Limited Liability Companies 551

## Chapter 13 Corporations: Organization, Stock Transactions, and Dividends 595

# What Successful Students Are Saying

In a recent survey of students who took financial and managerial accounting courses, students stated that, in order to be successful in these courses, students should (in order of importance):

- Complete assigned homework
- Attend class and pay attention during the lecture
- Study
- Ask for help or get a tutor
- Complete ungraded practice assignments or review exercises

☐ Did you read the chapter from the required textbook prior to attending class?
☐ Did you attend class?
☐ Did you take notes during class?
☐ Did you ask questions of the professor either during or after class when you did not understand a concept being taught?
☐ Did you complete all assigned homework?
☐ Did you complete ungraded practice assignments or review exercises to better learn and understand accounting concepts?
☐ Did you obtain an explanation from the professor for incorrect answers?
☐ Did you utilize additional resources provided such as demonstration videos & tutorials?

Successful students spent an average of 4 hours per week outside of class time studying, including completing assigned homework.

*You just need to put in the effort. If you work through the homework problems and show up to class, you will do well.*

*—Brandy J. Gibson, Business Administration Major Ivy Tech Community College*

*Do not put off homework – it is more important than you know – and when in need – ASK FOR HELP!!*

*—Sally Cross, Accounting Major Ivy Tech Community College*

*You need to attend every class and pay attention. Take good notes and do all the homework.*

*—Melinda Lallier, Accounting Major Community College of Rhode Island*

*Come to class every day – if you miss a class, you miss a lot of notes and example problems. Homework is vital and so is studying for tests – you need to learn the different formulas and equations.*

*—Shannon Green, General Business Major Community College of Rhode Island*

**Anyone can succeed at learning & understanding accounting concepts!**
**How? Preparation, time management, & practice!**

# Introduction to Accounting and Business

## Twitter

When two teams pair up for a game of football, there is often a lot of noise. The band plays, the fans cheer, and fireworks light up the scoreboard. Obviously, the fans are committed and care about the outcome of the game. Just like fans at a football game, the owners of a business want their business to "win" against their competitors in the marketplace. While having your football team win can be a source of pride, winning in the marketplace goes beyond pride and has many tangible benefits. Companies that are winners are better able to serve customers, provide good jobs for employees, and make money for their owners.

**Twitter** is one of the most visible companies on the Internet. It provides a real-time information network where members can post messages, called Tweets, of up to 140 characters for free. Millions post Tweets every day throughout the world.

Do you think Twitter is a successful company? Does it make money? How would you know? Accounting helps to answer these questions.

This textbook introduces you to accounting, the language of business. Chapter 1 begins by discussing what a business is, how it operates, and the role that accounting plays.

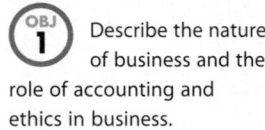

**OBJ 1** Describe the nature of business and the role of accounting and ethics in business.

# Nature of Business and Accounting

A **business**[1] is an organization in which basic resources (inputs), such as materials and labor, are assembled and processed to provide goods or services (outputs) to customers. Businesses come in all sizes, from a local coffee house to Starbucks, which sells over $10 billion of coffee and related products each year.

The objective of most businesses is to earn a **profit**. Profit is the difference between the amounts received from customers for goods or services and the amounts paid for the inputs used to provide the goods or services. This text focuses on businesses operating to earn a profit. However, many of the same concepts and principles also apply to not-for-profit organizations such as hospitals, churches, and government agencies.

## Types of Businesses

Three types of businesses operating for profit include service, merchandising, and manufacturing businesses. Some examples of each type of business follow:

- **Service businesses** provide services rather than products to customers.
    Delta Air Lines (transportation services)
    The Walt Disney Company (entertainment services)

- **Merchandising businesses** sell products they purchase from other businesses to customers.
    Walmart (general merchandise)
    Amazon.com (Internet books, music, videos)

[1] A complete glossary of terms appears at the end of the text.

- **Manufacturing businesses** change basic inputs into products that are sold to customers.

  Ford Motor Co. (cars, trucks, vans)

  Dell Inc. (personal computers)

## Role of Accounting in Business

The role of accounting in business is to provide information for managers to use in operating the business. In addition, accounting provides information to other users in assessing the economic performance and condition of the business.

Thus, **accounting** can be defined as an information system that provides reports to users about the economic activities and condition of a business. You could think of accounting as the "language of business." This is because accounting is the means by which businesses' financial information is communicated to users.

The process by which accounting provides information to users is as follows:

1. Identify users.
2. Assess users' information needs.
3. Design the accounting information system to meet users' needs.
4. Record economic data about business activities and events.
5. Prepare accounting reports for users.

As illustrated in Exhibit 1, users of accounting information can be divided into two groups: internal users and external users.

**Note:**
Accounting is an information system that provides reports to users about the economic activities and condition of a business.

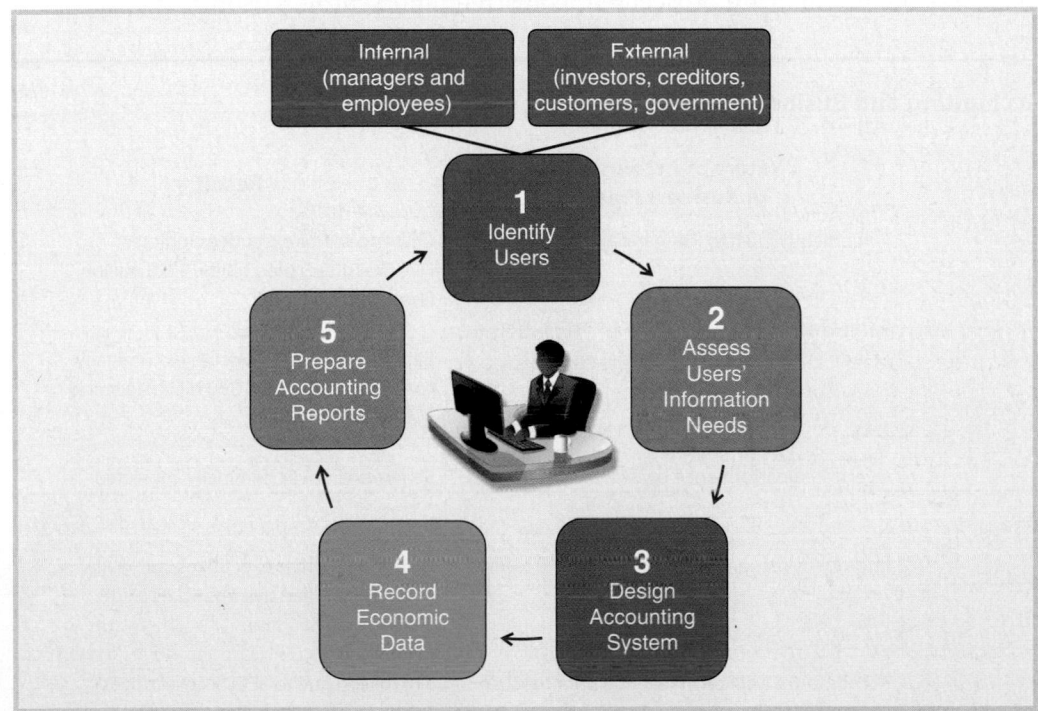

EXHIBIT 1

**Accounting as an Information System**

**Managerial Accounting**  Internal users of accounting information include managers and employees. These users are directly involved in managing and operating the business. The area of accounting that provides internal users with information is called **managerial accounting**, or **management accounting**.

The objective of managerial accounting is to provide relevant and timely information for managers' and employees' decision-making needs. Oftentimes, such information is sensitive and is not distributed outside the business. Examples of sensitive information might include information about customers, prices, and plans to expand the business. Managerial accountants employed by a business are employed in **private accounting**.

**Financial Accounting** External users of accounting information include investors, creditors, customers, and the government. These users are not directly involved in managing and operating the business. The area of accounting that provides external users with information is called **financial accounting**.

The objective of financial accounting is to provide relevant and timely information for the decision-making needs of users outside of the business. For example, financial reports on the operations and condition of the business are useful for banks and other creditors in deciding whether to lend money to the business. **General-purpose financial statements** are one type of financial accounting report that is distributed to external users. The term *general-purpose* refers to the wide range of decision-making needs that these reports are designed to serve. Later in this chapter, general-purpose financial statements are described and illustrated.

## Role of Ethics in Accounting and Business

The objective of accounting is to provide relevant, timely information for user decision making. Accountants must behave in an ethical manner so that the information they provide users will be trustworthy and, thus, useful for decision making. Managers and employees must also behave in an ethical manner in managing and operating a business. Otherwise, no one will be willing to invest in or loan money to the business.

**Ethics** are moral principles that guide the conduct of individuals. Unfortunately, business managers and accountants sometimes behave in an unethical manner. Many of the managers of the companies listed in Exhibit 2 engaged in accounting or business fraud. These ethical violations led to fines, firings, and lawsuits. In some cases, managers were criminally prosecuted, convicted, and sent to prison.

| EXHIBIT 2 | Accounting and Business Frauds |
| --- | --- |

| Company | Nature of Accounting or Business Fraud | Result |
| --- | --- | --- |
| Computer Associates International, Inc. | Fraudulently inflated its financial results. | CEO and senior executives indicted. Five executives pled guilty. $225 million fine. |
| Enron | Fraudulently inflated its financial results. | Bankrupcty. Senior executives criminally convicted. More than $60 billion in stock market losses. |
| HealthSouth | Overstated performance by $4 billion in false entries. | Senior executives criminally convicted. |
| Qwest Communications International, Inc. | Improperly recognized $3 billion in false receipts. | CEO and six other executives criminally convicted of "massive financial fraud." $250 million SEC fine. |
| Xerox Corporation | Recognized $3 billion in revenue prior to when it should have been recorded. | $10 million fine to SEC. Six executives forced to pay $22 million. |

What went wrong for the managers and companies listed in Exhibit 2? The answer normally involved one or both of the following two factors:

- *Failure of Individual Character.* Ethical managers and accountants are honest and fair. However, managers and accountants often face pressures from supervisors to meet company and investor expectations. In many of the cases in Exhibit 2, managers and accountants justified small ethical violations to avoid such pressures. However, these small violations became big violations as the company's financial problems became worse.

- *Culture of Greed and Ethical Indifference.* By their behavior and attitude, senior managers set the company culture. In most of the companies listed in Exhibit 2, the senior managers created a culture of greed and indifference to the truth.

As a result of the accounting and business frauds shown in Exhibit 2, Congress passed laws to monitor the behavior of accounting and business. For example, the **Sarbanes-Oxley Act (SOX)** was enacted. SOX established a new oversight body for the accounting profession called the **Public Company Accounting Oversight Board (PCAOB)**. In addition, SOX established standards for independence, corporate responsibility, and disclosure.

How does one behave ethically when faced with financial or other types of pressure? Guidelines for behaving ethically follow:[2]

1. Identify an ethical decision by using your personal ethical standards of honesty and fairness.
2. Identify the consequences of the decision and its effect on others.
3. Consider your obligations and responsibilities to those who will be affected by your decision.
4. Make a decision that is ethical and fair to those affected by it.

## Integrity, Objectivity, and Ethics in Business

### BERNIE MADOFF

In June 2009, Bernard L. "Bernie" Madoff was sentenced to 150 years in prison for defrauding thousands of investors in one of the biggest frauds in American history. Madoff's fraud started several decades earlier when he began a "Ponzi scheme" in his investment management firm, Bernard L. Madoff Investment Securities LLC.

In a Ponzi scheme, the investment manager uses funds received from new investors to pay a return to existing investors, rather than basing investment returns on the fund's actual performance. As long as the Investment manager is able to attract new investors, he or she will have new funds to pay existing investors and continue the fraud. While most Ponzi schemes collapse quickly when the investment manager runs out of new investors, Madoff's reputation, popularity, and personal contacts provided a steady stream of investors, which allowed the fraud to survive for decades.

## Opportunities for Accountants

Numerous career opportunities are available for students majoring in accounting. Currently, the demand for accountants exceeds the number of new graduates entering the job market. This is partly due to the increased regulation of business caused by the accounting and business frauds shown in Exhibit 2. Also, more and more businesses have come to recognize the importance and value of accounting information.

As indicated earlier, accountants employed by a business are employed in private accounting. Private accountants have a variety of possible career options within a company. Some of these career options are shown in Exhibit 3 along with their starting salaries. Accountants who provide audit services, called *auditors*, verify the accuracy of financial records, accounts, and systems. As shown in Exhibit 3, several private accounting careers have certification options.

Accountants and their staff who provide services on a fee basis are said to be employed in **public accounting**. In public accounting, an accountant may practice as an individual or as a member of a public accounting firm. Public accountants who have met a state's education, experience, and examination requirements may become **Certified Public Accountants (CPAs)**. CPAs typically perform general accounting,

| EXHIBIT 3 | Accounting Career Paths and Salaries | | | |

| Accounting Career Track | Description | Career Options | Annual Starting Salaries* | Certification |
| --- | --- | --- | --- | --- |
| Private Accounting | Accountants employed by companies, government, and not-for-profit entities. | Bookkeeper | $39,750 | |
| | | Payroll clerk | $38,250 | Certified Payroll Professional (CPP) |
| | | General accountant | $46,375 | |
| | | Budget analyst | $49,375 | |
| | | Cost accountant | $48,375 | Certified Management Accountant (CMA) |
| | | Internal auditor | $53,875 | Certified Internal Auditor (CIA) |
| | | Information technology auditor | $62,875 | Certified Information Systems Auditor (CISA) |
| Public Accounting | Accountants employed individually or within a public accounting firm in tax or audit services. | Local firms | $48,500 | Certified Public Accountant (CPA) |
| | | National firms | $58,625 | Certified Public Accountant (CPA) |

*Mean salaries of a reported range. Private accounting salaries are reported for large companies. Salaries may vary by region.
Source: Robert Half *2013 U.S. Salary Guide (Finance and Accounting)*, Robert Half International, Inc. (http://www.rhi.com/salaryguides)

audit, or tax services. As can be seen in Exhibit 3, CPAs have slightly better starting salaries than private accountants. Career statistics indicate, however, that these salary differences tend to disappear over time.

Because all functions within a business use accounting information, experience in private or public accounting provides a solid foundation for a career. Many positions in industry and in government agencies are held by individuals with accounting backgrounds.

# Business  Connection

## PATHWAYS COMMISSION

The Pathway Commission recently issued its study titled *Charting a National Strategy for the Next Generation of Accountants*. The Commission was made up of diverse members and was jointly sponsored by the American Institute of Certified Public Accountants (AICPA) and the American Accounting Association (AAA). The Commission emphasized the importance of accounting for a prosperous society and good decision making. The Commission also emphasized that accountants must be critical thinkers who are comfortable addressing the shades of grey required by accounting judgments.

Sources: *Charting a National Strategy for the Next Generation of Accountants*, The Pathways Commission, July 2012.

# Generally Accepted Accounting Principles

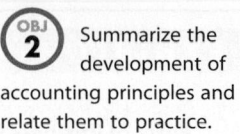

Summarize the development of accounting principles and relate them to practice.

If a company's management could record and report financial data as it saw fit, comparisons among companies would be difficult, if not impossible. Thus, financial accountants follow **generally accepted accounting principles (GAAP)** in preparing reports. These reports allow investors and other users to compare one company to another.

Accounting principles and concepts develop from research, accepted accounting practices, and pronouncements of regulators. Within the United States, the **Financial Accounting Standards Board (FASB)** has the primary responsibility for developing accounting principles. The FASB publishes *Statements of Financial Accounting Standards* as well as *Interpretations* of these Standards. In addition, the **Securities and Exchange Commission (SEC),** an agency of the U.S. government, has authority over the accounting and financial disclosures for companies whose shares of ownership (stock) are traded and sold to the public. The SEC normally accepts the accounting principles set forth by the FASB. However, the SEC may issue *Staff Accounting Bulletins* on accounting matters that may not have been addressed by the FASB.

See Appendix D for more information.

Many countries outside the United States use generally accepted accounting principles adopted by the **International Accounting Standards Board (IASB)**. The IASB issues *International Financial Reporting Standards (IFRSs)*. Differences currently exist between FASB and IASB accounting principles. However, the FASB and IASB are working together to reduce and eliminate these differences into a single set of accounting principles. Such a set of worldwide accounting principles would help facilitate investment and business in an increasingly global economy.

In this chapter and text, accounting principles and concepts are emphasized. It is through this emphasis on the "why" as well as the "how" that you will gain an understanding of accounting.

## International  Connection

**IFRS INTERNATIONAL FINANCIAL REPORTING STANDARDS (IFRS)**

IFRS are considered to be more "principles-based" than U.S. GAAP, which is considered to be more "rules-based." For example, U.S. GAAP consists of approximately 17,000 pages, which include numerous industry-specific accounting rules. In contrast, IFRS allow more judgment in deciding how business transactions are recorded. Many believe that the strong regulatory and litigation environment in the United States is the cause for the more rules-based GAAP approach. Regardless, IFRS and GAAP share many common principles.*

*Differences between U.S. GAAP and IFRS are further discussed and illustrated in Appendix D.

## Business Entity Concept

The **business entity concept** limits the economic data in an accounting system to data related directly to the activities of the business. In other words, the business is viewed as an entity separate from its owners, creditors, or other businesses. For example, the accountant for a business with one owner would record the activities of the business only and would not record the personal activities, property, or debts of the owner.

A business entity may take the form of a proprietorship, partnership, corporation, or limited liability company (LLC). Each of these forms and their major characteristics are listed in Exhibit 4.

**Note:**
Under the business entity concept, the activities of a business are recorded separately from the activities of its owners, creditors, or other businesses.

| EXHIBIT 4 | Forms of Business Entities |
|-----------|---------------------------|

| Form of Business Entity | Characteristics | Examples |
|-------------------------|-----------------|----------|
| **Proprietorship** is owned by one individual. | • 70% of business entities in the United States.<br>• Easy and inexpensive to organize.<br>• Resources are limited to those of the owner.<br>• Used by small businesses. | • A & B Painting |
| **Partnership** is owned by two or more individuals. | • 10% of business organizations in the United States (combined with limited liability companies).<br>• Combines the skills and resources of more than one person. | • Jones & Smith, Architects |
| **Corporation** is organized under state or federal statutes as a separate legal taxable entity. | • Generates 90% of business revenues.<br>• 20% of the business organizations in the United States.<br>• Ownership is divided into shares called stock.<br>• Can obtain large amounts of resources by issuing stock.<br>• Used by large businesses. | • **Apple**<br>• **Google**<br>• **Ford Motor Company** |
| **Limited liability company (LLC)** combines the attributes of a partnership and a corporation. | • 10% of business organizations in the United States (combined with partnerships).<br>• Often used as an alternative to a partnership.<br>• Has tax and legal liability advantages for owners. | • Mosel & Farmer, CPAs, LLC |

The three types of businesses discussed earlier—service, merchandising, and manufacturing—may be organized as proprietorships, partnerships, corporations, or limited liability companies. Because of the large amount of resources required to operate a manufacturing business, most manufacturers such as Ford Motor Company are corporations. Most large retailers such as Walmart and Home Depot are also corporations.

## Cost Concept

Under the **cost concept**, amounts are initially recorded in the accounting records at their cost or purchase price. To illustrate, assume that Aaron Publishers purchased the following building on February 20, 2014, for $150,000:

| | |
|---|---:|
| Price listed by seller on January 1, 2014 | $160,000 |
| Aaron Publishers' initial offer to buy on January 31, 2014 | 140,000 |
| Purchase price on February 20, 2014 | 150,000 |
| Estimated selling price on December 31, 2016 | 220,000 |
| Assessed value for property taxes, December 31, 2016 | 190,000 |

Under the cost concept, Aaron Publishers records the purchase of the building on February 20, 2014, at the purchase price of $150,000. The other amounts listed have no effect on the accounting records.

The fact that the building has an estimated selling price of $220,000 on December 31, 2016, indicates that the building has increased in value. However, to use the $220,000 in the accounting records would be to record an illusory or unrealized profit. If Aaron Publishers sells the building on January 9, 2018, for $240,000, a profit of $90,000 ($240,000 − $150,000) is then realized and recorded. The new owner would record $240,000 as its cost of the building.

The cost concept also involves the objectivity and unit of measure concepts. The **objectivity concept** requires that the amounts recorded in the accounting records be based on objective evidence. In exchanges between a buyer and a seller, both try to get the best price. Only the final agreed-upon amount is objective enough to be recorded in the accounting records. If amounts in the accounting records were constantly being revised upward or downward based on offers, appraisals, and opinions, accounting reports could become unstable and unreliable.

The **unit of measure concept** requires that economic data be recorded in dollars. Money is a common unit of measurement for reporting financial data and reports.

---

### Example Exercise 1-1    Cost Concept       OBJ 2

On August 25, Gallatin Repair Service extended an offer of $125,000 for land that had been priced for sale at $150,000. On September 3, Gallatin Repair Service accepted the seller's counteroffer of $137,000. On October 20, the land was assessed at a value of $98,000 for property tax purposes. On December 4, Gallatin Repair Service was offered $160,000 for the land by a national retail chain. At what value should the land be recorded in Gallatin Repair Service's records?

### Follow My Example 1-1

$137,000. Under the cost concept, the land should be recorded at the cost to Gallatin Repair Service.

Practice Exercises: PE 1-1A, PE 1-1B

---

## The Accounting Equation

OBJ 3   State the accounting equation and define each element of the equation.

The resources owned by a business are its **assets**. Examples of assets include cash, land, buildings, and equipment. The rights or claims to the assets are divided into two types: (1) the rights of creditors and (2) the rights of owners. The rights of creditors are the debts of the business and are called **liabilities**. The rights of the owners are called **owner's equity**. The following equation shows the relationship among assets, liabilities, and owner's equity:

**Assets = Liabilities + Owner's Equity**

This equation is called the **accounting equation**. Liabilities usually are shown before owner's equity in the accounting equation because creditors have first rights to the assets.

Given any two amounts, the accounting equation may be solved for the third unknown amount. To illustrate, if the assets owned by a business amount to $100,000 and the liabilities amount to $30,000, the owner's equity is equal to $70,000, computed as follows:

| Assets | − | Liabilities | = | Owner's Equity |
|--------|---|-------------|---|----------------|
| $100,000 | − | $30,000 | = | $70,000 |

---

## Business  Connection

### THE ACCOUNTING EQUATION

The accounting equation serves as the basic foundation for the accounting systems of all companies. From the smallest business, such as the local convenience store, to the largest business, such as The Coca-Cola Company, companies use the accounting equation. Some examples taken from recent financial reports of well-known companies follow:

| Company | Assets* | = | Liabilities | + | Owner's Equity |
|---------|---------|---|-------------|---|----------------|
| The Coca-Cola Company | $79,974 | = | $48,339 | + | $31,635 |
| DuPont | $49,736 | = | $39,648 | + | $10,088 |
| eBay | $37,074 | = | $16,209 | + | $20,865 |
| Google | $93,798 | = | $22,083 | + | $71,715 |
| McDonald's | $32,990 | = | $18,600 | + | $14,390 |
| Microsoft Corporation | $121,271 | − | $54,908 | + | $66,363 |
| Southwest Airlines | $18,596 | − | $11,604 | + | $6,992 |
| Walmart | $193,406 | = | $122,091 | + | $71,315 |

*Amounts are shown in millions of dollars.

**Example Exercise 1-2  Accounting Equation**

John Joos is the owner and operator of You're A Star, a motivational consulting business. At the end of its accounting period, December 31, 2015, You're A Star has assets of $800,000 and liabilities of $350,000. Using the accounting equation, determine the following amounts:

a. Owner's equity as of December 31, 2015.

b. Owner's equity as of December 31, 2016, assuming that assets increased by $130,000 and liabilities decreased by $25,000 during 2016.

**Follow My Example 1-2**

a.       Assets = Liabilities + Owner's Equity

      $800,000 = $350,000 + Owner's Equity

Owner's Equity = $450,000

b. First, determine the change in owner's equity during 2016 as follows:

       Assets = Liabilities + Owner's Equity

      $130,000 = −$25,000 + Owner's Equity

Owner's Equity = $155,000

Next, add the change in owner's equity during 2016 to the owner's equity on December 31, 2015 to arrive at owner's equity on December 31, 2016, as follows:

Owner's Equity on December 31, 2016 = $450,000 + $155,000 = $605,000

Practice Exercises: PE 1-2A, PE 1-2B

---

 Describe and illustrate how business transactions can be recorded in terms of the resulting change in the elements of the accounting equation.

**Note:**
**All business transactions can be stated in terms of changes in the elements of the accounting equation.**

# Business Transactions and the Accounting Equation

Paying a monthly bill, such as a telephone bill of $168, affects a business's financial condition because it now has less cash on hand. Such an economic event or condition that directly changes an entity's financial condition or its results of operations is a **business transaction**. For example, purchasing land for $50,000 is a business transaction. In contrast, a change in a business's credit rating does not directly affect cash or any other asset, liability, or owner's equity amount.

All business transactions can be stated in terms of changes in the elements of the accounting equation. How business transactions affect the accounting equation can be illustrated by using some typical transactions. As a basis for illustration, a business organized by Chris Clark is used.

Assume that on November 1, 2015, Chris Clark begins a business that will be known as **NetSolutions**. The first phase of Chris's business plan is to operate NetSolutions as a service business assisting individuals and small businesses in developing Web pages and installing computer software. Chris expects this initial phase of the business to last one to two years. During this period, Chris plans on gathering information on the software and hardware needs of customers. During the second phase of the business plan, Chris plans to expand NetSolutions into a personalized retailer of software and hardware for individuals and small businesses.

Each transaction during NetSolutions' first month of operations is described in the following paragraphs. The effect of each transaction on the accounting equation is then shown.

---

**Transaction A**  *Nov. 1, 2015  Chris Clark deposited $25,000 in a bank account in the name of NetSolutions.*

This transaction increases the asset cash (on the left side of the equation) by $25,000. To balance the equation, the owner's equity (on the right side of the equation) increases by the same amount. The equity of the owner is identified using the owner's name and "Capital," such as "Chris Clark, Capital."

The effect of this transaction on NetSolutions' accounting equation is as follows:

| Assets | = | Owner's Equity |
|---|---|---|
| Cash | = | Chris Clark, Capital |
| a. 25,000 | | 25,000 |

Since Chris Clark is the sole owner, NetSolutions is a proprietorship. Also, the preceding accounting equation is only for the business, NetSolutions. Under the business entity concept, Chris's personal assets, such as a home or personal bank account, and personal liabilities are excluded from the equation.

---

*Nov. 5, 2015  NetSolutions paid $20,000 for the purchase of land as a future building site.*            ***Transaction B***

The land is located in a business park with access to transportation facilities. Chris Clark plans to rent office space and equipment during the first phase of the business plan. During the second phase, Chris plans to build an office and a warehouse on the land.

The purchase of the land changes the makeup of the assets, but it does not change the total assets. The items in the equation prior to this transaction and the effect of the transaction follow. The new amounts are called *balances*.

| Assets | | = | Owner's Equity |
|---|---|---|---|
| Cash + | Land | = | Chris Clark, Capital |
| Bal. 25,000 | | | 25,000 |
| b. −20,000 | +20,000 | | |
| Bal. 5,000 | 20,000 | | 25,000 |

---

*Nov. 10, 2015   NetSolutions purchased supplies for $1,350 and agreed to pay the supplier in the near future.*            ***Transaction C***

You have probably used a credit card to buy clothing or other merchandise. In this type of transaction, you received clothing for a promise to pay your credit card bill in the future. That is, you received an asset and incurred a liability to pay a future bill. NetSolutions entered into a similar transaction by purchasing supplies for $1,350 and agreeing to pay the supplier in the near future. This type of transaction is called a purchase *on account* and is often described as follows: *Purchased supplies on account, $1,350.*

The liability created by a purchase on account is called an **account payable**. Items such as supplies that will be used in the business in the future are called **prepaid expenses**, which are assets. Thus, the effect of this transaction is to increase assets (Supplies) and liabilities (Accounts Payable) by $1,350, as follows:

| Assets | | | = | Liabilities + Owner's Equity | |
|---|---|---|---|---|---|
| | | | | Accounts + | Chris Clark, |
| Cash + | Supplies + | Land | = | Payable | Capital |
| Bal. 5,000 | | 20,000 | | | 25,000 |
| c. | +1,350 | | | +1,350 | |
| Bal. 5,000 | 1,350 | 20,000 | | 1,350 | 25,000 |

---

*Nov. 18, 2015   NetSolutions received cash of $7,500 for providing services to customers.*            ***Transaction D***

You may have earned money by painting houses or mowing lawns. If so, you received money for rendering services to a customer. Likewise, a business earns money by selling goods or services to its customers. This amount is called **revenue**.

During its first month of operations, NetSolutions received cash of $7,500 for providing services to customers. The receipt of cash increases NetSolutions' assets and also increases Chris Clark's equity in the business. The revenues of $7,500 are recorded in a Fees Earned column to the right of Chris Clark, Capital. The effect of this transaction is to increase Cash and Fees Earned by $7,500, as follows:

| | Assets | | | = | Liabilities + | Owner's Equity | |
|---|---|---|---|---|---|---|---|
| | | | | | Accounts | Chris Clark, | Fees |
| | Cash | + Supplies + | Land | | Payable + | Capital | + Earned |
| Bal. | 5,000 | 1,350 | 20,000 | = | 1,350 | 25,000 | |
| d. | +7,500 | | | | | | +7,500 |
| Bal. | 12,500 | 1,350 | 20,000 | | 1,350 | 25,000 | 7,500 |

Different terms are used for the various types of revenues. As illustrated for NetSolutions, revenue from providing services is recorded as **fees earned**. Revenue from the sale of merchandise is recorded as **sales**. Other examples of revenue include rent, which is recorded as **rent revenue**, and interest, which is recorded as **interest revenue**.

Instead of receiving cash at the time services are provided or goods are sold, a business may accept payment at a later date. Such revenues are described as *fees earned on account* or *sales on account*. For example, if NetSolutions had provided services on account instead of for cash, transaction (d) would have been described as follows: *Fees earned on account, $7,500.*

In such cases, the firm has an **account receivable**, which is a claim against the customer. An account receivable is an asset, and the revenue is earned and recorded as if cash had been received. When customers pay their accounts, Cash increases, and Accounts Receivable decreases.

---

**Transaction E**    *Nov. 30, 2015*    *NetSolutions paid the following expenses during the month: wages, $2,125; rent, $800; utilities, $450; and miscellaneous, $275.*

During the month, NetSolutions spent cash or used up other assets in earning revenue. Assets used in this process of earning revenue are called **expenses**. Expenses include supplies used and payments for employee wages, utilities, and other services.

NetSolutions paid the following expenses during the month: wages, $2,125; rent, $800; utilities, $450; and miscellaneous, $275. Miscellaneous expenses include small amounts paid for such items as postage, coffee, and newspapers. The effect of expenses is the opposite of revenues in that expenses reduce assets and owner's equity. Like fees earned, the expenses are recorded in columns to the right of Chris Clark, Capital. However, since expenses reduce owner's equity, the expenses are entered as negative amounts. The effect of this transaction is as follows:

| | Assets | | | = | Liabilities + | | Owner's Equity | | | | |
|---|---|---|---|---|---|---|---|---|---|---|---|
| | | | | | Accounts | Chris Clark, | Fees | Wages | Rent | Utilities | Misc. |
| | Cash | + Supplies + | Land | = | Payable + | Capital | + Earned − | Exp. − | Exp. − | Exp. − | Exp. |
| Bal. | 12,500 | 1,350 | 20,000 | | 1,350 | 25,000 | 7,500 | | | | |
| e. | −3,650 | | | | | | | −2,125 | −800 | −450 | −275 |
| Bal. | 8,850 | 1,350 | 20,000 | | 1,350 | 25,000 | 7,500 | −2,125 | −800 | −450 | −275 |

Businesses usually record each revenue and expense transaction as it occurs. However, to simplify, NetSolutions' revenues and expenses are summarized for the month in transactions (d) and (e).

---

**Transaction F**    *Nov. 30, 2015*    *NetSolutions paid creditors on account, $950.*

When you pay your monthly credit card bill, you decrease the cash and decrease the amount you owe to the credit card company. Likewise, when NetSolutions pays $950 to creditors during the month, it reduces assets and liabilities, as follows:

| | Assets | | = | Liabilities + | | | Owner's Equity | | | | |
|---|---|---|---|---|---|---|---|---|---|---|---|
| | | | | Accounts | Chris Clark, | Fees | Wages | Rent | Utilities | Misc. | |
| Cash | + Supplies + | Land | = | Payable + | Capital | + Earned − | Exp. − | Exp. − | Exp. − | Exp. | |
| Bal. 8,850 | 1,350 | 20,000 | | 1,350 | 25,000 | 7,500 | −2,125 | −800 | −450 | −275 | |
| f. −950 | | | | −950 | | | | | | | |
| Bal. 7,900 | 1,350 | 20,000 | | 400 | 25,000 | 7,500 | −2,125 | −800 | −450 | −275 | |

Paying an amount on account is different from paying an expense. The paying of an expense reduces owner's equity, as illustrated in transaction (e). Paying an amount on account reduces the amount owed on a liability.

*Nov. 30, 2015  Chris Clark determined that the cost of supplies on hand at the end of the month was $550.*  **Transaction G**

The cost of the supplies on hand (not yet used) at the end of the month is $550. Thus, $800 ($1,350 − $550) of supplies must have been used during the month. This decrease in supplies is recorded as an expense, as follows:

| | Assets | | = | Liabilities + | | | Owner's Equity | | | | |
|---|---|---|---|---|---|---|---|---|---|---|---|
| | | | | Accounts | Chris Clark, | Fees | Wages | Rent | Supplies | Utilities | Misc. |
| Cash | + Supplies + | Land | = | Payable + | Capital | + Earned − | Exp. − | Exp. − | Exp. − | Exp. − | Exp. |
| Bal. 7,900 | 1,350 | 20,000 | | 400 | 25,000 | 7,500 | −2,125 | −800 | | −450 | −275 |
| g. | −800 | | | | | | | | −800 | | |
| Bal. 7,900 | 550 | 20,000 | | 400 | 25,000 | 7,500 | −2,125 | −800 | −800 | −450 | −275 |

*Nov. 30, 2015  Chris Clark withdrew $2,000 from NetSolutions for personal use.*  **Transaction H**

At the end of the month, Chris Clark withdrew $2,000 in cash from the business for personal use. This transaction is the opposite of an investment in the business by the owner. Withdrawals by the owner should not be confused with expenses. Withdrawals *do not* represent assets or services used in the process of earning revenues. Instead, withdrawals are a distribution of capital to the owner. Owner withdrawals are identified by the owner's name and *Drawing*. For example, Chris's withdrawal is identified as Chris Clark, Drawing. Like expenses, withdrawals are recorded in a column to the right of Chris Clark, Capital. The effect of the $2,000 withdrawal is as follows:

| | Assets | | = | Liabilities + | | | | Owner's Equity | | | | | |
|---|---|---|---|---|---|---|---|---|---|---|---|---|---|
| | | | | Accounts | Chris Clark, | Chris Clark, | Fees | Wages | Rent | Supplies | Utilities | Misc. | |
| Cash + | Supp. + | Land | = | Payable + | Capital − | Drawing + | Earned − | Exp. − | Exp. − | Exp. − | Exp. − | Exp. | |
| Bal. 7,900 | 550 | 20,000 | | 400 | 25,000 | | 7,500 | −2,125 | −800 | −800 | −450 | −275 | |
| h. −2,000 | | | | | | −2,000 | | | | | | | |
| Bal. 5,900 | 550 | 20,000 | | 400 | 25,000 | −2,000 | 7,500 | −2,125 | −800 | −800 | −450 | −275 | |

## Summary

The transactions of **NetSolutions** are summarized in Exhibit 5. Each transaction is identified by letter, and the balance of each accounting equation element is shown after every transaction.

You should note the following:

- The effect of every transaction *is an increase or a decrease in one or more of the accounting equation elements.*
- The two sides of the accounting equation are *always equal.*
- The owner's equity is *increased by amounts invested by the owner* and is *decreased by withdrawals by the owner.* In addition, the owner's equity is *increased by revenues* and is *decreased by expenses.*

**EXHIBIT 5**   Summary of Transaction for NetSolutions

| | **Assets** | | | = | **Liabilities +** | | **Owner's Equity** | | | | | | |
|---|---|---|---|---|---|---|---|---|---|---|---|---|---|
| | Cash | + Supp. + | Land | = | Accounts Payable + | Chris Clark, Capital + | Chris Clark, Drawing − | Fees Earned + | Wages Exp. − | Rent Exp. − | Supplies Exp. − | Utilities Exp. − | Misc. Exp. |
| a. | +25,000 | | | | | +25,000 | | | | | | | |
| b. | −20,000 | | +20,000 | | | | | | | | | | |
| Bal. | 5,000 | | 20,000 | | | 25,000 | | | | | | | |
| c. | | +1,350 | | | +1,350 | | | | | | | | |
| Bal. | 5,000 | +1,350 | 20,000 | | +1,350 | 25,000 | | | | | | | |
| d. | +7,500 | | | | | | | +7,500 | | | | | |
| Bal. | 12,500 | 1,350 | 20,000 | | 1,350 | 25,000 | | 7,500 | | | | | |
| e. | −3,650 | | | | | | | | −2,125 | −800 | | −450 | −275 |
| Bal. | 8,850 | 1,350 | 20,000 | | 1,350 | 25,000 | | 7,500 | −2,125 | −800 | | −450 | −275 |
| f. | −950 | | | | −950 | | | | | | | | |
| Bal. | 7,900 | 1,350 | 20,000 | | 400 | 25,000 | | 7,500 | −2,125 | −800 | | −450 | −275 |
| g. | | −800 | | | | | | | | | −800 | | |
| Bal. | 7,900 | 550 | 20,000 | | 400 | 25,000 | | 7,500 | −2,125 | −800 | −800 | −450 | −275 |
| h. | −2,000 | | | | | | −2,000 | | | | | | |
| Bal. | 5,900 | 550 | 20,000 | | 400 | 25,000 | −2,000 | 7,500 | −2,125 | −800 | −800 | −450 | −275 |

Dynamic Exhibit

The four types of transactions affecting owner's equity are illustrated in Exhibit 6.

**EXHIBIT 6**

**Types of Transactions Affecting Owner's Equity**

Dynamic Exhibit

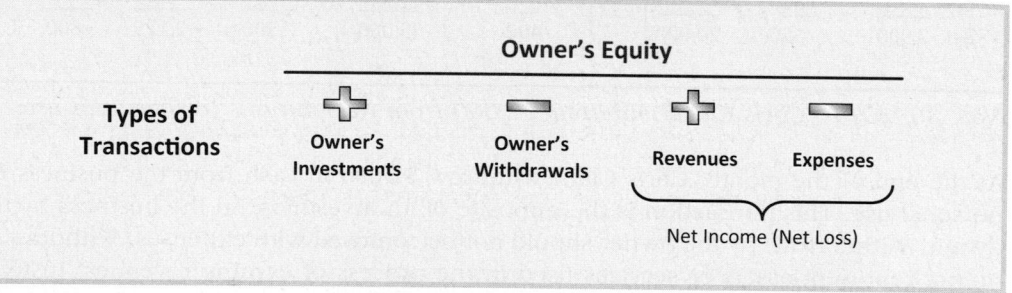

| | **Owner's Equity** | | | |
|---|---|---|---|---|
| Types of Transactions | Owner's Investments (+) | Owner's Withdrawals (−) | Revenues (+) | Expenses (−) |

Net Income (Net Loss)

## Example Exercise 1-3   Transactions   OBJ 4

Salvo Delivery Service is owned and operated by Joel Salvo. The following selected transactions were completed by Salvo Delivery Service during February:

1. Received cash from owner as additional investment, $35,000.
2. Paid creditors on account, $1,800.
3. Billed customers for delivery services on account, $11,250.
4. Received cash from customers on account, $6,740.
5. Paid cash to owner for personal use, $1,000.

Indicate the effect of each transaction on the accounting equation elements (Assets, Liabilities, Owner's Equity, Drawing, Revenue, and Expense). Also indicate the specific item within the accounting equation element that is affected. To illustrate, the answer to (1) follows:

(1) Asset (Cash) increases by $35,000; Owner's Equity (Joel Salvo, Capital) increases by $35,000.

### Follow My Example 1-3

(2) Asset (Cash) decreases by $1,800; Liability (Accounts Payable) decreases by $1,800.
(3) Asset (Accounts Receivable) increases by $11,250; Revenue (Delivery Service Fees) increases by $11,250.
(4) Asset (Cash) increases by $6,740; Asset (Accounts Receivable) decreases by $6,740.
(5) Asset (Cash) decreases by $1,000; Drawing (Joel Salvo, Drawing) increases by $1,000.

Practice Exercises: PE 1-3A, PE 1-3B

# Financial Statements

OBJ **5** Describe the financial statements of a proprietorship and explain how they interrelate.

After transactions have been recorded and summarized, reports are prepared for users. The accounting reports providing this information are called **financial statements**. The primary financial statements of a proprietorship are the income statement, the statement of owner's equity, the balance sheet, and the statement of cash flows. The order in which the financial statements are prepared and the nature of each statement are described in Exhibit 7.

**EXHIBIT 7**

**Financial Statements**

| Order Prepared | Financial Statement | Description of Statement |
|---|---|---|
| 1. | Income statement | A summary of the revenue and expenses *for a specific period of time*, such as a month or a year. |
| 2. | Statement of owner's equity | A summary of the changes in the owner's equity that have occurred *during a specific period of time*, such as a month or a year. |
| 3. | Balance sheet | A list of the assets, liabilities, and owner's equity *as of a specific date*, usually at the close of the last day of a month or a year. |
| 4. | Statement of cash flows | A summary of the cash receipts and cash payments for a *specific period of time*, such as a month or a year. |

The four financial statements and their interrelationships are illustrated in Exhibit 8, The data for the statements are taken from the summary of **NetSolutions'** transactions in Exhibit 5.

All financial statements are identified by the name of the business, the title of the statement, and the *date* or *period of time*. The data presented in the income statement, the statement of owner's equity, and the statement of cash flows are for a period of time. The data presented in the balance sheet are for a specific date.

## Income Statement

The income statement reports the revenues and expenses for a period of time, based on the **matching concept**. This concept is applied by *matching* the expenses incurred during a period with the revenue that those expenses generated. The excess of the revenue over the expenses is called **net income**, **net profit**, or **earnings**. If the expenses exceed the revenue, the excess is a **net loss**.

**Note:**
When revenues exceed expenses, it is referred to as *net income, net profit,* or *earnings.* When expenses exceed revenues, it is referred to as *net loss.*

The revenue and expenses for **NetSolutions** were shown in the equation as separate increases and decreases. Net income for a period increases the owner's equity (capital) for the period. A net loss decreases the owner's equity (capital) for the period.

The revenue, expenses, and the net income of $3,050 for NetSolutions are reported in the income statement in Exhibit 8. The order in which the expenses are listed in the income statement varies among businesses. Most businesses list expenses in order of size, beginning with the larger items. Miscellaneous expense is usually shown as the last item, regardless of the amount.

### Example Exercise 1-4  Income Statement

OBJ **5**

The revenues and expenses of Chickadee Travel Service for the year ended April 30, 2016, follow:

| | |
|---|---|
| Fees earned | $263,200 |
| Miscellaneous expense | 12,950 |
| Office expense | 63,000 |
| Wages expense | 131,700 |

Prepare an income statement for the year ended April 30, 2016.

*(Continued)*

**Follow My Example 1-4**

**Chickadee Travel Service**
**Income Statement**
**For the Year Ended April 30, 2016**

| | | |
|---|---:|---:|
| Fees earned................................ | | $263,200 |
| Expenses: | | |
|     Wages expense......................... | $131,700 | |
|     Office expense.......................... | 63,000 | |
|     Miscellaneous expense ................ | 12,950 | |
|       Total expenses ...................... | | 207,650 |
| Net income ............................... | | $ 55,550 |

Practice Exercises: PE 1-4A, PE 1-4B

## Statement of Owner's Equity

The statement of owner's equity reports the changes in the owner's equity for a period of time. It is prepared *after* the income statement because the net income or net loss for the period must be reported in this statement. Similarly, it is prepared *before* the balance sheet because the amount of owner's equity at the end of the period must be reported on the balance sheet. As a result, the statement of owner's equity is often viewed as the connecting link between the income statement and balance sheet.

Three types of transactions affected owner's equity of **NetSolutions** during November:

- the original investment of $25,000,
- the revenue and expenses that resulted in net income of $3,050 for the month, and
- a withdrawal of $2,000 by the owner.

The preceding information is summarized in the statement of owner's equity in Exhibit 8.

**Example Exercise 1-5** **Statement of Owner's Equity**  OBJ 5

Using the income statement for Chickadee Travel Service shown in Example Exercise 1-4, prepare a statement of owner's equity for the year ended April 30, 2016. Adam Cellini, the owner, invested an additional $50,000 in the business and withdrew cash of $30,000 for personal use during the year. The capital of Adam Cellini was $80,000 on May 1, 2015.

**Follow My Example 1-5**

**Chickadee Travel Service**
**Statement of Owner's Equity**
**For the Year Ended April 30, 2016**

| | | | |
|---|---:|---:|---:|
| Adam Cellini, capital, May 1, 2015 ....................................... | | | $ 80,000 |
| Additional investment by owner during year ......................... | | $ 50,000 | |
| Net income for the year .............................................. | | 55,550 | |
| | | $105,550 | |
| Less withdrawals .................................................... | | 30,000 | |
| Increase in owner's equity........................................... | | | 75,550 |
| Adam Cellini, capital, April 30, 2016.................................. | | | $155,550 |

Practice Exercises: PE 1-5A, PE 1-5B

## Balance Sheet

The balance sheet in Exhibit 8 reports the amounts of **NetSolutions'** assets, liabilities, and owner's equity as of November 30, 2015. The asset and liability amounts are taken from the last line of the summary of transactions in Exhibit 5. Chris Clark, Capital

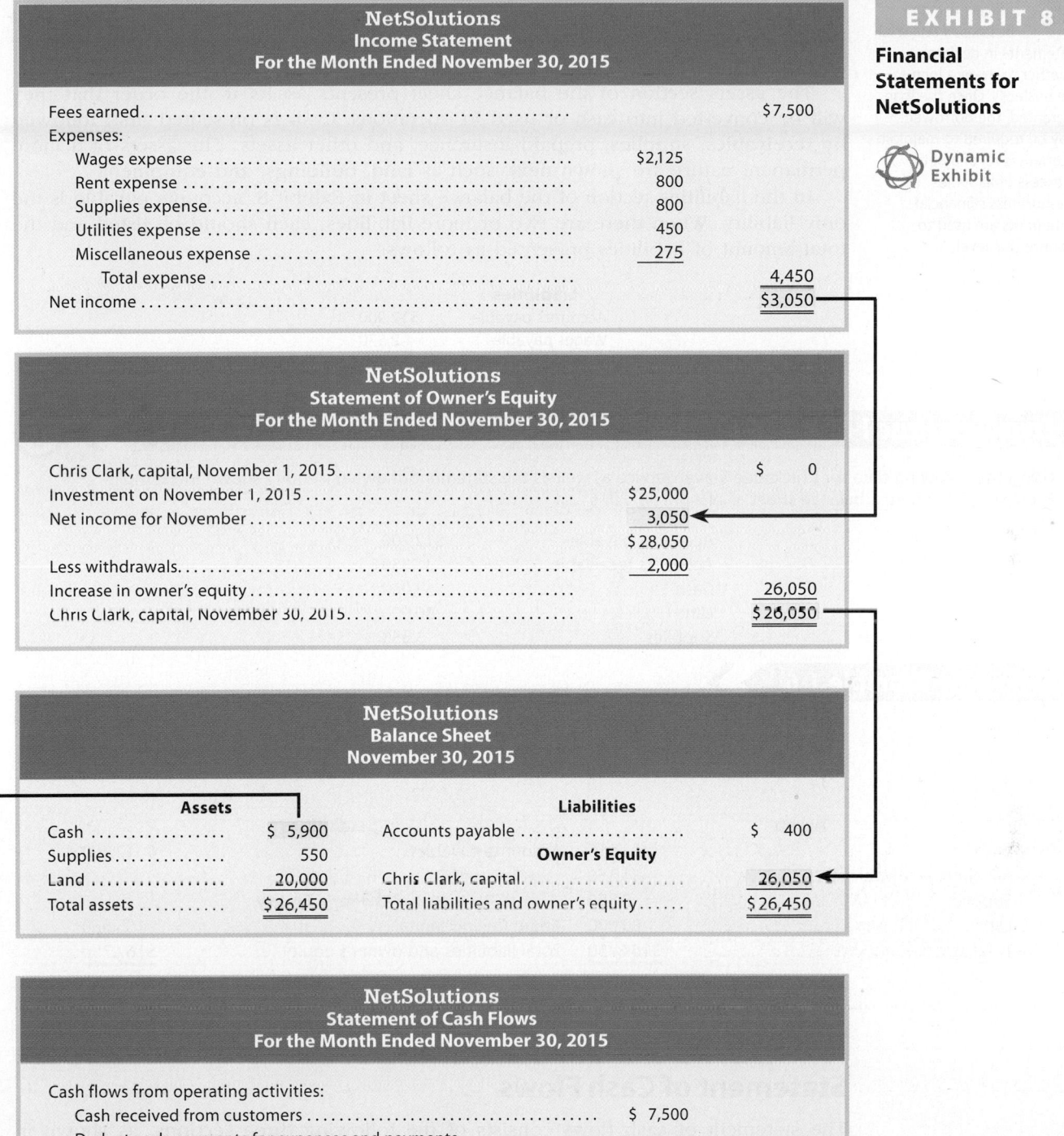

**EXHIBIT 8**

**Financial Statements for NetSolutions**

Dynamic Exhibit

**NetSolutions**
**Income Statement**
**For the Month Ended November 30, 2015**

| | | |
|---|---:|---:|
| Fees earned............................................... | | $7,500 |
| Expenses: | | |
| Wages expense ..................................... | $2,125 | |
| Rent expense ....................................... | 800 | |
| Supplies expense................................... | 800 | |
| Utilities expense ................................... | 450 | |
| Miscellaneous expense ............................ | 275 | |
| Total expense .................................. | | 4,450 |
| Net income ............................................. | | $3,050 |

**NetSolutions**
**Statement of Owner's Equity**
**For the Month Ended November 30, 2015**

| | | |
|---|---:|---:|
| Chris Clark, capital, November 1, 2015............................. | | $      0 |
| Investment on November 1, 2015 ................................. | $25,000 | |
| Net income for November ......................................... | 3,050 | |
| | $28,050 | |
| Less withdrawals..................................................... | 2,000 | |
| Increase in owner's equity......................................... | | 26,050 |
| Chris Clark, capital, November 30, 2015............................ | | $26,050 |

**NetSolutions**
**Balance Sheet**
**November 30, 2015**

| Assets | | Liabilities | |
|---|---:|---|---:|
| Cash ................. | $  5,900 | Accounts payable ...................... | $    400 |
| Supplies.............. | 550 | **Owner's Equity** | |
| Land ................. | 20,000 | Chris Clark, capital..................... | 26,050 |
| Total assets ........... | $26,450 | Total liabilities and owner's equity...... | $26,450 |

**NetSolutions**
**Statement of Cash Flows**
**For the Month Ended November 30, 2015**

| | | |
|---|---:|---:|
| Cash flows from operating activities: | | |
| Cash received from customers ...................................... | $ 7,500 | |
| Deduct cash payments for expenses and payments | | |
| to creditors ................................................. | (4,600) | |
| Net cash flow from operating activities ........................... | | $ 2,900 |
| Cash flows used for investing activities: | | |
| Cash payments for purchase of land................................ | | (20,000) |
| Cash flows from financing activities: | | |
| Cash received as owner's investment.............................. | $25,000 | |
| Deduct cash withdrawal by owner ................................ | (2,000) | |
| Net cash flows from financing activities ............................ | | 23,000 |
| Net increase in cash and November 30, 2015, cash balance ............ | | $ 5,900 |

Bank loan officers use a business's financial statements in deciding whether to grant a loan to the business. Once the loan is granted, the borrower may be required to maintain a certain level of assets in excess of liabilities. The business's financial statements are used to monitor this level.

as of November 30, 2015, is taken from the statement of owner's equity. The form of balance sheet shown in Exhibit 8 is called the **account form**. This is because it resembles the basic format of the accounting equation, with assets on the left side and the liabilities and owner's equity sections on the right side.[3]

The assets section of the balance sheet presents assets in the order that they will be converted into cash or used in operations. Cash is presented first, followed by receivables, supplies, prepaid insurance, and other assets. The assets of a more permanent nature are shown next, such as land, buildings, and equipment.

In the liabilities section of the balance sheet in Exhibit 8, accounts payable is the only liability. When there are two or more liabilities, each should be listed and the total amount of liabilities presented as follows:

| Liabilities | | |
|---|---|---|
| Accounts payable | $12,900 | |
| Wages payable | 2,570 | |
| Total liabilities | | $15,470 |

## Example Exercise 1-6 Balance Sheet

OBJ 5

Using the following data for Chickadee Travel Service as well as the statement of owner's equity shown in Example Exercise 1-5, prepare a balance sheet as of April 30, 2016.

| | |
|---|---|
| Accounts payable | $12,200 |
| Accounts receivable | 31,350 |
| Cash | 53,050 |
| Land | 80,000 |
| Supplies | 3,350 |

### Follow My Example 1-6

**Chickadee Travel Service**
**Balance Sheet**
**April 30, 2016**

| Assets | | Liabilities | |
|---|---|---|---|
| Cash | $ 53,050 | Accounts payable | $ 12,200 |
| Accounts receivable | 31,350 | | |
| Supplies | 3,350 | **Owner's Equity** | |
| Land | 80,000 | Adam Cellini, capital | 155,550 |
| Total assets | $167,750 | Total liabilities and owner's equity | $167,750 |

Practice Exercises: PE 1-6A, PE 1-6B

## Statement of Cash Flows

The statement of cash flows consists of the following three sections, as shown in Exhibit 8:

1. operating activities
2. investing activities
3. financing activities

Each of these sections is briefly described in this section.

**Cash Flows from Operating Activities** This section reports a summary of cash receipts and cash payments from operations. The net cash flow from operating activities normally differs from the amount of net income for the period. In Exhibit 8, **Net-Solutions** reported net cash flows from operating activities of $2,900 and net income

[3] An alternative form of balance sheet, called the *report form,* is illustrated in Chapter 6. It presents the liabilities and owner's equity sections below the assets section.

of $3,050. This difference occurs because revenues and expenses may not be recorded at the same time that cash is received from customers or paid to creditors.

**Cash Flows from Investing Activities** This section reports the cash transactions for the acquisition and sale of relatively permanent assets. Exhibit 8 reports that **NetSolutions** paid $20,000 for the purchase of land during November.

**Cash Flows from Financing Activities** This section reports the cash transactions related to cash investments by the owner, borrowings, and withdrawals by the owner. Exhibit 8 shows that Chris Clark invested $25,000 in **NetSolutions** and withdrew $2,000 during November.

**Preparing NetSolutions' Statement of Cash Flows** Preparing the statement of cash flows requires that each of the November cash transactions for **NetSolutions** be classified as an operating, investing, or financing activity. Using the summary of transactions shown in Exhibit 5, the November cash transactions for NetSolutions are classified as follows:

| Transaction | Amount | Cash Flow Activity |
|---|---|---|
| a. | $25,000 | Financing (Investment by Chris Clark) |
| b. | −20,000 | Investing (Purchase of land) |
| d. | 7,500 | Operating (Fees earned) |
| e. | −3,650 | Operating (Payment of expenses) |
| f. | −950 | Operating (Payment of account payable) |
| h. | −2,000 | Financing (Withdrawal by Chris Clark) |

Transactions (c) and (g) are not listed since they did not involve a cash receipt or payment. In addition, the payment of accounts payable in transaction (f) is classified as an operating activity because the account payable arose from the purchase of supplies, which are used in operations. Using the preceding classifications of November cash transactions, the statement of cash flows is prepared as shown in Exhibit 8.[4]

The ending cash balance shown on the statement of cash flows is also reported on the balance sheet as of the end of the period. To illustrate, the ending cash of $5,900 reported on the November statement of cash flows in Exhibit 8 is also reported as the amount of cash on hand in the November 30, 2015, balance sheet.

Since November is NetSolutions' first period of operations, the net cash flow for November and the November 30, 2015, cash balance are the same amount, $5,900, as shown in Exhibit 8. In later periods, NetSolutions will report in its statement of cash flows a beginning cash balance, an increase or a decrease in cash for the period, and an ending cash balance. For example, assume that for December NetSolutions has a decrease in cash of $3,835. The last three lines of NetSolutions' statement of cash flows for December would be as follows:

| | |
|---|---|
| Decrease in cash | $(3,835) |
| Cash as of December 1, 2015 | 5,900 |
| Cash as of December 31, 2015 | $ 2,065 |

**Example Exercise 1-7  Statement of Cash Flows**      OBJ 5

A summary of cash flows for Chickadee Travel Service for the year ended April 30, 2016, follows:

| | |
|---|---|
| Cash receipts: | |
| Cash received from customers.......................................... | $251,000 |
| Cash received from additional investment of owner .................... | 50,000 |
| Cash payments: | |
| Cash paid for expenses............................................... | 210,000 |
| Cash paid for land.................................................... | 80,000 |
| Cash paid to owner for personal use .................................. | 30,000 |

The cash balance as of May 1, 2015, was $72,050. Prepare a statement of cash flows for Chickadee Travel Service for the year ended April 30, 2016.

[4] This method of preparing the statement of cash flows is called the "direct method." This method and the indirect method are discussed further in Chapter 16.

*(Continued)*

**Follow My Example 1-7**

**Chickadee Travel Service**
**Statement of Cash Flows**
**For the Year Ended April 30, 2016**

| | | |
|---|---:|---:|
| Cash flows from operating activities: | | |
| Cash received from customers........................... | $ 251,000 | |
| Deduct cash payments for expenses..................... | (210,000) | |
| Net cash flows from operating activities................. | | $ 41,000 |
| Cash flows from investing activities: | | |
| Cash payments for purchase of land.................... | | (80,000) |
| Cash flows from financing activities: | | |
| Cash received from owner as investment................ | $ 50,000 | |
| Deduct cash withdrawals by owner...................... | (30,000) | |
| Net cash flows from financing activities ................. | | 20,000 |
| Net decrease in cash during year ........................... | | $(19,000) |
| Cash as of May 1, 2015 ..................................... | | 72,050 |
| Cash as of April 30, 2016 ................................... | | $ 53,050 |

Practice Exercises: PE 1-7A, PE 1-7B

## Interrelationships Among Financial Statements

Financial statements are prepared in the order of the income statement, statement of owner's equity, balance sheet, and statement of cash flows. This order is important because the financial statements are interrelated. These interrelationships for **NetSolutions** are shown in Exhibit 8 and are described in Exhibit 9.[5]

**EXHIBIT 9**    **Financial Statement Interrelationships**

| Financial Statements | Interrelationship | NetSolutions Example (Exhibit 8) |
|---|---|---|
| Income Statement *and* Statement of Owner's Equity | Net income or net loss reported on the income statement is also reported on the statement of owner's equity as either an addition (net income) to or deduction (net loss) from the beginning owner's equity and any additional investments by the owner during the period. | NetSolutions' net income of $3,050 for November is added to Chris Clark's investment of $25,000 on the statement of owner's equity. |
| Statement of Owner's Equity *and* Balance Sheet | Owner's capital at the end of the period reported on the statement of owner's equity is also reported on the balance sheet as owner's capital. | Chris Clark, Capital of $26,050 as of November 30, 2015, on the statement of owner's equity also appears on the November 30, 2015, balance sheet as Chris Clark, Capital. |
| Balance Sheet *and* Statement of Cash Flows | The cash reported on the balance sheet is also reported as the end-of-period cash on the statement of cash flows. | Cash of $5,900 reported on the balance sheet as of November 30, 2015, is also reported on the November statement of cash flows as the end-of-period cash. |

The preceding interrelationships are important in analyzing financial statements and the impact of transactions on a business. In addition, these interrelationships serve as a check on whether the financial statements are prepared correctly. For example, if the ending cash on the statement of cash flows does not agree with the balance sheet cash, then an error has occurred.

[5] Depending on the method of preparing the cash flows from operating activities section of the statement of cash flows, net income (or net loss) may also appear on the statement of cash flows. This interrelationship or method of preparing the statement of cash flows, called the "indirect method," is described and illustrated in Chapter 16.

# Financial Analysis and Interpretation: Ratio of Liabilities to Owner's Equity

OBJ 6 Describe and illustrate the use of the ratio of liabilities to owner's equity in evaluating a company's financial condition.

The basic financial statements illustrated in this chapter are useful to bankers, creditors, owners, and others in analyzing and interpreting the financial performance and condition of a company. Throughout this text, various tools and techniques that are often used to analyze and interpret a company's financial performance and condition are described and illustrated. The first such tool that is discussed is useful in analyzing the ability of a company to pay its creditors.

The relationship between liabilities and owner's equity, expressed as a **ratio of liabilities to owner's equity**, is computed as follows:

$$\text{Ratio of Liabilities to Owner's Equity} = \frac{\text{Total Liabilities}}{\text{Total Owner's Equity (or Total Stockholders' Equity)}}$$

**NetSolutions'** ratio of liabilities to owner's equity at the end of November is 0.015, computed as follows:

$$\text{Ratio of Liabilities to Owner's Equity} = \frac{\$400}{\$26,050} = 0.015 \text{ (Rounded)}$$

Corporations refer to total owner's equity as total stockholders' equity. Thus, total stockholders' equity is substituted for total owner's equity when computing this ratio.

To illustrate, recent balance sheet data (in millions) for Google Inc. and McDonald's Corporation follows:

|  | Recent Year | Prior Year |
|---|---|---|
| Google Inc. | | |
| Total liabilities | $22,083 | $14,429 |
| Total stockholders' equity | 71,715 | 58,145 |
| | | |
| McDonald's Corporation | | |
| Total liabilities | $18,600 | $17,341 |
| Total stockholders' equity | 14,390 | 14,634 |

The ratio of liabilities to stockholders' equity for Google and McDonald's for a recent year and the prior year is computed as follows:

|  | Recent Year* | Prior Year* |
|---|---|---|
| Google Inc. | | |
| Ratio of liabilities to stockholders' equity | 0.31 | 0.25 |
| | ($22,083 ÷ $71,715) | ($14,429 ÷ $58,145) |
| McDonald's Corporation | | |
| Ratio of liabilities to stockholders' equity | 1.29 | 1.18 |
| | ($18,600 ÷ $14,390) | ($17,341 ÷ $14,634) |

* Rounded to two decimal places.

The rights of creditors to a business's assets come before the rights of the owners or stockholders. Thus, the lower the ratio of liabilities to owner's equity, the better able the company is to withstand poor business conditions and to pay its obligations to creditors.

Google is unusual in that it has a very low amount of liabilities. Its ratio of liabilities to stockholders' equity of 0.31 in the recent year and 0.25 in the prior year is low. In contrast, McDonald's has more liabilities; its ratio of liabilities to stockholders' equity is 1.29 in the recent year and 1.18 in the prior year. Because McDonald's ratio of liabilities to stockholders' equity increased slightly, its creditors are slightly more at risk at the end of the recent year. Also, McDonald's creditors are more at risk than are Google's creditors. As well-established companies, however, the creditors of both companies are protected against the risk of nonpayment.

## Example Exercise 1-8    Ratio of Liabilities to Owner's Equity

OBJ 6

The following data were taken from Hawthorne Company's balance sheet:

|  | Dec. 31, 2016 | Dec. 31, 2015 |
|---|---|---|
| Total liabilities | $120,000 | $105,000 |
| Total owner's equity | 80,000 | 75,000 |

a.  Compute the ratio of liabilities to owner's equity.

b.  Has the creditors' risk increased or decreased from December 31, 2015, to December 31, 2016?

### Follow My Example 1-8

a.

|  | Dec. 31, 2016 | Dec. 31, 2015 |
|---|---|---|
| Total liabilities | $120,000 | $105,000 |
| Total owner's equity | 80,000 | 75,000 |
| Ratio of liabilities to owner's equity | 1.50 | 1.40 |
|  | ($120,000 ÷ $80,000) | ($105,000 ÷ $75,000) |

b.  Increased

Practice Exercises: PE 1-8A, PE 1-8B

# At a Glance 1

OBJ 1

**Describe the nature of a business and the role of accounting and ethics in business.**

**Key Points**    A business provides goods or services (outputs) to customers with the objective of earning a profit. Three types of businesses include service, merchandising, and manufacturing businesses.

Accounting is an information system that provides reports to users about the economic activities and condition of a business.

Ethics are moral principles that guide the conduct of individuals. Good ethical conduct depends on individual character and firm culture.

Accountants are engaged in private accounting or public accounting.

| Learning Outcomes | Example Exercises | Practice Exercises |
|---|---|---|
| • Distinguish among service, merchandising, and manufacturing businesses. |  |  |
| • Describe the role of accounting in business, and explain why accounting is called the "language of business." |  |  |
| • Define ethics, and list two factors affecting ethical conduct. |  |  |
| • Differentiate between private and public accounting. |  |  |

**Summarize the development of accounting principles and relate them to practice.**

**Key Points** Generally accepted accounting principles (GAAP) are used in preparing financial statements. Accounting principles and concepts develop from research, practice, and pronouncements of authoritative bodies.

The business entity concept views the business as an entity separate from its owners, creditors, or other businesses. Businesses may be organized as proprietorships, partnerships, corporations, and limited liability companies. The cost concept requires that purchases by a business be recorded in terms of actual cost. The objectivity concept requires that the accounting records and reports be based on objective evidence. The unit of measure concept requires that economic data be recorded in dollars.

| Learning Outcomes | Example Exercises | Practice Exercises |
|---|---|---|
| • Explain what is meant by generally accepted accounting principles. | | |
| • Describe how generally accepted accounting principles are developed. | | |
| • Describe and give an example of what is meant by the business entity concept. | | |
| • Describe the characteristics of a proprietorship, partnership, corporation, and limited liability company. | | |
| • Describe and give an example of what is meant by the cost concept. | **EE1-1** | **PE1-1A, 1-1B** |
| • Describe and give an example of what is meant by the objectivity concept. | | |
| • Describe and give an example of what is meant by the unit of measure concept. | | |

**State the accounting equation and define each element of the equation.**

**Key Points** The resources owned by a business and the rights or claims to these resources may be stated in the form of an equation, as follows: Assets = Liabilities + Owner's Equity

| Learning Outcomes | Example Exercises | Practice Exercises |
|---|---|---|
| • State the accounting equation. | | |
| • Define assets, liabilities, and owner's equity. | | |
| • Given two elements of the accounting equation, solve for the third element. | **EE1-2** | **PE1-2A, 1-2B** |

**Describe and illustrate how business transactions can be recorded in terms of the resulting change in the elements of the accounting equation.**

**Key Points** All business transactions can be stated in terms of the change in one or more of the three elements of the accounting equation.

| Learning Outcomes | Example Exercises | Practice Exercises |
|---|---|---|
| • Define a business transaction. | | |
| • Using the accounting equation as a framework, record transactions. | **EE1-3** | **PE1-3A, 1-3B** |

**Describe the financial statements of a proprietorship and explain how they interrelate.**

**Key Points**    The primary financial statements of a proprietorship are the income statement, the statement of owner's equity, the balance sheet, and the statement of cash flows. The income statement reports a period's net income or net loss, which is also reported on the statement of owner's equity. The ending owner's capital reported on the statement of owner's equity is also reported on the balance sheet. The ending cash balance is reported on the balance sheet and the statement of cash flows.

| Learning Outcomes | Example Exercises | Practice Exercises |
|---|---|---|
| • List and describe the financial statements of a proprietorship. | | |
| • Prepare an income statement. | EE1-4 | PE1-4A, 1-4B |
| • Prepare a statement of owner's equity. | EE1-5 | PE1-5A, 1-5B |
| • Prepare a balance sheet. | EE1-6 | PE1-6A, 1-6B |
| • Prepare a statement of cash flows. | EE1-7 | PE1-7A, 1-7B |
| • Explain how the financial statements of a proprietorship are interrelated. | | |

**Describe and illustrate the use of the ratio of liabilities to owner's equity in evaluating a company's financial condition.**

**Key Points**    A ratio useful in analyzing the ability of a business to pay its creditors is the ratio of liabilities to owner's (stockholders') equity. The lower the ratio of liabilities to owner's equity, the better able the company is to withstand poor business conditions and to pay its obligations to creditors.

| Learning Outcomes | Example Exercises | Practice Exercises |
|---|---|---|
| • Describe the usefulness of the ratio of liabilities to owner's (stockholders') equity. | | |
| • Compute the ratio of liabilities to owner's (stockholders') equity. | EE1-8 | PE1-8A, 1-8B |

# Key Terms

account form (18)
account payable (11)
account receivable (12)
accounting (3)
accounting equation (9)
assets (9)
balance sheet (15)
business (2)
business entity concept (7)
business transaction (10)
Certified Public Accountant (CPA) (5)

corporation (8)
cost concept (8)
earnings (15)
ethics (4)
expenses (12)
fees earned (12)
financial accounting (4)
Financial Accounting Standards Board (FASB) (7)
financial statements (15)
generally accepted accounting principles (GAAP) (7)

general-purpose financial statements (4)
income statement (15)
interest revenue (12)
International Accounting Standards Board (IASB) (7)
liabilities (9)
limited liability company (LLC) (8)
management (or managerial) accounting (3)
manufacturing business (3)
matching concept (15)

merchandising business (2)
net income (or net profit) (15)
net loss (15)
objectivity concept (8)
owner's equity (9)
partnership (8)
prepaid expenses (11)
private accounting (3)
profit (2)

proprietorship (8)
public accounting (5)
Public Company Accounting
   Oversight Board (PCAOB) (5)
ratio of liabilities to owner's
   (stockholders')
   equity (21)
rent revenue (12)
revenue (11)

sales (12)
Sarbanes-Oxley Act (SOX) (5)
Securities and Exchange
   Commission (SEC) (7)
service business (2)
statement of cash flows (15)
statement of owner's
   equity (15)
unit of measure concept (9)

# Illustrative Problem

Cecil Jameson, Attorney-at-Law, is a proprietorship owned and operated by Cecil Jameson. On July 1, 2015, the company has the following assets and liabilities: cash, $1,000; accounts receivable, $3,200; supplies, $850; land, $10,000; accounts payable, $1,530. Office space and office equipment are currently being rented, pending the construction of an office complex on land purchased last year. Business transactions during July are summarized as follows:

  a. Received cash from clients for services, $3,928.

  b. Paid creditors on account, $1,055.

  c. Received cash from Cecil Jameson as an additional investment, $3,700.

  d. Paid office rent for the month, $1,200.

  e. Charged clients for legal services on account, $2,025.

  f. Purchased supplies on account, $245.

  g. Received cash from clients on account, $3,000.

  h. Received invoice for paralegal services from Legal Aid Inc. for July (to be paid on August 10), $1,635.

  i. Paid the following: wages expense, $850; utilities expense, $325; answering service expense, $250; and miscellaneous expense, $75.

  j. Determined that the cost of supplies on hand was $980; therefore, the cost of supplies used during the month was $115.

  k. Jameson withdrew $1,000 in cash from the business for personal use.

## Instructions

1. Determine the amount of owner's equity (Cecil Jameson's capital) as of July 1, 2015.

2. State the assets, liabilities, and owner's equity as of July 1 in equation form similar to that shown in this chapter. In tabular form below the equation, indicate the increases and decreases resulting from each transaction and the new balances after each transaction.

3. Prepare an income statement for July, a statement of owner's equity for July, and a balance sheet as of July 31, 2015.

4. (Optional) Prepare a statement of cash flows for July.

## Solution

1.

                        Assets   Liabilities = Owner's Equity (Cecil Jameson, capital)
($1,000 + $3,200 + $850 + $10,000) − $1,530 = Owner's Equity (Cecil Jameson, capital)
                  $15,050 − $1,530 = Owner's Equity (Cecil Jameson, capital)
                         $13,520 = Owner's Equity (Cecil Jameson, capital)

2.

| | Cash | + | Accts. Rec. | + | Supp. | + | Land | = | Accts. Pay. | + | Cecil Jameson, Capital | − | Cecil Jameson, Drawing | + | Fees Earned | − | Paralegal Exp. | − | Rent Exp. | − | Wages Exp. | − | Utilities Exp. | − | Answering Service Exp. | − | Supp. Exp. | − | Misc. Exp. |
|---|---|---|---|---|---|---|---|---|---|---|---|---|---|---|---|---|---|---|---|---|---|---|---|---|---|---|---|---|---|
| **Assets** | | | | | | | | **= Liabilities +** | | | | | | | | **Owner's Equity** | | | | | | | | | | | | | |
| Bal. | 1,000 | | 3,200 | | 850 | | 10,000 | | 1,530 | | 13,520 | | | | | | | | | | | | | | | | | | |
| a. | +3,928 | | | | | | | | | | | | | | 3,928 | | | | | | | | | | | | | | |
| Bal. | 4,928 | | 3,200 | | 850 | | 10,000 | | 1,530 | | 13,520 | | | | 3,928 | | | | | | | | | | | | | | |
| b. | −1,055 | | | | | | | | −1,055 | | | | | | | | | | | | | | | | | | | | |
| Bal. | 3,873 | | 3,200 | | 850 | | 10,000 | | 475 | | 13,520 | | | | 3,928 | | | | | | | | | | | | | | |
| c. | +3,700 | | | | | | | | | | +3,700 | | | | | | | | | | | | | | | | | | |
| Bal. | 7,573 | | 3,200 | | 850 | | 10,000 | | 475 | | 17,220 | | | | 3,928 | | | | | | | | | | | | | | |
| d. | −1,200 | | | | | | | | | | | | | | | | | | −1,200 | | | | | | | | | | |
| Bal. | 6,373 | | 3,200 | | 850 | | 10,000 | | 475 | | 17,220 | | | | 3,928 | | | | −1,200 | | | | | | | | | | |
| e. | | | +2,025 | | | | | | | | | | | | +2,025 | | | | | | | | | | | | | | |
| Bal. | 6,373 | | 5,225 | | 850 | | 10,000 | | 475 | | 17,220 | | | | 5,953 | | | | −1,200 | | | | | | | | | | |
| f. | | | | | +245 | | | | +245 | | | | | | | | | | | | | | | | | | | | |
| Bal. | 6,373 | | 5,225 | | 1,095 | | 10,000 | | 720 | | 17,220 | | | | 5,953 | | | | −1,200 | | | | | | | | | | |
| g. | +3,000 | | −3,000 | | | | | | | | | | | | | | | | | | | | | | | | | | |
| Bal. | 9,373 | | 2,225 | | 1,095 | | 10,000 | | 720 | | 17,220 | | | | 5,953 | | | | −1,200 | | | | | | | | | | |
| h. | | | | | | | | | +1,635 | | | | | | | | −1,635 | | | | | | | | | | | | |
| Bal. | 9,373 | | 2,225 | | 1,095 | | 10,000 | | 2,355 | | 17,220 | | | | 5,953 | | −1,635 | | −1,200 | | | | | | | | | | |
| i. | −1,500 | | | | | | | | | | | | | | | | | | | | −850 | | −325 | | −250 | | | | −75 |
| Bal. | 7,873 | | 2,225 | | 1,095 | | 10,000 | | 2,355 | | 17,220 | | | | 5,953 | | −1,635 | | −1,200 | | −850 | | −325 | | −250 | | | | −75 |
| j. | | | | | −115 | | | | | | | | | | | | | | | | | | | | | | −115 | | |
| Bal. | 7,873 | | 2,225 | | 980 | | 10,000 | | 2,355 | | 17,220 | | | | 5,953 | | −1,635 | | −1,200 | | −850 | | −325 | | −250 | | −115 | | −75 |
| k. | −1,000 | | | | | | | | | | | | −1,000 | | | | | | | | | | | | | | | | |
| Bal. | 6,873 | | 2,225 | | 980 | | 10,000 | | 2,355 | | 17,220 | | −1,000 | | 5,953 | | −1,635 | | −1,200 | | −850 | | −325 | | −250 | | −115 | | −75 |

3.

### Cecil Jameson, Attorney-at-Law
### Income Statement
### For the Month Ended July 31, 2015

| | | |
|---|---:|---:|
| Fees earned | | **$5,953** |
| Expenses: | | |
| Paralegal expense | $1,635 | |
| Rent expense | 1,200 | |
| Wages expense | 850 | |
| Utilities expense | 325 | |
| Answering service expense | 250 | |
| Supplies expense | 115 | |
| Miscellaneous expense | 75 | |
| Total expenses | | 4,450 |
| Net income | | $1,503 |

### Cecil Jameson, Attorney-at-Law
### Statement of Owner's Equity
### For the Month Ended July 31, 2015

| | | |
|---|---:|---:|
| Cecil Jameson, capital, July 1, 2015 | | $13,520 |
| Additional investment by owner | $3,700 | |
| Net income for the month | 1,503 | |
| | $5,203 | |
| Less withdrawals | 1,000 | |
| Increase in owner's equity | | 4,203 |
| Cecil Jameson, capital, July 31, 2015 | | $17,723 |

*(Continued)*

**Cecil Jameson, Attorney-at-Law**
**Balance Sheet**
**July 31, 2015**

| Assets | | Liabilities | |
|---|---|---|---|
| Cash ................................ | $ 6,873 | Accounts payable ................. | $ 2,355 |
| Accounts receivable ............... | 2,225 | **Owner's Equity** | |
| Supplies........................... | 980 | Cecil Jameson, capital ............. | 17,723 |
| Land .............................. | 10,000 | Total liabilities and owner's | |
| Total assets ...................... | $20,078 | equity.......................... | $20,078 |

4. (Optional)

**Cecil Jameson, Attorney-at-Law**
**Statement of Cash Flows**
**For the Month Ended July 31, 2015**

| | | |
|---|---|---|
| Cash flows from operating activities: | | |
| Cash received from customers ..................................... | $ 6,928* | |
| Deduct cash payments for operating expenses.................... | (3,755)** | |
| Net cash flows from operating activities ........................... | | $ 3,173 |
| Cash flows from investing activities.................................... | | — |
| Cash flows from financing activities: | | |
| Cash received from owner as investment ......................... | $ 3,700 | |
| Deduct cash withdrawals by owner................................ | (1,000) | |
| Net cash flows from financing activities............................ | | 2,700 |
| Net increase in cash during year...................................... | | $ 5,873 |
| Cash as of July 1, 2015 ............................................... | | 1,000 |
| Cash as of July 31, 2015............................................... | | $ 6,873 |

*$6,928 = $3,928 + $3,000
**$3,755 = $1,055 + $1,200 + $1,500

# Discussion Questions

1. Name some users of accounting information.

2. What is the role of accounting in business?

3. Why are most large companies like Microsoft, PepsiCo, Caterpillar, and AutoZone organized as corporations?

4. Josh Reilly is the owner of Dispatch Delivery Service. Recently Josh paid interest of $4,500 on a personal loan of $75,000 that he used to begin the business. Should Dispatch Delivery Service record the interest payment? Explain.

5. On July 12, Reliable Repair Service extended an offer of $150,000 for land that had been priced for sale at $185,000. On September 3, Reliable Repair Service accepted the seller's counteroffer of $167,500. Describe how Reliable Repair Service should record the land.

6. a. Land with an assessed value of $750,000 for property tax purposes is acquired by a business for $900,000. Ten years later, the plot of land has an assessed value of $1,200,000 and the business receives an offer of $2,000,000 for it. Should the monetary amount assigned to the land in the business records now be increased?

   b. Assuming that the land acquired in (a) was sold for $2,125,000, how would the various elements of the accounting equation be affected?

7. Describe the difference between an account receivable and an account payable.

8. A business had revenues of $679,000 and operating expenses of $588,000. Did the business (a) incur a net loss or (b) realize net income?

9. A business had revenues of $640,000 and operating expenses of $715,000. Did the business (a) incur a net loss or (b) realize net income?

10. The financial statements are interrelated. (a) What item of financial or operating data appears on both the income statement and the statement of owner's equity? (b) What item appears on both the balance sheet and the statement of owner's equity? (c) What item appears on both the balance sheet and the statement of cash flows?

## Practice Exercises

EE 1-1 *p. 9*

SHOW
ME HOW

### PE 1-1A  Cost concept                                                     OBJ. 2

On February 22, Kountry Repair Service extended an offer of $200,000 for land that had been priced for sale at $250,000. On April 3, Kountry Repair Service accepted the seller's counteroffer of $230,000. On September 15, the land was assessed at a value of $185,000 for property tax purposes. On January 9 of the next year, Kountry Repair Service was offered $300,000 for the land by a national retail chain. At what value should the land be recorded in Kountry Repair Service's records?

EE 1-1 *p. 9*

SHOW
ME HOW

### PE 1-1B  Cost concept                                                     OBJ. 2

On March 31, Higgins Repair Service extended an offer of $415,000 for land that had been priced for sale at $460,000. On April 15, Higgins Repair Service accepted the seller's counteroffer of $437,500. On September 9, the land was assessed at a value of $375,000 for property tax purposes. On December 8, Higgins Repair Service was offered $475,000 for the land by a national retail chain. At what value should the land be recorded in Higgins Repair Service's records?

EE 1-2 *p. 10*

SHOW
ME HOW

### PE 1-2A  Accounting equation                                              OBJ. 3

Brock Hahn is the owner and operator of Dream-It LLC, a motivational consulting business. At the end of its accounting period, December 31, 2015, Dream-It has assets of $780,000 and liabilities of $150,000. Using the accounting equation, determine the following amounts:

a. Owner's equity as of December 31, 2015.

b. Owner's equity as of December 31, 2016, assuming that assets increased by $90,000 and liabilities increased by $25,000 during 2016.

EE 1-2 *p. 10*

SHOW
ME HOW

### PE 1-2B  Accounting equation                                              OBJ. 3

Fritz Evans is the owner and operator of Be-The-One, a motivational consulting business. At the end of its accounting period, December 31, 2015, Be-The-One has assets of $395,000 and liabilities of $97,000. Using the accounting equation, determine the following amounts:

a. Owner's equity as of December 31, 2015.

b. Owner's equity as of December 31, 2016, assuming that assets decreased by $65,000 and liabilities increased by $36,000 during 2016.

EE 1-3 *p. 14*

SHOW
ME HOW

### PE 1-3A  Transactions                                                     OBJ. 4

Arrowhead Delivery Service is owned and operated by Gates Deeter. The following selected transactions were completed by Arrowhead Delivery Service during August:

1. Received cash from owner as additional investment, $25,000.

2. Paid creditors on account, $3,750.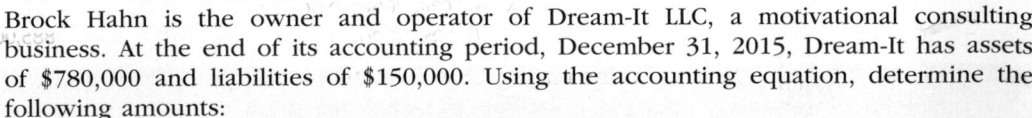

3. Billed customers for delivery services on account, $22,400.

4. Received cash from customers on account, $11,300.

5. Paid cash to owner for personal use, $6,000.

Indicate the effect of each transaction on the accounting equation elements (Assets, Liabilities, Owner's Equity, Drawing, Revenue, and Expense). Also indicate the specific item within the accounting equation element that is affected. To illustrate, the answer to (1) follows:

(1) Asset (Cash) increases by $25,000; Owner's Equity (Gates Deeter, Capital) increases by $25,000.

---

EE 1-3 *p. 14* **PE 1-3B    Transactions**                                                        OBJ. 4

SHOW
ME HOW

Interstate Delivery Service is owned and operated by Katie Wyer. The following selected transactions were completed by Interstate Delivery Service during May:

1. Received cash from owner as additional investment, $18,000. *Cash, Owners Capital*

2. Paid advertising expense, $4,850. *Cash, Accts payable Advertising expense*

3. Purchased supplies on account, $2,100. *Supplies, accts pay*

4. Billed customers for delivery services on account, $14,700. *Accts rece, fees earned*

5. Received cash from customers on account, $8,200. *Cash, fees earned Accts receivable*

Indicate the effect of each transaction on the accounting equation elements (Assets, Liabilities, Owner's Equity, Drawing, Revenue, and Expense). Also indicate the specific item within the accounting equation element that is affected. To illustrate, the answer to (1) follows:

(1) Asset (Cash) increases by $18,000; Owner's Equity (Katie Wyer, Capital) increases by $18,000.

---

EE 1-4 *p. 15* **PE 1-4A    Income statement**                                                     OBJ. 5

SHOW
ME HOW

The revenues and expenses of Ousel Travel Service for the year ended November 30, 2016, follow:

| | |
|---|---:|
| Fees earned | $1,475,000 |
| Office expense | 320,000 |
| Miscellaneous expense | 28,000 |
| Wages expense | 885,000 |

*242,000*

Prepare an income statement for the year ended November 30, 2016.

---

EE 1-4 *p. 15* **PE 1-4B    Income statement**                                                     OBJ. 5

SHOW
ME HOW

The revenues and expenses of Sentinel Travel Service for the year ended August 31, 2016, follow:

| | |
|---|---:|
| Fees earned | $750,000 |
| Office expense | 295,000 |
| Miscellaneous expense | 12,000 |
| Wages expense | 450,000 |

Prepare an income statement for the year ended August 31, 2016.

---

EE 1-5 *p. 16* **PE 1-5A    Statement of owner's equity**                                          OBJ. 5

SHOW
ME HOW

Using the income statement for Ousel Travel Service shown in Practice Exercise 1-4A, prepare a statement of owner's equity for the year ended November 30, 2016. Shane Ousel, the owner, invested an additional $50,000 in the business during the year and withdrew cash of $30,000 for personal use. Shane Ousel, capital as of December 1, 2015, was $666,000.

EE 1-5  *p. 16* **PE 1-5B   Statement of owner's equity**    **OBJ. 5**

SHOW
ME HOW

Using the income statement for Sentinel Travel Service shown in Practice Exercise 1-4B, prepare a statement of owner's equity for the year ended August 31, 2016. Barb Schroeder, the owner, invested an additional $36,000 in the business during the year and withdrew cash of $18,000 for personal use. Barb Schroeder, capital as of September 1, 2015, was $380,000.

EE 1-6  *p. 18* **PE 1-6A   Balance sheet**    **OBJ. 5**

SHOW
ME HOW

Using the following data for Ousel Travel Service as well as the statement of owner's equity shown in Practice Exercise 1-5A, prepare a balance sheet as of November 30, 2016:

| | |
|---|---|
| Accounts payable | $ 62,500 |
| Accounts receivable | 186,000 |
| Cash | 308,000 |
| Land | 480,000 |
| Supplies | 16,500 |

EE 1-6  *p. 18* **PE 1-6B   Balance sheet**    **OBJ. 5**

SHOW
ME HOW

Using the following data for Sentinel Travel Service as well as the statement of owner's equity shown in Practice Exercise 1-5B, prepare a balance sheet as of August 31, 2016:

| | |
|---|---|
| Accounts payable | $ 44,600 |
| Accounts receivable | 75,500 |
| Cash | 45,400 |
| Land | 310,000 |
| Supplies | 4,700 |

EE 1-7  *p. 19* **PE 1-7A   Statement of cash flows**    **OBJ. 5**

SHOW
ME HOW

A summary of cash flows for Ousel Travel Service for the year ended November 30, 2016, follows:

| | |
|---|---|
| Cash receipts: | |
| Cash received from customers | $1,465,000 |
| Cash received from additional investment of owner | 50,000 |
| Cash payments: | |
| Cash paid for operating expenses | 1,230,000 |
| Cash paid for land | 150,000 |
| Cash paid to owner for personal use | 30,000 |

The cash balance as of December 1, 2015, was $203,000.

Prepare a statement of cash flows for Ousel Travel Service for the year ended November 30, 2016.

EE 1-7  *p. 19* **PE 1-7B   Statement of cash flows**    **OBJ. 5**

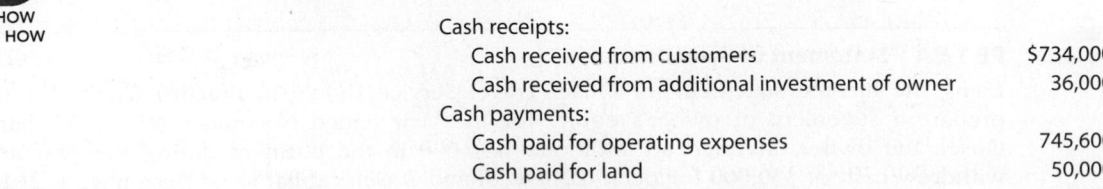
SHOW
ME HOW

A summary of cash flows for Sentinel Travel Service for the year ended August 31, 2016, follows:

| | |
|---|---|
| Cash receipts: | |
| Cash received from customers | $734,000 |
| Cash received from additional investment of owner | 36,000 |
| Cash payments: | |
| Cash paid for operating expenses | 745,600 |
| Cash paid for land | 50,000 |
| Cash paid to owner for personal use | 18,000 |

The cash balance as of September 1, 2015, was $89,000.

Prepare a statement of cash flows for Sentinel Travel Service for the year ended August 31, 2016.

EE 1-8 *p. 22*

SHOW
ME HOW

**PE 1-8A   Ratio of liabilities to owner's equity**                                OBJ. 6

The following data were taken from Mesa Company's balance sheet:

|  | Dec. 31, 2016 | Dec. 31, 2015 |
|---|---|---|
| Total liabilities | $547,800 | $518,000 |
| Total owner's equity | 415,000 | 370,000 |

a.  Compute the ratio of liabilities to owner's equity.

b.  Has the creditor's risk increased or decreased from December 31, 2015, to December 31, 2016?

EE 1-8 *p. 22*

SHOW
ME HOW

**PE 1-8B   Ratio of liabilities to owner's equity**                                OBJ. 6

The following data were taken from Alvarado Company's balance sheet:

|  | Dec. 31, 2016 | Dec. 31, 2015 |
|---|---|---|
| Total liabilities | $4,085,000 | $2,880,000 |
| Total owner's equity | 4,300,000 | 3,600,000 |

a.  Compute the ratio of liabilities to owner's equity.

b.  Has the creditor's risk increased or decreased from December 31, 2015, to December 31, 2016?

# Exercises

Internet Project

**EX 1-1   Types of businesses**                                                    OBJ. 1

The following is a list of well-known companies:

| | |
|---|---|
| 1. Alcoa Inc. | 9. Ford Motor Company |
| 2. Boeing | 10. Gap Inc. |
| 3. Caterpillar | 11. H&R Block |
| 4. Citigroup Inc. | 12. Hilton Hospitality, Inc. |
| 5. CVS | 13. Procter & Gamble |
| 6. Dow Chemical Company | 14. SunTrust |
| 7. eBay Inc. | 15. Walmart Stores, Inc. |
| 8. FedEx | |

a.  Indicate whether each of these companies is primarily a service, merchandise, or manufacturing business. If you are unfamiliar with the company, use the Internet to locate the company's home page or use the finance Web site of Yahoo (finance.yahoo.com).

b.  For which of the preceding companies is the accounting equation relevant?

**EX 1-2   Professional ethics**                                                    OBJ. 1

A fertilizer manufacturing company wants to relocate to Yellowstone County. A report from a fired researcher at the company indicates the company's product is releasing toxic by-products. The company suppressed that report. A later report commissioned by the company shows there is no problem with the fertilizer.

━━━▶ Should the company's chief executive officer reveal the content of the unfavorable report in discussions with Yellowstone County representatives? Discuss.

### EX 1-3   Business entity concept

OBJ. 2

Ozark Sports sells hunting and fishing equipment and provides guided hunting and fishing trips. Ozark Sports is owned and operated by Eric Griffith, a well-known sports enthusiast and hunter. Eric's wife, Linda, owns and operates Lake Boutique, a women's clothing store. Eric and Linda have established a trust fund to finance their children's college education. The trust fund is maintained by Missouri State Bank in the name of the children, Mark and Steffy.

a. For each of the following transactions, identify which of the entities listed should record the transaction in its records:

| Entities | |
|---|---|
| L | Lake Boutique |
| M | Missouri State Bank |
| O | Ozark Sports |
| X | None of the above |

1. Linda authorized the trust fund to purchase mutual fund shares.

2. Linda purchased two dozen spring dresses from a St. Louis designer for a special spring sale.

3. Eric paid a breeder's fee for an English springer spaniel to be used as a hunting guide dog.

4. Linda deposited a $2,000 personal check in the trust fund at Missouri State Bank.

5. Eric paid a local doctor for his annual physical, which was required by the workmen's compensation insurance policy carried by Ozark Sports.

6. Eric received a cash advance from customers for a guided hunting trip.

7. Linda paid her dues to the YWCA.

8. Linda donated several dresses from inventory for a local charity auction for the benefit of a women's abuse shelter.

9. Eric paid for dinner and a movie to celebrate their twelfth wedding anniversary.

10. Eric paid for an advertisement in a hunters' magazine.

b. What is a business transaction?

---

### EX 1-4   Accounting equation

OBJ. 3

✔ Starbucks, $5,109

SHOW
ME HOW

The total assets and total liabilities (in millions) of **Green Mountain Coffee Roasters, Inc.** and **Starbucks Corporation** follow:

| | Green Mountain | Starbucks |
|---|---|---|
| Assets | $3,616 | $8,219 |
| Liabilities | 1,345 | 3,110 |

Determine the owners' equity of each company.

---

### EX 1-5   Accounting equation

OBJ. 3

✔ Dollar Tree, $1,345

The total assets and total liabilities (in millions) of **Dollar Tree Inc.** and **Target Corporation** follow:

| | Dollar Tree | Target Corporation |
|---|---|---|
| Assets | $2,329 | $46,630 |
| Liabilities | 984 | 30,809 |

Determine the owners' equity of each company.

---

### EX 1-6   Accounting equation

OBJ. 3

✔ a. $1,271,000

SHOW
ME HOW

Determine the missing amount for each of the following:

| | Assets | = | Liabilities | + | Owner's Equity |
|---|---|---|---|---|---|
| a. | X | = | $376,000 | + | $895,000 |
| b. | $1,375,000 | = | X | + | $855,000 |
| c. | $863,500 | = | $211,000 | + | X |

### EX 1-7 Accounting equation

OBJ. 3, 4

Annie Rasmussen is the owner and operator of Go44, a motivational consulting business. At the end of its accounting period, December 31, 2015, Go44 has assets of $720,000 and liabilities of $180,000. Using the accounting equation and considering each case independently, determine the following amounts:

a. Annie Rasmussen, capital, as of December 31, 2015.

b. Annie Rasmussen, capital, as of December 31, 2016, assuming that assets increased by $96,500 and liabilities increased by $30,000 during 2016.

c. Annie Rasmussen, capital, as of December 31, 2016, assuming that assets decreased by $168,000 and liabilities increased by $15,000 during 2016.

d. Annie Rasmussen, capital, as of December 31, 2016, assuming that assets increased by $175,000 and liabilities decreased by $18,000 during 2016.

e. Net income (or net loss) during 2016, assuming that as of December 31, 2016, assets were $880,000, liabilities were $220,000, and there were no additional investments or withdrawals.

### EX 1-8 Asset, liability, and owner's equity items

OBJ. 3

Indicate whether each of the following is identified with (1) an asset, (2) a liability, or (3) owner's equity:

a. accounts payable

b. cash

c. fees earned

d. land

e. supplies

f. wages expense

### EX 1-9 Effect of transactions on accounting equation

OBJ. 4

Describe how the following business transactions affect the three elements of the accounting equation:

a. Invested cash in business.

b. Paid for utilities used in the business.

c. Purchased supplies for cash.

d. Purchased supplies on account.

e. Received cash for services performed.

### EX 1-10 Effect of transactions on accounting equation

OBJ. 4

a. A vacant lot acquired for $115,000 is sold for $298,000 in cash. What is the effect of the sale on the total amount of the seller's (1) assets, (2) liabilities, and (3) owner's equity?

b. Assume that the seller owes $80,000 on a loan for the land. After receiving the $298,000 cash in (a), the seller pays the $80,000 owed. What is the effect of the payment on the total amount of the seller's (1) assets, (2) liabilities, and (3) owner's equity?

c. ➤ Is it true that a transaction always affects at least two elements (Assets, Liabilities, or Owner's Equity) of the accounting equation? Explain.

### EX 1-11 Effect of transactions on owner's equity

OBJ. 4

Indicate whether each of the following types of transactions will either (a) increase owner's equity or (b) decrease owner's equity:

1. expenses

2. owner's investments

3. owner's withdrawals

4. revenues

### EX 1-12  Transactions

OBJ. 4

The following selected transactions were completed by Cota Delivery Service during July:

1. Received cash from owner as additional investment, $35,000.
2. Purchased supplies for cash, $1,100.
3. Paid rent for October, $4,500.
4. Paid advertising expense, $900.
5. Received cash for providing delivery services, $33,000.
6. Billed customers for delivery services on account, $58,000.
7. Paid creditors on account, $2,900.
8. Received cash from customers on account, $27,500.
9. Determined that the cost of supplies on hand was $300 and $8,600 of supplies had been used during the month.
10. Paid cash to owner for personal use, $2,500.

Indicate the effect of each transaction on the accounting equation by listing the numbers identifying the transactions, (1) through (10), in a column, and inserting at the right of each number the appropriate letter from the following list:

a.  Increase in an asset, decrease in another asset.

b.  Increase in an asset, increase in a liability.

c.  Increase in an asset, increase in owner's equity.

d.  Decrease in an asset, decrease in a liability.

e.  Decrease in an asset, decrease in owner's equity.

---

### EX 1-13  Nature of transactions

OBJ. 4

✔ d. $22,800

SHOW
ME HOW

Teri West operates her own catering service. Summary financial data for July are presented in equation form as follows. Each line designated by a number indicates the effect of a transaction on the equation. Each increase and decrease in owner's equity, except transaction (5), affects net income.

| | Assets | | | = Liabilities + | | Owner's Equity | | | |
|---|---|---|---|---|---|---|---|---|---|
| | Cash | + Supplies + | Land | = | Accounts Payable + | Teri West, Capital | − | Teri West, Drawing | + | Fees Earned − Expenses |

| | Cash | + Supplies + | Land | = | Accounts Payable + | Teri West, Capital | − | Teri West, Drawing | + Fees Earned | − Expenses |
|---|---|---|---|---|---|---|---|---|---|---|
| Bal. | 40,000 | 3,000 | 82,000 | | 7,500 | 117,500 | | | | |
| 1. | +71,800 | | | | | | | | +71,800 | |
| 2. | −15,000 | | +15,000 | | | | | | | |
| 3. | −47,500 | | | | | | | | | −47,500 |
| 4. | | +1,100 | | | +1,100 | | | | | |
| 5. | −5,000 | | | | | | | −5,000 | | |
| 6. | −4,000 | | | | −4,000 | | | | | |
| 7. | | −1,500 | | | | | | | | −1,500 |
| Bal. | 40,300 | 2,600 | 97,000 | | 4,600 | 117,500 | | −5,000 | 71,800 | −49,000 |

a.  Describe each transaction.

b.  What is the amount of the net increase in cash during the month?

c.  What is the amount of the net increase in owner's equity during the month?

d.  What is the amount of the net income for the month?

e.  How much of the net income for the month was retained in the business?

---

### EX 1-14  Net income and owner's withdrawals

OBJ. 5

The income statement of a proprietorship for the month of February indicates a net income of $17,500. During the same period, the owner withdrew $25,500 in cash from the business for personal use.

━━━━▶ Would it be correct to say that the business incurred a net loss of $8,000 during the month? Discuss.

**EX 1-15 Net income and owner's equity for four businesses** OBJ. 5

Four different proprietorships, Jupiter, Mars, Saturn, and Venus, show the same balance sheet data at the beginning and end of a year. These data, exclusive of the amount of owner's equity, are summarized as follows:

|  | Total Assets | Total Liabilities |
|---|---|---|
| Beginning of the year | $550,000 | $215,000 |
| End of the year | 844,000 | 320,000 |

On the basis of the preceding data and the following additional information for the year, determine the net income (or loss) of each company for the year. (*Hint:* First determine the amount of increase or decrease in owner's equity during the year.)

Jupiter: The owner had made no additional investments in the business and had made no withdrawals from the business.

Mars: The owner had made no additional investments in the business but had withdrawn $36,000.

Saturn: The owner had made an additional investment of $60,000 but had made no withdrawals.

Venus: The owner had made an additional investment of $60,000 and had withdrawn $36,000.

**EX 1-16 Balance sheet items** OBJ. 5

From the following list of selected items taken from the records of Bobcat Appliance Service as of a specific date, identify those that would appear on the balance sheet:

1. Accounts Receivable
2. Cash
3. Fees Earned
4. Land
5. Mary Bayern, Capital
6. Supplies
7. Supplies Expense
8. Utilities Expense
9. Wages Expense
10. Wages Payable

**EX 1-17 Income statement items** OBJ. 5

Based on the data presented in Exercise 1-16, identify those items that would appear on the income statement.

**EX 1-18 Statement of owner's equity** OBJ. 5

Financial information related to Udder Products Company, a proprietorship, for the month ended April 30, 2016, is as follows:

| | |
|---|---|
| Net income for April | $166,000 |
| Mark Kominksy's withdrawals during April | 25,000 |
| Mark Kominksy's capital, April 1, 2016 | 384,500 |

a. Prepare a statement of owner's equity for the month ended April 30, 2016.

b. ━━━▶ Why is the statement of owner's equity prepared before the April 30, 2016, balance sheet?

**EX 1-19 Income statement** OBJ. 5

Dairy Services was organized on August 1, 2016. A summary of the revenue and expense transactions for August follows:

| | |
|---|---|
| Fees earned | $783,000 |
| Wages expense | 550,000 |
| Rent expense | 35,000 |
| Supplies expense | 8,500 |
| Miscellaneous expense | 11,400 |

Prepare an income statement for the month ended August 31.

SHOW
ME HOW

### EX 1-20 Missing amounts from balance sheet and income statement data  OBJ. 5

One item is omitted in each of the following summaries of balance sheet and income statement data for the following four different proprietorships:

|  | Freeman | Heyward | Jones | Ramirez |
|---|---|---|---|---|
| **Beginning of the year:** | | | | |
| Assets | $ 900,000 | $490,000 | $115,000 | (d) |
| Liabilities | 360,000 | 260,000 | 81,000 | $120,000 |
| **End of the year:** | | | | |
| Assets | 1,260,000 | 675,000 | 100,000 | 270,000 |
| Liabilities | 330,000 | 220,000 | 80,000 | 136,000 |
| **During the year:** | | | | |
| Additional investment in the business | (a) | 150,000 | 10,000 | 55,000 |
| Withdrawals from the business | 75,000 | 32,000 | (c) | 39,000 |
| Revenue | 570,000 | (b) | 115,000 | 115,000 |
| Expenses | 240,000 | 128,000 | 122,500 | 128,000 |

Determine the missing amounts, identifying them by letter. (*Hint:* First determine the amount of increase or decrease in owner's equity during the year.)

### EX 1-21 Balance sheets, net income  OBJ. 5

SHOW
ME HOW

Financial information related to the proprietorship of Ebony Interiors for February and March 2016 is as follows:

|  | February 29, 2016 | March 31, 2016 |
|---|---|---|
| Accounts payable | $310,000 | $400,000 |
| Accounts receivable | 800,000 | 960,000 |
| Cash | 320,000 | 380,000 |
| Justin Berk, capital | ? | ? |
| Supplies | 30,000 | 35,000 |

a. Prepare balance sheets for Ebony Interiors as of February 29 and March 31, 2016.

b. Determine the amount of net income for March, assuming that the owner made no additional investments or withdrawals during the month.

c. Determine the amount of net income for March, assuming that the owner made no additional investments but withdrew $50,000 during the month.

### EX 1-22 Financial statements  OBJ. 5

Each of the following items is shown in the financial statements of **Exxon Mobil Corporation**:

1. Accounts payable
2. Cash equivalents
3. Crude oil inventory
4. Equipment
5. Exploration expenses
6. Income taxes payable
7. Investments
8. Long-term debt
9. Marketable securities
10. Notes and loans payable
11. Notes receivable
12. Operating expenses
13. Prepaid taxes
14. Sales
15. Selling expenses

a. Identify the financial statement (balance sheet or income statement) in which each item would appear.

b. Can an item appear on more than one financial statement?

c. Is the accounting equation relevant for Exxon Mobil Corporation?

### EX 1-23 Statement of cash flows  OBJ. 5

Indicate whether each of the following activities would be reported on the statement of cash flows as (a) an operating activity, (b) an investing activity, or (c) a financing activity:

1. Cash received from fees earned.
2. Cash paid for expenses.
3. Cash paid for land.
4. Cash paid to owner for personal use.

### EX 1-24  Statement of cash flows

**OBJ. 5**

A summary of cash flows for Ethos Consulting Group for the year ended May 31, 2016, follows:

| | |
|---|---|
| Cash receipts: | |
| Cash received from customers | $637,500 |
| Cash received from additional investment of owner | 62,500 |
| Cash payments: | |
| Cash paid for operating expenses | 475,000 |
| Cash paid for land | 90,000 |
| Cash paid to owner for personal use | 17,500 |

The cash balance as of June 1, 2015, was $58,000.

Prepare a statement of cash flows for Ethos Consulting Group for the year ended May 31, 2016.

### EX 1-25  Financial statements

**OBJ. 5**

✔ Correct amount of total assets is $51,500.

We-Sell Realty, organized August 1, 2016, is owned and operated by Omar Farah. How many errors can you find in the following statements for We-Sell Realty, prepared after its first month of operations?

**We-Sell Realty**
**Income Statement**
**August 31, 2016**

| | | |
|---|---:|---:|
| Sales commissions | | $140,000 |
| Expenses: | | |
| Office salaries expense | $87,000 | |
| Rent expense | 18,000 | |
| Automobile expense | 7,500 | |
| Miscellaneous expense | 2,200 | |
| Supplies expense | 1,150 | |
| Total expenses | | 115,850 |
| Net income | | $ 25,000 |

**Omar Farah**
**Statement of Owner's Equity**
**August 31, 2015**

| | | |
|---|---:|---:|
| Omar Farah, capital, August 1, 2016 | | $    0 |
| Less withdrawals during August | | 10,000 |
| | | $(10,000) |
| Investment on August 1, 2016 | | 15,000 |
| | | $  5,000 |
| Net income for August | | 25,000 |
| Omar Farah, capital, August 31, 2016 | | $ 30,000 |

**Balance Sheet**
**For the Month Ended August 31, 2016**

| Assets | | | Liabilities | |
|---|---:|---|---|---:|
| Cash | $ 8,900 | | Accounts receivable | $38,600 |
| Accounts payable | 22,350 | | Supplies | 4,000 |
| | | | **Owner's Equity** | |
| | | | Omar Farah, capital | 30,000 |
| Total assets | $31,250 | | Total liabilities and owner's equity | $72,600 |

SHOW
ME HOW

### EX 1-26 Ratio of liabilities to stockholders' equity

OBJ. 6

The Home Depot, Inc., is the world's largest home improvement retailer and one of the largest retailers in the United States based on net sales volume. The Home Depot operates over 2,200 Home Depot® stores that sell a wide assortment of building materials and home improvement and lawn and garden products.

The Home Depot recently reported the following balance sheet data (in millions):

| | Year 2 | Year 1 |
|---|---|---|
| Total assets | $40,518 | $40,125 |
| Total stockholders' equity | 22,620 | 21,236 |

a. Determine the total liabilities at the end of Years 2 and 1.

b. Determine the ratio of liabilities to stockholders' equity for Year 2 and Year 1. Round to two decimal places.

c. ➤ What conclusions regarding the margin of protection to the creditors can you draw from (b)?

### EX 1-27 Ratio of liabilities to stockholders' equity

OBJ. 6

Lowe's Companies Inc., a major competitor of The Home Depot in the home improvement business, operates over 1,700 stores. Lowe's recently reported the following balance sheet data (in millions):

| | Year 2 | Year 1 |
|---|---|---|
| Total assets | $33,559 | $33,699 |
| Total liabilities | 17,026 | 15,587 |

a. Determine the total stockholders' equity at the end of Years 2 and 1.

b. Determine the ratio of liabilities to stockholders' equity for Year 2 and Year 1. Round to two decimal places.

c. ➤ What conclusions regarding the risk to the creditors can you draw from (b)?

d. Using the balance sheet data for The Home Depot in Exercise 1-26, how does the ratio of liabilities to stockholders' equity of Lowe's compare to that of The Home Depot?

## Problems: Series A

✔ Cash bal. at end of
April: $39,785

SHOW
ME HOW

### PR 1-1A Transactions

OBJ. 4

On April 1 of the current year, Andrea Byrd established a business to manage rental property. She completed the following transactions during April:

a. Opened a business bank account with a deposit of $45,000 from personal funds.

b. Purchased office supplies on account, $2,000.

c. Received cash from fees earned for managing rental property, $8,500.

d. Paid rent on office and equipment for the month, $5,000.

e. Paid creditors on account, $1,375.

f. Billed customers for fees earned for managing rental property, $11,250.

g. Paid automobile expenses (including rental charges) for month, $840, and miscellaneous expenses, $900.

h. Paid office salaries, $3,600.

i. Determined that the cost of supplies on hand was $550; therefore, the cost of supplies used was $1,450.

j. Withdrew cash for personal use, $2,000.

### Instructions

1. Indicate the effect of each transaction and the balances after each transaction, using the following tabular headings:

| Assets | | | = Liabilities + | | | Owner's Equity | | | | | | |
|---|---|---|---|---|---|---|---|---|---|---|---|---|
| | Accounts | | Accounts | Andrea Byrd, | Andrea Byrd, | Fees | Rent | Salaries | Supplies | Auto | Misc. | |
| Cash + | Receivable + | Supplies = | Payable + | Capital | – Drawing | + Earned | – Expense | – Expense | – Expense | – Expense | – Expense | |

2. ➤ Briefly explain why the owner's investment and revenues increased owner's equity, while withdrawals and expenses decreased owner's equity.

3. Determine the net income for April.

4. How much did April's transactions increase or decrease Andrea Byrd's capital?

---

### PR 1-2A   Financial statements   OBJ. 5

✔ 1. Net income: $327,500

SHOW
ME HOW

The amounts of the assets and liabilities of Nordic Travel Agency at December 31, 2016, the end of the year, and its revenue and expenses for the year follow. The capital of Ian Eiscle, owner, was $670,000 on January 1, 2016, the beginning of the year. During the year, Ian withdrew $42,000.

| | | | |
|---|---:|---|---:|
| Accounts payable | $ 69,500 | Rent expense | $ 36,000 |
| Accounts receivable | 285,000 | Supplies | 5,500 |
| Cash | 190,500 | Supplies expense | 4,100 |
| Fees earned | 912,500 | Utilities expense | 28,500 |
| Land | 544,000 | Wages expense | 510,000 |
| Miscellaneous expense | 6,400 | | |

**Instructions**

1. Prepare an income statement for the year ended December 31, 2016.

2. Prepare a statement of owner's equity for the year ended December 31, 2016.

3. Prepare a balance sheet as of December 31, 2016.

4. What item appears on both the statement of owner's equity and the balance sheet?

---

### PR 1-3A   Financial statements   OBJ. 5

✔ 1. Net income: $31,200

Seth Feye established Reliance Financial Services on July 1, 2016. Reliance Financial Services offers financial planning advice to its clients. The effect of each transaction and the balances after each transaction for July follow:

| | Assets | | | = Liabilities + | | | Owner's Equity | | | | | | |
|---|---|---|---|---|---|---|---|---|---|---|---|---|---|
| | Cash | + Accounts Receivable | + Supplies = | Accounts Payable | + Seth Feye, Capital | – Seth Feye, Drawing | + Fees Earned | – Salaries Expense | – Rent Expense | Auto Expense | Supplies Expense | – Misc. Expense | |
| a. | +50,000 | | | | +50,000 | | | | | | | | |
| b. | | | +7,000 | +7,000 | | | | | | | | | |
| Bal. | 50,000 | | 7,000 | 7,000 | 50,000 | | | | | | | | |
| c. | –3,600 | | | –3,600 | | | | | | | | | |
| Bal. | 46,400 | | 7,000 | 3,400 | 50,000 | | | | | | | | |
| d. | 110,000 | | | | | | +110,000 | | | | | | |
| Bal. | 156,400 | | 7,000 | 3,400 | 50,000 | | 110,000 | | | | | | |
| e. | –33,000 | | | | | | | | –33,000 | | | | |
| Bal. | 123,400 | | 7,000 | 3,400 | 50,000 | | 110,000 | | –33,000 | | | | |
| f. | –20,800 | | | | | | | | | –16,000 | | –4,800 | |
| Bal. | 102,600 | | 7,000 | 3,400 | 50,000 | | 110,000 | | –33,000 | –16,000 | | –4,800 | |
| g. | –55,000 | | | | | | | –55,000 | | | | | |
| Bal. | 47,600 | | 7,000 | 3,400 | 50,000 | | 110,000 | –55,000 | –33,000 | –16,000 | | –4,800 | |
| h. | | | –4,500 | | | | | | | | –4,500 | | |
| Bal. | 47,600 | | 2,500 | 3,400 | 50,000 | | 110,000 | –55,000 | –33,000 | –16,000 | –4,500 | –4,800 | |
| i. | | +34,500 | | | | | + 34,500 | | | | | | |
| Bal. | 47,600 | 34,500 | 2,500 | 3,400 | 50,000 | | 144,500 | –55,000 | –33,000 | –16,000 | –4,500 | –4,800 | |
| j. | –15,000 | | | | | –15,000 | | | | | | | |
| Bal. | 32,600 | 34,500 | 2,500 | 3,400 | 50,000 | –15,000 | 144,500 | –55,000 | –33,000 | –16,000 | –4,500 | –4,800 | |

(*Continued*)

**Instructions**

1. Prepare an income statement for the month ended July 31, 2016.

2. Prepare a statement of owner's equity for the month ended July 31, 2016.

3. Prepare a balance sheet as of July 31, 2016.

4. *(Optional)* Prepare a statement of cash flows for the month ending July 31, 2016.

---

**PR 1-4A   Transactions; financial statements**                                OBJ. 4, 5

✔ 2. Net income: $27,350

On July 1, 2016, Pat Glenn established Half Moon Realty. Pat completed the following transactions during the month of July:

a. Opened a business bank account with a deposit of $25,000 from personal funds.

b. Purchased office supplies on account, $1,850.

c. Paid creditor on account, $1,200.

d. Earned sales commissions, receiving cash, $41,500.

e. Paid rent on office and equipment for the month, $3,600.

f. Withdrew cash for personal use, $4,000.

g. Paid automobile expenses (including rental charge) for month, $3,050, and miscellaneous expenses, $1,600.

h. Paid office salaries, $5,000.

i. Determined that the cost of supplies on hand was $950; therefore, the cost of supplies used was $900.

**Instructions**

1. Indicate the effect of each transaction and the balances after each transaction, using the following tabular headings:

| Assets | | = Liabilities + | | | | Owner's Equity | | | | | |
|--------|--------|--------|--------|--------|--------|--------|--------|--------|--------|--------|--------|
| Cash + Supplies = | | Accounts Payable + | Pat Glenn, Capital − | Pat Glenn, Drawing + | Sales Commissions − | Salaries Expense − | Rent Expense − | Auto Expense − | Supplies Expense − | Misc. Expense | |

2. Prepare an income statement for July, a statement of owner's equity for July, and a balance sheet as of July 31.

---

**PR 1-5A   Transactions; financial statements**                                OBJ. 4, 5

✔ 3. Net income: $63,775

D'Lite Dry Cleaners is owned and operated by Joel Palk. A building and equipment are currently being rented, pending expansion to new facilities. The actual work of dry cleaning is done by another company at wholesale rates. The assets and the liabilities of the business on July 1, 2016, are as follows: Cash, $45,000; Accounts Receivable, $93,000; Supplies, $7,000; Land, $75,000; Accounts Payable, $40,000. Business transactions during July are summarized as follows:

a. Joel Palk invested additional cash in the business with a deposit of $35,000 in the business bank account.

b. Paid $50,000 for the purchase of land adjacent to land currently owned by D'Lite Dry Cleaners as a future building site.

c. Received cash from cash customers for dry cleaning revenue, $32,125.

d. Paid rent for the month, $6,000.

e. Purchased supplies on account, $2,500.

f. Paid creditors on account, $22,800.

g. Charged customers for dry cleaning revenue on account, $84,750.

h. Received monthly invoice for dry cleaning expense for July (to be paid on August 10), $29,500.

i. Paid the following: wages expense, $7,500; truck expense, $2,500; utilities expense, $1,300; miscellaneous expense, $2,700.

j. Received cash from customers on account, $88,000.

k. Determined that the cost of supplies on hand was $5,900; therefore, the cost of supplies used during the month was $3,600.

l. Withdrew $12,000 cash for personal use.

**Instructions**

1. Determine the amount of Joel Palk's capital as of July 1 of the current year.

2. State the assets, liabilities, and owner's equity as of July 1 in equation form similar to that shown in this chapter. In tabular form below the equation, indicate increases and decreases resulting from each transaction and the new balances after each transaction.

3. Prepare an income statement for July, a statement of owner's equity for July, and a balance sheet as of July 31.

4. *(Optional)* Prepare a statement of cash flows for July.

---

✔ k. $750,000

**PR 1-6A    Missing amounts from financial statements**                                      OBJ. 5

The financial statements at the end of Wolverine Realty's first month of operations are as follows:

**Wolverine Realty**
**Income Statement**
**For the Month Ended April 30, 2016**

| | | |
|---|---:|---:|
| Fees earned.................................................... | | $      (a) |
| Expenses: | | |
| Wages expense ................................................ | $300,000 | |
| Rent expense ................................................. | 100,000 | |
| Supplies expense ............................................. | (b) | |
| Utilities expense ............................................. | 20,000 | |
| Miscellaneous expense ....................................... | 25,000 | |
| Total expenses............................................ | | 475,000 |
| Net income .................................................... | | $275,000 |

**Wolverine Realty**
**Statement of Owner's Equity**
**For the Month Ended April 30, 2016**

| | | |
|---|---:|---:|
| Dakota Rowe, capital, April 1, 2016 ................................ | | $      (c) |
| Investment on April 1, 2016....................................... | $375,000 | |
| Net income for April.............................................. | (d) | |
| | $      (e) | |
| Less withdrawals ................................................. | 125,000 | |
| Increase in owner's equity ........................................ | | (f) |
| Dakota Rowe, capital, April 30, 2016 .............................. | | $      (g) |

**Wolverine Realty**
**Balance Sheet**
**April 30, 2016**

| Assets | | Liabilities | |
|---|---:|---|---:|
| Cash .......................... | $462,500 | Accounts payable .............. | $100,000 |
| Supplies....................... | 12,500 | **Owner's Equity** | |
| Land .......................... | 150,000 | Dakota Rowe, capital ............ | (i) |
| Total assets ................... | $      (h) | Total liabilities and owner's equity | $      (j) |

*(Continued)*

**Wolverine Realty**
**Statement of Cash Flows**
**For the Month Ended April 30, 2016**

| | | |
|---|---|---|
| Cash flows from operating activities: | | |
| Cash received from customers.................................... | $      (k) | |
| Deduct cash payments for expenses and payments to creditors.... | (387,500) | |
| Net cash flows from operating activities ......................... | | $      (l) |
| Cash flows from investing activities: | | |
| Cash payments for acquisition of land ........................... | | (m) |
| Cash flows from financing activities: | | |
| Cash received as owner's investment ........................... | $      (n) | |
| Deduct cash withdrawal by owner............................. | (o) | |
| Net cash flows from financing activities......................... | | (p) |
| Net increase (decrease) in cash and April 30, 2016, cash balance ...... | | $      (q) |

**Instructions**

By analyzing the interrelationships among the four financial statements, determine the proper amounts for (a) through (q).

# Problems: Series B

## PR 1-1B   Transactions
**OBJ. 4**

✔ Cash bal. at end of March: $48,650

**SHOW ME HOW**

Amy Austin established an insurance agency on March 1 of the current year and completed the following transactions during March:

a.  Opened a business bank account with a deposit of $50,000 from personal funds.

b.  Purchased supplies on account, $4,000.

c.  Paid creditors on account, $2,300.

d.  Received cash from fees earned on insurance commissions, $13,800.

e.  Paid rent on office and equipment for the month, $5,000.

f.  Paid automobile expenses for month, $1,150, and miscellaneous expenses, $300.

g.  Paid office salaries, $2,500.

h.  Determined that the cost of supplies on hand was $2,700; therefore, the cost of supplies used was $1,300.

i.  Billed insurance companies for sales commissions earned, $12,500.

j.  Withdrew cash for personal use, $3,900.

**Instructions**

1.  Indicate the effect of each transaction and the balances after each transaction, using the following tabular headings:

| Assets | | | = Liabilities + | | Owner's Equity | | | | | | |
|---|---|---|---|---|---|---|---|---|---|---|---|
| Cash + | Accounts Receivable + | Supplies = | Accounts Payable + | Amy Austin, Capital − | Amy Austin, Drawing + | Fees Earned − | Rent Expense − | Salaries Expense − | Supplies Expense − | Auto Expense − | Misc. Expense |

2.  ⬛⬛⬛➤ Briefly explain why the owner's investment and revenues increased owner's equity, while withdrawals and expenses decreased owner's equity.

3.  Determine the net income for March.

4.  How much did March's transactions increase or decrease Amy Austin's capital?

✔ 1. Net income:
$200,000

**SHOW ME HOW**

### PR 1-2B  Financial statements

OBJ. 5

The amounts of the assets and liabilities of Wilderness Travel Service at April 30, 2016, the end of the year, and its revenue and expenses for the year follow. The capital of Harper Borg, owner, was $180,000 at May 1, 2015, the beginning of the year, and the owner withdrew $40,000 during the year.

| | | | |
|---|---|---|---|
| Accounts payable | $ 25,000 | Supplies | $ 9,000 |
| Accounts receivable | 210,000 | Supplies expense | 12,000 |
| Cash | 146,000 | Taxes expense | 10,000 |
| Fees earned | 875,000 | Utilities expense | 38,000 |
| Miscellaneous expense | 15,000 | Wages expense | 525,000 |
| Rent expense | 75,000 | | |

#### Instructions

1. Prepare an income statement for the year ended April 30, 2016.
2. Prepare a statement of owner's equity for the year ended April 30, 2016.
3. Prepare a balance sheet as of April 30, 2016.
4. What item appears on both the income statement and statement of owner's equity?

✔ 1. Net income:
$10,900

### PR 1-3B  Financial statements

OBJ. 5

Jose Loder established Bronco Consulting on August 1, 2016. The effect of each transaction and the balances after each transaction for August follow:

| | Assets | | | = | Liabilities | + | | Owner's Equity | | | | | | |
|---|---|---|---|---|---|---|---|---|---|---|---|---|---|---|
| | Cash | Accounts + Receivable | + Supplies | = | Accounts Payable | + | Jose Loder, Capital | Jose Loder, Drawing + | Fees Earned | Salaries – Expense | Rent – Expense | Auto – Expense | Supplies – Expense | Misc. – Expense |
| a. | +75,000 | | | | | | +75,000 | | | | | | | |
| b. | | | +9,000 | | +9,000 | | | | | | | | | |
| Bal. | 75,000 | | 9,000 | | 9,000 | | 75,000 | | | | | | | |
| c. | +92,000 | | | | | | | | +92,000 | | | | | |
| Bal. | 167,000 | | 9,000 | | 9,000 | | 75,000 | | 92,000 | | | | | |
| d. | −27,000 | | | | | | | | | | −27,000 | | | |
| Bal. | 140,000 | | 9,000 | | 9,000 | | 75,000 | | 92,000 | | −27,000 | | | |
| e. | −6,000 | | | | −6,000 | | | | | | | | | |
| Bal. | 134,000 | | 9,000 | | 3,000 | | 75,000 | | 92,000 | | 27,000 | | | |
| f. | | +33,000 | | | | | | | +33,000 | | | | | |
| Bal. | 134,000 | 33,000 | 9,000 | | 3,000 | | 75,000 | | 125,000 | | −27,000 | | | |
| g | −23,000 | | | | | | | | | | | −15,500 | | −7,500 |
| Bal. | 111,000 | 33,000 | 9,000 | | 3,000 | | 75,000 | | 125,000 | | −27,000 | −15,500 | | −7,500 |
| h | −58,000 | | | | | | | | | −58,000 | | | | |
| Bal. | 53,000 | 33,000 | 9,000 | | 3,000 | | 75,000 | | 125,000 | −58,000 | −27,000 | −15,500 | | −7,500 |
| i. | | | −6,100 | | | | | | | | | | −6,100 | |
| Bal. | 53,000 | 33,000 | 2,900 | | 3,000 | | 75,000 | | 125,000 | −58,000 | −27,000 | −15,500 | −6,100 | −7,500 |
| j. | −15,000 | | | | | | | −15,000 | | | | | | |
| Bal. | 38,000 | 33,000 | 2,900 | | 3,000 | | 75,000 | −15,000 | 125,000 | −58,000 | −27,000 | −15,500 | −6,100 | −7,500 |

#### Instructions

1. Prepare an income statement for the month ended August 31, 2016.
2. Prepare a statement of owner's equity for the month ended August 31, 2016.
3. Prepare a balance sheet as of August 31, 2016.
4. *(Optional)* Prepare a statement of cash flows for the month ending August 31, 2016.

✔ 2. Net income:
$10,850

### PR 1-4B  Transactions; financial statements

OBJ. 4, 5

On April 1, 2016, Maria Adams established Custom Realty. Maria completed the following transactions during the month of April:

*(Continued)*

a. Opened a business bank account with a deposit of $24,000 from personal funds.

b. Paid rent on office and equipment for the month, $3,600.

c. Paid automobile expenses (including rental charge) for month, $1,350, and miscellaneous expenses, $600.

d. Purchased office supplies on account, $1,200.

e. Earned sales commissions, receiving cash, $19,800.

f. Paid creditor on account, $750.

g. Paid office salaries, $2,500.

h. Withdrew cash for personal use, $3,500.

i. Determined that the cost of supplies on hand was $300; therefore, the cost of supplies used was $900.

**Instructions**

1. Indicate the effect of each transaction and the balances after each transaction, using the following tabular headings:

| Assets | | = Liabilities + | | | Owner's Equity | | | | | |
|---|---|---|---|---|---|---|---|---|---|---|
| | | Accounts | Maria Adams, | Maria Adams, | Sales | Rent | Salaries | Auto | Supplies | Misc. |
| Cash + Supplies | = | Payable + | Capital − | Drawing + | Commissions − | Expense − | Expense − | Expense − | Expense − | Expense |

2. Prepare an income statement for April, a statement of owner's equity for April, and a balance sheet as of April 30.

---

**PR 1-5B    Transactions; financial statements**                                    OBJ. 4, 5

✔ 3. Net income: $40,150

Bev's Dry Cleaners is owned and operated by Beverly Zahn. A building and equipment are currently being rented, pending expansion to new facilities. The actual work of dry cleaning is done by another company at wholesale rates. The assets and the liabilities of the business on November 1, 2016, are as follows: Cash, $39,000; Accounts Receivable, $80,000; Supplies, $11,000; Land, $50,000; Accounts Payable, $31,500. Business transactions during November are summarized as follows:

a. Beverly Zahn invested additional cash in the business with a deposit of $21,000 in the business bank account.

b. Purchased land adjacent to land currently owned by Bev's Dry Cleaners to use in the future as a parking lot, paying cash of $35,000.

c. Paid rent for the month, $4,000.

d. Charged customers for dry cleaning revenue on account, $72,000.

e. Paid creditors on account, $20,000.

f. Purchased supplies on account, $8,000.

g. Received cash from cash customers for dry cleaning revenue, $38,000.

h. Received cash from customers on account, $77,000.

i. Received monthly invoice for dry cleaning expense for November (to be paid on December 10), $29,450.

j. Paid the following: wages expense, $24,000; truck expense, $2,100; utilities expense, $1,800; miscellaneous expense, $1,300.

k. Determined that the cost of supplies on hand was $11,800; therefore, the cost of supplies used during the month was $7,200.

l. Withdrew $5,000 for personal use.

**Instructions**

1. Determine the amount of Beverly Zahn's capital as of November 1.

2. State the assets, liabilities, and owner's equity as of November 1 in equation form similar to that shown in this chapter. In tabular form below the equation, indicate increases and decreases resulting from each transaction and the new balances after each transaction.

3. Prepare an income statement for November, a statement of owner's equity for November, and a balance sheet as of November 30.

4. *(Optional)* Prepare a statement of cash flows for November.

---

**PR 1-6B   Missing amounts from financial statements**                                    OBJ. 5

✔ i. $208,000          The financial statements at the end of Atlas Realty's first month of operations follow:

**Atlas Realty**
**Income Statement**
**For the Month Ended May 31, 2016**

| | | |
|---|---:|---:|
| Fees earned.................................................... | | $400,000 |
| Expenses: | | |
|     Wages expense ............................................. | $  (a) | |
|     Rent expense ............................................. | 48,000 | |
|     Supplies expense ......................................... | 17,600 | |
|     Utilities expense ......................................... | 14,400 | |
|     Miscellaneous expense ...................................... | 4,800 | |
|       Total expenses........................................ | | 288,000 |
| Net income .................................................... | | $     (b) |

**Atlas Realty**
**Statement of Owner's Equity**
**For the Month Ended May 31, 2016**

| | | |
|---|---:|---:|
| LuAnn Martin, capital, May 1, 2016 ................................. | | $     (c) |
| Investment on May 1, 2016......................................... | $   (d) | |
| Net income for May .............................................. | (e) | |
| | $   (f) | |
| Less withdrawals ................................................ | (g) | |
| Increase in owner's equity ......................................... | | (h) |
| LuAnn Martin, capital, May 31, 2016 ............................... | | $     (i) |

**Atlas Realty**
**Balance Sheet**
**May 31, 2016**

| Assets | | Liabilities | |
|---|---:|---|---:|
| Cash ............................. | $123,200 | Accounts payable ................... | $48,000 |
| Supplies.......................... | 12,800 | **Owner's Equity** | |
| Land ............................. | (j) | LuAnn Martin, capital................ | (l) |
| Total assets ....................... | $    (k) | Total liabilities and owner's equity.... | $    (m) |

**Atlas Realty**
**Statement of Cash Flows**
**For the Month Ended May 31, 2016**

| | | |
|---|---:|---:|
| Cash flows from operating activities: | | |
|     Cash received from customers...................................... | $    (n) | |
|     Deduct cash payments for expenses and payments to creditors.... | (252,800) | |
|     Net cash flows from operating activities ......................... | | $     (o) |
| Cash flows from investing activities: | | |
|     Cash payments for acquisition of land ............................ | | (120,000) |
| Cash flows from financing activities: | | |
|     Cash received as owner's investment ........................... | $ 160,000 | |
|     Deduct cash withdrawal by owner.............................. | (64,000) | |
|     Net cash flows from financing activities......................... | | (p) |
| Net increase (decrease) in cash and May 31, 2016, cash balance....... | | $     (q) |

**Instructions**

By analyzing the interrelationships among the four financial statements, determine the proper amounts for (a) through (q).

## Continuing Problem

✔ 2. Net income: $1,340

Peyton Smith enjoys listening to all types of music and owns countless CDs. Over the years, Peyton has gained a local reputation for knowledge of music from classical to rap and the ability to put together sets of recordings that appeal to all ages.

During the last several months, Peyton served as a guest disc jockey on a local radio station. In addition, Peyton has entertained at several friends' parties as the host deejay.

On June 1, 2016, Peyton established a proprietorship known as PS Music. Using an extensive collection of music MP3 files, Peyton will serve as a disc jockey on a fee basis for weddings, college parties, and other events. During June, Peyton entered into the following transactions:

June 1. Deposited $4,000 in a checking account in the name of PS Music.
   2. Received $3,500 from a local radio station for serving as the guest disc jockey for June.
   2. Agreed to share office space with a local real estate agency, Pinnacle Realty. PS Music will pay one-fourth of the rent. In addition, PS Music agreed to pay a portion of the wages of the receptionist and to pay one-fourth of the utilities. Paid $800 for the rent of the office.
   4. Purchased supplies from City Office Supply Co. for $350. Agreed to pay $100 within 10 days and the remainder by July 5, 2016.
   6. Paid $500 to a local radio station to advertise the services of PS Music twice daily for two weeks.
   8. Paid $675 to a local electronics store for renting digital recording equipment.
   12. Paid $350 (music expense) to Cool Music for the use of its current music demos to make various music sets.
   13. Paid City Office Supply Co. $100 on account.
   16. Received $300 from a dentist for providing two music sets for the dentist to play for her patients.
   22. Served as disc jockey for a wedding party. The father of the bride agreed to pay $1,000 in July.
   25. Received $500 for serving as the disc jockey for a cancer charity ball hosted by the local hospital.
   29. Paid $240 (music expense) to Galaxy Music for the use of its library of music demos.
   30. Received $900 for serving as PS disc jockey for a local club's monthly dance.
   30. Paid Pinnacle Realty $400 for PS Music's share of the receptionist's wages for June.
   30. Paid Pinnacle Realty $300 for PS Music's share of the utilities for June.
   30. Determined that the cost of supplies on hand is $170. Therefore, the cost of supplies used during the month was $180.
   30. Paid for miscellaneous expenses, $415.
   30. Paid $1,000 royalties (music expense) to National Music Clearing for use of various artists' music during the month.
   30. Withdrew $500 of cash from PS Music for personal use.

### Instructions

1. Indicate the effect of each transaction and the balances after each transaction, using the following tabular headings:

| Assets | | | = | Liabilities + | | | | Owner's Equity | | | | | | | |
|---|---|---|---|---|---|---|---|---|---|---|---|---|---|---|---|
| Cash + | Accts. Rec. + | Supplies = | | Accounts Payable + | Peyton Smith, Capital – | Peyton Smith, Drawing + | Fees Earned – | Music Exp. – | Office Rent Exp. – | Equipment Rent Exp. – | Advertising Exp. – | Wages Exp. – | Utilities Exp. – | Supplies Exp. – | Misc. Exp. |

2. Prepare an income statement for PS Music for the month ended June 30, 2016.

3. Prepare a statement of owner's equity for PS Music for the month ended June 30, 2016.

4. Prepare a balance sheet for PS Music as of June 30, 2016.

# Cases & Projects

### CP 1-1  Ethics and professional conduct in business
**Group Project**

Colleen Fernandez, president of Rhino Enterprises, applied for a $175,000 loan from First Federal Bank. The bank requested financial statements from Rhino Enterprises as a basis for granting the loan. Colleen has told her accountant to provide the bank with a balance sheet. Colleen has decided to omit the other financial statements because there was a net loss during the past year.

In groups of three or four, discuss the following questions:

1. Is Colleen behaving in a professional manner by omitting some of the financial statements?

2. a. What types of information about their businesses would owners be willing to provide bankers? What types of information would owners not be willing to provide?

   b. What types of information about a business would bankers want before extending a loan?

   c. What common interests are shared by bankers and business owners?

---

### CP 1-2  Net income

On January 1, 2015, Dr. Marcie Cousins established Health-Wise Medical, a medical practice organized as a proprietorship. The following conversation occurred the following August between Dr. Cousins and a former medical school classmate, Dr. Avi Abu, at an American Medical Association convention in Seattle:

*Dr. Abu:* Marcie, good to see you again. Why didn't you call when you were in Miami? We could have had dinner together.

*Dr. Cousins:* Actually, I never made it to Miami this year. My husband and kids went up to our Vail condo twice, but I got stuck in Jacksonville. I opened a new consulting practice this January and haven't had any time for myself since.

*Dr. Abu:* I heard about it . . . Health . . . something . . . right?

*Dr. Cousins:* Yes, Health-Wise Medical.  My husband chose the name.

*Dr. Abu:* I've thought about doing something like that. Are you making any money? I mean, is it worth your time?

*Dr. Cousins:* You wouldn't believe it. I started by opening a bank account with $25,000, and my July bank statement has a balance of $80,000. Not bad for six months—all pure profit.

*Dr. Abu:* Maybe I'll try it in Miami! Let's have breakfast together tomorrow and you can fill me in on the details.

➤ Comment on Dr. Cousins' statement that the difference between the opening bank balance ($25,000) and the July statement balance ($80,000) is pure profit.

---

### CP 1-3  Transactions and financial statements

Lisa Duncan, a junior in college, has been seeking ways to earn extra spending money. As an active sports enthusiast, Lisa plays tennis regularly at the Phoenix Tennis Club, where her family has a membership. The president of the club recently approached Lisa with the proposal that she manage the club's tennis courts. Lisa's primary duty would be to supervise the operation of the club's four indoor and 10 outdoor courts, including court reservations.

In return for her services, the club would pay Lisa $325 per week, plus Lisa could keep whatever she earned from lessons. The club and Lisa agreed to a one-month trial, after which both would consider an arrangement for the remaining two years of Lisa's college career. On this basis, Lisa organized Serve-N-Volley. During September 2016, Lisa managed the tennis courts and entered into the following transactions:

a. Opened a business account by depositing $950.

b. Paid $300 for tennis supplies (practice tennis balls, etc.).

*(Continued)*

c. Paid $275 for the rental of video equipment to be used in offering lessons during September.

d. Arranged for the rental of two ball machines during September for $250. Paid $100 in advance, with the remaining $150 due October 1.

e. Received $1,750 for lessons given during September.

f. Received $600 in fees from the use of the ball machines during September.

g. Paid $800 for salaries of part-time employees who answered the telephone and took reservations while Lisa was giving lessons.

h. Paid $290 for miscellaneous expenses.

i. Received $1,300 from the club for managing the tennis courts during September.

j. Determined that the cost of supplies on hand at the end of the month totaled $180; therefore, the cost of supplies used was $120.

k. Withdrew $400 for personal use on September 30.

As a friend and accounting student, you have been asked by Lisa to aid her in assessing the venture.

1. Indicate the effect of each transaction and the balances after each transaction, using the following tabular headings:

| Assets | = | Liabilities + | | | Owner's Equity | | | | |
|---|---|---|---|---|---|---|---|---|---|
| Cash + Supplies = | | Accounts Payable + | Lisa Duncan, Capital − | Lisa Duncan, Drawing + | Fees Earned | Salaries − Expense − | Rent Expense − | Supplies Expense − | Misc. Expense |

2. Prepare an income statement for September.

3. Prepare a statement of owner's equity for September.

4. Prepare a balance sheet as of September 30.

5. a. Assume that Lisa Duncan could earn $10 per hour working 30 hours a week as a waitress. Evaluate which of the two alternatives, working as a waitress or operating Serve-N-Volley, would provide Lisa with the most income per month.

b. 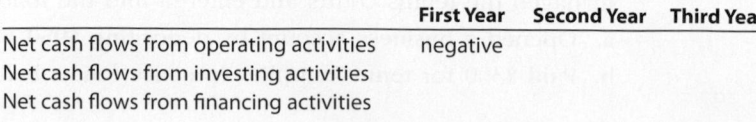 Discuss any other factors that you believe Lisa should consider before discussing a long-term arrangement with the Phoenix Tennis Club.

---

### CP 1-4 Certification requirements for accountants

Internet Project

By satisfying certain specific requirements, accountants may become certified as public accountants (CPAs), management accountants (CMAs), or internal auditors (CIAs). Find the certification requirements for one of these accounting groups by accessing one of the following Web sites:

| Site | Description |
|---|---|
| www.ais-cpa.com | This site lists the address and/or Internet link for each state's board of accountancy. Find your state's requirements. |
| www.imanet.org | This site lists the requirements for becoming a CMA. |
| www.theiia.org | This site lists the requirements for becoming a CIA. |

---

### CP 1-5 Cash flows

Amazon.com, an Internet retailer, was incorporated and began operation in the mid-90s. On the statement of cash flows, would you expect Amazon.com's net cash flows from operating, investing, and financing activities to be positive or negative for its first three years of operations? Use the following format for your answers, and briefly explain your logic.

| | First Year | Second Year | Third Year |
|---|---|---|---|
| Net cash flows from operating activities | negative | | |
| Net cash flows from investing activities | | | |
| Net cash flows from financing activities | | | |

## CP 1-6   Financial analysis

The now defunct **Enron Corporation**, once headquartered in Houston, Texas, provided products and services for natural gas, electricity, and communications to wholesale and retail customers. Enron's operations were conducted through a variety of subsidiaries and affiliates that involved transporting gas through pipelines, transmitting electricity, and managing energy commodities. The following data were taken from Enron's financial statements:

|  | In millions |
|---|---|
| Total revenues | $100,789 |
| Total costs and expenses | 98,836 |
| Operating income | 1,953 |
| Net income | 979 |
| Total assets | 65,503 |
| Total liabilities | 54,033 |
| Total owners' equity | 11,470 |
| Net cash flows from operating activities | 4,779 |
| Net cash flows from investing activities | (4,264) |
| Net cash flows from financing activities | 571 |
| Net increase in cash | 1,086 |

The market price of Enron's stock was approximately $83 per share when the prior financial statement data were taken. Before it went bankrupt, Enron's stock sold for $0.22 per share.

Review the preceding financial statement data and search the Internet for articles on Enron Corporation. Briefly explain why Enron's stock dropped so dramatically.

# Analyzing Transactions

## Apple Inc. ™

**E**very day it seems like we get an incredible amount of incoming e-mail messages—from friends, relatives, subscribed e-mail lists, and even spammers! But how do you organize all of these messages? You might create folders to sort messages by sender, topic, or project. Perhaps you use keyword search utilities. You might even use filters or rules to automatically delete spam or send messages from your best friend to a special folder. In any case, you are organizing information so that it is simple to retrieve and allows you to understand, respond, or refer to the messages.

In the same way that you organize your e-mail, companies develop an organized method for processing, recording, and summarizing financial transactions. For example, **Apple Inc.** has a huge volume of financial transactions, resulting from sales of its innovative computers, digital media (iTunes),

iPods, iPhones, and iPads. When Apple sells an iPad, a customer has the option of paying with credit card, a debit or check card, an Apple gift card, a financing arrangement, or cash. In order to analyze only the information related to Apple's cash transactions, the company must record or summarize all these similar sales using a single category or "cash" account. Similarly, Apple will record credit card payments for iPads and sales from financing arrangements in different accounts (records).

While Chapter 1 used the accounting equation (Assets = Liabilities + Owner's Equity) to analyze and record financial transactions, this chapter presents more practical and efficient recording methods that most companies use. In addition, this chapter discusses possible accounting errors that may occur, along with methods to detect and correct them.

**OBJ 1** Describe the characteristics of an account and a chart of accounts.
**Using Accounts to Record Transactions**
   Chart of Accounts

**OBJ 2** Describe and illustrate journalizing transactions using the double-entry accounting system.
**Double-Entry Accounting System**
   Balance Sheet Accounts
   Income Statement Accounts
   Owner Withdrawals
   Normal Balances                                                      EE 2-1
   Journalizing                                                         EE 2-2

**OBJ 3** Describe and illustrate the journalizing and posting of transactions to accounts.
**Posting Journal Entries to Accounts**                                EE 2-3
                                                                        EE 2-4
                                                                        EE 2-5

**OBJ 4** Prepare an unadjusted trial balance and explain how it can be used to discover errors.
**Trial Balance**
   Errors Affecting the Trial Balance                                  EE 2-6
   Errors Not Affecting the Trial Balance                              EE 2-7

**OBJ 5** Describe and illustrate the use of horizontal analysis in evaluating a company's performance and financial condition.
   Financial Analysis and Interpretation: Horizontal Analysis         EE 2-8

**At a Glance 2** ▶ Page 75

---

**OBJ 1** Describe the characteristics of an account and a chart of accounts.

# Using Accounts to Record Transactions

In Chapter 1, the November transactions for **NetSolutions** were recorded using the accounting equation format shown in Exhibit 1. However, this format is not efficient or practical for companies that have to record thousands or millions of transactions daily. As a result, accounting systems are designed to show the increases and decreases in each accounting equation element as a separate record. This record is called an **account**.

To illustrate, the Cash column of Exhibit 1 records the increases and decreases in cash. Likewise, the other columns in Exhibit 1 record the increases and decreases in the other accounting equation elements. Each of these columns can be organized into a separate account.

An account, in its simplest form, has three parts.

- A title, which is the name of the accounting equation element recorded in the account
- A space for recording increases in the amount of the element
- A space for recording decreases in the amount of the element

The account form that follows is called a **T account** because it resembles the letter T. The left side of the account is called the *debit* side, and the right side is called the *credit* side:[1]

| Title | |
|---|---|
| Left side *debit* | Right side *credit* |

---

[1] The terms *debit* and *credit* are derived from the Latin *debere* and *credere*.

| EXHIBIT 1 | NetSolutions' November Transactions |
| --- | --- |

| | Assets | | | = | Liabilities + | | Owner's Equity | | | | | | | |
| --- | --- | --- | --- | --- | --- | --- | --- | --- | --- | --- | --- | --- | --- | --- |
| | | | | | Accounts | | Chris Clark, | Chris Clark, | Fees | Wages | Rent | Supplies | Utilities | Misc. |
| | Cash | + Supp. + | Land | = | Payable | + | Capital – | Drawing + | Earned – | Exp. – | Exp. – | Exp. – | Exp. – | Exp. |
| a. | +25,000 | | | | | | +25,000 | | | | | | | |
| b. | –20,000 | | +20,000 | | | | | | | | | | | |
| Bal. | 5,000 | | 20,000 | | | | 25,000 | | | | | | | |
| c. | | +1,350 | | | +1,350 | | | | | | | | | |
| Bal. | 5,000 | 1,350 | 20,000 | | 1,350 | | 25,000 | | | | | | | |
| d. | +7,500 | | | | | | | | +7,500 | | | | | |
| Bal. | 12,500 | 1,350 | 20,000 | | 1,350 | | 25,000 | | 7,500 | | | | | |
| e. | –3,650 | | | | | | | | | –2,125 | –800 | | –450 | –275 |
| Bal. | 8,850 | 1,350 | 20,000 | | 1,350 | | 25,000 | | 7,500 | –2,125 | –800 | | –450 | –275 |
| f. | –950 | | | | –950 | | | | | | | | | |
| Bal. | 7,900 | 1,350 | 20,000 | | 400 | | 25,000 | | 7,500 | –2,125 | –800 | | –450 | –275 |
| g. | | –800 | | | | | | | | | | –800 | | |
| Bal. | 7,900 | 550 | 20,000 | | 400 | | 25,000 | | 7,500 | –2,125 | –800 | –800 | –450 | –275 |
| h. | –2,000 | | | | | | | –2,000 | | | | | | |
| Bal. | 5,900 | 550 | 20,000 | | 400 | | 25,000 | –2,000 | 7,500 | –2,125 | –800 | –800 | –450 | –275 |

The amounts shown in the Cash column of Exhibit 1 would be recorded in a cash account as follows:

**Cash**

| | | | | |
| --- | --- | --- | --- | --- |
| Debit Side of Account | (a) | 25,000 | (b) | 20,000 | Credit Side of Account |
| | (d) | 7,500 | (e) | 3,650 | |
| | | | (f) | 950 | |
| | | | (h) | 2,000 | |
| | Balance | 5,900 | | | |

Balance of Account ⟶

**Note:**
Amounts entered on the left side of an account are debits, and amounts entered on the right side of an account are credits.

Recording transactions in accounts must follow certain rules. For example, increases in assets are recorded on the **debit** (left side) of an account. Likewise, decreases in assets are recorded on the **credit** (right side) of an account. The excess of the debits of an asset account over its credits is the **balance of the account**.

To illustrate, the receipt (increase in Cash) of $25,000 in transaction (a) is entered on the debit (left) side of the cash account. The letter or date of the transaction is also entered into the account. That way, if any questions later arise related to the entry, the entry can be traced back to the underlying transaction data. In contrast, the payment (decrease in Cash) of $20,000 to purchase land in transaction (b) is entered on the credit (right) side of the account.

The balance of the cash account of $5,900 is the excess of the debits over the credits, computed as follows:

| | |
| --- | --- |
| Debits ($25,000 + $7,500) . . . . . . . . . . . . . . . . . . . . . . . . . . . . . . . . . . . . . . . . . . . . . . . . . . . . . . . . . . | $32,500 |
| Less credits ($20,000 + $3,650 + $950 + $2,000) . . . . . . . . . . . . . . . . . . . . . . . . . . . . . . . . . . . . . | 26,600 |
| Balance of Cash as of November 30, 2015 . . . . . . . . . . . . . . . . . . . . . . . . . . . . . . . . . . . . . . . . . . | $ 5,900 |

The balance of the cash account is inserted in the account, in the Debit column. In this way, the balance is identified as a debit balance.[2] This balance represents NetSolutions' cash on hand as of November 30, 2015. This balance of $5,900 is reported on the November 30, 2015, balance sheet for NetSolutions as shown in Exhibit 8 of Chapter 1.

In an actual accounting system, a more formal account form replaces the T account. Later in this chapter, a four-column account is illustrated. The T account, however, is

[2] The totals of the debit and credit columns may be shown separately in an account. When this is done, these amounts should be identified in some way so that they are not mistaken for entries or the ending balance of the account.

a simple way to illustrate the effects of transactions on accounts and financial statements. For this reason, T accounts are often used in business to explain transactions.

Each of the columns in Exhibit 1 can be converted into an account form in a similar manner as was done for the Cash column of Exhibit 1. However, as mentioned earlier, recording increases and decreases in accounts must follow certain rules. These rules are discussed after the chart of accounts is described.

## Chart of Accounts

A group of accounts for a business entity is called a **ledger**. A list of the accounts in the ledger is called a **chart of accounts**. The accounts are normally listed in the order in which they appear in the financial statements. The balance sheet accounts are listed first, in the order of assets, liabilities, and owner's equity. The income statement accounts are then listed in the order of revenues and expenses.

**Assets** **Assets** are resources owned by the business entity. These resources can be physical items, such as cash and supplies, or intangibles that have value. Examples of intangible assets include patent rights, copyrights, and trademarks. Assets also include accounts receivable, prepaid expenses (such as insurance), buildings, equipment, and land.

**Liabilities** **Liabilities** are debts owed to outsiders (creditors). Liabilities are often identified on the balance sheet by titles that include *payable*. Examples of liabilities include accounts payable, notes payable, and wages payable. Cash received before services are delivered creates a liability to perform the services. These future service commitments are called *unearned revenues*. Examples of unearned revenues include magazine subscriptions received by a publisher and tuition received at the beginning of a term by a college.

**Owner's equity** **Owner's equity** is the owner's right to the assets of the business after all liabilities have been paid. For a proprietorship, the owner's equity is represented by the balance of the owner's **capital account**. A **drawing** account represents the amount of withdrawals made by the owner.

**Revenues** **Revenues** are increases in assets and owner's equity as a result of selling services or products to customers. Examples of revenues include fees earned, fares earned, commissions revenue, and rent revenue.

---

# Business ⊕ Connection

## THE HIJACKING RECEIVABLE

A company's chart of accounts should reflect the basic nature of its operations. Occasionally, however, transactions take place that give rise to unusual accounts. The following is a story of one such account.

Before strict airport security was implemented across the United States, several airlines experienced hijacking incidents. One such incident occurred when a Southern Airways jet en route from Memphis to Miami was hijacked during a stopover in Birmingham, Alabama. The three hijackers boarded the plane in Birmingham armed with handguns and hand grenades. At gunpoint, the hijackers took the plane, the plane's crew, and the passengers to nine American cities, Toronto, and eventually to Havana, Cuba.

During the long flight, the hijackers demanded a ransom of $10 million. Southern Airways, however, was only able to come up with $2 million. Eventually, the pilot talked the hijackers into settling for the $2 million when the plane landed in Chattanooga for refueling.

Upon landing in Havana, the Cuban authorities arrested the hijackers and, after a brief delay, sent the plane, passengers, and crew back to the United States. The hijackers and the $2 million stayed in Cuba.

How did Southern Airways account for and report the hijacking payment in its subsequent financial statements? As you might have analyzed, the initial entry credited Cash for $2 million. The debit was to an account entitled "Hijacking Payment." This account was reported as a type of receivable under "other assets" on Southern Airways' balance sheet. The company maintained that it would be able to collect the cash from the Cuban government and that, therefore, a receivable existed. In fact, Southern Airways was later repaid $2 million by the Cuban government, which was, at that time, attempting to improve relations with the United States.

**Expenses** Expenses result from using up assets or consuming services in the process of generating revenues. Examples of expenses include wages expense, rent expense, utilities expense, supplies expense, and miscellaneous expense.

**Illustration of Chart of Accounts** A chart of accounts should meet the needs of a company's managers and other users of its financial statements. The accounts within the chart of accounts are numbered for use as references. A numbering system is normally used, so that new accounts can be added without affecting other account numbers.

Exhibit 2 is **NetSolutions'** chart of accounts that is used in this chapter. Additional accounts will be introduced in later chapters. In Exhibit 2, each account number has two digits. The first digit indicates the major account group of the ledger in which the account is located. Accounts beginning with 1 represent assets; 2, liabilities; 3, owner's equity; 4, revenue; and 5, expenses. The second digit indicates the location of the account within its group.

Procter & Gamble's account numbers have over 30 digits to reflect P&G's many different operations and regions.

---

**EXHIBIT 2**

**Chart of Accounts for NetSolutions**

| Balance Sheet Accounts | Income Statement Accounts |
|---|---|
| **1. Assets** | **4. Revenue** |
| 11  Cash | 41  Fees Earned |
| 12  Accounts Receivable | **5. Expenses** |
| 14  Supplies | 51  Wages Expense |
| 15  Prepaid Insurance | 52  Supplies Expense |
| 17  Land | 53  Rent Expense |
| 18  Office Equipment | 54  Utilities Expense |
| **2. Liabilities** | 59  Miscellaneous Expense |
| 21  Accounts Payable | |
| 23  Unearned Rent | |
| **3. Owner's Equity** | |
| 31  Chris Clark, Capital | |
| 32  Chris Clark, Drawing | |

---

Each of the columns in Exhibit 1 has been assigned an account number in the chart of accounts shown in Exhibit 2. In addition, Accounts Receivable, Prepaid Insurance, Office Equipment, and Unearned Rent have been added. These accounts will be used in recording NetSolutions' December transactions.

# Double-Entry Accounting System

All businesses use what is called the **double-entry accounting system**. This system is based on the accounting equation and requires:

- Every business transaction to be recorded in at least two accounts.
- The total debits recorded for each transaction to be equal to the total credits recorded.

**OBJ 2** Describe and illustrate journalizing transactions using the double-entry accounting system.

The double-entry accounting system also has specific **rules of debit and credit** for recording transactions in the accounts.

## Balance Sheet Accounts

The debit and credit rules for balance sheet accounts are as follows:

| Balance Sheet Accounts | | | | | |
|---|---|---|---|---|---|
| ASSETS<br>Asset Accounts | | = LIABILITIES<br>Liability Accounts | | + OWNER'S EQUITY<br>Owner's Equity Accounts | |
| Debit for<br>increases (+) | Credit for<br>decreases (−) | Debit for<br>decreases (−) | Credit for<br>increases (+) | Debit for<br>decreases (−) | Credit for<br>increases (+) |

## Income Statement Accounts

The debit and credit rules for income statement accounts are based on their relationship with owner's equity. As shown for balance sheet accounts, owner's equity accounts are increased by credits. Because revenues increase owner's equity, revenue accounts are increased by credits and decreased by debits. Because owner's equity accounts are decreased by debits, expense accounts are increased by debits and decreased by credits. Thus, the rules of debit and credit for revenue and expense accounts are as follows:

**Income Statement Accounts**

| Revenue Accounts | | Expense Accounts | |
|---|---|---|---|
| Debit for decreases (–) | Credit for increases (+) | Debit for increases (+) | Credit for decreases (–) |

## Owner Withdrawals

The debit and credit rules for recording owner withdrawals are based on the effect of owner withdrawals on owner's equity. Because an owner's withdrawals decrease owner's equity, the owner's drawing account is increased by debits. Likewise, the owner's drawing account is decreased by credits. Thus, the rules of debit and credit for the owner's drawing account are as follows:

**Drawing Account**

| Debit for increases (+) | Credit for decreases (–) |
|---|---|

## Normal Balances

The sum of the increases in an account is usually equal to or greater than the sum of the decreases in the account. Thus, the **normal balance of an account** is either a debit or credit depending on whether increases in the account are recorded as debits or credits. For example, because asset accounts are increased with debits, asset accounts normally have debit balances. Likewise, liability accounts normally have credit balances.

The rules of debit and credit and the normal balances of the various types of accounts are summarized in Exhibit 3. Debits and credits are sometimes abbreviated as Dr. for debit and Cr. for credit.

---

**EXHIBIT 3** **Rules of Debit and Credit, Normal Balances of Accounts**

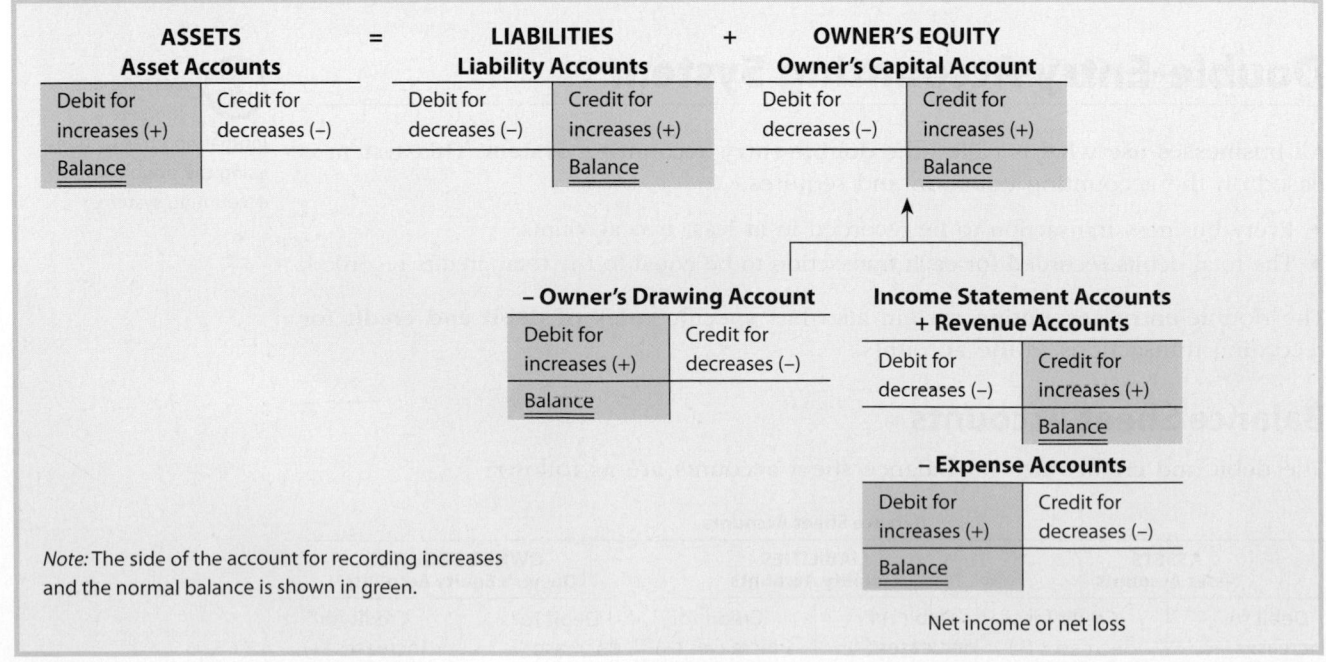

*Note:* The side of the account for recording increases and the normal balance is shown in green.

When an account normally having a debit balance has a credit balance, or vice versa, an error may have occurred or an unusual situation may exist. For example, a credit balance in the office equipment account could result only from an error. This is because a business cannot have more decreases than increases of office equipment. On the other hand, a debit balance in an accounts payable account could result from an overpayment.

## Example Exercise 2-1   Rules of Debit and Credit and Normal Balances

State for each account whether it is likely to have (a) debit entries only, (b) credit entries only, or (c) both debit and credit entries. Also, indicate its normal balance.

1.  Amber Saunders, Drawing
2.  Accounts Payable
3.  Cash

4.  Fees Earned
5.  Supplies
6.  Utilities Expense

## Follow My Example 2-1

1.  Debit entries only; normal debit balance
2.  Debit and credit entries; normal credit balance
3.  Debit and credit entries; normal debit balance

4.  Credit entries only; normal credit balance
5.  Debit and credit entries; normal debit balance
6.  Debit entries only; normal debit balance

Practice Exercises: PE 2-1A, PE 2-1B

## Journalizing

Using the rules of debit and credit, transactions are initially entered in a record called a **journal**. In this way, the journal serves as a record of when transactions occurred and were recorded. To illustrate, the November transactions of **NetSolutions** from Chapter 1 are used.

 A journal can be thought of as being similar to an individual's diary of significant day-to-day life events.

| | |
|---|---|
| *Nov. 1   Chris Clark deposited $25,000 in a bank account in the name of NetSolutions.* | *Transaction A* |

This transaction increases an asset account and increases an owner's equity account. It is recorded in the journal as an increase (debit) to Cash and an increase (credit) to Chris Clark, Capital.

*Analysis*

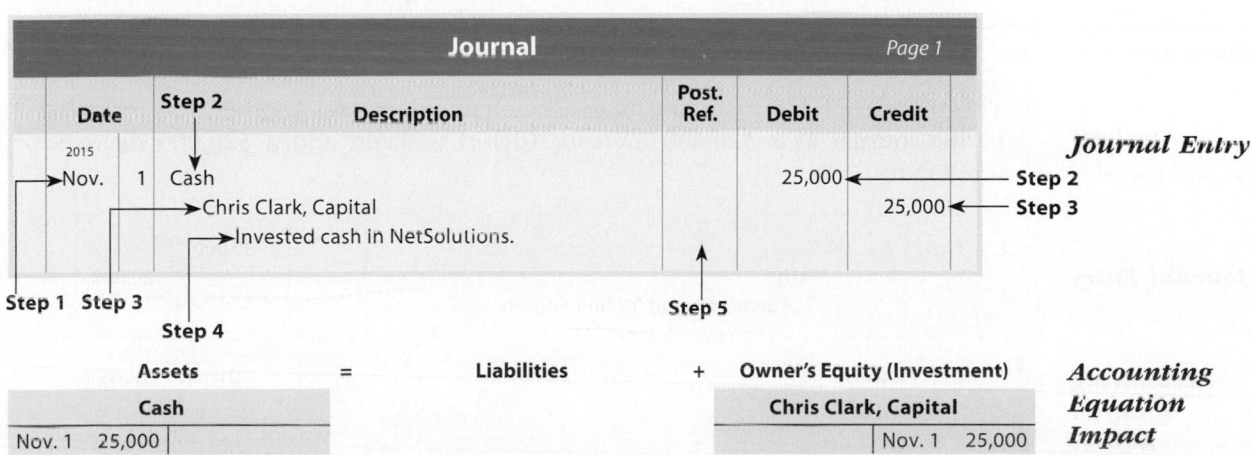

*Journal Entry*

*Accounting Equation Impact*

The transaction is recorded in the journal using the following steps:

- Step 1. The date of the transaction is entered in the Date column.
- Step 2. The title of the account to be debited is recorded in the left-hand margin under the Description column, and the amount to be debited is entered in the Debit column.

- Step 3. The title of the account to be credited is listed below and to the right of the debited account title, and the amount to be credited is entered in the Credit column.
- Step 4. A brief description may be entered below the credited account.
- Step 5. The Post. Ref. (Posting Reference) column is left blank when the journal entry is initially recorded. This column is used later in this chapter when the journal entry amounts are transferred to the accounts in the ledger.

The process of recording a transaction in the journal is called **journalizing**. The entry in the journal is called a **journal entry**.

The following is a useful method for analyzing and journalizing transactions:

- Step 1. Carefully read the description of the transaction to determine whether an asset, a liability, an owner's equity, a revenue, an expense, or a drawing account is affected.
- Step 2. For each account affected by the transaction, determine whether the account increases or decreases.
- Step 3. Determine whether each increase or decrease should be recorded as a debit or a credit, following the rules of debit and credit shown in Exhibit 3.
- Step 4. Record the transaction using a journal entry.

Exhibit 4 summarizes terminology that is often used in describing a transaction along with the related accounts that would be debited and credited.

---

**EXHIBIT 4**

**Transaction Terminology and Related Journal Entry Accounts**

| Common Transaction Terminology | Journal Entry Account | |
|---|---|---|
| | **Debit** | **Credit** |
| Received cash for services provided | Cash | Fees Earned |
| Services provided on account | Accounts Receivable | Fees Earned |
| Received cash on account | Cash | Accounts Receivable |
| Purchased on account | Asset account | Accounts Payable |
| Paid on account | Accounts Payable | Cash |
| Paid cash | Asset or expense account | Cash |
| Owner investments | Cash and/or other assets | (Owner's name), Capital |
| Owner withdrawals | (Owner's name), Drawing | Cash |

---

The remaining transactions of **NetSolutions** for November are analyzed and journalized next.

---

**Transaction B**   *Nov. 5*   *NetSolutions paid $20,000 for the purchase of land as a future building site.*

**Analysis**   This transaction increases one asset account and decreases another. It is recorded in the journal as a $20,000 increase (debit) to Land and a $20,000 decrease (credit) to Cash.

**Journal Entry**

| | | | | | |
|---|---|---|---|---|---|
| Nov. | 5 | Land | | 20,000 | |
| | | Cash | | | 20,000 |
| | | Purchased land for building site. | | | |

**Accounting Equation Impact**

| Assets | = | Liabilities | + | Owner's Equity |
|---|---|---|---|---|

| Land | |
|---|---|
| Nov. 5   20,000 | |

| Cash | |
|---|---|
| | Nov. 5   20,000 |

*Nov. 10 NetSolutions purchased supplies on account for $1,350.*          *Transaction C*

This transaction increases an asset account and increases a liability account. It is recorded in the journal as a $1,350 increase (debit) to Supplies and a $1,350 increase (credit) to Accounts Payable.          *Analysis*

| | | | | | |
|---|---|---|---|---|---|
| Nov. | 10 | Supplies | | 1,350 | |
| | | Accounts Payable | | | 1,350 |
| | | Purchased supplies on account. | | | |

*Journal Entry*

| Assets | = | Liabilities | + | Owner's Equity |
|---|---|---|---|---|
| **Supplies** | | **Accounts Payable** | | |
| Nov. 10   1,350 | | Nov. 10   1,350 | | |

*Accounting Equation Impact*

*Nov. 18 NetSolutions received cash of $7,500 from customers for services provided.*          *Transaction D*

This transaction increases an asset account and increases a revenue account. It is recorded in the journal as a $7,500 increase (debit) to Cash and a $7,500 increase (credit) to Fees Earned.          *Analysis*

| | | | | | |
|---|---|---|---|---|---|
| Nov. | 18 | Cash | | 7,500 | |
| | | Fees Earned | | | 7,500 |
| | | Received fees from customers. | | | |

*Journal Entry*

| Assets | = | Liabilities | + | Owner's Equity (Revenue) |
|---|---|---|---|---|
| **Cash** | | | | **Fees Earned** |
| Nov. 18   7,500 | | | | Nov. 18   7,500 |

*Accounting Equation Impact*

*Nov. 30 NetSolutions incurred the following expenses: wages, $2,125; rent, $800; utilities, $450; and miscellaneous, $275.*          *Transaction E*

This transaction increases various expense accounts and decreases an asset (Cash) account. You should note that regardless of the number of accounts, *the sum of the debits is always equal to the sum of the credits in a journal entry*. It is recorded in the journal with increases (debits) to the expense accounts (Wages Expense, $2,125; Rent Expense, $800; Utilities Expense, $450; and Miscellaneous Expense, $275) and a decrease (credit) to Cash, $3,650.          *Analysis*

| | | | | | |
|---|---|---|---|---|---|
| Nov. | 30 | Wages Expense | | 2,125 | |
| | | Rent Expense | | 800 | |
| | | Utilities Expense | | 450 | |
| | | Miscellaneous Expense | | 275 | |
| | | Cash | | | 3,650 |
| | | Paid expenses. | | | |

*Journal Entry*

| Assets | = | Liabilities | + | Owner's Equity (Expense) |
|---|---|---|---|---|
| **Cash** | | | | **Wages Expense** |
| | Nov. 30   3,650 | | | Nov. 30   2,125 |
| | | | | **Rent Expense** |
| | | | | Nov. 30   800 |
| | | | | **Utilities Expense** |
| | | | | Nov. 30   450 |
| | | | | **Miscellaneous Expense** |
| | | | | Nov. 30   275 |

*Accounting Equation Impact*

| | |
|---|---|
| *Transaction F* | Nov. 30  NetSolutions paid creditors on account, $950. |

**Analysis** — This transaction decreases a liability account and decreases an asset account. It is recorded in the journal as a $950 decrease (debit) to Accounts Payable and a $950 decrease (credit) to Cash.

**Journal Entry**

| Nov. | 30 | Accounts Payable | | 950 | |
|------|----|------------------|--|-----|--|
| | | Cash | | | 950 |
| | | Paid creditors on account. | | | |

**Accounting Equation Impact**

| Assets | = | Liabilities | + | Owner's Equity |
|--------|---|-------------|---|----------------|
| **Cash** | | **Accounts Payable** | | |
| Nov. 30    950 | | Nov. 30    950 | | |

---

| | |
|---|---|
| *Transaction G* | Nov. 30  Chris Clark determined that the cost of supplies on hand at November 30 was $550. |

**Analysis** — NetSolutions purchased $1,350 of supplies on November 10. Thus, $800 ($1,350 – $550) of supplies must have been used during November. This transaction is recorded in the journal as an $800 increase (debit) to Supplies Expense and an $800 decrease (credit) to Supplies.

**Journal Entry**

| Nov. | 30 | Supplies Expense | | 800 | |
|------|----|------------------|--|-----|--|
| | | Supplies | | | 800 |
| | | Supplies used during November. | | | |

**Accounting Equation Impact**

| Assets | = | Liabilities | + | Owner's Equity (Expense) |
|--------|---|-------------|---|--------------------------|
| **Supplies** | | | | **Supplies Expense** |
| Nov. 30    800 | | | | Nov. 30    800 |

---

| | |
|---|---|
| *Transaction H* | Nov. 30  Chris Clark withdrew $2,000 from NetSolutions for personal use. |

**Analysis** — This transaction decreases assets and owner's equity. This transaction is recorded in the journal as a $2,000 increase (debit) to Chris Clark, Drawing and a $2,000 decrease (credit) to Cash.

**Journal Entry**

| | Journal | | | Page 2 |
|--|---------|--|--|--------|

| Date | Description | Post. Ref. | Debit | Credit |
|------|-------------|------------|-------|--------|
| 2015 | | | | |
| Nov. 30 | Chris Clark, Drawing | | 2,000 | |
| | Cash | | | 2,000 |
| | Chris Clark withdrew cash for personal use. | | | |

**Accounting Equation Impact**

| Assets | = | Liabilities | + | Owner's Equity (Drawing) |
|--------|---|-------------|---|--------------------------|
| **Cash** | | | | **Chris Clark, Drawing** |
| Nov. 30    2,000 | | | | Nov. 30    2,000 |

---

## Integrity, Objectivity, and Ethics in Business

### WILL JOURNALIZING PREVENT FRAUD?

While journalizing transactions reduces the possibility of fraud, it by no means eliminates it. For example, embezzlement can be hidden within the double-entry book-keeping system by creating fictitious suppliers to whom checks are issued.

**Example Exercise 2-2 Journal Entry for Asset Purchase** OBJ 2

Prepare a journal entry for the purchase of a truck on June 3 for $42,500, paying $8,500 cash and the remainder on account.

**Follow My Example 2-2**

| June 3 | Truck............................................... | 42,500 | |
| | Cash........................................... | | 8,500 |
| | Accounts Payable............................. | | 34,000 |

Practice Exercises: PE 2-2A, PE 2-2B

# Posting Journal Entries to Accounts

OBJ 3 Describe and illustrate the journalizing and posting of transactions to accounts.

As illustrated, a transaction is first recorded in a journal. Periodically, the journal entries are transferred to the accounts in the ledger. The process of transferring the debits and credits from the journal entries to the accounts is called **posting**.

The December transactions of **NetSolutions** are used to illustrate posting from the journal to the ledger. By using the December transactions, an additional review of analyzing and journalizing transactions is provided.

*Dec. 1 NetSolutions paid a premium of $2,400 for an insurance policy for liability, theft, and fire. The policy covers a one-year period.*

*Transaction*

Advance payments of expenses, such as for insurance premiums, are called prepaid expenses. Prepaid expenses are assets. For NetSolutions, the asset purchased is insurance protection for 12 months. This transaction is recorded as a $2,400 increase (debit) to Prepaid Insurance and a $2,400 decrease (credit) to Cash.

*Analysis*

| Dec. | 1 | Prepaid Insurance | 15 | 2,400 | |
| | | Cash | 11 | | 2,400 |
| | | Paid premium on one-year policy. | | | |

*Journal Entry*

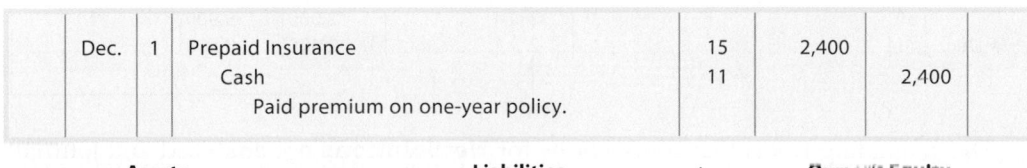

Assets = Liabilities + Owner's Equity

*Accounting Equation Impact*

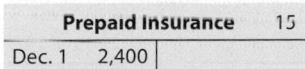

The posting of the preceding December 1 transaction is shown in Exhibit 5. Notice that the T account form is not used in Exhibit 5. In practice, the T account is usually replaced with a standard account form similar to that shown in Exhibit 5.

The debits and credits for each journal entry are posted to the accounts in the order in which they occur in the journal. To illustrate, the debit portion of the December 1 journal entry is posted to the prepaid account in Exhibit 5 using the following four steps:

- Step 1. The date (Dec. 1) of the journal entry is entered in the Date column of Prepaid Insurance.
- Step 2. The amount (2,400) is entered into the Debit column of Prepaid Insurance.
- Step 3. The journal page number (2) is entered in the Posting Reference (Post. Ref.) column of Prepaid Insurance.
- Step 4. The account number (15) is entered in the Posting Reference (Post. Ref.) column in the journal.

As shown in Exhibit 5, the credit portion of the December 1 journal entry is posted to the cash account in a similar manner.

| EXHIBIT 5 | Diagram of the Recording and Posting of a Debit and a Credit |
|---|---|

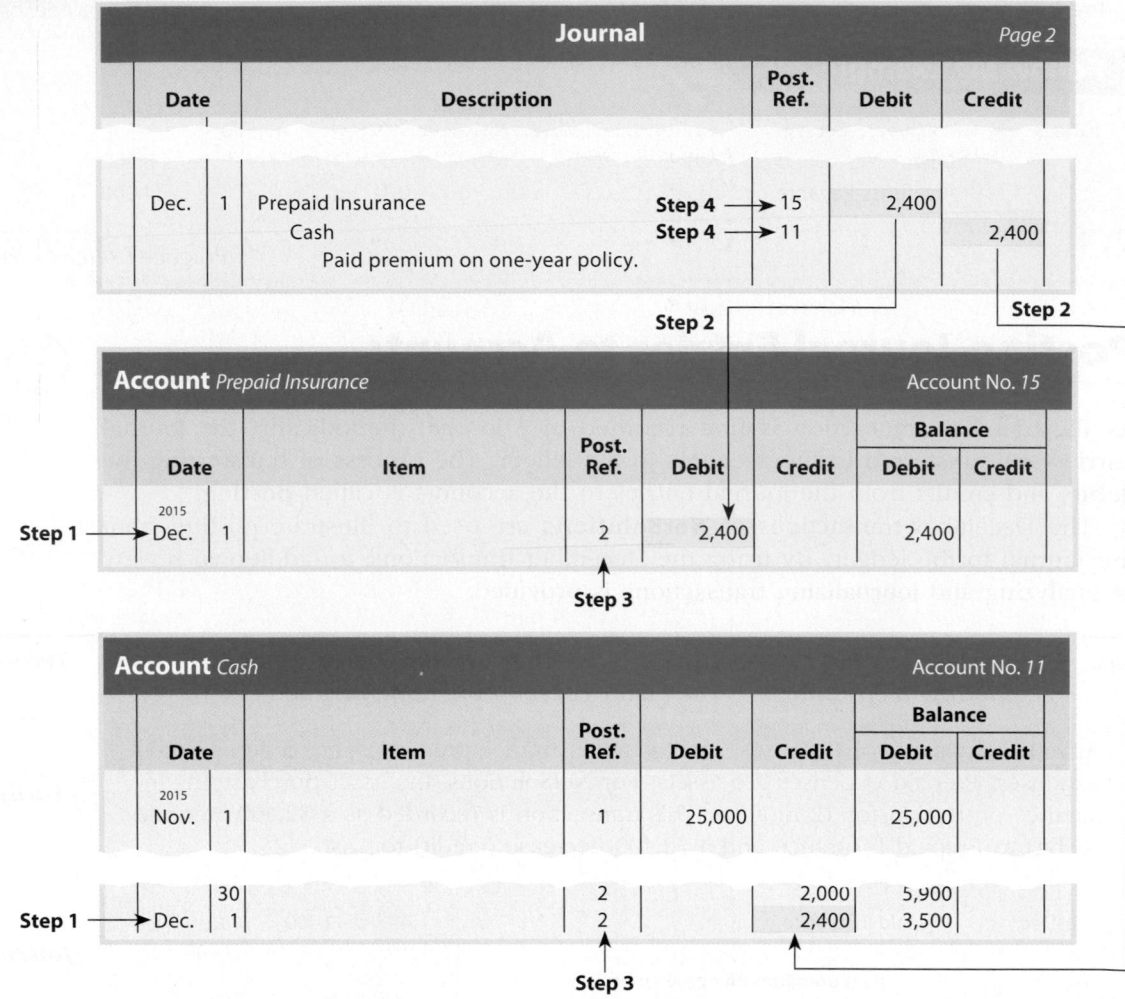

The remaining December transactions for **NetSolutions** are analyzed and journalized in the following paragraphs. These transactions are posted to the ledger later in this chapter (see Exhibit 6). To simplify, some of the December transactions are stated in summary form. For example, cash received for services is normally recorded on a daily basis. However, only summary totals are recorded at the middle and end of the month for NetSolutions.

**Transaction** **Dec. 1** *NetSolutions paid rent for December, $800. The company from which NetSolutions is renting its office space now requires the payment of rent on the first of each month, rather than at the end of the month.*

**Analysis** The advance payment of rent is an asset, much like the advance payment of the insurance premium in the preceding transaction. However, unlike the insurance premium, this prepaid rent will expire in one month. When an asset is purchased with the expectation that it will be used up in a short period of time, such as a month, it is normal to debit an expense account initially. This avoids having to transfer the balance from an asset account (Prepaid Rent) to an expense account (Rent Expense) at the end of the month. Thus, this transaction is recorded as an $800 increase (debit) to Rent Expense and an $800 decrease (credit) to Cash.

**Journal Entry**

| | | | | Debit | Credit |
|---|---|---|---|---|---|
| Dec. | 1 | Rent Expense | 53 | 800 | |
| | | Cash | 11 | | 800 |
| | | Paid rent for December. | | | |

| Assets | | = | Liabilities | + | Owner's Equity (Expense) | | Accounting |
|---|---|---|---|---|---|---|---|
| **Cash** | 11 | | | | **Rent Expense** | 53 | Equation |
| | Dec. 1 800 | | | | Dec. 1 800 | | Impact |

**Dec. 1** *NetSolutions received an offer from a local retailer to rent the land*      *Transaction*
*purchased on November 5. The retailer plans to use the land as a parking*
*lot for its employees and customers. NetSolutions agreed to rent the*
*land to the retailer for three months, with the rent payable in advance.*
*NetSolutions received $360 for three months' rent beginning December 1.*

By agreeing to rent the land and accepting the $360, NetSolutions has incurred an
obligation (liability) to the retailer. This obligation is to make the land available
for use for three months and not to interfere with its use. The liability created      *Analysis*
by receiving the cash in advance of providing the service is called **unearned**
**revenue**. As time passes, the unearned rent liability will decrease and will become revenue. Thus, this transaction is recorded as a $360 increase (debit) to
Cash and a $360 increase (credit) to Unearned Rent.

| Dec. | 1 | Cash | 11 | 360 | | |
|---|---|---|---|---|---|---|
| | | Unearned Rent | 23 | | 360 | *Journal Entry* |
| | | Received advance payment for three | | | | |
| | | months' rent on land. | | | | |

| Assets | | = | Liabilities | | + | Owner's Equity | Accounting |
|---|---|---|---|---|---|---|---|
| **Cash** | 11 | | **Unearned Rent** | 23 | | | Equation |
| Dec. 1 360 | | | Dec. 1 | 360 | | | Impact |

# Business Connection

## MICROSOFT'S UNEARNED REVENUE

Microsoft Corporation develops, manufactures, licenses, and supports a wide range of computer software products, including Windows 7®, Windows 8®, Word®, Excel®, and the Xbox® gaming system. When Microsoft sells its products, it also provides technical support and periodic updates on those products for a period of time. Thus, at the time of sale a portion of the proceeds is unearned (deferred) for these services. As time passes and services are provided to customers, Microsoft records a portion of its unearned (deferred) revenue as revenue.[3]

To illustrate, the following excerpts were taken from recent financial statement of Microsoft:

Unearned revenue comprises mainly unearned revenue from volume licensing programs, and payments for offerings for which we have been paid in advance and we earn the revenue when we provide the service or software or otherwise meet the revenue recogni-

tion criteria.... Also included in unearned revenue are payments for post-delivery support and consulting services to be performed in the future....

Unearned revenue (in millions) by segment:

| | June 30 current year | June 30 prior year |
|---|---|---|
| Windows Division | $ 2,086 | $ 2,444 |
| Server and Tools | 8,639 | 7,445 |
| Microsoft Business Division | 10,142 | 9,015 |
| Other segments | 1,532 | 1,155 |
| Total | $22,399 | $20,059 |

During the year, Microsoft recognized $44.25 billion in unearned revenue as revenue. At the same time, Microsoft recorded additional unearned revenue from the current period of $41.92 billion. Out of $77.8 billion in total revenue, Microsoft recognized $44.2 billion from unearned revenue, or 56% of total revenues. Thus, unearned revenues are a significant reporting item for Microsoft.

Source: Microsoft Corp., Form 10-K for the Fiscal Year Ended June 30, 2013.

**Dec. 4** *NetSolutions purchased office equipment on account from Executive*      *Transaction*
*Supply Co. for $1,800.*

The asset (Office Equipment) and liability accounts (Accounts Payable) increase.      *Analysis*
This transaction is recorded as an $1,800 increase (debit) to Office Equipment
and an $1,800 increase (credit) to Accounts Payable.

[3] Separating unearned revenue from the initial sale of a product or service is consistent with FASB Exposure Draft, Revenue Recognition (Topic 605), June 24, 2010, paras. 23, 35-36.

**Journal Entry**

| Dec. | 4 | Office Equipment | 18 | 1,800 | |
|---|---|---|---|---|---|
| | | Accounts Payable | 21 | | 1,800 |
| | | Purchased office equipment on account. | | | |

**Accounting Equation Impact**

| Assets | = | Liabilities | + | Owner's Equity |
|---|---|---|---|---|
| Office Equipment 18 | | Accounts Payable 21 | | |
| Dec. 4 1,800 | | Dec. 4 1,800 | | |

---

**Transaction** *Dec. 6 NetSolutions paid $180 for a newspaper advertisement.*

**Analysis** An expense increases, and an asset (Cash) decreases. Expense items that are expected to be minor in amount are normally included as part of the miscellaneous expense. This transaction is recorded as a $180 increase (debit) to Miscellaneous Expense and a $180 decrease (credit) to Cash.

**Journal Entry**

| Dec. | 6 | Miscellaneous Expense | 59 | 180 | |
|---|---|---|---|---|---|
| | | Cash | 11 | | 180 |
| | | Paid for newspaper advertisement. | | | |

**Accounting Equation Impact**

| Assets | = | Liabilities | + | Owner's Equity (Expense) |
|---|---|---|---|---|
| Cash 11 | | | | Miscellaneous Exp. 59 |
| Dec. 6 180 | | | | Dec. 6 180 |

---

**Transaction** *Dec. 11 NetSolutions paid creditors $400.*

**Analysis** A liability (Accounts Payable) and an asset (Cash) decrease. This transaction is recorded as a $400 decrease (debit) to Accounts Payable and a $400 decrease (credit) to Cash.

**Journal Entry**

| Dec. | 11 | Accounts Payable | 21 | 400 | |
|---|---|---|---|---|---|
| | | Cash | 11 | | 400 |
| | | Paid creditors on account. | | | |

**Accounting Equation Impact**

| Assets | = | Liabilities | + | Owner's Equity |
|---|---|---|---|---|
| Cash 11 | | Accounts Payable 21 | | |
| Dec. 11 400 | | Dec. 11 400 | | |

---

**Transaction** *Dec. 13 NetSolutions paid a receptionist and a part-time assistant $950 for two weeks' wages.*

**Analysis** This transaction is similar to the December 6 transaction, where an expense account is increased and Cash is decreased. This transaction is recorded as a $950 increase (debit) to Wages Expense and a $950 decrease (credit) to Cash.

**Journal Entry**

| | Journal | | | | Page 3 |
|---|---|---|---|---|---|
| **Date** | | **Description** | **Post. Ref.** | **Debit** | **Credit** |
| 2015 | | | | | |
| Dec. | 13 | Wages Expense | 51 | 950 | |
| | | Cash | 11 | | 950 |
| | | Paid two weeks' wages. | | | |

**Accounting Equation Impact**

| Assets | = | Liabilities | + | Owner's Equity (Expense) |
|---|---|---|---|---|
| Cash 11 | | | | Wages Expense 51 |
| Dec. 13 950 | | | | Dec. 13 950 |

# Business 🌐 Connection

## COMPUTERIZED ACCOUNTING SYSTEMS

Computerized accounting systems are widely used by even the smallest companies. These systems simplify the record-keeping process in that transactions are recorded in electronic forms. Forms used to bill customers for services provided are often completed using drop-down menus that list services that are normally provided to customers. An auto-complete entry feature may also be used

to fill in customer names. For example, type "ca" to display customers with names beginning with "Ca" (Caban, Cahill, Carey, and Caswell). And, to simplify data entry, entries are automatically posted to the ledger accounts when the electronic form is completed.

One popular accounting software package used by small- to medium-sized businesses is QuickBooks®. Some examples of using QuickBooks to record accounting transactions are illustrated and discussed in Chapter 5.

---

*Dec. 16   NetSolutions received $3,100 from fees earned for the first half of December.*      *Transaction*

An asset account (Cash) and a revenue account (Fees Earned) increase. This transaction is recorded as a $3,100 increase (debit) to Cash and a $3,100 increase (credit) to Fees Earned.      *Analysis*

| | Dec. | 16 | Cash | 11 | 3,100 | |
|---|---|---|---|---|---|---|
| | | | Fees Earned | 41 | | 3,100 |
| | | | Received fees from customers. | | | |

*Journal Entry*

| Assets | = | Liabilities | + | Owner's Equity (Revenue) |
|---|---|---|---|---|
| **Cash** 11 | | | | **Fees Earned** 41 |
| Dec. 16  3,100 | | | | Dec. 16  3,100 |

*Accounting Equation Impact*

---

*Dec. 16   Fees earned on account totaled $1,750 for the first half of December.*      *Transaction*

When a business agrees that a customer may pay for services provided at a later date, an **account receivable** is created. An account receivable is a claim against the customer. An account receivable is an asset, and the revenue is earned even though no cash has been received. Thus, this transaction is recorded as a $1,750 increase (debit) to Accounts Receivable and a $1,750 increase (credit) to Fees Earned.      *Analysis*

| | Dec. | 16 | Accounts Receivable | 12 | 1,750 | |
|---|---|---|---|---|---|---|
| | | | Fees Earned | 41 | | 1,750 |
| | | | Fees earned on account. | | | |

*Journal Entry*

| Assets | = | Liabilities | + | Owner's Equity (Revenue) |
|---|---|---|---|---|
| **Accounts Receivable** 12 | | | | **Fees Earned** 41 |
| Dec. 16  1,750 | | | | Dec. 16  1,750 |

*Accounting Equation Impact*

---

## Example Exercise 2-3   Journal Entry for Fees Earned      OBJ 3

Prepare a journal entry on August 7 for the fees earned on account, $115,000.

## Follow My Example 2-3

| Aug. 7 | Accounts Receivable...................................... | 115,000 | |
|---|---|---|---|
| | Fees Earned.......................................... | | 115,000 |

Practice Exercises: PE 2-3A, PE 2-3B

*Transaction*    Dec. 20   NetSolutions paid $900 to Executive Supply Co. on the $1,800 debt owed from the December 4 transaction.

*Analysis*    This is similar to the transaction of December 11. This transaction is recorded as a $900 decrease (debit) to Accounts Payable and a $900 decrease (credit) to Cash.

*Journal Entry*

| Dec. | 20 | Accounts Payable | 21 | 900 | |
| | |    Cash | 11 | | 900 |
| | |      Paid creditors on account. | | | |

*Accounting Equation Impact*

| Assets | = | Liabilities | + | Owner's Equity |
|---|---|---|---|---|

| **Cash** | 11 |
|---|---|
| | Dec. 20   900 |

| **Accounts Payable** | 21 |
|---|---|
| Dec. 20   900 | |

---

*Transaction*    Dec. 21   NetSolutions received $650 from customers in payment of their accounts.

*Analysis*    When customers pay amounts owed for services they have previously received, one asset increases and another asset decreases. This transaction is recorded as a $650 increase (debit) to Cash and a $650 decrease (credit) to Accounts Receivable.

*Journal Entry*

| Dec. | 21 | Cash | 11 | 650 | |
| | |    Accounts Receivable | 12 | | 650 |
| | |      Received cash from customers on account. | | | |

*Accounting Equation Impact*

| Assets | = | Liabilities | + | Owner's Equity |
|---|---|---|---|---|

| **Cash** | 11 |
|---|---|
| Dec. 21   650 | |

| **Accounts Receivable** | 12 |
|---|---|
| | Dec. 21   650 |

---

*Transaction*    Dec. 23   NetSolutions paid $1,450 for supplies.

*Analysis*    One asset account (Supplies) increases, and another asset account (Cash) decreases. This transaction is recorded as a $1,450 increase (debit) to Supplies and a $1,450 decrease (credit) to Cash.

*Journal Entry*

| Dec. | 23 | Supplies | 14 | 1,450 | |
| | |    Cash | 11 | | 1,450 |
| | |      Purchased supplies. | | | |

*Accounting Equation Impact*

| Assets | = | Liabilities | + | Owner's Equity |
|---|---|---|---|---|

| **Cash** | 11 |
|---|---|
| | Dec. 23   1,450 |

| **Supplies** | 14 |
|---|---|
| Dec. 23   1,450 | |

---

*Transaction*    Dec. 27   NetSolutions paid the receptionist and the part-time assistant $1,200 for two weeks' wages.

*Analysis*    This transaction is similar to the transaction of December 13. This transaction is recorded as a $1,200 increase (debit) to Wages Expense and a $1,200 decrease (credit) to Cash.

| Dec. | 27 | Wages Expense | 51 | 1,200 | |
| | | Cash | 11 | | 1,200 |
| | | Paid two weeks' wages. | | | |

*Journal Entry*

| Assets | = | Liabilities | + | Owner's Equity (Expense) |
| **Cash** 11 | | | | **Wages Expense** 51 |
| Dec. 27 1,200 | | | | Dec. 27 1,200 |

*Accounting Equation Impact*

---

*Dec. 31 NetSolutions paid its $310 telephone bill for the month.*

*Transaction*

This is similar to the transaction of December 6. This transaction is recorded as a $310 increase (debit) to Utilities Expense and a $310 decrease (credit) to Cash.

*Analysis*

| Dec. | 31 | Utilities Expense | 54 | 310 | |
| | | Cash | 11 | | 310 |
| | | Paid telephone bill. | | | |

*Journal Entry*

| Assets | = | Liabilities | + | Owner's Equity (Expense) |
| **Cash** 11 | | | | **Utilities Expense** 54 |
| Dec. 31 310 | | | | Dec. 31 310 |

*Accounting Equation Impact*

---

*Dec. 31 NetSolutions paid its $225 electric bill for the month.*

*Transaction*

This is similar to the preceding transaction. This transaction is recorded as a $225 increase (debit) to Utilities Expense and a $225 decrease (credit) to Cash.

*Analysis*

| Journal | | | | | Page 4 |
|---|---|---|---|---|---|
| Date | | Description | Post. Ref. | Debit | Credit |
| 2015 Dec. | 31 | Utilities Expense | 54 | 225 | |
| | | Cash | 11 | | 225 |
| | | Paid electric bill. | | | |

*Journal Entry*

| Assets | = | Liabilities | + | Owner's Equity (Expense) |
| **Cash** 11 | | | | **Utilities Expense** 54 |
| Dec. 31 225 | | | | Dec. 31 225 |

*Accounting Equation Impact*

---

*Dec. 31 NetSolutions received $2,870 from fees earned for the second half of December.*

*Transaction*

This is similar to the transaction of December 16. This transaction is recorded as a $2,870 increase (debit) to Cash and a $2,870 increase (credit) to Fees Earned.

*Analysis*

| Dec. | 31 | Cash | 11 | 2,870 | |
| | | Fees Earned | 41 | | 2,870 |
| | | Received fees from customers. | | | |

*Journal Entry*

| Assets | = | Liabilities | + | Owner's Equity (Revenue) |
| **Cash** 11 | | | | **Fees Earned** 41 |
| Dec. 31 2,870 | | | | Dec. 31 2,870 |

*Accounting Equation Impact*

| | | | | | | |
|---|---|---|---|---|---|---|
| *Transaction* | | *Dec. 31* | *Fees earned on account totaled $1,120 for the second half of December.* | | | |

| | |
|---|---|
| *Analysis* | This is similar to the transaction of December 16. This transaction is recorded as a $1,120 increase (debit) to Accounts Receivable and a $1,120 increase (credit) to Fees Earned. |

| | | | | | |
|---|---|---|---|---|---|
| *Journal Entry* | Dec. | 31 | Accounts Receivable | 12 | 1,120 |
| | | |    Fees Earned | 41 |      1,120 |
| | | |       Fees earned on account. | | |

*Accounting Equation Impact*

| Assets | = | Liabilities | + | Owner's Equity (Revenue) |
|---|---|---|---|---|
| **Accounts Receivable**   12 | | | | **Fees Earned**   41 |
| Dec. 31  1,120 | | | | Dec. 31  1,120 |

| | | | | |
|---|---|---|---|---|
| *Transaction* | | *Dec. 31* | *Chris Clark withdrew $2,000 for personal use.* | |

| | |
|---|---|
| *Analysis* | This transaction decreases owner's equity and assets. This transaction is recorded as a $2,000 increase (debit) to Chris Clark, Drawing and a $2,000 decrease (credit) to Cash. |

| | | | | | |
|---|---|---|---|---|---|
| *Journal Entry* | Dec. | 31 | Chris Clark, Drawing | 32 | 2,000 |
| | | |    Cash | 11 |      2,000 |
| | | |       Chris Clark withdrew cash for personal use. | | |

*Accounting Equation Impact*

| Assets | = | Liabilities | + | Owner's Equity (Drawing) |
|---|---|---|---|---|
| **Cash**   11 | | | | **Chris Clark, Drawing**   32 |
| Dec. 31  2,000 | | | | Dec. 31  2,000 |

---

## Example Exercise 2-4   Journal Entry for Owner's Withdrawal 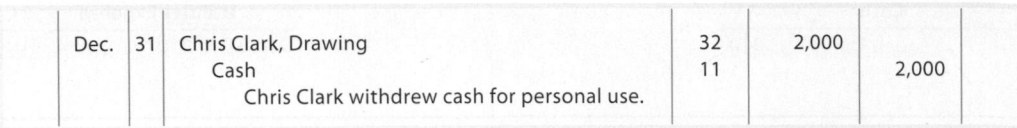   OBJ 3

Prepare a journal entry on December 29 for the payment of $12,000 to the owner of Smartstaff Consulting Services, Dominique Walsh, for personal use.

### Follow My Example 2-4

| | | | |
|---|---|---|---|
| Dec. 29 | Dominique Walsh, Drawing ............................... | 12,000 | |
| |    Cash.................................................... | | 12,000 |

Practice Exercises: PE 2-4A, PE 2-4B

---

## Example Exercise 2-5   Missing Amount from an Account    OBJ 3

On March 1, the cash account balance was $22,350. During March, cash receipts totaled $241,880, and the March 31 balance was $19,125. Determine the cash payments made during March.

### Follow My Example 2-5

Using the following T account, solve for the amount of cash payments (indicated by ? ):

| Cash | | | |
|---|---|---|---|
| Mar. 1 Bal. | 22,350 | ? | Cash payments |
| Cash receipts | 241,880 | | |
| Mar. 31 Bal. | 19,125 | | |

$19,125 = $22,350 + $241,880 − Cash payments

Cash payments = $22,350 + $241,880 − $19,125 = $245,105

Practice Exercises: PE 2-5A, PE 2-5B

Exhibit 6 shows the ledger for **NetSolutions** after the transactions for both November and December have been posted.

**EXHIBIT 6** | **Cash Receipts Journal for a Merchandising Business**

## Ledger

**Account** Cash — Account No. 11

| Date | Item | Post. Ref. | Debit | Credit | Balance Debit | Balance Credit |
|---|---|---|---|---|---|---|
| 2015 | | | | | | |
| Nov. 1 | | 1 | 25,000 | | 25,000 | |
| 5 | | 1 | | 20,000 | 5,000 | |
| 18 | | 1 | 7,500 | | 12,500 | |
| 30 | | 1 | | 3,650 | 8,850 | |
| 30 | | 1 | | 950 | 7,900 | |
| 30 | | 2 | | 2,000 | 5,900 | |
| Dec. 1 | | 2 | | 2,400 | 3,500 | |
| 1 | | 2 | | 800 | 2,700 | |
| 1 | | 2 | 360 | | 3,060 | |
| 6 | | 2 | | 180 | 2,880 | |
| 11 | | 2 | | 400 | 2,480 | |
| 13 | | 3 | | 950 | 1,530 | |
| 16 | | 3 | 3,100 | | 4,630 | |
| 20 | | 3 | | 900 | 3,730 | |
| 21 | | 3 | 650 | | 4,380 | |
| 23 | | 3 | | 1,450 | 2,930 | |
| 27 | | 3 | | 1,200 | 1,730 | |
| 31 | | 3 | | 310 | 1,420 | |
| 31 | | 4 | | 225 | 1,195 | |
| 31 | | 4 | 2,870 | | 4,065 | |
| 31 | | 4 | | 2,000 | 2,065 | |

**Account** Accounts Receivable — Account No. 12

| Date | Item | Post. Ref. | Debit | Credit | Balance Debit | Balance Credit |
|---|---|---|---|---|---|---|
| 2015 | | | | | | |
| Dec. 16 | | 3 | 1,750 | | 1,750 | |
| 21 | | 3 | | 650 | 1,100 | |
| 31 | | 4 | 1,120 | | 2,220 | |

**Account** Supplies — Account No. 14

| Date | Item | Post. Ref. | Debit | Credit | Balance Debit | Balance Credit |
|---|---|---|---|---|---|---|
| 2015 | | | | | | |
| Nov. 10 | | 1 | 1,350 | | 1,350 | |
| 30 | | 1 | | 800 | 550 | |
| Dec. 23 | | 3 | 1,450 | | 2,000 | |

**Account** Prepaid Insurance — Account No. 15

| Date | Item | Post. Ref. | Debit | Credit | Balance Debit | Balance Credit |
|---|---|---|---|---|---|---|
| 2015 | | | | | | |
| Dec. 1 | | 2 | 2,400 | | 2,400 | |

**Account** Land — Account No. 17

| Date | Item | Post. Ref. | Debit | Credit | Balance Debit | Balance Credit |
|---|---|---|---|---|---|---|
| 2015 | | | | | | |
| Nov. 5 | | 1 | 20,000 | | 20,000 | |

**Account** Office Equipment — Account No. 18

| Date | Item | Post. Ref. | Debit | Credit | Balance Debit | Balance Credit |
|---|---|---|---|---|---|---|
| 2015 | | | | | | |
| Dec. 4 | | 2 | 1,800 | | 1,800 | |

**Account** Accounts Payable — Account No. 21

| Date | Item | Post. Ref. | Debit | Credit | Balance Debit | Balance Credit |
|---|---|---|---|---|---|---|
| 2015 | | | | | | |
| Nov. 10 | | 1 | | 1,350 | | 1,350 |
| 30 | | 1 | 950 | | | 400 |
| Dec. 4 | | 2 | | 1,800 | | 2,200 |
| 11 | | 2 | 400 | | | 1,800 |
| 20 | | 3 | 900 | | | 900 |

**Account** Unearned Rent — Account No. 23

| Date | Item | Post. Ref. | Debit | Credit | Balance Debit | Balance Credit |
|---|---|---|---|---|---|---|
| 2015 | | | | | | |
| Dec. 1 | | 2 | | 360 | | 360 |

**Account** Chris Clark, Capital — Account No. 31

| Date | Item | Post. Ref. | Debit | Credit | Balance Debit | Balance Credit |
|---|---|---|---|---|---|---|
| 2015 | | | | | | |
| Nov. 1 | | 1 | | 25,000 | | 25,000 |

**Account** Chris Clark, Drawing — Account No. 32

| Date | Item | Post. Ref. | Debit | Credit | Balance Debit | Balance Credit |
|---|---|---|---|---|---|---|
| 2015 | | | | | | |
| Nov. 30 | | 2 | 2,000 | | 2,000 | |
| Dec. 31 | | 1 | 2,000 | | 4,000 | |

(Continued)

| EXHIBIT 6 | Cash Receipts Journal for a Merchandising Business (*Concluded*) |
|---|---|

**Account** Fees Earned — Account No. 41

| Date | Item | Post. Ref. | Debit | Credit | Balance Debit | Balance Credit |
|---|---|---|---|---|---|---|
| 2015 | | | | | | |
| Nov. 18 | | 1 | | 7,500 | | 7,500 |
| Dec. 16 | | 3 | | 3,100 | | 10,600 |
| 16 | | 3 | | 1,750 | | 12,350 |
| 31 | | 4 | | 2,870 | | 15,220 |
| 31 | | 4 | | 1,120 | | 16,340 |

**Account** Wages Expense — Account No. 51

| Date | Item | Post. Ref. | Debit | Credit | Balance Debit | Balance Credit |
|---|---|---|---|---|---|---|
| 2015 | | | | | | |
| Nov. 30 | | 1 | 2,125 | | 2,125 | |
| Dec. 13 | | 3 | 950 | | 3,075 | |
| 27 | | 3 | 1,200 | | 4,275 | |

**Account** Supplies Expense — Account No. 52

| Date | Item | Post. Ref. | Debit | Credit | Balance Debit | Balance Credit |
|---|---|---|---|---|---|---|
| 2015 | | | | | | |
| Nov. 30 | | 1 | 800 | | 800 | |

**Account** Rent Expense — Account No. 53

| Date | Item | Post. Ref. | Debit | Credit | Balance Debit | Balance Credit |
|---|---|---|---|---|---|---|
| 2015 | | | | | | |
| Nov. 30 | | 1 | 800 | | 800 | |
| Dec. 1 | | 2 | 800 | | 1,600 | |

**Account** Utilities Expense — Account No. 54

| Date | Item | Post. Ref. | Debit | Credit | Balance Debit | Balance Credit |
|---|---|---|---|---|---|---|
| 2015 | | | | | | |
| Nov. 30 | | 1 | 450 | | 450 | |
| Dec. 31 | | 3 | 310 | | 760 | |
| 31 | | 4 | 225 | | 985 | |

**Account** Miscellaneous Expense — Account No. 59

| Date | Item | Post. Ref. | Debit | Credit | Balance Debit | Balance Credit |
|---|---|---|---|---|---|---|
| 2015 | | | | | | |
| Nov. 30 | | 1 | 275 | | 275 | |
| Dec. 6 | | 2 | 180 | | 455 | |

**OBJ 4** Prepare an unadjusted trial balance and explain how it can be used to discover errors.

# Trial Balance

Errors may occur in posting debits and credits from the journal to the ledger. One way to detect such errors is by preparing a **trial balance**. Double-entry accounting requires that debits must always equal credits. The trial balance verifies this equality. The steps in preparing a trial balance are as follows:

- Step 1. List the name of the company, the title of the trial balance, and the date the trial balance is prepared.
- Step 2. List the accounts from the ledger, and enter their debit or credit balance in the Debit or Credit column of the trial balance.
- Step 3. Total the Debit and Credit columns of the trial balance.
- Step 4. Verify that the total of the Debit column equals the total of the Credit column.

The trial balance for **NetSolutions** as of December 31, 2015, is shown in Exhibit 7. The account balances in Exhibit 7 are taken from the ledger shown in Exhibit 6. Before a trial balance is prepared, each account balance in the ledger must be determined. When the standard account form is used as in Exhibit 6, the balance of each account appears in the balance column on the same line as the last posting to the account.

The trial balance shown in Exhibit 7 is titled an **unadjusted trial balance**. This is to distinguish it from other trial balances that will be prepared in later

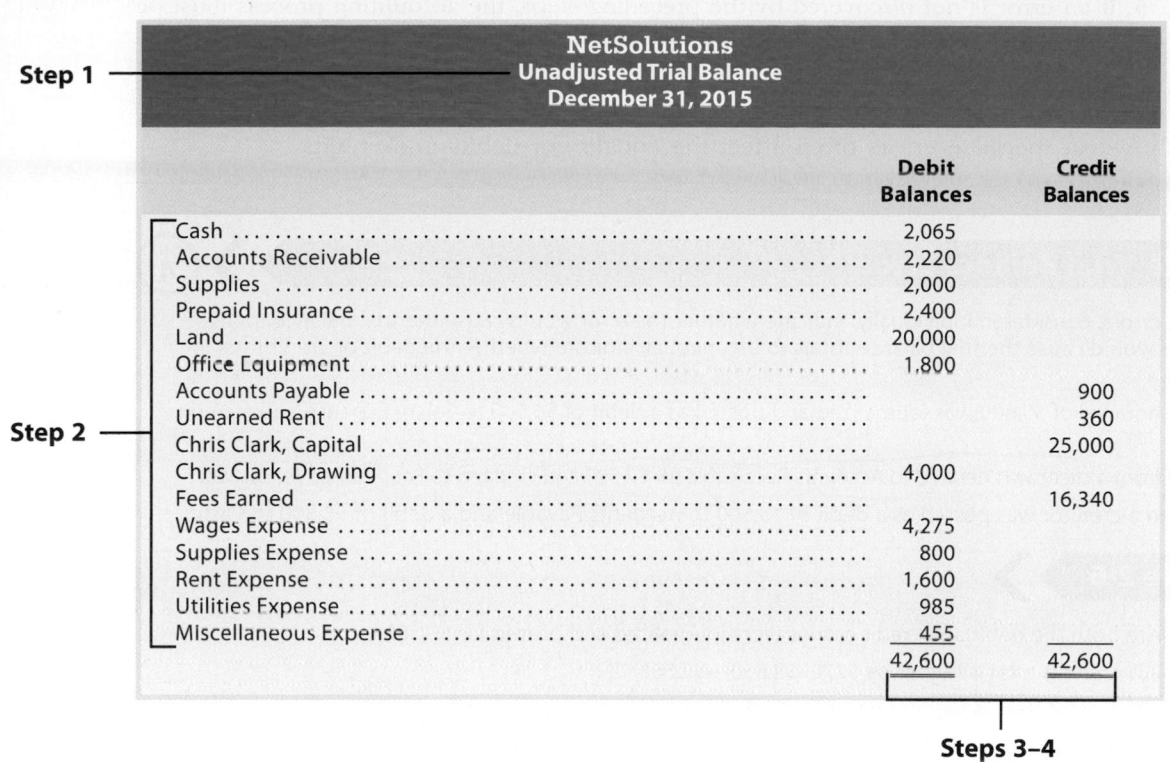

**Step 1**

**Step 2**

**Steps 3–4**

**EXHIBIT 7**

**Trial Balance**

| NetSolutions<br>Unadjusted Trial Balance<br>December 31, 2015 | Debit<br>Balances | Credit<br>Balances |
|---|---|---|
| Cash | 2,065 | |
| Accounts Receivable | 2,220 | |
| Supplies | 2,000 | |
| Prepaid Insurance | 2,400 | |
| Land | 20,000 | |
| Office Equipment | 1,800 | |
| Accounts Payable | | 900 |
| Unearned Rent | | 360 |
| Chris Clark, Capital | | 25,000 |
| Chris Clark, Drawing | 4,000 | |
| Fees Earned | | 16,340 |
| Wages Expense | 4,275 | |
| Supplies Expense | 800 | |
| Rent Expense | 1,600 | |
| Utilities Expense | 985 | |
| Miscellaneous Expense | 455 | |
| | 42,600 | 42,600 |

chapters. These other trial balances include an adjusted trial balance and a post-closing trial balance.[4]

## Errors Affecting the Trial Balance

If the trial balance totals are not equal, an error has occurred. In this case, the error must be found and corrected. A method useful in discovering errors is as follows:

1. If the difference between the Debit and Credit column totals is 10, 100, or 1,000, an error in addition may have occurred. In this case, re-add the trial balance column totals. If the error still exists, recompute the account balances.

2. If the difference between the Debit and Credit column totals can be evenly divisible by 2, the error may be due to the entering of a debit balance as a credit balance, or vice versa. In this case, review the trial balance for account balances of one-half the difference that may have been entered in the wrong column. For example, if the Debit column total is $20,640 and the Credit column total is $20,236, the difference of $404 ($20,640 − $20,236) may be due to a credit account balance of $202 that was entered as a debit account balance.

3. If the difference between the Debit and Credit column totals is evenly divisible by 9, trace the account balances back to the ledger to see if an account balance was incorrectly copied from the ledger. Two common types of copying errors are transpositions and slides. A **transposition** occurs when the order of the digits is copied incorrectly, such as writing $542 as $452 or $524. In a **slide**, the entire number is copied incorrectly one or more spaces to the right or the left, such as writing $542.00 as $54.20 or $5,420.00. In both cases, the resulting error will be evenly divisible by 9.

4. If the difference between the Debit and Credit column totals is not evenly divisible by 2 or 9, review the ledger to see if an account balance in the amount of the error has been omitted from the trial balance. If the error is not discovered, review the journal postings to see if a posting of a debit or credit may have been omitted.

5. If an error is not discovered by the preceding steps, the accounting process must be retraced, beginning with the last journal entry.

The trial balance does not provide complete proof of the accuracy of the ledger. It indicates only that the debits and the credits are equal. This proof is of value, however, because errors often affect the equality of debits and credits.

---

## Example Exercise 2-6  Trial Balance Errors

For each of the following errors, considered individually, indicate whether the error would cause the trial balance totals to be unequal. If the error would cause the trial balance totals to be unequal, indicate whether the debit or credit total is higher and by how much.

a. Payment of a cash withdrawal of $5,600 was journalized and posted as a debit of $6,500 to Salary Expense and a credit of $6,500 to Cash.

b. A fee of $2,850 earned from a client was debited to Accounts Receivable for $2,580 and credited to Fees Earned for $2,850.

c. A payment of $3,500 to a creditor was posted as a debit of $3,500 to Accounts Payable and a debit of $3,500 to Cash.

## Follow My Example 2-6

a. The totals are equal since both the debit and credit entries were journalized and posted for $6,500.

b. The totals are unequal. The credit total is higher by $270 ($2,850 − $2,580).

c. The totals are unequal. The debit total is higher by $7,000 ($3,500 + $3,500).

Practice Exercises: PE 2-6A, PE 2-6B

---

## Errors Not Affecting the Trial Balance

An error may occur that does not cause the trial balance totals to be unequal. Such an error may be discovered when preparing the trial balance or may be indicated by an unusual account balance. For example, a credit balance in the supplies account indicates an error has occurred. This is because a business cannot have "negative" supplies. When such errors are discovered, they should be corrected. If the error has already been journalized and posted to the ledger, a **correcting journal entry** is normally prepared.

To illustrate, assume that on May 5 a $12,500 purchase of office equipment on account was incorrectly journalized and posted as a debit to Supplies and a credit to Accounts Payable for $12,500. This posting of the incorrect entry is shown in the following T accounts:

*Incorrect:*

| Supplies | | Accounts Payable | |
|---|---|---|---|
| 12,500 | | | 12,500 |

Before making a correcting journal entry, it is best to determine the debit(s) and credit(s) that should have been recorded. These are shown in the following T accounts:

*Correct:*

| Office Equipment | | Accounts Payable | |
|---|---|---|---|
| 12,500 | | | 12,500 |

Comparing the two sets of T accounts shows that the incorrect debit to Supplies may be corrected by debiting Office Equipment for $12,500 and crediting Supplies for $12,500. The following correcting entry is then journalized and posted:

*Entry to Correct Error:*

| | | | | | |
|---|---|---|---|---|---|
| May | 31 | Office Equipment | 18 | 12,500 | |
| | | Supplies | 14 | | 12,500 |
| | | To correct erroneous debit | | | |
| | | to Supplies on May 5. See invoice | | | |
| | | from Bell Office Equipment Co. | | | |

## Example Exercise 2-7  Correcting Entries

The following errors took place in journalizing and posting transactions:

a.  A withdrawal of $6,000 by Cheri Ramey, owner of the business, was recorded as a debit to Office Salaries Expense and a credit to Cash.

b.  Utilities Expense of $4,500 paid for the current month was recorded as a debit to Miscellaneous Expense and a credit to Accounts Payable.

Journalize the entries to correct the errors. Omit explanations.

## Follow My Example 2-7

| | | | |
|---|---|---|---|
| a. | Cheri Ramey, Drawing............................ | 6,000 | |
| | Office Salaries Expense......................... | | 6,000 |
| b. | Accounts Payable ................................ | 4,500 | |
| | Miscellaneous Expense ......................... | | 4,500 |
| | Utilities Expense.................................. | 4,500 | |
| | Cash.......................................... | | 4,500 |

*Note:* The first entry in (b) reverses the incorrect entry, and the second entry records the correct entry. These two entries could also be combined into one entry; however, preparing two entries will make it easier for someone later to understand what happened and why the entries were necessary.

Practice Exercises: PE 2-7A, PE 2-7B

# Financial Analysis and Interpretation: Horizontal Analysis

Describe and illustrate the use of horizontal analysis in evaluating a company's performance and financial condition.

A single item in a financial statement, such as net income, is often useful in interpreting the financial performance of a company. However, a comparison with prior periods often makes the financial information even more useful. For example, comparing net income of the current period with the net income of the prior period will indicate whether the company's operating performance has improved.

In **horizontal analysis**, the amount of each item on a current financial statement is compared with the same item on an earlier statement. The increase or decrease in the *amount* of the item is computed together with the *percent* of increase or decrease. When two statements are being compared, the earlier statement is used as the base for computing the amount and the percent of change.

To illustrate, the horizontal analysis of two income statements for J. Holmes, Attorney-at-Law follows:

**J. Holmes, Attorney-at-Law**
**Income Statements**
**For the Years Ended December 31**

| | Year 2 | Year 1 | Increase (Decrease) Amount | Increase (Decrease) Percent |
|---|---|---|---|---|
| Fees earned | $187,500 | $150,000 | $37,500 | 25.0%* |
| Operating expenses: | | | | |
| Wages expense | $ 60,000 | $ 45,000 | $15,000 | 33.3 |
| Rent expense | 15,000 | 12,000 | 3,000 | 25.0 |
| Utilities expense | 12,500 | 9,000 | 3,500 | 38.9 |
| Supplies expense | 2,700 | 3,000 | (300) | (10.0) |
| Miscellaneous | | | | |
| expense | 2,300 | 1,800 | 500 | 27.8 |
| Total operating expenses | $ 92,500 | $ 70,800 | $21,700 | 30.6 |
| Net income | $ 95,000 | $ 79,200 | $15,800 | 19.9 |

*$37,500 ÷ $150,000

The horizontal analysis for J. Holmes, Attorney-at-Law, indicates both favorable and unfavorable trends. The increase in fees earned is a favorable trend, as is the decrease in supplies expense. Unfavorable trends include the increase in wages expense, utilities expense, and miscellaneous expense. These expenses increased the same as or faster than the increase in revenues, with total operating expenses increasing by 30.6%. Overall, net income increased by $15,800, or 19.9%, a favorable trend.

The significance of the various increases and decreases in the revenue and expense items should be investigated to see if operations could be further improved. For example, the increase in utilities expense of 38.9% was the result of renting additional office space for use by a part-time law student in performing paralegal services. This explains the increase in rent expense of 25.0% and the increase in wages expense of 33.3%. The increase in revenues of 25.0% reflects the fees generated by the new paralegal.

The preceding example illustrates how horizontal analysis can be useful in interpreting and analyzing the income statement. Horizontal analyses can also be performed for the balance sheet, the statement of owner's equity, and the statement of cash flows.

To illustrate, horizontal analysis for two recent years of Apple Inc.'s statements of cash flows (in millions) follows:

**Apple Inc.**
**Statements of Cash Flows**

| | Year 2 | Year 1 | Increase (Decrease) Amount | Increase (Decrease) Percent |
|---|---|---|---|---|
| Cash flows from operating activities | $ 50,856 | $ 37,529 | $13,327 | 35.5% |
| Cash flows used for investing activities | (48,227) | (40,419) | (7,808) | (19.3) |
| Cash flows from financing activities | (1,698) | 1,444 | (3,142) | (217.6) |
| Net increase (decrease) in cash | $ 931 | $ (1,446) | $ 2,377 | 164.4 |
| Beginning of the year balance of cash | 9,815 | 11,261 | (1,446) | (12.8) |
| End of the year balance of cash | $ 10,746 | $ 9,815 | $ 931 | 9.5 |

The horizontal analysis of cash flows for Apple Inc. indicates an increase in cash flows from operating activities of 35.5%, which is a favorable trend. At the same time, Apple increased the cash used in its investing activities by 19.3% and decreased the cash it received from financing activities by 217.6%. Overall, Apple had a 164.4% increase in cash for the year, which increased the end-of-the-year cash balance by 9.5%. In contrast, in the prior year Apple decreased its ending cash balance, which is the beginning cash balance of the current year, by 12.8%.

## Example Exercise 2-8   Horizontal Analysis

OBJ 5

Two income statements for McCorkle Company follow:

**McCorkle Company**
**Income Statements**
**For the Years Ended December 31**

|  | 2016 | 2015 |
|---|---|---|
| Fees earned | $210,000 | $175,000 |
| Operating expenses | 172,500 | 150,000 |
| Net income | $ 37,500 | $ 25,000 |

Prepare a horizontal analysis of McCorkle Company's income statements.

### Follow My Example 2-8

**McCorkle Company**
**Income Statements**
**For the Years Ended December 31**

|  | 2016 | 2015 | Increase (Decrease) Amount | Percent |
|---|---|---|---|---|
| Fees earned | $210,000 | $175,000 | $35,000 | 20% |
| Operating expenses | 172,500 | 150,000 | 22,500 | 15 |
| Net income | $ 37,500 | $ 25,000 | $12,500 | 50 |

Practice Exercises: PE 2-8A, PE 2-8B

# At a Glance 2

OBJ 1

### Describe the characteristics of an account and a chart of accounts.

**Key Points**   The simplest form of an account, a T account, has three parts: (1) a title, which is the name of the item recorded in the account; (2) a left side, called the debit side; and (3) a right side, called the credit side. Periodically, the debits in an account are added, the credits in the account are added, and the balance of the account is determined.

The system of accounts that make up a ledger is called a chart of accounts.

| Learning Outcomes | Example Exercises | Practice Exercises |
|---|---|---|
| • Record transactions in T accounts. |  |  |
| • Determine the balance of a T account. |  |  |
| • Prepare a chart of accounts for a proprietorship. |  |  |

**OBJ 2** Describe and illustrate journalizing transactions using the double-entry accounting system.

**Key Points** Transactions are initially entered in a record called a journal. The rules of debit and credit for recording increases or decreases in accounts are shown in Exhibit 3. Each transaction is recorded so that the sum of the debits is always equal to the sum of the credits. The normal balance of an account is indicated by the side of the account (debit or credit) that receives the increases.

| Learning Outcomes | Example Exercises | Practice Exercises |
|---|---|---|
| • Indicate the normal balance of an account. | EE2-1 | PE2-1A, 2-1B |
| • Journalize transactions using the rules of debit and credit. | EE2-2 | PE2-2A, 2-2B |

**OBJ 3** Describe and illustrate the journalizing and posting of transactions to accounts.

**Key Points** Transactions are journalized and posted to the ledger using the rules of debit and credit. The debits and credits for each journal entry are posted to the accounts in the order in which they occur in the journal.

| Learning Outcomes | Example Exercises | Practice Exercises |
|---|---|---|
| • Journalize transactions using the rules of debit and credit. | EE2-3 | PE2-3A, 2-3B |
| • Given other account data, determine the missing amount of an account entry. | EE2-4 | PE2-4A, 2-4B |
| • Post journal entries to a standard account. | EE2-5 | PE2-5A, 2-5B |
| • Post journal entries to a T account. | | |

**OBJ 4** Prepare an unadjusted trial balance and explain how it can be used to discover errors.

**Key Points** A trial balance is prepared by listing the accounts from the ledger and their balances. The totals of the Debit column and Credit column of the trial balance must be equal. If the two totals are not equal, an error has occurred. Errors may occur even though the trial balance totals are equal. Such errors may require a correcting journal entry.

| Learning Outcomes | Example Exercises | Practice Exercises |
|---|---|---|
| • Prepare an unadjusted trial balance. | EE2-6 | PE2-6A, 2-6B |
| • Discover errors that cause unequal totals in the trial balance. | EE2-7 | PE2-7A, 2-7B |
| • Prepare correcting journal entries for various errors. | | |

**Describe and illustrate the use of horizontal analysis in evaluating a company's performance and financial condition.**

**Key Points**    In horizontal analysis, the amount of each item on a current financial statement is compared with the same item on an earlier statement. The increase or decrease in the *amount* of the item is computed, together with the *percent* of increase or decrease. When two statements are being compared, the earlier statement is used as the base for computing the amount and the percent of change.

| Learning Outcomes | Example Exercises | Practice Exercises |
|---|---|---|
| • Describe horizontal analysis. | | |
| • Prepare a horizontal analysis report of a financial statement | EE2-8 | PE2-8A, 2-8B |

## Key Terms

account (52)
account receivable (65)
assets (54)
balance of the account (53)
capital account (54)
chart of accounts (54)
correcting journal entry (72)
credit (53)
debit (53)
double-entry accounting system (55)

drawing (54)
expenses (55)
horizontal analysis (73)
journal (57)
journal entry (58)
journalizing (58)
ledger (54)
liabilities (54)
normal balance of an account (56)
owner's equity (54)

posting (61)
revenues (54)
rules of debit and credit (55)
slide (71)
T account (52)
transposition (71)
trial balance (70)
unadjusted trial balance (70)
unearned revenue (63)

## Illustrative Problem

J. F. Outz, M.D., has been practicing as a cardiologist for three years. During April 2015, Outz completed the following transactions in her practice of cardiology:

Apr.  1.  Paid office rent for April, $800.

3.  Purchased equipment on account, $2,100.

5.  Received cash on account from patients, $3,150.

8.  Purchased X-ray film and other supplies on account, $245.

9.  One of the items of equipment purchased on April 3 was defective. It was returned with the permission of the supplier, who agreed to reduce the account for the amount charged for the item, $325.

12.  Paid cash to creditors on account, $1,250.

Apr. 17. Paid cash for renewal of a six-month property insurance policy, $370.

20. Discovered that the balances of the cash account and the accounts payable account as of April 1 were overstated by $200. A payment of that amount to a creditor in March had not been recorded. Journalize the $200 payment as of April 20.

24. Paid cash for laboratory analysis, $545.

27. Paid cash from business bank account for personal and family expenses, $1,250.

30. Recorded the cash received in payment of services (on a cash basis) to patients during April, $1,720.

30. Paid salaries of receptionist and nurses, $1,725.

30. Paid various utility expenses, $360.

30. Recorded fees charged to patients on account for services performed in April, $5,145.

30. Paid miscellaneous expenses, $132.

Outz's account titles, numbers, and balances as of April 1 (all normal balances) are listed as follows: Cash, 11, $4,123; Accounts Receivable, 12, $6,725; Supplies, 13, $290; Prepaid Insurance, 14, $465; Equipment, 18, $19,745; Accounts Payable, 22, $765; J. F. Outz, Capital, 31, $30,583; J. F. Outz, Drawing, 32, $0; Professional Fees, 41, $0; Salary Expense, 51, $0; Rent Expense, 53, $0; Laboratory Expense, 55, $0; Utilities Expense, 56, $0; Miscellaneous Expense, 59, $0.

## Instructions

1. Open a ledger of standard four-column accounts for Dr. Outz as of April 1. Enter the balances in the appropriate balance columns and place a check mark (✓) in the Posting Reference column. (*Hint:* Verify the equality of the debit and credit balances in the ledger before proceeding with the next instruction.)

2. Journalize each transaction in a two-column journal.

3. Post the journal to the ledger, extending the month-end balances to the appropriate balance columns after each posting.

4. Prepare an unadjusted trial balance as of April 30.

**Solution** 1., 2., and 3.

| Journal | | | | Page 27 |
|---|---|---|---|---|
| Date | Description | Post. Ref. | Debit | Credit |
| 2015 | | | | |
| Apr. 1 | Rent Expense | 53 | 800 | |
| | Cash | 11 | | 800 |
| | Paid office rent for April. | | | |
| 3 | Equipment | 18 | 2,100 | |
| | Accounts Payable | 22 | | 2,100 |
| | Purchased equipment on account. | | | |
| 5 | Cash | 11 | 3,150 | |
| | Accounts Receivable | 12 | | 3,150 |
| | Received cash on account. | | | |
| 8 | Supplies | 13 | 245 | |
| | Accounts Payable | 22 | | 245 |
| | Purchased supplies. | | | |
| 9 | Accounts Payable | 22 | 325 | |
| | Equipment | 18 | | 325 |
| | Returned defective equipment. | | | |
| 12 | Accounts Payable | 22 | 1,250 | |
| | Cash | 11 | | 1,250 |
| | Paid creditors on account. | | | |
| 17 | Prepaid Insurance | 14 | 370 | |
| | Cash | 11 | | 370 |
| | Renewed six-month property policy. | | | |
| 20 | Accounts Payable | 22 | 200 | |
| | Cash | 11 | | 200 |
| | Recorded March payment to creditor. | | | |

| Journal | | | | Page 28 |
|---|---|---|---|---|
| Date | Description | Post. Ref. | Debit | Credit |
| 2015 | | | | |
| Apr. 24 | Laboratory Expense | 55 | 545 | |
| | Cash | 11 | | 545 |
| | Paid for laboratory analysis. | | | |
| 27 | J. F. Outz, Drawing | 32 | 1,250 | |
| | Cash | 11 | | 1,250 |
| | J. F. Outz withdrew cash for personal use. | | | |
| 30 | Cash | 11 | 1,720 | |
| | Professional Fees | 41 | | 1,720 |
| | Received fees from patients. | | | |
| 30 | Salary Expense | 51 | 1,725 | |
| | Cash | 11 | | 1,725 |
| | Paid salaries. | | | |
| 30 | Utilities Expense | 56 | 360 | |
| | Cash | 11 | | 360 |
| | Paid utilities. | | | |
| 30 | Accounts Receivable | 12 | 5,145 | |
| | Professional Fees | 41 | | 5,145 |
| | Recorded fees earned on account. | | | |
| 30 | Miscellaneous Expense | 59 | 132 | |
| | Cash | 11 | | 132 |
| | Paid expenses. | | | |

**Account** Cash — Account No. 11

| | | | | | Balance | |
|---|---|---|---|---|---|---|
| Date | Item | Post. Ref. | Debit | Credit | Debit | Credit |
| 2015 | | | | | | |
| Apr. 1 | Balance | ✓ | | | 4,123 | |
| 1 | | 27 | | 800 | 3,323 | |
| 5 | | 27 | 3,150 | | 6,473 | |
| 12 | | 27 | | 1,250 | 5,223 | |
| 17 | | 27 | | 370 | 4,853 | |
| 20 | | 27 | | 200 | 4,653 | |
| 24 | | 28 | | 545 | 4,108 | |
| 27 | | 28 | | 1,250 | 2,858 | |
| 30 | | 28 | 1,720 | | 4,578 | |
| 30 | | 28 | | 1,725 | 2,853 | |
| 30 | | 28 | | 360 | 2,493 | |
| 30 | | 28 | | 132 | 2,361 | |

**Account** Accounts Receivable — Account No. 12

| | | | | | Balance | |
|---|---|---|---|---|---|---|
| Date | Item | Post. Ref. | Debit | Credit | Debit | Credit |
| 2015 | | | | | | |
| Apr. 1 | Balance | ✓ | | | 6,725 | |
| 5 | | 27 | | 3,150 | 3,575 | |
| 30 | | 28 | 5,145 | | 8,720 | |

**Account** Supplies — Account No. 13

| | | | | | Balance | |
|---|---|---|---|---|---|---|
| Date | Item | Post. Ref. | Debit | Credit | Debit | Credit |
| 2015 | | | | | | |
| Apr. 1 | Balance | ✓ | | | 290 | |
| 8 | | 27 | 245 | | 535 | |

**Account** *Prepaid Insurance* — Account No. 14

| Date | Item | Post. Ref. | Debit | Credit | Balance Debit | Balance Credit |
|------|------|-----------|-------|--------|-------|--------|
| 2015 | | | | | | |
| Apr. 1 | Balance | ✓ | | | 465 | |
| 17 | | 27 | 370 | | 835 | |

**Account** *Equipment* — Account No. 18

| Date | Item | Post. Ref. | Debit | Credit | Balance Debit | Balance Credit |
|------|------|-----------|-------|--------|-------|--------|
| 2015 | | | | | | |
| Apr. 1 | Balance | ✓ | | | 19,745 | |
| 3 | | 27 | 2,100 | | 21,845 | |
| 9 | | 27 | | 325 | 21,520 | |

**Account** *Accounts Payable* — Account No. 22

| Date | Item | Post. Ref. | Debit | Credit | Balance Debit | Balance Credit |
|------|------|-----------|-------|--------|-------|--------|
| 2015 | | | | | | |
| Apr. 1 | Balance | ✓ | | | | 765 |
| 3 | | 27 | | 2,100 | | 2,865 |
| 8 | | 27 | | 245 | | 3,110 |
| 9 | | 27 | 325 | | | 2,785 |
| 12 | | 27 | 1,250 | | | 1,535 |
| 20 | | 27 | 200 | | | 1,335 |

**Account** *J. F. Outz, Capital* — Account No. 31

| Date | Item | Post. Ref. | Debit | Credit | Balance Debit | Balance Credit |
|------|------|-----------|-------|--------|-------|--------|
| 2015 | | | | | | |
| Apr. 1 | Balance | ✓ | | | | 30,583 |

**Account** *J. F. Qutz, Drawing* — Account No. 32

| Date | Item | Post. Ref. | Debit | Credit | Balance Debit | Balance Credit |
|------|------|-----------|-------|--------|-------|--------|
| 2015 | | | | | | |
| Apr. 27 | | 28 | 1,250 | | 1,250 | |

**Account** *Professional Fees* — Account No. 41

| Date | Item | Post. Ref. | Debit | Credit | Balance Debit | Balance Credit |
|------|------|-----------|-------|--------|-------|--------|
| 2015 | | | | | | |
| Apr. 30 | | 28 | | 1,720 | | 1,720 |
| 30 | | 28 | | 5,145 | | 6,865 |

**Account** *Salary Expense* — Account No. 51

| Date | Item | Post. Ref. | Debit | Credit | Balance Debit | Balance Credit |
|------|------|-----------|-------|--------|-------|--------|
| 2015 | | | | | | |
| Apr. 30 | | 28 | 1,725 | | 1,725 | |

**Account** *Rent Expense* — Account No. 53

| Date | Item | Post. Ref. | Debit | Credit | Balance Debit | Balance Credit |
|------|------|-----------|-------|--------|-------|--------|
| 2015 | | | | | | |
| Apr. 1 | | 27 | 800 | | 800 | |

**Account** *Laboratory Expense* — Account No. 55

| Date | Item | Post. Ref. | Debit | Credit | Balance Debit | Balance Credit |
|------|------|-----------|-------|--------|-------|--------|
| 2015 | | | | | | |
| Apr. 24 | | 28 | 545 | | 545 | |

**Account** *Utilities Expense* — Account No. 56

| Date | Item | Post. Ref. | Debit | Credit | Balance Debit | Balance Credit |
|------|------|-----------|-------|--------|-------|--------|
| 2015 | | | | | | |
| Apr. 30 | | 28 | 360 | | 360 | |

**Account** *Miscellaneous Expense* — Account No. 59

| Date | Item | Post. Ref. | Debit | Credit | Balance Debit | Balance Credit |
|------|------|-----------|-------|--------|-------|--------|
| 2015 | | | | | | |
| Apr. 30 | | 28 | 132 | | 132 | |

4.

|  | J. F. Outz, M.D.<br>Unadjusted Trial Balance<br>April 30, 2015 | |
|---|---|---|
|  | Debit<br>Balances | Credit<br>Balances |
| Cash ........................................................ | 2,361 |  |
| Accounts Receivable........................................ | 8,720 |  |
| Supplies...................................................... | 535 |  |
| Prepaid Insurance .......................................... | 835 |  |
| Equipment................................................... | 21,520 |  |
| Accounts Payable .......................................... |  | 1,335 |
| J. F. Outz, Capital ......................................... |  | 30,583 |
| J. F. Outz, Drawing......................................... | 1,250 |  |
| Professional Fees........................................... |  | 6,865 |
| Salary Expense............................................. | 1,725 |  |
| Rent Expense ............................................... | 800 |  |
| Laboratory Expense ........................................ | 545 |  |
| Utilities Expense ........................................... | 360 |  |
| Miscellaneous Expense .................................... | 132 |  |
|  | 38,783 | 38,783 |

# Discussion Questions

1. What is the difference between an account and a ledger?

2. Do the terms *debit* and *credit* signify increase or decrease or can they signify either? Explain.

3. McIntyre Company adheres to a policy of depositing all cash receipts in a bank account and making all payments by check. The cash account as of December 31 has a credit balance of $1,850, and there is no undeposited cash on hand. (a) Assuming no errors occurred during journalizing or posting, what caused this unusual balance? (b) Is the $1,850 credit balance in the cash account an asset, a liability, owner's equity, a revenue, or an expense?

4. eCatalog Services Company performed services in October for a specific customer, for a fee of $7,890. Payment was received the following November. (a) Was the revenue earned in October or November? (b) What accounts should be debited and credited in (1) October and (2) November?

5. If the two totals of a trial balance are equal, does it mean that there are no errors in the accounting records? Explain.

6. Assume that a trial balance is prepared with an account balance of $8,900 listed as $9,800 and an account balance of $1,000 listed as $100. Identify the transposition and the slide.

7. Assume that when a purchase of supplies of $2,650 for cash was recorded, both the debit and the credit were journalized and posted as $2,560. (a) Would this error cause the trial balance to be out of balance? (b) Would the trial balance be out of balance if the $2,650 entry had been journalized correctly but the credit to Cash had been posted as $2,560?

8. Assume that Muscular Consulting erroneously recorded the payment of $7,500 of owner withdrawals as a debit to Salary Expense. (a) How would this error affect the equality of the trial balance? (b) How would this error affect the income statement, statement of owner's equity, and balance sheet?

9. Assume that Sunshine Realty Co. borrowed $300,000 from Columbia First Bank and Trust. In recording the transaction, Sunshine erroneously recorded the receipt as a debit to Cash, $300,000, and a credit to Fees Earned, $300,000. (a) How would this error affect the equality of the trial balance? (b) How would this error affect the income statement, statement of owner's equity, and balance sheet?

10. Checking accounts are one of the most common forms of deposits for banks. Assume that Surety Storage has a checking account at Ada Savings Bank. What type of account (asset, liability, owner's equity, revenue, expense, drawing) does the account balance of $11,375 represent from the viewpoint of (a) Surety Storage and (b) Ada Savings Bank?

# Practice Exercises

EE 2-1 *p. 57*

**PE 2-1A** **Rules of debit and credit and normal balances** **OBJ. 2**

State for each account whether it is likely to have (a) debit entries only, (b) credit entries only, or (c) both debit and credit entries. Also, indicate its normal balance.

1. Accounts Receivable
2. Commissions Earned
3. Notes Payable
4. Patricia Mayer, Capital
5. Rent Revenue
6. Wages Expense

EE 2-1 *p. 57*

**PE 2-1B** **Rules of debit and credit and normal balances** **OBJ. 2**

State for each account whether it is likely to have (a) debit entries only, (b) credit entries only, or (c) both debit and credit entries. Also, indicate its normal balance.

1. Accounts Payable
2. Cash
3. Del Robinson, Drawing
4. Miscellaneous Expense
5. Insurance Expense
6. Fees Earned

EE 2-2 *p. 61*

**PE 2-2A** **Journal entry for asset purchase** **OBJ. 2**

Prepare a journal entry for the purchase of office equipment on October 27 for $32,750, paying $6,550 cash and the remainder on account.

EE 2-2 *p. 61*

**PE 2-2B** **Journal entry for asset purchase** **OBJ. 2**

Prepare a journal entry for the purchase of office supplies on September 30 for $2,500, paying $800 cash and the remainder on account.

EE 2-3 *p. 65*

**PE 2-3A** **Journal entry for fees earned** **OBJ. 3**

Prepare a journal entry on March 16 for fees earned on account, $9,450.

EE 2-3 *p. 65*

**PE 2-3B** **Journal entry for fees earned** **OBJ. 3**

Prepare a journal entry on August 13 for cash received for services rendered, $9,000.

EE 2-4 *p. 68*

**PE 2-4A** **Journal entry for owner's withdrawal** **OBJ. 3**

Prepare a journal entry on December 23 for the withdrawal of $20,000 by Steve Buckley for personal use.

EE 2-4 *p. 68*

**PE 2-4B** **Journal entry for owner's withdrawal** **OBJ. 3**

Prepare a journal entry on June 30 for the withdrawal of $11,500 by Dawn Pierce for personal use.

SHOW
ME HOW

EE 2-5 *p. 68* **PE 2-5A    Missing amount from an account**                                    OBJ. 3

On July 1, the cash account balance was $37,450. During July, cash payments totaled $115,860 and the July 31 balance was $29,600. Determine the cash receipts during July.

SHOW
ME HOW

EE 2-5 *p. 68* **PE 2-5B    Missing amount from an account**                                    OBJ. 3

On August 1, the supplies account balance was $1,025. During August, supplies of $3,110 were purchased, and $1,324 of supplies were on hand as of August 31. Determine supplies expense for August.

SHOW
ME HOW

EE 2-6 *p. 72* **PE 2-6A    Trial balance errors**                                                OBJ. 4

For each of the following errors, considered individually, indicate whether the error would cause the trial balance totals to be unequal. If the error would cause the trial balance totals to be unequal, indicate whether the debit or credit total is higher and by how much.

a. The payment of an insurance premium of $5,400 for a three-year policy was debited to Prepaid Insurance for $5,400 and credited to Cash for $4,500.

b. A payment of $270 on account was debited to Accounts Payable for $720 and credited to Cash for $720.

c. A purchase of supplies on account for $1,600 was debited to Supplies for $1,600 and debited to Accounts Payable for $1,600.

EE 2-6 *p. 72* **PE 2-6B    Trial balance errors**                                                OBJ. 4

For each of the following errors, considered individually, indicate whether the error would cause the trial balance totals to be unequal. If the error would cause the trial balance totals to be unequal, indicate whether the debit or credit total is higher and by how much.

SHOW
ME HOW

a. The payment of cash for the purchase of office equipment of $12,900 was debited to Land for $12,900 and credited to Cash for $12,900.

b. The payment of $1,840 on account was debited to Accounts Payable for $184 and credited to Cash for $1,840.

c. The receipt of cash on account of $3,800 was recorded as a debit to Cash for $8,300 and a credit to Accounts Receivable for $3,800.

EE 2-7 *p. 73* **PE 2-7A    Correcting entries**                                                 OBJ. 4

The following errors took place in journalizing and posting transactions:

a. Rent expense of $4,650 paid for the current month was recorded as a debit to Miscellaneous Expense and a credit to Rent Expense.

SHOW
ME HOW

b. The payment of $3,700 from a customer on account was recorded as a debit to Cash and a credit to Accounts Payable.

Journalize the entries to correct the errors. Omit explanations.

SHOW
ME HOW

EE 2-7 *p. 73* **PE 2-7B    Correcting entries**                                                 OBJ. 4

The following errors took place in journalizing and posting transactions:

a. The receipt of $8,400 for services rendered was recorded as a debit to Accounts Receivable and a credit to Fees Earned.

b. The purchase of supplies of $2,500 on account was recorded as a debit to Office Equipment and a credit to Supplies.

Journalize the entries to correct the errors. Omit explanations.

EE 2-8 *p. 75* **PE 2-8A    Horizontal analysis**                                               OBJ. 5

Two income statements for Fuller Company follow:

*(Continued)*

SHOW
ME HOW

**Fuller Company**
**Income Statements**
**For Years Ended December 31**

|  | 2016 | 2015 |
|---|---|---|
| Fees earned | $680,000 | $850,000 |
| Operating expenses | 541,875 | 637,500 |
| Net income | $138,125 | $212,500 |

Prepare a horizontal analysis of Fuller Company's income statements.

EE 2-8 *p. 75*   **PE 2-8B   Horizontal analysis**                                OBJ. 5

SHOW
ME HOW

Two income statements for Paragon Company follow:

**Paragon Company**
**Income Statements**
**For Years Ended December 31**

|  | 2016 | 2015 |
|---|---|---|
| Fees earned | $1,416,000 | $1,200,000 |
| Operating expenses | 1,044,000 | 900,000 |
| Net income | $ 372,000 | $ 300,000 |

Prepare a horizontal analysis of Paragon Company's income statements.

# Exercises

## EX 2-1   Chart of accounts                                              OBJ. 1

The following accounts appeared in recent financial statements of **Delta Air Lines**:

| | |
|---|---|
| Accounts Payable | Flight Equipment |
| Advanced Payments for Equipment | Frequent Flyer (Obligations) |
| Air Traffic Liability | Fuel Inventory |
| Aircraft Fuel (Expense) | Landing Fees (Expense) |
| Aircraft Maintenance (Expense) | Parts and Supplies Inventories |
| Aircraft Rent (Expense) | Passenger Commissions (Expense) |
| Cargo Revenue | Passenger Revenue |
| Cash | Prepaid Expenses |
| Contract Carrier Arrangements (Expense) | Taxes Payable |

Identify each account as either a balance sheet account or an income statement account. For each balance sheet account, identify it as an asset, a liability, or owner's equity. For each income statement account, identify it as a revenue or an expense.

## EX 2-2   Chart of accounts                                              OBJ. 1

Innerscape Interiors is owned and operated by Jackie Vargo, an interior decorator. In the ledger of Innerscape Interiors, the first digit of the account number indicates its major account classification (1—assets, 2—liabilities, 3—owner's equity, 4—revenues, 5—expenses). The second digit of the account number indicates the specific account within each of the preceding major account classifications.

Match each account number with its most likely account in the list that follows. The account numbers are 11, 12, 13, 21, 31, 32, 41, 51, 52, and 53.

| | |
|---|---|
| Accounts Payable | Jackie Vargo, Drawing |
| Accounts Receivable | Land |
| Cash | Miscellaneous Expense |
| Fees Earned | Supplies Expense |
| Jackie Vargo, Capital | Wages Expense |

## EX 2-3   Chart of accounts                                              OBJ. 1

LeadCo School is a newly organized business that teaches people how to inspire and influence others. The list of accounts to be opened in the general ledger is as follows:

| | |
|---|---|
| Accounts Payable | Miscellaneous Expense |
| Accounts Receivable | Prepaid Insurance |
| Cash | Rent Expense |
| Equipment | Supplies |
| Fees Earned | Supplies Expense |
| Ivy Bishop, Capital | Unearned Rent |
| Ivy Bishop, Drawing | Wages Expense |

List the accounts in the order in which they should appear in the ledger of LeadCo School and assign account numbers. Each account number is to have two digits: the first digit is to indicate the major classification (1 for assets, etc.), and the second digit is to identify the specific account within each major classification (11 for Cash, etc.).

---

### EX 2-4   Rules of debit and credit                                OBJ. 1, 2

The following table summarizes the rules of debit and credit. For each of the items (a) through (l), indicate whether the proper answer is a debit or a credit.

| | Increase | Decrease | Normal Balance |
|---|---|---|---|
| Balance sheet accounts: | | | |
| Asset | (a) | (b) | Debit |
| Liability | (c) | Debit | (d) |
| Owner's equity: | | | |
| Capital | Credit | (e) | (f) |
| Drawing | (g) | (h) | (i) |
| Income statement accounts: | | | |
| Revenue | (j) | (k) | Credit |
| Expense | (l) | Credit | Debit |

---

### EX 2-5   Normal entries for accounts                                OBJ. 2

During the month, Gates Labs Co. has a substantial number of transactions affecting each of the following accounts. State for each account whether it is likely to have (a) debit entries only, (b) credit entries only, or (c) both debit and credit entries.

1. Accounts Payable
2. Accounts Receivable
3. Cash
4. Fees Earned
5. Insurance Expense
6. Miriam Ramsey, Drawing
7. Utilities Expense

---

### EX 2-6   Normal balances of accounts                                OBJ. 1, 2

Identify each of the following accounts of Kaiser Services Co. as asset, liability, owner's equity, revenue, or expense, and state in each case whether the normal balance is a debit or a credit:

a. Accounts Payable
b. Accounts Receivable
c. Bobby Lund, Capital
d. Bobby Lund, Drawing
e. Cash
f. Fees Earned
g. Office Equipment
h. Rent Expense
i. Supplies
j. Wages Expense

---

### EX 2-7   Transactions                                OBJ. 2

SHOW
ME HOW

Jardine Consulting Co. has the following accounts in its ledger: Cash; Accounts Receivable; Supplies; Office Equipment; Accounts Payable; Cammy Jardine, Capital; Cammy Jardine, Drawing; Fees Earned; Rent Expense; Advertising Expense; Utilities Expense; Miscellaneous Expense.

   Journalize the following selected transactions for March 2016 in a two-column journal. Journal entry explanations may be omitted.

*(Continued)*

Mar. 1. Paid rent for the month, $2,500.

3. Paid advertising expense, $675.

5. Paid cash for supplies, $1,250.

6. Purchased office equipment on account, $9,500.

10. Received cash from customers on account, $16,550.

15. Paid creditor on account, $3,180.

27. Paid cash for repairs to office equipment, $540.

30. Paid telephone bill for the month, $375.

31. Fees earned and billed to customers for the month, $49,770.

31. Paid electricity bill for the month, $830.

31. Withdrew cash for personal use, $1,750.

---

### EX 2-8 Journalizing and posting
**OBJ. 2, 3**

SHOW
ME HOW

On January 7, 2016, Captec Company purchased $4,175 of supplies on account. In Captec Company's chart of accounts, the supplies account is No. 15, and the accounts payable account is No. 21.

a. Journalize the January 7, 2016, transaction on page 33 of Captec Company's two-column journal. Include an explanation of the entry.

b. Prepare a four-column account for Supplies. Enter a debit balance of $2,200 as of January 1, 2016. Place a check mark (✓) in the Posting Reference column.

c. Prepare a four-column account for Accounts Payable. Enter a credit balance of $18,430 as of January 1, 2016. Place a check mark (✓) in the Posting Reference column.

d. Post the January 7, 2016, transaction to the accounts.

e. ▬▬▬▶ Do the rules of debit and credit apply to all companies?

---

### EX 2-9 Transactions and T accounts
**OBJ. 2, 3**

SHOW
ME HOW

The following selected transactions were completed during August of the current year:

1. Billed customers for fees earned, $73,900.

2. Purchased supplies on account, $1,960.

3. Received cash from customers on account, $62,770.

4. Paid creditors on account, $820.

a. Journalize these transactions in a two-column journal, using the appropriate number to identify the transactions. Journal entry explanations may be omitted.

b. Post the entries prepared in (a) to the following T accounts: Cash, Supplies, Accounts Receivable, Accounts Payable, Fees Earned. To the left of each amount posted in the accounts, place the appropriate number to identify the transactions.

c. ▬▬▬▶ Assume that the unadjusted trial balance on August 31 shows a credit balance for Accounts Receivable. Does this credit balance mean an error has occurred?

---

### EX 2-10 Cash account balance
**OBJ. 1, 2, 3**

During the month, Warwick Co. received $515,000 in cash and paid out $375,000 in cash.

a. ▬▬▬▶ Do the data indicate that Warwick Co. had net income of $140,000 during the month? Explain.

b. If the balance of the cash account is $200,000 at the end of the month, what was the cash balance at the beginning of the month?

---

### EX 2-11 Account balances
**OBJ. 1, 2, 3**

✔ c. $238,050

SHOW
ME HOW

a. During February, $186,500 was paid to creditors on account, and purchases on account were $201,400. Assuming the February 28 balance of Accounts Payable was $59,900, determine the account balance on February 1.

b. On October 1, the accounts receivable account balance was $115,800. During October, $449,600 was collected from customers on account. Assuming the October 31 balance was $130,770 determine the fees billed to customers on account during October.

c. On April 1, the cash account balance was $46,220. During April, cash receipts totaled $248,600 and the April 30 balance was $56,770. Determine the cash payments made during April.

---

SHOW
ME HOW

### EX 2-12 Capital account balance

OBJ. 1, 2

As of January 1, Terrace Waters, Capital, had a credit balance of $314,000. During the year, withdrawals totaled $10,000, and the business incurred a net loss of $320,000.

a. Compute the balance of Terrace Waters, Capital, as of the end of the year.

b. ➤ Assuming that there have been no recording errors, will the balance sheet prepared at December 31 balance? Explain.

---

### EX 2-13 Identifying transactions

OBJ. 1, 2

Wyoming Tours Co. is a travel agency. The nine transactions recorded by Wyoming Tours during June 2016, its first month of operations, are indicated in the following T accounts:

| Cash | | | | | Equipment | | | | Lorene Jones, Drawing | |
|---|---|---|---|---|---|---|---|---|---|---|
| (1) | 40,000 | (2) | 2,500 | (3) | 14,500 | | | (9) | 3,000 | |
| (7) | 8,700 | (3) | 4,000 | | | | | | | |
| | | (4) | 4,850 | | | | | | | |
| | | (6) | 5,500 | | | | | | | |
| | | (9) | 3,000 | | | | | | | |

| Accounts Receivable | | | | | Accounts Payable | | | | Service Revenue | |
|---|---|---|---|---|---|---|---|---|---|---|
| (5) | 13,800 | (7) | 8,700 | (6) | 5,500 | (3) | 10,500 | | (5) | 13,800 |

| Supplies | | | | | Lorene Jones, Capital | | | | Operating Expenses | |
|---|---|---|---|---|---|---|---|---|---|---|
| (2) | 2,500 | (8) | 1,100 | | | (1) | 40,000 | (4) | 4,850 | |
| | | | | | | | | (8) | 1,100 | |

Indicate for each debit and each credit: (a) whether an asset, liability, owner's equity, drawing, revenue, or expense account was affected and (b) whether the account was increased (+) or decreased (–). Present your answers in the following form, with transaction (1) given as an example:

| | Account Debited | | | Account Credited | |
|---|---|---|---|---|---|
| Transaction | Type | Effect | | Type | Effect |
| (1) | asset | + | | owner's equity | + |

---

### EX 2-14 Journal entries

OBJ. 1, 2

SHOW
ME HOW

Based upon the T accounts in Exercise 2-13, prepare the nine journal entries from which the postings were made. Journal entry explanations may be omitted.

---

✔ (a) Total of Debit
column: $58,800

SHOW
ME HOW

### EX 2-15 Trial balance

OBJ. 4

Based upon the data presented in Exercise 2-13, (a) prepare an unadjusted trial balance, listing the accounts in their proper order. (b) Based upon the unadjusted trial balance, determine the net income or net loss.

✔ Total of Credit
column: $925,000

SHOW
ME HOW

### EX 2-16 Trial balance

OBJ. 4

The accounts in the ledger of Hickory Furniture Company as of December 31, 2016, are listed in alphabetical order as follows. All accounts have normal balances. The balance of the cash account has been intentionally omitted.

*(Continued)*

| Accounts Payable | $ 42,770 | Notes Payable | $ 50,000 |
|---|---|---|---|
| Accounts Receivable | 116,900 | Prepaid Insurance | 21,600 |
| Cash | ? | Rent Expense | 48,000 |
| Elaine Wells, Capital | 75,000 | Supplies | 4,275 |
| Elaine Wells, Drawing | 24,000 | Supplies Expense | 6,255 |
| Fees Earned | 745,230 | Unearned Rent | 12,000 |
| Insurance Expense | 3,600 | Utilities Expense | 26,850 |
| Land | 50,000 | Wages Expense | 580,700 |
| Miscellaneous Expense | 9,500 | | |

Prepare an unadjusted trial balance, listing the accounts in their normal order and inserting the missing figure for cash.

---

### EX 2-17   Effect of errors on trial balance                           OBJ. 4

Indicate which of the following errors, each considered individually, would cause the trial balance totals to be unequal:

a. A fee of $21,000 earned and due from a client was not debited to Accounts Receivable or credited to a revenue account, because the cash had not been received.

b. A receipt of $11,300 from an account receivable was journalized and posted as a debit of $11,300 to Cash and a credit of $11,300 to Fees Earned.

c. A payment of $4,950 to a creditor was posted as a debit of $4,950 to Accounts Payable and a debit of $4,950 to Cash.

d. A payment of $5,000 for equipment purchased was posted as a debit of $500 to Equipment and a credit of $500 to Cash.

e. Payment of a cash withdrawal of $19,000 was journalized and posted as a debit of $1,900 to Salary Expense and a credit of $19,000 to Cash.

Indicate which of the preceding errors would require a correcting entry.

---

### EX 2-18   Errors in trial balance                                     OBJ. 4

✔ Total of Credit column: $525,000

The following preliminary unadjusted trial balance of Ranger Co., a sports ticket agency, does not balance:

**Ranger Co.**
**Unadjusted Trial Balance**
**August 31, 2016**

| | Debit Balances | Credit Balances |
|---|---|---|
| Cash | 77,600 | |
| Accounts Receivable | 37,750 | |
| Prepaid Insurance | | 12,000 |
| Equipment | 19,000 | |
| Accounts Payable | | 29,100 |
| Unearned Rent | | 10,800 |
| Carmen Meeks, Capital | 110,000 | |
| Carmen Meeks, Drawing | 13,000 | |
| Service Revenue | | 385,000 |
| Wages Expense | | 213,000 |
| Advertising Expense | 16,350 | |
| Miscellaneous Expense | | 18,400 |
| | 273,700 | 668,300 |

When the ledger and other records are reviewed, you discover the following: (1) the debits and credits in the cash account total $77,600 and $62,100, respectively; (2) a billing of $9,000 to a customer on account was not posted to the accounts receivable account; (3) a payment of $4,500 made to a creditor on account was not posted to the accounts payable account; (4) the balance of the unearned rent account is $5,400; (5) the correct balance of the equipment account is $190,000; and (6) each account has a normal balance. Prepare a corrected unadjusted trial balance.

**EX 2-19    Effect of errors on trial balance**                                    OBJ. 4

The following errors occurred in posting from a two-column journal:

1. A credit of $6,000 to Accounts Payable was not posted.

2. An entry debiting Accounts Receivable and crediting Fees Earned for $5,300 was not posted.

3. A debit of $2,700 to Accounts Payable was posted as a credit.

4. A debit of $480 to Supplies was posted twice.

5. A debit of $3,600 to Cash was posted to Miscellaneous Expense.

6. A credit of $780 to Cash was posted as $870.

7. A debit of $12,620 to Wages Expense was posted as $12,260.

Considering each case individually (i.e., assuming that no other errors had occurred), indicate: (a) by "yes" or "no" whether the trial balance would be out of balance; (b) if answer to (a) is "yes," the amount by which the trial balance totals would differ; and (c) whether the Debit or Credit column of the trial balance would have the larger total. Answers should be presented in the following form, with error (1) given as an example:

| | (a) | (b) | (c) |
|---|---|---|---|
| Error | Out of Balance | Difference | Larger Total |
| 1. | yes | $6,000 | debit |

**EX 2-20    Errors in trial balance**                                              OBJ. 4

Identify the errors in the following trial balance. All accounts have normal balances.

✔ Total of Credit
column: $1,040,000

SHOW
ME HOW

**Mascot Co.**
**Unadjusted Trial Balance**
**For the Month Ending July 31, 2016**

| | Debit Balances | Credit Balances |
|---|---|---|
| Cash ..................................................................... | 36,000 | |
| Accounts Receivable............................................... | | 112,600 |
| Prepaid Insurance ................................................... | 18,000 | |
| Equipment.............................................................. | 375,000 | |
| Accounts Payable ................................................... | 53,300 | |
| Salaries Payable....................................................... | | 7,500 |
| Samuel Parson, Capital ........................................... | | 297,200 |
| Samuel Parson, Drawing......................................... | | 17,000 |
| Service Revenue ..................................................... | | 682,000 |
| Salary Expense........................................................ | 396,800 | |
| Advertising Expense................................................ | | 73,000 |
| Miscellaneous Expense .......................................... | 11,600 | |
| | 1,189,300 | 1,189,300 |

**EX 2-21    Entries to correct errors**                                            OBJ. 4

SHOW
ME HOW

The following errors took place in journalizing and posting transactions:

a. Insurance of $18,000 paid for the current year was recorded as a debit to Insurance Expense and a credit to Prepaid Insurance.

b. A withdrawal of $10,000 by Brian Phillips, owner of the business, was recorded as a debit to Wages Expense and a credit to Cash.

Journalize the entries to correct the errors. Omit explanations.

**EX 2-22    Entries to correct errors**                                            OBJ. 4

SHOW
ME HOW

The following errors took place in journalizing and posting transactions:

a. Cash of $8,800 received on account was recorded as a debit to Fees Earned and a credit to Cash.

b. A $1,760 purchase of supplies for cash was recorded as a debit to Supplies Expense and a credit to Accounts Payable.

Journalize the entries to correct the errors. Omit explanations.

**EX 2-23    Horizontal analysis of income statement**                    OBJ. 5

The following data (in millions) are taken from the financial statements of Target Corporation:

SHOW
ME HOW

|  | Recent Year | Prior Year |
|---|---|---|
| Revenue | $69,865 | $67,390 |
| Operating expenses | 64,543 | 62,138 |
| Operating income | $ 5,322 | $ 5,252 |

a.  For Target Corporation, determine the amount of change in millions and the percent of change (round to one decimal place) from the prior year to the recent year for:

1.  Revenue

2.  Operating expenses

3.  Operating income

b.  ➡What conclusions can you draw from your analysis of the revenue and the total operating expenses?

**EX 2-24    Horizontal analysis of income statement**                    OBJ. 5

The following data (in millions) were taken from the financial statements of Walmart Stores, Inc:

|  | Recent Year | Prior Year |
|---|---|---|
| Revenue | $446,950 | $421,849 |
| Operating expenses | 420,392 | 396,307 |
| Operating income | $ 26,558 | $ 25,542 |

a.  For Walmart Stores, Inc., determine the amount of change in millions and the percent of change (round to one decimal place) from the prior year to the recent year for:

1.  Revenue

2.  Operating expenses

3.  Operating income

b.  ➡Comment on the results of your horizontal analysis in part (a).

c.  Based upon Exercise 2-23, compare and comment on the operating results of Target and Walmart for the recent year.

# Problems: Series A

**PR 2-1A    Entries into T accounts and trial balance**                    OBJ. 1, 2, 3, 4

✔ 3. Total of Debit
column: $80,650

Kimberly Manis, an architect, opened an office on January 1, 2016. During the month, she completed the following transactions connected with her professional practice:

a.  Transferred cash from a personal bank account to an account to be used for the business, $18,000.

b.  Paid January rent for office and workroom, $1,950.

c.  Purchased used automobile for $28,500, paying $5,700 cash and giving a note payable for the remainder.

d.  Purchased office and computer equipment on account, $4,500.

e.  Paid cash for supplies, $1,875.

f.  Paid cash for annual insurance policies, $3,600.

g.  Received cash from client for plans delivered, $13,650. ─ cash  + fee J

h.  Paid cash for miscellaneous expenses, $2,600. ─ misc Ex

i.  Paid cash to creditors on account, $3,000. ─ A/P    + cash

j.  Paid installment due on note payable, $950. ─ N/P    + cash

k.  Received invoice for blueprint service, due in February, $3,750. ─ blueprt + A/P

l.  Recorded fees earned on plans delivered, payment to be received in February, $21,900.   + A/P + fee

m.  Paid salary of assistants, $4,100. ─ salary   + cash   Expense

n.  Paid gas, oil, and repairs on automobile for January, $1,300.   ─ Auto E    + cash

## Instructions

1. Record these transactions directly in the following T accounts, without journalizing: Cash; Accounts Receivable; Supplies; Prepaid Insurance; Automobiles; Equipment; Notes Payable; Accounts Payable; Kimberly Manis, Capital; Professional Fees; Salary Expense; Blueprint Expense; Rent Expense; Automobile Expense; Miscellaneous Expense. To the left of the amount entered in the accounts, place the appropriate letter to identify the transaction.

2. Determine account balances of the T accounts. Accounts containing a single entry only (such as Prepaid Insurance) do not need a balance.

3. Prepare an unadjusted trial balance for Kimberly Manis, Architect, as of January 31, 2016.

4. Determine the net income or net loss for January.

---

**PR 2-2A** **Journal entries and trial balance** OBJ. 1, 2, 3, 4

✔ 4. c. $4,550

General Ledger

SHOW
ME HOW

On August 1, 2016, Bill Hudson established Heritage Realty, which completed the following transactions during the month:

a. Bill Hudson transferred cash from a personal bank account to an account to be used for the business, $30,000.

b. Paid rent on office and equipment for the month, $3,250.

c. Purchased supplies on account, $2,150.

d. Paid creditor on account, $875.

e. Earned sales commissions, receiving cash, $14,440.

f. Paid automobile expenses (including rental charge) for month, $1,580, and miscellaneous expenses, $650.

g. Paid office salaries, $3,000.

h. Determined that the cost of supplies used was $1,300.

i. Withdrew cash for personal use, $2,500.

## Instructions

1. Journalize entries for transactions (a) through (i), using the following account titles: Cash; Supplies; Accounts Payable; Bill Hudson, Capital; Bill Hudson, Drawing; Sales Commissions; Rent Expense; Office Salaries Expense; Automobile Expense; Supplies Expense; Miscellaneous Expense. Explanations may be omitted.

2. Prepare T accounts, using the account titles in (1). Post the journal entries to these accounts, placing the appropriate letter to the left of each amount to identify the transactions. Determine the account balances, after all posting is complete. Accounts containing only a single entry do not need a balance.

3. Prepare an unadjusted trial balance as of August 31, 2016.

4. Determine the following:

   a. Amount of total revenue recorded in the ledger.

   b. Amount of total expenses recorded in the ledger.

   c. Amount of net income for August.

5. Determine the increase or decrease in owner's equity for August.

---

**PR 2-3A** **Journal entries and trial balance** OBJ. 1, 2, 3, 4

✔ 3. Total of Credit column: $81,450

General Ledger

SHOW
ME HOW

On November 1, 2016, Patty Cosgrove established an interior decorating business, Classic Designs. During the month, Patty completed the following transactions related to the business:

Nov. 1. Patty transferred cash from a personal bank account to an account to be used for the business, $27,750.

1. Paid rent for period of November 1 to end of month, $4,000.

6. Purchased office equipment on account, $12,880.

8. Purchased a truck for $32,500 paying $6,500 cash and giving a note payable for the remainder.

10. Purchased supplies for cash, $1,860.

12. Received cash for job completed, $7,500.

(Continued)

Nov. 15. Paid annual premiums on property and casualty insurance, $2,400.

23. Recorded jobs completed on account and sent invoices to customers, $12,440.

24. Received an invoice for truck expenses, to be paid in November, $1,100.

*Enter the following transactions on Page 2 of the two-column journal:*

29. Paid utilities expense, $3,660.

29. Paid miscellaneous expenses, $1,700.

30. Received cash from customers on account, $8,000.

30. Paid wages of employees, $4,750.

30. Paid creditor a portion of the amount owed for equipment purchased on November 6, $6,220.

30. Withdrew cash for personal use, $2,000.

**Instructions**

1. Journalize each transaction in a two-column journal beginning on Page 1, referring to the following chart of accounts in selecting the accounts to be debited and credited. (Do not insert the account numbers in the journal at this time.) Explanations may be omitted.

| | | | |
|---|---|---|---|
| 11 | Cash | 31 | Patty Cosgrove, Capital |
| 12 | Accounts Receivable | 32 | Patty Cosgrove, Drawing |
| 13 | Supplies | 41 | Fees Earned |
| 14 | Prepaid Insurance | 51 | Wages Expense |
| 16 | Equipment | 53 | Rent Expense |
| 18 | Truck | 54 | Utilities Expense |
| 21 | Notes Payable | 55 | Truck Expense |
| 22 | Accounts Payable | 59 | Miscellaneous Expense |

2. Post the journal to a ledger of four-column accounts, inserting appropriate posting references as each item is posted. Extend the balances to the appropriate balance columns after each transaction is posted.

3. Prepare an unadjusted trial balance for Classic Designs as of November 30, 2016.

4. Determine the excess of revenues over expenses for November.

5. Can you think of any reason why the amount determined in (4) might not be the net income for November?

---

**PR 2-4A  Journal entries and trial balance**                    OBJ. 1, 2, 3, 4

✔ 4. Total of Debit column: $532,525

General Ledger

Elite Realty acts as an agent in buying, selling, renting, and managing real estate. The unadjusted trial balance on March 31, 2016, follows:

**Elite Realty**
**Unadjusted Trial Balance**
**March 31, 2016**

| | | Debit Balances | Credit Balances |
|---|---|---|---|
| 11 | Cash | 26,300 | |
| 12 | Accounts Receivable | 61,500 | |
| 13 | Prepaid Insurance | 3,000 | |
| 14 | Office Supplies | 1,800 | |
| 16 | Land | — | |
| 21 | Accounts Payable | | 14,000 |
| 22 | Unearned Rent | | — |
| 23 | Notes Payable | | — |
| 31 | Lester Wagner, Capital | | 46,000 |
| 32 | Lester Wagner, Drawing | 2,000 | |
| 41 | Fees Earned | | 240,000 |
| 51 | Salary and Commission Expense | 148,200 | |
| 52 | Rent Expense | 30,000 | |
| 53 | Advertising Expense | 17,800 | |
| 54 | Automobile Expense | 5,500 | |
| 59 | Miscellaneous Expense | 3,900 | |
| | | 300,000 | 300,000 |

The following business transactions were completed by Elite Realty during April 2016:

Apr.  1.  Paid rent on office for month, $6,500.

2.  Purchased office supplies on account, $2,300.

5.  Paid insurance premiums, $6,000.

10.  Received cash from clients on account, $52,300.

15.  Purchased land for a future building site for $200,000, paying $30,000 in cash and giving a note payable for the remainder.

17.  Paid creditors on account, $6,450.

20.  Returned a portion of the office supplies purchased on April 2, receiving full credit for their cost, $325.

23.  Paid advertising expense, $4,300.

*Enter the following transactions on Page 19 of the two-column journal:*

27.  Discovered an error in computing a commission; received cash from the salesperson for the overpayment, $2,500.

28.  Paid automobile expense (including rental charges for an automobile), $1,500.

29.  Paid miscellaneous expenses, $1,400.

30.  Recorded revenue earned and billed to clients during the month, $57,000.

30.  Paid salaries and commissions for the month, $11,900.

30.  Withdrew cash for personal use, $4,000.

30.  Rented land purchased on April 15 to local merchants association for use as a parking lot in May and June, during a street rebuilding program; received advance payment of $10,000.

### Instructions

1.  Record the April 1, 2016, balance of each account in the appropriate balance column of a four-column account, write *Balance* in the item section, and place a check mark (✓) in the Posting Reference column.

2.  Journalize the transactions for April in a two-column journal beginning on Page 18. Journal entry explanations may be omitted.

3.  Post to the ledger, extending the account balance to the appropriate balance column after each posting.

4.  Prepare an unadjusted trial balance of the ledger as of April 30, 2016.

5.  Assume that the April 30 transaction for salaries and commissions should have been $19,100. (a) Why did the unadjusted trial balance in (4) balance? (b) Journalize the correcting entry. (c) Is this error a transposition or slide?

---

**PR 2-5A**   **Corrected trial balance**                      **OBJ. 4**

✔ 1. Total of Debit column: $725,000

The Colby Group has the following unadjusted trial balance as of August 31, 2016:

**The Colby Group**
**Unadjusted Trial Balance**
**August 31, 2016**

| | Debit Balances | Credit Balances |
|---|---|---|
| Cash | 17,300 | |
| Accounts Receivable | 37,000 | |
| Supplies | 7,400 | |
| Prepaid Insurance | 1,900 | |
| Equipment | 196,000 | |
| Notes Payable | | 97,600 |
| Accounts Payable | | 26,000 |
| Terry Colby, Capital | | 129,150 |
| Terry Colby, Drawing | 56,000 | |
| Fees Earned | | 454,450 |
| Wages Expense | 270,000 | |
| Rent Expense | 51,800 | |
| Advertising Expense | 25,200 | |
| Miscellaneous Expense | 5,100 | |
| | 667,700 | 707,200 |

*(Continued)*

The debit and credit totals are not equal as a result of the following errors:

a. The cash entered on the trial balance was understated by $6,000.

b. A cash receipt of $5,600 was posted as a debit to Cash of $6,500.

c. A debit of $11,000 to Accounts Receivable was not posted.

d. A return of $150 of defective supplies was erroneously posted as a $1,500 credit to Supplies.

e. An insurance policy acquired at a cost of $1,200 was posted as a credit to Prepaid Insurance.

f. The balance of Notes Payable was understated by $20,000.

g. A credit of $4,800 in Accounts Payable was overlooked when determining the balance of the account.

h. A debit of $7,000 for a withdrawal by the owner was posted as a credit to Terry Colby, Capital.

i. The balance of $58,100 in Rent Expense was entered as $51,800 in the trial balance.

j. Gas, Electricity, and Water Expense, with a balance of $24,150, was omitted from the trial balance.

### Instructions

1. Prepare a corrected unadjusted trial balance as of August 31, 2016.

2. ▬▬▶ Does the fact that the unadjusted trial balance in (1) is balanced mean that there are no errors in the accounts? Explain.

## Problems: Series B

### PR 2-1B   Entries into T accounts and trial balance
OBJ. 1, 2, 3, 4

✔ 3. Total of Debit column: $69,550

Ken Jones, an architect, opened an office on April 1, 2016. During the month, he completed the following transactions connected with his professional practice:

a. Transferred cash from a personal bank account to an account to be used for the business, $18,000.

b. Purchased used automobile for $19,500, paying $2,500 cash and giving a note payable for the remainder.

c. Paid April rent for office and workroom, $3,150.

d. Paid cash for supplies, $1,450.

e. Purchased office and computer equipment on account, $6,500.

f. Paid cash for annual insurance policies on automobile and equipment, $2,400.

g. Received cash from a client for plans delivered, $12,000.

h. Paid cash to creditors on account, $1,800.

i. Paid cash for miscellaneous expenses, $375.

j. Received invoice for blueprint service, due in May, $2,500.

k. Recorded fees earned on plans delivered, payment to be received in May, $15,650.

l. Paid salary of assistant, $2,800.

m. Paid cash for miscellaneous expenses, $200.

n. Paid installment due on note payable, $300.

o. Paid gas, oil, and repairs on automobile for April, $550.

### Instructions

1. Record these transactions directly in the following T accounts, without journalizing: Cash; Accounts Receivable; Supplies; Prepaid Insurance; Automobiles; Equipment; Notes Payable; Accounts Payable; Ken Jones, Capital; Professional Fees; Rent Expense; Salary Expense; Blueprint Expense; Automobile Expense; Miscellaneous Expense. To the left of each amount entered in the accounts, place the appropriate letter to identify the transaction.

2. Determine account balances of the T accounts. Accounts containing a single entry only (such as Prepaid Insurance) do not need a balance.

3. Prepare an unadjusted trial balance for Ken Jones, Architect, as of April 30, 2016.

4. Determine the net income or net loss for April.

---

### PR 2-2B   Journal entries and trial balance

OBJ. 1, 2, 3, 4

✔ 4. c. $4,550

**General Ledger**

SHOW
ME HOW

On August 1, 2016, Rafael Masey established Planet Realty, which completed the following transactions during the month:

a. Rafael Masey transferred cash from a personal bank account to an account to be used for the business, $17,500.

b. Purchased supplies on account, $2,300.

c. Earned sales commissions, receiving cash, $13,300.

d. Paid rent on office and equipment for the month, $3,000.

e. Paid creditor on account, $1,150.

f. Withdrew cash for personal use, $1,800.

g. Paid automobile expenses (including rental charge) for month, $1,500, and miscellaneous expenses, $400.

h. Paid office salaries, $2,800.

i. Determined that the cost of supplies used was $1,050.

**Instructions**

1. Journalize entries for transactions (a) through (i), using the following account titles: Cash; Supplies; Accounts Payable; Rafael Masey, Capital; Rafael Masey, Drawing; Sales Commissions; Rent Expense; Office Salaries Expense; Automobile Expense; Supplies Expense; Miscellaneous Expense. Journal entry explanations may be omitted.

2. Prepare T accounts, using the account titles in (1). Post the journal entries to these accounts, placing the appropriate letter to the left of each amount to identify the transactions. Determine the account balances, after all posting is complete. Accounts containing only a single entry do not need a balance.

3. Prepare an unadjusted trial balance as of August 31, 2016.

4. Determine the following:

   a. Amount of total revenue recorded in the ledger.

   b. Amount of total expenses recorded in the ledger.

   c. Amount of net income for August.

5. Determine the increase or decrease in owner's equity for August.

---

### PR 2-3B   Journal entries and trial balance

OBJ. 1, 2, 3, 4

✔ 3. Total of Credit
column: $70,300

**General Ledger**

SHOW
ME HOW

On October 1, 2016, Jay Pryor established an interior decorating business, Pioneer Designs. During the month, Jay completed the following transactions related to the business:

Oct. 1. Jay transferred cash from a personal bank account to an account to be used for the business, $18,000.

4. Paid rent for period of October 4 to end of month, $3,000.

10. Purchased a used truck for $23,750, paying $3,750 cash and giving a note payable for the remainder.

13. Purchased equipment on account, $10,500.

14. Purchased supplies for cash, $2,100.

15. Paid annual premiums on property and casualty insurance, $3,600.

15. Received cash for job completed, $8,950.

*Enter the following transactions on Page 2 of the two-column journal:*

21. Paid creditor a portion of the amount owed for equipment purchased on October 13, $2,000.

24. Recorded jobs completed on account and sent invoices to customers, $14,150.

26. Received an invoice for truck expenses, to be paid in November, $700.

27. Paid utilities expense, $2,240.

(*Continued*)

Oct. 27. Paid miscellaneous expenses, $1,100.

    29. Received cash from customers on account, $7,600.

    30. Paid wages of employees, $4,800.

    31. Withdrew cash for personal use, $3,500.

**Instructions**

1. Journalize each transaction in a two-column journal beginning on Page 1, referring to the following chart of accounts in selecting the accounts to be debited and credited. (Do not insert the account numbers in the journal at this time.) Journal entry explanations may be omitted.

| | | | |
|---|---|---|---|
| 11 | Cash | 31 | Jay Pryor, Capital |
| 12 | Accounts Receivable | 32 | Jay Pryor, Drawing |
| 13 | Supplies | 41 | Fees Earned |
| 14 | Prepaid Insurance | 51 | Wages Expense |
| 16 | Equipment | 53 | Rent Expense |
| 18 | Truck | 54 | Utilities Expense |
| 21 | Notes Payable | 55 | Truck Expense |
| 22 | Accounts Payable | 59 | Miscellaneous Expense |

2. Post the journal to a ledger of four-column accounts, inserting appropriate posting references as each item is posted. Extend the balances to the appropriate balance columns after each transaction is posted.

3. Prepare an unadjusted trial balance for Pioneer Designs as of October 31, 2016.

4. Determine the excess of revenues over expenses for October.

5. ▬▬▬▶ Can you think of any reason why the amount determined in (4) might not be the net income for October?

**PR 2-4B    Journal entries and trial balance**                   OBJ. 1, 2, 3, 4

✔ 4. Total of Debit column: $945,000

[General Ledger]

Valley Realty acts as an agent in buying, selling, renting, and managing real estate. The unadjusted trial balance on July 31, 2016, follows:

**Valley Realty**
**Unadjusted Trial Balance**
**July 31, 2016**

| | | Debit Balances | Credit Balances |
|---|---|---:|---:|
| 11 | Cash | 52,500 | |
| 12 | Accounts Receivable | 100,100 | |
| 13 | Prepaid Insurance | 12,600 | |
| 14 | Office Supplies | 2,800 | |
| 16 | Land | — | |
| 21 | Accounts Payable | | 21,000 |
| 22 | Unearned Rent | | — |
| 23 | Notes Payable | | — |
| 31 | Cindy Getman, Capital | | 87,500 |
| 32 | Cindy Getman, Drawing | 44,800 | |
| 41 | Fees Earned | | 591,500 |
| 51 | Salary and Commission Expense | 385,000 | |
| 52 | Rent Expense | 49,000 | |
| 53 | Advertising Expense | 32,200 | |
| 54 | Automobile Expense | 15,750 | |
| 59 | Miscellaneous Expense | 5,250 | |
| | | 700,000 | 700,000 |

The following business transactions were completed by Valley Realty during August 2016:

Aug. 1. Purchased office supplies on account, $3,150.

    2. Paid rent on office for month, $7,200.

    3. Received cash from clients on account, $83,900.

Aug. 5. Paid insurance premiums, $12,000.

9. Returned a portion of the office supplies purchased on August 1, receiving full credit for their cost, $400.

17. Paid advertising expense, $8,000.

23. Paid creditors on account, $13,750.

*Enter the following transactions on Page 19 of the two-column journal:*

29. Paid miscellaneous expenses, $1,700.

30. Paid automobile expense (including rental charges for an automobile), $2,500.

31. Discovered an error in computing a commission during July; received cash from the salesperson for the overpayment, $2,000.

31. Paid salaries and commissions for the month, $53,000.

31. Recorded revenue earned and billed to clients during the month, $183,500.

31. Purchased land for a future building site for $75,000, paying $7,500 in cash and giving a note payable for the remainder.

31. Withdrew cash for personal use, $1,000.

31. Rented land purchased on August 31 to a local university for use as a parking lot during football season (September, October, and November); received advance payment of $5,000.

**Instructions**

1. Record the August 1 balance of each account in the appropriate balance column of a four-column account, write *Balance* in the item section, and place a check mark (✓) in the Posting Reference column.

2. Journalize the transactions for August in a two-column journal beginning on Page 18. Journal entry explanations may be omitted.

3. Post to the ledger, extending the account balance to the appropriate balance column after each posting.

4. Prepare an unadjusted trial balance of the ledger as of August 31, 2016.

5. Assume that the August 31 transaction for Cindy Getman's cash withdrawal should have been $10,000. (a) Why did the unadjusted trial balance in (4) balance? (b) Journalize the correcting entry. (c) Is this error a transposition or slide?

---

**PR 2-5B  Corrected trial balance**                                    OBJ. 4

✔ 1. Total of Debit column: $712,500

Tech Support Services has the following unadjusted trial balance as of January 31, 2016:

**Tech Support Services**
**Unadjusted Trial Balance**
**January 31, 2016**

|  | Debit Balances | Credit Balances |
|---|---|---|
| Cash | 25,550 | |
| Accounts Receivable | 44,050 | |
| Supplies | 6,660 | |
| Prepaid Insurance | 3,600 | |
| Equipment | 162,000 | |
| Notes Payable | | 75,000 |
| Accounts Payable | | 13,200 |
| Thad Engelberg, Capital | | 101,850 |
| Thad Engelberg, Drawing | 33,000 | |
| Fees Earned | | 534,000 |
| Wages Expense | 306,000 | |
| Rent Expense | 62,550 | |
| Advertising Expense | 23,850 | |
| Gas, Electricity, and Water Expense | 17,000 | |
| | 684,260 | 724,050 |

(*Continued*)

The debit and credit totals are not equal as a result of the following errors:

a.  The cash entered on the trial balance was overstated by $8,000.

b.  A cash receipt of $4,100 was posted as a debit to Cash of $1,400.

c.  A debit of $12,350 to Accounts Receivable was not posted.

d.  A return of $235 of defective supplies was erroneously posted as a $325 credit to Supplies.

e.  An insurance policy acquired at a cost of $3,000 was posted as a credit to Prepaid Insurance.

f.  The balance of Notes Payable was overstated by $21,000.

g.  A credit of $3,450 in Accounts Payable was overlooked when the balance of the account was determined.

h.  A debit of $6,000 for a withdrawal by the owner was posted as a debit to Thad Engelberg, Capital.

i.  The balance of $28,350 in Advertising Expense was entered as $23,850 in the trial balance.

j.  Miscellaneous Expense, with a balance of $4,600, was omitted from the trial balance.

**Instructions**

1.  Prepare a corrected unadjusted trial balance as of January 31, 2016.

2.  ━━━━▶ Does the fact that the unadjusted trial balance in (1) is balanced mean that there are no errors in the accounts? Explain.

# Continuing Problem

✔ **4. Total of Debit column: $40,750**

General Ledger

The transactions completed by PS Music during June 2016 were described at the end of Chapter 1. The following transactions were completed during July, the second month of the business's operations:

July  1.  Peyton Smith made an additional investment in PS Music by depositing $5,000 in PS Music's checking account.

1.  Instead of continuing to share office space with a local real estate agency, Peyton decided to rent office space near a local music store. Paid rent for July, $1,750.

1.  Paid a premium of $2,700 for a comprehensive insurance policy covering liability, theft, and fire. The policy covers a one-year period.

2.  Received $1,000 on account.

3.  On behalf of PS Music, Peyton signed a contract with a local radio station, KXMD, to provide guest spots for the next three months. The contract requires PS Music to provide a guest disc jockey for 80 hours per month for a monthly fee of $3,600. Any additional hours beyond 80 will be billed to KXMD at $40 per hour. In accordance with the contract, Peyton received $7,200 from KXMD as an advance payment for the first two months.

3.  Paid $250 on account.

4.  Paid an attorney $900 for reviewing the July 3 contract with KXMD. (Record as Miscellaneous Expense.)

5.  Purchased office equipment on account from Office Mart, $7,500.

8.  Paid for a newspaper advertisement, $200.

11.  Received $1,000 for serving as a disc jockey for a party.

13.  Paid $700 to a local audio electronics store for rental of digital recording equipment.

14.  Paid wages of $1,200 to receptionist and part-time assistant.

*Enter the following transactions on Page 2 of the two-column journal:*

July 16. Received $2,000 for serving as a disc jockey for a wedding reception.

18. Purchased supplies on account, $850.

21. Paid $620 to Upload Music for use of its current music demos in making various music sets.

22. Paid $800 to a local radio station to advertise the services of PS Music twice daily for the remainder of July.

23. Served as disc jockey for a party for $2,500. Received $750, with the remainder due August 4, 2016.

27. Paid electric bill, $915.

28. Paid wages of $1,200 to receptionist and part-time assistant.

29. Paid miscellaneous expenses, $540.

30. Served as a disc jockey for a charity ball for $1,500. Received $500, with the remainder due on August 9, 2016.

31. Received $3,000 for serving as a disc jockey for a party.

31. Paid $1,400 royalties (music expense) to National Music Clearing for use of various artists' music during July.

31. Withdrew $1,250 cash from PS Music for personal use.

PS Music's chart of accounts and the balance of accounts as of July 1, 2016 (all normal balances), are as follows:

| | | | | | |
|---|---|---|---|---|---|
| 11 | Cash | $3,920 | 41 | Fees Earned | $6,200 |
| 12 | Accounts Receivable | 1,000 | 50 | Wages Expense | 400 |
| 14 | Supplies | 170 | 51 | Office Rent Expense | 800 |
| 15 | Prepaid Insurance | — | 52 | Equipment Rent Expense | 675 |
| 17 | Office Equipment | — | 53 | Utilities Expense | 300 |
| 21 | Accounts Payable | 250 | 54 | Music Expense | 1,590 |
| 23 | Unearned Revenue | — | 55 | Advertising Expense | 500 |
| 31 | Peyton Smith, Capital | 4,000 | 56 | Supplies Expense | 180 |
| 32 | Peyton Smith, Drawing | 500 | 59 | Miscellaneous Expense | 415 |

### Instructions

1. Enter the July 1, 2016, account balances in the appropriate balance column of a four-column account. Write *Balance* in the Item column, and place a check mark (✓) in the Posting Reference column. (*Hint:* Verify the equality of the debit and credit balances in the ledger before proceeding with the next instruction.)

2. Analyze and journalize each transaction in a two-column journal beginning on Page 1, omitting journal entry explanations.

3. Post the journal to the ledger, extending the account balance to the appropriate balance column after each posting.

4. Prepare an unadjusted trial balance as of July 31, 2016.

## Cases & Projects

### CP 2-1  Ethics and professional conduct in business

At the end of the current month, Gil Frank prepared a trial balance for College App Services. The credit side of the trial balance exceeds the debit side by a significant amount. Gil has decided to add the difference to the balance of the miscellaneous expense account in order to complete the preparation of the current month's financial statements by a 5 o'clock deadline. Gil will look for the difference next week when he has more time.
━━━━━➤ Discuss whether Gil is behaving in a professional manner

### CP 2-2   Account for revenue

Bozeman College requires students to pay tuition each term before classes begin. Students who have not paid their tuition are not allowed to enroll or to attend classes.

What journal entry do you think Bozeman College would use to record the receipt of the students' tuition payments? Describe the nature of each account in the entry.

### CP 2-3   Record transactions

The following discussion took place between Tony Cork, the office manager of Hallmark Data Company, and a new accountant, Cassie Miles:

*Cassie:* I've been thinking about our method of recording entries. It seems that it's inefficient.

*Tony:* In what way?

*Cassie:* Well—correct me if I'm wrong—it seems like we have unnecessary steps in the process. We could easily develop a trial balance by posting our transactions directly into the ledger and bypassing the journal altogether. In this way, we could combine the recording and posting process into one step and save ourselves a lot of time. What do you think?

*Tony:* We need to have a talk.

➤ What should Tony say to Cassie?

### CP 2-4   Debits and credits
### Group Project

The following excerpt is from a conversation between Kate Purvis, the president and chief operating officer of Light House Company, and her neighbor, Dot Evers:

*Dot:* Kate, I'm taking a course in night school, "Intro to Accounting." I was wondering—could you answer a couple of questions for me?

*Kate:* Well, I will if I can.

*Dot:* Okay, our instructor says that it's critical we understand the basic concepts of accounting, or we'll never get beyond the first test. My problem is with those rules of debit and credit . . . you know, assets increase with debits, decrease with credits, etc.

*Kate:* Yes, pretty basic stuff. You just have to memorize the rules. It shouldn't be too difficult.

*Dot:* Sure, I can memorize the rules, but my problem is I want to be sure I understand the basic concepts behind the rules. For example, why can't assets be increased with credits and decreased with debits like revenue? As long as everyone did it that way, why not? It would seem easier if we had the same rules for all increases and decreases in accounts. Also, why is the left side of an account called the debit side? Why couldn't it be called something simple . . . like the "LE" for Left Entry? The right side could be called just "RE" for Right Entry. Finally, why are there just two sides to an entry? Why can't there be three or four sides to an entry?

In a group of four or five, select one person to play the role of Kate and one person to play the role of Dot.

1. ➤ After listening to the conversation between Kate and Dot, help Kate answer Dot's questions.

2. ➤ What information (other than just debit and credit journal entries) could the accounting system gather that might be useful to Kate in managing Light House Company?

### CP 2-5   Transactions and income statement

Cory Neece is planning to manage and operate Eagle Caddy Service at Canyon Lake Golf and Country Club during June through August 2016. Cory will rent a small maintenance building from the country club for $500 per month and will offer caddy services, including cart rentals, to golfers. Cory has had no formal training in record keeping.

Cory keeps notes of all receipts and expenses in a shoe box. An examination of Cory's shoe box records for June revealed the following:

June   1.   Transferred $2,000 from personal bank account to be used to operate the caddy service.

       1.   Paid rent expense to Canyon Lake Golf and Country Club, $500.

       2.   Paid for golf supplies (practice balls, etc.), $750.

June 3. Arranged for the rental of 40 regular (pulling) golf carts and 20 gasoline-driven carts for $3,000 per month. Paid $600 in advance, with the remaining $2,400 due June 20.

7. Purchased supplies, including gasoline, for the golf carts on account, $1,000. Canyon Lake Golf and Country Club has agreed to allow Cory to store the gasoline in one of its fuel tanks at no cost.

15. Received cash for services from June 1–15, $5,400.

17. Paid cash to creditors on account, $1,000.

20. Paid remaining rental on golf carts, $2,400.

22. Purchased supplies, including gasoline, on account, $850.

25. Accepted IOUs from customers on account, $1,800.

28. Paid miscellaneous expenses, $395.

30. Received cash for services from June 16–30, $4,200.

30. Paid telephone and electricity (utilities) expenses, $340.

30. Paid wages of part-time employees, $850.

30. Received cash in payment of IOUs on account, $1,500.

30. Determined the amount of supplies on hand at the end of June, $675.

Cory has asked you several questions concerning his financial affairs to date, and he has asked you to assist with his record keeping and reporting of financial data.

a. To assist Cory with his record keeping, prepare a chart of accounts that would be appropriate for Eagle Caddy Service.

b. Prepare an income statement for June in order to help Cory assess the profitability of Eagle Caddy Service. For this purpose, the use of T accounts may be helpful in analyzing the effects of each June transaction.

c. Based on Cory's records of receipts and payments, compute the amount of cash on hand on June 30. For this purpose, a T account for cash may be useful.

d. ━━━━▶ A count of the cash on hand on June 30 totaled $6,175. Briefly discuss the possible causes of the difference between the amount of cash computed in (c) and the actual amount of cash on hand.

---

### CP 2-6  Opportunities for accountants

**Internet Project**

The increasing complexity of the current business and regulatory environment has created an increased demand for accountants who can analyze business transactions and interpret their effects on the financial statements. In addition, a basic ability to analyze the effects of transactions is necessary to be successful in all fields of business as well as in other disciplines, such as law. To better understand the importance of accounting in today's environment, search the Internet or your local newspaper for job opportunities. One possible Internet site is www.careerbuilder.com. Then do one of the following:

1. Print a listing of one or two ads for accounting jobs. Alternatively, bring to class one or two newspaper ads for accounting jobs.

2. Print a listing of one or two ads for nonaccounting jobs for which some knowledge of accounting is preferred or necessary. Alternatively, bring to class one or two newspaper ads for such jobs.

# The Adjusting Process

## Pandora

Do you use an Internet-based music service such as **Pandora**? Using playlist-generating algorithms, Pandora predicts a listener's music preferences based on their initial music selections. Pandora selects music they think the listener will enjoy, including music of new artists that match the listener's preferences. Recently, Pandora developed similar comedy-generating algorithms that match a listener's preferences for comedy with more than 1,000 comedians.

Most of Pandora's services are offered free to listeners with only 12.5% of its revenues generated from subscription services. So, where do most of Pandora's revenues come from?

Pandora generates more than 85% of its revenues from selling advertising banners that surround the video displays on its tuner. By analyzing its listener interactions, Pandora identifies listener age, gender, zip code, and content preferences. These attributes can then be matched with advertiser needs and desires.

When should Pandora record revenue from its advertisers and subscribers? Revenue should be recorded when earned. Advertising revenue is earned as ads are displayed, while subscriber revenue is earned when the service has been delivered to the listener. As a result, companies like Pandora must update their accounting records for such items as unearned advertising and subscription revenue before preparing financial statements.

This chapter describes and illustrates the process by which companies update their accounting records before preparing financial statements. This discussion includes the adjustments for unearned revenues that exist at the end of the accounting period.

## Learning Objectives

After studying this chapter, you should be able to:

*Example Exercises*

**OBJ 1**
Describe the nature of the adjusting process.
**Nature of the Adjusting Process**
    The Adjusting Process      EE 3-1
    Types of Accounts Requiring Adjustment      EE 3-2

**OBJ 2**
Journalize entries for accounts requiring adjustment.
**Adjusting Entries**
    Prepaid Expenses      EE 3-3
    Unearned Revenues      EE 3-4
    Accrued Revenues      EE 3-5
    Accrued Expenses      EE 3-6
    Depreciation Expense      EE 3-7

**OBJ 3**
Summarize the adjustment process.
**Summary of Adjustment Process**      EE 3-8

**OBJ 4**
Prepare an adjusted trial balance.
**Adjusted Trial Balance**      EE 3-9

**OBJ 5**
Describe and illustrate the use of vertical analysis in evaluating a company's performance and financial condition.
**Financial Analysis and Interpretation: Vertical Analysis**      EE 3-10

**At a Glance 3**     Page 126

**OBJ 1**
Describe the nature of the adjusting process.

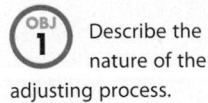

**American Airlines** uses the accrual basis of accounting. Revenues are recognized when passengers take flights, not when the passenger makes the reservation or pays for the ticket.

# Nature of the Adjusting Process

When preparing financial statements, the economic life of the business is divided into time periods. This **accounting period concept** requires that revenues and expenses be reported in the proper period. To determine the proper period, accountants use generally accepted accounting principles (GAAP), which requires the **accrual basis of accounting**.

Under the accrual basis of accounting, revenues are reported on the income statement in the period in which they are earned. For example, revenue is reported when the services are provided to customers. Cash may or may not be received from customers during this period. The accounting concept supporting this reporting of revenues is called the **revenue recognition concept**.

Under accrual accounting, revenues are recognized when services have been performed or products have been delivered to customers.[1] Revenue is measured as assets received, such as cash or accounts receivable, in exchange for a service or product. This process of recording revenues is called **revenue recognition**.

The accounting concept supporting reporting revenues and related expenses in the same period is called the **matching concept**. By matching revenues and expenses, net income or loss for the period is properly reported on the income statement.

Although GAAP requires the accrual basis of accounting, some businesses use the **cash basis of accounting**. Under the cash basis of accounting, revenues and expenses are reported on the income statement in the period in which cash is received or paid. For example, fees are recorded when cash is received from clients; likewise, wages are recorded when cash is paid to employees. The net income (or net loss) is the difference between the cash receipts (revenues) and the cash payments (expenses).

Small service businesses may use the cash basis because they have few receivables and payables. For example, attorneys, physicians, and real estate agents often use the cash basis. For them, the cash basis provides financial statements similar to those of the accrual basis. For most large businesses, however, the cash basis will not provide accurate financial statements for user needs. For this reason, the accrual basis is used in this text.

---

[1]Revenues may involve contracts with customers that have several elements or performance obligations. Recording of revenues under such contracts is described and illustrated in Appendix E Revenue Recognition.

# The Adjusting Process

At the end of the accounting period, many of the account balances in the ledger are reported in the financial statements without change. For example, the balances of the cash and land accounts are normally the amounts reported on the balance sheet.

Some accounts, however, require updating for the following reasons:[2]

- Some expenses are not recorded daily. For example, the daily use of supplies would require many entries with small amounts. Also, the amount of supplies on hand on a day-to-day basis is normally not needed.
- Some revenues and expenses are incurred as time passes rather than as separate transactions. For example, rent received in advance (unearned rent) expires and becomes revenue with the passage of time. Likewise, prepaid insurance expires and becomes an expense with the passage of time.
- Some revenues and expenses may be unrecorded. For example, a company may have provided services to customers that it has not billed or recorded at the end of the accounting period. Likewise, a company may not pay its employees until the next accounting period even though the employees have earned their wages in the current period.

The analysis and updating of accounts at the end of the period before the financial statements are prepared is called the **adjusting process**. The journal entries that bring the accounts up to date at the end of the accounting period are called **adjusting entries**. All adjusting entries affect at least one income statement account and one balance sheet account. Thus, an adjusting entry will *always* involve a revenue or an expense account *and* an asset or a liability account.

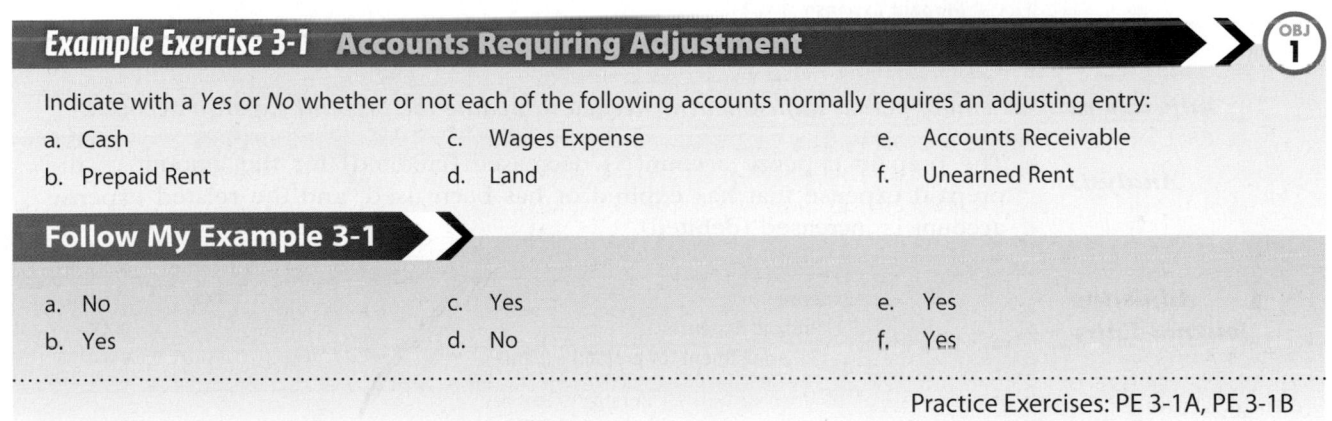

**Example Exercise 3-1   Accounts Requiring Adjustment**                          OBJ 1

Indicate with a *Yes* or *No* whether or not each of the following accounts normally requires an adjusting entry:

a.  Cash                     c.  Wages Expense            e.  Accounts Receivable
b.  Prepaid Rent             d.  Land                     f.  Unearned Rent

**Follow My Example 3-1**

a.  No                       c.  Yes                      e.  Yes
b.  Yes                      d.  No                       f,  Yes

Practice Exercises: PE 3-1A, PE 3-1B

## Types of Accounts Requiring Adjustment

The following basic types of accounts require adjusting entries:

- Prepaid expenses
- Unearned revenues
- Accrued revenues
- Accrued expenses

**Prepaid Expenses**  **Prepaid expenses** are the advance payment of *future* expenses and are recorded as assets when cash is paid. Prepaid expenses become expenses over time or during normal operations. To illustrate, the following transaction of **NetSolutions** from Chapter 2 is used:

> Dec. 1   NetSolutions paid $2,400 as a premium on a one-year insurance policy.

On December 1, the cash payment of $2,400 was recorded as a debit to Prepaid Insurance and credit to Cash for $2,400. At the end of December, only $200 ($2,400 ÷ 12 months)

[2] Under the cash basis of accounting, accounts do not require adjusting. This is because transactions are recorded only when cash is received or paid. Thus, the matching concept is not used under the cash basis.

of the insurance premium is expired and has become an expense. The remaining $2,200 of prepaid insurance will become an expense in future months. Thus, the $200 is insurance expense of December and should be recorded with an adjusting entry.

Other examples of prepaid expenses include supplies, prepaid advertising, and prepaid interest.

Exhibit 1 summarizes the nature of prepaid expenses.

---

| EXHIBIT 1 | **Prepaid Expenses** |
|---|---|

| *Transaction* | *Cash is paid in advance for an expense.* |
|---|---|
| *Analysis* | Advance payments of future expenses are recorded as assets when the cash is paid. The transaction is recorded as a debit to a prepaid expense account and a credit to the cash account. |

| *Journal Entry* | Prepaid Expense | | XXX | |
|---|---|---|---|---|
| | Cash | | | XXX |
| | Paid an expense in advance. | | | |

*Accounting Equation Impact*

| Assets | = | Liabilities | + | Owner's Equity |
|---|---|---|---|---|

| Cash | |
|---|---|
| | XXX |

| Prepaid Expense | |
|---|---|
| XXX | |

| *Adjustment* | *An end-of-period adjustment is needed to update the prepaid expense account.* |
|---|---|
| *Analysis* | The prepaid expense account is decreased (credited) for the amount of the prepaid expense that has expired or has been used, and the related expense account is increased (debited). |

| *Adjusting Journal Entry* | Expense | | XXX | |
|---|---|---|---|---|
| | Prepaid Expense | | | XXX |
| | Adjustment for prepaid expense. | | | |

*Accounting Equation Impact*

| Assets | = | Liabilities | + | Owner's Equity (Expense) |
|---|---|---|---|---|

| Prepaid Expense | | | Expense | |
|---|---|---|---|---|
| | XXX | | XXX | |

---

**Unearned Revenues**   **Unearned revenues** are the advance receipt of *future* revenues and are recorded as liabilities when cash is received. Unearned revenues become earned revenues over time or during normal operations. To illustrate, the following December 1 transaction of **NetSolutions** is used:

> Dec. 1   NetSolutions received $360 from a local retailer to rent land for three months.

On December 1, the cash receipt of $360 was recorded as a debit to Cash and a credit to Unearned Rent for $360. At the end of December, $120 ($360 divided by 3 months) of the unearned rent has been earned. The remaining $240 will become rent revenue in future months. Thus, the $120 is rent revenue of December and should be recorded with an adjusting entry.

Other examples of unearned revenues include tuition received in advance by a school, an annual retainer fee received by an attorney, premiums received in advance by an insurance company, and magazine subscriptions received in advance by a publisher.

Exhibit 2 summarizes the nature of unearned revenues.

---

### EXHIBIT 2    Unearned Revenues

*Cash is received for an unearned revenue.*        *Transaction*

Advance receipts for future services to be provided are recorded as liabilities when the cash is received. The transaction is recorded as a debit to the cash account and a credit to the unearned revenue account.        *Analysis*

| | | | | |
|---|---|---|---|---|
| Cash | | | XXX | |
| Unearned Revenue | | | | XXX |
| Received cash for unearned revenue. | | | | |

*Journal Entry*

| Assets | = | Liabilities | + | Owner's Equity |
|---|---|---|---|---|
| **Cash** | | **Unearned Revenue** | | |
| XXX | | | XXX | |

*Accounting Equation Impact*

*An end-of-period adjustment is needed to update the unearned revenue account.*        *Adjustment*

The unearned revenue account is decreased (debited) for the amount of the revenue that has been earned, and the related revenue account is increased (credited).        *Analysis*

| | | | | |
|---|---|---|---|---|
| Unearned Revenue | | | XXX | |
| Revenue | | | | XXX |
| Adjustment for unearned revenue. | | | | |

*Adjusting Journal Entry*

| Assets | = | Liabilities | + | Owner's Equity (Revenue) |
|---|---|---|---|---|
| | | **Unearned Revenue** | | **Revenue** |
| | | XXX | | XXX |

*Accounting Equation Impact*

---

**Accrued Revenues** Accrued revenues are unrecorded revenues that have been earned and for which cash has yet to be received. Fees for services that an attorney or a doctor has provided but not yet billed are accrued revenues. To illustrate, the following example involving **NetSolutions** and one of its customers is used:

> Dec. 15  NetSolutions signed an agreement with Dankner Co. under which NetSolutions will bill Dankner Co. on the fifteenth of each month for services rendered at the rate of $20 per hour.

From December 16–31, NetSolutions provided 25 hours of service to Dankner Co. Although the revenue of $500 (25 hours × $20) has been earned, it will not be billed until January 15. Likewise, cash of $500 will not be received until Dankner pays its bill. Thus, the $500 of accrued revenue and the $500 of fees earned should be recorded with an adjusting entry on December 31.

Other examples of accrued revenues include accrued interest on notes receivable and accrued rent on property rented to others.

Exhibit 3 summarizes the nature of accrued revenues.

---

| EXHIBIT 3 | **Accrued Revenues** |
|---|---|

*Transaction* — *Revenue has been earned but has not been recorded.*

*Analysis* — Revenues have been earned, but the revenue has not been recorded nor has cash been received. No journal entry has been recorded even though revenues have been earned.

*Journal Entry* — No entry has been recorded.

*Accounting Equation Impact* —

| Assets | = | Liabilities | + | Owner's Equity |
|---|---|---|---|---|

No impact, since the revenue has not been recorded.

*Adjustment* — *An end-of-period adjustment is needed to recognize accrued revenue.*

*Analysis* — An asset account is increased (debited) for the amount of the revenue that has been earned, and the related revenue account is increased (credited). The type of receivable account that is debited depends upon the type of revenue. For example, Accounts Receivable would be debited for fees earned. Interest Receivable would be debited for interest earned.

*Adjusting Journal Entry* —

| Asset (Receivable) | | | | XXX | |
|---|---|---|---|---|---|
| Revenue | | | | | XXX |
| Adjustment for accrued revenue. | | | | | |

*Accounting Equation Impact* —

| Assets | = | Liabilities | + | Owner's Equity (Revenue) |
|---|---|---|---|---|

| _____ Receivable | | Revenue |
|---|---|---|
| XXX | | XXX |

---

## Accrued Expenses

**Accrued expenses** are unrecorded expenses that have been incurred and for which cash has yet to be paid. Wages owed to employees at the end of a period but not yet paid are an accrued expense. To illustrate, the following example involving **NetSolutions** and its employees is used:

> Dec. 31   NetSolutions owes its employees wages of $250 for Monday and Tuesday, December 30 and 31.

NetSolutions paid wages of $950 on December 13 and $1,200 on December 27, 2015. These payments covered the biweekly pay periods that ended on those days. As of December 31, 2015, NetSolutions owes its employees wages of $250 for Monday and Tuesday, December 30 and 31. The wages of $250 will be paid on January 10, 2016; however, they are an expense of December. Thus, $250 of accrued wages should be recorded with an adjusting entry on December 31.

Other examples of accrued expenses include accrued interest on notes payable and accrued taxes.

Exhibit 4 summarizes the nature of accrued expenses.

| EXHIBIT 4 | **Accrued Expenses** | |
|---|---|---|

*An expense has been incurred but has not been recorded.* | *Transaction*

An expense has been incurred, but the expense has not been recorded nor has cash been paid. No journal entry has been recorded even though an expense has been incurred. | *Analysis*

| | | No entry has been recorded. | | | | *Journal Entry* |

| **Assets** | **=** | **Liabilities** | **+** | **Owner's Equity** | *Accounting Equation Impact* |
| No impact, since the expense has not been recorded. | | | | | |

*An end-of-period adjustment is needed to recognize the accrued expense.* | *Adjustment*

An expense account is increased (debited) for the amount of the expense that has been incurred, and the related liability account is increased (credited). The liability account that is credited depends upon the type of expense. For example, Wages Payable would be credited for wages expense. Interest Payable would be credited for interest expense. | *Analysis*

| | Expense | | XXX | | *Adjusting Journal Entry* |
| |     Liability (Payable) | | | XXX | |
| |       Adjustment for accrued expense. | | | | |

| **Assets** | **=** | **Liabilities** | **+** | **Owner's Equity (Expense)** | *Accounting Equation Impact* |
| | | **Payable** | | **Expense** | |
| | |      XXX | | XXX | |

**Accruals Versus Deferrals** As illustrated in Exhibit 3, accrued revenues are earned revenues that are unrecorded. The cash receipts for accrued revenues are normally received in the next accounting period. As illustrated in Exhibit 4, accrued expenses are expenses that have been incurred but are unrecorded. The cash payments for accrued expenses are normally paid in the next accounting period.

Prepaid expenses and unearned revenues are sometimes referred to as *deferrals*. This is because the recording of the related expense or revenue is deferred to a future period. Accrued revenues and accrued expenses are sometimes referred to as *accruals*. This is because the related revenue or expense should be recorded or accrued in the current period.

## Example Exercise 3-2  Type of Adjustment  OBJ. 1

Classify the following items as (1) prepaid expense, (2) unearned revenue, (3) accrued expense, or (4) accrued revenue:

a.  Wages owed but not yet paid.

b.  Supplies on hand.

c.  Fees received but not yet earned.

d.  Fees earned but not yet received.

## Follow My Example 3-2

a.  Accrued expense

b.  Prepaid expense

c.  Unearned revenue

d.  Accrued revenue

Practice Exercises: PE 3-2A, PE 3-2B

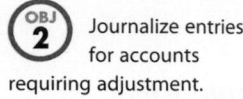

Journalize entries
for accounts
requiring adjustment.

# Adjusting Entries

To illustrate adjusting entries, the December 31, 2015, unadjusted trial balance of **NetSolutions**, shown in Exhibit 5, is used. An expanded chart of accounts for NetSolutions is shown in Exhibit 6. The additional accounts used in this chapter are highlighted. The rules of debit and credit shown in Exhibit 3 of Chapter 2 are used to record the adjusting entries.

**EXHIBIT 5**

**Unadjusted Trial
Balance for
NetSolutions**

| NetSolutions<br>Unadjusted Trial Balance<br>December 31, 2015 | | |
|---|---:|---:|
| | **Debit<br>Balances** | **Credit<br>Balances** |
| Cash .......................................................... | 2,065 | |
| Accounts Receivable ........................................ | 2,220 | |
| Supplies ...................................................... | 2,000 | |
| Prepaid Insurance .......................................... | 2,400 | |
| Land .......................................................... | 20,000 | |
| Office Equipment ........................................... | 1,800 | |
| Accounts Payable ........................................... | | 900 |
| Unearned Rent .............................................. | | 360 |
| Chris Clark, Capital ......................................... | | 25,000 |
| Chris Clark, Drawing ........................................ | 4,000 | |
| Fees Earned .................................................. | | 16,340 |
| Wages Expense .............................................. | 4,275 | |
| Supplies Expense ........................................... | 800 | |
| Rent Expense ................................................ | 1,600 | |
| Utilities Expense ............................................ | 985 | |
| Miscellaneous Expense ..................................... | 455 | |
| | 42,600 | 42,600 |

**EXHIBIT 6**

**Expanded Chart
of Accounts for
NetSolutions**

| **Balance Sheet Accounts** | **Income Statement Accounts** |
|---|---|
| **1. Assets** | **4. Revenue** |
| 11   Cash | 41   Fees Earned |
| 12   Accounts Receivable | 42   Rent Revenue |
| 14   Supplies | **5. Expenses** |
| 15   Prepaid Insurance | 51   Wages Expense |
| 17   Land | 52   Supplies Expense |
| 18   Office Equipment | 53   Rent Expense |
| 19   Accumulated Depreciation—Office Equipment | 54   Utilities Expense |
| **2. Liabilities** | 55   Insurance Expense |
| 21   Accounts Payable | 56   Depreciation Expense |
| 22   Wages Payable | 59   Miscellaneous Expense |
| 23   Unearned Rent | |
| **3. Owner's Equity** | |
| 31   Chris Clark, Capital | |
| 32   Chris Clark, Drawing | |

## Prepaid Expenses

**Supplies**  The December 31, 2015, unadjusted trial balance of **NetSolutions** indicates a balance in the supplies account of $2,000. In addition, the prepaid insurance account has a balance of $2,400. Each of these accounts requires an adjusting entry.

The balance in NetSolutions' supplies account on December 31 is $2,000. Some of these supplies (CDs, paper, envelopes, etc.) were used during December, and some are still on hand (not used). If either amount is known, the other can be determined. It is normally easier to determine the cost of the supplies on hand at the end of the month than to record daily supplies used.

Assuming that on December 31 the amount of supplies on hand is $760, the amount to be transferred from the asset account to the expense account is $1,240, computed as follows:

| | |
|---|---|
| Supplies available during December (balance of account) | $2,000 |
| Supplies on hand, December 31 | 760 |
| Supplies used (amount of adjustment) | $1,240 |

At the end of December, the supplies expense account is increased (debited) for $1,240, and the supplies account is decreased (credited) for $1,240 to record the supplies used during December. The adjusting journal entry and T accounts for Supplies and Supplies Expense are as follows:

**Journal**                                             *Page 5*

| Date | | Description | Post. Ref. | Debit | Credit |
|---|---|---|---|---|---|
| 2015 Dec. | 31 | Supplies Expense | 52 | 1,240 | |
| | | Supplies | 14 | | 1,240 |
| | | Supplies used ($2,000 – $760). | | | |

*Adjusting Journal Entry*

| Assets | = | Liabilities | + | Owner's Equity (Expense) |
|---|---|---|---|---|

| Supplies | | 14 |
|---|---|---|
| Bal. | 2,000 | Dec. 31  1,240 |
| Adj. Bal. | 760 | |

| Supplies Expense | | 52 |
|---|---|---|
| Bal. | 800 | |
| Dec. 31 | 1,240 | |
| Adj. Bal. | 2,040 | |

*Accounting Equation Impact*

The adjusting entry is shown in color in the T accounts to separate it from other transactions. After the adjusting entry is recorded and posted, the supplies account has a debit balance of $760. This balance is an asset that will become an expense in a future period.

**Prepaid Insurance** The debit balance of $2,400 in **NetSolutions**' prepaid insurance account represents a December 1 prepayment of insurance for 12 months. At the end of December, the insurance expense account is increased (debited), and the prepaid insurance account is decreased (credited) by $200, the insurance for one month. The adjusting journal entry and T accounts for Prepaid Insurance and Insurance Expense are as follows:

| Dec. | 31 | Insurance Expense | 55 | 200 | |
|---|---|---|---|---|---|
| | | Prepaid Insurance | 15 | | 200 |
| | | Insurance expired ($2,400 ÷ 12). | | | |

*Adjusting Journal Entry*

| Assets | = | Liabilities | + | Owner's Equity (Expense) |
|---|---|---|---|---|

| Prepaid Insurance | | 15 |
|---|---|---|
| Bal. | 2,400 | Dec. 31   200 |
| Adj. Bal. | 2,200 | |

| Insurance Expense | | 55 |
|---|---|---|
| Dec. 31 | 200 | |

*Accounting Equation Impact*

After the adjusting entry is recorded and posted, the prepaid insurance account has a debit balance of $2,200. This balance is an asset that will become an expense in future periods. The insurance expense account has a debit balance of $200, which is an expense of the current period.

If the preceding adjustments for supplies ($1,240) and insurance ($200) are not recorded, the financial statements prepared as of December 31 will be misstated. On the income statement, Supplies Expense and Insurance Expense will be understated by a total of $1,440 ($1,240 + $200), and net income will be overstated by $1,440. On the balance sheet, Supplies and Prepaid Insurance will be overstated by a total of $1,440. Because net income increases owner's equity, Chris Clark, Capital will also be overstated by $1,440 on the balance sheet. The effects of omitting these adjusting entries on the income statement and balance sheet are as follows:

|  | | Amount of Misstatement |
|---|---|---|
| Income Statement | | |
| Revenues correctly stated | | $ XXX |
| Expenses understated by | | (1,440) |
| Net income overstated by | (1) | $1,440 |
| | | |
| Balance Sheet | | |
| Assets overstated by | | $1,440 (2) |
| | | |
| Liabilities correctly stated | | $ XXX |
| Owner's equity overstated by | | 1,440 |
| Total liabilities and | | |
| owner's equity overstated by | | $1,440 |

Arrow (1) indicates the effect of the understated expenses on assets. Arrow (2) indicates the effect of the overstated net income on owner's equity.

Payments for prepaid expenses are sometimes made at the beginning of the period in which they will be *entirely used or consumed*. To illustrate, the following December 1 transaction of NetSolutions is used:

> Dec. 1 NetSolutions paid rent of $800 for the month.

On December 1, the rent payment of $800 represents Prepaid Rent. However, the Prepaid Rent expires daily, and at the end of December there will be no asset left. In such cases, the payment of $800 is recorded as Rent Expense rather than as Prepaid Rent. In this way, no adjusting entry is needed at the end of the period.[3]

## Example Exercise 3-3  Adjustment for Prepaid Expense     OBJ 2

The prepaid insurance account had a beginning balance of $6,400 and was debited for $3,600 of premiums paid during the year. Journalize the adjusting entry required at the end of the year, assuming the amount of unexpired insurance related to future periods is $3,250.

### Follow My Example 3-3

| | | |
|---|---|---|
| Insurance Expense ..................................................... | 6,750 | |
|    Prepaid Insurance ..................................................... | | 6,750 |
|       Insurance expired ($6,400 + $3,600 − $3,250). | | |

Practice Exercises: PE 3-3A, PE 3-3B

## Integrity, Objectivity, and Ethics in Business

**FREE ISSUE**

Office supplies are often available to employees on a "free issue" basis. This means that employees do not have to "sign" for the release of office supplies but merely obtain the necessary supplies from a local storage area as needed. Just because supplies are easily available, however, doesn't mean they can be taken for personal use. There are many instances where employees have been terminated for taking supplies home for personal use.

[3] An alternative treatment of recording the cost of supplies, rent, and other prepayments of expenses is discussed in an appendix that can be downloaded from the book's companion Web site (www.cengagebrain.com).

# Unearned Revenues

The December 31 unadjusted trial balance of **NetSolutions** indicates a balance in the unearned rent account of $360. This balance represents the receipt of three months' rent on December 1 for December, January, and February. At the end of December, one month's rent has been earned. Thus, the unearned rent account is decreased (debited) by $120, and the rent revenue account is increased (credited) by $120. The $120 represents the rental revenue for one month ($360 ÷ 3). The adjusting journal entry and T accounts are as follows:

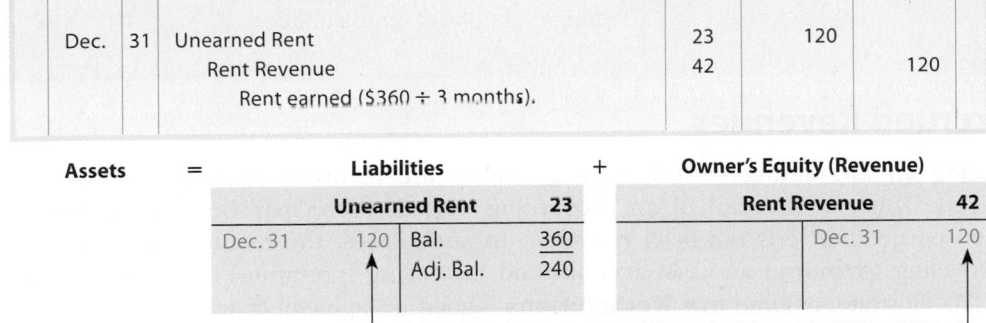

*Adjusting Journal Entry*

*Accounting Equation Impact*

After the adjusting entry is recorded and posted, the unearned rent account has a credit balance of $240. This balance is a liability that will become revenue in a future period. Rent Revenue has a balance of $120, which is revenue of the current period.[4]

If the preceding adjustment of unearned rent and rent revenue is not recorded, the financial statements prepared on December 31 will be misstated. On the income statement, Rent Revenue and the net income will be understated by $120. On the balance sheet, Unearned Rent will be overstated by $120, and Chris Clark, Capital will be understated by $120. The effects of omitting this adjusting entry are as follows:

 **Best Buy** sells extended warranty contracts with terms between 12 and 36 months. The receipts from sales of these contracts are reported as unearned revenue on Best Buy's balance sheet. Revenue is recorded as the contracts expire.

|  | Amount of Misstatement |
|---|---|
| **Income Statement** | |
| Revenues understated by | $ (120) |
| Expenses correctly stated | XXX |
| Net income understated by | $ (120) |
| | |
| **Balance Sheet** | |
| Assets correctly stated | $ XXX |
| | |
| Liabilities overstated by | $ 120 |
| Owner's equity understated by | (120) |
| Total liabilities and | |
| owner's equity correctly stated | $ XXX |

## Example Exercise 3-4 Adjustment for Unearned Revenue

OBJ 2

The balance in the unearned fees account, before adjustment at the end of the year, is $44,900. Journalize the adjusting entry required if the amount of unearned fees at the end of the year is $22,300.

### Follow My Example 3-4

| | | |
|---|---|---|
| Unearned Fees.................................................... | 22,600 | |
|    Fees Earned................................................ | | 22,600 |
|      Fees earned ($44,900 – $22,300). | | |

Practice Exercises: PE 3-4A, PE 3-4B

---

[4] An alternative treatment of recording revenues received in advance of their being earned is discussed in an appendix that can be downloaded from the book's companion Web site (www.cengagebrain.com).

# Business ⊕ Connection

## NATIONAL FITNESS CENTER: UPFRONT FEES

National Fitness Center imposes a nonrefundable up-front fee on some of its multiyear club memberships. Should the fee be recognized as revenue when the club receives the fee?

The upfront fee is like an advance payment made by customers for use of the club facilities. The company earns these fees over time as customers work out and use the facilities. Thus, the initial fee is unearned when received by the club and becomes earned revenue over time.[5] As a result, each month the club records revenue from club dues that are paid monthly as well as from a portion of upfront (prepaid) dues.

## Accrued Revenues

**RadioShack Corporation** is engaged in consumer electronics retailing. RadioShack accrues revenue for finance charges and late payment charges related to its credit operations.

During an accounting period, some revenues are recorded only when cash is received. Thus, at the end of an accounting period, there may be revenue that has been earned *but has not been recorded*. In such cases, the revenue is recorded by increasing (debiting) an asset account and increasing (crediting) a revenue account.

To illustrate, assume that **NetSolutions** signed an agreement with Dankner Co. on December 15. The agreement provides that NetSolutions will answer computer questions and render assistance to Dankner Co.'s employees. The services will be billed to Dankner Co. on the fifteenth of each month at a rate of $20 per hour. As of December 31, NetSolutions had provided 25 hours of assistance to Dankner Co. The revenue of $500 (25 hours × $20) will be billed on January 15. However, NetSolutions earned the revenue in December.

The claim against the customer for payment of the $500 is an account receivable (*an asset*). Thus, the accounts receivable account is increased (debited) by $500, and the fees earned account is increased (credited) by $500. The adjusting journal entry and T accounts are as follows:

**Adjusting Journal Entry**

| | | | | | | |
|---|---|---|---|---|---|---|
| Dec. | 31 | Accounts Receivable | | 12 | 500 | |
| | | Fees Earned | | 41 | | 500 |
| | | Accrued fees (25 hrs. × $20). | | | | |

**Accounting Equation Impact**

| **Assets** | = | **Liabilities** | + | **Owner's Equity (Revenue)** |
|---|---|---|---|---|
| **Accounts Receivable** 12 | | | | **Fees Earned** 41 |
| Bal. 2,220 | | | | Bal. 16,340 |
| Dec. 31 500 | | | | Dec. 31 500 |
| Adj. Bal. 2,720 | | | | Adj. Bal. 16,840 |

If the adjustment for the accrued revenue ($500) is not recorded, Fees Earned and the net income will be understated by $500 on the income statement. On the balance sheet, Accounts Receivable and Chris Clark, Capital will be understated by $500. The effects of omitting this adjusting entry are as follows:

| | **Amount of Misstatement** |
|---|---|
| Income Statement | |
| Revenues understated by | $ (500) |
| Expenses correctly stated | XXX |
| Net income understated by | $ (500) |
| Balance Sheet | |
| Assets understated by | $ (500) |
| | |
| Liabilities correctly stated | $ XXX |
| Owner's equity understated by | (500) |
| Total liabilities and | |
| owner's equity understated by | $ (500) |

[5]FASB Exposure Draft, Revenue Recognition (Topic 605), June 24, 2010, para. IG29–IG32.

**Example Exercise 3-5 Adjustment for Accrued Revenues**

At the end of the current year, $13,680 of fees have been earned but have not been billed to clients. Journalize the adjusting entry to record the accrued fees.

**Follow My Example 3-5**

| | | |
|---|---|---|
| Accounts Receivable..................................................... | 13,680 | |
| Fees Earned........................................................ | | 13,680 |
| Accrued fees. | | |

Practice Exercises: PE 3-5A, PE 3-5B

## Accrued Expenses

Some types of services used in earning revenues are paid for *after* the service has been performed. For example, wages expense is used hour by hour but is paid only daily, weekly, biweekly, or monthly. At the end of the accounting period, the amount of such *accrued* but unpaid items is an expense and a liability.

For example, if the last day of the employees' pay period is not the last day of the accounting period, an accrued expense (wages expense) and the related liability (wages payable) must be recorded by an adjusting entry. This adjusting entry is necessary so that expenses are properly matched to the period in which they were incurred in earning revenue.

To illustrate, **NetSolutions** pays its employees biweekly. During December, NetSolutions paid wages of $950 on December 13 and $1,200 on December 27. These payments covered pay periods ending on those days as shown in Exhibit 7.

**Callaway Golf Company**, a manufacturer of such innovative golf clubs as the "RAZR Hawk" driver, reports accrued warranty expense on its balance sheet.

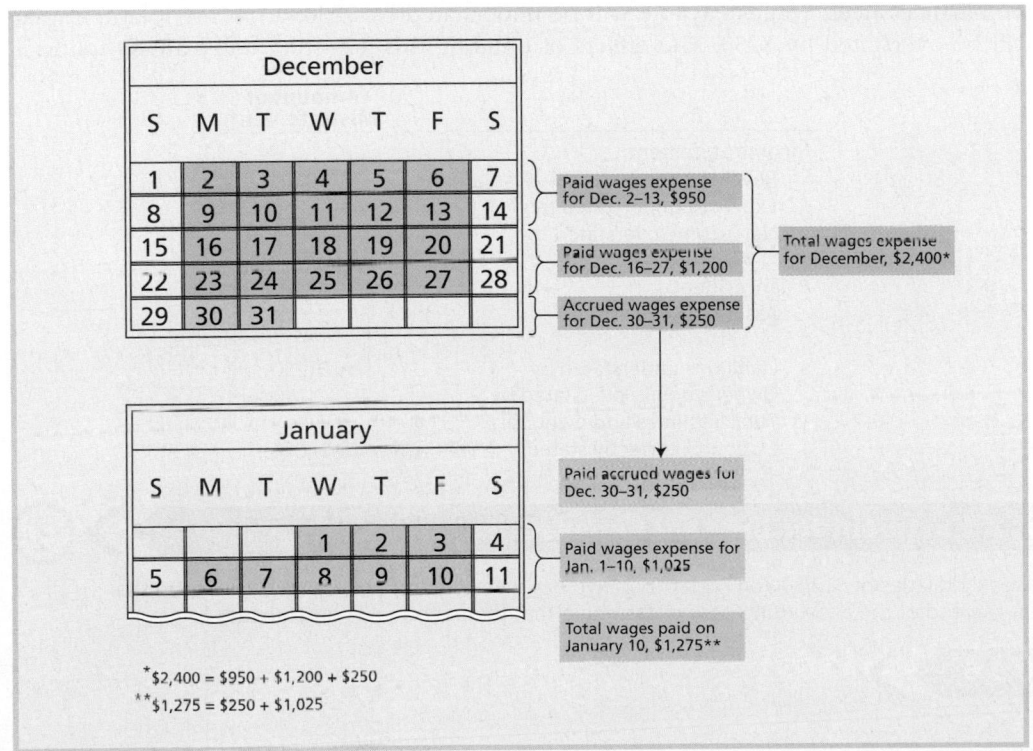

**EXHIBIT 7**

**Accrued Wages**

Dynamic Exhibit

As of December 31, NetSolutions owes $250 of wages to employees for Monday and Tuesday, December 30 and 31. Thus, the wages expense account is increased (debited) by $250, and the wages payable account is increased (credited) by $250. The adjusting journal entry and T accounts are as follows:

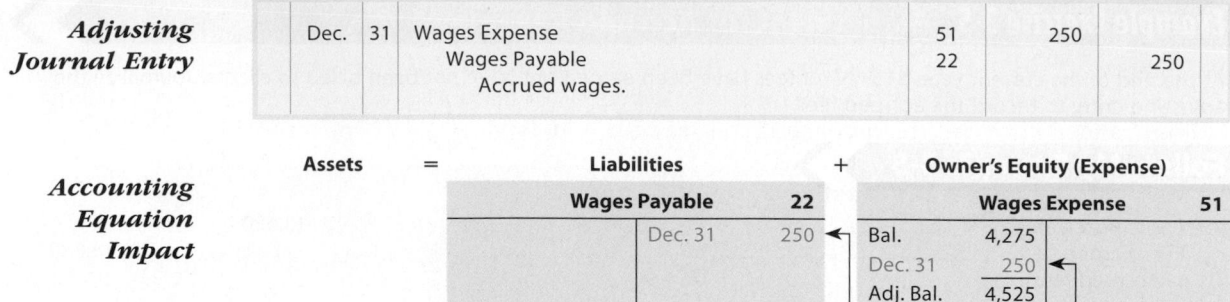

*Adjusting Journal Entry*

| | Dec. | 31 | Wages Expense | 51 | 250 | |
|---|---|---|---|---|---|---|
| | | | Wages Payable | 22 | | 250 |
| | | | Accrued wages. | | | |

*Accounting Equation Impact*

| Assets | = | Liabilities | + | Owner's Equity (Expense) |
|---|---|---|---|---|

| | | Wages Payable | 22 | | Wages Expense | 51 |
|---|---|---|---|---|---|---|
| | | Dec. 31 | 250 | Bal. | 4,275 | |
| | | | | Dec. 31 | 250 | |
| | | | | Adj. Bal. | 4,525 | |

After the adjusting entry is recorded and posted, the debit balance of the wages expense account is $4,525. This balance of $4,525 is the wages expense for two months, November and December. The credit balance of $250 in Wages Payable is the liability for wages owed on December 31.

As shown in Exhibit 7, NetSolutions paid wages of $1,275 on January 10. This payment includes the $250 of accrued wages recorded on December 31. Thus, on January 10, the wages payable account is decreased (debited) by $250. Also, the wages expense account is increased (debited) by $1,025 ($1,275 – $250), which is the wages expense for January 1–10. Finally, the cash account is decreased (credited) by $1,275. The journal entry for the payment of wages on January 10 follows:[6]

| | Jan. | 10 | Wages Expense | 51 | 1,025 | |
|---|---|---|---|---|---|---|
| | | | Wages Payable | 22 | 250 | |
| | | | Cash | 11 | | 1,275 |

If the adjustment for wages ($250) is not recorded, Wages Expense will be understated by $250, and the net income will be overstated by $250 on the income statement. On the balance sheet, Wages Payable will be understated by $250, and Chris Clark, Capital will be overstated by $250. The effects of omitting this adjusting entry are as follows:

| | Amount of Misstatement |
|---|---|
| Income Statement | |
| Revenues correctly stated | $ XXX |
| Expenses understated by | (250) |
| Net income overstated by | $ 250 |
| | |
| Balance Sheet | |
| Assets correctly stated | $ XXX |
| | |
| Liabilities understated by | $ (250) |
| Owner's equity overstated by | 250 |
| Total liabilities and owner's equity correctly stated | $ XXX |

## Example Exercise 3-6   Adjustment for Accrued Expense

OBJ 2

Sanregret Realty Co. pays weekly salaries of $12,500 on Friday for a five-day week ending on that day. Journalize the necessary adjusting entry at the end of the accounting period, assuming that the period ends on Thursday.

### Follow My Example 3-6

| Salaries Expense . . . . . . . . . . . . . . . . . . . . . . . . . . . . . . . . . . . . . . . . . . . . . . | 10,000 | |
|---|---|---|
| Salaries Payable . . . . . . . . . . . . . . . . . . . . . . . . . . . . . . . . . . . . . . . . . . . . . | | 10,000 |
| Accrued salaries [($12,500 ÷ 5 days) × 4 days]. | | |

Practice Exercises: PE 3-6A, PE 3-6B

[6] To simplify the subsequent recording of the following period's transactions, some accountants use what is known as reversing entries for certain types of adjustments. Reversing entries are discussed and illustrated in Appendix B at the end of the textbook.

# Depreciation Expense

**Fixed assets**, or **plant assets**, are physical resources that are owned and used by a business and are permanent or have a long life. Examples of fixed assets include land, buildings, and equipment. In a sense, fixed assets are a type of *long-term* prepaid expense. However, because of their unique nature and long life, they are discussed separately from other prepaid expenses.

Fixed assets, such as office equipment, are used to generate revenue much like supplies are used to generate revenue. Unlike supplies, however, there is no visible reduction in the quantity of the equipment. Instead, as time passes, the equipment loses its ability to provide useful services. This decrease in usefulness is called **depreciation**.

All fixed assets, except land, lose their usefulness and, thus, are said to **depreciate**. As a fixed asset depreciates, a portion of its cost should be recorded as an expense. This periodic expense is called **depreciation expense**.

The adjusting entry to record depreciation expense is similar to the adjusting entry for supplies used. The depreciation expense account is increased (debited) for the amount of depreciation. However, the fixed asset account is not decreased (credited). This is because both the original cost of a fixed asset and the depreciation recorded since its purchase are reported on the balance sheet. Instead, an account entitled **Accumulated Depreciation** is increased (credited).

Accumulated depreciation accounts are called **contra accounts**, or **contra asset accounts**. This is because accumulated depreciation accounts are deducted from their related fixed asset accounts on the balance sheet. The normal balance of a contra account is opposite to the account from which it is deducted. Because the normal balance of a fixed asset account is a debit, the normal balance of an accumulated depreciation account is a credit.

The normal titles for fixed asset accounts and their related contra asset accounts are as follows:

**Lowe's Companies, Inc.**, reported land, buildings, and store equipment at a cost of $34,332 million and accumulated depreciation of $12,362 million.

| Fixed Asset Account | Contra Asset Account |
| --- | --- |
| Land | None—Land is not depreciated. |
| Buildings | Accumulated Depreciation—Buildings |
| Store Equipment | Accumulated Depreciation—Store Equipment |
| Office Equipment | Accumulated Depreciation—Office Equipment |

The December 31, 2015, unadjusted trial balance of **NetSolutions** (Exhibit 5) indicates that NetSolutions owns two fixed assets: land and office equipment. Land does not depreciate; however, an adjusting entry is recorded for the depreciation of the office equipment for December. Assume that the office equipment depreciates $50 during December. The depreciation expense account is increased (debited) by $50, and the accumulated depreciation—office equipment account is increased (credited) by $50.[7] The adjusting journal entry and T accounts are as follows:

| | | | | | |
| --- | --- | --- | --- | --- | --- |
| Dec. | 31 | Depreciation Expense | 56 | 50 | |
| | | Accumulated Depreciation—Office Equip. | 19 | | 50 |
| | | Depreciation on office equipment. | | | |

*Adjusting Journal Entry*

| Assets | = Liabilities + | Owner's Equity (Expense) |
| --- | --- | --- |

| **Office Equipment** | 18 |
| --- | --- |
| Bal. | 1,800 | |

| **Depreciation Expense** | 56 |
| --- | --- |
| Dec. 31 | 50 | |

| **Accumulated Depr.—Office Equip.** | 19 |
| --- | --- |
| | Dec. 31 | 50 |

*Accounting Equation Impact*

After the adjusting journal entry is recorded and posted, the office equipment account still has a debit balance of $1,800. This is the original cost of the office equipment that

[7] Methods of computing depreciation expense are described and illustrated in Chapter 10.

was purchased on December 4. The accumulated depreciation—office equipment account has a credit balance of $50. The difference between these two balances is the cost of the office equipment that has not yet been depreciated. This amount, called the **book value of the asset** (or **net book value**), is computed as follows:

Book Value of Asset = Cost of the Asset – Accumulated Depreciation of Asset
Book Value of Office Equipment = Cost of Office Equipment – Accumulated Depr. of Office Equipment
= $1,800 – $50
= $1,750

The office equipment and its related accumulated depreciation are reported on the December 31, 2015, balance sheet as follows:

| Office equipment | $1,800 | |
| Less accumulated depreciation | 50 | $1,750 |

The market value of a fixed asset usually differs from its book value. This is because depreciation is an *allocation* method, not a *valuation* method. That is, depreciation allocates the cost of a fixed asset to expense over its estimated life. Depreciation does not measure changes in market values, which vary from year to year. Thus, on December 31, 2015, the market value of NetSolutions' office equipment could be more or less than $1,750.

If the adjustment for depreciation ($50) is not recorded, Depreciation Expense on the income statement will be understated by $50, and the net income will be overstated by $50. On the balance sheet, the book value of Office Equipment and Chris Clark, Capital will be overstated by $50. The effects of omitting the adjustment for depreciation are as follows:

| | Amount of Misstatement |
|---|---|
| Income Statement | |
| Revenues correctly stated | $ XX |
| Expenses understated by | (50) |
| Net income overstated by | $ 50 |
| | |
| Balance Sheet | |
| Assets overstated by | $ 50 |
| | |
| Liabilities correctly stated | $ XX |
| Owner's equity overstated by | 50 |
| Total liabilities and owner's equity overstated by | $ 50 |

---

### Example Exercise 3-7  Adjustment for Depreciation  OBJ 2

The estimated amount of depreciation on equipment for the current year is $4,250. Journalize the adjusting entry to record the depreciation.

### Follow My Example 3-7

| Depreciation Expense..................................................... | 4,250 | |
| Accumulated Depreciation—Equipment............................... | | 4,250 |
| Depreciation on equipment. | | |

Practice Exercises: PE 3-7A, PE 3-7B

---

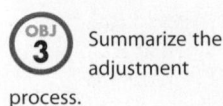

OBJ 3
Summarize the adjustment process.

## Summary of Adjustment Process

A summary of the basic types of adjusting entries is shown in Exhibit 8. The adjusting entries for **NetSolutions** are shown in Exhibit 9. The adjusting entries are dated as of the last day of the period. However, because collecting the adjustment data requires

| EXHIBIT 8 | Summary of Adjustments |
|---|---|

## PREPAID EXPENSES

| Examples | Reason for Adjustment | Adjusting Entry | | Examples from NetSolutions | | Financial Statement Impact if Adjusting Entry Is Omitted | |
|---|---|---|---|---|---|---|---|
| Supplies, prepaid insurance | Prepaid expenses (assets) have been used or consumed in the business operations. | Expense Asset | Dr. Cr. | Supplies Expense 1,240<br>  Supplies 1,240<br>Insurance Expense 200<br>  Prepaid Insurance 200 | | Income Statement:<br>  Revenues No effect<br>  Expenses Understated<br>  Net income Overstated<br>Balance Sheet:<br>  Assets Overstated<br>  Liabilities No effect<br>  Owner's equity Overstated<br>  (capital) | |

## UNEARNED REVENUES

| Unearned rent, magazine subscriptions received in advance, fees received in advance of services | Cash received before the services have been provided is recorded as a liability. Some services have been provided to the customer before the end of the accounting period. | Liability Revenue | Dr. Cr. | Unearned Rent 120<br>  Rent Revenue 120 | | Income Statement:<br>  Revenues Understated<br>  Expenses No effect<br>  Net income Understated<br>Balance Sheet:<br>  Assets No effect<br>  Liabilities Overstated<br>  Owner's equity Understated<br>  (capital) | |

## ACCRUED REVENUES

| Services performed but not billed, interest to be received | Services have been provided to the customer, but have not been billed or recorded. Interest has been earned, but has not been received or recorded. | Asset Revenue | Dr. Cr. | Accounts Receivable 500<br>  Fees Earned 500 | | Income Statement:<br>  Revenues Understated<br>  Expenses No effect<br>  Net income Understated<br>Balance Sheet:<br>  Assets Understated<br>  Liabilities No effect<br>  Owner's equity Understated<br>  (capital) | |

## ACCRUED EXPENSES

| Wages or salaries incurred but not paid, interest incurred but not paid | Expenses have been incurred, but have not been paid or recorded. | Expense Liability | Dr. Cr. | Wages Expense 250<br>  Wages Payable 250 | | Income Statement:<br>  Revenues No effect<br>  Expenses Understated<br>  Net income Overstated<br>Balance Sheet:<br>  Assets No effect<br>  Liabilities Understated<br>  Owner's equity Overstated<br>  (capital) | |

## DEPRECIATION

| Depreciation of equipment and buildings | Fixed assets depreciate as they are used or consumed in the business operations. | Expense Contra Asset | Dr. Cr. | Depreciation Expense 50<br>  Accum. Depreciation—<br>    Office Equipment 50 | | Income Statement:<br>  Revenues No effect<br>  Expenses Understated<br>  Net income Overstated<br>Balance Sheet:<br>  Assets Overstated<br>  Liabilities No effect<br>  Owner's equity Overstated<br>  (capital) | |

**EXHIBIT 9**

**Adjusting Entries— NetSolutions**

| | Journal | | | | Page 5 |
|---|---|---|---|---|---|
| **Date** | **Description** | **Post. Ref.** | **Debit** | **Credit** | |
| | Adjusting Entries | | | | |
| 2015 Dec. 31 | Supplies Expense | 52 | 1,240 | | |
| | Supplies | 14 | | 1,240 | |
| | Supplies used ($2,000 – $760). | | | | |
| 31 | Insurance Expense | 55 | 200 | | |
| | Prepaid Insurance | 15 | | 200 | |
| | Insurance expired ($2,400 ÷ 12 months). | | | | |
| 31 | Unearned Rent | 23 | 120 | | |
| | Rent Revenue | 42 | | 120 | |
| | Rent earned ($360 ÷ 3 months). | | | | |
| 31 | Accounts Receivable | 12 | 500 | | |
| | Fees Earned | 41 | | 500 | |
| | Accrued fees (25 hrs. × $20). | | | | |
| 31 | Wages Expense | 51 | 250 | | |
| | Wages Payable | 22 | | 250 | |
| | Accrued wages. | | | | |
| 31 | Depreciation Expense | 56 | 50 | | |
| | Accum. Depreciation—Office Equipment | 19 | | 50 | |
| | Depreciation on office equipment. | | | | |

An accountant may check whether all adjustments have been made by comparing current period adjustments with those of the prior period.

# Business Connection

## MICROSOFT CORPORATION

Microsoft Corporation develops, manufactures, licenses, and supports a wide range of computer software products, including Windows Vista®, Windows 7®, Windows XP®, Word®, Excel®, and the Xbox® gaming system. When Microsoft sells its products, it incurs an obligation to support its software with technical support and periodic updates. As a result, not all the revenue is earned on the date of sale; some of the revenue on the date of sale is unearned. The portion of revenue related to support services, such as updates and technical support, is earned as time passes and support is provided to customers. Thus, each year Microsoft makes adjusting entries transferring some of its unearned revenue to revenue. The following excerpts were taken from recent financial statements of Microsoft:

> The percentage of revenue recorded as unearned . . . ranges from approximately 15% to 25% of the sales price for Windows XP Home, approximately 5% to 15% of the sales price for Windows XP Professional, . . .

Unearned Revenue:

| | **Recent Year** | **Prior Year** |
|---|---|---|
| Unearned revenue (in millions) | $17,120 | $14,830 |

During the next year, Microsoft expects to record more than $15,722 million of unearned revenue as revenue. At the same time, Microsoft will record additional unearned revenue from current period sales.

time, the entries are usually recorded at a later date. An explanation is normally included with each adjusting entry.

NetSolutions' adjusting entries are posted to the ledger shown in Exhibit 10. The adjustments are highlighted in Exhibit 10 to distinguish them from other transactions.

## EXHIBIT 10 Ledger with Adjusting Entries—NetSolutions

### Account Cash — Account No. 11

| Date | Item | Post. Ref. | Debit | Credit | Balance Debit | Balance Credit |
|---|---|---|---|---|---|---|
| 2015 | | | | | | |
| Nov. 1 | | 1 | 25,000 | | 25,000 | |
| 5 | | 1 | | 20,000 | 5,000 | |
| 18 | | 1 | 7,500 | | 12,500 | |
| 30 | | 1 | | 3,650 | 8,850 | |
| 30 | | 1 | | 950 | 7,900 | |
| 30 | | 2 | | 2,000 | 5,900 | |
| Dec. 1 | | 2 | | 2,400 | 3,500 | |
| 1 | | 2 | | 800 | 2,700 | |
| 1 | | 2 | 360 | | 3,060 | |
| 6 | | 2 | | 180 | 2,880 | |
| 11 | | 2 | | 400 | 2,480 | |
| 13 | | 3 | | 950 | 1,530 | |
| 16 | | 3 | 3,100 | | 4,630 | |
| 20 | | 3 | | 900 | 3,730 | |
| 21 | | 3 | 650 | | 4,380 | |
| 23 | | 3 | | 1,450 | 2,930 | |
| 27 | | 3 | | 1,200 | 1,730 | |
| 31 | | 3 | | 310 | 1,420 | |
| 31 | | 4 | | 225 | 1,195 | |
| 31 | | 4 | 2,870 | | 4,065 | |
| 31 | | 4 | | 2,000 | 2,065 | |

### Account Accounts Receivable — Account No. 12

| Date | Item | Post. Ref. | Debit | Credit | Balance Debit | Balance Credit |
|---|---|---|---|---|---|---|
| 2015 | | | | | | |
| Dec. 16 | | 3 | 1,750 | | 1,750 | |
| 21 | | 3 | | 650 | 1,100 | |
| 31 | | 4 | 1,120 | | 2,220 | |
| 31 | Adjusting | 5 | 500 | | 2,720 | |

### Account Supplies — Account No. 14

| Date | Item | Post. Ref. | Debit | Credit | Balance Debit | Balance Credit |
|---|---|---|---|---|---|---|
| 2015 | | | | | | |
| Nov. 10 | | 1 | 1,350 | | 1,350 | |
| 30 | | 1 | | 800 | 550 | |
| Dec. 23 | | 3 | 1,450 | | 2,000 | |
| 31 | Adjusting | 5 | | 1,240 | 760 | |

### Account Prepaid Insurance — Account No. 15

| Date | Item | Post. Ref. | Debit | Credit | Balance Debit | Balance Credit |
|---|---|---|---|---|---|---|
| 2015 | | | | | | |
| Dec. 1 | | 2 | 2,400 | | 2,400 | |
| 31 | Adjusting | 5 | | 200 | 2,200 | |

### Account Land — Account No. 17

| Date | Item | Post. Ref. | Debit | Credit | Balance Debit | Balance Credit |
|---|---|---|---|---|---|---|
| 2015 | | | | | | |
| Nov. 5 | | 1 | 20,000 | | 20,000 | |

### Account Office Equipment — Account No. 18

| Date | Item | Post. Ref. | Debit | Credit | Balance Debit | Balance Credit |
|---|---|---|---|---|---|---|
| 2015 | | | | | | |
| Dec. 4 | | 2 | 1,800 | | 1,800 | |

### Account Accum. Depr.—Office Equip. — Account No. 19

| Date | Item | Post. Ref. | Debit | Credit | Balance Debit | Balance Credit |
|---|---|---|---|---|---|---|
| 2015 | | | | | | |
| Dec. 1 | Adjusting | 5 | | 50 | | 50 |

### Account Accounts Payable — Account No. 21

| Date | Item | Post. Ref. | Debit | Credit | Balance Debit | Balance Credit |
|---|---|---|---|---|---|---|
| 2015 | | | | | | |
| Nov. 10 | | 1 | | 1,350 | | 1,350 |
| 30 | | 1 | 950 | | | 400 |
| Dec. 4 | | 2 | | 1,800 | | 2,200 |
| 11 | | 2 | 400 | | | 1,800 |
| 20 | | 3 | 900 | | | 900 |

### Account Wages Payable — Account No. 22

| Date | Item | Post. Ref. | Debit | Credit | Balance Debit | Balance Credit |
|---|---|---|---|---|---|---|
| 2015 | | | | | | |
| Dec. 31 | Adjusting | 5 | | 250 | | 250 |

### Account Unearned Rent — Account No. 23

| Date | Item | Post. Ref. | Debit | Credit | Balance Debit | Balance Credit |
|---|---|---|---|---|---|---|
| 2015 | | | | | | |
| Dec. 1 | | 2 | | 360 | | 360 |
| 31 | Adjusting | 5 | 120 | | | 240 |

### Account Chris Clark, Capital — Account No. 31

| Date | Item | Post. Ref. | Debit | Credit | Balance Debit | Balance Credit |
|---|---|---|---|---|---|---|
| 2015 | | | | | | |
| Nov. 1 | | 1 | | 25,000 | | 25,000 |

(Continued)

**EXHIBIT 10**    **Ledger with Adjusting Entries—NetSolutions (*Concluded*)**

**Account** *Chris Clark, Drawing*    Account No. *32*

| Date | Item | Post. Ref. | Debit | Credit | Balance Debit | Balance Credit |
|------|------|------|-------|--------|-------|--------|
| 2015 | | | | | | |
| Nov. 30 | | 2 | 2,000 | | 2,000 | |
| Dec. 31 | | 4 | 2,000 | | 4,000 | |

**Account** *Fees Earned*    Account No. *41*

| Date | Item | Post. Ref. | Debit | Credit | Balance Debit | Balance Credit |
|------|------|------|-------|--------|-------|--------|
| 2015 | | | | | | |
| Nov. 18 | | 1 | | 7,500 | | 7,500 |
| Dec. 16 | | 3 | | 3,100 | | 10,600 |
| 16 | | 3 | | 1,750 | | 12,350 |
| 31 | | 4 | | 2,870 | | 15,220 |
| 31 | | 4 | | 1,120 | | 16,340 |
| 31 | Adjusting | 5 | | 500 | | 16,840 |

**Account** *Rent Revenue*    Account No. *42*

| Date | Item | Post. Ref. | Debit | Credit | Balance Debit | Balance Credit |
|------|------|------|-------|--------|-------|--------|
| 2015 | | | | | | |
| Dec. 31 | Adjusting | 5 | | 120 | | 120 |

**Account** *Wages Expense*    Account No. *51*

| Date | Item | Post. Ref. | Debit | Credit | Balance Debit | Balance Credit |
|------|------|------|-------|--------|-------|--------|
| 2015 | | | | | | |
| Nov. 30 | | 1 | 2,125 | | 2,125 | |
| Dec. 13 | | 3 | 950 | | 3,075 | |
| 27 | | 3 | 1,200 | | 4,275 | |
| 31 | Adjusting | 5 | 250 | | 4,525 | |

**Account** *Supplies Expense*    Account No. *52*

| Date | Item | Post. Ref. | Debit | Credit | Balance Debit | Balance Credit |
|------|------|------|-------|--------|-------|--------|
| 2015 | | | | | | |
| Nov. 30 | | 1 | 800 | | 800 | |
| Dec. 31 | Adjusting | 5 | 1,240 | | 2,040 | |

**Account** *Rent Expense*    Account No. *53*

| Date | Item | Post. Ref. | Debit | Credit | Balance Debit | Balance Credit |
|------|------|------|-------|--------|-------|--------|
| 2015 | | | | | | |
| Nov. 30 | | 1 | 800 | | 800 | |
| Dec. 1 | | 2 | 800 | | 1,600 | |

**Account** *Utilities Expense*    Account No. *54*

| Date | Item | Post. Ref. | Debit | Credit | Balance Debit | Balance Credit |
|------|------|------|-------|--------|-------|--------|
| 2015 | | | | | | |
| Nov. 30 | | 1 | 450 | | 450 | |
| Dec. 31 | | 3 | 310 | | 760 | |
| 31 | | 4 | 225 | | 985 | |

**Account** *Insurance Expense*    Account No. *55*

| Date | Item | Post. Ref. | Debit | Credit | Balance Debit | Balance Credit |
|------|------|------|-------|--------|-------|--------|
| 2015 | | | | | | |
| Dec. 31 | Adjusting | 5 | 200 | | 200 | |

**Account** *Depreciation Expense*    Account No. *56*

| Date | Item | Post. Ref. | Debit | Credit | Balance Debit | Balance Credit |
|------|------|------|-------|--------|-------|--------|
| 2015 | | | | | | |
| Dec. 31 | Adjusting | 5 | 50 | | 50 | |

**Account** *Miscellaneous Expense*    Account No. *59*

| Date | Item | Post. Ref. | Debit | Credit | Balance Debit | Balance Credit |
|------|------|------|-------|--------|-------|--------|
| 2015 | | | | | | |
| Nov. 30 | | 1 | 275 | | 275 | |
| Dec. 6 | | 2 | 180 | | 455 | |

## Example Exercise 3-8  Effect of Omitting Adjustments

For the year ending December 31, 2016, Mann Medical Co. mistakenly omitted adjusting entries for (1) $8,600 of unearned revenue that was earned, (2) earned revenue of $12,500 that was not billed, and (3) accrued wages of $2,900. Indicate the combined effect of the errors on (a) revenues, (b) expenses, and (c) net income for the year ended December 31, 2016.

### Follow My Example 3-8

a.  Revenues were understated by $21,100 ($8,600 + $12,500).
b.  Expenses were understated by $2,900.
c.  Net income was understated by $18,200 ($8,600 + $12,500 − $2,900).

Practice Exercises: PE 3-8A, PE 3-8B

## Adjusted Trial Balance

**OBJ 4** Prepare an adjusted trial balance.

After the adjusting entries are posted, an **adjusted trial balance** is prepared. The adjusted trial balance verifies the equality of the total debit and credit balances before the financial statements are prepared. If the adjusted trial balance does not balance, an error has occurred. However, as discussed in Chapter 2, errors may occur even though the adjusted trial balance totals agree. For example, if an adjusting entry were omitted, the adjusted trial balance totals would still agree.

Exhibit 11 shows the adjusted trial balance for **NetSolutions** as of December 31, 2015. Chapter 4 discusses how financial statements, including a classified balance sheet, are prepared from an adjusted trial balance.

| NetSolutions<br>Adjusted Trial Balance<br>December 31, 2015 | Debit<br>Balances | Credit<br>Balances |
|---|---|---|
| Cash | 2,065 | |
| Accounts Receivable | 2,720 | |
| Supplies | 760 | |
| Prepaid Insurance | 2,200 | |
| Land | 20,000 | |
| Office Equipment | 1,800 | |
| Accumulated Depreciation—Office Equipment | | 50 |
| Accounts Payable | | 900 |
| Wages Payable | | 250 |
| Unearned Rent | | 240 |
| Chris Clark, Capital | | 25,000 |
| Chris Clark, Drawing | 4,000 | |
| Fees Earned | | 16,840 |
| Rent Revenue | | 120 |
| Wages Expense | 4,525 | |
| Supplies Expense | 2,040 | |
| Rent Expense | 1,600 | |
| Utilities Expense | 985 | |
| Insurance Expense | 200 | |
| Depreciation Expense | 50 | |
| Miscellaneous Expense | 455 | |
| | 43,400 | 43,400 |

**EXHIBIT 11**

**Adjusted Trial Balance**

## Example Exercise 3-9   Effect of Errors on Adjusted Trial Balance

For each of the following errors, considered individually, indicate whether the error would cause the adjusted trial balance totals to be unequal. If the error would cause the adjusted trial balance totals to be unequal, indicate whether the debit or credit total is higher and by how much.

a.  The adjustment for accrued fees of $5,340 was journalized as a debit to Accounts Payable for $5,340 and a credit to Fees Earned of $5,340.

b.  The adjustment for depreciation of $3,260 was journalized as a debit to Depreciation Expense for $3,620 and a credit to Accumulated Depreciation for $3,260.

### Follow My Example 3-9

a.  The totals are equal even though the debit should have been to Accounts Receivable instead of Accounts Payable.

b.  The totals are unequal. The debit total is higher by $360 ($3,620 − $3,260).

Practice Exercises: PE 3-9A, PE 3-9B

Describe and illustrate the use of vertical analysis in evaluating a company's performance and financial condition.

# Financial Analysis and Interpretation: Vertical Analysis

Comparing each item in a financial statement with a total amount from the same statement is useful in analyzing relationships within the financial statement. **Vertical analysis** is the term used to describe such comparisons.

In vertical analysis of a balance sheet, each asset item is stated as a percent of the total assets. Each liability and owner's equity item is stated as a percent of total liabilities and owner's equity. In vertical analysis of an income statement, each item is stated as a percent of revenues or fees earned.

Vertical analysis is also useful for analyzing changes in financial statements over time. To illustrate, a vertical analysis of two years of income statements for J. Holmes, Attorney-at-Law, follows:

**J. Holmes, Attorney-at-Law**
**Income Statements**
**For the Years Ended December 31**

|  | Year 2 | | Year 1 | |
|---|---|---|---|---|
|  | Amount | Percent* | Amount | Percent* |
| Fees earned | $187,500 | 100.0% | $150,000 | 100.0% |
| Operating expenses: |  |  |  |  |
|   Wages expense | $ 60,000 | 32.0% | $ 45,000 | 30.0% |
|   Rent expense | 15,000 | 8.0 | 12,000 | 8.0 |
|   Utilities expense | 12,500 | 6.7 | 9,000 | 6.0 |
|   Supplies expense | 2,700 | 1.4 | 3,000 | 2.0 |
|   Miscellaneous expense | 2,300 | 1.2 | 1,800 | 1.2 |
|     Total operating expenses | $ 92,500 | 49.3% | $ 70,800 | 47.2% |
| Net income | $ 95,000 | 50.7% | $ 79,200 | 52.8% |

*Rounded to one decimal place

The preceding vertical analysis indicates both favorable and unfavorable trends affecting the income statement of J. Holmes, Attorney-at-Law. The increase in wages expense of 2% (32.0% − 30.0%) is an unfavorable trend, as is the increase in utilities expense of 0.7% (6.7% − 6.0%). A favorable trend is the decrease in supplies expense of 0.6% (2.0% − 1.4%). Rent expense and miscellaneous expense as a percent of fees earned were constant. The net result of these trends is that net income decreased as a percent of fees earned from 52.8% to 50.7%.

The analysis of the various percentages shown for J. Holmes, Attorney-at-Law, can be enhanced by comparisons with industry averages. Such averages are published by trade associations and financial information services. Any major differences between industry averages should be investigated.

Vertical analysis of operating income taken from two recent years of income statements for Pandora Media, Inc. follows:

**Pandora Media, Inc.**
**Income Statements**
**For the Years Ended January 31**

| | Year 2 | | Year 1 | |
| --- | --- | --- | --- | --- |
| | Amount* | Percent** | Amount* | Percent** |
| Revenues: | | | | |
| Advertising | $239,957 | 87.5% | $119,333 | 86.6% |
| Subscription services (other) | 34,383 | 12.5 | 18,431 | 13.4 |
| Total revenue | $274,340 | 100.0% | $137,764 | 100.0% |
| Expenses: | | | | |
| Cost of revenues | 22,759 | 8.3% | 11,559 | 8.4% |
| Marketing and selling | 65,010 | 23.7 | 36,250 | 26.3 |
| General and administrative | 35,428 | 12.9 | 14,183 | 10.3 |
| Content acquisition | 148,708 | 54.2 | 69,357 | 50.3 |
| Product development | 13,425 | 4.9 | 6,736 | 4.9 |
| Total expenses | $285,330 | 104.0% | $138,085 | 100.2% |
| Operating income (loss) | $ (10,990) | (4.0) | $ (321) | (0.2)% |

*In thousands
**Rounded to one decimal place

The preceding analysis illustrates the usefulness of vertical analysis. Since Year 2 revenues are almost twice those of Year 1, it is difficult to compare operating results using only dollar amounts. Vertical analysis, however, reveals that advertising revenue as a percent of total revenue in Year 2 increased 0.9% over that in Year 1, while subscription revenues fell by the same percent. In addition, expenses as a percent of total revenues increased 3.8% from Year 1 and to Year 2. Specifically, marketing and selling expenses declined from 26.3% to 23.7%, while general and administrative expenses increased from 10.3% to 12.9%. In addition, content acquisition costs, which include royalties paid to artists for playing their music, increased from 50.3% to 54.2%. As a result, the loss from operations increased from (0.2%) to (4.0%). There does not appear to be any major change in Pandora's overall operating performance from Year 1 to Year 2 except for increasing revenues and the related increase in expenses.

## Example Exercise 3-10  Vertical Analysis

OBJ 5

Two income statements for Fortson Company follow:

**Fortson Company**
**Income Statements**
**For the Years Ended December 31, 2016 and 2015**

| | 2016 | 2015 |
| --- | --- | --- |
| Fees earned | $425,000 | $375,000 |
| Operating expenses | 263,500 | 210,000 |
| Operating income | $161,500 | $165,000 |

a. Prepare a vertical analysis of Fortson Company's income statements.

b. Does the vertical analysis indicate a favorable or an unfavorable trend?

*(Continued)*

## Follow My Example 3-10

a.
**Fortson Company**
**Income Statements**
**For the Years Ended December 31, 2016 and 2015**

|  | 2016 | | 2015 | |
|  | Amount | Percent | Amount | Percent |
| --- | --- | --- | --- | --- |
| Fees earned | $425,000 | 100% | $375,000 | 100% |
| Operating expenses | 263,500 | 62 | 210,000 | 56 |
| Operating income | $161,500 | 38% | $165,000 | 44% |

b.   An unfavorable trend of increasing operating expenses and decreasing operating income is indicated.

Practice Exercises: PE 3-10A, PE 3-10B

# At a Glance 3

**OBJ 1**   Describe the nature of the adjusting process.

**Key Points**   The accrual basis of accounting requires that revenues are reported in the period in which they are earned and expenses are matched with the revenues they generate. The updating of accounts at the end of the accounting period is called the adjusting process. Each adjusting entry affects an income statement and balance sheet account. The four types of accounts requiring adjusting entries are prepaid expenses, unearned revenues, accrued revenues, and accrued expenses.

| Learning Outcomes | Example Exercises | Practice Exercises |
| --- | --- | --- |
| • Explain why accrual accounting requires adjusting entries. |  |  |
| • List accounts that do and do NOT require adjusting entries at the end of the accounting period. | EE3-1 | PE3-1A, 3-1B |
| • Give an example of a prepaid expense, unearned revenue, accrued revenue, and accrued expense. | EE3-2 | PE3-2A, 3-2B |

## Journalize entries for accounts requiring adjustment.

**Key Points**   At the end of the period, adjusting entries are needed for prepaid expenses, unearned revenues, accrued revenues, and accrued expenses. In addition, an adjusting entry is necessary to record depreciation on fixed assets.

| Learning Outcomes | Example Exercises | Practice Exercises |
|---|---|---|
| • Prepare an adjusting entry for a prepaid expense. | EE3-3 | PE3-3A, 3-3B |
| • Prepare an adjusting entry for an unearned revenue. | EE3-4 | PE3-4A, 3-4B |
| • Prepare an adjusting entry for an accrued revenue. | EE3-5 | PE3-5A, 3-5B |
| • Prepare an adjusting entry for an accrued expense. | EE3-6 | PE3-6A, 3-6B |
| • Prepare an adjusting entry for depreciation expense. | EE3-7 | PE3-7A, 3-7B |

## Summarize the adjustment process.

**Key Points**   A summary of adjustments, including the type of adjustment, reason for the adjustment, the adjusting entry, and the effect of omitting an adjustment on the financial statements, is shown in Exhibit 8.

| Learning Outcomes | Example Exercises | Practice Exercises |
|---|---|---|
| • Determine the effect on the income statement and balance sheet of omitting an adjusting entry for prepaid expense, unearned revenue, accrued revenue, accrued expense, and depreciation. | EE3-8 | PE3-8A, 3-8B |

## Prepare an adjusted trial balance.

**Key Points**   After all the adjusting entries have been posted, the equality of the total debit balances and total credit balances is verified by an adjusted trial balance.

| Learning Outcomes | Example Exercises | Practice Exercises |
|---|---|---|
| • Prepare an adjusted trial balance. | | |
| • Determine the effect of errors on the equality of the adjusted trial balance. | EE3-9 | PE3-9A, 3-9B |

## Describe and illustrate the use of vertical analysis in evaluating a company's performance and financial condition.

**Key Points**   Comparing each item on a financial statement with a total amount from the same statement is called vertical analysis. On the balance sheet, each asset is expressed as a percent of total assets, and each liability and owner's equity is expressed as a percent of total liabilities and owner's equity. On the income statement, each revenue and expense is expressed as a percent of total revenues or fees earned.

| Learning Outcomes | Example Exercises | Practice Exercises |
|---|---|---|
| • Describe vertical analysis. | | |
| • Prepare a vertical analysis report of a financial statement. | EE3-10 | PE3-10A, 3-10B |

# Key Terms

accounting period concept (104)
accrual basis of accounting (104)
accrued expenses (108)
accrued revenues (107)
Accumulated Depreciation (117)
adjusted trial balance (123)
adjusting entries (105)
adjusting process (105)

book value of the asset
  (or net book value) (118)
cash basis of accounting (104)
contra accounts (or contra
  asset accounts) (117)
depreciate (117)
depreciation (117)
depreciation expense (117)

fixed assets (or plant assets) (117)
matching concept (104)
prepaid expenses (105)
revenue recognition
  concept (104)
unearned revenues (106)
vertical analysis (124)

# Illustrative Problem

Three years ago, T. Roderick organized Harbor Realty. At July 31, 2016, the end of the current year, the unadjusted trial balance of Harbor Realty follows:

| Harbor Realty<br>Unadjusted Trial Balance<br>July 31, 2016 | | |
| --- | --- | --- |
| | **Debit Balances** | **Credit Balances** |
| Cash ....................................................... | 3,425 | |
| Accounts Receivable........................................... | 7,000 | |
| Supplies ..................................................... | 1,270 | |
| Prepaid Insurance ............................................ | 620 | |
| Office Equipment ............................................. | 51,650 | |
| Accumulated Depreciation—Office Equipment.................. | | 9,700 |
| Accounts Payable ............................................. | | 925 |
| Wages Payable ............................................... | | 0 |
| Unearned Fees................................................ | | 1,250 |
| T. Roderick, Capital .......................................... | | 29,000 |
| T. Roderick, Drawing.......................................... | 5,200 | |
| Fees Earned.................................................. | | 59,125 |
| Wages Expense .............................................. | 22,415 | |
| Depreciation Expense ........................................ | 0 | |
| Rent Expense ................................................ | 4,200 | |
| Utilities Expense ............................................. | 2,715 | |
| Supplies Expense............................................. | 0 | |
| Insurance Expense ........................................... | 0 | |
| Miscellaneous Expense ....................................... | 1,505 | |
| | 100,000 | 100,000 |

The data needed to determine year-end adjustments are as follows:

a. Supplies on hand at July 31, 2016, $380.

b. Insurance premiums expired during the year, $315.

c. Depreciation of equipment during the year, $4,950.

d. Wages accrued but not paid at July 31, 2016, $440.

e. Accrued fees earned but not recorded at July 31, 2016, $1,000.

f. Unearned fees on July 31, 2016, $750.

## Instructions

1. Prepare the necessary adjusting journal entries. Include journal entry explanations.

2. Determine the balance of the accounts affected by the adjusting entries, and prepare an adjusted trial balance.

## Solution

1.

| Journal | | | | | |
|---|---|---|---|---|---|
| **Date** | | **Description** | **Post. Ref.** | **Debit** | **Credit** |
| 2016 July | 31 | Supplies Expense | | 890 | |
| | | Supplies | | | 890 |
| | | Supplies used ($1,270 – $380). | | | |
| | 31 | Insurance Expense | | 315 | |
| | | Prepaid Insurance | | | 315 |
| | | Insurance expired. | | | |
| | 31 | Depreciation Expense | | 4,950 | |
| | | Accumulated Depreciation—Office Equipment | | | 4,950 |
| | | Depreciation expense. | | | |
| | 31 | Wages Expense | | 440 | |
| | | Wages Payable | | | 440 |
| | | Accrued wages. | | | |
| | 31 | Accounts Receivable | | 1,000 | |
| | | Fees Earned | | | 1,000 |
| | | Accrued fees. | | | |
| | 31 | Unearned Fees | | 500 | |
| | | Fees Earned | | | 500 |
| | | Fees earned ($1,250 – $750). | | | |

2.

| Harbor Realty<br>Adjusted Trial Balance<br>July 31, 2016 | Debit<br>Balances | Credit<br>Balances |
|---|---|---|
| Cash | 3,425 | |
| Accounts Receivable | 8,000 | |
| Supplies | 380 | |
| Prepaid Insurance | 305 | |
| Office Equipment | 51,650 | |
| Accumulated Depreciation—Office Equipment | | 14,650 |
| Accounts Payable | | 925 |
| Wages Payable | | 440 |
| Unearned Fees | | 750 |
| T. Roderick, Capital | | 29,000 |
| T. Roderick, Drawing | 5,200 | |
| Fees Earned | | 60,625 |
| Wages Expense | 22,855 | |
| Depreciation Expense | 4,950 | |
| Rent Expense | 4,200 | |
| Utilities Expense | 2,715 | |
| Supplies Expense | 890 | |
| Insurance Expense | 315 | |
| Miscellaneous Expense | 1,505 | |
| | 106,390 | 106,390 |

# Discussion Questions

1. How are revenues and expenses reported on the income statement under (a) the cash basis of accounting and (b) the accrual basis of accounting?

2. Is the matching concept related to (a) the cash basis of accounting or (b) the accrual basis of accounting?

3. Why are adjusting entries needed at the end of an accounting period?

4. What is the difference between *adjusting entries* and *correcting entries*?

5. Identify the four different categories of adjusting entries frequently required at the end of an accounting period.

6. If the effect of the debit portion of an adjusting entry is to increase the balance of an asset account, which of the following statements describes the effect of the credit portion of the entry?

   a. Increases the balance of a revenue account.

   b. Increases the balance of an expense account.

   c. Increases the balance of a liability account.

7. If the effect of the credit portion of an adjusting entry is to increase the balance of a liability account, which of the following statements describes the effect of the debit portion of the entry?

   a. Increases the balance of a revenue account.

   b. Increases the balance of an expense account.

   c. Increases the balance of an asset account.

8. Does every adjusting entry have an effect on determining the amount of net income for a period? Explain.

9. On November 1 of the current year, a business paid the November rent on the building that it occupies. (a) Do the rights acquired at November 1 represent an asset or an expense? (b) What is the justification for debiting Rent Expense at the time of payment?

10. (a) Explain the purpose of the two accounts: Depreciation Expense and Accumulated Depreciation. (b) What is the normal balance of each account? (c) Is it customary for the balances of the two accounts to be equal in amount? (d) In what financial statements, if any, will each account appear?

# Practice Exercises

EE 3-1 *p. 105*

**PE 3-1A   Accounts requiring adjustment**                                    **OBJ. 1**

Indicate with a Yes or No whether or not each of the following accounts normally requires an adjusting entry:

a. Accumulated Depreciation *yes*    c. Land *no*         e. Supplies *yes*

b. Frank Kent, Drawing *no*          d. Salaries Payable *yes*   f. Unearned Rent *yes*

EE 3-1 *p. 105*

**PE 3-1B   Accounts requiring adjustment**                                    **OBJ. 1**

Indicate with a Yes or No whether or not each of the following accounts normally requires an adjusting entry:

a. Building              c. Interest Expense          e. Nancy Palmer, Capital

b. Cash                  d. Miscellaneous Expense     f. Prepaid Insurance

EE 3-2 *p. 109*

**PE 3-2A   Type of adjustment**                                              **OBJ. 1**

Classify the following items as (1) prepaid expense, (2) unearned revenue, (3) accrued revenue, or (4) accrued expense:

a. Cash received for services not yet rendered *2*    c. Rent revenue earned but not received *3*

b. Insurance paid for the next year *1*               d. Salaries owed but not yet paid *4*

EE 3-2 *p. 109*

**PE 3-2B   Type of adjustment**                                              **OBJ. 1**

Classify the following items as (1) prepaid expense, (2) unearned revenue, (3) accrued revenue, or (4) accrued expense:

a. Cash received for use of land next month     c. Rent expense owed but not yet paid

b. Fees earned but not received                 d. Supplies on hand

EE 3-3 *p. 112*

**PE 3-3A   Adjustment for prepaid expense**                                  **OBJ. 2**

The supplies account had a beginning balance of $3,375 and was debited for $6,450 for supplies purchased during the year. Journalize the adjusting entry required at the end of the year, assuming the amount of supplies on hand is $2,980.

EE 3-3 *p. 112*

**PE 3-3B   Adjustment for prepaid expense**                                  **OBJ. 2**

The prepaid insurance account had a beginning balance of $9,600 and was debited for $12,900 of premiums paid during the year. Journalize the adjusting entry required at the end of the year, assuming the amount of unexpired insurance related to future periods is $7,360.

EE 3-4 *p. 113*

**PE 3-4A   Adjustment for unearned revenue**                                 **OBJ. 2**

The balance in the unearned fees account, before adjustment at the end of the year, is $272,500. Journalize the adjusting entry required, assuming the amount of unearned fees at the end of the year is $189,750.

EE 3-4 *p. 113*

**PE 3-4B   Adjustment for unearned revenue**                                 **OBJ. 2**

On June 1, 2016, Herbal Co. received $18,900 for the rent of land for 12 months. Journalize the adjusting entry required for unearned rent on December 31, 2016.

SHOW
ME HOW

EE 3-5 *p. 115* | **PE 3-5A** **Adjustment for accrued revenues** | **OBJ. 2**

At the end of the current year, $23,570 of fees have been earned but have not been billed to clients. Journalize the adjusting entry to record the accrued fees.

SHOW
ME HOW

EE 3-5 *p. 115* | **PE 3-5B** **Adjustment for accrued revenues** | **OBJ. 2**

At the end of the current year, $17,555 of fees have been earned but have not been billed to clients. Journalize the adjusting entry to record the accrued fees.

SHOW
ME HOW

EE 3-6 *p. 116* | **PE 3-6A** **Adjustment for accrued expense** | **OBJ. 2**

We-Sell Realty Co. pays weekly salaries of $11,800 on Friday for a five-day workweek ending on that day. Journalize the necessary adjusting entry at the end of the accounting period, assuming that the period ends on Wednesday.

SHOW
ME HOW

EE 3-6 *p. 116* | **PE 3-6B** **Adjustment for accrued expense** | **OBJ. 2**

Prospect Realty Co. pays weekly salaries of $27,600 on Monday for a six-day workweek ending the preceding Saturday. Journalize the necessary adjusting entry at the end of the accounting period, assuming that the period ends on Friday.

SHOW
ME HOW

EE 3-7 *p. 118* | **PE 3-7A** **Adjustment for depreciation** | **OBJ. 2**

The estimated amount of depreciation on equipment for the current year is $6,880. Journalize the adjusting entry to record the depreciation.

SHOW
ME HOW

EE 3-7 *p. 118* | **PE 3-7B** **Adjustment for depreciation** | **OBJ. 2**

The estimated amount of depreciation on equipment for the current year is $7,700. Journalize the adjusting entry to record the depreciation.

SHOW
ME HOW

EE 3-8 *p. 123* | **PE 3-8A** **Effect of omitting adjustments** | **OBJ. 3**

For the year ending August 31, 2016, Mammalia Medical Co. mistakenly omitted adjusting entries for (1) depreciation of $5,800, (2) fees earned that were not billed of $44,500, and (3) accrued wages of $7,300. Indicate the combined effect of the errors on (a) revenues, (b) expenses, and (c) net income for the year ended August 31, 2016.

SHOW
ME HOW

EE 3-8 *p. 123* | **PE 3-8B** **Effect of omitting adjustments** | **OBJ. 3**

For the year ending April 30, 2016, Urology Medical Services Co. mistakenly omitted adjusting entries for (1) $1,400 of supplies that were used, (2) unearned revenue of $6,600 that was earned, and (3) insurance of $9,000 that expired. Indicate the combined effect of the errors on (a) revenues, (b) expenses, and (c) net income for the year ended April 30, 2016.

SHOW
ME HOW

EE 3-9 *p. 124* | **PE 3-9A** **Effect of errors on adjusted trial balance** | **OBJ. 4**

For each of the following errors, considered individually, indicate whether the error would cause the adjusted trial balance totals to be unequal. If the error would cause the adjusted trial balance totals to be unequal, indicate whether the debit or credit total is higher and by how much.

a. The adjustment of $9,800 for accrued fees earned was journalized as a debit to Accounts Receivable for $9,800 and a credit to Fees Earned for $8,900.

b. The adjustment of depreciation of $3,600 was omitted from the end-of-period adjusting entries.

EE 3-9 p. 124

**PE 3-9B Effect of errors on adjusted trial balance** OBJ. 4

SHOW
ME HOW

For each of the following errors, considered individually, indicate whether the error would cause the adjusted trial balance totals to be unequal. If the error would cause the adjusted trial balance totals to be unequal, indicate whether the debit or credit total is higher and by how much.

a. The adjustment for accrued wages of $5,200 was journalized as a debit to Wages Expense for $5,200 and a credit to Accounts Payable for $5,200.

b. The entry for $1,125 of supplies used during the period was journalized as a debit to Supplies Expense of $1,125 and a credit to Supplies of $1,152.

EE 3-10 p. 125

**PE 3-10A Vertical analysis** OBJ. 5

**FAI**

SHOW
ME HOW

Two income statements for Hemlock Company follow:

| Hemlock Company Income Statements For Years Ended December 31 | | |
| --- | --- | --- |
| | **2016** | **2015** |
| Fees earned | $725,000 | $615,000 |
| Operating expenses | 435,000 | 356,700 |
| Operating income | $290,000 | $258,300 |

a. Prepare a vertical analysis of Hemlock Company's income statements.

b. ⬛━━━▶ Does the vertical analysis indicate a favorable or an unfavorable trend?

EE 3-10 p. 125

**PE 3-10B Vertical analysis** OBJ. 5

**FAI**

SHOW
ME HOW

Two income statements for Cornea Company follow:

| Cornea Company Income Statements For Years Ended December 31 | | |
| --- | --- | --- |
| | **2016** | **2015** |
| Fees earned | $1,640,000 | $1,300,000 |
| Operating expenses | 869,200 | 715,000 |
| Operating income | $ 770,800 | $ 585,000 |

a. Prepare a vertical analysis of Cornea Company's income statements.

b. ⬛━━━▶ Does the vertical analysis indicate a favorable or an unfavorable trend?

# Exercises

**EX 3-1 Classifying types of adjustments** OBJ. 1

Classify the following items as (a) prepaid expense, (b) unearned revenue, (c) accrued revenue, or (d) accrued expense:

1. A two-year premium paid on a fire insurance policy.
2. Fees earned but not yet received.
3. Fees received but not yet earned.
4. Salary owed but not yet paid.
5. Subscriptions received in advance by a magazine publisher.
6. Supplies on hand.
7. Taxes owed but payable in the following period.
8. Utilities owed but not yet paid.

### EX 3-2 Classifying adjusting entries

OBJ. 1

The following accounts were taken from the unadjusted trial balance of Orion Co., a congressional lobbying firm. Indicate whether or not each account would normally require an adjusting entry. If the account normally requires an adjusting entry, use the following notation to indicate the type of adjustment:

> AE—Accrued Expense
> AR—Accrued Revenue
> PE—Prepaid Expense
> UR—Unearned Revenue

To illustrate, the answer for the first account follows:

| Account | Answer |
|---|---|
| Accounts Receivable | Normally requires adjustment (AR). |
| Cash | |
| Interest Expense | |
| Interest Receivable | |
| Johann Atkins, Capital | |
| Land | |
| Office Equipment | |
| Prepaid Rent | |
| Supplies | |
| Unearned Fees | |
| Wages Expense | |

### EX 3-3 Adjusting entry for supplies

OBJ. 2

SHOW
ME HOW

The balance in the supplies account, before adjustment at the end of the year, is $5,330. Journalize the adjusting entry required if the amount of supplies on hand at the end of the year is $1,875.

### EX 3-4 Determining supplies purchased

OBJ. 2

SHOW
ME HOW

The supplies and supplies expense accounts at December 31, after adjusting entries have been posted at the end of the first year of operations, are shown in the following T accounts:

| Supplies | | | Supplies Expense | | |
|---|---|---|---|---|---|
| Bal. | 2,550 | | Bal. | 7,120 | |

Determine the amount of supplies purchased during the year.

### EX 3-5 Effect of omitting adjusting entry

OBJ. 2, 3

At March 31, the end of the first month of operations, the usual adjusting entry transferring prepaid insurance expired to an expense account is omitted. Which items will be incorrectly stated, because of the error, on (a) the income statement for March and (b) the balance sheet as of March 31? Also indicate whether the items in error will be overstated or understated.

### EX 3-6 Adjusting entries for prepaid insurance

OBJ. 2

SHOW
ME HOW

The balance in the prepaid insurance account, before adjustment at the end of the year, is $18,630. Journalize the adjusting entry required under each of the following *alternatives* for determining the amount of the adjustment: (a) the amount of insurance expired during the year is $15,300; (b) the amount of unexpired insurance applicable to future periods is $3,330.

SHOW
ME HOW

### EX 3-7 Adjusting entries for prepaid insurance                    OBJ. 2

The prepaid insurance account had a balance of $7,000 at the beginning of the year. The account was debited for $24,000 for premiums on policies purchased during the year. Journalize the adjusting entry required under each of the following *alternatives* for determining the amount of the adjustment: (a) the amount of unexpired insurance applicable to future periods is $8,500; (b) the amount of insurance expired during the year is $22,500.

SHOW
ME HOW

### EX 3-8 Adjusting entries for unearned fees                    OBJ. 2

The balance in the unearned fees account, before adjustment at the end of the year, is $36,950. Journalize the adjusting entry required if the amount of unearned fees at the end of the year is $14,440.

### EX 3-9 Effect of omitting adjusting entry                    OBJ. 2, 3

At the end of July, the first month of the business year, the usual adjusting entry transferring rent earned to a revenue account from the unearned rent account was omitted. Indicate which items will be incorrectly stated, because of the error, on (a) the income statement for July and (b) the balance sheet as of July 31. Also indicate whether the items in error will be overstated or understated.

SHOW
ME HOW

### EX 3-10 Adjusting entry for accrued fees                    OBJ. 2

At the end of the current year, $22,650 of fees have been earned but have not been billed to clients.

a. Journalize the adjusting entry to record the accrued fees.

b. ▬▬▬➤ If the cash basis rather than the accrual basis had been used, would an adjusting entry have been necessary? Explain.

SHOW
ME HOW

### EX 3-11 Adjusting entries for unearned and accrued fees                    OBJ. 2

The balance in the unearned fees account, before adjustment at the end of the year, is $97,770. Of these fees, $82,220 have been earned. In addition, $34,250 of fees have been earned but have not been billed. Journalize the adjusting entries (a) to adjust the unearned fees account and (b) to record the accrued fees.

### EX 3-12 Effect of omitting adjusting entry                    OBJ. 2, 3

The adjusting entry for accrued fees was omitted at October 31, the end of the current year. Indicate which items will be in error, because of the omission, on (a) the income statement for the current year and (b) the balance sheet as of October 31. Also indicate whether the items in error will be overstated or understated.

✔ a. Amount of entry: $9,960

### EX 3-13 Adjusting entries for accrued salaries                    OBJ. 2

Ocular Realty Co. pays weekly salaries of $16,600 on Friday for a five-day workweek ending on that day. Journalize the necessary adjusting entry at the end of the accounting period, assuming that the period ends (a) on Wednesday and (b) on Thursday.

SHOW
ME HOW

### EX 3-14 Determining wages paid                    OBJ. 2

The wages payable and wages expense accounts at May 31, after adjusting entries have been posted at the end of the first month of operations, are shown in the following T accounts:

| Wages Payable | | Wages Expense | |
|---|---|---|---|
| Bal. | 7,175 | Bal. 73,250 | |

Determine the amount of wages paid during the month.

### EX 3-15   Effect of omitting adjusting entry      OBJ. 2, 3

Accrued salaries owed to employees for October 30 and 31 are not considered in preparing the financial statements for the year ended October 31. Indicate which items will be erroneously stated, because of the error, on (a) the income statement for the year and (b) the balance sheet as of October 31. Also indicate whether the items in error will be overstated or understated.

### EX 3-16   Effect of omitting adjusting entry      OBJ. 2, 3

Assume that the error in Exercise 3-15 was not corrected and that the accrued salaries were included in the first salary payment in November. Indicate which items will be erroneously stated, because of failure to correct the initial error, on (a) the income statement for the month of November and (b) the balance sheet as of November 30.

✔ b. $67,000

SHOW
ME HOW

### EX 3-17   Adjusting entries for prepaid and accrued taxes      OBJ. 2

Art Imaging Company was organized on April 1 of the current year. On April 2, Art Imaging Company prepaid $54,000 to the city for taxes (license fees) for the *next* 12 months and debited the prepaid taxes account. Art Imaging Company is also required to pay in January an annual tax (on property) for the *previous* calendar year. The estimated amount of the property tax for the current year (April 1 to December 31) is $26,500.

a. Journalize the two adjusting entries required to bring the accounts affected by the two taxes up to date as of December 31, the end of the current year.

b. What is the amount of tax expense for the current year?

SHOW
ME HOW

### EX 3-18   Adjustment for depreciation      OBJ. 2

The estimated amount of depreciation on equipment for the current year is $10,650. Journalize the adjusting entry to record the depreciation.

SHOW
ME HOW

### EX 3-19   Determining fixed asset's book value      OBJ. 2

The balance in the equipment account is $28,650,000, and the balance in the accumulated depreciation—equipment account is $16,430,000.

a. What is the book value of the equipment?

b.  ⟶ Does the balance in the accumulated depreciation account mean that the equipment's loss of value is $16,430,000? Explain.

### EX 3-20   Book value of fixed assets      OBJ. 2

In a recent balance sheet, **Microsoft Corporation** reported *Property, Plant, and Equipment* of $19,231 million and *Accumulated Depreciation* of $10,962 million.

a. What was the book value of the fixed assets?

b.  ⟶ Would the book value of Microsoft Corporation's fixed assets normally approximate their fair market values?

### EX 3-21   Effects of errors on financial statements      OBJ. 2, 3

For a recent period, the balance sheet for **Costco Wholesale Corporation** reported accrued expenses of $2,890 million. For the same period, Costco reported income before income taxes of $2,767 million. Assume that the adjusting entry for $2,890 million of accrued expenses was not recorded at the end of the current period. What would have been the income (loss) before income taxes?

**EX 3-22**    **Effects of errors on financial statements**      OBJ. 2, 3

For a recent year, the balance sheet for **The Campbell Soup Company** includes accrued expenses of $598 million. The income before taxes for The Campbell Soup Company for the year was $1,106 million.

a. Assume the adjusting entry for $598 million of accrued expenses was not recorded at the end of the year. By how much would income before taxes have been misstated?

b. What is the percentage of the misstatement in (a) to the reported income of $1,106 million? Round to one decimal place.

**EX 3-23**    **Effects of errors on financial statements**      OBJ. 2, 3

✔ 1. a. Revenue understated, $34,900

The accountant for Healthy Life Company, a medical services consulting firm, mistakenly omitted adjusting entries for (a) unearned revenue earned during the year ($34,900) and (b) accrued wages ($12,770). Indicate the effect of each error, considered individually, on the income statement for the current year ended July 31. Also indicate the effect of each error on the July 31 balance sheet. Set up a table similar to the following, and record your answers by inserting the dollar amount in the appropriate spaces. Insert a zero if the error does not affect the item.

| | Error (a) | | Error (b) | |
|---|---|---|---|---|
| | Over-stated | Under-stated | Over-stated | Under-stated |
| 1. Revenue for the year would be | $ ____ | $ ____ | $ ____ | $ ____ |
| 2. Expenses for the year would be | $ ____ | $ ____ | $ ____ | $ ____ |
| 3. Net income for the year would be | $ ____ | $ ____ | $ ____ | $ ____ |
| 4. Assets at July 31 would be | $ ____ | $ ____ | $ ____ | $ ____ |
| 5. Liabilities at July 31 would be | $ ____ | $ ____ | $ ____ | $ ____ |
| 6. Owner's equity at July 31 would be | $ ____ | $ ____ | $ ____ | $ ____ |

**EX 3-24**    **Effects of errors on financial statements**      OBJ. 2, 3

If the net income for the current year had been $196,400 in Exercise 3-23, what would have been the correct net income if the proper adjusting entries had been made?

**EX 3-25**    **Adjusting entries for depreciation; effect of error**      OBJ. 2, 3

SHOW
ME HOW

On December 31, a business estimates depreciation on equipment used during the first year of operations to be $13,900.

a. Journalize the adjusting entry required as of December 31.

b. If the adjusting entry in (a) were omitted, which items would be erroneously stated on (1) the income statement for the year and (2) the balance sheet as of December 31?

**EX 3-26**    **Adjusting entries from trial balances**      OBJ. 4

SHOW
ME HOW

The unadjusted and adjusted trial balances for American Leaf Company on October 31, 2016, follow:

(Continued)

**American Leaf Company**
**Trial Balances**
**October 31, 2016**

| | Unadjusted | | Adjusted | |
|---|---|---|---|---|
| | Debit Balances | Credit Balances | Debit Balances | Credit Balances |
| Cash .......................................... | 16 | | 16 | |
| Accounts Receivable............................ | 38 | | 44 | |
| Supplies...................................... | 12 | | 10 | |
| Prepaid Insurance .............................. | 20 | | 8 | |
| Land ......................................... | 26 | | 26 | |
| Equipment..................................... | 40 | | 40 | |
| Accumulated Depreciation—Equipment ......... | | 8 | | 12 |
| Accounts Payable ............................. | | 26 | | 26 |
| Wages Payable................................. | | 0 | | 2 |
| Sloane Kissel, Capital .......................... | | 92 | | 92 |
| Sloane Kissel, Drawing.......................... | 8 | | 8 | |
| Fees Earned................................... | | 74 | | 80 |
| Wages Expense ................................ | 24 | | 26 | |
| Rent Expense .................................. | 8 | | 8 | |
| Insurance Expense ............................. | 0 | | 12 | |
| Utilities Expense .............................. | 4 | | 4 | |
| Depreciation Expense .......................... | 0 | | 4 | |
| Supplies Expense............................... | 0 | | 2 | |
| Miscellaneous Expense ......................... | 4 | | 4 | |
| | 200 | 200 | 212 | 212 |

Journalize the five entries that adjusted the accounts at October 31, 2016. None of the accounts were affected by more than one adjusting entry.

**EX 3-27** **Adjusting entries from trial balances** OBJ. 4

✔ Corrected trial balance totals, $369,000

The accountant for Eva's Laundry prepared the following unadjusted and adjusted trial balances. Assume that all balances in the unadjusted trial balance and the amounts of the adjustments are correct. Identify the errors in the accountant's adjusting entries, assuming that none of the accounts were affected by more than one adjusting entry.

**Eva's Laundry**
**Trial Balances**
**May 31, 2016**

| | Unadjusted | | Adjusted | |
|---|---|---|---|---|
| | Debit Balances | Credit Balances | Debit Balances | Credit Balances |
| Cash ........................................... | 7,500 | | 7,500 | |
| Accounts Receivable............................. | 18,250 | | 23,250 | |
| Laundry Supplies................................. | 3,750 | | 6,750 | |
| Prepaid Insurance* .............................. | 5,200 | | 1,600 | |
| Laundry Equipment .............................. | 190,000 | | 177,000 | |
| Accumulated Depreciation—Laundry Equipment.... | | 48,000 | | 48,000 |
| Accounts Payable ................................ | | 9,600 | | 9,600 |
| Wages Payable................................... | | | | 1,000 |
| Eva Bruns, Capital ............................... | | 110,300 | | 110,300 |
| Eva Bruns, Drawing............................... | 28,775 | | 28,775 | |
| Laundry Revenue................................. | | 182,100 | | 182,100 |
| Wages Expense .................................. | 49,200 | | 49,200 | |
| Rent Expense .................................... | 25,575 | | 25,575 | |
| Utilities Expense ................................ | 18,500 | | 18,500 | |
| Depreciation Expense ............................ | | | 13,000 | |
| Laundry Supplies Expense ........................ | | | 3,000 | |
| Insurance Expense ............................... | | | 600 | |
| Miscellaneous Expense ........................... | 3,250 | | 3,250 | |
| | 350,000 | 350,000 | 358,000 | 351,000 |

* $3,600 of insurance expired during the year.

### EX 3-28 Vertical analysis of income statement

OBJ. 5

**FAI**

The following data (in millions) are taken from recent financial statements of Nike Inc.:

|  | Year 2 | Year 1 |
|---|---|---|
| Net sales (revenues) | $24,128 | $20,862 |
| Net income | 2,223 | 2,133 |

a. Determine the amount of change (in millions) and percent of change in net income for Year 2. Round to one decimal place.

b. Determine the percentage relationship between net income and net sales (net income divided by net sales) for Year 2 and Year 1. Round to one decimal place.

c. ➤ What conclusions can you draw from your analysis?

### EX 3-29 Vertical analysis of income statement

OBJ. 5

**FAI**

The following income statement data (in millions) for Dell Inc. and Hewlett-Packard Company (HP) were taken from their recent annual reports:

|  | Dell | Hewlett-Packard |
|---|---|---|
| Net sales | $62,071 | $120,357 |
| Cost of goods sold (expense) | (48,260) | (92,385) |
| Operating expenses | (9,380) | (39,029) |
| Operating income (loss) | $ 4,431 | $ (11,057) |

a. Prepare a vertical analysis of the income statement for Dell. Round to one decimal place.

b. Prepare a vertical analysis of the income statement for HP. Round to one decimal place.

c. ➤ Based on (a) and (b), how does Dell compare to HP?

## Problems: Series A

### PR 3-1A Adjusting entries

OBJ. 2

SHOW
ME HOW

On March 31, 2016, the following data were accumulated to assist the accountant in preparing the adjusting entries for Potomac Realty:

a. The supplies account balance on March 31 is $5,620 The supplies on hand on March 31 are $1,290.

b. The unearned rent account balance on March 31 is $5,000 representing the receipt of an advance payment on March 1 of four months' rent from tenants.

c. Wages accrued but not paid at March 31 are $2,290.

d. Fees accrued but unbilled at March 31 are $16,825.

e. Depreciation of office equipment is $4,600.

**Instructions**

1. Journalize the adjusting entries required at March 31, 2016.

2. ➤ Briefly explain the difference between adjusting entries and entries that would be made to correct errors.

### PR 3-2A Adjusting entries

OBJ. 2, 3

SHOW
ME HOW

Selected account balances before adjustment for Alantic Coast Realty at July 31, 2016, the end of the current year, are as follows:

*(Continued)*

|  | Debits | Credits |
|---|---|---|
| Accounts Receivable | $ 75,000 | |
| Equipment | 345,700 | |
| Accumulated Depreciation—Equipment | | $112,500 |
| Prepaid Rent | 9,000 | |
| Supplies | 3,350 | |
| Wages Payable | | — |
| Unearned Fees | | 12,000 |
| Fees Earned | | 660,000 |
| Wages Expense | 325,000 | |
| Rent Expense | — | |
| Depreciation Expense | — | |
| Supplies Expense | — | |

Data needed for year-end adjustments are as follows:

a. Unbilled fees at July 31, $11,150.

b. Supplies on hand at July 31, $900.

c. Rent expired, $6,000.

d. Depreciation of equipment during year, $8,950.

e. Unearned fees at July 31, $2,000.

f. Wages accrued but not paid at July 31, $4,840.

### Instructions

1. Journalize the six adjusting entries required at July 31, based on the data presented.

2. What would be the effect on the income statement if adjustments (a) and (f) were omitted at the end of the year?

3. What would be the effect on the balance sheet if adjustments (a) and (f) were omitted at the end of the year?

4. What would be the effect on the "Net increase or decrease in cash" on the statement of cash flows if adjustments (a) and (f) were omitted at the end of the year?

---

**PR 3-3A  Adjusting entries**                                    OBJ. 2, 3

Reliable Repairs & Service, an electronics repair store, prepared the following unadjusted trial balance at the end of its first year of operations:

General Ledger

**Reliable Repairs & Service**
**Unadjusted Trial Balance**
**April 30, 2016**

|  | Debit Balances | Credit Balances |
|---|---|---|
| Cash ...................................................... | 10,350 | |
| Accounts Receivable............................. | 67,500 | |
| Supplies.................................................. | 16,200 | |
| Equipment.............................................. | 116,100 | |
| Accounts Payable .................................. | | 15,750 |
| Unearned Fees....................................... | | 18,000 |
| Karin Bickle, Capital ............................. | | 121,500 |
| Karin Bickle, Drawing........................... | 13,500 | |
| Fees Earned............................................ | | 294,750 |
| Wages Expense ...................................... | 94,500 | |
| Rent Expense .......................................... | 72,000 | |
| Utilities Expense .................................... | 51,750 | |
| Miscellaneous Expense ......................... | 8,100 | |
|  | 450,000 | 450,000 |

For preparing the adjusting entries, the following data were assembled:

a. Fees earned but unbilled on April 30 were $9,850.

b. Supplies on hand on April 30 were $4,660.

c. Depreciation of equipment was estimated to be $6,470 for the year.

d. The balance in unearned fees represented the April 1 receipt in advance for services to be provided. During April, $15,000 of the services were provided.

e. Unpaid wages accrued on April 30 were $5,200.

### Instructions

1. Journalize the adjusting entries necessary on April 30, 2016.

2. Determine the revenues, expenses, and net income of Reliable Service & Repairs before the adjusting entries.

3. Determine the revenues, expense, and net income of Reliable Service & Repairs after the adjusting entries.

4. Determine the effect of the adjusting entries on Karin Bickle, Capital.

---

### PR 3-4A Adjusting entries

OBJ. 2, 3, 4

General Ledger

Good Note Company specializes in the repair of music equipment and is owned and operated by Robin Stahl. On November 30, 2016, the end of the current year, the accountant for Good Note Company prepared the following trial balances:

**Good Note Company**
**Trial Balances**
**November 30, 2016**

| | Unadjusted | | Adjusted | |
|---|---|---|---|---|
| | Debit Balances | Credit Balances | Debit Balances | Credit Balances |
| Cash | 38,250 | | 38,250 | |
| Accounts Receivable | 89,500 | | 89,500 | |
| Supplies | 11,250 | | 2,400 | |
| Prepaid Insurance | 14,250 | | 3,850 | |
| Equipment | 290,450 | | 290,450 | |
| Accumulated Depreciation—Equipment | | 94,500 | | 106,100 |
| Automobiles | 129,500 | | 129,500 | |
| Accumulated Depreciation—Automobiles | | 54,750 | | 62,050 |
| Accounts Payable | | 24,930 | | 26,130 |
| Salaries Payable | | — | | 8,100 |
| Unearned Service Fees | | 18,000 | | 9,000 |
| Robin Stahl, Capital | | 324,020 | | 324,020 |
| Robin Stahl, Drawing | 75,000 | | 75,000 | |
| Service Fees Earned | | 733,800 | | 742,800 |
| Salary Expense | 516,900 | | 525,000 | |
| Rent Expense | 54,000 | | 54,000 | |
| Supplies Expense | — | | 8,850 | |
| Depreciation Expense—Equipment | — | | 11,600 | |
| Depreciation Expense—Automobiles | — | | 7,300 | |
| Utilities Expense | 12,900 | | 14,100 | |
| Taxes Expense | 8,175 | | 8,175 | |
| Insurance Expense | — | | 10,400 | |
| Miscellaneous Expense | 9,825 | | 9,825 | |
| | 1,250,000 | 1,250,000 | 1,278,200 | 1,278,200 |

### Instructions

Journalize the seven entries that adjusted the accounts at November 30. None of the accounts were affected by more than one adjusting entry.

### PR 3-5A    Adjusting entries and adjusted trial balances

OBJ. 2, 3, 4

Rowland Company is a small editorial services company owned and operated by Marlene Rowland. On August 31, 2016, the end of the current year, Rowland Company's accounting clerk prepared the following unadjusted trial balance:

**Rowland Company**
**Unadjusted Trial Balance**
**August 31, 2016**

|  | Debit Balances | Credit Balances |
|---|---|---|
| Cash ........................................................ | 7,500 | |
| Accounts Receivable........................................ | 38,400 | |
| Prepaid Insurance .......................................... | 7,200 | |
| Supplies..................................................... | 1,980 | |
| Land ........................................................ | 112,500 | |
| Building ..................................................... | 150,250 | |
| Accumulated Depreciation—Building......................... | | 87,550 |
| Equipment................................................... | 135,300 | |
| Accumulated Depreciation—Equipment ..................... | | 97,950 |
| Accounts Payable ........................................... | | 12,150 |
| Unearned Rent.............................................. | | 6,750 |
| Marlene Rowland, Capital.................................... | | 221,000 |
| Marlene Rowland, Drawing ................................. | 15,000 | |
| Fees Earned................................................. | | 324,600 |
| Salaries and Wages Expense................................. | 193,370 | |
| Utilities Expense ............................................ | 42,375 | |
| Advertising Expense......................................... | 22,800 | |
| Repairs Expense............................................. | 17,250 | |
| Miscellaneous Expense ..................................... | 6,075 | |
| | 750,000 | 750,000 |

The data needed to determine year-end adjustments are as follows:

a.  Unexpired insurance at August 31, $6,000.

b.  Supplies on hand at August 31, $480.

c.  Depreciation of building for the year, $7,500.

d.  Depreciation of equipment for the year, $4,150.

e.  Rent unearned at August 31, $1,550.

f.  Accrued salaries and wages at August 31, $3,200.

g.  Fees earned but unbilled on August 31, $11,330.

**Instructions**

1.  Journalize the adjusting entries using the following additional accounts: Salaries and Wages Payable; Rent Revenue; Insurance Expense; Depreciation Expense—Building; Depreciation Expense—Equipment; and Supplies Expense.

2.  Determine the balances of the accounts affected by the adjusting entries, and prepare an adjusted trial balance.

### PR 3-6A    Adjusting entries and errors

OBJ. 2, 3

At the end of April, the first month of operations, the following selected data were taken from the financial statements of Shelby Crawford, an attorney:

| | |
|---|---|
| Net income for April | $120,000 |
| Total assets at April 30 | 750,000 |
| Total liabilities at April 30 | 300,000 |
| Total owner's equity at April 30 | 450,000 |

In preparing the financial statements, adjustments for the following data were overlooked:

a.  Supplies used during April, $2,750.

b.  Unbilled fees earned at April 30, $23,700.

c.  Depreciation of equipment for April, $1,800.

d.  Accrued wages at April 30, $1,400.

**Instructions**

1. Journalize the entries to record the omitted adjustments.

2. Determine the correct amount of net income for April and the total assets, liabilities, and owner's equity at April 30. In addition to indicating the corrected amounts, indicate the effect of each omitted adjustment by setting up and completing a columnar table similar to the following. Adjustment (a) is presented as an example.

| | Net Income | Total Assets | = Total Liabilities | + Total Owner's Equity |
|---|---|---|---|---|
| Reported amounts | $120,000 | $750,000 | $300,000 | $450,000 |
| Corrections: | | | | |
| Adjustment (a) | –2,750 | –2,750 | 0 | –2,750 |
| Adjustment (b) | | | | |
| Adjustment (c) | | | | |
| Adjustment (d) | | | | |
| Corrected amounts | | | | |

## Problems: Series B

SHOW
ME HOW

**PR 3-1B   Adjusting entries**                                                        OBJ. 2

On May 31, 2016, the following data were accumulated to assist the accountant in preparing the adjusting entries for Oceanside Realty:

a. Fees accrued but unbilled at May 31 are $19,750.

b. The supplies account balance on May 31 is $12,300. The supplies on hand at May 31 are $4,150.

c. Wages accrued but not paid at May 31 are $2,700.

d. The unearned rent account balance at May 31 is $9,000, representing the receipt of an advance payment on May 1 of three months' rent from tenants.

e. Depreciation of office equipment is $3,200.

**Instructions**

1. Journalize the adjusting entries required at May 31, 2016.

2. ━━━▶ Briefly explain the difference between adjusting entries and entries that would be made to correct errors.

SHOW
ME HOW

**PR 3-2B   Adjusting entries**                                                        OBJ. 2, 3

Selected account balances before adjustment for Intuit Realty at November 30, the end of the current year, follow:

| | Debits | Credits |
|---|---|---|
| Accounts Receivable | $ 75,000 | |
| Equipment | 250,000 | |
| Accumulated Depreciation—Equipment | | $ 12,000 |
| Prepaid Rent | 12,000 | |
| Supplies | 3,170 | |
| Wages Payable | | — |
| Unearned Fees | | 10,000 |
| Fees Earned | | 400,000 |
| Wages Expense | 140,000 | |
| Rent Expense | — | |
| Depreciation Expense | — | |
| Supplies Expense | — | |

Data needed for year-end adjustments are as follows:

a. Supplies on hand at November 30, $550.

b. Depreciation of equipment during year, $1,675.

*(Continued)*

c.  Rent expired during year, $8,500.

d.  Wages accrued but not paid at November 30, $2,000.

e.  Unearned fees at November 30, $4,000.

f.  Unbilled fees at November 30, $5,380.

### Instructions

1.  Journalize the six adjusting entries required at November 30, based on the data presented.

2.  What would be the effect on the income statement if adjustments (b) and (e) were omitted at the end of the year?

3.  What would be the effect on the balance sheet if adjustments (b) and (e) were omitted at the end of the year?

4.  What would be the effect on the "Net increase or decrease in cash" on the statement of cash flows if adjustments (b) and (e) were omitted at the end of the year?

### PR 3-3B    Adjusting entries

OBJ. 2, 3

General Ledger

Crazy Mountain Outfitters Co., an outfitter store for fishing treks, prepared the following unadjusted trial balance at the end of its first year of operations:

**Crazy Mountain Outfitters Co.**
**Unadjusted Trial Balance**
**April 30, 2016**

|  | Debit Balances | Credit Balances |
|---|---|---|
| Cash | 11,400 | |
| Accounts Receivable | 72,600 | |
| Supplies | 7,200 | |
| Equipment | 112,000 | |
| Accounts Payable | | 12,200 |
| Unearned Fees | | 19,200 |
| Diana Keck, Capital | | 137,800 |
| Diana Keck, Drawing | 10,000 | |
| Fees Earned | | 305,800 |
| Wages Expense | 157,800 | |
| Rent Expense | 55,000 | |
| Utilities Expense | 42,000 | |
| Miscellaneous Expense | 7,000 | |
| | 475,000 | 475,000 |

For preparing the adjusting entries, the following data were assembled:

a.  Supplies on hand on April 30 were $1,380.

b.  Fees earned but unbilled on April 30 were $3,900.

c.  Depreciation of equipment was estimated to be $3,000 for the year.

d.  Unpaid wages accrued on April 30 were $2,475.

e.  The balance in unearned fees represented the April 1 receipt in advance for services to be provided. Only $14,140 of the services was provided between April 1 and April 30.

### Instructions

1.  Journalize the adjusting entries necessary on April 30, 2016.

2.  Determine the revenues, expenses, and net income of Crazy Mountain Outfitters Co. before the adjusting entries.

3.  Determine the revenues, expense, and net income of Crazy Mountain Outfitters Co. after the adjusting entries.

4.  Determine the effect of the adjusting entries on Diana Keck, Capital.

### PR 3-4B    Adjusting entries

OBJ. 2, 3, 4

General Ledger

The Signage Company specializes in the maintenance and repair of signs, such as billboards. On March 31, 2016, the accountant for The Signage Company prepared the following trial balances:

**The Signage Company**
**Trial Balances**
**March 31, 2016**

| | Unadjusted Debit Balances | Unadjusted Credit Balances | Adjusted Debit Balances | Adjusted Credit Balances |
|---|---|---|---|---|
| Cash .................................................. | 4,750 | | 4,750 | |
| Accounts Receivable................................. | 17,400 | | 17,400 | |
| Supplies ............................................. | 6,200 | | 2,175 | |
| Prepaid Insurance .................................... | 9,000 | | 1,150 | |
| Land .................................................. | 100,000 | | 100,000 | |
| Buildings ............................................ | 170,000 | | 170,000 | |
| Accumulated Depreciation—Buildings................ | | 51,500 | | 61,000 |
| Trucks ................................................ | 75,000 | | 75,000 | |
| Accumulated Depreciation—Trucks.................... | | 12,000 | | 17,000 |
| Accounts Payable .................................... | | 6,920 | | 8,750 |
| Salaries Payable...................................... | | — | | 1,400 |
| Unearned Service Fees................................ | | 10,500 | | 3,850 |
| Al Bosch, Capital .................................... | | 256,400 | | 256,400 |
| Al Bosch, Drawing.................................... | 7,500 | | 7,500 | |
| Service Fees Earned ................................. | | 162,680 | | 169,330 |
| Salary Expense....................................... | 80,000 | | 81,400 | |
| Depreciation Expense—Trucks ...................... | — | | 5,000 | |
| Rent Expense ........................................ | 11,900 | | 11,900 | |
| Supplies Expense..................................... | — | | 4,025 | |
| Utilities Expense ..................................... | 6,200 | | 8,030 | |
| Depreciation Expense—Buildings .................... | — | | 9,500 | |
| Taxes Expense ....................................... | 2,900 | | 2,900 | |
| Insurance Expense ................................... | — | | 7,850 | |
| Miscellaneous Expense .............................. | 9,150 | | 9,150 | |
| | 500,000 | 500,000 | 517,730 | 517,730 |

**Instructions**

Journalize the seven entries that adjusted the accounts at March 31. None of the accounts were affected by more than one adjusting entry.

**PR 3-5B    Adjusting entries and adjusted trial balances**          OBJ. 2, 3, 4

✔ 2. Total of Debit column: $420,300

General Ledger

Reece Financial Services Co., which specializes in appliance repair services, is owned and operated by Joni Reece. Reece Financial Services Co.'s accounting clerk prepared the following unadjusted trial balance at July 31, 2016:

**Reece Financial Services Co.**
**Unadjusted Trial Balance**
**July 31, 2016**

| | Debit Balances | Credit Balances |
|---|---|---|
| Cash ................................................... | 10,200 | |
| Accounts Receivable.................................... | 34,750 | |
| Prepaid Insurance ..................................... | 6,000 | |
| Supplies ............................................... | 1,725 | |
| Land ................................................... | 50,000 | |
| Building ............................................... | 155,750 | |
| Accumulated Depreciation—Building.................... | | 62,850 |
| Equipment............................................. | 45,000 | |
| Accumulated Depreciation—Equipment ................ | | 17,650 |
| Accounts Payable ..................................... | | 3,750 |
| Unearned Rent ........................................ | | 3,600 |
| Joni Reece, Capital .................................... | | 153,550 |
| Joni Reece, Drawing ................................... | 8,000 | |
| Fees Earned............................................ | | 158,600 |
| Salaries and Wages Expense............................ | 56,850 | |
| Utilities Expense ...................................... | 14,100 | |
| Advertising Expense ................................... | 7,500 | |
| Repairs Expense........................................ | 6,100 | |
| Miscellaneous Expense ................................ | 4,025 | |
| | 400,000 | 400,000 |

(Continued)

The data needed to determine year-end adjustments are as follows:

a. Depreciation of building for the year, $6,400.

b. Depreciation of equipment for the year, $2,800.

c. Accrued salaries and wages at July 31, $900.

d. Unexpired insurance at July 31, $1,500.

e. Fees earned but unbilled on July 31, $10,200.

f. Supplies on hand at July 31, $615.

g. Rent unearned at July 31, $300.

### Instructions

1. Journalize the adjusting entries using the following additional accounts: Salaries and Wages Payable; Rent Revenue; Insurance Expense; Depreciation Expense—Building; Depreciation Expense—Equipment; and Supplies Expense.

2. Determine the balances of the accounts affected by the adjusting entries and prepare an adjusted trial balance.

---

**✔ 2. Corrected net income: $128,700**

**PR 3-6B   Adjusting entries and errors**                                          **OBJ. 2, 3**

At the end of August, the first month of operations, the following selected data were taken from the financial statements of Tucker Jacobs, an attorney:

| | |
|---|---|
| Net income for August | $112,500 |
| Total assets at August 31 | 650,000 |
| Total liabilities at August 31 | 225,000 |
| Total owner's equity at August 31 | 425,000 |

In preparing the financial statements, adjustments for the following data were overlooked:

a. Unbilled fees earned at August 31, $31,900.

b. Depreciation of equipment for August, $7,500.

c. Accrued wages at August 31, $5,200.

d. Supplies used during August, $3,000.

### Instructions

1. Journalize the entries to record the omitted adjustments.

2. Determine the correct amount of net income for August and the total assets, liabilities, and owner's equity at August 31. In addition to indicating the corrected amounts, indicate the effect of each omitted adjustment by setting up and completing a columnar table similar to the following. Adjustment (a) is presented as an example.

| | Net Income | Total Assets | = Total Liabilities | + Total Owner's Equity |
|---|---|---|---|---|
| Reported amounts | $112,500 | $650,000 | $225,000 | $425,000 |
| Corrections: | | | | |
| Adjustment (a) | +31,900 | +31,900 | 0 | +31,900 |
| Adjustment (b) | _____ | _____ | _____ | _____ |
| Adjustment (c) | _____ | _____ | _____ | _____ |
| Adjustment (d) | _____ | _____ | _____ | _____ |
| Corrected amounts | | | | |

# Continuing Problem

**✔ 3. Total of Debit column: $42,340**

**General Ledger**

The unadjusted trial balance that you prepared for PS Music at the end of Chapter 2 should appear as follows:

**PS Music**
**Unadjusted Trial Balance**
**July 31, 2016**

| | Debit Balances | Credit Balances |
|---|---|---|
| Cash ........................................................... | 9,945 | |
| Accounts Receivable........................................... | 2,750 | |
| Supplies....................................................... | 1,020 | |
| Prepaid Insurance ............................................. | 2,700 | |
| Office Equipment ............................................. | 7,500 | |
| Accounts Payable ............................................. | | 8,350 |
| Unearned Revenue............................................. | | 7,200 |
| Peyton Smith, Capital.......................................... | | 9,000 |
| Peyton Smith, Drawing ........................................ | 1,750 | |
| Fees Earned................................................... | | 16,200 |
| Music Expense ................................................ | 3,610 | |
| Wages Expense ............................................... | 2,800 | |
| Office Rent Expense ........................................... | 2,550 | |
| Advertising Expense........................................... | 1,500 | |
| Equipment Rent Expense ...................................... | 1,375 | |
| Utilities Expense .............................................. | 1,215 | |
| Supplies Expense.............................................. | 180 | |
| Miscellaneous Expense ........................................ | 1,855 | |
| | 40,750 | 40,750 |

The data needed to determine adjustments are as follows:

a.  During July, PS Music provided guest disc jockeys for KXMD for a total of 115 hours. For information on the amount of the accrued revenue to be billed to KXMD, see the contract described in the July 3, 2016, transaction at the end of Chapter 2.

b.  Supplies on hand at July 31, $275.

c.  The balance of the prepaid insurance account relates to the July 1, 2016, transaction at the end of Chapter 2.

d.  Depreciation of the office equipment is $50.

e.  The balance of the unearned revenue account relates to the contract between PS Music and KXMD, described in the July 3, 2016, transaction at the end of Chapter 2.

f.  Accrued wages as of July 31, 2016, were $140.

**Instructions**

1.  Prepare adjusting journal entries. You will need the following additional accounts:

   18 Accumulated Depreciation—Office Equipment

   22 Wages Payable

   57 Insurance Expense

   58 Depreciation Expense

2.  Post the adjusting entries, inserting balances in the accounts affected.

3.  Prepare an adjusted trial balance.

# Cases & Projects

### CP 3-1  Ethics and professional conduct in business

Daryl Kirby opened Squid Realty Co. on January 1, 2015. At the end of the first year, the business needed additional capital. On behalf of Squid Realty Co., Daryl applied to Ocean National Bank for a loan of $375,000. Based on Squid Realty Co.'s financial statements, which had been prepared on a cash basis, the Ocean National Bank loan officer rejected the loan as too risky.

*(Continued)*

After receiving the rejection notice, Daryl instructed his accountant to prepare the financial statements on an accrual basis. These statements included $65,000 in accounts receivable and $25,000 in accounts payable. Daryl then instructed his accountant to record an additional $30,000 of accounts receivable for commissions on property for which a contract had been signed on December 28, 2015. The title to the property is to transfer on January 5, 2016, when an attorney formally records the transfer of the property to the buyer.

Daryl then applied for a $375,000 loan from Free Spirit Bank, using the revised financial statements. On this application, Daryl indicated that he had not previously been rejected for credit.

➤ Discuss the ethical and professional conduct of Daryl Kirby in applying for the loan from Free Spirit Bank.

### CP 3-2  Accrued revenue

The following is an excerpt from a conversation between Sonia Lopez and Pete Lemke just before they boarded a flight to Paris on **Delta Air Lines**. They are going to Paris to attend their company's annual sales conference.

*Sonia:* Pete, aren't you taking an introductory accounting course at college?

*Pete:* Yes, I decided it's about time I learned something about accounting. You know, our annual bonuses are based on the sales figures that come from the accounting department.

*Sonia:* I guess I never really thought about it.

*Pete:* You should think about it! Last year, I placed a $5,000,000 order on December 30. But when I got my bonus, the $5,000,000 sale wasn't included. They said it hadn't been shipped until January 9, so it would have to count in next year's bonus.

*Sonia:* A real bummer!

*Pete:* Right! I was counting on that bonus including the $5,000,000 sale.

*Sonia:* Did you complain?

*Pete:* Yes, but it didn't do any good. Julie, the head accountant, said something about matching revenues and expenses. Also, something about not recording revenues until the sale is final. I figure I'd take the accounting course and find out whether she's just messing with me.

*Sonia:* I never really thought about it. When do you think Delta Air Lines will record its revenues from this flight?

*Pete:* Hmmm . . . I guess it could record the revenue when it sells the ticket . . . or . . . when the boarding passes are scanned at the door . . . or . . . when we get off the plane . . . or when our company pays for the tickets . . . or . . . I don't know. I'll ask my accounting instructor.

➤ Discuss when Delta Air Lines should recognize the revenue from ticket sales to properly match revenues and expenses.

### CP 3-3  Adjustments and financial statements

Several years ago, your brother opened Magna Appliance Repairs. He made a small initial investment and added money from his personal bank account as needed. He withdrew money for living expenses at irregular intervals. As the business grew, he hired an assistant. He is now considering adding more employees, purchasing additional service trucks, and purchasing the building he now rents. To secure funds for the expansion, your brother submitted a loan application to the bank and included the most recent financial statements (which follow) prepared from accounts maintained by a part-time bookkeeper.

**Magna Appliance Repairs**
**Income Statement**
**For the Year Ended October 31, 2016**

| | | |
|---|---:|---:|
| Service revenue . . . . . . . . . . . . . . . . | | $675,000 |
| Less: Rent paid . . . . . . . . . . . . . . . . . | $187,200 | |
| Wages paid . . . . . . . . . . . . . . . | 148,500 | |
| Supplies paid . . . . . . . . . . . . . | 42,000 | |
| Utilities paid . . . . . . . . . . . . . . | 39,000 | |
| Insurance paid . . . . . . . . . . . . | 21,600 | |
| Miscellaneous payments. . . . | 54,600 | 492,900 |
| Net income . . . . . . . . . . . . . . . . . . . . | | $ 182,100 |

**Magna Appliance Repairs**
**Balance Sheet**
**October 31, 2016**

| Assets | |
|---|---:|
| Cash . . . . . . . . . . . . . . . . . . . . . . . . . . | $ 95,400 |
| Amounts due from customers . . . . | 112,500 |
| Truck . . . . . . . . . . . . . . . . . . . . . . . . . | 332,100 |
| Total assets . . . . . . . . . . . . . . . . . . . . | $540,000 |
| **Equities** | |
| Owner's capital . . . . . . . . . . . . . . . . | $540,000 |

After reviewing the financial statements, the loan officer at the bank asked your brother if he used the accrual basis of accounting for revenues and expenses. Your brother responded that he did and that is why he included an account for "Amounts Due from Customers." The loan officer then asked whether or not the accounts were adjusted prior to the preparation of the statements. Your brother answered that they had not been adjusted.

a. ━━━▶ Why do you think the loan officer suspected that the accounts had not been adjusted prior to the preparation of the statements?

b. Indicate possible accounts that might need to be adjusted before an accurate set of financial statements could be prepared.

---

**CP 3-4  Codes of ethics**

**Group Project**

Internet Project

Obtain a copy of your college or university's student code of conduct. In groups of three or four, answer the following questions:

1. Compare this code of conduct with the Institute of Management Accountants' *Statement of Ethical Professional Practice*, which can be obtained from the IMA Web site at www.imanet.org, and the American Institute of Certified Public Accountants' *Code of Professional Conduct*, which can be obtained from the AICPA Web site at www.aicpa.org.

2. One of your classmates asks you for permission to copy your homework, which your instructor will be collecting and grading for part of your overall term grade. Although your instructor has not stated whether one student may or may not copy another student's homework, is it ethical for you to allow your classmate to copy your homework? Is it ethical for your classmate to copy your homework?

# Completing the Accounting Cycle

## Zynga

**Z**ynga is a leading provider of social games with more than 240 million active players per month. Zynga's games, such as CityVille, FarmVille, CastleVille, and Café World, can be played on a variety of platforms including Facebook, Google Android, and Apple iOS.

Zynga was founded in 2007 and is named after CEO (Chief Executive Officer) Mark Pincus's dog. Zinga is an American Bulldog who is known for her human-like qualities, which include sitting on chairs and eating at the dinner table. Because she is playful, loyal, and lovable, Zinga is considered the guiding spirit of the company.

In developing its games, Zynga goes through a game development cycle that starts with the initial gaming concept, program development, and ends with testing and debugging errors. Businesses also go through a cycle of accounting activities that begins with

recording transactions and ends with preparing financial statements and getting the accounting records ready for recording the next period's transactions.

In Chapter 1, the initial accounting cycle for **NetSolutions** began with Chris Clark's investment in the business on November 1, 2015. The cycle continued with recording NetSolutions' transactions for November and December, as we discussed and illustrated in Chapters 1 and 2. In Chapter 3, the cycle continued when the adjusting entries for the two months ending December 31, 2015, were recorded. In this chapter, the cycle is completed for NetSolutions by preparing financial statements and getting the accounts ready for recording transactions of the next period.

*Source:* Zynga.com

**(OBJ 1)** Describe the flow of accounting information from the unadjusted trial balance into the adjusted trial balance and financial statements.
**Flow of Accounting Information** — EE 4-1

**(OBJ 2)** Prepare financial statements from adjusted account balances.
**Financial Statements**
   Income Statement
   Statement of Owner's Equity — EE 4-2
   Balance Sheet — EE 4-3

**(OBJ 3)** Prepare closing entries.
**Closing Entries**
   Journalizing and Posting Closing Entries — EE 4-4
   Post-Closing Trial Balance

**(OBJ 4)** Describe the accounting cycle.
**Accounting Cycle** — EE 4-5

**(OBJ 5)** Illustrate the accounting cycle for one period.
**Illustration of the Accounting Cycle**

**(OBJ 6)** Explain what is meant by the fiscal year and the natural business year.
**Fiscal Year**

**(OBJ 7)** Describe and illustrate the use of working capital and the current ratio in evaluating a company's financial condition.
**Financial Analysis and Interpretation: Working Capital and Current Ratio** — EE 4-6

**At a Glance  4 ▸** Page 184

---

**(OBJ 1)** Describe the flow of accounting information from the unadjusted trial balance into the adjusted trial balance and financial statements.

# Flow of Accounting Information

The process of adjusting the accounts and preparing financial statements is one of the most important in accounting. Using the **NetSolutions** illustration from Chapters 1–3 and an end-of-period spreadsheet, the flow of accounting data in adjusting accounts and preparing financial statements are summarized in Exhibit 1.

The end-of-period spreadsheet in Exhibit 1 begins with the unadjusted trial balance. The unadjusted trial balance verifies that the total of the debit balances equals the total of the credit balances. If the trial balance totals are unequal, an error has occurred. Any errors must be found and corrected before the end-of-period process can continue.

The adjustments for NetSolutions from Chapter 3 are shown in the Adjustments columns of the spreadsheet. Cross-referencing (by letters) the debit and credit of each adjustment is useful in reviewing the effect of the adjustments on the unadjusted account balances. The adjustments are normally entered in the order in which the data are assembled. If the titles of the accounts to be adjusted do not appear in the unadjusted trial balance, the accounts are inserted in their proper order in the Account Title column. The total of the Adjustments columns verifies that the total debits equal the total credits for the adjusting entries. The total of the Debit column must equal the total of the Credit column.

Many companies use **Microsoft's** Excel® software to prepare end-of-period spreadsheets.

The adjustments in the spreadsheet are added to or subtracted from the amounts in the Unadjusted Trial Balance columns to arrive at the amounts inserted in the Adjusted Trial Balance columns. In this way, the Adjusted Trial Balance columns of the spreadsheet illustrate the effect of the adjusting entries on the unadjusted accounts. The totals of the Adjusted Trial Balance columns verify that the totals of the debit and credit balances are equal after adjustment.

**EXHIBIT 1**

**End-of-Period Spreadsheet and Flow of Accounting Data, NetSolutions**

## NetSolutions
### Balance Sheet
### December 31, 2015

**Assets**

| | | | |
|---|---|---|---|
| Current assets: | | | |
| Cash | $ 2,065 | | |
| Accounts receivable | 2,720 | | |
| Supplies | 760 | | |
| Prepaid insurance | 2,200 | | |
| Total current assets | | $ 7,745 | |
| Property, plant, and equipment: | | | |
| Land | | $20,000 | |
| Office equipment | $1,800 | | |
| Less accum. depreciation | 50 | 1,750 | |
| Total property, plant, and equipment | | 21,750 | |
| Total assets | | $29,495 | |

**Liabilities**

| | | |
|---|---|---|
| Current liabilities: | | |
| Accounts payable | $900 | |
| Wages payable | 250 | |
| Unearned rent | 240 | |
| Total liabilities | | $ 1,390 |

**Owner's Equity**

| | | |
|---|---|---|
| Chris Clark, capital | | 28,105 |
| Total liabilities and owner's equity | | $29,495 |

## NetSolutions
### Statement of Owner's Equity
### For the Two Months Ended December 31, 2015

| | | |
|---|---|---|
| Chris Clark, capital, November 1, 2015 | | $ 0 |
| Investment on November 1, 2015 | $25,000 | |
| Net income for November and December | 7,105 | |
| | $32,105 | |
| Less withdrawals | 4,000 | |
| Increase in owner's equity | | 28,105 |
| Chris Clark, capital, December 31, 2015 | | $28,105 |

## NetSolutions
### Income Statement
### For the Two Months Ended December 31, 2015

| | | |
|---|---|---|
| Revenues: | | |
| Fees earned | $16,840 | |
| Rent revenue | 120 | |
| Total revenues | | $16,960 |
| Expenses: | | |
| Wages expense | $ 4,525 | |
| Supplies expense | 2,040 | |
| Rent expense | 1,600 | |
| Utilities expense | 985 | |
| Insurance expense | 200 | |
| Depreciation expense | 50 | |
| Miscellaneous expense | 455 | |
| Total expenses | | 9,855 |
| Net income | | $ 7,105 |

### NetSolutions
### End-of-Period Spreadsheet
### For the Two Months Ended December 31, 2015

| | Unadjusted Trial Balance | | Adjustments | | Adjusted Trial Balance | |
|---|---|---|---|---|---|---|
| Account Title | Dr. | Cr. | Dr. | Cr. | Dr. | Cr. |
| Cash | 2,065 | | | | 2,065 | |
| Accounts Receivable | 2,220 | | (d) 500 | | 2,720 | |
| Supplies | 2,000 | | | (a) 1,240 | 760 | |
| Prepaid Insurance | 2,400 | | | (b) 200 | 2,200 | |
| Land | 20,000 | | | | 20,000 | |
| Office Equipment | 1,800 | | | | 1,800 | |
| Accumulated Depreciation | | | | (f) 50 | | 50 |
| Accounts Payable | | 900 | | | | 900 |
| Wages Payable | | | | (e) 250 | | 250 |
| Unearned Rent | | 360 | (c) 120 | | | 240 |
| Chris Clark, Capital | | 25,000 | | | | 25,000 |
| Chris Clark, Drawing | 4,000 | | | | 4,000 | |
| Fees Earned | | 16,340 | | (d) 500 | | 16,840 |
| Rent Revenue | | | | (c) 120 | | 120 |
| Wages Expense | 4,275 | | (e) 250 | | 4,525 | |
| Supplies Expense | 800 | | (a) 1,240 | | 2,040 | |
| Rent Expense | 1,600 | | | | 1,600 | |
| Utilities Expense | 985 | | | | 985 | |
| Insurance Expense | | | (b) 200 | | 200 | |
| Depreciation Expense | | | (f) 50 | | 50 | |
| Miscellaneous Expense | 455 | | | | 455 | |
| | 42,600 | 42,600 | 2,360 | 2,360 | 43,400 | 43,400 |

Exhibit 1 illustrates the flow of accounts from the adjusted trial balance into the financial statements as follows:

1. The revenue and expense accounts (spreadsheet lines 20–28) flow into the income statement.
2. The owner's capital account, Chris Clark, Capital (spreadsheet line 18), and owner's drawing account, Chris Clark, Drawing (spreadsheet line 19), flow into the statement of owner's equity. The net income of $7,105 also flows into the statement of owner's equity from the income statement.
3. The asset and liability accounts (spreadsheet lines 8–17) flow into the balance sheet. The end-of-period owner's equity (Chris Clark, Capital of $28,105) also flows into the balance sheet from the statement of owner's equity.

To summarize, Exhibit 1 illustrates the process by which accounts are adjusted. In addition, Exhibit 1 illustrates how the adjusted accounts flow into the financial statements. The financial statements for NetSolutions can be prepared directly from Exhibit 1.

The spreadsheet in Exhibit 1 is not required. However, many accountants prepare such a spreadsheet, sometimes called a *work sheet*, as part of the normal end-of-period process. The primary advantage in doing so is that it allows managers and accountants to see the effect of adjustments on the financial statements. This is especially useful for adjustments that depend upon estimates. Such estimates and their effect on the financial statements are discussed in later chapters.[1]

## Example Exercise 4-1   Flow of Accounts into Financial Statements

The balances for the accounts that follow appear in the Adjusted Trial Balance columns of the end-of-period spreadsheet. Indicate whether each account would flow into the income statement, statement of owner's equity, or balance sheet.

1. Office Equipment
2. Utilities Expense
3. Accumulated Depreciation—Equipment
4. Unearned Rent

5. Fees Earned
6. Doug Johnson, Drawing
7. Rent Revenue
8. Supplies

### Follow My Example 4-1

1. Balance sheet
2. Income statement
3. Balance sheet
4. Balance sheet

5. Income statement
6. Statement of owner's equity
7. Income statement
8. Balance sheet

Practice Exercises: PE 4-1A, PE 4-1B

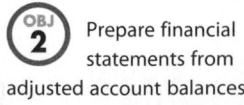

**OBJ 2** Prepare financial statements from adjusted account balances.

# Financial Statements

Using the adjusted trial balance shown in Exhibit 1, the financial statements for **NetSolutions** can be prepared. The income statement, the statement of owner's equity, and the balance sheet are shown in Exhibit 2.

## Income Statement

The income statement is prepared directly from the Adjusted Trial Balance columns of the Exhibit 1 spreadsheet, beginning with fees earned of $16,840. The expenses in the income statement in Exhibit 2 are listed in order of size, beginning with the larger items. Miscellaneous expense is the last item, regardless of its amount.

[1] The appendix to this chapter describes and illustrates how to prepare an end-of-period spreadsheet that includes financial statement columns.

| EXHIBIT 2 | **Financial Statements, NetSolutions** |

**NetSolutions**
**Income Statement**
**For the Two Months Ended December 31, 2015**

| | | |
|---|---:|---:|
| Fees earned.............................................. | $16,840 | |
| Rent revenue ........................................... | 120 | |
| Total revenues ...................................... | | $16,960 |
| Expenses: | | |
| Wages expense....................................... | $ 4,525 | |
| Supplies expense..................................... | 2,040 | |
| Rent expense ......................................... | 1,600 | |
| Utilities expense...................................... | 985 | |
| Insurance expense.................................... | 200 | |
| Depreciation expense................................ | 50 | |
| Miscellaneous expense ............................. | 455 | |
| Total expenses ................................... | | 9,855 |
| Net income .............................................. | | $ 7,105 |

**NetSolutions**
**Statement of Owner's Equity**
**For the Two Months Ended December 31, 2015**

| | | |
|---|---:|---:|
| Chris Clark, capital, November 1, 2015 ................................... | | $ 0 |
| Investment on November 1, 2015......................................... | $25,000 | |
| Net income for November and December .............................. | 7,105 | |
| | $32,105 | |
| Less withdrawals ..................................................... | 4,000 | |
| Increase in owner's equity ............................................ | | 28,105 |
| Chris Clark, capital, December 31, 2015 ................................. | | $28,105 |

**NetSolutions**
**Balance Sheet**
**December 31, 2015**

| Assets | | | Liabilities | | |
|---|---:|---:|---|---:|---:|
| Current assets: | | | Current liabilities: | | |
| Cash.................................. | $ 2,065 | | Accounts payable.................. | $900 | |
| Accounts receivable ................. | 2,720 | | Wages payable .................... | 250 | |
| Supplies ............................ | 760 | | Unearned rent..................... | 240 | |
| Prepaid insurance ................... | 2,200 | | Total liabilities...................... | | $ 1,390 |
| Total current assets............... | | $ 7,745 | | | |
| Property, plant, and equipment: | | | | | |
| Land.............................. | $20,000 | | | | |
| Office equipment......... $1,800 | | | | | |
| Less accum. depreciation... 50 | 1,750 | | **Owner's Equity** | | |
| Total property, plant, | | | Chris Clark, capital ................... | | 28,105 |
| and equipment ................. | | 21,750 | Total liabilities and | | |
| Total assets........................... | | $29,495 | owner's equity ..................... | | $29,495 |

# Integrity, Objectivity, and Ethics in Business

### CEO'S HEALTH?

How much and what information to disclose in financial statements and to investors presents a common ethical dilemma for managers and accountants. For example, Steve Jobs, co-founder and CEO of Apple Inc., had been diagnosed and treated for pancreatic cancer. Apple Inc. had insisted that the status of Steve Jobs's health was a "private" matter and did not have to be disclosed to investors. Apple maintained this position even though

Jobs was a driving force behind Apple's innovation and financial success.

However, in response to increasing investor concerns and speculation, Jobs released a letter on January 5, 2009, to investors on his health. The letter indicated that his recent weight loss was due to a hormone imbalance and not due to the recurrence of cancer. On October 5, 2011, Steve Jobs died at the age of 56.

## Statement of Owner's Equity

The first item presented on the statement of owner's equity is the balance of the owner's capital account at the beginning of the period. The amount listed as owner's capital in the spreadsheet, however, is not always the account balance at the beginning of the period. The owner may have invested additional assets in the business during the period. For the beginning balance and any additional investments, it is necessary to refer to the owner's capital account in the ledger. These amounts, along with the net income (or net loss) and the drawing account balance, are used to determine the ending owner's capital account balance.

The basic form of the statement of owner's equity is shown in Exhibit 2. For NetSolutions, the amount of drawings by the owner was less than the net income. If the owner's withdrawals had exceeded the net income, the difference between the two items would then be deducted from the beginning capital account balance. Other factors, such as additional investments or a net loss, also require some change in the form, as follows:

| | | |
|---|---:|---:|
| Allan Johnson, capital, January 1, 2015 | | $39,000 |
| Add: Investment during year | $ 6,000 | |
| Less: Net loss for year | (5,600) | |
| Withdrawals | (9,500) | |
| Decrease in owner's equity | | (9,100) |
| Allan Johnson, capital, December 31, 2015 | | $29,900 |

## Example Exercise 4-2  Statement of Owner's Equity

**OBJ 2**

Zack Gaddis owns and operates Gaddis Employment Services. On January 1, 2015, Zack Gaddis, Capital had a balance of $186,000. During the year, Zack invested an additional $40,000 and withdrew $25,000. For the year ended December 31, 2015, Gaddis Employment Services reported a net income of $18,750. Prepare a statement of owner's equity for the year ended December 31, 2015.

## Follow My Example 4-2

**Gaddis Employment Services**
**Statement of Owner's Equity**
**For the Year Ended December 31, 2015**

| | | |
|---|---:|---:|
| Zack Gaddis, capital, January 1, 2015............................ | | $186,000 |
| Add: Investment during 2015 .................................. | $40,000 | |
| Net income............................................. | 18,750 | |
| | $58,750 | |
| Less: Withdrawals............................................ | 25,000 | |
| Increase in owner's equity...................................... | | 33,750 |
| Zack Gaddis, capital, December 1, 2015 ...................... | | $219,750 |

Practice Exercises: PE 4-2A, PE 4-2B

# Balance Sheet

The balance sheet is prepared directly from the Adjusted Trial Balance columns of the Exhibit 1 spreadsheet, beginning with Cash of $2,065. The asset and liability amounts are taken from the spreadsheet. The owner's equity amount, however, is taken from the statement of owner's equity, as illustrated in Exhibit 2.

The balance sheet in Exhibit 2 shows subsections for assets and liabilities. Such a balance sheet is a *classified balance sheet*. These subsections are described next.

**Assets** Assets are commonly divided into two sections on the balance sheet: (1) current assets and (2) property, plant, and equipment.

*Current Assets* Cash and other assets that are expected to be converted to cash or sold or used up usually within one year or less, through the normal operations of the business, are called **current assets**. In addition to cash, the current assets may include notes receivable, accounts receivable, supplies, and other prepaid expenses.

**Notes receivable** are amounts that customers owe. They are written promises to pay the amount of the note and interest. Accounts receivable are also amounts customers owe, but they are less formal than notes. Accounts receivable normally result from providing services or selling merchandise on account. Notes receivable and accounts receivable are current assets because they are usually converted to cash within one year or less.

*Property, Plant, and Equipment* The property, plant, and equipment section may also be described as **fixed assets** or **plant assets**. These assets include equipment, machinery, buildings, and land. With the exception of land, as discussed in Chapter 3, fixed assets depreciate over a period of time. The original cost, accumulated depreciation, and book value of each major type of fixed asset are normally reported on the balance sheet or in the notes to the financial statements.

**Liabilities** Liabilities are the amounts the business owes to creditors. Liabilities are commonly divided into two sections on the balance sheet: (1) current liabilities and (2) long-term liabilities.

*Current Liabilities* Liabilities that will be due within a short time (usually one year or less) and that are to be paid out of current assets are called **current liabilities**. The most common liabilities in this group are notes payable and accounts payable. Other current liabilities may include Wages Payable, Interest Payable, Taxes Payable, and Unearned Fees.

*Long-Term Liabilities* Liabilities that will not be due for a long time (usually more than one year) are called **long-term liabilities**. If NetSolutions had long-term liabilities, they would be reported below the current liabilities. As long-term liabilities come due and are to be paid within one year, they are reported as current liabilities. If they are to be renewed rather than paid, they would continue to be reported as long term. When an asset is pledged as security for a liability, the obligation may be called a *mortgage note payable* or a *mortgage payable*.

**Owner's Equity** The owner's right to the assets of the business is presented on the balance sheet below the liabilities section. The owner's equity is added to the total liabilities, and this total must be equal to the total assets.

**Note:**
Two common classes of assets are current assets and property, plant, and equipment.

**Note:**
Two common classes of liabilities are current liabilities and long-term liabilities.

## Example Exercise 4-3 Classified Balance Sheet
OBJ 2

The following accounts appear in an adjusted trial balance of Hindsight Consulting. Indicate whether each account would be reported in the (a) current asset; (b) property, plant, and equipment; (c) current liability; (d) long-term liability; or (e) owner's equity section of the December 31, 2015, balance sheet of Hindsight Consulting.

1. Jason Corbin, Capital
2. Notes Receivable (due in six months)
3. Notes Payable (due in 10 years)
4. Land
5. Cash
6. Unearned Rent (three months)
7. Accumulated Depreciation—Equipment
8. Accounts Payable

*(Continued)*

# International  Connection

 INTERNATIONAL DIFFERENCES

Financial statements prepared under accounting practices in other countries often differ from those prepared under generally accepted accounting principles in the United States. This is to be expected because cultures and market structures differ from country to country.

To illustrate, **BMW Group** prepares its financial statements under International Financial Reporting Standards as adopted by the European Union. In doing so, BMW's balance sheet reports fixed assets first, followed by current assets. It also reports owner's equity before the liabilities. In contrast, balance sheets prepared under U.S. accounting principles report current assets followed by

fixed assets and current liabilities followed by long-term liabilities and owner's equity. The U.S. form of balance sheet is organized to emphasize creditor interpretation and analysis. For example, current assets and current liabilities are presented first to facilitate their interpretation and analysis by creditors. Likewise, to emphasize their importance, liabilities are reported before owner's equity.*

Regardless of these differences, the basic principles underlying the accounting equation and the double-entry accounting system are the same in Germany and the United States. Even though differences in recording and reporting exist, the accounting equation holds true: The total assets still equal the total liabilities and owner's equity.

*Examples of U.S. and IFRS financial statement reporting differences are further discussed and illustrated in Appendix D.

 Prepare closing entries.

# Closing Entries

As discussed in Chapter 3, the adjusting entries are recorded in the journal at the end of the accounting period. For **NetSolutions**, the adjusting entries are shown in Exhibit 9 of Chapter 3.

After the adjusting entries are posted to NetSolutions' ledger, shown in Exhibit 6, the ledger agrees with the data reported on the financial statements.

The balances of the accounts reported on the balance sheet are carried forward from year to year. Because they are relatively permanent, these accounts are called **permanent accounts** or **real accounts**. For example, Cash, Accounts Receivable, Equipment, Accumulated Depreciation, Accounts Payable, and Owner's Capital are permanent accounts.

The balances of the accounts reported on the income statement are not carried forward from year to year. Also, the balance of the owner's drawing account, which is reported on the statement of owner's equity, is not carried forward. Because these accounts report amounts for only one period, they are called **temporary accounts** or **nominal accounts**. Temporary accounts are not carried forward because they relate only to one period. For example, the Fees Earned of $16,840 and Wages Expense of $4,525 for NetSolutions shown in Exhibit 2 are for the two months ending December 31, 2015, and should not be carried forward to 2016.

At the beginning of the next period, temporary accounts should have zero balances. To achieve this, temporary account balances are transferred to permanent accounts at the end of the accounting period. The entries that transfer these balances are called **closing entries**. The transfer process is called the **closing process** and is sometimes referred to as **closing the books**.

**Note:**
Closing entries transfer the balances of temporary accounts to the owner's capital account.

The closing process involves the following four steps:

- Step 1. Revenue account balances are transferred to an account called Income Summary.
- Step 2. Expense account balances are transferred to an account called Income Summary.
- Step 3. The balance of Income Summary (net income or net loss) is transferred to the owner's capital account.
- Step 4. The balance of the owner's drawing account is transferred to the owner's capital account.

Exhibit 3 diagrams the closing process.

**EXHIBIT 3**

**The Closing Process**

**Income Summary** is a temporary account that is only used during the closing process. At the beginning of the closing process, Income Summary has no balance. During the closing process, Income Summary will be debited and credited for various amounts. At the end of the closing process, Income Summary will again have no balance. Because Income Summary has the effect of clearing the revenue and expense accounts of their balances, it is sometimes called a **clearing account**. Other titles used for this account include Revenue and Expense Summary, Profit and Loss Summary, and Income and Expense Summary.

**Note:**
The income summary account does not appear on the financial statements.

The four closing entries required in the closing process are as follows:

1. Debit each revenue account for its balance and credit Income Summary for the total revenue.
2. Credit each expense account for its balance and debit Income Summary for the total expenses.
3. Debit Income Summary for its balance (net income) and credit the owner's capital account.
4. Debit the owner's capital account for the balance of the drawing account and credit the drawing account.

In the case of a net loss, Income Summary will have a debit balance after the first two closing entries. In this case, credit Income Summary for the amount of its balance and debit the owner's capital account for the amount of the net loss.

Closing entries are recorded in the journal and are dated as of the last day of the accounting period. In the journal, closing entries are recorded immediately following the adjusting entries. The caption, *Closing Entries*, is often inserted above the closing entries to separate them from the adjusting entries.

It is possible to close the temporary revenue and expense accounts without using a clearing account such as Income Summary. In this case, the balances of the revenue and expense accounts are closed directly to the owner's capital account.

## Journalizing and Posting Closing Entries

A flowchart of the four closing entries for **NetSolutions** is shown in Exhibit 4. The balances in the accounts are those shown in the Adjusted Trial Balance columns of the end-of-period spreadsheet shown in Exhibit 1.

**EXHIBIT 4**   **Flowchart of Closing Entries for NetSolutions**

The closing entries for **NetSolutions** are shown in Exhibit 5. The account titles and balances for these entries may be obtained from the end-of-period spreadsheet, the adjusted trial balance, the income statement, the statement of owner's equity, or the ledger.

**EXHIBIT 5**

**Closing Entries, NetSolutions**

| | | | Journal | | | Page 6 |
|---|---|---|---|---|---|---|
| Date | | | Description | Post. Ref. | Debit | Credit |
| 2015 | | | Closing Entries | | | |
| Dec. | 31 | Fees Earned | | 41 | 16,840 | |
| | | Rent Revenue | | 42 | 120 | |
| | | Income Summary | | 33 | | 16,960 |
| | | | | | | |
| | 31 | Income Summary | | 33 | 9,855 | |
| | | Wages Expense | | 51 | | 4,525 |
| | | Supplies Expense | | 52 | | 2,040 |
| | | Rent Expense | | 53 | | 1,600 |
| | | Utilities Expense | | 54 | | 985 |
| | | Insurance Expense | | 55 | | 200 |
| | | Depreciation Expense | | 56 | | 50 |
| | | Miscellaneous Expense | | 59 | | 455 |
| | | | | | | |
| | 31 | Income Summary | | 33 | 7,105 | |
| | | Chris Clark, Capital | | 31 | | 7,105 |
| | | | | | | |
| | 31 | Chris Clark, Capital | | 31 | 4,000 | |
| | | Chris Clark, Drawing | | 32 | | 4,000 |

The closing entries are posted to NetSolutions' ledger as shown in Exhibit 6. Income Summary has been added to NetSolutions' ledger in Exhibit 6 as account number 33. After the closing entries are posted, NetSolutions' ledger has the following characteristics:

• The balance of Chris Clark, Capital of $28,105 agrees with the amount reported on the statement of owner's equity and the balance sheet.
• The revenue, expense, and drawing accounts will have zero balances.

As shown in Exhibit 6, the closing entries are normally identified in the ledger as "Closing." In addition, a line is often inserted in both balance columns after a closing entry is posted. This separates next period's revenue, expense, and withdrawal transactions from those of the current period. Next period's transactions will be posted directly below the closing entry.

---

## Example Exercise 4-4    Closing Entries

After the accounts have been adjusted at July 31, the end of the fiscal year, the following balances are taken from the ledger of Cabriolet Services Co.:

| | |
|---|---:|
| Terry Lambert, Capital | $615,850 |
| Terry Lambert, Drawing | 25,000 |
| Fees Earned | 380,450 |
| Wages Expense | 250,000 |
| Rent Expense | 65,000 |
| Supplies Expense | 18,250 |
| Miscellaneous Expense | 6,200 |

Journalize the four entries required to close the accounts.

### Follow My Example 4-4

| | | | | |
|---|---|---|---:|---:|
| July | 31 | Fees Earned | 380,450 | |
| | |    Income Summary | | 380,450 |
| | | | | |
| | 31 | Income Summary | 339,450 | |
| | |    Wages Expense | | 250,000 |
| | |    Rent Expense | | 65,000 |
| | |    Supplies Expense | | 18,250 |
| | |    Miscellaneous Expense | | 6,200 |
| | | | | |
| | 31 | Income Summary | 41,000 | |
| | |    Terry Lambert, Capital | | 41,000 |
| | | | | |
| | 31 | Terry Lambert, Capital | 25,000 | |
| | |    Terry Lambert, Drawing | | 25,000 |

Practice Exercises: PE 4-4A, PE 4-4B

---

## Post-Closing Trial Balance

A post-closing trial balance is prepared after the closing entries have been posted. The purpose of the post-closing (after closing) trial balance is to verify that the ledger is in balance at the beginning of the next period. The accounts and amounts should agree exactly with the accounts and amounts listed on the balance sheet at the end of the period. The post-closing trial balance for **NetSolutions** is shown in Exhibit 7.

**EXHIBIT 6** | **Ledger, NetSolutions**

### Account Cash — Account No. 11

| Date | Item | Post. Ref. | Debit | Credit | Balance Debit | Balance Credit |
|---|---|---|---|---|---|---|
| 2015 | | | | | | |
| Nov. 1 | | 1 | 25,000 | | 25,000 | |
| 5 | | 1 | | 20,000 | 5,000 | |
| 18 | | 1 | 7,500 | | 12,500 | |
| 30 | | 1 | | 3,650 | 8,850 | |
| 30 | | 1 | | 950 | 7,900 | |
| 30 | | 2 | | 2,000 | 5,900 | |
| Dec. 1 | | 2 | | 2,400 | 3,500 | |
| 1 | | 2 | | 800 | 2,700 | |
| 1 | | 2 | 360 | | 3,060 | |
| 6 | | 2 | | 180 | 2,880 | |
| 11 | | 2 | | 400 | 2,480 | |
| 13 | | 3 | | 950 | 1,530 | |
| 16 | | 3 | 3,100 | | 4,630 | |
| 20 | | 3 | | 900 | 3,730 | |
| 21 | | 3 | 650 | | 4,380 | |
| 23 | | 3 | | 1,450 | 2,930 | |
| 27 | | 3 | | 1,200 | 1,730 | |
| 31 | | 3 | | 310 | 1,420 | |
| 31 | | 4 | | 225 | 1,195 | |
| 31 | | 4 | 2,870 | | 4,065 | |
| 31 | | 4 | | 2,000 | 2,065 | |

### Account Accounts Receivable — Account No. 12

| Date | Item | Post. Ref. | Debit | Credit | Balance Debit | Balance Credit |
|---|---|---|---|---|---|---|
| 2015 | | | | | | |
| Dec. 16 | | 3 | 1,750 | | 1,750 | |
| 21 | | 3 | | 650 | 1,100 | |
| 31 | | 4 | 1,120 | | 2,220 | |
| 31 | Adjusting | 5 | 500 | | 2,720 | |

### Account Supplies — Account No. 14

| Date | Item | Post. Ref. | Debit | Credit | Balance Debit | Balance Credit |
|---|---|---|---|---|---|---|
| 2015 | | | | | | |
| Nov. 10 | | 1 | 1,350 | | 1,350 | |
| 30 | | 1 | | 800 | 550 | |
| Dec. 23 | | 3 | 1,450 | | 2,000 | |
| 31 | Adjusting | 5 | | 1,240 | 760 | |

### Account Prepaid Insurance — Account No. 15

| Date | Item | Post. Ref. | Debit | Credit | Balance Debit | Balance Credit |
|---|---|---|---|---|---|---|
| 2015 | | | | | | |
| Dec. 1 | | 2 | 2,400 | | 2,400 | |
| 31 | Adjusting | 5 | | 200 | 2,200 | |

### Account Land — Account No. 17

| Date | Item | Post. Ref. | Debit | Credit | Balance Debit | Balance Credit |
|---|---|---|---|---|---|---|
| 2015 | | | | | | |
| Nov. 5 | | 1 | 20,000 | | 20,000 | |

### Account Office Equipment — Account No. 18

| Date | Item | Post. Ref. | Debit | Credit | Balance Debit | Balance Credit |
|---|---|---|---|---|---|---|
| 2015 | | | | | | |
| Dec. 4 | | 2 | 1,800 | | 1,800 | |

### Account Accumulated Depreciation — Account No. 19

| Date | Item | Post. Ref. | Debit | Credit | Balance Debit | Balance Credit |
|---|---|---|---|---|---|---|
| 2015 | | | | | | |
| Dec. 31 | Adjusting | 5 | | 50 | | 50 |

### Account Accounts Payable — Account No. 21

| Date | Item | Post. Ref. | Debit | Credit | Balance Debit | Balance Credit |
|---|---|---|---|---|---|---|
| 2015 | | | | | | |
| Nov. 10 | | 1 | | 1,350 | | 1,350 |
| 30 | | 1 | 950 | | | 400 |
| Dec. 4 | | 2 | | 1,800 | | 2,200 |
| 11 | | 2 | 400 | | | 1,800 |
| 20 | | 3 | 900 | | | 900 |

### Account Wages Payable — Account No. 22

| Date | Item | Post. Ref. | Debit | Credit | Balance Debit | Balance Credit |
|---|---|---|---|---|---|---|
| 2015 | | | | | | |
| Dec. 31 | Adjusting | 5 | | 250 | | 250 |

### Account Unearned Rent — Account No. 23

| Date | Item | Post. Ref. | Debit | Credit | Balance Debit | Balance Credit |
|---|---|---|---|---|---|---|
| 2015 | | | | | | |
| Dec. 1 | | 2 | | 360 | | 360 |
| 31 | Adjusting | 5 | 120 | | | 240 |

### Account Chris Clark, Capital — Account No. 31

| Date | Item | Post. Ref. | Debit | Credit | Balance Debit | Balance Credit |
|---|---|---|---|---|---|---|
| 2015 | | | | | | |
| Nov. 1 | | 1 | | 25,000 | | 25,000 |
| Dec. 31 | Closing | 6 | | 7,105 | | 32,105 |
| 31 | Closing | 6 | 4,000 | | | 28,105 |

**EXHIBIT 6** **Ledger, NetSolutions (Concluded)**

**Account** Chris Clark, Drawing — Account No. 32

| Date | Item | Post. Ref. | Debit | Credit | Balance Debit | Balance Credit |
|------|------|-----------|-------|--------|-------|--------|
| 2015 | | | | | | |
| Nov. 30 | | 2 | 2,000 | | 2,000 | |
| Dec. 31 | | 4 | 2,000 | | 4,000 | |
| 31 | Closing | 6 | | 4,000 | — | — |

**Account** Income Summary — Account No. 33

| Date | Item | Post. Ref. | Debit | Credit | Balance Debit | Balance Credit |
|------|------|-----------|-------|--------|-------|--------|
| 2015 | | | | | | |
| Dec. 31 | Closing | 6 | | 16,960 | | 16,960 |
| 31 | Closing | 6 | 9,855 | | | 7,105 |
| 31 | Closing | 6 | 7,105 | | — | — |

**Account** Fees Earned — Account No. 41

| Date | Item | Post. Ref. | Debit | Credit | Balance Debit | Balance Credit |
|------|------|-----------|-------|--------|-------|--------|
| 2015 | | | | | | |
| Nov. 18 | | 1 | | 7,500 | | 7,500 |
| Dec. 16 | | 3 | | 3,100 | | 10,600 |
| 16 | | 3 | | 1,750 | | 12,350 |
| 31 | | 4 | | 2,870 | | 15,220 |
| 31 | | 4 | | 1,120 | | 16,340 |
| 31 | Adjusting | 5 | | 500 | | 16,840 |
| 31 | Closing | 6 | 16,840 | | — | — |

**Account** Rent Revenue — Account No. 42

| Date | Item | Post. Ref. | Debit | Credit | Balance Debit | Balance Credit |
|------|------|-----------|-------|--------|-------|--------|
| 2015 | | | | | | |
| Dec. 31 | Adjusting | 5 | | 120 | | 120 |
| 31 | Closing | 6 | 120 | | — | — |

**Account** Wages Expense — Account No. 51

| Date | Item | Post. Ref. | Debit | Credit | Balance Debit | Balance Credit |
|------|------|-----------|-------|--------|-------|--------|
| 2015 | | | | | | |
| Nov. 30 | | 1 | 2,125 | | 2,125 | |
| Dec. 13 | | 3 | 950 | | 3,075 | |
| 27 | | 3 | 1,200 | | 4,275 | |
| 31 | Adjusting | 5 | 250 | | 4,525 | |
| 31 | Closing | 6 | | 4,525 | — | — |

**Account** Supplies Expense — Account No. 52

| Date | Item | Post. Ref. | Debit | Credit | Balance Debit | Balance Credit |
|------|------|-----------|-------|--------|-------|--------|
| 2015 | | | | | | |
| Nov. 30 | | 1 | 800 | | 800 | |
| Dec. 31 | Adjusting | 5 | 1,240 | | 2,040 | |
| 31 | Closing | 6 | | 2,040 | — | — |

**Account** Rent Expense — Account No. 53

| Date | Item | Post. Ref. | Debit | Credit | Balance Debit | Balance Credit |
|------|------|-----------|-------|--------|-------|--------|
| 2015 | | | | | | |
| Nov. 30 | | 1 | 800 | | 800 | |
| Dec. 1 | | 2 | 800 | | 1,600 | |
| 31 | Closing | 6 | | 1,600 | — | — |

**Account** Utilities Expense — Account No. 54

| Date | Item | Post. Ref. | Debit | Credit | Balance Debit | Balance Credit |
|------|------|-----------|-------|--------|-------|--------|
| 2015 | | | | | | |
| Nov. 30 | | 1 | 450 | | 450 | |
| Dec. 31 | | 3 | 310 | | 760 | |
| 31 | | 4 | 225 | | 985 | |
| 31 | Closing | 6 | | 985 | — | — |

**Account** Insurance Expense — Account No. 55

| Date | Item | Post. Ref. | Debit | Credit | Balance Debit | Balance Credit |
|------|------|-----------|-------|--------|-------|--------|
| 2015 | | | | | | |
| Dec. 31 | Adjusting | 5 | 200 | | 200 | |
| 31 | Closing | 6 | | 200 | — | |

**Account** Depreciation Expense — Account No. 56

| Date | Item | Post. Ref. | Debit | Credit | Balance Debit | Balance Credit |
|------|------|-----------|-------|--------|-------|--------|
| 2015 | | | | | | |
| Dec. 31 | Adjusting | 5 | 50 | | 50 | |
| 31 | Closing | 6 | | 50 | — | — |

**Account** Miscellaneous Expense — Account No. 59

| Date | Item | Post. Ref. | Debit | Credit | Balance Debit | Balance Credit |
|------|------|-----------|-------|--------|-------|--------|
| 2015 | | | | | | |
| Nov. 30 | | 1 | 275 | | 275 | |
| Dec. 6 | | 2 | 180 | | 455 | |
| 31 | Closing | 6 | | 455 | — | — |

**EXHIBIT 7**

**Post-Closing Trial Balance, NetSolutions**

**NetSolutions**
**Post-Closing Trial Balance**
**December 31, 2015**

| | Debit Balances | Credit Balances |
|---|---|---|
| Cash........................................................... | 2,065 | |
| Accounts Receivable ...................................... | 2,720 | |
| Supplies ..................................................... | 760 | |
| Prepaid Insurance........................................... | 2,200 | |
| Land........................................................... | 20,000 | |
| Office Equipment ........................................... | 1,800 | |
| Accumulated Depreciation................................. | | 50 |
| Accounts Payable ........................................... | | 900 |
| Wages Payable............................................... | | 250 |
| Unearned Rent .............................................. | | 240 |
| Chris Clark, Capital ......................................... | | 28,105 |
| | 29,545 | 29,545 |

**OBJ 4** Describe the accounting cycle.

# Accounting Cycle

The accounting process that begins with analyzing and journalizing transactions and ends with the post-closing trial balance is called the **accounting cycle**. The steps in the accounting cycle are as follows:

- Step 1. Transactions are analyzed and recorded in the journal.
- Step 2. Transactions are posted to the ledger.
- Step 3. An unadjusted trial balance is prepared.
- Step 4. Adjustment data are assembled and analyzed.
- Step 5. An optional end-of-period spreadsheet is prepared.
- Step 6. Adjusting entries are journalized and posted to the ledger.
- Step 7. An adjusted trial balance is prepared.
- Step 8. Financial statements are prepared.
- Step 9. Closing entries are journalized and posted to the ledger.
- Step 10. A post-closing trial balance is prepared.[2]

**Example Exercise 4-5 Accounting Cycle**  **OBJ 4**

From the following list of steps in the accounting cycle, identify what two steps are missing:

a. Transactions are analyzed and recorded in the journal:

b. Transactions are posted to the ledger.

c. Adjustment data are assembled and analyzed.

d. An optional end-of-period spreadsheet is prepared.

e. Adjusting entries are journalized and posted to the ledger.

f. Financial statements are prepared.

g. Closing entries are journalized and posted to the ledger.

h. A post-closing trial balance is prepared.

**Follow My Example 4-5**

The following two steps are missing: (1) the preparation of an unadjusted trial balance and (2) the preparation of the adjusted trial balance. The unadjusted trial balance should be prepared after step (b). The adjusted trial balance should be prepared after step (e).

Practice Exercises: PE 4-5A, PE 4-5B

[2] Some accountants include the journalizing and posting of "reversing entries" as the last step in the accounting cycle. Because reversing entries are not required, they are described and illustrated in Appendix B at the end of the book.

Exhibit 8 illustrates the accounting cycle in graphic form. It also illustrates how the accounting cycle begins with the source documents for a transaction and flows through the accounting system and into the financial statements.

## Accounting Cycle Steps

**Step 1**  Transactions are analyzed and recorded in the journal.

**Step 2**  Transactions are posted to the ledger.

**Step 3**  An unadjusted trial balance is prepared.

**Step 4**  Adjustment data are assembled and analyzed.

**Step 5**  An optional end-of-period spreadsheet is prepared.

**Step 6**  Adjusting entries are journalized and posted to the ledger.

**Step 7**  An adjusted trial balance is prepared.

**Step 8**  Financial statements are prepared.

**Step 9**  Closing entries are journalized and posted to the ledger.

**Step 10**  A post-closing trial balance is prepared.

# Illustration of the Accounting Cycle

**OBJ 5** Illustrate the accounting cycle for one period.

In this section, the complete accounting cycle for one period is illustrated. Assume that for several years Kelly Pitney has operated a part-time consulting business from her home. As of April 1, 2016, Kelly decided to move to rented quarters and to operate the business on a full-time basis. The business will be known as Kelly Consulting. During April, Kelly Consulting entered into the following transactions:

Apr. 1. The following assets were received from Kelly Pitney: cash, $13,100; accounts receivable, $3,000; supplies, $1,400; and office equipment, $12,500. There were no liabilities received.

 1. Paid three months' rent on a lease rental contract, $4,800.

 2. Paid the premiums on property and casualty insurance policies, $1,800.

 4. Received cash from clients as an advance payment for services to be provided and recorded it as unearned fees, $5,000.

Apr. 5. Purchased additional office equipment on account from Office Station Co., $2,000.

6. Received cash from clients on account, $1,800.

10. Paid cash for a newspaper advertisement, $120.

12. Paid Office Station Co. for part of the debt incurred on April 5, $1,200.

12. Recorded services provided on account for the period April 1–12, $4,200.

14. Paid part-time receptionist for two weeks' salary, $750.

17. Recorded cash from cash clients for fees earned during the period April 1–16, $6,250.

18. Paid cash for supplies, $800.

20. Recorded services provided on account for the period April 13–20, $2,100.

24. Recorded cash from cash clients for fees earned for the period April 17–24, $3,850.

26. Received cash from clients on account, $5,600.

27. Paid part-time receptionist for two weeks' salary, $750.

29. Paid telephone bill for April, $130.

30. Paid electricity bill for April, $200.

30. Recorded cash from cash clients for fees earned for the period April 25–30, $3,050.

30. Recorded services provided on account for the remainder of April, $1,500.

30. Kelly withdrew $6,000 for personal use.

## Step 1. Analyzing and Recording Transactions in the Journal

The first step in the accounting cycle is to analyze and record transactions in the journal using the double-entry accounting system. As illustrated in Chapter 2, transactions are analyzed and journalized using the following steps:

- Step 1. Carefully read the description of the transaction to determine whether an asset, liability, owner's equity, revenue, expense, or drawing account is affected.
- Step 2. For each account affected by the transaction, determine whether the account increases or decreases.
- Step 3. Determine whether each increase or decrease should be recorded as a debit or a credit, following the rules of debit and credit shown in Exhibit 3 of Chapter 2.
- Step 4. Record the transaction using a journal entry.

The company's chart of accounts is useful in determining which accounts are affected by the transaction. The chart of accounts for Kelly Consulting is shown in Exhibit 9.

**EXHIBIT 9**

**Chart of Accounts for Kelly Consulting**

| | |
|---|---|
| 11 Cash | 31 Kelly Pitney, Capital |
| 12 Accounts Receivable | 32 Kelly Pitney, Drawing |
| 14 Supplies | 33 Income Summary |
| 15 Prepaid Rent | 41 Fees Earned |
| 16 Prepaid Insurance | 51 Salary Expense |
| 18 Office Equipment | 52 Rent Expense |
| 19 Accumulated Depreciation | 53 Supplies Expense |
| 21 Accounts Payable | 54 Depreciation Expense |
| 22 Salaries Payable | 55 Insurance Expense |
| 23 Unearned Fees | 59 Miscellaneous Expense |

After analyzing each of Kelly Consulting's transactions for April, the journal entries are recorded as shown in Exhibit 10.

## Step 2. Posting Transactions to the Ledger

Periodically, the transactions recorded in the journal are posted to the accounts in the ledger. The debits and credits for each journal entry are posted to the accounts in the

| Journal | | | Page 1 | |
|---|---|---|---|---|
| Date | Description | Post. Ref. | Debit | Credit |
| 2016 Apr. 1 | Cash | 11 | 13,100 | |
| | Accounts Receivable | 12 | 3,000 | |
| | Supplies | 14 | 1,400 | |
| | Office Equipment | 18 | 12,500 | |
| | Kelly Pitney, Capital | 31 | | 30,000 |
| 1 | Prepaid Rent | 15 | 4,800 | |
| | Cash | 11 | | 4,800 |
| 2 | Prepaid Insurance | 16 | 1,800 | |
| | Cash | 11 | | 1,800 |
| 4 | Cash | 11 | 5,000 | |
| | Unearned Fees | 23 | | 5,000 |
| 5 | Office Equipment | 18 | 2,000 | |
| | Accounts Payable | 21 | | 2,000 |
| 6 | Cash | 11 | 1,800 | |
| | Accounts Receivable | 12 | | 1,800 |
| 10 | Miscellaneous Expense | 59 | 120 | |
| | Cash | 11 | | 120 |
| 12 | Accounts Payable | 21 | 1,200 | |
| | Cash | 11 | | 1,200 |
| 12 | Accounts Receivable | 12 | 4,200 | |
| | Fees Earned | 41 | | 4,200 |
| 14 | Salary Expense | 51 | 750 | |
| | Cash | 11 | | 750 |

| Journal | | | Page 2 | |
|---|---|---|---|---|
| Date | Description | Post. Ref. | Debit | Credit |
| 2016 Apr. 17 | Cash | 11 | 6,250 | |
| | Fees Earned | 41 | | 6,250 |
| 18 | Supplies | 14 | 800 | |
| | Cash | 11 | | 800 |
| 20 | Accounts Receivable | 12 | 2,100 | |
| | Fees Earned | 41 | | 2,100 |
| 24 | Cash | 11 | 3,850 | |
| | Fees Earned | 41 | | 3,850 |
| 26 | Cash | 11 | 5,600 | |
| | Accounts Receivable | 12 | | 5,600 |
| 27 | Salary Expense | 51 | 750 | |
| | Cash | 11 | | 750 |
| 29 | Miscellaneous Expense | 59 | 130 | |
| | Cash | 11 | | 130 |

(Continued)

**EXHIBIT 10**

**Journal Entries for April, Kelly Consulting**

**EXHIBIT 10**

**Journal Entries for April, Kelly Consulting** (*Concluded*)

| | | Journal | | | Page 2 |
|---|---|---|---|---|---|
| Date | | Description | Post. Ref. | Debit | Credit |
| | 30 | Miscellaneous Expense | 59 | 200 | |
| | | Cash | 11 | | 200 |
| | 30 | Cash | 11 | 3,050 | |
| | | Fees Earned | 41 | | 3,050 . |
| | 30 | Accounts Receivable | 12 | 1,500 | |
| | | Fees Earned | 41 | | 1,500 |
| | 30 | Kelly Pitney, Drawing | 32 | 6,000 | |
| | | Cash | 11 | | 6,000 |

order in which they occur in the journal. As illustrated in Chapters 2 and 3, journal entries are posted to the accounts using the following four steps:

- Step 1. The date is entered in the Date column of the account.
- Step 2. The amount is entered into the Debit or Credit column of the account.
- Step 3. The journal page number is entered in the Posting Reference column.
- Step 4. The account number is entered in the Posting Reference (Post. Ref.) column in the journal.

The journal entries for Kelly Consulting have been posted to the ledger shown in Exhibit 18.

## Step 3. Preparing an Unadjusted Trial Balance

An unadjusted trial balance is prepared to determine whether any errors have been made in posting the debits and credits to the ledger. The unadjusted trial balance shown in Exhibit 11 does not provide complete proof of the accuracy of the ledger. It indicates only that the debits and the credits are equal. This proof is of value, however, because errors often affect the equality of debits and credits. If the two totals of a trial balance are not equal, an error has occurred that must be discovered and corrected.

The unadjusted account balances shown in Exhibit 11 were taken from Kelly Consulting's ledger shown in Exhibit 18, before any adjusting entries were recorded.

## Step 4. Assembling and Analyzing Adjustment Data

Before the financial statements can be prepared, the accounts must be updated. The four types of accounts that normally require adjustment include prepaid expenses, unearned revenue, accrued revenue, and accrued expenses. In addition, depreciation expense must be recorded for fixed assets other than land. The following data have been assembled on April 30, 2016, for analysis of possible adjustments for Kelly Consulting:

a. Insurance expired during April is $300.
b. Supplies on hand on April 30 are $1,350.
c. Depreciation of office equipment for April is $330.
d. Accrued receptionist salary on April 30 is $120.
e. Rent expired during April is $1,600.
f. Unearned fees on April 30 are $2,500.

**EXHIBIT 11**

**Unadjusted Trial Balance, Kelly Consulting**

**Kelly Consulting**
**Unadjusted Trial Balance**
**April 30, 2016**

| | Debit Balances | Credit Balances |
|---|---|---|
| Cash | 22,100 | |
| Accounts Receivable | 3,400 | |
| Supplies | 2,200 | |
| Prepaid Rent | 4,800 | |
| Prepaid Insurance | 1,800 | |
| Office Equipment | 14,500 | |
| Accumulated Depreciation | | 0 |
| Accounts Payable | | 800 |
| Salaries Payable | | 0 |
| Unearned Fees | | 5,000 |
| Kelly Pitney, Capital | | 30,000 |
| Kelly Pitney, Drawing | 6,000 | |
| Fees Earned | | 20,950 |
| Salary Expense | 1,500 | |
| Rent Expense | 0 | |
| Supplies Expense | 0 | |
| Depreciation Expense | 0 | |
| Insurance Expense | 0 | |
| Miscellaneous Expense | 450 | |
| | 56,750 | 56,750 |

## Step 5. Preparing an Optional End-of-Period Spreadsheet

Although an end-of-period spreadsheet is not required, it is useful in showing the flow of accounting information from the unadjusted trial balance to the adjusted trial balance. In addition, an end-of-period spreadsheet is useful in analyzing the impact of proposed adjustments on the financial statements. The end-of-period spreadsheet for Kelly Consulting is shown in Exhibit 12.

**EXHIBIT 12**

**End-of-Period Spreadsheet, Kelly Consulting**

| | A | B | C | D | E | F | G |
|---|---|---|---|---|---|---|---|
| 1 | | | | Kelly Consulting | | | |
| 2 | | | | End-of-Period Spreadsheet | | | |
| 3 | | | | For the Month Ended April 30, 2016 | | | |
| 4 | | Unadjusted | | | | Adjusted | |
| 5 | | Trial Balance | | Adjustments | | Trial Balance | |
| 6 | Account Title | Dr. | Cr. | Dr. | Cr. | Dr. | Cr. |
| 7 | | | | | | | |
| 8 | Cash | 22,100 | | | | 22,100 | |
| 9 | Accounts Receivable | 3,400 | | | | 3,400 | |
| 10 | Supplies | 2,200 | | | (b) 850 | 1,350 | |
| 11 | Prepaid Rent | 4,800 | | | (e) 1,600 | 3,200 | |
| 12 | Prepaid Insurance | 1,800 | | | (a) 300 | 1,500 | |
| 13 | Office Equipment | 14,500 | | | | 14,500 | |
| 14 | Accum. Depreciation | | | | (c) 330 | | 330 |
| 15 | Accounts Payable | | 800 | | | | 800 |
| 16 | Salaries Payable | | | | (d) 120 | | 120 |
| 17 | Unearned Fees | | 5,000 | (f) 2,500 | | | 2,500 |
| 18 | Kelly Pitney, Capital | | 30,000 | | | | 30,000 |
| 19 | Kelly Pitney, Drawing | 6,000 | | | | 6,000 | |
| 20 | Fees Earned | | 20,950 | | (f) 2,500 | | 23,450 |
| 21 | Salary Expense | 1,500 | | (d) 120 | | 1,620 | |
| 22 | Rent Expense | | | (e) 1,600 | | 1,600 | |
| 23 | Supplies Expense | | | (b) 850 | | 850 | |
| 24 | Depreciation Expense | | | (c) 330 | | 330 | |
| 25 | Insurance Expense | | | (a) 300 | | 300 | |
| 26 | Miscellaneous Expense | 450 | | | | 450 | |
| 27 | | 56,750 | 56,750 | 5,700 | 5,700 | 57,200 | 57,200 |
| 28 | | | | | | | |

| | | Journal | | | Page 3 |
|---|---|---|---|---|---|
| Date | | Description | Post. Ref. | Debit | Credit |
| 2016 Apr. 30 | | Adjusting Entries | | | |
| | | Insurance Expense | 55 | 300 | |
| | |     Prepaid Insurance | 16 | | 300 |
| | |         Expired insurance. | | | |
| | 30 | Supplies Expense | 53 | 850 | |
| | |     Supplies | 14 | | 850 |
| | |         Supplies used ($2,200 – $1,350). | | | |
| | 30 | Depreciation Expense | 54 | 330 | |
| | |     Accumulated Depreciation | 19 | | 330 |
| | |         Depreciation of office equipment. | | | |
| | 30 | Salary Expense | 51 | 120 | |
| | |     Salaries Payable | 22 | | 120 |
| | |         Accrued salary. | | | |
| | 30 | Rent Expense | 52 | 1,600 | |
| | |     Prepaid Rent | 15 | | 1,600 |
| | |         Rent expired during April. | | | |
| | 30 | Unearned Fees | 23 | 2,500 | |
| | |     Fees Earned | 41 | | 2,500 |
| | |         Fees earned ($5,000 – $2,500). | | | |

## Step 6. Journalizing and Posting Adjusting Entries

Based on the adjustment data shown in Step 4, adjusting entries for Kelly Consulting are prepared as shown in Exhibit 13. Each adjusting entry affects at least one income statement account and one balance sheet account. Explanations for each adjustment including any computations are normally included with each adjusting entry.

Each of the adjusting entries shown in Exhibit 13 is posted to Kelly Consulting's ledger shown in Exhibit 18. The adjusting entries are identified in the ledger as "Adjusting."

## Step 7. Preparing an Adjusted Trial Balance

After the adjustments have been journalized and posted, an adjusted trial balance is prepared to verify the equality of the total of the debit and credit balances. This is the last step before preparing the financial statements. If the adjusted trial balance does not balance, an error has occurred and must be found and corrected. The adjusted trial balance for Kelly Consulting as of April 30, 2016, is shown in Exhibit 14.

## Step 8. Preparing the Financial Statements

The most important outcome of the accounting cycle is the financial statements. The income statement is prepared first, followed by the statement of owner's equity and then the balance sheet. The statements can be prepared directly from the adjusted trial balance, the end-of-period spreadsheet, or the ledger. The net income or net loss shown on the income statement is reported on the statement of owner's equity along with any additional investments by the owner and any withdrawals. The ending owner's capital is reported on the balance sheet and is added with total liabilities to equal total assets.

The financial statements for Kelly Consulting are shown in Exhibit 15. Kelly Consulting earned net income of $18,300 for April. As of April 30, 2016, Kelly Consulting has total assets of $45,720, total liabilities of $3,420, and total owner's equity of $42,300.

**Kelly Consulting**
**Adjusted Trial Balance**
**April 30, 2016**

| | Debit Balances | Credit Balances |
|---|---|---|
| Cash ............................................................. | 22,100 | |
| Accounts Receivable ...................................... | 3,400 | |
| Supplies ........................................................ | 1,350 | |
| Prepaid Rent ................................................. | 3,200 | |
| Prepaid Insurance ......................................... | 1,500 | |
| Office Equipment .......................................... | 14,500 | |
| Accumulated Depreciation ............................ | | 330 |
| Accounts Payable .......................................... | | 800 |
| Salaries Payable ............................................ | | 120 |
| Unearned Fees .............................................. | | 2,500 |
| Kelly Pitney, Capital ...................................... | | 30,000 |
| Kelly Pitney, Drawing .................................... | 6,000 | |
| Fees Earned .................................................. | | 23,450 |
| Salary Expense .............................................. | 1,620 | |
| Rent Expense ................................................ | 1,600 | |
| Supplies Expense ........................................... | 850 | |
| Depreciation Expense .................................... | 330 | |
| Insurance Expense ........................................ | 300 | |
| Miscellaneous Expense .................................. | 450 | |
| | 57,200 | 57,200 |

**EXHIBIT 14**

**Adjusted Trial Balance, Kelly Consulting**

**Kelly Consulting**
**Income Statement**
**For the Month Ended April 30, 2016**

| | | |
|---|---|---|
| Fees earned ................................................... | | $23,450 |
| Expenses: | | |
| Salary expense .......................................... | $1,620 | |
| Rent expense ............................................ | 1,600 | |
| Supplies expense ...................................... | 850 | |
| Depreciation expense ............................... | 330 | |
| Insurance expense .................................... | 300 | |
| Miscellaneous expense ............................. | 450 | |
| Total expenses ...................................... | | 5,150 |
| Net income .................................................... | | $18,300 |

**EXHIBIT 15**

**Financial Statements, Kelly Consulting**

**Kelly Consulting**
**Statement of Owner's Equity**
**For the Month Ended April 30, 2016**

| | | |
|---|---|---|
| Kelly Pitney, capital, April 1, 2016 ..................... | | $    0 |
| Investment during the month .......................... | $30,000 | |
| Net income for the month ............................... | 18,300 | |
| | $48,300 | |
| Less withdrawals ........................................... | 6,000 | |
| Increase in owner's equity .............................. | | 42,300 |
| Kelly Pitney, capital, April 30, 2016 ................... | | $42,300 |

*(Continued)*

**EXHIBIT 15** **Financial Statements, Kelly Consulting (*Concluded*)**

### Kelly Consulting
### Balance Sheet
### April 30, 2016

| Assets | | | Liabilities | | |
|---|---|---|---|---|---|
| Current assets: | | | Current liabilities: | | |
| Cash | $22,100 | | Accounts payable | $ 800 | |
| Accounts receivable | 3,400 | | Salaries payable | 120 | |
| Supplies | 1,350 | | Unearned fees | 2,500 | |
| Prepaid rent | 3,200 | | Total liabilities | | $ 3,420 |
| Prepaid insurance | 1,500 | | | | |
| Total current assets | | $31,550 | | | |
| Property, plant, and equipment: | | | | | |
| Office equipment | $14,500 | | | | |
| Less accumulated depreciation | 330 | | **Owner's Equity** | | |
| Total property, plant, | | | Kelly Pitney, capital | | 42,300 |
| and equipment | | 14,170 | Total liabilities and | | |
| Total assets | | $45,720 | owner's equity | | $45,720 |

## Step 9. Journalizing and Posting Closing Entries

As described earlier in this chapter, four closing entries are required at the end of an accounting period. These four closing entries are as follows:

1. Debit each revenue account for its balance, and credit Income Summary for the total revenue.
2. Credit each expense account for its balance, and debit Income Summary for the total expenses.
3. Debit Income Summary for its balance, and credit the owner's capital account.
4. Debit the owner's capital account for the balance of the drawing account, and credit the drawing account.

The four closing entries for Kelly Consulting are shown in Exhibit 16. The closing entries are posted to Kelly Consulting's ledger as shown in Exhibit 18. After the closing entries are posted, Kelly Consulting's ledger has the following characteristics:

- The balance of Kelly Pitney, Capital of $42,300 agrees with the amount reported on the statement of owner's equity and the balance sheet.
- The revenue, expense, and drawing accounts will have zero balances.

The closing entries are normally identified in the ledger as "Closing." In addition, a line is often inserted in both balance columns after a closing entry is posted. This separates next period's revenue, expense, and withdrawal transactions from those of the current period.

## Step 10. Preparing a Post-Closing Trial Balance

A post-closing trial balance is prepared after the closing entries have been posted. The purpose of the post-closing trial balance is to verify that the ledger is in balance at the beginning of the next period. The accounts and amounts in the post-closing trial balance should agree exactly with the accounts and amounts listed on the balance sheet at the end of the period.

| | | | | | | | Journal | | | | | Page 4 |
|---|---|---|---|---|---|---|---|---|---|---|---|---|

| Date | | | Description | Post. Ref. | Debit | Credit |
|---|---|---|---|---|---|---|
| | | | Closing Entries | | | |
| 2016 Apr. | 30 | | Fees Earned | 41 | 23,450 | |
| | | | Income Summary | 33 | | 23,450 |
| | | | | | | |
| | 30 | | Income Summary | 33 | 5,150 | |
| | | | Salary Expense | 51 | | 1,620 |
| | | | Rent Expense | 52 | | 1,600 |
| | | | Supplies Expense | 53 | | 850 |
| | | | Depreciation Expense | 54 | | 330 |
| | | | Insurance Expense | 55 | | 300 |
| | | | Miscellaneous Expense | 59 | | 450 |
| | | | | | | |
| | 30 | | Income Summary | 33 | 18,300 | |
| | | | Kelly Pitney, Capital | 31 | | 18,300 |
| | | | | | | |
| | 30 | | Kelly Pitney, Capital | 31 | 6,000 | |
| | | | Kelly Pitney, Drawing | 32 | | 6,000 |

**EXHIBIT 16**

**Closing Entries, Kelly Consulting**

The post-closing trial balance for Kelly Consulting is shown in Exhibit 17. The balances shown in the post-closing trial balance are taken from the ending balances in the ledger shown in Exhibit 18. These balances agree with the amounts shown on Kelly Consulting's balance sheet in Exhibit 15.

| Kelly Consulting Post-Closing Trial Balance April 30, 2016 | Debit Balances | Credit Balances |
|---|---|---|
| Cash | 22,100 | |
| Accounts Receivable | 3,400 | |
| Supplies | 1,350 | |
| Prepaid Rent | 3,200 | |
| Prepaid Insurance | 1,500 | |
| Office Equipment | 14,500 | |
| Accumulated Depreciation | | 330 |
| Accounts Payable | | 800 |
| Salaries Payable | | 120 |
| Unearned Fees | | 2,500 |
| Kelly Pitney, Capital | | 42,300 |
| | 46,050 | 46,050 |

**EXHIBIT 17**

**Post-Closing Trial Balance, Kelly Consulting**

| EXHIBIT 18 | Ledger, Kelly Consulting |
|---|---|

## Ledger

### Account *Cash* — Account No. 11

| Date | Item | Post. Ref. | Debit | Credit | Balance Debit | Balance Credit |
|---|---|---|---|---|---|---|
| 2016 | | | | | | |
| Apr. 1 | | 1 | 13,100 | | 13,100 | |
| 1 | | 1 | | 4,800 | 8,300 | |
| 2 | | 1 | | 1,800 | 6,500 | |
| 4 | | 1 | 5,000 | | 11,500 | |
| 6 | | 1 | 1,800 | | 13,300 | |
| 10 | | 1 | | 120 | 13,180 | |
| 12 | | 1 | | 1,200 | 11,980 | |
| 14 | | 1 | | 750 | 11,230 | |
| 17 | | 2 | 6,250 | | 17,480 | |
| 18 | | 2 | | 800 | 16,680 | |
| 24 | | 2 | 3,850 | | 20,530 | |
| 26 | | 2 | 5,600 | | 26,130 | |
| 27 | | 2 | | 750 | 25,380 | |
| 29 | | 2 | | 130 | 25,250 | |
| 30 | | 2 | | 200 | 25,050 | |
| 30 | | 2 | 3,050 | | 28,100 | |
| 30 | | 2 | | 6,000 | 22,100 | |

### Account *Accounts Receivable* — Account No. 12

| Date | Item | Post. Ref. | Debit | Credit | Balance Debit | Balance Credit |
|---|---|---|---|---|---|---|
| 2016 | | | | | | |
| Apr. 1 | | 1 | 3,000 | | 3,000 | |
| 6 | | 1 | | 1,800 | 1,200 | |
| 12 | | 1 | 4,200 | | 5,400 | |
| 20 | | 2 | 2,100 | | 7,500 | |
| 26 | | 2 | | 5,600 | 1,900 | |
| 30 | | 2 | 1,500 | | 3,400 | |

### Account *Supplies* — Account No. 14

| Date | Item | Post. Ref. | Debit | Credit | Balance Debit | Balance Credit |
|---|---|---|---|---|---|---|
| 2016 | | | | | | |
| Apr. 1 | | 1 | 1,400 | | 1,400 | |
| 18 | | 2 | 800 | | 2,200 | |
| 30 | Adjusting | 3 | | 850 | 1,350 | |

### Account *Prepaid Rent* — Account No. 15

| Date | Item | Post. Ref. | Debit | Credit | Balance Debit | Balance Credit |
|---|---|---|---|---|---|---|
| 2016 | | | | | | |
| Apr. 1 | | 1 | 4,800 | | 4,800 | |
| 30 | Adjusting | 3 | | 1,600 | 3,200 | |

### Account *Prepaid Insurance* — Account No. 16

| Date | Item | Post. Ref. | Debit | Credit | Balance Debit | Balance Credit |
|---|---|---|---|---|---|---|
| 2016 | | | | | | |
| Apr. 2 | | 1 | 1,800 | | 1,800 | |
| 30 | Adjusting | 3 | | 300 | 1,500 | |

### Account *Office Equipment* — Account No. 18

| Date | Item | Post. Ref. | Debit | Credit | Balance Debit | Balance Credit |
|---|---|---|---|---|---|---|
| 2016 | | | | | | |
| Apr. 1 | | 1 | 12,500 | | 12,500 | |
| 5 | | 1 | 2,000 | | 14,500 | |

### Account *Accumulated Depreciation* — Account No. 19

| Date | Item | Post. Ref. | Debit | Credit | Balance Debit | Balance Credit |
|---|---|---|---|---|---|---|
| 2016 | | | | | | |
| Apr. 30 | Adjusting | 3 | | 330 | | 330 |

### Account *Accounts Payable* — Account No. 21

| Date | Item | Post. Ref. | Debit | Credit | Balance Debit | Balance Credit |
|---|---|---|---|---|---|---|
| 2016 | | | | | | |
| Apr. 5 | | 1 | | 2,000 | | 2,000 |
| 12 | | 1 | 1,200 | | | 800 |

### Account *Salaries Payable* — Account No. 22

| Date | Item | Post. Ref. | Debit | Credit | Balance Debit | Balance Credit |
|---|---|---|---|---|---|---|
| 2016 | | | | | | |
| Apr. 30 | Adjusting | 3 | | 120 | | 120 |

### Account *Unearned Fees* — Account No. 23

| Date | Item | Post. Ref. | Debit | Credit | Balance Debit | Balance Credit |
|---|---|---|---|---|---|---|
| 2016 | | | | | | |
| Apr. 4 | | 1 | | 5,000 | | 5,000 |
| 30 | Adjusting | 3 | 2,500 | | | 2,500 |

### Account *Kelly Pitney, Capital* — Account No. 31

| Date | Item | Post. Ref. | Debit | Credit | Balance Debit | Balance Credit |
|---|---|---|---|---|---|---|
| 2016 | | | | | | |
| Apr. 1 | | 1 | | 30,000 | | 30,000 |
| 30 | Closing | 4 | | 18,300 | | 48,300 |
| 30 | Closing | 4 | 6,000 | | | 42,300 |

| EXHIBIT 18 | Ledger, Kelly Consulting (*Concluded*) |
|---|---|

**Account** *Kelly Pitney, Drawing*  Account No. *32*

| Date | Item | Post. Ref. | Debit | Credit | Balance Debit | Balance Credit |
|---|---|---|---|---|---|---|
| 2016 Apr. 30 | | 2 | 6,000 | | 6,000 | |
| 30 | Closing | 4 | | 6,000 | — | — |

**Account** *Income Summary*  Account No. *33*

| Date | Item | Post. Ref. | Debit | Credit | Balance Debit | Balance Credit |
|---|---|---|---|---|---|---|
| 2016 Apr. 30 | Closing | 4 | | 23,450 | | 23,450 |
| 30 | Closing | 4 | 5,150 | | | 18,300 |
| 30 | Closing | 4 | 18,300 | | — | — |

**Account** *Fees Earned*  Account No. *41*

| Date | Item | Post. Ref. | Debit | Credit | Balance Debit | Balance Credit |
|---|---|---|---|---|---|---|
| 2016 Apr. 12 | | 1 | | 4,200 | | 4,200 |
| 17 | | 2 | | 6,250 | | 10,450 |
| 20 | | 2 | | 2,100 | | 12,550 |
| 24 | | 2 | | 3,850 | | 16,400 |
| 30 | | 2 | | 3,050 | | 19,450 |
| 30 | | 2 | | 1,500 | | 20,950 |
| 30 | Adjusting | 3 | | 2,500 | | 23,450 |
| 30 | Closing | 4 | 23,450 | | — | — |

**Account** *Salary Expense*  Account No. *51*

| Date | Item | Post. Ref. | Debit | Credit | Balance Debit | Balance Credit |
|---|---|---|---|---|---|---|
| 2016 Apr. 14 | | 1 | 750 | | 750 | |
| 27 | | 2 | 750 | | 1,500 | |
| 30 | Adjusting | 3 | 120 | | 1,620 | |
| 30 | Closing | 4 | | 1,620 | — | — |

**Account** *Rent Expense*  Account No. *52*

| Date | Item | Post. Ref. | Debit | Credit | Balance Debit | Balance Credit |
|---|---|---|---|---|---|---|
| 2016 Apr. 30 | Adjusting | 3 | 1,600 | | 1,600 | |
| 30 | Closing | 4 | | 1,600 | — | — |

**Account** *Supplies Expense*  Account No. *53*

| Date | Item | Post. Ref. | Debit | Credit | Balance Debit | Balance Credit |
|---|---|---|---|---|---|---|
| 2016 Apr. 30 | Adjusting | 3 | 850 | | 850 | |
| 30 | Closing | 4 | | 850 | — | — |

**Account** *Depreciation Expense*  Account No. *54*

| Date | Item | Post. Ref. | Debit | Credit | Balance Debit | Balance Credit |
|---|---|---|---|---|---|---|
| 2016 Apr. 30 | Adjusting | 3 | 330 | | 330 | |
| 30 | Closing | 4 | | 330 | — | — |

**Account** *Insurance Expense*  Account No. *55*

| Date | Item | Post. Ref. | Debit | Credit | Balance Debit | Balance Credit |
|---|---|---|---|---|---|---|
| 2016 Apr. 30 | Adjusting | 3 | 300 | | 300 | |
| 30 | Closing | 4 | | 300 | — | — |

**Account** *Miscellaneous Expense*  Account No. *59*

| Date | Item | Post. Ref. | Debit | Credit | Balance Debit | Balance Credit |
|---|---|---|---|---|---|---|
| 2016 Apr. 10 | | 1 | 120 | | 120 | |
| 29 | | 2 | 130 | | 250 | |
| 30 | | 2 | 200 | | 450 | |
| 30 | Closing | 4 | | 450 | — | — |

# Fiscal Year

The annual accounting period adopted by a business is known as its **fiscal year**. Fiscal years begin with the first day of the month selected and end on the last day of the following twelfth month. The period most commonly used is the calendar year. Other periods are not unusual, especially for businesses organized as corporations. For example, a corporation may adopt a fiscal year that ends when business activities have

**OBJ 6** Explain what is meant by the fiscal year and the natural business year.

reached the lowest point in its annual operating cycle. Such a fiscal year is called the **natural business year**. At the low point in its operating cycle, a business has more time to analyze the results of operations and to prepare financial statements.

Because companies with fiscal years often have highly seasonal operations, investors and others should be careful in interpreting partial-year reports for such companies. That is, you should expect the results of operations for these companies to vary significantly throughout the fiscal year.

The financial history of a business may be shown by a series of balance sheets and income statements for several fiscal years. If the life of a business is expressed by a line moving from left to right, the series of balance sheets and income statements may be graphed as shown in Exhibit 19.

---

**EXHIBIT 19** **Financial History of a Business**

---

# Business Connection

**CHOOSING A FISCAL YEAR**

CVS Caremark Corporation (CVS) operates more than 7,000 pharmacies throughout the United States and fills more than one billion prescriptions annually. CVS recently chose December 31 as its fiscal year-end and described its decision as follows:

.... our Board of Directors approved a change in our fiscal year-end ... to December 31 of each year to better reflect our position in the health care ... industry.

In contrast, most large retailers such as Walmart and Target use fiscal years ending January 31, when their operations are the slowest following the December holidays.

---

**OBJ 7** Describe and illustrate the use of working capital and the current ratio in evaluating a company's financial condition.

# Financial Analysis and Interpretation: Working Capital and Current Ratio

The ability to convert assets into cash is called **liquidity**, while the ability of a business to pay its debts is called **solvency**. Two financial measures for evaluating a business's short-term liquidity and solvency are working capital and the current ratio.

**Working capital** is the excess of the current assets of a business over its current liabilities, computed as follows:

$$\text{Working Capital} = \text{Current Assets} - \text{Current Liabilities}$$

Current assets are more liquid than long-term assets. Thus, an increase in a company's current assets increases or improves its liquidity. An increase in working capital increases or improves liquidity in the sense that current assets are available for uses other than paying current liabilities.

A positive working capital implies that the business is able to pay its current liabilities and is solvent. Thus, an increase in working capital increases or improves a company's short-term solvency.

To illustrate, **NetSolutions**' working capital at the end of 2015 is $6,355 computed as follows:

$$\text{Working Capital} = \text{Current Assets} - \text{Current Liabilities}$$
$$= \$7,745 - \$1,390$$
$$= \$6,355$$

This amount of working capital implies that NetSolutions is able to pay its current liabilities.

The **current ratio** is another means of expressing the relationship between current assets and current liabilities. The current ratio is computed by dividing current assets by current liabilities, as follows:

$$\text{Current Ratio} = \frac{\text{Current Assets}}{\text{Current Liabilities}}$$

To illustrate, the current ratio for **NetSolutions** at the end of 2015 is 5.6, computed as follows:

$$\text{Current Ratio} = \frac{\text{Current Assets}}{\text{Current Liabilities}}$$
$$= \frac{\$7,745}{\$1,390}$$
$$= 5.6 \text{ (Rounded)}$$

The current ratio is more useful than working capital in making comparisons across companies or with industry averages. To illustrate, the following data (in millions) were taken from recent financial statements of Electronic Arts Inc., Take-Two Interactive Software, Inc., and Zynga, Inc.:

|  | Electronic Arts | | Take-Two | | Zynga | |
|---|---|---|---|---|---|---|
|  | Year 2 | Year 1 | Year 2 | Year 1 | Year 2 | Year 1 |
| Current assets | $2,609 | $3,032 | $744 | $567 | $1,484 | $2,024 |
| Current liabilities | 2,120 | 2,001 | 219 | 231 | 509 | 669 |
| Working capital | $ 489 | $1,031 | $525 | $336 | $ 975 | $1,355 |
| Current ratio* | 1.23 | 1.52 | 3.40 | 2.45 | 2.92 | 3.03 |
|  | ($2,609 ÷ $2,120) | ($3,032 ÷ $2,001) | ($744 ÷ $219) | ($567 ÷ $231) | ($1,484 ÷ $509) | ($2,024 ÷ $669) |

* Rounded to two decimal places.

Electronic Arts has more than 3.5 times ($2,609 compared to $744) the current assets as does Take-Two and more than 1.7 times ($2,609 compared to $1,484) the current assets of Zynga. Such size differences makes meaningful comparisons difficult across companies. For this reason, ratios, such as the current ratio, are computed.

Although Electronic Arts is larger, Take-Two and Zynga have higher current ratios (3.40 and 2.45 for Take-Two; 2.92 and 3.03 for Zynga) than Electronic Arts. Overall, Take-Two and Zynga appear to be in a stronger short-term liquidity position than Electronic Arts. In addition, Electronics Arts' current ratio has decreased to 1.23 from 1.52, while Take-Two's current ratio has increased to 3.40 from 2.45 and Zynga's current ratio has decreased slightly to 2.92 from 3.03.

## Example Exercise 4-6   Working Capital and Current Ratio

Current assets and current liabilities for Fortson Company follow:

|  | 2016 | 2015 |
|---|---|---|
| Current assets | $310,500 | $262,500 |
| Current liabilities | 172,500 | 150,000 |

a.  Determine the working capital and current ratio for 2016 and 2015.

b.  Does the change in the current ratio from 2015 to 2016 indicate a favorable or an unfavorable trend?

### Follow My Example 4-6

a.

|  | 2016 | 2015 |
|---|---|---|
| Current assets | $310,500 | $262,500 |
| Current liabilities | 172,500 | 150,000 |
| Working capital | $138,000 | $112,500 |
| Current ratio | 1.80 | 1.75 |
|  | ($310,500 ÷ $172,500) | ($262,500 ÷ $150,000) |

b.  The change from 1.75 to 1.80 indicates a favorable trend.

Practice Exercises: PE 4-6A, PE 4-6B

# APPENDIX 1

# End-of-Period Spreadsheet

Accountants often use spreadsheets for analyzing and summarizing data. Such spreadsheets are not a formal part of the accounting records. This is in contrast to the chart of accounts, the journal, and the ledger, which are essential parts of an accounting system. Spreadsheets are usually prepared by using a computer program such as Microsoft's Excel.®

Exhibit 1 is an end-of-period spreadsheet used to summarize adjusting entries and their effects on the accounts. As illustrated in the chapter, the financial statements for NetSolutions can be prepared directly from the spreadsheet's Adjusted Trial Balance columns.

Some accountants prefer to expand the end-of-period spreadsheet shown in Exhibit 1 to include financial statement columns. Exhibits 20 through 24 illustrate the step-by-step process of how to prepare this expanded spreadsheet. As a basis for illustration, **NetSolutions** is used.

## Step 1. Enter the Title

The spreadsheet is started by entering the following data:

1.  Name of the business: *NetSolutions*
2.  Type of spreadsheet: *End-of-Period Spreadsheet*
3.  The period of time: *For the Two Months Ended December 31, 2015*

Exhibit 20 shows the preceding data entered for NetSolutions.

| EXHIBIT 20 | | **Spreadsheet with Unadjusted Trial Balance Entered** |

| | A | B | C | D | E | F | G | H | I | J | K |
|---|---|---|---|---|---|---|---|---|---|---|---|
| 1 | | | | NetSolutions | | | | | | | |
| 2 | | | | End-of-Period Spreadsheet | | | | | | | |
| 3 | | | | For the Two Months Ended December 31, 2015 | | | | | | | |
| 4 | | Unadjusted | | | | Adjusted | | | | | |
| 5 | | Trial Balance | | Adjustments | | Trial Balance | | Income Statement | | Balance Sheet | |
| 6 | Account Title | Dr. | Cr. | Dr. | Cr. | Dr. | Cr. | Dr. | Cr. | Dr. | Cr. |
| 7 | | | | | | | | | | | |
| 8 | Cash | 2,065 | | | | | | | | | |
| 9 | Accounts Receivable | 2,220 | | | | | | | | | |
| 10 | Supplies | 2,000 | | | | | | | | | |
| 11 | Prepaid Insurance | 2,400 | | | | | | | | | |
| 12 | Land | 20,000 | | | | | | | | | |
| 13 | Office Equipment | 1,800 | | | | | | | | | |
| 14 | Accumulated Depreciation | | | | | | | | | | |
| 15 | Accounts Payable | | 900 | | | | | | | | |
| 16 | Wages Payable | | | | | | | | | | |
| 17 | Unearned Rent | | 360 | | | | | | | | |
| 18 | Chris Clark, Capital | | 25,000 | | | | | | | | |
| 19 | Chris Clark, Drawing | 4,000 | | | | | | | | | |
| 20 | Fees Earned | | 16,340 | | | | | | | | |
| 21 | Rent Revenue | | | | | | | | | | |
| 22 | Wages Expense | 4,275 | | | | | | | | | |
| 23 | Supplies Expense | 800 | | | | | | | | | |
| 24 | Rent Expense | 1,600 | | | | | | | | | |
| 25 | Utilities Expense | 985 | | | | | | | | | |
| 26 | Insurance Expense | | | | | | | | | | |
| 27 | Depreciation Expense | | | | | | | | | | |
| 28 | Miscellaneous Expense | 455 | | | | | | | | | |
| 29 | | 42,600 | 42,600 | | | | | | | | |
| 30 | | | | | | | | | | | |

*The spreadsheet is used for summarizing the effects of adjusting entries. It also aids in preparing financial statements.*

*Closing Acc. (handwritten note beside rows 19–30)*

## Step 2. Enter the Unadjusted Trial Balance

Enter the unadjusted trial balance on the spreadsheet. The spreadsheet in Exhibit 20 shows the unadjusted trial balance for NetSolutions at December 31, 2015.

## Step 3. Enter the Adjustments

The adjustments for NetSolutions from Chapter 3 are entered in the Adjustments columns, as shown in Exhibit 21. Cross-referencing (by letters) the debit and credit of each adjustment is useful in reviewing the spreadsheet. It is also helpful for identifying the adjusting entries that need to be recorded in the journal. This cross-referencing process is sometimes referred to as *keying* the adjustments.

The adjustments are normally entered in the order in which the data are assembled. If the titles of the accounts to be adjusted do not appear in the unadjusted trial balance, the accounts are inserted in their proper order in the Account Title column.

The adjusting entries for NetSolutions that are entered in the Adjustments columns are as follows:

(a) **Supplies.** The supplies account has a debit balance of $2,000. The cost of the supplies on hand at the end of the period is $760. The supplies expense for December is the difference between the two amounts, or $1,240 ($2,000 – $760). The adjustment is entered as (1) $1,240 in the Adjustments Debit column on the same line as Supplies Expense and (2) $1,240 in the Adjustments Credit column on the same line as Supplies.

(b) **Prepaid Insurance.** The prepaid insurance account has a debit balance of $2,400. This balance represents the prepayment of insurance for 12 months beginning December 1. Thus, the insurance expense for December is $200 ($2,400 ÷ 12). The adjustment is entered as (1) $200 in the Adjustments Debit column on the same line as Insurance Expense and (2) $200 in the Adjustments Credit column on the same line as Prepaid Insurance.

| EXHIBIT 21 | Spreadsheet with Unadjusted Trial Balance and Adjustments |
| --- | --- |

| | A | B | C | D | E | F | G | H | I | J | K |
| --- | --- | --- | --- | --- | --- | --- | --- | --- | --- | --- | --- |
| 1 | | | | NetSolutions | | | | | | | |
| 2 | | | | End-of-Period Spreadsheet | | | | | | | |
| 3 | | | | For the Two Months Ended December 31, 2015 | | | | | | | |
| 4 | | Unadjusted | | | | Adjusted | | | | | |
| 5 | | Trial Balance | | Adjustments | | Trial Balance | | Income Statement | | Balance Sheet | |
| 6 | Account Title | Dr. | Cr. | Dr. | Cr. | Dr. | Cr. | Dr. | Cr. | Dr. | Cr. |
| 7 | | | | | | | | | | | |
| 8 | Cash | 2,065 | | | | | | | | | |
| 9 | Accounts Receivable | 2,220 | | (d) 500 | | | | | | | |
| 10 | Supplies | 2,000 | | | (a) 1,240 | | | | | | |
| 11 | Prepaid Insurance | 2,400 | | | (b) 200 | | | | | | |
| 12 | Land | 20,000 | | | | | | | | | |
| 13 | Office Equipment | 1,800 | | | | | | | | | |
| 14 | Accumulated Depreciation | | | | (f) 50 | | | | | | |
| 15 | Accounts Payable | | 900 | | | | | | | | |
| 16 | Wages Payable | | | | (e) 250 | | | | | | |
| 17 | Unearned Rent | | 360 | (c) 120 | | | | | | | |
| 18 | Chris Clark, Capital | | 25,000 | | | | | | | | |
| 19 | Chris Clark, Drawing | 4,000 | | | | | | | | | |
| 20 | Fees Earned | | 16,340 | | (d) 500 | | | | | | |
| 21 | Rent Revenue | | | | (c) 120 | | | | | | |
| 22 | Wages Expense | 4,275 | | (e) 250 | | | | | | | |
| 23 | Supplies Expense | 800 | | (a) 1,240 | | | | | | | |
| 24 | Rent Expense | 1,600 | | | | | | | | | |
| 25 | Utilities Expense | 985 | | | | | | | | | |
| 26 | Insurance Expense | | | (b) 200 | | | | | | | |
| 27 | Depreciation Expense | | | (f) 50 | | | | | | | |
| 28 | Miscellaneous Expense | 455 | | | | | | | | | |
| 29 | | 42,600 | 42,600 | 2,360 | 2,360 | | | | | | |
| 30 | | | | | | | | | | | |

> The adjustments on the spreadsheet are used in preparing the adjusting journal entries.

(c) **Unearned Rent.** The unearned rent account has a credit balance of $360. This balance represents the receipt of three months' rent, beginning with December. Thus, the rent revenue for December is $120 ($360 ÷ 3). The adjustment is entered as (1) $120 in the Adjustments Debit column on the same line as Unearned Rent and (2) $120 in the Adjustments Credit column on the same line as Rent Revenue.

(d) **Accrued Fees.** Fees accrued at the end of December but not recorded total $500. This amount is an increase in an asset and an increase in revenue. The adjustment is entered as (1) $500 in the Adjustments Debit column on the same line as Accounts Receivable and (2) $500 in the Adjustments Credit column on the same line as Fees Earned.

(e) **Wages.** Wages accrued but not paid at the end of December total $250. This amount is an increase in expenses and an increase in liabilities. The adjustment is entered as (1) $250 in the Adjustments Debit column on the same line as Wages Expense and (2) $250 in the Adjustments Credit column on the same line as Wages Payable.

(f) **Depreciation.** Depreciation of the office equipment is $50 for December. The adjustment is entered as (1) $50 in the Adjustments Debit column on the same line as Depreciation Expense and (2) $50 in the Adjustments Credit column on the same line as Accumulated Depreciation.

After the adjustments have been entered, the Adjustments columns are totaled to verify the equality of the debits and credits. The total of the Debit column must equal the total of the Credit column.

## Step 4. Enter the Adjusted Trial Balance

The adjusted trial balance is entered by combining the adjustments with the unadjusted balances for each account. The adjusted amounts are then extended to the Adjusted Trial Balance columns, as shown in Exhibit 22.

To illustrate, the cash amount of $2,065 is extended to the Adjusted Trial Balance Debit column since no adjustments affected Cash. Accounts Receivable has an initial

**EXHIBIT 22** Spreadsheet with Unadjusted Trial Balance, Adjustments, and Adjusted Trial Balance Entered

| | A | B | C | D | E | F | G | H | I | J | K |
|---|---|---|---|---|---|---|---|---|---|---|---|
| | | | | | | | | | | | |
| 1 | | | | NetSolutions | | | | | | | |
| 2 | | | | End-of-Period Spreadsheet | | | | | | | |
| 3 | | | | For the Two Months Ended December 31, 2015 | | | | | | | |
| 4 | | Unadjusted | | | | Adjusted | | | | | |
| 5 | | Trial Balance | | Adjustments | | Trial Balance | | Income Statement | | Balance Sheet | |
| 6 | Account Title | Dr. | Cr. | Dr. | Cr. | Dr. | Cr. | Dr. | Cr. | Dr. | Cr. |
| 7 | | | | | | | | | | | |
| 8 | Cash | 2,065 | | | | 2,065 | | | | | |
| 9 | Accounts Receivable | 2,220 | | (d) 500 | | 2,720 | | | | | |
| 10 | Supplies | 2,000 | | | (a) 1,240 | 760 | | | | | |
| 11 | Prepaid Insurance | 2,400 | | | (b) 200 | 2,200 | | | | | |
| 12 | Land | 20,000 | | | | 20,000 | | | | | |
| 13 | Office Equipment | 1,800 | | | | 1,800 | | | | | |
| 14 | Accumulated Depreciation | | | | (f) 50 | | 50 | | | | |
| 15 | Accounts Payable | | 900 | | | | 900 | | | | |
| 16 | Wages Payable | | | | (e) 250 | | 250 | | | | |
| 17 | Unearned Rent | | 360 | (c) 120 | | | 240 | | | | |
| 18 | Chris Clark, Capital | | 25,000 | | | | 25,000 | | | | |
| 19 | Chris Clark, Drawing | 4,000 | | | | 4,000 | | | | | |
| 20 | Fees Earned | | 16,340 | | (d) 500 | | 16,840 | | | | |
| 21 | Rent Revenue | | | | (c) 120 | | 120 | | | | |
| 22 | Wages Expense | 4,275 | | (e) 250 | | 4,525 | | | | | |
| 23 | Supplies Expense | 800 | | (a) 1,240 | | 2,040 | | | | | |
| 24 | Rent Expense | 1,600 | | | | 1,600 | | | | | |
| 25 | Utilities Expense | 985 | | | | 985 | | | | | |
| 26 | Insurance Expense | | | (b) 200 | | 200 | | | | | |
| 27 | Depreciation Expense | | | (f) 50 | | 50 | | | | | |
| 28 | Miscellaneous Expense | 455 | | | | 455 | | | | | |
| 29 | | 42,600 | 42,600 | 2,360 | 2,360 | 43,400 | 43,400 | | | | |
| 30 | | | | | | | | | | | |

> The adjusted trial balance amounts are determined by adding the adjustments to or subtracting the adjustments from the trial balance amounts. For example, the Wages Expense debit of $4,525 is the trial balance amount of $4,275 plus the $250 adjustment debit.

balance of $2,220 and a debit adjustment of $500. Thus, $2,720 ($2,220 + $500) is entered in the Adjusted Trial Balance Debit column for Accounts Receivable. The same process continues until all account balances are extended to the Adjusted Trial Balance columns.

After the accounts and adjustments have been extended, the Adjusted Trial Balance columns are totaled to verify the equality of debits and credits. The total of the Debit column must equal the total of the Credit column.

## Step 5. Extend the Accounts to the Income Statement and Balance Sheet Columns

The adjusted trial balance amounts are extended to the Income Statement and Balance Sheet columns. The amounts for revenues and expenses are extended to the Income Statement columns. The amounts for assets, liabilities, owner's capital, and drawings are extended to the Balance Sheet columns.[3]

The first account listed in the Adjusted Trial Balance columns is Cash with a debit balance of $2,065. Cash is an asset, is listed on the balance sheet, and has a debit balance. Therefore, $2,065 is extended to the Balance Sheet Debit column. The Fees Earned balance of $16,840 is extended to the Income Statement Credit column. The

[3] The balance of the dividends account is extended to the Balance Sheet columns because the spreadsheet does not have separate Statement of Owner's Equity columns.

**EXHIBIT 23**    **Spreadsheet with Amounts Extended to Income Statement and Balance Sheet Columns**

| | A | B | C | D | E | F | G | H | I | J | K |
|---|---|---|---|---|---|---|---|---|---|---|---|
| 1 | | | | | NetSolutions | | | | | | |
| 2 | | | | | End-of-Period Spreadsheet | | | | | | |
| 3 | | | | | For the Two Months Ended December 31, 2015 | | | | | | |
| 4 | | Unadjusted | | | | Adjusted | | | | | |
| 5 | | Trial Balance | | Adjustments | | Trial Balance | | Income Statement | | Balance Sheet | |
| 6 | Account Title | Dr. | Cr. | Dr. | Cr. | Dr. | Cr. | Dr. | Cr. | Dr. | Cr. |
| 7 | | | | | | | | | | | |
| 8 | Cash | 2,065 | | | | 2,065 | | | | 2,065 | |
| 9 | Accounts Receivable | 2,220 | | (d) 500 | | 2,720 | | | | 2,720 | |
| 10 | Supplies | 2,000 | | | (a) 1,240 | 760 | | | | 760 | |
| 11 | Prepaid Insurance | 2,400 | | | (b) 200 | 2,200 | | | | 2,200 | |
| 12 | Land | 20,000 | | | | 20,000 | | | | 20,000 | |
| 13 | Office Equipment | 1,800 | | | | 1,800 | | | | 1,800 | |
| 14 | Accumulated Depreciation | | | | (f) 50 | | 50 | | | | 50 |
| 15 | Accounts Payable | | 900 | | | | 900 | | | | 900 |
| 16 | Wages Payable | | | | (e) 250 | | 250 | | | | 250 |
| 17 | Unearned Rent | | 360 | (c) 120 | | | 240 | | | | 240 |
| 18 | Chris Clark, Capital | | 25,000 | | | | 25,000 | | | | 25,000 |
| 19 | Chris Clark, Drawing | 4,000 | | | | 4,000 | | | | 4,000 | |
| 20 | Fees Earned | | 16,340 | | (d) 500 | | 16,840 | | 16,840 | | |
| 21 | Rent Revenue | | | | (c) 120 | | 120 | | 120 | | |
| 22 | Wages Expense | 4,275 | | (e) 250 | | 4,525 | | 4,525 | | | |
| 23 | Supplies Expense | 800 | | (a) 1,240 | | 2,040 | | 2,040 | | | |
| 24 | Rent Expense | 1,600 | | | | 1,600 | | 1,600 | | | |
| 25 | Utilities Expense | 985 | | | | 985 | | 985 | | | |
| 26 | Insurance Expense | | | (b) 200 | | 200 | | 200 | | | |
| 27 | Depreciation Expense | | | (f) 50 | | 50 | | 50 | | | |
| 28 | Miscellaneous Expense | 455 | | | | 455 | | 455 | | | |
| 29 | | 42,600 | 42,600 | 2,360 | 2,360 | 43,400 | 43,400 | | | | |
| 30 | | | | | | | | | | | |

The revenue and expense amounts are extended to (entered in) the Income Statement columns.

The asset, liability, owner's capital, and drawing amounts are extended to (entered in) the Balance Sheet columns.

same process continues until all account balances have been extended to the proper columns, as shown in Exhibit 23.

## Step 6. Total the Income Statement and Balance Sheet Columns, Compute the Net Income or Net Loss, and Complete the Spreadsheet

After the account balances are extended to the Income Statement and Balance Sheet columns, each of the columns is totaled. The difference between the two Income Statement column totals is the amount of the net income or the net loss for the period. This difference (net income or net loss) will also be the difference between the two Balance Sheet column totals.

If the Income Statement Credit column total (total revenue) is greater than the Income Statement Debit column total (total expenses), the difference is the net income. If the Income Statement Debit column total is greater than the Income Statement Credit column total, the difference is a net loss.

As shown in Exhibit 24, the total of the Income Statement Credit column is $16,960, and the total of the Income Statement Debit column is $9,855. Thus, the net income for NetSolutions is $7,105, computed as follows:

| | |
|---|---|
| Total of Income Statement Credit column (revenues) | $16,960 |
| Total of Income Statement Debit column (expenses) | 9,855 |
| Net income (excess of revenues over expenses) | $ 7,105 |

The amount of the net income, $7,105, is entered in the Income Statement Debit column and the Balance Sheet Credit column. *Net income* is also entered in the Account Title column. Entering the net income of $7,105 in the Balance Sheet Credit column has the effect of transferring the net balance of the revenue and expense accounts to the retained earnings account.

If there was a net loss instead of net income, the amount of the net loss would be entered in the Income Statement Credit column and the Balance Sheet Debit column. *Net loss* would also be entered in the Account Title column.

---

**EXHIBIT 24**   **Completed Spreadsheet with Net Income Shown**

| | A | B | C | D | E | F | G | H | I | J | K |
|---|---|---|---|---|---|---|---|---|---|---|---|
| 1 | | | | | NetSolutions | | | | | | |
| 2 | | | | | End-of-Period Spreadsheet | | | | | | |
| 3 | | | | | For the Two Months Ended December 31, 2015 | | | | | | |
| 4 | | Unadjusted | | | | Adjusted | | | | | |
| 5 | | Trial Balance | | Adjustments | | Trial Balance | | Income Statement | | Balance Sheet | |
| 6 | Account Title | Dr. | Cr. | Dr. | Cr. | Dr. | Cr. | Dr. | Cr. | Dr. | Cr. |
| 7 | | | | | | | | | | | |
| 8 | Cash | 2,065 | | | | 2,065 | | | | 2,065 | |
| 9 | Accounts Receivable | 2,220 | | (d) 500 | | 2,720 | | | | 2,720 | |
| 10 | Supplies | 2,000 | | | (a) 1,240 | 760 | | | | 760 | |
| 11 | Prepaid Insurance | 2,400 | | | (b) 200 | 2,200 | | | | 2,200 | |
| 12 | Land | 20,000 | | | | 20,000 | | | | 20,000 | |
| 13 | Office Equipment | 1,800 | | | | 1,800 | | | | 1,800 | |
| 14 | Accumulated Depreciation | | | | (f) 50 | | 50 | | | | 50 |
| 15 | Accounts Payable | | 900 | | | | 900 | | | | 900 |
| 16 | Wages Payable | | | | (e) 250 | | 250 | | | | 250 |
| 17 | Unearned Rent | | 360 | (c) 120 | | | 240 | | | | 240 |
| 18 | Chris Clark, Capital | | 25,000 | | | | 25,000 | | | | 25,000 |
| 19 | Chris Clark, Drawing | 4,000 | | | | 4,000 | | | | 4,000 | |
| 20 | Fees Earned | | 16,340 | | (d) 500 | | 16,840 | | 16,840 | | |
| 21 | Rent Revenue | | | | (c) 120 | | 120 | | 120 | | |
| 22 | Wages Expense | 4,275 | | (e) 250 | | 4,525 | | 4,525 | | | |
| 23 | Supplies Expense | 800 | | (a) 1,240 | | 2,040 | | 2,040 | | | |
| 24 | Rent Expense | 1,600 | | | | 1,600 | | 1,600 | | | |
| 25 | Utilities Expense | 985 | | | | 985 | | 985 | | | |
| 26 | Insurance Expense | | | (b) 200 | | 200 | | 200 | | | |
| 27 | Depreciation Expense | | | (f) 50 | | 50 | | 50 | | | |
| 28 | Miscellaneous Expense | 455 | | | | 455 | | 455 | | | |
| 29 | | 42,600 | 42,600 | 2,360 | 2,360 | 43,400 | 43,400 | 9,855 | 16,960 | 33,545 | 26,440 |
| 30 | Net income | | | | | | | 7,105 | | | 7,105 |
| 31 | | | | | | | | 16,960 | 16,960 | 33,545 | 33,545 |
| 32 | | | | | | | | | | | |

The difference between the Income Statement column totals is the net income (or net loss) for the period The difference between the Balance Sheet column totals is also the net income (or net loss) for the period.

After the net income or net loss is entered on the spreadsheet, the Income Statement and Balance Sheet columns are totaled. The totals of the two Income Statement columns must now be equal. The totals of the two Balance Sheet columns must also be equal.

## Preparing the Financial Statements from the Spreadsheet

The spreadsheet can be used to prepare the income statement, the statement of owner's equity, and the balance sheet shown in Exhibit 2. The income statement is normally prepared directly from the spreadsheet. The expenses are listed in the income statement in Exhibit 2 in order of size, beginning with the larger items. Miscellaneous expense is the last item, regardless of its amount.

The first item normally presented on the statement of owner's equity is the balance of the owner's capital account at the beginning of the period. The amount listed as owner's capital in the spreadsheet, however, is not always the account balance at the beginning of the period. The owner may have invested additional assets in the business during the period. Thus, for the beginning balance and any additional investments, it is necessary to refer to the capital account in the ledger. These amounts, along with the net income (or net loss) and the drawing amount shown in the spreadsheet, are used to determine the ending capital account balance.

The balance sheet can be prepared directly from the spreadsheet columns except for the ending balance of owner's capital. The ending balance of owner's capital is taken from the statement of owner's equity.

When a spreadsheet is used, the adjusting and closing entries are normally not journalized or posted until after the spreadsheet and financial statements have been prepared. The data for the adjusting entries are taken from the Adjustments columns of the spreadsheet. The data for the first two closing entries are taken from the Income Statement columns of the spreadsheet. The amount for the third closing entry is the net income or net loss appearing at the bottom of the spreadsheet. The amount for the fourth closing entry is the drawing account balance that appears in the Balance Sheet Debit column of the spreadsheet.

# At a Glance 4

**Describe the flow of accounting information from the unadjusted trial balance into the adjusted trial balance and financial statements.**

**Key Points**   Exhibit 1 illustrates the end-of-period process by which accounts are adjusted and how the adjusted accounts flow into the financial statements.

| Learning Outcomes | Example Exercises | Practice Exercises |
|---|---|---|
| • Using an end-of-period spreadsheet, describe how the unadjusted trial balance accounts are affected by adjustments and how the adjusted trial balance accounts flow into the income statement and balance sheet. | EE4-1 | PE4-1A, 4-1B |

**Prepare financial statements from adjusted account balances.**

**Key Points** Using the end-of-period spreadsheet shown in Exhibit 1, the income statement and balance sheet for NetSolutions can be prepared. The statement of owner's equity is prepared by referring to transactions that have been posted to owner's capital accounts in the ledger. A classified balance sheet has sections for current assets; property, plant, and equipment; current liabilities; long-term liabilities; and owner's equity.

| Learning Outcomes | Example Exercises | Practice Exercises |
|---|---|---|
| • Describe how the net income or net loss from the period can be determined from an end-of-period spreadsheet. | | |
| • Prepare an income statement, a statement of owner's equity, and a balance sheet. | EE4-2 | PE4-2A, 4-2B |
| • Indicate how accounts would be reported on a classified balance sheet. | EE4-3 | PE4-3A, 4-3B |

**Prepare closing entries.**

**Key Points** Four entries are required in closing the temporary accounts. The first entry closes the revenue accounts to Income Summary. The second entry closes the expense accounts to Income Summary. The third entry closes the balance of Income Summary (net income or net loss) to the owner's capital account. The fourth entry closes the drawing account to the owner's capital account.

After the closing entries have been posted to the ledger, the balance in the capital account agrees with the amount reported on the statement of owner's equity and balance sheet. In addition, the revenue, expense, and drawing accounts will have zero balances.

| Learning Outcomes | Example Exercises | Practice Exercises |
|---|---|---|
| • Prepare the closing entry for revenues. | EE4-4 | PE4-4A, 4-4B |
| • Prepare the closing entry for expenses. | EE4-4 | PE4-4A, 4-4B |
| • Prepare the closing entry for transferring the balance of Income Summary to the owner's capital account. | EE4-4 | PE4-4A, 4-4B |
| • Prepare the closing entry for the owner's drawing account. | EE4-4 | PE4-4A, 4-4B |

**Describe the accounting cycle.**

**Key Points** The 10 basic steps of the accounting cycle are as follows:

1. Transactions are analyzed and recorded in the journal.
2. Transactions are posted to the ledger.
3. An unadjusted trial balance is prepared.
4. Adjustment data are assembled and analyzed.
5. An optional end-of-period spreadsheet is prepared.
6. Adjusting entries are journalized and posted to the ledger.
7. An adjusted trial balance is prepared.
8. Financial statements are prepared.
9. Closing entries are journalized and posted to the ledger.
10. A post-closing trial balance is prepared.

| Learning Outcomes | Example Exercises | Practice Exercises |
|---|---|---|
| • List the 10 steps of the accounting cycle. | EE4-5 | PE4-5A, 4-5B |
| • Determine whether any steps are out of order in a listing of accounting cycle steps. | | |
| • Determine whether there are any missing steps in a listing of accounting cycle steps. | | |

**Illustrate the accounting cycle for one period.**

**Key Points**   The complete accounting cycle for Kelly Consulting for the month of April is described and illustrated in this chapter.

| Learning Outcomes | Example Exercises | Practice Exercises |
|---|---|---|
| • Complete the accounting cycle for a period from beginning to end. | | |

**Explain what is meant by the fiscal year and the natural business year.**

**Key Points**   The annual accounting period adopted by a business is its fiscal year. A company's fiscal year that ends when business activities have reached the lowest point in its annual operating cycle is called the natural business year.

| Learning Outcomes | Example Exercises | Practice Exercises |
|---|---|---|
| • Explain why companies use a fiscal year that is different from the calendar year. | | |

**Describe and illustrate the use of working capital and the current ratio in evaluating a company's financial condition.**

**Key Points**   The ability to convert assets into cash is called liquidity, while the ability of a business to pay its debts is called solvency. Two financial measures for evaluating a business's short-term liquidity and solvency are working capital and the current ratio. Working capital is computed by subtracting current liabilities from current assets. An excess of current assets over current liabilities implies that the business is able to pay its current liabilities. The current ratio is computed by dividing current assets by current liabilities. The current ratio is more useful than working capital in making comparisons across companies or with industry averages.

| Learning Outcomes | Example Exercises | Practice Exercises |
|---|---|---|
| • Define liquidity and solvency. | | |
| • Compute working capital. | **EE4-6** | **PE4-6A, 4-6B** |
| • Compute the current ratio. | **EE4-6** | **PE4-6A, 4-6B** |

# Key Terms

accounting cycle (164)
clearing account (159)
closing entries (158)
closing process (158)
closing the books (158)
current assets (157)
current liabilities (157)

current ratio (177)
fiscal year (175)
fixed (plant) assets (157)
Income Summary (159)
liquidity (176)
long-term liabilities (157)
natural business year (176)

notes receivable (157)
real (permanent) accounts (158)
solvency (176)
temporary (nominal) accounts (158)
working capital (176)

## Illustrative Problem

Three years ago, T. Roderick organized Harbor Realty. At July 31, 2016, the end of the fiscal year, the following end-of-period spreadsheet was prepared:

| | A | B | C | D | E | F | G |
|---|---|---|---|---|---|---|---|
| 1 | | Harbor Realty | | | | | |
| 2 | | End-of-Period Spreadsheet | | | | | |
| 3 | | For the Year Ended July 31, 2016 | | | | | |
| 4 | | Unadjusted | | | | Adjusted | |
| 5 | | Trial Balance | | Adjustments | | Trial Balance | |
| 6 | Account Title | Dr. | Cr. | Dr. | Cr. | Dr. | Cr. |
| 7 | | | | | | | |
| 8 | Cash | 3,425 | | | | 3,425 | |
| 9 | Accounts Receivable | 7,000 | | (e) 1,000 | | 8,000 | |
| 10 | Supplies | 1,270 | | | (a) 890 | 380 | |
| 11 | Prepaid Insurance | 620 | | | (b) 315 | 305 | |
| 12 | Office Equipment | 51,650 | | | | 51,650 | |
| 13 | Accum. Depreciation | | 9,700 | | (c) 4,950 | | 14,650 |
| 14 | Accounts Payable | | 925 | | | | 925 |
| 15 | Unearned Fees | | 1,250 | (f) 500 | | | 750 |
| 16 | Wages Payable | | | | (d) 440 | | 440 |
| 17 | T. Roderick, Capital | | 29,000 | | | | 29,000 |
| 18 | T. Roderick, Drawing | 5,200 | | | | 5,200 | |
| 19 | Fees Earned | | 59,125 | | (c) 1,000 | | 60,625 |
| 20 | | | | | (f) 500 | | |
| 21 | Wages Expense | 22,415 | | (d) 440 | | 22,855 | |
| 22 | Depreciation Expense | | | (c) 4,950 | | 4,950 | |
| 23 | Rent Expense | 4,200 | | | | 4,200 | |
| 24 | Utilities Expense | 2,715 | | | | 2,715 | |
| 25 | Supplies Expense | | | (a) 890 | | 890 | |
| 26 | Insurance Expense | | | (b) 315 | | 315 | |
| 27 | Miscellaneous Expense | 1,505 | | | | 1,505 | |
| 28 | | 100,000 | 100,000 | 8,095 | 8,095 | 106,390 | 106,390 |
| 29 | | | | | | | |

## Instructions

1. Prepare an income statement, a statement of owner's equity (no additional investments were made during the year), and a balance sheet.

2. On the basis of the data in the end-of-period spreadsheet, journalize the closing entries.

## Solution

1.

| Harbor Realty<br>Income Statement<br>For the Year Ended July 31, 2016 | | |
|---|---|---|
| Fees earned.............................................................. | | $60,625 |
| Expenses: | | |
| Wages expense ....................................................... | $22,855 | |
| Depreciation expense ................................................ | 4,950 | |
| Rent expense ......................................................... | 4,200 | |
| Utilities expense ..................................................... | 2,715 | |
| Supplies expense ..................................................... | 890 | |
| Insurance expense ................................................... | 315 | |
| Miscellaneous expense ............................................... | 1,505 | |
| Total expenses.................................................... | | 37,430 |
| Net income ........................................................... | | $23,195 |

| Harbor Realty<br>Statement of Owner's Equity<br>For the Year Ended July 31, 2016 | | |
|---|---|---|
| T. Roderick, capital, August 1, 2015 ........................................... | | $29,000 |
| Net income for the year.................................................... | $23,195 | |
| Less withdrawals ......................................................... | 5,200 | |
| Increase in owner's equity ................................................ | | 17,995 |
| T. Roderick, capital, July 31, 2016 ........................................... | | $46,995 |

| Harbor Realty<br>Balance Sheet<br>July 31, 2016 | | | | | |
|---|---|---|---|---|---|
| **Assets** | | | **Liabilities** | | |
| Current assets: | | | Current liabilities: | | |
| Cash................................ | $ 3,425 | | Accounts payable.................. | $925 | |
| Accounts receivable ................. | 8,000 | | Unearned fees .................... | 750 | |
| Supplies ........................... | 380 | | Wages payable .................... | 440 | |
| Prepaid insurance ................... | 305 | | Total liabilities....................... | | $ 2,115 |
| Total current assets............... | | $12,110 | | | |
| Property, plant, and equipment: | | | | | |
| Office equipment.................... | $51,650 | | | | |
| Less accum. depreciation............ | 14,650 | | **Owner's Equity** | | |
| Total property, plant, | | | T. Roderick, capital.................. | | 46,995 |
| and equipment ................ | | 37,000 | Total liabilities and | | |
| Total assets.......................... | | $49,110 | owner's equity .................... | | $49,110 |

2.

| | | Journal | | | Page |
|---|---|---|---|---|---|
| **Date** | | **Description** | **Post. Ref.** | **Debit** | **Credit** |
| 2016 | | Closing Entries | | | |
| July | 31 | Fees Earned | | 60,625 | |
| | | Income Summary | | | 60,625 |
| | 31 | Income Summary | | 37,430 | |
| | | Wages Expense | | | 22,855 |
| | | Depreciation Expense | | | 4,950 |
| | | Rent Expense | | | 4,200 |
| | | Utilities Expense | | | 2,715 |
| | | Supplies Expense | | | 890 |
| | | Insurance Expense | | | 315 |
| | | Miscellaneous Expense | | | 1,505 |
| | 31 | Income Summary | | 23,195 | |
| | | T. Roderick, Capital | | | 23,195 |
| | 31 | T. Roderick, Capital | | 5,200 | |
| | | T. Roderick, Drawing | | | 5,200 |

# Discussion Questions

1. Why do some accountants prepare an end-of-period spreadsheet?

2. Describe the nature of the assets that compose the following sections of a balance sheet: (a) current assets, (b) property, plant, and equipment.

3. What is the difference between a current liability and a long-term liability?

4. What types of accounts are referred to as temporary accounts?

5. Why are closing entries required at the end of an accounting period?

6. What is the difference between adjusting entries and closing entries?

7. What is the purpose of the post-closing trial balance?

8. (a) What is the most important output of the accounting cycle? (b) Do all companies have an accounting cycle? Explain.

9. What is the natural business year?

10. Recent fiscal years for several well-known companies are as follows:

| Company | Fiscal Year Ending |
|---|---|
| JCPenney | January 27 |
| Limited Brands, Inc. | January 27 |
| Sears | January 27 |
| Target Corp. | January 27 |
| Home Depot | January 28 |
| Tiffany & Co. | January 30 |

What general characteristic shared by these companies explains why they do not have fiscal years ending December 31?

# Practice Exercises

EE 4-1 *p. 154*

### PE 4-1A Flow of accounts into financial statements
OBJ. 1

The balances for the accounts that follow appear in the Adjusted Trial Balance columns of the end-of-period spreadsheet. Indicate whether each account would flow into the income statement, statement of owner's equity, or balance sheet.

1. Accounts Receivable
2. Depreciation Expense—Equipment
3. Gene Cox, Capital (beginning of period)
4. Office Equipment

5. Rent Revenue
6. Supplies Expense
7. Unearned Revenue
8. Wages Payable

EE 4-1 *p. 154*

### PE 4-1B Flow of accounts into financial statements
OBJ. 1

The balances for the accounts that follow appear in the Adjusted Trial Balance columns of the end-of-period spreadsheet. Indicate whether each account would flow into the income statement, statement of owner's equity, or balance sheet.

1. Accumulated Depreciation—Building
2. Cash
3. Fees Earned
4. Insurance Expense

5. Prepaid Rent
6. Supplies
7. Tina Greer, Drawing
8. Wages Expense

EE 4-2 *p. 156*

### PE 4-2A Statement of owner's equity
OBJ. 2

Marcie Davies owns and operates Gemini Advertising Services. On January 1, 2015, Marcie Davies, Capital had a balance of $618,500. During the year, Marcie invested an additional $40,000 and withdrew $15,000. For the year ended December 31, 2015, Gemini Advertising Services reported a net income of $92,330. Prepare a statement of owner's equity for the year ended December 31, 2015.

EE 4-2 *p. 156*

### PE 4-2B Statement of owner's equity
OBJ. 2

Blake Knudson owns and operates Grab Bag Delivery Services. On January 1, 2015, Blake Knudson, Capital had a balance of $918,000. During the year, Blake made no additional investments and withdrew $15,000. For the year ended December 31, 2015, Grab Bag Delivery Services reported a net loss of $43,500. Prepare a statement of owner's equity for the year ended December 31, 2015.

EE 4-3 *p. 157*

### PE 4-3A Classified balance sheet
OBJ. 2

The following accounts appear in an adjusted trial balance of San Jose Consulting. Indicate whether each account would be reported in the (a) current asset; (b) property, plant, and equipment; (c) current liability; (d) long-term liability; or (e) owner's equity section of the December 31, 2015, balance sheet of San Jose Consulting.

1. Building
2. Nata Foust, Capital
3. Notes Payable (due in five years)
4. Prepaid Rent

5. Salaries Payable
6. Supplies
7. Taxes Payable
8. Unearned Service Fees

EE 4-3  *p. 157*
### PE 4-3B  Classified balance sheet
**OBJ. 2**

The following accounts appear in an adjusted trial balance of Kangaroo Consulting. Indicate whether each account would be reported in the (a) current asset; (b) property, plant, and equipment; (c) current liability; (d) long-term liability; or (e) owner's equity section of the December 31, 2015, balance sheet of Kangaroo Consulting.

1. Accounts Payable
2. Accounts Receivable
3. Accumulated Depreciation—Building
4. Cash
5. Lea Gabel, Capital
6. Note Payable (due in ten years)
7. Supplies
8. Wages Payable

EE 4-4  *p. 161*
### PE 4-4A  Closing entries
**OBJ. 3**

After the accounts have been adjusted at October 31, the end of the fiscal year, the following balances were taken from the ledger of Smart Delivery Services Co.:

| | |
|---|---:|
| Fraser Smart, Capital | $3,550,000 |
| Fraser Smart, Drawing | 40,000 |
| Fees Earned | 1,145,000 |
| Wages Expense | 740,000 |
| Rent Expense | 65,000 |
| Supplies Expense | 14,750 |
| Miscellaneous Expense | 8,800 |

Journalize the four entries required to close the accounts.

EE 4-4  *p. 161*
### PE 4-4B  Closing entries
**OBJ. 3**

After the accounts have been adjusted at April 30, the end of the fiscal year, the following balances were taken from the ledger of Nuclear Landscaping Co.:

| | |
|---|---:|
| Felix Godwin, Capital | $643,600 |
| Felix Godwin, Drawing | 10,500 |
| Fees Earned | 356,500 |
| Wages Expense | 283,100 |
| Rent Expense | 56,000 |
| Supplies Expense | 11,500 |
| Miscellaneous Expense | 13,000 |

Journalize the four entries required to close the accounts.

EE 4-5  *p. 164*
### PE 4-5A  Accounting cycle
**OBJ. 4**

From the following list of steps in the accounting cycle, identify what two steps are missing:

a. Transactions are analyzed and recorded in the journal.
b. An unadjusted trial balance is prepared.
c. Adjustment data are assembled and analyzed.
d. An optional end-of-period spreadsheet is prepared.
e. Adjusting entries are journalized and posted to the ledger.
f. An adjusted trial balance is prepared.
g. Closing entries are journalized and posted to the ledger.
h. A post-closing trial balance is prepared.

EE 4-5  *p. 164*
### PE 4-5B  Accounting cycle
**OBJ. 4**

From the following list of steps in the accounting cycle, identify what two steps are missing:

a. Transactions are analyzed and recorded in the journal.
b. Transactions are posted to the ledger.
c. An unadjusted trial balance is prepared.

(*Continued*)

d. An optional end-of-period spreadsheet is prepared.

e. Adjusting entries are journalized and posted to the ledger.

f. An adjusted trial balance is prepared.

g. Financial statements are prepared.

h. A post-closing trial balance is prepared.

---

EE 4-6 *p. 178*

SHOW
ME HOW

### PE 4-6A   Working capital and current ratio

**OBJ. 7**

Balance sheet data for HQ Properties Company follows:

|  | 2016 | 2015 |
|---|---|---|
| Current assets | $2,175,000 | $1,900,000 |
| Current liabilities | 1,500,000 | 1,250,000 |

a. Determine the working capital and current ratio for 2016 and 2015.

b. ➤ Does the change in the current ratio from 2015 to 2016 indicate a favorable or an unfavorable trend?

---

EE 4-6 *p. 178*

SHOW
ME HOW

### PE 4-6B   Working capital and current ratio

**OBJ. 7**

Balance sheet data for Brimstone Company follows:

|  | 2016 | 2015 |
|---|---|---|
| Current assets | $1,586,250 | $1,210,000 |
| Current liabilities | 705,000 | 550,000 |

a. Determine the working capital and current ratio for 2016 and 2015.

b. ➤ Does the change in the current ratio from 2015 to 2016 indicate a favorable or an unfavorable trend?

---

# Exercises

---

### EX 4-1   Flow of accounts into financial statements

**OBJ. 1, 2**

The balances for the accounts that follow appear in the Adjusted Trial Balance columns of the end-of-period spreadsheet. Indicate whether each account would flow into the income statement, statement of owner's equity, or balance sheet.

1. Accounts Payable
2. Accounts Receivable
3. Cash
4. Danny Reacher, Drawing
5. Fees Earned

6. Supplies
7. Unearned Rent
8. Utilities Expense
9. Wages Expense
10. Wages Payable

---

### EX 4-2   Classifying accounts

**OBJ. 1, 2**

Balances for each of the following accounts appear in an adjusted trial balance. Identify each as (a) asset, (b) liability, (c) revenue, or (d) expense.

1. Accounts Receivable
2. Equipment
3. Fees Earned
4. Insurance Expense
5. Prepaid Advertising
6. Prepaid Rent

7. Rent Revenue
8. Salary Expense
9. Salary Payable
10. Supplies
11. Supplies Expense
12. Unearned Rent

SHOW
ME HOW

### EX 4-3  Financial statements from the end-of-period spreadsheet

OBJ. 1, 2

Bamboo Consulting is a consulting firm owned and operated by Lisa Gooch. The following end-of-period spreadsheet was prepared for the year ended July 31, 2016:

| | A | B | C | D | E | F | G |
|---|---|---|---|---|---|---|---|
| 1 | | Bamboo Consulting | | | | | |
| 2 | | End-of-Period Spreadsheet | | | | | |
| 3 | | For the Year Ended July 31, 2016 | | | | | |
| 4 | | Unadjusted | | | | Adjusted | |
| 5 | | Trial Balance | | Adjustments | | Trial Balance | |
| 6 | Account Title | Dr. | Cr. | Dr. | Cr. | Dr. | Cr. |
| 7 | | | | | | | |
| 8 | Cash | 58,000 | | | | 58,000 | |
| 9 | Accounts Receivable | 106,200 | | | | 106,200 | |
| 10 | Supplies | 11,900 | | | (a) 7,500 | 4,400 | |
| 11 | Office Equipment | 515,000 | | | | 515,000 | |
| 12 | Accumulated Depreciation | | 28,000 | | (b) 5,600 | | 33,600 |
| 13 | Accounts Payable | | 20,500 | | | | 20,500 |
| 14 | Salaries Payable | | | | (c) 2,500 | | 2,500 |
| 15 | Lisa Gooch, Capital | | 516,700 | | | | 516,700 |
| 16 | Lisa Gooch, Drawing | 25,000 | | | | 25,000 | |
| 17 | Fees Earned | | 348,500 | | | | 348,500 |
| 18 | Salary Expense | 186,500 | | (c) 2,500 | | 189,000 | |
| 19 | Supplies Expense | | | (a) 7,500 | | 7,500 | |
| 20 | Depreciation Expense | | | (b) 5,600 | | 5,600 | |
| 21 | Miscellaneous Expense | 11,100 | | | | 11,100 | |
| 22 | | 913,700 | 913,700 | 15,600 | 15,600 | 921,800 | 921,800 |
| 23 | | | | | | | |

Based on the preceding spreadsheet, prepare an income statement, statement of owner's equity, and balance sheet for Bamboo Consulting.

SHOW
ME HOW

### EX 4-4  Financial statements from the end-of-period spreadsheet

OBJ. 1, 2

Elliptical Consulting is a consulting firm owned and operated by Jayson Neese. The following end-of-period spreadsheet was prepared for the year ended June 30, 2016:

| | A | B | C | D | E | F | G |
|---|---|---|---|---|---|---|---|
| 1 | | Elliptical Consulting | | | | | |
| 2 | | End-of-Period Spreadsheet | | | | | |
| 3 | | For the Year Ended June 30, 2016 | | | | | |
| 4 | | Unadjusted | | | | Adjusted | |
| 5 | | Trial Balance | | Adjustments | | Trial Balance | |
| 6 | Account Title | Dr. | Cr. | Dr. | Cr. | Dr. | Cr. |
| 7 | | | | | | | |
| 8 | Cash | 27,000 | | | | 27,000 | |
| 9 | Accounts Receivable | 53,500 | | | | 53,500 | |
| 10 | Supplies | 3,000 | | | (a) 2,100 | 900 | |
| 11 | Office Equipment | 30,500 | | | | 30,500 | |
| 12 | Accumulated Depreciation | | 4,500 | | (b) 1,500 | | 6,000 |
| 13 | Accounts Payable | | 3,300 | | | | 3,300 |
| 14 | Salaries Payable | | | | (c) 375 | | 375 |
| 15 | Jayson Neese, Capital | | 82,200 | | | | 82,200 |
| 16 | Jayson Neese, Drawing | 2,000 | | | | 2,000 | |
| 17 | Fees Earned | | 60,000 | | | | 60,000 |
| 18 | Salary Expense | 32,000 | | (c) 375 | | 32,375 | |
| 19 | Supplies Expense | | | (a) 2,100 | | 2,100 | |
| 20 | Depreciation Expense | | | (b) 1,500 | | 1,500 | |
| 21 | Miscellaneous Expense | 2,000 | | | | 2,000 | |
| 22 | | 150,000 | 150,000 | 3,975 | 3,975 | 151,875 | 151,875 |
| 23 | | | | | | | |

don't
close

close

Based on the preceding spreadsheet, prepare an income statement, statement of owner's equity, and balance sheet for Elliptical Consulting.

### EX 4-5 Income statement

OBJ. 2

The following account balances were taken from the adjusted trial balance for Laser Messenger Service, a delivery service firm, for the fiscal year ended April 30, 2016:

| | | | |
|---|---|---|---|
| Depreciation Expense | $ 8,650 | Rent Expense | $ 60,000 |
| Fees Earned | 674,000 | Salaries Expense | 336,900 |
| Insurance Expense | 1,500 | Supplies Expense | 4,100 |
| Miscellaneous Expense | 3,650 | Utilities Expense | 41,200 |

Prepare an income statement.

### EX 4-6 Income statement; net loss

OBJ. 2

The following revenue and expense account balances were taken from the ledger of Wholistic Health Services Co. after the accounts had been adjusted on February 29, 2016, the end of the fiscal year:

| | | | |
|---|---|---|---|
| Depreciation Expense | $ 7,500 | Service Revenue | $448,400 |
| Insurance Expense | 3,000 | Supplies Expense | 2,750 |
| Miscellaneous Expense | 8,150 | Utilities Expense | 33,900 |
| Rent Expense | 54,000 | Wages Expense | 360,000 |

Prepare an income statement.

### EX 4-7 Income statement

OBJ. 2

**FedEx Corporation** had the following revenue and expense account balances (in millions) for a recent year ending May 31:

| | | | |
|---|---|---|---|
| Depreciation Expense | $2,113 | Purchased Transportation | $ 6,335 |
| Fuel Expense | 4,956 | Rentals and Landing Fees | 2,487 |
| Maintenance and Repairs Expense | 1,980 | Revenues | 42,680 |
| Other Expense (Income) Net | 5,569 | Salaries and Employee Benefits | 16,099 |
| Provision for Income Taxes | 1,109 | | |

a. Prepare an income statement.

b. ➤ Compare your income statement with the income statement that is available at the FedEx Corporation Web site, (http://investors.fedex.com). Click on Annual Report and Download Annual Report. What similarities and differences do you see?

### EX 4-8 Statement of owner's equity

OBJ. 2

Apex Systems Co. offers its services to residents in the Seattle area. Selected accounts from the ledger of Apex Systems Co. for the fiscal year ended December 31, 2016, are as follows:

| Bart Nesbit, Capital | | | | Bart Nesbit, Drawing | | | |
|---|---|---|---|---|---|---|---|
| Dec. 31 | 90,000 | Jan. 1 (2016) | 1,375,000 | Mar. 31 | 22,500 | Dec. 31 | 90,000 |
| | | Dec. 31 | 355,000 | June 30 | 22,500 | | |
| | | | | Sept. 30 | 22,500 | | |
| | | | | Dec. 31 | 22,500 | | |

| Income Summary | | | |
|---|---|---|---|
| Dec. 31 | 1,415,000 | Dec. 31 | 1,770,000 |
| 31 | 355,000 | | |

Prepare a statement of owner's equity for the year.

### EX 4-9 Statement of owner's equity; net loss

OBJ. 2

Selected accounts from the ledger of Restoration Arts for the fiscal year ended April 30, 2016, are as follows:

| Doug Stone, Capital | | | | Doug Stone, Drawing | | | |
|---|---|---|---|---|---|---|---|
| Apr. 30 | 31,200 | May 1 (2015) | 475,500 | Sept. 30 | 1,250 | Apr. 30 | 5,000 |
| 30 | 5,000 | | | Dec. 31 | 1,250 | | |
| | | | | March 31 | 1,250 | | |
| | | | | June 30 | 1,250 | | |

**Income Summary**

| | | | |
|---|---|---|---|
| Apr. 30 | 197,000 | Apr. 30 | 165,800 |
| | | 30 | 31,200 |

Prepare a statement of owner's equity for the year.

---

### EX 4-10 Classifying assets

OBJ. 2

Identify each of the following as (a) a current asset or (b) property, plant, and equipment:

1. Accounts Receivable
2. Building
3. Cash
4. Equipment
5. Prepaid Insurance
6. Supplies

---

### EX 4-11 Balance sheet classification

OBJ. 2

At the balance sheet date, a business owes a mortgage note payable of $375,000, the terms of which provide for monthly payments of $1,250.

➤ Explain how the liability should be classified on the balance sheet.

---

### EX 4-12 Balance sheet

OBJ. 2

✔ Total assets: $775,000

SHOW ME HOW

Optimum Weight Loss Co. offers personal weight reduction consulting services to individuals. After all the accounts have been closed on November 30, 2016, the end of the fiscal year, the balances of selected accounts from the ledger of Optimum Weight Loss Co. are as follows:

| | | | |
|---|---|---|---|
| Accounts Payable | $ 37,700 | Prepaid Insurance | $ 7,200 |
| Accounts Receivable | 116,750 | Prepaid Rent | 21,000 |
| Accumulated Depreciation—Equipment | 186,400 | Salaries Payable | 9,000 |
| Cash | ? | Cheryl Viers, Capital | 710,300 |
| Equipment | 474,150 | Supplies | 4,800 |
| Land | 300,000 | Unearned Fees | 18,000 |

Prepare a classified balance sheet that includes the correct balance for Cash.

---

### EX 4-13 Balance sheet

OBJ. 2

✔ Corrected balance sheet, total assets: $625,000

List the errors you find in the following balance sheet. Prepare a corrected balance sheet.

**Labyrinth Services Co.**
**Balance Sheet**
**For the Year Ended August 31, 2016**

| Assets | | Liabilities | |
|---|---|---|---|
| Current assets: | | Current liabilities: | |
| Cash . . . . . . . . . . . . . . . . . . . . . | $ 18,500 | Accounts receivable . . . . . . . | $ 41,400 |
| Accounts payable . . . . . . . . | 31,300 | Accum. depr.   building . . . | 155,000 |
| Supplies . . . . . . . . . . . . . . . | 6,500 | Accum. depr.—equipment | 25,000 |
| Prepaid insurance . . . . . . . . | 16,600 | Net income . . . . . . . . . . . . . . | 118,200 |
| Land . . . . . . . . . . . . . . . . . . . . | 225,000 | Total liabilities . . . . . . . . . . . . . | $339,600 |
| Total current assets . . . . . | $297,900 | | |
| Property, plant, and equipment: | | **Owner's Equity** | |
| Building . . . . . . . . . . . . . . . . . | $400,000 | Wages payable . . . . . . . . . . . . | $ 6,500 |
| Equipment . . . . . . . . . . . . . . | 97,000 | Ruben Daniel, capital . . . . . . . . | 587,200 |
| Total property, plant, and equipment . . . . . . | 635,400 | Total owner's equity . . . . . . . . | 593,700 |
| Total assets . . . . . . . . . . . . . . . | $933,300 | Total liabilities and owner's equity . . . . . . . . . . . | $933,300 |

---

### EX 4-14 Identifying accounts to be closed

OBJ. 3

From the list that follows, identify the accounts that should be closed to Income Summary at the end of the fiscal year:

*(Continued)*

a. Accounts Payable

b. Accumulated Depreciation—Equipment

c. Depreciation Expense—Equipment

d. Equipment

e. Ellen Drake, Capital

f. Ellen Drake, Drawing

g. Fees Earned

h. Land

i. Supplies

j. Supplies Expense

k. Wages Expense

l. Wages Payable

---

### EX 4-15  Closing entries
**OBJ. 3**

Prior to its closing, Income Summary had total debits of $1,190,500 and total credits of $1,476,300.

➤ Briefly explain the purpose served by the income summary account and the nature of the entries that resulted in the $1,190,500 and the $1,476,300.

---

### EX 4-16  Closing entries with net income
**OBJ. 3**

SHOW
ME HOW

After all revenue and expense accounts have been closed at the end of the fiscal year, Income Summary has a debit of $798,400 and a credit of $955,300. At the same date, Debra Allen, Capital has a credit balance of $1,439,000, and Debra Allen, Drawing has a balance of $36,000. (a) Journalize the entries required to complete the closing of the accounts. (b) Determine the amount of Debra Allen, Capital at the end of the period.

---

### EX 4-17  Closing entries with net loss
**OBJ. 3**

SHOW
ME HOW

Mira Services Co. offers its services to individuals desiring to improve their personal images. After the accounts have been adjusted at October 31, the end of the fiscal year, the following balances were taken from the ledger of Mira Services Co.:

| | | | |
|---|---|---|---|
| Bonnie Mira, Capital | $910,000 | Rent Expense | $72,000 |
| Bonnie Mira, Drawing | 16,000 | Supplies Expense | 11,900 |
| Fees Earned | 519,300 | Miscellaneous Expense | 14,250 |
| Wages Expense | 488,000 | | |

Journalize the four entries required to close the accounts.

---

### EX 4-18  Identifying permanent accounts
**OBJ. 3**

Which of the following accounts will usually appear in the post-closing trial balance?

a. Accounts Payable

b. Accumulated Depreciation

c. Ben Crayton, Capital

d. Ben Crayton, Drawing

e. Cash

f. Depreciation Expense

g. Fees Earned

h. Office Equipment

i. Salaries Expense

j. Salaries Payable

k. Supplies

---

### EX 4-19  Post-closing trial balance
**OBJ. 3**

✔ Correct column totals, $300,000

SHOW
ME HOW

An accountant prepared the following post-closing trial balance:

**La Casa Services Co.**
**Post-Closing Trial Balance**
**March 31, 2016**

| | Debit Balances | Credit Balances |
|---|---|---|
| Cash | 46,540 | |
| Accounts Receivable | 122,260 | |
| Supplies | | 4,000 |
| Equipment | | 127,200 |
| Accumulated Depreciation—Equipment | 33,600 | |
| Accounts Payable | 52,100 | |
| Salaries Payable | | 6,400 |
| Unearned Rent | 9,000 | |
| Sonya Flynn, Capital | 198,900 | |
| | 462,400 | 137,600 |

Prepare a corrected post-closing trial balance. Assume that all accounts have normal balances and that the amounts shown are correct.

### EX 4-20 Steps in the accounting cycle    OBJ. 4

Rearrange the following steps in the accounting cycle in proper sequence:

a. A post closing trial balance is prepared.

b. Adjustment data are asssembled and analyzed.

c. Adjusting entries are journalized and posted to the ledger.

d. An adjusted trial balance is prepared.

e. An optional end-of-period spreadsheet is prepared.

f. An unadjusted trial balance is prepared.

g. Closing entries are journalized and posted to the ledger.

h. Financial statements are prepared.

i. Transactions are analyzed and recorded in the journal.

j. Transactions are posted to the ledger.

SHOW
ME HOW

### EX 4-21 Working capital and current ratio    OBJ. 7

The following data (in thousands) were taken from recent financial statements of Under Armour, Inc.:

|  | December 31 | |
|---|---|---|
|  | Year 2 | Year 1 |
| Current assets | $689,663 | $558,850 |
| Current liabilities | 183,607 | 149,147 |

a. Compute the working capital and the current ratio as of December 31, Year 2 and Year 1. Round to two decimal places.

b. ➤ What conclusions concerning the company's ability to meet its financial obligations can you draw from part (a)?

### EX 4-22 Working capital and current ratio    OBJ. 7

The following data (in thousands) were taken from recent financial statements of Starbucks Corporation:

|  | Year 2 | Year 1 |
|---|---|---|
| Current assets | $4,199,600 | $3,794,900 |
| Current liabilities | 2,209,200 | 2,075,800 |

a. Compute the working capital and the current ratio for Year 2 and Year 1. Round to two decimal places.

b. ➤ What conclusions concerning the company's ability to meet its financial obligations can you draw from part (a)?

### Appendix
### EX 4-23 Completing an end-of-period spreadsheet

List (a) through (j) in the order they would be performed in preparing and completing an end-of-period spreadsheet.

a. Add the Debit and Credit columns of the Unadjusted Trial Balance columns of the spreadsheet to verify that the totals are equal.

b. Add the Debit and Credit columns of the Balance Sheet and Income Statement columns of the spreadsheet to verify that the totals are equal.

(*Continued*)

c. Add or deduct adjusting entry data to trial balance amounts, and extend amounts to the Adjusted Trial Balance columns.

d. Add the Debit and Credit columns of the Adjustments columns of the spreadsheet to verify that the totals are equal.

e. Add the Debit and Credit columns of the Balance Sheet and Income Statement columns of the spreadsheet to determine the amount of net income or net loss for the period.

f. Add the Debit and Credit columns of the Adjusted Trial Balance columns of the spreadsheet to verify that the totals are equal.

g. Enter the adjusting entries into the spreadsheet, based on the adjustment data.

h. Enter the amount of net income or net loss for the period in the proper Income Statement column and Balance Sheet column.

i. Enter the unadjusted account balances from the general ledger into the Unadjusted Trial Balance columns of the spreadsheet.

j. Extend the adjusted trial balance amounts to the Income Statement columns and the Balance Sheet columns.

## Appendix
## EX 4-24    Adjustment data on an end-of-period spreadsheet

✔ Total debits of Adjustments column: $31

Alert Security Services Co. offers security services to business clients. The trial balance for Alert Security Services Co. has been prepared on the following end-of-period spreadsheet for the year ended October 31, 2016:

**Alert Security Services Co.**
**End-of-Period Spreadsheet**
**For the Year Ended October 31, 2016**

| Account Title | Unadjusted Trial Balance Dr. | Cr. | Adjustments Dr. | Cr. | Adjusted Trial Balance Dr. | Cr. |
|---|---|---|---|---|---|---|
| Cash | 12 | | | | | |
| Accounts Receivable | 90 | | | | | |
| Supplies | 8 | | | | | |
| Prepaid Insurance | 12 | | | | | |
| Land | 190 | | | | | |
| Equipment | 50 | | | | | |
| Accum. Depr.—Equipment | | 4 | | | | |
| Accounts Payable | | 36 | | | | |
| Wages Payable | | 0 | | | | |
| Brenda Schultz, Capital | | 260 | | | | |
| Brenda Schultz, Drawing | 8 | | | | | |
| Fees Earned | | 200 | | | | |
| Wages Expense | 110 | | | | | |
| Rent Expense | 12 | | | | | |
| Insurance Expense | 0 | | | | | |
| Utilities Expense | 6 | | | | | |
| Supplies Expense | 0 | | | | | |
| Depreciation Expense | 0 | | | | | |
| Miscellaneous Expense | 2 | | | | | |
| | 500 | 500 | | | | |

The data for year-end adjustments are as follows:
a. Fees earned, but not yet billed, $13.
b. Supplies on hand, $4.
c. Insurance premiums expired, $10.

d. Depreciation expense, $3.

e. Wages accrued, but not paid, $1.

Enter the adjustment data, and place the balances in the Adjusted Trial Balance columns.

---

**Appendix**
**EX 4-25 Completing an end-of-period spreadsheet**

✔ Net income: $65

Alert Security Services Co. offers security services to business clients. Complete the following end-of-period spreadsheet for Alert Security Services Co.:

**Alert Security Services Co.**
**End-of-Period Spreadsheet**
**For the Year Ended October 31, 2016**

| Account Title | Adjusted Trial Balance Dr. | Adjusted Trial Balance Cr. | Income Statement Dr. | Income Statement Cr. | Balance Sheet Dr. | Balance Sheet Cr. |
|---|---|---|---|---|---|---|
| Cash | 12 | | | | | |
| Accounts Receivable | 103 | | | | | |
| Supplies | 4 | | | | | |
| Prepaid Insurance | 2 | | | | | |
| Land | 190 | | | | | |
| Equipment | 50 | | | | | |
| Accum. Depr.—Equipment | | 7 | | | | |
| Accounts Payable | | 36 | | | | |
| Wages Payable | | 1 | | | | |
| Brenda Schultz, Capital | | 260 | | | | |
| Brenda Schultz, Drawing | 8 | | | | | |
| Fees Earned | | 213 | | | | |
| Wages Expense | 111 | | | | | |
| Rent Expense | 12 | | | | | |
| Insurance Expense | 10 | | | | | |
| Utilities Expense | 6 | | | | | |
| Supplies Expense | 4 | | | | | |
| Depreciation Expense | 3 | | | | | |
| Miscellaneous Expense | 2 | | | | | |
| | 517 | 517 | | | | |
| Net income (loss) | | | | | | |

---

**Appendix**
**EX 4-26 Financial statements from an end-of-period spreadsheet**

✔ Brenda Schultz, capital, October 31, 2016: $317

Based on the data in Exercise 4-25, prepare an income statement, statement of owner's equity, and balance sheet for Alert Security Services Co.

---

**Appendix**
**EX 4-27 Adjusting entries from an end-of-period spreadsheet**

Based on the data in Exercise 4-24, prepare the adjusting entries for Alert Security Services Co.

---

**Appendix**
**EX 4-28 Closing entries from an end-of-period spreadsheet**

Based on the data in Exercise 4-25, prepare the closing entries for Alert Security Services Co.

## Problems: Series A

### PR 4-1A Financial statements and closing entries

OBJ. 1, 2, 3

✔ 3. Total assets: $354,500

**General Ledger**

SHOW
ME HOW

Lamp Light Company maintains and repairs warning lights, such as those found on radio towers and lighthouses. Lamp Light Company prepared the following end-of-period spreadsheet at December 31, 2016, the end of the fiscal year:

| | A | B | C | D | E | F | G |
|---|---|---|---|---|---|---|---|
| 1 | | | | Lamp Light Company | | | |
| 2 | | | | End-of-Period Spreadsheet | | | |
| 3 | | | | For the Year Ended December 31, 2016 | | | |
| 4 | | Unadjusted | | | | Adjusted | |
| 5 | | Trial Balance | | Adjustments | | Trial Balance | |
| 6 | Account Title | Dr. | Cr. | Dr. | Cr. | Dr. | Cr. |
| 7 | | | | | | | |
| 8 | Cash | 10,800 | | | | 10,800 | |
| 9 | Accounts Receivable | 38,900 | | (a) 11,300 | | 50,200 | |
| 10 | Prepaid Insurance | 4,200 | | | (b) 3,000 | 1,200 | |
| 11 | Supplies | 2,730 | | | (c) 2,250 | 480 | |
| 12 | Land | 98,000 | | | | 98,000 | |
| 13 | Building | 400,000 | | | | 400,000 | |
| 14 | Accum. Depr.—Building | | 205,300 | | (d)10,100 | | 215,400 |
| 15 | Equipment | 101,000 | | | | 101,000 | |
| 16 | Accum. Depr.—Equipment | | 85,100 | | (e) 6,680 | | 91,780 |
| 17 | Accounts Payable | | 15,700 | | | | 15,700 |
| 18 | Salaries & Wages Payable | | | | (f) 4,900 | | 4,900 |
| 19 | Unearned Rent | | 2,100 | (g) 1,300 | | | 800 |
| 20 | Ted Hickman, Capital | | 203,100 | | | | 203,100 |
| 21 | Ted Hickman, Drawing | 10,000 | | | | 10,000 | |
| 22 | Fees Earned | | 363,700 | | (a)11,300 | | 375,000 |
| 23 | Rent Revenue | | | | (g) 1,300 | | 1,300 |
| 24 | Salaries & Wages Expense | 163,100 | | (f) 4,900 | | 168,000 | |
| 25 | Advertising Expense | 21,700 | | | | 21,700 | |
| 26 | Utilities Expense | 11,400 | | | | 11,400 | |
| 27 | Depr. Exp.—Building | | | (d) 10,100 | | 10,100 | |
| 28 | Repairs Expense | 8,850 | | | | 8,850 | |
| 29 | Depr. Exp.—Equipment | | | (e) 6,680 | | 6,680 | |
| 30 | Insurance Expense | | | (b) 3,000 | | 3,000 | |
| 31 | Supplies Expense | | | (c) 2,250 | | 2,250 | |
| 32 | Misc. Expense | 4,320 | | | | 4,320 | |
| 33 | | 875,000 | 875,000 | 39,530 | 39,530 | 907,980 | 907,980 |
| 34 | | | | | | | |

### Instructions

1. Prepare an income statement for the year ended December 31.

2. Prepare a statement of owner's equity for the year ended December 31. No additional investments were made during the year.

3. Prepare a balance sheet as of December 31.

4. Based upon the end-of-period spreadsheet, journalize the closing entries.

5. Prepare a post-closing trial balance.

### PR 4-2A Financial statements and closing entries

OBJ. 2, 3

✔ 1. Stacy Tanner, capital, June 30: $483,300

Finders Investigative Services is an investigative services firm that is owned and operated by Stacy Tanner. On June 30, 2016, the end of the fiscal year, the accountant for Finders Investigative Services prepared an end-of-period spreadsheet, a part of which follows:

| | A | F | G |
|---|---|---|---|
| 1 | Finders Investigative Services | | |
| 2 | End-of-Period Spreadsheet | | |
| 3 | For the Year Ended June 30, 2016 | | |
| 4 | | Adjusted | |
| 5 | | Trial Balance | |
| 6 | Account Title | Dr. | Cr. |
| 7 | | | |
| 8 | Cash | 28,000 | |
| 9 | Accounts Receivable | 69,600 | |
| 10 | Supplies | 4,600 | |
| 11 | Prepaid Insurance | 2,500 | |
| 12 | Building | 439,500 | |
| 13 | Accumulated Depreciation—Building | | 44,200 |
| 14 | Accounts Payable | | 11,700 |
| 15 | Salaries Payable | | 3,000 |
| 16 | Unearned Rent | | 2,000 |
| 17 | Stacy Tanner, Capital | | 373,800 |
| 18 | Stacy Tanner, Drawing | 12,000 | |
| 19 | Service Fees | | 718,000 |
| 20 | Rent Revenue | | 12,000 |
| 21 | Salaries Expense | 522,100 | |
| 22 | Rent Expense | 48,000 | |
| 23 | Supplies Expense | 10,800 | |
| 24 | Depreciation Expense—Building | 8,750 | |
| 25 | Utilities Expense | 7,150 | |
| 26 | Repairs Expense | 3,000 | |
| 27 | Insurance Expense | 2,500 | |
| 28 | Miscellaneous Expense | 6,200 | |
| 29 | | 1,164,700 | 1,164,700 |

## Instructions

1. Prepare an income statement, a statement of owner's equity (no additional investments were made during the year), and a balance sheet.

2. Journalize the entries that were required to close the accounts at June 30.

3. If Stacy Tanner, Capital has instead decreased $30,000 after the closing entries were posted, and the withdrawals remained the same, what would have been the amount of net income or net loss?

---

**PR 4-3A  T accounts, adjusting entries, financial statements, and closing entries; optional end-of-period spreadsheet**

OBJ. 2, 3

✔ 5. Net income:
$10,700

General Ledger

The unadjusted trial balance of Epicenter Laundry at June 30, 2016, the end of the fiscal year, follows:

**Epicenter Laundry**
**Unadjusted Trial Balance**
**June 30, 2016**

| | Debit Balances | Credit Balances |
|---|---|---|
| Cash | 11,000 | |
| Laundry Supplies | 21,500 | |
| Prepaid Insurance | 9,600 | |
| Laundry Equipment | 232,600 | |
| Accumulated Depreciation | | 125,400 |
| Accounts Payable | | 11,800 |
| Sophie Perez, Capital | | 105,600 |
| Sophie Perez, Drawing | 10,000 | |
| Laundry Revenue | | 232,200 |
| Wages Expense | 125,200 | |
| Rent Expense | 40,000 | |
| Utilities Expense | 19,700 | |
| Miscellaneous Expense | 5,400 | |
| | 475,000 | 475,000 |

(*Continued*)

The data needed to determine year-end adjustments are as follows:

a. Laundry supplies on hand at June 30 are $3,600.

b. Insurance premiums expired during the year are $5,700.

c. Depreciation of laundry equipment during the year is $6,500.

d. Wages accrued but not paid at June 30 are $1,100.

**Instructions**

1. For each account listed in the unadjusted trial balance, enter the balance in a T account. Identify the balance as "June 30 Bal." In addition, add T accounts for Wages Payable, Depreciation Expense, Laundry Supplies Expense, Insurance Expense, and Income Summary.

2. *(Optional)* Enter the unadjusted trial balance on an end-of-period spreadsheet and complete the spreadsheet. Add the accounts listed in part (1) as needed.

3. Journalize and post the adjusting entries. Identify the adjustments by "Adj." and the new balances as "Adj. Bal."

4. Prepare an adjusted trial balance.

5. Prepare an income statement, a statement of owner's equity (no additional investments were made during the year), and a balance sheet.

6. Journalize and post the closing entries. Identify the closing entries by "Clos."

7. Prepare a post-closing trial balance.

---

**PR 4-4A   Ledger accounts, adjusting entries, financial statements, and closing entries; optional spreadsheet**

OBJ. 2, 3

✔ 5. Net income: $51,150

The unadjusted trial balance of Lakota Freight Co. at March 31, 2016, the end of the year, follows:

**Lakota Freight Co.**
**Unadjusted Trial Balance**
**March 31, 2016**

| | | Debit Balances | Credit Balances |
|---|---|---|---|
| 11 | Cash | 12,000 | |
| 13 | Supplies | 30,000 | |
| 14 | Prepaid Insurance | 3,600 | |
| 16 | Equipment | 110,000 | |
| 17 | Accumulated Depreciation—Equipment | | 25,000 |
| 18 | Trucks | 60,000 | |
| 19 | Accumulated Depreciation—Trucks | | 15,000 |
| 21 | Accounts Payable | | 4,000 |
| 31 | Kaya Tarango, Capital | | 96,000 |
| 32 | Kaya Tarango, Drawing | 15,000 | |
| 41 | Service Revenue | | 160,000 |
| 51 | Wages Expense | 45,000 | |
| 53 | Rent Expense | 10,600 | |
| 54 | Truck Expense | 9,000 | |
| 59 | Miscellaneous Expense | 4,800 | |
| | | 300,000 | 300,000 |

The data needed to determine year-end adjustments are as follows:

a. Supplies on hand at March 31 are $7,500.

b. Insurance premiums expired during year are $1,800.

c. Depreciation of equipment during year is $8,350.

d. Depreciation of trucks during year is $6,200.

e. Wages accrued but not paid at March 31 are $600.

**Instructions**

1. For each account listed in the trial balance, enter the balance in the appropriate Balance column of a four-column account and place a check mark (✓) in the Posting Reference column.

2. *(Optional)* Enter the unadjusted trial balance on an end-of-period spreadsheet and complete the spreadsheet. Add the accounts listed in part (3) as needed.

3. Journalize and post the adjusting entries, inserting balances in the accounts affected. Record the adjusting entries on Page 26 of the journal. The following additional accounts from Lakota Freight Co.'s chart of accounts should be used: Wages Payable, 22; Supplies Expense, 52; Depreciation Expense—Equipment, 55; Depreciation Expense—Trucks, 56; Insurance Expense, 57.

4. Prepare an adjusted trial balance.

5. Prepare an income statement, a statement of owner's equity (no additional investments were made during the year), and a balance sheet.

6. Journalize and post the closing entries. Record the closing entries on Page 27 of the journal. (Income Summary is account #33 in the chart of accounts.) Indicate closed accounts by inserting a line in both Balance columns opposite the closing entry.

7. Prepare a post-closing trial balance.

---

**PR 4-5A   Complete accounting cycle**                             OBJ. 4, 5

✔ 8. Net income:
$33,475

For the past several years, Steffy Lopez has operated a part-time consulting business from his home. As of July 1, 2016, Steffy decided to move to rented quarters and to operate the business, which was to be known as Diamond Consulting, on a full-time basis. Diamond Consulting entered into the following transactions during July:

July 1. The following assets were received from Steffy Lopez: cash, $13,500; accounts receivable, $20,800; supplies, $3,200; and office equipment, $7,500. There were no liabilities received.

  1. Paid two months' rent on a lease rental contract, $4,800.

  2. Paid the premiums on property and casualty insurance policies, $4,500.

  4. Received cash from clients as an advance payment for services to be provided, and recorded it as unearned fees, $5,500.

  5. Purchased additional office equipment on account from Office Station Co., $6,500.

  6. Received cash from clients on account, $15,300.

  10. Paid cash for a newspaper advertisement, $400.

  12. Paid Office Station Co. for part of the debt incurred on July 5, $5,200.

  12. Recorded services provided on account for the period July 1–12, $13,300.

  14. Paid receptionist for two weeks' salary, $1,750.

*Record the following transactions on Page 2 of the journal:*

  17. Recorded cash from cash clients for fees earned during the period July 1–17, $9,450.

  18. Paid cash for supplies, $600.

  20. Recorded services provided on account for the period July 13–20, $6,650.

  24. Recorded cash from cash clients for fees earned for the period July 17–24, $4,000.

  26. Received cash from clients on account, $12,000.

  27. Paid receptionist for two weeks' salary, $1,750.

  29. Paid telephone bill for July, $325.

  31. Paid electricity bill for July, $675.

  31. Recorded cash from cash clients for fees earned for the period July 25–31, $5,200.

*(Continued)*

July 31. Recorded services provided on account for the remainder of July, $3,000.

31. Steffy withdrew $12,500 for personal use.

### Instructions

1. Journalize each transaction in a two-column journal starting on Page 1, referring to the following chart of accounts in selecting the accounts to be debited and credited. (Do not insert the account numbers in the journal at this time.)

| | | | |
|---|---|---|---|
| 11 | Cash | 31 | Steffy Lopez, Capital |
| 12 | Accounts Receivable | 32 | Steffy Lopez, Drawing |
| 14 | Supplies | 41 | Fees Earned |
| 15 | Prepaid Rent | 51 | Salary Expense |
| 16 | Prepaid Insurance | 52 | Rent Expense |
| 18 | Office Equipment | 53 | Supplies Expense |
| 19 | Accumulated Depreciation | 54 | Depreciation Expense |
| 21 | Accounts Payable | 55 | Insurance Expense |
| 22 | Salaries Payable | 59 | Miscellaneous Expense |
| 23 | Unearned Fees | | |

2. Post the journal to a ledger of four-column accounts.

3. Prepare an unadjusted trial balance.

4. At the end of July, the following adjustment data were assembled. Analyze and use these data to complete parts (5) and (6).

   a. Insurance expired during July is $375.

   b. Supplies on hand on July 31 are $1,525.

   c. Depreciation of office equipment for July is $750.

   d. Accrued receptionist salary on July 31 is $175.

   e. Rent expired during July is $2,400.

   f. Unearned fees on July 31 are $2,750.

5. *(Optional)* Enter the unadjusted trial balance on an end-of-period spreadsheet and complete the spreadsheet.

6. Journalize and post the adjusting entries. Record the adjusting entries on Page 3 of the journal.

7. Prepare an adjusted trial balance.

8. Prepare an income statement, a statement of owner's equity, and a balance sheet.

9. Prepare and post the closing entries. (Income Summary is account #33 in the chart of accounts.) Record the closing entries on Page 4 of the journal. Indicate closed accounts by inserting a line in both the Balance columns opposite the closing entry.

10. Prepare a post-closing trial balance.

## Problems: Series B

### PR 4-1B    Financial statements and closing entries                OBJ. 1, 2, 3

✔ 3. Total assets:
$342,425

General Ledger

SHOW
ME HOW

Last Chance Company offers legal consulting advice to prison inmates. Last Chance Company prepared the end-of-period spreadsheet that follows at June 30, 2016, the end of the fiscal year.

### Instructions

1. Prepare an income statement for the year ended June 30.

2. Prepare a statement of owner's equity for the year ended June 30. No additional investments were made during the year.

3. Prepare a balance sheet as of June 30.

4. On the basis of the end-of-period spreadsheet, journalize the closing entries.

5. Prepare a post-closing trial balance.

| | A | B | C | D | E | F | G |
|---|---|---|---|---|---|---|---|
| 1 | | | | Last Chance Company | | | |
| 2 | | | | End-of-Period Spreadsheet | | | |
| 3 | | | | For the Year Ended June 30, 2016 | | | |
| 4 | | Unadjusted | | | | Adjusted | |
| 5 | | Trial Balance | | Adjustments | | Trial Balance | |
| 6 | Account Title | Dr. | Cr. | Dr. | Cr. | Dr. | Cr. |
| 7 | | | | | | | |
| 8 | Cash | 5,100 | | | | 5,100 | |
| 9 | Accounts Receivable | 22,750 | | (a) 3,750 | | 26,500 | |
| 10 | Prepaid Insurance | 3,600 | | | (b) 1,300 | 2,300 | |
| 11 | Supplies | 2,025 | | | (c) 1,500 | 525 | |
| 12 | Land | 80,000 | | | | 80,000 | |
| 13 | Building | 340,000 | | | | 340,000 | |
| 14 | Accum. Depr.—Building | | 190,000 | | (d) 3,000 | | 193,000 |
| 15 | Equipment | 140,000 | | | | 140,000 | |
| 16 | Accum. Depr.—Equipment | | 54,450 | | (e) 4,550 | | 59,000 |
| 17 | Accounts Payable | | 9,750 | | | | 9,750 |
| 18 | Salaries & Wages Payable | | | | (f) 1,900 | | 1,900 |
| 19 | Unearned Rent | | 4,500 | (g) 3,000 | | | 1,500 |
| 20 | Tami Garrigan, Capital | | 361,300 | | | | 361,300 |
| 21 | Tami Garrigan, Drawing | 20,000 | | | | 20,000 | |
| 22 | Fees Earned | | 280,000 | | (a) 3,750 | | 283,750 |
| 23 | Rent Revenue | | | | (g) 3,000 | | 3,000 |
| 24 | Salaries & Wages Expense | 145,100 | | (f) 1,900 | | 147,000 | |
| 25 | Advertising Expense | 86,800 | | | | 86,800 | |
| 26 | Utilities Expense | 30,000 | | | | 30,000 | |
| 27 | Travel Expense | 18,750 | | | | 18,750 | |
| 28 | Depr. Exp.—Equipment | | | (e) 4,550 | | 4,550 | |
| 29 | Depr. Exp.—Building | | | (d) 3,000 | | 3,000 | |
| 30 | Supplies Expense | | | (c) 1,500 | | 1,500 | |
| 31 | Insurance Expense | | | (b) 1,300 | | 1,300 | |
| 32 | Misc. Expense | 5,875 | | | | 5,875 | |
| 33 | | 900,000 | 900,000 | 19,000 | 19,000 | 913,200 | 913,200 |
| 34 | | | | | | | |

## PR 4-2B Financial statements and closing entries

OBJ. 2, 3

✔ 1. Nicole Gorman, capital, October 31: $313,000

The Gorman Group is a financial planning services firm owned and operated by Nicole Gorman. As of October 31, 2016, the end of the fiscal year, the accountant for The Gorman Group prepared an end-of-period spreadsheet, part of which follows:

| | A | F | G |
|---|---|---|---|
| 1 | | The Gorman Group | |
| 2 | | End-of-Period Spreadsheet | |
| 3 | | For the Year Ended October 31, 2016 | |
| 4 | | Adjusted | |
| 5 | | Trial Balance | |
| 6 | Account Title | Dr. | Cr. |
| 7 | | | |
| 8 | Cash | 11,000 | |
| 9 | Accounts Receivable | 28,150 | |
| 10 | Supplies | 6,350 | |
| 11 | Prepaid Insurance | 9,500 | |
| 12 | Land | 75,000 | |
| 13 | Buildings | 250,000 | |
| 14 | Accumulated Depreciation—Buildings | | 117,200 |
| 15 | Equipment | 240,000 | |
| 16 | Accumulated Depreciation—Equipment | | 151,700 |
| 17 | Accounts Payable | | 33,300 |
| 18 | Salaries Payable | | 3,300 |
| 19 | Unearned Rent | | 1,500 |
| 20 | Nicole Gorman, Capital | | 220,000 |
| 21 | Nicole Gorman, Drawing | 20,000 | |
| 22 | Service Fees | | 468,000 |
| 23 | Rent Revenue | | 5,000 |
| 24 | Salaries Expense | 291,000 | |
| 25 | Depreciation Expense—Equipment | 17,500 | |
| 26 | Rent Expense | 15,500 | |
| 27 | Supplies Expense | 9,000 | |
| 28 | Utilities Expense | 8,500 | |
| 29 | Depreciation Expense—Buildings | 6,600 | |
| 30 | Repairs Expense | 3,450 | |
| 31 | Insurance Expense | 3,000 | |
| 32 | Miscellaneous Expense | 5,450 | |
| 33 | | 1,000,000 | 1,000,000 |

*(Continued)*

**Instructions**

1. Prepare an income statement, a statement of owner's equity (no additional investments were made during the year), and a balance sheet.

2. Journalize the entries that were required to close the accounts at October 31.

3. If the balance of Nicole Gorman, Capital had instead increased $115,000 after the closing entries were posted, and the withdrawals remained the same, what would have been the amount of net income or net loss?

---

**PR 4-3B  T accounts, adjusting entries, financial statements,**                **OBJ. 2, 3**
**and closing entries; optional end-of-period spreadsheet**

✔ 5. Net income: $27,350

General Ledger

The unadjusted trial balance of La Mesa Laundry at August 31, 2016, the end of the fiscal year, follows:

**La Mesa Laundry**
**Unadjusted Trial Balance**
**August 31, 2016**

|  | Debit Balances | Credit Balances |
|---|---|---|
| Cash | 3,800 | |
| Laundry Supplies | 9,000 | |
| Prepaid Insurance | 6,000 | |
| Laundry Equipment | 180,800 | |
| Accumulated Depreciation | | 49,200 |
| Accounts Payable | | 7,800 |
| Bobbi Downey, Capital | | 95,000 |
| Bobbi Downey, Drawing | 2,400 | |
| Laundry Revenue | | 248,000 |
| Wages Expense | 135,800 | |
| Rent Expense | 43,200 | |
| Utilities Expense | 16,000 | |
| Miscellaneous Expense | 3,000 | |
| | 400,000 | 400,000 |

The data needed to determine year-end adjustments are as follows:

a. Wages accrued but not paid at August 31 are $2,200.

b. Depreciation of equipment during the year is $8,150.

c. Laundry supplies on hand at August 31 are $2,000.

d. Insurance premiums expired during the year are $5,300.

**Instructions**

1. For each account listed in the unadjusted trial balance, enter the balance in a T account. Identify the balance as "Aug. 31 Bal." In addition, add T accounts for Wages Payable, Depreciation Expense, Laundry Supplies Expense, Insurance Expense, and Income Summary.

2. *(Optional)* Enter the unadjusted trial balance on an end-of-period spreadsheet and complete the spreadsheet. Add the accounts listed in part (1) as needed.

3. Journalize and post the adjusting entries. Identify the adjustments by "Adj." and the new balances as "Adj. Bal."

4. Prepare an adjusted trial balance.

5. Prepare an income statement, a statement of owner's equity (no additional investments were made during the year), and a balance sheet.

6. Journalize and post the closing entries. Identify the closing entries by "Clos."

7. Prepare a post-closing trial balance.

**PR 4-4B    Ledger accounts, adjusting entries, financial statements,**    OBJ. 2, 3
**and closing entries; optional end-of-period spreadsheet**

✔ 5. Net income:
$46,150

The unadjusted trial balance of Recessive Interiors at January 31, 2016, the end of the year, follows:

**Recessive Interiors**
**Unadjusted Trial Balance**
**January 31, 2016**

|    |    | Debit Balances | Credit Balances |
|----|----|---------------|-----------------|
| 11 | Cash ...................................................... | 13,100 | |
| 13 | Supplies..................................................... | 8,000 | |
| 14 | Prepaid Insurance ......................................... | 7,500 | |
| 16 | Equipment................................................ | 113,000 | |
| 17 | Accumulated Depreciation—Equipment ...................... | | 12,000 |
| 18 | Trucks...................................................... | 90,000 | |
| 19 | Accumulated Depreciation—Trucks........................... | | 27,100 |
| 21 | Accounts Payable .......................................... | | 4,500 |
| 31 | Jeanne McQuay, Capital .................................... | | 126,400 |
| 32 | Jeanne McQuay, Drawing .................................... | 3,000 | |
| 41 | Service Revenue ........................................... | | 155,000 |
| 51 | Wages Expense ............................................ | 72,000 | |
| 52 | Rent Expense .............................................. | 7,600 | |
| 53 | Truck Expense............................................. | 5,350 | |
| 59 | Miscellaneous Expense ..................................... | 5,450 | |
| | | 325,000 | 325,000 |

The data needed to determine year-end adjustments are as follows:

a. Supplies on hand at January 31 are $2,850.

b. Insurance premiums expired during the year are $3,150.

c. Depreciation of equipment during the year is $5,250.

d. Depreciation of trucks during the year is $4,000.

e. Wages accrued but not paid at January 31 are $900.

**Instructions**

1. For each account listed in the unadjusted trial balance, enter the balance in the appropriate Balance column of a four-column account and place a check mark (✓) in the Posting Reference column.

2. *(Optional)* Enter the unadjusted trial balance on an end-of-period spreadsheet and complete the spreadsheet. Add the accounts listed in part (3) as needed.

3. Journalize and post the adjusting entries, inserting balances in the accounts affected. Record the adjusting entries on Page 26 of the journal. The following additional accounts from Recessive Interiors' chart of accounts should be used: Wages Payable, 22; Depreciation Expense—Equipment, 54; Supplies Expense, 55; Depreciation Expense—Trucks, 56; Insurance Expense, 57.

4. Prepare an adjusted trial balance.

5. Prepare an income statement, a statement of owner's equity (no additional investments were made during the year), and a balance sheet.

6. Journalize and post the closing entries. Record the closing entries on Page 27 of the journal. (Income Summary is account #33 in the chart of accounts.) Indicate closed accounts by inserting a line in both Balance columns opposite the closing entry.

7. Prepare a post-closing trial balance.

**PR 4-5B    Complete accounting cycle**    OBJ. 4, 5

✔ 8. Net income:
$53,775

For the past several years, Jeff Horton has operated a part-time consulting business from his home. As of April 1, 2016, Jeff decided to move to rented quarters and to operate the

*(Continued)*

business, which was to be known as Rosebud Consulting, on a full-time basis. Rosebud Consulting entered into the following transactions during April:

Apr. 1. The following assets were received from Jeff Horton: cash, $20,000; accounts receivable, $14,700; supplies, $3,300; and office equipment, $12,000. There were no liabilities received.

1. Paid three months' rent on a lease rental contract, $6,000.

2. Paid the premiums on property and casualty insurance policies, $4,200.

4. Received cash from clients as an advance payment for services to be provided and recorded it as unearned fees, $9,400.

5. Purchased additional office equipment on account from Smith Office Supply Co., $8,000.

6. Received cash from clients on account, $11,700.

10. Paid cash for a newspaper advertisement, $350.

12. Paid Smith Office Supply Co. for part of the debt incurred on April 5, $6,400.

12. Recorded services provided on account for the period April 1–12, $21,900.

14. Paid receptionist for two weeks' salary, $1,650.

*Record the following transactions on Page 2 of the journal:*

17. Recorded cash from cash clients for fees earned during the period April 1–16, $6,600.

18. Paid cash for supplies, $725.

20. Recorded services provided on account for the period April 13–20, $16,800.

24. Recorded cash from cash clients for fees earned for the period April 17–24, $4,450.

26. Received cash from clients on account, $26,500.

27. Paid receptionist for two weeks' salary, $1,650.

29. Paid telephone bill for April, $540.

30. Paid electricity bill for April, $760.

30. Recorded cash from cash clients for fees earned for the period April 25–30, $5,160.

30. Recorded services provided on account for the remainder of April, $2,590.

30. Jeff withdrew $18,000 for personal use.

## Instructions

1. Journalize each transaction in a two-column journal starting on Page 1, referring to the following chart of accounts in selecting the accounts to be debited and credited. (Do not insert the account numbers in the journal at this time.)

| | | | |
|---|---|---|---|
| 11 | Cash | 31 | Jeff Horton, Capital |
| 12 | Accounts Receivable | 32 | Jeff Horton, Drawing |
| 14 | Supplies | 41 | Fees Earned |
| 15 | Prepaid Rent | 51 | Salary Expense |
| 16 | Prepaid Insurance | 52 | Supplies Expense |
| 18 | Office Equipment | 53 | Rent Expense |
| 19 | Accumulated Depreciation | 54 | Depreciation Expense |
| 21 | Accounts Payable | 55 | Insurance Expense |
| 22 | Salaries Payable | 59 | Miscellaneous Expense |
| 23 | Unearned Fees | | |

2. Post the journal to a ledger of four-column accounts.

3. Prepare an unadjusted trial balance.

4. At the end of April, the following adjustment data were assembled. Analyze and use these data to complete parts (5) and (6).

a. Insurance expired during April is $350.

b. Supplies on hand on April 30 are $1,225.

    c. Depreciation of office equipment for April is $400.

    d. Accrued receptionist salary on April 30 is $275.

    e. Rent expired during April is $2,000.

    f. Unearned fees on April 30 are $2,350.

5. *(Optional)* Enter the unadjusted trial balance on an end-of-period spreadsheet and complete the spreadsheet.

6. Journalize and post the adjusting entries. Record the adjusting entries on Page 3 of the journal.

7. Prepare an adjusted trial balance.

8. Prepare an income statement, a statement of owner's equity, and a balance sheet.

9. Prepare and post the closing entries. Record the closing entries on Page 4 of the journal. (Income Summary is account #33 in the chart of accounts.) Indicate closed accounts by inserting a line in both the Balance columns opposite the closing entry.

10. Prepare a post-closing trial balance.

# Continuing Problem

✔ **2. Net income:**
**$4,955**

General Ledger

The unadjusted trial balance of PS Music as of July 31, 2016, along with the adjustment data for the two months ended July 31, 2016, are shown in Chapter 3. Based upon the adjustment data, the following adjusted trial balance was prepared:

**PS Music**
**Adjusted Trial Balance**
**July 31, 2016**

| | Debit Balances | Credit Balances |
|---|---|---|
| Cash | 9,945 | |
| Accounts Receivable | 4,150 | |
| Supplies | 275 | |
| Prepaid Insurance | 2,475 | |
| Office Equipment | 7,500 | |
| Accumulated Depreciation—Office Equipment | | 50 |
| Accounts Payable | | 8,350 |
| Wages Payable | | 140 |
| Unearned Revenue | | 3,600 |
| Peyton Smith, Capital | | 9,000 |
| Peyton Smith, Drawing | 1,750 | |
| Fees Earned | | 21,200 |
| Music Expense | 3,610 | |
| Wages Expense | 2,940 | |
| Office Rent Expense | 2,550 | |
| Advertising Expense | 1,500 | |
| Equipment Rent Expense | 1,375 | |
| Utilities Expense | 1,215 | |
| Supplies Expense | 925 | |
| Insurance Expense | 225 | |
| Depreciation Expense | 50 | |
| Miscellaneous Expense | 1,855 | |
| | 42,340 | 42,340 |

**Instructions**

1. *(Optional)* Using the data from Chapter 3, prepare an end-of-period spreadsheet.

2. Prepare an income statement, a statement of owner's equity, and a balance sheet. (*Note:* Peyton Smith made investments in PS Music on June 1 and July 1, 2016.)

*(Continued)*

3. Journalize and post the closing entries. The income summary account is #33 in the ledger of PS Music. Indicate closed accounts by inserting a line in both Balance columns opposite the closing entry.

4. Prepare a post-closing trial balance.

# Comprehensive Problem 1

✔ 8. Net income,
$33,425

**General Ledger**

Kelly Pitney began her consulting business, Kelly Consulting, on April 1, 2016. The accounting cycle for Kelly Consulting for April, including financial statements, was illustrated in this chapter. During May, Kelly Consulting entered into the following transactions:

May 3. Received cash from clients as an advance payment for services to be provided and recorded it as unearned fees, $4,500.

5. Received cash from clients on account, $2,450.

9. Paid cash for a newspaper advertisement, $225.

13. Paid Office Station Co. for part of the debt incurred on April 5, $640.

15. Recorded services provided on account for the period May 1–15, $9,180.

16. Paid part-time receptionist for two weeks' salary including the amount owed on April 30, $750.

17. Recorded cash from cash clients for fees earned during the period May 1–16, $8,360.

*Record the following transactions on Page 6 of the journal:*

20. Purchased supplies on account, $735.

21. Recorded services provided on account for the period May 16–20, $4,820.

25. Recorded cash from cash clients for fees earned for the period May 17–23, $7,900.

27. Received cash from clients on account, $9,520.

28. Paid part-time receptionist for two weeks' salary, $750.

30. Paid telephone bill for May, $260.

31. Paid electricity bill for May, $810.

31. Recorded cash from cash clients for fees earned for the period May 26–31, $3,300.

31. Recorded services provided on account for the remainder of May, $2,650.

31. Kelly withdrew $10,500 for personal use.

**Instructions**

1. The chart of accounts for Kelly Consulting is shown in Exhibit 9, and the post-closing trial balance as of April 30, 2016, is shown in Exhibit 17. For each account in the post-closing trial balance, enter the balance in the appropriate Balance column of a four-column account. Date the balances May 1, 2016, and place a check mark (✓) in the Posting Reference column. Journalize each of the May transactions in a two-column journal starting on Page 5 of the journal and using Kelly Consulting's chart of accounts. (Do not insert the account numbers in the journal at this time.)

2. Post the journal to a ledger of four-column accounts.

3. Prepare an unadjusted trial balance.

4. At the end of May, the following adjustment data were assembled. Analyze and use these data to complete parts (5) and (6).

a. Insurance expired during May is $275.

b. Supplies on hand on May 31 are $715.

c. Depreciation of office equipment for May is $330.

d. Accrued receptionist salary on May 31 is $325.

e. Rent expired during May is $1,600.

f. Unearned fees on May 31 are $3,210.

5. *(Optional)* Enter the unadjusted trial balance on an end-of-period spreadsheet and complete the spreadsheet.

6. Journalize and post the adjusting entries. Record the adjusting entries on Page 7 of the journal.

7. Prepare an adjusted trial balance.

8. Prepare an income statement, a statement of owner's equity, and a balance sheet.

9. Prepare and post the closing entries. Record the closing entries on Page 8 of the journal. (Income Summary is account #33 in the chart of accounts.) Indicate closed accounts by inserting a line in both the Balance columns opposite the closing entry.

10. Prepare a post-closing trial balance.

# Cases & Projects

### CP 4-1    Ethics and professional conduct in business

Picasso Graphics is a graphics arts design consulting firm. Pablo Taylor, its treasurer and vice president of finance, has prepared a classified balance sheet as of July 31, 2016, the end of its fiscal year. This balance sheet will be submitted with Picasso Graphics' loan application to Paris Trust & Savings Bank.

In the Current Assets section of the balance sheet, Pablo reported a $56,000 receivable from Becky Holt, the president of Picasso Graphics, as a trade account receivable. Becky borrowed the money from Picasso Graphics in January 2014 for a down payment on a new home. She has orally assured Pablo that she will pay off the account receivable within the next year. Pablo reported the $56,000 in the same manner on the preceding year's balance sheet.

Evaluate whether it is acceptable for Pablo to prepare the July 31, 2016, balance sheet in this manner.

### CP 4-2    Financial statements

The following is an excerpt from a telephone conversation between Ben Simpson, president of Main Street Co., and Tami Lundgren, owner of Reliable Employment Co.:

*Ben:* Tami, you're going to have to do a better job of finding me a new computer programmer. That last guy was great at programming, but he didn't have any common sense.

*Tami:* What do you mean? The guy had a master's degree with straight A's.

*Ben:* Yes, well, last month he developed a new financial reporting system. He said we could do away with manually preparing an end-of-period spreadsheet and financial statements. The computer would automatically generate our financial statements with "a push of a button."

*Tami:* So what's the big deal? Sounds to me like it would save you time and effort.

*Ben:* Right! The balance sheet showed a minus for supplies!

*Tami:* Minus supplies? How can that be?

*Ben:* That's what I asked.

*Tami:* So, what did he say?

*Ben:* Well, after he checked the program, he said that it must be right. The minuses were greater than the pluses. . . .

*Tami:* Didn't he know that Supplies can't have a credit balance—it must have a debit balance?

*Ben:* He asked me what a debit and credit were.

*Tami:* I see your point.

1. Comment on (a) the desirability of computerizing Main Street Co.'s financial reporting system, (b) the elimination of the end-of-period spreadsheet in a computerized accounting system, and (c) the computer programmer's lack of accounting knowledge.

2. Explain to the programmer why Supplies could not have a credit balance.

## CP 4-3 Financial statements

Assume that you recently accepted a position with Five Star National Bank & Trust as an assistant loan officer. As one of your first duties, you have been assigned the responsibility of evaluating a loan request for $300,000 from West Gate Auto Co., a small proprietorship. In support of the loan application, Joan Whalen, owner, submitted a "Statement of Accounts" (trial balance) for the first year of operations ended October 31, 2016.

**West Gate Auto Co.**
**Statement of Accounts**
**October 31, 2016**

| | | |
|---|---:|---:|
| Cash | 5,000 | |
| Billings Due from Others | 40,000 | |
| Supplies (chemicals, etc.) | 7,500 | |
| Building | 222,300 | |
| Equipment | 50,000 | |
| Amounts Owed to Others | | 31,000 |
| Investment in Business | | 179,000 |
| Service Revenue | | 215,000 |
| Wages Expense | 75,000 | |
| Utilities Expense | 10,000 | |
| Rent Expense | 8,000 | |
| Insurance Expense | 6,000 | |
| Other Expenses | 1,200 | |
| | 425,000 | 425,000 |

1. ▬▬▶ Explain to Joan Whalen why a set of financial statements (income statement, statement of owner's equity, and balance sheet) would be useful to you in evaluating the loan request.

2. In discussing the "Statement of Accounts" with Joan Whalen, you discovered that the accounts had not been adjusted at October 31. Analyze the "Statement of Accounts" and indicate possible adjusting entries that might be necessary before an accurate set of financial statements could be prepared.

3. ▬▬▶ Assuming that an accurate set of financial statements will be submitted by Joan Whalen in a few days, what other considerations or information would you require before making a decision on the loan request?

## CP 4-4 Compare balance sheets

### Group Project

**Internet Project**

In groups of three or four, compare the balance sheets of two different companies, and present to the class a summary of the similarities and differences of the two companies. You may obtain the balance sheets you need from one of the following sources:

1. Your school or local library.

2. The investor relations department of each company.

3. The company's Web site on the Internet.

4. EDGAR (Electronic Data Gathering, Analysis, and Retrieval), the electronic archives of financial statements filed with the Securities and Exchange Commission.

SEC documents can be retrieved using the EdgarScan™ service at http://sec.gov. To obtain annual report information, under Filings & Forms click on "Search for Company Filings," click on "Company or fund name, ticker symbol, ..." type in the company name, and then click on "Find Companies." Click on the CIK related to the company name, search for Form 10-K, and click on "Retrieve Selected Findings." Finally, click on the "html" for the latest period and the related document.

PIXLAND/JUPITER IMAGES

# Accounting Systems

## Intuit Inc.

Whether you realize it or not, you likely interact with accounting systems. For example, your bank statement is a type of accounting system. When you make a deposit, the bank records an addition to your cash; when you withdraw cash, the bank records a reduction in your cash. Such a simple accounting system works well for a person with just a few transactions per month. However, over time, you may find that your financial affairs will become more complex and involve many different types of transactions, including investments and loan payments. At this point, relying on your bank statement may not be sufficient for managing your financial affairs. Personal financial planning software, such as **Intuit**'s Quicken, can be useful when your financial affairs become more complex.

What happens if you decide to begin a small business? Transactions expand to include customers, vendors, and employees. As a result, the accounting system will need to adjust to this complexity. Thus, many small businesses will use small business accounting software, such as Intuit's QuickBooks, as their first accounting system. As a business grows, more sophisticated accounting systems will be needed. Companies such as **SAP, Oracle, Microsoft,** and **Sage Software, Inc.,** offer accounting system solutions for businesses that become larger with more complex accounting needs.

Accounting systems used by large and small businesses employ the basic principles of the accounting cycle discussed in the previous chapters. However, these accounting systems include features that simplify the recording and summary process. In this chapter, we will discuss these simplifying procedures as they apply to both manual and computerized systems.

**OBJ 1**  Define and describe an accounting system.
Basic Accounting Systems

**OBJ 2**  Journalize and post transactions in a manual accounting system that uses subsidiary ledgers and special journals.
Manual Accounting Systems
    Subsidiary Ledgers
    Special Journals
    Revenue Journal      **EE 5-1**
    Cash Receipts Journal
    Accounts Receivable Control Account and Subsidiary Ledger      **EE 5-2**
    Purchases Journal      **EE 5-3**
    Cash Payments Journal
    Accounts Payable Control Account and Subsidiary Ledger      **EE 5-4**

**OBJ 3**  Describe and illustrate the use of a computerized accounting system.
Computerized Accounting Systems

**OBJ 4**  Describe the basic features of e-commerce.
E-Commerce

**OBJ 5**  Use segment analysis in evaluating the operating performance of a company.
Financial Analysis and Interpretation: Segment Analysis      **EE 5-5**

**At a Glance 5** ▶ Page 234

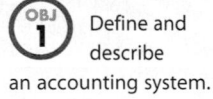

**OBJ 1** Define and describe an accounting system.

# Basic Accounting Systems

In Chapters 1–4, an accounting system for **NetSolutions** was described and illustrated. An **accounting system** is the methods and procedures for collecting, classifying, summarizing, and reporting a business's financial and operating information. Most accounting systems, however, are more complex than NetSolutions'. For example, Southwest Airlines's accounting system not only records basic transaction data but also records data on such items as ticket reservations, credit card collections, frequent-flier mileage, and aircraft maintenance.

As a business grows and changes, its accounting system also changes in a three-step process. This three-step process is as follows:

- Step 1. *Analyze* user information needs.
- Step 2. *Design* the system to meet the user needs.
- Step 3. *Implement* the system.

For NetSolutions, our analysis determined that Chris Clark needed financial statements for the new business. We designed the system, using a basic manual system that included a chart of accounts, a two-column journal, and a general ledger. Finally, we implemented the system to record transactions and prepare financial statements.

Once a system has been implemented, input from users is used to analyze and improve the system. For example, in later chapters, NetSolutions expands its chart of accounts to record more complex transactions.

The accounting system design consists of:

- internal controls and
- information processing methods.

**Internal controls** are the policies and procedures that protect assets from misuse, ensure that business information is accurate, and ensure that laws and regulations are being followed. Internal controls are discussed in Chapter 8.

*Processing methods* are the means by which the accounting system collects, summarizes, and reports accounting information. These methods may be either *manual* or *computerized*. In the following sections, manual accounting systems that use special journals and subsidiary ledgers are described and illustrated. This is followed by a discussion of computerized accounting systems.

# Manual Accounting Systems

 Journalize and post transactions in a manual accounting system that uses subsidiary ledgers and special journals.

Accounting systems are manual or computerized. Understanding a manual accounting system is useful in identifying relationships between accounting data and reports. Also, most computerized systems use principles from manual systems.

In prior chapters, the transactions for **NetSolutions** were manually recorded in an all-purpose (two-column) journal. The journal entries were then posted individually to the accounts in the ledger. Such a system is simple to use and easy to understand when there are a small number of transactions. However, when a business has a large number of *similar* transactions, using an all-purpose journal is inefficient and impractical. In such cases, subsidiary ledgers and special journals are useful.

## Subsidiary Ledgers

A large number of individual accounts with a common characteristic can be grouped together in a separate ledger called a **subsidiary ledger**. The primary ledger, which contains all of the balance sheet and income statement accounts, is then called the **general ledger**. Each subsidiary ledger is represented in the general ledger by a summarizing account, called a **controlling account**. The sum of the balances of the accounts in a subsidiary ledger must equal the balance of the related controlling account. Thus, a subsidiary ledger is a secondary ledger that supports a controlling account in the general ledger.

Two of the most common subsidiary ledgers are as follows:

- Accounts receivable subsidiary ledger
- Accounts payable subsidiary ledger

The **accounts receivable subsidiary ledger**, or *customers ledger*, lists the individual customer accounts in alphabetical order. The controlling account in the general ledger that summarizes the debits and credits to the individual customer accounts is Accounts Receivable.

The **accounts payable subsidiary ledger**, or *creditors ledger*, lists individual creditor accounts in alphabetical order. The related controlling account in the general ledger is Accounts Payable.

The relationship between the general ledger and the accounts receivable and accounts payable subsidiary ledgers is illustrated in Exhibit 1.

Many businesses use subsidiary ledgers for other accounts in addition to Accounts Receivable and Accounts Payable. For example, businesses often use an equipment subsidiary ledger to keep track of each item of equipment purchased, its cost, location, and other data.

## Special Journals

One method of processing transactions more efficiently in a manual system is to use special journals. **Special journals** are designed to record a single kind of transaction

**EXHIBIT 1** **General Ledger and Subsidiary Ledgers**

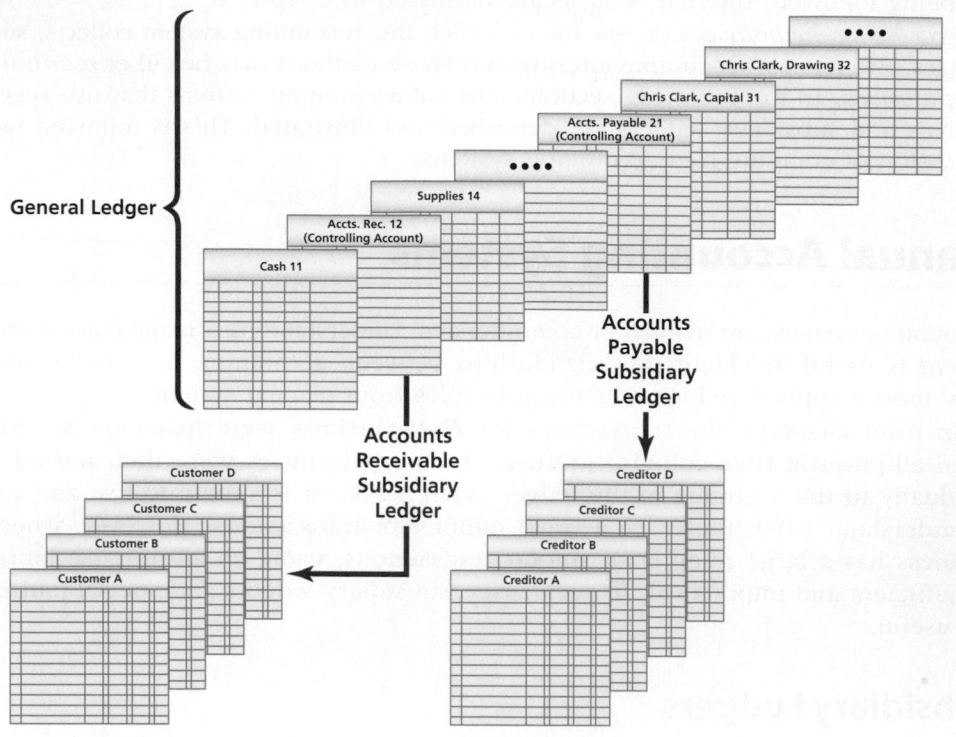

that occurs frequently. For example, since most businesses have many transactions in which cash is paid out, they will likely use a special journal for recording cash payments. Likewise, they will use another special journal for recording cash receipts.

The format and number of special journals that a business uses depends on the nature of the business. The common transactions and their related special journals used by small service businesses are as follows:

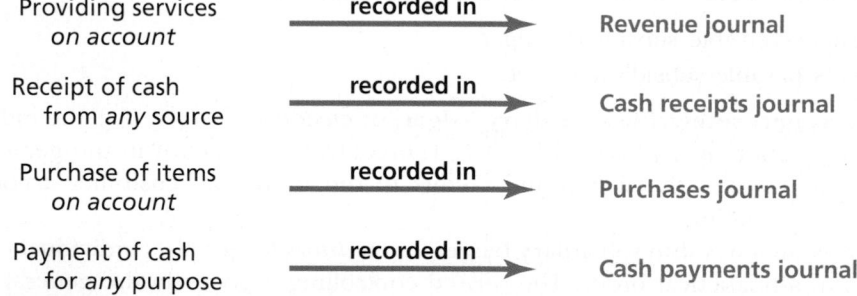

The all-purpose two-column journal, called the **general journal** or simply the *journal,* can be used for entries that do not fit into any of the special journals. For example, adjusting and closing entries are recorded in the general journal.

The following types of transactions, special journals, and subsidiary ledgers are described and illustrated for **NetSolutions**:

| Transaction | Special Journal | Subsidiary Ledger |
|---|---|---|
| Fees earned on account | Revenue journal | Accounts receivable subsidiary ledger |
| Cash receipts | Cash receipts journal | Accounts receivable subsidiary ledger |
| Purchases on account | Purchases journal | Accounts payable subsidiary ledger |
| Cash payments | Cash payments journal | Accounts payable subsidiary ledger |

As shown, transactions that are recorded in the revenue and cash receipts journals will affect the accounts receivable subsidiary ledger. Likewise, transactions that are recorded in the purchases and cash payments journals will affect the accounts payable subsidiary ledger.

We will assume that NetSolutions had the following selected general ledger balances on March 1, 2016:

| Account Number | Account | Balance |
|---|---|---|
| 11 | Cash | $6,200 |
| 12 | Accounts Receivable | 3,400 |
| 14 | Supplies | 2,500 |
| 18 | Office Equipment | 2,500 |
| 21 | Accounts Payable | 1,230 |

## Revenue Journal

*Fees earned on account* would be recorded in the **revenue journal**. *Cash fees earned* would be recorded in the cash receipts journal.

To illustrate the efficiency of using a revenue journal, an example for **NetSolutions** is used. Specifically, assume that NetSolutions recorded the following four revenue transactions for March in its general journal:

| Date | | | Description | Post. Ref. | Debit | Credit |
|---|---|---|---|---|---|---|
| 2016 | | | | | | |
| Mar. | 2 | | Accounts Receivable—Accessories By Claire | 12/✓ | 2,200 | |
| | | | Fees Earned | 41 | | 2,200 |
| | 6 | | Accounts Receivable—RapZone | 12/✓ | 1,750 | |
| | | | Fees Earned | 41 | | 1,750 |
| | 18 | | Accounts Receivable—Web Cantina | 12/✓ | 2,650 | |
| | | | Fees Earned | 41 | | 2,650 |
| | 27 | | Accounts Receivable—Accessories By Claire | 12/✓ | 3,000 | |
| | | | Fees Earned | 41 | | 3,000 |

For the preceding entries, NetSolutions recorded eight accounts and eight amounts. In addition, NetSolutions made 12 postings to the ledgers—four to Accounts Receivable in the general ledger, four to the accounts receivable subsidiary ledger (indicated by each check mark), and four to Fees Earned in the general ledger.

The preceding revenue transactions could be recorded more efficiently in a revenue journal, as shown in Exhibit 2. In each revenue transaction, the amount of the debit to Accounts Receivable is the same as the amount of the credit to Fees Earned. Thus, only a single amount column is necessary. The date, invoice number, customer name, and amount are entered separately for each transaction.

Revenues are normally recorded in the revenue journal when the company sends an invoice to the customer. An **invoice** is the bill that is sent to the customer by the company. Each invoice is normally numbered in sequence for future reference.

To illustrate, assume that on March 2 NetSolutions issued Invoice No. 615 to Accessories By Claire for fees earned of $2,200. This transaction is entered in the revenue journal, shown in Exhibit 2, by entering the following items:

1. Date column: *Mar. 2*
2. Invoice No. column: *615*
3. Account Debited column: *Accessories By Claire*
4. Accts. Rec. Dr./Fees Earned Cr. column: *2,200*

**EXHIBIT 2**    Revenue Journal

| | | | | | |
|---|---|---|---|---|---|
| **Revenue Journal** | | | | | *Page 35* |
| **Date** | **Invoice No.** | | **Account Debited** | **Post. Ref.** | **Accts. Rec. Dr. Fees Earned Cr.** |
| 2016 | | | | | |
| Mar. 2 | 615 | | Accessories By Claire | | 2,200 |
| 6 | 616 | | RapZone | | 1,750 |
| 18 | 617 | | Web Cantina | | 2,650 |
| 27 | 618 | | Accessories By Claire | | 3,000 |
| 31 | | | | | 9,600 |

The process of posting from a revenue journal, shown in Exhibit 3, is as follows:

- Step 1. Each transaction is posted individually to a customer account in the accounts receivable subsidiary ledger. Postings to customer accounts should be made on a regular basis. In this way, the customer's account will show a current balance. Since the balances in the customer accounts are usually debit balances, the three-column account form is shown in Exhibit 3.

    *To illustrate, Exhibit 3 shows the posting of the $2,200 debit to Accessories By Claire in the accounts receivable subsidiary ledger. After the posting, Accessories By Claire has a debit balance of $2,200.*

- Step 2. To provide a trail of the entries posted to the subsidiary and general ledger, the source of these entries is indicated in the Posting Reference column of each account by inserting the letter R (for revenue journal) and the page number of the revenue journal.

    *To illustrate, Exhibit 3 shows that after $2,200 is posted to Accessories By Claire's account, R35 is inserted into the Post. Ref. column of the account.*

- Step 3. To indicate that the transaction has been posted to the accounts receivable subsidiary ledger, a check mark (✓) is inserted in the Post. Ref. column of the revenue journal, as shown in Exhibit 3.

    *To illustrate, Exhibit 3 shows that a check mark (✓) has been inserted in the Post. Ref. column next to Accessories By Claire in the revenue journal to indicate that the $2,200 has been posted.*

- Step 4. A single monthly total is posted to Accounts Receivable and Fees Earned in the general ledger. This total is equal to the sum of the month's debits to the individual accounts in the subsidiary ledger. It is posted in the general ledger as a debit to Accounts Receivable and a credit to Fees Earned, as shown in Exhibit 3. The accounts receivable account number (12) and the fees earned account number (41) are then inserted below the total in the revenue journal to indicate that the posting is completed.

    *To illustrate, Exhibit 3 shows the monthly total of $9,600 was posted as a debit to Accounts Receivable (12) and as a credit to Fees Earned (41).*

Exhibit 3 illustrates the efficiency gained by using the revenue journal rather than the general journal. Specifically, all of the transactions for fees earned during the month are posted to the general ledger only once—at the end of the month.

**EXHIBIT 3**   Revenue Journal and Postings

### Revenue Journal — Page 35

| Date | Invoice No. | Account Debited | Post. Ref. | Accts. Rec. Dr. Fees Earned Cr. |
|---|---|---|---|---|
| 2016 | | | | |
| Mar. 2 | 615 | Accessories By Claire | ✓ | 2,200 |
| 6 | 616 | RapZone | ✓ | 1,750 |
| 18 | 617 | Web Cantina | ✓ | 2,650 |
| 27 | 618 | Accessories By Claire  **Step 3** | ✓ | 3,000 |
| 31 | | | | 9,600 |
| | | | | (12) (41) |

### General Ledger

**Account** Accounts Receivable                     Account No. 12

| Date | Item | Post. Ref. | Debit | Credit | Balance Debit | Balance Credit |
|---|---|---|---|---|---|---|
| 2016 | | | | | | |
| Mar. 1 | Balance | ✓ | | | 3,400 | |
| 31 | | R35 | 9,600 | | 13,000 | |

**Step 4**

**Account** Fees Earned                     Account No. 41

| Date | Item | Post. Ref. | Debit | Credit | Balance Debit | Balance Credit |
|---|---|---|---|---|---|---|
| 2016 | | | | | | |
| Mar. 31 | | R35 | | 9,600 | | 9,600 |

**Step 4**

### Accounts Receivable Subsidiary Ledger

**Name:** Accessories By Claire

| Date | Item | Post. Ref. | Debit | Credit | Balance |
|---|---|---|---|---|---|
| 2016 | | | | | |
| Mar. 2 | | R35 | 2,200 | | 2,200 |
| 27 | | R35 | 3,000 | | 5,200 |

**Step 2**          **Step 1**

**Name:** RapZone

| Date | Item | Post. Ref. | Debit | Credit | Balance |
|---|---|---|---|---|---|
| 2016 | | | | | |
| Mar. 6 | | R35 | 1,750 | | 1,750 |

**Name:** Web Cantina

| Date | Item | Post. Ref. | Debit | Credit | Balance |
|---|---|---|---|---|---|
| 2016 | | | | | |
| Mar. 1 | Balance | ✓ | | | 3,400 |
| 18 | | R35 | 2,650 | | 6,050 |

---

## Example Exercise 5-1   Revenue Journal          OBJ 2

The following revenue transactions occurred during December:

Dec. 5. Issued Invoice No. 302 to Butler Company for services provided on account, $5,000.
9. Issued Invoice No. 303 to JoJo Enterprises for services provided on account, $2,100.
15. Issued Invoice No. 304 to Salinas Inc. for services provided on account, $3,250.

Record these transactions in a revenue journal as illustrated in Exhibit 2.

## Follow My Example 5-1

### REVENUE JOURNAL

| Date | Invoice No. | Account Debited | Post. Ref. | Accts. Rec. Dr. Fees Earned Cr. |
|---|---|---|---|---|
| Dec. 5 | 302 | Butler Company | | 5,000 |
| 9 | 303 | JoJo Enterprises | | 2,100 |
| 15 | 304 | Salinas Inc. | | 3,250 |

Practice Exercises: PE 5-1A, PE 5-1B

## Cash Receipts Journal

All transactions that involve the receipt of cash are recorded in a **cash receipts journal**. The cash receipts journal for **NetSolutions** is shown in Exhibit 4.

This journal has a Cash Dr. column. The types of cash receipt transactions and their frequency determine the titles of the other columns. For example, NetSolutions often receives cash from customers on account. Thus, the cash receipts journal in Exhibit 4 has an Accounts Receivable Cr. column.

To illustrate, on March 19 Web Cantina made a payment of $3,400 on its account. This transaction is recorded in the cash receipts journal, shown in Exhibit 4, by entering the following items:

1. Date column: *Mar. 19*
2. Account Credited column: *Web Cantina*

**EXHIBIT 4** **Cash Receipts Journal and Postings**

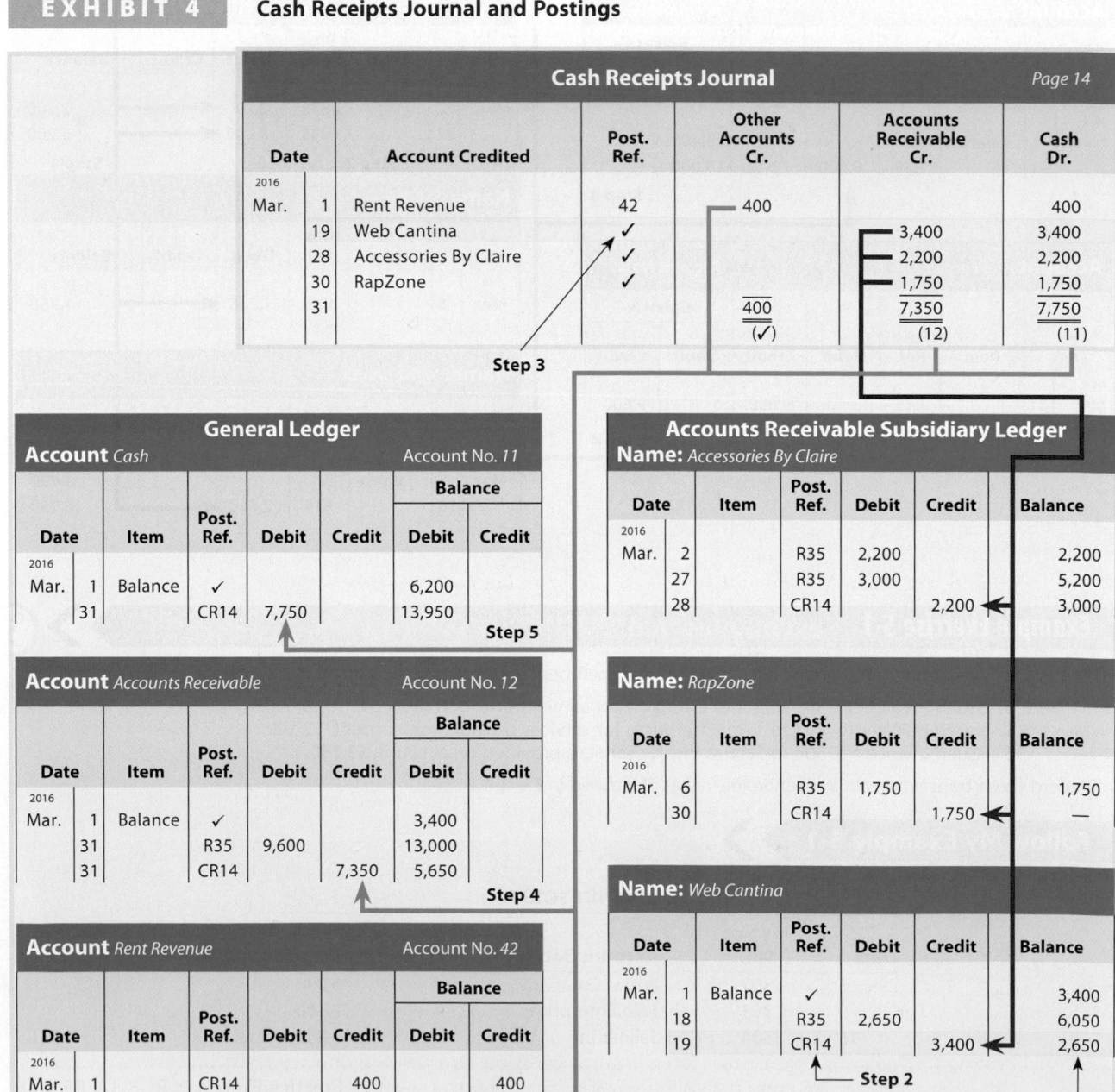

3. Accounts Receivable Cr. column: *3,400*

4. Cash Dr. column: *3,400*

The Other Accounts Cr. column in Exhibit 4 is used for recording credits to any account for which there is no special credit column. For example, NetSolutions received cash on March 1 for rent. Since no special column exists for Rent Revenue, Rent Revenue is entered in the Account Credited column. Thus, this transaction is recorded in the cash receipts journal, shown in Exhibit 4, by entering the following items:

1. Date column: *Mar. 1*

2. Account Credited column: *Rent Revenue*

3. Other Accounts Cr. column: *400*

4. Cash Dr. column: *400*

At the end of the month, all of the amount columns are totaled. The debits must equal the credits. If the debits do not equal the credits, an error has occurred. Before proceeding further, the error must be found and corrected.

The process of posting from the cash receipts journal, shown in Exhibit 4, is:

- Step 1. Each transaction involving the receipt of cash on account is posted individually to a customer account in the accounts receivable subsidiary ledger. Postings to customer accounts should be made on a regular basis. In this way, the customer's account will show a current balance.

  *To illustrate, Exhibit 4 shows on March 19 the receipt of $3,400 on account from Web Cantina. The posting of the $3,400 credit to Web Cantina in the accounts receivable subsidiary ledger is also shown in Exhibit 4. After the posting, Web Cantina has a debit balance of $2,650. If a posting results in a customer's account with a credit balance, the credit balance is indicated by an asterisk or parentheses in the Balance column. If an account's balance is zero, a line may be drawn in the Balance column.*

- Step 2. To provide a trail of the entries posted to the subsidiary ledger, the source of these entries is indicated in the Posting Reference column of each account by inserting the letters CR (for cash receipts journal) and the page number of the cash receipts journal.

  *To illustrate, Exhibit 4 shows that after $3,400 is posted to Web Cantina's account in the accounts receivable subsidiary ledger, CR14 is inserted into the Post. Ref. column of the account.*

- Step 3. To indicate that the transaction has been posted to the accounts receivable subsidiary ledger, a check mark (✓) is inserted in the Posting Reference column of the cash receipts journal.

  *To illustrate, Exhibit 4 shows that a check mark (✓) has been inserted in the Post. Ref. column next to Web Cantina to indicate that the $3,400 has been posted.*

- Step 4. A single monthly total of the Accounts Receivable Cr. column is posted to the accounts receivable general ledger account. This is the total cash received on account and is posted as a credit to Accounts Receivable. The accounts receivable account number (12) is then inserted below the Accounts Receivable Cr. column to indicate that the posting is complete.

  *To illustrate, Exhibit 4 shows the monthly total of $7,350 was posted as a credit to Accounts Receivable (12).*

- Step 5. A single monthly total of the Cash Dr. column is posted to the cash general ledger account. This is the total cash received during the month and is posted as a debit to Cash. The cash account number (11) is then inserted below the Cash Dr. column to indicate that the posting is complete.

  *To illustrate, Exhibit 4 shows the monthly total of $7,750 was posted as a debit to Cash (11).*

- Step 6. The accounts listed in the Other Accounts Cr. column are posted on a regular basis as a separate credit to each account. The account number is then inserted in the Post. Ref. column to indicate that the posting is complete. Because accounts in the Other Accounts Cr. column are posted individually, a check mark is placed below the column total at the end of the month to show that no further action is needed.

*To illustrate, Exhibit 4 shows that $400 was posted as a credit to Rent Revenue in the general ledger, and the rent revenue account number (42) was entered in the Post. Ref. column of the cash receipts journal. Also, at the end of the month a check mark (✓) is entered below the Other Accounts Cr. column to indicate that no further action is needed.*

## Accounts Receivable Control Account and Subsidiary Ledger

After all posting has been completed for the month, the balances in the accounts receivable subsidiary ledger should be totaled. This total can be summarized in a separate schedule of customer balances. The total should then be compared with the balance of the accounts receivable controlling account in the general ledger. If the controlling account and the subsidiary ledger do not agree, an error has occurred and must be located and corrected.

The total of **NetSolutions'** accounts receivable customer balances is $5,650. This total agrees with the balance of its accounts receivable controlling account on March 31, 2016, as follows:

| Accounts Receivable (Controlling) | | NetSolutions Accounts Receivable Customer Balances March 31, 2016 | |
|---|---|---|---|
| Balance, March 1, 2016 | $ 3,400 | Accessories By Claire | $3,000 |
| Total debits (from revenue journal) | 9,600 | RapZone | 0 |
| Total credits (from cash receipts journal) | (7,350) | Web Cantina | 2,650 |
| Balance, March 31, 2016 | $ 5,650 | Total accounts receivable | $5,650 |

Equal debit balances

### Example Exercise 5-2 Accounts Receivable Subsidiary Ledger

**OBJ 2**

The debits and credits from two transactions are presented in the following customer account:

NAME    *Sweet Tooth Confections*
ADDRESS    *1212 Lombard St.*

| Date | Item | Post. Ref. | Debit | Credit | Balance |
|---|---|---|---|---|---|
| July 1 | Balance | | | | 625 |
| 7 | Invoice 35 | R12 | 86 | | 711 |
| 31 | Invoice 31 | CR4 | | 122 | 589 |

Describe each transaction and the source of each posting.

### Follow My Example 5-2

July 7. Provided $86 of services on account to Sweet Tooth Confections, itemized on Invoice No. 35. Amount posted from Page 12 of the revenue journal.

31. Collected cash of $122 from Sweet Tooth Confections (Invoice No. 31). Amount posted from Page 4 of the cash receipts journal.

Practice Exercises: PE 5-2A, PE 5-2B

## Purchases Journal

All *purchases on account* are recorded in the **purchases journal**. *Cash purchases would be recorded in the cash payments journal.* The purchases journal for **NetSolutions** is shown in Exhibit 5.

The amounts purchased on account are recorded in the purchases journal in an Accounts Payable Cr. column. The items most often purchased on account determine the titles of the other columns. For example, NetSolutions often purchases supplies on account. Thus, the purchases journal in Exhibit 5 has a Supplies Dr. column.

| EXHIBIT 5 | Purchases Journal and Postings |
| --- | --- |

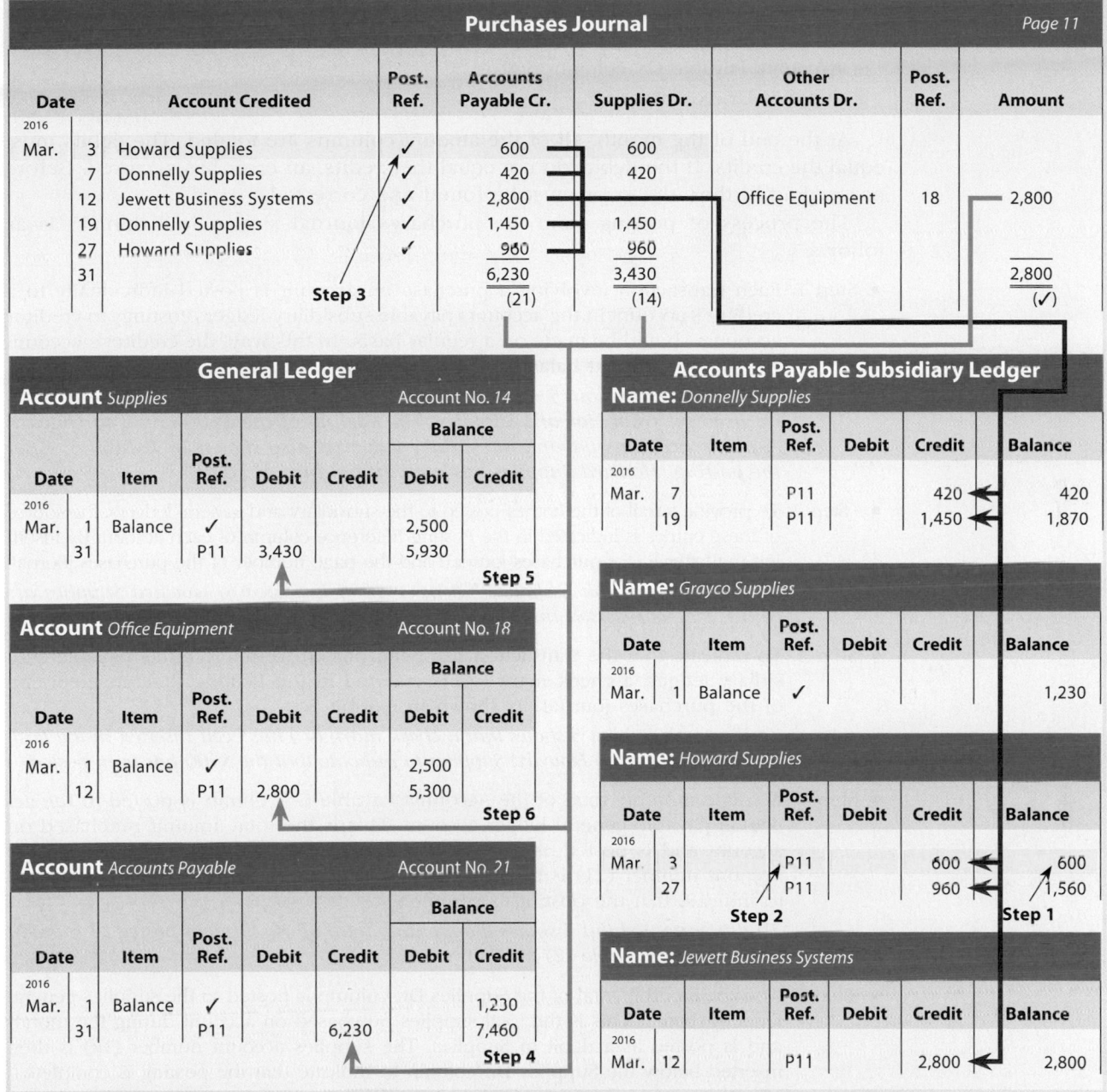

To illustrate, on March 3 NetSolutions purchased $600 of supplies on account from Howard Supplies. This transaction is recorded in the purchases journal, shown in Exhibit 5, by entering the following items:

1. Date column: *Mar. 3*
2. Account Credited column: *Howard Supplies*
3. Accounts Payable Cr. column: *600*
4. Supplies Dr. column: *600*

The Other Accounts Dr. column in Exhibit 5 is used to record purchases on account of any item for which there is no special debit column. The title of the account to be debited is entered in the Other Accounts Dr. column, and the amount is entered in the Amount column.

To illustrate, on March 3 NetSolutions purchased supplies on account from Howard Supplies for $600. This transaction is recorded in the purchases journal shown in Exhibit 5 by entering the following items:

1. Date column: *Mar. 3*
2. Account Credited column: *Howard Supplies*
3. Accounts Payable Cr. column: *600*
4. Supplies Dr. column: *600*

At the end of the month, all of the amount columns are totaled. The debits must equal the credits. If the debits do not equal the credits, an error has occurred. Before proceeding further, the error must be found and corrected.

The process of posting from the purchases journal shown in Exhibit 5 is as follows:

- Step 1. Each transaction involving a purchase on account is posted individually to a creditor's account in the accounts payable subsidiary ledger. Postings to creditor accounts should be made on a regular basis. In this way, the creditor's account will show a current balance.

    *To illustrate, Exhibit 5 shows on March 3 the purchase of supplies of $600 on account from Howard Supplies. The posting of the $600 credit to Howard Supplies accounts payable subsidiary ledger is also shown in Exhibit 5. After the posting, Howard Supplies has a credit balance of $600.*

- Step 2. To provide a trail of the entries posted to the subsidiary and general ledgers, the source of these entries is indicated in the Posting Reference column of each account by inserting the letter P (for purchases journal) and the page number of the purchases journal.

    *To illustrate, Exhibit 5 shows that after $600 is posted to Howard Supplies account, P11 is inserted into the Post. Ref. column of the account.*

- Step 3. To indicate that the transaction has been posted to the accounts payable subsidiary ledger, a check mark (✓) is inserted in the Posting Reference column of the purchases journal, as shown in Exhibit 5.

    *To illustrate, Exhibit 5 shows that a check mark (✓) has been inserted in the Post. Ref. column next to Howard Supplies to indicate that the $600 has been posted.*

- Step 4. A single monthly total of the Accounts Payable Cr. column is posted to the accounts payable general ledger account. This is the total amount purchased on account and is posted as a credit to Accounts Payable. The accounts payable account number (21) is then inserted below the Accounts Payable Cr. column to indicate that the posting is complete.

    *To illustrate, Exhibit 5 shows the monthly total of $6,230 was posted as a credit to Accounts Payable (21).*

- Step 5. A single monthly total of the Supplies Dr. column is posted to the supplies general ledger account. This is the total supplies purchased on account during the month and is posted as a debit to Supplies. The supplies account number (14) is then inserted below the Supplies Dr. column to indicate that the posting is complete.

    *To illustrate, Exhibit 5 shows the monthly total of $3,430 was posted as a debit to Supplies (14).*

- Step 6. The accounts listed in the Other Accounts Dr. column are posted on a regular basis as a separate debit to each account. The account number is then inserted in the Post. Ref. column to indicate that the posting is complete. Because accounts in the Other Accounts Dr. column are posted individually, a check mark is placed below the column total at the end of the month to show that no further action is needed.

    *To illustrate, Exhibit 5 shows that $2,800 was posted as a debit to Office Equipment in the general ledger, and the office equipment account number (18) was entered in the Post. Ref. column of the purchases journal. Also, at the end of the month, a check mark (✓) is entered below the Amount column to indicate no further action is needed.*

**Example Exercise 5-3  Purchases Journal**

The following purchase transactions occurred during October for Helping Hand Cleaners:

Oct. 11.    Purchased cleaning supplies for $235, on account, from General Supplies.
    19.    Purchased cleaning supplies for $110, on account, from Hubble Supplies.
    24.    Purchased office equipment for $850, on account, from Office Warehouse.

Record these transactions in a purchases journal as illustrated at the top of Exhibit 5.

**Follow My Example 5-3**

**PURCHASES JOURNAL**

| Date | Account Credited | Post. Ref. | Accounts Payable Cr. | Cleaning Supplies Dr. | Other Accounts Dr. | Post. Ref. | Amount |
|------|------------------|-----------|----------------------|-----------------------|--------------------|-----------|--------|
| Oct. 11 | General Supplies | | 235 | 235 | | | |
| 19 | Hubble Supplies | | 110 | 110 | | | |
| 24 | Office Warehouse | | 850 | | Office Equipment | | 850 |

Practice Exercises: PE 5-3A, PE 5-3B

## Cash Payments Journal

All transactions that involve the payment of cash are recorded in a **cash payments journal**. The cash payments journal for **NetSolutions** is shown in Exhibit 6.

The cash payments journal shown in Exhibit 6 has a Cash Cr. column. The kinds of transactions in which cash is paid and how often they occur determine the titles of the other columns. For example, NetSolutions often pays cash to creditors on account. Thus, the cash payments journal in Exhibit 6 has an Accounts Payable Dr. column. In addition, NetSolutions makes all payments by check. Thus, a check number is entered for each payment in the Ck. No. (Check Number) column to the right of the Date column. The check numbers are helpful in controlling cash payments and provide a useful cross-reference.

To illustrate, on March 15 NetSolutions issued Check No. 151 for $1,230 to Grayco Supplies for payment on its account. This transaction is recorded in the cash payments journal shown in Exhibit 6 by entering the following items:

1. Date column: *Mar. 15*
2. Ck. No. column: *151*
3. Account Debited column: *Grayco Supplies*
4. Accounts Payable Dr. column: *1,230*
5. Cash Cr. column: *1,230*

The Other Accounts Dr. column in Exhibit 6 is used for recording debits to any account for which there is no special debit column. For example, NetSolutions issued Check No. 150 on March 2 for $1,600 in payment of March rent. This transaction is recorded in the cash payments journal, shown in Exhibit 6, by entering these items:

1. Date column: *Mar. 2*
2. Ck. No. column: *150*
3. Account Debited column: *Rent Expense*
4. Other Accounts Dr. column: *1,600*
5. Cash Cr. column: *1,600*

At the end of the month, all of the amount columns are totaled. The debits must equal the credits. If the debits do not equal the credits, an error has occurred. Before proceeding further, the error must be found and corrected.

The process of posting from the cash payments journal, Exhibit 6, is as follows:

- Step 1. Each transaction involving the payment of cash on account is posted individually to a creditor account in the accounts payable subsidiary ledger. Postings to

**EXHIBIT 6** Cash Payments Journal and Postings

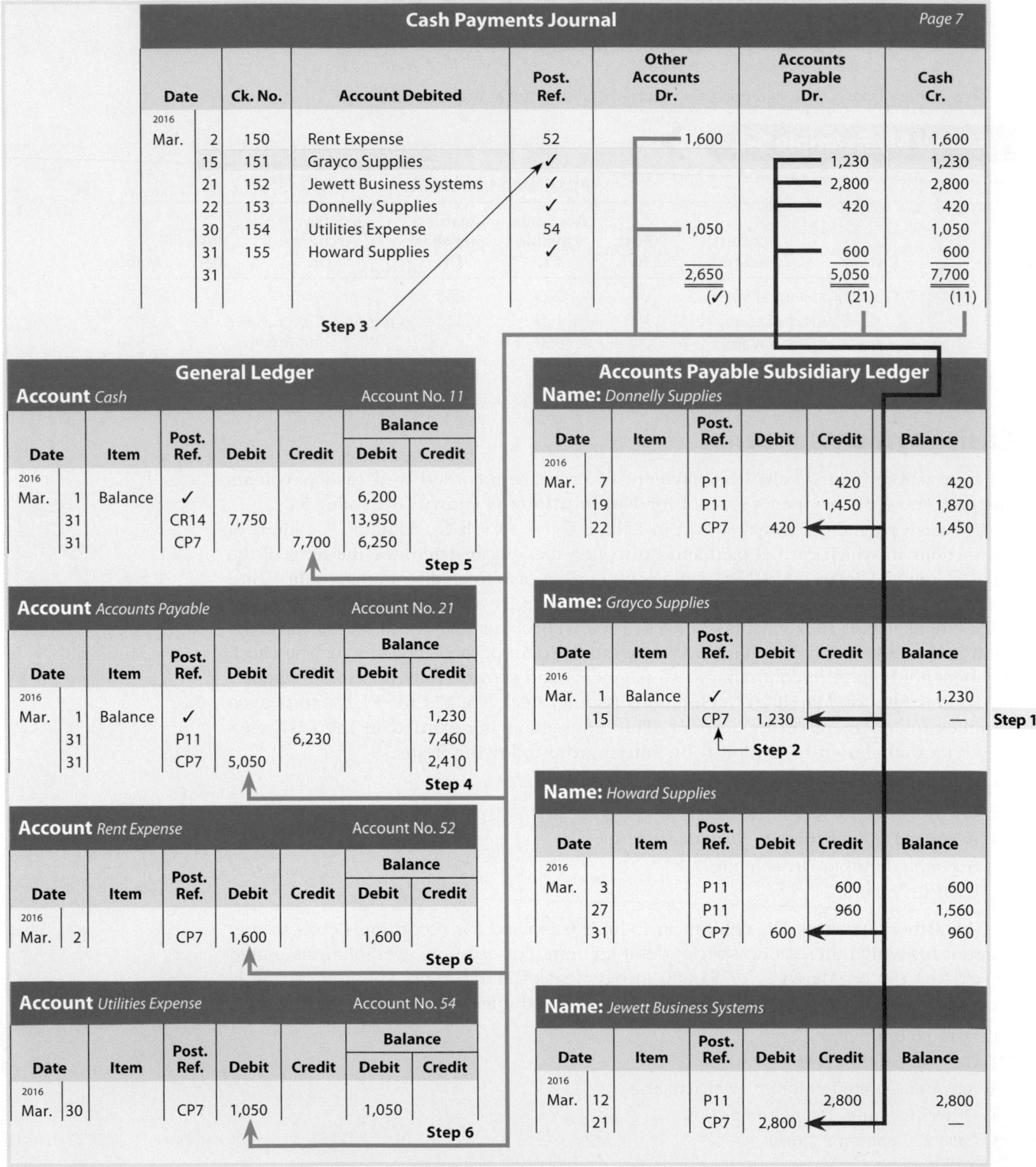

creditor accounts should be made on a regular basis. In this way, the creditor's account will show a current balance.

*To illustrate, Exhibit 6 shows on March 15 the payment of $1,230 on account to Grayco Supplies. The posting of the $1,230 debit to Grayco Supplies in the accounts payable subsidiary ledger is also shown in Exhibit 6. After the posting, Grayco Supplies has a zero balance.*

- Step 2. To provide a trail of the entries posted to the subsidiary and general ledgers, the source of these entries is indicated in the Posting Reference column of each account by inserting the letters CP (for cash payments journal) and the page number of the cash payments journal.

  *To illustrate, Exhibit 6 shows that after $1,230 is posted to Grayco Supplies account, CP7 is inserted into the Post. Ref. column of the account.*

- Step 3. To indicate that the transaction has been posted to the accounts payable subsidiary ledger, a check mark (✓) is inserted in the Posting Reference column of the cash payments journal.

  *To illustrate, Exhibit 6 shows that a check mark (✓) has been inserted in the Post. Ref. column next to Grayco Supplies to indicate that the $1,230 has been posted.*

- Step 4. A single monthly total of the Accounts Payable Dr. column is posted to the accounts payable general ledger account. This is the total cash paid on account and is posted as a debit to Accounts Payable. The accounts payable account number (21) is then inserted below the Accounts Payable Dr. column to indicate that the posting is complete.

  *To illustrate, Exhibit 6 shows the monthly total of $5,050 was posted as a debit to Accounts Payable (21).*

- Step 5. A single monthly total of the Cash Cr. column is posted to the cash general ledger account. This is the total cash payments during the month and is posted as a credit to Cash. The cash account number (11) is then inserted below the Cash Cr. column to indicate that the posting is complete.

  *To illustrate, Exhibit 6 shows the monthly total of $7,700 was posted as a credit to Cash (11).*

- Step 6. The accounts listed in the Other Accounts Dr. column are posted on a regular basis as a separate debit to each account. The account number is then inserted in the Post. Ref. column to indicate that the posting is complete. Because accounts in the Other Accounts Dr. column are posted individually, a check mark is placed below the column total at the end of the month to show that no further action is needed.

  *To illustrate, Exhibit 6 shows that $1,600 was posted as a debit to Rent Expense (52) and $1,050 was posted as a debit to Utilities Expense (54) in the general ledger. The account numbers (52 and 54, respectively) were entered in the Post. Ref. column of the cash payments journal. Also, at the end of the month, a check mark (✓) is entered below the Other Accounts Dr. column to indicate that no further action is needed.*

## Accounts Payable Control Account and Subsidiary Ledger

After all posting has been completed for the month, the balances in the accounts payable subsidiary ledger should be totaled. This total can be summarized in a separate schedule of creditor balances. The total should then be compared with the balance of the accounts payable controlling account in the general ledger. If the controlling account and the subsidiary ledger do not agree, an error has occurred, and must be located and corrected.

The total of **NetSolutions'** accounts payable creditor balances is $2,410. This total agrees with the balance of its accounts payable controlling account on March 31, 2016, as follows:

| Accounts Payable (Controlling) | | NetSolutions Accounts Payable Creditor Balances March 31, 2016 | |
|---|---|---|---|
| Balance, March 1, 2016 | $1,230 | Donnelly Supplies | $1,450 |
| Total credits (from purchases journal) | 6,230 | Grayco Supplies | 0 |
| Total debits | | Howard Supplies | 960 |
| (from cash payments journal) | (5,050) | Jewett Business Systems | 0 |
| Balance, March 31, 2016 | $2,410 | Total | $2,410 |

Equal credit balances

## Example Exercise 5-4  Accounts Payable Subsidiary Ledger

The debits and credits from two transactions are presented in the following creditor's (supplier's) account:

NAME   *Lassiter Services Inc.*
ADDRESS   *301 St. Bonaventure Ave.*

| Date | Item | Post. Ref. | Debit | Credit | Balance |
|---|---|---|---|---|---|
| Aug. 1 | Balance | | | | 320 |
| 12 | Invoice No. 101 | CP36 | 200 | | 120 |
| 22 | Invoice No. 106 | P16 | | 140 | 260 |

Describe each transaction and the source of each posting.

### Follow My Example 5-4

Aug. 12. Paid $200 to Lassiter Services Inc. on account (Invoice No. 101). Amount posted from Page 36 of the cash payments journal.

22. Purchased $140 of services on account from Lassiter Services Inc. itemized on Invoice No. 106. Amount posted from Page 16 of the purchases journal.

Practice Exercises: PE 5-4A, PE 5-4B

## Business  Connection

### ACCOUNTING SYSTEMS AND PROFIT MEASUREMENT

A Greek restaurant owner in Canada had his own system of accounting. He kept his accounts payable in a cigar box on the left-hand side of his cash register, his daily cash returns in the cash register, and his receipts for paid bills in another cigar box on the right. A truly "manual" system.

When his youngest son graduated as an accountant, he was appalled by his father's primitive methods. "I don't know how you can run a business that way," he said. "How do you know what your profits are?"

"Well, son," the father replied, "when I got off the boat from Greece, I had nothing but the pants I was wearing. Today, your brother is a doctor. You are an accountant. Your sister is a speech therapist. Your mother and I have a nice car, a city house, and a country home. We have a good business, and everything is paid for. . . ."

"So, you add all that together, subtract the pants, and there's your profit!"

## Computerized Accounting Systems

**OBJ 3** Define and illustrate the use of a computerized accounting system.

Computerized accounting systems are widely used by even the smallest of companies. Computerized accounting systems have the following three main advantages over manual systems:

- Computerized systems simplify the record-keeping process by recording transactions in electronic journals or forms and, at the same time, posting them electronically to general and subsidiary ledger accounts.
- Computerized systems are generally more accurate than manual systems.
- Computerized systems provide management with current account balance information to support decision making, since account balances are posted as the transactions occur.

The popular QuickBooks accounting software for small- to medium-sized businesses is used to illustrate a computerized accounting system for **NetSolutions**. To simplify, the illustration is limited to transactions involving revenue earned on account and the subsequent recording of cash collections. Exhibit 7 illustrates the use of QuickBooks for NetSolutions to record transactions as follows:

Large companies have their accounting systems integrated within the automated business systems of the firm. Such integrated software is termed ERP, or enterprise resource planning.

- Step 1. Record fees by completing an electronic invoice form and sending to customer (print and mail, or e-mail).

    Sales transactions are entered onto the computer screen using an electronic invoice form. The electronic form appears like a paper form with spaces, or fields, to input transaction data. The data spaces may have pull-down lists to ease data entry. After the form is completed, it is printed out and mailed, or e-mailed, to the customer.

    *To illustrate, on March 2, NetSolutions earned $2,200 on account from Accessories By Claire. As shown in Exhibit 7, Invoice No. 615 was created using an electronic form. Upon submitting the invoice form, QuickBooks automatically posts a $2,200 debit to the Accessories By Claire customer account and a credit to Fees Earned. An invoice is either e-mailed or printed for mailing to Accessories By Claire.*

- Step 2. Record collection of payment by completing a "receive payment" form.

    Upon collection from the customer, a "receive payment" electronic form is opened and completed. As with the "invoice form," data are input into the various spaces directly or by using pull-down lists.

    *To illustrate, a $2,200 payment was collected from Accessories By Claire on March 28. The $2,200 was applied to Invoice No. 615, as shown by the check mark (✓) next to the March 2 date at the bottom of the form in Exhibit 7. As shown at the bottom of the form, the March 27 invoice of $3,000 remains uncollected. When the screen is completed, a debit of $2,200 is automatically posted to the cash account, and a credit for $2,200 is posted to the Accessories By Claire account. This causes the balance of the Accessories By Claire account to be reduced from $5,200 to $3,000.*

- Step 3. Prepare reports.

    At any time, managers may request reports from the software. Three such reports include the following:

    - "Accounts Receivable Customer Balances" lists as of a specific date the accounts receivable balances by customer.

        *To illustrate, the Accounts Receivable Customer Balances report shown in Exhibit 7 for NetSolutions was generated as of March 31, 2016. The total of the balances of the Accounts Receivable Customer Balances report of $5,650 agrees with the accounts receivable subsidiary ledger balance total we illustrated using a manual system for NetSolutions in Exhibit 4.*

    - "Fees Earned by Customer" lists revenue by customer for the month. It is created from the electronic invoice form used in step 1.

        *To illustrate, the Fees Earned by Customer report shown in Exhibit 7 for NetSolutions is for the month of March 2016. The $9,600 of total fees earned by customer agree with the total of the revenue journal we illustrated using a manual system for NetSolutions in Exhibits 2 and 3.*

    - "Cash Receipts" lists the cash receipts during the month.

        *To illustrate, the Cash Receipts report shown in Exhibit 7 for NetSolutions is for the month of March 2016. The total cash receipts of $7,750 agree with the total of the Cash Dr. column of the cash receipts journal we illustrated using a manual system for NetSolutions in Exhibit 4.*

Quickbooks and other computerized accounting systems use electronic forms. Alternatively, some computerized systems use electronic special journals. Such journals are designed similar to those illustrated in the text. Additionally, electronic general journals are found in all computerized systems.

**EXHIBIT 7**   Revenue and Cash Receipts in QuickBooks

1. Record fees by completing an electronic invoice form and sending to customer (print and mail, or e-mail).

| Invoice | | | Date | Invoice No. |
|---|---|---|---|---|
| Bill To: | | | 03/02/16 | 615 |

Accessories By Claire
244 Grand Ave.
Des Moines, IA 50310

| | | | P.O. Number | Terms | |
|---|---|---|---|---|---|
| Item | Description | Quantity | Rate | Amount | Tax |
| Consulting | Computer consulting | 22 | 100.00 | 2,200.00 | |

| Customer Message | | no tax | 0.0% | 0.00 |
|---|---|---|---|---|
| | | | Total | 2,200.00 |

**Journal Entry Equivalent**

| | Dr. | Cr. |
|---|---|---|
| Accounts Receivable— | | |
| Accessories By Claire | 2,200 | |
| Fees Earned | | 2,200 |

Accessories By Claire  37¢
244 Grand Ave.
Des Moines, IA 50310

**Receive payment.**

2. Record collection of payment by completing a "receive payment" form.

| Customer Payment | | | Date | Balance |
|---|---|---|---|---|
| Amount | 2,200.00 | | 03/28/16 | 5,200.00 |
| Pmt. Method | | | | |
| Check No. | | | | |

Invoices paid (with this payment) and those still outstanding

| ✓ | Date | Type | Number | Job | Orig. Amt. | Disc. Date | Amt. Due | Payment |
|---|---|---|---|---|---|---|---|---|
| ✓ | 03/02/16 | Invoice | 615 | | 2,200.00 | | 2,200.00 | 2,200.00 |
| | 03/27/16 | Invoice | 618 | | 3,000.00 | | 3,000.00 | 0.00 |
| | Totals | | | | | | 5,200.00 | 2,200.00 |

Deposit: ○ Group with other undeposited funds
● Deposit to First Untion Bank

| Discount Info | Existing Credits: | 0.00 |
|---|---|---|
| | □ Apply Existing Credits? | |
| Clear Payments | Total to Apply: | 2,200.00 |
| | Unapplied Amount: | 0.00 |

**Journal Entry Equivalent**

| | Dr. | Cr. |
|---|---|---|
| Cash | 2,200 | |
| Accounts Receivable— | | |
| Accessories By Claire | | 2,200 |

3. Prepare reports.

| Dates: Custom Dates | From: 03/31/16 | To: 03/31/16 |
|---|---|---|

NetSolutions
Accounts Receivable Customer Balances
March 31, 2016

| | Mar 31, '16 |
|---|---|
| Accessories By Claire | 3,000.00 |
| Web Cantina | 2,650.00 |
| TOTAL | 5,650.00 |

| Dates: Custom Dates | From: 03/01/16 | To: 03/31/16 | Total By: A |
|---|---|---|---|

NetSolutions
Cash Receipts
March 2016

| Type | Date | Name | Amount |
|---|---|---|---|
| First Union Bank | | | |
| Sales Receipt | 03/01/16 | Rental Customer | 400.00 |
| Payment | 03/19/16 | Web Cantina | 3,400.00 |
| Payment | 03/28/16 | Accessories By Claire | 2,200.00 |
| Payment | 03/28/16 | RapZone | 1,750.00 |
| Total First Untion Bank | | | 7,750.00 |

| Dates: Custom Dates | From: 03/01/16 | To: 03/31/16 | □Hide Header □Collapse |
|---|---|---|---|

NetSolutions
Fees Earned by Customer
March 2016

| Type | Date | Num | Name | Amount |
|---|---|---|---|---|
| Service | | | | |
| Consulting | | | | |
| Invoice | 03/02/16 | 615 | Accessories By Claire | 2,200.00 |
| Invoice | 03/06/16 | 616 | RapZone | 1,750.00 |
| Invoice | 03/18/16 | 617 | Web Cantina | 2,650.00 |
| Invoice | 03/27/16 | 618 | Accessories By Claire | 3,000.00 |
| Total Consulting | | | | 9,600.00 |

# Business  Connection

## TURBOTAX

**Intuit** sells TurboTax®, one of the most popular tax preparation software products for individuals. Using this product, the tax return is prepared using electronic tax forms. Thus, the familiar Form 1040 is presented as an electronic form with data-entry fields provided for the various line items. The advantage of this approach is that all the arithmetic and linking between forms is done automatically. A change in one field automatically updates all other linked fields.

In using these tools, the computer prevents transactions in which the total debits do not equal the total credits. In such cases, an error screen will notify the user to correct data inputs. Likewise, the computer will not make posting or mathematical errors.

In this section, revenue and cash receipt transactions are illustrated for NetSolutions using QuickBooks accounting software. Similar illustrations could be provided for purchases and cash payment transactions. A complete illustration of a computerized accounting system is beyond the scope of this text. However, this chapter provides a solid foundation for applying accounting system concepts in either a manual or a computerized system.

# E-Commerce

 Describe the basic features of e-commerce.

Using the Internet to perform business transactions is termed **e-commerce**. The U.S. Census Bureau indicates that e-commerce represents more than $225 billion in retail sales, or more than 5% of all retail sales.[1] When transactions are between a company and a consumer, it is termed *B2C (business-to-consumer) e-commerce*. Examples of companies engaged in B2C e-commerce include Amazon.com, priceline.com Incorporated, and Apple Inc. The B2C business allows consumers to shop and receive goods at home, rather than going to the store. For example, Apple Inc. allows consumers to use its Web site to select and purchase Apple products for direct shipment to the home.

When transactions are conducted between two companies, it is termed *B2B (business-to-business) e-commerce*. Examples of companies engaged in B2B e-commerce include Cisco Systems, Inc., an Internet equipment manufacturer, and Union Pacific Corporation, a railroad. Union Pacific, for example, allows their business customers to order freight transportation services from their Web site.

 A new trend is toward "cloud" software solutions whereby the accounting system and data are stored and distributed over the Internet by a third party. Under this model, the software is "rented," while analysis, design, and implementation are largely provided by the software vendor.

The Internet creates opportunities for improving the speed and efficiency of transactions. As discussed, many companies are realizing these benefits of using e-commerce. Three additional areas where the Internet is being used for business purposes are as follows:

- **Supply chain management (SCM):** Internet applications to plan supply needs and coordinate them with suppliers.
- **Customer relationship management (CRM):** Internet applications to plan and coordinate marketing and sales effort.
- **Product life-cycle management (PLM):** Internet applications to plan and coordinate the product development and design process.

Many Web applications generate accounting transactions as they occur. For example, purchases using e-commerce shopping carts generate the accounting sales transaction.

## Integrity, Objectivity, and Ethics in Business

### ONLINE FRAUD

Fraud accounted for more than $3.4 billion in e-commerce losses in 2011, or approximately 1.0% of all online revenue. As a result, online retailers are using address verification and credit card security codes as additional security measures. Address verification matches the customer's address to the address on file with the credit card company, while the security code is the additional four-digit code designed to reduce fictitious credit card transactions. Online fraud has been decreasing the last several years as a result of these and other measures.

Source: 13th Annual CyberSource fraud survey, *CyberSource*, January 2012.

[1] Quarterly Retail E commerce Sales, *U.S. Census Bureau News*, U.S. Department of Commerce, February 15, 2013, p. 1.

As the Internet continues to become the preferred method of conducting business, new applications will be developed. Many of these applications will be linked to the accounting system as transactions flow inside and outside the organization.

OBJ 5 Use segment analysis in evaluating the operating performance of a company.

# Financial Analysis and Interpretation: Segment Analysis

Accounting systems often use computers to collect, classify, summarize, and report financial and operating information in a variety of ways. One way is to report revenue earned by different segments of business. Businesses may be segmented by region, by product or service, or by type of customer. Segment revenues are determined from the invoice data that are entered into the accounting system.

For example, Intuit Inc. uses invoice data from the accounting system to determine the amount of revenue earned by different products and services. Segment analysis uses horizontal and vertical comparisons to analyze the contributions of various segments to the total operating performance of a company. To illustrate, selected product and service segment revenue information from the notes to Intuit's financial statements for two recent fiscal years follows:

| Segment | Recent Year (in millions) | Prior Year (in millions) |
|---|---|---|
| Financial Management Solutions | $ 691 | $ 622 |
| Employee Management Solutions | 512 | 457 |
| Payment Solutions | 417 | 348 |
| Consumer Tax | 1,441 | 1,298 |
| Accounting Professionals | 423 | 399 |
| Financial Institutions | 362 | 346 |
| Other Businesses | 305 | 302 |
| Total revenues | $4,151 | $3,772 |

This segment information can be used to perform horizontal analysis using the prior year as the base year as follows:

| Segment | Recent Year (in millions) | Prior Year (in millions) | Increase (Decrease) Amount | Increase (Decrease) Percent |
|---|---|---|---|---|
| Financial Management Solutions | $ 691 | $ 622 | $ 69 | 11.1% |
| Employee Management Solutions | 512 | 457 | 55 | 12.0 |
| Payment Solutions | 417 | 348 | 69 | 19.8 |
| Consumer Tax | 1,441 | 1,298 | 143 | 11.0 |
| Accounting Professionals | 423 | 399 | 24 | 6.0 |
| Financial Institutions | 362 | 346 | 16 | 4.6 |
| Other Businesses | 305 | 302 | 3 | 1.0 |
| Total revenues | $4,151 | $3,772 | $379 | 10.0 |

Intuit Inc. increased total revenue by 10% between the two years. This increase came from strong revenue gains in the Financial Management Solutions, Employee Management Solutions, Payment Solutions, and Consumer Tax segments.

In addition, vertical analysis could be performed on the segment disclosures as follows:

| Segment | Recent Year Amount (in millions) | Percent | Prior Year Amount (in millions) | Percent |
|---|---|---|---|---|
| Financial Management Solutions | $ 691 | 16.6% | $ 622 | 16.5% |
| Employee Management Solutions | 512 | 12.3 | 457 | 12.1 |
| Payment Solutions | 417 | 10.1 | 348 | 9.2 |
| Consumer Tax | 1,441 | 34.7 | 1,298 | 34.4 |
| Accounting Professionals | 423 | 10.2 | 399 | 10.6 |
| Financial Institutions | 362 | 8.7 | 346 | 9.2 |
| Other Businesses | 305 | 7.4 | 302 | 8.0 |
| Total revenues | $4,151 | 100.0% | $3,772 | 100.0% |

The preceding analysis shows that revenue in the Financial Management Solutions, Employee Management Solutions, Payment Solutions, and Consumer Tax segments increased as a percent of total revenues between the two years. The remaining segments all decreased as a percent of total revenues between the two years.

Both analyses together show that the largest segment, Consumer Tax, has increased revenues by 11% and has increased the segment's share of total revenues from 34.4% to 34.7% across the two years. In addition, the remaining segments are all showing strong revenue growth.

## Example Exercise 5-5  Segment Analysis  OBJ 5

Morse Company does business in two regional segments: East and West. The following annual revenue information was determined from the accounting system's invoice information:

| Segment | 2016 | 2015 |
|---|---|---|
| East | $25,000 | $20,000 |
| West | 50,000 | 60,000 |
| Total revenues | $75,000 | $80,000 |

Prepare horizontal and vertical analyses of the segments.

## Follow My Example 5-5

Horizontal analysis:

| Segment | 2016 | 2015 | Increase (Decrease) Amount | Percent |
|---|---|---|---|---|
| East | $25,000 | $20,000 | $ 5,000 | 25.0% |
| West | 50,000 | 60,000 | (10,000) | (16.7) |
| Total revenues | $75,000 | $80,000 | $ (5,000) | (6.3) |

Vertical analysis:

| Segment | 2016 Amount | Percent | 2015 Amount | Percent |
|---|---|---|---|---|
| East | $25,000 | 33.3% | $20,000 | 25.0% |
| West | 50,000 | 66.7 | 60,000 | 75.0 |
| Total revenues | $75,000 | 100.0% | $80,000 | 100.0% |

Practice Exercises: PE 5-5A, PE 5-5B

# At a Glance 5

**OBJ 1**

## Define and describe an accounting system.

**Key Points**    An accounting system is the methods and procedures for collecting, classifying, summarizing, and reporting a business's financial information. The three steps through which an accounting system evolves are: (1) analysis of information needs, (2) design of the system, and (3) implementation of the system design.

| Learning Outcomes | Example Exercises | Practice Exercises |
|---|---|---|
| • Define an accounting system. | | |
| • Describe the three steps for designing an accounting system: (1) analysis, (2) design, and (3) implementation. | | |

**OBJ 2**

## Journalize and post transactions in a manual accounting system that uses subsidiary ledgers and special journals.

**Key Points**    Subsidiary ledgers may be used to maintain separate records for customers and creditors (vendors). A controlling account in the general ledger summarizes the subsidiary ledger accounts. The sum of the subsidiary ledger account balances must agree with the balance in the related controlling account.

| Learning Outcomes | Example Exercises | Practice Exercises |
|---|---|---|
| • Prepare a revenue journal and post services provided on account to individual customer accounts and the column total to the corresponding general ledger accounts. | EE5-1 | PE5-1A, 5-1B |
| • Prepare a cash receipts journal and post collections on account to individual customer accounts. Post Other Accounts column entries individually and special column totals to the corresponding general ledger accounts. | EE5-2 | PE5-2A, 5-2B |
| • Prepare a purchases journal and post amounts owed to individual creditor accounts. Post Other Accounts column entries individually and special column totals to the corresponding general ledger accounts. | EE5-3 | PE5-3A, 5-3B |
| • Prepare a cash payments journal and post the amounts paid to individual creditor accounts. Post Other Accounts column entries individually and special column totals to the corresponding general ledger accounts. | EE5-4 | PE5-4A, 5-4B |

## Describe and illustrate the use of a computerized accounting system.

**Key Points**    Computerized accounting systems are similar to manual systems. The main advantages of a computerized accounting system are the simultaneous recording and posting of transactions, high degree of accuracy, and timeliness of reporting.

| Learning Outcomes | Example Exercises | Practice Exercises |
|---|---|---|
| • Differentiate between a manual and a computerized accounting system. | | |
| • Illustrate revenue and cash receipts transactions using QuickBooks. | | |

## Describe the basic features of e-commerce.

**Key Points**    Using the Internet to perform business transactions is termed e-commerce. B2C e-commerce involves Internet transactions between a business and consumer, while B2B e-commerce involves Internet transactions between businesses. More elaborate e-commerce involves planning and coordinating suppliers, customers, and product design.

| Learning Outcome | Example Exercises | Practice Exercises |
|---|---|---|
| • Define e-commerce and describe the major trends in e-commerce. | | |

## Use segment analysis in evaluating the operating performance of a company.

**Key Points**    Businesses may be segmented by region, by product or service, or by type of customer. Segment revenues can be analyzed using horizontal and vertical analyses. Such analyses are useful to management for evaluating the causes of business performance.

| Learning Outcome | Example Exercises | Practice Exercises |
|---|---|---|
| • Prepare horizontal and vertical analyses for business segments. | **EE5-5** | **PE5-5A, 5-5B** |

# Key Terms

accounting system (214)
accounts payable subsidiary ledger (215)
accounts receivable subsidiary ledger (215)
cash payments journal (225)

cash receipts journal (220)
controlling account (215)
e-commerce (231)
general journal (216)
general ledger (215)
internal controls (215)

invoice (217)
purchases journal (222)
revenue journal (217)
special journals (215)
subsidiary ledger (215)

## Illustrative Problem

Selected transactions of O'Malley Co. for the month of May are as follows:

a.   May   1.   Issued Check No. 1001 in payment of rent for May, $1,200.

b.         2.   Purchased office supplies on account from McMillan Co., $3,600.

c.         4.   Issued Check No. 1003 in payment of freight charges on the supplies purchased on May 2, $320.

d.         8.   Provided services on account to Waller Co., Invoice No. 51, $4,500.

e.         9.   Issued Check No. 1005 for office supplies purchased, $450.

f.        10.   Received cash for office supplies sold to employees at cost, $120.

g.        11.   Purchased office equipment on account from Fender Office Products, $15,000.

h.        12.   Issued Check No. 1010 in payment of the supplies purchased from McMillan Co. on May 2, $3,600.

i.        16.   Provided services on account to Riese Co., Invoice No. 58, $8,000.

j.        18.   Received $4,500 from Waller Co. in payment of May 8 invoice.

k.        20.   Invested additional cash in the business, $10,000.

l.        25.   Provided services for cash, $15,900.

m.       30.   Issued Check No. 1040 for withdrawal of cash for personal use, $1,000.

n.        30.   Issued Check No. 1041 in payment of electricity and water invoices, $690.

o.        30.   Issued Check No. 1042 in payment of office and sales salaries for May, $15,800.

p.        31.   Journalized adjusting entries from the work sheet prepared for the fiscal year ended May 31.

O'Malley Co. maintains a revenue journal, a cash receipts journal, a purchases journal, a cash payments journal, and a general journal. In addition, accounts receivable and accounts payable subsidiary ledgers are used.

### Instructions

1.   Indicate the journal in which each of the preceding transactions, (a) through (p), would be recorded.

2.   Indicate whether an account in the accounts receivable or accounts payable subsidiary ledgers would be affected for each of the preceding transactions.

3.   Journalize transactions (b), (c), (d), (h), and (j) in the appropriate journals.

### Solution

| 1. | Journal | 2. | Subsidiary Ledger |
|----|---------|----|-------------------|
| a. | Cash payments journal | | |
| b. | Purchases journal | | Accounts payable ledger |
| c. | Cash payments journal | | |
| d. | Revenue journal | | Accounts receivable ledger |
| e. | Cash payments journal | | |
| f. | Cash receipts journal | | |
| g. | Purchases journal | | Accounts payable ledger |
| h. | Cash payments journal | | Accounts payable ledger |
| i. | Revenue journal | | Accounts receivable ledger |
| j. | Cash receipts journal | | Accounts receivable ledger |
| k. | Cash receipts journal | | |
| l. | Cash receipts journal | | |
| m. | Cash payments journal | | |
| n. | Cash payments journal | | |
| o. | Cash payments journal | | |
| p. | General journal | | |

3.

**Transaction (b):**

| | Purchases Journal | | | | | | |
|---|---|---|---|---|---|---|---|
| Date | Account Credited | Post. Ref. | Accounts Payable Cr. | Office Supplies Dr. | Other Accounts Dr. | Post. Ref. | Amount |
| May 2 | McMillan Co. | | 3,600 | 3,600 | | | |

**Transactions (c) and (h):**

| | | Cash Payments Journal | | | | |
|---|---|---|---|---|---|---|
| Date | Ck. No. | Account Debited | Post. Ref. | Other Accounts Dr. | Accounts Payable Dr. | Cash Cr. |
| May 4 | 1003 | Freight Expense | | 320 | | 320 |
| 12 | 1010 | McMillan Co. | | | 3,600 | 3,600 |

**Transaction (d):**

| | | Revenue Journal | | |
|---|---|---|---|---|
| Date | Invoice No. | Account Debited | Post. Ref. | Accts. Rec. Dr. Fees Earned Cr. |
| May 8 | 51 | Waller Co. | | 4,500 |

**Transaction (j):**

| | Cash Receipts Journal | | | | |
|---|---|---|---|---|---|
| Date | Account Credited | Post. Ref. | Other Accounts Cr. | Accounts Receivable Cr. | Cash Dr. |
| May 18 | Waller Co. | | | 4,500 | 4,500 |

# Discussion Questions

1. Why would a company maintain separate accounts receivable ledgers for each customer, as opposed to maintaining a single accounts receivable ledger for all customers?

2. What are the major advantages of the use of special journals?

3. In recording 400 fees earned on account during a single month, how many times will it be necessary to write Fees Earned (a) if each transaction, including fees earned, is recorded individually in a two-column general journal; (b) if each transaction for fees earned is recorded in a revenue journal?

4. How many postings to Fees Earned for the month would be needed in Discussion Question 3 if the procedure described in (a) had been used; if the procedure described in (b) had been used?

5. During the current month, the following errors occurred in recording transactions in the purchases journal or in posting from it:

  a. An invoice for $1,875 of supplies from Kelly Co. was recorded as having been received from Kelley Co., another supplier.
  b. A credit of $420 to Blackstone Company was posted as $240 in the subsidiary ledger.
  c. An invoice for equipment of $4,800 was recorded as $4,000.
  d. The Accounts Payable column of the purchases journal was overstated by $3,600.

  How will each error come to the bookkeeper's attention, other than by chance discovery?

6. Assuming the use of a two-column general journal, a purchases journal, and a cash payments journal as illustrated in this chapter, indicate the journal in which each of the following transactions should be recorded:

  a. Purchase of office supplies on account.
  b. Purchase of supplies for cash.
  c. Purchase of store equipment on account.
  d. Payment of cash on account to creditor.
  e. Payment of cash for office supplies.

7. What is an electronic form, and how is it used in a computerized accounting system?

8. Do computerized systems use controlling accounts to verify the accuracy of the subsidiary accounts?

9. What happens to the special journal in a computerized accounting system that uses electronic forms?

10. How would e-commerce improve the revenue/collection cycle?

# Practice Exercises

EE 5-1 *p. 219*

SHOW
ME HOW

**PE 5-1A   Revenue journal**                                OBJ. 2

The following revenue transactions occurred during November:

Oct.  4. Issued Invoice No. 162 to Dawkins Co. for services provided on account, $320.
   19. Issued Invoice No. 163 to City Electric Inc. for services provided on account, $245.
   25. Issued Invoice No. 164 to Matthews Co. for services provided on account, $515.

Record these three transactions into the following revenue journal format:

**REVENUE JOURNAL**

| Date | Invoice No. | Account Debited | Post. Ref. | Accts. Rec. Dr. Fees Earned Cr. |
|------|------------|-----------------|-----------|--------------------------------|
|      |            |                 |           |                                |

EE 5-1 *p. 219*

SHOW
ME HOW

**PE 5-1B   Revenue journal**                                OBJ. 2

The following revenue transactions occurred during April:

Apr.  6. Issued Invoice No. 78 to Lemon Co. for services provided on account, $1,240.
   11. Issued Invoice No. 79 to Hitchcock Inc. for services provided on account, $2,570.
   19. Issued Invoice No. 80 to Fletcher Inc. for services provided on account, $990.

Record these three transactions into the following revenue journal format:

**REVENUE JOURNAL**

| Date | Invoice No. | Account Debited | Post. Ref. | Accts. Rec. Dr. Fees Earned Cr. |
|------|------------|-----------------|-----------|--------------------------------|
|      |            |                 |           |                                |

EE 5-2 *p. 222*

SHOW
ME HOW

**PE 5-2A    Accounts receivable subsidiary ledger**    **OBJ. 2**

The debits and credits from two transactions are presented in the following customer account:

NAME    *Horizon Entertainment*
ADDRESS    *125 Wycoff Ave.*

| Date | Item | Post. Ref. | Debit | Credit | Balance |
|------|------|-----------|-------|--------|---------|
| Feb. 1 | Balance | ✓ | | | 280 |
| 22 | Invoice 422 | CR106 | *provided cash* | 120 | 160 |
| 27 | Invoice 445 | R92 | 170 | *collected cash* | 330 |

Describe each transaction and the source of each posting.

---

EE 5-2 *p. 222*

SHOW
ME HOW

**PE 5-2B    Accounts receivable subsidiary ledger**    **OBJ. 2**

The debits and credits from two transactions are presented in the following customer account:

NAME    *Moravian Products Inc.*
ADDRESS    *46 W. Main St.*

| Date | Item | Post. Ref. | Debit | Credit | Balance |
|------|------|-----------|-------|--------|---------|
| Aug. 1 | Balance | ✓ | | | 1,200 |
| 10 | Invoice 119 | R24 | 750 *provided* | | 1,950 |
| 17 | Invoice 106 | CR46 *ins, Acct Rec* | | 610 *collected* | 1,340 |

Describe each transaction and the source of each posting.

---

EE 5-3 *p. 225*

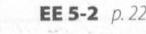

SHOW
ME HOW

**PE 5-3A    Purchases journal**    **OBJ. 2**

The following purchase transactions occurred during March for Celebration Catering Service:

Mar. 11. Purchased party supplies for $610, on account from Party Hearty Supplies Inc.

16. Purchased party supplies for $312, on account from Fun 4 All Supplies Inc.

27. Purchased office furniture for $2,480, on account from Office Space Inc.

Record these transactions in the following purchases journal format:

**PURCHASES JOURNAL**

| Date | Account Credited | Post. Ref. | Accounts Payable Cr. | Party Supplies Dr. | Other Accounts Dr. | Post. Ref. | Amount |
|------|------------------|-----------|---------------------|--------------------|--------------------|-----------|--------|
| | | | | | | | |

---

EE 5-3 *p. 225*

SHOW
ME HOW

**PE 5-3B    Purchases journal**    **OBJ. 2**

The following purchase transactions occurred during November for Manheim Inc.:

Nov. 6. Purchased office supplies for $330, on account from Carry Out Supply Inc.

14. Purchased office equipment for $1,950, on account from Zell Computer Inc.

22. Purchased office supplies for $195, on account from Carry Out Supply Inc.

Record these transactions in the following purchases journal format:

**PURCHASES JOURNAL**

| Date | Account Credited | Post. Ref. | Accounts Payable Cr. | Office Supplies Dr. | Other Accounts Dr. | Post. Ref. | Amount |
|------|------------------|-----------|---------------------|---------------------|--------------------|-----------|--------|
| | | | | | | | |

**EE 5-4** *p. 228*

**PE 5-4A** **Accounts payable subsidiary ledger** OBJ. 2

The debits and credits from two transactions are presented in the following supplier's (creditor's) account:

**NAME** *Migrant Technology*
**ADDRESS** *2199 Commerce Place*

| Date | Item | Post. Ref. | Debit | Credit | Balance |
|------|------|-----------|-------|--------|---------|
| Nov. 1 | Balance | | | | 9,400 |
| 11 | Invoice 85 | P8 | | 1,845 | 11,245 |
| 22 | Invoice 43 | CP46 | 3,270 | | 7,975 |

Describe each transaction and the source of each posting.

**EE 5-4** *p. 228*

**PE 5-4B** **Accounts payable subsidiary ledger** OBJ. 2

The debits and credits from two transactions are presented in the following supplier's (creditor's) account:

**NAME** *Colonial Inc.*
**ADDRESS** *5000 Grand Ave.*

| Date | Item | Post. Ref. | Debit | Credit | Balance |
|------|------|-----------|-------|--------|---------|
| Jan. 1 | Balance | | | | 92 |
| 11 | Invoice 122 | CP71 | 64 | | 28 |
| 26 | Invoice 139 | P55 | | 72 | 100 |

Describe each transaction and the source of each posting.

**EE 5-5** *p. 233*

**PE 5-5A** **Segment analysis** OBJ. 5

McHale Company does business in two customer segments, Retail and Wholesale. The following annual revenue information was determined from the accounting system's invoice information:

| | 2016 | 2015 |
|------|------|------|
| Retail | $126,000 | $120,000 |
| Wholesale | 150,000 | 164,000 |
| Total revenue | $276,000 | $284,000 |

Prepare a horizontal and vertical analysis of the segments. Round to one decimal place.

**EE 5-5** *p. 233*

**PE 5-5B** **Segment analysis** OBJ. 5

Back Country Life, Inc., does business in two product segments, Camping and Fishing. The following annual revenue information was determined from the accounting system's invoice information:

| | 2016 | 2015 |
|------|------|------|
| Camping | $280,000 | $240,000 |
| Fishing | 140,000 | 160,000 |
| Total revenue | $420,000 | $400,000 |

Prepare a horizontal and vertical analysis of the segments. Round to one decimal place.

# Exercises

### EX 5-1  Identify postings from revenue journal

OBJ. 2

Using the following revenue journal for Zeta Services Inc., identify each of the posting references, indicated by a letter, as representing (1) posting to general ledger accounts or (2) posting to subsidiary ledger accounts:

**REVENUE JOURNAL**

| Date | Invoice No. | Account Debited | Post. Ref. | Accounts Rec. Dr. Fees Earned Cr. |
|------|-------------|-----------------|------------|-----------------------------------|
| 2016 | | | | |
| Mar. 1 | 112 | Hazmat Safety Co. | (a) | $2,875 |
| 10 | 113 | Masco Co. | (b) | 980 |
| 20 | 114 | Eco-Systems | (c) | 1,700 |
| 27 | 115 | Sunrise Enterprises | (d) | 1,240 |
| 30 | | | | $6,795 |
| | | | | (e) |

### EX 5-2  Accounts receivable ledger

OBJ. 2

✔ d. Total accounts receivable, $7,275

SHOW
ME HOW

Based on the data presented in Exercise 5-1, assume that the beginning balances for the customer accounts were zero, except for Sunrise Enterprises, which had a $480 beginning balance. In addition, there were no collections during the period.

a. Set up a T account for Accounts Receivable and T accounts for the four accounts needed in the customer ledger.

b. Post to the T accounts.

c. Determine the balance in the accounts.

d. Prepare a listing of the accounts receivable customer balances as of March 31, 2016.

### EX 5-3  Identify journals

OBJ. 2

Assuming the use of a two-column (all-purpose) general journal, a revenue journal, and a cash receipts journal as illustrated in this chapter, indicate the journal in which each of the following transactions should be recorded:

a. Closing of drawing account at the end of the year.

b. Providing services for cash.

c. Sale of office supplies on account, at cost, to a neighboring business.

d. Receipt of cash from sale of office equipment.

e. Receipt of cash for rent.

f. Receipt of cash on account from a customer.

g. Providing services on account.

h. Investment of additional cash in the business by the owner.

i. Receipt of cash refund from overpayment of taxes.

j. Adjustment to record accrued salaries at the end of the year.

### EX 5-4  Identify journals

OBJ. 2

Assuming the use of a two-column (all-purpose) general journal, a purchases journal, and a cash payments journal as illustrated in this chapter, indicate the journal in which each of the following transactions should be recorded:

a. Purchase of office supplies for cash.

b. Advance payment of a one-year fire insurance policy on the office.

c. Purchase of office equipment for cash.

d. Adjustment to prepaid insurance at the end of the month.

(*Continued*)

e. Adjustment to prepaid rent at the end of the month. *general, no*

f. Adjustment to record accrued salaries at the end of the period. *gen, no*

g. Purchase of services on account. *purchase, yes*

h. Purchase of office supplies on account. *purchase, yes*

i. Adjustment to record depreciation at the end of the month. *general, no*

j. Payment of six months' rent in advance. *Cash pay, no*

k. Purchase of an office computer on account. *purchases, yes*

---

**EX 5-5 Identify transactions in accounts receivable subsidiary ledger**     **OBJ. 2**

The debits and credits from three related transactions are presented in the following customer's account taken from the accounts receivable subsidiary ledger:

**NAME**   *Mission Design*
**ADDRESS**   *1319 Elm Street*

| Date | Item | Post. Ref. | Debit | Credit | Balance |
|------|------|-----------|-------|--------|---------|
| 2016 | | | | | |
| Apr. 3 | | R44 | 740 | | 740 |
| 6 | | J11 | | 60 | 680 |
| 24 | | CR81 | | 680 | — |

Describe each transaction, and identify the source of each posting.

---

**EX 5-6 Prepare journal entries in a revenue journal**     **OBJ. 2**

SHOW
ME HOW

Global Services Company had the following transactions during the month of August:

Aug. 2. Issued Invoice No. 321 to Morgan Corp. for services rendered on account, $425.

3. Issued Invoice No. 322 to Mid States Inc. for services rendered on account, $260.

14. Issued Invoice No. 323 to Morgan Corp. for services rendered on account, $350.

22. Issued Invoice No. 324 to Rose Co. for services rendered on account, $690.

28. Collected Invoice No. 321 from Morgan Corp.

a. Record the August revenue transactions for Global Services Company into the following revenue journal format:

**REVENUE JOURNAL**

| Date | Invoice No. | Account Debited | Post. Ref. | Accts. Rec. Dr. Fees Earned Cr. |
|------|-------------|-----------------|-----------|--------------------------------|

b. What is the total amount posted to the accounts receivable and fees earned accounts from the revenue journal for August?

c. What is the August 31 balance of the Morgan Corp. customer account assuming a zero balance on August 1?

---

**EX 5-7 Posting a revenue journal**     **OBJ. 2, 3**

SHOW
ME HOW

The revenue journal for Sapling Consulting Inc. follows. The accounts receivable controlling account has a July 1, 2016, balance of $625 consisting of an amount due from Aladdin Co. There were no collections during July.

**REVENUE JOURNAL**     Page 12

| Date | Invoice No. | Account Debited | Post. Ref. | Accts. Rec. Dr. Fees Earned Cr. |
|------|-------------|-----------------|-----------|--------------------------------|
| 2016 | | | | |
| July 4 | 355 | Clearmark Co.............................. | | 1,890 |
| 9 | 356 | Life Star Inc............................. | | 3,410 |
| 18 | 357 | Aladdin Co. ............................. | | 950 |
| 22 | 359 | Clearmark Co............................. | | 3,660 |
| 31 | | | | 9,910 |

a. Prepare a T account for the accounts receivable customer accounts.

b. Post the transactions from the revenue journal to the customer accounts, and determine their ending balances.

c. Prepare T accounts for the accounts receivable and fees earned accounts. Post control totals to the two accounts, and determine the ending balances.

d. Prepare a schedule of the customer account balances to verify the equality of the sum of the customer account balances and the accounts receivable controlling account balance.

e. How might a computerized system differ from a revenue journal in recording revenue transactions?

---

✔ Accounts
Receivable balance,
August 31, $8,070

SHOW
ME HOW

### EX 5-8 Accounts receivable subsidiary ledger   OBJ. 2

The revenue and cash receipts journals for Mirage Productions Inc. follow. The accounts receivable control account has a August 1, 2016, balance of $4,230 consisting of an amount due from Celestial Studios Inc.

| REVENUE JOURNAL | | | | | Page 16 |
|---|---|---|---|---|---|
| **Date** | **Invoice No.** | **Account Debited** | **Post. Ref.** | | **Accts. Rec. Dr. Fees Earned Cr.** |
| 2016 | | | | | |
| Aug. 6 | 1 | Franklin Broadcasting Co. . . . . . . . . . . . . . . . . . . . . . . | ✓ | | 1,900 |
| 14 | 2 | Gold Coast Media Inc.. . . . . . . . . . . . . . . . . . . . . . . . | ✓ | | 5,100 |
| 22 | 3 | Franklin Broadcasting Co. . . . . . . . . . . . . . . . . . . . . | ✓ | | 2,350 |
| 25 | 4 | Celestial Studios Inc.. . . . . . . . . . . . . . . . . . . . . . . | ✓ | | 1,650 |
| 28 | 5 | Amber Communications Inc. . . . . . . . . . . . . . . . . . . | ✓ | | 4,070 |
| 31 | | | | | 15,070 |
| | | | | | (12) (41) |

| CASH RECEIPTS JOURNAL | | | | Page 36 |
|---|---|---|---|---|
| **Date** | **Account Credited** | **Post. Ref.** | **Fees Earned Cr.** | **Accts. Rec. Cr.** | **Cash Dr.** |
| 2016 | | | | | |
| Aug. 6 | Celestial Studios Inc. . . . . . . . . . . . . . . . . . . . . | ✓ | — | 4,230 | 4,230 |
| 11 | Fees Earned. . . . . . . . . . . . . . . . . . . . . . . . . . . | | 3,200 | | 3,200 |
| 18 | Franklin Broadcasting Co. . . . . . . . . . . . . . . . | ✓ | — | 1,900 | 1,900 |
| 28 | Gold Coast Media Inc. . . . . . . . . . . . . . . . . . | ✓ | — | 5,100 | 5,100 |
| 31 | | | 3,200 | 11,230 | 14,430 |
| | | | (41) | (12) | (11) |

Prepare a listing of the accounts receivable customer balances and verify that the total agrees with the ending balance of the accounts receivable controlling account.

---

SHOW
ME HOW

### EX 5-9 Revenue and cash receipts journals   OBJ. 2

Transactions related to revenue and cash receipts completed by Sycamore Inc. during the month of December 2016 are as follows:

Dec. 2. Issued Invoice No. 512 to Cadence Co., $775.

4. Received cash from CMI Inc., on account, for $230.

8. Issued Invoice No. 513 to Gabriel Co., $300.

12. Issued Invoice No. 514 to Ells Inc., $910.

19. Received cash from Ells Inc., on account, $605.

20. Issued Invoice No. 515 to Electronic Central Inc., $195.

28. Received cash from Marshall Inc. for services provided, $160.

29. Received cash from Cadence Co. for Invoice No. 512 of December 2.

31. Received cash from McCleary Co. for services provided, $110.

*(Continued)*

Prepare a single-column revenue journal and a cash receipts journal to record these transactions. Use the following column headings for the cash receipts journal: Fees Earned Cr., Accounts Receivable Cr., and Cash Dr. Place a check mark (✓) in the Post. Ref. column to indicate when the accounts receivable subsidiary ledger should be posted.

---

### EX 5-10 Revenue and cash receipts journals

OBJ. 2

✔ a. Revenue journal total, $8,700

Lasting Summer Inc. has $2,510 in the October 1 balance of the accounts receivable account consisting of $1,060 from Champion Co. and $1,450 from Wayfarer Co. Transactions related to revenue and cash receipts completed by Lasting Summer Inc. during the month of October 2016 are as follows:

Oct. 3. Issued Invoice No. 622 for services provided to Palace Corp., $2,890.

5. Received cash from Champion Co., on account, for $1,060.

8. Issued Invoice No. 623 for services provided to Sunny Style Inc., $1,940.

12. Received cash from Wayfarer Co., on account, for $1,450.

18. Issued Invoice No. 624 for services provided to Amex Services Inc., $2,970.

23. Received cash from Palace Corp. for Invoice No. 622 of October 3.

28. Issued Invoice No. 625 to Wayfarer Co., on account, for $900.

30. Received cash from Rogers Co. for services provided, $120.

a. Prepare a single-column revenue journal and a cash receipts journal to record these transactions. Use the following column headings for the cash receipts journal: Fees Earned Cr., Accounts Receivable Cr., and Cash Dr. Place a check mark (✓) in the Post. Ref. column to indicate when the accounts receivable subsidiary ledger should be posted.

b. Prepare a listing of the accounts receivable customer balances and verify that the total of the accounts receivable customer balances equals the balance of the accounts receivable controlling account on October 31, 2016.

c. Why does Lasting Summer Inc. use a subsidiary ledger for accounts receivable?

---

### EX 5-11 Identify postings from purchases journal

OBJ. 2

Using the following purchases journal, identify each of the posting references, indicated by a letter, as representing (1) a posting to a general ledger account, (2) a posting to a subsidiary ledger account, or (3) that no posting is required:

| | | | | | | | | |
|---|---|---|---|---|---|---|---|---|
| **PURCHASES JOURNAL** | | | | | | | | **Page 49** |
| Date | Account Credited | Post. Ref. | Accounts Payable Cr. | Store Supplies Dr. | Office Supplies Dr. | Other Accounts Dr. | Post. Ref. | Amount |
| 2016 | | | | | | | | |
| Jan. 4 | Coastal Equipment Co. | (a) | 5,325 | | | Warehouse Equipment | (g) | 5,325 |
| 6 | Arrow Supply Co. | (b) | 4,000 | | 4,000 | | | |
| 9 | Thorton Products | (c) | 1,875 | 1,600 | 275 | | | |
| 14 | Office Warehouse | (d) | 2,200 | | | Office Equipment | (h) | 2,200 |
| 20 | Office Warehouse | (e) | 6,000 | | | Store Equipment | (i) | 6,000 |
| 25 | Monroe Supply Co. | (f) | 2,740 | 2,740 | | | | |
| 30 | | | 22,140 | 4,340 | 4,275 | | | 13,525 |
| | | | (j) | (k) | (l) | | | (m) |

---

### EX 5-12 Identify postings from cash payments journal

OBJ. 2

Using the following cash payments journal, identify each of the posting references, indicated by a letter, as representing (1) a posting to a general ledger account, (2) a posting to a subsidiary ledger account, or (3) that no posting is required.

| CASH PAYMENTS JOURNAL | | | | | | Page 46 |
|---|---|---|---|---|---|---|
| Date | Ck. No. | Account Debited | Post. Ref. | Other Accounts Dr. | Accounts Payable Dr. | Cash Cr. |
| 2016 | | | | | | |
| July 3 | 611 | Energy Systems Co. | (a) | | 4,000 | 4,000 |
| 5 | 612 | Utilities Expense | (b) | 310 | | 310 |
| 10 | 613 | Prepaid Rent | (c) | 3,200 | | 3,200 |
| 16 | 614 | Flowers to Go, Inc. | (d) | | 1,250 | 1,250 |
| 19 | 615 | Advertising Expense | (e) | 640 | | 640 |
| 22 | 616 | Office Equipment | (f) | 3,600 | | 3,600 |
| 25 | 617 | Echo Co. | (g) | | 5,500 | 5,500 |
| 26 | 618 | Office Supplies | (h) | 250 | | 250 |
| 31 | 619 | Salaries Expense | (i) | 1,750 | | 1,750 |
| 31 | | | | 9,750 | 10,750 | 20,500 |
| | | | | (j) | (k) | (l) |

### EX 5-13 Identify transactions in accounts payable subsidiary ledger OBJ. 2

The debits and credits from three related transactions are presented in the following creditor's account taken from the accounts payable ledger:

**NAME** Apex Performance Co.
**ADDRESS** 101 W. Stratford Ave.

| Date | Item | Post. Ref. | Debit | Credit | Balance |
|---|---|---|---|---|---|
| 2016 | | | | | |
| May 6 | | P44 | | 12,000 | 12,000 |
| 14 | | J12 | 150 | | 11,850 |
| 16 | | CP23 | 11,850 | | — |

Describe each transaction, and identify the source of each posting.

### EX 5-14 Prepare journal entries in a purchases journal OBJ. 2

SHOW ME HOW

Protection Services Inc. had the following transactions during the month of June:

June 4. Purchased office supplies from Office Universe Inc. on account, $490.

9. Purchased office equipment on account from Tek Village Inc., $2,790.

16. Purchased office supplies from Office Universe Inc. on account, $140.

21. Purchased office supplies from Paper-to-Go Inc. on account, $225.

27. Paid invoice on June 4 purchase from Office Universe Inc.

a. Record the June purchase transactions for Protection Services Inc. in the following purchases journal format:

| PURCHASES JOURNAL | | | | | | |
|---|---|---|---|---|---|---|
| Date | Account Credited | Post. Ref. | Accts. Payable Cr. | Office Supplies Dr. | Other Accounts Dr. | Post. Ref. | Amount |

b. What is the total amount posted to the accounts payable and office supplies accounts from the purchases journal for June?

c. What is the June 30 balance of the Office Universe Inc. creditor account assuming a zero balance on June 1?

### EX 5-15 Posting a purchases journal OBJ. 2, 3

✔ d. Total, $5,840

The purchases journal for Newmark Exterior Cleaners Inc. follows. The accounts payable account has a March 1, 2016, balance of $580 for an amount owed to Nicely Co. There were no payments made on creditor invoices during March.

(*Continued*)

**PURCHASES JOURNAL**                                                                 Page *16*

| Date | | Account Credited | Post. Ref. | Accts. Payable Cr. | Cleaning Supplies Dr. | Other Accounts Dr. | Post. Ref. | Amount |
|---|---|---|---|---|---|---|---|---|
| 2015 | | | | | | | | |
| Mar. | 4 | Enviro-Wash Supplies Inc. | | 690 | 690 | | | |
| | 15 | Nicely Co. | | 325 | 325 | | | |
| | 20 | Office Mate Inc. | | 3,860 | | Office Equipment | | 3,860 |
| | 26 | Enviro-Wash Supplies Inc. | | 385 | 385 | | | |
| | 31 | | | 5,260 | 1,400 | | | 3,860 |

a. Prepare a T account for the accounts payable creditor accounts.

b. Post the transactions from the purchases journal to the creditor accounts, and determine their ending balances.

c. Prepare T accounts for the accounts payable control and cleaning supplies accounts. Post control totals to the two accounts, and determine their ending balances. Cleaning Supplies had a zero balance at the beginning of the month.

d. Prepare a schedule of the creditor account balances to verify the equality of the sum of the accounts payable creditor balances and the accounts payable controlling account balance.

e. How might a computerized accounting system differ from the use of a purchases journal in recording purchase transactions?

---

✔ Accts. Pay., June 30, $21,580

SHOW ME HOW

### EX 5-16 Accounts payable subsidiary ledger

OBJ. 2

The cash payments and purchases journals for Outdoor Artisan Landscaping Co. follow. The accounts payable control account has an June 1, 2016, balance of $2,230, consisting of an amount owed to Augusta Sod Co.

**CASH PAYMENTS JOURNAL**                                                      Page *31*

| Date | Ck. No. | Account Debited | Post. Ref. | Other Accounts Dr. | Accounts Payable Dr. | Cash Cr. |
|---|---|---|---|---|---|---|
| 2015 | | | | | | |
| June 4 | 203 | Augusta Sod Co. | ✓ | | 2,230 | 2,230 |
| 5 | 204 | Utilities Expense | 54 | 440 | | 440 |
| 15 | 205 | Home Centers Lumber Co. | ✓ | | 5,210 | 5,210 |
| 24 | 206 | Nu Lawn Fertilizer | ✓ | | 910 | 910 |
| 30 | | | | 440 | 8,350 | 8,790 |
| | | | | (✓) | (21) | (11) |

**PURCHASES JOURNAL**                                                          Page *22*

| Date | Account Credited | Post. Ref. | Accounts Payable Cr. | Landscaping Supplies Dr. | Other Accounts Dr. | Post. Ref. | Amount |
|---|---|---|---|---|---|---|---|
| 2015 | | | | | | | |
| June 3 | Home Centers Lumber Co. | ✓ | 5,210 | 5,210 | | | |
| 7 | Concrete Equipment Co. | ✓ | 6,700 | | Equipment | 18 | 6,700 |
| 14 | Nu Lawn Fertilizer | ✓ | 910 | 910 | | | |
| 24 | Augusta Sod Co. | ✓ | 6,450 | 6,450 | | | |
| 29 | Home Centers Lumber Co. | ✓ | 8,430 | 8,430 | | | |
| 30 | | | 27,700 | 21,000 | | | 6,700 |
| | | | (21) | (14) | | | (✓) |

Prepare a schedule of the accounts payable creditor balances, and determine that the total agrees with the ending balance of the accounts payable controlling account.

---

✔ Purchases journal, Accts. Pay., Total, $1,045

SHOW ME HOW

### EX 5-17 Purchases and cash payments journals

OBJ. 2

Transactions related to purchases and cash payments completed by Brite Way Cleaning Services Inc. during the month of May 2016 are as follows:

May 1. Issued Check No. 57 to Liquid Klean Supplies Inc. in payment of account, $395.

3. Purchased cleaning supplies on account from Sani-Fresh Products Inc., $220.

8. Issued Check No. 58 to purchase equipment from Carson Equipment Sales, $3,150.

May 12. Purchased cleaning supplies on account from Porter Products Inc., $400.

15. Issued Check No. 59 to Bowman Electrical Service in payment of account, $165.

18. Purchased supplies on account from Liquid Klean Supplies Inc., $275.

20. Purchased electrical repair services from Bowman Electrical Service on account, $150.

26. Issued Check No. 60 to Sani-Fresh Products Inc. in payment of May 3 invoice.

31. Issued Check No. 61 in payment of salaries, $6,500.

Prepare a purchases journal and a cash payments journal to record these transactions. The forms of the journals are similar to those illustrated in the text. Place a check mark (✓) in the Post. Ref. column to indicate when the accounts payable subsidiary ledger should be posted. Brite Way Cleaning Services Inc. uses the following accounts:

| | |
|---|---|
| Cash | 11 |
| Cleaning Supplies | 14 |
| Equipment | 18 |
| Accounts Payable | 21 |
| Salary Expense | 51 |
| Electrical Service Expense | 53 |

---

**EX 5-18   Purchases and cash payments journals**                                    OBJ. 2

Happy Tails Inc. has a June 1, 2016 accounts payable balance of $600, which consists of $360 due Labradore Inc. and $240 due Meow Mart Inc. Transactions related to purchases and cash payments completed by Happy Tails Inc. during the month of June 2016 are as follows:

June  4. Purchased pet supplies from Best Friend Supplies Inc. on account, $255,

6. Issued Check No. 345 to Labradore Inc. in payment of account, $360.

13. Purchased pet supplies from Poodle Pals Inc., $710.

18. Issued Check No. 346 to Meow Mart Inc. in payment of account, $240.

19. Purchased office equipment from Office Helper Inc. on account, $2,670.

23. Issued Check No. 347 to Best Friend Supplies Inc. in payment of account from purchase made on June 4.

27. Purchased pet supplies from Meow Mart Inc. on account, $400.

30. Issued Check No. 348 to Jennings Inc. for cleaning expenses, $65.

a. Prepare a purchases journal and a cash payments journal to record these transactions. The forms of the journals are similar to those used in the text. Place a check mark (✓) in the Post. Ref. column to indicate when the accounts payable subsidiary ledger should be posted. Happy Tails Inc. uses the following accounts:

| | |
|---|---|
| Cash | 11 |
| Pet Supplies | 14 |
| Office Equipment | 18 |
| Accounts Payable | 21 |
| Cleaning Expense | 54 |

b. Prepare a listing of accounts payable creditor balances on June 30, 2016. Verify that the total of the accounts payable creditor balances equals the balance of the accounts payable controlling account on June 30, 2016.

c. Why does Happy Tails Inc. use a subsidiary ledger for accounts payable?

---

**EX 5-19   Error in accounts payable subsidiary ledger**                              OBJ. 2

After Bunker Hill Assay Services Inc. had completed all postings for March in the current year (2016), the sum of the balances in the following accounts payable ledger did not agree with the $37,600 balance of the controlling account in the general ledger:

(Continued)

**NAME**  C. D. Greer and Son
**ADDRESS**  972 S. Tenth Street

| Date | Item | Post. Ref. | Debit | Credit | Balance |
|---|---|---|---|---|---|
| 2016 | | | | | |
| Mar. 17 | | P30 | | 3,750 | 3,750 |
| 27 | | P31 | | 12,000 | 15,750 |

**NAME**  Carbon Supplies Inc.
**ADDRESS**  1170 Mattis Avenue

| Date | Item | Post. Ref. | Debit | Credit | Balance |
|---|---|---|---|---|---|
| 2016 | | | | | |
| Mar. 1 | Balance | ✓ | | | 8,300 |
| 9 | | P30 | | 7,000 | 14,000 |
| 12 | | J7 | 300 | | 13,700 |
| 20 | | CP23 | 5,800 | | 7,900 |

**NAME**  Cutler and Powell
**ADDRESS**  717 Elm Street

| Date | Item | Post. Ref. | Debit | Credit | Balance |
|---|---|---|---|---|---|
| 2016 | | | | | |
| Mar. 1 | Balance | ✓ | | | 6,100 |
| 18 | | CP23 | 6,100 | | — |
| 29 | | P31 | | 7,800 | 7,800 |

**NAME**  Hudson Bay Minerals Co.
**ADDRESS**  1240 W. Main Street

| Date | Item | Post. Ref. | Debit | Credit | Balance |
|---|---|---|---|---|---|
| 2016 | | | | | |
| Mar. 1 | Balance | ✓ | | | 4,750 |
| 10 | | CP22 | 4,750 | | — |
| 17 | | P30 | | 3,700 | 3,700 |
| 25 | | J7 | 3,000 | | 1,700 |

**NAME**  Valley Power
**ADDRESS**  915 E. Walnut Street

| Date | Item | Post. Ref. | Debit | Credit | Balance |
|---|---|---|---|---|---|
| 2016 | | | | | |
| Mar. 5 | | P30 | | 3,150 | 3,150 |

Assuming that the controlling account balance of $36,600 has been verified as correct, (a) determine the error(s) in the preceding accounts and (b) prepare a listing of accounts payable creditor balances (from the corrected accounts payable subsidiary ledger).

---

**EX 5-20  Identify postings from special journals**                    OBJ. 2

Pinnacle Consulting Company makes most of its sales and purchases on credit. It uses the five journals described in this chapter (revenue, cash receipts, purchases, cash payments, and general journals). Identify the journal most likely used in recording the postings for selected transactions indicated by letter in the T accounts, as follows:

| | Cash | | | | | Prepaid Rent | |
|---|---|---|---|---|---|---|---|
| a. | 10,940 | b. | 6,500 | | | e. | 1,200 |
| | Accounts Receivable | | | | | Accounts Payable | |
| c. | 11,790 | a. | 10,940 | | b. | 6,500 | d. 7,400 |
| | Office Supplies | | | | | Fees Earned | |
| d. | 7,400 | | | | | c. | 11,790 |

| | Rent Expense | |
|---|---|---|
| e. | 1,200 | |

**EX 5-21  Cash receipts journal** OBJ. 2

The following cash receipts journal headings have been suggested for a small service firm. List the errors you find in the headings.

| | | | CASH RECEIPTS JOURNAL | | | Page 12 |
|---|---|---|---|---|---|---|
| Date | Account Credited | Post. Ref. | Fees Earned Cr. | Accts. Rec. Cr. | Cash Cr. | Other Accounts Dr. |

**EX 5-22  Computerized accounting systems** OBJ. 3

Most computerized accounting systems use electronic forms to record transaction information, such as the invoice form illustrated at the top of Exhibit 7 in this chapter.

a. Identify the key input fields (spaces) in an electronic invoice form.

b. What accounts are posted from an electronic invoice form?

c. Why aren't special journal totals posted to control accounts at the end of the month in an electronic accounting system?

**EX 5-23  Computerized accounting systems and e-commerce** OBJ. 3, 4

Apple Inc.'s iTunes® provides digital products, such as music, video, and software, which can be downloaded to portable devices such as the iPhone® and iPad®. Purchases made on iTunes are made with credit cards that are on file with the credit card processing company. Such transactions are considered cash transactions. Once the purchases are made, consumers can download the requested digital products to their portable devices for their enjoyment and the charges will show up on their credit card bills.

a. What kind of e-commerce application is described by Apple iTunes?

b. Assume you purchased 12 songs for $1.25 each on iTunes. Provide the journal entry generated by Apple's e-commerce application.

c. If a special journal were used, what type of special journal would be used to record this sales transaction?

d. If an electronic form were used, what type of electronic form would be used to record this sales transaction?

e. Would it be appropriate for Apple to use either special journals or electronic forms for sales transactions from iTunes? Explain.

**EX 5-24  E-commerce** OBJ. 4

For each of the following companies, determine what they primarily sell, and whether their e-commerce strategy is primarily business-to-consumer (B2C), business-to-business (B2B), or both. Use the Internet to investigate each company's site in conducting your research.

a. Amazon.com

b. Dell Inc.

c. DuPont

d. Intuit Inc.

e. L.L. Bean, Inc.

f. W.W. Grainger, Inc.

### EX 5-25  Segment revenue horizontal analysis
OBJ. 5

Starbucks Corporation reported the following geographical segment revenues for a recent and a prior fiscal year:

| | Recent Year (in millions, rounded) | Prior Year (in millions, rounded) |
|---|---|---|
| Americas | $ 9,936 | $ 9,065 |
| EMEA* | 1,141 | 1,047 |
| China/Asia Pacific | 721 | 552 |
| Channel Development** | 1,292 | 860 |
| Other | 209 | 176 |
| Total | $13,299 | $11,700 |

\* Europe, Middle East, and Africa
\*\* Sells packaged coffee and teas globally

a. Prepare a horizontal analysis of the segment data using the prior year as the base year. Round whole percents to one decimal place.

b. Prepare a vertical analysis of the segment data. Round whole percents to one decimal place.

c. What conclusions can be drawn from your analyses?

### EX 5-26  Segment revenue vertical analysis
OBJ. 5

News Corporation is one of the world's largest entertainment companies that includes Twentieth Century Fox films, Fox Broadcasting, Fox News, the FX, and various satellite, cable, and publishing properties. The company provided revenue disclosures by its major product segments in the notes to its financial statements as follows:

| Major Product Segments | For a Recent Year (in millions) |
|---|---|
| Cable Network Programming | $ 9,132 |
| Filmed Entertainment | 7,302 |
| Television | 4,734 |
| Direct Broadcast Satellite Television | 3,672 |
| Publishing | 8,248 |
| Other | 618 |
| Total revenues | $33,706 |

a. Provide a vertical analysis of the product segment revenue. Round whole percents to one decimal place.

b. Are the revenues of News Corporation diversified or concentrated within a product segment? Explain.

### EX 5-27  Segment revenue horizontal and vertical analyses
OBJ. 5

The comparative regional segment revenues for McDonald's Corporation are as follows:

| | Recent Year (in millions) | Prior Year (in millions) |
|---|---|---|
| United States | $ 8,814 | $ 8,528 |
| Europe | 10,827 | 10,886 |
| APMEA* | 6,391 | 6,020 |
| Other Countries & Corporate | 1,535 | 1,572 |
| Total revenues | $27,567 | $27,006 |

\* APMEA = Asia/Pacific, Middle East, Africa

a. Provide a horizontal analysis of the regional segment revenues using the prior year as the base year. Round whole percents to one decimal place.

b. Provide a vertical analysis of the regional segment revenues for both years. Round whole percents to one decimal place.

c. What conclusions can be drawn from your analyses?

# Problems: Series A

**✔ 1. Revenue journal, total fees earned, $1,170**

### PR 5-1A Revenue journal; accounts receivable subsidiary and general ledgers    OBJ. 2, 3

Sage Learning Centers was established on July 20, 2016, to provide educational services. The services provided during the remainder of the month are as follows:

July 21. Issued Invoice No. 1 to J. Dunlop for $115 on account.

22. Issued Invoice No. 2 to K. Tisdale for $350 on account.

24. Issued Invoice No. 3 to T. Quinn for $85 on account.

25. Provided educational services, $300, to K. Tisdale in exchange for educational supplies.

27. Issued Invoice No. 4 to F. Mintz for $225 on account.

30. Issued Invoice No. 5 to D. Chase for $170 on account.

30. Issued Invoice No. 6 to K. Tisdale for $120 on account.

31. Issued Invoice No. 7 to T. Quinn for $105 on account.

**Instructions**

1. Journalize the transactions for July, using a single-column revenue journal and a two-column general journal. Post to the following customer accounts in the accounts receivable ledger, and insert the balance immediately after recording each entry: D. Chase; J. Dunlop; F. Mintz; T. Quinn; K. Tisdale.

2. Post the revenue journal and the general journal to the following accounts in the general ledger, inserting the account balances only after the last postings:

    12  Accounts Receivable
    13  Supplies
    41  Fees Earned

3. a. What is the sum of the balances of the customer accounts in the subsidiary ledger at July 31?

    b. What is the balance of the accounts receivable controlling account at July 31?

4. Assume Sage Learning Centers began using a computerized accounting system to record the sales transactions on August 1. What are some of the benefits of the computerized system over the manual system?

### PR 5-2A Revenue and cash receipts journals; accounts receivable subsidiary and general ledgers    OBJ. 2, 3

**✔ 3. Total cash receipts, $37,600**

**SHOW ME HOW**

Transactions related to revenue and cash receipts completed by Albany Architects Co. during the period November 2–30, 2016, are as follows:

Nov. 2. Issued Invoice No. 793 to Ohr Co., $5,650. *Revenue, yes*

5. Received cash from Mendez Co. for the balance owed on its account. *Cash receipt, yes*

6. Issued Invoice No. 794 to Rahal Co., $2,450. *Revenue, yes*

13. Issued Invoice No. 795 to Shilo Co., $3,980. *Revenue, yes*

    Post revenue and collections to the accounts receivable subsidiary ledger. *Cash rec, yes*

15. Received cash from Rahal Co. for the balance owed on November 1. *Cash rec, yes*

16. Issued Invoice No. 796 to Rahal Co., $6,500. *Revenue, yes*

    Post revenue and collections to the accounts receivable subsidiary ledger.

19. Received cash from Ohr Co. for the balance due on invoice of November 2.

20. Received cash from Rahal Co. for balance due on invoice of November 6.

22. Issued Invoice No. 797 to Mendez Co., $8,040. *Revenue, yes*

25. Received $3,000 note receivable in partial settlement of the balance due on the Shilo Co. account. *General journal entry*

30. Recorded cash fees earned, $13,270. *Cash receipt, no (got paid immediately)*

    Post revenue and collections to the accounts receivable subsidiary ledger.

(*Continued*)

**Instructions**

1. Insert the following balances in the general ledger as of November 1:

| | | |
|---|---|---|
| 11 | Cash | $11,350 |
| 12 | Accounts Receivable | 16,230 |
| 14 | Notes Receivable | 6,000 |
| 41 | Fees Earned | — |

2. Insert the following balances in the accounts receivable subsidiary ledger as of November 1:

| | |
|---|---|
| Mendez Co. | $9,460 |
| Ohr Co. | — |
| Rahal Co. | 6,770 |
| Shilo Co. | — |

3. Prepare a single-column revenue journal (p. 40) and a cash receipts journal (p. 36). Use the following column headings for the cash receipts journal: Fees Earned Cr., Accounts Receivable Cr., and Cash Dr. The Fees Earned column is used to record cash fees. Insert a check mark (✓) in the Post. Ref. column when recording cash fees.

4. Using the two special journals and the two-column general journal (p. 1), journalize the transactions for November. Post to the accounts receivable subsidiary ledger, and insert the balances at the points indicated in the narrative of transactions. Determine the balance in the customer's account before recording a cash receipt.

5. Total each of the columns of the special journals, and post the individual entries and totals to the general ledger. Insert account balances after the last posting.

6. Determine that the sum of the customer balances agrees with the accounts receivable controlling account in the general ledger.

7. Why would an automated system omit postings to a controlling account as performed in step 5 for Accounts Receivable?

---

**PR 5-3A**  **Purchases, accounts payable subsidiary account, and accounts payable ledger**
                                                                                    OBJ. 2, 4

✔ 5b. $18,110

**General Ledger**

SHOW
ME HOW

Sterling Forest Landscaping designs and installs landscaping. The landscape designers and office staff use office supplies, while field supplies (rock, bark, etc.) are used in the actual landscaping. Purchases on account completed by Sterling Forest Landscaping during October 2016 are as follows:

Oct.  2. Purchased office supplies on account from Meade Co., $400.

5. Purchased office equipment on account from Peach Computers Co., $3,980.

9. Purchased office supplies on account from Executive Office Supply Co., $320.

13. Purchased field supplies on account from Yamura Co., $1,420.

14. Purchased field supplies on account from Omni Co., $2,940.

17. Purchased field supplies on account from Yamura Co., $1,890.

24. Purchased field supplies on account from Omni Co., $3,880.

29. Purchased office supplies on account from Executive Office Supply Co., $310.

31. Purchased field supplies on account from Omni Co., $1,800.

**Instructions**

1. Insert the following balances in the general ledger as of October 1:

| | | |
|---|---|---|
| 14 | Field Supplies | $ 5,920 |
| 15 | Office Supplies | 750 |
| 18 | Office Equipment | 12,300 |
| 21 | Accounts Payable | 1,170 |

2. Insert the following balances in the accounts payable subsidiary ledger as of October 1:

| | |
|---|---|
| Executive Office Supply Co. | $390 |
| Meade Co. | 780 |
| Omni Co. | — |
| Peach Computers Co. | — |
| Yamura Co. | — |

3. Journalize the transactions for October, using a purchases journal (p. 30) similar to the one illustrated in this chapter. Prepare the purchases journal with columns for Accounts Payable, Field Supplies, Office Supplies, and Other Accounts. Post to the creditor accounts in the accounts payable subsidiary ledger immediately after each entry.

4. Post the purchases journal to the accounts in the general ledger.

5. a. What is the sum of the creditor balances in the subsidiary ledger at October 31?

   b. What is the balance of the accounts payable controlling account at October 31?

6. What type of e-commerce application would be used to plan and coordinate transactions with suppliers?

---

### PR 5-4A Purchases and cash payments journals; accounts payable subsidiary and general ledgers

**OBJ. 2**

✔ 1. Total cash payments, $203,940

[General Ledger]

AquaFresh Water Testing Service was established on April 16, 2016. AquaFresh uses field equipment and field supplies (chemicals and other supplies) to analyze water for unsafe contaminants in streams, lakes, and ponds. Transactions related to purchases and cash payments during the remainder of April are as follows:

April 16. Issued Check No. 1 in payment of rent for the remainder of April, $3,500.

16. Purchased field supplies on account from Hydro Supply Co., $5,340.

16. Purchased field equipment on account from Pure Equipment Co., $21,450.

17. Purchased office supplies on account from Best Office Supply Co., $510.

19. Issued Check No. 2 in payment of field supplies, $3,340, and office supplies, $400.

   *Post the journals to the accounts payable subsidiary ledger.*

23. Purchased office supplies on account from Best Office Supply Co., $660.

23. Issued Check No. 3 to purchase land, $140,000.

24. Issued Check No. 4 to Hydro Supply Co. in payment of April 16 invoice, $5,340.

26. Issued Check No. 5 to Pure Equipment Co. in payment of April 16 invoice, $21,450.

   *Post the journals to the accounts payable subsidiary ledger.*

30. Acquired land in exchange for field equipment having a cost of $12,000.

30. Purchased field supplies on account from Hydro Supply Co., $7,650.

30. Issued Check No. 6 to Best Office Supply Co. in payment of April 17 invoice, $510.

30. Purchased the following from Pure Equipment Co. on account: field supplies, $1,340, and field equipment, $4,700.

30. Issued Check No. 7 in payment of salaries, $29,400.

   *Post the journals to the accounts payable subsidiary ledger.*

### Instructions

1. Journalize the transactions for April. Use a purchases journal and a cash payments journal, similar to those illustrated in this chapter, and a two-column general journal. Use debit columns for Field Supplies, Office Supplies, and Other Accounts in the purchases journal. Refer to the following partial chart of accounts:

| | | | |
|---|---|---|---|
| 11 | Cash | 19 | Land |
| 14 | Field Supplies | 21 | Accounts Payable |
| 15 | Office Supplies | 61 | Salary Expense |
| 17 | Field Equipment | 71 | Rent Expense |

At the points indicated in the narrative of transactions, post to the following accounts in the accounts payable subsidiary ledger:

Best Office Supply Co.
Hydro Supply Co.
Pure Equipment Co.

*(Continued)*

2. Post the individual entries (Other Accounts columns of the purchases journal and the cash payments journal and both columns of the general journal) to the appropriate general ledger accounts.

3. Total each of the columns of the purchases journal and the cash payments journal, and post the appropriate totals to the general ledger. (Because the problem does not include transactions related to cash receipts, the cash account in the ledger will have a credit balance.)

4. Prepare a schedule of the accounts payable creditor balances.

5. Why might AquaFresh consider using a subsidiary ledger for the field equipment?

---

✔ 2. Total cash receipts, $57,430

General Ledger

**PR 5-5A    All journals and general ledger; trial balance**                     OBJ. 2

The transactions completed by Revere Courier Company during December 2016, the first month of the fiscal year, were as follows:

Dec.  1. Issued Check No. 610 for December rent, $4,500.

2. Issued Invoice No. 940 to Capps Co., $1,980.

3. Received check for $5,100 from Trimble Co. in payment of account.

5. Purchased a vehicle on account from Boston Transportation, $39,500.

6. Purchased office equipment on account from Austin Computer Co., $4,800.

6. Issued Invoice No. 941 to Dawar Co., $5,680.

9. Issued Check No. 611 for fuel expense, $800.

10. Received check from Sing Co. in payment of $4,850 invoice.

10. Issued Check No. 612 for $360 to Office To Go Inc. in payment of invoice.

10. Issued Invoice No. 942 to Joy Co., $2,140.

11. Issued Check No. 613 for $3,240 to Essential Supply Co. in payment of account.

11. Issued Check No. 614 for $650 to Porter Co. in payment of account.

12. Received check from Capps Co. in payment of $1,980 invoice of December 2.

13. Issued Check No. 615 to Boston Transportation in payment of $39,500 balance of December 5.

16. Issued Check No. 616 for $40,900 for cash purchase of a vehicle.

16. Cash fees earned for December 1–16, $21,700.

17. Issued Check No. 617 for miscellaneous administrative expense, $600.

18. Purchased maintenance supplies on account from Essential Supply Co., $1,750.

19. Purchased the following on account from McClain Co.: maintenance supplies, $1,500; office supplies, $325.

20. Issued Check No. 618 in payment of advertising expense, $1,990.

20. Used $3,600 maintenance supplies to repair delivery vehicles.

23. Purchased office supplies on account from Office To Go Inc., $440.

24. Issued Invoice No. 943 to Sing Co., $6,400.

24. Issued Check No. 619 to S. Holmes as a personal withdrawal, $3,200.

25. Issued Invoice No. 944 to Dawar Co., $5,720.

25. Received check for $4,100 from Trimble Co. in payment of balance.

26. Issued Check No. 620 to Austin Computer Co. in payment of $4,800 invoice of December 6.

30. Issued Check No. 621 for monthly salaries as follows: driver salaries, $16,900; office salaries, $7,600.

31. Cash fees earned for December 17–31, $19,700.

31. Issued Check No. 622 in payment for office supplies, $310.

**Instructions**

1. Enter the following account balances in the general ledger as of December 1:

| | | | | | | |
|---|---|---|---|---|---|---|
| 11 | Cash | $160,900 | 32 | S. Holmes, Drawing | — |
| 12 | Accounts Receivable | 14,050 | 41 | Fees Earned | — |
| 14 | Maintenance Supplies | 10,850 | 51 | Driver Salaries Expense | — |
| 15 | Office Supplies | 4,900 | 52 | Maintenance Supplies Exp. | — |
| 16 | Office Equipment | 28,500 | 53 | Fuel Expense | — |
| 17 | Accum. Depr.—Office Equip. | 6,900 | 61 | Office Salaries Expense | — |
| 18 | Vehicles | 95,900 | 62 | Rent Expense | — |
| 19 | Accum. Depr.—Vehicles | 14,700 | 63 | Advertising Expense | — |
| 21 | Accounts Payable | 4,250 | 64 | Miscellaneous Administrative Expense | — |
| 31 | S. Holmes, Capital | 289,250 | | | |

2. Journalize the transactions for December 2016, using the following journals similar to those illustrated in this chapter: cash receipts journal (p. 31), purchases journal (p. 37, with columns for Accounts Payable, Maintenance Supplies, Office Supplies, and Other Accounts), single-column revenue journal (p. 35), cash payments journal (p. 34), and two-column general journal (p. 1). Assume that the daily postings to the individual accounts in the accounts payable subsidiary ledger and the accounts receivable subsidiary ledger have been made.

3. Post the appropriate individual entries to the general ledger.

4. Total each of the columns of the special journals, and post the appropriate totals to the general ledger; insert the account balances.

5. Prepare a trial balance.

# Problems: Series B

**PR 5-1B   Revenue journal; accounts receivable subsidiary and general ledgers   OBJ. 2, 3**

✔ 1. Revenue
journal, total fees
earned, $2,875

Guardian Security Services was established on January 15, 2016, to provide security services. The services provided during the remainder of the month are as follows:

Jan. 18. Issued Invoice No. 1 to Murphy Co. for $490 on account.

   20. Issued Invoice No. 2 to Qwik-Mart Co. for $340 on account.

   24. Issued Invoice No. 3 to Hopkins Co. for $750 on account.

   27. Issued Invoice No. 4 to Carson Co. for $680 on account.

   28. Issued Invoice No. 5 to Amber Waves Co. for $120 on account.

   28. Provided security services, $100, to Qwik-Mart Co. in exchange for supplies.

   30. Issued Invoice No. 6 to Qwik-Mart Co. for $200 on account.

   31. Issued Invoice No. 7 to Hopkins Co. for $295 on account.

**Instructions**

1. Journalize the transactions for January, using a single-column revenue journal and a two-column general journal. Post to the following customer accounts in the accounts receivable ledger, and insert the balance immediately after recording each entry: Amber Waves Co.; Carson Co.; Hopkins Co.; Murphy Co.; Qwik-Mart Co.

2. Post the revenue journal to the following accounts in the general ledger, inserting the account balances only after the last postings:

| | |
|---|---|
| 12 | Accounts Receivable |
| 14 | Supplies |
| 41 | Fees Earned |

3. a. What is the sum of the balances of the customer accounts in the subsidiary ledger at January 31?

   b. What is the balance of the accounts receivable controlling account at January 31?

(*Continued*)

4. Assume Guardian Security Services began using a computerized accounting system to record the sales transactions on February 1. What are some of the benefits of the computerized system over the manual system?

---

### PR 5-2B  Revenue and cash receipts journals; accounts receivable subsidiary and general ledgers

OBJ. 2, 3

✔ 3. Total cash receipts, $9,270

General Ledger

SHOW
ME HOW

Transactions related to revenue and cash receipts completed by Sterling Engineering Services during the period June 2–30, 2016, are as follows:

June  2. Issued Invoice No. 717 to Yee Co., $1,430.

3. Received cash from Auto-Flex Co. for the balance owed on its account.

7. Issued Invoice No. 718 to Cooper Development Co., $670.

10. Issued Invoice No. 719 to Ridge Communities, $2,840.

    *Post revenue and collections to the accounts receivable subsidiary ledger.*

14. Received cash from Cooper Development Co. for the balance owed on June 1.

16. Issued Invoice No. 720 to Cooper Development Co., $400.

    *Post revenue and collections to the accounts receivable subsidiary ledger.*

18. Received cash from Yee Co. for the balance due on invoice of June 2.

20. Received cash from Cooper Development Co. for invoice of June 7.

23. Issued Invoice No. 721 to Auto-Flex Co., $860.

30. Recorded cash fees earned, $4,520.

30. Received office equipment of $1,800 in partial settlement of balance due on the Ridge Communities account.

    *Post revenue and collections to the accounts receivable subsidiary ledger.*

### Instructions

1. Insert the following balances in the general ledger as of June 1:

    | 11 | Cash | $18,340 |
    |----|------|---------|
    | 12 | Accounts Receivable | 2,650 |
    | 18 | Office Equipment | 34,700 |
    | 41 | Fees Earned | — |

2. Insert the following balances in the accounts receivable subsidiary ledger as of June 1:

    | Auto-Flex Co. | $1,670 |
    |---------------|--------|
    | Cooper Development Co. | 980 |
    | Ridge Communities | — |
    | Yee Co. | — |

3. Prepare a single-column revenue journal (p. 40) and a cash receipts journal (p. 36). Use the following column headings for the cash receipts journal: Fees Earned Cr., Accounts Receivable Cr., and Cash Dr. The Fees Earned column is used to record cash fees. Insert a check mark (✓) in the Post. Ref. column when recording cash fees.

4. Using the two special journals and the two-column general journal (p. 1), journalize the transactions for June. Post to the accounts receivable subsidiary ledger, and insert the balances at the points indicated in the narrative of transactions. Determine the balance in the customer's account before recording a cash receipt.

5. Total each of the columns of the special journals, and post the individual entries and totals to the general ledger. Insert account balances after the last posting.

6. Determine that the sum of the customer accounts agrees with the accounts receivable controlling account in the general ledger.

7. Why would an automated system omit postings to a control account as performed in step 5 for Accounts Receivable?

### PR 5-3B Purchases, accounts payable account, and accounts payable subsidiary ledger

OBJ. 2, 4

✔ 5a. $31,300

General Ledger

SHOW
ME HOW

Plumb Line Surveyors provides survey work for construction projects. The office staff use office supplies, while surveying crews use field supplies. Purchases on account completed by Plumb Line Surveyors during May 2016 are as follows:

May 1. Purchased field supplies on account from Wendell Co., $3,240.

3. Purchased office supplies on account from Lassiter Co., $340.

8. Purchased field supplies on account from Tri Cities Supplies, $4,500.

12. Purchased field supplies on account from Wendell Co., $3,670.

15. Purchased office supplies on account from J-Mart Co., $500.

19. Purchased office equipment on account from Accu-Vision Supply Co., $8,150.

23. Purchased field supplies on account from Tri Cities Supplies, $2,450.

26. Purchased office supplies on account from J-Mart Co., $265.

30. Purchased field supplies on account from Tri Cities Supplies, $3,040.

**Instructions**

1. Insert the following balances in the general ledger as of May 1:

| 14 | Field Supplies | $ 6,200 |
|----|----------------|---------|
| 15 | Office Supplies | 1,490 |
| 18 | Office Equipment | 19,400 |
| 21 | Accounts Payable | 5,145 |

2. Insert the following balances in the accounts payable subsidiary ledger as of May 1:

| Accu-Vision Supply Co. | $3,900 |
|------------------------|--------|
| J-Mart Co. | 730 |
| Lassiter Co. | 515 |
| Tri Cities Supplies | — |
| Wendell Co. | — |

3. Journalize the transactions for May, using a purchases journal (p. 30) similar to the one illustrated in this chapter. Prepare the purchases journal with columns for Accounts Payable, Field Supplies, Office Supplies, and Other Accounts. Post to the creditor accounts in the accounts payable subsidiary ledger immediately after each entry.

4. Post the purchases journal to the accounts in the general ledger.

5. a. What is the sum of the creditor balances in the subsidiary ledger at May 31?

   b. What is the balance of the accounts payable controlling account at May 31?

6. What type of e-commerce application would be used to plan and coordinate transactions with suppliers?

### PR 5-4B Purchases and cash payments journals; accounts payable subsidiary and general ledgers

OBJ. 2

✔ 1. Total cash payments, $327,920

General Ledger

West Texas Exploration Co. was established on October 15, 2016, to provide oil-drilling services. West Texas uses field equipment (rigs and pipe) and field supplies (drill bits and lubricants) in its operations. Transactions related to purchases and cash payments during the remainder of October are as follows:

Oct. 16. Issued Check No. 1 in payment of rent for the remainder of October, $7,000.

16. Purchased field equipment on account from Petro Services Inc., $32,600.

17. Purchased field supplies on account from Midland Supply Co., $9,780.

18. Issued Check No. 2 in payment of field supplies, $4,570, and office supplies, $650.

20. Purchased office supplies on account from A-One Office Supply Co., $1,320.

   *Post the journals to the accounts payable subsidiary ledger.*

24. Issued Check No. 3 to Petro Services Inc., in payment of October 16 invoice.

*(Continued)*

Oct. 26. Issued Check No. 4 to Midland Supply Co. in payment of October 17 invoice.

28. Issued Check No. 5 to purchase land, $240,000.

28. Purchased office supplies on account from A-One Office Supply Co., $3,670.

*Post the journals to the accounts payable subsidiary ledger.*

30. Purchased the following from Petro Services Inc. on account: field supplies, $25,300 and office equipment, $5,500.

30. Issued Check No. 6 to A-One Office Supply Co. in payment of October 20 invoice.

30. Purchased field supplies on account from Midland Supply Co., $12,450.

31. Issued Check No. 7 in payment of salaries, $32,000.

31. Rented building for one year in exchange for field equipment having a cost of $15,000.

*Post the journals to the accounts payable subsidiary ledger.*

### Instructions

1. Journalize the transactions for October. Use a purchases journal and a cash payments journal, similar to those illustrated in this chapter, and a two-column general journal. Set debit columns for Field Supplies, Office Supplies, and Other Accounts in the purchases journal. Refer to the following partial chart of accounts:

| | | | |
|---|---|---|---|
| 11 | Cash | 18 | Office Equipment |
| 14 | Field Supplies | 19 | Land |
| 15 | Office Supplies | 21 | Accounts Payable |
| 16 | Prepaid Rent | 61 | Salary Expense |
| 17 | Field Equipment | 71 | Rent Expense |

At the points indicated in the narrative of transactions, post to the following subsidiary accounts in the accounts payable ledger:

A-One Office Supply Co.
Midland Supply Co.
Petro Services Inc.

2. Post the individual entries (Other Accounts columns of the purchases journal and the cash payments journal; both columns of the general journal) to the appropriate general ledger accounts.

3. Total each of the columns of the purchases journal and the cash payments journal, and post the appropriate totals to the general ledger. (Because the problem does not include transactions related to cash receipts, the cash account in the ledger will have a credit balance.)

4. Sum the balances of the accounts payable creditor balances.

5. Why might West Texas consider using a subsidiary ledger for the field equipment?

---

**PR 5-5B  All journals and general ledger; trial balance**                    OBJ. 2

✔ 2. Total cash receipts, $96,050

General Ledger

The transactions completed by AM Express Company during March 2016, the first month of the fiscal year, were as follows:

Mar. 1. Issued Check No. 205 for March rent, $2,450.

2. Purchased a vehicle on account from McIntyre Sales Co., $26,900.

3. Purchased office equipment on account from Office Mate Inc., $1,570.

5. Issued Invoice No. 91 to Ellis Co., $7,000.

6. Received check for $7,950 from Chavez Co. in payment of invoice.

7. Issued Invoice No. 92 to Trent Co., $9,840.

9. Issued Check No. 206 for fuel expense, $820.

10. Received check for $10,000 from Sajeev Co. in payment of invoice.

10. Issued Check No. 207 to Office City in payment of $450 invoice.

Mar. 10. Issued Check No. 208 to Bastille Co. in payment of $1,890 invoice.

11. Issued Invoice No. 93 to Jarvis Co., $7,200.

11. Issued Check No. 209 to Porter Co. in payment of $415 invoice.

12. Received check for $7,000 from Ellis Co. in payment of March 5 invoice.

13. Issued Check No. 210 to McIntyre Sales Co. in payment of $26,900 invoice of March 2.

16. Cash fees earned for March 1–16, $26,800.

16. Issued Check No. 211 for purchase of a vehicle, $28,500.

17. Issued Check No. 212 for miscellaneous administrative expense, $4,680.

18. Purchased maintenance supplies on account from Bastille Co., $2,430.

18. Received check for rent revenue on office space, $900.

19. Purchased the following on account from Master Supply Co.: maintenance supplies, $2,640, and office supplies, $1,500.

20. Issued Check No. 213 in payment of advertising expense, $8,590.

20. Used maintenance supplies with a cost of $4,400 to repair vehicles.

21. Purchased office supplies on account from Office City, $990.

24. Issued Invoice No. 94 to Sajeev Co., $9,200.

25. Received check for $14,000 from Chavez Co. in payment of invoice.

25. Issued Invoice No. 95 to Trent Co., $6,300.

26. Issued Check No. 214 to Office Mate Inc. in payment of $1,570 invoice of March 3.

27. Issued Check No. 215 to J. Wu as a personal withdrawal, $4,000.

30. Issued Check No. 216 in payment of driver salaries, $33,300.

31. Issued Check No. 217 in payment of office salaries, $21,200.

31. Issued Check No. 218 for office supplies, $600.

31. Cash fees earned for March 17–31, $29,400.

**Instructions**

1. Enter the following account balances in the general ledger as of March 1:

| | | | | | |
|---|---|---|---|---|---|
| 11 | Cash | $ 65,200 | 32 | J. Wu, Drawing | — |
| 12 | Accounts Receivable | 31,950 | 41 | Fees Earned | — |
| 14 | Maintenance Supplies | 7,240 | 42 | Rent Revenue | — |
| 15 | Office Supplies | 3,690 | 51 | Driver Salaries Expense | — |
| 16 | Office Equipment | 17,300 | 52 | Maintenance Supplies Expense | — |
| 17 | Accum. Depr.—Office Equip. | 4,250 | 53 | Fuel Expense | — |
| 18 | Vehicles | 62,400 | 61 | Office Salaries Expense | — |
| 19 | Accum. Depr.—Vehicles | 17,800 | 62 | Rent Expense | — |
| 21 | Accounts Payable | 2,755 | 63 | Advertising Expense | — |
| 31 | J. Wu, Capital | 162,975 | 64 | Miscellaneous Administrative Exp. | — |

2. Journalize the transactions for March 2016, using the following journals similar to those illustrated in this chapter: single-column revenue journal (p. 35), cash receipts journal (p. 31), purchases journal (p. 37, with columns for Accounts Payable, Maintenance Supplies, Office Supplies, and Other Accounts), cash payments journal (p. 34), and two-column general journal (p. 1). Assume that the daily postings to the individual accounts in the accounts payable subsidiary ledger and the accounts receivable subsidiary ledger have been made.

3. Post the appropriate individual entries to the general ledger.

4. Total each of the columns of the special journals, and post the appropriate totals to the general ledger; insert the account balances.

5. Prepare a trial balance.

## Cases & Projects

### CP 5-1 Ethics and professional conduct in business

Netbooks Inc. provides accounting applications for business customers on the Internet for a monthly subscription. Netbooks customers run their accounting system on the Internet; thus, the business data and accounting software reside on the servers of Netbooks Inc. The senior management of Netbooks believes that once a customer begins to use Netbooks, it would be very difficult to cancel the service. That is, customers are "locked in" because it would be difficult to move the business data from Netbooks to another accounting application, even though the customers own their own data. Therefore, Netbooks has decided to entice customers with an initial low monthly price that is half of the normal monthly rate for the first year of services. After a year, the price will be increased to the regular monthly rate. Netbooks management believes that customers will have to accept the full price because customers will be "locked in" after one year of use.

a. Discuss whether the half-price offer is an ethical business practice.

b. Discuss whether customer "lock in" is an ethical business practice.

### CP 5-2 Manual vs. computerized accounting systems

The following conversation took place between Durable Construction Co.'s bookkeeper, Kyle Byers, and the accounting supervisor, Sarah Nelson:

*Sarah:* Kyle, I'm thinking about bringing in a new computerized accounting system to replace our manual system. I guess this will mean that you will need to learn how to do computerized accounting.

*Kyle:* What does computerized accounting mean?

*Sarah:* I'm not sure, but you'll need to prepare for this new way of doing business.

*Kyle:* I'm not so sure we need a computerized system. I've been looking at some of the sample reports from the software vendor. It looks to me as if the computer will not add much to what we are already doing.

*Sarah:* What do you mean?

*Kyle:* Well, look at these reports. This Sales by Customer Report looks like our revenue journal, and the Deposit Detail Report looks like our cash receipts journal. Granted, the computer types them, so they look much neater than my special journals, but I don't see that we're gaining much from this change.

*Sarah:* Well, surely there's more to it than nice-looking reports. I've got to believe that a computerized system will save us time and effort someplace.

*Kyle:* I don't see how. We still need to key in transactions into the computer. If anything, there may be more work when it's all said and done.

➤ Do you agree with Kyle? Why might a computerized environment be preferred over the manual system?

### CP 5-3 Accounts receivable and accounts payable

A subsidiary ledger is used for accounts receivable and accounts payable. Thus, transactions that are made "on account" are posted to the individual customer or creditor accounts.

a. Why do companies use subsidiary ledgers for accounts payable and accounts receivable?

b. Identify another account that may benefit from using a subsidiary ledger.

### CP 5-4 Design of accounting systems

For the past few years, your client, Omni Care, has operated a small medical practice. Omni Care's current annual revenues are $945,000. Because the accountant has been spending more and more time each month recording all transactions in a two-column journal and preparing the financial statements, Omni Care is considering improving the accounting system by adding special journals and subsidiary ledgers. Omni Care has asked you to help with this project and has compiled the following information:

| Type of Transaction | Estimated Frequency per Month |
|---|---|
| Fees earned on account | 240 |
| Purchase of medical supplies on account | 190 |
| Cash receipts from patients on account | 175 |
| Cash payments on account | 160 |
| Cash receipts from patients at time services provided | 120 |
| Purchase of office supplies on account | 35 |
| Purchase of magazine subscriptions on account | 5 |
| Purchase of medical equipment on account | 4 |
| Cash payments for office salaries | 3 |
| Cash payments for utilities expense | 3 |

1. ▬▬▶ Briefly discuss the circumstances under which special journals would be used in place of a two-column (all-purpose) journal. Include in your answer your recommendations for Omni Care's medical practice.

2. Assume that Omni Care has decided to use a revenue journal and a purchases journal. Design the format for each journal, giving special consideration to the needs of the medical practice.

3. Which subsidiary ledgers would you recommend for the medical practice?

---

### CP 5-5  Internet-based accounting systems

**Internet Project**

Internet-based accounting software is a recent trend in business computing. Major software firms such as Oracle, SAP, and NetSuite are running their core products on the Internet using cloud computing. NetSuite is one of the most popular small business Internet-based accounting systems.

▬▬▶ Go to NetSuite Inc.'s Web site at www.netsuite.com. Read about the product from the site, and prepare a memo to management, defining Internet-based accounting. Also, outline the advantages and disadvantages of Internet-based accounting compared to running software on a company's internal computer network.

---

### CP 5-6  SCM and CRM

**Group Project**

**Internet Project**

The two leading software application providers for supply chain management (SCM) and customer relationship management (CRM) software are JDA and Salesforce.com, respectively. In groups of two or three, go to the Web site for each company (www.jda.com and www.salesforce.com, respectively) and list the services provided by each company's software.

# Accounting for Merchandising Businesses

## Dollar Tree Stores, Inc.

When you are low on cash but need to pick up party supplies, housewares, or other consumer items, where do you go? Many shoppers are turning to **Dollar Tree Stores, Inc.**, the nation's largest single price point dollar retailer with more than 4,000 stores in 48 states. For the fixed price of $1 on merchandise in its stores, Dollar Tree has worked hard providing "new treasures" every week for the entire family.

Despite the fact that items cost only $1, the accounting for a merchandiser, like Dollar Tree, is more complex than for a service company. This is because a service company sells only services and has no inventory. With Dollar Tree's locations and merchandise, the company must design its accounting system to not only record the receipt of goods for resale, but also to keep track of what merchandise is available for sale as well as where the merchandise is located. In addition, Dollar Tree must record the sales and costs of the goods sold for each of its stores. Finally, Dollar Tree must record such data as delivery costs, merchandise discounts, and merchandise returns.

This chapter focuses on the accounting principles and concepts for a merchandising business. In doing so, the basic differences between merchandiser and service company activities are highlighted. The financial statements of a merchandising business and accounting for merchandise transactions are also described and illustrated.

## Learning Objectives

---

**OBJ 1** Distinguish between the activities and financial statements of service and merchandising businesses.

# Nature of Merchandising Businesses

The activities of a service business differ from those of a merchandising business. These differences are reflected in the operating cycles of a service and merchandising business as well as in their financial statements.

## Operating Cycle

The **operating cycle** is the process by which a company spends cash, generates revenues, and receives cash either at the time the revenues are generated or later by collecting an accounts receivable. The operating cycle of a service and merchandising business differs in that a merchandising business must purchase merchandise for sale to customers. The operating cycle for a merchandise business is shown in Exhibit 1.

---

**EXHIBIT 1**

**The Operating Cycle for a Merchandising Business**

The time in days to complete an operating cycle differs significantly among merchandise businesses. Grocery stores normally have short operating cycles because of the nature of their merchandise. For example, many grocery items, such as milk, must be sold within their expiration dates of a week or two. In contrast, jewelry stores often carry expensive items that are often displayed months before being sold to customers.

## Financial Statements

The differences between service and merchandising businesses are also reflected in their financial statements. For example, these differences are illustrated in the following condensed income statements:

| Service Business | | Merchandising Business | |
| --- | --- | --- | --- |
| Fees earned | $XXX | Sales | $XXX |
| Operating expenses | –XXX | Cost of merchandise sold | –XXX |
| Net income | $XXX | Gross profit | $XXX |
| | | Operating expenses | –XXX |
| | | Net income | $XXX |

The revenue activities of a service business involve providing services to customers. On the income statement for a service business, the revenues from services are reported as *fees earned*. The operating expenses incurred in providing the services are subtracted from the fees earned to arrive at *net income*.

In contrast, the revenue activities of a merchandising business involve the buying and selling of merchandise. A merchandising business first purchases merchandise to sell to its customers. When this merchandise is sold, the revenue is reported as **sales**, and its cost is recognized as an expense. This expense is called the **cost of merchandise sold**. The cost of merchandise sold is subtracted from sales to arrive at gross profit. This amount is called **gross profit** because it is the profit *before* deducting operating expenses.

Merchandise on hand (not sold) at the end of an accounting period is called **merchandise inventory**. Merchandise inventory is reported as a current asset on the balance sheet.

## Business  Connection

### H&R BLOCK VERSUS THE HOME DEPOT

**H&R Block** is a service business that primarily offers tax planning and preparation to its customers. **The Home Depot** is a large home improvement retailer. The differences in the operations of a service and merchandise business are illustrated in their recent income statements, as shown.

As discussed in a later chapter, corporations are subject to income taxes. Thus, the income statements of H&R Block and The Home Depot report "income taxes" as a deduction from "income before income taxes" in arriving at net income. This is in contrast to a proprietorship, such as **NetSolutions**, which is not subject to income taxes.

**H&R Block**
**Condensed Income Statement**
**(in millions)**

| | |
| --- | --- |
| Revenue | $2,794 |
| Operating expenses | 2,235 |
| Operating income | $ 559 |
| Other expense (net) | 63 |
| Income before taxes | $ 496 |
| Income taxes | 230 |
| Net income | $ 266 |

**The Home Depot**
**Condensed Income Statement**
**(in millions)**

| | |
| --- | --- |
| Sales | $70,395 |
| Cost of merchandise sold | 46,133 |
| Gross profit | $24,262 |
| Operating expenses | 17,601 |
| Operating income | $ 6,661 |
| Other expense (net) | 593 |
| Income before taxes | $ 6,068 |
| Income taxes | 2,185 |
| Net income | $ 3,883 |

**Example Exercise 6-1** Gross Profit

OBJ 1

During the current year, merchandise is sold for $250,000 cash and for $975,000 on account. The cost of the merchandise sold is $735,000. What is the amount of the gross profit?

**Follow My Example 6-1**

The gross profit is $490,000 ($250,000 + $975,000 − $735,000).

Practice Exercises: PE 6-1A, PE 6-1B

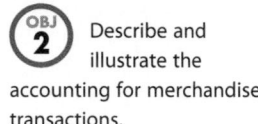

OBJ 2

Describe and illustrate the accounting for merchandise transactions.

# Merchandising Transactions

This section illustrates merchandise transactions for **NetSolutions** after it becomes a retailer of computer hardware and software. During 2015, Chris Clark implemented the second phase of NetSolutions' business plan. In doing so, Chris notified clients that beginning July 1, 2016, NetSolutions would no longer offer consulting services. Instead, it would become a retailer.

NetSolutions' business strategy is to offer personalized service to individuals and small businesses that are upgrading or purchasing new computer systems. NetSolutions' personal service includes a no-obligation, on-site assessment of the customer's computer needs. By providing personalized service and follow-up, Chris feels that NetSolutions can compete effectively against such retailers as Best Buy, Office Max, Office Depot, and Dell.

Merchandise transactions are recorded in the accounts, using the rules of debit and credit that are described and illustrated in Chapter 2. Most merchandising companies use computerized accounting systems with reports that are similar to special journals and subsidiary ledgers. For example, a computerized merchandise accounting system would typically produce sales and inventory reports. However, for the sake of simplicity, the journal entries in this chapter will be illustrated using a two-column general journal.

## Purchases Transactions

There are two systems for accounting for merchandise transactions: perpetual and periodic. In a **perpetual inventory system,** each purchase and sale of merchandise is recorded in the inventory account and related subsidiary ledger. In this way, the amount of merchandise available for sale and the amount sold are continuously (perpetually) updated in the inventory records. In a **periodic inventory system**, the inventory does not show the amount of merchandise available for sale and the amount sold. Instead, a listing of inventory on hand, called a **physical inventory**, is prepared at the end of the accounting period. This physical inventory is used to determine the cost of merchandise on hand at the end of the period and the cost of merchandise sold during the period.

Retailers, such as Best Buy, Sears Holding Corporation, and Walmart, and grocery store chains, such as Winn-Dixie Stores, Inc., and Kroger, use bar codes and optical scanners as part of their computerized inventory systems.

Most merchandise companies use computerized perpetual inventory systems. Such systems use bar codes or radio frequency identification codes embedded in a product. An optical scanner or radio frequency identification device is then used to read the product codes and track inventory on hand and sold.

Because computerized perpetual inventory systems are widely used, this chapter illustrates merchandise transactions using a perpetual inventory system. The periodic system is described and illustrated in an appendix at the end of this chapter.

Under the perpetual inventory system, cash purchases of merchandise are recorded as follows:

| Journal | | | | | Page 24 |
|---|---|---|---|---|---|
| **Date** | | **Description** | **Post. Ref.** | **Debit** | **Credit** |
| 2017 Jan. | 3 | Merchandise Inventory | | 2,510 | |
| | | Cash | | | 2,510 |
| | | Purchased inventory from Bowen Co. | | | |

Purchases of merchandise on account are recorded as follows:

| | | | | | |
|---|---|---|---|---|---|
| Jan. | 4 | Merchandise Inventory | | 9,250 | |
| | | Accounts Payable—Thomas Corporation | | | 9,250 |
| | | Purchased inventory on account. | | | |

The terms of purchases on account are normally indicated on the **invoice** or bill that the seller sends the buyer. An example of an invoice sent to NetSolutions by Alpha Technologies is shown in Exhibit 2.

---

| **Alpha Technologies** 1000 Matrix Blvd. San Jose, CA 95116-1000 | | **Invoice 106-8** |
|---|---|---|
| | | Made in U.S.A. |

| **SOLD TO** NetSolutions 5101 Washington Ave. Cincinnati, OH 45227-5101 | **CUSTOMER ORDER NO.** 412 | **ORDER DATE** Jan. 3, 2017 |
|---|---|---|
| **DATE SHIPPED** Jan. 5, 2017 | **HOW SHIPPED AND ROUTE** US Express Trucking Co. | **TERMS** 2/10, n/30 | **INVOICE DATE** Jan. 5, 2017 |
| **FROM** San Jose | **F.O.B.** Cincinnati | |

| **QUANTITY** | **DESCRIPTION** | **UNIT PRICE** | **AMOUNT** |
|---|---|---|---|
| 20 | HC9 Printer/Fax/Copiers | 150.00 | 3,000.00 |

**EXHIBIT 2**

**Invoice**

---

The terms for when payments for merchandise are to be made are called the **credit terms**. If payment is required on delivery, the terms are cash or net cash. Otherwise, the buyer is allowed an amount of time, known as the **credit period**, in which to pay. The credit period usually begins with the date of the sale as shown on the invoice.

If payment is due within a stated number of days after the invoice date, such as 30 days, the terms are net 30 days. These terms may be written as *n/30*.[1] If payment is due by the end of the month in which the sale was made, the terms are written as *n/eom*.

**Purchases Discounts** To encourage the buyer to pay before the end of the credit period, the seller may offer a discount. For example, a seller may offer a 2% discount if the buyer pays within 10 days of the invoice date. If the buyer does not take the

---

[1] The word *net* as used here does not have the usual meaning of a number after deductions have been subtracted, as in *net income*.

discount, the total invoice amount is due within 30 days. These terms are expressed as 2/10, n/30 and are read as "2% discount if paid within 10 days, net amount due within 30 days." The credit terms of 2/10, n/30 are summarized in Exhibit 3, using the invoice in Exhibit 2.

---

**EXHIBIT 3**     **Credit Terms**

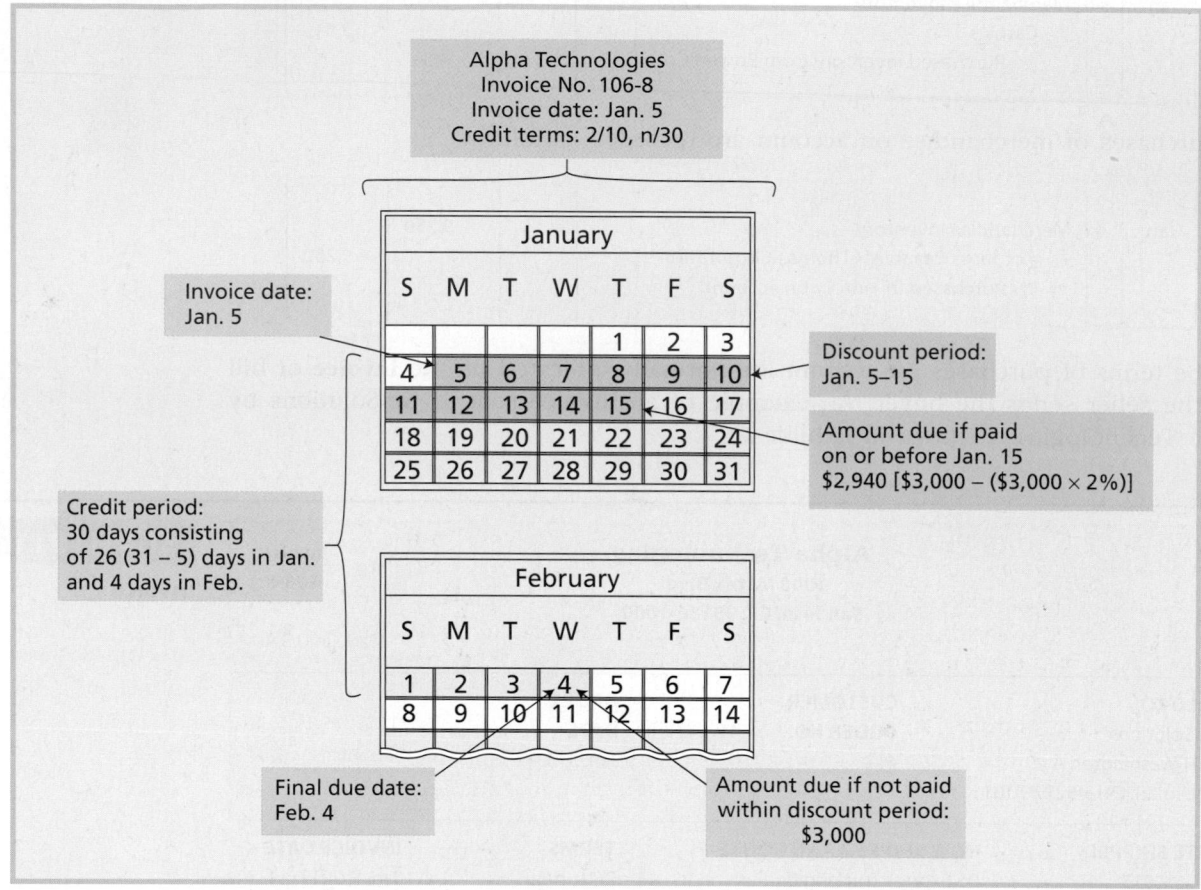

---

Discounts taken by the buyer for early payment of an invoice are called **purchases discounts**. Purchases discounts taken by a buyer reduce the cost of the merchandise purchased. Even if the buyer has to borrow to pay within a discount period, it is normally to the buyer's advantage to do so. For this reason, accounting systems are normally designed so that all available discounts are taken.

To illustrate, the invoice shown in Exhibit 2 is used. The last day of the discount period is January 15 (invoice date of January 5 plus 10 days). Assume that in order to pay the invoice on January 15, **NetSolutions** borrows $2,940, which is $3,000 less the discount of $60 ($3,000 × 2%). If an annual interest rate of 6% and a 360-day year is also assumed, the interest on the loan of $2,940 for the remaining 20 days of the credit period is $9.80 ($2,940 × 6% × 20 ÷ 360).[2]

The net savings to NetSolutions of taking the discount is $50.20, computed as follows:

| | |
|---|---:|
| Discount of 2% on $3,000 | $60.00 |
| Interest for 20 days at a rate of 6% on $2,940 | 9.80 |
| Savings from taking the discount | $50.20 |

The savings can also be seen by comparing the interest rate on the money *saved* by taking the discount and the interest rate on the money *borrowed* to take the

---

[2] To simplify computations and rounding, we use a 360-day year rather than a 365-year.

discount. The interest rate on the money saved in the prior example is estimated by converting 2% for 20 days to a yearly rate, as follows:

$$2\% \times \frac{360 \text{ days}}{20 \text{ days}} = 2\% \times 18 = 36\%$$

NetSolutions borrowed $2,940 at 6% to take the discount. If NetSolutions does not take the discount, it *pays* an estimated interest rate of 36% for using the $2,940 for the remaining 20 days of the credit period. Thus, buyers should normally take all available purchase discounts.

Since buyers normally take all purchases discounts, Merchandise Inventory is debited for the net purchase price under the perpetual inventory system. That is, the buyer debits Merchandise Inventory for the amount of the invoice less the discount.[3]

To illustrate, NetSolutions would record the Alpha Technologies invoice and its payment as follows:

| | | | | |
|---|---|---|---|---|
| Jan. | 5 | Merchandise Inventory | 2,940 | |
| | | Accounts Payable—Alpha Technologies | | 2,940 |
| | 15 | Accounts Payable—Alpha Technologies | 2,940 | |
| | | Cash | | 2,940 |

**Purchases Returns and Allowances** A buyer may request an allowance for merchandise that is returned (purchases return) or a price allowance (purchases allowance) for damaged or defective merchandise. From a buyer's perspective, such returns and allowances are called **purchases returns and allowances**. In both cases, the buyer normally sends the seller a debit memorandum to notify the seller of reasons for the return (purchase return) or to request a price reduction (purchase allowance).

A **debit memorandum**, often called a **debit memo**, is shown in Exhibit 4. A debit memo informs the seller of the amount the buyer proposes to *debit* to the account payable due the seller. It also states the reasons for the return or the request for the price allowance.

The buyer may use the debit memo as the basis for recording the return or allowance or wait for approval from the seller (creditor). In either case, the buyer debits Accounts Payable and credits Merchandise Inventory.

---

**NetSolutions**                                                   No. 18
5101 Washington Ave.
Cincinnati, OH 45227-5101

**DEBIT MEMO**

| **TO** | **DATE** |
|---|---|
| Maxim Systems | March 7, 2017 |
| 7519 East Wilson Ave. | |
| Seattle, WA 98101-7519 | |

**WE DEBITED YOUR ACCOUNT AS FOLLOWS**

| | | |
|---|---|---|
| 10 Server Network Interface Cards, your invoice No. 7291, are being returned via parcel post. Our order specified No. 825X. | @90.00 | 900.00 |

**EXHIBIT 4**

**Debit Memo**

---

[3] To simplify, we assume that all purchase discounts are taken.

To illustrate, **NetSolutions** records the return of the merchandise indicated in the debit memo in Exhibit 4 as follows:

| | | | | |
|---|---|---|---|---|
| Mar. | 7 | Accounts Payable—Maxim Systems | 900 | |
| | | Merchandise Inventory | | 900 |
| | | Debit Memo No. 18. | | |

Before paying an invoice, a buyer may return merchandise or be granted a price allowance for an invoice with a purchase discount. In this case, the amount of the return is recorded at its invoice amount less the discount.

To illustrate, assume the following data concerning a purchase of merchandise by NetSolutions on May 2:

May 2. Purchased $5,000 of merchandise on account from Delta Data Link, terms 2/10, n/30.

 4. Returned $1,000 of the merchandise purchased on May 2.

 12. Paid for the purchase of May 2 less the return and discount.

NetSolutions would record these transactions as follows:

| | | | | |
|---|---|---|---|---|
| May | 2 | Merchandise Inventory | 4,900 | |
| | | Accounts Payable—Delta Data Link | | 4,900 |
| | | Purchased merchandise. | | |
| | | [$5,000 – ($5,000 × 2%)] | | |
| | 4 | Accounts Payable—Delta Data Link | 980 | |
| | | Merchandise Inventory | | 980 |
| | | Returned portion of merch. purchased. | | |
| | | [$1,000 – ($1,000 × 2%)] | | |
| | 12 | Accounts Payable—Delta Data Link | 3,920 | |
| | | Cash | | 3,920 |
| | | ($4,900 – $980) | | |

## Example Exercise 6-2   Purchases Transactions                    OBJ 2

Rofles Company purchased merchandise on account from a supplier for $11,500, terms 2/10, n/30. Rofles Company returned $2,500 of the merchandise and received full credit.

a. If Rofles Company pays the invoice within the discount period, what is the amount of cash required for the payment?

b. Under a perpetual inventory system, what account is credited by Rofles Company to record the return?

## Follow My Example 6-2

a. $8,820. Purchase of $11,270 [$11,500 – ($11,500 × 2%)] less the return of $2,450 [$2,500 – ($2,500 × 2%)].

b. Merchandise Inventory

Practice Exercises: PE 6-2A, PE 6-2B

## Sales Transactions

Revenue from merchandise sales is usually recorded as *Sales*. Sometimes a business may use the title *Sales of Merchandise*.

**Cash Sales** A business may sell merchandise for cash. Cash sales are normally entered on a cash register and recorded in the accounts. To illustrate, assume that on March 3, **NetSolutions** sells merchandise for $1,800. These cash sales are recorded as follows:

| Journal | | | | | Page 25 |
|---|---|---|---|---|---|
| **Date** | | **Description** | **Post. Ref.** | **Debit** | **Credit** |
| 2017<br>Mar. | 3 | Cash | | 1,800 | |
| | |     Sales | | | 1,800 |
| | |         To record cash sales. | | | |

Using the perpetual inventory system, the cost of merchandise sold and the decrease in merchandise inventory are also recorded. In this way, the merchandise inventory account indicates the amount of merchandise on hand (not sold).

To illustrate, assume that the cost of merchandise sold on March 3 is $1,200. The entry to record the cost of merchandise sold and the decrease in the merchandise inventory is as follows:

| | | | | | |
|---|---|---|---|---|---|
| Mar. | 3 | Cost of Merchandise Sold | | 1,200 | |
| | |     Merchandise Inventory | | | 1,200 |
| | |         To record the cost of merchandise sold. | | | |

Sales may be made to customers using credit cards such as **MasterCard** or **VISA**. Such sales are recorded as cash sales. This is because these sales are normally processed by a clearinghouse that contacts the bank that issued the card. The issuing bank then electronically transfers cash directly to the retailer's bank account.[4] Thus, the retailer normally receives cash within a few days of making the credit card sale.

If customers use MasterCards to pay for their purchases, the sales would be recorded exactly as shown in the first March 3 entry illustrated in this section. Any processing fees charged by the clearinghouse or issuing bank are periodically recorded as an expense. This expense is normally reported on the income statement as an administrative expense. To illustrate, assume that NetSolutions paid credit card processing fees of $4,150 on March 31. These fees would be recorded as follows:

| | | | | | |
|---|---|---|---|---|---|
| Mar. | 31 | Credit Card Expense | | 4,150 | |
| | |     Cash | | | 4,150 |
| | |         To record service charges on credit<br>        card sales for the month. | | | |

Instead of using MasterCard or VISA, a customer may use a credit card that is not issued by a bank. For example, a customer might use an **American Express** card. If the seller uses a clearinghouse, the clearinghouse will collect the receivable and transfer the cash to the retailer's bank account, similar to the way it would have if the customer had used MasterCard or VISA. Large businesses, however, may not use a clearinghouse. In such cases, nonbank credit card sales must first be reported to the card company before cash is received. Thus, a receivable is created with the nonbank credit card company. However, because most retailers use clearinghouses to process both bank and nonbank credit cards, all credit card sales will be recorded as cash sales.

### Sales on Account

**Sales on Account** A business may sell merchandise on account. The seller records such sales as a debit to Accounts Receivable and a credit to Sales. An example of an entry for a **NetSolutions** sale on account of $18,000 follows. The cost of merchandise sold was $10,800.

A retailer may accept **MasterCard** or **VISA** but not **American Express**. Why? American Express Co.'s service fees are normally higher than MasterCard's or VISA's. As a result, some retailers choose not to accept American Express cards. The disadvantage of this practice is that the retailer may lose customers to competitors who do accept American Express cards.

---

[4] CyberSource is one of the major credit card clearinghouse. For a more detailed description of how credit card sales are processed, see the following CyberSource Web page: www.cybersource.com, click on Products & Services, click on Global Payment Services, and then click on Credit Card Processing.

| | | | | | |
|---|---|---|---|---|---|
| Mar. | 10 | Accounts Receivable—Digital Technologies | | 18,000 | |
| | | Sales | | | 18,000 |
| | | Invoice No. 7172. | | | |
| | | | | | |
| | 10 | Cost of Merchandise Sold | | 10,800 | |
| | | Merchandise Inventory | | | 10,800 |
| | | Cost of merch. sold on Invoice No. 7172. | | | |

**Customer Discounts** A seller may grant customers a variety of discounts, called **customer discounts**, as incentives to encourage customers to act in a way benefiting the seller. For example, a seller may offer customer discounts to encourage customers to purchase in volume or order early.

A common discount, called a **sales discount**, encourages customers to pay their invoice early. For example, a seller may offer credit terms of 2/10, n/30, which provides a 2% sales discount if the invoice is paid within 10 days. If not paid within 10 days, the total invoice amount is due within 30 days.[5]

To illustrate the accounting for sales discounts, assume that **NetSolutions** sold $18,000 of merchandise to Digital Technologies on March 10 with credit terms 2/10, n/30. The March 10 sale would be recorded as follows:[6]

| | | | | | |
|---|---|---|---|---|---|
| Mar. | 10 | Accounts Receivable—Digital Technologies | | 17,640 | |
| | | Sales [$18,000 – ($18,000 × 2%)] | | | 17,640 |

The sale to Digital Technologies is recorded by **NetSolutions** as $17,640, which is the invoice amount of $18,000 less the sales discount of $360 ($18,000 × 2%).[7]

The payment by Digital Technologies on March 19 is recorded as follows:[8]

| | | | | | |
|---|---|---|---|---|---|
| Mar. | 19 | Cash | | 17,640 | |
| | | Accounts Receivable—Digital Technologies | | | 17,640 |

**Customer Returns and Allowances** Merchandise sold may be returned to the seller (returns). In other cases, the seller may reduce the initial selling price (allowances). This might occur if the merchandise is defective, damaged during shipment, or does not meet the buyer's expectations. From a seller's perspective, these are termed **customer returns and allowances**, sometimes called *sales returns and allowances*.

To illustrate the accounting for customer returns and allowances, assume Schafer Co. had sales of $2,000,000 and related cost of merchandise sold of $1,400,000 for its first year of operations ending December 31, 2016. Schafer Co. provides customers a refund for any returned or damaged merchandise. At the end of the year, Schafer Co. estimates that customers will request refunds for 2% of sales and estimates that merchandise costing $25,000 will be returned.

On December 31, 2016, the following two adjusting journal entries must be recorded.[9]

| | | | | | |
|---|---|---|---|---|---|
| Dec. | 31 | Sales (2% × $2,000,000) | | 40,000 | |
| | | Customer Refunds Payable | | | 40,000 |
| | | | | | |
| | 31 | Estimated Returns Inventory | | 25,000 | 25,000 |
| | | Cost of Merchandise Sold | | | |

---

[5] From the buyer's perspective, a sales discount is referred to as a purchases discount, which was discussed earlier in this chapter.
[6] The accounting for customer discounts other than sales discounts is discussed in advanced accounting courses.
[7] This is consistent with *Revenue from Contracts with Customers, Topic 606, FASB Accounting Standards Update*, Financial Accounting Standards Board, Norwalk, CT, May 2014.
[8] To simplify, we assume buyers take all sales discounts.
[9] The accounting illustrated is based upon *Revenue from Contracts with Customers, Topic 606, FASB Accounting Standards Update*, Financial Accounting Standards Board, Norwalk, CT, May 2014.

The first adjusting entry reduces 2016 Sales by the amount of estimated refunds that may occur in 2017. Since 2% refunds are expected, Sales is debited for $40,000 (2% × $2,000,000). In addition, a liability is recorded for $40,000 by crediting Customer Refunds Payable for the estimated refunds expected to be paid in 2017.

The second adjusting entry debits the asset Estimated Returns Inventory for the $25,000 cost of the merchandise that is expected to be returned in 2017. In addition, Cost of Merchandise Sold is credited for $25,000 for the original cost recorded at the time of sale. The Estimated Returns Inventory account is used since the type of merchandise returned will not be known until the returns actually occur.

The preceding two adjusting entries ensure that current period sales are matched with the related cost of merchandise sold on the income statement. In addition, an asset for estimated returned inventory and a liability for customer refunds is reported on the balance sheet.

To continue the illustration, on January 15, 2017, Baker Company returned merchandise with a selling price of $3,000 for cash refund. The merchandise originally cost Schafer Co. $2,100.

Schafer Co. would record the return and refund with the following two entries.

| | | | | | |
|---|---|---|---|---|---|
| Jan. | 15 | Customer Refunds Payable | | 3,000 | |
| | | Cash | | | 3,000 |
| | 15 | Merchandise Inventory | | 2,100 | |
| | | Estimated Returns Inventory | | | 2,100 |

The first entry records the cash refund paid Baker Company of $3,000. The cash paid Baker also reduces the estimated liability for customer refunds payable. The second entry records the cost of the merchandise that was returned of $2,100. Since the type of merchandise is now known, Merchandise Inventory is debited and Estimated Returns Inventory is credited for $2,100.[10]

In some cases, a customer that is due a refund has an outstanding account receivable balance. In this case, the seller may credit the customer's accounts receivable rather than pay cash. When this is done, the seller normally sends the buyer a credit memorandum or credit memo indicating its intent to credit the customer's accounts receivable.

To illustrate, assume that Schafer Company issued the credit memo shown in Exhibit 5 to Blake & Sons. Exhibit 5 indicates that Schafer Company intends to credit Blake & Sons account receivable for $900 as an allowance for merchandise that was damaged in shipment. Blake & Sons has agreed to keep the merchandise and make any necessary repairs.

| Schafer Co. | No. 321 |
|---|---|
| 9004 Madison Road | |
| Bozeman, MT 59715 | |

**CREDIT MEMO**

| **TO** | **DATE** |
|---|---|
| Blake & Sons | March 4, 2017 |
| 7608 Melton Avenue | |
| Los Angeles, CA 90025-3942 | |

**WE CREDIT YOUR ACCOUNT AS FOLLOWS**

| Allowance for merchandise damaged in shipment | 900.00 |
|---|---|

**EXHIBIT 5**

**Credit Memo**

---

[10] Because of wear, tear, and damage, companies may segregate returned items from normal inventory by using a separate returns inventory account.

Schafer Co. would record issuance of the credit memo as follows:

| | | | | | |
|---|---|---|---|---|---|
| Mar. | 4 | Customer Refunds Payable | | 900 | |
| | | Accounts Receivable—Blake & Sons | | | 900 |

The preceding entry reduces the estimated liability Customer Refunds Payable, but credits Blake & Sons' accounts receivable instead of Cash. Since the merchandise was not returned, there is no need to record a second entry for merchandise inventory.

# Integrity, Objectivity, and Ethics in Business

### THE CASE OF THE FRAUDULENT PRICE TAGS

One of the challenges for a retailer is policing its sales return policy. There are many ways in which customers can unethically or illegally abuse such policies. In one case, a couple was accused of attaching Marshalls' store price tags to cheaper merchandise bought or obtained elsewhere. The couple then returned the cheaper goods and received the substantially higher refund amount. Company security officials discovered the fraud and had the couple arrested after they had allegedly bilked the company for more than $1 million.

## Example Exercise 6-3 Sales Transactions

Journalize the following merchandise transactions:

a. Sold merchandise on account, $7,500, with terms 2/10, n/30. The cost of the merchandise sold was $5,625.

b. Received payment less the discount.

### Follow My Example 6-3

| | | | |
|---|---|---|---|
| a. | Accounts Receivable [$7,500 – ($7,500 × 2%)] ........................... | 7,350 | |
| | Sales ..................................................................... | | 7,350 |
| | Cost of Merchandise Sold ................................................ | 5,625 | |
| | Merchandise Inventory ................................................... | | 5,625 |
| b. | Cash ...................................................................... | 7,350 | |
| | Accounts Receivable ..................................................... | | 7,350 |

Practice Exercises: PE 6-3A, PE 6-3B

## Freight

Purchases and sales of merchandise often involve freight. The terms of a sale indicate when ownership (title and control) of the merchandise passes from the seller to the buyer. This point determines whether the buyer or the seller pays the freight costs.[11]

**Note:**
The buyer bears the freight costs if the shipping terms are FOB shipping point.

The ownership of the merchandise may pass to the buyer when the seller delivers the merchandise to the freight carrier. In this case, the terms are said to be **FOB (free on board) shipping point**. This term means that the buyer pays the freight costs from the shipping point to the final destination. Such costs are part of the buyer's total cost of purchasing inventory and are added to the cost of the inventory by debiting Merchandise Inventory.

[11] The passage of title also determines whether the buyer or seller must pay other costs, such as the cost of insurance, while the merchandise is in transit.

To illustrate, assume that on June 10, **NetSolutions** purchased merchandise as follows:

June 10. Purchased merchandise from Magna Data, $900, terms FOB shipping point.
  10. Paid freight of $50 on June 10 purchase from Magna Data.

NetSolutions would record these two transactions as follows:

| | | | | |
|---|---|---|---|---|
| June | 10 | Merchandise Inventory | 900 | |
| | | Accounts Payable—Magna Data | | 900 |
| | | Purchased merchandise, terms FOB shipping point. | | |
| | 10 | Merchandise Inventory | 50 | |
| | | Cash | | 50 |
| | | Paid shipping cost on merchandise purchased. | | |

The ownership of the merchandise may pass to the buyer when the buyer receives the merchandise. In this case, the terms are said to be **FOB (free on board) destination**. This term means that the seller pays the freight costs from the shipping point to the buyer's final destination. When the seller pays the delivery charges, the seller debits Delivery Expense or Freight Out. Delivery Expense is reported on the seller's income statement as a selling expense.

To illustrate, assume that **NetSolutions** sells merchandise as follows:

June 15. Sold merchandise to Kranz Company on account, $700, terms FOB destination. The cost of the merchandise sold is $480.
  15. NetSolutions pays freight of $40 on the sale of June 15.

NetSolutions records the sale, the cost of the sale, and the freight cost as follows:

| | | | | |
|---|---|---|---|---|
| June | 15 | Accounts Receivable—Kranz Company | 700 | |
| | | Sales | | 700 |
| | | Sold merchandise, terms FOB destination. | | |
| | 15 | Cost of Merchandise Sold | 480 | |
| | | Merchandise Inventory | | 480 |
| | | Recorded cost of merchandise sold to Kranz Company. | | |
| | 15 | Delivery Expense | 40 | |
| | | Cash | | 40 |
| | | Paid shipping cost on merchandise sold. | | |

The seller may prepay the freight, even though the terms are FOB shipping point. The seller will then add the freight to the invoice. The buyer debits Merchandise Inventory for the total amount of the invoice, including the freight. Any discount terms would not apply to the prepaid freight.

To illustrate, assume that **NetSolutions** sells merchandise as follows:

June 20. Sold merchandise to Planter Company on account, $800, terms FOB shipping point. NetSolutions paid freight of $45, which was added to the invoice. The cost of the merchandise sold is $360.

**Note:**
The seller bears the freight costs if the shipping terms are FOB destination.

Sometimes FOB shipping point and FOB destination are expressed in terms of a specific location at which the title to the merchandise passes to the buyer. For example, if **Toyota Motor Corporation**'s assembly plant in Osaka, Japan, sells automobiles to a dealer in Chicago, FOB shipping point is expressed as FOB Osaka. Likewise, FOB destination is expressed as FOB Chicago.

NetSolutions records the sale, the cost of the sale, and the freight as follows:

| | | | | | |
|---|---|---|---|---|---|
| June | 20 | Accounts Receivable—Planter Company | | 800 | |
| | | Sales | | | 800 |
| | | Sold merchandise, terms FOB shipping point. | | | |
| | | | | | |
| | 20 | Cost of Merchandise Sold | | 360 | |
| | | Merchandise Inventory | | | 360 |
| | | Recorded cost of merchandise sold to | | | |
| | | Planter Company. | | | |
| | | | | | |
| | 20 | Accounts Receivable—Planter Company | | 45 | |
| | | Cash | | | 45 |
| | | Prepaid shipping cost on merchandise sold. | | | |

Shipping terms, the passage of title (control), and whether the buyer or seller is to pay the freight costs are summarized in Exhibit 6.

---

**EXHIBIT 6**     **Freight Terms**

**Example Exercise 6-4 Freight Terms**

Determine the amount to be paid in full settlement of each of the two invoices, (a) and (b), assuming that credit for returns and allowances was received prior to payment and that all invoices were paid within the discount period.

| | Merchandise | Freight Paid by Seller | Freight Terms | Returns and Allowances |
|---|---|---|---|---|
| a. | $4,500 | $200 | FOB shipping point, 1/10, n/30 | $ 800 |
| b. | 5,000 | 60 | FOB destination, 2/10, n/30 | 2,500 |

**Follow My Example 6-4**

a. $3,863. Purchase of $4,455 [$4,500 – ($4,500 × 1%)] less return of $792 [$800 – ($800 × 1%)] plus $200 of shipping.

b. $2,450. Purchase of $4,900 [$5,000 – ($5,000 × 2%)] less return of $2,450 [$2,500 – ($2,500 × 2%)].

Practice Exercises: PE 6-4A, PE 6-4B

## Summary: Recording Merchandise Inventory Transactions

Recording merchandise inventory transactions under the perpetual inventory system has been described and illustrated in the preceding sections. These transactions involved purchases, purchases returns and allowances, freight, cost of merchandise sold (from sales), and customer returns. Exhibit 7 summarizes how these transactions are recorded in T account form.

**EXHIBIT 7**

Recording Merchandise Inventory Transactions

**Merchandise Inventory**

| Purchases (net of discounts) | XXX | Purchases returns and allowances (net of discounts) | XXX |
| Freight for merchandise purchased FOB shipping point | XXX | Cost of merchandise sold | XXX |
| Customer returns | XXX | | |

**Estimated Returns Inventory**

| Adjusting entry for estimated customer returns | XXX | Customer returns | XXX |

**Cost of Merchandise Sold**

| Cost of merchandise sold | XXX | Adjusting entry for estimated customer returns | XXX |

## Dual Nature of Merchandise Transactions

Each merchandising transaction affects a buyer and a seller. In the illustration shown in Exhibit 8, the same transactions for a seller and buyer are recorded. In Exhibit 8, the seller is Scully Company and the buyer is Burton Co.

| EXHIBIT 8 | Illustration of Merchandise Inventory Transactions for Seller and Buyer |

| Transaction | Scully Company (Seller) | | Burton Co. (Buyer) | |
|---|---|---|---|---|
| **July 1.** Scully Company sold merchandise on account to Burton Co., $7,500, terms FOB shipping point, n/45. The cost of the merchandise sold was $4,500. | Accounts Receivable—Burton Co. ...     Sales............................ <br><br> Cost of Merchandise Sold..........     Merchandise Inventory.......... | 7,500 <br> 7,500 <br><br> 4,500 <br> 4,500 | Merchandise Inventory ...........     Accounts Payable—Scully Co. ... | 7,500 <br> 7,500 |
| **July 2.** Burton Co. paid freight of $150 on July 1 purchase from Scully Company. | No journal entry. | | Merchandise Inventory ...........     Cash........................... | 150 <br> 150 |
| **July 5.** Scully Company sold merchandise on account to Burton Co., $5,000, terms FOB destination, n/30. The cost of the merchandise sold was $3,500. | Accounts Receivable—Burton Co. ...     Sales............................ <br><br> Cost of Merchandise Sold..........     Merchandise Inventory.......... | 5,000 <br> 5,000 <br><br> 3,500 <br> 3,500 | Merchandise Inventory ...........     Accounts Payable—Scully Co. ... | 5,000 <br> 5,000 |
| **July 7.** Scully Company paid freight of $250 for delivery of merchandise sold to Burton Co. on July 5. | Delivery Expense ..................     Cash............................ | 250 <br> 250 | No journal entry. | |
| **July 15.** Scully Company received payment from Burton Co. for purchase of July 5. | Cash ..............................     Accounts Receivable—Burton Co. | 5,000 <br> 5,000 | Accounts Payable—Scully Co. .....     Cash........................... | 5,000 <br> 5,000 |
| **July 18.** Scully Company sold merchandise on account to Burton Co.,$12,000, terms FOB shipping point, 2/10, n/eom. Scully Company prepaid freight of $500, which was added to the invoice. The cost of the merchandise sold was $7,200. | Accounts Receivable—Burton Co. ...     Sales............................ <br><br> Accounts Receivable—Burton Co. ...     Cash............................ <br><br> Cost of Merchandise Sold..........     Merchandise Inventory.......... | 11,760 <br> 11,760 <br><br> 500 <br> 500 <br><br> 7,200 <br> 7,200 | Merchandise Inventory ...........     Accounts Payable—Scully Co. ... | 12,260 <br> 12,260 |
| **July 28.** Scully Company received payment from Burton Co. for purchase of July 18. | Cash ..............................     Accounts Receivable—Burton Co. | 12,260 <br> 12,260 | Accounts Payable—Scully Co. .....     Cash........................... | 12,260 <br> 12,260 |

## Example Exercise 6-5  Transactions for Buyer and Seller

Sievert Co. sold merchandise to Bray Co. on account, $11,500, terms 2/15, n/30. The cost of the merchandise sold is $6,900. Journalize the entries for Sievert Co. and Bray Co. for the sale, purchase, and payment of amount due.

### Follow My Example 6-5

Sievert Co. journal entries:

| | | |
|---|---|---|
| Accounts Receivable [$11,500 – ($11,500 × 2%)] | 11,270 | |
| Sales | | 11,270 |
| Cost of Merchandise Sold | 6,900 | |
| Merchandise Inventory | | 6,900 |
| Cash | 11,270 | |
| Accounts Receivable—Bray Co. | | 11,270 |

Bray Co. journal entries:

| | | |
|---|---|---|
| Merchandise Inventory [$11,500 – ($11,500 × 2%)] | 11,270 | |
| Accounts Payable | | 11,270 |
| Accounts Payable—Sievert Co. | 11,270 | |
| Cash | | 11,270 |

Practice Exercises: PE 6-5A, PE 6-5B

## Chart of Accounts for a Merchandising Business

The chart of accounts for a merchandising business should reflect the types of merchandise transactions described and illustrated earlier in this chapter. The chart of accounts for **NetSolutions** is shown in Exhibit 9. The accounts related to merchandising transactions are highlighted.[12]

| Balance Sheet Accounts | Income Statement Accounts |
|---|---|
| **100 Assets** | **400 Revenues** |
| 110  Cash | 410  Sales |
| 112  Accounts Receivable | **500 Costs and Expenses** |
| 115  Merchandise Inventory | 510  Cost of Merchandise Sold |
| 116  Office Supplies | 520  Sales Salaries Expense |
| 117  Prepaid Insurance | 521  Advertising Expense |
| 120  Land | 522  Depreciation Expense— |
| 123  Store Equipment | Store Equipment |
| 124  Accumulated Depreciation— | 523  Delivery Expense |
| Store Equipment | 529  Miscellaneous Selling Expense |
| 125  Office Equipment | 530  Office Salaries Expense |
| 126  Accumulated Depreciation— | 531  Rent Expense |
| Office Equipment | 532  Depreciation Expense— |
| | Office Equipment |
| **200 Liabilities** | 533  Insurance Expense |
| 210  Accounts Payable | 534  Office Supplies Expense |
| 211  Salaries Payable | 539  Misc. Administrative Expense |
| 212  Unearned Rent | **600 Other Income** |
| 215  Notes Payable | 610  Rent Revenue |
| **300 Owner's Equity** | **700 Other Expense** |
| 310  Chris Clark, Capital | 710  Interest Expense |
| 311  Chris Clark, Drawing | |
| 312  Income Summary | |

**EXHIBIT 9**

**Chart of Accounts for NetSolutions, a Merchandising Business**

[12] To simplify, we assume NetSolutions does not accept customer returns and allowances.

As shown in Exhibit 9, NetSolutions' chart of accounts consists of three-digit account numbers. The first digit indicates the major financial statement classification (1 for assets, 2 for liabilities, and so on). The second digit indicates the subclassification (e.g., 11 for current assets, 12 for noncurrent assets, etc.). The third digit identifies the specific account (e.g., 110 for Cash, 123 for Store Equipment, etc.). Using a three-digit numbering system makes it easier to add new accounts as they are needed.

## Sales Taxes and Trade Discounts

Sales of merchandise often involve sales taxes. Also, the seller may offer buyers trade discounts.

**Sales Taxes** Almost all states levy a tax on sales of merchandise.[13] The liability for the sales tax is incurred when the sale is made.

At the time of a cash sale, the seller collects the sales tax. When a sale is made on account, the seller charges the tax to the buyer by debiting Accounts Receivable. The seller credits the sales account for the amount of the sale and credits the tax to Sales Tax Payable. For example, the seller would record a sale of $100 on account, subject to a tax of 6%, as follows:

| | | | | | |
|---|---|---|---|---|---|
| Aug. | 12 | Accounts Receivable—Lemon Co. | | 106 | |
| | | Sales | | | 100 |
| | | Sales Tax Payable | | | 6 |
| | | Invoice No. 339. | | | |

On a regular basis, the seller pays to the taxing authority (state) the amount of the sales tax collected. The seller records such a payment as follows:

| | | | | | |
|---|---|---|---|---|---|
| Sept. | 15 | Sales Tax Payable | | 2,900 | |
| | | Cash | | | 2,900 |
| | | Payment for sales taxes collected | | | |
| | | during August. | | | |

## Business Connection

### SALES TAXES

While there is no federal sales tax, most states have enacted statewide sales taxes. In addition, many states allow counties and cities to collect a "local option" sales tax. Delaware, Montana, New Hampshire, and Oregon have no state or local sales taxes. Tennessee (9.45%), Washington (8.8%), and Louisiana (8.75%) have the highest average combined rates (including state and local option taxes). Several towns in Tuscaloosa County, Alabama, have the highest combined rates in the United States of 11%, while Chicago, Illinois, has the highest combined city rate of 10.25%.

What about companies that sell merchandise through the Internet? The general rule is that if the company ships merchandise to a customer in a state where the company does not have a physical location, no sales tax is due. For example, a customer in Montana who purchases merchandise online from a New York retailer (and no physical location in Montana) does not have to pay sales tax to either Montana or New York.

Source: The Sales Tax Clearinghouse at www.thestc.com/FAQ.stm.

**Trade Discounts** Wholesalers are companies that sell merchandise to other businesses rather than to the public. Many wholesalers publish sales catalogs. Rather than updating their catalogs, wholesalers may publish price updates. These updates may include large discounts from the catalog list prices. In addition, wholesalers often offer

[13] Businesses that purchase merchandise for resale to others are normally exempt from paying sales taxes on their purchases. Only final buyers of merchandise normally pay sales taxes.

special discounts to government agencies or businesses that order large quantities. Such discounts are called **trade discounts**.

Sellers and buyers do not normally record the list prices of merchandise and trade discounts in their accounts. For example, assume that an item has a list price of $1,000 and a 40% trade discount. The seller records the sale of the item at $600 [$1,000 less the trade discount of $400 ($1,000 × 40%)]. Likewise, the buyer records the purchase at $600.

# Financial Statements for a Merchandising Business

Although merchandising transactions affect the balance sheet in reporting inventory, they primarily affect the income statement. An income statement for a merchandising business is normally prepared using either a multiple-step or single-step format.

OBJ **3** Describe and illustrate the financial statements of a merchandising business.

## Multiple-Step Income Statement

The 2017 income statement for **NetSolutions** is shown in Exhibit 10.[14] This form of income statement, called a **multiple-step income statement**, contains several sections, subsections, and subtotals.

| NetSolutions Income Statement For the Year Ended December 31, 2017 | | | |
|---|---:|---:|---:|
| Sales | | | $708,255 |
| Cost of merchandise sold | | | 525,305 |
| Gross profit | | | $182,950 |
| Operating expenses: | | | |
| Selling expenses: | | | |
| Sales salaries expense | $53,430 | | |
| Advertising expense | 10,860 | | |
| Depreciation expense—store equipment | 3,100 | | |
| Delivery expense | 2,800 | | |
| Miscellaneous selling expense | 630 | | |
| Total selling expenses | | $ 70,820 | |
| Administrative expenses: | | | |
| Office salaries expense | $21,020 | | |
| Rent expense | 8,100 | | |
| Depreciation expense—office equipment | 2,490 | | |
| Insurance expense | 1,910 | | |
| Office supplies expense | 610 | | |
| Miscellaneous administrative expense | 760 | | |
| Total administrative expenses | | 34,890 | |
| Total operating expenses | | | 105,710 |
| Income from operations | | | $ 77,240 |
| Other income and expense: | | | |
| Rent revenue | | $ 600 | |
| Interest expense | | (2,440) | (1,840) |
| Net income | | | $ 75,400 |

**EXHIBIT 10**

**Multiple-Step Income Statement**

[14] The NetSolutions income statement for 2017 is used because it allows a better illustration of the computation of the cost of merchandise sold in the appendix to this chapter.

**Sales** The total amount of sales to customers for cash and on account is reported in this section. NetSolutions reported sales of $708,255 for the year ended December 31, 2017.

**Cost of Merchandise Sold** As shown in Exhibit 10, NetSolutions reported cost of merchandise sold of $525,305 during 2017. This amount is the cost of merchandise sold to customers. Cost of merchandise sold may also be reported as *cost of goods sold* or *cost of sales*.

**Gross Profit** The excess of sales over cost of merchandise sold is gross profit. As shown in Exhibit 10, NetSolutions reported gross profit of $182,950 in 2017.

**Income from Operations** **Income from operations**, sometimes called *operating income*, is determined by subtracting operating expenses from gross profit. Operating expenses are normally classified as either selling expenses or administrative expenses.

 For many merchandising businesses, the cost of merchandise sold is usually the largest expense. For example, the approximate percentage of cost of merchandise sold to sales is 64% for **JCPenney** and 66% for **The Home Depot**.

**Selling expenses** are incurred directly in the selling of merchandise. Examples of selling expenses include sales salaries, store supplies used, depreciation of store equipment, delivery expense, and advertising.

**Administrative expenses**, sometimes called **general expenses**, are incurred in the administration or general operations of the business. Examples of administrative expenses include office salaries, depreciation of office equipment, and office supplies used.

Each selling and administrative expense may be reported separately as shown in Exhibit 10. However, many companies report selling, administrative, and operating expenses as single line items, as follows for NetSolutions:

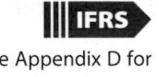 See Appendix D for more information.

| | | |
|---|---:|---:|
| Gross profit | | $182,950 |
| Operating expenses: | | |
| Selling expenses | $70,820 | |
| Administrative expenses | 34,890 | |
| Total operating expenses | | 105,710 |
| Income from operations | | $ 77,240 |

**Other Income and Expense** Other income and expense items are not related to the primary operations of the business. **Other income** is revenue from sources other than the primary operating activity of a business. Examples of other income include income from interest, rent, and gains resulting from the sale of fixed assets. **Other expense** is an expense that cannot be traced directly to the normal operations of the business. Examples of other expenses include interest expense and losses from disposing of fixed assets.

Other income and other expense are offset against each other on the income statement. If the total of other income exceeds the total of other expense, the difference is added to income from operations to determine net income. If the reverse is true, the difference is subtracted from income from operations. The other income and expense items of NetSolutions are reported as follows and in Exhibit 10:

| | | |
|---|---:|---:|
| Income from operations | | $77,240 |
| Other income and expense: | | |
| Rent revenue | $ 600 | |
| Interest expense | (2,440) | (1,840) |
| Net income | | $75,400 |

## Single-Step Income Statement

An alternate form of income statement is the **single-step income statement**. As shown in Exhibit 11, the income statement for **NetSolutions** deducts the total of all expenses *in one step* from the total of all revenues.

The single-step form emphasizes total revenues and total expenses in determining net income. A criticism of the single-step form is that gross profit and income from operations are not reported.

| NetSolutions<br>Income Statement<br>For the Year Ended December 31, 2017 | | |
|---|---:|---:|
| Revenues: | | |
| Sales | | $708,255 |
| Rent revenue | | 600 |
| Total revenues | | $708,855 |
| Expenses: | | |
| Cost of merchandise sold | $525,305 | |
| Selling expenses | 70,820 | |
| Administrative expenses | 34,890 | |
| Interest expense | 2,440 | |
| Total expenses | | 633,455 |
| Net income | | $ 75,400 |

**EXHIBIT 11**

**Single-Step Income Statement**

## Statement of Owner's Equity

The statement of owner's equity for **NetSolutions** is shown in Exhibit 12. This statement is prepared in the same manner as for a service business.

| NetSolutions<br>Statement of Owner's Equity<br>For the Year Ended December 31, 2017 | | |
|---|---:|---:|
| Chris Clark, capital, January 1, 2017 | | $153,800 |
| Net income for the year | $75,400 | |
| Less withdrawals | 18,000 | |
| Increase in owner's equity | | 57,400 |
| Chris Clark, capital, December 31, 2017 | | $211,200 |

**EXHIBIT 12**

**Statement of Owner's Equity for Merchandising Business**

## Balance Sheet

The balance sheet may be presented with assets on the left-hand side and the liabilities and owner's equity on the right-hand side. This form of the balance sheet is called the **account form.** The balance sheet may also be presented in a downward sequence in three sections. This form of balance sheet is called the **report form.** The report form of balance sheet for **NetSolutions** is shown in Exhibit 13. In Exhibit 13, merchandise inventory is reported as a current asset and the current portion of the note payable of $5,000 is reported as a current liability.

**EXHIBIT 13**

**Report Form of Balance Sheet**

| NetSolutions<br>Balance Sheet<br>December 31, 2017 | | | |
|---|---|---|---|
| **Assets** | | | |
| Current assets: | | | |
| Cash.......................................... | | $52,950 | |
| Accounts receivable ........................... | | 91,080 | |
| Merchandise inventory ........................ | | 62,150 | |
| Office supplies .................................. | | 480 | |
| Prepaid insurance ............................. | | 2,650 | |
| Total current assets......................... | | | $209,310 |
| Property, plant, and equipment: | | | |
| Land ........................................... | | $20,000 | |
| Store equipment .............................. | $27,100 | | |
| Less accumulated depreciation............... | 5,700 | 21,400 | |
| Office equipment................................ | $15,570 | | |
| Less accumulated depreciation............... | 4,720 | 10,850 | |
| Total property, plant, and equipment....... | | | 52,250 |
| Total assets ........................................ | | | $261,560 |
| **Liabilities** | | | |
| Current liabilities: | | | |
| Accounts payable .............................. | | $22,420 | |
| Note payable (current portion) ................... | | 5,000 | |
| Salaries payable................................. | | 1,140 | |
| Unearned rent ................................. | | 1,800 | |
| Total current liabilities....................... | | | $ 30,360 |
| Long-term liabilities: | | | |
| Note payable (final payment due in ten years) ..... | | | 20,000 |
| Total liabilities ...................................... | | | $ 50,360 |
| **Owner's Equity** | | | |
| Chris Clark, capital .................................. | | | 211,200 |
| Total liabilities and owner's equity................... | | | $261,560 |

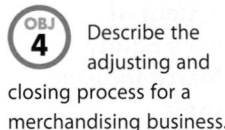

OBJ **4**   Describe the adjusting and closing process for a merchandising business.

# The Adjusting and Closing Process

Thus far, the recording of transactions, chart of accounts, and financial statements for a merchandising business (NetSolutions) have been described and illustrated. In the remainder of this chapter, the adjusting and closing process for a merchandising business will be described. In this discussion, the focus will be on the elements of the accounting cycle that differ from those of a service business.

## Adjusting Entry for Inventory Shrinkage

Under the perpetual inventory system, the merchandise inventory account is continually updated for purchase and sales transactions. As a result, the balance of the merchandise inventory account is the amount of merchandise available for sale at that point in time. However, retailers normally experience some loss of inventory due to shoplifting, employee theft, or errors. Thus, the physical inventory on hand at the end of the accounting period is usually less than the balance of Merchandise Inventory. This difference is called **inventory shrinkage** or **inventory shortage**.

To illustrate, **NetSolutions'** inventory records indicate the following on December 31, 2017:

| | |
|---|---|
| Account balance of Merchandise Inventory | $63,950 |
| Physical merchandise inventory on hand | 62,150 |
| Inventory shrinkage | $ 1,800 |

At the end of the accounting period, inventory shrinkage is recorded by the following adjusting entry:

| | | | | |
|---|---|---|---|---|
| | | Adjusting Entry | | |
| Dec. | 31 | Cost of Merchandise Sold | 1,800 | |
| | | Merchandise Inventory | | 1,800 |
| | | Inventory shrinkage ($63,950 – $62,150). | | |

After the preceding entry is recorded, the balance of Merchandise Inventory agrees with the physical inventory on hand at the end of the period. Since inventory shrinkage cannot be totally eliminated, it is considered a normal cost of operations. If, however, the amount of the shrinkage is unusually large, it may be disclosed separately on the income statement. In such cases, the shrinkage may be recorded in a separate account, such as Loss from Merchandise Inventory Shrinkage.

# Integrity, Objectivity, and Ethics in Business

### THE COST OF EMPLOYEE THEFT

One survey reported that the 24 largest U.S. retail store chains have lost more than $6 billion to shoplifting and employee theft. The stores apprehended over 1 million shoplifters and dishonest employees and recovered more than $161 million from these thieves. Approximately 1 out of every 36 employees was apprehended for theft from his or her employer. Each dishonest employee stole approximately 6 times the amount stolen by shoplifters ($665.77 versus $113.30).

Source: Jack L. Hayes International, 24th Annual Retail Theft Survey, 2012.

## Example Exercise 6-6   Inventory Shrinkage

OBJ 4

Pulmonary Company's perpetual inventory records indicate that $382,800 of merchandise should be on hand on March 31, 2016. The physical inventory indicates that $371,250 of merchandise is actually on hand. Journalize the adjusting entry for the inventory shrinkage for Pulmonary Company for the year ended March 31, 2016. Assume that the inventory shrinkage is a normal amount.

## Follow My Example 6-6

| | | | |
|---|---|---|---|
| Mar. 31 | Cost of Merchandise Sold ..................................... | 11,550 | |
| | Merchandise Inventory......................................... | | 11,550 |
| | Inventory shrinkage ($382,800 – $371,250). | | |

Practice Exercises: PE 6-6A, PE 6-6B

# Closing Entries

The closing entries for a merchandising business are similar to those for a service business. The four closing entries for a merchandising business are as follows:

1. Debit each temporary account with a credit balance, such as Sales, for its balance and credit Income Summary.
2. Credit each temporary account with a debit balance, such as the various expenses, and debit Income Summary. Since Cost of Merchandise Sold is a temporary account with a debit balance, it is credited for its balance.

3. Debit Income Summary for the amount of its balance (net income) and credit the owner's capital account. The accounts debited and credited are reversed if there is a net loss.

4. Debit the owner's capital account for the balance of the drawing account and credit the drawing account.

The four closing entries for **NetSolutions** follow:

| | | **Journal** | | | *Page 29* |
|---|---|---|---|---|---|
| **Date** | | **Item** | **Post. Ref.** | **Debit** | **Credit** |
| 2017 | | Closing Entries | | | |
| Dec. | 31 | Sales | 410 | 708,255 | |
| | | Rent Revenue | 610 | 600 | |
| | | Income Summary | 312 | | 708,855 |
| | | | | | |
| | 31 | Income Summary | 312 | 633,455 | |
| | | Cost of Merchandise Sold | 510 | | 525,305 |
| | | Sales Salaries Expense | 520 | | 53,430 |
| | | Advertising Expense | 521 | | 10,860 |
| | | Depr. Expense—Store Equipment | 522 | | 3,100 |
| | | Delivery Expense | 523 | | 2,800 |
| | | Miscellaneous Selling Expense | 529 | | 630 |
| | | Office Salaries Expense | 530 | | 21,020 |
| | | Rent Expense | 531 | | 8,100 |
| | | Depr. Expense—Office Equipment | 532 | | 2,490 |
| | | Insurance Expense | 533 | | 1,910 |
| | | Office Supplies Expense | 534 | | 610 |
| | | Misc. Administrative Expense | 539 | | 760 |
| | | Interest Expense | 710 | | 2,440 |
| | | | | | |
| | 31 | Income Summary | 312 | 75,400 | |
| | | Chris Clark, Capital | 310 | | 75,400 |
| | | | | | |
| | 31 | Chris Clark, Capital | 310 | 18,000 | |
| | | Chris Clark, Drawing | 311 | | 18,000 |

NetSolutions' income summary account after the closing entries have been posted is as follows:

| **Account** *Income Summary* | | | | | | | **Account No.** *312* |
|---|---|---|---|---|---|---|---|
| | | | **Post. Ref.** | | | **Balance** | |
| **Date** | | **Item** | | **Debit** | **Credit** | **Debit** | **Credit** |
| 2017 | | | | | | | |
| Dec. | 31 | Revenues | 29 | | 708,855 | | 708,855 |
| | 31 | Expenses | 29 | 633,455 | | | 75,400 |
| | 31 | Net income | 29 | 75,400 | | — | — |

After the closing entries are posted to the accounts, a post-closing trial balance is prepared. The only accounts that should appear on the post-closing trial balance are the asset, contra asset, liability, and owner's capital accounts with balances. These are the same accounts that appear on the end-of-period balance sheet. If the two totals of the trial balance columns are not equal, an error has occurred that must be found and corrected.

# Financial Analysis and Interpretation: Ratio of Sales to Assets

OBJ 5

Describe and illustrate the use of the ratio of sales to assets in evaluating a company's operating performance.

The **ratio of sales to assets** measures how effectively a business is using its assets to generate sales. A high ratio indicates an effective use of assets. The assets used in computing the ratio may be the total assets at the end of the year, the average of the total assets at the beginning and end of the year, or the average of the monthly assets. For our purposes, the average of the total assets at the beginning and end of the year is used.

The ratio of sales to assets is computed as follows:

$$\text{Ratio of Sales to Assets} = \frac{\text{Sales}}{\text{Average Total Assets}}$$

To illustrate the use of this ratio, the following data (in millions) were taken from recent annual reports of Dollar Tree, Inc.:

|  | Year 2 | Year 1 |
|---|---|---|
| Total revenues (sales) | $6,631 | $5,882 |
| Total assets: |  |  |
| Beginning of year | 2,381 | 2,290 |
| End of year | 2,328 | 2,381 |

The ratios of sales to assets for each year are as follows:

|  | Year 2 | Year 1 |
|---|---|---|
| Ratio of sales to assets* | 2.82 | 2.52 |
|  | $6,631 ÷ [($2,381 + $2,328) ÷ 2] | $5,882 ÷ [($2,290 + $2,381) ÷ 2] |

*Rounded to two decimal places.

Based on the preceding ratios, Dollar Tree improved its ratio of sales to assets from 2.52 in Year 1 to 2.82 in Year 2. Thus, Dollar Tree improved the utilization of its assets to generate sales in Year 2.

Using the ratio of sales to assets for comparisons to competitors and with industry averages could also be beneficial in interpreting Dollar Tree's use of its assets. For example, the following data (in millions) were taken from recent annual reports of Dollar General Corporation:

|  | Year 2 |
|---|---|
| Total revenues (sales) | $14,807 |
| Total assets: |  |
| Beginning of year | 9,546 |
| End of year | 9,689 |

Dollar General's ratio of sales to assets for Year 2 is as follows:

|  | Year 2 |
|---|---|
| Ratio of sales to assets* | 1.54 |
|  | $14,807 ÷ [($9,546 + $9,689) ÷ 2] |

*Rounded to two decimal places.

Comparing Dollar General's Year 2 ratio of 1.54 to Dollar Tree's Year 2 ratio of 2.82 implies that Dollar Tree is using its assets more efficiently than is Dollar General.

## Example Exercise 6-7 Ratio of Sales to Assets
OBJ 5

Financial statement data for the years ending December 31, 2016 and 2015, for Gilbert Company follow:

|  | 2016 | 2015 |
|---|---|---|
| Sales | $1,305,000 | $962,500 |
| Total assets: |  |  |
| Beginning of year | 840,000 | 700,000 |
| End of year | 900,000 | 840,000 |

a. Determine the ratio of sales to assets for 2016 and 2015.

b. Does the change in the ratio of sales to assets from 2015 to 2016 indicate a favorable or an unfavorable trend?

## Follow My Example 6-7

a.

|  | 2016 | 2015 |
|---|---|---|
| Ratio of sales to assets | 1.50 | 1.25 |
|  | $1,305,000 ÷ [($840,000 + $900,000) ÷ 2] | $962,500 ÷ [($700,000 + $840,000) ÷ 2] |

b. The change from 1.25 to 1.50 indicates a favorable trend in using assets to generate sales.

Practice Exercises: PE 6-7A, PE 6-7B

# A P P E N D I X

# The Periodic Inventory System

Throughout this chapter, the perpetual inventory system was used to record purchases and sales of merchandise. Not all merchandise businesses, however, use the perpetual inventory system. For example, small merchandise businesses, such as a local hardware store, may use a manual accounting system. A manual perpetual inventory system is time consuming and costly to maintain. In this case, the periodic inventory system may be used.

Under the periodic inventory system, purchases are normally recorded at their invoice amount. If the invoice is paid within the discount period, the discount is recorded in a separate account called Purchases Discounts. Likewise, purchases returns are recorded in a separate account called Purchases Returns and Allowances.

## Chart of Accounts Under the Periodic Inventory System

The chart of accounts for **NetSolutions** under a periodic inventory system is shown in Exhibit 14. The accounts used to record transactions under the periodic inventory system are highlighted in Exhibit 14.

| Balance Sheet Accounts | Income Statement Accounts |
|---|---|
| **100 Assets** | **400 Revenues** |
| 110 Cash | 410 Sales |
| 111 Notes Receivable | **500 Costs and Expenses** |
| 112 Accounts Receivable | 510 Purchases |
| 115 Merchandise Inventory | 511 Purchases Returns and |
| 116 Office Supplies |     Allowances |
| 117 Prepaid Insurance | 512 Purchases Discounts |
| 120 Land | 513 Freight In |
| 123 Store Equipment | 520 Sales Salaries Expense |
| 124 Accumulated Depreciation— | 521 Advertising Expense |
|     Store Equipment | 522 Depreciation Expense— |
| 125 Office Equipment |     Store Equipment |
| 126 Accumulated Depreciation— | 523 Delivery Expense |
|     Office Equipment | 529 Miscellaneous Selling Expense |
| **200 Liabilities** | 530 Office Salaries Expense |
| 210 Accounts Payable | 531 Rent Expense |
| 211 Salaries Payable | 532 Depreciation Expense— |
| 212 Unearned Rent |     Office Equipment |
| 215 Notes Payable | 533 Insurance Expense |
| | 534 Office Supplies Expense |
| **300 Owner's Equity** | 539 Misc. Administrative Expense |
| 310 Chris Clark, Capital | **600 Other Income** |
| 311 Chris Clark, Drawing | 610 Rent Revenue |
| 312 Income Summary | **700 Other Expense** |
| | 710 Interest Expense |

**EXHIBIT 14**

**Chart of Accounts Under the Periodic Inventory System**

## Recording Merchandise Transactions Under the Periodic Inventory System

Using the periodic inventory system, purchases of inventory are not recorded in the merchandise inventory account. Instead, purchases, purchases discounts, and purchases returns and allowances accounts are used. In addition, the sales of merchandise are not recorded in the inventory account. Thus, there is no detailed record of the amount of inventory on hand at any given time. At the end of the period, a physical count of merchandise inventory on hand is taken. This physical count is used to determine the cost of merchandise sold as will be illustrated later.

The use of purchases, purchases discounts, purchases returns and allowances, and freight in accounts are described in this section.

**Purchases** Purchases of inventory are recorded in a purchases account rather than in the merchandise inventory account. Purchases is debited for the invoice amount of a purchase.

**Purchases Discounts** Purchases discounts are normally recorded in a separate purchases discounts account. The balance of the purchases discounts account is reported as a deduction from Purchases for the period. Thus, Purchases Discounts is a contra (or offsetting) account to Purchases.

**Purchases Returns and Allowances** Purchases returns and allowances are recorded in a similar manner as purchases discounts. A separate purchases returns and allowances account is used to record returns and allowances. Purchases returns and allowances are reported as a deduction from Purchases for the period. Thus, Purchases Returns and Allowances is a contra (or offsetting) account to Purchases.

**Freight In** When merchandise is purchased FOB shipping point, the buyer pays for the freight. Under the periodic inventory system, freight paid when purchasing merchandise FOB shipping point is debited to Freight In, Transportation In, or a similar account.

The preceding periodic inventory accounts and their effect on the cost of merchandise purchased are summarized as follows:

| Account | Entry to Increase | Normal Balance | Effect on Cost of Merchandise Purchased |
|---|---|---|---|
| Purchases | Debit | Debit | Increases |
| Purchases Discounts | Credit | Credit | Decreases |
| Purchases Returns and Allowances | Credit | Credit | Decreases |
| Freight In | Debit | Debit | Increases |

Exhibit 15 illustrates the recording of merchandise transactions using the periodic system.

## Adjusting Process Under the Periodic Inventory System

The adjusting process is the same under the periodic and perpetual inventory systems except for the inventory shrinkage adjustment. The ending merchandise inventory is determined by a physical count under both systems.

Under the perpetual inventory system, the ending inventory physical count is compared to the balance of Merchandise Inventory. The difference is the amount of inventory shrinkage. The inventory shrinkage is then recorded as a debit to Cost of Merchandise Sold and a credit to Merchandise Inventory.

Under the periodic inventory system, the merchandise inventory account is not kept up to date for purchases and sales. As a result, the inventory shrinkage cannot be directly determined. Instead, any inventory shrinkage is included indirectly in the computation of the cost of merchandise sold as shown in Exhibit 14. This is a major disadvantage of the periodic inventory system. That is, under the periodic inventory system, inventory shrinkage is not separately determined.

When the periodic inventory system is used, the cost of merchandise sold is determined as shown in Exhibit 16.

| Transaction | Periodic Inventory System | | |
|---|---|---|---|
| **June 5.** Purchased $30,000 of merchandise on account, terms 2/10, n/30. | Purchases . . . . . . . . . . . . . . . . . . . . . . Accounts Payable . . . . . . . . . . | 30,000 | 30,000 |
| **June 8.** Returned merchandise purchased on account on June 5, $500. | Accounts Payable . . . . . . . . . . . . . . Purchases Returns and Allowances . . . . . . . . . . . . . . | 500 | 500 |
| **June 15.** Paid for purchase of June 5, less return of $500 and discount of $590 [($30,000 – $500) × 2%]. | Accounts Payable . . . . . . . . . . . . . . Cash . . . . . . . . . . . . . . . . . . . . . . Purchases Discounts . . . . . . . . | 29,500 | 28,910 590 |
| **June 18.** Sold merchandise on account, $12,500, 1/10, n/30. The cost of the merchandise sold was $9,000. | Accounts Receivable [$12,500 – ($12,500 × 1%)] . . . . . . . . . . . . Sales . . . . . . . . . . . . . . . . . . . . . . | 12,375 | 12,375 |
| **June 22.** Purchased merchandise, $15,000, terms FOB shipping point, 2/15, n/30, with prepaid freight of $750 added to the invoice. | Purchases . . . . . . . . . . . . . . . . . . . . . . Freight In . . . . . . . . . . . . . . . . . . . . . Accounts Payable . . . . . . . . . . | 15,000 750 | 15,750 |
| **June 28.** Received payment on account from June 18 sale | Cash . . . . . . . . . . . . . . . . . . . . . . . . Accounts Receivable . . . . . . . . | 12,375 | 12,375 |
| **June 29.** Received $19,600 from cash sales. The cost of the merchandise sold was $13,800. | Cash . . . . . . . . . . . . . . . . . . . . . . . . Sales . . . . . . . . . . . . . . . . . . . . . . | 19,600 | 19,600 |

**EXHIBIT 15**

**Transactions Using the Periodic Inventory System**

# Financial Statements Under the Periodic Inventory System

The financial statements are similar under the perpetual and periodic inventory systems. When the multiple-step format of income statement is used, the cost of merchandise sold may be reported as shown in Exhibit 16.

| | | | |
|---|---|---|---|
| Merchandise Inventory, January 1, 2017 . . . . . . . . . . . . . . . . . . . . . . | | | $ 59,700 |
| Purchases . . . . . . . . . . . . . . . . . . . . . . . . . . . . . . . . . . . . . . . . . . . . | | $521,980 | |
| Less: Purchases returns and allowances . . . . . . . . . . . . . . . . . . . . . | $9,100 | | |
| Purchases discounts . . . . . . . . . . . . . . . . . . . . . . . . . . . . . . . . | 2,525 | 11,625 | |
| Net purchases . . . . . . . . . . . . . . . . . . . . . . . . . . . . . . . . . . . . . . . . . . | | $510,355 | |
| Add freight in . . . . . . . . . . . . . . . . . . . . . . . . . . . . . . . . . . . . . . . . . | | 17,400 | |
| Cost of merchandise purchased . . . . . . . . . . . . . . . . . . . . . . . . . | | | 527,755 |
| Merchandise available for sale . . . . . . . . . . . . . . . . . . . . . . . . . . . . . | | | $587,455 |
| Less merchandise inventory, December 31, 2017 . . . . . . . . . . . . . | | | 62,150 |
| Cost of merchandise sold . . . . . . . . . . . . . . . . . . . . . . . . . . . . . . . . . | | | $525,305 |

**EXHIBIT 16**

**Determining Cost of Merchandise Sold Using the Periodic System**

# Closing Entries Under the Periodic Inventory System

The closing entries differ in the periodic inventory system in that there is no cost of merchandise sold account to close to Income Summary. Instead, the purchases,

purchases discounts, purchases returns and allowances, and freight in accounts are closed to Income Summary. In addition, the merchandise inventory account is adjusted to the end-of-period physical inventory count during the closing process.

The four closing entries under the periodic inventory system are as follows:

1. Debit each temporary account with a credit balance, such as Sales, for its balance and credit Income Summary. Since Purchases Discounts and Purchases Returns and Allowances are temporary accounts with credit balances, they are debited for their balances. In addition, Merchandise Inventory is debited for its end-of-period balance based on the end-of-period physical inventory.

2. Credit each temporary account with a debit balance, such as the various expenses, and debit Income Summary. Since Freight In is a temporary account with a debit balance, it is credited for its balance. In addition, Merchandise Inventory is credited for its balance as of the beginning of the period.

3. Debit Income Summary for the amount of its balance (net income) and credit the owner's capital account. The accounts debited and credited are reversed if there is a net loss.

4. Debit the owner's capital account for the balance of the drawing account and credit the drawing account.

The four closing entries for **NetSolutions** under the periodic inventory system follow:

| Journal | | | | | |
|---|---|---|---|---|---|
| **Date** | | **Item** | **Post. Ref.** | **Debit** | **Credit** |
| 2017 | | Closing Entries | | | |
| Dec. | 31 | Merchandise Inventory | 115 | 62,150 | |
| | | Sales | 410 | 708,255 | |
| | | Purchases Returns and Allowances | 511 | 9,100 | |
| | | Purchases Discounts | 512 | 2,525 | |
| | | Rent Revenue | 610 | 600 | |
| | | Income Summary | 312 | | 782,630 |
| | | | | | |
| | 31 | Income Summary | 312 | 707,230 | |
| | | Merchandise Inventory | 115 | | 59,700 |
| | | Purchases | 510 | | 521,980 |
| | | Freight In | 513 | | 17,400 |
| | | Sales Salaries Expense | 520 | | 53,430 |
| | | Advertising Expense | 521 | | 10,860 |
| | | Depreciation Expense—Store Equipment | 522 | | 3,100 |
| | | Delivery Expense | 523 | | 2,800 |
| | | Miscellaneous Selling Expense | 529 | | 630 |
| | | Office Salaries Expense | 530 | | 21,020 |
| | | Rent Expense | 531 | | 8,100 |
| | | Depreciation Expense—Office Equipment | 532 | | 2,490 |
| | | Insurance Expense | 533 | | 1,910 |
| | | Office Supplies Expense | 534 | | 610 |
| | | Miscellaneous Administrative Expense | 539 | | 760 |
| | | Interest Expense | 710 | | 2,440 |
| | | | | | |
| | 31 | Income Summary | 312 | 75,400 | |
| | | Chris Clark, Capital | 310 | | 75,400 |
| | | | | | |
| | 31 | Chris Clark, Capital | 310 | 18,000 | |
| | | Chris Clark, Drawing | 311 | | 18,000 |

In the first closing entry, Merchandise Inventory is debited for $62,150. This is the ending physical inventory count on December 31, 2017. In the second closing entry, Merchandise Inventory is credited for its January 1, 2017, balance of $59,700. In this way, the closing entries highlight the importance of the beginning and ending balances of Merchandise Inventory in determining the cost of merchandise sold, as shown in Exhibit 16. After the closing entries are posted, Merchandise Inventory will have a balance of $62,150. This is the amount reported on the December 31, 2017, balance sheet.

In the preceding closing entries, the periodic accounts are highlighted. Under the perpetual inventory system, the highlighted periodic inventory accounts are replaced by the cost of merchandise sold account.

# At a Glance 6

**OBJ 1**

### Distinguish between the activities and financial statements of service and merchandising businesses.

**Key Points**   Merchandising businesses purchase merchandise for selling to customers. On a merchandising business's income statement, revenue from selling merchandise is reported as sales. The cost of the merchandise sold is subtracted from sales to arrive at gross profit. The operating expenses are subtracted from gross profit to arrive at net income. Merchandise inventory, which is merchandise not sold, is reported as a current asset on the balance sheet.

| Learning Outcomes | Example Exercises | Practice Exercises |
|---|---|---|
| • Describe how the activities of a service and a merchandising business differ. | | |
| • Describe the differences between the income statements of a service and a merchandising business. | | |
| • Compute gross profit. | EE6-1 | PE6-1A, 6-1B |
| • Describe how merchandise inventory is reported on the balance sheet. | | |

**Key Points**    Purchases of merchandise for cash or on account are recorded as merchandise inventory. Discounts for early payment of purchases on account are purchases discounts. Purchases of merchandise inventory subject to purchase discounts are recorded net of the discount. Price adjustments or returned merchandise are purchases returns. Price adjustments or returned merchandise are recorded net of any purchase discount.

Sales of merchandise for cash or on account are recorded as sales. The cost of merchandise sold and the reduction in merchandise inventory are also recorded at the time of sale.

A seller may grant customers a variety of discounts, called customer discounts. A sales discount encourages customer to pay their invoice early. Sales subject to a sales discount are recorded net of the discount.

A seller may pay a customer a refund or grant a price allowance for returned or damaged merchandise, called customer returns and allowances. At the end of the accounting period, a seller must record two adjusting entries for expected returns and allowances. The first adjusting entry debits Sales and credits Customer Refunds Payable. The second entry debits Estimated Returns Inventory and credits Cost of Merchandise Sold. When merchandise is returned for a refund, Customer Refunds Payable is debited and Cash is credited for the amount of the refund. The returned merchandise is recorded as a debit to Merchandise Inventory and credit to Estimated Returns Inventory. When a customer doesn't return merchandise, but is granted an allowance Customer Refunds Payable is debited and either Cash, if the customer has already paid for the merchandise, or Account Receivable is credited.

When merchandise is shipped FOB shipping point, the buyer pays the freight and debits Merchandise Inventory. When merchandise is shipped FOB destination, the seller pays the freight and debits Delivery Expense or Freight Out. Merchandise transactions can be summarized in T account form as shown in Exhibit 7. Each merchandising transaction affects a buyer and a seller. The chart of accounts for a merchandising business (NetSolutions) is shown in Exhibit 9. The liability for sales tax is incurred when the sale is made and is recorded by the seller as a credit to the sales tax payable account. Trade discounts are discounts off the list price of merchandise.

| Learning Outcomes | Example Exercises | Practice Exercises |
|---|---|---|
| • Prepare journal entries to record the purchases of merchandise for cash. | | |
| • Prepare journal entries to record the purchases of merchandise on account. | EE6-2 | PE6-2A, 6-2B |
| • Prepare journal entries to record purchases discounts and purchases returns and allowances. | EE6-2 | PE6-2A, 6-2B |
| • Prepare journal entries to record sales of merchandise for cash or using a credit card. | | |
| • Prepare journal entries to record sales of merchandise on account. | EE6-3 | PE6-3A, 6-3B |
| • Prepare journal entries to record sales discounts and customer returns and allowances. | EE6-3 | PE6-3A, 6-3B |
| • Prepare journal entries for freight from the point of view of the buyer and seller. | | |
| • Determine the total cost of the purchase of merchandise under differing freight terms. | EE6-4 | PE6-4A, 6-4B |
| • Record the same merchandise transactions for the buyer and seller. | EE6-5 | PE6-5A, 6-5B |
| • Prepare a chart of accounts for a merchandising business. | | |
| • Determine the cost of merchandise purchased when a trade discount is offered by the seller. | | |
| • Record sales transactions involving sales taxes and trade discounts. | | |

**Describe and illustrate the financial statements of a merchandising business.**

**Key Points** The multiple-step income statement of a merchandiser reports sales. The cost of the merchandise sold is subtracted from sales to determine the gross profit. Operating income is determined by subtracting selling and administrative expenses from gross profit. Net income is determined by adding or subtracting the net of other income and expense. The income statement may also be reported in a single-step form.

The statement of owner's equity is similar to that for a service business.

The balance sheet reports merchandise inventory at the end of the period as a current asset.

| Learning Outcomes | Example Exercises | Practice Exercises |
|---|---|---|
| • Prepare a multiple-step income statement for a merchandising business. | | |
| • Prepare a single-step income statement. | | |
| • Prepare a statement of owner's equity for a merchandising business. | | |
| • Prepare a report form of balance sheet for a merchandising business. | | |

**Describe the adjusting and closing process for a merchandising business.**

**Key Points** The normal adjusting entry for inventory shrinkage is to debit Cost of Merchandise Sold and credit Merchandise Inventory.

The closing entries for a merchandising business are similar to those for a service business except that the cost of merchandise sold is also closed to Income Summary.

| Learning Outcomes | Example Exercises | Practice Exercises |
|---|---|---|
| • Prepare the adjusting journal entry for inventory shrinkage. | EE6-6 | PE6-6A, 6-6B |
| • Prepare the closing entries for a merchandising business. | | |

**Describe and illustrate the use of the ratio of sales to assets in evaluating a company's operating performance.**

**Key Points** The ratio of sales to assets measures how effectively a business is using its assets to generate sales. A high ratio indicates an effective use of assets. Using the average of the total assets at the beginning and end of the year, the ratio is computed as follows:

$$\text{Ratio of Sales to Assets} = \frac{\text{Sales}}{\text{Average Total Assets}}$$

| Learning Outcomes | Example Exercises | Practice Exercises |
|---|---|---|
| • Interpret a high ratio of sales to assets. | | |
| • Compute the ratio of sales to assets. | EE6-7 | PE6-7A, 6-7B |

## Key Terms

account form (283)

administrative expenses (general expenses) (282)

cost of merchandise sold (265)

credit memorandum (credit memo) (273)

credit period (267)

credit terms (267)

customer discounts (272)

customer returns and allowances (272)

debit memorandum (debit memo) (269)

FOB (free on board) destination (275)

FOB (free on board) shipping point (274)

gross profit (265)

income from operations (operating income) (282)

inventory shrinkage (inventory shortage) (284)

invoice (267)

merchandise inventory (265)

multiple-step income statement (281)

operating cycle (264)

other expense (282)

other income (282)

periodic inventory system (266)

perpetual inventory system (266)

physical inventory (266)

purchases discounts (268)

purchases returns and allowances (269)

ratio of sales to assets (287)

report form (283)

sales (265)

sales discounts (272)

selling expenses (282)

single-step income statement (283)

trade discounts (281)

## Illustrative Problem

The following transactions were completed by Montrose Company during May of the current year. Montrose Company uses a perpetual inventory system.

May  3.  Purchased merchandise on account from Floyd Co., $4,000, terms FOB shipping point, 2/10, n/30, with prepaid freight of $120 added to the invoice.

5.  Purchased merchandise on account from Kramer Co., $8,500, terms FOB destination, 1/10, n/30.

6.  Sold merchandise on account to C. F. Howell Co., list price $4,000, trade discount 30%, terms 2/10, n/30. The cost of the merchandise sold was $1,125.

8.  Purchased office supplies for cash, $150.

10.  Returned merchandise purchased on May 5 from Kramer Co., $1,300.

13.  Paid Floyd Co. on account for purchase of May 3.

14.  Purchased merchandise for cash, $10,500.

15.  Paid Kramer Co. on account for purchase of May 5, less return of May 10.

16.  Received cash on account from sale of May 6 to C. F. Howell Co.

19.  Sold merchandise on MasterCard credit cards, $2,450. The cost of the merchandise sold was $980.

22.  Sold merchandise for cash to Comer Co., $3,480. The cost of the merchandise sold was $1,400.

24.  Sold merchandise on account to Smith Co., $4,350. The cost of the merchandise sold was $1,750.

25.  Refunded Comer Co. $1,480 for returned merchandise from sale on May 22. The cost of the returned merchandise was $600.

31.  Paid a service processing fee of $140 for MasterCard sales.

## Instructions

1. Journalize the preceding transactions.

2. Journalize the adjusting entry for merchandise inventory shrinkage, $3,750.

## Solution

| | | | | | |
|---|---|---|---|---|---|
| 1. | May | 3 | Merchandise Inventory [$4,000 – ($4,000 × 2%)] + $120 | 4,040 | |
| | | | Accounts Payable—Floyd Co. | | 4,040 |
| | | 5 | Merchandise Inventory [$8,500 – ($8,500 × 1%)] | 8,415 | |
| | | | Accounts Payable—Kramer Co. | | 8,415 |
| | | 6 | Accounts Receivable—C. F. Howell Co. | 2,744 | |
| | | | Sales | | 2,744 |
| | | | [$4,000 – (30% × $4,000)] = $2,800 | | |
| | | | [$2,800 – ($2,800 × 2%)] = $2,744 | | |
| | | 6 | Cost of Merchandise Sold | 1,125 | |
| | | | Merchandise Inventory | | 1,125 |
| | | 8 | Office Supplies | 150 | |
| | | | Cash | | 150 |
| | | 10 | Accounts Payable—Kramer Co. [$1,300 – ($1,300 × 1%)] | 1,287 | |
| | | | Merchandise Inventory | | 1,300 |
| | | 13 | Accounts Payable—Floyd Co. | 4,040 | |
| | | | Cash | | 4,040 |
| | | 14 | Merchandise Inventory | 10,500 | |
| | | | Cash | | 10,500 |
| | | 15 | Accounts Payable—Kramer Co. ($8,415 – $1,287) | 7,128 | |
| | | | Cash | | 7,128 |
| | | 16 | Cash | 2,744 | |
| | | | Accounts Receivable—C. F. Howell Co. | | 2,744 |
| | | 19 | Cash | 2,450 | |
| | | | Sales | | 2,450 |
| | | 19 | Cost of Merchandise Sold | 980 | |
| | | | Merchandise Inventory | | 980 |
| | | 22 | Cash | 3,480 | |
| | | | Sales | | 3,480 |
| | | 22 | Cost of Merchandise Sold | 1,400 | |
| | | | Merchandise Inventory | | 1,400 |
| | | 24 | Accounts Receivable—Smith Co. | 4,350 | |
| | | | Sales | | 4,350 |
| | | 24 | Cost of Merchandise Sold | 1,750 | |
| | | | Merchandise Inventory | | 1,750 |
| | | 25 | Customers Refunds Payable | 1,480 | |
| | | | Cash | | 1,480 |
| | | 25 | Merchandise Inventory | 600 | |
| | | | Estimated Returns Inventory | | 600 |
| | | 31 | Credit Card Expense | 140 | |
| | | | Cash | | 140 |
| 2. | May | 31 | Cost of Merchandise Sold | 3,750 | |
| | | | Merchandise Inventory | | 3,750 |
| | | | Inventory shrinkage. | | |

# Discussion Questions

1. What distinguishes a merchandising business from a service business?

2. Can a business earn a gross profit but incur a net loss? Explain.

3. The credit period during which the buyer of merchandise is allowed to pay usually begins with what date?

4. What is the meaning of (a) 1/15, n/60; (b) n/30; (c) n/eom?

5. How are sales to customers using MasterCard and VISA recorded?

6. What is the nature of (a) a credit memo issued by the seller of merchandise, (b) a debit memo issued by the buyer of merchandise?

7. Who bears the freight when the terms of sale are (a) FOB shipping point, (b) FOB destination?

8. Name three accounts that would normally appear in the chart of accounts of a merchandising business but would not appear in the chart of accounts of a service business.

9. Audio Outfitter Inc., which uses a perpetual inventory system, experienced a normal inventory shrinkage of $13,675. What accounts would be debited and credited to record the adjustment for the inventory shrinkage at the end of the accounting period?

10. Assume that Audio Outfitter Inc. in Discussion Question 9 experienced an abnormal inventory shrinkage of $98,600. Audio Outfitter Inc. has decided to record the abnormal inventory shrinkage so that it would be separately disclosed on the income statement. What account would be debited for the abnormal inventory shrinkage?

# Practice Exercises

EE 6-1 *p. 266*   **PE 6-1A   Gross profit**                                  OBJ. 1

During the current year, merchandise is sold for $615,000 cash and $4,110,000 on account. The cost of the merchandise sold is $2,835,000. What is the amount of the gross profit?

EE 6-1 *p. 266*   **PE 6-1B   Gross profit**                                  OBJ. 1

During the current year, merchandise is sold for $18,300 cash and $295,700 on account. The cost of the merchandise sold is $188,000. What is the amount of the gross profit?

EE 6-2 *p. 270*   **PE 6-2A   Purchases transactions**                        OBJ. 2

Halibut Company purchased merchandise on account from a supplier for $18,600, terms 2/10, n/30. Halibut Company returned $5,000 of the merchandise and received full credit.

a. If Halibut Company pays the invoice within the discount period, what is the amount of cash required for the payment?

b. What account is credited by Halibut Company to record the return?

EE 6-2 *p. 270*   **PE 6-2B   Purchases transactions**                        OBJ. 2

Hoffman Company purchased merchandise on account from a supplier for $65,000, terms 1/10, n/30. Hoffman Company returned $7,500 of the merchandise and received full credit.

a. If Hoffman Company pays the invoice within the discount period, what is the amount of cash required for the payment?

b. What account is debited by Hoffman Company to record the return?

SHOW
ME HOW

EE 6-3 *p. 274*

SHOW
ME HOW

**PE 6-3A Sales transactions** OBJ. 2

Journalize the following merchandise transactions:

a. Sold merchandise on account, $72,500 with terms 2/10, n/30. The cost of the merchandise sold was $43,500.

b. Received payment less the discount.

EE 6-3 *p. 274*

SHOW
ME HOW

**PE 6-3B Sales transactions** OBJ. 2

Journalize the following merchandise transactions:

a. Sold merchandise on account, $92,500 with terms 1/10, n/30. The cost of the merchandise sold was $55,500.

b. Received payment less the discount.

EE 6-4 *p. 277*

SHOW
ME HOW

**PE 6-4A Freight terms** OBJ. 2

Determine the amount to be paid in full settlement of each of two invoices, (a) and (b), assuming that credit for returns and allowances was received prior to payment and that all invoices were paid within the discount period.

| | Merchandise | Freight Paid by Seller | Freight Terms | Returns and Allowances |
|---|---|---|---|---|
| a. | $ 90,000 | $1,000 | FOB shipping point, 1/10, n/30 | $15,000 |
| b. | 110,000 | 1,575 | FOB destination, 2/10, n/30 | 8,500 |

EE 6-4 *p. 277*

SHOW
ME HOW

**PE 6-4B Freight terms** OBJ. 2

Determine the amount to be paid in full settlement of each of two invoices, (a) and (b), assuming that credit for returns and allowances was received prior to payment and that all invoices were paid within the discount period.

| | Merchandise | Freight Paid by Seller | Freight Terms | Returns and Allowances |
|---|---|---|---|---|
| a. | $36,000 | $800 | FOB destination, 1/10, n/30 | $4,000 |
| b. | 44,900 | 375 | FOB shipping point, 2/10, n/30 | 2,400 |

EE 6-5 *p. 279*

SHOW
ME HOW

**PE 6-5A Transactions for buyer and seller** OBJ. 2

Sather Co. sold merchandise to Boone Co. on account, $31,800, terms 2/15, n/30. The cost of the merchandise sold is $19,000. Journalize the entries for Sather Co. and Boone Co. for the sale, purchase, and payment of amount due.

EE 6-5 *p. 279*

SHOW
ME HOW

**PE 6-5B Transactions for buyer and seller** OBJ. 2

Shore Co. sold merchandise to Blue Star Co. on account, $112,000, terms FOB shipping point, 2/10, n/30. The cost of the merchandise sold is $67,200. Shore Co. paid freight of $1,800. Journalize the entries for Shore Co. and Blue Star Co. for the sale, purchase, and payment of amount due.

EE 6-6 *p. 285*

SHOW
ME HOW

**PE 6-6A Inventory shrinkage** OBJ. 4

Castle Furnishings Company's perpetual inventory records indicate that $675,400 of merchandise should be on hand on November 30, 2016. The physical inventory indicates that $663,800 of merchandise is actually on hand. Journalize the adjusting entry for the inventory shrinkage for Castle Furnishings Company for the year ended November 30, 2016. Assume that the inventory shrinkage is a normal amount.

EE 6-6 *p. 285*

SHOW
ME HOW

### PE 6-6B Inventory shrinkage

OBJ. 4

Hahn Flooring Company's perpetual inventory records indicate that $1,333,150 of merchandise should be on hand on December 31, 2016. The physical inventory indicates that $1,309,900 of merchandise is actually on hand. Journalize the adjusting entry for the inventory shrinkage for Hahn Flooring Company for the year ended December 31, 2016. Assume that the inventory shrinkage is a normal amount.

EE 6-7 *p. 288*

SHOW
ME HOW

### PE 6-7A Ratio of sales to assets

OBJ. 5

Financial statement data for years ending December 31 for Latchkey Company follows:

|  | 2016 | 2015 |
| --- | --- | --- |
| Sales | $1,734,000 | $1,645,000 |
| Total assets: |  |  |
| Beginning of year | 480,000 | 460,000 |
| End of year | 540,000 | 480,000 |

a. Determine the ratio of sales to assets for 2016 and 2015.

b. ⟶ Does the change in the ratio of sales to assets from 2015 to 2016 indicate a favorable or an unfavorable trend?

EE 6-7 *p. 288*

SHOW
ME HOW

### PE 6-7B Ratio of sales to assets

OBJ. 5

Financial statement data for years ending December 31 for Edison Company follows:

|  | 2016 | 2015 |
| --- | --- | --- |
| Sales | $1,884,000 | $1,562,000 |
| Total assets: |  |  |
| Beginning of year | 770,000 | 650,000 |
| End of year | 800,000 | 770,000 |

a. Determine the ratio of sales to assets for 2016 and 2015.

b. ⟶ Does the change in the ratio of sales to assets from 2015 to 2016 indicate a favorable or an unfavorable trend?

## Exercises

### EX 6-1 Determining gross profit

OBJ. 1

During the current year, merchandise is sold for $4,885,000. The cost of the merchandise sold is $3,028,700.

a. What is the amount of the gross profit?

b. Compute the gross profit percentage (gross profit divided by sales).

c. ⟶ Will the income statement necessarily report a net income? Explain.

### EX 6-2 Determining cost of merchandise sold

OBJ. 1

For a recent year, Best Buy reported sales of $50,705 million. Its gross profit was $12,573 million. What was the amount of Best Buy's cost of merchandise sold?

SHOW
ME HOW

### EX 6-3 Purchase-related transactions

OBJ. 2

The Stationery Company purchased merchandise on account from a supplier for $28,900, terms 1/10, n/30. The Stationery Company returned $6,100 of the merchandise and received full credit.

a. What is the amount of cash required for the payment?

b. Under a perpetual inventory system, what account is credited by The Stationery Company to record the return?

---

### EX 6-4 Purchase-related transactions OBJ. 2

A retailer is considering the purchase of 250 units of a specific item from either of two suppliers. Their offers are as follows:

Supplier One: $400 a unit, total of $100,000, 1/10, n/30, no charge for freight.

Supplier Two: $399 a unit, total of $99,750, 2/10, n/30, plus freight of $975.

Which of the two offers, Supplier One or Supplier Two, yields the lower price?

---

### EX 6-5 Purchase-related transactions OBJ. 2

The debits and credits from four related transactions are presented in the following T accounts. Describe each transaction.

| Cash | | | | Accounts Payable | | | |
|---|---|---|---|---|---|---|---|
| | | (2) | 300 | (3) | 3,920 | (1) | 20,580 |
| | | (4) | 16,660 | (4) | 16,660 | | |

| Merchandise Inventory | | | |
|---|---|---|---|
| (1) | 20,580 | (3) | 3,920 |
| (2) | 300 | | |

---

### EX 6-6 Purchase-related transactions OBJ. 2

✔ (c) Cash, cr. $64,680

SHOW
ME HOW

Warwick's Co., a women's clothing store, purchased $75,000 of merchandise from a supplier on account, terms FOB destination, 2/10, n/30. Warwick's returned $9,000 of the merchandise, receiving a credit memo, and then paid the amount due within the discount period. Journalize Warwick's entries to record (a) the purchase, (b) the merchandise return, and (c) the payment.

---

### EX 6-7 Purchase-related transactions OBJ. 2

✔ (e) Cash, dr. $1,425

SHOW
ME HOW

Journalize entries for the following related transactions of South Coast Heating & Air Company:

a. Purchased $48,000 of merchandise from Atlas Co. on account, terms 1/10, n/30.

b. Paid the amount owed on the invoice within the discount period.

c. Discovered that $7,500 of the merchandise purchased in (a) was defective and returned items, receiving credit.

d. Purchased $6,000 of merchandise from Atlas Co. on account, terms n/30.

e. Received a refund from Atlas Co. for return in (c) less the purchase in (d).

---

### EX 6-8 Sales-related transactions, including the use of credit cards OBJ. 2

SHOW
ME HOW

Journalize the entries for the following transactions:

a. Sold merchandise for cash, $30,000. The cost of the merchandise sold was $18,000.

b. Sold merchandise on account, $258,000. The cost of the merchandise sold was $154,800.

c. Sold merchandise to customers who used MasterCard and VISA, $160,000. The cost of the merchandise sold was $96,000.

d. Sold merchandise to customers who used American Express, $72,000. The cost of the merchandise sold was $43,200.

e. Received an invoice from National Clearing House Credit Co. for $8,800, representing a service fee paid for processing MasterCard, VISA, and American Express sales.

### EX 6-9 Customer returns and allowances

**OBJ. 2**

Zell Company had sales of $1,800,000 and related cost of merchandise sold of $1,150,000 for its first year of operations ending December 31, 2016. Zell Company provides customers a refund for any returned or damaged merchandise. At the end of the year, Zell Company estimates that customers will request refunds for 1.5% of sales and estimates that merchandise costing $16,000 will be returned. Assume that on February 3, 2017 Anderson Co. returned merchandise with a selling price of $5,000 for a cash refund. The returned merchandise originally cost Zell Company $3,100. (a) Journalize the adjusting entries on December 31, 2016 to record the expected customer returns. (b) Journalize the entries to record the returned merchandise and cash refund to Anderson Co.

### EX 6-10 Sales-related transactions

**OBJ. 2**

SHOW
ME HOW

After the amount due on a sale of $28,000, terms 2/10, n/eom, is received from a customer within the discount period, the seller consents to the return of the entire shipment for a cash refund. The cost of the merchandise returned was $16,800. (a) What is the amount of the refund owed to the customer? (b) Journalize the entries made by the seller to record the return and the refund.

### EX 6-11 Sales-related transactions

**OBJ. 2**

The debits and credits for three related transactions are presented in the following T accounts. Describe each transaction.

| | Cash | | | Sales | |
|---|---|---|---|---|---|
| (5) | 39,200 | | | (1) | 41,160 |

| | Accounts Receivable | | | | Cost of Merchandise Sold | |
|---|---|---|---|---|---|---|
| (1) | 41,160 | (3) | 1,960 | (2) | 25,200 | |
| | | (5) | 39,200 | | | |

| | Merchandise Inventory | | |
|---|---|---|---|
| (4) | 1,200 | (2) | 25,200 |

| | Estimated Returns Inventory | |
|---|---|---|
| | | (4) | 1,200 |

| | Customer Refunds Payable | |
|---|---|---|
| (3) | 1,960 | |

### EX 6-12 Sales-related transactions

**OBJ. 2**

✔ c. $57,470

SHOW
ME HOW

Merchandise is sold on account to a customer for $56,500, terms FOB shipping point, 2/10, n/30. The seller paid the freight of $2,100. Determine the following: (a) amount of the sale, (b) amount debited to Accounts Receivable, and (c) amount received within the discount period.

### EX 6-13 Determining amounts to be paid on invoices

**OBJ. 2**

✔ a. $22,500

SHOW
ME HOW

Determine the amount to be paid in full settlement of each of the following invoices, assuming that credit for returns and allowances was received prior to payment and that all invoices were paid within the discount period:

| | Merchandise | Freight Paid by Seller | | Customer Returns and Allowances |
|---|---|---|---|---|
| a. | $27,000 | — | FOB destination, n/30 | $4,500 |
| b. | 18,600 | $475 | FOB shipping point, 2/10, n/30 | 3,000 |
| c. | 8,400 | — | FOB shipping point, 1/10, n/30 | 700 |
| d. | 48,300 | 900 | FOB shipping point, 2/10, n/30 | 6,500 |
| e. | 33,000 | — | FOB destination, 1/10, n/30 | — |

### EX 6-14  Sales-related transactions

Showcase Co., a furniture wholesaler, sells merchandise to Balboa Co. on account, $254,500, terms n/30. The cost of the merchandise sold is $152,700. Showcase Co. issues a credit memo for $30,000 for merchandise returned prior to Balboa Co. paying the original invoice. The cost of the merchandise returned is $17,500. Journalize Showcase Co.'s entries for (a) the sale, including the cost of the merchandise sold, (b) the credit memo, including the cost of the returned merchandise, and (c) the receipt of the check for the amount due from Balboa Co.

### EX 6-15  Purchase-related transactions

Based on the data presented in Exercise 6-14, journalize Balboa Co.'s entries for (a) the purchase, (b) the return of the merchandise for credit, and (c) the payment of the invoice.

### EX 6-16  Chart of accounts

Monet Paints Co. is a newly organized business with a list of accounts arranged in alphabetical order, as follows:

| | |
|---|---|
| Accounts Payable | Merchandise Inventory |
| Accounts Receivable | Miscellaneous Administrative Expense |
| Accumulated Depreciation—Office Equipment | Miscellaneous Selling Expense |
| Accumulated Depreciation—Store Equipment | Notes Payable |
| Advertising Expense | Office Equipment |
| Cash | Office Salaries Expense |
| Cost of Merchandise Sold | Office Supplies |
| Delivery Expense | Office Supplies Expense |
| Depreciation Expense—Office Equipment | Prepaid Insurance |
| Depreciation Expense—Store Equipment | Rent Expense |
| Income Summary | Salaries Payable |
| Insurance Expense | Sales |
| Interest Expense | Sales Salaries Expense |
| Kailey Garner, Capital | Store Equipment |
| Kailey Garner, Drawing | Store Supplies |
| Land | Store Supplies Expense |

Construct a chart of accounts, assigning account numbers and arranging the accounts in balance sheet and income statement order, as illustrated in Exhibit 9. Each account number is three digits: the first digit is to indicate the major classification (1 for assets, and so on); the second digit is to indicate the subclassification (11 for current assets, and so on); and the third digit is to identify the specific account (110 for Cash, 112 for Accounts Receivable, 114 for Merchandise Inventory, 115 for Store Supplies, and so on).

### EX 6-17  Sales tax

A sale of merchandise on account for $36,000 is subject to an 8% sales tax. (a) Should the sales tax be recorded at the time of sale or when payment is received? (b) What is the amount of the sale? (c) What is the amount debited to Accounts Receivable? (d) What is the title of the account to which the $2,880 ($36,000 × 8%) is credited?

### EX 6-18  Sales tax transactions

Journalize the entries to record the following selected transactions:

a. Sold $62,800 of merchandise on account, subject to a sales tax of 5%. The cost of the merchandise sold was $37,500.

b. Paid $39,650 to the state sales tax department for taxes collected.

### EX 6-19  Normal balances of merchandise accounts

What is the normal balance of the following accounts: (a) Cost of Merchandise Sold, (b) Customer Refunds Payable, (c) Delivery Expense, (d) Estimated Returns Inventory, (e) Merchandise Inventory, (f) Sales, (g) Sales Tax Payable.

SHOW
ME HOW

### EX 6-20 Income statement and accounts for merchandiser
OBJ. 3

For the fiscal year, sales were $25,565,000 and the cost of merchandise sold was $15,400,000.

a. What was the amount of gross profit?

b. If total operating expenses were $4,550,000, could you determine net income?

c. Is Customer Refunds Payable an asset, liability, or owner's equity account and what is its normal balance?

d. Is Estimated Returns Inventory an asset, liability, or owner's equity account and what is its normal balance?

### EX 6-21 Income statement for merchandiser
OBJ. 3

The following expenses were incurred by a merchandising business during the year. In which expense section of the income statement should each be reported: (a) selling, (b) administrative, or (c) other?

1. Advertising expense

2. Depreciation expense on store equipment

3. Insurance expense on office equipment

4. Interest expense on notes payable

5. Rent expense on office building

6. Salaries of office personnel

7. Salary of sales manager

8. Sales supplies used

SHOW
ME HOW

### EX 6-22 Determining amounts for items omitted from income statement
OBJ. 3

Two items are omitted in each of the following four lists of income statement data. Determine the amounts of the missing items, identifying them by letter.

| | | | | | | | |
|---|---|---|---|---|---|---|---|
| Sales | $463,400 | | (b) | $1,295,000 | | (d) | |
| Cost of merchandise sold | (a) | | 410,000 | (c) | | 900,000 | |
| Gross profit | 83,500 | | $277,500 | 275,000 | | 600,000 | |

✔ a. Net income:
$1,345,000

SHOW
ME HOW

### EX 6-23 Multiple-step income statement
OBJ. 3

On October 31, 2016, the balances of the accounts appearing in the ledger of Prestige Furnishings Company, a furniture wholesaler, are as follows:

| | | | |
|---|---|---|---|
| Accumulated Depreciation—Building | $ 750,000 | Merchandise Inventory | $ 980,000 |
| Administrative Expenses | 540,000 | Notes Payable | 250,000 |
| Building | 2,500,000 | Office Supplies | 20,000 |
| Cash | 175,000 | Salaries Payable | 8,000 |
| Cost of Merchandise Sold | 3,800,000 | Sales | 6,410,000 |
| Interest Expense | 10,000 | Selling Expenses | 715,000 |
| Jan Brown, Capital | 1,587,000 | Store Supplies | 90,000 |
| Jan Brown, Drawing | 175,000 | | |

a. Prepare a multiple-step income statement for the year ended October 31, 2016.

b. ━━━▶ Compare the major advantages and disadvantages of the multiple-step and single-step forms of income statements.

**EX 6-24 Multiple-step income statement** OBJ. 3

Identify the errors in the following income statement:

| Curbstone Company | | |
|---|---|---|
| Income Statement | | |
| For the Year Ended August 31, 2016 | | |
| Sales .................................................. | | $8,595,000 |
| Cost of merchandise sold ................................ | | 6,110,000 |
| Income from operations .................................. | | $2,485,000 |
| Expenses: | | |
| Selling expenses........................................ | $ 800,000 | |
| Administrative expenses ............................... | 575,000 | |
| Delivery expense ...................................... | 425,000 | |
| Total expenses ...................................... | | 1,800,000 |
| | | $ 685,000 |
| Other expense: | | |
| Interest revenue....................................... | | 45,000 |
| Gross profit........................................... | | $ 640,000 |

✔ Net income:
$1,277,500

SHOW
ME HOW

SHOW
ME HOW

**EX 6-25 Single-step income statement** OBJ. 3

Summary operating data for Custom Wire & Tubing Company during the year ended April 30, 2016, are as follows: cost of merchandise sold, $6,100,000; administrative expenses, $740,000; interest expense, $25,000; rent revenue, $60,000; sales, $9,332,500; and selling expenses, $1,250,000. Prepare a single-step income statement.

**EX 6-26 Adjusting entry for merchandise inventory shrinkage** OBJ. 4

Paragon Tire Co.'s perpetual inventory records indicate that $2,780,000 of merchandise should be on hand on March 31, 2016. The physical inventory indicates that $2,734,800 of merchandise is actually on hand. Journalize the adjusting entry for the inventory shrinkage for Paragon Tire Co. for the year ended March 31, 2016.

**EX 6-27 Closing the accounts of a merchandiser** OBJ. 4

From the following list, identify the accounts that should be closed to Income Summary at the end of the fiscal year under a perpetual inventory system: (a) Accounts Payable, (b) Advertising Expense, (c) Cost of Merchandise Sold, (d) Merchandise Inventory, (e) Sales, (f) Supplies, (g) Supplies Expense, (h) Valery Lavine, Drawing, (i) Wages Payable.

**EX 6-28 Closing entries; net income** OBJ. 4

Based on the data presented in Exercise 6-23, journalize the closing entries.

### EX 6-29 Closing entries

OBJ. 4

On July 31, 2016, the balances of the accounts appearing in the ledger of Serbian Interiors Company, a furniture wholesaler, are as follows:

| | | | |
|---|---|---|---|
| Accumulated Depr.—Building | $365,000 | Notes Payable | $ 100,000 |
| Administrative Expenses | 440,000 | Sales | 1,437,000 |
| Building | 810,000 | Sales Tax Payable | 4,500 |
| Cash | 78,000 | Selling Expenses | 160,000 |
| Cost of Merchandise Sold | 775,000 | Store Supplies | 16,000 |
| Interest Expense | 6,000 | Store Supplies Expense | 21,500 |
| Peter Bronsky, Capital | 530,000 | | |
| Peter Bronsky, Drawing | 15,000 | | |
| Merchandise Inventory | 115,000 | | |

Prepare the July 31, 2016, closing entries for Serbian Interiors Company.

### EX 6-30 Ratio of sales to assets

OBJ. 5

The Home Depot reported the following data (in millions) in its recent financial statements:

SHOW
ME HOW

| | Year 2 | Year 1 |
|---|---|---|
| Sales | $70,395 | $67,997 |
| Total assets at the end of the year | 40,518 | 40,125 |
| Total assets at the beginning of the year | 40,125 | 40,877 |

a. Determine the ratio of sales to assets for The Home Depot for Year 2 and Year 1. Round to two decimal places.

b. ━━━▶ What conclusions can be drawn from these ratios concerning the trend in the ability of The Home Depot to effectively use its assets to generate sales?

### EX 6-31 Ratio of sales to assets

OBJ. 5

Kroger, a national supermarket chain, reported the following data (in millions) in its financial statements for a recent year:

| | |
|---|---|
| Total revenue | $90,374 |
| Total assets at end of year | 23,476 |
| Total assets at beginning of year | 23,505 |

a. Compute the ratio of sales to assets. Round to two decimal places.

b. ━━━▶ Tiffany & Co. is a large North American retailer of jewelry, with a ratio of sales to assets of 0.92. Why would Tiffany's ratio of sales to assets be lower than that of Kroger?

### Appendix
### EX 6-32 Rules of debit and credit for periodic inventory accounts

Complete the following table by indicating for (a) through (g) whether the proper answer is debit or credit:

| Account | Increase | Decrease | Normal Balance |
|---|---|---|---|
| Purchases | debit | (a) | (b) |
| Purchases Discounts | credit | (c) | credit |
| Purchases Returns and Allowances | (d) | (e) | (f) |
| Freight In | debit | (g) | debit |

**Appendix**
## EX 6-33   Journal entries using the periodic inventory system

The following selected transactions were completed by Air Systems Company during January of the current year. Air Systems Company uses the periodic inventory system.

Jan. 2.  Purchased $18,200 of merchandise on account, FOB shipping point, terms 2/15, n/30.

5.  Paid freight of $190 on the January 2 purchase.

6.  Returned $2,750 of the merchandise purchased on January 2.

13.  Sold merchandise on account, $37,300, FOB destination, 1/10, n/30. The cost of merchandise sold was $22,400.

15.  Paid freight of $215 for the merchandise sold on January 13.

17.  Paid for the purchase of January 2 less the return and discount.

23.  Received payment on account for the sale of January 13 less the discount.

Journalize the entries to record the transactions of Air Systems Company.

**Appendix**
## EX 6-34   Identify items missing in determining cost of merchandise sold

For (a) through (d), identify the items designated by X and Y.

a.  Purchases − (X + Y) = Net purchases.

b.  Net purchases + X = Cost of merchandise purchased.

c.  Merchandise inventory (beginning) + Cost of merchandise purchased = X.

d.  Merchandise available for sale − X = Cost of merchandise sold.

**Appendix**
## EX 6-35   Cost of merchandise sold and related Items

✔ a. Cost of merchandise sold, $3,551,600

The following data were extracted from the accounting records of Harkins Company for the year ended April 30, 2016:

| | |
|---|---:|
| Merchandise inventory, May 1, 2015 | $ 380,000 |
| Merchandise inventory, April 30, 2016 | 415,000 |
| Purchases | 3,800,000 |
| Purchases returns and allowances | 150,000 |
| Purchases discounts | 80,000 |
| Sales | 5,850,000 |
| Freight in | 16,600 |

a.  Prepare the cost of merchandise sold section of the income statement for the year ended April 30, 2016, using the periodic inventory system.

b.  Determine the gross profit to be reported on the income statement for the year ended April 30, 2016.

c.  ━━━▶ Would gross profit be different if the perpetual inventory system was used instead of the periodic inventory system?

**Appendix**
## EX 6-36   Cost of merchandise sold

Based on the following data, determine the cost of merchandise sold for November:

| | |
|---|---:|
| Merchandise inventory, November 1 | $ 28,000 |
| Merchandise inventory, November 30 | 31,500 |
| Purchases | 475,000 |
| Purchases returns and allowances | 15,000 |
| Purchases discounts | 9,000 |
| Freight in | 7,000 |

**Appendix**
### EX 6-37 Cost of merchandise sold

Based on the following data, determine the cost of merchandise sold for July:

| | |
|---|---|
| Merchandise inventory, July 1 | $ 190,850 |
| Merchandise inventory, July 31 | 160,450 |
| Purchases | 1,126,000 |
| Purchases returns and allowances | 46,000 |
| Purchases discounts | 23,000 |
| Freight in | 17,500 |

✔ Correct cost of merchandise sold, $1,033,300

**Appendix**
### EX 6-38 Cost of merchandise sold

Identify the errors in the following schedule of the cost of merchandise sold for the year ended May 31, 2016:

Cost of merchandise sold:

| | | | |
|---|---|---|---|
| Merchandise inventory, May 31, 2016 | | | $ 105,000 |
| Purchases | | $1,110,000 | |
| Plus: Purchases returns and allowances | $55,000 | | |
| Purchases discounts | 30,000 | 85,000 | |
| Gross purchases | | $1,195,000 | |
| Less freight in | | 22,000 | |
| Cost of merchandise purchased | | | 1,173,000 |
| Merchandise available for sale | | | $1,278,000 |
| Less merchandise inventory, June 1, 2015 | | | 91,300 |
| Cost of merchandise sold | | | $1,186,700 |

**Appendix**
### Ex 6-39 Closing entries using periodic inventory system

United Rug Company is a small rug retailer owned and operated by Pat Kirwan. After the accounts have been adjusted on December 31, the following selected account balances were taken from the ledger:

| | |
|---|---|
| Advertising Expense | $ 36,000 |
| Depreciation Expense | 13,000 |
| Freight In | 17,000 |
| Merchandise Inventory, December 1 | 375,000 |
| Merchandise Inventory, December 31 | 460,000 |
| Miscellaneous Expense | 9,000 |
| Purchases | 1,760,000 |
| Purchases Discounts | 35,000 |
| Purchases Returns and Allowances | 45,000 |
| Pat Kirwan, Drawing | 65,000 |
| Salaries Expense | 375,000 |
| Sales | 2,220,000 |

Journalize the closing entries on December 31.

# Problems: Series A

**General Ledger**

---

### PR 6-1A Purchase-related transactions using perpetual inventory system OBJ. 2

The following selected transactions were completed by Capers Company during October of the current year:

Oct. 1. Purchased merchandise from UK Imports Co., $14,448, terms FOB destination, n/30.

3. Purchased merchandise from Hoagie Co., $9,950, terms FOB shipping point, 2/10, n/eom. Prepaid freight of $220 was added to the invoice.

4. Purchased merchandise from Taco Co., $13,650, terms FOB destination, 2/10, n/30.

6. Issued debit memo to Taco Co. for $4,550 of merchandise returned from purchase on October 4.

13. Paid Hoagie Co. for invoice of October 3.

14. Paid Taco Co. for invoice of October 4, less debit memo of October 6.

19. Purchased merchandise from Veggie Co., $27,300, terms FOB shipping point, n/eom.

19. Paid freight of $400 on October 19 purchase from Veggie Co.

20. Purchased merchandise from Caesar Salad Co., $22,000, terms FOB destination, 1/10, n/30.

30. Paid Caesar Salad Co. for invoice of October 20.

31. Paid UK Imports Co. for invoice of October 1.

31. Paid Veggie Co. for invoice of October 19.

**Instructions**

Journalize the entries to record the transactions of Capers Company for October.

---

### PR 6-2A Sales-related transactions using perpetual inventory system OBJ. 2

**General Ledger**

SHOW
ME HOW

The following selected transactions were completed by Amsterdam Supply Co., which sells office supplies primarily to wholesalers and occasionally to retail customers:

Mar. 2. Sold merchandise on account to Equinox Co., $18,900, terms FOB destination, 1/10, n/30. The cost of the merchandise sold was $13,300.

3. Sold merchandise for $11,350 plus 6% sales tax to retail cash customers. The cost of merchandise sold was $7,000.

4. Sold merchandise on account to Empire Co., $55,400, terms FOB shipping point, n/eom. The cost of merchandise sold was $33,200.

5. Sold merchandise for $30,000 plus 6% sales tax to retail customers who used MasterCard. The cost of merchandise sold was $19,400.

12. Received check for amount due from Equinox Co. for sale on March 2.

14. Sold merchandise to customers who used American Express cards, $13,700. The cost of merchandise sold was $8,350.

16. Sold merchandise on account to Targhee Co., $27,500, terms FOB shipping point, 1/10, n/30. The cost of merchandise sold was $16,000.

18. Issued credit memo for $4,800 to Targhee Co. for merchandise returned from sale on March 16. The cost of the merchandise returned was $2,900.

19. Sold merchandise on account to Vista Co., $8,250, terms FOB shipping point, 2/10, n/30. Added $75 to the invoice for prepaid freight. The cost of merchandise sold was $5,000.

26. Received check for amount due from Targhee Co. for sale on March 16 less credit memo of March 18.

*(Continued)*

Mar. 28. Received check for amount due from Vista Co. for sale of March 19.

31. Received check for amount due from Empire Co. for sale of March 4.

31. Paid Fleetwood Delivery Service $5,600 for merchandise delivered during March to customers under shipping terms of FOB destination.

Apr. 3. Paid City Bank $940 for service fees for handling MasterCard and American Express sales during March.

15. Paid $6,544 to state sales tax division for taxes owed on sales.

**Instructions**

Journalize the entries to record the transactions of Amsterdam Supply Co.

---

**PR 6-3A   Sales-related and purchase-related transactions using perpetual inventory system**    OBJ. 2

General Ledger

SHOW
ME HOW

The following were selected from among the transactions completed by Babcock Company during November of the current year:

Nov. 3. Purchased merchandise on account from Moonlight Co., list price $85,000, trade discount 25%, terms FOB destination, 2/10, n/30.

4. Sold merchandise for cash, $37,680. The cost of the merchandise sold was $22,600.

5. Purchased merchandise on account from Papoose Creek Co., $47,500, terms FOB shipping point, 2/10, n/30, with prepaid freight of $810 added to the invoice.

6. Returned $13,500 ($18,000 list price less trade discount of 25%) of merchandise purchased on November 3 from Moonlight Co.

8. Sold merchandise on account to Quinn Co., $15,600 with terms n/15. The cost of the merchandise sold was $9,400.

13. Paid Moonlight Co. on account for purchase of November 3, less return of November 6.

14. Sold merchandise on VISA, $236,000. The cost of the merchandise sold was $140,000.

15. Paid Papoose Creek Co. on account for purchase of November 5.

23. Received cash on account from sale of November 8 to Quinn Co.

24. Sold merchandise on account to Rabel Co., $56,900, terms 1/10, n/30. The cost of the merchandise sold was $34,000.

28. Paid VISA service fee of $3,540.

30. Paid Quinn Co. a cash refund of $6,000 for returned merchandise from sale of November 8. The cost of the returned merchandise was $3,300.

**Instructions**

Journalize the transactions.

---

**PR 6-4A   Sales-related and purchase-related transactions for seller and buyer using perpetual inventory system**    OBJ. 2

The following selected transactions were completed during August between Summit Company and Beartooth Co.:

Aug. 1. Summit Company sold merchandise on account to Beartooth Co., $48,000, terms FOB destination, 2/15, n/eom. The cost of the merchandise sold was $28,800.

2. Summit Company paid freight of $1,150 for delivery of merchandise sold to Beartooth Co. on August 1.

5. Summit Company sold merchandise on account to Beartooth Co., $66,000, terms FOB shipping point, n/eom. The cost of the merchandise sold was $40,000.

9. Beartooth Co. paid freight of $2,300 on August 5 purchase from Summit Company.

Aug. 15. Summit Company sold merchandise on account to Beartooth Co., $58,700, terms FOB shipping point, 1/10, n/30. Summit Company paid freight of $1,675, which was added to the invoice. The cost of the merchandise sold was $35,000.

   16. Beartooth Co. paid Summit Company for purchase of August 1.

   25. Beartooth Co. paid Summit Company on account for purchase of August 15.

   31. Beartooth Co. paid Summit Company on account for purchase of August 5.

### Instructions
Journalize the August transactions for (1) Summit Company and (2) Beartooth Co.

---

### PR 6-5A  Multiple-step income statement and report form of balance sheet  OBJ. 3

✔ 1. Net income
$943,400

**General Ledger**

The following selected accounts and their current balances appear in the ledger of Clairemont Co. for the fiscal year ended May 31, 2016:

| | | | |
|---|---|---|---|
| Cash | $ 240,000 | Kristina Marble, Drawing | $ 100,000 |
| Accounts Receivable | 966,000 | Sales | 11,343,000 |
| Merchandise Inventory | 1,712,500 | Cost of Merchandise Sold | 7,850,000 |
| Office Supplies | 13,500 | Sales Salaries Expense | 916,000 |
| Prepaid Insurance | 8,000 | Advertising Expense | 550,000 |
| Office Equipment | 830,000 | Depreciation Expense— | |
| Accumulated Depreciation— | |   Store Equipment | 140,000 |
|   Office Equipment | 550,000 | Miscellaneous Selling Expense | 38,000 |
| Store Equipment | 3,600,000 | Office Salaries Expense | 650,000 |
| Accumulated Depreciation— | | Rent Expense | 94,000 |
|   Store Equipment | 1,820,000 | Depreciation Expense— | |
| Accounts Payable | 366,000 |   Office Equipment | 50,000 |
| Salaries Payable | 41,500 | Insurance Expense | 48,000 |
| Note Payable | | Office Supplies Expense | 28,100 |
|   (final payment due 2022) | 300,000 | Miscellaneous Administrative Exp. | 14,500 |
| Kristina Marble, Capital | 3,449,100 | Interest Expense | 21,000 |

### Instructions
1. Prepare a multiple-step income statement.

2. Prepare a statement of owner's equity.

3. Prepare a report form of balance sheet, assuming that the current portion of the note payable is $50,000.

4. ➡ Briefly explain (a) how multiple-step and single-step income statements differ and (b) how report-form and account-form balance sheets differ.

---

### PR 6-6A  Single-step income statement and account form of balance sheet  OBJ. 3

✔ 3. Total assets:
$5,000,000

Selected accounts and related amounts for Clairemont Co. for the fiscal year ended May 31, 2016, are presented in Problem 6-5A.

### Instructions
1. Prepare a single-step income statement in the format shown in Exhibit 11.

2. Prepare a statement of owner's equity.

3. Prepare an account form of balance sheet, assuming that the current portion of the note payable is $50,000.

4. Prepare closing entries as of May 31, 2016.

**Appendix**

**PR 6-7A    Purchase-related transactions using periodic inventory system**

Selected transactions for Capers Company during October of the current year are listed in Problem 6-1A.

**Instructions**

Journalize the entries to record the transactions of Capers Company for October using the periodic inventory system.

**Appendix**

**PR 6-8A    Sales-related and purchase-related transactions using periodic inventory system**

Selected transactions for Babcock Company during November of the current year are listed in Problem 6-3A.

**Instructions**

Journalize the entries to record the transactions of Babcock Company for November using the periodic inventory system.

**Appendix**

**PR 6-9A    Sales-related and purchase-related transactions for buyer and seller using periodic inventory system**

Selected transactions during August between Summit Company and Beartooth Co. are listed in Problem 6-4A.

**Instructions**

Journalize the entries to record the transactions for (1) Summit Company and (2) Beartooth Co., assuming that both companies use the periodic inventory system.

**Appendix**

**PR 6-10A    Periodic inventory accounts, multiple-step income statement, closing entries**

✔ 2. Net income, $180,000

On December 31, 2016, the balances of the accounts appearing in the ledger of Wyman Company are as follows:

| | | | |
|---|---|---|---|
| Cash | $ 13,500 | Purchases | $2,650,000 |
| Accounts Receivable | 72,000 | Purchases Returns and Allowances | 93,000 |
| Merchandise Inventory, | | Purchases Discounts | 37,000 |
| January 1, 2016 | 257,000 | Freight In | 48,000 |
| Office Supplies | 3,000 | Sales Salaries Expense | 300,000 |
| Prepaid Insurance | 4,500 | Advertising Expense | 45,000 |
| Land | 150,000 | Delivery Expense | 9,000 |
| Store Equipment | 270,000 | Depreciation Expense— | |
| Accumulated Depreciation— | | Store Equipment | 6,000 |
| Store Equipment | 55,900 | Miscellaneous Selling Expense | 12,000 |
| Office Equipment | 78,500 | Office Salaries Expense | 175,000 |
| Accumulated Depreciation— | | Rent Expense | 28,000 |
| Office Equipment | 16,000 | Insurance Expense | 3,000 |
| Accounts Payable | 27,800 | Office Supplies Expense | 2,000 |
| Salaries Payable | 3,000 | Depreciation Expense— | |
| Unearned Rent | 8,300 | Office Equipment | 1,500 |
| Notes Payable | 50,000 | Miscellaneous Administrative Expense | 3,500 |
| Shirley Wyman, Capital | 580,500 | Rent Revenue | 7,000 |
| Shirley Wyman, Drawing | 25,000 | Interest Expense | 2,000 |
| Sales | 3,280,000 | | |

**Instructions**

1. ━━━━▶ Does Wyman Company use a periodic or perpetual inventory system? Explain.

2. Prepare a multiple-step income statement for Wyman Company for the year ended December 31, 2016. The merchandise inventory as of December 31, 2016, was $305,000.

3. Prepare the closing entries for Wyman Company as of December 31, 2016.

4. What would be the net income if the perpetual inventory system had been used?

# Problems: Series B

### PR 6-1B    Purchase-related transactions using perpetual inventory system    OBJ. 2

The following selected transactions were completed by Niles Co. during March of the current year:

Mar.  1.  Purchased merchandise from Haas Co., $43,250, terms FOB shipping point, 2/10, n/eom. Prepaid freight of $650 was added to the invoice.

  5.  Purchased merchandise from Whitman Co., $19,175, terms FOB destination, n/30.

  10.  Paid Haas Co. for invoice of March 1.

  13.  Purchased merchandise from Jost Co., $15,550, terms FOB destination, 2/10, n/30.

  14.  Issued debit memo to Jost Co. for $3,750 of merchandise returned from purchase on March 13.

  18.  Purchased merchandise from Fairhurst Company, $13,560, terms FOB shipping point, n/eom.

  18.  Paid freight of $140 on March 18 purchase from Fairhurst Company.

  19.  Purchased merchandise from Bickle Co., $6,500, terms FOB destination, 2/10, n/30.

  23.  Paid Jost Co. for invoice of March 13, less debit memo of March 14.

  29.  Paid Bickle Co. for invoice of March 19.

  31.  Paid Fairhurst Company for invoice of March 18.

  31.  Paid Whitman Co. for invoice of March 5.

**Instructions**

Journalize the entries to record the transactions of Niles Co. for March.

### PR 6-2B    Sales-related transactions using perpetual inventory system    OBJ. 2

SHOW
ME HOW

The following selected transactions were completed by Green Lawn Supplies Co., which sells irrigation supplies primarily to wholesalers and occasionally to retail customers:

July  1.  Sold merchandise on account to Landscapes Co., $33,450, terms FOB shipping point, n/eom. The cost of merchandise sold was $20,000.

  2.  Sold merchandise for $86,000 plus 8% sales tax to retail cash customers. The cost of merchandise sold was $51,600.

  5.  Sold merchandise on account to Peacock Company, $17,500, terms FOB destination, 1/10, n/30. The cost of merchandise sold was $10,000.

  8.  Sold merchandise for $112,000 plus 8% sales tax to retail customers who used VISA cards. The cost of merchandise sold was $67,200.

  13.  Sold merchandise to customers who used MasterCard cards, $96,000. The cost of merchandise sold was $57,600.

  14.  Sold merchandise on account to Loeb Co., $16,000, terms FOB shipping point, 1/10, n/30. The cost of merchandise sold was $9,000.

  15.  Received check for amount due from Peacock Company for sale on July 5.

  16.  Issued credit memo for $3,000 to Loeb Co. for merchandise returned from sale on July 14. The cost of the merchandise returned was $1,800.

  18.  Sold merchandise on account to Jennings Company, $11,350, terms FOB shipping point, 2/10, n/30. Paid $475 for freight and added it to the invoice. The cost of merchandise sold was $6,800.

  24.  Received check for amount due from Loeb Co. for sale on July 14 less credit memo of July 16.

  28.  Received check for amount due from Jennings Company for sale of July 18.

  31.  Paid Black Lab Delivery Service $8,550 for merchandise delivered during July to customers under shipping terms of FOB destination.

(Continued)

July 31. Received check for amount due from Landscapes Co. for sale of July 1.

Aug. 3. Paid Hays Federal Bank $3,770 for service fees for handling MasterCard and VISA sales during July.

10. Paid $41,260 to state sales tax division for taxes owed on sales.

**Instructions**

Journalize the entries to record the transactions of Green Lawn Supplies Co.

**PR 6-3B    Sales-related and purchase-related transactions using perpetual    OBJ. 2
inventory system**

SHOW
ME HOW

The following were selected from among the transactions completed by Essex Company during July of the current year:

July  3. Purchased merchandise on account from Hamling Co., list price $72,000, trade discount 15%, terms FOB shipping point, 2/10, n/30, with prepaid freight of $1,450 added to the invoice.

5. Purchased merchandise on account from Kester Co., $33,450, terms FOB destination, 2/10, n/30.

6. Sold merchandise on account to Parsley Co., $36,000, terms n/15. The cost of the merchandise sold was $25,000.

7. Returned $6,850 of merchandise purchased on July 5 from Kester Co.

13. Paid Hamling Co. on account for purchase of July 3.

15. Paid Kester Co. on account for purchase of July 5, less return of July 7.

21. Received cash on account from sale of July 6 to Parsley Co.

21. Sold merchandise on MasterCard, $108,000. The cost of the merchandise sold was $64,800.

22. Sold merchandise on account to Tabor Co., $16,650, terms 2/10, n/30. The cost of the merchandise sold was $10,000.

23. Sold merchandise for cash, $91,200. The cost of the merchandise sold was $55,000.

28. Paid Parsley Co. a cash refund of $7,150 for returned merchandise from sale of July 6. The cost of the returned merchandise was $4,250.

31. Paid MasterCard service fee of $1,650.

**Instructions**

Journalize the transactions.

**PR 6-4B    Sales-related and purchase-related transactions for seller and buyer    OBJ. 2
using perpetual inventory system**

The following selected transactions were completed during April between Swan Company and Bird Company:

Apr.  2. Swan Company sold merchandise on account to Bird Company, $32,000, terms FOB shipping point, 2/10, n/30. Swan Company paid freight of $330, which was added to the invoice. The cost of the merchandise sold was $19,200.

8. Swan Company sold merchandise on account to Bird Company, $49,500, terms FOB destination, 1/15, n/eom. The cost of the merchandise sold was $29,700.

8. Swan Company paid freight of $710 for delivery of merchandise sold to Bird Company on April 8.

12. Bird Company paid Swan Company for purchase of April 2.

23. Bird Company paid Swan Company for purchase of April 8.

24. Swan Company sold merchandise on account to Bird Company, $67,350, terms FOB shipping point, n/eom. The cost of the merchandise sold was $40,400.

Apr. 26. Bird Company paid freight of $875 on April 24 purchase from Swan Company.

30. Bird Company paid Swan Company on account for purchase of April 24.

**Instructions**

Journalize the April transactions for (1) Swan Company and (2) Bird Company.

---

**PR 6-5B    Multiple-step income statement and report form of balance sheet**    OBJ. 3

✔ 1. Net income:
$1,340,000

**General Ledger**

The following selected accounts and their current balances appear in the ledger of Kanpur Co. for the fiscal year ended June 30, 2016:

| | | | |
|---|---|---|---|
| Cash | $ 92,000 | Gerri Faber, Drawing | $ 300,000 |
| Accounts Receivable | 450,000 | Sales | 8,925,000 |
| Merchandise Inventory | 375,000 | Cost of Merchandise Sold | 5,620,000 |
| Office Supplies | 10,000 | Sales Salaries Expense | 850,000 |
| Prepaid Insurance | 12,000 | Advertising Expense | 420,000 |
| Office Equipment | 220,000 | Depreciation Expense— | |
| Accumulated Depreciation— | | Store Equipment | 33,000 |
| Office Equipment | 58,000 | Miscellaneous Selling Expense | 18,000 |
| Store Equipment | 650,000 | Office Salaries Expense | 540,000 |
| Accumulated Depreciation— | | Rent Expense | 48,000 |
| Store Equipment | 87,500 | Insurance Expense | 24,000 |
| Accounts Payable | 48,500 | Depreciation Expense— | |
| Salaries Payable | 4,000 | Office Equipment | 10,000 |
| Note Payable | | Office Supplies Expense | 4,000 |
| (final payment due 2032) | 140,000 | Miscellaneous Administrative Exp. | 6,000 |
| Gerri Faber, Capital | 431,000 | Interest Expense | 12,000 |

**Instructions**

1. Prepare a multiple-step income statement.

2. Prepare a statement of owner's equity.

3. Prepare a report form of balance sheet, assuming that the current portion of the note payable is $7,000.

4. ▸ Briefly explain (a) how multiple-step and single-step income statements differ and (b) how report-form and account-form balance sheets differ.

---

**PR 6-6B    Single-step income statement and account form of balance sheet**    OBJ. 3

✔ 3. Total assets:
$1,663,500

Selected accounts and related amounts for Kanpur Co. for the fiscal year ended June 30, 2016, are presented in Problem 6-5B.

**Instructions**

1. Prepare a single-step income statement in the format shown in Exhibit 11.

2. Prepare a statement of owner's equity.

3. Prepare an account form of balance sheet, assuming that the current portion of the note payable is $7,000.

4. Prepare closing entries as of June 30, 2016.

---

**Appendix**
**PR 6-7B    Purchase-related transactions using periodic inventory system**

Selected transactions for Niles Co. during March of the current year are listed in Problem 6-1B.

**Instructions**

Journalize the entries to record the transactions of Niles Co. for March using the periodic inventory system.

**Appendix**

**PR 6-8B** **Sales-related and purchase-related transactions using periodic inventory system**

Selected transactions for Essex Company during July of the current year are listed in Problem 6-3B.

**Instructions**

Journalize the entries to record the transactions of Essex Company for July using the periodic inventory system.

**Appendix**

**PR 6-9B** **Sales-related and purchase-related transactions for buyer and seller using periodic inventory system**

Selected transactions during April between Swan Company and Bird Company are listed in Problem 6-4B.

**Instructions**

Journalize the entries to record the transactions for (1) Swan Company and (2) Bird Company assuming that both companies use the periodic inventory system.

**Appendix**

**PR 6-10B** **Periodic inventory accounts, multiple-step income statement, closing entries**

✔ 2. Net income, $1,200,000

On June 30, 2016, the balances of the accounts appearing in the ledger of Simkins Company are as follows:

| | | | |
|---|---:|---|---:|
| Cash | $ 125,000 | Purchases | $4,100,000 |
| Accounts Receivable | 340,000 | Purchases Returns and Allowances | 32,000 |
| Merchandise Inventory, July 1, 2015 | 415,000 | Purchases Discounts | 13,000 |
| Office Supplies | 9,000 | Freight In | 45,000 |
| Prepaid Insurance | 18,000 | Sales Salaries Expense | 580,000 |
| Land | 300,000 | Advertising Expense | 315,000 |
| Store Equipment | 550,000 | Delivery Expense | 18,000 |
| Accumulated Depreciation— | | Depreciation Expense— | |
| Store Equipment | 190,000 | Store Equipment | 12,000 |
| Office Equipment | 250,000 | Miscellaneous Selling Expense | 28,000 |
| Accumulated Depreciation— | | Office Salaries Expense | 375,000 |
| Office Equipment | 110,000 | Rent Expense | 43,000 |
| Accounts Payable | 85,000 | Insurance Expense | 17,000 |
| Salaries Payable | 9,000 | Office Supplies Expense | 5,000 |
| Unearned Rent | 6,000 | Depreciation Expense— | |
| Notes Payable | 50,000 | Office Equipment | 4,000 |
| Amy Gant, Capital | 825,000 | Miscellaneous Administrative Expense | 16,000 |
| Amy Gant, Drawing | 275,000 | Rent Revenue | 32,500 |
| Sales | 6,590,000 | Interest Expense | 2,500 |

**Instructions**

1. ▬▬▬▶ Does Simkins Company use a periodic or perpetual inventory system? Explain.

2. Prepare a multiple-step income statement for Simkins Company for the year ended June 30, 2016. The merchandise inventory as of June 30, 2016, was $508,000.

3. Prepare the closing entries for Simkins Company as of June 30, 2016.

4. What would be the net income if the perpetual inventory system had been used?

## Continuing Problem

✔ 8. Net income:
$741,855

Palisade Creek Co. is a merchandising business that uses the perpetual inventory system. The account balances for Palisade Creek Co. as of May 1, 2016 (unless otherwise indicated), are as follows:

| | | |
|---|---|---:|
| 110 | Cash | $   83,600 |
| 112 | Accounts Receivable | 233,900 |
| 115 | Merchandise Inventory | 624,400 |
| 116 | Estimated Returns Inventory | 28,000 |
| 117 | Prepaid Insurance | 16,800 |
| 118 | Store Supplies | 11,400 |
| 123 | Store Equipment | 569,500 |
| 124 | Accumulated Depreciation—Store Equipment | 56,700 |
| 210 | Accounts Payable | 96,600 |
| 211 | Salaries Payable | — |
| 212 | Customers Refunds Payable | 50,000 |
| 310 | Lynn Tolley, Capital, June 1, 2015 | 685,300 |
| 311 | Lynn Tolley, Drawing | 135,000 |
| 312 | Income Summary | — |
| 410 | Sales | 5,069,000 |
| 510 | Cost of Merchandise Sold | 2,823,000 |
| 520 | Sales Salaries Expense | 664,800 |
| 521 | Advertising Expense | 281,000 |
| 522 | Depreciation Expense | — |
| 523 | Store Supplies Expense | — |
| 529 | Miscellaneous Selling Expense | 12,600 |
| 530 | Office Salaries Expense | 382,100 |
| 531 | Rent Expense | 83,700 |
| 532 | Insurance Expense | — |
| 539 | Miscellaneous Administrative Expense | 7,800 |

During May, the last month of the fiscal year, the following transactions were completed:

May   1. Paid rent for May, $5,000.

3. Purchased merchandise on account from Martin Co., terms 2/10, n/30, FOB shipping point, $36,000.

4. Paid freight on purchase of May 3, $600.

6. Sold merchandise on account to Korman Co., terms 2/10, n/30, FOB shipping point, $68,500. The cost of the merchandise sold was $41,000.

7. Received $22,300 cash from Halstad Co. on account.

10. Sold merchandise for cash, $54,000. The cost of the merchandise sold was $32,000.

13. Paid for merchandise purchased on May 3.

15. Paid advertising expense for last half of May, $11,000.

16. Received cash from sale of May 6.

19. Purchased merchandise for cash, $18,700.

19. Paid $33,450 to Buttons Co. on account.

20. Paid Korman Co. a cash refund of $13,230 for returned merchandise from sale of May 6. The invoice amount of the returned merchandise was $13,500 and the cost of the returned merchandise was $8,000.

*Record the following transactions on Page 21 of the journal:*

20. Sold merchandise on account to Crescent Co., terms 1/10, n/30, FOB shipping point, $110,000. The cost of the merchandise sold was $70,000.

21. For the convenience of Crescent Co., paid freight on sale of May 20, $2,300.

21. Received $42,900 cash from Gee Co. on account.

*(Continued)*

May 21. Purchased merchandise on account from Osterman Co., terms 1/10, n/30, FOB destination, $88,000.

24. Returned of damaged merchandise purchased on May 21, receiving a credit memo from the seller for $5,000.

26. Refunded cash on sales made for cash, $7,500. The cost of the merchandise returned was $4,800.

28. Paid sales salaries of $56,000 and office salaries of $29,000.

29. Purchased store supplies for cash, $2,400.

30. Sold merchandise on account to Turner Co., terms 2/10, n/30, FOB shipping point, $78,750. The cost of the merchandise sold was $47,000.

30. Received cash from sale of May 20 plus freight paid on May 21.

31. Paid for purchase of May 21, less return of May 24.

## Instructions

1. Enter the balances of each of the accounts in the appropriate balance column of a four-column account. Write *Balance* in the item section, and place a check mark (✓) in the Posting Reference column. Journalize the transactions for July, starting on Page 20 of the journal.

2. Post the journal to the general ledger, extending the month-end balances to the appropriate balance columns after all posting is completed. In this problem, you are not required to update or post to the accounts receivable and accounts payable subsidiary ledgers.

3. Prepare an unadjusted trial balance.

4. At the end of May, the following adjustment data were assembled. Analyze and use these data to complete (5) and (6).

| | | | |
|---|---|---:|---:|
| a. | Merchandise inventory on May 31 | | $570,000 |
| b. | Insurance expired during the year | | 12,000 |
| c. | Store supplies on hand on May 31 | | 4,000 |
| d. | Depreciation for the current year | | 14,000 |
| e. | Accrued salaries on May 31: | | |
| | Sales salaries | $7,000 | |
| | Office salaries | 6,600 | 13,600 |

f. The adjustment for customer returns and allowances is $60,000 for sales and $35,000 for cost of merchandise sold.

5. *(Optional)* Enter the unadjusted trial balance on a 10-column end-of-period spreadsheet (work sheet), and complete the spreadsheet.

6. Journalize and post the adjusting entries. Record the adjusting entries on Page 22 of the journal.

7. Prepare an adjusted trial balance.

8. Prepare an income statement, a statement of owner's equity, and a balance sheet.

9. Prepare and post the closing entries. Record the closing entries on Page 23 of the journal. Indicate closed accounts by inserting a line in both the Balance columns opposite the closing entry. Insert the new balance in the owner's capital account.

10. Prepare a post-closing trial balance.

# Cases & Projects

### CP 6-1 Ethics and professional conduct in business

On April 18, 2016, Bontanica Company, a garden retailer, purchased $9,800 of seed, terms 2/10, n/30, from Whitetail Seed Co. Even though the discount period had expired, Shelby Davey subtracted the discount of $196 when he processed the documents for payment on May 1, 2016.

━━━━━▶ Discuss whether Shelby Davey behaved in a professional manner by subtracting the discount, even though the discount period had expired.

### CP 6-2 Purchases discounts and accounts payable

Rustic Furniture Co. is owned and operated by Cam Pfeifer. The following is an excerpt from a conversation between Cam Pfeifer and Mitzi Wheeler, the chief accountant for Rustic Furniture Co:

*Cam:* Mitzi, I've got a question about this recent balance sheet.

*Mitzi:* Sure, what's your question?

*Cam:* Well, as you know, I'm applying for a bank loan to finance our new store in Garden Grove, and I noticed that the accounts payable are listed as $320,000.

*Mitzi:* That's right. Approximately $275,000 of that represents amounts due our suppliers, and the remainder is miscellaneous payables to creditors for utilities, office equipment, supplies, etc.

*Cam:* That's what I thought. But as you know, we normally receive a 2% discount from our suppliers for earlier payment, and we always try to take the discount.

*Mitzi:* That's right. I can't remember the last time we missed a discount.

*Cam:* Well, in that case, it seems to me the accounts payable should be listed minus the 2% discount. Let's list the accounts payable due suppliers as $314,500, rather than $320,000. Every little bit helps. You never know. It might make the difference between getting the loan and not.

▶ How would you respond to Cam Pfeifer's request?

### CP 6-3 Determining cost of purchase

The following is an excerpt from a conversation between Mark Loomis and Krista Huff. Mark is debating whether to buy a stereo system from Tru-Sound Systems, a locally owned electronics store, or Wholesale Stereo, an online electronics company.

*Mark:* Krista, I don't know what to do about buying my new stereo.

*Krista:* What's the problem?

*Mark:* Well, I can buy it locally at Tru-Sound Systems for $1,175.00. However, Wholesale Stereo has the same system listed for $1,200.00.

*Krista:* What's the big deal? Buy it from Tru-Sound Systems.

*Mark:* It's not quite that simple. Wholesale Stereo charges $49.99 for shipping and handling. If I have them send it next-day air, it'll cost $89.99 for shipping and handling.

*Krista:* So?

*Mark:* But, that's not all. Tru-Sound Systems will give an additional 2% discount if I pay cash. Otherwise, they will let me use my VISA, or I can pay it off in three monthly installments. In addition, if I buy it from Tru-Sound Systems, I have to pay 9% sales tax. I won't have to pay sales tax if I buy it from Wholesale Stereo, since they are out of state.

*Krista:* Anything else???

*Mark:* Well . . . Wholesale Stereo says I have to charge it on my VISA. They don't accept checks.

*Krista:* I am not surprised. Many online stores don't accept checks.

*Mark:* I give up. What would you do?

1. Assuming that Wholesale Stereo doesn't charge sales tax on the sale to Mark, which company is offering the best buy?

2. ▶ What might be some considerations other than price that might influence Mark's decision on where to buy the stereo system?

**CP 6-4   Sales discounts**

Your sister operates Watercraft Supply Company, an online boat parts distributorship that is in its third year of operation. The following income statement was recently prepared for the year ended October 31, 2016:

**Watercraft Supply Company**
**Income Statement**
**For the Year Ended October 31, 2016**

| | | |
|---|---:|---:|
| Revenues: | | |
| Sales............................................................. | | $1,350,000 |
| Interest revenue ................................................ | | 15,000 |
| Total revenues........................................... | | $1,365,000 |
| Expenses: | | |
| Cost of merchandise sold........................................ | $810,000 | |
| Selling expenses................................................ | 140,000 | |
| Administrative expenses ......................................... | 90,000 | |
| Interest expense................................................ | 4,000 | |
| Total expenses ........................................... | | 1,044,000 |
| Net income ..................................................... | | $ 321,000 |

Your sister is considering a proposal to increase net income by offering sales discounts of 2/15, n/30, and by shipping all merchandise FOB shipping point. Currently, no sales discounts are allowed and merchandise is shipped FOB destination. It is estimated that these credit terms will increase sales by 10%. The ratio of the cost of merchandise sold to sales is expected to be 60%. All selling and administrative expenses are expected to remain unchanged, except for store supplies, miscellaneous selling, office supplies, and miscellaneous administrative expenses, which are expected to increase proportionately with increased sales. The amounts of these preceding items for the year ended October 31, 2016, were as follows:

| | |
|---|---:|
| Store supplies expense | $12,000 |
| Miscellaneous selling expense | 6,000 |
| Office supplies expense | 3,000 |
| Miscellaneous administrative expense | 2,500 |

The other income and other expense items will remain unchanged. The shipment of all merchandise FOB shipping point will eliminate all delivery expenses, which for the year ended October 31, 2016, were $12,000.

1.  Prepare a projected single-step income statement for the year ending October 31, 2017, based on the proposal. Assume all sales are collected within the discount period.

2.  a.  ➤ Based on the projected income statement in (1), would you recommend the implementation of the proposed changes?

    b.  ➤ Describe any possible concerns you may have related to the proposed changes described in (1).

**CP 6-5   Shopping for a television**

**Group Project**

Assume that you are planning to purchase a 55-inch LED, LCD flat-screen television. In groups of three or four, determine the lowest cost for the television, considering the available alternatives and the advantages and disadvantages of each alternative. For example, you could purchase locally, through mail order, or through an Internet shopping service. Consider such factors as delivery charges, interest-free financing, discounts, coupons, and availability of warranty services. Prepare a report for presentation to the class.

# Inventories

## Best Buy

Assume that in September you purchased a Sony HDTV from **Best Buy**. At the same time, you purchased a Denon surround sound system for $399.99. You liked your surround sound so well that in November you purchased an identical Denon system on sale for $349.99 for your bedroom TV. Over the holidays, you moved to a new apartment and in the process of unpacking discovered that one of the Denon surround sound systems was missing. Luckily, your renters or homeowners insurance policy will cover the theft; but the insurance company needs to know the cost of the system that was stolen.

The Denon systems were identical. However, to respond to the insurance company, you will need to identify which system was stolen. Was it the first system, which cost $399.99, or was it the second system, which cost $349.99? Whichever assumption you make may determine the amount that you receive from the insurance company.

Merchandising businesses such as Best Buy make similar assumptions when identical merchandise is purchased at different costs. For example, Best Buy may have purchased thousands of Denon surround sound systems over the past year at different costs. At the end of a period, some of the Denon systems will still be in inventory, and some will have been sold. But which costs relate to the sold systems, and which costs relate to the Denon systems still in inventory? Best Buy's assumption about inventory costs can involve large dollar amounts and, thus, can have a significant impact on the financial statements. For example, Best Buy reported $5,731 million of inventory and net loss of $1,231 million for a recent year.

This chapter discusses such issues as how to determine the cost of merchandise in inventory and the cost of merchandise sold. However, this chapter begins by discussing the importance of control over inventory.

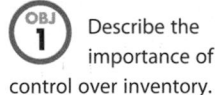
**OBJ 1** Describe the importance of control over inventory.

# Control of Inventory

Two primary objectives of control over inventory are as follows:[1]

- Safeguarding the inventory from damage or theft.
- Reporting inventory in the financial statements.

## Safeguarding Inventory

Controls for safeguarding inventory begin as soon as the inventory is ordered. The following documents are often used for inventory control:

- Purchase order
- Receiving report
- Vendor's invoice

The **purchase order** authorizes the purchase of the inventory from an approved vendor. As soon as the inventory is received, a receiving report is completed. The **receiving report** establishes an initial record of the receipt of the inventory. To make sure the inventory received is what was ordered, the receiving report is compared

[1] Additional controls used by businesses are described and illustrated in Chapter 8, "Sarbanes-Oxley, Internal Control, and Cash."

with the purchase order. The price, quantity, and description of the item on the purchase order and receiving report are then compared to the vendor's invoice. If the receiving report, purchase order, and vendor's invoice agree, the inventory is recorded in the accounting records. If any differences exist, they should be investigated and reconciled.

Recording inventory using a perpetual inventory system is also an effective means of control. The amount of inventory is always available in the **subsidiary inventory ledger**. This helps keep inventory quantities at proper levels. For example, comparing inventory quantities with maximum and minimum levels allows for the timely reordering of inventory and prevents ordering excess inventory.

Finally, controls for safeguarding inventory should include security measures to prevent damage and customer or employee theft. Some examples of security measures include the following:

- Storing inventory in areas that are restricted to only authorized employees
- Locking high-priced inventory in cabinets
- Using two-way mirrors, cameras, security tags, and guards

### Reporting Inventory

A **physical inventory** or *count of inventory* should be taken near year-end to make sure that the quantity of inventory reported in the financial statements is accurate. After the quantity of inventory on hand is determined, the cost of the inventory is assigned for reporting in the financial statements. Most companies assign costs to inventory using one of three inventory cost flow assumptions. If a physical count is not possible or inventory records are not available, the inventory cost may be estimated as described in the appendix at the end of this chapter.

 **Best Buy** uses scanners to screen customers as they leave the store for merchandise that has not been purchased. In addition, Best Buy stations greeters at the store's entrance to keep customers from bringing in bags that can be used to shoplift merchandise.

 **OBJ 2** Describe three inventory cost flow assumptions and how they impact the income statement and balance sheet.

## Inventory Cost Flow Assumptions

An accounting issue arises when identical units of merchandise are acquired at different unit costs during a period. In such cases, when an item is sold, it is necessary to determine its cost using a cost flow assumption and related inventory costing method. Three common cost flow assumptions and related inventory costing methods are shown in Exhibit 1.

**EXHIBIT 1**    **Cost Flow Assumptions**

To illustrate, assume that three identical units of merchandise are purchased during May, as follows:

|  |  |  | Units | Cost |
|---|---|---|---|---|
| May | 10 | Purchase | 1 | $ 9 |
|  | 18 | Purchase | 1 | 13 |
|  | 24 | Purchase | 1 | 14 |
| Total |  |  | 3 | $36 |

Average cost per unit: $12 ($36 ÷ 3 units)

Assume that one unit is sold on May 30 for $20. Depending upon which unit was sold, the gross profit varies from $11 to $6, computed as follows:

|  | May 10 Unit Sold | May 18 Unit Sold | May 24 Unit Sold |
|---|---|---|---|
| Sales | $20 | $20 | $20 |
| Cost of merchandise sold | 9 | 13 | 14 |
| Gross profit | $11 | $ 7 | $ 6 |
| Ending inventory | $27 | $23 | $22 |
|  | ($13 + $14) | ($9 + $14) | ($9 + $13) |

Under the **specific identification inventory cost flow method**, the unit sold is identified with a specific purchase. The ending inventory is made up of the remaining units on hand. Thus, the gross profit, cost of merchandise sold, and ending inventory can vary as illustrated. For example, if the May 18 unit was sold, the cost of merchandise sold is $13, the gross profit is $7, and the ending inventory is $23.

The specific identification method is normally used by automobile dealerships, jewelry stores, and art galleries.

The specific identification method is not practical unless each inventory unit can be separately identified. For example, an automobile dealer may use the specific identification method because each automobile has a unique serial number. However, most businesses cannot identify each inventory unit separately. In such cases, one of the following three inventory cost flow methods is used.

✓ Under the **first-in, first-out (FIFO) inventory cost flow method**, the first units purchased are assumed to be sold and the ending inventory is made up of the most recent purchases. In the preceding example, the May 10 unit would be assumed to have been sold. Thus, the gross profit would be $11, and the ending inventory would be $27 ($13 + $14).

✓ Under the **last-in, first-out (LIFO) inventory cost flow method**, the last units purchased are assumed to be sold and the ending inventory is made up of the first purchases. In the preceding example, the May 24 unit would be assumed to have been sold. Thus, the gross profit would be $6, and the ending inventory would be $22 ($9 + $13).

Under the **weighted average inventory cost flow method**, sometimes called the *average cost flow method*, the cost of the units sold and in ending inventory is a weighted average of the purchase costs. The purchase costs are weighted by the quantities purchased at each cost, thus the term *weighted average*. In the preceding example, the cost of the unit sold would be $12 ($36 ÷ 3 units), the gross profit would be $8 ($20 – $12), and the ending inventory would be $24 ($12 × 2 units). In this example, the purchase costs are weighted equally, since the same quantity (one) was purchased at each cost.

The three inventory cost flow methods, FIFO, LIFO, and weighted average, are shown in Exhibit 2. The frequency with which the FIFO, LIFO, and weighted average methods are used is shown in Exhibit 3.

EXHIBIT 2 **Inventory Costing Methods**

## Purchases

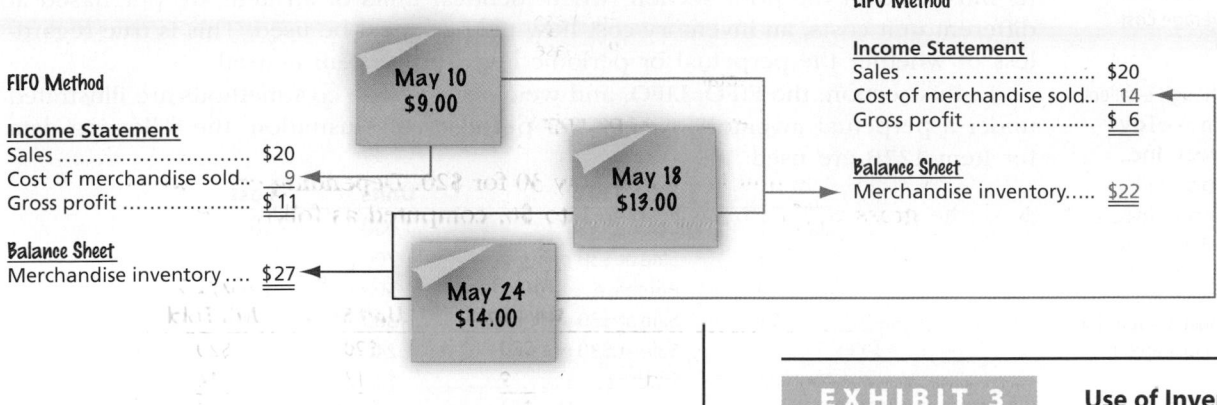

**FIFO Method**

Income Statement
Sales ............................ $20
Cost of merchandise sold.. 9
Gross profit .................... $11

Balance Sheet
Merchandise inventory .... $27

**LIFO Method**

Income Statement
Sales ............................ $20
Cost of merchandise sold.. 14
Gross profit .................... $ 6

Balance Sheet
Merchandise inventory..... $22

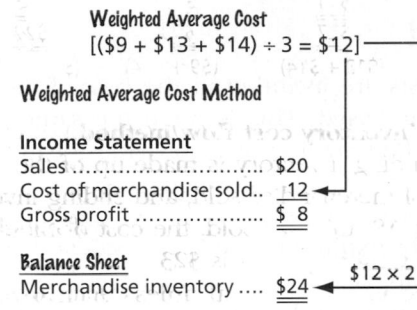

Weighted Average Cost
[($9 + $13 + $14) ÷ 3 = $12]

Weighted Average Cost Method

Income Statement
Sales ............................ $20
Cost of merchandise sold.. 12
Gross profit .................... $ 8

Balance Sheet
Merchandise inventory .... $24    $12 × 2

EXHIBIT 3    **Use of Inventory Costing Methods***

*Firms may be counted more than once for using multiple methods.
Source: *Accounting Trends and Techniques*, 66th edition, 2012
(New York: American Institute of Certified Public Accountants).

---

## Example Exercise 7-1   Cost Flow Methods

The following three identical units of Item QBM are purchased during February:

|          |    | Item QBM  | Units | Cost  |
|----------|----|-----------|-------|-------|
| Feb.     | 8  | Purchase  | 1     | $ 45  |
|          | 15 | Purchase  | 1     | 48    |
|          | 26 | Purchase  | 1     | 51    |
|          | Total |        | 3     | $144  |
|          | Average cost per unit | | | $ 48 ($144 ÷ 3 units) |

Assume that one unit is sold on February 27 for $70.

Determine the gross profit for February and ending inventory on February 28 using the (a) first-in, first-out (FIFO); (b) last-in, first-out (LIFO); and (c) weighted average cost methods.

### Follow My Example 7-1

|                                        | Gross Profit        | Ending Inventory    |
|----------------------------------------|---------------------|---------------------|
| a. First-in, first-out (FIFO)........... | $25 ($70 − $45)     | $99 ($48 + $51)     |
| b. Last-in, first-out (LIFO)........... | $19 ($70 − $51)     | $93 ($45 + $48)     |
| c. Weighted average cost ............. | $22 ($70 − $48)     | $96 ($48 × 2)       |

Practice Exercises: PE 7-1A, PE 7-1B

**OBJ 3**  Determine the cost of inventory under the perpetual inventory system, using the FIFO, LIFO, and weighted average cost methods.

Although e-tailers, such as **eToys Direct, Inc.,** Amazon.com, and Furniture.com, Inc., don't have retail stores, they still take possession of inventory in warehouses. Thus, they must account for inventory as illustrated in this chapter.

# Inventory Costing Methods Under a Perpetual Inventory System

As illustrated in the prior section, when identical units of an item are purchased at different unit costs, an inventory cost flow method must be used. This is true regardless of whether the perpetual or periodic inventory system is used.

In this section, the FIFO, LIFO, and weighted average cost methods are illustrated under a perpetual inventory system. For purposes of illustration, the following data for Item 127B are used:

| Item 127B | | Units | Cost |
|---|---|---|---|
| Jan. 1 | Inventory | 1,000 | $20.00 |
| 4 | Sale at $30 per unit | 700 | |
| 10 | Purchase | 500 | 22.40 |
| 22 | Sale at $30 per unit | 360 | |
| 28 | Sale at $30 per unit | 240 | |
| 30 | Purchase | 600 | 23.30 |

## First-In, First-Out Method

When the FIFO method is used, costs are included in the cost of merchandise sold in the order in which they were purchased. This is often the same as the physical flow of the merchandise. Thus, the FIFO method often provides results that are about the same as those that would have been obtained using the specific identification method. For example, grocery stores shelve milk and other perishable products by expiration dates. Products with early expiration dates are stocked in front. In this way, the oldest products (earliest purchases) are sold first.

To illustrate, Exhibit 4 shows the use of FIFO under a perpetual inventory system for Item 127B. The journal entries and the subsidiary inventory ledger for Item 127B are shown in Exhibit 4 as follows:

1. The beginning balance on January 1 is $20,000 (1,000 units at a unit cost of $20).
2. On January 4, 700 units were sold at a price of $30 each for sales of $21,000 (700 units at a selling price of $30 per unit). The cost of merchandise sold is $14,000 (700 units at a unit cost of $20). After the sale, there remains $6,000 of inventory (300 units at a unit cost of $20).

**EXHIBIT 4**    **Entries and Perpetual Inventory Account (FIFO)**

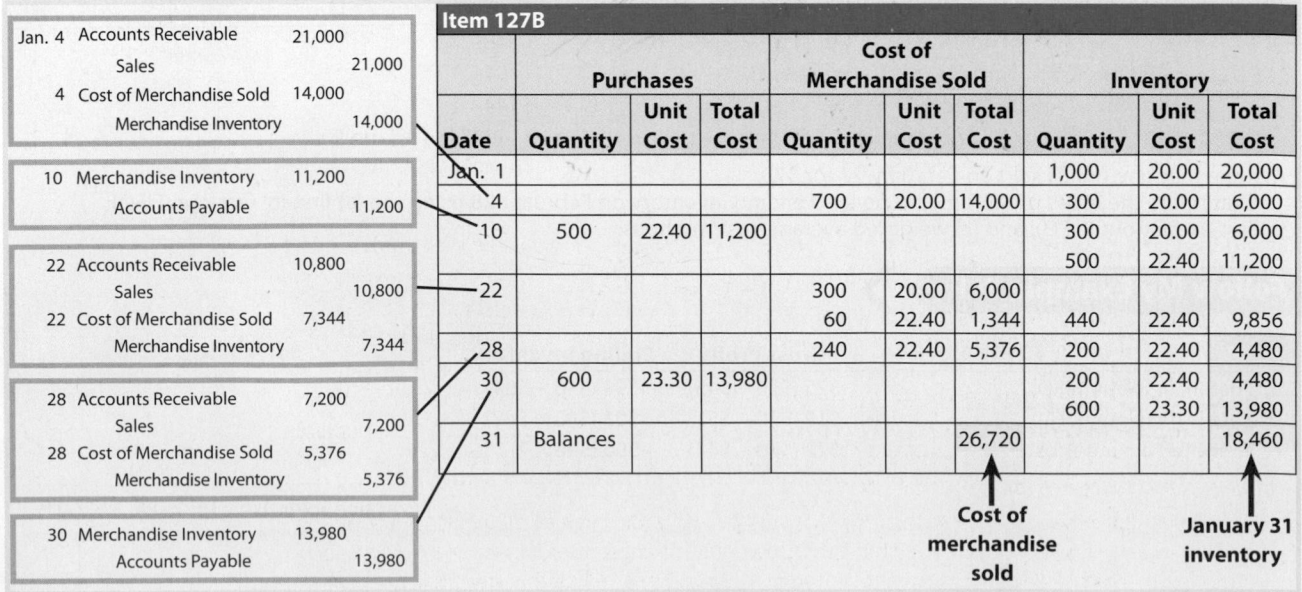

| | Jan. 4 | Accounts Receivable | 21,000 | |
|---|---|---|---|---|
| | | Sales | | 21,000 |
| | 4 | Cost of Merchandise Sold | 14,000 | |
| | | Merchandise Inventory | | 14,000 |
| | 10 | Merchandise Inventory | 11,200 | |
| | | Accounts Payable | | 11,200 |
| | 22 | Accounts Receivable | 10,800 | |
| | | Sales | | 10,800 |
| | 22 | Cost of Merchandise Sold | 7,344 | |
| | | Merchandise Inventory | | 7,344 |
| | 28 | Accounts Receivable | 7,200 | |
| | | Sales | | 7,200 |
| | 28 | Cost of Merchandise Sold | 5,376 | |
| | | Merchandise Inventory | | 5,376 |
| | 30 | Merchandise Inventory | 13,980 | |
| | | Accounts Payable | | 13,980 |

**Item 127B**

| | | Purchases | | | Cost of Merchandise Sold | | | Inventory | | |
|---|---|---|---|---|---|---|---|---|---|---|
| Date | Quantity | Unit Cost | Total Cost | Quantity | Unit Cost | Total Cost | Quantity | Unit Cost | Total Cost |
| Jan. 1 | | | | | | | 1,000 | 20.00 | 20,000 |
| 4 | | | | 700 | 20.00 | 14,000 | 300 | 20.00 | 6,000 |
| 10 | 500 | 22.40 | 11,200 | | | | 300 | 20.00 | 6,000 |
| | | | | | | | 500 | 22.40 | 11,200 |
| 22 | | | | 300 | 20.00 | 6,000 | | | |
| | | | | 60 | 22.40 | 1,344 | 440 | 22.40 | 9,856 |
| 28 | | | | 240 | 22.40 | 5,376 | 200 | 22.40 | 4,480 |
| 30 | 600 | 23.30 | 13,980 | | | | 200 | 22.40 | 4,480 |
| | | | | | | | 600 | 23.30 | 13,980 |
| 31 | Balances | | | | | 26,720 | | | 18,460 |

Cost of merchandise sold

January 31 inventory

3. On January 10, $11,200 is purchased (500 units at a unit cost of $22.40). After the purchase, the inventory is reported on two lines, $6,000 (300 units at a unit cost of $20.00) from the beginning inventory and $11,200 (500 units at a unit cost of $22.40) from the January 10 purchase.

4. On January 22, 360 units are sold at a price of $30 each for sales of $10,800 (360 units at a selling price of $30 per unit). Using FIFO, the cost of merchandise sold of $7,344 consists of $6,000 (300 units at a unit cost of $20.00) from the beginning inventory plus $1,344 (60 units at a unit cost of $22.40) from the January 10 purchase. After the sale, there remains $9,856 of inventory (440 units at a unit cost of $22.40) from the January 10 purchase.

5. The January 28 sale and January 30 purchase are recorded in a similar manner.

6. The ending balance on January 31 is $18,460. This balance is made up of two layers of inventory as follows:

| | Date of Purchase | Quantity | Unit Cost | Total Cost |
|---|---|---|---|---|
| Layer 1: | Jan. 10 | 200 | $22.40 | $ 4,480 |
| Layer 2: | Jan. 30 | 600 | 23.30 | 13,980 |
| Total | | 800 | | $18,460 |

## Example Exercise 7-2  Perpetual Inventory Using FIFO

OBJ 3

Beginning inventory, purchases, and sales for Item ER27 are as follows:

Dynamic Exhibit

| Nov. | 1 | Inventory | 40 units at $5 |
|---|---|---|---|
| | 5 | Sale | 30 units |
| | 11 | Purchase | 70 units at $7 |
| | 21 | Sale | 36 units |

Assuming a perpetual inventory system and using the first-in, first-out (FIFO) method, determine (a) the cost of merchandise sold on November 21 and (b) the inventory on November 30.

### Follow My Example 7-2

a. Cost of merchandise sold (November 21):

| 10 units at $5 | $ 50 |
|---|---|
| 26 units at $7 | 182 |
| 36 units | $232 |

b. Inventory, November 30:
$308 (44 units × $7)

Practice Exercises: PE 7-2A, PE 7-2B

## Last-In, First-Out Method

When the LIFO method is used, the cost of the units sold is the cost of the most recent purchases. The LIFO method was originally used in those rare cases where the units sold were taken from the most recently purchased units. However, for tax purposes, LIFO is now widely used even when it does not represent the physical flow of units. The tax impact of LIFO is discussed later in this chapter.

◀ **IFRS** ‖‖‖

See Appendix D for more information.

To illustrate, Exhibit 5 shows the use of LIFO under a perpetual inventory system for Item 127B. The journal entries and the subsidiary inventory ledger for Item 127B are shown in Exhibit 5 as follows:

1. The beginning balance on January 1 is $20,000 (1,000 units at a unit of cost of $20.00).

2. On January 4, 700 units were sold at a price of $30 each for sales of $21,000 (700 units at a selling price of $30 per unit). The cost of merchandise sold is $14,000 (700 units at a unit cost of $20). After the sale, there remains $6,000 of inventory (300 units at a unit cost of $20).

3. On January 10, $11,200 is purchased (500 units at a unit cost of $22.40). After the purchase, the inventory is reported on two lines, $6,000 (300 units at a unit cost of $20.00) from the beginning inventory and $11,200 (500 units at $22.40 per unit) from the January 10 purchase.

4. On January 22, 360 units are sold at a price of $30 each for sales of $10,800 (360 units at a selling price of $30 per unit). Using LIFO, the cost of merchandise sold is $8,064 (360 units at unit cost of $22.40) from the January 10 purchase. After the sale, there remains

| EXHIBIT 5 | **Entries and Perpetual Inventory Account (LIFO)** |

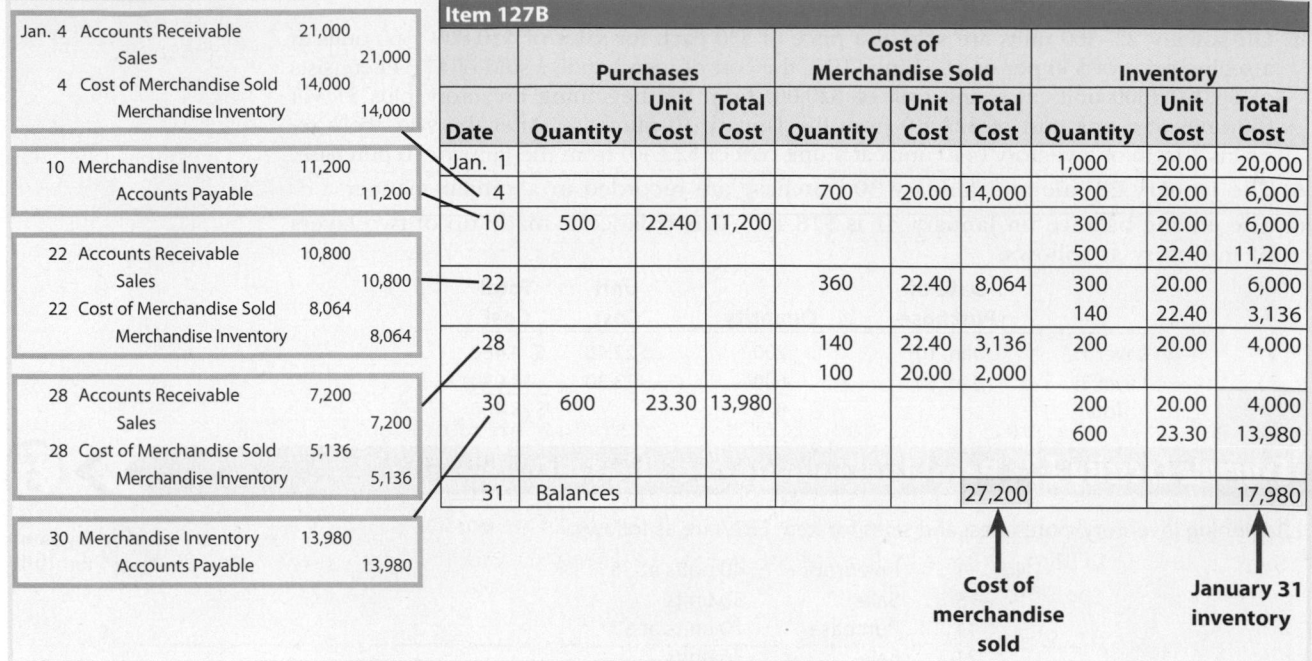

Jan. 4 Accounts Receivable    21,000
      Sales                    21,000
   4 Cost of Merchandise Sold    14,000
      Merchandise Inventory       14,000

   10 Merchandise Inventory    11,200
      Accounts Payable           11,200

   22 Accounts Receivable    10,800
      Sales                    10,800
   22 Cost of Merchandise Sold    8,064
      Merchandise Inventory       8,064

   28 Accounts Receivable    7,200
      Sales                    7,200
   28 Cost of Merchandise Sold    5,136
      Merchandise Inventory       5,136

   30 Merchandise Inventory    13,980
      Accounts Payable           13,980

**Item 127B**

| | Purchases | | | Cost of Merchandise Sold | | | Inventory | | |
|---|---|---|---|---|---|---|---|---|---|
| Date | Quantity | Unit Cost | Total Cost | Quantity | Unit Cost | Total Cost | Quantity | Unit Cost | Total Cost |
| Jan. 1 | | | | | | | 1,000 | 20.00 | 20,000 |
| 4 | | | | 700 | 20.00 | 14,000 | 300 | 20.00 | 6,000 |
| 10 | 500 | 22.40 | 11,200 | | | | 300 | 20.00 | 6,000 |
| | | | | | | | 500 | 22.40 | 11,200 |
| 22 | | | | 360 | 22.40 | 8,064 | 300 | 20.00 | 6,000 |
| | | | | | | | 140 | 22.40 | 3,136 |
| 28 | | | | 140 | 22.40 | 3,136 | 200 | 20.00 | 4,000 |
| | | | | 100 | 20.00 | 2,000 | | | |
| 30 | 600 | 23.30 | 13,980 | | | | 200 | 20.00 | 4,000 |
| | | | | | | | 600 | 23.30 | 13,980 |
| 31 | Balances | | | | | 27,200 | | | 17,980 |

Cost of merchandise sold

January 31 inventory

$9,136 of inventory consisting of $6,000 (300 units at a unit cost of $20.00) from the beginning inventory and $3,136 (140 units at a unit cost of $22.40) from the January 10 purchase.

5. The January 28 sale and January 30 purchase are recorded in a similar manner.

6. The ending balance on January 31 is $17,980. This balance is made up of two layers of inventory as follows:

| | Date of Purchase | Quantity | Unit Cost | Total Cost |
|---|---|---|---|---|
| Layer 1: | Beg. inv. (Jan. 1) | 200 | $20.00 | $ 4,000 |
| Layer 2: | Jan. 30 | 600 | 23.30 | 13,980 |
| | Total | 800 | | $17,980 |

When the LIFO method is used, the subsidiary inventory ledger is sometimes maintained in units only. The units are converted to dollars when the financial statements are prepared at the end of the period.

## *Example Exercise 7-3* **Perpetual Inventory Using LIFO**

OBJ 3

Beginning inventory, purchases, and sales for Item ER27 are as follows:

| Nov. | 1 | Inventory | 40 units at $5 |
|---|---|---|---|
| | 5 | Sale | 30 units |
| | 11 | Purchase | 70 units at $7 |
| | 21 | Sale | 36 units |

Dynamic Exhibit

Assuming a perpetual inventory system and using the last-in, first-out (LIFO) method, determine (a) the cost of the merchandise sold on November 21 and (b) the inventory on November 30.

## **Follow My Example 7-3**

a. Cost of merchandise sold (November 21):
    $252 (36 units × $7)

b. Inventory, November 30:

| 10 units at $5 | $ 50 |
|---|---|
| 34 units at $7 | 238 |
| 44 units | $288 |

Practice Exercises: PE 7-3A, PE 7-3B

# International 🌐 Connection

||| **IFRS** ▶ INTERNATIONAL FINANCIAL REPORTING STANDARDS (IFRS)

IFRS permit the first-in, first-out and weighted average cost methods but prohibit the last-in, first-out (LIFO) method for determining inventory costs. Since LIFO is used in the United States, adoption of IFRS could have a significant impact on many U.S. companies. For example, Caterpillar Inc. uses LIFO. For a recent year, Caterpillar reported that its inventories would have been $2,750 million higher if FIFO had been used. Since Caterpillar reported profits of $5,681 million for the year, the adoption of IFRS would have significantly affected net income if IFRS and FIFO had been used.*

*Differences between U.S. GAAP and IFRS are further discussed and illustrated in Appendix D.

## Weighted Average Cost Method

When the weighted average cost method is used in a perpetual inventory system, a weighted average unit cost for each item is computed each time a purchase is made. This unit cost is used to determine the cost of each sale until another purchase is made and a new average is computed. This technique is called a *moving average*.

To illustrate, Exhibit 6 shows the use of weighted average under a perpetual inventory system for Item 127B.

---

**EXHIBIT 6** **Entries and Perpetual Inventory Account (Weighted Average)**

Jan. 4 Accounts Receivable 21,000
      Sales 21,000
    4 Cost of Merchandise Sold 14,000
      Merchandise Inventory 14,000

   10 Merchandise Inventory 11,200
      Accounts Payable 11,200

   22 Accounts Receivable 10,800
      Sales 10,800
   22 Cost of Merchandise Sold 7,740
      Merchandise Inventory 7,740

   28 Accounts Receivable 7,200
      Sales 7,200
   28 Cost of Merchandise Sold 5,160
      Merchandise Inventory 5,160

   30 Merchandise Inventory 13,980
      Accounts Payable 13,980

**Item 127B**

| | Purchases | | | Cost of Merchandise Sold | | | Inventory | | |
|---|---|---|---|---|---|---|---|---|---|
| Date | Quantity | Unit Cost | Total Cost | Quantity | Unit Cost | Total Cost | Quantity | Unit Cost | Total Cost |
| Jan. 1 | | | | | | | 1,000 | 20.00 | 20,000 |
| 4 | | | | 700 | 20.00 | 14,000 | 300 | 20.00 | 6,000 |
| 10 | 500 | 22.40 | 11,200 | | | | 800 | 21.50 | 17,200 |
| 22 | | | | 360 | 21.50 | 7,740 | 440 | 21.50 | 9,460 |
| 28 | | | | 240 | 21.50 | 5,160 | 200 | 21.50 | 4,300 |
| 30 | 600 | 23.30 | 13,980 | | | | 800 | 22.85 | 18,280 |
| 31 | Balances | | | | | 26,900 | 800 | 22.85 | 18,280 |

Cost of merchandise sold

January 31 inventory

---

The journal entries and the subsidiary inventory ledger for Item 127B are shown in Exhibit 6 as follows:

1. The beginning balance on January 1 is $20,000 (1,000 units at a unit cost of $20).
2. On January 4, 700 units were sold at a price of $30 each for sales of $21,000 (700 units at a selling price of $30 per unit). The cost of merchandise sold is $14,000 (700 units at a unit cost of $20.00). After the sale, there remains $6,000 of inventory (300 units at a unit cost of $20.00).
3. On January 10, $11,200 is purchased (500 units at a unit cost of $22.40). After the purchase, the weighted average unit cost of $21.50 is determined by dividing the total

cost of the inventory on hand of $17,200 ($6,000 + $11,200) by the total quantity of inventory on hand of 800 (300 + 500) units. Thus, after the purchase, the inventory consists of 800 units at $21.50 per unit for a total cost of $17,200.

4. On January 22, 360 units are sold at a price of $30 each for sales of $10,800 (360 units at a selling price of $30 per unit). Using weighted average, the cost of merchandise sold is $7,740 (360 units × $21.50 per unit). After the sale, there remains $9,460 of inventory (440 units × $21.50 per unit).

5. The January 28 sale and January 30 purchase are recorded in a similar manner.

6. The ending balance on January 31 is $18,280 (800 units × $22.85 per unit).

---

### Example Exercise 7-4   Perpetual Inventory Using Weighted Average

Beginning inventory, purchases, and sales for ER27 are as follows:

| Nov. | 1  | Inventory | 40 units at $5 |
|------|----|-----------|----------------|
|      | 5  | Sale      | 30 units       |
|      | 11 | Purchase  | 70 units at $7 |
|      | 21 | Sale      | 36 units       |

Dynamic Exhibit

Assuming a perpetual inventory system using the weighted average method, determine (a) the weighted average unit cost after the November 11 purchase, (b) the cost of the merchandise sold on November 21, and (c) the inventory on November 30.

### Follow My Example 7-4

a.  Weighted average unit cost: $6.75
    Inventory total cost after purchase on November 21:

|               | **Cost** |
|---------------|----------|
| 10 units at $5 | $  50   |
| 70 units at $7 | 490     |
| 80 units       | $540    |

Weighted average unit cost = $6.75 ($540 ÷ 80 units)

b.  Cost of merchandise sold (November 21):
    $243 (36 units × $6.75)

c.  Inventory, November 30:
    $297 (44 units at $6.75)

Practice Exercises: PE 7-4A, PE 7-4B

---

## Computerized Perpetual Inventory Systems

A perpetual inventory system may be used in a manual accounting system. However, if there are many inventory transactions, such a system is costly and time consuming. In almost all cases, perpetual inventory systems are computerized.

Computerized perpetual inventory systems are useful to managers in controlling and managing inventory. For example, fast-selling items can be reordered before the stock runs out. Sales patterns can also be analyzed to determine when to mark down merchandise or when to restock seasonal merchandise. Finally, inventory data can be used in evaluating advertising campaigns and sales promotions.

**OBJ 4**
Determine the cost of inventory under the periodic inventory system, using the FIFO, LIFO, and weighted average cost methods.

## Inventory Costing Methods Under a Periodic Inventory System

When the periodic inventory system is used, only revenue is recorded each time a sale is made. No entry is made at the time of the sale to record the cost of the merchandise sold. At the end of the accounting period, a physical inventory is taken to determine the cost of the inventory and the cost of the merchandise sold.[2]

---

[2] Determining the cost of merchandise sold using the periodic system was illustrated in the appendix to Chapter 6.

Like the perpetual inventory system, a cost flow assumption must be made when identical units are acquired at different unit costs during a period. In such cases, the FIFO, LIFO, or weighted average cost method is used.

## First-In, First-Out Method

To illustrate the use of the FIFO method in a periodic inventory system, we use the same data for Item 127B as in the perpetual inventory example. The beginning inventory and purchases of Item 127B in January are as follows:

| Jan. | 1 | Inventory | 1,000 units at | $20.00 | $20,000 |
|------|---|-----------|----------------|--------|---------|
|      | 10 | Purchase | 500 units at | 22.40 | 11,200 |
|      | 30 | Purchase | 600 units at | 23.30 | 13,980 |
| Available for sale during month | | | 2,100 | | $45,180 |

The physical count on January 31 shows that 800 units are on hand. Using the FIFO method, the cost of the merchandise on hand at the end of the period is made up of the most recent costs. The cost of the 800 units in the ending inventory on January 31 is determined as follows:

| Most recent costs, January 30 purchase | 600 units at | $23.30 | $13,980 |
|---|---|---|---|
| Next most recent costs, January 10 purchase | 200 units at | $22.40 | 4,480 |
| Inventory, January 31 | 800 units | | $18,460 |

Deducting the cost of the January 31 inventory of $18,460 from the cost of merchandise available for sale of $45,180 yields the cost of merchandise sold of $26,720, computed as follows:

| Beginning inventory, January 1 | $20,000 |
|---|---|
| Purchases ($11,200 + $13,980) | 25,180 |
| Cost of merchandise available for sale in January | $45,180 |
| Less ending inventory, January 31 | 18,460 |
| Cost of merchandise sold | $26,720 |

The $18,460 cost of the ending merchandise inventory on January 31 is made up of the most recent costs. The $26,720 cost of merchandise sold is made up of the beginning inventory and the earliest costs. Exhibit 7 shows the relationship of the cost of merchandise sold for January and the ending inventory on January 31.

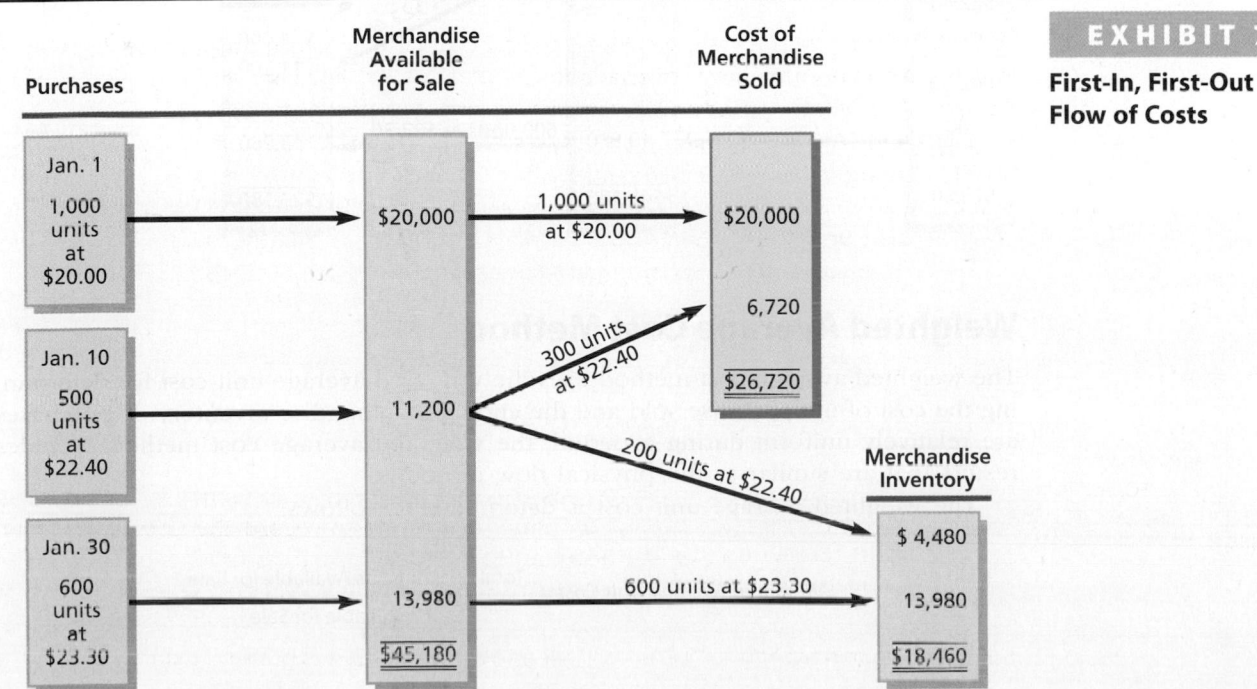

**EXHIBIT 7**

**First-In, First-Out Flow of Costs**

## Last-In, First-Out Method

See Appendix D for more information.

When the LIFO method is used, the cost of merchandise on hand at the end of the period is made up of the earliest costs. Based on the same data as in the FIFO example, the cost of the 800 units in ending inventory on January 31 is $16,000, which consists of 800 units from the beginning inventory at a cost of $20.00 per unit.

Deducting the cost of the January 31 inventory of $16,000 from the cost of merchandise available for sale of $45,180 yields the cost of merchandise sold of $29,180, computed as follows:

| | |
|---|---:|
| Beginning inventory, January 1 | $20,000 |
| Purchases ($11,200 + $13,980) | 25,180 |
| Cost of merchandise available for sale in January | $45,180 |
| Less ending inventory, January 31 | 16,000 |
| Cost of merchandise sold | $29,180 |

The $16,000 cost of the ending merchandise inventory on January 31 is made up of the earliest costs. The $29,180 cost of merchandise sold is made up of the most recent costs. Exhibit 8 shows the relationship of the cost of merchandise sold for January and the ending inventory on January 31.

### EXHIBIT 8

**Last-In, First-Out Flow of Costs**

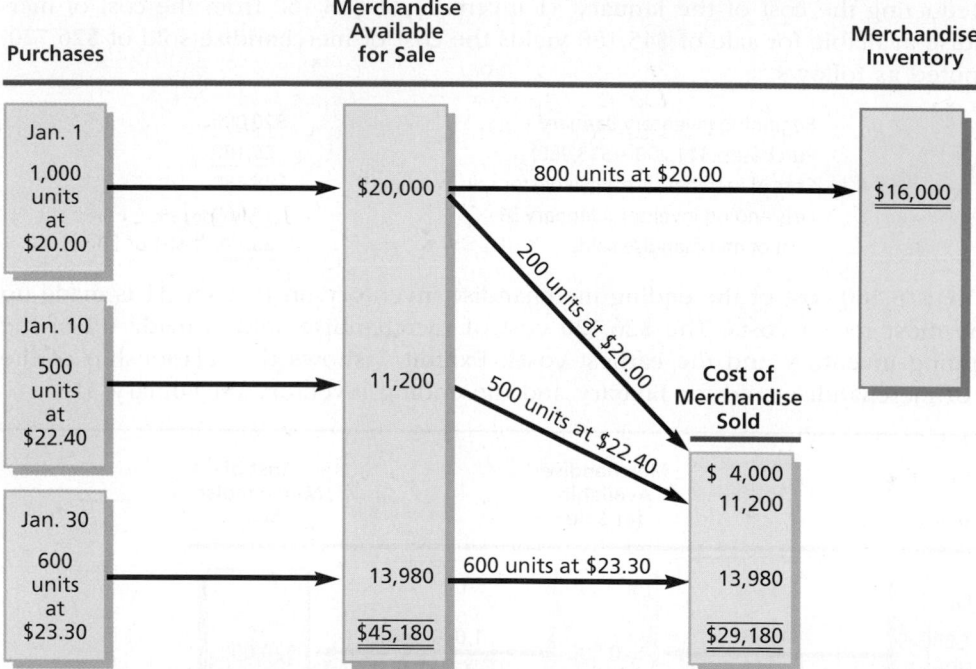

## Weighted Average Cost Method

The weighted average cost method uses the weighted average unit cost for determining the cost of merchandise sold and the ending merchandise inventory. If purchases are relatively uniform during a period, the weighted average cost method provides results that are similar to the physical flow of goods.

The weighted average unit cost is determined as follows:

$$\text{Weighted Average Unit Cost} = \frac{\text{Total Cost of Units Available for Sale}}{\text{Units Available for Sale}}$$

To illustrate, the data for Item 127B is used as follows:

$$\text{Weighted Average Unit Cost} = \frac{\text{Total Cost of Units Available for Sale}}{\text{Units Available for Sale}} = \frac{\$45,180}{2,100 \text{ units}}$$

$$= \$21.51 \text{ per unit (Rounded)}$$

The cost of the January 31 ending inventory is as follows:

Inventory, January 31: $17,208 (800 units × $21.51)

Deducting the cost of the January 31 inventory of $17,208 from the cost of merchandise available for sale of $45,180 yields the cost of merchandise sold of $27,972, computed as follows:

| | |
|---|---|
| Beginning inventory, January 1 | $20,000 |
| Purchases ($11,200 + $13,980) | 25,180 |
| Cost of merchandise available for sale in January | $45,180 |
| Less ending inventory, January 31 | 17,208 |
| Cost of merchandise sold | $27,972 |

---

## Example Exercise 7-5  Periodic Inventory Using FIFO, LIFO, and Weighted Average Cost Methods

OBJ 4

The units of an item available for sale during the year were as follows:

| | | | | |
|---|---|---|---|---|
| Jan. | 1 | Inventory | 6 units at $50 | $ 300 |
| Mar. | 20 | Purchase | 14 units at $55 | 770 |
| Oct. | 30 | Purchase | 20 units at $62 | 1,240 |
| | | Available for sale | 40 units | $2,310 |

There are 16 units of the item in the physical inventory at December 31. The periodic inventory system is used. Determine the inventory cost using (a) the first-in, first-out (FIFO) method; (b) the last-in, first-out (LIFO) method; and (c) the weighted average cost method.

### Follow My Example 7-5

a. First-in, first-out (FIFO) method: $992 = (16 units × $62)
b. Last-in, first-out (LIFO) method: $850 = (6 units × $50) + (10 units × $55)
c. Weighted average cost method: $924 (16 units × $57.75), where average cost = $57.75 = $2,310 ÷ 40 units

Practice Exercises: PE 7-5A, PE 7-5B

---

# Comparing Inventory Costing Methods

OBJ 5 Compare and contrast the use of the three inventory costing methods.

A different cost flow is assumed for the FIFO, LIFO, and weighted average inventory cost flow methods. As a result, the three methods normally yield different amounts for the following:

• Cost of merchandise sold
• Gross profit
• Net income
• Ending merchandise inventory

See Appendix D for
more information.

Using the perpetual inventory system illustration with sales of $39,000 (1,300 units ×
$30), the following differences are apparent:[3]

**Partial Income Statements**

|  | First-In, First-Out | Weighted Average Cost | Last-In, First-Out |
|---|---|---|---|
| Sales | $39,000 | $39,000 | $39,000 |
| Cost of merchandise sold: | 26,720 | 26,900 | 27,200 |
| Gross profit | $12,280 | $12,100 | $11,800 |
| Merchandise Inventory, Jan. 31 | $18,460 | $18,280 | $17,980 |

The preceding differences show the effect of increasing costs (prices). If costs
(prices) remain the same, all three methods would yield the same results. However,
costs (prices) normally do change. The effects of changing costs (prices) on the FIFO
and LIFO methods are summarized in Exhibit 9. The weighted average cost method
will always yield results between those of FIFO and LIFO.

---

**EXHIBIT 9**

**Effects of Changing
Costs (Prices):
FIFO and LIFO Cost
Methods**

|  | **+ Increasing Costs (Prices)** | | **− Decreasing Costs (Prices)** | |
|---|---|---|---|---|
|  | ▲ Highest Amount | ▼ Lowest Amount | ▲ Highest Amount | ▼ Lowest Amount |
| Cost of merchandise sold | LIFO | FIFO | FIFO | LIFO |
| Gross profit | FIFO | LIFO | LIFO | FIFO |
| Net income | FIFO | LIFO | LIFO | FIFO |
| Ending merchandise inventory | FIFO | LIFO | LIFO | FIFO |

---

FIFO reports higher gross profit and net income than the LIFO method when
costs (prices) are increasing, as shown in Exhibit 9. However, in periods of rapidly
rising costs, the inventory that is sold must be replaced at increasingly higher costs.
In such cases, the larger FIFO gross profit and net income are sometimes called
*inventory profits* or *illusory profits*.

During a period of increasing costs, LIFO matches more recent costs against
sales on the income statement. Thus, it can be argued that the LIFO method more
nearly matches current costs with current revenues. LIFO also offers an income
tax savings during periods of increasing costs. This is because LIFO reports the
lowest amount of gross profit and, thus, taxable net income.[4] However, under
LIFO, the ending inventory on the balance sheet may be quite different from
its current replacement cost. In such cases, the financial statements normally
include a note that estimates what the inventory would have been if FIFO had
been used.

The weighted average cost method is, in a sense, a compromise between FIFO
and LIFO. The effect of cost (price) trends is averaged in determining the cost of
merchandise sold and the ending inventory.

---

[3] Similar results would also occur when comparing inventory costing methods under a periodic inventory system.
[4] A proposal currently exists to not allow the use of LIFO for tax purposes.

## Integrity, Objectivity, and Ethics in Business

**WHERE'S THE BONUS?**

Managers are often given bonuses based on reported earnings numbers. This can create a conflict. LIFO can improve the value of the company through lower taxes. However, in periods of rising costs (prices), LIFO also produces a lower earnings number and, therefore, lower management bonuses. Ethically, managers should select accounting procedures that will maximize the value of the firm, rather than their own compensation. Compensation specialists can help avoid this ethical dilemma by adjusting the bonus plan for the accounting procedure differences.

# Reporting Merchandise Inventory in the Financial Statements

**OBJ 6** Describe and illustrate the reporting of merchandise inventory in the financial statements.

Cost is the primary basis for valuing and reporting inventories in the financial statements. However, inventory may be valued at other than cost in the following cases:

1. The cost of replacing items in inventory is below the recorded cost.
2. The inventory cannot be sold at normal prices due to imperfections, style changes, spoilage, damage, obsolescence, or other causes.

## Valuation at Lower of Cost or Market

If the market is lower than the purchase cost, the **lower-of-cost-or-market (LCM) method** is used to value the inventory. *Market,* as used in *lower of cost or market,* is the **net realizable value** of the merchandise.[5] Net realizable value is determined as follows:

See Appendix D for more information.

Net Realizable Value = Estimated Selling Price – Direct Costs of Disposal

Direct costs of disposal include selling expenses such as special advertising or sales commissions.

To illustrate, assume the following data about an item of damaged merchandise:

| | |
|---|---|
| Original cost | $1,000 |
| Estimated selling price | 800 |
| Estimated selling expenses | 150 |

In applying LCM, the market value of the merchandise is $650, computed as follows:

Market Value (Net Realizable Value) = $800 – $150 = $650

Thus, the merchandise would be valued at $650, which is the lower of its cost of $1,000 and its market value of $650.

The lower-of-cost-or-market method can be applied in one of three ways. The cost, market price, and any declines could be determined for the following:

- Each item in the inventory
- Each major class or category of inventory
- Total inventory as a whole

The amount of any price decline is included in the cost of merchandise sold. This, in turn, reduces gross profit and net income in the period in which the price declines occur. This matching of price declines to the period in which they occur is the primary advantage of using the lower-of-cost-or-market method.

[5] The FASB has issued a Proposed Accounting Standards Update that uses net realizable value as market. Proposed Accounting Standards Update, *Inventory (Topic 3330): Simplifying the Measurement of Inventory,* July 15, 2014, FASB.

To illustrate, assume the following data for 400 identical units of Item A in inventory on December 31, 2016:

| | |
|---|---|
| Cost per unit | $10.25 |
| Market value (net realizable value) per unit | 9.50 |

Since the market value of Item A is $9.50 per unit, $9.50 is used under the lower-of-cost-or-market method.

Exhibit 10 illustrates applying the lower-of-cost-or-market method to each inventory item (Echo, Foxtrot, Sierra, Tango). As applied on an item-by-item basis, the total lower-of-cost-or-market is $15,070, which is a market decline of $450 ($15,520 − $15,070). This market decline of $450 is included in the cost of merchandise sold.

In Exhibit 10, Items Echo, Foxtrot, Sierra, and Tango could be viewed as a class of inventory items. If the lower-of-cost-or-market method is applied to the class, the inventory would be valued at $15,472, which is a market decline of $48 ($15,520 − $15,472). Likewise, if Items Echo, Foxtrot, Sierra, and Tango make up the total inventory, the lower-of-cost-or-market method as applied to the total inventory would be the same amount, $15,472.

---

**EXHIBIT 10**

**Determining Inventory at Lower of Cost or Market (LCM)**

| | A | B | C | D | E | F | G |
|---|---|---|---|---|---|---|---|
| 1 | | | | Market Value | | | |
| 2 | | Inventory | Cost per | per Unit | | Total | |
| 3 | Item | Quantity | Unit | (Net Realizable Value) | Cost | Market | LCM |
| 4 | Echo | 400 | $10.25 | $ 9.50 | $ 4,100 | $ 3,800 | $ 3,800 |
| 5 | Foxtrot | 120 | 22.50 | 24.10 | 2,700 | 2,892 | 2,700 |
| 6 | Sierra | 600 | 8.00 | 7.75 | 4,800 | 4,650 | 4,650 |
| 7 | Tango | 280 | 14.00 | 14.75 | 3,920 | 4,130 | 3,920 |
| 8 | Total | | | | $15,520 | $15,472 | $15,070 |
| 9 | | | | | | | |

---

**Example Exercise 7-6    Lower-of-Cost-or-Market Method**

On the basis of the following data, determine the value of the inventory at the lower of cost or market. Apply lower of cost or market to each inventory item as shown in Exhibit 10.

| Item | Inventory Quantity | Cost per Unit | Market Value per Unit (Net Realizable Value) |
|---|---|---|---|
| C17Y | 10 | $ 39 | $40 |
| B563 | 7 | 110 | 98 |

**Follow My Example 7-6**

| | A | B | C | D | E | F | G |
|---|---|---|---|---|---|---|---|
| 1 | | | | Market Value | | | |
| 2 | | Inventory | Cost per | per Unit | | Total | |
| 3 | Item | Quantity | Unit | (Net Realizable Value) | Cost | Market | LCM |
| 4 | C17Y | 10 | $ 39 | $40 | $ 390 | $ 400 | $ 390 |
| 5 | B563 | 7 | 110 | 98 | 770 | 686 | 686 |
| 6 | Total | | | | $1,160 | $1,086 | $1,076 |
| 7 | | | | | | | |

Practice Exercises: PE 7-6A, PE 7-6B

## Business  Connection

## Merchandise Inventory on the Balance Sheet

Merchandise inventory is usually reported in the Current Assets section of the balance sheet. In addition to this amount, the following are reported:

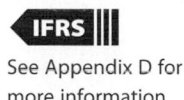

See Appendix D for more information.

- The method of determining the cost of the inventory (FIFO, LIFO, or weighted average)
- The method of valuing the inventory (cost or the lower of cost or market)

The financial statement reporting for the topics covered in Chapters 7–15 are illustrated using excerpts from the financial statements of **Mornin' Joe**. Mornin' Joe is a fictitious company that offers drip and espresso coffee in a coffeehouse setting. The complete financial statements of Mornin' Joe are illustrated at the end of Chapter 15.

The balance sheet presentation for merchandise inventory for Mornin' Joe is as follows:

| Mornin' Joe | | |
| Balance Sheet | | |
| December 31, 2016 | | |
| --- | --- | --- |
| Current assets: | | |
| Cash and cash equivalents ....................................... | | $235,000 |
| Trading investments (at cost) .................................... | $420,000 | |
| Plus valuation allowance on trading investments .............. | 45,000 | 465,000 |
| Accounts receivable ............................................ | $305,000 | |
| Less allowance for doubtful accounts ........................ | 12,300 | 292,700 |
| Merchandise inventory—at lower of cost | | |
| (first-in, first-out method) or market ......................... | | 120,000 |

It is not unusual for a large business to use different costing methods for segments of its inventories. Also, a business may change its inventory costing method. In such cases, the effect of the change and the reason for the change are disclosed in the financial statements.

## Effect of Inventory Errors on the Financial Statements

Any errors in merchandise inventory will affect the balance sheet and income statement. Some reasons that inventory errors may occur include the following:

- Physical inventory on hand was miscounted.
- Costs were incorrectly assigned to inventory. For example, the FIFO, LIFO, or weighted average cost method was incorrectly applied.
- Inventory in transit was incorrectly included or excluded from inventory.
- Consigned inventory was incorrectly included or excluded from inventory.

Inventory errors often arise from merchandise that is in transit at year-end. As discussed in Chapter 6, shipping terms determine when the title to merchandise passes. When goods are purchased or sold *FOB shipping point*, title passes to the buyer when the goods are shipped. When the terms are *FOB destination*, title passes to the buyer when the goods are received.

To illustrate, assume that SysExpress ordered the following merchandise from American Products:

| | |
|---|---|
| Date ordered: | December 27, 2015 |
| Amount: | $10,000 |
| Terms: | FOB shipping point, 2/10, n/30 |
| Date shipped by seller: | December 30 |
| Date delivered: | January 3, 2016 |

When SysExpress counts its physical inventory on December 31, 2015, the merchandise is still in transit. In such cases, it would be easy for SysExpress to not include the $10,000 of merchandise in its December 31 physical inventory. However, since the merchandise was purchased *FOB shipping point*, SysExpress owns the merchandise. Thus, it should be included in the December 31 inventory, even though it is not on hand. Likewise, any merchandise *sold* by SysExpress *FOB destination* is still SysExpress's inventory, even if it is in transit to the buyer on December 31.

Inventory errors often arise from **consigned inventory**. Manufacturers sometimes ship merchandise to retailers who act as the manufacturer's selling agent. The manufacturer, called the **consignor**, retains title until the goods are sold. Such merchandise is said to be shipped *on consignment* to the retailer, called the **consignee**. Any unsold merchandise at year-end is a part of the manufacturer's (consignor's) inventory, even though the merchandise is in the hands of the retailer (consignee). At year-end, it would be easy for the retailer (consignee) to incorrectly include the consigned merchandise in its physical inventory. Likewise, the manufacturer (consignor) should include consigned inventory in its physical inventory, even though the inventory is not on hand.

**Income Statement Effects** Inventory errors will misstate the income statement amounts for cost of merchandise sold, gross profit, and net income. The effects of inventory errors on the current period's income statement are summarized in Exhibit 11.

---

**EXHIBIT 11**

**Effect of Inventory Errors on Current Period's Income Statement**

| | Income Statement Effect | | |
|---|---|---|---|
| **Inventory Error** | **Cost of Merchandise Sold** | **Gross Profit** | **Net Income** |
| Beginning inventory is: | | | |
| Understated ↓ | Understated ↓ | ↑ Overstated | ↑ Overstated |
| ↑ Overstated | ↑ Overstated | Understated ↓ | Understated ↓ |
| Ending inventory is: | | | |
| Understated ↓ | ↑ Overstated | Understated ↓ | Understated ↓ |
| ↑ Overstated | Understated ↓ | ↑ Overstated | ↑ Overstated |

---

To illustrate, the income statements of SysExpress shown in Exhibit 12 are used.[6] On December 31, 2015, assume that SysExpress incorrectly records its physical inventory as $50,000 instead of the correct amount of $60,000. Thus, the December 31, 2015, inventory is understated by $10,000 ($60,000 – $50,000). As a result, the cost of merchandise sold is overstated by $10,000. The gross profit and the net income for the year will also be understated by $10,000.

The December 31, 2015, merchandise inventory becomes the January 1, 2016, inventory. Thus, the beginning inventory for 2016 is understated by $10,000. As a result, the cost of merchandise sold is understated by $10,000 for 2016. The gross profit and net income for 2016 will be overstated by $10,000.

As shown in Exhibit 12, because the ending inventory of one period is the beginning inventory of the next period, the effects of inventory errors carry forward to the next period. Specifically, if uncorrected, the effects of inventory errors reverse themselves in the next period. In Exhibit 12, the combined net income for the two years of $525,000 is correct, even though the 2015 and 2016 income statements were incorrect.

---

[6] The effect of inventory errors will be illustrated using the periodic system. This is because it is easier to see the impact of inventory errors on the income statement using the periodic system. The effect of inventory errors would be the same under the perpetual inventory system.

**EXHIBIT 12**    **Effects of Inventory Errors on Two Years' Income Statements**

**SysExpress**
**Income Statement**
**For the Years Ended December 31, 2015 and 2016**

| | 2015 | | 2016 | |
| --- | --- | --- | --- | --- |
| | **Correct** | **Incorrect** | **Incorrect** | **Correct** |
| Sales | $980,000 | $980,000 | $1,100,000 | $1,100,000 |
| Merchandise inventory, January 1 | $ 55,000 | $ 55,000 | $ 50,000 | $ 60,000 |
| Purchases | 650,000 | 650,000 | 700,000 | 700,000 |
| Merchandise available for sale | $705,000 | $705,000 | $750,000 | $760,000 |
| Less merchandise inventory, December 31 | 60,000 | 50,000 | 70,000 | 70,000 |
| Cost of merchandise sold | 645,000 | 655,000 | 680,000 | 690,000 |
| Gross profit | $335,000 | $325,000 | $ 420,000 | $ 410,000 |
| Operating expenses | 100,000 | 100,000 | 120,000 | 120,000 |
| Net income | $235,000 | $225,000 | $ 300,000 | $ 290,000 |

$10,000
Understatement
of Net Income

$10,000
Overstatement
of Net Income

Net Effect Is Zero for Two Years
The inventory errors reverse (or cancel) so that the combined net
income for the two years of $525,000 ($225,000 + $300,000) is correct.

**Balance Sheet Effects** Inventory errors misstate the merchandise inventory, current assets, total assets, and owner's equity on the balance sheet. The effects of inventory errors on the current period's balance sheet are summarized in Exhibit 13.

**EXHIBIT 13**

**Effect of Inventory Errors on Current Period's Balance Sheet**

| | Balance Sheet Effect | | | |
| --- | --- | --- | --- | --- |
| **Ending Inventory Error** | **Merchandise Inventory** | **Current Assets** | **Total Assets** | **Owner's Equity (Capital)** |
| Understated ▾ | Understated ▾ | Understated ▾ | Understated ▾ | Understated ▾ |
| ▴ Overstated | ▴ Overstated | ▴ Overstated | ▴ Overstated | ▴ Overstated |

For the SysExpress illustration shown in Exhibit 12, the December 31, 2015, ending inventory was understated by $10,000. As a result, the merchandise inventory, current assets, and total assets would be understated by $10,000 on the December 31, 2015, balance sheet. Because the ending physical inventory is understated, the cost of merchandise sold for 2015 will be overstated by $10,000. Thus, the gross profit and the net income for 2015 are understated by $10,000. Because the net income is closed to owner's equity (capital) at the end of the period, the owner's equity on the December 31, 2015, balance sheet is also understated by $10,000.

Inventory errors reverse themselves within two years. As a result, the balance sheet will be correct as of December 31, 2016. Using the SysExpress illustration from Exhibit 12, these effects are summarized as follows:

|  | Amount of Misstatement | |
| --- | --- | --- |
| Balance Sheet: | December 31, 2015 | December 31, 2016 |
| Merchandise inventory overstated (understated) | $(10,000) | Correct |
| Current assets overstated (understated) | (10,000) | Correct |
| Total assets overstated (understated) | (10,000) | Correct |
| Owner's equity overstated (understated) | (10,000) | Correct |
|  |  |  |
| Income Statement: | 2015 | 2016 |
| Cost of merchandise sold overstated (understated) | $ 10,000 | $(10,000) |
| Gross profit overstated (understated) | (10,000) | 10,000 |
| Net income overstated (understated) | (10,000) | 10,000 |

## Example Exercise 7-7   Effect of Inventory Errors
OBJ 6

Zula Repair Shop incorrectly counted its December 31, 2016, inventory as $250,000 instead of the correct amount of $220,000. Indicate the effect of the misstatement on Zula's December 31, 2016, balance sheet and income statement for the year ended December 31, 2016.

### Follow My Example 7-7

|  | Amount of Misstatement Overstatement (Understatement) |
| --- | --- |
| Balance Sheet: |  |
| Merchandise inventory overstated ........................................ | $ 30,000 |
| Current assets overstated ................................................... | 30,000 |
| Total assets overstated ...................................................... | 30,000 |
| Owner's equity overstated .................................................. | 30,000 |
|  |  |
| Income Statement: |  |
| Cost of merchandise sold understated .................................... | $(30,000) |
| Gross profit overstated ...................................................... | 30,000 |
| Net income overstated ....................................................... | 30,000 |

Practice Exercises: PE 7-7A, PE 7-7B

OBJ 7 Describe and illustrate the inventory turnover and the number of days' sales in inventory in analyzing the efficiency and effectiveness of inventory management.

# Financial Analysis and Interpretation: Inventory Turnover and Number of Days' Sales in Inventory

A merchandising business should keep enough inventory on hand to meet its customers' needs. A failure to do so may result in lost sales. However, too much inventory ties up funds that could be used to improve operations. Also, excess inventory increases expenses such as storage and property taxes. Finally, excess inventory increases the risk of losses due to price declines, damage, or changes in customer tastes.

Two measures to analyze the efficiency and effectiveness of inventory management are:

- inventory turnover and
- number of days' sales in inventory.

**Inventory turnover** measures the relationship between the cost of merchandise sold and the amount of inventory carried during the period. It is computed as follows:

$$\text{Inventory Turnover} = \frac{\text{Cost of Merchandise Sold}}{\text{Average Inventory}}$$

## Business Connection

### RAPID INVENTORY AT COSTCO

Costco Wholesale Corporation operates more than 500 membership warehouses that offer members low prices on a limited selection of nationally branded and selected private label products. Costco emphasizes high sales volumes and rapid inventory turnover. This enables Costco to operate profitably at lower gross margins than traditional wholesalers, discount retailers, and supermarkets.

In addition, Costco's rapid inventory turnover allows it to conserve its working capital, described as follows:

*Because of our high sales volume and rapid inventory turnover, we generally have the opportunity to sell and be paid for inventory before we are required to pay . . . our merchandise vendors. . . . As sales increase and inventory turnover becomes more rapid, a greater percentage of inventory is financed through payment terms provided by suppliers rather than by our working capital.*

Source: Costco Wholesale Corporation, *Form 10-K For the Fiscal Year Ended September 1, 2013.*

To illustrate, inventory turnover for Best Buy is computed from the following data (in millions) taken from two recent annual reports:

|  | For the Year Ended | |
|---|---|---|
|  | Year 2 | Year 1 |
| Cost of merchandise sold | $38,132 | $37,206 |
| Inventories: | | |
| Beginning of year | 5,897 | 5,486 |
| End of year | 5,731 | 5,897 |
| Average inventory:* | | |
| ($5,897 + $5,731) ÷ 2 | 5,814.0 | |
| ($5,486 + $5,897) ÷ 2 | | 5,691.5 |
| Inventory turnover:* | | |
| $38,132 ÷ $5,814.0 | 6.6 | |
| $37,206 ÷ $5,691.5 | | 6.5 |

* Rounded to one decimal place.

Generally, the larger the inventory turnover the more efficient and effective the company is in managing inventory. In the preceding example, inventory turnover increased slightly from 6.5 to 6.6 during Year 2, and thus Best Buy's inventory efficiency increased during Year 2.

The **number of days' sales in inventory** measures the length of time it takes to acquire, sell, and replace the inventory. It is computed as follows:

$$\text{Number of Days' Sales in Inventory} = \frac{\text{Average Inventory}}{\text{Average Daily Cost of Merchandise Sold}}$$

The average daily cost of merchandise sold is determined by dividing the cost of merchandise sold by 365.[6] Based upon the preceding data, the number of days' sales in inventory for Best Buy is computed as follows:

|  | For the Year Ended | |
|---|---|---|
|  | Year 2 | Year 1 |
| Cost of merchandise sold | $38,132 | $37,206 |
| Average daily cost of merchandise sold:* | | |
| $38,132 ÷ 365 days | 104.5 | |
| $37,206 ÷ 365 days | | 101.9 |
| Average inventory:* | | |
| ($5,897 + $5,731) ÷ 2 | 5,814.0 | |
| ($5,486 + $5,897) ÷ 2 | | 5,691.5 |
| Number of days' sales in inventory:* | | |
| $5,814.0 ÷ $104.5 | 55.6 days | |
| $5,691.5 ÷ $101.9 | | 55.9 days |

* Rounded to one decimal place.

[6] We use 365 days for all computations involving real world companies and data. We do this to highlight differences among companies and because computations using real world data normally require rounding.

Generally, the lower the number of days' sales in inventory, the more efficient and effective the company is in managing inventory. As shown previously, the number of days' sales in inventory decreased slightly from 55.9 to 55.6 during Year 2, and thus Best Buy's inventory management improved. This is consistent with the increase in inventory turnover during the year.

As with most financial ratios, differences exist among industries. To illustrate, Zale Corporation is a large retailer of fine jewelry in the United States. Because jewelry doesn't sell as rapidly as Best Buy's consumer electronics, Zale's inventory turnover and number of days' sales in inventory should be significantly different than Best Buy's. For a recent year, this is confirmed as follows:

|  | Best Buy | Zale |
| --- | --- | --- |
| Inventory turnover | 6.6 | 1.2 |
| Number of days' sales in inventory | 55.6 days | 294.7 days |

## Example Exercise 7-8  Inventory Turnover and Number of Days' Sales in Inventory

OBJ 7

Financial statement data for years ending December 31 for Beadle Company follows:

|  | 2016 | 2015 |
| --- | --- | --- |
| Cost of merchandise sold | $877,500 | $615,000 |
| Inventories: |  |  |
| Beginning of year | 225,000 | 185,000 |
| End of year | 315,000 | 225,000 |

a.  Determine the inventory turnover for 2016 and 2015.

b.  Determine the number of days' sales in inventory for 2016 and 2015, using 365 days.

c.  Does the change in the inventory turnover and the number of days' sales in inventory from 2015 to 2016 indicate a favorable or an unfavorable trend?

## Follow My Example 7-8

a.  Inventory turnover:

|  | 2016 | 2015 |
| --- | --- | --- |
| Average inventory: |  |  |
| ($225,000 + $315,000) ÷ 2 | $270,000 |  |
| ($185,000 + $225,000) ÷ 2 |  | $205,000 |
| Inventory turnover: |  |  |
| $877,500 ÷ $270,000 | 3.25 |  |
| $615,000 ÷ $205,000 |  | 3.00 |

b.  Number of days' sales in inventory:

|  | 2016 | 2015 |
| --- | --- | --- |
| Average daily cost of merchandise sold: |  |  |
| $877,500 ÷ 365 days | $2,404 |  |
| $615,000 ÷ 365 days |  | $1,685 |
| Average inventory: |  |  |
| ($225,000 + $315,000) ÷ 2 | $270,000 |  |
| ($185,000 + $225,000) ÷ 2 |  | $205,000 |
| Number of days' sales in inventory: |  |  |
| $270,000 ÷ $2,404 | 112.3 days |  |
| $205,000 ÷ $1,685 |  | 121.7 days |

c.  The increase in the inventory turnover from 3.00 to 3.25 and the decrease in the number of days' sales in inventory from 121.7 days to 112.3 days indicate favorable trends in managing inventory.

Practice Exercises: PE 7-8A, PE 7-8B

# A P P E N D I X

# Estimating Inventory Cost

A business may need to estimate the amount of inventory for the following reasons:

- Perpetual inventory records are not maintained.
- A disaster such as a fire or flood has destroyed the inventory records and the inventory.
- Monthly or quarterly financial statements are needed, but a physical inventory is taken only once a year.

This appendix describes and illustrates two widely used methods of estimating inventory cost.

## Retail Method of Inventory Costing

The **retail inventory method** of estimating inventory cost requires costs and retail prices to be maintained for the merchandise available for sale. A ratio of cost to retail price is then used to convert ending inventory at retail to estimate the ending inventory cost.

The retail inventory method is applied as follows:

- Step 1. Determine the total merchandise available for sale at cost and retail.
- Step 2. Determine the ratio of the cost to retail of the merchandise available for sale.
- Step 3. Determine the ending inventory at retail by deducting the sales from the merchandise available for sale at retail.
- Step 4. Estimate the ending inventory cost by multiplying the ending inventory at retail by the cost to retail ratio.

Exhibit 14 illustrates the retail inventory method.

| | A | B | C |
|---|---|---|---|
| 1 | | Cost | Retail |
| 2 | Merchandise inventory, January 1 | $19,400 | $ 36,000 |
| 3 | Purchases in January (net) | 42,600 | 64,000 |
| Step 1 → 4 | Merchandise available for sale | $62,000 | $100,000 |
| Step 2 → 5 | Ratio of cost to retail price: $\frac{\$62,000}{\$100,000} = 62\%$ | | |
| 6 | Sales for January | | 70,000 |
| Step 3 → 7 | Merchandise inventory, January 31, at retail | | $ 30,000 |
| Step 4 → 8 | Merchandise Inventory, January 31, at estimated cost | | |
| 9 | ($30,000 × 62%) | | $ 18,600 |
| 10 | | | |

**EXHIBIT 14**

**Determining Inventory by the Retail Method**

When estimating the cost to retail ratio, the mix of items in the ending inventory is assumed to be the same as the merchandise available for sale. If the ending inventory is made up of different classes of merchandise, cost to retail ratios may be developed for each class of inventory.

An advantage of the retail method is that it provides inventory figures for preparing monthly statements. Department stores and similar retailers often determine gross profit and operating income each month but may take a physical inventory only once or twice a year. Thus, the retail method allows management to monitor operations more closely.

The retail method may also be used as an aid in taking a physical inventory. In this case, the items are counted and recorded at their retail (selling) prices instead of their costs. The physical inventory at retail is then converted to cost by using the cost to retail ratio.

## Gross Profit Method of Inventory Costing

The **gross profit method** uses the estimated gross profit for the period to estimate the inventory at the end of the period. The gross profit is estimated from the preceding year, adjusted for any current-period changes in the cost and sales prices.

The gross profit method is applied as follows:

- Step 1. Determine the merchandise available for sale at cost.
- Step 2. Determine the estimated gross profit by multiplying the sales by the gross profit percentage.
- Step 3. Determine the estimated cost of merchandise sold by deducting the estimated gross profit from the sales.
- Step 4. Estimate the ending inventory cost by deducting the estimated cost of merchandise sold from the merchandise available for sale.

Exhibit 15 illustrates the gross profit method.

### EXHIBIT 15

**Estimating Inventory by Gross Profit Method**

| | A | B | C |
|---|---|---|---|
| 1 | | | Cost |
| 2 | Merchandise inventory, January 1 | | $ 57,000 |
| 3 | Purchases in January (net) | | 180,000 |
| Step 1 → 4 | Merchandise available for sale | | $237,000 |
| 5 | Sales for January | $250,000 | |
| Step 2 → 6 | Less estimated gross profit ($250,000 × 30%) | 75,000 | |
| Step 3 → 7 | Estimated cost of merchandise sold | | 175,000 |
| Step 4 → 8 | Estimated merchandise inventory, January 31 | | $ 62,000 |
| 9 | | | |

The gross profit method is useful for estimating inventories for monthly or quarterly financial statements. It is also useful in estimating the cost of merchandise destroyed by fire or other disasters.

# At a Glance 7

### OBJ 1
### Describe the importance of control over inventory.

**Key Points**  Two objectives of inventory control are safeguarding the inventory and properly reporting it in the financial statements. The perpetual inventory system and physical count enhance control over inventory.

| Learning Outcomes | Example Exercises | Practice Exercises |
|---|---|---|
| • Describe controls for safeguarding inventory. | | |
| • Describe how a perpetual inventory system enhances control over inventory. | | |
| • Describe why taking a physical inventory enhances control over inventory. | | |

**Describe three inventory cost flow assumptions and how they impact the income statement and balance sheet.**

**Key Points** The three common inventory cost flow assumptions used in business are the (1) first-in, first-out method (FIFO); (2) last-in, first-out method (LIFO); and (3) weighted average cost method. The cost flow assumption affects the income statement and balance sheet.

| Learning Outcomes | Example Exercises | Practice Exercises |
|---|---|---|
| • Describe the FIFO, LIFO, and weighted average cost flow methods. | | |
| • Describe how the choice of a cost flow method affects the income statement and balance sheet. | EE7-1 | PE7-1A, 7-1B |

**Determine the cost of inventory under the perpetual inventory system, using the FIFO, LIFO, and weighted average cost methods.**

**Key Points** In a perpetual inventory system, the number of units and the cost of each type of merchandise are recorded in a subsidiary inventory ledger, with a separate account for each type of merchandise.

| Learning Outcomes | Example Exercises | Practice Exercises |
|---|---|---|
| • Determine the cost of inventory and the cost of merchandise sold, using a perpetual inventory system under the FIFO method. | EE7-2 | PE7-2A, 7-2B |
| • Determine the cost of inventory and the cost of merchandise sold, using a perpetual inventory system under the LIFO method. | EE7-3 | PE7-3A, 7-3B |
| • Determine the cost of inventory and the cost of merchandise sold, using a perpetual inventory system under the weighted average cost method. | EE7-4 | PE7-4A, 7-4B |

**Determine the cost of inventory under the periodic inventory system, using the FIFO, LIFO, and weighted average cost methods.**

**Key Points** In a periodic inventory system, a physical inventory is taken to determine the cost of the inventory and the cost of merchandise sold.

| Learning Outcomes | Example Exercises | Practice Exercises |
|---|---|---|
| • Determine the cost of inventory and the cost of merchandise sold, using a periodic inventory system under the FIFO method. | EE7-5 | PE7-5A, 7-5B |
| • Determine the cost of inventory and the cost of merchandise sold, using a periodic inventory system under the LIFO method. | EE7-5 | PE7-5A, 7-5B |
| • Determine the cost of inventory and the cost of merchandise sold, using a periodic inventory system under the weighted average cost method. | EE7-5 | PE7-5A, 7-5B |

**Compare and contrast the use of the three inventory costing methods.**

**Key Points** The three inventory costing methods will normally yield different amounts for (1) the ending inventory, (2) the cost of merchandise sold for the period, and (3) the gross profit (and net income) for the period.

| Learning Outcomes | Example Exercises | Practice Exercises |
|---|---|---|
| • Indicate which inventory cost flow method will yield the highest and lowest ending inventory and net income during periods of increasing prices. | | |
| • Indicate which inventory cost flow method will yield the highest and lowest ending inventory and net income during periods of decreasing prices. | | |

**Describe and illustrate the reporting of merchandise inventory in the financial statements.**

**Key Points** The lower of cost or market is used to value inventory. The market value is the net realizable value of the merchandise.

Merchandise inventory is usually presented in the Current Assets section of the balance sheet, following receivables. The method of determining the cost and valuing the inventory is reported.

Errors in reporting inventory based on the physical inventory will affect the balance sheet and income statement.

| Learning Outcomes | Example Exercises | Practice Exercises |
|---|---|---|
| • Determine inventory using lower of cost or market. | EE7-6 | PE7-6A, 7-6B |
| • Prepare the Current Assets section of the balance sheet that includes inventory. | | |
| • Determine the effect of inventory errors on the balance sheet and income statement. | EE7-7 | PE7-7A, 7-7B |

**Describe and illustrate the inventory turnover and the number of days' sales in inventory in analyzing the efficiency and effectiveness of inventory management.**

**Key Points** Two measures to analyze the efficiency and effectiveness of inventory management are (1) inventory turnover and (2) number of days' sales in inventory

| Learning Outcomes | Example Exercises | Practice Exercises |
|---|---|---|
| • Describe the use of inventory turnover and number of days' sales in inventory in analyzing how well a company manages inventory. | | |
| • Compute the inventory turnover. | EE7-8 | PE7-8A, 7-8B |
| • Compute the number of days' sales in inventory. | EE7-8 | PE7-8A, 7-8B |

# Key Terms

consigned inventory (338)

consignee (338)

consignor (338)

first-in, first-out (FIFO)
inventory cost flow
method (324)

gross profit method (344)

inventory turnover (340)

last-in, first-out (LIFO) inventory
cost flow method (324)

lower-of-cost-or-market
(LCM) method (335)

net realizable value (336)

number of days' sales in
inventory (341)

physical inventory (323)

purchase order (322)

receiving report (322)

retail inventory method (343)

specific identification inventory
cost flow method (324)

subsidiary inventory ledger (323)

weighted average inventory
cost flow method (324)

# Illustrative Problem

Stewart Co.'s beginning inventory and purchases during the year ended December 31, 2016, were as follows:

|  |  | Unit | Units Cost | Total Cost |
|---|---|---|---|---|
| January 1 | Inventory | 1,000 | $50.00 | $ 50,000 |
| March 10 | Purchase | 3,000 | 52.00 | 156,000 |
| June 25 | Sold 1,600 units |  |  |  |
| August 30 | Purchase | 2,600 | 55.00 | 143,000 |
| October 5 | Sold 4,000 units |  |  |  |
| November 26 | Purchase | 1,000 | 57.68 | 57,680 |
| December 31 | Sold 800 units |  |  |  |
| Total |  | 7,600 |  | $406,680 |

## Instructions

1. Determine the cost of inventory on December 31, 2016, using the perpetual inventory system and each of the following inventory costing methods:
   a. first-in, first-out
   b. last-in, first-out
   c. weighted average

2. Determine the cost of inventory on December 31, 2016, using the periodic inventory system and each of the following inventory costing methods:
   a. first-in, first-out
   b. last-in, first-out
   c. weighted average cost

3. (Appendix) Assume that during the fiscal year ended December 31, 2016, sales were $530,000 and the estimated gross profit rate was 36%. Estimate the ending inventory at December 31, 2016, using the gross profit method.

## Solution

1. The perpetual inventory ledgers follow:
   a. First-in, first-out method: $68,680 ($11,000 + $57,680)
   b. Last-in, first-out method: $61,536 ($50,000 + $11,536)
   c. Weighted average cost method: $66,600 (1,200 units × $55.50)

2. a. First-in, first-out method:

| 1,000 units at $57.68 | $57,680 |
|---|---|
| 200 units at $55.00 | 11,000 |
| 1,200 units | $68,680 |

   b. Last-in, first-out method:

| 1,000 units at $50.00 | $50,000 |
|---|---|
| 200 units at $52.00 | 10,400 |
| 1,200 units | $60,400 |

   c. Weighted average cost method:

   Weighted average cost per unit. ($406,680 ÷ 7,600 units = $53.51 (Rounded)
   Inventory, December 31, 2016: 1,200 units at $53.51 = $64,212

1. a. First-in, first-out method: $68,680 ($11,000 + $57,680)

| Date | Purchases | | | Cost of Merchandise Sold | | | Inventory | | |
|---|---|---|---|---|---|---|---|---|---|
| | Quantity | Unit Cost | Total Cost | Quantity | Unit Cost | Total Cost | Quantity | Unit Cost | Total Cost |
| 2016 | | | | | | | | | |
| Jan. 1 | | | | | | | 1,000 | 50.00 | 50,000 |
| Mar. 10 | 3,000 | 52.00 | 156,000 | | | | 1,000 | 50.00 | 50,000 |
| | | | | | | | 3,000 | 52.00 | 156,000 |
| June 25 | | | | 1,000 | 50.00 | 50,000 | 2,400 | 52.00 | 124,800 |
| | | | | 600 | 52.00 | 31,200 | | | |
| Aug. 30 | 2,600 | 55.00 | 143,000 | | | | 2,400 | 52.00 | 124,800 |
| | | | | | | | 2,600 | 55.00 | 143,000 |
| Oct. 5 | | | | 2,400 | 52.00 | 124,800 | 1,000 | 55.00 | 55,000 |
| | | | | 1,600 | 55.00 | 88,000 | | | |
| Nov. 26 | 1,000 | 57.68 | 57,680 | | | | 1,000 | 55.00 | 55,000 |
| | | | | | | | 1,000 | 57.68 | 57,680 |
| Dec. 31 | | | | 800 | 55.00 | 44,000 | 200 | 55.00 | 11,000 |
| | | | | | | | 1,000 | 57.68 | 57,680 |
| 31 | Balances | | | | | 338,000 | | | 68,680 |

b. Last-in, first-out method: $61,536 ($50,000 + $11,536)

| Date | Purchases | | | Cost of Merchandise Sold | | | Inventory | | |
|---|---|---|---|---|---|---|---|---|---|
| | Quantity | Unit Cost | Total Cost | Quantity | Unit Cost | Total Cost | Quantity | Unit Cost | Total Cost |
| 2016 | | | | | | | | | |
| Jan. 1 | | | | | | | 1,000 | 50.00 | 50,000 |
| Mar. 10 | 3,000 | 52.00 | 156,000 | | | | 1,000 | 50.00 | 50,000 |
| | | | | | | | 3,000 | 52.00 | 156,000 |
| June 25 | | | | 1,600 | 52.00 | 83,200 | 1,000 | 50.00 | 50,000 |
| | | | | | | | 1,400 | 52.00 | 72,800 |
| Aug. 30 | 2,600 | 55.00 | 143,000 | | | | 1,000 | 50.00 | 50,000 |
| | | | | | | | 1,400 | 52.00 | 72,800 |
| | | | | | | | 2,600 | 55.00 | 143,000 |
| Oct. 5 | | | | 2,600 | 55.00 | 143,000 | 1,000 | 50.00 | 50,000 |
| | | | | 1,400 | 52.00 | 72,800 | | | |
| Nov. 26 | 1,000 | 57.68 | 57,680 | | | | 1,000 | 50.00 | 50,000 |
| | | | | | | | 1,000 | 57.68 | 57,680 |
| Dec. 31 | | | | 800 | 57.68 | 46,144 | 1,000 | 50.00 | 50,000 |
| | | | | | | | 200 | 57.68 | 11,536 |
| 31 | Balances | | | | | 345,144 | | | 61,536 |

c. Weighted average cost method: $66,600 (1,200 units × $55.50)

| Date | Purchases | | | Cost of Merchandise Sold | | | Inventory | | |
|---|---|---|---|---|---|---|---|---|---|
| | Quantity | Unit Cost | Total Cost | Quantity | Unit Cost | Total Cost | Quantity | Unit Cost | Total Cost |
| Jan. 1 | | | | | | | 1,000 | 50.00 | 50,000 |
| Mar. 10 | 3,000 | 52.00 | 156,000 | | | | 4,000 | 51.50 | 206,000 |
| June 25 | | | | 1,600 | 51.50 | 82,400 | 2,400 | 51.50 | 123,600 |
| Aug. 30 | 2,600 | 55.00 | 143,000 | | | | 5,000 | 53.32 | 266,600 |
| Oct. 5 | | | | 4,000 | 53.32 | 213,280 | 1,000 | 53.32 | 53,320 |
| Nov. 26 | 1,000 | 57.68 | 57,680 | | | | 2,000 | 55.50 | 111,000 |
| Dec. 31 | | | | 800 | 55.50 | 44,400 | 1,200 | 55.50 | 66,600 |
| 31 | Balances | | | | | 340,080 | 1,200 | 55.50 | 66,600 |

3. (Appendix)

| | | |
|---|---:|---:|
| Merchandise inventory, January 1, 2016.................. | | $ 50,000 |
| Purchases (net)........................................... | | 356,680 |
| Merchandise available for sale ........................... | | $406,680 |
| Sales ..................................................... | $530,000 | |
| Less estimated gross profit ($530,000 × 36%)............. | 190,800 | |
| Estimated cost of merchandise sold....................... | | 339,200 |
| Estimated merchandise inventory, December 31, 2016 .... | | $ 67,480 |

# Discussion Questions

1. Before inventory purchases are recorded, the receiving report should be reconciled to what documents?

2. Why is it important to periodically take a physical inventory when using a perpetual inventory system?

3. Do the terms *FIFO, LIFO, and weighted average* refer to techniques used in determining quantities of the various classes of merchandise on hand? Explain.

4. If merchandise inventory is being valued at cost and the price level is decreasing, which of the three methods of costing—FIFO, LIFO, or weighted average cost—will yield (a) the highest inventory cost, (b) the lowest inventory cost, (c) the highest gross profit, and (d) the lowest gross profit?

5. Which of the three methods of inventory costing—FIFO, LIFO, or weighted average cost—will in general yield an inventory cost most nearly approximating current replacement cost?

6. If inventory is being valued at cost and the price level is steadily rising, which of the three methods of costing—FIFO, LIFO, or weighted average cost—will yield the lowest annual income tax expense? Explain.

7. Using the following data, how should the merchandise be valued under lower of cost or market?

| | |
|---|---|
| Original cost | $1,350 |
| Estimated selling price | 1,475 |
| Selling expenses | 180 |

8. The inventory at the end of the year was understated by $14,750. (a) Did the error cause an overstatement or an understatement of the gross profit for the year? (b) Which items on the balance sheet at the end of the year were overstated or understated as a result of the error?

9. Hutch Co. sold merchandise to Bibbins Company on May 31, FOB shipping point. If the merchandise is in transit on May 31, the end of the fiscal year, which company would report it in its financial statements? Explain.

10. A manufacturer shipped merchandise to a retailer on a consignment basis. If the merchandise is unsold at the end of the period, in whose inventory should the merchandise be included?

# Practice Exercises

EE 7-1 *p. 325*

SHOW ME HOW

**PE 7-1A Cost flow methods** OBJ. 2

The following three identical units of Item BZ1810 are purchased during November:

| Item BZ1810 | | Units | Cost |
|---|---|---|---:|
| Nov. | 2 Purchase | 1 | $ 55 |
| | 14 Purchase | 1 | 57 |
| | 28 Purchase | 1 | 62 |
| | Total | 3 | $174 |
| | Average cost per unit | | $ 58 ($174 ÷ 3 units) |

Assume that one unit is sold on November 30 for $90.

Determine the gross profit for November and ending inventory on November 30 using the (a) first-in, first-out (FIFO); (b) last-in, first-out (LIFO); and (c) weighted average cost methods.

*(Continued)*

EE 7-1 *p. 325* **PE 7-1B Cost flow methods** OBJ. 2

The following three identical units of Item Beta are purchased during June:

| | Item Beta | Units | Cost |
|---|---|---|---|
| June 2 | Purchase | 1 | $ 50 |
| 12 | Purchase | 1 | 60 |
| 23 | Purchase | 1 | 70 |
| | Total | 3 | $180 |
| | Average cost per unit | | $ 60 ($180 ÷ 3 units) |

Assume that one unit is sold on June 27 for $110.

Determine the gross profit for June and ending inventory on June 30 using the (a) first-in, first-out (FIFO); (b) last-in, first-out (LIFO); and (c) weighted average cost methods.

EE 7-2 *p. 327* **PE 7-2A Perpetual inventory using FIFO** OBJ. 3

Beginning inventory, purchases, and sales for Item ProX2 are as follows:

| Jan. | 1 | Inventory | 60 units at $100 |
|---|---|---|---|
| | 9 | Sale | 35 units |
| | 13 | Purchase | 50 units at $110 |
| | 25 | Sale | 48 units |

Assuming a perpetual inventory system and using the first-in, first-out (FIFO) method, determine (a) the cost of merchandise sold on January 25 and (b) the inventory on January 31.

EE 7-2 *p. 327* **PE 7-2B Perpetual inventory using FIFO** OBJ. 3

Beginning inventory, purchases, and sales for Item Delta are as follows:

| July | 1 | Inventory | 50 units at $15 |
|---|---|---|---|
| | 7 | Sale | 44 units |
| | 15 | Purchase | 90 units at $18 |
| | 24 | Sale | 40 units |

Assuming a perpetual inventory system and using the first-in, first-out (FIFO) method, determine (a) the cost of merchandise sold on July 24 and (b) the inventory on July 31.

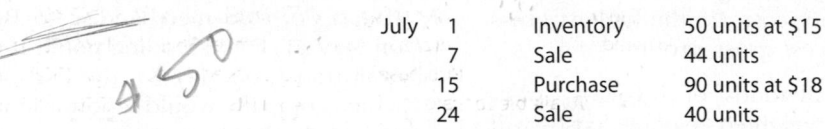

EE 7-3 *p. 328* **PE 7-3A Perpetual inventory using LIFO** OBJ. 3

Beginning inventory, purchases, and sales for Item Zebra 9x are as follows:

| April | 1 | Inventory | 420 units at $8 |
|---|---|---|---|
| | 10 | Sale | 300 units |
| | 18 | Purchase | 280 units at $9 |
| | 27 | Sale | 250 units |

Assuming a perpetual inventory system and using the last-in, first-out (LIFO) method, determine (a) the cost of merchandise sold on April 27 and (b) the inventory on April 30.

EE 7-3 *p. 328* **PE 7-3B Perpetual inventory using LIFO** OBJ. 3

Beginning inventory, purchases, and sales for Item Foxtrot are as follows:

| Mar. | 1 | Inventory | 270 units at $18 |
|---|---|---|---|
| | 8 | Sale | 225 units |
| | 15 | Purchase | 375 units at $20 |
| | 27 | Sale | 240 units |

Assuming a perpetual inventory system and using the last-in, first-out (LIFO) method, determine (a) the cost of merchandise sold on March 27 and (b) the inventory on March 31.

EE 7-4 *p. 330*

SHOW
ME HOW

### PE 7-4A Perpetual inventory using weighted average OBJ. 3

Beginning inventory, purchases, and sales for 30xT are as follows:

| May | 1 | Inventory | 50 units at $80 |
|-----|----|-----------|-----------------|
| | 12 | Sale | 35 units |
| | 23 | Purchase | 60 units at $90 |
| | 26 | Sale | 55 units |

Assuming a perpetual inventory system and using the weighted average method, determine (a) the weighted average unit cost after the May 23 purchase, (b) the cost of the merchandise sold on May 26, and (c) the inventory on May 31.

EE 7-4 *p. 330*

SHOW
ME HOW

### PE 7-4B Perpetual inventory using weighted average OBJ. 3

Beginning inventory, purchases, and sales for WCS12 are as follows:

| Oct. | 1 | Inventory | 300 units at $8 |
|------|----|-----------|-----------------|
| | 13 | Sale | 175 units |
| | 22 | Purchase | 375 units at $10 |
| | 29 | Sale | 280 units |

Assuming a perpetual inventory system and using the weighted average method, determine (a) the weighted average unit cost after the October 22 purchase, (b) the cost of the merchandise sold on October 29, and (c) the inventory on October 31.

EE 7-5 *p. 333*

SHOW
ME HOW

### PE 7-5A Periodic inventory using FIFO, LIFO, and weighted average cost methods OBJ. 4

The units of an item available for sale during the year were as follows:

| Jan. | 1 | Inventory | 12 units at $5,400 | $ 64,800 |
|------|----|-----------|--------------------|----------|
| Aug. | 7 | Purchase | 18 units at $6,000 | 108,000 |
| Dec. | 11 | Purchase | 15 units at $6,480 | 97,200 |
| | | Available for sale | 45 units | $270,000 |

There are 14 units of the item in the physical inventory at December 31. The periodic inventory system is used. Determine the inventory cost using (a) the first-in, first-out (FIFO) method; (b) the last-in, first-out (LIFO) method; and (c) the weighted average cost method.

EE 7-5 *p. 333*

SHOW
ME HOW

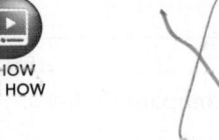

### PE 7-5B Periodic inventory using FIFO, LIFO, and weighted average cost methods OBJ. 4

The units of an item available for sale during the year were as follows:

| Jan. | 1 | Inventory | 20 units at $360 | $ 7,200 |
|------|----|-----------|------------------|---------|
| Aug. | 13 | Purchase | 260 units at $342 | 88,920 |
| Nov. | 30 | Purchase | 40 units at $357 | 14,280 |
| | | Available for sale | 320 units | $110,400 |

There are 57 units of the item in the physical inventory at December 31. The periodic inventory system is used. Determine the inventory cost using (a) the first-in, first-out (FIFO) method; (b) the last-in, first-out (LIFO) method; and (c) the weighted average cost method.

EE 7-6 *p. 336*

SHOW
ME HOW

### PE 7-6A Lower-of-cost-or-market method OBJ. 6

On the basis of the following data, determine the value of the inventory at the lower of cost or market. Apply lower of cost or market to each inventory item, as shown in Exhibit 10.

| Item | Inventory Quantity | Cost per Unit | Market Value per Unit (Net Realizable Value) |
|------|--------------------|---------------|----------------------------------------------|
| Raven 10 | 1,200 | $115 | $112 |
| Dove 23 | 6,500 | 17 | 22 |

EE 7-6 *p. 336*

### PE 7-6B    Lower-of-cost-or-market method                                    OBJ. 6

On the basis of the following data, determine the value of the inventory at the lower of cost or market. Apply lower of cost or market to each inventory item, as shown in Exhibit 10.

| Item | Inventory Quantity | Cost per Unit | Market Value per Unit (Net Realizable Value) |
|---|---|---|---|
| JFW1 | 6,330 | $10 | $11 |
| SAW9 | 1,140 | 36 | 34 |

EE 7-7 *p. 340*

### PE 7-7A    Effect of inventory errors                                        OBJ. 6

During the taking of its physical inventory on August 31, 2016, Kate Interiors Company incorrectly counted its inventory as $366,900 instead of the correct amount of $378,500. Indicate the effect of the misstatement on Kate Interiors' August 31, 2016, balance sheet and income statement for the year ended August 31, 2016.

EE 7-7 *p. 340*

### PE 7-7B    Effect of inventory errors                                        OBJ. 6

During the taking of its physical inventory on December 31, 2016, Waterjet Bath Company incorrectly counted its inventory as $728,660 instead of the correct amount of $719,880. Indicate the effect of the misstatement on Waterjet Bath's December 31, 2016, balance sheet and income statement for the year ended December 31, 2016.

EE 7-8 *p. 342*

### PE 7-8A    Inventory turnover and number of days' sales in inventory         OBJ. 7

Financial statement data for years ending December 31 for Holland Company follows:

| | 2016 | 2015 |
|---|---|---|
| Cost of merchandise sold | $4,504,500 | $3,715,200 |
| Inventories: | | |
| Beginning of year | 788,000 | 760,000 |
| End of year | 850,000 | 788,000 |

a. Determine the inventory turnover for 2016 and 2015.

b. Determine the number of days' sales in inventory for 2016 and 2015. Use 365 days and round to one decimal place.

c. Does the change in inventory turnover and the number of days' sales in inventory from 2015 to 2016 indicate a favorable or an unfavorable trend?

EE 7-8 *p. 342*

### PE 7-8B    Inventory turnover and number of days' sales in inventory         OBJ. 7

Financial statement data for years ending December 31 for Tango Company follows:

| | 2016 | 2015 |
|---|---|---|
| Cost of merchandise sold | $3,864,000 | $4,001,500 |
| Inventories: | | |
| Beginning of year | 770,000 | 740,000 |
| End of year | 840,000 | 770,000 |

a. Determine the inventory turnover for 2016 and 2015.

b. Determine the number of days' sales in inventory for 2016 and 2015. Use 365 days and round to one decimal place.

c. Does the change in inventory turnover and the number of days' sales in inventory from 2015 to 2016 indicate a favorable or an unfavorable trend?

# Exercises

### EX 7-1 Control of inventories
OBJ. 1

Triple Creek Hardware Store currently uses a periodic inventory system. Kevin Carlton, the owner, is considering the purchase of a computer system that would make it feasible to switch to a perpetual inventory system.

Kevin is unhappy with the periodic inventory system because it does not provide timely information on inventory levels. Kevin has noticed on several occasions that the store runs out of good-selling items, while too many poor-selling items are on hand.

Kevin is also concerned about lost sales while a physical inventory is being taken. Triple Creek Hardware currently takes a physical inventory twice a year. To minimize distractions, the store is closed on the day inventory is taken. Kevin believes that closing the store is the only way to get an accurate inventory count.

Will switching to a perpetual inventory system strengthen Triple Creek Hardware's control over inventory items? Will switching to a perpetual inventory system eliminate the need for a physical inventory count? Explain.

### EX 7-2 Control of inventories
OBJ. 1

Hardcase Luggage Shop is a small retail establishment located in a large shopping mall. This shop has implemented the following procedures regarding inventory items:

a. Because the shop carries mostly high-quality, designer luggage, all inventory items are tagged with a control device that activates an alarm if a tagged item is removed from the store.

b. Because the display area of the store is limited, only a sample of each piece of luggage is kept on the selling floor. Whenever a customer selects a piece of luggage, the salesclerk gets the appropriate piece from the store's stockroom. Because all salesclerks need access to the stockroom, it is not locked. The stockroom is adjacent to the break room used by all mall employees.

c. Whenever Hardcase Luggage Shop receives a shipment of new inventory, the items are taken directly to the stockroom. Hardcase's accountant uses the vendor's invoice to record the amount of inventory received.

State whether each of these procedures is appropriate or inappropriate. If it is inappropriate, state why.

### EX 7-3 Perpetual inventory using FIFO
OBJ. 2, 3

✔ Inventory balance, June 30, $29,920

SHOW ME HOW

Beginning inventory, purchases, and sales data for portable DVD players are as follows:

| June | 1 | Inventory | 240 units at $78 |
|------|----|-----------|------------------|
| | 10 | Sale | 180 units |
| | 15 | Purchase | 280 units at $80 |
| | 20 | Sale | 220 units |
| | 24 | Sale | 90 units |
| | 30 | Purchase | 320 units at $86 |

The business maintains a perpetual inventory system, costing by the first-in, first-out method.

a. Determine the cost of the merchandise sold for each sale and the inventory balance after each sale, presenting the data in the form illustrated in Exhibit 4.

b. Based upon the preceding data, would you expect the inventory to be higher or lower using the last-in, first-out method?

### EX 7-4 Perpetual inventory using LIFO
OBJ. 2, 3

✔ Inventory balance, June 30, $29,860

SHOW ME HOW

Assume that the business in Exercise 7-3 maintains a perpetual inventory system, costing by the last-in, first-out method. Determine the cost of merchandise sold for each sale and the inventory balance after each sale, presenting the data in the form illustrated in Exhibit 5.

✔ Inventory balance,
May 31, $20,160

SHOW
ME HOW

✔ Inventory balance,
May 31, $21,120

SHOW
ME HOW

✔ b. $22,000

SHOW
ME HOW

✔ Total Cost of
Merchandise Sold,
$1,758,750

SHOW
ME HOW

✔ Total Cost of
Merchandise Sold,
$154,400

**EX 7-5**  **Perpetual inventory using LIFO**  OBJ. 2, 3

Beginning inventory, purchases, and sales data for prepaid cell phones for May are as follows:

| Inventory | | Purchases | | Sales | |
|---|---|---|---|---|---|
| May 1 | 1,550 units at $44 | May 10 | 720 units at $45 | May 12 | 1,200 units |
| | | 20 | 1,200 units at $48 | 14 | 830 units |
| | | | | 31 | 1,000 units |

a. Assuming that the perpetual inventory system is used, costing by the LIFO method, determine the cost of merchandise sold for each sale and the inventory balance after each sale, presenting the data in the form illustrated in Exhibit 5.

b. Based upon the preceding data, would you expect the inventory to be higher or lower using the first-in, first-out method?

**EX 7-6**  **Perpetual inventory using FIFO**  OBJ. 2, 3

Assume that the business in Exercise 7-5 maintains a perpetual inventory system, costing by the first-in, first-out method. Determine the cost of merchandise sold for each sale and the inventory balance after each sale, presenting the data in the form illustrated in Exhibit 4.

**EX 7-7**  **FIFO and LIFO costs under perpetual inventory system**  OBJ. 2, 3

The following units of an item were available for sale during the year:

| | |
|---|---|
| Beginning inventory | 3,600 units at $4.00 |
| Sale | 2,400 units at $8.00 |
| First purchase | 8,000 units at $4.20 |
| Sale | 6,000 units at $8.00 |
| Second purchase | 7,500 units at $4.40 |
| Sale | 5,500 units at $8.00 |

The firm uses the perpetual inventory system, and there are 5,200 units of the item on hand at the end of the year. What is the total cost of the ending inventory according to (a) FIFO, (b) LIFO?

**EX 7-8**  **Weighted average cost flow method under perpetual inventory system**  OBJ. 3

The following units of a particular item were available for sale during the calendar year:

| | | | |
|---|---|---|---|
| Jan. | 1 | Inventory | 10,000 units at $75.00 |
| Mar. | 18 | Sale | 8,000 units |
| May | 2 | Purchase | 18,000 units at $77.50 |
| Aug. | 9 | Sale | 15,000 units |
| Oct. | 20 | Purchase | 7,000 units at $80.25 |

The firm uses the weighted average cost method with a perpetual inventory system. Determine the cost of merchandise sold for each sale and the inventory balance after each sale. Present the data in the form illustrated in Exhibit 6.

**EX 7-9**  **Weighted average cost flow method under perpetual inventory system**  OBJ. 3

The following units of a particular item were available for sale during the calendar year:

| | | | |
|---|---|---|---|
| Jan. | 1 | Inventory | 4,000 units at $20 |
| Apr. | 19 | Sale | 2,500 units |
| June | 30 | Purchase | 6,000 units at $24 |
| Sept. | 2 | Sale | 4,500 units |
| Nov. | 15 | Purchase | 1,000 units at $25 |

The firm uses the weighted average cost method with a perpetual inventory system. Determine the cost of merchandise sold for each sale and the inventory balance after each sale. Present the data in the form illustrated in Exhibit 6.

### EX 7-10  Perpetual inventory using FIFO
OBJ. 3

**✔ Total Cost of Merchandise Sold, $152,000**

Assume that the business in Exercise 7-9 maintains a perpetual inventory system. Determine the cost of merchandise sold for each sale and the inventory balance after each sale, assuming the first-in, first-out method. Present the data in the form illustrated in Exhibit 4.

### EX 7-11  Perpetual inventory using LIFO
OBJ. 3

**✔ Total Cost of Merchandise Sold, $158,000**

Assume that the business in Exercise 7-9 maintains a perpetual inventory system. Determine the cost of merchandise sold for each sale and the inventory balance after each sale, assuming the last-in, first-out method. Present the data in the form illustrated in Exhibit 5.

### EX 7-12  Periodic inventory by three methods
OBJ. 2, 4

**✔ b. $13,280**

**SHOW ME HOW**

The units of an item available for sale during the year were as follows:

| Jan. | 1 | Inventory | 200 units at $60 |
| Feb. | 17 | Purchase | 275 units at $64 |
| July | 21 | Purchase | 300 units at $68 |
| Nov. | 23 | Purchase | 225 units at $70 |

There are 220 units of the item in the physical inventory at December 31. The periodic inventory system is used. Determine the inventory cost by (a) the first-in, first-out method, (b) the last-in, first-out method, and (c) the weighted average cost method.

### EX 7-13  Periodic inventory by three methods; cost of merchandise sold
OBJ. 2, 4

**✔ a. Inventory, $6,228**

**SHOW ME HOW**

The units of an item available for sale during the year were as follows:

| Jan. | 1 | Inventory | 90 units at $54 |
| Mar. | 10 | Purchase | 112 units at $55 |
| Aug. | 30 | Purchase | 100 units at $58 |
| Dec. | 12 | Purchase | 98 units at $60 |

There are 104 units of the item in the physical inventory at December 31. The periodic inventory system is used. Determine the inventory cost and the cost of merchandise sold by three methods, presenting your answers in the following form:

| | Cost | |
| Inventory Method | Merchandise Inventory | Merchandise Sold |
| --- | --- | --- |
| a. First-in, first-out | $ | $ |
| b. Last-in, first-out | | |
| c. Weighted average cost | | |

### EX 7-14  Comparing inventory methods
OBJ. 5

Assume that a firm separately determined inventory under FIFO and LIFO and then compared the results.

a. In each space that follows, place the correct sign [less than (<), greater than (>), or equal (=)] for each comparison, assuming periods of rising prices.

| 1. FIFO inventory | _____ | LIFO inventory |
| 2. FIFO cost of goods sold | _____ | LIFO cost of goods sold |
| 3. FIFO net income | _____ | LIFO net income |
| 4. FIFO income taxes | _____ | LIFO income taxes |

b. Why would management prefer to use LIFO over FIFO in periods of rising prices?

SHOW
ME HOW

### EX 7-15 Lower-of-cost-or-market inventory

OBJ. 6

On the basis of the following data, determine the value of the inventory at the lower of cost or market. Assemble the data in the form illustrated in Exhibit 10.

| Commodity | Inventory Quantity | Cost per Unit | Market Value per Unit (Net Realizable Value) |
|---|---|---|---|
| Ash | 80 | $140 | $125 |
| Aspen | 120 | 90 | 112 |
| Beech | 30 | 75 | 74 |
| Maple | 75 | 88 | 86 |
| Oak | 60 | 140 | 145 |

### EX 7-16 Merchandise inventory on the balance sheet

OBJ. 6

Based on the data in Exercise 7-15 and assuming that cost was determined by the FIFO method, show how the merchandise inventory would appear on the balance sheet.

### EX 7-17 Effect of errors in physical inventory

OBJ. 6

Missouri River Supply Co. sells canoes, kayaks, whitewater rafts, and other boating supplies. During the taking of its physical inventory on December 31, 2016, Missouri River Supply incorrectly counted its inventory as $233,400 instead of the correct amount of $238,600.

a. State the effect of the error on the December 31, 2016, balance sheet of Missouri River Supply.

b. State the effect of the error on the income statement of Missouri River Supply for the year ended December 31, 2016.

c. If uncorrected, what would be the effect of the error on the 2017 income statement?

d. If uncorrected, what would be the effect of the error on the December 31, 2017, balance sheet?

### EX 7-18 Effect of errors in physical inventory

OBJ. 6

Fonda Motorcycle Shop sells motorcycles, ATVs, and other related supplies and accessories. During the taking of its physical inventory on December 31, 2016, Fonda Motorcycle Shop incorrectly counted its inventory as $337,500 instead of the correct amount of $328,850.

a. State the effect of the error on the December 31, 2016, balance sheet of Fonda Motorcycle Shop.

b. State the effect of the error on the income statement of Fonda Motorcycle Shop for the year ended December 31, 2016.

c. If uncorrected, what would be the effect of the error on the 2017 income statement?

d. If uncorrected, what would be the effect of the error on the December 31, 2017, balance sheet?

### EX 7-19 Error in inventory

OBJ. 6

During 2016, the accountant discovered that the physical inventory at the end of 2015 had been understated by $42,750. Instead of correcting the error, however, the accountant assumed that the error would balance out (correct itself) in 2016.

➤ Are there any flaws in the accountant's assumption? Explain.

### EX 7-20 Inventory turnover

OBJ. 7

SHOW
ME HOW

The following data (in thousands) were taken from recent annual reports of Apple Inc., a manufacturer of personal computers and related products, and American Greetings Corporation, a manufacturer and distributor of greeting cards and related products:

| | Apple | American Greetings |
|---|---|---|
| Cost of goods sold | $87,846,000 | $741,645 |
| Inventory, end of year | 791,000 | 208,945 |
| Inventory, beginning of the year | 776,000 | 179,730 |

a. Determine the inventory turnover for Apple and American Greetings. Round to one decimal place.

b. Would you expect American Greetings' inventory turnover to be higher or lower than Apple's? Why?

---

**EX 7-21  Inventory turnover and number of days' sales in inventory**    OBJ. 7

Kroger, Safeway Inc., and Whole Foods Markets, Inc. are three grocery chains in the United States. Inventory management is an important aspect of the grocery retail business. Recent balance sheets for these three companies indicated the following merchandise inventory information:

✔ a. Kroger, 26 days' sales in inventory

SHOW ME HOW

| | Merchandise Inventory | |
|---|---|---|
| | End of Year (in millions) | Beginning of Year (in millions) |
| Kroger | $5,114 | $4,966 |
| Safeway | 2,470 | 2,623 |
| Whole Foods | 374 | 337 |

The cost of goods sold for each company was:

| | Cost of Goods Sold (in millions) |
|---|---|
| Kroger | $71,494 |
| Safeway | 31,837 |
| Whole Foods | 11,699 |

a. Determine the number of days' sales in inventory (use 365 days and round to the nearest day) and the inventory turnover (round to one decimal place) for the three companies.

b. Interpret your results in part (a).

c. If Kroger had Whole Foods' number of days' sales in inventory, how much additional cash flow (rounded to nearest million) would have been generated from the smaller inventory relative to its actual average inventory position?

---

**Appendix**
**EX 7-22  Retail method**

A business using the retail method of inventory costing determines that merchandise inventory at retail is $1,235,000. If the ratio of cost to retail price is 54%, what is the amount of inventory to be reported on the financial statements?

---

**Appendix**
**EX 7-23  Retail method**

A business using the retail method of inventory costing determines that merchandise inventory at retail is $396,400. If the ratio of cost to retail price is 61%, what is the amount of inventory to be reported on the financial statements?

---

**Appendix**
**EX 7-24  Retail method**

A business using the retail method of inventory costing determines that merchandise inventory at retail is $775,000. If the ratio of cost to retail price is 66%, what is the amount of inventory to be reported on the financial statements?

**Appendix**
**EX 7-25   Retail method**

On the basis of the following data, estimate the cost of the merchandise inventory at June 30 by the retail method:

|  |  | Cost | Retail |
|---|---|---|---|
| June 1 | Merchandise inventory | $ 165,000 | $ 275,000 |
| June 1–30 | Purchases (net) | 2,361,500 | 3,800,000 |
| June 1–30 | Sales |  | 3,550,000 |

**Appendix**
**EX 7-26   Gross profit method**

✔ a. Merchandise
destroyed: $414,000

The merchandise inventory was destroyed by fire on December 13. The following data were obtained from the accounting records:

|  |  |  |
|---|---|---|
| Jan. 1 | Merchandise inventory | $ 350,000 |
| Jan. 1–Dec. 13 | Purchases (net) | 2,950,000 |
|  | Sales | 4,440,000 |
|  | Estimated gross profit rate | 35% |

a.  Estimate the cost of the merchandise destroyed.

b.  Briefly describe the situations in which the gross profit method is useful.

**Appendix**
**EX 7-27   Gross profit method**

Based on the following data, estimate the cost of the ending merchandise inventory:

| Sales | $9,250,000 |
|---|---|
| Estimated gross profit rate | 36% |
|  |  |
| Beginning merchandise inventory | $  180,000 |
| Purchases (net) | 5,945,000 |
| Merchandise available for sale | $6,125,000 |

**Appendix**
**EX 7-28   Gross profit method**

Based on the following data, estimate the cost of the ending merchandise inventory:

| Sales | $1,450,000 |
|---|---|
| Estimated gross profit rate | 42% |
|  |  |
| Beginning merchandise inventory | $  100,000 |
| Purchases (net) | 860,000 |
| Merchandise available for sale | $  960,000 |

# Problems: Series A

**PR 7-1A   FIFO perpetual inventory**                                    OBJ. 2, 3

✔ 3. $2,286,750

The beginning inventory at Funky Party Supplies and data on purchases and sales for a three-month period ending March 31, 2016, are as follows:

| Date |  | Transaction | Number of Units | Per Unit | Total |
|---|---|---|---|---|---|
| Jan. | 1 | Inventory | 2,500 | $60.00 | $150,000 |
|  | 10 | Purchase | 7,500 | 68.00 | 510,000 |
|  | 28 | Sale | 3,750 | 120.00 | 450,000 |
|  | 30 | Sale | 1,250 | 120.00 | 150,000 |

SHOW
ME HOW

| Date | | Transaction | Number of Units | Per Unit | Total |
|---|---|---|---|---|---|
| Feb. | 5 | Sale | 500 | $120.00 | $ 60,000 |
| | 10 | Purchase | 18,000 | 70.00 | 1,260,000 |
| | 16 | Sale | 9,000 | 125.00 | 1,125,000 |
| | 28 | Sale | 8,500 | 125.00 | 1,062,500 |
| Mar. | 5 | Purchase | 15,000 | 71.60 | 1,074,000 |
| | 14 | Sale | 10,000 | 125.00 | 1,250,000 |
| | 25 | Purchase | 2,500 | 72.00 | 180,000 |
| | 30 | Sale | 8,750 | 125.00 | 1,093,750 |

**Instructions**

1. Record the inventory, purchases, and cost of merchandise sold data in a perpetual inventory record similar to the one illustrated in Exhibit 4, using the first-in, first-out method.

2. Determine the total sales and the total cost of merchandise sold for the period. Journalize the entries in the sales and cost of merchandise sold accounts. Assume that all sales were on account.

3. Determine the gross profit from sales for the period.

4. Determine the ending inventory cost as of March 31, 2016.

5. Based upon the preceding data, would you expect the inventory using the last-in, first-out method to be higher or lower?

---

✔ 2. Gross profit, $2,252,250

**PR 7-2A    LIFO perpetual inventory**    OBJ. 2, 3

The beginning inventory at Funky Party Supplies and data on purchases and sales for a three-month period are shown in Problem 7-1A.

**SHOW ME HOW**

**Instructions**

1. Record the inventory, purchases, and cost of merchandise sold data in a perpetual inventory record similar to the one illustrated in Exhibit 5, using the last-in, first-out method.

2. Determine the total sales, the total cost of merchandise sold, and the gross profit from sales for the period.

3. Determine the ending inventory cost as of March 31, 2016.

---

✔ 2. Gross profit, $2,284,250

**PR 7-3A    Weighted average cost method with perpetual inventory**    OBJ. 2, 3

The beginning inventory for Funky Party Supplies and data on purchases and sales for a three-month period are shown in Problem 7-1A.

**Instructions**

1. Record the inventory, purchases, and cost of merchandise sold data in a perpetual inventory record similar to the one illustrated in Exhibit 6, using the weighted average cost method.

2. Determine the total sales, the total cost of merchandise sold, and the gross profit from sales for the period.

3. Determine the ending inventory cost as of March 31, 2016.

---

✔ 2. Inventory, $235,000

**PR 7-4A    Periodic inventory by three methods**    OBJ. 2, 3

The beginning inventory for Funky Party Supplies and data on purchases and sales for a three-month period are shown in Problem 7-1A.

**Instructions**

1. Determine the inventory on March 31, 2016, and the cost of goods sold for the three-month period, using the first-in, first-out method and the periodic inventory system.

2. Determine the inventory on March 31, 2016, and the cost of goods sold for the three-month period, using the last-in, first-out method and the periodic inventory system.

(*Continued*)

3. Determine the inventory on March 31, 2016, and the cost of goods sold for the three-month period, using the weighted average cost method and the periodic inventory system. Round the weighted average unit cost to the nearest cent.

4. Compare the gross profit and the March 31, 2016, inventories, using the following column headings:

| | FIFO | LIFO | Weighted Average |
|---|---|---|---|
| Sales | | | |
| Cost of merchandise sold | | | |
| Gross profit | | | |
| Inventory, March 31, 2016 | | | |

## PR 7-5A  Periodic inventory by three methods

**OBJ. 2, 4**

✔ 1. $10,700

Dymac Appliances uses the periodic inventory system. Details regarding the inventory of appliances at November 1, 2015, purchases invoices during the next 12 months, and the inventory count at October 31, 2016, are summarized as follows:

| | | Purchases Invoices | | | |
|---|---|---|---|---|---|
| Model | Inventory, November 1 | 1st | 2nd | 3rd | Inventory Count, October 31 |
| A10 | — | 4 at $ 64 | 4 at $ 70 | 4 at $ 76 | 6 |
| B15 | 8 at $176 | 4 at 158 | 3 at 170 | 6 at 184 | 8 |
| E60 | 3 at 75 | 3 at 65 | 15 at 68 | 9 at 70 | 5 |
| G83 | 7 at 242 | 6 at 250 | 5 at 260 | 10 at 259 | 9 |
| J34 | 12 at 240 | 10 at 246 | 16 at 267 | 16 at 270 | 15 |
| M90 | 2 at 108 | 2 at 110 | 3 at 128 | 3 at 130 | 5 |
| Q70 | 5 at 160 | 4 at 170 | 4 at 175 | 7 at 180 | 8 |

## Instructions

1. Determine the cost of the inventory on October 31, 2016, by the first-in, first-out method. Present data in columnar form, using the following headings:

| Model | Quantity | Unit Cost | Total Cost |
|---|---|---|---|

If the inventory of a particular model comprises one entire purchase plus a portion of another purchase acquired at a different unit cost, use a separate line for each purchase.

2. Determine the cost of the inventory on October 31, 2016, by the last-in, first-out method, following the procedures indicated in (1).

3. Determine the cost of the inventory on October 31, 2016, by the weighted average cost method, using the columnar headings indicated in (1).

4. ▬▬▶ Discuss which method (FIFO or LIFO) would be preferred for income tax purposes in periods of (a) rising prices and (b) declining prices.

## PR 7-6A  Lower-of-cost-or-market inventory

**OBJ. 6**

✔ Total LCM, $39,873

Data on the physical inventory of Ashwood Products Company as of December 31, 2016, follows:

| Description | Inventory Quantity | Market Value per Unit (Net Realizable Value) |
|---|---|---|
| B12 | 38 | $ 57 |
| E41 | 18 | 180 |
| G19 | 33 | 126 |
| L88 | 18 | 550 |
| N94 | 400 | 7 |
| P24 | 90 | 18 |
| R66 | 8 | 250 |
| T33 | 140 | 20 |
| Z16 | 15 | 752 |

Quantity and cost data from the last purchases invoice of the year and the next-to-the-last purchases invoice are summarized as follows:

| Description | Last Purchases Invoice | | Next-to-the-Last Purchases Invoice | |
|---|---|---|---|---|
| | Quantity Purchased | Unit Cost | Quantity Purchased | Unit Cost |
| B12 | 30 | $ 60 | 30 | $ 59 |
| E41 | 35 | 178 | 20 | 180 |
| G19 | 20 | 128 | 25 | 129 |
| L88 | 10 | 563 | 10 | 560 |
| N94 | 500 | 8 | 500 | 7 |
| P24 | 80 | 22 | 50 | 21 |
| R66 | 5 | 248 | 4 | 260 |
| T33 | 100 | 21 | 100 | 19 |
| Z16 | 10 | 750 | 9 | 745 |

## Instructions

Determine the inventory at cost and also at the lower of cost or market, using the first-in, first-out method. Record the appropriate unit costs on the inventory sheet, and complete the pricing of the inventory. When there are two different unit costs applicable to an item, proceed as follows:

1. Draw a line through the quantity, and insert the quantity and unit cost of the last purchase.

2. On the following line, insert the quantity and unit cost of the next-to-the-last purchase.

3. Total the cost and market columns and insert the lower of the two totals in the Lower of C or M column. The first item on the inventory sheet has been completed as an example.

**Inventory Sheet**
**December 31, 2016**

| Description | Inventory Quantity | Cost per Unit | Market Value per Unit (Net Realizable Value) | Total Cost | Total Market | Lower of C or M |
|---|---|---|---|---|---|---|
| B12 | 3̶8̶ 30 | $60 | $57 | $1,800 | $1,710 | |
| | 8 | 59 | 57 | 472 | 456 | |
| | | | | $2,272 | $2,166 | $2,166 |

## Appendix
### PR 7-7A  Retail method; gross profit method

✔ 1. $483,600

Selected data on merchandise inventory, purchases, and sales for Celebrity Tan Co. and Ranchworks Co. are as follows:

| | Cost | Retail |
|---|---|---|
| **Celebrity Tan** | | |
| Merchandise inventory, August 1 | $ 300,000 | $ 575,000 |
| Transactions during August: | | |
| Purchases (net) | 2,149,000 | 3,375,000 |
| Sales | | 3,170,000 |
| | | |
| **Ranchworks Co.** | | |
| Merchandise inventory, March 1 | $ 880,000 | |
| Transactions during March through November: | | |
| Purchases (net) | 9,500,000 | |
| Sales | 15,800,000 | |
| Estimated gross profit rate | 38% | |

*(Continued)*

**Instructions**

1. Determine the estimated cost of the merchandise inventory of Celebrity Tan Co. on August 31 by the retail method, presenting details of the computations.

2. a. Estimate the cost of the merchandise inventory of Ranchworks Co. on November 30 by the gross profit method, presenting details of the computations.

   b. Assume that Ranchworks Co. took a physical inventory on November 30 and discovered that $369,750 of merchandise was on hand. What was the estimated loss of inventory due to theft or damage during March through November?

# Problems: Series B

### PR 7-1B   FIFO perpetual inventory                                      OBJ. 2, 3

✔ 3. $214,474

SHOW
ME HOW

The beginning inventory of merchandise at Dunne Co. and data on purchases and sales for a three-month period ending June 30, 2016, are as follows:

| Date | | Transaction | Number of Units | Per Unit | Total |
|---|---|---|---|---|---|
| Apr. | 3 | Inventory | 25 | $1,200 | $ 30,000 |
| | 8 | Purchase | 75 | 1,240 | 93,000 |
| | 11 | Sale | 40 | 2,000 | 80,000 |
| | 30 | Sale | 30 | 2,000 | 60,000 |
| May | 8 | Purchase | 60 | 1,260 | 75,600 |
| | 10 | Sale | 50 | 2,000 | 100,000 |
| | 19 | Sale | 20 | 2,000 | 40,000 |
| | 28 | Purchase | 80 | 1,260 | 100,800 |
| June | 5 | Sale | 40 | 2,250 | 90,000 |
| | 16 | Sale | 25 | 2,250 | 56,250 |
| | 21 | Purchase | 35 | 1,264 | 44,240 |
| | 28 | Sale | 44 | 2,250 | 99,000 |

**Instructions**

1. Record the inventory, purchases, and cost of merchandise sold data in a perpetual inventory record similar to the one illustrated in Exhibit 4, using the first-in, first-out method.

2. Determine the total sales and the total cost of merchandise sold for the period. Journalize the entries in the sales and cost of merchandise sold accounts. Assume that all sales were on account.

3. Determine the gross profit from sales for the period.

4. Determine the ending inventory cost on June 30, 2016.

5. Based upon the preceding data, would you expect the inventory using the last-in, first-out method to be higher or lower?

### PR 7-2B   LIFO perpetual inventory                                      OBJ. 2, 3

✔ 2. Gross profit,
$213,170

SHOW
ME HOW

The beginning inventory for Dunne Co. and data on purchases and sales for a three-month period are shown in Problem 7-1B.

**Instructions**

1. Record the inventory, purchases, and cost of merchandise sold data in a perpetual inventory record similar to the one illustrated in Exhibit 5, using the last-in, first-out method.

2. Determine the total sales, the total cost of merchandise sold, and the gross profit from sales for the period.

3. Determine the ending inventory cost on June 30, 2016.

### PR 7-3B     Weighted average cost method with perpetual inventory     OBJ. 2, 3

The beginning inventory for Dunne Co. and data on purchases and sales for a three-month period are shown in Problem 7-1B.

#### Instructions

1. Record the inventory, purchases, and cost of merchandise sold data in a perpetual inventory record similar to the one illustrated in Exhibit 6, using the weighted average cost method.

2. Determine the total sales, the total cost of merchandise sold, and the gross profit from sales for the period.

3. Determine the ending inventory cost on June 30, 2016.

### PR 7-4B     Periodic inventory by three methods     OBJ. 2, 3

The beginning inventory for Dunne Co. and data on purchases and sales for a three-month period are shown in Problem 7-1B.

#### Instructions

1. Determine the inventory on June 30, 2016, and the cost of goods sold for the three-month period, using the first-in, first-out method and the periodic inventory system.

2. Determine the inventory on June 30, 2016, and the cost of goods sold for the three-month period, using the last-in, first-out method and the periodic inventory system.

3. Determine the inventory on June 30, 2016, and the cost of goods sold for the three-month period, using the weighted average cost method and the periodic inventory system. Round the weighted average unit cost to the dollar.

4. Compare the gross profit and June 30, 2016, inventories using the following column headings:

|  | FIFO | LIFO | Weighted Average |
|---|---|---|---|
| Sales |  |  |  |
| Cost of merchandise sold |  |  |  |
| Gross profit |  |  |  |
| Inventory, June 30, 2016 |  |  |  |

### PR 7-5B     Periodic inventory by three methods     OBJ. 2, 4

Pappa's Appliances uses the periodic inventory system. Details regarding the inventory of appliances at January 1, 2016, purchases invoices during the year, and the inventory count at December 31, 2016, are summarized as follows:

| Model | Inventory, January 1 | Purchases Invoices 1st | 2nd | 3rd | Inventory Count, December 31 |
|---|---|---|---|---|---|
| C55 | 3 at $1,040 | 3 at $1,054 | 3 at $1,060 | 3 at $1,070 | 4 |
| D11 | 9 at 639 | 7 at 645 | 6 at 666 | 6 at 675 | 11 |
| F32 | 5 at 240 | 3 at 260 | 1 at 260 | 1 at 280 | 2 |
| H29 | 6 at 305 | 3 at 310 | 3 at 316 | 4 at 317 | 4 |
| K47 | 6 at 520 | 8 at 531 | 4 at 549 | 6 at 542 | 8 |
| S33 | — | 4 at 222 | 4 at 232 | — | 2 |
| X74 | 4 at 35 | 6 at 36 | 8 at 37 | 7 at 39 | 7 |

#### Instructions

1. Determine the cost of the inventory on December 31, 2016, by the first-in, first-out method. Present data in columnar form, using the following headings:

| Model | Quantity | Unit Cost | Total Cost |
|---|---|---|---|

(*Continued*)

If the inventory of a particular model comprises one entire purchase plus a portion of another purchase acquired at a different unit cost, use a separate line for each purchase.

2. Determine the cost of the inventory on December 31, 2016, by the last-in, first-out method, following the procedures indicated in (1).

3. Determine the cost of the inventory on December 31, 2016, by the weighted average cost method, using the columnar headings indicated in (1).

4. ➤ Discuss which method (FIFO or LIFO) would be preferred for income tax purposes in periods of (a) rising prices and (b) declining prices.

---

**PR 7-6B   Lower-of-cost-or-market inventory**                                     OBJ. 6

✔ Total LCM, $41,873

Data on the physical inventory of Katus Products Co. as of December 31, 2016, follows:

| Description | Inventory Quantity | Market Value per Unit (Net Realizable Value) |
|---|---|---|
| A54 | 37 | $ 56 |
| C77 | 24 | 178 |
| F66 | 30 | 132 |
| H83 | 21 | 545 |
| K12 | 375 | 5 |
| Q58 | 90 | 18 |
| S36 | 8 | 235 |
| V97 | 140 | 20 |
| Y88 | 17 | 744 |

Quantity and cost data from the last purchases invoice of the year and the next-to-the-last purchases invoice are summarized as follows:

| Description | Last Purchases Invoice | | Next-to-the-Last Purchases Invoice | |
|---|---|---|---|---|
| | Quantity Purchased | Unit Cost | Quantity Purchased | Unit Cost |
| A54 | 30 | $ 60 | 40 | $ 58 |
| C77 | 25 | 174 | 15 | 180 |
| F66 | 20 | 130 | 15 | 128 |
| H83 | 6 | 547 | 15 | 540 |
| K12 | 500 | 6 | 500 | 7 |
| Q58 | 75 | 25 | 80 | 26 |
| S36 | 5 | 256 | 4 | 260 |
| V97 | 100 | 17 | 115 | 16 |
| Y88 | 10 | 750 | 8 | 740 |

**Instructions**

Determine the inventory at cost and also at the lower of cost or market, using the first-in, first-out method. Record the appropriate unit costs on the inventory sheet, and complete the pricing of the inventory. When there are two different unit costs applicable to an item:

1. Draw a line through the quantity, and insert the quantity and unit cost of the last purchase.

2. On the following line, insert the quantity and unit cost of the next-to-the-last purchase.

3. Total the cost and market columns and insert the lower of the two totals in the Lower of C or M column. The first item on the inventory sheet has been completed as an example.

**Inventory Sheet**
**December 31, 2016**

| Description | Unit Inventory Quantity | Cost per Unit | Market Value per Unit (Net Realizable Value) | Total | | |
|---|---|---|---|---|---|---|
| | | | | Cost | Market | LCM |
| A54 | 3̶7̶ 30 | 60 | $56 | $1,800 | $1,680 | |
| | 7 | 58 | 56 | 406 | 392 | |
| | | | | $2,206 | $2,072 | $2,072 |

**Appendix**
**PR 7-7B Retail method; gross profit method**

✔ 1. $630,000

Selected data on merchandise inventory, purchases, and sales for Jaffe Co. and Coronado Co. are as follows:

| | Cost | Retail |
|---|---|---|
| **Jaffe Co.** | | |
| Merchandise inventory, February 1 | $ 400,000 | $ 615,000 |
| Transactions during February: | | |
| Purchases (net) | 4,055,000 | 5,325,000 |
| Sales | | 5,100,000 |
| | | |
| **Coronado Co.** | | |
| Merchandise inventory, May 1 | $ 400,000 | |
| Transactions during May thru October: | | |
| Purchases (net) | 3,150,000 | |
| Sales | 4,750,000 | |
| Estimated gross profit rate | 35% | |

**Instructions**

1. Determine the estimated cost of the merchandise inventory of Jaffe Co. on February 28 by the retail method, presenting details of the computations.

2. a. Estimate the cost of the merchandise inventory of Coronado Co. on October 31 by the gross profit method, presenting details of the computations.

   b. Assume that Coronado Co. took a physical inventory on October 31 and discovered that $366,500 of merchandise was on hand. What was the estimated loss of inventory due to theft or damage during May thru October?

# Cases & Projects

### CP 7-1 Ethics and professional conduct in business

Anstead Co. is experiencing a decrease in sales and operating income for the fiscal year ending October 31, 2016. Ryan Frazier, controller of Anstead Co., has suggested that all orders received before the end of the fiscal year be shipped by midnight, October 31, 2016, even if the shipping department must work overtime. Because Anstead Co. ships all merchandise FOB shipping point, it would record all such shipments as sales for the year ending October 31, 2016, thereby offsetting some of the decreases in sales and operating income.
Discuss whether Ryan Frazier is behaving in a professional manner.

### CP 7-2 LIFO and inventory flow

The following is an excerpt from a conversation between Paula Marlo, the warehouse manager for Musick Foods Wholesale Co., and its accountant, Mike Hayes. Musick Foods operates a large regional warehouse that supplies produce and other grocery products to grocery stores in smaller communities.

*Paula:* Mike, can you explain what's going on here with these monthly statements?

*Mike:* Sure, Paula. How can I help you?

*Paula:* I don't understand this last-in, first-out inventory procedure. It just doesn't make sense.

*Mike:* Well, what it means is that we assume that the last goods we receive are the first ones sold. So the inventory consists of the items we purchased first.

*Paula:* Yes, but that's my problem. It doesn't work that way! We always distribute the oldest produce first. Some of that produce is perishable! We can't keep any of it very long or it'll spoil.

*(Continued)*

*Mike:* Paula, you don't understand. We only *assume* that the products we distribute are the last ones received. We don't actually have to distribute the goods in this way.

*Paula:* I always thought that accounting was supposed to show what really happened. It all sounds like "make believe" to me! Why not report what really happens?

 Respond to Paula's concerns.

## CP 7-3  Costing inventory

Golden Eagle Company began operations in 2016 by selling a single product. Data on purchases and sales for the year were as follows:

**Purchases:**

| Date | Units Purchased | Unit Cost | Total Cost |
|------|-----------------|-----------|------------|
| April 6 | 31,000 | $36.60 | $1,134,600 |
| May 18 | 33,000 | 39.00 | 1,287,000 |
| June 6 | 40,000 | 39.60 | 1,584,000 |
| July 10 | 40,000 | 42.00 | 1,680,000 |
| August 10 | 27,200 | 42.75 | 1,162,800 |
| October 25 | 12,800 | 43.50 | 556,800 |
| November 4 | 8,000 | 44.85 | 358,800 |
| December 10 | 8,000 | 48.00 | 384,000 |
|  | 200,000 |  | $8,148,000 |

**Sales:**

| | |
|---|---|
| April | 16,000 units |
| May | 16,000 |
| June | 20,000 |
| July | 24,000 |
| August | 28,000 |
| September | 28,000 |
| October | 18,000 |
| November | 10,000 |
| December | 8,000 |
| Total units | 168,000 |
| Total sales | $10,000,000 |

On January 4, 2017, the president of the company, Connie Kilmer, asked for your advice on costing the 32,000-unit physical inventory that was taken on December 31, 2016. Moreover, since the firm plans to expand its product line, she asked for your advice on the use of a perpetual inventory system in the future.

1. Determine the cost of the December 31, 2016, inventory under the periodic system, using the (a) first-in, first-out method, (b) last-in, first-out method, and (c) weighted average cost method.

2. Determine the gross profit for the year under each of the three methods in (1).

3. a. ▬▬▬▶ Explain varying viewpoints why each of the three inventory costing methods may best reflect the results of operations for 2016.

   b. ▬▬▬▶ Which of the three inventory costing methods may best reflect the replacement cost of the inventory on the balance sheet as of December 31, 2016?

   c. ▬▬▬▶ Which inventory costing method would you choose to use for income tax purposes? Why?

   d. ▬▬▬▶ Discuss the advantages and disadvantages of using a perpetual inventory system. From the data presented in this case, is there any indication of the adequacy of inventory levels during the year?

## CP 7-4  Inventory ratios for Dell and HP

 **FAI**

Dell Inc. and Hewlett-Packard Development Company, L.P. (HP) are both manufacturers of computer equipment and peripherals. However, the two companies follow two different strategies. Dell follows primarily a build-to-order strategy, where the consumer orders the computer from a Web page. The order is then manufactured and shipped to the customer within days of the order. In contrast, HP follows a build-to-stock strategy, where the computer is first built for inventory, then sold from inventory to retailers, such as **Best Buy**. The two strategies can be seen in the difference between the inventory turnover and number of days' sales in inventory ratios for the two companies. The following financial statement information is provided for Dell and HP for a recent fiscal year (in millions):

|  | Dell | HP |
| --- | --- | --- |
| Inventory, beginning of period | $ 1,301 | $ 7,490 |
| Inventory, end of period | 1,404 | 6,317 |
| Cost of goods sold | 48,260 | 92,385 |

a. Determine the inventory turnover ratio and the number of days' sales in inventory ratio for each company. Use 365 days and round to one decimal place.

b. Interpret the difference between the ratios for the two companies.

---

### CP 7-5  Comparing inventory ratios for two companies

**Tiffany Co.** is a high-end jewelry retailer, while **Amazon.com** uses its e-commerce services, features, and technologies to sell its products through the Internet. Recent balance sheet inventory disclosures for Tiffany and Amazon.com (in millons) are as follows:

|  | End-of-Period Inventory | Beginning-of-Period Inventory |
| --- | --- | --- |
| Tiffany Co. | $2,073 | $1,625 |
| Amazon.com | 6,031 | 4,992 |

The cost of merchandise sold reported by each company was as follows:

|  | Tiffany Co. | Amazon.com |
| --- | --- | --- |
| Cost of merchandise sold | $1,492 | $45,971 |

a. Determine the inventory turnover and number of days' sales in inventory for Tiffany and Amazon.com. Use 365 days and round to two decimal places.

b. Interpret your results.

---

### CP 7-6  Comparing inventory ratios for three companies

The general merchandise retail industry has a number of segments represented by the following companies:

| Company Name | Merchandise Concept |
| --- | --- |
| Costco Wholesale Corporation | Membership warehouse |
| Walmart | Discount general merchandise |
| JCPenney | Department store |

For a recent year, the following cost of merchandise sold and beginning and ending inventories have been provided from corporate annual reports (in millions) for these three companies:

|  | Costco | Walmart | JCPenney |
| --- | --- | --- | --- |
| Cost of merchandise sold | $86,823 | $335,127 | $11,042 |
| Merchandise inventory, beginning | 6,638 | 36,437 | 3,213 |
| Merchandise inventory, ending | 7,096 | 40,714 | 2,916 |

a. Determine the inventory turnover ratio for all three companies. Round to one decimal place.

b. Determine the number of days' sales in inventory for all three companies. Use 365 days and round to one decimal place.

c. Interpret these results based on each company's merchandise concept.

# Sarbanes-Oxley, Internal Control, and Cash

## eBay Inc.

Controls are a part of your everyday life. At one extreme, laws are used to limit your behavior. For example, speed limits are designed to control your driving for traffic safety. In addition, you may also use many nonlegal controls. For example, you can keep credit card receipts in order to compare your transactions to the monthly credit card statement. Comparing receipts to the monthly statement is a control designed to catch mistakes made by the credit card company. In addition, banks give you a personal identification number (PIN) as a control against unauthorized access to your cash if you lose your automated teller machine (ATM) card. Dairies use freshness dating on their milk containers as a control to prevent the purchase or sale of soured milk. As you can see, you use and encounter controls every day.

Just as there are many examples of controls throughout society, businesses must also implement controls to help guide the behavior of their managers, employees, and customers. For example, **eBay Inc.** maintains an Internet-based marketplace for the sale of goods and services. Using eBay's online platform, buyers and sellers can browse, buy, and sell a wide variety of items including antiques and used cars. However, in order to maintain the integrity and trust of its buyers and sellers, eBay must have controls to ensure that buyers pay for their items and sellers don't misrepresent their items or fail to deliver sales. One such control eBay uses is a feedback forum that establishes buyer and seller reputations. A prospective buyer or seller can view the member's reputation and feedback comments before completing a transaction. Dishonest or unfair trading can lead to a negative reputation and even suspension or cancellation of the member's ability to trade on eBay.

This chapter discusses controls that can be included in accounting systems to provide reasonable assurance that the financial statements are reliable. Controls to discover and prevent errors to a bank account are also discussed. This chapter begins by discussing the Sarbanes-Oxley Act and its impact on controls and financial reporting.

**OBJ 1** Describe the Sarbanes-Oxley Act and its impact on internal controls and financial reporting.

# Sarbanes-Oxley Act

During recent financial scandals, stockholders, creditors, and other investors lost billions of dollars.[1] As a result, the U.S. Congress passed the **Sarbanes-Oxley Act**. This act is one of the most important laws affecting U.S. companies in recent history. The purpose of Sarbanes-Oxley is to maintain public confidence and trust in the financial reporting of companies.

Sarbanes-Oxley applies only to companies whose stock is traded on public exchanges, referred to as *publicly held companies*. However, Sarbanes-Oxley highlighted the importance of assessing the financial controls and reporting of all companies. As a result, companies of all sizes have been influenced by Sarbanes-Oxley.

Sarbanes-Oxley emphasizes the importance of effective internal control.[2] **Internal control** is defined as the procedures and processes used by a company to:

- Safeguard its assets.
- Process information accurately.
- Ensure compliance with laws and regulations.

Sarbanes-Oxley requires companies to maintain effective internal controls over the recording of transactions and the preparing of financial statements. Such controls

---

[1] Exhibit 2 in Chapter 1 briefly summarizes these scandals.
[2] Sarbanes-Oxley also has important implications for corporate governance and the regulation of the public accounting profession. This chapter, however, focuses on the internal control implications of Sarbanes-Oxley.

are important because they deter fraud and prevent misleading financial statements as shown in Exhibit 1.

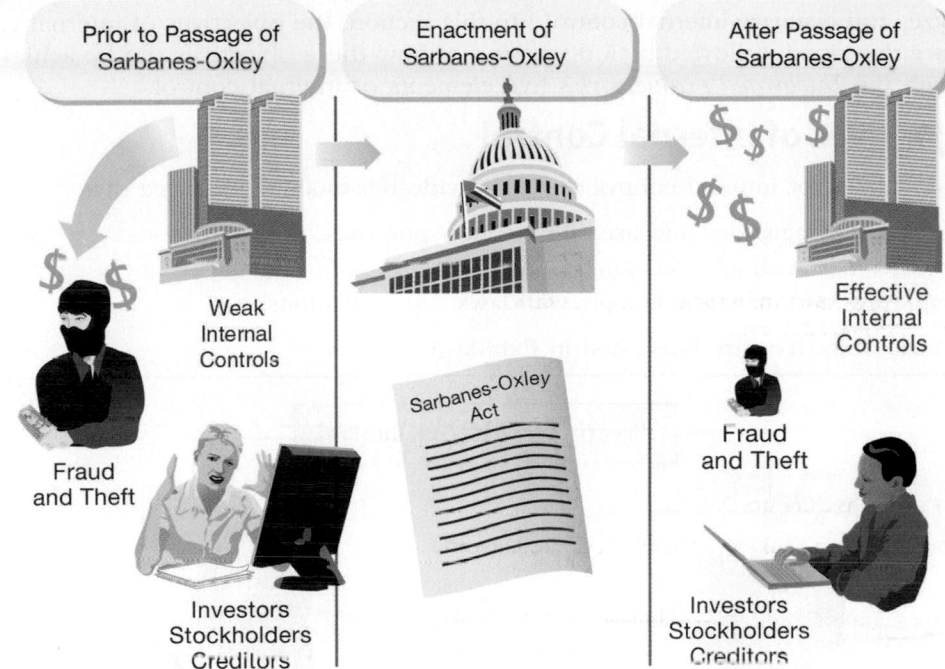

EXHIBIT 1

**Effect of Sarbanes-Oxley**

Sarbanes-Oxley also requires companies and their independent accountants to report on the effectiveness of the company's internal controls.[3] These reports are required to be filed with the company's annual 10-K report with the Securities and Exchange Commission. Companies are also encouraged to include these reports in their annual reports to stockholders. An example of such a report by the management of **Nike** is shown in Exhibit 2.

EXHIBIT 2

**Sarbanes-Oxley Report of Nike**

### Management's Annual Report on Internal Control Over Financial Reporting

Management is responsible for establishing and maintaining adequate internal control over financial reporting....

Under the supervision and with the participation of our Chief Executive Officer and Chief Financial Officer, our management conducted an evaluation of the effectiveness of our internal control over financial reporting based upon the framework in *Internal Control—Integrated Framework* issued by the Committee of Sponsoring Organizations of the Treadway Commission. Based on that evaluation, our management concluded that our internal control over financial reporting is effective....

PricewaterhouseCoopers LLP, an independent registered public accounting firm, has audited . . . the effectiveness of our internal control over financial reporting . . . as stated in their report....

MARK G. PARKER
Chief Executive Officer and President

DONALD W. BLAIR
Chief Financial Officer

*Source:* Nike, *Form 10-K For the Fiscal Year Ended May 31, 2013.*

Exhibit 2 indicates that Nike based its evaluation of internal controls on *Internal Control—Integrated Framework*, which was issued by the Committee of Sponsoring Organizations (COSO) of the Treadway Commission. This framework is the standard by which companies design, analyze, and evaluate internal controls. For this reason, this framework is used as the basis for discussing internal controls.

 Information on *Internal Control—Integrated Framework* can be found on COSO's Web site at http://www.coso.org/.

[3] These reporting requirements are required under Section 404 of the act. As a result, these requirements and reports are often referred to as 404 requirements and 404 reports.

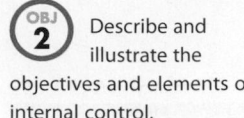

Describe and illustrate the objectives and elements of internal control.

# Internal Control

*Internal Control—Integrated Framework* is the standard by which companies design, analyze, and evaluate internal control.[4] In this section, the objectives of internal control are described, followed by a discussion of how these objectives can be achieved through the *Integrated Framework's* five elements of internal control.

## Objectives of Internal Control

The objectives of internal control are to provide reasonable assurance that:

- Assets are safeguarded and used for business purposes.
- Business information is accurate.
- Employees and managers comply with laws and regulations.

These objectives are illustrated in Exhibit 3.

**EXHIBIT 3**

**Objectives of Internal Control**

Safeguarded Assets | Accurate Information | Compliance with Laws and Regulations

Internal control can safeguard assets by preventing theft, fraud, misuse, or misplacement. A serious concern of internal control is preventing employee fraud. **Employee fraud** is the intentional act of deceiving an employer for personal gain. Such fraud may range from minor overstating of a travel expense report to stealing millions of dollars. Employees stealing from a business often adjust the accounting records in order to hide their fraud. Thus, employee fraud usually affects the accuracy of business information.

Accurate information is necessary to successfully operate a business. Businesses must also comply with laws, regulations, and financial reporting standards. Examples of such standards include environmental regulations, safety regulations, and generally accepted accounting principles (GAAP).

## Business  Connection

**EMPLOYEE FRAUD**

The Association of Fraud Examiners estimates that 5% of annual revenues worldwide or more than $3.5 trillion is lost to employee fraud. A common cash receipts em-

ployee fraud can occur when employees accept cash payments from customers, do not record the sale, and then pocket the cash. A common cash payments employee fraud can occur when employees bill their employer for false services or personal items.

Source: *2012 Report to the Nation on Occupational Fraud and Abuse*, Association of Fraud Examiners.

## Elements of Internal Control

The three internal control objectives can be achieved by applying the five **elements of internal control** set forth by the *Integrated Framework*.[5] These elements are as follows:

- Control environment
- Risk assessment

[4] *Internal Control—Integrated Framework* by the Committee of Sponsoring Organizations of the Treadway Commission, 2013.
[5] Ibid., pp. 12–14.

- Control procedures
- Monitoring
- Information and communication

The elements of internal control are illustrated in Exhibit 4.

**EXHIBIT 4**

**Elements of Internal Control**

In Exhibit 4, the elements of internal control form an umbrella over the business to protect it from control threats. The control environment is the size of the umbrella. Risk assessment, control procedures, and monitoring are the fabric of the umbrella, which keep it from leaking. Information and communication connect the umbrella to management.

## Control Environment

The **control environment** is the overall attitude of management and employees about the importance of controls. Three factors influencing a company's control environment include the following, as shown in Exhibit 5:

- Management's philosophy and operating style
- The company's organizational structure
- The company's personnel policies

**EXHIBIT 5**     **Control Environment**

Management's philosophy and operating style relates to whether management emphasizes the importance of internal controls. An emphasis on controls and adherence to control policies creates an effective control environment. In contrast, overemphasizing operating goals and tolerating deviations from control policies creates an ineffective control environment.

The business's organizational structure is the framework for planning and controlling operations. For example, a retail store chain might organize each of its stores as separate business units. Each store manager has full authority over pricing and other operating activities. In such a structure, each store manager has the responsibility for establishing an effective control environment.

The business's personnel policies involve the hiring, training, evaluation, compensation, and promotion of employees. In addition, job descriptions, employee codes of ethics, and conflict-of-interest policies are part of the personnel policies. Such policies can enhance the internal control environment if they provide reasonable assurance that only competent, honest employees are hired and retained.

## Risk Assessment

All businesses face risks such as changes in customer requirements, competitive threats, regulatory changes, and changes in economic factors. Management should identify such risks, analyze their significance, assess their likelihood of occurring, and take any necessary actions to minimize them.

## Control Procedures

Control procedures provide reasonable assurance that business goals will be achieved, including the prevention of fraud. Control procedures, which constitute one of the most important elements of internal control, include the following as shown in Exhibit 6:

- Competent personnel, rotating duties, and mandatory vacations
- Separating responsibilities for related operations
- Separating operations, custody of assets, and accounting
- Proofs and security measures

---

**EXHIBIT 6**

**Internal Control Procedures**

**Competent Personnel, Rotating Duties, and Mandatory Vacations** A successful company needs competent employees who are able to perform the duties that they are assigned. Procedures should be established for properly training and supervising employees. It is also advisable to rotate duties of accounting personnel and mandate vacations for all employees. In this way, employees are encouraged to adhere to procedures. Cases of employee fraud are often discovered when a long-term employee, who never took vacations, missed work because of an illness or another unavoidable reason.

**Separating Responsibilities for Related Operations** The responsibility for related operations should be divided among two or more people. This decreases the possibility of errors and fraud. For example, if the same person orders supplies, verifies the receipt of the supplies, and pays the supplier, the following abuses may occur:

- Orders may be placed on the basis of friendship with a supplier, rather than on price, quality, and other objective factors.
- The quantity and quality of supplies received may not be verified; thus, the company may pay for supplies not received or that are of poor quality.
- Supplies may be stolen by the employee.
- The validity and accuracy of invoices may not be verified; hence, the company may pay false or inaccurate invoices.

For the preceding reasons, the responsibilities for purchasing, receiving, and paying for supplies should be divided among three persons or departments.

**Separating Operations, Custody of Assets, and Accounting** The responsibilities for operations, custody of assets, and accounting should be separated. In this way, the accounting records serve as an independent check on the operating managers and the employees who have custody of assets.

To illustrate, employees who handle cash receipts should not record cash receipts in the accounting records. To do so would allow employees to borrow or steal cash and hide the theft in the accounting records. Likewise, operating managers should not also record the results of operations. To do so would allow the managers to distort the accounting reports to show favorable results, which might allow them to receive larger bonuses.

**Proofs and Security Measures** Proofs and security measures are used to safeguard assets and ensure reliable accounting data. Proofs involve procedures such as authorization, approval, and reconciliation. For example, an employee planning to travel on company business may be required to complete a "travel request" form for a manager's authorization and approval.

## Integrity, Objectivity, and Ethics in Business

**TIPS ON PREVENTING EMPLOYEE FRAUD IN SMALL COMPANIES**

- Do not have the same employee write company checks and keep the books. Look for payments to vendors you don't know or payments to vendors whose names appear to be misspelled.
- If your business has a computer system, restrict access to accounting files as much as possible. Also, keep a backup copy of your accounting files and store it at an off-site location.
- Be wary of anybody working in finance who declines to take vacations. They may be afraid that a replacement will uncover fraud.

- Require and monitor supporting documentation (such as vendor invoices) before signing checks.
- Track the number of credit card bills you sign monthly.
- Limit and monitor access to important documents and supplies, such as blank checks and signature stamps.
- Check W-2 forms against your payroll annually to make sure you're not carrying any fictitious employees.
- Rely on yourself, not on your accountant, to spot fraud.

Source: Steve Kaufman, "Embezzlement Common at Small Companies," Knight-Ridder Newspapers, reported in *Athens Daily News/Athens Banner-Herald*, March 10, 1996, p. 4D.

Documents used for authorization and approval should be prenumbered, accounted for, and safeguarded. Prenumbering of documents helps prevent transactions from being recorded more than once or not at all. In addition, accounting for and safeguarding prenumbered documents helps prevent fraudulent transactions from being recorded. For example, blank checks are prenumbered and safeguarded. Once a payment has been properly authorized and approved, the checks are filled out and issued.

Reconciliations are also an important control. Later in this chapter, the use of bank reconciliations as an aid in controlling cash is described and illustrated.

Security measures involve measures to safeguard assets. For example, cash on hand should be kept in a cash register or safe. Inventory not on display should be stored in a locked storeroom or warehouse. Accounting records such as the accounts receivable subsidiary ledger should also be safeguarded to prevent their loss. For example, electronically maintained accounting records should be safeguarded with access codes and backed up so that any lost or damaged files could be recovered if necessary.

## Monitoring

Monitoring the internal control system is used to locate weaknesses and improve controls. Monitoring often includes observing employee behavior and the accounting system for indicators of control problems. Some such indicators are shown in Exhibit 7.[6]

 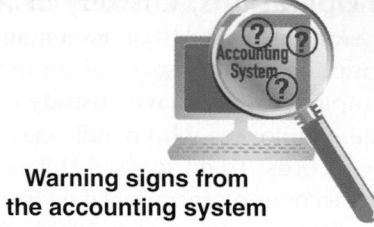

**Warning signs with regard to people**

- Abrupt change in lifestyle (without winning the lottery).
- Close social relationships with suppliers.
- Refusing to take a vacation.
- Frequent borrowing from other employees.
- Excessive use of alcohol or drugs.

**Warning signs from the accounting system**

- Missing documents or gaps in transaction numbers (could mean documents are being used for fraudulent transactions).
- An unusual increase in customer refunds (refunds may be phony).
- Differences between daily cash receipts and bank deposits (could mean receipts are being pocketed before being deposited).
- Sudden increase in slow payments (employee may be pocketing the payments).
- Backlog in recording transactions (possibly an attempt to delay detection of fraud).

Evaluations of controls are often performed when there are major changes in strategy, senior management, business structure, or operations. Internal auditors, who are independent of operations, usually perform such evaluations. Internal auditors are also responsible for day-to-day monitoring of controls. External auditors also evaluate and report on internal control as part of their annual financial statement audit.

## Information and Communication

Information and communication is an essential element of internal control. Information about the control environment, risk assessment, control procedures, and monitoring is used by management for guiding operations and ensuring compliance with reporting, legal, and regulatory requirements. Management also uses external

---

[6] Edwin C. Bliss, "Employee Theft," *Boardroom Reports,* July 15, 1994, pp. 5–6.

information to assess events and conditions that impact decision making and external reporting. For example, management uses pronouncements of the Financial Accounting Standards Board (FASB) to assess the impact of changes in reporting standards on the financial statements.

---

### Example Exercise 8-1  Internal Control Elements

Identify each of the following as relating to (a) the control environment, (b) risk assessment, or (c) control procedures:

1. Mandatory vacations
2. Personnel policies
3. Report of outside consultants on future market changes

### Follow My Example 8-1

1. (c) control procedures
2. (a) the control environment
3. (b) risk assessment

Practice Exercises: PE 8-1A, PE 8-1B

---

## Limitations of Internal Control

Internal control systems can provide only reasonable assurance for safeguarding assets, processing accurate information, and compliance with laws and regulations. In other words, internal controls are not a guarantee. This is due to the following factors:

- The human element of controls
- Cost-benefit considerations

The *human element* recognizes that controls are applied and used by humans. As a result, human errors can occur because of fatigue, carelessness, confusion, or misjudgment. For example, an employee may unintentionally shortchange a customer or miscount the amount of inventory received from a supplier. In addition, two or more employees may collude together to defeat or circumvent internal controls. This latter case often involves fraud and the theft of assets. For example, the cashier and the accounts receivable clerk might collude to steal customer payments on account.

*Cost-benefit considerations* recognize that the cost of internal controls should not exceed their benefits. For example, retail stores could eliminate shoplifting by searching all customers before they leave the store. However, such a control procedure would upset customers and result in lost sales. Instead, retailers use cameras or signs saying, "*We prosecute all shoplifters.*"

## Cash Controls over Receipts and Payments

**OBJ 3** Describe and illustrate the application of internal controls to cash.

**Cash** includes coins, currency (paper money), checks, and money orders. Money on deposit with a bank or other financial institution that is available for withdrawal is also considered cash. Normally, you can think of cash as anything that a bank would accept for deposit in your account. For example, a check made payable to you could normally be deposited in a bank and, thus, is considered cash.

Businesses usually have several bank accounts. For example, a business might have one bank account for general cash payments and another for payroll. A separate ledger account is normally used for each bank account. For example, a bank account at City Bank could be identified in the ledger as *Cash in Bank—City Bank*. To simplify, this chapter assumes that a company has only *one* bank account, which is identified in the ledger as *Cash*.

Cash is the asset most likely to be stolen or used improperly in a business. For this reason, businesses must carefully control cash and cash transactions.

## Control of Cash Receipts

To protect cash from theft and misuse, a business must control cash from the time it is received until it is deposited in a bank. Businesses normally receive cash from two main sources.

- Customers purchasing products or services
- Customers making payments on account

**Cash Received from Cash Sales** An important control to protect cash received in over-the-counter sales is a cash register. The use of a cash register to control cash is shown in Exhibit 8.

A cash register controls cash as follows:

1. At the beginning of every work shift, each cash register clerk is given a cash drawer containing a predetermined amount of cash. This amount is used for making change for customers and is sometimes called a *change fund*.
2. When a salesperson enters the amount of a sale, the cash register displays the amount to the customer. This allows the customer to verify that the clerk has charged the correct amount. The customer also receives a cash receipt.
3. At the end of the shift, the clerk and the supervisor count the cash in the clerk's cash drawer. The amount of cash in each drawer should equal the beginning amount of cash plus the cash sales for the day.
4. The supervisor takes the cash to the Cashier's Department where it is placed in a safe.
5. The supervisor forwards the clerk's cash register receipts to the Accounting Department.
6. The cashier prepares a bank deposit ticket.
7. The cashier deposits the cash in the bank, or the cash is picked up by an armored car service, such as Wells Fargo.
8. The Accounting Department summarizes the cash receipts and records the day's cash sales.
9. When cash is deposited in the bank, the bank normally stamps a duplicate copy of the deposit ticket with the amount received. This bank receipt is returned to the Accounting Department, where it is compared to the total amount that should have been deposited. This control helps ensure that all the cash is deposited and that no cash is lost or stolen on the way to the bank. Any shortages are thus promptly detected.

Salespersons may make errors in making change for customers or in ringing up cash sales. As a result, the amount of cash on hand may differ from the amount of cash sales. Such differences are recorded in a **cash short and over account**.

To illustrate, assume the following cash register data for May 3:

| | |
|---|---|
| Cash register total for cash sales | $35,690 |
| Cash receipts from cash sales | 35,668 |

The cash sales, receipts, and shortage of $22 ($35,690 – $35,668) would be recorded as follows:

| May | 3 | Cash | | 35,668 | |
|-----|---|------|---|--------|---|
| | | Cash Short and Over | | 22 | |
| | |     Sales | | | 35,690 |

If there had been cash over, Cash Short and Over would have been credited for the overage. At the end of the accounting period, a debit balance in Cash Short and Over is included in miscellaneous expense on the income statement. A credit balance is included in the Other Income section. If a salesperson consistently has large cash short and over amounts, the supervisor may require the clerk to take additional training.

**Cash Received in the Mail** Cash is received in the mail when customers pay their bills. This cash is usually in the form of checks and money orders. Most companies design their invoices so that customers return a portion of the invoice, called a *remittance advice*, with their payment. Remittance advices may be used to control cash received in the mail as follows:

1. An employee opens the incoming mail and compares the amount of cash received with the amount shown on the remittance advice. If a customer does not return a remittance advice, the employee prepares one. The remittance advice serves as a record of the cash initially received. It also helps ensure that the posting to the customer's account is for the amount of cash received.
2. The employee opening the mail stamps checks and money orders "For Deposit Only" in the bank account of the business.
3. The remittance advices and their summary totals are delivered to the Accounting Department.
4. All cash and money orders are delivered to the Cashier's Department.
5. The cashier prepares a bank deposit ticket.
6. The cashier deposits the cash in the bank, or the cash is picked up by an armored car service, such as Wells Fargo.
7. An accounting clerk records the cash received and posts the amounts to the customer accounts.
8. When cash is deposited in the bank, the bank normally stamps a duplicate copy of the deposit ticket with the amount received. This bank receipt is returned to the Accounting Department, where it is compared to the total amount that should have been deposited. This control helps ensure that all cash is deposited and that no cash is lost or stolen on the way to the bank. Any shortages are thus promptly detected.

Separating the duties of the Cashier's Department, which handles cash, and the Accounting Department, which records cash, is a control. If Accounting Department employees both handle and record cash, an employee could steal cash and change the accounting records to hide the theft.

**Cash Received by EFT** Cash may also be received from customers through **electronic funds transfer (EFT)**. For example, customers may authorize automatic electronic transfers from their checking accounts to pay monthly bills for such items as cell phone, Internet, and electric services. In such cases, the company sends the customer's bank a signed form from the customer authorizing the monthly electronic transfers. Each month, the company notifies the customer's bank of the amount of the transfer and the date the transfer should take place. On the due date, the company records the electronic transfer as a receipt of cash to its bank account and posts the amount paid to the customer's account.

Companies encourage customers to use EFT for the following reasons:

- EFTs cost less than receiving cash payments through the mail.
- EFTs enhance internal controls over cash, since the cash is received directly by the bank without any employees handling cash.
- EFTs reduce late payments from customers and speed up the processing of cash receipts.

## Control of Cash Payments

**Howard Schultz & Associates (HS&A)** specializes in reviewing cash payments for its clients. HS&A searches for errors, such as duplicate payments, failures to take discounts, and inaccurate computations. Amounts recovered for clients range from thousands to millions of dollars.

The control of cash payments should provide reasonable assurance that:

- Payments are made for only authorized transactions.
- Cash is used effectively and efficiently. For example, controls should ensure that all available purchase discounts are taken.

In a small business, an owner/manager may authorize payments based on personal knowledge. In a large business, however, purchasing goods, inspecting the goods received, and verifying the invoices are usually performed by different employees. These duties must be coordinated to ensure that proper payments are made to creditors. One system used for this purpose is the voucher system.

**Voucher System** A **voucher system** is a set of procedures for authorizing and recording liabilities and cash payments. A **voucher** is any document that serves as proof of authority to pay cash or issue an electronic funds transfer. An invoice that has been approved for payment could be considered a voucher. In many businesses, however, a voucher is a special form used to record data about a liability and the details of its payment.

In a manual system, a voucher is normally prepared after all necessary supporting documents have been received. For the purchase of goods, a voucher is supported by the supplier's invoice, a purchase order, and a receiving report. After a voucher is prepared, it is submitted for approval. Once approved, the voucher is recorded in the accounts and filed by due date. Upon payment, the voucher is recorded in the same manner as the payment of an account payable.

In a computerized system, data from the supporting documents (such as purchase orders, receiving reports, and suppliers' invoices) are entered directly into computer files. At the due date, the checks are automatically generated and mailed to creditors. At that time, the voucher is electronically transferred to a paid voucher file.

**Cash Paid by EFT** Cash can also be paid by electronic funds transfer (EFT) systems. For example, you can withdraw cash from your bank account using an ATM machine. Your withdrawal is a type of EFT transfer.

Companies also use EFT transfers. For example, many companies pay their employees via EFT. Under such a system, employees authorize the deposit of their payroll checks directly into their checking accounts. Each pay period, the company transfers the employees' net pay to their checking accounts through the use of EFT. Many companies also use EFT systems to pay their suppliers and other vendors.

# Bank Accounts

**OBJ 4** Describe the nature of a bank account and its use in controlling cash.

A major reason that companies use bank accounts is for internal control. Some of the control advantages of using bank accounts are as follows:

- Bank accounts reduce the amount of cash on hand.
- Bank accounts provide an independent recording of cash transactions. Reconciling the balance of the cash account in the company's records with the cash balance according to the bank is an important control.
- Use of bank accounts facilitates the transfer of funds using EFT systems.

## Bank Statement

Banks usually maintain a record of all checking account transactions. A summary of all transactions, called a **bank statement**, is mailed, usually each month, to the company (depositor) or made available online. The bank statement shows the beginning balance, additions, deductions, and the ending balance. A typical bank statement is shown in Exhibit 9.

Checks or copies of the checks listed in the order that they were paid by the bank may accompany the bank statement. If paid checks are returned, they are stamped "Paid," together with the date of payment. Many banks no longer return checks or check copies. Instead, the check payment information is available online.

**EXHIBIT 9**

**Bank Statement**

```
                        MEMBER FDIC                                    PAGE    1

VALLEY NATIONAL BANK                        ACCOUNT NUMBER    1627042
OF LOS ANGELES
                                            FROM  6/30/15    TO  7/31/15
LOS ANGELES, CA 90020-4253    (310)555-5151
                                            BALANCE            4,218.60

                                        22 DEPOSITS           13,749.75

                                        52 WITHDRAWALS        14,698.57
       POWER NETWORKING
       1000 Belkin Street                 3 OTHER DEBITS
       Los Angeles, CA 90014-1000           AND CREDITS          90.00CR

                                            NEW BALANCE        3,359.78


* – – CHECKS AND OTHER DEBITS – – – – – – – – * – – – – – – – – DEPOSITS – * – DATE * BALANCE *

  No. 850   819.40    No. 852  122.54              585.75    07/01   3,862.41
  No. 854   369.50    No. 853   20.15              421.53    07/02   3,894.29
  No. 851   600.00    No. 856  190.70              781.30    07/03   3,884.89
  No. 855    25.93    No. 857   52.50                        07/04   3,806.46
  No. 860   921.20    No. 858  160.00              662.50    07/05   3,387.76
  No. 862    91.07    NSF      300.00              503.18    07/07   3,499.87
```

```
  No. 880    32.26    No. 877  535.09          ACH 932.00    07/29   4,136.66
  No. 881    21.10    No. 879  732.26              705.21    07/30   4,088.51
  No. 882   126.20    SC        18.00          MS  408.00    07/30   4,352.31
  No. 874    26.12    ACH    1,615.13              648.72    07/31   3,359.78

        EC — ERROR CORRECTION          ACH    AUTOMATED CLEARING HOUSE
        MS — MISCELLANEOUS
        NSF — NOT SUFFICIENT FUNDS      SC — SERVICE CHARGE
  * * *                          * * *                          * * *

        THE RECONCILEMENT OF THIS STATEMENT WITH YOUR RECORDS IS ESSENTIAL.
        ANY ERROR OR EXCEPTION SHOULD BE REPORTED IMMEDIATELY.
```

The company's checking account balance *in the bank records* is a liability. Thus, in the bank's records, the company's account has a credit balance. Because the bank statement is prepared from the bank's point of view, a credit memo entry on the bank statement indicates an increase (a credit) to the company's account. Likewise, a debit memo entry on the bank statement indicates a decrease (a debit) in the company's account. This relationship is shown in Exhibit 10.

**EXHIBIT 10**

**Checking Account: Company and Bank Perspectives**

A bank makes credit entries (issues credit memos) for the following:

- Deposits made by electronic funds transfer (EFT)
- Collections of notes receivable for the company
- Proceeds for a loan made to the company by the bank
- Interest earned on the company's account
- Correction (if any) of bank errors

A bank makes debit entries (issues debit memos) for the following:

- Payments made by electronic funds transfer (EFT)
- Service charges
- Customer checks returned for not sufficient funds
- Correction (if any) of bank errors

Customers' checks returned for not sufficient funds, called *NSF checks*, are customer checks that were initially deposited but were not paid by the customer's bank. Because the company's bank credited the customer's check to the company's account when it was deposited, the bank debits the company's account (issues a debit memo) when the check is returned without payment.

The reason for a credit or debit memo entry is indicated on the bank statement. Exhibit 9 identifies the following types of credit and debit memo entries:

- EC: Error correction to correct bank error
- NSF: Not sufficient funds check
- SC: Service charge
- ACH: Automated clearing house entry for electronic funds transfer
- MS: Miscellaneous item such as collection of a note receivable on behalf of the company or receipt of a loan by the company from the bank

The preceding list includes the notation "ACH" for electronic funds transfers. ACH is a network for clearing electronic funds transfers among individuals, companies, and banks.[7] Because electronic funds transfers may be either deposits or payments, ACH entries may indicate either a debit or credit entry to the company's account. Likewise, entries to correct bank errors and miscellaneous items may indicate a debit or credit entry to the company's account.

## Example Exercise 8-2 Items on Company's Bank Statement

**OBJ 4**

The following items may appear on a bank statement:

1. NSF check
2. EFT deposit
3. Service charge
4. Bank correction of an error from recording a $400 check as $40

Using the following format, indicate whether the item would appear as a debit or credit memo on the bank statement and whether the item would increase or decrease the balance of the company's account:

| Item No. | Appears on the Bank Statement as a Debit or Credit Memo | Increases or Decreases the Balance of the Company's Bank Account |
|---|---|---|

## Follow My Example 8-2

| Item No. | Appears on the Bank Statement as a Debit or Credit Memo | Increases or Decreases the Balance of the Company's Bank Account |
|---|---|---|
| 1 | debit memo | decreases |
| 2 | credit memo | increases |
| 3 | debit memo | decreases |
| 4 | debit memo | decreases |

Practice Exercises: PE 8-2A, PE 8-2B

[7] For further information on ACH, go to www.nacha.org/. Click on "ACH Network" and then click on "Intro to the ACH Network."

## Using the Bank Statement as a Control over Cash

The bank statement is a primary control that a company uses over cash. A company uses the bank's statement by comparing the company's recording of cash transactions to those recorded by the bank.

The cash balance shown by a bank statement is usually different from the company's cash balance, as shown in Exhibit 11.

| Bank Statement | | |
|---|---|---|
| Beginning balance | | $ 4,218.60 |
| Additions: | | |
| Deposits | $13,749.75 | |
| Miscellaneous | 408.00 | 14,157.75 |
| Deductions: | | |
| Checks | $14,698.57 | |
| NSF check | 300.00 | |
| Service charge | 18.00 | (15,016.57) |
| Ending balance | | $ 3,359.78 |

| Power Networking Records | |
|---|---|
| Beginning balance | $ 4,227.60 |
| Deposits | 14,565.95 |
| Checks | (16,243.56) |
| Ending balance | $ 2,549.99 |

**EXHIBIT 11**

**Power Networking's Records and Bank Statement**

Power Networking should determine the reason for the difference in these two amounts.

Differences between the company and bank balance may arise because of a delay by either the company or bank in recording transactions. For example, there is normally a time lag of one or more days between the date a check is written and the date that it is paid by the bank. Likewise, there is normally a time lag between when the company mails a deposit to the bank (or uses the night depository) and when the bank receives and records the deposit.

Differences may also arise because the bank has debited or credited the company's account for transactions that the company will not know about until the bank statement is received. Finally, differences may arise from errors made by either the company or the bank. For example, the company may incorrectly post to Cash a check written for $4,500 as $450. Likewise, a bank may incorrectly record the amount of a check.

## Bank Reconciliation

A **bank reconciliation** is an analysis of the items and amounts that result in the cash balance reported in the bank statement to differ from the balance of the cash account in the ledger. The adjusted cash balance determined in the bank reconciliation is reported on the balance sheet.

A bank reconciliation is usually divided into two sections as follows:

1. The *bank section* begins with the cash balance according to the bank statement and ends with the *adjusted balance*.

2. The *company section* begins with the cash balance according to the company's records and ends with the *adjusted balance*.

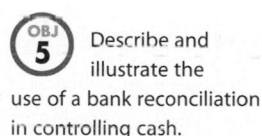

**OBJ 5**  Describe and illustrate the use of a bank reconciliation in controlling cash.

The *adjusted balance* from bank and company sections must be equal. The format of the bank reconciliation follows:

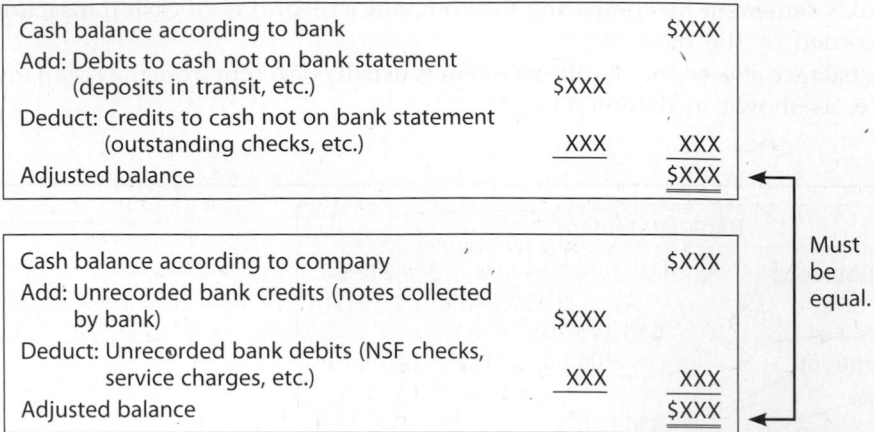

| Cash balance according to bank | | $XXX |
| Add: Debits to cash not on bank statement (deposits in transit, etc.) | $XXX | |
| Deduct: Credits to cash not on bank statement (outstanding checks, etc.) | XXX | XXX |
| Adjusted balance | | $XXX |

| Cash balance according to company | | $XXX |
| Add: Unrecorded bank credits (notes collected by bank) | $XXX | |
| Deduct: Unrecorded bank debits (NSF checks, service charges, etc.) | XXX | XXX |
| Adjusted balance | | $XXX |

Must be equal.

A bank reconciliation is prepared using steps illustrated in Exhibit 12.

---

## EXHIBIT 12

**How to Prepare a Bank Reconciliation**

### Bank Section of Reconciliation

- Step 1. Enter the *Cash balance according to bank* from the ending cash balance according to the bank statement.
- Step 2. *Add deposits not recorded by the bank.*

    Identify deposits not recorded by the bank by comparing each deposit listed on the bank statement with unrecorded deposits appearing in the preceding period's reconciliation and with the current period's deposits.

    Examples: Deposits in transit at the end of the period.
- Step 3. *Deduct outstanding checks that have not been paid by the bank.*

    Identify outstanding checks by comparing paid checks with outstanding checks appearing on the preceding period's reconciliation and with recorded checks.

    Examples: Outstanding checks at the end of the period.
- Step 4. Determine the *Adjusted balance* by adding Step 2 and deducting Step 3.

### Company Section of Reconciliation

- Step 5. Enter the *Cash balance according to company* from the ending cash balance in the ledger.
- Step 6. *Add credit memos that have not been recorded.*

    Identify the bank credit memos that have not been recorded by comparing the bank statement credit memos to entries in the journal.

    Examples: A note receivable and interest that the bank has collected for the company.
- Step 7. *Deduct debit memos that have not been recorded.*

    Identify the bank debit memos that have not been recorded by comparing the bank statement debit memos to entries in the journal.

    Examples: Customers' not sufficient funds (NSF) checks; bank service charges.
- Step 8. Determine the *Adjusted balance* by adding Step 6 and deducting Step 7.

### Verify That Adjusted Balances Are Equal

- Step 9. Verify that the adjusted balances determined in Steps 4 and 8 are equal.

The adjusted balances in the bank and company sections of the reconciliation must be equal. If the balances are not equal, an item has been overlooked and must be found.

Sometimes, the adjusted balances are not equal because either the company or the bank has made an error. In such cases, the error is often discovered by comparing the amount of each item (deposit and check) on the bank statement with that in the company's records.

Any bank or company errors discovered should be added to or deducted from the bank or company section of the reconciliation, depending on the nature of the error. For example, assume that the bank incorrectly recorded a company check for $50 as $500. This bank error of $450 ($500 − $50) would be added to the bank balance in the bank section of the reconciliation. In addition, the bank would be notified of the error so that it could be corrected. On the other hand, assume that the company recorded a deposit of $1,200 as $2,100. This company error of $900 ($2,100 − $1,200) would be deducted from the cash balance in the company section of the bank reconciliation. The company would later correct the error using a journal entry.

To illustrate, the bank statement for Power Networking in Exhibit 9 is used. This bank statement shows a balance of $3,359.78 as of July 31. The cash balance in Power Networking's ledger on the same date is $2,549.99. Using the preceding steps, the following reconciling items were identified:

Step 2.  Deposit of July 31, not recorded on bank statement: $816.20
Step 3.  Outstanding checks:

| | |
|---|---|
| Check No. 812 | $1,061.00 |
| Check No. 878 | 435.39 |
| Check No. 883 | 48.60 |
| Total | $1,544.99 |

Step 6.  Note receivable of $400 plus interest of $8 collected by bank not recorded in the journal as indicated by a credit memo of $408.
Step 7.  Check from customer (Thomas Ivey) for $300 returned by bank because of insufficient funds (NSF) as indicated by a debit memo of $300.00.
Bank service charges of $18, not recorded in the journal as indicated by a debit memo of $18.00.

In addition, an error of $9 was discovered. This error occurred when Check No. 879 for $732.26 to Taylor Co., on account, was recorded in the company's journal as $723.26.

The bank reconciliation, based on the Exhibit 9 bank statement and the preceding reconciling items, is shown in Exhibit 13.

**EXHIBIT 13**   **Bank Reconciliation for Power Networking**

Power Networking
Bank Reconciliation
July 31, 2015

| | | | |
|---|---|---|---|
| Step 1 | Cash balance according to bank statement | | $3,359.78 |
| Step 2 | Add deposit of July 31, not recorded by bank | | 816.20 |
| | | | $4,175.98 |
| Step 3 | Deduct outstanding checks: | | |
| | No. 812 | $1,061.00 | |
| | No. 878 | 435.39 | |
| | No. 883 | 48.60 | 1,544.99 |
| Step 4 | Adjusted balance | | $2,630.99 |
| Step 5 | Cash balance according to Power Networking | | $2,549.99 |
| Step 6 | Add note and interest collected by bank | | 408.00 |
| | | | $2,957.99 |
| Step 7 | Deduct: Check returned because of insufficient funds | $ 300.00 | |
| | Bank service charge | 18.00 | |
| | Error in recording Check No. 879 | 9.00 | 327.00 |
| Step 8 | Adjusted balance | | $2,630.99 |

Step 9

The company's records do not need to be updated for any items in the *bank section* of the reconciliation. This section begins with the cash balance according to the bank statement. However, the bank should be notified of any errors that need to be corrected.

The company's records do need to be updated for any items in the *company section* of the bank reconciliation. The company's records are updated using journal entries. For example, journal entries should be made for any unrecorded bank memos and any company errors.

The journal entries for Power Networking, based on the bank reconciliation shown in Exhibit 13, are as follows:

| | | | | | |
|------|----|-------------------------------|-----|-----|
| July | 31 | Cash | 408 | |
| | | Notes Receivable | | 400 |
| | | Interest Revenue | | 8 |
| | | | | |
| | 31 | Accounts Receivable—Thomas Ivey | 300 | |
| | | Miscellaneous Expense | 18 | |
| | | Accounts Payable—Taylor Co. | 9 | |
| | | Cash | | 327 |

After the preceding journal entries are recorded and posted, the cash account will have a debit balance of $2,630.99. This cash balance agrees with the adjusted balance shown on the bank reconciliation. This is the amount of cash on July 31 and is the amount that is reported on Power Networking's July 31 balance sheet.

Businesses may reconcile their bank accounts in a slightly different format from that shown in Exhibit 13. Regardless, the objective is to control cash by reconciling the company's records with the bank statement. In doing so, any errors or misuse of cash may be detected.

To enhance internal control, the bank reconciliation should be prepared by an employee who does not take part in or record cash transactions. Otherwise, mistakes may occur, and it is more likely that cash will be stolen or misapplied. For example, an employee who handles cash and also reconciles the bank statement could steal a cash deposit, omit the deposit from the accounts, and omit it from the reconciliation.

Bank reconciliations are also an important part of computerized systems where deposits and checks are stored in electronic files and records. Some systems use computer software to determine the difference between the bank statement and company cash balances. The software then adjusts for deposits in transit and outstanding checks. Any remaining differences are reported for further analysis.

## Example Exercise 8-3  Bank Reconciliation

The following data were gathered to use in reconciling the bank account of Photo Op:

| | |
|---|---|
| Balance per bank......................................................................... | $14,500 |
| Balance per company records.......................................................... | 13,875 |
| Bank service charges .................................................................... | 75 |
| Deposit in transit ......................................................................... | 3,750 |
| NSF check................................................................................... | 800 |
| Outstanding checks ...................................................................... | 5,250 |

a. What is the adjusted balance on the bank reconciliation?

b. Journalize any necessary entries for Photo Op based on the bank reconciliation.

*(Continued)*

**Follow My Example 8-3** ▶▶

a.   $13,000, computed as follows:

Bank section of reconciliation: $14,500 + $3,750 − $5,250 = $13,000
Company section of reconciliation: $13,875 − $75 − $800 = $13,000

b.   Accounts Receivable. . . . . . . . . . . . . . . . . . . . . . . . . . . . . . . . . . . . . . . . . . . . . . . . . . . . . . .          800
    Miscellaneous Expense . . . . . . . . . . . . . . . . . . . . . . . . . . . . . . . . . . . . . . . . . . . . . . . . . . .           75
        Cash. . . . . . . . . . . . . . . . . . . . . . . . . . . . . . . . . . . . . . . . . . . . . . . . . . . . . . . . . . . . . . . . . .                             875

Practice Exercises: PE 8-3A, PE 8-3B

## Integrity, Objectivity, and Ethics in Business

**BANK ERROR IN YOUR FAVOR**

It is possible that you may have a bank error in your favor, such as a misposted deposit. Such errors are not a case of "found money," as in the Monopoly® game. Bank control systems quickly discover most errors and make automatic adjustments. Even so, you have a legal responsibility to report the error and return the money to the bank.

# Special-Purpose Cash Funds

 **OBJ 6**  Describe the accounting for special-purpose cash funds.

A company often has to pay small amounts for such items as postage, office supplies, or minor repairs. Although small, such payments may occur often enough to total a significant amount. Thus, it is desirable to control such payments. However, writing a check for each small payment is not practical. Instead, a special cash fund, called a **petty cash fund**, is used.

A petty cash fund is established by estimating the amount of payments needed from the fund during a period, such as a week or a month. A check is then written and cashed for this amount. The money obtained from cashing the check is then given to an employee, called the *petty cash custodian*. The petty cash custodian disburses monies from the fund as needed. For control purposes, the company may place restrictions on the maximum amount and the types of payments that can be made from the fund. Each time money is paid from petty cash, the custodian records the details on a petty cash receipts form.

The petty cash fund is normally replenished at periodic intervals, when it is depleted, or reaches a minimum amount. When a petty cash fund is replenished, the accounts debited are determined by summarizing the petty cash receipts. A check is then written for this amount, payable to Petty Cash.

To illustrate, assume that a petty cash fund of $500 is established on August 1. The entry to record this transaction is as follows:

| | | | | | |
|---|---|---|---|---|---|
| Aug. | 1 | Petty Cash | | 500 | |
| | |    Cash | | | 500 |

The only time Petty Cash is debited is when the fund is initially established, as shown in the preceding entry, or when the fund is being increased. The only time Petty Cash is credited is when the fund is being decreased.

At the end of August, the petty cash receipts indicate expenditures for the following items:

| | |
|---|---:|
| Office supplies | $380 |
| Postage (debit Office Supplies) | 22 |
| Store supplies | 35 |
| Miscellaneous administrative expense | 30 |
| Total | $467 |

The entry to replenish the petty cash fund on August 31 is as follows:

| | | | | |
|---|---|---|---:|---:|
| Aug. | 31 | Office Supplies | 402 | |
| | | Store Supplies | 35 | |
| | | Miscellaneous Administrative Expense | 30 | |
| | | Cash | | 467 |

Petty Cash is not debited when the fund is replenished. Instead, the accounts affected by the petty cash disbursements are debited, as shown in the preceding entry. Replenishing the petty cash fund restores the fund to its original amount of $500.

Companies often use other cash funds for special needs, such as payroll or travel expenses. Such funds are called **special-purpose funds**. For example, each salesperson might be given $1,000 for travel-related expenses. Periodically, each salesperson submits an expense report, and the fund is replenished. Special-purpose funds are established and controlled in a manner similar to that of the petty cash fund.

## Example Exercise 8-4 Petty Cash Fund

OBJ 6

Prepare journal entries for each of the following:

a. Issued a check to establish a petty cash fund of $500.

b. The amount of cash in the petty cash fund is $120. Issued a check to replenish the fund, based on the following summary of petty cash receipts: office supplies, $300, and miscellaneous administrative expense, $75. Record any missing funds in the cash short and over account.

### Follow My Example 8-4

| | | |
|---|---:|---:|
| a. Petty Cash......................................................... | 500 | |
| Cash............................................................... | | 500 |
| b. Office Supplies.................................................. | 300 | |
| Miscellaneous Administrative Expense............................. | 75 | |
| Cash Short and Over............................................. | 5 | |
| Cash............................................................... | | 380 |

Practice Exercises: PE 8-4A, PE 8-4B

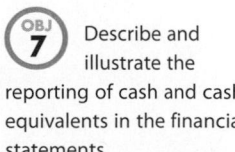

OBJ 7

Describe and illustrate the reporting of cash and cash equivalents in the financial statements.

# Financial Statement Reporting of Cash

Cash is normally listed as the first asset in the Current Assets section of the balance sheet. Most companies present only a single cash amount on the balance sheet by combining all their bank and cash fund accounts.

A company may temporarily have excess cash. In such cases, the company normally invests in highly liquid investments in order to earn interest. These investments are called **cash equivalents**.[8] Examples of cash equivalents include U.S. Treasury bills, notes issued by major corporations (referred to as *commercial paper*), and money

---

[8] To be classified as a cash equivalent, according to FASB *Accounting Standards Codification*, Section 305.10, the investment is expected to be converted to cash within three months.

market funds. In such cases, companies usually report *Cash and cash equivalents* as one amount on the balance sheet.

The balance sheet presentation for cash for **Mornin' Joe** follows:

| Mornin' Joe<br>Balance Sheet<br>December 31, 2016 | |
|---|---|
| **Assets** | |
| Current assets: | |
| Cash and cash equivalents ................................ | $235,000 |

Banks may require that companies maintain minimum cash balances in their bank accounts. Such a balance is called a **compensating balance**. This is often required by the bank as part of a loan agreement or line of credit. A *line of credit* is a preapproved amount the bank is willing to lend to a customer upon request. Compensating balance requirements are normally disclosed in notes to the financial statements.

# Financial Analysis and Interpretation: Ratio of Cash to Monthly Cash Expenses

**OBJ 8** Describe and illustrate the use of the ratio of cash to monthly cash expenses to assess the ability of a company to continue in business.

**FAI**

For startup companies or companies in financial distress, cash is critical for survival. In their first few years, startup companies often report losses and negative net cash flows from operations. Moreover, companies in financial distress can also report losses and negative cash flows from operations. In such cases, the **ratio of cash to monthly cash expenses** is useful for assessing how long a company can continue to operate without:

- Additional financing, or
- Generating positive cash flows from operations

The ratio of cash to monthly cash expenses is computed as follows:

$$\text{Ratio of Cash to Monthly Cash Expenses} = \frac{\text{Cash as of Year-End}}{\text{Monthly Cash Expenses}}$$

The cash, including any cash equivalents, is taken from the balance sheet as of year-end. The monthly cash expenses, sometimes called *cash burn*, are estimated from the operating activities section of the statement of cash flows as follows:

$$\text{Monthly Cash Expenses} = \frac{\text{Negative Cash Flow from Operations}}{12}$$

To illustrate, Ocean Power Technologies, Inc., develops and markets systems that generate electricity from the rising and falling of ocean waves. The following data (in thousands) were taken from recent financial statements of Ocean Power Technologies:

| | For Years Ended April 29 | | | |
|---|---|---|---|---|
| | **Year 4** | **Year 3** | **Year 2** | **Year 1** |
| Cash and cash equivalents at year-end | $ 9,353 | $4,376 | $4,237 | $ 12,268 |
| Cash flow from operations | (13,915) | (18,770) | (15,771) | (16,708) |

Based on the preceding data, the monthly cash expenses and ratio of cash to monthly cash expenses are computed as follows:

| | **For Years Ended April 29** | | | |
| --- | --- | --- | --- | --- |
| | **Year 4** | **Year 3** | **Year 2** | **Year 1** |
| Monthly cash expenses:* | | | | |
| $13,915 ÷ 12................................. | $1,160 | | | |
| $18,770 ÷ 12................................. | | $1,564 | | |
| $15,771 ÷ 12................................. | | | $1,314 | |
| $16,708 ÷ 12................................. | | | | $1,392 |
| Ratio of cash to monthly cash expenses:** | | | | |
| $9,353 ÷ $1,160............................ | 8.1 months | | | |
| $4,376 ÷ $1,564............................ | | 2.8 months | | |
| $4,237 ÷ $1,314............................ | | | 3.2 months | |
| $12,268 ÷ $1,392........................... | | | | 8.8 months |

*Rounded to nearest dollar.

**Rounded to one decimal place.

The preceding computations indicate that Ocean Power had 8.8 months of cash available at the end of Year 1 to continue its operations. However, at the end of Year 1 Ocean Power also had short-term investments totaling almost $29 million. These investments had maturities greater than three months and, thus, were not included as cash equivalents. In addition, Ocean Power had more than $40 million of long-term investments at the end of Year 1. These short- and long-term investments were generated from issuing stock of almost $91 million two years earlier.

At the end of Year 2, Ocean Power had 3.2 months of cash available to continue its operations. During Year 2, Ocean Power sold short-term investments of almost $8 million to continue its operations. At the end of Year 3, Ocean Power had 2.8 months of cash available to continue its operations. During Year 3, Ocean Power sold short-term investments of $19 million to continue its operations. At the end of Year 4, Ocean Power had 8.1 months of cash available to continue its operations. During Year 4, Ocean Power sold short-term investments of almost $20 million to continue its operations.

The preceding analysis indicates that Ocean Power has generated negative cash flows from operations in each of the last four years. During each of the last four years, Ocean Power has been selling short-term investments, which were purchased from funds received by issuing stock, to finance its operations. At the end of Year 4, Ocean Power had no long-term investments and a little more than $22 million left in short-term investments. Unless Ocean Power can generate positive cash flows from operations in the next several years, it will have to raise additional funds from borrowing or issuing stock. On a favorable note, negative cash flows from operations decreased from $1,564 in Year 3 to $1,160 in Year 4.

## Example Exercise 8-5 Ratio of Cash to Monthly Cash Expenses OBJ 8

Financial data for Chapman Company follows:

| | **For Year Ended December 31, 2016** |
| --- | --- |
| Cash on December 31, 2016 | $ 102,000 |
| Cash flow from operations | (144,000) |

a. Compute the ratio of cash to monthly cash expenses.

b. Interpret the results computed in (a).

*(Continued)*

### Follow My Example 8-5

a.   Monthly Cash Expenses $= \dfrac{\text{Negative Cash Flow from Operations}}{12} = \dfrac{\$144,000}{12} = \$12,000$ per month

$\dfrac{\text{Ratio of Cash to}}{\text{Monthly Cash Expenses}} = \dfrac{\text{Cash as of Year-End}}{\text{Monthly Cash Expenses}} = \dfrac{\$102,000}{\$12,000 \text{ per month}} = 8.5$ months

b.   The preceding computations indicate that Chapman Company has 8.5 months of cash remaining as of December 31, 2016. To continue operations beyond 8.5 months, Chapman Company will need to generate positive cash flows from operations or raise additional financing from its owners or by issuing debt.

Practice Exercises: PE 8-5A, PE 8-5B

## Business  Connection

### MICROSOFT CORPORATION

Microsoft Corporation develops, manufactures, licenses, and supports software products for computing devices. Microsoft software products include computer operating systems, such as Windows®, and application software, such as Microsoft Word® and Excel®. Microsoft is actively involved in the video game market through its Xbox® and is also involved in online products and services.

Microsoft is known for its strong cash position. The following recent balance sheet of Microsoft reported more than $63 billion of cash and short-term investments:

**Balance Sheet**
**(In millions)**

**Assets**

Current assets:

| | |
|---|---:|
| Cash and equivalents............................................. | $ 6,938 |
| Short-term investments ........................................ | 56,102 |
| Total cash and short-term investments...................... | $63,040 |

The cash and cash equivalents of $6,938 million are further described in the notes to the financial statements, as follows:

Cash and equivalents:

| | |
|---|---:|
| Cash ................................................................ | $2,019 |
| Mutual funds...................................................... | 820 |
| Commercial paper ............................................... | 96 |
| U.S. government and agency securities....................... | 561 |
| Foreign government bonds ..................................... | 575 |
| Certificates of deposit.......................................... | 342 |
| Corporate notes and bonds ................................... | 2,525 |
| Total cash and equivalents..................................... | $6,938 |

Source: Microsoft Corporation, *Form 10-K For the Fiscal Year Ended June 30, 2012.*

# At a Glance 8

**OBJ 1** Describe the Sarbanes-Oxley Act and its impact on internal controls and financial reporting.

**Key Points** Sarbanes-Oxley requires companies to maintain strong and effective internal controls and to report on the effectiveness of the internal controls.

| Learning Outcomes | Example Exercises | Practice Exercises |
|---|---|---|
| • Describe why Congress passed Sarbanes-Oxley. | | |
| • Describe the purpose of Sarbanes-Oxley. | | |
| • Define internal control. | | |

**OBJ 2** Describe and illustrate the objectives and elements of internal control.

**Key Points** The objectives of internal control are to provide reasonable assurance that (1) assets are safeguarded and used for business purposes, (2) business information is accurate, and (3) the company is complying with laws and regulations. The elements of internal control are the control environment, risk assessment, control procedures, monitoring, and information and communication.

| Learning Outcomes | Example Exercises | Practice Exercises |
|---|---|---|
| • List the objectives of internal control. | | |
| • List the elements of internal control. | | |
| • Describe each element of internal control and factors influencing each element. | **EE8-1** | **PE8-1A, 8-1B** |

**OBJ 3** Describe and illustrate the application of internal controls to cash.

**Key Points** A cash register is a control for protecting cash received in over-the-counter sales. A remittance advice is a control for cash received through the mail. Separating the duties of handling cash and recording cash is also a control. A voucher system is a control system for cash payments. Many companies use electronic funds transfers for cash receipts and cash payments.

| Learning Outcomes | Example Exercises | Practice Exercises |
|---|---|---|
| • Describe and give examples of controls for cash received from cash sales, cash received in the mail, and cash received by EFT. | | |
| • Describe and give examples of controls for cash payments made using a voucher system and cash payments made by EFT. | | |

**OBJ 4** Describe the nature of a bank account and its use in controlling cash.

**Key Points** Bank accounts control cash by reducing the amount of cash on hand and facilitating the transfer of cash between businesses and locations. In addition, the bank statement allows a business to reconcile the cash transactions recorded in the accounting records to those recorded by the bank.

| Learning Outcomes | Example Exercises | Practice Exercises |
|---|---|---|
| • Describe how the use of bank accounts helps control cash. | **EE8-2** | **PE8-2A, 8-2B** |
| • Describe a bank statement and provide examples of items that appear on a bank statement as debit and credit memos. | | |

**OBJ 5** Describe and illustrate the use of a bank reconciliation in controlling cash.

**Key Points** A bank reconciliation is prepared using the nine steps as summarized in Exhibit 12. The items in the company section of a bank reconciliation must be journalized on the company's records.

| Learning Outcomes | Example Exercises | Practice Exercises |
|---|---|---|
| • Describe a bank reconciliation. | | |
| • Prepare a bank reconciliation. | **EE8-3** | **PE8-3A, 8-3B** |
| • Journalize any necessary entries on the company's records, based on the bank reconciliation. | **EE8-3** | **PE8-3A, 8-3B** |

**OBJ 6** Describe the accounting for special-purpose cash funds.

**Key Points** Special-purpose cash funds, such as a petty cash fund or travel funds, are used by businesses to meet specific needs. Each fund is established by cashing a check for the amount of cash needed. At periodic intervals, the fund is replenished and the disbursements recorded.

| Learning Outcomes | Example Exercises | Practice Exercises |
|---|---|---|
| • Describe the use of special-purpose cash funds. | | |
| • Journalize the entry to establish a petty cash fund. | **EE8-4** | **PE8-4A, 8-4B** |
| • Journalize the entry to replenish a petty cash fund. | **EE8-4** | **PE8-4A, 8-4B** |

**OBJ 7** Describe and illustrate the reporting of cash and cash equivalents in the financial statements.

**Key Points** Cash is listed as the first asset in the Current assets section of the balance sheet. Companies that have invested excess cash in highly liquid investments usually report *Cash and cash equivalents* on the balance sheet.

| Learning Outcomes | Example Exercises | Practice Exercises |
|---|---|---|
| • Describe the reporting of cash and cash equivalents in the financial statements. | | |
| • Illustrate the reporting of cash and cash equivalents in the financial statements. | | |

**OBJ 8**

**Describe and illustrate the use of the ratio of cash to monthly cash expenses to assess the ability of a company to continue in business.**

**Key Points** The ratio of cash to monthly cash expenses is useful for assessing how long a company can continue to operate without (1) additional financing or (2) generating positive cash flows from operations.

| Learning Outcomes | Example Exercises | Practice Exercises |
|---|---|---|
| • Describe the use of the ratio of cash to monthly cash expenses. | | |
| • Compute the ratio of cash to monthly cash expenses. | EE8-5 | PE8-5A, 8-5B |

# Key Terms

bank reconciliation (383)
bank statement (380)
cash (377)
cash equivalents (388)
cash short and over account (378)
compensating balance (389)

control environment (373)
electronic funds transfer (EFT) (379)
elements of internal control (372)
employee fraud (372)
internal control (370)
petty cash fund (387)

ratio of cash to monthly
   cash expenses (389)
Sarbanes-Oxley Act (370)
special-purpose funds (388)
voucher (380)
voucher system (380)

# Illustrative Problem

The bank statement for Urethane Company for June 30, 2015, indicates a balance of $9,293.11. All cash receipts are deposited each evening in a night depository, after banking hours. The accounting records indicate the following summary data for cash receipts and payments for June:

| | |
|---|---|
| Cash balance as of June 1 | $ 3,943.50 |
| Total cash receipts for June | 28,971.60 |
| Total amount of checks issued in June | 28,388.85 |

Comparing the bank statement and the accompanying canceled checks and memos with the records reveals the following reconciling items:

a. The bank had collected for Urethane Company $1,030 on a note left for collection. The face amount of the note was $1,000.

b. A deposit of $1,852.21, representing receipts of June 30, had been made too late to appear on the bank statement.

c. Checks outstanding totaled $5,265.27.

d. A check drawn for $139 had been incorrectly charged by the bank as $157.

e. A check for $370 returned with the statement had been recorded in the company's records as $730. The check was for the payment of an obligation to Avery Equipment Company for the purchase of office supplies on account.

f. Bank service charges for June amounted to $18.20.

### Instructions

1. Prepare a bank reconciliation for June.

2. Journalize the entries that should be made by Urethane Company.

### Solution

1.

| Urethane Company Bank Reconciliation June 30, 2015 | | |
|---|---:|---:|
| Cash balance according to bank statement . . . . . . . . . . . . . . . . . . . . . . . . . . . . . . . . |  | $ 9,293.11 |
| Add: Deposit of June 30 not recorded by bank . . . . . . . . . . . . . . . . . . . . . . . . . . | $1,852.21 |  |
| Bank error in charging check as $157 |  |  |
| instead of $139 . . . . . . . . . . . . . . . . . . . . . . . . . . . . . . . . . . . . . . . | 18.00 | 1,870.21 |
|  |  | $11,163.32 |
| Deduct: Outstanding checks. . . . . . . . . . . . . . . . . . . . . . . . . . . . . . . . . . . . . . |  | 5,265.27 |
| Adjusted balance . . . . . . . . . . . . . . . . . . . . . . . . . . . . . . . . . . . . . . . . . . . . |  | $ 5,898.05 |
|  |  |  |
| Cash balance according to company's records  . . . . . . . . . . . . . . . . . . . . . . . |  | $ 4,526.25* |
| Add: Proceeds of note collected by bank, |  |  |
| including $30 interest. . . . . . . . . . . . . . . . . . . . . . . . . . . . . . . . . . . . . . | $1,030.00 |  |
| Error in recording check . . . . . . . . . . . . . . . . . . . . . . . . . . . . . . . . . . . . . . | 360.00 | 1,390.00 |
|  |  | $ 5,916.25 |
| Deduct: Bank service charges . . . . . . . . . . . . . . . . . . . . . . . . . . . . . . . . . . . . . . . |  | 18.20 |
| Adjusted balance . . . . . . . . . . . . . . . . . . . . . . . . . . . . . . . . . . . . . . . . . . . . |  | $ 5,898.05 |
| *$3,943.50 + $28,971.60 − $28,388.85 |  |  |

2.

| | | | | |
|---|---|---|---:|---:|
| June | 30 | Cash | 1,390.00 | |
| | | Notes Receivable | | 1,000.00 |
| | | Interest Revenue | | 30.00 |
| | | Accounts Payable—Avery Equipment Company | | 360.00 |
| | | | | |
| | 30 | Miscellaneous Administrative Expense | 18.20 | |
| | | Cash | | 18.20 |

# Discussion Questions

1. (a) Name and describe the five elements of internal control. (b) Is any one element of internal control more important than another?

2. Why should the employee who handles cash receipts not have the responsibility for maintaining the accounts receivable records? Explain.

3. The ticket seller at a movie theater doubles as a ticket taker for a few minutes each day while the ticket taker is on a break. Which control procedure of a business's system of internal control is violated in this situation?

4. Why should the responsibility for maintaining the accounting records be separated from the responsibility for operations? Explain.

5. Assume that Brooke Miles, accounts payable clerk for West Coast Design Inc., stole $48,350 by paying fictitious invoices for goods that were never received. The clerk set up accounts in the names of the fictitious companies and cashed the checks at a local bank. Describe a control procedure that would have prevented or detected the fraud.

6. Before a voucher for the purchase of merchandise is approved for payment, supporting documents should be compared to verify the accuracy of the liability. Give an example of supporting documents for the purchase of merchandise.

7. The balance of Cash is likely to differ from the bank statement balance. What two factors are likely to be responsible for the difference?

8. What is the purpose of preparing a bank reconciliation?

9. Knott Inc. has a petty cash fund of $750. (a) Since the petty cash fund is only $750, should Knott Inc. implement controls over petty cash? (b) What controls, if any, could be used for the petty cash fund?

10. (a) How are cash equivalents reported in the financial statements? (b) What are some examples of cash equivalents?

# Practice Exercises

**EE 8-1** *p. 377*

**PE 8-1A Internal control elements** OBJ. 2

Identify each of the following as relating to (a) the control environment, (b) control procedures, or (c) information and communication:

1. Organizational structure
2. Report of company's conformity with environmental laws and regulations
3. Proofs and security measures

**EE 8-1** *p. 377*

**PE 8-1B Internal control elements** OBJ. 2

Identify each of the following as relating to (a) the control environment, (b) control procedures, or (c) monitoring:

1. Hiring of external auditors to review the adequacy of controls
2. Personnel policies
3. Safeguarding inventory in a locked warehouse

**EE 8-2** *p. 382*

**PE 8-2A Items on company's bank statement** OBJ. 4

The following items may appear on a bank statement:

1. Bank correction of an error from recording a $6,200 deposit as $2,600
2. EFT payment
3. Note collected for company
4. Service charge

Using the following format, indicate whether each item would appear as a debit or credit memo on the bank statement and whether the item would increase or decrease the balance of the company's account:

| Item No. | Appears on the Bank Statement as a Debit or Credit Memo | Increases or Decreases the Balance of the Company's Bank Account |
| --- | --- | --- |

EE 8-2 *p. 382*

**PE 8-2B** **Items on company's bank statement** OBJ. 4

The following items may appear on a bank statement:

1. Bank correction of an error from posting another customer's check (disbursement) to the company's account
2. EFT deposit
3. Loan proceeds
4. NSF check

Using the following format, indicate whether each item would appear as a debit or credit memo on the bank statement and whether the item would increase or decrease the balance of the company's account:

| Item No. | Appears on the Bank Statement as a Debit or Credit Memo | Increases or Decreases the Balance of the Company's Bank Account |
|---|---|---|
| | | |

EE 8-3 *p. 386*

**PE 8-3A** **Bank reconciliation** OBJ. 5

The following data were gathered to use in reconciling the bank account of Eves Company:

| | |
|---|---|
| Balance per bank | $9,350 |
| Balance per company records | 8,510 |
| Bank service charges | 35 |
| Deposit in transit | 2,350 |
| NSF check | 1,875 |
| Outstanding checks | 5,100 |

a. What is the adjusted balance on the bank reconciliation?

b. Journalize any necessary entries for Eves Company based on the bank reconciliation.

EE 8-3 *p. 387*

**PE 8-3B** **Bank reconciliation** OBJ. 5

The following data were gathered to use in reconciling the bank account of Conway Company:

| | |
|---|---|
| Balance per bank | $23,900 |
| Balance per company records | 8,700 |
| Bank service charges | 50 |
| Deposit in transit | 5,500 |
| Note collected by bank with $450 interest | 9,450 |
| Outstanding checks | 11,300 |

a. What is the adjusted balance on the bank reconciliation?

b. Journalize any necessary entries for Conway Company based on the bank reconciliation.

EE 8-4 *p. 388*

**PE 8-4A** **Petty cash fund** OBJ. 6

Prepare journal entries for each of the following:

a. Issued a check to establish a petty cash fund of $750.

b. The amount of cash in the petty cash fund is $115. Issued a check to replenish the fund, based on the following summary of petty cash receipts: repair expense, $515 and miscellaneous selling expense, $88. Record any missing funds in the cash short and over account.

EE 8-4 *p. 388*

**PE 8-4B** **Petty cash fund** OBJ. 6

Prepare journal entries for each of the following:

a. Issued a check to establish a petty cash fund of $900.

b. The amount of cash in the petty cash fund is $115. Issued a check to replenish the fund, based on the following summary of petty cash receipts: store supplies, $550 and miscellaneous selling expense, $200. Record any missing funds in the cash short and over account.

EE 8-5 *p. 390*

SHOW
ME HOW

### PE 8-5A Ratio of cash to monthly cash expenses OBJ. 8

Financial data for Otto Company follows:

| | For Year Ended December 31, 2016 |
|---|---|
| Cash on December 31, 2016 | $ 69,350 |
| Cash flow from operations | (114,000) |

a. Compute the ratio of cash to monthly cash expenses.

b. Interpret the results computed in (a).

EE 8-5 *p. 391*

SHOW
ME HOW

### PE 8-5B Ratio of cash to monthly cash expenses OBJ. 8

Financial data for Bonita Company follows:

| | For Year Ended December 31, 2016 |
|---|---|
| Cash on December 31, 2016 | $ 187,180 |
| Cash flow from operations | (458,400) |

a. Compute the ratio of cash to monthly cash expenses.

b. Interpret the results computed in (a).

## Exercises

### EX 8-1 Sarbanes-Oxley internal control report OBJ. 1

Internet Project

Using Wikipedia (www.wikipedia.com), look up the entry for Sarbanes-Oxley Act. Look over the table of contents and find the section that describes Section 404.

➤ What does Section 404 require of management's internal control report?

### EX 8-2 Internal controls OBJ. 2, 3

Faith Cassen has recently been hired as the manager of Gibraltar Coffee Shop. Gibraltar Coffee Shop is a national chain of franchised coffee shops. During her first month as store manager, Faith encountered the following internal control situations:

a. Faith caught an employee putting a case of 1,000 single-serving tea bags in his car. Not wanting to create a scene, Faith smiled and said, "I don't think you're putting those tea bags on the right shelf. Don't they belong inside the coffee shop?" The employee returned the tea bags to the stockroom.

b. Gibraltar Coffee Shop has one cash register. Prior to Faith's joining the coffee shop, each employee working on a shift would take a customer order, accept payment, and then prepare the order. Faith made one employee on each shift responsible for taking orders and accepting the customer's payment. Other employees prepare the orders.

c. Because only one employee uses the cash register, that employee is responsible for counting the cash at the end of the shift and verifying that the cash in the drawer matches the amount of cash sales recorded by the cash register. Faith expects each cashier to balance the drawer to the penny *every* time—no exceptions.

➤ State whether you agree or disagree with Faith's method of handling each situation and explain your answer.

### EX 8-3 Internal controls OBJ. 2, 3

Ramona's Clothing is a retail store specializing in women's clothing. The store has established a liberal return policy for the holiday season in order to encourage gift purchases. Any item purchased during November and December may be returned through January 31, with a receipt, for cash or exchange. If the customer does not have a receipt, cash will still be refunded for any item under $75. If the item is more than $75, a check is mailed to the customer.

Whenever an item is returned, a store clerk completes a return slip, which the customer signs. The return slip is placed in a special box. The store manager visits the return counter approximately once every two hours to authorize the return slips. Clerks are instructed to place the returned merchandise on the proper rack on the selling floor as soon as possible.

This year, returns at Ramona's Clothing have reached an all-time high. There are a large number of returns under $75 without receipts.

a. ➤How can sales clerks employed at Ramona's Clothing use the store's return policy to steal money from the cash register?

b. ➤What internal control weaknesses do you see in the return policy that make cash thefts easier?

c. ➤Would issuing a store credit in place of a cash refund for all merchandise returned without a receipt reduce the possibility of theft? List some advantages and disadvantages of issuing a store credit in place of a cash refund.

d. ➤Assume that Ramona's Clothing is committed to the current policy of issuing cash refunds without a receipt. What changes could be made in the store's procedures regarding customer refunds in order to improve internal control?

---

**EX 8-4  Internal controls for bank lending**                    OBJ. 2, 3

Pacific Bank provides loans to businesses in the community through its Commercial Lending Department. Small loans (less than $100,000) may be approved by an individual loan officer, while larger loans (greater than $100,000) must be approved by a board of loan officers. Once a loan is approved, the funds are made available to the loan applicant under agreed-upon terms. Pacific Bank has instituted a policy whereby its president has the individual authority to approve loans up to $5,000,000. The president believes that this policy will allow flexibility to approve loans to valued clients much quicker than under the previous policy.

➤As an internal auditor of Pacific Bank, how would you respond to this change in policy?

---

**EX 8-5  Internal controls**                                     OBJ. 2, 3

One of the largest losses in history from unauthorized securities trading involved a securities trader for the French bank, **Societe Generale**. The trader was able to circumvent internal controls and create more than $7 billion in trading losses in six months. The trader apparently escaped detection by using knowledge of the bank's internal control systems learned from a previous back-office monitoring job. Much of this monitoring involved the use of software to monitor trades. In addition, traders were usually kept to tight trading limits. Apparently, these controls failed in this case.

➤ What general weaknesses in Societe Generale's internal controls contributed to the occurrence and size of the losses?

---

**EX 8-6  Internal controls**                                     OBJ. 2, 3

An employee of **JHT Holdings, Inc.**, a trucking company, was responsible for resolving roadway accident claims under $25,000. The employee created fake accident claims and wrote settlement checks of between $5,000 and $25,000 to friends or acquaintances acting as phony "victims." One friend recruited subordinates at his place of work to cash some of the checks. Beyond this, the JHT employee also recruited lawyers, whom he paid to represent both the trucking company and the fake victims in the bogus accident settlements. When the lawyers cashed the checks, they allegedly split the money with the corrupt JHT employee. This fraud went undetected for two years.

➤ Why would it take so long to discover such a fraud?

---

**EX 8-7  Internal controls**                                     OBJ. 2, 3

All-Around Sound Co. discovered a fraud whereby one of its front office administrative employees used company funds to purchase goods, such as computers, digital cameras, and other electronic items for her own use. The fraud was discovered when employees noticed an increase in delivery frequency from vendors and the use of unusual vendors. After some investigation, it was discovered that the employee would alter the description or change the quantity on an invoice in order to explain the cost on the bill.

➤ What general internal control weaknesses contributed to this fraud?

### EX 8-8 Financial statement fraud

OBJ. 2, 3

A former chairman, CFO, and controller of Donnkenny, Inc., an apparel company that makes sportswear for Pierre Cardin and Victoria Jones, pleaded guilty to financial statement fraud. These managers used false journal entries to record fictitious sales, hid inventory in public warehouses so that it could be recorded as "sold," and required sales orders to be backdated so that the sale could be moved back to an earlier period. The combined effect of these actions caused $25 million out of $40 million in quarterly sales to be phony.

a. ▬▬▬▶ Why might control procedures listed in this chapter be insufficient in stopping this type of fraud?

b. ▬▬▬▶ How could this type of fraud be stopped?

### EX 8-9 Internal control of cash receipts

OBJ. 2, 3

The procedures used for over-the-counter receipts are as follows. At the close of each day's business, the sales clerks count the cash in their respective cash drawers, after which they determine the amount recorded by the cash register and prepare the memo cash form, noting any discrepancies. An employee from the cashier's office counts the cash, compares the total with the memo, and takes the cash to the cashier's office.

a. ▬▬▬▶ Indicate the weak link in internal control.

b. ▬▬▬▶ How can the weakness be corrected?

### EX 8-10 Internal control of cash receipts

OBJ. 2, 3

Sergio Flores works at the drive-through window of Big & Bad Burgers. Occasionally, when a drive-through customer orders, Sergio fills the order and pockets the customer's money. He does not ring up the order on the cash register.

▬▬▬▶ Identify the internal control weaknesses that exist at Big & Bad Burgers, and discuss what can be done to prevent this theft.

### EX 8-11 Internal control of cash receipts

OBJ. 2, 3

The mailroom employees send all remittances and remittance advices to the cashier. The cashier deposits the cash in the bank and forwards the remittance advices and duplicate deposit slips to the Accounting Department.

a. ▬▬▬▶ Indicate the weak link in internal control in the handling of cash receipts.

b. ▬▬▬▶ How can the weakness be corrected?

### EX 8-12 Entry for cash sales; cash short

OBJ. 2, 3

The actual cash received from cash sales was $33,854 and the amount indicated by the cash register total was $33,866. Journalize the entry to record the cash receipts and cash sales.

SHOW
ME HOW

### EX 8-13 Entry for cash sales; cash over

OBJ. 2, 3

The actual cash received from cash sales was $51,175 and the amount indicated by the cash register total was $50,997. Journalize the entry to record the cash receipts and cash sales.

SHOW
ME HOW

### EX 8-14 Internal control of cash payments

OBJ. 2, 3

Abbe Co. is a small merchandising company with a manual accounting system. An investigation revealed that in spite of a sufficient bank balance, a significant amount of available cash discounts had been lost because of failure to make timely payments. In addition, it was discovered that the invoices for several purchases had been paid twice.

▬▬▬▶ Outline procedures for the payment of vendors' invoices so that the possibilities of losing available cash discounts and of paying an invoice a second time will be minimized.

**EX 8-15     Internal control of cash payments**                                    OBJ. 2, 3

Paragon Tech Company, a communications equipment manufacturer, recently fell victim to a fraud scheme developed by one of its employees. To understand the scheme, it is necessary to review Paragon Tech's procedures for the purchase of services.

The purchasing agent is responsible for ordering services (such as repairs to a photocopy machine or office cleaning) after receiving a service requisition from an authorized manager. However, because no tangible goods are delivered, a receiving report is not prepared. When the Accounting Department receives an invoice billing Paragon Tech for a service call, the accounts payable clerk calls the manager who requested the service in order to verify that it was performed.

The fraud scheme involves Mae Jansma, the manager of plant and facilities. Mae arranged for her uncle's company, Radiate Systems, to be placed on Paragon Tech's approved vendor list. Mae did not disclose the family relationship.

On several occasions, Mae would submit a requisition for services to be provided by Radiate Systems. However, the service requested was really not needed, and it was never performed. Radiate Systems would bill Paragon Tech for the service and then split the cash payment with Mae.

➤ Explain what changes should be made to Paragon Tech's procedures for ordering and paying for services in order to prevent such occurrences in the future.

---

**EX 8-16     Bank reconciliation**                                          OBJ. 5

Identify each of the following reconciling items as: (a) an addition to the cash balance according to the bank statement, (b) a deduction from the cash balance according to the bank statement, (c) an addition to the cash balance according to the company's records, or (d) a deduction from the cash balance according to the company's records. (None of the transactions reported by bank debit and credit memos have been recorded by the company.)

1.  Bank service charges, $75.

2.  Check of a customer returned by bank to company because of insufficient funds, $880.

3.  Check for $275 incorrectly recorded by the company as $725.

4.  Check for $100 incorrectly charged by bank as $1,000.

5.  Deposit in transit, $5,550.

6.  Outstanding checks, $10,350.

7.  Note collected by bank, $12,720.

---

**EX 8-17     Entries based on bank reconciliation**                            OBJ. 5

Which of the reconciling items listed in Exercise 8-16 require an entry in the company's accounts?

---

**EX 8-18     Bank reconciliation**                                          OBJ. 5

✔ Adjusted balance: $22,545

SHOW ME HOW

The following data were accumulated for use in reconciling the bank account of Zek's Co. for May 2016:

1.  Cash balance according to the company's records at May 31, 2016, $22,110.

2.  Cash balance according to the bank statement at May 31, 2016, $29,650.

3.  Checks outstanding, $13,875.

4.  Deposit in transit, not recorded by bank, $6,770.

5.  A check for $50 in payment of an account was erroneously recorded in the check register as $500.

6.  Bank debit memo for service charges, $15.

a.  Prepare a bank reconciliation, using the format shown in Exhibit 13.

b.  If the balance sheet were prepared for Zek's Co. on May 31, 2016, what amount should be reported for cash?

c.  Must a bank reconciliation always balance (reconcile)?

### EX 8-19 Entries for bank reconciliation

OBJ. 5

Using the data presented in Exercise 8-18, journalize the entry or entries that should be made by the company.

### EX 8-20 Entries for note collected by bank

OBJ. 5

Accompanying a bank statement for Santee Company is a credit memo for $15,120 representing the principal ($14,000) and interest ($1,120) on a note that had been collected by the bank. The company had been notified by the bank at the time of the collection but had made no entries. Journalize the entry that should be made by the company to bring the accounting records up to date.

### EX 8-21 Bank reconciliation

OBJ. 5

An accounting clerk for Chesner Co. prepared the following bank reconciliation:

**Chesner Co.**
**Bank Reconciliation**
**July 31, 2016**

| | | |
|---|---:|---:|
| Cash balance according to company's records ...................... | | $11,100 |
| Add: Outstanding checks ......................................... | $ 3,585 | |
| Error by Chesner Co. in recording Check | | |
| No. 1056 as $950 instead of $590 ........................... | 360 | |
| Note for $12,000 collected by bank, including interest .......... | 12,480 | 16,425 |
| | | $27,525 |
| Deduct: Deposit in transit on July 31............................. | $ 7,200 | |
| Bank service charges ....................................... | 25 | 7,225 |
| Cash balance according to bank statement........................ | | $20,300 |

a. From the data in this bank reconciliation, prepare a new bank reconciliation for Chesner Co., using the format shown in the illustrative problem.

b. If a balance sheet were prepared for Chesner Co. on July 31, 2016, what amount should be reported for cash?

### EX 8-22 Bank reconciliation

OBJ. 5

✔ Corrected adjusted balance: $19,780

Identify the errors in the following bank reconciliation:

**Poway Co.**
**Bank Reconciliation**
**For the Month Ended June 30, 2016**

| | | | |
|---|---:|---:|---:|
| Cash balance according to bank statement......................... | | | $16,185 |
| Add outstanding checks: | | | |
| No. 1067...................................................... | | $ 575 | |
| 1106......................................................... | | 470 | |
| 1110......................................................... | | 1,050 | |
| 1113......................................................... | | 910 | 3,005 |
| | | | $19,190 |
| Deduct deposit of June 30, not recorded by bank................... | | | 6,600 |
| Adjusted balance............................................... | | | $12,590 |
| Cash balance according to company's records ...................... | | | $ 8,985 |
| Add: Proceeds of note collected by bank: | | | |
| Principal...................................................... | $6,000 | | |
| Interest....................................................... | 300 | $6,300 | |
| Service charges ............................................... | | 15 | 6,315 |
| | | | $15,300 |
| Deduct: Check returned because of insufficient funds............... | | $ 890 | |
| Error in recording June 17 deposit of $7,150 as $1,750 ....... | | 5,400 | 6,290 |
| Adjusted balance................................................ | | | $ 9,010 |

SHOW
ME HOW

**EX 8-23    Using bank reconciliation to determine cash receipts stolen**    OBJ. 2, 3, 5

Alaska Impressions Co. records all cash receipts on the basis of its cash register tapes. Alaska Impressions Co. discovered during October 2016 that one of its sales clerks had stolen an undetermined amount of cash receipts by taking the daily deposits to the bank. The following data have been gathered for October:

| | |
|---|---:|
| Cash in bank according to the general ledger | $11,680 |
| Cash according to the October 31, 2016, bank statement | 13,275 |
| Outstanding checks as of October 31, 2016 | 3,670 |
| Bank service charge for October | 40 |
| Note receivable, including interest collected by bank in October | 2,100 |

No deposits were in transit on October 31.

a.  Determine the amount of cash receipts stolen by the sales clerk.

b.  What accounting controls would have prevented or detected this theft?

**EX 8-24    Petty cash fund entries**    OBJ. 6

Journalize the entries to record the following:

a.  Check No. 245-13 is issued to establish a petty cash fund of $1,100.

SHOW
ME HOW

b.  The amount of cash in the petty cash fund is now $115. Check No. 271-13 is issued to replenish the fund, based on the following summary of petty cash receipts: office supplies, $614; miscellaneous selling expense, $200; miscellaneous administrative expense, $145. (Because the amount of the check to replenish the fund plus the balance in the fund do not equal $1,100, record the discrepancy in the cash short and over account.)

**EX 8-25    Variation in cash flows**    OBJ. 7

Mattel, Inc., designs, manufactures, and markets toy products worldwide. Mattel's toys include Barbie™ fashion dolls and accessories, Hot Wheels™, and Fisher-Price brands. For a recent year, Mattel reported the following net cash flows from operating activities (in thousands):

| | |
|---|---:|
| First quarter ending March 30 | $ 171,506 |
| Second quarter ending June 29 | (232,557) |
| Third quarter ending September 29 | (40,109) |
| Fourth quarter ending December 30 | 986,778 |

  Explain why Mattel reported negative net cash flows from operating activities during the second and third quarters and a large positive cash flow for the fourth quarter, with overall net positive cash flow for the year.

**EX 8-26    Cash to monthly cash expenses ratio**    OBJ. 8

SHOW
ME HOW

During 2016, El Dorado Inc. has monthly cash expenses of $168,500. On December 31, 2016, the cash balance is $1,415,400.

a.  Compute the ratio of cash to monthly cash expenses.

b.   Based on (a), what are the implications for El Dorado Inc.?

**EX 8-27    Cash to monthly cash expenses ratio**    OBJ. 8

SHOW
ME HOW

Capstone Turbine Corporation produces and sells turbine generators for such applications as charging electric, hybrid vehicles. Capstone Turbine reported the following financial data for a recent year (in thousands):

| | |
|---|---:|
| Net cash flows from operating activities | $(21,438) |
| Cash and cash equivalents | 49,952 |

a.  Determine the monthly cash expenses. Round to one decimal place.

b.  Determine the ratio of cash to monthly cash expenses. Round to one decimal place.

c.  Based on your analysis, do you believe that Capstone Turbine will remain in business?

### EX 8-28   Cash to monthly cash expenses ratio

**OBJ. 8**

Amicus Therapeutics, Inc., is a biopharmaceutical company that develops drugs for the treatment of various diseases, including Parkinson's disease. Amicus Therapeutics reported the following financial data (in thousands) for three recent years:

SHOW
ME HOW

| | For Years Ended December 31 | | |
| --- | --- | --- | --- |
| | Year 3 | Year 2 | Year 1 |
| Cash and cash equivalents | $ 25,668 | $29,572 | $ 19,339 |
| Net cash flows from operations | (49,422) | (13,983) | (43,371) |

a. Determine the monthly cash expenses for Year 3, Year 2, and Year 1. Round to one decimal place.

b. Determine the ratio of cash to monthly cash expenses for Year 3, Year 2, and Year 1 as of December 31. Round to one decimal place.

c. ➤ Based on (a) and (b), comment on Amicus Therapeutics' ratio of cash to monthly operating expenses for Year 3, Year 2, and Year 1.

## Problems: Series A

### PR 8-1A   Evaluating internal control of cash

**OBJ. 2, 3**

The following procedures were recently installed by Raspberry Creek Company:

a. After necessary approvals have been obtained for the payment of a voucher, the treasurer signs and mails the check. The treasurer then stamps the voucher and supporting documentation as paid and returns the voucher and supporting documentation to the accounts payable clerk for filing.

b. The accounts payable clerk prepares a voucher for each disbursement. The voucher along with the supporting documentation is forwarded to the treasurer's office for approval.

c. Along with petty cash expense receipts for postage, office supplies, etc., several post-dated employee checks are in the petty cash fund.

d. At the end of the day, cash register clerks are required to use their own funds to make up any cash shortages in their registers.

e. At the end of each day, all cash receipts are placed in the bank's night depository.

f. At the end of each day, an accounting clerk compares the duplicate copy of the daily cash deposit slip with the deposit receipt obtained from the bank.

g. All mail is opened by the mail clerk, who forwards all cash remittances to the cashier. The cashier prepares a listing of the cash receipts and forwards a copy of the list to the accounts receivable clerk for recording in the accounts.

h. The bank reconciliation is prepared by the cashier, who works under the supervision of the treasurer.

**Instructions**

➤ Indicate whether each of the procedures of internal control over cash represents (1) a strength or (2) a weakness. For each weakness, indicate why it exists.

### PR 8-2A   Transactions for petty cash, cash short and over

**OBJ. 3, 6**

Cactus Restoration Company completed the following selected transactions during May 2016:

SHOW
ME HOW

Oct.  1.   Established a petty cash fund of $750.

12.   The cash sales for the day, according to the cash register records, totaled $12,440 The actual cash received from cash sales was $12,465.

31.   Petty cash on hand was $157. Replenished the petty cash fund for the following disbursements, each evidenced by a petty cash receipt:

Oct. 3. Store supplies, $390.

7. Express charges on merchandise sold, $35 (Delivery Expense).

9. Office supplies, $16.

13. Office supplies, $22.

19. Postage stamps, $12 (Office Supplies).

21. Repair to office file cabinet lock, $15 (Miscellaneous Administrative Expense).

22. Postage due on special delivery letter, $27 (Miscellaneous Administrative Expense).

24. Express charges on merchandise sold, $55 (Delivery Expense).

30. Office supplies, $6.

Oct. 31. The cash sales for the day, according to the cash register records, totaled $18,820. The actual cash received from cash sales was $18,780.

31. Decreased the petty cash fund by $100.

### Instructions
Journalize the transactions.

---

**PR 8-3A    Bank reconciliation and entries**                                OBJ. 5

✔ 1. Adjusted balance: $114,960

**General Ledger**

SHOW
ME HOW

The cash account for Capstone Medical Co. at November 30, 2016, indicated a balance of $89,620. The bank statement indicated a balance of $128,660 on November 30, 2016. Comparing the bank statement and the accompanying canceled checks and memos with the records revealed the following reconciling items:

a. Checks outstanding totaled $32,700.

b. A deposit of $18,550, representing receipts of November 30, had been made too late to appear on the bank statement.

c. The bank collected $26,750 on a $25,000 note, including interest of $1,750.

d. A check for $1,500 returned with the statement had been incorrectly recorded by Capstone Medical Co. as $150. The check was for the payment of an obligation to ABC Supply Co. for a purchase on account.

e. A check drawn for $490 had been erroneously charged by the bank as $940.

f. Bank service charges for November amounted to $60.

### Instructions
1. Prepare a bank reconciliation.

2. Journalize the necessary entries. The accounts have not been closed.

3. If a balance sheet were prepared for Capstone Medical Co. on November 30, 2016, what amount should be reported as cash?

---

**PR 8-4A    Bank reconciliation and entries**                                OBJ. 5

✔ 1. Adjusted balance: $39,475

**General Ledger**

SHOW
ME HOW

The cash account for Brentwood Bike Co. at May 1, 2016, indicated a balance of $34,250. During May, the total cash deposited was $140,300, and checks written totaled $138,880. The bank statement indicated a balance of $43,525 on May 31. Comparing the bank statement, the canceled checks, and the accompanying memos with the records revealed the following reconciling items:

a. Checks outstanding totaled $6,440. ✓

b. A deposit of $1,850 representing receipts of May 31, had been made too late to appear on the bank statement.

c. The bank had collected for Brentwood Bike Co. $5,250 on a note left for collection. The face of the note was $5,000.

d. A check for $390 returned with the statement had been incorrectly charged by the bank as $930.

*(Continued)*

e. A check for $210 returned with the statement had been recorded by Brentwood Bike Co. as $120. The check was for the payment of an obligation to Adkins Co. on account.

f. Bank service charges for May amounted to $30.

g. A check for $1,325 from Jennings Co. was returned by the bank due to insufficient funds.

**Instructions**

1. Prepare a bank reconciliation as of May 31.

2. Journalize the necessary entries. The accounts have not been closed.

3. If a balance sheet were prepared for Brentwood Bike Co. on May 31, 2016, what amount should be reported as cash?

---

✔ 1. Adjusted balance: $13,216

### PR 8-5A  Bank reconciliation and entries

OBJ. 5

Beeler Furniture Company deposits all cash receipts each Wednesday and Friday in a night depository, after banking hours. The data required to reconcile the bank statement as of June 30 have been taken from various documents and records and are reproduced as follows. The sources of the data are printed in capital letters. All checks were written for payments on account.

CASH ACCOUNT:

| | |
|---|---|
| Balance as of June 1 | $9,317.40 |
| CASH RECEIPTS FOR MONTH OF JUNE | $9,223.76 |

DUPLICATE DEPOSIT TICKETS:

Date and amount of each deposit in June:

| Date | Amount | Date | Amount | Date | Amount |
|---|---|---|---|---|---|
| June 1 | $1,080.50 | June 10 | $ 996.61 | June 22 | $ 897.34 |
| 3 | 854.17 | 15 | 882.95 | 24 | 947.21 |
| 8 | 840.50 | 17 | 1,606.74 | 30 | 1,117.74 |

CHECKS WRITTEN:

Number and amount of each check issued in June:

| Check No. | Amount | Check No. | Amount | Check No. | Amount |
|---|---|---|---|---|---|
| 740 | $237.50 | 747 | Void | 754 | $ 449.75 |
| 741 | 495.15 | 748 | $450.90 | 755 | 272.75 |
| 742 | 501.90 | 749 | 640.13 | 756 | 113.95 |
| 743 | 761.30 | 750 | 276.77 | 757 | 407.95 |
| 744 | 506.88 | 751 | 299.37 | 758 | 259.60 |
| 745 | 117.25 | 752 | 537.01 | 759 | 901.50 |
| 746 | 298.66 | 753 | 380.95 | 760 | 486.39 |
| Total amount of checks issued in June | | | | | $8,395.66 |

BANK RECONCILIATION FOR PRECEDING MONTH:

**Beeler Furniture Company**
**Bank Reconciliation**
**May 31, 2016**

| | | |
|---|---|---|
| Cash balance according to bank statement........................ | | $ 9,447.20 |
| Add deposit for May 31, not recorded by bank...................... | | 690.25 |
| | | $10,137.45 |
| Deduct outstanding checks: | | |
| No. 731 ........................................... | $162.15 | |
| 736 ............................................ | 345.95 | |
| 738 ............................................ | 251.40 | |
| 739 ............................................ | 60.55 | 820.05 |
| Adjusted balance.................................... | | $ 9,317.40 |
| Cash balance according to company's records ...................... | | $ 9,352.50 |
| Deduct service charges ............................................ | | 35.10 |
| Adjusted balance.................................... | | $ 9,317.40 |

**Instructions**

1. Prepare a bank reconciliation as of June 30. If errors in recording deposits or checks are discovered, assume that the errors were made by the company. Assume that all deposits are from cash sales. All checks are written to satisfy accounts payable.

2. Journalize the necessary entries. The accounts have not been closed.

3. What is the amount of Cash that should appear on the balance sheet as of June 30?

4. ➤ Assume that a canceled check for $390 has been incorrectly recorded by the bank as $930. Briefly explain how the error would be included in a bank reconciliation and how it should be corrected.

JUNE BANK STATEMENT:

|  | | | MEMBER FDIC | | PAGE 1 |
|---|---|---|---|---|---|

A N B
**AMERICAN NATIONAL BANK OF CHICAGO**

CHICAGO, IL 60603 (312) 441-1239

ACCOUNT NUMBER

FROM 6/01/2016 TO 6/30/2016

| | | |
|---|---|---|
| BALANCE | | 9,447.20 |
| 9 DEPOSITS | | 8,691.77 |
| 20 WITHDRAWALS | | 7,899.26 |
| 4 OTHER DEBITS AND CREDITS | | 3,085.00CR |
| NEW BALANCE | | 13,624.71 |

BEELER FURNITURE COMPANY

\* – – – CHECKS AND OTHER DEBITS – – – \* – – DEPOSITS – – \* – DATE – \* – – BALANCE – – \*

| | | | | DEPOSITS | DATE | BALANCE |
|---|---|---|---|---|---|---|
| No.731 | 162.15 | No.736 | 345.95 | 690.25 | 6/01 | 9,629.35 |
| No.739 | 60.55 | No.740 | 237.50 | 1,080.50 | 6/02 | 10,411.80 |
| No.741 | 495.15 | No.742 | 501.90 | 854.17 | 6/04 | 10,268.92 |
| No.743 | 671.30 | No.744 | 506.88 | 840.50 | 6/09 | 9,931.24 |
| No.745 | 117.25 | No.746 | 298.66 | MS 3,500.00 | 6/09 | 13,015.33 |
| No.748 | 450.90 | No.749 | 640.13 | MS 210.00 | 6/09 | 12,134.30 |
| No.750 | 276.77 | No.751 | 299.37 | 896.61 | 6/11 | 12,454.77 |
| No.752 | 537.01 | No.753 | 380.95 | 882.95 | 6/16 | 12,419.76 |
| No.754 | 449.75 | No.755 | 272.75 | 1,606.74 | 6/18 | 13,304.00 |
| No.757 | 407.95 | No.760 | 486.39 | 897.34 | 6/23 | 13,307.00 |
| | | | | 942.71 | 6/25 | 14,249.71 |
| | | NSF | 550.00 | | 6/28 | 13,699.71 |
| | | SC | 75.00 | | 6/30 | 13,624.71 |

EC — ERROR CORRECTION          OD — OVERDRAFT
MS — MISCELLANEOUS             PS — PAYMENT STOPPED
NSF — NOT SUFFICIENT FUNDS     SC — SERVICE CHARGE

\* \* \*                    \* \* \*                    \* \* \*

THE RECONCILEMENT OF THIS STATEMENT WITH YOUR RECORDS IS ESSENTIAL.
ANY ERROR OR EXCEPTION SHOULD BE REPORTED IMMEDIATELY.

# Problems: Series B

## PR 8-1B    Evaluating internal control of cash

OBJ. 2, 3

The following procedures were recently installed by The China Shop:

a. All sales are rung up on the cash register, and a receipt is given to the customer. All sales are recorded on a record locked inside the cash register.

b. Each cashier is assigned a separate cash register drawer to which no other cashier has access.

c. At the end of a shift, each cashier counts the cash in his or her cash register, unlocks the cash register record, and compares the amount of cash with the amount on the record to determine cash shortages and overages.

*(Continued)*

d. Checks received through the mail are given daily to the accounts receivable clerk for recording collections on account and for depositing in the bank.

e. Vouchers and all supporting documents are perforated with a PAID designation after being paid by the treasurer.

f. Disbursements are made from the petty cash fund only after a petty cash receipt has been completed and signed by the payee.

g. The bank reconciliation is prepared by the cashier.

### Instructions

Indicate whether each of the procedures of internal control over cash represents (1) a strength or (2) a weakness. For each weakness, indicate why it exists.

---

SHOW
ME HOW

**PR 8-2B** **Transactions for petty cash, cash short and over** OBJ. 3, 6

Cedar Springs Company completed the following selected transactions during June 2016:

June 1. Established a petty cash fund of $1,000.

    12. The cash sales for the day, according to the cash register records, totaled $9,440. The actual cash received from cash sales was $9,506.

    30. Petty cash on hand was $46. Replenished the petty cash fund for the following disbursements, each evidenced by a petty cash receipt:

      June 2. Store supplies, $375.

         10. Express charges on merchandise purchased, $105 (Merchandise Inventory).

         14. Office supplies, $85.

         15. Office supplies, $90.

         18. Postage stamps, $33 (Office Supplies).

         20. Repair to fax, $100 (Miscellaneous Administrative Expense).

         21. Repair to office door lock, $25 (Miscellaneous Administrative Expense).

         22. Postage due on special delivery letter, $9 (Miscellaneous Administrative Expense).

         28. Express charges on merchandise purchased, $110 (Merchandise Inventory).

    30. The cash sales for the day, according to the cash register records, totaled $13,390. The actual cash received from cash sales was $13,350.

    30. Increased the petty cash fund by $200.

### Instructions

Journalize the transactions.

---

✔ 1. Adjusted balance: $24,305

General Ledger

SHOW
ME HOW

**PR 8-3B** **Bank reconciliation and entries** OBJ. 5

The cash account for Stone Systems at July 31, 2016, indicated a balance of $17,750. The bank statement indicated a balance of $33,650 on July 31, 2016. Comparing the bank statement and the accompanying canceled checks and memos with the records reveals the following reconciling items:

a. Checks outstanding totaled $17,865.

b. A deposit of $9,150, representing receipts of July 31, had been made too late to appear on the bank statement.

c. The bank had collected $6,095 on a note left for collection. The face of the note was $5,750.

d. A check for $390 returned with the statement had been incorrectly recorded by Stone Systems as $930. The check was for the payment of an obligation to Holland Co. for the purchase of office supplies on account.

e. A check drawn for $1,810 had been incorrectly charged by the bank as $1,180.

f. Bank service charges for July amounted to $80.

### Instructions

1. Prepare a bank reconciliation.

2. Journalize the necessary entries. The accounts have not been closed.

3. If a balance sheet were prepared for Stone Systems on July 31, 2014, what amount should be reported as cash?

### PR 8-4B   Bank reconciliation and entries

OBJ. 5

✔ 1. Adjusted
balance: $78,535

General Ledger

SHOW
ME HOW

The cash account for Collegiate Sports Co. on November 1, 2016, indicated a balance of $81,145. During November, the total cash deposited was $293,150, and checks written totaled $307,360. The bank statement indicated a balance of $112,675 on November 30, 2016. Comparing the bank statement, the canceled checks, and the accompanying memos with the records revealed the following reconciling items:

a.  Checks outstanding totaled $41,840.

b.  A deposit of $12,200, representing receipts of November 30, had been made too late to appear on the bank statement.

c.  A check for $7,250 had been incorrectly charged by the bank as $2,750.

d.  A check for $760 returned with the statement had been recorded by Collegiate Sports Co. as $7,600. The check was for the payment of an obligation to Ramirez Co. on account.

e.  The bank had collected for Collegiate Sports Co. $7,385 on a note left for collection. The face of the note was $7,000.

f.  Bank service charges for November amounted to $125.

g.  A check for $2,500 from Hallen Academy was returned by the bank because of insufficient funds.

#### Instructions

1.  Prepare a bank reconciliation as of November 30.

2.  Journalize the necessary entries. The accounts have not been closed.

3.  If a balance sheet were prepared for Collegiate Sports Co. on November 30, 2014, what amount should be reported as cash?

### PR 8-5B   Bank reconciliation and entries

OBJ. 5

✔ 1. Adjusted balance:
$11,494

Sunshine Interiors deposits all cash receipts each Wednesday and Friday in a night depository, after banking hours. The data required to reconcile the bank statement as of July 31 have been taken from various documents and records and are reproduced as follows. The sources of the data are printed in capital letters. All checks were written for payments on account.

BANK RECONCILIATION FOR PRECEDING MONTH (DATED JUNE 30):

| | | |
|---|---:|---:|
| Cash balance according to bank statement............................ | | $ 9,422.80 |
| Add deposit of June 30, not recorded by bank........................ | | 780.80 |
| | | $10,203.60 |
| Deduct outstanding checks: | | |
| No. 580 ..................................................... | $310.10 | |
| No. 602 ..................................................... | 85.50 | |
| No. 612 ..................................................... | 92.50 | |
| No. 613 ..................................................... | 137.50 | 625.60 |
| Adjusted balance........................................... | | $ 9,578.00 |
| Cash balance according to company's records ....................... | | $ 9,605.70 |
| Deduct service charges ........................................... | | 27.70 |
| Adjusted balance........................................... | | $ 9,578.00 |
| CASH ACCOUNT: | | |
| Balance as of July 1 ......................................... | | $ 9,578.00 |
| CASH RECEIPTS FOR MONTH OF JULY | | 6,465.42 |

DUPLICATE DEPOSIT TICKETS:

Date and amount of each deposit in July:

| Date | Amount | Date | Amount | Date | Amount |
|---|---|---|---|---|---|
| July 2 | $569.50 | July 12 | $580.70 | July 23 | $ 713.45 |
| 5 | 701.80 | 16 | 600.10 | 26 | 601.50 |
| 9 | 819.24 | 19 | 701.26 | 31 | 1,177.87 |

(Continued)

CHECKS WRITTEN:

Number and amount of each check issued in July:

| Check No. | Amount | Check No. | Amount | Check No. | Amount |
|---|---|---|---|---|---|
| 614 | $243.50 | 621 | $309.50 | 628 | $ 837.70 |
| 615 | 350.10 | 622 | Void | 629 | 329.90 |
| 616 | 279.90 | 623 | Void | 630 | 882.80 |
| 617 | 395.50 | 624 | 707.01 | 631 | 1,081.56 |
| 618 | 435.40 | 625 | 158.63 | 632 | 325.40 |
| 619 | 320.10 | 626 | 550.03 | 633 | 310.08 |
| 620 | 238.87 | 627 | 381.73 | 634 | 241.71 |
| Total amount of checks issued in July | | | | | $8,379.42 |

JULY BANK STATEMENT:

| | | | MEMBER FDIC | | PAGE 1 |
|---|---|---|---|---|---|

AB
AMERICAN NATIONAL BANK
OF DETROIT

DETROIT, MI 48201-2500    (313) 933-8547

ACCOUNT NUMBER

FROM 7/01/2016 TO 7/31/2016

| BALANCE | 9,422.80 |
|---|---|
| 9 DEPOSITS | 6,086.35 |
| 20 WITHDRAWALS | 7,656.74 |
| 4 OTHER DEBITS AND CREDITS | 3,749.00CR |
| NEW BALANCE | 11,601.41 |

SUNSHINE INTERIORS

*----- CHECKS AND OTHER DEBITS -----*- DEPOSITS -*-DATE-*-BALANCE-*

| No.580 | 310.10 | No.612 | 92.50 | | 780.80 | 07/01 | 9,801.00 |
|---|---|---|---|---|---|---|---|
| No.602 | 85.50 | No.614 | 243.50 | | 569.50 | 07/03 | 10,041.50 |
| No.615 | 350.10 | No.616 | 279.90 | | 701.80 | 07/06 | 10,113.30 |
| No.617 | 395.50 | No.618 | 435.40 | | 819.24 | 07/11 | 10,101.64 |
| No.619 | 320.10 | No.620 | 238.87 | | 580.70 | 07/13 | 10,123.37 |
| No.621 | 309.50 | No.624 | 707.01 | MS 4,000.00 | | 07/14 | 13,106.86 |
| No.625 | 158.63 | No.626 | 550.03 | MS 160.00 | | 07/14 | 12,558.20 |
| No.627 | 318.73 | No.629 | 329.90 | | 600.10 | 07/17 | 12,509.67 |
| No.630 | 882.80 | No.631 | 1,081.56 | NSF 375.00 | | 07/20 | 10,170.31 |
| No.632 | 325.40 | No.634 | 241.71 | | 701.26 | 07/21 | 10,304.46 |
| | | | | | 731.45 | 07/24 | 11,035.91 |
| | | | | | 601.50 | 07/28 | 11,637.41 |
| | | SC | 36.00 | | | 07/31 | 11,601.41 |

EC — ERROR CORRECTION        OD — OVERDRAFT

MS — MISCELLANEOUS           PS — PAYMENT STOPPED

NSF — NOT SUFFICIENT FUNDS   SC — SERVICE CHARGE

* * *                    * * *                    * * *

THE RECONCILEMENT OF THIS STATEMENT WITH YOUR RECORDS IS ESSENTIAL.
ANY ERROR OR EXCEPTION SHOULD BE REPORTED IMMEDIATELY.

## Instructions

1. Prepare a bank reconciliation as of July 31. If errors in recording deposits or checks are discovered, assume that the errors were made by the company. Assume that all deposits are from cash sales. All checks are written to satisfy accounts payable.

2. Journalize the necessary entries. The accounts have not been closed.

3. What is the amount of Cash that should appear on the balance sheet as of July 31?

4. ➤ Assume that a canceled check for $180 has been incorrectly recorded by the bank as $1,800. Briefly explain how the error would be included in a bank reconciliation and how it should be corrected.

# Cases & Projects

### CP 8-1  Ethics and professional conduct in business

During the preparation of the bank reconciliation for Building Concepts Co., Joel Kimmel, the assistant controller, discovered that Lone Peak National Bank incorrectly recorded a $3,290 check written by Building Concepts Co. as $329. Joel has decided not to notify the bank but wait for the bank to detect the error. Joel plans to record the $2,961 error as Other Income if the bank fails to detect the error within the next three months.

➤ Discuss whether Joel is behaving in a professional manner.

### CP 8-2  Internal controls

The following is an excerpt from a conversation between two sales clerks, Jean Moen and Sara Cheney. Jean and Sara are employed by Turpin Meadows Electronics, a locally owned and operated electronics retail store.

*Jean:* Did you hear the news?

*Sara:* What news?

*Jean:* Neal and Linda were both arrested this morning.

*Sara:* What? Arrested? You're putting me on!

*Jean:* No, really! The police arrested them first thing this morning. Put them in handcuffs, read them their rights—the whole works. It was unreal!

*Sara:* What did they do?

*Jean:* Well, apparently they were filling out merchandise refund forms for fictitious customers and then taking the cash.

*Sara:* I guess I never thought of that. How did they catch them?

*Jean:* The store manager noticed that returns were twice that of last year and seemed to be increasing. When he confronted Neal, he became flustered and admitted to taking the cash, apparently more than $9,000 in just three months. They're going over the last six months' transactions to try to determine how much Linda stole. She apparently started stealing first.

➤ Suggest appropriate control procedures that would have prevented or detected the theft of cash.

### CP 8-3  Internal controls

The following is an excerpt from a conversation between the store manager of Wholesome Grocery Stores, Kara Dahl, and Lynn Shutes, president of Wholesome Grocery Stores:

*Lynn:* Kara, I'm concerned about this new scanning system.

*Kara:* What's the problem?

*Lynn:* Well, how do we know the clerks are ringing up all the merchandise?

*Kara:* That's one of the strong points about the system. The scanner automatically rings up each item, based on its bar code. We update the prices daily, so we're sure that the sale is rung up for the right price.

*Lynn:* That's not my concern. What keeps a clerk from pretending to scan items and then simply not charging his friends? If his friends were buying 10–15 items, it would be easy for the clerk to pass through several items with his finger over the bar code or just pass the merchandise through the scanner with the wrong side showing. It would look normal for anyone observing. In the old days, we at least could hear the cash register ringing up each sale.

*Kara:* I see your point.

➤ Suggest ways that Wholesome Grocery Stores could prevent or detect the theft of merchandise as described.

### CP 8-4   Ethics and professional conduct in business

Doris Tidwell and Jo Yost are both cash register clerks for Fuller's Organic Markets. Tom Ward is the store manager for Fuller's Organic Markets. The following is an excerpt of a conversation between Doris and Jo:

*Doris:* Jo, how long have you been working for Fuller's Organic Markets?

*Jo:* Almost five years this April. You just started two weeks ago . . . right?

*Doris:* Yes. Do you mind if I ask you a question?

*Jo:* No, go ahead.

*Doris:* What I want to know is, have they always had this rule that if your cash register is short at the end of the day, you have to make up the shortage out of your own pocket?

*Jo:* Yes, as long as I've been working here.

*Doris:* Well, it's the pits. Last week I had to pay in almost $40.

*Jo:* It's not that big a deal. I just make sure that I'm not short at the end of the day.

*Doris:* How do you do that?

*Jo:* I just shortchange a few customers early in the day. There are a few jerks that deserve it anyway. Most of the time, their attention is elsewhere, and they don't think to check their change.

*Doris:* What happens if you're over at the end of the day?

*Jo:* Tom lets me keep it as long as it doesn't get to be too large. I've not been short in over a year. I usually clear about $20 to $30 extra per day.

➤ Discuss this case from the viewpoint of proper controls and professional behavior.

### CP 8-5   Bank reconciliation and internal control

The records of Parker Company indicate a July 31, 2016 cash balance of $10,400, which includes undeposited receipts for July 30 and 31. The cash balance on the bank statement as of July 31 is $10,575. This balance includes a note of $2,250 plus $150 interest collected by the bank but not recorded in the journal. Checks outstanding on July 31 were as follows: No. 2670, $1,050; No. 3679, $675; No. 3690, $1,650; No. 5148, $225; No. 5149, $750; and No. 5151, $800.

On July 25, the cashier resigned, effective at the end of the month. Before leaving on July 31, the cashier prepared the following bank reconciliation:

| | | |
|---|---:|---:|
| Cash balance per books, July 31 . . . . . . . . . . . . . . . . . . . . . . . . . . . . . . . . . | | $10,400 |
| Add outstanding checks: | | |
| No. 5148 . . . . . . . . . . . . . . . . . . . . . . . . . . . . . . . . . . . . . . . . . . . . . . . . . . . | $225 | |
| 5149 . . . . . . . . . . . . . . . . . . . . . . . . . . . . . . . . . . . . . . . . . . . . . . . . . . . | 750 | |
| 5151 . . . . . . . . . . . . . . . . . . . . . . . . . . . . . . . . . . . . . . . . . . . . . . . . . . . | 800 | 1,675 |
| | | $12,075 |
| Less undeposited receipts . . . . . . . . . . . . . . . . . . . . . . . . . . . . . . . . . . . . . | | 1,500 |
| Cash balance per bank, July 31 . . . . . . . . . . . . . . . . . . . . . . . . . . . . . . . . . | | $10,575 |
| Deduct unrecorded note with interest . . . . . . . . . . . . . . . . . . . . . . . . . . . | | 2,400 |
| True cash, July 31. . . . . . . . . . . . . . . . . . . . . . . . . . . . . . . . . . . . . . . . . . . . | | $ 8,175 |

> *Calculator Tape of Outstanding Checks:*
> 0*
> 225+
> 750+
> 800+
> 1,675*

Subsequently, the owner of Parker Company discovered that the cashier had stolen an unknown amount of undeposited receipts, leaving only $1,500 to be deposited on July 31. The owner, a close family friend, has asked your help in determining the amount that the former cashier has stolen.

1. Determine the amount the cashier stole from Parker Company. Show your computations in good form.
2. How did the cashier attempt to conceal the theft?
3. a. Identify two major weaknesses in internal controls that allowed the cashier to steal the undeposited cash receipts.

   b. ━━━━▶Recommend improvements in internal controls so that similar types of thefts of undeposited cash receipts can be prevented.

---

### CP 8-6   Observe internal controls over cash

**Group Project**

Select a business in your community and observe its internal controls over cash receipts and cash payments. The business could be a bank or a bookstore, restaurant, department store, or other retailer. In groups of three or four, identify and discuss the similarities and differences in each business's cash internal controls.

---

### CP 8-7   Cash to monthly cash expenses ratio

TearLab Corp. is a health care company that specializes in developing diagnostic devices for eye disease. TearLab reported the following data (in thousands) for three recent years:

|  | For Years Ended December 31 | | |
|---|---|---|---|
|  | **Year 3** | **Year 2** | **Year 1** |
| Cash and cash equivalents | $ 2,807 | $ 2,726 | $   106 |
| Net cash flows from operations | (5,974) | (4,540) | (4,098) |

1. Determine the monthly cash expenses for Year 3, Year 2, and Year 1. Round to one decimal place.
2. Determine the ratio of cash to monthly cash expenses as of December 31, for Year 3, Year 2, and Year 1. Round to one decimal place.
3. ━━━━▶Based on (1) and (2), comment on TearLab's ratio of cash to monthly operating expenses for Year 3, Year 2, and Year 1.

# Receivables

## Oakley, Inc.

The sale and purchase of merchandise involves the exchange of goods for cash. However, the point at which cash actually changes hands varies with the transaction. Consider transactions by **Oakley, Inc.**, a worldwide leader in the design, development, manufacture, and distribution of premium sunglasses, goggles, prescription eyewear, apparel, footwear, and accessories. Not only does the company sell its products through three different company-owned retail chains, but it also has approximately 10,000 independent distributors.

If you were to buy a pair of sunglasses at an Oakley Vault, which is one of the company's retail outlet stores, you would have to pay cash or use a credit card to pay for the glasses be-

fore you left the store. However, Oakley allows its distributors to purchase sunglasses "on account." These sales on account are recorded as receivables due from the distributors.

As an individual, you also might build up a trusted financial history with a local company or department store that would allow you to purchase merchandise on account. Like Oakley's distributors, your purchase on account would be recorded as an account receivable. Such credit transactions facilitate sales and are a significant current asset for many businesses.

This chapter describes common classifications of receivables, illustrates how to account for uncollectible receivables, and demonstrates the reporting of receivables on the balance sheet.

## Learning Objectives

**At a Glance 9**     Page 433

---

**OBJ 1** Describe the common classes of receivables.

# Classification of Receivables

The receivables that result from sales on account are normally accounts receivable or notes receivable. The term **receivables** includes all money claims against other entities, including people, companies, and other organizations. Receivables are usually a significant portion of the total current assets.

## Accounts Receivable

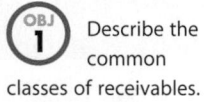

A recent balance sheet of **Caterpillar Inc.** reported that receivables made up more than 56% of its current assets.

The most common transaction creating a receivable is selling merchandise or services on account (on credit). The receivable is recorded as a debit to Accounts Receivable. Such **accounts receivable** are normally collected within a short period, such as 30 or 60 days. They are classified on the balance sheet as a current asset.

## Notes Receivable

**Notes receivable** are amounts that customers owe for which a formal, written instrument of credit has been issued. If notes receivable are expected to be collected within a year, they are classified on the balance sheet as a current asset.

Notes are often used for credit periods of more than 60 days. For example, an automobile dealer may require a down payment at the time of sale and accept a note or a series of notes for the remainder. Such notes usually provide for monthly payments.

Notes may also be used to settle a customer's account receivable. Notes and accounts receivable that result from sales transactions are sometimes called *trade receivables*. In this chapter, all notes and accounts receivable are from sales transactions.

## Other Receivables

*Other receivables* include interest receivable, taxes receivable, and receivables from officers or employees. Other receivables are normally reported separately on the balance sheet. If they are expected to be collected within one year, they are classified as current assets. If collection is expected beyond one year, they are classified as noncurrent assets and reported under the caption *Investments*.

# Uncollectible Receivables

In prior chapters, the accounting for sales of merchandise or services on account (on credit) was described and illustrated. A major issue that has not yet been discussed is that some customers will not pay their accounts. That is, some accounts receivable will be uncollectible.

Companies may shift the risk of uncollectible receivables to other companies. For example, some retailers do not accept sales on account but will only accept cash or credit cards. Such policies shift the risk to the credit card companies.

Companies may also sell their receivables. This is often the case when a company issues its own credit card. For example, Macy's and JCPenney issue their own credit cards. Selling receivables is called *factoring* the receivables. The buyer of the receivables is called a *factor*. An advantage of factoring is that the company selling its receivables immediately receives cash for operating and other needs. Also, depending on the factoring agreement, some of the risk of uncollectible accounts is shifted to the factor.

Regardless of how careful a company is in granting credit, some credit sales will be uncollectible. The operating expense recorded from uncollectible receivables is called **bad debt expense**, *uncollectible accounts expense*, or *doubtful accounts expense*.

There is no general rule for when an account becomes uncollectible. Some indications that an account may be uncollectible include the following:

- The receivable is past due.
- The customer does not respond to the company's attempts to collect.
- The customer files for bankruptcy.
- The customer closes its business.
- The company cannot locate the customer.

If a customer doesn't pay, a company may turn the account over to a collection agency. After the collection agency attempts to collect payment, any remaining balance in the account is considered worthless.

The two methods of accounting for uncollectible receivables are as follows:

- The **direct write-off method** records bad debt expense only when an account is determined to be worthless.
- The **allowance method** records bad debt expense by estimating uncollectible accounts at the end of the accounting period.

The direct write-off method is often used by small companies and companies with few receivables.[1] Generally accepted accounting principles (GAAP), however, require companies with a large amount of receivables to use the allowance method. As a result, most well-known companies such as General Electric, Pepsi, Intel, and FedEx use the allowance method.

# Direct Write-Off Method for Uncollectible Accounts

Under the direct write-off method, Bad Debt Expense is not recorded until the customer's account is determined to be worthless. At that time, the customer's account receivable is written off.

[1] The direct write-off method is also required for federal income tax purposes.

Describe the accounting for uncollectible receivables.

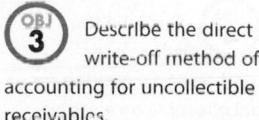

**Adams, Stevens & Bradley, Ltd.** is a collection agency that operates on a contingency basis. That is, its fees are based on what it collects.

Describe the direct write-off method of accounting for uncollectible receivables.

To illustrate, assume that a $4,200 account receivable from D. L. Ross has been determined to be uncollectible. The entry to write off the account is as follows:

| | | | | |
|---|---|---|---|---|
| May | 10 | Bad Debt Expense | 4,200 | |
| | | Accounts Receivable—D. L. Ross | | 4,200 |

An account receivable that has been written off may be collected later. In such cases, the account is reinstated by an entry that reverses the write-off entry. The cash received in payment is then recorded as a receipt on account.

To illustrate, assume that the D. L. Ross account of $4,200 written off on May 10 is later collected on November 21. The reinstatement and receipt of cash is recorded as follows:

| | | | | |
|---|---|---|---|---|
| Nov. | 21 | Accounts Receivable—D. L. Ross | 4,200 | |
| | | Bad Debt Expense | | 4,200 |
| | 21 | Cash | 4,200 | |
| | | Accounts Receivable—D. L. Ross | | 4,200 |

The direct write-off method is used by businesses that sell most of their goods or services for cash or through the acceptance of MasterCard or VISA, which are re-corded as cash sales. In such cases, receivables are a small part of the current assets and any bad debt expense is small. Examples of such businesses are a restaurant, a convenience store, and a small retail store.

## Example Exercise 9-1   Direct Write-Off Method

Journalize the following transactions, using the direct write-off method of accounting for uncollectible receivables:

July 9.   Received $1,200 from Jay Burke and wrote off the remainder owed of $3,900 as uncollectible.
Oct. 11.   Reinstated the account of Jay Burke and received $3,900 cash in full payment.

## Follow My Example 9-1

| | | | |
|---|---|---|---|
| July 9 | Cash ...................................................... | 1,200 | |
| | Bad Debt Expense............................................. | 3,900 | |
| | Accounts Receivable—Jay Burke ........................... | | 5,100 |
| Oct. 11 | Accounts Receivable—Jay Burke.............................. | 3,900 | |
| | Bad Debt Expense............................................ | | 3,900 |
| 11 | Cash ...................................................... | 3,900 | |
| | Accounts Receivable—Jay Burke ........................... | | 3,900 |

Practice Exercises: PE 9-1A, PE 9-1B

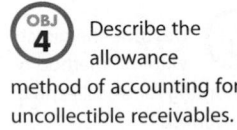

Describe the allowance method of accounting for uncollectible receivables.

# Allowance Method for Uncollectible Accounts

The allowance method estimates the uncollectible accounts receivable at the end of the accounting period. Based on this estimate, Bad Debt Expense is recorded by an adjusting entry.

To illustrate, assume that **ExTone Company** began operations August 1. As of the end of its accounting period on December 31, 2015, ExTone has an accounts receivable balance of $200,000. This balance includes some past due accounts. Based on industry averages, ExTone estimates that $30,000 of the December 31 accounts receivable will be uncollectible. However, on December 31, ExTone doesn't know which customer accounts will be uncollectible. Thus, specific customer accounts cannot be decreased or credited. Instead, a contra asset account, **Allowance for Doubtful Accounts**, is credited for the estimated bad debts.

Using the $30,000 estimate, the following adjusting entry is made on December 31:

| 2015 | | | | |
|------|----|----------------------------------------|--------|--------|
| Dec. | 31 | Bad Debt Expense | 30,000 | |
| | | Allowance for Doubtful Accounts | | 30,000 |
| | | Uncollectible accounts estimate. | | |

The preceding adjusting entry affects the income statement and balance sheet. On the income statement, the $30,000 of Bad Debt Expense will be matched against the related revenues of the period. On the balance sheet, the value of the receivables is reduced to the amount that is expected to be collected or realized. This amount, $170,000 ($200,000 – $30,000), is called the **net realizable value** of the receivables.

After the preceding adjusting entry is recorded, Accounts Receivable still has a debit balance of $200,000. This balance is the total amount owed by customers on account on December 31 as supported by the accounts receivable subsidiary ledger. The accounts receivable contra account, Allowance for Doubtful Accounts, has a credit balance of $30,000.

**Note:**
The adjusting entry reduces receivables to their net realizable value and matches the uncollectible expense with revenues.

## Integrity, Objectivity, and Ethics in Business

### SELLER BEWARE

A company in financial distress will still try to purchase goods and services on account. In these cases, rather than "buyer beware," it is more like "seller beware." Sellers must be careful in advancing credit to such companies because trade creditors have low priority for cash payments in the event of bankruptcy. To help suppliers, third-party services specialize in evaluating court actions and payment decisions of financially distressed companies.

## Write-Offs to the Allowance Account

When a customer's account is identified as uncollectible, it is written off against the allowance account. This requires the company to remove the specific accounts receivable and an equal amount from the allowance account.

To illustrate, on January 21, 2016, John Parker's account of $6,000 with **ExTone Company** is written off as follows:

| 2016 | | | | |
|------|----|----------------------------------------|-------|-------|
| Jan. | 21 | Allowance for Doubtful Accounts | 6,000 | |
| | | Accounts Receivable—John Parker | | 6,000 |

At the end of a period, Allowance for Doubtful Accounts will normally have a balance. This is because Allowance for Doubtful Accounts is based on an estimate. As a result, the total write-offs to the allowance account during the period will rarely equal the balance of the account at the beginning of the period. The allowance account will have a credit balance at the end of the period if the write-offs during the period are less than the beginning balance. It will have a debit balance if the write-offs exceed the beginning balance.

Exhibit 1 illustrates the allowance method where the adjusting entry increases the Allowance for Doubtful Accounts (fills the bucket) while writing off accounts decreases the Allowance for Doubtful Accounts (empties the bucket).

| EXHIBIT 1 | The Allowance Method |

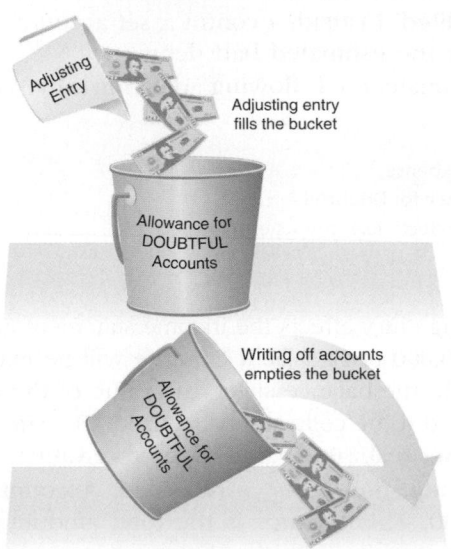

Adjusting entry fills the bucket

Allowance for DOUBTFUL Accounts

Writing off accounts empties the bucket

Allowance for DOUBTFUL Accounts

To illustrate, assume that during 2016 **ExTone Company** writes off $26,750 of uncollectible accounts, including the $6,000 account of John Parker recorded on January 21. Allowance for Doubtful Accounts will have a credit balance of $3,250 ($30,000 − $26,750), computed as follows:

**ALLOWANCE FOR DOUBTFUL ACCOUNTS**

|  |  |  |  |  |  |  |  |
|---|---|---|---|---|---|---|---|
| Total accounts written off $26,750 | Jan. | 21 | 6,000 | Jan. 1 | Balance | | 30,000 |
| | Feb. | 2 | 3,900 | | | | |
| | ⋮ | | ⋮ | Dec. 31 | Unadjusted balance | | 3,250 |

If ExTone had written off $32,100 in accounts receivable during 2016, Allowance for Doubtful Accounts would have a debit balance of $2,100, computed as follows:

**ALLOWANCE FOR DOUBTFUL ACCOUNTS**

|  |  |  |  |  |  |  |  |
|---|---|---|---|---|---|---|---|
| | | | | Jan. 1 | Balance | | 30,000 |
| Total accounts written off $32,100 | Jan. | 21 | 6,000 | | | | |
| | Feb. | 2 | 3,900 | | | | |
| | ⋮ | | ⋮ | | | | |
| Dec. 31 | Unadjusted balance | | 2,100 | | | | |

The allowance account balances (credit balance of $3,250 and debit balance of $2,100) in the preceding illustrations are *before* the end-of-period adjusting entry. After the end-of-period adjusting entry is recorded, Allowance for Doubtful Accounts should always have a credit balance.

An account receivable that has been written off against the allowance account may be collected later. Like the direct write-off method, the account is reinstated by an entry that reverses the write-off entry. The cash received in payment is then recorded as a receipt on account.

To illustrate, assume that Nancy Smith's account of $5,000, which was written off on April 2, is collected later on June 10. **ExTone Company** records the reinstatement and the collection as follows:

| | | | | | |
|---|---|---|---|---|---|
| June | 10 | Accounts Receivable—Nancy Smith | | 5,000 | |
| | | Allowance for Doubtful Accounts | | | 5,000 |
| | 10 | Cash | | 5,000 | |
| | | Accounts Receivable—Nancy Smith | | | 5,000 |

**Example Exercise 9-2** Allowance Method

OBJ 4

Journalize the following transactions, using the allowance method of accounting for uncollectible receivables:

July 9. Received $1,200 from Jay Burke and wrote off the remainder owed of $3,900 as uncollectible.
Oct. 11. Reinstated the account of Jay Burke and received $3,900 cash in full payment.

**Follow My Example 9-2**

| | | | |
|---|---|---|---|
| July 9 | Cash .......................................... | 1,200 | |
| | Allowance for Doubtful Accounts............................ | 3,900 | |
| |     Accounts Receivable—Jay Burke .......................... | | 5,100 |
| Oct. 11 | Accounts Receivable—Jay Burke............................. | 3,900 | |
| |     Allowance for Doubtful Accounts........................ | | 3,900 |
| 11 | Cash .......................................... | 3,900 | |
| |     Accounts Receivable—Jay Burke .......................... | | 3,900 |

Practice Exercises: PE 9-2A, PE 9-2B

## Estimating Uncollectibles

The allowance method requires an estimate of uncollectible accounts at the end of the period. This estimate is normally based on past experience, industry averages, and forecasts of the future.

The two methods used to estimate uncollectible accounts are as follows:

- Percent of sales method.
- Analysis of receivables method.

**Percent of Sales Method** Since accounts receivable are created by credit sales, uncollectible accounts can be estimated as a percent of credit sales. If the portion of credit sales to sales is relatively constant, the percent may be applied to total sales.

# Business 🌎 Connection

## ALLOWANCE PERCENTAGES ACROSS COMPANIES

The percent of the allowance for doubtful accounts to total accounts receivable will vary across companies and industries. For example, the following percentages were computed from recent annual reports:

HCA's higher percentage of allowance for doubtful accounts to total accounts receivable is due in part because Medicare reimbursements are often less than the amounts billed patients.

| Company | Industry | Percent of Allowance for Doubtful Accounts to Total Accounts Receivable |
|---|---|---|
| Apple Inc. | Computer and technology products | 1.0% |
| Boeing | Aerospace and airplanes | 1.0 |
| Delta Air Lines | Transportation services | 2.1 |
| HCA Inc. | Health services | 50.9 |
| Sears | Retail | 3.9 |

To illustrate, assume the following data for **ExTone Company** on December 31, 2016, before any adjustments:

| | |
|---|---|
| Balance of Accounts Receivable | $ 240,000 |
| Balance of Allowance for Doubtful Accounts | 3,250 (Cr.) |
| Total credit sales | 3,000,000 |
| Bad debt as a percent of credit sales | ¾% |

Bad Debt Expense of $22,500 is estimated as follows:

Bad Debt Expense = Credit Sales × Bad Debt as a Percent of Credit Sales
Bad Debt Expense = $3,000,000 × ¾% = $22,500

The adjusting entry for uncollectible accounts on December 31, 2016, is as follows:

| | | | | |
|---|---|---|---|---|
| Dec. | 31 | Bad Debt Expense | 22,500 | |
| | | Allowance for Doubtful Accounts | | 22,500 |
| | | Uncollectible accounts estimate | | |
| | | ($3,000,000 × ¾% = $22,500). | | |

After the adjusting entry is posted to the ledger, Bad Debt Expense will have an adjusted balance of $22,500. Allowance for Doubtful Accounts will have an adjusted balance of $25,750 ($3,250 + $22,500). Both T accounts follow:

**BAD DEBT EXPENSE**

| | | | |
|---|---|---|---|
| Dec. 31 | Adjusting entry | 22,500 | ← |
| Dec. 31 | Adjusted balance | 22,500 | |

**ALLOWANCE FOR DOUBTFUL ACCOUNTS**

| | | | | | |
|---|---|---|---|---|---|
| | | | | Jan. 1 | Balance | 30,000 |
| Total accounts written off $26,750 | Jan. 21 | 6,000 | | | |
| | Feb. 2 | 3,900 | | | |
| | ⋮ | ⋮ | | | |
| | | | Dec. 31 | Unadjusted balance | 3,250 |
| | | | Dec. 31 | Adjusting entry | 22,500 ← |
| | | | Dec. 31 | Adjusted balance | 25,750 |

Under the percent of sales method, the amount of the adjusting entry is the amount estimated for Bad Debt Expense. This estimate is credited to whatever the unadjusted balance is for Allowance for Doubtful Accounts.

To illustrate, assume that in the preceding example the unadjusted balance of Allowance for Doubtful Accounts on December 31, 2016, had been a $2,100 debit balance instead of a $3,250 credit balance. The adjustment would still have been $22,500. However, the December 31, 2016, ending adjusted balance of Allowance for Doubtful Accounts would have been $20,400 ($22,500 – $2,100).

**Note:**
The estimate based on sales is added to any balance in Allowance for Doubtful Accounts.

## Example Exercise 9-3 Percent of Sales Method

OBJ 4

At the end of the current year, Accounts Receivable has a balance of $800,000; Allowance for Doubtful Accounts has a credit balance of $7,500; and sales for the year total $3,500,000. Bad debt expense is estimated at ½ of 1% of sales.

Determine (a) the amount of the adjusting entry for uncollectible accounts; (b) the adjusted balances of Accounts Receivable, Allowance for Doubtful Accounts, and Bad Debt Expense; and (c) the net realizable value of accounts receivable.

## Follow My Example 9-3

 Dynamic Exhibit

a. $17,500 ($3,500,000 × 0.005)

| | Adjusted Balance |
|---|---|
| b. Accounts Receivable ..................................................... | $800,000 |
| Allowance for Doubtful Accounts ($7,500 + $17,500) ...................... | 25,000 |
| Bad Debt Expense.......................................................... | 17,500 |

c. $775,000 ($800,000 – $25,000)

Practice Exercises: PE 9-3A, PE 9-3B

**Analysis of Receivables Method** The analysis of receivables method is based on the assumption that the longer an account receivable is outstanding, the less likely that it will be collected. The analysis of receivables method is applied as follows:

- Step 1. The due date of each account receivable is determined.
- Step 2. The number of days each account is past due is determined. This is the number of days between the due date of the account and the date of the analysis.
- Step 3. Each account is placed in an aged class according to its days past due. Typical aged classes include the following:

  Not past due

  1–30 days past due

  31–60 days past due

  61–90 days past due

  91–180 days past due

  181–365 days past due

  Over 365 days past due

- Step 4. The totals for each aged class are determined.
- Step 5. The total for each aged class is multiplied by an estimated percentage of uncollectible accounts for that class.
- Step 6. The estimated total of uncollectible accounts is determined as the sum of the uncollectible accounts for each aged class.

The preceding steps are summarized in an aging schedule, and this overall process is called **aging the receivables**.

To illustrate, assume that **ExTone Company** uses the analysis of receivables method instead of the percent of sales method. ExTone prepared an aging schedule for its accounts receivable of $240,000 as of December 31, 2016, as shown in Exhibit 2.

---

**EXHIBIT 2**     **Aging of Receivables Schedule, December 31, 2016**

|  | | A | B | C | D | E | F | G | H | I |
|---|---|---|---|---|---|---|---|---|---|---|
| | 1 | | | **Not** | | | **Days Past Due** | | | |
| | 2 | | | **Past** | | | | | | **Over** |
| | 3 | **Customer** | **Balance** | **Due** | **1–30** | **31–60** | **61–90** | **91–180** | **181–365** | **365** |
| | 4 | Ashby & Co. | 1,500 | | | 1,500 | | | | |
| | 5 | B. T. Barr | 6,100 | | | | | | 3,500 | 2,600 | |
| Steps 1–3 | 6 | Brock Co. | 4,700 | 4,700 | | | | | | |
| | 21 | | | | | | | | | |
| | 22 | Saxon Woods Co. | 600 | | | | | 600 | | |
| Step 4 ⟶ | 23 | Total | 240,000 | 125,000 | 64,000 | 13,100 | 8,900 | 5,000 | 10,000 | 14,000 |
| Step 5 ⟶ | 24 | Percent uncollectible | | | 2% | 5% | 10% | 20% | 30% | 50% | 80% |
| Step 6 ⟶ | 25 | Estimate of uncollectible accounts | 26,490 | 2,500 | 3,200 | 1,310 | 1,780 | 1,500 | 5,000 | 11,200 |

---

Assume that ExTone sold merchandise to Saxon Woods Co. on August 29 with terms 2/10, n/30. Thus, the due date (Step 1) of Saxon Woods' account is September 28, computed as follows:

| | |
|---|---|
| Credit terms, net | 30 days |
| Less: Aug. 29 to Aug. 31 | 2 days |
| Days in September | 28 days |

As of December 31, Saxon Woods' account is 94 days past due (Step 2), computed as follows:

| | |
|---|---|
| Number of days past due in September | 2 days (30 – 28) |
| Number of days past due in October | 31 days |
| Number of days past due in November | 30 days |
| Number of days past due in December | 31 days |
| Total number of days past due | 94 days |

Exhibit 2 shows that the $600 account receivable for Saxon Woods Co. was placed in the 91–180 days past due class (Step 3).

The total for each of the aged classes is determined (Step 4). Exhibit 2 shows that $125,000 of the accounts receivable are not past due, while $64,000 are 1–30 days past due. ExTone applies a different estimated percentage of uncollectible accounts to the totals of each of the aged classes (Step 5). As shown in Exhibit 2, the percent is 2% for accounts not past due, while the percent is 80% for accounts over 365 days past due.

The sum of the estimated uncollectible accounts for each aged class (Step 6) is the estimated uncollectible accounts on December 31, 2016. This is the desired adjusted balance for Allowance for Doubtful Accounts. For ExTone, this amount is $26,490, as shown in Exhibit 2.

Comparing the estimate of $26,490 with the unadjusted balance of the allowance account determines the amount of the adjustment for Bad Debt Expense. For ExTone, the unadjusted balance of the allowance account is a credit balance of $3,250. The amount to be added to this balance is therefore $23,240 ($26,490 – $3,250). The adjusting entry is as follows:

**Note:**

The estimate based on receivables is compared to the balance in the allowance account to determine the amount of the adjusting entry.

| | | | | |
|---|---|---|---|---|
| Dec. | 31 | Bad Debt Expense | 23,240 | |
| | | Allowance for Doubtful Accounts | | 23,240 |
| | | Uncollectible accounts estimate | | |
| | | ($26,490 – $3,250). | | |

After the preceding adjusting entry is posted to the ledger, Bad Debt Expense will have an adjusted balance of $23,240. Allowance for Doubtful Accounts will have an adjusted balance of $26,490, and the net realizable value of the receivables is $213,510 ($240,000 – $26,490). Both T accounts follow:

**BAD DEBT EXPENSE**

| | | |
|---|---|---|
| Dec. 31 | Adjusting entry | 23,240 |
| Dec. 31 | Adjusted balance | 23,240 |

**ALLOWANCE FOR DOUBTFUL ACCOUNTS**

| | | |
|---|---|---|
| Dec. 31 | Unadjusted balance | 3,250 |
| Dec. 31 | Adjusting entry | 23,240 |
| Dec. 31 | Adjusted balance | 26,490 |

Under the analysis of receivables method, the amount of the adjusting entry is the amount that will yield an adjusted balance for Allowance for Doubtful Accounts equal to that estimated by the aging schedule.

To illustrate, if the unadjusted balance of the allowance account had been a debit balance of $2,100, the amount of the adjustment would have been $28,590 ($26,490 + $2,100). In this case, Bad Debt Expense would have an adjusted balance of $28,590. However, the adjusted balance of Allowance for Doubtful Accounts would still have been $26,490. After the adjusting entry is posted, both T accounts follow:

**BAD DEBT EXPENSE**

| | | |
|---|---|---|
| Dec. 31 | Adjusting entry | 28,590 |
| Dec. 31 | Adjusted balance | 28,590 |

**ALLOWANCE FOR DOUBTFUL ACCOUNTS**

| | | |
|---|---|---|
| Dec. 31 | Unadjusted balance | 2,100 |

| | | |
|---|---|---|
| Dec. 31 | Adjusting entry | 28,590 |
| Dec. 31 | Adjusted balance | 26,490 |

## Example Exercise 9-4 Analysis of Receivables Method

At the end of the current year, Accounts Receivable has a balance of $800,000; Allowance for Doubtful Accounts has a credit balance of $7,500; and sales for the year total $3,500,000. Using the aging method, the balance of Allowance for Doubtful Accounts is estimated as $30,000.

Determine (a) the amount of the adjusting entry for uncollectible accounts; (b) the adjusted balances of Accounts Receivable, Allowance for Doubtful Accounts, and Bad Debt Expense; and (c) the net realizable value of accounts receivable.

### Follow My Example 9-4

a. $22,500 ($30,000 – $7,500)

|  | Adjusted Balance |
|---|---|
| b. Accounts Receivable | $800,000 |
| Allowance for Doubtful Accounts | 30,000 |
| Bad Debt Expense | 22,500 |

c. $770,000 ($800,000 – $30,000)

Practice Exercises: PE 9-4A, PE 9-4B

## Comparing Estimation Methods

Both the percent of sales and analysis of receivables methods estimate uncollectible accounts. However, each method has a slightly different focus and financial statement emphasis.

Under the percent of sales method, Bad Debt Expense is the focus of the estimation process. The percent of sales method places more emphasis on matching revenues and expenses and, thus, emphasizes the income statement. That is, the amount of the adjusting entry is based on the estimate of Bad Debt Expense for the period. Allowance for Doubtful Accounts is then credited for this amount.

Under the analysis of receivables method, Allowance for Doubtful Accounts is the focus of the estimation process. The analysis of receivables method places more emphasis on the net realizable value of the receivables and, thus, emphasizes the balance sheet. That is, the amount of the adjusting entry is the amount that will yield an adjusted balance for Allowance for Doubtful Accounts equal to that estimated by the aging schedule. Bad Debt Expense is then debited for this amount.

Exhibit 3 summarizes these differences between the percent of sales and the analysis of receivables methods. Exhibit 3 also shows the results of the **ExTone Company** illustration for the percent of sales and analysis of receivables methods. The amounts shown in Exhibit 3 assume an unadjusted credit balance of $3,250 for Allowance for

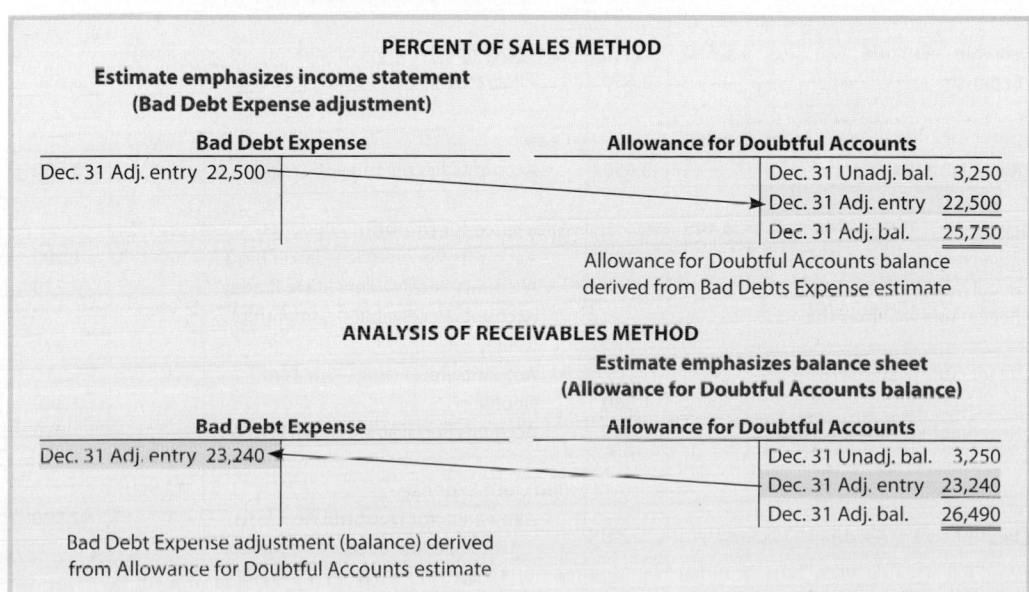

**PERCENT OF SALES METHOD**

Estimate emphasizes income statement
(Bad Debt Expense adjustment)

| Bad Debt Expense | Allowance for Doubtful Accounts |
|---|---|
| Dec. 31 Adj. entry 22,500 | Dec. 31 Unadj. bal. 3,250 |
| | Dec. 31 Adj. entry 22,500 |
| | Dec. 31 Adj. bal. 25,750 |

Allowance for Doubtful Accounts balance
derived from Bad Debts Expense estimate

**ANALYSIS OF RECEIVABLES METHOD**

Estimate emphasizes balance sheet
(Allowance for Doubtful Accounts balance)

| Bad Debt Expense | Allowance for Doubtful Accounts |
|---|---|
| Dec. 31 Adj. entry 23,240 | Dec. 31 Unadj. bal. 3,250 |
| | Dec. 31 Adj. entry 23,240 |
| | Dec. 31 Adj. bal. 26,490 |

Bad Debt Expense adjustment (balance) derived
from Allowance for Doubtful Accounts estimate

**EXHIBIT 3**

**Difference Between Estimation Methods**

Dynamic Exhibit

Doubtful Accounts. While the methods normally yield different amounts for any one period, over several periods the amounts should be similar.

## Comparing Direct Write-Off and Allowance Methods

**OBJ 5** Compare the direct write-off and allowance methods of accounting for uncollectible accounts.

Journal entries for the direct write-off and allowance methods are illustrated and compared in this section. As a basis for illustration, the following transactions, taken from the records of Hobbs Company for the year ending December 31, 2015, are used:

Mar. 1. Wrote off account of C. York, $3,650.

Apr. 12. Received $2,250 as partial payment on the $5,500 account of Cary Bradshaw. Wrote off the remaining balance as uncollectible.

June 22. Received the $3,650 from C. York, which had been written off on March 1. Reinstated the account and recorded the cash receipt.

Sept. 7. Wrote off the following accounts as uncollectible (record as one journal entry):

| Jason Bigg | $1,100 | Stanford Noonan | $1,360 |
| Steve Bradey | 2,220 | Aiden Wyman | 990 |
| Samantha Neeley | 775 | | |

Dec. 31. Hobbs Company uses the percent of credit sales method of estimating uncollectible expenses. Based on past history and industry averages, 1.25% of credit sales are expected to be uncollectible. Hobbs recorded $3,400,000 of credit sales during 2015.

Exhibit 4 illustrates the journal entries for Hobbs using the direct write-off and allowance methods. Using the direct write-off method, there is no adjusting entry on December 31 for uncollectible accounts. In contrast, the allowance method records an adjusting entry for estimated uncollectible accounts of $42,500.

**EXHIBIT 4** **Comparing Direct Write-Off and Allowance Methods**

| 2015 | | Direct Write-Off Method | | | Allowance Method | | |
|---|---|---|---|---|---|---|---|
| Mar. | 1 | Bad Debt Expense | 3,650 | | Allowance for Doubtful Accounts | 3,650 | |
| | | Accounts Receivable—C. York | | 3,650 | Accounts Receivable—C. York | | 3,650 |
| Apr. | 12 | Cash | 2,250 | | Cash | 2,250 | |
| | | Bad Debt Expense | 3,250 | | Allowance for Doubtful Accounts | 3,250 | |
| | | Accounts Receivable—Cary Bradshaw | | 5,500 | Accounts Receivable—Cary Bradshaw | | 5,500 |
| June | 22 | Accounts Receivable—C. York | 3,650 | | Accounts Receivable—C. York | 3,650 | |
| | | Bad Debt Expense | | 3,650 | Allowance for Doubtful Accounts | | 3,650 |
| | 22 | Cash | 3,650 | | Cash | 3,650 | |
| | | Accounts Receivable—C. York | | 3,650 | Accounts Receivable—C. York | | 3,650 |
| Sept. | 7 | Bad Debt Expense | 6,445 | | Allowance for Doubtful Accounts | 6,445 | |
| | | Accounts Receivable—Jason Bigg | | 1,100 | Accounts Receivable—Jason Bigg | | 1,100 |
| | | Accounts Receivable—Steve Bradey | | 2,220 | Accounts Receivable—Steve Bradey | | 2,220 |
| | | Accounts Receivable—Samantha Neeley | | 775 | Accounts Receivable—Samantha Neeley | | 775 |
| | | Accounts Receivable—Stanford Noonan | | 1,360 | Accounts Receivable—Stanford Noonan | | 1,360 |
| | | Accounts Receivable—Aiden Wyman | | 990 | Accounts Receivable—Aiden Wyman | | 990 |
| Dec. | 31 | No Entry | | | Bad Debt Expense | 42,500 | |
| | | | | | Allowance for Doubtful Accounts | | 42,500 |
| | | | | | Uncollectible accounts estimate ($3,400,000 × 0.0125 = $42,500). | | |

The primary differences between the direct write-off and allowance methods are summarized in Exhibit 5.

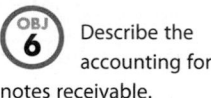

**EXHIBIT 5**

**Direct Write-Off and Allowance Methods**

| | Direct Write-Off Method | Allowance Method |
|---|---|---|
| Bad debt expense is recorded | When the specific customer accounts are determined to be uncollectible. | Using estimate based on (1) a percent of sales or (2) an analysis of receivables. |
| Allowance account | No allowance account is used. | The allowance account is used. |
| Primary users | Small companies and companies with few receivables. | Large companies and those with a large amount of receivables. |

# Notes Receivable

**OBJ 6** Describe the accounting for notes receivable.

A note has some advantages over an account receivable. By signing a note, the debtor recognizes the debt and agrees to pay it according to its terms. Thus, a note is a stronger legal claim.

## Characteristics of Notes Receivable

A promissory note is a written promise to pay the face amount, usually with interest, on demand or at a date in the future.[2] Characteristics of a promissory note are as follows:

1. The *maker* is the party making the promise to pay.
2. The *payee* is the party to whom the note is payable.
3. The *face amount* is the amount for which the note is written on its face.
4. The *issuance date* is the date a note is issued.
5. The *due date* or *maturity date* is the date the note is to be paid.
6. The *term* of a note is the amount of time between the issuance and due dates.
7. The *interest rate* is that rate of interest that must be paid on the face amount for the term of the note.

Exhibit 6 illustrates a promissory note. The maker of the note is Selig Company, and the payee is Pearland Company. The face value of the note is $2,000, the interest rate is 10%, and the issuance date is March 16, 2015. The term of the note is 90 days, which results in a due date of June 14, 2015, computed as follows and shown in Exhibit 7:

| | |
|---|---|
| Days in March | 31 days |
| Minus issuance date of note | 16 |
| Days remaining in March | 15 days |
| Add days in April | 30 |
| Add days in May | 31 |
| Add days in June (due date of June 14) | 14 |
| Term of note | 90 days |

The interest on a note is computed as follows:

$$\text{Interest} = \text{Face Amount} \times \text{Interest Rate} \times (\text{Term} \div 360 \text{ days})$$

The interest rate is stated on an annual (yearly) basis, while the term is expressed as days. Thus, the interest on the note in Exhibit 6 is computed as follows:

$$\text{Interest} = \$2,000 \times 10\% \times (90 \div 360) = \$50$$

To simplify, 360 days per year will be used. In practice, companies such as banks and mortgage companies use the exact number of days in a year, 365.

---

[2] You may see references to non-interest-bearing notes. Such notes are not widely used and carry an assumed or implicit interest rate.

| EXHIBIT 6 | Promissory Note |
|---|---|

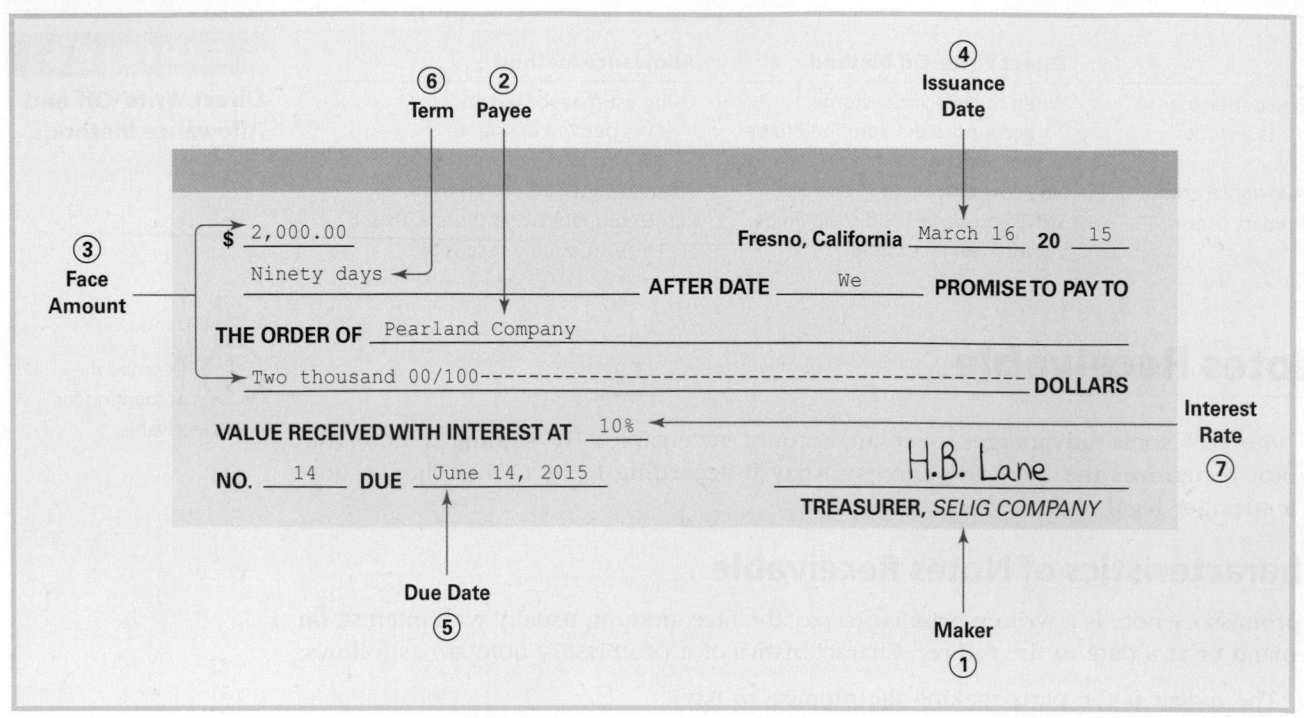

The **maturity value** is the amount that must be paid at the due date of the note, which is the sum of the face amount and the interest. The maturity value of the note in Exhibit 6 is $2,050 ($2,000 + $50).

| EXHIBIT 7 | Determining Due Date of Promissory Note |
|---|---|

## Accounting for Notes Receivable

A promissory note may be received by a company from a customer to replace an account receivable. In such cases, the promissory note is recorded as a note receivable.[3]

To illustrate, assume that a company accepts a 30-day, 12% note dated November 21, 2016, in settlement of the account of W. A. Bunn Co., which is past due and has a balance of $6,000. The company records the receipt of the note as follows:

| | | | | | |
|---|---|---|---|---|---|
| Nov. | 21 | Notes Receivable—W. A. Bunn Co. | | 6,000 | |
| | | Accounts Receivable—W. A. Bunn Co. | | | 6,000 |

[3] The accounting for notes payable is described and illustrated in Chapter 14.

At the due date, the company records the receipt of $6,060 ($6,000 face amount plus $60 interest) as follows:

| Dec. | 21 | Cash | | 6,060 | |
|------|----|------|--|-------|--|
| | | Notes Receivable—W. A. Bunn Co. | | | 6,000 |
| | | Interest Revenue | | | 60 |
| | | [$6,060 = $6,000 + ($6,000 × 12% × 30 ÷ 360)]. | | | |

If the maker of a note fails to pay the note on the due date, the note is a **dishonored note receivable**. A company that holds a dishonored note transfers the face amount of the note plus any interest due back to an accounts receivable account. For example, assume that the $6,000, 30-day, 12% note received from W. A. Bunn Co. and recorded on November 21 is dishonored. The company holding the note transfers the note and interest back to the customer's account as follows:

| Dec. | 21 | Accounts Receivable—W. A. Bunn Co. | | 6,060 | |
|------|----|-----------------------------------|--|-------|--|
| | | Notes Receivable—W. A. Bunn Co. | | | 6,000 |
| | | Interest Revenue | | | 60 |

The company has earned the interest of $60, even though the note is dishonored. If the account receivable is uncollectible, the company will write off $6,060 against Allowance for Doubtful Accounts.

A company receiving a note should record an adjusting entry for any accrued interest at the end of the period. For example, assume that Crawford Company issues a $4,000, 90-day, 12% note dated December 1, 2016, to settle its account receivable. If the accounting period ends on December 31, the company receiving the note would record the following entries:

| 2016 | | | | | |
|------|----|------|--|-------|--|
| Dec. | 1 | Notes Receivable—Crawford Company | | 4,000 | |
| | | Accounts Receivable—Crawford Company | | | 4,000 |
| | | | | | |
| | 31 | Interest Receivable | | 40 | |
| | | Interest Revenue | | | 40 |
| | | Accrued interest | | | |
| | | ($4,000 × 12% × 30 ÷ 360). | | | |
| | | | | | |
| 2017 | | | | | |
| Mar. | 1 | Cash | | 4,120 | |
| | | Notes Receivable—Crawford Company | | | 4,000 |
| | | Interest Receivable | | | 40 |
| | | Interest Revenue | | | 80 |
| | | Total interest of $120 | | | |
| | | ($4,000 × 12% × 90 ÷ 360). | | | |

The interest revenue account is closed at the end of each accounting period. The amount of interest revenue is normally reported in the Other Income section of the income statement.

## Example Exercise 9-5 Note Receivable

OBJ 6

Same Day Surgery Center received a 120-day, 6% note for $40,000, dated March 14, from a patient on account.

a. Determine the due date of the note.

b. Determine the maturity value of the note.

c. Journalize the entry to record the receipt of the payment of the note at maturity.

(Continued)

a. The due date of the note is July 12, determined as follows:

| | |
|---|---|
| March | 17 days (31 – 14) |
| April | 30 days |
| May | 31 days |
| June | 30 days |
| July | 12 days |
| Total | 120 days |

b. $40,800 [$40,000 + ($40,000 × 6% × 120 ÷ 360)]

c. July 12   Cash ................................................. 40,800
              Notes Receivable............................................ 40,000
              Interest Revenue........................................... 800

Practice Exercises: PE 9-5A, PE 9-5B

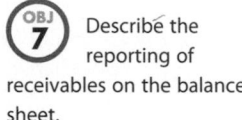

## OBJ 7
Describe the reporting of receivables on the balance sheet.

# Reporting Receivables on the Balance Sheet

All receivables that are expected to be realized in cash within a year are reported in the Current assets section of the balance sheet. Current assets are normally reported in the order of their liquidity, beginning with cash and cash equivalents.

The balance sheet presentation for receivables for **Mornin' Joe** follows:

| Mornin' Joe | | |
|---|---|---|
| Balance Sheet | | |
| December 31, 2016 | | |
| **Assets** | | |
| Current assets: | | |
| Cash and cash equivalents .................................. | | $235,000 |
| Trading investments (at cost).............................. | $420,000 | |
| Plus valuation allowance for trading investments ......... | 45,000 | 465,000 |
| Accounts receivable ....................................... | $305,000 | |
| Less allowance for doubtful accounts.................... | 12,300 | 292,700 |

In Mornin' Joe's financial statements, the allowance for doubtful accounts is subtracted from accounts receivable. Some companies report receivables at their net realizable value with a note showing the amount of the allowance.

Other disclosures related to receivables are reported either on the face of the financial statements or in the financial statement notes. Such disclosures include the market (fair) value of the receivables. In addition, if unusual credit risks exist within the receivables, the nature of the risks are disclosed. For example, if the majority of the receivables are due from one customer or are due from customers located in one area of the country or one industry, these facts are disclosed.[4]

## OBJ 8
Describe and illustrate the use of accounts receivable turnover and number of days' sales in receivables to evaluate a company's efficiency in collecting its receivables.

**FAI**

# Financial Analysis and Interpretation: Accounts Receivable Turnover and Number of Days' Sales in Receivables

Two financial measures that are especially useful in evaluating efficiency in collecting receivables are the following:

- the accounts receivable turnover
- the number of days' sales in receivables

[4] FASB Accounting Standards Codification, Section 210-10-50.

The **accounts receivable turnover** measures how frequently during the year the accounts receivable are being converted to cash. For example, with credit terms of n/30, the accounts receivable should turn over about 12 times per year.

The accounts receivable turnover is computed as follows:[5]

$$\text{Accounts Receivable Turnover} = \frac{\text{Sales}}{\text{Average Accounts Receivable}}$$

The average accounts receivable can be determined by using monthly data or by simply adding the beginning and ending accounts receivable balances and dividing by two. For example, using the following financial data (in millions) for FedEx, the Year 2 and Year 1 accounts receivable turnover is 8.2 in Year 2 and 8.0 in Year 1, computed as follows:

| | Year 2 | Year 1 |
|---|---|---|
| Sales | $42,680 | $39,304 |
| Accounts receivable: | | |
| Beginning of year | 5,191 | 4,692 |
| End of year | 5,237 | 5,191 |
| Average accounts receivable:* | | |
| ($5,191 + $5,237) ÷ 2 | 5,214.0 | |
| ($4,692 + $5,191) ÷ 2 | | 4,941.5 |
| Accounts receivable turnover:* | | |
| $42,680 ÷ $5,214 | 8.2 | |
| $39,304 ÷ $4,941.5 | | 8.0 |

* Rounded to one decimal place.

The **number of days' sales in receivables** is an estimate of the length of time the accounts receivable have been outstanding. With credit terms of n/30, the number of days' sales in receivables should be about 30 days. It is computed as follows:

$$\text{Number of Days' Sales in Receivables} = \frac{\text{Average Accounts Receivable}}{\text{Average Daily Sales}}$$

Average daily sales are determined by dividing sales by 365 days.[6] For example, using the preceding data for FedEx, the number of days' sales in receivables is 44.6 and 45.9 for Year 2 and Year 1, computed as follows:

| | Year 2 | Year 1 |
|---|---|---|
| Average daily sales:* | | |
| $42,680 ÷ 365 | 116.9 | |
| $39,304 ÷ 365 | | 107.7 |
| Number of days' sales in receivables:* | | |
| $5,214.0 ÷ 116.9 | 44.6 | |
| $4,941.5 ÷ 107.7 | | 45.9 |

* Rounded to one decimal place.

The number of days' sales in receivables confirms that FedEx's efficiency in collecting accounts receivable increased from Year 1 to Year 2. Generally, the efficiency in collecting accounts receivable has improved when the accounts receivable turnover increases or the number of days' sales in receivables decreases.

**Example Exercise 9-6 Accounts Receivable Turnover and Number of Days' Sales in Receivables**

OBJ 8

Financial statement data for years ending December 31 for Osterman Company follows:

| | 2016 | 2015 |
|---|---|---|
| Sales | $4,284,000 | $3,040,000 |
| Accounts receivable: | | |
| Beginning of year | 550,000 | 400,000 |
| End of year | 640,000 | 550,000 |

(Continued)

[5] If known, credit sales can be used in the numerator. However, because credit sales are not normally disclosed to external users, most analysts use sales in the numerator.
[6] We use 365 days for all computations involving real world companies and data. We do this to highlight differences among companies and because computations using real world data normally require rounding.

## Follow My Example 9-6

a.  Determine the accounts receivable turnover for 2016 and 2015.

b.  Determine the number of days' sales in receivables for 2016 and 2015. Use 365 days and round to one decimal place.

c.  Does the change in accounts receivable turnover and the number of days' sales in receivable from 2015 to 2016 indicate a favorable or an unfavorable trend?

a.  Accounts receivable turnover:

|  | 2016 | 2015 |
|---|---|---|
| Average accounts receivable: | | |
| ($550,000 + $640,000) ÷ 2 .................... | $595,000 | |
| ($400,000 + $550,000) ÷ 2 .................... | | $475,000 |
| Accounts receivable turnover: | | |
| $4,284,000 ÷ $595,000........................ | 7.2 | |
| $3,040,000 ÷ $475,000........................ | | 6.4 |

b.  Number of days' sales in receivables:

|  | 2016 | 2015 |
|---|---|---|
| Average daily sales: | | |
| $4,284,000 ÷ 365 days ........................ | $11,737.0 | |
| $3,040,000 ÷ 365 days ........................ | | $8,328.8 |
| Number of days' sales in receivables: | | |
| $595,000 ÷ $11,737.0........................ | 50.7 days | |
| $475,000 ÷ $8,328.8 ........................ | | 57.0 days |

c.  The increase in the accounts receivable turnover from 6.4 to 7.2 and the decrease in the number of days' sales in receivables from 57.0 days to 50.7 days indicate favorable trends in the efficiency of collecting accounts receivable.

Practice Exercises: PE 9-6A, PE 9-6B

# Business  Connection

### DELTA AIR LINES

**Delta Air Lines** is a major air carrier that services cities throughout the United States and the world. In its operations, Delta generates accounts receivable as reported in the following note to its financial statements:

*Our accounts receivable are generated largely from the sale of passenger airline tickets and cargo transportation services. The majority of these sales are processed through major credit card companies, resulting in accounts receivable. . . .*

*We also have receivables from the sale of mileage credits under our SkyMiles Program to participating airlines and non-airline businesses such as credit card companies, hotels, and car rental agencies. The credit risk associated with our receivables is minimal.*

In a recent, balance sheet, Delta reported the following accounts receivable (in millions):

|  | Dec. 31, Year 2 | Dec. 31, Year 1 |
|---|---|---|
| Current Assets: | | |
| ⋮ | | |
| Accounts receivable, net of an allowance for uncollectible accounts of $36 at December 31 (Year 2) and $33 at December 31 (Year 1) | $1,693 | $1,563 |

Source: Delta Air Lines, Inc., *Form 10-K For the Fiscal Year Ended December 31, 2012.*

# At a Glance 9

**OBJ 1**

### Describe the common classes of receivables.

**Key Points** *Receivables* includes all money claims against other entities. Receivables are normally classified as accounts receivable, notes receivable, or other receivables.

| Learning Outcomes | Example Exercises | Practice Exercises |
|---|---|---|
| • Define the term *receivables*. | | |
| • List some common classifications of receivables. | | |

**OBJ 2**

### Describe the accounting for uncollectible receivables.

**Key Points** The operating expense recorded from uncollectible receivables is called *bad debt expense*. The two methods of accounting for uncollectible receivables are the direct write-off method and the allowance method.

| Learning Outcomes | Example Exercises | Practice Exercises |
|---|---|---|
| • Describe how a company may shift the risk of uncollectible receivables to other companies. | | |
| • List factors that indicate an account receivable is uncollectible. | | |
| • Describe two methods of accounting for uncollectible accounts receivable. | | |

**OBJ 3**

### Describe the direct write-off method of accounting for uncollectible receivables.

**Key Points** Under the direct write-off method, the entry to write off an account debits Bad Debt Expense and credits Accounts Receivable. Neither an allowance account nor an adjusting entry is needed at the end of the period.

| Learning Outcomes | Example Exercises | Practice Exercises |
|---|---|---|
| • Prepare journal entries to write off an account, using the direct write-off method. | EE9-1 | PE9-1A, 9-1B |
| • Prepare journal entries for the reinstatement and collection of an account previously written off. | EE9-1 | PE9-1A, 9-1B |

**Describe the allowance method of accounting for uncollectible receivables.**

**Key Points** Under the allowance method, an adjusting entry is made for uncollectible accounts. When an account is determined to be uncollectible, it is written off against the allowance account. The allowance account is a contra asset account that normally has a credit balance after the adjusting entry has been posted.

The estimate of uncollectibles may be based on a percent of sales or an analysis of receivables. Exhibit 3 compares and contrasts these two methods.

| Learning Outcomes | Example Exercises | Practice Exercises |
|---|---|---|
| • Prepare journal entries to write off an account, using the allowance method. | EE9-2 | PE9-2A, 9-2B |
| • Prepare journal entries for the reinstatement and collection of an account previously written off. | EE9-2 | PE9-2A, 9-2B |
| • Determine the adjustment, bad debt expense, and net realizable value of accounts receivable, using the percent of sales method. | EE9-3 | PE9-3A, 9-3B |
| • Determine the adjustment, bad debt expense, and net realizable value of accounts receivable, using the analysis of receivables method. | EE9-4 | PE9-4A, 9-4B |

**Compare the direct write-off and allowance methods of accounting for uncollectible accounts.**

**Key Points** Exhibit 4 illustrates the differences between the direct write-off and allowance methods of accounting for uncollectible accounts.

| Learning Outcomes | Example Exercises | Practice Exercises |
|---|---|---|
| • Describe the differences in accounting for uncollectible accounts under the direct write-off and allowance methods. | | |
| • Record journal entries, using the direct write-off and allowance methods. | | |

**Describe the accounting for notes receivable.**

**Key Points** A note received to settle an account receivable is recorded as a debit to Notes Receivable and a credit to Accounts Receivable. When a note is paid at maturity, Cash is debited, Notes Receivable is credited, and Interest Revenue is credited. If the maker of a note fails to pay, the dishonored note is recorded by debiting an account receivable for the amount due from the maker of the note.

| Learning Outcomes | Example Exercises | Practice Exercises |
|---|---|---|
| • Describe the characteristics of a note receivable. | | |
| • Determine the due date and maturity value of a note receivable. | EE9-5 | PE9-5A, 9-5B |
| • Prepare journal entries for the receipt of the payment of a note receivable. | EE9-5 | PE9-5A, 9-5B |
| • Prepare a journal entry for the dishonored note receivable. | | |

**Describe the reporting of receivables on the balance sheet.**

**Key Points**    All receivables that are expected to be realized in cash within a year are reported in the Current Assets section of the balance sheet. In addition to the allowance for doubtful accounts, additional receivable disclosures include the market (fair) value and unusual credit risks.

| Learning Outcomes | Example Exercises | Practice Exercises |
|---|---|---|
| • Describe how receivables are reported in the Current Assets section of the balance sheet. | | |
| • Describe the disclosures related to receivables that should be reported in the financial statements. | | |

**Describe and illustrate the use of accounts receivable turnover and number of days' sales in receivables to evaluate a company's efficiency in collecting its receivables.**

**Key Points**    Two financial measures that are especially useful in evaluating efficiency in collecting receivables are (1) the accounts receivable turnover and (2) the number of days' sales in receivables. Generally, the efficiency in collecting accounts receivable has improved when the accounts receivable turnover increases or there is a decrease in the number of days' sales in receivables.

| Learning Outcomes | Example Exercises | Practice Exercises |
|---|---|---|
| • Describe two measures of the efficiency of managing receivables. | | |
| • Compute and interpret the accounts receivable turnover and the number of days' sales in receivables. | EE9-6 | PE9-6A, 9-6B |

# Key Terms

accounts receivable (416)
accounts receivable turnover (431)
aging the receivables (423)
Allowance for Doubtful Accounts (419)

allowance method (417)
bad debt expense (417)
direct write-off method (417)
dishonored note receivable (429)
maturity value (428)

net realizable value (419)
notes receivable (416)
number of days' sales in receivables (431)
receivables (416)

## Illustrative Problem

Ditzler Company, a construction supply company, uses the allowance method of accounting for uncollectible accounts receivable. Selected transactions completed by Ditzler Company are as follows:

Feb.  1.  Sold merchandise on account to Ames Co., $8,000. The cost of the merchandise sold was $4,500.

Mar. 15.  Accepted a 60-day, 12% note for $8,000 from Ames Co. on account.

Apr.  9.  Wrote off a $2,500 account from Dorset Co. as uncollectible.

    21.  Loaned $7,500 cash to Jill Klein, receiving a 90-day, 14% note.

May 14.  Received the interest due from Ames Co. and a new 90-day, 14% note as a renewal of the loan. (Record both the debit and the credit to the notes receivable account.)

June 13.  Reinstated the account of Dorset Co., written off on April 9, and received $2,500 in full payment.

July  20.  Jill Klein dishonored her note.

Aug. 12.  Received from Ames Co. the amount due on its note of May 14.

    19.  Received from Jill Klein the amount owed on the dishonored note, plus interest for 30 days at 15%, computed on the maturity value of the note.

Dec. 16.  Accepted a 60-day, 12% note for $12,000 from Global Company on account.

    31.  It is estimated that 3% of the credit sales of $1,375,000 for the year ended December 31 will be uncollectible.

### Instructions

1. Journalize the transactions.

2. Journalize the adjusting entry to record the accrued interest on December 31 on the Global Company note.

## Solution

1.

| | | | | |
|---|---|---|---|---|
| Feb. | 1 | Accounts Receivable—Ames Co. | 8,000.00 | |
| | |    Sales | | 8,000.00 |
| | 1 | Cost of Merchandise Sold | 4,500.00 | |
| | |    Merchandise Inventory | | 4,500.00 |
| Mar. | 15 | Notes Receivable—Ames Co. | 8,000.00 | |
| | |    Accounts Receivable—Ames Co. | | 8,000.00 |
| Apr. | 9 | Allowance for Doubtful Accounts | 2,500.00 | |
| | |    Accounts Receivable—Dorset Co. | | 2,500.00 |
| | 21 | Notes Receivable—Jill Klein | 7,500.00 | |
| | |    Cash | | 7,500.00 |
| May | 14 | Notes Receivable—Ames Co. | 8,000.00 | |
| | | Cash | 160.00 | |
| | |    Notes Receivable—Ames Co. | | 8,000.00 |
| | |    Interest Revenue | | 160.00 |
| June | 13 | Accounts Receivable—Dorset Co. | 2,500.00 | |
| | |    Allowance for Doubtful Accounts | | 2,500.00 |
| | 13 | Cash | 2,500.00 | |
| | |    Accounts Receivable—Dorset Co. | | 2,500.00 |
| July | 20 | Accounts Receivable—Jill Klein | 7,762.50 | |
| | |    Notes Receivable—Jill Klein | | 7,500.00 |
| | |    Interest Revenue | | 262.50 |
| Aug. | 12 | Cash | 8,280.00 | |
| | |    Notes Receivable—Ames Co. | | 8,000.00 |
| | |    Interest Revenue | | 280.00 |
| | 19 | Cash | 7,859.53 | |
| | |    Accounts Receivable—Jill Klein | | 7,762.50 |
| | |    Interest Revenue | | 97.03 |
| | |      ($7,762.50 × 15% × 30 ÷ 360). | | |
| Dec. | 16 | Notes Receivable—Global Company | 12,000.00 | |
| | |    Accounts Receivable—Global Company | | 12,000.00 |
| | 31 | Bad Debt Expense | 41,250.00 | |
| | |    Allowance for Doubtful Accounts | | 41,250.00 |
| | |      Uncollectible accounts estimate | | |
| | |      ($1,375,000 × 3%). | | |

2.

| | | | | |
|---|---|---|---|---|
| Dec. | 31 | Interest Receivable | 60.00 | |
| | |    Interest Revenue | | 60.00 |
| | |      Accrued interest | | |
| | |      ($12,000 × 12% × 15 ÷ 360). | | |

## Discussion Questions

1. What are the three classifications of receivables?

2. Dan's Hardware is a small hardware store in the rural township of Twin Bridges. It rarely extends credit to its customers in the form of an account receivable. The few customers who are allowed to carry accounts receivable are long-time residents of Twin Bridges with a history of doing business at Dan's Hardware. What method of accounting for uncollectible receivables should Dan's Hardware use? Why?

3. What kind of an account (asset, liability, etc.) is Allowance for Doubtful Accounts, and is its normal balance a debit or a credit?

4. After the accounts are adjusted and closed at the end of the fiscal year, Accounts Receivable has a balance of $673,400, and Allowance for Doubtful Accounts has a balance of $11,900. Describe how the accounts receivable and the allowance for doubtful accounts are reported on the balance sheet.

5. A firm has consistently adjusted its allowance account at the end of the fiscal year by adding a fixed percent of the period's sales on account. After seven years, the balance in Allowance for Doubtful Accounts has become very large in relationship to the balance in Accounts Receivable. Give two possible explanations.

6. Which of the two methods of estimating uncollectibles provides for the most accurate estimate of the current net realizable value of the receivables?

7. Neptune Company issued a note receivable to Sailfish Company. (a) Who is the payee? (b) What is the title of the account used by Sailfish Company in recording the note?

8. If a note provides for payment of principal of $85,000 and interest at the rate of 6%, will the interest amount to $5,100? Explain.

9. The maker of a $240,000, 6%, 90-day note receivable failed to pay the note on the due date of November 30. What accounts should be debited and credited by the payee to record the dishonored note receivable?

10. The note receivable dishonored in Discussion Question 9 is paid on December 30 by the maker, plus interest for 30 days at 9%. What entry should be made to record the receipt of the payment?

## Practice Exercises

EE 9-1  p. 418  **PE 9-1A** **Direct write-off method**                OBJ. 3

Journalize the following transactions, using the direct write-off method of accounting for uncollectible receivables:

June  2. Received $1,200 from Melissa Crone and wrote off the remainder owed of $4,000 as uncollectible.

Oct.  9. Reinstated the account of Melissa Crone and received $4,000 cash in full payment.

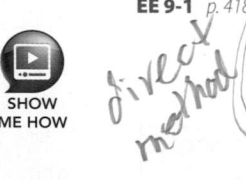

EE 9-1  p. 418  **PE 9-1B** **Direct write-off method** *on phone*           OBJ. 3

Journalize the following transactions, using the direct write-off method of accounting for uncollectible receivables:

Oct.  2. Received $600 from Rachel Elpel and wrote off the remainder owed of $1,350 as uncollectible.

Dec. 20. Reinstated the account of Rachel Elpel and received $1,350 cash in full payment.

SHOW
ME HOW

**EE 9-2** *p. 421*   **PE 9-2A   Allowance method**   **OBJ. 4**

Journalize the following transactions, using the allowance method of accounting for uncollectible receivables:

June   2.  Received $1,200 from Melissa Crone and wrote off the remainder owed of $4,000 as uncollectible.

Oct.   9.  Reinstated the account of Melissa Crone and received $4,000 cash in full payment.

SHOW
ME HOW

**EE 9-2** *p. 421*   **PE 9-2B   Allowance method**   ~~on phone~~   **OBJ. 4**

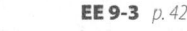
*indirect method*

Journalize the following transactions, using the allowance method of accounting for uncollectible receivables:

Oct.   2.  Received $600 from Rachel Elpel and wrote off the remainder owed of $1,350 as uncollectible.

Dec. 20.  Reinstated the account of Rachel Elpel and received $1,350 cash in full payment.

SHOW
ME HOW

**EE 9-3** *p. 422*   **PE 9-3A   Percent of sales method**   **OBJ. 4**

At the end of the current year, Accounts Receivable has a balance of $1,975,000; Allowance for Doubtful Accounts has a credit balance of $19,670; and sales for the year total $28,550,000. Bad debt expense is estimated at ¾ of 1% of sales.

Determine (a) the amount of the adjusting entry for uncollectible accounts; (b) the adjusted balances of Accounts Receivable, Allowance for Doubtful Accounts, and Bad Debt Expense; and (c) the net realizable value of accounts receivable.

SHOW
ME HOW

**EE 9-3** *p. 422*   **PE 9-3B   Percent of sales method**   **OBJ. 4**

At the end of the current year, Accounts Receivable has a balance of $3,460,000; Allowance for Doubtful Accounts has a debit balance of $12,500; and sales for the year total $46,300,000. Bad debt expense is estimated at ½ of 1% of sales.

Determine (a) the amount of the adjusting entry for uncollectible accounts; (b) the adjusted balances of Accounts Receivable, Allowance for Doubtful Accounts, and Bad Debt Expense; and (c) the net realizable value of accounts receivable.

SHOW
ME HOW

**EE 9-4** *p. 425*   **PE 9-4A   Analysis of receivables method**   **OBJ. 4**

At the end of the current year, Accounts Receivable has a balance of $1,975,000; Allowance for Doubtful Accounts has a credit balance of $19,670; and sales for the year total $28,550,000. Using the aging method, the balance of Allowance for Doubtful Accounts is estimated as $225,000.

Determine (a) the amount of the adjusting entry for uncollectible accounts; (b) the adjusted balances of Accounts Receivable, Allowance for Doubtful Accounts, and Bad Debt Expense; and (c) the net realizable value of accounts receivable.

SHOW
ME HOW

**EE 9-4** *p. 425*   **PE 9-4B   Analysis of receivables method**   **OBJ. 4**

At the end of the current year, Accounts Receivable has a balance of $3,460,000; Allowance for Doubtful Accounts has a debit balance of $12,500; and sales for the year total $46,300,000. Using the aging method, the balance of Allowance for Doubtful Accounts is estimated as $245,000.

Determine (a) the amount of the adjusting entry for uncollectible accounts; (b) the adjusted balances of Accounts Receivable, Allowance for Doubtful Accounts, and Bad Debt Expense; and (c) the net realizable value of accounts receivable.

SHOW
ME HOW

**EE 9-5** *p. 429*   **PE 9-5A   Note receivable**   **OBJ. 6**

Guzman Company received a 60-day, 5% note for $54,000 dated July 12 from a customer on account.

a.  Determine the due date of the note.

b.  Determine the maturity value of the note.

c.  Journalize the entry to record the receipt of the payment of the note at maturity.

SHOW
ME HOW

EE 9-5 *p.429*

SHOW
ME HOW

**PE 9-5B** **Note receivable** OBJ. 6

Prefix Supply Company received a 120-day, 8% note for $450,000, dated April 9 from a customer on account.

a. Determine the due date of the note.

b. Determine the maturity value of the note.

c. Journalize the entry to record the receipt of the payment of the note at maturity.

---

EE 9-6 *p.431*

SHOW
ME HOW

**PE 9-6A** **Accounts receivable turnover and number of days' sales in receivables** OBJ. 8

Financial statement data for years ending December 31 for Chiro-Solutions Company follows:

| | 2016 | 2015 |
|---|---|---|
| Sales | $2,912,000 | $2,958,000 |
| Accounts receivable: | | |
| Beginning of year | 300,000 | 280,000 |
| End of year | 340,000 | 300,000 |

a. Determine the accounts receivable turnover for 2016 and 2015.

b. Determine the number of days' sales in receivables for 2016 and 2015. Use 365 days and round to one decimal place.

c. Does the change in accounts receivable turnover and the number of days' sales in receivables from 2015 to 2016 indicate a favorable or an unfavorable trend?

---

EE 9-6 *p.431*

SHOW
ME HOW

**PE 9-6B** **Accounts receivable turnover and number of days' sales in receivables** OBJ. 8

Financial statement data for years ending December 31 for Robinhood Company follows:

| | 2016 | 2015 |
|---|---|---|
| Sales | $7,906,000 | $6,726,000 |
| Accounts receivable: | | |
| Beginning of year | 600,000 | 540,000 |
| End of year | 580,000 | 600,000 |

a. Determine the accounts receivable turnover for 2016 and 2015.

b. Determine the number of days' sales in receivables for 2016 and 2015. Use 365 days and round to one decimal place.

c. Does the change in accounts receivable turnover and the number of days' sales in receivables from 2015 to 2016 indicate a favorable or an unfavorable trend?

---

# Exercises

---

**EX 9-1** **Classifications of receivables** OBJ. 1

Boeing is one of the world's major aerospace firms with operations involving commercial aircraft, military aircraft, missiles, satellite systems, and information and battle management systems. As of a recent year, Boeing had $2,788 million of receivables involving U.S. government contracts and $903 million of receivables involving commercial aircraft customers, such as Delta Air Lines and United Airlines.

Should Boeing report these receivables separately in the financial statements or combine them into one overall accounts receivable amount? Explain.

✔ a. 17.1%

### EX 9-2 Nature of uncollectible accounts

OBJ. 2

**MGM Resorts International** owns and operates hotels and casinos including the MGM Grand and the Bellagio in Las Vegas, Nevada. As of a recent year, MGM reported accounts receivable of $592,937,000 and allowance for doubtful accounts of $101,207,000 **Johnson & Johnson** manufactures and sells a wide range of healthcare products including Band-Aids and Tylenol. As of a recent year, Johnson & Johnson reported accounts receivable of $11,775,000,000 and allowance for doubtful accounts of $466,000,000.

a. Compute the percentage of the allowance for doubtful accounts to the accounts receivable for MGM Resorts International. Round to one decimal place.

b. Compute the percentage of the allowance for doubtful accounts to the accounts receivable for Johnson & Johnson. Round to one decimal place.

c. ▬▬▶ Discuss possible reasons for the difference in the two ratios computed in (a) and (b).

### EX 9-3 Entries for uncollectible accounts, using direct write-off method

OBJ. 3

Journalize the following transactions in the accounts of Midwest Medical Co., a medical equipment company that uses the direct write-off method of accounting for uncollectible receivables:

Feb. 3. Sold merchandise on account to Dr. Jill Hall, $17,340. The cost of the merchandise sold was $9,500.

Sept.10. Received $5,000 from Dr. Jill Hall and wrote off the remainder owed on the sale of February 3 as uncollectible.

Dec. 21. Reinstated the account of Dr. Jill Hall that had been written off on September 10 and received $12,340 cash in full payment.

### EX 9-4 Entries for uncollectible receivables, using allowance method

OBJ. 4

Journalize the following transactions in the accounts of Dining Interiors Company, a restaurant supply company that uses the allowance method of accounting for uncollectible receivables:

Apr. 2. Sold merchandise on account to Peking Palace Co., $41,900. The cost of the merchandise sold was $24,850.

June 9. Received $10,000 from Peking Palace Co. and wrote off the remainder owed on the sale of April 2 as uncollectible.

Oct. 31. Reinstated the account of Peking Palace Co. that had been written off on June 9 and received $31,900 cash in full payment.

### EX 9-5 Entries to write off accounts receivable

OBJ. 3, 4

Creative Solutions Company, a computer consulting firm, has decided to write off the $11,750 balance of an account owed by a customer, Wil Treadwell. Journalize the entry to record the write-off, assuming that (a) the direct write-off method is used and (b) the allowance method is used.

### EX 9-6 Providing for doubtful accounts

OBJ. 4

✔ a. $115,125

✔ b. $148,000

At the end of the current year, the accounts receivable account has a debit balance of $1,400,000 and sales for the year total $15,350,000. Determine the amount of the adjusting entry to provide for doubtful accounts under each of the following assumptions:

a. The allowance account before adjustment has a debit balance of $23,000. Bad debt expense is estimated at ¾ of 1% of sales.

b. The allowance account before adjustment has a debit balance of $23,000. An aging of the accounts in the customer ledger indicates estimated doubtful accounts of $125,000.

c. The allowance account before adjustment has a credit balance of $14,500. Bad debt expense is estimated at ½ of 1% of sales.

d. The allowance account before adjustment has a credit balance of $14,500. An aging of the accounts in the customer ledger indicates estimated doubtful accounts of $180,000.

✔ Avalanche Auto,
84 days

### EX 9-7   Number of days past due                                          OBJ. 4

Toot Auto Supply distributes new and used automobile parts to local dealers throughout the Midwest. Toot's credit terms are n/30. As of the end of business on October 31, the following accounts receivable were past due:

| Account | Due Date | Amount |
|---|---|---|
| Avalanche Auto | August 8 | $12,000 |
| Bales Auto | October 11 | 2,400 |
| Derby Auto Repair | June 23 | 3,900 |
| Lucky's Auto Repair | September 2 | 6,600 |
| Pit Stop Auto | September 19 | 1,100 |
| Reliable Auto Repair | July 15 | 9,750 |
| Trident Auto | August 24 | 1,800 |
| Valley Repair & Tow | May 17 | 4,000 |

Determine the number of days each account is past due as of October 31.

### EX 9-8   Aging of receivables schedule                                     OBJ. 4

SHOW
ME HOW

The accounts receivable clerk for Waddell Industries prepared the following partially completed aging of receivables schedule as of the end of business on August 31:

|  | A | B | C | D | E | F | G |
|---|---|---|---|---|---|---|---|
| 1 |  |  | Not |  | Days Past Due |  |  |
| 2 |  |  | Past |  |  |  | Over |
| 3 | Customer | Balance | Due | 1–30 | 31–60 | 61–90 | 90 |
| 4 | Acme Industries Inc. | 3,000 | 3,000 |  |  |  |  |
| 5 | Alliance Company | 4,500 |  | 4,500 |  |  |  |
| 21 | Zollinger Company | 5,000 |  |  | 5,000 |  |  |
| 22 | Subtotals | 1,050,000 | 600,000 | 220,000 | 115,000 | 85,000 | 30,000 |

The following accounts were unintentionally omitted from the aging schedule and not included in the preceding subtotals:

| Customer | Balance | Due Date |
|---|---|---|
| Builders Industries | $44,500 | May 1 |
| Elkhorn Company | 21,000 | June 20 |
| Granite Creek Inc. | 7,500 | July 13 |
| Lockwood Company | 14,000 | September 9 |
| Teton Company | 13,000 | August 7 |

a. Determine the number of days past due for each of the preceding accounts as of August 31.

b. Complete the aging of receivables schedule by adding the omitted accounts to the bottom of the schedule and updating the totals.

### EX 9-9   Estimating allowance for doubtful accounts                        OBJ. 4

✔ Allowance for
doubtful accounts,
$142,815

Waddell Industries has a past history of uncollectible accounts, as follows. Estimate the allowance for doubtful accounts, based on the aging of receivables schedule you completed in Exercise 9-8.

SHOW
ME HOW

| Age Class | Percent Uncollectible |
|---|---|
| Not past due | 3% |
| 1–30 days past due | 4 |
| 31–60 days past due | 15 |
| 61–90 days past due | 35 |
| Over 90 days past due | 80 |

SHOW
ME HOW

### EX 9-10 Adjustment for uncollectible accounts

OBJ. 4

Using data in Exercise 9-9, assume that the allowance for doubtful accounts for Waddell Industries has a credit balance of $6,350 before adjustment on August 31. Journalize the adjusting entry for uncollectible accounts as of August 31.

SHOW
ME HOW

### EX 9-11 Estimating doubtful accounts

OBJ. 4

Selby's Bike Co. is a wholesaler of motorcycle supplies. An aging of the company's accounts receivable on December 31, 2016, and a historical analysis of the percentage of uncollectible accounts in each age category are as follows:

| Age Interval | Balance | Percent Uncollectible |
|---|---|---|
| Not past due | $1,250,000 | ¾% |
| 1–30 days past due | 500,000 | 3 |
| 31–60 days past due | 190,000 | 5 |
| 61–90 days past due | 60,000 | 15 |
| 91–180 days past due | 36,000 | 40 |
| Over 180 days past due | 24,000 | 80 |
| | $2,060,000 | |

Estimate what the proper balance of the allowance for doubtful accounts should be as of December 31, 2016.

SHOW
ME HOW

### EX 9-12 Entry for uncollectible accounts

OBJ. 4

Using the data in Exercise 9-11, assume that the allowance for doubtful accounts for Selby's Bike Co. had a debit balance of $7,200 as of December 31, 2016.

Journalize the adjusting entry for uncollectible accounts as of December 31, 2016.

### EX 9-13 Entries for bad debt expense under the direct write-off and allowance methods

OBJ. 5

✔ c. $8,225 higher

SHOW
ME HOW

The following selected transactions were taken from the records of Shipway Company for the first year of its operations ending December 31, 2016:

Apr. 13. Wrote off account of Dean Sheppard, $8,450.

May 15. Received $500 as partial payment on the $7,100 account of Dan Pyle. Wrote off the remaining balance as uncollectible.

July 27. Received $8,450 from Dean Sheppard, whose account had been written off on April 13. Reinstated the account and recorded the cash receipt.

Dec. 31. Wrote off the following accounts as uncollectible (record as one journal entry):

| | |
|---|---|
| Paul Chapman | $2,225 |
| Duane DeRosa | 3,550 |
| Teresa Galloway | 4,770 |
| Ernie Klatt | 1,275 |
| Marty Richey | 1,690 |

31. If necessary, record the year-end adjusting entry for uncollectible accounts.

a. Journalize the transactions for 2016 under the direct write-off method.

b. Journalize the transactions for 2016 under the allowance method. Shipway Company uses the percent of credit sales method of estimating uncollectible accounts expense. Based on past history and industry averages, ¾% of credit sales are expected to be uncollectible. Shipway Company recorded $3,778,000 of credit sales during 2016.

c. ➤ How much higher (lower) would Shipway Company's net income have been under the direct write-off method than under the allowance method?

**EX 9-14**   **Entries for bad debt expense under the direct write-off and allowance methods**                                                                       **OBJ. 5**

SHOW
ME HOW

The following selected transactions were taken from the records of Rustic Tables Company for the year ending December 31, 2016:

June   8. Wrote off account of Kathy Quantel, $8,440.

Aug. 14. Received $3,000 as partial payment on the $12,500 account of Rosalie Oakes. Wrote off the remaining balance as uncollectible.

Oct. 16. Received the $8,440 from Kathy Quantel, whose account had been written off on June 8. Reinstated the account and recorded the cash receipt.

Dec. 31. Wrote off the following accounts as uncollectible (record as one journal entry):

| | |
|---|---:|
| Wade Dolan | $4,600 |
| Greg Gagne | 3,600 |
| Amber Kisko | 7,150 |
| Shannon Poole | 2,975 |
| Niki Spence | 6,630 |

   31. If necessary, record the year-end adjusting entry for uncollectible accounts.

a. Journalize the transactions for 2016 under the direct write-off method.

b. Journalize the transactions for 2016 under the allowance method, assuming that the allowance account had a beginning balance of $36,000 on January 1, 2016, and the company uses the analysis of receivables method. Rustic Tables Company prepared the following aging schedule for its accounts receivable:

| Aging Class (Number of Days Past Due) | Receivables Balance on December 31 | Estimated Percent of Uncollectible Accounts |
|---|---:|:---:|
| 0–30 days | $320,000 | 1% |
| 31–60 days | 110,000 | 3 |
| 61–90 days | 24,000 | 10 |
| 91–120 days | 18,000 | 33 |
| More than 120 days | 43,000 | 75 |
| Total receivables | $515,000 | |

c. ━━━▶ How much higher (lower) would Rustic Tables' 2016 net income have been under the direct write-off method than under the allowance method?

---

**EX 9-15**   **Effect of doubtful accounts on net income**                                        **OBJ. 5**

During its first year of operations, Mack's Plumbing Supply Co. had sales of $3,250,000, wrote off $27,800 of accounts as uncollectible using the direct write-off method, and reported net income of $487,500. Determine what the net income would have been if the allowance method had been used, and the company estimated that 1% of sales would be uncollectible.

---

**EX 9-16**   **Effect of doubtful accounts on net income**                                        **OBJ. 5**

Using the data in Exercise 9-15, assume that during the second year of operations Mack's Plumbing Supply Co. had sales of $4,100,000, wrote off $34,000 of accounts as uncollectible using the direct write-off method, and reported net income of $600,000.

a. Determine what net income would have been in the second year if the allowance method (using 1% of sales) had been used in both the first and second years.

b. Determine what the balance of the allowance for doubtful accounts would have been at the end of the second year if the allowance method had been used in both the first and second years.

**EX 9-17** **Entries for bad debt expense under the direct write-off and allowance** OBJ. 5
methods

✔ c. $9,375 higher

SHOW
ME HOW

Casebolt Company wrote off the following accounts receivable as uncollectible for the first year of its operations ending December 31, 2016:

| Customer | Amount |
|---|---|
| Shawn Brooke | $ 4,650 |
| Eve Denton | 5,180 |
| Art Malloy | 11,050 |
| Cassie Yost | 9,120 |
| Total | $30,000 |

a. Journalize the write-offs for 2016 under the direct write-off method.

b. Journalize the write-offs for 2016 under the allowance method. Also, journalize the adjusting entry for uncollectible accounts. The company recorded $5,250,000 of credit sales during 2016. Based on past history and industry averages, ¾% of credit sales are expected to be uncollectible.

c. How much higher (lower) would Casebolt Company's 2016 net income have been under the direct write-off method than under the allowance method?

**EX 9-18** **Entries for bad debt expense under the direct write-off and allowance** OBJ. 5
methods

Seaforth International wrote off the following accounts receivable as uncollectible for the year ending December 31, 2016:

| Customer | Amount |
|---|---|
| Kim Abel | $ 21,550 |
| Lee Drake | 33,925 |
| Jenny Green | 27,565 |
| Mike Lamb | 19,460 |
| Total | $102,500 |

The company prepared the following aging schedule for its accounts receivable on December 31, 2016:

| Aging Class (Number of Days Past Due) | Receivables Balance on December 31 | Estimated Percent of Uncollectible Accounts |
|---|---|---|
| 0–30 days | $ 715,000 | 1% |
| 31–60 days | 310,000 | 2 |
| 61–90 days | 102,000 | 15 |
| 91–120 days | 76,000 | 30 |
| More than 120 days | 97,000 | 60 |
| Total receivables | $1,300,000 | |

a. Journalize the write-offs for 2016 under the direct write-off method.

b. Journalize the write-offs and the year-end adjusting entry for 2016 under the allowance method, assuming that the allowance account had a beginning balance of $95,000 on January 1, 2016, and the company uses the analysis of receivables method.

c. How much higher (lower) would Seaforth International's 2016 net income have been under the allowance method than under the direct write-off method?

SHOW
ME HOW

### EX 9-19    Determine due date and interest on notes                                    OBJ. 6

Determine the due date and the amount of interest due at maturity on the following notes dated in 2016:

|     | Date of Note | Face Amount | Interest Rate | Term of Note |
|-----|--------------|-------------|---------------|--------------|
| a.  | January 3*   | $80,000     | 6%            | 120 days     |
| b.  | February 20* | 27,000      | 4             | 30 days      |
| c.  | May 24       | 62,500      | 8             | 45 days      |
| d.  | August 30    | 30,000      | 5             | 90 days      |
| e.  | October 4    | 40,000      | 7             | 90 days      |

* February 2016 has 29 days.

SHOW
ME HOW

### EX 9-20    Entries for notes receivable                                                 OBJ. 6

Master Designs Decorators issued a 180-day, 6% note for $75,000, dated May 14, 2016, to Morgan Furniture Company on account.

a.  Determine the due date of the note.

b.  Determine the maturity value of the note.

c.  Journalize the entries to record the following: (1) receipt of the note by Morgan Furniture and (2) receipt of payment of the note at maturity.

### EX 9-21    Entries for notes receivable                                                 OBJ. 6

The series of seven transactions recorded in the following T accounts were related to a sale to a customer on account and the receipt of the amount owed. Briefly describe each transaction.

| | CASH | | | | NOTES RECEIVABLE | | |
|---|---|---|---|---|---|---|---|
| (7) | 61,509 | | | (5) | 60,000 | (6) | 60,000 |

| | ACCOUNTS RECEIVABLE | | | | SALES RETURNS AND ALLOWANCES | |
|---|---|---|---|---|---|---|
| (1) | 75,000 | (3) | 15,000 | (3) | 15,000 | |
| (6) | 60,600 | (5) | 60,000 | | | |
| | | (7) | 60,600 | | | |

| | MERCHANDISE INVENTORY | | | | COST OF MERCHANDISE SOLD | | |
|---|---|---|---|---|---|---|---|
| (4) | 9,000 | (2) | 45,000 | (2) | 45,000 | (4) | 9,000 |

| | SALES | | | INTEREST REVENUE | |
|---|---|---|---|---|---|
| | | (1) | 75,000 | (6) | 600 |
| | | | | (7) | 909 |

SHOW
ME HOW

### EX 9-22    Entries for notes receivable, including year-end entries                     OBJ. 6

The following selected transactions were completed by Zippy Do Co., a supplier of zippers for clothing:

2015

Dec.  3.  Received from Chicago Clothing & Bags Co., on account, a $36,000, 90-day, 6% note dated December 3.

      31.  Recorded an adjusting entry for accrued interest on the note of December 3.

      31.  Recorded the closing entry for interest revenue.

2016

Mar.  2.  Received payment of note and interest from Chicago Clothing & Bags Co.

Journalize the entries to record the transactions.

**EX 9-23 Entries for receipt and dishonor of note receivable** OBJ. 6

Journalize the following transactions of Trapper Jon's Productions:

June 23 Received a $48,000, 90-day, 8% note dated June 23 from Radon Express Co. on account.

Sept. 21 The note is dishonored by Radon Express Co.

Oct. 21 Received the amount due on the dishonored note plus interest for 30 days at 10% on the total amount charged to Radon Express Co. on September 21.

**EX 9-24 Entries for receipt and dishonor of notes receivable** OBJ. 4, 6

Journalize the following transactions in the accounts of Safari Games Co., which operates a riverboat casino:

Apr. 18. Received a $60,000, 30-day, 7% note dated April 18 from Glenn Cross on account.

30. Received a $42,000, 60-day, 8% note dated April 30 from Rhoni Melville on account.

May 18. The note dated April 18 from Glenn Cross is dishonored, and the customer's account is charged for the note, including interest.

June 29. The note dated April 30 from Rhoni Melville is dishonored, and the customer's account is charged for the note, including interest.

Aug. 16. Cash is received for the amount due on the dishonored note dated April 18 plus interest for 90 days at 8% on the total amount debited to Glenn Cross on May 18.

Oct. 22. Wrote off against the allowance account the amount charged to Rhoni Melville on June 29 for the dishonored note dated April 30.

**EX 9-25 Receivables on the balance sheet** OBJ. 7

List any errors you can find in the following partial balance sheet:

**Napa Vino Company**
**Balance Sheet**
**December 31, 2016**

| Assets | | |
|---|---|---|
| Current assets: | | |
| Cash | | $ 78,500 |
| Notes receivable | $ 300,000 | |
| Less interest receivable | 4,500 | 295,500 |
| Accounts receivable | $1,200,000 | |
| Plus allowance for doubtful accounts | 11,500 | 1,211,500 |

**EX 9-26 Accounts receivable turnover and days' sales in receivables** OBJ. 8

Polo Ralph Lauren Corporation designs, markets, and distributes a variety of apparel, home decor, accessory, and fragrance products. The company's products include such brands as Polo by Ralph Lauren, Ralph Lauren Purple Label, Ralph Lauren, Polo Jeans Co., and Chaps. Polo Ralph Lauren reported the following (in thousands) for two recent years:

| | For the Period Ending | |
|---|---|---|
| | Year 2 | Year 1 |
| Sales | $6,859,500 | $5,660,300 |
| Accounts receivable | 690,000 | 592,700 |

✔ a. Year 2: 10.7

SHOW
ME HOW

FAI

SHOW
ME HOW

*(Continued)*

Assume that accounts receivable (in millions) were $486,200 at the beginning of Year 1.

a. Compute the accounts receivable turnover for Year 2 and Year 1. Round to one decimal place.

b. Compute the days' sales in receivables for Year 2 and Year 1. Use 365 days and round to one decimal place.

c. ━━━━▸What conclusions can be drawn from these analyses regarding Ralph Lauren's efficiency in collecting receivables?

---

**EX 9-27   Accounts receivable turnover and days' sales in receivables**          OBJ. 8

✔ a. Year 2: 10.3

H.J. Heinz Company was founded in 1869 at Sharpsburg, Pennsylvania, by Henry J. Heinz. The company manufactures and markets food products throughout the world, including ketchup, condiments and sauces, frozen food, pet food, soups, and tuna. For two recent years, H.J. Heinz reported the following (in thousands):

|                     | Year 2      | Year 1      |
|---------------------|-------------|-------------|
| Sales               | $11,649,079 | $10,706,588 |
| Accounts receivable | 993,510     | 1,265,032   |

Assume that the accounts receivable (in thousands) were $1,045,338 at the beginning of Year 1.

a. Compute the accounts receivable turnover for Year 2 and Year 1. Round to one decimal place.

b. Compute the days' sales in receivables at the end of Year 2 and Year 1. Use 365 days and round to one decimal place.

c. ━━━━▸What conclusions can be drawn from these analyses regarding Heinz's efficiency in collecting receivables?

---

**EX 9-28   Accounts receivable turnover and days' sales in receivables**          OBJ. 8

The Limited Brands Inc. sells women's clothing and personal health care products through specialty retail stores including Victoria's Secret and Bath & Body Works stores. The Limited Brands reported the following (in millions) for two recent years:

|                     | Year 2   | Year 1  |
|---------------------|----------|---------|
| Sales               | $10,364  | $9,613  |
| Accounts receivable | 269      | 267     |

Assume that accounts receivable (in millions) were $249 at the beginning of Year 1.

a. Compute the accounts receivable turnover for Year 2 and Year 1. Round to one decimal place.

b. Compute the day's sales in receivables for Year 2 and Year 1. Use 365 days and round to one decimal place.

c. What conclusions can be drawn from these analyses regarding The Limited Brands' efficiency in collecting receivables?

---

**EX 9-29   Accounts receivable turnover**          OBJ. 8

Use the data in Exercises 9-27 and 9-28 to analyze the accounts receivable turnover ratios of H.J. Heinz Company and The Limited Brands Inc.

a. Compute the average accounts receivable turnover ratio for The Limited Brands Inc. and H.J. Heinz Company for the years shown in Exercises 9-27 and 9-28.

b. ━━━━▸Does The Limited Brands or H.J. Heinz Company have the higher average accounts receivable turnover ratio?

c. ━━━━▸Explain the logic underlying your answer in (b).

## Problems: Series A

✔ 3. $1,749,300

General Ledger

SHOW
ME HOW

### PR 9-1A  Entries related to uncollectible accounts                    OBJ. 4

The following transactions were completed by The Irvine Company during the current fiscal year ended December 31:

Feb.   8. Received 40% of the $18,000 balance owed by DeCoy Co., a bankrupt business, and wrote off the remainder as uncollectible.

May 27. Reinstated the account of Seth Nelsen, which had been written off in the preceding year as uncollectible. Journalized the receipt of $7,350 cash in full payment of Seth's account.

Aug. 13. Wrote off the $6,400 balance owed by Kat Tracks Co., which has no assets.

Oct. 31. Reinstated the account of Crawford Co., which had been written off in the preceding year as uncollectible. Journalized the receipt of $3,880 cash in full payment of the account.

Dec. 31. Wrote off the following accounts as uncollectible (compound entry): Newbauer Co., $7,190; Bonneville Co., $5,500; Crow Distributors, $9,400; Fiber Optics, $1,110.

       31. Based on an analysis of the $1,785,000 of accounts receivable, it was estimated that $35,700 will be uncollectible. Journalized the adjusting entry.

#### Instructions

1. Record the January 1 credit balance of $26,000 in a T account for Allowance for Doubtful Accounts.

2. Journalize the transactions. Post each entry that affects the following selected T accounts and determine the new balances:

Allowance for Doubtful Accounts<br>Bad Debt Expense

3. Determine the expected net realizable value of the accounts receivable as of December 31.

4. Assuming that instead of basing the provision for uncollectible accounts on an analysis of receivables, the adjusting entry on December 31 had been based on an estimated expense of ¼ of 1% of the sales of $18,200,000 for the year, determine the following:

   a.  Bad debt expense for the year.

   b.  Balance in the allowance account after the adjustment of December 31.

   c.  Expected net realizable value of the accounts receivable as of December 31.

### PR 9-2A  Aging of receivables; estimating allowance for doubtful accounts   OBJ. 4

✔ 3. $121,000

Trophy Fish Company supplies flies and fishing gear to sporting goods stores and outfitters throughout the western United States. The accounts receivable clerk for Trophy Fish prepared the following partially completed aging of receivables schedule as of the end of business on December 31, 2015:

|   | A | B | C | D | E | F | G | H |
|---|---|---|---|---|---|---|---|---|
| 1 |   |   | Not |   | Days Past Due |   |   |   |
| 2 |   |   | Past |   |   |   |   |   |
| 3 | **Customer** | **Balance** | **Due** | **1–30** | **31–60** | **61–90** | **91–120** | **Over 120** |
| 4 | ΛΛΛ Outfitters | 20,000 | 20,000 |   |   |   |   |   |
| 5 | Brown Trout Fly Shop | 7,500 |   |   | 7,500 |   |   |   |
|   |   |   |   |   |   |   |   |   |
| 30 | Zigs Fish Adventures | 4,000 |   | 4,000 |   |   |   |   |
| 31 | Subtotals | 1,300,000 | 750,000 | 290,000 | 120,000 | 40,000 | 20,000 | 80,000 |

*(Continued)*

The following accounts were unintentionally omitted from the aging schedule:

| Customer | Due Date | Balance |
|---|---|---|
| Adams Sports & Flies | May   22, 2015 | $5,000 |
| Blue Dun Flies | Oct.   10, 2015 | 4,900 |
| Cicada Fish Co. | Sept.  29, 2015 | 8,400 |
| Deschutes Sports | Oct.   20, 2015 | 7,000 |
| Green River Sports | Nov.   7, 2015 | 3,500 |
| Smith River Co. | Nov.  28, 2015 | 2,400 |
| Western Trout Company | Dec.   7, 2015 | 6,800 |
| Wolfe Sports | Jan.   20, 2016 | 4,400 |

Trophy Fish has a past history of uncollectible accounts by age category, as follows:

| Age Class | Percent Uncollectible |
|---|---|
| Not past due | 1% |
| 1–30 days past due | 2 |
| 31–60 days past due | 10 |
| 61–90 days past due | 30 |
| 91–120 days past due | 40 |
| Over 120 days past due | 80 |

## Instructions

1. Determine the number of days past due for each of the preceding accounts.

2. Complete the aging of receivables schedule by adding the omitted accounts to the bottom of the schedule and updating the totals.

3. Estimate the allowance for doubtful accounts, based on the aging of receivables schedule.

4. Assume that the allowance for doubtful accounts for Trophy Fish Company has a debit balance of $3,600 before adjustment on December 31, 2015. Journalize the adjusting entry for uncollectible accounts.

5. Assume that the adjusting entry in (4) was inadvertently omitted, how would the omission affect the balance sheet and income statement?

---

**PR 9-3A   Compare two methods of accounting for uncollectible receivables**   OBJ. 3, 4, 5

✔ 1. Year 4: Balance of allowance account, end of year, $15,050

Call Systems Company, a telephone service and supply company, has just completed its fourth year of operations. The direct write-off method of recording bad debt expense has been used during the entire period. Because of substantial increases in sales volume and the amount of uncollectible accounts, the company is considering changing to the allowance method. Information is requested as to the effect that an annual provision of 1% of sales would have had on the amount of bad debt expense reported for each of the past four years. It is also considered desirable to know what the balance of Allowance for Doubtful Accounts would have been at the end of each year. The following data have been obtained from the accounts:

| Year | Sales | Uncollectible Accounts Written Off | 1st | 2nd | 3rd | 4th |
|---|---|---|---|---|---|---|
| | | | Year of Origin of Accounts Receivable Written Off as Uncollectible | | | |
| 1st | $   900,000 | $ 4,500 | $4,500 | | | |
| 2nd | 1,250,000 | 9,600 | 3,000 | $6,600 | | |
| 3rd | 1,500,000 | 12,800 | 1,000 | 3,700 | $8,100 | |
| 4th | 2,200,000 | 16,550 | | 1,500 | 4,300 | $10,750 |

**Instructions**

1. Assemble the desired data, using the following column headings:

| | Bad Debt Expense | | | |
|---|---|---|---|---|
| Year | Expense Actually Reported | Expense Based on Estimate | Increase (Decrease) in Amount of Expense | Balance of Allowance Account, End of Year |

2. ➤ Experience during the first four years of operations indicated that the receivables were either collected within two years or had to be written off as uncollectible. Does the estimate of 1% of sales appear to be reasonably close to the actual experience with uncollectible accounts originating during the first two years? Explain.

---

**PR 9-4A   Details of notes receivable and related entries**                  OBJ. 6

Flush Mate Co. wholesales bathroom fixtures. During the current fiscal year, Flush Mate Co. received the following notes:

✔ 1. Note 2: Due date, June 22; Interest due at maturity, $360

SHOW ME HOW

| | Date | Face Amount | Term | Interest Rate |
|---|---|---|---|---|
| 1. | Mar. 6 | $80,000 | 45 days | 5% |
| 2. | Apr. 23 | 24,000 | 60 days | 9 |
| 3. | July 20 | 42,000 | 120 days | 6 |
| 4. | Sept. 6 | 54,000 | 90 days | 7 |
| 5. | Nov. 29 | 27,000 | 60 days | 6 |
| 6. | Dec. 30 | 72,000 | 30 days | 5 |

**Instructions**

1. Determine for each note (a) the due date and (b) the amount of interest due at maturity, identifying each note by number.
2. Journalize the entry to record the dishonor of Note (3) on its due date.
3. Journalize the adjusting entry to record the accrued interest on Notes (5) and (6) on December 31.
4. Journalize the entries to record the receipt of the amounts due on Notes (5) and (6) in January.

---

**PR 9-5A   Notes receivable entries**                  OBJ. 6

The following data relate to notes receivable and interest for CGH Cable Co., a cable manufacturer and supplier. (All notes are dated as of the day they are received.)

Apr. 10. Received a $144,000, 5%, 60-day note on account.

May 15. Received a $270,000, 7%, 120-day note on account.

June  9. Received $145,200 on note of April 10.

Aug. 22. Received a $150,000, 4%, 45-day note on account.

Sept. 12. Received $276,300 on note of May 15.

   30. Received a $210,000, 8%, 60-day note on account.

Oct.  6. Received $150,750 on note of August 22.

   18. Received a 120,000, 5%, 60-day note on account.

Nov. 29. Received $212,800 on note of September 30.

Dec. 17. Received $121,000 on note of October 18.

**Instructions**

Journalize the entries to record the transactions.

### PR 9-6A Sales and notes receivable transactions

OBJ. 6

The following were selected from among the transactions completed by Caldemeyer Co. during the current year. Caldemeyer Co. sells and installs home and business security systems.

Jan. 3. Loaned $18,000 cash to Trina Gelhaus, receiving a 90-day, 8% note.

Feb. 10. Sold merchandise on account to Bradford & Co., $24,000. The cost of the merchandise sold was $14,400.

13. Sold merchandise on account to Dry Creek Co., $60,000. The cost of merchandise sold was $54,000.

Mar. 12. Accepted a 60-day, 7% note for $24,000 from Bradford & Co. on account.

14. Accepted a 60-day, 9% note for $60,000 from Dry Creek Co. on account.

Apr. 3. Received the interest due from Trina Gelhaus and a new 120-day, 9% note as a renewal of the loan of January 3. (Record both the debit and the credit to the notes receivable account.)

May 11. Received from Bradford & Co. the amount due on the note of March 12.

13. Dry Creek Co. dishonored its note dated March 14.

July 12. Received from Dry Creek Co. the amount owed on the dishonored note, plus interest for 60 days at 12% computed on the maturity value of the note.

Aug. 1. Received from Trina Gelhaus the amount due on her note of April 3.

Oct. 5. Sold merchandise on account to Halloran Co., $13,500. The cost of the merchandise sold was $8,100.

15. Received from Halloran Co. the amount of the invoice of October 5, less 2% discount.

#### Instructions

Journalize the entries to record the transactions.

## Problems: Series B

### PR 9-1B Entries related to uncollectible accounts

OBJ. 4

The following transactions were completed by The Wild Trout Gallery during the current fiscal year ended December 31:

Jan. 19. Reinstated the account of Arlene Gurley, which had been written off in the preceding year as uncollectible. Journalized the receipt of $2,660 cash in full payment of Arlene's account.

Apr. 3. Wrote off the $12,750 balance owed by Premier GS Co., which is bankrupt.

July 16. Received 25% of the $22,000 balance owed by Hayden Co., a bankrupt business, and wrote off the remainder as uncollectible.

Nov. 23. Reinstated the account of Harry Carr, which had been written off two years earlier as uncollectible. Recorded the receipt of $4,000 cash in full payment.

Dec. 31. Wrote off the following accounts as uncollectible (compound entry): Cavey Co., $3,300; Fogle Co., $8,100; Lake Furniture, $11,400; Melinda Shryer, $1,200.

31. Based on an analysis of the $2,350,000 of accounts receivable, it was estimated that $60,000 will be uncollectible. Journalized the adjusting entry.

#### Instructions

1. Record the January 1 credit balance of $50,000 in a T account for Allowance for Doubtful Accounts.

2. Journalize the transactions. Post each entry that affects the following T accounts and determine the new balances:

Allowance for Doubtful Accounts

Bad Debt Expense

3. Determine the expected net realizable value of the accounts receivable as of December 31.

4. Assuming that instead of basing the provision for uncollectible accounts on an analysis of receivables, the adjusting entry on December 31 had been based on an estimated expense of ½ of 1% of the sales of $15,800,000 for the year, determine the following:

   a. Bad debt expense for the year.

   b. Balance in the allowance account after the adjustment of December 31.

   c. Expected net realizable value of the accounts receivable as of December 31.

---

**PR 9-2B Aging of receivables; estimating allowance for doubtful accounts**     **OBJ. 4**

✔ 3. $123,235

Wig Creations Company supplies wigs and hair care products to beauty salons throughout Texas and the Southwest. The accounts receivable clerk for Wig Creations prepared the following partially completed aging of receivables schedule as of the end of business on December 31, 2015:

|  | A | B | C | D | E | F | G | H |
|---|---|---|---|---|---|---|---|---|
| 1 |  |  | **Not** | | **Days Past Due** | | | |
| 2 |  |  | **Past** |  |  |  |  |  |
| 3 | **Customer** | **Balance** | **Due** | **1–30** | **31–60** | **61–90** | **91–120** | **Over 120** |
| 4 | ABC Beauty | 15,000 | 15,000 |  |  |  |  |  |
| 5 | Angel Wigs | 8,000 |  |  | 8,000 |  |  |  |
| 30 | Zodiac Beauty | 3,000 |  | 3,000 |  |  |  |  |
| 31 | Subtotals | 875,000 | 415,000 | 210,000 | 112,000 | 55,000 | 18,000 | 65,000 |

The following accounts were unintentionally omitted from the aging schedule:

| Customer | Due Date | Balance |
|---|---|---|
| Arcade Beauty | Aug. 17, 2015 | $10,000 |
| Creative Images | Oct. 30, 2015 | 8,500 |
| Excel Hair Products | July 3, 2015 | 7,500 |
| First Class Hair Care | Sept. 8, 2015 | 6,600 |
| Golden Images | Nov. 23, 2015 | 3,600 |
| Oh That Hair | Nov. 29, 2015 | 1,400 |
| One Stop Hair Designs | Dec. 7, 2015 | 4,000 |
| Visions Hair & Nail | Jan. 11, 2016 | 9,000 |

Wig Creations has a past history of uncollectible accounts by age category, as follows:

| Age Class | Percent Uncollectible |
|---|---|
| Not past due | 1% |
| 1–30 days past due | 4 |
| 31–60 days past due | 16 |
| 61–90 days past due | 25 |
| 91–120 days past due | 40 |
| Over 120 days past due | 80 |

**Instructions**

1. Determine the number of days past due for each of the preceding accounts.

2. Complete the aging of receivables schedule by adding the omitted accounts to the bottom of the schedule and updating the totals.

*(Continued)*

3. Estimate the allowance for doubtful accounts, based on the aging of receivables schedule.

4. Assume that the allowance for doubtful accounts for Wig Creations has a credit balance of $7,375 before adjustment on December 31, 2015. Journalize the adjustment for uncollectible accounts.

5. Assume that the adjusting entry in (4) was inadvertently omitted, how would the omission affect the balance sheet and income statement?

---

**PR 9-3B**  **Compare two methods of accounting for uncollectible receivables**    OBJ. 3, 4, 5

✔ 1. Year 4: Balance of allowance account, end of year, $32,550

Digital Depot Company, which operates a chain of 40 electronics supply stores, has just completed its fourth year of operations. The direct write-off method of recording bad debt expense has been used during the entire period. Because of substantial increases in sales volume and the amount of uncollectible accounts, the firm is considering changing to the allowance method. Information is requested as to the effect that an annual provision of ¼% of sales would have had on the amount of bad debt expense reported for each of the past four years. It is also considered desirable to know what the balance of Allowance for Doubtful Accounts would have been at the end of each year. The following data have been obtained from the accounts:

| | | | Year of Origin of Accounts Receivable Written Off as Uncollectible | | | |
| | | Uncollectible Accounts | | | | |
| Year | Sales | Written Off | 1st | 2nd | 3rd | 4th |
|------|-------|-------------|-----|-----|-----|-----|
| 1st | $12,500,000 | $18,000 | $18,000 | | | |
| 2nd | 14,800,000 | 30,200 | 9,000 | $21,200 | | |
| 3rd | 18,000,000 | 39,900 | 3,600 | 9,300 | $27,000 | |
| 4th | 24,000,000 | 52,600 | | 5,100 | 12,500 | $35,000 |

**Instructions**

1. Assemble the desired data, using the following column headings:

| | Bad Debt Expense | | | |
| | Expense Actually Reported | Expense Based on Estimate | Increase (Decrease) in Amount of Expense | Balance of Allowance Account, End of Year |
| Year | | | | |
|------|---|---|---|---|

2. ▬▬▶ Experience during the first four years of operations indicated that the receivables were either collected within two years or had to be written off as uncollectible. Does the estimate of ¼% of sales appear to be reasonably close to the actual experience with uncollectible accounts originating during the first two years? Explain.

---

**PR 9-4B**  **Details of notes receivable and related entries**    OBJ. 6

✔ 1. Note 1: Due date, Feb. 13; Interest due at maturity, $110

Gen-X Ads Co. produces advertising videos. During the current fiscal year, Gen-X Ads Co. received the following notes:

SHOW
ME HOW

| | Date | Face Amount | Term | Interest Rate |
|---|------|-------------|------|---------------|
| 1. | Jan. 14 | $33,000 | 30 days | 4% |
| 2. | Mar. 9 | 60,000 | 45 days | 7 |
| 3. | July 12 | 48,000 | 90 days | 5 |
| 4. | Aug. 23 | 16,000 | 75 days | 6 |
| 5. | Nov. 15 | 36,000 | 60 days | 8 |
| 6. | Dec. 10 | 24,000 | 60 days | 6 |

**Instructions**

1. Determine for each note (a) the due date and (b) the amount of interest due at maturity, identifying each note by number.

2. Journalize the entry to record the dishonor of Note (3) on its due date.

3. Journalize the adjusting entry to record the accrued interest on Notes (5) and (6) on December 31.

4. Journalize the entries to record the receipt of the amounts due on Notes (5) and (6) in January and February.

---

**PR 9-5B   Notes receivable entries**                                   OBJ. 6

The following data relate to notes receivable and interest for Owens Co., a financial services company. (All notes are dated as of the day they are received.)

Mar.  8. Received a $33,000, 5%, 60-day note on account.

31. Received an $80,000, 7%, 90-day note on account.

May  7. Received $33,275 on note of March 8.

16. Received a $72,000, 7%, 90-day note on account.

June 11. Received a $36,000, 6%, 45-day note on account.

29. Received $81,400 on note of March 31.

July 26. Received $36,270 on note of June 11.

Aug.  4. Received a $48,000, 9%, 120-day note on account.

14. Received $73,260 on note of May 16.

Dec.  2. Received $49,440 on note of August 4.

**Instructions**

Journalize the entries to record the transactions.

---

**PR 9-6B   Sales and notes receivable transactions**                    OBJ. 6

General Ledger

The following were selected from among the transactions completed during the current year by Danix Co., an appliance wholesale company:

Jan. 21. Sold merchandise on account to Black Tie Co., $28,000. The cost of merchandise sold was $16,800.

Mar. 18. Accepted a 60-day, 6% note for $28,000 from Black Tie Co. on account.

May 17. Received from Black Tie Co. the amount due on the note of March 18.

June 15. Sold merchandise on account to Pioneer Co. for $17,700. The cost of merchandise sold was $10,600.

21. Loaned $18,000 cash to JR Stutts, receiving a 30-day, 8% note.

25. Received from Pioneer Co. the amount due on the invoice of June 15, less 1% discount.

July 21. Received the interest due from JR Stutts and a new 60-day, 9% note as a renewal of the loan of June 21. (Record both the debit and the credit to the notes receivable account.)

Sept.19. Received from JR Stutts the amount due on her note of July 21.

22. Sold merchandise on account to Wycoff Co., $20,000. The cost of merchandise sold was $12,000.

Oct. 14. Accepted a 30-day, 6% note for $20,000 from Wycoff Co. on account.

Nov. 13. Wycoff Co. dishonored the note dated October 14.

Dec. 28. Received from Wycoff Co. the amount owed on the dishonored note, plus interest for 45 days at 8% computed on the maturity value of the note.

**Instructions**

Journalize the entries to record the transactions.

## Cases & Projects

### CP 9-1 Ethics and professional conduct in business

Bev Wynn, vice president of operations for Dillon County Bank, has instructed the bank's computer programmer to use a 365-day year to compute interest on depository accounts (liabilities). Bev also instructed the programmer to use a 360-day year to compute interest on loans (assets).

➤ Discuss whether Bev is behaving in a professional manner.

### CP 9-2 Estimate uncollectible accounts

For several years, Xtreme Co.'s sales have been on a "cash only" basis. On January 1, 2013, however, Xtreme Co. began offering credit on terms of n/30. The amount of the adjusting entry to record the estimated uncollectible receivables at the end of each year has been ½ of 1% of credit sales, which is the rate reported as the average for the industry. Credit sales and the year-end credit balances in Allowance for Doubtful Accounts for the past four years are as follows:

| Year | Credit Sales | Allowance for Doubtful Accounts |
|------|-------------|-------------------------------|
| 2013 | $4,000,000 | $ 5,000 |
| 2014 | 4,400,000 | 8,250 |
| 2015 | 4,800,000 | 10,200 |
| 2016 | 5,100,000 | 14,400 |

Laurie Jones, president of Xtreme Co., is concerned that the method used to account for and write off uncollectible receivables is unsatisfactory. She has asked for your advice in the analysis of past operations in this area and for recommendations for change.

1. Determine the amount of (a) the addition to Allowance for Doubtful Accounts and (b) the accounts written off for each of the four years.

2. a. ➤ Advise Laurie Jones as to whether the estimate of ½ of 1% of credit sales appears reasonable.

   b. ➤ Assume that after discussing (a) with Laurie Jones, she asked you what action might be taken to determine what the balance of Allowance for Doubtful Accounts should be at December 31, 2016, and what possible changes, if any, you might recommend in accounting for uncollectible receivables. How would you respond?

### CP 9-3 Accounts receivable turnover and days' sales in receivables

Best Buy is a specialty retailer of consumer electronics, including personal computers, entertainment software, and appliances. Best Buy operates retail stores in addition to the Best Buy, Media Play, On Cue, and Magnolia Hi-Fi Web sites. For two recent years, Best Buy reported the following (in millions):

| | Year 2 | Year 1 |
|---|--------|--------|
| Sales | $50,705 | $49,747 |
| Accounts receivable at end of year | 2,288 | 2,348 |

Assume that the accounts receivable (in millions) were $2,020 at the beginning of fiscal Year 1.

1. Compute the accounts receivable turnover for Year 2 and Year 1. Round to one decimal place.

2. Compute the days' sales in receivables at the end of Year 2 and Year 1. Use 365 days and round to one decimal place.

3.  What conclusions can be drawn from (1) and (2) regarding Best Buy's efficiency in collecting receivables?

4.  What assumption did we make about sales for the Best Buy ratio computations that might distort the ratios and therefore cause the ratios not to be comparable for Year 2 and Year 1?

---

### CP 9-4 Accounts receivable turnover and days' sales in receivables

**Apple Inc.** designs, manufactures, and markets personal computers and related personal computing and communicating solutions for sale primarily to education, creative, consumer, and business customers. Substantially all of the company's sales over the last five years are from sales of its Macs, iPods, iPads, and related software and peripherals. For two recent fiscal years, Apple reported the following (in millions):

|  | Year 2 | Year 1 |
|---|---|---|
| Sales | $156,508 | $108,249 |
| Accounts receivable at end of year | 21,275 | 13,731 |

Assume that the accounts receivable (in millions) were $11,560 at the beginning of fiscal Year 1.

1. Compute the accounts receivable turnover for Year 2 and Year 1. Round to one decimal place.

2. Compute the days' sales in receivables at the end of Year 2 and Year 1. Use 365 days and round to one decimal place.

3.  What conclusions can be drawn from (1) and (2) regarding Apple's efficiency in collecting receivables?

---

### CP 9-5 Accounts receivable turnover and days' sales in receivables

**Costco Wholesale Corporation** operates membership warehouses that sell a variety of branded and private label products. Headquartered in Issaquah, Washington, it also sells merchandise online in the United States (Costco.com) and in Canada (Costco.ca). For two recent years, Costco reported the following (in millions):

|  | Year 2 | Year 1 |
|---|---|---|
| Sales | $99,137 | $88,915 |
| Accounts receivable at end of year | 1,576 | 1,455 |

Assume that the accounts receivable (in thousands) were $1,321 at the beginning of Year 1.

1. Compute the accounts receivable turnover for Year 2 and Year 1. Round to one decimal place.

2. Compute the days' sales in receivables at the end of Year 2 and Year 1. Use 365 days and round to one decimal place.

3.  What conclusions can be drawn from (1) and (2) regarding Costco's efficiency in collecting receivables?

4.  Given the nature of Costco's operations, do you believe Costco's accounts receivable turnover ratio would be higher or lower than a typical manufacturing company, such as **H.J. Heinz Company**? Explain.

### CP 9-6 Accounts receivable turnover

The accounts receivable turnover ratio will vary across companies, depending on the nature of the company's operations. For example, an accounts receivable turnover of 6 for a retailer is unacceptable but might be excellent for a manufacturer of specialty milling equipment. A list of well-known companies follows:

| | | |
|---|---|---|
| Alcoa Inc. | The Coca-Cola Company | Kroger |
| AutoZone, Inc. | Delta Air Lines | Procter & Gamble |
| Barnes & Noble, Inc. | The Home Depot | Walmart |
| Caterpillar | IBM | Whirlpool Corporation |

1. Categorize each of the preceding companies as to whether its turnover ratio is likely to be above or below 15.

2. ➤ Based on (1), identify a characteristic of companies with accounts receivable turnover ratios above 15.

# Fixed Assets and Intangible Assets

## McDonald's

**M**cDonald's began in 1940 in San Bernardino, California, as a Bar-B-Q restaurant operated by two brothers, Dick and Mac McDonald. In 1954, Ray Kroc visited the restaurant and convinced the McDonald brothers to let him franchise its operations nationwide. Ray Kroc opened his first McDonald's in Des Plaines, Illinois, in 1955, with its distinguishing, newly designed Golden Arches. Today, McDonald's operates in 119 countries, has more than 34,000 restaurants, employs more than 400,000 people, has sold more than 250 billion hamburgers, and generates yearly revenues in excess of $27.5 billion.

Would you like to own and operate a McDonald's restaurant? McDonald's grants twenty-year franchises to individuals who want to become owner/operators of a restaurant. Individuals may purchase either an existing or a new restaurant. When opening a new restaurant, the owner must invest in the store equipment, signs, seating, and décor. The company normally owns the land and the building. McDonald's also provides training for its owner/operators. In return, the company is paid a monthly service charge, which is either a fixed amount or a percent of sales. The total cost of opening a new restaurant may exceed several million dollars.

Obviously, the decision to open a McDonald's restaurant is a major commitment with long-lasting implications. This chapter discusses the accounting for investments in long-term, fixed assets such as a new restaurant. This accounting addresses such issues as how much of the investment should be recorded as an asset, how much should be written off as an expense each year, and how the disposal of a fixed asset should be recorded. Finally, accounting for natural resources, such as mineral deposits, and intangible assets, such as patents and copyrights, are discussed.

*Source:* http://www.aboutmcdonalds.com

**OBJ 1** Define, classify, and account for the cost of fixed assets.

# Nature of Fixed Assets

**Fixed assets** are long-term or relatively permanent assets such as equipment, machinery, buildings, and land. Other descriptive titles for fixed assets are *plant assets* or *property, plant, and equipment*. Fixed assets have the following characteristics:

- They exist physically and, thus, are *tangible* assets.
- They are owned and used by the company in its normal operations.
- They are not offered for sale as part of normal operations.

Exhibit 1 shows the percent of fixed assets to total assets for some select companies. As shown in Exhibit 1, fixed assets are often a significant portion of the total assets of a company.

**EXHIBIT 1**

**Fixed Assets as a Percent of Total Assets—Selected Companies**

| | Fixed Assets as a Percent of Total Assets |
|---|---|
| Alcoa Inc.......................................................... | 47% |
| Exxon Mobil Corporation......................................... | 68 |
| Ford Motor Company ............................................. | 22 |
| Kroger.............................................................. | 62 |
| Office Depot Inc. ................................................. | 21 |
| United Parcel Service, Inc........................................ | 46 |
| Verizon Communications......................................... | 39 |
| Walgreen Co. ..................................................... | 36 |
| Walmart............................................................ | 58 |

## Classifying Costs

A cost that has been incurred may be classified as a fixed asset, an investment, or an expense. Exhibit 2 shows how to determine the proper classification of a cost and how it should be recorded.

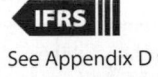

See Appendix D for more information.

**EXHIBIT 2**

**Classifying Costs**

As shown in Exhibit 2, classifying a cost involves the following steps:

- Step 1.   Is the purchased item long-lived?

    If *yes*, the item is recorded as an asset on the balance sheet, either as a fixed asset or an investment. Proceed to Step 2.

    If *no*, the item is classified and recorded as an *expense*.

- Step 2.   Is the asset used in normal operations?

    If *yes*, the asset is classified and recorded as a *fixed asset*.

    If *no*, the asset is classified and recorded as an *investment*.

Items that are classified and recorded as fixed assets include land, buildings, or equipment. Such assets normally last more than a year and are used in the normal operations. However, standby equipment for use during peak periods or when other equipment breaks down is still classified as a fixed asset, even though it is not used very often. In contrast, fixed assets that have been abandoned or are no longer used in operations are not classified as fixed assets.

Although fixed assets may be sold, they should not be offered for sale as part of normal operations. For example, cars and trucks offered for sale by an automotive dealership are not fixed assets of the dealership. On the other hand, a tow truck used in the normal operations of the dealership is a fixed asset of the dealership.

Investments are long-lived assets that are not used in the normal operations and are held for future resale. Such assets are reported on the balance sheet in a section entitled *Investments*. For example, undeveloped land acquired for future resale would be classified and reported as an investment, not land.

## The Cost of Fixed Assets

In addition to purchase price, the costs of acquiring fixed assets include all amounts spent getting the asset in place and ready for use. For example, freight costs and the costs of installing equipment are part of the asset's total cost.

Exhibit 3 summarizes some of the common costs of acquiring fixed assets. These costs are recorded by debiting the related fixed asset account, such as Land,[1] Building, Land Improvements, or Machinery and Equipment.

---

**EXHIBIT 3**　　**Costs of Acquiring Fixed Assets**

### Building

- Architects' fees
- Engineers' fees
- Insurance costs incurred during construction
- Interest on money borrowed to finance construction
- Sales taxes
- Repairs (purchase of existing building)
- Reconditioning (purchase of existing building)
- Modifying for use
- Permits from government agencies

### Machinery & Equipment

- Sales taxes
- Freight
- Installation
- Repairs (purchase of used equipment)
- Reconditioning (purchase of used equipment)
- Insurance while in transit
- Assembly
- Modifying for use
- Testing for use
- Permits from government agencies

### Land

- Purchase price
- Sales taxes
- Permits from government agencies
- Broker's commissions
- Title fees
- Surveying fees
- Delinquent real estate taxes
- Removing unwanted building less any salvage
- Grading and leveling

### Land Improvements

- Trees and shrubs
- Fences
- Outdoor lighting
- Paved parking areas or walkways

---

Only costs necessary for preparing the fixed asset for use are included as a cost of the asset. Unnecessary costs that do not increase the asset's usefulness are recorded as an expense. For example, the following costs are included as an expense:

- Vandalism
- Mistakes in installation
- Uninsured theft
- Damage during unpacking and installing
- Fines for not obtaining proper permits from governmental agencies

A company may incur costs associated with constructing a fixed asset such as a new building. The direct costs incurred in the construction, such as labor and

---

[1] As discussed here, land is assumed to be used only as a location or site and not for its mineral deposits or other natural resources.

materials, should be capitalized as a debit to an account entitled *Construction in Progress*. When the construction is complete, the costs are reclassified by crediting Construction in Progress and debiting the proper fixed asset account such as Building. For some companies, construction in progress can be significant.

 **Intel Corporation** reported in a recent annual report construction in progress of $8.2 billion, which was 29% of its total fixed assets.

**IFRS**

See Appendix D for more information.

## Capital and Revenue Expenditures

Once a fixed asset has been acquired and placed into service, costs may be incurred for ordinary maintenance and repairs. In addition, costs may be incurred for improving an asset or for extraordinary repairs that extend the asset's useful life. Costs that benefit only the current period are called **revenue expenditures**. Costs that improve the asset or extend its useful life are **capital expenditures**.

### Ordinary Maintenance and Repairs
Costs related to the ordinary maintenance and repairs of a fixed asset are recorded as an expense of the current period. Such expenditures are *revenue expenditures* and are recorded as increases to Repairs and Maintenance Expense. For example, $300 paid for a tune-up of a delivery truck is recorded as follows:

|  |  | Repairs and Maintenance Expense | 300 |  |
|  |  | Cash |  | 300 |

### Asset Improvements
After a fixed asset has been placed into service, costs may be incurred to improve the asset. For example, the service value of a delivery truck might be improved by adding a $5,500 hydraulic lift to allow for easier and quicker loading of cargo. Such costs are *capital expenditures* and are recorded as increases to the fixed asset account. In the case of the hydraulic lift, the expenditure is recorded as follows:

|  |  | Delivery Truck | 5,500 |  |
|  |  | Cash |  | 5,500 |

Because the cost of the delivery truck has increased, depreciation for the truck will also change over its remaining useful life.

### Extraordinary Repairs
After a fixed asset has been placed into service, costs may be incurred to extend the asset's useful life. For example, the engine of a forklift that is near the end of its useful life may be overhauled at a cost of $4,500, extending its useful life by eight years. Such costs are *capital expenditures* and are recorded as a decrease in an accumulated depreciation account. In the case of the forklift, the expenditure is recorded as follows:

|  |  | Accumulated Depreciation—Forklift | 4,500 |  |
|  |  | Cash |  | 4,500 |

Because the forklift's remaining useful life has changed, depreciation for the forklift will also change based on the new book value of the forklift.

## Integrity, Objectivity, and Ethics in Business

**CAPITAL CRIME**

One of the largest alleged accounting frauds in history involved the improper accounting for capital expenditures. WorldCom, the second largest telecommunications company in the United States at the time, improperly treated maintenance expenditures on its telecommunications network as capital expenditures. As a result, the company had to restate its prior years' earnings downward by nearly $4 billion to correct this error. The company declared bankruptcy within months of disclosing the error, and the CEO was sentenced to 25 years in prison.

The accounting for revenue and capital expenditures is summarized in Exhibit 4.

## EXHIBIT 4    Revenue and Capital Expenditures

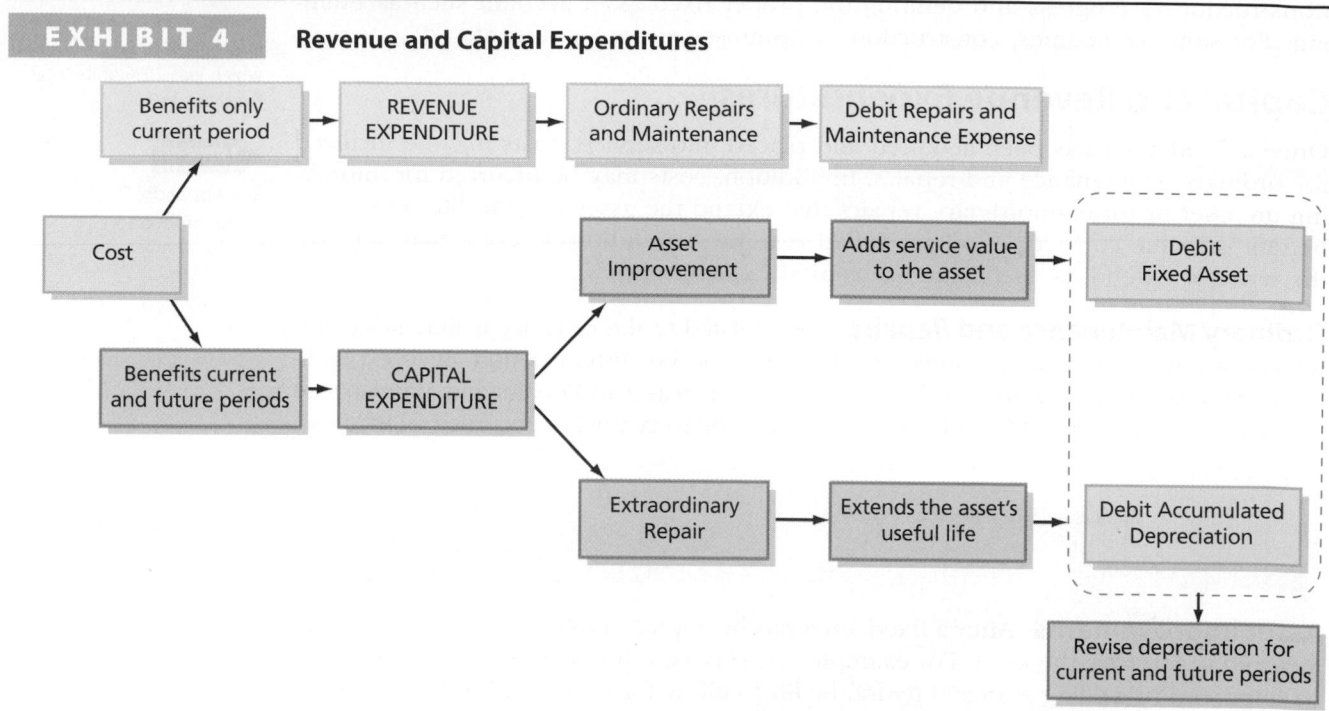

## Example Exercise 10-1   Capital and Revenue Expenditures

 OBJ 1

On June 18, GTS Co. paid $1,200 to upgrade a hydraulic lift and $45 for an oil change for one of its delivery trucks. Journalize the entries for the hydraulic lift upgrade and oil change expenditures.

### Follow My Example 10-1

| June 18 | Delivery Truck ........................................................... | 1,200 | |
| | Cash........................................................... | | 1,200 |
| | | | |
| 18 | Repairs and Maintenance Expense ............................................ | 45 | |
| | Cash........................................................... | | 45 |

Practice Exercises: PE 10-1A, PE 10-1B

## Leasing Fixed Assets

A *lease* is a contract for the use of an asset for a period of time. Leases are often used in business. For example, automobiles, computers, medical equipment, buildings, and airplanes are often leased.

The two parties to a lease contract are as follows:

- The *lessor* is the party who owns the asset.
- The *lessee* is the party to whom the rights to use the asset are granted by the lessor.

**Delta Air Lines** leases facilities, aircraft, and equipment.

See Appendix D for more information.

Under a lease contract, the lessee pays rent on a periodic basis for the lease term. An advantage of leasing an asset is that the lessee has access to an asset without having to spend funds or obtain financing to buy the asset. In addition, expenses such as maintenance and repair costs may be the responsibility of the lessor. Finally, the risk of incurring additional cost because the asset becomes obsolete before the end of its useful life can be mitigated by leasing an asset.

The accounting for leases is currently the focus of a joint project by the Financial Accounting Standards (FASB) and the International Accounting Standards Board (IASB) to merge U.S. and international standards.[2] Under the proposed standard lessors and lessees would be required to record assets and liabilities related to certain long-term lease contracts.

For purposes of this text, we assume that leases are short-term and not extending beyond one year. Thus, lease payments are recorded as rent by debiting Rent Expense and crediting Cash. The lease terms, such as a renewal option, may be disclosed in the notes to the financial statements. The asset rentals described in the earlier chapters of this text were accounted for in this manner.

# Accounting for Depreciation

**OBJ 2** Compute depreciation, using the following methods: straight-line method, units-of-output method, and double-declining-balance method.

Over time, fixed assets, with the exception of land, lose their ability to provide services. Thus, the costs of fixed assets such as equipment and buildings should be recorded as an expense over their useful lives. This periodic recording of the cost of fixed assets as an expense is called **depreciation**. Because land has an unlimited life, it is not depreciated.

The adjusting entry to record depreciation debits Depreciation Expense and credits a contra asset account entitled *Accumulated Depreciation* or *Allowance for Depreciation*. The use of a contra asset account allows the original cost to remain unchanged in the fixed asset account.

**Note:**
**The adjusting entry to record depreciation debits Depreciation Expense and credits Accumulated Depreciation.**

Depreciation can be caused by physical or functional factors.

* *Physical depreciation* factors include wear and tear during use or from exposure to weather.
* *Functional depreciation* factors include obsolescence and changes in customer needs that cause the asset to no longer provide services for which it was intended. For example, equipment may become obsolete due to changing technology.

Two common misunderstandings that exist about depreciation as used in accounting include:

* Depreciation does not measure a decline in the market value of a fixed asset. Instead, depreciation is an allocation of a fixed asset's cost to expense over the asset's useful life. Thus, the book value of a fixed asset (cost less accumulated depreciation) usually does not agree with the asset's market value. This is justified in accounting because a fixed asset is for use in a company's operations rather than for resale.
* Depreciation does not provide cash to replace fixed assets as they wear out. This misunderstanding may occur because depreciation, unlike most expenses, does not require an outlay of cash when it is recorded.

## Factors in Computing Depreciation Expense

Three factors determine the depreciation expense for a fixed asset. These three factors are as follows:

* The asset's initial cost
* The asset's expected useful life
* The asset's estimated residual value

The initial *cost* of a fixed asset is determined using the concepts discussed and illustrated earlier in this chapter.

The *expected useful life* of a fixed asset is estimated at the time the asset is placed into service. Estimates of expected useful lives are available from industry trade associations. The Internal Revenue Service also publishes guidelines for useful lives, which may be helpful for financial reporting purposes. However, it is not uncommon for different companies to use a different useful life for similar assets.

The **residual value** of a fixed asset at the end of its useful life is estimated at the time the asset is placed into service. Residual value is sometimes referred to as *scrap value, salvage value,* or *trade-in value.* The difference between a fixed asset's initial cost

The cost and related accumulated depletion of mineral rights are normally shown as part of the Fixed Assets section of the balance sheet. The mineral rights may be shown net of depletion on the face of the balance sheet. In such cases, a supporting note discloses the accumulated depletion.

**OBJ 7** Describe and illustrate the fixed asset turnover ratio to assess the efficiency of a company's use of its fixed assets.

# Financial Analysis and Interpretation: Fixed Asset Turnover Ratio

A measure of a company's efficiency in using its fixed assets to generate revenue is the fixed asset turnover ratio. The **fixed asset turnover ratio** measures the number of dollars of sales earned per dollar of fixed assets. It is computed as follows:

$$\text{Fixed Asset Turnover Ratio} = \frac{\text{Sales}}{\text{Average Book Value of Fixed Assets}}$$

To illustrate, the following data (in millions) were taken from recent financial statements of **Starbucks Corporation**:

|  | Year 2 | Year 1 |
|---|---|---|
| Sales | $13,300 | $11,700 |
| Fixed assets (net): |  |  |
| Beginning of year | 2,355 | 2,417 |
| End of year | 2,659 | 2,355 |

Starbucks' fixed asset turnover ratios for Year 2 and Year 1 are computed as follows:

|  | Year 2 | Year 1 |
|---|---|---|
| Sales | $13,300 | $11,700 |
| Average fixed assets | $2,507 | $2,386 |
|  | [($2,355 + $2,659) ÷ 2] | [($2,417 + $2,355) ÷ 2] |
| Fixed asset turnover ratio* | 5.31 | 4.90 |
|  | ($13,300 ÷ $2,507) | ($11,700 ÷ $2,386) |

*Rounded to two decimal places.

## Business Connection

### HUB-AND-SPOKE OR POINT-TO-POINT?

**Southwest Airlines Co.** uses a simple fare structure, featuring low, unrestricted, unlimited, everyday coach fares. These fares are made possible by Southwest's use of a point-to-point, rather than a hub-and-spoke, business approach.

**United Airlines, Inc., Delta Air Lines**, and **American Airlines** employ a hub-and-spoke approach in which an airline establishes major hubs that serve as connecting links to other cities. For example, Delta has major connecting hubs in Atlanta and Salt Lake City.

In contrast, Southwest focuses on nonstop, point-to-point service between selected cities. As a result, Southwest minimizes connections, delays, and total trip time. This operating approach permits Southwest to achieve high utilization of its fixed assets, such as its 737 aircraft.

The higher the fixed asset turnover, the more efficiently a company is using its fixed assets in generating sales. For example, in Year 2 Starbucks earned $5.31 of sales for every dollar of fixed assets, which is more than $4.90 of sales for every dollar of fixed assets it earned in Year 1. Thus, Starbucks used its fixed assets more efficiently in Year 2.

As illustrated for Starbucks, the fixed asset turnover ratio can be compared across time for a single company. In addition, the ratio can be compared across companies. For example, the fixed asset turnover ratio for a number of different companies and industries is shown in Exhibit 13.

**EXHIBIT 13**

**Fixed Asset Turnover Ratio Examples**

| Company (industry) | Fixed Asset Turnover Ratio |
| --- | --- |
| Comcast Corporation (cable) | 2.38 |
| Google (Internet) | 4.68 |
| Manpower Inc. (temporary employment) | 115.10 |
| Norfolk Southern Corporation (railroad) | 0.44 |
| Ruby Tuesday, Inc. (restaurant) | 1.33 |
| Southwest Airlines Co. (airline) | 1.37 |

The smaller ratios are associated with companies that require large fixed asset investments. The larger fixed asset turnover ratios are associated with firms that are more labor intensive and require smaller fixed asset investments.

## Example Exercise 10-9  Fixed Asset Turnover Ratio

OBJ 7

Financial statement data for years ending December 31 for Broadwater Company follows:

| | 2016 | 2015 |
| --- | --- | --- |
| Sales | $2,862,000 | $2,025,000 |
| Fixed assets: | | |
| Beginning of year | 750,000 | 600,000 |
| End of year | 840,000 | 750,000 |

a. Determine the fixed asset turnover ratio for 2016 and 2015.

b. Does the change in the fixed asset turnover ratio from 2015 to 2016 indicate a favorable or an unfavorable trend?

## Follow My Example 10-9

a. Fixed asset turnover:

| | 2016 | 2015 |
| --- | --- | --- |
| Sales | $2,862,000 | $2,025,000 |
| Fixed assets: | | |
| Beginning of year | $750,000 | $600,000 |
| End of year | $840,000 | $750,000 |
| Average fixed assets | $795,000 | $675,000 |
| | [($750,000 + $840,000) ÷ 2] | [($600,000 + $750,000) ÷ 2] |
| Fixed asset turnover | 3.6 | 3.0 |
| | ($2,862,000 ÷ $795,000) | ($2,025,000 ÷ $675,000) |

b. The increase in the fixed asset turnover ratio from 3.0 to 3.6 indicates a favorable trend in the efficiency of using fixed assets to generate sales.

Practice Exercises: PE 10-9A, PE 10-9B

# A P P E N D I X

## Exchanging Similar Fixed Assets

Old equipment is often traded in for new equipment having a similar use. In such cases, the seller allows the buyer an amount for the old equipment traded in. This amount, called the **trade-in allowance**, may be either greater or less than the book value of the old equipment. The remaining balance—the amount owed—is either paid in cash or recorded as a liability. It is normally called **boot**, which is its tax name.

Accounting for the exchange of similar assets depends on whether the transaction has *commercial substance*.[9] An exchange has commercial substance if future cash flows change as a result of the exchange. If an exchange of similar assets has commercial substance, a gain or loss is recognized. In such cases, the exchange is accounted for similar to that of a sale of a fixed asset. The gain or loss is determined as the difference between the fair market value (trade-in allowance) of the asset given up (exchanged) and its book value. Alternatively, the gain or loss can be determined as the difference between the fair market value of the new asset received and the assets given up in the exchange (cash and book value of the old asset).

## Gain on Exchange

To illustrate a gain on an exchange of similar assets, assume the following:

*Similar equipment acquired (new):*

| | |
|---|---:|
| Price (fair market value) of new equipment | $5,000 |
| Trade-in allowance on old equipment | 1,100 |
| Cash paid at June 19, date of exchange | $3,900 |

*Equipment traded in (old):*

| | |
|---|---:|
| Cost of old equipment | $4,000 |
| Accumulated depreciation at date of exchange | 3,200 |
| Book value at June 19, date of exchange | $ 800 |

The entry to record this exchange and payment of cash is as follows:

| | | | |
|---|---|---:|---:|
| June 19 | Accumulated Depreciation—Equipment | 3,200 | |
| | Equipment (new equipment) | 5,000 | |
| | Equipment (old equipment) | | 4,000 |
| | Cash | | 3,900 |
| | Gain on Exchange of Equipment | | 300 |

The gain on the exchange, $300, is the difference between the fair market value (trade-in allowance) of the asset given up (exchanged) of $1,100 and its book value of $800, computed as follows:

| | |
|---|---:|
| Fair market value (trade-in allowance) of old equipment | $1,100 |
| Less book value of old equipment | 800 |
| Gain on exchange of assets | $ 300 |

[9] *FASB Accounting Standards Codification*, Section 360-10-30.

Ethan Bert Crocker
Mrs. Cobia
16 Feb. 2017

Proper Ethics

Ethics are important to not only the
business world, but our physical world
as well. How can one be trusted? They
are trusted by their moral character. Nothing
shows moral character like practicing
proper ethics.

The gain on the exchange, $300, can also be determined as the difference between the fair market value of the new asset of $5,000 and the book value of the old asset traded in of $800 plus the cash paid of $3,900, computed as follows:

| | | |
|---|---|---|
| Price (fair market value) of new equipment ......................... | | $5,000 |
| Less assets given up in exchange: | | |
|     Book value of old equipment ($4,000 – $3,200) ................. | $ 800 | |
|     Cash paid on the exchange ..................................... | 3,900 | 4,700 |
| Gain on exchange of assets........................................ | | $ 300 |

## Loss on Exchange

To illustrate a loss on an exchange of similar assets, assume that instead of a trade-in allowance of $1,100, a trade-in allowance of only $675 was allowed in the preceding example. In this case, the cash paid on the exchange is $4,325, computed as follows:

| | |
|---|---|
| Price (fair market value) of new equipment ............................ | $5,000 |
| Trade-in allowance of old equipment.................................... | 675 |
| Cash paid at June 19, date of exchange ................................ | $4,325 |

The entry to record this exchange and payment of cash is as follows:

| | | | |
|---|---|---|---|
| June 19 | Accumulated Depreciation—Equipment............... | 3,200 | |
| | Equipment (new equipment)......................... | 5,000 | |
| | Loss on Exchange of Equipment...................... | 125 | |
| |     Equipment (old equipment) ....................... | | 4,000 |
| |     Cash .............................................. | | 4,325 |

The loss on the exchange, $125, is the difference between the fair market value (trade-in allowance) of the asset given up (exchanged) of $675 and its book value of $800, computed as follows:

| | |
|---|---|
| Fair market value (trade-in allowance) of old equipment ........................ | $ 675 |
| Less book value of old equipment............................................... | 800 |
| Loss on exchange of assets .................................................... | $(125) |

The loss on the exchange, $125, can also be determined as the difference between the fair market value of the new asset of $5,000 and the book value of the old asset traded in of $800 plus the cash paid of $4,325, computed as follows:

| | | |
|---|---|---|
| Price (fair market value) of new equipment ........................... | | $5,000 |
| Less assets given up in exchange: | | |
|     Book value of old equipment ($4,000 – $3,200) .................. | $ 800 | |
|     Cash paid on the exchange ..................................... | 4,325 | 5,125 |
| Loss on exchange of assets........................................... | | $ (125) |

In those cases where an asset exchange *lacks commercial substance*, no gain is recognized on the exchange. Instead, the cost of the new asset is adjusted for any gain. For example, in the first illustration, the gain of $300 would be subtracted from the purchase price of $5,000 and the new asset would be recorded at $4,700. Accounting for the exchange of assets that lack commercial substance is discussed in more advanced accounting texts.[10]

---

[10] The exchange of similar assets also involves complex tax issues which are discussed in advanced accounting courses.

# At a Glance 10

**OBJ 1**

## Define, classify, and account for the cost of fixed assets.

**Key Points**   Fixed assets are long-term tangible assets used in the normal operations of the business such as equipment, buildings, and land. The initial cost of a fixed asset includes all amounts spent to get the asset in place and ready for use. Revenue expenditures include ordinary repairs and maintenance. Capital expenditures include asset improvements and extraordinary repairs.

| Learning Outcomes | Example Exercises | Practice Exercises |
|---|---|---|
| • Define *fixed assets*. | | |
| • List the types of costs that should be included in the cost of a fixed asset. | | |
| • Provide examples of ordinary repairs, asset improvements, and extraordinary repairs. | | |
| • Prepare journal entries for ordinary repairs, asset improvements, and extraordinary repairs. | EE10-1 | PE10-1A, 10-1B |

**OBJ 2**

## Compute depreciation, using the following methods: straight-line method, units-of-output method, and double-declining-balance method.

**Key Points**   All fixed assets except land should be depreciated over time. Three factors are considered in determining depreciation: (1) the fixed asset's initial cost, (2) the useful life of the asset, and (3) the residual value of the asset.

   Depreciation may be determined using the straight-line, units-of-output, and double-declining-balance methods. Depreciation may be revised into the future for changes in an asset's useful life or residual value.

| Learning Outcomes | Example Exercises | Practice Exercises |
|---|---|---|
| • Define and describe *depreciation*. | | |
| • List the factors used in determining depreciation. | | |
| • Compute straight-line depreciation. | EE10-2 | PE10-2A, 10-2B |
| • Compute units-of-output depreciation. | EE10-3 | PE10-3A, 10-3B |
| • Compute double-declining-balance depreciation. | EE10-4 | PE10-4A, 10-4B |
| • Compute revised depreciation for a change in an asset's useful life and residual value. | EE10-5 | PE10-5A, 10-5B |

**OBJ 3**

## Journalize entries for the disposal of fixed assets.

**Key Points**   When discarding a fixed asset, any depreciation for the current period should be recorded, and the book value of the asset is then removed from the accounts.

   When a fixed asset is sold, the book value is removed, and the cash or other asset received is recorded. If the selling price is more than the book value of the asset, the transaction results in a gain. If the selling price is less than the book value, there is a loss.

| Learning Outcomes | Example Exercises | Practice Exercises |
|---|---|---|
| • Prepare the journal entry for discarding a fixed asset. | | |
| • Prepare journal entries for the sale of a fixed asset. | EE10-6 | PE10-6A, 10-6B |

**Compute depletion and journalize the entry for depletion.**

**Key Points** The amount of periodic depletion is computed by multiplying the quantity of minerals extracted during the period by a depletion rate. The depletion rate is computed by dividing the cost of the mineral deposit by its estimated total units of resource. The entry to record depletion debits a depletion expense account and credits an accumulated depletion account.

| Learning Outcomes | Example Exercises | Practice Exercises |
|---|---|---|
| • Define and describe *depletion*. | | |
| • Compute a depletion rate. | **EE10-7** | **PE10-7A, 10-7B** |
| • Prepare the journal entry to record depletion. | **EE10-7** | **PE10-7A, 10-7B** |

**Describe the accounting for intangible assets, such as patents, copyrights, and goodwill.**

**Key Points** Long-term assets such as patents, copyrights, trademarks, and goodwill are intangible assets. The cost of patents and copyrights should be amortized over the years of the asset's expected usefulness by debiting an expense account and crediting the intangible asset account. Trademarks and goodwill are not amortized but are written down only upon impairment.

| Learning Outcomes | Example Exercises | Practice Exercises |
|---|---|---|
| • Define, describe, and provide examples of *intangible assets*. | | |
| • Prepare a journal entry for the purchase of an intangible asset. | | |
| • Prepare a journal entry to amortize the costs of patents and copyrights. | **EE10-8** | **PE10-8A, 10-8B** |
| • Prepare the journal entry to record the impairment of goodwill. | **EE10-8** | **PE10-8A, 10-8B** |

**Describe how depreciation expense is reported in an income statement and prepare a balance sheet that includes fixed assets and intangible assets.**

**Key Points** The amount of depreciation expense and the depreciation methods used should be disclosed in the financial statements. Each major class of fixed assets should be disclosed, along with the related accumulated depreciation. Intangible assets are usually presented in a separate section following fixed assets. Each major class of intangible assets should be disclosed net of the amortization recorded to date.

| Learning Outcomes | Example Exercises | Practice Exercises |
|---|---|---|
| • Describe and illustrate how fixed assets are reported on the income statement and balance sheet. | | |
| • Describe and illustrate how intangible assets are reported on the income statement and balance sheet. | | |

**OBJ 7**

**Describe and illustrate the fixed asset turnover ratio to assess the efficiency of a company's use of its fixed assets.**

**Key Points** A measure of a company's efficiency in using its fixed assets to generate sales is the fixed asset turnover ratio. The fixed asset turnover ratio measures the number of dollars of sales earned per dollar of fixed assets and is computed by dividing sales by the average book value of fixed assets.

| Learning Outcomes | Example Exercises | Practice Exercises |
|---|---|---|
| • Describe a measure of the efficiency of a company's use of fixed assets to generate revenue. | EE10-9 | PE10-9A, 10-9B |
| • Compute and interpret the fixed asset turnover ratio. | | |

# Key Terms

accelerated depreciation method (469)
amortization (476)
book value (469)
boot (482)
capital expenditures (463)
capital lease (464)
copyright (477)

depletion (475)
depreciation (465)
double-declining-balance method (469)
fixed asset turnover ratio (480)
fixed assets (460)
goodwill (477)
intangible assets (476)

operating lease (465)
patents (476)
residual value (465)
revenue expenditures (463)
straight-line method (467)
trade-in allowance (482)
trademark (477)
units-of-output method (468)

# Illustrative Problem

McCollum Company, a furniture wholesaler, acquired new equipment at a cost of $150,000 at the beginning of the fiscal year. The equipment has an estimated life of five years and an estimated residual value of $12,000. Ellen McCollum, the president, has requested information regarding alternative depreciation methods.

## Instructions

1. Determine the annual depreciation for each of the five years of estimated useful life of the equipment, the accumulated depreciation at the end of each year, and the book value of the equipment at the end of each year by (a) the straight-line method and (b) the double-declining-balance method.

2. Assume that the equipment was depreciated under the double-declining-balance method. In the first week of the fifth year, the equipment was sold for $10,000. Journalize the entry to record the sale.

## Solution

1.

| | Year | Depreciation Expense | Accumulated Depreciation, End of Year | Book Value, End of Year |
|---|---|---|---|---|
| a. | 1 | $27,600* | $ 27,600 | $122,400 |
| | 2 | 27,600 | 55,200 | 94,800 |
| | 3 | 27,600 | 82,800 | 67,200 |
| | 4 | 27,600 | 110,400 | 39,600 |
| | 5 | 27,600 | 138,000 | 12,000 |

*$27,600 = ($150,000 − $12,000) ÷ 5

| b. | 1 | $60,000** | $ 60,000 | $90,000 |
|---|---|---|---|---|
| | 2 | 36,000 | 96,000 | 54,000 |
| | 3 | 21,600 | 117,600 | 32,400 |
| | 4 | 12,960 | 130,560 | 19,440 |
| | 5 | 7,440*** | 138,000 | 12,000 |

**$60,000 = $150,000 × 40%
***The asset is not depreciated below the estimated residual value of $12,000.
$7,440 = $150,000 − $130,560 − $12,000

2.

| | | Cash | | 10,000 | |
|---|---|---|---|---|---|
| | | Accumulated Depreciation—Equipment | | 130,560 | |
| | | Loss on Sale of Equipment | | 9,440 | |
| | | Equipment | | | 150,000 |

# Discussion Questions

1. O'Neil Office Supplies has a fleet of automobiles and trucks for use by salespersons and for delivery of office supplies and equipment. Collins Auto Sales Co. has automobiles and trucks for sale. Under what caption would the automobiles and trucks be reported in the balance sheet of (a) O'Neil Office Supplies and (b) Collins Auto Sales Co.?

2. Bullwinkle Co. acquired an adjacent vacant lot with the hope of selling it in the future at a gain. The lot is not intended to be used in Bullwinkle business operations. Where should such real estate be listed in the balance sheet?

3. Alpine Company solicited bids from several contractors to construct an addition to its office building. The lowest bid received was for $1,200,000. Alpine Company decided to construct the addition itself at a cost of $1,100,000. What amount should be recorded in the building account?

4. Distinguish between the accounting for capital expenditures and revenue expenditures.

5. Immediately after a used truck is acquired, a new motor is installed at a total cost of $3,850. Is this a capital expenditure or a revenue expenditure?

6. Keyser Company purchased a machine that has a manufacturer's suggested life of 20 years. The company plans to use the machine on a special project that will last 12 years. At the completion of the project, the machine will be sold. Over how many years should the machine be depreciated?

7. Is it necessary for a business to use the same method of computing depreciation (a) for all classes of its depreciable assets and (b) for financial statement purposes and in determining income taxes?

8. a. Under what conditions is the use of an accelerated depreciation method most appropriate?
   b. Why is an accelerated depreciation method often used for income tax purposes?
   c. What is the Modified Accelerated Cost Recovery System (MACRS), and under what conditions is it used?

9. For some of the fixed assets of a business, the balance in Accumulated Depreciation is exactly equal to the cost of the asset. (a) Is it permissible to record additional depreciation on the assets if they are still useful to the business? Explain. (b) When should an entry be made to remove the cost and the accumulated depreciation from the accounts?

10. a. Over what period of time should the cost of a patent acquired by purchase be amortized?
    b. In general, what is the required accounting treatment for research and development costs?
    c. How should goodwill be amortized?

## Practice Exercises

EE 10-1 *p. 464*

SHOW
ME HOW

**PE 10-1A   Capital and revenue expenditures**                                    OBJ. 1

On August 7, Green River Inflatables Co. paid $1,675 to install a hydraulic lift and $40 for an air filter for one of its delivery trucks. Journalize the entries for the new lift and air filter expenditures.

EE 10-1 *p. 464*

SHOW
ME HOW

**PE 10-1B   Capital and revenue expenditures**                                    OBJ. 1

On February 14, Garcia Associates Co. paid $2,300 to repair the transmission on one´of its delivery vans. In addition, Garcia Associates paid $450 to install a GPS system in its van. Journalize the entries for the transmission and GPS system expenditures.

EE 10-2 *p. 467*

SHOW
ME HOW

**PE 10-2A   Straight-line depreciation**                                          OBJ. 2

Equipment acquired at the beginning of the year at a cost of $340,000 has an estimated residual value of $45,000 and an estimated useful life of 10 years. Determine (a) the depreciable cost, (b) the straight-line rate, and (c) the annual straight-line depreciation.

EE 10-2 *p. 467*

SHOW
ME HOW

**PE 10-2B   Straight-line depreciation**                                          OBJ. 2

A building acquired at the beginning of the year at a cost of $1,450,000 has an estimated residual value of $300,000 and an estimated useful life of 10 years. Determine (a) the depreciable cost, (b) the straight-line rate, and (c) the annual straight-line depreciation.

EE 10-3 *p. 468*

SHOW
ME HOW

**PE 10-3A   Units-of-output depreciation**                                        OBJ. 2

A tractor acquired at a cost of $420,000 has an estimated residual value of $30,000, has an estimated useful life of 25,000 hours, and was operated 1,850 hours during the year. Determine (a) the depreciable cost, (b) the depreciation rate, and (c) the units-of-output depreciation for the year.

EE 10-3 *p. 468*

SHOW
ME HOW

**PE 10-3B   Units-of-output depreciation**                                        OBJ. 2

A truck acquired at a cost of $69,000 has an estimated residual value of $12,000, has an estimated useful life of 300,000 miles, and was driven 77,000 miles during the year. Determine (a) the depreciable cost, (b) the depreciation rate, and (c) the units-of-output depreciation for the year.

EE 10-4 *p. 470*

SHOW
ME HOW

**PE 10-4A   Double-declining-balance depreciation**                               OBJ. 2

Equipment acquired at the beginning of the year at a cost of $175,000 has an estimated residual value of $12,000 and an estimated useful life of 10 years. Determine (a) the double-declining-balance rate and (b) the double-declining-balance depreciation for the first year.

EE 10-4 *p. 470*

SHOW
ME HOW

**PE 10-4B   Double-declining-balance depreciation**                               OBJ. 2

A building acquired at the beginning of the year at a cost of $1,375,000 has an estimated residual value of $250,000 and an estimated useful life of 40 years. Determine (a) the double-declining-balance rate and (b) the double-declining-balance depreciation for the first year.

EE 10-5  *p. 473*  **PE 10-5A   Revision of depreciation**    OBJ. 2

SHOW
ME HOW

A truck with a cost of $82,000 has an estimated residual value of $16,000, has an estimated useful life of 12 years, and is depreciated by the straight-line method. (a) Determine the amount of the annual depreciation. (b) Determine the book value at the end of the seventh year of use. (c) Assuming that at the start of the eighth year the remaining life is estimated to be six years and the residual value is estimated to be $12,000, determine the depreciation expense for each of the remaining six years.

EE 10-5  *p. 473*  **PE 10-5B   Revision of depreciation**    OBJ. 2

SHOW
ME HOW

Equipment with a cost of $180,000 has an estimated residual value of $14,400, has an estimated useful life of 16 years, and is depreciated by the straight-line method. (a) Determine the amount of the annual depreciation. (b) Determine the book value at the end of the tenth year of use. (c) Assuming that at the start of the eleventh year the remaining life is estimated to be eight years and the residual value is estimated to be $10,500, determine the depreciation expense for each of the remaining eight years.

EE 10-6  *p. 475*  **PE 10-6A   Sale of equipment**    OBJ. 3

SHOW
ME HOW

Equipment was acquired at the beginning of the year at a cost of $465,000. The equipment was depreciated using the straight-line method based on an estimated useful life of 15 years and an estimated residual value of $45,000.

a.  What was the depreciation for the first year?

b.  Assuming the equipment was sold at the end of the eighth year for $235,000, determine the gain or loss on the sale of the equipment.

c.  Journalize the entry to record the sale.

EE 10-6  *p. 475*  **PE 10-6B   Sale of equipment**    OBJ. 3

SHOW
ME HOW

Equipment was acquired at the beginning of the year at a cost of $600,000. The equipment was depreciated using the double-declining-balance method based on an estimated useful life of 16 years and an estimated residual value of $60,000.

a.  What was the depreciation for the first year?

b.  Assuming the equipment was sold at the end of the second year for $480,000, determine the gain or loss on the sale of the equipment.

c.  Journalize the entry to record the sale.

EE 10-7  *p. 476*  **PE 10-7A   Depletion**    OBJ. 4

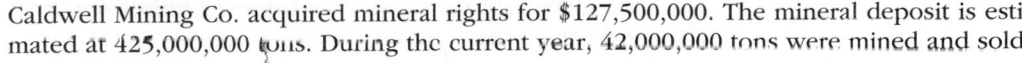
SHOW
ME HOW

Caldwell Mining Co. acquired mineral rights for $127,500,000. The mineral deposit is estimated at 425,000,000 tons. During the current year, 42,000,000 tons were mined and sold.

a.  Determine the depletion rate.

b.  Determine the amount of depletion expense for the current year.

c.  Journalize the adjusting entry on December 31 to recognize the depletion expense.

EE 10-7  *p. 476*  **PE 10-7B   Depletion**    OBJ. 4

SHOW
ME HOW

Glacier Mining Co. acquired mineral rights for $494,000,000. The mineral deposit is estimated at 475,000,000 tons. During the current year, 31,500,000 tons were mined and sold.

a.  Determine the depletion rate.

b.  Determine the amount of depletion expense for the current year.

c.  Journalize the adjusting entry on December 31 to recognize the depletion expense.

EE 10-8 *p. 479*

SHOW
ME HOW

**PE 10-8A    Impaired goodwill and amortization of patent**    OBJ. 5

On December 31, it was estimated that goodwill of $4,000,000 was impaired. In addition, a patent with an estimated useful economic life of 15 years was acquired for $900,000 on August 1.

a.  Journalize the adjusting entry on December 31 for the impaired goodwill.

b.  Journalize the adjusting entry on December 31 for the amortization of the patent rights.

---

EE 10-8 *p. 479*

SHOW
ME HOW

**PE 10-8B    Impaired goodwill and amortization of patent**    OBJ. 5

On December 31, it was estimated that goodwill of $6,000,000 was impaired. In addition, a patent with an estimated useful economic life of 12 years was acquired for $1,500,000 on April 1.

a.  Journalize the adjusting entry on December 31 for the impaired goodwill.

b.  Journalize the adjusting entry on December 31 for the amortization of the patent rights.

---

EE 10-9 *p. 481*

**FAI**

SHOW
ME HOW

**PE 10-9A    Fixed asset turnover ratio**    OBJ. 7

Financial statement data for years ending December 31 for DePuy Company follows:

|  | 2016 | 2015 |
|---|---|---|
| Sales | $5,510,000 | $4,880,000 |
| Fixed assets: | | |
| Beginning of year | 1,600,000 | 1,450,000 |
| End of year | 2,200,000 | 1,600,000 |

a.  Determine the fixed asset turnover ratio for 2016 and 2015.

b.  Does the change in the fixed asset turnover ratio from 2015 to 2016 indicate a favorable or an unfavorable trend?

---

EE 10-9 *p. 481*

**FAI**

SHOW
ME HOW

**PE 10-9B    Fixed asset turnover ratio**    OBJ. 7

Financial statement data for years ending December 31 for Davenport Company follows:

|  | 2016 | 2015 |
|---|---|---|
| Sales | $1,668,000 | $1,125,000 |
| Fixed assets: | | |
| Beginning of year | 670,000 | 580,000 |
| End of year | 720,000 | 670,000 |

a.  Determine the fixed asset turnover ratio for 2016 and 2015.

b.  Does the change in the fixed asset turnover ratio from 2015 to 2016 indicate a favorable or an unfavorable trend?

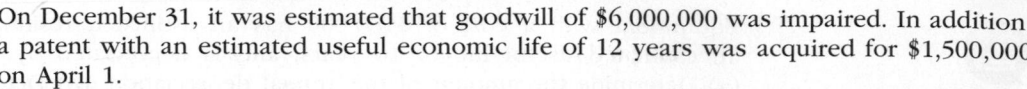

# Exercises

**EX 10-1    Costs of acquiring fixed assets**    OBJ. 1

Melinda Stoffers owns and operates ABC Print Co. During February, ABC Print Co. incurred the following costs in acquiring two printing presses. One printing press was new, and the other was bought from a business that recently filed for bankruptcy.

Costs related to new printing press:

1.  Fee paid to factory representative for installation

2.  Freight

3.  Insurance while in transit

4.  New parts to replace those damaged in unloading

5. Sales tax on purchase price
6. Special foundation

Costs related to used printing press:

7. Fees paid to attorney to review purchase agreement
8. Freight
9. Installation
10. Repair of damage incurred in reconditioning the press
11. Replacement of worn-out parts
12. Vandalism repairs during installation

a. Indicate which costs incurred in acquiring the new printing press should be debited to the asset account.

b. Indicate which costs incurred in acquiring the used printing press should be debited to the asset account.

---

**EX 10-2    Determining cost of land**                                          OBJ. 1

Bridger Ski Co. has developed a tract of land into a ski resort. The company has cut the trees, cleared and graded the land and hills, and constructed ski lifts. (a) Should the tree cutting, land clearing, and grading costs of constructing the ski slopes be debited to the land account? (b) If such costs are debited to Land, should they be depreciated?

---

**EX 10-3    Determining cost of land**                                          OBJ. 1

✔ $196,900

SHOW
ME HOW

Northwest Delivery Company acquired an adjacent lot to construct a new warehouse, paying $75,000 and giving a short-term note for $90,000. Legal fees paid were $2,500, delinquent taxes assumed were $22,400, and fees paid to remove an old building from the land were $14,500. Materials salvaged from the demolition of the building were sold for $7,500. A contractor was paid $660,000 to construct a new warehouse. Determine the cost of the land to be reported on the balance sheet.

---

**EX 10-4    Capital and revenue expenditures**                                  OBJ. 1

Warner Freight Lines Co. incurred the following costs related to trucks and vans used in operating its delivery service:

1. Changed the oil and greased the joints of all the trucks and vans.
2. Changed the radiator fluid on a truck that had been in service for the past four years.
3. Installed a hydraulic lift to a van.
4. Installed security systems on four of the newer trucks.
5. Overhauled the engine on one of the trucks purchased three years ago.
6. Rebuilt the transmission on one of the vans that had been driven 40,000 miles. The van was no longer under warranty.
7. Removed a two-way radio from one of the trucks and installed a new radio with a greater range of communication.
8. Repaired a flat tire on one of the vans.
9. Replaced a truck's suspension system with a new suspension system that allows for the delivery of heavier loads.
10. Tinted the back and side windows of one of the vans to discourage theft of contents.

Classify each of the costs as a capital expenditure or a revenue expenditure.

---

**EX 10-5 Capital and revenue expenditures**                                OBJ. 1

Jackie Fox owns and operates Platinum Transport Co. During the past year, Jackie incurred the following costs related to an 18-wheel truck:

1. Changed engine oil.
2. Installed a television in the sleeping compartment of the truck.
3. Installed a wind deflector on top of the cab to increase fuel mileage.
4. Modified the factory-installed turbo charger with a special-order kit designed to add 50 more horsepower to the engine performance.
5. Replaced a headlight that had burned out.
6. Replaced a shock absorber that had worn out.
7. Replaced fog and cab light bulbs.
8. Replaced the hydraulic brake system that had begun to fail during his latest trip through the Rocky Mountains.
9. Removed the old CB radio and replaced it with a newer model with a greater range.
10. Replaced the old radar detector with a newer model that is fastened to the truck with a locking device that prevents its removal.

Classify each of the costs as a capital expenditure or a revenue expenditure.

---

SHOW
ME HOW

**EX 10-6 Capital and revenue expenditures**                                OBJ. 1

Quality Move Company made the following expenditures on one of its delivery trucks:

Mar. 20.  Replaced the transmission at a cost of $1,890.

June 11.  Paid $1,350 for installation of a hydraulic lift.

Nov. 30.  Paid $55 to change the oil and air filter.

Prepare journal entries for each expenditure.

---

**EX 10-7 Nature of depreciation**                                OBJ. 2

Tri-City Ironworks Co. reported $44,500,000 for equipment and $29,800,000 for accumulated depreciation—equipment on its balance sheet.

Does this mean (a) that the replacement cost of the equipment is $44,500,000 and (b) that $29,800,000 is set aside in a special fund for the replacement of the equipment? Explain.

---

✔ c. 10%

**EX 10-8 Straight-line depreciation rates**                                OBJ. 2

Convert each of the following estimates of useful life to a straight-line depreciation rate, stated as a percentage: (a) 4 years, (b) 8 years, (c) 10 years, (d) 16 years, (e) 25 years, (f) 40 years, (g) 50 years.

---

✔ $2,600

SHOW
ME HOW

**EX 10-9 Straight-line depreciation**                                OBJ. 2

A refrigerator used by a meat processor has a cost of $48,000, an estimated residual value of $9,000, and an estimated useful life of 15 years. What is the amount of the annual depreciation computed by the straight-line method?

---

✔ $702

SHOW
ME HOW

**EX 10-10 Depreciation by units-of-output method**                                OBJ. 2

A diesel-powered tractor with a cost of $180,000 and estimated residual value of $18,000 is expected to have a useful operating life of 36,000 hours. During February, the tractor was operated 156 hours. Determine the depreciation for the month.

✔ a. Truck #1, credit to Accumulated Depreciation, $5,460

SHOW
ME HOW

**EX 10-11    Depreciation by units-of-output method**                    OBJ. 2

Prior to adjustment at the end of the year, the balance in Trucks is $296,900 and the balance in Accumulated Depreciation—Trucks is $99,740. Details of the subsidiary ledger are as follows:

| Truck No. | Cost | Estimated Residual Value | Estimated Useful Life | Accumulated Depreciation at Beginning of Year | Miles Operated During Year |
|---|---|---|---|---|---|
| 1 | $80,000 | $15,000 | 250,000 miles | — | 21,000 miles |
| 2 | 54,000 | 6,000 | 300,000 | $14,400 | 33,500 |
| 3 | 72,900 | 10,900 | 200,000 | 60,140 | 8,000 |
| 4 | 90,000 | 22,800 | 240,000 | 25,200 | 22,500 |

a.  Determine the depreciation rates per mile and the amount to be credited to the accumulated depreciation section of each of the subsidiary accounts for the miles operated during the current year.

b.  Journalize the entry to record depreciation for the year.

**EX 10-12    Depreciation by two methods**                              OBJ. 2

✔ a. $4,800

SHOW
ME HOW

A John Deere tractor acquired on January 4 at a cost of $120,000 has an estimated useful life of 25 years. Assuming that it will have no residual value, determine the depreciation for each of the first two years (a) by the straight-line method and (b) by the double-declining-balance method.

**EX 10-13    Depreciation by two methods**                              OBJ. 2

✔ a. $3,250

SHOW
ME HOW

A storage tank acquired at the beginning of the fiscal year at a cost of $75,000 has an estimated residual value of $10,000 and an estimated useful life of 20 years. Determine the following: (a) the amount of annual depreciation by the straight-line method and (b) the amount of depreciation for the first and second years computed by the double-declining-balance method.

**EX 10-14    Partial-year depreciation**                                OBJ. 2

✔ a. First year, $3,000

SHOW
ME HOW

Sandblasting equipment acquired at a cost of $40,000 has an estimated residual value of $8,000 and an estimated useful life of eight years. It was placed into service on April 1 of the current fiscal year, which ends on December 31. Determine the depreciation for the current fiscal year and for the following fiscal year by (a) the straight-line method and (b) the double-declining-balance method.

**EX 10-15    Revision of depreciation**                                 OBJ. 2

✔ a. $23,750

SHOW
ME HOW

A building with a cost of $1,200,000 has an estimated residual value of $250,000, has an estimated useful life of 40 years, and is depreciated by the straight-line method. (a) What is the amount of the annual depreciation? (b) What is the book value at the end of the twenty-eighth year of use? (c) If at the start of the twenty-ninth year it is estimated that the remaining life is 10 years and that the residual value is $180,000 what is the depreciation expense for each of the remaining 10 years?

**EX 10-16    Capital expenditure and depreciation**                     OBJ. 1, 2

✔ b. Depreciation Expense, $800

Willow Creek Company purchased and installed carpet in its new general offices on April 30 for a total cost of $18,000. The carpet is estimated to have a 15 year useful life and no residual value.

a.  Prepare the journal entry necessary for recording the purchase of the new carpet.

b.  Record the December 31 adjusting entry for the partial-year depreciation expense for the carpet, assuming that Willow Creek Company uses the straight-line method.

### EX 10-17 Entries for sale of fixed asset

**OBJ. 3**

Equipment acquired on January 8, 2013, at a cost of $140,000, has an estimated useful life of 16 years, has an estimated residual value of $8,000, and is depreciated by the straight-line method.

a. What was the book value of the equipment at December 31, 2016, the end of the year?

b. Assuming that the equipment was sold on July 1, 2017, for $96,700, journalize the entries to record (1) depreciation for the six months until the sale date, and (2) the sale of the equipment.

✔ b. $357,500

### EX 10-18 Disposal of fixed asset

**OBJ. 3**

Equipment acquired on January 6, 2013, at a cost of $425,000, has an estimated useful life of 16 years and an estimated residual value of $65,000

a. What was the annual amount of depreciation for the years 2013, 2014, and 2015 using the straight-line method of depreciation?

b. What was the book value of the equipment on January 1, 2016?

c. Assuming that the equipment was sold on January 3, 2016, for $340,000, journalize the entry to record the sale.

d. Assuming that the equipment had been sold on January 3, 2016, for $372,500 instead of $340,000, journalize the entry to record the sale.

✔ a. $3,885,000

### EX 10-19 Depletion entries

**OBJ. 4**

Big Sky Mining Co. acquired mineral rights for $42,000,000. The mineral deposit is estimated at 20,000,000 tons. During the current year, 1,850,000 tons were mined and sold.

a. Determine the amount of depletion expense for the current year.

b. Journalize the adjusting entry to recognize the depletion expense.

✔ a. $105,500

### EX 10-20 Amortization entries

**OBJ. 5**

Smith Company acquired patent rights on January 6, 2013, for $882,000. The patent has a useful life equal to its legal life of nine years. On January 3, 2016, Smith successfully defended the patent in a lawsuit at a cost of $45,000.

a. Determine the patent amortization expense for the year ended December 31, 2016.

b. Journalize the adjusting entry to recognize the amortization.

### EX 10-21 Book value of fixed assets

**OBJ. 6**

Apple Inc. designs, manufactures, and markets personal computers and related software. Apple also manufactures and distributes music players (iPod) and mobile phones (iPhone) along with related accessories and services, including online distribution of third-party music, videos, and applications. The following information was taken from a recent annual report of Apple:

Property, Plant, and Equipment (in millions):

|  | Current Year | Preceding Year |
|---|---|---|
| Land and buildings | $ 2,439 | $2,059 |
| Machinery, equipment, and internal-use software | 15,743 | 6,926 |
| Office furniture and equipment | 241 | 184 |
| Other fixed assets related to leases | 3,464 | 2,599 |
| Accumulated depreciation and amortization | 6,435 | 3,991 |

a. Compute the book value of the fixed assets for the current year and the preceding year and explain the differences, if any.

b. ━━━▶ Would you normally expect Apple's book value of fixed assets to increase or decrease during the year?

### EX 10-22 Balance sheet presentation

OBJ. 6

List the errors you find in the following partial balance sheet:

**Burnt Red Company**
**Balance Sheet**
**December 31, 2016**

**Assets**

Total current assets.................................................... $350,000

| Property, plant, and equipment: | Replacement Cost | Accumulated Depreciation | Book Value |
|---|---|---|---|
| Land........................................ | $ 250,000 | $ 50,000 | $200,000 |
| Buildings................................... | 450,000 | 160,000 | 290,000 |
| Factory equipment ....................... | 375,000 | 140,000 | 235,000 |
| Office equipment.......................... | 125,000 | 60,000 | 65,000 |
| Patents .................................... | 90,000 | — | 90,000 |
| Goodwill ................................... | 60,000 | 10,000 | 50,000 |
| Total property, plant, and equipment ........ | $1,350,000 | $420,000 | $930,000 |

### EX 10-23 Fixed asset turnover ratio

OBJ. 7

**Verizon Communications** is a major telecommunications company in the United States. Two recent balance sheets for Verizon disclosed the following information regarding fixed assets:

| | Year 2 (in millions) | Year 1 (in millions) |
|---|---|---|
| Plant, property, and equipment | $209,575 | $215,626 |
| Less accumulated depreciation | 120,933 | 127,192 |
| | $ 88,642 | $ 88,434 |

Verizon's revenue for Year 2 was $115,846 million. Assume the fixed asset turnover for the telecommunications industry averages approximately 1.10.

a. Determine Verizon's fixed asset turnover ratio for Year 2. Round to two decimal places.

b. ➤ Interpret Verizon's fixed asset turnover ratio.

### EX 10-24 Fixed asset turnover ratio

OBJ. 7

The following table shows the revenue and average net fixed assets (in millions) for a recent fiscal year for **Best Buy** and **RadioShack**:

| | Revenue | Average Net Fixed Assets |
|---|---|---|
| Best Buy | $50,705 | $3,647 |
| RadioShack | 4,258 | 255 |

a. Compute the fixed asset turnover for each company. Round to two decimal places.

b. Which company uses its fixed assets more efficiently? Explain.

### Appendix
### EX 10-25 Asset traded for similar asset

✔ a. $185,000

A printing press priced at a fair market value of $275,000 is acquired in a transaction that has commercial substance by trading in a similar press and paying cash for the difference between the trade-in allowance and the price of the new press.

a. Assuming that the trade-in allowance is $90,000, what is the amount of cash given?

b. Assuming that the book value of the press traded in is $68,000, what is the gain or loss on the exchange?

**Appendix**

**EX 10-26   Asset traded for similar asset**

✔ b. $18,500 loss

Assume the same facts as in Exercise 10-25, except that the book value of the press traded in is $108,500. (a) What is the amount of cash given? (b) What is the gain or loss on the exchange?

**Appendix**

**EX 10-27   Entries for trade of fixed asset**

On July 1, Twin Pines Co., a water distiller, acquired new bottling equipment with a list price (fair market value) of $220,000. Twin Pines received a trade-in allowance (fair market value) of $45,000 on the old equipment of a similar type and paid cash of $175,000. The following information about the old equipment is obtained from the account in the equipment ledger: cost, $180,000; accumulated depreciation on December 31, the end of the preceding fiscal year, $120,000; annual depreciation, $12,000. Assuming the exchange has commercial substance, journalize the entries to record (a) the current depreciation of the old equipment to the date of trade-in and (b) the exchange transaction on July 1.

**Appendix**

**EX 10-28   Entries for trade of fixed asset**

On October 1, Bentley Delivery Services acquired a new truck with a list price (fair market value) of $75,000. Bentley Delivery received a trade-in allowance (fair market value) of $24,000 on an old truck of similar type and paid cash of $51,000. The following information about the old truck is obtained from the account in the equipment ledger: cost, $56,000; accumulated depreciation on December 31, the end of the preceding fiscal year, $35,000; annual depreciation, $7,000. Assuming the exchange has commercial substance, journalize the entries to record (a) the current depreciation of the old truck to the date of trade-in and (b) the transaction on October 1.

# Problems: Series A

**PR 10-1A   Allocating payments and receipts to fixed asset accounts**          OBJ. 1

✔ Land, $400,000

The following payments and receipts are related to land, land improvements, and buildings acquired for use in a wholesale ceramic business. The receipts are identified by an asterisk.

| | | |
|---|---|---:|
| a. | Fee paid to attorney for title search | $   2,500 |
| b. | Cost of real estate acquired as a plant site: Land | 285,000 |
| | Building | 55,000 |
| c. | Delinquent real estate taxes on property, assumed by purchaser | 15,500 |
| d. | Cost of razing and removing building | 5,000 |
| e. | Proceeds from sale of salvage materials from old building | 4,000* |
| f. | Special assessment paid to city for extension of water main to the property | 29,000 |
| g. | Architect's and engineer's fees for plans and supervision | 60,000 |
| h. | Premium on one-year insurance policy during construction | 6,000 |
| i. | Cost of filling and grading land | 12,000 |
| j. | Money borrowed to pay building contractor | 900,000* |
| k. | Cost of repairing windstorm damage during construction | 5,500 |
| l. | Cost of paving parking lot to be used by customers | 32,000 |
| m. | Cost of trees and shrubbery planted | 11,000 |
| n. | Cost of floodlights installed on parking lot | 2,000 |
| o. | Cost of repairing vandalism damage during construction | 2,500 |
| p. | Proceeds from insurance company for windstorm and vandalism damage | 7,500* |
| q. | Payment to building contractor for new building | 800,000 |
| r. | Interest incurred on building loan during construction | 34,500 |
| s. | Refund of premium on insurance policy (h) canceled after 11 months | 500* |

## Instructions

1. Assign each payment and receipt to Land (unlimited life), Land Improvements (limited life), Building, or Other Accounts. Indicate receipts by an asterisk. Identify each item by letter and list the amounts in columnar form, as follows:

| Item | Land | Land Improvements | Building | Other Accounts |
|------|------|-------------------|----------|----------------|

2. Determine the amount debited to Land, Land Improvements, and Building.

3. ⟶ The costs assigned to the land, which is used as a plant site, will not be depreciated, while the costs assigned to land improvements will be depreciated. Explain this seemingly contradictory application of the concept of depreciation.

4. What would be the effect on the income statement and balance sheet if the cost of filling and grading land of $12,000 [payment (i)] was incorrectly classified as Land Improvements rather than Land? Assume Land Improvements are depreciated over a 20-year life using the double-declining-balance method.

---

### PR 10-2A Comparing three depreciation methods OBJ. 2

✔ 1. a. 2014: straight-line depreciation, $28,000

SHOW ME HOW

Monte's Coffee Company purchased packaging equipment on January 5, 2014, for $90,000. The equipment was expected to have a useful life of three years, or 20,000 operating hours, and a residual value of $6,000. The equipment was used for 8,900 hours during 2014, 7,100 hours in 2015, and 4,000 hours in 2016.

#### Instructions

1. Determine the amount of depreciation expense for the years ended December 31, 2014, 2015, and 2016 by (a) the straight-line method, (b) the units-of-output method, and (c) the double-declining-balance method. Also determine the total depreciation expense for the three years by each method. The following columnar headings are suggested for recording the depreciation expense amounts:

| | Depreciation Expense | | |
|------|----------------------|-----------------|----------------------------|
| Year | Straight-Line Method | Units-of-Output Method | Double-Declining-Balance Method |

2. What method yields the highest depreciation expense for 2014?

3. What method yields the most depreciation over the three-year life of the equipment?

---

### PR 10-3A Depreciation by three methods; partial years OBJ. 2

✔ a. 2014: $65,250

Perdue Company purchased equipment on April 1, 2014, for $270,000. The equipment was expected to have a useful life of three years, or 18,000 operating hours, and a residual value of $9,000. The equipment was used for 7,500 hours during 2014, 5,500 hours in 2015, 4,000 hours in 2016, and 1,000 hours in 2017.

#### Instructions

Determine the amount of depreciation expense for the years ended December 31, 2014, 2015, 2016, and 2017, by (a) the straight-line method, (b) the units-of-output method, and (c) the double-declining-balance method.

---

### PR 10-4A Depreciation by two methods; sale of fixed asset OBJ. 2, 3

✔ 1. b. Year 1: $320,000 depreciation expense

General Ledger

New lithographic equipment, acquired at a cost of $800,000 at the beginning of a fiscal year, has an estimated useful life of five years and an estimated residual value of $90,000. The manager requested information regarding the effect of alternative methods on the amount of depreciation expense each year. On the basis of the data presented to the manager, the double-declining-balance method was selected.

In the first week of the fifth year, the equipment was sold for $135,000.

#### Instructions

1. Determine the annual depreciation expense for each of the estimated five years of use, the accumulated depreciation at the end of each year, and the book value of the equipment at the end of each year by (a) the straight-line method and (b) the

(*Continued*)

double-declining-balance method. The following columnar headings are suggested for each schedule:

| Year | Depreciation Expense | Accumulated Depreciation, End of Year | Book Value, End of Year |
|------|---------------------|----------------------------------------|--------------------------|

2. Journalize the entry to record the sale.

3. Journalize the entry to record the sale, assuming that the equipment was sold for $88,750 instead of $135,000.

---

**PR 10-5A** **Transactions for fixed assets, including sale** OBJ. 1, 2, 3

General Ledger

The following transactions, adjusting entries, and closing entries were completed by Legacy Furniture Co. during a three-year period. All are related to the use of delivery equipment. The double-declining-balance method of depreciation is used.

**2014**

Jan.  4.  Purchased a used delivery truck for $28,000, paying cash.

Nov.  2.  Paid garage $675 for miscellaneous repairs to the truck.

Dec. 31.  Recorded depreciation on the truck for the year. The estimated useful life of the truck is four years, with a residual value of $5,000 for the truck.

**2015**

Jan.  6.  Purchased a new truck for $48,000, paying cash.

Apr.  1.  Sold the used truck for $15,000. (Record depreciation to date in 2015 for the truck.)

June 11.  Paid garage $450 for miscellaneous repairs to the truck.

Dec. 31.  Record depreciation for the new truck. It has an estimated residual value of $9,000 and an estimated life of five years.

**2016**

July  1.  Purchased a new truck for $54,000, paying cash.

Oct.  2.  Sold the truck purchased January 6, 2015, for $16,750. (Record depreciation to date for 2016 for the truck.)

Dec. 31.  Recorded depreciation on the remaining truck. It has an estimated residual value of $12,000 and an estimated useful life of eight years.

**Instructions**

Journalize the transactions and the adjusting entries.

---

**PR 10-6A** **Amortization and depletion entries** OBJ. 4, 5

✔ 1. a. $352,000

Data related to the acquisition of timber rights and intangible assets during the current year ended December 31 are as follows:

a. Timber rights on a tract of land were purchased for $1,600,000 on February 22. The stand of timber is estimated at 5,000,000 board feet. During the current year, 1,100,000 board feet of timber were cut and sold.

b. On December 31, the company determined that $3,750,000 of goodwill was impaired.

c. Governmental and legal costs of $6,600,000 were incurred on April 3 in obtaining a patent with an estimated economic life of 12 years. Amortization is to be for three-fourths of a year.

**Instructions**

1. Determine the amount of the amortization, depletion, or impairment for the current year for each of the foregoing items.

2. Journalize the adjusting entries required to record the amortization, depletion, or impairment for each item.

## Problems: Series B

### PR 10-1B  Allocating payments and receipts to fixed asset accounts

OBJ. 1

✔ Land, $860,000

The following payments and receipts are related to land, land improvements, and buildings acquired for use in a wholesale apparel business. The receipts are identified by an asterisk.

| | | |
|---|---|---:|
| a. | Fee paid to attorney for title search | $ 3,600 |
| b. | Cost of real estate acquired as a plant site: Land | 720,000 |
| | Building | 60,000 |
| c. | Finder's fee paid to real estate agency | 23,400 |
| d. | Delinquent real estate taxes on property, assumed by purchaser | 15,000 |
| e. | Architect's and engineer's fees for plans and supervision | 75,000 |
| f. | Cost of removing building purchased with land in (b) | 10,000 |
| g. | Proceeds from sale of salvage materials from old building | 3,400* |
| h. | Cost of filling and grading land | 18,000 |
| i. | Premium on one-year insurance policy during construction | 8,400 |
| j. | Money borrowed to pay building contractor | 800,000* |
| k. | Special assessment paid to city for extension of water main to the property | 13,400 |
| l. | Cost of repairing windstorm damage during construction | 3,000 |
| m. | Cost of repairing vandalism damage during construction | 2,000 |
| n. | Cost of trees and shrubbery planted | 14,000 |
| o. | Cost of paving parking lot to be used by customers | 21,600 |
| p. | Interest incurred on building loan during construction | 40,000 |
| q. | Proceeds from insurance company for windstorm and vandalism damage | 4,500* |
| r. | Payment to building contractor for new building | 800,000 |
| s. | Refund of premium on insurance policy (i) canceled after 10 months | 1,400* |

#### Instructions

1. Assign each payment and receipt to Land (unlimited life), Land Improvements (limited life), Building, or Other Accounts. Indicate receipts by an asterisk. Identify each item by letter and list the amounts in columnar form, as follows:

| Item | Land | Land Improvements | Building | Other Accounts |
|------|------|-------------------|----------|----------------|

2. Determine the amount debited to Land, Land Improvements, and Building.

3. ➤ The costs assigned to the land, which is used as a plant site, will not be depreciated, while the costs assigned to land improvements will be depreciated. Explain this seemingly contradictory application of the concept of depreciation.

4. What would be the effect on the income statement and balance sheet if the cost of paving the parking lot of $21,600 [payment (o)] was incorrectly classified as Land rather than Land Improvements? Assume Land Improvements are depreciated over a 10-year life using the double-declining-balance method.

### PR 10-2B  Comparing three depreciation methods

OBJ. 2

✔ 1. a. 2015: straight-line depreciation, $71,250

Waylander Coatings Company purchased waterproofing equipment on January 6, 2015, for $320,000. The equipment was expected to have a useful life of four years, or 20,000 operating hours, and a residual value of $35,000. The equipment was used for 7,200 hours during 2015, 6,400 hours in 2016, 4,400 hours in 2017, and 2,000 hours in 2018.

SHOW
ME HOW

#### Instructions

1. Determine the amount of depreciation expense for the years ended December 31, 2015, 2016, 2017, and 2018, by (a) the straight-line method, (b) the units-of-output method, and (c) the double-declining-balance method. Also determine the total depreciation expense for the four years by each method. The following columnar headings are suggested for recording the depreciation expense amounts:

| | Depreciation Expense | | |
|---|---|---|---|
| Year | Straight-Line Method | Units-of-Output Method | Double-Declining-Balance Method |

*(Continued)*

2. What method yields the highest depreciation expense for 2015?

3. What method yields the most depreciation over the four-year life of the equipment?

---

**PR 10-3B   Depreciation by three methods; partial years**                              OBJ. 2

✔ a. 2014, $8,400

Layton Company purchased tool sharpening equipment on October 1, 2014, for $108,000. The equipment was expected to have a useful life of three years, or 12,000 operating hours, and a residual value of $7,200. The equipment was used for 1,350 hours during 2014, 4,200 hours in 2015, 3,650 hours in 2016, and 2,800 hours in 2017.

**Instructions**

Determine the amount of depreciation expense for the years ended December 31, 2014, 2015, 2016, and 2017, by (a) the straight-line method, (b) the units-of-output method, and (c) the double-declining-balance method.

---

**PR 10-4B   Depreciation by two methods; sale of fixed asset**                        OBJ. 2, 3

✔ 1. b. Year 1, $55,000
depreciation expense

**General Ledger**

New tire retreading equipment, acquired at a cost of $110,000 at the beginning of a fiscal year, has an estimated useful life of four years and an estimated residual value of $7,500. The manager requested information regarding the effect of alternative methods on the amount of depreciation expense each year. On the basis of the data presented to the manager, the double-declining-balance method was selected.

In the first week of the fourth year, the equipment was sold for $18,000.

**Instructions**

1. Determine the annual depreciation expense for each of the estimated four years of use, the accumulated depreciation at the end of each year, and the book value of the equipment at the end of each year by (a) the straight-line method and (b) the double-declining-balance method. The following columnar headings are suggested for each schedule:

| Year | Depreciation Expense | Accumulated Depreciation, End of Year | Book Value, End of Year |
|------|----------------------|---------------------------------------|-------------------------|

2. Journalize the entry to record the sale.

3. Journalize the entry to record the sale, assuming that the equipment sold for $10,500 instead of $18,000.

---

**PR 10-5B   Transactions for fixed assets, including sale**                          OBJ. 1, 2, 3

**General Ledger**

The following transactions, adjusting entries, and closing entries were completed by Robinson Furniture Co. during a three-year period. All are related to the use of delivery equipment. The double-declining-balance method of depreciation is used.

**2014**

Jan.   8. Purchased a used delivery truck for $24,000, paying cash.

Mar.   7. Paid garage $900 for changing the oil, replacing the oil filter, and tuning the engine on the delivery truck.

Dec. 31. Recorded depreciation on the truck for the fiscal year. The estimated useful life of the truck is four years, with a residual value of $4,000 for the truck.

**2015**

Jan.   9. Purchased a new truck for $50,000, paying cash.

Feb. 28. Paid garage $250 to tune the engine and make other minor repairs on the used truck.

Apr. 30. Sold the used truck for $9,500. (Record depreciation to date in 2015 for the truck.)

Dec. 31. Record depreciation for the new truck. It has an estimated residual value of $12,000 and an estimated life of eight years.

2016

Sept. 1. Purchased a new truck for $58,500, paying cash.

4. Sold the truck purchased January 9, 2015, for $36,000. (Record depreciation to date for 2016 for the truck.)

Dec. 31. Recorded depreciation on the remaining truck. It has an estimated residual value of $16,000 and an estimated useful life of 10 years.

**Instructions**

Journalize the transactions and the adjusting entries.

---

✔ b. $150,000

**PR 10-6B   Amortization and depletion entries**                          OBJ. 4, 5

Data related to the acquisition of timber rights and intangible assets during the current year ended December 31 are as follows:

a. On December 31, the company determined that $3,400,000 of goodwill was impaired.

b. Governmental and legal costs of $4,800,000 were incurred on September 30 in obtaining a patent with an estimated economic life of eight years. Amortization is to be for one-fourth year.

c. Timber rights on a tract of land were purchased for $2,975,000 on February 4. The stand of timber is estimated at 12,500,000 board feet. During the current year, 4,150,000 board feet of timber were cut and sold.

**Instructions**

1. Determine the amount of the amortization, depletion, or impairment for the current year for each of the foregoing items.

2. Journalize the adjusting entries to record the amortization, depletion, or impairment for each item.

---

# Cases & Projects

**CP 10-1   Ethics and professional conduct in business**

Dave Elliott, CPA, is an assistant to the controller of Lyric Consulting Co. In his spare time, Dave also prepares tax returns and performs general accounting services for clients. Frequently, Dave performs these services after his normal working hours, using Lyric Consulting Co.'s computers and laser printers. Occasionally, Dave's clients will call him at the office during regular working hours.

━━━━━▶ Discuss whether Dave is performing in a professional manner.

**CP 10-2   Financial vs. tax depreciation**

The following is an excerpt from a conversation between two employees of WXT Technologies, Nolan Sears and Stacy Mays. Nolan is the accounts payable clerk, and Stacy is the cashier.

*Nolan:* Stacy, could I get your opinion on something?

*Stacy:* Sure, Nolan.

*Nolan:* Do you know Rita, the fixed assets clerk?

*Stacy:* I know who she is, but I don't know her real well. Why?

*Nolan:* Well, I was talking to her at lunch last Monday about how she liked her job, etc. You know, the usual . . . and she mentioned something about having to keep two sets of books . . . one for taxes and one for the financial statements. That can't be good accounting, can it? What do you think?

*Stacy:* Two sets of books? It doesn't sound right.

*Nolan:* It doesn't seem right to me either. I was always taught that you had to use generally accepted accounting principles. How can there be two sets of books? What can be the difference between the two?

━━━━━▶ How would you respond to Nolan and Stacy if you were Rita?

### CP 10-3   Effect of depreciation on net income

Tuttle Construction Co. specializes in building replicas of historic houses. Tim Newman, president of Tuttle Construction, is considering the purchase of various items of equipment on July 1, 2014, for $400,000. The equipment would have a useful life of five years and no residual value. In the past, all equipment has been leased. For tax purposes, Tim is considering depreciating the equipment by the straight-line method. He discussed the matter with his CPA and learned that, although the straight-line method could be elected, it was to his advantage to use the Modified Accelerated Cost Recovery System (MACRS) for tax purposes. He asked for your advice as to which method to use for tax purposes.

1.  Compute depreciation for each of the years (2014, 2015, 2016, 2017, 2018, and 2019) of useful life by (a) the straight-line method and (b) MACRS. In using the straight-line method, one-half year's depreciation should be computed for 2014 and 2019. Use the MACRS rates presented in Exhibit 9.

2.  Assuming that income before depreciation and income tax is estimated to be $750,000 uniformly per year and that the income tax rate is 40%, compute the net income for each of the years 2014, 2015, 2016, 2017, 2018, and 2019 if (a) the straight-line method is used and (b) MACRS is used.

3.   What factors would you present for Tim's consideration in the selection of a depreciation method?

### CP 10-4   Applying for patents, copyrights, and trademarks

**Group Project**

Go to the Internet and review the procedures for applying for a patent, a copyright, and a trademark. You may find information available on Wikipedia (Wikipedia.org) useful for this purpose. Prepare a brief written summary of these procedures.

### CP 10-5   Fixed asset turnover: three industries

 **FAI**

The following table shows the revenues and average net fixed assets for a recent fiscal year for three different companies from three different industries: retailing, manufacturing, and communications.

|  | Revenues (in millions) | Average Net Fixed Assets (in millions) |
| --- | --- | --- |
| Walmart | $446,950 | $110,101 |
| Occidental Petroleum Corporation | 24,172 | 48,874 |
| Comcast Corporation | 62,570 | 27,396 |

a.  For each company, determine the fixed asset turnover ratio. Round to two decimal places.

b.  Explain Walmart's ratio relative to the other two companies.

# Current Liabilities and Payroll

## Starbucks

**B**uying goods on credit is essential for businesses to run efficiently. The use of credit makes transactions more convenient and improves buying power. For *individuals*, the most common form of short-term credit is a credit card. Credit cards allow individuals to purchase items before they are paid for, while removing the need for individuals to carry large amounts of cash. They also provide documentation of purchases through a monthly credit card statement.

Short-term credit is also used by *businesses* to make purchasing items for manufacture or resale more convenient. It also gives the business control over the payment for goods and services. When **Starbucks** opened its first coffee shop in 1971, it relied on short-term trade credit, or accounts payable,

to purchase ingredients for its coffee shop in Seattle's historic Pike Place Market. Today, Starbucks still relies on accounts payable and short-term trade credit, which also gives them control over cash payments by separating the purchase function from the payment function. Thus, the employee responsible for purchasing the ingredients is separated from the employee responsible for paying for the purchase. This separation of duties can help prevent unauthorized purchases or payments.

In addition to accounts payable, a business like Starbucks can also have current liabilities related to payroll, payroll taxes, employee benefits, short-term notes, unearned revenue, and contingencies. This chapter discusses each of these types of current liabilities.

## Learning Objectives

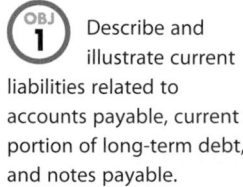

**OBJ 1** Describe and illustrate current liabilities related to accounts payable, current portion of long-term debt, and notes payable.

# Current Liabilities

When a company or a bank advances *credit*, it is making a loan. The company or bank is called a *creditor* (or *lender*). The individuals or companies receiving the loan are called *debtors* (or *borrowers*).

Debt is recorded as a liability by the debtor. *Long-term liabilities* are debts due beyond one year. Thus, a 30-year mortgage used to purchase property is a long-term liability. *Current liabilities* are debts that will be paid out of current assets and are due within one year.

Three types of current liabilities are discussed in this section—accounts payable, the current portion of long-term debt, and short-term notes payable.

## Accounts Payable

Accounts payable transactions have been described and illustrated in earlier chapters. These transactions involve a variety of purchases on account, including the purchase of merchandise and supplies. For most companies, accounts payable is the largest current liability. Exhibit 1 shows the accounts payable balance as a percent of total current liabilities for a number of companies.

| Company | Accounts Payable as a Percent of Total Current Liabilities |
|---|---|
| Alcoa Inc............................................................................................... | 45% |
| Chevron Corp......................................................................................... | 67 |
| Gap Inc. ................................................................................................ | 50 |
| IBM ........................................................................................................ | 18 |
| Verizon Communications, Inc............................................................... | 60 |
| Walgreen Corp....................................................................................... | 50 |

**EXHIBIT 1**

**Accounts Payable as a Percent of Total Current Liabilities**

## Current Portion of Long-Term Debt

Long-term liabilities are often paid back in periodic payments, called *installments*. Such installments that are due *within* the coming year are classified as a current liability. The installments due *after* the coming year are classified as a long-term liability.

To illustrate, **The Coca-Cola Company** reported the following debt payments schedule (in millions):[1]

| Fiscal year ending | |
|---|---|
| 2013 | $ 1,577 |
| 2014 | 2,633 |
| 2015 | 2,451 |
| 2016 | 1,705 |
| 2017 | 1,439 |
| Thereafter | 6,508 |
| Total principal payments | $16,313 |

The debt of $1,577 due in 2013 would be reported as a current liability on the December 31, 2012 balance sheet. The remaining debt of $14,736 ($16,313 – $1,577) would be reported as a long-term liability on the balance sheet.

## Short-Term Notes Payable

Notes may be issued to purchase merchandise or other assets. Notes may also be issued to creditors to satisfy an account payable created earlier.[2]

To illustrate, assume that Nature's Sunshine Company issued a 90-day, 12% note for $1,000, dated August 1, 2015, to Murray Co. for a $1,000 overdue account. The entry to record the issuance of the note is as follows:

| | | | | | |
|---|---|---|---|---|---|
| Aug. | 1 | Accounts Payable—Murray Co. | | 1,000 | |
| | | Notes Payable | | | 1,000 |
| | | Issued a 90-day, 12% note on account. | | | |

When the note matures, the entry to record the payment of $1,000 plus $30 interest ($1,000 × 12% × 90 ÷ 360) is as follows:

| | | | | | |
|---|---|---|---|---|---|
| Oct. | 30 | Notes Payable | | 1,000 | |
| | | Interest Expense | | 30 | |
| | | Cash | | | 1,030 |
| | | Paid principal and interest due on note. | | | |

[1] The Coca-Cola Company, *Form 10-K For the Fiscal Year Ended December 31, 2012.*

[2] The accounting for notes received to satisfy an account receivable was described and illustrated in Chapter 9, *Receivables.*

The interest expense is reported in the Other Expense section of the income statement for the year ended December 31, 2015. The interest expense account is closed at December 31.

Each note transaction affects a debtor (borrower) and creditor (lender). The following illustration shows how the same transactions are recorded by the debtor and creditor. In this illustration, the debtor (borrower) is Bowden Co., and the creditor (lender) is Coker Co.

| | Bowden Co. (Borrower) | | Coker Co. (Creditor) | |
|---|---|---|---|---|
| **May 1.** Bowden Co. purchased merchandise on account from Coker Co., $10,000, 2/10, n/30. The merchandise cost Coker Co. $7,500. | Merchandise Inventory    10,000 <br>    Accounts Payable | 10,000 | Accounts Receivable    10,000 <br>    Sales <br><br> Cost of Merchandise Sold    7,500 <br>    Merchandise Inventory | 10,000 <br><br><br> 7,500 |
| **May 31.** Bowden Co. issued a 60-day, 12% note for $10,000 to Coker Co. on account. | Accounts Payable    10,000 <br>    Notes Payable | 10,000 | Notes Receivable    10,000 <br>    Accounts Receivable | 10,000 |
| **July 30.** Bowden Co. paid Coker Co. the amount due on the note of May 31. Interest: $10,000 × 12% × 60 ÷ 360. | Notes Payable    10,000 <br> Interest Expense    200 <br>    Cash | 10,200 | Cash    10,200 <br>    Interest Revenue <br>    Notes Receivable | 200 <br> 10,000 |

A company may also borrow from a bank by issuing a note. To illustrate, assume that on September 19 Iceburg Company borrowed cash from First National Bank by issuing a $4,000, 90-day, 15% note to the bank. The entry to record the issuance of the note and the cash proceeds is as follows:

| | | | | | |
|---|---|---|---|---|---|
| Sept. | 19 | Cash | | 4,000 | |
| | |    Notes Payable | | | 4,000 |
| | |    Issued a 90-day, 15% note to First National Bank. | | | |

On the due date of the note (December 18), Iceburg Company owes First National Bank $4,000 plus interest of $150 ($4,000 × 15% × 90 ÷ 360). The entry to record the payment of the note is as follows:

| | | | | | |
|---|---|---|---|---|---|
| Dec. | 18 | Notes Payable | | 4,000 | |
| | | Interest Expense | | 150 | |
| | |    Cash | | | 4,150 |
| | |    Paid principal and interest due on note. | | | |

In some cases, a *discounted note* may be issued rather than an interest-bearing note. A discounted note has the following characteristics:

- The interest rate on the note is called the *discount rate*.
- The amount of interest on the note, called the *discount*, is computed by multiplying the discount rate times the face amount of the note.
- The debtor (borrower) receives the face amount of the note less the discount, called the *proceeds*.
- The debtor must repay the face amount of the note on the due date.

To illustrate, assume that on August 10, Cary Company issues a $20,000, 90-day discounted note to Western National Bank. The discount rate is 15%, and the amount of the discount is $750 ($20,000 × 15% × 90 ÷ 360). Thus, the proceeds received by Cary Company are $19,250. The entry by Cary Company is as follows:

| Aug. | 10 | Cash | | 19,250 | |
| | | Interest Expense | | 750 | |
| | |    Notes Payable | | | 20,000 |
| | |       Issued a 90-day discounted note to Western | | | |
| | |       National Bank at a 15% discount rate. | | | |

The entry when Cary Company pays the discounted note on November 8 is as follows:[3]

| Nov. | 8 | Notes Payable | | 20,000 | |
| | |    Cash | | | 20,000 |
| | |       Paid note due. | | | |

Other current liabilities that have been discussed in earlier chapters include accrued expenses, unearned revenue, and interest payable. The accounting for wages and salaries, termed *payroll accounting*, is discussed next.

---

**Example Exercise 11-1  Proceeds from Notes Payable**

On July 1, Bella Salon Company borrowed cash from Best Bank by issuing a 60-day note with a face amount of $60,000.

a.  Determine the proceeds of the note, assuming the note carries an interest rate of 6%.

b.  Determine the proceeds of the note, assuming the note is discounted at 6%.

Dynamic Exhibit

**Follow My Example 11-1**

a.  $60,000

b.  $59,400 [$60,000 − ($60,000 × 6% × 60 ÷ 360)]

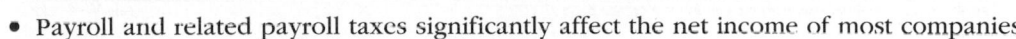

Practice Exercises: PE 11-1A, PE 11-1B

---

# Payroll and Payroll Taxes

 Determine employer liabilities for payroll, including liabilities arising from employee earnings and deductions from earnings.

In accounting, **payroll** refers to the amount paid to employees for services they provided during the period. A company's payroll is important for the following reasons:

- Payroll and related payroll taxes significantly affect the net income of most companies.
- Payroll is subject to federal and state regulations.
- Good employee morale requires payroll to be paid timely and accurately.

## Liability for Employee Earnings

*Salary* usually refers to payment for managerial and administrative services. Salary is normally expressed in terms of a month or a year. *Wages* usually refers to payment for employee manual labor. The rate of wages is normally stated on an hourly or a weekly basis. The salary or wage of an employee may be increased by bonuses, commissions, profit sharing, or cost-of-living adjustments.

**Note:**
Employee salaries and wages are expenses to an employer.

Companies engaged in interstate commerce must follow the Fair Labor Standards Act. This act, sometimes called the Federal Wage and Hour Law, requires employers to pay a minimum rate of 1½ times the regular rate for all hours worked in excess of 40 hours per week. Exemptions are provided for executive, administrative, and some supervisory positions. Increased rates for working overtime, nights, or holidays are common, even when not required by law. These rates may be as much as twice the regular rate.

---

[3] If the accounting period ends before a discounted note is paid, an adjusting entry should record the prepaid (deferred) interest that is not yet an expense. This deferred interest would be deducted from Notes Payable in the Current Liabilities section of the balance sheet.

To illustrate computing an employee's earnings, assume that **John T. McGrath** is a salesperson employed by **McDermott Supply Co.** McGrath's regular rate is $34 per hour, and any hours worked in excess of 40 hours per week are paid at 1½ times the regular rate. McGrath worked 42 hours for the week ended December 27. His earnings of $1,462 for the week are computed as follows:

| | |
|---|---|
| Earnings at regular rate (40 hrs. × $34) | $1,360 |
| Earnings at overtime rate [2 hrs. × ($34 × 1½)] | 102 |
| Total earnings | $1,462 |

## Deductions from Employee Earnings

The total earnings of an employee for a payroll period, including any overtime pay, are called **gross pay**. From this amount is subtracted one or more *deductions* to arrive at the **net pay**. Net pay is the amount paid the employee. The deductions normally include federal, state, and local income taxes, medical insurance, and pension contributions.

**Income Taxes** Employers normally withhold a portion of employee earnings for payment of the employees' federal income tax. Each employee authorizes the amount to be withheld by completing an "Employee's Withholding Allowance Certificate," called a W-4. Exhibit 2 is the W-4 form submitted by **John T. McGrath**.

---

**EXHIBIT 2**

**Employee's Withholding Allowance Certificate (W-4 Form)**

---

On the W-4, an employee indicates marital status and the number of withholding allowances. A single employee may claim one withholding allowance. A married employee may claim an additional allowance for a spouse. An employee may also claim an allowance for each dependent other than a spouse. Each allowance reduces the federal income tax withheld from the employee's pay. Exhibit 2 indicates that McGrath is single and, thus, claimed one withholding allowance.

The federal income tax withheld depends on each employee's gross pay and W-4 allowance. Withholding tables issued by the Internal Revenue Service (IRS) are used to determine amounts to withhold. Exhibit 3 is an example of an IRS wage withholding table for a single person who is paid weekly.[4]

In Exhibit 3, each row is the employee's wages after deducting the employee's withholding allowances. Each year, the amount of the standard withholding allowance is determined by the IRS. For ease of computation and because this amount changes each year, we assume that the standard withholding allowance to be deducted in Exhibit 3 for a single person paid weekly is $75.[5] Thus, if two withholding allowances are claimed, $150 ($75 × 2) is deducted.

[4] IRS withholding tables are also available for married employees and for pay periods other than weekly.

[5] The actual IRS standard withholding allowance changes every year and was $75.00 for 2013.

**EXHIBIT 3**

**Wage Bracket Withholding Table**

**Table for Percentage Method of Withholding WEEKLY Payroll Period**

**(a) SINGLE person (including head of household)—**
If the amount of wages (after subtracting withholding allowances) is:
The amount of income tax to withhold is:
Not over $42 . . . . . . . . . . . . . . . . . . . . . $0

| Over— | But not over— | | of excess over— |
|---|---|---|---|
| $42 | —$214 . . | $0.00 plus 10% | —$42 |
| $214 | —$739 . . | $17.20 plus 15% | —$214 |
| $739 | —$1,732 . . | $95.95 plus 25% | —$739 |
| $1,732 | —$3,566 . . | $344.20 plus 28% | —$1,732 |
| $3,566 | —$7,703 . . | $857.72 plus 33% | —$3,566 |
| $7,703 | —$7,735 . . | $2,222.93 plus 35% | —$7,703 |
| $7,735 | . . . . . . . . . . . . . . | $2,234.13 plus 39.6% | —$7,735 |

← McGrath wage bracket

Source: Publication 15, Employer's Tax Guide, Internal Revenue Service, 2013.

To illustrate, **John T. McGrath** made $1,462 for the week ended December 27. McGrath's W-4 claims one withholding allowance of $75. Thus, the wages used in determining McGrath's withholding bracket in Exhibit 3 are $1,387 ($1,462 – $75).

After the person's withholding wage bracket has been computed, the federal income tax to be withheld is determined as follows:

- Step 1. Locate the proper withholding wage bracket in Exhibit 3.

  *McGrath's wages after deducting one standard IRS withholding allowance are $1,387 ($1,462 – $75). Therefore, the wage bracket for McGrath is $739–$1,732.*

- Step 2. Compute the withholding for the proper wage bracket using the directions in the two right-hand columns in Exhibit 3.

  *For McGrath's wage bracket, the withholding is computed as "$95.95 plus 25% of the excess over $739." Hence, McGrath's withholding is $257.95, computed as follows:*

| | |
|---|---|
| Initial withholding from wage bracket | $ 95.95 |
| Plus [25% × ($1,387 – $739)] | 162.00 |
| Total withholding | $257.95 |

Employers may also be required to withhold state or city income taxes. The amounts to be withheld are determined on state-by-state and city-by-city bases.

Residents of certain cities including Detroit, the District of Columbia, and New York City must pay a city income tax in addition to their federal and state income taxes.

## Example Exercise 11-2 Federal Income Tax Withholding

OBJ 2

Karen Dunn's weekly gross earnings for the present week were $2,250. Dunn has two exemptions. Using the wage bracket withholding table in Exhibit 3 with a $75 standard withholding allowance for each exemption, what is Dunn's federal income tax withholding?

## Follow My Example 11-2

| | | |
|---|---|---|
| Total wage payment. . . . . . . . . . . . . . . . . . . . . . . . . . . . . . . . . . . . . . . . . . . . . . . . . . . . . | | $ 2,250 |
| One allowance (provided by IRS). . . . . . . . . . . . . . . . . . . . . . . . . . . . . . . . . . . . . . . . . . . | $75 | |
| Multiplied by allowances claimed on Form W-4 . . . . . . . . . . . . . . . . . . . . . . . . . . . . . . . . | × 2 | 150 |
| Amount subject to withholding. . . . . . . . . . . . . . . . . . . . . . . . . . . . . . . . . . . . . . . . . . . . . | | $ 2,100 |
| Initial withholding from wage bracket in Exhibit 3. . . . . . . . . . . . . . . . . . . . . . . . . . . . . . | | $344.20 |
| Plus additional withholding: 28% of excess over $1,732 . . . . . . . . . . . . . . . . . . . . . . . . | | 103.04* |
| Federal income tax withholding. . . . . . . . . . . . . . . . . . . . . . . . . . . . . . . . . . . . . . . . . . . . . | | $447.24 |

*28% × ($2,100 – $1,732)

Practice Exercises: PE 11-2A, PE 11-2B

**FICA Tax** Employers are required by the Federal Insurance Contributions Act (FICA) to withhold a portion of the earnings of each employee. The **FICA tax** withheld contributes to the following two federal programs:

- *Social security*, which provides payments for retirees, survivors, and disability insurance.
- *Medicare*, which provides health insurance for senior citizens.

The amount withheld from each employee is based on the employee's earnings *paid* in the *calendar* year. The withholding tax rates and maximum earnings subject to tax are often revised by Congress.[6] To simplify, this chapter assumes the following rates and earnings subject to tax:

- Social security: 6% on all earnings
- Medicare: 1.5% on all earnings

To illustrate, assume that **John T. McGrath**'s earnings for the week ending December 27 are $1,462 and the total FICA tax to be withheld is $109.65, computed as follows:

| | | |
|---|---:|---:|
| Earnings subject to 6% social security tax | | $1,462 |
| Social security tax rate | | × 6% |
|    Social security tax | | $ 87.72 |
| Earnings subject to 1.5% Medicare tax | | $1,462 |
| Medicare tax rate | | × 1.5% |
|    Medicare tax | | 21.93 |
| Total FICA tax | | $109.65 |

**Other Deductions** Employees may choose to have additional amounts deducted from their gross pay. For example, an employee may authorize deductions for retirement savings, for charitable contributions, or life insurance. A union contract may also require the deduction of union dues.

## Computing Employee Net Pay

Gross earnings less payroll deductions equals *net pay*, sometimes called *take-home pay*. Assuming that **John T. McGrath** authorized deductions for retirement savings and for a United Fund contribution, McGrath's net pay for the week ended December 27 is $1,069.40, computed as follows:

| | | |
|---|---:|---:|
| Gross earnings for the week | | $1,462.00 |
| Deductions: | | |
|    Social security tax | $ 87.72 | |
|    Medicare tax | 21.93 | |
|    Federal income tax | 257.95 | |
|    Retirement savings | 20.00 | |
|    United Fund | 5.00 | |
|      Total deductions | | 392.60 |
| Net pay | | $1,069.40 |

**Example Exercise 11-3** **Employee Net Pay** OBJ 2

Karen Dunn's weekly gross earnings for the week ending December 3 were $2,250, and her federal income tax withholding was $447.24. Assuming the social security rate is 6% and Medicare is 1.5%, what is Dunn's net pay?

**Follow My Example 11-3**

| | | |
|---|---:|---:|
| Total wage payment | | $2,250.00 |
| Less: Federal income tax withholding | $447.24 | |
|    Social security tax ($2,250 × 6%) | 135.00 | |
|    Medicare tax ($2,250 × 1.5%) | 33.75 | 615.99 |
| Net pay | | $1,634.01 |

Practice Exercises: PE 11-3A, PE 11-3B

[6] For 2013, the social security tax rate was 6.2% and the Medicare tax rate was 1.45%. Earnings subject to the social security tax are limited to an annual threshold amount, but for text examples and problems, assume all accumulated annual earnings are below this threshold and subject to the tax.

## Liability for Employer's Payroll Taxes

Employers are subject to the following payroll taxes for amounts paid their employees:

- *FICA Tax:* Employers must match the employee's FICA tax contribution.
- *Federal Unemployment Compensation Tax (FUTA):* This employer tax provides for temporary payments to those who become unemployed. The tax collected by the federal government is allocated among the states for use in state programs rather than paid directly to employees. Congress often revises the FUTA tax rate and maximum earnings subject to tax.
- *State Unemployment Compensation Tax (SUTA):* This employer tax also provides temporary payments to those who become unemployed. The FUTA and SUTA programs are closely coordinated, with the states distributing the unemployment checks.[7] SUTA tax rates and earnings subject to tax vary by state.[8]

The preceding employer taxes are an operating expense of the company. Exhibit 4 summarizes the responsibility for employee and employer payroll taxes.

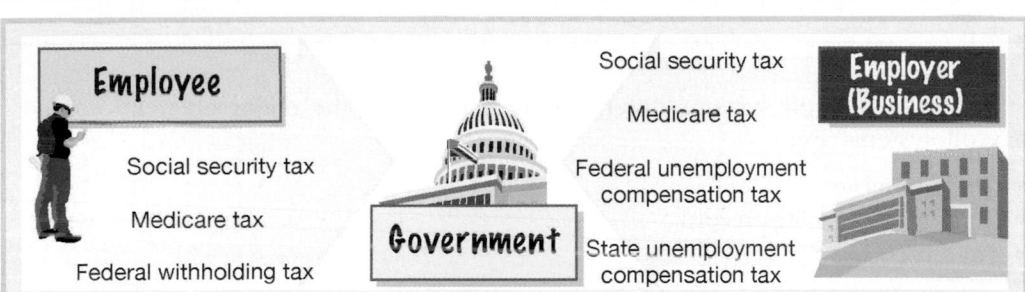

**EXHIBIT 4**

**Responsibility for Tax Payments**

 **Business**  **Connection**

### THE MOST YOU WILL EVER PAY

In 1936, the Social Security Board described how the tax was expected to affect a worker's pay, as follows:

*The taxes called for in this law will be paid both by your employer and by you. For the next 3 years you will pay maybe 15 cents a week, maybe 25 cents a week, maybe 30 cents or more, according to what you earn. That is to say, during the next 3 years, beginning January 1, 1937, you will pay 1 cent for every dollar you earn, and at the same time your employer will pay 1 cent for every dollar you earn, up to $3,000 a year. . . .*

*. . . Beginning in 1940 you will pay, and your employer will pay, 1½ cents for each dollar you earn, up to $3,000 a year . . . and then beginning in 1943, you will pay 2 cents, and so will your employer, for every dollar you earn for the next three years. After that, you and your employer will each pay half a cent more for 3 years, and finally, beginning in 1949, . . . you and your employer will each pay 3 cents on each dollar you earn, up to $3,000 a year. That is the most you will ever pay.*

The rate on January 1, 2013, was 7.65 cents per dollar earned (7.65%). The social security portion was 6.20% on the first $110,100 of earnings. The Medicare portion was 1.45% on all earnings.

Source: Arthur Lodge, "That Is the Most You Will Ever Pay," *Journal of Accountancy*, October 1985, p. 44.

## Accounting Systems for Payroll and Payroll Taxes

**OBJ 3** Describe payroll accounting systems that use a payroll register, employee earnings records, and a general journal.

Payroll systems should be designed to:

- Pay employees accurately and timely.
- Meet regulatory requirements of federal, state, and local agencies.
- Provide useful data for management decision-making needs.

[7] This rate may be reduced to 0.8% for credits for state unemployment compensation tax.

[8] For 2013, the maximum state rate credited against the federal unemployment rate was 5.4% of the first $7,000 of each employee's earnings during a calendar year.

| EXHIBIT 5 | **Payroll Register** |
|---|---|

| | | | Earnings | | | |
|---|---|---|---|---|---|---|
| | **Employee Name** | **Total Hours** | **Regular** | **Overtime** | **Total** | |
| 1 | Abrams, Julie S. | 40 | 500.00 | | 500.00 | 1 |
| 2 | Elrod, Fred G. | 44 | 392.00 | 58.80 | 450.80 | 2 |
| 3 | Gomez, Jose C. | 40 | 840.00 | | 840.00 | 3 |
| 4 | **McGrath, John T.** | **42** | **1,360.00** | **102.00** | **1,462.00** | 4 |
| 25 | Wilkes, Glenn K. | 40 | 480.00 | | 480.00 | 25 |
| 26 | Zumpano, Michael W. | 40 | 600.00 | | 600.00 | 26 |
| 27 | Total | | 13,328.00 | 574.00 | 13,902.00 | 27 |
| 28 | | | | | | 28 |

Although payroll systems differ among companies, the major elements of most payroll systems are:

- Payroll register
- Employee's earnings record
- Payroll checks

## Payroll Register

The **payroll register** is a multicolumn report used for summarizing the data for each payroll period. Although payroll registers vary by company, a payroll register normally includes the following columns:

- Employee name
- Total hours worked
- Regular earnings
- Overtime earnings
- Total gross earnings
- Social security tax withheld
- Medicare tax withheld

- Federal income tax withheld
- Retirement savings withheld
- Miscellaneous items withheld
- Total withholdings
- Net pay
- Check number of payroll check issued
- Accounts debited for payroll expense

Exhibit 5 illustrates a payroll register for **McDermott Supply Co.** The two right-hand columns of the payroll register indicate the accounts debited for the payroll expense. These columns are often referred to as the *payroll distribution*.

**Recording Employees' Earnings** The column totals of the payroll register provide the basis for recording the journal entry for payroll. The entry based on the payroll register in Exhibit 5 follows:

| | | | | | |
|---|---|---|---|---|---|
| Dec. | 27 | Sales Salaries Expense | | 11,122.00 | |
| | | Office Salaries Expense | | 2,780.00 | |
| | | Social Security Tax Payable | | | 834.12 |
| | | Medicare Tax Payable | | | 208.53 |
| | | Employees Federal Income Tax Payable | | | 3,332.00 |
| | | Retirement Savings Deductions Payable | | | 680.00 |
| | | United Fund Deductions Payable | | | 520.00 |
| | | Salaries Payable | | | 8,327.35 |
| | | Payroll for week ended December 27. | | | |

| EXHIBIT 5 | (Concluded) |

| | Deductions Withheld | | | | | | | Paid | | Accounts Debited | | |
|---|---|---|---|---|---|---|---|---|---|---|---|---|
| | Social Security Tax | Medicare Tax | Federal Income Tax | Retirement Savings | Misc. | | Total | Net Pay | Check No. | Sales Salaries Expense | Office Salaries Expense | |
| 1 | 30.00 | 7.50 | 48.85 | 20.00 | UF | 10.00 | 116.35 | 383.65 | 6857 | 500.00 | | 1 |
| 2 | 27.05 | 6.76 | 30.22 | | UF | 50.00 | 114.03 | 336.77 | 6858 | | 450.80 | 2 |
| 3 | 50.40 | 12.60 | 83.70 | 25.00 | UF | 10.00 | 181.70 | 658.30 | 6859 | 840.00 | | 3 |
| 4 | 87.72 | 21.93 | 257.95 | 20.00 | UF | 5.00 | 392.60 | 1,069.40 | 6860 | 1,462.00 | | 4 |
| 25 | 28.80 | 7.20 | 45.85 | 10.00 | | | 91.85 | 388.15 | 6880 | 480.00 | | 25 |
| 26 | 36.00 | 9.00 | 63.85 | 5.00 | UF | 2.00 | 115.85 | 484.15 | 6881 | | 600.00 | 26 |
| 27 | 834.12 | 208.53 | 3,332.00 | 680.00 | UF | 520.00 | 5,574.65 | 8,327.35 | | 11,122.00 | 2,780.00 | 27 |
| 28 | | | | | | | | | | | | 28 |

Miscellaneous Deductions: UF—United Fund

**Recording and Paying Payroll Taxes** Payroll taxes are recorded as liabilities when the payroll is *paid* to employees. In addition, employers compute and report payroll taxes on a *calendar-year* basis, which may differ from the company's fiscal year.

**Note:**
Payroll taxes become a liability to the employer when the payroll is paid.

## Example Exercise 11-4 Journalize Period Payroll

The payroll register of Chen Engineering Services indicates $900 of social security withheld and $225 of Medicare tax withheld on total salaries of $15,000 for the period. Federal withholding for the period totaled $2,925.

Provide the journal entry for the period's payroll.

### Follow My Example 11-4

| | | |
|---|---|---|
| Salaries Expense | 15,000 | |
| Social Security Tax Payable | | 900 |
| Medicare Tax Payable | | 225 |
| Employees Federal Income Tax Payable | | 2,925 |
| Salaries Payable | | 10,950 |

Practice Exercises: PE 11-4A, PE 11-4B

On December 27, McDermott Supply has the following payroll data:

| | |
|---|---|
| Sales salaries | $11,122 |
| Office salaries owed | 2,780 |
| Wages owed employees on December 27 | $13,902 |
| Wages subject to payroll taxes: | |
| Social security tax (6%) | $13,902 |
| Medicare tax (1.5%) | 13,902 |
| State (5.4%) and federal (0.8%) unemployment compensation tax | 2,710 |

Employers must match the employees' social security and Medicare tax contributions. In addition, the employer must pay state unemployment compensation tax (SUTA) of 5.4% and federal unemployment compensation tax (FUTA) of 0.8%. When payroll is paid on December 27, these payroll taxes are computed as follows:

| | |
|---|---|
| Social security tax | $ 834.12 ($13,902 × 6%, and from Social Security Tax column of Exhibit 5) |
| Medicare tax | 208.53 ($13,902 × 1.5%, and from Medicare Tax column of Exhibit 5) |
| SUTA | 146.34 ($2,710 × 5.4%) |
| FUTA | 21.68 ($2,710 × 0.8%) |
| Total payroll taxes | $1,210.67 |

The entry to journalize the payroll tax expense for Exhibit 5 follows:

| | | | | |
|---|---|---|---|---|
| Dec. | 27 | Payroll Tax Expense | 1,210.67 | |
| | | Social Security Tax Payable | | 834.12 |
| | | Medicare Tax Payable | | 208.53 |
| | | State Unemployment Tax Payable | | 146.34 |
| | | Federal Unemployment Tax Payable | | 21.68 |
| | | Payroll taxes for week ended December 27. | | |

The preceding entry records a liability for each payroll tax. When the payroll taxes are paid, an entry is recorded debiting the payroll tax liability accounts and crediting Cash.

---

## Example Exercise 11-5   Journalize Payroll Tax

OBJ 3

The payroll register of Chen Engineering Services indicates $900 of social security withheld and $225 of Medicare tax withheld on total salaries of $15,000 for the period. Earnings of $5,250 are subject to state and federal unemployment compensation taxes at the federal rate of 0.8% and the state rate of 5.4%.

Provide the journal entry to record the payroll tax expense for the period.

*(Continued)*

---

**EXHIBIT 6**

**Employee's Earnings Record**

**John T. McGrath**
**1830 4th St.**
**Clinton, IA 52732-6142**        **PHONE: 555-3148**

| SINGLE | NUMBER OF WITHHOLDING ALLOWANCES: 1 | PAY RATE: | $1,360.00 Per Week |
|---|---|---|---|
| OCCUPATION: | Salesperson | EQUIVALENT HOURLY RATE: $34 | |

| | | | | Earnings | | |
|---|---|---|---|---|---|---|
| | Period Ending | Total Hours | Regular Earnings | Overtime Earnings | Total Earnings | Total |
| 42 | SEPT. 27 | 53 | 1,360.00 | 663.00 | 2,023.00 | 75,565.00 | 42 |
| 43 | THIRD QUARTER | | 17,680.00 | 7,605.00 | 25,285.00 | | 43 |
| 44 | OCT. 4 | 51 | 1,360.00 | 561.00 | 1,921.00 | 77,486.00 | 44 |
| 50 | NOV. 15 | 50 | 1,360.00 | 510.00 | 1,870.00 | 89,382.00 | 50 |
| 51 | NOV. 22 | 53 | 1,360.00 | 663.00 | 2,023.00 | 91,405.00 | 51 |
| 52 | NOV. 29 | 47 | 1,360.00 | 357.00 | 1,717.00 | 93,122.00 | 52 |
| 53 | DEC. 6 | 53 | 1,360.00 | 663.00 | 2,023.00 | 95,145.00 | 53 |
| 54 | DEC.13 | 52 | 1,360.00 | 612.00 | 1,972.00 | 97,117.00 | 54 |
| 55 | DEC. 20 | 51 | 1,360.00 | 561.00 | 1,921.00 | 99,038.00 | 55 |
| 56 | DEC. 27 | 42 | 1,360.00 | 102.00 | 1,462.00 | 100,500.00 | 56 |
| 57 | FOURTH QUARTER | | 17,680.00 | 7,255.00 | 24,935.00 | | 57 |
| 58 | YEARLY TOTAL | | 70,720.00 | 29,780.00 | 100,500.00 | | 58 |

**Follow My Example 11-5** ▶▶

| | | |
|---|---|---|
| Payroll Tax Expense . . . . . . . . . . . . . . . . . . . . . . . . . . . . . . . . . . . . . . . . . . . . . . | 1,450.50 | |
|    Social Security Tax Payable. . . . . . . . . . . . . . . . . . . . . . . . . . . . . . . . . . . . . . | | 900.00 |
|    Medicare Tax Payable . . . . . . . . . . . . . . . . . . . . . . . . . . . . . . . . . . . . . . . . . . | | 225.00 |
|    State Unemployment Tax Payable. . . . . . . . . . . . . . . . . . . . . . . . . . . . . . . . . | | 283.50* |
|    Federal Unemployment Tax Payable . . . . . . . . . . . . . . . . . . . . . . . . . . . . . | | 42.00** |

\*$5,250 × 5.4%
\*\*$5,250 × 0.8%

Practice Exercises: PE 11-5A, PE 11-5B

## Employee's Earnings Record

Each employee's earnings to date must be determined at the end of each payroll period. This total is necessary for computing the employee's social security tax withholding and the employer's payroll taxes. Thus, detailed payroll records must be kept for each employee. This record is called an **employee's earnings record**.

Exhibit 6 shows a portion of **John T. McGrath**'s employee's earnings record. An employee's earnings record and the payroll register are interrelated. For example, McGrath's earnings record for December 27 can be traced to the fourth line of the payroll register in Exhibit 5.

**EXHIBIT 6** (Concluded)

**SOC. SEC. NO.: 381-48-9120**  **EMPLOYEE NO.: 814**

**DATE OF BIRTH: February 15, 1982**

**DATE EMPLOYMENT TERMINATED:**

| | Social Security Tax | Medicare Tax | Federal Income Tax | Retirement Savings | Other | | Total | Net Amount | Check No. | |
|---|---|---|---|---|---|---|---|---|---|---|
| 42 | 121.38 | 30.35 | 404.68 | 20.00 | | | 576.41 | 1,446.59 | 6175 | 42 |
| 43 | 1,517.10 | 379.28 | 5,391.71 | 260.00 | UF | 40.00 | 7,588.09 | 17,696.91 | | 43 |
| 44 | 115.26 | 28.82 | 376.12 | 20.00 | | | 540.20 | 1,380.80 | 6225 | 44 |
| 50 | 112.20 | 28.05 | 361.84 | 20.00 | | | 522.09 | 1,347.91 | 6530 | 50 |
| 51 | 121.38 | 30.35 | 404.68 | 20.00 | | | 576.41 | 1,446.59 | 6582 | 51 |
| 52 | 103.02 | 25.76 | 321.70 | 20.00 | | | 470.48 | 1,246.52 | 6640 | 52 |
| 53 | 121.38 | 30.35 | 404.68 | 20.00 | UF | 5.00 | 581.41 | 1,441.59 | 6688 | 53 |
| 54 | 118.32 | 29.58 | 390.40 | 20.00 | | | 558.30 | 1,413.70 | 6743 | 54 |
| 55 | 115.26 | 28.82 | 376.12 | 20.00 | | | 540.20 | 1,380.80 | 6801 | 55 |
| 56 | 87.72 | 21.93 | 257.95 | 20.00 | UF | 5.00 | 392.60 | 1,069.40 | 6860 | 56 |
| 57 | 1,496.10 | 374.03 | 5,293.71 | 260.00 | UF | 15.00 | 7,438.84 | 17,496.16 | | 57 |
| 58 | 6,030.00 | 1,507.50 | 21,387.65 | 1,040.00 | UF | 100.00 | 30,065.15 | 70,434.85 | | 58 |

**Deductions** span columns Social Security Tax through Total; **Paid** spans Net Amount and Check No.

As shown in Exhibit 6, an employee's earnings record has quarterly and yearly totals. These totals are used for tax, insurance, and other reports. For example, one such report is the Wage and Tax Statement, commonly called a *W-2*. This form is provided annually to each employee as well as to the Social Security Administration. The W-2 shown in Exhibit 7 is based on **John T. McGrath**'s employee's earnings record shown in Exhibit 6.

---

| **EXHIBIT 7** | **Employee's Wage and Tax Statement (W-2 Form)** |

| 22222 | Void ☐ | **a** Employee's social security number 381-48-9120 | For Official Use Only ▶ OMB No. 1545-0008 | | |
|---|---|---|---|---|---|
| **b** Employer identification number (EIN) 61-8436524 | | | **1** Wages, tips, other compensation 100,500.00 | **2** Federal income tax withheld 21,387.65 | |
| **c** Employer's name, address, and ZIP code McDermott Supply Co. 415 5th Ave. So. Dubuque, IA 52736-0142 | | | **3** Social security wages 100,500.00 | **4** Social security tax withheld 6,030.00 | |
| | | | **5** Medicare wages and tips 100,500.00 | **6** Medicare tax withheld 1,507.50 | |
| | | | **7** Social security tips | **8** Allocated tips | |
| **d** Control number | | | **9** | **10** Dependent care benefits | |
| **e** Employee's first name and initial John T. | Last name McGrath | Suff. | **11** Nonqualified plans | **12a** See instructions for box 12 | |
| 1830 4th St. Clinton, IA 52732-6142 | | | **13** Statutory employee ☐  Retirement plan ☐  Third-party sick pay ☐ | **12b** | |
| | | | **14** Other | **12c** | |
| | | | | **12d** | |
| **f** Employee's address and ZIP code | | | | | |
| **15** State IA  Employer's state ID number | **16** State wages, tips, etc. | **17** State income tax | **18** Local wages, tips, etc. | **19** Local income tax | **20** Locality name Dubuque |

**Form W-2** Wage and Tax Statement **2014**

Copy A For Social Security Administration — Send this entire page with Form W-3 to the Social Security Administration; photocopies are **not** acceptable.

Department of the Treasury—Internal Revenue Service

**For Privacy Act and Paperwork Reduction Act Notice, see the separate instructions.**

Cat. No. 10134D

**Do Not Cut, Fold, or Staple Forms on This Page**

---

## Payroll Checks

Companies pay employees either by electronic funds transfer or by issuing *payroll checks*. With electronic funds transfers, the employee's net pay is electronically deposited into their bank account each period. Later, the employees receive a payroll statement summarizing how the net pay was computed. A payroll statement for the electronic funds transfer of **John T. McGrath**'s pay is shown in Exhibit 8. Each payroll check includes a detachable statement showing how the net pay was computed, which is typically identical to the payroll statement accompanying electronic funds transfers (EFTs).

Most companies use a special payroll bank account to disburse payroll. In such cases, payroll is processed as follows:

1. The total net pay for the period is determined from the payroll register.
2. The company authorizes an electronic funds transfer (EFT) from its regular bank account to the special payroll bank account for the total net pay.
3. Individual EFTs or payroll checks are disbursed from the payroll account.
4. The numbers of the individual payroll disbursements are inserted in the payroll register.

**EXHIBIT 8**

**Payroll Statement**

| McDermott Supply Co. | | | |
|---|---|---|---|
| 415 5th Ave. So. | John T. McGrath | Check Number: 6860 | |
| Dubuque, IA 52736-0142 | 1830 4th St. | Pay Period Ending: 12/27/14 | |
| | Clinton, IA 52732-6142 | | |

| HOURS & EARNINGS | | TAXES & DEDUCTIONS | | |
|---|---|---|---|---|
| DESCRIPTION | AMOUNT | DESCRIPTION | CURRENT AMOUNT | Y-T-D AMOUNT |
| Rate of Pay Reg. | 34 | Social Security Tax | 87.72 | 6,030.00 |
| Rate of Pay O.T. | 51 | Medicare Tax | 21.93 | 1,507.50 |
| Hours Worked Reg. | 40 | Fed. Income Tax | 257.95 | 21,387.65 |
| Hours Worked O.T. | 2 | U.S. Savings Bonds | 20.00 | 1,040.00 |
| | | United Fund | 5.00 | 100.00 |
| Net Pay | 1,069.40 | | | |
| Total Gross Pay | 1,462.00 | Total | 392.60 | 30,365.15 |
| Total Gross Y-T-D | 100,500.00 | | | |

An advantage of using a separate payroll bank account is that reconciling the bank statements is simplified. In addition, a payroll bank account establishes control over payroll checks and, thus, prevents their theft or misuse.

## Computerized Payroll System

The inputs into a payroll system may be classified as:

- *Constants:* Data that remain unchanged from payroll to payroll

  Examples: Employee names, social security numbers, marital status, number of income tax withholding allowances, rates of pay, tax rates, and withholding tables

- *Variables:* Data that change from payroll to payroll

  Examples: Number of hours or days worked for each employee, accrued days of sick leave, vacation credits, total earnings to date, and total taxes withheld

In a computerized accounting system, constants are stored within a payroll file. The variables are input each pay period by a payroll clerk. In some systems, employees swipe their identification (ID) cards when they report for and leave from work. In such cases, the hours worked by each employee are automatically updated.

A computerized payroll system also maintains electronic versions of the payroll register and employee earnings records. Payroll system outputs, such as payroll checks, electronic funds transfers, and tax records, are automatically produced each pay period.

## Internal Controls for Payroll Systems

The cash payment controls described in Chapter 8 also apply to payrolls. Some examples of payroll controls include the following:

- If a check-signing machine is used, blank payroll checks and access to the machine should be restricted to prevent their theft or misuse.
- The hiring and firing of employees should be properly authorized and approved in writing.
- All changes in pay rates should be properly authorized and approved in writing.
- Employees should be observed when arriving for work to verify that employees are "checking in" for work only once and only for themselves. Employees may "check in" for work by using a time card or by swiping their employee ID card.
- Payroll checks should be distributed by someone other than employee supervisors.
- A special payroll bank account should be used.

# Integrity, Objectivity, and Ethics in Business

**$8 MILLION FOR 18 MINUTES OF WORK**

Computer system controls can be very important in issuing payroll checks. In one case, a Detroit schoolteacher was paid $4,015,625 after deducting $3,884,375 in payroll deductions for 18 minutes of overtime work. The error was caused by a computer glitch when the teacher's employee identification number was substituted incorrectly in the "hourly wage" field and wasn't caught by the payroll software. After six days, the error was discovered, and the money was returned. "One of the things that came with (the software) is a fail-safe that prevents that. It doesn't work," a financial officer said. The district has since installed a program to flag any paycheck exceeding $10,000.

Source: Associated Press, September 27, 2002.

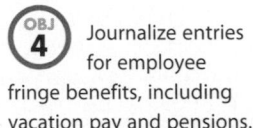

Journalize entries for employee fringe benefits, including vacation pay and pensions.

# Employees' Fringe Benefits

Many companies provide their employees benefits in addition to salary and wages earned. Such **fringe benefits** may include vacation, medical, and retirement benefits.

The cost of employee fringe benefits is recorded as an expense by the employer. To match revenues and expenses, the estimated cost of fringe benefits is recorded as an expense during the period in which the employees earn the benefits.

## Vacation Pay

**Note:**
**Vacation pay becomes the employer's liability as the employee earns vacation rights.**

Most employers provide employees vacations, sometimes called *compensated absences*. The liability to pay for employee vacations could be accrued as a liability at the end of each pay period. However, many companies wait and record an adjusting entry for accrued vacation at the end of the year.

To illustrate, assume that employees earn one day of vacation for each month worked. The estimated vacation pay for the year ending December 31 is $325,000. The adjusting entry for the accrued vacation is as follows:

| | | | | |
|---|---|---|---|---|
| Dec. | 31 | Vacation Pay Expense | 325,000 | |
| | | Vacation Pay Payable | | 325,000 |
| | | Accrued vacation pay for the year. | | |

Employees may be required to take all their vacation time within one year. In such cases, any accrued vacation pay will be paid within one year. Thus, the vacation pay payable is reported as a current liability on the balance sheet. If employees are allowed to accumulate their vacation pay, the estimated vacation pay payable that will *not* be taken within a year is reported as a long-term liability.

When employees take vacations, the liability for vacation pay is decreased by debiting Vacation Pay Payable. Salaries or Wages Payable and the other related payroll accounts for taxes and withholdings are credited.

## Pensions

A **pension** is a cash payment to retired employees. Pension rights are accrued by employees as they work, based on the employer's pension plan. Two basic types of pension plans are defined contribution and defined benefit plans.[9]

**Defined Contribution Plans** In a **defined contribution plan**, the company invests contributions on behalf of the employee during the employee's working years. Normally, the employee and employer contribute to the plan. The employee's pension depends on the total contributions and the investment returns earned on those contributions.

One of the more popular defined contribution plans is the 401k plan. Under this plan, employees contribute a portion of their gross pay to investments, such as mutual funds. A 401k plan offers employees two advantages.

- The employee contribution is deducted before taxes.
- The contributions and related earnings are not taxed until withdrawn at retirement.

In most cases, the employer matches some portion of the employee's contribution. The employer's cost is debited to *Pension Expense*. To illustrate, assume that Heaven Scent Perfumes Company contributes 10% of employee monthly salaries to an employee 401k plan. Assuming $500,000 of monthly salaries, the journal entry to record the monthly contribution is as follows:

| Dec. | 31 | Pension Expense | 50,000 | |
|------|----|-----------------|--------|--------|
| | | Cash | | 50,000 |
| | | Contributed 10% of monthly salaries to pension plan. | | |

**Defined Benefit Plans** In a **defined benefit plan**, the company pays the employee a fixed annual pension based on a formula. The formula is normally based on such factors as the employee's years of service, age, and past salary.

In a defined benefit plan, the employer is obligated to pay for (fund) the employee's future pension benefits. As a result, many companies are replacing their defined benefit plans with defined contribution plans.

The pension cost of a defined benefit plan is debited to *Pension Expense*. Cash is credited for the amount contributed (funded) by the employer. Any unfunded amount is credited to *Unfunded Pension Liability*.

To illustrate, assume that the defined benefit plan of Hinkle Co. requires an annual pension cost of $80,000. This annual contribution is based on estimates of Hinkle's future pension liabilities. On December 31, Hinkle Co. pays $60,000 to the pension fund. The entry to record the payment and the unfunded liability is as follows:

| Dec. | 31 | Pension Expense | 80,000 | |
|------|----|-----------------|--------|--------|
| | | Cash | | 60,000 |
| | | Unfunded Pension Liability | | 20,000 |
| | | Annual pension cost and contribution. | | |

If the unfunded pension liability is to be paid within one year, it is reported as a current liability on the balance sheet. Any portion of the unfunded pension liability that will be paid beyond one year is a long-term liability.

[9] The accounting for pensions is complex due to the uncertainties of estimating future pension liabilities. These estimates depend on such factors as employee life expectancies, employee turnover, expected employee compensation levels, and investment income on pension contributions. Additional accounting and disclosures related to pensions are covered in advanced accounting courses.

**Example Exercise 11-6** **Vacation Pay and Pension Benefits**

OBJ 4

Manfield Services Company provides its employees vacation benefits and a defined contribution pension plan. Employees earned vacation pay of $44,000 for the period. The pension plan requires a contribution to the plan administrator equal to 8% of employee salaries. Salaries were $450,000 during the period.

Provide the journal entry for the (a) vacation pay and (b) pension benefit.

**Follow My Example 11-6**

a.  Vacation Pay Expense ...................................................... 44,000
        Vacation Pay Payable...............................................            44,000
            Vacation pay accrued for the period.

b.  Pension Expense ........................................................ 36,000
        Cash ...............................................................            36,000
            Pension contribution, 8% of $450,000 salary.

Practice Exercises: PE 11-6A, PE 11-6B

## Postretirement Benefits Other than Pensions

Employees may earn rights to other postretirement benefits from their employer. Such benefits may include dental care, eye care, medical care, life insurance, tuition assistance, tax services, and legal services.

The accounting for other postretirement benefits is similar to that of defined benefit pension plans. The estimate of the annual benefits expense is recorded by debiting *Postretirement Benefits Expense*. If the benefits are fully funded, Cash is credited for the same amount. If the benefits are not fully funded, a postretirement benefits plan liability account is also credited.

The financial statements should disclose the nature of the postretirement benefit liabilities. These disclosures are usually included as notes to the financial statements. Additional accounting and disclosures for postretirement benefits are covered in advanced accounting courses.

## Current Liabilities on the Balance Sheet

Accounts payable, the current portion of long-term debt, notes payable, and any other debts that are due within one year are reported as current liabilities on the balance sheet. The balance sheet presentation of current liabilities for **Mornin' Joe** follows:

| Mornin' Joe<br>Balance Sheet<br>December 31, 2016 | | |
|---|---:|---:|
| **Liabilities** | | |
| Current liabilities: | | |
|     Accounts payable ......................................... | $133,000 | |
|     Notes payable (current portion) ........................... | 200,000 | |
|     Salaries and wages payable .............................. | 42,000 | |
|     Payroll taxes payable .................................... | 16,400 | |
|     Interest payable.......................................... | 40,000 | |
|         Total current liabilities................................ | | $431,400 |

## Business  Connection

# Contingent Liabilities

Some liabilities may arise from past transactions only if certain events occur in the future. These *potential* liabilities are called **contingent liabilities**.

The accounting for contingent liabilities depends on the following two factors:

- *Likelihood of occurring:* Probable, reasonably possible, or remote
- *Measurement:* Estimable or not estimable

The likelihood that the event creating the liability occurring is classified as *probable*, *reasonably possible*, or *remote*. The ability to estimate the potential liability is classified as *estimable* or *not estimable*.

## Probable and Estimable

If a contingent liability is *probable* and the amount of the liability can be *reasonably estimated*, it is recorded and disclosed. The liability is recorded by debiting an expense and crediting a liability.

To illustrate, assume that during June a company sold a product for $60,000 that includes a 36-month warranty for repairs.[10] The average cost of repairs over the warranty period is estimated at 5% of the sales price. The entry to record the estimated product warranty expense for June is as follows:

| | | | | |
|---|---|---|---|---|
| June | 30 | Product Warranty Expense | 3,000 | |
| | | Product Warranty Payable | | 3,000 |
| | | Warranty expense for June, 5% × $60,000. | | |

The preceding entry records warranty expense in the same period in which the sale is recorded. In this way, warranty expense is matched with the related revenue (sales).

If the product is repaired under warranty, the repair costs are recorded by debiting *Product Warranty Payable* and crediting *Cash, Supplies, Wages Payable*, or other appropriate accounts. Thus, if a $200 part is replaced under warranty on August 16, the entry is as follows:

| | | | | |
|---|---|---|---|---|
| Aug. | 16 | Product Warranty Payable | 200 | |
| | | Supplies | | 200 |
| | | Replaced defective part under warranty. | | |

**OBJ 5**  Describe the accounting treatment for contingent liabilities and journalize entries for product warranties.

The estimated costs of warranty work on new car sales are a contingent liability for Ford Motor Company.

[10] This discussion is limited to a discussion of assurance type warranties. A more detailed discussion of the types of warranties and their accounting is covered in intermediate and advanced accounting texts.

## Example Exercise 11-7 Estimated Warranty Liability

Cook-Rite Co. sold $140,000 of kitchen appliances during August under a six-month warranty. The cost to repair defects under the warranty is estimated at 6% of the sales price. On September 12, a customer required a $200 part replacement plus $90 of labor under the warranty.

Provide the journal entry for (a) the estimated warranty expense on August 31 for August sales, and (b) the September 12 warranty work.

## Follow My Example 11-7

| | | |
|---|---|---|
| a. Product Warranty Expense ........................................................ | 8,400 | |
|     Product Warranty Payable...................................................... | | 8,400 |
|         To record warranty expense for August, 6% × $140,000. | | |
| b. Product Warranty Payable....................................................... | 290 | |
|     Supplies ............................................................... | | 200 |
|     Wages Payable.......................................................... | | 90 |
|         Replaced defective part under warranty. | | |

Practice Exercises: PE 11-7A, PE 11-7B

## Probable and Not Estimable

A contingent liability may be probable, but cannot be estimated. In this case, the contingent liability is disclosed in the notes to the financial statements. For example, a company may have accidentally polluted a local river by dumping waste products. At the end of the period, the cost of the cleanup and any fines may not be able to be estimated.

## Reasonably Possible

A contingent liability may be only possible. For example, a company may have lost a lawsuit for infringing on another company's patent rights. However, the verdict is under appeal and the company's lawyers feel that the verdict will be reversed or significantly reduced. In this case, the contingent liability is disclosed in the notes to the financial statements.

## Remote

A contingent liability may be remote. For example, a ski resort may be sued for injuries incurred by skiers. In most cases, the courts have found that a skier accepts the risk of injury when participating in the activity. Thus, unless the ski resort is grossly negligent, the resort will not incur a liability for ski injuries. In such cases, no disclosure needs to be made in the notes to the financial statements. The accounting treatment of contingent liabilities is summarized in Exhibit 9.

Common examples of contingent liabilities disclosed in notes to the financial statements are litigation, environmental matters, guarantees, and contingencies from the sale of receivables.

An example of a recent contingent liability disclosure from Google Inc. follows:[11]

*We have had patent, copyright, and trademark infringement lawsuits filed against us claiming that certain of our products, services, and technologies, including Android, Google Search, Google AdWords, Google AdSense, Google Books, Google News, Google Image Search, Google Chrome, Google Talk, Google Voice, Motorola devices and YouTube, infringe the intellectual property rights of others. Adverse results in these lawsuits may include awards of substantial monetary damages, costly royalty or licensing agreements, or orders preventing us from offering certain*

---

[11] Google Inc., *Form 10-K For the Fiscal Year Ended December 31, 2012.*

| EXHIBIT 9 | Accounting Treatment of Contingent Liabilities |

**Likelihood of Occurring**     **Measurement**     **Accounting Treatment**

Contingency → Probable → Estimable → Record and Disclose Liability

Probable → Not Estimable → Disclose Liability

Contingency → Reasonably Possible → Disclose Liability

Contingency → Remote → None

*features, functionalities, products, or services, and may also cause us to change our business practices, and require development of non-infringing products or technologies, which could result in a loss of revenues for us and otherwise harm our business. . . .*

*With respect to our outstanding legal matters, based on our current knowledge, we believe that the amount or range of reasonably possible loss will not, either individually or in the aggregate, have a material adverse effect on our business, consolidated financial position, results of operations, or cash flows. However, the outcome of such legal matters is inherently unpredictable and subject to significant uncertainties. . . .*

Professional judgment is necessary in distinguishing between classes of contingent liabilities. This is especially the case when distinguishing between probable and reasonably possible contingent liabilities.

# Financial Analysis and Interpretation: Quick Ratio

**OBJ 6** Describe and illustrate the use of the quick ratio in analyzing a company's ability to pay its current liabilities.

**Current position analysis** helps creditors evaluate a company's ability to pay its current liabilities. This analysis is based on the following three measures:

- Working capital
- Current ratio
- Quick ratio

Working capital and the current ratio were discussed in Chapter 4 and are computed as follows:

$$\text{Working Capital} = \text{Current Assets} - \text{Current Liabilities}$$

$$\text{Current Ratio} = \frac{\text{Current Assets}}{\text{Current Liabilities}}$$

While these two measures can be used to evaluate a company's ability to pay its current liabilities, they do not provide insight into the company's ability to pay these liabilities within a short period of time. This is because some current assets, such as inventory, cannot be converted into cash as quickly as other current assets, such as cash and accounts receivable.

The **quick ratio** overcomes this limitation by measuring the "instant" debt-paying ability of a company and is computed as follows:

$$\text{Quick Ratio} = \frac{\text{Quick Assets}}{\text{Current Liabilities}}$$

**Quick assets** are cash and other current assets that can be easily converted to cash. This normally includes cash, temporary investments, and accounts receivable. To illustrate, consider the following data for TechSolutions, Inc., at the end of 2015:

| | |
|---|---:|
| Current assets: | |
| Cash | $2,020 |
| Temporary investments | 3,400 |
| Accounts receivable | 1,600 |
| Inventory | 2,000 |
| Other current assets | 160 |
| Total current assets | $9,180 |
| | |
| Current liabilities: | |
| Accounts payable | $3,000 |
| Other current liabilities | 2,400 |
| Total current liabilities | $5,400 |
| | |
| Working capital (current assets – current liabilities) | $3,780 |
| Current ratio (current assets ÷ current liabilities) | 1.7 |

The quick ratio for TechSolutions, Inc., is computed as follows:

$$\text{Quick Ratio} = \frac{\$2,020 + \$3,400 + \$1,600}{\$5,400} = 1.3$$

The quick ratio of 1.3 indicates that the company has more than enough quick assets to pay its current liabilities in a short period of time. A quick ratio below 1.0 would indicate that the company does not have enough quick assets to cover its current liabilities.

Like the current ratio, the quick ratio is particularly useful in making comparisons across companies. To illustrate, the following selected balance sheet data (excluding ratios) were taken from recent financial statements of **Panera Bread Company** and **Starbucks Corporation** (in thousands):

| | Panera Bread | Starbucks |
|---|---:|---:|
| Current assets: | | |
| Cash and cash equivalents | $297,141 | $1,188,600 |
| Temporary investments | — | 848,400 |
| Accounts receivable | 86,262 | 485,900 |
| Inventory | 19,714 | 1,241,500 |
| Other current assets | 75,725 | 435,200 |
| Total current assets | $478,842 | $4,199,600 |
| | | |
| Current liabilities: | | |
| Accounts payable | $ 9,371 | $ 389,100 |
| Other current liabilities | 268,169 | 1,820,700 |
| Total current liabilities | $277,540 | $2,209,800 |
| | | |
| Working capital (current assets – current liabilities) | $201,302 | $1,989,800 |
| Current ratio (current assets ÷ current liabilities) | 1.7 | 1.9 |
| Quick ratio (quick assets ÷ current liabilities)* | 1.4 | 1.1 |

*The quick ratio for each company is computed as follows:
 Panera Bread: ($297,141 + $86,262) ÷ $277,540 = 1.4
 Starbucks: ($1,188,600 + $848,400 + $485,900) ÷ $2,209,800 = 1.1

Starbucks is larger than Panera Bread and has more than nine times the amount of working capital. Such size differences make working capital comparisons between companies difficult. In contrast, the current and quick ratios provide better comparisons across companies. In this example, Starbucks has a slightly higher current ratio than Panera Bread. However, Starbucks' 1.1 quick ratio reveals that it has just enough quick assets to cover its current liabilities, while Panera Bread's quick ratio of 1.4 indicates that the company has more than enough quick assets to meet its current liabilities.

## Example Exercise 11-8  Quick Ratio

OBJ 6

Sayer Company reported the following current assets and current liabilities for the years ended December 31, 2016 and 2015:

|  | 2016 | 2015 |
|---|---|---|
| Cash | $1,250 | $1,000 |
| Temporary investments | 1,925 | 1,650 |
| Accounts receivable | 1,775 | 1,350 |
| Inventory | 1,900 | 1,700 |
| Accounts payable | 2,750 | 2,500 |

a.   Compute the quick ratio for 2016 and 2015.

b.   Interpret the company's quick ratio across the two time periods.

## Follow My Example 11-8

a.   December 31, 2016:
     Quick Ratio = Quick Assets ÷ Current Liabilities
     $\quad\quad\quad\quad$ = ($1,250 + $1,925 + $1,775) ÷ $2,750
     $\quad\quad\quad\quad$ = 1.8

     December 31, 2015:
     Quick Ratio = Quick Assets ÷ Current Liabilities
     $\quad\quad\quad\quad$ = ($1,000 + $1,650 + $1,350) ÷ $2,500
     $\quad\quad\quad\quad$ = 1.6

b.   The quick ratio of Sayer Company has improved from 1.6 in 2015 to 1.8 in 2016. This increase is the result of a large increase in the three types of quick assets (cash, temporary investments, and accounts receivable) compared to a relatively smaller increase in the current liability, accounts payable.

Practice Exercises: PE 11-8A, PE 11-8B

# At a Glance 11

**OBJ 1**

### Describe and illustrate current liabilities related to accounts payable, current portion of long-term debt, and notes payable.

**Key Points**   Current liabilities are obligations that are to be paid out of current assets and are due within a short time, usually within one year. The three primary types of current liabilities are accounts payable, notes payable, and the current portion of long-term debt.

| Learning Outcomes | Example Exercises | Practice Exercises |
|---|---|---|
| • Identify and define the most frequently reported current liabilities on the balance sheet. | | |
| • Determine the interest from interest-bearing and discounted notes payable. | EE11-1 | PE11-1A, 11-1B |

**OBJ 2**

### Determine employer liabilities for payroll, including liabilities arising from employee earnings and deductions from earnings.

**Key Points**   An employer's liability for payroll is determined from employee total earnings, including overtime pay. From this amount, employee deductions are subtracted to arrive at the net pay to be paid to each employee. Most employers also incur liabilities for payroll taxes, such as social security tax, Medicare tax, federal unemployment compensation tax, and state unemployment compensation tax.

| Learning Outcomes | Example Exercises | Practice Exercises |
|---|---|---|
| • Compute the federal withholding tax from a wage bracket withholding table. | EE11-2 | PE11-2A, 11-2B |
| • Compute employee net pay, including deductions for social security and Medicare tax. | EE11-3 | PE11-3A, 11-3B |

**OBJ 3**

### Describe payroll accounting systems that use a payroll register, employee earnings records, and a general journal.

**Key Points**   The payroll register is used in assembling and summarizing the data needed for each payroll period. The payroll register is supported by a detailed payroll record for each employee, called an *employee's earnings record*.

| Learning Outcomes | Example Exercises | Practice Exercises |
|---|---|---|
| • Journalize the employee's earnings, net pay, and payroll liabilities from the payroll register. | EE11-4 | PE11-4A, 11-4B |
| • Journalize the payroll tax expense. | | |
| • Describe elements of a payroll system, including the employee's earnings record, payroll checks, and internal controls. | EE11-5 | PE11-5A, 11-5B |

**Journalize entries for employee fringe benefits, including vacation pay and pensions.**

**Key Points** Fringe benefits are expenses of the period in which the employees earn the benefits. Fringe benefits are recorded by debiting an expense account and crediting a liability account.

| Learning Outcomes | Example Exercises | Practice Exercises |
|---|---|---|
| • Journalize vacation pay. | EE11-6 | PE11-6A, 11-6B |
| • Distinguish and journalize defined contribution and defined benefit pension plans. | EE11-6 | PE11-6A, 11-6B |

**Describe the accounting treatment for contingent liabilities and journalize entries for product warranties.**

**Key Points** A contingent liability is a potential obligation that results from a past transaction but depends on a future event. The accounting for contingent liabilities is summarized in Exhibit 9.

| Learning Outcomes | Example Exercises | Practice Exercises |
|---|---|---|
| • Describe the accounting for contingent liabilities. | | |
| • Journalize estimated warranty obligations and services granted under warranty. | EE11-7 | PE11-7A, 11-7B |

**Describe and illustrate the use of the quick ratio in analyzing a company's ability to pay its current liabilities.**

**Key Points** The quick ratio is a measure of a company's ability to pay current liabilities within a short period of time. The quick ratio is computed by dividing quick assets by current liabilities. Quick assets include cash, temporary investments, accounts receivable, and other current assets that can be easily converted into cash. A quick ratio exceeding 1.0 is usually desirable.

| Learning Outcomes | Example Exercises | Practice Exercises |
|---|---|---|
| • Describe the quick ratio. | | |
| • Compute and evaluate the quick ratio. | EE11-8 | PE11-8A, 11-8B |

# Key Terms

contingent liabilities (521)
current position analysis (523)
defined benefit plan (519)
defined contribution plan (519)
employee's earnings record (515)

FICA tax (510)
fringe benefits (518)
gross pay (508)
net pay (508)
payroll (507)

payroll register (512)
pension (518)
quick assets (524)
quick ratio (524)

## Illustrative Problem

Selected transactions of Taylor Company, completed during the fiscal year ended December 31, are as follows:

Mar.  1.  Purchased merchandise on account from Kelvin Co., $20,000.

Apr. 10.  Issued a 60-day, 12% note for $20,000 to Kelvin Co. on account.

June  9.  Paid Kelvin Co. the amount owed on the note of April 10.

Aug.  1.  Issued a $50,000, 90-day note to Harold Co. in exchange for a building. Harold Co. discounted the note at 15%.

Oct. 30.  Paid Harold Co. the amount due on the note of August 1.

Dec. 27.  Journalized the entry to record the biweekly payroll. A summary of the payroll record follows:

| Salary distribution: | | |
|---|---|---|
| Sales | $63,400 | |
| Officers | 36,600 | |
| Office | 10,000 | $110,000 |
| Deductions: | | |
| Social security tax | $ 6,600 | |
| Medicare tax | 1,650 | |
| Federal income tax withheld | 17,600 | |
| State income tax withheld | 4,950 | |
| Savings bond deductions | 850 | |
| Medical insurance deductions | 1,120 | 32,770 |
| Net amount | | $ 77,230 |

    27.  Journalized the entry to record payroll taxes for social security and Medicare from the biweekly payroll.

    30.  Issued a check in payment of liabilities for employees' federal income tax of $17,600, social security tax of $13,200, and Medicare tax of $3,300.

    31.  Issued a check for $9,500 to the pension fund trustee to fully fund the pension cost for December.

    31.  Journalized an entry to record the employees' accrued vacation pay, $36,100.

    31.  Journalized an entry to record the estimated accrued product warranty liability, $37,240.

### Instructions

Journalize the preceding transactions.

## Solution

| | | | | |
|---|---|---|---|---|
| Mar. | 1 | Merchandise Inventory | 20,000 | |
| | | Accounts Payable—Kelvin Co. | | 20,000 |
| | | | | |
| Apr. | 10 | Accounts Payable—Kelvin Co. | 20,000 | |
| | | Notes Payable | | 20,000 |
| | | | | |
| June | 9 | Notes Payable | 20,000 | |
| | | Interest Expense | 400 | |
| | | Cash | | 20,400 |
| | | | | |
| Aug. | 1 | Building | 48,125 | |
| | | Interest Expense | 1,875 | |
| | | Notes Payable | | 50,000 |
| | | | | |
| Oct. | 30 | Notes Payable | 50,000 | |
| | | Cash | | 50,000 |
| | | | | |
| Dec. | 27 | Sales Salaries Expense | 63,400 | |
| | | Officers Salaries Expense | 36,600 | |
| | | Office Salaries Expense | 10,000 | |
| | | Social Security Tax Payable | | 6,600 |
| | | Medicare Tax Payable | | 1,650 |
| | | Employees Federal Income Tax Payable | | 17,600 |
| | | Employees State Income Tax Payable | | 4,950 |
| | | Bond Deductions Payable | | 850 |
| | | Medical Insurance Payable | | 1,120 |
| | | Salaries Payable | | 77,230 |
| | | | | |
| | 27 | Payroll Tax Expense | 8,250 | |
| | | Social Security Tax Payable | | 6,600 |
| | | Medicare Tax Payable | | 1,650 |
| | | | | |
| | 30 | Employees Federal Income Tax Payable | 17,600 | |
| | | Social Security Tax Payable | 13,200 | |
| | | Medicare Tax Payable | 3,300 | |
| | | Cash | | 34,100 |
| | | | | |
| | 31 | Pension Expense | 9,500 | |
| | | Cash | | 9,500 |
| | | Fund pension cost. | | |
| | | | | |
| | 31 | Vacation Pay Expense | 36,100 | |
| | | Vacation Pay Payable | | 36,100 |
| | | Accrue vacation pay. | | |
| | | | | |
| | 31 | Product Warranty Expense | 37,240 | |
| | | Product Warranty Payable | | 37,240 |
| | | Accrue warranty expense. | | |

# Discussion Questions

1. Does a discounted note payable provide credit without interest? Discuss.

2. Employees are subject to taxes withheld from their paychecks.
   a. List the federal taxes withheld from most employee paychecks.
   b. Give the title of the accounts credited by amounts withheld.

3. Why are deductions from employees' earnings classified as liabilities for the employer?

4. For each of the following payroll-related taxes, indicate whether they generally apply to (a) employees only, (b) employers only, or (c) both employees and employers:
   1. Federal income tax
   2. Medicare tax
   3. Social security tax
   4. Federal unemployment compensation tax
   5. State unemployment compensation tax

5. What are the principal reasons for using a special payroll bank account?

6. In a payroll system, what types of input data are referred to as (a) constants and (b) variables?

7. To match revenues and expenses properly, should the expense for employee vacation pay be recorded in the period during which the vacation privilege is earned or during the period in which the vacation is taken? Discuss.

8. Explain how a defined contribution pension plan works.

9. When should the liability associated with a product warranty be recorded? Discuss.

10. **General Motors Corporation** reported $2.6 billion of product warranties in the Current Liabilities section of a recent balance sheet. How would costs of repairing a defective product be recorded?

# Practice Exercises

**EE 11-1** *p. 507* | **PE 11-1A  Proceeds from notes payable** | **OBJ. 1**

On October 12, Belleville Co. borrowed cash from Texas Bank by issuing a 30-day note with a face amount of $70,000.
a. Determine the proceeds of the note, assuming the note carries an interest rate of 6%.
b. Determine the proceeds of the note, assuming the note is discounted at 6%.

**EE 11-1** *p. 507* | **PE 11-1B  Proceeds from notes payable** | **OBJ. 1**

On January 26, Nyree Co. borrowed cash from Conrad Bank by issuing a 45-day note with a face amount of $150,000.
a. Determine the proceeds of the note, assuming the note carries an interest rate of 10%.
b. Determine the proceeds of the note, assuming the note is discounted at 10%.

**EE 11-2** *p. 509* | **PE 11-2A  Federal income tax withholding** | **OBJ. 2**

Lily Flower's weekly gross earnings for the present week were $2,500. Flower has two exemptions. Using the wage bracket withholding table in Exhibit 3 with a $75 standard withholding allowance for each exemption, what is Flower's federal income tax withholding?

SHOW
ME HOW

EE 11-2  *p. 509*    **PE 11-2B**    **Federal income tax withholding**    **OBJ. 2**

Marsha Mellow's weekly gross earnings for the present week were $1,250. Mellow has one exemption. Using the wage bracket withholding table in Exhibit 3 with a $75 standard withholding allowance for each exemption, what is Mellow's federal income tax withholding?

SHOW
ME HOW

EE 11-3  *p. 510*    **PE 11-3A**    **Employee net pay**    **OBJ. 2**

Lily Flower's weekly gross earnings for the week ended October 20 were $2,500, and her federal income tax withholding was $517.24. Assuming the social security rate is 6% and Medicare is 1.5% of all earnings, what is Flower's net pay?

SHOW
ME HOW

EE 11-3  *p. 510*    **PE 11-3B**    **Employee net pay**    **OBJ. 2**

Marsha Mellow's weekly gross earnings for the week ended May 23 were $1,250, and her federal income tax withholding was $204.95. Assuming the social security rate is 6% and Medicare is 1.5% of all earnings, what is Mellow's net pay?

EE 11-4  *p. 513*    **PE 11-4A**    **Journalize period payroll**    **OBJ. 3**

The payroll register of Konrath Co. indicates $13,200 of social security withheld and $3,300 of Medicare tax withheld on total salaries of $220,000 for the period. Federal withholding for the period totaled $43,560.

Provide the journal entry for the period's payroll.

SHOW
ME HOW

EE 11-4  *p. 513*    **PE 11-4B**    **Journalize period payroll**    **OBJ. 3**

The payroll register of Longboat Co. indicates $5,400 of social security withheld and $1,350 of Medicare tax withheld on total salaries of $90,000 for the period. Retirement savings withheld from employee paychecks were $5,400 for the period. Federal withholding for the period totaled $17,820.

Provide the journal entry for the period's payroll.

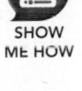

SHOW
ME HOW

EE 11-5  *p. 514*    **PE 11-5A**    **Journalize payroll tax**    **OBJ. 3**

The payroll register of Konrath Co. indicates $13,200 of social security withheld and $3,300 of Medicare tax withheld on total salaries of $220,000 for the period. Earnings of $35,000 are subject to state and federal unemployment compensation taxes at the federal rate of 0.8% and the state rate of 5.4%.

Provide the journal entry to record the payroll tax expense for the period.

SHOW
ME HOW

EE 11-5  *p. 514*    **PE 11-5B**    **Journalize payroll tax**    **OBJ. 3**

The payroll register of Longboat Co. indicates $5,400 of social security withheld and $1,350 of Medicare tax withheld on total salaries of $90,000 for the period. Earnings of $10,000 are subject to state and federal unemployment compensation taxes at the federal rate of 0.8% and the state rate of 5.4%.

Provide the journal entry to record the payroll tax expense for the period.

SHOW
ME HOW

EE 11-6  *p. 520*    **PE 11-6A**    **Vacation pay and pension benefits**    **OBJ. 4**

Fukushima Company provides its employees with vacation benefits and a defined contribution pension plan. Employees earned vacation pay of $19,500 for the period. The pension plan requires a contribution to the plan administrator equal to 6% of employee salaries. Salaries were $260,000 during the period, and the full amount due was contributed to the pension plan administrator.

Provide the journal entry for the (a) vacation pay and (b) pension benefit.

EE 11-6 p. 520

SHOW
ME HOW

### PE 11-6B  Vacation pay and pension benefits

OBJ. 4

Regling Company provides its employees vacation benefits and a defined benefit pension plan. Employees earned vacation pay of $35,000 for the period. The pension formula calculated a pension cost of $201,250. Only $175,000 was contributed to the pension plan administrator.

Provide the journal entry for the (a) vacation pay and (b) pension benefit.

EE 11-7 p. 522

SHOW
ME HOW

### PE 11-7A  Estimated warranty liability

OBJ. 5

Chloe Co. sold $300,000 of equipment during January under a one-year warranty. The cost to repair defects under the warranty is estimated at 5% of the sales price. On June 20, a customer required a $90 part replacement, plus $42 of labor under the warranty.

Provide the journal entry for (a) the estimated warranty expense on January 31 for January sales, and (b) the June 20 warranty work.

EE 11-7 p. 522

SHOW
ME HOW

### PE 11-7B  Estimated warranty liability

OBJ. 5

Quantas Industries sold $325,000 of consumer electronics during July under a nine-month warranty. The cost to repair defects under the warranty is estimated at 4.5% of the sales price. On November 11, a customer was given $220 cash under terms of the warranty.

Provide the journal entry for (a) the estimated warranty expense on July 31 for July sales, and (b) the November 11 cash payment.

EE 11-8 p. 525

**FAI**

SHOW
ME HOW

### PE 11-8A  Quick ratio

OBJ. 6

Nabors Company reported the following current assets and liabilities for December 31 for two recent years:

|  | Dec. 31, Current Year | Dec. 31, Previous Year |
| --- | --- | --- |
| Cash | $ 650 | $ 680 |
| Temporary investments | 1,500 | 1,550 |
| Accounts receivable | 700 | 770 |
| Inventory | 1,250 | 1,400 |
| Accounts payable | 2,375 | 2,000 |

a. Compute the quick ratio on December 31 of both years.

b. Interpret the company's quick ratio. Is the quick ratio improving or declining?

EE 11-8 p. 525

**FAI**

SHOW
ME HOW

### PE 11-8B  Quick ratio

OBJ. 6

Adieu Company reported the following current assets and liabilities for December 31 for two recent years:

|  | Dec. 31, Current Year | Dec. 31, Previous Year |
| --- | --- | --- |
| Cash | $1,000 | $1,140 |
| Temporary investments | 1,200 | 1,400 |
| Accounts receivable | 800 | 910 |
| Inventory | 2,200 | 2,300 |
| Accounts payable | 1,875 | 2,300 |

a. Compute the quick ratio on December 31 of both years.

b. Interpret the company's quick ratio. Is the quick ratio improving or declining?

## Exercises

✔ Total current
liabilities, $1,929,750

SHOW
ME HOW

### EX 11-1  Current liabilities

OBJ. 1

Bon Nebo Co. sold 25,000 annual subscriptions of *Bjorn 20XX* for $85 during December 2016. These new subscribers will receive monthly issues, beginning in January 2017. In addition, the business had taxable income of $840,000 during the first calendar quarter of 2017. The federal tax rate is 40%. A quarterly tax payment will be made on April 12, 2017.

Prepare the Current Liabilities section of the balance sheet for Bon Nebo Co. on March 31, 2017.

**EX 11-2  Entries for discounting notes payable**  OBJ. 1

Griffin Enterprises issues a $660,000, 45-day, 4% note to Romo Industries for merchandise inventory.

a. Journalize Griffin Enterprises' entries to record:

 1. the issuance of the note.

 2. the payment of the note at maturity.

b. Journalize Romo Industries' entries to record:

 1. the receipt of the note.

 2. the receipt of the payment of the note at maturity.

**EX 11-3  Evaluating alternative notes**  OBJ. 1

A borrower has two alternatives for a loan: (1) issue a $360,000, 60-day, 5% note or (2) issue a $360,000, 60-day note that the creditor discounts at 5%.

a. Calculate the amount of the interest expense for each option.

b. Determine the proceeds received by the borrower in each situation.

c. ➤ Which alternative is more favorable to the borrower? Explain.

**EX 11-4  Entries for notes payable**  OBJ. 1

A business issued a 45-day, 6% note for $210,000 to a creditor on account. Journalize the entries to record (a) the issuance of the note and (b) the payment of the note at maturity, including interest.

**EX 11-5  Entries for discounted note payable**  OBJ. 1

A business issued a 60-day note for $75,000 to a creditor on account. The note was discounted at 7%. Journalize the entries to record (a) the issuance of the note and (b) the payment of the note at maturity.

**EX 11-6  Fixed asset purchases with note**  OBJ. 1

On June 30, Collins Management Company purchased land for $400,000 and a building for $560,000, paying $360,000 cash and issuing a 5% note for the balance, secured by a mortgage on the property. The terms of the note provide for 20 semiannual payments of $30,000 on the principal plus the interest accrued from the date of the preceding payment. Journalize the entry to record (a) the transaction on June 30, (b) the payment of the first installment on December 31, and (c) the payment of the second installment the following June 30.

**EX 11-7  Current portion of long-term debt**  OBJ. 1

PepsiCo, Inc., reported the following information about its long-term debt in the notes to a recent financial statement (in millions):

Long-term debt is comprised of the following:

| | December 31 | |
| --- | --- | --- |
| | Current Year | Previous Year |
| Total long term-debt | $28,359 | $26,773 |
| Less current portion | (4,815) | (6,205) |
| Long-term debt | $23,544 | $20,568 |

a. How much of the long-term debt was disclosed as a current liability on the current year's December 31 balance sheet?

b. How much did the total current liabilities change between the preceding year and the current year as a result of the current portion of long-term debt?

c. If PepsiCo did not issue additional long-term debt next year, what would be the total long-term debt on December 31 of the upcoming year?

### EX 11-8   Calculate payroll

**OBJ. 2**

An employee earns $32 per hour and 1.5 times that rate for all hours in excess of 40 hours per week. Assume that the employee worked 55 hours during the week. Assume further that the social security tax rate was 6.0%, the Medicare tax rate was 1.5%, and federal income tax to be withheld was $398.

a.  Determine the gross pay for the week.

b.  Determine the net pay for the week.

### EX 11-9   Calculate payroll

**OBJ. 2**

Diego Company has three employees—a consultant, a computer programmer, and an administrator. The following payroll information is available for each employee:

|  | Consultant | Computer Programmer | Administrator |
|---|---|---|---|
| Regular earnings rate | $3,800 per week | $38 per hour | $42 per hour |
| Overtime earnings rate* | Not applicable | 2 times hourly rate | 1.5 times hourly rate |
| Number of withholding allowances | 1 | 2 | 2 |

\* For hourly employees, overtime is paid for hours worked in excess of 40 hours per week.

For the current pay period, the computer programmer worked 55 hours and the administrator worked 52 hours. The federal income tax withheld for all three employees, who are single, can be determined from the wage bracket withholding table in Exhibit 3 in the chapter. Assume further that the social security tax rate was 6.0%, the Medicare tax rate was 1.5%, and one withholding allowance is $75.

Determine the gross pay and the net pay for each of the three employees for the current pay period.

### EX 11-10   Summary payroll data

**OBJ. 2, 3**

In the following summary of data for a payroll period, some amounts have been intentionally omitted:

| | | |
|---|---|---|
| Earnings: | | |
| 1.  At regular rate | | ? |
| 2.  At overtime rate | | $80,000 |
| 3.  Total earnings | | ? |
| Deductions: | | |
| 4.  Social security tax | 32,400 | |
| 5.  Medicare tax | 8,100 | |
| 6.  Income tax withheld | 135,000 | |
| 7.  Medical insurance | 18,900 | |
| 8.  Union dues | ? | |
| 9.  Total deductions | | 201,150 |
| 10.  Net amount paid | | 338,850 |
| Accounts debited: | | |
| 11.  Factory Wages | | 285,000 |
| 12.  Sales Salaries | | ? |
| 13.  Office Salaries | | 120,000 |

a.  Calculate the amounts omitted in lines (1), (3), (8), and (12).

b.  Journalize the entry to record the payroll accrual.

c.  Journalize the entry to record the payment of the payroll.

### EX 11-11   Payroll tax entries

**OBJ. 3**

According to a summary of the payroll of Murtagh Co., $750,000 was subject to the 6.0% social security tax and the 1.5% Medicare tax. Also, $50,000 was subject to state and federal unemployment taxes.

a.  Calculate the employer's payroll taxes, using the following rates: state unemployment, 5.4%; federal unemployment, 0.8%.

b.  Journalize the entry to record the accrual of payroll taxes.

SHOW
ME HOW

### EX 11-12   Payroll entries

OBJ. 3

The payroll register for Proctor Company for the week ended February 14 indicated the following:

| | |
|---|---:|
| Salaries | $1,500,000 |
| Social security tax withheld | 90,000 |
| Medicare tax withheld | 22,500 |
| Federal income tax withheld | 300,000 |

In addition, state and federal unemployment taxes were calculated at the rate of 5.4% and 0.8%, respectively, on $270,000 of salaries.

a. Journalize the entry to record the payroll for the week of February 14.

b. Journalize the entry to record the payroll tax expense incurred for the week of February 14.

SHOW
ME HOW

### EX 11-13   Payroll entries

OBJ. 3

Widmer Company had gross wages of $240,000 during the week ended June 17. The amount of wages subject to social security tax was $240,000, while the amount of wages subject to federal and state unemployment taxes was $35,000. Tax rates are as follows:

| | |
|---|---:|
| Social security | 6.0% |
| Medicare | 1.5% |
| State unemployment | 5.4% |
| Federal unemployment | 0.8% |

The total amount withheld from employee wages for federal taxes was $48,000.

a. Journalize the entry to record the payroll for the week of June 17.

b. Journalize the entry to record the payroll tax expense incurred for the week of June 17.

### EX 11-14   Payroll internal control procedures

OBJ. 3

Big Howie's Hot Dog Stand is a fast-food restaurant specializing in hot dogs and hamburgers. The store employs 8 full-time and 12 part-time workers. The store's weekly payroll averages $5,600 for all 20 workers.

Big Howie's Hot Dog Stand uses a personal computer to assist in preparing paychecks. Each week, the store's accountant collects employee time cards and enters the hours worked into the payroll program. The payroll program calculates each employee's pay and prints a paycheck. The accountant uses a check-signing machine to sign the paychecks. Next, the restaurant's owner authorizes the transfer of funds from the restaurant's regular bank account to the payroll account.

For the week of May 12, the accountant accidentally recorded 100 hours worked instead of 40 hours for one of the full-time employees.

Does Big Howie's Hot Dog Stand have internal controls in place to catch this error? If so, how will this error be detected?

### EX 11-15   Internal control procedures

OBJ. 3

Dave's Scooters is a small manufacturer of specialty scooters. The company employs 14 production workers and four administrative persons. The following procedures are used to process the company's weekly payroll:

a. Whenever an employee receives a pay raise, the supervisor must fill out a wage adjustment form, which is signed by the company president. This form is used to change the employee's wage rate in the payroll system.

b. All employees are required to record their hours worked by clocking in and out on a time clock. Employees must clock out for lunch break. Due to congestion around the time clock area at lunch time, management has not objected to having one employee clock in and out for an entire department.

(*Continued*)

c. Whenever a salaried employee is terminated, Personnel authorizes Payroll to remove the employee from the payroll system. However, this procedure is not required when an hourly worker is fired. Hourly employees only receive a paycheck if their time cards show hours worked. The computer automatically drops an employee from the payroll system when that employee has six consecutive weeks with no hours worked.

d. Paychecks are signed by using a check-signing machine. This machine is located in the main office so that it can be easily accessed by anyone needing a check signed.

e. Dave's Scooters maintains a separate checking account for payroll checks. Each week, the total net pay for all employees is transferred from the company's regular bank account to the payroll account.

State whether each of the procedures is appropriate or inappropriate, after considering the principles of internal control. If a procedure is inappropriate, describe the appropriate procedure.

---

### EX 11-16  Accrued vacation pay                                        OBJ. 4

SHOW
ME HOW

A business provides its employees with varying amounts of vacation per year, depending on the length of employment. The estimated amount of the current year's vacation pay is $42,000.

a. Journalize the adjusting entry required on January 31, the end of the first month of the current year, to record the accrued vacation pay.

b. How is the vacation pay reported on the company's balance sheet? When is this amount removed from the company's balance sheet?

---

### EX 11-17  Pension plan entries                                        OBJ. 4

SHOW
ME HOW

Yuri Co. operates a chain of gift shops. The company maintains a defined contribution pension plan for its employees. The plan requires quarterly installments to be paid to the funding agent, Whims Funds, by the fifteenth of the month following the end of each quarter. Assume that the pension cost is $365,000 for the quarter ended December 31.

a. Journalize the entries to record the accrued pension liability on December 31 and the payment to the funding agent on January 15.

b. How does a defined contribution plan differ from a defined benefit plan?

---

### EX 11-18  Defined benefit pension plan terms                          OBJ. 4

In a recent year's financial statements, Procter & Gamble showed an unfunded pension liability of $5,599 million and a periodic pension cost of $434 million.

Explain the meaning of the $5,599 million unfunded pension liability and the $434 million periodic pension cost.

---

### EX 11-19  Accrued product warranty                                    OBJ. 5

SHOW
ME HOW

Lowe Manufacturing Co. warrants its products for one year. The estimated product warranty is 4% of sales. Assume that sales were $560,000 for January. In February, a customer received warranty repairs requiring $140 of parts and $95 of labor.

a. Journalize the adjusting entry required at January 31, the end of the first month of the current fiscal year, to record the accrued product warranty.

b. Journalize the entry to record the warranty work provided in February.

---

### EX 11-20  Accrued product warranty                                    OBJ. 5

General Motors Corporation (GM) disclosed estimated product warranty payable for comparative years as follows:

|  | (in millions) | |
| --- | --- | --- |
|  | Year 2 | Year 1 |
| Current estimated product warranty payable | $3,059 | $2,884 |
| Noncurrent estimated product warranty payable | 4,327 | 4,147 |
| Total | $7,386 | $7,031 |

Presume that GM's sales were $135,592 million in Year 2 and that the total paid on warranty claims during Year 2 was $3,000 million.

a. ➤ Why are short- and long-term estimated warranty liabilities separately disclosed?

b. Provide the journal entry for the Year 2 product warranty expense.

c. What two conditions must be met in order for a product warranty liability to be reported in the financial statements?

---

### EX 11-21   Contingent liabilities
**OBJ. 5**

Several months ago, Ayers Industries Inc. experienced a hazardous materials spill at one of its plants. As a result, the Environmental Protection Agency (EPA) fined the company $240,000. The company is contesting the fine. In addition, an employee is seeking $220,000 in damages related to the spill. Lastly, a homeowner has sued the company for $310,000. The homeowner lives 35 miles from the plant but believes that the incident has reduced the home's resale value by $310,000.

Ayers' legal counsel believes that it is probable that the EPA fine will stand. In addition, counsel indicates that an out-of-court settlement of $125,000 has recently been reached with the employee. The final papers will be signed next week. Counsel believes that the homeowner's case is much weaker and will be decided in favor of Ayers. Other litigation related to the spill is possible, but the damage amounts are uncertain.

a. Journalize the contingent liabilities associated with the hazardous materials spill. Use the account "Damage Awards and Fines" to recognize the expense for the period.

b. ➤ Prepare a note disclosure relating to this incident.

---

### EX 11-22   Quick ratio
**OBJ. 6**

✔ a. Current year: 1.2

Gmeiner Co. had the following current assets and liabilities on December 31 of two recent years:

| | Current Year | Previous Year |
|---|---|---|
| Current assets: | | |
| Cash | $ 486,000 | $ 500,000 |
| Accounts receivable | 210,000 | 200,000 |
| Inventory | 375,000 | 350,000 |
| Total current assets | $1,071,000 | $1,050,000 |
| Current liabilities: | | |
| Current portion of long-term debt | $ 145,000 | $ 110,000 |
| Accounts payable | 175,000 | 150,000 |
| Accrued and other current liabilities | 260,000 | 240,000 |
| Total current liabilities | $ 580,000 | $ 500,000 |

a. Determine the quick ratio for December 31 of both years.

b. ➤ Interpret the change in the quick ratio between the two balance sheet dates.

---

### EX 11-23   Quick ratio
**OBJ. 6**

✔ a. Apple, 1.3

The current assets and current liabilities for Apple Inc. and Dell, Inc., are as follows at the end of a recent fiscal period:

| | Apple Inc. (in millions) | Dell, Inc. (in millions) |
|---|---|---|
| Current assets: | | |
| Cash and cash equivalents | $10,746 | $12,569 |
| Short-term investments | 18,383 | 208 |
| Accounts receivable | 21,275 | 9,842 |
| Inventories | 791 | 1,382 |
| Other current assets* | 6,458 | 3,967 |
| Total current assets | $57,653 | $27,968 |
| Current liabilities: | | |
| Accounts payable | $32,589 | $15,223 |
| Accrued and other current liabilities | 5,953 | 8,216 |
| Total current liabilities | $38,542 | $23,439 |

*These represent prepaid expense and other nonquick current assets.

(*Continued*)

a. Determine the quick ratio for both companies. (Round to one decimal place.)

b. Interpret the quick ratio difference between the two companies.

# Problems: Series A

## PR 11-1A   Liability transactions                                    OBJ. 1, 5

The following items were selected from among the transactions completed by Pioneer Co. during the current year:

Mar.  1. Purchased merchandise on account from Galston Co., $360,000, terms n/30.

31. Issued a 30-day, 5% note for $360,000 to Galston Co., on account.

Apr. 30. Paid Galston Co. the amount owed on the note of March 31.

June  1. Borrowed $180,000 from Pilati Bank, issuing a 45-day, 4% note.

July   1. Purchased tools by issuing a $210,000, 60-day note to Zegna Co., which discounted the note at the rate of 7%.

16. Paid Pilati Bank the interest due on the note of June 1 and renewed the loan by issuing a new 30-day, 6.5% note for $180,000. (Journalize both the debit and credit to the notes payable account.)

Aug. 15. Paid Pilati Bank the amount due on the note of July 16.

30. Paid Zegna Co. the amount due on the note of July 1.

Dec.  1. Purchased office equipment from Taylor Co. for $500,000, paying $120,000 and issuing a series of ten 6% notes for $38,000 each, coming due at 30-day intervals.

22. Settled a product liability lawsuit with a customer for $310,000, payable in January. Pioneer accrued the loss in a litigation claims payable account.

31. Paid the amount due Taylor Co. on the first note in the series issued on December 1.

### Instructions

1. Journalize the transactions.

2. Journalize the adjusting entry for each of the following accrued expenses at the end of the current year:

   a. Product warranty cost, $27,500.

   b. Interest on the nine remaining notes owed to Taylor Co.

---

✔ 1. (b) Dr. Payroll
Tax Expense, $52,795

## PR 11-2A   Entries for payroll and payroll taxes                     OBJ. 2, 3

The following information about the payroll for the week ended December 30 was obtained from the records of Qualitech Co.:

| Salaries: | | Deductions: | |
|---|---|---|---|
| Sales salaries | $350,000 | Income tax withheld | $118,800 |
| Warehouse salaries | 180,000 | Social security tax withheld | 40,500 |
| Office salaries | 145,000 | Medicare tax withheld | 10,125 |
| | $675,000 | U.S. savings bonds | 14,850 |
| | | Group insurance | 12,150 |
| | | | $196,425 |

Tax rates assumed:

Social security, 6%

Medicare, 1.5%

State unemployment (employer only), 5.4%

Federal unemployment (employer only), 0.8%

**Instructions**

1. Assuming that the payroll for the last week of the year is to be paid on December 31, journalize the following entries:

   a. December 30, to record the payroll.

   b. December 30, to record the employer's payroll taxes on the payroll to be paid on December 31. Of the total payroll for the last week of the year, $35,000 is subject to unemployment compensation taxes.

2. Assuming that the payroll for the last week of the year is to be paid on January 5 of the following fiscal year, journalize the following entries:

   a. December 30, to record the payroll.

   b. January 5, to record the employer's payroll taxes on the payroll to be paid on January 5. Because it is a new fiscal year, all $675,000 in salaries is subject to unemployment compensation taxes.

---

**PR 11-3A   Wage and tax statement data on employer FICA tax**     OBJ. 2, 3

✔ 2. (e) $28,574.96

Ehrlich Co. began business on January 2, 2015. Salaries were paid to employees on the last day of each month, and social security tax, Medicare tax, and federal income tax were withheld in the required amounts. An employee who is hired in the middle of the month receives half the monthly salary for that month. All required payroll tax reports were filed, and the correct amount of payroll taxes was remitted by the company for the calendar year. Early in 2016, before the Wage and Tax Statements (Form W-2) could be prepared for distribution to employees and for filing with the Social Security Administration, the employees' earnings records were inadvertently destroyed.

None of the employees resigned or were discharged during the year, and there were no changes in salary rates. The social security tax was withheld at the rate of 6.0% and Medicare tax at the rate of 1.5%. Data on dates of employment, salary rates, and employees' income taxes withheld, which are summarized as follows, were obtained from personnel records and payroll records:

| Employee | Date First Employed | Monthly Salary | Monthly Income Tax Withheld |
|---|---|---|---|
| Arnett | Nov. 16 | $ 5,500 | $  944 |
| Cruz | Jan. 2 | 4,800 | 833 |
| Edwards | Oct. 1 | 8,000 | 1,592 |
| Harvin | Dec. 1 | 6,000 | 1,070 |
| Nicks | Feb. 1 | 10,000 | 2,350 |
| Shiancoe | Mar. 1 | 11,600 | 2,600 |
| Ward | Nov. 16 | 5,220 | 876 |

**Instructions**

1. Calculate the amounts to be reported on each employee's Wage and Tax Statement (Form W-2) for 2015, arranging the data in the following form:

| Employee | Gross Earnings | Federal Income Tax Withheld | Social Security Tax Withheld | Medicare Tax Withheld |
|---|---|---|---|---|

2. Calculate the following employer payroll taxes for the year: (a) social security; (b) Medicare; (c) state unemployment compensation at 5.4% on the first $10,000 of each employee's earnings; (d) federal unemployment compensation at 0.8% on the first $10,000 of each employee's earnings; (e) total.

### PR 11-4A Payroll register

The following data for Throwback Industries Inc. relate to the payroll for the week ended December 9, 2016:

| Employee | Hours Worked | Hourly Rate | Weekly Salary | Federal Income Tax | U.S. Savings Bonds |
|---|---|---|---|---|---|
| Aaron | 46 | $68.00 | | $750.20 | $100 |
| Cobb | 41 | 62.00 | | 537.68 | 110 |
| Clemente | 48 | 70.00 | | 832.64 | 120 |
| DiMaggio | 35 | 56.00 | | 366.04 | 0 |
| Griffey, Jr. | 45 | 62.00 | | 641.84 | 130 |
| Mantle | | | $1,800 | 342.45 | 120 |
| Robinson | 36 | 54.00 | | 382.56 | 130 |
| Williams | | | 2,000 | 398.24 | 125 |
| Vaughn | 42 | 62.00 | | 584.72 | 50 |

Employees Mantle and Williams are office staff, and all of the other employees are sales personnel. All sales personnel are paid 1½ times the regular rate for all hours in excess of 40 hours per week. The social security tax rate is 6.0%, and Medicare tax is 1.5% of each employee's annual earnings. The next payroll check to be used is No. 901.

### Instructions

1. Prepare a payroll register for Throwback Industries Inc. for the week ended December 9, 2016. Use the following columns for the payroll register: Employee, Total Hours, Regular Earnings, Overtime Earnings, Total Earnings, Social Security Tax, Medicare Tax, Federal Income Tax, U.S. Savings Bonds, Total Deductions, Net Pay, Ck. No., Sales Salaries Expense, and Office Salaries Expense.

2. Journalize the entry to record the payroll for the week.

### PR 11-5A Payroll accounts and year-end entries

The following accounts, with the balances indicated, appear in the ledger of Garcon Co. on December 1 of the current year:

| | | | | | |
|---|---|---|---|---|---|
| 211 | Salaries Payable | — | 218 | Bond Deductions Payable | $ 3,400 |
| 212 | Social Security Tax Payable | $ 9,273 | 219 | Medical Insurance Payable | 27,000 |
| 213 | Medicare Tax Payable | 2,318 | 411 | Operations Salaries Expense | 950,000 |
| 214 | Employees Federal Income Tax Payable | 15,455 | 511 | Officers Salaries Expense | 600,000 |
| 215 | Employees State Income Tax Payable | 13,909 | 512 | Office Salaries Expense | 150,000 |
| 216 | State Unemployment Tax Payable | 1,400 | 519 | Payroll Tax Expense | 137,951 |
| 217 | Federal Unemployment Tax Payable | 500 | | | |

The following transactions relating to payroll, payroll deductions, and payroll taxes occurred during December:

Dec. 2. Issued Check No. 410 for $3,400 to Jay Bank to purchase U.S. savings bonds for employees.

2. Issued Check No. 411 to Jay Bank for $27,046 in payment of $9,273 of social security tax, $2,318 of Medicare tax, and $15,455 of employees' federal income tax due.

13. Journalized the entry to record the biweekly payroll. A summary of the payroll record follows:

| | | |
|---|---|---|
| Salary distribution: | | |
| Operations | $43,200 | |
| Officers | 27,200 | |
| Office | 6,800 | $77,200 |
| Deductions: | | |
| Social security tax | $ 4,632 | |
| Medicare tax | 1,158 | |
| Federal income tax withheld | 15,440 | |
| State income tax withheld | 3,474 | |
| Savings bond deductions | 1,700 | |
| Medical insurance deductions | 4,500 | 30,904 |
| Net amount | | $46,296 |

Dec. 13. Issued Check No. 420 in payment of the net amount of the biweekly payroll.

13. Journalized the entry to record payroll taxes on employees' earnings of December 13: social security tax, $4,632; Medicare tax, $1,158; state unemployment tax, $350; federal unemployment tax, $125.

16. Issued Check No. 424 to Jay Bank for $27,020, in payment of $9,264 of social security tax, $2,316 of Medicare tax, and $15,440 of employees' federal income tax due.

19. Issued Check No. 429 to Sims-Walker Insurance Company for $31,500 in payment of the semiannual premium on the group medical insurance policy.

27. Journalized the entry to record the biweekly payroll. A summary of the payroll record follows:

| Salary distribution: | | |
|---|---|---|
| Operations | $42,800 | |
| Officers | 28,000 | |
| Office | 7,000 | $77,800 |
| Deductions: | | |
| Social security tax | $ 4,668 | |
| Medicare tax | 1,167 | |
| Federal income tax withheld | 15,404 | |
| State income tax withheld | 3,501 | |
| Savings bond deductions | 1,700 | 26,440 |
| Net amount | | $51,360 |

27. Issued Check No. 541 in payment of the net amount of the biweekly payroll.

27. Journalized the entry to record payroll taxes on employees' earnings of December 27: social security tax, $4,668; Medicare tax, $1,167; state unemployment tax, $225; federal unemployment tax, $75.

27. Issued Check No. 543 for $20,884 to State Department of Revenue in payment of employees' state income tax due on December 31.

31. Issued Check No. 545 to Jay Bank for $3,400 to purchase U.S. savings bonds for employees.

31. Paid $45,000 to the employee pension plan. The annual pension cost is $60,000. (Record both the payment and unfunded pension liability.)

**Instructions**

1. Journalize the transactions.

2. Journalize the following adjusting entries on December 31:

   a. Salaries accrued: operations salaries, $8,560; officers salaries, $5,600; office salaries, $1,400. The payroll taxes are immaterial and are not accrued.

   b. Vacation pay, $15,000.

# Problems: Series B

---

**PR 11-1B    Liability transactions**                                      OBJ. 1, 5

General Ledger

SHOW
ME HOW

The following items were selected from among the transactions completed by Aston Martin Inc. during the current year:

Apr. 15. Borrowed $225,000 from Audi Company, issuing a 30-day, 6% note for that amount.

May  1. Purchased equipment by issuing a $320,000, 180-day note to Spyder Manufacturing Co., which discounted the note at the rate of 6%.

15. Paid Audi Company the interest due on the note of April 15 and renewed the loan by issuing a new 60-day, 8% note for $225,000. (Record both the debit and credit to the notes payable account.)

July 14. Paid Audi Company the amount due on the note of May 15.

*(Continued)*

Aug. 16. Purchased merchandise on account from Exige Co., $90,000, terms, n/30.

Sept.15. Issued a 45-day, 6% note for $90,000 to Exige Co., on account.

Oct. 28. Paid Spyder Manufacturing Co. the amount due on the note of May 1.

  30. Paid Exige Co. the amount owed on the note of September 15.

Nov. 16. Purchased store equipment from Gallardo Co. for $450,000, paying $50,000 and issuing a series of twenty 9% notes for $20,000 each, coming due at 30-day intervals.

Dec. 16. Paid the amount due Gallardo Co. on the first note in the series issued on November 16.

  28. Settled a personal injury lawsuit with a customer for $87,500, to be paid in January. Aston Martin Inc. accrued the loss in a litigation claims payable account.

**Instructions**

1. Journalize the transactions.

2. Journalize the adjusting entry for each of the following accrued expenses at the end of the current year:

   a. Product warranty cost, $26,800.

   b. Interest on the 19 remaining notes owed to Gallardo Co.

---

**PR 11-2B   Entries for payroll and payroll taxes**                                    OBJ. 2, 3

✔ 1. (b) Dr. Payroll Tax Expense, $90,735

General Ledger

The following information about the payroll for the week ended December 30 was obtained from the records of Saine Co.:

| Salaries: | | Deductions: | |
|---|---:|---|---:|
| Sales salaries | $ 625,000 | Income tax withheld | $232,260 |
| Warehouse salaries | 240,000 | Social security tax withheld | 71,100 |
| Office salaries | 320,000 | Medicare tax withheld | 17,775 |
| | $1,185,000 | U.S. savings bonds | 35,500 |
| | | Group insurance | 53,325 |
| | | | $409,960 |

Tax rates assumed:
  Social security, 6%
  Medicare, 1.5%
  State unemployment (employer only), 5.4%
  Federal unemployment (employer only), 0.8%

**Instructions**

1. Assuming that the payroll for the last week of the year is to be paid on December 31, journalize the following entries:

   a. December 30, to record the payroll.

   b. December 30, to record the employer's payroll taxes on the payroll to be paid on December 31. Of the total payroll for the last week of the year, $30,000 is subject to unemployment compensation taxes.

2. Assuming that the payroll for the last week of the year is to be paid on January 4 of the following fiscal year, journalize the following entries:

   a. December 30, to record the payroll.

   b. January 4, to record the employer's payroll taxes on the payroll to be paid on January 4. Because it is a new fiscal year, all $1,185,000 in salaries is subject to unemployment compensation taxes.

---

**PR 11-3B   Wage and tax statement data and employer FICA tax**                        OBJ. 2, 3

✔ 2. (e) $25,136.13

Jocame Inc. began business on January 2, 2015. Salaries were paid to employees on the last day of each month, and social security tax, Medicare tax, and federal income tax were withheld in the required amounts. An employee who is hired in the middle of the month receives half the monthly salary for that month. All required payroll tax reports were filed, and the correct amount of payroll taxes was remitted by the company for the calendar year. Early in 2016, before the Wage and Tax Statements (Form W-2) could be prepared for distribution to employees and for filing with the Social Security Administration, the employees' earnings records were inadvertently destroyed.

None of the employees resigned or were discharged during the year, and there were no changes in salary rates. The social security tax was withheld at the rate of 6.0% and Medicare tax at the rate of 1.5% on salary. Data on dates of employment, salary rates, and employees' income taxes withheld, which are summarized as follows, were obtained from personnel records and payroll records:

| Employee | Date First Employed | Monthly Salary | Monthly Income Tax Withheld |
|---|---|---|---|
| Addai | July 16 | $ 8,160 | $1,704 |
| Kasay | June 1 | 3,600 | 533 |
| McGahee | Feb. 16 | 6,420 | 1,238 |
| Moss | Jan. 1 | 4,600 | 783 |
| Stewart | Dec. 1 | 4,500 | 758 |
| Tolbert | Nov. 16 | 3,250 | 446 |
| Wells | May 1 | 10,500 | 2,359 |

### Instructions

1. Calculate the amounts to be reported on each employee's Wage and Tax Statement (Form W-2) for 2015, arranging the data in the following form:

| Employee | Gross Earnings | Federal Income Tax Withheld | Social Security Tax Withheld | Medicare Tax Withheld |
|---|---|---|---|---|

2. Calculate the following employer payroll taxes for the year: (a) social security; (b) Medicare; (c) state unemployment compensation at 5.4% on the first $10,000 of each employee's earnings; (d) federal unemployment compensation at 0.8% on the first $10,000 of each employee's earnings; (e) total.

---

**PR 11-4B  Payroll register**                  OBJ. 2, 3

✔ 1. Total net pay, $16,592.58

The following data for Flexco Inc. relate to the payroll for the week ended December 9, 2016:

| Employee | Hours Worked | Hourly Rate | Weekly Salary | Federal Income Tax | U.S. Savings Bonds |
|---|---|---|---|---|---|
| Carlton | 52 | $50.00 | | $667.00 | $ 60 |
| Grove | | | $4,000 | 860.00 | 100 |
| Johnson | 36 | 52.00 | | 355.68 | 0 |
| Koufax | 45 | 58.00 | | 578.55 | 44 |
| Maddux | 37 | 45.00 | | 349.65 | 62 |
| Seaver | | | 3,200 | 768.00 | 120 |
| Spahn | 46 | 52.00 | | 382.20 | 0 |
| Winn | 48 | 50.00 | | 572.00 | 75 |
| Young | 43 | 54.00 | | 480.60 | 80 |

Employees Grove and Seaver are office staff, and all of the other employees are sales personnel. All sales personnel are paid 1½ times the regular rate for all hours in excess of 40 hours per week. The social security tax rate is 6.0% of each employee's annual earnings, and Medicare tax is 1.5% of each employee's annual earnings. The next payroll check to be used is No. 328.

### Instructions

1. Prepare a payroll register for Flexco Inc. for the week ended December 9, 2016. Use the following columns for the payroll register: Employee, Total Hours, Regular Earnings, Overtime Earnings, Total Earnings, Social Security Tax, Medicare Tax, Federal Income Tax, U.S. Savings Bonds, Total Deductions, Net Pay, Ck. No., Sales Salaries Expense, and Office Salaries Expense.

2. Journalize the entry to record the payroll for the week.

**PR 11-5B** **Payroll accounts and year-end entries**                    OBJ. 2, 3, 4

The following accounts, with the balances indicated, appear in the ledger of Codigo Co. on December 1 of the current year:

| | | | | | |
|---|---|---|---|---|---|
| 101 | Salaries Payable | — | 108 | Bond Deductions Payable | $ 2,300 |
| 102 | Social Security Tax Payable | $2,913 | 109 | Medical Insurance Payable | 2,520 |
| 103 | Medicare Tax Payable | 728 | 201 | Sales Salaries Expense | 700,000 |
| 104 | Employees Federal Income Tax Payable | 4,490 | 301 | Officers Salaries Expense | 340,000 |
| 105 | Employees State Income Tax Payable | 4,078 | 401 | Office Salaries Expense | 125,000 |
| 106 | State Unemployment Tax Payable | 1,260 | 408 | Payroll Tax Expense | 59,491 |
| 107 | Federal Unemployment Tax Payable | 360 | | | |

The following transactions relating to payroll, payroll deductions, and payroll taxes occurred during December:

Dec.  1. Issued Check No. 815 to Aberderas Insurance Company for $2,520, in payment of the semiannual premium on the group medical insurance policy.

   1. Issued Check No. 816 to Alvarez Bank for $8,131, in payment for $2,913 of social security tax, $728 of Medicare tax, and $4,490 of employees' federal income tax due.

   2. Issued Check No. 817 for $2,300 to Alvarez Bank to purchase U.S. savings bonds for employees.

   12. Journalized the entry to record the biweekly payroll. A summary of the payroll record follows:

| | | |
|---|---|---|
| Salary distribution: | | |
| Sales | $14,500 | |
| Officers | 7,100 | |
| Office | 2,600 | $24,200 |
| Deductions: | | |
| Social security tax | $ 1,452 | |
| Medicare tax | 363 | |
| Federal income tax withheld | 4,308 | |
| State income tax withheld | 1,089 | |
| Savings bond deductions | 1,150 | |
| Medical insurance deductions | 420 | 8,782 |
| Net amount | | $15,418 |

   12. Issued Check No. 822 in payment of the net amount of the biweekly payroll.

   12. Journalized the entry to record payroll taxes on employees' earnings of December 12: social security tax, $1,452; Medicare tax, $363; state unemployment tax, $315; federal unemployment tax, $90.

   15. Issued Check No. 830 to Alvarez Bank for $7,938, in payment of $2,904 of social security tax, $726 of Medicare tax, and $4,308 of employees' federal income tax due.

   26. Journalized the entry to record the biweekly payroll. A summary of the payroll record follows:

| | | |
|---|---|---|
| Salary distribution: | | |
| Sales | $14,250 | |
| Officers | 7,250 | |
| Office | 2,750 | $24,250 |
| Deductions: | | |
| Social security tax | $ 1,455 | |
| Medicare tax | 364 | |
| Federal income tax withheld | 4,317 | |
| State income tax withheld | 1,091 | |
| Savings bond deductions | 1,150 | 8,377 |
| Net amount | | $15,873 |

   26. Issued Check No. 840 for the net amount of the biweekly payroll.

Dec. 26. Journalized the entry to record payroll taxes on employees' earnings of December 26: social security tax, $1,455; Medicare tax, $364; state unemployment tax, $150; federal unemployment tax, $40.

30. Issued Check No. 851 for $6,258 to State Department of Revenue, in payment of employees' state income tax due on December 31.

30. Issued Check No. 852 to Alvarez Bank for $2,300 to purchase U.S. savings bonds for employees.

31. Paid $55,400 to the employee pension plan. The annual pension cost is $65,500. (Record both the payment and the unfunded pension liability.)

### Instructions

1. Journalize the transactions.

2. Journalize the following adjusting entries on December 31:

    a. Salaries accrued: sales salaries, $4,275; officers salaries, $2,175; office salaries, $825. The payroll taxes are immaterial and are not accrued.

    b. Vacation pay, $13,350.

## Comprehensive Problem 3

✔ 5. Total assets, $3,569,300

[General Ledger]

Selected transactions completed by Kornett Company during its first fiscal year ended December 31, 2016, were as follows:

Jan. 3. Issued a check to establish a petty cash fund of $4,500.

Feb. 26. Replenished the petty cash fund, based on the following summary of petty cash receipts: office supplies, $1,680; miscellaneous selling expense, $570; miscellaneous administrative expense, $880.

Apr. 14. Purchased $31,300 of merchandise on account, terms 1/10, n/30. The perpetual inventory system is used to account for inventory.

May 13. Paid the invoice of April 14 after the discount period had passed.

17. Received cash from daily cash sales for $21,200. The amount indicated by the cash register was $21,240.

June 2. Received a 60-day, 8% note for $180,000 on the Ryanair account.

Aug. 1. Received amount owed on June 2 note, plus interest at the maturity date.

24. Received $7,600 on the Finley account and wrote off the remainder owed on a $9,000 accounts receivable balance. (The allowance method is used in accounting for uncollectible receivables.)

Sept. 15. Reinstated the Finley account written off on August 24 and received $1,400 cash in full payment.

15. Purchased land by issuing a $670,000, 90-day note to Zahorik Co., which discounted it at 9%.

Oct. 17. Sold office equipment in exchange for $135,000 cash plus receipt of a $100,000, 90-day, 9% note. The equipment had a cost of $320,000 and accumulated depreciation of $64,000 as of October 17.

*(Continued)*

Nov. 30. Journalized the monthly payroll for November, based on the following data:

| Salaries | | Deductions | |
|---|---|---|---|
| Sales salaries | $135,000 | Income tax withheld | $39,266 |
| Office salaries | 77,250 | Social security tax withheld | 12,735 |
| | $212,250 | Medicare tax withheld | 3,184 |

| Unemployment tax rates: | |
|---|---|
| State unemployment | 5.4% |
| Federal unemployment | 0.8% |
| Amount subject to unemployment taxes: | |
| State unemployment | $5,000 |
| Federal unemployment | 5,000 |

30. Journalized the employer's payroll taxes on the payroll.

Dec. 14. Journalized the payment of the September 15 note at maturity.

31. The pension cost for the year was $190,400, of which $139,700 was paid to the pension plan trustee.

## Instructions

1. Journalize the selected transactions.

2. Based on the following data, prepare a bank reconciliation for December of the current year:

   a. Balance according to the bank statement at December 31, $283,000.

   b. Balance according to the ledger at December 31, $245,410.

   c. Checks outstanding at December 31, $68,540.

   d. Deposit in transit, not recorded by bank, $29,500.

   e. Bank debit memo for service charges, $750.

   f. A check for $12,700 in payment of an invoice was incorrectly recorded in the accounts as $12,000.

3. Based on the bank reconciliation prepared in (2), journalize the entry or entries to be made by Kornett Company.

4. Based on the following selected data, journalize the adjusting entries as of December 31 of the current year:

   a. Estimated uncollectible accounts at December 31, $16,000, based on an aging of accounts receivable. The balance of Allowance for Doubtful Accounts at December 31 was $2,000 (debit).

   b. The physical inventory on December 31 indicated an inventory shrinkage of $3,300.

   c. Prepaid insurance expired during the year, $22,820.

   d. Office supplies used during the year, $3,920.

   e. Depreciation is computed as follows:

| Asset | Cost | Residual Value | Acquisition Date | Useful Life in Years | Depreciation Method Used |
|---|---|---|---|---|---|
| Buildings | $900,000 | $ 0 | January 2 | 50 | Double-declining-balance |
| Office Equip. | 246,000 | 26,000 | January 3 | 5 | Straight-line |
| Store Equip. | 112,000 | 12,000 | July 1 | 10 | Straight-line |

   f. A patent costing $48,000 when acquired on January 2 has a remaining legal life of 10 years and is expected to have value for eight years.

   g. The cost of mineral rights was $546,000. Of the estimated deposit of 910,000 tons of ore, 50,000 tons were mined and sold during the year.

   h. Vacation pay expense for December, $10,500.

   i. A product warranty was granted beginning December 1 and covering a one-year period. The estimated cost is 4% of sales, which totaled $1,900,000 in December.

   j. Interest was accrued on the note receivable received on October 17.

5. Based on the following information and the post-closing trial balance that follows, prepare a balance sheet in report form at December 31 of the current year:

The merchandise inventory is stated at cost by the LIFO method.

The product warranty payable is a current liability.

Vacation pay payable:

| | |
|---|---|
| Current liability | $7,140 |
| Long-term liability | 3,360 |

The unfunded pension liability is a long-term liability.

Notes payable:

| | |
|---|---|
| Current liability | $ 70,000 |
| Long-term liability | 630,000 |

**Kornett Company**
**Post-Closing Trial Balance**
**December 31, 2016**

| | Debit Balances | Credit Balances |
|---|---|---|
| Petty Cash | 4,500 | |
| Cash | 243,960 | |
| Notes Receivable | 100,000 | |
| Accounts Receivable | 470,000 | |
| Allowance for Doubtful Accounts | | 16,000 |
| Merchandise Inventory | 320,000 | |
| Interest Receivable | 1,875 | |
| Prepaid Insurance | 45,640 | |
| Office Supplies | 13,400 | |
| Land | 654,925 | |
| Buildings | 900,000 | |
| Accumulated Depreciation—Buildings | | 36,000 |
| Office Equipment | 246,000 | |
| Accumulated Depreciation—Office Equipment | | 44,000 |
| Store Equipment | 112,000 | |
| Accumulated Depreciation—Store Equipment | | 5,000 |
| Mineral Rights | 546,000 | |
| Accumulated Depletion | | 30,000 |
| Patents | 42,000 | |
| Social Security Tax Payable | | 25,470 |
| Medicare Tax Payable | | 4,710 |
| Employees Federal Income Tax Payable | | 40,000 |
| State Unemployment Tax Payable | | 270 |
| Federal Unemployment Tax Payable | | 40 |
| Salaries Payable | | 157,000 |
| Accounts Payable | | 131,600 |
| Interest Payable | | 28,000 |
| Product Warranty Payable | | 76,000 |
| Vacation Pay Payable | | 10,500 |
| Unfunded Pension Liability | | 50,700 |
| Notes Payable | | 700,000 |
| J. Kornett, Capital | | 2,345,010 |
| | 3,700,300 | 3,700,300 |

## Cases & Projects

General Ledger

### CP 11-1 Ethics and professional conduct in business

Tonya Latirno is a certified public accountant (CPA) and staff accountant for Kennedy and Kennedy, a local CPA firm. It had been the policy of the firm to provide a holiday bonus equal to two weeks' salary to all employees. The firm's new management team announced on November 15 that a bonus equal to only one week's salary would be made available to employees this year. Tonya thought that this policy was unfair because she and her co-workers planned on the full two-week bonus. The two-week bonus had been given for 10 straight years, so it seemed as though the firm had breached an implied commitment. Thus, Tonya decided that she would make up the lost bonus week by working an extra six hours of overtime per week over the next five weeks until the end of the year. Kennedy and Kennedy's policy is to pay overtime at 150% of straight time.

Tonya's supervisor was surprised to see overtime being reported, because there is generally very little additional or unusual client service demands at the end of the calendar year. However, the overtime was not questioned, because firm employees are on the "honor system" in reporting their overtime.

➤ Discuss whether the firm is acting in an ethical manner by changing the bonus. Is Tonya behaving in an ethical manner?

### CP 11-2 Recognizing pension expense

The annual examination of Felton Company's financial statements by its external public accounting firm (auditors) is nearing completion. The following conversation took place between the controller of Felton Company (Francie) and the audit manager from the public accounting firm (Sumana):

*Sumana:* You know, Francie, we are about to wrap up our audit for this fiscal year. Yet, there is one item still to be resolved.

*Francie:* What's that?

*Sumana:* Well, as you know, at the beginning of the year, Felton began a defined benefit pension plan. This plan promises your employees an annual payment when they retire, using a formula based on their salaries at retirement and their years of service. I believe that a pension expense should be recognized this year, equal to the amount of pension earned by your employees.

*Francie:* Wait a minute. I think you have it all wrong. The company doesn't have a pension expense until it actually pays the pension in cash when the employee retires. After all, some of these employees may not reach retirement, and if they don't, the company doesn't owe them anything.

*Sumana:* You're not really seeing this the right way. The pension is earned by your employees during their working years. You actually make the payment much later—when they retire. It's like one long accrual—much like incurring wages in one period and paying them in the next. Thus, I think that you should recognize the expense in the period the pension is earned by the employees.

*Francie:* Let me see if I've got this straight. I should recognize an expense this period for something that may or may not be paid to the employees in 20 or 30 years, when they finally retire. How am I supposed to determine what the expense is for the current year? The amount of the final retirement depends on many uncertainties: salary levels, employee longevity, mortality rates, and interest earned on investments to fund the pension. I don't think that an amount can be determined, even if I accepted your arguments.

➤ Evaluate Sumana's position. Is she right or is Francie correct?

### CP 11-3 Ethics and professional conduct in business

Marvin Turner was discussing summer employment with Tina Song, president of Motown Construction Service:

*Tina:* I'm glad that you're thinking about joining us for the summer. We could certainly use the help.

*Marvin:* Sounds good. I enjoy outdoor work, and I could use the money to help with next year's school expenses.

*Tina:* I've got a plan that can help you out on that. As you know, I'll pay you $14 per hour, but in addition, I'd like to pay you with cash. Since you're only working for the summer, it really doesn't make sense for me to go to the trouble of formally putting you on our payroll system. In fact, I do some jobs for my clients on a strictly cash basis, so it would be easy to just pay you that way.

*Marvin:* Well, that's a bit unusual, but I guess money is money.

*Tina:* Yeah, not only that, it's tax-free!

*Marvin:* What do you mean?

*Tina:* Didn't you know? Any money that you receive in cash is not reported to the IRS on a W-2 form; therefore, the IRS doesn't know about the income—hence, it's the same as tax-free earnings.

a. ━━━▶ Why does Tina Song want to conduct business transactions using cash (not check or credit card)?

b. ━━━▶ How should Marvin respond to Tina's suggestion?

### CP 11-4   Payroll forms

### Group Project

Payroll accounting involves the use of government-supplied forms to account for payroll taxes. Three common forms are the W-2, Form 940, and Form 941. Form a team with three of your classmates and retrieve copies of each of these forms. They may be obtained from a local IRS office, a library, or downloaded from the Internet at www.irs.gov (go to forms and publications). ━━━▶ Briefly describe the purpose of each of the three forms.

### CP 11-5   Contingent liabilities

Altria Group, Inc., has more than 12 pages dedicated to describing contingent liabilities in the notes to recent financial statements. These pages include extensive descriptions of multiple contingent liabilities. Use the Internet to research Altria Group, Inc., at www.altria.com.

a. What are the major business units of Altria Group?

b. Based on your understanding of this company, why would Altria Group require more than 12 pages of contingency disclosure?

# Accounting for Partnerships and Limited Liability Companies

## Boston Basketball Partners LLC

**B**oston Basketball Partners (BBP) LLC are the owners of the Boston Celtics NBA basketball franchise. The letters "LLC" stand for *limited liability company*. Unlike sole proprietorships illustrated in prior chapters, an LLC is a business form that normally has multiple owners. BBP LLC is led by Wic Grousbeck, a former venture fund manager from Boston, with the assistance of more than 15 other owners. Grousbeck called investing in the Celtics "a chance of a lifetime." Surprisingly, Grousbeck claims "money would not be the first priority." Even so, *Forbes* estimates the team is now worth $730 million, which is more than twice what BBP LLC originally paid, while ranking the Celtics as the fourth most valuable team in the NBA. So, Grousbeck must be doing something right. Grousbeck and his team have turned their venture capital skills toward the Celtics. Some of

their innovations off the court include building a cable partnership, using technology to evaluate seat usage, and adding advertising sponsors. On the court, they pioneered the "three superstars to win" strategy with Rondo, Garnett, and Allen.

So why would BBP LLC choose the LLC form of organization?

The entity form chosen by a business has an important impact on the owners' legal liability, taxation, and ability to raise money. The four major forms of business entities discussed in this text are the proprietorship, partnership, limited liability company, and corporation. Proprietorships have been discussed in prior chapters. Partnerships and limited liability companies will be discussed in this chapter, and corporations will be introduced in the next chapter.

**OBJ 1** Describe the characteristics of proprietorships, partnerships, and limited liability companies.

# Proprietorships, Partnerships, and Limited Liability Companies

The four most common legal forms for organizing and operating a business are as follows:

- Proprietorship
- Corporation
- Partnership
- Limited liability company

In this section, the characteristics of proprietorships, partnerships, and limited liability companies are described. The characteristics of corporations are described in Chapter 13.

## Proprietorships

A *proprietorship* is a company owned by a single individual. The most common proprietorships are professional service providers, such as lawyers, architects, realtors, and physicians.

Characteristics of proprietorships include the following:

- *Simple to form.* There are no legal restrictions or forms to file.
- *No limitation on legal liability.* The owner is personally liable for any debts or legal claims against the business. Thus, creditors can take the personal assets of the owner if the business debts exceed the owner's investment in the company.

The **Internal Revenue Service (IRS)** estimates that proprietorships file 70% of business tax returns, but earn only 5% of all business revenues.

- *Not taxable*. For federal income tax purposes, a proprietorship is not taxed. Instead, the proprietorship's income or loss is "passed through" to the owner's individual income tax return.[1]
- *Limited life*. When the owner dies or retires, the proprietorship ceases to exist.
- *Limited ability to raise capital (funds)*. The ability to raise capital (funds) is limited to what the owner can provide from personal resources or through borrowing.

## Partnerships

A **partnership** is an association of two or more persons who own and manage a business for profit.[2] Partnerships are less widely used than proprietorships.

Characteristics of a partnership include the following:

- *Moderately complex to form*. A partnership is often formed with a partnership agreement. A **partnership agreement** includes matters such as amounts to be invested, limits on withdrawals, distributions of income and losses, and admission and withdrawal of partners. Thus, an attorney is often used in forming a partnership.
- *No limitation on legal liability*. The partners are personally liable for any debts or legal claims against the partnership. Therefore, creditors can take the personal assets of the partners if the business debts exceed the partners' investment in the business.
- *Not taxable*. For federal income tax purposes, a partnership is not taxed. Instead, the partnership's income or loss is "passed through" to the partners' individual income tax returns. However, partnerships must still report revenues, expenses, and income or loss annually to the Internal Revenue Service.
- *Limited life*. When a partner dies or retires, the partnership ceases to exist. Likewise, the admission of a new partner dissolves the old partnership, and a new partnership must be formed if operations are to continue.
- *Limited ability to raise capital (funds)*. The ability to raise capital (funds) for the partnership is limited to what the partners can provide from personal resources or through borrowing.

> **Note:**
> A partnership is a nontaxable entity that has a limited life and unlimited liability.

In addition to those characteristics, some unique aspects of partnerships are:

- *Co-ownership of partnership property*. The property invested in a partnership by a partner becomes the joint property of all the partners. When a partnership is dissolved, each partner's share of the partnership assets is the balance in their capital account.
- *Mutual agency*. Each partner is an agent of the partnership and may act on behalf of the entire partnership. Thus, any liabilities created by one partner become liabilities of all the partners.
- *Participation in income*. Net income and net loss are distributed among the partners according to their partnership agreement. If the partnership agreement does not provide for distribution of income and losses, then income and losses are divided equally among the partners.

## Business ✦ Connection

### BREAKING UP IS HARD TO DO

Former partners of Adam Carolla filed court papers accusing the star of The Adam Carolla Show (adamcarolla.com) of a breach of their partnership agreement. They claimed the partnership agreement gave 30% ownership to Donny Misraje, 10% to Sandy Ganz, and 60% to Carolla. The suit alleges that Carolla began his popular podcast with the help of his partners at a time when future success of the venture was risky and unknown.

The former partners claim to have given up jobs, invested money and equipment, and provided expertise to launch the show. Once the show achieved success, the former partners claim Carolla unfairly kicked them out of the partnership. The court will, in part, use the partnership agreement to help settle this dispute. A partnership agreement helps protect the interests of all parties to a business venture.

*Source:* Radar Staff, "Best Friend Sues Adam Carolla Over Hit Podcast Show," January 18, 2013.

---

[1] The proprietor's statement of income is included on Schedule C of the individual 1040 tax return.
[2] The definition of a partnership is included in the Uniform Partnership Act, which has been adopted by most states.

## Limited Liability Companies

 Many companies have joint ventures organized as LLCs. For example, **Walt Disney Company** has a 42% interest in **A&E Television Networks, LLC.**

A **limited liability company (LLC)** is a form of legal entity that provides limited liability to its owners but is treated as a partnership for tax purposes. Thus, the LLC organizational form is popular for small businesses.

Characteristics of an LLC include the following:

- *Moderately complex to form.* An LLC requires an agreement among the owners, who are called members. The *operating agreement* includes matters such as amounts to be invested, limits on withdrawals, distributions of income and losses, and admission and withdrawal of members. An attorney is normally used in forming an LCC.

- *Limited legal liability.* The members have *limited liability* even if they are active in the company. Thus, the members' personal assets are legally protected against creditor claims made against the LLC. That is, only the members' investments in the company are subject to claims of creditors.

- *Not taxable.* An LLC may elect to be treated as a partnership for tax purposes. In this way, income passes through the LLC and is taxed on the individual members' tax returns.[3]

- *Unlimited life.* Most LLC operating agreements specify continuity of life for the LLC, even when a member withdraws or new members join the LLC.

- *Moderate ability to raise capital (funds).* Because of their limited liability, LLCs are attractive to many investors, thus allowing for greater access to capital (funds) than is normally the case in a partnership.

An LLC may elect to operate as a *member-managed* or a *manager-managed* company. In a member-managed LLC, individual members may legally bind the LLC, like partners bind a partnership. In a manager-managed LLC, only authorized members may legally bind the LLC. Thus, in a manager-managed LLC, members may share in the income of the LLC without concern for managing the company.

## Comparing Proprietorships, Partnerships, and Limited Liability Companies

Exhibit 1 summarizes the characteristics of proprietorships, partnerships, and limited liability companies.

---

**EXHIBIT 1**   Characteristics of Proprietorships, Partnerships, and Limited Liability Companies

| Organizational Form | Complexity of Formation | Legal Liability | Taxation | Limitation on Life of Entity | Access to Capital |
|---|---|---|---|---|---|
| Proprietorship | Simple | No limitation | Nontaxable (pass-through) entity | Limited | Limited |
| Partnership | Moderate | No limitation | Nontaxable (pass-through) entity | Limited | Limited |
| Limited Liability Company | Moderate | Limited liability | Nontaxable (pass-through) entity by election | Unlimited | Moderate |

---

# Business Connection

### ORGANIZATIONAL FORMS IN THE ACCOUNTING INDUSTRY

The four major accounting firms, KPMG LLP, Ernst & Young, PricewaterhouseCoopers, and Deloitte & Touche, all began as partnerships. This form was legally required due to the theory of mutual agency. That is, the partnership form was thought to create public trust by requiring all partners to be jointly liable and responsible for each other's judgments. In addition, investment in the partnerships was limited to practicing accountants. This prevented any pressures from outside investors affecting professional decisions.

As these firms grew and the risk increased, all of these firms were allowed to change, by law, to limited liability partnerships (LLPs). Thus, while remaining a partnership, the liability of the partners was limited to their investment in the firm. The LLP form is very similar to an LLC, except that investment is restricted to professionals.

---

[3] An LLC may also be taxed as a separate entity. However, doing so would remove these tax benefits, making this a less common election.

# Forming a Partnership and Dividing Income

**OBJ 2** Describe and illustrate the accounting for forming a partnership and for dividing the net income and net loss of a partnership.

Most of the day-to-day accounting for a partnership or an LLC is similar to that illustrated in earlier chapters. However, the formation, division of net income or net loss, dissolution, and liquidation of partnerships and LLCs give rise to unique transactions.

In the remainder of this chapter, the unique transactions for partnerships and LLCs are described and illustrated. The accounting for an LLC is the same as a partnership, except that the terms *member* and *members' equity* are used rather than *partner* or *owners' capital*. For this reason, the journal entries for an LLC are shown alongside the partnership entries.

## Forming a Partnership

In forming a partnership, the investments of each partner are recorded in separate entries. The assets contributed by a partner are debited to the partnership asset accounts. If any liabilities are assumed by the partnership, the partnership liability accounts are credited. The partner's capital account is credited for the net amount.

To illustrate, assume that Joseph Stevens and Earl Foster, owners of competing hardware stores, agree to combine their businesses in a partnership. Stevens agrees to contribute the following:

| | | | |
|---|---|---|---|
| Cash | $ 7,200 | Office equipment | $2,500 |
| Accounts receivable | 16,300 | Allowance for doubtful accounts | 1,500 |
| Merchandise inventory | 28,700 | Accounts payable | 2,600 |
| Store equipment | 5,400 | | |

The entry to record the assets and liabilities contributed by Stevens is as follows:

| LLC | | |
|---|---|---|
| Cash | 7,200 | |
| Accounts Receivable | 16,300 | |
| Merchandise Inventory | 28,700 | |
| Store Equipment | 5,400 | |
| Office Equipment | 2,500 | |
| Allowance for Doubtful Accounts | | 1,500 |
| Accounts Payable | | 2,600 |
| Joseph Stevens, Member Equity | | 56,000 |

| | | | | |
|---|---|---|---|---|
| Apr. | 1 | Cash | 7,200 | |
| | | Accounts Receivable | 16,300 | |
| | | Merchandise Inventory | 28,700 | |
| | | Store Equipment | 5,400 | |
| | | Office Equipment | 2,500 | |
| | | Allowance for Doubtful Accounts | | 1,500 |
| | | Accounts Payable | | 2,600 |
| | | Joseph Stevens, Capital | | 56,000 |

In the preceding entry, the noncash assets are recorded at values agreed upon by the partners. These values are normally based on current market values. As a result, the book value of the assets contributed by the partners normally differs from that recorded by the new partnership.

To illustrate, the store equipment contributed by Stevens may have had a book value of $3,500 in Stevens' ledger (cost of $10,000 less accumulated depreciation of $6,500). However, the store equipment is recorded at its current market value of $5,400 in the preceding entry. The contributions of Foster would be recorded in an entry similar to the entry for Stevens.

**Example Exercise 12-1** **Journalize Partner's Original Investment**  **OBJ 1**

Reese Howell contributed equipment, inventory, and $34,000 cash to a partnership. The equipment had a book value of $23,000 and a market value of $29,000. The inventory had a book value of $60,000, but only had a market value of $15,000, due to obsolescence. The partnership also assumed a $12,000 note payable owed by Howell that was used originally to purchase the equipment.

Provide the journal entry for Howell's contribution to the partnership.

*(Continued)*

**Follow My Example 12-1**

| | | |
|---|---|---|
| Cash............................................................................. | 34,000 | |
| Inventory...................................................................... | 15,000 | |
| Equipment .................................................................... | 29,000 | |
|     Notes Payable ........................................................... | | 12,000 |
|     Reese Howell, Capital ................................................... | | 66,000 |

Practice Exercises: PE 12-1A, PE 12-1B

## Dividing Income

Income or losses of the partnership are divided as specified in the partnership agreement. If there is no specification or agreement, income and losses are divided equally.

Common methods of dividing partnership income are based on:

- Services of the partners
- Services and investments of the partners

**Services of Partners** One method of dividing partnership income is based on the services provided by each partner to the partnership. These services are often recognized by partner salary allowances. Such allowances reflect differences in partners' abilities and time devoted to the partnership. Since partners are not employees, such allowances are recorded as divisions of net income and are credited to the partners' capital accounts.

To illustrate, assume that the partnership agreement of Jennifer Stone and Crystal Mills provides for the following:

| | **Monthly Salary Allowance** |
|---|---|
| Jennifer Stone | $5,000 |
| Crystal Mills | 4,000 |
| | |
| Remaining net income: | Divided Equally |

The division of income may be reported at the bottom of the partnership income statement. Using this format, the division of $150,000 of net income would be reported on the bottom of the partnership income statement as follows:

| | | | |
|---|---|---|---|
| Net income ................................................................... | | | $150,000 |

Division of net income:

| | **J. Stone** | **C. Mills** | **Total** |
|---|---|---|---|
| Annual salary allowance (mo. × 12) | $60,000 | $48,000 | $108,000 |
| Remaining income | 21,000 | 21,000 | 42,000 |
| Net income | $81,000 | $69,000 | $150,000 |

A closing entry is used to record the division of net income, even if the partners do not withdraw the amounts of their salary allowances. The entry for closing Income Summary and dividing net income is as follows:

**LLC**

| | | |
|---|---|---|
| Income Summary | 150,000 | |
|    Jennifer Stone, Member Equity | | 81,000 |
|    Crystal Mills, Member Equity | | 69,000 |

| | | | | | |
|---|---|---|---|---|---|
| Dec. | 31 | Income Summary | | 150,000 | |
| | |    Jennifer Stone, Capital | | | 81,000 |
| | |    Crystal Mills, Capital | | | 69,000 |

If Stone and Mills withdraw their salary allowances monthly, the withdrawals are debited to their drawing accounts. At the end of the year, the drawing account debit balances of $60,000 and $48,000 are then closed to the partners' capital accounts.

**Services of Partners and Investments** A partnership agreement may divide income based upon salary allowances, as discussed, and also based upon interest on capital balances of each partner. In this way, partners with more invested in the partnership are rewarded by receiving more of the partnership income. One such method of dividing partnership income would be as follows:

1. Partner salary allowances
2. Interest on capital investments
3. Any remaining income equally

To illustrate, assume that the partnership agreement for Stone and Mills provides for the following:

1.

| | **Monthly Salary Allowance** |
|---|---|
| Jennifer Stone | $5,000 |
| Crystal Mills | 4,000 |

2.   Interest of 12% on each partner's capital balance as of January 1.

| | |
|---|---|
| Capital, Jennifer Stone, January 1 | $160,000 |
| Capital, Crystal Mills, January 1 | 120,000 |

3.   Remaining income: Divided Equally

The $150,000 net income for the year is divided as follows:

Net income . . . . . . . . . . . . . . . . . . . . . . . . . . . . . . . . . . . . . . . . . . . . . . . . . . . . . . .   $150,000

Division of net income:

| | **J. Stone** | **C. Mills** | **Total** |
|---|---|---|---|
| Annual salary allowance | $60,000 | $48,000 | $108,000 |
| Interest allowance | 19,200[1] | 14,400[2] | 33,600 |
| Total | $79,200 | $62,400 | $141,600 |
| Remaining income | 4,200 | 4,200 | 8,400 |
| Net income | $83,400 | $66,600 | $150,000 |

[1]12% × $160,000
[2]12% × $120,000

The entry for closing Income Summary and dividing net income is as follows:

| LLC | | |
|---|---|---|
| *Income Summary* | *150,000* | |
| *Jennifer Stone, Member Equity* | | *83,400* |
| *Crystal Mills, Member Equity* | | *66,600* |

| | | | | | |
|---|---|---|---|---|---|
| Dec. | 31 | Income Summary | | 150,000 | |
| | | Jennifer Stone, Capital | | | 83,400 |
| | | Crystal Mills, Capital | | | 66,600 |

# Integrity, Objectivity, and Ethics in Business

**TYRANNY OF THE MAJORITY**

Some partnerships involve the contribution of money by one partner and the contribution of effort and expertise by another. This can create a conflict between the two partners, because one works and the other doesn't. Without a properly developed partnership agreement, the working partner could take income in the form of a salary allowance, leaving little for the investor partner. Thus, partnership agreements often require all partners to agree on salary allowances provided to working partners.

**Allowances Exceed Net Income** In the preceding example, the net income is $150,000. The total of the salary ($108,000) and interest ($33,600) allowances is $141,600. Thus, the net income exceeds the salary and interest allowances. In some cases, however, the net income may be less than the total of the allowances. In this case, the remaining net income to divide is a *negative* amount. This negative amount is divided among the partners as though it were a net loss.

To illustrate, assume the same salary and interest allowances as in the preceding example, but that the net income is $100,000. In this case, the total of the allowances of $141,600 exceeds the net income by $41,600 ($100,000 − $141,600). This amount is divided equally between Stone and Mills. Thus, $20,800 ($41,600 ÷ 2) is deducted from each partner's share of the allowances. The final division of net income between Stone and Mills is as follows:

Net income .................................................................... $100,000

Division of net income:

|  | J. Stone | C. Mills | Total |
|---|---|---|---|
| Annual salary allowance | $60,000 | $48,000 | $108,000 |
| Interest allowance | 19,200 | 14,400 | 33,600 |
| Total | $79,200 | $62,400 | $141,600 |
| Deduct excess of allowances over income | 20,800 | 20,800 | 41,600 |
| Net income[4] | $58,400 | $41,600 | $100,000 |

The entry for closing Income Summary and dividing net income is as follows:

**LLC**

| Income Summary | 100,000 | |
|---|---|---|
|    Jennifer Stone, Member Equity | | 58,400 |
|    Crystal Mills, Member Equity | | 41,600 |

| Dec. | 31 | Income Summary | 100,000 | |
|---|---|---|---|---|
| | |    Jennifer Stone, Capital | | 58,400 |
| | |    Crystal Mills, Capital | | 41,600 |

---

## Example Exercise 12-2   Dividing Partnership Net Income

OBJ 2

Dynamic Exhibit

Steve Prince and Chelsy Bernard formed a partnership, dividing income as follows:

1.  Annual salary allowance to Prince of $42,000.

2.  Interest of 9% on each partner's capital balance on January 1.

3.  Any remaining net income divided equally.

Prince and Bernard had $20,000 and $150,000 in their January 1 capital balances, respectively. Net income for the year was $240,000.

How much net income should be distributed to Prince and Bernard?

## Follow My Example 12-2

|  | S. Prince | C. Bernard | Total |
|---|---|---|---|
| Annual salary allowance........................................ | $ 42,000 | $ 0 | $ 42,000 |
| Interest allowance .......................................... | 1,800[1] | 13,500[2] | 15,300 |
|    Total ................................................. | $ 43,800 | $ 13,500 | $ 57,300 |
| Remaining income.......................................... | 91,350[3] | 91,350 | 182,700 |
| Net income ............................................... | $135,150 | $104,850 | $240,000 |

[1] $20,000 × 9%

[2] $150,000 × 9%

[3] ($240,000 − $42,000 − $15,300) × 50%

Practice Exercises: PE 12-2A, PE 12-2B

---

[4] In the event of a net loss, the amount deducted from the total allowances would be the "excess of allowances over loss" or the sum of the net loss and the allowances, divided according to the sharing ratio.

# Partner Admission and Withdrawal

**OBJ 3**  Describe and illustrate the accounting for partner admission and withdrawal.

Many partnerships provide for admitting new partners and for partner withdrawals by amending the existing partnership agreement. In this way, the company may continue operating without having to form a new partnership and prepare a new partnership agreement.

## Admitting a Partner

As shown in Exhibit 2, a person may be admitted to a partnership by either of the following:

- Purchasing an interest from one or more of the existing partners
- Contributing assets to the partnership

**EXHIBIT 2**

**Two Methods for Admitting a Partner**

When a new partner is admitted by *purchasing an interest* from one or more of the existing partners, the total assets and the total owners' equity of the partnership are not affected. The capital (equity) of the new partner is recorded by transferring capital (equity) from the existing partners.

When a new partner is admitted by *contributing assets* to the partnership, the total assets and the total owners' equity of the partnership are increased. The capital (equity) of the new partner is recorded as the amount of assets contributed to the partnership by the new partner.

**Purchasing an Interest from Existing Partners**  When a new partner is admitted by purchasing an interest from one or more of the existing partners, the transaction is between the new and existing partners acting as individuals. The admission of the new partner is recorded by transferring owners' equity amounts from the capital accounts of the selling partners to the capital account of the new partner.

To illustrate, assume that on June 1 Tom Andrews and Nathan Bell each sell one-fifth of their partnership equity of Bring It Consulting to Joe Canter for $10,000 in cash. On June 1, the partnership has net assets of $100,000 and both existing partners have capital balances of $50,000 each. This transaction is between Andrews, Bell, and Canter. The only entry required by Bring It Consulting is to record the transfer of capital (equity) from Andrews and Bell to Canter, as follows:

| LLC | | |
|---|---|---|
| *Tom Andrews, Member Equity* | *10,000* | |
| *Nathan Bell, Member Equity* | *10,000* | |
| *Joe Canter, Member Equity* | | *20,000* |

| | | | | | |
|---|---|---|---|---|---|
| June | 1 | Tom Andrews, Capital | | 10,000 | |
| | | Nathan Bell, Capital | | 10,000 | |
| | | Joe Canter, Capital | | | 20,000 |

The effect of the transaction on the partnership accounts is as follows:

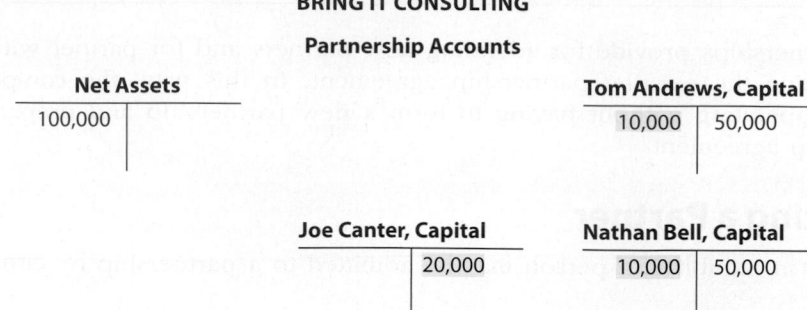

**BRING IT CONSULTING**

**Partnership Accounts**

| Net Assets | | Tom Andrews, Capital | |
|---|---|---|---|
| 100,000 | | 10,000 | 50,000 |

| Joe Canter, Capital | | Nathan Bell, Capital | |
|---|---|---|---|
| | 20,000 | 10,000 | 50,000 |

After Canter is admitted to Bring It Consulting, the total owners' equity is still $100,000. Canter has a one-fifth (20%) interest and a capital balance of $20,000. Andrews and Bell each own two-fifths (40%) interest and have capital balances of $40,000 each.

Even though Canter has a one-fifth (20%) interest in the partnership, he may not be entitled to a one-fifth share of the partnership net income. The division of the net income or net loss is made according to the new or amended partnership agreement.

The preceding entry is not affected by the amount paid by Canter for the one-fifth interest. For example, if Canter had paid $15,000 to Andrews and Bell instead of $10,000, the entry would still be the same. This is because the transaction is between Andrews, Bell, and Canter, rather than the partnership. Any gain or loss by Andrews and Bell on the sale of their partnership interest is theirs as individuals and does not affect the partnership.

**Contributing Assets to a Partnership** When a new partner is admitted by contributing assets to the partnership, the total assets and the total owners' equity of the partnership are increased. This is because the transaction is between the new partner and the partnership.

To illustrate, assume that instead of purchasing a one-fifth ownership in Bring It Consulting directly from Tom Andrews and Nathan Bell, Joe Canter contributes $20,000 cash to Bring It Consulting for ownership equity of $20,000. The entry to record this transaction is as follows:

**LLC**

| Cash | 20,000 | |
|---|---|---|
|    Joe Canter, Member Equity | | 20,000 |

| | June | 1 | Cash | 20,000 | |
|---|---|---|---|---|---|
| | | |    Joe Canter, Capital | | 20,000 |

The effect of the transaction on the partnership accounts is as follows:

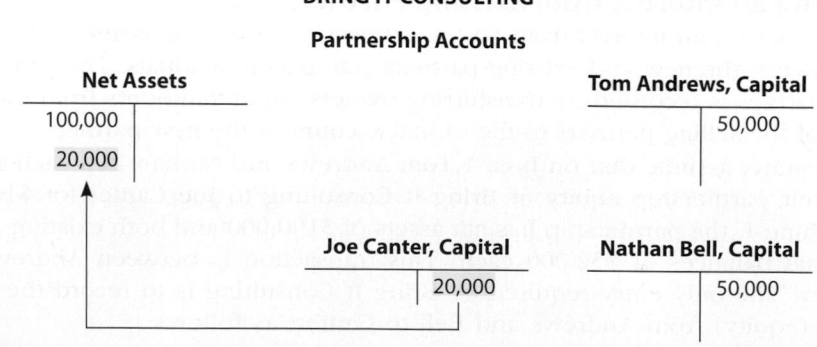

**BRING IT CONSULTING**

**Partnership Accounts**

| Net Assets | | Tom Andrews, Capital | |
|---|---|---|---|
| 100,000 | | | 50,000 |
| 20,000 | | | |

| Joe Canter, Capital | | Nathan Bell, Capital | |
|---|---|---|---|
| | 20,000 | | 50,000 |

After the admission of Canter, the net assets and total owners' equity of Bring It Consulting increase to $120,000, of which Joe Canter has a $20,000 interest. In contrast, in the prior example, the net assets and total owners' equity of Bring It Consulting did not change from $100,000.

**Revaluation of Assets** Before a new partner is admitted, the balances of a partnership's asset accounts should be stated at current values. If necessary, the accounts should be adjusted. Any net adjustment (increase or decrease) in asset values is divided among the capital accounts of the existing partners, similar to the division of income.

To illustrate, assume that in the preceding example the balance of the merchandise inventory account is $14,000 and the current replacement value is $17,000. If Andrews and Bell share net income equally, the revaluation is recorded as follows:

| **LLC** | | |
|---|---|---|
| Merchandise Inventory | 3,000 | |
|     Tom Andrews, Member Equity | | 1,500 |
|     Nathan Bell, Member Equity | | 1,500 |

| June | 1 | Merchandise Inventory | 3,000 | |
|---|---|---|---|---|
| | |     Tom Andrews, Capital | | 1,500 |
| | |     Nathan Bell, Capital | | 1,500 |

Failure to adjust the partnership accounts for current values before admission of a new partner may result in the new partner sharing in asset gains or losses that arose in prior periods.

---

## Example Exercise 12-3   Revaluing and Contributing Assets to a Partnership

Blake Nelson invested $45,000 in the Lawrence & Kerry partnership for ownership equity of $45,000. Prior to the investment, land was revalued to a market value of $260,000 from a book value of $200,000. Lynne Lawrence and Tim Kerry share net income in a 1:2 ratio.
a. Provide the journal entry for the revaluation of land.
b. Provide the journal entry to admit Nelson.

### Follow My Example 12-3

| a. Land............................................................... | 60,000 | |
|---|---|---|
|     Lynne Lawrence, Capital ....................................................... | | 20,000 |
|     Tim Kerry, Capital.............................................................. | | 40,000 |

[1] $60,000 × 1/3
[2] $60,000 × 2/3

| b. Cash............................................................... | 45,000 | |
|---|---|---|
|     Blake Nelson, Capital ......................................................... | | 45,000 |

Practice Exercises: PE 12-3A, PE 12-3B

---

**Partner Bonuses** A new partner may pay existing partners a bonus to join a partnership. In other cases, existing partners may pay a new partner a bonus to join the partnership.

Bonuses are usually paid because of higher than normal profits the new or existing partners are expected to contribute in the future. For example, a new partner may bring special qualities or skills to the partnership. Celebrities such as actors, musicians, or sports figures often provide name recognition that is expected to increase a partnership's profits.

Partner bonuses are illustrated in Exhibit 3. Existing partners receive a bonus when the ownership interest received by the new partner is less than the amount paid. In

**Bonus to Existing Partners**

Ownership Interest is less than amount paid

Bonus

New Partner     Existing Partners

**Bonus to New Partner**

Ownership Interest is greater than amount paid

Bonus

New Partner     Existing Partners

**EXHIBIT 3**

**Partner Bonuses**

contrast, the new partner receives a bonus when the ownership interest received by the new partner is greater than the amount paid.

To illustrate, assume that on March 1 the partnership of Marsha Jenkins and Helen Kramer is considering a new partner, Alex Diaz. After the assets of the partnership have been adjusted to current market values, the capital balances of Jenkins and Kramer are as follows:

| | |
|---|---|
| Marsha Jenkins, Capital | $20,000 |
| Helen Kramer, Capital | 24,000 |
| Total owners' equity *before* admitting Diaz | $44,000 |

Jenkins and Kramer agree to admit Diaz to the partnership for $31,000. In return, Diaz will receive a one-third equity in the partnership and will share equally with Jenkins and Kramer in partnership income or losses. In this case, Diaz is paying Jenkins and Kramer a $6,000 bonus to join the partnership, computed as follows:

| | |
|---|---|
| Marsha Jenkins, Capital | $20,000 |
| Helen Kramer, Capital | 24,000 |
| Diaz's contribution | 31,000 |
| Total owners' equity *after* admitting Diaz | $75,000 |
| Diaz's equity interest after admission | × 1/3 |
| Alex Diaz, Capital | $25,000 |
| | |
| Diaz's contribution | $31,000 |
| Alex Diaz, Capital | 25,000 |
| Bonus paid to Jenkins and Kramer | $ 6,000 |

The $6,000 bonus paid by Diaz increases Jenkins's and Kramer's capital accounts. It is distributed to the capital accounts of Jenkins and Kramer according to their income-sharing ratio.[5] Assuming that Jenkins and Kramer share profits and losses equally, the entry to record the admission of Diaz to the partnership is as follows:

| **LLC** | | |
|---|---|---|
| *Cash* | *31,000* | |
| *Alex Diaz, Member Equity* | | *25,000* |
| *Marsha Jenkins, Member Equity* | | *3,000* |
| *Helen Kramer, Member Equity* | | *3,000* |

| Mar. | 1 | Cash | 31,000 | |
|---|---|---|---|---|
| | | Alex Diaz, Capital | | 25,000 |
| | | Marsha Jenkins, Capital | | 3,000 |
| | | Helen Kramer, Capital | | 3,000 |

Existing partners may agree to pay the new partner a bonus to join a partnership. To illustrate, assume that after adjusting assets to market values, the capital balances of Janice Cowen and Steve Dodd are as follows:

| | |
|---|---|
| Janice Cowen, Capital | $ 80,000 |
| Steve Dodd, Capital | 40,000 |
| Total owners' equity *before* admitting Chou | $120,000 |

Cowen and Dodd agree to admit Ellen Chou to the partnership on June 1 for an investment of $30,000. In return, Chou will receive a one-fourth equity interest in the partnership and will share in one-fourth of the profits and losses. In this case, Cowen and Dodd are paying Chou a $7,500 bonus to join the partnership, computed as follows:

| | |
|---|---|
| Janice Cowen, Capital | $ 80,000 |
| Steve Dodd, Capital | 40,000 |
| Chou's contribution | 30,000 |
| Total owners' equity *after* admitting Chou | $150,000 |
| Chou's equity interest after admission | × 1/4 |
| Ellen Chou, Capital | $ 37,500 |
| Ellen Chou, Capital | $ 37,500 |
| Chou's contribution | 30,000 |
| Bonus paid to Chou | $ 7,500 |

[5] Another method used to record the admission of partners attributes goodwill rather than a bonus to the partners. This method is discussed in advanced accounting textbooks.

The $7,500 bonus paid to Chou decreases Cowen's and Dodd's capital accounts. It is distributed to the capital accounts of Cowen and Dodd according to their income-sharing ratio. Assuming that the income-sharing ratio of Cowen and Dodd was 2:1 before the admission of Chou, the entry to record the admission of Chou to the partnership is as follows:

| LLC | | |
|---|---|---|
| Cash | 30,000 | |
| Janice Cowen, Member Equity | 5,000[1] | |
| Steve Dodd, Member Equity | 2,500[2] | |
|    Ellen Chou, Member Equity | | 37,500 |

| June | 1 | Cash | 30,000 | |
|---|---|---|---|---|
| | | Janice Cowen, Capital | 5,000[1] | |
| | | Steve Dodd, Capital | 2,500[2] | |
| | |    Ellen Chou, Capital | | 37,500 |

[1] $7,500 × 2/3

[2] $7,500 × 1/3

---

## Example Exercise 12-4   Partner Bonus

 Dynamic Exhibit

Lowman has a capital balance of $51,000 after adjusting assets to fair market value. Conrad contributes $24,000 to receive a 30% interest in a new partnership with Lowman.
   Determine the amount and recipient of the partner bonus.

### Follow My Example 12-4

| | |
|---|---|
| Equity of Lowman...................................................... | $51,000 |
| Conrad's contribution................................................ | 24,000 |
|    Total equity after admitting Conrad.......................... | $75,000 |
| Conrad's equity interest............................................. | × 30% |
| Conrad's equity after admission.................................. | $22,500 |
| Conrad's contribution................................................ | $24,000 |
| Conrad's equity after admission.................................. | 22,500 |
| Bonus paid to Lowman.............................................. | $ 1,500 |

Practice Exercises: PE 12-4A, PE 12-4B

---

# Withdrawal of a Partner

A partner may retire or withdraw from a partnership. In such cases, the withdrawing partner's interest is normally sold to the:

- Existing partners or
- Partnership

If the *existing partners* purchase the withdrawing partner's interest, the purchase and sale of the partnership interest is between the partners as individuals. The only entry on the partnership's records is to debit the capital account of the partner withdrawing and to credit the capital account of the partner or partners buying the additional interest.

If the *partnership purchases* the withdrawing partner's interest, the assets and the owners' equity of the partnership are reduced by the purchase price. Before the purchase, the asset accounts should be adjusted to current values. The net amount of any adjustment should be divided among the capital accounts of the partners according to their income-sharing ratio.

The entry to record the purchase debits the capital account of the withdrawing partner and credits Cash for the amount of the purchase. If not enough partnership cash is available to pay the withdrawing partner, a liability may be created (credited) for the amount owed the withdrawing partner.

 A partner generally cannot withdraw without permission of the remaining partners, nor can a partner be forced to withdraw by the other partners. In this sense, a partnership is like a marriage, "for better or for worse."

## Death of a Partner

When a partner dies, the partnership accounts should be closed as of the date of death. The net income for the current period should then be determined and divided among the partners' capital accounts. The asset accounts should also be adjusted to current values and the amount of any adjustment divided among the capital accounts of the partners.

After the income is divided and any assets revalued, an entry is recorded to close the deceased partner's capital account. The entry debits the deceased partner's capital account for its balance and credits a liability account, which is payable to the deceased's estate. The remaining partner or partners may then decide to continue the business or liquidate it.

Describe and illustrate the accounting for liquidating a partnership.

# Liquidating Partnerships

When a partnership goes out of business, it sells the assets, pays the creditors, and distributes the remaining cash or other assets to the partners. This winding-up process is called the **liquidation** of the partnership. Although *liquidating* refers to the payment of liabilities, it includes the entire winding-up process.

When the partnership goes out of business and the normal operations are discontinued, the accounts should be adjusted and closed. The only accounts remaining open will be the asset, contra asset, liability, and owners' equity accounts.

The liquidation process is illustrated in Exhibit 4. The steps in the liquidation process are as follows:

- Step 1. Sell the partnership assets. This step is called **realization.**

- Step 2. Distribute any gains or losses from realization to the partners based on their income-sharing ratio.

**Note:**

In liquidation, cash is distributed to partners according to their capital balances.

- Step 3. Pay the claims of creditors, using the cash from the step 1 realization.

- Step 4. Distribute the remaining cash to the partners based on the balances in their capital accounts.

**EXHIBIT 4**

**Steps in Liquidating a Partnership**

To illustrate, assume that Farley, Green, and Hall decide to liquidate their partnership. On April 9, after discontinuing business operations of the partnership and closing the accounts, the following trial balance is prepared:

| Farley, Green, and Hall Post-Closing Trial Balance April 9, 2016 | Debit Balances | Credit Balances |
|---|---|---|
| Cash | 11,000 | |
| Noncash Assets | 64,000 | |
| Liabilities | | 9,000 |
| Jean Farley, Capital | | 22,000 |
| Brad Green, Capital | | 22,000 |
| Alice Hall, Capital | | 22,000 |
| | 75,000 | 75,000 |

Farley, Green, and Hall share income and losses in a ratio of 5:3:2 (50%, 30%, 20%). To simplify, assume that all noncash assets are sold in a single transaction and that all liabilities are paid at one time. In addition, Noncash Assets and Liabilities will be used as account titles in place of the various asset, contra asset, and liability accounts.

## Gain on Realization

Assume that Farley, Green, and Hall sell all noncash assets for $72,000. Thus, a gain of $8,000 ($72,000 – $64,000) is realized. The partnership is liquidated during April as follows:

- Step 1. Sale of assets: $72,000 is realized from sale of all the noncash assets.

- Step 2. Division of gain: The gain of $8,000 is distributed to Farley, Green, and Hall in the income-sharing ratio of 5:3:2. Thus, the partner capital accounts are credited as follows:

| | |
|---|---|
| Farley | $4,000 ($8,000 × 50%) |
| Green | 2,400 ($8,000 × 30%) |
| Hall | 1,600 ($8,000 × 20%) |

- Step 3. Payment of liabilities: Creditors are paid $9,000.

- Step 4. Distribution of cash to partners: The remaining cash of $74,000 is distributed to the partners according to their capital balances as follows:

| | |
|---|---|
| Farley | $26,000 |
| Green | 24,400 |
| Hall | 23,600 |

A **statement of partnership liquidation**, which summarizes the liquidation process, is shown in Exhibit 5.

**EXHIBIT 5** Statement of Partnership Liquidation: Gain on Realization

| Farley, Green, and Hall Statement of Partnership Liquidation For Period April 10–30, 2016 | | | | | | Capital | | |
|---|---|---|---|---|---|---|---|---|
| | Cash | + | Noncash Assets | = Liabilities | + | Farley (50%) | + Green (30%) | + Hall (20%) |
| Balances before realization | $11,000 | | $64,000 | $9,000 | | $22,000 | $22,000 | $22,000 |
| Sale of assets and division of gain | +72,000 | | –64,000 | | | + 4,000 | + 2,400 | + 1,600 |
| Balances after realization | $83,000 | | $  0 | $9,000 | | $26,000 | $24,400 | $23,600 |
| Payment of liabilities | – 9,000 | | | –9,000 | | | | |
| Balances after payment of liabilities | $74,000 | | $  0 | $  0 | | $26,000 | $24,400 | $23,600 |
| Cash distributed to partners | –74,000 | | | | | –26,000 | –24,400 | –23,600 |
| Final balances | $  0 | | $  0 | $  0 | | $  0 | $  0 | $  0 |

Steps 1–2 →
Step 3 →
Step 4 →

The entries to record the steps in the liquidating process are as follows:

Sale of assets (Step 1):

| LLC | | |
|---|---|---|
| Cash | 72,000 | |
|    Noncash Assets | | 64,000 |
|    Gain on Realization | | 8,000 |

| | Cash | 72,000 | |
|---|---|---|---|
| |    Noncash Assets | | 64,000 |
| |    Gain on Realization | | 8,000 |

Division of gain (Step 2):

| LLC | | |
|---|---|---|
| Gain on Realization | 8,000 | |
|    Jean Farley, Member Equity | | 4,000 |
|    Brad Green, Member Equity | | 2,400 |
|    Alice Hall, Member Equity | | 1,600 |

| | Gain on Realization | 8,000 | |
|---|---|---|---|
| |    Jean Farley, Capital | | 4,000 |
| |    Brad Green, Capital | | 2,400 |
| |    Alice Hall, Capital | | 1,600 |

Payment of liabilities (Step 3):

| LLC | | |
|---|---|---|
| Liabilities | 9,000 | |
|    Cash | | 9,000 |

| | Liabilities | 9,000 | |
|---|---|---|---|
| |    Cash | | 9,000 |

Distribution of cash to partners (Step 4):

| LLC | | |
|---|---|---|
| Jean Farley, Member Equity | 26,000 | |
| Brad Green, Member Equity | 24,400 | |
| Alice Hall, Member Equity | 23,600 | |
|    Cash | | 74,000 |

| | Jean Farley, Capital | 26,000 | |
|---|---|---|---|
| | Brad Green, Capital | 24,400 | |
| | Alice Hall, Capital | 23,600 | |
| |    Cash | | 74,000 |

As shown in Exhibit 5, *the cash is distributed to the partners based on the balances of their capital accounts.* These balances are determined after the gain on realization has been divided among the partners and the liabilities paid. *The income-sharing ratio should not be used as a basis for distributing the cash to partners.*

## Loss on Realization

Assume that Farley, Green, and Hall sell all noncash assets for $44,000. Thus, a loss of $20,000 ($64,000 – $44,000) is realized. The liquidation of the partnership is as follows:

- Step 1. Sale of assets: $44,000 is realized from the sale of all the noncash assets.

- Step 2. Division of loss: The loss of $20,000 is distributed to Farley, Green, and Hall in the income-sharing ratio of 5:3:2. Thus, the partner capital accounts are debited as follows:

| Farley | $10,000 ($20,000 × 50%) |
|---|---|
| Green | 6,000 ($20,000 × 30%) |
| Hall | 4,000 ($20,000 × 20%) |

- Step 3. Payment of liabilities: Creditors are paid $9,000.

- Step 4. Distribution of cash to partners: The remaining cash of $46,000 is distributed to the partners according to their capital balances as follows:

| | |
|---|---|
| Farley | $12,000 |
| Green | 16,000 |
| Hall | 18,000 |

The steps in liquidating the partnership are summarized in the statement of partnership liquidation shown in Exhibit 6.

---

**EXHIBIT 6**  **Statement of Partnership Liquidation: Loss on Realization**

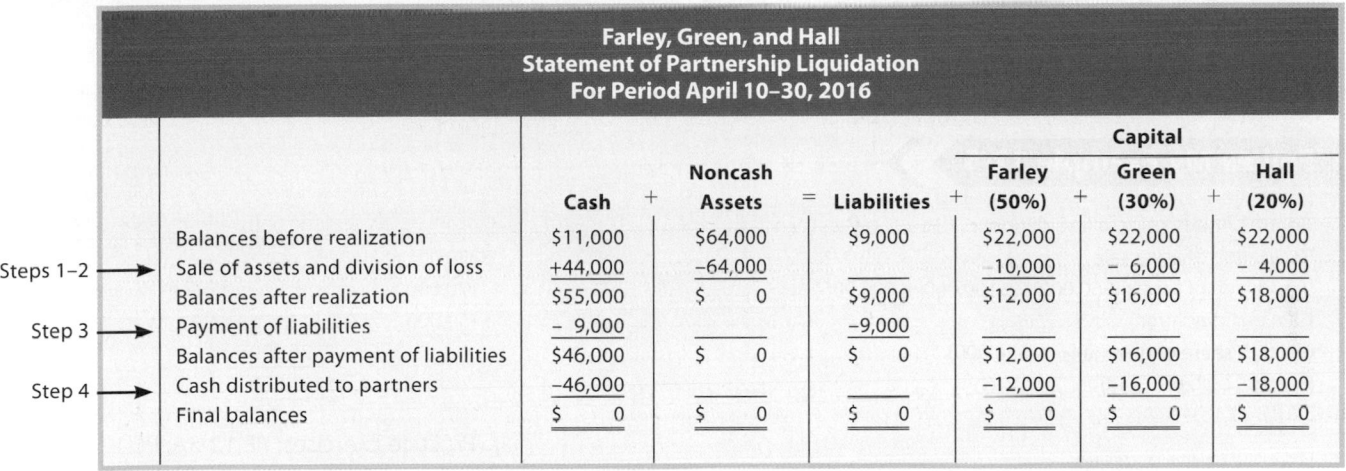

| | Cash + | Noncash Assets = | Liabilities + | Farley (50%) + | Green (30%) + | Hall (20%) |
|---|---|---|---|---|---|---|
| | | | | | **Capital** | |
| Balances before realization | $11,000 | $64,000 | $9,000 | $22,000 | $22,000 | $22,000 |
| Sale of assets and division of loss | +44,000 | −64,000 | | −10,000 | − 6,000 | − 4,000 |
| Balances after realization | $55,000 | $ 0 | $9,000 | $12,000 | $16,000 | $18,000 |
| Payment of liabilities | − 9,000 | | −9,000 | | | |
| Balances after payment of liabilities | $46,000 | $ 0 | $ 0 | $12,000 | $16,000 | $18,000 |
| Cash distributed to partners | −46,000 | | | −12,000 | −16,000 | −18,000 |
| Final balances | $ 0 | $ 0 | $ 0 | $ 0 | $ 0 | $ 0 |

Farley, Green, and Hall
Statement of Partnership Liquidation
For Period April 10–30, 2016

Steps 1–2 → Sale of assets and division of loss
Step 3 → Payment of liabilities
Step 4 → Cash distributed to partners

The entries to liquidate the partnership are as follows:

### Sale of assets (Step 1):

**LLC**

| | | |
|---|---|---|
| Cash | 44,000 | |
| Loss on Realization | 20,000 | |
| Noncash Assets | | 64,000 |

| | | |
|---|---|---|
| Cash | 44,000 | |
| Loss on Realization | 20,000 | |
| Noncash Assets | | 64,000 |

### Division of loss (Step 2):

**LLC**

| | | |
|---|---|---|
| Jean Farley, Member Equity | 10,000 | |
| Brad Green, Member Equity | 6,000 | |
| Alice Hall, Member Equity | 4,000 | |
| Loss on Realization | | 20,000 |

| | | |
|---|---|---|
| Jean Farley, Capital | 10,000 | |
| Brad Green, Capital | 6,000 | |
| Alice Hall, Capital | 4,000 | |
| Loss on Realization | | 20,000 |

### Payment of liabilities (Step 3):

**LLC**

| | | |
|---|---|---|
| Liabilities | 9,000 | |
| Cash | | 9,000 |

| | | |
|---|---|---|
| Liabilities | 9,000 | |
| Cash | | 9,000 |

Distribution of cash to partners (Step 4):

| LLC | | | | | | | |
|---|---|---|---|---|---|---|---|
| Jean Farley, Member Equity | 12,000 | | | Jean Farley, Capital | | 12,000 | |
| Brad Green, Member Equity | 16,000 | | | Brad Green, Capital | | 16,000 | |
| Alice Hall, Member Equity | 18,000 | | | Alice Hall, Capital | | 18,000 | |
| Cash | | 46,000 | | Cash | | | 46,000 |

## Example Exercise 12-5  Liquidating Partnerships  OBJ 4

Prior to liquidating their partnership, Todd and Gentry had capital accounts of $50,000 and $100,000, respectively. Prior to liquidation, the partnership had no other cash assets than what was realized from the sale of assets. These assets were sold for $220,000. The partnership had $20,000 of liabilities. Todd and Gentry share income and losses equally. Determine the amount received by Gentry as a final distribution from the liquidation of the partnership.

### Follow My Example 12-5

| | | |
|---|---|---|
| Gentry's equity prior to liquidation............................................ | | $100,000 |
| Realization of asset sale........................................................ | $220,000 | |
| Book value of assets ($50,000 + $100,000 + $20,000)....................... | 170,000 | |
| Gain on liquidation ............................................................. | $ 50,000 | |
| Gentry's share of gain (50% × $50,000)..................................... | | 25,000 |
| Gentry's cash distribution...................................................... | | $125,000 |

Practice Exercises: PE 12-5A, PE 12-5B

## Loss on Realization—Capital Deficiency

The share of a loss on realization may be greater than the balance in a partner's capital account. The resulting debit balance in the capital account is called a **deficiency**. It represents a claim of the partnership against the partner.

To illustrate, assume that Farley, Green, and Hall sell all noncash assets for $10,000. Thus, a loss of $54,000 ($64,000 − $10,000) is realized. The liquidation of the partnership is as follows:

- Step 1. Sale of assets: $10,000 is realized from the sale of all the noncash assets.

- Step 2. Division of loss: The loss of $54,000 is distributed to Farley, Green, and Hall in the income-sharing ratio of 5:3:2. The partner capital accounts are debited as follows:

| Farley | $27,000 ($54,000 × 50%) |
|---|---|
| Green | 16,200 ($54,000 × 30%) |
| Hall | 10,800 ($54,000 × 20%) |

- Step 3. Payment of liabilities: Creditors are paid $9,000.

- Step 4. Distribution of cash to partners: The share of the loss allocated to Farley, $27,000 (50% × $54,000), exceeds the $22,000 balance in her capital account. This $5,000 deficiency represents an amount that Farley owes the partnership. Assuming that Farley pays the deficiency, the cash of $17,000 is distributed to the partners according to their capital balances as follows:

| Farley | $ 0 |
|---|---|
| Green | 5,800 |
| Hall | 11,200 |

The steps in liquidating the partnership are summarized in the statement of partnership liquidation shown in Exhibit 7.

| EXHIBIT 7 | Statement of Partnership Liquidation: Loss on Realization—Capital Deficiency |
| --- | --- |

**Farley, Green, and Hall**
**Statement of Partnership Liquidation**
**For Period April 10–30, 2016**

| | Cash + | Noncash Assets = | Liabilities + | Capital | | |
| --- | --- | --- | --- | --- | --- | --- |
| | | | | Farley (50%) + | Green (30%) + | Hall (20%) |
| Balances before realization | $11,000 | $64,000 | $9,000 | $22,000 | $22,000 | $22,000 |
| Sale of assets and division of loss | +10,000 | −64,000 | | −27,000 | −16,200 | −10,800 |
| Balances after realization | $21,000 | $ 0 | $9,000 | $(5,000) | $ 5,800 | $11,200 |
| Payment of liabilities | − 9,000 | | −9,000 | | | |
| Balances after payment of liabilities | $12,000 | $ 0 | $ 0 | $(5,000) | $ 5,800 | $11,200 |
| Receipt of deficiency | + 5,000 | | | + 5,000 | | |
| Balances | $17,000 | $ 0 | $ 0 | $ 0 | $ 5,800 | $11,200 |
| Cash distributed to partners | −17,000 | | | | − 5,800 | −11,200 |
| Final balances | $ 0 | $ 0 | $ 0 | $ 0 | $ 0 | $ 0 |

Steps 1–2 → Sale of assets and division of loss / Balances after realization

Step 3 → Payment of liabilities

Step 4 → Receipt of deficiency / Balances / Cash distributed to partners

The entries to liquidate the partnership are as follows:

### Sale of assets (Step 1):

**LLC**

| | | |
| --- | --- | --- |
| Cash | 10,000 | |
| Loss on Realization | 54,000 | |
| Noncash Assets | | 64,000 |

| | | |
| --- | --- | --- |
| Cash | 10,000 | |
| Loss on Realization | 54,000 | |
| Noncash Assets | | 64,000 |

### Division of loss (Step 2):

**LLC**

| | | |
| --- | --- | --- |
| Jean Farley, Member Equity | 27,000 | |
| Brad Green, Member Equity | 16,200 | |
| Alice Hall, Member Equity | 10,800 | |
| Loss on Realization | | 54,000 |

| | | |
| --- | --- | --- |
| Jean Farley, Capital | 27,000 | |
| Brad Green, Capital | 16,200 | |
| Alice Hall, Capital | 10,800 | |
| Loss on Realization | | 54,000 |

### Payment of liabilities (Step 3):

**LLC**

| | | |
| --- | --- | --- |
| Liabilities | 9,000 | |
| Cash | | 9,000 |

| | | |
| --- | --- | --- |
| Liabilities | 9,000 | |
| Cash | | 9,000 |

### Receipt of deficiency (Step 4):

**LLC**

| | | |
| --- | --- | --- |
| Cash | 5,000 | |
| Jean Farley, Member Equity | | 5,000 |

| | | |
| --- | --- | --- |
| Cash | 5,000 | |
| Jean Farley, Capital | | 5,000 |

Distribution of cash to partners (Step 4):

| LLC | | |
|---|---|---|
| Brad Green, Member Equity | 5,800 | |
| Alice Hall, Member Equity | 11,200 | |
| Cash | | 17,000 |

| | Brad Green, Capital | 5,800 | |
|---|---|---|---|
| | Alice Hall, Capital | 11,200 | |
| | Cash | | 17,000 |

If the deficient partner does not pay the partnership the deficiency, there will not be sufficient partnership cash to pay the remaining partners in full. Any uncollected deficiency becomes a loss to the partnership and is divided among the remaining partners' capital balances based on their income-sharing ratio. The cash balance will then equal the sum of the capital account balances. The cash can then be distributed to the remaining partners, based on the balances of their capital accounts.

To illustrate, assume that in the preceding example Farley could not pay her deficiency. The deficiency would be allocated to Green and Hall based on their income-sharing ratio of 3:2. The remaining cash of $12,000 would then be distributed to Green ($2,800) and Hall ($9,200), computed as follows:

| | Capital Balances *Before* Deficiency | Allocated (Deficiency) | Capital Balances *After* Deficiency |
|---|---|---|---|
| Farley | $ (5,000) | $ 5,000 | $ 0 |
| Green | 5,800 | (3,000)* | 2,800 |
| Hall | 11,200 | (2,000)** | 9,200 |
| Total | $12,000 | | $12,000 |

\*$3,000 = ($5,000 × 3/5) or ($5,000 × 60%)
\*\*$2,000 = ($5,000 × 2/5) or ($5,000 × 40%)

The entries to allocate Farley's deficiency and distribute the cash are as follows:

Allocation of deficiency (Step 4):

| LLC | | |
|---|---|---|
| Brad Green, Member Equity | 3,000 | |
| Alice Hall, Member Equity | 2,000 | |
| Jean Farley, Member Equity | | 5,000 |

| | Brad Green, Capital | 3,000 | |
|---|---|---|---|
| | Alice Hall, Capital | 2,000 | |
| | Jean Farley, Capital | | 5,000 |

Distribution of cash to partners (Step 4):

| LLC | | |
|---|---|---|
| Brad Green, Member Equity | 2,800 | |
| Alice Hall, Member Equity | 9,200 | |
| Cash | | 12,000 |

| | Brad Green, Capital | 2,800 | |
|---|---|---|---|
| | Alice Hall, Capital | 9,200 | |
| | Cash | | 12,000 |

## Example Exercise 12-6 Liquidating Partnerships—Deficiency

Prior to liquidating their partnership, Short and Bain had capital accounts of $20,000 and $80,000, respectively. The partnership assets were sold for $40,000. The partnership had no liabilities. Short and Bain share income and losses equally.
  a. Determine the amount of Short's deficiency.
  b. Determine the amount distributed to Bain, assuming Short is unable to satisfy the deficiency.

**Follow My Example 12-6**

| a. | | |
|---|---|---|
| Short's equity prior to liquidation | | $ 20,000 |
| Realization of asset sale | $ 40,000 | |
| Book value of assets ($20,000 + $80,000) | 100,000 | |
| Loss on liquidation | $ 60,000 | |
| Short's share of loss (50% × $60,000) | | 30,000 |
| Short's deficiency | | $(10,000) |

b. $40,000 ($80,000 – $30,000 share of loss – $10,000 Short deficiency)

Practice Exercises: PE 12-6A, PE 12-6B

## Statement of Partnership Equity

OBJ 5 Prepare the statement of partnership equity.

Reporting changes in partnership capital accounts is similar to that for a proprietorship. The primary difference is that there is a capital account for each partner. The changes in partner capital accounts for a period of time are reported in a **statement of partnership equity**.

Exhibit 8 illustrates a statement of partnership equity for Investors Associates, a partnership of Dan Cross and Kelly Baker. Each partner's capital account is shown as a separate column. The partner capital accounts may change due to capital additions, net income, or withdrawals.

| Investors Associates<br>Statement of Partnership Equity<br>For the Year Ended December 31, 2016 | | | |
|---|---|---|---|
| | Dan Cross, Capital | Kelly Baker, Capital | Total Partnership Capital |
| Balance, January 1, 2016 | $245,000 | $365,000 | $610,000 |
| Capital additions | 50,000 | | 50,000 |
| Net income for the year | 40,000 | 80,000 | 120,000 |
| Less partner withdrawals | (5,000) | (15,000) | (50,000) |
| Balance, December 31, 2016 | $330,000 | $400,000 | $730,000 |

**EXHIBIT 8**

**Statement of Partnership Equity**

The equity reporting for an LLC is similar to that of a partnership. Instead of a statement of partnership capital, a statement of members' equity is prepared. The **statement of members' equity** reports the changes in member equity for a period. The statement is similar to Exhibit 8, except that the columns represent member equity rather than partner equity.

## Financial Analysis and Interpretation: Revenue per Employee

OBJ 6 Analyze and interpret employee efficiency.

Many partnerships and LLCs operate as service-oriented enterprises. This is the case for many professions, such as medical, advertising, and accounting. The performance of such firms can be measured by the amount of net income per partner, as illustrated in this chapter. Another measure used to assess the performance of a service-oriented business is revenue per employee.

**Revenue per employee** is a measure of the efficiency of the business in generating revenues. It is computed as follows:

$$\text{Revenue per Employee} = \frac{\text{Revenue}}{\text{Number of Employees}}$$

In a partnership, the number of partners may be included with employees, or partners may be evaluated separately. Generally, the higher the revenue per employee, the more efficient the company is in generating revenue from its employees. In evaluating revenue per employee, changes over time as well as comparisons with industry peers or averages are often used.

To illustrate comparisons over time, assume Washburn & Lovett, CPAs, has the following information for two years:

|  | 2017 | 2016 |
|---|---|---|
| Revenues | $220,000,000 | $180,000,000 |
| Number of employees | 1,600 | 1,500 |

For Washburn & Lovett, the revenue per employee ratio is computed for 2017 and 2016 as follows:

$$\text{Revenue per employee, 2017: } \frac{\$220,000,000}{1,600 \text{ employees}} = \$137,500 \text{ per employee}$$

$$\text{Revenue per employee, 2016: } \frac{\$180,000,000}{1,500 \text{ employees}} = \$120,000 \text{ per employee}$$

Washburn & Lovett increased revenues by $40,000,000 ($220,000,000 – $180,000,000), or 22.2% ($40,000,000 ÷ $180,000,000) from 2016 to 2017. The number of employees increased by 100, or 6.7% (100 employees ÷ 1,500 employees) between the two years. Thus, the firm increased revenues at a rate faster than the increase in employees. As a result, the revenue per employee improved from $120,000 to $137,500 between the two years, suggesting improved efficiency in generating revenues.

To illustrate comparison within an industry, the revenue per employee for **Starbucks** and **McDonald's** for a recent year are as computed as follows:

$$\text{Starbucks: } \frac{\$13,299,500,000}{160,000 \text{ employees}} = \$83,122 \text{ per employee}$$

$$\text{McDonald's: } \frac{\$27,567,000,000}{440,000 \text{ employees}} = \$62,652 \text{ per employee}$$

Starbucks is able to generate more revenues per employee than is McDonald's. Many factors may explain this difference, including relative employee efficiency, extent of part-time workforce, and product pricing.

## *Example Exercise 12-7* Revenue per Employee

OBJ 6

AccuTax, CPAs earned $4,200,000 during 2016 using 20 employees. During 2017, the firm grew revenues to $4,560,000 and expanded the staff to 24 employees.

a. Determine the revenue per employee for each year.
b. Interpret the results.

### Follow My Example 12-7

a. 2016: $\dfrac{\$4,200,000}{20 \text{ employees}} = \$210,000$ per employee

2017: $\dfrac{\$4,560,000}{24 \text{ employees}} = \$190,000$ per employee

b. While AccuTax grew revenues by $360,000 ($4,560,000 – $4,200,000), or 8.6% ($360,000 ÷ $4,200,000), the number of employees expanded by 4, or 20% (4/20). The growth in revenue was less than the growth in the number of employees; thus, the revenue per employee declined between the two years. The firm was less efficient in generating revenues from its employees in 2017.

Practice Exercises: PE 12-7A, PE 12-7B

# At a Glance 12

**1** **Describe the characteristics of proprietorships, partnerships, and limited liability companies.**

**Key Points** The advantages and disadvantages of proprietorships, partnerships, and limited liability companies are summarized in Exhibit 1.

| Learning Outcomes | Example Exercises | Practice Exercises |
|---|---|---|
| • Identify the advantages and disadvantages of proprietorships, partnerships, and limited liability companies. | | |

**2** **Describe and illustrate the accounting for forming a partnership and for dividing the net income and net loss of a partnership.**

**Key Points** When a partnership is formed, accounts are debited for contributed assets and credited for assumed liabilities, and the partner's capital account is credited for the net amount. The net income of a partnership may be divided among the partners on the basis of services rendered, interest earned on the capital account balance, and the income-sharing ratio.

| Learning Outcomes | Example Exercises | Practice Exercises |
|---|---|---|
| • Journalize the initial formation of a partnership and establish partner capital. | EE12-1 | PE12-1A, 12-1B |
| • Determine and journalize the income distributed to each partner. | EE12-2 | PE12-2A, 12-2B |

**3** **Describe and illustrate the accounting for partner admission and withdrawal.**

**Key Points** Partnership assets should be restated to current values prior to the admission or withdrawal of a partner. A new partner may be admitted into a partnership by either purchasing an interest from an existing partner or by purchasing an interest directly from the partnership.

| Learning Outcomes | Example Exercises | Practice Exercises |
|---|---|---|
| • Prepare for partner admission by revaluing assets to approximate current values. | EE12-3 | PE12-3A, 12-3B |
| • Distinguish between partner admission through purchase from an existing partner or purchase from the partnership. | EE12-3 | PE12-3A, 12-3B |
| • Determine partner bonuses. | EE12-4 | PE12-4A, 12-4B |

**Describe and illustrate the accounting for liquidating a partnership.**

**Key Points** A partnership is liquidated by the (1) sale of partnership assets (realization), (2) distribution of gain or loss on realization to the partners, (3) payments to creditors, and (4) distribution of the remaining cash to partners according to their capital account balances. A partner may be deficient when the amount of loss distribution exceeds the capital balance.

| Learning Outcomes | Example Exercises | Practice Exercises |
|---|---|---|
| • Apply the four steps of liquidating a partnership for either gain or loss on realization. | EE12-5 | PE12-5A, 12-5B |
| • Apply the four steps of partnership liquidation when there is a partner deficiency. | EE12-6 | PE12-6A, 12-6B |

**Prepare the statement of partnership equity.**

**Key Points** A statement of partnership equity reports the changes in partnership equity from capital additions, net income, and withdrawals.

| Learning Outcomes | Example Exercises | Practice Exercises |
|---|---|---|
| • Prepare a statement of partnership equity. | | |

**Analyze and interpret employee efficiency.**

**Key Points** The revenue per employee ratio is calculated as the total annual revenues divided by the total employees. This ratio measures the total revenue earned by each employee and, thus, is a measure of the efficiency of each employee in revenue terms. The ratio is often used to measure efficiency trends over time and across similar firms.

| Learning Outcomes | Example Exercises | Practice Exercises |
|---|---|---|
| • Analyze and interpret the revenue per employee ratio. | EE12-7 | PE12-7A, 12-7B |

# Key Terms

deficiency (568)
limited liability company (LLC) (554)
liquidation (564)
partnership (553)

partnership agreement (553)
realization (564)
revenue per employee (571)
statement of members' equity (571)

statement of partnership equity (571)
statement of partnership liquidation (565)

# Illustrative Problem

Radcliffe, Sonders, and Towers, who share in income and losses in the ratio of 2:3:5, decided to discontinue operations as of April 30, 2016, and liquidate their partnership. After the accounts were closed on April 30, 2016, the following trial balance was prepared:

|  | Radcliffe, Sonders, and Towers<br>Post-Closing Trial Balance<br>April 30, 2016 | |
| --- | --- | --- |
|  | Debit<br>Balances | Credit<br>Balances |
| Cash ...................................................... | 5,900 |  |
| Noncash Assets ........................................ | 109,900 |  |
| Liabilities ................................................ |  | 26,800 |
| Radcliffe, Capital ..................................... |  | 14,600 |
| Sonders, Capital....................................... |  | 27,900 |
| Towers, Capital......................................... |  | 46,500 |
|  | 115,800 | 115,800 |

Between May 1 and May 18, the noncash assets were sold for $27,400, and the liabilities were paid.

## Instructions

1. Assuming that the partner with the capital deficiency pays the entire amount owed to the partnership, prepare a statement of partnership liquidation.

2. Journalize the entries to record (a) the sale of the assets, (b) the division of loss on the sale of the assets, (c) the payment of the liabilities, (d) the receipt of the deficiency, and (e) the distribution of cash to the partners.

## Solution

1.

| | | | | | Capital | | |
| --- | --- | --- | --- | --- | --- | --- | --- |
| Radcliffe, Sonders, and Towers<br>Statement of Partnership Liquidation<br>For Period May 1–18, 2016 | | | | | | | |
| | Cash | + | Noncash<br>Assets | = Liabilities + | Radcliffe<br>(20%) + | Sonders<br>(30%) + | Towers<br>(50%) |
| Balances before realization | $ 5,900 | | $109,900 | $26,800 | $14,600 | $27,900 | $46,500 |
| Sale of assets and division of loss | +27,400 | | −109,900 | | −16,500 | −24,750 | −41,250 |
| Balances after realization | $33,300 | | $ 0 | $26,800 | $ (1,900) | $ 3,150 | $ 5,250 |
| Payment of liabilities | −26,800 | | | −26,800 | | | |
| Balances after payment of liabilities | $ 6,500 | | $ 0 | $ 0 | $ (1,900) | $ 3,150 | $ 5,250 |
| Receipt of deficiency | + 1,900 | | | | + 1,900 | | |
| Balances | $ 8,400 | | $ 0 | $ 0 | $ 0 | $ 3,150 | $ 5,250 |
| Cash distributed to partners | − 8,400 | | | | | − 3,150 | − 5,250 |
| Final balances | $ 0 | | $ 0 | $ 0 | $ 0 | $ 0 | $ 0 |

2.a.

| | | | |
|---|---|---|---|
| Cash | | 27,400 | |
| Loss on Realization | | 82,500 | |
| Noncash Assets | | | 109,900 |

b.

| | | | |
|---|---|---|---|
| Radcliffe, Capital | | 16,500 | |
| Sonders, Capital | | 24,750 | |
| Towers, Capital | | 41,250 | |
| Loss on Realization | | | 82,500 |

c.

| | | | |
|---|---|---|---|
| Liabilities | | 26,800 | |
| Cash | | | 26,800 |

d.

| | | | |
|---|---|---|---|
| Cash | | 1,900 | |
| Radcliffe, Capital | | | 1,900 |

e.

| | | | |
|---|---|---|---|
| Sonders, Capital | | 3,150 | |
| Towers, Capital | | 5,250 | |
| Cash | | | 8,400 |

# Discussion Questions

1. What are the main advantages of (a) proprietorships, (b) partnerships, and (c) limited liability companies?

2. What are the disadvantages of a partnership over a limited liability company form of organization for a profit-making business?

3. Emilio Alvarez and Graciela Zavala joined together to form a partnership. Is it possible for them to lose a greater amount than the amount of their investment in the partnership? Explain.

4. What are the major features of a partnership agreement for a partnership, or an operating agreement for a limited liability company?

5. Josiah Barlow, Patty DuMont, and Owen Maholic are contemplating the formation of a partnership. According to the partnership agreement, Barlow is to invest $60,000 and devote one-half time, DuMont is to invest $40,000 and devote three-fourths time, and Maholic is to make no investment and devote full time. Would Maholic be correct in assuming

that, since he is not contributing any assets to the firm, he is risking nothing? Explain.

6. During the current year, Marsha Engles withdrew $4,000 monthly from the partnership of Engles and Cox Water Management Consultants. Is it possible that her share of partnership net income for the current year might be more or less than $48,000? Explain.

7. a. What accounts are debited and credited to record a partner's cash withdrawal in lieu of salary?

   b. The articles of partnership provide for a salary allowance of $6,000 per month to partner C. If C withdrew only $4,000 per month, would

this affect the division of the partnership net income?

   c. At the end of the fiscal year, what accounts are debited and credited to record the division of net income among partners?

8. Explain the difference between the admission of a new partner to a partnership (a) by purchase of an interest from another partner and (b) by contribution of assets to the partnership.

9. Why is it important to state all partnership assets in terms of current prices at the time of the admission of a new partner?

10. Why might a partnership pay a bonus to a newly admitted partner?

# Practice Exercises

EE 12-1 p. 555

SHOW
ME HOW

**PE 12-1A  Journalizing partner's original investment** OBJ. 2

Catrina Santana contributed a patent, accounts receivable, and $23,000 cash to a partnership. The patent had a book value of $8,000. However, the technology covered by the patent appeared to have significant market potential. Thus, the patent was appraised at $85,000. The accounts receivable control account was $38,000, with an allowance for doubtful accounts of $2,000. The partnership also assumed a $10,000 account payable owed to a Santana supplier.
Provide the journal entry for Santana's contribution to the partnership.

EE 12-1 p. 555

SHOW
ME HOW

**PE 12-1B  Journalizing partner's original investment** OBJ. 2

Austin Fisher contributed land, inventory, and $36,000 cash to a partnership. The land had a book value of $120,000 and a market value of $175,000. The inventory had a book value of $50,000 and a market value of $42,000. The partnership also assumed a $35,000 note payable owed by Fisher that was used originally to purchase the land.
Provide the journal entry for Fisher's contribution to the partnership.

EE 12-2 p. 558

SHOW
ME HOW

**PE 12-2A  Dividing partnership net income** OBJ. 2

Han Lee and Monica Andrews formed a partnership, dividing income as follows:

1. Annual salary allowance to Lee of $32,000.

2. Interest of 4% on each partner's capital balance on January 1.

3. Any remaining net income divided to Lee and Andrews, 2:1.

Lee and Andrews had $80,000 and $150,000, respectively, in their January 1 capital balances. Net income for the year was $64,000.
How much net income should be distributed to Lee and Andrews?

EE 12-2 p. 558

SHOW
ME HOW

**PE 12-2B  Dividing partnership net income** OBJ. 2

John Prado and Ayana Nicks formed a partnership, dividing income as follows:

1. Annual salary allowance to Prado, $10,000 and Nicks, $28,000.

2. Interest of 5% on each partner's capital balance on January 1.

3. Any remaining net income divided equally.

*(Continued)*

Prado and Nicks had $20,000 and $50,000, respectively, in their January 1 capital balances. Net income for the year was $30,000.

How much net income should be distributed to Prado and Nicks?

**EE 12-3** *p. 561*

**PE 12-3A** **Revaluing and contributing assets to a partnership** **OBJ. 3**

Aasif Safar purchased one-half of Michael Thorton's interest in the Vale and Thorton partnership for $34,000. Prior to the investment, land was revalued to a market value of $150,000 from a book value of $80,000. Tony Vale and Michael Thorton share net income equally. Thorton had a capital balance of $28,000 prior to these transactions.

a. Provide the journal entry for the revaluation of land.

b. Provide the journal entry to admit Safar.

**EE 12-3** *p. 561*

**PE 12-3B** **Revaluing and contributing assets to a partnership** **OBJ. 3**

Demarco Lee invested $60,000 in the Camden and Sayler partnership for ownership equity of $60,000. Prior to the investment, equipment was revalued to a market value of $39,000 from a book value of $30,000. Kevin Camden and Chloe Sayler share net income in a 2:1 ratio.

a. Provide the journal entry for the revaluation of equipment.

b. Provide the journal entry to admit Lee.

**EE 12-4** *p. 563*

**PE 12-4A** **Partner bonus** **OBJ. 3**

Bellows has a capital balance of $200,000 after adjusting assets to fair market value. Rodriguez contributes $340,000 to receive a 60% interest in a new partnership with Bellows.
Determine the amount and recipient of the partner bonus.

**EE 12-4** *p. 563*

**PE 12-4B** **Partner bonus** **OBJ. 3**

Hiro has a capital balance of $75,000 after adjusting assets to fair market value. Marone contributes $20,000 to receive a 40% interest in a new partnership with Hiro.
Determine the amount and recipient of the partner bonus.

**EE 12-5** *p. 568*

**PE 12-5A** **Liquidating partnerships** **OBJ. 4**

Prior to liquidating their partnership, Parker and Xi had capital accounts of $40,000 and $75,000, respectively. Prior to liquidation, the partnership had no cash assets other than what was realized from the sale of assets. These partnership assets were sold for $155,000. The partnership had $10,000 of liabilities. Parker and Xi share income and losses equally. Determine the amount received by Parker as a final distribution from liquidation of the partnership.

**EE 12-5** *p. 568*

**PE 12-5B** **Liquidating partnerships** **OBJ. 4**

Prior to liquidating their partnership, Manning and Adamo had capital accounts of $240,000 and $150,000, respectively. Prior to liquidation, the partnership had no cash assets other than what was realized from the sale of assets. These partnership assets were sold for $410,000. The partnership had $80,000 of liabilities. Manning and Adamo share income and losses equally. Determine the amount received by Manning as a final distribution from liquidation of the partnership.

**EE 12-6** *p. 570*

**PE 12-6A** **Liquidating partnerships—deficiency** **OBJ. 4**

Prior to liquidating their partnership, Wakefield and Barns had capital accounts of $105,000 and $55,000, respectively. The partnership assets were sold for $40,000. The partnership had no liabilities. Wakefield and Barns share income and losses equally.

a. Determine the amount of Barns' deficiency.

b. Determine the amount distributed to Wakefield, assuming Barns is unable to satisfy the deficiency.

EE 12-6 *p. 570*

**PE 12-6B   Liquidating partnerships—deficiency**    **OBJ. 4**

Prior to liquidating their partnership, Bonilla and Perez had capital accounts of $185,000 and $245,000, respectively. The partnership assets were sold for $30,000. The partnership had no liabilities. Bonilla and Perez share income and losses equally.

a. Determine the amount of Bonilla's deficiency.

b. Determine the amount distributed to Perez, assuming Bonilla is unable to satisfy the deficiency.

EE 12-7 *p. 572*

**PE 12-7A   Revenue per employee**    **OBJ. 6**

Niles and Cohen, CPAs earned $12,375,000 during 2016 using 75 employees. During 2017, the firm grew revenues to $15,400,000 and expanded the staff to 88 employees.

a. Determine the revenue per employee for each year.

b. Interpret the results.

EE 12-7 *p. 572*

**PE 12-7B   Revenue per employee**    **OBJ. 6**

Eclipse Architects earned $1,800,000 during 2016 using 12 employees. During 2017, the firm reduced revenues to $1,440,000 and reduced the staff to nine employees.

a. Determine the revenue per employee for each year.

b. Interpret the results.

# Exercises

**EX 12-1   Recording partner's original investment**    **OBJ. 2**

LaTasha Nabors and Chelsey Rollins decide to form a partnership by combining the assets of their separate businesses. Nabors contributes the following assets to the partnership: cash, $24,000; accounts receivable with a face amount of $160,000 and an allowance for doubtful accounts of $4,200; merchandise inventory with a cost of $92,000; and equipment with a cost of $136,000 and accumulated depreciation of $45,000.

The partners agree that $6,000 of the accounts receivable are completely worthless and are not to be accepted by the partnership, that $4,800 is a reasonable allowance for the uncollectibility of the remaining accounts, that the merchandise inventory is to be recorded at the current market price of $104,300, and that the equipment is to be valued at $84,500.

Journalize the partnership's entry to record Nabor's investment.

**EX 12-2   Recording partner's original investment**    **OBJ. 2**

Melissa Myers and Hugo Hernandez form a partnership by combining assets of their former businesses. The following balance sheet information is provided by Myers, sole proprietorship:

| | | |
|---|---:|---:|
| Cash | | $ 75,000 |
| Accounts receivable | $135,000 | |
| Less: Allowance for doubtful accounts | 7,200 | 127,800 |
| Land | | 215,000 |
| Equipment | $ 78,000 | |
| Less: Accumulated depreciation—equipment | 41,000 | 37,000 |
| Total assets | | $454,800 |
| Accounts payable | | $ 24,800 |
| Notes payable | | 84,000 |
| Melissa Myers, capital | | 346,000 |
| Total liabilities and owner's equity | | $454,800 |

*(Continued)*

Myers obtained appraised values for the land and equipment as follows:

| | |
|---|---|
| Land | $300,000 |
| Equipment | 32,700 |

An analysis of the accounts receivable indicated that the allowance for doubtful accounts should be increased to $9,200.

Journalize the partnership's entry for Myers' investment.

---

**EX 12-3 Dividing partnership income** OBJ. 2

✔ b. Taylor, $187,500

SHOW
ME HOW

Brittany Taylor and Piper Albright formed a partnership, investing $210,000 and $70,000, respectively. Determine their participation in the year's net income of $250,000 under each of the following independent assumptions: (a) no agreement concerning division of net income; (b) divided in the ratio of original capital investment; (c) interest at the rate of 5% allowed on original investments and the remainder divided in the ratio of 2:3; (d) salary allowances of $30,000 and $40,000, respectively, and the balance divided equally; (e) allowance of interest at the rate of 5% on original investments, salary allowances of $30,000 and $40,000, respectively, and the remainder divided equally.

---

**EX 12-4 Dividing partnership income** OBJ. 2

✔ c. Taylor, $43,300

SHOW
ME HOW

Determine the income participation of Taylor and Albright, according to each of the five assumptions as to income division listed in Exercise 12-3, if the year's net income is $96,000.

---

**EX 12-5 Dividing partnership net loss** OBJ. 2

Leigh Meadows and Luke Kowalski formed a partnership in which the partnership agreement provided for salary allowances of $35,000 and $25,000, respectively. Determine the division of a $30,000 net loss for the current year, assuming remaining income or losses are shared equally by the two partners.

---

**EX 12-6 Negotiating income-sharing ratio** OBJ. 2

Sixty-year-old Wanda Davis retired from her computer consulting business in Boston and moved to Florida. There she met 27-year-old Ava Jain, who had just graduated from Eldon Community College with an associate degree in computer science. Wanda and Ava formed a partnership called D&J Computer Consultants. Wanda contributed $50,000 for startup costs and devoted one-half time to the business. Ava devoted full time to the business. The monthly drawings were $2,500 for Wanda and $5,000 for Ava.

At the end of the first year of operations, the two partners disagreed on the division of net income. Wanda reasoned that the division should be equal. Although she devoted only one-half time to the business, she contributed all of the startup funds. Ava reasoned that the income-sharing ratio should be 2:1 in her favor because she devoted full time to the business and her monthly drawings were twice those of Wanda.

a. Can you identify any flaws in the partners' reasoning regarding the income-sharing ratio?

b. How could an income-sharing agreement resolve this dispute?

---

**EX 12-7 Dividing LLC income** OBJ. 2

✔ a. Farley, $86,800

Martin Farley and Ashley Clark formed a limited liability company with an operating agreement that provided a salary allowance of $40,000 and $30,000 to each member, respectively. In addition, the operating agreement specified an income-sharing ratio of 3:2. The two members withdrew amounts equal to their salary allowances.

a. Determine the division of $148,000 net income for the year.

b. Provide journal entries to close the (1) income summary and (2) drawing accounts for the two members.

c. If the net income were less than the sum of the salary allowances, how would income be divided between the two members of the LLC?

**EX 12-8 LLC net income and statement of members' equity** OBJ. 2, 5

✔ a. Sanders, $138,500

Marvel Media, LLC, has three members: WLKT Partners, Madison Sanders, and Observer Newspaper, LLC. On January 1, 2016, the three members had equity of $200,000, $40,000, and $160,000, respectively. WLKT Partners contributed an additional $50,000 to Marvel Media, LLC, on June 1, 2016. Madison Sanders received an annual salary allowance of $55,000 during 2016. The members' equity accounts are also credited with 10% interest on each member's January 1 capital balance. Any remaining income is to be shared in the ratio of 4:3:3 among the three members. The net income for Marvel Media, LLC, for 2016 was $360,000. Amounts equal to the salary and interest allowances were withdrawn by the members.

a. Determine the division of income among the three members.

b. Prepare the journal entry to close the net income and withdrawals to the individual member equity accounts.

c. Prepare a statement of members' equity for 2016.

d. What are the advantages of an income-sharing agreement for the members of this LLC?

---

**EX 12-9 Partner income and withdrawal journal entries** OBJ. 2

The notes to the annual report for **KPMG LLP** (U.K.) indicated the following policies regarding the partners' capital:

The allocation of profits to those who were partners during the financial year occurs following the finalization of the annual financial statements. During the year, partners receive monthly drawings and, from time to time, additional profit distributions. Both the monthly drawings and profit distributions represent payments on account of current year profits and are reclaimable from partners until profits have been allocated.

Assume that the partners draw £50 million per month for 2016 and the net income for the year is £740 million. Journalize the partner capital and partner drawing control accounts in the following requirements.

a. Provide the journal entry for the monthly partner drawing for January.

b. Provide the journal entry to close the income summary account at the end of the year.

c. Provide the journal entry to close the drawing account at the end of the year.

d. Why would partner drawings be considered "reclaimable" until profits have been allocated?

---

**EX 12-10 Admitting new partners** OBJ. 3

SHOW
ME HOW

Hope Abrams and Crystal Santori are partners who share in the income equally and have capital balances of $180,000 and $62,500, respectively. Abrams, with the consent of Santori, sells one-third of her interest to David Cruz. What entry is required by the partnership if the sales price is (a) $60,000? (b) $80,000?

---

**EX 12-11 Admitting new partners who buy an interest and contribute assets** OBJ. 3

✔ b. Henry, $112,000

SHOW
ME HOW

The capital accounts of Trent Henry and Paul Chavez have balances of $140,000 and $90,000, respectively. LeAnne Gilbert and Jen Faber are to be admitted to the partnership. Gilbert buys one-fifth of Henry's interest for $30,000 and one-fourth of Chavez's interest for $20,000. Faber contributes $75,000 cash to the partnership, for which she is to receive an ownership equity of $75,000.

a. Journalize the entries to record the admission of (1) Gilbert and (2) Faber.

b. What are the capital balances of each partner after the admission of the new partners?

---

**EX 12-12 Admitting new partner who contributes assets** OBJ. 3

✔ b. Neel, $35,000

After the tangible assets have been adjusted to current market prices, the capital accounts of Brad Paulson and Drew Webster have balances of $45,000 and $60,000, respectively.

*(Continued)*

Austin Neel is to be admitted to the partnership, contributing $30,000 cash to the partnership, for which he is to receive an ownership equity of $35,000. All partners share equally in income.

a. Journalize the entry to record the admission of Neel, who is to receive a bonus of $5,000.

b. What are the capital balances of each partner after the admission of the new partner?

c. Why are tangible assets adjusted to current market prices, prior to admitting a new partner?

---

**EX 12-13  Admitting new partner with bonus**                                    OBJ. 3

Cody Jenkins and Jun Ito formed a partnership to provide landscaping services. Jenkins and Ito shared profits and losses equally. After all the tangible assets have been adjusted to current market prices, the capital accounts of Cody Jenkins and Jun Ito have balances of $72,000 and $38,000, respectively. Valeria Solano has expertise with using the computer to prepare landscape designs, cost estimates, and renderings. Jenkins and Ito deem these skills useful; thus, Solano is admitted to the partnership at a 30% interest for a purchase price of $30,000.

a. Determine the recipient and amount of the partner bonus.

b. Provide the journal entry to admit Solano into the partnership.

c. Why would a bonus be paid in this situation?

---

✔ b. (2) Bonus paid to Lin, $7,500

**EX 12-14  Admitting a new LLC member with bonus**                                OBJ. 3

Alert Medical, LLC, consists of two doctors, Abrams and Lipscomb, who share in all income and losses according to a 2:3 income-sharing ratio. Dr. Lin has been asked to join the LLC. Prior to admitting Lin, the assets of Alert Medical were revalued to reflect their current market values. The revaluation resulted in medical equipment being increased by $40,000. Prior to the revaluation, the equity balances for Abrams and Lipscomb were $154,000 and $208,000, respectively.

a. Provide the journal entry for the asset revaluation.

b. Provide the journal entry for the bonus under the following independent situations:

1. Lin purchased a 30% interest in Alert Medical, LLC, for $228,000.

2. Lin purchased a 25% interest in Alert Medical, LLC, for $124,000.

---

✔ b. (1) Bonus paid to Ortiz, $9,600

**EX 12-15  Admitting new partner with bonus**                                     OBJ. 3

L. Bowers and V. Lipscomb are partners in Elegant Event Consultants. Bowers and Lipscomb share income equally. M. Ortiz will be admitted to the partnership. Prior to the admission, equipment was revalued downward by $8,000. The capital balances of each partner are $96,000 and $40,000, respectively, prior to the revaluation.

a. Provide the journal entry for the asset revaluation.

b. Provide the journal entry for Ortiz's admission under the following independent situations:

1. Ortiz purchased a 20% interest for $20,000.

2. Ortiz purchased a 30% interest for $60,000.

---

✔ Dennis Overton, Capital, Dec. 31, 2016, $226,400

**EX 12-16  Partner bonuses, statement of partners' equity**                       OBJ. 2, 3, 5

The partnership of Angel Investor Associates began operations on January 1, 2016, with contributions from two partners as follows:

| | |
|---|---|
| Dennis Overton | $180,000 |
| Ben Testerman | 120,000 |

The following additional partner transactions took place during the year:

1. In early January, Randy Campbell is admitted to the partnership by contributing $75,000 cash for a 20% interest.

2. Net income of $150,000 was earned in 2016. In addition, Dennis Overton received a salary allowance of $40,000 for the year. The three partners agree to an income-sharing ratio equal to their capital balances after admitting Campbell.

3. The partners' withdrawals are equal to half of the increase in their capital balances from salary allowance and income.

Prepare a statement of partnership equity for the year ended December 31, 2016.

---

SHOW
ME HOW

### EX 12-17 Withdrawal of partner OBJ. 3

Justin Marley is to retire from the partnership of Marley and Associates as of March 31, the end of the current fiscal year. After closing the accounts, the capital balances of the partners are as follows: Justin Marley, $140,000; Cherrie Ford, $70,000; and LaMarcus Rollins, $60,000. They have shared net income and net losses in the ratio of 3:2:2. The partners agree that the merchandise inventory should be increased by $15,500, and the allowance for doubtful accounts should be increased by $1,500. Marley agrees to accept a note for $100,000 in partial settlement of his ownership equity. The remainder of his claim is to be paid in cash. Ford and Rollins are to share equally in the net income or net loss of the new partnership.

Journalize the entries to record (a) the adjustment of the assets to bring them into agreement with current market prices and (b) the withdrawal of Marley from the partnership.

---

✔ a. 3:7

### EX 12-18 Statement of members' equity, admitting new member OBJ. 2, 3, 5

The statement of members' equity for Bonanza, LLC, follows:

**Bonanza, LLC**
**Statement of Members' Equity**
**For the Years Ended December 31, 2016 and 2017**

| | Idaho Properties, LLC, Member Equity | Silver Streams, LLC, Member Equity | Thomas Dunn, Member Equity | Total Members' Equity |
|---|---|---|---|---|
| Members' equity, January 1, 2016 | $273,000 | $307,000 | | $ 580,000 |
| Net income | 57,000 | 133,000 | | 190,000 |
| Members' equity, December 31, 2016 | $330,000 | $440,000 | | $ 770,000 |
| Dunn contribution, January 1, 2017 | 3,000 | 7,000 | $220,000 | 230,000 |
| Net income | 62,500 | 137,500 | 50,000 | 250,000 |
| Less member withdrawals | (32,000) | (48,000) | (40,000) | (120,000) |
| Members' equity, December 31, 2017 | $363,500 | $536,500 | $230,000 | $1,130,000 |

a. What was the income-sharing ratio in 2016?

b. What was the income-sharing ratio in 2017?

c. How much cash did Thomas Dunn contribute to Bonanza, LLC, for his interest?

d. Why do the member equity accounts of Idaho Properties, LLC, and Silver Streams, LLC, have positive entries for Thomas Dunn's contribution?

e. What percentage interest of Bonanza did Thomas Dunn acquire?

f. Why are withdrawals less than net income?

---

✔ a. $11,000 loss

### EX 12-19 Distribution of cash upon liquidation OBJ. 4

Hewitt and Patel are partners, sharing gains and losses equally. They decide to terminate their partnership. Prior to realization, their capital balances are $28,000 and $18,000, respectively. After all noncash assets are sold and all liabilities are paid, there is a cash balance of $35,000.

a. What is the amount of a gain or loss on realization?

b. How should the gain or loss be divided between Hewitt and Patel?

c. How should the cash be divided between Hewitt and Patel?

### EX 12-20 Distribution of cash upon liquidation

OBJ. 4

✔ Oliver, $30,000

David Oliver and Umar Ansari, with capital balances of $28,000 and $35,000, respectively, decide to liquidate their partnership. After selling the noncash assets and paying the liabilities, there is $67,000 of cash remaining. If the partners share income and losses equally, how should the cash be distributed?

### EX 12-21 Liquidating partnerships—capital deficiency

OBJ. 4

✔ b. $97,500

Lewis, Zapata, and Fowler share equally in net income and net losses. After the partnership sells all assets for cash, divides the losses on realization, and pays the liabilities, the balances in the capital accounts are as follows: Lewis, $73,500 Cr.; Zapata, $41,000 Cr.; Fowler, $17,000 Dr.

a. What term is applied to the debit balance in Fowler's capital account?

b. What is the amount of cash on hand?

c. Journalize the transaction that must take place for Lewis and Zapata to receive cash in the liquidation process equal to their capital account balances.

### EX 12-22 Distribution of cash upon liquidation

OBJ. 4

✔ a. Bray, $550

Bray, Lincoln, and Mapes arranged to import and sell orchid corsages for a university dance. They agreed to share equally the net income or net loss of the venture. Bray and Lincoln advanced $225 and $300 of their own respective funds to pay for advertising and other expenses. After collecting for all sales and paying creditors, the partnership has $1,500 in cash.

a. How should the money be distributed?

b. Assuming that the partnership has only $300 instead of $1,500, do any of the three partners have a capital deficiency? If so, how much?

### EX 12-23 Liquidating partnerships—capital deficiency

OBJ. 4

Nettles, King, and Tanaka are partners sharing income 3:2:1. After the firm's loss from liquidation is distributed, the capital account balances were: Nettles, $15,000 Dr.; King, $46,000 Cr.; and Tanaka, $71,000 Cr. If Nettles is personally bankrupt and unable to pay any of the $15,000, what will be the amount of cash received by King and Tanaka upon liquidation?

### EX 12-24 Statement of partnership liquidation

OBJ. 4, 5

After closing the accounts on July 1, prior to liquidating the partnership, the capital account balances of Gold, Porter, and Sims are $55,000, $45,000, and $20,000, respectively. Cash, noncash assets, and liabilities total $56,000, $96,000, and $32,000, respectively. Between July 1 and July 29, the noncash assets are sold for $90,000, the liabilities are paid, and the remaining cash is distributed to the partners. The partners share net income and loss in the ratio of 3:2:1. Prepare a statement of partnership liquidation for the period July 1–29, 2016.

SHOW
ME HOW

### EX 12-25 Statement of LLC liquidation

OBJ. 4, 5

Lester, Torres, and Hearst are members of Arcadia Sales, LLC, sharing income and losses in the ratio of 2:2:1, respectively. The members decide to liquidate the limited liability company. The members' equity prior to liquidation and asset realization on August 1, 2016, are as follows:

| | |
|---|---|
| Lester | $ 49,000 |
| Torres | 61,000 |
| Hearst | 27,000 |
| Total | $137,000 |

In winding up operations during the month of August, noncash assets with a book value of $146,000 are sold for $158,000, and liabilities of $35,000 are satisfied. Prior to realization, Arcadia Sales has a cash balance of $26,000.

a. Prepare a statement of LLC liquidation.

b. Provide the journal entry for the final cash distribution to members.

c. What is the role of the income- and loss-sharing ratio in liquidating a LLC?

---

✔ b. Alvarez, Capital, Dec. 31, $54,000

### EX 12-26  Partnership entries and statement of partners' equity                    OBJ. 2, 5

The capital accounts of Angel Alvarez and Emma Allison have balances of $47,000 and $73,000, respectively, on January 1, 2016, the beginning of the fiscal year. On March 10, Alvarez invested an additional $8,000. During the year, Alvarez and Allison withdrew $32,000 and $39,000, respectively, and net income for the year was $62,000. The articles of partnership make no reference to the division of net income.

a. Journalize the entries to close (1) the income summary account and (2) the drawing accounts.

b. Prepare a statement of partnership equity for the current year for the partnership of Alvarez and Allison.

---

### EX 12-27  Revenue per professional staff                                          OBJ. 6

The accounting firm of Deloitte & Touche is the largest international accounting firm in the world as ranked by total revenues. For two recent years, Deloitte & Touche reported the following for its U.S. operations:

|                                                   | Current Year | Previous Year |
|---------------------------------------------------|--------------|---------------|
| Revenue (in billions)                             | $13.1        | $11.9         |
| Number of professional staff (including partners) | 46,243       | 41,187        |

a. For the current and previous years, determine the revenue per professional staff.

b. Interpret the trend between the two years.

---

### EX 12-28  Revenue per employee                                                    OBJ. 6

Superior Cleaning Services, LLC, provides cleaning services for office buildings. The firm has 10 members in the LLC, which did not change between 2016 and 2017. During 2017, the business terminated two commercial contracts. The following revenue and employee information is provided:

|                                          | 2017     | 2016     |
|------------------------------------------|----------|----------|
| Revenues (in thousands)                  | $16,200  | $18,400  |
| Number of employees (excluding members)  | 150      | 200      |

a. For 2017 and 2016, determine the revenue per employee (excluding members).

b. Interpret the trend between the two years.

---

# Problems: Series A

---

✔ 3. Keene net income, $41,900

General Ledger

SHOW ME HOW

### PR 12-1A  Entries and balance sheet for partnership                                OBJ. 2

On March 1, 2016, Eric Keene and Abigail McKee form a partnership. Keene agrees to invest $21,100 in cash and merchandise inventory valued at $55,900. McKee invests certain business assets at valuations agreed upon, transfers business liabilities, and contributes sufficient cash to bring her total capital to $60,000. Details regarding the book values of the business assets and liabilities, and the agreed valuations, follow:

(*Continued*)

|  | McKee's Ledger Balance | Agreed-Upon Valuation |
|---|---|---|
| Accounts Receivable | $18,900 | $18,000 |
| Allowance for Doubtful Accounts | 1,200 | 1,500 |
| Equipment | 83,500 ⎫ | 54,900 |
| Accumulated Depreciation—Equipment | 29,800 ⎭ |  |
| Accounts Payable | 15,000 | 15,000 |
| Notes Payable (current) | 36,000 | 36,000 |

The partnership agreement includes the following provisions regarding the division of net income: interest on original investments at 10%, salary allowances of $22,500 (Keene) and $30,400 (McKee), and the remainder equally.

### Instructions

1. Journalize the entries to record the investments of Keene and McKee in the partnership accounts.

2. Prepare a balance sheet as of March 1, 2016, the date of formation of the partnership of Keene and McKee.

3. After adjustments and the closing of revenue and expense accounts at February 28, 2017, the end of the first full year of operations, the income summary account has a credit balance of $90,000, and the drawing accounts have debit balances of $28,000 (Keene) and $30,400 (McKee). Journalize the entries to close the income summary account and the drawing accounts at February 28, 2017.

---

**PR 12-2A  Dividing partnership income**                                      OBJ. 2

✔ 1. f. Morrison net income, $40,400

SHOW
ME HOW

Morrison and Amato have decided to form a partnership. They have agreed that Morrison is to invest $150,000 and that Amato is to invest $50,000. Morrison is to devote one-half time to the business and Amato is to devote full time. The following plans for the division of income are being considered:

a. Equal division.

b. In the ratio of original investments.

c. In the ratio of time devoted to the business.

d. Interest of 12% on original investments and the remainder equally.

e. Interest of 12% on original investments, salary allowances of $30,000 to Morrison and $64,000 to Amato, and the remainder equally.

f. Plan (e), except that Amato is also to be allowed a bonus equal to 20% of the amount by which net income exceeds the total salary allowances.

### Instructions

For each plan, determine the division of the net income under each of the following assumptions: (1) net income of $105,000 and (2) net income of $180,000. Present the data in tabular form, using the following columnar headings:

| Plan | $105,000 | | $180,000 | |
|---|---|---|---|---|
|  | Morrison | Amato | Morrison | Amato |

---

**PR 12-3A  Financial statements for partnership**                            OBJ. 2, 5

✔ 2. Dec. 31 capital—Yost, $125,000

The ledger of Tyler Lambert and Jayla Yost, attorneys-at-law, contains the following accounts and balances after adjustments have been recorded on December 31, 2016:

**Lambert and Yost**
**Trial Balance**
**December 31, 2016**

| | Debit Balances | Credit Balances |
|---|---|---|
| Cash | 34,000 | |
| Accounts Receivable | 47,800 | |
| Supplies | 2,000 | |
| Land | 120,000 | |
| Building | 157,500 | |
| Accumulated Depreciation—Building | | 67,200 |
| Office Equipment | 63,600 | |
| Accumulated Depreciation—Office Equipment | | 21,700 |
| Accounts Payable | | 27,900 |
| Salaries Payable | | 5,100 |
| Tyler Lambert, Capital | | 135,000 |
| Tyler Lambert, Drawing | 50,000 | |
| Jayla Yost, Capital | | 88,000 |
| Jayla Yost, Drawing | 60,000 | |
| Professional Fees | | 395,300 |
| Salary Expense | 154,500 | |
| Depreciation Expense—Building | 15,700 | |
| Property Tax Expense | 12,000 | |
| Heating and Lighting Expense | 8,500 | |
| Supplies Expense | 6,000 | |
| Depreciation Expense—Office Equipment | 5,000 | |
| Miscellaneous Expense | 3,600 | |
| | 740,200 | 740,200 |

The balance in Yost's capital account includes an additional investment of $10,000 made on April 10, 2016.

**Instructions**

1. Prepare an income statement for 2016, indicating the division of net income. The partnership agreement provides for salary allowances of $45,000 to Lambert and $54,700 to Yost, allowances of 10% on each partner's capital balance at the beginning of the fiscal year, and equal division of the remaining net income or net loss.

2. Prepare a statement of partnership equity for 2016.

3. Prepare a balance sheet as of the end of 2016.

---

**PR 12-4A** **Admitting new partner** OBJ. 3

✔ 3. Total assets, $326,300

General Ledger

Musa Moshref and Shaniqua Hollins have operated a successful firm for many years, sharing net income and net losses equally. Taylor Anderson is to be admitted to the partnership on July 1 of the current year, in accordance with the following agreement:

a. Assets and liabilities of the old partnership are to be valued at their book values as of June 30, except for the following:

- Accounts receivable amounting to $2,500 are to be written off, and the allowance for doubtful accounts is to be increased to 5% of the remaining accounts.

- Merchandise inventory is to be valued at $76,600.

- Equipment is to be valued at $155,700.

b. Anderson is to purchase $70,000 of the ownership interest of Hollins for $75,000 cash and to contribute another $45,000 cash to the partnership for a total ownership equity of $115,000.

(*Continued*)

The post-closing trial balance of Moshref and Hollins as of June 30 is as follows:

**Moshref and Hollins**
**Post-Closing Trial Balance**
**June 30, 2016**

| | Debit Balances | Credit Balances |
|---|---|---|
| Cash | 8,000 | |
| Accounts Receivable | 42,500 | |
| Allowance for Doubtful Accounts | | 1,600 |
| Merchandise Inventory | 72,000 | |
| Prepaid Insurance | 3,000 | |
| Equipment | 180,500 | |
| Accumulated Depreciation—Equipment | | 43,100 |
| Accounts Payable | | 21,300 |
| Notes Payable (current) | | 35,000 |
| Musa Moshref, Capital | | 120,000 |
| Shaniqua Hollins, Capital | | 85,000 |
| | 306,000 | 306,000 |

**Instructions**

1. Journalize the entries as of June 30 to record the revaluations, using a temporary account entitled Asset Revaluations. The balance in the accumulated depreciation account is to be eliminated. After journalizing the revaluations, close the balance of the asset revaluations account to the capital accounts of Musa Moshref and Shaniqua Hollins.

2. Journalize the additional entries to record Anderson's entrance to the partnership on July 1, 2016.

3. Present a balance sheet for the new partnership as of July 1, 2016.

---

**PR 12-5A    Statement of partnership liquidation**                                      **OBJ. 4**

After the accounts are closed on February 3, 2016, prior to liquidating the partnership, the capital accounts of William Gerloff, Joshua Chu, and Courtney Jewett are $19,300, $4,500, and $22,300, respectively. Cash and noncash assets total $5,200 and $55,900, respectively. Amounts owed to creditors total $15,000. The partners share income and losses in the ratio of 2:1:1. Between February 3 and February 28, the noncash assets are sold for $34,300, the partner with the capital deficiency pays the deficiency to the partnership, and the liabilities are paid.

**Instructions**

1. Prepare a statement of partnership liquidation, indicating (a) the sale of assets and division of loss, (b) the payment of liabilities, (c) the receipt of the deficiency (from the appropriate partner), and (d) the distribution of cash.

2. Assume the partner with the capital deficiency declares bankruptcy and is unable to pay the deficiency. Journalize the entries to (a) allocate the partner's deficiency and (b) distribute the remaining cash.

---

**PR 12-6A    Statement of partnership liquidation**                                      **OBJ. 4**

On November 1, 2016, the firm of Sails, Welch, and Greenberg decided to liquidate their partnership. The partners have capital balances of $58,000, $72,000, and $10,000, respectively. The cash balance is $32,000, the book values of noncash assets total $128,000, and liabilities total $20,000. The partners share income and losses in the ratio of 2:2:1.

**Instructions**

1. Prepare a statement of partnership liquidation, covering the period November 1–30, 2016, for each of the following independent assumptions:

    a. All of the noncash assets are sold for $156,000 in cash, the creditors are paid, and the remaining cash is distributed to the partners.

b. All of the noncash assets are sold for $55,000 in cash, the creditors are paid, the partner with the debit capital balance pays the amount owed to the firm, and the remaining cash is distributed to the partners.

2. Assume the partner with the capital deficiency in part (b) declares bankruptcy and is unable to pay the deficiency. Journalize the entries to (a) allocate the partner's deficiency and (b) distribute the remaining cash.

## Problems: Series B

✔ 3. Lang net income, $63,400

**General Ledger**

SHOW
ME HOW

### PR 12-1B   Entries and balance sheet for partnership                          OBJ. 2

On April 1, 2015, Whitney Lang and Eli Capri form a partnership. Lang agrees to invest $18,000 cash and merchandise inventory valued at $50,000. Capri invests certain business assets at valuations agreed upon, transfers business liabilities, and contributes sufficient cash to bring his total capital to $120,000. Details regarding the book values of the business assets and liabilities, and the agreed valuations, follow:

|  | Capri's Ledger Balance | Agreed-Upon Balance |
|---|---|---|
| Accounts Receivable | $45,700 | $43,400 |
| Allowance for Doubtful Accounts | 3,200 | 3,500 |
| Merchandise Inventory | 31,500 | 28,900 |
| Equipment | 89,500 ⎫ | 63,400 |
| Accumulated Depreciation—Equipment | 19,000 ⎭ |  |
| Accounts Payable | 23,400 | 23,400 |
| Notes Payable (current) | 15,000 | 15,000 |

The partnership agreement includes the following provisions regarding the division of net income: interest of 10% on original investments, salary allowances of $36,000 (Lang) and $22,000 (Capri), and the remainder equally.

### Instructions

1. Journalize the entries to record the investments of Lang and Capri in the partnership accounts.

2. Prepare a balance sheet as of April 1, 2015, the date of formation of the partnership of Lang and Capri.

3. After adjustments and the closing of revenue and expense accounts at March 31, 2016, the end of the first full year of operations, the income summary account has a credit balance of $118,000, and the drawing accounts have debit balances of $40,000 (Lang) and $30,000 (Capri). Journalize the entries to close the income summary account and the drawing accounts at March 31, 2016.

✔ 1. f. Howell net income, $254,550

SHOW
ME HOW

### PR 12-2B   Dividing partnership income                                         OBJ. 2

Dylan Howell and Demond Nickles have decided to form a partnership. They have agreed that Howell is to invest $50,000 and that Nickles is to invest $75,000. Howell is to devote full time to the business, and Nickles is to devote one-half time. The following plans for the division of income are being considered:

a. Equal division.

b. In the ratio of original investments.

c. In the ratio of time devoted to the business.

d. Interest of 10% on original investments and the remainder in the ratio of 3:2.

e. Interest of 10% on original investments, salary allowances of $38,000 to Howell and $19,000 to Nickles, and the remainder equally.

f. Plan (e), except that Howell is also to be allowed a bonus equal to 20% of the amount by which net income exceeds the total salary allowances.

*(Continued)*

## Instructions

For each plan, determine the division of the net income under each of the following assumptions: (1) net income of $420,000 and (2) net income of $150,000. Present the data in tabular form, using the following columnar headings:

| | $420,000 | | $150,000 | |
|---|---|---|---|---|
| Plan | Howell | Nickles | Howell | Nickles |

---

✔ 2. Dec. 31 capital—
Xue, $179,100

### PR 12-3B Financial statements for partnerships

**OBJ. 2, 5**

The ledger of Camila Ramirez and Ping Xue, attorneys-at-law, contains the following accounts and balances after adjustments have been recorded on December 31, 2016:

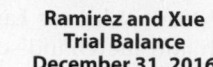

**Ramirez and Xue**
**Trial Balance**
**December 31, 2016**

| | Debit Balances | Credit Balances |
|---|---|---|
| Cash | 70,300 | |
| Accounts Receivable | 33,600 | |
| Supplies | 5,800 | |
| Land | 128,000 | |
| Building | 175,000 | |
| Accumulated Depreciation—Building | | 80,000 |
| Office Equipment | 42,000 | |
| Accumulated Depreciation—Office Equipment | | 25,300 |
| Accounts Payable | | 12,400 |
| Salaries Payable | | 10,000 |
| Camila Ramirez, Capital | | 125,000 |
| Camila Ramirez, Drawing | 35,000 | |
| Ping Xue, Capital | | 155,000 |
| Ping Xue, Drawing | 50,000 | |
| Professional Fees | | 555,300 |
| Salary Expense | 384,900 | |
| Depreciation Expense—Building | 12,900 | |
| Heating and Lighting Expense | 10,500 | |
| Depreciation Expense—Office Equipment | 6,300 | |
| Property Tax Expense | 3,200 | |
| Supplies Expense | 3,000 | |
| Miscellaneous Expense | 2,500 | |
| | 963,000 | 963,000 |

The balance in Xue's capital account includes an additional investment of $20,000 made on May 5, 2016.

## Instructions

1. Prepare an income statement for the current fiscal year, indicating the division of net income. The partnership agreement provides for salary allowances of $50,000 to Ramirez and $65,000 to Xue, allowances of 12% on each partner's capital balance at the beginning of the fiscal year, and equal division of the remaining net income or net loss.

2. Prepare a statement of partnership equity for 2016.

3. Prepare a balance sheet as of the end of 2016.

---

### PR 12-4B Admitting new partner

**OBJ. 3**

✔ 3. Total assets,
$173,900

Brian Caldwell and Adriana Estrada have operated a successful firm for many years, sharing net income and net losses equally. Kris Mays is to be admitted to the partnership on September 1 of the current year, in accordance with the following agreement:

General Ledger

a. Assets and liabilities of the old partnership are to be valued at their book values as of August 31, except for the following:

- Accounts receivable amounting to $1,500 are to be written off, and the allowance for doubtful accounts is to be increased to 5% of the remaining accounts.
- Merchandise inventory is to be valued at $46,800.
- Equipment is to be valued at $64,500.

b. Mays is to purchase $26,000 of the ownership interest of Estrada for $30,000 cash and to contribute $32,000 cash to the partnership for a total ownership equity of $58,000.

The post-closing trial balance of Caldwell and Estrada as of August 31 follows:

**Caldwell and Estrada**
**Post-Closing Trial Balance**
**August 31, 2016**

| | Debit Balances | Credit Balances |
|---|---|---|
| Cash | 12,300 | |
| Accounts Receivable | 19,500 | |
| Allowance for Doubtful Accounts | | 600 |
| Merchandise Inventory | 42,500 | |
| Prepaid Insurance | 1,200 | |
| Equipment | 67,500 | |
| Accumulated Depreciation—Equipment | | 15,500 |
| Accounts Payable | | 8,900 |
| Notes Payable (current) | | 15,000 |
| Brian Caldwell, Capital | | 55,000 |
| Adriana Estrada, Capital | | 48,000 |
| | 143,000 | 143,000 |

## Instructions

1. Journalize the entries as of August 31 to record the revaluations, using a temporary account entitled Asset Revaluations. The balance in the accumulated depreciation account is to be eliminated. After journalizing the revaluations, close the balance of the asset revaluations account to the capital accounts of Brian Caldwell and Adriana Estrada.

2. Journalize the additional entries to record Mays' entrance to the partnership on September 1, 2016.

3. Present a balance sheet for the new partnership as of September 1, 2016.

---

**PR 12-5B** **Statement of partnership liquidation** **OBJ. 4**

After the accounts are closed on April 10, 2016, prior to liquidating the partnership, the capital accounts of Zach Fairchild, Austin Lowes, and Amber Howard are $42,000, $7,500, and $36,500, respectively. Cash and noncash assets total $23,500 and $84,500, respectively. Amounts owed to creditors total $22,000. The partners share income and losses in the ratio of 1:1:2. Between April 10 and April 30, the noncash assets are sold for $48,500, the partner with the capital deficiency pays the deficiency to the partnership, and the liabilities are paid.

## Instructions

1. Prepare a statement of partnership liquidation, indicating (a) the sale of assets and division of loss, (b) the payment of liabilities, (c) the receipt of the deficiency (from the appropriate partner), and (d) the distribution of cash.

2. Assume the partner with the capital deficiency declares bankruptcy and is unable to pay the deficiency. Journalize the entries to (a) allocate the partner's deficiency and (b) distribute the remaining cash.

### PR 12-6B   Statement of partnership liquidation                OBJ. 4

On August 3, 2016, the firm of Chapelle, Rock, and Pryor decided to liquidate their partnership. The partners have capital balances of $14,000, $102,000, and $86,000, respectively. The cash balance is $65,000, the book values of noncash assets total $167,000, and liabilities total $30,000. The partners share income and losses in the ratio of 1:2:2.

### Instructions

1. Prepare a statement of partnership liquidation, covering the period August 3–29, 2016, for each of the following independent assumptions:

   a. All of the noncash assets are sold for $217,000 in cash, the creditors are paid, and the remaining cash is distributed to the partners.

   b. All of the noncash assets are sold for $72,000 in cash, the creditors are paid, the partner with the debit capital balance pays the amount owed to the firm, and the remaining cash is distributed to the partners.

2. Assume the partner with the capital deficiency in part (b) declares bankruptcy and is unable to pay the deficiency. Journalize the entries to (a) allocate the partner's deficiency and (b) distribute the remaining cash.

## Cases & Projects

### CP 12-1   Partnership agreement

Taye Barrow, M.D., and James Robbins, M.D., are sole owners of two medical practices that operate in the same medical building. The two doctors agree to combine assets and liabilities of the two businesses to form a partnership. The partnership agreement calls for dividing income equally between the two doctors. After several months, the following conversation takes place between the two doctors:

*Barrow:* I've noticed that your patient load has dropped over the last couple of months. When we formed our partnership, we were seeing about the same number of patients per week. However, now our patient records show that you have been seeing about half as many patients as I have. Are there any issues that I should be aware of?

*Robbins:* There's nothing going on. When I was working on my own, I was really putting in the hours. One of the reasons I formed this partnership was to enjoy life a little more and scale back a little bit.

*Barrow:* I see. Well, I find that I'm working as hard as I did when I was on my own, yet making less than I did previously. Essentially, you're sharing in half of my billings and I'm sharing in half of yours. Since you are working much less than I am, I end up on the short end of the bargain.

*Robbins:* Well, I don't know what to say. An agreement is an agreement. The partnership is based on a 50/50 split. That's what a partnership is all about.

*Barrow:* If that's so, then it applies equally well on the effort end of the equation as on the income end.

    ▸ Discuss whether Robbins is acting in an ethical manner. How could Barrow renegotiate the partnership agreement to avoid this dispute?

### CP 12-2   Dividing partnership income

Terry Willard and Jasmine Hill decide to form a partnership. Willard will contribute $300,000 to the partnership, while Hill will contribute only $30,000. However, Hill will be responsible for running the day-to-day operations of the partnership, which are anticipated to require about 45 hours per week. In contrast, Willard will only work five hours per week for the partnership. The two partners are attempting to determine a formula for dividing partnership net income. Willard believes the partners should divide income in the ratio of 7:3, favoring Willard, since Willard provides the majority of the capital. Hill believes the income should be divided 7:3, favoring Hill, since Hill provides the majority of effort in running the partnership business.

    ▸ How would you advise the partners in developing a method for dividing income?

### CP 12-3 Revenue per employee

The following table shows key operating statistics for the four largest public accounting firms:

| | U.S. Net Revenues (in millions) | No. of Partners |
|---|---|---|
| Deloitte & Touche | $13,067 | 2,949 |
| PwC | 9,552 | 2,350 |
| Ernst & Young | 8,200 | 2,500 |
| KPMG | 5,753 | 1,775 |

Source: The 2013 *Accounting Today* Top 100 Firms.

a. Determine the revenue per partner for each firm. Round to the nearest dollar.

b. Interpret the differences between the firms in terms of your answer in (a) and the table information.

### CP 12-4 Partnership agreement

General Ledger

Lindsey Wilson has agreed to invest $200,000 into an LLC with Lacy Lovett and Justin Lassiter. Lovett and Lassiter will not invest any money but will provide effort and expertise to the LLC. Lovett and Lassiter have agreed that the net income of the LLC should be divided so that Wilson is to receive a 10% preferred return on her capital investment prior to any remaining income being divided equally among the partners. In addition, Lovett and Lassiter have suggested that the operating agreement be written so that all matters are settled by majority vote, with each partner having a one-third voting interest in the LLC. If you were providing Lindsey Wilson counsel, what might you suggest in forming the final agreement?

# Corporations: Organization, Stock Transactions, and Dividends

## *Google*

If you purchase a share of stock from **Google**, you own a small interest in the company. You may request a Google stock certificate as an indication of your ownership.

Google is one of the most visible companies on the Internet. Many of us cannot visit the Web without using Google to power a search or to retrieve our e-mail using Google's gmail. Yet Google's Internet tools are free to online browsers. Google generates most of its revenue through online advertising.

Purchasing a share of stock from Google may be a great gift idea for the "hard-to-shop-for person." However, a stock certificate represents more than just a picture that you can frame. In fact, the stock certificate is a document that reflects legal ownership of the future financial prospects of Google. In addition, as a shareholder, it represents your claim against the assets and earnings of the corporation.

If you are purchasing Google stock as an investment, you should analyze Google's financial statements and management's plans for the future. For example, Google first offered its stock to the public on August 19, 2004, for $100 per share. Google's stock recently sold for more than $1,000 per share, even though it pays no dividends. In addition, Google recently expanded into developing and offering free software platforms for mobile devices such as cell phones. For example, your cell phone may use Google's Android™ operating system. So, should you purchase Google stock?

This chapter describes and illustrates the nature of corporations, including the accounting for stock and dividends. This discussion will aid you in making decisions such as whether or not to buy stock in a company.

**OBJ 1**
Describe the nature of the corporate form of organization.
**Nature of a Corporation**
    Characteristics of a Corporation
    Forming a Corporation

**OBJ 2**
Describe the two main sources of stockholders' equity.
**Stockholders' Equity**

**OBJ 3**
Describe and illustrate the characteristics of stock, classes of stock, and entries for issuing stock.
**Paid-In Capital from Issuing Stock**
    Characteristics of Stock
    Classes of Stock                           EE 13-1
    Issuing Stock                              EE 13-2
    Premium on Stock                      EE 13-2
    No-Par Stock                             EE 13-2

**OBJ 4**
Describe and illustrate the accounting for cash dividends and stock dividends.
**Accounting for Dividends**
    Cash Dividends                           EE 13-3
    Stock Dividends                        EE 13-4

**OBJ 5**
Describe and illustrate the accounting for treasury stock transactions.
**Treasury Stock Transactions**                EE 13-5

**OBJ 6**
Describe and illustrate the reporting of stockholders' equity.
**Reporting Stockholders' Equity**
    Stockholders' Equity on the Balance Sheet         EE 13-6
    Reporting Retained Earnings              EE 13-7
    Statement of Stockholders' Equity
    Reporting Stockholders' Equity for Mornin' Joe

**OBJ 7**
Describe the effect of stock splits on corporate financial statements.
**Stock Splits**

**OBJ 8**
Describe and illustrate the use of earnings per share in evaluating a company's profitability.
**Financial Analysis and Interpretation: Earnings per Share**    EE 13-8

**At a Glance 13**   ▶ Page 617

---

**OBJ 1** Describe the nature of the corporate form of organization.

# Nature of a Corporation

Most large businesses are organized as corporations. As a result, corporations generate more than 90% of the total business dollars in the United States. In contrast, most small businesses are organized as proprietorships, partnerships, or limited liability companies.

## Characteristics of a Corporation

A corporation was defined in the Dartmouth College case of 1819, in which Chief Justice Marshall of the U.S. Supreme Court stated: "A corporation is an artificial being, invisible, intangible, and existing only in contemplation of the law."

A *corporation* is a legal entity, distinct and separate from the individuals who create and operate it. As a legal entity, a corporation may acquire, own, and dispose of property in its own name. It may also incur liabilities and enter into contracts. Most importantly, it can sell shares of ownership, called **stock**. This characteristic gives corporations the ability to raise large amounts of capital.

The **stockholders** or *shareholders* who own the stock own the corporation. They can buy and sell stock without affecting the corporation's operations or continued existence. Corporations whose shares of stock are traded in public markets are called *public corporations*. Corporations whose shares are not traded publicly are usually owned by a small group of investors and are called *nonpublic* or *private corporations*.

The stockholders of a corporation have *limited liability*. This means that creditors usually may not go beyond the assets of the corporation to satisfy their claims. Thus, the financial loss that a stockholder may suffer is limited to the amount invested.

The stockholders control a corporation by electing a *board of directors*. This board meets periodically to establish corporate policies. It also selects the chief executive officer (CEO) and other major officers to manage the corporation's day-to-day affairs. Exhibit 1 shows the organizational structure of a corporation.

**EXHIBIT 1**

**Organizational Structure of a Corporation**

As a separate entity, a corporation is subject to taxes. For example, corporations must pay federal income taxes on their income.[1] Thus, corporate income that is distributed to stockholders in the form of *dividends* has already been taxed. In turn, stockholders must pay income taxes on the dividends they receive. This *double taxation* of corporate earnings is a major disadvantage of the corporate form. The advantages and disadvantages of the corporate form are listed in Exhibit 2.

**Note:**
Corporations have a separate legal existence, transferable units of ownership, and limited stockholder liability.

**EXHIBIT 2** Advantages and Disadvantages of the Corporate Form

| Advantages | Explanation |
|---|---|
| Separate legal existence | A corporation exists separately from its owners. |
| Continuous life | A corporation's life is separate from its owners; therefore, it exists indefinitely. |
| Raising large amounts of capital | The corporate form is suited for raising large amounts of money from shareholders. |
| Ownership rights are easily transferable | A corporation sells shares of ownership, called *stock*. The stockholders of a public company can transfer their shares of stock to other stockholders through stock markets, such as the New York Stock Exchange. |
| Limited liability | A corporation's creditors usually may not go beyond the assets of the corporation to satisfy their claims. Thus, the financial loss that a stockholder may suffer is limited to the amount invested. |

| Disadvantages | Explanation |
|---|---|
| Owner is separate from management | Stockholders control management through a board of directors. The board of directors should represent shareholder interests; however, the board is often more closely tied to management than to shareholders. As a result, the board of directors and management may not always behave in the best interests of stockholders. |
| Double taxation of dividends | As a separate legal entity, a corporation is subject to taxation. Thus, net income distributed as dividends will be taxed once at the corporation level, and then again at the individual level. |
| Regulatory costs | Corporations must satisfy many requirements, such as those required by the Sarbanes-Oxley Act. |

# Forming a Corporation

The first step in forming a corporation is to file an *application of incorporation* with the state. State incorporation laws differ, and corporations often organize in those states with the more favorable laws. For this reason, more than half of the largest companies are incorporated in Delaware. Exhibit 3 lists some corporations, their states of incorporation, and the location of their headquarters.

After the application of incorporation has been approved, the state grants a *charter* or *articles of incorporation*. The articles of incorporation formally create the corporation.[2] The corporate management and board of directors then prepare a set of *bylaws*, which are the rules and procedures for conducting the corporation's affairs.

---

[1] A majority of states also require corporations to pay income taxes.

[2] The articles of incorporation may also restrict a corporation's activities in certain areas, such as owning certain types of real estate, conducting certain types of business activities, or purchasing its own stock.

**EXHIBIT 3**

**Examples of
Corporations and
their States of
Incorporation**

| Corporation | State of Incorporation | Headquarters |
|---|---|---|
| Caterpillar | Delaware | Peoria, IL |
| Delta Air Lines | Delaware | Atlanta, GA |
| The Dow Chemical Company | Delaware | Midland, MI |
| Google | Delaware | Mountain View, CA |
| General Electric Company | New York | Fairfield, CT |
| The Home Depot | Delaware | Atlanta, GA |
| Kellogg Company | Delaware | Battle Creek, MI |
| R.J. Reynolds Tobacco Company | Delaware | Winston-Salem, NC |
| Starbucks Corporation | Washington | Seattle, WA |
| Sun Microsystems, Inc. | Delaware | Palo Alto, CA |
| 3M | Delaware | St. Paul, MN |
| The Washington Post Company | Delaware | Washington, D.C. |
| Whirlpool Corporation | Delaware | Benton Harbor, MI |

Costs may be incurred in organizing a corporation. These costs include legal fees, taxes, state incorporation fees, license fees, and promotional costs. Such costs are debited to an expense account entitled *Organizational Expenses*.

To illustrate, a corporation's organizing costs of $8,500 on January 5 are recorded as follows:

| | | | | |
|---|---|---|---|---|
| Jan. | 5 | Organizational Expenses | 8,500 | |
| | | Cash | | 8,500 |
| | | Paid costs of organizing the corporation. | | |

# Stockholders' Equity

Describe the two main sources of stockholders' equity.

The owners' equity in a corporation is called **stockholders' equity**, *shareholders' equity, shareholders' investment,* or *capital.* On the balance sheet, stockholders' equity is reported by its following two main sources, as shown in Exhibit 4:

- Capital contributed to the corporation by the stockholders, called **paid-in capital** or *contributed capital.*
- Net income retained in the business, called **retained earnings**.

**EXHIBIT 4**

**Sources of
Stockholders' Equity**

A Stockholders' Equity section of a balance sheet follows:[3]

**Stockholders' Equity**

| | | |
|---|---|---|
| Paid-in capital: | | |
| Common stock | $330,000 | |
| Retained earnings | 80,000 | |
| Total stockholders' equity | | $410,000 |

[3] The reporting of stockholders' equity is further discussed and illustrated later in this chapter.

The paid-in capital contributed by the stockholders is recorded in separate accounts for each class of stock. If there is only one class of stock, the account is entitled *Common Stock* or *Capital Stock*.

*Retained earnings* is a corporation's cumulative net income that has not been distributed as dividends. **Dividends** are distributions of a corporation's earnings to stockholders. Sometimes retained earnings that are not distributed as dividends are referred to in the financial statements as *earnings retained for use in the business* and *earnings reinvested in the business*.

Net income increases retained earnings, while a net loss and dividends decrease retained earnings. The net increase or decrease in retained earnings for a period is recorded by the following closing entries:

1. The balance of Income Summary (the net income or net loss) is transferred to Retained Earnings. For net income, Income Summary is debited and Retained Earnings is credited. For a net loss, Retained Earnings is debited and Income Summary is credited.
2. The balance of the dividends account, which is similar to the drawing account for a proprietorship, is transferred to Retained Earnings. Retained Earnings is debited and Dividends is credited for the balance of the dividends account.

Most companies generate net income. In addition, most companies do not pay out all of their net income in dividends. As a result, Retained Earnings normally has a credit balance. However, in some cases, a debit balance in Retained Earnings may occur. A debit balance in Retained Earnings is called a **deficit**. Such a balance results from accumulated net losses. In the Stockholders' Equity section, a deficit is deducted from paid-in capital in determining total stockholders' equity.

The balance of Retained Earnings does not represent surplus cash or cash left over for dividends. This is because cash generated from operations is normally used to improve or expand operations. As cash is used, its balance decreases; however, the balance of the retained earnings account is unaffected. As a result, over time the balance in Retained Earnings becomes less and less related to the balance of Cash.

# Paid-In Capital from Issuing Stock

The two main sources of stockholders' equity are paid-in capital (or contributed capital) and retained earnings. The main source of paid-in capital is from issuing stock.

## Characteristics of Stock

The number of shares of stock that a corporation is *authorized* to issue is stated in its charter. The term *issued* refers to the shares issued to the stockholders. A corporation may reacquire some of the stock that it has issued. The stock remaining in the hands of stockholders is then called **outstanding stock**. The relationship between authorized, issued, and outstanding stock is shown in Exhibit 5.

Upon request, corporations may issue stock certificates to stockholders to document their ownership. Printed on a stock certificate is the name of the company, the name of

**OBJ 3** Describe and illustrate the characteristics of stock, classes of stock, and entries for issuing stock.

**Authorized**
**Issued**
**Outstanding**

**Number of shares authorized, issued, and outstanding**

**EXHIBIT 5**

**Authorized, Issued, and Outstanding Stock**

the stockholder, and the number of shares owned. The stock certificate may also indicate a dollar amount assigned to each share of stock, called **par value**. Stock may be issued without par, in which case it is called *no-par stock*. In some states, the board of directors of a corporation is required to assign a *stated value* to no-par stock.

Corporations have limited liability, and thus, creditors have no claim against stockholders' personal assets. To protect creditors, however, some states require corporations to maintain a minimum amount of paid-in capital. This minimum amount, called *legal capital*, usually includes the par or stated value of the shares issued.

The major rights that accompany ownership of a share of stock are as follows:

- The right to vote in matters concerning the corporation.
- The right to share in distributions of earnings.
- The right to share in assets upon liquidation.

These stock rights normally vary with the class of stock.

## Classes of Stock

Dynamic Exhibit

**Note:**
The two primary classes of paid-in capital are common stock and preferred stock.

When only one class of stock is issued, it is called **common stock**. Each share of common stock has equal rights.

A corporation may also issue one or more classes of stock with various preference rights such as a preference to dividends. Such a stock is called a **preferred stock**. The dividend rights of preferred stock are stated either as dollars per share or as a percent of par. For example, a $50 par value preferred stock with a $4 per share dividend may be described as either:[4]

preferred $4 stock, $50 par

or

preferred 8% stock, $50 par

As shown in Exhibit 6, preferred stockholders have first rights (preference) to any dividends, and thus, they have a greater chance of receiving dividends than common stockholders. However, since dividends are normally based on earnings, a corporation cannot guarantee dividends even to preferred stockholders.

---

**EXHIBIT 6**

**Dividend Preferences**

The payment of dividends is authorized by the corporation's board of directors. When authorized, the directors are said to have *declared* a dividend.

**Cumulative preferred stock** has a right to receive regular dividends that were not declared (paid) in prior years. Noncumulative preferred stock does not have this right.

Cumulative preferred stock dividends that have not been paid in prior years are said to be **in arrears**. Any preferred dividends in arrears must be paid before any common stock dividends are paid. In addition, any dividends in arrears are normally disclosed in notes to the financial statements.

To illustrate, assume that a corporation has issued the following preferred and common stock:

1,000 shares of cumulative preferred $4 stock, $50 par
4,000 shares of common stock, $15 par

---

[4] In some cases, preferred stock may receive additional dividends if certain conditions are met. Such stock, called *participating preferred stock*, is not often issued.

The corporation was organized on January 1, 2014, and paid no dividends in 2014 and 2015. In 2016, the corporation paid $22,000 in dividends, of which $12,000 was paid to preferred stockholders and $10,000 was paid to common stockholders, computed as follows:

| | | |
|---|---:|---:|
| Total dividends paid | | $22,000 |
| Preferred stockholders: | | |
| 2014 dividends in arrears (1,000 shares × $4) | $4,000 | |
| 2015 dividends in arrears (1,000 shares × $4) | 4,000 | |
| 2016 dividend (1,000 shares × $4) | 4,000 | |
| Total preferred dividends paid | | (12,000) |
| Dividends available to common stockholders | | $10,000 |

As a result, preferred stockholders received $12.00 per share ($12,000 ÷ 1,000 shares) in dividends, while common stockholders received $2.50 per share ($10,000 ÷ 4,000 shares).

In addition to dividend preference, preferred stock may be given preferences to assets if the corporation goes out of business and is liquidated. However, claims of creditors must be satisfied first. Preferred stockholders are next in line to receive any remaining assets, followed by the common stockholders.

## Example Exercise 13-1  Dividends per Share

OBJ 3

Sandpiper Company has 20,000 shares of cumulative preferred 1% stock of $100 par and 100,000 shares of $50 par common stock. The following amounts were distributed as dividends:

| | |
|---|---|
| Year 1 | $10,000 |
| Year 2 | 45,000 |
| Year 3 | 80,000 |

Determine the dividends per share for preferred and common stock for each year.

### Follow My Example 13-1

| | Year 1 | Year 2 | Year 3 |
|---|---:|---:|---:|
| Amount distributed | $10,000 | $45,000 | $80,000 |
| Preferred dividend (20,000 shares) | 10,000 | 30,000* | 20,000 |
| Common dividend (100,000 shares) | $    0 | $15,000 | $60,000 |
| *($10,000 + $20,000) | | | |
| Dividends per share: | | | |
| Preferred stock | $0.50 | $1.50 | $1.00 |
| Common stock | None | $0.15 | $0.60 |

Practice Exercises: PE 13-1A, PE 13-1B

## Issuing Stock

A separate account is used for recording the amount of each class of stock issued to investors in a corporation. For example, assume that a corporation is authorized to issue 10,000 shares of $100 par preferred stock and 100,000 shares of $20 par common stock. The corporation issued 5,000 shares of preferred stock and 50,000

Dynamic Exhibit

shares of common stock at par for cash. The corporation's entry to record the stock issue is as follows:[5]

| | | | | | |
|---|---|---|---|---|---|
| | Cash | | 1,500,000 | | |
| | Preferred Stock | | | 500,000 | |
| | Common Stock | | | 1,000,000 | |
| | Issued preferred stock and common stock at par for cash. | | | | |

Stock is often issued by a corporation at a price other than its par. The price at which stock is sold depends on a variety of factors, such as the following:

- The financial condition, earnings record, and dividend record of the corporation.
- Investor expectations of the corporation's potential earning power.
- General business and economic conditions and expectations.

If stock is issued (sold) for a price that is more than its par, the stock has been sold at a **premium**. For example, if common stock with a par of $50 is sold for $60 per share, the stock has sold at a premium of $10.

If stock is issued (sold) for a price that is less than its par, the stock has been sold at a **discount**. For example, if common stock with a par of $50 is sold for $45 per share, the stock has sold at a discount of $5. Many states do not permit stock to be sold at a discount. In other states, stock may be sold at a discount in only unusual cases. Because stock is rarely sold at a discount, it is not illustrated.

In order to distribute dividends, financial statements, and other reports, a corporation must keep track of its stockholders. Large public corporations normally use a financial institution, such as a bank, for this purpose.[6] In such cases, the financial institution is referred to as a *transfer agent* or *registrar*.

## Premium on Stock

When stock is issued at a premium, Cash is debited for the amount received. Common Stock or Preferred Stock is credited for the par amount. The excess of the amount paid over par is part of the paid-in capital. An account entitled *Paid-In Capital in Excess of Par* is credited for this amount.

To illustrate, assume that Caldwell Company issues 2,000 shares of $50 par preferred stock for cash at $55. The entry to record this transaction is as follows:

| | | | | | |
|---|---|---|---|---|---|
| | Cash | | 110,000 | | |
| | Preferred Stock | | | 100,000 | |
| | Paid-In Capital in Excess of Par—Preferred Stock | | | 10,000 | |
| | Issued $50 par preferred stock at $55. | | | | |

When stock is issued in exchange for assets other than cash, such as land, buildings, and equipment, the assets acquired are recorded at their fair market value. If this value cannot be determined, the fair market price of the stock issued is used.

To illustrate, assume that a corporation acquired land with a fair market value that cannot be determined. In exchange, the corporation issued 10,000 shares of its

---

[5] The accounting for investments in stocks from the point of view of the investor is discussed in Chapter 15.

[6] Small corporations may use a subsidiary ledger, called a *stockholders ledger.* in this case, the stock accounts (Preferred Stock and Common Stock) are controlling accounts for the subsidiary ledger.

$10 par common stock. If the stock has a market price of $12 per share, the transaction is recorded as follows:

| | | | | |
|---|---|---|---|---|
| Land | | | 120,000 | |
| | Common Stock | | | 100,000 |
| | Paid-In Capital in Excess of Par | | | 20,000 |
| | | Issued $10 par common stock, valued | | |
| | | at $12 per share, for land. | | |

## No-Par Stock

In most states, no-par preferred and common stock may be issued. When no-par stock is issued, Cash is debited and Common Stock is credited for the proceeds. As no-par stock is issued over time, this entry is the same even if the issuing price varies.

To illustrate, assume that on January 9, a corporation issues 10,000 shares of no-par common stock at $40 a share. On June 27, the corporation issues an additional 1,000 shares at $36. The entries to record these issuances of the no-par stock are as follows:

| | | | | | |
|---|---|---|---|---|---|
| Jan. | 9 | Cash | | 400,000 | |
| | | Common Stock | | | 400,000 |
| | | Issued 10,000 shares of no-par | | | |
| | | common stock at $40. | | | |
| June | 27 | Cash | | 36,000 | |
| | | Common Stock | | | 36,000 |
| | | Issued 1,000 shares of no-par | | | |
| | | common stock at $36. | | | |

In some states, no-par stock may be assigned a *stated value per share*. The stated value is recorded like a par value. Any excess of the proceeds over the stated value is credited to *Paid-In Capital in Excess of Stated Value*.

To illustrate, assume that in the preceding example the no-par common stock is assigned a stated value of $25. The issuance of the stock on January 9 and June 27 is recorded as follows:

| | | | | | |
|---|---|---|---|---|---|
| Jan. | 9 | Cash | | 400,000 | |
| | | Common Stock | | | 250,000 |
| | | Paid-In Capital in Excess of Stated Value | | | 150,000 |
| | | Issued 10,000 shares of no-par common stock | | | |
| | | at $40; stated value, $25. | | | |
| June | 27 | Cash | | 36,000 | |
| | | Common Stock | | | 25,000 |
| | | Paid-In Capital in Excess of Stated Value | | | 11,000 |
| | | Issued 1,000 shares of no-par common stock | | | |
| | | at $36; stated value, $25. | | | |

# Business  Connection

## GOOGLE INC.

Some excepts from Google's bylaws follow:

### ARTICLE I—CORPORATE OFFICES

#### 1.1 REGISTERED OFFICE.
The registered office of Google Inc. shall be fixed in the corporation's certificate of incorporation. ...

#### 1.2 OTHER OFFICES.
The corporation's Board of Directors (the "Board") may at any time establish other offices at any place or places where the corporation is qualified to do business.

### ARTICLE II—MEETINGS OF STOCKHOLDERS

#### 2.2 ANNUAL MEETING.
The annual meeting of stockholders shall be held each year on a date and at a time designated by the Board. At the annual meeting, directors shall be elected and any other proper business may be transacted.

#### 2.4 NOTICE OF STOCKHOLDERS' MEETINGS.
All notices of meetings of stockholders shall be sent ... not less than ten (10) nor more than sixty (60) days before the date of the meeting to each stockholder entitled to vote at such meeting. ... The notice shall specify the place, if any, date and hour of the meeting, the means of remote communication, if any, by which stockholders and proxy holders may be deemed to be present in person and vote at such meeting. ...

#### 2.8 ADMINISTRATION OF THE MEETING.
Meetings of stockholders shall be presided over by the chairman of the Board. ...

### ARTICLE V—OFFICERS

#### 5.1 OFFICERS.
The officers of the corporation shall be a chief executive officer, one or more presidents (at the discretion of the Board), a chairman of the Board and a secretary. The corporation may also have, at the discretion of the Board, a vice chairman of the Board, a chief financial officer, a treasurer, one or more vice presidents, one or more assistant vice presidents, one or more assistant treasurers, one or more assistant secretaries, and any such other officers as may be appointed in accordance with the provisions of these bylaws.

#### 5.6 CHAIRMAN OF THE BOARD.
The chairman of the Board shall be a member of the Board and, if present, preside at meetings of the Board. ...

#### 5.7 CHIEF EXECUTIVE OFFICER.
Subject to the control of the Board, ... the chief executive officer shall, together with the president or presidents of the corporation, have general supervision, direction, and control of the business and affairs of the corporation. ... The chief executive officer shall ... preside at all meetings of the stockholders.

#### 5.11 CHIEF FINANCIAL OFFICER.
The chief financial officer shall keep and maintain ... adequate and correct books and records of accounts of the properties and business transactions of the corporation, including accounts of its assets, liabilities, receipts, disbursements, gains, losses, capital, retained earnings and shares. ...

#### 5.12 TREASURER.
The treasurer shall deposit all moneys and other valuables in the name and to the credit of the corporation. ...

Source: http://investor.google.com/corporate/bylaws.html

---

## Example Exercise 13-2  Entries for Issuing Stock

On March 6, Limerick Corporation issued for cash 15,000 shares of no-par common stock at $30. On April 13, Limerick issued at par 1,000 shares of preferred 4% stock, $40 par for cash. On May 19, Limerick issued for cash 15,000 shares of 4%, $40 par preferred stock at $42.

Journalize the entries to record the March 6, April 13, and May 19 transactions.

### Follow My Example 13-2

| | | | | |
|---|---|---|---:|---:|
| Mar. 6 | Cash | | 450,000 | |
| | Common Stock | | | 450,000 |
| | (15,000 shares × $30). | | | |
| Apr. 13 | Cash | | 40,000 | |
| | Preferred Stock | | | 40,000 |
| | (1,000 shares × $40). | | | |
| May 19 | Cash | | 630,000 | |
| | Preferred Stock | | | 600,000 |
| | Paid-In Capital in Excess of Par | | | 30,000 |
| | (15,000 shares × $42). | | | |

Practice Exercises: PE 13-2A, PE 13-2B

# Accounting for Dividends

 **OBJ 4** Describe and illustrate the accounting for cash dividends and stock dividends.

When a board of directors declares a cash dividend, it authorizes the distribution of cash to stockholders. When a board of directors declares a stock dividend, it authorizes the distribution of its stock. In both cases, declaring a dividend reduces the retained earnings of the corporation.[7]

## Cash Dividends

A cash distribution of earnings by a corporation to its shareholders is a **cash dividend**. Although dividends may be paid in other assets, cash dividends are the most common.

Three conditions for a cash dividend are as follows:

- Sufficient retained earnings
- Sufficient cash
- Formal action by the board of directors

# International Connection

**IFRS**  **IFRS FOR SMEs**

In 2010, the International Accounting Standards Board (IASB) issued a set of accounting standards specifically designed for small- and medium-sized enterprises (SMEs) called International Financial Reporting Standards (IFRS) for SMEs. SMEs in the United States are private companies and such small corporations that they do not report to the Securities and Exchange Commission (SEC). IFRS for SMEs consist of only 230 pages, compared to 2,700 pages for full IFRS. These standards are designed to be cost effective for SMEs. Thus, IFRS for SMEs require fewer disclosures and contain no industry-specific standards or exceptions.

The American Institute of CPAs (AICPA) has accepted IFRS for SMEs as part of U.S. generally accepted accounting principles (GAAP) for private companies not reporting to the SEC. If users, such as bankers and investors, accept these financial statements, IFRS for SMEs may become popular in the United States.*

*Differences between U.S. GAAP and IFRS are further discussed and illustrated in Appendix D.

There must be a sufficient (large enough) balance in Retained Earnings to declare a cash dividend. That is, the balance of Retained Earnings must be large enough so that the dividend does not create a debit balance in the retained earnings account. However, a large Retained Earnings balance does not mean that there is cash available to pay dividends. This is because the balances of Cash and Retained Earnings are often unrelated.

Even if there are sufficient retained earnings and cash, a corporation's board of directors is not required to pay dividends. Nevertheless, many corporations pay quarterly cash dividends to make their stock more attractive to investors. *Special* or *extra dividends* may also be paid when a corporation experiences higher than normal profits.

Three dates included in a dividend announcement are as follows:

1. Date of declaration
2. Date of record
3. Date of payment

 **Microsoft Corporation** declared a dividend of $0.28 per share on November 19, 2013, to common stockholders of record as of February 20, 2014, payable on March 13, 2014.

The *date of declaration* is the date the board of directors formally authorizes the payment of the dividend. On this date, the corporation incurs the liability to pay the amount of the dividend.

The *date of record* is the date the corporation uses to determine which stockholders will receive the dividend. During the period of time between the date of declaration and

---

[7] In rare cases, when a corporation is reducing its operations or going out of business, a dividend may be a distribution of paid-in capital. Such a dividend is called a *liquidating dividend*.

the date of record, the stock price is quoted as selling *with-dividends*. This means that any investors purchasing the stock before the date of record will receive the dividend.

The *date of payment* is the date the corporation will pay the dividend to the stockholders who owned the stock on the date of record. During the period of time between the record date and the payment date, the stock price is quoted as selling *ex-dividends*. This means that since the date of record has passed, any new investors will not receive the dividend.

To illustrate, assume that on October 1, Hiber Corporation declares the following cash dividends with a date of record of November 10 and a date of payment of December 2:

|  | Dividend per Share | Total Dividends |
|---|---|---|
| Preferred stock, $100 par, 5,000 shares outstanding.................... | $2.50 | $12,500 |
| Common stock, $10 par, 100,000 shares outstanding .................. | $0.30 | 30,000 |
| Total ................................................................ |  | $42,500 |

On October 1, the declaration date, Hiber Corporation records the following entry:

**Declaration Date**

| Oct. | 1 | Cash Dividends | 42,500 | |
|---|---|---|---|---|
|  |  | Cash Dividends Payable | | 42,500 |
|  |  | Declared cash dividends. | | |

**Date of Record**

On November 10, the date of record, no entry is necessary. This date merely determines which stockholders will receive the dividends.

On December 2, the date of payment, Hiber Corporation records the payment of the dividends as follows:

**Date of Payment**

| Dec. | 2 | Cash Dividends Payable | 42,500 | |
|---|---|---|---|---|
|  |  | Cash | | 42,500 |
|  |  | Paid cash dividends. | | |

At the end of the accounting period, the balance in Cash Dividends will be transferred to Retained Earnings as part of the closing process. This closing entry debits Retained Earnings and credits Cash Dividends for the balance of the cash dividends account. If the cash dividends have not been paid by the end of the period, Cash Dividends Payable will be reported on the balance sheet as a current liability.

---

## Example Exercise 13-3 Entries for Cash Dividends

OBJ 4

The important dates in connection with a cash dividend of $75,000 on a corporation's common stock are February 26, March 30, and April 2. Journalize the entries required on each date.

### Follow My Example 13-3

| Feb. 26 | Cash Dividends........................................... | 75,000 | |
|---|---|---|---|
|  | Cash Dividends Payable................................ | | 75,000 |
| Mar. 30 | No entry required. | | |
| Apr. 2 | Cash Dividends Payable.................................. | 75,000 | |
|  | Cash................................................ | | 75,000 |

Practice Exercises: PE 13-3A, PE 13-3B

## Integrity, Objectivity, and Ethics in Business

### THE PROFESSOR WHO KNEW TOO MUCH

A major Midwestern university released a quarterly "American Customer Satisfaction Index" based on its research of customers of popular U.S. products and services. Before the release of the index to the public, the professor in charge of the research bought and sold stocks of some of the companies in the report. The professor was quoted as saying that he thought it was important to test his theories of customer satisfaction with "real" [his own] money.

Is this proper or ethical? Apparently, the dean of the Business School didn't think so. In a statement to the press, the dean stated: "I have instructed anyone affiliated with the (index) not to make personal use of information gathered in the course of producing the quarterly index, prior to the index's release to the general public, and they [the researchers] have agreed."

Sources: Jon E. Hilsenrath and Dan Morse, "Researcher Uses Index to Buy, Short Stocks," *The Wall Street Journal*, February 18, 2003; and Jon E. Hilsenrath, "Satisfaction Theory: Mixed Results," *The Wall Street Journal*, February 19, 2003.

## Stock Dividends

A **stock dividend** is a distribution of shares of stock to stockholders. Stock dividends are normally declared only on common stock and issued to common stockholders.

A stock dividend affects only stockholders' equity. Specifically, the amount of the stock dividend is transferred from Retained Earnings to Paid In Capital. The amount transferred is normally the fair value (market price) of the shares issued in the stock dividend.[8]

To illustrate, assume that the stockholders' equity accounts of Hendrix Corporation as of December 15 are as follows:

| | |
|---|---|
| Common Stock, $20 par (2,000,000 shares issued) | $40,000,000 |
| Paid-In Capital in Excess of Par—Common Stock | 9,000,000 |
| Retained Earnings | 26,600,000 |

On December 15, Hendrix Corporation declares a stock dividend of 5% or 100,000 shares (2,000,000 shares × 5%) to be issued on January 10 to stockholders of record on December 31. The market price of the stock on December 15 (the date of declaration) is $31 per share.

The entry to record the stock dividend is as follows:

| | | | | |
|---|---|---|---|---|
| Dec. | 15 | Stock Dividends | 3,100,000 | |
| | | Stock Dividends Distributable | | 2,000,000 |
| | | Paid-In Capital in Excess of Par—Common Stock | | 1,100,000 |
| | | Declared 5% (100,000 shares) stock dividend on $20 par common stock with a market price of $31 per share. | | |

After the preceding entry is recorded, Stock Dividends will have a debit balance of $3,100,000. Like cash dividends, the stock dividends account is closed to Retained Earnings at the end of the accounting period. This closing entry debits Retained Earnings and credits Stock Dividends.

At the end of the period, the *stock dividends distributable* and *paid-in capital in excess of par—common stock* accounts are reported in the Paid-In Capital section of the balance sheet. Thus, the effect of the preceding stock dividend is to transfer $3,100,000 of retained earnings to paid-in capital.

[8] The use of fair market value is justified as long as the number of shares issued for the stock dividend is small (less than 25% of the shares outstanding).

On January 10, the stock dividend is distributed to stockholders by issuing 100,000 shares of common stock. The issuance of the stock is recorded by the following entry:

| | | | | |
|---|---|---|---|---|
| Jan. | 10 | Stock Dividends Distributable | 2,000,000 | |
| | | Common Stock | | 2,000,000 |
| | | Issued stock as stock dividend. | | |

A stock dividend does not change the assets, liabilities, or total stockholders' equity of a corporation. Likewise, a stock dividend does not change an individual stockholder's proportionate interest (equity) in the corporation.

To illustrate, assume a stockholder owns 1,000 of a corporation's 10,000 shares outstanding. If the corporation declares a 6% stock dividend, the stockholder's proportionate interest will not change, computed as follows:

| | Before Stock Dividend | After Stock Dividend |
|---|---|---|
| Total shares issued | 10,000 | 10,600 [10,000 + (10,000 × 6%)] |
| Number of shares owned | 1,000 | 1,060 [1,000 + (1,000 × 6%)] |
| Proportionate ownership | 10% (1,000 ÷ 10,000) | 10% (1,060 ÷ 10,600) |

## Example Exercise 13-4  Entries for Stock Dividends

Vienna Highlights Corporation has 150,000 shares of $100 par common stock outstanding. On June 14, Vienna Highlights declared a 4% stock dividend to be issued August 15 to stockholders of record on July 1. The market price of the stock was $110 per share on June 14.
   Journalize the entries required on June 14, July 1, and August 15.

### Follow My Example 13-4

| | | | |
|---|---|---|---|
| June 14 | Stock Dividends (150,000 × 4% × $110) | 660,000 | |
| | Stock Dividends Distributable (6,000 × $100) | | 600,000 |
| | Paid-In Capital in Excess of Par—Common Stock ($660,000 – $600,000) | | 60,000 |
| July 1 | No entry required. | | |
| Aug. 15 | Stock Dividends Distributable | 600,000 | |
| | Common Stock | | 600,000 |

Practice Exercises: PE 13-4A, PE 13-4B

Describe and illustrate the accounting for treasury stock transactions.

The 2012 edition of *Accounting Trends & Techniques* indicated that 68.2% of the companies surveyed reported treasury stock.

Dynamic Exhibit

# Treasury Stock Transactions

**Treasury stock** is stock that a corporation has issued and then reacquired. A corporation may reacquire (purchase) its own stock for a variety of reasons, including the following:

- To provide shares for resale to employees
- To reissue as bonuses to employees, or
- To support the market price of the stock

The *cost method* is normally used for recording the purchase and resale of treasury stock.[9] Using the cost method, *Treasury Stock* is debited for the cost (purchase price) of the stock. When the stock is resold, Treasury Stock is credited for its cost. Any difference between the cost and the selling price is debited or credited to *Paid-In Capital from Sale of Treasury Stock*.

---

[9] Another method that is infrequently used, called the *par value method*, is discussed in advanced accounting texts.

To illustrate, assume that a corporation has the following paid-in capital on January 1:

| | |
|---|---|
| Common stock, $25 par (20,000 shares authorized and issued) | $500,000 |
| Excess of issue price over par | 150,000 |
| | $650,000 |

On February 13, the corporation purchases 1,000 shares of its common stock at $45 per share. The entry to record the purchase of the treasury stock is as follows:

| | | | | |
|---|---|---|---|---|
| Feb. | 13 | Treasury Stock | 45,000 | |
| | | Cash | | 45,000 |
| | | Purchased 1,000 shares of treasury stock at $45. | | |

On April 29, the corporation sells 600 shares of the treasury stock for $60. The entry to record the sale is as follows:

| | | | | |
|---|---|---|---|---|
| Apr. | 29 | Cash | 36,000 | |
| | | Treasury Stock | | 27,000 |
| | | Paid-In Capital from Sale of Treasury Stock | | 9,000 |
| | | Sold 600 shares of treasury stock at $60. | | |

A sale of treasury stock may result in a decrease in paid-in capital. To the extent that Paid-In Capital from Sale of Treasury Stock has a credit balance, it is debited for any such decrease. Any remaining decrease is then debited to the retained earnings account.

To illustrate, assume that on October 4, the corporation sells the remaining 400 shares of treasury stock for $40 per share. The entry to record the sale is as follows:

| | | | | |
|---|---|---|---|---|
| Oct. | 4 | Cash | 16,000 | |
| | | Paid-In Capital from Sale of Treasury Stock | 2,000 | |
| | | Treasury Stock | | 18,000 |
| | | Sold 400 shares of treasury stock at $40. | | |

The preceding October 4 entry decreases paid-in capital by $2,000. Because Paid-In Capital from Sale of Treasury Stock has a credit balance of $9,000, the entire $2,000 was debited to Paid-In Capital from Sale of Treasury Stock.

No dividends (cash or stock) are paid on the shares of treasury stock. To do so would result in the corporation earning dividend revenue from itself.

## Example Exercise 13-5 Entries for Treasury Stock

OBJ 5

On May 3, Buzz Off Corporation reacquired 3,200 shares of its common stock at $42 per share. On July 22, Buzz Off sold 2,000 of the reacquired shares at $47 per share. On August 30, Buzz Off sold the remaining shares at $40 per share. Journalize the transactions of May 3, July 22, and August 30.

### Follow My Example 13-5

| | | | | |
|---|---|---|---|---|
| May | 3 | Treasury Stock (3,200 × $42)............................................ | 134,400 | |
| | | Cash............................................................. | | 134,400 |
| July | 22 | Cash (2,000 × $47) ..................................... | 94,000 | |
| | | Treasury Stock (2,000 × $42)....................... | | 84,000 |
| | | Paid-In Capital from Sale of Treasury Stock [2,000 × ($47 – $42)] .................... | | 10,000 |
| Aug. | 30 | Cash (1,200 × $40) ..................................... | 48,000 | |
| | | Paid-In Capital from Sale of Treasury Stock [1,200 × ($42 – $40)] ................. | 2,400 | |
| | | Treasury Stock (1,200 × $42)....................... | | 50,400 |

Practice Exercises: PE 13-5A, PE 13-5B

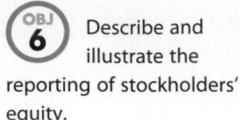

Describe and illustrate the reporting of stockholders' equity.

# Reporting Stockholders' Equity

As with other sections of the balance sheet, alternative terms and formats may be used in reporting stockholders' equity. Also, changes in retained earnings and paid-in capital may be reported in separate statements or notes to the financial statements.

## Stockholders' Equity on the Balance Sheet

Exhibit 7 shows two methods for reporting stockholders' equity for the December 31, 2016, balance sheet for Telex Inc.

- Method 1. Each class of stock is reported, followed by its related paid-in capital accounts. Retained earnings is then reported followed by a deduction for treasury stock.
- Method 2. The stock accounts are reported, followed by the paid-in capital reported as a single item, Additional paid-in capital. Retained earnings is then reported followed by a deduction for treasury stock.

**EXHIBIT 7** **Stockholders' Equity Section of a Balance Sheet**

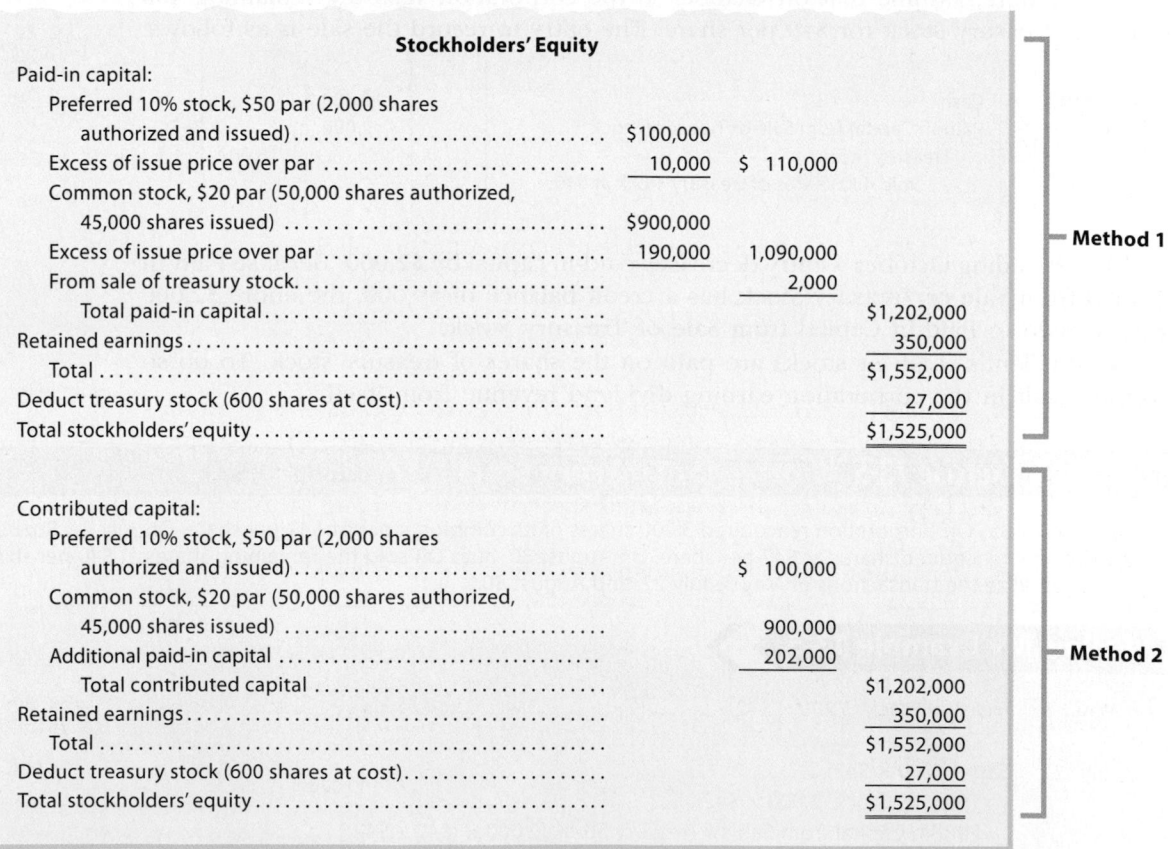

| Telex Inc. |
| Balance Sheet |
| December 31, 2016 |

**Stockholders' Equity**

Paid-in capital:

| | | | |
|---|---|---|---|
| Preferred 10% stock, $50 par (2,000 shares authorized and issued) | $100,000 | | |
| Excess of issue price over par | 10,000 | $ 110,000 | |
| Common stock, $20 par (50,000 shares authorized, 45,000 shares issued) | $900,000 | | |
| Excess of issue price over par | 190,000 | 1,090,000 | |
| From sale of treasury stock | | 2,000 | |
| Total paid-in capital | | | $1,202,000 |
| Retained earnings | | | 350,000 |
| Total | | | $1,552,000 |
| Deduct treasury stock (600 shares at cost) | | | 27,000 |
| Total stockholders' equity | | | $1,525,000 |

**Method 1**

Contributed capital:

| | | | |
|---|---|---|---|
| Preferred 10% stock, $50 par (2,000 shares authorized and issued) | $ 100,000 | | |
| Common stock, $20 par (50,000 shares authorized, 45,000 shares issued) | 900,000 | | |
| Additional paid-in capital | 202,000 | | |
| Total contributed capital | | $1,202,000 | |
| Retained earnings | | 350,000 | |
| Total | | $1,552,000 | |
| Deduct treasury stock (600 shares at cost) | | 27,000 | |
| Total stockholders' equity | | $1,525,000 | |

**Method 2**

Significant changes in stockholders' equity during a period may also be presented in a statement of stockholders' equity or in the notes to the financial statements. The statement of stockholders' equity is illustrated later in this section.

Relevant rights and privileges of the various classes of stock outstanding should also be reported.[10] Examples include dividend and liquidation preferences, conversion rights, and redemption rights. Such information may be disclosed on the face of the balance sheet or in the notes to the financial statements.

## *Example Exercise 13-6* Reporting Stockholders' Equity

Using the following accounts and balances, prepare the Stockholders' Equity section of the balance sheet. Forty thousand shares of common stock are authorized, and 5,000 shares have been reacquired.

| | |
|---|---|
| Common Stock, $50 par | $1,500,000 |
| Paid-In Capital from Sale of Treasury Stock | 44,000 |
| Paid-In Capital in Excess of Par | 160,000 |
| Retained Earnings | 4,395,000 |
| Treasury Stock | 120,000 |

### Follow My Example 13-6

**Stockholders' Equity**

| | | |
|---|---|---|
| Paid-in capital: | | |
| Common stock, $50 par | | |
| (40,000 shares authorized, 30,000 shares issued)..................... | $1,500,000 | |
| Excess of issue price over par........................................ | 160,000 | $1,660,000 |
| From sale of treasury stock............................................... | | 44,000 |
| Total paid-in capital.................................................. | | $1,704,000 |
| Retained earnings.......................................................... | | 4,395,000 |
| Total...................................................................... | | $6,099,000 |
| Deduct treasury stock (5,000 shares at cost) .............................. | | 120,000 |
| Total stockholders' equity ................................................ | | $5,979,000 |

Practice Exercises: PE 13-6A, PE 13-6B

## Reporting Retained Earnings

Changes in retained earnings may be reported using one of the following:

- Separate retained earnings statement
- Combined income and retained earnings statement
- Statement of stockholders' equity

Changes in retained earnings may be reported in a separate retained earnings statement. When a separate **retained earnings statement** is prepared, the beginning balance of retained earnings is reported. The net income is then added (or net loss is subtracted) and any dividends are subtracted to arrive at the ending retained earnings for the period.

To illustrate, a retained earnings statement for Telex Inc. is shown in Exhibit 8.

| Telex Inc.<br>Retained Earnings Statement<br>For the Year Ended December 31, 2016 | | | |
|---|---|---|---|
| Retained earnings, January 1, 2016 .......................... | | | $245,000 |
| Net income .............................................. | | $180,000 | |
| Less dividends: | | | |
| Preferred stock dividends............................. | $10,000 | | |
| Common stock dividends............................. | 65,000 | 75,000 | |
| Increase in retained earnings............................... | | | 105,000 |
| Retained earnings, December 31, 2016...................... | | | $350,000 |

**EXHIBIT 8**

**Retained Earnings Statement**

[10] *FASB Accounting Standards Codification*, Section 505-10-50

Changes in retained earnings may also be reported in combination with the income statement. This format emphasizes net income as the connecting link between the income statement and ending retained earnings. Because this format is not often used, we do not illustrate it.

Changes in retained earnings may also be reported in a statement of stockholders' equity. An example of reporting changes in retained earnings in a statement of stockholders' equity for Telex Inc. is shown in Exhibit 9.

---

### Example Exercise 13-7  Retained Earnings Statement

**OBJ 6**

Dry Creek Cameras Inc. reported the following results for the year ending March 31, 2016:

| | |
|---|---:|
| Retained earnings, April 1, 2015 | $3,338,500 |
| Net income | 461,500 |
| Cash dividends declared | 80,000 |
| Stock dividends declared | 120,000 |

Prepare a retained earnings statement for the fiscal year ended March 31, 2016.

### Follow My Example 13-7

**Dry Creek Cameras Inc.**
Retained Earnings Statement
For the Year Ended March 31, 2016

| | | |
|---|---:|---:|
| Retained earnings, April 1, 2015 . . . . . . . . . . . . . . . . . . . . . . . . . . . . . . . . . . . . | | $3,338,500 |
| Net income . . . . . . . . . . . . . . . . . . . . . . . . . . . . . . . . . . . . . . . . . . . . . . . | $461,500 | |
| Less dividends declared . . . . . . . . . . . . . . . . . . . . . . . . . . . . . . . . . . . . . . . | 200,000 | |
| Increase in retained earnings . . . . . . . . . . . . . . . . . . . . . . . . . . . . . . . . . . . | | 261,500 |
| Retained earnings, March 31, 2016 . . . . . . . . . . . . . . . . . . . . . . . . . . . . . . | | $3,600,000 |

Practice Exercises: PE 13-7A, PE 13-7B

---

**Restrictions** The use of retained earnings for payment of dividends may be restricted by action of a corporation's board of directors. Such **restrictions**, sometimes called *appropriations,* remain part of the retained earnings.

Restrictions of retained earnings are classified as:

- *Legal.* State laws may require a restriction of retained earnings.

    Example: States may restrict retained earnings by the amount of treasury stock purchased. In this way, legal capital cannot be used for dividends.

- *Contractual.* A corporation may enter into contracts that require restrictions of retained earnings.

    Example: A bank loan may restrict retained earnings so that money for repaying the loan cannot be used for dividends.

- *Discretionary.* A corporation's board of directors may restrict retained earnings voluntarily.

    Example: The board may restrict retained earnings and, thus, limit dividend distributions so that more money is available for expanding the business.

Restrictions of retained earnings must be disclosed in the financial statements. Such disclosures are usually included in the notes to the financial statements.

**Prior Period Adjustments** An error may arise from a mathematical mistake or from a mistake in applying accounting principles. Such errors may not be discovered within the same period in which they occur. In such cases, the effect of the error should not affect the current period's net income. Instead, the correction of the error, called a **prior period adjustment**, is reported in the retained earnings statement. Such corrections are reported as an adjustment to the beginning balance of retained earnings.[11]

---

[11] Prior period adjustments are illustrated in advanced texts.

## Statement of Stockholders' Equity

When the only change in stockholders' equity is due to net income or net loss and dividends, a retained earnings statement is sufficient. However, when a corporation also has changes in stock and paid-in capital accounts, a **statement of stockholders' equity** is normally prepared.

A statement of stockholders' equity is normally prepared in a columnar format. Each column is a major stockholders' equity classification. Changes in each classification are then described in the left-hand column. Exhibit 9 illustrates a statement of stockholders' equity for Telex Inc.

---

**EXHIBIT 9**     **Statement of Stockholders' Equity**

**Telex Inc.**
**Statement of Stockholders' Equity**
**For the Year Ended December 31, 2016**

| | Preferred Stock | Common Stock | Additional Paid-In Capital | Retained Earnings | Treasury Stock | Total |
|---|---|---|---|---|---|---|
| Balance, January 1, 2016 . . . . . . . . . . . . . . . . | $100,000 | $850,000 | $177,000 | $245,000 | $(17,000) | $1,355,000 |
| Net income . . . . . . . . . . . . . . . . . . . . . . . . . . . . . | | | | 180,000 | | 180,000 |
| Dividends on preferred stock. . . . . . . . . . . | | | | (10,000) | | (10,000) |
| Dividends on common stock . . . . . . . . . . . . | | | | (65,000) | | (65,000) |
| Issuance of additional common stock . . . . | | 50,000 | 25,000 | | | 75,000 |
| Purchase of treasury stock . . . . . . . . . . . . . . | | | | | (10,000) | (10,000) |
| Balance, December 31, 2016 . . . . . . . . . . . . | $100,000 | $900,000 | $202,000 | $350,000 | $(27,000) | $1,525,000 |

---

## Reporting Stockholders' Equity for Mornin' Joe

**Mornin' Joe** reports stockholders' equity in its balance sheet. Mornin' Joe also includes a retained earnings statement and statement of stockholders' equity in its financial statements.

The Stockholders' Equity section of Mornin' Joe's balance sheet as of December 31, 2016, follows:

**Mornin' Joe**
**Balance Sheet**
**December 31, 2016**

**Stockholders' Equity**

| | | |
|---|---|---|
| Paid-in capital: | | |
| Preferred 10% stock, $50 par (6,000 shares authorized and issued) . . . . . . . . . . . . . . . . . . . . . . . . . . . . . . . . | $ 300,000 | |
| Excess of issue price over par . . . . . . . . . . . . . . . . . . . . . . . . . . . . | 50,000 | $ 350,000 |
| Common stock, $20 par (50,000 shares authorized, 45,000 shares issued) . . . . . . . . . . . . . . . . . . . . . . . . . . . . . . | $ 900,000 | |
| Excess of issue price over par . . . . . . . . . . . . . . . . . . . . . . . . . . . . | 1,450,000 | 2,350,000 |
| Total paid-in capital . . . . . . . . . . . . . . . . . . . . . . . . . . . . . . . . . | | $2,700,000 |
| Retained earnings . . . . . . . . . . . . . . . . . . . . . . . . . . . . . . . . . . . . . . . | | 1,200,300 |
| Total . . . . . . . . . . . . . . . . . . . . . . . . . . . . . . . . . . . . . . . . . . | | $3,900,300 |
| Deduct treasury stock (1,000 shares at cost) . . . . . . . . . . . . . . . . . . . | | 46,000 |
| Total stockholders' equity . . . . . . . . . . . . . . . . . . . . . . . . . . . . . . . . . | | $3,854,300 |
| Total liabilities and stockholders' equity . . . . . . . . . . . . . . . . . . . | | $6,169,700 |

Mornin' Joe's retained earnings statement for the year ended December 31, 2016, is as follows:

| Mornin' Joe<br>Retained Earnings Statment<br>For the Year Ended December 31, 2016 | | | |
|---|---|---|---|
| Retained earnings, January 1, 2016 . . . . . . . . . . . . . . . . . | | | $  852,700 |
| Net income . . . . . . . . . . . . . . . . . . . . . . . . . . . . . . . . . . . . . | | $421,600 | |
| Less dividends: | | | |
| Preferred stock . . . . . . . . . . . . . . . . . . . . . . . . . . . . . . . | $30,000 | | |
| Common stock . . . . . . . . . . . . . . . . . . . . . . . . . . . . . . . | 44,000 | 74,000 | |
| Increase in retained earnings. . . . . . . . . . . . . . . . . . . . . | | | 347,600 |
| Retained earnings, December 31, 2016. . . . . . . . . . . . . | | | $1,200,300 |

The statement of stockholders' equity for Mornin' Joe follows:

| Mornin' Joe<br>Statement of Stockholders' Equity<br>For the Year Ended December 31, 2016 | | | | | | |
|---|---|---|---|---|---|---|
| | Preferred<br>Stock | Common<br>Stock | Additional<br>Paid-In<br>Capital | Retained<br>Earnings | Treasury<br>Stock | Total |
| Balance, January 1, 2016 . . . . . . . . . . . | $300,000 | $800,000 | $1,325,000 | $  852,700 | $(36,000) | $3,241,700 |
| Net income . . . . . . . . . . . . . . . . . . . . . . | | | | 421,600 | | 421,600 |
| Dividends on preferred stock. . . . . . . | | | | (30,000) | | (30,000) |
| Dividends on common stock . . . . . . . | | | | (44,000) | | (44,000) |
| Issuance of additional | | | | | | |
| common stock . . . . . . . . . . . . . . . | | 100,000 | 175,000 | | | 275,000 |
| Purchase of treasury stock . . . . . . . . . | | | | | (10,000) | (10,000) |
| Balance, December 31, 2016 . . . . . . . | $300,000 | $900,000 | $1,500,000 | $1,200,300 | $(46,000) | $3,854,300 |

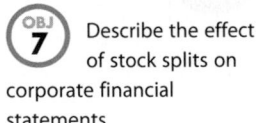

**OBJ 7** Describe the effect of stock splits on corporate financial statements.

Dynamic Exhibit

# Stock Splits

A **stock split** is a process by which a corporation reduces the par or stated value of its common stock and issues a proportionate number of additional shares. A stock split applies to all common shares including the unissued, issued, and treasury shares.

A major objective of a stock split is to reduce the market price per share of the stock. This attracts more investors and broadens the types and numbers of stockholders.

To illustrate, assume that Rojek Corporation has 10,000 shares of $100 par common stock outstanding with a current market price of $150 per share. The board of directors declares the following stock split:

1. Each common shareholder will receive 5 shares for each share held. This is called a 5-for-l stock split. As a result, 50,000 shares (10,000 shares × 5) will be outstanding.
2. The par of each share of common stock will be reduced to $20 ($100÷5).

The par value of the common stock outstanding is $1,000,000 both before and after the stock split as shown in Exhibit 10 and computed as follows:

| | Before Split | After Split |
|---|---|---|
| Number of shares | 10,000 | 50,000 |
| Par value per share | × $100 | × $20 |
| Total | $1,000,000 | $1,000,000 |

In addition, each Rojek Corporation shareholder owns the same total par amount of stock before and after the stock split. For example, a stockholder who owned 4 shares of $100 par stock before the split (total par of $400) would own 20 shares of

**EXHIBIT 10**

**Stock Split: Before and After**

$20 par stock after the split (total par of $400). Only the number of shares and the par value per share have changed.

Because there are more shares outstanding after the stock split, the market price of the stock should decrease. For example, in the preceding example, there would be 5 times as many shares outstanding after the split. Thus, the market price of the stock would be expected to fall from $150 to about $30 ($150 ÷ 5).

Stock splits do not require a journal entry because only the par (or stated) value and number of shares outstanding have changed. However, the details of stock splits are normally disclosed in the notes to the financial statements.

**Note:**
A stock split does not require a journal entry.

---

## Business ⊗ Connection

### BUFFETT ON STOCK SPLITS

Warren E. Buffett, chairman and chief executive officer of **Berkshire Hathaway Inc.**, opposes stock splits on the basis that they add no value to the company. Since its inception, Berkshire Hathaway has never declared a stock split on its primary (Class A) common stock. As a result, Berkshire Hathaway's Class A common stock sells well above $170,000 per share, which is the most expensive stock on the New York Stock Exchange. Such a high price doesn't bother Buffet because he believes that high stock prices attract more sophisticated and long-term investors and discourage stock speculators and short-term investors.

In contrast, **Microsoft Corporation** has split its stock nine times since it went public in 1986. As a result, one share of Microsoft purchased in 1986 is equivalent to 288 shares today, which would be worth more than $10,000.

---

# Financial Analysis and Interpretation: Earnings per Share

 **OBJ 8** Describe and illustrate the use of earnings per share in evaluating a company's profitability.

Net income is often used by investors and creditors in evaluating a company's profitability. However, net income by itself is difficult to use in comparing companies of different sizes. Also, trends in net income may be difficult to evaluate if there have been significant changes in a company's stockholders' equity. Thus, the profitability of companies is often expressed as earnings per share.

**Earnings per common share (EPS)**, sometimes called *basic earnings per share*, is the net income per share of common stock outstanding during a period.[12] Corporations whose stock is traded in a public market must report earnings per common share on their income statements.

Earnings per share is computed as follows:

$$\text{Earnings per Share} = \frac{\text{Net Income} - \text{Preferred Dividends}}{\text{Average Number of Common Shares Outstanding}}$$

If a company has preferred stock outstanding, any preferred dividends are subtracted from net income. This is because the numerator represents only those earnings available to the common shareholders.

[12] For complex capital structures, earnings per share assuming dilution may also be reported as described in Chapter 17.

---

st...

N...
A...

Ea...

su...
sh...
p...

in...
y...

G...

Ea...

W...

Ea...

### Example Exercise 13-8

Financial statement data fo...

Net income .
Preferred div
Average num

a. Determine earnings per
b. Does the change in the

### Follow My Example

a.

2016:

Earnings per Share = —————————
Avera...

2015:

Earnings per Share = —————————
Avera...

b. The increase in the earn...

---

**OBJ 4** Describe and illustrate the accounting for cash dividends and stock dividends.

**Key Points** The entry to record a declaration of cash dividends debits Dividends and credits Dividends Payable. When a stock dividend is declared, Stock Dividends is debited for the fair value of the stock to be issued. Stock Dividends Distributable is credited for the par or stated value of the common stock to be issued. The difference between the fair value of the stock and its par or stated value is credited to Paid-In Capital in Excess of Par—Common Stock. When the stock is issued on the date of payment, Stock Dividends Distributable is debited and Common Stock is credited for the par or stated value of the stock issued.

| Learning Outcomes | Example Exercises | Practice Exercises |
|---|---|---|
| • Journalize the entries for the declaration and payment of cash dividends. | EE13-3 | PE13-3A, 13-3B |
| • Journalize the entries for the declaration and payment of stock dividends. | EE13-4 | PE13-4A, 13-4B |

**OBJ 5** Describe and illustrate the accounting for treasury stock transactions.

**Key Points** When a corporation buys its own stock, the cost method of accounting is normally used. Treasury Stock is debited for its cost, and Cash is credited. If the stock is resold, Treasury Stock is credited for its cost and any difference between the cost and the selling price is normally debited or credited to Paid-In Capital from Sale of Treasury Stock.

| Learning Outcomes | Example Exercises | Practice Exercises |
|---|---|---|
| • Define treasury stock. | | |
| • Describe the accounting for treasury stock. | | |
| • Journalize entries for the purchase and sale of treasury stock. | EE13-5 | PE13-5A, 13-5B |

**OBJ 6** Describe and illustrate the reporting of stockholders' equity.

**Key Points** Two alternatives for reporting stockholders' equity are shown in Exhibit 7. Changes in retained earnings are reported in a retained earnings statement, as shown in Exhibit 8. Restrictions to retained earnings should be disclosed. Any prior period adjustments are reported in the retained earnings statement. Changes in stockholders' equity may be reported on a statement of stockholders' equity, as shown in Exhibit 9.

| Learning Outcomes | Example Exercises | Practice Exercises |
|---|---|---|
| • Prepare the Stockholders' Equity section of the balance sheet. | EE13-6 | PE13-6A, 13-6B |
| • Prepare a retained earnings statement. | EE13-7 | PE13-7A, 13-7B |
| • Describe retained earnings restrictions and prior period adjustments. | | |
| • Prepare a statement of stockholders' equity. | | |

**OBJ 7**

## Describe the effect of stock splits on corporate financial statements.

**Key Points** When a corporation reduces the par or stated value of its common stock and issues a proportionate number of additional shares, a stock split has occurred. There are no changes in the balances of any accounts, and no entry is required for a stock split.

| Learning Outcomes | Example Exercises | Practice Exercises |
|---|---|---|
| • Define and give an example of a stock split. | | |
| • Describe the accounting for and effects of a stock split on the financial statements. | | |

**OBJ 8**

## Describe and illustrate the use of earnings per share in evaluating a company's profitability.

**Key Points** The profitability of companies is often expressed as earnings per share. Earnings per share is computed by subtracting preferred dividends from net income and dividing by the average number of common shares outstanding.

| Learning Outcomes | Example Exercises | Practice Exercises |
|---|---|---|
| • Describe the use of earnings per share in evaluating a company's profitability. | | |
| • Compute and interpret earnings per share. | EE13-8 | PE13-8A, 13-8B |

# Key Terms

cash dividend (605)
common stock (600)
cumulative preferred
    stock (600)
deficit (599)
discount (602)
dividends (599)
earnings per common
    share (EPS) (615)

in arrears (600)
outstanding stock (599)
paid-in capital (598)
par value (600)
preferred stock (600)
premium (602)
prior period adjustments (612)
restrictions (612)
retained earnings (598)

retained earnings statement (611)
statement of stockholders'
    equity (613)
stock (596)
stock dividend (607)
stock split (614)
stockholders (596)
stockholders' equity (598)
treasury stock (608)

# Illustrative Problem

Altenburg Inc. is a lighting fixture wholesaler located in Arizona. During its current fiscal year, ended December 31, 2016, Altenburg Inc. completed the following selected transactions:

Feb.   3.   Purchased 2,500 shares of its own common stock at $26, recording the stock at cost. (Prior to the purchase, there were 40,000 shares of $20 par common stock outstanding.)

May   1.   Declared a semiannual dividend of $1 on the 10,000 shares of preferred stock and a $0.30 dividend on the common stock to stockholders of record on May 31, payable on June 15.

June 15.   Paid the cash dividends.

Sept. 23.   Sold 1,000 shares of treasury stock at $28, receiving cash.

Nov.   1.   Declared semiannual dividends of $1 on the preferred stock and $0.30 on the common stock. In addition, a 5% common stock dividend was declared on the common stock outstanding, to be capitalized at the fair market value of the common stock, which is estimated at $30.

Dec.   1.   Paid the cash dividends and issued the certificates for the common stock dividend.

## Instructions

Journalize the entries to record the transactions for Altenburg Inc.

## Solution

| 2016 | | | | |
|------|---|---|---|---|
| Feb. | 3 | Treasury Stock | 65,000 | |
| | |    Cash | | 65,000 |
| | | | | |
| May | 1 | Cash Dividends | 21,250 | |
| | |    Cash Dividends Payable | | 21,250 |
| | |       (10,000 × $1) + [(40,000 − 2,500) × $0.30]. | | |
| | | | | |
| June | 15 | Cash Dividends Payable | 21,250 | |
| | |    Cash | | 21,250 |
| | | | | |
| Sept. | 23 | Cash | 28,000 | |
| | |    Treasury Stock | | 26,000 |
| | |    Paid-In Capital from Sale of Treasury Stock | | 2,000 |
| | | | | |
| Nov. | 1 | Cash Dividends | 21,550 | |
| | |    Cash Dividends Payable | | 21,550 |
| | |       (10,000 × $1) + [(40,000 − 1,500) × $0.30]. | | |
| | | | | |
| | 1 | Stock Dividends | 57,750* | |
| | |    Stock Dividends Distributable | | 38,500 |
| | |    Paid-In Capital in Excess of | | |
| | |      Par—Common Stock | | 19,250 |
| | |       *(40,000 − 1,500) × 5% × $30. | | |
| | | | | |
| Dec. | 1 | Cash Dividends Payable | 21,550 | |
| | | Stock Dividends Distributable | 38,500 | |
| | |    Cash | | 21,550 |
| | |    Common Stock | | 38,500 |

# Discussion Questions

1. Of two corporations organized at approximately the same time and engaged in competing businesses, one issued $80 par common stock, and the other issued $1 par common stock. Do the par designations provide any indication as to which stock is preferable as an investment? Explain.

2. A stockbroker advises a client to "buy preferred stock. ... With that type of stock, ... [you] will never have to worry about losing the dividends." Is the broker right?

3. A corporation with both preferred stock and common stock outstanding has a substantial credit balance in its retained earnings account at the beginning of the current fiscal year. Although net income for the current year is sufficient to pay the preferred dividend of $150,000 each quarter and a common dividend of $90,000 each quarter, the board of directors declares dividends only on the preferred stock. Suggest possible reasons for passing the dividends on the common stock.

4. An owner of 2,500 shares of Simmons Company common stock receives a stock dividend of 50 shares.

   a. What is the effect of the stock dividend on the stockholder's proportionate interest (equity) in the corporation?

   b. How does the total equity of 2,550 shares compare with the total equity of 2,500 shares before the stock dividend?

5. a. Where should a declared but unpaid cash dividend be reported on the balance sheet?

   b. Where should a declared but unissued stock dividend be reported on the balance sheet?

6. A corporation reacquires 60,000 shares of its own $10 par common stock for $3,000,000, recording it at cost.

   a. What effect does this transaction have on revenue or expense of the period?

   b. What effect does it have on stockholders' equity?

7. The treasury stock in Discussion Question 6 is resold for $3,750,000.

   a. What is the effect on the corporation's revenue of the period?

   b. What is the effect on stockholders' equity?

8. What are the three classifications of restrictions of retained earnings, and how are such restrictions normally reported on the financial statements?

9. Indicate how prior period adjustments would be reported on the financial statements presented only for the current period.

10. What is the primary purpose of a stock split?

# Practice Exercises

EE 13-1  *p. 601*

SHOW
ME HOW

**PE 13-1A   Dividends per share**                                                                      **OBJ. 3**

National Furniture Company has 25,000 shares of cumulative preferred 2% stock, $75 par and 200,000 shares of $10 par common stock. The following amounts were distributed as dividends:

| | |
|---|---|
| Year 1 | $25,000 |
| Year 2 | 88,000 |
| Year 3 | 95,500 |

Determine the dividends per share for preferred and common stock for each year.

EE 13-1 *p. 601*

**PE 13-1B   Dividends per share**                                                  OBJ. 3

Zero Calories Company has 16,000 shares of cumulative preferred 1% stock, $40 par and 80,000 shares of $150 par common stock. The following amounts were distributed as dividends:

| | |
|---|---|
| Year 1 | $ 21,600 |
| Year 2 | 4,000 |
| Year 3 | 100,800 |

Determine the dividends per share for preferred and common stock for each year.

EE 13-2 *p. 604*

**PE 13-2A   Entries for issuing stock**                                            OBJ. 3

On August 26, Mountain Realty Inc. issued for cash 120,000 shares of no-par common stock (with a stated value of $5) at $8. On October 1, Mountain Realty Inc. issued at par value 40,000 shares of preferred 1% stock, $10 par for cash. On November 30, Mountain Realty Inc. issued for cash 18,000 shares of preferred 1% stock, $10 par at $13.

  Journalize the entries to record the August 26, October 1, and November 30 transactions.

EE 13-2 *p. 604*

**PE 13-2B   Entries for issuing stock**                                            OBJ. 3

On January 22, Zentric Corporation issued for cash 180,000 shares of no-par common stock at $4. On February 14, Zentric Corporation issued at par value 44,000 shares of preferred 2% stock, $55 par for cash. On August 30, Zentric Corporation issued for cash 9,000 shares of preferred 2% stock, $55 par at $60.

  Journalize the entries to record the January 22, February 14, and August 30 transactions.

EE 13-3 *p. 606*

**PE 13-3A   Entries for cash dividends**                                           OBJ. 4

The declaration, record, and payment dates in connection with a cash dividend of $710,000 on a corporation's common stock are June 15, August 10, and September 15. Journalize the entries required on each date.

EE 13-3 *p. 606*

**PE 13-3B   Entries for cash dividends**                                           OBJ. 4

The declaration, record, and payment dates in connection with a cash dividend of $480,000 on a corporation's common stock are February 1, March 18, and May 1. Journalize the entries required on each date.

EE 13-4 *p. 608*

**PE 13-4A   Entries for stock dividends**                                          OBJ. 4

Olde Wine Corporation has 250,000 shares of $40 par common stock outstanding. On February 15, Olde Wine Corporation declared a 2% stock dividend to be issued May 2 to stockholders of record on March 27. The market price of the stock was $52 per share on February 15.

  Journalize the entries required on February 15, March 27, and May 2.

EE 13-4 *p. 608*

**PE 13-4B   Entries for stock dividends**                                          OBJ. 4

Antique Buggy Corporation has 820,000 shares of $35 par common stock outstanding. On June 8, Antique Buggy Corporation declared a 5% stock dividend to be issued August 12 to stockholders of record on July 13. The market price of the stock was $63 per share on June 8.

  Journalize the entries required on June 8, July 13, and August 12.

EE 13-5 *p. 609*

**PE 13-5A   Entries for treasury stock**                                           OBJ. 5

On January 31, Wilderness Resorts Inc. reacquired 22,500 shares of its common stock at $31 per share. On April 20, Wilderness Resorts sold 12,800 of the reacquired shares at $40 per share. On October 4, Wilderness Resorts sold the remaining shares at $28 per share.

  Journalize the transactions of January 31, April 20, and October 4.

EE 13-5 *p. 609*    **PE 13-5B   Entries for treasury stock**                          OBJ. 5

On May 27, Hydro Clothing Inc. reacquired 75,000 shares of its common stock at $8 per share. On August 3, Hydro Clothing sold 54,000 of the reacquired shares at $11 per share. On November 14, Hydro Clothing sold the remaining shares at $7 per share.

Journalize the transactions of May 27, August 3, and November 14.

EE 13-6 *p. 611*    **PE 13-6A   Reporting stockholders' equity**                      OBJ. 6

Using the following accounts and balances, prepare the Stockholders' Equity section of the balance sheet. Two hundred fifty thousand shares of common stock are authorized, and 17,500 shares have been reacquired.

| | |
|---|---:|
| Common Stock, $60 par | $12,000,0000 |
| Paid-In Capital from Sale of Treasury Stock | 320,000 |
| Paid-In Capital in Excess of Par—Common Stock | 3,200,000 |
| Retained Earnings | 18,500,000 |
| Treasury Stock | 1,137,500 |

EE 13-6 *p. 611*    **PE 13-6B   Reporting stockholders' equity**                      OBJ. 6

Using the following accounts and balances, prepare the Stockholders' Equity section of the balance sheet. Five-hundred thousand shares of common stock are authorized, and 40,000 shares have been reacquired.

| | |
|---|---:|
| Common Stock, $120 par | $48,000,000 |
| Paid-In Capital from Sale of Treasury Stock | 4,500,000 |
| Paid-In Capital in Excess of Par—Common Stock | 6,400,000 |
| Retained Earnings | 63,680,000 |
| Treasury Stock | 5,200,000 |

EE 13-7 *p. 612*    **PE 13-7A   Retained earnings statement**                         OBJ. 6

Rockwell Inc. reported the following results for the year ended June 30, 2016:

| | |
|---|---:|
| Retained earnings, July 1, 2015 | $3,900,000 |
| Net income | 714,000 |
| Cash dividends declared | 100,000 |
| Stock dividends declared | 50,000 |

Prepare a retained earnings statement for the fiscal year ended June 30, 2016.

EE 13-7 *p. 612*    **PE 13-7B   Retained earnings statement**                         OBJ. 6

Noric Cruises Inc. reported the following results for the year ended October 31, 2016:

| | |
|---|---:|
| Retained earnings, November 1, 2015 | $12,400,000 |
| Net income | 2,350,000 |
| Cash dividends declared | 175,000 |
| Stock dividends declared | 300,000 |

Prepare a retained earnings statement for the fiscal year ended October 31, 2016.

EE 13-8 *p. 616*    **PE 13-8A   Earnings per share**                                   OBJ. 8

Financial statement data for the years ended December 31 for Dovetail Corporation follows:

| | 2016 | 2015 |
|---|---:|---:|
| Net income | $448,750 | $376,000 |
| Preferred dividends | $40,000 | $40,000 |
| Average number of common shares outstanding | 75,000 shares | 60,000 shares |

a.  Determine the earnings per share for 2016 and 2015.

b.  Does the change in the earnings per share from 2015 to 2016 indicate a favorable or an unfavorable trend?

EE 13-8  *p. 616*

SHOW
ME HOW

**FAI**

### PE 13-8B   Earnings per share

**OBJ. 8**

Financial statement data for the years ended December 31 for Black Bull Inc. follows:

|  | 2016 | 2015 |
|---|---|---|
| Net income | $2,485,700 | $1,538,000 |
| Preferred dividends | $50,000 | $50,000 |
| Average number of common shares outstanding | 115,000 shares | 80,000 shares |

a.  Determine the earnings per share for 2016 and 2015.

b.  Does the change in the earnings per share from 2015 to 2016 indicate a favorable or an unfavorable trend?

## Exercises

✔ Preferred stock,
1st year: $2.25

SHOW
ME HOW

### EX 13-1   Dividends per share

**OBJ. 3**

Triple Z Inc., a developer of radiology equipment, has stock outstanding as follows: 12,000 shares of cumulative preferred 2% stock, $150 par and 50,000 shares of $10 par common. During its first four years of operations, the following amounts were distributed as dividends: first year, $27,000; second year, $60,000; third year, $80,000; fourth year, $90,000. Calculate the dividends per share on each class of stock for each of the four years.

### EX 13-2   Dividends per share

**OBJ. 3**

✔ Preferred stock,
1st year: $0.90

Lightfoot Inc., a software development firm, has stock outstanding as follows: 40,000 shares of cumulative preferred 1% stock, $125 par, and 100,000 shares of $150 par common. During its first four years of operations, the following amounts were distributed as dividends: first year, $36,000; second year, $58,000; third year, $75,000; fourth year, $124,000. Calculate the dividends per share on each class of stock for each of the four years.

### EX 13-3   Entries for issuing par stock

**OBJ. 3**

SHOW
ME HOW

On April 20, Gallatin County Rocks Inc., a marble contractor, issued for cash 75,000 shares of $45 par common stock at $54, and on August 7, it issued for cash 20,000 shares of preferred stock, $10 par at $12.

a.  Journalize the entries for April 20 and August 7.

b.  What is the total amount invested (total paid-in capital) by all stockholders as of August 7?

### EX 13-4   Entries for issuing no-par stock

**OBJ. 3**

SHOW
ME HOW

On May 15, Helena Carpet Inc., a carpet wholesaler, issued for cash 750,000 shares of no-par common stock (with a stated value of $1.50) at $4, and on June 30, it issued for cash 17,500 shares of preferred stock, $50 par at $60.

a.  Journalize the entries for May 15 and June 30, assuming that the common stock is to be credited with the stated value.

b.  What is the total amount invested (total paid-in capital) by all stockholders as of June 30?

### EX 13-5   Issuing stock for assets other than cash

**OBJ. 3**

SHOW
ME HOW

On July 11, American Lift Corporation, a wholesaler of hydraulic lifts, acquired land in exchange for 5,000 shares of $5 par common stock with a current market price of $32. Journalize the entry to record the transaction.

### EX 13-6   Selected stock transactions

**OBJ. 3**

Alpha Sounds Corp., an electric guitar retailer, was organized by Michele Kirby, Paul Glenn, and Gretchen Northway. The charter authorized 1,000,000 shares of common stock with a par of $1. The following transactions affecting stockholders' equity were completed during the first year of operations:

a.  Issued 100,000 shares of stock at par to Paul Glenn for cash.

b.  Issued 3,000 shares of stock at par to Michele Kirby for promotional services provided in connection with the organization of the corporation, and issued 45,000 shares of stock at par to Michele Kirby for cash.

c. Purchased land and a building from Gretchen Northway in exchange for stock issued at par. The building is mortgaged for $180,000 for 20 years at 6%, and there is accrued interest of $5,200 on the mortgage note at the time of the purchase. It is agreed that the land is to be priced at $60,000 and the building at $225,000 and that Gretchen Northway's equity will be exchanged for stock at par. The corporation agreed to assume responsibility for paying the mortgage note and the accrued interest.

Journalize the entries to record the transactions.

---

**EX 13-7  Issuing stock**                                                                    **OBJ. 3**

Willow Creek Nursery, with an authorization of 75,000 shares of preferred stock and 200,000 shares of common stock, completed several transactions involving its stock on October 1, the first day of operations. The trial balance at the close of the day follows:

| | | |
|---|---:|---:|
| Cash | 3,780,000 | |
| Land | 840,000 | |
| Buildings | 2,380,000 | |
| Preferred 1% Stock, $80 par | | 2,800,000 |
| Paid-In Capital in Excess of Par—Preferred Stock | | 420,000 |
| Common Stock, $30 par | | 3,600,000 |
| Paid-In Capital in Excess of Par—Common Stock | | 180,000 |
| | 7,000,000 | 7,000,000 |

All shares within each class of stock were sold at the same price. The preferred stock was issued in exchange for the land and buildings.

Journalize the two entries to record the transactions summarized in the trial balance.

---

**EX 13-8  Issuing stock**                                                                    **OBJ. 3**

SHOW
ME HOW

Occupational Products Inc., a wholesaler of office products, was organized on March 1 of the current year, with an authorization of 25,000 shares of preferred 2% stock, $100 par and 500,000 shares of $10 par common stock. The following selected transactions were completed during the first year of operations:

Mar.  1.  Issued 220,000 shares of common stock at par for cash.

       1.  Issued 500 shares of common stock at par to an attorney in payment of legal fees for organizing the corporation.

May 31.  Issued 70,000 shares of common stock in exchange for land, buildings, and equipment with fair market prices of $150,000, $560,000 and $165,000 respectively.

July  1.  Issued 18,000 shares of preferred stock at $110 for cash.

         Journalize the transactions.

---

**EX 13-9  Entries for cash dividends**                                                        **OBJ. 4**

SHOW
ME HOW

The declaration, record, and payment dates in connection with a cash dividend of $135,000 on a corporation's common stock are January 12, March 13, and April 12. Journalize the entries required on each date.

---

**EX 13-10  Entries for stock dividends**                                                      **OBJ. 4**

✔ b. (1) $3,000,000
(3) $36,500,000

SHOW
ME HOW

Senior Life Co. is an HMO for businesses in the Portland area. The following account balances appear on the balance sheet of Senior Life Co.: Common stock (800,000 shares authorized; 500,000 shares issued), $4 par, $2,000,000; Paid-in capital in excess of par—common stock, $1,000,000; and Retained earnings, $33,500,000. The board of directors declared a 2% stock dividend when the market price of the stock was $13 a share. Senior Life Co. reported no income or loss for the current year.

a. Journalize the entries to record (1) the declaration of the dividend, capitalizing an amount equal to market value, and (2) the issuance of the stock certificates.

b. Determine the following amounts before the stock dividend was declared: (1) total paid-in capital, (2) total retained earnings, and (3) total stockholders' equity.

c. Determine the following amounts after the stock dividend was declared and closing entries were recorded at the end of the year: (1) total paid-in capital, (2) total retained earnings, and (3) total stockholders' equity.

### EX 13-11    Treasury stock transactions                                                OBJ. 5

✔ b. $170,000 credit

SHOW
ME HOW

Mystic Lake Inc. bottles and distributes spring water. On July 9 of the current year, Mystic Lake reacquired 40,000 shares of its common stock at $44 per share. On September 22, Mystic Lake Inc. sold 30,000 of the reacquired shares at $50 per share. The remaining 10,000 shares were sold at $43 per share on November 23.

a. Journalize the transactions of July 9, September 22, and November 23.

b. What is the balance in Paid-In Capital from Sale of Treasury Stock on December 31 of the current year?

c. ➤ For what reasons might Mystic Lake have purchased the treasury stock?

---

### EX 13-12    Treasury stock transactions                                                OBJ. 5, 6

✔ b. $57,000 credit

SHOW
ME HOW

Lawn Smart Inc. develops and produces spraying equipment for lawn maintenance and industrial uses. On May 29 of the current year, Lawn Smart Inc. reacquired 18,000 shares of its common stock at $20 per share. On August 11, 13,500 of the reacquired shares were sold at $24 per share, and on October 30, 3,000 of the reacquired shares were sold at $21.

a. Journalize the transactions of May 29, August 11, and October 30.

b. What is the balance in Paid-In Capital from Sale of Treasury Stock on December 31 of the current year?

c. What is the balance in Treasury Stock on December 31 of the current year?

d. How will the balance in Treasury Stock be reported on the balance sheet?

---

### EX 13-13    Treasury stock transactions                                                OBJ. 5, 6

✔ b. $55,500 credit

Biscayne Bay Water Inc. bottles and distributes spring water. On May 14 of the current year, Biscayne Bay Water Inc. reacquired 23,500 shares of its common stock at $75 per share. On September 6, Biscayne Bay Water Inc. sold 14,000 of the reacquired shares at $81 per share. The remaining 9,500 shares were sold at $72 per share on November 30.

a. Journalize the transactions of May 14, September 6, and November 30.

b. What is the balance in Paid-In Capital from Sale of Treasury Stock on December 31 of the current year?

c. Where will the balance in Paid-In Capital from Sale of Treasury Stock be reported on the balance sheet?

d. ➤ For what reasons might Biscayne Bay Water Inc. have purchased the treasury stock?

---

### EX 13-14    Reporting paid-in capital                                                  OBJ. 6

✔ Total paid-in capital, $13,615,000

The following accounts and their balances were selected from the unadjusted trial balance of Point Loma Group Inc., a freight forwarder, at October 31, the end of the current fiscal year:

| | |
|---|---:|
| Common Stock, no par, $14 stated value | $ 4,480,000 |
| Paid-In Capital from Sale of Treasury Stock | 45,000 |
| Paid-In Capital in Excess of Par—Preferred Stock | 210,000 |
| Paid-In Capital in Excess of Stated Value—Common Stock | 480,000 |
| Preferred 2% Stock, $120 par | 8,400,000 |
| Retained Earnings | 39,500,000 |

Prepare the Paid-In Capital portion of the Stockholders' Equity section of the balance sheet using Method 1 of Exhibit 7. There are 375,000 shares of common stock authorized and 85,000 shares of preferred stock authorized.

**EX 13-15  Stockholders' Equity section of balance sheet**  OBJ. 6

✔ Total stockholders' equity, $23,676,000

The following accounts and their balances appear in the ledger of Goodale Properties Inc. on June 30 of the current year:

| | |
|---|---|
| Common Stock, $45 par | $ 3,060,000 |
| Paid-In Capital from Sale of Treasury Stock | 115,000 |
| Paid-In Capital in Excess of Par—Common Stock | 272,000 |
| Retained Earnings | 20,553,000 |
| Treasury Stock | 324,000 |

Prepare the Stockholders' Equity section of the balance sheet as of June 30. Eighty thousand shares of common stock are authorized, and 9,000 shares have been reacquired.

**EX 13-16  Stockholders' Equity section of balance sheet**  OBJ. 6

✔ Total stockholders' equity, $89,100,000

Specialty Auto Racing Inc. retails racing products for BMWs, Porsches, and Ferraris. The following accounts and their balances appear in the ledger of Specialty Auto Racing Inc. on July 31, the end of the current year:

| | |
|---|---|
| Common Stock, $36 par | $10,080,000 |
| Paid-In Capital from Sale of Treasury Stock—Common | 340,000 |
| Paid-In Capital in Excess of Par—Common Stock | 420,000 |
| Paid-In Capital in Excess of Par—Preferred Stock | 384,000 |
| Preferred 1% Stock, $150 par | 7,200,000 |
| Retained Earnings | 71,684,000 |
| Treasury Stock—Common | 1,008,000 |

Fifty thousand shares of preferred and 300,000 shares of common stock are authorized. There are 24,000 shares of common stock held as treasury stock.

Prepare the Stockholders' Equity section of the balance sheet as of July 31, the end of the current year using Method 1 of Exhibit 7.

**EX 13-17  Retained earnings statement**  OBJ. 6

✔ Retained earnings, January 31, $64,210,000

Sumter Pumps Corporation, a manufacturer of industrial pumps, reports the following results for the year ended January 31, 2016:

| | |
|---|---|
| Retained earnings, February 1, 2015 | $59,650,000 |
| Net Income | 8,160,000 |
| Cash dividends declared | 1,000,000 |
| Stock dividends declared | 2,600,000 |

SHOW ME HOW

Prepare a retained earnings statement for the fiscal year ended January 31, 2016.

**EX 13-18  Stockholders' Equity section of balance sheet**  OBJ. 6

✔ Corrected total stockholders' equity, $122,800,000

List the errors in the following Stockholders' Equity section of the balance sheet prepared as of the end of the current year:

**Stockholders' Equity**

| | | |
|---|---|---|
| Paid-in capital: | | |
| Preferred 2% stock, $80 par | | |
| (125,000 shares authorized and issued) | $10,000,000 | |
| Excess of issue price over par | 500,000 | $ 10,500,000 |
| Retained earnings | | 96,700,000 |
| Treasury stock (75,000 shares at cost) | | 1,755,000 |
| Dividends payable | | 430,000 |
| Total paid-in capital | | $ 109,385,000 |
| Common stock, $20 par (1,000,000 shares | | |
| authorized, 825,000 shares issued) | | 17,655,000 |
| Organizing costs | | 300,000 |
| Total stockholders' equity | | $127,340,000 |

✔ Total stockholders' equity, Dec. 31, $21,587,000

**EX 13-19  Statement of stockholders' equity**  OBJ. 6

The stockholders' equity T accounts of I-Cards Inc. for the fiscal year ended December 31, 2016, are as follows. Prepare a statement of stockholders' equity for the fiscal year ended December 31, 2016.

**COMMON STOCK**

|  |  |  |  |
|---|---|---|---|
|  | Jan.  1 | Balance | 4,800,000 |
|  | Apr. 14 | Issued |  |
|  |  | 30,000 shares | 1,200,000 |
|  | Dec. 31 | Balance | 6,000,000 |

**PAID-IN CAPITAL IN EXCESS OF PAR**

|  |  |  |  |
|---|---|---|---|
|  | Jan.  1 | Balance | 960,000 |
|  | Apr. 14 | Issued |  |
|  |  | 30,000 shares | 300,000 |
|  | Dec. 31 | Balance | 1,260,000 |

**TREASURY STOCK**

|  |  |  |
|---|---|---|
| Aug.  7 | Purchased |  |
|  | 12,000 shares | 552,000 |

**RETAINED EARNINGS**

| Mar.  31 | Dividend | 69,000 | Jan.  1 | Balance | 11,375,000 |
|---|---|---|---|---|---|
| June 30 | Dividend | 69,000 | Dec. 31 | Closing |  |
| Sept. 30 | Dividend | 69,000 |  | (net income) | 3,780,000 |
| Dec.  31 | Dividend | 69,000 | Dec. 31 | Balance | 14,879,000 |

SHOW
ME HOW

**EX 13-20  Effect of stock split**  OBJ. 7

Copper Grill Restaurant Corporation wholesales ovens and ranges to restaurants throughout the Southwest. Copper Grill Restaurant Corporation, which had 50,000 shares of common stock outstanding, declared a 3-for-1 stock split.

a.  What will be the number of shares outstanding after the split?

b.  If the common stock had a market price of $210 per share before the stock split, what would be an approximate market price per share after the split?

**EX 13-21  Effect of cash dividend and stock split**  OBJ. 4, 7

Indicate whether the following actions would (+) increase, (–) decrease, or (0) not affect Indigo Inc.'s total assets, liabilities, and stockholders' equity:

|  | Assets | Liabilities | Stockholders' Equity |
|---|---|---|---|
| (1)  Authorizing and issuing stock certificates in a stock split | | | |
| (2)  Declaring a stock dividend | | | |
| (3)  Issuing stock certificates for the stock dividend declared in (2) | | | |
| (4)  Declaring a cash dividend | | | |
| (5)  Paying the cash dividend declared in (4) | | | |

**EX 13-22  Selected dividend transactions, stock split**  OBJ. 4, 7

Selected transactions completed by Canyon Ferry Boating Corporation during the current fiscal year are as follows:

Jan.   8. Split the common stock 2 for 1 and reduced the par from $80 to $40 per share. After the split, there were 150,000 common shares outstanding.

Apr. 30. Declared semiannual dividends of $0.75 on 18,000 shares of preferred stock and $0.28 on the common stock payable on July 1.

July 1. Paid the cash dividends.

Oct. 31. Declared semiannual dividends of $0.75 on the preferred stock and $0.14 on the common stock (before the stock dividend). In addition, a 5% common stock dividend was declared on the common stock outstanding. The fair market value of the common stock is estimated at $52.

Dec. 31. Paid the cash dividends and issued the certificates for the common stock dividend.

Journalize the transactions.

---

**EX 13-23  EPS**                                                                                  OBJ. 8

Junkyard Arts, Inc., had earnings of $316,000 for 2016. The company had 40,000 shares of common stock outstanding during the year. In addition, the company issued 15,000 shares of $50 par value preferred stock on January 9, 2016. The preferred stock has a dividend of $1.60 per share. There were no transactions in either common or preferred stock during 2016.

Determine the basic earnings per share for Junkyard Arts.

---

**EX 13-24  EPS**                                                                                  OBJ. 8

Pacific Gas and Electric Company is a large gas and electric utility operating in northern and central California. Three recent years of financial data for Pacific Gas and Electric Company are as follows:

|  | Year 3 | Year 2 | Year 1 |
|---|---|---|---|
| | **Fiscal Years Ended (in millions)** | | |
| Net income | $830 | $858 | $1,113 |
| Preferred dividends | $14 | $14 | $14 |
| Average number of common shares outstanding | 424 | 401 | 382 |

a. Determine the earnings per share for fiscal Year 3, Year 2, and Year 1. Round to the nearest cent.

b. Evaluate the growth in earnings per share for the three years in comparison to the growth in net income for the three years.

---

**EX 13-25  EPS**                                                                                  OBJ. 8

For a recent year, OfficeMax and Staples are two companies competing in the retail office supply business. OfficeMax had a net income of $34,894,000, while Staples had a net loss of $210,706,000. OfficeMax had preferred stock of $28,726,000 with preferred dividends of $2,123,000. Staples had no preferred stock. The average outstanding common shares for each company were as follows:

|  | **Average Number of Common Shares Outstanding** |
|---|---|
| OfficeMax | 85,881,000 |
| Staples | 669,479,000 |

a. Determine the earnings per share for each company. Round to the nearest cent.

b. Evaluate the relative profitability of the two companies.

## Problems: Series A

### PR 13-1A  Dividends on preferred and common stock

OBJ. 3

Sunbird Theatre Inc. owns and operates movie theaters throughout Florida and Georgia. Sunbird Theatre Inc. has declared the following annual dividends over a six-year period: 2011, $20,000; 2012, $36,000; 2013, $70,000; 2014, $90,000; 2015, $100,000 and 2016, $150,000. During the entire period ended December 31 of each year, the outstanding stock of the company was composed of 100,000 shares of cumulative, preferred 1% stock, $30 par, and 400,000 shares of common stock, $20 par.

**Instructions**

1. Calculate the total dividends and the per-share dividends declared on each class of stock for each of the six years. There were no dividends in arrears on January 1, 2011. Summarize the data in tabular form, using the following column headings:

| Year | Total Dividends | Preferred Dividends | | Common Dividends | |
|------|-----------------|-------|-----------|-------|-----------|
|      |                 | Total | Per Share | Total | Per Share |
| 2011 | $ 20,000 | | | | |
| 2012 | 36,000 | | | | |
| 2013 | 70,000 | | | | |
| 2014 | 90,000 | | | | |
| 2015 | 102,000 | | | | |
| 2016 | 150,000 | | | | |

2. Calculate the average annual dividend per share for each class of stock for the six-year period.

3. Assuming a market price per share of $37.50 for the preferred stock and $30.00 for the common stock, calculate the average annual percentage return on initial shareholders' investment, based on the average annual dividend per share (a) for preferred stock and (b) for common stock.

### PR 13-2A  Stock transactions for corporate expansion

OBJ. 3

On December 1 of the current year, the following accounts and their balances appear in the ledger of Latte Corp., a coffee processor:

| | |
|---|---|
| Preferred 2% Stock, $50 par (250,000 shares authorized, 80,000 shares issued) . . . . . . . . . . . . . . . . . . . . . . . . . . . . . . . . . . . . . . . . . . . . . . | $ 4,000,000 |
| Paid-In Capital in Excess of Par—Preferred Stock . . . . . . . . . . . . . . . . . . . . . . . . . . . . | 560,000 |
| Common Stock, $35 par (1,000,000 shares authorized, 400,000 shares issued) . . . . . . . . . . . . . . . . . . . . . . . . . . . . . . . . . . . . . . . . . . . . . . . . | 14,000,000 |
| Paid-In Capital in Excess of Par—Common Stock . . . . . . . . . . . . . . . . . . . . . . . . . . . . | 1,200,000 |
| Retained Earnings. . . . . . . . . . . . . . . . . . . . . . . . . . . . . . . . . . . . . . . . . . . . . . . . . . . . . . . | 180,000,000 |

At the annual stockholders' meeting on March 31, the board of directors presented a plan for modernizing and expanding plant operations at a cost of approximately $11,000,000. The plan provided (a) that a building, valued at $3,375,000, and the land on which it is located, valued at $1,500,000, be acquired in accordance with preliminary negotiations by the issuance of 125,000 shares of common stock, (b) that 40,000 shares of the unissued preferred stock be issued through an underwriter, and (c) that the corporation borrow $4,000,000. The plan was approved by the stockholders and accomplished by the following transactions:

May 11.  Issued 125,000 shares of common stock in exchange for land and a building, according to the plan.

20.  Issued 40,000 shares of preferred stock, receiving $52 per share in cash.

31.  Borrowed $4,000,000 from Laurel National, giving a 5% mortgage note.

**Instructions**

Journalize the entries to record the May transactions.

**PR 13-3A    Selected stock transactions**                                    OBJ. 3, 4, 5

The following selected accounts appear in the ledger of EJ Construction Inc. at the beginning of the current fiscal year:

| | |
|---|---:|
| Preferred 1% Stock, $50 par (100,000 shares authorized, 80,000 shares issued) | $ 4,000,000 |
| Paid-In Capital in Excess of Par—Preferred Stock | 175,000 |
| Common Stock, $3 par (5,000,000 shares authorized, 2,000,000 shares issued) | 6,000,000 |
| Paid-In Capital in Excess of Par—Common Stock | 1,500,000 |
| Retained Earnings | 32,350,000 |

During the year, the corporation completed a number of transactions affecting the stockholders' equity. They are summarized as follows:

a.  Issued 500,000 shares of common stock at $8, receiving cash.

b.  Issued 10,000 shares of preferred 1% stock at $60.

c.  Purchased 50,000 shares of treasury common for $7 per share.

d.  Sold 20,000 shares of treasury common for $9 per share.

e.  Sold 5,000 shares of treasury common for $6 per share.

f.  Declared cash dividends of $0.50 per share on preferred stock and $0.08 per share on common stock.

g.  Paid the cash dividends.

**Instructions**

Journalize the entries to record the transactions. Identify each entry by letter.

**PR 13-4A    Entries for selected corporate transactions**                    OBJ. 3, 4, 5, 6

Morrow Enterprises Inc. manufactures bathroom fixtures. The stockholders' equity accounts of Morrow Enterprises Inc., with balances on January 1, 2016, are as follows:

| | |
|---|---:|
| Common Stock, $20 stated value (500,000 shares authorized, 375,000 shares issued) | $ 7,500,000 |
| Paid-In Capital in Excess of Stated Value—Common Stock | 825,000 |
| Retained Earnings | 33,600,000 |
| Treasury Stock (25,000 shares, at cost) | 450,000 |

The following selected transactions occurred during the year:

Jan. 22.  Paid cash dividends of $0.08 per share on the common stock. The dividend had been properly recorded when declared on December 1 of the preceding fiscal year for $28,000.

Apr. 10.  Issued 75,000 shares of common stock for $24 per share.

June  6.  Sold all of the treasury stock for $26 per share.

July  5.  Declared a 4% stock dividend on common stock, to be capitalized at the market price of the stock, which is $25 per share.

Aug. 15.  Issued the certificates for the dividend declared on July 5.

Nov. 23.  Purchased 30,000 shares of treasury stock for $19 per share.

Dec. 28.  Declared a $0.10-per-share dividend on common stock.

    31.  Closed the credit balance of the income summary account, $1,125,000.

    31.  Closed the two dividends accounts to Retained Earnings.

*(Continued)*

**Instructions**

1. Enter the January 1 balances in T accounts for the stockholders' equity accounts listed. Also prepare T accounts for the following: Paid-In Capital from Sale of Treasury Stock; Stock Dividends Distributable; Stock Dividends; Cash Dividends.

2. Journalize the entries to record the transactions, and post to the eight selected accounts.

3. Prepare a retained earnings statement for the year ended December 31, 2016.

4. Prepare the Stockholders' Equity section of the December 31, 2016, balance sheet.

---

**PR 13-5A Entries for selected corporate transactions** OBJ. 3, 4, 5, 7

✔ Oct. 1, cash dividends, $202,800

General Ledger

Selected transactions completed by Primo Discount Corporation during the current fiscal year are as follows:

Jan. 9. Split the common stock 3 for 1 and reduced the par from $75 to $25 per share. After the split, there were 1,200,000 common shares outstanding.

Feb. 28. Purchased 40,000 shares of the corporation's own common stock at $28, recording the stock at cost.

May 1. Declared semiannual dividends of $0.80 on 75,000 shares of preferred stock and $0.12 on the common stock to stockholders of record on June 1, payable on July 10.

July 10. Paid the cash dividends.

Sept. 7. Sold 30,000 shares of treasury stock at $34, receiving cash.

Oct. 1. Declared semiannual dividends of $0.80 on the preferred stock and $0.12 on the common stock (before the stock dividend). In addition, a 2% common stock dividend was declared on the common stock outstanding. The fair market value of the common stock is estimated at $36.

Dec. 1. Paid the cash dividends and issued the certificates for the common stock dividend.

**Instructions**

Journalize the transactions.

---

# Problems: Series B

---

**PR 13-1B Dividends on preferred and common stock** OBJ. 3

✔ 1. Common dividends in 2013: $25,000

SHOW
ME HOW

Yosemite Bike Corp. manufactures mountain bikes and distributes them through retail outlets in California, Oregon, and Washington. Yosemite Bike Corp. has declared the following annual dividends over a six-year period ended December 31 of each year: 2011, $24,000; 2012, $10,000; 2013, $126,000; 2014, $100,000; 2015, $125,000; and 2016, $125,000. During the entire period, the outstanding stock of the company was composed of 25,000 shares of cumulative preferred 2% stock, $90 par, and 100,000 shares of common stock, $4 par.

**Instructions**

1. Determine the total dividends and the per-share dividends declared on each class of stock for each of the six years. There were no dividends in arrears on January 1, 2011. Summarize the data in tabular form, using the following column headings:

| Year | Total Dividends | Preferred Dividends | | Common Dividends | |
|------|-----------------|---------------------|-----------|------------------|-----------|
| | | Total | Per Share | Total | Per Share |
| 2011 | $ 24,000 | | | | |
| 2012 | 10,000 | | | | |
| 2013 | 126,000 | | | | |
| 2014 | 100,000 | | | | |
| 2015 | 125,000 | | | | |
| 2016 | 125,000 | | | | |

2. Determine the average annual dividend per share for each class of stock for the six-year period.

3. Assuming a market price of $100 for the preferred stock and $5 for the common stock, calculate the average annual percentage return on initial shareholders' investment, based on the average annual dividend per share (a) for preferred stock and (b) for common stock.

---

**PR 13-2B** **Stock transaction for corporate expansion**   OBJ. 3

General Ledger

Pulsar Optics produces medical lasers for use in hospitals. The accounts and their balances appear in the ledger of Pulsar Optics on April 30 of the current year as follows:

| | |
|---|---:|
| Preferred 1% Stock, $120 par (300,000 shares authorized, 36,000 shares issued) | $ 4,320,000 |
| Paid-In Capital in Excess of Par—Preferred Stock | 180,000 |
| Common Stock, $15 par (2,000,000 shares authorized, 1,400,000 shares issued) | 21,000,000 |
| Paid-In Capital in Excess of Par—Common Stock | 3,500,000 |
| Retained Earnings | 78,000,000 |

At the annual stockholders' meeting on August 5, the board of directors presented a plan for modernizing and expanding plant operations at a cost of approximately $9,000,000. The plan provided (a) that the corporation borrow $1,500,000, (b) that 20,000 shares of the unissued preferred stock be issued through an underwriter, and (c) that a building, valued at $4,150,000, and the land on which it is located, valued at $800,000, be acquired in accordance with preliminary negotiations by the issuance of 300,000 shares of common stock. The plan was approved by the stockholders and accomplished by the following transactions:

Oct. 9. Borrowed $1,500,000 from St. Peter City Bank, giving a 4% mortgage note.

17. Issued 20,000 shares of preferred stock, receiving $126 per share in cash.

28. Issued 300,000 shares of common stock in exchange for land and a building, according to the plan.

**Instructions**

Journalize the entries to record the October transactions.

---

**PR 13-3B** **Selected stock transactions**   OBJ. 3, 4, 5

✔ f. Cash dividends, $234,775

General Ledger

SHOW
ME HOW

Diamondback Welding & Fabrication Corporation sells and services pipe welding equipment in Illinois. The following selected accounts appear in the ledger of Diamondback Welding & Fabrication Corporation at the beginning of the current fiscal year:

| | |
|---|---:|
| Preferred 2% Stock, $80 par (100,000 shares authorized, 60,000 shares issued) | $ 4,800,000 |
| Paid-In Capital in Excess of Par—Preferred Stock | 210,000 |
| Common Stock, $9 par (3,000,000 shares authorized, 1,750,000 shares issued) | 15,750,000 |
| Paid-In Capital in Excess of Par—Common Stock | 1,400,000 |
| Retained Earnings | 52,840,000 |

During the year, the corporation completed a number of transactions affecting the stockholders' equity. They are summarized as follows:

a. Purchased 87,500 shares of treasury common for $8 per share.

b. Sold 55,000 shares of treasury common for $11 per share.

c. Issued 20,000 shares of preferred 2% stock at $84.

d. Issued 400,000 shares of common stock at $13, receiving cash.

*(Continued)*

e. Sold 18,000 shares of treasury common for $7.50 per share.

f. Declared cash dividends of $1.60 per share on preferred stock and $0.05 per share on common stock.

g. Paid the cash dividends.

**Instructions**

Journalize the entries to record the transactions. Identify each entry by letter.

---

**PR 13-4B**   **Entries for selected corporate transactions**   OBJ. 3, 4, 5, 6

✔ 4. Total stockholders' equity, $11,262,432

General Ledger

Nav-Go Enterprises Inc. produces aeronautical navigation equipment. The stockholders' equity accounts of Nav-Go Enterprises Inc., with balances on January 1, 2016, are as follows:

| | |
|---|---:|
| Common Stock, $5 stated value (900,000 shares authorized, 620,000 shares issued) ........................................... | $3,100,000 |
| Paid-In Capital in Excess of Stated Value—Common Stock ............ | 1,240,000 |
| Retained Earnings ................................................ | 4,875,000 |
| Treasury Stock (48,000 shares, at cost) .............................. | 288,000 |

The following selected transactions occurred during the year:

Jan. 15. Paid cash dividends of $0.06 per share on the common stock. The dividend had been properly recorded when declared on December 1 of the preceding fiscal year for $34,320.

Mar. 15. Sold all of the treasury stock for $6.75 per share.

Apr. 13. Issued 200,000 shares of common stock for $8 per share.

June 14. Declared a 3% stock dividend on common stock, to be capitalized at the market price of the stock, which is $7.50 per share.

July 16. Issued the certificates for the dividend declared on June 14.

Oct. 30. Purchased 50,000 shares of treasury stock for $6 per share.

Dec. 30. Declared a $0.08-per-share dividend on common stock.

     31. Closed the credit balance of the income summary account, $775,000.

     31. Closed the two dividends accounts to Retained Earnings.

**Instructions**

1. Enter the January 1 balances in T accounts for the stockholders' equity accounts listed. Also prepare T accounts for the following: Paid-In Capital from Sale of Treasury Stock; Stock Dividends Distributable; Stock Dividends; Cash Dividends.

2. Journalize the entries to record the transactions, and post to the eight selected accounts.

3. Prepare a retained earnings statement for the year ended December 31, 2016.

4. Prepare the Stockholders' Equity section of the December 31, 2016, balance sheet.

---

**PR 13-5B**   **Entries for selected corporate transactions**   OBJ. 3, 4, 5, 7

✔ Sept. 1, Cash dividends, $95,200

General Ledger

West Yellowstone Outfitters Corporation manufactures and distributes leisure clothing. Selected transactions completed by West Yellowstone Outfitters during the current fiscal year are as follows:

Jan. 15. Split the common stock 4 for 1 and reduced the par from $120 to $30 per share. After the split, there were 800,000 common shares outstanding.

Mar. 1. Declared semiannual dividends of $0.25 on 100,000 shares of preferred stock and $0.07 on the 800,000 shares of $30 par common stock to stockholders of record on March 31, payable on April 30.

Apr. 30. Paid the cash dividends.

May 31. Purchased 60,000 shares of the corporation's own common stock at $32, recording the stock at cost.

Aug. 17. Sold 40,000 shares of treasury stock at $38, receiving cash.

Sept. 1. Declared semiannual dividends of $0.25 on the preferred stock and $0.09 on the common stock (before the stock dividend). In addition, a 1% common stock dividend was declared on the common stock outstanding, to be capitalized at the fair market value of the common stock, which is estimated at $40.

Oct. 31. Paid the cash dividends and issued the certificates for the common stock dividend.

### Instructions
Journalize the transactions.

## Cases & Projects

### CP 13-1 Board of directors' actions

Bernie Ebbers, the CEO of WorldCom, a major telecommunications company, was having personal financial troubles. Ebbers pledged a large stake of his WorldCom stock as security for some personal loans. As the price of WorldCom stock sank, Ebbers' bankers threatened to sell his stock in order to protect their loans. To avoid having his stock sold, Ebbers asked the board of directors of WorldCom to loan him nearly $400 million of corporate assets at 2.5% interest to pay off his bankers. The board agreed to lend him the money.

➥ Comment on the decision of the board of directors in this situation.

### CP 13-2 Ethics and professional conduct in business

Lou Hoskins and Shirley Crothers are organizing Red Lodge Metals Unlimited Inc. to undertake a high-risk gold-mining venture in Canada. Lou and Shirley tentatively plan to request authorization for 400,000,000 shares of common stock to be sold to the general public. Lou and Shirley have decided to establish par of $0.03 per share in order to appeal to a wide variety of potential investors. Lou and Shirley feel that investors would be more willing to invest in the company if they received a large quantity of shares for what might appear to be a "bargain" price.

➥ Discuss whether Lou and Shirley are behaving in a professional manner.

### CP 13-3 Issuing stock

Epstein Engineering Inc. began operations on January 5, 2016, with the issuance of 500,000 shares of $80 par common stock. The sole stockholders of Epstein Engineering Inc. are Barb Abrams and Dr. Amber Epstein, who organized Epstein Engineering Inc.

*(Continued)*

with the objective of developing a new flu vaccine. Dr. Epstein claims that the flu vaccine, which is nearing the final development stage, will protect individuals against 90% of the flu types that have been medically identified. To complete the project, Epstein Engineering Inc. needs $25,000,000 of additional funds. The local banks have been unwilling to loan the funds because of the lack of sufficient collateral and the riskiness of the business.

The following is a conversation between Barb Abrams, the chief executive officer of Epstein Engineering Inc., and Amber Epstein, the leading researcher:

*Barb:* What are we going to do? The banks won't loan us any more money, and we've got to have $25 million to complete the project. We are so close! It would be a disaster to quit now. The only thing I can think of is to issue additional stock. Do you have any suggestions?

*Amber:* I guess you're right. But if the banks won't loan us any more money, how do you think we can find any investors to buy stock?

*Barb:* I've been thinking about that. What if we promise the investors that we will pay them 5% of sales until they have received an amount equal to what they paid for the stock?

*Amber:* What happens when we pay back the $25 million? Do the investors get to keep the stock? If they do, it'll dilute our ownership.

*Barb:* How about, if after we pay back the $25 million, we make them turn in their stock for $120 per share? That's one and one-half times what they paid for it, plus they would have already gotten all their money back. That's a $120 profit per share for the investors.

*Amber:* It could work. We get our money, but don't have to pay any interest, dividends, or the $80 per share until we start generating sales. At the same time, the investors could get their money back plus $120 per share profit.

*Barb:* We'll need current financial statements for the new investors. I'll get our accountant working on them and contact our attorney to draw up a legally binding contract for the new investors. Yes, this could work.

In late 2016, the attorney and the various regulatory authorities approved the new stock offering, and 312,500 shares of common stock were privately sold to new investors at the stock's par of $80.

In preparing financial statements for 2016, Barb Abrams and Dan Fisher, the controller for Epstein Engineering Inc., have the following conversation:

*Dan:* Barb, I've got a problem.

*Barb:* What's that, Dan?

*Dan:* Issuing common stock to raise that additional $25 million was a great idea. But . . .

*Barb:* But what?

*Dan:* I've got to prepare the 2016 annual financial statements, and I am not sure how to classify the common stock.

*Barb:* What do you mean? It's common stock.

*Dan:* I'm not so sure. I called the auditor and explained how we are contractually obligated to pay the new stockholders 5% of sales until $80 per share is paid. Then, we may be obligated to pay them $120 per share.

*Barb:* So . . .

*Dan:* So the auditor thinks that we should classify the additional issuance of $25 million as debt, not stock! And, if we put the $25 million on the balance sheet as debt, we will violate our other loan agreements with the banks. And, if these agreements are violated, the banks may call in all our debt immediately. If they do that, we are in deep trouble. We'll probably have to file for bankruptcy. We just don't have the cash to pay off the banks.

1. ➡ Discuss the arguments for and against classifying the issuance of the $25 million of stock as debt.

2. ➡ What do you think might be a practical solution to this classification problem?

### CP 13-4 Interpret stock exchange listing

The following stock exchange data for **Microsoft Corporation** were taken from the **Yahoo!** Finance Web site on November 29, 2013:

Microsoft Corporation (MSFT)

| | | | |
|---|---|---|---|
| Last Trade: | 38.13 | Prev. Clos: | 37.60 |
| Trade Time: | 1:00 PM EST | 1y Target Est: | 36.32 |
| | | Day's Range: | 37.82–38.29 |
| | | 52wk Range: | 26.26–38.29 |
| | | Volume: | 22,090,428 |
| | | Div & Yield: | 1.12 (3.00%) |

a. If you owned 500 shares of Mircosoft, what amount would you receive as a quarterly dividend?

b. Compute the percentage increase in price from the Previous Close to the Last Trade. Round to two decimal places.

c. What is Microsoft's percentage change in market price from the 52-week low to the Last Trade on November 29, 2013? Round to one decimal place.

d. If you bought 500 shares of Microsoft at the Last Trade price on November 29, 2013, how much would it cost, and who gets the money?

---

### CP 13-5 Dividends

Motion Designs Inc. has paid quarterly cash dividends since 2005. These dividends have steadily increased from $0.05 per share to the latest dividend declaration of $0.50 per share. The board of directors would like to continue this trend and is hesitant to suspend or decrease the amount of quarterly dividends. Unfortunately, sales dropped sharply in the fourth quarter of 2016 because of worsening economic conditions and increased competition. As a result, the board is uncertain as to whether it should declare a dividend for the last quarter of 2016.

On October 1, 2016, Motion Designs Inc. borrowed $4,000,000 from Valley National Bank to use in modernizing its retail stores and to expand its product line in reaction to its competition. The terms of the 10-year, 6% loan require Motion Designs Inc. to:

a. Pay monthly interest on the last day of the month.

b. Pay $400,000 of the principal each October 1, beginning in 2017.

c. Maintain a current ratio (current assets ÷ current liabilities) of 2.

d. Maintain a minimum balance (a compensating balance) of $100,000 in its Valley National Bank account.

*(Continued)*

On December 31, 2016, $1,000,000 of the $4,000,000 loan had been disbursed in modernization of the retail stores and in expansion of the product line. Motion Designs Inc.'s balance sheet as of December 31, 2016, follows:

**Motion Designs Inc.**
**Balance Sheet**
**December 31, 2016**

**Assets**

| | | | |
|---|---|---|---|
| Current assets: | | | |
| Cash | | $ 250,000 | |
| Marketable securities | | 3,000,000 | |
| Accounts receivable | $ 800,000 | | |
| Less allowance for doubtful accounts | 50,000 | 750,000 | |
| Merchandise inventory | | 2,980,000 | |
| Prepaid expenses | | 20,000 | |
| Total current assets | | | $ 7,000,000 |
| Property, plant, and equipment: | | | |
| Land | | $1,500,000 | |
| Buildings | $5,050,000 | | |
| Less accumulated depreciation | 1,140,000 | 3,910,000 | |
| Equipment | $3,320,000 | | |
| Less accumulated depreciation | 730,000 | 2,590,000 | |
| Total property, plant, and equipment | | | 8,000,000 |
| Total assets | | | $15,000,000 |

**Liabilities**

| | | | |
|---|---|---|---|
| Current liabilities: | | | |
| Accounts payable | | $ 1,590,000 | |
| Notes payable (Valley National Bank) | | 400,000 | |
| Salaries payable | | 10,000 | |
| Total current liabilities | | $2,000,000 | |
| Long-term liabilities: | | | |
| Notes payable (Valley National Bank) | | 3,600,000 | |
| Total liabilities | | | $ 5,600,000 |

**Stockholders' Equity**

| | | | |
|---|---|---|---|
| Paid-in capital: | | | |
| Common stock, $25 par (200,000 shares authorized, 180,000 shares issued) | | $ 4,500,000 | |
| Excess of issue price over par | | 270,000 | |
| Total paid-in capital | | $4,770,000 | |
| Retained earnings | | 4,630,000 | |
| Total stockholders' equity | | | 9,400,000 |
| Total liabilities and stockholders' equity | | | $15,000,000 |

The board of directors is scheduled to meet January 10, 2017, to discuss the results of operations for 2016 and to consider the declaration of dividends for the fourth quarter of 2016. The chairman of the board has asked for your advice on the declaration of dividends.

1. ━━━▶ What factors should the board consider in deciding whether to declare a cash dividend?

2. ━━━▶ The board is considering the declaration of a stock dividend instead of a cash dividend. Discuss the issuance of a stock dividend from the point of view of (a) a stockholder and (b) the board of directors.

### CP 13-6  Profiling a corporation

### Group Project

Select a public corporation you are familiar with or which interests you. Using the Internet, develop a short (1 to 2 pages) profile of the corporation. Include in your profile the following information:

1. Name of the corporation.

2. State of incorporation.

3. Nature of its operations.

4. Total assets for the most recent balance sheet.

5. Total revenues for the most recent income statement.

6. Net income for the most recent income statement.

7. Classes of stock outstanding.

8. Market price of the stock outstanding.

9. High and low price of the stock for the past year.

10. Cash dividends paid for each share of stock during the past year.

In groups of three or four, discuss each corporate profile. Select one of the corporations, assuming that your group has $100,000 to invest in its stock. Summarize why your group selected the corporation it did and how financial accounting information may have affected your decision. Keep track of the performance of your corporation's stock for the remainder of the term.

*Note:* Most major corporations maintain "home pages" on the Internet. This home page provides a variety of information on the corporation and often includes the corporation's financial statements. In addition, the New York Stock Exchange Web site (www.nyse .com) includes links to the home pages of many listed companies that can be assessed by clicking on "Listings Directory." Financial statements can also be accessed using EDGAR, the electronic archives of financial statements filed with the Securities and Exchange Commission (SEC).

SEC documents can also be retrieved using the EdgarScan™ service at www.sec .gov/edgar/searchedgar/companysearch.html. To obtain annual report information, key in a company name in the appropriate space. Edgar will list the reports available to you for the company you've selected. Select the most recent annual report filing, identified as a 10-K or 10-K405.

# Long-Term Liabilities: Bonds and Notes

## Dick's Sporting Goods

**M**ost of us don't have enough money in our bank accounts to buy a house or a car by simply writing a check. Just imagine if you had to save the entire purchase price of a house before you could buy it! To help us make these types of purchases, banks will typically lend us the money, as long as we agree to repay the loan with interest in smaller future payments. Loans such as this, or long-term debt, allow us to purchase assets such as houses and cars today, which benefit us over the long term.

The use of debt can also help a business reach its objectives. Most businesses have to borrow money in order to acquire assets that they will use to generate income. For example, in 1948 Dick Stack borrowed $300 from his grandmother to start a sporting goods store in Binghamton, New York. Over the years the business grew, and in the early 1990s, **Dick's Sporting Goods** used long-term debt to transform itself from a small business to a Fortune 500 company with more than 450 stores across the United States.

While debt can help companies like Dick's Sporting Goods grow to achieve financial success, too much debt can be a financial burden that may even lead to bankruptcy. Just like individuals, businesses must manage debt wisely. In this chapter, we will discuss the nature of, accounting for, and analysis of, long-term debt.

**OBJ 1** Compute the potential impact of long-term borrowing on earnings per share.

# Financing Corporations

Corporations finance their operations using the following sources:

- Short-term debt, such as purchasing goods or services on account.
- Long-term debt, such as issuing bonds or notes payable.
- Equity, such as issuing common or preferred stock.

Short-term debt, including the purchase of goods and services on account and the issuance of short-term notes payable, was discussed in Chapter 11. Issuing equity in the form of common or preferred stock was discussed in Chapter 13. This chapter focuses on the use of long-term debt such as bonds and notes payable to finance a company's operations.

A **bond** is a form of an interest-bearing note. Like a note, a bond requires periodic interest payments, with the face amount to be repaid at the maturity date. For example, a 12% bond requires the company issuing the bond to pay 12% interest on the face amount of the bonds every year. As creditors of the corporation, bondholder claims on the corporation's assets rank ahead of stockholders.

One of the main factors that influences the decision to issue debt or equity is the effect that various financing alternatives will have on earnings per share. **Earnings per share (EPS)** measures the income earned by each share of common stock. It is computed as follows:[1]

$$\text{Earnings per Share} = \frac{\text{Net Income} - \text{Preferred Dividends}}{\text{Number of Common Shares Outstanding}}$$

---

[1] Earnings per share is also discussed in the *Financial Analysis and Interpretation* section of Chapter 13 and in Chapter 17.

To illustrate the effects that issuing debt can have on earnings per share, consider the following alternative plans for financing Boz Corporation, a $4,000,000 company:

|  | Plan 1 | | Plan 2 | | Plan 3 | |
| --- | --- | --- | --- | --- | --- | --- |
|  | **Amount** | **Percent** | **Amount** | **Percent** | **Amount** | **Percent** |
| Issue 12% bonds | — | 0% | — | 0% | $2,000,000 | 50% |
| Issue preferred 9% stock, $50 par value | — | 0 | $2,000,000 | 50 | 1,000,000 | 25 |
| Issue common stock, $10 par value | $4,000,000 | 100 | 2,000,000 | 50 | 1,000,000 | 25 |
| Total amount of financing | $4,000,000 | 100% | $4,000,000 | 100% | $4,000,000 | 100% |

The company must choose one of these plans. Each plan finances some of the corporation's operations by issuing common stock. However, the percentage financed by common stock varies from 100% (Plan 1) to 25% (Plan 3).

Assume the following data for Boz Corporation:

- Earnings before interest and income taxes are $800,000.
- The tax rate is 40%.
- All bonds or stocks are issued at their par or face amount.

The effect of the preceding financing plans on Boz's net income and earnings per share is shown in Exhibit 1.

|  | Plan 1 | Plan 2 | Plan 3 |
| --- | --- | --- | --- |
| 12% bonds | — | — | $2,000,000 |
| Preferred 9% stock, $50 par | — | $2,000,000 | 1,000,000 |
| Common stock, $10 par | $4,000,000 | 2,000,000 | 1,000,000 |
| Total | $4,000,000 | $4,000,000 | $4,000,000 |
| Earnings before interest and income tax | $ 800,000 | $ 800,000 | $ 800,000 |
| Deduct interest on bonds | — | — | 240,000[a] |
| Income before income tax | $ 800,000 | $ 800,000 | $ 560,000 |
| Deduct income tax | 320,000[b] | 320,000[b] | 224,000[b] |
| Net income | $ 480,000 | $ 480,000 | $ 336,000 |
| Dividends on preferred stock | — | 180,000[c] | 90,000[c] |
| Available for dividends on common stock | $ 480,000 | $ 300,000 | $ 246,000 |
| Shares of common stock outstanding | ÷ 400,000[d] | ÷ 200,000[d] | ÷ 100,000[d] |
| Earnings per share on common stock | $ 1.20 | $ 1.50 | $ 2.46 |

[a] $2,000,000 bonds × 12%
[b] Income before income tax × 40%
[c] Preferred stock × 9%
[d] Common stock ÷ $10 par value per share

**EXHIBIT 1**

**Effect of Alternative Financing Plans— $800,000 Earnings**

 Dynamic Exhibit

Exhibit 1 indicates that when earnings are strong, Plan 3 has the highest earnings per share, making it the most attractive for common shareholders. This is because the company is generating more than enough net income to cover the bond interest. If the estimated earnings are more than $800,000, the difference between the earnings per share to common stockholders under Plans 1 and 3 is even greater.[2]

Lower earnings, however, have the opposite effect. If earnings are reduced to $440,000, as illustrated in Exhibit 2, Plans 1 and 2 become more attractive to common stockholders. This is because more of the company's earnings are being used to pay bond interest, leaving less net income attributable to common stockholders.

---

[2] The higher earnings per share under Plan 3 is due to a finance concept known as *leverage*. This concept is discussed further in Chapter 17.

**EXHIBIT 2**

**Effect of Alternative Financing Plans— $440,000 Earnings**

Dynamic Exhibit

| | Plan 1 | Plan 2 | Plan 3 |
|---|---|---|---|
| 12% bonds.......................................... | — | — | $2,000,000 |
| Preferred 9% stock, $50 par.......................... | — | $2,000,000 | 1,000,000 |
| Common stock, $10 par............................ | $4,000,000 | 2,000,000 | 1,000,000 |
| Total ............................................. | $4,000,000 | $4,000,000 | $4,000,000 |
| Earnings before interest and income tax.............. | $ 440,000 | $ 440,000 | $ 440,000 |
| Deduct interest on bonds........................... | — | — | 240,000 |
| Income before income tax......................... | $ 440,000 | $ 440,000 | $ 200,000 |
| Deduct income tax ................................. | 176,000 | 176,000 | 80,000 |
| Net income ...................................... | $ 264,000 | $ 264,000 | $ 120,000 |
| Dividends on preferred stock ...................... | — | 180,000 | 90,000 |
| Available for dividends on common stock............. | $ 264,000 | $ 84,000 | $ 30,000 |
| Shares of common stock outstanding................. | ÷ 400,000 | ÷ 200,000 | ÷ 100,000 |
| Earnings per share on common stock ................ | $ 0.66 | $ 0.42 | $ 0.30 |

In addition to earnings per share, the corporation should consider other factors in deciding among the financing plans. For example, if bonds are issued, the interest and the face value of the bonds at maturity must be paid. If these payments are not made, the bondholders could seek court action and force the company into bankruptcy. In contrast, a corporation is not legally obligated to pay dividends on preferred or common stock.

---

**Example Exercise 14-1** **Alternative Financing Plans**                                OBJ 1

Gonzales Co. is considering the following alternative plans for financing its company:

| | Plan 1 | Plan 2 |
|---|---|---|
| Issue 10% bonds (at face value) | — | $2,000,000 |
| Issue common stock, $10 par | $3,000,000 | 1,000,000 |

Income tax is estimated at 40% of income.

Determine the earnings per share of common stock under the two alternative financing plans, assuming income before bond interest and income tax is $750,000.

**Follow My Example 14-1**

| | Plan 1 | Plan 2 |
|---|---|---|
| Earnings before bond interest and income tax | $750,000 | $750,000 |
| Deduct interest on bonds | 0 | 200,000[2] |
| Income before income tax | $750,000 | $550,000 |
| Deduct income tax | 300,000[1] | 220,000[3] |
| Net income | $450,000 | $330,000 |
| Dividends on preferred stock | 0 | 0 |
| Available for dividends on common stock | $450,000 | $330,000 |
| Shares of common stock outstanding | ÷300,000 | ÷100,000 |
| Earnings per share on common stock | $ 1.50 | $ 3.30 |

[1]$750,000 × 40%    [2]$2,000,000 × 10%    [3]$550,000 × 40%

Practice Exercises: PE 14-1A, PE 14-1B

---

OBJ 2

Describe the characteristics and terminology of bonds payable.

# Nature of Bonds Payable

Corporate bonds normally differ in face amount, interest rates, interest payment dates, and maturity dates. Bonds also differ in other ways such as whether corporate assets are pledged in support of the bonds.

# Bond Characteristics and Terminology

A bond issue is normally divided into a number of individual bonds. The face amount of each bond is called the *principal*. This is the amount that must be repaid on the dates the bonds mature. The principal is usually $1,000, or a multiple of $1,000. The interest on bonds may be payable annually, semiannually, or quarterly. Most bonds pay interest semiannually.

The underlying contract between the company issuing bonds and the bondholders is called a **bond indenture**. This contract can be written in different ways, depending on the financing needs of the company. The two most common types of bonds are term bonds and serial bonds. When all bonds of an issue mature at the same time, they are called *term bonds*. If the bonds mature over several dates, they are called *serial bonds*. For example, one-tenth of an issue of $1,000,000 bonds, or $100,000, may mature 16 years from the issue date, another $100,000 in the 17th year, and so on.

There are also a variety of more complicated bond structures. For example, *convertible bonds* may be exchanged for shares of common stock, and *callable bonds* may be redeemed by the corporation prior to maturity. These bonds are discussed in intermediate and advanced accounting texts.

# Proceeds from Issuing Bonds

When a corporation issues bonds, the proceeds received for the bonds depend on:

- The face amount of the bonds, which is the amount due at the maturity date.
- The interest rate on the bonds.
- The market rate of interest for similar bonds.

The face amount and the interest rate on the bonds are identified in the bond indenture. The interest rate to be paid on the face amount of the bond is called the **contract rate** or *coupon rate*.

The **market rate of interest**, sometimes called the **effective rate of interest**, is the rate determined from sales and purchases of similar bonds. The market rate of interest is affected by a variety of factors, including investors' expectations of current and future economic conditions.

By comparing the market and contract rates of interest, it can be determined whether the bonds will sell for more than, less than, or at their face amount, as shown in Exhibit 3.

---

| **EXHIBIT 3** | **Issuing Bonds at a Discount, at Face Amount, and at a Premium** |
|---|---|

**If:** Market Rate > Contract Rate    **If:** Market Rate = Contract Rate    **If:** Market Rate < Contract Rate

 < $1,000 Bond     = $1,000 Bond    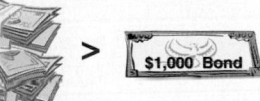 > $1,000 Bond

Less than $1,000                  $1,000                      More than $1,000

**Then:** Selling Price < Face Amount    **Then:** Selling Price = Face Amount    **Then:** Selling Price > Face Amount

Sold at a DISCOUNT              Sold at FACE AMOUNT              Sold at a PREMIUM

---

If the market rate equals the contract rate, bonds will sell at the **face amount**.

If the market rate is greater than the contract rate, the bonds will sell for less than their face value. The face amount of the bonds less the selling price is called a **discount**. A bond sells at a discount because buyers are not willing to pay the full face amount for bonds with a contract rate that is lower than the market rate.

**Dow Chemical Company's** 9.00% bonds, maturing in 2021, sold for 129.97 on February 26, 2013.

If the market rate is less than the contract rate, the bonds will sell for more than their face value. The selling price of the bonds less the face amount is called a **premium**. A bond sells at a premium because buyers are willing to pay more than the face amount for bonds with a contract rate that is higher than the market rate.

The price of a bond is quoted as a percentage of the bond's face value. For example, a $1,000 bond quoted at 98 could be purchased or sold for $980 ($1,000 × 0.98). Likewise, bonds quoted at 109 could be purchased or sold for $1,090 ($1,000 × 1.09).

## Business Connection

### U.S. GOVERNMENT DEBT

Like many corporations, the U.S. government issues debt to finance its operations. The debt is issued by the U.S. Treasury Department in the form of U.S. Treasury bills, notes, and bonds, which have the following characteristics:

| | Issued at | Interest Paid | Maturity |
|---|---|---|---|
| U.S. Treasury bills | Discount | None | 1 year or less |
| U.S. Treasury notes | Face value | Semiannual | 1 to 10 years |
| U.S. Treasury bonds | Face value | Semiannual | 10 years or more |

At the end of 2013, total U.S. government debt issued by the federal government was estimated to be $17,548 billion. The Congressional Budget Office estimated that this amount would grow to $21,325 billion by 2017.

Source: Historical Tables: Budget of the U.S. Government, Fiscal Year 2013, U.S. Office of Management and Budget.

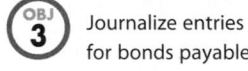

**OBJ 3** Journalize entries for bonds payable.

# Accounting for Bonds Payable

Bonds may be issued at their face amount, a discount, or a premium. When bonds are issued at less or more than their face amount, the discount or premium must be amortized over the life of the bonds. At the maturity date, the face amount must be repaid. In some situations, a corporation may redeem bonds before their maturity date by repurchasing them from investors.

## Bonds Issued at Face Amount

If the market rate of interest is equal to the contract rate of interest, the bonds will sell for their face amount or at a price of 100. To illustrate, assume that on January 1, 2015, Eastern Montana Communications Inc. issued the following bonds:

| | |
|---|---|
| Face amount .................................... | $100,000 |
| Contract rate of interest ......................... | 12% |
| Interest paid semiannually on June 30 and December 31. | |
| Term of bonds .................................. | 5 years |
| Market rate of interest ........................... | 12% |

Since the contract rate of interest and the market rate of interest are the same, the bonds will sell at their face amount. The entry to record the issuance of the bonds is as follows:

| | 2015 | | | | | |
|---|---|---|---|---|---|---|
| | Jan. | 1 | Cash | | 100,000 | |
| | | | Bonds Payable | | | 100,000 |
| | | | Issued $100,000 bonds payable at face amount. | | | |

Every six months (on June 30 and December 31) after the bonds are issued, interest of $6,000 ($100,000 × 12% × ½ year) is paid. The first interest payment on June 30, 2015, is recorded as follows:

| 2015 | | | | | |
|---|---|---|---|---|---|
| June | 30 | Interest Expense | | 6,000 | |
| | | Cash | | | 6,000 |
| | | Paid six months' interest on bonds. | | | |

At the maturity date, the payment of the principal of $100,000 is recorded as follows:

| 2019 | | | | | |
|---|---|---|---|---|---|
| Dec. | 31 | Bonds Payable | | 100,000 | |
| | | Cash | | | 100,000 |
| | | Paid bond principal at maturity date. | | | |

## Example Exercise 14-2  Issuing Bonds at Face Amount  OBJ 3

On January 1, the first day of the fiscal year, a company issues a $1,000,000, 6%, five-year bond that pays semiannual interest of $30,000 ($1,000,000 × 6% × ½ year), receiving cash of $1,000,000. Journalize the entries to record (a) the issuance of the bonds at their face amount, (b) the first interest payment on June 30, and (c) the payment of the principal on the maturity date.

### Follow My Example 14-2

a.
Cash ....................................................... 1,000,000
    Bonds Payable ............................................... 1,000,000

b.
Interest Expense ................................................ 30,000
    Cash ....................................................... 30,000

c.
Bonds Payable ................................................. 1,000,000
    Cash ....................................................... 1,000,000

Practice Exercises: PE 14-2A, PE 14-2B

## Bonds Issued at a Discount

If the market rate of interest is greater than the contract rate of interest, the bonds will sell for less than their face amount. This is because investors are not willing to pay the full face amount for bonds that pay a lower contract rate of interest than the rate they could earn on similar bonds (market rate). The difference between the face amount and the selling price of the bonds is the bond discount.[3]

**Note:** Bonds will sell at a discount when the market rate of interest is higher than the contract rate.

To illustrate, assume that on January 1, 2015, Western Wyoming Distribution Inc. issued the following bonds:

| | |
|---|---|
| Face amount ............................. | $100,000 |
| Contract rate of interest ................. | 12% |
| Interest paid semiannually on June 30 and December 31. | |
| Term of bonds............................ | 5 years |
| Market rate of interest ................... | 13% |

[3] The price that investors are willing to pay for the bonds depends on present value concepts. Present value concepts, including the computation of bond prices, are described and illustrated in Appendix 1 at the end of this chapter.

Because the contract rate of interest is less than the market rate of interest, the bonds will sell at less than their face amount. Assuming the bonds sell for $96,406, the entry to record the issuance of the bonds is as follows:

| | | | | | |
|---|---|---|---|---|---|
| 2015<br>Jan. | 1 | Cash | | 96,406 | |
| | | Discount on Bonds Payable | | 3,594 | |
| | |     Bonds Payable | | | 100,000 |
| | |         Issued $100,000 bonds at discount. | | | |

The $96,406 is the amount investors are willing to pay for bonds that have a lower contract rate of interest (12%) than the market rate (13%). The discount is the market's way of adjusting the contract rate of interest to the higher market rate of interest.

The account, Discount on Bonds Payable, is a contra account to Bonds Payable and has a normal debit balance. It is subtracted from Bonds Payable to determine the carrying amount (or book value) of the bonds payable. The **carrying amount** of bonds payable is the face amount of the bonds less any unamortized discount or plus any unamortized premium. Thus, after the preceding entry, the carrying amount of the bonds payable is $96,406 ($100,000 − $3,594).

## Example Exercise 14-3 Issuing Bonds at a Discount

OBJ 3

On the first day of the fiscal year, a company issues a $1,000,000, 6%, five-year bond that pays semiannual interest of $30,000 ($1,000,000 × 6% × ½), receiving cash of $936,420. Journalize the entry to record the issuance of the bonds.

### Follow My Example 14-3

Cash . . . . . . . . . . . . . . . . . . . . . . . . . . . . . . . . . . . . . . . . . . . . . . . . 936,420
Discount on Bonds Payable . . . . . . . . . . . . . . . . . . . . . . . . . . . . . 63,580
    Bonds Payable . . . . . . . . . . . . . . . . . . . . . . . . . . . . . . . . . . . . . . . . . 1,000,000

Practice Exercises: PE 14-3A, PE 14-3B

## Amortizing a Bond Discount

Every period, a portion of the bond discount must be reduced and added to interest expense to reflect the passage of time. This process, called **amortization**, increases the contract rate of interest on a bond to the market rate of interest that existed on the date the bonds were issued. The entry to amortize a bond discount is as follows:

| | | | | | |
|---|---|---|---|---|---|
| | | Interest Expense | | XXX | |
| | |     Discount on Bonds Payable | | | XXX |

The preceding entry may be made annually as an adjusting entry, or it may be combined with the semiannual interest payment. In the latter case, the entry would be as follows:

| | | | | | |
|---|---|---|---|---|---|
| | | Interest Expense | | XXX | |
| | |     Discount on Bonds Payable | | | XXX |
| | |     Cash (amount of semiannual interest) | | | XXX |

The two methods of computing the amortization of a bond discount are:

- *Straight-line method*
- *Effective interest rate method,* sometimes called the *interest method*

The **effective interest rate method** is required by generally accepted accounting principles. However, the straight-line method may be used if the results do not differ significantly from the interest method. The straight-line method is used in this chapter. The effective interest rate method is described and illustrated in Appendix 2 at the end of this chapter.

The straight-line method provides equal amounts of amortization each period. To illustrate, amortization of the Western Wyoming Distribution bond discount of $3,594 is computed as follows:

| | |
|---|---|
| Discount on bonds payable ................. | $3,594 |
| Term of bonds ............................. | 5 years |
| Semiannual amortization .................... | $359.40 ($3,594 ÷ 10 periods) |

The combined entry to record the first interest payment and the amortization of the discount is as follows:

| 2015 | | | | | |
|---|---|---|---|---|---|
| June | 30 | Interest Expense | 6,359.40 | |
| | | Discount on Bonds Payable | | 359.40 |
| | | Cash | | 6,000.00 |
| | | Paid semiannual interest and | | |
| | | amortized $^{1}/_{10}$ of bond discount. | | |

The preceding entry is made on each interest payment date. Thus, the amount of the semiannual interest expense on the bonds ($6,359.40) remains the same over the life of the bonds.

The effect of the discount amortization is to increase the interest expense from $6,000.00 to $6,359.40 on every semiannual interest payment date. In effect, this increases the contract rate of interest from 12% to a rate of interest that approximates the market rate of 13%. In addition, as the discount is amortized, the carrying amount of the bonds increases until it equals the face amount of the bonds on the maturity date.

**Example Exercise 14-4  Discount Amortization**   OBJ 3

Using the bond from Example Exercise 14-3, Journalize the first interest payment and the amortization of the related bond discount.

**Follow My Example 14-4**

| | | |
|---|---|---|
| Interest Expense ................................................ | 36,358 | |
| Discount on Bonds Payable ............................................ | | 6,358 |
| Cash ...................................................... | | 30,000 |
| Paid interest and amortized the bond discount ($63,580 ÷ 10). | | |

Practice Exercises: PE 14-4A, PE 14-4B

## Bonds Issued at a Premium

If the market rate of interest is less than the contract rate of interest, the bonds will sell for more than their face amount. This is because investors are willing to pay more for bonds that pay a higher contract rate of interest than the rate they could earn on similar bonds (market rate).

**Note:**
Bonds will sell at a premium when the market rate of interest is less than the contract rate.

To illustrate, assume that on January 1, 2015, Northern Idaho Transportation Inc. issued the following bonds:

| | |
|---|---|
| Face amount ................................. | $100,000 |
| Contract rate of interest ..................... | 12% |
| Interest paid semiannually on | |
| June 30 and December 31. | |
| Term of bonds ............................. | 5 years |
| Market rate of interest ....................... | 11% |

Because the contract rate of interest is more than the market rate of interest, the bonds will sell for more than their face amount. Assuming the bonds sell for $103,769, the entry to record the issuance of the bonds is as follows:

| 2015 Jan. | 1 | Cash | 103,769 | |
|---|---|---|---|---|
| | | Bonds Payable | | 100,000 |
| | | Premium on Bonds Payable | | 3,769 |
| | | Issued $100,000 bonds at a premium. | | |

The $3,769 premium is the extra amount investors are willing to pay for bonds that have a higher contract rate of interest (12%) than the market rate (11%). The premium is the market's way of adjusting the contract rate of interest to the lower market rate of interest.

The account, Premium on Bonds Payable, has a normal credit balance. It is added to Bonds Payable to determine the carrying amount (or book value) of the bonds payable. Thus, after the preceding entry, the carrying amount of the bonds payable is $103,769 ($100,000 + $3,769).

## Example Exercise 14-5 Issuing Bonds at a Premium

OBJ 3

On the first day of the fiscal year, a company issues a $2,000,000, 12%, five-year bond that pays semiannual interest of $120,000 ($2,000,000 × 12% × ½), receiving cash of $2,154,440. Journalize the bond issuance.

### Follow My Example 14-5

| Cash ........................................................ | 2,154,440 | |
|---|---|---|
| Premium on Bonds Payable ................................ | | 154,440 |
| Bonds Payable ............................................. | | 2,000,000 |

Practice Exercises: PE 14-5A, PE 14-5B

## Amortizing a Bond Premium

Like bond discounts, a bond premium must be amortized over the life of the bond. The amortization of a bond premium decreases the contract rate of interest on a bond to the market rate of interest that existed on the date the bonds were issued. The amortization can be computed using either the straight-line or the effective interest rate method. The entry to amortize a bond premium is as follows:

| | | Premium on Bonds Payable | XXX | |
|---|---|---|---|---|
| | | Interest Expense | | XXX |

The preceding entry may be made annually as an adjusting entry, or it may be combined with the semiannual interest payment. In the latter case, it would be:

| | | Interest Expense | XXX | |
|---|---|---|---|---|
| | | Premium on Bonds Payable | XXX | |
| | | Cash (amount of semiannual interest) | | XXX |

To illustrate, amortization of the preceding premium of $3,769 is computed as follows using the straight-line method:

| | |
|---|---|
| Premium on bonds payable................... | $3,769 |
| Term of bonds............................... | 5 years |
| Semiannual amortization .................... | $376.90 ($3,769 ÷ 10 periods) |

The combined entry to record the first interest payment and the amortization of the premium is as follows:

| | | | | | |
|---|---|---|---|---|---|
| 2015 | | | | | |
| June | 30 | Interest Expense | | 5,623.10 | |
| | | Premium on Bonds Payable | | 376.90 | |
| | | Cash | | | 6,000.00 |
| | | Paid semiannual interest and amortized ¹/₁₀ of bond premium. | | | |

The preceding entry is made on each interest payment date. Thus, the amount of the semiannual interest expense ($5,623.10) on the bonds remains the same over the life of the bonds.

The effect of the premium amortization is to decrease the interest expense from $6,000.00 to $5,623.10. In effect, this decreases the rate of interest from 12% to a rate of interest that approximates the market rate of 11%. In addition, as the premium is amortized, the carrying amount of the bonds decreases until it equals the face amount of bonds on the maturity date.

## Example Exercise 14-6  Premium Amortization

OBJ 3

Using the bond from Example Exercise 14-5, journalize the first interest payment and the amortization of the related bond premium.

### Follow My Example 14-6

| | | |
|---|---|---|
| Interest Expense ...................................................... | 104,556 | |
| Premium on Bonds Payable ......................................... | 15,444 | |
| Cash............................................................... | | 120,000 |
| Paid interest and amortized the bond premium ($154,440 ÷ 10). | | |

Practice Exercises: PE 14-6A, PE 14-6B

## Business Connection

### BOND RATINGS

When purchasing bonds, investors are very interested in understanding how likely it is that the bond issuer will be able to repay the bond principal and associated interest. To help them assess this likelihood, independent rating agencies review and grade the financial condition of companies that issue bonds. For example, the Standard & Poor's rating agency rates bonds on a scale from D (lowest) to AAA (highest). Bonds with a rating of BBB- or higher are called *investment*

*grade* because they are issued by companies in sound financial condition and are considered to be reasonably safe investments. Bonds issued by companies in relatively weak financial condition receive ratings below BBB-, reflecting the higher potential for default or nonpayment. These lesser quality bonds are referred to as *non-investment grade* or *junk* bonds. The market rate of interest on junk bonds is much higher than the market rate on investment grade bonds, which compensates bond investors for junk bonds' higher risk of default.

## Bond Redemption

A corporation may redeem or call bonds before they mature. This is often done when the market rate of interest declines below the contract rate of interest. In such cases, the corporation may issue new bonds at a lower interest rate and use the proceeds to redeem the original bond issue.

*Callable bonds* can be redeemed by the issuing corporation within the period of time and at the price stated in the bond indenture. Normally, the call price is above the face value. A corporation may also redeem its bonds by purchasing them on the open market.[4]

A corporation usually redeems its bonds at a price different from the carrying amount (or book value) of the bonds. A gain or loss may be realized on a bond redemption as follows:

- A *gain* is recorded if the price paid for redemption is below the bond carrying amount.
- A *loss* is recorded if the price paid for the redemption is above the carrying amount.

Gains and losses on the redemption of bonds are reported in the *Other income (loss)* section of the income statement.

To illustrate, assume that on June 30, 2015, a corporation has the following bond issue:

| | |
|---|---|
| Face amount of bonds | $100,000 |
| Premium on bonds payable | 4,000 |

On June 30, 2015, the corporation redeemed one-fourth ($25,000) of these bonds in the market for $24,000. The entry to record the redemption is as follows:

| | | | | | |
|---|---|---|---|---|---|
| 2015 | | | | | |
| June | 30 | Bonds Payable | | 25,000 | |
| | | Premium on Bonds Payable | | 1,000 | |
| | | Cash | | | 24,000 |
| | | Gain on Redemption of Bonds | | | 2,000 |
| | | Redeemed $25,000 bonds for $24,000. | | | |

In the preceding entry, only the portion of the premium related to the redeemed bonds ($4,000 × 25% = $1,000) is written off. The difference between the carrying amount of the bonds redeemed, $26,000 ($25,000 + $1,000), and the redemption price, $24,000, is recorded as a gain.

Assume that the corporation calls the remaining $75,000 of outstanding bonds, which are held by a private investor, for $79,500 on July 1, 2015. The entry to record the redemption is as follows:

| | | | | | |
|---|---|---|---|---|---|
| 2015 | | | | | |
| July | 1 | Bonds Payable | | 75,000 | |
| | | Premium on Bonds Payable | | 3,000 | |
| | | Loss on Redemption of Bonds | | 1,500 | |
| | | Cash | | | 79,500 |
| | | Redeemed $75,000 bonds for $79,500. | | | |

---

### Example Exercise 14-7 Redemption of Bonds Payable

OBJ 3

A $500,000 bond issue on which there is an unamortized discount of $40,000 is redeemed for $475,000. Journalize the redemption of the bonds.

---

[4] Some bond indentures require the corporation issuing the bonds to transfer cash to a special cash fund, called a *sinking fund,* over the life of the bond. Such funds help assure investors that there will be adequate cash to pay the bonds at their maturity date.

**Follow My Example 14-7** ▶▶

| | | |
|---|---|---|
| Bonds Payable ....................................................... | 500,000 | |
| Loss on Redemption of Bonds ..................................... | 15,000 | |
| Discount on Bonds Payable ...................................... | | 40,000 |
| Cash ................................................................. | | 475,000 |

Practice Exercises: PE 14-7A, PE 14-7B

# Installment Notes

**OBJ 4** Describe and illustrate the accounting for installment notes.

Corporations often finance their operations by issuing bonds payable. As an alternative, corporations may issue a different kind of notes payable called installment notes. An **installment note** is a debt that requires the borrower to make equal periodic payments to the lender for the term of the note. Unlike bonds, each note payment includes the following:

- Payment of a portion of the amount initially borrowed, called the *principal*
- Payment of interest on the outstanding balance

At the end of the note's term, the principal will have been repaid in full.

Installment notes are often used to purchase specific assets such as equipment, and are often secured by the purchased asset. When a note is secured by an asset, it is called a **mortgage note**. If the borrower fails to pay a mortgage note, the lender has the right to take possession of the pledged asset and sell it to pay off the debt. Mortgage notes are typically issued by an individual bank.

 Individuals typically use mortgage notes when buying a house or car.

## Issuing an Installment Note

When an installment note is issued, an entry is recorded debiting Cash and crediting Notes Payable. To illustrate, assume that Lewis Company issues the following installment note to City National Bank on January 1, 2015:

| | |
|---|---|
| Principal amount of note .......................... | $24,000 |
| Interest rate ....................................... | 6% |
| Term of note ....................................... | 5 years |
| Annual payments .................................. | $5,698[5] |

The entry to record the issuance of the note is as follows:

| 2015 | | | | | |
|---|---|---|---|---|---|
| Jan. | 1 | Cash | | 24,000 | |
| | | Notes Payable | | | 24,000 |
| | | Issued installment note for cash. | | | |

## Annual Payments

The preceding note payable requires Lewis Company to repay the principal and interest in equal payments of $5,698 beginning December 31, 2015, for each of the next five years. Unlike bonds, however, each installment note payment includes an interest and principal component.

The interest portion of an installment note payment is computed by multiplying the interest rate by the carrying amount (book value) of the note at the beginning of the period. The principal portion of the payment is then computed as the difference between the total installment note payment (cash paid) and the interest component. These computations are illustrated in Exhibit 4 (rounded to the nearest dollar).

[5] The amount of the annual payment is calculated by using the present value concepts discussed in Appendix 1 at the end of this chapter. The annual payment of $5,698 is computed by dividing the $24,000 loan amount by the present value of an annuity of $1 for five periods at 6% (4.21236) from Exhibit 10 (rounded to the nearest dollar).

| EXHIBIT 4 | **Amortization of Installment Notes** |
| --- | --- |

| | A | B | C | D | E |
| --- | --- | --- | --- | --- | --- |
| **For the Year Ending** | **January 1 Carrying Amount** | **Note Payment (cash paid)** | **Interest Expense (6% of January 1 Note Carrying Amount)** | **Decrease in Notes Payable (B – C)** | **December 31 Carrying Amount (A – D)** |
| December 31, 2015 | $24,000 | $ 5,698 | $ 1,440 (6% of $24,000) | $ 4,258 | $19,742 |
| December 31, 2016 | 19,742 | 5,698 | 1,185 (6% of $19,742) | 4,513 | 15,229 |
| December 31, 2017 | 15,229 | 5,698 | 914 (6% of $15,229) | 4,784 | 10,445 |
| December 31, 2018 | 10,445 | 5,698 | 627 (6% of $10,445) | 5,071 | 5,374 |
| December 31, 2019 | 5,374 | 5,698 | 324* (6% of $5,374) | 5,374 | 0 |
| | | **$28,490** | **$4,490** | **$24,000** | |

*Rounded ($5,374 – $5,698).

1. The January 1, 2015, carrying value (Column A) equals the amount borrowed from the bank. The January 1 balance in the following years equals the December 31 balance from the prior year.

2. The note payment (Column B) remains constant at $5,698, the annual cash payment required by the bank.

3. The interest expense (Column C) is computed at 6% of the installment note carrying amount at the beginning of each year. As a result, the interest expense decreases each year.

4. Notes payable decreases each year by the amount of the principal repayment (Column D). The principal repayment is computed by subtracting the interest expense (Column C) from the total payment (Column B). The principal repayment (Column D) increases each year as the interest expense decreases (Column C).

5. The carrying amount on December 31 (Column E) of the note decreases from $24,000, the initial amount borrowed, to $0 at the end of the five years.

The entry to record the first payment on December 31, 2015, is as follows:

| 2015 Dec. | 31 | Interest Expense | 1,440 | |
| --- | --- | --- | --- | --- |
| | | Notes Payable | 4,258 | |
| | | Cash | | 5,698 |
| | | Paid principal and interest on installment note. | | |

The entry to record the second payment on December 31, 2016, is as follows:

| 2016 Dec. | 31 | Interest Expense | 1,185 | |
| --- | --- | --- | --- | --- |
| | | Notes Payable | 4,513 | |
| | | Cash | | 5,698 |
| | | Paid principal and interest on installment note. | | |

As the prior entries show, the cash payment is the same in each year. The interest and principal repayment, however, change each year. This is because the carrying amount (book value) of the note decreases each year as principal is repaid, which decreases the interest component the next period.

The entry to record the final payment on December 31, 2019, is as follows:

| 2019 Dec. | 31 | Interest Expense | 324 | |
| --- | --- | --- | --- | --- |
| | | Notes Payable | 5,374 | |
| | | Cash | | 5,698 |
| | | Paid principal and interest on installment note. | | |

After the final payment, the carrying amount on the note is zero, indicating that the note has been paid in full. Any assets that secure the note would then be released by the bank.

---

**Example Exercise 14-8  Journalizing Installment Notes**

On the first day of the fiscal year, a company issues a $30,000, 10%, five-year installment note that has annual payments of $7,914. The first note payment consists of $3,000 of interest and $4,914 of principal repayment.

a.  Journalize the entry to record the issuance of the installment note.

b.  Journalize the first annual note payment.

**Follow My Example 14-8**

    a.
    Cash ...................................................... 30,000
        Notes Payable .........................................         30,000

    b.
    Interest Expense........................................... 3,000
    Notes Payable............................................. 4,914
        Cash...................................................         7,914

Practice Exercises: PE 14-8A, PE 14-8B

---

## Integrity, Objectivity, and Ethics in Business

**THE RATINGS GAME**

In February 2013, the United States Justice Department filed a lawsuit against the three main credit rating agencies (Moody's, Standard & Poor's, and Fitch) for inflating their ratings on highly risk bond issuances between 2004 and 2007. During this time period, the three ratings agencies gave their highest rating (AAA) to debt securities that were, in fact, highly risky. During the financial crisis of 2008, most of these bonds experienced significant drops in value, leaving investors with huge losses. The Justice Department lawsuit alleges that the ratings agencies were aware of the high risks associated with these bonds but inflated their ratings because of the large fee they received for providing a rating on these bonds. At the time of this writing, the lawsuit was pending.

Source: "U.S. vs. S&P: The Rating Game," *The Chicago Tribune*, February 6, 2013.

---

## Reporting Long-Term Liabilities

 Describe and illustrate the reporting of long-term liabilities, including bonds and notes payable.

Bonds payable and notes payable are reported as liabilities on the balance sheet. Any portion of the bonds or notes that is due within one year is reported as a current liability. Any remaining bonds or notes are reported as a long-term liability.

Any unamortized premium is reported as an addition to the face amount of the bonds. Any unamortized discount is reported as a deduction from the face amount of the bonds. A description of the bonds and notes should also be reported either on the face of the financial statements or in the accompanying notes.

The reporting of bonds and notes payable for **Mornin' Joe** follows:

| Mornin' Joe<br>Balance Sheet<br>December 31, 2016 | | |
|---|---|---|
| Current liabilities: | | |
| Accounts payable | $133,000 | |
| Notes payable (current portion) | 200,000 | |
| Salaries and wages payable | 42,000 | |
| Payroll taxes payable | 16,400 | |
| Interest payable | 40,000 | |
| Total current liabilities | | $ 431,400 |
| Long-term liabilities: | | |
| Bonds payable, 8%, due December 31, 2030 | $500,000 | |
| Less unamortized discount | 16,000 | $ 484,000 |
| Notes payable | | 1,400,000 |
| Total long-term liabilities | | $1,884,000 |
| Total liabilities | | $2,315,400 |

**OBJ 6** Describe and illustrate how the number of times interest charges are earned is used to evaluate a company's financial condition.

# Financial Analysis and Interpretation: Number of Times Interest Charges Are Earned

As we have discussed, the assets of a company are subject to the (1) claims of creditors and (2) the rights of owners. As creditors, bondholders are primarily concerned with the company's ability to make its periodic interest payments and repay the face amount of the bonds at maturity.

Analysts assess the risk that bondholders will not receive their interest payments by computing the **number of times interest charges are earned** during the year as follows:

$$\text{Number of Times Interest Charges Are Earned} = \frac{\text{Income Before Income Tax} + \text{Interest Expense}}{\text{Interest Expense}}$$

This ratio computes the number of times interest payments could be paid out of current period earnings, measuring the company's ability to make its interest payments. Because interest payments reduce income tax expense, the ratio is computed using income before tax.

To illustrate, the following data were taken from a recent annual report of The Coca-Cola Company (in thousands):

| | |
|---|---|
| Interest expense | $ 733,000 |
| Income before income tax | 14,243,000 |

The number of times interest charges are earned for The Coca-Cola Company is computed as follows:

$$\text{Number of Times Interest Charges Are Earned} = \frac{\$14,243,000 + \$733,000}{\$733,000} = 20.43$$

Compare this to the number of times interest charges are earned for United Continental Holdings (an airline), and Verizon Communications (a telecommunications company) which follow (in thousands):

|  | Coca-Cola | United Continental | Verizon Communications |
|---|---|---|---|
| Interest expense | $733,000 | $783,000 | $2,523,000 |
| Income before income tax expense | $14,243,000 | $250,000 | $12,684,000 |
| Number of times interest charges are earned | 20.43 | 1.32 | 6.03 |

Coca-Cola's number of times interest charges are earned is 20.43, indicating that the company generates enough income before taxes to pay (cover) its interest payments 20.43 times. As a result, debtholders have extremely good protection in the event of an earnings decline. Compare this to United Continental, which only generates enough income before taxes to pay (cover) its interest payments 1.32 times. A small decrease in United Continental's earnings could jeopardize the payment of interest. Verizon Communications falls in between, with a ratio of 6.03.

## Example Exercise 14-9 Number of Times Interest Charges Are Earned

Harris Industries reported the following on the company's income statement in 2016 and 2015:

|  | 2016 | 2015 |
|---|---|---|
| Interest expense | $ 200,000 | $180,000 |
| Income before income tax expense | 1,000,000 | 720,000 |

a. Determine the number of times interest charges were earned for 2016 and 2015.
b. Is the number of times interest charges are earned improving or declining?

## Follow My Example 14-9

a. 2016:

$$\text{Number of times interest charges are earned: } \frac{\$1,000,000 + \$200,000}{\$200,000} = 6.0$$

2015:

$$\text{Number of times interest charges are earned: } \frac{\$720,000 + \$180,000}{\$180,000} = 5.0$$

b. The number of times interest charges are earned has increased from 5.0 in 2015 to 6.0 in 2016. Thus, the debtholders have improved confidence in the company's ability to make its interest payments.

Practice Exercises: PE 14-9A, PE 14-9B

# APPENDIX 1

# Present Value Concepts and Pricing Bonds Payable

When a corporation issues bonds, the price that investors are willing to pay for the bonds depends on the following:

- The face amount of the bonds, which is the amount due at the maturity date.
- The periodic interest to be paid on the bonds.
- The market rate of interest.

An investor determines how much to pay for the bonds by computing the present value of the bond's future cash receipts, using the market rate of interest. A bond's future cash receipts include its face value at maturity and the periodic interest payments.

## Present Value Concepts

The concept of present value is based on the time value of money. The *time value of money concept* recognizes that cash received today is worth more than the same amount of cash to be received in the future.

To illustrate, what would you rather have: $1,000 today or $1,000 one year from now? You would rather have the $1,000 today because it could be invested to earn interest. For example, if the $1,000 could be invested to earn 10% per year, the $1,000 will accumulate to $1,100 ($1,000 plus $100 interest) in one year. In this sense, you can think of the $1,000 in hand today as the **present value** of $1,100 to be received a year from today. This present value is illustrated in Exhibit 5.

---

**EXHIBIT 5**    **Present Value and Future Value**

Present value of $1,100
to be received one
year from today

Future value of $1,000
received one
year ago

$1,000    (Interest rate of 10%)    $1,100

Jan. 1, 2015

Dec. 31, 2015

---

A related concept to present value is **future value**. To illustrate, using the preceding example illustrated in Exhibit 5, the $1,100 to be received on December 31, 2015, is the *future value* of $1,000 on January 1, 2015, assuming an interest rate of 10%.

**Present Value of an Amount**    To illustrate the present value of an amount, assume that $1,000 is to be received in one year. If the market rate of interest is 10%, the present value of the $1,000 is $909.09 ($1,000 ÷ 1.10). This present value is illustrated in Exhibit 6.

---

**EXHIBIT 6**    **Present Value of an Amount to Be Received in One Year**

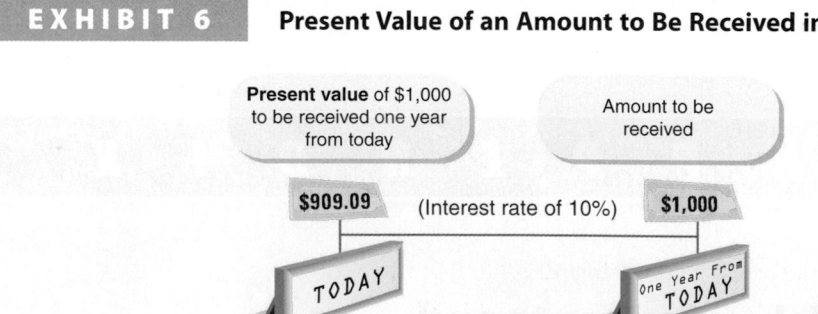

Present value of $1,000
to be received one year
from today

Amount to be
received

$909.09    (Interest rate of 10%)    $1,000

TODAY

One Year From
TODAY

---

If the $1,000 is to be received in two years, with interest of 10% compounded at the end of the first year, the present value is $826.45 ($909.09 ÷ 1.10).[6] This present value is illustrated in Exhibit 7.

[6] Note that the future value of $826.45 in two years, at an interest rate of 10% compounded annually, is $1,000.

**EXHIBIT 7**      **Present Value of an Amount to Be Received in Two Years**

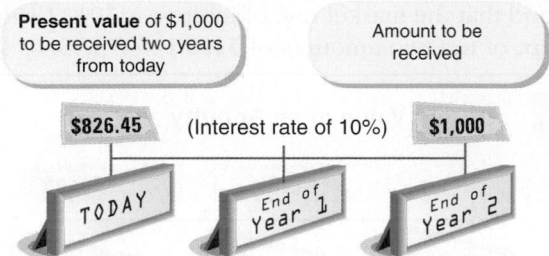

The present value of an amount to be received in the future can be determined by a series of divisions as illustrated in Exhibits 5, 6, and 7. In practice, however, it is easier to use a table of present values.

The *present value of $1* table is used to find the present value factor for $1 to be received after a number of periods in the future. The amount to be received is then multiplied by this factor to determine its present value.

To illustrate, Exhibit 8 is a partial table of the present value of $1.[7] Exhibit 8 indicates that the present value of $1 to be received in two years with a market rate of interest of 10% a year is 0.82645. Multiplying $1,000 to be received in two years by 0.82645 yields $826.45 ($1,000 × 0.82645). This amount is the same amount computed earlier. In Exhibit 8, the Periods column represents the number of compounding periods, and the percentage columns represent the compound interest rate per period. Thus, the present value factor from Exhibit 8 for 12% for five years is 0.56743. If the interest is compounded semiannually, the interest rate is 6% (12% ÷ 2), and the number of periods is 10 (5 years × 2 times per year). Thus, the present value factor from Exhibit 8 for 6% and 10 periods is 0.55839.

 Spreadsheet software and business calculators have built-in present value functions that can also be used to calculate present values.

**EXHIBIT 8**      **Present Value of $1 at Compound Interest**

| Periods | 4% | 4½% | 5% | 5½% | 6% | 6½% | 7% | 10% | 11% | 12% | 13% |
|---|---|---|---|---|---|---|---|---|---|---|---|
| 1 | 0.96154 | 0.956940 | 0.95238 | 0.94787 | 0.94340 | 0.93897 | 0.93458 | 0.90909 | 0.90090 | 0.89286 | 0.88496 |
| 2 | 0.92456 | 0.915730 | 0.90703 | 0.89845 | 0.89000 | 0.88166 | 0.87344 | 0.82645 | 0.81162 | 0.79719 | 0.78315 |
| 3 | 0.88900 | 0.876300 | 0.86384 | 0.85161 | 0.83962 | 0.82785 | 0.81630 | 0.75131 | 0.73119 | 0.71178 | 0.69305 |
| 4 | 0.85480 | 0.838560 | 0.82270 | 0.80722 | 0.79209 | 0.77732 | 0.76290 | 0.68301 | 0.65873 | 0.63552 | 0.61332 |
| 5 | 0.82193 | 0.802450 | 0.78353 | 0.76513 | 0.74726 | 0.72988 | 0.71299 | 0.62092 | 0.59345 | 0.56743 | 0.54276 |
| 6 | 0.79031 | 0.767900 | 0.74622 | 0.72525 | 0.70496 | 0.68533 | 0.66634 | 0.56447 | 0.53464 | 0.50663 | 0.48032 |
| 7 | 0.75992 | 0.734830 | 0.71068 | 0.68744 | 0.66506 | 0.64351 | 0.62275 | 0.51316 | 0.48166 | 0.45235 | 0.42506 |
| 8 | 0.73069 | 0.703190 | 0.67684 | 0.65160 | 0.62741 | 0.60423 | 0.58201 | 0.46651 | 0.43393 | 0.40388 | 0.37616 |
| 9 | 0.70259 | 0.672900 | 0.64461 | 0.61763 | 0.59190 | 0.56735 | 0.54393 | 0.42410 | 0.39092 | 0.36061 | 0.33288 |
| 10 | 0.67556 | 0.643930 | 0.61391 | 0.58543 | 0.55839 | 0.53273 | 0.50835 | 0.38554 | 0.35218 | 0.32197 | 0.29459 |

Some additional examples using Exhibit 8 follow:

| | Number of Periods | Interest Rate | Present Value of $1 Factor from Exhibit 8 |
|---|---|---|---|
| 10% for *two* years compounded *annually* | 2 | 10% | 0.82645 |
| 10% for *two* years compounded *semiannually* | 4 | 5% | 0.82270 |
| 10% for *three* years compounded *semiannually* | 6 | 5% | 0.74622 |
| 12% for *five* years compounded *semiannually* | 10 | 6% | 0.55839 |

[7] To simplify the illustrations and homework assignments, the tables presented in this chapter are limited to 10 periods for a small number of interest rates, and the amounts are carried to only five decimal places. Computer programs and business function calculators can be used to determine present values for any number of interest rates, decimal places, or periods. More complete interest tables are presented in Appendix A of the text.

**Present Value of the Periodic Receipts** A series of equal cash receipts spaced equally in time is called an **annuity**. The **present value of an annuity** is the sum of the present values of each cash receipt. To illustrate, assume that $100 is to be received annually for two years and that the market rate of interest is 10%. Using Exhibit 8, the present value of the receipt of the two amounts of $100 is $173.55, as shown in Exhibit 9.

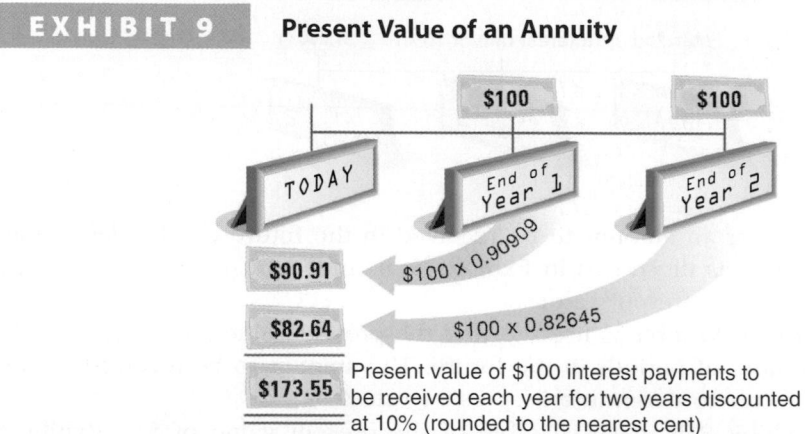

**EXHIBIT 9**  **Present Value of an Annuity**

Present value of $100 interest payments to be received each year for two years discounted at 10% (rounded to the nearest cent)

Instead of using present value of $1 tables to determine the present value of each cash flow separately, such as in Exhibit 8, the present value of an annuity can be computed in a single step. Using a value from the *present value of an annuity of $1* table in Exhibit 10, the present value of the entire annuity can be calculated by multiplying the equal cash payment times the appropriate present value of an annuity of $1.

**EXHIBIT 10**  **Present Value of an Annuity of $1 at Compound Interest**

| Periods | 4% | 4½% | 5% | 5½% | 6% | 6½% | 7% | 10% | 11% | 12% | 13% |
|---|---|---|---|---|---|---|---|---|---|---|---|
| 1 | 0.96154 | 0.95694 | 0.95238 | 0.94787 | 0.94340 | 0.93897 | 0.93458 | 0.90909 | 0.90090 | 0.89286 | 0.88496 |
| 2 | 1.88609 | 1.87267 | 1.85941 | 1.84632 | 1.83339 | 1.82063 | 1.80802 | 1.73554 | 1.71252 | 1.69005 | 1.66810 |
| 3 | 2.77509 | 2.74896 | 2.72325 | 2.69793 | 2.67301 | 2.64848 | 2.62432 | 2.48685 | 2.44371 | 2.40183 | 2.36115 |
| 4 | 3.62990 | 3.58753 | 3.54595 | 3.50515 | 3.46511 | 3.42580 | 3.38721 | 3.16987 | 3.10245 | 3.03735 | 2.97447 |
| 5 | 4.45182 | 4.38998 | 4.32948 | 4.27028 | 4.21236 | 4.15568 | 4.10020 | 3.79079 | 3.69590 | 3.60478 | 3.51723 |
| 6 | 5.24214 | 5.15787 | 5.07569 | 4.99553 | 4.91732 | 4.84101 | 4.76654 | 4.35526 | 4.23054 | 4.11141 | 3.99755 |
| 7 | 6.00205 | 5.89270 | 5.78637 | 5.68297 | 5.58238 | 5.48452 | 5.38929 | 4.86842 | 4.71220 | 4.56376 | 4.42261 |
| 8 | 6.73274 | 6.59589 | 6.46321 | 6.33457 | 6.20979 | 6.08875 | 5.97130 | 5.33493 | 5.14612 | 4.96764 | 4.79677 |
| 9 | 7.43533 | 7.26879 | 7.10782 | 6.95220 | 6.80169 | 6.65610 | 6.51523 | 5.75902 | 5.53705 | 5.32825 | 5.13166 |
| 10 | 8.11090 | 7.91272 | 7.72173 | 7.53763 | 7.36009 | 7.18883 | 7.02358 | 6.14457 | 5.88923 | 5.65022 | 5.42624 |

To illustrate, the present value of $100 to be received at the end of each of the next two years at 10% compound interest per period is $173.55 ($100 × 1.73554). This amount is the same amount computed previously using the present value of $1.

## Pricing Bonds

The selling price of a bond is the sum of the present values of:

• The face amount of the bonds due at the maturity date
• The periodic interest to be paid on the bonds

The market rate of interest is used to compute the present value of both the face amount and the periodic interest.

To illustrate the pricing of bonds, assume that Southern Utah Communications Inc. issued the following bond on January 1, 2015:

| | |
|---|---|
| Face amount ................................................................ | $100,000 |
| Contract rate of interest ............................................... | 12% |
| Interest paid semiannually on June 30 and December 31. | |
| Term of bonds................................................................ | 5 years |

**Market Rate of Interest of 12%** Assuming a market rate of interest of 12%, the bonds would sell for their face amount. As shown by the following present value computations, the bonds would sell for $100,000:

Present value of face amount of $100,000 due in five years,
    at 12% compounded semiannually: $100,000 × 0.55839
      (present value of $1 for 10 periods at 6% from Exhibit 8).................................    $ 55,839
Present value of 10 semiannual interest payments of $6,000,
    at 12% compounded semiannually: $6,000 × 7.36009
      (present value of an annuity of $1 for 10 periods at 6% from Exhibit 10)...................    44,161
Total present value of bonds.........................................................................    $100,000

**Market Rate of Interest of 13%** Assuming a market rate of interest of 13%, the bonds would sell at a discount. As shown by the following present value computations, the bonds would sell for $96,406:[8]

Present value of face amount of $100,000 due in five years,
    at 13% compounded semiannually: $100,000 × 0.53273
      (present value of $1 for 10 periods at 6½% from Exhibit 8).................................    $53,273
Present value of 10 semiannual interest payments of $6,000,
    at 13% compounded semiannually: $6,000 × 7.18883
      (present value of an annuity of $1 for 10 periods at 6½% from Exhibit 10).................    43,133
Total present value of bonds.........................................................................    $96,406

**Market Rate of Interest of 11%** Assuming a market rate of interest of 11%, the bonds would sell at a premium. As shown by the following present value computations, the bonds would sell for $103,769:

Present value of face amount of $100,000 due in five years,
    at 11% compounded semiannually: $100,000 × 0.58543
      (present value of $1 for 10 periods at 5½% from Exhibit 8).................................    $ 58,543
Present value of 10 semiannual interest payments of $6,000,
    at 11% compounded semiannually: $6,000 × 7.53763
      (present value of an annuity of $1 for 10 periods at 5½% from Exhibit 10).................    45,226
Total present value of bonds.........................................................................    $103,769

As shown, the selling price of the bond varies with the present value of the bond's face amount at maturity, interest payments, and the market rate of interest.

# A P P E N D I X  2

# Effective Interest Rate Method of Amortization

The effective interest rate method of amortization provides for a constant *rate* of interest over the life of the bonds. As the discount or premium is amortized, the carrying amount of the bonds changes. As a result, interest expense also changes each period. This is in contrast to the straight-line method, which provides for a constant *amount* of interest expense each period.

[8] Some corporations issue bonds called zero-coupon bonds that provide for only the payment of the face amount at maturity. Such bonds sell for large discounts. In this example, such a bond would sell for $53,273, which is the present value of the face amount.

The interest rate used in the effective interest rate method of amortization, sometimes called the *interest method*, is the market rate on the date the bonds are issued. The carrying amount of the bonds is multiplied by this interest rate to determine the interest expense for the period. The difference between the interest expense and the interest payment is the amount of discount or premium to be amortized for the period.

## Amortization of Discount by the Interest Method

To illustrate, the following data taken from the chapter illustration of issuing bonds at a discount are used:

| | |
|---|---:|
| Face value of 12%, five-year bonds, interest compounded semiannually.................... | $100,000 |
| Present value of bonds at effective (market) rate of interest of 13% ........................ | 96,406 |
| Discount on bonds payable........................................................ | $ 3,594 |

Exhibit 11 illustrates the interest method for the preceding bonds. Exhibit 11 begins with six columns. The first column is not lettered. The remaining columns are lettered A through E. The exhibit was then prepared as follows:

- Step 1. List the interest payments dates in the first column, which for the preceding bond are 10 interest payment dates (semiannual interest over five years). Also, list on the first line the initial amount of discount in Column D and the initial carrying amount (selling price) of the bonds in Column E.
- Step 2. List in Column A the semiannual interest payments, which for the preceding bond are $6,000 ($100,000 × 6%).
- Step 3. Compute the interest expense in Column B by multiplying the bond carrying amount at the beginning of each period times 6½%, which is the semiannual effective interest (market) rate (13% ÷ 2).
- Step 4. In Column C, compute the discount to be amortized each period by subtracting the interest payment in Column A ($6,000) from the interest expense for the period shown in Column B.
- Step 5. Compute the remaining unamortized discount by subtracting the amortized discount in Column C for the period from the unamortized discount at the beginning of the period in Column D.
- Step 6. Compute the bond carrying amount at the end of the period by subtracting the unamortized discount at the end of the period in Column D from the face amount of the bonds ($100,000).

Steps 3–6 are repeated for each interest payment.

---

**EXHIBIT 11**   **Amortization of Discount on Bonds Payable**

| Interest Payment Date | A Interest Paid (6% of Face Amount) | B Interest Expense (6½% of Bond Carrying Amount) | C Discount Amortization (B – A) | D Unamortized Discount (D – C) | E Bond Carrying Amount ($100,000 – D) |
|---|---|---|---|---|---|
| | | | | $3,594 | $ 96,406 |
| June 30, 2015 | $6,000 | $6,266 (6½% of $96,406) | $266 | 3,328 | 96,672 |
| Dec. 31, 2015 | 6,000 | 6,284 (6½% of $96,672) | 284 | 3,044 | 96,956 |
| June 30, 2016 | 6,000 | 6,302 (6½% of $96,956) | 302 | 2,742 | 97,258 |
| Dec. 31, 2016 | 6,000 | 6,322 (6½% of $97,258) | 322 | 2,420 | 97,580 |
| June 30, 2017 | 6,000 | 6,343 (6½% of $97,580) | 343 | 2,077 | 97,923 |
| Dec. 31, 2017 | 6,000 | 6,365 (6½% of $97,923) | 365 | 1,712 | 98,288 |
| June 30, 2018 | 6,000 | 6,389 (6½% of $98,288) | 389 | 1,323 | 98,677 |
| Dec. 31, 2018 | 6,000 | 6,414 (6½% of $98,677) | 414 | 909 | 99,091 |
| June 30, 2019 | 6,000 | 6,441 (6½% of $99,091) | 441 | 468 | 99,532 |
| Dec. 31, 2019 | 6,000 | 6,470 (6½% of $99,532) | 468* | — | 100,000 |

*Cannot exceed unamortized discount.

As shown in Exhibit 11, the interest expense increases each period as the carrying amount of the bond increases. Also, the unamortized discount decreases each period to zero at the maturity date. Finally, the carrying amount of the bonds increases from $96,406 to $100,000 (the face amount) at maturity.

The entry to record the first interest payment on June 30, 2015, and the related discount amortization is as follows:

| 2015 | | | | |
|---|---|---|---|---|
| June | 30 | Interest Expense | 6,266 | |
| | | Discount on Bonds Payable | | 266 |
| | | Cash | | 6,000 |
| | | Paid semiannual interest and amortized bond discount for ½ year. | | |

If the amortization is recorded only at the end of the year, the amount of the discount amortized on December 31, 2015, would be $550. This is the sum of the first two semiannual amortization amounts ($266 and $284) from Exhibit 11.

## Amortization of Premium by the Interest Method

To illustrate, the following data taken from the chapter illustration of issuing bonds at a premium are used:

Present value of bonds at effective (market) rate of interest of 11%........................... $103,769
Face value of 12%, five-year bonds, interest compounded semiannually..................... 100,000
Premium on bonds payable....................................................................... $ 3,769

Exhibit 12 illustrates the interest method for the preceding bonds. Exhibit 12 begins with six columns. The first column is not lettered. The remaining columns are lettered A through E. The exhibit was then prepared as follows:

- Step 1. List the number of interest payments in the first column, which for the preceding bond are 10 interest payments (semiannual interest over five years). Also, list on the first line the initial amount of premium in Column D and the initial carrying amount of the bonds in Column E.
- Step 2. List in Column A the semiannual interest payments, which for the preceding bond are $6,000 ($100,000 × 6%).

**EXHIBIT 12**   Amortization of Premium on Bonds Payable

| Interest Payment Date | A<br>Interest Paid<br>(6% of Face<br>Amount) | B<br>Interest Expense<br>(5½% of Bond<br>Carrying Amount) | C<br>Premium<br>Amortization<br>(A – B) | D<br>Unamortized<br>Premium<br>(D – C) | E<br>Bond Carrying<br>Amount<br>($100,000 + D) |
|---|---|---|---|---|---|
| | | | | $3,769 | $103,769 |
| June 30, 2015 | $6,000 | $5,707 (5½% of $103,769) | $293 | 3,476 | 103,476 |
| Dec. 31, 2015 | 6,000 | 5,691 (5½% of $103,476) | 309 | 3,167 | 103,167 |
| June 30, 2016 | 6,000 | 5,674 (5½% of $103,167) | 326 | 2,841 | 102,841 |
| Dec. 31, 2016 | 6,000 | 5,656 (5½% of $102,841) | 344 | 2,497 | 102,497 |
| June 30, 2017 | 6,000 | 5,637 (5½% of $102,497) | 363 | 2,134 | 102,134 |
| Dec. 31, 2017 | 6,000 | 5,617 (5½% of $102,134) | 383 | 1,751 | 101,751 |
| June 30, 2018 | 6,000 | 5,596 (5½% of $101,751) | 404 | 1,347 | 101,347 |
| Dec. 31, 2018 | 6,000 | 5,574 (5½% of $101,347) | 426 | 921 | 100,921 |
| June 30, 2019 | 6,000 | 5,551 (5½% of $100,921) | 449 | 472 | 100,472 |
| Dec. 31, 2019 | 6,000 | 5,526 (5½% of $100,472) | 472* | — | 100,000 |

*Cannot exceed unamortized premium.

- Step 3. Compute the interest expense in Column B by multiplying the bond carrying amount at the beginning of each period times 5½%, which is the semiannual effective interest (market) rate (11% ÷ 2).
- Step 4. In Column C, compute the premium to be amortized each period by subtracting the interest expense for the period shown in Column B from the interest payment in Column A ($6,000).
- Step 5. Compute the remaining unamortized premium by subtracting the amortized premium in Column C for the period from the unamortized premium at the beginning of the period in Column D.
- Step 6. Compute the bond carrying amount at the end of the period by adding the unamortized premium at the end of the period in Column D to the face amount of the bonds ($100,000).

Steps 3–6 are repeated for each interest payment.

As shown in Exhibit 12, the interest expense decreases each period as the carrying amount of the bond decreases. Also, the unamortized premium decreases each period to zero at the maturity date. Finally, the carrying amount of the bonds decreases from $103,769 to $100,000 (the face amount) at maturity.

The entry to record the first interest payment on June 30, 2015, and the related premium amortization is as follows:

| 2015 | | | | | |
|------|----|----------------------------------|-------|-------|
| June | 30 | Interest Expense | 5,707 | |
| | | Premium on Bonds Payable | 293 | |
| | | Cash | | 6,000 |
| | | Paid semiannual interest and amortized | | |
| | | bond premium for ½ year. | | |

If the amortization is recorded only at the end of the year, the amount of the premium amortized on December 31, 2015, would be $602. This is the sum of the first two semiannual amortization amounts ($293 and $309) from Exhibit 12.

# At a Glance 14

OBJ
1

**Compute the potential impact of long-term borrowing on earnings per share.**

**Key Points**   Corporations can finance their operations by issuing short-term debt, long-term debt, or equity. One of the many factors that influence a corporation's decision on whether it should issue long-term debt or equity is the effect each alternative has on earnings per share.

| Learning Outcomes | Example Exercises | Practice Exercises |
|-------------------|-------------------|--------------------|
| • Define the concept of a bond. | | |
| • Calculate and compare the effect of alternative long-term financing plans on earnings per share. | EE14-1 | PE14-1A, 14-1B |

## Describe the characteristics and terminology of bonds payable.

**Key Points**    A corporation that issues bonds enters into a contract, or bond indenture.

When a corporation issues bonds, the price that buyers are willing to pay for the bonds depends on (1) the face amount of the bonds, (2) the periodic interest to be paid on the bonds, and (3) the market rate of interest.

| Learning Outcomes | Example Exercises | Practice Exercises |
|---|---|---|
| • Define the characteristics of a bond. | | |
| • Describe the various types of bonds. | | |
| • Describe the factors that determine the price of a bond. | | |

## Journalize entries for bonds payable.

**Key Points**    The journal entry for issuing bonds payable debits Cash and credits Bonds Payable. Any difference between the face amount of the bonds and the selling price is debited to Discount on Bonds Payable or credited to Premium on Bonds Payable when the bonds are issued. The discount or premium on bonds payable is amortized to interest expense over the life of the bonds.

At the maturity date, the entry to record the repayment of the face value of a bond is a debit to Bonds Payable and a credit to Cash.

When a corporation redeems bonds before they mature, Bonds Payable is debited for the face amount of the bonds, the premium (discount) on bonds payable account is debited (credited) for its unamortized balance, Cash is credited, and any gain or loss on the redemption is recorded.

| Learning Outcomes | Example Exercises | Practice Exercises |
|---|---|---|
| • Journalize the issuance of bonds at face value and the payment of periodic interest. | EE14-2 | PE14-2A, 14-2B |
| • Journalize the issuance of bonds at a discount. | EE14-3 | PE14-3A, 14-3B |
| • Journalize the amortization of a bond discount. | EE14-4 | PE14-4A, 14-4B |
| • Journalize the issuance of bonds at a premium. | EE14-5 | PE14-5A, 14-5B |
| • Journalize the amortization of a bond premium. | EE14-6 | PE14-6A, 14-6B |
| • Describe bond redemptions. | | |
| • Journalize the redemption of bonds payable | EE14-7 | PE14-7A, 14-7B |

## Describe and illustrate the accounting for installment notes.

**Key Points**    An installment note requires the borrower to make equal periodic payments to the lender for the term of the note. Unlike bonds, the annual payment in an installment note consists of both principal and interest. The journal entry for the annual payment debits Interest Expense and Notes Payable and credits Cash for the amount of the payment. After the final payment, the carrying amount on the note is zero.

| Learning Outcomes | Example Exercises | Practice Exercises |
|---|---|---|
| • Define the characteristics of an installment note. | | |
| • Journalize the issuance of installment notes. | EE14-8 | PE14-8A, 14-8B |
| • Journalize the annual payment for an installment note. | | |

**Describe and illustrate the reporting of long-term liabilities, including bonds and notes payable.**

**Key Points** Bonds payable and notes payable are usually reported as long-term liabilities. If the balance sheet date is within one year, they are reported as current liabilities. A discount on bonds should be reported as a deduction from the related bonds payable. A premium on bonds should be reported as an addition to related bonds payable.

| Learning Outcome | Example Exercises | Practice Exercises |
|---|---|---|
| • Illustrate the balance sheet presentation of bonds payable and notes payable. | | |

**Describe and illustrate how the number of times interest charges are earned is used to evaluate a company's financial condition.**

**Key Points** The number of times interest charges are earned measures the risk to bondholders that a company will not be able to make its interest payments. It is computed by dividing income before income tax plus interest expense by interest expense. This ratio measures the number of times interest payments could be paid (covered) by current period earnings.

| Learning Outcomes | Example Exercises | Practice Exercises |
|---|---|---|
| • Describe and compute the number of times interest charges are earned. | **EE14-9** | **PE14-9A, 14-9B** |
| • Interpret the number of times interest charges are earned. | | |

# Key Terms

amortization (648)
annuity (660)
bond (642)
bond indenture (645)
carrying amount (648)
contract rate (645)
discount (645)

earnings per share (EPS) (642)
effective interest rate method (648)
effective rate of interest (645)
face amount (645)
future value (658)
installment note (653)

market rate of interest (645)
mortgage notes (653)
number of times interest charges are earned (656)
premium (646)
present value (658)
present value of annuity (660)

# Illustrative Problem

The fiscal year of Russell Inc., a manufacturer of acoustical supplies, ends December 31. Selected transactions for the period 2015 through 2022, involving bonds payable issued by Russell Inc., are as follows:

2015

June 30. Issued $2,000,000 of 25-year, 7% callable bonds dated June 30, 2015, for cash of $1,920,000. Interest is payable semiannually on June 30 and December 31.

Dec. 31. Paid the semiannual interest on the bonds. The bond discount is amortized annually in a separate journal entry.

31. Recorded straight-line amortization of $1,600 of discount on the bonds.

31. Closed the interest expense account.

2016

June 30. Paid the semiannual interest on the bonds. The bond discount is amortized annually in a separate journal entry.

Dec. 31. Paid the semiannual interest on the bonds. The bond discount is amortized annually in a separate journal entry.

31. Recorded straight-line amortization of $3,200 of discount on the bonds.

31. Closed the interest expense account.

2022

June 30. Recorded the redemption of the bonds, which were called at 101.5. The balance in the bond discount account is $57,600 after the payment of interest and amortization of discount have been recorded. (Record the redemption only.)

## Instructions

1. Journalize entries to record the preceding transactions.

2. Determine the amount of interest expense for 2015 and 2016.

3. Determine the carrying amount of the bonds as of December 31, 2016.

## Solution

1.

| | | | | | |
|---|---|---|---|---|---|
| 2015 | | | | | |
| June | 30 | Cash | | 1,920,000 | |
| | | Discount on Bonds Payable | | 80,000 | |
| | | Bonds Payable | | | 2,000,000 |
| Dec. | 31 | Interest Expense | | 70,000 | |
| | | Cash | | | 70,000 |
| | 31 | Interest Expense | | 1,600 | |
| | | Discount on Bonds Payable | | | 1,600 |
| | | Amortization of discount from July 1 to December 31. | | | |
| | 31 | Income Summary | | 71,600 | |
| | | Interest Expense | | | 71,600 |
| 2016 | | | | | |
| June | 30 | Interest Expense | | 70,000 | |
| | | Cash | | | 70,000 |
| Dec. | 31 | Interest Expense | | 70,000 | |
| | | Cash | | | 70,000 |
| | 31 | Interest Expense | | 3,200 | |
| | | Discount on Bonds Payable | | | 3,200 |
| | | Amortization of discount from January 1 to December 31. | | | |
| | 31 | Income Summary | | 143,200 | |
| | | Interest Expense | | | 143,200 |
| 2022 | | | | | |
| June | 30 | Bonds Payable | | 2,000,000 | |
| | | Loss on Redemption of Bonds Payable | | 87,600 | |
| | | Discount on Bonds Payable | | | 57,600 |
| | | Cash | | | 2,030,000 |

2. a. 2015: $71,600 = $70,000 + $1,600

  b. 2016: $143,200 = $70,000 + $70,000 + $3,200

3.
| | |
|---|---:|
| Initial carrying amount of bonds | $1,920,000 |
| Discount amortized on December 31, 2015 | 1,600 |
| Discount amortized on December 31, 2016 | 3,200 |
| Carrying amount of bonds, December 31, 2016 | $1,924,800 |

# Discussion Questions

1. Describe the two distinct obligations incurred by a corporation when issuing bonds.

2. Explain the meaning of each of the following terms as they relate to a bond issue: (a) convertible, and (b) callable.

3. If you asked your broker to purchase for you a 12% bond when the market interest rate for such bonds was 11%, would you expect to pay more or less than the face amount for the bond? Explain.

4. A corporation issues $26,000,000 of 9% bonds to yield interest at the rate of 7%. (a) Was the amount of cash received from the sale of the bonds greater or less than $26,000,000? (b) Identify the following amounts as they relate to the bond issue: (1) face amount, (2) market or effective rate of interest, (3) contract rate of interest, and (4) maturity amount.

5. If bonds issued by a corporation are sold at a discount, is the market rate of interest greater or less than the contract rate?

6. The following data relate to a $2,000,000, 8% bond issued for a selected semiannual interest period:

| | |
|---|---:|
| Bond carrying amount at beginning of period | $2,125,000 |
| Interest paid during period | 160,000 |
| Interest expense allocable to the period | 148,750 |

(a) Were the bonds issued at a discount or at a premium? (b) What is the unamortized amount of the discount or premium account at the beginning of the period? (c) What account was debited to amortize the discount or premium?

7. Bonds Payable has a balance of $5,000,000 and Discount on Bonds Payable has a balance of $150,000. If the issuing corporation redeems the bonds at 98, is there a gain or loss on the bond redemption?

8. What is a mortgage note?

9. Fleeson Company needs additional funds to purchase equipment for a new production facility and is considering either issuing bonds payable or borrowing the money from a local bank in the form of an installment note. How does an installment note differ from a bond payable?

10. In what section of the balance sheet would a bond payable be reported if: (a) it is payable within one year and (b) it is payable beyond one year?

# Practice Exercises

EE 14-1 *p. 644*   **PE 14-1A   Alternative financing plans**   **OBJ. 1**

SHOW
ME HOW

Owen Co. is considering the following alternative financing plans:

| | Plan 1 | Plan 2 |
|---|---:|---:|
| Issue 7% bonds (at face value) | $5,000,000 | $3,400,000 |
| Issue preferred $1 stock, $20 par | — | 3,600,000 |
| Issue common stock, $25 par | 5,000,000 | 3,000,000 |

Income tax is estimated at 40% of income.

Determine the earnings per share of common stock, assuming income before bond interest and income tax is $750,000.

EE 14-1 *p. 644*

SHOW
ME HOW

**PE 14-1B   Alternative financing plans**                                OBJ. 1

Brower Co. is considering the following alternative financing plans:

|                                          | Plan 1      | Plan 2      |
|------------------------------------------|-------------|-------------|
| Issue 10% bonds (at face value)          | $4,000,000  | $2,500,000  |
| Issue preferred $2.50 stock, $25 par     | —           | 3,000,000   |
| Issue common stock, $10 par              | 4,000,000   | 2,500,000   |

Income tax is estimated at 40% of income.

Determine the earnings per share of common stock, assuming income before bond interest and income tax is $2,000,000.

---

EE 14-2 *p. 647*

SHOW
ME HOW

**PE 14-2A   Issuing bonds at face amount**                                OBJ. 3

On January 1, the first day of the fiscal year, a company issues a $500,000, 5%, 10-year bond that pays semiannual interest of $12,500 ($500,000 × 5% × ½ year), receiving cash of $500,000. Journalize the entries to record (a) the issuance of the bonds, (b) the first interest payment on June 30, and (c) the payment of the principal on the maturity date.

---

EE 14-2 *p. 647*

SHOW
ME HOW

**PE 14-2B   Issuing bonds at face amount**                                OBJ. 3

On January 1, the first day of the fiscal year, a company issues a $800,000, 4%, 10-year bond that pays semiannual interest of $16,000 ($800,000 × 4% × ½ year), receiving cash of $800,000. Journalize the entries to record (a) the issuance of the bonds, (b) the first interest payment on June 30, and (c) the payment of the principal on the maturity date.

---

EE 14-3 *p. 648*

SHOW
ME HOW

**PE 14-3A   Issuing bonds at a discount**                                OBJ. 3

On the first day of the fiscal year, a company issues a $1,200,000, 9%, five-year bond that pays semiannual interest of $54,000 ($1,200,000 × 9% × ½), receiving cash of $1,153,670. Journalize the bond issuance.

---

EE 14-3 *p. 648*

SHOW
ME HOW

**PE 14-3B   Issuing bonds at a discount**                                OBJ. 3

On the first day of the fiscal year, a company issues a $3,000,000, 11%, five-year bond that pays semiannual interest of $165,000 ($3,000,000 × 11% × ½), receiving cash of $2,889,599. Journalize the bond issuance.

---

EE 14-4 *p. 649*

SHOW
ME HOW

**PE 14-4A   Discount amortization**                                OBJ. 3

Using the bond from Practice Exercise 14-3A, journalize the first interest payment and the amortization of the related bond discount. Round to the nearest dollar.

---

EE 14-4 *p. 649*

SHOW
ME HOW

**PE 14-4B   Discount amortization**                                OBJ. 3

Using the bond from Practice Exercise 14-3B, journalize the first interest payment and the amortization of the related bond discount. Round to the nearest dollar.

---

EE 14-5 *p. 650*

SHOW
ME HOW

**PE 14-5A   Issuing bonds at a premium**                                OBJ. 3

On the first day of the fiscal year, a company issues a $2,000,000, 8%, five-year bond that pays semiannual interest of $80,000 ($2,000,000 × 8% × ½), receiving cash of $2,170,604. Journalize the bond issuance.

---

EE 14-5 *p. 650*

SHOW
ME HOW

**PE 14-5B   Issuing bonds at a premium**                                OBJ. 3

On the first day of the fiscal year, a company issues an $8,000,000, 11%, five-year bond that pays semiannual interest of $440,000 ($8,000,000 × 11% × ½), receiving cash of $8,308,869. Journalize the bond issuance.

EE 14-6 *p. 651*

### PE 14-6A Premium amortization
OBJ. 3

Using the bond from Practice Exercise 14-5A, journalize the first interest payment and the amortization of the related bond premium. Round to the nearest dollar.

EE 14-6 *p. 651*

### PE 14-6B Premium amortization
OBJ. 3

Using the bond from Practice Exercise 14-5B, journalize the first interest payment and the amortization of the related bond premium. Round to the nearest dollar.

EE 14-7 *p. 652*

### PE 14-7A Redemption of bonds payable
OBJ. 3

A $1,500,000 bond issue on which there is an unamortized discount of $70,100 is redeemed for $1,455,000. Journalize the redemption of the bonds.

EE 14-7 *p. 652*

### PE 14-7B Redemption of bonds payable
OBJ. 3

A $500,000 bond issue on which there is an unamortized premium of $67,000 is redeemed for $490,000. Journalize the redemption of the bonds.

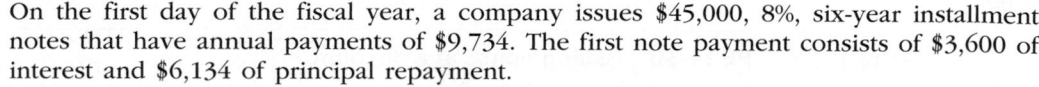

EE 14-8 *p. 655*

### PE 14-8A Journalizing installment notes
OBJ. 4

On the first day of the fiscal year, a company issues $65,000, 6%, five-year installment notes that have annual payments of $15,431. The first note payment consists of $3,900 of interest and $11,531 of principal repayment.

a. Journalize the entry to record the issuance of the installment notes.

b. Journalize the first annual note payment.

EE 14-8 *p. 655*

### PE 14-8B Journalizing installment notes
OBJ. 4

On the first day of the fiscal year, a company issues $45,000, 8%, six-year installment notes that have annual payments of $9,734. The first note payment consists of $3,600 of interest and $6,134 of principal repayment.

a. Journalize the entry to record the issuance of the installment notes.

b. Journalize the first annual note payment.

**FAI**

EE 14-9 *p. 657*

### PE 14-9A Number of times interest charges are earned
OBJ. 6

Berry Company reported the following on the company's income statement in 2016 and 2015:

|  | 2016 | 2015 |
|---|---|---|
| Interest expense | $ 320,000 | $ 300,000 |
| Income before income tax expense | 3,200,000 | 3,600,000 |

a. Determine the number of times interest charges are earned for 2016 and 2015. Round to one decimal place.

b. Is the number of times interest charges are earned improving or declining?

**FAI**

EE 14-9 *p. 657*

### PE 14-9B Number of times interest charges are earned
OBJ. 6

Averill Products Inc. reported the following on the company's income statement in 2016 and 2015:

|  | 2016 | 2015 |
|---|---|---|
| Interest expense | $ 440,000 | $ 400,000 |
| Income before income tax expense | 5,544,000 | 4,400,000 |

a. Determine the number of times interest charges are earned for 2016 and 2015. Round to one decimal place.

b. Is the number of times interest charges are earned improving or declining?

## Exercises

### EX 14-1   Effect of financing on earnings per share   OBJ. 1

Domanico Co., which produces and sells biking equipment, is financed as follows:

| | |
|---|---|
| Bonds payable, 8% (issued at face amount) | $10,000,000 |
| Preferred 5% stock, $10 par | 10,000,000 |
| Common stock, $20 par | 10,000,000 |

Income tax is estimated at 40% of income.

Determine the earnings per share of common stock, assuming that the income before bond interest and income tax is (a) $10,500,000, (b) $11,800,000, and (c) $13,000,000.

### EX 14-2   Evaluate alternative financing plans   OBJ. 1

Based on the data in Exercise 14-1, what factors other than earnings per share should be considered in evaluating these alternative financing plans?

### EX 14-3   Corporate financing   OBJ. 1

The financial statements for Nike, Inc., are presented in Appendix C at the end of the text. What is the major source of financing for Nike?

### EX 14-4   Bond price   OBJ. 3

United States Steel's 7.375% bonds due in 2020 were reported as selling for 103.00.

Were the bonds selling at a premium or at a discount? Why is United States Steel able to sell its bonds at this price?

### EX 14-5   Entries for issuing bonds   OBJ. 3

Gabriel Co. produces and distributes semiconductors for use by computer manufacturers. Gabriel Co. issued $600,000 of 10-year, 8% bonds on May 1 of the current year at face value, with interest payable on May 1 and November 1. The fiscal year of the company is the calendar year. Journalize the entries to record the following selected transactions for the current year:

May   1. Issued the bonds for cash at their face amount.

Nov.   1. Paid the interest on the bonds.

Dec. 31. Recorded accrued interest for two months.

### EX 14-6   Entries for issuing bonds and amortizing discount by straight-line method   OBJ. 2, 3

On the first day of its fiscal year, Pretender Company issued $18,500,000 of five-year, 10% bonds to finance its operations of producing and selling home improvement products. Interest is payable semiannually. The bonds were issued at a market (effective) interest rate of 12%, resulting in Pretender Company receiving cash of $17,138,298.

a. Journalize the entries to record the following:

1. Issuance of the bonds.

2. First semiannual interest payment. The bond discount is combined with the semiannual interest payment. (Round your answer to the nearest dollar.)

3. Second semiannual interest payment. The bond discount is combined with the semiannual interest payment. (Round your answer to the nearest dollar.)

b. Determine the amount of the bond interest expense for the first year.

c. Explain why the company was able to issue the bonds for only $17,138,298 rather than for the face amount of $18,500,000.

SHOW
ME HOW

### EX 14-7 Entries for issuing bonds and amortizing premium by straight-line method OBJ. 2, 3

Lerner Corporation wholesales repair products to equipment manufacturers. On April 1, 2016, Lerner Corporation issued $12,000,000 of five-year, 8% bonds at a market (effective) interest rate of 6%, receiving cash of $13,023,576. Interest is payable semiannually on April 1 and October 1. Journalize the entries to record the following:

a. Issuance of bonds on April 1, 2016.

b. First interest payment on October 1, 2016, and amortization of bond premium for six months, using the straight-line method. (Round to the nearest dollar.)

c. Explain why the company was able to issue the bonds for $13,023,576 rather than for the face amount of $12,000,000.

SHOW
ME HOW

### EX 14-8 Entries for issuing and calling bonds; loss OBJ. 3

Adele Corp., a wholesaler of music equipment, issued $22,000,000 of 20-year, 7% callable bonds on March 1, 2016 at their face amount, with interest payable on March 1 and September 1. The fiscal year of the company is the calendar year. Journalize the entries to record the following selected transactions:

2016

Mar. 1. Issued the bonds for cash at their face amount.

Sept. 1. Paid the interest on the bonds.

2020

Sept. 1. Called the bond issue at 102, the rate provided in the bond indenture. (Omit entry for payment of interest.)

SHOW
ME HOW

### EX 14-9 Entries for issuing and calling bonds; gain OBJ. 3

Emil Corp. produces and sells wind-energy-driven engines. To finance its operations, Emil Corp. issued $15,000,000 of 20-year, 9% callable bonds on May 1, 2016 at their face amount, with interest payable on May 1 and November 1. The fiscal year of the company is the calendar year. Journalize the entries to record the following selected transactions:

2016

May 1. Issued the bonds for cash at their face amount.

Nov. 1. Paid the interest on the bonds.

2022

Nov. 1. Called the bond issue at 96, the rate provided in the bond indenture. (Omit entry for payment of interest.)

SHOW
ME HOW

### EX 14-10 Entries for installment note transactions OBJ. 4

On the first day of the fiscal year, Shiller Company borrowed $85,000 by giving a seven-year, 7% installment note to Soros Bank. The note requires annual payments of $15,772, with the first payment occurring on the last day of the fiscal year. The first payment consists of interest of $5,950 and principal repayment of $9,822.

a. Journalize the entries to record the following:

1. Issued the installment note for cash on the first day of the fiscal year.

2. Paid the first annual payment on the note.

b. Explain how the notes payable would be reported on the balance sheet at the end of the first year.

SHOW
ME HOW

### EX 14-11 Entries for installment note transactions

**OBJ. 4**

On January 1, 2016, Hebron Company issued a $175,000, five-year, 8% installment note to Ventsam Bank. The note requires annual payments of $43,380, beginning on December 31, 2016. Journalize the entries to record the following:

2016

Jan.  1. Issued the note for cash at its face amount.

Dec. 31. Paid the annual payment on the note, which consisted of interest of $14,000 and principal of $29,830.

2019

Dec. 31. Paid the annual payment on the note, included $6,253 of interest. The remainder of the payment reduced the principal balance on the note.

SHOW
ME HOW

### EX 14-12 Entries for installment note transactions

**OBJ. 4**

On January 1, 2016, Bryson Company obtained a $147,750, four-year, 7% installment note from Campbell Bank. The note requires annual payments of $43,620, beginning on December 31, 2016.

a. Prepare an amortization table for this installment note, similar to the one presented in Exhibit 4.

b. Journalize the entries for the issuance of the note and the four annual note payments.

c. Describe how the annual note payment would be reported in the 2016 income statement.

### EX 14-13 Reporting bonds

**OBJ. 5**

At the beginning of the current year, two bond issues (Simmons Industries 7% 20-year bonds and Hunter Corporation 8% 10-year bonds) were outstanding. During the year, the Simmons Industries bonds were redeemed and a significant loss on the redemption of bonds was reported as an extraordinary item on the income statement. At the end of the year, the Hunter Corporation bonds were reported as a noncurrent liability. The maturity date on the Hunter Corporation bonds was early in the following year.

➤ Identify the flaws in the reporting practices related to the two bond issues.

### EX 14-14 Number of times interest charges are earned

**OBJ. 6**

The following data were taken from recent annual reports of **Southwest Airlines**, which operates a low-fare airline service to more than 50 cities in the United States:

|  | Current Year | Preceding Year |
|---|---|---|
| Interest expense | $147,000,000 | $194,000,000 |
| Income before income tax | 685,000,000 | 323,000,000 |

a. Determine the number of times interest charges are earned for the current and preceding years. Round to one decimal place.

b. ➤ What conclusions can you draw?

### EX 14-15 Number of times interest charges are earned

**OBJ. 6**

Loomis, Inc. reported the following on the company's income statement in 2016 and 2015:

|  | 2016 | 2015 |
|---|---|---|
| Interest expense | $ 13,500,000 | $ 16,000,000 |
| Income before income tax expense | 310,500,000 | 432,000,000 |

a. Determine the number of times interest charges were earned for 2016 and 2015. Round to one decimal place.

b. ➤ Is the number of times interest charges are earned improving or declining?

**EX 14-16** **Number of times interest charges are earned**                                   OBJ. 6

Iacouva Company reported the following on the company's income statement for 2016 and 2015:

|                          | 2016        | 2015        |
|--------------------------|-------------|-------------|
| Interest expense         | $5,000,000  | $5,000,000  |
| Income before income tax | 3,500,000   | 6,000,000   |

a. Determine the number of times interest charges are earned for 2016 and 2015. Round to one decimal place.

b. ━━━━▶ What conclusions can you draw?

**Appendix 1**
**EX 14-17** **Present value of amounts due**

Tommy John is going to receive $1,000,000 in three years. The current market rate of interest is 10%.

a. Using the present value of $1 table in Exhibit 8, determine the present value of this amount compounded annually.

b. Why is the present value less than the $1,000,000 to be received in the future?

**Appendix 1**
**EX 14-18** **Present value of an annuity**

Determine the present value of $200,000 to be received at the end of each of four years, using an interest rate of 7%, compounded annually, as follows:

a. By successive computations, using the present value table in Exhibit 8.

b. By using the present value table in Exhibit 10.

c. Why is the present value of the four $200,000 cash receipts less than the $800,000 to be received in the future?

**Appendix 1**
**EX 14-19** **Present value of an annuity**

✔ $40,395,063

On January 1, 2016, you win $50,000,000 in the state lottery. The $50,000,000 prize will be paid in equal installments of $6,250,000 over eight years. The payments will be made on December 31 of each year, beginning on December 31, 2016. If the current interest rate is 5%, determine the present value of your winnings. Use the present value tables in Appendix A.

**Appendix 1**
**EX 14-20** **Present value of an annuity**

Assume the same data as in Exercise 14–19, except that the current interest rate is 12%.

━━━━▶ Will the present value of your winnings using an interest rate of 12% be more than the present value of your winnings using an interest rate of 5%? Why or why not?

**Appendix 1**
**EX 14-21** **Present value of bonds payable; discount**

Pinder Co. produces and sells high-quality video equipment. To finance its operations, Pinder Co. issued $25,000,000 of five-year, 7% bonds, with interest payable semiannually, at a market (effective) interest rate of 9%. Determine the present value of the bonds payable, using the present value tables in Exhibits 8 and 10. Round to the nearest dollar.

**Appendix 1**
**EX 14-22** **Present value of bonds payable; premium**

✔ $45,323,443

Moss Co. issued $42,000,000 of five-year, 11% bonds, with interest payable semiannually, at a market (effective) interest rate of 9%. Determine the present value of the bonds payable using the present value tables in Exhibits 8 and 10. Round to the nearest dollar.

**Appendix 2**
**EX 14-23 Amortize discount by interest method**

✔ b. $3,923,959

On the first day of its fiscal year, Ebert Company issued $50,000,000 of 10-year, 7% bonds to finance its operations. Interest is payable semiannually. The bonds were issued at a market (effective) interest rate of 9%, resulting in Ebert Company receiving cash of $43,495,895. The company uses the interest method.

a. Journalize the entries to record the following:

1. Sale of the bonds.

2. First semiannual interest payment, including amortization of discount. Round to the nearest dollar.

3. Second semiannual interest payment, including amortization of discount. Round to the nearest dollar.

b. Compute the amount of the bond interest expense for the first year.

c. Explain why the company was able to issue the bonds for only $43,495,895 rather than for the face amount of $50,000,000.

**Appendix 2**
**EX 14-24 Amortize premium by interest method**

✔ b. $1,662,619

Shunda Corporation wholesales parts to appliance manufacturers. On January 1, 2016, Shunda Corporation issued $22,000,000 of five-year, 9% bonds at a market (effective) interest rate of 7%, receiving cash of $23,829,684. Interest is payable semiannually. Shunda Corporation's fiscal year begins on January 1. The company uses the interest method.

a. Journalize the entries to record the following:

1. Sale of the bonds.

2. First semiannual interest payment, including amortization of premium. Round to the nearest dollar.

3. Second semiannual interest payment, including amortization of premium. Round to the nearest dollar.

b. Determine the bond interest expense for the first year.

c. Explain why the company was able to issue the bonds for $23,829,684 rather than for the face amount of $22,000,000.

**Appendix 1 and Appendix 2**
**EX 14-25 Compute bond proceeds, amortizing premium by interest method, and interest expense**

✔ a. $37,702,483
✔ c. $225,620

Ware Co. produces and sells motorcycle parts. On the first day of its fiscal year, Ware Co. issued $35,000,000 of five-year, 12% bonds at a market (effective) interest rate of 10%, with interest payable semiannually. Compute the following, presenting figures used in your computations:

a. The amount of cash proceeds from the sale of the bonds. Use the tables of present values in Exhibits 8 and 10. Round to the nearest dollar.

b. The amount of premium to be amortized for the first semiannual interest payment period, using the interest method. Round to the nearest dollar.

c. The amount of premium to be amortized for the second semiannual interest payment period, using the interest method. Round to the nearest dollar.

d. The amount of the bond interest expense for the first year.

**Appendix 1 and Appendix 2**
**EX 14-26 Compute bond proceeds, amortizing discount by interest method, and interest expense**

✔ a. $71,167,524
✔ b. $670,051

Boyd Co. produces and sells aviation equipment. On the first day of its fiscal year, Boyd Co. issued $80,000,000 of five-year, 9% bonds at a market (effective) interest rate of 12%, with interest payable semiannually. Compute the following, presenting figures used in your computations:

*(Continued)*

a. The amount of cash proceeds from the sale of the bonds. Use the tables of present values in Exhibits 8 and 10. Round to the nearest dollar.

b. The amount of discount to be amortized for the first semiannual interest payment period, using the interest method. Round to the nearest dollar.

c. The amount of discount to be amortized for the second semiannual interest payment period, using the interest method. Round to the nearest dollar.

d. The amount of the bond interest expense for the first year.

# Problems: Series A

### PR 14-1A  Effect of financing on earnings per share
OBJ. 1

✔ 1. Plan 3: $1.44

Three different plans for financing an $18,000,000 corporation are under consideration by its organizers. Under each of the following plans, the securities will be issued at their par or face amount, and the income tax rate is estimated at 40% of income:

|  | Plan 1 | Plan 2 | Plan 3 |
|---|---|---|---|
| 8% Bonds | — | — | $ 9,000,000 |
| Preferred 4% stock, $20 par | — | $ 9,000,000 | 4,500,000 |
| Common stock, $10 par | $18,000,000 | 9,000,000 | 4,500,000 |
| Total | $18,000,000 | $18,000,000 | $18,000,000 |

#### Instructions

1. Determine the earnings per share of common stock for each plan, assuming that the income before bond interest and income tax is $2,100,000.

2. Determine the earnings per share of common stock for each plan, assuming that the income before bond interest and income tax is $1,050,000.

3. ➤ Discuss the advantages and disadvantages of each plan.

### PR 14-2A  Bond discount, entries for bonds payable transactions
OBJ. 2, 3

✔ 3. $1,232,685

General Ledger

SHOW
ME HOW

On July 1, 2016, Merideth Industries Inc. issued $28,500,000 of 10-year, 8% bonds at a market (effective) interest rate of 9%, receiving cash of $26,646,292. Interest on the bonds is payable semiannually on December 31 and June 30. The fiscal year of the company is the calendar year.

#### Instructions

1. Journalize the entry to record the amount of cash proceeds from the issuance of the bonds on July 1, 2016.

2. Journalize the entries to record the following:

a. The first semiannual interest payment on December 31, 2016, and the amortization of the bond discount, using the straight-line method. (Round to the nearest dollar.)

b. The interest payment on June 30, 2017, and the amortization of the bond discount, using the straight-line method. (Round to the nearest dollar.)

3. Determine the total interest expense for 2016.

4. Will the bond proceeds always be less than the face amount of the bonds when the contract rate is less than the market rate of interest?

5. (Appendix 1) Compute the price of $26,646,292 received for the bonds by using the present value tables in Appendix A at the end of the text. (Round to the nearest dollar.)

### PR 14-3A  Bond premium, entries for bonds payable transactions
OBJ. 2, 3

✔ 3. $2,600,141

General Ledger

Saverin Inc. produces and sells outdoor equipment. On July 1, 2016, Saverin Inc. issued $62,500,000 of 10-year, 9% bonds at a market (effective) interest rate of 8%, receiving cash of $66,747,178. Interest on the bonds is payable semiannually on December 31 and June 30. The fiscal year of the company is the calendar year.

**Instructions**

1. Journalize the entry to record the amount of cash proceeds from the issuance of the bonds on July 1, 2016.

2. Journalize the entries to record the following:

   a. The first semiannual interest payment on December 31, 2016, and the amortization of the bond premium, using the straight-line method. (Round to the nearest dollar.)

   b. The interest payment on June 30, 2017, and the amortization of the bond premium, using the straight-line method. (Round to the nearest dollar.)

3. Determine the total interest expense for 2016.

4. Will the bond proceeds always be greater than the face amount of the bonds when the contract rate is greater than the market rate of interest?

5. (Appendix 1) Compute the price of 66,747,178 received for the bonds by using the present value tables in Appendix A at the end of the text. (Round to the nearest dollar.)

---

**PR 14-4A** **Entries for bonds payable and installment note transactions** OBJ. 3, 4

✔ 3. $64,317,346

General Ledger

SHOW
ME HOW

The following transactions were completed by Winklevoss Inc., whose fiscal year is the calendar year:

**2016**

July    1. Issued $74,000,000 of 20-year, 11% callable bonds dated July 1, 2016, at a market (effective) rate of 13%, receiving cash of $63,532,267. Interest is payable semiannually on December 31 and June 30.

Oct.    1. Borrowed $200,000 by issuing a six-year, 6% installment note to Nicks Bank. The note requires annual payments of $40,673, with the first payment occurring on September 30, 2017.

Dec. 31. Accrued $3,000 of interest on the installment note. The interest is payable on the date of the next installment note payment.

      31. Paid the semiannual interest on the bonds. The bond discount amortization of $261,693 is combined with the semiannual interest payment.

      31. Closed the interest expense account.

**2017**

June 30. Paid the semiannual interest on the bonds. The bond discount amortization of $261,693 is combined with the semiannual interest payment.

Sept. 30. Paid the annual payment on the note, which consisted of interest of $12,000 and principal of $28,673.

Dec. 31. Accrued $2,570 of interest on the installment note. The interest is payable on the date of the next installment note payment.

      31. Paid the semiannual interest on the bonds. The bond discount amortization of $261,693 is combined with the semiannual interest payment.

      31. Closed the interest expense account.

**2018**

June 30. Recorded the redemption of the bonds, which were called at 98. The balance in the bond discount account is $9,420,961 after payment of interest and amortization of discount have been recorded. (Record the redemption only.)

Sept. 30. Paid the second annual payment on the note, which consisted of interest of $10,280 and principal of $30,393.

**Instructions**

1. Journalize the entries to record the foregoing transactions. Round all amounts to the nearest dollar.

2. Indicate the amount of the interest expense in (a) 2016 and (b) 2017.

3. Determine the carrying amount of the bonds as of December 31, 2017.

**Appendix 1 and Appendix 2**
**PR 14-5A    Bond discount, entries for bonds payable transactions, interest method of amortizing bond discount**

✔ 3. $1,199,083

On July 1, 2016, Merideth Industries Inc. issued $28,500,000 of 10-year, 8% bonds at a market (effective) interest rate of 9%, receiving cash of $26,646,292. Interest on the bonds is payable semiannually on December 31 and June 30. The fiscal year of the company is the calendar year.

**Instructions**

1. Journalize the entry to record the amount of cash proceeds from the issuance of the bonds.

2. Journalize the entries to record the following:

    a. The first semiannual interest payment on December 31, 2016, and the amortization of the bond discount, using the interest method. (Round to the nearest dollar.)

    b. The interest payment on June 30, 2017, and the amortization of the bond discount, using the interest method. (Round to the nearest dollar.)

3. Determine the total interest expense for 2016.

---

**Appendix 1 and Appendix 2**
**PR 14-6A    Bond premium, entries for bonds payable transactions, interest method of amortizing bond premium**

✔ 3. $2,669,887

Saverin, Inc. produces and sells outdoor equipment. On July 1, 2016, Saverin, Inc. issued $62,500,000 of 10-year, 9% bonds at a market (effective) interest rate of 8%, receiving cash of $66,747,178. Interest on the bonds is payable semiannually on December 31 and June 30. The fiscal year of the company is the calendar year.

**Instructions**

1. Journalize the entry to record the amount of cash proceeds from the issuance of the bonds.

2. Journalize the entries to record the following:

    a. The first semiannual interest payment on December 31, 2016, and the amortization of the bond premium, using the interest method. (Round to the nearest dollar.)

    b. The interest payment on June 30, 2017, and the amortization of the bond premium, using the interest method. (Round to the nearest dollar.)

3. Determine the total interest expense for 2016.

# Problems: Series B

**PR 14-1B    Effect of financing on earnings per share**                OBJ. 1

✔ 1. Plan 3: $2.84

Three different plans for financing an $80,000,000 corporation are under consideration by its organizers. Under each of the following plans, the securities will be issued at their par or face amount, and the income tax rate is estimated at 40% of income:

|  | Plan 1 | Plan 2 | Plan 3 |
|---|---|---|---|
| 9% Bonds | — | — | $40,000,000 |
| Preferred 5% stock, $25 par | — | $40,000,000 | 20,000,000 |
| Common stock, $20 par | $80,000,000 | 40,000,000 | 20,000,000 |
| Total | $80,000,000 | $80,000,000 | $80,000,000 |

**Instructions**

1. Determine for each plan the earnings per share of common stock, assuming that the income before bond interest and income tax is $10,000,000.

2. Determine for each plan the earnings per share of common stock, assuming that the income before bond interest and income tax is $6,000,000.

3. ──────▶ Discuss the advantages and disadvantages of each plan.

**PR 14-2B**   **Bond discount, entries for bonds payable transactions**   OBJ. 2, 3

On July 1, 2016, Livingston Corporation, a wholesaler of manufacturing equipment, issued $46,000,000 of 20-year, 10% bonds at a market (effective) interest rate of 11%, receiving cash of $42,309,236. Interest on the bonds is payable semiannually on December 31 and June 30. The fiscal year of the company is the calendar year.

**Instructions**

1. Journalize the entry to record the amount of cash proceeds from the issuance of the bonds on July 1, 2016.

2. Journalize the entries to record the following:

   a. The first semiannual interest payment on December 31, 2016, and the amortization of the bond discount, using the straight-line method. (Round to the nearest dollar.)

   b. The interest payment on June 30, 2017, and the amortization of the bond discount, using the straight-line method. (Round to the nearest dollar.)

3. Determine the total interest expense for 2016.

4. Will the bond proceeds always be less than the face amount of the bonds when the contract rate is less than the market rate of interest?

5. *(Appendix 1)* Compute the price of $42,309,236 received for the bonds by using the present value tables in Appendix A at the end of the text. (Round to the nearest dollar.)

---

**PR 14-3B**   **Bond premium, entries for bonds payable transactions**   OBJ. 2, 3

Rodgers Corporation produces and sells football equipment. On July 1, 2016, Rodgers Corporation issued $65,000,000 of 10-year, 12% bonds at a market (effective) interest rate of 10%, receiving cash of $73,100,469. Interest on the bonds is payable semiannually on December 31 and June 30. The fiscal year of the company is the calendar year.

**Instructions**

1. Journalize the entry to record the amount of cash proceeds from the issuance of the bonds on July 1, 2016.

2. Journalize the entries to record the following:

   a. The first semiannual interest payment on December 31, 2016, and the amortization of the bond premium, using the straight-line method. (Round to the nearest dollar.)

   b. The interest payment on June 30, 2017, and the amortization of the bond premium, using the straight-line method. (Round to the nearest dollar.)

3. Determine the total interest expense for 2016.

4. Will the bond proceeds always be greater than the face amount of the bonds when the contract rate is greater than the market rate of interest?

5. *(Appendix 1)* Compute the price of $73,100,469 received for the bonds by using the present value tables in Appendix A at the end of the text. (Round to the nearest dollar.)

---

**PR 14-4B**   **Entries for bonds payable and installment note transactions**   OBJ. 3, 4

The following transactions were completed by Montague Inc., whose fiscal year is the calendar year:

2016

July   1.   Issued $55,000,000 of 10-year, 9% callable bonds dated July 1, 2016, at a market (effective) rate of 7%, receiving cash of $62,817,040. Interest is payable semiannually on December 31 and June 30.

Oct.   1.   Borrowed $450,000 by issuing a six-year, 8% installment note to Intexicon Bank. The note requires annual payments of $97,342, with the first payment occurring on September 30, 2017.

Dec. 31.   Accrued $9,000 of interest on the installment note. The interest is payable on the date of the next installment note payment.

       31.   Paid the semiannual interest on the bonds. The bond discount amortization of $390,852 is combined with the semiannual interest payment.

       31.   Closed the interest expense account.

*(Continued)*

2017

June 30. Paid the semiannual interest on the bonds. The bond discount amortization of $390,852 is combined with the semiannual interest payment.

Sept. 30. Paid the annual payment on the note, which consisted of interest of $36,000 and principal of $61,342.

Dec. 31. Accrued $7,773 of interest on the installment note. The interest is payable on the date of the next installment note payment.

31. Paid the semiannual interest on the bonds. The bond discount amortization of $390,852 is combined with the semiannual interest payment.

31. Closed the interest expense account.

2018

June 30. Recorded the redemption of the bonds, which were called at 103. The balance in the bond premium account is $6,253,632 after payment of interest and amortization of premium have been recorded. (Record the redemption only.)

Sept. 30. Paid the second annual payment on the note, which consisted of interest of $31,093 and principal of $66,249.

**Instructions**

1. Journalize the entries to record the foregoing transactions.

2. Indicate the amount of the interest expense in (a) 2016 and (b) 2017.

3. Determine the carrying amount of the bonds as of December 31, 2017.

---

**Appendix 1 and Appendix 2**
**PR 14-5B   Bond discount, entries for bonds payable transactions, interest method of amortizing bond discount**

✔ 3. $2,327,008

On July 1, 2016, Livingston Corporation, a wholesaler of manufacturing equipment, issued $46,000,000 of 20-year, 10% bonds at a market (effective) interest rate of 11%, receiving cash of $42,309,236. Interest on the bonds is payable semiannually on December 31 and June 30. The fiscal year of the company is the calendar year.

**Instructions**

1. Journalize the entry to record the amount of cash proceeds from the issuance of the bonds.

2. Journalize the entries to record the following:

   a. The first semiannual interest payment on December 31, 2016, and the amortization of the bond discount, using the interest method. (Round to the nearest dollar.)

   b. The interest payment on June 30, 2017, and the amortization of the bond discount, using the interest method. (Round to the nearest dollar.)

3. Determine the total interest expense for 2016.

---

**Appendix 1 and Appendix 2**
**PR 14-6B   Bond premium, entries for bonds payable transactions, interest method of amortizing bond premium**

✔ 3. $3,655,023

Rodgers Corporation produces and sells football equipment. On July 1, 2016, Rodgers Corporation issued $65,000,000 of 10-year, 12% bonds at a market (effective) interest rate of 10%, receiving cash of $73,100,469. Interest on the bonds is payable semiannually on December 31 and June 30. The fiscal year of the company is the calendar year.

**Instructions**

1. Journalize the entry to record the amount of cash proceeds from the issuance of the bonds.

2. Journalize the entries to record the following:

   a. The first semiannual interest payment on December 31, 2016, and the amortization of the bond premium, using the interest method. (Round to the nearest dollar.)

   b. The interest payment on June 30, 2017, and the amortization of the bond premium, using the interest method. (Round to the nearest dollar.)

3. Determine the total interest expense for 2016.

## Cases & Projects

### CP 14-1    General Electric bond issuance

**General Electric Capital**, a division of **General Electric**, uses long-term debt extensively. In a recent year, GE Capital issued $11 billion in long-term debt to investors, then within days filed legal documents to prepare for another $50 billion long-term debt issue. As a result of the $50 billion filing, the price of the initial $11 billion offering declined (due to higher risk of more debt).

> *Bill Gross, a manager of a bond investment fund, "denounced a 'lack in candor' related to GE's recent debt deal. 'It was the most recent and most egregious example of how bondholders are mistreated.' Gross argued that GE was not forthright when GE Capital recently issued $11 billion in bonds, one of the largest issues ever from a U.S. corporation. What bothered Gross is that three days after the issue the company announced its intention to sell as much as $50 billion in additional debt, warrants, preferred stock, guarantees, letters of credit and promissory notes at some future date."*

➤ In your opinion, did GE Capital act unethically by selling $11 billion of long-term debt without telling those investors that a few days later it would be filing documents to prepare for another $50 billion debt offering?

*Source:* Jennifer Ablan, "Gross Shakes the Bond Market; GE Calms It, a Bit," *Barron's*, March 25, 2002.

### CP 14-2    Ethics and professional conduct in business

Solar Industries develops and produces high-efficiency solar panels. The company has an outstanding $10,000,000, 30-year, 10% bond issue dated July 1, 2011. The bond issue is due June 30, 2040. Some bond indentures require the corporation issuing the bonds to transfer cash to a special cash fund, called a sinking fund, over the life of the bond. Such funds help assure investors that there will be adequate cash to pay the bonds at their maturity date.

The bond indenture requires a bond sinking fund, which has a balance of $1,200,000 as of July 1, 2016. The company is currently experiencing a shortage of funds due to a recent acquisition. Bob Lachgar, the company's treasurer, is considering using the funds from the bond sinking fund to cover payroll and other bills that are coming due at the end of the month. Bob's brother-in-law, a trustee of Solar's sinking fund, has indicated a willingness to allow Bob to use the funds from the sinking fund to temporarily meet the company's cash needs.

➤ Discuss whether Bob's proposal is appropriate.

### CP 14-3    Present values

Alex Kelton recently won the jackpot in the Colorado lottery while he was visiting his parents. When he arrived at the lottery office to collect his winnings, he was offered the following three payout options:

a.  Receive $100,000,000 in cash today.

b.  Receive $25,000,000 today and $9,000,000 per year for eight years, with the first payment being received one year from today.

c.  Receive $15,000,000 per year for 10 years, with the first payment being received one year from today.

➤ Assuming that the effective rate of interest is 7%, which payout option should Alex select? Use the present value tables in Appendix A. Explain your answer and provide any necessary supporting calculations.

### CP 14-4    Preferred stock vs. bonds

Xentec Inc. has decided to expand its operations to owning and operating golf courses. The following is an excerpt from a conversation between the chief executive officer, Peter Kilgallon, and the vice president of finance, Dan Baron:

*Peter:* Dan, have you given any thought to how we're going to manage the acquisition of Sweeping Bluff Golf Course?

*Dan:* Well, the two basic options, as I see it, are to issue either preferred stock or bonds. The equity market is a little depressed right now. The rumor is that the Federal Reserve Bank's going to increase the interest rates either this month or next.

*Peter:* Yes, I've heard the rumor. The problem is that we can't wait around to see what's going to happen. We'll have to move on this next week if we want any chance to complete the acquisition of Sweeping Bluff Golf Course.

*Dan:* Well, the bond market is strong right now. Maybe we should issue debt this time around.

*Peter:* That's what I would have guessed as well. Sweeping Bluff Golf Course's financial statements look pretty good, except for the volatility of its income and cash flows. But that's characteristic of the industry.

➤ Discuss the advantages and disadvantages of issuing preferred stock versus bonds.

---

### CP 14-5  Financing business expansion

You hold a 25% common stock interest in YouOwnIt, a family-owned construction equipment company. Your sister, who is the manager, has proposed an expansion of plant facilities at an expected cost of $26,000,000. Two alternative plans have been suggested as methods of financing the expansion. Each plan is briefly described as follows:

Plan 1.   Issue $26,000,000 of 20-year, 8% notes at face amount.

Plan 2.   Issue an additional 550,000 shares of $10 par common stock at $20 per share, and $15,000,000 of 20-year, 8% notes at face amount.

The balance sheet as of the end of the previous fiscal year is as follows:

**YouOwnIt, Inc.**
**Balance Sheet**
**December 31, 2016**

| Assets | |
| --- | --- |
| Current assets | $15,000,000 |
| Property, plant, and equipment | 22,500,000 |
| Total assets | $37,500,000 |
| **Liabilities and Stockholders' Equity** | |
| Liabilities | $11,250,000 |
| Common stock, $10 | 4,000,000 |
| Paid-in capital in excess of par | 500,000 |
| Retained earnings | 21,750,000 |
| Total liabilities and stockholders' equity | $37,500,000 |

Net income has remained relatively constant over the past several years. The expansion program is expected to increase yearly income before bond interest and income tax from $2,667,000 in the previous year to $5,000,000 for this year. Your sister has asked you, as the company treasurer, to prepare an analysis of each financing plan.

1.  Prepare a table indicating the expected earnings per share on the common stock under each plan. Assume an income tax rate of 40%. Round to the nearest cent.

2.  a. ➤ Discuss the factors that should be considered in evaluating the two plans.

    b. ➤ Which plan offers the greater benefit to the present stockholders? Give reasons for your opinion.

---

### CP 14-6  Number of times interest charges are earned

  The following financial data (in thousands) were taken from recent financial statements of Staples, Inc.:

| | Year 3 | Year 2 | Year 1 |
| --- | --- | --- | --- |
| Interest expense | $ 173,751 | $ 214,824 | $ 237,025 |
| Earnings before taxes | 1,459,141 | 1,356,595 | 1,155,894 |

1.  What is the number of times interest charges are earned for Staples in Year 3, Year 2, and Year 1? (Round your answers to one decimal place.)

2.  Evaluate this ratio for Staples.

# Investments and Fair Value Accounting

## The Coca-Cola Company

You invest cash to earn more cash. For example, you could deposit cash in a bank account to earn interest. You could also invest cash in preferred or common stocks and in corporate or U.S. government notes and bonds.

Preferred and common stock can be purchased through a stock exchange, such as the **New York Stock Exchange (NYSE)**. Preferred stock is purchased primarily with the expectation of earning dividends. Common stock is purchased with the expectation of earning dividends or realizing gains from a price increase in the stock.

Corporate and U.S. government bonds can also be purchased through a bond exchange. Bonds are purchased with the primary expectation of earning interest revenue.

Companies make investments for many of the same reasons that you would as an individual. For example,

**The Coca-Cola Company** has invested approximately $3.1 billion of available cash in stocks and bonds. These investments are held by The Coca-Cola Company for interest, dividends, and expected price increases.

Unlike most individuals, however, companies also purchase significant amounts of the outstanding common stock of other companies for strategic reasons. For example, The Coca-Cola Company has more than $9 billion invested in companies where they own between 20% and 50% of the outstanding shares. The vast majority of these investments are in independent bottlers, who bottle and distribute Coca-Cola products.

Investments in debt and equity securities give rise to a number of accounting issues. These issues are described and illustrated in this chapter.

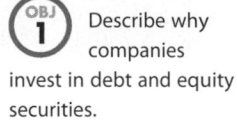

**OBJ 1** Describe why companies invest in debt and equity securities.

# Why Companies Invest

Most companies generate cash from their operations. This cash can be used for the following purposes:

- Investing in current operations
- Investing in temporary investments to earn additional revenue
- Investing in long-term investments in stock of other companies for strategic reasons

## Investing Cash in Current Operations

Cash is often used to support the current operating activities of a company. For example, cash may be used to replace worn-out equipment or to purchase new, more efficient and productive equipment. In addition, cash may be reinvested in the company to expand its current operations. For example, a retailer based in the northwest United States might decide to expand by opening stores in the Midwest.

To support its current level of operations, a company also uses cash to pay:

- expenses.
- suppliers of merchandise and other assets.
- interest to creditors.
- dividends to stockholders.

The accounting for the use of cash in current operations has been described and illustrated in earlier chapters. For example, Chapter 10, "Fixed Assets and Intangible Assets," illustrated the use of cash for purchasing property, plant, and equipment.

In this chapter, we describe and illustrate the use of cash for investing in temporary investments and the stock of other companies.

## Investing Cash in Temporary Investments

A company may temporarily have excess cash that is not needed for use in its current operations. This is often the case when a company has a seasonal operating cycle. For example, a significant portion of the annual merchandise sales of a retailer occurs during the fall holiday season. As a result, retailers often experience a large increase in cash during this period, which is not needed until the spring buying season.

Instead of letting excess cash remain idle in a checking account, most companies invest their excess cash in temporary investments. In doing so, companies invest in securities such as:

- **Debt securities**, which are notes and bonds that pay interest and have a fixed maturity date.
- **Equity securities**, which are preferred and common stock that represent ownership in a company and do not have a fixed maturity date.

Investments in debt and equity securities, termed **investments** or *temporary investments*, are reported in the Current Assets section of the balance sheet.

The primary objective of investing in temporary investments is to:

- earn interest revenue.
- receive dividends.
- realize gains from increases in the market price of the securities.

Investments in certificates of deposit and other securities that do not normally change in value are disclosed on the balance sheet as *cash and cash equivalents*. Such investments are held primarily for their interest revenue.

## Investing Cash in Long-Term Investments

A company may invest cash in the debt or equity of another company as a long-term investment. Long-term investments may be held for the same investment objectives as temporary investments. However, long-term investments often involve the purchase of a significant portion of the stock of another company. Such investments usually have a strategic purpose, such as:

 In 2012, **Dell Computer** purchased **Quest Software** for $2.4 billion. The acquisition allowed Dell to competitively expand into the software sector.

- *Reduction of costs*: When one company buys another company, the combined company may be able to reduce administrative expenses. For example, a combined company does not need two chief executive officers (CEOs) or chief financial officers (CFOs).
- *Replacement of management*: If the purchased company has been mismanaged, the acquiring company may replace the company's management and, thus, improve operations and profits.
- *Expansion*: The acquiring company may purchase a company because it has a complementary product line, territory, or customer base. The new combined company may be able to serve customers better than the two companies could separately.
- *Integration*: A company may integrate operations by acquiring a supplier or customer. Acquiring a supplier may provide a more stable or uninterrupted supply of resources. Acquiring a customer may also provide a market for the company's products or services.

## Accounting for Debt Investments

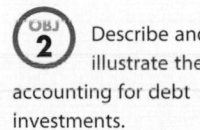 Describe and illustrate the accounting for debt investments.

Debt securities include notes and bonds issued by corporations and governmental organizations. Most companies invest excess cash in bonds as investments to earn interest revenue.

The accounting for bond investments[1] includes recording the following:

- Purchase of bonds
- Interest revenue
- Sale of bonds

## Purchase of Bonds

The purchase of bonds is recorded by debiting an investments account for the purchase price of the bonds, including any brokerage commissions. (A *brokerage commission* is the fee charged by the agent who arranges the transaction between the buyer and seller.) If the bonds are purchased between interest dates, the purchase price includes accrued interest since the last interest payment. This is because the seller has earned the accrued interest, but the buyer will receive the accrued interest when it is paid.

To illustrate, assume that Homer Company purchases $18,000 of U.S. Treasury bonds at their face amount on March 17, 2016, plus accrued interest for 45 days. The bonds have an interest rate of 6%, payable on July 31 and January 31.

The entry to record the purchase of the U.S. Treasury bonds is as follows:

| 2016 | | | | |
|---|---|---|---|---|
| Mar. | 17 | Investments—U.S. Treasury Bonds | 18,000 | |
| | | Interest Receivable | 135 | |
| | | Cash | | 18,135 |
| | | Purchased $18,000, 6% U.S. Treasury bonds. | | |

Because Homer Company purchased the bonds on March 17, it is also purchasing the accrued interest for 45 days (January 31 to March 17), as shown in Exhibit 1. The accrued interest of $135 is computed as follows:[2]

$$\text{Accrued Interest} = \$18,000 \times 6\% \times (45 \div 360) = \$135$$

The accrued interest is recorded by debiting Interest Receivable for $135. Investments is debited for the purchase price of the bonds of $18,000.

---

**EXHIBIT 1**

**Interest Timeline**

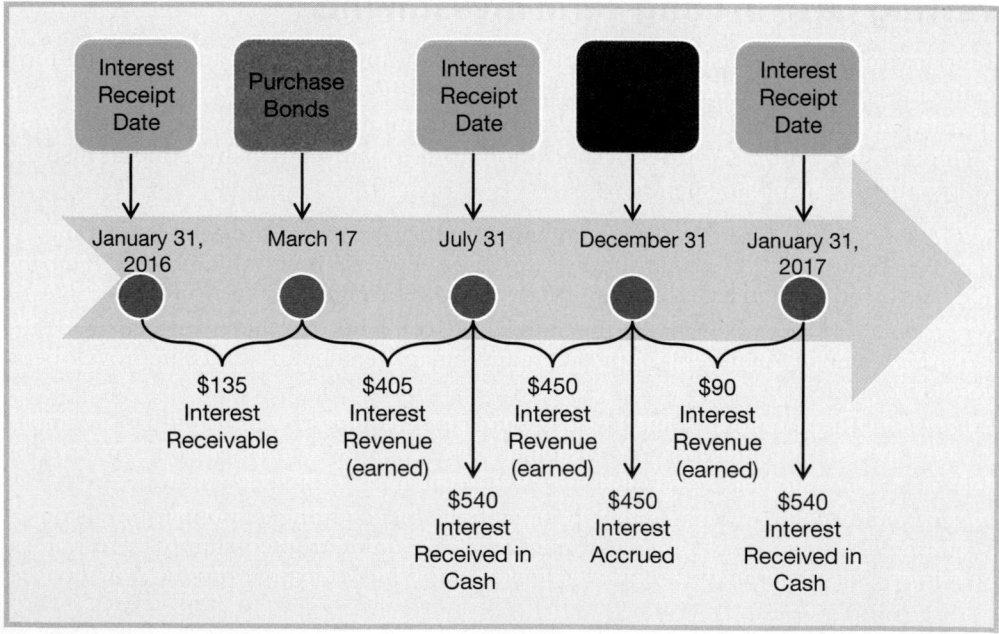

## Interest Revenue

On July 31, Homer Company receives a semiannual interest payment of $540 ($18,000 × 6% × ½). The $540 interest includes the $135 accrued interest that Homer Company purchased with the bonds on March 17. Thus, Homer has earned $405 ($540 − $135) of interest revenue since purchasing the bonds, as shown in Exhibit 1.

---

[1] Debt investments may also include installment notes and short-term notes. The accounting for these debt investments is covered in intermediate and advanced accounting courses.

[2] To simplify, a 360-day year is used to compute interest.

The receipt of the interest on July 31 is recorded as follows:

| 2016 July | 31 | Cash | | 540 | |
|---|---|---|---|---|---|
| | | Interest Receivable | | | 135 |
| | | Interest Revenue | | | 405 |
| | | Received semiannual interest. | | | |

Homer Company's accounting period ends on December 31. Thus, an adjusting entry must be made to accrue interest for five months (August 1 to December 31) of $450 ($18,000 × 6% × $\frac{5}{12}$), as shown in Exhibit 1. The adjusting entry to record the accrued interest is as follows:

| 2016 Dec. | 31 | Interest Receivable | | 450 | |
|---|---|---|---|---|---|
| | | Interest Revenue | | | 450 |
| | | Accrued 5 months of interest. | | | |

For the year ended December 31, 2016, Homer Company would report Interest Revenue of $855 ($405 + $450) as part of Other Income on its income statement.

The receipt of the semiannual interest of $540 on January 31, 2017, is recorded as follows:

| 2017 Jan. | 31 | Cash | | 540 | |
|---|---|---|---|---|---|
| | | Interest Revenue | | | 90 |
| | | Interest Receivable | | | 450 |
| | | Received semiannual interest | | | |

## Sale of Bonds

The sale of a bond investment normally results in a gain or loss. If the proceeds from the sale exceed the book value (cost) of the bonds, then a gain is recorded. If the proceeds are less than the book value (cost) of the bonds, a loss is recorded.

To illustrate, on January 31, 2017, Homer Company sells the Treasury bonds at 98, which is a price equal to 98% of their face amount. The sale results in a loss of $360, computed as follows:

| | |
|---|---|
| Proceeds from sale | $17,640* |
| Less book value (cost) of the bonds | 18,000 |
| Loss on sale of bonds | $ (360) |
| *$18,000 × 98% | |

The entry to record the sale is as follows:

| 2017 Jan. | 31 | Cash | | 17,640 | |
|---|---|---|---|---|---|
| | | Loss on Sale of Investment | | 360 | |
| | | Investments   U.S. Treasury Bonds | | | 18,000 |
| | | Sold U.S. Treasury bonds. | | | |

There is no accrued interest upon the sale because the interest payment date is also January 31. If the sale were between interest dates, interest accrued since the last interest payment date would be added to the sale proceeds and credited to Interest Revenue. The loss on the sale of bond investments is reported as part of Other Income (Loss) on Homer Company's income statement.

## Example Exercise 15-1 Bond Investment Transactions

OBJ 2

Journalize the entries to record the following selected bond investment transactions for Fly Company:

1. Purchased for cash $40,000 of Tyler Company 10% bonds at 100 plus accrued interest of $320.
2. Received the first semiannual interest.
3. Sold $30,000 of the bonds at 102 plus accrued interest of $110.

### Follow My Example 15-1

| | | | |
|---|---|---|---|
| 1. | Investments—Tyler Company Bonds ............................. | 40,000 | |
| | Interest Receivable ............................................... | 320 | |
| | Cash ......................................................... | | 40,320 |
| 2. | Cash ......................................................... | 2,000* | |
| | Interest Receivable ............................................. | | 320 |
| | Interest Revenue .............................................. | | 1,680 |
| | *$40,000 × 10% × ½ | | |
| 3. | Cash ......................................................... | 30,710* | |
| | Interest Revenue .............................................. | | 110 |
| | Gain on Sale of Investments..................................... | | 600 |
| | Investments—Tyler Company Bonds ........................... | | 30,000 |

| | |
|---|---|
| *Sale proceeds ($30,000 × 102%) .............................. | $30,600 |
| Accrued interest ............................................... | 110 |
| Total proceeds from sale ....................................... | $30,710 |

Practice Exercises: PE 15-1A, PE 15-1B

---

OBJ 3

Describe and illustrate the accounting for equity investments.

# Accounting for Equity Investments

A company may invest in the preferred or common stock of another company. The company investing in another company's stock is the **investor**. The company whose stock is purchased is the **investee**.

The percent of the investee's outstanding stock purchased by the investor determines the degree of control that the investor has over the investee. This, in turn, determines the accounting method used to record the stock investment, as shown in Exhibit 2.

---

**EXHIBIT 2**

**Stock Investments**

| Percent of Outstanding Stock Owned by Investor | Degree of Control of Investor over Investee | Accounting Method |
|---|---|---|
| Less than 20% | No control | Cost method |
| Between 20% and 50% | Significant influence | Equity method |
| Greater than 50% | Control | Consolidation |

## Cost Method: Less Than 20% Ownership

If the investor purchases less than 20% of the outstanding stock of the investee, the investor is considered to have no control over the investee. In this case, it is assumed that the investor purchased the stock primarily to earn dividends or to realize gains on price increases of the stock.

Investments of less than 20% of the investee's outstanding stock are accounted for using the **cost method**. Under the cost method, entries are recorded for the following transactions:

- Purchase of stock
- Receipt of dividends
- Sale of stock

**Purchase of Stock** The purchase of stock is recorded at its cost. Any brokerage commissions are included as part of the cost.

To illustrate, assume that on May 1, Bart Company purchases 2,000 shares of Lisa Company common stock at $49.90 per share plus a brokerage commission of $200. The entry to record the purchase of the stock is as follows:

| | | | | | |
|---|---|---|---|---|---|
| May | 1 | Investments—Lisa Company Stock | | 100,000 | |
| | | Cash | | | 100,000 |
| | | Purchased 2,000 shares of Lisa Company | | | |
| | | common stock [($49.90 × 2,000 | | | |
| | | shares) + $200]. | | | |

**Receipt of Dividends** On July 31, Bart Company receives a dividend of $0.40 per share from Lisa Company. The entry to record the receipt of the dividend is as follows:

| | | | | | |
|---|---|---|---|---|---|
| July | 31 | Cash | | 800 | |
| | | Dividend Revenue | | | 800 |
| | | Received dividend on Lisa Company | | | |
| | | common stock (2,000 shares × $0.40). | | | |

Dividend Revenue is reported as part of Other Income on Bart Company's income statement.

**Sale of Stock** The sale of a stock investment normally results in a gain or loss. A gain is recorded if the proceeds from the sale exceed the book value (cost) of the stock. A loss is recorded if the proceeds from the sale are less than the book value (cost).

To illustrate, on September 1, Bart Company sells 1,500 shares of Lisa Company stock for $54.50 per share, less a $160 commission. The sale results in a gain of $6,590, computed as follows:

| | |
|---|---|
| Proceeds from sale | $81,590* |
| Book value (cost) of the stock | 75,000** |
| Gain on sale | $ 6,590 |

*($54.50 × 1,500 shares) − $160
**($100,000 ÷ 2,000 shares) × 1,500 shares

The entry to record the sale is as follows:

| | | | | | |
|---|---|---|---|---|---|
| Sept. | 1 | Cash | | 81,590 | |
| | | Gain on Sale of Investments | | | 6,590 |
| | | Investments—Lisa Company Stock | | | 75,000 |
| | | Sold 1,500 shares of Lisa Company | | | |
| | | common stock. | | | |

The gain on the sale of investments is reported as part of Other Income on Bart Company's income statement.

**Example Exercise 15-2** **Stock Investment Transactions**

On September 1, 1,500 shares of Monroe Company are acquired at a price of $24 per share plus a $40 brokerage commission. On October 14, a $0.60-per-share dividend was received on the Monroe Company stock. On November 11, 750 shares (half) of Monroe Company stock were sold for $20 per share, less a $45 brokerage commission. Prepare the journal entries for the original purchase, dividend, and sale.

**Follow My Example 15-2**

| | | | |
|---|---|---|---|
| Sept. 1 | Investments—Monroe Company Stock .................... | 36,040* | |
| | Cash ..................................................... | | 36,040 |
| | *(1,500 shares × $24 per share) + $40 | | |
| Oct. 14 | Cash ..................................................... | 900* | |
| | Dividend Revenue ...................................... | | 900 |
| | *$0.60 per share × 1,500 shares | | |
| Nov. 11 | Cash ..................................................... | 14,955* | |
| | Loss on Sale of Investments .............................. | 3,065 | |
| | Investments—Monroe Company Stock ................. | | 18,020** |
| | *(750 shares × $20) – $45 | | |
| | **$36,040 × ½ | | |

Practice Exercises: PE 15-2A, PE 15-2B

## Equity Method: Between 20%–50% Ownership

If the investor purchases between 20% and 50% of the outstanding stock of the investee, the investor is considered to have a *significant influence* over the investee. In this case, it is assumed that the investor purchased the stock primarily for strategic reasons, such as developing a supplier relationship.

Investments of between 20% and 50% of the investee's outstanding stock are accounted for using the **equity method**. Under the equity method, the stock is recorded initially at its cost, including any brokerage commissions. This is the same as under the cost method.

Under the equity method, the investment account is adjusted for the investor's share of the net income and dividends of the investee. These adjustments are as follows:

- *Net Income:* The investor records its share of the net income of the investee as an increase in the investment account. Its share of any net loss is recorded as a decrease in the investment account.

- *Dividends:* The investor's share of cash dividends received from the investee decreases the investment account.

**Purchase of Stock** To illustrate, assume that Simpson Inc. purchased its 40% interest in Flanders Corporation's common stock on January 2, 2016, for $350,000. The entry to record the purchase is as follows:

| | | | | |
|---|---|---|---|---|
| 2016 Jan. | 2 | Investment in Flanders Corporation Stock | 350,000 | |
| | | Cash | | 350,000 |
| | | Purchased 40% of Flanders Corporation stock. | | |

**Recording Investee Net Income** For the year ended December 31, 2016, Flanders Corporation reported net income of $105,000. Under the equity method, Simpson Inc. (the investor) records its share of Flanders net income, as follows:

| 2016 | | | | | |
|------|----|--------------------------------------------------------------|---|--------|--------|
| Dec. | 31 | Investment in Flanders Corporation Stock | | 42,000 | |
| | | Income of Flanders Corporation | | | 42,000 |
| | | Recorded 40% share of Flanders | | | |
| | | Corporation net income, $105,000 × 40%. | | | |

Income of Flanders Corporation is reported on Simpson Inc.'s income statement. Depending on its significance, it may be reported separately or as part of *Other Income*. If Flanders had a loss during the period, then the journal entry would be a debit to Loss of Flanders Corporation and a credit to the investment account.

**Recording Investee Dividends** During the year, Flanders Corporation declared and paid cash dividends of $45,000. Under the equity method, Simpson Inc. (the investor) records its share of Flanders dividends as follows:

| 2016 | | | | | |
|------|----|--------------------------------------------------------------|---|--------|--------|
| Dec. | 31 | Cash | | 18,000 | |
| | | Investment in Flanders Corporation Stock | | | 18,000 |
| | | Recorded 40% share of Flanders | | | |
| | | Corporation dividends, $45,000 × 40%. | | | |

The effect of recording 40% of Flanders Corporation's net income and dividends is to increase the investment account by $24,000 ($42,000 − $18,000). Thus, Investment in Flanders Corporation Stock increases from $350,000 to $374,000, as shown in Exhibit 3.

Under the equity method, the investment account reflects the investor's proportional changes in the net book value of the investee. For example, Flanders Corporation's net book value increased by $60,000 (net income of $105,000 less dividends of $45,000) during the year. As a result, Simpson Inc.'s share of Flanders' net book value increased by $24,000 ($60,000 × 40%). Investments accounted for under the equity method are classified on the balance sheet as noncurrent assets.

**Sale of Stock** Under the equity method, a gain or loss is normally recorded from the sale of an investment. A gain is recorded if the proceeds exceed the *book value* of the investment. A loss is recorded if the proceeds are less than the *book value* of the investment.

To illustrate, if Simpson Inc. sold Flanders Corporation's stock on January 1, 2017, for $400,000, a gain of $26,000 would be reported, computed as follows:

| | |
|------------------------------|----------|
| Proceeds from sale | $400,000 |
| Book value of stock investment | 374,000 |
| Gain on sale | $ 26,000 |

The entry to record the sale is as follows:

| 2017 Jan. | 1 | Cash | 400,000 | |
|---|---|---|---|---|
| | | Investment in Flanders Corporation Stock | | 374,000 |
| | | Gain on Sale of Flanders Corporation Stock | | 26,000 |
| | | Sold Flanders Corporation stock. | | |

## Example Exercise 15-3   Equity Method

On January 2, Olson Company acquired 35% of the outstanding stock of Bryant Company for $140,000. For the year ended December 31, Bryant Company earned income of $44,000 and paid dividends of $20,000. Prepare the entries for Olson Company for the purchase of the stock, the share of Bryant income, and the dividends received from Bryant Company.

### Follow My Example 15-3

| Jan. 2 | Investment in Bryant Company Stock......................... | 140,000 | |
|---|---|---|---|
| | Cash ...................................................... | | 140,000 |
| Dec. 31 | Investment in Bryant Company Stock......................... | 15,400* | |
| | Income of Bryant Company .............................. | | 15,400 |
| | *Recorded 35% of Bryant income, 35% × $44,000 | | |
| Dec. 31 | Cash ...................................................... | 7,000* | |
| | Investment in Bryant Company Stock..................... | | 7,000 |
| | *Recorded 35% of Bryant's $20,000 dividend, 35% × $20,000 | | |

Practice Exercises: PE 15-3A, PE 15-3B

## Consolidation: More Than 50% Ownership

If the investor purchases more than 50% of the outstanding stock of the investee, the investor is considered to have *control* over the investee. In this case, it is assumed that the investor purchased the stock of the investee primarily for strategic reasons.

The purchase of more than 50% ownership of the investee's stock is termed a **business combination**. Companies may combine in order to produce more efficiently, diversify product lines, expand geographically, or acquire know-how.

A corporation owning all or a majority of the voting stock of another corporation is called a **parent company**. The corporation that is controlled is called the **subsidiary company**.

Parent and subsidiary corporations often continue to maintain separate accounting records and prepare their own financial statements. In such cases, at the end of the year, the financial statements of the parent and subsidiary are combined and reported as a single company. These combined financial statements are called **consolidated financial statements**. Such statements are normally identified by adding *and Subsidiary(ies)* to the name of the parent corporation or by adding *Consolidated* to the statement title.

To the external stakeholders of the parent company, consolidated financial statements are more meaningful than separate statements for each corporation. This is because the parent company, in substance, controls the subsidiaries. The accounting for business combinations, including preparing consolidated financial statements, is described and illustrated in advanced accounting courses and textbooks.

## Business Connection

**MORE CASH MEANS MORE INVESTMENTS FOR DRUG COMPANIES**

Patented drugs are the life blood of the pharmaceutical industry. Drug companies with extensive portfolios of patented drugs generate huge cash flows from operating activities. As a result, these companies often have vast amounts of cash on hand to invest in other companies.

Near the end of 2012, the five biggest drug makers had in excess of $70 billion in cash and investments. Many analysts anticipated that these companies would use this excess cash to acquire smaller biotechnology and drug companies for their patented drugs and their ongoing research activities.

Source: "Mergers and Acquisitions on the Rise in 2013 as Big Pharma Companies Hold Record Amounts of Cash on Hand," *Five Star Equities Market Research Report*. Feb. 7, 2013.

# Valuing and Reporting Investments

**OBJ 4**

Describe and illustrate valuing and reporting investments in the financial statements.

Debt and equity securities are *financial assets* that are often traded on public exchanges such as the New York Stock Exchange. As a result, their market value can be observed and, thus, objectively determined. For this reason, generally accepted accounting principles (GAAP) allows some debt securities, and requires equity securities where there is less than a 20% ownership interest to be valued in the accounting records and financial statements at their fair market values.

These securities are classified as follows:

- Trading securities
- Available-for-sale securities
- Held-to-maturity securities

## Trading Securities

**Trading securities** are debt and equity securities that are purchased to earn short-term profits from changes in their market prices. Trading securities are often held by banks, mutual funds, insurance companies, and other financial institutions.

Because trading securities are held as a short-term investment, they are reported as a current asset on the balance sheet. Trading securities are valued as a portfolio (group) of securities using the securities' fair values. **Fair value** is the market price that the company would receive for a security if it were sold. A change in the fair value of the portfolio (group) of trading securities is recognized as an **unrealized gain or loss** for the period.

**SunTrust Banks Inc.** holds over $6 billion in trading securities as current assets.

To illustrate, assume Maggie Company purchased a portfolio of trading securities during 2016. On December 31, 2016, the cost and fair values of the securities were as follows:

| Name | Number of Shares | Total Cost | Total Fair Value |
|---|---|---|---|
| Armour Company | 400 | $ 5,000 | $ 7,200 |
| Maven, Inc. | 500 | 11,000 | 7,500 |
| Polaris Co. | 200 | 8,000 | 10,600 |
| Total | | $24,000 | $25,300 |

The portfolio of trading securities is reported at its fair value of $25,300. An adjusting entry is made to record the increase in the fair value of $1,300 ($25,300 – $24,000). In order to maintain a record of the original cost of the securities, a valuation account, called *Valuation Allowance for Trading Investments*, is debited for $1,300, and Unrealized Gain on Trading Investments is credited for $1,300.[3] The adjusting entry on

December 31, 2016, to record the fair value of the portfolio of trading securities is as follows:

| 2016 Dec. | 31 | Valuation Allowance for Trading Investments | 1,300 | |
|---|---|---|---|---|
| | | Unrealized Gain on Trading Investments | | 1,300 |
| | | To record increase in fair value of trading securities. | | |

Unrealized Gain on Trading Investments is reported on the income statement. Depending on its significance, it may be reported separately or as Other Income on the income statement. The valuation allowance is reported on the December 31, 2016, balance sheet as follows:

**Maggie Company**
**Balance Sheet (selected items)**
**December 31, 2016**

| | | |
|---|---|---|
| Current assets: | | |
| Cash........................................................ | | $120,000 |
| Trading investments (at cost)............................... | $24,000 | |
| Plus valuation allowance for trading investments ............ | 1,300 | |
| Trading investments (at fair value) ......................... | | 25,300 |

If the fair value of the portfolio of trading securities was less than the cost, then the adjustment would debit Unrealized Loss on Trading Investments and credit Valuation Allowance for Trading Investments for the difference. Unrealized Loss on Trading Investments would be reported on the income statement as Other Expenses. Valuation Allowance for Trading Investments would be shown on the balance sheet as a *deduction* from Trading Investments (at cost).

Over time, the valuation allowance account is adjusted to reflect the difference between the cost and the fair value of the portfolio. Thus, increases in the valuation allowance account from the beginning of the period will result in an adjustment to record an unrealized gain, similar to the preceding journal entry. Likewise, decreases in the valuation allowance account from the beginning of the period will result in an adjustment to record an unrealized loss.

**Example Exercise 15-4** **Valuing Trading Securities at Fair Value**  **OBJ 4**

On January 1, 2016, Valuation Allowance for Trading Investments had a zero balance. On December 31, 2016, the cost of the trading securities portfolio was $79,200, and the fair value was $76,800. Prepare the December 31, 2016, adjusting journal entry to record the unrealized gain or loss on trading investments.

**Follow My Example 15-4**

| 2016 | | | |
|---|---|---|---|
| Dec. 31 | Unrealized Loss on Trading Investments....................... | 2,400 | |
| | Valuation Allowance for Trading Investments............... | | 2,400* |
| | To record decrease in fair value of trading investments. | | |

| *Trading investments at fair value, December 31, 2016 | $ 76,800 |
|---|---|
| Less trading investments at cost, December 31, 2016 | 79,200 |
| Unrealized loss on trading investments | $ (2,400) |

Practice Exercises: PE 15-4A, PE 15-4B

[3] We assume that the valuation allowance account has a beginning balance of zero to simplify our illustrations.

## Integrity, Objectivity, and Ethics in Business

### SOCIALLY RESPONSIBLE INVESTING

Socially responsible investing is a growing trend in the United States and Europe that focuses on making investments to improve society. Socially responsible investors attempt to balance investment return with social good by seeking out investments in companies that (1) are environmentally friendly, (2) do not infringe on human rights in the production of a product or provision of a service, and (3) are anti-discriminatory. In some situations, socially responsible investors target emerging markets to both generate a return and help overcome social challenges. In addition, some socially responsible investors refuse to invest in companies that produce alcohol, tobacco, or weapons.

## Available-for-Sale Securities

**Available-for-sale securities** are debt and equity securities that are neither held for trading, held to maturity, nor held for strategic reasons. The accounting for available-for-sale securities is similar to the accounting for trading securities, except for the reporting of changes in fair values. Specifically, changes in the fair values of *trading securities* are reported as an unrealized gain or loss on the income statement. In contrast, changes in the fair values of *available-for-sale securities* are reported as part of stockholders' equity and, thus, excluded from the income statement.

> **Google, Inc.** holds over $34 billion in available-for-sale securities as current assets.

To illustrate, assume that Maggie Company purchased the three securities during 2016 as available-for-sale securities instead of trading securities. On December 31, 2016, the cost and fair values of the securities were as follows:

| Name | Number of Shares | Total Cost | Total Fair Value |
|---|---|---|---|
| Armour Company | 400 | $ 5,000 | $ 7,200 |
| Maven, Inc. | 500 | 11,000 | 7,500 |
| Polaris Co. | 200 | 8,000 | 10,600 |
| Total | | $24,000 | $25,300 |

The portfolio of available-for-sale securities is reported at its fair value of $25,300. An adjusting entry is made to record the increase in fair value of $1,300 ($25,300 – $24,000). In order to maintain a record of the original cost of the securities, a valuation account, called *Valuation Allowance for Available-for-Sale Investments*, is debited for $1,300. This account is similar to the valuation account used for trading securities.

Unlike trading securities, the December 31, 2016, adjusting entry credits a stockholders' equity account instead of an income statement account.[4] The $1,300 increase in fair value is credited to Unrealized Gain (Loss) on Available-for-Sale Investments.

The adjusting entry on December 31, 2016, to record the fair value of the portfolio of available-for-sale securities is as follows:

| | | | | | |
|---|---|---|---|---|---|
| 2016<br>Dec. | 31 | Valuation Allowance for Available-for-Sale Investments | | 1,300 | |
| | |     Unrealized Gain (Loss) on Available-for-Sale Investments | | | 1,300 |
| | |         To record increase in fair value of available-for-sale investments. | | | |

---

[4] This is a rare exception to the rule that every adjusting entry must affect an income statement and a balance sheet account.

A credit balance in Unrealized Gain (Loss) on Available-for-Sale Investments is added to stockholders' equity, while a debit balance is subtracted from stockholders' equity.

The valuation allowance and the unrealized gain are reported on the December 31, 2016, balance sheet as follows:

| | | |
|---|---|---|
| **Maggie Company** | | |
| **Balance Sheet** | | |
| **December 31, 2016** | | |
| Current assets: | | |
| Cash.................................................. | | $120,000 |
| Available-for-sale investments (at cost)............................. | $24,000 | |
| Plus valuation allowance for available-for-sale investments............ | 1,300 | |
| Available-for-sale investments (at fair value)......................... | | 25,300 |
| **Equal** | | |
| Stockholders' equity: | | |
| Common stock..................................................... | | $ 10,000 |
| Paid-in capital in excess of par....................................... | | 150,000 |
| Retained earnings.................................................. | | 250,000 |
| Unrealized gain (loss) on available-for-sale investments .............. | | 1,300 |
| Total stockholders' equity ........................................... | | $411,300 |

As shown, Unrealized Gain (Loss) on Available-for-Sale Investments is reported as an addition to stockholders' equity. In future years, the cumulative effects of unrealized gains and losses are reported in this account. Because 2014 was the first year that Maggie Company purchased available-for-sale securities, the unrealized gain is reported as the balance of Unrealized Gain (Loss) on Available-for-Sale Investments. This treatment is supported under the theory that available-for-sale securities will be held longer than trading securities, so changes in fair value over time have a greater opportunity to cancel out. Thus, these changes are not reported on the income statement, as is the case with trading securities.

If the fair value was less than the cost, then the adjustment would debit Unrealized Gain (Loss) on Available-for-Sale Investments and credit Valuation Allowance for Available-for-Sale Investments for the difference. Unrealized Gain (Loss) on Trading Investments would be reported in the Stockholders' Equity section as a negative item. Valuation Allowance for Available-for-Sale Investments would be shown on the balance sheet as a deduction from Available-for-Sale Investments (at cost).

Over time, the valuation allowance account is adjusted to reflect the difference between the cost and the fair value of the portfolio. Thus, increases in the valuation allowance from the beginning of the period will result in an adjustment to record an increase in the valuation and unrealized gain (loss) accounts, similar to the journal entry illustrated earlier. Likewise, decreases in the valuation allowance from the beginning of the period will result in an adjustment to record decreases in the valuation and unrealized gain (loss) accounts.

**Example Exercise 15-5** Valuing Available-for-Sale Securities at Fair Value

On January 1, 2016, Valuation Allowance for Available-for-Sale Investments had a zero balance. On December 31, 2016, the cost of the available-for-sale securities was $45,700, and the fair value was $50,000.

Prepare the adjusting entry to record the unrealized gain or loss for available-for-sale investments on December 31, 2016.

**Follow My Example 15-5**

| 2016 | | | |
|---|---|---|---|
| Dec. 31 | Valuation Allowance for Available-for-Sale Investments . . . . . . . . . . . . . . . . . | 4,300* | |
| | Unrealized Gain (Loss) on Available-for-Sale Investments . . . . . . . . . . . . | | 4,300 |
| | To record increase in fair value of available-for-sale securities. | | |

| | |
|---|---|
| *Available-for-sale investments at fair value, December 31, 2016 | $50,000 |
| Less available-for-sale investments at cost, December 31, 2016 | 45,700 |
| Unrealized gain (loss) on available-for-sale investments | $ 4,300 |

Practice Exercises: PE 15-5A, PE 15-5B

## Held-to-Maturity Securities

Held-to-maturity securities are debt investments, such as notes or bonds, that a company intends to hold until their maturity date. Held-to-maturity securities are primarily purchased to earn interest revenue.

If a held-to-maturity security will mature within a year, it is reported as a current asset on the balance sheet. Held-to-maturity securities maturing beyond a year are reported as noncurrent assets.

Only securities with maturity dates, such as corporate notes and bonds, are classified as held-to-maturity securities. Equity securities are not held-to-maturity securities because they have no maturity date.

Held-to-maturity bond investments are recorded at their cost, including any brokerage commissions, as illustrated earlier in this chapter. If the interest rate on the bonds differs from the market rate of interest, the bonds may be purchased at a premium or discount. In such cases, the premium or discount is amortized over the life of the bonds.

Held-to-maturity bond investments are reported on the balance sheet at their amortized cost. The accounting for held-to-maturity investments, including premium and discount amortization, is described in advanced accounting texts.

## Summary

Exhibit 4 summarizes the valuation and balance sheet reporting of trading, available-for-sale, and held-to-maturity securities.

**Summary of Valuing and Reporting of Investments**

| | Trading Securities | Available-for-Sale Securities | Held-to-Maturity Securities |
|---|---|---|---|
| Valued at: | **Fair Value** | **Fair Value** | **Amortized Cost** |
| Changes in valuation are reported as: | Unrealized gain or loss in the income statement as Other income (loss). | Accumulated unrealized gain or loss is reported in stockholders' equity on the balance sheet. | Not applicable. Held-to-Maturity Securities are reported at cost.* |
| Reported on the balance sheet as: | Cost of investments plus or minus valuation allowance. | Cost of investments plus or minus valuation allowance. | Amortized cost of investment. |
| Classified on balance sheet as: | A current asset. | Either as a current or noncurrent asset, depending on management's intent. | Either as a current or noncurrent asset, depending on remaining term to maturity. |

*Premium or discount amortization is reported as part of interest revenue on the income statement.

Common stock investments in trading and available-for-sale securities are normally less than 20% of the outstanding common stock of the investee. The portfolios are reported at fair value using the valuation allowance account, while the individual securities are accounted for using the cost method. Investments between 20% and 50% of the outstanding common stock of the investee are accounted for using the equity method illustrated earlier in this chapter. Equity method investments are classified as noncurrent assets on the balance sheet.

The balance sheet reporting for the investments of **Mornin' Joe** follows:

| Mornin' Joe<br>Balance Sheet<br>December 31, 2016 | | | |
|---|---|---|---|
| **Assets** | | | |
| Current assets: | | | |
| Cash and cash equivalents ............................. | | | $235,000 |
| Trading investments (at cost) .......................... | $420,000 | | |
| Plus valuation allowance for trading investments ..... | 45,000 | 465,000 | |
| Accounts receivable .................................... | $305,000 | | |
| Less allowance for doubtful accounts ................ | 12,300 | 292,700 | |
| Merchandise inventory—at lower of cost | | | |
| (first-in, first-out method) or market ................. | | 120,000 | |
| Prepaid insurance ...................................... | | 24,000 | |
| Total current assets................................ | | | $1,136,700 |
| Investments: | | | |
| Investment in AM Coffee (equity method) ............... | | | 565,000 |
| Property, plant, and equipment: | | | |

Mornin' Joe invests in trading securities and does not have investments in held-to-maturity or available-for-sale securities. Mornin' Joe also owns 40% of AM Coffee Corporation, which is accounted for using the equity method. Mornin' Joe intends to keep its investment in AM Coffee indefinitely for strategic reasons; thus, its investment in AM Coffee is classified as a noncurrent asset. Such investments are normally reported before property, plant, and equipment.

Mornin' Joe reported an Unrealized Gain on Trading Investments of $5,000 and Equity Income in AM Coffee of $57,000 in the Other Income and Expense section of its income statement, as follows:

| Mornin' Joe<br>Income Statement<br>For the Year Ended December 31, 2016 | | | |
|---|---|---|---|
| Revenue from sales: | | | |
| Sales ............................................. | | $5,450,000 | |
| Less: Sales returns and allowances .............. | $26,500 | | |
| Sales discounts .......................... | 21,400 | 47,900 | |
| Sales ............................................. | | | $5,402,100 |
| Cost of merchandise sold ......................... | | | 2,160,000 |
| Gross profit ....................................... | | | $3,242,100 |
| | | | |
| Total operating expenses ....................... | | | 2,608,700 |
| Income from operations .......................... | | | $ 633,400 |
| Other income and expense: | | | |
| Interest revenue ............................... | | $ 18,000 | |
| Interest expense ............................... | | (136,000) | |
| Loss on disposal of fixed asset ................. | | (23,000) | |
| Unrealized gain on trading investments ......... | | 5,000 | |
| Equity income in AM Coffee .................... | | 57,000 | (79,000) |
| Income before income taxes ...................... | | | $ 554,400 |
| Income tax expense ............................... | | | 132,800 |
| Net income ....................................... | | | $ 421,600 |

---

## Business ⊕ Connection

### WARREN BUFFETT: THE SAGE OF OMAHA

Beginning in 1962, Warren Buffett, one of the world's wealthiest and most successful investors, began buying shares of Berkshire Hathaway. He eventually took control of the company and transformed it from a textile manufacturing company into an investment holding company. Today, Berkshire Hathaway holds more than $125 billion in cash and cash equivalents, equity securities, and debt securities. Berkshire's largest holdings include The Coca-Cola Company, American Express, Wells Fargo, and Procter & Gamble. Berkshire Class A common stock trades near $155,000 per share, the highest priced share on the New York Stock Exchange. These shares would have given an investor more than a 1,800% return since 1990.

Buffett compares his investment style to hitting a baseball: "Ted Williams, one of the greatest hitters in the game, stated, 'my argument is, to be a good hitter, you've got to get a good ball to hit. It's the first rule of the book. If I have to bite at stuff that is out of my happy zone, I'm not a .344 hitter. I might only be a .250 hitter.'" Buffett states, "Charlie (Buffett's partner) and I agree and will try to wait for (investment) opportunities that are well within our 'happy zone.'" One of Buffet's recent "happy zone" investments was the acquisition of Burlington Northern Santa Fe Railroad for $34 billion.

Warren Buffett as the CEO of Berkshire Hathaway earns a salary of only $100,000 per year, which is the lowest CEO salary for a company of its size in the United States. However, he personally owns approximately 38% of the company, making him worth more than $40 billion. What will Buffett do with this wealth? He has decided to give nearly all of it to philanthropic causes through the Bill and Melinda Gates Foundation.

Source: Warren E. Buffett, *The Essays of Warren Buffett: Lessons for Corporate America*, edited by Lawrence A. Cunningham, p. 234.

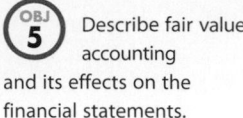

Describe fair value accounting and its effects on the financial statements.

# Fair Value Accounting

Fair value is the price that would be received from selling an asset. Fair value assumes that this transaction occurs under *normal* business conditions.

As illustrated earlier, generally accepted accounting principles require trading and available-for-sale investments to be recorded at their fair value. This differs from the traditional historical cost measurement basis, which records assets such as inventory and property, plant, and equipment at their purchase price. As a result, financial statements include some assets that are reported at their historical cost (inventory, property, plant, and equipment), and other assets that are reported at their fair value (trading, and available-for-sale securities).

Over the past several decades, the financial statements of companies in most industries have included more fair value measures. This is partially due to the Financial Accounting Standards Board's increased willingness to apply fair value to certain assets and transactions. As the ability to measure fair value becomes more reliable, a greater number of assets and transactions are likely to be reported at fair value. A more detailed discussion of fair value is provided in intermediate and advanced financial accounting courses.

## Effect of Fair Value Accounting on the Financial Statements

The use of fair values for valuing assets and liabilities affects the financial statements. Specifically, the balance sheet and income statement could be affected.

**Balance Sheet** When an asset is reported at its fair value, any difference between the asset's original cost or prior period's fair value must be recorded. As we illustrated for trading and available-for-sale securities, this difference is reported in a valuation allowance. The account, Valuation Allowance for Trading Investments, was used earlier in this chapter to adjust trading securities to their fair values.

Available-for-sale securities are reported at fair value in the balance sheet. Changes in their fair values are not recognized on the income statement, but are included as part of stockholders' equity through the comprehensive income and accumulated other comprehensive income accounts. These accounts are described in the appendix to this chapter.

**Income Statement** Trading securities are also reported at fair value in the balance sheet. However, instead of recording the changes in the fair values of trading securities as part of stockholders' equity, the unrealized gains or losses are reported on the income statement.

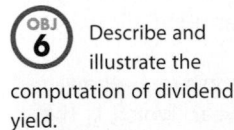

Describe and illustrate the computation of dividend yield.

# Financial Analysis and Interpretation: Dividend Yield

The **dividend yield** measures the rate of return to stockholders, based on cash dividends. Dividend yield is most often computed for common stock because preferred stock has a stated dividend rate. In contrast, the cash dividends paid on common stock normally vary with the profitability of the corporation.

The dividend yield is computed as follows:

$$\text{Dividend Yield} = \frac{\text{Dividends per Share of Common Stock}}{\text{Market Price per Share of Common Stock}}$$

To illustrate, the market price of The Coca-Cola Company was $40.69 on March 26, 2013. During the preceding year, The Coca-Cola Company had paid dividends of $1.05 per share. Thus, the dividend yield of The Coca-Cola Company's common stock is computed as follows:

$$\text{Dividend Yield} = \frac{\text{Dividends per Share of Common Stock}}{\text{Market Price per Share of Common Stock}} = \frac{\$1.05}{\$40.69} = 2.6\%$$

The Coca-Cola Company pays a dividend yield of slightly less than 2.6%. The dividend yield is first a function of a company's profitability, or ability to pay a dividend. For example, many banks nearly eliminated their dividends during the banking crisis of 2008 because they had significant losses. The Coca-Cola Company has sufficient profitability to pay a dividend. Secondly, a company's dividend yield is a function of management's alternative use of funds. If a company has sufficient growth opportunities, funds may be directed toward internal investment, rather than toward paying dividends.

The dividend yield will vary from day to day because the market price of a corporation's stock varies day to day. Current dividend yields are provided with news service quotations of market prices, such as The Wall Street Journal or Yahoo! Finance.

Recent dividend yields for some selected companies are as follows:

| Company | Dividend Yield (%) |
| --- | --- |
| Facebook | None |
| Best Buy | 2.20 |
| Coca-Cola Company | 2.60 |
| Duke Energy | 4.30 |
| Google | None |
| Hewlett-Packard | 2.10 |
| Microsoft | 2.80 |
| Verizon Communications | 4.10 |

As can be seen, the dividend yield varies widely across firms. Growth firms tend to retain their earnings to fund future growth. Thus, Facebook and Google pay no dividends, and Hewlett-Packard has a relatively small dividend. Common stockholders of these companies expect to earn most of their return from stock price appreciation. In contrast, Duke Energy and Verizon Communications are regulated utilities that provide a return to common stockholders mostly through dividends. Best Buy, Coca-Cola, and Microsoft provide a mix of dividends and expected stock price appreciation to their common stockholders.

**Example Exercise 15-6  Dividend Yield**                    OBJ 6

On March 11, 2016, Sheldon Corporation had a market price of $58 per share of common stock. For the previous year, Sheldon paid an annual dividend of $2.90 per share. Compute the dividend yield for Sheldon Corporation.

**Follow My Example 15-6**

$$\text{Dividend Yield} = \frac{\text{Dividends per Share of Common Stock}}{\text{Market Price per Share of Common Stock}}$$

$$\text{Dividend Yield} = \frac{\$2.90}{\$58} = 0.05, \text{ or } 5\%$$

Practice Exercises: PE 15-6A, PE 15-6B

# A P P E N D I X

## Comprehensive Income

**Comprehensive income** is defined as all changes in stockholders' equity during a period, except those resulting from dividends and stockholders' investments. Comprehensive income is computed by adding or subtracting *other comprehensive income* to (from) net income, as follows:

| | |
|---|---|
| Net income | $XXX |
| Other comprehensive income | XXX |
| Comprehensive income | $XXX |

**Other comprehensive income** items include unrealized gains and losses on available-for-sale securities as well as other items such as foreign currency and pension liability adjustments. The *cumulative* effect of other comprehensive income is reported on the balance sheet, as **accumulated other comprehensive income**.

Companies are required to report comprehensive income in the financial statements in one of the following two ways:

- On the income statement, or
- In a separate statement of comprehensive income that immediately follows the income statement.

In the earlier illustration, Maggie Company had reported an unrealized gain of $1,300 on available-for-sale investments. This unrealized gain would be reported in the Stockholders' Equity section of Maggie's 2016 balance sheet, as follows:

**Maggie Company**
**Balance Sheet**
**December 31, 2016**

| | |
|---|---|
| Stockholders' equity: | |
| Common stock. . . . . . . . . . . . . . . . . . . . . . . . . . . . . . . . . . . . . . . . . . . . . . . . . . . | $ 10,000 |
| Paid-in capital in excess of par . . . . . . . . . . . . . . . . . . . . . . . . . . . . . . . . . . . . . . | 150,000 |
| Retained earnings. . . . . . . . . . . . . . . . . . . . . . . . . . . . . . . . . . . . . . . . . . . . . . . . . | 250,000 |
| Unrealized gain (loss) on available-for-sale investments. . . . . . . . . . . . . . . . . . . . . . . | 1,300 |
| Total stockholders' equity . . . . . . . . . . . . . . . . . . . . . . . . . . . . . . . . . . . . . . . . . . . . | $411,300 |

Alternatively, Maggie Company could have reported the unrealized gain as part of accumulated other comprehensive income as follows:

| Maggie Company<br>Balance Sheet<br>December 31, 2016 | | |
| --- | --- | --- |
| Stockholders' equity: | | |
| Common stock.......................................................... | $ 10,000 | |
| Paid-in capital in excess of par .................................. | 150,000 | |
| Retained earnings.................................................... | 250,000 | |
| Accumulated other comprehensive income: | | |
| Unrealized gain on available-for-sale investments.............................. | 1,300 | |
| Total stockholders' equity ........................................ | $411,300 | |

# At a Glance 15

## Describe why companies invest in debt and equity securities.

**Key Points**  Cash can be used to (1) invest in current operations, (2) invest to earn additional revenue in marketable securities, or (3) invest in marketable securities for strategic reasons.

| Learning Outcomes | Example Exercises | Practice Exercises |
| --- | --- | --- |
| • Describe the ways excess cash is used by a business. | | |
| • Describe the purpose of temporary investments. | | |
| • Describe the strategic purpose of long-term investments. | | |

## Describe and illustrate the accounting for debt investments.

**Key Points**  The accounting for debt investments includes recording the purchase, interest revenue, and sale of the debt. Both the purchase and sale date may include accrued interest.

| Learning Outcomes | Example Exercises | Practice Exercises |
| --- | --- | --- |
| • Prepare journal entries to record the purchase of a debt investment, including accrued interest. | EE15-1 | PE15-1A, 15-1B |
| • Prepare journal entries for interest revenue from debt investments. | EE15-1 | PE15-1A, 15-1B |
| • Prepare journal entries to record the sale of a debt investment at a gain or loss. | EE15-1 | PE15-1A, 15-1B |

## Describe and illustrate the accounting for equity investments.

**Key Points** The accounting for equity investments differs, depending on the degree of control. Accounting for investments of less than 20% of the outstanding stock (no control) of the investee includes recording the purchase of stock, the receipt of dividends, and the sale of stock at a gain or loss. Investments of 20%–50% of the outstanding stock of an investee are considered to have significant influence and accounted for under the *equity method*. An investment for more than 50% of the outstanding stock of an investee is treated as a *business combination* and accounted for using *consolidated financial statements*.

| Learning Outcomes | Example Exercises | Practice Exercises |
|---|---|---|
| • Describe the accounting for less than 20%, 20%–50%, and greater than 50% investments. | | |
| • Prepare journal entries to record the purchase of a stock investment. | **EE15-2** | **PE15-2A, 15-2B** |
| • Prepare journal entries for the receipt of dividends. | **EE15-2** | **PE15-2A, 15-2B** |
| • Prepare journal entries for the sale of a stock investment at a gain or loss. | **EE15-2** | **PE15-2A, 15-2B** |
| • Prepare journal entries for the equity earnings of an equity method investee. | **EE15-3** | **PE15-3A, 15-3B** |
| • Prepare journal entries for the dividends received from an equity method investee. | **EE15-3** | **PE15-3A, 15-3B** |
| • Describe a business combination, parent company, and subsidiary company. | | |
| • Describe consolidated financial statements. | | |

## Describe and illustrate valuing and reporting investments in the financial statements.

**Key Points** Debt and equity security investments of 20%–50% of the outstanding stock (not control) are classified as either (1) trading securities, (2) available-for-sale securities, or (3) held-to-maturity securities for reporting and valuation purposes. *Trading securities* are valued at *fair value*, with unrealized gains and losses reported on the income statement. *Available-for-sale securities* are reported at fair value with unrealized gains or losses reported in the Stockholders' Equity section of the balance sheet. *Held-to-maturity* investments are valued at amortized cost.

| Learning Outcomes | Example Exercises | Practice Exercises |
|---|---|---|
| • Describe trading securities, held-to-maturity securities, and available-for-sale securities. | | |
| • Prepare journal entries to record the change in the fair value of a trading security portfolio. | **EE15-4** | **PE15-4A, 15-4B** |
| • Describe and illustrate the reporting of trading securities on the balance sheet. | | |
| • Prepare journal entries to record the change in fair value of an available-for-sale security portfolio. | **EE15-5** | **PE15-5A, 15-5B** |
| • Describe and illustrate the reporting of available-for-sale securities on the balance sheet. | | |
| • Describe the accounting for held-to-maturity debt securities. | | |

**Describe fair value accounting and its effects on the financial statements.**

**Key Points** There is a trend toward fair value accounting in generally accepted accounting principles. Fair value is the price that would be received to sell an asset.

| Learning Outcomes | Example Exercises | Practice Exercises |
|---|---|---|
| • Describe fair value accounting. | | |
| • Describe how fair value accounting impacts the balance sheet and income statement. | | |

**Describe and illustrate the computation of dividend yield.**

**Key Points** The dividend yield measures the cash return from common dividends as a percent of the market price of the common stock. The ratio is computed as dividends per share of common stock divided by the market price per share of common stock.

| Learning Outcomes | Example Exercises | Practice Exercises |
|---|---|---|
| • Compute dividend yield. | EE15-6 | PE15-6A, 15-6B |
| • Describe how dividend yield measures the return to stockholders from dividends. | | |

# Key Terms

accumulated other comprehensive income (702)
available-for-sale securities (695)
business combination (692)
comprehensive income (702)
consolidated financial statements (692)
cost method (689)

debt securities (685)
dividend yield (700)
equity method (690)
equity securities (685)
fair value (693)
held-to-maturity securities (697)
investee (688)

investments (685)
investor (688)
other comprehensive income (702)
parent company (692)
subsidiary company (692)
trading securities (693)
unrealized gain or loss (693)

# Illustrative Problem

The following selected investment transactions were completed by Rosewell Company during 2016, its first year of operations:

2016

Jan. 11. Purchased 800 shares of Bryan Company stock as an available-for-sale security at $23 per share plus an $80 brokerage commission.

Feb. 6. Purchased $40,000 of 8% U.S. Treasury bonds at their face amount plus accrued interest for 36 days. The bonds pay interest on January 1 and July 1. The bonds were classified as held-to-maturity securities.

**2016**

Mar. 3. Purchased 1,900 shares of Cohen Company stock as a trading security at $48 per share plus a $152 brokerage commission.

Apr. 5. Purchased 2,400 shares of Lyons Inc. stock as an available-for-sale security at $68 per share plus a $120 brokerage commission.

May 12. Purchased 200,000 shares of Myers Company at $37 per share plus an $8,000 brokerage commission. Myers Company has 800,000 common shares issued and outstanding. The equity method was used for this investment.

July 1. Received semiannual interest on bonds purchased on February 6.

Aug. 29. Sold 1,200 shares of Cohen Company stock at $61 per share less a $90 brokerage commission.

Oct. 5. Received an $0.80-per-share dividend on Bryan Company stock.

Nov. 11. Received a $1.10-per-share dividend on Myers Company stock.

16. Purchased 3,000 shares of Morningside Company stock as a trading security for $52 per share plus a $150 brokerage commission.

Dec. 31. Accrued interest on U.S. Treasury bonds.

31. Myers Company earned $1,200,000 during the year. Rosewell recorded its share of Myers Company earnings, using the equity method.

31. Prepared adjusting entries for the portfolios of trading and available-for-sale securities, based upon the following fair values (stock prices):

| | |
|---|---|
| Bryan Company | $21 |
| Cohen Company | 43 |
| Lyons Inc. | 88 |
| Myers Company | 40 |
| Morningside Company | 45 |

## Instructions

1. Journalize the preceding transactions.

2. Prepare the balance sheet disclosure for Rosewell Company's investments on December 31, 2016. Assume held-to-maturity investments are classified as noncurrent assets.

## Solution

1.

| 2016 | | | | | |
|---|---|---|---|---|---|
| Jan. | 11 | Investments—Bryan Company | | 18,480* | |
| | | Cash | | | 18,480 |
| | | *(800 shares × $23 per share) + $80 | | | |

| | | | | | |
|---|---|---|---|---|---|
| Feb. | 6 | Investments—U.S. Treasury Bonds | | 40,000 | |
| | | Interest Receivable | | 320* | |
| | | Cash | | | 40,320 |
| | | *$40,000 × 8% × (36 days ÷ 360 days) | | | |

| | | | | | |
|---|---|---|---|---|---|
| Mar. | 3 | Investments—Cohen Company | | 91,352* | |
| | | Cash | | | 91,352 |
| | | *(1,900 shares × $48 per share) + $152 | | | |

| | | | | |
|---|---|---|---|---|
| 2016 Apr. | 5 | Investments—Lyons Inc. | 163,320* | |
| | | Cash | | 163,320 |
| | | *(2,400 shares × $68 per share) + $120 | | |

| | | | | |
|---|---|---|---|---|
| May | 12 | Investment in Myers Company | 7,408,000* | |
| | | Cash | | 7,408,000 |
| | | *(200,000 shares × $37 per share) + $8,000 | | |

| | | | | |
|---|---|---|---|---|
| July | 1 | Cash | 1,600* | |
| | | Interest Receivable | | 320 |
| | | Interest Revenue | | 1,280 |
| | | *$40,000 × 8% × ½ | | |

| | | | | |
|---|---|---|---|---|
| Aug. | 29 | Cash | 73,110* | |
| | | Investments—Cohen Company | | 57,696** |
| | | Gain on Sale of Investments | | 15,414 |
| | | *(1,200 shares × $61 per share) – $90 | | |
| | | **1,200 shares × ($91,352 ÷ 1,900 shares) | | |

| | | | | |
|---|---|---|---|---|
| Oct. | 5 | Cash | 640 | |
| | | Dividend Revenue | | 640 |
| | | *800 shares × $0.80 per share | | |

| | | | | |
|---|---|---|---|---|
| Nov. | 11 | Cash | 220,000 | |
| | | Investment in Myers Company Stock | | 220,000 |
| | | *200,000 shares × $1.10 per share | | |

| | | | | |
|---|---|---|---|---|
| Nov. | 16 | Investments—Morningside Company | 156,150* | |
| | | Cash | | 156,150 |
| | | *(3,000 shares × $52 per share) + $150 | | |

| | | | | |
|---|---|---|---|---|
| Dec. | 31 | Interest Receivable | 1,600 | |
| | | Interest Revenue | | 1,600 |
| | | Accrued interest, $40,000 × 8% × ½. | | |

| | | | | |
|---|---|---|---|---|
| Dec. | 31 | Investment in Myers Company Stock | 300,000 | |
| | | Income of Myers Company | | 300,000 |
| | | Recorded equity income, | | |
| | | $1,200,000 × (200,000 shares ÷ 800,000 shares). | | |

| | | | | | |
|---|---|---|---|---|---|
| 2016<br>Dec. | 31 | Unrealized Loss on Trading Investments | | 24,706 | |
| | | Valuation Allowance for Trading Investments | | | 24,706 |
| | | Recorded decease in fair value of trading<br>investments, $165,100 – $189,806. | | | |

| Name | Number of Shares | Total Cost | Total Fair Value |
|---|---|---|---|
| Cohen Company | 700 | $ 33,656 | $ 30,100* |
| Morningside Company | 3,000 | 156,150 | 135,000** |
| Total | | $189,806 | $165,100 |

*700 shares × $43 per share
**3,000 shares × $45 per share

*Note*: Myers Company is valued using the equity method; thus, the fair value is not used.

| | | | | | |
|---|---|---|---|---|---|
| Dec. | 31 | Valuation Allowance for Available-for-Sale<br>Investments | | 46,200 | |
| | | Unrealized Gain (Loss) on Available-for-<br>Sale Investments | | | 46,200 |
| | | Recorded increase in fair value of available-<br>for-sale investments, $228,000 – $181,800. | | | |

| Name | Number of Shares | Total Cost | Total Fair Value |
|---|---|---|---|
| Bryan Company | 800 | $ 18,480 | $ 16,800* |
| Lyons Inc. | 2,400 | 163,320 | 211,200** |
| Total | | $181,800 | $228,000 |

*800 shares × $21 per share
**2,400 shares × $88 per share

2.

### Rosewell Company
### Balance Sheet (Selected)
### December 31, 2016

| | | |
|---|---|---|
| Current assets: | | |
| Cash . . . . . . . . . . . . . . . . . . . . . . . . . . . . . . . . . . . . . . . . . . . . . . . . . . . . . | | $ XXX,XXX |
| Trading investments (at cost) . . . . . . . . . . . . . . . . . . . . . . . . . . . . . . | $189,806 | |
| Less valuation allowance for trading investments . . . . . . . . . . . . | 24,706 | |
| Trading investments at fair value. . . . . . . . . . . . . . . . . . . . . . . . . . . | | 165,100 |
| Available-for-sale investments (at cost) . . . . . . . . . . . . . . . . . . . . . | $181,800 | |
| Plus valuation allowance for available-for-sale investments . . . . | 46,200 | |
| Available-for-sale investments at fair value . . . . . . . . . . . . . . . . . | | 228,000 |
| Investments: | | |
| Held-to-maturity investments . . . . . . . . . . . . . . . . . . . . . . . . . . . . . | | 40,000 |
| Investment in Myers Company (equity method). . . . . . . . . . . . . . . | | 7,488,000 |
| | | |
| Stockholders' equity: | | |
| Common stock . . . . . . . . . . . . . . . . . . . . . . . . . . . . . . . . . . . . . . . . . . | | $ XX,XXX |
| Paid-in capital in excess of par . . . . . . . . . . . . . . . . . . . . . . . . . . . . . | | XXX,XXX |
| Retained earnings . . . . . . . . . . . . . . . . . . . . . . . . . . . . . . . . . . . . . . . . | | XXX,XXX |
| Plus unrealized gain (loss) on available-for-sale investments . . . | | 46,200 |
| Total stockholders' equity . . . . . . . . . . . . . . . . . . . . . . . . . . . . . . . . . . . . | | $ XXX,XXX |

# Discussion Questions

1. Why might a business invest cash in temporary investments?

2. What causes a gain or loss on the sale of a bond investment?

3. When is the equity method the appropriate accounting for equity investments?

4. How does the accounting for a dividend received differ between the cost method and the equity method?

5. If an investor owns more than 50% of an investee, how is the investment treated on the investor's financial statements?

6. What is the major difference in the accounting for a portfolio of trading securities and a portfolio of available-for-sale securities?

7. If Valuation Allowance for Available-for-Sale Investments has a credit balance, how is it treated on the balance sheet?

8. How would a debit balance in Unrealized Gain (Loss) on Available-for-Sale Investments be reported in the financial statements?

9. What are the factors contributing to the trend toward fair value accounting?

10. How are the balance sheet and income statement affected by fair value accounting?

# Practice Exercises

**EE 15-1** *p. 688*  **PE 15-1A   Bond investment transactions**                                    OBJ. 2

SHOW
ME HOW

Journalize the entries to record the following selected bond investment transactions for Hall Trust:

a. Purchased for cash $300,000 of Oates City 4% bonds at 100 plus accrued interest of $3,000.

b. Received first semiannual interest payment.

c. Sold $150,000 of the bonds at 97 plus accrued interest of $500.

**EE 15-1** *p. 688*  **PE 15-1B   Bond investment transactions**                                    OBJ. 2

SHOW
ME HOW

Journalize the entries to record the following selected bond investment transactions for Starks Products:

a. Purchased for cash $120,000 of Iceline, Inc. 5% bonds at 100 plus accrued interest of $1,000.

b. Received first semiannual interest payment.

c. Sold $60,000 of the bonds at 101 plus accrued interest of $500.

**EE 15-2** *p. 690*  **PE 15-2A   Stock investment transactions**                                    OBJ. 3

SHOW
ME HOW

On February 10, 15,000 shares of Sting Company are acquired at a price of $25 per share plus a $150 brokerage commission. On April 12, a $0.40-per-share dividend was received on the Sting Company stock. On May 29, 6,000 shares of the Sting Company stock were sold for $32 per share less a $120 brokerage commission. Prepare the journal entries for the original purchase, the dividend, and the sale under the cost method.

**EE 15-2** *p. 690*  **PE 15-2B   Stock investment transactions**                                    OBJ. 3

SHOW
ME HOW

On September 12, 2,000 shares of Aspen Company are acquired at a price of $50 per share plus a $200 brokerage commission. On October 15, a $0.50-per-share dividend was received on the Aspen Company stock. On November 10, 1,200 shares of the Aspen Company stock were sold for $42 per share less a $150 brokerage commission. Prepare the journal entries for the original purchase, the dividend, and the sale under the cost method.

EE 15-3 *p. 692*

**PE 15-3A    Equity method**                                            OBJ. 3

On January 2, Peyroux Company acquired 35% of the outstanding stock of Gruden Company for $625,000. For the year ended December 31, Gruden Company earned income of $110,000 and paid dividends of $26,000. Prepare the entries for Peyroux Company for the purchase of the stock, the share of Gruden income, and the dividends received from Gruden Company.

EE 15-3 *p. 692*

**PE 15-3B   Equity method**                                             OBJ. 3

On January 2, Yorkshire Company acquired 40% of the outstanding stock of Fain Company for $500,000. For the year ended December 31, Fain Company earned income of $140,000 and paid dividends of $50,000. Prepare the entries for Yorkshire Company for the purchase of the stock, the share of Fain income, and the dividends received from Fain Company.

EE 15-4 *p. 694*

**PE 15-4A    Valuing trading securities at fair value**                  OBJ. 4

On January 1, 2016, Valuation Allowance for Trading Investments had a zero balance. On December 31, 2016, the cost of the trading securities portfolio was $385,000, and the fair value was $357,400. Prepare the December 31, 2016, adjusting journal entry to record the unrealized gain or loss on trading investments.

EE 15-4 *p. 694*

**PE 15-4B   Valuing trading securities at fair value**                   OBJ. 4

On January 1, 2016, Valuation Allowance for Trading Investments had a zero balance. On December 31, 2016, the cost of the trading securities portfolio was $41,500, and the fair value was $46,300. Prepare the December 31, 2016, adjusting journal entry to record the unrealized gain or loss on trading investments.

EE 15-5 *p. 697*

**PE 15-5A    Valuing available-for-sale securities at fair value**       OBJ. 4

On January 1, 2016, Valuation Allowance for Available-for-Sale Investments had a zero balance. On December 31, 2016, the cost of the available-for-sale securities was $78,400, and the fair value was $72,600. Prepare the adjusting entry to record the unrealized gain or loss on available-for-sale investments on December 31, 2016.

EE 15-5 *p. 697*

**PE 15-5B   Valuing available-for-sale securities at fair value**        OBJ. 4

On January 1, 2016, Valuation Allowance for Available-for-Sale Investments had a zero balance. On December 31, 2016, the cost of the available-for-sale securities was $24,260, and the fair value was $26,350. Prepare the adjusting entry to record the unrealized gain or loss on available-for-sale investments on December 31, 2016.

EE 15-6 *p. 701*

**PE 15-6A    Dividend yield**                                           OBJ. 6

On June 30, 2016, Setzer Corporation had a market price of $100 per share of common stock. For the previous year, Setzer paid an annual dividend of $4.00. Compute the dividend yield for Setzer Corporation.

EE 15-6 *p. 701*

**PE 15-6B   Dividend yield**                                            OBJ. 6

On October 23, 2016, Wilkerson Company had a market price of $40 per share of common stock. For the previous year, Wilkerson paid an annual dividend of $1.20. Compute the dividend yield for Wilkerson Company.

## Exercises

**EX 15-1    Entries for investment in bonds, interest, and sale of bonds**    OBJ. 2

Parilo Company acquired $170,000 of Makofske Co., 5% bonds on May 1, 2016, at their face amount. Interest is paid semiannually on May 1 and November 1. On November 1, 2016, Parilo Company sold $50,000 of the bonds for 96.

Journalize entries to record the following:

a.  The initial acquisition of the bonds on May 1.

b.  The semiannual interest received on November 1.

c. The sale of the bonds on November 1.

d. The accrual of $1,000 interest on December 31, 2016.

---

### EX 15-2 Entries for investments in bonds, interest, and sale of bonds OBJ. 2

Kalyagin Investments acquired $220,000 of Jerris Corp., 7% bonds at their face amount on October 1, 2016. The bonds pay interest on October 1 and April 1. On April 1, 2017, Kalyagin sold $80,000 of Jerris Corp. bonds at 103.

Journalize the entries to record the following:

a. The initial acquisition of the Jerris Corp. bonds on October 1, 2016.

b. The adjusting entry for three months of accrued interest earned on the Jerris Corp. bonds on December 31, 2016.

c. The receipt of semiannual interest on April 1, 2017.

d. The sale of $80,000 of Jerris Corp. bonds on April 1, 2017, at 103.

---

### EX 15-3 Entries for investment in bonds, interest, and sale of bonds OBJ. 2

✔ Oct. 31, Loss on sale of investments, $400

Bocelli Co. purchased $120,000 of 6%, 20-year Sanz County bonds on May 11, 2016, directly from the county, at their face amount plus accrued interest. The bonds pay semiannual interest on April 1 and October 1. On October 31, 2016, Bocelli Co. sold $30,000 of the Sanz County bonds at 99 plus $150 accrued interest, less a $100 brokerage commission.

Provide journal entries for the following:

a. The purchase of the bonds on May 11, plus 40 days of accrued interest.

b. Semiannual interest on October 1.

c. Sale of the bonds on October 31.

d. Adjusting entry for accrued interest of $1,365 on December 31, 2016.

---

### EX 15-4 Entries for investment in bonds, interest, and sale of bonds OBJ. 2

✔ Aug. 29, Loss on sale of investments, $700

The following bond investment transactions were completed during 2016 by Starks Company:

Jan. 31. Purchased 75, $1,000 government bonds at 100 plus 30 days' accrued interest. The bonds pay 6% annual interest on July 1 and January 1.

July 1. Received semiannual interest on bond investment.

Aug. 29. Sold 35, $1,000 bonds at 98 plus $350 accrued interest.

a. Journalize the entries for these transactions.

b. Provide the December 31, 2016, adjusting journal entry for semiannual interest earned on the bonds.

---

### EX 15-5 Interest on bond investments OBJ. 2

On April 1, 2016, Rizzo Company purchased $80,000 of 4.5%, 20-year Energizer Company bonds at their face amount plus one month's accrued interest. The bonds pay interest on March 1 and September 1. On November 1, 2016, Rizzo Company sold $30,000 of the Energizer Company bonds acquired on April 1, plus two months' accrued interest. On December 31, 2016, four months' interest was accrued for the remaining bonds.

Determine the interest earned by Rizzo Company on Energizer Company bonds for 2016.

---

### EX 15-6 Entries for investment in stock, receipt of dividends, and sale of shares OBJ. 3

✔ c. Gain on sale of investments, $17,755

On March 4, Breen Corporation acquired 7,500 shares of the 200,000 outstanding shares of Melton Co. common stock at $40 plus commission charges of $175. On June 15, a cash dividend of $2.10 per share was received. On October 12, 3,000 shares were sold at $46, less commission charges of $175.

Using the cost method, journalize the entries for (a) the purchase of stock, (b) the receipt of dividends, and (c) the sale of 3,000 shares.

SHOW ME HOW

### EX 15-7 Entries for investment in stock, receipt of dividends, and sale of shares   OBJ. 3

The following equity investment transactions were completed by Chung Company in 2016:

Mar.  4.  Purchased 4,000 shares of Jas Company for a price of $50 per share plus a brokerage commission of $100.

May 12.  Received a quarterly dividend of $0.75 per share on the Jas Company investment.

June 17.  Sold 1,400 shares for a price of $44 per share less a brokerage commission of $80.

Journalize the entries for these transactions.

### EX 15-8 Entries for stock investments, dividends, and sale of stock   OBJ. 3

Yerbury Corp. manufactures construction equipment. Journalize the entries to record the following selected equity investment transactions completed by Yerbury during 2016:

Feb.  2.  Purchased for cash 5,300 shares of Wong Inc. stock for $20 per share plus a $110 brokerage commission.

Mar.  6.  Received dividends of $0.30 per share on Wong Inc. stock.

June  7.  Purchased 2,000 shares of Wong Inc. stock for $26 per share plus a $125 brokerage commission.

July  26.  Sold 6,000 shares of Wong Inc. stock for $35 per share less a $100 brokerage commission. Yerbury assumes that the first investments purchased are the first investments sold.

Sept. 25.  Received dividends of $0.40 per share on Wong Inc. stock.

### EX 15-9 Entries for stock investments, dividends, and sale of stock   OBJ. 3

Seamus Industries Inc. buys and sells investments as part of its ongoing cash management. The following investment transactions were completed during the year:

Feb. 24.  Acquired 1,000 shares of Tett Co. stock for $85 per share plus a $150 brokerage commission.

May 16.  Acquired 2,500 shares of Issacson Co. stock for $36 per share plus a $100 commission.

July 14.  Sold 400 shares of Tett Co. stock for $100 per share less a $75 brokerage commission.

Aug. 12.  Sold 750 shares of Issacson Co. stock for $32.50 per share less an $80 brokerage commission.

Oct. 31.  Received dividends of $0.40 per share on Tett Co. stock.

Journalize the entries for these transactions.

### EX 15-10 Equity method for stock investment   OBJ. 3

At a total cost of $6,300,000, Veravo Corporation acquired 210,000 shares of Strado Corp. common stock as a long-term investment. Veravo Corporation uses the equity method of accounting for this investment. Strado Corp. has 700,000 shares of common stock outstanding, including the shares acquired by Veravo Corporation.

a.  Journalize the entries by Veravo Corporation to record the following information:

1.  Strado Corp. reports net income of $860,000 for the current period.

2.  A cash dividend of $0.32 per common share is paid by Strado Corp. during the current period.

b.  ⬤━━━▶ Why is the equity method appropriate for the Strado Corp. investment?

✔ b. $5,400,500

SHOW
ME HOW

### EX 15-11 Equity method for stock investment

OBJ. 3

On January 4, 2016, Spandella Company purchased 175,000 shares of Filington Company directly from one of the founders for a price of $30 per share. Filington has 500,000 shares outstanding, including the Penman shares. On July 2, 2016, Filington paid $620,000 in total dividends to its shareholders. On December 31, 2016, Filington reported a net income of $1,050,000 for the year. Spandella uses the equity method in accounting for its investment in Filington.

a. Provide the Spandella Inc. journal entries for the transactions involving its investment in Filington Inc. during 2016.

b. Determine the December 31, 2016, balance of the Investment in Filington Company. Stock account.

### EX 15-12 Equity method for stock investment with loss

OBJ. 3

On January 6, 2016, Bulldog Co. purchased 34% of the outstanding stock of Gator Co. for $212,000. Gator Co. paid total dividends of $24,000 to all shareholders on June 30. Gator had a net loss of $56,000 for 2016.

a. Journalize Bulldog's purchase of the stock, receipt of the dividends, and the adjusting entry for the equity loss in Gator Co. stock.

b. Compute the balance of Investment in Gator Co. Stock on December 31, 2016.

c. How does valuing an investment under the equity method differ from valuing an investment at fair value?

### EX 15-13 Equity method for stock investment

OBJ. 3

Hawkeye Company's balance sheet reported, under the equity method, its long-term investment in Raven Company for comparative years as follows:

|  | Dec. 31, 2017 | Dec. 31, 2016 |
|---|---|---|
| Investment in Raven Company stock (in millions) | $281 | $264 |

In addition, the 2017 Hawkeye Company income statement disclosed equity earnings in the Raven Company investment as $25 million. Hawkeye Company neither purchased nor sold Raven Company stock during 2017. The fair value of the Raven Company stock investment on December 31, 2017, was $310 million.

Explain the change in Investment in Raven Company Stock from December 31, 2016, to December 31, 2017.

### EX 15-14 Missing statement items, trading investments

OBJ. 4

✔ g. $6,000

JED Capital Inc. makes investments in trading securities. Selected income statement items for the years ended December 31, 2016 and 2017, plus selected items from comparative balance sheets, are as follows:

**JED Capital Inc.**
**Selected Income Statement Items**
**For the Years Ended December 31, 2016 and 2017**

|  | 2016 | 2017 |
|---|---|---|
| Operating income | a. | e. |
| Unrealized gain (loss) | b. | $(11,000) |
| Net income | c. | 28,000 |

**JED Capital Inc.**
**Selected Balance Sheet Items**
**December 31, 2015, 2016, and 2017**

|  | Dec. 31, 2015 | Dec. 31, 2016 | Dec. 31, 2017 |
|---|---|---|---|
| Trading investments, at cost | $144,000 | $168,000 | $205,000 |
| Valuation allowance for trading investments | (12,000) | 17,000 | g. |
| Trading investments, at fair value | d. | f. | h. |
| Retained earnings | $210,000 | $245,000 | i. |

There were no dividends.

Determine the missing lettered items.

SHOW
ME HOW

### EX 15-15  Fair value journal entries, trading investments                OBJ. 3, 4

The investments of Charger Inc. include a single investment: 14,500 shares of Raiders Inc. common stock purchased on February 24, 2016, for $38 per share including brokerage commission. These shares were classified as trading securities. As of the December 31, 2016, balance sheet date, the share price had increased to $42 per share.

a. Journalize the entries to acquire the investment on February 24, and record the adjustment to fair value on December 31, 2016.

b. How is the unrealized gain or loss for trading investments reported on the financial statements?

SHOW
ME HOW

### EX 15-16  Fair value journal entries, trading investments                OBJ. 3, 4

Jets Bancorp Inc. purchased a portfolio of trading securities during 2016. The cost and fair value of this portfolio on December 31, 2016, was as follows:

| Name | Number of Shares | Total Cost | Total Fair Value |
|---|---|---|---|
| Dolphins Inc. | 1,400 | $28,000 | $30,800 |
| Marino Company | 1,200 | 30,000 | 27,600 |
| Namath Company | 800 | 28,000 | 26,400 |
| Total | | $86,000 | $84,800 |

On May 10, 2017, Jets Bancorp Inc. purchased 1,000 shares of Giants Inc. at $24 per share plus a $150 brokerage commission.

Provide the journal entries to record the following:

a. The adjustment of the trading security portfolio to fair value on December 31, 2016.

b. The May 10, 2017, purchase of Giants Inc. stock.

✔ a. Dec. 31, 2016,
Unrealized gain on
trading investments,
$17,500

### EX 15-17  Fair value journal entries, trading investments                OBJ. 3, 4

Last Unguaranteed Financial Inc. purchased the following trading securities during 2016, its first year of operations:

| Name | Number of Shares | Cost |
|---|---|---|
| Arden Enterprises Inc. | 5,000 | $150,000 |
| French Broad Industries Inc. | 2,750 | 66,000 |
| Pisgah Construction Inc. | 1,600 | 104,000 |
| Total | | $320,000 |

The market price per share for the trading security portfolio on December 31, 2016, was as follows:

| | Market Price per Share, Dec. 31, 2016 |
|---|---|
| Arden Enterprises Inc. | $34 |
| French Broad Industries Inc. | 26 |
| Pisgah Construction Inc. | 60 |

a. Provide the journal entry to adjust the trading security portfolio to fair value on December 31, 2016.

b. Assume the market prices of the portfolio were the same on December 31, 2017, as they were on December 31, 2016. What would be the journal entry to adjust the portfolio to fair value?

### EX 15-18  Balance sheet presentation, trading investments                OBJ. 4

The income statement for Delta-tec Inc. for the year ended December 31, 2016, was as follows:

**Delta-tec Inc.**
**Income Statement (selected items)**
**For the Year Ended December 31, 2016**

| | |
|---|---|
| Income from operations | $299,700 |
| Gain on sale of investments | 17,800 |
| Less unrealized loss on trading investments | 72,500 |
| Net income | $245,000 |

The balance sheet dated December 31, 2015, showed a Retained Earnings balance of $825,000. During 2016, the company purchased trading investments for the first time at a cost of $346,000. In addition, trading investments with a cost of $66,000 were sold at a gain during 2016. The company paid $65,000 in dividends during 2016.

a. Determine the December 31, 2016, Retained Earnings balance.

b. Provide the December 31, 2016, balance sheet presentation for Trading Investments.

---

**EX 15-19   Missing statement items, available-for-sale securities**                       **OBJ. 4**

✔ f. $(11,000)

Highland Industries Inc. makes investments in available-for-sale securities. Selected income statement items for the years ended December 31, 2016 and 2017, plus selected items from comparative balance sheets, are as follows:

**Highland Industries Inc.**
**Selected Income Statement Items**
**For the Years Ended December 31, 2016 and 2017**

|  | 2016 | 2017 |
|---|---|---|
| Operating income | a. | g. |
| Gain (loss) from sale of investments | $7,500 | $(12,000) |
| Net income (loss) | b. | (21,000) |

**Highland Industries Inc.**
**Selected Balance Sheet Items**
**December 31, 2015, 2016, and 2017**

|  | Dec. 31, 2015 | Dec. 31, 2016 | Dec. 31, 2017 |
|---|---|---|---|
| **Assets** | | | |
| Available-for-sale investments, at cost | $ 90,000 | $ 86,000 | $102,000 |
| Valuation allowance for available-for-sale investments | 12,000 | (11,000) | h. |
| Available-for-sale investments, at fair value | c. | e. | i. |
| **Stockholders' Equity** | | | |
| Unrealized gain (loss) on available-for-sale investments | d. | f. | (16,400) |
| Retained earnings | $175,400 | $220,000 | j. |

There were no dividends.
    Determine the missing lettered items.

---

**EX 15-20   Fair value journal entries, available-for-sale investments**                    **OBJ. 3, 4**

The investments of Steelers Inc. include a single investment: 33,100 shares of Bengals Inc. common stock purchased on September 12, 2016, for $13 per share including brokerage commission. These shares were classified as available-for-sale securities. As of the December 31, 2016, balance sheet date, the share price declined to $11 per share.

a. Journalize the entries to acquire the investment on September 12 and record the adjustment to fair value on December 31, 2016.

b. How is the unrealized gain or loss for available-for-sale investments disclosed on the financial statements?

---

**EX 15-21   Fair value journal entries, available-for-sale investments**                    **OBJ. 3, 4**

Hurricane Inc. purchased a portfolio of available-for-sale securities in 2016, its first year of operations. The cost and fair value of this portfolio on December 31, 2016, was as follows:

| Name | Number of Shares | Total Cost | Total Fair Value |
|---|---|---|---|
| Tornado Inc. | 800 | $14,000 | $15,600 |
| Tsunami Corp. | 1,250 | 31,250 | 35,000 |
| Typhoon Corp. | 2,140 | 43,870 | 42,800 |
| Total | | $89,120 | $93,400 |

*(Continued)*

On June 12, 2017, Hurricane purchased 1,450 shares of Rogue Wave Inc. at $45 per share plus a $100 brokerage commission.

a. Provide the journal entries to record the following:

1. The adjustment of the available-for-sale security portfolio to fair value on December 31, 2016.

2. The June 12, 2017, purchase of Rogue Wave Inc. stock.

b. How are unrealized gains and losses treated differently for available-for-sale securities than for trading securities?

---

**EX 15-22  Fair value journal entries, available-for-sale investments**  OBJ. 3, 4

Storm, Inc. purchased the following available-for-sale securities during 2016, its first year of operations:

| Name | Number of Shares | Cost |
|---|---|---|
| Dust Devil, Inc. | 1,900 | $ 81,700 |
| Gale Co. | 850 | 68,000 |
| Whirlwind Co. | 2,850 | 114,000 |
| Total | | $263,700 |

The market price per share for the available-for-sale security portfolio on December 31, 2016, was as follows:

| | Market Price per Share, Dec. 31, 2016 |
|---|---|
| Dust Devil, Inc. | $40 |
| Gale Co. | 75 |
| Whirlwind Co. | 42 |

a. Provide the journal entry to adjust the available-for-sale security portfolio to fair value on December 31, 2016.

b. Describe the income statement impact from the December 31, 2016, journal entry.

---

**EX 15-23  Balance sheet presentation of available-for-sale investments**  OBJ. 4

During 2016, its first year of operations, Galileo Company purchased two available-for-sale investments as follows:

| Security | Shares Purchased | Cost |
|---|---|---|
| Hawking Inc. | 900 | $44,000 |
| Pavlov Co. | 1,780 | 38,000 |

Assume that as of December 31, 2016, the Hawking Inc. stock had a market value of $50 per share, and the Pavlov Co. stock had a market value of $24 per share. Galileo Company had net income of $300,000, and paid no dividends for the year ended December 31, 2016. All of the available-for-sale investments are classified as current assets.

a. Prepare the Current Assets section of the balance sheet presentation for the available-for-sale investments.

b. Prepare the Stockholders' Equity section of the balance sheet to reflect the earnings and unrealized gain (loss) for the available-for-sale investments.

---

**EX 15-24  Balance sheet presentation of available-for-sale investments**  OBJ. 4

During 2016, Copernicus Corporation held a portfolio of available-for-sale securities having a cost of $185,000. There were no purchases or sales of investments during the year. The market values at the beginning and end of the year were $225,000 and $160,000, respectively. The net income for 2016 was $180,000, and no dividends were paid during the year. The Stockholders' Equity section of the balance sheet was as follows on December 31, 2015:

**Copernicus Corporation**
**Stockholders' Equity**
**December 31, 2015**

| | |
|---|---:|
| Common stock | $ 50,000 |
| Paid-in capital in excess of par | 250,000 |
| Retained earnings | 340,000 |
| Unrealized gain (loss) on available-for-sale investments | 40,000 |
| Total | $680,000 |

Prepare the Stockholders' Equity section of the balance sheet for December 31, 2016.

---

**EX 15-25   Dividend yield**                                  **OBJ. 6**

At the market close on March 28 of a recent year, **McDonald's Corporation** had a closing stock price of $99.69. In addition, McDonald's Corporation had a dividend per share of $2.87 during the previous year.

    Determine McDonald's Corporation's dividend yield. (Round to one decimal place.)

---

**EX 15-26   Dividend yield**                                  **OBJ. 6**

✔ a. Dec. 31, current year, 3.00%

The market price for **Microsoft Corporation** closed at $26.71 and $25.96 on December 31, current year, and previous year, respectively. The dividends per share were $0.80 for current year and $0.64 for previous year.

a. Determine the dividend yield for Microsoft on December 31, current year, and previous year. (Round percentages to two decimal places.)

b. Interpret these measures.

---

**EX 15-27   Dividend yield**                                  **OBJ. 6**

**eBay Inc.** developed a Web-based marketplace at www.ebay.com, in which individuals can buy and sell a variety of items. eBay also acquired **PayPal**, an online payments system that allows businesses and individuals to send and receive online payments securely. In a recent annual report, eBay published the following dividend policy:

*We have never paid cash dividends on our stock and currently anticipate that we will continue to retain any future earnings for the foreseeable future.*

    Given eBay's dividend policy, why would an investor be attracted to its stock?

---

**Appendix**
**EX 15-28   Comprehensive income**

On May 12, 2016, Chewco Co. purchased 2,000 shares of Jedi Inc. for $112 per share, including the brokerage commission. The Jedi investment was classified as an available-for-sale security. On December 31, 2016, the fair value of Jedi Inc. was $124 per share. The net income of Chewco Co. was $50,000 for 2016.

    Compute the comprehensive income for Chewco Co. for the year ended December 31, 2016.

---

**Appendix**
**EX 15-29   Comprehensive income**

On December 31, 2015, Valur Co. had the following available-for-sale investment disclosure within the Current Assets section of the balance sheet:

| | |
|---|---:|
| Available-for-sale investments (at cost) | $145,000 |
| Plus valuation allowance for available-for-sale investments | 40,000 |
| Available-for-sale investments (at fair value) | $185,000 |

There were no purchases or sales of available-for-sale investments during 2016. On December 31, 2016, the fair value of the available-for-sale investment portfolio was $200,000. The net income of Valur Co. was $210,000 for 2016.

    Compute the comprehensive income for Valur Co. for the year ended December 31, 2016.

## Problems: Series A

General Ledger

SHOW
ME HOW

### PR 15-1A  Debt investment transactions, available-for-sale valuation

OBJ. 2, 4

Gaelic Industries Inc. is an athletic footware company that began operations on January 1, 2016. The following transactions relate to debt investments acquired by Gaelic Industries Inc., which has a fiscal year ending on December 31:

**2016**

May  1.  Purchased $75,000 of Avery Co. 7%, 15-year bonds at their face amount plus accrued interest of $875. The bonds pay interest semiannually on March 1 and September 1.

     16.  Purchased $60,000 of Clawhammer 6%, 10-year bonds at their face amount plus accrued interest of $150. The bonds pay interest semiannually on May 1 and November 1.

Sept.  1.  Received semiannual interest on the Avery Co. bonds.

      30.  Sold $30,000 of Avery Co. bonds at 98 plus accrued interest of $175.

Nov.  1.  Received semiannual interest on the Clawhammer bonds.

Dec.  31.  Accrued $1,050 interest on the Avery Co. bonds.

      31.  Accrued $600 interest on the Clawhammer bonds.

**2017**

Mar.  1.  Received semiannual interest on the Avery Co. bonds.

May  1.  Received semiannual interest on the Clawhammer bonds.

**Instructions**

1. Journalize the entries to record these transactions.

2. If the bond portfolio is classified as available for sale, what impact would this have on financial statement disclosure?

### PR 15-2A  Stock investment transactions, trading securities

OBJ. 3, 4

Scofield Financial Co. is a regional insurance company that began operations on January 1, 2016. The following transactions relate to trading securities acquired by Scofield Financial Co., which has a fiscal year ending on December 31:

**2016**

Mar. 14.  Purchased 5,000 shares of Wilkomm Inc. as a trading security at $40 per share plus a brokerage commission of $500.

Apr. 24.  Purchased 1,800 shares of McMarsh Inc. as a trading security at $50 plus a brokerage commission of $198.

June  1.  Sold 2,600 shares of Wilkomm Inc. for $38 per share less a $100 brokerage commission.

      30.  Received an annual dividend of $0.35 per share on Wilkomm Inc. stock.

Dec. 31.  The portfolio of trading securities was adjusted to fair values of $38 and $49 per share for Wilkomm Inc. and McMarsh Inc., respectively.

**2017**

Apr.  4.  Purchased 3,500 shares of Daley Inc. as a trading security at $30 per share plus a $175 brokerage commission.

June 28.  Received an annual dividend of $0.40 per share on Wilkomm Inc. stock.

Sept.  9.  Sold 700 shares of Daley Inc. for $32 per share less a $50 brokerage commission.

Dec. 31.  The portfolio of trading securities had a cost of $270,578 and a fair value of $350,000, requiring a debit balance in Valuation Allowance for Trading Investments of $79,422 ($350,000 − $270,578). Thus, the credit balance from December 31, 2016, is to be adjusted to the new balance.

**Instructions**

1. Journalize the entries to record these transactions.

2. Prepare the investment-related current asset balance sheet presentation for Scofield Financial Co. on December 31, 2017.

3. How are unrealized gains or losses on trading investments presented in the financial statements of Scofield Financial Co.?

---

**PR 15-3A    Stock investment transactions, equity method and available-for-sale**    OBJ. 3, 4
**securities**

Forte Inc. produces and sells theater set designs and costumes. The company began operations on January 1, 2016. The following transactions relate to securities acquired by Forte Inc., which has a fiscal year ending on December 31:

**2016**

Jan. 22. Purchased 22,000 shares of Sankal Inc. as an available-for-sale security at $18 per share, including the brokerage commission.

Mar. 8. Received a cash dividend of $0.22 per share on Sankal Inc. stock.

Sept. 8. A cash dividend of $0.25 per share was received on the Sankal stock.

Oct. 17. Sold 3,000 shares of Sankal Inc. stock at $16 per share, less a brokerage commission of $75.

Dec. 31. Sankal Inc. is classified as an available-for-sale investment and is adjusted to a fair value of $25 per share. Use the valuation allowance for available-for-sale investments account in making the adjustment.

**2017**

Jan. 10. Purchased an influential interest in Imboden Inc. for $720,000 by purchasing 96,000 shares directly from the estate of the founder of Imboden Inc. There are 300,000 shares of Imboden Inc. stock outstanding.

Mar. 10. Received a cash dividend of $0.30 per share on Sankal Inc. stock.

Sept. 12. Received a cash dividend of $0.25 per share plus an extra dividend of $0.05 per share on Sankal Inc. stock.

Dec. 31. Received $57,600 of cash dividends on Imboden Inc. stock. Imboden Inc. reported net income of $450,000 in 2017. Forte Inc. uses the equity method of accounting for its investment in Imboden Inc.

31. Sankal Inc. is classified as an available-for-sale investment and is adjusted to a fair value of $22 per share. Use the valuation allowance for available-for-sale investments account in making the adjustment for the decrease in fair value from $25 to $22 per share.

**Instructions**

1. Journalize the entries to record these transactions.

2. Prepare the investment-related asset and stockholders' equity balance sheet presentation for Forte Inc. on December 31, 2017, assuming the Retained Earnings balance on December 31, 2017, is $389,000.

---

**PR 15-4A    Investment reporting**    OBJ. 2, 3, 4

✔ h. $(5,800)

O'Brien Industries Inc. is a book publisher. The comparative unclassified balance sheets for December 31, 2017 and 2016 follow. Selected missing balances are shown by letters.

*(Continued)*

**O'Brien Industries Inc.**
**Balance Sheet**
**December 31, 2017 and 2016**

|  | Dec. 31, 2017 | Dec. 31, 2016 |
|---|---|---|
| Cash | $233,000 | $220,000 |
| Accounts receivable (net) | 136,530 | 138,000 |
| Available-for-sale investments (at cost)—Note 1 | a. | 103,770 |
| Less valuation allowance for available-for-sale investments | b. | 2,500 |
| Available-for-sale investments (fair value) | $ c. | $101,270 |
| Interest receivable | $ d. | — |
| Investment in Jolly Roger Co. stock—Note 2 | e. | $ 77,000 |
| Office equipment (net) | 115,000 | 130,000 |
| Total assets | $ f. | $666,270 |
| Accounts payable | $ 69,400 | $ 65,000 |
| Common stock | 70,000 | 70,000 |
| Excess of issue price over par | 225,000 | 225,000 |
| Retained earnings | g. | 308,770 |
| Unrealized gain (loss) on available-for-sale investments | h. | (2,500) |
| Total liabilities and stockholders' equity | $ i. | $666,270 |

Note 1. Investments are classified as available for sale. The investments at cost and fair value on December 31, 2016, are as follows:

| | No. of Shares | Cost per Share | Total Cost | Total Fair Value |
|---|---|---|---|---|
| Bernard Co. stock | 2,250 | $17 | $ 38,250 | $ 37,500 |
| Chadwick Co. stock | 1,260 | 52 | 65,520 | 63,770 |
| | | | $103,770 | $101,270 |

Note 2. The investment in Jolly Roger Co. stock is an equity method investment representing 30% of the outstanding shares of Jolly Roger Co.

The following selected investment transactions occurred during 2017:

May 5. Purchased 3,080 shares of Gozar Inc. at $30 per share including brokerage commission. Gozar Inc. is classified as an available-for-sale security.

Oct. 1. Purchased $40,000 of Nightline Co. 6%, 10-year bonds at 100. The bonds are classified as available for sale. The bonds pay interest on October 1 and April 1.

9. Dividends of $12,500 are received on the Jolly Roger Co. investment.

Dec. 31. Jolly Roger Co. reported a total net income of $112,000 for 2017. O'Brien Industries Inc. recorded equity earnings for its share of Jolly Roger Co. net income.

31. Accrued three months of interest on the Nightline bonds.

31. Adjusted the available-for-sale investment portfolio to fair value, using the following fair value per-share amounts:

| Available-for-Sale Investments | Fair Value |
|---|---|
| Bernard Co. stock | $15.40 per share |
| Chadwick Co. stock | $46.00 per share |
| Gozar Inc. stock | $32.00 per share |
| Nightline Co. bonds | $98 per $100 of face amount |

31. Closed the O'Brien Industries Inc. net income of $146,230. O'Brien Industries Inc. paid no dividends during the year.

**Instructions**

Determine the missing letters in the unclassified balance sheet. Provide appropriate supporting calculations.

# Problems: Series B

General Ledger

SHOW
ME HOW

**PR 15-1B    Debt investment transactions, available-for-sale valuation**    OBJ. 2, 4

Rekya Mart Inc. is a general merchandise retail company that began operations on January 1, 2016. The following transactions relate to debt investments acquired by Rekya Mart Inc., which has a fiscal year ending on December 31:

2016

Apr.   1.   Purchased $90,000 of Smoke Bay 6%, 10-year bonds at their face amount plus accrued interest of $900. The bonds pay interest semiannually on February 1 and August 1.

May   16.   Purchased $42,000 of Geotherma Co. 4%, 12-year bonds at their face amount plus accrued interest of $70. The bonds pay interest semiannually on May 1 and November 1.

Aug.   1.   Received semiannual interest on the Smoke Bay bonds.

Sept.   1.   Sold $12,000 of Smoke Bay bonds at 101 plus accrued interest of $60.

Nov.   1.   Received semiannual interest on the Geotherma Co. bonds.

Dec.   31.   Accrued $1,950 interest on the Smoke Bay bonds.

31.   Accrued $280 interest on the Geotherma Co. bonds.

2017

Feb.   1.   Received semiannual interest on the Smoke Bay bonds.

May   1.   Received semiannual interest on the Geotherma Co. bonds.

### Instructions

1. Journalize the entries to record these transactions.

2. If the bond portfolio is classified as available for sale, what impact would this have on financial statement disclosure?

---

**PR 15-2B   Stock investment transactions, trading securities**          **OBJ. 3, 4**

Zeus Investments Inc. is a regional investment company that began operations on January 1, 2016. The following transactions relate to trading securities acquired by Zeus Investments Inc., which has a fiscal year ending on December 31:

2016

Feb.   14.   Purchased 4,800 shares of Apollo Inc. as a trading security at $26 per share plus a brokerage commission of $192.

Apr.   1.   Purchased 2,300 shares of Ares Inc. as a trading security at $19 per share plus a brokerage commission of $92.

June   1.   Sold 600 shares of Apollo Inc. for $32 per share less a $100 brokerage commission.

27.   Received an annual dividend of $0.20 per share on Apollo Inc. stock.

Dec.   31.   The portfolio of trading securities was adjusted to fair values of $33 and $18.50 per share for Apollo Inc. and Ares Inc., respectively.

2017

Mar.   14.   Purchased 1,200 shares of Athena Inc. as a trading security at $65 per share plus a $120 brokerage commission.

June   26.   Received an annual dividend of $0.21 per share on Apollo Inc. stock.

July   30.   Sold 480 shares of Athena Inc. for $60 per share less a $50 brokerage commission.

Dec.   31.   The portfolio of trading securities had a cost of $200,032 and a fair value of $188,000, requiring a credit balance in Valuation Allowance for Trading Investments of $12,032 ($200,032 − $188,000). Thus, the debit balance from December 31, 2014, is to be adjusted to the new balance.

### Instructions

1. Journalize the entries to record these transactions.

2. Prepare the investment-related current asset balance sheet presentation for Zeus Investments Inc. on December 31, 2017.

3. How are unrealized gains or losses on trading investments presented in the financial statements of Zeus Investments Inc.?

**PR 15-3B** **Stock investment transactions, equity method and available-for-sale** OBJ. 3, 4
**securities**

Glacier Products Inc. is a wholesaler of rock climbing gear. The company began operations on January 1, 2016. The following transactions relate to securities acquired by Glacier Products Inc., which has a fiscal year ending on December 31:

**2016**

Jan. 18. Purchased 9,000 shares of Malmo Inc. as an available-for-sale investment at $40 per share, including the brokerage commission.

July 22. A cash dividend of $3.00 per share was received on the Malmo stock.

Oct. 5. Sold 500 shares of Malmo Inc. stock at $58.00 per share, less a brokerage commission of $100.

Dec. 18. Received a regular cash dividend of $3.00 per share on Malmo Inc. stock.

31. Malmo Inc. is classified as an available-for-sale investment and is adjusted to a fair value of $36.00 per share. Use the valuation allowance for available-for-sale investments account in making the adjustment.

**2017**

Jan. 25. Purchased an influential interest in Helsi Co. for $800,000 by purchasing 75,000 shares directly from the estate of the founder of Helsi. There are 250,000 shares of Helsi Co. stock outstanding.

July 16. Received a cash dividend of $3.00 per share on Malmo Inc. stock.

Dec. 16. Received a cash dividend of $3.00 per share plus an extra dividend of $0.20 per share on Malmo Inc. stock.

31. Received $38,000 of cash dividends on Helsi Co. stock. Helsi Co. reported net income of $170,000 in 2015. Glacier Products Inc. uses the equity method of accounting for its investment in Helsi Co.

31. Malmo Inc. is classified as an available-for-sale investment and is adjusted to a fair value of $44 per share. Use the valuation allowance for available-for-sale investments account in making the adjustment for the increase in fair value from $36 to $44 per share.

**Instructions**

1. Journalize the entries to record the preceding transactions.

2. Prepare the investment-related asset and stockholders' equity balance sheet presentation for Glacier Products Inc. on December 31, 2017, assuming the Retained Earnings balance on December 31, 2017, is $700,000.

**PR 15-4B** **Investment reporting** OBJ. 2, 3, 4

✔ b. $4,680

Teasdale Inc. manufactures and sells commercial and residential security equipment. The comparative unclassified balance sheets for December 31, 2017 and 2016 are provided below. Selected missing balances are shown by letters.

**Teasdale Inc.**
**Balance Sheet**
**December 31, 2017 and 2016**

| | Dec. 31, 2017 | Dec. 31, 2016 |
|---|---|---|
| Cash | $160,000 | $156,000 |
| Accounts receivable (net) | 115,000 | 108,000 |
| Available-for-sale investments (at cost)—Note 1 | a. | 91,200 |
| Plus valuation allowance for available-for-sale investments | b. | 8,776 |
| Available-for-sale investments (fair value) | $ c. | $ 99,976 |
| Interest receivable | $ d. | — |
| Investment in Wright Co. stock—Note 2 | e. | $ 69,200 |
| Office equipment (net) | 96,000 | 105,000 |
| Total assets | $ f. | $538,176 |
| Accounts payable | $ 91,000 | $ 72,000 |
| Common stock | 80,000 | 80,000 |
| Excess of issue price over par | 250,000 | 250,000 |
| Retained earnings | g. | 127,400 |
| Unrealized gain (loss) on available-for-sale investments | h. | 8,776 |
| Total liabilities and stockholders' equity | $ i. | $538,176 |

Note 1. Investments are classified as available for sale. The investments at cost and fair value on December 31, 2016, are as follows:

| | No. of Shares | Cost per Share | Total Cost | Total Fair Value |
|---|---|---|---|---|
| Alvarez Inc. stock | 960 | $38.00 | $36,480 | $39,936 |
| Hirsch Inc. stock | 1,900 | 28.80 | 54,720 | 60,040 |
| | | | $91,200 | $99,976 |

Note 2. The Investment in Wright Co. stock is an equity method investment representing 30% of the outstanding shares of Wright Co.

The following selected investment transactions occurred during 2017:

Mar. 18.  Purchased 800 shares of Richter Inc. at $40 including brokerage commission. Richter is classified as an available-for-sale security.

July 12.  Dividends of $12,000 are received on the Wright Co. investment.

Oct.   1.  Purchased $24,000 of Toon Co. 4%, 10-year bonds at 100. The bonds are classified as available for sale. The bonds pay interest on October 1 and April 1.

Dec. 31.  Wright Co. reported a total net income of $80,000 for 2017. Teasdale recorded equity earnings for its share of Wright Co. net income.

31.  Accrued interest for three months on the Toon Co. bonds purchased on October 1.

31.  Adjusted the available-for-sale investment portfolio to fair value, using the following fair value per-share amounts:

| Available-for-Sale Investments | Fair Value |
|---|---|
| Alvarez Inc. stock | $41.50 per share |
| Hirsch Inc. stock | $26.00 per share |
| Richter Inc. stock | $48.00 per share |
| Toon Co. bonds | 101 per $100 of face amount |

31.  Closed the Teasdale Inc. net income of $51,240. Teasdale Inc. paid no dividends during the year.

**Instructions**

Determine the missing letters in the unclassified balance sheet. Provide appropriate supporting calculations.

# Comprehensive Problem 4

 General Ledger

Selected transactions completed by Equinox Products Inc. during the fiscal year ended December 31, 2016, were as follows:

a.  Issued 15,000 shares of $20 par common stock at $30, receiving cash.

b.  Issued 4,000 shares of $80 par preferred 5% stock at $100, receiving cash.

c.  Issued $500,000 of 10-year, 5% bonds at 104, with interest payable semiannually.

d.  Declared a quarterly dividend of $0.50 per share on common stock and $1.00 per share on preferred stock. On the date of record, 100,000 shares of common stock were outstanding, no treasury shares were held, and 20,000 shares of preferred stock were outstanding.

e.  Paid the cash dividends declared in (d).

f.  Purchased 7,500 shares of Solstice Corp. at $40 per share, plus a $150 brokerage commission. The investment is classified as an available-for-sale investment.

g.  Purchased 8,000 shares of treasury common stock at $33 per share.

h.  Purchased 40,000 shares of Pinkberry Co. stock directly from the founders for $24 per share. Pinkberry has 125,000 shares issued and outstanding. Equinox Products Inc. treated the investment as an equity method investment.

i.  Declared a $1.00 quarterly cash dividend per share on preferred stock. On the date of record, 20,000 shares of preferred stock had been issued.

(*Continued*)

j. Paid the cash dividends to the preferred stockholders.

k. Received $27,500 dividend from Pinkberry Co. investment in (h).

l. Purchased $90,000 of Dream Inc. 10-year, 5% bonds, directly from the issuing company, at their face amount plus accrued interest of $375. The bonds are classified as a held-to-maturity long-term investment.

m. Sold, at $38 per share, 2,600 shares of treasury common stock purchased in (g).

n. Received a dividend of $0.60 per share from the Solstice Corp. investment in (f).

o. Sold 1,000 shares of Solstice Corp. at $45, including commission.

p. Recorded the payment of semiannual interest on the bonds issued in (c) and the amortization of the premium for six months. The amortization is determined using the straight-line method.

q. Accrued interest for three months on the Dream Inc. bonds purchased in (l).

r. Pinkberry Co. recorded total earnings of $240,000. Equinox Products recorded equity earnings for its share of Pinkberry Co. net income.

s. The fair value for Solstice Corp. stock was $39.02 per share on December 31, 2016. The investment is adjusted to fair value, using a valuation allowance account. Assume Valuation Allowance for Available-for-Sale Investments had a beginning balance of zero.

### Instructions

1. Journalize the selected transactions.

2. After all of the transactions for the year ended December 31, 2016, had been posted [including the transactions recorded in part (1) and all adjusting entries], the data that follows were taken from the records of Equinox Products Inc.

   a. Prepare a multiple-step income statement for the year ended December 31, 2016, concluding with earnings per share. In computing earnings per share, assume that the average number of common shares outstanding was 100,000 and preferred dividends were $100,000. (Round earnings per share to the nearest cent.)

   b. Prepare a retained earnings statement for the year ended December 31, 2016.

   c. Prepare a balance sheet in report form as of December 31, 2016.

| Income statement data: | |
| --- | --- |
| Advertising expense | $ 150,000 |
| Cost of merchandise sold | 3,700,000 |
| Delivery expense | 30,000 |
| Depreciation expense—office buildings and equipment | 30,000 |
| Depreciation expense—store buildings and equipment | 100,000 |
| Dividend revenue | 4,500 |
| Gain on sale of investment | 4,980 |
| Income from Pinkberry Co. investment | 76,800 |
| Income tax expense | 140,500 |
| Interest expense | 21,000 |
| Interest revenue | 2,720 |
| Miscellaneous administrative expense | 7,500 |
| Miscellaneous selling expense | 14,000 |
| Office rent expense | 50,000 |
| Office salaries expense | 170,000 |
| Office supplies expense | 10,000 |
| Sales | 5,254,000 |
| Sales commissions | 185,000 |
| Sales salaries expense | 385,000 |
| Store supplies expense | 21,000 |

| Retained earnings and balance sheet data: | |
| --- | --- |
| Accounts payable | $ 194,300 |
| Accounts receivable | 545,000 |
| Accumulated depreciation—office buildings and equipment | 1,580,000 |
| Accumulated depreciation—store buildings and equipment | 4,126,000 |
| Allowance for doubtful accounts | 8,450 |

| | |
|---|---:|
| Available-for-sale investments (at cost) | $ 260,130 |
| Bonds payable, 5%, due 2024 | 500,000 |
| Cash | 246,000 |
| Common stock, $20 par (400,000 shares authorized; 100,000 shares issued, 94,600 outstanding) | 2,000,000 |
| Dividends: | |
|    Cash dividends for common stock | 155,120 |
|    Cash dividends for preferred stock | 100,000 |
| Goodwill | 500,000 |
| Income tax payable | 44,000 |
| Interest receivable | 1,125 |
| Investment in Pinkberry Co. stock (equity method) | 1,009,300 |
| Investment in Dream Inc. bonds (long term) | 90,000 |
| Merchandise inventory (December 31, 2016), at lower of cost (FIFO) or market | 778,000 |
| Office buildings and equipment | 4,320,000 |
| Paid-in capital from sale of treasury stock | 13,000 |
| Excess of issue price over par—common stock | 886,800 |
| Excess of issue price over par—preferred stock | 150,000 |
| Preferred 5% stock, $80 par (30,000 shares authorized; 20,000 shares issued) | 1,600,000 |
| Premium on bonds payable | 19,000 |
| Prepaid expenses | 27,400 |
| Retained earnings, January 1, 2016 | 9,319,725 |
| Store buildings and equipment | 12,560,000 |
| Treasury stock (5,400 shares of common stock at cost of $33 per share) | 178,200 |
| Unrealized gain (loss) on available-for-sale investments | (6,500) |
| Valuation allowance for available-for-sale investments | (6,500) |

# Cases & Projects

## CP 15-1  Benefits of fair value

On July 16, 1998, Wyatt Corp. purchased 40 acres of land for $350,000. The land has been held for a future plant site until the current date, December 31, 2016. On December 18, 2016, TexoPete Inc. purchased 40 acres of land for $2,000,000 to be used for a distribution center. The TexoPete land is located next to the Wyatt Corp. land. Thus, both Wyatt Corp. and TexoPete Inc. own nearly identical pieces of land.

1. What are the valuations of land on the balance sheets of Wyatt Corp. and TexoPete Inc. using generally accepted accounting principles?

2. How might fair value accounting aid comparability when evaluating these two companies?

**|||IFRS▶**

## CP 15-2  International fair value accounting

*International Financial Reporting Standard No. 16* provides companies the option of valuing property, plant, and equipment at either historical cost or fair value. If fair value is selected, then the property, plant, and equipment must be revalued periodically to fair value. Under fair value, if there is an increase in the value of the property, plant, and equipment during the reporting period, then the increase is credited to stockholders' equity. However, if there is a decrease in fair value, then the decrease is reported as an expense for the period.

How is the international accounting treatment for changes in fair value for property, plant, and equipment similar to investments?

### CP 15-3 Ethics and fair value measurement

Financial assets include stocks and bonds. These are fairly simple securities that can often be valued using quoted market prices. However, there are more complex financial instruments that do not have quoted market prices. These complex securities must still be valued on the balance sheet at fair value. Generally accepted accounting principles require that the reporting entity use assumptions in valuing investments when market prices or critical valuation inputs are unobservable.

What are the ethical considerations in making subjective valuations of these complex financial instruments?

### CP 15-4 Warren Buffett and "look-through" earnings

Berkshire Hathaway, the investment holding company of Warren Buffett, reports its "less than 20% ownership" investments according to generally accepted accounting principles. However, it also provides additional disclosures that it terms "look-through" earnings.

Warren Buffett states,

> Many of these companies (in the less than 20%-owned category) pay out relatively small proportions of their earnings in dividends. This means that only a small proportion of their earning power is recorded in our own current operating earnings. But, while our reported operating earnings reflect only the dividends received from such companies, our economic well-being is determined by their earnings, not their dividends.

> The value to Berkshire Hathaway of retained earnings (of our investees) is not determined by whether we own 100%, 50%, 20%, or 1% of the businesses in which they reside.... Our perspective on such "forgotten-but-not-gone" earnings is simple: the way they are accounted for is of no importance, but their ownership and subsequent utilization is all-important. We care not whether the auditors hear a tree fall in the forest; we do care who owns the tree and what's next done with it.

> I believe the best way to think about our earnings is in terms of "look-through" results, calculated as follows: Take $250 million, which is roughly our share of the operating earnings retained by our investees (<20% ownership holdings); subtract... incremental taxes we would have owed had that $250 million been paid to us in dividends; then add the remainder, $220 million, to our reported earnings of $371 million. Thus, our "look-through" earnings were about $590 million.

Source: Warren Buffett, *The Essays of Warren Buffett: Lessons for Corporate America*, edited by Lawrence A. Cunningham, pp. 180–183 (excerpted).

1. What are look-through earnings?

2. Why does Warren Buffett favor look-through earnings?

### CP 15-5 Reporting investments

### Group Project

In groups of three or four, find the latest annual report for Microsoft Corporation. The annual report can be found on the company's Web site at www.microsoft.com/msft/default.mspx.

The notes to the financial statements include details of Microsoft's investments. Find the notes that provide details of its investments (Note 4) and the income from its investments (Note 3).

From these disclosures, answer the following questions:

1. What is the total cost of investments?

2. What is the fair value (recorded value) of investments?

3. What is the total unrealized gain from investments?

4. What is the total unrealized loss from investments?

5. What percent of total investments (at fair value) are:

   a. Cash and equivalents

   b. Short-term investments

   c. Equity and other investments (long term)

6. What was the total combined dividend and interest revenue?

7. What was the recognized net gain or loss from sale of investments?

# Mornin' Joe

Financial Statements for Mornin' Joe

Financial Statements for Mornin' Joe International

# Financial Statements for Mornin' Joe

The financial statements of **Mornin' Joe** follow. Mornin' Joe is a fictitious coffeehouse chain featuring drip and espresso coffee in a café setting. The financial statements of Mornin' Joe are provided to illustrate the complete financial statements of a corporation, using the terms, formats, and reporting illustrated throughout this text. In addition, excerpts of the Mornin' Joe financial statements are used to illustrate the financial reporting presentation for the topics discussed in Chapters 7–15. Thus, you can refer to the complete financial statements in Exhibits 1, 2, 3, and 4 here or the excerpts in Chapters 7–15.

---

**EXHIBIT 1**

**Income Statement for Mornin' Joe**

### Mornin' Joe
### Income Statement
### For the Year Ended December 31, 2016

| | | | |
|---|---|---|---|
| Revenue from sales: | | | |
| Sales | | $5,450,000 | |
| Less: Sales returns and allowances | $ 26,500 | | |
| Sales discounts | 21,400 | 47,900 | |
| Sales | | | $5,402,100 |
| Cost of merchandise sold | | | 2,160,000 |
| Gross profit | | | $3,242,100 |
| Operating expenses | | | |
| Selling expenses: | | | |
| Wages expense | $825,000 | | |
| Advertising expense | 678,900 | | |
| Depreciation expense—buildings | 124,300 | | |
| Miscellaneous selling expense | 26,500 | | |
| Total selling expense | | $ 1,654,700 | |
| Administrative expenses: | | | |
| Office salaries expense | $325,000 | | |
| Rent expense | 425,600 | | |
| Payroll tax expense | 110,000 | | |
| Depreciation expense—office equipment | 68,900 | | |
| Bad debt expense | 14,000 | | |
| Amortization expense | 10,500 | | |
| Total administrative expenses | | 954,000 | |
| Total operating expenses | | | 2,608,700 |
| Income from operations | | | $ 633,400 |
| Other income and expense: | | | |
| Interest revenue | | $ 18,000 | |
| Interest expense | | (136,000) | |
| Loss on disposal of fixed asset | | (23,000) | |
| Unrealized gain on trading investments | | 5,000 | |
| Equity income in AM Coffee | | 57,000 | (79,000) |
| Income before income taxes | | | $ 554,400 |
| Income tax expense | | | 132,800 |
| Net income | | | $ 421,600 |
| | | | |
| Basic earnings per share [($421,600 – $30,000 ) ÷ 44,000 shares issued and outstanding] | | | $ 8.90 |

**EXHIBIT 2**

**Balance Sheet for Mornin' Joe**

**Mornin' Joe**
**Balance Sheet**
**December 31, 2016**

### Assets

| | | |
|---|---:|---:|
| **Current assets:** | | |
| Cash and cash equivalents.......................... | | $ 235,000 |
| Trading investments (at cost) ...................... | $ 420,000 | |
| Plus valuation allowance for trading investments ... | 45,000 | 465,000 |
| Accounts receivable ............................. | $ 305,000 | |
| Less allowance for doubtful accounts .......... | 12,300 | 292,700 |
| Merchandise inventory—at lower of cost (first-in, first-out method) or market ........... | | 120,000 |
| Prepaid insurance ................................ | | 24,000 |
| Total current assets ........................... | | $1,136,700 |
| **Investments:** | | |
| Investment in AM Coffee (equity method) .......... | | 565,000 |
| **Property, plant, and equipment:** | | |
| Land............................................ | | $1,850,000 |
| Buildings ...................................... | $2,650,000 | |
| Less accumulated depreciation .............. | 420,000 | 2,230,000 |
| Office equipment ................................ | $ 350,000 | |
| Less accumulated depreciation .............. | 102,000 | 248,000 |
| Total property, plant, and equipment ....... | | 4,328,000 |
| **Intangible assets:** | | |
| Patents .......................................... | | 140,000 |
| Total assets .......................................... | | $6,169,700 |

### Liabilities

| | | |
|---|---:|---:|
| **Current liabilities:** | | |
| Accounts payable ................................. | $ 133,000 | |
| Notes payable (current portion).................... | 200,000 | |
| Salaries and wages payable........................ | 42,000 | |
| Payroll taxes payable ............................. | 16,400 | |
| Interest payable ................................. | 40,000 | |
| Total current liabilities ........................ | | $ 431,400 |
| **Long-term liabilities:** | | |
| Bonds payable, 8%, due December 31, 2032 ........ | $ 500,000 | |
| Less unamortized discount.................... | 16,000 | $ 484,000 |
| Notes payable .................................... | | 1,400,000 |
| Total long-term liabilities...................... | | $1,884,000 |
| Total liabilities ....................................... | | $2,315,400 |

### Stockholders' Equity

| | | |
|---|---:|---:|
| **Paid-in capital:** | | |
| Preferred 10% stock, $50 par (6,000 shares authorized and issued)........................ | $ 300,000 | |
| Excess of issue price over par ..................... | 50,000 | $ 350,000 |
| Common stock, $20 par (50,000 shares authorized, 45,000 shares issued) .............. | $ 900,000 | |
| Excess of issue price over par ..................... | 1,450,000 | 2,350,000 |
| Total paid-in capital.......................... | | $2,700,000 |
| Retained earnings ..................................... | | 1,200,300 |
| Total ............................................. | | $3,900,300 |
| Deduct treasury stock (1,000 shares at cost)............ | | 46,000 |
| Total stockholders' equity ............................ | | $3,854,300 |
| Total liabilities and stockholders' equity ............... | | $6,169,700 |

**EXHIBIT 3**

**Retained Earnings Statement for Mornin' Joe**

| Mornin' Joe Retained Earnings Statement For the Year Ended December 31, 2016 | | | |
|---|---|---|---|
| Retained earnings, January 1, 2016...................... | | | $ 852,700 |
| Net income........................................... | | $421,600 | |
| Less dividends: | | | |
| Preferred stock .................................... | $30,000 | | |
| Common stock .................................... | 44,000 | 74,000 | |
| Increase in retained earnings .......................... | | | 347,600 |
| Retained earnings, December 31, 2016 ................. | | | $1,200,300 |

**EXHIBIT 4**    **Statement of Stockholders' Equity for Mornin' Joe**

| Mornin' Joe Statement of Stockholders' Equity For the Year Ended December 31, 2016 | | | | | | |
|---|---|---|---|---|---|---|
| | Preferred Stock | Common Stock | Additional Paid-In Capital | Retained Earnings | Treasury Stock | Total |
| Balance, January 1, 2016.................... | $300,000 | $800,000 | $1,325,000 | $852,700 | $(36,000) | $3,241,700 |
| Net income.................................. | | | | 421,600 | | 421,600 |
| Dividends on preferred stock .............. | | | | (30,000) | | (30,000) |
| Dividends on common stock............... | | | | (44,000) | | (44,000) |
| Issuance of additional common stock..... | | 100,000 | 175,000 | | | 275,000 |
| Purchase of treasury stock.................. | | | | | (10,000) | (10,000) |
| Balance, December 31, 2016 ............... | $300,000 | $900,000 | $1,500,000 | $1,200,300 | $(46,000) | $3,854,300 |

# Financial Statements for Mornin' Joe International

Mornin' Joe is planning to expand operations to various places around the world. Financing for this expansion will come from foreign banks. While financial statements prepared under U.S. GAAP may be appropriate for U.S. operations, financial statements prepared for foreign bankers should be prepared using international accounting standards.

The European Union (EU) has developed accounting standards similar in structure to U.S. standards. Its accounting standards board is called the International Accounting Standards Board (IASB). The IASB issues accounting standards that are termed *International Financial Reporting Standards (IFRS)*. The intent of the IASB is to create a set of financial standards that can be used by public companies worldwide, not just in the EU.

Currently, the EU countries and more than 100 other countries around the world have adopted or are planning to adopt IFRS. As a result, there are efforts under way to converge U.S. GAAP with IFRS so as to harmonize accounting standards around the world.

## Key Reporting Differences between IFRS and U.S. GAAP

The financial statements of Mornin' Joe International using IFRS are presented in Exhibits 1, 2, and 3. This illustration highlights reporting and terminology differences between IFRS and U.S. GAAP. Differences in recording transactions under IFRS and U.S. GAAP are discussed in Appendix D and in various International Connection boxes throughout the text.

The Mornin' Joe International financial statements in Exhibits 5, 6, and 7 are simplified and illustrate only portions of IFRS that are appropriate for introductory accounting. The financial statements are presented in euros (€) for demonstration purposes only. The euro is the standard currency of the European Union. The euro is translated at a 1:1 ratio from the dollar to simplify comparisons. Throughout the illustration, call-outs and end notes to each statement are used to highlight the differences between financial statements prepared under IFRS and under U.S. GAAP.

## Statements of Comprehensive Income versus Income Statements

Exhibit 5 illustrates the statement of comprehensive income for **Mornin' Joe International** and shows key differences from the income statements prepared under U.S. GAAP.

**EXHIBIT 5**    **Statement of Comprehensive Income for Mornin' Joe International**

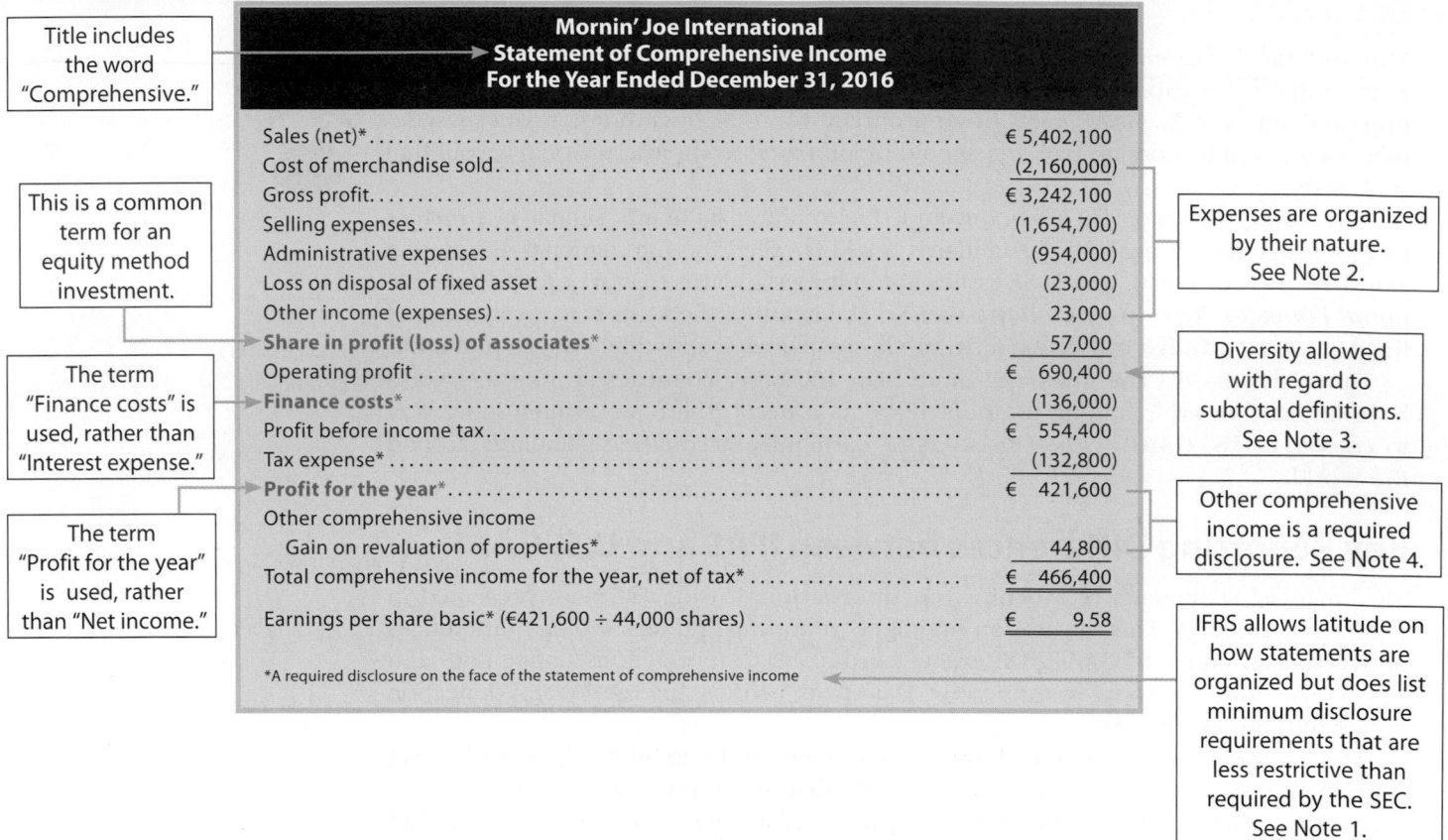

Title includes the word "Comprehensive."

This is a common term for an equity method investment.

The term "Finance costs" is used, rather than "Interest expense."

The term "Profit for the year" is used, rather than "Net income."

**Mornin' Joe International**
**Statement of Comprehensive Income**
**For the Year Ended December 31, 2016**

| | |
|---|---:|
| Sales (net)*........................................ | € 5,402,100 |
| Cost of merchandise sold........................ | (2,160,000) |
| Gross profit....................................... | € 3,242,100 |
| Selling expenses.................................. | (1,654,700) |
| Administrative expenses ......................... | (954,000) |
| Loss on disposal of fixed asset ................. | (23,000) |
| Other income (expenses)......................... | 23,000 |
| Share in profit (loss) of associates*............ | 57,000 |
| Operating profit ................................. | € 690,400 |
| Finance costs*.................................... | (136,000) |
| Profit before income tax......................... | € 554,400 |
| Tax expense*..................................... | (132,800) |
| Profit for the year*.............................. | € 421,600 |
| Other comprehensive income | |
|    Gain on revaluation of properties*.......... | 44,800 |
| Total comprehensive income for the year, net of tax*........ | € 466,400 |
| | |
| Earnings per share basic* (€421,600 ÷ 44,000 shares) ........ | € 9.58 |

*A required disclosure on the face of the statement of comprehensive income

Expenses are organized by their nature. See Note 2.

Diversity allowed with regard to subtotal definitions. See Note 3.

Other comprehensive income is a required disclosure. See Note 4.

IFRS allows latitude on how statements are organized but does list minimum disclosure requirements that are less restrictive than required by the SEC. See Note 1.

1. IFRS statements are often more summarized than U.S. GAAP statements. To compensate, IFRS requires specific disclosures on the face of the financial statements (denoted *) and additional disclosures in the footnotes to the financial statements. Because additions and subtractions are grouped together in sections of IFRS statements, parentheses are used to indicate subtractions.

2. Expenses in an IFRS income statement are classified by either their nature or function. The nature of an expense is how the expense would naturally be recorded in a journal entry reflecting the economic benefit received for that expense. Examples include salaries, depreciation, advertising, and utilities. The function of an expense identifies the purpose of the expense, such as a selling expense or an administrative expense.

   IFRS does not permit the natural and functional classifications to be mixed together on the same statement. That is, all expenses must be classified by either nature or function. However, if a functional classification of expenses is used, a footnote to the income statement must show the natural classification of expenses. To illustrate, because **Mornin' Joe International** uses the functional classification of expenses in its income statement, it must also show the following natural classification of expenses in a footnote:

| | | |
|---|---:|---|
| Cost of product | €2,100,000 | The cost of product purchased for resale |
| Employee benefits expense | 1,260,000 | Required natural disclosure |
| Depreciation and amortization expense | 203,700 | Required natural disclosure |
| Rent expense | 425,600 | |
| Advertising expense | 678,900 | |
| Other expenses | 58,500 | |
| Total natural expenses | €4,726,700 | |

3. IFRS provides flexibility with regard to line items, headings, and subtotals on the income statement. There is less flexibility under U.S. GAAP for public companies.

4. IFRS requires the reporting of other comprehensive income (see appendix to Chapter 15) either on the income statement (see Exhibit 5) or in a separate statement. U.S. GAAP has a similar disclosure treatment. For **Mornin' Joe International**, other comprehensive income consists of the restatement of café locations to fair value (see Note 6 for more details).

5. Under IFRS, there is no standard format for the balance sheet (statement of financial position, see Exhibit 6). A typical format for European Union companies is to begin the asset section of the balance sheet with noncurrent assets. This is followed by current assets listed in reverse order of liquidity. That is, the asset side of the balance sheet is reported in reverse order of liquidity from least liquid to most liquid. Listing noncurrent assets first emphasizes the going concern nature of the entity.

    The liability and owners' equity side of the balance sheet is also reported differently than under U.S. GAAP. Specifically, owners' equity is reported first followed by noncurrent liabilities and current liabilities. Listing equity first emphasizes the going concern nature of the entity and the long-term financial interest of the owners in the business.

6. Under IFRS, property, plant, and equipment (PP&E) may be measured at historical cost or fair value. If fair value is used, the revaluation must be for similar classifications of PP&E but need not be for all PP&E. This departs from U.S. GAAP, which requires PP&E to be measured at historical cost. **Mornin' Joe International** restated its Land and Buildings to fair value because the café sites have readily available real estate market prices. Land and buildings are included together because their fair values are not separable. The office equipment remains at historical cost because it does not have a readily available market price. The increase in fair value is recorded by reducing accumulated depreciation and recognizing the gain as other comprehensive income. This element of other comprehensive income is accumulated in stockholders' equity under the heading Property revaluation reserve.* This treatment is similar (with different titles) to the U.S. GAAP treatment of unrealized gains (losses) from available-for-sale securities. For Mornin' Joe International, there is an increase in the property revaluation reserve of €44,800. This amount is the only difference between Mornin' Joe's U.S. GAAP net income, total assets, and total stockholders' equity and Mornin' Joe International's IFRS total comprehensive income, total assets, and total stockholders' equity.

7. **Mornin' Joe International** recently acquired a coffee plantation. This is an example of a biological asset. IFRS requires separate reporting of biological assets (principally agricultural assets) at fair value.

8. Inventories are valued at lower of cost or market; however, "market" is defined as net realizable value under IFRS. U.S. GAAP defines "market" as replacement cost under most conditions. In addition, IFRS prohibits LIFO cost valuation.

9. Under IFRS, some elements of other comprehensive income and owner's equity are often aggregated under the term "reserves." In contrast, under U.S. GAAP, "reserve" is used to identify a liability. IFRS also does not require separate disclosure of treasury stock as does U.S. GAAP. Specifically, treasury stock may be reported as a reduction of a reserve, a reduction of a stock premium, or as a separate item.

10. The term *provision* is used to denote a liability under IFRS, whereas this term often indicates an expense under U.S. GAAP. For example, *Provision for income taxes* means *Income tax expense* under U.S. GAAP, whereas it would mean *Income taxes payable* under IFRS.

11. Under U.S. GAAP, other comprehensive income items must be included as changes in accumulated other comprehensive income in the statement of changes in stockholders' equity (see Exhibit 7). IFRS allows for similar treatment, with wider latitude for terminology, such as *Property Revaluation Reserve* illustrated by the column title here. In this illustration, treasury stock is included as part of a reserve (Reserve for Own Shares). As discussed in Note 9, under U.S. GAAP the term *reserve* denotes a liability.

## Statements of Financial Position versus Balance Sheets

Exhibit 6 illustrates the statement of financial position for **Mornin' Joe International** and shows key differences from the balance sheets prepared under U.S. GAAP.

---

**EXHIBIT 6**    Statement of Financial Position for Mornin' Joe International

| | Mornin' Joe International | | |
|---|---|---|---|
| | **Statement of Financial Position** | | |
| | **December 31, 2016** | | |

**Preferred title for the "Balance Sheet."** →

| | | | |
|---|---:|---:|---:|
| **Assets** | | | |
| **Noncurrent assets** | | | |
| Property, plant, and equipment* | | | |
| Land and buildings at fair value . . . . . . . . . . . . | €4,180,000 | | |
| Less: Accumulated depreciation . . . . . . . . . . . | 375,200 | €3,804,800 | |
| Office equipment at cost . . . . . . . . . . . . . . . . . . | € 350,000 | | |
| Less: Accumulated depreciation . . . . . . . . . . . | 102,000 | 248,000 | |
| Biological assets at fair value* . . . . . . . . . . . . . . | | 320,000 | |
| Patents at amortized cost* . . . . . . . . . . . . . . . . . . | | 140,000 | |
| Investment in AM Coffee (equity method)* . . . . . . | | 565,000 | |
| Total noncurrent assets . . . . . . . . . . . . . . . . . . . | | | €5,077,800 |
| **Current assets** | | | |
| Prepaid insurance . . . . . . . . . . . . . . . . . . . . . . . | | € 24,000 | |
| Merchandise inventory—**at lower of cost** | | | |
| **(first-in, first-out) or realizable value*** . . | | 120,000 | |
| Accounts receivable (net of allowance | | | |
| for doubtful accounts)* . . . . . . . . . . . . . . . . . | | 292,700 | |
| **Financial assets at fair value through** | | | |
| **profit or loss*** . . . . . . . . . . . . . . . . . . . . . . . . | | 465,000 | |
| Cash and cash equivalents* . . . . . . . . . . . . . . . | | 235,000 | |
| Total current assets . . . . . . . . . . . . . . . . . . . . | | | 1,136,700 |
| **Total assets*** . . . . . . . . . . . . . . . . . . . . . . . . . . . . . | | | €6,214,500 |
| **Equity attributable to owners** | | | |
| Preferred 10% stock, €50 par (6,000 shares | | | |
| authorized and issued)* . . . . . . . . . . . . . . . . . | | € 300,000 | |
| Common stock, €20 par (50,000 shares | | | |
| authorized, 45,000 shares issued)* . . . . . . . . . . | | 900,000 | |
| **Share premium*** . . . . . . . . . . . . . . . . . . . . . . . . . . | | 1,500,000 | |
| **Reserves*** . . . . . . . . . . . . . . . . . . . . . . . . . . . . . . . | | (1,200) | |
| Retained earnings* . . . . . . . . . . . . . . . . . . . . . . . . | | 1,200,300 | |
| Total equity attributable to owners* . . . . . . . . | | | €3,899,100 |
| **Liabilities** | | | |
| **Noncurrent liabilities*** | | | |
| Bonds payable, 8%, due December 31, 2032 | | | |
| (net of discount) . . . . . . . . . . . . . . . . . . . . . . . . | | € 484,000 | |
| Notes payable . . . . . . . . . . . . . . . . . . . . . . . . . . . . | | 1,400,000 | |
| Total noncurrent liabilities . . . . . . . . . . . . . . . . | | | €1,884,000 |
| **Current liabilities** | | | |
| Accounts payable* . . . . . . . . . . . . . . . . . . . . . . . . | | € 133,000 | |
| Loans* . . . . . . . . . . . . . . . . . . . . . . . . . . . . . . . . . . . | | 200,000 | |
| **Employee provisions*** . . . . . . . . . . . . . . . . . . . . . . | | 58,400 | |
| Interest payable . . . . . . . . . . . . . . . . . . . . . . . . . . | | 40,000 | |
| Total current liabilities . . . . . . . . . . . . . . . . . . . | | | 431,400 |
| Total liabilities* . . . . . . . . . . . . . . . . . . . . . . . . | | | €2,315,400 |
| **Total equity and liabilities*** . . . . . . . . . . . . . . . . . | | | €6,214,500 |

*Required disclosures. Footnotes provide additional subclassification detail.

**Side annotations:**

- "Biological assets" are a required disclosure at fair value. See Note 7.
- Inventory valuation. See Note 8.
- International terminology for "Trading investments." Same accounting treatment.
- International terminology for "Excess of issue price over par."
- Other comprehensive items and treasury stock. See Note 9.
- Employee provisions are wages, salaries, and payroll taxes payable. See Note 10.
- Sub-classifications of PP&E may be valued at fair value. See Note 6.
- Reverse liquidity account order. See Note 5.
- Equities listed first, then liabilities. See Note 5.
- Noncurrent liabilities listed prior to current liabilities.

## Statements of Changes in Equity versus Statements of Stockholders' Equity

Exhibit 7 illustrates the statement of changes in equity for **Mornin' Joe International** and shows key differences from the statements of stockholders' equity prepared under U.S. GAAP.

**EXHIBIT 7**    Statement of Changes in Equity for Mornin' Joe International

**Mornin' Joe International**
**Statement of Changes in Equity**
**For the Year Ended December 31, 2016**

| | Preferred Stock | Common Stock | Share Premium | Reserves: Property Revaluation Reserve | Reserves: Reserve for Own Shares | Retained Earnings | Total Equity Attributable to Owners |
|---|---|---|---|---|---|---|---|
| Balance, January 1, 2016 | €300,000 | €800,000 | €1,325,000 | € 0 | (€36,000) | € 852,700 | €3,241,700 |
| Profit for the year | | | | | | 421,600 | 421,600 |
| **Other comprehensive income** | | | | | | | |
| Property revaluation (gain) | | | | 44,800 | | | 44,800 |
| Total comprehensive income | | | | €44,800 | | € 421,600 | € 466,400 |
| **Contributions by and distributions to owners** | | | | | | | |
| Dividends on preferred stock | | | | | | (30,000) | (30,000) |
| Dividends on common stock | | | | | | (44,000) | (44,000) |
| Issuance of additional common stock | | 100,000 | 175,000 | | | | 275,000 |
| Purchase of own shares | | | | | (10,000) | | (10,000) |
| **Total contributions and distributions to owners** | € 0 | €100,000 | € 175,000 | € 0 | (€10,000) | (€ 74,000) | € 191,000 |
| Balance, December 31, 2016 | €300,000 | €900,000 | €1,500,000 | €44,800 | (€46,000) | €1,200,300 | €3,899,100 |

"Reserves," see Notes 9 and 11.

# Discussion Questions

1. Contrast U.S. GAAP financial statement terms with their differing IFRS terms.

2. What is the difference between classifying an expense by nature or function?

3. If a functional expense classification is used for the statement of comprehensive income, what must also be disclosed?

4. How is the term "provision" used differently under IFRS than under U.S. GAAP?

5. What are two main differences in inventory valuation under IFRS compared to U.S. GAAP?

6. What is a "biological asset"?

7. What is the most significant IFRS departure from U.S. GAAP for valuing property, plant, and equipment?

8. What is a "share premium"?

9. How is the term "reserve" used under IFRS, and how does it differ from its meaning under U.S. GAAP?

10. How is treasury stock reported under IFRS? How does this differ from its treatment under U.S. GAAP?

### IFRS Activity 1

**Unilever Group** is a global company that markets a wide variety of products, including Lever® soap, Breyer's® ice cream, and Hellman's® mayonnaise. A recent income statement and statement of comprehensive income for the Dutch company, Unilever Group, follow:

| Unilever Group Consolidated Income Statement For the Year Ended December 31 (in millions of euros) | |
| --- | --- |
| Turnover | €51,324 |
| Operating profit | 6,989 |
| After (charging)/crediting: | |
| Non-core items | (73) |
| Net finance costs | (397) |
| Finance income | 136 |
| Finance costs | (526) |
| Pensions and similar obligations | (7) |
| Share of net profit/(loss) of joint ventures and associations | 105 |
| Other income from non-current investments | (14) |
| Profit before taxation | € 6,683 |
| Taxation | (1,735) |
| Net profit | € 4,948 |
| Earnings per share—basic | €   1.58 |
| Earnings per share—diluted | €   1.54 |

| Consolidated Statement of Comprehensive Income For the Year Ended December 31 | |
| --- | --- |
| Fair value gains (losses), net of tax | € (125) |
| Actuarial gains (losses) on pensions, net of tax | (644) |
| Currency retranslation gains (losses), net of tax | (316) |
| Net income (expense) recognized directly into equity | €(1,085) |
| Net profit | 4,948 |
| Total comprehensive income | €3,863 |

a. What do you think is meant by "turnover"?

b. How does Unilever's income statement presentation differ significantly from that of Mornin' Joe?

c. How is the total for net finance costs presented differently than would be typically found under U.S. GAAP?

**IFRS Activity 2**

The following is a recent consolidated statement of financial position on December 31 of a recent year for **LVMH**, a French company that markets the Louis Vuitton® and Moët Hennessy® brands:

| LVMH Statement of Financial Position December 31 (in millions of euros) | |
| --- | --- |
| **Assets** | |
| Brands and other intangible assets—net | €11,510 |
| Goodwill—net | 7,806 |
| Property, plant, and equipment—net | 8,769 |
| Investment in associates | 163 |
| Non-current available for sale financial assets | 6,004 |
| Other non-current assets | 524 |
| Deferred tax | 881 |
| **Non-current assets** | €35,657 |
| Inventories | € 8,080 |
| Trade accounts receivable | 1,985 |
| Income taxes | 201 |
| Other current assets | 1,811 |
| Cash and cash equivalents | 2,196 |
| **Current assets** | €14,273 |
| **TOTAL ASSETS** | €49,930 |
| **Liabilities and Equity** | |
| Share capital | € 152 |
| Share premium | 3,848 |
| Treasury shares | (414) |
| Revaluation reserves | 2,819 |
| Other reserves | 14,393 |
| Cumulative translation adjustment | 342 |
| Net profit, group share | 3,424 |
| **Equity, group share** | €24,564 |
| Minority interests | 1,102 |
| **Total equity** | €25,666 |
| Long-term borrowings | € 3,836 |
| Provisions | 1,530 |
| Deferred tax | 3,960 |
| Other non-current liabilities | 5,456 |
| **Total non-current liabilities** | €14,782 |
| Short-term borrowings | € 2,976 |
| Trade accounts payable | 3,134 |
| Income taxes payable | 442 |
| Provisions | 335 |
| Other current liabilities | 2,595 |
| **Total current liabilities** | € 9,482 |
| **TOTAL LIABILITIES AND EQUITY** | €49,930 |

a. Identify presentation differences between the balance sheet of LVMH and a balance sheet prepared under U.S. GAAP. Use the Mornin' Joe balance sheet (Exhibit 2) as an example of a U.S. GAAP balance sheet. (Ignore minority interests and cumulative translation adjustment.)

b. Compare the terms used in this balance sheet with the terms used by Mornin' Joe (Exhibit 2), using the table that follows:

| LVMH Term | Mornin' Joe U.S. GAAP Term |
|---|---|
| Statement of financial position | |
| Share capital | |
| Share premium | |
| Other reserves | |
| Provisions | |

c. What does the "Revaluation reserves" in the Equity section of the balance sheet represent?

**IFRS IFRS Activity 3**

Under U.S. GAAP, LIFO is an acceptable inventory method. Financial statement information for three companies that use LIFO follows. All table numbers are in millions of dollars.

| | LIFO Inventory | FIFO Inventory (from notes) | Impact on Net Income from Using LIFO Rather than FIFO (from notes) | Total Current Assets | Net Income as Reported |
|---|---|---|---|---|---|
| Exxon | $9,852 | $31,200 | $317 | $58,984 | $30,460 |
| Kroger | 4,966 | 5,793 | (57) | 7,621 | 1,116 |
| Ford Motor* | 5,917 | 6,782 | 4 | 34,368 | 4,690 |

*Autos and trucks only

Assume these companies adopted IFRS, and thus were required to use FIFO, rather than LIFO.

a. Prepare a table with the following columns:

| (1) | (2) | (3) | (4) |
|---|---|---|---|
| FIFO less LIFO | IFRS Net Income | $\dfrac{\text{(FIFO less LIFO)}}{\text{Total Current Assets}}$ | $\dfrac{\text{IFRS Net Income (Col. 2)}}{\text{Reported Net Income}}$ |

(1) Difference between FIFO and LIFO inventory valuation.

(2) Revised IFRS net income using FIFO.

(3) Difference between FIFO and LIFO inventory valuation as a percent of total current assets.

(4) Revised IFRS net income as a percent of the reported net income.

b. Complete the table for the three companies.

c. For which company would a change to IFRS for inventory valuation have the largest percentage impact on total current assets (Col. 3)?

d. For which company would a change to IFRS for inventory valuation have the largest percentage impact on net income (Col. 4)?

e. Why might Kroger have a negative impact on net income from using LIFO, while the other two companies have a positive impact on net income from using LIFO?

# Statement of Cash Flows

## *National Beverage Co.*

**S**uppose you were to receive $100 from an event. Would it make a difference what the event was? Yes, it would! If you received $100 for your birthday, then it's a gift. If you received $100 as a result of working part time for a week, then it's the result of your effort. If you received $100 as a loan, then it's money that you will have to pay back in the future. If you received $100 as a result of selling your iPod, then it's the result of selling an asset. Thus, $100 received can be associated with different types of events, and these events have different meanings to you, and different implications for your future. You would much rather receive a $100 gift than take out a $100 loan. Likewise, company stakeholders view inflows and outflows of cash differently, depending on their source.

Companies are required to report information about the events causing a change in cash over a period of time. This information is reported in the statement of cash flows. One such company is **National Beverage**, which is an alternative beverage company, known for its innovative soft drinks, enhanced juices and waters, and fortified powders and supplements. You have probably seen the company's **Shasta** and **Faygo** soft drinks, or **LaCroix**, **Everfresh**, and **Crystal Bay** drinks at your local grocery or convenience store. As with any company, cash is important to National Beverage. Without cash, National Beverage would be unable to expand its brands, distribute its product, support extreme sports, or provide a return for its owners. Thus, its managers are concerned about the sources and uses of cash.

In previous chapters, we have used the income statement, balance sheet, statement of retained earnings, and other information to analyze the effects of management decisions on a business's financial position and operating performance. In this chapter, we focus on the events causing a change in cash by presenting the preparation and use of the statement of cash flows.

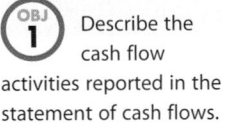
**(OBJ 1)** Describe the cash flow activities reported in the statement of cash flows.

# Reporting Cash Flows

The **statement of cash flows** reports a company's cash inflows and outflows for a period.[1] The statement of cash flows provides useful information about a company's ability to do the following:

- Generate cash from operations
- Maintain and expand its operating capacity
- Meet its financial obligations
- Pay dividends

The statement of cash flows is used by managers in evaluating past operations and in planning future investing and financing activities. It is also used by external users such as investors and creditors to assess a company's profit potential and ability to pay its debt and pay dividends.

The statement of cash flows reports three types of cash flow activities, as follows:

**Note:**
The statement of cash flows reports cash flows from operating, investing, and financing activities.

1. **Cash flows from operating activities** are the cash flows from transactions that affect the net income of the company.

    Example: Purchase and sale of merchandise by a retailer.

2. **Cash flows from investing activities** are the cash flows from transactions that affect investments in the noncurrent assets of the company.

    Example: Purchase and sale of fixed assets, such as equipment and buildings.

[1] As used in this chapter, *cash* refers to cash and cash equivalents. Examples of cash equivalents include short-term, highly liquid investments, such as money market accounts, bank certificates of deposit, and U.S. Treasury bills.

3. **Cash flows from financing activities** are the cash flows from transactions that affect the debt and equity of the company.

Example: Issuing or retiring equity and debt securities.

The cash flows are reported in the statement of cash flows as follows:

| | |
|---|---|
| Cash flows from operating activities | $XXX |
| Cash flows from investing activities | XXX |
| Cash flows from financing activities | XXX |
| Net increase or decrease in cash for the period | $XXX |
| Cash at the beginning of the period | XXX |
| Cash at the end of the period | $XXX |

The ending cash on the statement of cash flows equals the cash reported on the company's balance sheet at the end of the year.

Exhibit 1 illustrates the sources (increases) and uses (decreases) of cash by each of the three cash flow activities. A *source* of cash causes the cash flow to increase and is called a *cash inflow*. A *use* of cash causes cash flow to decrease and is called *cash outflow*.

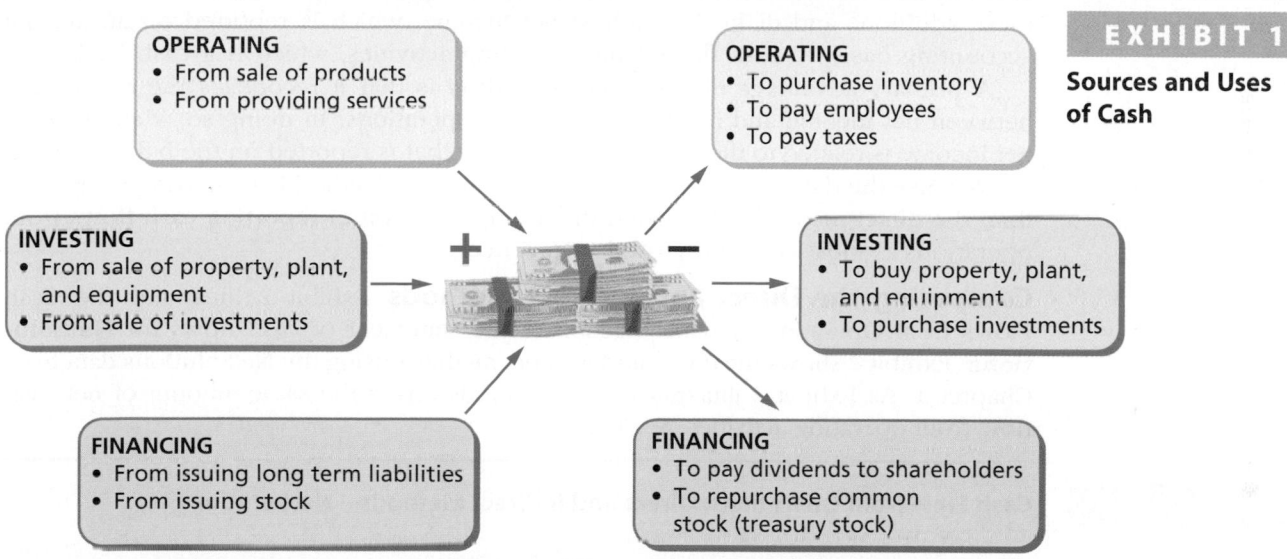

**EXHIBIT 1**

**Sources and Uses of Cash**

## Cash Flows from Operating Activities

Cash flows from operating activities reports the cash inflows and outflows from a company's day-to-day operations. Companies may select one of two alternative methods for reporting cash flows from operating activities in the statement of cash flows:

 In fiscal 2012, Google Inc. generated $16.6 billion in net cash flow from operating activities.

- The direct method
- The indirect method

Both methods result in the same amount of cash flows from operating activities. They differ in the way they report cash flows from operating activities.

**The Direct Method** The **direct method** reports operating cash inflows (receipts) and cash outflows (payments) as follows:

| | | |
|---|---|---|
| Cash flows from operating activities: | | |
| Cash received from customers | | $XXX |
| Less: Cash payments for merchandise | $XXX | |
| Cash payments for operating expenses | XXX | |
| Cash payments for interest | XXX | |
| Cash payments for income taxes | XXX | XXX |
| Net cash flow from operating activities | | $XXX |

The primary operating cash inflow is cash received from customers. The primary operating cash outflows are cash payments for merchandise, operating expenses, interest, and income tax payments. The cash received from operating activities less the cash payments for operating activities is the net cash flow from operating activities.

The primary advantage of the direct method is that it *directly* reports cash receipts and cash payments in the statement of cash flows. Its primary disadvantage is that these data may not be readily available in the accounting records. Thus, the direct method is normally more costly to prepare and, as a result, is used infrequently in practice.

**The Indirect Method** The **indirect method** reports cash flows from operating activities by beginning with net income and adjusting it for revenues and expenses that do not involve the receipt or payment of cash, as follows:

Cash flows from operating activities:
Net income — $XXX
Adjustments to reconcile net income to net
cash flow from operating activities — XXX
Net cash flow from operating activities — $XXX

The adjustments to reconcile net income to net cash flow from operating activities include such items as depreciation and gains or losses on fixed assets. Changes in current operating assets and liabilities such as accounts receivable or accounts payable are also added or deducted, depending on their effect on cash flows. In effect, these additions and deductions adjust net income, which is reported on an accrual accounting basis, to cash flows from operating activities, which is a cash basis.

A primary advantage of the indirect method is that it reconciles the differences between net income and net cash flows from operations. In doing so, it shows how net income is related to the ending cash balance that is reported on the balance sheet.

Because the data are readily available, the indirect method is less costly to prepare than the direct method. As a result, the indirect method of reporting cash flows from operations is most commonly used in practice.

**Comparing the Direct and Indirect Methods** Exhibit 2 illustrates the Cash Flows from Operating Activities section of the statement of cash flows for **NetSolutions**. Exhibit 2 shows the direct and indirect methods using the NetSolutions data from Chapter 1. As Exhibit 2 illustrates, both methods report the same amount of net cash flow from operating activities, $2,900.

---

**EXHIBIT 2**     **Cash Flow from Operations: Direct and Indirect Methods—NetSolutions**

**Direct Method**
Cash flows from operating activities:
Cash received from customers.................... $7,500
Deduct cash payments for expenses
and payments to creditors ..................... 4,600
Net cash flow from operating activities ........... $2,900

**Indirect Method**
Cash flows from operating activities:
Net income .................................... $3,050
Add increase in accounts payable.............. 400
$3,450
Deduct increase in supplies ................... 550
Net cash flow from operating activities ........ $2,900

the same

---

# Business Connection

## CASH CRUNCH!

In late 2011, American Airlines' deteriorating cash flow situation forced the company to file for bankruptcy. At the time, the airline had generated $235 million in net cash flow from operating activities for the nine-month period ending September 31, 2011, while spending $1.1 billion on additional property, plant, and equipment. The property, plant, and equipment purchases were paid for by issuing additional debt. By Thanksgiving 2011, it became clear that the company's weak net cash flow from operating activities would not be sufficient to pay off the airline's massive debt. On November 29, 2011, the airline filed for bankruptcy. In February 2013, American and U.S. Airways announced plans to merge, creating the largest airline in the world.

Source: M. Curriden and N. Posgate, "American Airlines bankruptcy, merger deals were complex, expensive," *Dallas Morning News*, February 17, 2013.

## Cash Flows from Investing Activities

Cash flows from investing activities show the cash inflows and outflows related to changes in a company's long-term assets. Cash flows from investing activities are reported on the statement of cash flows as follows:

Cash flows from investing activities:
| | | |
|---|---|---|
| Cash inflows from investing activities | $XXX | |
| Less cash used for investing activities | XXX | |
| Net cash flows from investing activities | | $XXX |

Cash inflows from investing activities normally arise from selling fixed assets, investments, and intangible assets. Cash outflows normally include payments to purchase fixed assets, investments, and intangible assets.

## Cash Flows from Financing Activities

Cash flows from financing activities show the cash inflows and outflows related to changes in a company's long-term liabilities and stockholders' equity. Cash flows from financing activities are reported on the statement of cash flows as follows:

Cash flows from financing activities:
| | | |
|---|---|---|
| Cash inflows from financing activities | $XXX | |
| Less cash used for financing activities | XXX | |
| Net cash flow from financing activities | | $XXX |

Cash inflows from financing activities normally arise from issuing long-term debt or equity securities. For example, issuing bonds, notes payable, preferred stock, and common stock creates cash inflows from financing activities. Cash outflows from financing activities include paying cash dividends, repaying long-term debt, and acquiring treasury stock.

In March 2013, U.S. companies in the S&P 500 index were expected to pay $300 billion in dividends to Investors during 2013.

## Noncash Investing and Financing Activities

A company may enter into transactions involving investing and financing activities that do not *directly* affect cash. For example, a company may issue common stock to retire long-term debt. Although this transaction does not directly affect cash, it does eliminate future cash payments for interest and for paying the bonds when they mature. Because such transactions *indirectly* affect cash flows, they are reported in a separate section of the statement of cash flows. This section usually appears at the bottom of the statement of cash flows.

## Format of the Statement of Cash Flows

The statement of cash flows presents the cash flows generated by, or used for, the three activities previously discussed: operating, investing, and financing. These three activities are always reported in the same order, following the format illustrated in Exhibit 3.

---

**COMPANY NAME**
**Statement of Cash Flows**
**For the Year Ended xxxx**

| | | |
|---|---|---|
| **Cash flows from operating activities** | | |
| (List of individual items, as illustrated in Exhibit 1) .......................... | XXX | |
| Net cash flows from operating activities ................................. | | $XXX |
| **Cash flows from investing activities** | | |
| (List of individual items, as illustrated in Exhibit 1) .......................... | XXX | |
| Net cash flows from (used for) investing activities .................... | | XXX |
| **Cash flows from financing activities** | | |
| (List of individual items, as illustrated in Exhibit 1) .......................... | XXX | |
| Net cash flows from (used for) financing activities..................... | | XXX |
| **Increase (decrease) in cash** ........................................... | | $XXX |
| **Cash at the beginning of the period** ................................... | | XXX |
| **Cash at the end of the period** ........................................ | | $XXX |
| **Noncash investing and financing activites** ............................ | | $XXX |

**EXHIBIT 3**

**Format of the Statement of Cash Flows**

**Example Exercise 16-1** **Classifying Cash Flows**

Identify whether each of the following would be reported as an operating, investing, or financing activity in the statement of cash flows:

a. Purchase of patent

b. Payment of cash dividend

c. Disposal of equipment

d. Cash sales

e. Purchase of treasury stock

f. Payment of wages expense

**Follow My Example 16-1**

a. Investing

b. Financing

c. Investing

d. Operating

e. Financing

f. Operating

Practice Exercises: PE 16-1A, PE 16-1B

## No Cash Flow per Share

**Cash flow per share** is sometimes reported in the financial press. As reported, cash flow per share is normally computed as *cash flow from operations divided by the number of common shares outstanding*. However, such reporting may be misleading because of the following:

- Users may misinterpret cash flow per share as the per-share amount available for dividends. This would not be the case if the cash generated by operations is required for repaying loans or for reinvesting in the business.
- Users may misinterpret cash flow per share as equivalent to (or better than) earnings per share.

For these reasons, the financial statements, including the statement of cash flows, should not report cash flow per share.

**OBJ 2** Prepare a statement of cash flows, using the indirect method.

# Preparing the Statement of Cash Flows—
# The Indirect Method

The indirect method of reporting cash flows from operating activities uses the logic that a change in any balance sheet account (including cash) can be analyzed in terms of changes in the other balance sheet accounts. Thus, by analyzing changes in noncash balance sheet accounts, any change in the cash account can be *indirectly* determined.

To illustrate, the accounting equation can be solved for cash as follows:

Assets = Liabilities + Stockholders' Equity

Cash + Noncash Assets = Liabilities + Stockholders' Equity

Cash = Liabilities + Stockholders' Equity − Noncash Assets

Therefore, any change in the cash account can be determined by analyzing changes in the liability, stockholders' equity, and noncash asset accounts as follows:

*Change* in Cash = *Change* in Liabilities + *Change* in Stockholders' Equity − *Change* in Noncash Assets

Under the indirect method, there is no order in which the balance sheet accounts must be analyzed. However, net income (or net loss) is the first amount reported on the statement of cash flows. Because net income (or net loss) is a component of any change in Retained Earnings, the first account normally analyzed is Retained Earnings.

To illustrate the indirect method, the income statement and comparative balance sheets for **Rundell Inc.**, shown in Exhibit 4, are used. Ledger accounts and other data supporting the income statement and balance sheet are presented as needed.[2]

**EXHIBIT 4**

**Income Statement and Comparative Balance Sheet**

## Rundell Inc.
### Income Statement
### For the Year Ended December 31, 2016

| | | |
|---|---:|---:|
| Sales | | $1,180,000 |
| Cost of merchandise sold | | 790,000 |
| Gross profit | | $ 390,000 |
| Operating expenses: | | |
| Depreciation expense | $ 7,000 | |
| Other operating expenses | 196,000 | |
| Total operating expenses | | 203,000 |
| Income from operations | | $ 187,000 |
| Other income: | | |
| Gain on sale of land | $ 12,000 | |
| Other expense: | | |
| Interest expense | 8,000 | 4,000 |
| Income before income tax | | $ 191,000 |
| Income tax expense | | 83,000 |
| Net income | | $ 108,000 |

## Rundell Inc.
### Comparative Balance Sheet
### December 31, 2016 and 2015

| | 2016 | 2015 | Increase Decrease* |
|---|---:|---:|---:|
| **Assets** | | | |
| Cash | $ 97,500 | $ 26,000 | $ 71,500 |
| Accounts receivable (net) | 74,000 | 65,000 | 9,000 |
| Inventories | 172,000 | 180,000 | 8,000* |
| Land | 80,000 | 125,000 | 45,000* |
| Building | 260,000 | 200,000 | 60,000 |
| Accumulated depreciation—building | (65,300) | (58,300) | 7,000** |
| Total assets | $618,200 | $537,700 | $ 80,500 |
| **Liabilities** | | | |
| Accounts payable (merchandise creditors) | $ 43,500 | $ 46,700 | $ 3,200* |
| Accrued expenses payable (operating expenses) | 26,500 | 24,300 | 2,200 |
| Income taxes payable | 7,900 | 8,400 | 500* |
| Dividends payable | 14,000 | 10,000 | 4,000 |
| Bonds payable | 100,000 | 150,000 | 50,000* |
| Total liabilities | $191,900 | $239,400 | $ 47,500* |
| **Stockholders' Equity** | | | |
| Common stock ($2 par) | $ 24,000 | $ 16,000 | $ 8,000 |
| Paid-in capital in excess of par | 120,000 | 80,000 | 40,000 |
| Retained earnings | 282,300 | 202,300 | 80,000 |
| Total stockholders' equity | $426,300 | $298,300 | $128,000 |
| Total liabilities and stockholders' equity | $618,200 | $537,700 | $ 80,500 |

**There is a $7,000 increase to Accumulated Depreciation—Building, which is a contra asset account. As a result, the $7,000 increase in this account must be subtracted in summing to the increase in Total assets of $80,500.

[2] An appendix that discusses using a spreadsheet (work sheet) as an aid in assembling data for the statement of cash flows is presented at the end of this chapter. This appendix illustrates the use of this spreadsheet in reporting cash flows from operating activities using the indirect method.

## Retained Earnings

The comparative balance sheet for **Rundell Inc.** shows that retained earnings increased $80,000 during the year. The retained earnings account that follows indicates how this change occurred:

| **Account** *Retained Earnings* | | | | | Account No. | |
|---|---|---|---|---|---|---|
| | | | | | **Balance** | |
| **Date** | | **Item** | **Debit** | **Credit** | **Debit** | **Credit** |
| 2016 Jan. | 1 | Balance | | | | 202,300 |
| Dec. | 31 | Net income | | 108,000 | | 310,300 |
| | 31 | Cash dividends | 28,000 | | | 282,300 |

The retained earnings account indicates that the $80,000 ($108,000 − $28,000) change resulted from net income of $108,000 and cash dividends of $28,000. The net income of $108,000 is the first amount reported in the Cash Flows from Operating Activities section.

## Adjustments to Net Income

The net income of $108,000 reported by **Rundell Inc.** does not equal the cash flows from operating activities for the period. This is because net income is determined using the accrual method of accounting.

Under the accrual method of accounting, revenues and expenses are recorded at different times from when cash is received or paid. For example, merchandise may be sold on account and the cash received at a later date. Likewise, insurance premiums may be paid in the current period but expensed in a following period.

Thus, under the indirect method, adjustments to net income must be made to determine cash flows from operating activities. The typical adjustments to net income are shown in Exhibit 5.[3]

---

**EXHIBIT 5**

**Adjustments to Net Income (Loss) Using the Indirect Method**

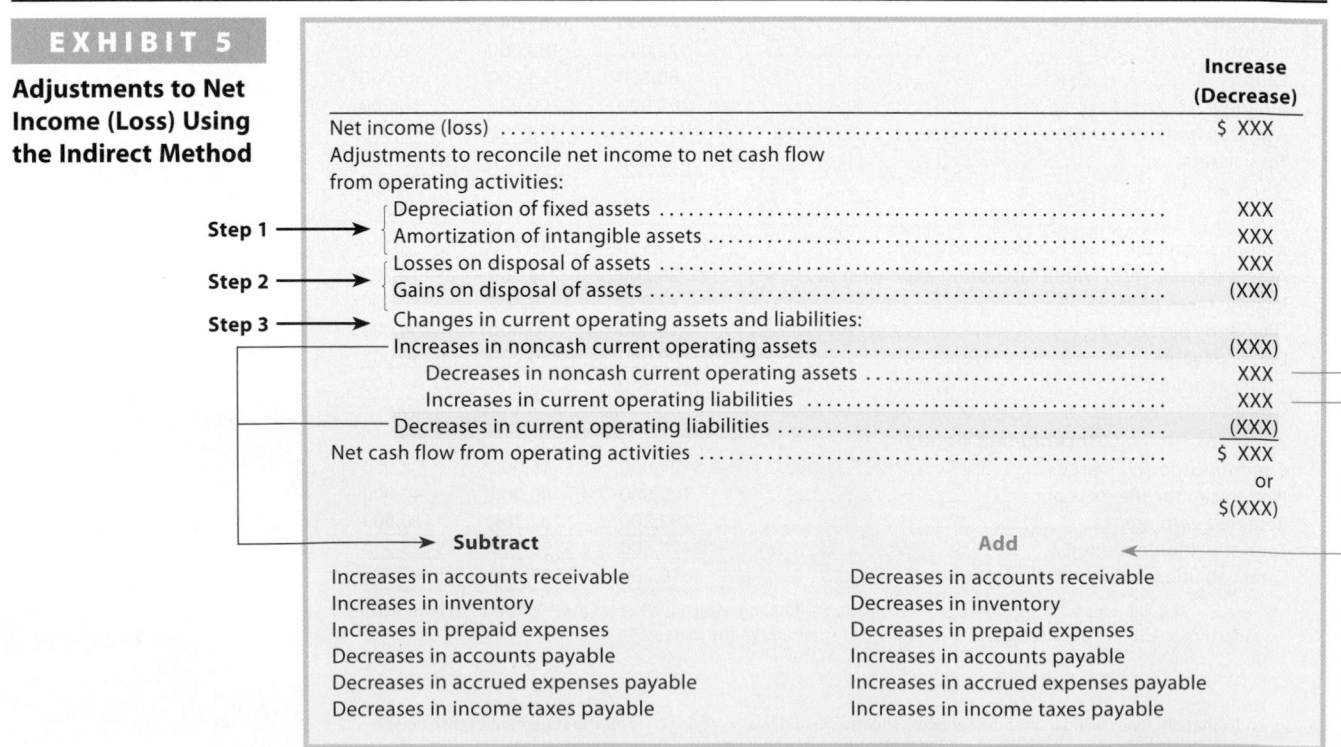

---

[3] Other items that also require adjustments to net income to obtain cash flows from operating activities include amortization of bonds payable discounts (add), losses on debt retirement (add), amortization of bonds payable premiums (deduct), and gains on retirement of debt (deduct).

Net income is normally adjusted to cash flows from operating activities, using the following steps:

- Step 1. Expenses that do not affect cash are added. Such expenses decrease net income but do not involve cash payments and, thus, are added to net income.

    Example: Depreciation of fixed assets and amortization of intangible assets are added to net income.

- Step 2. Losses on the disposal of assets are added and gains on the disposal of assets are deducted. The disposal (sale) of assets is an investing activity rather than an operating activity. However, such losses and gains are reported as part of net income. As a result, any *losses* on disposal of assets are *added* back to net income. Likewise, any *gains* on disposal of assets are *deducted* from net income.

    Example: Land costing $100,000 is sold for $90,000. The loss of $10,000 is added back to net income.

- Step 3. Changes in current operating assets and liabilities are added or deducted as follows:

    - Increases in noncash current operating assets are deducted.
    - Decreases in noncash current operating assets are added.
    - Increases in current operating liabilities are added.
    - Decreases in current operating liabilities are deducted.

    Example: A sale of $10,000 on account increases sales, accounts receivable, and net income by $10,000. However, cash is not affected. Thus, the $10,000 increase in accounts receivable is deducted. Similar adjustments are required for the changes in the other current asset and liability accounts, such as inventory, prepaid expenses, accounts payable, accrued expenses payable, and income taxes payable, as shown in Exhibit 5.

---

## Example Exercise 16-2  Adjustments to Net Income—Indirect Method

Omni Corporation's accumulated depreciation increased by $12,000, while $3,400 of patent amortization was recognized between balance sheet dates. There were no purchases or sales of depreciable or intangible assets during the year. In addition, the income statement showed a gain of $4,100 from the sale of land. Reconcile Omni's net income of $50,000 to net cash flow from operating activities.

### Follow My Example 16-2

| | |
|---|---:|
| Net income .......................................................... | $50,000 |
| Adjustments to reconcile net income to net cash flow from operating activities: | |
| Depreciation ....................................................... | 12,000 |
| Amortization of patents ......................................... | 3,400 |
| Gain from sale of land ........................................... | (4,100) |
| Net cash flow from operating activities ........................ | $61,300 |

Practice Exercises: PE 16-2A, PE 16-2B

---

The Cash Flows from Operating Activities section of **Rundell Inc.'s** statement of cash flows is shown in Exhibit 6.

Rundell's net income of $108,000 is converted to cash flows from operating activities of $100,500 as follows:

Step 1.  Add depreciation of $7,000.

**EXHIBIT 6**

**Net Cash Flow From Operating Activities— Indirect Method**

Cash flows from operating activities:

| | |
|---|---|
| Net income | $108,000 |

Adjustments to reconcile net income to net cash flow from operating activities:

Step 1 → Depreciation ............................................................. 7,000
Step 2 → Gain on sale of land .................................................. (12,000)

Changes in current operating assets and liabilities:

Step 3 →
Increase in accounts receivable ................................... (9,000)
Decrease in inventories........................................... 8,000
Decrease in accounts payable ..................................... (3,200)
Increase in accrued expenses payable ........................... 2,200
Decrease in income taxes payable ............................... (500)

Net cash flow from operating activities ....................................... $100,500

Analysis: The comparative balance sheet in Exhibit 4 indicates that Accumulated Depreciation—Building increased by $7,000. The following account indicates that depreciation for the year was $7,000 for the building:

**Account** *Accumulated Depreciation—Building*                    Account No.

| Date | | Item | Debit | Credit | Balance Debit | Balance Credit |
|---|---|---|---|---|---|---|
| 2016 Jan. | 1 | Balance | | | | 58,300 |
| Dec. | 31 | Depreciation for year | | 7,000 | | 65,300 |

Step 2.  Deduct the gain on the sale of land of $12,000.

Analysis: The income statement in Exhibit 4 reports a gain of $12,000 from the sale of land. The proceeds, which include the gain, are reported in the Investing section of the statement of cash flows.[4] Thus, the gain of $12,000 is deducted from net income in determining cash flows from operating activities.

Step 3.  Add and deduct changes in current operating assets and liabilities excluding cash.

Analysis: The increases and decreases in the current operating asset and current liability accounts excluding cash are as follows:

| Accounts | December 31 2016 | December 31 2015 | Increase Decrease* |
|---|---|---|---|
| Accounts Receivable (net) | $ 74,000 | $ 65,000 | $9,000 |
| Inventories | 172,000 | 180,000 | 8,000* |
| Accounts Payable (merchandise creditors) | 43,500 | 46,700 | 3,200* |
| Accrued Expenses Payable (operating expenses) | 26,500 | 24,300 | 2,200 |
| Income Taxes Payable | 7,900 | 8,400 | 500* |

*Accounts receivable (net):* The $9,000 increase is deducted from net income. This is because the $9,000 increase in accounts receivable indicates that sales on account were $9,000 more than the cash received from customers. Thus, sales (and net income) includes $9,000 that was not received in cash during the year.

*Inventories:* The $8,000 decrease is added to net income. This is because the $8,000 decrease in inventories indicates that the cost of merchandise *sold* exceeds the cost of the merchandise *purchased* during the year by $8,000. In other words, the cost of merchandise sold includes $8,000 of goods from inventory that were not purchased (used cash) during the year.

*Accounts payable (merchandise creditors):* The $3,200 decrease is deducted from net income. This is because a decrease in accounts payable indicates that the cash

[4] The reporting of the proceeds (cash flows) from the sale of land as part of investing activities is discussed later in this chapter.

*payments* to merchandise creditors exceed the merchandise *purchased on account* by $3,200. Therefore, the cost of merchandise sold is $3,200 less than the cash paid to merchandise creditors during the year.

*Accrued expenses payable (operating expenses):* The $2,200 increase is added to net income. This is because an increase in accrued expenses payable indicates that operating expenses exceed the cash payments for operating expenses by $2,200. In other words, operating expenses reported on the income statement include $2,200 that did not require a cash outflow during the year.

*Income taxes payable:* The $500 decrease is deducted from net income. This is because a decrease in income taxes payable indicates that taxes paid exceed the amount of taxes incurred during the year by $500. In other words, the amount reported on the income statement for income tax expense is less than the amount paid by $500.

---

**Example Exercise 16-3  Changes in Current Operating Assets and Liabilities—Indirect Method**

OBJ 2

Victor Corporation's current operating assets and liabilities from the company's comparative balance sheet were as follows:

|  | Dec. 31, 2016 | Dec. 31, 2015 |
|---|---|---|
| Accounts receivable | $ 6,500 | $ 4,900 |
| Inventory | 12,300 | 15,000 |
| Accounts payable | 4,800 | 5,200 |
| Dividends payable | 5,000 | 4,000 |

Adjust Victor's net income of $70,000 for changes in operating assets and liabilities to arrive at cash flows from operating activities.

**Follow My Example 16-3**

| | |
|---|---|
| Net income ................................................................... | $70,000 |
| Adjustments to reconcile net income to net cash flow from operating activities: | |
| Changes in current operating assets and liabilities: | |
| Increase in accounts receivable ................................................ | (1,600) |
| Decrease in inventory ......................................................... | 2,700 |
| Decrease in accounts payable ................................................. | (400) |
| Net cash flow from operating activities ........................................ | $70,700 |

*Note:* The change in dividends payable impacts the cash paid for dividends, which is disclosed under financing activities.

........................................................................................

Practice Exercises: PE 16-3A, PE 16-3B

---

Using the preceding analyses, Rundell's net income of $108,000 is converted to cash flows from operating activities of $100,500 as shown in Exhibit 6.

---

# Integrity, Objectivity, and Ethics in Business

### CREDIT POLICY AND CASH FLOW

Investors frequently use net cash flow from operating activities to assess a company's financial health. If a company is financially healthy, net cash flow from operating activities should be roughly consistent with accrual basis net income. Questions arise, however, when a company's net cash flow from operating activities significantly lags net income. There are two scenarios which can cause this to happen:

• Sales on account are never collected in cash.

• Large cash purchases for inventory are never sold, or sell at a very slow pace.

Both of these scenarios increase net income, without a corresponding increase in net cash flow from operating activities. Prudent investors are often skeptical when they observe these scenarios and tend to avoid these types of investments until the cash flows become clear.

Source: Argersinger, M., "How Companies Fake It (With Cash Flow)," *Daily Finance Investor Center*, July 17, 2011.

**Example Exercise 16-4** **Cash Flows from Operating Activities—Indirect Method**

OBJ 2

Omicron Inc. reported the following data:

| | |
|---|---:|
| Net income | $120,000 |
| Depreciation expense | 12,000 |
| Loss on disposal of equipment | 15,000 |
| Increase in accounts receivable | 5,000 |
| Decrease in accounts payable | 2,000 |

Prepare the Cash Flows from Operating Activities section of the statement of cash flows, using the indirect method.

**Follow My Example 16-4**

| | |
|---|---:|
| Cash flows from operating activities: | |
| Net income | $120,000 |
| Adjustments to reconcile net income to net cash flow from operating activities: | |
| Depreciation expense | 12,000 |
| Loss on disposal of equipment | 15,000 |
| Changes in current operating assets and liabilities: | |
| Increase in accounts receivable | (5,000) |
| Decrease in accounts payable | (2,000) |
| Net cash flow from operating activities | $140,000 |

Practice Exercises: PE 16-4A, PE 16-4B

## Dividends

The retained earnings account of **Rundell Inc.** indicates cash dividends of $28,000 were declared during the year. However, the following dividends payable account indicates that only $24,000 of dividends were paid during the year:

**Account** *Dividends Payable*                                                  Account No.

| Date | | Item | Debit | Credit | Balance Debit | Balance Credit |
|---|---|---|---:|---:|---:|---:|
| 2016 | | | | | | |
| Jan. | 1 | Balance | | | | 10,000 |
| | 10 | Cash paid | 10,000 | | — | — |
| June | 20 | Dividends declared | | 14,000 | | 14,000 |
| July | 10 | Cash paid | 14,000 | | — | — |
| Dec. | 20 | Dividends declared | | 14,000 | | 14,000 |

Because dividend payments are a financing activity, the dividend payment of $24,000 is reported in the Financing Activities section of the statement of cash flows, as follows:

| | |
|---|---:|
| Cash flows from financing activities: | |
| Cash paid for dividends | $24,000 |

## Common Stock

The common stock account of **Rundell Inc.** increased by $8,000, and the paid-in capital in excess of par—common stock account increased by $40,000, as follows:

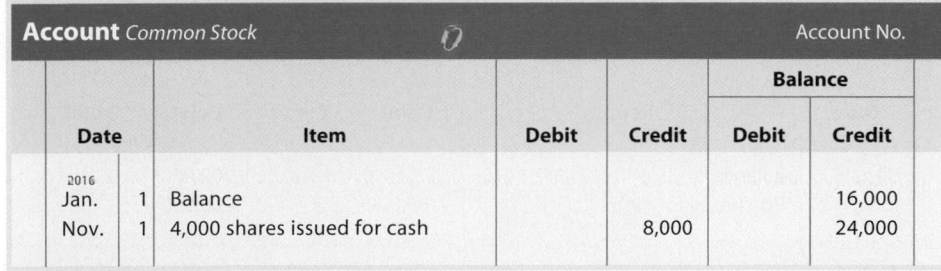

| Account Common Stock | | | Debit | Credit | Balance | |
|---|---|---|---|---|---|---|
| Date | | Item | | | Debit | Credit |
| 2016 | | | | | | |
| Jan. | 1 | Balance | | | | 16,000 |
| Nov. | 1 | 4,000 shares issued for cash | | 8,000 | | 24,000 |

| Account Paid-In Capital in Excess of Par—Common Stock | | | Debit | Credit | Balance | |
|---|---|---|---|---|---|---|
| Date | | Item | | | Debit | Credit |
| 2016 | | | | | | |
| Jan. | 1 | Balance | | | | 80,000 |
| Nov. | 1 | 4,000 shares issued for cash | | 40,000 | | 120,000 |

These increases were from issuing 4,000 shares of common stock for $12 per share. This cash inflow is reported in the Financing Activities section as follows:

> Cash flows from financing activities:
>     Cash received from sale of common stock .................... $48,000

## Bonds Payable

The bonds payable account of **Rundell Inc.** decreased by $50,000, as follows:

| Account Bonds Payable | | | Debit | Credit | Balance | |
|---|---|---|---|---|---|---|
| Date | | Item | | | Debit | Credit |
| 2016 | | | | | | |
| Jan. | 1 | Balance | | | | 150,000 |
| June | 1 | Retired by payment of cash | | | | |
| | | at face amount | 50,000 | | | 100,000 |

This decrease is from retiring the bonds by a cash payment for their face amount. This cash outflow is reported in the Financing Activities section as follows:

> Cash flows from financing activities:
>     Cash paid to retire bonds payable ........................... $50,000

## Building

The building account of **Rundell Inc.** increased by $60,000, and the accumulated depreciation—building account increased by $7,000, as follows:

| Account Building | | | | | Account No. | | |
|---|---|---|---|---|---|---|---|
| | | | | | **Balance** | | |
| **Date** | | **Item** | **Debit** | **Credit** | **Debit** | **Credit** | |
| 2016 Jan. | 1 | Balance | | | 200,000 | | |
| Dec. | 27 | Purchased for cash | 60,000 | | 260,000 | | |

| Account Accumulated Depreciation—Building | | | | | Account No. | | |
|---|---|---|---|---|---|---|---|
| | | | | | **Balance** | | |
| **Date** | | **Item** | **Debit** | **Credit** | **Debit** | **Credit** | |
| 2016 Jan. | 1 | Balance | | | | 58,300 | |
| Dec. | 31 | Depreciation for the year | | 7,000 | | 65,300 | |

The purchase of a building for cash of $60,000 is reported as an outflow of cash in the Investing Activities section as follows:

> Cash flows from investing activities:
> Cash paid for purchase of building . . . . . . . . . . . . . . . . . . . . . . . . .     $60,000

The credit in the accumulated depreciation—building account represents depreciation expense for the year. This depreciation expense of $7,000 on the building was added to net income in determining cash flows from operating activities, as reported in Exhibit 6.

## Land

The $45,000 decline in the land account of **Rundell Inc.** was from two transactions, as follows:

| Account Land | | | | | Account No. | | |
|---|---|---|---|---|---|---|---|
| | | | | | **Balance** | | |
| **Date** | | **Item** | **Debit** | **Credit** | **Debit** | **Credit** | |
| 2016 Jan. | 1 | Balance | | | 125,000 | | |
| June | 8 | Sold for $72,000 cash | | 60,000 | 65,000 | | |
| Oct. | 12 | Purchased for $15,000 cash | 15,000 | | 80,000 | | |

The June 8 transaction is the sale of land with a cost of $60,000 for $72,000 in cash. The $72,000 proceeds from the sale are reported in the Investing Activities section as follows:

> Cash flows from investing activities:
> Cash received from sale of land . . . . . . . . . . . . . . . . . . . . . . . . . . . . .     $72,000

The proceeds of $72,000 include the $12,000 gain on the sale of land and the $60,000 cost (book value) of the land. As shown in Exhibit 6, the $12,000 gain is deducted from net income in the Cash Flows from Operating Activities section. This is so that the $12,000 cash inflow related to the gain is not included twice as a cash inflow.

The October 12 transaction is the purchase of land for cash of $15,000. This transaction is reported as an outflow of cash in the Investing Activities section as follows:

Cash flows from investing activities:
Cash paid for purchase of land .............................. $15,000

---

## Example Exercise 16-5   Land Transactions on the Statement of Cash Flows

OBJ 2

Alpha Corporation purchased land for $125,000. Later in the year, the company sold a different piece of land with a book value of $165,000 for $200,000. How are the effects of these transactions reported on the statement of cash flows?

### Follow My Example 16-5

The gain on the sale of the land is deducted from net income, as follows:

Gain on sale of land ........................................................... $ (35,000)

The purchase and sale of land is reported as part of cash flows from investing activities, as follows:

Cash received from sale of land ................................................... $200,000
Cash paid for purchase of land ................................................... (125,000)

Practice Exercises: PE 16-5A, PE 16-5B

---

## Preparing the Statement of Cash Flows

The statement of cash flows for **Rundell Inc.**, using the indirect method, is shown in Exhibit 7. The statement of cash flows indicates that cash increased by $71,500 during the year. The most significant increase in net cash flows ($100,500) was from operating activities. The most significant use of cash ($26,000) was for financing activities. The ending balance of cash on December 31, 2016, is $97,500. This ending cash balance is also reported on the December 31, 2016, balance sheet shown in Exhibit 4.

**EXHIBIT 7**

**Statement of Cash Flows—Indirect Method**

**Rundell Inc.**
**Statement of Cash Flows**
**For the Year Ended December 31, 2016**

| | | | |
|---|---|---:|---:|
| Cash flows from operating activities: | | | |
| Net income........................................... | | $108,000 | |
| Adjustments to reconcile net income to net cash flow from operating activities: | | | |
| Depreciation ....................................... | | 7,000 | |
| Gain on sale of land............................ | | (12,000) | |
| Changes in current operating assets and liabilities: | | | |
| Increase in accounts receivable.................. | | (9,000) | |
| Decrease in inventories.......................... | | 8,000 | |
| Decrease in accounts payable ................... | | (3,200) | |
| Increase in accrued expenses payable........... | | 2,200 | |
| Decrease in income taxes payable .............. | | (500) | |
| Net cash flow from operating activities ................ | | | $100,500 |
| Cash flows from investing activities: | | | |
| Cash received from sale of land ........................ | | $ 72,000 | |
| Less: Cash paid for purchase of land .................... | $15,000 | | |
| Cash paid for purchase of building ................ | 60,000 | 75,000 | |
| Net cash flow used for investing activities.............. | | | (3,000) |
| Cash flows from financing activities: | | | |
| Cash received from sale of common stock............... | | $ 48,000 | |
| Less: Cash paid to retire bonds payable ............... | $50,000 | | |
| Cash paid for dividends......................... | 24,000 | 74,000 | |
| Net cash flow used for financing activities ............ | | | (26,000) |
| Increase in cash ...................................... | | | $ 71,500 |
| Cash at the beginning of the year........................ | | | 26,000 |
| Cash at the end of the year........................... | | | $ 97,500 |

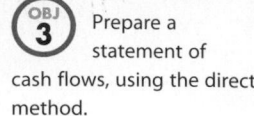

OBJ **3** Prepare a statement of cash flows, using the direct method.

# Preparing the Statement of Cash Flows—The Direct Method

The direct method reports cash flows from operating activities as follows:

| | | |
|---|---:|---:|
| Cash flows from operating activities: | | |
| Cash received from customers .................................... | | $ XXX |
| Less: Cash payments for merchandise ........................... | $ XXX | |
| Cash payments for operating expenses ...................... | XXX | |
| Cash payments for interest ................................. | XXX | |
| Cash payments for income taxes ........................... | XXX | XXX |
| Net cash flow from operating activities .......................... | | $ XXX |

The Cash Flows from Investing and Financing Activities sections of the statement of cash flows are exactly the same under both the direct and indirect methods. The amount of net cash flow from operating activities is also the same, but the manner in which it is reported is different.

Under the direct method, the income statement is adjusted to cash flows from operating activities as shown in Exhibit 8.

---

**EXHIBIT 8**

**Converting Income Statement to Cash Flows from Operating Activities using the Direct Method**

| Income Statement | Adjusted to | Cash Flows from Operating Activities |
|---|:---:|---|
| Sales | → | Cash received from customers |
| Cost of merchandise sold | → | Cash payments for merchandise |
| Operating expenses: | | |
|    Depreciation expense | N/A | N/A |
|    Other operating expenses | → | Cash payments for operating expenses |
| Gain on sale of land | N/A | N/A |
| Interest expense | → | Cash payments for interest |
| Income tax expense | → | Cash payments for income taxes |
| Net income | → | Net cash flow from operating activities |

N/A—Not applicable

---

As shown in Exhibit 8, depreciation expense is not adjusted or reported as part of cash flows from operating activities. This is because depreciation expense does not involve a cash outflow. The gain on the sale of the land is also not adjusted and is not reported as part of cash flows from operating activities. This is because the cash flow from operating activities is determined directly, rather than by reconciling net income. The cash proceeds from the sale of the land are reported as an investing activity.

To illustrate the direct method, the income statement and comparative balance sheet for Rundell Inc., shown in Exhibit 4, are used.

## Cash Received from Customers

The income statement (shown in Exhibit 4) of **Rundell Inc.** reports sales of $1,180,000. To determine the cash received from customers, the $1,180,000 is adjusted for any increase or decrease in accounts receivable. The adjustment is summarized in Exhibit 9.

---

**EXHIBIT 9**

**Determining the Cash Received from Customers**

The cash received from customers is $1,171,000, computed as follows:

| | |
|---|---|
| Sales | $1,180,000 |
| Less increase in accounts receivable | 9,000 |
| Cash received from customers | $1,171,000 |

The increase of $9,000 in accounts receivable (shown in Exhibit 4) during 2016 indicates that sales on account exceeded cash received from customers by $9,000. In other words, sales include $9,000 that did not result in a cash inflow during the year. Thus, $9,000 is deducted from sales to determine the cash received from customers.

**Example Exercise 16-6** **Cash Received from Customers—Direct Method** OBJ 3

Sales reported on the income statement were $350,000. The accounts receivable balance declined $8,000 over the year. Determine the amount of cash received from customers.

**Follow My Example 16-6**

| | |
|---|---|
| Sales................................................... | $350,000 |
| Add decrease in accounts receivable ............................ | 8,000 |
| Cash received from customers..................................... | $358,000 |

Practice Exercises: PE 16-6A, PE 16-6B

## Cash Payments for Merchandise

The income statement (shown in Exhibit 4) for **Rundell Inc.** reports cost of merchandise sold of $790,000. To determine the cash payments for merchandise, the $790,000 is adjusted for any increases or decreases in inventories and accounts payable. Assuming the accounts payable are owed to merchandise suppliers, the adjustment is summarized in Exhibit 10.

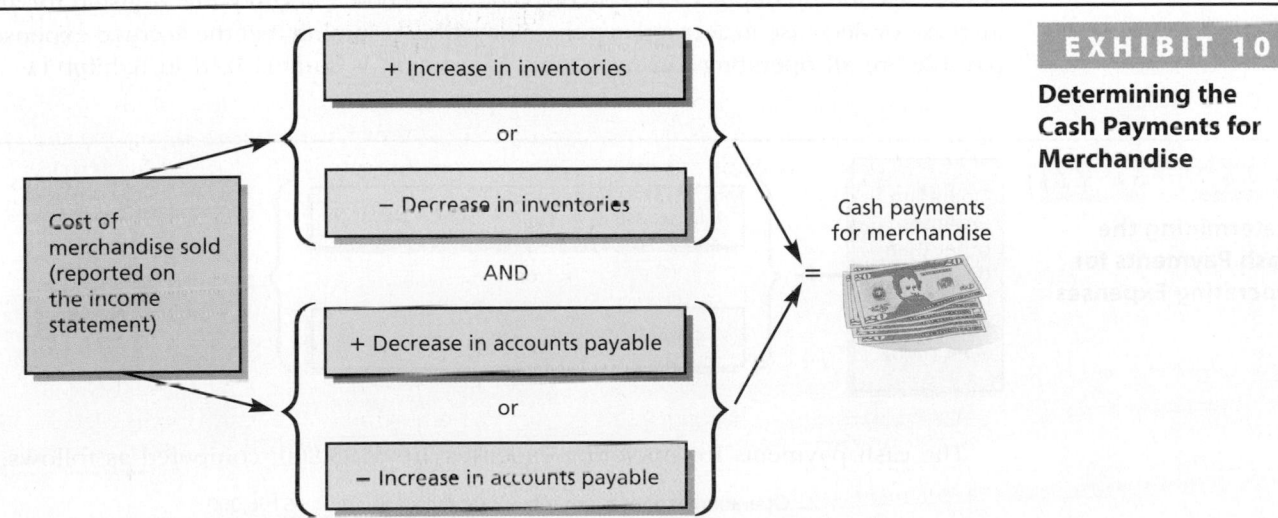

**EXHIBIT 10**

**Determining the Cash Payments for Merchandise**

The cash payments for merchandise are $785,200, computed as follows:

| | |
|---|---|
| Cost of merchandise sold | $790,000 |
| Deduct decrease in inventories | (8,000) |
| Add decrease in accounts payable | 3,200 |
| Cash payments for merchandise | $785,200 |

The $8,000 decrease in inventories (from Exhibit 4) indicates that the merchandise sold exceeded the cost of the merchandise purchased by $8,000. In other words, the cost of merchandise sold includes $8,000 of goods sold from inventory that did not require a cash outflow during the year. Thus, $8,000 is deducted from the cost of merchandise sold in determining the cash payments for merchandise.

The $3,200 decrease in accounts payable (from Exhibit 4) indicates that cash payments for merchandise were $3,200 more than the purchases on account during 2016. Therefore, $3,200 is added to the cost of merchandise sold in determining the cash payments for merchandise.

## Example Exercise 16-7 Cash Payments for Merchandise—Direct Method OBJ 3

The cost of merchandise sold reported on the income statement was $145,000. The accounts payable balance increased by $4,000, and the inventory balance increased by $9,000 over the year. Determine the amount of cash paid for merchandise.

### Follow My Example 16-7

| | |
|---|---:|
| Cost of merchandise sold............................................................ | $145,000 |
| Add increase in inventories........................................................ | 9,000 |
| Deduct increase in accounts payable ........................................... | (4,000) |
| Cash paid for merchandise ......................................................... | $150,000 |

Practice Exercises: PE 16-7A, PE 16-7B

## Cash Payments for Operating Expenses

The income statement for **Rundell Inc.** (from Exhibit 4) reports total operating expenses of $203,000, which includes depreciation expense of $7,000. Because depreciation expense does not require a cash outflow, it is omitted from cash payments for operating expenses.

To determine the cash payments for operating expenses, the other operating expenses (excluding depreciation) of $196,000 ($203,000 − $7,000) are adjusted for any increase or decrease in accrued expenses payable. Assuming that the accrued expenses payable are all operating expenses, this adjustment is summarized in Exhibit 11.

**EXHIBIT 11**

**Determining the Cash Payments for Operating Expenses**

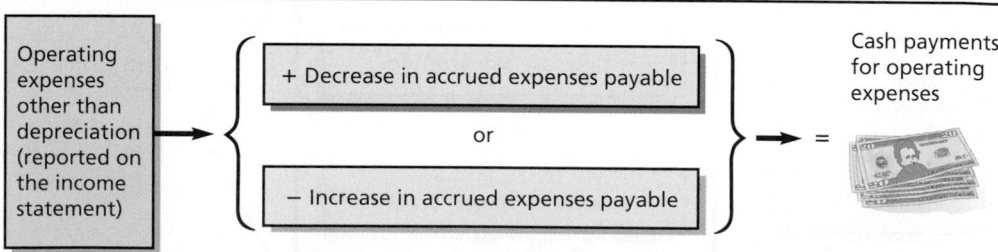

The cash payments for operating expenses are $193,800, computed as follows:

| | |
|---|---:|
| Operating expenses other than depreciation | $196,000 |
| Deduct increase in accrued expenses payable | (2,200) |
| Cash payments for operating expenses | $193,800 |

The increase in accrued expenses payable (from Exhibit 4) indicates that the cash payments for operating expenses were $2,200 less than the amount reported for operating expenses during the year. Thus, $2,200 is deducted from the operating expenses in determining the cash payments for operating expenses.

## Gain on Sale of Land

The income statement for **Rundell Inc.** (from Exhibit 4) reports a gain of $12,000 on the sale of land. The sale of land is an investing activity. Thus, the proceeds from the sale, which include the gain, are reported as part of the cash flows from investing activities.

## Interest Expense

The income statement for **Rundell Inc.** (from Exhibit 4) reports interest expense of $8,000. To determine the cash payments for interest, the $8,000 is adjusted for any increases or decreases in interest payable. The adjustment is summarized in Exhibit 12.

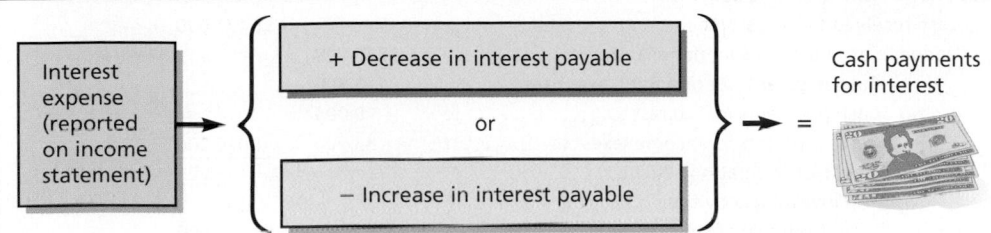

The comparative balance sheet of Rundell in Exhibit 4 indicates no interest payable. This is because the interest expense on the bonds payable is paid on June 1 and December 31. Because there is no interest payable, no adjustment of the interest expense of $8,000 is necessary.

## Cash Payments for Income Taxes

The income statement for **Rundell Inc.** (from Exhibit 3) reports income tax expense of $83,000. To determine the cash payments for income taxes, the $83,000 is adjusted for any increases or decreases in income taxes payable. The adjustment is summarized in Exhibit 13.

The cash payments for income taxes are $83,500, computed as follows:

| | |
|---|---|
| Income tax expense | $83,000 |
| Add decrease in income taxes payable | 500 |
| Cash payments for income taxes | $83,500 |

The $500 decrease in income taxes payable (from Exhibit 4) indicates that the cash payments for income taxes were $500 more than the amount reported for income tax expense during 2016. Thus, $500 is added to the income tax expense in determining the cash payments for income taxes.

# Reporting Cash Flows from Operating Activities—Direct Method

The statement of cash flows for **Rundell Inc.**, using the direct method for reporting cash flows from operating activities, is shown in Exhibit 14. The portions of the statement that differ from those prepared under the indirect method are highlighted.

---

**EXHIBIT 14**

**Statement of Cash Flows—Direct Method**

**Rundell Inc.**
**Statement of Cash Flows**
**For the Year Ended December 31, 2016**

| | | | |
|---|---:|---:|---:|
| Cash flows from operating activities: | | | |
| Cash received from customers ........................ | | $1,171,000 | |
| Deduct: Cash payments for merchandise.............. | $785,200 | | |
| Cash payments for operating expenses........ | 193,800 | | |
| Cash payments for interest ................... | 8,000 | | |
| Cash payments for income taxes .............. | 83,500 | 1,070,500 | |
| Net cash flow from operating activities ............... | | | $100,500 |
| Cash flows from investing activities: | | | |
| Cash received from sale of land ........................ | | $ 72,000 | |
| Less: Cash paid for purchase of land ................... | $ 15,000 | | |
| Cash paid for purchase of building ............... | 60,000 | 75,000 | |
| Net cash flow used for investing activities............. | | | (3,000) |
| Cash flows from financing activities: | | | |
| Cash received from sale of common stock.............. | | $ 48,000 | |
| Less: Cash paid to retire bonds payable ................ | $ 50,000 | | |
| Cash paid for dividends ......................... | 24,000 | 74,000 | |
| Net cash flow used for financing activities ............. | | | (26,000) |
| Increase in cash ......................................... | | | $ 71,500 |
| Cash at the beginning of the year........................ | | | 26,000 |
| Cash at the end of the year............................... | | | $ 97,500 |
| **Schedule Reconciling Net Income with Cash** | | | |
| **Flows from Operating Activities:** | | | |
| Cash flows from operating activities: | | | |
| Net income........................................... | | | $108,000 |
| Adjustments to reconcile net income to net cash | | | |
| flow from operating activities: | | | |
| Depreciation .................................... | | | 7,000 |
| Gain on sale of land............................. | | | (12,000) |
| Changes in current operating assets and | | | |
| liabilities: | | | |
| Increase in accounts receivable ............... | | | (9,000) |
| Decrease in inventory ........................ | | | 8,000 |
| Decrease in accounts payable................. | | | (3,200) |
| Increase in accrued expenses payable ......... | | | 2,200 |
| Decrease in income taxes payable............. | | | (500) |
| Net cash flow from operating activities ................ | | | $100,500 |

---

Exhibit 14 also includes the separate schedule reconciling net income and net cash flow from operating activities. This schedule is included in the statement of cash flows when the direct method is used. This schedule is similar to the Cash Flows from Operating Activities section prepared under the indirect method.

# International Connection

 **IFRS FOR STATEMENT OF CASH FLOWS**

The statement of cash flows is required under International Financial Reporting Standards (IFRS). The statement of cash flows under IFRS is similar to that reported under U.S. GAAP in that the statement has separate sections for operating, investing, and financing activities. Like U.S. GAAP, IFRS also allow the use of either the indirect or direct method of reporting cash flows from operating activities. IFRS differ from U.S. GAAP in some minor areas, including:

- Interest paid can be reported as either an operating or a financing activity, while interest received can be reported as either an operating or an investing activity. In contrast, U.S. GAAP reports interest paid or received as an operating activity.
- Dividends paid can be reported as either an operating or a financing activity, while dividends received can be reported as either an operating or an investing activity. In contrast, U.S. GAAP reports dividends paid as a financing activity and dividends received as an operating activity.
- Cash flows to pay taxes are reported as a separate line in the operating activities, in contrast to U.S. GAAP, which does not require a separate line disclosure.

* IFRS are further discussed and illustrated in this chapter and in Appendix D.

# Financial Analysis and Interpretation: Free Cash Flow

 Describe and illustrate the use of free cash flow in evaluating a company's cash flow.

A valuable tool for evaluating the cash flows of a business is free cash flow. **Free cash flow** measures the operating cash flow available to a company to use after purchasing the property, plant, and equipment (PP&E) necessary to maintain current productive capacity.[5] It is computed as follows:

| | |
|---|---|
| Cash flow from operating activities | $XXX |
| Less: Investments in PP&E needed to maintain current production | XXX |
| Free cash flow | $XXX |

Analysts often use free cash flow, rather than cash flows from operating activities, to measure the financial strength of a business. Industries such as airlines, railroads, and telecommunications companies must invest heavily in new equipment to remain competitive. Such investments can significantly reduce free cash flow. For example, Verizon Communications Inc.'s free cash flow is approximately 51% of the cash flow from operating activities. In contrast, Apple Inc.'s free cash flow is approximately 89% of the cash flow from operating activities.

To illustrate, the cash flow from operating activities for Research in Motion, Inc., maker of BlackBerry® smartphones, was $2,912 million in a recent fiscal year. The statement of cash flows indicated that the cash invested in property, plant, and equipment was $902 million. Assuming that the amount invested in property, plant, and equipment is necessary to maintain productive capacity, free cash flow would be computed as follows (in millions):

| | |
|---|---|
| Cash flow from operating activities | $2,912 |
| Less: Investments in PP&E needed to maintain current production | 902 |
| Free cash flow | $2,010 |

Research in Motion's free cash flow was 69% of cash flow from operations and more than 10% of sales. Compare this to the calculation of free cash flows for Apple Inc.

[5] Productive capacity is the number of goods the company is currently producing and selling.

(a computer company), The Coca-Cola Company (a beverage company), and Verizon Communications, Inc. (a telecommunications company), that follows (in millions):

| | Apple Inc. | The Coca-Cola Company | Verizon Communications, Inc. |
|---|---|---|---|
| Sales | $156,508 | $48,017 | $115,846 |
| Cash flow from operating activities | 50,856 | 10,645 | 31,486 |
| Less: Investments in PP&E needed to maintain current production | 8,295 | 2,870 | 16,175 |
| Free cash flow | $ 42,561 | $ 7,775 | $ 15,311 |
| Free cash flow as a percentage of cash flow from operations | 84% | 73% | 49% |
| Free cash flow as a percentage of sales | 27% | 16% | 13% |

Positive free cash flow is considered favorable. A company that has free cash flow is able to fund internal growth, retire debt, pay dividends, and benefit from financial flexibility. A company with no free cash flow is unable to maintain current productive capacity. Lack of free cash flow can be an early indicator of liquidity problems. As one analyst notes, "Free cash flow gives the company firepower to reduce debt and ultimately generate consistent, actual income."[6]

## Example Exercise 16-8  Free Cash Flow

OBJ 4

Omnicron Inc. reported the following on the company's cash flow statement in 2016 and 2015:

| | 2016 | 2015 |
|---|---|---|
| Net cash flow from operating activities | $140,000 | $120,000 |
| Net cash flow used for investing activities | (120,000) | (80,000) |
| Net cash flow used for financing activities | (20,000) | (32,000) |

Seventy-five percent of the net cash flow used for investing activities was used to replace existing capacity.

a. Determine Omnicron's free cash flow.

b. Has Omnicron's free cash flow improved or declined from 2015 to 2016?

## Follow My Example 16-8

a.

| | 2016 | 2015 |
|---|---|---|
| Net cash flow from operating activities | $140,000 | $120,000 |
| Less: Investments in fixed assets to maintain current production | 90,000[1] | 60,000[2] |
| Free cash flow | $ 50,000 | $ 60,000 |

[1] $120,000 × 75%
[2] $80,000 × 75%

b. The change from $60,000 to $50,000 indicates an unfavorable trend.

Practice Exercises: PE 16-8A, PE 16-8B

[6] Jill Krutick, *Fortune*, March 30, 1998, p. 106.

# A P P E N D I X

# Spreadsheet (Work Sheet) for Statement of Cash Flows—The Indirect Method

A spreadsheet (work sheet) may be used in preparing the statement of cash flows. However, whether or not a spreadsheet (work sheet) is used, the concepts presented in this chapter are not affected.

The data for **Rundell Inc.**, presented in Exhibit 4 are used as a basis for illustrating the spreadsheet (work sheet) for the indirect method. The steps in preparing this spreadsheet (work sheet), shown in Exhibit 15, are as follows:

- Step 1.　List the title of each balance sheet account in the Accounts column.
- Step 2.　For each balance sheet account, enter its balance as of December 31, 2015, in the first column and its balance as of December 31, 2016, in the last column. Place the credit balances in parentheses.
- Step 3.　Add the December 31, 2015 and 2016 column totals, which should total to zero.
- Step 4.　Analyze the change during the year in each noncash account to determine its net increase (decrease) and classify the change as affecting cash flows from operating activities, investing activities, financing activities, or noncash investing and financing activities.
- Step 5.　Indicate the effect of the change on cash flows by making entries in the Transactions columns.
- Step 6.　After all noncash accounts have been analyzed, enter the net increase (decrease) in cash during the period.
- Step 7.　Add the Debit and Credit Transactions columns. The totals should be equal.

## Analyzing Accounts

In analyzing the noncash accounts (Step 4), try to determine the type of cash flow activity (operating, investing, or financing) that led to the change in the account. As each noncash account is analyzed, an entry (Step 5) is made on the spreadsheet (work sheet) for the type of cash flow activity that caused the change. After all noncash accounts have been analyzed, an entry (Step 6) is made for the increase (decrease) in cash during the period.

The entries made on the spreadsheet are not posted to the ledger. They are only used in preparing and summarizing the data on the spreadsheet.

The order in which the accounts are analyzed is not important. However, it is more efficient to begin with Retained Earnings and proceed upward in the account listing.

## Retained Earnings

The spreadsheet (work sheet) shows a Retained Earnings balance of $202,300 at December 31, 2015, and $282,300 at December 31, 2016. Thus, Retained Earnings increased $80,000 during the year. This increase is from the following:

- Net Income of $108,000
- Declaring cash dividends of $28,000

To identify the cash flows from these activities, two entries are made on the spreadsheet.

**EXHIBIT 15** **End-of-Period Spreadsheet (Work Sheet) for Statement of Cash Flows—Indirect Method**

Step 2

| | A | B | C | D | E | F | G |
|---|---|---|---|---|---|---|---|
| 1 | Rundell Inc. | | | | | | |
| 2 | End-of-Period Spreadsheet (Work Sheet) for Statement of Cash Flows | | | | | | |
| 3 | For the Year Ended December 31, 2016 | | | | | | |
| 4 | Accounts | Balance, | | Transactions | | | Balance, |
| 5 | | Dec. 31, 2015 | | Debit | | Credit | Dec. 31, 2016 |
| 6 | Cash | 26,000 | (o) | 71,500 | | | 97,500 |
| 7 | Accounts receivable (net) | 65,000 | (n) | 9,000 | | | 74,000 |
| 8 | Inventories | 180,000 | | | (m) | 8,000 | 172,000 |
| 9 | Land | 125,000 | (k) | 15,000 | (l) | 60,000 | 80,000 |
| 10 | Building | 200,000 | (j) | 60,000 | | | 260,000 |
| 11 | Accumulated depreciation—building | (58,300) | | | (i) | 7,000 | (65,300) |
| 12 | Accounts payable (merchandise creditors) | (46,700) | (h) | 3,200 | | | (43,500) |
| 13 | Accrued expenses payable (operating expenses) | (24,300) | | | (g) | 2,200 | (26,500) |
| 14 | Income taxes payable | (8,400) | (f) | 500 | | | (7,900) |
| 15 | Dividends payable | (10,000) | | | (e) | 4,000 | (14,000) |
| 16 | Bonds payable | (150,000) | (d) | 50,000 | | | (100,000) |
| 17 | Common stock | (16,000) | | | (c) | 8,000 | (24,000) |
| 18 | Paid-in capital in excess of par | (80,000) | | | (c) | 40,000 | (120,000) |
| 19 | Retained earnings | (202,300) | (b) | 28,000 | (a) | 108,000 | (282,300) |
| 20 | Totals | 0 | | 237,200 | | 237,200 | 0 |
| 21 | Operating activities: | | | | | | |
| 22 | Net income | | (a) | 108,000 | | | |
| 23 | Depreciation of building | | (i) | 7,000 | | | |
| 24 | Gain on sale of land | | | | (l) | 12,000 | |
| 25 | Increase in accounts receivable | | | | (n) | 9,000 | |
| 26 | Decrease in inventories | | (m) | 8,000 | | | |
| 27 | Decrease in accounts payable | | | | (h) | 3,200 | |
| 28 | Increase in accrued expenses payable | | (g) | 2,200 | | | |
| 29 | Decrease in income taxes payable | | | | (f) | 500 | |
| 30 | Investing activities: | | | | | | |
| 31 | Sale of land | | (l) | 72,000 | | | |
| 32 | Purchase of land | | | | (k) | 15,000 | |
| 33 | Purchase of building | | | | (j) | 60,000 | |
| 34 | Financing activities: | | | | | | |
| 35 | Issued common stock | | (c) | 48,000 | | | |
| 36 | Retired bonds payable | | | | (d) | 50,000 | |
| 37 | Declared cash dividends | | | | (b) | 28,000 | |
| 38 | Increase in dividends payable | | (e) | 4,000 | | | |
| 39 | Net increase in cash | | | | (o) | 71,500 | |
| 40 | Totals | | | 249,200 | | 249,200 | |

Step 1

Step 3 → (row 20, B) | Step 3 ← (row 20, G)

Steps 4–7

The $108,000 is reported on the statement of cash flows as part of cash flows from operating activities. Thus, an entry is made in the Transactions columns on the spreadsheet, as follows:

(a)  Operating Activities—Net Income................................  108,000
        Retained Earnings.............................................          108,000

The preceding entry accounts for the net income portion of the change to Retained Earnings. It also identifies the cash flow in the bottom portion of the spreadsheet as related to operating activities.

The $28,000 of dividends is reported as a financing activity on the statement of cash flows. Thus, an entry is made in the Transactions columns on the spreadsheet, as follows:

| | | | |
|---|---|---|---|
| (b) | Retained Earnings............................................... | 28,000 | |
| | Financing Activities—Declared Cash Dividends ................. | | 28,000 |

The preceding entry accounts for the dividends portion of the change to Retained Earnings. It also identifies the cash flow in the bottom portion of the spreadsheet as related to financing activities. The $28,000 of declared dividends will be adjusted later for the actual amount of cash dividends paid during the year.

## Other Accounts

The entries for the other noncash accounts are made in the spreadsheet in a manner similar to entries (a) and (b). A summary of these entries follows:

| | | | |
|---|---|---|---|
| (c) | Financing Activities—Issued Common Stock....................... | 48,000 | |
| | Common Stock .............................................. | | 8,000 |
| | Paid-In Capital in Excess of Par—Common Stock ............... | | 40,000 |
| (d) | Bonds Payable ............................................... | 50,000 | |
| | Financing Activities—Retired Bonds Payable................... | | 50,000 |
| (e) | Financing Activities—Increase in Dividends Payable.............. | 4,000 | |
| | Dividends Payable ........................................... | | 4,000 |
| (f) | Income Taxes Payable ........................................ | 500 | |
| | Operating Activities—Decrease in Income Taxes Payable ........ | | 500 |
| (g) | Operating Activities—Increase in Accrued Expenses Payable ....... | 2,200 | |
| | Accrued Expenses Payable ................................... | | 2,200 |
| (h) | Accounts Payable ............................................ | 3,200 | |
| | Operating Activities—Decrease in Accounts Payable ............ | | 3,200 |
| (i) | Operating Activities—Depreciation of Building ................... | 7,000 | |
| | Accumulated Depreciation—Building .......................... | | 7,000 |
| (j) | Building .................................................... | 60,000 | |
| | Investing Activities—Purchase of Building ..................... | | 60,000 |
| (k) | Land........................................................ | 15,000 | |
| | Investing Activities—Purchase of Land......................... | | 15,000 |
| (l) | Investing Activities—Sale of Land.............................. | 72,000 | |
| | Operating Activities—Gain on Sale of Land .................... | | 12,000 |
| | Land........................................................ | | 60,000 |
| (m) | Operating Activities—Decrease in Inventories.................... | 8,000 | |
| | Inventories.................................................. | | 8,000 |
| (n) | Accounts Receivable ......................................... | 9,000 | |
| | Operating Activities—Increase in Accounts Receivable.......... | | 9,000 |
| (o) | Cash........................................................ | 71,500 | |
| | Net Increase in Cash.......................................... | | 71,500 |

After all the balance sheet accounts are analyzed and the entries made on the spreadsheet (work sheet), all the operating, investing, and financing activities are identified in the bottom portion of the spreadsheet. The accuracy of the entries is verified by totaling the Debit and Credit Transactions columns. The totals of the columns should be equal.

## Preparing the Statement of Cash Flows

The statement of cash flows prepared from the spreadsheet is identical to the statement in Exhibit 7. The data for the three sections of the statement are obtained from the bottom portion of the spreadsheet.

# At a Glance 16

**Describe the cash flow activities reported in the statement of cash flows.**

**Key Points**   The statement of cash flows reports cash receipts and cash payments by three types of activities: operating activities, investing activities, and financing activities. Cash flows from operating activities reports the cash inflows and outflows from a company's day-to-day operations. Cash flows from investing activities reports the cash inflows and outflows related to changes in a company's long-term assets. Cash flows from financing activities reports the cash inflows and outflows related to changes in a company's long-term liabilities and stockholders' equity. Investing and financing for a business may be affected by transactions that do not involve cash. The effect of such transactions should be reported in a separate schedule accompanying the statement of cash flows.

| Learning Outcome | Example Exercises | Practice Exercises |
|---|---|---|
| • Classify transactions that either provide or use cash into either operating, investing, or financing activities. | EE16-1 | PE16-1A, 16-1B |

**Prepare a statement of cash flows, using the indirect method.**

**Key Points**   The indirect method reports cash flows from operating activities by adjusting net income for revenues and expenses that do not involve the receipt or payment of cash. Noncash expenses such as depreciation are added back to net income. Gains and losses on the disposal of assets are added to or deducted from net income. Changes in current operating assets and liabilities are added to or subtracted from net income, depending on their effect on cash. Cash flows from investing activities and cash flows from financing activities are reported below cash flows from operating activities in the statement of cash flows.

| Learning Outcomes | Example Exercises | Practice Exercises |
|---|---|---|
| • Determine cash flows from operating activities under the indirect method by adjusting net income for noncash expenses and gains and losses from asset disposals. | EE16-2 | PE16-2A, 16-2B |
| • Determine cash flows from operating activities under the indirect method by adjusting net income for changes in current operating assets and liabilities. | EE16-3 | PE16-3A, 16-3B |
| • Prepare the Cash Flows from Operating Activities section of the statement of cash flows, using the indirect method. | EE16-4 | PE16-4A, 16-4B |
| • Prepare the Cash Flows from Investing Activities and Cash Flows from Financing Activities sections of the statement of cash flows. | EE16-5 | PE16-5A, 16-5B |

### Prepare a statement of cash flows, using the direct method.

**Key Points** The amount of cash flows from operating activities is the same under both the direct and indirect methods, but the manner in which cash flows operating activities is reported is different. The direct method reports cash flows from operating activities by major classes of operating cash receipts and cash payments. The difference between the major classes of total operating cash receipts and total operating cash payments is the net cash flow from operating activities. The Cash Flows from Investing and Financing Activities sections of the statement are the same under both the direct and indirect methods.

| Learning Outcome | Example Exercises | Practice Exercises |
|---|---|---|
| • Prepare the cash flows from operating activities section of the statement of cash flows under the direct method. | EE16-6<br>EE16-7 | PE16-6A, 16-6B<br>PE16-7A, 16-7B |

### Describe and illustrate the use of free cash flow in evaluating a company's cash flow.

**Key Points** Free cash flow measures the operating cash flow available for company use after purchasing the fixed assets that are necessary to maintain current productive capacity. It is calculated by subtracting these fixed asset purchases from net cash flow from operating activities. A company with strong free cash flow is able to fund internal growth, retire debt, pay dividends, and enjoy financial flexibility. A company with weak free cash flow has much less financial flexibility.

| Learning Outcomes | Example Exercises | Practice Exercises |
|---|---|---|
| • Describe free cash flow. | | |
| • Calculate and evaluate free cash flow. | EE16-8 | PE16-8A, 16-8B |

# Key Terms

cash flow per share (744)
cash flows from financing activities (741)
cash flows from investing activities (740)

cash flows from operating activities (740)
direct method (741)
free cash flow (759)

indirect method (742)
statement of cash flows (740)

# Illustrative Problem

The comparative balance sheet of Dowling Company for December 31, 2016 and 2015, is as follows:

## Dowling Company
### Comparative Balance Sheet
### December 31, 2016 and 2015

| | 2016 | 2015 |
|---|---|---|
| **Assets** | | |
| Cash | $ 140,350 | $ 95,900 |
| Accounts receivable (net) | 95,300 | 102,300 |
| Inventories | 165,200 | 157,900 |
| Prepaid expenses | 6,240 | 5,860 |
| Investments (long-term) | 35,700 | 84,700 |
| Land | 75,000 | 90,000 |
| Buildings | 375,000 | 260,000 |
| Accumulated depreciation—buildings | (71,300) | (58,300) |
| Machinery and equipment | 428,300 | 428,300 |
| Accumulated depreciation—machinery and equipment | (148,500) | (138,000) |
| Patents | 58,000 | 65,000 |
| Total assets | $1,159,290 | $1,093,660 |
| | | |
| **Liabilities and Stockholders' Equity** | | |
| Accounts payable (merchandise creditors) | $ 43,500 | $ 46,700 |
| Accrued expenses payable (operating expenses) | 14,000 | 12,500 |
| Income taxes payable | 7,900 | 8,400 |
| Dividends payable | 14,000 | 10,000 |
| Mortgage note payable, due 2023 | 40,000 | 0 |
| Bonds payable | 150,000 | 250,000 |
| Common stock, $30 par | 450,000 | 375,000 |
| Excess of issue price over par—common stock | 66,250 | 41,250 |
| Retained earnings | 373,640 | 349,810 |
| Total liabilities and stockholders' equity | $1,159,290 | $1,093,660 |

The income statement for Dowling Company follows:

## Dowling Company
### Income Statement
### For the Year Ended December 31, 2016

| | | |
|---|---|---|
| Sales | | $1,100,000 |
| Cost of merchandise sold | | 710,000 |
| Gross profit | | $ 390,000 |
| Operating expenses: | | |
| Depreciation expense | $ 23,500 | |
| Patent amortization | 7,000 | |
| Other operating expenses | 196,000 | |
| Total operating expenses | | 226,500 |
| Income from operations | | $ 163,500 |
| Other income: | | |
| Gain on sale of investments | $ 11,000 | |
| Other expense: | | |
| Interest expense | 26,000 | (15,000) |
| Income before income tax | | $ 148,500 |
| Income tax expense | | 50,000 |
| Net income | | $ 98,500 |

An examination of the accounting records revealed the following additional information applicable to 2016:

a. Land costing $15,000 was sold for $15,000.

b. A mortgage note was issued for $40,000.

c. A building costing $115,000 was constructed.

d. 2,500 shares of common stock were issued at $40 in exchange for the bonds payable.

e. Cash dividends declared were $74,670.

## Instructions

1. Prepare a statement of cash flows, using the indirect method of reporting cash flows from operating activities.

2. Prepare a statement of cash flows, using the direct method of reporting cash flows from operating activities.

## Solution

1.

| Dowling Company<br>Statement of Cash Flows—Indirect Method<br>For the Year Ended December 31, 2016 | | | |
|---|---|---|---|
| Cash flows from operating activities: | | | |
| Net income | | $ 98,500 | |
| Adjustments to reconcile net income to net cash flow from operating activities: | | | |
| Depreciation | | 23,500 | |
| Amortization of patents | | 7,000 | |
| Gain on sale of investments | | (11,000) | |
| Changes in current operating assets and liabilities: | | | |
| Decrease in accounts receivable | | 7,000 | |
| Increase in inventories | | (7,300) | |
| Increase in prepaid expenses | | (380) | |
| Decrease in accounts payable | | (3,200) | |
| Increase in accrued expenses payable | | 1,500 | |
| Decrease in income taxes payable | | (500) | |
| Net cash flow from operating activities | | | $115,120 |
| Cash flows from investing activities: | | | |
| Cash received from sale of: | | | |
| Investments | $60,000[1] | | |
| Land | 15,000 | $ 75,000 | |
| Less: Cash paid for construction of building | | 115,000 | |
| Net cash flow used for investing activities | | | (40,000) |
| Cash flows from financing activities: | | | |
| Cash received from issuing mortgage note payable | | $ 40,000 | |
| Less: Cash paid for dividends | | 70,670[2] | |
| Net cash flow used for financing activities | | | (30,670) |
| Increase in cash | | | $ 44,450 |
| Cash at the beginning of the year | | | 95,900 |
| Cash at the end of the year | | | $140,350 |
| | | | |
| **Schedule of Noncash Investing and Financing Activities:** | | | |
| Issued common stock to retire bonds payable | | | $100,000 |

[1] $60,000 = $11,000 gain + $49,000 (decrease in investments)

[2] $70,670 = $74,670 − $4,000 (increase in dividends)

2.

| Dowling Company<br>Statement of Cash Flows—Direct Method<br>For the Year Ended December 31, 2016 | | | |
|---|---|---|---|
| Cash flows from operating activities: | | | |
| Cash received from customers[1]........................ | | $1,107,000 | |
| Deduct: Cash paid for merchandise[2]................... | $720,500 | | |
| Cash paid for operating expenses[3]............. | 194,880 | | |
| Cash paid for interest expense ................ | 26,000 | | |
| Cash paid for income tax[4].................... | 50,500 | 991,880 | |
| Net cash flow from operating activities ............... | | | $115,120 |
| Cash flows from investing activities: | | | |
| Cash received from sale of: | | | |
| Investments...................................... | $ 60,000[5] | | |
| Land........................................... | 15,000 | $ 75,000 | |
| Less: Cash paid for construction of building............ | | 115,000 | |
| Net cash flow used for investing activities.............. | | | (40,000) |
| Cash flows from financing activities: | | | |
| Cash received from issuing mortgage note payable..... | | $ 40,000 | |
| Less: Cash paid for dividends[6]........................ | | 70,670 | |
| Net cash flow used for financing activities ............. | | | (30,670) |
| Increase in cash ............................................ | | | $ 44,450 |
| Cash at the beginning of the year........................ | | | 95,900 |
| Cash at the end of the year................................ | | | $140,350 |
| | | | |
| **Schedule of Noncash Investing and** | | | |
| **Financing Activities:** | | | |
| Issued common stock to retire bonds payable.......... | | | $100,000 |
| **Schedule Reconciling Net Income with Cash Flows** | | | |
| **from Operating Activities[7]** | | | |

Computations:

[1]$1,100,000 + $7,000 = $1,107,000
[2]$710,000 + $3,200 + $7,300 = $720,500
[3]$196,000 + $380 – $1,500 = $194,880
[4]$50,000 + $500 = $50,500
[5]$60,000 = $11,000 gain + $49,000 (decrease in investments)
[6]$74,670 + $10,000 – $14,000 = $70,670
[7]The content of this schedule is the same as the Operating Activities section of part (1) of this solution and is not reproduced here for the sake of brevity.

# Discussion Questions

1. What is the principal disadvantage of the direct method of reporting cash flows from operating activities?

2. What are the major advantages of the indirect method of reporting cash flows from operating activities?

3. A corporation issued $2,000,000 of common stock in exchange for $2,000,000 of fixed assets. Where would this transaction be reported on the statement of cash flows?

4. A retail business, using the accrual method of accounting, owed merchandise creditors (accounts payable) $320,000 at the beginning of the year and $350,000 at the end of the year. How would the $30,000 increase be used to adjust net income in determining the amount of cash flows from operating activities by the indirect method? Explain.

5. If salaries payable was $100,000 at the beginning of the year and $75,000 at the end of the year, should $25,000 decrease be added to or deducted from income to determine the amount of cash flows from operating activities by the indirect method? Explain.

6. A long-term investment in bonds with a cost of $500,000 was sold for $600,000 cash. (a) What was the gain or loss on the sale? (b) What was the effect of the transaction on cash flows? (c) How should the transaction be reported on the statement of cash flows if cash flows from operating activities are reported by the indirect method?

7. A corporation issued $2,000,000 of 20-year bonds for cash at 98. How would the transaction be reported on the statement of cash flows?

8. Fully depreciated equipment costing $50,000 was discarded. What was the effect of the transaction on cash flows if (a) $15,000 cash is received for the equipment, (b) no cash is received for the equipment?

9. For the current year, Packers Company decided to switch from the indirect method to the direct method for reporting cash flows from operating activities on the statement of cash flows. Will the change cause the amount of net cash flow from operating activities to be larger, smaller, or the same as if the indirect method had been used? Explain.

10. Name five common major classes of operating cash receipts or operating cash payments presented on the statement of cash flows when the cash flows from operating activities are reported by the direct method.

# Practice Exercises

EE 16-1 *p. 744*
## PE 16-1A  Classifying cash flows
OBJ. 1

Identify whether each of the following would be reported as an operating, investing, or financing activity on the statement of cash flows:

SHOW ME HOW

a. Repurchase of common stock
b. Cash received from customers
c. Payment of accounts payable

d. Retirement of bonds payable
e. Purchase of equipment
f. Purchase of inventory for cash

EE 16-1 *p. 744*
## PE 16-1B  Classifying cash flows
OBJ. 1

Identify whether each of the following would be reported as an operating, investing, or financing activity on the statement of cash flows:

SHOW ME HOW

a. Purchase of investments
b. Disposal of equipment
c. Payment for selling expenses

d. Collection of accounts receivable
e. Cash sales
f. Issuance of bonds payable

EE 16-2 *p. 747*
## PE 16-2A  Adjustments to net income—indirect method
OBJ. 2

Pearl Corporation's accumulated depreciation—furniture account increased by $8,400, while $3,080 of patent amortization was recognized between balance sheet dates. There were no purchases or sales of depreciable or intangible assets during the year. In addition, the income statement showed a loss of $4,480 from the sale of land. Reconcile a net income of $120,400 to net cash flow from operating activities.

SHOW ME HOW

EE 16-2 *p. 747*
## PE 16-2B  Adjustments to net income—indirect method
OBJ. 2

Ya Wen Corporation's accumulated depreciation—equipment account increased by $8,750, while $3,250 of patent amortization was recognized between balance sheet dates. There were no purchases or sales of depreciable or intangible assets during the year. In addition, the income statement showed a gain of $18,750 from the sale of investments. Reconcile a net income of $175,000 to net cash flow from operating activities.

SHOW ME HOW

EE 16-3 *p. 749*

SHOW
ME HOW

**PE 16-3A    Changes in current operating assets and liabilities—indirect method**    **OBJ. 2**

Alpenrose Corporation's comparative balance sheet for current assets and liabilities was as follows:

|  | Dec. 31, 2016 | Dec. 31, 2015 |
|---|---|---|
| Accounts receivable | $27,000 | $32,400 |
| Inventory | 18,000 | 15,480 |
| Accounts payable | 16,200 | 14,220 |
| Dividends payable | 49,500 | 53,100 |

*[handwritten: people paid us] [handwritten: Paid out, use] [handwritten: source of cash, add] [handwritten: Financing, use]*

Adjust net income of $207,000 for changes in operating assets and liabilities to arrive at net cash flow from operating activities.

EE 16-3 *p. 749*

SHOW
ME HOW

**PE 16-3B    Changes in current operating assets and liabilities—indirect method**    **OBJ. 2**

Huluduey Corporation's comparative balance sheet for current assets and liabilities was as follows:

|  | Dec. 31, 2016 | Dec. 31, 2015 |
|---|---|---|
| Accounts receivable | $18,000 | $14,400 |
| Inventory | 34,800 | 29,700 |
| Accounts payable | 27,600 | 20,700 |
| Dividends payable | 8,400 | 10,800 |

*[handwritten: use, use, source annotations and "people borrowing money", "Financing"]*

Adjust net income of $160,000 for changes in operating assets and liabilities to arrive at net cash flow from operating activities.

EE 16-4 *p. 750*

SHOW
ME HOW

**PE 16-4A    Cash flows from operating activities—indirect method**    **OBJ. 2**

Pettygrove Inc. reported the following data:

| | |
|---|---|
| Net income | $405,000 |
| Depreciation expense | 45,000 |
| Gain on disposal of equipment | 36,900 |
| Decrease in accounts receivable | 25,200 |
| Decrease in accounts payable | 6,480 |

Prepare the Cash Flows from Operating Activities section of the statement of cash flows, using the indirect method.

EE 16-4 *p. 750*

SHOW
ME HOW

**PE 16-4B    Cash flows from operating activities—indirect method**    **OBJ. 2**

Staley Inc. reported the following data:

| | |
|---|---|
| Net income | $280,000 |
| Depreciation expense | 48,000 |
| Loss on disposal of equipment | 19,520 |
| Increase in accounts receivable | 17,280 |
| Increase in accounts payable | 8,960 |

*[handwritten: use, "if decrease, source", source]*

Prepare the Cash Flows from Operating Activities section of the statement of cash flows, using the indirect method.

EE 16-5 *p. 753*

SHOW
ME HOW

**PE 16-5A    Land transactions on the statement of cash flows**    **OBJ. 2**

Milo Corporation purchased land for $540,000. Later in the year, the company sold a different piece of land with a book value of $270,000 for $180,000. How are the effects of these transactions reported on the statement of cash flows?

EE 16-5  *p. 753*   **PE 16-5B   Land transactions on the statement of cash flows**   **OBJ. 2**

IZ Corporation purchased land for $400,000. Later in the year, the company sold a different piece of land with a book value of $200,000 for $240,000. How are the effects of these transactions reported on the statement of cash flows?

SHOW
ME HOW

EE 16-6  *p. 755*   **PE 16-6A   Cash received from customers—direct method**   **OBJ. 3**

Sales reported on the income statement were $480,000. The accounts receivable balance increased $54,000 over the year. Determine the amount of cash received from customers.

SHOW
ME HOW

EE 16-6  *p. 755*   **PE 16-6B   Cash received from customers—direct method**   **OBJ. 3**

Sales reported on the income statement were $112,000. The accounts receivable balance decreased $10,500 over the year. Determine the amount of cash received from customers.

SHOW
ME HOW

EE 16-7  *p. 756*   **PE 16-7A   Cash payments for merchandise—direct method**   **OBJ. 3**

The cost of merchandise sold reported on the income statement was $770,000. The accounts payable balance decreased $44,000, and the inventory balance decreased by $66,000 over the year. Determine the amount of cash paid for merchandise.

SHOW
ME HOW

EE 16-7  *p. 756*   **PE 16-7B   Cash payments for merchandise—direct method**   **OBJ. 3**

The cost of merchandise sold reported on the income statement was $240,000. The accounts payable balance increased $12,000, and the inventory balance increased by $19,200 over the year. Determine the amount of cash paid for merchandise.

SHOW
ME HOW

EE 16-8  *p. 760*   **PE 16-8A   Free cash flow**   **OBJ. 4**

McMahon Inc. reported the following on the company's statement of cash flows in 2016 and 2015:

|  | 2016 | 2015 |
|---|---|---|
| Net cash flow from operating activities | $ 294,000 | $ 280,000 |
| Net cash flow used for investing activities | (224,000) | (252,000) |
| Net cash flow used for financing activities | (63,000) | (42,000) |

SHOW
ME HOW

Seventy percent of the net cash flow used for investing activities was used to replace existing capacity.

a. Determine McMahon's free cash flow for both years.

b. Has McMahon's free cash flow improved or declined from 2015 to 2016?

EE 16-8  *p. 760*   **PE 16-8B   Free cash flow**   **OBJ. 4**

Dillin Inc. reported the following on the company's statement of cash flows in 2016 and 2015:

|  | 2016 | 2015 |
|---|---|---|
| Net cash flow from operating activities | $ 476,000 | $ 455,000 |
| Net cash flow used for investing activities | (427,000) | (378,000) |
| Net cash flow used for financing activities | (42,000) | (58,800) |

SHOW
ME HOW

Eighty percent of the net cash flow used for investing activities was used to replace existing capacity.

a. Determine Dillin's free cash flow for both years.

b. Has Dillin's free cash flow improved or declined from 2015 to 2016?

## Exercises

### EX 16-1    Cash flows from operating activities—net loss

OBJ. 1

On its income statement for a recent year, United Continental Holdings, Inc., the parent company of United Airlines, reported a net *loss* of $723 million from operations. On its statement of cash flows, it reported $935 million of cash flows from operating activities.

➤ Explain this apparent contradiction between the loss and the positive cash flows.

### EX 16-2    Effect of transactions on cash flows

OBJ. 1

✔ a. Cash payment, $525,000

State the effect (cash receipt or payment and amount) of each of the following transactions, considered individually, on cash flows:

a. Retired $500,000 of bonds, on which there was $5,000 of unamortized discount, for $525,000.

b. Sold 6,000 shares of $20 par common stock for $30 per share.

c. Sold equipment with a book value of $98,200 for $117,500.

d. Purchased land for $322,000 cash.

e. Purchased a building by paying $75,000 cash and issuing a $62,500 mortgage note payable.

f. Sold a new issue of $300,000 of bonds at 101.

g. Purchased 2,500 shares of $40 par common stock as treasury stock at $50 per share.

h. Paid dividends of $2.00 per share. There were 50,000 shares issued and 10,000 shares of treasury stock.

### EX 16-3    Classifying cash flows

OBJ. 1

Identify the type of cash flow activity for each of the following events (operating, investing, or financing):

a. Net income

b. Paid cash dividends

c. Issued common stock

d. Issued bonds

e. Redeemed bonds *use*

f. Sold long-term investments *source*

g. Purchased treasury stock *F, use*

h. Sold equipment *I, source*

i. Issued preferred stock *F, source*

j. Purchased buildings *I, use*

k. Purchased patents *I, use*

### EX 16-4    Cash flows from operating activities—indirect method

OBJ. 2

Indicate whether each of the following would be added to or deducted from net income in determining net cash flow from operating activities by the indirect method:

a. Decrease in merchandise inventory

b. Increase in accounts receivable

c. Increase in accounts payable

d. Loss on retirement of long-term debt

e. Depreciation of fixed assets

f. Decrease in notes receivable due in 60 days from customers

g. Increase in salaries payable

h. Decrease in prepaid expenses

i. Amortization of patent

j. Increase in notes payable due in 120 days to vendors

k. Gain on disposal of fixed assets

**EX 16-5    Cash flows from operating activities—indirect method**    OBJ. 1, 2

The net income reported on the income statement for the current year was $400,000. Depreciation recorded on store equipment for the year amounted to $16,000. Balances of the current asset and current liability accounts at the beginning and end of the year are as follows:

|  | End of Year | Beginning of Year |
|---|---|---|
| Cash | $41,600 | $38,400 |
| Accounts receivable (net) | 30,400 | 28,000 |
| Merchandise inventory | 40,000 | 44,000 |
| Prepaid expenses | 4,800 | 3,600 |
| Accounts payable (merchandise creditors) | 40,000 | 36,000 |
| Wages payable | 21,200 | 24,000 |

a. Prepare the Cash Flows from Operating Activities section of the statement of cash flows, using the indirect method.

b. ▬▬▶ Briefly explain why net cash flow from operating activities is different than net income.

**EX 16-6    Cash flows from operating activities—indirect method**    OBJ. 1, 2

The net income reported on the income statement for the current year was $320,000. Depreciation recorded on equipment and a building amounted to $96,000 for the year. Balances of the current asset and current liability accounts at the beginning and end of the year are as follows:

|  | End of Year | Beginning of Year |
|---|---|---|
| Cash | $ 89,600 | $ 96,000 |
| Accounts receivable (net) | 112,000 | 118,400 |
| Inventories | 224,000 | 200,000 |
| Prepaid expenses | 12,800 | 14,400 |
| Accounts payable (merchandise creditors) | 96,000 | 104,000 |
| Salaries payable | 16,000 | 13,600 |

a. Prepare the Cash Flows from Operating Activities section of the statement of cash flows, using the indirect method.

b. ▬▬▶ If the direct method had been used, would the net cash flow from operating activities have been the same? Explain.

**EX 16-7    Cash flows from operating activities—indirect method**    OBJ. 1, 2

The income statement disclosed the following items for 2016:

| Depreciation expense | $ 57,600 |
|---|---|
| Gain on disposal of equipment | 33,600 |
| Net income | 508,000 |

Balances of the current assets and current liability accounts changed between December 31, 2015, and December 31, 2016, as follows:

*Add sources*
*subt uses*

|  | Increase (Decrease) |
|---|---|
| Accounts receivable | – $8,960 – use |
| Inventory | + (5,120) – source |
| Prepaid insurance | + (1,920) source. |
| Accounts payable | – (6,080) use |
| Income taxes payable | 1,410 source |
| Dividends payable | 2,200 |

a. Prepare the Cash Flows from Operating Activities section of the statement of cash flows, using the indirect method.

b. ▬▬▶ Briefly explain why net cash flows from operating activities is different than net income.

**EX 16-8    Determining cash payments to stockholders**                          OBJ. 2

The board of directors declared cash dividends totaling $585,000 during the current year. The comparative balance sheet indicates dividends payable of $167,625 at the beginning of the year and $146,250 at the end of the year. What was the amount of cash payments to stockholders during the year?

**EX 16-9    Reporting changes in equipment on statement of cash flows**          OBJ. 2

An analysis of the general ledger accounts indicates that office equipment, which cost $202,500 and on which accumulated depreciation totaled $84,375 on the date of sale, was sold for $101,250 during the year. Using this information, indicate the items to be reported on the statement of cash flows.

**EX 16-10    Reporting changes in equipment on statement of cash flows**         OBJ. 2

An analysis of the general ledger accounts indicates that delivery equipment, which cost $80,000 and on which accumulated depreciation totaled $36,000 on the date of sale, was sold for $37,200 during the year. Using this information, indicate the items to be reported on the statement of cash flows.

**EX 16-11    Reporting land transactions on statement of cash flows**            OBJ. 2

On the basis of the details of the following fixed asset account, indicate the items to be reported on the statement of cash flows:

ACCOUNT *Land*                                                        ACCOUNT NO.

| Date | | Item | Debit | Credit | Balance Debit | Balance Credit |
|---|---|---|---|---|---|---|
| 2016 | | | | | | |
| Jan. | 1 | Balance | | | 868,000 | |
| Mar. | 12 | Purchased for cash | 104,300 | | 972,300 | |
| Oct. | 4 | Sold for $95,550 | | 63,840 | 908,460 | |

**EX 16-12    Reporting stockholders' equity items on statement of cash flows**   OBJ. 2

On the basis of the following stockholders' equity accounts, indicate the items, exclusive of net income, to be reported on the statement of cash flows. There were no unpaid dividends at either the beginning or the end of the year.

ACCOUNT *Common Stock, $40 par*                                       ACCOUNT NO.

| Date | | Item | Debit | Credit | Balance Debit | Balance Credit |
|---|---|---|---|---|---|---|
| 2016 | | | | | | |
| Jan. | 1 | Balance, 120,000 shares | | | | 4,800,000 |
| Apr. | 2 | 30,000 shares issued for cash | | 1,200,000 | | 6,000,000 |
| June | 30 | 4,400-share stock dividend | | 176,000 | | 6,176,000 |

ACCOUNT *Paid-In Capital in Excess of Par—Common Stock*               ACCOUNT NO.

| Date | | Item | Debit | Credit | Balance Debit | Balance Credit |
|---|---|---|---|---|---|---|
| 2016 | | | | | | |
| Jan. | 1 | Balance | | | | 360,000 |
| Apr. | 2 | 30,000 shares issued for cash | | 720,000 | | 1,080,000 |
| June | 30 | Stock dividend | | 114,400 | | 1,194,400 |

ACCOUNT *Retained Earnings*                                              ACCOUNT NO.

| Date | | Item | Debit | Credit | Balance Debit | Balance Credit |
|---|---|---|---|---|---|---|
| 2016 | | | | | | |
| Jan. | 1 | Balance | | | | 2,000,000 |
| June | 30 | Stock dividend | 290,440 | | | 1,709,560 |
| Dec. | 30 | Cash dividend | 463,200 | | | 1,246,360 |
| | 31 | Net income | | 1,440,000 | | 2,686,360 |

---

**EX 16-13   Reporting land acquisition for cash and mortgage note on statement of      OBJ. 2
cash flows**

On the basis of the details of the following fixed asset account, indicate the items to be reported on the statement of cash flows:

ACCOUNT *Land*                                                          ACCOUNT NO.

| Date | | Item | Debit | Credit | Balance Debit | Balance Credit |
|---|---|---|---|---|---|---|
| 2016 | | | | | | |
| Jan. | 1 | Balance | | | 156,000 | |
| Feb. | 10 | Purchased for cash | 246,000 | | 402,000 | |
| Nov. | 20 | Purchased with long-term mortgage note | 324,000 | | 726,000 | |

---

**EX 16-14   Reporting issuance and retirement of long-term debt      OBJ. 2**

On the basis of the details of the following bonds payable and related discount accounts, indicate the items to be reported in the Financing Activities section of the statement of cash flows, assuming no gain or loss on retiring the bonds:

ACCOUNT *Bonds Payable*                                                ACCOUNT NO.

| Date | | Item | Debit | Credit | Balance Debit | Balance Credit |
|---|---|---|---|---|---|---|
| 2016 | | | | | | |
| Jan. | 1 | Balance | | | | 750,000 |
| | 2 | Retire bonds | 150,000 | | | 600,000 |
| June | 30 | Issue bonds | | 450,000 | | 1,050,000 |

ACCOUNT *Discount on Bonds Payable*                                    ACCOUNT NO.

| Date | | Item | Debit | Credit | Balance Debit | Balance Credit |
|---|---|---|---|---|---|---|
| 2016 | | | | | | |
| Jan. | 1 | Balance | | | 33,750 | |
| | 2 | Retire bonds | | 12,000 | 21,750 | |
| June | 30 | Issue bonds | 30,000 | | 51,750 | |
| Dec. | 31 | Amortize discount | | 2,625 | 49,125 | |

✔ Net income,
$341,770

SHOW
ME HOW

---

**EX 16-15   Determining net income from net cash flow from operating activities**   OBJ. 2

Curwen Inc. reported net cash flow from operating activities of $357,500 on its statement of cash flows for the year ended December 31, 2016. The following information was reported in the Cash Flows from Operating Activities section of the statement of cash flows, using the indirect method:

| | |
|---|---:|
| Decrease in income taxes payable | $ 7,700 |
| Decrease in inventories | 19,140 |
| Depreciation | 29,480 |
| Gain on sale of investments | 13,200 |
| Increase in accounts payable | 5,280 |
| Increase in prepaid expenses | 2,970 |
| Increase in accounts receivable | 14,300 |

a. Determine the net income reported by Curwen Inc. for the year ended December 31, 2016.

b. ━━━▶ Briefly explain why Curwen's net income is different than net cash flow from operating activities.

---

✔ Net cash flow
from operating
activities, $42,174

**EX 16-16   Cash flows from operating activities—indirect method**   OBJ. 2

Selected data derived from the income statement and balance sheet of National Beverage Co. for a recent year are as follows:

| | |
|---|---:|
| Income statement data (in thousands): | |
| Net earnings (loss) | $43,993 |
| Losses on inventory write-down and fixed assets | 7 |
| Depreciation expense | 10,174 |
| Stock-based compensation expense (noncash) | 290 |
| Balance sheet data (in thousands): | |
| Increase in accounts receivable | 5,679 |
| Increase in inventory | 7,509 |
| Decrease in prepaid expenses | 2,239 |
| Decrease in accounts payable and other current liabilities | 1,341 |

a. Prepare the Cash Flows from Operating Activities section of the statement of cash flows, using the indirect method for National Beverage Co.

b. ━━━▶ Interpret your results in part (a).

---

✔ Net cash flow from
operating activities,
$150

SHOW
ME HOW

**EX 16-17   Statement of cash flows—indirect method**   OBJ. 2

The comparative balance sheet of Pelican Joe Industries Inc. for December 31, 2016 and 2015, is as follows:

| | Dec. 31, 2016 | Dec. 31, 2015 |
|---|---:|---:|
| **Assets** | | |
| Cash | $ 490 | $ 160 |
| Accounts receivable (net) | 280 | 200 |
| Inventories | 175 | 110 |
| Land | 400 | 450 |
| Equipment | 225 | 175 |
| Accumulated depreciation—equipment | (60) | (30) |
| Total assets | $1,510 | $1,065 |
| **Liabilities and Stockholders' Equity** | | |
| Accounts payable (merchandise creditors) | $ 175 | $ 160 |
| Dividends payable | 30 | — |
| Common stock, $10 par | 100 | 50 |
| Paid-in capital: Excess of issue price over par—common stock | 250 | 125 |
| Retained earnings | 955 | 730 |
| Total liabilities and stockholders' equity | $1,510 | $1,065 |

The following additional information is taken from the records:

1. Land was sold for $125.    $125 - 50 = 75$
2. Equipment was acquired for cash.   use
3. There were no disposals of equipment during the year.
4. The common stock was issued for cash.
5. There was a $325 credit to Retained Earnings for net income.
6. There was an $100 debit to Retained Earnings for cash dividends declared.

a. Prepare a statement of cash flows, using the indirect method of presenting cash flows from operating activities.

b. ➤➤➤ Was Pelican Joe Industries Inc. net cash flow from operations more or less than net income? What is the source of this difference?

---

**EX 16-18   Statement of cash flows—indirect method**                    OBJ. 2

List the errors you find in the following statement of cash flows. The cash balance at the beginning of the year was $240,000. All other amounts are correct, except the cash balance at the end of the year.

**Shasta Inc.**
**Statement of Cash Flows**
**For the Year Ended December 31, 2016**

| | | | |
|---|---:|---:|---:|
| Cash flows from operating activities: | | | |
| Net income ............................................ | | $360,000 | |
| Adjustments to reconcile net income to net | | | |
| cash flow from operating activities: | | | |
| Depreciation...................................... | | 100,800 | |
| Gain on sale of investments........................ | | 17,280 | |
| Changes in current operating assets and liabilities: | | | |
| Increase in accounts receivable..................... | | 27,360 | |
| Increase in inventories............................. | | (36,000) | |
| Increase in accounts payable....................... | | (3,600) | |
| Decrease in accrued expenses payable.............. | | (2,400) | |
| Net cash flow from operating activities ................... | | | $463,440 |
| Cash flows from investing activities: | | | |
| Cash received from sale of investments .................. | | $240,000 | |
| Less: Cash paid for purchase of land ,,,,,,,,......... | $259,200 | | |
| Cash paid for purchase of equipment................ | 432,000 | 691,200 | |
| Net cash flow used for investing activities................ | | | (415,200) |
| Cash flows from financing activities: | | | |
| Cash received from sale of common stock................ | | $312,000 | |
| Cash paid for dividends............................... | | 132,000 | |
| Net cash flow from financing activities.................... | | | 180,000 |
| Increase in cash ........................................... | | | $ 47,760 |
| Cash at the end of the year................................ | | | 192,240 |
| Cash at the beginning of the year.......................... | | | $240,000 |

---

**EX 16-19   Cash flows from operating activities—direct method**            OBJ. 3

✔ a. $801,900

The cash flows from operating activities are reported by the direct method on the statement of cash flows. Determine the following:

a. If sales for the current year were $753,500 and accounts receivable decreased by $48,400 during the year, what was the amount of cash received from customers?

b. If income tax expense for the current year was $50,600 and income tax payable decreased by $5,500 during the year, what was the amount of cash payments for income taxes?

c. ➤➤➤ Briefly explain why the cash received from customers in (a) is different than sales.

**EX 16-20** **Cash paid for merchandise purchases** OBJ. 3

The cost of merchandise sold for Kohl's Corporation for a recent year was $11,625 million. The balance sheet showed the following current account balances (in millions):

| | Balance, End of Year | Balance, Beginning of Year |
|---|---|---|
| Merchandise inventories | $3,199 | $3,036 |
| Accounts payable | 1,233 | 1,138 |

Determine the amount of cash payments for merchandise.

**EX 16-21** **Determining selected amounts for cash flows from operating** OBJ. 3
**activities—direct method**

✔ a. $1,025,800

Selected data taken from the accounting records of Ginis Inc. for the current year ended December 31 are as follows:

| | Balance, December 31 | Balance, January 1 |
|---|---|---|
| Accrued expenses payable (operating expenses) | $ 12,650 | $ 14,030 |
| Accounts payable (merchandise creditors) | 96,140 | 105,800 |
| Inventories | 178,020 | 193,430 |
| Prepaid expenses | 7,360 | 8,970 |

During the current year, the cost of merchandise sold was $1,031,550, and the operating expenses other than depreciation were $179,400. The direct method is used for presenting the cash flows from operating activities on the statement of cash flows.

Determine the amount reported on the statement of cash flows for (a) cash payments for merchandise and (b) cash payments for operating expenses.

**EX 16-22** **Cash flows from operating activities—direct method** OBJ. 3

✔ Net cash flow from operating activities, $96,040

The income statement of Booker T Industries Inc. for the current year ended June 30 is as follows:

| | | |
|---|---|---|
| Sales | | $511,000 |
| Cost of merchandise sold | | 290,500 |
| Gross profit | | $220,500 |
| Operating expenses: | | |
| Depreciation expense | $ 39,200 | |
| Other operating expenses | 105,000 | |
| Total operating expenses | | 144,200 |
| Income before income tax | | $ 76,300 |
| Income tax expense | | 21,700 |
| Net income | | $ 54,600 |

Changes in the balances of selected accounts from the beginning to the end of the current year are as follows:

| | Increase (Decrease) |
|---|---|
| Accounts receivable (net) | ($11,760) |
| Inventories | 3,920 |
| Prepaid expenses | (3,780) |
| Accounts payable (merchandise creditors) | (7,980) |
| Accrued expenses payable (operating expenses) | 1,260 |
| Income tax payable | (2,660) |

a. Prepare the Cash Flows from Operating Activities section of the statement of cash flows, using the direct method.

b. ━━━▶ What does the direct method show about a company's cash flows from operating activities that is not shown using the indirect method?

### EX 16-23 Cash flows from operating activities—direct method OBJ. 3

The income statement for Rhino Company for the current year ended June 30 and balances of selected accounts at the beginning and the end of the year are as follows:

| | | |
|---|---|---|
| Sales | | $445,500 |
| Cost of merchandise sold | | 154,000 |
| Gross profit | | $291,500 |
| Operating expenses: | | |
| Depreciation expense | $ 38,500 | |
| Other operating expenses | 115,280 | |
| Total operating expenses | | 153,780 |
| Income before income tax | | $137,720 |
| Income tax expense | | 39,600 |
| Net income | | $ 98,120 |

| | End of Year | Beginning of Year |
|---|---|---|
| Accounts receivable (net) | $36,300 | $31,240 |
| Inventories | 92,400 | 80,300 |
| Prepaid expenses | 14,520 | 15,840 |
| Accounts payable (merchandise creditors) | 67,540 | 62,700 |
| Accrued expenses payable (operating expenses) | 19,140 | 20,900 |
| Income tax payable | 4,400 | 4,400 |

Prepare the Cash Flows from Operating Activities section of the statement of cash flows, using the direct method.

### EX 16-24 Free cash flow OBJ. 4

SHOW
ME HOW

Sweeter Enterprises Inc. has cash flows from operating activities of $539,000. Cash flows used for investments in property, plant, and equipment totaled $210,000, of which 75% of this investment was used to replace existing capacity.

a. Determine the free cash flow for Sweeter Enterprises Inc.

b. ➡ How might a lender use free cash flow to determine whether or not to give Sweeter Enterprises Inc. a loan?

### EX 16-25 Free cash flow OBJ. 4

The financial statements for Nike, Inc., are provided in Appendix C at the end of the text.

a. Determine the free cash flow for the most recent fiscal year. Assume that 90% of the additions to property, plant, and equipment were used to maintain productive capacity. Round to the nearest thousand dollars.

b. ➡ How might a lender use free cash flow to determine whether or not to give Nike, Inc., a loan?

c. ➡ Would you feel comfortable giving Nike a loan, based on the free cash flow calculated in (a)?

### EX 16-26 Free cash flow OBJ. 4

Lovato Motors Inc. has cash flows from operating activities of $720,000. Cash flows used for investments in property, plant, and equipment totaled $440,000, of which 85% of this investment was used to replace existing capacity.

Determine the free cash flow for Lovato Motors Inc.

## Problems: Series A

### PR 16-1A Statement of cash flows—indirect method
OBJ. 2

The comparative balance sheet of Cromme Inc. for December 31, 2016 and 2015, is shown as follows:

| | Dec. 31, 2016 | Dec. 31, 2015 |
|---|---|---|
| **Assets** | | |
| Cash | $ 625,760 | $ 585,920 |
| Accounts receivable (net) | 227,840 | 208,960 |
| Inventories | 641,760 | 617,120 |
| Investments | 0 | 240,000 |
| Land | 328,000 | 0 |
| Equipment | 705,120 | 553,120 |
| Accumulated depreciation—equipment | (166,400) | (148,000) |
| Total assets | $2,362,080 | $2,057,120 |
| **Liabilities and Stockholders' Equity** | | |
| Accounts payable (merchandise creditors) | $ 424,480 | $ 404,960 |
| Accrued expenses payable (operating expenses) | 42,240 | 52,640 |
| Dividends payable | 24,000 | 19,200 |
| Common stock, $4 par | 150,000 | 100,000 |
| Paid-in capital: Excess of issue price over par—common stock | 417,500 | 280,000 |
| Retained earnings | 1,303,860 | 1,200,320 |
| Total liabilities and stockholders' equity | $2,362,080 | $2,057,120 |

Additional data obtained from an examination of the accounts in the ledger for 2016 are as follows:

a. The investments were sold for $280,000 cash.

b. Equipment and land were acquired for cash.

c. There were no disposals of equipment during the year.

d. The common stock was issued for cash.

e. There was a $199,540 credit to Retained Earnings for net income.

f. There was a $96,000 debit to Retained Earnings for cash dividends declared.

**Instructions**

Prepare a statement of cash flows, using the indirect method of presenting cash flows from operating activities.

### PR 16-2A Statement of cash flows—indirect method
OBJ. 2

The comparative balance sheet of Del Ray Enterprises Inc. at December 31, 2016 and 2015, is as follows:

| | Dec. 31, 2016 | Dec. 31, 2015 |
|---|---|---|
| **Assets** | | |
| Cash | $ 146,600 | $ 179,800 |
| Accounts receivable (net) | 224,600 | 242,000 |
| Merchandise inventory | 321,600 | 299,200 |
| Prepaid expenses | 13,400 | 9,600 |
| Equipment | 655,000 | 537,000 |
| Accumulated depreciation—equipment | (170,800) | (132,200) |
| Total assets | $1,190,400 | $1,135,400 |
| **Liabilities and Stockholders' Equity** | | |
| Accounts payable (merchandise creditors) | $ 250,200 | $ 237,600 |
| Mortgage note payable | 0 | 336,000 |
| Common stock, $10 par | 74,000 | 24,000 |
| Paid-in capital: Excess of issue price over par—common stock | 470,000 | 320,000 |
| Retained earnings | 396,200 | 217,800 |
| Total liabilities and stockholders' equity | $1,190,400 | $1,135,400 |

Additional data obtained from the income statement and from an examination of the accounts in the ledger for 2016 are as follows:

a.  Net income, $332,000

b.  Depreciation reported on the income statement, $83,400

c.  Equipment was purchased at a cost of $162,800 and fully depreciated equipment costing $44,800 was discarded, with no salvage realized.

d.  The mortgage note payable was not due until 2018 but the terms permitted earlier payment without penalty.

e.  10,000 shares of common stock were issued at $20 for cash.

f.  Cash dividends declared and paid, $153,600

## Instructions

Prepare a statement of cash flows, using the indirect method of presenting cash flows from operating activities.

---

**PR 16-3A   Statement of cash flows—indirect method**                    OBJ. 2

The comparative balance sheet of Whitman Co. at December 31, 2016 and 2015, is as follows:

✔ Net cash flow from operating activities, $(169,600)

| | Dec. 31, 2016 | Dec. 31, 2015 |
|---|---|---|
| **Assets** | | |
| Cash | $ 918,000 | $ 964,800 |
| Accounts receivable (net) | 828,900 | 761,940 |
| Inventories | 1,268,460 | 1,162,980 |
| Prepaid expenses | 29,340 | 35,100 |
| Land | 315,900 | 479,700 |
| Buildings | 1,462,500 | 900,900 |
| Accumulated depreciation—buildings | (408,600) | (382,320) |
| Equipment | 512,280 | 454,680 |
| Accumulated depreciation—equipment | (141,300) | (158,760) |
| Total assets | $4,785,480 | $4,219,020 |
| **Liabilities and Stockholders' Equity** | | |
| Accounts payable (merchandise creditors) | $ 922,500 | $ 958,320 |
| Bonds payable | 270,000 | 0 |
| Common stock, $25 par | 317,000 | 117,000 |
| Paid-in capital: Excess of issue price over par—common stock | 758,000 | 558,000 |
| Retained earnings | 2,517,980 | 2,585,700 |
| Total liabilities and stockholders' equity | $4,785,480 | $4,219,020 |

The noncurrent asset, noncurrent liability, and stockholders' equity accounts for 2016 are as follows:

**ACCOUNT** Land                                               **ACCOUNT NO.**

| Date | | Item | Debit | Credit | Balance Debit | Balance Credit |
|---|---|---|---|---|---|---|
| 2016 | | | | | | |
| Jan. | 1 | Balance | | | 479,700 | |
| Apr. | 20 | Realized $151,200 cash from sale | | 163,800 | 315,900 | |

**ACCOUNT** Buildings                                          **ACCOUNT NO.**

| Date | | Item | Debit | Credit | Balance Debit | Balance Credit |
|---|---|---|---|---|---|---|
| 2016 | | | | | | |
| Jan. | 1 | Balance | | | 900,900 | |
| Apr. | 20 | Acquired for cash | 561,600 | | 1,462,500 | |

*(Continued)*

ACCOUNT *Accumulated Depreciation—Buildings*                ACCOUNT NO.

| Date | | Item | Debit | Credit | Balance Debit | Balance Credit |
|---|---|---|---|---|---|---|
| 2016 | | | | | | |
| Jan. | 1 | Balance | | | | 382,320 |
| Dec. | 31 | Depreciation for year | | 26,280 | | 408,600 |

ACCOUNT *Equipment*                ACCOUNT NO.

| Date | | Item | Debit | Credit | Balance Debit | Balance Credit |
|---|---|---|---|---|---|---|
| 2016 | | | | | | |
| Jan. | 1 | Balance | | | 454,680 | |
| | 26 | Discarded, no salvage | | 46,800 | 407,880 | |
| Aug. | 11 | Purchased for cash | 104,400 | | 512,280 | |

ACCOUNT *Accumulated Depreciation—Equipment*                ACCOUNT NO.

| Date | | Item | Debit | Credit | Balance Debit | Balance Credit |
|---|---|---|---|---|---|---|
| 2016 | | | | | | |
| Jan. | 1 | Balance | | | | 158,760 |
| | 26 | Equipment discarded | 46,800 | | | 111,960 |
| Dec. | 31 | Depreciation for year | | 29,340 | | 141,300 |

ACCOUNT *Bonds Payable*                ACCOUNT NO.

| Date | | Item | Debit | Credit | Balance Debit | Balance Credit |
|---|---|---|---|---|---|---|
| 2016 | | | | | | |
| May | 1 | Issued 20-year bonds | | 270,000 | | 270,000 |

ACCOUNT *Common Stock, $25 par*                ACCOUNT NO.

| Date | | Item | Debit | Credit | Balance Debit | Balance Credit |
|---|---|---|---|---|---|---|
| 2016 | | | | | | |
| Jan. | 1 | Balance | | | | 117,000 |
| Dec. | 7 | Issued 8,000 shares of common stock for $50 per share | | 200,000 | | 317,000 |

ACCOUNT *Paid-In Capital in Excess of Par—Common Stock*                ACCOUNT NO.

| Date | | Item | Debit | Credit | Balance Debit | Balance Credit |
|---|---|---|---|---|---|---|
| 2016 | | | | | | |
| Jan. | 1 | Balance | | | | 558,000 |
| Dec. | 7 | Issued 8,000 shares of common stock for $50 per share | | 200,000 | | 758,000 |

**ACCOUNT** *Retained Earnings*                                    **ACCOUNT NO.**

| Date | | Item | Debit | Credit | Balance Debit | Balance Credit |
|------|---|------|-------|--------|-------|--------|
| 2016 | | | | | | |
| Jan. | 1 | Balance | | | | 2,585,700 |
| Dec. | 31 | Net loss | 35,320 | | | 2,550,380 |
| | 31 | Cash dividends | 32,400 | | | 2,517,980 |

**Instructions**

Prepare a statement of cash flows, using the indirect method of presenting cash flows from operating activities.

## PR 16-4A  Statement of cash flows—direct method                OBJ. 3

✔ Net cash flow from operating activities, $293,600

General Ledger

SHOW
ME HOW

The comparative balance sheet of Canace Products Inc. for December 31, 2016 and 2015, is as follows:

| | Dec. 31, 2016 | Dec. 31, 2015 |
|---|---|---|
| **Assets** | | |
| Cash | $ 643,400 | $ 679,400 |
| Accounts receivable (net) | 566,800 | 547,400 |
| Inventories | 1,011,000 | 982,800 |
| Investments | 0 | 240,000 |
| Land | 520,000 | 0 |
| Equipment | 880,000 | 680,000 |
| Accumulated depreciation | (244,400) | (200,400) |
| Total assets | $3,376,800 | $2,929,200 |
| **Liabilities and Stockholders' Equity** | | |
| Accounts payable (merchandise creditors) | $ 771,800 | $ 748,400 |
| Accrued expenses payable (operating expenses) | 63,400 | 70,800 |
| Dividends payable | 8,800 | 6,400 |
| Common stock, $2 par | 56,000 | 32,000 |
| Paid-in capital: Excess of issue price over par—common stock | 408,000 | 192,000 |
| Retained earnings | 2,068,800 | 1,879,600 |
| Total liabilities and stockholders' equity | $3,376,800 | $2,929,200 |

The income statement for the year ended December 31, 2016, is as follows:

| | | |
|---|---|---|
| Sales | | $5,980,000 |
| Cost of merchandise sold | | 2,452,000 |
| Gross profit | | $3,528,000 |
| Operating expenses: | | |
| Depreciation expense | $ 44,000 | |
| Other operating expenses | 3,100,000 | |
| Total operating expenses | | 3,144,000 |
| Operating income | | $ 384,000 |
| Other expense: | | |
| Loss on sale of investments | | (64,000) |
| Income before income tax | | $ 320,000 |
| Income tax expense | | 102,800 |
| Net Income | | $ 217,200 |

Additional data obtained from an examination of the accounts in the ledger for 2016 are as follows:

a. Equipment and land were acquired for cash.

b. There were no disposals of equipment during the year.

*(Continued)*

c. The investments were sold for $176,000 cash.

d. The common stock was issued for cash.

e. There was a $28,000 debit to Retained Earnings for cash dividends declared.

**Instructions**

Prepare a statement of cash flows, using the direct method of presenting cash flows from operating activities.

---

**PR 16-5A    Statement of cash flows—direct method applied to PR 16-1A**    OBJ. 3

✔ Net cash flow from operating activities, $143,540

The comparative balance sheet of Cromme Inc. for December 31, 2016 and 2015, is as follows:

|  | Dec. 31, 2016 | Dec. 31, 2015 |
|---|---|---|
| **Assets** | | |
| Cash | $ 625,760 | $ 585,920 |
| Accounts receivable (net) | 227,840 | 208,960 |
| Inventories | 641,760 | 617,120 |
| Investments | 0 | 240,000 |
| Land | 328,000 | 0 |
| Equipment | 705,120 | 553,120 |
| Accumulated depreciation—equipment | (166,400) | (148,000) |
| Total assets | $2,362,080 | $2,057,120 |
| **Liabilities and Stockholders' Equity** | | |
| Accounts payable (merchandise creditors) | $ 424,480 | $ 404,960 |
| Accrued expenses payable (operating expenses) | 42,240 | 52,640 |
| Dividends payable | 24,000 | 19,200 |
| Common stock, $2 par | 150,000 | 100,000 |
| Paid-in capital: Excess of issue price over par—common stock | 417,500 | 280,000 |
| Retained earnings | 1,303,860 | 1,200,320 |
| Total liabilities and stockholders' equity | $2,362,080 | $2,057,120 |

The income statement for the year ended December 31, 2016, is as follows:

| | | |
|---|---|---|
| Sales | | $5,372,559 |
| Cost of merchandise sold | | 3,306,190 |
| Gross profit | | $2,066,369 |
| Operating expenses: | | |
| Depreciation expense | $ 18,400 | |
| Other operating expenses | 1,755,402 | |
| Total operating expenses | | 1,773,802 |
| Operating income | | $ 292,567 |
| Other income: | | |
| Gain on sale of investments | | 40,000 |
| Income before income tax | | $ 332,567 |
| Income tax expense | | 133,027 |
| Net income | | $ 199,540 |

Additional data obtained from an examination of the accounts in the ledger for 2016 are as follows:

a. The investments were sold for $280,000 cash.

b. Equipment and land were acquired for cash.

c. There were no disposals of equipment during the year.

d. The common stock was issued for cash.

e. There was a $96,000 debit to Retained Earnings for cash dividends declared.

**Instructions**

Prepare a statement of cash flows, using the direct method of presenting cash flows from operating activities.

## Problems: Series B

✔ Net cash flow from
operating activities,
$154,260

SHOW
ME HOW

### PR 16-1B  Statement of cash flows—indirect method                OBJ. 2

The comparative balance sheet of Merrick Equipment Co. for December 31, 2016 and 2015, is as follows:

|  | Dec. 31, 2016 | Dec. 31, 2015 |
|---|---|---|
| **Assets** | | |
| Cash ...................................................... | $ 70,720 | $ 47,940 |
| Accounts receivable (net) ..................................... | 207,230 | 188,190 |
| Inventories ................................................. | 298,520 | 209,850 |
| Investments ................................................ | 0 | 102,000 |
| Land ...................................................... | 295,800 | 0 |
| Equipment.................................................. | 438,600 | 358,020 |
| Accumulated depreciation—equipment ...................... | (99,110) | (84,320) |
| Total assets ......................................... | $1,211,760 | $901,680 |
| **Liabilities and Stockholders' Equity** | | |
| Accounts payable (merchandise creditors) ...................... | $ 205,700 | $194,140 |
| Accrued expenses payable (operating expenses) ............... | 30,600 | 26,860 |
| Dividends payable........................................... | 25,500 | 20,400 |
| Common stock, $1 par........................................ | 202,000 | 102,000 |
| Paid-in capital: Excess of issue price over par—common stock ............ | 354,000 | 204,000 |
| Retained earnings........................................... | 393,960 | 354,280 |
| Total liabilities and stockholders' equity..................... | $1,211,760 | $901,680 |

Additional data obtained from an examination of the accounts in the ledger for 2016 are as follows:

a.  Equipment and land were acquired for cash.

b.  There were no disposals of equipment during the year.

c.  The investments were sold for $91,800 cash.

d.  The common stock was issued for cash.

e.  There was a $141,680 credit to Retained Earnings for net income.

f.  There was a $102,000 debit to Retained Earnings for cash dividends declared.

**Instructions**

Prepare a statement of cash flows, using the indirect method of presenting cash flows from operating activities.

✔ Net cash flow from
operating activities,
$561,400

SHOW
ME HOW

### PR 16-2B  Statement of cash flows—indirect method                OBJ. 2

The comparative balance sheet of Harris Industries Inc. at December 31, 2016 and 2015, is as follows:

|  | Dec. 31, 2016 | Dec. 31, 2015 |
|---|---|---|
| **Assets** | | |
| Cash ...................................................... | $ 443,240 | $ 360,920 |
| Accounts receivable (net) ............................... | 665,280 | 592,200 |
| Inventories ............................................ | 887,880 | 1,022,560 |
| Prepaid expenses ...................................... | 31,640 | 25,200 |
| Land ................................................. | 302,400 | 302,400 |
| Buildings ............................................. | 1,713,600 | 1,134,000 |
| Accumulated depreciation—buildings..................... | (466,200) | (414,540) |
| Machinery and equipment............................... | 781,200 | 781,200 |
| Accumulated depreciation—machinery and equipment..... | (214,200) | (191,520) |
| Patents ............................................... | 106,960 | 112,000 |
| Total assets ....................................... | $4,251,800 | $3,724,420 |

*(Continued)*

**Liabilities and Stockholders' Equity**

| | | |
|---|---:|---:|
| Accounts payable (merchandise creditors) . . . . . . . . . . . . . . . . . | $ 837,480 | $ 927,080 |
| Dividends payable. . . . . . . . . . . . . . . . . . . . . . . . . . . . . . . . . . . . | 32,760 | 25,200 |
| Salaries payable. . . . . . . . . . . . . . . . . . . . . . . . . . . . . . . . . . . . . | 78,960 | 87,080 |
| Mortgage note payable, due 2017 . . . . . . . . . . . . . . . . . . . . . . . | 224,000 | 0 |
| Bonds payable . . . . . . . . . . . . . . . . . . . . . . . . . . . . . . . . . . . . . . | 0 | 390,000 |
| Common stock, $5 par. . . . . . . . . . . . . . . . . . . . . . . . . . . . . . . . | 200,400 | 50,400 |
| Paid-in capital: Excess of issue price over par—common stock. . . . . . | 366,000 | 126,000 |
| Retained earnings. . . . . . . . . . . . . . . . . . . . . . . . . . . . . . . . . . . . | 2,512,200 | 2,118,660 |
| Total liabilities and stockholders' equity. . . . . . . . . . . . . . . | $4,251,800 | $3,724,420 |

An examination of the income statement and the accounting records revealed the following additional information applicable to 2016:

a. Net income, $524,580.

b. Depreciation expense reported on the income statement: buildings, $51,660; machinery and equipment, $22,680.

c. Patent amortization reported on the income statement, $5,040.

d. A building was constructed for $579,600.

e. A mortgage note for $224,000 was issued for cash.

f. 30,000 shares of common stock were issued at $13 in exchange for the bonds payable.

g. Cash dividends declared, $131,040.

**Instructions**

Prepare a statement of cash flows, using the indirect method of presenting cash flows from operating activities.

---

**PR 16-3B    Statement of cash flows—indirect method**                                    OBJ. 2

✔ Net cash flow from operating activities, $162,800

The comparative balance sheet of Coulson, Inc. at December 31, 2016 and 2015, is as follows:

| | Dec. 31, 2016 | Dec. 31, 2015 |
|---|---:|---:|
| **Assets** | | |
| Cash . . . . . . . . . . . . . . . . . . . . . . . . . . . . . . . . . . . . . . . . . . . . . . | $ 300,600 | $ 337,800 |
| Accounts receivable (net) . . . . . . . . . . . . . . . . . . . . . . . . . . . . . | 704,400 | 609,600 |
| Inventories . . . . . . . . . . . . . . . . . . . . . . . . . . . . . . . . . . . . . . . . . | 918,600 | 865,800 |
| Prepaid expenses . . . . . . . . . . . . . . . . . . . . . . . . . . . . . . . . . . . | 18,600 | 26,400 |
| Land . . . . . . . . . . . . . . . . . . . . . . . . . . . . . . . . . . . . . . . . . . . . . . | 990,000 | 1,386,000 |
| Buildings . . . . . . . . . . . . . . . . . . . . . . . . . . . . . . . . . . . . . . . . . . | 1,980,000 | 990,000 |
| Accumulated depreciation—buildings. . . . . . . . . . . . . . . . . . . . | (397,200) | (366,000) |
| Equipment . . . . . . . . . . . . . . . . . . . . . . . . . . . . . . . . . . . . . . . . | 660,600 | 529,800 |
| Accumulated depreciation—equipment . . . . . . . . . . . . . . . . . . | (133,200) | (162,000) |
| Total assets . . . . . . . . . . . . . . . . . . . . . . . . . . . . . . . . . . . | $5,042,400 | $4,217,400 |
| **Liabilities and Stockholders' Equity** | | |
| Accounts payable (merchandise creditors) . . . . . . . . . . . . . . . . . | $ 594,000 | $ 631,200 |
| Income taxes payable . . . . . . . . . . . . . . . . . . . . . . . . . . . . . . . | 26,400 | 21,600 |
| Bonds payable . . . . . . . . . . . . . . . . . . . . . . . . . . . . . . . . . . . . . | 330,000 | 0 |
| Common stock, $20 par. . . . . . . . . . . . . . . . . . . . . . . . . . . . . . . | 320,000 | 180,000 |
| Paid-in capital: Excess of issue price over par—common stock . . . . . . | 950,000 | 810,000 |
| Retained earnings. . . . . . . . . . . . . . . . . . . . . . . . . . . . . . . . . . . | 2,822,000 | 2,574,600 |
| Total liabilities and stockholders' equity. . . . . . . . . . . . . . . | $5,042,400 | $4,217,400 |

The noncurrent asset, noncurrent liability, and stockholders' equity accounts for 2016 are as follows:

**ACCOUNT** *Land*                                      **ACCOUNT NO.**

| Date | | Item | Debit | Credit | Balance Debit | Balance Credit |
|---|---|---|---|---|---|---|
| 2016 | | | | | | |
| Jan. | 1 | Balance | | | 1,386,000 | |
| Apr. | 20 | Realized $456,000 cash from sale | | 396,000 | 990,000 | |

**ACCOUNT** *Buildings*                                 **ACCOUNT NO.**

| Date | | Item | Debit | Credit | Balance Debit | Balance Credit |
|---|---|---|---|---|---|---|
| 2016 | | | | | | |
| Jan. | 1 | Balance | | | 990,000 | |
| Apr. | 20 | Acquired for cash | 990,000 | | 1,980,000 | |

**ACCOUNT** *Accumulated Depreciation—Buildings*        **ACCOUNT NO.**

| Date | | Item | Debit | Credit | Balance Debit | Balance Credit |
|---|---|---|---|---|---|---|
| 2016 | | | | | | |
| Jan. | 1 | Balance | | | | 366,000 |
| Dec. | 31 | Depreciation for year | | 31,200 | | 397,200 |

**ACCOUNT** *Equipment*                                 **ACCOUNT NO.**

| Date | | Item | Debit | Credit | Balance Debit | Balance Credit |
|---|---|---|---|---|---|---|
| 2016 | | | | | | |
| Jan. | 1 | Balance | | | 529,800 | |
| | 26 | Discarded, no salvage | | 66,000 | 463,800 | |
| Aug. | 11 | Purchased for cash | 196,800 | | 660,600 | |

**ACCOUNT** *Accumulated Depreciation—Equipment*        **ACCOUNT NO.**

| Date | | Item | Debit | Credit | Balance Debit | Balance Credit |
|---|---|---|---|---|---|---|
| 2016 | | | | | | |
| Jan. | 1 | Balance | | | | 162,000 |
| | 26 | Equipment discarded | 66,000 | | | 96,000 |
| Dec. | 31 | Depreciation for year | | 37,200 | | 133,200 |

**ACCOUNT** *Bonds Payable*                             **ACCOUNT NO.**

| Date | | Item | Debit | Credit | Balance Debit | Balance Credit |
|---|---|---|---|---|---|---|
| 2016 | | | | | | |
| May | 1 | Issued 20-year bonds | | 330,000 | | 330,000 |

*(Continued)*

ACCOUNT *Common Stock, $20 par*                                ACCOUNT NO.

| Date | | Item | Debit | Credit | Balance Debit | Balance Credit |
|---|---|---|---|---|---|---|
| 2016 | | | | | | |
| Jan. | 1 | Balance | | | | 180,000 |
| Dec. | 7 | Issued 7,000 shares of common stock for $40 per share | | 140,000 | | 320,000 |

ACCOUNT *Paid-In Capital in Excess of Par—Common Stock*          ACCOUNT NO.

| Date | | Item | Debit | Credit | Balance Debit | Balance Credit |
|---|---|---|---|---|---|---|
| 2016 | | | | | | |
| Jan. | 1 | Balance | | | | 810,000 |
| Dec. | 7 | Issued 7,000 shares of common stock for $40 per share | | 140,000 | | 950,000 |

ACCOUNT *Retained Earnings*                                    ACCOUNT NO.

| Date | | Item | Debit | Credit | Balance Debit | Balance Credit |
|---|---|---|---|---|---|---|
| 2016 | | | | | | |
| Jan. | 1 | Balance | | | | 2,574,600 |
| Dec. | 31 | Net income | | 326,600 | | 2,901,200 |
| | 31 | Cash dividends | 79,200 | | | 2,822,000 |

## Instructions

Prepare a statement of cash flows, using the indirect method of presenting cash flows from operating activities.

---

**PR 16-4B    Statement of cash flows—direct method**                OBJ. 3

The comparative balance sheet of Martinez Inc. for December 31, 2016 and 2015, is as follows:

✔ Net cash flow from operating activities, $509,220

General Ledger

SHOW
ME HOW

| | Dec. 31, 2016 | Dec. 31, 2015 |
|---|---|---|
| **Assets** | | |
| Cash ..................................................... | $ 661,920 | $ 683,100 |
| Accounts receivable (net) ................................ | 992,640 | 914,400 |
| Inventories ............................................... | 1,394,400 | 1,363,800 |
| Investments ............................................. | 0 | 432,000 |
| Land ..................................................... | 960,000 | 0 |
| Equipment................................................ | 1,224,000 | 984,000 |
| Accumulated depreciation—equipment .................... | (481,500) | (368,400) |
| Total assets ........................................ | $4,751,460 | $4,008,900 |
| **Liabilities and Stockholders' Equity** | | |
| Accounts payable (merchandise creditors) ................. | $1,080,000 | $ 966,600 |
| Accrued expenses payable (operating expenses) ........... | 67,800 | 79,200 |
| Dividends payable........................................ | 100,800 | 91,200 |
| Common stock, $5 par ................................... | 130,000 | 30,000 |
| Paid-in capital: Excess of issue price over par—common stock ...... | 950,000 | 450,000 |
| Retained earnings....................................... | 2,422,860 | 2,391,900 |
| Total liabilities and stockholders' equity................. | $4,751,460 | $4,008,900 |

The income statement for the year ended December 31, 2016, is as follows:

| | | |
|---|---|---|
| Sales | | $4,512,000 |
| Cost of merchandise sold | | 2,352,000 |
| Gross profit | | $2,160,000 |
| Operating expenses: | | |
| Depreciation expense | $ 113,100 | |
| Other operating expenses | 1,344,840 | |
| Total operating expenses | | 1,457,940 |
| Operating income | | $ 702,060 |
| Other income: | | |
| Gain on sale of investments | | 156,000 |
| Income before income tax | | $ 858,060 |
| Income tax expense | | 299,100 |
| Net income | | $ 558,960 |

Additional data obtained from an examination of the accounts in the ledger for 2016 are as follows:

a.  Equipment and land were acquired for cash.

b.  There were no disposals of equipment during the year.

c.  The investments were sold for $588,000 cash.

d.  The common stock was issued for cash.

e.  There was a $528,000 debit to Retained Earnings for cash dividends declared.

**Instructions**

Prepare a statement of cash flows, using the direct method of presenting cash flows from operating activities.

---

**PR 16-5B  Statement of cash flows—direct method applied to PR 16-1B**　　　**OBJ. 3**

✔ Net cash flow from operating activities, $154,260

The comparative balance sheet of Merrick Equipment Co. for Dec. 31, 2016 and 2015, is:

| | Dec. 31, 2016 | Dec. 31, 2015 |
|---|---|---|
| **Assets** | | |
| Cash | $ 70,720 | $ 47,940 |
| Accounts receivable (net) | 207,230 | 188,190 |
| Inventories | 298,520 | 289,850 |
| Investments | 0 | 102,000 |
| Land | 295,800 | 0 |
| Equipment | 438,600 | 358,020 |
| Accumulated depreciation—equipment | (99,110) | (81,320) |
| Total assets | $1,211,760 | $ 901,680 |
| **Liabilities and Stockholders' Equity** | | |
| Accounts payable (merchandise creditors) | $ 205,700 | $ 194,140 |
| Accrued expenses payable (operating expenses) | 30,600 | 26,860 |
| Dividends payable | 25,500 | 20,400 |
| Common stock, $1 par | 202,000 | 102,000 |
| Paid-in capital: Excess of issue price over par—common stock | 354,000 | 204,000 |
| Retained earnings | 393,960 | 354,280 |
| Total liabilities and stockholders' equity | $1,211,760 | $ 901,680 |

*(Continued)*

# Financial Statement Analysis

## Nike, Inc.

**"J**ust do it." These three words identify one of the most recognizable brands in the world, **Nike**. While this phrase inspires athletes to "compete and achieve their potential," it also defines the company.

Nike began in 1964 as a partnership between University of Oregon track coach Bill Bowerman and one of his former student-athletes, Phil Knight. The two began by selling shoes imported from Japan out of the back of Knight's car to athletes at track and field events. As sales grew, the company opened retail outlets, calling itself **Blue Ribbon Sports**. The company also began to develop its own shoes. In 1971, the company commissioned a graphic design student at Portland State University to develop the swoosh logo for a fee of $35. In 1978, the company changed its name to Nike, and in 1980, it sold its first shares of stock to the public.

Nike would have been a great company to invest in at the time. If you had invested in Nike's common stock back in 1990,

you would have paid $5.00 per share. As of April 2011, Nike's stock was worth $109.23 per share. Unfortunately, you can't invest using hindsight.

How can you select companies in which to invest? Like any significant purchase, you should do some research to guide your investment decision. If you were buying a car, for example, you might go to **Edmunds.com** to obtain reviews, ratings, prices, specifications, options, and fuel economies to evaluate different vehicles. In selecting companies to invest in, you can use financial analysis to gain insight into a company's past performance and future prospects. This chapter describes and illustrates common financial data that can be analyzed to assist you in making investment decisions such as whether or not to invest in Nike's stock.

*Source: www.nikebiz.com/.*

After studying this chapter, you should be able to:

*Example Exercises*

**OBJ 1**
Describe basic financial statement analytical methods.
**Basic Analytical Methods**
   Horizontal Analysis — EE 17-1
   Vertical Analysis — EE 17-2
   Common-Sized Statements
   Other Analytical Measures

**OBJ 2**
Use financial statement analysis to assess the solvency of a business.
**Liquidity and Solvency Analysis**
   Current Position Analysis — EE 17-3
   Accounts Receivable Analysis — EE 17-4
   Inventory Analysis — EE 17-5
   Ratio of Fixed Assets to Long-Term Liabilities
   Ratio of Liabilities to Stockholders' Equity — EE 17-6
   Number of Times Interest Charges Are Earned — EE 17-7

**OBJ 3**
Use financial statement analysis to assess the profitability of a business.
**Profitability Analysis**
   Ratio of Sales to Assets — EE 17-8
   Rate Earned on Total Assets — EE 17-9
   Rate Earned on Stockholders' Equity
   Rate Earned on Common Stockholders' Equity — EE 17-10
   Earnings per Share on Common Stock
   Price-Earnings Ratio — EE 17-11
   Divdends per Share
   Divdend Yield
   Summary of Analytical Measures

**OBJ 4**
Describe the contents of corporate annual reports.
**Corporate Annual Reports**
   Management Discussion and Analysis
   Report on Internal Control
   Report on Fairness of the Financial Statements

**At a Glance 17** ▶ Page 821

---

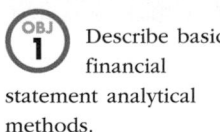

**OBJ 1** Describe basic financial statement analytical methods.

# Basic Analytical Methods

Users analyze a company's financial statements using a variety of analytical methods. Three such methods are:

- Horizontal analysis
- Vertical analysis
- Common-sized statements

## Horizontal Analysis

The analysis of increases and decreases in the amount and percentage of comparative financial statement items is called **horizontal analysis**. Each item on the most recent statement is compared with the same item on one or more earlier statements in terms of the following:

- *Amount* of increase or decrease
- *Percent* of increase or decrease

When comparing statements, the earlier statement is normally used as the base year for computing increases and decreases.

Exhibit 1 illustrates horizontal analysis for the December 31, 2016 and 2015, balance sheets of **Lincoln Company**. In Exhibit 1, the December 31, 2015, balance sheet (the earliest year presented) is used as the base year.

Exhibit 1 indicates that total assets decreased by $91,000 (7.4%), liabilities decreased by $133,000 (30.0%), and stockholders' equity increased by $42,000 (5.3%). Since the long-term investments account decreased by $82,500, it appears that most of the decrease in long-term liabilities of $100,000 was achieved through the sale of long-term investments.

**EXHIBIT 1**

**Comparative Balance Sheet—Horizontal Analysis**

### Lincoln Company
### Comparative Balance Sheet
### December 31, 2016 and 2015

| | Dec. 31, 2016 | Dec. 31, 2015 | Increase (Decrease) Amount | Percent |
|---|---|---|---|---|
| **Assets** | | | | |
| Current assets..................................... | $ 550,000 | $ 533,000 | $ 17,000 | 3.2% |
| Long-term investments........................... | 95,000 | 177,500 | (82,500) | (46.5%) |
| Property, plant, and equipment (net) ............. | 444,500 | 470,000 | (25,500) | (5.4%) |
| Intangible assets .................................. | 50,000 | 50,000 | — | — |
| Total assets ...................................... | $1,139,500 | $1,230,500 | $ (91,000) | (7.4%) |
| **Liabilities** | | | | |
| Current liabilities................................. | $ 210,000 | $ 243,000 | $ (33,000) | (13.6%) |
| Long-term liabilities.............................. | 100,000 | 200,000 | (100,000) | (50.0%) |
| Total liabilities ................................... | $ 310,000 | $ 443,000 | $(133,000) | (30.0%) |
| **Stockholders' Equity** | | | | |
| Preferred 6% stock, $100 par ...................... | $ 150,000 | $ 150,000 | — | — |
| Common stock, $10 par........................... | 500,000 | 500,000 | — | — |
| Retained earnings................................. | 179,500 | 137,500 | $ 42,000 | 30.5% |
| Total stockholders' equity......................... | $ 829,500 | $ 787,500 | $ 42,000 | 5.3% |
| Total liabilities and stockholders' equity............ | $1,139,500 | $1,230,500 | $ (91,000) | (7.4%) |

The balance sheets in Exhibit 1 may be expanded or supported by a separate schedule that includes the individual asset and liability accounts. For example, Exhibit 2 is a supporting schedule of **Lincoln Company**'s current asset accounts.

**EXHIBIT 2**

**Comparative Schedule of Current Assets—Horizontal Analysis**

### Lincoln Company
### Comparative Schedule of Current Assets
### December 31, 2016 and 2015

| | Dec. 31, 2016 | Dec. 31, 2015 | Increase (Decrease) Amount | Percent |
|---|---|---|---|---|
| Cash ............................................ | $ 90,500 | $ 64,700 | $ 25,800 | 39.9% |
| Temporary investments........................... | 75,000 | 60,000 | 15,000 | 25.0% |
| Accounts receivable (net) ......................... | 115,000 | 120,000 | (5,000) | (4.2%) |
| Inventories ...................................... | 264,000 | 283,000 | (19,000) | (6.7%) |
| Prepaid expenses ................................ | 5,500 | 5,300 | 200 | 3.8% |
| Total current assets.............................. | $550,000 | $533,000 | $ 17,000 | 3.2% |

Exhibit 2 indicates that while cash and temporary investments increased, accounts receivable and inventories decreased. The decrease in accounts receivable could be caused by improved collection policies, which would increase cash. The decrease in inventories could be caused by increased sales.

Exhibit 3 illustrates horizontal analysis for the 2016 and 2015 income statements of **Lincoln Company**. Exhibit 3 indicates an increase in sales of $298,000, or 24.8%. However, the percentage increase in sales of 24.8% was accompanied by an even greater percentage increase in the cost of goods (merchandise) sold of 27.2%.[1] Thus, gross profit increased by only 19.7% rather than by the 24.0% increase in sales.

---

| **EXHIBIT 3** | Lincoln Company |||||
|---|---|---|---|---|---|
| **Comparative Income Statement— Horizontal Analysis** | Comparative Income Statement For the Years Ended December 31, 2016 and 2015 |||||

| | | | Increase (Decrease) ||
|---|---|---|---|---|
| | **2016** | **2015** | **Amount** | **Percent** |
| Sales | $1,498,000 | $1,200,000 | $298,000 | 24.8% |
| Cost of goods sold | 1,043,000 | 820,000 | 223,000 | 27.2% |
| Gross profit | $ 455,000 | $ 380,000 | $ 75,000 | 19.7% |
| Selling expenses | $ 191,000 | $ 147,000 | $ 44,000 | 29.9% |
| Administrative expenses | 104,000 | 97,400 | 6,600 | 6.8% |
| Total operating expenses | $ 295,000 | $ 244,400 | $ 50,600 | 20.7% |
| Income from operations | $ 160,000 | $ 135,600 | $ 24,400 | 18.0% |
| Other income | 8,500 | 11,000 | (2,500) | (22.7%) |
| | $ 168,500 | $ 146,600 | $ 21,900 | 14.9% |
| Other expense (interest) | 6,000 | 12,000 | (6,000) | (50.0%) |
| Income before income tax | $ 162,500 | $ 134,600 | $ 27,900 | 20.7% |
| Income tax expense | 71,500 | 58,100 | 13,400 | 23.1% |
| Net income | $ 91,000 | $ 76,500 | $ 14,500 | 19.0% |

Exhibit 3 also indicates that selling expenses increased by 29.9%. Thus, the 24.8% increases in sales could have been caused by an advertising campaign, which increased selling expenses. Administrative expenses increased by only 6.8%, total operating expenses increased by 20.7%, and income from operations increased by 18.0%. Interest expense decreased by 50.0%. This decrease was probably caused by the 50.0% decrease in long-term liabilities (Exhibit 1). Overall, net income increased by 19.0%, a favorable result.

Exhibit 4 illustrates horizontal analysis for the 2016 and 2015 retained earnings statements of **Lincoln Company**. Exhibit 4 indicates that retained earnings increased by 30.5% for the year. The increase is due to net income of $91,000 for the year, less dividends of $49,000.

---

| **EXHIBIT 4** | Lincoln Company |||||
|---|---|---|---|---|---|
| **Comparative Retained Earnings Statement— Horizontal Analysis** | Comparative Retained Earnings Statement For the Years Ended December 31, 2016 and 2015 |||||

| | | | Increase (Decrease) ||
|---|---|---|---|---|
| | **2016** | **2015** | **Amount** | **Percent** |
| Retained earnings, January 1 | $137,500 | $100,000 | $37,500 | 37.5% |
| Net income for the year | 91,000 | 76,500 | 14,500 | 19.0% |
| Total | $228,500 | $176,500 | $52,000 | 29.5% |
| Dividends: | | | | |
| On preferred stock | $ 9,000 | $ 9,000 | — | — |
| On common stock | 40,000 | 30,000 | $10,000 | 33.3% |
| Total | $ 49,000 | $ 39,000 | $10,000 | 25.6% |
| Retained earnings, December 31 | $179,500 | $137,500 | $42,000 | 30.5% |

[1] The term *cost of goods sold* is often used in practice in place of *cost of merchandise sold*. Such usage is followed in this chapter.

## Example Exercise 17-1 Horizontal Analysis

OBJ 1

The comparative cash and accounts receivable balances for a company follow:

|  | Dec. 31, 2016 | Dec. 31, 2015 |
|---|---|---|
| Cash | $62,500 | $50,000 |
| Accounts receivable (net) | 74,400 | 80,000 |

Based on this information, what is the amount and percentage of increase or decrease that would be shown on a balance sheet with horizontal analysis?

## Follow My Example 17-1

Cash              $12,500 increase ($62,500 – $50,000), or 25%

Accounts receivable  $5,600 decrease ($74,400 – $80,000), or (7%)

Practice Exercises: PE 17-1A, PE 17-1B

## Vertical Analysis

The percentage analysis of the relationship of each component in a financial statement to a total within the statement is called **vertical analysis**. Although vertical analysis is applied to a single statement, it may be applied on the same statement over time. This enhances the analysis by showing how the percentages of each item have changed over time.

In vertical analysis of the balance sheet, the percentages are computed as follows:

- Each asset item is stated as a percent of the total assets.
- Each liability and stockholders' equity item is stated as a percent of the total liabilities and stockholders' equity.

Exhibit 5 illustrates the vertical analysis of the December 31, 2016 and 2015, balance sheets of **Lincoln Company**. Exhibit 5 indicates that current assets have increased from 43.3% to 48.3% of total assets. Long-term investments decreased from 14.4% to 8.3% of total assets. Stockholders' equity increased from 64.0% to 72.8%, with a comparable decrease in liabilities.

**EXHIBIT 5**

Comparative Balance Sheet— Vertical Analysis

### Lincoln Company
### Comparative Balance Sheet
### December 31, 2016 and 2015

|  | Dec. 31, 2016 | | Dec. 31, 2015 | |
|---|---|---|---|---|
|  | Amount | Percent | Amount | Percent |
| **Assets** | | | | |
| Current assets.............................. | $ 550,000 | 48.3% | $ 533,000 | 43.3% |
| Long-term investments...................... | 95,000 | 8.3 | 177,500 | 14.4 |
| Property, plant, and equipment (net) ......... | 444,500 | 39.0 | 470,000 | 38.2 |
| Intangible assets ........................... | 50,000 | 4.4 | 50,000 | 4.1 |
| Total assets ................................ | $1,139,500 | 100.0% | $1,230,500 | 100.0% |
| **Liabilities** | | | | |
| Current liabilities........................... | $ 210,000 | 18.4% | $ 243,000 | 19.7% |
| Long-term liabilities........................ | 100,000 | 8.8 | 200,000 | 16.3 |
| Total liabilities ............................ | $ 310,000 | 27.2% | $ 443,000 | 36.0% |
| **Stockholders' Equity** | | | | |
| Preferred 6% stock, $100 par ................ | $ 150,000 | 13.2% | $ 150,000 | 12.2% |
| Common stock, $10 par..................... | 500,000 | 43.9 | 500,000 | 40.6 |
| Retained earnings........................... | 179,500 | 15.7 | 137,500 | 11.2 |
| Total stockholders' equity ................... | $ 829,500 | 72.8% | $ 787,500 | 64.0% |
| Total liabilities and stockholders' equity ....... | $1,139,500 | 100.0% | $1,230,500 | 100.0% |

In a vertical analysis of the income statement, each item is stated as a percent of sales. Exhibit 6 illustrates the vertical analysis of the 2016 and 2015 income statements of **Lincoln Company**.

| EXHIBIT 6 | | |
|---|---|---|
| **Comparative Income Statement—Vertical Analysis** | | |

**Lincoln Company**
**Comparative Income Statement**
**For the Years Ended December 31, 2016 and 2015**

| | 2016 Amount | 2016 Percent | 2015 Amount | 2015 Percent |
|---|---|---|---|---|
| Sales | $1,498,000 | 100.0% | $1,200,000 | 100.0% |
| Cost of goods sold | 1,043,000 | 69.6 | 820,000 | 68.3 |
| Gross profit | $ 455,000 | 30.4% | $ 380,000 | 31.7% |
| Selling expenses | $ 191,000 | 12.8% | $ 147,000 | 12.3% |
| Administrative expenses | 104,000 | 6.9 | 97,400 | 8.1 |
| Total operating expenses | $ 295,000 | 19.7% | $ 244,400 | 20.4% |
| Income from operations | $ 160,000 | 10.7% | $ 135,600 | 11.3% |
| Other income | 8,500 | 0.6 | 11,000 | 0.9 |
| | $ 168,500 | 11.3% | $ 146,600 | 12.2% |
| Other expense (interest) | 6,000 | 0.4 | 12,000 | 1.0 |
| Income before income tax | $ 162,500 | 10.9% | $ 134,600 | 11.2% |
| Income tax expense | 71,500 | 4.8 | 58,100 | 4.8 |
| Net income | $ 91,000 | 6.1% | $ 76,500 | 6.4% |

Exhibit 6 indicates a decrease in the gross profit rate from 31.7% in 2015 to 30.4% in 2016. Although this is only a 1.3 percentage point (31.7% – 30.4%) decrease, in dollars of potential gross profit, it represents a decrease of $19,474 (1.3% × $1,498,000) based on 2016 sales. Thus, a small percentage decrease can have a large dollar effect.

## Example Exercise 17-2 Vertical Analysis

OBJ 1

Income statement information for Lee Corporation follows:

| Sales | $100,000 |
|---|---|
| Cost of goods sold | 65,000 |
| Gross profit | $ 35,000 |

Prepare a vertical analysis of the income statement for Lee Corporation.

## Follow My Example 17-2

| | Amount | Percentage | |
|---|---|---|---|
| Sales | $100,000 | 100% | ($100,000 ÷ $100,000) |
| Cost of goods sold | 65,000 | 65 | ($65,000 ÷ $100,000) |
| Gross profit | $ 35,000 | 35% | ($35,000 ÷ $100,000) |

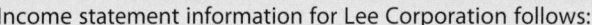

Practice Exercises: PE 17-2A, PE 17-2B

## Common-Sized Statements

In a **common-sized statement**, all items are expressed as percentages, with no dollar amounts shown. Common-sized statements are often useful for comparing one company with another or for comparing a company with industry averages.

Exhibit 7 illustrates common-sized income statements for **Lincoln Company** and Madison Corporation. Exhibit 7 indicates that Lincoln has a slightly higher rate of gross profit (30.4%) than Madison (30.0%). However, Lincoln has a higher percentage of selling expenses (12.8%) and administrative expenses (6.9%) than does Madison (11.5% and 4.1%). As a result, the income from operations of Lincoln (10.7%) is less than that of Madison (14.4%).

| | Lincoln Company | Madison Corporation |
|---|---|---|
| Sales | 100.0% | 100.0% |
| Cost of goods sold | 69.6 | 70.0 |
| Gross profit | 30.4% | 30.0% |
| Selling expenses | 12.8% | 11.5% |
| Administrative expenses | 6.9 | 4.1 |
| Total operating expenses | 19.7% | 15.6% |
| Income from operations | 10.7% | 14.4% |
| Other income | 0.6 | 0.6 |
| | 11.3% | 15.0% |
| Other expense (interest) | 0.4 | 0.5 |
| Income before income tax | 10.9% | 14.5% |
| Income tax expense | 4.8 | 5.5 |
| Net income | 6.1% | 9.0% |

The unfavorable difference of 3.7 (14.4% − 10.7%) percentage points in income from operations would concern the managers and other stakeholders of Lincoln. The underlying causes of the difference should be investigated and possibly corrected. For example, Lincoln may decide to outsource some of its administrative duties so that its administrative expenses are more comparative to that of Madison.

## Other Analytical Measures

Other relationships may be expressed in ratios and percentages. Often, these relationships are compared within the same statement and, thus, are a type of vertical analysis. Comparing these items with items from earlier periods is a type of horizontal analysis.

Analytical measures are not a definitive conclusion. They are only guides in evaluating financial and operating data. Many other factors, such as trends in the industry and general economic conditions, should also be considered when analyzing a company.

# Liquidity and Solvency Analysis

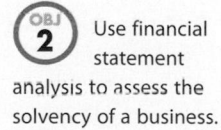
**OBJ 2** Use financial statement analysis to assess the solvency of a business.

All users of financial statements are interested in the ability of a company to do the following:

• Maintain liquidity and solvency
• Earn income, called **profitability**

The ability of a company to convert assets into cash is called **liquidity**, while the ability of a company to pay its debts is called **solvency**. Liquidity, solvency, and profitability are interrelated. For example, a company that cannot convert assets into cash may have difficulty taking advantage of profitable courses of action requiring immediate cash outlays. Likewise, a company that cannot pay its debts will have difficulty obtaining credit. A lack of credit will, in turn, limit the company's ability to purchase merchandise or expand operations, which decreases its profitability

Liquidity and solvency are normally assessed using the following:

- Current position analysis
  - Working capital
  - Current ratio
  - Quick ratio

One popular printed source for industry ratios is *Annual Statement Studies* from Risk Management Association. Online analysis is available from Zacks Investment Research site at www.zacks.com.

- Accounts receivable analysis
  - Accounts receivable turnover
  - Number of days' sales in receivables

- Inventory analysis
  - Inventory turnover
  - Number of days' sales in inventory

- The ratio of fixed assets to long-term liabilities
- The ratio of liabilities to stockholders' equity
- The number of times interest charges are earned

The Lincoln Company financial statements presented earlier are used to illustrate the preceding analyses.

## Current Position Analysis

A company's ability to pay its current liabilities is called **current position analysis**. It is a solvency measure of special interest to short-term creditors and includes the computation and analysis of the following:

- Working capital
- Current ratio
- Quick ratio

**Working Capital** A company's **working capital** is computed as follows:

$$\text{Working Capital} = \text{Current Assets} - \text{Current Liabilities}$$

To illustrate, the working capital for **Lincoln Company** for 2016 and 2015 is computed as follows:

|  | 2016 | 2015 |
|---|---|---|
| Current assets | $550,000 | $533,000 |
| Less current liabilities | 210,000 | 243,000 |
| Working capital | $340,000 | $290,000 |

The working capital is used to evaluate a company's ability to pay current liabilities. A company's working capital is often monitored monthly, quarterly, or yearly by creditors and other debtors. However, it is difficult to use working capital to compare companies of different sizes. For example, working capital of $250,000 may be adequate for a local hardware store, but it would be inadequate for The Home Depot.

**Current Ratio** The **current ratio**, sometimes called the *working capital ratio*, is computed as follows:

$$\text{Current Ratio} = \frac{\text{Current Assets}}{\text{Current Liabilities}}$$

To illustrate, the current ratio for **Lincoln Company** is computed as follows:

|  | 2016 | 2015 |
|---|---|---|
| Current assets | $550,000 | $533,000 |
| Current liabilities | $210,000 | $243,000 |
| Current ratio | 2.6 ($550,000 ÷ $210,000) | 2.2 ($533,000 ÷ $243,000) |

The current ratio is a more reliable indicator of a company's ability to pay its current liabilities than is working capital, and it is much easier to compare across companies. To illustrate, assume that as of December 31, 2016, the working capital of a competitor is much greater than $340,000, but its current ratio is only 1.3. Considering these facts alone, Lincoln, with its current ratio of 2.6, is in a more favorable position to obtain short-term credit than the competitor, which has the greater amount of working capital.

**Quick Ratio** One limitation of working capital and the current ratio is that they do not consider the types of current assets a company has and how easily they can be turned in to cash. Because of this, two companies may have the same working capital and current ratios but differ significantly in their ability to pay their current liabilities.

To illustrate, the current assets and liabilities for **Lincoln Company** and Jefferson Corporation as of December 31, 2016, are as follows:

|  | Lincoln Company | Jefferson Corporation |
|---|---|---|
| Current assets: |  |  |
| Cash | $ 90,500 | $ 45,500 |
| Temporary investments | 75,000 | 25,000 |
| Accounts receivable (net) | 115,000 | 90,000 |
| Inventories | 264,000 | 380,000 |
| Prepaid expenses | 5,500 | 9,500 |
| Total current assets | $550,000 | $550,000 |
| Total current assets | $550,000 | $550,000 |
| Less current liabilities | 210,000 | 210,000 |
| Working capital | $340,000 | $340,000 |
| Current ratio ($550,000 ÷ $210,000) | 2.6 | 2.6 |

Lincoln and Jefferson both have a working capital of $340,000 and current ratios of 2.6. Jefferson, however, has more of its current assets in inventories. These inventories must be sold and the receivables collected before all the current liabilities can be paid. This takes time. In addition, if the market for its product declines, Jefferson may have difficulty selling its inventory. This, in turn, could impair its ability to pay its current liabilities.

In contrast, Lincoln's current assets contain more cash, temporary investments, and accounts receivable, which can easily be converted to cash. Thus, Lincoln is in a stronger current position than Jefferson to pay its current liabilities.

A ratio that measures the "instant" debt-paying ability of a company is the **quick ratio**, sometimes called the *acid-test ratio*. The quick ratio is computed as follows:

$$\text{Quick Ratio} = \frac{\text{Quick Assets}}{\text{Current Liabilities}}$$

**Quick assets** are cash and other current assets that can be easily converted to cash. Quick assets normally include cash, temporary investments, and receivables but exclude inventories and prepaid assets.

To illustrate, the quick ratio for **Lincoln Company** is computed as follows:

|  | 2016 | 2015 |
|---|---|---|
| Quick assets: |  |  |
| Cash | $ 90,500 | $ 64,700 |
| Temporary investments | 75,000 | 60,000 |
| Accounts receivable (net) | 115,000 | 120,000 |
| Total quick assets | $280,500 | $244,700 |
| Current liabilities | $210,000 | $243,000 |
| Quick ratio | 1.3 ($280,500 ÷ $210,000) | 1.0 ($244,700 ÷ $243,000) |

## Example Exercise 17-3 Current Position Analysis

OBJ 2

The following items are reported on a company's balance sheet:

| | |
|---|---|
| Cash | $300,000 |
| Temporary investments | 100,000 |
| Accounts receivable (net) | 200,000 |
| Inventory | 200,000 |
| Accounts payable | 400,000 |

Determine (a) the current ratio and (b) the quick ratio.

## Follow My Example 17-3

a.  Current Ratio = Current Assets ÷ Current Liabilities

= ($300,000 + $100,000 + $200,000 + $200,000) ÷ $400,000

= 2.0

b.  Quick Ratio = Quick Assets ÷ Current Liabilities

= ($300,000 + $100,000 + $200,000) ÷ $400,000

= 1.5

Practice Exercises: PE 17-3A, PE 17-3B

## Accounts Receivable Analysis

A company's ability to collect its accounts receivable is called **accounts receivable analysis**. It includes the computation and analysis of the following:

• Accounts receivable turnover
• Number of days' sales in receivables

Collecting accounts receivable as quickly as possible improves a company's liquidity. In addition, the cash collected from receivables may be used to improve or expand operations. Quick collection of receivables also reduces the risk of uncollectible accounts.

**Accounts Receivable Turnover** The **accounts receivable turnover** is computed as follows:

$$\text{Accounts Receivable Turnover} = \frac{\text{Sales}^2}{\text{Average Accounts Receivable}}$$

To illustrate, the accounts receivable turnover for **Lincoln Company** for 2016 and 2015 is computed as follows. Lincoln's accounts receivable balance at the beginning of 2015 is $140,000.

| | 2016 | 2015 |
|---|---|---|
| Sales | $1,498,000 | $1,200,000 |
| Accounts receivable (net): | | |
| Beginning of year | $  120,000 | $  140,000 |
| End of year | 115,000 | 120,000 |
| Total | $  235,000 | $  260,000 |
| | | |
| Average accounts receivable | $117,500 ($235,000 ÷ 2) | $130,000 ($260,000 ÷ 2) |
| Accounts receivable turnover | 12.7 ($1,498,000 ÷ $117,500) | 9.2 ($1,200,000 ÷ $130,000) |

The increase in Lincoln's accounts receivable turnover from 9.2 to 12.7 indicates that the collection of receivables has improved during 2016. This may be due to a change in how credit is granted, collection practices, or both.

---

[2] If known, *credit* sales should be used in the numerator. Because credit sales are not normally known by external users, we use sales in the numerator.

For Lincoln, the average accounts receivable was computed using the accounts receivable balance at the beginning and the end of the year. When sales are seasonal and, thus, vary throughout the year, monthly balances of receivables are often used. Also, if sales on account include notes receivable as well as accounts receivable, notes and accounts receivable are normally combined for analysis.

**Number of Days' Sales in Receivables** The **number of days' sales in receivables** is computed as follows:

$$\text{Number of Days' Sales in Receivables} = \frac{\text{Average Accounts Receivable}}{\text{Average Daily Sales}}$$

where

$$\text{Average Daily Sales} = \frac{\text{Sales}}{365 \text{ days}}$$

To illustrate, the number of days' sales in receivables for **Lincoln Company** is computed as follows:

|  | **2016** | **2015** |
|---|---|---|
| Average accounts receivable | $117,500 ($235,000 ÷ 2) | $130,000 ($260,000 ÷ 2) |
| Average daily sales | $4,104 ($1,498,000 ÷ 365) | $3,288 ($1,200,000 ÷ 365) |
| Number of days' sales in receivables | 28.6 ($117,500 ÷ $4,104) | 39.5 ($130,000 ÷ $3,288) |

The number of days' sales in receivables is an estimate of the time (in days) that the accounts receivable have been outstanding. The number of days' sales in receivables is often compared with a company's credit terms to evaluate the efficiency of the collection of receivables.

To illustrate, if Lincoln's credit terms are 2/10, n/30, then Lincoln was very *inefficient* in collecting receivables in 2015. In other words, receivables should have been collected in 30 days or less but were being collected in 39.5 days. Although collections improved during 2016 to 28.6 days, there is probably still room for improvement. On the other hand, if Lincoln's credit terms are n/45, then there is probably little room for improving collections.

---

**Example Exercise 17-4** **Accounts Receivable Analysis** OBJ 2

A company reports the following:

| Sales | $960,000 |
|---|---|
| Average accounts receivable (net) | 48,000 |

Determine (a) the accounts receivable turnover and (b) the number of days' sales in receivables. Round to one decimal place.

**Follow My Example 17-4**

a. Accounts Receivable Turnover = Sales ÷ Average Accounts Receivable

= $960,000 ÷ $48,000

= 20.0

b. Number of Days' Sales in Receivables = Average Accounts Receivable ÷ Average Daily Sales

= $48,000 ÷ ($960,000 ÷ 365) = $48,000 ÷ $2,630

= 18.3 days

Practice Exercises: PE 17-4A, PE 17-4B

# Inventory Analysis

A company's ability to manage its inventory effectively is evaluated using **inventory analysis**. It includes the computation and analysis of the following:

- Inventory turnover
- Number of days' sales in inventory

Excess inventory decreases liquidity by tying up funds (cash) in inventory. In addition, excess inventory increases insurance expense, property taxes, storage costs, and other related expenses. These expenses further reduce funds that could be used elsewhere to improve or expand operations.

Excess inventory also increases the risk of losses because of price declines or obsolescence of the inventory. On the other hand, a company should keep enough inventory in stock so that it doesn't lose sales because of lack of inventory.

**Inventory Turnover** The **inventory turnover** is computed as follows:

$$\text{Inventory Turnover} = \frac{\text{Cost of Goods Sold}}{\text{Average Inventory}}$$

To illustrate, the inventory turnover for **Lincoln Company** for 2016 and 2015 is computed as follows. Lincoln's inventory balance at the beginning of 2015 is $311,000.

|  | **2016** | **2015** |
|---|---|---|
| Cost of goods sold | $1,043,000 | $820,000 |
| Inventories: |  |  |
| Beginning of year | $ 283,000 | $311,000 |
| End of year | 264,000 | 283,000 |
| Total | $ 547,000 | $594,000 |
| Average inventory | $273,500 ($547,000 ÷ 2) | $297,000 ($594,000 ÷ 2) |
| Inventory turnover | 3.8 ($1,043,000 ÷ $273,500) | 2.8 ($820,000 ÷ $297,000) |

The increase in Lincoln's inventory turnover from 2.8 to 3.8 indicates that the management of inventory has improved in 2016. The inventory turnover improved because of an increase in the cost of goods sold, which indicates more sales and a decrease in the average inventories.

What is considered a good inventory turnover varies by type of inventory, companies, and industries. For example, grocery stores have a higher inventory turnover than jewelers or furniture stores. Likewise, within a grocery store, perishable foods have a higher turnover than the soaps and cleansers.

**Number of Days' Sales in Inventory** The **number of days' sales in inventory** is computed as follows:

$$\text{Number of Days' Sales in Inventory} = \frac{\text{Average Inventory}}{\text{Average Daily Cost of Goods Sold}}$$

where

$$\text{Average Daily Cost of Goods Sold} = \frac{\text{Cost of Goods Sold}}{365 \text{ days}}$$

To illustrate, the number of days' sales in inventory for **Lincoln Company** is computed as follows:

|  | **2016** | **2015** |
|---|---|---|
| Average inventory | $273,500 ($547,000 ÷ 2) | $297,000 ($594,000 ÷ 2) |
| Average daily cost of goods sold | $2,858 ($1,043,000 ÷ 365) | $2,247 ($820,000 ÷ 365) |
| Number of days' sales in inventory | 95.7 ($273,500 ÷ $2,858) | 132.2 ($297,000 ÷ $2,247) |

The number of days' sales in inventory is a rough measure of the length of time it takes to purchase, sell, and replace the inventory. Lincoln's number of days' sales in inventory improved from 132.2 days to 95.7 days during 2016. This is a major improvement in managing inventory.

**Example Exercise 17-5  Inventory Analysis**                                     OBJ 2

A company reports the following:

| | |
|---|---|
| Cost of goods sold | $560,000 |
| Average inventory | 112,000 |

Determine (a) the inventory turnover and (b) the number of days' sales in inventory. Round to one decimal place.

**Follow My Example 17-5**

a.  Inventory Turnover = Cost of Goods Sold ÷ Average Inventory

         = $560,000 ÷ $112,000

         = 5.0

b.  Number of Days' Sales in Inventory = Average Inventory ÷ Average Daily Cost of Goods Sold

                          = $112,000 ÷ ($560,000 ÷ 365) = $112,000 ÷ $1,534

                          = 73.0 days

Practice Exercises: PE 17-5A, PE 17-5B

## Ratio of Fixed Assets to Long-Term Liabilities

The **ratio of fixed assets to long-term liabilities** provides a measure of whether noteholders or bondholders will be paid. Because fixed assets are often pledged as security for long-term notes and bonds, it is computed as follows:

$$\text{Ratio of Fixed Assets to Long-Term Liabilities} = \frac{\text{Fixed Assets (net)}}{\text{Long-Term Liabilities}}$$

To illustrate, the ratio of fixed assets to long-term liabilities for **Lincoln Company** is computed as follows:

| | 2016 | 2015 |
|---|---|---|
| Fixed assets (net) | $444,500 | $470,000 |
| Long-term liabilities | $100,000 | $200,000 |
| Ratio of fixed assets to long-term liabilities | 4.4 ($444,500 ÷ $100,000) | 2.4 ($470,000 ÷ $200,000) |

During 2016, Lincoln's ratio of fixed assets to long-term liabilities increased from 2.4 to 4.4. This increase was due primarily to Lincoln paying off one-half of its long-term liabilities in 2016.

## Ratio of Liabilities to Stockholders' Equity

The **ratio of liabilities to stockholders' equity** measures how much of the company is financed by debt and equity. It is computed as follows:

$$\text{Ratio of Liabilities to Stockholders' Equity} = \frac{\text{Total Liabilities}}{\text{Total Stockholders' Equity}}$$

To illustrate, the ratio of liabilities to stockholders' equity for **Lincoln Company** is computed as follows:

| | 2016 | 2015 |
|---|---|---|
| Total liabilities | $310,000 | $443,000 |
| Total stockholders' equity | $829,500 | $787,500 |
| Ratio of liabilities to stockholders' equity | 0.4 ($310,000 ÷ $829,500) | 0.6 ($443,000 ÷ $787,500) |

Lincoln's ratio of liabilities to stockholders' equity decreased from 0.6 to 0.4 during 2016. This is an improvement and indicates that Lincoln's creditors have an adequate margin of safety.

## Example Exercise 17-6 Long-Term Solvency Analysis

OBJ 2

The following information was taken from Acme Company's balance sheet:

| | |
|---|---|
| Fixed assets (net) | $1,400,000 |
| Long-term liabilities | 400,000 |
| Total liabilities | 560,000 |
| Total stockholders' equity | 1,400,000 |

Determine the company's (a) ratio of fixed assets to long-term liabilities and (b) ratio of liabilities to total stockholders' equity.

## Follow My Example 17-6

a. Ratio of Fixed Assets to Long-Term Liabilities = Fixed Assets ÷ Long-Term Liabilities

= $1,400,000 ÷ $400,000

= 3.5

b. Ratio of Liabilities to Total Stockholders' Equity = Total Liabilities ÷ Total Stockholders' Equity

= $560,000 ÷ $1,400,000

= 0.4

Practice Exercises: PE 17-6A, PE 17-6B

## Number of Times Interest Charges Are Earned

The **number of times interest charges are earned**, sometimes called the *fixed charge coverage ratio*, measures the risk that interest payments will not be made if earnings decrease. It is computed as follows:

$$\text{Number of Times Interest Charges Are Earned} = \frac{\text{Income Before Income Tax} + \text{Interest Expense}}{\text{Interest Expense}}$$

Interest expense is paid before income taxes. In other words, interest expense is deducted in determining taxable income and, thus, income tax. For this reason, income *before taxes* is used in computing the number of times interest charges are earned.

The *higher* the ratio the more likely interest payments will be paid if earnings decrease. To illustrate, the number of times interest charges are earned for **Lincoln Company** is computed as follows:

| | 2016 | 2015 |
|---|---|---|
| Income before income tax | $162,500 | $134,600 |
| Add interest expense | 6,000 | 12,000 |
| Amount available to pay interest | $168,500 | $146,600 |
| Number of times interest charges are earned | 28.1 ($168,500 ÷ $6,000) | 12.2 ($146,600 ÷ $12,000) |

The number of times interest charges are earned improved from 12.2 to 28.1 during 2016. This indicates that Lincoln has sufficient earnings to pay interest expense.

The number of times interest charges are earned can be adapted for use with dividends on preferred stock. In this case, the *number of times preferred dividends are earned* is computed as follows:

$$\text{Number of Times Preferred Dividends Are Earned} = \frac{\text{Net Income}}{\text{Preferred Dividends}}$$

Since dividends are paid after taxes, net income is used in computing the number of times preferred dividends are earned. The *higher* the ratio, the more likely preferred dividend payments will be paid if earnings decrease.

**Example Exercise 17-7   Times Interest Charges Are Earned**

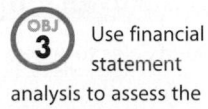

A company reports the following:

| | |
|---|---|
| Income before income tax | $250,000 |
| Interest expense | 100,000 |

Determine the number of times interest charges are earned.

**Follow My Example 17-7**

Number of Times Interest Charges Are Earned = (Income Before Income Tax + Interest Expense) ÷ Interest Expense
= ($250,000 + $100,000) ÷ $100,000
= 3.5

Practice Exercises: PE 17-7A, PE 17-7B

# Profitability Analysis

Profitability analysis focuses on the ability of a company to earn profits. This ability is reflected in the company's operating results, as reported in its income statement. The ability to earn profits also depends on the assets the company has available for use in its operations, as reported in its balance sheet. Thus, income statement and balance sheet relationships are often used in evaluating profitability.

Common profitability analyses include the following:

- Ratio of sales to assets
- Rate earned on total assets
- Rate earned on stockholders' equity
- Rate earned on common stockholders' equity
- Earnings per share on common stock
- Price-earnings ratio
- Dividends per share
- Dividend yield

**OBJ 3** Use financial statement analysis to assess the profitability of a business.

**Note:**
**Profitability analysis focuses on the relationship between operating results and the resources available to a business.**

## Ratio of Sales to Assets

The **ratio of sales to assets** measures how effectively a company uses its assets. It is computed as follows:

$$\text{Ratio of Sales to Assets} = \frac{\text{Sales}}{\substack{\text{Average Total Assets} \\ \text{(excluding long-term investments)}}}$$

Note that any long-term investments are excluded in computing the ratio of sales to assets. This is because long-term investments are unrelated to normal operations and sales.

To illustrate, the ratio of sales to assets for **Lincoln Company** is computed as follows. Total assets (excluding long-term investments) are $1,010,000 at the beginning of 2015.

| | 2016 | 2015 |
|---|---|---|
| Sales | $1,498,000 | $1,200,000 |
| Total assets (excluding long-term investments): | | |
| Beginning of year | $1,053,000* | $1,010,000 |
| End of year | 1,044,500** | 1,053,000* |
| Total | $2,097,500 | $2,063,000 |
| | | |
| Average total assets | $1,048,750 ($2,097,500 ÷ 2) | $1,031,500 ($2,063,000 ÷ 2) |
| Ratio of sales to assets | 1.4 ($1,498,000 ÷ $1,048,750) | 1.2 ($1,200,000 : $1,031,500) |

*($1,230,500 – $177,500)
**($1,139,500 – $95,000)

For Lincoln, the average total assets was computed using total assets (excluding long-term investments) at the beginning and end of the year. The average total assets could also be based on monthly or quarterly averages.

The ratio of sales to assets indicates that Lincoln's use of its operating assets has improved in 2016. This was primarily due to the increase in sales in 2016.

---

**Example Exercise 17-8** **Sales to Assets**      OBJ 3

A company reports the following:

| | |
|---|---|
| Sales | $2,250,000 |
| Average total assets | 1,500,000 |

Determine the ratio of sales to assets.

**Follow My Example 17-8**

Ratio of Sales to Assets = Sales ÷ Average Total Assets
    = $2,250,000 ÷ $1,500,000
    = 1.5

Practice Exercises: PE 17-8A, PE 17-8B

---

## Rate Earned on Total Assets

The **rate earned on total assets** measures the profitability of total assets, without considering how the assets are financed. In other words, this rate is not affected by the portion of assets financed by creditors or stockholders. It is computed as follows:

$$\text{Rate Earned on Total Assets} = \frac{\text{Net Income} + \text{Interest Expense}}{\text{Average Total Assets}}$$

The rate earned on total assets is computed by adding interest expense to net income. By adding interest expense to net income, the effect of whether the assets are financed by creditors (debt) or stockholders (equity) is eliminated. Because net income includes any income earned from long-term investments, the average total assets includes long-term investments as well as the net operating assets.

To illustrate, the rate earned on total assets by **Lincoln Company** is computed as follows. Total assets are $1,187,500 at the beginning of 2015.

| | 2016 | 2015 |
|---|---|---|
| Net income | $ 91,000 | $ 76,500 |
| Plus interest expense | 6,000 | 12,000 |
|    Total | $ 97,000 | $ 88,500 |
| Total assets: | | |
|    Beginning of year | $1,230,500 | $1,187,500 |
|    End of year | 1,139,500 | 1,230,500 |
|    Total | $2,370,000 | $2,418,000 |
| Average total assets | $1,185,000 ($2,370,000 ÷ 2) | $1,209,000 ($2,418,000 ÷ 2) |
| Rate earned on total assets | 8.2% ($97,000 ÷ $1,185,000) | 7.3% ($88,500 ÷ $1,209,000) |

The rate earned on total assets improved from 7.3% to 8.2% during 2016.

The *rate earned on operating assets* is sometimes computed when there are large amounts of nonoperating income and expense. It is computed as follows:

$$\text{Rate Earned on Operating Assets} = \frac{\text{Income from Operations}}{\text{Average Operating Assets}}$$

Because Lincoln Company does not have a significant amount of nonoperating income and expense, the rate earned on operating assets is not illustrated.

**Example Exercise 17-9  Rate Earned on Total Assets**

OBJ 3

A company reports the following income statement and balance sheet information for the current year:

| | |
|---|---:|
| Net income | $ 125,000 |
| Interest expense | 25,000 |
| Average total assets | 2,000,000 |

Determine the rate earned on total assets.

**Follow My Example 17-9**

Rate Earned on Total Assets = (Net Income + Interest Expense) ÷ Average Total Assets
$$= (\$125{,}000 + \$25{,}000) \div \$2{,}000{,}000$$
$$= \$150{,}000 \div \$2{,}000{,}000$$
$$= 7.5\%$$

Practice Exercises: PE 17-9A, PE 17-9B

## Rate Earned on Stockholders' Equity

The **rate earned on stockholders' equity** measures the rate of income earned on the amount invested by the stockholders. It is computed as follows:

$$\text{Rate Earned on Stockholders' Equity} = \frac{\text{Net Income}}{\text{Average Total Stockholders' Equity}}$$

To illustrate, the rate earned on stockholders' equity for **Lincoln Company** is computed as follows. Total stockholders' equity is $750,000 at the beginning of 2015.

| | 2016 | 2015 |
|---|---|---|
| Net income | $ 91,000 | $ 76,500 |
| Stockholders' equity: | | |
| Beginning of year | $ 787,500 | $ 750,000 |
| End of year | 829,500 | 787,500 |
| Total | $1,617,000 | $1,537,500 |
| | | |
| Average stockholders' equity | $808,500 ($1,617,000 ÷ 2) | $768,750 ($1,537,500 ÷ 2) |
| Rate earned on stockholders' equity | 11.3% ($91,000 ÷ $808,500) | 10.0% ($76,500 ÷ $768,750) |

The rate earned on stockholders' equity improved from 10.0% to 11.3% during 2016.

**Leverage** involves using debt to increase the return on an investment. The rate earned on stockholders' equity is normally higher than the rate earned on total assets. This is because of the effect of leverage.

For **Lincoln Company**, the effect of leverage for 2016 is 3.1% and for 2015 is 2.7% computed as follows:

| | 2016 | 2015 |
|---|---|---|
| Rate earned on stockholders' equity | 11.3% | 10.0% |
| Less rate earned on total assets | 8.2 | 7.3 |
| Effect of leverage | 3.1% | 2.7% |

Exhibit 8 shows the 2016 and 2015 effects of leverage for Lincoln.

## Rate Earned on Common Stockholders' Equity

The **rate earned on common stockholders' equity** measures the rate of profits earned on the amount invested by the common stockholders. It is computed as follows:

$$\text{Rate Earned on Common Stockholders' Equity} = \frac{\text{Net Income} - \text{Preferred Dividends}}{\text{Average Common Stockholders' Equity}}$$

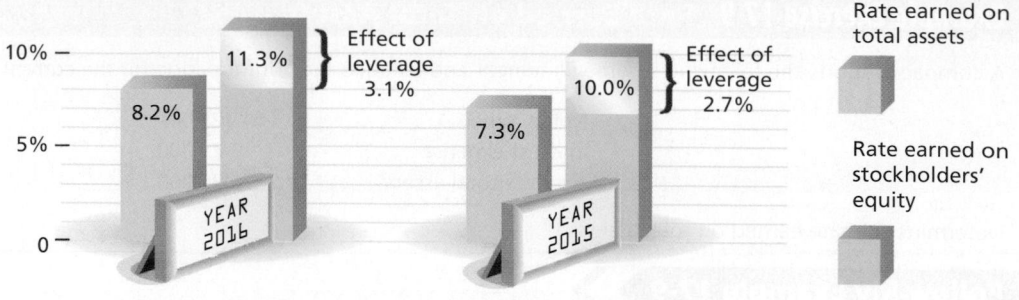

**EXHIBIT 8**

**Effect of Leverage**

Because preferred stockholders rank ahead of the common stockholders in their claim on earnings, any preferred dividends are subtracted from net income in computing the rate earned on common stockholders' equity.

**Lincoln Company** had $150,000 of 6% preferred stock outstanding on December 31, 2016 and 2015. Thus, preferred dividends of $9,000 ($150,000 × 6%) are deducted from net income. Lincoln's common stockholders' equity is determined as follows:

|  | December 31 | | |
|---|---|---|---|
|  | **2016** | **2015** | **2014** |
| Common stock, $10 par | $500,000 | $500,000 | $500,000 |
| Retained earnings | 179,500 | 137,500 | 100,000 |
| Common stockholders' equity | $679,500 | $637,500 | $600,000 |

The retained earnings on December 31, 2014, of $100,000 is the same as the retained earnings on January 1, 2015, as shown in Lincoln's retained earnings statement in Exhibit 4.

Using this information, the rate earned on common stockholders' equity for Lincoln is computed as follows:

|  | **2016** | **2015** |
|---|---|---|
| Net income | $ 91,000 | $ 76,500 |
| Less preferred dividends | 9,000 | 9,000 |
| Total | $ 82,000 | $ 67,500 |
| Common stockholders' equity: |  |  |
| Beginning of year | $ 637,500 | $ 600,000 |
| End of year | 679,500* | 637,500** |
| Total | $1,317,000 | $1,237,500 |
| Average common stockholders' equity | $658,500 ($1,317,000 ÷ 2) | $618,750 ($1,237,500 ÷ 2) |
| Rate earned on common stockholders' equity | 12.5% ($82,000 ÷ $658,500) | 10.9% ($67,500 ÷ $618,750) |

*($829,500 – $150,000)
**($787,500 – $150,000)

Lincoln's rate earned on common stockholders' equity improved from 10.9% to 12.5% in 2016. This rate differs from the rates earned by Lincoln on total assets and stockholders' equity, which follow:

|  | 2016 | 2015 |
|---|---|---|
| Rate earned on total assets | 8.2% | 7.3% |
| Rate earned on stockholders' equity | 11.3% | 10.0% |
| Rate earned on common stockholders' equity | 12.5% | 10.9% |

These rates differ because of leverage, as discussed in the preceding section.

**Example Exercise 17-10    Common Stockholders' Profitability Analysis**

OBJ 3

A company reports the following:

| | |
|---|---:|
| Net income | $ 125,000 |
| Preferred dividends | 5,000 |
| Average stockholders' equity | 1,000,000 |
| Average common stockholders' equity | 800,000 |

Determine (a) the rate earned on stockholders' equity and (b) the rate earned on common stockholders' equity.

**Follow My Example 17-10**

a.  Rate Earned on Stockholders' Equity = Net Income ÷ Average Stockholders' Equity

$$= \$125,000 \div \$1,000,000$$

$$= 12.5\%$$

b.  Rate Earned on Common Stockholders' Equity = (Net Income − Preferred Dividends) ÷ Average
Common Stockholders' Equity

$$= (\$125,000 - \$5,000) \div \$800,000$$

$$= 15\%$$

Practice Exercises: PE 17-10A, PE 17-10B

# Earnings per Share on Common Stock

**Earnings per share (EPS) on common stock** measures the share of profits that are earned by a share of common stock. Earnings per share must be reported in the income statement. As a result, earnings per share (EPS) is often reported in the financial press. It is computed as follows:

$$\text{Earnings per Share (EPS) on Common Stock} = \frac{\text{Net Income} - \text{Preferred Dividends}}{\text{Shares of Common Stock Outstanding}}$$

When preferred and common stock are outstanding, preferred dividends are subtracted from net income to determine the income related to the common shares.

To illustrate, the earnings per share (EPS) of common stock for **Lincoln Company** is computed as follows:

| | 2016 | 2015 |
|---|---|---|
| Net income | $91,000 | $76,500 |
| Preferred dividends | 9,000 | 9,000 |
| Total | $82,000 | $67,500 |
| Shares of common stock outstanding | 50,000 | 50,000 |
| Earnings per share on common stock | $1.64 ($82,000 ÷ 50,000) | $1.35 ($67,500 ÷ 50,000) |

Lincoln had $150,000 of 6% preferred stock outstanding on December 31, 2016 and 2015. Thus, preferred dividends of $9,000 ($150,000 × 6%) are deducted from net income in computing earnings per share on common stock.

Lincoln did not issue any additional shares of common stock in 2016. If Lincoln had issued additional shares in 2016, a weighted average of common shares outstanding during the year would have been used.

Lincoln's earnings per share (EPS) on common stock improved from $1.35 to $1.64 during 2016.

Lincoln Company has a simple capital structure with only common stock and preferred stock outstanding. Many corporations, however, have complex capital structures with various types of equity securities outstanding, such as convertible preferred stock,

stock options, and stock warrants. In such cases, the possible effects of such securities on the shares of common stock outstanding are considered in reporting earnings per share. These possible effects are reported separately as *earnings per common share assuming dilution* or *diluted earnings per share*. This topic is described and illustrated in advanced accounting courses and textbooks.

## Price-Earnings Ratio

The **price-earnings (P/E) ratio** on common stock measures a company's future earnings prospects. It is often quoted in the financial press and is computed as follows:

$$\text{Price-Earnings (P/E) Ratio} = \frac{\text{Market Price per Share of Common Stock}}{\text{Earnings per Share on Common Stock}}$$

To illustrate, the price-earnings (P/E) ratio for **Lincoln Company** is computed as follows:

|  | 2016 | 2015 |
|---|---|---|
| Market price per share of common stock | $41.00 | $27.00 |
| Earnings per share on common stock | $1.64 | $1.35 |
| Price-earnings ratio on common stock | 25 ($41 ÷ $1.64) | 20 ($27 ÷ $1.35) |

The price-earnings ratio improved from 20 to 25 during 2016. In other words, a share of common stock of Lincoln was selling for 20 times earnings per share at the end of 2015. At the end of 2016, the common stock was selling for 25 times earnings per share. This indicates that the market expects Lincoln to experience favorable earnings in the future.

---

### Example Exercise 17-11 Earnings per Share and Price-Earnings Ratio

 OBJ 3

A company reports the following:

| | |
|---|---|
| Net income | $250,000 |
| Preferred dividends | $15,000 |
| Shares of common stock outstanding | 20,000 |
| Market price per share of common stock | $35.25 |

a. Determine the company's earnings per share on common stock.

b. Determine the company's price-earnings ratio. Round to one decimal place.

### Follow My Example 17-11

a. Earnings per Share on Common Stock = (Net Income – Preferred Dividends) ÷ Shares of Common Stock Outstanding

= ($250,000 – $15,000) ÷ 20,000

= $11.75

b. Price-Earnings Ratio = Market Price per Share of Common Stock ÷ Earnings per Share on Common Stock

= $35.25 ÷ $11.75

= 3.0

Practice Exercises: PE 17-11A, PE 17-11B

---

## Dividends per Share

**Dividends per share** measures the extent to which earnings are being distributed to common shareholders. It is computed as follows:

$$\text{Dividends per Share} = \frac{\text{Dividends on Common Stock}}{\text{Shares of Common Stock Outstanding}}$$

To illustrate, the dividends per share for **Lincoln Company** are computed as follows:

|  | 2016 | 2015 |
|---|---|---|
| Dividends on common stock | $40,000 | $30,000 |
| Shares of common stock outstanding | 50,000 | 50,000 |
| Dividends per share of common stock | $0.80 ($40,000 ÷ 50,000) | $0.60 ($30,000 ÷ 50,000) |

The dividends per share of common stock increased from $0.60 to $0.80 during 2016. Dividends per share are often reported with earnings per share. Comparing the two per-share amounts indicates the extent to which earnings are being retained for use in operations. To illustrate, the dividends and earnings per share for **Lincoln Company** are shown in Exhibit 9.

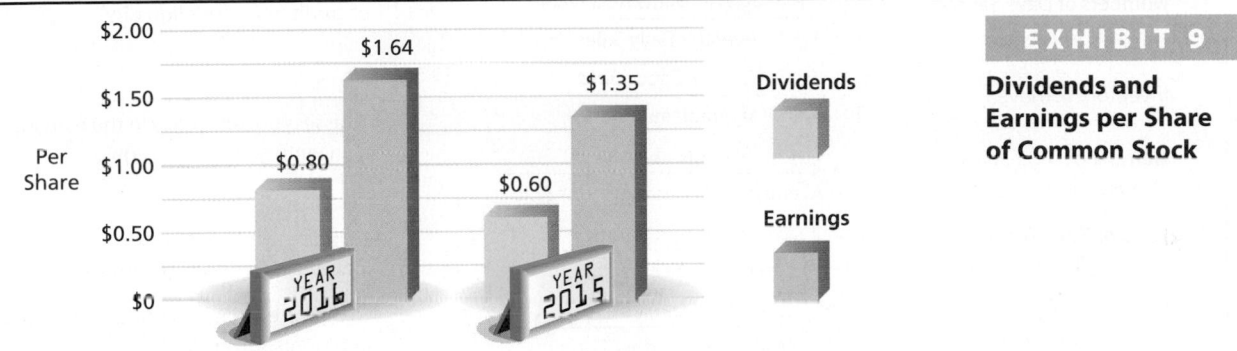

**EXHIBIT 9**

**Dividends and Earnings per Share of Common Stock**

## Dividend Yield

The **dividend yield** on common stock measures the rate of return to common stockholders from cash dividends. It is of special interest to investors whose objective is to earn revenue (dividends) from their investment. It is computed as follows:

 The dividends per share, dividend yield, and P/E ratio of a common stock are normally quoted on the daily listing of stock prices in *The Wall Street Journal* and on Yahoo!'s finance Web site.

$$\text{Dividend Yield} = \frac{\text{Dividends per Share of Common Stock}}{\text{Market Price per Share of Common Stock}}$$

To illustrate, the dividend yield for **Lincoln Company** is computed as follows:

|  | 2016 | 2015 |
|---|---|---|
| Dividends per share of common stock | $0.80 | $0.60 |
| Market price per share of common stock | $41.00 | $27.00 |
| Dividend yield on common stock | 2.0% ($0.80 ÷ $41) | 2.2% ($0.60 ÷ $27) |

The dividend yield declined slightly from 2.2% to 2.0% in 2016. This decline was primarily due to the increase in the market price of Lincoln's common stock.

## Summary of Analytical Measures

Exhibit 10 shows a summary of the solvency and profitability measures discussed in this chapter. The type of industry and the company's operations usually affect which measures are used. In many cases, additional measures are used for a specific industry. For example, airlines use *revenue per passenger mile* and *cost per available seat* as profitability measures. Likewise, hotels use *occupancy rates* as a profitability measure.

The analytical measures shown in Exhibit 10 are a useful starting point for analyzing a company's solvency and profitability. However, they are not a substitute for sound judgment. For example, the general economic and business environment should always be considered in analyzing a company's future prospects. In addition, any trends and interrelationships among the measures should be carefully studied.

| EXHIBIT 10 | Summary of Analytical Measures |
| --- | --- |

| | Method of Computation | Use |
| --- | --- | --- |
| **Liquidity and Solvency Measures** | | |
| Working Capital | Current Assets – Current Liabilities | To indicate the ability to meet currently maturing obligations (measures solvency) |
| Current Ratio | $\dfrac{\text{Current Assets}}{\text{Current Liabilities}}$ | |
| Quick Ratio | $\dfrac{\text{Quick Assets}}{\text{Current Liabilities}}$ | To indicate instant debt-paying ability (measures solvency) |
| Accounts Receivable Turnover | $\dfrac{\text{Sales}}{\text{Average Accounts Receivable}}$ | To assess the efficiency in collecting receivables and in the management of credit (measures liquidity) |
| Numbers of Days' Sales in Receivables | $\dfrac{\text{Average Accounts Receivable}}{\text{Average Daily Sales}}$ | |
| Inventory Turnover | $\dfrac{\text{Cost of Goods Sold}}{\text{Average Inventory}}$ | To assess the efficiency in the management of inventory (measures liquidity) |
| Number of Days' Sales in Inventory | $\dfrac{\text{Average Inventory}}{\text{Average Daily Cost of Goods Sold}}$ | |
| Ratio of Fixed Assets to Long-Term Liabilities | $\dfrac{\text{Fixed Assets (net)}}{\text{Long-Term Liabilities}}$ | To indicate the margin of safety to long-term creditors (measures solvency) |
| Ratio of Liabilities to Stockholders' Equity | $\dfrac{\text{Total Liabilities}}{\text{Total Stockholders' Equity}}$ | To indicate the margin of safety to creditors (measures solvency) |
| Number of Times Interest Charges Are Earned | $\dfrac{\text{Income Before Income Tax} + \text{Interest Expense}}{\text{Interest Expense}}$ | To assess the risk to debtholders in terms of number of times interest charges were earned (measures solvency) |
| Number of Times Preferred Dividends Are Earned | $\dfrac{\text{Net Income}}{\text{Preferred Dividends}}$ | To assess the risk to preferred stockholders in terms of the number of times preferred dividends were earned (measures solvency) |
| **Profitability Measures** | | |
| Ratio of Sales to Assets | $\dfrac{\text{Sales}}{\text{Average Total Assets (excluding long-term investments)}}$ | To assess the effectiveness in the use of assets |
| Rate Earned on Total Assets | $\dfrac{\text{Net Income} + \text{Interest Expense}}{\text{Average Total Assets}}$ | To assess the profitability of the assets |
| Rate Earned on Stockholders' Equity | $\dfrac{\text{Net Income}}{\text{Average Total Stockholders' Equity}}$ | To assess the profitability of the investment by stockholders |
| Rate Earned on Common Stockholders' Equity | $\dfrac{\text{Net Income} - \text{Preferred Dividends}}{\text{Average Common Stockholders' Equity}}$ | To assess the profitability of the investment by common stockholders |
| Earnings per Share (EPS) on Common Stock | $\dfrac{\text{Net Income} - \text{Preferred Dividends}}{\text{Shares of Common Stock Outstanding}}$ | |
| Price-Earnings (P/E) Ratio | $\dfrac{\text{Market Price per Share of Common Stock}}{\text{Earnings per Share on Common Stock}}$ | To indicate future earnings prospects, based on the relationship between market value of common stock and earnings |
| Dividends per Share | $\dfrac{\text{Dividends on Common Stock}}{\text{Shares of Common Stock Outstanding}}$ | To indicate the extent to which earnings are being distributed to common stockholders |
| Dividend Yield | $\dfrac{\text{Dividends per Share of Common Stock}}{\text{Market Price per Share of Common Stock}}$ | To indicate the rate of return to common stockholders in terms of dividends |

# Integrity, Objectivity, and Ethics in Business

## CHARACTERISTICS OF FINANCIAL STATEMENT FRAUD

Each year the Association of Certified Fraud Examiners conducts a worldwide survey examining the characteristics of corporate fraud. The most recent study found that:

- 43.3% of frauds were detected by a tip from an employee or someone close to the company;
- Frauds committed by owners and executives tended to be much larger than those caused by employees;

- Most people who are caught committing fraud are first time offenders with clean employment histories; and
- In 81% of the cases, the person committing the fraud displayed one or more behavioral red flags such as living beyond their means, financial difficulties, and excessive control issues.

Fraud examiners can use these trends to help them narrow their focus when searching for fraud.

Source: 2012 Report to the Nations, Association of Certified Fraud Examiners, 2012.

# Corporate Annual Reports

**OBJ 4** Describe the contents of corporate annual reports.

Public corporations issue annual reports summarizing their operating activities for the past year and plans for the future. Such annual reports include the financial statements and the accompanying notes. In addition, annual reports normally include the following sections:

- Management discussion and analysis
- Report on internal control
- Report on fairness of the financial statements

See Appendix D for more information.

## Management Discussion and Analysis

**Management's Discussion and Analysis (MD&A)** is required in annual reports filed with the Securities and Exchange Commission. It includes management's analysis of current operations and its plans for the future. Typical items included in the MD&A are as follows:

- Management's analysis and explanations of any significant changes between the current and prior years' financial statements.
- Important accounting principles or policies that could affect interpretation of the financial statements, including the effect of changes in accounting principles or the adoption of new accounting principles.
- Management's assessment of the company's liquidity and the availability of capital to the company.
- Significant risk exposures that might affect the company.
- Any "off-balance-sheet" arrangements such as leases not included directly in the financial statements. Such arrangements are discussed in advanced accounting courses and textbooks.

## Report on Internal Control

The Sarbanes-Oxley Act of 2002 requires a report on internal control by management. The report states management's responsibility for establishing and maintaining internal control. In addition, management's assessment of the effectiveness of internal controls over financial reporting is included in the report.

Sarbanes-Oxley also requires a public accounting firm to verify management's conclusions on internal control. Thus, two reports on internal control, one by management and one by a public accounting firm, are included in the annual report. In some situations, these may be combined into a single report on internal control.

## Report on Fairness of the Financial Statements

All publicly held corporations are required to have an independent audit (examination) of their financial statements. The Certified Public Accounting (CPA) firm that conducts the audit renders an opinion, called the *Report of Independent Registered Public Accounting Firm*, on the fairness of the statements.

An opinion stating that the financial statements present fairly the financial position, results of operations, and cash flows of the company is said to be an *unqualified opinion*, sometimes called a *clean opinion*. Any report other than an unqualified opinion raises a "red flag" for financial statement users and requires further investigation as to its cause.

The annual report of Nike Inc. is shown in Appendix C. The Nike report includes the financial statements as well as the MD&A Report on Internal Control and the Report on Fairness of the Financial Statements.

## Integrity, Objectivity, and Ethics in Business

**BUY LOW, SELL HIGH**

Research analysts work for banks, brokerages, or other financial institutions. Their job is to estimate the value of a company's common stock by reviewing and evaluating the company's business model, strategic plan, and financial performance. Based on this analysis, the analyst develops an estimate of a stock's value, which is called its *fundamental value*. Analysts then advise their clients to "buy" or "sell" a company's stock based on the following guidelines:

| | |
|---|---|
| Current market price is greater than fundamental value | Sell |
| Current market price is lower than fundamental value | Buy |

If analysts are doing their job well, their clients will enjoy large returns by buying stocks at low prices and selling them at high prices.

# APPENDIX

# Unusual Items on the Income Statement

Generally accepted accounting principles require that unusual items be reported separately on the income statement. This is because such items do not occur frequently and are typically unrelated to current operations. Without separate reporting of these items, users of the financial statements might be misled about current and future operations.

Unusual items on the income statement are classified as one of the following:

- Affecting the *current period* income statement
- Affecting a *prior period* income statement

## Unusual Items Affecting the Current Period's Income Statement

Unusual items affecting the current period's income statement include the following:

- Discontinued operations
- Extraordinary items

These items are reported separately on the income statement for any period in which they occur.

**Discontinued Operations** A company may discontinue a component of its operations by selling or abandoning the component's operations. For example, a retailer might decide to sell its product only online and, thus, discontinue selling its merchandise at its retail outlets (stores).

If the discontinued component is (1) the result of a strategic shift and (2) has a major effect on the entity's operations and financial results, any gain or loss on discontinued operations is reported on the income statement as a *Gain (or loss) from discontinued operations*. It is reported immediately following *Income from continuing operations*.

To illustrate, assume that Jones Corporation produces and sells electrical products, hardware supplies, and lawn equipment. Because of a lack of profits, Jones discontinues its electrical products operation and sells the remaining inventory and other assets at a loss of $100,000. Exhibit 11 illustrates the reporting of the loss on discontinued operations.[3]

| | |
|---|---:|
| **Jones Corporation** | |
| **Income Statement** | |
| **For the Year Ended December 31, 2016** | |
| Sales | $12,350,000 |
| Cost of merchandise sold | 5,800,000 |
| Gross profit | $ 6,550,000 |
| Selling and administrative expenses | 5,240,000 |
| Income from continuing operations before income tax | $ 1,310,000 |
| Income tax expense | 620,000 |
| Income from continuing operations | $ 690,000 |
| Loss on discontinued operations | 100,000 |
| Income before extraordinary items | $ 590,000 |
| Extraordinary items: | |
| Gain on condemnation of land | 150,000 |
| Net income | $ 740,000 |

**EXHIBIT 11**

**Unusual Items in the Income Statement**

In addition, a note to the financial statements should describe the operations sold, including the date operations were discontinued, and details about the assets, liabilities, income, and expenses of the discontinued component.

**Extraordinary Items** An **extraordinary item** is defined as an event or a transaction that has both of the following characteristics:

- Unusual in nature
- Infrequent in occurrence

Gains and losses from natural disasters such as floods, earthquakes, and fires are normally reported as extraordinary items, provided that they occur infrequently. Gains or losses from land or buildings taken (condemned) for public use are also reported as extraordinary items.

Any gain or loss from extraordinary items is reported on the income statement as *Gain (or loss) from extraordinary item*. It is reported immediately following *Income from continuing operations* and any *Gain (or loss) on discontinued operations*.

To illustrate, assume that land owned by Jones Corporation was taken for public use (condemned) by the local government. The condemnation of the land resulted in a gain of $150,000. Exhibit 11 illustrates the reporting of the extraordinary gain.[4,5]

---

[3] The gain or loss on discontinued operations is reported net of any tax effects. To simplify, the tax effects are not specifically identified in Exhibit 11.

[4] The gain or loss on extraordinary operations is reported net of any tax effects.

[5] At the time of this writing, the Financial Accounting Standards Board had released an exposure draft, which proposes eliminating extraordinary items as a separate line item on the income statement. The outcome of this proposal was uncertain at the time of this writing.

**Reporting Earnings per Share** Earnings per common share should be reported separately for discontinued operations and extraordinary items. To illustrate, a partial income statement for Jones Corporation is shown in Exhibit 12. The company has 200,000 shares of common stock outstanding.

Exhibit 12 reports earnings per common share for income from continuing operations, discontinued operations, and extraordinary items. However, only earnings per share for income from continuing operations and net income are required by generally accepted accounting principles. The other per-share amounts may be presented in the notes to the financial statements.

| EXHIBIT 12 | Jones Corporation |
| --- | --- |
| **Income Statement with Earnings per Share** | **Income Statement**<br>**For the Year Ended December 31, 2016** |

| | |
| --- | --- |
| Earnings per common share: | |
| Income from continuing operations................................................. | $3.45 |
| Loss on discontinued operations ..................................................... | 0.50 |
| Income before extraordinary items ................................................. | $2.95 |
| Extraordinary items: | |
| Gain on condemnation of land ..................................................... | 0.75 |
| Net income ...................................................................... | $3.70 |

## Unusual Items Affecting the Prior Period's Income Statement

An unusual item may occur that affects a prior period's income statement. Two such items are as follows:

- Errors in applying generally accepted accounting principles
- Changes from one generally accepted accounting principle to another

If an error is discovered in a prior period's financial statement, the prior-period statement and all following statements are restated and thus corrected.

A company may change from one generally accepted accounting principle to another. In this case, the prior-period financial statements are restated as if the new accounting principle had always been used.[5]

For both of the preceding items, the current-period earnings are not affected. That is, only the earnings reported in prior periods are restated. However, because the prior earnings are restated, the beginning balance of Retained Earnings may also have to be restated. This, in turn, may cause the restatement of other balance sheet accounts. Illustrations of these types of adjustments and restatements are provided in advanced accounting courses.

[5] Changes from one acceptable depreciation method to another acceptable depreciation method are an exception to this general rule and are to be treated prospectively as a change in estimate, as discussed in Chapter 10.

# At a Glance 17

## 1 Describe basic financial statement analytical methods.

**Key Points** The basic financial statements provide much of the information users need to make economic decisions. Analytical procedures are used to compare items on a current financial statement with related items on earlier statements, or to examine relationships within a financial statement.

| Learning Outcomes | Example Exercises | Practice Exercises |
|---|---|---|
| • Prepare a vertical analysis from a company's financial statements. | EE17-1 | PE17-1A, 17-1B |
| • Prepare a horizontal analysis from a company's financial statements. | EE17-2 | PE17-2A, 17-2B |
| • Prepare common-sized financial statements. | | |

## 2 Use financial statement analysis to assess the solvency of a business.

**Key Points** All users of financial statements are interested in the ability of a business to convert assets into cash (liquidity), pay its debts (solvency), and earn income (profitability). Liquidity, solvency, and profitability are interrelated. Liquidity and solvency are normally assessed by examining the following: current position analysis, accounts receivable analysis, inventory analysis, the ratio of fixed assets to long-term liabilities, the ratio of liabilities to stockholders' equity, and the number of times interest charges are earned.

| Learning Outcomes | Example Exercises | Practice Exercises |
|---|---|---|
| • Determine working capital. | | |
| • Compute and interpret the current ratio. | EE17-3 | PE17-3A, 17-3B |
| • Compute and interpret the quick ratio. | EE17-3 | PE17-3A, 17-3B |
| • Compute and interpret accounts receivable turnover. | EE17-4 | PE17-4A, 17-4B |
| • Compute and interpret the number of days' sales in receivables. | EE17-4 | PE17-4A, 17-4B |
| • Compute and interpret inventory turnover. | EE17-5 | PE17-5A, 17-5B |
| • Compute and interpret the number of days' sales in inventory. | EE17-5 | PE17-5A, 17-5B |
| • Compute and interpret the ratio of fixed assets to long-term liabilities. | EE17-6 | PE17-6A, 17-6B |
| • Compute and interpret the ratio of liabilities to stockholders' equity. | EE17-6 | PE17-6A, 17-6B |
| • Compute and interpret the number of times interest charges are earned. | EE17-7 | PE17-7A, 17-7B |

**Use financial statement analysis to assess the profitability of a business.**

**Key Points**   Profitability analysis focuses on the ability of a company to earn profits. This ability is reflected in the company's operating results as reported on the income statement and resources available as reported on the balance sheet. Major analyses include the ratio of sales to assets, the rate earned on total assets, the rate earned on stockholders' equity, the rate earned on common stockholders' equity, earnings per share on common stock, the price-earnings ratio, dividends per share, and dividend yield.

| Learning Outcomes | Example Exercises | Practice Exercises |
|---|---|---|
| • Compute and interpret the ratio of sales to assets. | EE17-8 | PE17-8A, 17-8B |
| • Compute and interpret the rate earned on total assets. | EE17-9 | PE17-9A, 17-9B |
| • Compute and interpret the rate earned on stockholders' equity. | EE17-10 | PE17-10A, 17-10B |
| • Compute and interpret the rate earned on common stockholders' equity. | EE17-10 | PE17-10A, 17-10B |
| • Compute and interpret the earnings per share on common stock. | EE17-11 | PE17-11A, 17-11B |
| • Compute and interpret the price-earnings ratio. | EE17-11 | PE17-11A, 17-11B |
| • Compute and interpret the dividends per share and dividend yield. | | |
| • Describe the uses and limitations of analytical measures. | | |

**Describe the contents of corporate annual reports.**

**Key Points**   Corporations normally issue annual reports to their stockholders and other interested parties. Such reports summarize the corporation's operating activities for the past year and plans for the future.

| Learning Outcome | Example Exercises | Practice Exercises |
|---|---|---|
| • Describe the elements of a corporate annual report. | | |

# Key Terms

accounts receivable analysis (804)
accounts receivable turnover (804)
common-sized statement (800)
current position analysis (802)
current ratio (802)
dividend yield (815)
dividends per share (814)
earnings per share (EPS) on common stock (813)
extraordinary item (819)
horizontal analysis (796)
inventory analysis (806)
inventory turnover (806)

leverage (811)
liquidity (801)
Management's Discussion and Analysis (MD&A) (817)
number of days' sales in inventory (806)
number of days' sales in receivables (805)
number of times interest charges are earned (808)
price-earnings (P/E) ratio (814)
profitability (801)
quick assets (803)
quick ratio (803)

rate earned on common stockholders' equity (811)
rate earned on stockholders' equity (811)
rate earned on total assets (810)
ratio of fixed assets to long-term liabilities (807)
ratio of liabilities to stockholders' equity (807)
ratio of sales to assets (809)
solvency (801)
vertical analysis (799)
working capital (802)

# Illustrative Problem

Rainbow Paint Co.'s comparative financial statements for the years ending December 31, 2016 and 2015, are as follows. The market price of Rainbow Paint Co.'s common stock was $25 on December 31, 2016, and $30 on December 31, 2015.

| Rainbow Paint Co.<br>Comparative Income Statement<br>For the Years Ended December 31, 2016 and 2015 | | |
|---|---|---|
| | **2016** | **2015** |
| Sales | $5,000,000 | $3,200,000 |
| Cost of goods sold | 3,400,000 | 2,080,000 |
| Gross profit | $1,600,000 | $1,120,000 |
| Selling expenses | $ 650,000 | $ 464,000 |
| Administrative expenses | 325,000 | 224,000 |
| Total operating expenses | $ 975,000 | $ 688,000 |
| Income from operations | $ 625,000 | $ 432,000 |
| Other income | 25,000 | 19,200 |
| | $ 650,000 | $ 451,200 |
| Other expense (interest) | 105,000 | 64,000 |
| Income before income tax | $ 545,000 | $ 387,200 |
| Income tax expense | 300,000 | 176,000 |
| Net income | $ 245,000 | $ 211,200 |

| Rainbow Paint Co.<br>Comparative Retained Earnings Statement<br>For the Years Ended December 31, 2016 and 2015 | | |
|---|---|---|
| | **2016** | **2015** |
| Retained earnings, January 1 | $723,000 | $581,800 |
| Add net income for year | 245,000 | 211,200 |
| Total | $968,000 | $793,000 |
| Deduct dividends: | | |
| On preferred stock | $ 40,000 | $ 40,000 |
| On common stock | 45,000 | 30,000 |
| Total | $ 85,000 | $ 70,000 |
| Retained earnings, December 31 | $883,000 | $723,000 |

### Rainbow Paint Co.
### Comparative Balance Sheet
### December 31, 2016 and 2015

|  | Dec. 31, 2016 | Dec. 31, 2015 |
|---|---|---|
| **Assets** | | |
| Current assets: | | |
| Cash...................................................... | $ 175,000 | $ 125,000 |
| Temporary investments...................................... | 150,000 | 50,000 |
| Accounts receivable (net) ................................... | 425,000 | 325,000 |
| Inventories............................................... | 720,000 | 480,000 |
| Prepaid expenses.......................................... | 30,000 | 20,000 |
| Total current assets...................................... | $1,500,000 | $1,000,000 |
| Long-term investments........................................ | 250,000 | 225,000 |
| Property, plant, and equipment (net) ........................... | 2,093,000 | 1,948,000 |
| Total assets ............................................... | $3,843,000 | $3,173,000 |
| **Liabilities** | | |
| Current liabilities............................................ | $ 750,000 | $ 650,000 |
| Long-term liabilities: | | |
| Mortgage note payable, 10%, due 2017 ....................... | $ 410,000 | — |
| Bonds payable, 8%, due 2020................................ | 800,000 | $ 800,000 |
| Total long-term liabilities ................................ | $1,210,000 | $ 800,000 |
| Total liabilities ............................................. | $1,960,000 | $1,450,000 |
| **Stockholders' Equity** | | |
| Preferred 8% stock, $100 par ................................. | $ 500,000 | $ 500,000 |
| Common stock, $10 par....................................... | 500,000 | 500,000 |
| Retained earnings........................................... | 883,000 | 723,000 |
| Total stockholders' equity ................................ | $1,883,000 | $1,723,000 |
| Total liabilities and stockholders' equity......................... | $3,843,000 | $3,173,000 |

## Instructions

Determine the following measures for 2016:

1. Working capital

2. Current ratio

3. Quick ratio

4. Accounts receivable turnover

5. Number of days' sales in receivables

6. Inventory turnover

7. Number of days' sales in inventory

8. Ratio of fixed assets to long-term liabilities

9. Ratio of liabilities to stockholders' equity

10. Number of times interest charges are earned

11. Number of times preferred dividends are earned

12. Ratio of sales to assets

13. Rate earned on total assets

14. Rate earned on stockholders' equity

15. Rate earned on common stockholders' equity

16. Earnings per share on common stock

17. Price-earnings ratio

18. Dividends per share

19. Dividend yield

## Solution

(Ratios are rounded to the nearest single digit after the decimal point.)

1. Working capital: $750,000
   $1,500,000 − $750,000

2. Current ratio: 2.0
   $1,500,000 ÷ $750,000

3. Quick ratio: 1.0
   $750,000 ÷ $750,000

4. Accounts receivable turnover: 13.3
   $5,000,000 ÷ [($425,000 + $325,000) ÷ 2]

5. Number of days' sales in receivables: 27.4 days
   $5,000,000 ÷ 365 days = $13,699
   $375,000 ÷ $13,699

6. Inventory turnover: 5.7
   $3,400,000 ÷ [($720,000 + $480,000) ÷ 2]

7. Number of days' sales in inventory: 64.4 days
   $3,400,000 ÷ 365 days = $9,315
   $600,000 ÷ $9,315

8. Ratio of fixed assets to long-term liabilities: 1.7
   $2,093,000 ÷ $1,210,000

9. Ratio of liabilities to stockholders' equity: 1.0
   $1,960,000 ÷ $1,883,000

10. Number of times interest charges are earned: 6.2
    ($545,000 + $105,000) ÷ $105,000

11. Number of times preferred dividends are earned: 6.1
    $245,000 ÷ $40,000

12. Ratio of sales to assets: 1.5
    $5,000,000 ÷ [($3,593,000 + $2,948,000) ÷ 2]

13. Rate earned on total assets: 10.0%
    ($245,000 + $105,000) ÷ [($3,843,000 + $3,173,000) ÷ 2]

14. Rate earned on stockholders' equity: 13.6%
    $245,000 ÷ [($1,883,000 + $1,723,000) ÷ 2]

15. Rate earned on common stockholders' equity: 15.7%
    ($245,000 − $40,000) ÷ [($1,383,000 + $1,223,000) ÷ 2]

16. Earnings per share on common stock: $4.10
    ($245,000 − $40,000) ÷ 50,000 shares

17. Price-earnings ratio: 6.1
    $25 ÷ $4.10

18. Dividends per share: $0.90
    $45,000 ÷ 50,000 shares

19. Dividend yield: 3.6%
    $0.90 ÷ $25

# Discussion Questions

1. What is the difference between horizontal and vertical analysis of financial statements?

2. What is the advantage of using comparative statements for financial analysis rather than statements for a single date or period?

3. The current year's amount of net income (after income tax) is 25% larger than that of the preceding year. Does this indicate an improved operating performance? Discuss.

4. How would the current and quick ratios of a service business compare?

5. a. Why is it advantageous to have a high inventory turnover?
   b. Is it possible to have a high inventory turnover and a high number of days' sales in inventory? Discuss.

6. What do the following data taken from a comparative balance sheet indicate about the company's ability to borrow additional funds on a long-term basis in the current year as compared to the preceding year?

| | Current Year | Preceding Year |
| --- | --- | --- |
| Fixed assets (net) | $1,260,000 | $1,360,000 |
| Total long-term liabilities | 300,000 | 400,000 |

7. a. How does the rate earned on total assets differ from the rate earned on stockholders' equity?
   b. Which ratio is normally higher? Explain.

8. Kroger, a grocery store, recently had a price-earnings ratio of 13.7, while the average price-earnings ratio in the grocery store industry was 22.5. What might explain this difference?

9. The dividend yield of Suburban Propane was 7.7% in a recent year, and the dividend yield of Google was 0% in the same year. What might explain the difference between these ratios?

10. Describe two reports provided by independent auditors in the annual report to shareholders.

# Practice Exercises

SHOW
ME HOW

EE 17-1 *p. 799*

## PE 17-1A   Horizontal analysis

OBJ. 1

The comparative temporary investments and inventory balances of a company follow.

| | Current Year | Previous Year |
| --- | --- | --- |
| Temporary investments | $59,280 | $52,000 |
| Inventory | 70,680 | 76,000 |

Based on this information, what is the amount and percentage of increase or decrease that would be shown in a balance sheet with horizontal analysis?

SHOW
ME HOW

EE 17-1 *p. 799*

## PE 17-1B   Horizontal analysis

OBJ. 1

The comparative accounts payable and long-term debt balances for a company follow.

| | Current Year | Previous Year |
| --- | --- | --- |
| Accounts payable | $111,000 | $100,000 |
| Long-term debt | 132,680 | 124,000 |

Based on this information, what is the amount and percentage of increase or decrease that would be shown in a balance sheet with horizontal analysis?

EE 17-2 *p. 800*

SHOW
ME HOW

## PE 17-2A Vertical analysis

OBJ. 1

Income statement information for Axiom Corporation follows:

| | |
|---|---|
| Sales | $725,000 |
| Cost of goods sold | 391,500 |
| Gross profit | 333,500 |

Prepare a vertical analysis of the income statement for Axiom Corporation.

EE 17-2 *p. 800*

SHOW
ME HOW

## PE 17-2B Vertical analysis

OBJ. 1

Income statement information for Einsworth Corporation follows:

| | |
|---|---|
| Sales | $1,200,000 |
| Cost of goods sold | 780,000 |
| Gross profit | 420,000 |

Prepare a vertical analysis of the income statement for Einsworth Corporation.

EE 17-3 *p. 804*

SHOW
ME HOW

## PE 17-3A Current position analysis

OBJ. 2

The following items are reported on a company's balance sheet:

| | |
|---|---|
| Cash | $160,000 |
| Marketable securities | 75,000 |
| Accounts receivable (net) | 65,000 |
| Inventory | 140,000 |
| Accounts payable | 200,000 |

Determine (a) the current ratio and (b) the quick ratio. Round to one decimal place.

EE 17-3 *p. 804*

SHOW
ME HOW

## PE 17-3B Current position analysis

OBJ. 2

The following items are reported on a company's balance sheet:

| | |
|---|---|
| Cash | $210,000 |
| Marketable securities | 120,000 |
| Accounts receivable (net) | 110,000 |
| Inventory | 160,000 |
| Accounts payable | 200,000 |

Determine (a) the current ratio and (b) the quick ratio. Round to one decimal place.

EE 17-4 *p. 805*

SHOW
ME HOW

## PE 17-4A Accounts receivable analysis

OBJ. 2

A company reports the following:

| | |
|---|---|
| Sales | $832,000 |
| Average accounts receivable (net) | 80,000 |

Determine (a) the accounts receivable turnover and (b) the number of days' sales in receivables. Round to one decimal place.

EE 17-4 *p. 805*

SHOW
ME HOW

## PE 17-4B Accounts receivable analysis

OBJ. 2

A company reports the following:

| | |
|---|---|
| Sales | $3,150,000 |
| Average accounts receivable (net) | 210,000 |

Determine (a) the accounts receivable turnover and (b) the number of days' sales in receivables. Round to one decimal place.

EE 17-5 *p. 807*

SHOW
ME HOW

**PE 17-5A** **Inventory analysis** OBJ. 2

A company reports the following:

| | |
|---|---|
| Cost of goods sold | $630,000 |
| Average inventory | 90,000 |

Determine (a) the inventory turnover and (b) the number of days' sales in inventory. Round to one decimal place.

---

EE 17-5 *p. 807*

SHOW
ME HOW

**PE 17-5B** **Inventory analysis** OBJ. 2

A company reports the following:

| | |
|---|---|
| Cost of goods sold | $435,000 |
| Average inventory | 72,500 |

Determine (a) the inventory turnover and (b) the number of days' sales in inventory. Round to one decimal place.

---

EE 17-6 *p. 808*

SHOW
ME HOW

**PE 17-6A** **Long-term solvency analysis** OBJ. 2

The following information was taken from Kellman Company's balance sheet:

| | |
|---|---|
| Fixed assets (net) | $2,000,000 |
| Long-term liabilities | 800,000 |
| Total liabilities | 1,000,000 |
| Total stockholders' equity | 625,000 |

Determine the company's (a) ratio of fixed assets to long-term liabilities and (b) ratio of liabilities to stockholders' equity.

---

EE 17-6 *p. 808*

SHOW
ME HOW

**PE 17-6B** **Long-term solvency analysis** OBJ. 2

The following information was taken from Charu Company's balance sheet:

| | |
|---|---|
| Fixed assets (net) | $860,000 |
| Long-term liabilities | 200,000 |
| Total liabilities | 600,000 |
| Total stockholders' equity | 250,000 |

Determine the company's (a) ratio of fixed assets to long-term liabilities and (b) ratio of liabilities to stockholders' equity.

---

EE 17-7 *p. 809*

SHOW
ME HOW

**PE 17-7A** **Times interest charges are earned** OBJ. 2

A company reports the following:

| | |
|---|---|
| Income before income tax | $4,000,000 |
| Interest expense | 400,000 |

Determine the number of times interest charges are earned.

---

EE17-7 *p. 809*

SHOW
ME HOW

**PE 17-7B** **Times interest charges are earned** OBJ. 2

A company reports the following:

| | |
|---|---|
| Income before income tax | $8,000,000 |
| Interest expense | 500,000 |

Determine the number of times interest charges are earned.

---

EE 17-8 *p. 810*

SHOW
ME HOW

**PE 17-8A** **Sales to assets** OBJ. 3

A company reports the following:

| | |
|---|---|
| Sales | $1,800,000 |
| Average total assets (excluding long-term investments) | 1,125,000 |

Determine the ratio of sales to assets.

EE 17-8 *p. 810*

SHOW
ME HOW

**PE 17-8B   Sales to assets**                                                         OBJ. 3

A company reports the following:

| | |
|---|---|
| Sales | $4,400,000 |
| Average total assets (excluding long-term investments) | 2,000,000 |

Determine the ratio of sales to assets.

---

EE 17-9 *p. 811*

SHOW
ME HOW

**PE 17-9A   Rate earned on total assets**                                             OBJ. 3

A company reports the following income statement and balance sheet information for the current year:

| | |
|---|---|
| Net income | $ 250,000 |
| Interest expense | 100,000 |
| Average total assets | 2,500,000 |

Determine the rate earned on total assets.

---

EE 17-9 *p. 811*

SHOW
ME HOW

**PE 17-9B   Rate earned on total assets**                                             OBJ. 3

A company reports the following income statement and balance sheet information for the current year:

| | |
|---|---|
| Net income | $ 410,000 |
| Interest expense | 90,000 |
| Average total assets | 5,000,000 |

Determine the rate earned on total assets.

---

EE 17-10 *p. 813*

SHOW
ME HOW

**PE 17-10A   Common stockholders' profitability analysis**                            OBJ. 3

A company reports the following:

| | |
|---|---|
| Net income | $ 375,000 |
| Preferred dividends | 75,000 |
| Average stockholders' equity | 2,500,000 |
| Average common stockholders' equity | 1,875,000 |

Determine (a) the rate earned on stockholders' equity and (b) the rate earned on common stockholders' equity. Round to one decimal place.

---

EE 17-10 *p. 813*

SHOW
ME HOW

**PE 17-10B   Common stockholders' profitability analysis**                            OBJ. 3

A company reports the following:

| | |
|---|---|
| Net income | $1,000,000 |
| Preferred dividends | 50,000 |
| Average stockholders' equity | 6,250,000 |
| Average common stockholders' equity | 3,800,000 |

Determine (a) the rate earned on stockholders' equity and (b) the rate earned on common stockholders' equity. Round to one decimal place.

---

EE 17-11 *p. 814*

SHOW
ME HOW

**PE 17-11A   Earnings per share and price-earnings ratio**                            OBJ. 3

A company reports the following:

| | |
|---|---|
| Net income | $185,000 |
| Preferred dividends | $25,000 |
| Shares of common stock outstanding | 100,000 |
| Market price per share of common stock | $20 |

a. Determine the company's earnings per share on common stock.

b. Determine the company's price-earnings ratio.

EE 17-11  p. 814

SHOW
ME HOW

**PE 17-11B   Earnings per share and price-earnings ratio**                     **OBJ. 3**

A company reports the following:

| | |
|---|---|
| Net income | $410,000 |
| Preferred dividends | $60,000 |
| Shares of common stock outstanding | 50,000 |
| Market price per share of common stock | $84 |

a. Determine the company's earnings per share on common stock.

b. Determine the company's price-earnings ratio.

# Exercises

**EX 17-1   Vertical analysis of income statement**                              **OBJ. 1**

✔ a. Current year net
income: $175,000; 7.0%
of sales

SHOW
ME HOW

Not on
Test

Revenue and expense data for Gresham Inc. for two recent years are as follows:

| | Current Year | % | Previous Year | % |
|---|---|---|---|---|
| Sales | $2,500,000 | | $2,350,000 | |
| Cost of goods sold = Gross Profit | 1,500,000 | | 1,292,500 | |
| Selling expenses | 300,000 | | 376,000 | |
| Administrative expenses | 375,000 | | 305,500 | |
| Income tax expense | 150,000 | | 141,000 | |

a. Prepare an income statement in comparative form, stating each item for both years as a percent of sales. Round to one decimal place.

b. Comment on the significant changes disclosed by the comparative income statement.

**EX 17-2   Vertical analysis of income statement**                              **OBJ. 1**

✔ a. Current fiscal year
income from continuing
operations, 13.0% of
revenues

The following comparative income statement (in thousands of dollars) for the two recent fiscal years was adapted from the annual report of **Speedway Motorsports, Inc.**, owner and operator of several major motor speedways, such as the Atlanta, Texas, and Las Vegas Motor Speedways.

| | Current Year | Previous Year |
|---|---|---|
| Revenues: | | |
| Admissions | $116,034 | $130,239 |
| Event-related revenue | 151,562 | 163,621 |
| NASCAR broadcasting revenue | 192,662 | 185,394 |
| Other operating revenue | 29,902 | 26,951 |
| Total revenue | $490,160 | $506,205 |
| Expenses and other: | | |
| Direct expense of events | $101,402 | $106,204 |
| NASCAR purse and sanction fees | 122,950 | 120,146 |
| Other direct expenses | 18,908 | 20,352 |
| General and administrative | 183,215 | 241,223 |
| Total expenses and other | $426,475 | $487,925 |
| Income from continuing operations | $ 63,685 | $ 18,280 |

a. Prepare a comparative income statement for these two years in vertical form, stating each item as a percent of revenues. Round to one decimal place.

b. Comment on the significant changes.

✔ a. Tannenhill net
income: $120,000; 3.0%
of sales

SHOW
ME HOW

**EX 17-3   Common-sized income statement**                                      **OBJ. 1**

Revenue and expense data for the current calendar year for Tannenhill Company and for the electronics industry are as follows. The Tannenhill Company data are expressed in dollars. The electronics industry averages are expressed in percentages.

| | Tannenhill Company | Electronics Industry Average |
|---|---|---|
| Sales | $4,000,000 | 100.0% |
| Cost of goods sold | 2,120,000 | 60.0 |
| Gross profit | $1,880,000 | 40.0% |
| Selling expenses | $1,080,000 | 24.0% |
| Administrative expenses | 640,000 | 14.0 |
| Total operating expenses | $1,720,000 | 38.0% |
| Operating income | $ 160,000 | 2.0% |
| Other income | 120,000 | 3.0 |
| | $ 280,000 | 5.0% |
| Other expense | 80,000 | 2.0 |
| Income before income tax | $ 200,000 | 3.0% |
| Income tax expense | 80,000 | 2.0 |
| Net income | $ 120,000 | 1.0% |

a. Prepare a common-sized income statement comparing the results of operations for Tannenhill Company with the industry average. Round to one decimal place.

b. ➤ As far as the data permit, comment on significant relationships revealed by the comparisons.

---

**EX 17-4** **Vertical analysis of balance sheet** OBJ. 1

✔ Retained earnings, Current year, 40.0%

SHOW
ME HOW

Balance sheet data for Novak Company on December 31, the end of two recent fiscal years, follows:

| | Current Year | Previous Year |
|---|---|---|
| Current assets | $1,300,000 | $ 945,000 |
| Property, plant, and equipment | 3,000,000 | 3,150,000 |
| Intangible assets | 700,000 | 405,000 |
| Current liabilities | 1,000,000 | 720,000 |
| Long-term liabilities | 1,500,000 | 1,575,000 |
| Common stock | 500,000 | 495,000 |
| Retained earnings | 2,000,000 | 1,710,000 |

Prepare a comparative balance sheet for both years, stating each asset as a percent of total assets and each liability and stockholders' equity item as a percent of the total liabilities and stockholders' equity. Round to one decimal place.

---

**EX 17-5** **Horizontal analysis of the income statement** OBJ. 1

✔ a. Net income increase, 80.0%

SHOW
ME HOW

Income statement data for Moreno Company for two recent years ended December 31, are as follows:

| | Current Year | Previous Year |
|---|---|---|
| Sales | $1,120,000 | $1,000,000 |
| Cost of goods sold | 971,250 | 875,000 |
| Gross profit | $ 148,750 | $ 125,000 |
| Selling expenses | $ 71,250 | $ 62,500 |
| Administrative expenses | 56,000 | 50,000 |
| Total operating expenses | $ 127,250 | $ 112,500 |
| Income before income tax | $ 21,500 | $ 12,500 |
| Income tax expense | 8,000 | 5,000 |
| Net Income | $ 13,500 | $ 7,500 |

a. Prepare a comparative income statement with horizontal analysis, indicating the increase (decrease) for the current year when compared with the previous year. Round to one decimal place.

b. ➤ What conclusions can be drawn from the horizontal analysis?

### EX 17-6 Current position analysis

OBJ. 2

The following data were taken from the balance sheet of Gostkowski Company at the end of two recent fiscal years:

|  | Current Year | Previous Year |
| --- | --- | --- |
| Cash | $ 480,000 | $ 392,000 |
| Marketable securities | 576,000 | 411,600 |
| Accounts and notes receivable (net) | 384,000 | 316,400 |
| Inventories | 408,000 | 333,200 |
| Prepaid expenses | 552,000 | 506,800 |
| Total current assets | $2,400,000 | $1,960,000 |
| Accounts and notes payable (short-term) | $ 600,000 | $ 525,000 |
| Accrued liabilities | 200,000 | 175,000 |
| Total current liabilities | $ 800,000 | $ 700,000 |

a. Determine for each year (1) the working capital, (2) the current ratio, and (3) the quick ratio. Round ratios to one decimal place.

b. ▬▬▶What conclusions can be drawn from these data as to the company's ability to meet its currently maturing debts?

### EX 17-7 Current position analysis

OBJ. 2

PepsiCo, Inc., the parent company of Frito-Lay snack foods and Pepsi beverages, had the following current assets and current liabilities at the end of two recent years:

|  | Current Year (in millions) | Previous Year (in millions) |
| --- | --- | --- |
| Cash and cash equivalents | $ 6,297 | $4,067 |
| Short-term investments, at cost | 322 | 358 |
| Accounts and notes receivable, net | 7,041 | 6,912 |
| Inventories | 3,581 | 3,827 |
| Prepaid expenses and other current assets | 1,479 | 2,277 |
| Short-term obligations | 4,815 | 6,205 |
| Accounts payable | 12,274 | 11,949 |

a. Determine the (1) current ratio and (2) quick ratio for both years. Round to one decimal place.

b. ▬▬▶What conclusions can you draw from these data?

### EX 17-8 Current position analysis

OBJ. 2

The bond indenture for the 10-year, 9% debenture bonds issued January 2, 2015, required working capital of $100,000, a current ratio of 1.5, and a quick ratio of 1.0 at the end of each calendar year until the bonds mature. At December 31, 2016, the three measures were computed as follows:

| 1. Current assets: |  |  |
| --- | --- | --- |
| Cash......................................... | $102,000 |  |
| Temporary investments ...................... | 48,000 |  |
| Accounts and notes receivable (net)........... | 120,000 |  |
| Inventories.................................. | 36,000 |  |
| Prepaid expenses............................ | 24,000 |  |
| Intangible assets ........................... | 124,800 |  |
| Property, plant, and equipment............... | 55,200 |  |
| Total current assets (net) .................. |  | $510,000 |
| Current liabilities: |  |  |
| Accounts and short-term notes payable ....... | $ 96,000 |  |
| Accrued liabilities........................... | 204,000 |  |
| Total current liabilities .................... |  | 300,000 |
| Working capital ............................. |  | $210,000 |
| 2. Current ratio .................................. | 1.7 | $510,000 ÷ $300,000 |
| 3. Quick ratio.................................... | 1.2 | $115,200 ÷ $ 96,000 |

a. List the errors in the determination of the three measures of current position analysis.

b. ▬▬▬▶ Is the company satisfying the terms of the bond indenture?

---

### EX 17-9  Accounts receivable analysis

OBJ. 2

✔ a. Accounts receivable turnover, 2016, 7.0

SHOW
ME HOW

The following data are taken from the financial statements of Krawcheck Inc. Terms of all sales are 2/10, n/55.

|  | 2016 | 2015 | 2014 |
|---|---|---|---|
| Accounts receivable, end of year | $ 500,000 | $ 475,000 | $440,000 |
| Sales on account | 3,412,500 | 2,836,500 | |

a. For 2015 and 2016, determine (1) the accounts receivable turnover and (2) the number of days' sales in receivables. Round to the nearest dollar and one decimal place.

b. ▬▬▬▶ What conclusions can be drawn from these data concerning accounts receivable and credit policies?

---

### EX 17-10  Accounts receivable analysis

OBJ. 2

Xavier Stores Company and Lestrade Stores Inc. are large retail department stores. Both companies offer credit to their customers through their own credit card operations. Information from the financial statements for both companies for two recent years is as follows (all numbers are in millions):

|  | Xavier | Lestrade |
|---|---|---|
| Merchandise sales | $8,500,000 | $4,585,000 |
| Credit card receivables—beginning | 820,000 | 600,000 |
| Credit card receviables—ending | 880,000 | 710,000 |

a. Determine the (1) accounts receivable turnover and (2) the number of days' sales in receivables for both companies. Round to one decimal place.

b. ▬▬▬▶ Compare the two companies with regard to their credit card policies.

---

### EX 17-11  Inventory analysis

OBJ. 2

✔ a. Inventory turnover, current year, 7.5

SHOW
ME HOW

The following data were extracted from the income statement of Saleh Inc.:

|  | Current Year | Previous Year |
|---|---|---|
| Sales | $12,750,000 | $13,284,000 |
| Beginning inventories | 840,000 | 800,000 |
| Cost of goods sold | 6,375,000 | 7,380,000 |
| Ending inventories | 860,000 | 840,000 |

a. Determine for each year (1) the inventory turnover and (2) the number of days' sales in inventory. Round to the nearest dollar and one decimal place.

b. ▬▬▬▶ What conclusions can be drawn from these data concerning the inventories?

---

### EX 17-12  Inventory analysis

OBJ. 2

✔ a. Dell inventory turnover, 32.1

Dell Inc. and Hewlett-Packard Company (HP) compete with each other in the personal computer market. Dell's primary strategy is to assemble computers to customer orders, rather than for inventory. Thus, for example, Dell will build and deliver a computer within four days of a customer entering an order on a Web page. Hewlett-Packard, on the other hand, builds some computers prior to receiving an order, then sells from this inventory once an order is received. Selected financial information for both companies from a recent year's financial statements follows (in millions):

|  | Dell Inc. | Hewlett-Packard Company |
|---|---|---|
| Sales | $56,940 | $120,357 |
| Cost of goods sold | 44,754 | 92,385 |
| Inventory, beginning of period | 1,382 | 6,317 |
| Inventory, end of period | 1,404 | 7,490 |

a. Determine for both companies (1) the inventory turnover and (2) the number of days' sales in inventory. Round to one decimal place.

b. ━━━━▶Interpret the inventory ratios by considering Dell's and Hewlett-Packard's operating strategies.

---

**EX 17-13 Ratio of liabilities to stockholders' equity and number of times interest** OBJ. 2
**charges are earned**

✔ a. Ratio of liabilities to stockholders' equity, current year, 0.9

The following data were taken from the financial statements of Hunter Inc. for December 31 of two recent years:

|  | Current Year | Previous Year |
| --- | --- | --- |
| Accounts payable | $ 924,000 | $ 800,000 |
| Current maturities of serial bonds payable | 200,000 | 200,000 |
| Serial bonds payable, 10%, issued 2009, due 2019 | 1,000,000 | 1,200,000 |
| Common stock, $10 par value | 250,000 | 250,000 |
| Paid-in capital in excess of par | 1,250,000 | 1,250,000 |
| Retained earnings | 860,000 | 500,000 |

The income before income tax was $480,000 and $420,000 for the current and previous years, respectively.

a. Determine the ratio of liabilities to stockholders' equity at the end of each year. Round to one decimal place.

b. Determine the number of times the bond interest charges are earned during the year for both years. Round to one decimal place.

c. ━━━━▶What conclusions can be drawn from these data as to the company's ability to meet its currently maturing debts?

---

**EX 17-14 Ratio of liabilities to stockholders' equity and number of times interest** OBJ. 2
**charges are earned**

✔ a. Hasbro, 1.9

Hasbro and Mattel, Inc., are the two largest toy companies in North America. Condensed liabilities and stockholders' equity from a recent balance sheet are shown for each company as follows (in thousands):

|  | Hasbro | Mattel |
| --- | --- | --- |
| Current liabilities | $ 960,435 | $ 1,716,012 |
| Long-term debt | 1,396,421 | 1,100,000 |
| Deferred liabilities | 461,152 | 643,729 |
| Total liabilities | $ 2,818,008 | $ 3,459,741 |
| Shareholders' equity: |  |  |
| Common stock | $ 104,847 | $ 441,369 |
| Additional paid in capital | 655,943 | 1,727,682 |
| Retained earnings | 3,354,545 | 3,515,181 |
| Accumulated other comprehensive loss and other equity items | (72,307) | (464,486) |
| Treasury stock, at cost | (2,535,649) | (2,152,702) |
| Total stockholders' equity | $ 1,507,379 | $ 3,067,044 |
| Total liabilities and stockholders' equity | $ 4,325,387 | $ 6,526,785 |

The income from operations and interest expense from the income statement for each company were as follows (in thousands):

|  | Hasbro | Mattel |
| --- | --- | --- |
| Income from operations (before income tax) | $453,402 | $945,045 |
| Interest expense | 117,403 | 88,835 |

a. Determine the ratio of liabilities to stockholders' equity for both companies. Round to one decimal place.

b. Determine the number of times interest charges are earned for both companies. Round to one decimal place.

c. ━━━━▶Interpret the ratio differences between the two companies.

**EX 17-15 Ratio of liabilities to stockholders' equity and ratio of fixed assets to long-term liabilities** OBJ. 2

✔ a. Mondelez International, Inc., 1.3

Recent balance sheet information for two companies in the food industry, Mondelez International, Inc., and The Hershey Company, is as follows (in thousands of dollars):

|  | Mondelez | Hershey |
|---|---|---|
| Net property, plant, and equipment | $10,010,000 | $1,674,071 |
| Current liabilities | 14,873,000 | 1,471,110 |
| Long-term debt | 15,574,000 | 1,530,967 |
| Other long-term liabilities | 12,816,000 | 716,013 |
| Stockholders' equity | 32,215,000 | 1,036,749 |

a. Determine the ratio of liabilities to stockholders' equity for both companies. Round to one decimal place.

b. Determine the ratio of fixed assets to long-term liabilities for both companies. Round to one decimal place.

c. ━━━▶ Interpret the ratio differences between the two companies.

---

**EX 17-16 Ratio of sales to assets** OBJ. 3

✔ a. YRC Worldwide, 1.5

Three major segments of the transportation industry are motor carriers, such as YRC Worldwide; railroads, such as Union Pacific; and transportation arrangement services, such as C.H. Robinson Worldwide Inc. Recent financial statement information for these three companies is shown as follows (in thousands of dollars):

|  | YRC Worldwide | Union Pacific | C.H. Robinson Worldwide Inc. |
|---|---|---|---|
| Sales | $4,334,640 | $16,965,000 | $9,274,305 |
| Average total assets | 2,812,504 | 42,636,000 | 1,914,974 |

a. Determine the ratio of sales to assets for all three companies. Round to one decimal place.

b. ━━━▶ Assume that the ratio of sales to assets for each company represents their respective industry segment. Interpret the differences in the ratio of sales to assets in terms of the operating characteristics of each of the respective segments.

---

**EX 17-17 Profitability ratios** OBJ. 3

✔ a. Rate earned on total assets, 2016, 12.0%

The following selected data were taken from the financial statements of Robinson Inc. for December 31, 2016, 2015 and 2014:

|  | December 31 | | |
|---|---|---|---|
|  | 2016 | 2015 | 2014 |
| Total assets ......................................... | $4,800,000 | $4,400,000 | $4,000,000 |
| Notes payable (8% interest) ......................... | 2,250,000 | 2,250,000 | 2,250,000 |
| Common stock...................................... | 250,000 | 250,000 | 250,000 |
| Preferred 4% stock, $100 par | | | |
| (no change during year) ........................... | 500,000 | 500,000 | 500,000 |
| Retained earnings.................................. | 1,574,000 | 1,222,000 | 750,000 |

**SHOW ME HOW**

The 2016 net income was $372,000, and the 2015 net income was $492,000. No dividends on common stock were declared between 2014 and 2016.

a. Determine the rate earned on total assets, the rate earned on stockholders' equity, and the rate earned on common stockholders' equity for the years 2015 and 2016. Round to one decimal place.

b. ━━━▶ What conclusions can be drawn from these data as to the company's profitability?

### EX 17-18 Profitability ratios

OBJ. 3

Ralph Lauren Corp. sells men's apparel through company-owned retail stores. Recent financial information for Ralph Lauren follows (all numbers in thousands):

|  | Fiscal Year 3 | Fiscal Year 2 |  |
|---|---|---|---|
| Net income | $567,600 | $479,500 |  |
| Interest expense | 18,300 | 22,200 |  |
|  | **Fiscal Year 3** | **Fiscal Year 2** | **Fiscal Year 1** |
| Total assets (at end of fiscal year) | $4,981,100 | $4,648,900 | $4,356,500 |
| Total stockholders' equity (at end of fiscal year) | 3,304,700 | 3,116,600 | 2,735,100 |

Assume the apparel industry average rate earned on total assets is 8.0%, and the average rate earned on stockholders' equity is 10.0% for the year ended April 2, Year 3.

a. Determine the rate earned on total assets for Ralph Lauren for fiscal Years 2 and 3. Round to one digit after the decimal place.

b. Determine the rate earned on stockholders' equity for Ralph Lauren for fiscal Years 2 and 3. Round to one decimal place.

c. ▬▬▶ Evaluate the two-year trend for the profitability ratios determined in (a) and (b).

d. ▬▬▶ Evaluate Ralph Lauren's profit performance relative to the industry.

### EX 17-19 Six measures of solvency or profitability

OBJ. 2, 3

The following data were taken from the financial statements of Gates Inc. for the current fiscal year. Assuming that long-term investments totaled $3,000,000 throughout the year and that total assets were $7,000,000 at the beginning of the current fiscal year, determine the following: (a) ratio of fixed assets to long-term liabilities, (b) ratio of liabilities to stockholders' equity, (c) ratio of sales to assets, (d) rate earned on total assets, (e) rate earned on stockholders' equity, and (f) rate earned on common stockholders' equity. Round to one decimal place.

| | | | |
|---|---|---|---|
| Property, plant, and equipment (net) . . . . . . . . . . . . . . . . . . . . . | | | $ 3,200,000 |
| Liabilities: | | | |
|    Current liabilities. . . . . . . . . . . . . . . . . . . . . . . . . . . . . . . . . . . | | $1,000,000 | |
|    Mortgage note payable, 6%, issued 2005, due 2021 . . . . . . | | 2,000,000 | |
|    Total liabilities . . . . . . . . . . . . . . . . . . . . . . . . . . . . . . . . . . . | | | $ 3,000,000 |
| Stockholders' equity: | | | |
|    Preferred $10 stock, $100 par (no change during year) . . . | | | $ 1,000,000 |
|    Common stock, $10 par (no change during year) . . . . . . . . | | | 2,000,000 |
| Retained earnings: | | | |
|    Balance, beginning of year. . . . . . . . . . . . . . . . . . . . . . . . . . | $1,570,000 | | |
|    Net income . . . . . . . . . . . . . . . . . . . . . . . . . . . . . . . . . . . . . . | 930,000 | $2,500,000 | |
|    Preferred dividends . . . . . . . . . . . . . . . . . . . . . . . . . . . . . . . | $ 100,000 | | |
|    Common dividends . . . . . . . . . . . . . . . . . . . . . . . . . . . . . . . . | 400,000 | 500,000 | |
|    Balance, end of year . . . . . . . . . . . . . . . . . . . . . . . . . . . . . . . | | | 2,000,000 |
| Total stockholders' equity . . . . . . . . . . . . . . . . . . . . . . . . . . . . . | | | $ 5,000,000 |
| Sales . . . . . . . . . . . . . . . . . . . . . . . . . . . . . . . . . . . . . . . . . . . . . . | | | $18,900,000 |
| Interest expense . . . . . . . . . . . . . . . . . . . . . . . . . . . . . . . . . . . . | | | $ 120,000 |

### EX 17-20 Six measures of solvency or profitability

OBJ. 2, 3

The balance sheet for Garcon Inc. at the end of the current fiscal year indicated the following:

| | |
|---|---|
| Bonds payable, 8% (issued in 2006, due in 2026) | $5,000,000 |
| Preferred $4 stock, $50 par | 2,500,000 |
| Common stock, $10 par | 5,000,000 |

Income before income tax was $3,000,000, and income taxes were $1,200,000 for the current year. Cash dividends paid on common stock during the current year totaled $1,200,000. The common stock was selling for $32 per share at the end of the year. Determine each of the following: (a) number of times bond interest charges are earned, (b) number of times preferred dividends are earned, (c) earnings per share on common stock, (d) price-earnings ratio, (e) dividends per share of common stock, and (f) dividend yield. Round to one decimal place, except earnings per share, which should be rounded to two decimal places.

---

**EX 17-21    Earnings per share, price-earnings ratio, dividend yield**    OBJ. 3

✔ b. Price-earnings ratio, 15.0

SHOW
ME HOW

The following information was taken from the financial statements of Tolbert Inc. for December 31 of the current fiscal year:

| | |
|---|---|
| Common stock, $20 par (no change during the year) | $10,000,000 |
| Preferred $4 stock, $40 par (no change during the year) | 2,500,000 |

The net income was $1,750,000 and the declared dividends on the common stock were $1,125,000 for the current year. The market price of the common stock is $45 per share.

For the common stock, determine (a) the earnings per share, (b) the price-earnings ratio, (c) the dividends per share, and (d) the dividend yield. Round to one decimal place, except earnings per share, which should be rounded to two decimal places.

---

**EX 17-22    Price-earnings ratio; dividend yield**    OBJ. 3

The table that follows shows the stock price, earnings per share, and dividends per share for three companies for a recent year:

| | Price | Earnings per Share | Dividends per Share |
|---|---|---|---|
| Deere & Co. | $ 86.20 | $ 8.71 | $2.04 |
| Google | 873.32 | 36.75 | 0.00 |
| The Coca-Cola Company | 39.79 | 1.97 | 1.02 |

a. Determine the price-earnings ratio and dividend yield for the three companies. Round to one decimal place.

b. ➤ Explain the differences in these ratios across the three companies.

---

**Appendix**

**EX 17-23    Earnings per share, extraordinary item**

✔ b. Earnings per share on common stock, $7.60

The net income reported on the income statement of Cutler Co. was $4,000,000. There were 500,000 shares of $10 par common stock and 100,000 shares of $2 preferred stock outstanding throughout the current year. The income statement included two extraordinary items: an $800,000 gain from condemnation of land and a $400,000 loss arising from flood damage, both after applicable income tax. Determine the per-share figures for common stock for (a) income before extraordinary items and (b) net income.

---

**Appendix**

**EX 17-24    Extraordinary item**

Assume that the amount of each of the following items is material to the financial statements. Classify each item as either normally recurring (NR) or extraordinary (E).

a. Loss on the disposal of equipment considered to be obsolete because of the development of new technology.

b. Uninsured loss on building due to hurricane damage. The building was purchased by the company in 1910 and had not previously incurred hurricane damage.

c. Gain on sale of land condemned by the local government for a public works project.

d. Uninsured flood loss. (Flood insurance is unavailable because of periodic flooding in the area.)

e. Interest revenue on notes receivable.

f. Uncollectible accounts expense.

g. Loss on sale of investments in stocks and bonds.

**Appendix**

**EX 17-25 Income statement and earnings per share for extraordinary items and discontinued operations**

Apex Inc. reports the following for a recent year:

| | |
|---|---|
| Income from continuing operations before income tax | $1,000,000 |
| Extraordinary property loss from hurricane | $140,000* |
| Loss from discontinued operations | $240,000* |
| Weighted average number of shares outstanding | 20,000 |
| Applicable tax rate | 40% |

*Net of any tax effect.

a. Prepare a partial income statement for Apex Inc., beginning with income from continuing operations before income tax.

b. Calculate the earnings per common share for Apex Inc., including per-share amounts for unusual items.

**Appendix**

**EX 17-26 Unusual items**

Discuss whether Colston Company correctly reported the following items in the financial statements:

a. In a recent year, the company discovered a clerical error in the prior year's accounting records. As a result, the reported net income for the previous year was overstated by $45,000. The company corrected this error by restating the prior-year financial statements.

b. In a recent year, the company voluntarily changed its method of accounting for long-term construction contracts from the percentage of completion method to the completed contract method. Both methods are acceptable under generally acceptable accounting principles. The cumulative effect of this change was reported as a separate component of income in the current period income statement.

# Problems: Series A

**PR 17-1A Horizontal analysis of income statement** OBJ. 1

✔ 1. Sales, 12.5% increase

General Ledger

SHOW ME HOW

For 2016, Clapton Company reported a decline in net income. At the end of the year, S. Hand, the president, is presented with the following condensed comparative income statement:

**Clapton Company**
**Comparative Income Statement**
**For the Years Ended December 31, 2016 and 2015**

| | 2016 | 2015 |
|---|---|---|
| Sales | $6,750,000 | $6,000,000 |
| Cost of goods sold | 2,480,000 | 2,000,000 |
| Gross profit | $4,270,000 | $4,000,000 |
| Selling expenses | $1,260,000 | $1,000,000 |
| Administrative expenses | 625,000 | 500,000 |
| Total operating expenses | $1,885,000 | $1,500,000 |
| Income from operations | $2,385,000 | $2,500,000 |
| Other income | 110,000 | 100,000 |
| Income before income tax | $2,495,000 | $2,600,000 |
| Income tax expense | 60,000 | 50,000 |
| Net income | $2,435,000 | $2,550,000 |

**Instructions**

1. Prepare a comparative income statement with horizontal analysis for the two-year period, using 2015 as the base year. Round to one decimal place.

2. ➤ To the extent the data permit, comment on the significant relationships revealed by the horizontal analysis prepared in (1).

---

**PR 17-2A  Vertical analysis of income statement**  OBJ. 1

✔ 1. Net income, 2016, 13.0%

**General Ledger**

For 2016, Indigo Company initiated a sales promotion campaign that included the expenditure of an additional $39,000 for advertising. At the end of the year, Lumi Neer, the president, is presented with the following condensed comparative income statement:

**Indigo Company**
**Comparative Income Statement**
**For the Years Ended December 31, 2016 and 2015**

|  | 2016 | 2015 |
|---|---|---|
| Sales | $820,000 | $600,000 |
| Cost of goods sold | 311,600 | 240,000 |
| Gross profit | $508,400 | $360,000 |
| Selling expenses | $164,000 | $108,000 |
| Administrative expenses | 57,400 | 54,000 |
| Total operating expenses | $221,400 | $162,000 |
| Income from operations | $287,000 | $198,000 |
| Other income | 65,600 | 48,000 |
| Income before income tax | $352,600 | $246,000 |
| Income tax expense | 246,000 | 180,000 |
| Net income | $106,600 | $ 66,000 |

**Instructions**

1. Prepare a comparative income statement for the two-year period, presenting an analysis of each item in relationship to sales for each of the years. Round to one decimal place.

2. ➤ To the extent the data permit, comment on the significant relationships revealed by the vertical analysis prepared in (1).

---

**PR 17-3A  Effect of transactions on current position analysis**  OBJ. 2

✔ 2. c. Current ratio, 2.0

Data pertaining to the current position of Forte Company are as follows:

| | |
|---|---|
| Cash | $412,500 |
| Marketable securities | 187,500 |
| Accounts and notes receivable (net) | 300,000 |
| Inventories | 700,000 |
| Prepaid expenses | 50,000 |
| Accounts payable | 200,000 |
| Notes payable (short-term) | 250,000 |
| Accrued expenses | 300,000 |

**Instructions**

1. Compute (a) the working capital, (b) the current ratio, and (c) the quick ratio. Round to one decimal place.

2. List the following captions on a sheet of paper:

| Transaction | Working Capital | Current Ratio | Quick Ratio |
|---|---|---|---|

Compute the working capital, the current ratio, and the quick ratio after each of the following transactions, and record the results in the appropriate columns. *Consider each transaction separately* and assume that only that transaction affects the data given. Round to one decimal place.

a. Sold marketable securities at no gain or loss, $70,000.

b. Paid accounts payable, $125,000.

c. Purchased goods on account, $110,000.

d. Paid notes payable, $100,000.

e. Declared a cash dividend, $150,000.

f. Declared a common stock dividend on common stock, $50,000.

g. Borrowed cash from bank on a long-term note, $225,000.

h. Received cash on account, $125,000.

i. Issued additional shares of stock for cash, $600,000.

j. Paid cash for prepaid expenses, $10,000.

---

**PR 17-4A    Nineteen measures of solvency and profitability** OBJ. 2, 3

✔ 5. Number of days'
sales in receivables, 36.5

The comparative financial statements of Bettancort Inc. are as follows. The market price of Bettancort Inc. common stock was $71.25 on December 31, 2016.

**Bettancort Inc.**
**Comparative Retained Earnings Statement**
**For the Years Ended December 31, 2016 and 2015**

| | 2016 | 2015 |
|---|---|---|
| Retained earnings, January 1 | $2,655,000 | $2,400,000 |
| Add net income for year | 300,000 | 280,000 |
| Total | $2,955,000 | $2,680,000 |
| Deduct dividends: | | |
| On preferred stock | $ 15,000 | $ 15,000 |
| On common stock | 10,000 | 10,000 |
| Total | $ 25,000 | $ 25,000 |
| Retained earnings, December 31 | $2,930,000 | $2,655,000 |

**Bettancort Inc.**
**Comparative Income Statement**
**For the Years Ended December 31, 2016 and 2015**

| | 2016 | 2015 |
|---|---|---|
| Sales | $1,200,000 | $1,000,000 |
| Cost of goods sold | 500,000 | 475,000 |
| Gross profit | $ 700,000 | $ 525,000 |
| Selling expenses | $ 240,000 | $ 200,000 |
| Administrative expenses | 180,000 | 150,000 |
| Total operating expenses | $ 420,000 | $ 350,000 |
| Income from operations | $ 280,000 | $ 175,000 |
| Other income | 166,000 | 225,000 |
| | $ 446,000 | $ 400,000 |
| Other expense (interest) | 66,000 | 60,000 |
| Income before income tax | $ 380,000 | $ 340,000 |
| Income tax expense | 80,000 | 60,000 |
| Net income | $ 300,000 | $ 280,000 |

**Bettancort Inc.**
**Comparative Balance Sheet**
**December 31, 2016 and 2015**

| | Dec. 31, 2016 | Dec. 31, 2015 |
|---|---|---|
| **Assets** | | |
| Current assets: | | |
| Cash .......................................................... | $ 450,000 | $ 400,000 |
| Marketable securities........................................... | 300,000 | 260,000 |
| Accounts receivable (net)....................................... | 130,000 | 110,000 |
| Inventories ................................................... | 67,000 | 58,000 |
| Prepaid expenses ............................................. | 153,000 | 139,000 |
| Total current assets ...................................... | $1,100,000 | $ 967,000 |
| Long-term investments.......................................... | 2,350,000 | 2,200,000 |
| Property, plant, and equipment (net) ............................ | 1,320,000 | 1,188,000 |
| Total assets .................................................. | $4,770,000 | $4,355,000 |
| **Liabilities** | | |
| Current liabilities.............................................. | $ 440,000 | $ 400,000 |
| Long-term liabilities: | | |
| Mortgage note payable, 8%, due 2021 ........................... | $ 100,000 | $ 0 |
| Bonds payable, 5%, due 2017 ................................... | 1,000,000 | 1,000,000 |
| Total long-term liabilities .................................. | $1,100,000 | $1,000,000 |
| Total liabilities ............................................... | $1,540,000 | $1,400,000 |
| **Stockholders' Equity** | | |
| Preferred $0.75 stock, $10 par .................................. | $ 200,000 | $ 200,000 |
| Common stock, $10 par.......................................... | 100,000 | 100,000 |
| Retained earnings.............................................. | 2,930,000 | 2,655,000 |
| Total stockholders' equity................................... | $3,230,000 | $2,955,000 |
| Total liabilities and stockholders' equity......................... | $4,770,000 | $4,355,000 |

## Instructions

Determine the following measures for 2016, rounding to one decimal place:

1. Working capital
2. Current ratio
3. Quick ratio
4. Accounts receivable turnover
5. Number of days' sales in receivables
6. Inventory turnover
7. Number of days' sales in inventory
8. Ratio of fixed assets to long-term liabilities
9. Ratio of liabilities to stockholders' equity
10. Number of times interest charges are earned
11. Number of times preferred dividends are earned
12. Ratio of sales to assets
13. Rate earned on total assets
14. Rate earned on stockholders' equity
15. Rate earned on common stockholders' equity
16. Earnings per share on common stock
17. Price-earnings ratio
18. Dividends per share of common stock
19. Dividend yield

**PR 17-5A    Solvency and profitability trend analysis**                                    **OBJ. 2, 3**

Addai Company has provided the following comparative information:

|                                           | 2016      | 2015      | 2014      | 2013      | 2012      |
|-------------------------------------------|-----------|-----------|-----------|-----------|-----------|
| Net income                                | $ 273,406 | $ 367,976 | $ 631,176 | $ 884,000 | $ 800,000 |
| Interest expense                          | 616,047   | 572,003   | 528,165   | 495,000   | 440,000   |
| Income tax expense                        | 31,749    | 53,560    | 106,720   | 160,000   | 200,000   |
| Total assets (ending balance)             | 4,417,178 | 4,124,350 | 3,732,443 | 3,338,500 | 2,750,000 |
| Total stockholders' equity (ending balance) | 3,706,557 | 3,433,152 | 3,065,176 | 2,434,000 | 1,550,000 |
| Average total assets                      | 4,270,764 | 3,928,396 | 3,535,472 | 3,044,250 | 2,475,000 |
| Average total stockholders' equity        | 3,569,855 | 3,249,164 | 2,749,588 | 1,992,000 | 1,150,000 |

You have been asked to evaluate the historical performance of the company over the last five years.

Selected industry ratios have remained relatively steady at the following levels for the last five years:

|                                              | 2012–2016 |
|----------------------------------------------|-----------|
| Rate earned on total assets                  | 28%       |
| Rate earned on stockholders' equity          | 18%       |
| Number of times interest charges are earned  | 2.7       |
| Ratio of liabilities to stockholders' equity | 0.4       |

**Instructions**

1. Prepare four line graphs with the ratio on the vertical axis and the years on the horizontal axis for the following four ratios (rounded to one decimal place):

   a. Rate earned on total assets

   b. Rate earned on stockholders' equity

   c. Number of times interest charges are earned

   d. Ratio of liabilities to stockholders' equity

   Display both the company ratio and the industry benchmark on each graph. That is, each graph should have two lines.

2. ➤ Prepare an analysis of the graphs in (1).

# Problems: Series B

**PR 17-1B    Horizontal analysis of income statement**                                    **OBJ. 1**

✔ 1. Sales,
30.0% increase

General Ledger

SHOW
ME HOW

For 2016, Macklin Inc. reported a significant increase in net income. At the end of the year, John Mayer, the president, is presented with the following condensed comparative income statement:

**Macklin Inc.**
**Comparative Income Statement**
**For the Years Ended December 31, 2016 and 2015**

|                          | 2016     | 2015     |
|--------------------------|----------|----------|
| Sales                    | $910,000 | $700,000 |
| Cost of goods sold       | 441,000  | 350,000  |
| Gross profit             | $469,000 | $350,000 |
| Selling expenses         | $ 139,150 | $115,000 |
| Administrative expenses  | 99,450   | 85,000   |
| Total operating expenses | $238,600 | $200,000 |
| Income from operations   | $230,400 | $150,000 |
| Other income             | 65,000   | 50,000   |
| Income before income tax | $295,400 | $200,000 |
| Income tax expense       | 65,000   | 50,000   |
| Net income               | $230,400 | $150,000 |

## Instructions

1. Prepare a comparative income statement with horizontal analysis for the two-year period, using 2015 as the base year. Round to one decimal place.

2. ━━━▶ To the extent the data permit, comment on the significant relationships revealed by the horizontal analysis prepared in (1).

---

**PR 17-2B** **Vertical analysis of income statement**                    OBJ. 1

✔ 1. Net income, 2015, 14.0%

**General Ledger**

For 2016, Fielder Industries Inc. initiated a sales promotion campaign that included the expenditure of an additional $40,000 for advertising. At the end of the year, Leif Grando, the president, is presented with the following condensed comparative income statement:

**Fielder Industries Inc.**
**Comparative Income Statement**
**For the Years Ended December 31, 2016 and 2015**

|  | 2016 | 2015 |
|---|---|---|
| Sales ........................................................... | $1,300,000 | $1,180,000 |
| Cost of goods sold................................................ | 682,500 | 613,600 |
| Gross profit ..................................................... | $ 617,500 | $ 566,400 |
| Selling expenses ................................................. | $ 260,000 | $ 188,800 |
| Adminstrative expenses ........................................... | 169,000 | 177,000 |
| Total operating expenses ......................................... | $ 429,000 | $ 365,800 |
| Income from operations ........................................... | $ 188,500 | $ 200,600 |
| Other income.................................................... | 78,000 | 70,800 |
| Income before income tax ........................................ | $ 266,500 | $ 271,400 |
| Income tax expense .............................................. | 117,000 | 106,200 |
| Net income ..................................................... | $ 149,500 | $ 165,200 |

## Instructions

1. Prepare a comparative income statement for the two-year period, presenting an analysis of each item in relationship to sales for each of the years. Round to one decimal place.

2. ━━━▶ To the extent the data permit, comment on the significant relationships revealed by the vertical analysis prepared in (1).

---

**PR 17-3B** **Effect of transactions on current position analysis**                    OBJ. 2

✔ 2. g. Quick ratio, 1.6

Data pertaining to the current position of Lucroy Industries Inc. are as follows:

| | |
|---|---|
| Cash | $ 800,000 |
| Marketable securities | 550,000 |
| Accounts and notes receivable (net) | 850,000 |
| Inventories | 700,000 |
| Prepaid expenses | 300,000 |
| Accounts payable | 1,200,000 |
| Notes payable (short-term) | 700,000 |
| Accrued expenses | 100,000 |

## Instructions

1. Compute (a) the working capital, (b) the current ratio, and (c) the quick ratio. Round to one decimal place.

2. List the following captions on a sheet of paper:

| Transaction | Working Capital | Current Ratio | Quick Ratio |
|---|---|---|---|

Compute the working capital, the current ratio, and the quick ratio after each of the following transactions, and record the results in the appropriate columns. *Consider each transaction separately* and assume that only that transaction affects the data given. Round to one decimal place.

a. Sold marketable securities at no gain or loss, $500,000.

b. Paid accounts payable, $287,500.

c. Purchased goods on account, $400,000.

d. Paid notes payable, $125,000.

e. Declared a cash dividend, $325,000.

f. Declared a common stock dividend on common stock, $150,000.

g. Borrowed cash from bank on a long-term note, $1,000,000.

h. Received cash on account, $75,000.

i. Issued additional shares of stock for cash, $2,000,000.

j. Paid cash for prepaid expenses, $200,000.

---

**✔ 9. Ratio of liabilities to stockholders' equity, 0.4**

**PR 17-4B    Nineteen measures of solvency and profitability**        OBJ. 2, 3

The comparative financial statements of Stargel Inc. are as follows. The market price of Stargel Inc. common stock was $119.70 on December 31, 2016.

**Stargel Inc.**
**Comparative Retained Earnings Statement**
**For the Years Ended December 31, 2016 and 2015**

|  | 2016 | 2015 |
|---|---|---|
| Retained earnings, January 1 | $5,375,000 | $4,545,000 |
| Add net income for year | 900,000 | 925,000 |
| Total | $6,275,000 | $5,470,000 |
| Deduct dividends: |  |  |
| On preferred stock | $ 45,000 | $ 45,000 |
| On common stock | 50,000 | 50,000 |
| Total | $ 95,000 | $ 95,000 |
| Retained earnings, December 31 | $6,180,000 | $5,375,000 |

**Stargel Inc.**
**Comparative Income Statement**
**For the Years Ended December 31, 2016 and 2015**

|  | 2016 | 2015 |
|---|---|---|
| Sales | $10,000,000 | $9,400,000 |
| Cost of goods sold | 5,350,000 | 4,950,000 |
| Gross profit | $ 4,650,000 | $4,450,000 |
| Selling expenses | $ 2,000,000 | $1,880,000 |
| Administrative expenses | 1,500,000 | 1,410,000 |
| Total operating expenses | $ 3,500,000 | $3,290,000 |
| Income from operations | $ 1,150,000 | $1,160,000 |
| Other income | 150,000 | 140,000 |
|  | $ 1,300,000 | $1,300,000 |
| Other expense (interest) | 170,000 | 150,000 |
| Income before income tax | $ 1,130,000 | $1,150,000 |
| Income tax expense | 230,000 | 225,000 |
| Net income | $ 900,000 | $ 925,000 |

**Stargel Inc.**
**Comparative Balance Sheet**
**December 31, 2016 and 2015**

| | Dec. 31, 2016 | Dec. 31, 2015 |
|---|---|---|
| **Assets** | | |
| Current assets: | | |
| Cash...................................................... | $ 500,000 | $ 400,000 |
| Marketable securities ............................................ | 1,010,000 | 1,000,000 |
| Accounts receivable (net)....................................... | 740,000 | 510,000 |
| Inventories........................................................ | 1,190,000 | 950,000 |
| Prepaid expenses............................................ | 250,000 | 229,000 |
| Total current assets.......................... | $3,690,000 | $3,089,000 |
| Long-term investments......................................... | 2,350,000 | 2,300,000 |
| Property, plant, and equipment (net) ............................. | 3,740,000 | 3,366,000 |
| Total assets ...................................................... | $9,780,000 | $8,755,000 |
| **Liabilities** | | |
| Current liabilities............................................. | $ 900,000 | $ 880,000 |
| Long-term liabilities: | | |
| Mortgage note payable, 8.8%, due 2021.......................... | $ 200,000 | $ 0 |
| Bonds payable, 9%, due 2017.................................... | 1,500,000 | 1,500,000 |
| Total long-term liabilities ..................................... | $1,700,000 | $1,500,000 |
| Total liabilities ...................................................... | $2,600,000 | $2,380,000 |
| **Stockholders' Equity** | | |
| Preferred $0.90 stock, $10 par ...................................... | $ 500,000 | $ 500,000 |
| Common stock, $5 par......................................... | 500,000 | 500,000 |
| Retained earnings............................................. | 6,180,000 | 5,375,000 |
| Total stockholders' equity....................................... | $7,180,000 | $6,375,000 |
| Total liabilities and stockholders' equity............................. | $9,780,000 | $8,755,000 |

## Instructions

Determine the following measures for 2016, rounding to one decimal place, except per-share amounts, which should be rounded to the nearest penny:

1. Working capital
2. Current ratio
3. Quick ratio
4. Accounts receivable turnover
5. Number of days' sales in receivables
6. Inventory turnover
7. Number of days' sales in inventory
8. Ratio of fixed assets to long-term liabilities
9. Ratio of liabilities to stockholders' equity
10. Number of times interest charges are earned
11. Number of times preferred dividends are earned
12. Ratio of sales to assets
13. Rate earned on total assets
14. Rate earned on stockholders' equity
15. Rate earned on common stockholders' equity
16. Earnings per share on common stock
17. Price-earnings ratio
18. Dividends per share of common stock
19. Dividend yield

**PR 17-5B   Solvency and profitability trend analysis**                OBJ. 2, 3

Crosby Company has provided the following comparative information:

| | 2016 | 2015 | 2014 | 2013 | 2012 |
|---|---|---|---|---|---|
| Net income | $ 5,571,720 | $ 3,714,480 | $ 2,772,000 | $ 1,848,000 | $ 1,400,000 |
| Interest expense | 1,052,060 | 891,576 | 768,600 | 610,000 | 500,000 |
| Income tax expense | 1,225,572 | 845,222 | 640,320 | 441,600 | 320,000 |
| Total assets (ending balance) | 29,378,491 | 22,598,839 | 17,120,333 | 12,588,480 | 10,152,000 |
| Total stockholders' equity (ending balance) | 18,706,200 | 13,134,480 | 9,420,000 | 6,648,000 | 4,800,000 |
| Average total assets | 25,988,665 | 19,859,586 | 14,854,406 | 11,370,240 | 8,676,000 |
| Average total stockholders' equity | 15,920,340 | 11,277,240 | 8,034,000 | 5,724,000 | 4,100,000 |

You have been asked to evaluate the historical performance of the company over the last five years.

Selected industry ratios have remained relatively steady at the following levels for the last five years:

| | 2012–2016 |
|---|---|
| Rate earned on total assets | 19% |
| Rate earned on stockholders' equity | 26% |
| Number of times interest charges are earned | 3.4 |
| Ratio of liabilities to stockholders' equity | 1.4 |

**Instructions**

1. Prepare four line graphs with the ratio on the vertical axis and the years on the horizontal axis for the following four ratios (rounded to one decimal place):

   a. Rate earned on total assets

   b. Rate earned on stockholders' equity

   c. Number of times interest charges are earned

   d. Ratio of liabilities to stockholders' equity

   Display both the company ratio and the industry benchmark on each graph. That is, each graph should have two lines.

2. ➤ Prepare an analysis of the graphs in (1).

# Nike, Inc., Problem

## Financial Statement Analysis

The financial statements for Nike, Inc., are presented in Appendix C at the end of the text. The following additional information (in thousands) is available:

| | |
|---|---|
| Accounts receivable at May 31, 2010 | $ 3,138 |
| Inventories at May 31, 2010 | 2,715 |
| Total assets at May 31, 2010 | 14,998 |
| Stockholders' equity at May 31, 2010 | 9,843 |

**Instructions**

1. Determine the following measures for the fiscal years ended May 31, 2013 (fiscal 2012), and May 31, 2012 (fiscal 2011), rounding to one decimal place.

   a. Working capital

   b. Current ratio

   c. Quick ratio

   d. Accounts receivable turnover

   e. Number of days' sales in receivables

   f. Inventory turnover

   g. Number of days' sales in inventory

   h. Ratio of liabilities to stockholders' equity

   i. Ratio of sales to assets

j. Rate earned on total assets, assuming interest expense is $23 million for the year ending May 31, 2013, and $31 million for the year ending May 31, 2012

k. Rate earned on common stockholders' equity

l. Price-earnings ratio, assuming that the market price was $61.66 per share on May 31, 2013, and $53.10 per share on May 31, 2012

m. Percentage relationship of net income to sales

2. ➤ What conclusions can be drawn from these analyses?

# Cases & Projects

## CP 17-1 Analysis of financing corporate growth

Assume that the president of Freeman Industries Inc. made the following statement in the Annual Report to Shareholders:

"The founding family and majority shareholders of the company do not believe in using debt to finance future growth. The founding family learned from hard experience during Prohibition and the Great Depression that debt can cause loss of flexibility and eventual loss of corporate control. The company will not place itself at such risk. As such, all future growth will be financed either by stock sales to the public or by internally generated resources."

➤ As a public shareholder of this company, how would you respond to this policy?

## CP 17-2 Receivables and inventory turnover

Rodgers Industries Inc. has completed its fiscal year on December 31. The auditor, Josh McCoy, has approached the CFO, Aaron Mathews, regarding the year-end receivables and inventory levels of Rodgers Industries. The following conversation takes place:

*Josh:* We are beginning our audit of Rodgers Industries and have prepared ratio analyses to determine if there have been significant changes in operations or financial position. This helps us guide the audit process. This analysis indicates that the inventory turnover has decreased from 5.1 to 2.7, while the accounts receivable turnover has decreased from 11 to 7. Could you explain this change in operations?

*Aaron:* There is little need for concern. The inventory represents computers that we were unable to sell during the holiday buying season. We are confident, however, that we will be able to sell these computers as we move into the next fiscal year.

*Josh:* What gives you this confidence?

*Aaron:* We will increase our advertising and provide some very attractive price concessions to move these machines. We have no choice. Newer technology is already out there, and we have to unload this inventory.

*Josh:* ... and the receivables?

*Aaron:* As you may be aware, the company is under tremendous pressure to expand sales and profits. As a result, we lowered our credit standards to our commercial customers so that we would be able to sell products to a broader customer base. As a result of this policy change, we have been able to expand sales by 35%.

*Josh:* Your responses have not been reassuring to me.

*Aaron:* I'm a little confused. Assets are good, right? Why don't you look at our current ratio? It has improved, hasn't it? I would think that you would view that very favorably.

➤ Why is Josh concerned about the inventory and accounts receivable turnover ratios and Aaron's responses to them? What action may Josh need to take? How would you respond to Aaron's last comment?

## CP 17-3 Vertical analysis

The condensed income statements through income from operations for Dell Inc. and Apple Inc. for recent fiscal years follow (numbers in millions of dollars):

| | Dell Inc. | Apple Inc. |
|---|---|---|
| Sales | $56,940 | $156,508 |
| Cost of sales | 44,754 | 87,846 |
| Gross profit | $12,186 | $68,662 |
| Selling, general, and administrative expenses | $ 8,102 | $10,040 |
| Research and development | 1,072 | 3,381 |
| Operating expenses | $ 9,174 | $13,421 |
| Income from operations | $ 3,012 | $55,241 |

➤ Prepare comparative common-sized statements, rounding percents to one decimal place. Interpret the analyses.

### CP 17-4 Profitability and stockholder ratios

Deere & Co. manufactures and distributes farm and construction machinery that it sells around the world. In addition to its manufacturing operations, Deere & Co.'s credit division loans money to customers to finance the purchase of their farm and construction equipment.

The following information is available for three recent years (in millions except per-share amounts):

|  | Year 3 | Year 2 | Year 1 |
|---|---|---|---|
| Net income (loss) | $3,064.7 | $2,799.9 | $1,865.0 |
| Preferred dividends | $0.00 | $0.00 | $0.00 |
| Interest expense | $782.8 | $759.4 | $811.4 |
| Shares outstanding for computing earnings per share | 397 | 417 | 424 |
| Cash dividend per share | $1.79 | $1.52 | $1.16 |
| Average total assets | $52,237 | $45,737 | $42,200 |
| Average stockholders' equity | $6,821 | $6,545 | $5,555 |
| Average stock price per share | $79.27 | $80.48 | $61.18 |

1. Calculate the following ratios for each year (Round percentages to one decimal place):
   a. Rate earned on total assets
   b. Rate earned on stockholders' equity
   c. Earnings per share
   d. Dividend yield
   e. Price-earnings ratio
2. What is the ratio of average liabilities to average stockholders' equity for Year 3?
3. Based on these data, evaluate Deere & Co.'s performance.

### CP 17-5 Comprehensive profitability and solvency analysis

Marriott International, Inc., and Hyatt Hotels Corporation are two major owners and managers of lodging and resort properties in the United States. Abstracted income statement information for the two companies is as follows for a recent year:

|  | Marriott (in millions) | Hyatt (in millions) |
|---|---|---|
| Operating profit before other expenses and interest | $ 677 | $ 39 |
| Other income (expenses) | 54 | 118 |
| Interest expense | (180) | (54) |
| Income before income taxes | $ 551 | $103 |
| Income tax expense | 93 | 37 |
| Net income | $ 458 | $ 66 |

Balance sheet information is as follows:

|  | Marriott (in millions) | Hyatt (in millions) |
|---|---|---|
| Total liabilities | $7,398 | $2,125 |
| Total stockholders' equity | 1,585 | 5,118 |
| Total liabilities and stockholders' equity | $8,983 | $7,243 |

The average liabilities, average stockholders' equity, and average total assets were as follows:

|  | Marriott (in millions) | Hyatt (in millions) |
|---|---|---|
| Average total liabilities | $7,095 | $2,132 |
| Average total stockholders' equity | 1,364 | 5,067 |
| Average total assets | 8,458 | 7,199 |

1. Determine the following ratios for both companies (round to one decimal place after the whole percent):
   a. Rate earned on total assets
   b. Rate earned on stockholders' equity
   c. Number of times interest charges are earned
   d. Ratio of liabilities to stockholders' equity
2. ⟶ Analyze and compare the two companies, using the information in (1).

# Managerial Accounting Concepts and Principles

## Washburn Guitars

**P**aul Stanley, guitarist for the legendary rock band **KISS**, has entertained millions of fans playing his guitar. His guitar was built by quality craftsmen at **Washburn Guitars** in Chicago. Washburn Guitars is well-known in the music industry and has been in business for more than 120 years.

Staying in business for 120 years requires a thorough understanding of how to manufacture high-quality guitars. In addition, it requires knowledge of how to account for the costs of making guitars. For example, Washburn needs cost information to answer the following questions:

- How much should be charged for its guitars?
- How many guitars does it have to sell in a year to cover its costs and earn a profit?

- How many employees should the company have working on each stage of the manufacturing process?
- How would purchasing automated equipment affect the costs of its guitars?

This chapter introduces managerial accounting concepts that are useful in addressing these questions.

This chapter begins by describing managerial accounting and its relationship to financial accounting. Following this overview, the management process is described along with the role of managerial accounting in this process. Finally, characteristics of managerial accounting reports, managerial accounting terms, and uses of managerial accounting information are described and illustrated.

**OBJ 1** Describe managerial accounting and the role of managerial accounting in a business.

# Managerial Accounting

Managers make numerous decisions during the day-to-day operations of a business and in planning for the future. Managerial accounting provides much of the information used for these decisions.

Some examples of managerial accounting information along with the chapter in which it is described and illustrated follow:

- Classifying manufacturing and other costs and reporting them in the financial statements (Chapter 18)
- Determining the cost of manufacturing a product or providing a service (Chapters 19 and 20)
- Estimating the behavior of costs for various levels of activity and assessing cost-volume-profit relationships (Chapter 21)
- Planning for the future by preparing budgets (Chapter 22)
- Evaluating manufacturing costs by comparing actual with expected results (Chapter 23)
- Evaluating decentralized operations by comparing actual and budgeted costs as well as computing various measures of profitability (Chapter 24)
- Evaluating special decision-making situations by comparing differential revenues and costs, and allocating product costs using activity-based costing (Chapter 25)
- Evaluating alternative proposals for long-term investments in fixed assets (Chapter 26)

## Differences Between Managerial and Financial Accounting

Accounting information is often divided into two types: financial and managerial. Exhibit 1 shows the relationship between financial accounting and managerial accounting.

**EXHIBIT 1** **Financial Accounting and Managerial Accounting**

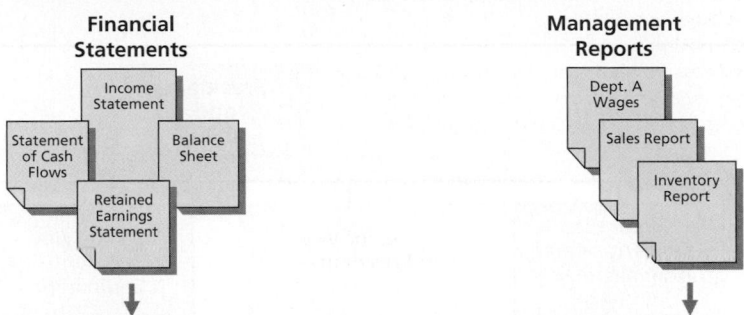

| | Financial Statements | Management Reports |
| --- | --- | --- |
| **Users of Information** | External users and company management | Management |
| **Nature of Information** | Objective | Objective and subjective |
| **Guidelines for Preparation** | Prepared according to GAAP | Prepared according to management needs |
| **Timeliness of Reporting** | Prepared at fixed intervals | Prepared at fixed intervals and on an as-needed basis |
| **Focus of Reporting** | Company as a whole | Company as a whole or segment |

**Financial accounting** information is reported at fixed intervals (monthly, quarterly, yearly) in general-purpose financial statements. These financial statements—the income statement, retained earnings statement, balance sheet, and statement of cash flows—are prepared according to generally accepted accounting principles (GAAP). These statements are used by external users such as the following:

- Shareholders
- Creditors
- Government agencies
- The general public

Managers of a company also use general-purpose financial statements. For example, in planning future operations, managers often begin by evaluating the current income statement and statement of cash flows.

**Managerial accounting** information is designed to meet the specific needs of a company's management. This information includes the following:

- Historical data, which provide *objective measures* of past operations
- Estimated data, which provide *subjective estimates* about future decisions

Management uses both types of information in directing daily operations, planning future operations, and developing business strategies.

Unlike the financial statements prepared in financial accounting, managerial accounting reports do *not* always have to be:

- Prepared according to generally accepted accounting principles (GAAP). This is because *only* the company's management uses the information. Also, in many cases, GAAP are not relevant to the specific decision-making needs of management.
- Prepared at fixed intervals (monthly, quarterly, yearly). Although some management reports are prepared at fixed intervals, most reports are prepared as management needs the information.
- Prepared for the business as a whole. Most management reports are prepared for products, projects, sales territories, or other segments of the company.

## The Management Accountant in the Organization

In most companies, departments or similar organizational units are assigned responsibilities for specific functions or activities. The operating structure of a company can be shown in an *organization chart*.

Exhibit 2 is a partial organization chart for Callaway Golf Company, the manufacturer and distributor of golf clubs, clothing, and other products.

**EXHIBIT 2**

**Partial Organization Chart for Callaway Golf Company**

The departments in a company can be viewed as having either of the following:

- Line responsibilities
- Staff responsibilities

A **line department** is directly involved in providing goods or services to the customers of the company. For Callaway Golf (shown in Exhibit 2), the following occupy line positions:

- Senior Vice President—Equipment
- Plant Manager—Chicopee, MA Plant
- Senior Vice President—Callaway Brand
- Managing Director, Callaway Golf Europe

Individuals in these positions are responsible for manufacturing and selling Callaway's products.

A **staff department** provides services, assistance, and advice to the departments with line or other staff responsibilities. A staff department has no direct authority over a line department. For Callaway Golf (Exhibit 2), the following are staff positions:

The terms *line* and *staff* may be applied to service organizations. For example, the line positions in a hospital would be the nurses, doctors, and other caregivers. Staff positions would include admissions and records.

- Senior VP—Chief Administrative Officer
- Vice President, Human Resources
- Chief Financial Officer
- Controller

In most companies, the **controller** is the chief management accountant. The controller's staff consists of a variety of other accountants who are responsible for specialized accounting functions such as the following:

- Systems and procedures
- General accounting
- Budgets and budget analysis
- Special reports and analysis
- Taxes
- Cost accounting

Experience in managerial accounting is often an excellent training ground for senior management positions. This is not surprising because accounting touches all phases of a company's operations.

## Managerial Accounting in the Management Process

As a staff department, managerial accounting supports management and the management process. The **management process** has the following five basic phases, as shown in Exhibit 3:

- Planning
- Directing
- Controlling
- Improving
- Decision making

As Exhibit 3 illustrates, the five phases interact with one another.

**EXHIBIT 3**

**The Management Process**

**Planning** Management uses **planning** in developing the company's **objectives (goals)** and translating these objectives into courses of action. For example, a company may set an objective to increase market share by 15% by introducing three new products. The actions to achieve this objective might be as follows:

- Increase the advertising budget
- Open a new sales territory
- Increase the research and development budget

   Planning may be classified as follows:

- **Strategic planning**, which is developing long term actions to achieve the company's objectives. These long-term actions are called **strategies**, which often involve periods of 5 to 10 years.
- **Operational planning**, which develops short-term actions for managing the day-to-day operations of the company.

**Directing** The process by which managers run day-to-day operations is called **directing**. An example of directing is a production supervisor's efforts to keep the production line moving without interruption (downtime). A credit manager's development of guidelines for assessing the ability of potential customers to pay their bills is also an example of directing.

**Controlling** Monitoring operating results and comparing actual results with the expected results is **controlling**. This **feedback** allows management to isolate areas for further investigation and possible remedial action. It may also lead to revising future plans. This philosophy of controlling by comparing actual and expected results is called **management by exception**.

**Improving** Feedback is also used by managers to support continuous process improvement. **Continuous process improvement** is the philosophy of continually improving employees, business processes, and products. The objective of continuous improvement is to eliminate the *source* of problems in a process. In this way, the right products (services) are delivered in the right quantities at the right time.

**Decision Making** Inherent in each of the preceding management processes is **decision making**. In managing a company, management must continually decide among alternative actions. For example, in directing operations, managers must decide on an operating structure, training procedures, and staffing of day-to-day operations.

Managerial accounting supports managers in all phases of the management process. For example, accounting reports comparing actual and expected operating results help managers plan and improve current operations. Such a report might compare the actual and expected costs of defective materials. If the cost of defective materials is unusually high, management might decide to change suppliers.

---

### Example Exercise 18-1    Management Process

**OBJ 1**

Three phases of the management process are planning, controlling, and improving. Match the following descriptions to the proper phase:

| Phase of management process | Description |
|---|---|
| Planning | a. Monitoring the operating results of implemented plans and comparing the actual results with expected results. |
| Controlling | b. Rejects solving individual problems with temporary solutions that fail to address the root cause of the problem. |
| Improving | c. Used by management to develop the company's objectives. |

#### Follow My Example 18-1

Planning (c), Controlling (a), and Improving (b).

Practice Exercises: PE 18-1A, PE 18-1B

---

## Integrity, Objectivity, and Ethics in Business

### ENVIRONMENTAL MANAGERIAL ACCOUNTING

Throughout the last decade, environmental issues have become an increasingly important part of the business environment for most companies. Companies and managers must now consider the environmental impact of their business decisions in the same way that they would consider other operational issues. To help managers make sound business decisions, the emerging field of environmental management accounting focuses on calculating the environmental-related costs of business decisions. Environmental managerial accountants evaluate a variety of issues such as the volume and level of emissions, the estimated costs of different levels of emissions, and the impact that environmental costs have on product cost. Managers use these results to consider clearly the environmental effects of their business decisions.

---

**OBJ 2**
Describe and illustrate the following costs: direct and indirect costs; direct materials, direct labor, and factory overhead costs; and product and period costs.

# Manufacturing Operations: Costs and Terminology

The operations of a business can be classified as service, merchandising, or manufacturing. The accounting for service and merchandising businesses has been described and illustrated in earlier chapters. For this reason, the remaining chapters of this text focus primarily on manufacturing businesses. Most of the managerial accounting concepts discussed, however, also apply to service and merchandising businesses.

As a basis for illustration of manufacturing operations, a guitar manufacturer, **Legend Guitars**, is used. Exhibit 4 is an overview of Legend's guitar manufacturing operations.

---

**EXHIBIT 4**     **Guitar-Making Operations of Legend Guitars**

Customer Places Order     Materials     Cutting Function     Assembly Function     Finished Guitar

Legend's guitar-making process begins when a customer places an order for a guitar. Once the order is accepted, the manufacturing process begins by obtaining the necessary materials. An employee then cuts the body and neck of the guitar out of raw lumber. Once the wood is cut, the body and neck of the guitar are assembled. When the assembly is complete, the guitar is painted and finished.

## Direct and Indirect Costs

A **cost** is a payment of cash or the commitment to pay cash in the future for the purpose of generating revenues. For example, cash (or credit) used to purchase equipment is the cost of the equipment. If equipment is purchased by exchanging assets other than cash, the current market value of the assets given up is the cost of the equipment purchased.

In managerial accounting, costs are classified according to the decision-making needs of management. For example, costs are often classified by their relationship to a segment of operations, called a **cost object**. A cost object may be a product, a sales territory, a department, or an activity, such as research and development. Costs identified with cost objects are either direct costs or indirect costs.

**Direct costs** are identified with and can be traced to a cost object. For example, as shown in Exhibit 5, the cost of wood (materials) used by **Legend Guitars** in manufacturing a guitar is a direct cost of the guitar.

---

**Materials**                    **Cost Object: Guitar**

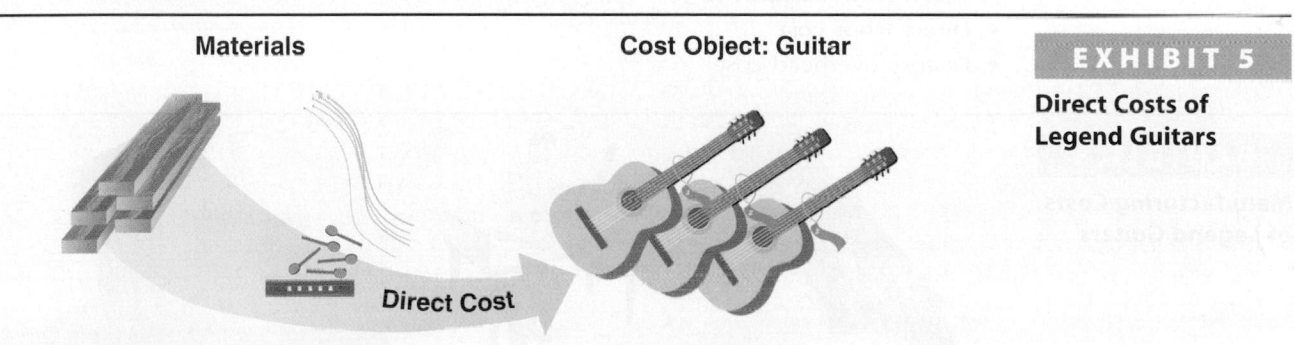

**Direct Cost**

**EXHIBIT 5**

**Direct Costs of Legend Guitars**

---

**Indirect costs** cannot be identified with or traced to a cost object. For example, as shown in Exhibit 6, the salaries of the **Legend Guitars** production supervisors are indirect costs of producing a guitar. Although the production supervisors contribute to the production of a guitar, their salaries cannot be identified with or traced to any individual guitar.

**EXHIBIT 6**

**Indirect Costs of
Legend Guitars**

Depending on the cost object, a cost may be either a direct or an indirect cost. For example, the salaries of production supervisors are indirect costs when the cost object is an individual guitar. If, however, the cost object is Legend Guitars' overall production process, then the salaries of production supervisors are direct costs.

This process of classifying a cost as direct or indirect is illustrated in Exhibit 7.

**EXHIBIT 7**

**Classifying Direct
and Indirect Costs**

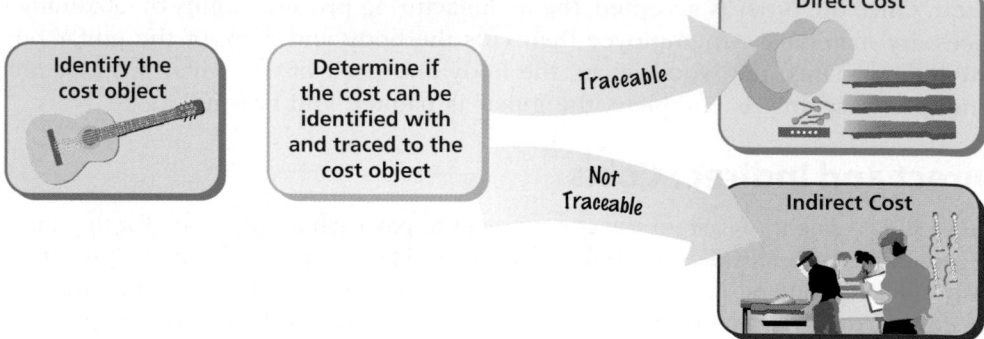

## Manufacturing Costs

The cost of a manufactured product includes the cost of materials used in making the product. In addition, the cost of a manufactured product includes the cost of converting the materials into a finished product. For example, **Legend Guitars** uses employees and machines to convert wood (and other supplies) into finished guitars. Thus, as shown in Exhibit 8, the cost of a finished guitar (the cost object) includes the following:

- Direct materials cost
- Direct labor cost
- Factory overhead cost

**EXHIBIT 8**

**Manufacturing Costs
of Legend Guitars**

**Direct Materials       Direct Labor       Factory Overhead**

**Direct Materials Cost** Manufactured products begin with raw materials that are converted into finished products. The cost of any material that is an integral part of the finished product is classified as a **direct materials cost**. For **Legend Guitars**, direct materials cost includes the cost of the wood used in producing each guitar. Other examples of direct materials costs include the cost of electronic components for a television, silicon wafers for microcomputer chips, and tires for an automobile.

To be classified as a direct materials cost, the cost must be *both* of the following:

- An integral part of the finished product
- A significant portion of the total cost of the product

For Legend, the cost of the guitar strings is not a direct materials cost. This is because the cost of guitar strings is an insignificant part of the total cost of each guitar. Instead, the cost of guitar strings is classified as a factory overhead cost, which is discussed later.

**Direct Labor Cost** Most manufacturing processes use employees to convert materials into finished products. The cost of employee wages that is an integral part of the finished product is classified as **direct labor cost**. For **Legend Guitars**, direct labor cost includes the wages of the employees who cut each guitar out of raw lumber and assemble it. Other examples of direct labor costs include mechanics' wages for repairing an automobile, machine operators' wages for manufacturing tools, and assemblers' wages for assembling a laptop computer.

Like a direct materials cost, a direct labor cost must meet *both* of the following criteria:

- An integral part of the finished product
- A significant portion of the total cost of the product

For Legend, the wages of the janitors who clean the factory are not a direct labor cost. This is because janitorial costs are not an integral part or a significant cost of each guitar. Instead, janitorial costs are classified as a factory overhead cost, which is discussed next.

**Factory Overhead Cost** Costs other than direct materials and direct labor that are incurred in the manufacturing process are combined and classified as **factory overhead cost**. Factory overhead is sometimes called **manufacturing overhead** or **factory burden**.

All factory overhead costs are indirect costs of the product. Some factory overhead costs include the following:

- Heating and lighting the factory
- Repairing and maintaining factory equipment
- Property taxes on factory buildings and land
- Insurance on factory buildings
- Depreciation on factory plant and equipment

Factory overhead cost also includes materials and labor costs that do not enter directly into the finished product. Examples include the cost of oil used to lubricate machinery and the wages of janitorial and supervisory employees. Also, if the costs of direct materials or direct labor are not a significant portion of the total product cost, these costs may be classified as factory overhead costs.

 As manufacturing processes have become more automated, direct labor costs have become so small that in some situations they are included as part of factory overhead.

For **Legend Guitars**, the costs of guitar strings and janitorial wages are factory overhead costs. Additional factory overhead costs of making guitars are as follows:

- Sandpaper
- Buffing compound
- Glue
- Power (electricity) to run the machines
- Depreciation of the machines and building
- Salaries of production supervisors

**Example Exercise 18-2** **Direct Materials, Direct Labor, and Factory Overhead**

Identify the following costs as direct materials (DM), direct labor (DL), or factory overhead (FO) for a baseball glove manufacturer:

a. Leather used to make a baseball glove

b. Coolants for machines that sew baseball gloves

c. Wages of assembly line employees

d. Ink used to print a player's autograph on a baseball glove

*(Continued)*

**Follow My Example 18-2**

a. DM
b. FO
c. DL
d. FO

Practice Exercises: PE 18-2A, PE 18-2B

**Prime Costs and Conversion Costs** Direct materials, direct labor, and factory overhead costs may be grouped together for analysis and reporting. Two such common groupings are as follows:

- **Prime costs**, which consist of direct materials and direct labor costs
- **Conversion costs**, which consist of direct labor and factory overhead costs

Conversion costs are the costs of converting the materials into a finished product. Direct labor is both a prime cost and a conversion cost, as shown in Exhibit 9.

**EXHIBIT 9**

**Prime Costs and Conversion Costs**

**Example Exercise 18-3** **Prime and Conversion Costs** OBJ 2

Identify the following costs as a prime cost (P), conversion cost (C), or both (B) for a baseball glove manufacturer:
a. Leather used to make a baseball glove
b. Coolants for machines that sew baseball gloves
c. Wages of assembly line employees
d. Ink used to print a player's autograph on a baseball glove

**Follow My Example 18-3**

a. P
b. C
c. B
d. C

Practice Exercises: PE 18-3A, PE 18-3B

**Note:**
Product costs consist of direct materials, direct labor, and factory overhead costs.

**Product Costs and Period Costs** For financial reporting purposes, costs are classified as product costs or period costs.

- **Product costs** consist of manufacturing costs: direct materials, direct labor, and factory overhead.
- **Period costs** consist of selling and administrative expenses. *Selling expenses* are incurred in marketing the product and delivering the product to customers. *Administrative*

*expenses* are incurred in managing the company and are not directly related to the manufacturing or selling functions.

Examples of product costs and period costs for **Legend Guitars** are presented in Exhibit 10.

---

**EXHIBIT 10**     **Examples of Product Costs and Period Costs—Legend Guitars**

## Product (Manufacturing) Costs

**Direct Materials Cost**
• Wood used in neck and body

**Direct Labor Cost**
• Wages of saw operator
• Wages of employees who assemble the guitar

**Factory Overhead**
• Guitar strings
• Wages of janitor
• Power to run the machines
• Depreciation expense—factory building
• Sandpaper and buffing materials
• Glue used in assembly of the guitar
• Salary of production supervisors

## Period (Nonmanufacturing) Costs

**Selling Expenses**
• Advertising expenses
• Sales salaries expenses
• Commissions expenses

**Administrative Expenses**
• Office salaries expense
• Office supplies expense
• Depreciation expense—office building and equipment

---

To facilitate control, selling and administrative expenses may be reported by level of responsibility. For example, selling expenses may be reported by products, salespersons, departments, divisions, or territories. Likewise, administrative expenses may be reported by areas such as human resources, computer services, legal, accounting, or finance.

The impact on the financial statements of product and period costs is summarized in Exhibit 11. As product costs are incurred, they are recorded and reported on the balance sheet as *inventory*. When the inventory is sold, the cost of the manufactured product sold is reported as *cost of goods sold* on the income statement. Period costs are reported as *expenses* on the income statement in the period in which they are incurred and, thus, never appear on the balance sheet.

---

**EXHIBIT 11**

**Product Costs, Period Costs, and the Financial Statements**

## Example Exercise 18-4  Product and Period Costs

Identify the following costs as a product cost or a period cost for a baseball glove manufacturer:

a.  Leather used to make a baseball glove

b.  Cost of endorsement from a professional baseball player

c.  Office supplies used at the company headquarters

d.  Ink used to print a player's autograph on the baseball glove

### Follow My Example 18-4

a.  Product cost

b.  Period cost

c.  Period cost

d.  Product cost

Practice Exercises: PE 18-4A, PE 18-4B

## Business  Connection

### OVERHEAD COSTS

Defense contractors such as General Dynamics, Boeing, and Lockheed Martin sell products such as airplanes, ships, and military equipment to the U.S. Department of Defense. Building large products such as these requires a significant investment in facilities and tools, all of which are classified as factory overhead costs. As a result, factory overhead costs are a much larger portion of the cost of goods sold for defense contractors than it is in other industries. For example, a U.S. General Accounting Office study of six defense contractors found that overhead costs were almost one-third of the price of the final product. This is more than three times greater than the factory overhead costs for a laptop computer, which are typically about 10% of the price of the final product.

## Financial Statements for a Manufacturing Business

**OBJ 3** Describe and illustrate the following statements for a manufacturing business: balance sheet, statement of cost of goods manufactured, and income statement.

The retained earnings and cash flow statements for a manufacturing business are similar to those illustrated in earlier chapters for service and merchandising businesses. However, the balance sheet and income statement for a manufacturing business are more complex. This is because a manufacturer makes the products that it sells and, thus, must record and report product costs. The reporting of product costs primarily affects the balance sheet and the income statement.

### Balance Sheet for a Manufacturing Business

A manufacturing business reports three types of inventory on its balance sheet as follows:

• **Materials inventory** (sometimes called raw materials inventory). This inventory consists of the costs of the direct and indirect materials that have not entered the manufacturing process.

  Examples for **Legend Guitars**: Wood, guitar strings, glue, sandpaper

• **Work in process inventory.** This inventory consists of the direct materials, direct labor, and factory overhead costs for products that have entered the manufacturing process, but are not yet completed (in process).

  Example for Legend: Unfinished (partially assembled) guitars

- **Finished goods inventory.** This inventory consists of completed (or finished) products that have not been sold.

  Example for Legend: Unsold guitars

Exhibit 12 illustrates the reporting of inventory on the balance sheet for a merchandising and a manufacturing business. MusicLand Stores, Inc., a retailer of musical instruments, reports only Merchandise Inventory. In contrast, **Legend Guitars**, a manufacturer of guitars, reports Finished Goods, Work in Process, and Materials inventories. In both balance sheets, inventory is reported in the Current Assets section.

**EXHIBIT 12**

**Balance Sheet Presentation of Inventory in Manufacturing and Merchandising Companies**

### MusicLand Stores, Inc.
#### Balance Sheet
#### December 31, 2016

| | |
|---|---:|
| Current assets: | |
| Cash............................................................. | $ 25,000 |
| Accounts receivable (net)................................... | 85,000 |
| Merchandise inventory..................................... | 142,000 |
| Supplies...................................................... | 10,000 |
| Total current assets.................................. | $ 262,000 |

### Legend Guitars
#### Balance Sheet
#### December 31, 2016

| | | |
|---|---:|---:|
| Current assets: | | |
| Cash............................................. | | $ 21,000 |
| Accounts receivable (net)....................... | | 120,000 |
| Inventories: | | |
| Finished goods............................... | $62,500 | |
| Work in process.............................. | 24,000 | |
| Materials..................................... | 35,000 | 121,500 |
| Supplies.......................................... | | 2,000 |
| Total current assets.......................... | | $ 264,500 |

## Income Statement for a Manufacturing Business

The income statements for merchandising and manufacturing businesses differ primarily in the reporting of the cost of merchandise (goods) *available for sale* and *sold* during the period. These differences are shown in Exhibit 13.

**EXHIBIT 13**

**Income Statements for Merchandising and Manufacturing Businesses**

### Merchandising Business

#### Income Statement

| | | |
|---|---:|---:|
| Sales | | $XXX |
| Beginning merchandise inventory | $XXX | |
| Plus net purchases | XXX | |
| Merchandise available for sale | $XXX | |
| Less ending merchandise inventory | XXX | |
| Cost of merchandise sold | | XXX |
| Gross profit | | $XXX |

### Manufacturing Business

#### Income Statement

| | | |
|---|---:|---:|
| Sales | | $XXX |
| Beginning finished goods inventory | $XXX | |
| Plus cost of goods manufactured | XXX | |
| Cost of finished goods available for sale | $XXX | |
| Less ending finished goods inventory | XXX | |
| Cost of goods sold | | XXX |
| Gross profit | | $XXX |

A merchandising business purchases merchandise ready for resale to customers. The total cost of the **merchandise available for sale** during the period is determined as follows:

$$\text{Beginning Merchandise Inventory} + \text{Net Purchases} = \text{Merchandise Available for Sale}$$

The **cost of merchandise sold** is determined as follows:

$$\text{Cost of Merchandise Available for Sale} - \text{Ending Merchandise Inventory} = \text{Cost of Merchandise Sold}$$

A manufacturer makes the products it sells, using direct materials, direct labor, and factory overhead. The total cost of making products that are available for sale during the period is called the **cost of goods manufactured**.

The **cost of finished goods available for sale** is determined as follows:

$$\text{Beginning Finished Goods Inventory} + \text{Cost of Goods Manufactured During the Period} = \text{Cost of Finished Goods Available for Sale}$$

The **cost of goods sold** is determined as follows:

$$\text{Cost of Finished Goods Available for Sale} - \text{Ending Finished Goods Inventory} = \text{Cost of Goods Sold}$$

*Cost of goods manufactured* is required to determine the *cost of goods sold* and, thus, to prepare the income statement. The cost of goods manufactured is often determined by preparing a **statement of cost of goods manufactured**.[1] This statement summarizes the cost of goods manufactured during the period, as follows:

**Statement of Cost of Goods Manufactured**

| | | |
|---|---|---|
| Beginning work in process inventory........... | | $XXX |
| Direct materials: | | |
|     Beginning materials inventory.............. | $XXX | |
|     Purchases................................... | XXX | |
|     Cost of materials available for use........... | $XXX | |
|     Less ending materials inventory ............ | XXX | |
|         Cost of direct materials used ............ | | $XXX |
| Direct labor ................................... | | XXX |
| Factory overhead............................... | | XXX |
| Total manufacturing costs incurred ............ | | XXX |
| Total manufacturing costs ..................... | | $XXX |
| Less ending work in process inventory ......... | | XXX |
| **Cost of goods manufactured** ................. | | $XXX |

To illustrate, the following data for **Legend Guitars** are used:

| | Jan. 1, 2016 | Dec. 31, 2016 |
|---|---|---|
| Inventories: | | |
|     Materials.................................... | $ 65,000 | $ 35,000 |
|     Work in process ........................... | 30,000 | 24,000 |
|     Finished goods............................. | 60,000 | 62,500 |
| Total inventories................................ | $155,000 | $121,500 |
| Manufacturing costs incurred during 2016: | | |
|     Materials purchased........................ | | $100,000 |
|     Direct labor ............................... | | 110,000 |
|     Factory overhead: | | |
|         Indirect labor .......................... | $ 24,000 | |
|         Depreciation on factory equipment ..... | 10,000 | |
|         Factory supplies and utility costs ........ | 10,000 | 44,000 |
| Total ......................................... | | $254,000 |
| Sales.......................................... | | $366,000 |
| Selling expenses............................... | | 20,000 |
| Administrative expenses....................... | | 15,000 |

[1] Chapters 19 and 20 describe and illustrate the use of job order and process cost systems. As will be discussed, these systems do not require a statement of cost of goods manufactured.

The statement of cost of goods manufactured is prepared using the following three steps:

- Step 1. Determine the *cost of materials used.*
- Step 2. Determine the *total manufacturing costs incurred.*
- Step 3. Determine the *cost of goods manufactured.*

Exhibit 14 summarizes how manufacturing costs flow to the income statement and balance sheet of a manufacturing business.

**EXHIBIT 14**

**Flow of Manufacturing Costs**

Using the data for **Legend Guitars**, the steps for determining the cost of materials used, total manufacturing costs incurred, and cost of goods manufactured are computed as follows:

Step 1. The *cost of materials used* in production is determined as follows:

| | |
|---|---:|
| Materials inventory, January 1, 2016 | $ 65,000 |
| Add materials purchased | 100,000 |
| Cost of materials available for use | $ 165,000 |
| Less materials inventory, December 31, 2016 | 35,000 |
| Cost of direct materials used | $ 130,000 |

The January 1, 2016 (beginning), materials inventory of $65,000 is added to the cost of materials purchased of $100,000 to yield the $165,000 total cost of materials that are available for use during 2016. Deducting the December 31, 2016 (ending), materials inventory of $35,000 yields the $130,000 cost of direct materials used in production.

Step 2. The *total manufacturing costs incurred* is determined as follows:

| | |
|---|---:|
| Direct materials used in production (Step 1) | $ 130,000 |
| Direct labor | 110,000 |
| Factory overhead | 44,000 |
| Total manufacturing costs incurred | $284,000 |

The total manufacturing costs incurred in 2016 of $284,000 are determined by adding the direct materials used in production (Step 1), the direct labor cost, and the factory overhead costs.

Step 3. The *cost of goods manufactured* is determined as follows:

| | |
|---|---:|
| Work in process inventory, January 1, 2016 | $ 30,000 |
| Total manufacturing costs incurred (Step 2) | 284,000 |
| Total manufacturing costs | $314,000 |
| Less work in process inventory, December 31, 2016 | 24,000 |
| Cost of goods manufactured | $290,000 |

The cost of goods manufactured of $290,000 is determined by adding the total manufacturing costs incurred (Step 2) to the January 1, 2016 (beginning), work in process inventory of $30,000. This yields total manufacturing costs of $314,000. The December 31, 2016 (ending), work in process inventory of $24,000 is then deducted to determine the cost of goods manufactured of $290,000.

The income statement and statement of cost of goods manufactured for **Legend Guitars** are shown in Exhibit 15.

**EXHIBIT 15**

**Manufacturing Company—Income Statement with Statement of Cost of Goods Manufactured**

Dynamic Exhibit

### Legend Guitars
### Income Statement
### For the Year Ended December 31, 2016

| | | |
|---|---:|---:|
| Sales | | $366,000 |
| Cost of goods sold: | | |
| Finished goods inventory, January 1, 2016 | $ 60,000 | |
| Cost of goods manufactured | 290,000 | |
| Cost of finished goods available for sale | $350,000 | |
| Less finished goods inventory, December 31, 2016 | 62,500 | |
| Cost of goods sold | | 287,500 |
| Gross profit | | $ 78,500 |
| Operating expenses: | | |
| Selling expenses | $ 20,000 | |
| Administrative expenses | 15,000 | |
| Total operating expenses | | 35,000 |
| Net income | | $ 43,500 |

### Legend Guitars
### Statement of Cost of Goods Manufactured
### For the Year Ended December 31, 2016

| | | | |
|---|---:|---:|---:|
| Work in process inventory, January 1, 2016 | | | $ 30,000 |
| Direct materials: | | | |
| Materials inventory, January 1, 2016 | $ 65,000 | | |
| Purchases | 100,000 | | |
| Cost of materials available for use | $165,000 | | |
| Less materials inventory, December 31, 2016 | 35,000 | | |
| Cost of direct materials used | | $130,000 | |
| Direct labor | | 110,000 | |
| Factory overhead: | | | |
| Indirect labor | $ 24,000 | | |
| Depreciation on factory equipment | 10,000 | | |
| Factory supplies and utility costs | 10,000 | | |
| Total factory overhead | | 44,000 | |
| Total manufacturing costs incurred | | | 284,000 |
| Total manufacturing costs | | | $314,000 |
| Less work in process inventory, December 31, 2016 | | | 24,000 |
| Cost of goods manufactured | | | $290,000 |

## Example Exercise 18-5   Cost of Goods Sold, Cost of Goods Manufactured

OBJ 3

Gauntlet Company has the following information for January:

| | |
|---|---|
| Cost of direct materials used in production | $25,000 |
| Direct labor | 35,000 |
| Factory overhead | 20,000 |
| Work in process inventory, January 1 | 30,000 |
| Work in process inventory, January 31 | 25,000 |
| Finished goods inventory, January 1 | 15,000 |
| Finished goods inventory, January 31 | 12,000 |

For January, determine (a) the cost of goods manufactured and (b) the cost of goods sold.

### Follow My Example 18-5

| | | | |
|---|---|---|---|
| a. | Work in process inventory, January 1............................... | | $ 30,000 |
| | Cost of direct materials used in production.......................... | $ 25,000 | |
| | Direct labor........................................................ | 35,000 | |
| | Factory overhead................................................... | 20,000 | |
| | Total manufacturing costs incurred during January.................. | | 80,000 |
| | Total manufacturing costs .......................................... | | $110,000 |
| | Less work in process inventory, January 31.......................... | | 25,000 |
| | Cost of goods manufactured......................................... | | $ 85,000 |
| | | | |
| b. | Finished goods inventory, January 1 ................................ | $ 15,000 | |
| | Cost of goods manufactured......................................... | 85,000 | |
| | Cost of finished goods available for sale............................ | $100,000 | |
| | Less finished goods inventory, January 31........................... | 12,000 | |
| | Cost of goods sold................................................. | $ 88,000 | |

Practice Exercises: PE 18-5A, PE 18-5B

# Uses of Managerial Accounting

OBJ 4 Describe the uses of managerial accounting information.

As mentioned earlier, managerial accounting provides information and reports for managers to use in operating a business. Some examples of how managerial accounting could be used by **Legend Guitars** include the following:

- The cost of manufacturing each guitar could be used to determine its selling price.
- Comparing the costs of guitars over time can be used to monitor and control the cost of direct materials, direct labor, and factory overhead.
- Performance reports could be used to identify any large amounts of scrap or employee downtime. For example, large amounts of unusable wood (scrap) after the cutting process should be investigated to determine the underlying cause. Such scrap may be caused by saws that have not been properly maintained.
- A report could analyze the potential efficiencies and dollar savings of purchasing a new computerized saw to speed up the production process.
- A report could analyze how many guitars need to be sold to cover operating costs and expenses. Such information could be used to set monthly selling targets and bonuses for sales personnel.

As the prior examples illustrate, managerial accounting information can be used for a variety of purposes. In the remaining chapters of this text, we examine these and other areas of managerial accounting.

## Service ▶ 🛎 ◀ Focus

### MANAGERIAL ACCOUNTING IN THE SERVICE INDUSTRY

All businesses can benefit from managerial accounting, whether they manufacture a product or provide a service. Service businesses such as professional service firms, restaurants, maintenance companies, and airlines need managerial accounting information to direct daily operations, plan future operations, and develop business strategies.

For example, The Walt Disney Company relies heavily on managerial accounting to manage its operations. Disney uses budgets and financial forecasts to plan costs and allocate resources between its various business units.

Based on these budgets and financial forecasts, Disney directs its operations by determining how to staff its theme parks and off cycle its theme park rides for maintenance. Operations are controlled by a variety of qualitative and quantitative metrics that provide feedback on the efficiency and quality of the customer experience. To ensure the best guest experience, Disney Theme Parks manages operations in small business units to maximize management ownership and responsibility. The results of Disney's deployment and use of managerial accounting have been impressive. The Walt Disney Company is typically ranked number 1 in *Fortune*'s listing of the 10 most admired companies for quality.

## At a Glance 18

**OBJ 1**

**Describe managerial accounting and the role of managerial accounting in a business.**

**Key Points** Managerial accounting is a staff function that supports the management process by providing reports to aid management in planning, directing, controlling, improving, and decision making. This differs from financial accounting, which provides information to users outside of the organization. Managerial accounting reports are designed to meet the specific needs of management and aid management in planning long-term strategies and running the day-to-day operations.

| Learning Outcomes | Example Exercises | Practice Exercises |
|---|---|---|
| • Describe the differences between financial accounting and managerial accounting. | | |
| • Describe the role of the management accountant in the organization. | | |
| • Describe the role of managerial accounting in the management process. | EE18-1 | PE18-1A, 18-1B |

**2** **Describe and illustrate the following costs: direct and indirect costs; direct materials, direct labor, and factory overhead costs; and product and period costs.**

**Key Points** Manufacturing companies use machinery and labor to convert materials into a finished product. A direct cost can be directly traced to a finished product, while an indirect cost cannot. The cost of a finished product is made up of three components: direct materials, direct labor, and factory overhead.

These three manufacturing costs can be categorized into prime costs (direct materials and direct labor) or conversion costs (direct labor and factory overhead). Product costs consist of the elements of manufacturing cost—direct materials, direct labor, and factory overhead—while period costs consist of selling and administrative expenses.

| Learning Outcomes | Example Exercises | Practice Exercises |
|---|---|---|
| • Describe a cost object. | | |
| • Classify a cost as a direct or an indirect cost for a cost object. | | |
| • Describe direct materials cost. | EE18-2 | PE18-2A, 18-2B |
| • Describe direct labor cost. | EE18-2 | PE18-2A, 18-2B |
| • Describe factory overhead cost. | EE18-2 | PE18-2A, 18-2B |
| • Describe prime costs and conversion costs. | EE18-3 | PE18-3A, 18-3B |
| • Describe product costs and period costs. | EE18-4 | PE18-4A, 18-4B |

**3** **Describe and illustrate the following statements for a manufacturing business: balance sheet, statement of cost of goods manufactured, and income statement.**

**Key Points** The financial statements of manufacturing companies differ from those of merchandising companies. Manufacturing company balance sheets report three types of inventory: materials, work in process, and finished goods. The income statement of manufacturing companies reports the cost of goods sold, which is the total manufacturing cost of the goods sold. The income statement is supported by the statement of cost of goods manufactured, which provides the details of the cost of goods manufactured during the period.

| Learning Outcomes | Example Exercises | Practice Exercises |
|---|---|---|
| • Describe materials inventory. | | |
| • Describe work in process inventory. | | |
| • Describe finished goods inventory. | | |
| • Describe the differences between merchandising and manufacturing company balance sheets. | | |
| • Prepare a statement of cost of goods manufactured. | EE18-5 | PE18-5A, 18-5B |
| • Prepare an income statement for a manufacturing company. | EE18-5 | PE18-5A, 18-5B |

**4** **Describe the uses of managerial accounting information.**

**Key Points** Managers need information to guide their decision making. Managerial accounting provides a variety of information and reports that help managers run the operations of their business.

| Learning Outcome | Example Exercises | Practice Exercises |
|---|---|---|
| • Describe examples of how managerial accounting aids managers in decision making. | | |

# Key Terms

continuous process improvement (854)
controller (852)
controlling (853)
conversion costs (858)
cost (855)
cost object (855)
cost of finished goods available for sale (862)
cost of goods manufactured (862)
cost of goods sold (862)
cost of merchandise sold (862)
decision making (854)
direct costs (855)
direct labor cost (857)

direct materials cost (856)
directing (853)
factory burden (857)
factory overhead cost (857)
feedback (853)
financial accounting (851)
finished goods inventory (861)
indirect costs (855)
line department (852)
management by exception (853)
management process (853)
managerial accounting (851)
manufacturing overhead (857)
materials inventory (860)

merchandise available for sale (862)
objectives (goals) (853)
operational planning (853)
period costs (858)
planning (853)
prime costs (858)
product costs (858)
staff department (852)
statement of cost of goods manufactured (862)
strategic planning (853)
strategies (853)
work in process inventory (860)

# Illustrative Problem

The following is a list of costs that were incurred in producing this textbook:

a. Insurance on the factory building and equipment

b. Salary of the vice president of finance

c. Hourly wages of printing press operators during production

d. Straight-line depreciation on the printing presses used to manufacture the text

e. Electricity used to run the presses during the printing of the text

f. Sales commissions paid to textbook representatives for each text sold

g. Paper on which the text is printed

h. Book covers used to bind the pages

i. Straight-line depreciation on an office building

j. Salaries of staff used to develop artwork for the text

k. Glue used to bind pages to cover

## Instructions

With respect to the manufacture and sale of this text, classify each cost as either a product cost or a period cost. Indicate whether each product cost is a direct materials cost, a direct labor cost, or a factory overhead cost. Indicate whether each period cost is a selling expense or an administrative expense.

## Solution

| | Product Cost | | | Period Cost | |
|---|---|---|---|---|---|
| Cost | Direct Materials Cost | Direct Labor Cost | Factory Overhead Cost | Selling Expense | Administrative Expense |
| a. | | | X | | |
| b. | | | | | X |
| c. | | X | | | |
| d. | | | X | | |
| e. | | | X | | |
| f. | | | | X | |
| g. | X | | | | |
| h. | X | | | | |
| i. | | | | | X |
| j. | | | X | | |
| k. | | | X | | |

# Discussion Questions

1. What are the major differences between managerial accounting and financial accounting?

2. a. Differentiate between a department with line responsibility and a department with staff responsibility.

   b. In an organization that has a Sales Department and a Personnel Department, among others, which of the two departments has (1) line responsibility and (2) staff responsibility?

3. What manufacturing cost term is used to describe the cost of materials that are an integral part of the manufactured end product?

4. Distinguish between prime costs and conversion costs.

5. What is the difference between a product cost and a period cost?

6. Name the three inventory accounts for a manufacturing business, and describe what each balance represents at the end of an accounting period.

7. In what order should the three inventories of a manufacturing business be presented on the balance sheet?

8. What are the three categories of manufacturing costs included in the cost of finished goods and the cost of work in process?

9. For a manufacturer, what is the description of the account that is comparable to a merchandising business's cost of merchandise sold?

10. How does the Cost of Goods Sold section of the income statement differ between merchandising and manufacturing companies?

# Practice Exercises

EE 18-1 *p. 854*

SHOW ME HOW

## PE 18-1A  Management process

OBJ. 1

Three phases of the management process are controlling, planning, and decision making. Match the following descriptions to the proper phase:

| Phase of management process | Description |
|---|---|
| Controlling | a. Monitoring the operating results of implemented plans and comparing the actual results with expected results |
| Planning | b. Inherent in planning, directing, controlling, and improving |
| Decision making | c. Long-range courses of action |

SHOW
ME HOW

EE 18-1 *p. 854* **PE 18-1B Management process** OBJ. 1

Three phases of the management process are planning, directing, and controlling. Match the following descriptions to the proper phase:

| Phase of management process | Description |
| --- | --- |
| Planning | a. Developing long-range courses of action to achieve goals. |
| Directing | b. Isolating significant departures from plans for further investigation and possible remedial action. It may lead to a revision of future plans. |
| Controlling | c. Process by which managers, given their assigned levels of responsibilities, run day-to-day operations. |

SHOW
ME HOW

EE 18-2 *p. 857* **PE 18-2A Direct materials, direct labor, and factory overhead** OBJ. 2

Identify the following costs as direct materials (DM), direct labor (DL), or factory overhead (FO) for an automobile manufacturer:

a. Wages of employees that operate painting equipment  DL

b. Wages of the plant supervisor  FOH

c. Steel  DM

d. Oil used for assembly line machinery  FOH

EE 18-2 *p. 857* **PE 18-2B Direct materials, direct labor, and factory overhead** OBJ. 2

Identify the following costs as direct materials (DM), direct labor (DL), or factory overhead (FO) for a magazine publisher:

a. Staples used to bind magazines

b. Wages of printing machine employees

c. Maintenance on printing machines

d. Paper used in the magazine

SHOW
ME HOW

EE 18-3 *p. 858* **PE 18-3A Prime and conversion costs** OBJ. 2

Identify the following costs as a prime cost (P), conversion cost (C), or both (B) for an automobile manufacturer:

a. Wages of employees that operate painting equipment  DL, Both

b. Wages of the plant manager  FOH

c. Steel

d. Oil used for assembly line machinery

SHOW
ME HOW

EE 18-3 *p. 858* **PE 18-3B Prime and conversion costs** OBJ. 2

Identify the following costs as a prime cost (P), conversion cost (C), or both (B) for a magazine publisher:

a. Paper used for the magazine

b. Wages of printing machine employees

c. Glue used to bind magazine

d. Maintenance on printing machines

SHOW
ME HOW

EE 18-4 *p. 860* **PE 18-4A Product and period costs** OBJ. 2

Identify the following costs as a product cost or a period cost for an automobile manufacturer:

a. Steel  Prod. C

b. Wages of employees that operate painting equipment  Prg DL

c. Rent on office building  Per, Adm

d. Sales staff salaries  Per, selling

**EE 18-4** *p. 860* **PE 18-4B** **Product and period costs** OBJ. 2

SHOW
ME HOW

Identify the following costs as a product cost or a period cost for a magazine publisher:

a. Sales salaries

b. Paper used for the magazine

c. Maintenance on printing machines

d. Depreciation expense—corporate headquarters

---

**EE 18-5** *p. 865* **PE 18-5A** **Cost of goods sold, cost of goods manufactured** OBJ. 3

SHOW
ME HOW

Timbuk 3 Company has the following information for March:

| | |
|---|---|
| Cost of direct materials used in production | $21,000 |
| Direct labor | 54,250 |
| Factory overhead | 35,000 |
| Work in process inventory, March 1 | 87,500 |
| Work in process inventory, March 31 | 92,750 |
| Finished goods inventory, March 1 | 36,750 |
| Finished goods inventory, March 31 | 42,000 |

For March, determine (a) the cost of goods manufactured and (b) the cost of goods sold.

---

**EE 18-5** *p. 865* **PE 18-5B** **Cost of goods sold, cost of goods manufactured** OBJ. 3

SHOW
ME HOW

Ebony Company has the following information for July:

| | |
|---|---|
| Cost of direct materials used In production | $67,200 |
| Direct labor | 88,000 |
| Factory overhead | 44,800 |
| Work in process inventory, July 1 | 32,800 |
| Work in process inventory, July 31 | 29,600 |
| Finished goods inventory, July 1 | 37,600 |
| Finished goods inventory, July 31 | 27,200 |

For July, determine (a) the cost of goods manufactured and (b) the cost of goods sold.

# Exercises

**EX 18-1** **Classifying costs as materials, labor, or factory overhead** OBJ. 2

Indicate whether each of the following costs of an automobile manufacturer would be classified as direct materials cost, direct labor cost, or factory overhead cost:

a. Depreciation of robotic assembly line equipment

b. V8 automobile engine

c. Steering wheel

d. Wheels

e. Painting safety masks for employees working in the paint room

f. Salary of test driver

g. Glass used in the vehicle's windshield

h. Wages of assembly line worker

### EX 18-2 Classifying costs as materials, labor, or factory overhead

OBJ. 2

Indicate whether the following costs of Procter & Gamble, a maker of consumer products, would be classified as direct materials cost, direct labor cost, or factory overhead cost:

a. Plant manager salary for the Iowa City, Iowa, plant

b. Maintenance supplies

c. Salary of process engineers

d. Wages paid to Packaging Department employees in the Bear River City, Utah, paper products plant

e. Scents and fragrances used in making soaps and detergents

f. Wages of production line employees at the Pineville, Louisiana, soap and detergent plant

g. Depreciation on assembly line in the Mehoopany, Pennsylvania, paper products plant

h. Packaging materials

i. Resins for body wash products

j. Depreciation on the Auburn, Maine, manufacturing plant

### EX 18-3 Classifying costs as factory overhead

OBJ. 2

Which of the following items are properly classified as part of factory overhead for Ford Motor Company, a maker of heavy automobiles and trucks?

a. Plant manager's salary at Buffalo, New York, stamping plant, which manufactures auto and truck subassemblies

b. Depreciation on Flat Rock, Michigan, assembly plant

c. Dividends paid to shareholders

d. Machine lubricant used to maintain the assembly line at the Louisville, Kentucky, assembly plant

e. Leather to be used on vehicles that have leather interiors

f. Depreciation on mechanical robots used on the assembly line

g. Consultant fees for a study of production line efficiency

h. Dealership sales incentives

i. Vice president of human resources's salary

j. Property taxes on the Detriot, Michigan, headquarters building

### EX 18-4 Classifying costs as product or period costs

OBJ. 2

For apparel manufacturer Abercrombie & Fitch, Inc., classify each of the following costs as either a product cost or a period cost:

a. Research and development costs

b. Depreciation on sewing machines

c. Fabric used during production

d. Depreciation on office equipment

e. Advertising expenses

f. Repairs and maintenance costs for sewing machines

g. Salary of production quality control supervisor

h. Utility costs for office building

i. Sales commissions

j. Salaries of distribution center personnel

k. Wages of sewing machine operators

l. Factory janitorial supplies

m. Chief financial officer's salary

n. Travel costs of media relations employees

o. Factory supervisors' salaries

p. Oil used to lubricate sewing machines

q. Property taxes on factory building and equipment

**EX 18-5    Concepts and terminology**                              OBJ. 1, 2

From the choices presented in parentheses, choose the appropriate term for completing each of the following sentences:

a.  Advertising costs are usually viewed as (period, product) costs.

b.  Feedback is often used to (improve, direct) operations.

c.  Payments of cash or the commitment to pay cash in the future for the purpose of generating revenues are (costs, expenses).

d.  A product, sales territory, department, or activity to which costs are traced is called a (direct cost, cost object).

e.  The balance sheet of a manufacturer would include an account for (cost of goods sold, work in process inventory).

f.  Factory overhead costs combined with direct labor costs are called (prime, conversion) costs.

g.  The implementation of automatic, robotic factory equipment normally (increases, decreases) the direct labor component of product costs.

---

**EX 18-6    Concepts and terminology**                              OBJ. 1, 2

From the choices presented in parentheses, choose the appropriate term for completing each of the following sentences:

a.  The phase of the management process that uses process information to eliminate the source of problems in a process so that the process delivers the correct product in the correct quantities is called (directing, improving).

b.  Direct labor costs combined with factory overhead costs are called (prime, conversion) costs.

c.  The salaries of sales people are normally considered a (period, product) cost.

d.  The plant manager's salary would be considered (direct, indirect) to the product.

e.  Long-term plans are called (strategic, operational) plans.

f.  Materials for use in production are called (supplies, materials inventory).

g.  An example of factory overhead is (electricity used to run assembly line, CEO salary).

---

**EX 18-7    Classifying costs in a service company**                OBJ. 2

A partial list of the costs for Wisconsin and Minnesota Railroad, a short hauler of freight, follows. Classify each cost as either indirect or direct. For purposes of classifying each cost, use the train as the cost object.

a.  Cost to lease (rent) railroad cars

b.  Cost of track and bed (ballast) replacement

c.  Diesel fuel costs

d.  Cost to lease (rent) train locomotives

e.  Depreciation of terminal facilities

f.  Maintenance costs of right of way, bridges, and buildings

g.  Salaries of dispatching and communications personnel

h.  Headquarters information technology support staff salaries

i.  Safety training costs

j.  Wages of train engineers

k.  Wages of switch and classification yard personnel

l.  Costs of accident cleanup

### EX 18-8 Classifying costs

OBJ. 2, 3

The following report was prepared for evaluating the performance of the plant manager of Marching Ants Inc. Evaluate and correct this report.

**Marching Ants Inc.**
**Manufacturing Costs**
**For the Quarter Ended June 30, 2016**

| | |
|---|---:|
| Materials used in production (including $56,200 of indirect materials) .......................... | $ 607,500 |
| Direct labor (including $84,400 maintenance salaries)........ | 562,500 |
| Factory overhead: | |
|     Supervisor salaries ...................................... | 517,500 |
|     Heat, light, and power................................... | 140,650 |
|     Sales salaries ......................................... | 348,750 |
|     Promotional expenses.................................... | 315,000 |
|     Insurance and property taxes—plant ..................... | 151,900 |
|     Insurance and property taxes—corporate offices .......... | 219,400 |
|     Depreciation—plant and equipment ..................... | 123,750 |
|     Depreciation—corporate offices ........................ | 90,000 |
| Total ................................................. | $3,076,950 |

### EX 18-9 Financial statements of a manufacturing firm

OBJ. 3

✔ a. Net income, $129,230

SHOW ME HOW

The following events took place for Video Wave Manufacturing Company during January 2016, the first month of its operations as a producer of digital video monitors:

a. Purchased $133,200 of materials.
b. Used $94,080 of direct materials in production.
c. Incurred $180,320 of direct labor wages.
d. Incurred $211,680 of factory overhead.
e. Transferred $425,320 of work in process to finished goods.
f. Sold goods with a cost of $365,000.
g. Earned revenues of $652,000.
h. Incurred $86,520 of selling expense.
i. Incurred $71,250 of administrative expense.

Using the information given, complete the following:

a. Prepare the January 2016 income statement for Video Wave Manufacturing Company.
b. Determine the inventory balances at the end of the first month of operations.

### EX 18-10 Manufacturing company balance sheet

OBJ. 3

SHOW ME HOW

Partial balance sheet data for Flat Top Company at December 31, 2016, are as follows:

| | | | |
|---|---:|---|---:|
| Finished goods inventory | $ 40,250 | Supplies | $ 71,300 |
| Prepaid insurance | 27,500 | Materials inventory | 87,500 |
| Accounts receivable | 105,000 | Cash | 112,000 |
| Work in process inventory | 157,500 | | |

Prepare the Current Assets section of Flat Top Company's balance sheet at December 31, 2016.

### EX 18-11 Cost of direct materials used in production for a manufacturing company

OBJ. 3

SHOW ME HOW

Rextacular Manufacturing Company reported the following materials data for the month ending June 30, 2016:

| | |
|---|---:|
| Materials purchased | $828,000 |
| Materials inventory, June 1 | 279,000 |
| Materials inventory, June 30 | 252,000 |

Determine the cost of direct materials used in production by Rextacular during the month ended June 30, 2016.

**EX 18-12   Cost of goods manufactured for a manufacturing company**                OBJ. 3

Two items are omitted from each of the following three lists of cost of goods manufactured statement data. Determine the amounts of the missing items, identifying them by letter.

|  |  |  |  |
|---|---|---|---|
| Work in process inventory, August 1 | $ 22,400 | $ 50,400 | (e) |
| Total manufacturing costs incurred during August | 156,800 | (c) | 58,800 |
| Total manufacturing costs | (a) | $294,000 | $68,600 |
| Work in process inventory, August 31 | 33,600 | 67,200 | (f) |
| Cost of goods manufactured | (b) | (d) | $60,200 |

**EX 18-13   Cost of goods manufactured for a manufacturing company**                OBJ. 3

SHOW
ME HOW

The following information is available for Ethtridge Manufacturing Company for the month ending January 31, 2016:

| | |
|---|---|
| Cost of direct materials used in production | $390,000 |
| Direct labor | 336,000 |
| Work in process inventory, January 1 | 162,000 |
| Work in process inventory, January 31 | 170,400 |
| Total factory overhead | 234,000 |

Determine Ethtridge's cost of goods manufactured for the month ended January 31, 2016.

**EX 18-14   Income statement for a manufacturing company**                OBJ. 3

Two items are omitted from each of the following three lists of cost of goods sold data from a manufacturing company income statement. Determine the amounts of the missing items, identifying them by letter.

|  |  |  |  |
|---|---|---|---|
| Finished goods inventory, June 1 | $ 61,600 | $ 46,200 | (e) |
| Cost of goods manufactured | 329,000 | (c) | 484,800 |
| Cost of finished goods available for sale | (a) | $260,400 | $540,000 |
| Finished goods inventory, June 30 | 72,800 | 61,600 | (f) |
| Cost of goods sold | (b) | (d) | $513,600 |

**EX 18-15   Statement of cost of goods manufactured for a manufacturing company**  OBJ. 3

Cost data for Mix-A-Lot Manufacturing Company for the month ended March 31, 2016, are as follows:

| Inventories | March 1 | March 31 |
|---|---|---|
| Materials | $315,000 | $277,200 |
| Work in process | 214,200 | 239,400 |
| Finished goods | 163,800 | 189,000 |

| | |
|---|---|
| Direct labor | $567,000 |
| Materials purchased during May | 604,800 |
| Factory overhead incurred during May: | |
| Indirect labor | 60,480 |
| Machinery depreciation | 36,000 |
| Heat, light, and power | 12,600 |
| Supplies | 10,080 |
| Property taxes | 8,820 |
| Miscellaneous costs | 16,380 |

a.  Prepare a cost of goods manufactured statement for March 2016.

b.  Determine the cost of goods sold for March 2016.

**EX 18-16** **Cost of goods sold, profit margin, and net income for a manufacturing company** OBJ. 3

✔ a. Cost of goods sold, $457,450

The following information is available for Crouching Alligator Manufacturing Company for the month ending October 31, 2016:

| | |
|---|---|
| Cost of goods manufactured | $450,000 |
| Selling expenses | 144,500 |
| Administrative expenses | 75,900 |
| Sales | 911,250 |
| Finished goods inventory, July 1 | 101,250 |
| Finished goods inventory, July 31 | 93,800 |

For the month ended October 31, 2016, determine Crouching Alligator's (a) cost of goods sold, (b) gross profit, and (c) net income.

**EX 18-17** **Cost flow relationships** OBJ. 3

✔ a. $330,000

The following information is available for the first month of operations of Bahadir Company, a manufacturer of mechanical pencils:

| | |
|---|---|
| Sales | $792,000 |
| Gross profit | 462,000 |
| Cost of goods manufactured | 396,000 |
| Indirect labor | 171,600 |
| Factory depreciation | 26,400 |
| Materials purchased | 244,200 |
| Total manufacturing costs for the period | 455,400 |
| Materials inventory, ending | 33,000 |

Using the information given, determine the following missing amounts:

a. Cost of goods sold

b. Finished goods inventory at the end of the month

c. Direct materials cost

d. Direct labor cost

e. Work in process inventory at the end of the month

**EX 18-18** **Uses of managerial accounting in a service company**

Priceline.com allows customers to bid on hotel rooms by "naming their price." This "name your price" process allows customers to obtain a better rate on a hotel room than they might be able to obtain by reserving their room directly from the hotel. The hotel can also benefit from this transaction by filling empty hotel rooms during periods of low occupancy.

Natalie Mooney bids $85 for a night's stay at the Hotel Monaco in Seattle on Saturday August 10. The Hotel Monaco is not fully booked that evening and would likely accept any reasonable bids. How might the Hotel Monaco use managerial accounting information to decide whether or not to accept Natalie's bid?

# Problems: Series A

**PR 18-1A** **Classifying costs** OBJ. 2

The following is a list of costs that were incurred in the production and sale of large commercial airplanes:

a. Salary of chief compliance officer of company *Per , Adm*

b. Power used by painting equipment *Prod, FOH*

c. Instrument panel installed in the airplane cockpit *Prod, DM*

d. Annual bonus paid to the chief operating officer of the company *Per, Adm*

e. Turbo-charged airplane engine *Pro, DM*

f. Interior trim material used throughout the airplane cabin *Pro, DM*

g. Cost of normal scrap from production of airplane body *Pro, FOH*

h. Hourly wages of employees that assemble the airplane *Pro, DL*

i. Salary of the marketing department personnel *Per, Selling Ex*

j. Cost of paving the headquarters employee parking lot *Per, Adm*

k. Cost of electrical wiring throughout the airplane *Pro, DM*

l. Cost of electronic guidance system installed in the airplane cockpit *Pro, PM*

m. Salary of plant manager *Pro, FOH*

n. Cost of miniature replicas of the airplane used to promote and market the airplane *Per, Sell*

o. Human resources department costs for the year *Per, Adm*

p. Metal used for producing the airplane body *Pro, DM*

q. Annual fee to a celebrity to promote the aircraft *Per, Sell*

r. Hydraulic pumps used in the airplane's flight control system *Pro, DM*

s. Yearly cost of the maintenance contract for robotic equipment *Pro, FOH*

t. Prebuilt leather seats installed in the first-class cabin *Pro, PM*

u. Depreciation on factory equipment *Pro, FOH*

v. Special advertising campaign in *Aviation World* magazine *Per, Sell*

w. Oil to lubricate factory equipment *Pro, FOH*

x. Masks for use by painters in painting the airplane body *Pro, FOH*

y. Decals for cockpit door, the cost of which is immaterial to the cost of the final product *Pro, FOH*

z. Salary of chief financial officer *Per, Adm*

**Instructions**

Classify each cost as either a product cost or a period cost. Indicate whether each product cost is a direct materials cost, a direct labor cost, or a factory overhead cost. Indicate whether each period cost is a selling expense or an administrative expense. Use the following tabular headings for your answer, placing an "X" in the appropriate column:

| | Product Costs | | | Period Costs | |
|---|---|---|---|---|---|
| Cost | Direct Materials Cost | Direct Labor Cost | Factory Overhead Cost | Selling Expense | Administrative Expense |

---

**PR 18-2A   Classifying costs**                                                    OBJ. 2

The following is a list of costs incurred by several businesses:

a. Cost of fabric used by clothing manufacturer

b. Maintenance and repair costs for factory equipment

c. Rent for a warehouse used to store work in process and finished products

d. Wages of production quality control personnel

e. Oil lubricants for factory plant and equipment

f. Depreciation of robot used to assemble a product

g. Travel costs of marketing executives to annual sales meeting

h. Depreciation of copying machines used by the Marketing Department

i. Fees charged by collection agency on past-due customer accounts

j. Electricity used to operate factory machinery

k. Maintenance costs for factory equipment

l. Pens, paper, and other supplies used by the Accounting Department in preparing various managerial reports

m. Charitable contribution to United Fund

n. Depreciation of microcomputers used in the factory to coordinate and monitor the production schedules

o. Fees paid to lawn service for office grounds upkeep

(Continued)

p. Cost of sewing machine needles used by a shirt manufacturer

q. Cost of plastic for a telephone being manufactured

r. Telephone charges by president's office

s. Cost of 30-second television commercial

t. Surgeon's fee for heart bypass surgery

u. Depreciation of tools used in production

v. Wages of a machine operator on the production line

w. Salary of the vice president of manufacturing operations

x. Factory janitorial supplies

### Instructions

Classify each of the preceding costs as a product cost or period cost. Indicate whether each product cost is a direct materials cost, a direct labor cost, or a factory overhead cost. Indicate whether each period cost is a selling expense or an administrative expense. Use the following tabular headings for preparing your answer, placing an "X" in the appropriate column:

| | Product Costs | | | Period Costs | |
| --- | --- | --- | --- | --- | --- |
| Cost | Direct Materials Cost | Direct Labor Cost | Factory Overhead Cost | Selling Expense | Administrative Expense |

### PR 18-3A  Cost classifications for a service company

OBJ. 2

A partial list of Foothills Medical Center's costs follows:

a. Cost of patient meals

b. Nurses' salaries

c. Depreciation of X-ray equipment

d. Utility costs of the hospital

e. Salary of intensive care personnel

f. Cost of X-ray test

g. Operating room supplies used on patients (catheters, sutures, etc.)

h. Salary of the nutritionist

i. General maintenance of the hospital

j. Cost of new heart wing

k. Cost of drugs used for patients

l. Cost of advertising hospital services on television

m. Cost of improvements on the employee parking lot

n. Cost of intravenous solutions used for patients

o. Training costs for nurses

p. Cost of laundry services for operating room personnel

q. Doctor's fee

r. Overtime incurred in the Patient Records Department due to a computer failure

s. Cost of blood tests

t. Cost of maintaining the staff and visitors' cafeteria

u. Depreciation on patient rooms

### Instructions

1. What would be Foothills Medical Center's most logical definition for the final cost object?

2. Identify whether each of the costs is to be classified as direct or indirect. For purposes of classifying each cost as direct or indirect, use the patient as the cost object.

**PR 18-4A  Manufacturing income statement, statement of cost of goods manufactured**   OBJ. 2, 3

Several items are omitted from the income statement and cost of goods manufactured statement data for two different companies for the month of December 2016:

| | Prius Company | Volt Company |
|---|---|---|
| Materials inventory, December 1 | $ 280,280 | $ 177,000 |
| Materials inventory, December 31 | (a) | 180,000 |
| Materials purchased | 712,800 | 342,000 |
| Cost of direct materials used in production | 752,400 | (a) |
| Direct labor | 1,058,400 | (b) |
| Factory overhead | 327,600 | 180,000 |
| Total manufacturing costs incurred during December | (b) | 1,035,000 |
| Total manufacturing costs | 2,678,400 | 1,477,500 |
| Work in process inventory, December 1 | 540,000 | 442,500 |
| Work in process inventory, December 31 | 453,600 | (c) |
| Cost of goods manufactured | (c) | 1,024,500 |
| Finished goods inventory, December 1 | 475,200 | 204,000 |
| Finished goods inventory, December 31 | 496,800 | (d) |
| Sales | 4,140,000 | 1,675,500 |
| Cost of goods sold | (d) | 1,051,500 |
| Gross profit | (e) | (e) |
| Operating expenses | 540,000 | (f) |
| Net income | (f) | 384,000 |

**Instructions**

1. Determine the amounts of the missing items, identifying them by letter.

2. Prepare Volt Company's statement of cost of goods manufactured for December.

3. Prepare Volt Company's income statement for December.

**PR 18-5A  Statement of cost of goods manufactured and income statement for a manufacturing company**   OBJ. 2, 3

SHOW ME HOW

The following information is available for The NewQuest Corporation for 2016:

| Inventories | January 1 | December 31 |
|---|---|---|
| Materials | $351,000 | $436,800 |
| Work in process | 631,800 | 592,800 |
| Finished goods | 608,400 | 576,000 |

| | |
|---|---|
| Advertising expense | $ 296,400 |
| Depreciation expense—office equipment | 42,120 |
| Depreciation expense—factory equipment | 56,160 |
| Direct labor | 670,800 |
| Heat, light, and power—factory | 22,460 |
| Indirect labor | 78,750 |
| Materials purchased | 659,800 |
| Office salaries expense | 185,000 |
| Property taxes—factory | 18,500 |
| Property taxes—office building | 32,400 |
| Rent expense—factory | 32,000 |
| Sales | 3,010,000 |
| Sales salaries expense | 420,000 |
| Supplies—factory | 15,400 |
| Miscellaneous costs—factory | 9,500 |

**Instructions**

1. Prepare the 2016 statement of cost of goods manufactured.

2. Prepare the 2016 income statement.

## Problems: Series B

**PR 18-1B    Classifying costs**                                                      OBJ. 2

The following is a list of costs that were incurred in the production and sale of lawn mowers:

a. Premiums on insurance policy for factory buildings

b. Tires for lawn mowers

c. Filter for spray gun used to paint the lawn mowers

d. Paint used to coat the lawn mowers, the cost of which is immaterial to the cost of the final product

e. Plastic for outside housing of lawn mowers

f. Salary of factory supervisor

g. Hourly wages of operators of robotic machinery used in production

h. Engine oil used in mower engines prior to shipment

i. Salary of vice president of marketing

j. Property taxes on the factory building and equipment

k. Cost of advertising in a national magazine

l. Gasoline engines used for lawn mowers

m. Electricity used to run the robotic machinery

n. Straight-line depreciation on the robotic machinery used to manufacture the lawn mowers

o. Salary of quality control supervisor who inspects each lawn mower before it is shipped

p. Attorney fees for drafting a new lease for headquarters offices

q. Payroll taxes on hourly assembly line employees

r. Telephone charges for company controller's office

s. Steering wheels for lawn mowers

t. Factory cafeteria cashier's wages

u. Cash paid to outside firm for janitorial services for factory

v. Maintenance costs for new robotic factory equipment, based on hours of usage

w. Cost of boxes used in packaging lawn mowers

x. License fees for use of patent for lawn mower blade, based on the number of lawn mowers produced

y. Steel used in producing the lawn mowers

z. Commissions paid to sales representatives, based on the number of lawn mowers sold

### Instructions

Classify each cost as either a product cost or a period cost. Indicate whether each product cost is a direct materials cost, a direct labor cost, or a factory overhead cost. Indicate whether each period cost is a selling expense or an administrative expense. Use the following tabular headings for your answer, placing an "X" in the appropriate column:

| | Product Costs | | | Period Costs | |
| --- | --- | --- | --- | --- | --- |
| Cost | Direct Materials Cost | Direct Labor Cost | Factory Overhead Cost | Selling Expense | Administrative Expense |

**PR 18-2B Classifying costs**

The following is a list of costs incurred by several businesses:

a. Salary of quality control supervisor

b. Packing supplies for products sold. These supplies are a very small portion of the total cost of the product.

c. Factory operating supplies

d. Depreciation of factory equipment

e. Hourly wages of warehouse laborers

f. Wages of company controller's secretary

g. Maintenance and repair costs for factory equipment

h. Paper used by commercial printer

i. Entertainment expenses for sales representatives

j. Protective glasses for factory machine operators

k. Sales commissions

l. Cost of hogs for meat processor

m. Cost of telephone operators for a toll-free hotline to help customers operate products

n. Hard drives for a microcomputer manufacturer

o. Lumber used by furniture manufacturer

p. Wages of a machine operator on the production line

q. First-aid supplies for factory workers

r. Tires for an automobile manufacturer

s. Paper used by Computer Department in processing various managerial reports

t. Seed for grain farmer

u. Health insurance premiums paid for factory workers

v. Costs of operating a research laboratory

w. Costs for television advertisement

x. Executive bonus for vice president of marketing

**Instructions**

Classify each of the preceding costs as a product cost or period cost. Indicate whether each product cost is a direct materials cost, a direct labor cost, or a factory overhead cost. Indicate whether each period cost is a selling expense or an administrative expense. Use the following tabular headings for preparing your answer. Place an "X" in the appropriate column.

| | Product Costs | | | Period Costs | |
| --- | --- | --- | --- | --- | --- |
| Cost | Direct Materials Cost | Direct Labor Cost | Factory Overhead Cost | Selling Expense | Administrative Expense |

**PR 18-3B Cost classifications for a service company**

A partial list of The Grand Hotel's costs follows:

a. Cost to mail a customer survey

b. Wages of convention setup employees

c. Pay-per-view movie rental costs (in rooms)

d. Cost of food

e. Cost of room mini-bar supplies

f. Training for hotel restaurant servers

g. Cost to paint lobby

*(Continued)*

h. Cost of laundering towels and bedding

i. Champagne for guests

j. Salary of the hotel manager

k. Depreciation of the hotel

l. Cost of valet parking

m. Wages of bellhops

n. Cost to replace lobby furniture

o. Cost of advertising in local newspaper

p. Wages of desk clerks

q. Wages of maids

r. Cost of new carpeting

s. Guest room telephone costs for long-distance calls

t. Cost of soaps and shampoos for rooms

u. Utility cost

v. Wages of kitchen employees

w. General maintenance supplies

### Instructions

1. What would be The Grand Hotel's most logical definition for the final cost object?

2. Identify whether each of the costs is to be classified as direct or indirect. For purposes of classifying each cost as direct or indirect, use the hotel guest as the cost object.

---

**PR 18-4B    Manufacturing income statement, statement of cost of goods manufactured**                OBJ. 2, 3

✔1. c. On Company, $800,800

Several items are omitted from the income statement and cost of goods manufactured statement data for two different companies for the month of December 2016:

|  | On Company | Off Company |
|---|---|---|
| Materials inventory, December 1 | $ 65,800 | $ 195,300 |
| Materials inventory, December 31 | (a) | 91,140 |
| Materials purchased | 282,800 | (a) |
| Cost of direct materials used in production | 317,800 | (b) |
| Direct labor | 387,800 | 577,220 |
| Factory overhead | 148,400 | 256,060 |
| Total manufacturing costs incurred in December | (b) | 1,519,000 |
| Total manufacturing costs | 973,000 | 1,727,320 |
| Work in process inventory, December 1 | 119,000 | 208,320 |
| Work in process inventory, December 31 | 172,200 | (c) |
| Cost of goods manufactured | (c) | 1,532,020 |
| Finished goods inventory, December 1 | 224,000 | 269,080 |
| Finished goods inventory, December 31 | 197,400 | (d) |
| Sales | 1,127,000 | 1,944,320 |
| Cost of goods sold | (d) | 1,545,040 |
| Gross profit | (e) | (e) |
| Operating expenses | 117,600 | (f) |
| Net income | (f) | 164,920 |

### Instructions

1. Determine the amounts of the missing items, identifying them by letter.

2. Prepare On Company's statement of cost of goods manufactured for December.

3. Prepare On Company's income statement for December.

**PR 18-5B   Statement of cost of goods manufactured and income statement for a**   OBJ. 2, 3
**manufacturing company**

✔1. Cost of goods
manufactured,
$367,510

SHOW
ME HOW

The following information is available for Shanika Company for 2016:

| Inventories | January 1 | December 31 |
| --- | --- | --- |
| Materials | $ 77,350 | $ 95,550 |
| Work in process | 109,200 | 96,200 |
| Finished goods | 113,750 | 100,100 |
| | | |
| Advertising expense | | $ 68,250 |
| Depreciation expense—office equipment | | 22,750 |
| Depreciation expense—factory equipment | | 14,560 |
| Direct labor | | 186,550 |
| Heat, light, and power—factory | | 5,850 |
| Indirect labor | | 23,660 |
| Materials purchased | | 123,500 |
| Office salaries expense | | 77,350 |
| Property taxes—factory | | 4,095 |
| Property taxes—headquarters building | | 13,650 |
| Rent expense—factory | | 6,825 |
| Sales | | 864,500 |
| Sales salaries expense | | 136,500 |
| Supplies—factory | | 3,250 |
| Miscellaneous costs—factory | | 4,420 |

**Instructions**

1. Prepare the 2016 statement of cost of goods manufactured.

2. Prepare the 2016 income statement.

# Cases & Projects

### CP 18-1   Ethics and professional conduct in business

H. Jeckel Manufacturing Company allows employees to purchase, at cost, manufacturing materials, such as metal and lumber, for personal use. To purchase materials for personal use, an employee must complete a materials requisition form, which must then be approved by the employee's immediate supervisor. Fred Rubble, an assistant cost accountant, charges the employee an amount based on H. Jeckel's net purchase cost.

Fred Rubble is in the process of replacing a deck on his home and has requisitioned lumber for personal use, which has been approved in accordance with company policy. In computing the cost of the lumber, Fred reviewed all the purchase invoices for the past year. He then used the lowest price to compute the amount due the company for the lumber.

➤Discuss whether Fred behaved in an ethical manner.

### CP 18-2   Financial versus managerial accounting

The following statement was made by the vice president of finance of The Muppet Company: "The managers of a company should use the same information as the shareholders of the firm. When managers use the same information in guiding their internal operations as shareholders use in evaluating their investments, the managers will be aligned with the stockholders' profit objectives."

➤Respond to the vice president's statement.

### CP 18-3 Managerial accounting in the management process

For each of the following managers, describe how managerial accounting could be used to satisfy strategic or operational objectives:

1. ➤The vice president of the Information Systems Division of a bank.
2. ➤A hospital administrator.
3. ➤The chief executive officer of a food company. The food company is divided into three divisions: Nonalcoholic Beverages, Snack Foods, and Fast Food Restaurants.
4. ➤The manager of the local campus copy shop.

### CP 18-4 Classifying costs

Geek Chic Company provides computer repair services for the community. Obie Won's computer was not working, and he called Geek Chic for a home repair visit. Geek Chic Company's technician arrived at 2:00 P.M. to begin work. By 4:00 P.M. the problem was diagnosed as a failed circuit board. Unfortunately, the technician did not have a new circuit board in the truck because the technician's previous customer had the same problem, and a board was used on that visit. Replacement boards were available back at Geek Chic Company's shop. Therefore, the technician drove back to the shop to retrieve a replacement board. From 4:00 to 5:00 P.M., Geek Chic Company's technician drove the round trip to retrieve the replacement board from the shop.

At 5:00 P.M. the technician was back on the job at Obie's home. The replacement procedure is somewhat complex because a variety of tests must be performed once the board is installed. The job was completed at 6:00 P.M.

Obie's repair bill showed the following:

| | |
|---|---|
| Circuit board | $100 |
| Labor charges | 300 |
| Total | $400 |

Obie was surprised at the size of the bill and asked for some greater detail supporting the calculations. Geek Chic Company responded with the following explanations:

| Cost of materials: | |
|---|---|
| Purchase price of circuit board | $ 80 |
| Markup on purchase price to cover storage and handling | 20 |
| Total materials charge | $100 |

The labor charge per hour is detailed as follows:

| | |
|---|---|
| 2:00–3:00 P.M. | $ 70 |
| 3:00–4:00 P.M. | 60 |
| 4:00–5:00 P.M. | 80 |
| 5:00–6:00 P.M. | 90 |
| Total labor charge | $300 |

Further explanations in the differences in the hourly rates are as follows:

| First hour: | |
|---|---|
| Base labor rate . . . . . . . . . . . . . . . . . . . . . . . . . . . . . . . . . . . . . . | $42 |
| Fringe benefits . . . . . . . . . . . . . . . . . . . . . . . . . . . . . . . . . . . . . . | 10 |
| Overhead (other than storage and handling) . . . . . . . . . . . . | 8 |
| Total base labor rate . . . . . . . . . . . . . . . . . . . . . . . . . . . . . | $60 |
| Additional charge for first hour of any job to cover the cost of vehicle depreciation, fuel, and employee time in transit. A 30-minute transit time is assumed. . . . . . . . . . . . . | 10 |
| | $70 |

Third hour:

| | |
|---|---|
| Base labor rate . . . . . . . . . . . . . . . . . . . . . . . . . . . . . . . . . . . . . . . | $60 |
| The trip back to the shop includes vehicle depreciation and fuel; therefore, a charge was added to the hourly rate to cover these costs. The round trip took an hour. . . . . . . . . . | 20 |
| | $80 |

Fourth hour:

| | |
|---|---|
| Base labor rate . . . . . . . . . . . . . . . . . . . . . . . . . . . . . . . . . . . . . . . | $60 |
| Overtime premium for time worked in excess of an eight-hour day (starting at 5:00 P.M.) is equal to 1.5 times the base rate. . . . . . . . . . . . . . . . . . . . . . . . . . . . . . . . . . . . . . . . . . . . . . . | 30 |
| | $90 |

1. ━━━▶If you were in Obie's position, how would you respond to the bill? Are there parts of the bill that appear incorrect to you? If so, what argument would you employ to convince Geek Chic Company that the bill is too high?

2. Use the headings that follow to construct a table. Fill in the table by first listing the costs identified in the activity in the left-hand column. For each cost, place a check mark in the appropriate column identifying the correct cost classification. Assume that each service call is a job.

| Cost | Direct Materials | Direct Labor | Overhead |
|---|---|---|---|

## CP 18-5   Using managerial accounting information

The following situations describe decision scenarios that could use managerial accounting information:

1. The manager of High Times Restaurant wishes to determine the price to charge for various lunch plates.

2. By evaluating the cost of leftover materials, the plant manager of a precision tool facility wishes to determine how effectively the plant is being run.

3. The division controller of West Coast Supplies needs to determine the cost of products left in inventory.

4. The manager of the Maintenance Department of a large manufacturing company wishes to plan next year's anticipated expenditures.

━━━▶For each situation, discuss how managerial accounting information could be used.

## CP 18-6   Classifying costs

**Group Project**

With a group of students, visit a local copy and graphics shop or a pizza restaurant. As you observe the operation, consider the costs associated with running the business. As a group, identify as many costs as you can and classify them according to the following table headings:

| Cost | Direct Materials | Direct Labor | Overhead | Selling Expenses |
|---|---|---|---|---|

# Job Order Costing

## Paul Stanley's Guitar

**A**s we discussed in Chapter 18, Paul Stanley of the legendary rock band **KISS** uses a custom-made guitar built by **Washburn Guitars**. In fact, Paul Stanley designed his guitar in partnership with Washburn Guitars, as have other rock stars like Dan Donnegan of the rock band **Disturbed**. Washburn's guitars are precision instruments that require high-quality materials and careful craftsmanship. As a result, amateurs and professionals are willing to pay between $1,100 and $10,000 for a PS (Paul Stanley) Series guitar. In order for Washburn to stay in business, the purchase price of the guitar must be greater than the cost of producing the guitar. So, how does Washburn determine the cost of producing a guitar?

Costs associated with creating a guitar include materials such as wood and strings, the wages of employees who build the guitar, and factory overhead. To determine the purchase price of Paul Stanley's guitar, Washburn identifies and records the costs that go into the guitar during each step of the manufacturing process. As the guitar moves through the production process, the costs of direct materials, direct labor, and factory overhead are recorded. When the guitar is complete, the costs that have been recorded are added up to determine the cost of Paul Stanley's unique guitar. The company then prices the guitar to achieve a level of profit greater than the cost of the guitar. This chapter introduces the principles of accounting systems that accumulate costs in the same manner as they were for Paul Stanley's guitar.

NEIL LUPIN/REDFERNS/GETTY IMAGES

## Learning Objectives

After studying this chapter, you should be able to:

*Example Exercises*

**1** Describe cost accounting systems used by manufacturing businesses.
Cost Accounting Systems Overview

**2** Describe and illustrate a job order cost accounting system.
Job Order Cost Systems for Manufacturing Businesses

| | |
|---|---|
| Materials | EE 19-1 |
| Factory Labor | EE 19-2 |
| Factory Overhead | EE 19-3, 19-4 |
| Work in Process | EE 19-5 |
| Finished Goods | |
| Sales and Cost of Goods Sold | EE 19-6 |
| Period Costs | |
| Summary of Cost Flows for Legend Guitars | |

**3** Describe the use of job order cost information for decision making.
Job Order Costing for Decision Making

**4** Describe the flow of costs for a service business that uses a job order cost accounting system.
Job Order Cost Systems for Professional Service Businesses

**At a Glance 19** ▶ Page 904

**1** Describe cost accounting systems used by manufacturing businesses.

# Cost Accounting Systems Overview

**Cost accounting systems** measure, record, and report product costs. Managers use product costs for setting product prices, controlling operations, and developing financial statements.

The two main types of cost accounting systems for manufacturing operations are:

- Job order cost systems
- Process cost systems

**Warner Bros.** and other movie studios use job order cost systems to accumulate movie production and distribution costs. Costs such as actor salaries, production costs, movie print costs, and marketing costs are accumulated in a job account for a particular movie.

A **job order cost system** provides product costs for each quantity of product that is manufactured. Each quantity of product that is manufactured is called a *job*. Job order cost systems are often used by companies that manufacture custom products for customers or batches of similar products. Manufacturers that use a job order cost system are sometimes called *job shops*. An example of a job shop would be an apparel manufacturer, such as Levi Strauss & Co., or a guitar manufacturer, such as Washburn Guitars.

A **process cost system** provides product costs for each manufacturing department or process. Process cost systems are often used by companies that manufacture units of a product that are indistinguishable from each other and are manufactured using a continuous production process. Examples would be oil refineries, paper producers, chemical processors, and food processors.

Job order and process cost systems are widely used. A company may use a job order cost system for some of its products and a process cost system for other products.

The process cost system is illustrated in Chapter 20. The job order cost system is illustrated in this chapter. As a basis for illustration, **Legend Guitars**, a manufacturer of guitars, is used. Exhibit 1 provides a summary of Legend Guitars' manufacturing operations, which were described in Chapter 18.

**EXHIBIT 1**

**Summary of Legend Guitars' Manufacturing Operations**

| **Manufacturing Operations** | |
| --- | --- |
| Cutting | Employees cut the body and neck of the guitar out of wood. |
| Assembling | Employees assemble and finish the guitars. |
| **Product Costs** | |
| Direct materials | The cost of material that is an integral part of and a significant portion of the total cost of the final product. The cost of wood used in the neck and body of the guitars. |
| Direct labor | The cost of employee wages that are an integral part of and a significant portion of the total cost of the final product. Employee wages for cutting and assembling. |
| Factory overhead | Costs other than direct materials and direct labor that are incurred in the manufacturing process. The cost of guitar strings, glue, sandpaper, buffing compound, paint, salaries of production supervisors, janitorial salaries, and factory utilities. |
| **Inventories** | |
| Materials | Includes the cost of direct and indirect materials used to produce the guitars. Direct materials include the cost of wood used in the neck and body of the guitars. Indirect materials include guitar strings, glue, sandpaper, buffing compound, varnish, and paint. |
| Work in process | Includes the product costs of units that have entered the manufacturing process but have not been completed. For example, the product costs of guitars for which the neck and body have been cut but not yet assembled. |
| Finished goods | Includes the cost of completed (or finished) products that have not been sold. The product costs assigned to completed guitars that have not yet been sold. |

# Job Order Cost Systems for Manufacturing Businesses

**OBJ 2** Describe and illustrate a job order cost accounting system.

A job order cost system records and summarizes manufacturing costs by jobs. The flow of manufacturing costs in a job order system is illustrated in Exhibit 2.

**EXHIBIT 2** **Flow of Manufacturing Costs**

- Direct Labor
- Factory Overhead

Materials Storeroom    Production Process    Warehouse    Music Store

Job No. 72   Job No. 71    Job No. 70   Job No. 69

Materials Inventory ⟶ Work in Process ⟶ Finished Goods ⟶ Cost of Goods Sold

Exhibit 2 indicates that although the materials for Jobs 71 and 72 have been added, both jobs are still in the production process. Thus, Jobs 71 and 72 are part of *Work in Process Inventory*. In contrast, Exhibit 2 indicates that Jobs 69 and 70 have been completed. Thus, Jobs 69 and 70 are part of *Finished Goods Inventory*. Exhibit 2 also indicates that when finished guitars are sold to music stores, their costs become part of *Cost of Goods Sold*.

In a job order cost accounting system, perpetual inventory controlling accounts and subsidiary ledgers are maintained for materials, work in process, and finished goods inventories as shown in Exhibit 3.

**EXHIBIT 3**     **Inventory Ledger Accounts**

## Materials

The materials account in the general ledger is a controlling account. A separate account for each type of material is maintained in a subsidiary **materials ledger**.

Exhibit 4 shows **Legend Guitars**' materials ledger account for maple. Increases (debits) and decreases (credits) to the account are as follows:

- Increases (debits) are based on *receiving reports* such as Receiving Report No. 196 for $10,500, which is supported by the supplier's invoice.
- Decreases (credits) are based on *materials requisitions* such as Requisition No. 672 for $2,000 for Job 71 and Requisition No. 704 for $11,000 for Job 72.

**EXHIBIT 4**

**Materials Information and Cost Flows**

Receiving Report No. 196 ← Supplier Invoice $10,500

**a.**

**MATERIALS LEDGER ACCOUNT**

MATERIAL: No. 8 Wood—Maple     ORDER POINT: 500 ft.

| | RECEIVED | | | ISSUED | | | BALANCE | | |
|---|---|---|---|---|---|---|---|---|---|
| Rec. Report No. | Quantity | Amount | Mat. Req. No. | Quantity | Amount | Date | Quantity | Unit Price | Amount |
| | | | | | | Dec. 1 | 600 | $10.00 | $ 6,000 |
| | | | 672 | 200 | $ 2,000 | 4 | 400 | 10.00 | 4,000 |
| 196 | 750 | $10,500 | | | | 8 | 400 | 10.00 | 4,000 |
| | | | | | | | 750 | 14.00 | 10,500 |
| | | | 704 | 900 | 11,000 | 12 | 250 | 14.00 | 3,500 |

**Materials Requisitions**

**b.**

**MATERIALS REQUISITION**

REQUISITION NO.: 672
JOB NO.: 71

| Description | Quantity Issued | Unit Price | Amount |
|---|---|---|---|
| No. 8 Wood—Maple | 200 | $10.00 | $2,000 |
| Total Issued | | | $2,000 |

**b.**

**MATERIALS REQUISITION**

REQUISITION NO.: 704
JOB NO.: 72

| Description | Quantity Issued | Unit Price | Amount |
|---|---|---|---|
| No. 8 Wood—Maple | 400 | $10.00 | $ 4,000 |
| No. 8 Wood—Maple | 500 | 14.00 | 7,000 |
| Total Issued | | | $11,000 |

**Job Cost Sheets**

**b.**

Job 71
20 units of Jazz Series guitars

| Balance, Dec. 1 | $3,000 |
|---|---|
| Direct Materials | 2,000 |
| Direct Labor | |
| Factory Overhead | |

**b.**

Job 72
60 units of American Series guitars

| Direct Materials | $11,000 |
|---|---|
| Direct Labor | |
| Factory Overhead | |

A **receiving report** is prepared when materials that have been ordered are received and inspected. The quantity received and the condition of the materials are entered on the receiving report. When the supplier's invoice is received, it is compared to the receiving report. If there are no discrepancies, a journal entry is made to record the purchase. The journal entry to record the supplier's invoice related to Receiving Report No. 196 in Exhibit 4 is as follows:

| | | | | |
|---|---|---|---|---|
| a. | Materials | | 10,500 | |
| | Accounts Payable | | | 10,500 |
| | Materials purchased during December. | | | |

The storeroom releases materials for use in manufacturing when a **materials requisition** is received. Examples of materials requisitions are shown in Exhibit 4.

The materials requisitions for each job serve as the basis for recording materials used. For direct materials, the quantities and amounts from the materials requisitions are posted to job cost sheets. **Job cost sheets**, which are also illustrated in Exhibit 4, make up the work in process subsidiary ledger.

Exhibit 4 shows the posting of $2,000 of direct materials to Job 71 and $11,000 of direct materials to Job 72.[1] Job 71 is an order for 20 units of Jazz Series guitars, while Job 72 is an order for 60 units of American Series guitars.

A summary of the materials requisitions is used as a basis for the journal entry recording the materials used for the month. For direct materials, this entry increases (debits) Work in Process and decreases (credits) Materials as follows:

| | | | | |
|---|---|---|---|---|
| b. | Work in Process | | 13,000 | |
| | Materials | | | 13,000 |
| | Materials requisitioned to jobs | | | |
| | ($2,000 + $11,000). | | | |

Many companies use computerized information processes to record the use of materials. In such cases, storeroom employees electronically record the release of materials, which automatically updates the materials ledger and job cost sheets.

## Integrity, Objectivity, and Ethics in Business

**PHONY INVOICE SCAMS**

A popular method for defrauding a company is to issue a phony invoice. The scam begins by initially contacting the target firm to discover details of key business contacts, business operations, and products. The swindler then uses this information to create a fictitious invoice.

The invoice will include names, figures, and other details to give it the appearance of legitimacy. This type of scam can be avoided if invoices are matched with receiving documents prior to issuing a check.

[1] To simplify, Exhibit 4 and this chapter use the first-in, first-out cost flow method.

## Example Exercise 19-1 Issuance of Materials

OBJ 2

On March 5, Hatch Company purchased 400 units of raw materials at $14 per unit. On March 10, raw materials were requisitioned for production as follows: 200 units for Job 101 at $12 per unit and 300 units for Job 102 at $14 per unit. Journalize the entry on March 5 to record the purchase and on March 10 to record the requisition from the materials storeroom.

## Follow My Example 19-1

| | | | | |
|---|---|---|---|---|
| Mar. | 5 | Materials......................................................... | 5,600 | |
| | | Accounts Payable .......................................... | | 5,600 |
| | | $5,600 = 400 × $14 | | |
| | 10 | Work in Process ................................................... | 6,600* | |
| | | Materials........................................................ | | 6,600 |

| | | |
|---|---|---|
| *Job 101 | $2,400 = 200 × $12 | |
| Job 102 | 4,200 = 300 × $14 | |
| Total | $6,600 | |

Practice Exercises: PE 19-1A, PE 19-1B

## Factory Labor

When employees report for work, they may use *electronic badges, clock cards,* or *in-and-out cards* to clock in. When employees work on an individual job, they use **time tickets** to record the amount of time they have worked on a specific job. Exhibit 5 illustrates time tickets for Jobs 71 and 72 at **Legend Guitars**.

**EXHIBIT 5**

**Labor Information and Cost Flows**

Dynamic Exhibit

Exhibit 5 shows that on December 13, 2016, D. McInnis spent six hours working on Job 71 at an hourly rate of $10 for a cost of $60 (6 hrs. × $10). Exhibit 5 also indicates that a total of 350 hours was spent by employees on Job 71 during December for a total cost of $3,500. This total direct labor cost of $3,500 is posted to the job cost sheet for Job 71, as shown in Exhibit 5.

Likewise, Exhibit 5 shows that on December 26, 2016, S. Andrews spent eight hours on Job 72 at an hourly rate of $15 for a cost of $120 (8 hrs. × $15). A total of 500 hours was spent by employees on Job 72 during December for a total cost of $7,500. This total direct labor cost of $7,500 is posted to the job cost sheet for Job 72, as shown in Exhibit 5.

A summary of the time tickets is used as the basis for the journal entry recording direct labor for the month. This entry increases (debits) Work in Process and increases (credits) Wages Payable, as follows:

| | | | | |
|---|---|---|---|---|
| c. | Work in Process | | 11,000 | |
| | Wages Payable | | | 11,000 |
| | Factory labor used in production of jobs ($3,500 + $7,500). | | | |

As with direct materials, many businesses use computerized information processing to record direct labor. In such cases, employees may log their time directly into computer terminals at their workstations. In other cases, employees may be issued magnetic cards, much like credit cards, to log in and out of work assignments.

---

## Example Exercise 19-2  Direct Labor Costs

OBJ 2

During March, Hatch Company accumulated 800 hours of direct labor costs on Job 101 and 600 hours on Job 102. The total direct labor was incurred at a rate of $16 per direct labor hour for Job 101 and $12 per direct labor hour for Job 102. Journalize the entry to record the flow of labor costs into production during March.

### Follow My Example 19-2

| | | | | |
|---|---|---|---|---|
| Work in Process ..................................................... | | 20,000* | |
| Wages Payable..................................................... | | | 20,000 |

| | | |
|---|---|---|
| *Job 101 | $12,800 = 800 hrs. × $16 | |
| Job 102 | 7,200 = 600 hrs. × $12 | |
| Total | $20,000 | |

Practice Exercises: PE 19-2A, PE 19-2B

---

## Business 🌎 Connection

### BMW'S FACTORY LABOR EXPERIMENT

In 2007, managers at Bavarian Motorworks (BMW) began to worry about the increasing age of their workforce. The average age of manufacturing plant workers was expected to increase from 39 to 47 by 2017. To plan for this change, BMW conducted an experiment by altering the age makeup of workers on one of the company's production lines to match the average age anticipated in 2017. In addition, the company made 70 changes to the production line to reduce the chance of error and physical strain. The changes resulted in a 7% improvement in productivity and a 2% decrease in employee absences from work. The company now uses the line as a model of quality and productivity for the rest of the company.

Source: C. Loch, F. Sting, N. Bauer, and H. Mauermann, "How BMW Is Defusing the Demographic Time Bomb," *Harvard Business Review*, March 2010.

## Factory Overhead

Factory overhead includes all manufacturing costs except direct materials and direct labor. Factory overhead costs come from a variety of sources, including the following:

- *Indirect materials* comes from a summary of materials requisitions.
- *Indirect labor* comes from the salaries of production supervisors and the wages of other employees such as janitors.
- *Factory power* comes from utility bills.
- *Factory depreciation* comes from Accounting Department computations of depreciation.

To illustrate the recording of factory overhead, assume that **Legend Guitars** incurred $4,600 of overhead during December, which included $500 of indirect materials, $2,000 of indirect labor, $900 of utilities, and $1,200 of factory depreciation. The $500 of indirect materials consisted of $200 of glue and $300 of sandpaper. The entry to record the factory overhead is as follows:

| | | | | | |
|---|---|---|---|---|---|
| d. | Factory Overhead | | | 4,600 | |
| | Materials | | | | 500 |
| | Wages Payable | | | | 2,000 |
| | Utilities Payable | | | | 900 |
| | Accumulated Depreciation | | | | 1,200 |
| | Factory overhead incurred in production. | | | | |

### Example Exercise 19-3 Factory Overhead Costs

**OBJ 2**

During March, Hatch Company incurred factory overhead costs as follows: indirect materials, $800; indirect labor, $3,400; utilities cost, $1,600; and factory depreciation, $2,500. Journalize the entry to record the factory overhead incurred during March.

### Follow My Example 19-3

| | | |
|---|---|---|
| Factory Overhead .................................................... | 8,300 | |
| Materials........................................................ | | 800 |
| Wages Payable.................................................. | | 3,400 |
| Utilities Payable................................................ | | 1,600 |
| Accumulated Depreciation—Factory ................................ | | 2,500 |

Practice Exercises: PE 19-3A, PE 19-3B

**Allocating Factory Overhead** Factory overhead is different from direct labor and direct materials in that it is *indirectly* related to the jobs. That is, factory overhead costs cannot be identified with or traced to specific jobs. For this reason, factory overhead costs are allocated to jobs. The process by which factory overhead or other costs are assigned to a cost object, such as a job, is called **cost allocation**.

The factory overhead costs are *allocated* to jobs using a common measure related to each job. This measure is called an **activity base**, *allocation base*, or *activity driver*. The activity base used to allocate overhead should reflect the consumption or use of factory overhead costs. Three common activity bases used to allocate factory overhead costs are direct labor hours, direct labor cost, and machine hours.

**Predetermined Factory Overhead Rate** Factory overhead costs are normally allocated or *applied* to jobs using a **predetermined factory overhead rate**. The predetermined factory overhead rate is computed as follows:

$$\text{Predetermined Factory Overhead Rate} = \frac{\text{Estimated Total Factory Overhead Costs}}{\text{Estimated Activity Base}}$$

To illustrate, assume that **Legend Guitars** estimates the total factory overhead cost as $50,000 for the year and the activity base as 10,000 direct labor hours. The predetermined factory overhead rate of $5 per direct labor hour is computed as follows:

$$\text{Predetermined Factory Overhead Rate} = \frac{\$50,000}{10,000 \text{ direct labor hours}} = \$5 \text{ per direct labor hour}$$

As illustrated, the predetermined overhead rate is computed using *estimated* amounts at the beginning of the period. This is because managers need timely information on the product costs of each job. If a company waited until all overhead costs were known at the end of the period, the allocated factory overhead would be accurate, but not timely. Only through timely reporting can managers adjust manufacturing methods or product pricing.

Many companies are using a method for accumulating and allocating factory overhead costs. This method, called **activity-based costing**, uses a different overhead rate for each type of factory overhead activity, such as inspecting, moving, and machining. Activity-based costing is discussed and illustrated in Chapter 25.

**Applying Factory Overhead to Work in Process** **Legend Guitars** applies factory overhead using a rate of $5 per direct labor hour. The factory overhead applied to each job is recorded in the job cost sheets, as shown in Exhibit 6.

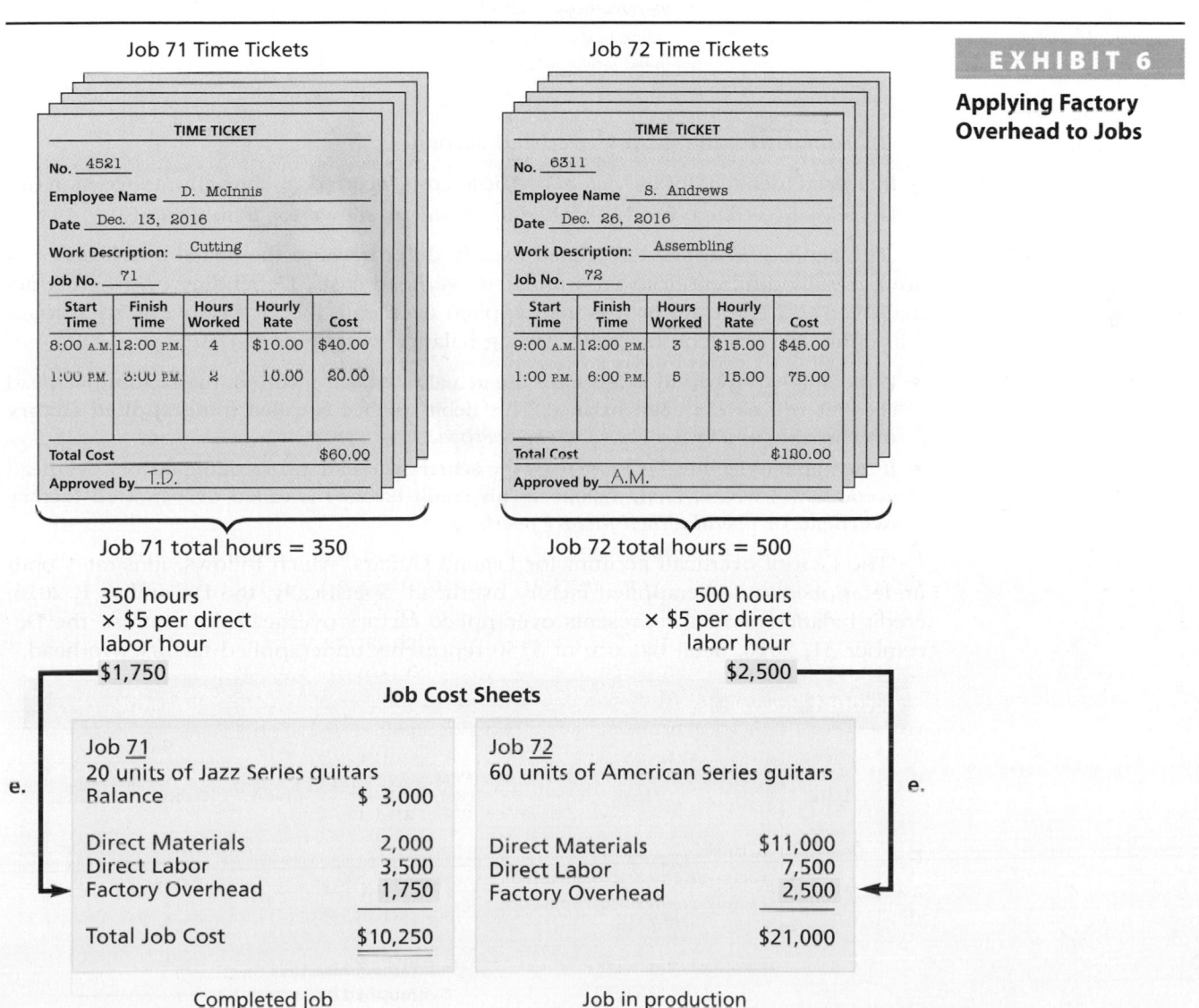

**EXHIBIT 6**

**Applying Factory Overhead to Jobs**

Exhibit 6 shows that 850 direct labor hours were used in Legend Guitars' December operations. Based on the time tickets, 350 hours can be traced to Job 71, and 500 hours can be traced to Job 72.

Using a factory overhead rate of $5 per direct labor hour, $4,250 of factory overhead is applied as follows:

| | Direct Labor Hours | Factory Overhead Rate | Factory Overhead Applied |
|---|---|---|---|
| Job 71 | 350 | $5 | $1,750 (350 hrs. × $5) |
| Job 72 | 500 | $5 | 2,500 (500 hrs. × $5) |
| Total | 850 | | $4,250 |

As shown in Exhibit 6, the applied overhead is posted to each job cost sheet. Factory overhead of $1,750 is posted to Job 71, which results in a total product cost on December 31, 2016, of $10,250. Factory overhead of $2,500 is posted to Job 72, which results in a total product cost on December 31, 2016, of $21,000.

The journal entry to apply factory overhead increases (debits) Work in Process and credits Factory Overhead. This journal entry to apply overhead to Jobs 71 and 72 is as follows:

| | | | | |
|---|---|---|---|---|
| e. | Work in Process | | 4,250 | |
| | Factory Overhead | | | 4,250 |
| | Factory overhead applied to jobs according to the predetermined overhead rate (850 hrs. × $5). | | | |

To summarize, the factory overhead account is:

- Increased (debited) for the *actual overhead* costs incurred, as shown for transaction (d).
- Decreased (credited) for the *applied overhead*, as shown for transaction (e).

The actual and applied overhead usually differ because the actual overhead costs are normally different from the estimated overhead costs. Depending on whether actual overhead is greater or less than applied overhead, the factory overhead account will either have a debit or credit ending balance as follows:

- If the applied overhead is *less than* the actual overhead incurred, the factory overhead account will have a debit balance. This debit balance is called **underapplied factory overhead** or *underabsorbed factory overhead*.
- If the applied overhead is *more than* the actual overhead incurred, the factory overhead account will have a credit balance. This credit balance is called **overapplied factory overhead** or *overabsorbed factory overhead*.

The factory overhead account for Legend Guitars, which follows, illustrates both underapplied and overapplied factory overhead. Specifically, the December 1, 2016, credit balance of $200 represents overapplied factory overhead. In contrast, the December 31, 2016, debit balance of $150 represents underapplied factory overhead.

| **Account** Factory Overhead | | | | | | *Account No.* | |
|---|---|---|---|---|---|---|---|
| | | | | | | **Balance** | |
| **Date** | | **Item** | **Post. Ref.** | **Debit** | **Credit** | **Debit** | **Credit** |
| 2016 Dec. | 1 | Balance | | | | | 200 |
| | 31 | Factory overhead cost incurred | | 4,600 | | 4,400 | |
| | 31 | Factory overhead cost applied | | | 4,250 | 150 | |

Underapplied balance ————
Overapplied balance ————

If the balance of factory overhead (either underapplied or overapplied) becomes large, the balance and related overhead rate should be investigated. For example, a large balance could be caused by changes in manufacturing methods. In this case, the factory overhead rate should be revised.

---

### Example Exercise 19-4 Applying Factory Overhead

OBJ 2

Hatch Company estimates that total factory overhead costs will be $100,000 for the year. Direct labor hours are estimated to be 25,000. For Hatch Company, (a) determine the predetermined factory overhead rate using direct labor hours as the activity base, (b) determine the amount of factory overhead applied to Jobs 101 and 102 in March, using the data on direct labor hours from Example Exercise 19-2, and (c) prepare the journal entry to apply factory overhead to both jobs in March according to the predetermined overhead rate.

### Follow My Example 19-4

a.  $4.00 per direct labor hour = $100,000 ÷ 25,000 direct labor hours

b.  Job 101      $3,200 = 800 hours × $4.00 per hour

    Job 102       2,400 = 600 hours × $4.00 per hour

    Total        $5,600

c.  Work in Process . . . . . . . . . . . . . . . . . . . . . . . . . . . . . . . . . . . . . . . . .      5,600

       Factory Overhead . . . . . . . . . . . . . . . . . . . . . . . . . . . . . . . . . . . .                  5,600

Practice Exercises: PE 19-4A, PE 19-4B

---

**Disposal of Factory Overhead Balance** During the year, the balance in the factory overhead account is carried forward and reported as a deferred debit or credit on the monthly (interim) balance sheets. However, any balance in the factory overhead account should not be carried over to the next year. This is because any such balance applies only to operations of the current year.

If the estimates for computing the predetermined overhead rate are reasonably accurate, the ending balance of Factory Overhead should be relatively small. For this reason, the balance of Factory Overhead at the end of the year is disposed of by transferring it to the cost of goods sold account as follows:[2]

- If there is an ending debit balance (underapplied overhead) in the factory overhead account, it is disposed of by the entry that follows:

| | | | | |
|---|---|---|---|---|
| Cost of Goods Sold | | | XXX | |
|   Factory Overhead | | | | XXX |
|     Transfer of underapplied | | | | |
|     overhead to cost of goods sold. | | | | |

- If there is an ending credit balance (overapplied overhead) in the factory overhead account, it is disposed of by the entry that follows:

| | | | | |
|---|---|---|---|---|
| Factory Overhead | | | XXX | |
|   Cost of Goods Sold | | | | XXX |
|     Transfer of overapplied | | | | |
|     overhead to cost of goods sold. | | | | |

---

[2] An ending balance in the factory overhead account may also be allocated among the work in process, finished goods, and cost of goods sold accounts. This brings these accounts into agreement with the actual costs incurred. This approach is rarely used and is only required for large ending balances in the factory overhead account. For this reason, it will not be used in this text.

To illustrate, the journal entry to dispose of **Legend Guitars'** December 31, 2016, underapplied overhead balance of $150 is as follows:

| | | | | |
|---|---|---|---|---|
| f. | Cost of Goods Sold | | 150 | |
| | Factory Overhead | | | 150 |
| | Closed underapplied factory overhead to cost of goods sold. | | | |

## Work in Process

During the period, Work in Process is increased (debited) for the following:

- Direct materials cost
- Direct labor cost
- Applied factory overhead cost

To illustrate, the work in process account for **Legend Guitars** is shown in Exhibit 7. The balance of Work in Process on December 1, 2016 (beginning balance), was $3,000. As shown in Exhibit 7, this balance relates to Job 71, which was the only job in process on this date. During December, Work in Process was debited for the following:

- Direct materials cost of $13,000 [transaction (b)], based on materials requisitions.
- Direct labor cost of $11,000 [transaction (c)], based on time tickets.
- Applied factory overhead of $4,250 [transaction (e)], based on the predetermined overhead rate of $5 per direct labor hour.

The preceding Work in Process debits are supported by the detail postings to job cost sheets for Jobs 71 and 72, as shown in Exhibit 7.

---

**EXHIBIT 7**

**Job Cost Sheets and the Work in Process Controlling Account**

**Job Cost Sheets**

| Job 71 | |
|---|---|
| 20 units of Jazz Series guitars | |
| Balance | $ 3,000 |
| Direct Materials | 2,000 |
| Direct Labor | 3,500 |
| Factory Overhead | 1,750 |
| Total Job Cost | $10,250 |
| Unit Cost | $512.50 |

| Job 72 | |
|---|---|
| 60 units of American Series guitars | |
| Direct Materials | $11,000 |
| Direct Labor | 7,500 |
| Factory Overhead | 2,500 |
| Total Job Cost | $21,000 |

**Account** *Work in Process*                                   *Account No.*

| | Date | | Item | Post. Ref. | Debit | Credit | Balance Debit | Balance Credit |
|---|---|---|---|---|---|---|---|---|
| g. | 2016 Dec. | 1 | Balance | | | | 3,000 | |
| | | 31 | Direct materials | | 13,000 | | 16,000 | |
| | | 31 | Direct labor | | 11,000 | | 27,000 | |
| | | 31 | Factory overhead | | 4,250 | | 31,250 | |
| | | 31 | Jobs completed—Job 71 | | | 10,250 | 21,000 | |

During December, Job 71 was completed. Upon completion, the product costs (direct materials, direct labor, factory overhead) are totaled. This total is divided by the number of units produced to determine the cost per unit. Thus, the 20 Jazz Series guitars produced as Job 71 cost $512.50 ($10,250 ÷ 20) per guitar.

After completion, Job 71 is transferred from Work in Process to Finished Goods by the following entry:

| | | | | |
|---|---|---|---|---|
| | g. | Finished Goods | 10,250 | |
| | | Work in Process | | 10,250 |
| | | Job 71 completed in December. | | |

Job 72 was started in December but was not completed by December 31, 2016. Thus, Job 72 is still part of work in process on December 31, 2016. As shown in Exhibit 7, the balance of the job cost sheet for Job 72 ($21,000) is also the December 31, 2016, balance of Work in Process.

## Example Exercise 19-5  Job Costs  OBJ 2

At the end of March, Hatch Company had completed Jobs 101 and 102. Job 101 is for 500 units, and Job 102 is for 1,000 units. Using the data from Example Exercises 19-1, 19-2, and 19-4, determine (a) the balance on the job cost sheets for Jobs 101 and 102 at the end of March and (b) the cost per unit for Jobs 101 and 102 at the end of March.

### Follow My Example 19-5

a.

| | Job 101 | Job 102 |
|---|---|---|
| Direct materials | $ 2,400 | $ 4,200 |
| Direct labor | 12,800 | 7,200 |
| Factory overhead | 3,200 | 2,400 |
| Total costs | $18,400 | $13,800 |

b. Job 101 $36.80 = $18,400 ÷ 500 units
   Job 102 $13.80 = $13,800 ÷ 1,000 units

Practice Exercises: PE 19-5A, PE 19-5B

## Finished Goods

The finished goods account is a controlling account for the subsidiary **finished goods ledger** or *stock ledger*. Each account in the finished goods ledger contains cost data for the units manufactured, units sold, and units on hand.

Exhibit 8 illustrates the finished goods ledger account for **Legend Guitars'** Jazz Series guitars.

**ITEM:** *Jazz Series guitars*

| Manufactured | | | Shipped | | | Balance | | | |
|---|---|---|---|---|---|---|---|---|---|
| Job Order No. | Quantity | Amount | Ship Order No. | Quantity | Amount | Date | Quantity | Amount | Unit Cost |
| | | | | | | Dec. 1 | 40 | $20,000 | $500.00 |
| | | | 643 | 40 | $20,000 | 9 | — | — | — |
| 71 | 20 | $10,250 | | | | 31 | 20 | 10,250 | 512.50 |

**EXHIBIT 8**

**Finished Goods Ledger Account**

Exhibit 8 indicates that there were 40 Jazz Series guitars on hand on December 1, 2016. During the month, 20 additional Jazz guitars were completed and transferred to Finished Goods from the completion of Job 71. In addition, the beginning inventory of 40 Jazz guitars was sold during the month.

## Sales and Cost of Goods Sold

During December, **Legend Guitars** sold 40 Jazz Series guitars for $850 each, generating total sales of $34,000 ($850 × 40 guitars). Exhibit 8 indicates that the cost of these guitars was $500 per guitar or a total cost of $20,000 ($500 × 40 guitars). The entries to record the sale and related cost of goods sold are as follows:

| | | | | |
|---|---|---|---|---|
| h. | Accounts Receivable | | 34,000 | |
| | Sales | | | 34,000 |
| | Revenue received from guitars sold on account. | | | |

| | | | | |
|---|---|---|---|---|
| i. | Cost of Goods Sold | | 20,000 | |
| | Finished Goods | | | 20,000 |
| | Cost of 40 Jazz Series guitars sold. | | | |

In a job order cost accounting system, the preparation of a statement of cost of goods manufactured, which was discussed in Chapter 18, is not necessary. This is because job order costing uses the perpetual inventory system and, thus, the cost of goods sold can be directly determined from the finished goods ledger as illustrated in Exhibit 8.

**Example Exercise 19-6** **Cost of Goods Sold**

OBJ 2

Nejedly Company completed 80,000 units during the year at a cost of $680,000. The beginning finished goods inventory was 10,000 units at $80,000. Determine the cost of goods sold for 60,000 units, assuming a FIFO cost flow.

**Follow My Example 19-6**

$505,000 = $80,000 + (50,000 × $8.50*)
*Cost per unit of goods produced during the year = $8.50 = $680,000 ÷ 80,000 units

Practice Exercises: PE 19-6A, PE 19-6B

## Period Costs

Period costs are used in generating revenue during the current period but are not involved in the manufacturing process. As discussed in Chapter 18, *period costs* are recorded as expenses of the current period as either selling or administrative expenses.

Selling expenses are incurred in marketing the product and delivering sold products to customers. Administrative expenses are incurred in managing the company but are not related to the manufacturing or selling functions. During December, **Legend Guitars** recorded the following selling and administrative expenses:

| | | | | |
|---|---|---|---|---|
| j. | Sales Salaries Expense | | 2,000 | |
| | Office Salaries Expense | | 1,500 | |
| | Salaries Payable | | | 3,500 |
| | Recorded December period costs. | | | |

## Summary of Cost Flows for Legend Guitars

Exhibit 9 shows the cost flows through the manufacturing accounts of **Legend Guitars** for December.

**EXHIBIT 9** Flow of Manufacturing Costs for Legend Guitars

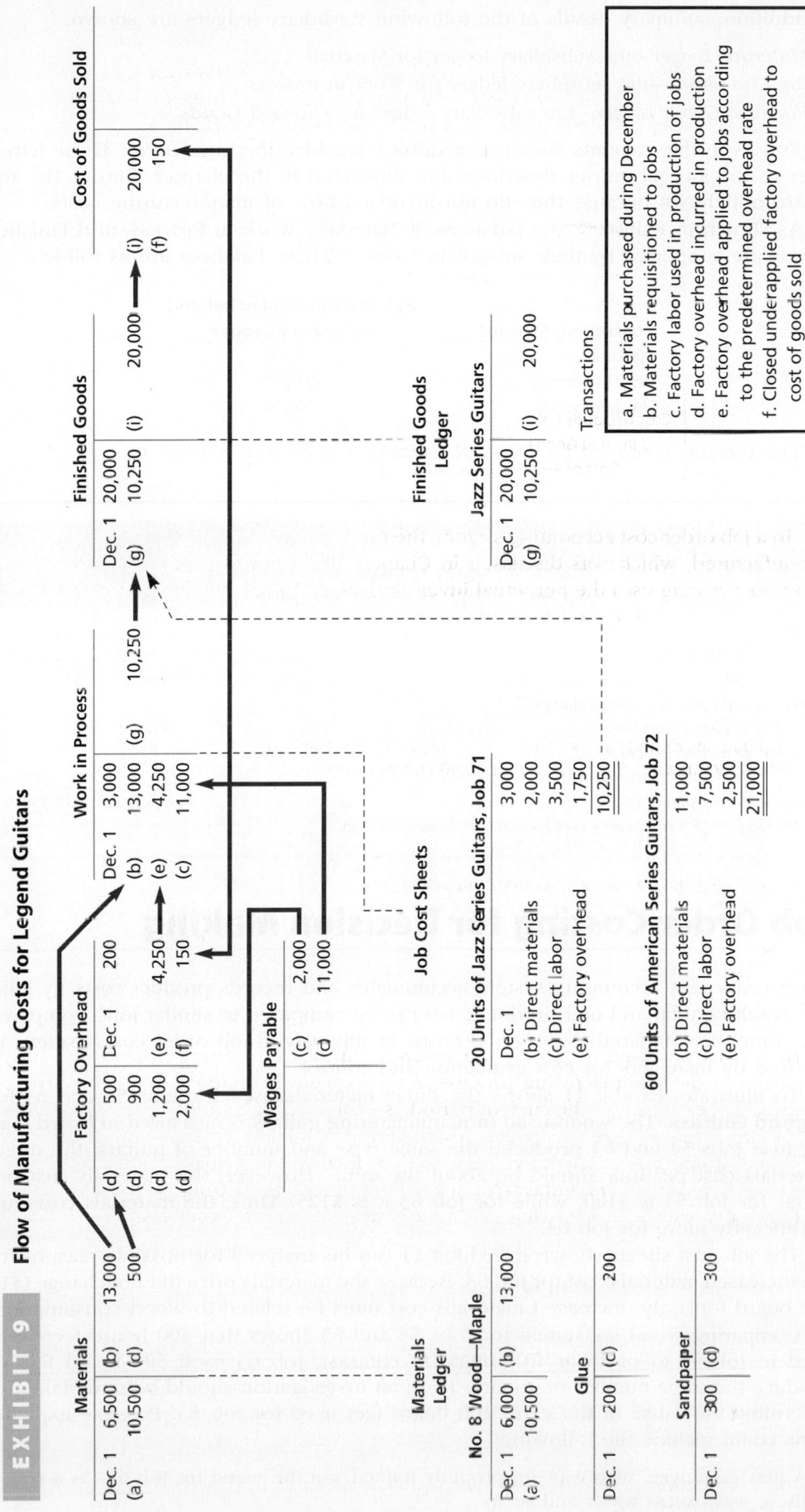

**Materials**

| | | | | |
|---|---|---|---|---|
| Dec. 1 | 6,500 | (b) | 13,000 | |
| (a) | 10,500 | (d) | 500 | |

**Materials Ledger**

**No. 8 Wood—Maple**

| | | | |
|---|---|---|---|
| Dec. 1 | 6,000 | (b) | 13,000 |
| (a) | 10,500 | | |

**Glue**

| | | | |
|---|---|---|---|
| Dec. 1 | 200 | (c) | 200 |

**Sandpaper**

| | | |
|---|---|---|
| Dec. 1 | 300 | (d) 300 |

**Factory Overhead**

| | | | | |
|---|---|---|---|---|
| (d) | 500 | Dec. 1 | 500 | |
| (d) | 900 | | | |
| (d) | 1,200 | (e) | 4,250 | |
| (d) | 2,000 | (f) | 150 | |

**Wages Payable**

| | | | |
|---|---|---|---|
| | | (c) | 2,000 |
| | | (d | 11,000 |

**Work in Process**

| | | | | |
|---|---|---|---|---|
| Dec. 1 | 3,000 | (g) | 10,250 | |
| (b) | 13,000 | | | |
| (e) | 4,250 | | | |
| (c) | 11,000 | | | |

**Job Cost Sheets**

**20 Units of Jazz Series Guitars, Job 71**

| | |
|---|---|
| Dec. 1 | 3,000 |
| (b) Direct materials | 2,000 |
| (c) Direct labor | 3,500 |
| (e) Factory overhead | 1,750 |
| | 10,250 |

**60 Units of American Series Guitars, Job 72**

| | |
|---|---|
| (b) Direct materials | 11,000 |
| (c) Direct labor | 7,500 |
| (e) Factory overhead | 2,500 |
| | 21,000 |

**Finished Goods**

| | | | | |
|---|---|---|---|---|
| Dec. 1 | 20,000 | (i) | 20,000 | |
| (g) | 10,250 | | | |

**Finished Goods Ledger**

**Jazz Series Guitars**

| | | | |
|---|---|---|---|
| Dec. 1 | 20,000 | (i) | 20,000 |
| (g) | 10,250 | | |

**Cost of Goods Sold**

| | | |
|---|---|---|
| (i) | 20,000 | |
| (f) | 150 | |

**Transactions**

a. Materials purchased during December
b. Materials requisitioned to jobs
c. Factory labor used in production of jobs
d. Factory overhead incurred in production
e. Factory overhead applied to jobs according to the predetermined overhead rate
f. Closed underapplied factory overhead to cost of goods sold
g. Job 71 completed in December
h. Sold 40 Jazz Series guitars on account (not shown)
i. Cost of 40 Jazz Series guitars sold
j. Recorded December period costs (not shown)

In addition, summary details of the following subsidiary ledgers are shown:

- *Materials Ledger*—the subsidiary ledger for Materials.
- *Job Cost Sheets*—the subsidiary ledger for Work in Process.
- *Finished Goods Ledger*—the subsidiary ledger for Finished Goods.

Entries in the accounts shown in Exhibit 9 are identified by letters. These letters refer to the journal entries described and illustrated in the chapter. Entries (h) and (j) are not shown because they do not involve a flow of manufacturing costs.

As shown in Exhibit 9, the balances of Materials, Work in Process, and Finished Goods are supported by their subsidiary ledgers. These balances are as follows:

| Controlling Account | Balance and Total of Related Subsidiary Ledger |
|---|---|
| Materials | $ 3,500 |
| Work in Process | 21,000 |
| Finished Goods | 10,250 |

The income statement for **Legend Guitars** is shown in Exhibit 10.

---

**EXHIBIT 10**

**Income Statement of Legend Guitars**

| Legend Guitars<br>Income Statement<br>For the Month Ended December 31, 2016 | | |
|---|---:|---:|
| Sales | | $34,000 |
| Cost of goods sold | | 20,150* |
| Gross profit | | $13,850 |
| Selling and administrative expenses: | | |
|    Sales salaries expense | $2,000 | |
|    Office salaries expense | 1,500 | |
|      Total selling and administrative expenses | | 3,500 |
| Income from operations | | $10,350 |
| *$20,150 = ($500 × 40 guitars) + $150 underapplied factory overhead | | |

---

## Job Order Costing for Decision Making

**OBJ 3** Describe the use of job order cost information for decision making.

A job order cost accounting system accumulates and records product costs by jobs. The resulting total and unit product costs can be compared to similar jobs, compared over time, or compared to expected costs. In this way, a job order cost system can be used by managers for cost evaluation and control.

To illustrate, Exhibit 11 shows the direct materials used for Jobs 54 and 63 for **Legend Guitars**. The wood used in manufacturing guitars is measured in board feet. Because Jobs 54 and 63 produced the same type and number of guitars, the direct materials cost per unit should be about the same. However, the materials cost per guitar for Job 54 is $100, while for Job 63 it is $125. Thus, the materials costs are significantly more for Job 63.

The job cost sheets shown in Exhibit 11 can be analyzed for possible reasons for the increased materials cost for Job 63. Because the materials price did not change ($10 per board foot), the increased materials cost must be related to wood consumption.

Comparing wood consumed for Jobs 54 and 63 shows that 400 board feet were used in Job 54 to produce 40 guitars. In contrast, Job 63 used 500 board feet to produce the same number of guitars. Thus, an investigation should be undertaken to determine the cause of the extra 100 board feet used for Job 63. Possible explanations could include the following:

Major electric utilities such as **Tennessee Valley Authority**, **Consolidated Edison Inc.**, and **Pacific Gas and Electric Company** use job order accounting to control the costs associated with major repairs and overhauls that occur during maintenance shutdowns.

- A new employee, who was not properly trained, cut the wood for Job 63. As a result, there was excess waste and scrap.

**Job 54**
Item: 40 Jazz Series guitars

| | Materials Quantity (board feet) | Materials Price | Materials Amount |
|---|---|---|---|
| Direct materials: | | | |
| No. 8 Wood—Maple | 400 | $10.00 | $4,000 |
| Direct materials per guitar | | | $ 100* |
| *$4,000 ÷ 40 | | | |

**Job 63**
Item: 40 Jazz Series guitars

| | Materials Quantity (board feet) | Materials Price | Materials Amount |
|---|---|---|---|
| Direct materials: | | | |
| No. 8 Wood—Maple | 500 | $10.00 | $5,000 |
| Direct materials per guitar | | | $ 125* |
| *$5,000 ÷ 40 | | | |

**EXHIBIT 11**

**Comparing Data from Job Cost Sheets**

- The wood used for Job 63 was purchased from a new supplier. The wood was of poor quality, which created excessive waste and scrap.
- The cutting tools needed repair and were not properly maintained. As a result, the wood was miscut, which created excessive waste and scrap.
- The instructions attached to the job were incorrect. The wood was cut according to the instructions. The incorrect instructions were discovered later in assembly. As a result, the wood had to be recut and the initial cuttings scrapped.

# Job Order Cost Systems for Professional Service Businesses

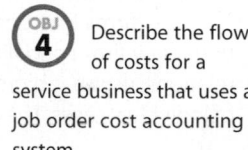 Describe the flow of costs for a service business that uses a job order cost accounting system.

A job order cost accounting system may be used for a professional service business. For example, an advertising agency, an attorney, and a physician each provide services to individual customers, clients, or patients. In such cases, the customer, client, or patient can be viewed as a job for which costs are accumulated and reported.

The primary product costs for a service business are direct labor and overhead costs. Any materials or supplies used in rendering services are normally insignificant. As a result, materials and supply costs are included as part of the overhead cost.

Like a manufacturing business, direct labor and overhead costs of rendering services to clients are accumulated in a work in process account. Work in Process is supported by a cost ledger with a job cost sheet for each client.

When a job is completed and the client is billed, the costs are transferred to a cost of services account. Cost of Services is similar to the cost of merchandise sold account for a merchandising business or the cost of goods sold account for a manufacturing business. A finished goods account and related finished goods ledger are not necessary. This is because the revenues for the services are recorded only after the services are provided.

In practice, other considerations unique to service businesses may need to be considered. For example, a service business may bill clients on a weekly or monthly basis rather than when a job is completed. In such cases, a portion of the costs related to each billing is transferred from the work in process account to the cost of services account. A service business may also bill clients for services in advance, which would be accounted for as deferred revenue until the services are completed.

The flow of costs through a service business using a job order cost accounting system is shown in Exhibit 12.

**EXHIBIT 12**  **Flow of Costs Through a Service Business**

 **Service** 🔔 **Focus**

### JOB ORDER COSTING IN A LAW FIRM

Law firms typically use job order costing to track the costs of individual legal cases or client engagements. The costs of each job are accumulated in a job cost sheet, just as in a manufacturing firm. However, because a law firm is a service firm, there are no direct materials costs. The primary cost comes from the direct labor of the professional staff.

Law firms like, **Constangy, Brooks, and Smith**, a national law firm specializing in employment law and labor relations, uses a job order costing system to track the cost of individual cases. The direct labor costs of the professional staff are determined by multiplying the time that each attorney spends on an individual case by the attorney's hourly billing rate. Billing rates vary depending on the rank of the attorney doing the work. In addition, any costs that can be directly attributed to a specific engagement are added to the engagement's job cost sheet. For example, if a case requires the legal team to travel to another city to interview witnesses, the cost of that travel is added to the job cost sheet for that specific client. Indirect costs, such as support staff, office supplies, and office rent, are accumulated as overhead costs and allocated to individual jobs using an activity base, such as professional service hours.

## At a Glance 19

 **OBJ 1**

**Describe cost accounting systems used by manufacturing businesses.**

**Key Points**  A cost accounting system accumulates product costs. The two primary cost accounting systems are the job order and the process cost systems. Job order cost systems accumulate costs for each quantity of product that passes through the factory. Process cost systems accumulate costs for each department or process within the factory.

| Learning Outcomes | Example Exercises | Practice Exercises |
|---|---|---|
| • Describe a cost accounting system. | | |
| • Describe a job order cost system. | | |
| • Describe a process cost system. | | |

**2** **Describe and illustrate a job order cost accounting system.**

**Key Points** A job order cost system accumulates costs for each quantity of product, or "job," that passes through the factory. Direct materials, direct labor, and factory overhead are accumulated on the job cost sheet, which is the subsidiary cost ledger for each job. Direct materials and direct labor are assigned to individual jobs, based on the quantity used. Factory overhead costs are assigned to each job, based on an activity base that reflects the use of factory overhead costs.

| Learning Outcomes | Example Exercises | Practice Exercises |
|---|---|---|
| • Describe the flow of materials and how materials costs are assigned. | | |
| • Prepare the journal entry to record materials used in production. | **EE19-1** | **PE19-1A, 19-1B** |
| • Describe how factory labor hours are recorded and how labor costs are assigned. | | |
| • Prepare the journal entry to record factory labor used in production. | **EE19-2** | **PE19-2A, 19-2B** |
| • Describe and illustrate how factory overhead costs are accumulated and assigned. | **EE19-3** **EE19-4** | **PE19-3A, 19-3B** **PE19-4A, 19-4B** |
| • Compute the predetermined overhead rate. | **EE19-4** | **PE19-4A, 19-4B** |
| • Describe and illustrate how to dispose of the balance in the factory overhead account. | | |
| • Describe and illustrate how costs are accumulated for work in process and finished goods inventories. | **EE19-5** | **PE19-5A, 19-5B** |
| • Describe how costs are assigned to the cost of goods sold. | **EE19-6** | **PE19-6A, 19-6B** |
| • Describe and illustrate the flow of costs. | | |

**3** **Describe the use of job order cost information for decision making.**

**Key Points** Job order cost systems can be used to evaluate cost performance. Unit costs can be compared over time to determine if product costs are staying within expected ranges.

| Learning Outcome | Example Exercises | Practice Exercises |
|---|---|---|
| • Describe and illustrate how job cost sheets can be used to investigate possible reasons for increased product costs. | | |

**4** **Describe the flow of costs for a service business that uses a job order cost accounting system.**

**Key Points** Job order cost accounting systems can be used by service businesses to plan and control operations. Because the product is a service, the focus is on direct labor and overhead costs. The costs of providing a service are accumulated in a work in process account and transferred to a cost of services account upon completion.

| Learning Outcome | Example Exercises | Practice Exercises |
|---|---|---|
| • Describe how service businesses use a job order cost system. | | |

# Key Terms

activity base (894)
activity-based costing (895)
cost accounting systems (888)
cost allocation (894)
finished goods ledger (899)
job cost sheets (891)

job order cost system (888)
materials ledger (890)
materials requisition (891)
overapplied factory overhead (896)
predetermined factory
  overhead rate (894)

process cost system (888)
receiving report (891)
time tickets (892)
underapplied factory
  overhead (896)

# Illustrative Problem

Wildwing Entertainment Inc. is a manufacturer that uses a job order cost system. The following data summarize the operations related to production for March, the first month of operations:

a. Materials purchased on account, $15,500.

b. Materials requisitioned and labor used:

|  | Materials | Factory Labor |
|---|---|---|
| Job No. 100 | $2,650 | $1,770 |
| Job No. 101 | 1,240 | 650 |
| Job No. 102 | 980 | 420 |
| Job No. 103 | 3,420 | 1,900 |
| Job No. 104 | 1,000 | 500 |
| Job No. 105 | 2,100 | 1,760 |
| For general factory use | 450 | 650 |

c. Factory overhead costs incurred on account, $2,700.

d. Depreciation of machinery, $1,750.

e. Factory overhead is applied at a rate of 70% of direct labor cost.

f. Jobs completed: Nos. 100, 101, 102, 104.

g. Jobs 100, 101, and 102 were shipped, and customers were billed for $8,100, $3,800, and $3,500, respectively.

## Instructions

1. Journalize the entries to record these transactions.

2. Determine the account balances for Work in Process and Finished Goods.

3. Prepare a schedule of unfinished jobs to support the balance in the work in process account.

4. Prepare a schedule of completed jobs on hand to support the balance in the finished goods account.

## Solution

1. a. Materials      15,500

        Accounts Payable      15,500

   b. Work in Process      11,390

        Materials      11,390

        Work in Process      7,000

        Wages Payable      7,000

        Factory Overhead      1,100

        Materials      450

        Wages Payable      650

   c. Factory Overhead      2,700

        Accounts Payable      2,700

   d. Factory Overhead      1,750

        Accumulated Depreciation—Machinery      1,750

   e. Work in Process      4,900

        Factory Overhead (70% of $7,000)      4,900

   f. Finished Goods      11,548

        Work in Process      11,548

Computation of the cost of jobs finished:

| Job | Direct Materials | Direct Labor | Factory Overhead | Total |
|---|---|---|---|---|
| Job No. 100 | $2,650 | $1,770 | $1,239 | $ 5,659 |
| Job No. 101 | 1,240 | 650 | 455 | 2,345 |
| Job No. 102 | 980 | 420 | 294 | 1,694 |
| Job No. 104 | 1,000 | 500 | 350 | 1,850 |
| | | | | $11,548 |

   g. Accounts Receivable      15,400

        Sales      15,400

        Cost of Goods Sold      9,698

        Finished Goods      9,698

Cost of jobs sold computation:

| | |
|---|---|
| Job No. 100 | $5,659 |
| Job No. 101 | 2,345 |
| Job No. 102 | 1,694 |
| | $9,698 |

2. Work in Process: $11,742 ($11,390 + $7,000 + $4,900 − $11,548)

   Finished Goods: $1,850 ($11,548 − $9,698)

3.

**Schedule of Unfinished Jobs**

| Job | Direct Materials | Direct Labor | Factory Overhead | Total |
|---|---|---|---|---|
| Job No. 103 | $3,420 | $1,900 | $1,330 | $ 6,650 |
| Job No. 105 | 2,100 | 1,760 | 1,232 | 5,092 |
| Balance of Work in Process, March 31 | | | | $11,742 |

4.

**Schedule of Completed Jobs**

Job No. 104:

| | |
|---|---|
| Direct materials | $1,000 |
| Direct labor | 500 |
| Factory overhead | 350 |
| Balance of Finished Goods, March 31 | $1,850 |

# Discussion Questions

1. a. Name two principal types of cost accounting systems.

   b. Which system provides for a separate record of each particular quantity of product that passes through the factory?

   c. Which system accumulates the costs for each department or process within the factory?

2. What kind of firm would use a job order cost system?

3. Which account is used in the job order cost system to accumulate direct materials, direct labor, and factory overhead applied to production costs for individual jobs?

4. What document is the source for (a) debiting the accounts in the materials ledger and (b) crediting the accounts in the materials ledger?

5. What is a job cost sheet?

6. What is the difference between a clock card and time ticket?

7. Discuss how the predetermined factory overhead rate can be used in job order cost accounting to assist management in pricing jobs.

8. a. How is a predetermined factory overhead rate calculated?

   b. Name three common bases used in calculating the rate.

9. a. What is (1) overapplied factory overhead and (2) underapplied factory overhead?

   b. If the factory overhead account has a debit balance, was factory overhead underapplied or overapplied?

   c. If the factory overhead account has a credit balance at the end of the first month of the fiscal year, where will the amount of this balance be reported on the interim balance sheet?

10. Describe how a job order cost system can be used for professional service businesses.

# Practice Exercises

EE 19-1 *p. 892*

SHOW
ME HOW

**PE 19-1A    Issuance of materials**                                    OBJ. 2

On April 6, Almerinda Company purchased on account 60,000 units of raw materials at $12 per unit. On April 21, raw materials were requisitioned for production as follows: 25,000 units for Job 50 at $10 per unit and 27,000 units for Job 51 at $12 per unit. Journalize the entry on April 6 to record the purchase and on April 21 to record the requisition from the materials storeroom.

EE 19-1 *p. 892*

SHOW
ME HOW

**PE 19-1B    Issuance of materials**                                    OBJ. 2

On August 4, Rothchild Company purchased on account 12,000 units of raw materials at $14 per unit. On August 24, raw materials were requisitioned for production as follows: 5,000 units for Job 40 at $8 per unit and 6,200 units for Job 42 at $14 per unit. Journalize the entry on August 4 to record the purchase and on August 24 to record the requisition from the materials storeroom.

EE 19-2 *p. 893*

SHOW
ME HOW

**PE 19-2A   Direct labor costs**                                                    OBJ. 2

During April, Almerinda Company accumulated 20,000 hours of direct labor costs on Job 50 and 24,000 hours on Job 51. The total direct labor was incurred at a rate of $20.00 per direct labor hour for Job 50 and $22.00 per direct labor hour for Job 51. Journalize the entry to record the flow of labor costs into production during April.

EE 19-2 *p. 893*

SHOW
ME HOW

**PE 19-2B   Direct labor costs**                                                    OBJ. 2

During August, Rothchild Company accumulated 3,500 hours of direct labor costs on Job 40 and 4,200 hours on Job 42. The total direct labor was incurred at a rate of $25.00 per direct labor hour for Job 40 and $23.50 per direct labor hour for Job 42. Journalize the entry to record the flow of labor costs into production during August.

EE 19-3 *p. 894*

SHOW
ME HOW

**PE 19-3A   Factory overhead costs**                                                OBJ. 2

During April, Almerinda Company incurred factory overhead costs as follows: indirect materials, $42,000; indirect labor, $90,000; utilities cost, $16,000; and factory depreciation, $54,000. Journalize the entry to record the factory overhead incurred during April.

EE 19-3 *p. 894*

SHOW
ME HOW

**PE 19-3B   Factory overhead costs**                                                OBJ. 2

During August, Rothchild Company incurred factory overhead costs as follows: indirect materials, $17,500; indirect labor, $22,000; utilities cost, $9,600; and factory depreciation, $17,500. Journalize the entry to record the factory overhead incurred during August.

EE 19-4 *p. 897*

SHOW
ME HOW

**PE 19-4A   Applying factory overhead**                                             OBJ. 2

Almerinda Company estimates that total factory overhead costs will be $1,750,000 for the year. Direct labor hours are estimated to be 500,000. For Almerinda Company, (a) determine the predetermined factory overhead rate using direct labor hours as the activity base, (b) determine the amount of factory overhead applied to Jobs 50 and 51 in April using the data on direct labor hours from Practice Exercise 19-2A, and (c) prepare the journal entry to apply factory overhead to both jobs in April according to the predetermined overhead rate.

EE 19-4 *p. 897*

SHOW
ME HOW

**PE 19-4B   Applying factory overhead**                                             OBJ. 2

Rothchild Company estimates that total factory overhead costs will be $810,000 for the year. Direct labor hours are estimated to be 90,000. For Rothchild Company, (a) determine the predetermined factory overhead rate using direct labor hours as the activity base, (b) determine the amount of factory overhead applied to Jobs 40 and 42 in August using the data on direct labor hours from Practice Exercise 19-2B, and (c) prepare the journal entry to apply factory overhead to both jobs in August according to the predetermined overhead rate.

EE 19-5 *p. 899*

SHOW
ME HOW

**PE 19-5A   Job costs**                                                             OBJ. 2

At the end of April, Almerinda Company had completed Jobs 50 and 51. Job 50 is for 23,040 units, and Job 51 is for 26,000 units. Using the data from Practice Exercises 19-1A, 19-2A, and 19-4A, determine (a) the balance on the job cost sheets for Jobs 50 and 51 at the end of April and (b) the cost per unit for Jobs 50 and 51 at the end of April.

EE 19-5 *p. 899*

SHOW
ME HOW

**PE 19-5B   Job costs**                                                             OBJ. 2

At the end of August, Rothchild Company had completed Jobs 40 and 42. Job 40 is for 10,000 units, and Job 42 is for 11,000 units. Using the data from Practice Exercises 19-1B, 19-2B, and 19-4B, determine (a) the balance on the job cost sheets for Jobs 40 and 42 at the end of August and (b) the cost per unit for Jobs 40 and 42 at the end of August.

EE 19-6 *p. 900*

**PE 19-6A    Cost of goods sold**                                              OBJ. 2

Hosmer Company completed 312,000 units during the year at a cost of $7,800,000. The beginning finished goods inventory was 22,000 units at $440,000. Determine the cost of goods sold for 325,000 units, assuming a FIFO cost flow.

EE 19-6 *p. 900*

**PE 19-6B    Cost of goods sold**                                              OBJ. 2

Skeleton Company completed 200,000 units during the year at a cost of $3,000,000. The beginning finished goods inventory was 25,000 units at $310,000. Determine the cost of goods sold for 210,000 units, assuming a FIFO cost flow.

# Exercises

**EX 19-1    Transactions in a job order cost system**                          OBJ. 2

Five selected transactions for the current month are indicated by letters in the following T accounts in a job order cost accounting system:

| Materials | | Work in Process | |
|---|---|---|---|
| (a) | | (a) | (d) |
| | | (b) | |
| | | (c) | |

| Wages Payable | | Finished Goods | |
|---|---|---|---|
| | (b) | (d) | (e) |

| Factory Overhead | | Cost of Goods Sold | |
|---|---|---|---|
| (a) | (c) | (e) | |
| (b) | | | |

Describe each of the five transactions.

**EX 19-2    Cost flow relationships**                                          OBJ. 2

✔ b. $1,005,200

The following information is available for the first month of operations of Kellman Inc., a manufacturer of art and craft items:

| | |
|---|---|
| Sales | $3,600,000 |
| Gross profit | 650,000 |
| Indirect labor | 216,000 |
| Indirect materials | 120,000 |
| Other factory overhead | 45,000 |
| Materials purchased | 1,224,000 |
| Total manufacturing costs for the period | 2,640,000 |
| Materials inventory, end of period | 98,800 |

Using this information, determine the following missing amounts:

a.  Cost of goods sold

b.  Direct materials cost

c.  Direct labor cost

### EX 19-3  Cost of materials issuances under the FIFO method                OBJ. 2

An incomplete subsidiary ledger of materials inventory for May is as follows:

| RECEIVED | | | ISSUED | | | BALANCE | | | |
|---|---|---|---|---|---|---|---|---|---|
| Receiving Report Number | Quantity | Unit Price | Materials Requisition Number | Quantity | Amount | Date | Quantity | Unit Price | Amount |
| | | | | | | May 1 | 285 | $30.00 | $8,550 |
| 40 | 130 | $32.00 | | | | May 4 | ___ | ___ | ___ |
| | | | 91 | 365 | | May 10 | ___ | ___ | ___ |
| 44 | 110 | 38.00 | | | | May 21 | ___ | ___ | ___ |
| | | | 97 | 100 | | May 27 | ___ | ___ | ___ |

a. Complete the materials issuances and balances for the materials subsidiary ledger under FIFO.

b. Determine the materials inventory balance at the end of May.

c. Journalize the summary entry to transfer materials to work in process.

d. ▬▬▬► Explain how the materials ledger might be used as an aid in maintaining inventory quantities on hand.

SHOW
ME HOW

### EX 19-4  Entry for issuing materials                OBJ. 2

Materials issued for the current month are as follows:

*(handwritten: direct - working process / indirect - FDA process)*

| Requisition No. | Material | Job No. | Amount |
|---|---|---|---|
| 201 | Aluminum | 500 | $88,700 |
| 202 | Plastic | 503 | 27,600 |
| 203 | Rubber | 504 | 3,650 |
| 204 | Glue | Indirect | 2,250 |
| 205 | Steel | 510 | 38,750 |

Journalize the entry to record the issuance of materials.

### EX 19-5  Entries for materials                OBJ. 2

SHOW
ME HOW

Eclectic Ergonomics Company manufactures designer furniture. Eclectic Ergonomics uses a job order cost system. Balances on April 1 from the materials ledger are as follows:

| | |
|---|---|
| Fabric | $ 67,500 |
| Polyester filling | 20,200 |
| Lumber | 150,000 |
| Glue | 6,550 |

The materials purchased during April are summarized from the receiving reports as follows:

| | |
|---|---|
| Fabric | $338,400 |
| Polyester filling | 470,400 |
| Lumber | 902,400 |
| Glue | 32,400 |

Materials were requisitioned to individual jobs as follows:

| | Fabric | Polyester Filling | Lumber | Glue | Total |
|---|---|---|---|---|---|
| Job 81 | $127,400 | $160,800 | $401,200 | | $ 689,400 |
| Job 82 | 97,200 | 145,200 | 375,000 | | 617,400 |
| Job 83 | 91,200 | 118,400 | 210,000 | | 419,600 |
| Factory overhead—indirect materials | | | | $34,000 | 34,000 |
| Total | $315,800 | $424,400 | $986,200 | $34,800 | $1,761,200 |

*(Continued)*

The glue is not a significant cost, so it is treated as indirect materials (factory overhead).

a. Journalize the entry to record the purchase of materials in April.

b. Journalize the entry to record the requisition of materials in April.

c. Determine the April 30 balances that would be shown in the materials ledger accounts.

SHOW
ME HOW

### EX 19-6 Entry for factory labor costs
OBJ. 2

A summary of the time tickets for the current month follows:

| Job No. | Amount | Job No. | Amount |
|---|---|---|---|
| 100 | $ 3,860 | Indirect | $ 6,340 |
| 101 | 4,300 | 111 | 7,120 |
| 104 | 24,500 | 115 | 7,400 |
| 108 | 18,600 | 117 | 32,000 |

Journalize the entry to record the factory labor costs.

### EX 19-7 Entry for factory labor costs
OBJ. 2

The weekly time tickets indicate the following distribution of labor hours for three direct labor employees:

| | Hours | | | |
|---|---|---|---|---|
| | Job 301 | Job 302 | Job 303 | Process Improvement |
| Tom Couro | 10 | 15 | 13 | 2 |
| David Clancy | 12 | 12 | 14 | 2 |
| Jose Cano | 11 | 13 | 15 | 1 |

The direct labor rate earned per hour by the three employees is as follows:

| | |
|---|---|
| Tom Couro | $32 |
| David Clancy | 36 |
| Jose Cano | 28 |

The process improvement category includes training, quality improvement, and other indirect tasks.

a. Journalize the entry to record the factory labor costs for the week.

b. Assume that Jobs 301 and 302 were completed but not sold during the week and that Job 303 remained incomplete at the end of the week. How would the direct labor costs for all three jobs be reflected on the financial statements at the end of the week?

SHOW
ME HOW

### EX 19-8 Entries for direct labor and factory overhead
OBJ. 2

Dash Industries Inc. manufactures recreational vehicles. Dash uses a job order cost system. The time tickets from April jobs are summarized as follows:

| | |
|---|---|
| Job 201 | $5,250 |
| Job 202 | 6,100 |
| Job 203 | 4,280 |
| Job 204 | 5,620 |
| Factory supervision | 2,785 |

Factory overhead is applied to jobs on the basis of a predetermined overhead rate of $25 per direct labor hour. The direct labor rate is $50 per hour.

a. Journalize the entry to record the factory labor costs.

b. Journalize the entry to apply factory overhead to production for April.

### EX 19-9  Factory overhead rates, entries, and account balance

OBJ. 2

Tiny Biggs Company operates two factories. The company applies factory overhead to jobs on the basis of machine hours in Factory 1 and on the basis of direct labor hours in Factory 2. Estimated factory overhead costs, direct labor hours, and machine hours are as follows:

|  | Factory 1 | Factory 2 |
|---|---|---|
| Estimated factory overhead cost for fiscal year beginning September 1 | $1,456,000 | $954,000 |
| Estimated direct labor hours for year |  | 26,500 |
| Estimated machine hours for year | 52,000 |  |
| Actual factory overhead costs for September | $117,600 | $102,350 |
| Actual direct labor hours for September |  | 2,795 |
| Actual machine hours for September | 4,250 |  |

a. Determine the factory overhead rate for Factory 1.

b. Determine the factory overhead rate for Factory 2.

c. Journalize the entries to apply factory overhead to production in each factory for September.

d. Determine the balances of the factory overhead accounts for each factory as of September 30, and indicate whether the amounts represent overapplied or under-applied factory overhead.

### EX 19-10  Predetermined factory overhead rate

OBJ. 2

Spring Street Engine Shop uses a job order cost system to determine the cost of performing engine repair work. Estimated costs and expenses for the coming period are as follows:

| | |
|---|---|
| Engine parts | $ 875,000 |
| Shop direct labor | 660,000 |
| Shop and repair equipment depreciation | 44,500 |
| Shop supervisor salaries | 138,000 |
| Shop property taxes | 27,500 |
| Shop supplies | 10,000 |
| Advertising expense | 22,100 |
| Administrative office salaries | 73,500 |
| Administrative office depreciation expense | 8,600 |
| Total costs and expenses | $1,859,200 |

The average shop direct labor rate is $30 per hour.

Determine the predetermined shop overhead rate per direct labor hour.

### EX 19-11  Predetermined factory overhead rate

OBJ. 2

Poehling Medical Center has a single operating room that is used by local physicians to perform surgical procedures. The cost of using the operating room is accumulated by each patient procedure and includes the direct materials costs (drugs and medical devices), physician surgical time, and operating room overhead. On January 1 of the current year, the annual operating room overhead is estimated to be:

| | |
|---|---|
| Disposable supplies | $299,600 |
| Depreciation expense | 75,000 |
| Utilities | 32,000 |
| Nurse salaries | 278,500 |
| Technician wages | 126,900 |
| Total operating room overhead | $812,000 |

(*Continued*)

The overhead costs will be assigned to procedures, based on the number of surgical room hours. Poehling Medical Center expects to use the operating room an average of eight hours per day, seven days per week. In addition, the operating room will be shut down two weeks per year for general repairs.

a. Determine the predetermined operating room overhead rate for the year.

b. Bill Harris had a five-hour procedure on January 22. How much operating room overhead would be charged to his procedure, using the rate determined in part (a)?

c. During January, the operating room was used 240 hours. The actual overhead costs incurred for January were $67,250. Determine the overhead under- or overapplied for the period.

---

**EX 19-12   Entry for jobs completed; cost of unfinished jobs**          OBJ. 2

✔ b. $95,200

SHOW
ME HOW

The following account appears in the ledger prior to recognizing the jobs completed in August:

| Work in Process | |
| --- | --- |
| Balance, August 1 | $ 60,000 |
| Direct materials | 325,000 |
| Direct labor | 462,000 |
| Factory overhead | 210,000 |

Jobs finished during August are summarized as follows:

| | | | |
| --- | --- | --- | --- |
| Job 210 | $197,800 | Job 224 | $ 160,000 |
| Job 216 | 240,000 | Job 230 | 364,000 |

a. Journalize the entry to record the jobs completed.

b. Determine the cost of the unfinished jobs at August 31.

---

**EX 19-13   Entries for factory costs and jobs completed**          OBJ. 2

✔ d. $73,750

Old School Publishing Inc. began printing operations on January 1. Jobs 301 and 302 were completed during the month, and all costs applicable to them were recorded on the related cost sheets. Jobs 303 and 304 are still in process at the end of the month, and all applicable costs except factory overhead have been recorded on the related cost sheets. In addition to the materials and labor charged directly to the jobs, $8,000 of indirect materials and $12,400 of indirect labor were used during the month. The cost sheets for the four jobs entering production during the month are as follows, in summary form:

| Job 301 | | Job 302 | |
| --- | --- | --- | --- |
| Direct materials | $10,000 | Direct materials | $20,000 |
| Direct labor | 8,000 | Direct labor | 17,000 |
| Factory overhead | 6,000 | Factory overhead | 12,750 |
| Total | $24,000 | Total | $49,750 |

| Job 303 | | Job 304 | |
| --- | --- | --- | --- |
| Direct materials | $24,000 | Direct materials | $14,000 |
| Direct labor | 18,000 | Direct labor | 12,000 |
| Factory overhead | — | Factory overhead | — |

Journalize the summary entry to record each of the following operations for January (one entry for each operation):

a. Direct and indirect materials used.

b. Direct and indirect labor used.

c. Factory overhead applied to all four jobs (a single overhead rate is used based on direct labor cost).

d. Completion of Jobs 301 and 302.

### EX 19-14    Financial statements of a manufacturing firm    OBJ. 2

The following events took place for Chi-Lite Inc. during June 2016, the first month of operations as a producer of road bikes:

- Purchased $400,000 of materials.
- Used $343,750 of direct materials in production.
- Incurred $295,000 of direct labor wages.
- Applied factory overhead at a rate of 75% of direct labor cost.
- Transferred $815,000 of work in process to finished goods.
- Sold goods with a cost of $789,000.
- Sold goods for $1,400,000.
- Incurred $316,000 of selling expenses.
- Incurred $125,000 of administrative expenses.

a. Prepare the June income statement for Chi-Lite. Assume that Chi-Lite uses the perpetual inventory method.

b. Determine the inventory balances at the end of the first month of operations.

### EX 19-15    Decision making with job order costs    OBJ. 3

Alvarez Manufacturing Inc. is a job shop. The management of Alvarez Manufacturing Inc. uses the cost information from the job sheets to assess cost performance. Information on the total cost, product type, and quantity of items produced is as follows:

| Date | Job No. | Product | Quantity | Amount |
| --- | --- | --- | --- | --- |
| Jan. 2 | 1 | TT | 520 | $16,120 |
| Jan. 15 | 22 | SS | 1,610 | 20,125 |
| Feb. 3 | 30 | SS | 1,420 | 25,560 |
| Mar. 7 | 41 | TT | 670 | 15,075 |
| Mar. 24 | 49 | SLK | 2,210 | 22,100 |
| May 19 | 58 | SLK | 2,550 | 31,875 |
| June 12 | 65 | TT | 620 | 10,540 |
| Aug. 18 | 78 | SLK | 3,110 | 48,205 |
| Sept. 2 | 82 | SS | 1,210 | 16,940 |
| Nov. 14 | 92 | TT | 750 | 8,250 |
| Dec. 12 | 98 | SLK | 2,700 | 52,650 |

a. Develop a graph for *each* product (three graphs), with Job Number (in date order) on the horizontal axis and Unit Cost on the vertical axis. Use this information to determine Alvarez Manufacturing Inc.'s cost performance over time for the three products.

b. ▬▬▬▶What additional information would you require in order to investigate Alvarez Manufacturing Inc.'s cost performance more precisely?

### EX 19-16    Decision making with job order costs    OBJ. 3

Raneri Trophies Inc. uses a job order cost system for determining the cost to manufacture award products (plaques and trophies). Among the company's products is an engraved plaque that is awarded to participants who complete a training program at a local business. The company sells the plaques to the local business for $80 each.

Each plaque has a brass plate engraved with the name of the participant. Engraving requires approximately 30 minutes per name. Improperly engraved names must be redone. The plate is screwed to a walnut backboard. This assembly takes approximately 15 minutes per unit. Improper assembly must be redone using a new walnut backboard.

*(Continued)*

During the first half of the year, Raneri had two separate plaque orders. The job cost sheets for the two separate jobs indicated the following information:

| Job 101 | May 4 | | |
|---|---|---|---|
| | **Cost per Unit** | **Units** | **Job Cost** |
| Direct materials: | | | |
| Wood | $20/unit | 40 units | $ 800 |
| Brass | 15/unit | 40 units | 600 |
| Engraving labor | 20/hr. | 20 hrs. | 400 |
| Assembly labor | 30/hr. | 10 hrs. | 300 |
| Factory overhead | 10/hr. | 30 hrs. | 300 |
| | | | $2,400 |
| Plaques shipped | | | ÷ 40 |
| Cost per plaque | | | $ 60 |

| Job 105 | June 10 | | |
|---|---|---|---|
| | **Cost per Unit** | **Units** | **Job Cost** |
| Direct materials: | | | |
| Wood | $20/unit | 34 units | $ 680 |
| Brass | 15/unit | 34 units | 510 |
| Engraving labor | 20/hr. | 17 hrs. | 340 |
| Assembly labor | 30/hr. | 8.5 hrs. | 255 |
| Factory overhead | 10/hr. | 25.5 hrs. | 255 |
| | | | $2,040 |
| Plaques shipped | | | ÷ 30 |
| Cost per plaque | | | $ 68 |

a. Why did the cost per plaque increase from $60 to $68?

b. What improvements would you recommend for Raneri Trophies Inc.?

---

**EX 19-17** **Job order cost accounting for a service company** OBJ. 4

✔ b. Underapplied, $5,530

The law firm of Furlan and Benson accumulates costs associated with individual cases, using a job order cost system. The following transactions occurred during July:

July 3. Charged 175 hours of professional (lawyer) time to the Obsidian Co. breech of contract suit to prepare for the trial, at a rate of $150 per hour.

10. Reimbursed travel costs to employees for depositions related to the Obsidian case, $12,500.

14. Charged 260 hours of professional time for the Obsidian trial at a rate of $185 per hour.

18. Received invoice from consultants Wadsley and Harden for $30,000 for expert testimony related to the Obsidian trial.

27. Applied office overhead at a rate of $62 per professional hour charged to the Obsidian case.

31. Paid administrative and support salaries of $28,500 for the month.

31. Used office supplies for the month, $4,000.

31. Paid professional salaries of $74,350 for the month.

31. Billed Obsidian $172,500 for successful defense of the case.

a. Provide the journal entries for each of these transactions.

b. How much office overhead is over- or underapplied?

c. Determine the gross profit on the Obsidian case, assuming that over- or underapplied office overhead is closed monthly to cost of services.

### EX 19-18   Job order cost accounting for a service company OBJ. 4

✔ d. Dr. Cost of
Services, $2,827,750

The Fly Company provides advertising services for clients across the nation. The Fly Company is presently working on four projects, each for a different client. The Fly Company accumulates costs for each account (client) on the basis of both direct costs and allocated indirect costs. The direct costs include the charged time of professional personnel and media purchases (air time and ad space). Overhead is allocated to each project as a percentage of media purchases. The predetermined overhead rate is 65% of media purchases.

On August 1, the four advertising projects had the following accumulated costs:

|  | August 1 Balances |
| --- | --- |
| Vault Bank | $270,000 |
| Take Off Airlines | 80,000 |
| Sleepy Tired Hotels | 210,000 |
| Tastee Beverages | 115,000 |
| Total | $675,000 |

During August, The Fly Company incurred the following direct labor and media purchase costs related to preparing advertising for each of the four accounts:

|  | Direct Labor | Media Purchases |
| --- | --- | --- |
| Vault Bank | $ 190,000 | $ 710,000 |
| Take Off Airlines | 85,000 | 625,000 |
| Sleepy Tired Hotels | 372,000 | 455,000 |
| Tastee Beverages | 421,000 | 340,000 |
| Total | $1,068,000 | $2,130,000 |

At the end of August, both the Vault Bank and Take Off Airlines campaigns were completed. The costs of completed campaigns are debited to the cost of services account.

Journalize the summary entry to record each of the following for the month:

a. Direct labor costs

b. Media purchases

c. Overhead applied

d. Completion of Vault Bank and Take Off Airlines campaigns

## Problems: Series A

### PR 19-1A   Entries for costs in a job order cost system OBJ. 2

General Ledger

SHOW
ME HOW

DiSalvio Co. uses a job order cost system. The following data summarize the operations related to production for May:

a. Materials purchased on account, $634,000.

b. Materials requisitioned, $646,200, of which $74,500 was for general factory use.

c. Factory labor used, $660,200, of which $91,200 was indirect.

d. Other costs incurred on account for factory overhead, $147,500; selling expenses, $234,000; and administrative expenses, $146,400.

e. Prepaid expenses expired for factory overhead were $29,200; for selling expenses, $26,800; and for administrative expenses, $18,000.

f. Depreciation of office building was $84,600; of office equipment, $43,340; and of factory equipment, $32,000.

g. Factory overhead costs applied to jobs, $362,000.

h. Jobs completed, $1,002,000.

i. Cost of goods sold, $890,000.

**Instructions**

Journalize the entries to record the summarized operations.

**PR 19-2A    Entries and schedules for unfinished jobs and completed jobs**      OBJ. 2

Tybee Industries Inc. uses a job order cost system. The following data summarize the operations related to production for January 2016, the first month of operations:

a.  Materials purchased on account, $29,800.

b.  Materials requisitioned and factory labor used:

| Job | Materials | Factory Labor |
| --- | --- | --- |
| 301 | $ 2,960 | $2,775 |
| 302 | 3,620 | 3,750 |
| 303 | 2,400 | 1,875 |
| 304 | 8,100 | 6,860 |
| 305 | 5,100 | 5,250 |
| 306 | 3,750 | 3,340 |
| For general factory use | 1,080 | 4,100 |

c.  Factory overhead costs incurred on account, $5,500.

d.  Depreciation of machinery and equipment, $1,980.

e.  The factory overhead rate is $54 per machine hour. Machine hours used:

| Job | Machine Hours |
| --- | --- |
| 301 | 25 |
| 302 | 36 |
| 303 | 30 |
| 304 | 72 |
| 305 | 40 |
| 306 | 25 |
| Total | 228 |

f.  Jobs completed: 301, 302, 303 and 305.

g.  Jobs were shipped and customers were billed as follows: Job 301, $8,250; Job 302, $11,200; Job 303, $15,000.

**Instructions**

1.  Journalize the entries to record the summarized operations.

2.  Post the appropriate entries to T accounts for Work in Process and Finished Goods, using the identifying letters as transaction codes. Insert memo account balances as of the end of the month.

3.  Prepare a schedule of unfinished jobs to support the balance in the work in process account.

4.  Prepare a schedule of completed jobs on hand to support the balance in the finished goods account.

**PR 19-3A    Job order cost sheet**      OBJ. 2, 3

Remnant Carpet Company sells and installs commercial carpeting for office buildings. Remnant Carpet Company uses a job order cost system. When a prospective customer asks for a price quote on a job, the estimated cost data are inserted on an unnumbered job cost sheet. If the offer is accepted, a number is assigned to the job, and the costs incurred are recorded in the usual manner on the job cost sheet. After the job is completed, reasons for the variances between the estimated and actual costs are noted on the sheet. The data are then available to management in evaluating the efficiency of operations and in preparing quotes on future jobs. On October 1, 2016, Remnant Carpet Company gave Jackson Consulting an estimate of $9,450 to carpet the consulting firm's newly leased office. The estimate was based on the following data:

Estimated direct materials:

| | |
|---|---|
| 200 meters at $35 per meter .................................... | $7,000 |

Estimated direct labor:

| | |
|---|---|
| 16 hours at $20 per hour ....................................... | 320 |
| Estimated factory overhead (75% of direct labor cost) .............. | 240 |
| Total estimated costs ............................................. | $7,560 |
| Markup (25% of production costs) ................................ | 1,890 |
| Total estimate ................................................... | $9,450 |

On October 3, Jackson Consulting signed a purchase contract, and the delivery and installation was completed on October 10.

The related materials requisitions and time tickets are summarized as follows:

| Materials Requisition No. | Description | Amount |
|---|---|---|
| 112 | 140 meters at $35 | $4,900 |
| 114 | 68 meters at $35 | 2,380 |

| Time Ticket No. | Description | Amount |
|---|---|---|
| H10 | 10 hours at $20 | $200 |
| H11 | 10 hours at $20 | 200 |

### Instructions

1. Complete that portion of the job order cost sheet that would be prepared when the estimate is given to the customer.

2. ➤ Record the costs incurred, and prepare a job order cost sheet. Comment on the reasons for the variances between actual costs and estimated costs. For this purpose, assume that the additional meters of material used in the job were spoiled, the factory overhead rate has proven to be satisfactory, and an inexperienced employee performed the work.

---

### PR 19-4A   Analyzing manufacturing cost accounts

OBJ. 2

✔ G. $751,870

Fire Rock Company manufactures designer paddle boards in a wide variety of sizes and styles. The following incomplete ledger accounts refer to transactions that are summarized for June:

**Materials**

| | | | | | | |
|---|---|---|---|---|---|---|
| June | 1 | Balance | 82,500 | June 30 | Requisitions | (A) |
| | 30 | Purchases | 330,000 | | | |

**Work in Process**

| | | | | | | |
|---|---|---|---|---|---|---|
| June | 1 | Balance | (B) | June 30 | Completed jobs | (F) |
| | 30 | Materials | (C) | | | |
| | 30 | Direct labor | (D) | | | |
| | 30 | Factory overhead applied | (E) | | | |

**Finished Goods**

| | | | | | | |
|---|---|---|---|---|---|---|
| June | 1 | Balance | 0 | June 30 | Cost of goods sold | (G) |
| | 30 | Completed jobs | (F) | | | |

**Wages Payable**

| | | | | | | |
|---|---|---|---|---|---|---|
| | | | | June 30 | Wages incurred | 330,000 |

**Factory Overhead**

| | | | | | | |
|---|---|---|---|---|---|---|
| June | 1 | Balance | 33,000 | June 30 | Factory overhead applied | (E) |
| | 30 | Indirect labor | (H) | | | |
| | 30 | Indirect materials | 44,000 | | | |
| | 30 | Other overhead | 237,500 | | | |

*(Continued)*

In addition, the following information is available:

a. Materials and direct labor were applied to six jobs in June:

| Job No. | Style | Quantity | Direct Materials | Direct Labor |
|---|---|---|---|---|
| 201 | T100 | 550 | $ 55,000 | $ 41,250 |
| 202 | T200 | 1,100 | 93,500 | 71,500 |
| 203 | T400 | 550 | 38,500 | 22,000 |
| 204 | S200 | 660 | 82,500 | 69,300 |
| 205 | T300 | 480 | 60,000 | 48,000 |
| 206 | S100 | 380 | 22,000 | 12,400 |
| | Total | 3,720 | $351,500 | $264,450 |

b. Factory overhead is applied to each job at a rate of 140% of direct labor cost.

c. The June 1 Work in Process balance consisted of two jobs, as follows:

| Job No. | Style | Work in Process, June 1 |
|---|---|---|
| Job 201 | T100 | $16,500 |
| Job 202 | T200 | 44,000 |
| Total | | $60,500 |

d. Customer jobs completed and units sold in June were as follows:

| Job No. | Style | Completed in June | Units Sold in June |
|---|---|---|---|
| 201 | T100 | X | 440 |
| 202 | T200 | X | 880 |
| 203 | T400 | | 0 |
| 204 | S200 | X | 570 |
| 205 | T300 | X | 420 |
| 206 | S100 | | 0 |

## Instructions

1. Determine the missing amounts associated with each letter. Provide supporting calculations by completing a table with the following headings:

| Job No. | Quantity | June 1 Work in Process | Direct Materials | Direct Labor | Factory Overhead | Total Cost | Unit Cost | Units Sold | Cost of Goods Sold |
|---|---|---|---|---|---|---|---|---|---|

2. Determine the June 30 balances for each of the inventory accounts and factory overhead.

---

**PR 19-5A  Flow of costs and income statement**                                  OBJ. 2

✔ 1. Income from operations, $432,000

Ginocera Inc. is a designer, manufacturer, and distributor of low-cost, high-quality stainless steel kitchen knives. A new kitchen knife series called the Kitchen Ninja was released for production in early 2016. In January, the company spent $600,000 to develop a late-night advertising infomercial for the new product. During 2016, the company spent $1,400,000 promoting the product through these infomercials, and $800,000 in legal costs. The knives were ready for manufacture on January 1, 2016.

Ginocera uses a job order cost system to accumulate costs associated with the kitchen knife. The unit direct materials cost for the knife is:

| | |
|---|---|
| Hardened steel blanks (used for knife shaft and blade) | $4.00 |
| Wood (for handle) | 1.50 |
| Packaging | 0.50 |

The production process is straightforward. First, the hardened steel blanks, which are purchased directly from a raw material supplier, are stamped into a single piece of metal that includes both the blade and the shaft. The stamping machine requires one hour per 250 knives.

After the knife shafts are stamped, they are brought to an assembly area where an employee attaches the handle to the shaft and packs the knife into a decorative box. The direct labor cost is $0.50 per unit.

The knives are sold to stores. Each store is given promotional materials, such as posters and aisle displays. Promotional materials cost $60 per store. In addition, shipping costs average $0.20 per knife.

Total completed production was 1,200,000 units during the year. Other information is as follows:

| | |
|---|---|
| Number of customers (stores) | 60,000 |
| Number of knives sold | 1,120,000 |
| Wholesale price (to store) per knife | $16 |

Factory overhead cost is applied to jobs at the rate of $800 per stamping machine hour after the knife blanks are stamped. There were an additional 25,000 stamped knives, handles, and cases waiting to be assembled on December 31, 2016.

### Instructions

1. Prepare an annual income statement for the Kitchen Ninja knife series, including supporting calculations, from the information provided.

2. Determine the balances in the work in process and finished goods inventories for the Kitchen Ninja knife series on December 31, 2016.

# Problems: Series B

**General Ledger**

SHOW
ME HOW

**PR 19-1B    Entries for costs in a job order cost system**          OBJ. 2

Royal Technology Company uses a job order cost system. The following data summarize the operations related to production for March:

a. Materials purchased on account, $770,000. _indirect material_

DM b. Materials requisitioned, $680,000, of which $75,800 was for general factory use.

c. Factory labor used, $756,000, of which $182,000 was indirect. (FOH)

d. Other costs incurred on account for factory overhead, $245,000; selling expenses, $171,500; and administrative expenses, $110,600.

e. Prepaid expenses expired for factory overhead were $24,500; for selling expenses, $28,420; and for administrative expenses, $16,660.

f. Depreciation of factory equipment was $49,500; of office equipment, $61,800; and of office building, $14,900.

g. Factory overhead costs applied to jobs, $568,500.

h. Jobs completed, $1,500,000.

i. Cost of goods sold, $1,375,000.     _Sell on account for 3,000,000,000_

**Instruction**

Journalize the entries to record the summarized operations.

**PR 19-2B    Entries and schedules for unfinished jobs and completed jobs**     OBJ. 2

✔ 3. Work in Process
balance, $127,880

**General Ledger**

Hildreth Company uses a job order cost system. The following data summarize the operations related to production for April 2016, the first month of operations:

a. Materials purchased on account, $147,000.

b. Materials requisitioned and factory labor used:

| Job No. | Materials | Factory Labor |
|---|---|---|
| 101 | $19,320 | $19,500 |
| 102 | 23,100 | 28,140 |
| 103 | 13,440 | 14,000 |
| 104 | 38,200 | 36,500 |
| 105 | 18,050 | 15,540 |
| 106 | 18,000 | 18,700 |
| For general factory use | 9,000 | 20,160 |

*(Continued)*

c. Factory overhead costs incurred on account, $6,000.

d. Depreciation of machinery and equipment, $4,100.

e. The factory overhead rate is $40 per machine hour. Machine hours used:

| Job | Machine Hours |
|---|---|
| 101 | 154 |
| 102 | 160 |
| 103 | 126 |
| 104 | 238 |
| 105 | 160 |
| 106 | 174 |
| Total | 1,012 |

f. Jobs completed: 101, 102, 103, and 105.

g. Jobs were shipped and customers were billed as follows: Job 101, $62,900; Job 102, $80,700; Job 105, $45,500.

**Instructions**

1. Journalize the entries to record the summarized operations.

2. Post the appropriate entries to T accounts for Work in Process and Finished Goods, using the identifying letters as transaction codes. Insert memo account balances as of the end of the month.

3. Prepare a schedule of unfinished jobs to support the balance in the work in process account.

4. Prepare a schedule of completed jobs on hand to support the balance in the finished goods account.

---

**PR 19-3B**    **Job order cost sheet**                                        OBJ. 2, 3

Stretch and Trim Carpet Company sells and installs commercial carpeting for office buildings. Stretch and Trim Carpet Company uses a job order cost system. When a prospective customer asks for a price quote on a job, the estimated cost data are inserted on an unnumbered job cost sheet. If the offer is accepted, a number is assigned to the job, and the costs incurred are recorded in the usual manner on the job cost sheet. After the job is completed, reasons for the variances between the estimated and actual costs are noted on the sheet. The data are then available to management in evaluating the efficiency of operations and in preparing quotes on future jobs. On May 9, Stretch and Trim gave Lunden Consulting an estimate of $18,044 to carpet the consulting firm's newly leased office. The estimate was based on the following data:

| | |
|---|---|
| Estimated direct materials: | |
|     400 meters at $32 per meter | $12,800 |
| Estimated direct labor: | |
|     30 hours at $20 per hour | 600 |
| Estimated factory overhead (80% of direct labor cost) | 480 |
| Total estimated costs | $13,880 |
| Markup (30% of production costs) | 4,164 |
| Total estimate | $18,044 |

On May 10, Lunden Consulting signed a purchase contract, and the carpet was delivered and installed on May 15.

The related materials requisitions and time tickets are summarized as follows:

| Materials Requisition No. | Description | Amount |
|---|---|---|
| 132 | 360 meters at $32 | $11,520 |
| 134 | 50 meters at $32 | 1,600 |

| Time Ticket No. | Description | Amount |
|---|---|---|
| H9 | 18 hours at $19 | $342 |
| H12 | 18 hours at $19 | 342 |

**Instructions**

1. Complete that portion of the job order cost sheet that would be prepared when the estimate is given to the customer. (Round factory overhead applied to the nearest dollar.)

2. ➤ Record the costs incurred, and prepare a job order cost sheet. Comment on the reasons for the variances between actual costs and estimated costs. For this purpose, assume that the additional meters of material used in the job were spoiled, the factory overhead rate has proven to be satisfactory, and an inexperienced employee performed the work.

**PR 19-4B    Analyzing manufacturing cost accounts**                              OBJ. 2

✔ G. $700,284

Clapton Company manufactures custom guitars in a wide variety of styles. The following incomplete ledger accounts refer to transactions that are summarized for May:

**Materials**

| May | 1 | Balance | 105,600 | May 31 | Requisitions | (A) |
| | 31 | Purchases | 500,000 | | | |

**Work in Process**

| May | 1 | Balance | (B) | May 31 | Completed jobs | (F) |
| | 31 | Materials | (C) | | | |
| | 31 | Direct labor | (D) | | | |
| | 31 | Factory overhead applied | (E) | | | |

**Finished Goods**

| May | 1 | Balance | 0 | May 31 | Cost of goods sold | (G) |
| | 31 | Completed jobs | (F) | | | |

**Wages Payable**

| | | | | May 31 | Wages incurred | 396,000 |

**Factory Overhead**

| May | 1 | Balance | 26,400 | May 31 | Factory overhead applied | (E) |
| | 31 | Indirect labor | (H) | | | |
| | 31 | Indirect materials | 15,400 | | | |
| | 31 | Other overhead | 122,500 | | | |

In addition, the following information is available:

a. Materials and direct labor were applied to six jobs in May:

| Job No. | Style | Quantity | Direct Materials | Direct Labor |
|---|---|---|---|---|
| 101 | AF1 | 330 | $ 82,500 | $ 59,400 |
| 102 | AF3 | 380 | 105,400 | 72,600 |
| 103 | AF2 | 500 | 132,000 | 110,000 |
| 104 | VY1 | 400 | 66,000 | 39,600 |
| 105 | VY2 | 660 | 118,800 | 66,000 |
| 106 | AF4 | 330 | 66,000 | 30,800 |
| | Total | 2,600 | $570,700 | $378,400 |

b. Factory overhead is applied to each job at a rate of 50% of direct labor cost.

c. The May 1 Work in Process balance consisted of two jobs, as follows:

| Job No. | Style | Work in Process, May 1 |
|---|---|---|
| Job 101 | AF1 | $26,400 |
| Job 102 | AF3 | 46,000 |
| Total | | $72,400 |

*(Continued)*

d. Customer jobs completed and units sold in May were as follows:

| Job No. | Style | Completed in May | Units Sold in May |
|---|---|---|---|
| 101 | AF1 | X | 264 |
| 102 | AF3 | X | 360 |
| 103 | AF2 | | 0 |
| 104 | VY1 | X | 384 |
| 105 | VY2 | X | 530 |
| 106 | AF4 | | 0 |

## Instructions

1. Determine the missing amounts associated with each letter. Provide supporting calculations by completing a table with the following headings:

| Job No. | Quantity | May 1 Work in Process | Direct Materials | Direct Labor | Factory Overhead | Total Cost | Unit Cost | Units Sold | Cost of Goods Sold |
|---|---|---|---|---|---|---|---|---|---|

2. Determine the May 31 balances for each of the inventory accounts and factory overhead.

---

## PR 19-5B Flow of costs and income statement

OBJ. 2

Technology Accessories Inc. is a designer, manufacturer, and distributor of accessories for consumer electronic products. Early in 2016, the company began production of a leather cover for tablet computers, called the iLeather. The cover is made of stitched leather with a velvet interior and fits snuggly around most tablet computers. In January, $750,000 was spent on developing marketing and advertising materials. For the first six months of 2016, the company spent $1,400,000 promoting the iLeather. The product was ready for manufacture on January 21, 2016.

Technology Accessories Inc. uses a job order cost system to accumulate costs for the iLeather. Direct materials unit costs for the iLeather are as follows:

| Leather | $10.00 |
|---|---|
| Velvet | 5.00 |
| Packaging | 0.40 |
| Total | $15.40 |

The actual production process for the iLeather is fairly straightforward. First, leather is brought to a cutting and stitching machine. The machine cuts the leather and stitches an exterior edge into the product. The machine requires one hour per 125 iLeathers.

After the iLeather is cut and stitched, it is brought to assembly, where assembly personnel affix the velvet interior and pack the iLeather for shipping. The direct labor cost for this work is $0.50 per unit.

The completed packages are then sold to retail outlets through a sales force. The sales force is compensated by a 20% commission on the wholesale price for all sales.

Total completed production was 500,000 units during the year. Other information is as follows:

| Number of iLeather units sold in 2016 | 460,000 |
|---|---|
| Wholesale price per unit | $40 |

Factory overhead cost is applied to jobs at the rate of $1,250 per machine hour. There were an additional 22,000 cut and stitched iLeathers waiting to be assembled on December 31, 2016.

## Instructions

1. Prepare an annual income statement for the iLeather product, including supporting calculations, from the information provided.

2. Determine the balances in the finished goods and work in process inventories for the iLeather product on December 31, 2016.

# Cases & Projects

---

### CP 19-1 Managerial analysis

The controller of the plant of Minsky Company prepared a graph of the unit costs from the job cost reports for Product One. The graph appeared as follows:

How would you interpret this information? What further information would you request?

---

### CP 19-2 Job order decision making and rate deficiencies

RIRA Company makes attachments, such as backhoes and grader and bulldozer blades, for construction equipment. The company uses a job order cost system. Management is concerned about cost performance and evaluates the job cost sheets to learn more about the cost effectiveness of the operations. To facilitate a comparison, the cost sheet for Job 206 (50 backhoe buckets completed in October) was compared with Job 228, which was for 75 backhoe buckets completed in December. The two job cost sheets follow:

**Job 206**

| | Item: 50 backhoe buckets | | | | |
|---|---|---|---|---|---|
| Materials: | **Direct Materials Quantity** | × | **Direct Materials Price** | = | **Amount** |
| Steel (tons) | 105 | | $1,200 | | $126,000 |
| Steel components (pieces) | 630 | | 7 | | 4,410 |
| Total materials | | | | | $130,410 |
| | **Direct Labor Hours** | × | **Direct Labor Rate** | = | **Amount** |
| Direct labor: | | | | | |
| Foundry | 400 | | $22.50 | | $ 9,000 |
| Welding | 550 | | 27.00 | | 14,850 |
| Shipping | 180 | | 18.00 | | 3,240 |
| Total direct labor | 1,130 | | | | $ 27,090 |
| | **Direct Total Labor Cost** | × | **Factory Overhead Rate** | = | **Amount** |
| Factory overhead | | | | | |
| (200% of direct labor dollars) | $27,090 | × | 200% | | $ 54,180 |
| Total cost | | | | | $ 211,680 |
| Total units | | | | | ÷ 50 |
| Unit cost (rounded) | | | | | $4,233.60 |

*(Continued)*

**Job 228**

| Item: 75 backhoe buckets | | | | |
|---|---|---|---|---|
| | **Direct Materials Quantity** | × | **Direct Materials Price** | = **Amount** |
| Materials: | | | | |
| Steel (tons) | 195 | | $1,100 | $214,500 |
| Steel components (pieces) | 945 | | 7 | 6,615 |
| Total materials | | | | $221,115 |

| | **Direct Labor Hours** | × | **Direct Labor Rate** | = **Amount** |
|---|---|---|---|---|
| Direct labor: | | | | |
| Foundry | 750 | | $22.50 | $ 16,875 |
| Welding | 1,050 | | 27.00 | 28,350 |
| Shipping | 375 | | 18.00 | 6,750 |
| Total direct labor | 2,175 | | | $ 51,975 |

| | **Direct Total Labor Cost** | × | **Factory Overhead Rate** | = **Amount** |
|---|---|---|---|---|
| Factory overhead | | | | |
| (200% of direct labor dollars) | $51,975 | × | 200% | $ 103,950 |
| Total cost | | | | $ 377,040 |
| Total units | | | | ÷ 75 |
| Unit cost | | | | $5,027.20 |

Management is concerned with the increase in unit costs over the months from October to December. To understand what has occurred, management interviewed the purchasing manager and quality manager.

*Purchasing Manager:* Prices have been holding steady for our raw materials during the first half of the year. I found a new supplier for our bulk steel that was willing to offer a better price than we received in the past. I saw these lower steel prices and jumped at them, knowing that a reduction in steel prices would have a very favorable impact on our costs.

*Quality Manager:* Something happened around mid-year. All of a sudden, we were experiencing problems with respect to the quality of our steel. As a result, we've been having all sorts of problems on the shop floor in our foundry and welding operation.

1. Analyze the two job cost sheets, and identify why the unit costs have changed for the backhoe buckets. Complete the following schedule to help you in your analysis:

| Item | Input Quantity per Unit—Job 206 | Input Quantity per Unit—Job 228 |
|---|---|---|
| Steel | | |
| Foundry labor | | |
| Welding labor | | |

2. ▬▬▶How would you interpret what has happened in light of your analysis and the interviews?

### CP 19-3   Factory overhead rate

Salvo Inc., a specialized equipment manufacturer, uses a job order costing system. The overhead is allocated to jobs on the basis of direct labor hours. The overhead rate is now $1,500 per direct labor hour. The design engineer thinks that this is illogical. The design engineer has stated the following:

Our accounting system doesn't make any sense to me. It tells me that every labor hour carries an additional burden of $1,500. This means that direct labor makes up only 6% of our total product cost, yet it drives all our costs.
In addition, these rates give my design engineers incentives to "design out" direct labor by using machine technology. Yet, over the past years as we have had less and less direct labor, the overhead rate keeps going up and up. I won't be surprised if next year the rate is $2,000 per direct labor hour. I'm also concerned because small errors in our estimates of the direct labor content can have a large impact on our estimated costs. Just a 30-minute error in our

estimate of assembly time is worth $750. Small mistakes in our direct labor time estimates really swing our bids around. I think this puts us at a disadvantage when we are going after business.

1. ▬▬▬▶What is the engineer's concern about the overhead rate going "up and up"?
2. ▬▬▬▶What did the engineer mean about the large overhead rate being a disadvantage when placing bids and seeking new business?
3. ▬▬▬▶What do you think is a possible solution?

---

### CP 19-4 Recording manufacturing costs

Todd Lay just began working as a cost accountant for Enteron Industries Inc., which manufactures gift items. Todd is preparing to record summary journal entries for the month. Todd begins by recording the factory wages as follows:

| | | |
|---|---|---|
| Wages Expense | 60,000 | |
| Wages Payable | | 60,000 |

Then the factory depreciation:

| | | |
|---|---|---|
| Depreciation Expense—Factory Machinery | 20,000 | |
| Accumulated Depreciation—Factory Machinery | | 20,000 |

Todd's supervisor, Jeff Fastow, walks by and notices the entries. The following conversation takes place:

*Jeff:* That's a very unusual way to record our factory wages and depreciation for the month.

*Todd:* What do you mean? This is exactly the way we were taught to record wages and depreciation in school. You know, debit an expense and credit Cash or payables, or in the case of depreciation, credit Accumulated Depreciation.

*Jeff:* Well, it's not the credits I'm concerned about. It's the debits—I don't think you've recorded the debits correctly. I wouldn't mind if you were recording the administrative wages or office equipment depreciation this way, but I've got real questions about recording factory wages and factory machinery depreciation this way.

*Todd:* Now I'm really confused. You mean this is correct for administrative costs, but not for factory costs? Well, what am I supposed to do—and why?

1. ▬▬▬▶Play the role of Jeff and answer Todd's questions.
2. ▬▬▬▶Why would Jeff accept the journal entries if they were for administrative costs?

---

### CP 19-5 Predetermined overhead rates

As an assistant cost accountant for Mississippi Industries, you have been assigned to review the activity base for the predetermined factory overhead rate. The president, Tony Favre, has expressed concern that the over- or underapplied overhead has fluctuated excessively over the years.

An analysis of the company's operations and use of the current overhead rate (direct labor cost) has narrowed the possible alternative overhead bases to direct labor cost and machine hours. For the past five years, the following data have been gathered:

| | 2016 | 2015 | 2014 | 2013 | 2012 |
|---|---|---|---|---|---|
| Actual overhead | $ 790,000 | $ 870,000 | $ 935,000 | $ 845,000 | $ 760,000 |
| Applied overhead | 777,000 | 882,000 | 924,000 | 840,000 | 777,000 |
| (Over-) underapplied overhead | $ 13,000 | $ (12,000) | $ 11,000 | $ 5,000 | $ (17,000) |
| Direct labor cost | $3,885,000 | $4,410,000 | $4,620,000 | $4,200,000 | $3,885,000 |
| Machine hours | 93,000 | 104,000 | 111,000 | 100,400 | 91,600 |

1. Calculate a predetermined factory overhead rate for each alternative base, assuming that rates would have been determined by relating the total amount of factory overhead for the past five years to the base.

2. For each of the past five years, determine the over- or underapplied overhead, based on the two predetermined overhead rates developed in part (1).

3. ▬▬▬▶Which predetermined overhead rate would you recommend? Discuss the basis for your recommendation.

# Process Cost Systems

## Dreyer's Ice Cream

In making ice cream, an electric ice cream maker is used to mix ingredients, which include milk, cream, sugar, and flavoring. After the ingredients are added, the mixer is packed with ice and salt to cool the ingredients, and it is then turned on.

After mixing for half of the required time, would you have ice cream? Of course not, because the ice cream needs to mix longer to freeze. Now, assume that you ask the question:

*What costs have I incurred so far in making ice cream?*

The answer to this question requires knowing the cost of the ingredients and electricity. The ingredients are added at the beginning; thus, all the ingredient costs have been incurred. Because the mixing is only half complete, only 50% of the electricity cost has been incurred. Therefore, the answer to the preceding question is:

*All the materials costs and half the electricity costs have been incurred.*

These same cost concepts apply to larger ice cream processes like those of **Dreyer's Ice Cream** (a subsidiary of **Nestlé**), manufacturer of Dreyer's® and Edy's® ice cream. Dreyer's mixes ingredients in 3,000-gallon vats in much the same way you would with an electric ice cream maker. Dreyer's also records the costs of the ingredients, labor, and factory overhead used in making ice cream. These costs are used by managers for decisions such as setting prices and improving operations.

This chapter describes and illustrates process cost systems that are used by manufacturers such as Dreyer's. In addition, the use of cost of production reports in decision making is described. Finally, just-in-time cost systems are discussed.

**OBJ 1** Describe process cost systems.

# Process Cost Systems

A **process manufacturer** produces products that are indistinguishable from each other using a continuous production process. For example, an oil refinery processes crude oil through a series of steps to produce a barrel of gasoline. One barrel of gasoline, the product, cannot be distinguished from another barrel. Other examples of process manufacturers include paper producers, chemical processors, aluminum smelters, and food processors.

## Integrity, Objectivity, and Ethics in Business

**ON BEING GREEN**

Process manufacturing often involves significant energy and material resources, which can be harmful to the environment. Thus, many process manufacturing companies, such as chemical, electronic, and metal processors, must address environmental issues. Companies, such as DuPont, Intel, Apple, and Alcoa, are at the forefront of providing environmental solutions for their products and processes.

For example, Apple provides free recycling programs for Macs®, iPhones®, and iPads®. Apple recovers more than 90% by weight of the original product in reusable components, glass, and plastic. You can even receive a free gift card for voluntarily recycling an older Apple product.

Source: Apple Web site.

The cost accounting system used by process manufacturers is called the **process cost system.** A process cost system records product costs for each manufacturing department or process.

In contrast, a job order manufacturer produces custom products for customers or batches of similar products. For example, a custom printer produces wedding invitations, graduation announcements, or other special print items that are tailored to the specifications of each customer. Each item manufactured is unique to itself. Other examples of job order manufacturers include furniture manufacturers, shipbuilders, and home builders.

As described and illustrated in Chapter 19, the cost accounting system used by job order manufacturers is called the *job order cost system.* A job order cost system records product cost for each job, using job cost sheets.

Some examples of process and job order companies and their products are shown in Exhibit 1.

| Process Manufacturing Companies | | Job Order Companies | |
|---|---|---|---|
| **Company** | **Product** | **Company** | **Product** |
| Pepsi | soft drinks | Walt Disney | movies |
| Alcoa | aluminum | Nike, Inc. | athletic shoes |
| Intel | computer chip | Nicklaus Design | golf courses |
| Apple | iPhone | Heritage Log Homes | log homes |
| Hershey Foods | chocolate bars | DDB Advertising Agency | advertising |

**EXHIBIT 1**

**Examples of Process Cost and Job Order Companies**

## Comparing Job Order and Process Cost Systems

Process and job order cost systems are similar in that each system:

- Records and summarizes product costs.
- Classifies product costs as direct materials, direct labor, and factory overhead.
- Allocates factory overhead costs to products.
- Uses perpetual inventory system for materials, work in process, and finished goods.
- Provides useful product cost information for decision making.

Process and job costing systems are different in several ways. As a basis for illustrating these differences, the cost systems for **Frozen Delight** and **Legend Guitars** are used.

Exhibit 2 illustrates the process cost system for Frozen Delight, an ice cream manufacturer. As a basis for comparison, Exhibit 2 also illustrates the job order cost system for Legend Guitars, a custom guitar manufacturer. Legend Guitars was described and illustrated in Chapters 18 and 19.

Exhibit 2 indicates that Frozen Delight manufactures ice cream, using two departments:

- The Mixing Department mixes the ingredients, using large vats.
- The Packaging Department puts the ice cream into cartons for shipping to customers.

Because each gallon of ice cream is similar, product costs are recorded in each department's work in process account. As shown in Exhibit 2, Frozen Delight accumulates (records) the cost of making ice cream in *work in process accounts* for the Mixing and Packaging departments. The product costs of making a gallon of ice cream include:

- *Direct materials costs,* which include milk, cream, sugar, and packing cartons. All materials costs are added at the beginning of the process for both the Mixing Department and the Packaging Department.

**EXHIBIT 2**   **Process Cost and Job Order Cost Systems**

- *Direct labor costs,* which are incurred by employees in each department who run the equipment and load and unload product.

- *Factory overhead costs,* which include the utility costs (power) and depreciation on the equipment.

When the Mixing Department completes the mixing process, its product costs are transferred to the Packaging Department. When the Packaging Department completes its process, the product costs are transferred to Finished Goods. In this way, the cost of the product (a gallon of ice cream) accumulates across the entire production process.

In contrast, Exhibit 2 shows that Legend Guitars accumulates (records) product costs by jobs, using a job cost sheet for each type of guitar. Thus, Legend Guitars uses just one work in process account. As each job is completed, its product costs are transferred to Finished Goods.

In a job order cost system, the work in process at the end of the period is the sum of the job cost sheets for partially completed jobs. In a process cost system, the work in process at the end of the period is the sum of the costs remaining in each department account at the end of the period.

## Example Exercise 20-1 Job Order versus Process Costing

OBJ 1

Which of the following industries would normally use job order costing systems, and which would normally use process costing systems?

| | |
|---|---|
| Home construction | Computer chips |
| Beverages | Cookies |
| Military aircraft | Video game design and production |

### Follow My Example 20-1

| | |
|---|---|
| Home construction | Job order |
| Beverages | Process |
| Military aircraft | Job order |
| Computer chips | Process |
| Cookies | Process |
| Video game design and production | Job order |

Practice Exercises: PE 20-1A, PE 20-1B

## Cost Flows for a Process Manufacturer

Exhibit 3 illustrates the *physical flow* of materials for **Frozen Delight**. Ice cream is made in a manufacturing plant in much the same way you would make it at home, except on a larger scale.

---

### EXHIBIT 3    Physical Flows for a Process Manufacturer

In the Mixing Department, direct materials in the form of milk, cream, and sugar are placed into a vat. An employee fills each vat, sets the cooling temperature, and sets the mix speed. The vat is cooled as the direct materials are being mixed by agitators (paddles). Factory overhead includes equipment depreciation and indirect materials.

In the Packaging Department, the ice cream is received from the Mixing Department in a form ready for packaging. The Packaging Department uses direct labor and factory overhead to package the ice cream into one-gallon containers. The ice cream is then transferred to finished goods, where it is frozen and stored in refrigerators prior to shipment to customers.

The *cost flows* in a process cost accounting system are similar to the *physical flow* of materials illustrated in Exhibit 3. The cost flows for **Frozen Delight** are illustrated in Exhibit 4 as follows:

Materials costs can be as high as 70% of the total product costs for many process manufacturers.

a. The cost of materials purchased is recorded in the materials account.

b. The cost of direct materials used by the Mixing and Packaging departments is recorded in the work in process accounts for each department.

**EXHIBIT 4** Cost Flows for a Process Manufacturer—Frozen Delight

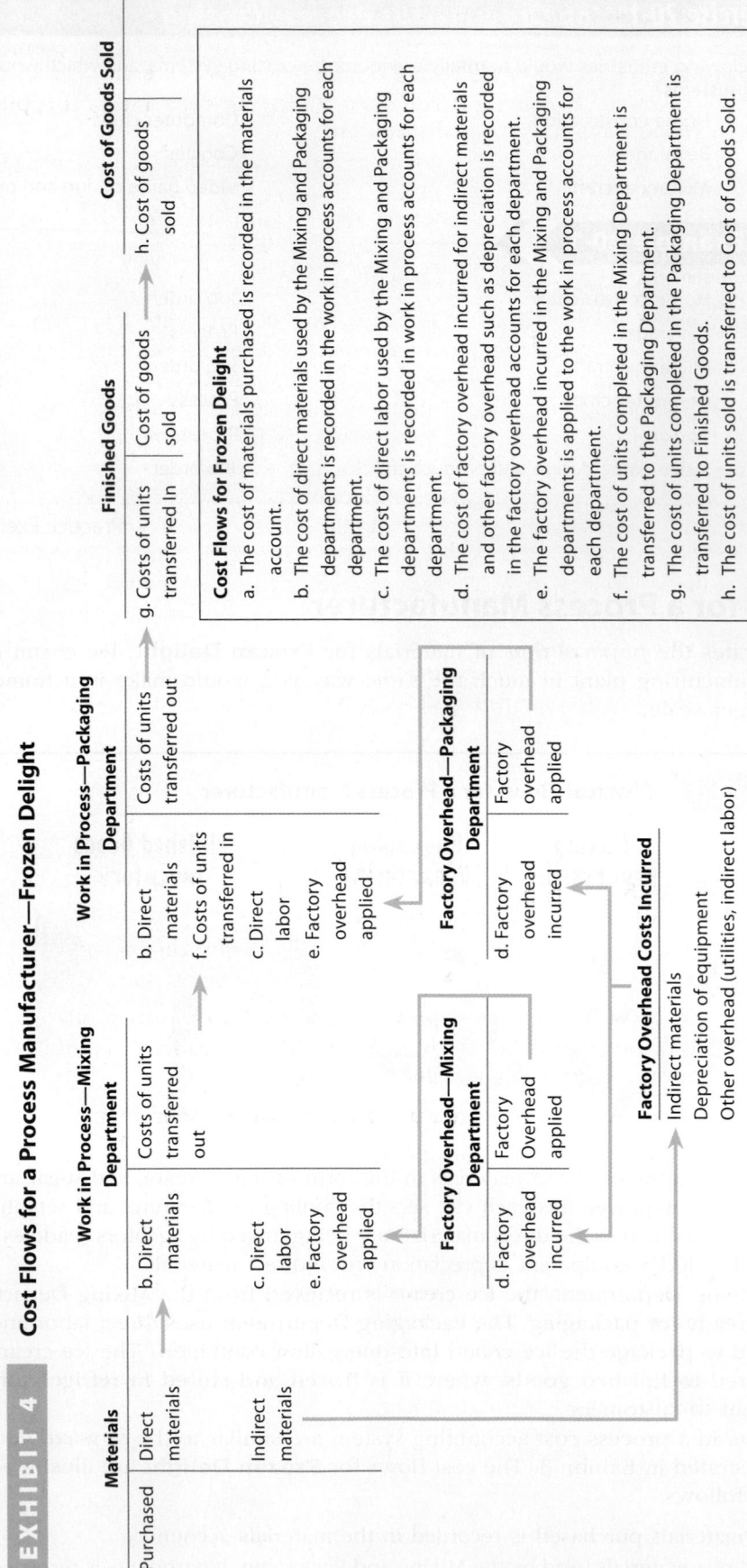

**Cost Flows for Frozen Delight**

a. The cost of materials purchased is recorded in the materials account.

b. The cost of direct materials used by the Mixing and Packaging departments is recorded in the work in process accounts for each department.

c. The cost of direct labor used by the Mixing and Packaging departments is recorded in work in process accounts for each department.

d. The cost of factory overhead incurred for indirect materials and other factory overhead such as depreciation is recorded in the factory overhead accounts for each department.

e. The factory overhead incurred in the Mixing and Packaging departments is applied to the work in process accounts for each department.

f. The cost of units completed in the Mixing Department is transferred to the Packaging Department.

g. The cost of units completed in the Packaging Department is transferred to Finished Goods.

h. The cost of units sold is transferred to Cost of Goods Sold.

c. The cost of direct labor used by the Mixing and Packaging departments is recorded in work in process accounts for each department.

d. The cost of factory overhead incurred for indirect materials and other factory overhead such as depreciation is recorded in the factory overhead accounts for each department.

e. The factory overhead incurred in the Mixing and Packaging departments is applied to the work in process accounts for each department.

f. The cost of units completed in the Mixing Department is transferred to the Packaging Department.

g. The cost of units completed in the Packaging Department is transferred to Finished Goods.

h. The cost of units sold is transferred to Cost of Goods Sold.

As shown in Exhibit 4, the Mixing and Packaging departments have separate factory overhead accounts. The factory overhead costs incurred for indirect materials, depreciation, and other overhead are debited to each department's factory overhead account. The overhead is applied to work in process by debiting each department's work in process account and crediting the department's factory overhead account.

Exhibit 4 illustrates how the Mixing and Packaging departments have separate work in process accounts. Each work in process account is debited for direct materials, direct labor, and applied factory overhead. In addition, the work in process account for the Packaging Department is debited for the cost of the units transferred in from the Mixing Department. Each work in process account is credited for the cost of the units transferred to the next department.

Lastly, Exhibit 4 shows that the finished goods account is debited for the cost of the units transferred from the Packaging Department. The finished goods account is credited for the cost of the units sold, which is debited to the cost of goods sold account.

# Cost of Production Report

**OBJ 2** Prepare a cost of production report.

In a process cost system, the cost of units transferred out of each processing department must be determined along with the cost of any partially completed units remaining in the department. The report that summarizes these costs is a cost of production report.

The **cost of production report** summarizes the production and cost data for a department as follows:

- The units the department is accountable for and the disposition of those units.
- The product costs incurred by the department and the allocation of those costs between completed (transferred out) and partially completed units.

A cost of production report is prepared using the following four steps:

- Step 1. Determine the units to be assigned costs.
- Step 2. Compute equivalent units of production.
- Step 3. Determine the cost per equivalent unit.
- Step 4. Allocate costs to units transferred out and partially completed units.

Preparing a cost of production report requires making a cost flow assumption. Like merchandise inventory, costs can be assumed to flow through the manufacturing process, using the first-in, first-out (FIFO), last in, first-out (LIFO), or average cost methods. Because the **first-in, first-out (FIFO) method** is often the same as the physical flow of units, the FIFO method is used in this chapter.[1]

---

[1] The average cost method is illustrated in an appendix to this chapter.

To illustrate, a cost of production report for the Mixing Department of **Frozen Delight** for July 2016 is prepared. The July data for the Mixing Department are as follows:

| | | |
|---|---:|---:|
| Inventory in process, July 1, 5,000 gallons: | | |
| Direct materials cost, for 5,000 gallons ..................... | $5,000 | |
| Conversion costs, for 5,000 gallons, 70% completed ......... | 1,225 | |
| Total inventory in process, July 1........................... | | $ 6,225 |
| Direct materials cost for July, 60,000 gallons .................. | | 66,000 |
| Direct labor cost for July...................................... | | 10,500 |
| Factory overhead applied for July ............................ | | 7,275 |
| Total production costs to account for ..................... | | $90,000 |
| Gallons transferred to Packaging in July (includes | | |
| units in process on July 1), 62,000 gallons ................. | | ? |
| Inventory in process, July 31, 3,000 gallons, | | |
| 25% completed as to conversion costs .................... | | ? |

By preparing a cost of production report, the cost of the gallons transferred to the Packaging Department in July and the ending work in process inventory in the Mixing Department are determined. These amounts are indicated by question marks (?).

## Step 1: Determine the Units to Be Assigned Costs

The first step is to determine the units to be assigned costs. A unit can be any measure of completed production, such as tons, gallons, pounds, barrels, or cases. For **Frozen Delight**, a unit is a gallon of ice cream.

The Mixing Department is accountable for 65,000 gallons of direct materials during July, computed as follows:

| | |
|---|---:|
| Total units (gallons) charged to production: | |
| In process, July 1 | 5,000 gallons |
| Received from materials storage | 60,000 |
| Total units (gallons) accounted for | 65,000 gallons |

For July, the following three groups of units (gallons) are assigned costs:

- Group 1.  Units (gallons) in beginning work in process inventory on July 1.
- Group 2.  Units (gallons) started and completed during July.
- Group 3.  Units (gallons) in ending work in process inventory on July 31.

Exhibit 5 illustrates these groups of units (gallons) in the Mixing Department for July. The 5,000 gallons of beginning inventory were completed and transferred to the Packaging Department. During July, 60,000 gallons of material were started (entered into mixing). Of the 60,000 gallons started in July, 3,000 gallons were incomplete on July 31. Thus, 57,000 gallons (60,000 – 3,000) were started and completed in July.

The total units (gallons) to be assigned costs for July are summarized as follows:

| | | |
|---|---|---:|
| Group 1 | Inventory in process, July 1, completed in July | 5,000 gallons |
| Group 2 | Started and completed in July | 57,000 |
| | Transferred out to the Packaging Department in July | 62,000 gallons |
| Group 3 | Inventory in process, July 31 | 3,000 |
| | Total units (gallons) to be assigned costs | 65,000 gallons |

The total gallons to be assigned costs (65,000) equal the total gallons accounted for (65,000) by the Mixing Department.

**EXHIBIT 5**

**July Units to Be Costed—Mixing Department**

60,000 Gallons Started in July

57,000 Gallons Started and Completed in July

5,000 Gallons Beginning Inventory

3,000 Gallons Ending inventory

Group 1

Group 2

Group 3

65,000 Gallons to Be Assigned Costs

## Example Exercise 20-2  Units to Be Assigned Costs

OBJ 2

Rocky Springs Beverage Company has two departments, Blending and Bottling. The Bottling Department received 57,000 liters from the Blending Department. During the period, the Bottling Department completed 58,000 liters, including 4,000 liters of work in process at the beginning of the period. The ending work in process was 3,000 liters. How many liters were started and completed during the period?

## Follow My Example 20-2

54,000 liters started and completed (58,000 completed – 4,000 beginning work in process), or (57,000 started – 3,000 ending work in process)

Practice Exercises: PE 20-2A, PE 20-2B

## Step 2: Compute Equivalent Units of Production

**Whole units** are the number of units in production during a period, whether completed or not. **Equivalent units of production** are the portion of whole units that are complete with respect to materials or conversion (direct labor and factory overhead) costs.

To illustrate, assume that a 1,000-gallon batch (vat) of ice cream at **Frozen Delight** is only 40% complete in the mixing process on May 31. Thus, the batch is only 40% complete as to conversion costs such as power. In this case, the whole units and equivalent units of production are as follows:

|  | Whole Units | Equivalent Units |
| --- | --- | --- |
| Materials costs | 1,000 gallons | 1,000 gallons |
| Conversion costs | 1,000 gallons | 400 gallons (1,000 × 40%) |

Because the materials costs are all added at the beginning of the process, the materials costs are 100% complete for the 1,000-gallon batch of ice cream. Thus, the whole units and equivalent units for materials costs are 1,000 gallons. However, because the batch is only 40% complete as to conversion costs, the equivalent units for conversion costs are 400 gallons.

Equivalent units for materials and conversion costs are usually determined separately as shown earlier. This is because materials and conversion costs normally enter production at different times and rates. In contrast, direct labor and factory overhead normally enter production at the same time and rate. For this reason, direct labor and factory overhead are combined as conversion costs in computing equivalent units.

**Materials Equivalent Units** To compute equivalent units for materials, it is necessary to know how materials are added during the manufacturing process. In the case of **Frozen Delight**, all the materials are added at the beginning of the mixing process. Thus, the equivalent units for materials in July are computed as follows:

| | | Total Whole Units | Percent Materials Added in July | Equivalent Units for Direct Materials |
|---|---|---|---|---|
| Group 1 | Inventory in process, July 1 .......................... | 5,000 | 0% | 0 |
| Group 2 | Started and completed in July | | | |
| | (62,000 − 5,000) ................................. | 57,000 | 100% | 57,000 |
| | Transferred out to Packaging | | | |
| | Department in July ......................... | 62,000 | — | 57,000 |
| Group 3 | Inventory in process, July 31 ........................ | 3,000 | 100% | 3,000 |
| | Total gallons to be assigned cost ................ | 65,000 | | 60,000 |

As shown, the whole units for the three groups of units determined in Step 1 are listed in the first column. The percent of materials added in July is then listed. The equivalent units are determined by multiplying the whole units by the percent of materials added.

To illustrate, the July 1 inventory (Group 1) has 5,000 gallons of whole units, which are complete as to materials. That is, all the direct materials for the 5,000 gallons in process on July 1 were added in June. Thus, the percent of materials added in July is zero, and the equivalent units added in July are zero.

The 57,000 gallons started and completed in July (Group 2) are 100% complete as to materials. Thus, the equivalent units for the gallons started and completed in July are 57,000 (57,000 × 100%) gallons. The 3,000 gallons in process on July 31 (Group 3) are also 100% complete as to materials because all materials are added at the beginning of the process. Therefore, the equivalent units for the inventory in process on July 31 are 3,000 (3,000 × 100%) gallons.

The equivalent units for direct materials for **Frozen Delight** are summarized in Exhibit 6.

---

**EXHIBIT 6**    **Direct Materials Equivalent Units**

**60,000 Total Equivalent Units of Materials Cost in July**

## Example Exercise 20-3 Equivalent Units of Materials Cost

OBJ 2

The Bottling Department of Rocky Springs Beverage Company had 4,000 liters in the beginning work in process inventory (30% complete). During the period, 58,000 liters were completed. The ending work in process inventory was 3,000 liters (60% complete). What are the total equivalent units for direct materials if materials are added at the beginning of the process?

### Follow My Example 20-3

Total equivalent units for direct materials are 57,000, computed as follows:

| | Total Whole Units | Percent Materials Added in Period | Equivalent Units for Direct Materials |
|---|---|---|---|
| Inventory in process, beginning of period | 4,000 | 0% | 0 |
| Started and completed during the period | 54,000* | 100% | 54,000 |
| Transferred out of Bottling (completed) | 58,000 | — | 54,000 |
| Inventory in process, end of period | 3,000 | 100% | 3,000 |
| Total units to be assigned costs | 61,000 | | 57,000 |

*(58,000 − 4,000)

Practice Exercises: PE 20-3A, PE 20-3B

**Conversion Equivalent Units** To compute equivalent units for conversion costs, it is necessary to know how direct labor and factory overhead enter the manufacturing process. Direct labor, utilities, and equipment depreciation are often incurred uniformly during processing. For this reason, it is assumed that **Frozen Delight** incurs conversion costs evenly throughout its manufacturing process. Thus, the equivalent units for conversion costs in July are computed as follows:

| | | Total Whole Units | Percent Conversion Completed in July | Equivalent Units for Conversion |
|---|---|---|---|---|
| Group 1 | Inventory in process, July 1 (70% completed) . . . . . . . | 5,000 | 30% | 1,500 |
| Group 2 | Started and completed in July (62,000 − 5,000) . . . . | 57,000 | 100% | 57,000 |
| | Transferred out to Packaging Department in July . . . . . . . . . . . . . . . . . . . . . . . . . | 62,000 | — | 58,500 |
| Group 3 | Inventory in process, July 31 (25% completed) . . . . . . | 3,000 | 25% | 750 |
| | Total gallons to be assigned cost . . . . . . . . . . . . . . . | 65,000 | | 59,250 |

As shown, the whole units for the three groups of units determined in Step 1 are listed in the first column. The percent of conversion costs added in July is then listed. The equivalent units are determined by multiplying the whole units by the percent of conversion costs added.

To illustrate, the July 1 inventory has 5,000 gallons of whole units (Group 1), which are 70% complete as to conversion costs. During July, the remaining 30% (100% − 70%) of conversion costs was added. Therefore, the equivalent units of conversion costs added in July are 1,500 (5,000 × 30%) gallons.

The 57,000 gallons started and completed in July (Group 2) are 100% complete as to conversion costs. Thus, the equivalent units of conversion costs for the gallons started and completed in July are 57,000 (57,000 × 100%) gallons.

The 3,000 gallons in process on July 31 (Group 3) are 25% complete as to conversion costs. Hence, the equivalent units for the inventory in process on July 31 are 750 (3,000 × 25%) gallons.

The equivalent units for conversion costs for **Frozen Delight** are summarized in Exhibit 7.

**EXHIBIT 7** **Conversion Equivalent Units**

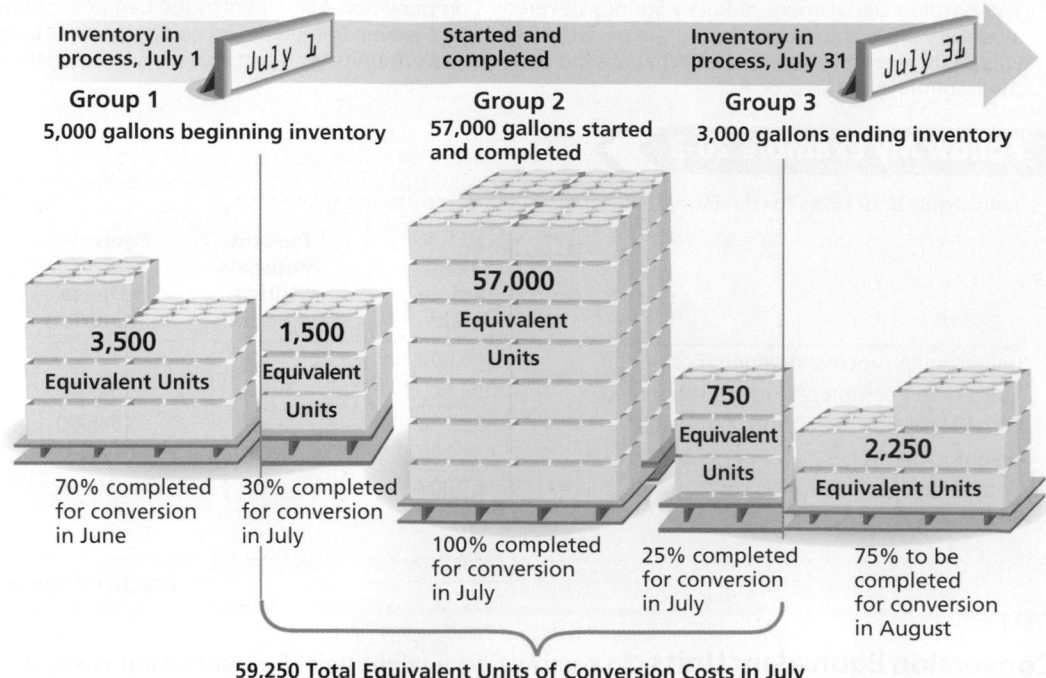

59,250 Total Equivalent Units of Conversion Costs in July

---

## Example Exercise 20-4 Equivalent Units of Conversion Costs

OBJ 2

The Bottling Department of Rocky Springs Beverage Company had 4,000 liters in the beginning work in process inventory (30% complete). During the period, 58,000 liters were completed. The ending work in process inventory was 3,000 liters (60% complete). What are the total equivalent units for conversion costs?

### Follow My Example 20-4

|  | Total Whole Units | Percent Conversion Completed in Period | Equivalent Units for Conversion |
|---|---|---|---|
| Inventory in process, beginning of period | 4,000 | 70% | 2,800 |
| Started and completed during the period | 54,000* | 100% | 54,000 |
| Transferred out of Bottling (completed) | 58,000 | — | 56,800 |
| Inventory in process, end of period | 3,000 | 60% | 1,800 |
| Total units to be assigned costs | 61,000 | | 58,600 |

*(58,000 − 4,000)

Practice Exercises: PE 20-4A, PE 20-4B

---

## Step 3: Determine the Cost per Equivalent Unit

The next step in preparing the cost of production report is to compute the cost per equivalent unit for direct materials and conversion costs. The **cost per equivalent unit** for direct materials and conversion costs is computed as follows:

$$\text{Direct Materials Cost per Equivalent Unit} = \frac{\text{Total Direct Materials Cost for the Period}}{\text{Total Equivalent Units of Direct Materials}}$$

$$\text{Conversion Cost per Equivalent Unit} = \frac{\text{Total Conversion Costs for the Period}}{\text{Total Equivalent Units of Conversion Costs}}$$

The July direct materials and conversion cost equivalent units for **Frozen Delight**'s Mixing Department from Step 2 are as follows:

| | | Equivalent Units | |
| --- | --- | --- | --- |
| | | **Direct Materials** | **Conversion** |
| Group 1 | Inventory in process, July 1 ................................. | 0 | 1,500 |
| Group 2 | Started and completed in July (62,000 – 5,000) ............. | 57,000 | 57,000 |
| | Transferred out to Packaging Department in July ....... | 57,000 | 58,500 |
| Group 3 | Inventory in process, July 31 ................................ | 3,000 | 750 |
| | Total gallons to be assigned cost ...................... | 60,000 | 59,250 |

The direct materials and conversion costs incurred by Frozen Delight in July are as follows:

| | | |
| --- | --- | --- |
| Direct materials ................................................ | | $66,000 |
| Conversion costs: | | |
| Direct labor................................................ | $10,500 | |
| Factory overhead ........................................... | 7,275 | 17,775 |
| Total product costs incurred in July....................... | | $83,775 |

The direct materials and conversion costs per equivalent unit are $1.10 and $0.30 per gallon, computed as follows:

$$\text{Direct Materials Cost per Equivalent Unit} = \frac{\text{Total Direct Materials Cost for the Period}}{\text{Total Equivalent Units of Direct Materials}}$$

$$\text{Direct Materials Cost per Equivalent Unit} = \frac{\$66,000}{60,000 \text{ gallons}} = \$1.10 \text{ per gallon}$$

$$\text{Conversion Cost per Equivalent Unit} = \frac{\text{Total Conversion Costs for the Period}}{\text{Total Equivalent Units of Conversion Costs}}$$

$$\text{Conversion Cost per Equivalent Unit} = \frac{\$17,775}{59,250 \text{ gallons}} = \$0.30 \text{ per gallon}$$

The preceding costs per equivalent unit are used in Step 4 to allocate the direct materials and conversion costs to the completed and partially completed units.

---

## Example Exercise 20-5   Cost per Equivalent Unit

OBJ 2

The cost of direct materials transferred into the Bottling Department of Rocky Springs Beverage Company is $22,800. The conversion cost for the period in the Bottling Department is $8,790. The total equivalent units for direct materials and conversion are 57,000 liters and 58,600 liters, respectively. Determine the direct materials and conversion costs per equivalent unit.

## Follow My Example 20-5

$$\text{Direct Materials Cost per Equivalent Unit} = \frac{\$22,800}{57,000 \text{ liters}} = \$0.40 \text{ per liter}$$

$$\text{Conversion Cost per Equivalent Unit} = \frac{\$8,790}{58,600 \text{ liters}} = \$0.15 \text{ per liter}$$

Practice Exercises: PE 20-5A, PE 20-5B

---

# Step 4: Allocate Costs to Units Transferred Out and Partially Completed Units

Product costs must be allocated to the units transferred out and the partially completed units on hand at the end of the period. The product costs are allocated using the costs per equivalent unit for materials and conversion costs that were computed in Step 3.

The total production costs to be assigned for **Frozen Delight** in July are $90,000, computed as follows:

| | |
|---|---:|
| Inventory in process, July 1, 5,000 gallons: | |
|    Direct materials cost, for 5,000 gallons ..................................... | $ 5,000 |
|    Conversion costs, for 5,000 gallons, 70% completed ...................... | 1,225 |
|    Total inventory in process, July 1 .......................................... | $ 6,225 |
| Direct materials cost for July, 60,000 gallons ................................. | 66,000 |
| Direct labor cost for July .................................................. | 10,500 |
| Factory overhead applied for July ........................................... | 7,275 |
|    Total production costs to account for ..................................... | $90,000 |

The units to be assigned these costs follow. The costs to be assigned these units are indicated by question marks (?).

| | | Units | Total Cost |
|---|---|---|---|
| Group 1 | Inventory in process, July 1, completed in July........ | 5,000 gallons | ? |
| Group 2 | Started and completed in July ....................... | 57,000 | ? |
| | Transferred out to the Packaging | | |
| | Department in July ........................... | 62,000 gallons | ? |
| Group 3 | Inventory in process, July 31 ........................ | 3,000 | ? |
| | Total......................................... | 65,000 gallons | $90,000 |

## Group 1: Inventory in Process on July 1

The 5,000 gallons of inventory in process on July 1 (Group 1) were completed and transferred out to the Packaging Department in July. The cost of these units of $6,675 is determined as follows:

| | Direct Materials Costs | Conversion Costs | Total Costs |
|---|---|---|---|
| Inventory in process, July 1 balance .................. | | | $6,225 |
| Equivalent units for completing the | | | |
|    July 1 in-process inventory ....................... | 0 | 1,500 | |
| Cost per equivalent unit ............................ | × $1.10 | × $0.30 | |
| Cost of completed July 1 in-process inventory........ | 0 | $450 | 450 |
| Cost of July 1 in-process inventory | | | |
|    transferred to Packaging Department ............ | | | $6,675 |

As shown, $6,225 of the cost of the July 1 in-process inventory of 5,000 gallons was carried over from June. This cost plus the cost of completing the 5,000 gallons in July was transferred to the Packaging Department during July. The cost of completing the 5,000 gallons during July is $450. The $450 represents the conversion costs necessary to complete the remaining 30% of the processing. There were no direct materials costs added in July because all the materials costs had been added in June. Thus, the cost of the 5,000 gallons in process on July 1 (Group 1) transferred to the Packaging Department is $6,675.

## Group 2: Started and Completed

The 57,000 units started and completed in July (Group 2) incurred all (100%) of their direct materials and conversion costs in July. Thus, the cost of the 57,000 gallons started and completed is $79,800, computed by multiplying 57,000 gallons by the costs per equivalent unit for materials and conversion costs as follows:

| | Direct Materials Costs | Conversion Costs | Total Costs |
|---|---|---|---|
| Units started and completed in July.................. | 57,000 gallons | 57,000 gallons | |
| Cost per equivalent unit ............................ | × $1.10 | × $0.30 | |
| Cost of the units started | | | |
|    and completed in July........................... | $62,700 | $17,100 | $79,800 |

The total cost of $86,475 transferred to the Packaging Department in July is the sum of the beginning inventory cost and the costs of the units started and completed in July, computed as follows:

| | | |
|---|---|---:|
| Group 1 | Cost of July 1 in-process inventory | $ 6,675 |
| Group 2 | Cost of the units started and completed in July | 79,800 |
| | Total costs transferred to Packaging Department in July | $86,475 |

## Group 3: Inventory in Process on July 31

The 3,000 gallons in process on July 31 (Group 3) incurred all their direct materials costs and 25% of their conversion costs in July. The cost of these partially completed units of $3,525 is computed as follows:

|  | Direct Materials Costs | Conversion Costs | Total Costs |
|---|---|---|---|
| Equivalent units in ending inventory | 3,000 gallons | 750 gallons | |
| Cost per equivalent unit | × $1.10 | × $0.30 | |
| Cost of July 31 in-process inventory | $3,300 | $225 | $3,525 |

The 3,000 gallons in process on July 31 received all (100%) of their materials in July. Therefore, the direct materials cost incurred in July is $3,300 (3,000 × $1.10). The conversion costs of $225 represent the cost of the 750 (3,000 × 25%) equivalent gallons multiplied by the cost of $0.30 per equivalent unit for conversion costs. The sum of the direct materials cost ($3,300) and the conversion costs ($225) equals the total cost of the July 31 work in process inventory of $3,525 ($3,300 + $225).

To summarize, the total manufacturing costs for Frozen Delight in July were assigned as follows. In doing so, the question marks (?) for the costs to be assigned to units in Groups 1, 2, and 3 have been answered.

|  |  | Units | Total Cost |
|---|---|---|---|
| Group 1 | Inventory in process, July 1, completed in July | 5,000 gallons | $ 6,675 |
| Group 2 | Started and completed in July | 57,000 | 79,800 |
| | Transferred out to the Packaging Department in July | 62,000 gallons | $86,475 |
| Group 3 | Inventory in process, July 31 | 3,000 | 3,525 |
| | Total | 65,000 gallons | $90,000 |

---

## Example Exercise 20-6  Cost of Units Transferred Out and Ending Work in Process

**OBJ 2**

The costs per equivalent unit of direct materials and conversion in the Bottling Department of Rocky Springs Beverage Company are $0.40 and $0.15, respectively. The equivalent units to be assigned costs are as follows:

|  | Equivalent Units | |
|---|---|---|
|  | Direct Materials | Conversion |
| Inventory in process, beginning of period | 0 | 2,800 |
| Started and completed during the period | 54,000 | 54,000 |
| Transferred out of Bottling (completed) | 54,000 | 56,800 |
| Inventory in process, end of period | 3,000 | 1,800 |
| Total units to be assigned costs | 57,000 | 58,600 |

The beginning work in process inventory had a cost of $1,860. Determine the cost of units transferred out and the ending work in process inventory.

### Follow My Example 20-6

|  | Direct Materials Costs | | Conversion Costs | Total Costs |
|---|---|---|---|---|
| Inventory in process, beginning of period | | | | $ 1,860 |
| Inventory in process, beginning of period | 0 | + | 2,800 × $0.15 | 420 |
| Started and completed during the period | 54,000 × $0.40 | + | 54,000 × $0.15 | 29,700 |
| Transferred out of Bottling (completed) | | | | $31,980 |
| Inventory in process, end of period | 3,000 × $0.40 | + | 1,800 × $0.15 | 1,470 |
| Total costs assigned by the Bottling Department | | | | $33,450 |
| Completed and transferred out of production | $31,980 | | | |
| Inventory in process, ending | $ 1,470 | | | |

Practice Exercises: PE 20-6A, PE 20-6B

# Preparing the Cost of Production Report

A cost of production report is prepared for each processing department at periodic intervals. The report summarizes the following production quantity and cost data:

- The units for which the department is accountable and the disposition of those units
- The production costs incurred by the department and the allocation of those costs between completed (transferred out) and partially completed units

Using Steps 1–4, the July cost of production report for **Frozen Delight**'s Mixing Department is shown in Exhibit 8. During July, the Mixing Department was accountable for 65,000 units (gallons). Of these units, 62,000 units were completed and transferred to the Packaging Department. The remaining 3,000 units are partially completed and are part of the in-process inventory as of July 31.

The Mixing Department was responsible for $90,000 of production costs during July. The cost of goods transferred to the Packaging Department in July was $86,475. The remaining cost of $3,525 is part of the in-process inventory as of July 31.

---

**EXHIBIT 8**    **Cost of Production Report for Frozen Delight's Mixing Department—FIFO**

| | A | B | C | D | E | |
|---|---|---|---|---|---|---|
| 1 | | | Frozen Delight | | | |
| 2 | | Cost of Production Report—Mixing Department | | | | |
| 3 | | For the Month Ended July 31, 2016 | | | | Step 1 |
| 4 | | | | | | Step 2 |
| 5 | | | Whole Units | Equivalent Units | | |
| 6 | **UNITS** | | | Direct Materials | Conversion | |
| 7 | Units charged to production: | | | | | |
| 8 | Inventory in process, July 1 | | 5,000 | | | |
| 9 | Received from materials storeroom | | 60,000 | | | |
| 10 | Total units accounted for by the Mixing Department | | 65,000 | | | |
| 11 | | | | | | |
| 12 | Units to be assigned costs: | | | | | |
| 13 | Inventory in process, July 1 (70% completed) | | 5,000 | 0 | 1,500 | |
| 14 | Started and completed in July | | 57,000 | 57,000 | 57,000 | |
| 15 | Transferred to Packaging Department in July | | 62,000 | 57,000 | 58,500 | |
| 16 | Inventory in process, July 31 (25% completed) | | 3,000 | 3,000 | 750 | |
| 17 | Total units to be assigned costs | | 65,000 | 60,000 | 59,250 | |
| 18 | | | | | | |
| 19 | | | | | Costs | |
| 20 | **COSTS** | | | Direct Materials | Conversion | Total |
| 21 | | | | | | |
| 22 | Costs per equivalent unit: | | | | | |
| 23 | Total costs for July in Mixing Department | | | $ 66,000 | $ 17,775 | |
| 24 | Total equivalent units (from Step 2) | | | ÷ 60,000 | ÷ 59,250 | |
| 25 | Cost per equivalent unit | | | $ 1.10 | $ 0.30 | |
| 26 | | | | | | Step 3 |
| 27 | Costs assigned to production: | | | | | |
| 28 | Inventory in process, July 1 | | | | | $ 6,225 |
| 29 | Costs incurred in July | | | | | 83,775[a] |
| 30 | Total costs accounted for by the Mixing Department | | | | | $90,000 |
| 31 | | | | | | |
| 32 | | | | | | |
| 33 | Cost allocated to completed and partially | | | | | |
| 34 | completed units: | | | | | |
| 35 | Inventory in process, July 1—balance | | | | | $ 6,225 |
| 36 | To complete inventory in process, July 1 | | | $ 0 + | $ 450[b] = | 450 |
| 37 | Cost of completed July 1 work in process | | | | | $ 6,675 |
| 38 | Started and completed in July | | | 62,700[c] + | 17,100[d] = | 79,800 |
| 39 | Transferred to Packaging Department in July | | | | | $86,475 |
| 40 | Inventory in process, July 31 | | | $ 3,300[e] + | $ 225[f] = | 3,525 |
| 41 | Total costs assigned by the Mixing Department | | | | | $90,000 |
| 42 | | | | | | |

[a]$66,000 + $10,500 + $7,275 = $83,775   [b]1,500 units × $0.30 = $450   [c]57,000 units × $1.10 = $62,700   [d]57,000 units × $0.30 = $17,100
[e]3,000 units × $1.10 = $3,300   [f]750 units × $0.30 = $225

# Journal Entries for a Process Cost System

The journal entries to record the cost flows and transactions for a process cost system are illustrated in this section. As a basis for illustration, the July transactions for **Frozen Delight** are used. To simplify, the entries are shown in summary form, even though many of the transactions would be recorded daily.

a. Purchased materials, including milk, cream, sugar, packaging, and indirect materials on account, $88,000.

| | | | | |
|---|---|---|---|---|
| a. | Materials | | 88,000 | |
| | Accounts Payable | | | 88,000 |

b. The Mixing Department requisitioned milk, cream, and sugar, $66,000. This is the total amount from the original July data. Packaging materials of $8,000 were requisitioned by the Packaging Department. Indirect materials for the Mixing and Packaging departments were $4,125 and $3,000, respectively.

| | | | | |
|---|---|---|---|---|
| b. | Work in Process—Mixing | | 66,000 | |
| | Work in Process—Packaging | | 8,000 | |
| | Factory Overhead—Mixing | | 4,125 | |
| | Factory Overhead—Packaging | | 3,000 | |
| | Materials | | | 81,125 |

c. Incurred direct labor in the Mixing and Packaging departments of $10,500 and $12,000, respectively.

| | | | | |
|---|---|---|---|---|
| c. | Work in Process—Mixing | | 10,500 | |
| | Work in Process—Packaging | | 12,000 | |
| | Wages Payable | | | 22,500 |

d. Recognized equipment depreciation for the Mixing and Packaging departments of $3,350 and $1,000, respectively.

| | | | | |
|---|---|---|---|---|
| d. | Factory Overhead—Mixing | | 3,350 | |
| | Factory Overhead—Packaging | | 1,000 | |
| | Accumulated Depreciation—Equipment | | | 4,350 |

e. Applied factory overhead to Mixing and Packaging departments of $7,275 and $3,500, respectively.

| | | | | |
|---|---|---|---|---|
| e. | Work in Process—Mixing | | 7,275 | |
| | Work in Process—Packaging | | 3,500 | |
| | Factory Overhead—Mixing | | | 7,275 |
| | Factory Overhead—Packaging | | | 3,500 |

f. Transferred costs of $86,475 from the Mixing Department to the Packaging Department per the cost of production report in Exhibit 8.

| | | | | |
|---|---|---|---|---|
| f. | Work in Process—Packaging | | 86,475 | |
| | Work in Process—Mixing | | | 86,475 |

g. Transferred goods of $106,000 out of the Packaging Department to Finished Goods according to the Packaging Department cost of production report (not illustrated).

| | | | |
|---|---|---|---|
| g. | Finished Goods—Ice Cream | 106,000 | |
| | Work in Process—Packaging | | 106,000 |

h. Recorded the cost of goods sold out of the finished goods inventory of $107,000.

| | | | |
|---|---|---|---|
| h. | Cost of Goods Sold | 107,000 | |
| | Finished Goods—Ice Cream | | 107,000 |

Exhibit 9 shows the flow of costs for each transaction. The highlighted amounts in Exhibit 9 were determined from assigning the costs in the Mixing Department. These amounts were computed and are shown at the bottom of the cost of production report for the Mixing Department in Exhibit 8. Likewise, the amount transferred out of the Packaging Department to Finished Goods would have also been determined from a cost of production report for the Packaging Department.

---

**EXHIBIT 9** **Frozen Delight's Cost Flows**

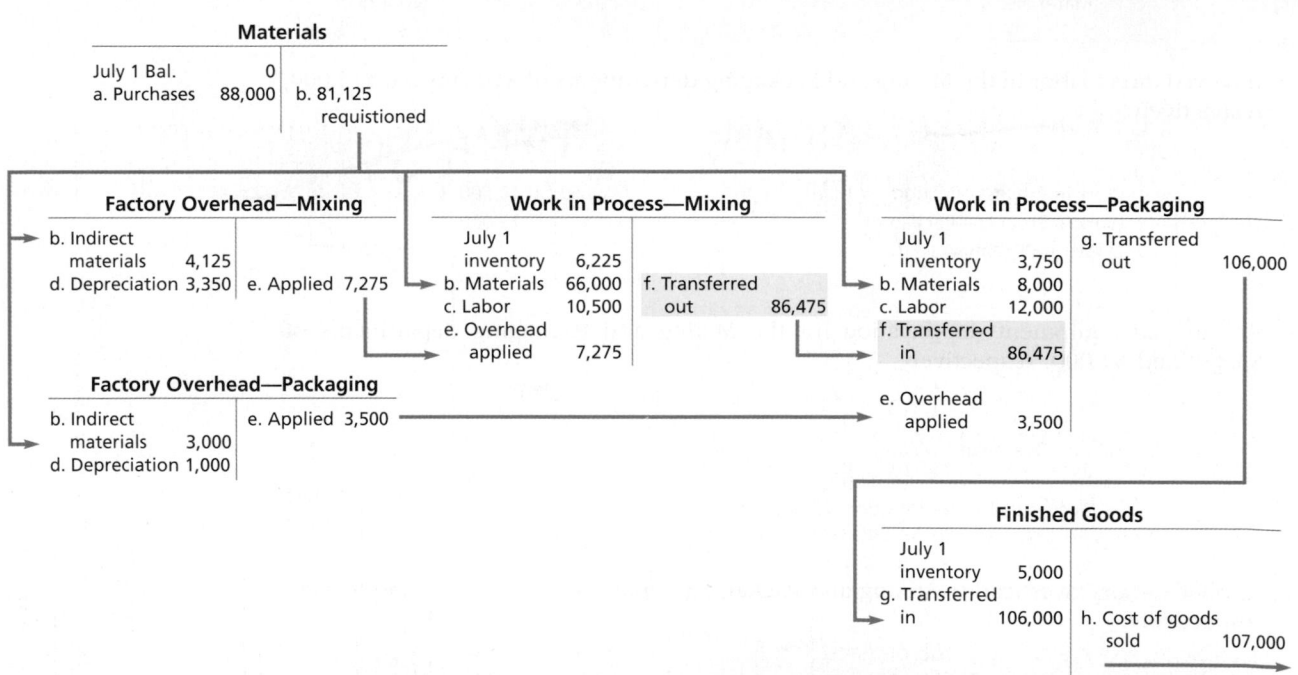

The ending inventories for Frozen Delight are reported on the July 31 balance sheet as follows:

| | |
|---|---|
| Materials | $ 6,875 |
| Work in Process—Mixing Department | 3,525 |
| Work in Process—Packaging Department | 7,725 |
| Finished Goods | 4,000 |
| Total inventories | $22,125 |

The $3,525 balance of Work in Process—Mixing Department is the amount determined from the bottom of the cost of production report in Exhibit 8.

## Example Exercise 20-7 Process Cost Journal Entries

The cost of materials transferred into the Bottling Department of Rocky Springs Beverage Company is $22,800, including $20,000 from the Blending Department and $2,800 from the materials storeroom. The conversion cost for the period in the Bottling Department is $8,790 ($3,790 factory overhead applied and $5,000 direct labor). The total cost transferred to Finished Goods for the period was $31,980. The Bottling Department had a beginning inventory of $1,860.

a. Journalize (1) the cost of transferred-in materials, (2) conversion costs, and (3) the costs transferred out to Finished Goods.
b. Determine the balance of Work in Process—Bottling at the end of the period.

### Follow My Example 20-7

a. 1. Work in Process—Bottling............................................... 22,800
      Work in Process—Blending............................................ 20,000
      Materials...................................................... 2,800
  2. Work in Process—Bottling............................................ 8,790
      Factory Overhead—Bottling......................................... 3,790
      Wages Payable.................................................... 5,000
  3. Finished Goods....................................................... 31,980
      Work in Process—Bottling.......................................... 31,980
b. $1,470 ($1,860 + $22,800 + $8,790 − $31,980)

Practice Exercises: PE 20-7A, PE 20-7B

# Service  Focus

## COSTING THE POWER STACK

Process costing can also be used in service businesses where the nature of the service is uniform across all units. Examples include electricity generation, wastewater treatment, and natural gas transmission. To illustrate, in generating electricity, the unit of production is called a *megawatt hour*, where each megawatt hour is the same across all sources of generation.

Unlike product manufacturing, service companies often do not have inventory. For example, in generating electricity, the electricity cannot be stored. Thus, electric companies such as **Duke Energy Corporation** match the production of electricity to the demand in real time. Electric companies use what is called the *power stack* to match power supply to demand by arranging generating facilities in order of cost per megawatt hour. The least cost per megawatt hour facilities satisfy initial demand at the bottom of the stack, while the highest cost per megawatt hour power sources are placed at top of the stack to satisfy peak loads, as illustrated in the following graph:

The cost per megawatt hour is determined using process costing by accumulating the conversion costs such as equipment depreciation, labor, and maintenance plus the cost of fuel for each facility. These costs are divided by the megawatt hours generated. Because there are no inventories, the additional complexity of equivalent units is avoided. The resulting cost per megawatt hour by facility is used to develop the power stack.

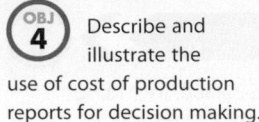

Describe and illustrate the use of cost of production reports for decision making.

# Using the Cost of Production Report for Decision Making

The cost of production report is often used by managers for decisions involving the control and improvement of operations. To illustrate, cost of production reports for **Frozen Delight** and **Holland Beverage Company** are used. Finally, the computation and use of yield are discussed.

## Frozen Delight

The cost of production report for the Mixing Department is shown in Exhibit 8. The cost per equivalent unit for June can be determined from the beginning inventory. The original Frozen Delight data indicate that the July 1 inventory in process of $6,225 consists of the following costs:

| | |
|---|---|
| Direct materials cost, 5,000 gallons | $5,000 |
| Conversion costs, 5,000 gallons, 70% completed | 1,225 |
| Total inventory in process, July 1 | $6,225 |

Using the preceding data, the June costs per equivalent unit of materials and conversion costs can be determined as follows:

$$\text{Direct Materials Cost per Equivalent Unit} = \frac{\text{Total Direct Materials Cost for the Period}}{\text{Total Equivalent Units of Direct Materials}}$$

$$\text{Direct Materials Cost per Equivalent Unit} = \frac{\$5,000}{5,000 \text{ gallons}} = \$1.00 \text{ per gallon}$$

$$\text{Conversion Cost per Equivalent Unit} = \frac{\text{Total Conversion Costs for the Period}}{\text{Total Equivalent Units of Conversion Costs}}$$

$$\text{Conversion Cost per Equivalent Unit} = \frac{\$1,225}{(5,000 \times 70\%) \text{ gallons}} = \$0.35 \text{ per gallon}$$

In July, the cost per equivalent unit of materials increased by $0.10 per gallon, while the cost per equivalent unit for conversion costs decreased by $0.05 per gallon, computed as follows:

| | July* | June | Increase (Decrease) |
|---|---|---|---|
| Cost per equivalent unit for direct materials | $1.10 | $1.00 | $0.10 |
| Cost per equivalent unit for conversion costs | 0.30 | 0.35 | (0.05) |

*From Exhibit 8

Frozen Delight's management could use the preceding analysis as a basis for investigating the increase in the direct materials cost per equivalent unit and the decrease in the conversion cost per equivalent unit.

## Holland Beverage Company

A cost of production report may be prepared showing more cost categories beyond just direct materials and conversion costs. This greater detail can help managers isolate problems and seek opportunities for improvement.

To illustrate, the Blending Department of Holland Beverage Company prepared cost of production reports for April and May. To simplify, assume that the Blending Department had no beginning or ending work in process inventory in either month. That is, all units started were completed in each month. The cost of production reports showing multiple cost categories for April and May in the Blending Department are as follows:

| | A | B | C |
|---|---|---|---|
| 1 | **Cost of Production Reports** | | |
| 2 | **Holland Beverage Company—Blending Department** | | |
| 3 | **For the Months Ended April 30 and May 31, 2016** | | |
| 4 | | April | May |
| 5 | Direct materials | $ 20,000 | $ 40,600 |
| 6 | Direct labor | 15,000 | 29,400 |
| 7 | Energy | 8,000 | 20,000 |
| 8 | Repairs | 1,000 | 0,000 |
| 9 | Tank cleaning | 3,000 | 8,000 |
| 10 | Total | $ 50,000 | $106,000 |
| 11 | Units completed | ÷100,000 | ÷200,000 |
| 12 | Cost per unit | $    0.50 | $    0.53 |
| 13 | | | |

The May results indicate that total unit costs have increased from $0.50 to $0.53, or 6% in May. To determine the possible causes for this increase, the cost of production report is restated in per-unit terms by dividing the costs by the number of units completed, as follows:

| | A | B | C | D |
|---|---|---|---|---|
| 1 | | **Blending Department** | | |
| 2 | | **Per-Unit Expense Comparisons** | | |
| 3 | | April | May | % Change |
| 4 | Direct materials | $0.200 | $0.203 | 1.50% |
| 5 | Direct labor | 0.150 | 0.147 | −2.00% |
| 6 | Energy | 0.080 | 0.100 | 25.00% |
| 7 | Repairs | 0.040 | 0.040 | 0.00% |
| 8 | Tank cleaning | 0.030 | 0.040 | 33.33% |
| 9 | Total | $0.500 | $0.530 | 6.00% |
| 10 | | | | |

Both energy and tank cleaning per-unit costs have increased significantly in May. These increases should be further investigated. For example, the increase in energy may be due to the machines losing fuel efficiency. This could lead management to repair the machines. The tank cleaning costs could be investigated in a similar fashion.

## Yield

In addition to unit costs, managers of process manufacturers are also concerned about yield. The **yield** is computed as follows:

$$\text{Yield} = \frac{\text{Quantity of Material Output}}{\text{Quantity of Material Input}}$$

To illustrate, assume that 1,000 pounds of sugar enter the Packaging Department, and 980 pounds of sugar were packed. The yield is 98%, computed as follows:

$$\text{Yield} = \frac{\text{Quantity of Material Output}}{\text{Quantity of Material Input}} = \frac{980 \text{ pounds}}{1,000 \text{ pounds}} = 98\%$$

Thus, two percent (100% − 98%) or 20 pounds of sugar were lost or spilled during the packing process. Managers can investigate significant changes in yield over time or significant differences in yield from industry standards.

**Example Exercise 20-8** Using Process Costs for Decision Making

The cost of energy consumed in producing good units in the Bottling Department of Rocky Springs Beverage Company was $4,200 and $3,700 for March and April, respectively. The number of equivalent units produced in March and April was 70,000 liters and 74,000 liters, respectively. Evaluate the change in the cost of energy between the two months.

**Follow My Example 20-8**

$$\text{Energy cost per liter, March} = \frac{\$4,200}{70,000 \text{ liters}} = \$0.06$$

$$\text{Energy cost per liter, April} = \frac{\$3,700}{74,000 \text{ liters}} = \$0.05$$

The cost of energy has improved by 1 cent per liter between March and April.

Practice Exercises: PE 20-8A, PE 20-8B

 Compare just-in-time processing with traditional manufacturing processing.

# Just-in-Time Processing

The objective of most manufacturers is to produce products with high quality, low cost, and instant availability. In attempting to achieve this objective, many manufacturers have implemented just-in-time processing. **Just-in-time (JIT) processing** is a management approach that focuses on reducing time and cost and eliminating poor quality. A JIT system obtains efficiencies and flexibility by reorganizing the traditional production process.

## Traditional Production Process

A traditional manufacturing process for a furniture manufacturer is shown in Exhibit 10. The product (chair) moves through seven processes. In each process, workers are assigned a specific job, which is performed repeatedly as unfinished products are received from the preceding department. The product moves from process to process as each function or step is completed.

**EXHIBIT 10** **Traditional Production Line**

For the furniture maker in Exhibit 10, the product (chair) moves through the following processes:

1. In the Cutting Department, the wood is cut to design specifications.
2. In the Drilling Department, the wood is drilled to design specifications.
3. In the Sanding Department, the wood is sanded.
4. In the Staining Department, the wood is stained.
5. In the Varnishing Department, varnish and other protective coatings are applied.

6. In the Upholstery Department, fabric and other materials are added.

7. In the Assembly Department, the product (chair) is assembled.

In the traditional production process, supervisors enter materials into manufacturing so as to keep all the manufacturing departments (processes) operating. Some departments, however, may process materials more rapidly than others. In addition, if one department stops because of machine breakdowns, for example, the preceding departments usually continue production in order to avoid idle time. In such cases, a buildup of work in process inventories results in some departments.

## Just-in-Time Production Process

In a just-in-time system, processing functions are combined into work centers, sometimes called **manufacturing cells**. For example, the seven departments illustrated in Exhibit 10 might be reorganized into the following three work centers:

1. Work Center 1 performs the cutting, drilling, and sanding functions.

2. Work Center 2 performs the staining and varnishing functions.

3. Work Center 3 performs the upholstery and assembly functions.

The preceding JIT manufacturing process is illustrated in Exhibit 11.

---

**EXHIBIT 11**  **Just-in-Time Production Line**

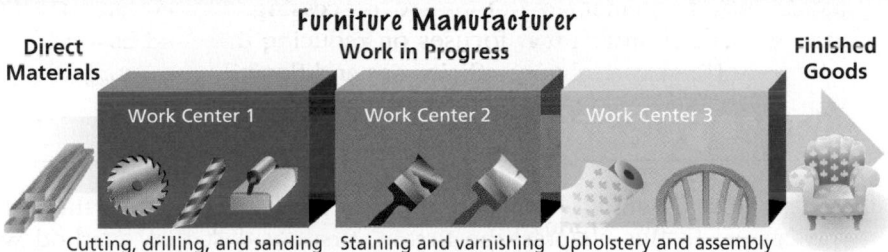

**Furniture Manufacturer**

Direct Materials — Work in Progress — Finished Goods

Work Center 1 | Work Center 2 | Work Center 3

Cutting, drilling, and sanding  Staining and varnishing  Upholstery and assembly

---

In traditional manufacturing, a worker typically performs only one function. However, in JIT manufacturing, work centers complete several functions. Thus, workers are often cross-trained to perform more than one function. Research has indicated that workers who perform several functions identify better with the end product. This creates pride in the product and improves quality and productivity.

The activities supporting the manufacturing process are called *service activities*. For example, repair and maintenance of manufacturing equipment are service activities. In a JIT manufacturing process, service activities may be assigned to individual work centers, rather than to centralized service departments. For example, each work center may be assigned responsibility for the repair and maintenance of its machinery and equipment. This creates an environment in which workers gain a better understanding of the production process and their machinery. In turn, workers tend to take better care of the machinery, which decreases repairs and maintenance costs, reduces machine downtime, and improves product quality.

In a JIT system, the product is often placed on a movable carrier that is centrally located in the work center. After the workers in a work center have completed their activities with the product, the entire carrier and any additional materials are moved just in time to satisfy the demand or need of the next work center. In this sense, the product is said to be "pulled through." Each work center is connected to other work centers through information contained on a Kanban, which is a Japanese term for cards.

In summary, the primary objective of JIT systems is to increase the efficiency of operations. This is achieved by eliminating waste and simplifying the production process. At the same time, JIT systems emphasize continually improving the manufacturing process and product quality.

 Before **Caterpillar** implemented JIT, a transmission traveled 10 miles through the factory and required 1,000 pieces of paper to support the manufacturing process. After implementing JIT, a transmission travels only 200 feet and requires only 10 pieces of paper.

## Business Connection

### RADICAL IMPROVEMENT: JUST IN TIME FOR PULASKI'S CUSTOMERS

Pulaski Furniture Corporation embraced just-in-time manufacturing principles and revolutionized its business. The company wanted to "be easier to do business with" by offering its customers smaller shipments more frequently. It was able to accomplish this by taking the following steps:

- Mapping processes to properly align labor, machines, and materials
- Eliminating 100 feet of conveyor line

- Moving machines into manufacturing cells
- Reducing manufacturing run sizes by simplifying the product design
- Making every product more frequently in order to reduce the customer's waiting time for a product

As a result of these just-in-time changes, the company significantly improved its inventory position while simultaneously improving its shipping times to the customer. Its lumber inventory was reduced by 25%, finished goods inventory was reduced by 40%, and work in process inventory was reduced by 50%. At the same time, customers' shipment waiting times were shortened from months to weeks.

Source: Jeff Linville, "Pulaski's Passion for Lean Plumps up Dealer Service," *Furniture Today,* June 2006.

# APPENDIX

# Average Cost Method

A cost flow assumption must be used as product costs flow through manufacturing processes. In this chapter, the first-in, first-out cost flow method was used for the Mixing Department of Frozen Delight. In this appendix, the average cost flow method is illustrated for **S&W Ice Cream Company (S&W)**.

## Determining Costs Using the Average Cost Method

S&W's operations are similar to those of Frozen Delight. Like Frozen Delight, S&W mixes direct materials (milk, cream, sugar) in refrigerated vats and has two manufacturing departments, Mixing and Packaging.

The manufacturing data for the Mixing Department for July 2016 are as follows:

| | |
|---|---:|
| Inventory in process, July 1, 5,000 gallons (70% completed)................ | $ 6,200 |
| Direct materials cost incurred in July, 60,000 gallons....................... | 66,000 |
| Direct labor cost incurred in July........................................... | 10,500 |
| Factory overhead applied in July........................................... | 6,405 |
|     Total production costs to account for................................. | $89,105 |
| | |
| Cost of goods transferred to Packaging in July (includes units in process on July 1), 62,000 gallons ............................................ | ? |
| Cost of work in process inventory, July 31, 3,000 gallons, 25% completed as to conversion costs......................................... | ? |

Using the average cost method, the objective is to allocate the total costs of production of $89,105 to the following:

- The 62,000 gallons completed and transferred to the Packaging Department
- The 3,000 gallons in the July 31 (ending) work in process inventory

The preceding costs show two question marks. These amounts are determined by preparing a cost of production report, using the following four steps:

- Step 1. Determine the units to be assigned costs.
- Step 2. Compute equivalent units of production.
- Step 3. Determine the cost per equivalent unit.
- Step 4. Allocate costs to transferred out and partially completed units.

Under the average cost method, all production costs (materials and conversion costs) are combined together for determining equivalent units and cost per equivalent unit.

### Step 1: Determine the Units to Be Assigned Costs
The first step is to determine the units to be assigned costs. A unit can be any measure of completed production, such as tons, gallons, pounds, barrels, or cases. For **S&W**, a unit is a gallon of ice cream.

S&W's Mixing Department had 65,000 gallons of direct materials to account for during July, as shown here.

Total gallons to account for:
| | |
|---|---|
| Inventory in process, July 1 ..................................................... | 5,000 gallons |
| Received from materials storeroom .............................................. | 60,000 |
| Total units to account for by the Packaging Department ....................... | 65,000 gallons |

There are two groups of units to be assigned costs for the period.

| | |
|---|---|
| Group 1 | Units completed and transferred out |
| Group 2 | Units in the July 31 (ending) work in process inventory |

During July, the Mixing Department completed and transferred 62,000 gallons to the Packaging Department. Of the 60,000 gallons started in July, 57,000 (60,000 − 3,000) gallons were completed and transferred to the Packaging Department. Thus, the ending work in process inventory consists of 3,000 gallons.

The total units (gallons) to be assigned costs for S&W can be summarized as follows:

| | | |
|---|---|---|
| Group 1 | Units transferred out to the Packaging Department in July | 62,000 gallons |
| Group 2 | Inventory in process, July 31 ........................................... | 3,000 |
| | Total gallons to be assigned costs................................... | 65,000 gallons |

The total units (gallons) to be assigned costs (65,000 gallons) equal the total units to account for (65,000 gallons).

### Step 2: Compute Equivalent Units of Production
**S&W** has 3,000 gallons of whole units in the work in process inventory for the Mixing Department on July 31. Because these units are 25% complete, the number of equivalent units in process in the Mixing Department on July 31 is 750 gallons (3,000 gallons × 25%). Because the units transferred to the Packaging Department have been completed, the whole units (62,000 gallons) transferred are the same as the equivalent units transferred.

The total equivalent units of production for the Mixing Department are determined by adding the equivalent units in the ending work in process inventory to the units transferred and completed during the period, computed as follows:

| | |
|---|---|
| Equivalent units completed and transferred to the Packaging Department during July ......................... | 62,000 gallons |
| Equivalent units in ending work in process, July 31 .............. | 750 |
| Total equivalent units ....................................... | 62,750 gallons |

### Step 3: Determine the Cost per Equivalent Unit
Because materials and conversion costs are combined under the average cost method, the cost per equivalent unit is determined by dividing the total production costs by the total equivalent units of production as follows:

$$\text{Cost per Equivalent Unit} = \frac{\text{Total Production Costs}}{\text{Total Equivalent Units}}$$

$$\text{Cost per Equivalent Unit} = \frac{\text{Total Production Costs}}{\text{Total Equivalent Units}} = \frac{\$89,105}{62,750 \text{ gallons}} = \$1.42$$

The cost per equivalent unit is used in Step 4 to allocate the production costs to the completed and partially completed units.

### Step 4: Allocate Costs to Transferred Out and Partially Completed Units

The cost of transferred and partially completed units is determined by multiplying the cost per equivalent unit times the equivalent units of production. For **S&W**'s Mixing Department, these costs are determined as follows:

| | | |
|---|---|---|
| Group 1 | Transferred out to the Packaging Department (62,000 gallons × $1.42) ...... | $88,040 |
| Group 2 | Inventory in process, July 31 (3,000 gallons × 25% × $1.42)................ | 1,065 |
| | Total production costs assigned ......................................... | $89,105 |

## The Cost of Production Report

The July cost of production report for **S&W**'s Mixing Department is shown in Exhibit 12. This cost of production report summarizes the following:

- The units for which the department is accountable and the disposition of those units
- The production costs incurred by the department and the allocation of those costs between completed and partially completed units

---

**EXHIBIT 12**  **Cost of Production Report for S&W's Mixing Department—Average Cost**

| | A | B | C |
|---|---|---|---|
| 1 | S&W Ice Cream Company | | |
| 2 | Cost of Production Report—Mixing Department | | |
| 3 | For the Month Ended July 31, 2016 | | |
| 4 | UNITS | | |
| 5 | | Whole Units | Equivalent Units |
| 6 | | | of Production |
| 7 | Units to account for during production: | | |
| 8 | Inventory in process, July 1 | 5,000 | |
| 9 | Received from materials storeroom | 60,000 | |
| 10 | Total units accounted for by the Mixing Department | 65,000 | |
| 11 | | | |
| 12 | Units to be assigned costs: | | |
| 13 | Transferred to Packaging Department in July | 62,000 | 62,000 |
| 14 | Inventory in process, July 31 (25% completed) | 3,000 | 750 |
| 15 | Total units to be assigned costs | 65,000 | 62,750 |
| 16 | | | |
| 17 | COSTS | | Costs |
| 18 | | | |
| 19 | Cost per equivalent unit: | | |
| 20 | Total production costs for July in Mixing Department | | $89,105 |
| 21 | Total equivalent units (from Step 2) | | ÷62,750 |
| 22 | Cost per equivalent unit | | $   1.42 |
| 23 | | | |
| 24 | Costs assigned to production: | | |
| 25 | Inventory in process, July 1 | | $  6,200 |
| 26 | Direct materials, direct labor, and factory overhead incurred in July | | 82,905 |
| 27 | Total costs accounted for by the Mixing Department | | $89,105 |
| 28 | | | |
| 29 | | | |
| 30 | Costs allocated to completed and partially completed units: | | |
| 31 | Transferred to Packaging Department in July (62,000 gallons × $1.42) | | $88,040 |
| 32 | Inventory in process, July 31 (3,000 gallons × 25% × $1.42) | | 1,065 |
| 33 | Total costs assigned by the Mixing Department | | $89,105 |
| 34 | | | |

Step 1 · Step 2 (rows 3–5)
Step 3 (rows 19–27)
Step 4 (rows 31–33)

# At a Glance 20

**1 Describe process cost systems.**

**Key Points**   The process cost system is best suited for industries that mass produce identical units of a product. Costs are charged to processing departments, rather than to jobs as with the job order cost system. These costs are transferred from one department to the next until production is completed.

| Learning Outcomes | Example Exercises | Practice Exercises |
|---|---|---|
| • Identify the characteristics of a process manufacturer. | | |
| • Compare and contrast the job order cost system with the process cost system. | EE20-1 | PE20-1A, 20-1B |
| • Describe the physical and cost flows of a process manufacturer. | | |

**2 Prepare a cost of production report.**

**Key Points**   Manufacturing costs must be allocated between the units that have been completed and those that remain within the department. This allocation is accomplished by allocating costs using equivalent units of production.

| Learning Outcomes | Example Exercises | Practice Exercises |
|---|---|---|
| • Determine the whole units charged to production and to be assigned costs. | EE20-2 | PE20-2A, 20-2B |
| • Compute the equivalent units with respect to materials. | EE20-3 | PE20-3A, 20-3B |
| • Compute the equivalent units with respect to conversion. | EE20-4 | PE20-4A, 20-4B |
| • Compute the costs per equivalent unit. | EE20-5 | PE20-5A, 20-5B |
| • Allocate the costs to beginning inventory, units started and completed, and ending inventory. | EE20-6 | PE20-6A, 20-6B |
| • Prepare a cost of production report. | | |

**3 Journalize entries for transactions using a process cost system.**

**Key Points**   Prepare the summary journal entries for materials, labor, applied factory overhead, and transferred costs incurred in production.

| Learning Outcomes | Example Exercises | Practice Exercises |
|---|---|---|
| • Prepare journal entries for process costing transactions. | EE20-7 | PE20-7A, 20-7B |
| • Summarize cost flows in T account form. | | |
| • Compute the ending inventory balances. | | |

**Describe and illustrate the use of cost of production reports for decision making.**

**Key Points** The cost of production report provides information for controlling and improving operations. The report(s) can provide details of a department for a single period, or over a period of time.
Yield measures the quantity of output of production relative to the inputs.

| Learning Outcomes | Example Exercises | Practice Exercises |
|---|---|---|
| • Prepare and evaluate a report showing the change in costs per unit by cost category for comparative periods. | **EE20-8** | **PE20-8A, 20-8B** |
| • Compute and interpret yield. | | |

**Compare just-in-time processing with traditional manufacturing processing.**

**Key Points** The just-in-time processing philosophy focuses on reducing time, cost, and poor quality within the process.

**Learning Outcome**

• Identify the characteristics of a just-in-time process.

# Key Terms

cost of production report (935)
cost per equivalent unit (940)
equivalent units of production (937)
first-in, first-out (FIFO) method (935)

just-in-time (JIT) processing (950)
manufacturing cells (951)
process cost system (931)
process manufacturer (930)

whole units (937)
yield (949)

# Illustrative Problem

Southern Aggregate Company manufactures concrete by a series of four processes. All materials are introduced in Crushing. From Crushing, the materials pass through Sifting, Baking, and Mixing, emerging as finished concrete. All inventories are costed by the first-in, first-out method.

The balances in the accounts Work in Process—Mixing and Finished Goods were as follows on May 1, 2016:

Inventory in Process—Mixing (2,000 units, 1/4 completed)      $13,700
Finished Goods (1,800 units at $8.00 a unit)                         14,400

The following costs were charged to Work in Process—Mixing during May:

| | |
|---|---:|
| Direct materials transferred from Baking: 15,200 units at | |
| $6.50 a unit | $98,800 |
| Direct labor | 17,200 |
| Factory overhead | 11,780 |

During May, 16,000 units of concrete were completed, and 15,800 units were sold. Inventories on May 31 were as follows:

Inventory in Process—Mixing: 1,200 units, 1/2 completed
Finished Goods: 2,000 units

## Instructions

1. Prepare a cost of production report for the Mixing Department.

2. Determine the cost of goods sold (indicate number of units and unit costs).

3. Determine the finished goods inventory, May 31, 2016.

## Solution

1.

| | A | B | C | D | E |
|---|---|---|---|---|---|
| 1 | | Southern Aggregate Company | | | |
| 2 | | Cost of Production Report—Mixing Department | | | |
| 3 | | For the Month Ended May 31, 2016 | | | |
| 4 | | | | Equivalent Units | |
| 5 | **UNITS** | Whole Units | Direct Materials | Conversion | |
| 6 | Units charged to production: | | | | |
| 7 | Inventory in process, May 1 | 2,000 | | | |
| 8 | Received from Baking | 15,200 | | | |
| 9 | Total units accounted for by the Mixing Department | 17,200 | | | |
| 10 | | | | | |
| 11 | Units to be assigned costs: | | | | |
| 12 | Inventory in process, May 1 (25% completed) | 2,000 | 0 | 1,500 | |
| 13 | Started and completed in May | 14,000 | 14,000 | 14,000 | |
| 14 | Transferred to finished goods in May | 16,000 | 14,000 | 15,500 | |
| 15 | Inventory in process, May 31 (50% completed) | 1,200 | 1,200 | 600 | |
| 16 | Total units to be assigned costs | 17,200 | 15,200 | 16,100 | |
| 17 | | | | | |
| 18 | | | | Costs | |
| 19 | **COSTS** | | Direct Materials | Conversion | Total |
| 20 | Unit costs: | | | | |
| 21 | Total costs for May in Mixing | | $ 98,800 | $ 28,980 | |
| 22 | Total equivalent units (row 16) | | ÷15,200 | ÷16,100 | |
| 23 | Cost per equivalent unit | | $ 6.50 | $ 1.80 | |
| 24 | | | | | |
| 25 | Costs assigned to production: | | | | |
| 26 | Inventory in process, May 1 | | | | $ 13,700 |
| 27 | Costs incurred in May | | | | 127,780 |
| 28 | Total costs accounted for by the Mixing Department | | | | $141,480 |
| 29 | | | | | |
| 30 | Cost allocated to completed and partially | | | | |
| 31 | completed units: | | | | |
| 32 | Inventory in process, May 1—balance | | | | $ 13,700 |
| 33 | To complete inventory in process, May 1 | | $ 0 | $ 2,700ᵃ | 2,700 |
| 34 | Cost of completed May 1 work in process | | | | $ 16,400 |
| 35 | Started and completed in May | | 91,000ᵇ | 25,200ᶜ | 116,200 |
| 36 | Transferred to finished goods in May | | | | $132,600 |
| 37 | Inventory in process, May 31 | | 7,800ᵈ | 1,080ᵉ | 8,880 |
| 38 | Total costs assigned by the Mixing Department | | | | $141,480 |
| 39 | | | | | |

ᵃ1,500 × $1.80 = $2,700  ᵇ14,000 × $6.50 = $91,000  ᶜ14,000 × $1.80 = $25,200  ᵈ1,200 × $6.50 = $7,800  ᵉ600 × $1.80 = $1,080

2. Cost of goods sold:

| | | |
|---|---:|---|
| 1,800 units at $8.00 | $ 14,400 | (from finished goods beginning inventory) |
| 2,000 units at $8.20* | 16,400 | (from inventory in process beginning inventory) |
| 12,000 units at $8.30** | 99,600 | (from May production started and completed) |
| 15,800 units | $130,400 | |

*($13,700 + $2,700) ÷ 2,000
**$116,200 ÷ 14,000

3. Finished goods inventory, May 31:

2,000 units at $8.30   $16,600

# Discussion Questions

1. Which type of cost system, process or job order, would be best suited for each of the following: (a) TV assembler, (b) building contractor, (c) automobile repair shop, (d) paper manufacturer, (e) custom jewelry manufacturer? Give reasons for your answers.

2. In job order cost accounting, the three elements of manufacturing cost are charged directly to job orders. Why is it not necessary to charge manufacturing costs in process cost accounting to job orders?

3. In a job order cost system, direct labor and factory overhead applied are debited to individual jobs. How are these items treated in a process cost system and why?

4. Why is the cost per equivalent unit often determined separately for direct materials and conversion costs?

5. What is the purpose for determining the cost per equivalent unit?

6. Rameriz Company is a process manufacturer with two production departments, Blending and Filling. All direct materials are introduced in Blending from the materials store area. What is included in the cost transferred to Filling?

7. What is the most important purpose of the cost of production report?

8. How are cost of production reports used for controlling and improving operations?

9. How is "yield" determined for a process manufacturer?

10. How does just-in-time processing differ from the conventional manufacturing process?

# Practice Exercises

---

SHOW
ME HOW

**EE 20-1** *p. 933*

**PE 20-1A   Job order versus process costing**                   **OBJ. 1**

Which of the following industries would typically use job order costing, and which would typically use process costing?

| Dentist | Movie studio |
| Gasoline refining | Paper manufacturing |
| Flour mill | Custom printing |

---

SHOW
ME HOW

**EE 20-1** *p. 933*

**PE 20-1B   Job order versus process costing**                   **OBJ. 1**

Which of the following industries would typically use job order costing, and which would typically use process costing?

| Steel manufactuirng | Computer chip manufacturing |
| Business consulting | Candy making |
| Web designer | Designer clothes manufacturing |

---

SHOW
ME HOW

**EE 20-2** *p. 937*

**PE 20-2A   Units to be assigned costs**                   **OBJ. 2**

Lilac Skin Care Company consists of two departments, Blending and Filling. The Filling Department received 45,000 ounces from the Blending Department. During the period, the Filling Department completed 42,800 ounces, including 4,000 ounces of work in process at the beginning of the period. The ending work in process inventory was 6,200 ounces. How many ounces were started and completed during the period?

*finished – beginning =*

---

SHOW
ME HOW

**EE 20-2** *p. 937*

**PE 20-2B   Units to be assigned costs**                   **OBJ. 2**

Keystone Steel Company has two departments, Casting and Rolling. In the Rolling Department, ingots from the Casting Department are rolled into steel sheet. The Rolling Department received 8,500 tons from the Casting Department. During the period, the Rolling Department completed 7,900 tons, including 400 tons of work in process at the beginning of the period. The ending work in process inventory was 1,000 tons. How many tons were started and completed during the period?

---

SHOW
ME HOW

**EE 20-3** *p. 939*

**PE 20-3A   Equivalent units of materials cost**                   **OBJ. 2**

The Filling Department of Lilac Skin Care Company had 4,000 ounces in beginning work in process inventory (70% complete). During the period, 42,800 ounces were completed. The ending work in process inventory was 6,200 ounces (40% complete). What are the total equivalent units for direct materials if materials are added at the beginning of the process?

---

SHOW
ME HOW

**EE 20-3** *p. 939*

**PE 20-3B   Equivalent units of materials cost**                   **OBJ. 2**

The Rolling Department of Keystone Steel Company had 400 tons in beginning work in process inventory (20% complete). During the period, 7,900 tons were completed. The ending work in process inventory was 1,000 tons (30% complete). What are the total equivalent units for direct materials if materials are added at the beginning of the process?

---

SHOW
ME HOW

**EE 20-4** *p. 940*

**PE 20-4A   Equivalent units of conversion costs**                   **OBJ. 2**

The Filling Department of Lilac Skin Care had 4,000 ounces in beginning work in process inventory (70% complete). During the period, 42,800 ounces were completed. The ending work in process inventory was 6,200 ounces (40% complete). What are the total equivalent units for conversion costs?

EE 20-4  *p. 940*    **PE 20-4B   Equivalent units of conversion costs**                    **OBJ. 2**

The Rolling Department of Keystone Steel Company had 400 tons in beginning work in process inventory (20% complete). During the period, 7,900 tons were completed. The ending work in process inventory was 1,000 tons (30% complete). What are the total equivalent units for conversion costs?

EE 20-5  *p. 941*    **PE 20-5A   Cost per equivalent unit**                              **OBJ. 2**

The cost of direct materials transferred into the Filling Department of Lilac Skin Care Company is $20,250. The conversion cost for the period in the Filling Department is $6,372. The total equivalent units for direct materials and conversion are 45,000 ounces and 42,480 ounces, respectively. Determine the direct materials and conversion costs per equivalent unit.

EE 20-5  *p. 941*    **PE 20-5B   Cost per equivalent unit**                              **OBJ. 2**

The cost of direct materials transferred into the Rolling Department of Keystone Steel Company is $510,000. The conversion cost for the period in the Rolling Department is $81,200. The total equivalent units for direct materials and conversion are 8,500 tons and 8,120 tons, respectively. Determine the direct materials and conversion costs per equivalent unit.

EE 20-6  *p. 943*    **PE 20-6A   Cost of units transferred out and ending work in process**    **OBJ. 2**

The costs per equivalent unit of direct materials and conversion in the Filling Department of Lilac Skin Care Company are $0.45 and $0.15, respectively. The equivalent units to be assigned costs are as follows:

|  | Equivalent Units | |
|---|---|---|
|  | **Direct Materials** | **Conversion** |
| Inventory in process, beginning of period | 0 | 1,200 |
| Started and completed during the period | 38,800 | 38,800 |
| Transferred out of Filling (completed) | 38,800 | 40,000 |
| Inventory in process, end of period | 6,200 | 2,480 |
| Total units to be assigned costs | 45,000 | 42,480 |

The beginning work in process inventory had a cost of $25,000. Determine the cost of completed and transferred-out production and the ending work in process inventory.

EE 20-6  *p. 943*    **PE 20-6B   Cost of units transferred out and ending work in process**    **OBJ. 2**

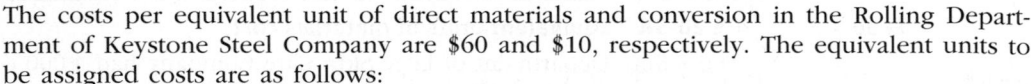

The costs per equivalent unit of direct materials and conversion in the Rolling Department of Keystone Steel Company are $60 and $10, respectively. The equivalent units to be assigned costs are as follows:

|  | Equivalent Units | |
|---|---|---|
|  | **Direct Materials** | **Conversion** |
| Inventory in process, beginning of period | 0 | 320 |
| Started and completed during the period | 7,500 | 7,500 |
| Transferred out of Rolling (completed) | 7,500 | 7,820 |
| Inventory in process, end of period | 1,000 | 300 |
| Total units to be assigned costs | 8,500 | 8,120 |

The beginning work in process inventory had a cost of $25,000. Determine the cost of completed and transferred-out production and the ending work in process inventory.

EE 20-7  *p. 947*    **PE 20-7A   Process cost journal entries**                          **OBJ. 3**

The cost of materials transferred into the Filling Department of Lilac Skin Care Company is $20,250, including $6,000 from the Blending Department and $14,250 from the materials storeroom. The conversion cost for the period in the Filling Department is $6,372

($1,600 factory overhead applied and $4,772 direct labor). The total cost transferred to Finished Goods for the period was $25,660. The Filling Department had a beginning inventory of $2,200.

a. Journalize (1) the cost of transferred-in materials, (2) conversion costs, and (3) the costs transferred out to Finished Goods.

b. Determine the balance of Work in Process—Filling at the end of the period.

---

**EE 20-7** *p. 947*

SHOW
ME HOW

**PE 20-7B    Process cost journal entries**                                          **OBJ. 3**

The cost of materials transferred into the Rolling Department of Keystone Steel Company is $510,000 from the Casting Department. The conversion cost for the period in the Rolling Department is $81,200 ($54,700 factory overhead applied and $26,500 direct labor). The total cost transferred to Finished Goods for the period was $553,200. The Rolling Department had a beginning inventory of $25,000.

a. Journalize (1) the cost of transferred-in materials, (2) conversion costs, and (3) the costs transferred out to Finished Goods.

b. Determine the balance of Work in Process—Rolling at the end of the period.

---

**EE 20-8** *p. 950*

SHOW
ME HOW

**PE 20-8A    Using process costs for decision making**                               **OBJ. 4**

The costs of energy consumed in producing good units in the Baking Department of Pan Company were $14,875 and $14,615 for June and July, respectively. The number of equivalent units produced in June and July was 42,500 pounds and 39,500 pounds, respectively. Evaluate the change in the cost of energy between the two months.

---

**EE 20-8** *p. 950*

SHOW
ME HOW

**PE 20-8B    Using process costs for decision making**                               **OBJ. 4**

The costs of materials consumed in producing good units in the Forming Department of Thomas Company were $76,000 and $77,350 for September and October, respectively. The number of equivalent units produced in September and October was 800 tons and 850 tons, respectively. Evaluate the change in the cost of materials between the two months.

---

# Exercises

---

**EX 20-1    Entries for materials cost flows in a process cost system**              **OBJ. 1, 3**

The Hershey Foods Company manufactures chocolate confectionery products. The three largest raw materials are cocoa, sugar, and dehydrated milk. These raw materials first go into the Blending Department. The blended product is then sent to the Molding Department, where the bars of candy are formed. The candy is then sent to the Packing Department, where the bars are wrapped and boxed. The boxed candy is then sent to the distribution center, where it is eventually sold to food brokers and retailers.

Show the accounts debited and credited for each of the following business events:

a. Materials used by the Blending Department

b. Transfer of blended product to the Molding Department

c. Transfer of chocolate to the Packing Department

d. Transfer of boxed chocolate to the distribution center

e. Sale of boxed chocolate

---

**EX 20-2    Flowchart of accounts related to service and processing departments**    **OBJ. 1**

Alcoa Inc. is the world's largest producer of aluminum products. One product that Alcoa manufactures is aluminum sheet products for the aerospace industry. The entire output of the Smelting Department is transferred to the Rolling Department. Part of the fully processed goods from the Rolling Department are sold as rolled sheet, and the remainder of the goods are transferred to the Converting Department for further processing into sheared sheet.

*(Continued)*

Prepare a chart of the flow of costs from the processing department accounts into the finished goods accounts and then into the cost of goods sold account. The relevant accounts are as follows:

| | |
|---|---|
| Cost of Goods Sold | Finished Goods—Rolled Sheet |
| Materials | Finished Goods—Sheared Sheet |
| Factory Overhead—Smelting Department | Work in Process—Smelting Department |
| Factory Overhead—Rolling Department | Work in Process—Rolling Department |
| Factory Overhead—Converting Department | Work in Process—Converting Department |

**SHOW ME HOW**

---

### EX 20-3  Entries for flow of factory costs for process cost system    OBJ. 1, 3

**Domino Foods, Inc.**, manufactures a sugar product by a continuous process, involving three production departments—Refining, Sifting, and Packing. Assume that records indicate that direct materials, direct labor, and applied factory overhead for the first department, Refining, were $372,000, $143,000, and $98,400, respectively. Also, work in process in the Refining Department at the beginning of the period totaled $29,400, and work in process at the end of the period totaled $28,700.

Journalize the entries to record (a) the flow of costs into the Refining Department during the period for (1) direct materials, (2) direct labor, and (3) factory overhead, and (b) the transfer of production costs to the second department, Sifting.

---

### EX 20-4  Factory overhead rate, entry for applying factory overhead, and    OBJ. 1, 3
### factory overhead account balance

✔ a. 140%

**SHOW ME HOW**

The chief cost accountant for Fizzy Fruit Beverage Co. estimated that total factory overhead cost for the Blending Department for the coming fiscal year beginning April 1 would be $147,000, and total direct labor costs would be $105,000. During April, the actual direct labor cost totaled $12,000, and factory overhead cost incurred totaled $17,050.

a. What is the predetermined factory overhead rate based on direct labor cost?

b. Journalize the entry to apply factory overhead to production for April.

c. What is the April 30 balance of the account Factory Overhead—Blending Department?

d. Does the balance in part (c) represent over- or underapplied factory overhead?

---

### EX 20-5  Equivalent units of production    OBJ. 2

✔ Direct materials, 14,050 units

**SHOW ME HOW**

The Converting Department of Soft Touch Towel and Tissue Company had 790 units in work in process at the beginning of the period, which were 60% complete. During the period, 13,700 units were completed and transferred to the Packing Department. There were 1,140 units in process at the end of the period, which were 25% complete. Direct materials are placed into the process at the beginning of production. Determine the number of equivalent units of production with respect to direct materials and conversion costs.

---

### EX 20-6  Equivalent units of production    OBJ. 2

✔ a. Conversion, 96,720 units

**SHOW ME HOW**

Units of production data for the two departments of Pacific Cable and Wire Company for November of the current fiscal year are as follows:

| | Drawing Department | Winding Department |
|---|---|---|
| Work in process, November 1 | 5,000 units, 40% completed | 3,200 units, 80% completed |
| Completed and transferred to next processing department during November | 95,000 units | 95,100 units |
| Work in process, November 30 | 6,200 units, 60% completed | 3,100 units, 15% completed |

If all direct materials are placed in process at the beginning of production, determine the direct materials and conversion equivalent units of production for November for (a) the Drawing Department and (b) the Winding Department.

### EX 20-7 Equivalent units of production

OBJ. 2

The following information concerns production in the Baking Department for August. All direct materials are placed in process at the beginning of production.

| ACCOUNT *Work in Process—Baking Department* | | | | ACCOUNT NO. | |
|---|---|---|---|---|---|
| | | | | Balance | |
| Date | Item | Debit | Credit | Debit | Credit |
| Aug. 1 | Bal., 5,000 units, ⅖ completed | | | 8,000 | |
| 31 | Direct materials, 204,000 units | 306,000 | | 314,000 | |
| 31 | Direct labor | 35,500 | | 349,500 | |
| 31 | Factory overhead | 29,076 | | 378,576 | |
| 31 | Goods finished, 196,000 units | | 356,580 | 21,996 | |
| 31 | Bal. ? units, ⅗ completed | | | 21,996 | |

a. Determine the number of units in work in process inventory at the end of the month.

b. Determine the equivalent units of production for direct materials and conversion costs in August.

### EX 20-8 Costs per equivalent unit

OBJ. 2, 4

a. Based upon the data in Exercise 20-7, determine the following:

1. Direct materials cost per equivalent unit.
2. Conversion cost per equivalent unit.
3. Cost of the beginning work in process completed during August.
4. Cost of units started and completed during August.
5. Cost of the ending work in process.

b. Assuming that the direct materials cost is the same for July and August, did the conversion cost per equivalent unit increase, decrease, or remain the same in August?

### EX 20-9 Equivalent units of production

OBJ. 2

Kellogg Company manufactures cold cereal products, such as *Frosted Flakes*. Assume that the inventory in process on March 1 for the Packing Department included 1,200 pounds of cereal in the packing machine hopper (enough for 800 24-oz. boxes), and 800 empty 24-oz. boxes held in the package carousel of the packing machine. During March, 65,400 boxes of 24-oz. cereal were packaged. Conversion costs are incurred when a box is filled with cereal. On March 31, the packing machine hopper held 900 pounds of cereal, and the package carousel held 600 empty 24-oz. (1½-pound) boxes. Assume that once a box is filled with cereal, it is immediately transferred to the finished goods warehouse.

Determine the equivalent units of production for cereal, boxes, and conversion costs for March. An equivalent unit is defined as "pounds" for cereal and "24-oz. boxes" for boxes and conversion costs.

### EX 20-10 Costs per equivalent unit

OBJ. 2

Georgia Products Inc. completed and transferred 89,000 particle board units of production from the Pressing Department. There was no beginning inventory in process in the department. The ending in process inventory was 2,400 units, which were ⅗ complete as to conversion cost. All materials are added at the beginning of the process. Direct materials cost incurred was $219,360, direct labor cost incurred was 28,100, and factory overhead applied was $12,598.

Determine the following for the Pressing Department:

a. Total conversion cost

b. Conversion cost per equivalent unit

c. Direct materials cost per equivalent unit

### EX 20-22 Decision making

OBJ. 4

Pix Paper Inc. produces photographic paper for printing digital images. One of the processes for this operation is a coating (solvent spreading) operation, where chemicals are coated onto paper stock. There has been some concern about the cost performance of this operation. As a result, you have begun an investigation. You first discover that all materials and conversion prices have been stable for the last six months. Thus, increases in prices for inputs are not an explanation for increasing costs. However, you have discovered three possible problems from some of the operating personnel whose quotes follow:

*Operator 1:* "I've been keeping an eye on my operating room instruments. I feel as though our energy consumption is becoming less efficient."

*Operator 2:* "Every time the coating machine goes down, we produce waste on shutdown and subsequent startup. It seems like during the last half year we have had more unscheduled machine shutdowns than in the past. Thus, I feel as though our yields must be dropping."

*Operator 3:* "My sense is that our coating costs are going up. It seems to me like we are spreading a thicker coating than we should. Perhaps the coating machine needs to be recalibrated."

The Coating Department had no beginning or ending inventories for any month during the study period. The following data from the cost of production report are made available:

| | A | B | C | D | E | F | G |
|---|---|---|---|---|---|---|---|
| 1 | | January | February | March | April | May | June |
| 2 | Paper stock | $67,200 | $63,840 | $60,480 | $64,512 | $57,120 | $53,760 |
| 3 | Coating | $11,520 | $11,856 | $12,960 | $15,667 | $16,320 | $18,432 |
| 4 | Conversion cost (incl. energy) | $38,400 | $36,480 | $34,560 | $36,864 | $32,640 | $30,720 |
| 5 | Pounds input to the process | 100,000 | 95,000 | 90,000 | 96,000 | 85,000 | 80,000 |
| 6 | Pounds transferred out | 96,000 | 91,200 | 86,400 | 92,160 | 81,600 | 76,800 |
| 7 | | | | | | | |

a. Prepare a table showing the paper cost per output pound, coating cost per output pound, conversion cost per output pound, and yield (pounds transferred out/pounds input) for each month.

b. ━━━▶ Interpret your table results.

### EX 20-23 Just-in-time manufacturing

OBJ. 5

The following are some quotes provided by a number of managers at Hawkeye Machining Company regarding the company's planned move toward a just-in-time manufacturing system:

*Director of Sales:* I'm afraid we'll miss some sales if we don't keep a large stock of items on hand just in case demand increases. It only makes sense to me to keep large inventories in order to assure product availability for our customers.

*Director of Purchasing:* I'm very concerned about moving to a just-in-time system for materials. What would happen if one of our suppliers were unable to make a shipment? A supplier could fall behind in production or have a quality problem. Without some safety stock in our materials, our whole plant would shut down.

*Director of Manufacturing:* If we go to just-in-time, I think our factory output will drop. We need in-process inventory in order to "smooth out" the inevitable problems that occur during manufacturing. For example, if a machine that is used to process a product breaks down, it would starve the next machine if I don't have in-process inventory between the two machines. If I have in-process inventory, then I can keep the next operation busy while I fix the broken machine. Thus, the in-process inventories give me a safety valve that I can use to keep things running when things go wrong.

━━━▶ How would you respond to these managers?

### Appendix
### EX 20-24 Equivalent units of production: average cost method

✔ a. 17,000

The Converting Department of Tender Soft Tissue Company uses the average cost method and had 1,900 units in work in process that were 60% complete at the beginning of the period. During the period, 15,800 units were completed and transferred to the Packing Department. There were 1,200 units in process that were 30% complete at the end of the period.

a. Determine the number of whole units to be accounted for and to be assigned costs for the period.

b. Determine the number of equivalent units of production for the period.

**Appendix**
**EX 20-25 Equivalent units of production: average cost method**

✔ a. 12,100 units to be accounted for

Units of production data for the two departments of Atlantic Cable and Wire Company for July of the current fiscal year are as follows:

|  | Drawing Department | Winding Department |
|---|---|---|
| Work in process, July 1 | 500 units, 50% completed | 350 units, 30% completed |
| Completed and transferred to next processing department during July | 11,400 units | 10,950 units |
| Work in process, July 31 | 700 units, 55% completed | 800 units, 25% completed |

Each department uses the average cost method.

a. Determine the number of whole units to be accounted for and to be assigned costs and the equivalent units of production for the Drawing Department.

b. Determine the number of whole units to be accounted for and to be assigned costs and the equivalent units of production for the Winding Department.

**Appendix**
**EX 20-26 Equivalent units of production: average cost method**

✔ a. 3,100

The following information concerns production in the Finishing Department for May. The Finishing Department uses the average cost method.

**ACCOUNT** *Work in Process—Finishing Department*　　　　　**ACCOUNT NO.**

|  |  | Item | Debit | Credit | Balance Debit | Balance Credit |
|---|---|---|---|---|---|---|
| May | 1 | Bal., 4,200 units, 70% completed |  |  | 36,500 |  |
|  | 31 | Direct materials, 23,600 units | 125,800 |  | 162,300 |  |
|  | 31 | Direct labor | 75,400 |  | 237,700 |  |
|  | 31 | Factory overhead | 82,675 |  | 320,375 |  |
|  | 31 | Goods transferred, 24,700 units |  | 308,750 | 11,625 |  |
|  | 31 | Bal., ? units, 30% completed |  |  | 11,625 |  |

a. Determine the number of units in work in process inventory at the end of the month.

b. Determine the number of whole units to be accounted for and to be assigned costs and the equivalent units of production for May.

**Appendix**
**EX 20-27 Equivalent units of production and related costs**

✔ b. 8,820 units

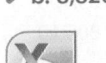

The charges to Work in Process—Baking Department for a period as well as information concerning production are as follows. The Baking Department uses the average cost method, and all direct materials are placed in process during production.

**Work in Process—Baking Department**

| Bal., 900 units, 40% completed | 2,466 | To Finished Goods, 8,100 units | ? |
|---|---|---|---|
| Direct materials, 8,400 units | 34,500 |  |  |
| Direct labor | 16,200 |  |  |
| Factory overhead | 8,574 |  |  |
| Bal., 1,200 units, 60% completed | ? |  |  |

Determine the following:

a. The number of whole units to be accounted for and to be assigned costs

b. The number of equivalent units of production

c. The cost per equivalent unit

d. The cost of units transferred to Finished Goods

e. The cost of units in ending Work in Process

## Appendix
### EX 20-28    Cost per equivalent unit: average cost method

✔ a. $26.00

The following information concerns production in the Forging Department for June. The Forging Department uses the average cost method.

**ACCOUNT** *Work in Process—Forging Department*        **ACCOUNT NO.**

| Date | | Item | Debit | Credit | Balance Debit | Balance Credit |
|------|---|------|-------|--------|-------|--------|
| June | 1 | Bal., 500 units, 40% completed | | | 5,000 | |
| | 30 | Direct materials, 3,700 units | 49,200 | | 54,200 | |
| | 30 | Direct labor | 25,200 | | 79,400 | |
| | 30 | Factory overhead | 25,120 | | 104,520 | |
| | 30 | Goods transferred, 3,600 units | | ? | ? | |
| | 30 | Bal., 600 units, 70% completed | | | ? | |

a. Determine the cost per equivalent unit.

b. Determine cost of units transferred to Finished Goods.

c. Determine the cost of units in ending Work in Process.

## Appendix
### EX 20-29    Cost of production report: average cost method

✔ Cost per equivalent unit, $3.60

The increases to Work in Process—Roasting Department for Highlands Coffee Company for May 2016 as well as information concerning production are as follows:

| | |
|---|---|
| Work in process, May 1, 1,150 pounds, 40% completed | $ 1,700 |
| Coffee beans added during May, 10,900 pounds | 28,600 |
| Conversion costs during May | 12,504 |
| Work in process, May 31, 800 pounds, 80% completed | — |
| Goods finished during May, 11,250 pounds | — |

Prepare a cost of production report, using the average cost method.

## Appendix
### EX 20-30    Cost of production report: average cost method

✔ Cost per equivalent unit, $9.00

Prepare a cost of production report for the Cutting Department of Dalton Carpet Company for January 2016. Use the average cost method with the following data:

| | |
|---|---|
| Work in process, January 1, 3,400 units, 75% completed | $ 23,000 |
| Materials added during January from Weaving Department, 64,000 units | 366,200 |
| Direct labor for January | 105,100 |
| Factory overhead for January | 80,710 |
| Goods finished during January (includes goods in process, January 1), 63,500 units | — |
| Work in process, January 31, 3,900 units, 10% completed | — |

# Problems: Series A

### PR 20-1A    Entries for process cost system                    OBJ. 1, 3

✔ 2. Materials October 31 balance, $5,900

General Ledger

SHOW
ME HOW

FloorMate Carpet Company manufactures carpets. Fiber is placed in process in the Spinning Department, where it is spun into yarn. The output of the Spinning Department is transferred to the Tufting Department, where carpet backing is added at the beginning of the process and the process is completed. On October 1, FloorMate Carpet Company had the following inventories:

| | |
|---|---|
| Finished Goods | $5,600 |
| Work in Process—Spinning Department | 1,500 |
| Work in Process—Tufting Department | 2,300 |
| Materials | 4,800 |

Departmental accounts are maintained for factory overhead, and both have zero balances on October 1.

Manufacturing operations for October are summarized as follows:

| | | |
|---|---|---|
| a. | Materials purchased on account .................................................. | $ 84,900 |
| b. | Materials requisitioned for use: | |
| | Fiber—Spinning Department .................................................. | $ 43,600 |
| | Carpet backing—Tufting Department ......................................... | 34,100 |
| | Indirect materials—Spinning Department .................................... | 3,200 |
| | Indirect materials—Tufting Department ...................................... | 2,900 |
| c. | Labor used: | |
| | Direct labor—Spinning Department........................................... | $ 26,300 |
| | Direct labor—Tufting Department............................................. | 17,900 |
| | Indirect labor—Spinning Department ........................................ | 12,100 |
| | Indirect labor—Tufting Department .......................................... | 11,700 |
| d. | Depreciation charged on fixed assets: | |
| | Spinning Department .......................................................... | $ 5,300 |
| | Tufting Department............................................................ | 3,400 |
| e. | Expired prepaid factory insurance: | |
| | Spinning Department .......................................................... | $ 1,200 |
| | Tufting Department............................................................ | 1,000 |
| f. | Applied factory overhead: | |
| | Spinning Department .......................................................... | $ 22,000 |
| | Tufting Department............................................................ | 18,700 |
| g. | Production costs transferred from Spinning Department to Tufting Department ........ | $ 88,000 |
| h. | Production costs transferred from Tufting Department to Finished Goods .............. | $159,000 |
| i. | Cost of goods sold during the period .......................................... | $160,500 |

*Handwritten notes: "WIP", "fackory overhead", "sales on acct were #3,000"*

### Instructions

1. Journalize the entries to record the operations, identifying each entry by letter.

2. Compute the October 31 balances of the inventory accounts.

3. Compute the October 31 balances of the factory overhead accounts.

---

### PR 20-2A Cost of production report

**OBJ. 2, 4**

✔ 1. Conversion cost per equivalent unit, $0.80

Fresh Mountain Coffee Company roasts and packs coffee beans. The process begins by placing coffee beans into the Roasting Department. From the Roasting Department, coffee beans are then transferred to the Packing Department. The following is a partial work in process account of the Roasting Department at March 31, 2016:

**ACCOUNT** *Work in Process—Roasting Department*  **ACCOUNT NO.**

| Date | | Item | Debit | Credit | Balance Debit | Balance Credit |
|---|---|---|---|---|---|---|
| Mar. | 1 | Bal., 1,500 units, 30% completed | | | 6,150 | |
| | 31 | Direct materials, 22,300 units | 86,970 | | 93,120 | |
| | 31 | Direct labor | 11,900 | | 105,020 | |
| | 31 | Factory overhead | 5,772 | | 110,792 | |
| | 31 | Goods transferred, 21,700 units | | ? | | |
| | 31 | Bal., ? units, 40% completed | | | ? | |

### Instructions

1. Prepare a cost of production report, and identify the missing amounts for Work in Process—Roasting Department.

2. Assuming that the March 1 work in process inventory includes $5,700 of direct materials, determine the increase or decrease in the cost per equivalent unit for direct materials and conversion between February and March.

**PR 20-3A** **Equivalent units and related costs; cost of production report; entries**   OBJ. 2, 3, 4

✔ 2. Transferred to Packaging Dept., $40,183

White Diamond Flour Company manufactures flour by a series of three processes, beginning with wheat grain being introduced in the Milling Department. From the Milling Department, the materials pass through the Sifting and Packaging departments, emerging as packaged refined flour.

The balance in the account Work in Process—Sifting Department was as follows on July 1, 2016:

| Work in Process—Sifting Department (900 units, ⅗ completed): | |
| --- | --- |
| Direct materials (900 × $2.05) | $1,845 |
| Conversion (900 × ⅗ × $0.40) | 216 |
| | $2,061 |

The following costs were charged to Work in Process—Sifting Department during July:

| Direct materials transferred from Milling Department: | |
| --- | --- |
| 15,700 units at $2.15 a unit | $33,755 |
| Direct labor | 4,420 |
| Factory overhead | 2,708 |

During July, 15,500 units of flour were completed. Work in Process—Sifting Department on July 31 was 1,100 units, ⅘ completed.

**Instructions**

1. Prepare a cost of production report for the Sifting Department for July.

2. Journalize the entries for costs transferred from Milling to Sifting and the costs transferred from Sifting to Packaging.

3. Determine the increase or decrease in the cost per equivalent unit from June to July for direct materials and conversion costs.

4. ▬▬▶ Discuss the uses of the cost of production report and the results of part (3).

---

**PR 20-4A** **Work in process account data for two months; cost of production reports**   OBJ. 1, 2, 3, 4

✔ 1. c. Transferred to finished goods in April, $49,818

Hearty Soup Co. uses a process cost system to record the costs of processing soup, which requires the cooking and filling processes. Materials are entered from the cooking process at the beginning of the filling process. The inventory of Work in Process—Filling on April 1 and debits to the account during April 2016 were as follows: 

| Bal., 800 units, 30% completed: | |
| --- | --- |
| Direct materials (800 × $4.30) | $ 3,440 |
| Conversion (800 × 30% × $1.75) | 420 |
| | $ 3,860 |

| | |
| --- | --- |
| From Cooking Department, 7,800 units | $34,320 |
| Direct labor | 8,562 |
| Factory overhead | 6,387 |

During April, 800 units in process on April 1 were completed, and of the 7,800 units entering the department, all were completed except 550 units that were 90% completed.

Charges to Work in Process—Filling for May were as follows:

| | |
| --- | --- |
| From Cooking Department, 9,600 units | $44,160 |
| Direct labor | 12,042 |
| Factory overhead | 6,878 |

During May, the units in process at the beginning of the month were completed, and of the 9,600 units entering the department, all were completed except 300 units that were 35% completed.

**Instructions**

1. Enter the balance as of April 1, 2016, in a four-column account for Work in Process—Filling. Record the debits and the credits in the account for April. Construct a cost of production report, and present computations for determining (a) equivalent units of production for materials and conversion, (b) costs per equivalent unit, (c) cost of goods

finished, differentiating between units started in the prior period and units started and finished in April, and (d) work in process inventory.

2. Provide the same information for May by recording the May transactions in the four-column work in process account. Construct a cost of production report, and present the May computations (a through d) listed in part (1).

3. ━━━▶ Comment on the change in costs per equivalent unit for March through May for direct materials and conversion costs.

## Appendix
### PR 20-5A Cost of production report: average cost method

✔ Cost per equivalent unit, $2.70

Sunrise Coffee Company roasts and packs coffee beans. The process begins in the Roasting Department. From the Roasting Department, the coffee beans are transferred to the Packing Department. The following is a partial work in process account of the Roasting Department at December 31, 2016:

**ACCOUNT** *Work in Process—Roasting Department*     **ACCOUNT NO.**

| Date | | Item | Debit | Credit | Balance Debit | Balance Credit |
|---|---|---|---|---|---|---|
| Dec. | 1 | Bal., 10,500 units, 75% completed | | | 21,000 | |
| | 31 | Direct materials, 210,400 units | 246,800 | | 267,800 | |
| | 31 | Direct labor | 135,700 | | 403,500 | |
| | 31 | Factory overhead | 168,630 | | 572,130 | |
| | 31 | Goods transferred, 208,900 units | | ? | ? | |
| | 31 | Bal., ? units, 25% completed | | | ? | |

### Instructions
Prepare a cost of production report, using the average cost method, and identify the missing amounts for Work in Process—Roasting Department.

# Problems: Series B

### PR 20-1B Entries for process cost system                        OBJ. 1, 3

✔ 2. Materials
July 31 balance, $11,390

**General Ledger**

SHOW
ME HOW

Preston & Grover Soap Company manufactures powdered detergent. Phosphate is placed in process in the Making Department, where it is turned into granulars. The output of Making is transferred to the Packing Department, where packaging is added at the beginning of the process. On July 1, Preston & Grover Soap Company had the following inventories:

| | |
|---|---|
| Finished Goods | $13,500 |
| Work in Process—Making | 6,790 |
| Work in Process—Packing | 7,350 |
| Materials | 5,100 |

Departmental accounts are maintained for factory overhead, which both have zero balances on July 1.

Manufacturing operations for July are summarized as follows:

| | |
|---|---|
| a. Materials purchased on account | $149,800 |
| b. Materials requisitioned for use: | |
| Phosphate—Making Department | $105,700 |
| Packaging—Packing Department | 31,300 |
| Indirect materials—Making Department | 4,980 |
| Indirect materials—Packing Department | 1,530 |

*(Continued)*

c. Labor used:

| | |
|---|---:|
| Direct labor—Making Department | $ 32,400 |
| Direct labor—Packing Department | 40,900 |
| Indirect labor—Making Department | 15,400 |
| Indirect labor—Packing Department | 18,300 |

d. Depreciation charged on fixed assets:

| | |
|---|---:|
| Making Department | $ 10,700 |
| Packing Department | 7,900 |

e. Expired prepaid factory insurance:

| | |
|---|---:|
| Making Department | $ 2,000 |
| Packing Department | 1,500 |

f. Applied factory overhead:

| | |
|---|---:|
| Making Department | $ 32,570 |
| Packing Department | 30,050 |

g. Production costs transferred from Making Department to Packing Department ..... $166,790

h. Production costs transferred from Packing Department to Finished Goods.......... $263,400

i. Cost of goods sold during the period ........................................... $265,200

### Instructions

1. Journalize the entries to record the operations, identifying each entry by letter.

2. Compute the July 31 balances of the inventory accounts.

3. Compute the July 31 balances of the factory overhead accounts.

---

**✔ 1. Conversion cost per equivalent unit, $6.00**

**PR 20-2B   Cost of production report**       **OBJ. 2, 4**

Bavarian Chocolate Company processes chocolate into candy bars. The process begins by placing direct materials (raw chocolate, milk, and sugar) into the Blending Department. All materials are placed into production at the beginning of the blending process. After blending, the milk chocolate is then transferred to the Molding Department, where the milk chocolate is formed into candy bars. The following is a partial work in process account of the Blending Department at October 31, 2016:

| | ACCOUNT *Work in Process—Blending Department* | | | ACCOUNT NO. | |
|---|---|---|---|---|---|
| | | | | **Balance** | |
| **Date** | **Item** | **Debit** | **Credit** | **Debit** | **Credit** |
| Oct. 1 | Bal., 2,300 units, ⅗ completed | | | 46,368 | |
| 31 | Direct materials, 26,000 units | 429,000 | | 475,368 | |
| 31 | Direct labor | 100,560 | | 575,928 | |
| 31 | Factory overhead | 48,480 | | 624,408 | |
| 31 | Goods transferred, 25,700 units | | ? | | |
| 31 | Bal., ? units, ⅕ completed | | | ? | |

### Instructions

1. Prepare a cost of production report, and identify the missing amounts for Work in Process—Blending Department.

2. Assuming that the October 1 work in process inventory includes direct materials of $38,295, determine the increase or decrease in the cost per equivalent unit for direct materials and conversion between September and October.

**PR 20-3B    Equivalent units and related costs; cost of production report; entries**                    OBJ. 2, 3, 4

✔ 2. Transferred to finished goods, $705,376

Dover Chemical Company manufactures specialty chemicals by a series of three processes, all materials being introduced in the Distilling Department. From the Distilling Department, the materials pass through the Reaction and Filling departments, emerging as finished chemicals.

The balance in the account Work in Process—Filling was as follows on January 1, 2016:

Work in Process—Filling Department
(3,400 units, 60% completed):

| | |
|---|---:|
| Direct materials (3,400 × $9.58) | $32,572 |
| Conversion (3,400 × 60% × $3.90) | 7,956 |
| | $40,528 |

The following costs were charged to Work in Process—Filling during January:

| | |
|---|---:|
| Direct materials transferred from Reaction Department: 52,300 units at $9.50 a unit | $496,850 |
| Direct labor | 101,560 |
| Factory overhead | 95,166 |

During January, 53,000 units of specialty chemicals were completed. Work in Process—Filling Department on January 31 was 2,700 units, 30% completed.

**Instructions**

1. Prepare a cost of production report for the Filling Department for January.

2. Journalize the entries for costs transferred from Reaction to Filling and the costs transferred from Filling to Finished Goods.

3. Determine the increase or decrease in the cost per equivalent unit from December to January for direct materials and conversion costs.

4. 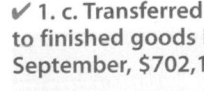 Discuss the uses of the cost of production report and the results of part (3).

---

**PR 20-4B    Work in process account data for two months; cost of production reports**                    OBJ. 1, 2, 3, 4

✔ 1. c. Transferred to finished goods in September, $702,195

Pittsburgh Aluminum Company uses a process cost system to record the costs of manufacturing rolled aluminum, which consists of the smelting and rolling processes. Materials are entered from smelting at the beginning of the rolling process. The inventory of Work in Process—Rolling on September 1, 2016, and debits to the account during September were as follows:

Bal., 2,600 units, ¼ completed:

| | |
|---|---:|
| Direct materials (2,600 × $15.50) | $40,300 |
| Conversion (2,600 × ¼ × $8.50) | 5,525 |
| | $45,825 |

| | |
|---|---:|
| From Smelting Department, 28,900 units | 462,400 |
| Direct labor | 158,920 |
| Factory overhead | 101,402 |

During September, 2,600 units in process on September 1 were completed, and of the 28,900 units entering the department, all were completed except 2,900 units that were ⅘ completed.

Charges to Work in Process—Rolling for October were as follows:

| | |
|---|---:|
| From Smelting Department, 31,000 units | $511,500 |
| Direct labor | 162,850 |
| Factory overhead | 104,494 |

During October, the units in process at the beginning of the month were completed, and of the 31,000 units entering the department, all were completed except 2,000 units that were ⅖ completed.

(*Continued*)

**Instructions**

1. Enter the balance as of September 1, 2016, in a four-column account for Work in Process—Rolling. Record the debits and the credits in the account for September. Construct a cost of production report and present computations for determining (a) equivalent units of production for materials and conversion, (b) costs per equivalent unit, (c) cost of goods finished, differentiating between units started in the prior period and units started and finished in September, and (d) work in process inventory.

2. Provide the same information for October by recording the October transactions in the four-column work in process account. Construct a cost of production report, and present the October computations (a through d) listed in part (1).

3. ➡ Comment on the change in costs per equivalent unit for August through October for direct materials and conversion cost.

---

**Appendix**
**PR 20-5B   Cost of production report: average cost method**

✔ Transferred to
Packaging Dept.,
$54,000

Blue Ribbon Flour Company manufactures flour by a series of three processes, beginning in the Milling Department. From the Milling Department, the materials pass through the Sifting and Packaging departments, emerging as packaged refined flour.

The balance in the account Work in Process—Sifting Department was as follows on May 1, 2016:

| | |
|---|---|
| Work in Process—Sifting Department (1,500 units, 75% completed) | $3,400 |

The following costs were charged to Work in Process—Sifting Department during May:

| | |
|---|---|
| Direct materials transferred from Milling Department: 18,300 units | $32,600 |
| Direct labor | 14,560 |
| Factory overhead | 7,490 |

During May, 18,000 units of flour were completed and transferred to finished goods. Work in Process—Sifting Department on May 31 was 1,800 units, 75% completed.

**Instructions**

Prepare a cost of production report for the Sifting Department for May, using the average cost method.

---

# Cases & Projects

---

**CP 20-1   Ethics and professional conduct in business**

Assume you are the division controller for Auntie M's Cookie Company. Auntie M has introduced a new chocolate chip cookie called Full of Chips, and it is a success. As a result, the product manager responsible for the launch of this new cookie was promoted to division vice president and became your boss. A new product manager, Bishop, has been brought in to replace the promoted manager. Bishop notices that the Full of Chips cookie uses a lot of chips, which increases the cost of the cookie. As a result, Bishop has ordered that the amount of chips used in the cookies be reduced by 10%. The manager believes that a 10% reduction in chips will not adversely affect sales but will reduce costs and, hence, improve margins. The increased margins would help Bishop meet profit targets for the period.

You are looking over some cost of production reports segmented by cookie line. You notice that there is a drop in the materials costs for Full of Chips. On further investigation, you discover why the chip costs have declined (fewer chips). Both you and Bishop report to the division vice president, who was the original product manager for Full of Chips. You are trying to decide what to do, if anything.

➡ Discuss the options you might consider.

**CP 20-2 Accounting for materials costs**

In papermaking operations for companies such as **International Paper Company**, wet pulp is fed into paper machines, which press and dry pulp into a continuous sheet of paper. The paper is formed at very high speeds (60 mph). Once the paper is formed, the paper is rolled onto a reel at the back end of the paper machine. One of the characteristics of papermaking is the creation of "broke" paper. Broke is paper that fails to satisfy quality standards and is therefore rejected for final shipment to customers. Broke is recycled back to the beginning of the process by combining the recycled paper with virgin (new) pulp material. The combination of virgin pulp and recycled broke is sent to the paper machine for papermaking. Broke is fed into this recycle process continuously from all over the facility.

In this industry, it is typical to charge the papermaking operation with the cost of direct materials, which is a mixture of virgin materials and broke. Broke has a much lower cost than does virgin pulp. Therefore, the more broke in the mixture, the lower the average cost of direct materials to the department. Papermaking managers will frequently comment on the importance of broke for keeping their direct materials costs down.

a. ▬▬▶ How do you react to this accounting procedure?

b. ▬▬▶ What "hidden costs" are not considered when accounting for broke as described?

**CP 20-3 Analyzing unit costs**

Midstate Containers Inc. manufactures cans for the canned food industry. The operations manager of a can manufacturing operation wants to conduct a cost study investigating the relationship of tin content in the material (can stock) to the energy cost for enameling the cans. The enameling was necessary to prepare the cans for labeling. A higher percentage of tin content in the can stock increases the cost of material. The operations manager believed that a higher tin content in the can stock would reduce the amount of energy used in enameling. During the analysis period, the amount of tin content in the steel can stock was increased for every month, from April to September. The following operating reports were available from the controller:

|   | A | B | C | D | E | F | G |
|---|---|---|---|---|---|---|---|
| 1 |  | April | May | June | July | August | September |
| 2 | Energy | $ 14,000 | $ 34,800 | $ 33,000 | $ 21,700 | $ 28,800 | $ 33,000 |
| 3 | Materials | 13,000 | 28,800 | 24,200 | 14,000 | 17,100 | 16,000 |
| 4 | Total cost | $ 27,000 | $ 63,600 | $ 57,200 | $ 35,700 | $ 45,900 | $ 49,000 |
| 5 | Units produced | ÷50,000 | ÷120,000 | ÷110,000 | ÷ 70,000 | ÷ 90,000 | ÷100,000 |
| 6 | Cost per unit | $ 0.54 | $ 0.53 | $ 0.52 | $ 0.51 | $ 0.51 | $ 0.49 |
| 7 |  |  |  |  |  |  |  |

Differences in materials unit costs were entirely related to the amount of tin content.

▬▬▶ Interpret this information and report to the operations manager your recommendations with respect to tin content.

**CP 20-4 Decision making**

Jamarcus Bradshaw, plant manager of Georgia Paper Company's papermaking mill, was looking over the cost of production reports for July and August for the Papermaking Department. The reports revealed the following:

|  | July | August |
|---|---|---|
| Pulp and chemicals........................ | $295,600 | $304,100 |
| Conversion cost............................ | 146,000 | 149,600 |
| Total cost,................................ | $441,600 | $453,700 |
| Number of tons ............................ | ÷ 1,200 | ÷ 1,130 |
| Cost per ton .............................. | $ 368 | $ 401.50 |

*(Continued)*

Jamarcus was concerned about the increased cost per ton from the output of the department. As a result, he asked the plant controller to perform a study to help explain these results. The controller, Leann Brunswick, began the analysis by performing some interviews of key plant personnel in order to understand what the problem might be. Excerpts from an interview with Len Tyson, a paper machine operator, follow:

*Len:* We have two papermaking machines in the department. I have no data, but I think paper machine No. 1 is applying too much pulp and, thus, is wasting both conversion and materials resources. We haven't had repairs on paper machine No. 1 in a while. Maybe this is the problem.

*Leann:* How does too much pulp result in wasted resources?

*Len:* Well, you see, if too much pulp is applied, then we will waste pulp material. The customer will not pay for the extra weight. Thus, we just lose that amount of material. Also, when there is too much pulp, the machine must be slowed down in order to complete the drying process. This results in a waste of conversion costs.

*Leann:* Do you have any other suspicions?

*Len:* Well, as you know, we have two products—green paper and yellow paper. They are identical except for the color. The color is added to the papermaking process in the paper machine. I think that during August these two color papers have been behaving very differently. I don't have any data, but it just seems as though the amount of waste associated with the green paper has increased.

*Leann:* Why is this?

*Len:* I understand that there has been a change in specifications for the green paper, starting near the beginning of August. This change could be causing the machines to run poorly when making green paper. If this is the case, the cost per ton would increase for green paper.

Leann also asked for a database printout providing greater detail on August's operating results.

September 9                                                     Requested by: Leann Brunswick
Papermaking Department—August detail

| | A | B | C | D | E | F |
|---|---|---|---|---|---|---|
| 1 | Production | | | | | |
| 2 | Run | Paper | | Material | Conversion | |
| 3 | Number | Machine | Color | Costs | Costs | Tons |
| 4 | 1 | 1 | Green | 40,300 | 18,300 | 150 |
| 5 | 2 | 1 | Yellow | 41,700 | 21,200 | 140 |
| 6 | 3 | 1 | Green | 44,600 | 22,500 | 150 |
| 7 | 4 | 1 | Yellow | 36,100 | 18,100 | 120 |
| 8 | 5 | 2 | Green | 38,300 | 18,900 | 160 |
| 9 | 6 | 2 | Yellow | 33,900 | 15,200 | 140 |
| 10 | 7 | 2 | Green | 35,600 | 18,400 | 130 |
| 11 | 8 | 2 | Yellow | 33,600 | 17,000 | 140 |
| 12 | | Total | | 304,100 | 149,600 | 1,130 |
| 13 | | | | | | |

Assuming that you're Leann Brunswick, write a memo to Jamarcus Bradshaw with a recommendation to management. You should analyze the August data to determine whether the paper machine or the paper color explains the increase in the unit cost from July. Include any supporting schedules that are appropriate.

---

**CP 20-5   Process costing companies**

**Group Project**

The following categories represent typical process manufacturing industries:

| | |
|---|---|
| Beverages | Metals |
| Chemicals | Petroleum refining |
| Food | Pharmaceuticals |
| Forest and paper products | Soap and cosmetics |

In groups of two or three, for each category identify one company (following your instructor's specific instructions) and determine the following:

1. Typical products manufactured by the selected company, including brand names

2. Typical raw materials used by the selected company

3. Types of processes used by the selected company

Use annual reports, the Internet, or library resources in doing this activity.

# Cost Behavior and Cost-Volume-Profit Analysis

## *Ford Motor Company*

**M**aking a profit isn't easy for U.S. auto manufacturers like the **Ford Motor Company.** The cost of materials, labor, equipment, and advertising make it very expensive to produce cars and trucks.

How many cars does Ford need to produce and sell to break even? The answer depends on the relationship between Ford's sales revenue and costs. Some of Ford's costs, like direct labor and materials, will change in direct proportion to the number of vehicles that are built. Other costs, such as the costs of manufacturing equipment, are fixed and do not change with the number of vehicles that are produced. Ford will break even when it generates enough sales revenue to cover both its fixed and variable costs.

During the depths of the 2009 recession, Ford renegotiated labor contracts with their employees. These renegotiations reduced the direct labor cost incurred to build each car, which lowered the number of cars that the company needed to sell to break even by 45%.

As with Ford, understanding how costs behave, and the relationship between costs, profits, and volume, is important for all businesses. This chapter discusses commonly used methods for classifying costs according to how they change and techniques for determining how many units must be sold for a company to break even. Techniques that management can use to evaluate costs in order to make sound business decisions are also discussed.

*Source:* J. Booton, "Moody's Upgrades Ford's Credit Rating, Returns Blue Oval Trademark," Fox Business, May 22, 2012.

**At a Glance 21**   Page 1007

**OBJ 1** Classify costs as variable costs, fixed costs, or mixed costs.

# Cost Behavior

**Cost behavior** is the manner in which a cost changes as a related activity changes. The behavior of costs is useful to managers for a variety of reasons. For example, knowing how costs behave allows managers to predict profits as sales and production volumes change. Knowing how costs behave is also useful for estimating costs, which affects a variety of decisions such as whether to replace a machine.

Understanding the behavior of a cost depends on the following:

- Identifying the activities that cause the cost to change. These activities are called **activity bases** (or *activity drivers*).

- Specifying the range of activity over which the changes in the cost are of interest. This range of activity is called the **relevant range**.

To illustrate, assume that a hospital is concerned about planning and controlling patient food costs. A good activity base is the number of patients who *stay* overnight in the hospital. The number of patients who are *treated* is not as good an activity base because some patients are outpatients and, thus, do not consume food. Once an activity base is identified, food costs can then be analyzed over the range of the number of patients who normally stay in the hospital (the relevant range).

Costs are normally classified as variable costs, fixed costs, or mixed costs.

# Variable Costs

**Variable costs** are costs that vary in proportion to changes in the activity base. When the activity base is units produced, direct materials and direct labor costs are normally classified as variable costs.

To illustrate, assume that Jason Sound Inc. produces stereo systems. The parts for the stereo systems are purchased from suppliers for $10 per unit and are assembled by Jason Sound. For Model JS-12, the direct materials costs for the relevant range of 5,000 to 30,000 units of production are as follows:

| Number of Units of Model JS-12 Produced | Direct Materials Cost per Unit | Total Direct Materials Cost |
|---|---|---|
| 5,000 units | $10 | $ 50,000 |
| 10,000 | 10 | 100,000 |
| 15,000 | 10 | 150,000 |
| 20,000 | 10 | 200,000 |
| 25,000 | 10 | 250,000 |
| 30,000 | 10 | 300,000 |

As shown, variable costs have the following characteristics:

- *Cost per unit* remains the same regardless of changes in the activity base. For Jason Sound, units produced is the activity base. For Model JS-12, the cost per unit is $10.
- *Total cost* changes in proportion to changes in the activity base. For Model JS-12, the direct materials cost for 10,000 units ($100,000) is twice the direct materials cost for 5,000 units ($50,000).

Exhibit 1 illustrates how the variable costs for direct materials for Model JS-12 behave in total and on a per-unit basis as production changes.

---

**EXHIBIT 1**    **Variable Cost Graphs**

Dynamic Exhibit

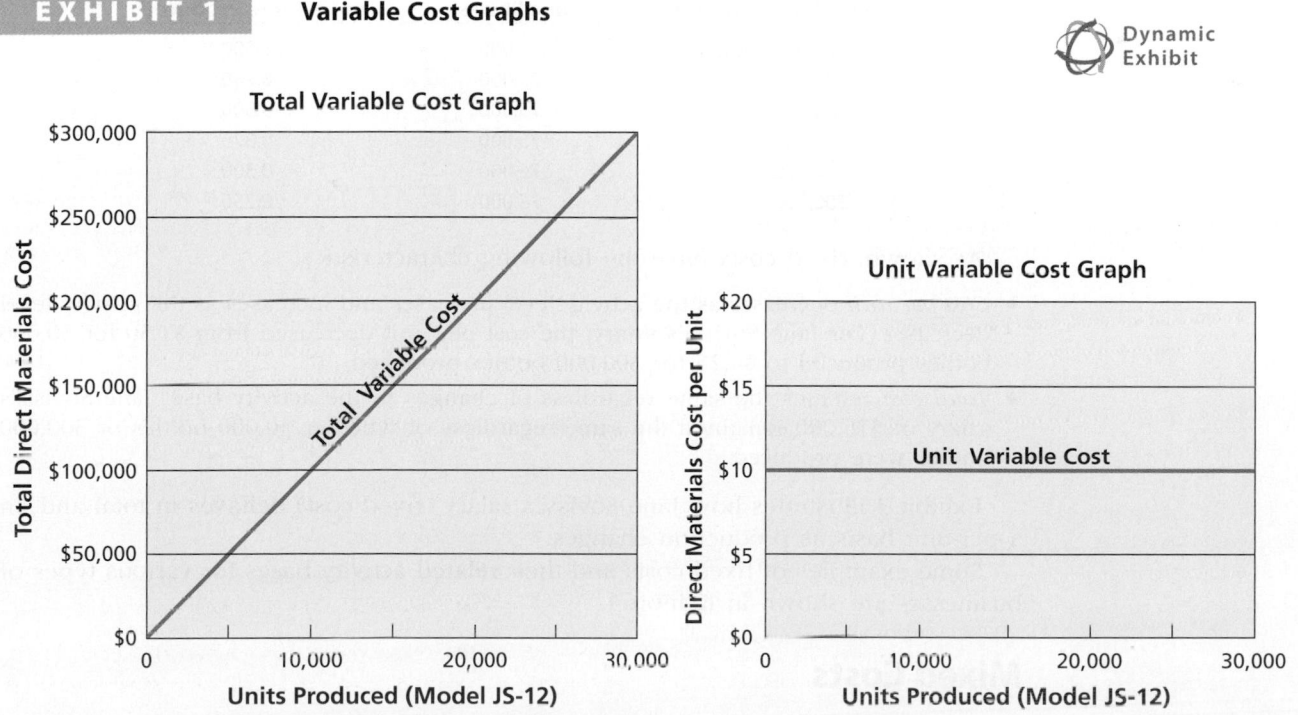

Some examples of variable costs and their related activity bases for various types of businesses are shown in Exhibit 2.

**EXHIBIT 2** **Variable Costs and Their Activity Bases**

| Type of Business | Cost | Activity Base |
|---|---|---|
| University | Instructor salaries | Number of classes |
| Passenger airline | Fuel | Number of miles flown |
| Manufacturing | Direct materials | Number of units produced |
| Hospital | Nurse wages | Number of patients |
| Hotel | Maid wages | Number of guests |
| Bank | Teller wages | Number of banking transactions |

## Fixed Costs

**Fixed costs** are costs that remain the same in total dollar amount as the activity base changes. When the activity base is units produced, many factory overhead costs such as straight-line depreciation are classified as fixed costs.

To illustrate, assume that Minton Inc. manufactures, bottles, and distributes perfume. The production supervisor is Jane Sovissi, who is paid a salary of $75,000 per year. For the relevant range of 50,000 to 300,000 bottles of perfume, the total fixed cost of $75,000 does not vary as production increases. As a result, the fixed cost per bottle decreases as the units produced increase. This is because the fixed cost is spread over a larger number of bottles, as follows:

| Number of Bottles of Perfume Produced | Total Salary for Jane Sovissi | Salary per Bottle of Perfume Produced |
|---|---|---|
| 50,000 bottles | $75,000 | $1.500 |
| 100,000 | 75,000 | 0.750 |
| 150,000 | 75,000 | 0.500 |
| 200,000 | 75,000 | 0.375 |
| 250,000 | 75,000 | 0.300 |
| 300,000 | 75,000 | 0.250 |

As shown, fixed costs have the following characteristics:

- *Cost per unit* decreases as the activity level increases and increases as the activity level decreases. For Jane Sovissi's salary, the cost per unit decreased from $1.50 for 50,000 bottles produced to $0.25 for 300,000 bottles produced.

- *Total cost* remains the same regardless of changes in the activity base. Jane Sovissi's salary of $75,000 remained the same regardless of whether 50,000 bottles or 300,000 bottles were produced.

Exhibit 3 illustrates how Jane Sovissi's salary (fixed cost) behaves in total and on a per-unit basis as production changes.

Some examples of fixed costs and their related activity bases for various types of businesses are shown in Exhibit 4.

## Mixed Costs

A salesperson's compensation can be a mixed cost comprised of a salary (fixed portion) plus a commission as a percent of sales (variable portion).

**Mixed costs** are costs that have characteristics of both a variable and a fixed cost. Mixed costs are sometimes called *semivariable* or *semifixed costs*.

To illustrate, assume that Simpson Inc. manufactures sails, using rented machinery. The rental charges are as follows:

Rental Charge = $15,000 per year + $1 for each hour used in excess of 10,000 hours

EXHIBIT 3     **Fixed Cost Graphs**

Dynamic
Exhibit

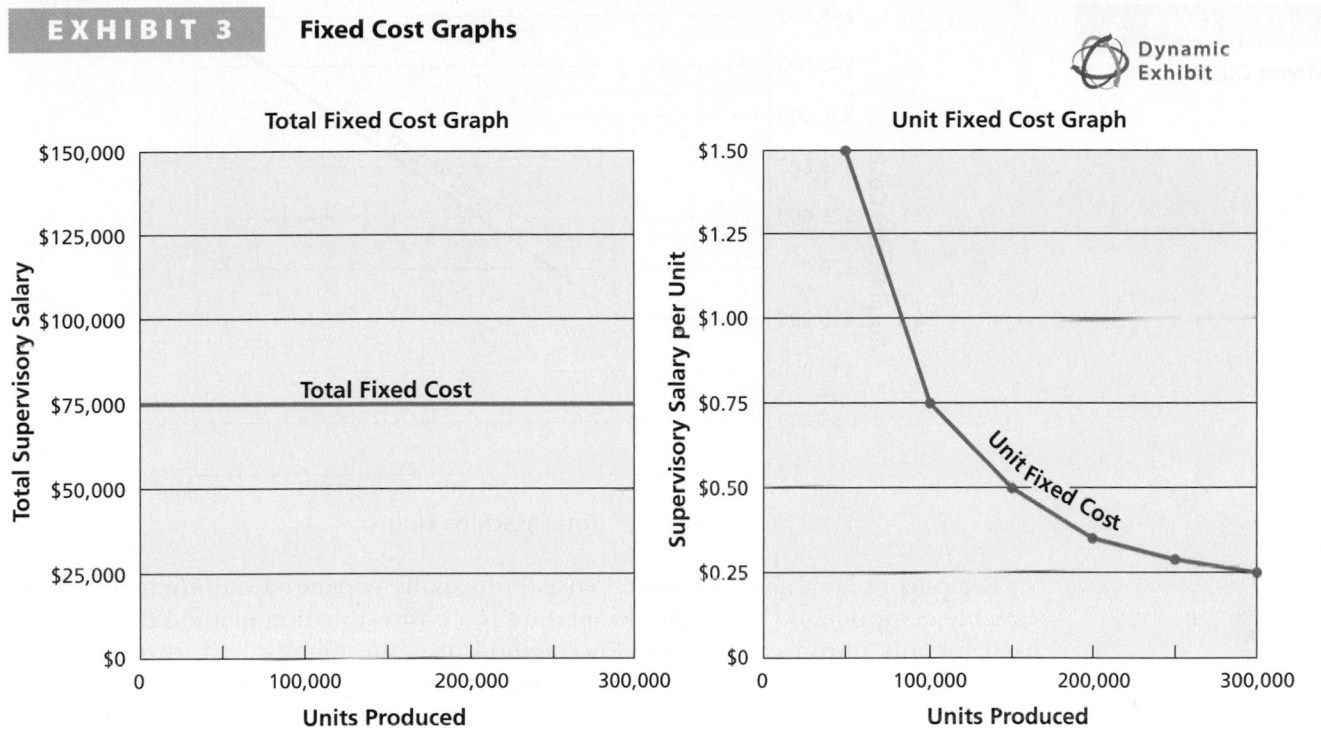

EXHIBIT 4     **Fixed Costs and Their Activity Bases**

| Type of Business | Fixed Cost | Activity Base |
|---|---|---|
| University | Building (straight-line) depreciation | Number of students |
| Passenger airline | Airplane (straight-line) depreciation | Number of miles flown |
| Manufacturing | Plant manager salary | Number of units produced |
| Hospital | Property insurance | Number of patients |
| Hotel | Property taxes | Number of guests |
| Bank | Branch manager salary | Number of customer accounts |

The rental charges for various hours used within the relevant range of 8,000 hours to 40,000 hours are as follows:

| Hours Used | Rental Charge |
|---|---|
| 8,000 hours | $15,000 |
| 12,000 | $17,000 {$15,000 + [(12,000 hrs. – 10,000 hrs.) × $1]} |
| 20,000 | $25,000 {$15,000 + [(20,000 hrs. – 10,000 hrs.) × $1]} |
| 40,000 | $45,000 {$15,000 + [(40,000 hrs. – 10,000 hrs.) × $1]} |

Exhibit 5 illustrates the preceding mixed cost behavior.

**EXHIBIT 5**

**Mixed Costs**

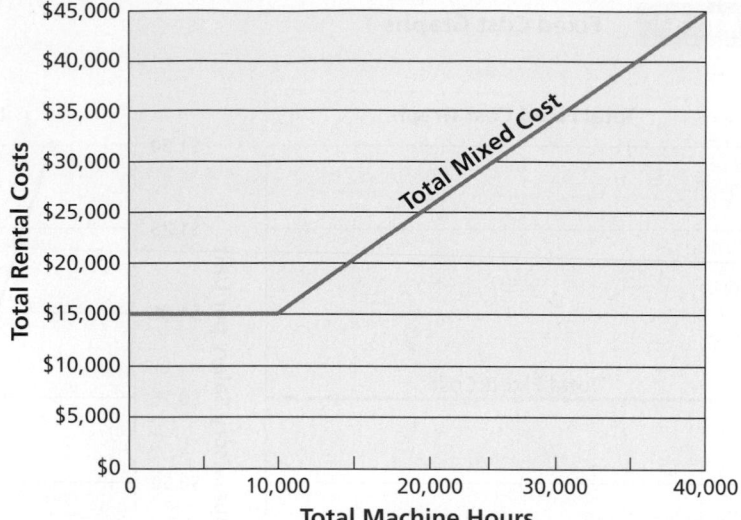

For purposes of analysis, mixed costs are usually separated into their fixed and variable components. The **high-low method** is a cost estimation method that may be used for this purpose.[1] The high-low method uses the highest and lowest activity levels and their related costs to estimate the variable cost per unit and the fixed cost.

To illustrate, assume that the Equipment Maintenance Department of Kason Inc. incurred the following costs during the past five months:

| | Units Produced | Total Cost |
|---|---|---|
| June | 1,000 units | $45,550 |
| July | 1,500 | 52,000 |
| August | 2,100 | 61,500 |
| September | 1,800 | 57,500 |
| October | 750 | 41,250 |

The number of units produced is the activity base, and the relevant range is the units produced between June and October. For Kason, the difference between the units produced and the total costs at the highest and lowest levels of production are as follows:

| | Units Produced | Total Cost |
|---|---|---|
| Highest level | 2,100 units | $61,500 |
| Lowest level | 750 | 41,250 |
| Difference | 1,350 units | $20,250 |

The total fixed cost does not change with changes in production. Thus, the $20,250 difference in the total cost is the change in the total variable cost. Dividing this difference of $20,250 by the difference in production is an estimate of the variable cost per unit. For Kason, this estimate is $15, computed as follows:

$$\text{Variable Cost per Unit} = \frac{\text{Difference in Total Cost}}{\text{Difference in Units Produced}}$$

$$= \frac{\$20,250}{1,350 \text{ units}} = \$15 \text{ per unit}$$

The fixed cost is estimated by subtracting the total variable costs from the total costs for the units produced, as follows:

$$\text{Fixed Cost} = \text{Total Costs} - (\text{Variable Cost per Unit} \times \text{Units Produced})$$

[1] Other methods of estimating costs, such as the scattergraph method and the least squares method, are discussed in cost accounting textbooks.

The fixed cost is the same at the highest and the lowest levels of production, as follows for Kason:

Highest level (2,100 units)

Fixed Cost = Total Costs – (Variable Cost per Unit × Units Produced)
= $61,500 – ($15 × 2,100 units)
= $61,500 – $31,500
= $30,000

Lowest level (750 units)

Fixed Cost = Total Costs – (Variable Cost per Unit × Units Produced)
= $41,250 – ($15 × 750 units)
= $41,250 – $11,250
= $30,000

Using the variable cost per unit and the fixed cost, the total equipment maintenance cost for Kason can be computed for various levels of production as follows:

Total Cost = (Variable Cost per Unit × Units Produced) + Fixed Costs
= ($15 × Units Produced) + $30,000

To illustrate, the estimated total cost of 2,000 units of production is $60,000, computed as follows:

Total Cost = ($15 × Units Produced) + $30,000
= ($15 × 2,000 units) + $30,000 = $30,000 + $30,000
= $60,000

## Example Exercise 21-1  High-Low Method

**OBJ 1**

The manufacturing costs of Alex Industries for the first three months of the year follow:

|  | Total Cost | Production |
|---|---|---|
| January | $ 80,000 | 1,000 units |
| February | 125,000 | 2,500 |
| March | 100,000 | 1,800 |

Using the high-low method, determine (a) the variable cost per unit and (b) the total fixed cost.

## Follow My Example 21-1

a.  $30 per unit = ($125,000 – $80,000) ÷ (2,500 – 1,000)
b.  $50,000 = $125,000 – ($30 × 2,500), or $80,000 – ($30 × 1,000)

Practice Exercises: PE 21-1A, PE 21-1B

## Summary of Cost Behavior Concepts

The cost behavior of variable costs and fixed costs is summarized in Exhibit 6.

| | Effect of Changing Activity Level | |
|---|---|---|
| **Cost** | **Total Amount** | **Per-Unit Amount** |
| Variable | Increases and decreases proportionately with activity level. | Remains the same regardless of activity level. |
| Fixed | Remains the same regardless of activity level. | Increases and decreases inversely with activity level. |

**EXHIBIT 6**

**Variable and Fixed Cost Behavior**

Mixed costs contain a fixed cost component that is incurred even if nothing is produced. For analysis, the fixed and variable cost components of mixed costs are separated using the high-low method.

Exhibit 7 provides some examples of variable, fixed, and mixed costs for the activity base of *units produced*.

| **EXHIBIT 7** | Variable Costs | Fixed Costs | Mixed Costs |
|---|---|---|---|
| **Variable, Fixed, and Mixed Cost** | • Direct materials | • Straight-line depreciation | • Quality Control Department salaries |
| | • Direct labor | • Property taxes | • Purchasing Department salaries |
| | • Electricity expense | • Production supervisor salaries | • Maintenance expenses |
| | • Supplies | • Insurance expense | • Warehouse expenses |

One method of reporting variable and fixed costs is called **variable costing** or *direct costing*. Under variable costing, only the variable manufacturing costs (direct materials, direct labor, and variable factory overhead) are included in the product cost. The fixed factory overhead is treated as an expense of the period in which it is incurred. Variable costing is described and illustrated in the appendix to this chapter.

# Business ⟩ 🌍 ⟨ Connection

## FRANCHISING

Many restaurant chains such as McDonald's, Wendy's, Dunkin' Donuts, and Fatburger operate as franchises. In a franchise, the restaurant chain (called the *franchisor*) sells the right to sell products using its trademark or brand name to a franchisee. The franchisee typically pays an initial franchise fee, which is a fixed cost. In addition,

the franchisee must normally make royalty payments to the franchisor based on a percentage of sales revenues, which is a variable cost. Prior to signing a franchise agreement, most franchisees conduct a break-even analysis to determine how much sales volume their franchise must generate to earn a profit. For example, McDonald's franchises require an initial investment of more than $500,000 and typically take several years to break even.

Source: B. Beshel, *An Introduction to Franchising*, IFA Educational Foundation, 2000.

**OBJ 2** Compute the contribution margin, the contribution margin ratio, and the unit contribution margin.

# Cost-Volume-Profit Relationships

**Cost-volume-profit analysis** is the examination of the relationships among selling prices, sales and production volume, costs, expenses, and profits. Cost-volume-profit analysis is useful for managerial decision making. Some of the ways cost-volume-profit analysis may be used include the following:

- Analyzing the effects of changes in selling prices on profits
- Analyzing the effects of changes in costs on profits
- Analyzing the effects of changes in volume on profits
- Setting selling prices
- Selecting the mix of products to sell
- Choosing among marketing strategies

## Contribution Margin

Contribution margin is especially useful because it provides insight into the profit potential of a company. **Contribution margin** is the excess of sales over variable costs, computed as follows:

$$\text{Contribution Margin} = \text{Sales} - \text{Variable Costs}$$

To illustrate, assume the following data for Lambert Inc.:

| | |
|---|---|
| Sales | 50,000 units |
| Sales price per unit | $20 per unit |
| Variable cost per unit | $12 per unit |
| Fixed costs | $300,000 |

Exhibit 8 illustrates an income statement for Lambert prepared in a contribution margin format.

**EXHIBIT 8**

**Contribution Margin Income Statement Format**

| | |
|---|---:|
| Sales (50,000 units × $20) | $1,000,000 |
| Variable costs (50,000 units × $12) | 600,000 |
| Contribution margin (50,000 units × $8) | $ 400,000 |
| Fixed costs | 300,000 |
| Income from operations | $ 100,000 |

Lambert's contribution margin of $400,000 is available to cover the fixed costs of $300,000. Once the fixed costs are covered, any additional contribution margin increases income from operations.

## Contribution Margin Ratio

Contribution margin can also be expressed as a percentage. The **contribution margin ratio**, sometimes called the *profit-volume ratio*, indicates the percentage of each sales dollar available to cover fixed costs and to provide income from operations. The contribution margin ratio is computed as follows:

$$\text{Contribution Margin Ratio} = \frac{\text{Contribution Margin}}{\text{Sales}}$$

The contribution margin ratio is 40% for Lambert Inc., computed as follows:

$$\text{Contribution Margin Ratio} = \frac{\$400,000}{\$1,000,000} = 40\%$$

The contribution margin ratio is most useful when the increase or decrease in sales volume is measured in sales *dollars*. In this case, the change in sales dollars multiplied by the contribution margin ratio equals the change in income from operations, computed as follows:

Change in Income from Operations = Change in Sales Dollars × Contribution Margin Ratio

To illustrate, if Lambert adds $80,000 in sales from the sale of an additional 4,000 units, its income from operations will increase by $32,000, computed as follows:

Change in Income from Operations = Change in Sales Dollars × Contribution Margin Ratio
Change in Income from Operations = $80,000 × 40% = $32,000

The preceding analysis is confirmed by the contribution margin income statement of Lambert that follows:

| | |
|---|---:|
| Sales (54,000 units × $20) | $1,080,000 |
| Variable costs (54,000 units × $12) | 648,000* |
| Contribution margin (54,000 units × $8) | $ 432,000** |
| Fixed costs | 300,000 |
| Income from operations | $ 132,000 |

*$1,080,000 × 60%
**$1,080,000 × 40%

A room night at **Hilton Hotels** has a high contribution margin. The high contribution margin per room night is necessary to cover the high fixed costs of the hotel.

Income from operations increased from $100,000 to $132,000 when sales increased from $1,000,000 to $1,080,000. Variable costs as a percentage of sales are equal to 100% minus the contribution margin ratio. Thus, in the preceding income statement, the variable costs are 60% (100% – 40%) of sales, or $648,000 ($1,080,000 × 60%). The total contribution margin, $432,000, can also be computed directly by multiplying the total sales by the contribution margin ratio ($1,080,000 × 40%).

In the preceding analysis, factors other than sales volume, such as variable cost per unit and sales price, are assumed to remain constant. If such factors change, their effect must also be considered.

The contribution margin ratio is also useful in developing business strategies. For example, assume that a company has a high contribution margin ratio and is producing below 100% of capacity. In this case, a large increase in income from operations can be expected from an increase in sales volume. Therefore, the company might consider implementing a special sales campaign to increase sales. In contrast, a company with a small contribution margin ratio will probably want to give more attention to reducing costs before attempting to promote sales.

## Unit Contribution Margin

The unit contribution margin is also useful for analyzing the profit potential of proposed decisions. The **unit contribution margin** is computed as follows:

Unit Contribution Margin = Sales Price per Unit – Variable Cost per Unit

To illustrate, if Lambert Inc.'s unit selling price is $20 and its variable cost per unit is $12, the unit contribution margin is $8, computed as follows:

Unit Contribution Margin = Sales Price per Unit – Variable Cost per Unit
Unit Contribution Margin = $20 – $12 = $8

The unit contribution margin is most useful when the increase or decrease in sales volume is measured in sales *units* (quantities). In this case, the change in sales volume (units) multiplied by the unit contribution margin equals the change in income from operations, computed as follows:

Change in Income from Operations = Change in Sales Units × Unit Contribution Margin

To illustrate, assume that Lambert's sales could be increased by 15,000 units, from 50,000 units to 65,000 units. Lambert's income from operations would increase by $120,000 (15,000 units × $8), computed as follows:

Change in Income from Operations = Change in Sales Units × Unit Contribution Margin
Change in Income from Operations = 15,000 units × $8 = $120,000

The preceding analysis is confirmed by the contribution margin income statement of Lambert that follows, which shows that income increased to $220,000 when 65,000 units are sold. The income statement in Exhibit 8 indicates income of $100,000 when 50,000 units are sold. Thus, selling an additional 15,000 units increases income by $120,000 ($220,000 – $100,000).

| | |
|---|---:|
| Sales (65,000 units × $20) | $1,300,000 |
| Variable costs (65,000 units × $12) | 780,000 |
| Contribution margin (65,000 units × $8) | $ 520,000 |
| Fixed costs | 300,000 |
| Income from operations | $ 220,000 |

Unit contribution margin analysis is useful information for managers. For example, in the preceding illustration, Lambert could spend up to $120,000 for special advertising or other product promotions to increase sales by 15,000 units and still increase income by $100,000, the $220,000 increase in sales minus the $120,000 cost of special advertising.

**Example Exercise 21-2** **Contribution Margin**

Molly Company sells 20,000 units at $12 per unit. Variable costs are $9 per unit, and fixed costs are $25,000. Determine the (a) contribution margin ratio, (b) unit contribution margin, and (c) income from operations.

**Follow My Example 21-2**

a.  25% = ($12 – $9) ÷ $12, or ($240,000 – $180,000) ÷ $240,000
b.  $3 per unit = $12 – $9
c.

| | | |
|---|---|---|
| Sales | $240,000 | (20,000 units × $12 per unit) |
| Variable costs | 180,000 | (20,000 units × $9 per unit) |
| Contribution margin | $ 60,000 | [20,000 units × ($12 – $9)] |
| Fixed costs | 25,000 | |
| Income from operations | $ 35,000 | |

Practice Exercises: PE 21-2A, PE 21-2B

# Mathematical Approach to Cost-Volume-Profit Analysis

**OBJ 3** Determine the break-even point and sales necessary to achieve a target profit.

The mathematical approach to cost-volume-profit analysis uses equations to determine the following:

• Sales necessary to break even
• Sales necessary to make a target or desired profit

## Break-Even Point

The **break-even point** is the level of operations at which a company's revenues and expenses are equal, as shown in Exhibit 9. At break-even, a company reports neither income nor a loss from operations.

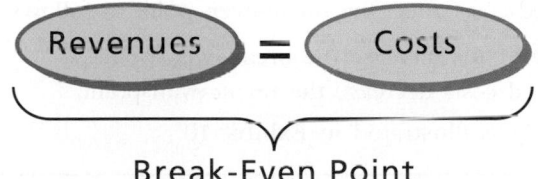

Break-Even Point

**EXHIBIT 9**

**Break-Even Point**

The break-even point in *sales units* is computed as follows:

$$\text{Break-Even Sales (units)} = \frac{\text{Fixed Costs}}{\text{Unit Contribution Margin}}$$

To illustrate, assume the following data for Baker Corporation:

| | |
|---|---|
| Fixed costs | $90,000 |
| Unit selling price | $25 |
| Unit variable cost | 15 |
| Unit contribution margin | $10 |

The break-even point for Baker is 9,000 units, computed as follows:

$$\text{Break-Even Sales (units)} = \frac{\text{Fixed Costs}}{\text{Unit Contribution Margin}} = \frac{\$90,000}{\$10} = 9,000 \text{ units}$$

The following income statement for Baker verifies the break-even point of 9,000 units:

| | |
|---|---|
| Sales (9,000 units × $25) | $225,000 |
| Variable costs (9,000 units × $15) | 135,000 |
| Contribution margin | $ 90,000 |
| Fixed costs | 90,000 |
| Income from operations | $ 0 |

As shown in Baker's income statement, the break-even point is $225,000 (9,000 units × $25) of sales. The break-even point in *sales dollars* can be determined directly as follows:

$$\text{Break-Even Sales (dollars)} = \frac{\text{Fixed Costs}}{\text{Contribution Margin Ratio}}$$

The contribution margin ratio can be computed using the unit contribution margin and unit selling price as follows:

$$\text{Contribution Margin Ratio} = \frac{\text{Unit Contribution Margin}}{\text{Unit Selling Price}}$$

The contribution margin ratio for Baker is 40%, computed as follows:

$$\text{Contribution Margin Ratio} = \frac{\text{Unit Contribution Margin}}{\text{Unit Selling Price}} = \frac{\$10}{\$25} = 40\%$$

Thus, the break-even sales dollars for Baker of $225,000 can be computed directly as follows:

$$\text{Break-Even Sales (dollars)} = \frac{\text{Fixed Costs}}{\text{Contribution Margin Ratio}} = \frac{\$90,000}{40\%} = \$225,000$$

The break-even point is affected by changes in the fixed costs, unit variable costs, and the unit selling price.

### Effect of Changes in Fixed Costs
Fixed costs do not change in total with changes in the level of activity. However, fixed costs may change because of other factors such as advertising campaigns, changes in property tax rates, or changes in factory supervisors' salaries.

Changes in fixed costs affect the break-even point as follows:

- Increases in fixed costs increase the break-even point.
- Decreases in fixed costs decrease the break-even point.

This relationship is illustrated in Exhibit 10.

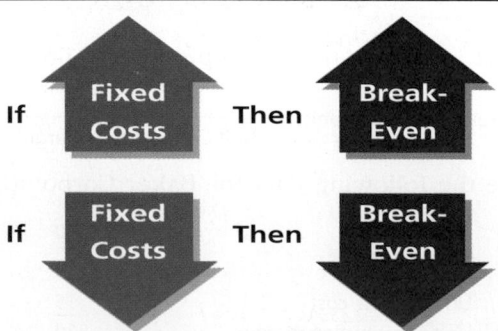

To illustrate, assume that Bishop Co. is evaluating a proposal to budget an additional $100,000 for advertising. The data for Bishop follows:

| | Current | Proposed |
|---|---|---|
| Unit selling price | $90 | $90 |
| Unit variable cost | 70 | 70 |
| Unit contribution margin | $20 | $20 |
| | | |
| Fixed costs | $600,000 | $700,000 |

Bishop's break-even point *before* the additional advertising expense of $100,000 is 30,000 units, computed as follows:

$$\text{Break-Even Sales (units)} = \frac{\text{Fixed Costs}}{\text{Unit Contribution Margin}} = \frac{\$600,000}{\$20} = 30,000 \text{ units}$$

Bishop's break-even point *after* the additional advertising expense of $100,000 is 35,000 units, computed as follows:

$$\text{Break-Even Sales (units)} = \frac{\text{Fixed Costs}}{\text{Unit Contribution Margin}} = \frac{\$700,000}{\$20} = 35,000 \text{ units}$$

As shown for Bishop, the $100,000 increase in advertising (fixed costs) requires an additional 5,000 units (35,000 – 30,000) of sales to break even.[2] In other words, an increase in sales of 5,000 units is required in order to generate an additional $100,000 of total contribution margin (5,000 units × $20) to cover the increased fixed costs.

### Effect of Changes in Unit Variable Costs
Unit variable costs do not change with changes in the level of activity. However, unit variable costs may be affected by other factors such as changes in the cost per unit of direct materials, changes in the wage rate for direct labor, or changes in the sales commission paid to salespeople.

Changes in unit variable costs affect the break-even point as follows:

- Increases in unit variable costs increase the break-even point.
- Decreases in unit variable costs decrease the break-even point.

This relationship is illustrated in Exhibit 11.

**EXHIBIT 11**

**Effect of Change in Unit Variable Cost on Break-Even Point**

To illustrate, assume that Park Co. is evaluating a proposal to pay an additional 2% commission on sales to its salespeople as an incentive to increase sales. The data for Park follows:

|  | Current | Proposed |
|---|---|---|
| Unit selling price | $250 | $250 |
| Unit variable cost | 145 | 150* |
| Unit contribution margin | $105 | $100 |
| Fixed costs | $840,000 | $840,000 |

*$150 = $145 + (2% × $250 unit selling price).

Park's break-even point *before* the additional 2% commission is 8,000 units, computed as follows:

$$\text{Break-Even Sales (units)} = \frac{\text{Fixed Costs}}{\text{Unit Contribution Margin}} = \frac{\$840,000}{\$105} = 8,000 \text{ units}$$

[2] The increase of 5,000 units can also be computed by dividing the increase in fixed costs of $100,000 by the unit contribution margin, $20, as follows: 5,000 units = $100,000 ÷ $20.

If the 2% sales commission proposal is adopted, unit variable costs will increase by \$5 (\$250 × 2%), from \$145 to \$150 per unit. This increase in unit variable costs will decrease the unit contribution margin from \$105 to \$100 (\$250 − \$150). Thus, Park's break-even point *after* the additional 2% commission is 8,400 units, computed as follows:

$$\text{Break-Even Sales (units)} = \frac{\text{Fixed Costs}}{\text{Unit Contribution Margin}} = \frac{\$840,000}{\$100} = 8,400 \text{ units}$$

As shown for Park, an additional 400 units of sales will be required in order to break even. This is because if 8,000 units are sold, the new unit contribution margin of \$100 provides only \$800,000 (8,000 units × \$100) of contribution margin. Thus, \$40,000 more contribution margin is necessary to cover the total fixed costs of \$840,000. This additional \$40,000 of contribution margin is provided by selling 400 more units (400 units × \$100).

## Effect of Changes in Unit Selling Price
Changes in the unit selling price affect the unit contribution margin and, thus, the break-even point. Specifically, changes in the unit selling price affect the break-even point as follows:

- Increases in the unit selling price decrease the break-even point.
- Decreases in the unit selling price increase the break-even point.

This relationship is illustrated in Exhibit 12.

**Effect of Change in Unit Selling Price on Break-Even Point**

To illustrate, assume that Graham Co. is evaluating a proposal to increase the unit selling price of its product from \$50 to \$60. The data for Graham follows:

|  | Current | Proposed |
| --- | --- | --- |
| Unit selling price | \$50 | \$60 |
| Unit variable cost | 30 | 30 |
| Unit contribution margin | \$20 | \$30 |
| Fixed costs | \$600,000 | \$600,000 |

Graham's break-even point *before* the price increase is 30,000 units, computed as follows:

$$\text{Break-Even Sales (units)} = \frac{\text{Fixed Costs}}{\text{Unit Contribution Margin}} = \frac{\$600,000}{\$20} = 30,000 \text{ units}$$

The increase of \$10 per unit in the selling price increases the unit contribution margin by \$10. Thus, Graham's break-even point *after* the price increase is 20,000 units, computed as follows:

$$\text{Break-Even Sales (units)} = \frac{\text{Fixed Costs}}{\text{Unit Contribution Margin}} = \frac{\$600,000}{\$30} = 20,000 \text{ units}$$

As shown for Graham, the price increase of $10 increased the unit contribution margin by $10, which decreased the break-even point by 10,000 units (30,000 units – 20,000 units).

## Summary of Effects of Changes on Break-Even Point

The break-even point in sales changes in the same direction as changes in the variable cost per unit and fixed costs. In contrast, the break-even point in sales changes in the opposite direction as changes in the unit selling price. These changes on the break-even point in sales are summarized in Exhibit 13.

| Type of Change | Direction of Change | Effect of Change on Break-Even Sales |
|---|---|---|
| Fixed cost | ↑ ↓ | ↑ ↓ |
| Unit variable cost | ↑ ↓ | ↑ ↓ |
| Unit selling price | ↑ ↓ | ↓ ↑ |

**EXHIBIT 13**

**Effects of Changes in Selling Price and Costs on Break-Even Point.**

---

## Example Exercise 21-3  Break-Even Point

OBJ 3

Nicolas Enterprises sells a product for $60 per unit. The variable cost is $35 per unit, while fixed costs are $80,000. Determine the (a) break-even point in sales units and (b) break-even point in sales units if the selling price were increased to $67 per unit.

### Follow My Example 21-3

a.  3,200 units = $80,000 ÷ ($60 – $35)
b.  2,500 units = $80,000 ÷ ($67 – $35)

Practice Exercises: PE 21-3A, PE 21-3B

---

## Business ⊕ Connection

### BREAKING EVEN IN THE AIRLINE INDUSTRY

Airlines have high fixed costs and operate in a very competitive industry. As a result, many airlines struggle to break even. In the late 2000s, many of the major airlines were unable to break even and filed bankruptcy. After emerging from bankruptcy, several airlines merged in an attempt to reduce their cost structure and become more competitive. As the table shows, airlines like United Airlines, Southwest Airlines, Delta Air Lines, and American Airlines still face challenges in breaking even, as a small change in ticket prices determines whether an airline is able to break even.

| | United | Southwest | Delta | American |
|---|---|---|---|---|
| Average one-way airfare per passenger* | $269.56 | $141.14 | $209.60 | $208.50 |
| Average cost per passenger* | 240.25 | 133.68 | 184.88 | 209.67 |

* Airfare and cost data obtained from AirlineFinancials.com

## Target Profit

At the break-even point, sales and costs are exactly equal. However, the goal of most companies is to make a profit.

By modifying the break-even equation, the sales required to earn a target or desired amount of profit may be computed. For this purpose, target profit is added to the break-even equation, as follows:

$$\text{Sales (units)} = \frac{\text{Fixed Costs} + \text{Target Profit}}{\text{Unit Contribution Margin}}$$

To illustrate, assume the following data for Waltham Co.:

| | |
|---|---:|
| Fixed costs | $200,000 |
| Target profit | 100,000 |
| | |
| Unit selling price | $75 |
| Unit variable cost | 45 |
| Unit contribution margin | $30 |

The sales necessary for Waltham to earn the target profit of $100,000 would be 10,000 units, computed as follows:

$$\text{Sales (units)} = \frac{\text{Fixed Costs} + \text{Target Profit}}{\text{Unit Contribution Margin}} = \frac{\$200,000 + \$100,000}{\$30} = 10,000 \text{ units}$$

The following income statement for Waltham verifies this computation:

| | |
|---|---:|
| Sales (10,000 units × $75) | $750,000 |
| Variable costs (10,000 units × $45) | 450,000 |
| Contribution margin (10,000 units × $30) | $300,000 |
| Fixed costs | 200,000 |
| Income from operations | $100,000 ← Target profit |

As shown in the income statement for Waltham, sales of $750,000 (10,000 units × $75) are necessary to earn the target profit of $100,000. The sales of $750,000 needed to earn the target profit of $100,000 can be computed directly using the contribution margin ratio, computed as follows:

$$\text{Contribution Margin Ratio} = \frac{\text{Unit Contribution Margin}}{\text{Unit Selling Price}} = \frac{\$30}{\$75} = 40\%$$

$$\text{Sales (dollars)} = \frac{\text{Fixed Costs} + \text{Target Profit}}{\text{Contribution Margin Ratio}}$$

$$= \frac{\$200,000 + \$100,000}{40\%} = \frac{\$300,000}{40\%} = \$750,000$$

---

### Example Exercise 21-4   Target Profit

Forest Company sells a product for $140 per unit. The variable cost is $60 per unit, and fixed costs are $240,000. Determine the (a) break-even point in sales units and (b) the sales units required to achieve a target profit of $50,000.

### Follow My Example 21-4

a.   3,000 units = $240,000 ÷ ($140 − $60)
b.   3,625 units = ($240,000 + $50,000) ÷ ($140 − $60)

Practice Exercises: PE 21-4A, PE 21-4B

## Integrity, Objectivity, and Ethics in Business

### ORPHAN DRUGS

Each year, pharmaceutical companies develop new drugs that cure a variety of physical conditions. In order to be profitable, drug companies must sell enough of a product for a reasonable price to exceed break even. Break-even points, however, create a problem for drugs, called "orphan drugs," targeted at rare diseases. These drugs are typically expensive to develop and have low sales volumes, making it impossible to achieve break even. To ensure that orphan drugs are not overlooked, Congress passed the Orphan Drug Act, which provides incentives for pharmaceutical companies to develop drugs for rare diseases that might not generate enough sales to reach break even. The program has been a great success. Since 1982, more than 200 orphan drugs have come to market, including Jacobus Pharmaceuticals Company, Inc.'s drug for the treatment of tuberculosis and Novartis AG's drug for the treatment of Paget's disease.

# Graphic Approach to Cost-Volume-Profit Analysis

**OBJ 4** Using a cost-volume-profit chart and a profit-volume chart, determine the break-even point and sales necessary to achieve a target profit.

Cost-volume-profit analysis can be presented graphically as well as in equation form. Many managers prefer the graphic form because the operating profit or loss for different levels can be easily seen.

## Cost-Volume-Profit (Break-Even) Chart

A **cost-volume-profit chart**, sometimes called a *break-even chart*, graphically shows sales, costs, and the related profit or loss for various levels of units sold. It assists in understanding the relationship among sales, costs, and operating profit or loss.

To illustrate, the cost-volume-profit chart in Exhibit 14 is based on the following data for Munoz Co.:

| | |
|---|---:|
| Total fixed costs | $100,000 |
| Unit selling price | $50 |
| Unit variable cost | 30 |
| Unit contribution margin | $20 |

The cost-volume-profit chart in Exhibit 14 is constructed using the following steps:

- Step 1. Volume in units of sales is indicated along the horizontal axis. The range of volume shown is the relevant range in which the company expects to operate. Dollar amounts of total sales and total costs are indicated along the vertical axis.

- Step 2. A total sales line is plotted by connecting the point at zero on the left corner of the graph to a second point on the chart. The second point is determined by multiplying the maximum number of units in the relevant range, which is found on the far right of the horizontal axis, by the unit sales price. A line is then drawn through both of these points. This is the total sales line. For Munoz, the maximum number of units in the relevant range is 10,000. The second point on the line is determined by multiplying the 10,000 units by the $50 unit selling price to get the second point for the total sales line of $500,000 (10,000 units × $50). The sales line is drawn upward to the right from zero through the $500,000 point at the end of the relevant range.

- Step 3. A total cost line is plotted by beginning with total fixed costs on the vertical axis. A second point is determined by multiplying the maximum number of units in the relevant range, which is found on the far right of the horizontal axis by the unit variable costs and adding the total fixed costs. A line is then drawn through both of these points. This is the total cost line. For Munoz, the maximum number of units in the relevant range is 10,000. The second point on the line is determined by multiplying the 10,000 units by the $30 unit variable cost and then adding the $100,000 total fixed costs to get the second point for the total estimated costs of $400,000 [(10,000 units × $30) + $100,000]. The cost line is drawn upward to the right from $100,000 on the vertical axis through the $400,000 point at the end of the relevant range.

- Step 4. The break-even point is the intersection point of the total sales and total cost lines. A vertical dotted line drawn downward at the intersection point indicates the units of sales at the break-even point. A horizontal dotted line drawn to the left at the intersection point indicates the sales dollars and costs at the break-even point.

---

**EXHIBIT 14**

**Cost-Volume-Profit Chart**

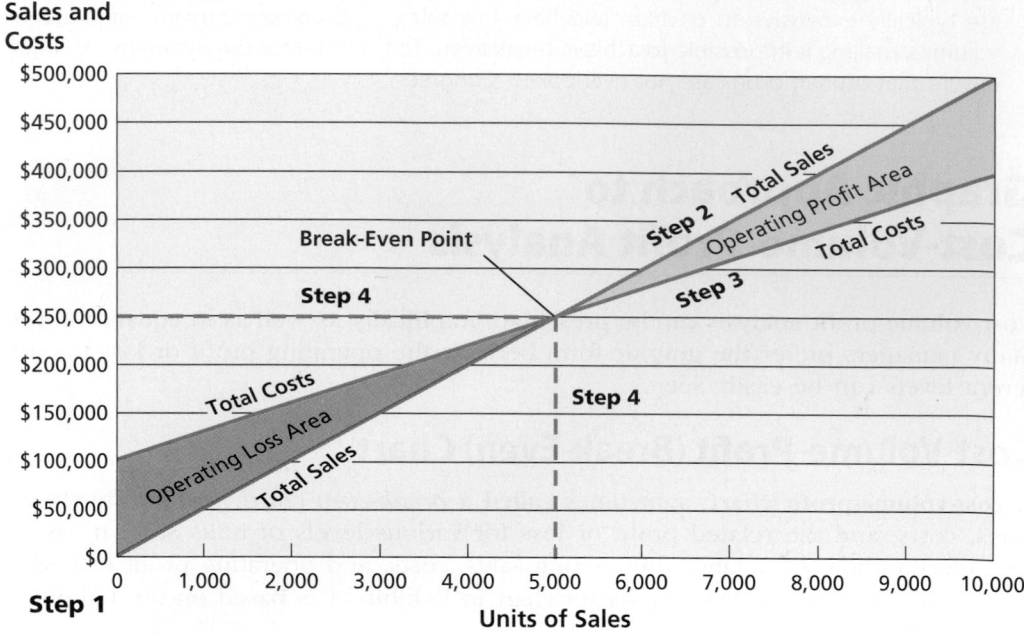

In Exhibit 14, the break-even point for Munoz is $250,000 of sales, which represents sales of 5,000 units. Operating profits will be earned when sales levels are to the right of the break-even point (*operating profit area*). Operating losses will be incurred when sales levels are to the left of the break-even point (*operating loss area*).

Changes in the unit selling price, total fixed costs, and unit variable costs can be analyzed by using a cost-volume-profit chart. Using the data in Exhibit 14, assume that Munoz is evaluating a proposal to reduce fixed costs by $20,000. In this case, the total fixed costs would be $80,000 ($100,000 − $20,000).

Under this scenario, the total sales line is not changed, but the total cost line will change. As shown in Exhibit 15, the total cost line is redrawn, starting at the $80,000 point (total fixed costs) on the vertical axis. The second point is determined by multiplying the maximum number of units in the relevant range, which is found on the far right of the horizontal axis, by the unit variable costs and adding the fixed costs. For Munoz, this is the total estimated cost for 10,000 units, which is $380,000 [(10,000 units × $30) + $80,000]. The cost line is drawn upward to the right from $80,000 on the vertical axis through the $380,000 point. The revised cost-volume-profit chart in Exhibit 15 indicates that the break-even point for Munoz decreases to $200,000 and 4,000 units of sales.

## Profit-Volume Chart

Another graphic approach to cost-volume-profit analysis is the profit-volume chart. The **profit-volume chart** plots only the difference between total sales and total costs (or profits). In this way, the profit-volume chart allows managers to determine the operating profit (or loss) for various levels of units sold.

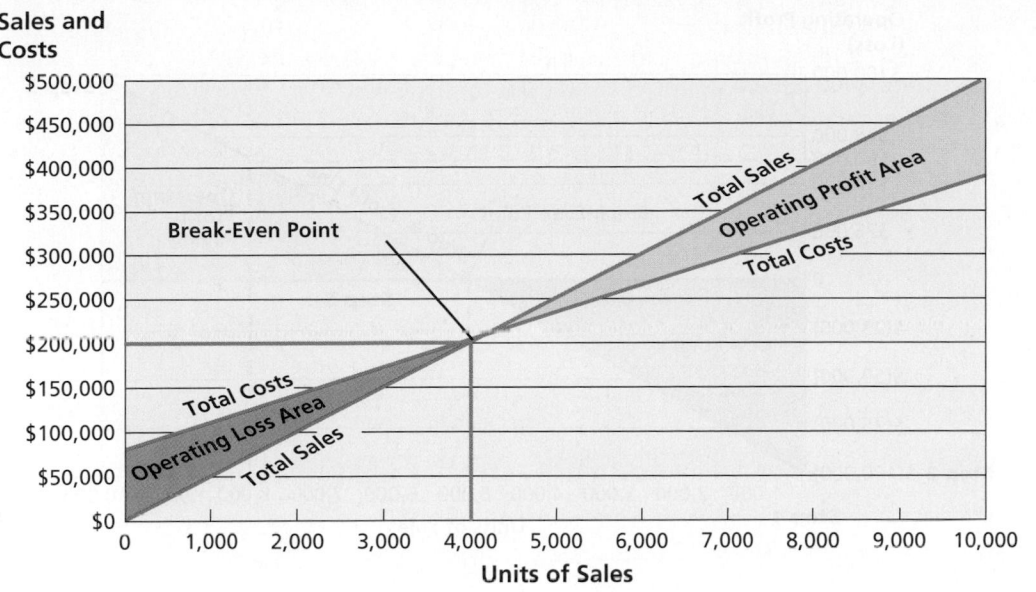

**Revised Cost-Volume-Profit Chart**

To illustrate, the profit-volume chart for Munoz Co. in Exhibit 16 is based on the same data as used in Exhibit 14. These data are as follows:

| | |
|---|---|
| Total fixed costs | $100,000 |
| Unit selling price | $50 |
| Unit variable cost | 30 |
| Unit contribution margin | $20 |

The maximum operating loss is equal to the fixed costs of $100,000. Assuming that the maximum units that can be sold within the relevant range is 10,000 units, the maximum operating profit is $100,000, computed as follows:

| | |
|---|---|
| Sales (10,000 units × $50)............................................................ | $500,000 |
| Variable costs (10,000 units × $30) ............................................... | 300,000 |
| Contribution margin (10,000 units × $20)........................................ | $200,000 |
| Fixed costs ............................................................................ | 100,000 |
| Operating profit........................................................................ | $100,000 ← Maximum profit |

The profit-volume chart in Exhibit 16 is constructed using the following steps:

- Step 1. Volume in units of sales is indicated along the horizontal axis. The range of volume shown is the relevant range in which the company expects to operate. In Exhibit 16, the maximum units of sales is 10,000 units. Dollar amounts indicating operating profits and losses are shown along the vertical axis.
- Step 2. A point representing the maximum operating loss is plotted on the vertical axis at the left. This loss is equal to the total fixed costs at the zero level of sales. Thus, the maximum operating loss is equal to the fixed costs of $100,000.
- Step 3. A point representing the maximum operating profit within the relevant range is plotted on the right. Assuming that the maximum unit sales within the relevant range is 10,000 units, the maximum operating profit is $100,000.
- Step 4. A diagonal profit line is drawn connecting the maximum operating loss point with the maximum operating profit point.
- Step 5. The profit line intersects the horizontal zero operating profit line at the break-even point in units of sales. The area indicating an operating profit is identified to the right of the intersection, and the area indicating an operating loss is identified to the left of the intersection.

**EXHIBIT 16**

**Profit-Volume Chart**

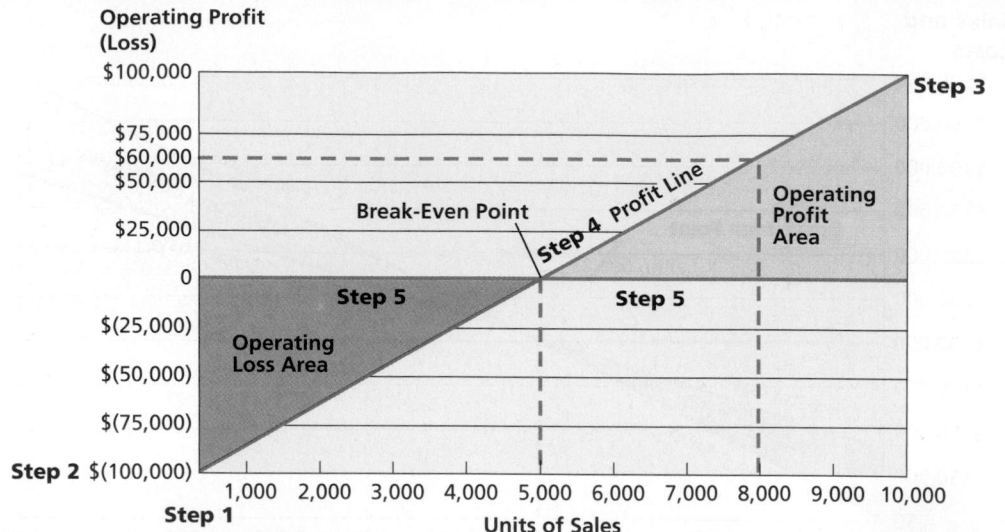

In Exhibit 16, the break-even point for Munoz is 5,000 units of sales, which is equal to total sales of $250,000 (5,000 units × $50). Operating profit will be earned when sales levels are to the right of the break-even point (*operating profit area*). Operating losses will be incurred when sales levels are to the left of the break-even point (*operating loss area*). For example, at sales of 8,000 units, an operating profit of $60,000 will be earned, as shown in Exhibit 16.

The effect of changes in the unit selling price, total fixed costs, and unit variable costs on profit can be analyzed using a profit-volume chart. Using the data in Exhibit 16, consider the effect that a $20,000 increase in fixed costs will have on profit. In this case, the total fixed costs will increase to $120,000 ($100,000 + $20,000), and the maximum operating loss will also increase to $120,000. At the maximum sales of 10,000 units, the maximum operating profit would be $80,000, computed as follows:

| | |
|---|---|
| Sales (10,000 units × $50) | $500,000 |
| Variable costs (10,000 units × $30) | 300,000 |
| Contribution margin (10,000 units × $20) | $200,000 |
| Fixed costs | 120,000 |
| Operating profit | $ 80,000 ← Revised maximum profit |

A revised profit-volume chart is constructed by plotting the maximum operating loss and maximum operating profit points and drawing the revised profit line. The original and the revised profit-volume charts for Munoz are shown in Exhibit 17.

The revised profit-volume chart indicates that the break-even point for Munoz is 6,000 units of sales. This is equal to total sales of $300,000 (6,000 units × $50). The operating loss area of the chart has increased, while the operating profit area has decreased.

## Use of Computers in Cost-Volume-Profit Analysis

With computers, the graphic approach and the mathematical approach to cost-volume-profit analysis are easy to use. Managers can vary assumptions regarding selling prices, costs, and volume and can observe the effects of each change on the break-even point and profit. Such an analysis is called a *"what if"* analysis or *sensitivity* analysis.

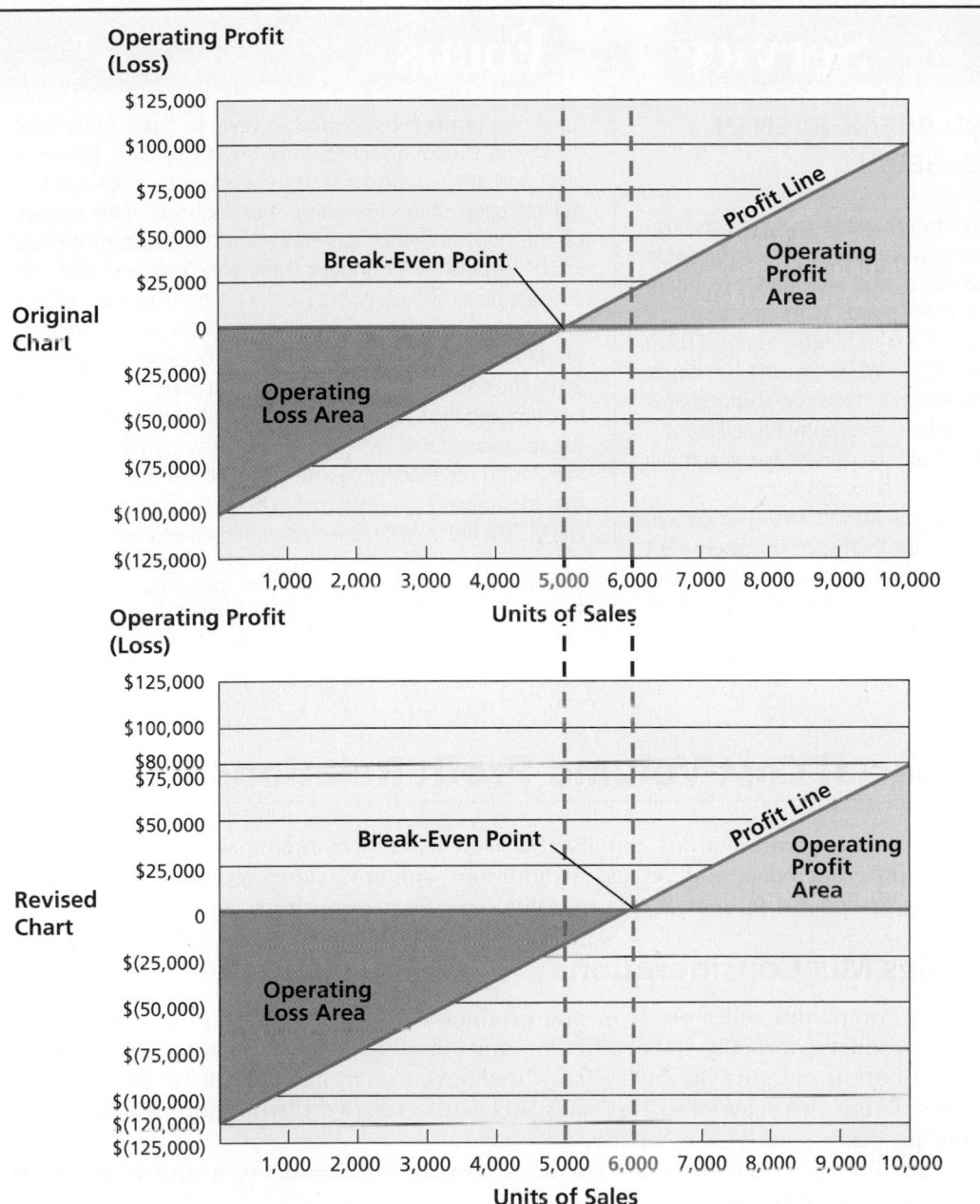

**EXHIBIT 17**

**Original Profit-Volume Chart and Revised Profit-Volume Chart**

## Assumptions of Cost-Volume-Profit Analysis

Cost-volume-profit analysis depends on several assumptions. The primary assumptions are as follows:

- Total sales and total costs can be represented by straight lines.
- Within the relevant range of operating activity, the efficiency of operations does not change.
- Costs can be divided into fixed and variable components.
- The sales mix is constant.
- There is no change in the inventory quantities during the period.

These assumptions simplify cost-volume-profit analysis. Because they are often valid for the relevant range of operations, cost-volume-profit analysis is useful for decision making.[3]

[3] The impact of violating these assumptions is discussed in advanced accounting texts.

## Service 🔔 Focus

### PROFIT, LOSS, AND BREAK-EVEN IN MAJOR LEAGUE BASEBALL

Major League Baseball is a tough game and a tough business. Ticket prices (unit selling price), player salaries (variable costs), stadium fees (fixed costs), and attendance (volume) converge to make it difficult for teams to make a profit, or at least break even. So, which major league baseball team was the most profitable in 2013? Well, it wasn't the World Champion Boston Red Sox. Nor was it the star-studded New York Yankees. Then, it had to be the recently turned around Los Angeles Angels, right? Not even close. It was actually the worst team in baseball—the Houston Astros.

Just how profitable were the Astros? They earned $99 million in 2013, which was more than the combined 2013 profits of the six most recent World Series champions. How could the team with the worst record in baseball since 2005

have one of the most profitable years in baseball history? By paying careful attention to costs and volume. Between 2011 and 2013, the Astros cut their player payroll from $56 million to less than $13 million. That's right, all of the players on the Houston Astros baseball team combined, made less in 2013 than Alex Rodriguez (New York Yankees), Cliff Lee (Philadelphia Phillies), Prince Fielder (Detroit Tigers), and Tim Lincecum (San Francisco Giants) made individually. While attendance at Astros games has dropped by around 20% since 2011, the cost reductions from reduced player salaries have far outpaced the drop in attendance, making the 2013 Astros the most profitable team in baseball history. While no one likes losing baseball games, the Houston Astros have shown that focusing on the relationship between cost and volume can yield a hefty profit, even when they aren't winning.

Source: D. Alexander, "2013 Houston Astros: Baseball's Worst Team Is The Most Profitable In History," *Forbes,* August 26, 2013.

**OBJ 5** Compute the break-even point for a company selling more than one product, the operating leverage, and the margin of safety.

## Special Cost-Volume-Profit Relationships

Cost-volume-profit analysis can also be used when a company sells several products with different costs and prices. In addition, operating leverage and the margin of safety are useful in analyzing cost-volume-profit relationships.

### Sales Mix Considerations

Many companies sell more than one product at different selling prices. In addition, the products normally have different unit variable costs and, thus, different unit contribution margins. In such cases, break-even analysis can still be performed by considering the sales mix. The **sales mix** is the relative distribution of sales among the products sold by a company.

To illustrate, assume that Cascade Company sold Products A and B during the past year, as follows:

| Total fixed costs | $200,000 | |
|---|---|---|
| | **Product A** | **Product B** |
| Unit selling price ................ | $90 | $140 |
| Unit variable cost................ | 70 | 95 |
| Unit contribution margin ........ | $20 | $ 45 |
| Units sold ...................... | 8,000 | 2,000 |
| Sales mix....................... | 80% | 20% |

The sales mix for Products A and B is expressed as a percentage of total units sold. For Cascade, a total of 10,000 (8,000 + 2,000) units were sold during the year. Therefore, the sales mix is 80% (8,000 ÷ 10,000) for Product A and 20% for Product B (2,000 ÷ 10,000), as shown in Exhibit 18. The sales mix could also be expressed as the ratio 80:20.

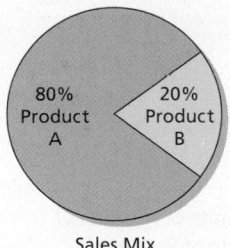

Sales Mix

**EXHIBIT 18**

**Multiple Product Sales Mix**

For break-even analysis, it is useful to think of Products A and B as components of one overall enterprise product called E. The unit selling price of E equals the sum of the unit selling prices of each product multiplied by its sales mix percentage. Likewise, the unit variable cost and unit contribution margin of E equal the sum of the unit variable costs and unit contribution margins of each product multiplied by its sales mix percentage.

For Cascade, the unit selling price, unit variable cost, and unit contribution margin for E are computed as follows:

| Product E | Product A | Product B |
|---|---|---|
| Unit selling price of E | $100 = ($90 × 0.8) | + ($140 × 0.2) |
| Unit variable cost of E | 75 = ($70 × 0.8) | + ($95 × 0.2) |
| Unit contribution margin of E | $ 25 = ($20 × 0.8) | + ($45 × 0.2) |

Cascade has total fixed costs of $200,000. The break-even point of 8,000 units of E can be determined as follows using the unit selling price, unit variable cost, and unit contribution margin of E:

$$\text{Break-Even Sales (units) for E} = \frac{\text{Fixed Costs}}{\text{Unit Contribution Margin}} = \frac{\$200,000}{\$25} = 8,000 \text{ units}$$

Because the sales mix for Products A and B is 80% and 20% respectively, the break-even quantity of A is 6,400 units (8,000 units × 80%) and B is 1,600 units (8,000 units × 20%). The preceding break-even analysis is verified in Exhibit 19.

**EXHIBIT 19**

**Break-Even Sales: Multiple Products**

|  | Product A | Product B | Total |
|---|---|---|---|
| Sales: |  |  |  |
| 6,400 units × $90 | $576,000 |  | $576,000 |
| 1,600 units × $140 |  | $224,000 | 224,000 |
| Total sales | $576,000 | $224,000 | $800,000 |
| Variable costs: |  |  |  |
| 6,400 units × $70 | $448,000 |  | $448,000 |
| 1,600 units × $95 |  | $152,000 | 152,000 |
| Total variable costs | $448,000 | $152,000 | $600,000 |
| Contribution margin | $128,000 | $ 72,000 | $200,000 |
| Fixed costs |  |  | 200,000 |
| Income from operations |  |  | $ 0 |

Break-even point

The effects of changes in the sales mix on the break-even point can be determined by assuming a different sales mix. The break-even point of E can then be recomputed.

## Example Exercise 21-5  Sales Mix and Break-Even Analysis

OBJ 5

Megan Company has fixed costs of $180,000. The unit selling price, variable cost per unit, and contribution margin per unit for the company's two products are as follows:

| Product | Selling Price | Variable Cost per Unit | Contribution Margin per Unit |
|---|---|---|---|
| Q | $160 | $100 | $60 |
| Z | 100 | 80 | 20 |

The sales mix for products Q and Z is 75% and 25%, respectively. Determine the break-even point in units of Q and Z.

*(Continued)*

**Follow My Example 21-5**

Unit selling price of E:     [($160 × 0.75) + ($100 × 0.25)] = $145
Unit variable cost of E:     [($100 × 0.75) + ($80 × 0.25)]  =   95
Unit contribution margin of E:                              $ 50

Break-Even Sales (units) for E = $180,000 ÷ $50 = 3,600 units
Break-Even Sales (units) for Q = 3,600 units of E × 75%  = 2,700 units of Product Q
Break-Even Sales (units) for Z = 3,600 units of E × 25%  = 900 units of Product Z

Practice Exercises: PE 21-5A, PE 21-5B

## Operating Leverage

The relationship between a company's contribution margin and income from operations is measured by **operating leverage**. A company's operating leverage is computed as follows:

$$\text{Operating Leverage} = \frac{\text{Contribution Margin}}{\text{Income from Operations}}$$

The difference between contribution margin and income from operations is fixed costs. Thus, companies with high fixed costs will normally have high operating leverage. Examples of such companies include airline and automotive companies, like Ford Motor Company. Low operating leverage is normal for companies that are labor intensive, such as professional service companies, which have low fixed costs.

To illustrate operating leverage, assume the following data for Jones Inc. and Wilson Inc.:

|  | Jones Inc. | Wilson Inc. |
|---|---|---|
| Sales | $400,000 | $400,000 |
| Variable costs | 300,000 | 300,000 |
| Contribution margin | $100,000 | $100,000 |
| Fixed costs | 80,000 | 50,000 |
| Income from operations | $ 20,000 | $ 50,000 |

As shown, Jones and Wilson have the same sales, the same variable costs, and the same contribution margin. However, Jones has larger fixed costs than Wilson and, thus, a higher operating leverage. The operating leverage for each company is computed as follows:

Jones Inc.

$$\text{Operating Leverage} = \frac{\text{Contribution Margin}}{\text{Income from Operations}} = \frac{\$100,000}{\$20,000} = 5$$

Wilson Inc.

$$\text{Operating Leverage} = \frac{\text{Contribution Margin}}{\text{Income from Operations}} = \frac{\$100,000}{\$50,000} = 2$$

Operating leverage can be used to measure the impact of changes in sales on income from operations. Using operating leverage, the effect of changes in sales on income from operations is computed as follows:

$$\frac{\text{Percent Change in}}{\text{Income from Operations}} = \frac{\text{Percent Change in}}{\text{Sales}} \times \frac{\text{Operating}}{\text{Leverage}}$$

To illustrate, assume that sales increased by 10%, or $40,000 ($400,000 × 10%), for Jones and Wilson. The percent increase in income from operations for Jones and Wilson is computed as follows:

Jones Inc.

$$\frac{\text{Percent Change in}}{\text{Income from Operations}} = \frac{\text{Percent Change in}}{\text{Sales}} \times \frac{\text{Operating}}{\text{Leverage}}$$

$$= 10\% \times 5 = 50\%$$

Wilson Inc.

$$\frac{\text{Percent Change in}}{\text{Income from Operations}} = \frac{\text{Percent Change in}}{\text{Sales}} \times \frac{\text{Operating}}{\text{Leverage}}$$

$$= 10\% \times 2 = 20\%$$

As shown, Jones's income from operations increases by 50%, while Wilson's income from operations increases by only 20%. The validity of this analysis is shown in the following income statements for Jones and Wilson based on the 10% increase in sales:

|  | Jones Inc. | Wilson Inc. |
|---|---|---|
| Sales | $440,000 | $440,000 |
| Variable costs | 330,000 | 330,000 |
| Contribution margin | $110,000 | $110,000 |
| Fixed costs | 80,000 | 50,000 |
| Income from operations | $ 30,000 | $ 60,000 |

The preceding income statements indicate that Jones's income from operations increased from $20,000 to $30,000, a 50% increase ($10,000 ÷ $20,000). In contrast, Wilson's income from operations increased from $50,000 to $60,000, a 20% increase ($10,000 ÷ $50,000).

Because even a small increase in sales will generate a large percentage increase in income from operations, Jones might consider ways to increase sales. Such actions could include special advertising or sales promotions. In contrast, Wilson might consider ways to increase operating leverage by reducing variable costs.

The impact of a change in sales on income from operations for companies with high and low operating leverage is summarized in Exhibit 20.

| Operating Leverage | Percentage Impact on Income from Operations from a Change in Sales |
|---|---|
| High | Large |
| Low | Small |

**EXHIBIT 20**

**Effect of Operating Leverage on Income from Operations**

## Example Exercise 21-6  Operating Leverage

**OBJ 5**

Tucker Company reports the following data:

| | |
|---|---|
| Sales | $750,000 |
| Variable costs | 500,000 |
| Contribution margin | $250,000 |
| Fixed costs | 187,500 |
| Income from operations | $ 62,500 |

Determine Tucker Company's operating leverage.

### Follow My Example 21-6

$$\text{Operating Leverage} = \frac{\text{Contribution Margin}}{\text{Income from Operations}} = \frac{\$250,000}{\$62,500} = 4.0$$

Practice Exercises: PE 21-6A, PE 21-6B

## Margin of Safety

The **margin of safety** indicates the possible decrease in sales that may occur before an operating loss results. Thus, if the margin of safety is low, even a small decline in sales revenue may result in an operating loss.

The margin of safety may be expressed in the following ways:

- Dollars of sales
- Units of sales
- Percent of current sales

To illustrate, assume the following data:

| | |
|---|---|
| Sales | $250,000 |
| Sales at the break-even point | 200,000 |
| Unit selling price | 25 |

The margin of safety in dollars of sales is $50,000 ($250,000 − $200,000). The margin of safety in units is 2,000 units ($50,000 ÷ $25). The margin of safety expressed as a percent of current sales is 20%, computed as follows:

$$\text{Margin of Safety} = \frac{\text{Sales} - \text{Sales at Break-Even Point}}{\text{Sales}}$$

$$= \frac{\$250,000 - \$200,000}{\$250,000} = \frac{\$50,000}{\$250,000} = 20\%$$

Therefore, the current sales may decline $50,000, 2,000 units, or 20% before an operating loss occurs.

### Example Exercise 21-7  Margin of Safety

OBJ 5

Rachel Company has sales of $400,000, and the break-even point in sales dollars is $300,000. Determine the company's margin of safety as a percent of current sales.

### Follow My Example 21-7

$$\text{Margin of Safety} = \frac{\text{Sales} - \text{Sales at Break-Even Point}}{\text{Sales}} = \frac{\$400,000 - \$300,000}{\$400,000} = \frac{\$100,000}{\$400,000} = 25\%$$

Practice Exercises: PE 21-7A, PE 21-7B

# APPENDIX

# Variable Costing

The cost of manufactured products consists of direct materials, direct labor, and factory overhead. The reporting of all these costs in financial statements is called **absorption costing**. Absorption costing is required under generally accepted accounting principles for financial statements distributed to external users. However, alternative reports may be prepared for decision-making purposes by managers and other internal users. One such alternative reporting is *variable costing* or *direct costing*.

In *variable costing*, the cost of goods manufactured is composed only of variable costs. Thus, the cost of goods manufactured consists of direct materials, direct labor, and *variable* factory overhead.

In a variable costing income statement, *fixed* factory overhead costs do not become a part of the cost of goods manufactured. Instead, fixed factory overhead costs are treated as a period expense. The differences between absorption and variable cost of goods manufactured is summarized in Exhibit 21.

| Cost of Goods Manufactured | |
|---|---|
| **Absorption Costing** | **Variable Costing** |
| Direct materials | Direct materials |
| Direct labor | Direct labor |
| Variable factory overhead | Variable factory overhead |
| Fixed factory overhead | |

**EXHIBIT 21**

**Absorption Versus Variable Cost of Goods Manufactured**

The form of a variable costing income statement is as follows:

| | | |
|---|---|---|
| Sales | | $XXX |
| Variable cost of goods sold | | XXX |
| Manufacturing margin | | $XXX |
| Variable selling and administrative expenses | | XXX |
| Contribution margin | | $XXX |
| Fixed costs: | | |
| Fixed manufacturing costs | $XXX | |
| Fixed selling and administrative expenses | XXX | XXX |
| Income from operations | | $XXX |

*Manufacturing margin* is the excess of sales over variable cost of goods sold.

Manufacturing Margin = Sales – Variable Cost of Goods Sold

*Variable cost of goods sold* consists of direct materials, direct labor, and variable factory overhead for the units sold. *Contribution margin* is the excess of manufacturing margin over variable selling and administrative expenses.

Contribution Margin = Manufacturing Margin – Variable Selling and Administrative Expenses

Subtracting fixed costs from contribution margin yields *income from operations*.

Income from Operations = Contribution Margin – Fixed Costs

The variable costing income statement facilitates managerial decision making because manufacturing margin and contribution margin are reported directly. As illustrated in this chapter, contribution margin is used in break-even analysis and other analyses.

To illustrate the variable costing income statement, assume that Martinez Co. manufactures 15,000 units, which are sold at a price of $50. The related costs and expenses for Martinez are as follows:

| | Total Cost | Number of Units | Unit Cost |
|---|---|---|---|
| Manufacturing costs: | | | |
| Variable......................................... | $375,000 | 15,000 | $25 |
| Fixed ........................................... | 150,000 | 15,000 | 10 |
| Total......................................... | $525,000 | | $35 |
| | | | |
| Selling and administrative expenses: | | | |
| Variable ($5 per unit sold) ........................ | $ 75,000 | | |
| Fixed ........................................... | 50,000 | | |
| Total......................................... | $125,000 | | |

Exhibit 22 shows the variable costing income statement prepared for Martinez. The computations are shown in parentheses.

| EXHIBIT 22 | | | |
|---|---|---|---|
| **Variable Costing Income Statement** | Sales (15,000 × $50) .................................................. | | $750,000 |
| | Variable cost of goods sold (15,000 × $25)........................... | | 375,000 |
| | Manufacturing margin ................................................ | | $375,000 |
| | Variable selling and administrative expenses (15,000 × $5).......... | | 75,000 |
| | Contribution margin .................................................. | | $300,000 |
| | Fixed costs: | | |
| |     Fixed manufacturing costs ...................................... | $150,000 | |
| |     Fixed selling and administrative expenses ...................... | 50,000 | 200,000 |
| | Income from operations .............................................. | | $100,000 |

Exhibit 23 illustrates the absorption costing income statement prepared for Martinez. The absorption costing income statement does not distinguish between variable and fixed costs. All manufacturing costs are included in the cost of goods sold. Deducting the cost of goods sold from sales yields the *gross profit*. Deducting the selling and administrative expenses from gross profit yields the *income from operations*.

| EXHIBIT 23 | | |
|---|---|---|
| **Absorption Costing Income Statement** | Sales (15,000 × $50) ................................................. | $750,000 |
| | Cost of goods sold (15,000 × $35) ................................... | 525,000 |
| | Gross profit ......................................................... | $225,000 |
| | Selling and administrative expenses ($75,000 + $50,000) ............ | 125,000 |
| | Income from operations .............................................. | $100,000 |

The relationship between variable and absorption costing *income from operations* is summarized in Exhibit 24.

**EXHIBIT 24**   **Relationship Between Variable and Absorption Costing Income**

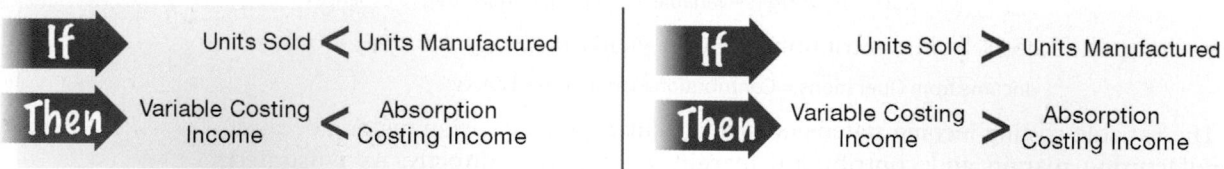

In Exhibits 22 and 23, Martinez manufactured and sold 15,000 units. Thus, the variable and absorption costing income statements reported the same income from operations of $100,000. However, assume that only 12,000 units of the 15,000 units Martinez manufactured were sold. Exhibit 25 shows the related variable and absorption costing income statements.

Exhibit 25 shows a $30,000 ($70,000 – $40,000) difference in income from operations. This difference is due to the fixed manufacturing costs. All of the $150,000 of fixed manufacturing costs is included as a period expense in the variable costing statement. However, the 3,000 units of ending inventory in the absorption costing statement include $30,000 (3,000 units × $10) of fixed manufacturing costs. By being included in inventory, this $30,000 is thus excluded from the current cost of goods sold. Thus, the absorption costing income from operations is $30,000 higher than the income from operations for variable costing.

A similar analysis could be used to illustrate that income from operations under variable costing is greater than income from operations under absorption costing when the units manufactured are less than the units sold.

Under absorption costing, increases or decreases in income from operations can result from changes in inventory levels. For example, for Martinez, a 3,000 increase in ending inventory created a $30,000 increase in income from operations under absorption

**EXHIBIT 25**

**Units Manufactured Exceed Units Sold**

**Variable Costing Income Statement**

| | | |
|---|---:|---:|
| Sales (12,000 × $50) | | $600,000 |
| Variable cost of goods sold: | | |
| Variable cost of goods manufactured (15,000 × $25) | $375,000 | |
| Less ending inventory (3,000 × $25) | 75,000 | |
| Variable cost of goods sold | | 300,000 |
| Manufacturing margin | | $300,000 |
| Variable selling and administrative expenses (12,000 × $5) | | 60,000 |
| Contribution margin | | $240,000 |
| Fixed costs: | | |
| Fixed manufacturing costs | $150,000 | |
| Fixed selling and administrative expenses | 50,000 | 200,000 |
| Income from operations | | $ 40,000 |

**Absorption Costing Income Statement**

| | | |
|---|---:|---:|
| Sales (12,000 × $50) | | $600,000 |
| Cost of goods sold: | | |
| Cost of goods manufactured (15,000 × $35) | $525,000 | |
| Less ending inventory (3,000 × $35) | 105,000 | |
| Cost of goods sold | | 420,000 |
| Gross profit | | $180,000 |
| Selling and administrative expenses [(12,000 × $5) + $50,000] | | 110,000 |
| Income from operations | | $ 70,000 |

costing. Such increases (decreases) could be misinterpreted by managers using absorption costing as operating efficiencies (inefficiencies). This is one of the reasons that variable costing is often used by managers for cost control, product pricing, and production planning. Such uses of variable costing are discussed in advanced accounting texts.

# At a Glance 21

**OBJ 1**

**Classify costs as variable costs, fixed costs, or mixed costs.**

**Key Points**    Variable costs vary in proportion to changes in the level of activity. Fixed costs remain the same in total dollar amount as the level of activity changes. Mixed costs are comprised of both fixed and variable costs.

| Learning Outcomes | Example Exercises | Practice Exercises |
|---|:---:|:---:|
| • Describe variable costs. | | |
| • Describe fixed costs. | | |
| • Describe mixed costs. | | |
| • Separate mixed costs, using the high-low method. | EE21-1 | PE21-1A, 21-1B |

**Compute the contribution margin, the contribution margin ratio, and the unit contribution margin.**

**Key Points** Contribution margin is the excess of sales revenue over variable costs and can be expressed as a ratio (contribution margin ratio) or a dollar amount (unit contribution margin).

| Learning Outcomes | Example Exercises | Practice Exercises |
|---|---|---|
| • Describe the contribution margin. | | |
| • Compute the contribution margin ratio. | EE21-2 | PE21-2A, 21-2B |
| • Compute the unit contribution margin. | EE21-2 | PE21-2A, 21-2B |

**Determine the break-even point and sales necessary to achieve a target profit.**

**Key Points** The break-even point is the point at which a business's revenues exactly equal costs. The mathematical approach to cost-volume-profit analysis uses the unit contribution margin concept and mathematical equations to determine the break-even point and the volume necessary to achieve a target profit.

| Learning Outcomes | Example Exercises | Practice Exercises |
|---|---|---|
| • Compute the break-even point in units. | EE21-3 | PE21-3A, 21-3B |
| • Describe how changes in fixed costs affect the break-even point. | | |
| • Describe how changes in unit variable costs affect the break-even point. | | |
| • Describe how a change in the unit selling price affects the break-even point. | EE21-3 | PE21-3A, 21-3B |
| • Modify the break-even equation to compute the unit sales required to earn a target profit. | EE21-4 | PE21-4A, 21-4B |

**Using a cost-volume-profit chart and a profit-volume chart, determine the break-even point and sales necessary to achieve a target profit.**

**Key Points** Graphical methods can be used to determine the break-even point and the volume necessary to achieve a target profit. A cost-volume-profit chart focuses on the relationship among costs, sales, and operating profit or loss. The profit-volume chart focuses on profits rather than on revenues and costs.

| Learning Outcomes | Example Exercises | Practice Exercises |
|---|---|---|
| • Describe how to construct a cost-volume-profit chart. | | |
| • Determine the break-even point, using a cost-volume-profit chart. | | |
| • Describe how to construct a profit-volume chart. | | |
| • Determine the break-even point, using a profit-volume chart. | | |
| • Describe factors affecting the reliability of cost-volume-profit analysis. | | |

**OBJ 5**

**Compute the break-even point for a company selling more than one product, the operating leverage, and the margin of safety.**

**Key Points**   Cost-volume-profit relationships can be used for analyzing (1) sales mix, (2) operating leverage, and (3) margin of safety.

| Learning Outcomes | Example Exercises | Practice Exercises |
|---|---|---|
| • Compute the break-even point for a mix of products. | **EE21-5** | **PE21-5A, 21-5B** |
| • Compute operating leverage. | **EE21-6** | **PE21-6A, 21-6B** |
| • Compute the margin of safety. | **EE21-7** | **PE21-7A, 21-7B** |

# Key Terms

absorption costing (1004)
activity bases (drivers) (980)
break-even point (989)
contribution margin (986)
contribution margin
  ratio (987)
cost behavior (980)

cost-volume-profit
  analysis (986)
cost-volume-profit chart (995)
fixed costs (982)
high-low method (984)
margin of safety (1004)
mixed costs (982)

operating leverage (1002)
profit-volume chart (996)
relevant range (980)
sales mix (1000)
unit contribution margin (988)
variable costing (986)
variable costs (981)

# Illustrative Problem

Wyatt Inc. expects to maintain the same inventories at the end of the year as at the beginning of the year. The estimated fixed costs for the year are $288,000, and the estimated variable costs per unit are $14. It is expected that 60,000 units will be sold at a price of $20 per unit. Maximum sales within the relevant range are 70,000 units.

### Instructions

1.  What is (a) the contribution margin ratio and (b) the unit contribution margin?

2.  Determine the break-even point in units.

3.  Construct a cost-volume-profit chart, indicating the break-even point.

4.  Construct a profit-volume chart, indicating the break-even point.

5.  What is the margin of safety?

### Solution

1.  a.   $\text{Contribution Margin Ratio} = \dfrac{\text{Sales} - \text{Variable Costs}}{\text{Sales}}$

$$= \frac{(60{,}000 \text{ units} \times \$20) - (60{,}000 \text{ units} \times \$14)}{(60{,}000 \text{ units} \times \$20)}$$

$$= \frac{\$1,200,000 - \$840,000}{\$1,200,000} = \frac{\$360,000}{\$1,200,000}$$

$$= 30\%$$

    b.  Unit Contribution Margin = Unit Selling Price − Unit Variable Costs

$$= \$20 - \$14 = \$6$$

2.  Break-Even Sales (units) = $\dfrac{\text{Fixed Costs}}{\text{Unit Contribution Margin}}$

$$= \frac{\$288,000}{\$6} = 48,000 \text{ units}$$

3.  **Sales and Costs**

4.  **Operating Profit (Loss)**

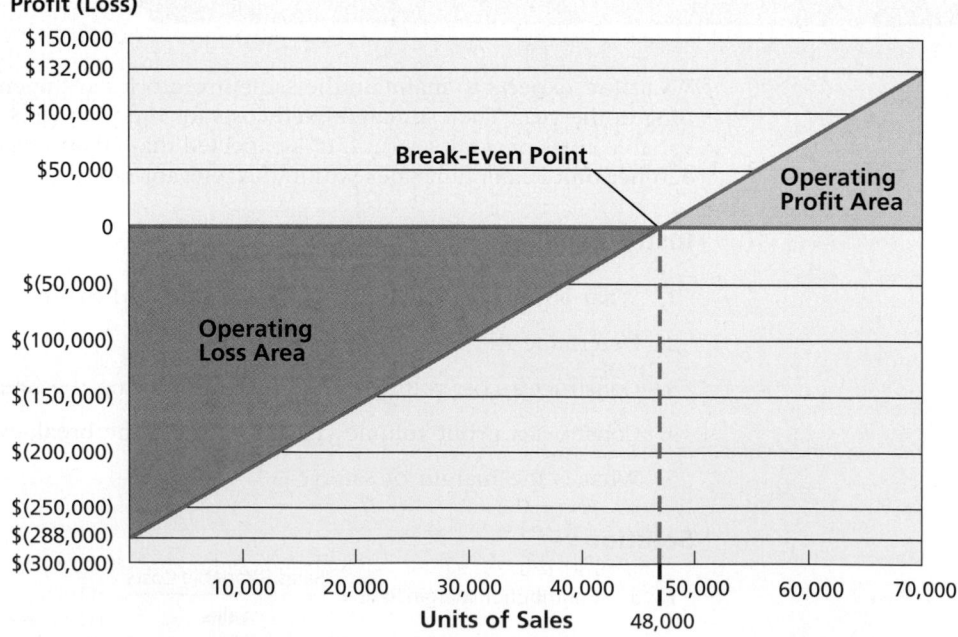

5. Margin of safety:

| | |
|---|---|
| Expected sales (60,000 units × $20) | $1,200,000 |
| Break-even point (48,000 units × $20) | 960,000 |
| Margin of safety | $ 240,000 |

or

$$\text{Margin of Safety (units)} = \frac{\text{Margin of Safety (dollars)}}{\text{Unit Selling Price}}$$

or

12,000 units ($240,000 ÷ $20)

or

$$\text{Margin of Safety} = \frac{\text{Sales} - \text{Sales at Break-Even Point}}{\text{Sales}}$$

$$= \frac{\$240,000}{\$1,200,000} = 20\%$$

# Discussion Questions

1. Describe how total variable costs and unit variable costs behave with changes in the level of activity.

2. Which of the following costs would be classified as variable and which would be classified as fixed, if units produced is the activity base?

   a. Direct materials costs

   b. Electricity costs of $0.35 per kilowatt-hour

3. Describe how total fixed costs and unit fixed costs behave with changes in the level of activity.

4. In applying the high-low method of cost estimation to mixed costs, how is the total fixed cost estimated?

5. If fixed costs increase, what would be the impact on the (a) contribution margin? (b) income from operations?

6. An examination of the accounting records of Clowney Company disclosed a high contribution margin ratio and production at a level below maximum capacity. Based on this information, suggest a likely means of improving income from operations. Explain.

7. If the unit cost of direct materials is decreased, what effect will this change have on the break-even point?

8. Both Austin Company and Hill Company had the same unit sales, total costs, and income from operations for the current fiscal year; yet, Austin Company had a lower break-even point than Hill Company. Explain the reason for this difference in break-even points.

9. How does the sales mix affect the calculation of the break-even point?

10. What does operating leverage measure, and how is it computed?

# Practice Exercises

EE 21-1 *p. 985*   **PE 21-1A   High-low method**                                                    **OBJ. 1**

The manufacturing costs of Lightfoot Industries for three months of the year follow:

SHOW
ME HOW

| | Total Costs | Units Produced |
|---|---|---|
| January | $640,000 | 30,000 units |
| February | 900,000 | 40,000 |
| March | 350,000 | 12,500 |

Using the high-low method, determine (a) the variable cost per unit and (b) the total fixed cost.

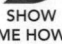
SHOW
ME HOW

EE 21-1 *p. 985*     **PE 21-1B**    **High-low method**           **OBJ. 1**

The manufacturing costs of Carrefour Enterprises for the first three months of the year follow:

|  | Total Costs | Units Produced |
|---|---|---|
| June | $300,000 | 2,700 units |
| July | 440,000 | 5,500 |
| August | 325,000 | 3,500 |

Using the high-low method, determine (a) the variable cost per unit and (b) the total fixed cost.

SHOW
ME HOW

EE 21-2 *p. 985*     **PE 21-2A**    **Contribution margin**           **OBJ. 2**

Michigan Company sells 10,000 units at $100 per unit. Variable costs are $75 per unit, and fixed costs are $125,000. Determine (a) the contribution margin ratio, (b) the unit contribution margin, and (c) income from operations.

EE 21-2 *p. 989*     **PE 21-2B**    **Contribution margin**           **OBJ. 2**

Weidner Company sells 22,000 units at $30 per unit. Variable costs are $24 per unit, and fixed costs are $40,000. Determine (a) the contribution margin ratio, (b) the unit contribution margin, and (c) income from operations.

SHOW
ME HOW

EE 21-3 *p. 993*     **PE 21-3A**    **Break-even point**           **OBJ. 3**

Santana sells a product for $115 per unit. The variable cost is $75 per unit, while fixed costs are $65,000. Determine (a) the break-even point in sales units and (b) the break-even point if the selling price were increased to $125 per unit.

SHOW
ME HOW

EE 21-3 *p. 993*     **PE 21-3B**    **Break-even point**           **OBJ. 3**

Elrod Inc. sells a product for $75 per unit. The variable cost is $45 per unit, while fixed costs are $48,000. Determine (a) the break-even point in sales units and (b) the break-even point if the selling price were increased to $95 per unit.

EE 21-4 *p. 994*     **PE 21-4A**    **Target profit**           **OBJ. 3**

Versa Inc. sells a product for $100 per unit. The variable cost is $75 per unit, and fixed costs are $45,000. Determine (a) the break-even point in sales units and (b) the break-even point in sales units if the company desires a target profit of $25,000.

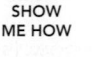
SHOW
ME HOW

EE 21-4 *p. 994*     **PE 21-4B**    **Target profit**           **OBJ. 3**

Scrushy Company sells a product for $150 per unit. The variable cost is $110 per unit, and fixed costs are $200,000. Determine (a) the break-even point in sales units and (b) the break-even point in sales units if the company desires a target profit of $50,000.

SHOW
ME HOW

EE 21-5 *p. 1002*     **PE 21-5A**    **Sales mix and break-even analysis**           **OBJ. 5**

Wide Open Industries Inc. has fixed costs of $475,000. The unit selling price, variable cost per unit, and contribution margin per unit for the company's two products follow:

| Product | Selling Price | Variable Cost per Unit | Contribution Margin per Unit |
|---|---|---|---|
| AA | $145 | $105 | $40 |
| BB | 110 | 75 | 35 |

SHOW
ME HOW

The sales mix for products AA and BB is 60% and 40%, respectively. Determine the break-even point in units of AA and BB.

EE 21-5 *p. 1002*

**PE 21-5B   Sales mix and break-even analysis**                                      OBJ. 5

Einhorn Company has fixed costs of $105,000. The unit selling price, variable cost per unit, and contribution margin per unit for the company's two products follow:

| Product | Selling Price | Variable Cost per Unit | Contribution Margin per Unit |
|---------|---------------|------------------------|------------------------------|
| QQ | $50 | $35 | $15 |
| ZZ | 60 | 30 | 30 |

The sales mix for products QQ and ZZ is 40% and 60%, respectively. Determine the break-even point in units of QQ and ZZ.

EE 21-6 *p. 1003*

**PE 21-6A   Operating leverage**                                                     OBJ. 5

SungSam Enterprises reports the following data:

| | |
|---|---|
| Sales | $340,000 |
| Variable costs | 180,000 |
| Contribution margin | $160,000 |
| Fixed costs | 80,000 |
| Income from operations | $ 80,000 |

Determine SungSam Enterprises's operating leverage.

EE 21-6 *p. 1003*

**PE 21-6B   Operating leverage**                                                     OBJ. 5

Westminster Co. reports the following data:

| | |
|---|---|
| Sales | $875,000 |
| Variable costs | 425,000 |
| Contribution margin | $450,000 |
| Fixed costs | 150,000 |
| Income from operations | $300,000 |

Determine Westminster Co.'s operating leverage.

EE 21-7 *p. 1004*

**PE 21-7A   Margin of safety**                                                       OBJ. 5

Melton Inc. has sales of $1,750,000, and the break-even point in sales dollars is $875,000. Determine the company's margin of safety as a percent of current sales.

EE 21-7 *p. 1004*

**PE 21-7B   Margin of safety**                                                       OBJ. 5

Junck Company has sales of $550,000, and the break-even point in sales dollars is $385,000. Determine the company's margin of safety as a percent of current sales.

# Exercises

**EX 21-1   Classify costs**                                                          OBJ. 1

Following is a list of various costs incurred in producing replacement automobile parts. With respect to the production and sale of these auto parts, classify each cost as either variable, fixed, or mixed.

1. Oil used in manufacturing equipment
2. Plastic
3. Property taxes, $165,000 per year on factory building and equipment
4. Salary of plant manager
5. Cost of labor for hourly workers
6. Packaging
7. Factory cleaning costs, $6,000 per month
8. Metal

9. Rent on warehouse, $10,000 per month plus $25 per square foot of storage used

10. Property insurance premiums, $3,600 per month plus $0.01 for each dollar of property over $1,200,000

11. Straight-line depreciation on the production equipment

12. Hourly wages of machine operators

13. Electricity costs, $0.20 per kilowatt-hour

14. Computer chip (purchased from a vendor)

15. Pension cost, $1.00 per employee hour on the job

---

**EX 21-2   Identify cost graphs**                                              OBJ. 1

The following cost graphs illustrate various types of cost behavior:

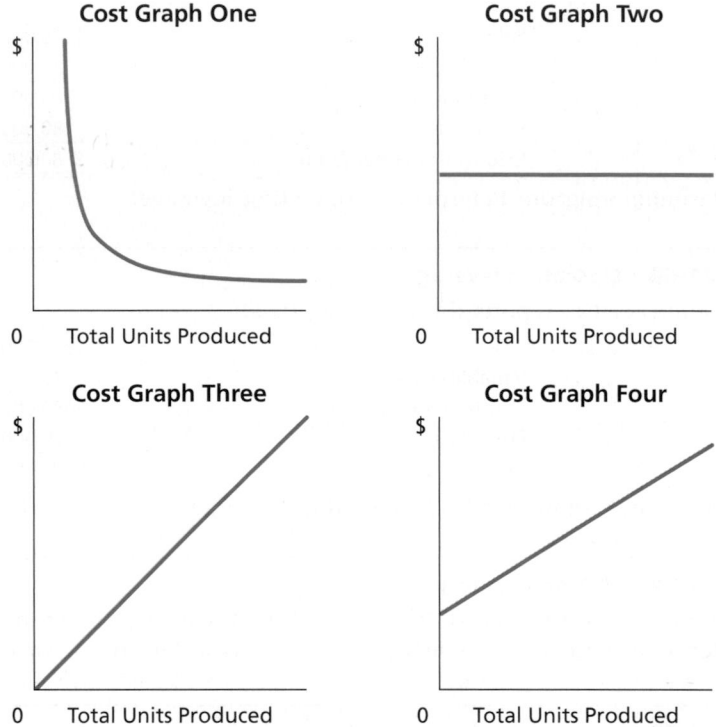

For each of the following costs, identify the cost graph that best illustrates its cost behavior as the number of units produced increases:

a. Total direct materials cost

b. Electricity costs of $1,000 per month plus $0.10 per kilowatt-hour

c. Per-unit cost of straight-line depreciation on factory equipment

d. Salary of quality control supervisor, $20,000 per month

e. Per-unit direct labor cost

---

**EX 21-3   Identify activity bases**                                           OBJ. 1

For a major university, match each cost in the following table with the activity base most appropriate to it. An activity base may be used more than once or not used at all.

Cost:
1. Financial aid office salaries
2. Office supplies
3. Instructor salaries
4. Housing personnel wages
5. Student records office salaries
6. Admissions office salaries

Activity Base:
a. Number of enrollment applications
b. Number of students
c. Student credit hours
d. Number of enrolled students and alumni
e. Number of financial aid applications
f. Number of students living on campus

**EX 21-4 Identify activity bases** OBJ. 1

From the following list of activity bases for an automobile dealership, select the base that would be most appropriate for each of these costs: (1) preparation costs (cleaning, oil, and gasoline costs) for each car received, (2) salespersons' commission of 5% of the sales price for each car sold, and (3) administrative costs for ordering cars.

a. Number of cars sold

b. Dollar amount of cars ordered

c. Number of cars ordered

d. Number of cars on hand

e. Number of cars received

f. Dollar amount of cars sold

g. Dollar amount of cars received

h. Dollar amount of cars on hand

**EX 21-5 Identify fixed and variable costs** OBJ. 1

Intuit Inc. develops and sells software products for the personal finance market, including popular titles such as Quickbooks® and TurboTax®. Classify each of the following costs and expenses for this company as either variable or fixed to the number of units produced and sold:

a. Packaging costs

b. Sales commissions

c. Property taxes on general offices

d. Shipping expenses

e. Straight-line depreciation of computer equipment

f. President's salary

g. Salaries of software developers

h. Salaries of human resources personnel

i. Wages of telephone order assistants

j. CDs

k. Users' guides

**EX 21-6 Relevant range and fixed and variable costs** OBJ. 1

✔ a. $1.25

SHOW
ME HOW

Quigley Inc. manufactures memory chips for electronic toys within a relevant range of 200,000 to 600,000 memory chips per year. Within this range, the following partially completed manufacturing cost schedule has been prepared:

| Components produced | 200,000 | 400,000 | 600,000 |
|---|---|---|---|
| Total costs: | | | |
| Total variable costs | $ 250,000 | (d) | (j) |
| Total fixed costs | 600,000 | (e) | (k) |
| Total costs | $850,000 | (f) | (l) |
| Cost per unit: | | | |
| Variable cost per unit | (a) | (g) | (m) |
| Fixed cost per unit | (b) | (h) | (n) |
| Total cost per unit | (c) | (i) | (o) |

Complete the cost schedule, identifying each cost by the appropriate letter (a) through (o).

**EX 21-7 High-low method** OBJ. 1

✔ a. $24.00 per unit

SHOW
ME HOW

Diamond Inc. has decided to use the high-low method to estimate the total cost and the fixed and variable cost components of the total cost. The data for various levels of production are as follows:

| Units Produced | Total Costs |
|---|---|
| 12,000 | $424,000 |
| 15,000 | 496,000 |
| 21,000 | 640,000 |

a. Determine the variable cost per unit and the total fixed cost.

b. Based on part (a), estimate the total cost for 17,000 units of production.

---

### EX 21-8 High-low method for a service company
OBJ. 1

Boston Railroad decided to use the high-low method and operating data from the past six months to estimate the fixed and variable components of transportation costs. The activity base used by Boston Railroad is a measure of railroad operating activity, termed "gross-ton miles," which is the total number of tons multiplied by the miles moved.

|  | Transportation Costs | Gross-Ton Miles |
| --- | --- | --- |
| January | $1,776,000 | 560,000 |
| February | 2,700,000 | 1,000,000 |
| March | 1,650,000 | 500,000 |
| April | 1,860,000 | 600,000 |
| May | 1,440,000 | 400,000 |
| June | 1,566,000 | 460,000 |

Determine the variable cost per gross-ton mile and the total fixed cost.

---

### EX 21-9 Contribution margin ratio
OBJ. 2

a. Segar Company budgets sales of $3,200,000, fixed costs of $700,000, and variable costs of $2,240,000. What is the contribution margin ratio for Segar Company?

b. If the contribution margin ratio for Domino Company is 35%, sales were $2,100,000, and fixed costs were $400,000, what was the income from operations?

---

### EX 21-10 Contribution margin and contribution margin ratio
OBJ. 2

For a recent year, McDonald's company-owned restaurants had the following sales and expenses (in millions):

| | |
| --- | --- |
| Sales | $18,602.5 |
| Food and packaging | $ 6,318.2 |
| Payroll | 4,710.3 |
| Occupancy (rent, depreciation, etc.) | 4,195.2 |
| General, selling, and administrative expenses | 2,445.2 |
| | 17,668.9 |
| Income from operations | $ 933.6 |

Assume that the variable costs consist of food and packaging, payroll, and 40% of the general, selling, and administrative expenses.

a. What is McDonald's contribution margin? Round to the nearest tenth of a million (one decimal place).

b. What is McDonald's contribution margin ratio? Round to one decimal place.

c. How much would income from operations increase if same-store sales increased by $900 million for the coming year, with no change in the contribution margin ratio or fixed costs? Round your answer to the nearest tenth of a million (one decimal place).

---

### EX 21-11 Break-even sales and sales to realize income from operations
OBJ. 3

For the current year ended March 31, Benatar Company expects fixed costs of $1,250,000, a unit variable cost of $140, and a unit selling price of $100.

a. Compute the anticipated break-even sales (units).

b. Compute the sales (units) required to realize income from operations of $150,000.

### EX 21-12 Break-even sales

OBJ. 3

Anheuser-Busch InBev Companies, Inc., reported the following operating information for a recent year (in millions):

| | |
|---|---|
| Net sales | $39,758 |
| Cost of goods sold | $16,447 |
| Selling, general and administration | 10,578 |
| | $27,025 |
| Income from operations | $12,733* |

*Before special items

In addition, assume that Anheuser-Busch InBev sold 320 million barrels of beer during the year. Assume that variable costs were 70% of the cost of goods sold and 40% of selling, general, and administration expenses. Assume that the remaining costs are fixed. For the following year, assume that Anheuser-Busch InBev expects pricing, variable costs per barrel, and fixed costs to remain constant, except that new distribution and general office facilities are expected to increase fixed costs by $400 million.

a. Compute the break-even number of barrels for the current year. *Note:* For the selling price per barrel and variable costs per barrel, round to the nearest cent.  Also, round the break-even to the nearest barrel.

b. Compute the anticipated break-even number of barrels for the following year.

### EX 21-13 Break-even sales

OBJ. 3

Currently, the unit selling price of a product is $160, the unit variable cost is $120, and the total fixed costs are $725,000. A proposal is being evaluated to increase the unit selling price to $170.

a. Compute the current break-even sales (units).

b. Compute the anticipated break-even sales (units), assuming that the unit selling price is increased and all costs remain constant.

SHOW
ME HOW

### EX 21-14 Break-even analysis

OBJ. 3

The Junior League of Yadkinville, California, collected recipes from members and published a cookbook entitled *Food for Everyone*. The book will sell for $18 per copy. The chairwoman of the cookbook development committee estimated that the club needed to sell 2,000 books to break even on its $4,000 investment. What is the variable cost per unit assumed in the Junior League's analysis?

### EX 21-15 Break-even analysis

OBJ. 3

Media outlets such as ESPN and Fox Sports often have Web sites that provide in-depth coverage of news and events. Portions of these Web sites are restricted to members who pay a monthly subscription to gain access to exclusive news and commentary. These Web sites typically offer a free trial period to introduce viewers to the Web site. Assume that during a recent fiscal year, ESPN.com spent $4,200,000 on a promotional campaign for the ESPN.com Web site that offered two free months of service for new subscribers. In addition, assume the following information:

| | |
|---|---|
| Number of months an average new customer stays with the service (including the two free months) | 14 months |
| Revenue per month per customer subscription | $10.00 |
| Variable cost per month per customer subscription | $5.00 |

Determine the number of new customer accounts needed to break even on the cost of the promotional campaign. In forming your answer, (1) treat the cost of the promotional campaign as a fixed cost, and (2) treat the revenue less variable cost per account for the subscription period as the unit contribution margin.

### EX 21-16    Break-even analysis for a service company                    OBJ. 3

Sprint Nextel is one of the largest digital wireless service providers in the United States. In a recent year, it had approximately 32.5 million direct subscribers (accounts) that generated revenue of $35,345 million. Costs and expenses for the year were as follows (in millions):

| | |
|---|---:|
| Cost of revenue | $20,841 |
| Selling, general, and administrative expenses | 9,765 |
| Depreciation | 2,239 |

Assume that 70% of the cost of revenue and 30% of the selling, general, and administrative expenses are variable to the number of direct subscribers (accounts).

a. What is Sprint Nextel's break-even number of accounts, using the data and assumptions given? Round units (accounts) and per-account amounts to one decimal place.

b. How much revenue per account would be sufficient for Sprint Nextel to break even if the number of accounts remained constant?

### EX 21-17    Cost-volume-profit chart                    OBJ. 4

✔ b. $1,500,000

For the coming year, Loudermilk Inc. anticipates fixed costs of $600,000, a unit variable cost of $75, and a unit selling price of $125. The maximum sales within the relevant range are $2,500,000.

a. Construct a cost-volume-profit chart.

b. Estimate the break-even sales (dollars) by using the cost-volume-profit chart constructed in part (a).

c. ➤ What is the main advantage of presenting the cost-volume-profit analysis in graphic form rather than equation form?

### EX 21-18    Profit-volume chart                    OBJ. 4

✔ b. $400,000

Using the data for Loudermilk Inc. in Exercise 21-17, (a) determine the maximum possible operating loss, (b) compute the maximum possible operating profit, (c) construct a profit-volume chart, and (d) estimate the break-even sales (units) by using the profit-volume chart constructed in part (c).

### EX 21-19    Break-even chart                    OBJ. 4

Name the following chart, and identify the items represented by the letters (a) through (f):

**EX 21-20  Break-even chart**                                                OBJ. 4

Name the following chart, and identify the items represented by the letters (a) through (f):

**EX 21-21  Sales mix and break-even sales**                                  OBJ. 5

✔ a. 15,500 units

SHOW
ME HOW

Dragon Sports Inc. manufactures and sells two products, baseball bats and baseball gloves. The fixed costs are $620,000, and the sales mix is 40% bats and 60% gloves. The unit selling price and the unit variable cost for each product are as follows:

| Products | Unit Selling Price | Unit Variable Cost |
|----------|-------------------|--------------------|
| Bats     | $ 90              | $50                |
| Gloves   | 105               | 65                 |

a.  Compute the break-even sales (units) for the overall product, E.

b.  How many units of each product, baseball bats and baseball gloves, would be sold at the break-even point?

**EX 21-22  Break-even sales and sales mix for a service company**           OBJ. 5

✔ a. 60 seats

Zero Turbulence Airline provides air transportation services between Los Angeles, California, and Kona, Hawaii. A single Los Angeles to Kona round-trip flight has the following operating statistics:

| | |
|---|---|
| Fuel | $7,000 |
| Flight crew salaries | 3,200 |
| Airplane depreciation | 3,480 |
| Variable cost per passenger—business class | 140 |
| Variable cost per passenger—economy class | 120 |
| Round-trip ticket price—business class | 800 |
| Round-trip ticket price—economy class | 300 |

It is assumed that the fuel, crew salaries, and airplane depreciation are fixed, regardless of the number of seats sold for the round-trip flight.

a.  Compute the break-even number of seats sold on a single round-trip flight for the overall product, E. Assume that the overall product mix is 10% business class and 90% economy class tickets.

b.  How many business class and economy class seats would be sold at the break-even point?

**EX 21-23 Margin of safety** OBJ. 5

✔ a. (2) 20%

SHOW
ME HOW

a. If Canace Company, with a break-even point at $960,000 of sales, has actual sales of $1,200,000, what is the margin of safety expressed (1) in dollars and (2) as a percentage of sales?

b. If the margin of safety for Canace Company was 20%, fixed costs were $1,875,000, and variable costs were 80% of sales, what was the amount of actual sales (dollars)? (*Hint:* Determine the break-even in sales dollars first.)

**EX 21-24 Break-even and margin of safety relationships** OBJ. 5

At a recent staff meeting, the management of Boost Technologies Inc. was considering discontinuing the Rocket Man line of electronic games from the product line. The chief financial analyst reported the following current monthly data for the Rocket Man:

| | |
|---|---|
| Units of sales | 420,000 |
| Break-even units | 472,500 |
| Margin of safety in units | 29,400 |

➤ For what reason would you question the validity of these data?

**EX 21-25 Operating leverage** OBJ. 5

✔ a. Beck, 5.0

Beck Inc. and Bryant Inc. have the following operating data:

| | Beck Inc. | Bryant Inc. |
|---|---|---|
| Sales | $1,250,000 | $2,000,000 |
| Variable costs | 750,000 | 1,250,000 |
| Contribution margin | $ 500,000 | $ 750,000 |
| Fixed costs | 400,000 | 450,000 |
| Income from operations | $ 100,000 | $ 300,000 |

a. Compute the operating leverage for Beck Inc. and Bryant Inc.

b. How much would income from operations increase for each company if the sales of each increased by 20%?

c. ➤ Why is there a difference in the increase in income from operations for the two companies? Explain.

**Appendix**
**EX 21-26 Items on variable costing income statement**

In the following equations, based on the variable costing income statement, identify the items designated by X:

a. Net Sales – X = Manufacturing Margin

b. Manufacturing Margin – X = Contribution Margin

c. Contribution Margin – X = Income from Operations

**Appendix**
**EX 21-27 Variable costing income statement**

✔ a. Contribution
margin, $1,934,400

On July 31, 2016, the end of the first month of operations, Rhys Company prepared the following income statement, based on the absorption costing concept:

| | | |
|---|---|---|
| Sales (96,000 units) | | $4,440,000 |
| Cost of goods sold: | | |
| Cost of goods manufactured | $3,120,000 | |
| Less ending inventory (24,000 units) | 624,000 | |
| Cost of goods sold | | 2,496,000 |
| Gross profit | | $1,944,000 |
| Selling and administrative expenses | | 288,000 |
| Income from operations | | $1,656,000 |

a. Prepare a variable costing income statement, assuming that the fixed manufacturing costs were $132,000 and the variable selling and administrative expenses were $115,200.

b. Reconcile the absorption costing income from operations of $1,656,000 with the variable costing income from operations determined in (a).

**Appendix**
**EX 21-28 Absorption costing income statement**

On June 30, 2016, the end of the first month of operations, Tudor Manufacturing Co. prepared the following income statement, based on the variable costing concept:

| | | |
|---|---:|---:|
| Sales (420,000 units) .................................................... | | $7,450,000 |
| Variable cost of goods sold: | | |
|    Variable cost of goods manufactured (500,000 units × $14 per unit) ..... | $7,000,000 | |
|    Less ending inventory (80,000 units × $14 per unit) .................... | 1,120,000 | |
|       Variable cost of goods sold ....................................... | | 5,880,000 |
| Manufacturing margin .................................................... | | $1,570,000 |
| Variable selling and administrative expenses............................. | | 80,000 |
| Contribution margin ..................................................... | | $1,490,000 |
| Fixed costs: | | |
|    Fixed manufacturing costs ........................................... | $ 160,000 | |
|    Fixed selling and administrative expenses ........................... | 75,000 | 235,000 |
| Income from operations.................................................. | | $1,255,000 |

a. Prepare an absorption costing income statement.

b. Reconcile the variable costing income from operations of $1,255,000 with the absorption costing income from operations determined in (a).

# Problems: Series A

**PR 21-1A Classify costs** OBJ. 1

Seymour Clothing Co. manufactures a variety of clothing types for distribution to several major retail chains. The following costs are incurred in the production and sale of blue jeans:

a. Shipping boxes used to ship orders

b. Consulting fee of $200,000 paid to industry specialist for marketing advice

c. Straight-line depreciation on sewing machines

d. Salesperson's salary, $10,000 plus 2% of the total sales

e. Fabric

f. Dye

g. Thread

h. Salary of designers

i. Brass buttons

j. Legal fees paid to attorneys in defense of the company in a patent infringement suit, $50,000 plus $87 per hour

k. Insurance premiums on property, plant, and equipment, $70,000 per year plus $5 per $30,000 of insured value over $8,000,000

l. Rental costs of warehouse, $5,000 per month plus $4 per square foot of storage used

m. Supplies

n. Leather for patches identifying the brand on individual pieces of apparel

o. Rent on plant equipment, $50,000 per year

p. Salary of production vice president

q. Janitorial services, $2,200 per month

r. Wages of machine operators

s. Electricity costs of $0.10 per kilowatt-hour

t. Property taxes on property, plant, and equipment

**Instructions**

Classify the preceding costs as either fixed, variable, or mixed. Use the following tabular headings and place an X in the appropriate column. Identify each cost by letter in the cost column.

| Cost | Fixed Cost | Variable Cost | Mixed Cost |
|---|---|---|---|

**PR 21-2A  Break-even sales under present and proposed conditions**  OBJ. 2, 3

BeeGee Company, operating at full capacity, sold 150,000 units at a price of $116 per unit during the current year. Its income statement is as follows:

| | | |
|---|---|---|
| Sales | | $17,400,000 |
| Cost of goods sold | | 6,000,000 |
| Gross profit | | $11,400,000 |
| Expenses: | | |
| Selling expenses | $4,000,000 | |
| Administrative expenses | 3,000,000 | |
| Total expenses | | 7,000,000 |
| Income from operations | | $ 4,400,000 |

The division of costs between variable and fixed is as follows:

| | Variable | Fixed |
|---|---|---|
| Cost of goods sold | 80% | 20% |
| Selling expenses | 75% | 25% |
| Administrative expenses | 70% | 30% |

Management is considering a plant expansion program for the following year that will permit an increase of $3,625,000 in yearly sales. The expansion will increase fixed costs by $1,000,000 but will not affect the relationship between sales and variable costs.

**Instructions**

1. Determine the total variable costs and the total fixed costs for the current year.

2. Determine (a) the unit variable cost and (b) the unit contribution margin for the current year.

3. Compute the break-even sales (units) for the current year.

4. Compute the break-even sales (units) under the proposed program for the following year.

5. Determine the amount of sales (units) that would be necessary under the proposed program to realize the $4,400,000 of income from operations that was earned in the current year.

6. Determine the maximum income from operations possible with the expanded plant.

7. If the proposal is accepted and sales remain at the current level, what will the income or loss from operations be for the following year?

8. ━━━▶ Based on the data given, would you recommend accepting the proposal? Explain.

**PR 21-3A  Break-even sales and cost-volume-profit chart**  OBJ. 3, 4

✔ 1. 12,000 units

For the coming year, Cleves Company anticipates a unit selling price of $100, a unit variable cost of $60, and fixed costs of $480,000.

**Instructions**

1. Compute the anticipated break-even sales (units).

2. Compute the sales (units) required to realize a target profit of $240,000.

3. Construct a cost-volume-profit chart, assuming maximum sales of 20,000 units within the relevant range.

4. Determine the probable income (loss) from operations if sales total 16,000 units.

**PR 21-4A  Break-even sales and cost-volume-profit chart**  OBJ. 3, 4

✔ 1. 1,000 units

Last year, Hever Inc. had sales of $500,000, based on a unit selling price of $250. The variable cost per unit was $175, and fixed costs were $75,000. The maximum sales within Hever Inc.'s relevant range are 2,500 units. Hever Inc. is considering a proposal to spend an additional $33,750 on billboard advertising during the current year in an attempt to increase sales and utilize unused capacity.

**Instructions**

1. Construct a cost-volume-profit chart indicating the break-even sales for last year. Verify your answer, using the break-even equation.

2. Using the cost-volume-profit chart prepared in part (1), determine (a) the income from operations for last year and (b) the maximum income from operations that could have been realized during the year. Verify your answers using the mathematical approach to cost-volume-profit analysis.

3. Construct a cost-volume-profit chart indicating the break-even sales for the current year, assuming that a noncancellable contract is signed for the additional billboard advertising. No changes are expected in the unit selling price or other costs. Verify your answer, using the break-even equation.

4. Using the cost-volume-profit chart prepared in part (3), determine (a) the income from operations if sales total 2,000 units and (b) the maximum income from operations that could be realized during the year. Verify your answers using the mathematical approach to cost-volume-profit analysis.

---

### PR 21-5A   Sales mix and break-even sales

**OBJ. 5**

✔ 1. 4,030 units

Data related to the expected sales of laptops and tablets for Tech Products Inc. for the current year, which is typical of recent years, are as follows:

| Products | Unit Selling Price | Unit Variable Cost | Sales Mix |
|---|---|---|---|
| Laptops | $1,600 | $800 | 40% |
| Tablets | 850 | 350 | 60% |

The estimated fixed costs for the current year are $2,498,600.

**Instructions**

1. Determine the estimated units of sales of the overall (total) product, E, necessary to reach the break-even point for the current year.

2. Based on the break-even sales (units) in part (1), determine the unit sales of both laptops and tablets for the current year.

3. ▬▬▬▶ Assume that the sales mix was 50% laptops and 50% tablets. Compare the break-even point with that in part (1). Why is it so different?

---

### PR 21-6A   Contribution margin, break-even sales, cost-volume-profit chart, margin of safety, and operating leverage   OBJ. 2, 3, 4, 5

✔ 2. 25%

Wolsey Industries Inc. expects to maintain the same inventories at the end of 2016 as at the beginning of the year. The total of all production costs for the year is therefore assumed to be equal to the cost of goods sold. With this in mind, the various department heads were asked to submit estimates of the costs for their departments during the year. A summary report of these estimates is as follows:

| | Estimated Fixed Cost | Estimated Variable Cost (per unit sold) |
|---|---|---|
| Production costs: | | |
| Direct materials............................. | — | $ 46 |
| Direct labor ................................. | — | 40 |
| Factory overhead........................... | $200,000 | 20 |
| Selling expenses: | | |
| Sales salaries and commissions............. | 110,000 | 8 |
| Advertising................................. | 40,000 | — |
| Travel ...................................... | 12,000 | — |
| Miscellaneous selling expense ............. | 7,600 | 1 |
| Administrative expenses: | | |
| Office and officers' salaries ................. | 132,000 | — |
| Supplies..................................... | 10,000 | 4 |
| Miscellaneous administrative expense ........ | 13,400 | 1 |
| Total ....................................... | $525,000 | $120 |

It is expected that 21,875 units will be sold at a price of $160 a unit. Maximum sales within the relevant range are 27,000 units.

**Instructions**

1. Prepare an estimated income statement for 2016.

2. What is the expected contribution margin ratio?

3. Determine the break-even sales in units and dollars.

4. Construct a cost-volume-profit chart indicating the break-even sales.

5. What is the expected margin of safety in dollars and as a percentage of sales?

6. Determine the operating leverage.

## Problems: Series B

### PR 21-1B   Classify costs                                                OBJ. 1

Cromwell Furniture Company manufactures sofas for distribution to several major retail chains. The following costs are incurred in the production and sale of sofas:

a. Fabric for sofa coverings

b. Wood for framing the sofas

c. Legal fees paid to attorneys in defense of the company in a patent infringement suit, $25,000 plus $160 per hour

d. Salary of production supervisor

e. Cartons used to ship sofas

f. Rent on experimental equipment, $50 for every sofa produced

g. Straight-line depreciation on factory equipment

h. Rental costs of warehouse, $30,000 per month

i. Property taxes on property, plant, and equipment

j. Insurance premiums on property, plant, and equipment, $25,000 per year plus $25 per $25,000 of insured value over $16,000,000

k. Springs

l. Consulting fee of $120,000 paid to efficiency specialists

m. Electricity costs of $0.13 per kilowatt-hour

n. Salesperson's salary, $80,000 plus 4% of the selling price of each sofa sold

o. Foam rubber for cushion fillings

p. Janitorial supplies, $2,500 per month

q. Employer's FICA taxes on controller's salary of $180,000

r. Salary of designers

s. Wages of sewing machine operators

t. Sewing supplies

### Instructions

Classify the preceding costs as either fixed, variable, or mixed. Use the following tabular headings and place an X in the appropriate column. Identify each cost by letter in the cost column.

| Cost | Fixed Cost | Variable Cost | Mixed Cost |
| --- | --- | --- | --- |

### PR 21-2B   Break-even sales under present and proposed conditions        OBJ. 2, 3

Howard Industries Inc., operating at full capacity, sold 64,000 units at a price of $45 per unit during the current year. Its income statement is as follows:

✔ 3. 29,375 units

SHOW
ME HOW

| | | |
| --- | --- | --- |
| Sales ............................. | | $2,880,000 |
| Cost of goods sold ................... | | 1,400,000 |
| Gross profit ......................... | | $1,480,000 |
| Expenses: | | |
| Selling expenses ................... | $400,000 | |
| Administrative expenses............ | 387,500 | |
| Total expenses.................... | | 787,500 |
| Income from operations .............. | | $ 692,500 |

The division of costs between variable and fixed is as follows:

| | Variable | Fixed |
| --- | --- | --- |
| Cost of goods sold | 75% | 25% |
| Selling expenses | 60% | 40% |
| Administrative expenses | 80% | 20% |

Management is considering a plant expansion program for the following year that will permit an increase of $900,000 in yearly sales. The expansion will increase fixed costs by $212,500 but will not affect the relationship between sales and variable costs.

**Instructions**

1. Determine the total fixed costs and the total variable costs for the current year.

2. Determine (a) the unit variable cost and (b) the unit contribution margin for the current year.

3. Compute the break-even sales (units) for the current year.

4. Compute the break-even sales (units) under the proposed program for the following year.

5. Determine the amount of sales (units) that would be necessary under the proposed program to realize the $692,500 of income from operations that was earned in the current year.

6. Determine the maximum income from operations possible with the expanded plant.

7. If the proposal is accepted and sales remain at the current level, what will the income or loss from operations be for the following year?

8. ━━━▶ Based on the data given, would you recommend accepting the proposal? Explain.

---

✔ 1. 20,000 units

**PR 21-3B   Break-even sales and cost-volume-profit chart**               **OBJ. 3, 4**

For the coming year, Culpeper Products Inc. anticipates a unit selling price of $150, a unit variable cost of $110, and fixed costs of $800,000.

**Instructions**

1. Compute the anticipated break-even sales (units).

2. Compute the sales (units) required to realize income from operations of $300,000.

3. Construct a cost-volume-profit chart, assuming maximum sales of 40,000 units within the relevant range.

4. Determine the probable income (loss) from operations if sales total 32,000 units.

---

✔ 1. 3,000 units

**PR 21-4B   Break-even sales and cost-volume-profit chart**               **OBJ. 3, 4**

Last year, Parr Co. had sales of $900,000, based on a unit selling price of $200. The variable cost per unit was $125, and fixed costs were $225,000. The maximum sales within Parr Co.'s relevant range are 7,500 units. Parr Co. is considering a proposal to spend an additional $112,500 on billboard advertising during the current year in an attempt to increase sales and utilize unused capacity.

**Instructions**

1. Construct a cost-volume-profit chart indicating the break-even sales for last year. Verify your answer, using the break-even equation.

2. Using the cost-volume-profit chart prepared in part (1), determine (a) the income from operations for last year and (b) the maximum income from operations that could have been realized during the year. Verify your answers arithmetically.

3. Construct a cost-volume-profit chart indicating the break-even sales for the current year, assuming that a noncancellable contract is signed for the additional billboard advertising. No changes are expected in the selling price or other costs. Verify your answer, using the break-even equation.

4. Using the cost-volume-profit chart prepared in part (3), determine (a) the income from operations if sales total 6,000 units and (b) the maximum income from operations that could be realized during the year. Verify your answers arithmetically.

---

✔ 1. 4,500 units

**PR 21-5B   Sales mix and break-even sales**               **OBJ. 5**

Data related to the expected sales of two types of frozen pizzas for Norfolk Frozen Foods Inc. for the current year, which is typical of recent years, are as follows:

| Products | Unit Selling Price | Unit Variable Cost | Sales Mix |
|---|---|---|---|
| 12" Pizza | $12 | $3 | 30% |
| 16" Pizza | 15 | 4 | 70% |

The estimated fixed costs for the current year are $46,800.

**Instructions**

1. Determine the estimated units of sales of the overall (total) product, E, necessary to reach the break-even point for the current year.

2. Based on the break-even sales (units) in part (1), determine the unit sales of both the 12″ pizza and 16″ pizza for the current year.

3. ➤ Assume that the sales mix was 50% 12″ pizza and 50% 16″ pizza. Compare the break-even point with that in part (1). Why is it so different?

✔ 3. 8,000 units

**PR 21-6B** **Contribution margin, break-even sales, cost-volume-profit chart,** OBJ. 2, 3, 4, 5
**margin of safety, and operating leverage**

Belmain Co. expects to maintain the same inventories at the end of 2016 as at the beginning of the year. The total of all production costs for the year is therefore assumed to be equal to the cost of goods sold. With this in mind, the various department heads were asked to submit estimates of the costs for their departments during the year. A summary report of these estimates is as follows:

|  | Estimated Fixed Cost | Estimated Variable Cost (per unit sold) |
|---|---|---|
| Production costs: | | |
| Direct materials | — | $50.00 |
| Direct labor | — | 30.00 |
| Factory overhead | $ 350,000 | 6.00 |
| Selling expenses: | | |
| Sales salaries and commissions | 340,000 | 4.00 |
| Advertising | 116,000 | — |
| Travel | 4,000 | — |
| Miscellaneous selling expense | 2,300 | 1.00 |
| Administrative expenses: | | |
| Office and officers' salaries | 325,000 | — |
| Supplies | 6,000 | 4.00 |
| Miscellaneous administrative expense | 8,700 | 1.00 |
| Total | $1,152,000 | $96.00 |

It is expected that 12,000 units will be sold at a price of $240 a unit. Maximum sales within the relevant range are 18,000 units.

**Instructions**

1. Prepare an estimated income statement for 2016.

2. What is the expected contribution margin ratio?

3. Determine the break-even sales in units and dollars.

4. Construct a cost-volume-profit chart indicating the break-even sales.

5. What is the expected margin of safety in dollars and as a percentage of sales?

6. Determine the operating leverage.

# Cases & Projects

**CP 21-1** **Ethics and professional conduct in business**

Edward Seymour is a financial consultant to Cornish Inc., a real estate syndicate. Cornish Inc. finances and develops commercial real estate (office buildings). The completed projects are then sold as limited partnership interests to individual investors. The syndicate makes a profit on the sale of these partnership interests. Edward provides financial information for the offering prospectus, which is a document that provides the financial and legal details of the limited partnership offerings. In one of the projects, the bank has financed the construction of a commercial office building at a rate of 10% for the first four years, after which time the rate jumps to 15% for the remaining 20 years of the mortgage. The interest costs are one of the major ongoing costs of a real estate project. Edward has reported prominently in the prospectus that the break-even occupancy for the first four years is 65%. This is the amount of office space that must be leased to cover the interest and general upkeep costs over the first four years. The 65% break-even is very low and thus communicates a low risk to potential investors. Edward uses the 65% break-even rate as a major marketing tool in selling the limited partnership interests. Buried in the fine print of the prospectus is additional information that would allow an astute investor to determine that the break-even occupancy will jump to 95% after the fourth year because of the contracted increase in the mortgage interest rate. Edward believes prospective investors are adequately informed as to the risk of the investment.

━━━━▶ Comment on the ethical considerations of this situation.

---

### CP 21-2   Break-even sales, contribution margin

"For a student, a grade of 65 percent is nothing to write home about. But for the airline . . . [industry], filling 65 percent of the seats . . . is the difference between profit and loss.

The [economy] might be just strong enough to sustain all the carriers on a cash basis, but not strong enough to bring any significant profitability to the industry. . . . For the airlines . . ., the emphasis will be on trying to consolidate routes and raise ticket prices. . . ."

Source: Edwin McDowell, "Empty Seats, Empty Beds, Empty Pockets," *The New York Times,* January 6, 1992, p. C3.

━━━━▶ The airline industry is notorious for boom and bust cycles. Why is airline profitability very sensitive to these cycles? Do you think that during a down cycle the strategy to consolidate routes and raise ticket prices is reasonable? What would make this strategy succeed or fail? Why?

---

### CP 21-3   Break-even analysis

Somerset Inc. has finished a new video game, *Snowboard Challenge*. Management is now considering its marketing strategies. The following information is available:

| | |
|---|---|
| Anticipated sales price per unit . . . . . . . . . . . . . . . . . . . . . . | $80 |
| Variable cost per unit* . . . . . . . . . . . . . . . . . . . . . . . . . . . . . | $35 |
| Anticipated volume . . . . . . . . . . . . . . . . . . . . . . . . . . . . . . . . | 1,000,000 units |
| Production costs . . . . . . . . . . . . . . . . . . . . . . . . . . . . . . . . . . . | $20,000,000 |
| Anticipated advertising . . . . . . . . . . . . . . . . . . . . . . . . . . . . . | $15,000,000 |

*The cost of the video game, packaging, and copying costs.

Two managers, James Hamilton and Thomas Seymour, had the following discussion of ways to increase the profitability of this new offering:

*James:* I think we need to think of some way to increase our profitability. Do you have any ideas?

*Thomas:* Well, I think the best strategy would be to become aggressive on price.

*James:* How aggressive?

*Thomas:* If we drop the price to $60 per unit and maintain our advertising budget at $15,000,000, I think we will generate total sales of 2,000,000 units.

*James:* I think that's the wrong way to go. You're giving too much up on price. Instead, I think we need to follow an aggressive advertising strategy.

*Thomas:* How aggressive?

*James:* If we increase our advertising to a total of $25,000,000, we should be able to increase sales volume to 1,400,000 units without any change in price.

*Thomas:* I don't think that's reasonable. We'll never cover the increased advertising costs.

━━━━▶ Which strategy is best: Do nothing? Follow the advice of Thomas Seymour? Or follow James Hamilton's strategy?

**CP 21-4 Variable costs and activity bases in decision making**

The owner of Warwick Printing, a printing company, is planning direct labor needs for the upcoming year. The owner has provided you with the following information for next year's plans:

|  | One Color | Two Color | Three Color | Four Color | Total |
|---|---|---|---|---|---|
| Number of banners | 212 | 274 | 616 | 698 | 1,800 |

Each color on the banner must be printed one at a time. Thus, for example, a four-color banner will need to be run through the printing operation four separate times. The total production volume last year was 800 banners, as follows:

|  | One Color | Two Color | Three Color | Total |
|---|---|---|---|---|
| Number of banners | 180 | 240 | 380 | 800 |

As you can see, the four-color banner is a new product offering for the upcoming year. The owner believes that the expected 1,000-unit increase in volume from last year means that direct labor expenses should increase by 125% (1,000 ÷ 800). What do you think?

**CP 21-5 Variable costs and activity bases in decision making**

Sales volume has been dropping at Mumford Industries. During this time, however, the Shipping Department manager has been under severe financial constraints. The manager knows that most of the Shipping Department's effort is related to pulling inventory from the warehouse for each order and performing the paperwork. The paperwork involves preparing shipping documents for each order. Thus, the pulling and paperwork effort associated with each sales order is essentially the same, regardless of the size of the order. The Shipping Department manager has discussed the financial situation with senior management. Senior management has responded by pointing out that sales volume has been dropping, so that the amount of work in the Shipping Department should be dropping. Thus, senior management told the Shipping Department manager that costs should be decreasing in the department.

The Shipping Department manager prepared the following information:

| Month | Sales Volume | Number of Customer Orders | Sales Volume per Order |
|---|---|---|---|
| January | $472,000 | 1,180 | 400 |
| February | 475,800 | 1,220 | 390 |
| March | 456,950 | 1,235 | 370 |
| April | 425,000 | 1,250 | 340 |
| May | 464,750 | 1,430 | 325 |
| June | 421,200 | 1,350 | 312 |
| July | 414,000 | 1,380 | 300 |
| August | 430,700 | 1,475 | 292 |

Given this information, how would you respond to senior management?

**CP 21-6 Break-even analysis**

**Group Project**

Break-even analysis is one of the most fundamental tools for managing any kind of business unit. Consider the management of your university or college. In a group, brainstorm some applications of break-even analysis at your university or college. Identify three areas where break-even analysis might be used. For each area, identify the revenues, variable costs, and fixed costs that would be used in the calculation.

# Budgeting

## Hendrick Motorsport

**Y**ou may have financial goals for your life. To achieve these goals, it is necessary to plan for future expenses. For example, you may consider taking a part-time job to save money for school expenses for the coming school year. How much money would you need to earn and save in order to pay these expenses? One way to find an answer to this question would be to prepare a budget. A budget would show an estimate of your expenses associated with school, such as tuition, fees, and books. In addition, you would have expenses for day-to-day living, such as rent, food, and clothing. You might also have expenses for travel and entertainment. Once the school year begins, you can use the budget as a tool for guiding your spending priorities during the year.

The budget is used in businesses in much the same way it can be used in personal life. For example, **Hendrick Motorsport**, featuring drivers Dale Earnhardt, Jr., Jeff Gordon, and Jimmy Johnson, uses budget information to remain one of the most valuable racing teams in NASCAR. Hendrick uses budgets to keep revenues greater than expenses. For example, Hendrick plans revenues from car sponsorships and winnings. Primary and secondary sponsorships (car decals) can provide as much as 70% of the revenues for a typical race team. Costs include salaries, engines, tires, cars, travel, and research and development. In addition, star drivers such as Dale Earnhardt, Jr. can earn as much as $28 million in salary, winnings, and endorsements. Overall, Hendrick is estimated to earn $179 million in revenues and $16.6 million in operating income from their four race teams. The budget provides the company with a "game plan" for the year. In this chapter, you will see how budgets can be used for financial planning and control.

*Source:* Kurt Badenhausen, "Hendrick Motorsports Tops list of Nascar's Most Valuable Teams," *Forbes*, March 13, 2013. Bob Pockrass, "NASCAR's Highest Paid drivers make their money from a variety of sources," *Sporting News*, December 4, 2012. Ed Hilton, "Under the Hood at Hendrick Motorsports", *Chicago Tribune*, July 13, 2007.

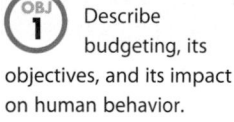

**(OBJ 1)** Describe budgeting, its objectives, and its impact on human behavior.

# Nature and Objectives of Budgeting

**Budgets** play an important role for organizations of all sizes and forms. For example, budgets are used in managing the operations of government agencies, churches, hospitals, and other nonprofit organizations. Individuals and families also use budgeting in managing their financial affairs. This chapter describes and illustrates budgeting for a manufacturing company.

## Objectives of Budgeting

Budgeting involves (1) establishing specific goals, (2) executing plans to achieve the goals, and (3) periodically comparing actual results with the goals. In doing so, budgeting affects the following managerial functions:

- Planning
- Directing
- Controlling

The relationships of these activities are illustrated in Exhibit 1.

*Planning* involves setting goals to guide decisions and help motivate employees. The planning process often identifies where operations can be improved.

*Directing* involves decisions and actions to achieve budgeted goals. A budgetary unit of a company is called a **responsibility center**. Each responsibility center is led by a manager who has the authority and responsibility for achieving the center's budgeted goals.

**Planning, Directing, and Controlling**

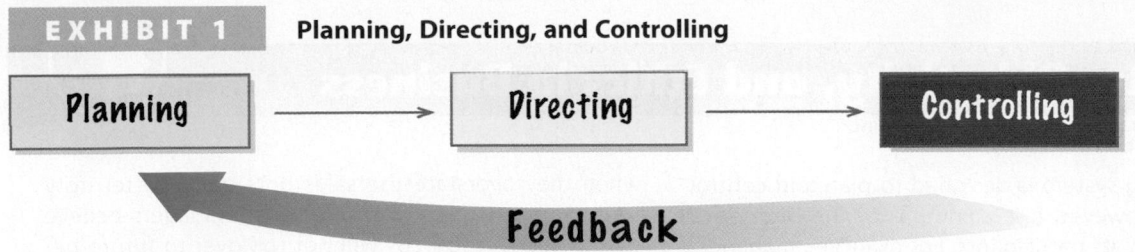

*Controlling* involves comparing actual performance against the budgeted goals. Such comparisons provide feedback to managers and employees about their performance. If necessary, responsibility centers can use such feedback to adjust their activities in the future.

## Human Behavior and Budgeting

Human behavior problems can arise in the budgeting process in the following situations:

- Budgeted goals are set too tight, which are very hard or impossible to achieve.
- Budgeted goals are set too loose, which are very easy to achieve.
- Budgeted goals conflict with the objectives of the company and employees.

These behavior problems are illustrated in Exhibit 2.

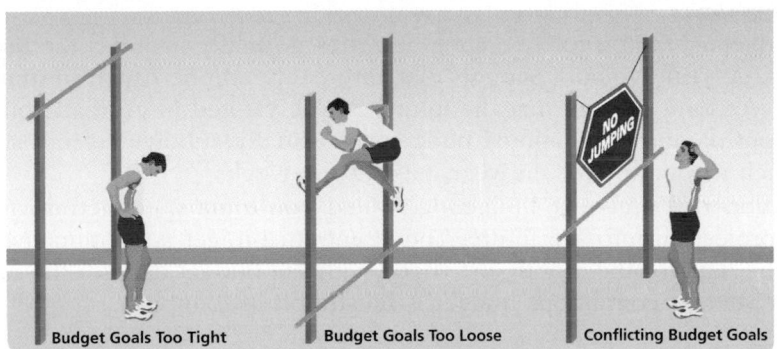

Budget Goals Too Tight     Budget Goals Too Loose     Conflicting Budget Goals

**Human Behavior Problems in Budgeting**

**Setting Budget Goals Too Tightly** Employees and managers may become discouraged if budgeted goals are set too high. That is, if budgeted goals are viewed as unrealistic or unachievable, the budget may have a negative effect on the ability of the company to achieve its goals.

Reasonable, attainable goals are more likely to motivate employees and managers. For this reason, it is important for employees and managers to be involved in the budgeting process. Involving employees in the budgeting process provides them with a sense of control and, thus, more of a commitment in meeting budgeted goals.

**Setting Budget Goals Too Loosely** Although it is desirable to establish attainable goals, it is undesirable to plan budget goals that are too easy. Such budget "padding" is termed **budgetary slack**. Managers may plan slack in their budgets to provide a "cushion" for unexpected events. However, slack budgets may create inefficiency by reducing the budgetary incentive to trim spending.

**Setting Conflicting Budget Goals** Goal conflict occurs when the employees' or managers' self-interest differs from the company's objectives or goals. To illustrate, assume that the sales department manager is given an increased sales goal and as a result accepts customers who are poor credit risks. Thus, while the sales department might meet sales goals, the overall firm may suffer reduced profitability from bad debts.

# Integrity, Objectivity, and Ethics in Business

**BUDGET GAMES**

The budgeting system is designed to plan and control a business. However, it is common for the budget to be "gamed" by its participants. For example, managers may pad their budgets with excess resources. In this way, the managers have additional resources for unexpected events during the period. If the budget is being used to establish the incentive plan, then sales managers have incentives to understate the sales potential of a territory to ensure hitting their quotas. Other times, managers engage in "land grabbing," which occurs when they overstate the sales potential of a territory to guarantee access to resources. If managers believe that unspent resources will not roll over to future periods, then they may be encouraged to "spend it or lose it," causing wasteful expenditures. These types of problems can be partially overcome by separating the budget into planning and incentive components. This is why many organizations have two budget processes, one for resource planning and another, more challenging budget, for motivating managers.

---

**OBJ 2**  Describe the basic elements of the budget process, the two major types of budgeting, and the use of computers in budgeting.

# Budgeting Systems

Budgeting systems vary among companies and industries. For example, the budget system used by **Ford Motor Company** differs from that used by **Delta Air Lines**. However, the basic budgeting concepts discussed in this section apply to all types of businesses and organizations.

The budgetary period for operating activities normally includes the fiscal year of a company. A year is short enough that future operations can be estimated fairly accurately, yet long enough that the future can be viewed in a broad context. However, for control purposes, annual budgets are usually subdivided into shorter time periods, such as quarters of the year, months, or weeks.

A variation of fiscal-year budgeting, called **continuous budgeting**, maintains a 12-month projection into the future. The 12-month budget is continually revised by replacing the data for the month just ended with the budget data for the same month in the next year. A continuous budget is illustrated in Exhibit 3.

---

**EXHIBIT 3**    **Continuous Budgeting**

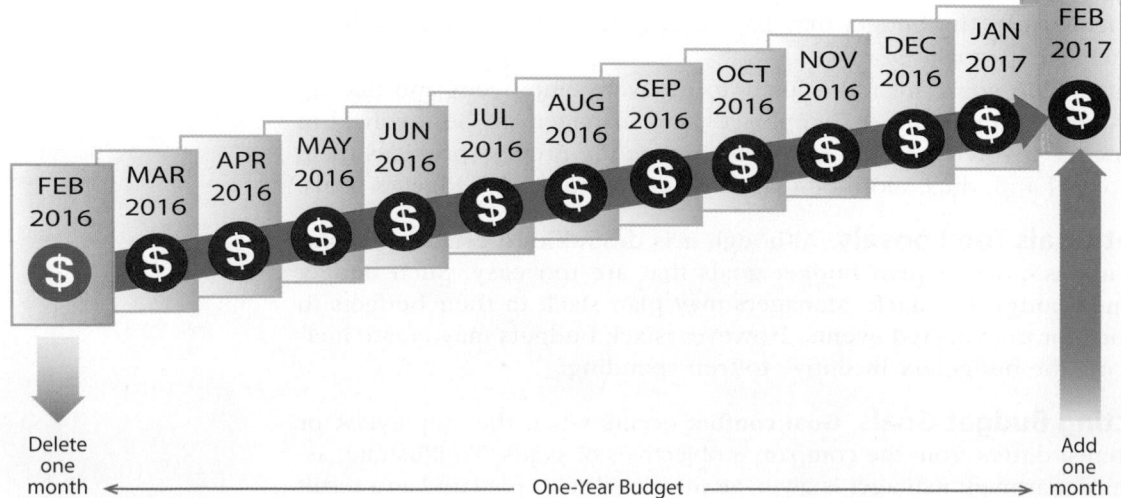

Delete one month ← ——————— One-Year Budget ——————— → Add one month

Developing an annual budget usually begins several months prior to the end of the current year. This responsibility is normally assigned to a budget committee. Such a committee often consists of the budget director, the controller, the treasurer, the production manager, and the sales manager. The budget process is monitored and summarized by the Accounting Department, which reports to the committee.

There are several methods of developing budget estimates. One method, called **zero-based budgeting**, requires managers to estimate sales, production, and other operating data as though operations are being started for the first time. This approach has the benefit of taking a fresh view of operations each year. A more common approach is to start with last year's budget and revise it for actual results and expected changes for the coming year. Two major budgets using this approach are the static budget and the flexible budget.

## Static Budget

A **static budget** shows the expected results of a responsibility center for only one activity level. Once the budget has been determined, it is not changed, even if the activity changes. Static budgeting is used by many service companies, governmental entities, and for some functions of manufacturing companies, such as purchasing, engineering, and accounting.

To illustrate, the static budget for the Assembly Department of Colter Manufacturing Company is shown in Exhibit 4.

| | A | B |
|---|---|---|
| 1 | Colter Manufacturing Company | |
| 2 | Assembly Department Budget | |
| 3 | For the Year Ending July 31, 2016 | |
| 4 | Direct labor | $40,000 |
| 5 | Electric power | 5,000 |
| 6 | Supervisor salaries | 15,000 |
| 7 | Total department costs | $60,000 |

**EXHIBIT 4**

**Static Budget**

A disadvantage of static budgets is that they do not adjust for changes in activity levels. For example, assume that the Assembly Department of Colter Manufacturing spent $70,800 for the year ended July 31, 2016. Thus, the Assembly Department spent $10,800 ($70,800 − $60,000), or 18% ($10,800 ÷ $60,000) more than budgeted. Is this good news or bad news?

The first reaction is that this is bad news and the Assembly Department was inefficient in spending more than budgeted. However, assume that the Assembly Department's budget was based on plans to assemble 8,000 units during the year. If 10,000 units were actually assembled, the additional $10,800 spent in excess of budget might be good news. That is, the Assembly Department assembled 25% (2,000 units ÷ 8,000 units) more than planned for only 18% more cost. In this case, a static budget may not be useful for controlling costs.

# Service 🛎 Focus

## FILM BUDGETING

Service businesses, like film and entertainment, use budgets as a roadmap to control expenses. In film production, the budget is a valuable tool to manage the tension between creative expression and cost.

The film budget is a static budget that can be divided into three major categories:

- above the line
- below the line
- post-production costs

The *above the line* costs include costs attributed to creative talent, such as the lead cast's and director's salaries and script fees. The *below the line* costs include the remaining costs to create the film, including location, costume, and prop rentals; permits; and other production costs. The *post-production costs* include the costs to complete the film, including editing, sound, and special effects. Marketing has a separate budget.

The total cost of the film is influenced by many decisions, including the cost of story rights, location, star quality of creative talent, union representation in the production crew, music, and special effects. Even a low-budget Indie (independent) documentary could easily have a budget of more than $1 million. In contrast, a special effect-laden Hollywood film could have a budget in excess of $200 million.

## Flexible Budget

**Note:**

Flexible budgets show expected results for several activity levels.

Unlike static budgets, **flexible budgets** show the expected results of a responsibility center for several activity levels. A flexible budget is, in effect, a series of static budgets for different levels of activity.

To illustrate, a flexible budget for the Assembly Department of Colter Manufacturing Company is shown in Exhibit 5.

**EXHIBIT 5**

**Flexible Budget**

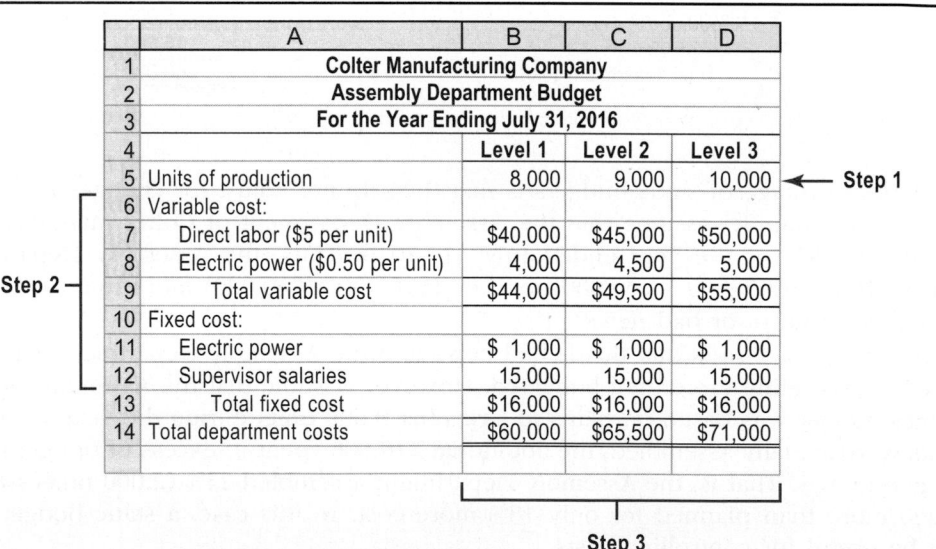

|  | A | B | C | D |
|---|---|---|---|---|
| 1 | Colter Manufacturing Company | | | |
| 2 | Assembly Department Budget | | | |
| 3 | For the Year Ending July 31, 2016 | | | |
| 4 | | Level 1 | Level 2 | Level 3 |
| 5 | Units of production | 8,000 | 9,000 | 10,000 |
| 6 | Variable cost: | | | |
| 7 | Direct labor ($5 per unit) | $40,000 | $45,000 | $50,000 |
| 8 | Electric power ($0.50 per unit) | 4,000 | 4,500 | 5,000 |
| 9 | Total variable cost | $44,000 | $49,500 | $55,000 |
| 10 | Fixed cost: | | | |
| 11 | Electric power | $ 1,000 | $ 1,000 | $ 1,000 |
| 12 | Supervisor salaries | 15,000 | 15,000 | 15,000 |
| 13 | Total fixed cost | $16,000 | $16,000 | $16,000 |
| 14 | Total department costs | $60,000 | $65,500 | $71,000 |

Step 1 ← row 5
Step 2 ← rows 6–12
Step 3

A flexible budget is constructed as follows:

- Step 1. Identify the relevant activity levels. The relevant levels of activity could be expressed in units, machine hours, direct labor hours, or some other activity base. In Exhibit 5, the levels of activity are 8,000, 9,000, and 10,000 units of production.
- Step 2. Identify the fixed and variable cost components of the costs being budgeted. In Exhibit 5, the electric power cost is separated into its fixed cost ($1,000 per year) and variable cost ($0.50 per unit). The direct labor is a variable cost, and the supervisor salaries are all fixed costs.
- Step 3. Prepare the budget for each activity level by multiplying the variable cost per unit by the activity level and then adding the monthly fixed cost.

With a flexible budget, actual costs can be compared to the budgeted costs for actual activity. To illustrate, assume that the Assembly Department spent $70,800 to produce 10,000 units. Exhibit 5 indicates that the Assembly Department was *under* budget by $200 ($71,000 – $70,800).

Under the static budget in Exhibit 4, the Assembly Department was $10,800 *over* budget. This comparison is illustrated in Exhibit 6.

The flexible budget for the Assembly Department is much more accurate and useful than the static budget. This is because the flexible budget adjusts for changes in the level of activity. Flexible budgets can be used in service businesses when the variable costs can be associated to an activity. For example, hospital room expenses are related to number of patients, or transportation fuel costs are related to number of miles.

---

| **EXHIBIT 6** | **Static and Flexible Budgets** |

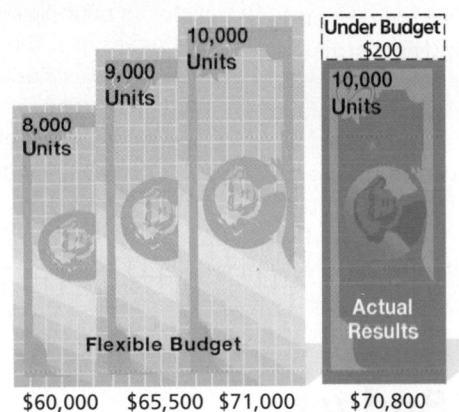

---

> **Example Exercise 22-1** **Flexible Budgeting** OBJ 2

At the beginning of the period, the Assembly Department budgeted direct labor of $45,000 and supervisor salaries of $30,000 for 5,000 hours of production. The department actually completed 6,000 hours of production. Determine the budget for the department, assuming that it uses flexible budgeting.

> **Follow My Example 22-1**

| | |
|---|---:|
| Variable cost: | |
| Direct labor (6,000 hours × $9* per hour) .......................................... | $54,000 |
| Fixed cost: | |
| Supervisor salaries............................................................ | 30,000 |
| Total department costs ....................................................... | $84,000 |

*$45,000 ÷ 5,000 hours

Practice Exercises: PE 22-1A, PE 22-1B

## Computerized Budgeting Systems

In developing budgets, companies use a variety of computerized approaches. Two of the most popular computerized approaches use:

- Spreadsheet software such as Microsoft Excel
- Integrated budget and planning (B&P) software systems

Spreadsheets ease budget preparation by summarizing budget information in linked spreadsheets across the organization. In addition, the impact of proposed changes in various assumptions or operating alternatives can be analyzed on a spreadsheet.

**Fujitsu**, a Japanese technology company, used B&P to reduce its budgeting process from 6–8 weeks down to 10–15 days.

B&P software systems use the Web (Intranet) to link thousands of employees together during the budget process. Employees can input budget data onto Web pages that are integrated and summarized throughout the company. In this way, a company can quickly and consistently integrate top-level strategies and goals to lower-level operational goals.

## Business 🌐 Connection

### BUILD VERSUS HARVEST

Budgeting systems are not "one size fits all" solutions but must adapt to the underlying business conditions. For example, a business can adopt either a build strategy or a harvest strategy. A *build* strategy is one where the business is designing, launching, and growing new products and markets. Apple, Inc.'s iPad® is an example of a product managed under a build strategy. A *harvest* strategy is often employed for business units with mature products enjoying high market share in low-growth industries. H.J. Heinz Company's ketchup and P&G's *Ivory* soap are examples of such products. A build strategy often has greater uncertainty, unpredictability, and change than a harvest

strategy. The difference between these strategies implies different budgeting approaches.

The build strategy should employ a budget approach that is flexible to the uncertainty of the business. Thus, budgets should adapt to changing conditions by allowing periodic revisions and flexible targets. The budget serves as a short-term planning tool to guide management in executing an uncertain and evolving product market strategy.

In a harvest strategy, the business is often much more stable and is managed to maximize profitability and cash flow. Because cost control is much more important in this strategy, the budget is used to restrict the actions of managers.

**OBJ 3** Describe the master budget for a manufacturing company.

# Master Budget

The **master budget** is an integrated set of operating and financial budgets for a period of time. Most companies prepare a master budget on a yearly basis. Exhibit 7 shows that the operating budgets can be used to prepare a budgeted income statement, while the financial budgets provide information for a budgeted balance sheet.

**EXHIBIT 7**

**Master Budget for a Manufacturing Company**

Operating Budgets

Sales budget
Cost of goods sold budget:
  Production budget
  Direct materials purchases budget
  Direct labor cost budget
  Factory overhead budget
Selling and administrative expense budget

⎬ Budgeted Income Statement

Financial Budgets

Cash budget
Capital expenditures budget

⎬ Budgeted Balance Sheet

The master budget begins with preparing the operating budgets, which form the budgeted income statement. Exhibit 8 shows the relationships among the operating budgets leading to an income statement budget.

EXHIBIT 8

**Operating Budgets**

# Operating Budgets

Prepare the basic operating budgets for a manufacturing company.

The integrated operating budgets that support the income statement budget are illustrated for **Elite Accessories Inc.**, a small manufacturing company of personal accessories.

## Sales Budget

The **sales budget** begins by estimating the quantity of sales. The prior year's sales are often used as a starting point. These sales quantities are then revised for such factors as planned advertising and promotion, projected pricing changes, and expected industry and general economic conditions.

Once sales quantities are estimated, the budgeted sales revenue can be determined as follows:

Budgeted Revenue = Expected Sales Volume × Expected Unit Sales Price

To illustrate, **Elite Accessories Inc.** manufactures wallets and handbags that are sold in two regions, the East and West regions. Elite Accessories estimates the following sales volumes and prices for 2016:

|  | East Region Sales Volume | West Region Sales Volume | Unit Selling Price |
|---|---|---|---|
| Wallets | 287,000 | 241,000 | $12 |
| Handbags | 156,400 | 123,600 | 25 |

Exhibit 9 illustrates the sales budget for Elite Accessories based on the preceding data.

**EXHIBIT 9**

**Sales Budget**

| | A | B | C | D |
|---|---|---|---|---|
| 1 | Elite Accessories Inc. | | | |
| 2 | Sales Budget | | | |
| 3 | For the Year Ending December 31, 2016 | | | |
| 4 | | Unit Sales | Unit Selling | |
| 5 | **Product and Region** | Volume | Price | Total Sales |
| 6 | Wallet: | | | |
| 7 | East | 287,000 | $12.00 | $ 3,444,000 |
| 8 | West | 241,000 | 12.00 | 2,892,000 |
| 9 | Total | 528,000 | | $ 6,336,000 |
| 10 | | | | |
| 11 | Handbag: | | | |
| 12 | East | 156,400 | $25.00 | $ 3,910,000 |
| 13 | West | 123,600 | 25.00 | 3,090,000 |
| 14 | Total | 280,000 | | $ 7,000,000 |
| 15 | | | | |
| 16 | Total revenue from sales | | | $13,336,000 |

## Production Budget

The production budget should be integrated with the sales budget to ensure that production and sales are kept in balance during the year. The **production budget** estimates the number of units to be manufactured to meet budgeted sales and desired inventory levels. The budgeted units to be produced are determined as follows:

| | |
|---|---|
| Expected units to be sold | XXX units |
| Plus desired units in ending inventory | + XXX |
| Less estimated units in beginning inventory | – XXX |
| Total units to be produced | XXX units |

**Elite Accessories Inc.** expects the following inventories of wallets and handbags:

| | Estimated Inventory, January 1, 2016 | Desired Inventory, December 31, 2016 |
|---|---|---|
| Wallets | 88,000 | 80,000 |
| Handbags | 48,000 | 60,000 |

Exhibit 10 illustrates the production budget for Elite Accessories.

**EXHIBIT 10**

**Production Budget**

| | A | B | C |
|---|---|---|---|
| 1 | Elite Accessories Inc. | | |
| 2 | Production Budget | | |
| 3 | For the Year Ending December 31, 2016 | | |
| 4 | | Units | |
| 5 | | Wallet | Handbag |
| 6 | Expected units to be sold (from Exhibit 9) | 528,000 | 280,000 |
| 7 | Plus desired ending inventory, December 31, 2016 | 80,000 | 60,000 |
| 8 | Total | 608,000 | 340,000 |
| 9 | Less estimated beginning inventory, January 1, 2016 | 88,000 | 48,000 |
| 10 | Total units to be produced | 520,000 | 292,000 |

**Example Exercise 22-2**  **Production Budget**

Landon Awards Co. projected sales of 45,000 brass plaques for 2016. The estimated January 1, 2016, inventory is 3,000 units, and the desired December 31, 2016, inventory is 5,000 units. What is the budgeted production (in units) for 2016?

| | |
|---|---:|
| Expected units to be sold............................................................ | 45,000 |
| Plus desired ending inventory, December 31, 2016............................... | 5,000 |
| Total.......................................................................... | 50,000 |
| Less estimated beginning inventory, January 1, 2016............................. | 3,000 |
| Total units to be produced ....................................................... | 47,000 |

Practice Exercises: PE 22-2A, PE 22-2B

## Direct Materials Purchases Budget

The direct materials purchases budget should be integrated with the production budget to ensure that production is not interrupted during the year. The **direct materials purchases budget** estimates the quantities of direct materials to be purchased to support budgeted production and desired inventory levels and can be developed in three steps.

**Step 1** Determine the budgeted direct material required for production, which is computed as follows:

Budgeted Direct Material  =  Budgeted Production Volume  ×  Direct Material Quantity
Required for Production            (from Exhibit 10)                 Expected per Unit

To illustrate, **Elite Accessories Inc.** uses leather and lining in producing wallets and handbags. The quantity of direct materials expected to be used for each unit of product is as follows:

| **Wallet** | **Handbag** |
|---|---|
| Leather: 0.30 sq. yd. per unit | Leather: 1.25 sq. yds. per unit |
| Lining: 0.10 sq. yd. per unit | Lining: 0.50 sq. yd. per unit |

For the wallet, the direct material required for production is computed as follows:

Leather: 520,000 units × 0.30 sq. yd. per unit = 156,000 sq. yds.
Lining: 520,000 units × 0.10 sq. yd. per unit = 52,000 sq. yds.

For the handbag, the direct material required for production is computed as follows:

Leather: 292,000 units × 1.25 sq. yd. per unit = 365,000 sq. yds.
Lining: 292,000 units × 0.50 sq. yd. per unit = 146,000 sq. yds.

**Step 2** The budgeted material required for production is adjusted for beginning and ending inventories to determine the direct materials to be purchased for each material, as follows:

| | |
|---|---|
| Materials required for production (Step 1) | XXX |
| Plus desired ending materials inventory | +XXX |
| Less estimated beginning materials inventory | −XXX |
| Direct material quantity to be purchased | XXX |

**Step 3** The budgeted direct materials to be purchased is computed as follows:

Budgeted Direct Material  =  Direct Material Quantity to be Purchased × Unit Price
to be Purchased                      (Step 2)

**Complete Direct Materials Purchases Budget** The following inventory and unit price information for **Elite Accessories Inc.** is expected:

| | Estimated<br>Direct Materials Inventory,<br>January 1, 2016 | Desired<br>Direct Materials Inventory,<br>December 31, 2016 |
|---|---|---|
| Leather | 18,000 sq. yds. | 20,000 sq. yds. |
| Lining | 15,000 sq. yds. | 12,000 sq. yds. |

The estimated price per square yard of leather and lining during 2016 follows:

|  | Price per Square Yard |
|---|---|
| Leather | $4.50 |
| Lining | 1.20 |

Exhibit 11 illustrates the complete direct materials purchases budget for Elite Accessories by combining all three steps into a single schedule.

**EXHIBIT 11**

**Direct Materials Purchases Budget**

|  | A | B | C | D | E |
|---|---|---|---|---|---|
| 1 | | Elite Accessories Inc. | | | |
| 2 | | Direct Materials Purchases Budget | | | |
| 3 | | For the Year Ending December 31, 2016 | | | |
| 4 | | | Direct Materials | | |
| 5 | | | Leather | Lining | Total |
| 6 | Square yards required for production: | | | | |
| 7 | Wallet (Note A) | | 156,000 | 52,000 | |
| 8 | Handbag (Note B) | | 365,000 | 146,000 | |
| 9 | Plus desired inventory, December 31, 2016 | | 20,000 | 12,000 | |
| 10 | Total | | 541,000 | 210,000 | |
| 11 | Less estimated inventory, January 1, 2016 | | 18,000 | 15,000 | |
| 12 | Total square yards to be purchased | | 523,000 | 195,000 | |
| 13 | Unit price (per square yard) | | × $4.50 | × $1.20 | |
| 14 | Total direct materials to be purchased | | $2,353,500 | $234,000 | $2,587,500 |
| 15 | | | | | |
| 16 | Note A: Leather: 520,000 units × 0.30 sq. yd. per unit = 156,000 sq. yds. | | | | |
| 17 | Lining: 520,000 units × 0.10 sq. yd. per unit = 52,000 sq. yds. | | | | |
| 18 | | | | | |
| 19 | Note B: Leather: 292,000 units × 1.25 sq. yds. per unit = 365,000 sq. yds. | | | | |
| 20 | Lining: 292,000 units × 0.50 sq. yd. per unit = 146,000 sq. yds. | | | | |

Step 1. (rows 7–8)  Step 2. (rows 9–12)  Step 3. (rows 13–14)

The timing of the direct materials purchases should be coordinated between the purchasing and production departments so that production is not interrupted.

**Example Exercise 22-3  Direct Materials Purchases Budget**  OBJ 4

Landon Awards Co. budgeted production of 47,000 brass plaques in 2016. Brass sheet is required to produce a brass plaque. Assume 96 square inches of brass sheet are required for each brass plaque. The estimated January 1, 2016, brass sheet inventory is 240,000 square inches. The desired December 31, 2016, brass sheet inventory is 200,000 square inches. If brass sheet costs $0.12 per square inch, determine the direct materials purchases budget for 2016.

**Follow My Example 22-3**

| | |
|---|---|
| Square inches required for production: Brass sheet (47,000 × 96 sq. in.) | 4,512,000 |
| Plus desired ending inventory, December 31, 2016 | 200,000 |
| Total | 4,712,000 |
| Less estimated beginning inventory, January 1, 2016 | 240,000 |
| Total square inches to be purchased | 4,472,000 |
| Unit price (per square inch) | × $0.12 |
| Total direct materials to be purchased | $536,640 |

Practice Exercises: PE 22-3A, PE 22-3B

## Direct Labor Cost Budget

The **direct labor cost budget** estimates the direct labor hours and related cost needed to support budgeted production. Production managers study work methods to provide estimates used in preparing the direct labor cost budget.

The direct labor cost budget for each department is determined in two steps, as follows.

**Step 1** Determine the budgeted direct labor hours required for production, which is computed as follows:

Budgeted Direct Labor = Budgeted Production Volume × Direct Labor Hours Expected
Hours Required for          (from Exhibit 10)                    per Unit
Production

To illustrate, **Elite Accessories Inc.**'s production managers estimate the following direct labor hours are needed to produce a wallet and handbag:

| Wallet | Handbag |
|---|---|
| Cutting Department: 0.10 hr. per unit | Cutting Department: 0.15 hr. per unit |
| Sewing Department: 0.25 hr. per unit | Sewing Department: 0.40 hr. per unit |

Thus, for the wallet, the budgeted direct labor hours required for production is computed as follows:

Cutting: 520,000 units × 0.10 hr. per unit = 52,000 direct labor hours
Sewing: 520,000 units × 0.25 hr. per unit = 130,000 direct labor hours

For the handbag, the budgeted direct labor hours required for production is computed as follows:

Cutting: 292,000 units × 0.15 hr. per unit = 43,800 direct labor hours
Sewing: 292,000 units × 0.40 hr. per unit – 116,800 direct labor hours

**Step 2** Determine the total direct labor cost as follows:

Direct Labor Cost = Direct Labor Required for Production (Step 1) × Hourly Rate

The estimated direct labor hourly rates for the Cutting and Sewing departments for **Elite Accessories, Inc.** during 2016 follow:

| | Hourly Rate |
|---|---|
| Cutting Department | $12 |
| Sewing Department | 15 |

**Complete Direct Labor Cost Budget** Exhibit 12 illustrates the direct labor cost budget by combining both steps for **Elite Accessories Inc.**

| | A | B | C | D | E |
|---|---|---|---|---|---|
| 1 | | Elite Accessories Inc. | | | |
| 2 | | Direct Labor Cost Budget | | | |
| 3 | | For the Year Ending December 31, 2016 | | | |
| 4 | | | Cutting | Sewing | Total |
| 5 | Hours required for production: | | | | |
| 6 | | Wallet (Note A) | 52,000 | 130,000 | |
| 7 | | Handbag (Note B) | 43,800 | 116,800 | |
| 8 | | Total | 95,800 | 246,800 | |
| 9 | Hourly rate | | ⊁ $12.00 | ⊁ $15.00 | |
| 10 | Total direct labor cost | | $1,149,600 | $3,702,000 | $4,851,600 |
| 11 | | | | | |
| 12 | Note A: | Cutting Department: 520,000 units × 0.10 hr. per unit = 52,000 hrs. | | | |
| 13 | | Sewing Department: 520,000 units × 0.25 hr. per unit = 130,000 hrs. | | | |
| 14 | | | | | |
| 15 | Note B: | Cutting Department: 292,000 units × 0.15 hr. per unit = 43,800 hrs. | | | |
| 16 | | Sewing Department: 292,000 units × 0.40 hr. per unit = 116,800 hrs. | | | |

Step 1. — rows 6, 7, 8
Step 2. — rows 9, 10

**EXHIBIT 12**

**Direct Labor Cost Budget**

The direct labor needs should be coordinated between the production and personnel departments so that there will be enough labor available for production.

---

### Example Exercise 22-4  Direct Labor Cost Budget

**OBJ 4**

Landon Awards Co. budgeted production of 47,000 brass plaques in 2016. Each plaque requires engraving. Assume that 12 minutes are required to engrave each plaque. If engraving labor costs $11.00 per hour, determine the direct labor cost budget for 2016.

### Follow My Example 22-4

Hours required for engraving:
| | |
|---|---:|
| Brass plaque (47,000 × 12 min.) ................................................... | 564,000 min. |
| Convert minutes to hours ...................................................... | ÷ 60 min. |
| Engraving hours ................................................................ | 9,400 hrs. |
| Hourly rate ..................................................................... | × $11.00 |
| Total direct labor cost.......................................................... | $103,400 |

Practice Exercises: PE 22-4A, PE 22-4B

---

## Factory Overhead Cost Budget

The **factory overhead cost budget** estimates the cost for each item of factory overhead needed to support budgeted production.

Exhibit 13 illustrates the factory overhead cost budget for **Elite Accessories Inc.**

**EXHIBIT 13**

**Factory Overhead Cost Budget**

| | A | B |
|---|---|---|
| 1 | Elite Accessories Inc. | |
| 2 | Factory Overhead Cost Budget | |
| 3 | For the Year Ending December 31, 2016 | |
| 4 | Indirect factory wages | $ 732,800 |
| 5 | Supervisor salaries | 360,000 |
| 6 | Power and light | 306,000 |
| 7 | Depreciation of plant and equipment | 288,000 |
| 8 | Indirect materials | 182,800 |
| 9 | Maintenance | 140,280 |
| 10 | Insurance and property taxes | 79,200 |
| 11 | Total factory overhead cost | $2,089,080 |

The factory overhead cost budget shown in Exhibit 13 may be supported by departmental schedules. Such schedules normally separate factory overhead costs into fixed and variable costs to better enable department managers to monitor and evaluate costs during the year.

The factory overhead cost budget should be integrated with the production budget to ensure that production is not interrupted during the year.

## Cost of Goods Sold Budget

The **cost of goods sold budget** is prepared by integrating the following budgets:

- Direct materials purchases budget (Exhibit 11)
- Direct labor cost budget (Exhibit 12)
- Factory overhead cost budget (Exhibit 13)

In addition, the estimated and desired inventories for direct materials, work in process, and finished goods must be integrated into the cost of goods sold budget.

**Elite Accessories Inc.** expects the following direct materials, work in process, and finished goods inventories:

| | Estimated Inventory, January 1, 2016 | Desired Inventory, December 31, 2016 |
|---|---|---|
| Direct materials: | | |
| Leather | $ 81,000 (18,000 sq. yds. × $4.50) | $ 90,000 (20,000 sq. yds. × $4.50) |
| Lining | 18,000 (15,000 sq. yds. × $1.20) | 14,400 (12,000 sq. yds. × $1.20) |
| Total direct materials | $ 99,000 | $ 104,400 |
| Work in process | $ 214,400 | $ 220,000 |
| Finished goods | $1,095,600 | $1,565,000 |

The cost of goods sold budget for Elite Accessories in Exhibit 14 indicates that total manufacturing costs of $9,522,780 are budgeted to be incurred in 2016. Of this total, $2,582,100 is budgeted for direct materials, $4,851,600 is budgeted for direct labor, and $2,089,080 is budgeted for factory overhead. After considering work in process inventories, the total budgeted cost of goods manufactured and transferred to finished goods during 2016 is $9,517,180. Based on expected sales, the budgeted cost of goods sold is $9,047,780.

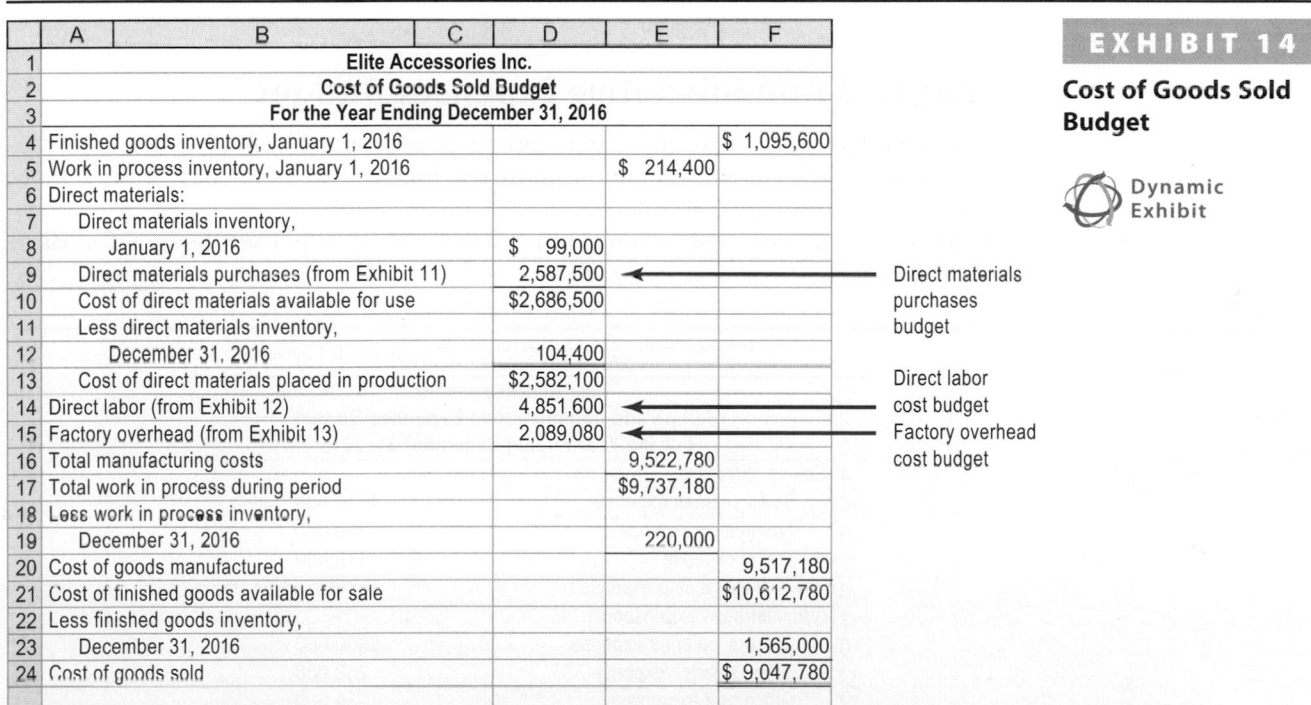

**EXHIBIT 14**

**Cost of Goods Sold Budget**

Dynamic Exhibit

| | A | B | C | D | E | F |
|---|---|---|---|---|---|---|
| 1 | | Elite Accessories Inc. | | | | |
| 2 | | Cost of Goods Sold Budget | | | | |
| 3 | | For the Year Ending December 31, 2016 | | | | |
| 4 | Finished goods inventory, January 1, 2016 | | | | | $ 1,095,600 |
| 5 | Work in process inventory, January 1, 2016 | | | | $ 214,400 | |
| 6 | Direct materials: | | | | | |
| 7 | Direct materials inventory, | | | | | |
| 8 | January 1, 2016 | | | $ 99,000 | | |
| 9 | Direct materials purchases (from Exhibit 11) | | | 2,587,500 | | |
| 10 | Cost of direct materials available for use | | | $2,686,500 | | |
| 11 | Less direct materials inventory, | | | | | |
| 12 | December 31, 2016 | | | 104,400 | | |
| 13 | Cost of direct materials placed in production | | | $2,582,100 | | |
| 14 | Direct labor (from Exhibit 12) | | | 4,851,600 | | |
| 15 | Factory overhead (from Exhibit 13) | | | 2,089,080 | | |
| 16 | Total manufacturing costs | | | | 9,522,780 | |
| 17 | Total work in process during period | | | | $9,737,180 | |
| 18 | Less work in process inventory, | | | | | |
| 19 | December 31, 2016 | | | | 220,000 | |
| 20 | Cost of goods manufactured | | | | | 9,517,180 |
| 21 | Cost of finished goods available for sale | | | | | $10,612,780 |
| 22 | Less finished goods inventory, | | | | | |
| 23 | December 31, 2016 | | | | | 1,565,000 |
| 24 | Cost of goods sold | | | | | $ 9,047,780 |

Direct materials purchases budget

Direct labor cost budget
Factory overhead cost budget

---

**Example Exercise 22-5  Cost of Goods Sold Budget**  OBJ 4

Prepare a cost of goods sold budget for Landon Awards Co. using the information in Example Exercises 22-3 and 22-4. Assume the estimated inventories on January 1, 2016, for finished goods and work in process were $54,000 and $47,000, respectively. Also assume the desired inventories on December 31, 2016, for finished goods and work in process were $50,000 and $49,000, respectively. Factory overhead was budgeted for $126,000.

*(Continued)*

**Follow My Example 22-5**

| | | | |
|---|---|---|---|
| Finished goods inventory, January 1, 2016 ........................... | | | $ 54,000 |
| Work in process inventory, January 1, 2016 ......................... | | $ 47,000 | |
| Direct materials: | | | |
|    Direct materials inventory, January 1, 2014 | | | |
|      (240,000 × $0.12, from EE 22-3) ............................. | $ 28,800 | | |
|    Direct materials purchases (from EE 22-3)....................... | 536,640 | | |
|    Cost of direct materials available for use....................... | $565,440 | | |
|    Less direct materials inventory, December 31, 2016 | | | |
|      (200,000 × $0.12, from EE 22-3) ............................. | 24,000 | | |
|    Cost of direct materials placed in production................... | $541,440 | | |
| Direct labor (from EE 22-4)........................................... | 103,400 | | |
| Factory overhead .................................................... | 126,000 | | |
| Total manufacturing costs ........................................... | | 770,840 | |
| Total work in process during period................................. | | $817,840 | |
| Less work in process inventory, December 31, 2016 ................. | | 49,000 | |
| Cost of goods manufactured........................................ | | | 768,840 |
| Cost of finished goods available for sale............................ | | | $822,840 |
| Less finished goods inventory, December 31, 2016 .................. | | | 50,000 |
| Cost of goods sold.................................................. | | | $772,840 |

Practice Exercises: PE 22-5A, PE 22-5B

## Selling and Administrative Expenses Budget

The sales budget is often used as the starting point for the selling and administrative expenses budget. For example, a budgeted increase in sales may require more advertising expenses.

Exhibit 15 illustrates the selling and administrative expenses budget for **Elite Accessories Inc.**

**EXHIBIT 15**

**Selling and Administrative Expenses Budget**

| | A | B | C |
|---|---|---|---|
| 1 | Elite Accessories Inc. | | |
| 2 | Selling and Administrative Expenses Budget | | |
| 3 | For the Year Ending December 31, 2016 | | |
| 4 | Selling expenses: | | |
| 5 |   Sales salaries expense | $715,000 | |
| 6 |   Advertising expense | 360,000 | |
| 7 |   Travel expense | 115,000 | |
| 8 |     Total selling expenses | | $1,190,000 |
| 9 | Administrative expenses: | | |
| 10 |   Officers' salaries expense | $360,000 | |
| 11 |   Office salaries expense | 258,000 | |
| 12 |   Office rent expense | 34,500 | |
| 13 |   Office supplies expense | 17,500 | |
| 14 |   Miscellaneous administrative expenses | 25,000 | |
| 15 |     Total administrative expenses | | 695,000 |
| 16 | Total selling and administrative expenses | | $1,885,000 |
| | | | |

The selling and administrative expenses budget shown in Exhibit 15 is normally supported by departmental schedules. For example, an advertising expense schedule for the Marketing Department could include the advertising media to be used (newspaper, direct mail, television), quantities (column inches, number of pieces, minutes), and related costs per unit.

## Budgeted Income Statement

The budgeted income statement for **Elite Accessories Inc.** in Exhibit 16 is prepared by integrating the following budgets:

- Sales budget (Exhibit 9)
- Cost of goods sold budget (Exhibit 14)
- Selling and administrative expenses budget (Exhibit 15)

In addition, estimates of other income, other expense, and income tax are also integrated into the budgeted income statement.

This budget summarizes the budgeted operating activities of the company. In doing so, the budgeted income statement allows management to assess the effects of estimated sales, costs, and expenses on profits for the year.

---

**EXHIBIT 16**    **Budgeted Income Statement**

| | A | B | C | |
|---|---|---|---|---|
| 1 | Elite Accessories Inc. | | | |
| 2 | Budgeted Income Statement | | | |
| 3 | For the Year Ending December 31, 2016 | | | |
| 4 | Revenue from sales (from Exhibit 9) | | $13,336,000 | ← Sales budget |
| 5 | Cost of goods sold (from Exhibit 14) | | 9,047,780 | ← Cost of goods sold budget |
| 6 | | | | |
| 7 | Gross profit | | $ 4,288,220 | |
| 8 | Selling and administrative expenses: | | | |
| 9 | Selling expenses (from Exhibit 15) | $1,190,000 | | Selling and administrative expenses budget |
| 10 | Administrative expenses (from Exhibit 15) | 695,000 | | |
| 11 | Total selling and administrative expenses | | 1,885,000 | |
| 12 | Income from operations | | $ 2,403,220 | |
| 13 | Other income: | | | |
| 14 | Interest revenue | $   98,000 | | |
| 15 | Other expenses: | | | |
| 16 | Interest expense | 90,000 | 8,000 | |
| 17 | Income before income tax | | $ 2,411,220 | |
| 18 | Income tax | | 600,000 | |
| 19 | Net income | | $ 1,811,220 | |

---

# Financial Budgets

While the operating budgets reflect the operating activities of the company, the financial budgets reflect the financing and investing activities. In this section, the following financial budgets are described and illustrated:

- Cash budget
- Capital expenditures budget

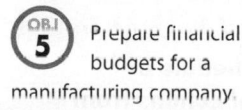

**OBJ 5**  Prepare financial budgets for a manufacturing company.

## Cash Budget

The **cash budget** estimates the expected receipts (inflows) and payments (outflows) of cash for a period of time. The cash budget is integrated with the various operating budgets. In addition, the capital expenditures budget, dividends, and equity or long-term debt financing plans of the company affect the cash budget.

**Note:**
The cash budget presents the expected receipts and payments of cash for a period of time.

To illustrate, a monthly cash budget for January, February, and March 2016 for **Elite Accessories Inc.** is prepared. The preparation of the cash budget begins by estimating cash receipts.

### Estimated Cash Receipts

The primary source of estimated cash receipts is from cash sales and collections on account. In addition, cash receipts may be obtained from plans to issue equity or debt financing as well as other sources such as interest revenue.

To estimate cash receipts from cash sales and collections on account, a *schedule of collections from sales* is prepared. To illustrate, the following data for **Elite Accessories Inc.** are used:

|  | January | February | March |
|---|---|---|---|
| Sales: | | | |
| Budgeted sales.................................... | $1,080,000 | $1,240,000 | $970,000 |
| Accounts Receivable: | | | |
| Accounts receivable January 1, 2016............... | $480,000 | | |
| Receipts from sales on account: | | | |
| From prior month's sales on account............... | 40% | | |
| From current month's sales on account............. | 60 | | |
| | 100% | | |

The budgeted cash collected for any month is the sum of the cash collected from previous month's sales and the cash collected from current month's sales. To illustrate, the cash collected in February is 40% of cash collected on sales in January ($1,080,000 × 40%) added to 60% of cash collected on sales in February ($1,240,000 × 60%), shown as follows:

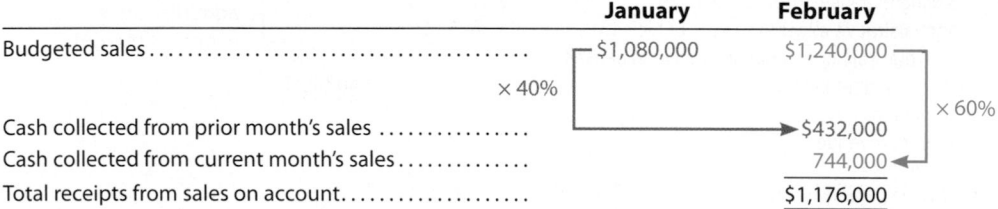

|  | January | February |
|---|---|---|
| Budgeted sales......................................... | $1,080,000 | $1,240,000 |
| × 40% | | |
| Cash collected from prior month's sales ................ | | $432,000 |
| Cash collected from current month's sales.............. | | 744,000 |
| Total receipts from sales on account................... | | $1,176,000 |

× 60%

Using the preceding data, Exhibit 17 shows the schedule of collections from sales for Elite Accessories for all three months. To simplify, it is assumed that all accounts receivable are collected and there are no cash sales.

**EXHIBIT 17**

**Schedule of Collections from Sales**

| | A | B | C | D | E |
|---|---|---|---|---|---|
| 1 | | Elite Accessories Inc. | | | |
| 2 | | Schedule of Collections from Sales | | | |
| 3 | | For the Three Months Ending March 31, 2016 | | | |
| 4 | | | January | February | March |
| 5 | Cash collected from prior month's sales—Note A | | 480,000 | 432,000 | 496,000 |
| 6 | Cash collected from current month's sales—Note B | | 648,000 | 744,000 | 582,000 |
| 7 | Total receipts from sales on account | | $1,128,000 | $1,176,000 | $1,078,000 |
| 8 | | | | | |
| 9 | Note A: | $480,000, given as January 1, 2016, Accounts Receivable balance | | | |
| 10 | | $432,000 = $1,080,000 × 40% | | | |
| 11 | | $496,000 = $1,240,000 × 40% | | | |
| 12 | | | | | |
| 13 | Note B: | $648,000 = $1,080,000 × 60% | | | |
| 14 | | $744,000 = $1,240,000 × 60% | | | |
| 15 | | $582,000 = $970,000 × 60% | | | |
| | | | | | |

### Estimated Cash Payments

Estimated cash payments must be budgeted for operating costs and expenses such as manufacturing costs, selling expenses, and administrative expenses. In addition, estimated cash payments may be planned for capital expenditures, dividends, interest payments, or long-term debt payments.

To estimate cash payments for manufacturing costs, a *schedule of payments for manufacturing costs* is prepared. To illustrate, the following data for **Elite Accessories Inc.** are used:

| | January | February | March |
|---|---|---|---|
| **Manufacturing Costs:** | | | |
| Budgeted manufacturing costs ........................... | $840,000 | $780,000 | $812,000 |
| Depreciation on machines included | | | |
| in manufacturing costs ................................. | 24,000 | 24,000 | 24,000 |
| **Accounts Payable:** | | | |
| Accounts payable, January 1, 2016 ....................... | $190,000 | | |
| **Payments of manufacturing costs on account:** | | | |
| From prior month's manufacturing costs ................. | 25% | | |
| From current month's manufacturing costs ............... | 75 | | |
| | 100% | | |

The budgeted cash payments for any month are the sum of the cash paid from previous month's manufacturing costs (less depreciation) and the cash paid from current month's manufacturing costs (less depreciation). To illustrate, the cash paid in February is 25% of manufacturing costs (less depreciation) in January [($840,000 – $24,000) × 25%] added to 75% of cash paid on manufacturing costs (less depreciation) in February [($780,000 – $24,000) × 75%], computed as follows:

| | January | February |
|---|---|---|
| Budgeted manufacturing costs | $840,000 | $780,000 |
| Less: depreciation on machines | 24,000 | 24,000 |
| Manufacturing costs (less depreciation) | $816,000 | $756,000 |
| | × 25% | |
| Payments of prior month's manufacturing costs (less depreciation) | | $204,000 | × 75% |
| Payments of current month's manufacturing costs (less depreciation) | | 567,000 |
| Total payments | | $771,000 |

Using the preceding data, Exhibit 18 shows the schedule of payments for manufacturing costs for Elite Accessories for all three months.

| | A | B | C | D | E |
|---|---|---|---|---|---|
| 1 | | Elite Accessories Inc. | | | |
| 2 | | Schedule of Payments for Manufacturing Costs | | | |
| 3 | | For the Three Months Ending March 31, 2016 | | | |
| 4 | | | January | February | March |
| 5 | Payments of prior month's manufacturing costs | | | | |
| 6 | {[25% × previous month's manufacturing costs | | | | |
| 7 | (less depreciation)]—Note A} | | $190,000 | $204,000 | $189,000 |
| 8 | Payments of current month's manufacturing costs | | | | |
| 9 | {[75% × current month's manufacturing costs | | | | |
| 10 | (less depreciation)]—Note B} | | 612,000 | 567,000 | 591,000 |
| 11 | Total payments | | $802,000 | $771,000 | $780,000 |
| 12 | | | | | |
| 13 | Note A: $190,000, given as January 1, 2016, Accounts Payable balance | | | | |
| 14 | | $204,000 = ($840,000 – $24,000) × 25% | | | |
| 15 | | $189,000 = ($780,000 – $24,000) × 25% | | | |
| 16 | | | | | |
| 17 | Note B: $612,000 = ($840,000 – $24,000) × 75% | | | | |
| 18 | | $567,000 = ($780,000 – $24,000) × 75% | | | |
| 19 | | $591,000 = ($812,000 – $24,000) × 75% | | | |

**EXHIBIT 18**

**Schedule of Payments for Manufacturing Costs**

**Completing the Cash Budget**  The cash budget is structured for a budget period as follows:

*Budget Period:*

| | |
|---|---|
| Estimated cash receipts | |
| − Estimated cash payments | |
| Cash increase (decrease) | |
| + Cash balance at the beginning of the month | |
| Cash balance at the end of the month | ⟶ Becomes the beginning balance for the next period |
| − Minimum cash balance | |
| Excess (deficiency) | |

The budgeted balance at the end of the period is determined by adding the net increase (decrease) for the period to the beginning cash balance. The ending balance is compared to a minimum cash balance to support operations as determined by management. Any difference between the ending balance and the minimum cash balance represents an excess or deficiency that may require management action.

To illustrate, assume the following additional data for **Elite Accessories Inc.**:

| | |
|---|---|
| Cash balance on January 1, 2016 | $225,000 |
| Quarterly taxes paid on March 31, 2016 | 150,000 |
| Quarterly interest expense paid on January 10, 2016 | 22,500 |
| Quarterly interest revenue received on March 21, 2016 | 24,500 |
| Sewing equipment purchased in February 2016 | 274,000 |
| Selling and administrative expenses (paid in month incurred): | |

| January | February | March |
|---|---|---|
| $160,000 | $165,000 | $145,000 |

The cash budget for Elite Accessories is shown in Exhibit 19.

The estimated cash receipts include the total receipts from sales on account (Exhibit 17). The estimated cash payments include the cash payments from manufacturing costs (Exhibit 18). Other receipts and payments are provided by the additional information. Additionally, assume the minimum cash balance is $340,000.

---

**EXHIBIT 19**

**Cash Budget**

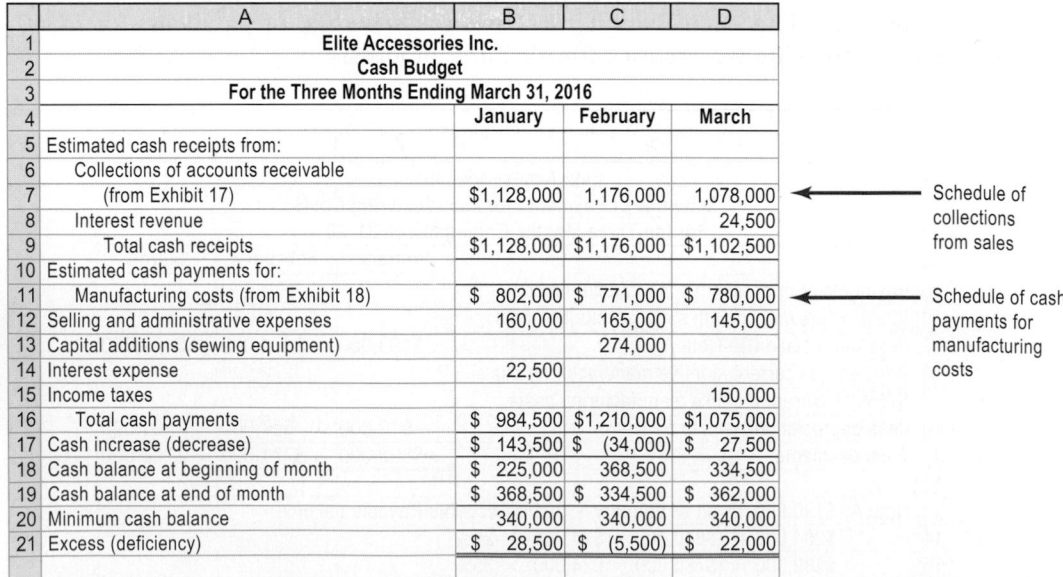

| | A | B | C | D |
|---|---|---|---|---|
| 1 | Elite Accessories Inc. | | | |
| 2 | Cash Budget | | | |
| 3 | For the Three Months Ending March 31, 2016 | | | |
| 4 | | January | February | March |
| 5 | Estimated cash receipts from: | | | |
| 6 | Collections of accounts receivable | | | |
| 7 | (from Exhibit 17) | $1,128,000 | 1,176,000 | 1,078,000 |
| 8 | Interest revenue | | | 24,500 |
| 9 | Total cash receipts | $1,128,000 | $1,176,000 | $1,102,500 |
| 10 | Estimated cash payments for: | | | |
| 11 | Manufacturing costs (from Exhibit 18) | $ 802,000 | $ 771,000 | $ 780,000 |
| 12 | Selling and administrative expenses | 160,000 | 165,000 | 145,000 |
| 13 | Capital additions (sewing equipment) | | 274,000 | |
| 14 | Interest expense | 22,500 | | |
| 15 | Income taxes | | | 150,000 |
| 16 | Total cash payments | $ 984,500 | $1,210,000 | $1,075,000 |
| 17 | Cash increase (decrease) | $ 143,500 | $ (34,000) | $ 27,500 |
| 18 | Cash balance at beginning of month | $ 225,000 | 368,500 | 334,500 |
| 19 | Cash balance at end of month | $ 368,500 | $ 334,500 | $ 362,000 |
| 20 | Minimum cash balance | 340,000 | 340,000 | 340,000 |
| 21 | Excess (deficiency) | $ 28,500 | $ (5,500) | $ 22,000 |

*Schedule of collections from sales* (→ row 7)

*Schedule of cash payments for manufacturing costs* (→ row 11)

Exhibit 19 indicates that Elite Accessories expects a cash excess at the end of January of $28,500. This excess could be invested in temporary income-producing securities such as U.S. Treasury bills or notes. In contrast, the estimated cash deficiency at the end of February of $5,500 might require Elite Accessories to borrow cash from its bank.

---

**Example Exercise 22-6   Cash Budget**

Landon Awards Co. collects 25% of its sales on account in the month of the sale and 75% in the month following the sale. If sales on account are budgeted to be $100,000 for March and $126,000 for April, what are the budgeted cash receipts from sales on account for April?

**Follow My Example 22-6**

|  | April |
| --- | --- |
| Collections from March sales (75% × $100,000)..................................... | $ 75,000 |
| Collections from April sales (25% × $126,000) ...................................... | 31,500 |
| Total receipts from sales on account ................................................ | $106,500 |

Practice Exercises: PE 22-6A, PE 22-6B

---

## Capital Expenditures Budget

The **capital expenditures budget** summarizes plans for acquiring fixed assets. Such expenditures are necessary as machinery and other fixed assets wear out or become obsolete. In addition, purchasing additional fixed assets may be necessary to meet increasing demand for the company's product.

To illustrate, a five-year capital expenditures budget for **Elite Accessories Inc.** is shown in Exhibit 20.

|  | A | B | C | D | E | F |
| --- | --- | --- | --- | --- | --- | --- |
| 1 | | Elite Accessories Inc. | | | | |
| 2 | | Capital Expenditures Budget | | | | |
| 3 | | For the Five Years Ending December 31, 2020 | | | | |
| 4 | Item | 2016 | 2017 | 2018 | 2019 | 2020 |
| 5 | Machinery—Cutting Department | $400,000 | | | $280,000 | $360,000 |
| 6 | Machinery—Sewing Department | 274,000 | $200,000 | $560,000 | 200,000 | |
| 7 | Office equipment | | | 90,000 | | 60,000 |
| 8 | Total | $674,000 | $350,000 | $560,000 | $480,000 | $420,000 |

**EXHIBIT 20**

**Capital Expenditures Budget**

As shown in Exhibit 20, capital expenditures budgets are often prepared for five to ten years into the future. This is necessary because fixed assets often must be ordered years in advance. Likewise, it could take years to construct new buildings or other production facilities.

The capital expenditures budget should be integrated with the operating and financing budgets. For example, depreciation of new manufacturing equipment affects the factory overhead cost budget. The plans for financing the capital expenditures also affect the cash budget.

## Budgeted Balance Sheet

The budgeted balance sheet is prepared based on the operating and financial budgets of the master budget. The budgeted balance sheet is dated as of the end of the budget period and is similar to a normal balance sheet except that estimated amounts are used. For this reason, a budgeted balance sheet for Elite Accessories Inc. is not illustrated.

# At a Glance 22

## 1  Describe budgeting, its objectives, and its impact on human behavior.

**Key Points**  Budgeting involves (1) establishing plans (planning), (2) directing operations (directing), and (3) evaluating performance (controlling). In addition, budgets should be established to avoid human behavior problems.

| Learning Outcomes | Example Exercises | Practice Exercises |
|---|---|---|
| • Describe the planning, directing, controlling, and feedback elements of the budget process. | | |
| • Describe the behavioral issues associated with tight goals, loose goals, and goal conflict. | | |

## 2  Describe the basic elements of the budget process, the two major types of budgeting, and the use of computers in budgeting.

**Key Points**  The budget estimates received by the budget committee should be carefully studied, analyzed, revised, and integrated. The static and flexible budgets are two major budgeting approaches. Computers can be used to make the budget process more efficient and organizationally integrated.

| Learning Outcomes | Example Exercises | Practice Exercises |
|---|---|---|
| • Describe a static budget and explain when it might be used. | | |
| • Describe and prepare a flexible budget and explain when it might be used. | EE22-1 | PE22-1A, 22-1B |
| • Describe the role of computers in the budget process. | | |

## 3  Describe the master budget for a manufacturing company.

**Key Points**  The master budget consists of operating and financial budgets.

| Learning Outcome | Example Exercises | Practice Exercises |
|---|---|---|
| • Illustrate the connection between the major operating and financial budgets. | | |

**Prepare the basic operating budgets for a manufacturing company.**

**Key Points** The basic operating budgets are the sales budget, production budget, direct materials purchases budget, direct labor cost budget, factory overhead cost budget, cost of goods sold budget, and selling and administrative expenses budget. These can then be combined to prepare an income statement budget.

| Learning Outcomes | Example Exercises | Practice Exercises |
|---|---|---|
| • Prepare a sales budget. | | |
| • Prepare a production budget. | EE22-2 | PE22-2A, 22-2B |
| • Prepare a direct materials purchases budget. | EE22-3 | PE22-3A, 22-3B |
| • Prepare a direct labor cost budget. | EE22-4 | PE22-4A, 22-4B |
| • Prepare a factory overhead cost budget. | | |
| • Prepare a cost of goods sold budget. | EE22-5 | PE22-5A, 22-5B |
| • Prepare a selling and administrative expenses budget. | | |
| • Prepare an income statement budget. | | |

**Prepare financial budgets for a manufacturing company.**

**Key Points** The cash budget and capital expenditures budget are financial budgets showing the investing and financing activities of the firm.

| Learning Outcomes | Example Exercises | Practice Exercises |
|---|---|---|
| • Prepare cash receipts and cash payments schedules. | EE22-6 | PE22-6A, 22-6B |
| • Prepare a cash budget. | | |
| • Prepare a capital expenditures budget. | | |

# Key Terms

budget (1030)
budgetary slack (1031)
capital expenditures budget (1049)
cash budget (1045)
continuous budgeting (1032)
cost of goods sold budget (1042)

direct labor cost budget (1040)
direct materials purchases budget (1039)
factory overhead cost budget (1042)
flexible budget (1034)
goal conflict (1031)

master budget (1036)
production budget (1038)
responsibility center (1030)
sales budget (1037)
static budget (1033)
zero-based budgeting (1033)

# Illustrative Problem

Selected information concerning sales and production for Cabot Co. for July 2016 are summarized as follows:

a. Estimated sales:

Product K: 40,000 units at $30 per unit
Product L: 20,000 units at $65 per unit

b. Estimated inventories, July 1, 2016:

| Material A: | 4,000 lbs. | Product K: | 3,000 units at $17 per unit | $ 51,000 |
| Material B: | 3,500 lbs. | Product L: | 2,700 units at $35 per unit | 94,500 |
| | | Total | | $145,500 |

There were no work in process inventories estimated for July 1, 2016.

c. Desired inventories at July 31, 2016:

| Material A: | 3,000 lbs. | Product K: | 2,500 units at $17 per unit | $ 42,500 |
| Material B: | 2,500 lbs. | Product L: | 2,000 units at $35 per unit | 70,000 |
| | | Total | | $112,500 |

There were no work in process inventories desired for July 31, 2016.

d. Direct materials used in production:

| | Product K | Product L |
| --- | --- | --- |
| Material A: | 0.7 lb. per unit | 3.5 lbs. per unit |
| Material B: | 1.2 lbs. per unit | 1.8 lbs. per unit |

e. Unit costs for direct materials:

Material A: $4.00 per lb.
Material B: $2.00 per lb.

f. Direct labor requirements:

| | Department 1 | Department 2 |
| --- | --- | --- |
| Product K | 0.4 hr. per unit | 0.15 hr. per unit |
| Product L | 0.6 hr. per unit | 0.25 hr. per unit |

g.

| | Department 1 | Department 2 |
| --- | --- | --- |
| Direct labor rate | $12.00 per hr. | $16.00 per hr. |

h. Estimated factory overhead costs for July:

| Indirect factory wages | $200,000 |
| Depreciation of plant and equipment | 40,000 |
| Power and light | 25,000 |
| Indirect materials | 34,000 |
| Total | $299,000 |

## Instructions

1. Prepare a sales budget for July.

2. Prepare a production budget for July.

3. Prepare a direct materials purchases budget for July.

4. Prepare a direct labor cost budget for July.

5. Prepare a cost of goods sold budget for July.

## Solution

1.

| | A | B | C | D |
|---|---|---|---|---|
| 1 | | Cabot Co. | | |
| 2 | | Sales Budget | | |
| 3 | | For the Month Ending July 31, 2016 | | |
| 4 | **Product** | **Unit Sales Volume** | **Unit Selling Price** | **Total Sales** |
| 5 | Product K | 40,000 | $30.00 | $1,200,000 |
| 6 | Product L | 20,000 | 65.00 | 1,300,000 |
| 7 | Total revenue from sales | | | $2,500,000 |

2.

| | A | B | C |
|---|---|---|---|
| 1 | | Cabot Co. | |
| 2 | | Production Budget | |
| 3 | | For the Month Ending July 31, 2016 | |
| 4 | | Units | |
| 5 | | **Product K** | **Product L** |
| 6 | Sales | 40,000 | 20,000 |
| 7 | Plus desired inventories at July 31, 2016 | 2,500 | 2,000 |
| 8 | Total | 42,500 | 22,000 |
| 9 | Less estimated inventories, July 1, 2016 | 3,000 | 2,700 |
| 10 | Total production | 39,500 | 19,300 |

3.

| | A | B | C | D | E | F | G |
|---|---|---|---|---|---|---|---|
| 1 | | | Cabot Co. | | | | |
| 2 | | | Direct Materials Purchases Budget | | | | |
| 3 | | | For the Month Ending July 31, 2016 | | | | |
| 4 | | | Direct Materials | | | | |
| 5 | | | **Material A** | | **Material B** | | **Total** |
| 6 | Units required for production: | | | | | | |
| 7 | Product K (39,500 × lbs. per unit) | | 27,650 | lbs.* | 47,400 | lbs.* | |
| 8 | Product L (19,300 × lbs. per unit) | | 67,550 | ** | 34,740 | ** | |
| 9 | Plus desired units of inventory, | | | | | | |
| 10 | July 31, 2016 | | 3,000 | | 2,500 | | |
| 11 | Total | | 98,200 | lbs. | 84,640 | lbs. | |
| 12 | Less estimated units of inventory, | | | | | | |
| 13 | July 1, 2016 | | 4,000 | | 3,500 | | |
| 14 | Total units to be purchased | | 94,200 | lbs. | 81,140 | lbs. | |
| 15 | Unit price | | × $4.00 | | × $2.00 | | |
| 16 | Total direct materials purchases | | $376,800 | | $162,280 | | $539,080 |
| 17 | | | | | | | |
| 18 | *27,650 − 39,500 × 0.7    47,400 = 39,500 × 1.2 | | | | | | |
| 19 | **67,550 = 19,300 × 3.5    34,740 = 19,300 × 1.8 | | | | | | |

4.

| | A | B | C | D | E | F | G |
|---|---|---|---|---|---|---|---|
| 1 | | | Cabot Co. | | | | |
| 2 | | | Direct Labor Cost Budget | | | | |
| 3 | | | For the Month Ending July 31, 2016 | | | | |
| 4 | | | Department 1 | | Department 2 | | Total |
| 5 | Hours required for production: | | | | | | |
| 6 | Product K (39,500 × hrs. per unit) | | 15,800 | * | 5,925 | * | |
| 7 | Product L (19,300 × hrs. per unit) | | 11,580 | ** | 4,825 | ** | |
| 8 | Total | | 27,380 | | 10,750 | | |
| 9 | Hourly rate | | ×$12.00 | | ×$16.00 | | |
| 10 | Total direct labor cost | | $328,560 | | $172,000 | | $500,560 |
| 11 | | | | | | | |
| 12 | *15,800 = 39,500 × 0.4 | 5,925 = 39,500 × 0.15 | | | | | |
| 13 | **11,580 = 19,300 × 0.6 | 4,825 = 19,300 × 0.25 | | | | | |

5.

| | A | B | C | D |
|---|---|---|---|---|
| 1 | Cabot Co. | | | |
| 2 | Cost of Goods Sold Budget | | | |
| 3 | For the Month Ending July 31, 2016 | | | |
| 4 | Finished goods inventory, July 1, 2016 | | | $ 145,500 |
| 5 | Direct materials: | | | |
| 6 | Direct materials inventory, July 1, 2016 (Note A) | | $ 23,000 | |
| 7 | Direct materials purchases | | 539,080 | |
| 8 | Cost of direct materials available for use | | $562,080 | |
| 9 | Less direct materials inventory, July 31, 2016 (Note B) | | 17,000 | |
| 10 | Cost of direct materials placed in production | | $545,080 | |
| 11 | Direct labor | | 500,560 | |
| 12 | Factory overhead | | 299,000 | |
| 13 | Cost of goods manufactured | | | 1,344,640 |
| 14 | Cost of finished goods available for sale | | | $1,490,140 |
| 15 | Less finished goods inventory, July 31, 2016 | | | 112,500 |
| 16 | Cost of goods sold | | | $1,377,640 |
| 17 | | | | |
| 18 | Note A: | | | |
| 19 | Material A    4,000 lbs.    at $4.00 per lb. | $16,000 | | |
| 20 | Material B    3,500 lbs.    at $2.00 per lb. | 7,000 | | |
| 21 | Direct materials inventory, July 1, 2016 | $23,000 | | |
| 22 | | | | |
| 23 | Note B: | | | |
| 24 | Material A    3,000 lbs.    at $4.00 per lb. | $12,000 | | |
| 25 | Material B    2,500 lbs.    at $2.00 per lb. | 5,000 | | |
| 26 | Direct materials inventory, July 31, 2016 | $17,000 | | |

# Discussion Questions

1. What are the three major objectives of budgeting?

2. Briefly describe the type of human behavior problems that might arise if budget goals are set too tightly.

3. What behavioral problems are associated with setting a budget too loosely?

4. What behavioral problems are associated with establishing conflicting goals within the budget?

5. Under what circumstances would a static budget be appropriate?

6. How do computerized budgeting systems aid firms in the budgeting process?

7. Why should the production requirements set forth in the production budget be carefully coordinated with the sales budget?

8. Why should the timing of direct materials purchases be closely coordinated with the production budget?

9. a. Discuss the purpose of the cash budget.

b. If the cash for the first quarter of the fiscal year indicates excess cash at the end of each of the first two months, how might the excess cash be used?

10. Give an example of how the capital expenditures budget affects other operating budgets.

# Practice Exercises

EE 22-1 p. 1035

SHOW
ME HOW

**PE 22-1A    Flexible budgeting**                                                   OBJ. 2

At the beginning of the period, the Assembly Department budgeted direct labor of $112,000 and property tax of $12,000 for 7,000 hours of production. The department actually completed 7,500 hours of production. Determine the budget for the department, assuming that it uses flexible budgeting.

EE 22-1 p. 1035

SHOW
ME HOW

**PE 22-1B    Flexible budgeting**                                                   OBJ. 2

At the beginning of the period, the Fabricating Department budgeted direct labor of $9,280 and equipment depreciation of $2,300 for 640 hours of production. The department actually completed 600 hours of production. Determine the budget for the department, assuming that it uses flexible budgeting.

EE 22-2 p. 1038

SHOW
ME HOW

**PE 22-2A    Production budget**                                                    OBJ. 4

MyLife Chronicles Inc. projected sales of 240,000 diaries for 2016. The estimated January 1, 2016, inventory is 19,900 units, and the desired December 31, 2016, inventory is 18,800 units. What is the budgeted production (in units) for 2016?

EE 22-2 p. 1038

SHOW
ME HOW

**PE 22-2B    Production budget**                                                    OBJ. 4

Magnolia Candle Inc. projected sales of 75,000 candles for 2016. The estimated January 1, 2016, inventory is 3,500 units, and the desired December 31, 2016, inventory is 2,700 units. What is the budgeted production (in units) for 2016?

EE 22-3 p. 1040

SHOW
ME HOW

**PE 22-3A    Direct materials purchases budget**                                    OBJ. 4

MyLife Chronicles Inc. budgeted production of 238,900 diaries in 2016. Paper is required to produce a diary. Assume five square yards of paper are required for each diary. The estimated January 1, 2016, paper inventory is 32,400 square yards. The desired December 31, 2016, paper inventory is 30,800 square yards. If paper costs $0.30 per square yard, determine the direct materials purchases budget for 2016.

EE 22-3 p. 1040

SHOW
ME HOW

**PE 22-3B    Direct materials purchases budget**                                    OBJ. 4

Magnolia Candle Inc. budgeted production of 74,200 candles in 2016. Wax is required to produce a candle. Assume eight ounces (one-half of a pound) of wax is required for each candle. The estimated January 1, 2016, wax inventory is 2,500 pounds. The desired December 31, 2016, wax inventory is 2,100 pounds. If candle wax costs $4.10 per pound, determine the direct materials purchases budget for 2016.

EE 22-4 *p. 1042*

SHOW
ME HOW

### PE 22-4A Direct labor cost budget
OBJ. 4

MyLife Chronicles Inc. budgeted production of 238,900 diaries in 2016. Each diary requires assembly. Assume that six minutes are required to assemble each diary. If assembly labor costs $12.00 per hour, determine the direct labor cost budget for 2016.

EE 22-4 *p. 1042*

SHOW
ME HOW

### PE 22-4B Direct labor cost budget
OBJ. 4

Magnolia Candle Inc. budgeted production of 74,200 candles in 2016. Each candle requires molding. Assume that 12 minutes are required to mold each candle. If molding labor costs $14.00 per hour, determine the direct labor cost budget for 2016.

EE 22-5 *p. 1043*

SHOW
ME HOW

### PE 22-5A Cost of goods sold budget
OBJ. 4

Prepare a cost of goods sold budget for MyLife Chronicles Inc. using the information in Practice Exercises 22-3A and 22-4A. Assume the estimated inventories on January 1, 2016, for finished goods and work in process were $25,000 and $19,000, respectively. Also assume the desired inventories on December 31, 2016, for finished goods and work in process were $31,500 and $16,700, respectively. Factory overhead was budgeted at $197,100.

EE 22-5 *p. 1043*

SHOW
ME HOW

### PE 22-5B Cost of goods sold budget
OBJ. 4

Prepare a cost of goods sold budget for Magnolia Candle Inc. using the information in Practice Exercises 22-3B and 22-4B. Assume the estimated inventories on January 1, 2016, for finished goods and work in process were $9,800 and $3,600, respectively. Also assume the desired inventories on December 31, 2016, for finished goods and work in process were $12,900 and $3,500, respectively. Factory overhead was budgeted at $109,600.

EE 22-6 *p. 1049*

SHOW
ME HOW

### PE 22-6A Cash budget
OBJ. 5

MyLife Chronicles Inc. collects 30% of its sales on account in the month of the sale and 70% in the month following the sale. If sales on account are budgeted to be $170,000 for June and $200,000 for July, what are the budgeted cash receipts from sales on account for July?

EE 22-6 *p. 1049*

SHOW
ME HOW

### PE 22-6B Cash budget
OBJ. 5

Magnolia Candle Inc. pays 10% of its purchases on account in the month of the purchase and 90% in the month following the purchase. If purchases are budgeted to be $11,900 for March and $12,700 for April, what are the budgeted cash payments for purchases on account for April?

# Exercises

✔ a. December 31 cash
balance, $3,000

SHOW
ME HOW

### EX 22-1 Personal budget
OBJ. 2, 5

At the beginning of the 2016 school year, Katherine Malloy decided to prepare a cash budget for the months of September, October, November, and December. The budget must plan for enough cash on December 31 to pay the spring semester tuition, which is the same as the fall tuition. The following information relates to the budget:

| | |
|---|---:|
| Cash balance, September 1 (from a summer job)..................... | $5,750 |
| Purchase season football tickets in September...................... | 210 |
| Additional entertainment for each month.......................... | 275 |
| Pay fall semester tuition in September ............................ | 3,700 |
| Pay rent at the beginning of each month.......................... | 600 |
| Pay for food each month......................................... | 235 |
| Pay apartment deposit on September 2 (to be returned December 15) .... | 500 |
| Part-time job earnings each month (net of taxes) ................... | 1,400 |

a. Prepare a cash budget for September, October, November, and December.

b. Are the four monthly budgets that are presented prepared as static budgets or flexible budgets?

c. ━━━► What are the budget implications for Katherine Malloy?

---

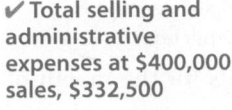

✔ Total selling and administrative expenses at $400,000 sales, $332,500

SHOW
ME HOW

### EX 22-2  Flexible budget for selling and administrative expenses for a service company

OBJ. 2, 4

Cloud Productivity Inc. uses flexible budgets that are based on the following data:

| | |
|---|---|
| Sales commissions ......................................... | 14% of sales |
| Advertising expense........................................ | 18% of sales |
| Miscellaneous administrative expense ...................... | $6,500 per month plus 12% of sales |
| Office salaries expense ..................................... | $28,000 per month |
| Customer support expenses................................. | $12,000 per month plus 20% of sales |
| Research and development expense........................ | $30,000 per month |

Prepare a flexible selling and administrative expenses budget for March 2016 for sales volumes of $400,000, $500,000, and $600,000.

---

✔ b. Excess of actual over budget for March, $25,000

SHOW
ME HOW

### EX 22-3  Static budget versus flexible budget

OBJ. 2, 4

The production supervisor of the Machining Department for Rodriguez Company agreed to the following monthly static budget for the upcoming year:

**Rodriguez Company**
**Machining Department**
**Monthly Production Budget**

| | |
|---|---|
| Wages...................................................... | $384,000 |
| Utilities..................................................... | 36,000 |
| Depreciation............................................... | 60,000 |
| Total ................................................. | $480,000 |

The actual amount spent and the actual units produced in the first three months of 2016 in the Machining Department were as follows:

| | Amount Spent | Units Produced |
|---|---|---|
| January | $400,000 | 90,000 |
| February | 440,000 | 100,000 |
| March | 470,000 | 110,000 |

The Machining Department supervisor has been very pleased with this performance because actual expenditures for January–March have been less than the monthly static budget of $480,000. However, the plant manager believes that the budget should not remain fixed for every month but should "flex" or adjust to the volume of work that is produced in the Machining Department. Additional budget information for the Machining Department is as follows:

| | |
|---|---|
| Wages per hour | $16.00 |
| Utility cost per direct labor hour | $1.50 |
| Direct labor hours per unit | 0.20 |
| Planned monthly unit production | 120,000 |

a. Prepare a flexible budget for the actual units produced for January, February, and March in the Machining Department. Assume depreciation is a fixed cost.

b. ━━━► Compare the flexible budget with the actual expenditures for the first three months. What does this comparison suggest?

SHOW
ME HOW

### EX 22-4 Flexible budget for Assembly Department

OBJ. 2

Steelcase Inc. is one of the largest manufacturers of office furniture in the United States. In Grand Rapids, Michigan, it assembles filing cabinets in an Assembly Department. Assume the following information for the Assembly Department:

| | |
|---|---|
| Direct labor per filing cabinet ....................................... | 12 minutes |
| Supervisor salaries ................................................. | $150,000 per month |
| Depreciation....................................................... | $24,500 per month |
| Direct labor rate................................................... | $22 per hour |

Prepare a flexible budget for 18,000, 20,000, and 22,000 filing cabinets for the month of August 2016 in the Assembly Department, similar to Exhibit 5.

SHOW
ME HOW

### EX 22-5 Production budget

OBJ. 4

True Tab Inc. produces a small and large version of its popular electronic scale. The anticipated unit sales for the scales by sales region are as follows:

| | Small Scale | Large Scale |
|---|---|---|
| North Region unit sales | 38,000 | 67,000 |
| South Region unit sales | 43,000 | 79,000 |
| Total | 81,000 | 146,000 |

The finished goods inventory estimated for July 1, 2017, for the small and large scale models is 1,800 and 2,200 units, respectively. The desired finished goods inventory for July 31, 2017, for the small and large scale models is 1,500 and 2,500 units, respectively.

Prepare a production budget for the small and large scales for the month ended July 31, 2017.

SHOW
ME HOW

### EX 22-6 Sales and production budgets

OBJ. 4

SoundLab Inc. manufactures two models of speakers, DL and XL. Based on the following production and sales data for September 2016, prepare (a) a sales budget and (b) a production budget:

| | DL | XL |
|---|---|---|
| Estimated inventory (units), September 1 ..................... | 340 | 92 |
| Desired inventory (units), September 30 ..................... | 300 | 101 |
| Expected sales volume (units): | | |
| East Region............................................. | 2,560 | 1,080 |
| West Region ............................................ | 2,310 | 930 |
| Unit sales price........................................... | $190 | $300 |

### EX 22-7 Professional fees earned budget for a service company

OBJ. 4

Rollins and Cohen, CPAs, offer three types of services to clients: auditing, tax, and small business accounting. Based on experience and projected growth, the following billable hours have been estimated for the year ending December 31, 2016:

| | Billable Hours |
|---|---|
| Audit Department: | |
| Staff........................................................ | 22,400 |
| Partners .................................................... | 7,900 |
| Tax Department: | |
| Staff........................................................ | 13,200 |
| Partners .................................................... | 5,500 |
| Small Business Accounting Department: | |
| Staff........................................................ | 3,000 |
| Partners .................................................... | 600 |

The average billing rate for staff is $150 per hour, and the average billing rate for partners is $320 per hour. Prepare a professional fees earned budget for Rollins and Cohen, CPAs, for the year ending December 31, 2016, using the following column headings and showing the estimated professional fees by type of service rendered:

| Billable Hours | Hourly Rate | Total Revenue |
| --- | --- | --- |

### EX 22-8 Professional labor cost budget for a service company OBJ. 4

✔ Staff total labor cost, $1,737,000

Based on the data in Exercise 22-7 and assuming that the average compensation per hour for staff is $45 and for partners is $140, prepare a professional labor cost budget for each department for Rollins and Cohen, CPAs, for the year ending December 31, 2016. Use the following column headings:

| Staff | Partners |
| --- | --- |

### EX 22-9 Direct materials purchases budget OBJ. 4

✔ Total cheese purchases, $35,448

SHOW ME HOW

Romano's Frozen Pizza Inc. has determined from its production budget the following estimated production volumes for 12" and 16" frozen pizzas for September 2016:

| | Units | |
| --- | --- | --- |
| | 12" Pizza | 16" Pizza |
| Budgeted production volume | 5,300 | 8,900 |

There are three direct materials used in producing the two types of pizza. The quantities of direct materials expected to be used for each pizza are as follows:

| | 12" Pizza | 16" Pizza |
| --- | --- | --- |
| Direct materials: | | |
| Dough | 0.70 lb. per unit | 1.50 lbs. per unit |
| Tomato | 0.40 | 0.70 |
| Cheese | 0.60 | 1.30 |

In addition, Romano's has determined the following information about each material:

| | Dough | Tomato | Cheese |
| --- | --- | --- | --- |
| Estimated inventory, September 1, 2016 | 520 lbs. | 200 lbs. | 295 lbs. |
| Desired Inventory, September 30, 2016 | 580 lbs. | 185 lbs. | 315 lbs. |
| Price per pound | $0.80 | $1.60 | $2.40 |

Prepare September's direct materials purchases budget for Romano's Frozen Pizza Inc.

### EX 22-10 Direct materials purchases budget OBJ. 4

✔ Concentrate budgeted purchases, $47,400

Coca-Cola Enterprises is the largest bottler of Coca-Cola® in Western Europe. The company purchases Coke® and Sprite® concentrate from The Coca-Cola Company, dilutes and mixes the concentrate with carbonated water, and then fills the blended beverage into cans or plastic two-liter bottles. Assume that the estimated production for Coke and Sprite two-liter bottles at the Wakefield, UK, bottling plant are as follows for the month of May:

| Coke | 153,000 two-liter bottles |
| --- | --- |
| Sprite | 86,500 two-liter bottles |

In addition, assume that the concentrate costs $75 per pound for both Coke and Sprite and is used at a rate of 0.15 pound per 100 liters of carbonated water in blending Coke and 0.10 pound per 100 liters of carbonated water in blending Sprite. Assume that two liters of carbonated water are used for each two-liter bottle of finished product. Assume further that two-liter bottles cost $0.08 per bottle and carbonated water costs $0.06 per liter.

Prepare a direct materials purchases budget for May 2016, assuming inventories are ignored, because there are no changes between beginning and ending inventories for concentrate, bottles, and carbonated water.

✔ Total steel
belt purchases,
$291,200

### EX 22-11   Direct materials purchases budget

OBJ. 4

Anticipated sales for Safety Grip Company were 42,000 passenger car tires and 19,000 truck tires. Rubber and steel belts are used in producing passenger car and truck tires as follows:

|  | Passenger Car | Truck |
|---|---|---|
| Rubber | 35 lbs. per unit | 78 lbs. per unit |
| Steel belts | 5 lbs. per unit | 8 lbs. per unit |

The purchase prices of rubber and steel are $1.20 and $0.80 per pound, respectively. The desired ending inventories of rubber and steel belts are 40,000 and 10,000 pounds, respectively. The estimated beginning inventories for rubber and steel belts are 46,000 and 8,000 pounds, respectively.

Prepare a direct materials purchases budget for Safety Grip Company for the year ended December 31, 2016.

✔ Total direct labor
cost, Assembly,
$31,080

### EX 22-12   Direct labor cost budget

OBJ. 4

Ace Racket Company manufactures two types of tennis rackets, the Junior and Pro Striker models. The production budget for July for the two rackets is as follows:

|  | Junior | Pro Striker |
|---|---|---|
| Production budget | 1,500 units | 6,200 units |

Both rackets are produced in two departments, Forming and Assembly. The direct labor hours required for each racket are estimated as follows:

|  | Forming Department | Assembly Department |
|---|---|---|
| Junior | 0.16 hour per unit | 0.24 hour per unit |
| Pro Striker | 0.20 hour per unit | 0.30 hour per unit |

The direct labor rate for each department is as follows:

| Forming Department | $18.00 per hour |
|---|---|
| Assembly Department | $14.00 per hour |

Prepare the direct labor cost budget for July 2016.

✔ Average weekday
total, $2,640

### EX 22-13   Direct labor budget for a service business

OBJ. 4

Ambassador Suites Inc. operates a downtown hotel property that has 300 rooms. On average, 80% of Ambassador Suites' rooms are occupied on weekdays, and 40% are occupied during the weekend. The manager has asked you to develop a direct labor budget for the housekeeping and restaurant staff for weekdays and weekends. You have determined that the housekeeping staff requires 30 minutes to clean each occupied room. The housekeeping staff is paid $14 per hour. The housekeeping labor cost is fully variable to the number of occupied rooms. The restaurant has six full-time staff (eight-hour day) on duty, regardless of occupancy. However, for every 60 occupied rooms, an additional person is brought in to work in the restaurant for the eight-hour day. The restaurant staff is paid $12 per hour.

Determine the estimated housekeeping, restaurant, and total direct labor cost for an average weekday and average weekend day. Format the budget in two columns, labeled as weekday and weekend day.

✔ a. Total production
of 501 Jeans, 53,300

### EX 22-14   Production and direct labor cost budgets

OBJ. 4

Levi Strauss & Co. manufactures slacks and jeans under a variety of brand names, such as Dockers® and 501 Jeans®. Slacks and jeans are assembled by a variety of different sewing operations. Assume that the sales budget for Dockers and 501 Jeans shows estimated sales of 23,600 and 53,100 pairs, respectively, for May 2016. The finished goods inventory is assumed as follows:

|  | Dockers | 501 Jeans |
|---|---|---|
| May 1 estimated inventory | 670 | 1,660 |
| May 31 desired inventory | 420 | 1,860 |

Assume the following direct labor data per 10 pairs of Dockers and 501 Jeans for four different sewing operations:

| | Direct Labor per 10 Pairs | |
|---|---|---|
| | **Dockers** | **501 Jeans** |
| Inseam | 18 minutes | 9 minutes |
| Outerseam | 20 | 14 |
| Pockets | 6 | 9 |
| Zipper | 12 | 6 |
| Total | 56 minutes | 38 minutes |

a. Prepare a production budget for May. Prepare the budget in two columns: Dockers® and 501 Jeans®.

b. Prepare the May direct labor cost budget for the four sewing operations, assuming a $13 wage per hour for the inseam and outerseam sewing operations and a $15 wage per hour for the pocket and zipper sewing operations. Prepare the direct labor cost budget in four columns: inseam, outerseam, pockets, and zipper.

---

### EX 22-15  Factory overhead cost budget
**OBJ. 4**

Sweet Tooth Candy Company budgeted the following costs for anticipated production for August 2016:

| | | | |
|---|---|---|---|
| Advertising expenses | $232,000 | Production supervisor wages | $135,000 |
| Manufacturing supplies | 14,000 | Production control wages | 32,000 |
| Power and light | 48,000 | Executive officer salaries | 310,000 |
| Sales commissions | 298,000 | Materials management wages | 39,000 |
| Factory insurance | 30,000 | Factory depreciation | 22,000 |

Prepare a factory overhead cost budget, separating variable and fixed costs. Assume that factory insurance and depreciation are the only fixed factory costs.

---

### EX 22-16  Cost of goods sold budget
**OBJ. 4**

Delaware Chemical Company uses oil to produce two types of plastic products, P1 and P2. Delaware budgeted 35,000 barrels of oil for purchase in June for $90 per barrel. Direct labor budgeted in the chemical process was $240,000 for June. Factory overhead was budgeted $400,000 during June. The inventories on June 1 were estimated to be:

| | |
|---|---|
| Oil | $15,200 |
| P1 | 8,300 |
| P2 | 8,600 |
| Work in process | 12,900 |

The desired inventories on June 30 were:

| | |
|---|---|
| Oil | $16,100 |
| P1 | 9,400 |
| P2 | 7,900 |
| Work in process | 13,500 |

Use the preceding information to prepare a cost of goods sold budget for June 2017.

---

### EX 22-17  Cost of goods sold budget
**OBJ. 4**

The controller of MingWare Ceramics Inc. wishes to prepare a cost of goods sold budget for September. The controller assembled the following information for constructing the cost of goods sold budget:

| Direct materials: | Enamel | Paint | Porcelain | Total |
|---|---|---|---|---|
| Total direct materials purchases budgeted for September | $36,780 | $6,130 | $145,500 | $188,410 |
| Estimated inventory, September 1, 2016 | 1,240 | 950 | 4,250 | 6,440 |
| Desired inventory, September 30, 2016 | 1,890 | 1,070 | 5,870 | 8,830 |

| Direct labor cost: | Kiln Department | | Decorating Department | Total |
|---|---|---|---|---|
| Total direct labor cost budgeted for September | $47,900 | | $145,700 | $193,600 |

| Finished goods inventories: | Dish | Bowl | Figurine | Total |
|---|---|---|---|---|
| Estimated inventory, September 1, 2016 | $5,780 | $3,080 | $2,640 | $11,500 |
| Desired inventory, September 30, 2016 | 3,710 | 2,670 | 3,290 | 9,670 |

| Work in process inventories: | |
|---|---|
| Estimated inventory, September 1, 2016 | $3,400 |
| Desired inventory, September 30, 2016 | 1,990 |

| Budgeted factory overhead costs for September: | |
|---|---|
| Indirect factory wages | $ 81,900 |
| Depreciation of plant and equipment | 14,300 |
| Power and light | 5,200 |
| Indirect materials | 4,100 |
| Total | $105,500 |

Use the preceding information to prepare a cost of goods sold budget for September 2016.

---

### EX 22-18   Schedule of cash collections of accounts receivable                     OBJ. 5

✔ Total cash collected in July, $163,050

SHOW
ME HOW

Pet Place Supplies Inc., a pet wholesale supplier, was organized on May 1, 2016. Projected sales for each of the first three months of operations are as follows:

| | |
|---|---|
| May | $134,000 |
| June | 155,000 |
| July | 169,000 |

All sales are on account. Sixty-five percent of sales are expected to be collected in the month of the sale, 30% in the month following the sale, and the remainder in the second month following the sale.

Prepare a schedule indicating cash collections from sales for May, June, and July.

---

### EX 22-19   Schedule of cash collections of accounts receivable                     OBJ. 5

✔ Total cash collected in October, $62,550

OfficeMart Inc. has "cash and carry" customers and credit customers. OfficeMart estimates that 25% of monthly sales are to cash customers, while the remaining sales are to credit customers. Of the credit customers, 30% pay their accounts in the month of sale, while the remaining 70% pay their accounts in the month following the month of sale. Projected sales for the next three months of 2016 are as follows:

| | |
|---|---|
| October | $58,000 |
| November | 65,000 |
| December | 72,000 |

The Accounts Receivable balance on September 30, 2016, was $35,000.

Prepare a schedule of cash collections from sales for October, November, and December.

---

### EX 22-20   Schedule of cash payments for a service company                     OBJ. 5

✔ Total cash payments in May, $58,490

Horizon Financial Inc. was organized on February 28, 2016. Projected selling and administrative expenses for each of the first three months of operations are as follows:

| | |
|---|---|
| March | $52,400 |
| April | 64,200 |
| May | 68,900 |

Depreciation, insurance, and property taxes represent $9,000 of the estimated monthly expenses. The annual insurance premium was paid on February 28, and property taxes for the year will be paid in June. Seventy percent of the remainder of the expenses are expected to be paid in the month in which they are incurred, with the balance to be paid in the following month.

Prepare a schedule indicating cash payments for selling and administrative expenses for March, April, and May.

### EX 22-21   Schedule of cash payments for a service company

**OBJ. 5**

✔ Total cash
payments in March,
$113,740

EastGate Physical Therapy Inc. is planning its cash payments for operations for the first quarter (January–March), 2017. The Accrued Expenses Payable balance on January 1 is $15,000. The budgeted expenses for the next three months are as follows:

|  | January | February | March |
|---|---|---|---|
| Salaries | $56,900 | $ 68,100 | $ 72,200 |
| Utilities | 2,400 | 2,600 | 2,500 |
| Other operating expenses | 32,300 | 41,500 | 44,700 |
| Total | $91,600 | $112,200 | $119,400 |

Other operating expenses include $3,000 of monthly depreciation expense and $500 of monthly insurance expense that was prepaid for the year on May 1 of the previous year. Of the remaining expenses, 70% are paid in the month in which they are incurred, with the remainder paid in the following month. The Accrued Expenses Payable balance on January 1 relates to the expenses incurred in December.

Prepare a schedule of cash payments for operations for January, February, and March.

### EX 22-22   Capital expenditures budget

**OBJ. 5**

✔ Total capital
expenditures in
2016, $4,000,000

On January 1, 2016, the controller of Omicron Inc. is planning capital expenditures for the years 2016–2019. The following interviews helped the controller collect the necessary information for the capital expenditures budget:

*Director of Facilities:* A construction contract was signed in late 2015 for the construction of a new factory building at a contract cost of $10,000,000. The construction is scheduled to begin in 2016 and be completed in 2017.

*Vice President of Manufacturing:* Once the new factory building is finished, we plan to purchase $1.5 million in equipment in late 2017. I expect that an additional $200,000 will be needed early in the following year (2018) to test and install the equipment before we can begin production. If sales continue to grow, I expect we'll need to invest another $1,000,000 in equipment in 2019.

*Chief Operating Officer:* We have really been growing lately. I wouldn't be surprised if we need to expand the size of our new factory building in 2019 by at least 35%. Fortunately, we expect inflation to have minimal impact on construction costs over the next four years. Additionally, I would expect the cost of the expansion to be proportional to the size of the expansion.

*Director of Information Systems:* We need to upgrade our information systems to wireless network technology. It doesn't make sense to do this until after the new factory building is completed and producing product. During 2018, once the factory is up and running, we should equip the whole facility with wireless technology. I think it would cost us $800,000 today to install the technology. However, prices have been dropping by 25% per year, so it should be less expensive at a later date.

*Chief Financial Officer:* I am excited about our long-term prospects. My only short-term concern is managing our cash flow while we expend the $4,000,000 of construction costs on the portion of the new factory building scheduled to be completed in 2016.

Use this interview information to prepare a capital expenditures budget for Omicron Inc. for the years 2016–2019.

## Problems: Series A

### PR 22-1A   Forecast sales volume and sales budget

**OBJ. 4**

✔ 3. Total revenue
from sales, $878,403

For 2016, Raphael Frame Company prepared the sales budget that follows.

At the end of December 2016, the following unit sales data were reported for the year:

| | Unit Sales | |
|---|---|---|
| | 8" × 10" Frame | 12" × 16" Frame |
| East | 8,755 | 3,686 |
| Central | 6,510 | 3,090 |
| West | 12,348 | 5,616 |

**Raphael Frame Company**
**Sales Budget**
**For the Year Ending December 31, 2016**

| Product and Area | Unit Sales Volume | Unit Selling Price | Total Sales |
|---|---|---|---|
| 8" × 10" Frame: | | | |
| East .............................. | 8,500 | $16 | $136,000 |
| Central ........................... | 6,200 | 16 | 99,200 |
| West ............................. | 12,600 | 16 | 201,600 |
| Total ........................... | 27,300 | | $436,800 |
| 12" × 16" Frame: | | | |
| East .............................. | 3,800 | $30 | $114,000 |
| Central ........................... | 3,000 | 30 | 90,000 |
| West ............................. | 5,400 | 30 | 162,000 |
| Total ........................... | 12,200 | | $366,000 |
| Total revenue from sales ............... | | | $802,800 |

For the year ending December 31, 2017, unit sales are expected to follow the patterns established during the year ending December 31, 2016. The unit selling price for the 8" × 10" frame is expected to increase to $17 and the unit selling price for the 12" × 16" frame is expected to increase to $32, effective January 1, 2017.

**Instructions**

1. Compute the increase or decrease of actual unit sales for the year ended December 31, 2016, over budget. Place your answers in a columnar table with the following format:

| | Unit Sales, Year Ended 2016 | | Increase (Decrease) Actual Over Budget | |
|---|---|---|---|---|
| | Budget | Actual Sales | Amount | Percent |
| 8" × 10" Frame: | | | | |
| East ............................. | | | | |
| Central .......................... | | | | |
| West ............................. | | | | |
| 12" × 16" Frame: | | | | |
| East ............................. | | | | |
| Central .......................... | | | | |
| West ............................. | | | | |

2. Assuming that the increase or decrease in actual sales to budget indicated in part (1) is to continue in 2017, compute the unit sales volume to be used for preparing the sales budget for the year ending December 31, 2017. Place your answers in a columnar table similar to that in part (1) but with the following column heads. Round budgeted units to the nearest unit.

| 2016 Actual Units | Percentage Increase (Decrease) | 2017 Budgeted Units (rounded) |
|---|---|---|

3. Prepare a sales budget for the year ending December 31, 2017.

**PR 22-2A** **Sales, production, direct materials purchases, and direct labor cost budgets** OBJ. 4

✔ 3. Total direct materials purchases, $771,490

The budget director of Gourmet Grill Company requests estimates of sales, production, and other operating data from the various administrative units every month. Selected information concerning sales and production for July 2016 is summarized as follows:

a. Estimated sales for July by sales territory:

Maine:

| Backyard Chef ..................................... | 310 units at $700 per unit |
| Master Chef...................................... | 150 units at $1,200 per unit |

Vermont:

| Backyard Chef ..................................... | 240 units at $750 per unit |
| Master Chef...................................... | 110 units at $1,300 per unit |

New Hampshire:

Backyard Chef ........................................ 360 units at $750 per unit

Master Chef........................................ 180 units at $1,400 per unit

b. Estimated inventories at July 1:

| Direct materials: | | Finished products: | |
|---|---|---|---|
| Grates......................... | 290 units | Backyard Chef ............ | 30 units |
| Stainless steel.................. | 1,500 lbs. | Master Chef............... | 32 units |
| Burner subassemblies .......... | 170 units | | |
| Shelves...................... | 340 units | | |

c. Desired inventories at July 31:

| Direct materials: | | Finished products: | |
|---|---|---|---|
| Grates......................... | 340 units | Backyard Chef ............ | 40 units |
| Stainless steel.................. | 1,800 lbs. | Master Chef............... | 22 units |
| Burner subassemblies .......... | 155 units | | |
| Shelves...................... | 315 units | | |

d. Direct materials used in production:

In manufacture of Backyard Chef:

| | |
|---|---|
| Grates................................................. | 3 units per unit of product |
| Stainless steel.......................................... | 24 lbs. per unit of product |
| Burner subassemblies .................................. | 2 units per unit of product |
| Shelves................................................ | 4 units per unit of product |

In manufacture of Master Chef:

| | |
|---|---|
| Grates................................................. | 6 units per unit of product |
| Stainless steel.......................................... | 42 lbs. per unit of product |
| Burner subassemblies .................................. | 4 units per unit of product |
| Shelves................................................ | 5 units per unit of product |

e. Anticipated purchase price for direct materials:

| Grates..................... | $15 per unit | Burner subassemblies ......... | 110 per unit |
|---|---|---|---|
| Stainless steel.............. | $6 per lb. | Shelves...................... | $10 per unit |

f. Direct labor requirements:

Backyard Chef:

| | |
|---|---|
| Stamping Department......................................... | 0.50 hr. at $17 per hr. |
| Forming Department.......................................... | 0.60 hr. at $15 per hr. |
| Assembly Department........................................ | 1.0 hr. at $14 per hr. |

Master Chef:

| | |
|---|---|
| Stamping Department......................................... | 0.60 hr. at $17 per hr. |
| Forming Department.......................................... | 0.80 hr. at $15 per hr. |
| Assembly Department ...................................... | 1.50 hrs. at $14 per hr. |

**Instructions**

1. Prepare a sales budget for July.

2. Prepare a production budget for July.

3. Prepare a direct materials purchases budget for July.

4. Prepare a direct labor cost budget for July.

---

**PR 22-3A  Budgeted income statement and supporting budgets**          OBJ. 4

✔ 4. Total direct labor cost in Fabrication Dept., $29,216

The budget director of Feathered Friends Inc., with the assistance of the controller, treasurer, production manager, and sales manager, has gathered the following data for use in developing the budgeted income statement for December 2016:

a. Estimated sales for December:

| | |
|---|---|
| Bird house............................................. | 3,200 units at $50 per unit |
| Bird feeder............................................ | 3,000 units at $70 per unit |

b. Estimated inventories at December 1:

| Direct materials: | | Finished products: | |
|---|---|---|---|
| Wood ........ | 200 ft. | Bird house....... | 320 units at $27 per unit |
| Plastic........ | 240 lbs. | Bird feeder....... | 270 units at $40 per unit |

c. Desired inventories at December 31:

| Direct materials: | | Finished products: | |
|---|---|---|---|
| Wood ........ | 220 ft. | Bird house....... | 290 units at $27 per unit |
| Plastic........ | 200 lbs. | Bird feeder....... | 250 units at $41 per unit |

d. Direct materials used in production:

| In manufacture of Bird House: | | In manufacture of Bird Feeder: | |
|---|---|---|---|
| Wood ............ | 0.80 ft. per unit of product | Wood ........... | 1.20 ft. per unit of product |
| Plastic............ | 0.50 lb. per unit of product | Plastic........... | 0.75 lb. per unit of product |

e. Anticipated cost of purchases and beginning and ending inventory of direct materials:

| Wood ........................ | $7.00 per ft. | Plastic................. | $1.00 per lb. |
|---|---|---|---|

f. Direct labor requirements:

Bird House:

| Fabrication Department ....................................... | 0.20 hr. at $16 per hr. |
|---|---|
| Assembly Department........................................ | 0.30 hr. at $12 per hr. |

Bird Feeder:

| Fabrication Department ....................................... | 0.40 hr. at $16 per hr. |
|---|---|
| Assembly Department........................................ | 0.35 hr. at $12 per hr. |

g. Estimated factory overhead costs for December:

| Indirect factory wages | $75,000 | Power and light | $6,000 |
|---|---|---|---|
| Depreciation of plant and equipment | 23,000 | Insurance and property tax | 5,000 |

h. Estimated operating expenses for December:

| Sales salaries expense | $70,000 |
|---|---|
| Advertising expense | 18,000 |
| Office salaries expense | 21,000 |
| Depreciation expense—office equipment | 600 |
| Telephone expense—selling | 550 |
| Telephone expense—administrative | 250 |
| Travel expense—selling | 4,000 |
| Office supplies expense | 200 |
| Miscellaneous administrative expense | 400 |

i. Estimated other income and expense for December:

| Interest revenue | $200 |
|---|---|
| Interest expense | 122 |

j. Estimated tax rate: 30%

**Instructions**

1. Prepare a sales budget for December.
2. Prepare a production budget for December.
3. Prepare a direct materials purchases budget for December.
4. Prepare a direct labor cost budget for December.
5. Prepare a factory overhead cost budget for December.
6. Prepare a cost of goods sold budget for December. Work in process at the beginning of December is estimated to be $29,000, and work in process at the end of December is estimated to be $35,400.
7. Prepare a selling and administrative expenses budget for December.
8. Prepare a budgeted income statement for December.

### PR 22-4A  Cash budget

OBJ. 5

The controller of Sonoma Housewares Inc. instructs you to prepare a monthly cash budget for the next three months. You are presented with the following budget information:

| | May | June | July |
|---|---|---|---|
| Sales | $86,000 | $90,000 | $95,000 |
| Manufacturing costs | 34,000 | 39,000 | 44,000 |
| Selling and administrative expenses | 15,000 | 16,000 | 22,000 |
| Capital expenditures | | | 80,000 |

The company expects to sell about 10% of its merchandise for cash. Of sales on account, 70% are expected to be collected in the month following the sale and the remainder the following month (second month following sale). Depreciation, insurance, and property tax expense represent $3,500 of the estimated monthly manufacturing costs. The annual insurance premium is paid in September, and the annual property taxes are paid in November. Of the remainder of the manufacturing costs, 80% are expected to be paid in the month in which they are incurred and the balance in the following month.

Current assets as of May 1 include cash of $33,000, marketable securities of $40,000, and accounts receivable of $90,000 ($72,000 from April sales and $18,000 from March sales). Sales on account for March and April were $60,000 and $72,000, respectively. Current liabilities as of May 1 include $6,000 of accounts payable incurred in April for manufacturing costs. All selling and administrative expenses are paid in cash in the period they are incurred. An estimated income tax payment of $14,000 will be made in June. Sonoma's regular quarterly dividend of $5,000 is expected to be declared in June and paid in July. Management desires to maintain a minimum cash balance of $30,000.

**Instructions**

1. Prepare a monthly cash budget and supporting schedules for May, June, and July 2016.

2. ━━━➤ On the basis of the cash budget prepared in part (1), what recommendation should be made to the controller?

### PR 22-5A  Budgeted income statement and balance sheet

OBJ. 4, 5

As a preliminary to requesting budget estimates of sales, costs, and expenses for the fiscal year beginning January 1, 2017, the following tentative trial balance as of December 31, 2016, is prepared by the Accounting Department of Regina Soap Co.:

| | | |
|---|---|---|
| Cash | $ 85,000 | |
| Accounts Receivable | 125,600 | |
| Finished Goods | 69,300 | |
| Work in Process | 32,500 | |
| Materials | 48,900 | |
| Prepaid Expenses | 2,600 | |
| Plant and Equipment | 325,000 | |
| Accumulated Depreciation—Plant and Equipment | | $156,200 |
| Accounts Payable | | 62,000 |
| Common Stock, $10 par | | 180,000 |
| Retained Earnings | | 290,700 |
| | $688,900 | $688,900 |

Factory output and sales for 2017 are expected to total 200,000 units of product, which are to be sold at $5.00 per unit. The quantities and costs of the inventories at December 31, 2017, are expected to remain unchanged from the balances at the beginning of the year.

Budget estimates of manufacturing costs and operating expenses for the year are summarized as follows:

| | Estimated Costs and Expenses | |
|---|---|---|
| | Fixed (Total for Year) | Variable (Per Unit Sold) |
| Cost of goods manufactured and sold: | | |
| Direct materials | — | $1.10 |
| Direct labor | — | 0.65 |
| Factory overhead: | | |
| Depreciation of plant and equipment | $40,000 | — |
| Other factory overhead | 12,000 | 0.40 |
| Selling expenses: | | |
| Sales salaries and commissions | 46,000 | 0.45 |
| Advertising | 64,000 | — |
| Miscellaneous selling expense | 6,000 | 0.25 |
| Administrative expenses: | | |
| Office and officers salaries | 72,400 | 0.12 |
| Supplies | 5,000 | 0.10 |
| Miscellaneous administrative expense | 4,000 | 0.05 |

Balances of accounts receivable, prepaid expenses, and accounts payable at the end of the year are not expected to differ significantly from the beginning balances. Federal income tax of $30,000 on 2017 taxable income will be paid during 2017. Regular quarterly cash dividends of $0.15 per share are expected to be declared and paid in March, June, September, and December on 18,000 shares of common stock outstanding. It is anticipated that fixed assets will be purchased for $75,000 cash in May.

**Instructions**

1. Prepare a budgeted income statement for 2017.
2. Prepare a budgeted balance sheet as of December 31, 2017, with supporting calculations.

# Problems: Series B

### PR 22-1B  Forecast sales volume and sales budget

OBJ. 4

✔ 3. Total revenue from sales, $2,148,950

Sentinel Systems Inc. prepared the following sales budget for 2016:

**Sentinel Systems Inc.**
**Sales Budget**
**For the Year Ending December 31, 2016**

| Product and Area | Unit Sales Volume | Unit Selling Price | Total Sales |
|---|---|---|---|
| Home Alert System: | | | |
| United States | 1,700 | $200 | $ 340,000 |
| Europe | 580 | 200 | 116,000 |
| Asia | 450 | 200 | 90,000 |
| Total | 2,730 | | $ 546,000 |
| Business Alert System: | | | |
| United States | 980 | $750 | $ 735,000 |
| Europe | 350 | 750 | 262,500 |
| Asia | 240 | 750 | 180,000 |
| Total | 1,570 | | $1,177,500 |
| Total revenue from sales | | | $1,723,500 |

At the end of December 2016, the following unit sales data were reported for the year:

| | Unit Sales | |
|---|---|---|
| | **Home Alert System** | **Business Alert System** |
| United States | 1,734 | 1,078 |
| Europe | 609 | 329 |
| Asia | 432 | 252 |

For the year ending December 31, 2017, unit sales are expected to follow the patterns established during the year ending December 31, 2016. The unit selling price for the Home Alert System is expected to increase to $250, and the unit selling price for the Business Alert System is expected to be decreased to $820, effective January 1, 2017.

### Instructions

1. Compute the increase or decrease of actual unit sales for the year ended December 31, 2016, over budget. Place your answers in a columnar table with the following format:

| | Unit Sales, Year Ended 2016 | | Increase (Decrease) Actual Over Budget | |
|---|---|---|---|---|
| | **Budget** | **Actual Sales** | **Amount** | **Percent** |
| Home Alert System: | | | | |
| United States ................... | | | | |
| Europe ...................... | | | | |
| Asia ......................... | | | | |
| Business Alert System: | | | | |
| United States ................... | | | | |
| Europe ...................... | | | | |
| Asia ......................... | | | | |

2. Assuming that the increase or decrease in actual sales to budget indicated in part (1) is to continue in 2017, compute the unit sales volume to be used for preparing the sales budget for the year ending December 31, 2017. Place your answers in a columnar table similar to that in part (1) but with the following column heads. Round budgeted units to the nearest unit.

| 2016 Actual Units | Percentage Increase (Decrease) | 2017 Budgeted Units (rounded) |
|---|---|---|

3. Prepare a sales budget for the year ending December 31, 2017.

---

✔ **3. Total direct materials purchases, $987,478**

**PR 22-2B    Sales, production, direct materials purchases, and direct labor cost budgets**   OBJ. 4

The budget director of Royal Furniture Company requests estimates of sales, production, and other operating data from the various administrative units every month. Selected information concerning sales and production for February 2016 is summarized as follows:

a. Estimated sales of King and Prince chairs for February by sales territory:

Northern Domestic:

King......................................... 610 units at $780 per unit
Prince....................................... 750 units at $550 per unit

Southern Domestic:

King......................................... 340 units at $780 per unit
Prince....................................... 440 units at $550 per unit

International:

King......................................... 360 units at $850 per unit
Prince....................................... 290 units at $600 per unit

b. Estimated inventories at February 1:

| Direct materials: | | Finished products: | |
|---|---|---|---|
| Fabric ................... | 420 sq. yds. | King.................... | 90 units |
| Wood ................... | 580 linear ft. | Prince ................. | 25 units |
| Filler ................... | 250 cu. ft. | | |
| Springs.................. | 660 units | | |

1959-2000

# Performance Evaluation Using Variances from Standard Costs

## BMW Group—Mini Cooper

When you play a sport, you are evaluated with respect to how well you perform compared to a standard or to a competitor. In bowling, for example, your score is compared to a perfect score of 300 or to the scores of your competitors. In this class, you are compared to performance standards. These standards are often described in terms of letter grades, which provide a measure of how well you achieved the class objectives. In your job, you are also evaluated according to performance standards.

Just as your class performance is evaluated, managers are evaluated according to goals and plans. For example, **BMW Group** uses manufacturing standards at its automobile assembly plants to guide performance. The Mini Cooper, a BMW Group car, is manufactured in a modern facility in Oxford, England. There are

a number of performance targets used in this plant. For example, the bodyshell is welded by more than 250 robots so as to be two to three times stiffer than rival cars. In addition, the bodyshell dimensions are tested to the accuracy of the width of a human hair. Such performance standards are not surprising given the automotive racing background of John W. Cooper, the designer of the original Mini Cooper.

If you want to get a view of the BMW manufacturing process, go to the BMW Web site and search the phrase "How an automobile is born."

Performance is often measured as the difference between actual results and planned results. In this chapter, we will discuss and illustrate the ways in which business performance is evaluated.

## Standards

**Standards** are performance goals. Manufacturing companies normally use **standard cost** for each of the three following product costs:

- Direct materials
- Direct labor
- Factory overhead

Accounting systems that use standards for product costs are called **standard cost systems**. Standard cost systems enable management to determine the following:

- How much a product *should* cost (standard cost)
- How much it does cost (actual cost)

When actual costs are compared with standard costs, the exceptions or cost variances are reported. This reporting by the *principle of exceptions* allows management to focus on correcting the cost variances.

## Setting Standards

The standard-setting process normally requires the joint efforts of accountants, engineers, and other management personnel. The accountant converts the results of judgments and process studies into dollars and cents. Engineers with the aid of operation managers identify the materials, labor, and machine requirements needed to produce the product. For example, engineers estimate direct materials by studying the product specifications and estimating normal spoilage. Time and motion studies may be used to determine the direct labor required for each manufacturing operation. Engineering studies may also be used to determine standards for factory overhead, such as the amount of power needed to operate machinery.

## Types of Standards

Standards imply an acceptable level of production efficiency. One of the major objectives in setting standards is to motivate employees to achieve efficient operations.

**Ideal standards**, or *theoretical standards*, are standards that can be achieved only under perfect operating conditions, such as no idle time, no machine breakdowns, and no materials spoilage. Such standards may have a negative impact on performance because they may be viewed by employees as unrealistic.

**Currently attainable standards**, sometimes called *normal standards*, are standards that can be attained with reasonable effort. Such standards, which are used by most companies, allow for normal production difficulties and mistakes. When reasonable standards are used, employees focus more on cost and are more likely to put forth their best efforts.

An example from the game of golf illustrates the distinction between ideal and normal standards. In golf, *par* is an ideal standard for most players. Each player's USGA (United States Golf Association) handicap is the player's normal standard. The motivation of average players is to beat their handicaps because beating par is unrealistic for most players.

## Reviewing and Revising Standards

Standard costs should be periodically reviewed to ensure that they reflect current operating conditions. Standards should not be revised, however, just because they differ from actual costs. For example, the direct labor standard would not be revised just because employees are unable to meet properly set standards. On the other hand, standards should be revised when prices, product designs, labor rates, or manufacturing methods change.

## Integrity, Objectivity, and Ethics in Business

**COMPANY REPUTATION: THE BEST OF THE BEST**

Harris Interactive annually ranks American corporations in terms of reputation. The ranking is based on how respondents rate corporations on 20 attributes in six major areas. The six areas are emotional appeal, products and services, financial performance, workplace environment, social responsibility, and vision and leadership. What are the five highest ranked companies in its 2013 survey? The five highest (best) ranked companies were Amazon.com, Apple Inc., The Walt Disney Company, Google, and Johnson & Johnson.

Source: Harris Interactive, February 2012.

## Criticisms of Standard Costs

Some criticisms of using standard costs for performance evaluation include the following:

- Standards limit operating improvements by discouraging improvement beyond the standard.
- Standards are too difficult to maintain in a dynamic manufacturing environment, resulting in "stale standards."
- Standards can cause employees to lose sight of the larger objectives of the organization by focusing only on efficiency improvement.
- Standards can cause employees to unduly focus on their own operations to the possible harm of other operations that rely on them.

Regardless of these criticisms, standards are used widely. In addition, standard costs are only one part of the performance evaluation system used by most companies. As discussed in this chapter, other nonfinancial performance measures are often used to supplement standard costs, with the result that many of the preceding criticisms are overcome.

---

**Business**  **Connection**

### STANDARD COSTING IN ACTION: EXPANDING BREWING OPERATIONS

In 2011, U.S. west coast craft brewers Sierra Nevada (CA) and New Belgium (CO) announced plans to expand their brewing operations to the Asheville, North Carolina, area. Both companies considered the standard cost of their product when making the decision to expand, and in selecting Asheville as their east coast location. The standard price of direct materials includes the cost of shipping direct materials to the manufacturers' place

of business. The Asheville location was desirable when considering these costs.

In addition, New Belgium projected that their Fort Collins, Colorado, brewery would reach maximum capacity in three to five years. While operating at 100% capacity creates a favorable overhead volume variance, exceeding 100% of capacity makes it very difficult to meet customer demand. Thus, New Belgium felt adding a new brewery prior to reaching 100% capacity at Fort Collins was supported. In both cases, standard costing was used to support the expansion and location decisions.

Sources: H. Dornbusch, "The Case For Low Mileage Beer," Brewers Association.org; J. McCurry, "Hops City: Beer Culture Comes to a Head in the Asheville Region," *Site Selection*, July 2012; J. Shikes, "New Belgium, maker of Fat Tire, plans a second brewery on the East Coast," *Denver Westward*, May 19, 2011.

---

Describe and illustrate how standards are used in budgeting.

## Budgetary Performance Evaluation

As discussed in Chapter 22, the master budget assists a company in planning, directing, and controlling performance. The control function, or budgetary performance evaluation, compares the actual performance against the budget.

To illustrate, **Western Rider Inc.**, a manufacturer of blue jeans, uses standard costs in its budgets. The standards for direct materials, direct labor, and factory overhead are separated into the following two components:

- Standard price
- Standard quantity

The standard cost per unit for direct materials, direct labor, and factory overhead is computed as follows:

Standard Cost per Unit = Standard Price × Standard Quantity

Western Rider's standard costs per unit for its XL jeans are shown in Exhibit 1.

| Manufacturing Costs | Standard Price | × | Standard Quantity per Pair | = | Standard Cost per Pair of XL Jeans |
|---|---|---|---|---|---|
| Direct materials | $5.00 per sq. yd. | | 1.5 sq. yds. | | $ 7.50 |
| Direct labor | $9.00 per hr. | | 0.80 hr. per pair | | 7.20 |
| Factory overhead | $6.00 per hr. | | 0.80 hr. per pair | | 4.80 |
| Total standard cost per pair | | | | | $19.50 |

**EXHIBIT 1**

**Standard Cost for XL Jeans**

As shown in Exhibit 1, the standard cost per pair of XL jeans is $19.50, which consists of $7.50 for direct materials, $7.20 for direct labor, and $4.80 for factory overhead.

The standard price and standard quantity are separated for each product cost. For example, Exhibit 1 indicates that for each pair of XL jeans, the standard price for direct materials is $5.00 per square yard and the standard quantity is 1.5 square yards. The standard price and quantity are separated because the department responsible for their control is normally different. For example, the direct materials price per square yard is controlled by the Purchasing Department, and the direct materials quantity per pair is controlled by the Production Department.

As illustrated in Chapter 22, the master budget is prepared based on planned sales and production. The budgeted costs for materials purchases, direct labor, and factory overhead are determined by multiplying their standard costs per unit by the planned level of production. Budgeted (standard) costs are then compared to actual costs during the year for control purposes.

## Budget Performance Report

The differences between actual and standard costs are called **cost variances**. A **favorable cost variance** occurs when the actual cost is less than the standard cost. An **unfavorable cost variance** occurs when the actual cost exceeds the standard cost. These cost variances are illustrated in Exhibit 2.

| Favorable Cost Variance | Unfavorable Cost Variance |
|---|---|
| Actual cost < Standard cost at actual volumes | Actual cost > Standard cost at actual volumes |

**EXHIBIT 2**

**Cost Variances**

The report that summarizes actual costs, standard costs, and the differences for the units produced is called a **budget performance report**. To illustrate, assume that **Western Rider Inc.** produced the following pairs of jeans during June:

| | |
|---|---|
| XL jeans produced and sold | 5,000 pairs |
| Actual costs incurred in the june: | |
| Direct materials | $ 40,150 |
| Direct labor | 38,500 |
| Factory overhead | 22,400 |
| Total costs incurred | $101,050 |

Exhibit 3 illustrates the budget performance report for June for Western Rider.

The budget performance report shown in Exhibit 3 is based on the actual units produced in June of 5,000 XL jeans. Even though 6,000 XL jeans might have been *planned* for production, the budget performance report is based on *actual* production.

**EXHIBIT 3**     **Budget Performance Report**

| | | **Western Rider Inc.** | |
| | | **Budget Performance Report** | |
| | | **For the Month Ended June 30, 2016** | |

| Manufacturing Costs | Actual Costs | Standard Cost at Actual Volume (5,000 pairs of XL Jeans)* | Cost Variance— (Favorable) Unfavorable |
|---|---|---|---|
| Direct materials......................... | $ 40,150 | $37,500 | $ 2,650 |
| Direct labor ............................ | 38,500 | 36,000 | 2,500 |
| Factory overhead ...................... | 22,400 | 24,000 | (1,600) |
|    Total manufacturing costs............ | $101,050 | $97,500 | $ 3,550 |

*5,000 pairs × $7.50 per pair = $37,500
5,000 pairs × $7.20 per pair = $36,000
5,000 pairs × $4.80 per pair = $24,000

## Manufacturing Cost Variances

The **total manufacturing cost variance** is the difference between total standard costs and total actual cost for the units produced. As shown in Exhibit 3, the total manufacturing cost unfavorable variance is $3,550, which consists of an unfavorable direct materials cost variance of $2,650, and unfavorable direct labor cost variance of $2,500, and a favorable factory overhead cost variance of $1,600.

For control purposes, each product cost variance is separated into two additional variances as shown in Exhibit 4.

**EXHIBIT 4**     **Manufacturing Cost Variances**

The total direct materials variance is separated into a *price* variance and a *quantity* variance. This is because standard and actual direct materials costs are computed as follows:

| | | |
|---|---|---|
| Actual Direct Materials Cost | = Actual Price | × Actual Quantity |
| Standard Direct Materials Cost | = Standard Price | × Standard Quantity |
| Direct Materials Cost Variance | = Price Difference | + Quantity Difference |

Thus, the actual and standard direct materials costs may differ because of a price difference (variance), a quantity difference (variance), or both.

Likewise, the total direct labor variance is separated into a *rate* variance and a *time* variance. This is because standard and actual direct labor costs are computed as follows:

Actual Direct Labor Cost = Actual Rate × Actual Time

Standard Direct Labor Cost = Standard Rate × Standard Time

Direct Labor Cost Variance = Rate Difference + Time Difference

Therefore, the actual and standard direct labor costs may differ because of a rate difference (variance), a time difference (variance), or both.

The total factory overhead variance is separated into a *controllable* variance and a *volume* variance. Because factory overhead has fixed and variable cost elements, it uses different variances than direct materials and direct labor, which are variable costs.

In the next sections, the price and quantity variances for direct materials, the rate and time variances for direct labor, and the controllable and volume variances for factory overhead are further described and illustrated.

# Direct Materials and Direct Labor Variances

OBJ **3** Compute and interpret direct materials and direct labor variances.

As indicated in the prior section, the total direct materials and direct labor variances are separated into the direct materials cost and direct labor cost variances for analysis and control purposes. These variances are illustrated in Exhibit 5.

**EXHIBIT 5**

**Direct Materials and Direct Labor Cost Variances**

As a basis for illustration, the variances for Western Rider's June operations shown in Exhibit 3 are used.

## Direct Materials Variances

During June, **Western Rider Inc.** reported an unfavorable total direct materials cost variance of $2,650 for the production of 5,000 XL style jeans, as shown in Exhibit 3. This variance was based on the following actual and standard costs:

| | |
|---|---|
| Actual costs | $40,150 |
| Standard costs | 37,500 |
| Total direct materials cost variance | $ 2,650 |

The actual costs incurred of $40,150 consist of the following:

Actual Direct Materials Cost = Actual Price × Actual Quantity
= ($5.50 per sq. yd.) × (7,300 sq. yds.)
= $40,150

The standard costs of $37,500 consist of the following:

$$\text{Standard Direct Materials Cost} = \text{Standard Price} \times \text{Standard Quantity}$$
$$= \$5.00 \text{ per sq. yd.} \times 7{,}500 \text{ sq. yds.}$$
$$= \$37{,}500$$

The standard price of $5.00 per square yard is taken from Exhibit 1. In addition, Exhibit 1 indicates that 1.5 square yards is the standard quantity of materials for producing one pair of XL jeans. Thus, 7,500 (5,000 × 1.5) square yards is the standard quantity of materials for producing 5,000 pairs of XL jeans.

Comparing the actual and standard cost computations indicates that the total direct materials unfavorable cost variance of $2,650 is caused by the following:

- A price per square yard of $0.50 ($5.50 – $5.00) more than standard
- A quantity usage of 200 square yards (7,300 sq. yds. – 7,500 sq. yds.) less than standard

The impact of these differences from standard is reported and analyzed as a direct materials *price* variance and direct materials *quantity* variance.

### Direct Materials Price Variance
The **direct materials price variance** is computed as follows:

$$\text{Direct Materials Price Variance} = (\text{Actual Price} - \text{Standard Price}) \times \text{Actual Quantity}$$

If the actual price per unit exceeds the standard price per unit, the variance is unfavorable. This positive amount (unfavorable variance) can be thought of as increasing costs (a debit). If the actual price per unit is less than the standard price per unit, the variance is favorable. This negative amount (favorable variance) can be thought of as decreasing costs (a credit).

To illustrate, the direct materials price variance for **Western Rider Inc.** for June is $3,650 (unfavorable), computed as follows:[1]

$$\text{Direct Materials Price Variance} = (\text{Actual Price} - \text{Standard Price}) \times \text{Actual Quantity}$$
$$= (\$5.50 - \$5.00) \times 7{,}300 \text{ sq. yds.}$$
$$= \$3{,}650 \text{ Unfavorable Variance}$$

### Direct Materials Quantity Variance
The **direct materials quantity variance** is computed as follows:

$$\text{Direct Materials Quantity Variance} = (\text{Actual Quantity} - \text{Standard Quantity}) \times \text{Standard Price}$$

If the actual quantity for the units produced exceeds the standard quantity, the variance is unfavorable. This positive amount (unfavorable variance) can be thought of as increasing costs (a debit). If the actual quantity for the units produced is less than the standard quantity, the variance is favorable. This negative amount (favorable variance) can be thought of as decreasing costs (a credit).

To illustrate, the direct materials quantity variance for **Western Rider Inc.** for June is $1,000 (favorable), computed as follows:

$$\text{Direct Materials Quantity Variance} = (\text{Actual Quantity} - \text{Standard Quantity}) \times \text{Standard Price}$$
$$= (7{,}300 \text{ sq. yds.} - 7{,}500 \text{ sq. yds.}) \times \$5.00$$
$$= -\$1{,}000 \text{ Favorable Variance}$$

### Direct Materials Variance Relationships
The relationship among the *total* direct materials cost variance, the direct materials *price* variance, and the direct materials *quantity* variance is shown in Exhibit 6.

### Reporting Direct Materials Variances
The direct materials quantity variances should be reported to the manager responsible for the variance. For example, an unfavorable quantity variance might be caused by either of the following:

- Equipment that has not been properly maintained
- Low-quality (inferior) direct materials

---

[1] To simplify, it is assumed that there is no change in the beginning and ending materials inventories. Thus, the amount of materials budgeted for production equals the amount purchased.

**EXHIBIT 6**

**Direct Materials Variance Relationships**

Dynamic Exhibit

In the first case, the Operating Department responsible for maintaining the equipment should be held responsible for the variance. In the second case, the Purchasing Department should be held responsible.

Not all variances are controllable. For example, an unfavorable materials price variance might be due to market-wide price increases. In this case, there is nothing the Purchasing Department might have done to avoid the unfavorable variance. On the other hand, if materials of the same quality could have been purchased from another supplier at the standard price, the variance was controllable.

## Service ▲ Focus

### STANDARD COSTING IN THE RESTAURANT INDUSTRY

Many restaurants use standard costs to manage their business. Food costs are typically the largest expense for a restaurant. As a result, many restaurants use food quantity standards to control food costs by establishing the amount of food that is served to a customer. For example, Red Lobster restaurants, a division of Darden Restuarants, Inc., establishes food quantity standards for the number of shrimp, scallops, or clams on a seafood plate.

The second largest cost to most restaurants is labor cost. Many restaurants base their labor cost standards on the labor cost percentage, which is the ratio of total labor cost to total sales. This ratio helps the restaurants of Darden Restaurants, Inc., including the Olive Garden and Red Lobster, control and monitor labor costs. Focusing on this metric has paid off in recent years, as Darden's labor cost percentage dropped from 33.1% of sales in 2010, to 30.4% in the first quarter of 2013. This disciplined focus on food and labor cost standards has helped Darden increase earnings by 4% in the first quarter of 2013.

Source: N. Irwin, "What Olive Garden and Red Lobster tell us about the economy," *The Washington Post*, September 21, 2012.

## Example Exercise 23-1  Direct Materials Variances

Tip Top Corp. produces a product that requires six standard pounds per unit. The standard price is $4.50 per pound. If 3,000 units required 18,500 pounds, which were purchased at $4.35 per pound, what is the direct materials (a) price variance, (b) quantity variance, and (c) cost variance?

(Continued)

## Direct Labor Variances

 The **Internal Revenue Service** publishes a time standard for completing a tax return. The average 1040EZ return is expected to require eight hours to prepare.

During June, **Western Rider Inc.** reported an unfavorable total direct labor cost variance of $2,500 for the production of 5,000 XL style jeans, as shown in Exhibit 3. This variance was based on the following actual and standard costs:

| | |
|---|---|
| Actual costs | $38,500 |
| Standard costs | 36,000 |
| Total direct labor cost variance | $ 2,500 |

The actual costs incurred of $38,500 consist of the following:

Actual Direct Labor Cost = Actual Rate per Hour × Actual Time
= $10.00 per hr. × 3,850 hrs.
= $38,500

The standard costs of $36,000 consist of the following:

Standard Direct Labor Cost = Standard Rate per Hour × Standard Time
= $9.00 per hr. × 4,000 hrs.
= $36,000

The standard rate of $9.00 per direct labor hour is taken from Exhibit 1. In addition, Exhibit 1 indicates that 0.80 hour is the standard time required for producing one pair of XL jeans. Thus, 4,000 (5,000 units × 0.80 hr.) direct labor hours is the standard for producing 5,000 pairs of XL jeans.

Comparing the actual and standard cost computations indicates that the total direct labor unfavorable cost variance of $2,500 is caused by the following:

- A rate of $1.00 per hour ($10.00 – $9.00) more than standard
- A quantity of 150 hours (4,000 hrs. – 3,850 hrs.) less than standard

The impact of these differences from standard is reported and analyzed as a direct labor *rate* variance and a direct labor *time* variance.

### Direct Labor Rate Variance
The **direct labor rate variance** is computed as follows:

Direct Labor Rate Variance = (Actual Rate per Hour – Standard Rate per Hour) × Actual Hours

If the actual rate per hour exceeds the standard rate per hour, the variance is unfavorable. This positive amount (unfavorable variance) can be thought of as increasing costs (a debit). If the actual rate per hour is less than the standard rate per hour, the variance is favorable. This negative amount (favorable variance) can be thought of as decreasing costs (a credit).

To illustrate, the direct labor rate variance for **Western Rider Inc.** in June is $3,850 (unfavorable), computed as follows:

Direct Labor Rate Variance = (Actual Rate per Hour – Standard Rate per Hour) × Actual Hours
= ($10.00 – $9.00) × 3,850 hours
= $3,850 Unfavorable Variance

### Direct Labor Time Variance

The **direct labor time variance** is computed as follows:

Direct Labor Time Variance = (Actual Direct Labor Hours – Standard Direct Labor Hours)
× Standard Rate per Hour

If the actual direct labor hours for the units produced exceeds the standard direct labor hours, the variance is unfavorable. This positive amount (unfavorable variance) can be thought of as increasing costs (a debit). If the actual direct labor hours for the units produced is less than the standard direct labor hours, the variance is favorable. This negative amount (favorable variance) can be thought of as decreasing costs (a credit).

To illustrate, the direct labor time variance for **Western Rider Inc.** for June is $1,350 (favorable) computed as follows:

Direct Labor Time Variance = (Actual Direct Labor Hours – Standard Direct Labor Hours)
× Standard Rate per Hour
= (3,850 hours – 4,000 direct labor hours) × $9.00
= – $1,350 Favorable Variance

### Direct Labor Variance Relationships

The relationships among the *total* direct labor cost variance, the direct labor *rate* variance, and the direct labor *time* variance is shown in Exhibit 7.

### EXHIBIT 7

**Direct Labor Variance Relationships**

Dynamic Exhibit

### Reporting Direct Labor Variances

Production supervisors are normally responsible for controlling direct labor cost. For example, an investigation could reveal the following causes for unfavorable rate and time variances:

- An unfavorable rate variance may be caused by the improper scheduling and use of employees. In such cases, skilled, highly paid employees may be used in jobs that are normally performed by unskilled, lower-paid employees. In this case, the unfavorable rate variance should be reported to the managers who schedule work assignments.

- An unfavorable time variance may be caused by a shortage of skilled employees. In such cases, there may be an abnormally high turnover rate among skilled employees. In this case, production supervisors with high turnover rates should be questioned as to why their employees are quitting.

**Direct Labor Standards for Nonmanufacturing Activities** Direct labor time standards can also be developed for use in administrative, selling, and service activities. This is most appropriate when the activity involves a repetitive task that produces a common output. In these cases, the use of standards is similar to that for a manufactured product.

To illustrate, standards could be developed for customer service personnel who process sales orders. A standard time for processing a sales order (the output) could be developed and used to control sales order processing costs. Similar standards could be developed for computer help desk operators, nurses, and insurance application processors.

When labor-related activities are not repetitive, direct labor time standards are less commonly used. For example, the time spent by a senior executive or the work of a research and development scientist would not normally be controlled using time standards.

---

**Example Exercise 23-2** **Direct Labor Variances**

Tip Top Corp. produces a product that requires 2.5 standard hours per unit at a standard hourly rate of $12 per hour. If 3,000 units required 7,420 hours at an hourly rate of $12.30 per hour, what is the (a) direct labor rate variance, (b) direct labor time variance, and (c) total direct labor cost variance?

**Follow My Example 23-2** >>

a. Direct labor rate variance:
   ($12.30 − $12.00) × 7,420 hours = $2,226 (unfavorable)

b. Direct labor time variance:
   (7,420 hours − 7,500 hours*) × $12.00 = −$960 (favorable)

c. Total direct labor cost variance:**
   $2,226 − $960 = $1,266 (unfavorable)

*3,000 units × 2.5 hours
** Also computed as follows:
   ($12.30 × 7,420 hours) − ($12.00 × 7,500 hours)
   $91,266 − $90,000 = $1,266 (unfavorable)

Practice Exercises: PE 23-2A, PE 23-2B

---

OBJ **4** Compute and interpret factory overhead controllable and volume variances.

# Factory Overhead Variances

Factory overhead costs are analyzed differently than direct labor and direct materials costs. This is because factory overhead costs have fixed and variable cost elements. For example, indirect materials and factory supplies normally behave as a variable cost as units produced changes. In contrast, straight-line plant depreciation on factory machinery is a fixed cost.

Factory overhead costs are budgeted and controlled by separating factory overhead into fixed and variable components. Doing so allows the preparation of flexible budgets and the analysis of factory overhead controllable and volume variances.

## The Factory Overhead Flexible Budget

The preparation of a flexible budget was described and illustrated in Chapter 22. Exhibit 8 illustrates a flexible factory overhead budget for **Western Rider Inc.** for June 2016.

| | A | B | C | D | E |
|---|---|---|---|---|---|
| 1 | Western Rider Inc. | | | | |
| 2 | Factory Overhead Cost Budget | | | | |
| 3 | For the Month Ending June 30, 2016 | | | | |
| 4 | Percent of normal capacity | 80% | 90% | 100% | 110% |
| 5 | Units produced | 5,000 | 5,625 | 6,250 | 6,875 |
| 6 | Direct labor hours (0.80 hr. per unit) | 4,000 | 4,500 | 5,000 | 5,500 |
| 7 | Budgeted factory overhead: | | | | |
| 8 | Variable costs: | | | | |
| 9 | Indirect factory wages | $ 8,000 | $ 9,000 | $10,000 | $11,000 |
| 10 | Power and light | 4,000 | 4,500 | 5,000 | 5,500 |
| 11 | Indirect materials | 2,400 | 2,700 | 3,000 | 3,300 |
| 12 | Total variable cost | $14,400 | $16,200 | $18,000 | $19,800 |
| 13 | Fixed costs: | | | | |
| 14 | Supervisory salaries | $ 5,500 | $ 5,500 | $ 5,500 | $ 5,500 |
| 15 | Depreciation of plant | | | | |
| 16 | and equipment | 4,500 | 4,500 | 4,500 | 4,500 |
| 17 | Insurance and property taxes | 2,000 | 2,000 | 2,000 | 2,000 |
| 18 | Total fixed cost | $12,000 | $12,000 | $12,000 | $12,000 |
| 19 | Total factory overhead cost | $26,400 | $28,200 | $30,000 | $31,800 |
| 20 | | | | | |
| 21 | Factory overhead rate per direct labor hour, $30,000 ÷ 5,000 hours = $6.00 | | | | |

**EXHIBIT 8**

**Factory Overhead Cost Budget Indicating Standard Factory Overhead Rate**

Exhibit 8 indicates that the budgeted factory overhead rate for Western Rider is $6.00, computed as follows:

$$\text{Factory Overhead Rate} = \frac{\text{Budgeted Factory Overhead at Normal Capacity}}{\text{Normal Productive Capacity}}$$

$$= \frac{\$30,000}{5,000 \text{ direct labor hrs.}} = \$6.00 \text{ per direct labor hr.}$$

The normal productive capacity is expressed in terms of an activity base such as direct labor hours, direct labor cost, or machine hours. For Western Rider, 100% of normal capacity is 5,000 direct labor hours. The budgeted factory overhead cost at 100% of normal capacity is $30,000, which consists of variable overhead of $18,000 and fixed overhead of $12,000.

For analysis purposes, the budgeted factory overhead rate is subdivided into a variable factory overhead rate and a fixed factory overhead rate. For Western Rider, the variable overhead rate is $3.60 per direct labor hour, and the fixed overhead rate is $2.40 per direct labor hour, computed as follows:

$$\text{Variable Factory Overhead Rate} = \frac{\text{Budgeted Variable Overhead at Normal Capacity}}{\text{Normal Productive Capacity}}$$

$$= \frac{\$18,000}{5,000 \text{ direct labor hrs.}} = \$3.60 \text{ per direct labor hr.}$$

$$\text{Fixed Factory Overhead Rate} = \frac{\text{Budgeted Fixed Overhead at Normal Capacity}}{\text{Normal Productive Capacity}}$$

$$= \frac{\$12,000}{5,000 \text{ direct labor hrs.}} = \$2.40 \text{ per direct labor hr.}$$

To summarize, the budgeted factory overhead rates for Western Rider Inc. are as follows:

| | |
|---|---|
| Variable factory overhead rate | $3.60 |
| Fixed factory overhead rate | 2.40 |
| Total factory overhead rate | $6.00 |

As mentioned previously, factory overhead variances can be separated into a controllable variance and a volume variance as discussed in the next sections.

## Variable Factory Overhead Controllable Variance

The variable factory overhead **controllable variance** is the difference between the actual variable overhead costs and the budgeted variable overhead for actual production. It is computed as follows:

$$\text{Variable Factory Overhead Controllable Variance} = \text{Actual Variable Factory Overhead} - \text{Budgeted Variable Factory Overhead}$$

If the actual variable overhead is less than the budgeted variable overhead, the variance is favorable. If the actual variable overhead exceeds the budgeted variable overhead, the variance is unfavorable.

The **budgeted variable factory overhead** is the standard variable overhead for the *actual* units produced. It is computed as follows:

$$\text{Budgeted Variable Factory Overhead} = \text{Standard Hours for Actual Units Produced} \times \text{Variable Factory Overhead Rate}$$

To illustrate, the budgeted variable overhead for **Western Rider Inc.** for June, when 5,000 units of XL jeans were produced, is $14,400, computed as follows:

$$\begin{aligned}
\text{Budgeted Variable Factory Overhead} &= \text{Standard Hours for Actual Units Produced} \\
&\quad \times \text{Variable Factory Overhead Rate} \\
&= 4{,}000 \text{ direct labor hrs.} \times \$3.60 \\
&= \$14{,}400
\end{aligned}$$

The preceding computation is based on the fact that Western Rider produced 5,000 XL jeans, which requires a standard of 4,000 (5,000 units × 0.8 hr.) direct labor hours. The variable factory overhead rate of $3.60 was computed earlier. Thus, the budgeted variable factory overhead is $14,400 (4,000 direct labor hrs. × $3.60).

During June, assume that Western Rider incurred the following actual factory overhead costs:

|  | **Actual Costs in June** |
| --- | --- |
| Variable factory overhead | $10,400 |
| Fixed factory overhead | 12,000 |
| Total actual factory overhead | $22,400 |

Based on the actual variable factory overhead incurred in June, the variable factory overhead controllable variance is a $4,000 favorable variance, computed as follows:

$$\begin{aligned}
\text{Variable Factory Overhead Controllable Variance} &= \text{Actual Variable Factory Overhead} - \text{Budgeted Variable Factory Overhead} \\
&= \$10{,}400 - \$14{,}400 \\
&= -\$4{,}000 \text{ Favorable Variance}
\end{aligned}$$

The variable factory overhead controllable variance indicates the ability to keep the factory overhead costs within the budget limits. Because variable factory overhead costs are normally controllable at the department level, responsibility for controlling this variance usually rests with department supervisors.

**Example Exercise 23-3  Factory Overhead Controllable Variance**

Tip Top Corp. produced 3,000 units of product that required 2.5 standard hours per unit. The standard variable overhead cost per unit is $2.20 per hour. The actual variable factory overhead was $16,850. Determine the variable factory overhead controllable variance.

**Follow My Example 23-3**

Variable Factory Overhead Controllable Variance = Actual Variable Factory Overhead − Budgeted Variable Factory Overhead

= $16,850 − [(3,000 units × 2.5 hrs.) × $2.20]
= $16,850 − $16,500
= $350 (unfavorable)

Practice Exercises: PE 23-3A, PE 23-3B

## Fixed Factory Overhead Volume Variance

Western Rider's budgeted factory overhead is based on a 100% normal capacity of 5,000 direct labor hours, as shown in Exhibit 8. This is the expected capacity that management believes will be used under normal business conditions. Exhibit 8 indicates that the 5,000 direct labor hours is less than the total available capacity of 110%, which is 5,500 direct labor hours.

The fixed factory overhead **volume variance** is the difference between the budgeted fixed overhead at 100% of normal capacity and the standard fixed overhead for the actual units produced. It is computed as follows:

$$\text{Fixed Factory Overhead Volume Variance} = \left(\begin{array}{c}\text{Standard Hours for 100\% of Normal Capacity}\end{array} - \begin{array}{c}\text{Standard Hours for Actual Units Produced}\end{array}\right) \times \text{Fixed Factory Overhead Rate}$$

The volume variance measures the use of fixed overhead resources (plant and equipment). The interpretation of an unfavorable and a favorable fixed factory overhead volume variance is as follows:

- *Unfavorable* fixed factory overhead volume variance. The actual units produced is *less than* 100% of normal capacity; thus, the company used its fixed overhead resources (plant and equipment) less than would be expected under normal operating conditions.
- *Favorable* fixed factory overhead volume variance. The actual units produced is *more than* 100% of normal capacity; thus, the company used its fixed overhead resources (plant and equipment) more than would be expected under normal operating conditions.

To illustrate, the fixed factory overhead volume variance for **Western Rider Inc.** is a $2,400 unfavorable variance, computed as follows:

$$\text{Fixed Factory Overhead Volume Variance} = \left(\begin{array}{c}\text{Standard Hours for 100\% of Normal Capacity}\end{array} - \begin{array}{c}\text{Standard Hours for Actual Units Produced}\end{array}\right) \times \text{Fixed Factory Overhead Rate}$$

$$= \left(\begin{array}{c}5{,}000\text{ direct labor hrs.}\end{array} - \begin{array}{c}4{,}000\text{ direct labor hrs.}\end{array}\right) \times \$2.40$$

$$= \$2{,}400 \text{ Unfavorable Variance}$$

Because Western Rider produced 5,000 XL jeans during June, the standard for the actual units produced is 4,000 (5,000 units × 0.80) direct labor hours. This is 1,000 hours less than the 5,000 standard hours of normal capacity. The fixed overhead rate of $2.40 was computed earlier. Thus, the unfavorable fixed factory overhead volume variance is $2,400 (1,000 direct labor hrs. × $2.40).

Exhibit 9 illustrates graphically the fixed factory overhead volume variance for **Western Rider Inc.** The budgeted fixed overhead does not change and is $12,000 at all levels of production. At 100% of normal capacity (5,000 direct labor hours), the standard fixed overhead line intersects the budgeted fixed costs line. For production levels *more than* 100% of normal capacity (5,000 direct labor hours), the volume variance is *favorable*. For production levels *less than* 100% of normal capacity (5,000 direct labor hours), the volume variance is *unfavorable*.

**EXHIBIT 9**

**Graph of Fixed Overhead Volume Variance**

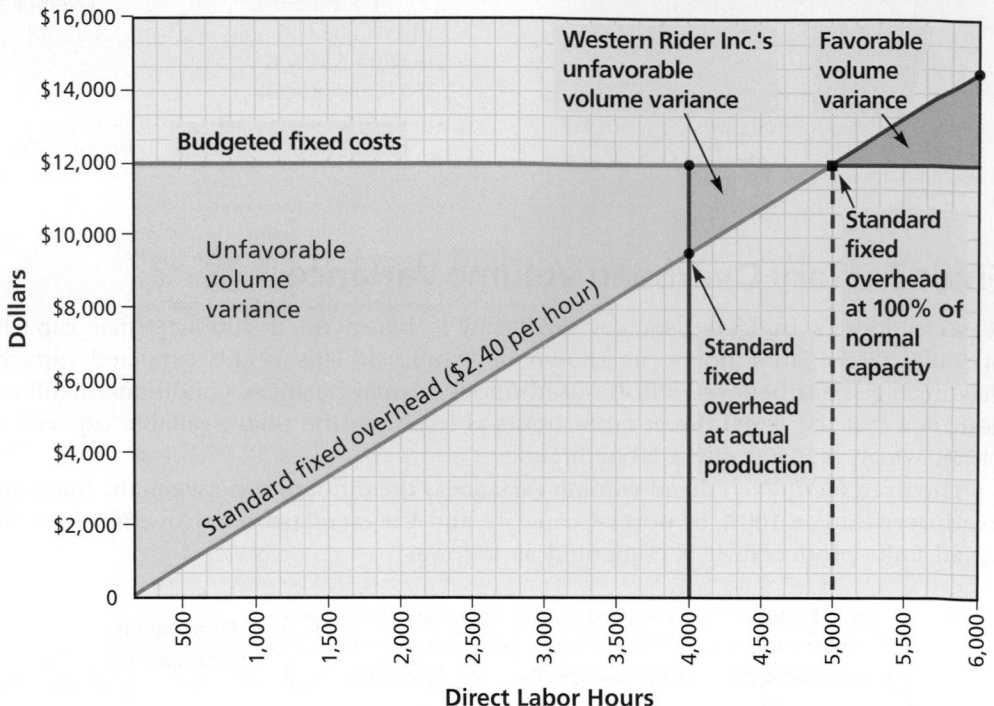

Exhibit 9 indicates that Western Rider's fixed factory overhead volume variance is unfavorable in June because the actual production is 4,000 direct labor hours, or 80% of normal volume. The unfavorable volume variance of $2,400 can be viewed as the cost of the unused capacity (1,000 direct labor hours).

An unfavorable volume variance may be due to factors such as the following:

- Failure to maintain an even flow of work
- Machine breakdowns
- Work stoppages caused by lack of materials or skilled labor
- Lack of enough sales orders to keep the factory operating at normal capacity

Management should determine the causes of the unfavorable variance and consider taking corrective action. For example, a volume variance caused by an uneven flow of work could be remedied by changing operating procedures. Lack of sales orders may be corrected through increased advertising.

Favorable volume variances may not always be desirable. For example, in an attempt to create a favorable volume variance, manufacturing managers might run the factory above the normal capacity. However, if the additional production cannot be sold, it must be stored as inventory, which would incur storage costs.

**Example Exercise 23-4** **Factory Overhead Volume Variance** ⟩⟩⟩

Tip Top Corp. produced 3,000 units of product that required 2.5 standard hours per unit. The standard fixed overhead cost per unit is $0.90 per hour at 8,000 hours, which is 100% of normal capacity. Determine the fixed factory overhead volume variance.

**Follow My Example 23-4** ▸▸

Fixed Factory Overhead Volume Variance = (Standard Hours for 100% of Normal Capacity − Standard Hours for Actual Units Produced) × Fixed Factory Overhead Rate
= [8,000 hrs. − (3,000 units × 2.5 hrs.)] × $0.90
= (8,000 hrs. − 7,500 hrs.) × $0.90
= $450 (unfavorable)

Practice Exercises: PE 23-4A, PE 23-4B

## Reporting Factory Overhead Variances

The total factory overhead cost variance can also be determined as the sum of the variable factory overhead controllable and fixed factory overhead volume variances, computed as follows for **Western Rider Inc.**:

| | |
|---|---|
| Variable factory overhead controllable variance | −$4,000 Favorable Variance |
| Fixed factory overhead volume variance | 2,400 Unfavorable Variance |
| Total factory overhead cost variance | −$1,600 Favorable Variance |

A **factory overhead cost variance report** is useful to management in controlling factory overhead costs. Budgeted and actual costs for variable and fixed factory overhead along with the related controllable and volume variances are reported by each cost element.

Exhibit 10 illustrates a factory overhead cost variance report for Western Rider Inc. for June.

| | A | B | C | D | E |
|---|---|---|---|---|---|
| 1 | | Western Rider Inc. | | | |
| 2 | | Factory Overhead Cost Variance Report | | | |
| 3 | | For the Month Ending June 30, 2016 | | | |
| 4 | Productive capacity for the month (100% of normal) | | 5,000 hours | | |
| 5 | Actual production for the month | | 4,000 hours | | |
| 6 | | | | | |
| 7 | | Budget | | | |
| 8 | | (at Actual | | Variances | |
| 9 | | Production) | Actual | Favorable | Unfavorable |
| 10 | Variable factory overhead costs: | | | | |
| 11 | Indirect factory wages | $ 8,000 | $ 5,100 | $2,900 | |
| 12 | Power and light | 4,000 | 4,200 | | $ 200 |
| 13 | Indirect materials | 2,400 | 1,100 | 1,300 | |
| 14 | Total variable factory | | | | |
| 15 | overhead cost | $14,400 | $10,400 | | |
| 16 | Fixed factory overhead costs: | | | | |
| 17 | Supervisory salaries | $ 5,500 | $ 5,500 | | |
| 18 | Depreciation of plant and | | | | |
| 19 | equipment | 4,500 | 4,500 | | |
| 20 | Insurance and property taxes | 2,000 | 2,000 | | |
| 21 | Total fixed factory | | | | |
| 22 | overhead cost | $12,000 | $12,000 | | |
| 23 | Total factory overhead cost | $26,400 | $22,400 | | |
| 24 | Total controllable variances | | | $4,200 | $ 200 |
| 25 | | | | | |
| 26 | | | | | |
| 27 | Net controllable variance—favorable | | | | $4,000 |
| 28 | Volume variance—unfavorable: | | | | |
| 29 | Capacity not used at the standard rate for fixed | | | | |
| 30 | factory overhead—1,000 × $2.40 | | | | 2,400 |
| 31 | Total factory overhead cost variance—favorable | | | | $1,600 |

**EXHIBIT 10**

**Factory Overhead Cost Variance Report**

## Factory Overhead Account

To illustrate, the applied factory overhead for **Western Rider Inc.** for the 5,000 XL jeans produced in June is $24,000, computed as follows:

$$\text{Applied Factory Overhead} = \frac{\text{Standard Hours for Actual}}{\text{Units Produced}} \times \frac{\text{Total Factory}}{\text{Overhead Rate}}$$

= (5,000 jeans × 0.80 direct labor hr. per pair of jeans) × $6.00

= 4,000 direct labor hrs. × $6.00 = $24,000

The total actual factory overhead for Western Rider, as shown in Exhibit 10, was $22,400. Thus, the total factory overhead cost variance for Western Rider for June is a $1,600 favorable variance, computed as follows:

$$\frac{\text{Total Factory Overhead}}{\text{Cost Variance}} = \text{Actual Factory Overhead} - \text{Applied Factory Overhead}$$

= $22,400 − $24,000 = −$1,600 Favorable Variance

At the end of the period, the factory overhead account normally has a balance. A debit balance in Factory Overhead represents underapplied overhead. Underapplied overhead occurs when actual factory overhead costs exceed the applied factory overhead. A credit balance in Factory Overhead represents overapplied overhead. Overapplied overhead occurs when actual factory overhead costs are less than the applied factory overhead.

The difference between the actual factory overhead and the applied factory overhead is the total factory overhead cost variance. Thus, underapplied and overapplied factory overhead account balances represent the following total factory overhead cost variances:

- *Underapplied* Factory Overhead = *Unfavorable* Total Factory Overhead Cost Variance
- *Overapplied* Factory Overhead = *Favorable* Total Factory Overhead Cost Variance

The factory overhead account for **Western Rider Inc.** for the month ending June 30, 2016, is as follows:

**Factory Overhead**

| | | | |
|---|---|---|---|
| Actual factory overhead | 22,400 | 24,000 | Applied factory overhead |
| ($10,400 + $12,000) | | | (4,000 hrs. × $6.00 per hr.) |
| | | Bal., June 30  1,600 | Overapplied factory overhead |

The $1,600 overapplied factory overhead account balance and the favorable total factory overhead cost variance shown in Exhibit 10 are the same.

The variable factory overhead controllable variance and the volume variance can be computed by comparing the factory overhead account with the budgeted total overhead for the actual level produced, as shown in Exhibit 11.

The controllable and volume variances are determined as follows:

- The difference between the actual overhead incurred and the budgeted overhead is the *controllable* variance.
- The difference between the applied overhead and the budgeted overhead is the *volume* variance.

If the actual factory overhead exceeds (is less than) the budgeted factory overhead, the controllable variance is unfavorable (favorable). In contrast, if the applied factory overhead is less than (exceeds) the budgeted factory overhead, the volume variance is unfavorable (favorable).

| EXHIBIT 11 | Factory Overhead Variances |

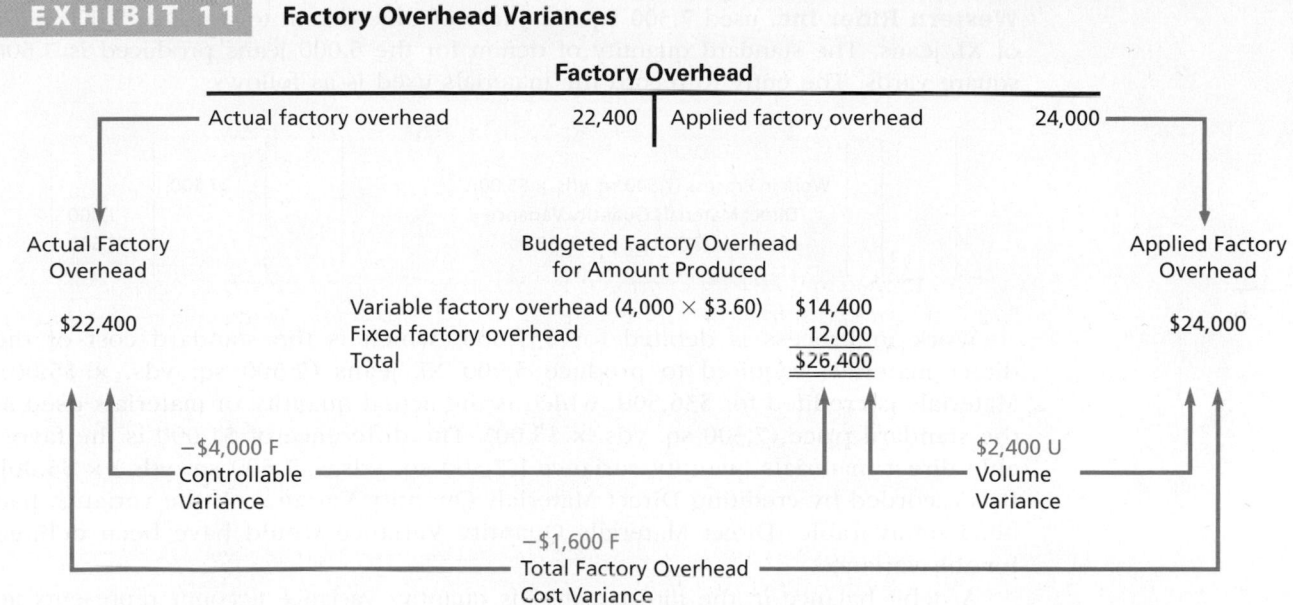

# Recording and Reporting Variances from Standards

OBJ **5** Journalize the entries for recording standards in the accounts and prepare an income statement that includes variances from standard.

Standard costs may be used as a management tool to control costs separately from the accounts in the general ledger. However, many companies include standard costs in their accounts. One method for doing so records standard costs and variances at the same time the actual product costs are recorded.

To illustrate, assume that **Western Rider Inc.** purchased, on account, the 7,300 square yards of blue denim used at $5.50 per square yard. The standard price for direct materials is $5.00 per square yard. The entry to record the purchase and the unfavorable direct materials price variance is as follows:

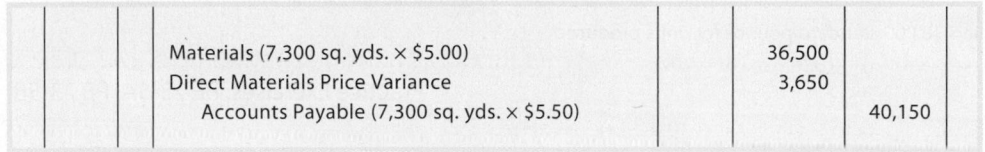

| | | | | |
|---|---|---|---|---|
| Materials (7,300 sq. yds. × $5.00) | | | 36,500 | |
| Direct Materials Price Variance | | | 3,650 | |
| Accounts Payable (7,300 sq. yds. × $5.50) | | | | 40,150 |

The materials account is debited for the *actual quantity* purchased at the *standard price*, $36,500 (7,300 square yards × $5.00). Accounts Payable is credited for the $40,150 actual cost and the amount due the supplier. The difference of $3,650 is the unfavorable direct materials price variance [($5.50 – $5.00) × 7,300 sq. yds.]. It is recorded by debiting Direct Materials Price Variance. If the variance had been favorable, Direct Materials Price Variance would have been credited for the variance.

A debit balance in the direct materials price variance account represents an unfavorable variance. Likewise, a credit balance in the direct materials price variance account represents a favorable variance.

The direct materials quantity variance is recorded in a similar manner. For example, **Western Rider Inc.** used 7,300 square yards of blue denim to produce 5,000 pairs of XL jeans. The standard quantity of denim for the 5,000 jeans produced is 7,500 square yards. The entry to record the materials used is as follows:

| | | |
|---|---|---|
| Work in Process (7,500 sq. yds. × $5.00) | 37,500 | |
| Direct Materials Quantity Variance | | 1,000 |
| Materials (7,300 sq. yds. × $5.00) | | 36,500 |

Work in Process is debited for $37,500, which is the standard cost of the direct materials required to produce 5,000 XL jeans (7,500 sq. yds. × $5.00). Materials is credited for $36,500, which is the actual quantity of materials used at the standard price (7,300 sq. yds. × $5.00). The difference of $1,000 is the favorable direct materials quantity variance [(7,300 sq. yds. − 7,500 sq. yds.) × $5.00]. It is recorded by crediting Direct Materials Quantity Variance. If the variance had been unfavorable, Direct Materials Quantity Variance would have been debited for the variance.

A debit balance in the direct materials quantity variance account represents an unfavorable variance. Likewise, a credit balance in the direct materials quantity variance account represents a favorable variance.

## Example Exercise 23-5 Standard Cost Journal Entries

Tip Top Corp. produced 3,000 units that require six standard pounds per unit at the $4.50 standard price per pound. The company actually used 18,500 pounds in production. Journalize the entry to record the standard direct materials used in production.

### Follow My Example 23-5

| | | |
|---|---|---|
| Work in Process (18,000* pounds × $4.50) .......................................... | 81,000 | |
| Direct Materials Quantity Variance [(18,500 pounds − 18,000 pounds) × $4.50] ....... | 2,250 | |
| Materials (18,500 pounds × $4.50) ................................................ | | 83,250 |

*3,000 units × 6 pounds per unit = 18,000 standard pounds for units produced

Practice Exercises: PE 23-5A, PE 23-5B

The journal entries to record the standard costs and variances for *direct labor* are similar to those for direct materials. These entries are summarized as follows:

- Work in Process is debited for the standard cost of direct labor.
- Wages Payable is credited for the actual direct labor cost incurred.
- Direct Labor Rate Variance is debited for an unfavorable variance and credited for a favorable variance.
- Direct Labor Time Variance is debited for an unfavorable variance and credited for a favorable variance.

As illustrated in the prior section, the factory overhead account already incorporates standard costs and variances into its journal entries. That is, Factory Overhead is debited for actual factory overhead and credited for applied (standard) factory overhead. The ending balance of factory overhead (overapplied or underapplied) is the total factory overhead cost variance. By comparing the actual factory overhead with the budgeted factory overhead, the controllable variance can be determined. By comparing the budgeted factory overhead with the applied factory overhead, the volume variance can be determined.

When goods are completed, Finished Goods is debited and Work in Process is credited for the standard cost of the product transferred.

At the end of the period, the balances of each of the variance accounts indicate the net favorable or unfavorable variance for the period. These variances may be reported in an income statement prepared for management's use.

Exhibit 12 is an example of an income statement for **Western Rider Inc.** that includes variances. In Exhibit 12, a sales price of $28 per pair of jeans, selling expenses of $14,500, and administrative expenses of $11,225 are assumed.

### EXHIBIT 12
**Variance from Standards in Income Statement**

**Western Rider Inc.**
**Income Statement**
**For the Month Ended June 30, 2016**

| | Favorable | Unfavorable | |
|---|---|---|---|
| Sales ................................................ | | | $140,000[1] |
| Cost of goods sold—at standard...................... | | | 97,500[2] |
| Gross profit—at standard ........................... | | | $ 42,500 |
| Less variances from standard cost: | | | |
| Direct materials price............................ | | $ 3,650 | |
| Direct materials quantity ........................ | $1,000 | | |
| Direct labor rate................................. | | 3,850 | |
| Direct labor time................................. | 1,350 | | |
| Factory overhead controllable..................... | 4,000 | | |
| Factory overhead volume.......................... | | 2,400 | 3,550 |
| Gross profit....................................... | | | $ 38,950 |
| Operating expenses: | | | |
| Selling expenses ................................. | | $14,500 | |
| Administrative expenses.......................... | | 11,225 | 25,725 |
| Income before income tax .......................... | | | $ 13,225 |

[1]5,000 × $28
[2]$37,500 + $36,000 + $24,000 (from Exhibit 3), or 5,000 × $19.50 (from Exhibit 1)

The income statement shown in Exhibit 12 is for internal use by management. That is, variances are not reported to external users. Thus, the variances shown in Exhibit 12 must be transferred to other accounts in preparing an income statement for external users.

In preparing an income statement for external users, the balances of the variance accounts are normally transferred to Cost of Goods Sold. However, if the variances are significant or if many of the products manufactured are still in inventory, the variances should be allocated to Work in Process, Finished Goods, and Cost of Goods Sold. Such an allocation, in effect, converts these account balances from standard cost to actual cost.

### Example Exercise 23-6  Income Statement with Variances

OBJ 5

Prepare an income statement for the year ended December 31, 2016, through gross profit for Tip Top Corp. using the variance data in Example Exercises 23-1 through 23-4. Assume Tip Top sold 3,000 units at $100 per unit.

*(Continued)*

**Follow My Example 23-6**

**Tip Top Corp.**
**Income Statement through Gross Profit**
**For the Year Ended December 31, 2016**

| | | | Favorable | Unfavorable | |
|---|---|---|---|---|---|
| Sales (3,000 units × $100) | | | | | $300,000 |
| Cost of goods sold—at standard | | | | | 194,250* |
| Gross profit—at standard | | | | | $105,750 |
| | | | **Favorable** | **Unfavorable** | |
| Less variances from standard cost: | | | | | |
| Direct materials price (EE23-1) | | | $2,775 | | |
| Direct materials quantity (EE23-1) | | | | $2,250 | |
| Direct labor rate (EE23-2) | | | | 2,226 | |
| Direct labor time (EE23-2) | | | 960 | | |
| Factory overhead controllable (EE23-3) | | | | 350 | |
| Factory overhead volume (EE23-4) | | | | 450 | 1,541 |
| Gross profit—actual | | | | | $104,209 |

| | | |
|---|---|---|
| *Direct materials (3,000 units × 6 lbs. × $4.50) | $ 81,000 | |
| Direct labor (3,000 units × 2.5 hrs. × $12.00) | 90,000 | |
| Factory overhead [3,000 units × 2.5 hrs. × ($2.20 + $0.90)] | 23,250 | |
| Cost of goods sold at standard | $194,250 | |

Practice Exercises: PE 23-6A, PE 23-6B

**OBJ 6** Describe and provide examples of nonfinancial performance measures.

# Nonfinancial Performance Measures

Many companies supplement standard costs and variances from standards with nonfinancial performance measures. A **nonfinancial performance measure** expresses performance in a measure other than dollars. For example, airlines use on-time performance, percent of bags lost, and number of customer complaints as nonfinancial performance measures. Such measures are often used to evaluate the time, quality, or quantity of a business activity.

Using financial and nonfinancial performance measures aids managers and employees in considering multiple performance objectives. Such measures often bring additional perspectives, such as quality of work, to evaluating performance. Some examples of nonfinancial performance measures are shown in Exhibit 13.

**EXHIBIT 13**

**Nonfinancial Performance Measures**

- Inventory turnover
- Percent on-time delivery
- Elapsed time between a customer order and product delivery
- Customer preference rankings compared to competitors
- Response time to a service call
- Time to develop new products
- Employee satisfaction
- Number of customer complaints

Nonfinancial measures are often linked to either the inputs or outputs of an activity or process. A **process** is a sequence of activities for performing a task. The relationship between an activity or a process and its inputs and outputs is shown in Exhibit 14.

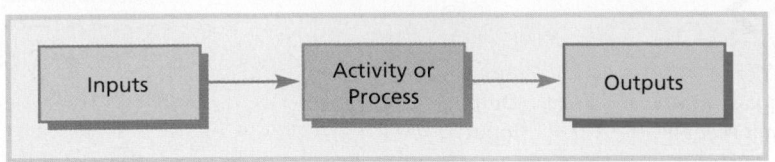

EXHIBIT 14

**Relationship Between a Process and Its Inputs and Outputs**

To illustrate, the counter service activity of a fast-food restaurant is used. The inputs/outputs for providing counter service at a fast-food restaurant are shown in Exhibit 15.

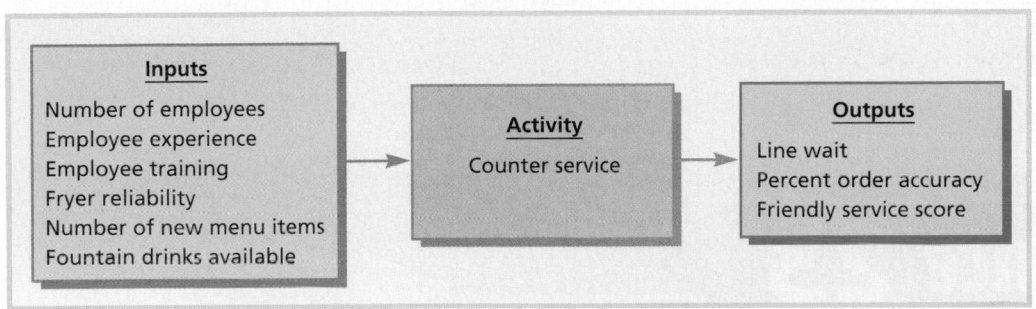

EXHIBIT 15

**Inputs / Outputs for a Fast-Food Restaurant**

The customer service outputs of the counter service activity include the following:

- Line wait for the customer
- Percent order accuracy in serving the customer
- Friendly service experience for the customer

Some of the inputs that impact the customer service outputs include the following:

- Number of employees
- Employee experience
- Employee training
- Fryer (and other cooking equipment) reliability
- Number of new menu items
- Fountain drink availability

A fast-food restaurant can develop a set of linked nonfinancial performance measures across inputs and outputs. The output measures tell management how the activity is performing, such as keeping the line wait to a minimum. The input measures are used to improve the output measures. For example, if the customer line wait is too long, then improving employee training or hiring more employees could improve the output (decrease customer line wait).

**Example Exercise 23-7 Activity Inputs and Outputs**

OBJ 6

The following are inputs and outputs to the baggage claim process of an airline:

Baggage handler training
Time customers wait for returned baggage
Maintenance of baggage handling equipment
Number of baggage handlers
Number of damaged bags
On-time flight performance

Identify whether each is an input or output to the baggage claim process.

*(Continued)*

**Follow My Example 23-7**

| | |
|---|---|
| Baggage handler training | Input |
| Time customers wait for returned baggage | Output |
| Maintenance of baggage handling equipment | Input |
| Number of baggage handlers | Input |
| Number of damaged bags | Output |
| On-time flight performance | Input |

Practice Exercises: PE 23-7A, PE 23-7B

# At a Glance 23

**Describe the types of standards and how they are established.**

**Key Points** Standards represent performance goals that can be compared to actual results in evaluating performance. Standards are established so that they are neither too high nor too low, but are attainable.

| Learning Outcomes | Example Exercises | Practice Exercises |
|---|---|---|
| • Define *ideal* and *currently attainable standards* and explain how they are used in setting standards. | | |
| • Describe some of the criticisms of the use of standards. | | |

**Describe and illustrate how standards are used in budgeting.**

**Key Points** Budgets are prepared by multiplying the standard cost per unit by the planned production. To measure performance, the standard cost per unit is multiplied by the actual number of units produced, and the actual results are compared with the standard cost at actual volumes (cost variance).

| Learning Outcomes | Example Exercises | Practice Exercises |
|---|---|---|
| • Compute the standard cost per unit of production for materials, labor, and factory overhead. | | |
| • Compute the direct materials, direct labor, and factory overhead cost variances. | | |
| • Prepare a budget performance report. | | |

**Compute and interpret direct materials and direct labor variances.**

**Key Points** The direct materials cost variance can be separated into direct materials price and quantity variances. The direct labor cost variance can be separated into direct labor rate and time variances.

| Learning Outcomes | Example Exercises | Practice Exercises |
|---|---|---|
| • Compute and interpret direct materials price and quantity variances. | EE23-1 | PE23-1A, 23-1B |
| • Compute and interpret direct labor rate and time variances. | EE23-2 | PE23-2A, 23-2B |
| • Describe and illustrate how time standards are used in nonmanufacturing settings. | | |

**Compute and interpret factory overhead controllable and volume variances.**

**Key Points** The factory overhead cost variance can be separated into a variable factory overhead controllable variance and a fixed factory overhead volume variance.

| Learning Outcomes | Example Exercises | Practice Exercises |
|---|---|---|
| • Prepare a factory overhead flexible budget. | | |
| • Compute and interpret the variable factory overhead controllable variance. | EE23-3 | PE23-3A, 23-3B |
| • Compute and interpret the fixed factory overhead volume variance. | EE23-4 | PE23-4A, 23-4B |
| • Prepare a factory overhead cost variance report. | | |
| • Evaluate factory overhead variances, using a T account. | | |

**Journalize the entries for recording standards in the accounts and prepare an income statement that includes variances from standard.**

**Key Points** Standard costs and variances can be recorded in the accounts at the same time the manufacturing costs are recorded in the accounts. Work in Process is debited at standard. Under a standard cost system, the cost of goods sold will be reported at standard cost. Manufacturing variances can be disclosed on the income statement to adjust the gross profit at standard to the actual gross profit.

| Learning Outcomes | Example Exercises | Practice Exercises |
|---|---|---|
| • Journalize the entries to record the purchase and use of direct materials at standard, recording favorable or unfavorable variances. | EE23-5 | PE23-5A, 23-5B |
| • Prepare an income statement, disclosing favorable and unfavorable direct materials, direct labor, and factory overhead variances. | EE23-6 | PE23-6A, 23-6B |

**Describe and provide examples of nonfinancial performance measures.**

**Key Points**   Many companies use a combination of financial and nonfinancial measures in order for multiple perspectives to be incorporated in evaluating performance. Nonfinancial measures are often used in conjunction with the inputs or outputs of a process or an activity.

| Learning Outcomes | Example Exercises | Practice Exercises |
|---|---|---|
| • Define, provide the rationale for, and provide examples of nonfinancial performance measures. | | |
| • Identify nonfinancial inputs and outputs of an activity. | EE23-7 | PE23-7A, 23-7B |

# Key Terms

budget performance report (1081)
budgeted variable factory overhead (1090)
controllable variance (1090)
cost variance (1090)
currently attainable standards (1079)
direct labor rate variance (1086)
direct labor time variance (1087)

direct materials price variance (1084)
direct materials quantity variance (1084)
factory overhead cost variance report (1093)
favorable cost variance (1081)
ideal standards (1079)
nonfinancial performance measure (1098)

process (1098)
standard cost (1078)
standard cost systems (1078)
standards (1078)
total manufacturing cost variance (1082)
unfavorable cost variance (1081)
volume variance (1091)

# Illustrative Problem

Hawley Inc. manufactures designer iPod cases for national distribution. The standard costs for the manufacture of Folk Art style baskets were as follows:

| | Standard Costs | Actual Costs |
|---|---|---|
| Direct materials | 1,500 lbs. at $35 | 1,600 lbs. at $32 |
| Direct labor | 4,800 hrs. at $11 | 4,500 hrs. at $11.80 |
| Factory overhead | Rates per labor hour, based on 100% of normal capacity of 5,500 labor hrs.: | |
| | Variable cost, $2.40 | $12,300 variable cost |
| | Fixed cost, $3.50 | $19,250 fixed cost |

## Instructions

1. Determine the direct materials price variance, direct materials quantity variance, and total direct materials cost variance for the designer iPod cases.

2. Determine the direct labor rate variance, direct labor time variance, and total direct labor cost variance for the designer iPod cases.

3. Determine the variable factory overhead controllable variance, fixed factory overhead volume variance, and total factory overhead cost variance for the designer iPod cases.

## Solution

1.

### Direct Materials Cost Variance

**Price variance:**

Direct Materials Price Variance = (Actual Price – Standard Price) × Actual Quantity

= ($32 per lb. – $35 per lb.) × 1,600 lbs.

= –$4,800 Favorable Variance

**Quantity variance:**

Direct Materials Quantity Variance = (Actual Quantity – Standard Quantity) × Standard Price

= (1,600 lbs. – 1,500 lbs.) × $35 per lb.

= $3,500 Unfavorable Variance

**Total direct materials cost variance:**

Direct Materials Cost Variance = Direct Materials Quantity Variance + Direct Materials Price Variance

= $3,500 + ($4,800)

= –$1,300 Favorable Variance

2.

### Direct Labor Cost Variance

**Rate variance:**

Direct Labor Rate Variance = (Actual Rate per Hour – Standard Rate per Hour) × Actual Hours

= ($11.80 – $11.00) × 4,500 hrs.

= $3,600 Unfavorable Variance

**Time variance:**

Direct Labor Time Variance = (Actual Direct Labor Hours – Standard Direct Labor Hours) ×

Standard Rate per Hour

= (4,500 hrs. – 4,800 hrs.) × $11.00 per hour

= –$3,300 Favorable Variance

**Total direct labor cost variance:**

Direct Labor Cost Variance = Direct Labor Time Variance + Direct Labor Rate Variance

= ($3,300) + $3,600

= $300 Unfavorable Variance

3.

### Factory Overhead Cost Variance

**Variable factory overhead controllable variance:**

Variable Factory Overhead = Actual Variable Factory Overhead – Budgeted Variable
Controllable Variance    Factory Overhead

= $12,300 – $11,520*

= $780 Unfavorable Variance

*4,800 hrs. × $2.40 per hour

**Fixed factory overhead volume variance:**

$$\text{Fixed Factory Overhead Volume Variance} = \left( \begin{array}{c} \text{Standard Hours for 100\%} \\ \text{of Normal Capacity} \end{array} - \begin{array}{c} \text{Standard Hours for} \\ \text{Actual Units Produced} \end{array} \right) \times \begin{array}{c} \text{Fixed Factory} \\ \text{Overhead Rate} \end{array}$$

= (5,500 hrs. – 4,800 hrs.) × $3.50 per hr.

= $2,450 Unfavorable Variance

**Total factory overhead cost variance:**

$$\text{Factory Overhead Cost Variance} = \begin{array}{c} \text{Variable Factory Overhead} \\ \text{Controllable Variance} \end{array} + \begin{array}{c} \text{Fixed Factory Overhead} \\ \text{Volume Variance} \end{array}$$

= $780 + $2,450

= $3,230 Unfavorable Variance

# Discussion Questions

1. What are the basic objectives in the use of standard costs?

2. What is meant by reporting by the "principle of exceptions," as the term is used in reference to cost control?

3. What are the two variances between the actual cost and the standard cost for direct materials?

4. The materials cost variance report for Nickols Inc. indicates a large favorable materials price variance and a significant unfavorable materials quantity variance. What might have caused these offsetting variances?

5. a. What are the two variances between the actual cost and the standard cost for direct labor?

   b. Who generally has control over the direct labor cost variances?

6. A new assistant controller recently was heard to remark: "All the assembly workers in this plant are covered by union contracts, so there should be no labor variances." Was the controller's remark correct? Discuss.

7. Would the use of standards be appropriate in a nonmanufacturing setting, such as a fast-food restaurant?

8. a. Describe the two variances between the actual costs and the standard costs for factory overhead.

   b. What is a factory overhead cost variance report?

9. If variances are recorded in the accounts at the time the manufacturing costs are incurred, what does a debit balance in Direct Materials Price Variance represent?

10. Briefly explain why firms might use nonfinancial performance measures.

# Practice Exercises

SHOW
ME HOW

EE 23-1 *p.1085*  **PE 23-1A   Direct materials variances**                    OBJ. 3

Lo-bed Company produces a product that requires two standard gallons per unit. The standard price is $20.00 per gallon. If 4,000 units required 8,200 gallons, which were purchased at $19.75 per gallon, what is the direct materials (a) price variance, (b) quantity variance, and (c) cost variance?

SHOW
ME HOW

EE 23-1 *p.1085*  **PE 23-1B   Direct materials variances**                    OBJ. 3

Dvorak Company produces a product that requires five standard pounds per unit. The standard price is $2.50 per pound. If 1,000 units required 4,500 pounds, which were purchased at $3.00 per pound, what is the direct materials (a) price variance, (b) quantity variance, and (c) cost variance?

SHOW
ME HOW

EE 23-2 *p.1088*  **PE 23-2A   Direct labor variances**                        OBJ. 3

Lo-bed Company produces a product that requires four standard hours per unit at a standard hourly rate of $28.00 per hour. If 4,000 units required 16,750 hours at an hourly rate of $28.40 per hour, what is the direct labor (a) rate variance, (b) time variance, and (c) cost variance?

EE 23-2 *p.1088*

### PE 23-2B   Direct labor variances
OBJ. 3

Dvorak Company produces a product that requires three standard hours per unit at a standard hourly rate of $17 per hour. If 1,000 units required 2,800 hours at an hourly rate of $16.50 per hour, what is the direct labor (a) rate variance, (b) time variance, and (c) cost variance?

EE 23-3 *p.1091*

### PE 23-3A   Factory overhead controllable variance
OBJ. 4

Lo-bed Company produced 4,000 units of product that required four standard hours per unit. The standard variable overhead cost per unit is $3.00 per hour. The actual variable factory overhead was $51,240. Determine the variable factory overhead controllable variance.

EE 23-3 *p.1091*

### PE 23-3B   Factory overhead controllable variance
OBJ. 4

Dvorak Company produced 1,000 units of product that required three standard hours per unit. The standard variable overhead cost per unit is $1.40 per hour. The actual variable factory overhead was $4,000. Determine the variable factory overhead controllable variance.

EE 23-4 *p.1092*

### PE 23-4A   Factory overhead volume variance
OBJ. 4

Lo-bed Company produced 4,000 units of product that required four standard hours per unit. The standard fixed overhead cost per unit is $1.20 per hour at 16,400 hours, which is 100% of normal capacity. Determine the fixed factory overhead volume variance.

EE 23-4 *p.1092*

### PE 23-4B   Factory overhead volume variance
OBJ. 4

Dvorak Company produced 1,000 units of product that required three standard hours per unit. The standard fixed overhead cost per unit is $0.60 per hour at 3,500 hours, which is 100% of normal capacity. Determine the fixed factory overhead volume variance.

EE 23-5 *p. 1096*

### PE 23-5A   Standard cost journal entries
OBJ. 5

Lo-bed Company produced 4,000 units that require two standard gallons per unit at $20.00 standard price per gallon. The company actually used 8,200 gallons in production. Journalize the entry to record the standard direct materials used in production.

EE 23-5 *p. 1096*

### PE 23-5B   Standard cost journal entries
OBJ. 5

Dvorak Company produced 1,000 units that require five standard pounds per unit at $2.50 standard price per pound. The company actually used 4,500 pounds in production. Journalize the entry to record the standard direct materials used in production.

EE 23-6 *p. 1097*

### PE 23-6A   Income statement with variances
OBJ. 5

Prepare a 2016 income statement through gross profit for Lo-bed Company, using the variance data in Practice Exercises 23-1A, 23-2A, 23-3A, and 23-4A. Assume Lo-bed sold 4,000 units at $250 per unit.

EE 23-6 *p. 1097*

### PE 23-6B   Income statement with variances
OBJ. 5

Prepare a 2016 income statement through gross profit for Dvorak Company, using the variance data in Practice Exercises 23-1B, 23-2B, 23-3B, and 23-4B. Assume Dvorak sold 1,000 units at $90 per unit.

SHOW
ME HOW

EE 23-7  *p. 1099*   **PE 23-7A   Activity inputs and outputs**                                    **OBJ. 6**

The following are inputs and outputs to the copying process of a copy shop:

Number of employee errors
Number of times paper supply runs out
Copy machine downtime (broken)
Number of pages copied per hour
Number of customer complaints
Percent jobs done on time

Identify whether each is an input or output to the copying process.

SHOW
ME HOW

EE 23-7  *p. 1099*   **PE 23-7B   Activity inputs and outputs**                                    **OBJ. 6**

The following are inputs and outputs to the cooking process of a restaurant:

Number of times ingredients are missing
Number of customer complaints
Number of hours kitchen equipment is down for repairs
Number of server order mistakes
Percent of meals prepared on time
Number of unexpected cook absences

Identify whether each is an input or output to the cooking process.

# Exercises

SHOW
ME HOW

**EX 23-1   Standard direct materials cost per unit**                                    **OBJ. 2**

Choco La Ti-Da Company produces chocolate bars. The primary materials used in producing chocolate bars are cocoa, sugar, and milk. The standard costs for a batch of chocolate (4,500 bars) are as follows:

| Ingredient | Quantity | Price |
|---|---|---|
| Cocoa | 510 lbs. | $1.50 per lb. |
| Sugar | 160 lbs. | $0.50 per lb. |
| Milk | 100 gal. | $3.25 per gal. |

Determine the standard direct materials cost per bar of chocolate.

SHOW
ME HOW

**EX 23-2   Standard product cost**                                    **OBJ. 2**

Wood You Lie To Me Furniture Company manufactures designer home furniture. Wood You Lie To Me uses a standard cost system. The direct labor, direct materials, and factory overhead standards for an unfinished dining room table are as follows:

| | | |
|---|---|---|
| Direct labor: | standard rate | $24.00 per hr. |
| | standard time per unit | 4.0 hrs. |
| Direct materials (oak): | standard price | $22.00 per bd. ft. |
| | standard quantity | 32 bd. ft. |
| Variable factory overhead: | standard rate | $3.00 per direct labor hr. |
| Fixed factory overhead: | standard rate | $2.00 per direct labor hr. |

a.   Determine the standard cost per dining room table.

b.   ━━━▶ Why would Wood You Lie To Me Furniture Company use a standard cost system?

### EX 23-3  Budget performance report

OBJ. 2

Genie in a Bottle Company (GBC) manufactures plastic two-liter bottles for the beverage industry. The cost standards per 100 two-liter bottles are as follows:

| Cost Category | Standard Cost per 100 Two-Liter Bottles |
|---|---|
| Direct labor | $ 2.00 |
| Direct materials | 9.10 |
| Factory overhead | 0.55 |
| Total | $11.65 |

At the beginning of July, GBC management planned to produce 400,000 bottles. The actual number of bottles produced for July was 406,000 bottles. The actual costs for July of the current year were as follows:

| Cost Category | Actual Cost for the Month Ended July 31 |
|---|---|
| Direct labor | $ 7,540 |
| Direct materials | 35,750 |
| Factory overhead | 2,680 |
| Total | $45,970 |

a. Prepare the July manufacturing standard cost budget (direct labor, direct materials, and factory overhead) for GBC, assuming planned production.

b. Prepare a budget performance report for manufacturing costs, showing the total cost variances for direct materials, direct labor, and factory overhead for July.

c. ▬▬▬▬▶ Interpret the budget performance report.

### EX 23-4  Direct materials variances

OBJ. 3

The following data relate to the direct materials cost for the production of 4,000 automobile tires:

| | | |
|---|---|---|
| Actual: | 72,500 lbs. at $3.30 | |
| Standard: | 75,160 lbs. at $3.15 | |

a. Determine the direct materials price variance, direct materials quantity variance, and total direct materials cost variance.

b. ▬▬▬▬▶ To whom should the variances be reported for analysis and control?

### EX 23-5  Direct materials variances

OBJ. 3

The Silicone Engine Inc. produces wrist-worn tablet computers. The company uses Thin Film Crystal (TFC) LCD displays for its products. Each tablet uses one display. The company produced 580 tablets during December. However, due to LCD defects, the company actually used 600 LCD displays during December. Each display has a standard cost of $15.00. Six hundred LCD displays were purchased for December production at a cost of $8,550.

Determine the price variance, quantity variance, and total direct materials cost variance for December.

### EX 23-6  Standard direct materials cost per unit from variance data

OBJ. 2, 3

The following data relating to direct materials cost for October of the current year are taken from the records of Good Clean Fun Inc., a manufacturer of organic toys:

| | |
|---|---|
| Quantity of direct materials used | 3,000 lbs. |
| Actual unit price of direct materials | $5.50 per lb. |
| Units of finished product manufactured | 1,400 units |
| Standard direct materials per unit of finished product | 2 lbs. |
| Direct materials quantity variance—unfavorable | $1,000 |
| Direct materials price variance—unfavorable | $1,500 |

Determine the standard direct materials cost per unit of finished product, assuming that there was no inventory of work in process at either the beginning or the end of the month.

SHOW
ME HOW

### EX 23-7   Standard product cost, direct materials variance                                    OBJ. 2, 3

H.J. Heinz Company uses standards to control its materials costs. Assume that a batch of ketchup (3,128 pounds) has the following standards:

|                | Standard Quantity | Standard Price    |
|----------------|-------------------|-------------------|
| Whole tomatoes | 4,000 lbs.        | $ 0.60 per lb.    |
| Vinegar        | 260 gal.          | 2.25 per gal.     |
| Corn syrup     | 25 gal.           | 28.00 per gal.    |
| Salt           | 100 lbs.          | 2.25 per lb.      |

The actual materials in a batch may vary from the standard due to tomato characteristics. Assume that the actual quantities of materials for batch K-111 were as follows:

4,250 lbs. of tomatoes
275 gal. of vinegar
22 gal. of corn syrup
90 lbs. of salt

a.  Determine the standard unit materials cost per pound for a standard batch.

b.  Determine the direct materials quantity variance for batch K-111. Round your answer to the nearest cent.

✔ a. Rate variance,
$4,225 F

SHOW
ME HOW

### EX 23-8   Direct labor variances                                                              OBJ. 3

The following data relate to labor cost for production of 20,000 cellular telephones:

|           |                      |
|-----------|----------------------|
| Actual:   | 8,450 hrs. at $22.50 |
| Standard: | 8,400 hrs. at $23.00 |

a.  Determine the direct labor rate variance, direct labor time variance, and total direct labor cost variance.

b.  ➤ Discuss what might have caused these variances.

✔ a. Time variance,
$525 U

SHOW
ME HOW

### EX 23-9   Direct labor variances                                                              OBJ. 3, 5

Reincarnation Bicycle Company manufactures commuter bicycles from recycled materials. The following data for April of the current year are available:

|                                  |                |
|----------------------------------|----------------|
| Quantity of direct labor used    | 1,530 hrs.     |
| Actual rate for direct labor     | $17.00 per hr. |
| Bicycles completed in April      | 500            |
| Standard direct labor per bicycle| 3 hrs.         |
| Standard rate for direct labor   | $17.50 per hr. |

a.  Determine the direct labor rate variance, time variance, and total direct labor cost variance.

b.  How much direct labor should be debited to Work in Process?

✔ a. Cutting
Department rate
variance, $638
favorable

### EX 23-10   Direct labor variances                                                             OBJ. 3

The Greeson Clothes Company produced 25,000 units during June of the current year. The Cutting Department used 6,380 direct labor hours at an actual rate of $10.90 per hour. The Sewing Department used 9,875 direct labor hours at an actual rate of $11.12 per hour. Assume there were no work in process inventories in either department at the beginning or end of the month. The standard labor rate is $11.00. The standard labor time for the Cutting and Sewing departments is 0.25 hour and 0.4 hour per unit, respectively.

a.  Determine the direct labor rate, direct labor time, and total direct labor cost variance for the (1) Cutting Department and (2) Sewing Department.

b.  ➤ Interpret your results.

✔ a. $2,400

### EX 23-11 Direct labor standards for nonmanufacturing expenses OBJ. 3

Englert Hospital began using standards to evaluate its Admissions Department. The standard was broken into two types of admissions as follows:

| Type of Admission | Standard Time to Complete Admission Record |
|---|---|
| Unscheduled admission | 30 min. |
| Scheduled admission | 15 min. |

The unscheduled admission took longer because name, address, and insurance information needed to be determined and verified at the time of admission. Information was collected on scheduled admissions prior to the admissions, which was less time consuming.

The Admissions Department employs four full-time people (40 productive hours per week, with no overtime) at $15 per hour. For the most recent week, the department handled 140 unscheduled and 350 scheduled admissions.

a. How much was actually spent on labor for the week?

b. What are the standard hours for the actual volume for the week?

c. Calculate a time variance, and report how well the department performed for the week.

### EX 23-12 Direct labor standards for a service company OBJ. 2, 3

One of the operations in the United States Postal Service is a mechanical mail sorting operation. In this operation, letter mail is sorted at a rate of 1.5 letters per second. The letter is mechanically sorted from a three-digit code input by an operator sitting at a keyboard. The manager of the mechanical sorting operation wishes to determine the number of temporary employees to hire for December. The manager estimates that there will be an additional 24,192,000 pieces of mail in December, due to the upcoming holiday season.

Assume that the sorting operators are temporary employees. The union contract requires that temporary employees be hired for one month at a time. Each temporary employee is hired to work 160 hours in the month.

a. How many temporary employees should the manager hire for December?

b. If each temporary employee earns a standard $16.40 per hour, what would be the labor time variance if the actual number of additional letters sorted in December was 23,895,000?

### Ex 23-13 Direct labor variances for a service company

Hit-n-Run Food Trucks, Inc. owns and operates food trucks (mobile kitchens) throughout the west coast. The company's employees have varying wage levels depending on their experience and length of time with the company. Employees work eight hour shifts and are assigned to a truck each day based on labor needs to support the daily menu. One of their trucks, Jose O'Brien's Mobile Fiesta, specializes in Irish-Mexican fusion cuisine. The truck offers a single menu item which changes daily. On November 11, the truck prepared 200 of its most popular item, the Irish Breakfast Enchiladas. The following data are available for that day:

| | |
|---|---|
| Quantity of direct labor used | 24 hrs. |
| (3 employees, working 8 hour shifts) | |
| Actual rate for direct labor | $15.00 per hr. |
| Standard direct labor per meal | 0.1 hr. |
| Standard rate for direct labor | $15.50 per hr. |

a. Determine the direct labor rate variance, direct labor time variance, and the total direct labor cost variance.

b. Discuss what might have caused these variances.

✔ Direct materials
quantity variance,
$1,100 U

SHOW
ME HOW

**EX 23-14   Direct materials and direct labor variances**     **OBJ. 3**

At the beginning of June, Bezco Toy Company budgeted 5,000 toy action figures to be manufactured in June at standard direct materials and direct labor costs as follows:

| | |
|---|---:|
| Direct materials | $50,000 |
| Direct labor | 36,000 |
| Total | $86,000 |

The standard materials price is $4.00 per pound. The standard direct labor rate is $18.00 per hour. At the end of June, the actual direct materials and direct labor costs were as follows:

| | |
|---|---:|
| Actual direct materials | $49,600 |
| Actual direct labor | 34,020 |
| Total | $83,620 |

There were no direct materials price or direct labor rate variances for June. In addition, assume no changes in the direct materials inventory balances in June. Bezco Toy Company actually produced 4,850 units during June.

Determine the direct materials quantity and direct labor time variances.

✔ Total factory
overhead, 22,000
hrs., $443,600

**EX 23-15   Flexible overhead budget**     **OBJ. 4**

Leno Manufacturing Company prepared the following factory overhead cost budget for the Press Department for October of the current year, during which it expected to require 20,000 hours of productive capacity in the department:

| | | |
|---|---:|---:|
| Variable overhead cost: | | |
| Indirect factory labor | $180,000 | |
| Power and light | 12,000 | |
| Indirect materials | 64,000 | |
| Total variable overhead cost | | $256,000 |
| Fixed overhead cost: | | |
| Supervisory salaries | $ 80,000 | |
| Depreciation of plant and equipment | 50,000 | |
| Insurance and property taxes | 32,000 | |
| Total fixed overhead cost | | 162,000 |
| Total factory overhead cost | | $418,000 |

Assuming that the estimated costs for November are the same as for October, prepare a flexible factory overhead cost budget for the Press Department for November for 18,000, 20,000, and 22,000 hours of production.

**EX 23-16   Flexible overhead budget**     **OBJ. 4**

Wiki Wiki Company has determined that the variable overhead rate is $4.50 per direct labor hour in the Fabrication Department. The normal production capacity for the Fabrication Department is 10,000 hours for the month. Fixed costs are budgeted at $60,000 for the month.

a.  Prepare a monthly factory overhead flexible budget for 9,000, 10,000, and 11,000 hours of production.

b.  How much overhead would be applied to production if 9,000 hours were used in the department during the month?

**EX 23-17   Factory overhead cost variances**                                      OBJ. 4

The following data relate to factory overhead cost for the production of 10,000 computers:

| | | | |
|---|---|---|---|
| Actual: | Variable factory overhead | | $262,000 |
| | Fixed factory overhead | | 90,000 |
| Standard: | 14,000 hrs. at $25 | | 350,000 |

If productive capacity of 100% was 15,000 hours and the total factory overhead cost budgeted at the level of 14,000 standard hours was $356,000, determine the variable factory overhead controllable variance, fixed factory overhead volume variance, and total factory overhead cost variance. The fixed factory overhead rate was $6.00 per hour.

**EX 23-18   Factory overhead cost variances**                                      OBJ. 4

Blumen Textiles Corporation began April with a budget for 90,000 hours of production in the Weaving Department. The department has a full capacity of 100,000 hours under normal business conditions. The budgeted overhead at the planned volumes at the beginning of April was as follows:

| | |
|---|---|
| Variable overhead | $540,000 |
| Fixed overhead | 240,000 |
| Total | $780,000 |

The actual factory overhead was $782,000 for April. The actual fixed factory overhead was as budgeted. During April, the Weaving Department had standard hours at actual production volume of 92,500 hours.

a.  Determine the variable factory overhead controllable variance.

b.  Determine the fixed factory overhead volume variance.

**EX 23-19   Factory overhead variance corrections**                                OBJ. 4

The data related to Shunda Enterprises Inc.'s factory overhead cost for the production of 100,000 units of product are as follows:

| | | |
|---|---|---|
| Actual: | Variable factory overhead | $458,000 |
| | Fixed factory overhead | 494,000 |
| Standard: | 132,000 hrs. at $7.30 ($3.50 for variable factory overhead) | 963,600 |

Productive capacity at 100% of normal was 130,000 hours, and the factory overhead cost budgeted at the level of 132,000 standard hours was $956,000. Based on these data, the chief cost accountant prepared the following variance analysis:

| | | |
|---|---|---|
| Variable factory overhead controllable variance: | | |
| Actual variable factory overhead cost incurred | $458,000 | |
| Budgeted variable factory overhead for 132,000 hours | 462,000 | |
| Variance—favorable | | −$ 4,000 |
| Fixed factory overhead volume variance: | | |
| Normal productive capacity at 100% | 130,000 hrs. | |
| Standard for amount produced | 132,000 | |
| Productive capacity not used | 2,000 hrs. | |
| Standard variable factory overhead rate | × $7.30 | |
| Variance—unfavorable | | 14,600 |
| Total factory overhead cost variance—unfavorable | | $10,600 |

Identify the errors in the factory overhead cost variance analysis.

### EX 23-20 Factory overhead cost variance report OBJ. 4

Tannin Products Inc. prepared the following factory overhead cost budget for the Trim Department for July of the current year, during which it expected to use 20,000 hours for production:

| Variable overhead cost: | | |
|---|---|---|
|    Indirect factory labor | $46,000 | |
|    Power and light | 12,000 | |
|    Indirect materials | 20,000 | |
|      Total variable overhead cost | | $ 78,000 |
| Fixed overhead cost: | | |
|    Supervisory salaries | $54,500 | |
|    Depreciation of plant and equipment | 40,000 | |
|    Insurance and property taxes | 35,500 | |
|      Total fixed overhead cost | | 130,000 |
|    Total factory overhead cost | | $208,000 |

Tannin has available 25,000 hours of monthly productive capacity in the Trim Department under normal business conditions. During July, the Trim Department actually used 22,000 hours for production. The actual fixed costs were as budgeted. The actual variable overhead for July was as follows:

| Actual variable factory overhead cost: | |
|---|---|
|    Indirect factory labor | $49,700 |
|    Power and light | 13,000 |
|    Indirect materials | 24,000 |
|      Total variable cost | $86,700 |

Construct a factory overhead cost variance report for the Trim Department for July.

### EX 23-21 Recording standards in accounts OBJ. 5

Cioffi Manufacturing Company incorporates standards in its accounts and identifies variances at the time the manufacturing costs are incurred. Journalize the entries to record the following transactions:

a. Purchased 2,450 units of copper tubing on account at $52.00 per unit. The standard price is $48.50 per unit.

b. Used 1,900 units of copper tubing in the process of manufacturing 200 air conditioners. Ten units of copper tubing are required, at standard, to produce one air conditioner.

### EX 23-22 Recording standards in accounts OBJ. 5

The Assembly Department produced 5,000 units of product during March. Each unit required 2.20 standard direct labor hours. There were 11,500 actual hours used in the Assembly Department during March at an actual rate of $17.60 per hour. The standard direct labor rate is $18.00 per hour. Assuming direct labor for a month is paid on the fifth day of the following month, journalize the direct labor in the Assembly Department on March 31.

### EX 23-23 Income statement indicating standard cost variances OBJ. 5

The following data were taken from the records of Griggs Company for December 2016:

| | |
|---|---|
| Administrative expenses | $100,800 |
| Cost of goods sold (at standard) | 550,000 |
| Direct materials price variance—unfavorable | 1,680 |
| Direct materials quantity variance—favorable | 560 |
| Direct labor rate variance—favorable | 1,120 |
| Direct labor time variance—unfavorable | 490 |
| Variable factory overhead controllable variance—favorable | 210 |
| Fixed factory overhead volume variance—unfavorable | 3,080 |
| Interest expense | 2,940 |
| Sales | 868,000 |
| Selling expenses | 125,000 |

Prepare an income statement for presentation to management.

**EX 23-24    Nonfinancial performance measures**                                    OBJ. 6

Diamond Inc. is an Internet retailer of woodworking equipment. Customers order woodworking equipment from the company, using an online catalog. The company processes these orders and delivers the requested product from its warehouse. The company wants to provide customers with an excellent purchase experience in order to expand the business through favorable word-of-mouth advertising and to drive repeat business. To help monitor performance, the company developed a set of performance measures for its order placement and delivery process:

Average computer response time to customer "clicks"
Dollar amount of returned goods
Elapsed time between customer order and product delivery
Maintenance dollars divided by hardware investment
Number of customer complaints divided by the number of orders
Number of misfilled orders divided by the number of orders
Number of orders per warehouse employee
Number of page faults or errors due to software programming errors
Number of software fixes per week
Server (computer) downtime
Training dollars per programmer

a.  For each performance measure, identify it as either an input or output measure related to the "order placement and delivery" process.

b.  ➡️Provide an explanation for each performance measure.

**EX 23-25    Nonfinancial performance measures**                                    OBJ. 6

Alpha University wishes to monitor the efficiency and quality of its course registration process.

a.  Identify three input and three output measures for this process.

b.  ➡️Why would Alpha University use nonfinancial measures for monitoring this process?

## Problems: Series A

**PR 23-1A    Direct materials and direct labor variance analysis**                  OBJ. 2, 3

✔ c. Direct labor time variance, $1,260 U

SHOW
ME HOW

Fancy Fixture Company manufactures faucets in a small manufacturing facility. The faucets are made from brass. Manufacturing has 100 employees. Each employee presently provides 40 hours of labor per week. Information about a production week is as follows:

| | |
|---|---:|
| Standard wage per hr. | $21.00 |
| Standard labor time per faucet | 20 min. |
| Standard number of lbs. of brass | 5 lbs. |
| Standard price per lb. of brass | $2.80 |
| Actual price per lb. of brass | $2.72 |
| Actual lbs. of brass used during the week | 59,875 lbs. |
| Number of faucets produced during the week | 11,820 |
| Actual wage per hr. | $21.40 |
| Actual hrs. for the week | 4,000 hrs. |

**Instructions**

Determine (a) the standard cost per unit for direct materials and direct labor; (b) the direct materials price variance, direct materials quantity variance, and total direct materials cost variance; and (c) the direct labor rate variance, direct labor time variance, and total direct labor cost variance.

---

**PR 23-2A** **Flexible budgeting and variance analysis** OBJ. 1, 2, 3

I Love My Chocolate Company makes dark chocolate and light chocolate. Both products require cocoa and sugar. The following planning information has been made available:

| | Standard Amount per Case | | |
| | Dark Chocolate | Light Chocolate | Standard Price per Pound |
| --- | --- | --- | --- |
| Cocoa | 12 lbs. | 8 lbs. | $7.25 |
| Sugar | 10 lbs. | 14 lbs. | 1.40 |
| Standard labor time | 0.50 hr. | 0.60 hr. | |

| | Dark Chocolate | Light Chocolate |
| --- | --- | --- |
| Planned production | 4,700 cases | 11,000 cases |
| Standard labor rate | $15.50 per hr. | $15.50 per hr. |

I Love My Chocolate Company does not expect there to be any beginning or ending inventories of cocoa or sugar. At the end of the budget year, I Love My Chocolate Company had the following actual results:

| | Dark Chocolate | Light Chocolate |
| --- | --- | --- |
| Actual production (cases) | 5,000 | 10,000 |
| | Actual Price per Pound | Actual Pounds Purchased and Used |
| Cocoa | $7.33 | 140,300 |
| Sugar | 1.35 | 188,000 |
| | Actual Labor Rate | Actual Labor Hours Used |
| Dark chocolate | $15.25 per hr. | 2,360 |
| Light chocolate | 15.80 per hr. | 6,120 |

**Instructions**

1. Prepare the following variance analyses for both chocolates and the total, based on the actual results and production levels at the end of the budget year:

   a. Direct materials price, quantity, and total variance.

   b. Direct labor rate, time, and total variance.

2. ▬▬▶Why are the standard amounts in part (1) based on the actual production for the year instead of the planned production for the year?

---

**PR 23-3A** **Direct materials, direct labor, and factory overhead cost variance** OBJ. 3, 4
**analysis**

Adamantane Inc. processes a base chemical into plastic. Standard costs and actual costs for direct materials, direct labor, and factory overhead incurred for the manufacture of 15,000 units of product were as follows:

| | Standard Costs | Actual Costs |
| --- | --- | --- |
| Direct materials | 5,000 lbs. at $50.00 | 4,950 lbs. at $50.60 |
| Direct labor | 3,000 hrs. at $25.00 | 2,945 hrs. at $25.60 |
| Factory overhead | Rates per direct labor hr., based on 100% of normal capacity of 3,200 direct labor hrs.: | |
| | Variable cost, $5.50 | $16,680 variable cost |
| | Fixed cost, $4.00 | $12,800 fixed cost |

Each unit requires 0.2 hour of direct labor.

**Instructions**

Determine (a) the direct materials price variance, direct materials quantity variance, and total direct materials cost variance; (b) the direct labor rate variance, direct labor time variance, and total direct labor cost variance; and (c) the variable factory overhead controllable variance, fixed factory overhead volume variance, and total factory overhead cost variance.

**PR 23-4A   Factory overhead cost variance report**                                   OBJ. 4

Tiger Equipment Inc., a manufacturer of construction equipment, prepared the following factory overhead cost budget for the Welding Department for May of the current year. The company expected to operate the department at 100% of normal capacity of 8,400 hours.

| | | |
|---|---:|---:|
| Variable costs: | | |
| Indirect factory wages | $30,240 | |
| Power and light | 20,160 | |
| Indirect materials | 16,800 | |
| Total variable cost | | $ 67,200 |
| Fixed costs: | | |
| Supervisory salaries | $20,000 | |
| Depreciation of plant and equipment | 36,200 | |
| Insurance and property taxes | 15,200 | |
| Total fixed cost | | 71,400 |
| Total factory overhead cost | | $138,600 |

During May, the department operated at 8,860 standard hours, and the factory overhead costs incurred were indirect factory wages, $32,400; power and light, $21,000; indirect materials, $18,250; supervisory salaries, $20,000; depreciation of plant and equipment, $36,200; and insurance and property taxes, $15,200.

**Instructions**

Prepare a factory overhead cost variance report for May. To be useful for cost control, the budgeted amounts should be based on 8,860 hours.

**PR 23-5A   Standards for nonmanufacturing expenses**                                OBJ. 3, 6

CodeHead Software Inc. does software development. One important activity in software development is writing software code. The manager of the WordPro Development Team determined that the average software programmer could write 25 lines of code in an hour. The plan for the first week in May called for 4,650 lines of code to be written on the Word-Pro product. The WordPro Team has five programmers. Each programmer is hired from an employment firm that requires temporary employees to be hired for a minimum of a 40-hour week. Programmers are paid $32.00 per hour. The manager offered a bonus if the team could generate more lines for the week, without overtime. Due to a project emergency, the programmers wrote more code in the first week of May than planned. The actual amount of code written in the first week of May was 5,650 lines, without overtime. As a result, the bonus caused the average programmer's hourly rate to increase to $40.00 per hour during the first week in May.

**Instructions**

1. If the team generated 4,650 lines of code according to the original plan, what would have been the labor time variance?

2. What was the actual labor time variance as a result of generating 5,650 lines of code?

3. What was the labor rate variance as a result of the bonus?

4. ▬▬▶Are there any performance-related issues that the labor time and rate variances fail to consider? Explain.

5. The manager is trying to determine if a better decision would have been to hire a temporary programmer to meet the higher programming demand in the first week of May, rather than paying out the bonus. If another employee was hired from the employment firm, what would have been the labor time variance in the first week?

6. ▬▬▶Which decision is better, paying the bonus or hiring another programmer?

## Problems: Series B

✔ c. Rate variance,
$200 F

SHOW
ME HOW

### PR 23-1B Direct materials and direct labor variance analysis

OBJ. 2, 3

Lenni Clothing Co. manufactures clothing in a small manufacturing facility. Manufacturing has 25 employees. Each employee presently provides 40 hours of productive labor per week. Information about a production week is as follows:

| | |
|---|---|
| Standard wage per hr. | $12.00 |
| Standard labor time per unit | 12 min. |
| Standard number of yds. of fabric per unit | 5.0 yds. |
| Standard price per yd. of fabric | $5.00 |
| Actual price per yd. of fabric | $5.10 |
| Actual yds. of fabric used during the week | 26,200 yds. |
| Number of units produced during the week | 5,220 |
| Actual wage per hr. | $11.80 |
| Actual hrs. for the week | 1,000 hrs. |

#### Instructions

Determine (a) the standard cost per unit for direct materials and direct labor; (b) the price variance, quantity variance, and total direct materials cost variance; and (c) the rate variance, time variance, and total direct labor cost variance.

### PR 23-2B Flexible budgeting and variance analysis

OBJ. 1, 2, 3

✔ 1. a. Direct
materials price
variance, $12,220 U

I'm Really Cold Coat Company makes women's and men's coats. Both products require filler and lining material. The following planning information has been made available:

| | Standard Amount per Unit | | |
|---|---|---|---|
| | Women's Coats | Men's Coats | Standard Price per Unit |
| Filler | 4.0 lbs. | 5.20 lbs. | $2.00 per lb. |
| Liner | 7.00 yds. | 9.40 yds. | 8.00 per yd. |
| Standard labor time | 0.40 hr. | 0.50 hr. | |

| | Women's Coats | Men's Coats |
|---|---|---|
| Planned production | 5,000 units | 6,200 units |
| Standard labor rate | $14.00 per hr. | $13.00 per hr. |

I'm Really Cold Coat Company does not expect there to be any beginning or ending inventories of filler and lining material. At the end of the budget year, I'm Really Cold Coat Company experienced the following actual results:

| | Women's Coats | Men's Coats |
|---|---|---|
| Actual production | 4,400 | 5,800 |
| | **Actual Price per Unit** | **Actual Quantity Purchased and Used** |
| Filler | $1.90 per lb. | 48,000 |
| Liner | 8.20 per yd. | 85,100 |
| | **Actual Labor Rate** | **Actual Labor Hours Used** |
| Women's coats | $14.10 per hr. | 1,825 |
| Men's coats | 13.30 per hr. | 2,800 |

The expected beginning inventory and desired ending inventory were realized.

#### Instructions

1. Prepare the following variance analyses for both coats and the total, based on the actual results and production levels at the end of the budget year:

    a. Direct materials price, quantity, and total variance.

    b. Direct labor rate, time, and total variance.

2. ▬▬▬►Why are the standard amounts in part (1) based on the actual production at the end of the year instead of the planned production at the beginning of the year?

### PR 23-3B  Direct materials, direct labor, and factory overhead cost variance analysis

**OBJ. 3, 4**

✔ a. Direct materials price variance, $10,100 U

Road Gripper Tire Co. manufactures automobile tires. Standard costs and actual costs for direct materials, direct labor, and factory overhead incurred for the manufacture of 4,160 tires were as follows:

|  | Standard Costs | Actual Costs |
|---|---|---|
| Direct materials | 100,000 lbs. at $6.40 | 101,000 lbs. at $6.50 |
| Direct labor | 2,080 hrs. at $15.75 | 2,000 hrs. at $15.40 |
| Factory overhead | Rates per direct labor hr., based on 100% of normal capacity of 2,000 direct labor hrs.: |  |
|  | Variable cost, $4.00 | $8,200 variable cost |
|  | Fixed cost, $6.00 | $12,000 fixed cost |

Each tire requires 0.5 hour of direct labor.

**Instructions**

Determine (a) the direct materials price variance, direct materials quantity variance, and total direct materials cost variance; (b) the direct labor rate variance, direct labor time variance, and total direct labor cost variance; and (c) the variable factory overhead controllable variance, fixed factory overhead volume variance, and total factory overhead cost variance.

### PR 23-4B  Factory overhead cost variance report

**OBJ. 4**

✔ Controllable variance, $1,450 F

General Ledger

Feeling Better Medical Inc., a manufacturer of disposable medical supplies, prepared the following factory overhead cost budget for the Assembly Department for October of the current year. The company expected to operate the department at 100% of normal capacity of 30,000 hours.

| | | |
|---|---|---|
| Variable costs: | | |
| Indirect factory wages | $247,500 | |
| Power and light | 189,000 | |
| Indirect materials | 52,500 | |
| Total variable cost | | $489,000 |
| Fixed costs: | | |
| Supervisory salaries | $126,000 | |
| Depreciation of plant and equipment | 70,000 | |
| Insurance and property taxes | 44,000 | |
| Total fixed cost | | 240,000 |
| Total factory overhead cost | | $729,000 |

During October, the department operated at 28,500 hours, and the factory overhead costs incurred were indirect factory wages, $234,000; power and light, $178,500; indirect materials, $50,600; supervisory salaries, $126,000; depreciation of plant and equipment, $70,000; and insurance and property taxes, $44,000.

**Instructions**

Prepare a factory overhead cost variance report for October. To be useful for cost control, the budgeted amounts should be based on 28,500 hours.

### PR 23-5B  Standards for nonmanufacturing expenses for a service company

**OBJ. 3, 6**

✔ 2. $161 F

The Radiology Department provides imaging services for Emergency Medical Center. One important activity in the Radiology Department is transcribing digitally recorded analyses of images into a written report. The manager of the Radiology Department determined that the average transcriptionist could type 700 lines of a report in an hour. The plan for the first week in May called for 81,900 typed lines to be written. The Radiology Department has three transcriptionists. Each transcriptionist is hired from an employment firm that requires temporary employees to be hired for a minimum of a 40-hour week. Transcriptionists are

*(Continued)*

paid $23.00 per hour. The manager offered a bonus if the department could type more lines for the week, without overtime. Due to high service demands, the transcriptionists typed more lines in the first week of May than planned. The actual amount of lines typed in the first week of May was 88,900 lines, without overtime. As a result, the bonus caused the average transcriptionist hourly rate to increase to $30.00 per hour during the first week in May.

### Instructions

1. If the department typed 81,900 lines according to the original plan, what would have been the labor time variance?

2. What was the labor time variance as a result of typing 88,900 lines?

3. What was the labor rate variance as a result of the bonus?

4. The manager is trying to determine if a better decision would have been to hire a temporary transcriptionist to meet the higher typing demands in the first week of May, rather than paying out the bonus. If another employee was hired from the employment firm, what would have been the labor time variance in the first week?

5. ━━━▶Which decision is better, paying the bonus or hiring another transcriptionist?

6. ━━━▶Are there any performance-related issues that the labor time and rate variances fail to consider? Explain.

## Comprehensive Problem 5

Genuine Spice Inc. began operations on January 1, 2016. The company produces eight-ounce bottles of hand and body lotion called *Eternal Beauty*. The lotion is sold wholesale in 12-bottle cases for $100 per case. There is a selling commission of $20 per case. The January direct materials, direct labor, and factory overhead costs are as follows:

### DIRECT MATERIALS

| | Cost Behavior | Units per Case | Cost per Unit | Direct Materials Cost per Case |
|---|---|---|---|---|
| Cream base | Variable | 100 ozs. | $0.02 | $ 2.00 |
| Natural oils | Variable | 30 ozs. | 0.30 | 9.00 |
| Bottle (8-oz.) | Variable | 12 bottles | 0.50 | 6.00 |
| | | | | $17.00 |

### DIRECT LABOR

| Department | Cost Behavior | Time per Case | Labor Rate per Hour | Direct Labor Cost per Case |
|---|---|---|---|---|
| Mixing | Variable | 20 min. | $18.00 | $6.00 |
| Filling | Variable | 5 | 14.40 | 1.20 |
| | | 25 min. | | $7.20 |

### FACTORY OVERHEAD

| | Cost Behavior | Total Cost |
|---|---|---|
| Utilities | Mixed | $ 600 |
| Facility lease | Fixed | 14,000 |
| Equipment depreciation | Fixed | 4,300 |
| Supplies | Fixed | 660 |
| | | $19,560 |

### Part A—Break-Even Analysis

The management of Genuine Spice Inc. wishes to determine the number of cases required to break even per month. The utilities cost, which is part of factory overhead, is a mixed cost. The following information was gathered from the first six months of operation regarding this cost:

| 2016 | Case Production | Utility Total Cost |
|---|---|---|
| January | 500 | $600 |
| February | 800 | 660 |
| March | 1,200 | 740 |
| April | 1,100 | 720 |
| May | 950 | 690 |
| June | 1,025 | 705 |

### Instructions

1. Determine the fixed and variable portion of the utility cost using the high-low method.
2. Determine the contribution margin per case.
3. Determine the fixed costs per month, including the utility fixed cost from part (1).
4. Determine the break-even number of cases per month.

✔ 2. $55.60

### Part B—August Budgets

During July of the current year, the management of Genuine Spice Inc. asked the controller to prepare August manufacturing and income statement budgets. Demand was expected to be 1,500 cases at $100 per case for August. Inventory planning information is provided as follows:

Finished Goods Inventory:

| | Cases | Cost |
|---|---|---|
| Estimated finished goods inventory, August 1, 2016 | 300 | $12,000 |
| Desired finished goods inventory, August 31, 2016 | 175 | 7,000 |

Materials Inventory:

| | Cream Base (ozs.) | Oils (ozs.) | Bottles (bottles) |
|---|---|---|---|
| Estimated materials inventory, August 1, 2016 | 250 | 290 | 600 |
| Desired materials inventory, August 31, 2016 | 1,000 | 360 | 240 |

There was negligible work in process inventory assumed for either the beginning or end of the month; thus, none was assumed. In addition, there was no change in the cost per unit or estimated units per case operating data from January.

### Instructions

5. Prepare the August production budget.
6. Prepare the August direct materials purchases budget.
7. Prepare the August direct labor budget. Round the hours required for production to the nearest hour.
8. Prepare the August factory overhead budget.
9. Prepare the August budgeted income statement, including selling expenses.

✔ 6. Bottles purchased, $8,070

### Part C—August Variance Analysis

During September of the current year, the controller was asked to perform variance analyses for August. The January operating data provided the standard prices, rates, times, and quantities per case. There were 1,500 actual cases produced during August, which was 250 more cases than planned at the beginning of the month. Actual data for August were as follows:

| | Actual Direct Materials Price per Unit | Actual Direct Materials Quantity per Case |
|---|---|---|
| Cream base | $0.016 per oz. | 102 ozs. |
| Natural oils | $0.32 per oz. | 31 ozs. |
| Bottle (8-oz.) | $0.42 per bottle | 12.5 bottles |

| | Actual Direct Labor Rate | Actual Direct Labor Time per Case |
|---|---|---|
| Mixing | $18.20 | 19.50 min. |
| Filling | 14.00 | 5.60 min. |

| | |
|---|---|
| Actual variable overhead | $305.00 |
| Normal volume | 1,600 cases |

The prices of the materials were different than standard due to fluctuations in market prices. The standard quantity of materials used per case was an ideal standard. The Mixing Department used a higher grade labor classification during the month, thus causing the actual labor rate to exceed standard. The Filling Department used a lower grade labor classification during the month, thus causing the actual labor rate to be less than standard.

**Instructions**

10. Determine and interpret the direct materials price and quantity variances for the three materials.

✔ 11. Mixing time variance, $216 F

11. Determine and interpret the direct labor rate and time variances for the two departments. Round hours to the nearest hour.

✔ 12. $5 U

12. Determine and interpret the factory overhead controllable variance.

13. Determine and interpret the factory overhead volume variance.

14. Why are the standard direct labor and direct materials costs in the calculations for parts (10) and (11) based on the actual 1,500-case production volume rather than the planned 1,250 cases of production used in the budgets for parts (6) and (7)?

# Cases & Projects

**CP 23-1  Ethics and professional conduct in business using nonmanufacturing standards**

Dash Riprock is a cost analyst with Safe Insurance Company. Safe is applying standards to its claims payment operation. Claims payment is a repetitive operation that could be evaluated with standards. Dash used time and motion studies to identify an ideal standard of 36 claims processed per hour. The Claims Processing Department manager, Henry Tudor, has rejected this standard and has argued that the standard should be 30 claims processed per hour. Henry and Dash were unable to agree, so they decided to discuss this matter openly at a joint meeting with the vice president of operations, who would arbitrate a final decision. Prior to the meeting, Dash wrote the following memo to the VP:

To:  Anne Boleyn, Vice President of Operations
From:  Dash Riprock
Re:  Standards in the Claims Processing Department

As you know, Henry and I are scheduled to meet with you to discuss our disagreement with respect to the appropriate standards for the Claims Processing Department. I have conducted time and motion studies and have determined that the ideal standard is 36 claims processed per hour. Henry argues that 30 claims processed per hour would be more appropriate. I believe he is trying to "pad" the budget with some slack. I'm not sure what he is trying to get away with, but I believe a tight standard will drive efficiency up in his area. I hope you will agree when we meet with you next week.

➤ Discuss the ethical and professional issues in this situation.

## CP 23-2 Nonfinancial performance measures

The senior management of Tungston Company has proposed the following three performance measures for the company:

1. Net income as a percent of stockholders' equity

2. Revenue growth

3. Employee satisfaction

   Management believes these three measures combine both financial and nonfinancial measures and are thus superior to using just financial measures.

━━━▶What advice would you give Tungston Company for improving its performance measurement system?

## CP 23-3 Variance interpretation

You have been asked to investigate some cost problems in the Assembly Department of Ruthenium Electronics Co., a consumer electronics company. To begin your investigation, you have obtained the following budget performance report for the department for the last quarter:

**Ruthenium Electronics Co.—Assembly Department**
**Quarterly Budget Performance Report**

|  | Standard Quantity at Standard Rates | Actual Quantity at Standard Rates | Quantity Variances |
|---|---|---|---|
| Direct labor | $157,500 | $227,500 | $ 70,000 U |
| Direct materials | 297,500 | 385,000 | 87,500 U |
| Total | $455,000 | $612,500 | $157,500 U |

The following reports were also obtained:

**Ruthenium Electronics Co.—Purchasing Department**
**Quarterly Budget Performance Report**

|  | Actual Quantity at Standard Rates | Actual Quantity at Actual Rates | Price Variance |
|---|---|---|---|
| Direct materials | $437,500 | $385,000 | –$52,500 F |

**Ruthenium Electronics Co.—Fabrication Department**
**Quarterly Budget Performance Report**

|  | Standard Quantity at Standard Rates | Actual Quantity at Standard Rates | Quantity Variances |
|---|---|---|---|
| Direct labor | $245,000 | $203,000 | –$42,000 F |
| Direct materials | 140,000 | 140,000 | 0 |
| Total | $385,000 | $343,000 | –$42,000 F |

You also interviewed the Assembly Department supervisor. Excerpts from the interview follow:

Q: What explains the poor performance in your department?

A: Listen, you've got to understand what it's been like in this department recently. Lately, it seems no matter how hard we try, we can't seem to make the standards. I'm not sure what is going on, but we've been having a lot of problems lately.

Q: What kind of problems?

A: Well, for instance, all this quarter we've been requisitioning purchased parts from the material storeroom, and the parts just didn't fit together very well. I'm not sure what is going on, but during most of this quarter we've had to scrap and sort purchased parts—just to get our assemblies put together. Naturally, all this takes time and material. And that's not all.

Q: Go on.

A: All this quarter, the work that we've been receiving from the Fabrication Department has been shoddy. I mean, maybe around 20% of the stuff that comes in from Fabrication just can't be assembled. The fabrication is all wrong. As a result, we've had to scrap and rework a lot of the stuff. Naturally, this has just shot our quantity variances.

━━━▶Interpret the variance reports in light of the comments by the Assembly Department supervisor.

### CP 23-4  Variance interpretation

Vanadium Audio Inc. is a small manufacturer of electronic musical instruments. The plant manager received the following variable factory overhead report for the period:

|  | Actual | Budgeted Variable Factory Overhead at Actual Production | Controllable Variance |
|---|---|---|---|
| Supplies | $ 42,000 | $ 39,780 | $ 2,220 U |
| Power and light | 52,500 | 50,900 | 1,600 U |
| Indirect factory wages | 39,100 | 30,600 | 8,500 U |
| Total | $133,600 | $121,280 | $12,320 U |

Actual units produced: 15,000 (90% of practical capacity)

The plant manager is not pleased with the $12,320 unfavorable variable factory overhead controllable variance and has come to discuss the matter with the controller. The following discussion occurred:

*Plant Manager:* I just received this factory report for the latest month of operation. I'm not very pleased with these figures. Before these numbers go to headquarters, you and I will need to reach an understanding.

*Controller:* Go ahead, what's the problem?

*Plant Manager:* What's the problem? Well, everything. Look at the variance. It's too large. If I understand the accounting approach being used here, you are assuming that my costs are variable to the units produced. Thus, as the production volume declines, so should these costs. Well, I don't believe that these costs are variable at all. I think they are fixed costs. As a result, when we operate below capacity, the costs really don't go down at all. I'm being penalized for costs I have no control over at all. I need this report to be redone to reflect this fact. If anything, the difference between actual and budget is essentially a volume variance. Listen, I know that you're a team player. You really need to reconsider your assumptions on this one.

➤If you were in the controller's position, how would you respond to the plant manager?

### CP 23-5  Nonmanufacturing performance measures—government

Internet Project

#### Group Project

Municipal governments are discovering that you can control only what you measure. As a result, many municipal governments are introducing nonfinancial performance measures to help improve municipal services. In a group, use the Google search engine to perform a search for "municipal government performance measurement." Google will provide a list of Internet sites that outline various city efforts in using nonfinancial performance measures. As a group, report on the types of measures used by one of the cities from the search.

# Performance Evaluation for Decentralized Operations

## Caterpillar, Inc.

**H**ave you ever wondered why large retail stores like **Macy's**, **JC Penney**, and **Sears** are divided into departments? Organizing into departments allows retailers to provide products and expertise in specialized areas while offering a wide range of products. Departments also allow companies to assign responsibility for financial performance. This information can be used to make product decisions, evaluate operations, and guide company strategy. Strong departmental performance might be attributable to a good department manager, while weak departmental performance may be the result of a product mix that has low customer appeal. By tracking departmental performance, companies can identify and reward excellent performance and take corrective action in departments that are performing poorly.

Like retailers, most businesses organize into operational units, such as divisions and departments. For example, **Caterpillar, Inc.**, manufactures a variety of equipment and machinery and is organized into a number of different segments, including Construction Industries, Resource Industries, and Power Systems. The Construction Industries Segment manufactures construction equipment such as tractors, dump trucks, and loaders. The Resource Industries segment makes equipment for the mining industry, such as off-highway and mining trucks. The Power Systems segment manufactures equipment that is used to generate power, such as engines and turbines for power plants.

Managers at Caterpillar, Inc., are responsible for running their business segment. Each segment is evaluated on segment profit, which excludes certain expense items from the calculation of profit that are not within the control of the business segment. The company uses segment profit to determine how to allocate resources between business segments and to plan and control the company's operations.

In this chapter, the role of accounting in assisting managers in planning and controlling organizational units, such as departments, divisions, and stores, is described and illustrated.

**OBJ 1**
Describe the advantages and disadvantages of decentralized operations.
**Centralized and Decentralized Operations**
  Advantages of Decentralization
  Disadvantages of Decentralization
  Responsibility Accounting

**OBJ 2**
Prepare a responsibility accounting report for a cost center.
**Responsibility Accounting for Cost Centers**

EE 24-1

**OBJ 3**
Prepare responsibility accounting reports for a profit center.
**Responsibility Accounting for Profit Centers**
  Service Department Charges
  Profit Center Reporting

EE 24-2
EE 24-3

**OBJ 4**
Compute and interpret the rate of return on investment, the residual income, and the balanced scorecard for an investment center.
**Responsibility Accounting for Investment Centers**
  Rate of Return on Investment
  Residual Income
  The Balanced Scorecard

EE 24-4
EE 24-5

**OBJ 5**
Describe and illustrate how the market price, negotiated price, and cost price approaches to transfer pricing may be used by decentralized segments of a business.
**Transfer Pricing**
  Market Price Approach
  Negotiated Price Approach
  Cost Price Approach

EE 24-6

**At a Glance 24** ▶ Page 1142

---

Describe the advantages and disadvantages of decentralized operations.

# Centralized and Decentralized Operations

In a *centralized* company, all major planning and operating decisions are made by top management. For example, a one-person, owner-manager-operated company is centralized because all plans and decisions are made by one person. In a small owner-manager-operated business, centralization may be desirable. This is because the owner-manager's close supervision ensures that the business will be operated in the way the owner-manager wishes.

In a *decentralized* company, managers of separate divisions or units are delegated operating responsibility. The division (unit) managers are responsible for planning and controlling the operations of their divisions. Divisions are often structured around products, customers, or regions.

The proper amount of decentralization for a company depends on the company's unique circumstances. For example, in some companies, division managers have authority over all operations, including fixed asset purchases. In other companies, division managers have authority over profits but not fixed asset purchases.

## Advantages of Decentralization

For large companies, it is difficult for top management to:

- Maintain daily contact with all operations, and
- Maintain operating expertise in all product lines and services

In such cases, delegating authority to managers closest to the operations usually results in better decisions. These managers often anticipate and react to operating data more quickly than could top management. These managers can also focus their attention on becoming "experts" in their area of operation.

Decentralized operations provide excellent training for managers. Delegating responsibility allows managers to develop managerial experience early in their careers. This helps a company retain managers, some of whom may be later promoted to top management positions.

Managers of decentralized operations often work closely with customers. As a result, they tend to identify with customers and, thus, are often more creative in suggesting operating and product improvements. This helps create good customer relations.

## Disadvantages of Decentralization

A primary disadvantage of decentralized operations is that decisions made by one manager may negatively affect the profits of the company. For example, managers of divisions whose products compete with one another might start a price war that decreases the profits of both divisions and, thus, the overall company.

Another disadvantage of decentralized operations is that assets and expenses may be duplicated across divisions. For example, each manager of a product line might have a separate sales force and office support staff.

The advantages and disadvantages of decentralization are summarized in Exhibit 1.

---

**Advantages of Decentralization**

- Allows managers closest to the operations to make decisions
- Provides excellent training for managers
- Allows managers to become experts in their area of operation
- Helps retain managers
- Improves creativity and customer relations

**Disadvantages of Decentralization**

- Decisions made by managers may negatively affect the profits of the company
- Duplicates assets and expenses

**EXHIBIT 1**

**Advantages and Disadvantages of Decentralized Operations**

---

## Business 🌐 Connection

### STEVE JOBS: CENTRALIZED OPERATIONS AT APPLE

Apple Inc.'s meteoric rise from a second-tier computer maker in the early 2000s to the standard for all things technology by the end of the decade was no accident. The company's success was the result of a centralized operation, where Apple CEO Steve Jobs had ultimate control over the company's strategic and operational decisions. As Andrew Keen noted

in his interview of Job's biographer, Walter Isaacson, it was Jobs' "obsessive end-to-end control of products—from chip manufacture to the retail experience—that most defined Steve's remarkable tenure as Apple CEO." This centralized business model also drove Apple's success. Unfortunately, Steve Jobs died in October 2011, creating a void at the top of the company's centralized operation. Since Job's death, Apple has struggled with how to adapt its highly successful centralized business model to the loss of the person that controlled the company's decisions.

Source: A. Keen, "Keen On ... Walter Isaacson: Sometimes It's Nice to Be In The Hands of a Control Freak," *AOLTech.com*, December 19, 2011.

## Responsibility Accounting

In a decentralized business, accounting assists managers in evaluating and controlling their areas of responsibility, called *responsibility centers*. **Responsibility accounting** is the process of measuring and reporting operating data by responsibility center.

Three types of responsibility centers are as follows:

- *Cost centers,* which have responsibility over costs
- *Profit centers,* which have responsibility over revenues and costs
- *Investment centers,* which have responsibility over revenues, costs, and investment in assets

**OBJ 2** Prepare a responsibility accounting report for a cost center.

# Responsibility Accounting for Cost Centers

A **cost center** manager has responsibility for controlling costs. For example, the supervisor of the Power Department has responsibility for the costs of providing power. A cost center manager does not make decisions concerning sales or the amount of fixed assets invested in the center.

Cost centers may vary in size from a small department to an entire manufacturing plant. In addition, cost centers may exist within other cost centers. For example, an entire university or college could be viewed as a cost center, and each college and department within the university could also be a cost center, as shown in Exhibit 2.

**EXHIBIT 2**     **Cost Centers in a University**

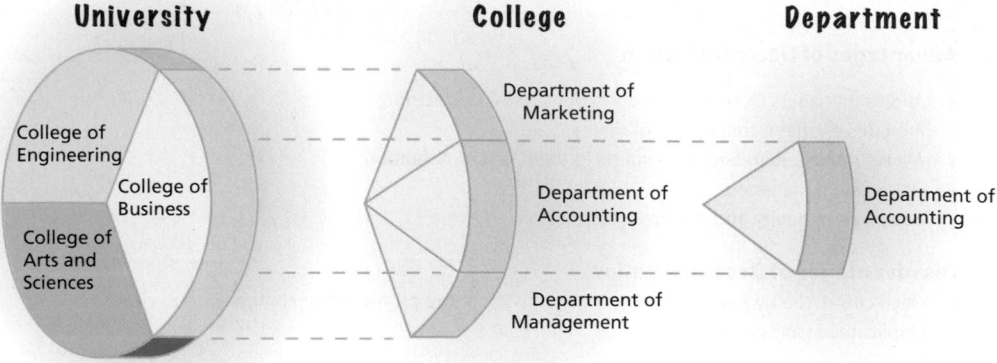

Responsibility accounting for cost centers focuses on the controlling and reporting of costs. Budget performance reports that report budgeted and actual costs are normally prepared for each cost center.

Exhibit 3 illustrates budget performance reports for the following cost centers:

- Vice President, Production
- Manager, Plant A
- Supervisor, Department 1—Plant A

Exhibit 3 shows how cost centers are often linked together within a company. For example, the budget performance report for Department 1—Plant A supports the report for Plant A, which supports the report for the vice president of production.

The reports in Exhibit 3 show the budgeted costs and actual costs along with the differences. Each difference is classified as either *over* budget or *under* budget. Such reports allow cost center managers to focus on areas of significant differences.

For example, the supervisor for Department 1 of Plant A can focus on why the materials cost was over budget. The supervisor might discover that excess materials were scrapped. This could be due to such factors as machine malfunctions, improperly trained employees, or low-quality materials.

As shown in Exhibit 3, responsibility accounting reports are usually more summarized for higher levels of management. For example, the budget performance report for the manager of Plant A shows only administration and departmental data. This report enables the plant manager to identify the departments responsible for major differences. Likewise, the report for the vice president of production summarizes the cost data for each plant.

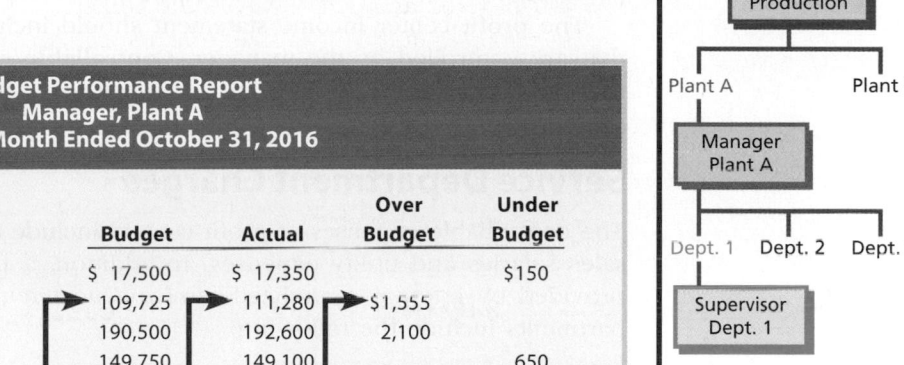

**EXHIBIT 3**

**Responsibility Accounting Reports for Cost Centers**

### Budget Performance Report
### Vice President, Production
### For the Month Ended October 31, 2016

|  | Budget | Actual | Over Budget | Under Budget |
|---|---|---|---|---|
| Administration | $ 19,500 | $ 19,700 | $ 200 | |
| Plant A | 467,475 | 470,330 | 2,855 | |
| Plant B | 395,225 | 394,300 | | $925 |
| | $882,200 | $884,330 | $3,055 | $925 |

### Budget Performance Report
### Manager, Plant A
### For the Month Ended October 31, 2016

|  | Budget | Actual | Over Budget | Under Budget |
|---|---|---|---|---|
| Administration | $ 17,500 | $ 17,350 | | $150 |
| Department 1 | 109,725 | 111,280 | $1,555 | |
| Department 2 | 190,500 | 192,600 | 2,100 | |
| Department 3 | 149,750 | 149,100 | | 650 |
| | $467,475 | $470,330 | $3,655 | $800 |

### Budget Performance Report
### Supervisor, Department 1—Plant A
### For the Month Ended October 31, 2016

|  | Budget | Actual | Over Budget | Under Budget |
|---|---|---|---|---|
| Factory wages | $ 58,100 | $ 58,000 | | $100 |
| Materials | 32,500 | 34,225 | $1,725 | |
| Supervisory salaries | 6,400 | 6,400 | | |
| Power and light | 5,750 | 5,690 | | 60 |
| Depreciation of plant and equipment | 4,000 | 4,000 | | |
| Maintenance | 2,000 | 1,990 | | 10 |
| Insurance and property taxes | 975 | 975 | | |
| | $109,725 | $111,280 | $1,725 | $170 |

---

## Example Exercise 24-1 Budgetary Performance for Cost Center

**OBJ 2**

Nuclear Power Company's costs were over budget by $24,000. The company is divided into North and South regions. The North Region's costs were under budget by $2,000. Determine the amount that the South Region's costs were over or under budget.

### Follow My Example 24-1

$26,000 over budget ($24,000 + $2,000)

Practice Exercises: PE 24-1A, PE 24-1B

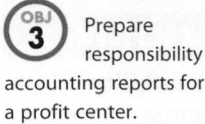

Prepare responsibility accounting reports for a profit center.

# Responsibility Accounting for Profit Centers

A **profit center** manager has the responsibility and authority for making decisions that affect revenues and costs and, thus, profits. Profit centers may be divisions, departments, or products.

The manager of a profit center does not make decisions concerning the fixed assets invested in the center. However, profit centers are an excellent training assignment for new managers.

Responsibility accounting for profit centers focuses on reporting revenues, expenses, and income from operations. Thus, responsibility accounting reports for profit centers take the form of income statements.

The profit center income statement should include only revenues and expenses that are controlled by the manager. **Controllable revenues** are revenues earned by the profit center. **Controllable expenses** are costs that can be influenced (controlled) by the decisions of profit center managers.

## Service Department Charges

The controllable expenses of profit centers include *direct operating expenses* such as sales salaries and utility expenses. In addition, a profit center may incur expenses provided by internal centralized *service departments*. Examples of such service departments include the following:

- Research and Development
- Legal
- Telecommunications
- Information and Computer Systems
- Facilities Management
- Purchasing
- Advertising
- Payroll Accounting
- Transportation
- Human Resources

Employees of **IBM** speak of "green money" and "blue money." Green money comes from customers. Blue money comes from providing services to other IBM departments via service department charges. IBM employees note that blue money is easier to earn than green money; yet from the stockholders' perspective, green money is the only money that counts.

Service department charges are *indirect* expenses to a profit center. They are similar to the expenses that would be incurred if the profit center purchased the services from outside the company. A profit center manager has control over service department expenses if the manager is free to choose how much service is used. In such cases, **service department charges** are allocated to profit centers based on the usage of the service by each profit center.

To illustrate, Nova Entertainment Group (NEG), a diversified entertainment company, is used. NEG has the following two operating divisions organized as profit centers:

- Theme Park Division
- Movie Production Division

The revenues and direct operating expenses for the two divisions follow. The operating expenses consist of direct expenses, such as the wages and salaries of a division's employees.

| | Theme Park Division | Movie Production Division |
| --- | --- | --- |
| Revenues | $6,000,000 | $2,500,000 |
| Operating expenses | 2,495,000 | 405,000 |

NEG's service departments and the expenses they incurred for the year ended December 31, 2016, are as follows:

| | |
| --- | --- |
| Purchasing | $400,000 |
| Payroll Accounting | 255,000 |
| Legal | 250,000 |
| Total | $905,000 |

An activity base for each service department is used to charge service department expenses to the Theme Park and Movie Production divisions. The activity base for each service department is a measure of the services performed. For NEG, the service department activity bases are as follows:

| Department | Activity Base |
|---|---|
| Purchasing | Number of purchase requisitions |
| Payroll Accounting | Number of payroll checks |
| Legal | Number of billed hours |

The use of services by the Theme Park and Movie Production divisions is as follows:

| Division | Service Usage Purchasing | Payroll Accounting | Legal |
|---|---|---|---|
| Theme Park | 25,000 purchase requisitions | 12,000 payroll checks | 100 billed hrs. |
| Movie Production | 15,000 | 3,000 | 900 |
| Total | 40,000 purchase requisitions | 15,000 payroll checks | 1,000 billed hrs. |

The rates at which services are charged to each division are called *service department charge rates*. These rates are computed as follows:

$$\text{Service Department Charge Rate} = \frac{\text{Service Department Expense}}{\text{Total Service Department Usage}}$$

NEG's service department charge rates are computed as follows:

$$\text{Purchasing Charge Rate} = \frac{\$400,000}{40,000 \text{ purchase requisitions}} = \$10 \text{ per purchase requisition}$$

$$\text{Payroll Charge Rate} = \frac{\$255,000}{15,000 \text{ payroll checks}} = \$17 \text{ per payroll check}$$

$$\text{Legal Charge Rate} = \frac{\$250,000}{1,000 \text{ billed hrs.}} = \$250 \text{ per hr.}$$

The services used by each division are multiplied by the service department charge rates to determine the service charges for each division, computed as follows:

$$\text{Service Department Charge} = \text{Service Usage} \times \text{Service Department Charge Rate}$$

Exhibit 4 illustrates the service department charges and related computations for NEG's Theme Park and Movie Production divisions.

**EXHIBIT 4**

**Service Department Charges to NEG Divisions**

**Nova Entertainment Group**
**Service Department Charges to NEG Divisions**
**For the Year Ended December 31, 2016**

| Service Department | Theme Park Division | Movie Production Division |
|---|---|---|
| Purchasing (Note A) | $250,000 | $150,000 |
| Payroll Accounting (Note B) | 204,000 | 51,000 |
| Legal (Note C) | 25,000 | 225,000 |
| Total service department charges | $479,000 | $426,000 |

Note A:
25,000 purchase requisitions × $10 per purchase requisition = $250,000
15,000 purchase requisitions × $10 per purchase requisition = $150,000

Note B:
12,000 payroll checks × $17 per check = $204,000
3,000 payroll checks × $17 per check = $51,000

Note C:
100 hours × $250 per hour = $25,000
900 hours × $250 per hour = $225,000

The differences in the service department charges between the two divisions can be explained by the nature of their operations and, thus, usage of services. For example, the Theme Park Division employs many part-time employees who are paid weekly. As a result, the Theme Park Division requires 12,000 payroll checks and incurs a $204,000 payroll service department charge (12,000 × $17). In contrast, the Movie Production Division has more permanent employees who are paid monthly. Thus, the Movie Production Division requires only 3,000 payroll checks and incurs a payroll service department charge of $51,000 (3,000 × $17).

## Example Exercise 24-2 Service Department Charges

OBJ 3

The centralized legal department of Johnson Company has expenses of $600,000. The department has provided a total of 2,000 hours of service for the period. The East Division has used 500 hours of legal service during the period, and the West Division has used 1,500 hours. How much should each division be charged for legal services?

### Follow My Example 24-2

**East Division Service Charge for Legal Department:**
$150,000 = 500 billed hours × ($600,000 ÷ 2,000 hours)

**West Division Service Charge for Legal Department:**
$450,000 = 1,500 billed hours × ($600,000 ÷ 2,000 hours)

Practice Exercises: PE 24-2A, PE 24-2B

## Profit Center Reporting

The divisional income statements for NEG are shown in Exhibit 5.

**EXHIBIT 5**

**Divisional Income Statements—NEG**

| | | Theme Park Division | Movie Production Division |
|---|---|---|---|
| **Nova Entertainment Group** | | | |
| **Divisional Income Statements** | | | |
| **For the Year Ended December 31, 2016** | | | |
| Revenues* | | $6,000,000 | $2,500,000 |
| Operating expenses | | 2,495,000 | 405,000 |
| Income from operations before service department charges | | $3,505,000 | $2,095,000 |
| Less service department charges: | | | |
| Purchasing | | $ 250,000 | $ 150,000 |
| Payroll Accounting | | 204,000 | 51,000 |
| Legal | | 25,000 | 225,000 |
| Total service department charges | | $ 479,000 | $ 426,000 |
| Income from operations | | $3,026,000 | $1,669,000 |

*For a profit center that sells products, the income statement would show: Net sales – Cost of goods sold = Gross profit. The operating expenses would be deducted from the gross profit to get the income from operations before service department charges.

In evaluating the profit center manager, the income from operations should be compared over time to a budget. However, it should not be compared across profit centers because the profit centers are usually different in terms of size, products, and customers.

**Example Exercise 24-3 Income from Operations for Profit Center**

Using the data for Johnson Company from Example Exercise 24-2 along with the following data, determine the divisional income from operations for the East and West divisions:

|  | East Division | West Division |
| --- | --- | --- |
| Sales | $3,000,000 | $8,000,000 |
| Cost of goods sold | 1,650,000 | 4,200,000 |
| Selling expenses | 850,000 | 1,850,000 |

**Follow My Example 24-3**

|  | East Division | West Division |
| --- | --- | --- |
| Net sales......................................................................... | $3,000,000 | $8,000,000 |
| Cost of goods sold ......................................................... | 1,650,000 | 4,200,000 |
| Gross profit..................................................................... | $1,350,000 | $3,800,000 |
| Selling expenses ............................................................. | 850,000 | 1,850,000 |
| Income from operations before service department charges .................... | $ 500,000 | $1,950,000 |
| Service department charges.............................................. | 150,000 | 450,000 |
| Income from operations.................................................... | $ 350,000 | $1,500,000 |

Practice Exercises: PE 24-3A, PE 24-3B

# Responsibility Accounting for Investment Centers

**OBJ 4** Compute and interpret the rate of return on investment, the residual income, and the balanced scorecard for an investment center.

An **investment center** manager has the responsibility and the authority to make decisions that affect not only costs and revenues but also the assets invested in the center. Investment centers are often used in diversified companies organized by divisions. In such cases, the divisional manager has authority similar to that of a chief operating officer or president of a company.

Because investment center managers have responsibility for revenues and expenses, *income from operations* is part of investment center reporting. In addition, because the manager has responsibility for the assets invested in the center, the following two additional measures of performance are used:

- Rate of return on investment
- Residual income

To illustrate, DataLink Inc., a cellular phone company with three regional divisions, is used. Condensed divisional income statements for the Northern, Central, and Southern divisions of DataLink are shown in Exhibit 6.

| DataLink Inc.<br>Divisional Income Statements<br>For the Year Ended December 31, 2016 | | | |
| --- | --- | --- | --- |
|  | Northern<br>Division | Central<br>Division | Southern<br>Division |
| Revenues ....................................... | $560,000 | $672,000 | $750,000 |
| Operating expenses............................ | 336,000 | 470,400 | 562,500 |
| Income from operations before service |  |  |  |
| department charges ......................... | $224,000 | $201,600 | $187,500 |
| Service department charges.................... | 154,000 | 117,600 | 112,500 |
| Income from operations........................ | $ 70,000 | $ 84,000 | $ 75,000 |

**EXHIBIT 6**

Divisional Income Statements— DataLink Inc.

Using only income from operations, the Central Division is the most profitable division. However, income from operations does not reflect the amount of assets invested in each center. For example, the Central Division could have twice as many assets as the Northern Division. For this reason, performance measures that consider the amount of invested assets, such as the rate of return on investment and residual income, are used.

## Rate of Return on Investment

Because investment center managers control the amount of assets invested in their centers, they should be evaluated based on the use of these assets. One measure that considers the amount of assets invested is the **rate of return on investment (ROI)** or *rate of return on assets*. It is computed as follows:

$$\text{Rate of Return on Investment (ROI)} = \frac{\text{Income from Operations}}{\text{Invested Assets}}$$

The rate of return on investment is useful because the three factors subject to control by divisional managers (revenues, expenses, and invested assets) are considered. The higher the rate of return on investment, the better the division is using its assets to generate income. In effect, the rate of return on investment measures the income (return) on each dollar invested. As a result, the rate of return on investment can be used as a common basis for comparing divisions with each other.

To illustrate, the invested assets of DataLink's three divisions are as follows:

| | **Invested Assets** |
|---|---|
| Northern Division | $350,000 |
| Central Division | 700,000 |
| Southern Division | 500,000 |

Using the income from operations for each division shown in Exhibit 6, the rate of return on investment for each division is computed as follows:

Northern Division:

$$\text{Rate of Return on Investment} = \frac{\text{Income from Operations}}{\text{Invested Assets}} = \frac{\$70,000}{\$350,000} = 20\%$$

Central Division:

$$\text{Rate of Return on Investment} = \frac{\text{Income from Operations}}{\text{Invested Assets}} = \frac{\$84,000}{\$700,000} = 12\%$$

Southern Division:

$$\text{Rate of Return on Investment} = \frac{\text{Income from Operations}}{\text{Invested Assets}} = \frac{\$75,000}{\$500,000} = 15\%$$

Although the Central Division generated the largest income from operations, its rate of return on investment (12%) is the lowest. Hence, relative to the assets invested, the Central Division is the least profitable division. In comparison, the rate of return on investment of the Northern Division is 20%, and the Southern Division is 15%.

To analyze differences in the rate of return on investment across divisions, the **DuPont formula** for the rate of return on investment is often used.[1] The DuPont formula views the rate of return on investment as the product of the following two factors:

- **Profit margin**, which is the ratio of income from operations to sales.
- **Investment turnover**, which is the ratio of sales to invested assets.

[1] The DuPont formula was created by a financial executive of E. I. du Pont de Nemours and Company in 1919.

Using the DuPont formula, the rate of return on investment is expressed as follows:

Rate of Return on Investment = Profit Margin × Investment Turnover

$$\text{Rate of Return on Investment} = \frac{\text{Income from Operations}}{\text{Sales}} \times \frac{\text{Sales}}{\text{Invested Assets}}$$

The DuPont formula is useful in evaluating divisions. This is because the profit margin and the investment turnover reflect the following underlying operating relationships of each division:

- Profit margin indicates *operating profitability* by computing the rate of profit earned on each sales dollar.
- Investment turnover indicates *operating efficiency* by computing the number of sales dollars generated by each dollar of invested assets.

If a division's profit margin increases, and all other factors remain the same, the division's rate of return on investment will increase. For example, a division might add more profitable products to its sales mix and, thus, increase its operating profit, profit margin, and rate of return on investment.

If a division's investment turnover increases, and all other factors remain the same, the division's rate of return on investment will increase. For example, a division might attempt to increase sales through special sales promotions and thus increase operating efficiency, investment turnover, and rate of return on investment.

The rate of return on investment, profit margin, and investment turnover operate in relationship to one another. Specifically, more income can be earned by either increasing the investment turnover, increasing the profit margin, or both.

Using the DuPont formula yields the same rate of return on investment for each of DataLink's divisions, computed as follows:

$$\text{Rate of Return on Investment} = \frac{\text{Income from Operations}}{\text{Sales}} \times \frac{\text{Sales}}{\text{Invested Assets}}$$

Northern Division:

$$\text{Rate of Return on Investment} = \frac{\$70,000}{\$560,000} \times \frac{\$560,000}{\$350,000} = 12.5\% \times 1.6 = 20\%$$

Central Division:

$$\text{Rate of Return on Investment} = \frac{\$84,000}{\$672,000} \times \frac{\$672,000}{\$700,000} = 12.5\% \times 0.96 = 12\%$$

Southern Division:

$$\text{Rate of Return on Investment} = \frac{\$75,000}{\$750,000} \times \frac{\$750,000}{\$500,000} = 10\% \times 1.5 = 15\%$$

The Northern and Central divisions have the same profit margins of 12.5%. However, the Northern Division's investment turnover of 1.6 is larger than that of the Central Division's turnover of 0.96. By using its invested assets more efficiently, the Northern Division's rate of return on investment of 20% is 8 percentage points higher than the Central Division's rate of return of 12%.

The Southern Division's profit margin of 10% and investment turnover of 1.5 are lower than those of the Northern Division. The product of these factors results in a return on investment of 15% for the Southern Division, compared to 20% for the Northern Division.

Even though the Southern Division's profit margin is lower than the Central Division's, its higher turnover of 1.5 results in a rate of return of 15%, which is greater than the Central Division's rate of return of 12%.

To increase the rate of return on investment, the profit margin and investment turnover for a division may be analyzed. For example, assume that the Northern Division is in a highly competitive industry in which the profit margin cannot be easily increased. As a result, the division manager might focus on increasing the investment turnover.

To illustrate, assume that the revenues of the Northern Division could be increased by $56,000 through increasing operating expenses, such as advertising, to $385,000. The Northern Division's income from operations will increase from $70,000 to $77,000, computed as follows:

| | |
|---|---:|
| Revenues ($560,000 + $56,000) | $616,000 |
| Operating expenses | 385,000 |
| Income from operations before service department charges | $231,000 |
| Service department charges | 154,000 |
| Income from operations | $ 77,000 |

The rate of return on investment for the Northern Division, using the DuPont formula, is recomputed as follows:

$$\text{Rate of Return on Investment} = \frac{\$77,000}{\$616,000} \times \frac{\$616,000}{\$350,000} = 12.5\% \times 1.76 = 22\%$$

Although the Northern Division's profit margin remains the same (12.5%), the investment turnover has increased from 1.6 to 1.76, an increase of 10% (0.16 ÷ 1.6). The 10% increase in investment turnover increases the rate of return on investment by 10% (from 20% to 22%).

The rate of return on investment is also useful in deciding where to invest additional assets or expand operations. For example, DataLink should give priority to expanding operations in the Northern Division because it earns the highest rate of return on investment. In other words, an investment in the Northern Division will return 20 cents (20%) on each dollar invested. In contrast, investments in the Central and Southern divisions will earn only 12 cents and 15 cents, respectively, per dollar invested.

A disadvantage of the rate of return on investment as a performance measure is that it may lead divisional managers to reject new investments that could be profitable for the company as a whole. To illustrate, assume the following rates of return for the Northern Division of DataLink:

| | |
|---|---|
| Current rate of return on investment | 20% |
| Minimum acceptable rate of return on investment set by top management | 10% |
| Expected rate of return on investment for new project | 14% |

If the manager of the Northern Division invests in the new project, the Northern Division's overall rate of return will decrease from 20% due to averaging. Thus, the division manager might decide to reject the project, even though the new project's expected rate of return of 14% exceeds DataLink's minimum acceptable rate of return of 10%.

---

## Example Exercise 24-4 Profit Margin, Investment Turnover, and ROI  OBJ 4

Campbell Company has income from operations of $35,000, invested assets of $140,000, and sales of $437,500. Use the DuPont formula to compute the rate of return on investment and show (a) the profit margin, (b) the investment turnover, and (c) the rate of return on investment.

### Follow My Example 24-4

a.  Profit Margin = $35,000 ÷ $437,500 = 8%

b.  Investment Turnover = $437,500 ÷ $140,000 = 3.125

c.  Rate of Return on Investment = 8% × 3.125 = 25%

Practice Exercises: PE 24-4A, PE 24-4B

# Residual Income

Residual income is useful in overcoming some of the disadvantages of the rate of return on investment. **Residual income** is the excess of income from operations over a minimum acceptable income from operations, as shown in Exhibit 7.

**EXHIBIT 7**

**Residual Income**

| | |
|---|---|
| Income from operations | $XXX |
| Less minimum acceptable income from operations as a percent of invested assets | XXX |
| Residual income | $XXX |

The minimum acceptable income from operations is computed by multiplying the company minimum rate of return by the invested assets. The minimum rate is set by top management, based on such factors as the cost of financing.

To illustrate, assume that DataLink Inc. has established 10% as the minimum acceptable rate of return on divisional assets. The residual incomes for the three divisions are shown in Exhibit 8.

**EXHIBIT 8**

**Residual Income—DataLink, Inc.**

| | Northern Division | Central Division | Southern Division |
|---|---|---|---|
| Income from operations | $70,000 | $84,000 | $75,000 |
| Less minimum acceptable income from operations as a percent of invested assets: | | | |
| $350,000 × 10% | 35,000 | | |
| $700,000 × 10% | | 70,000 | |
| $500,000 × 10% | | | 50,000 |
| Residual income | $35,000 | $14,000 | $25,000 |

As shown in Exhibit 8, the Northern Division has more residual income ($35,000) than the other divisions, even though it has the least amount of income from operations ($70,000). This is because the invested assets are less for the Northern Division than for the other divisions.

The major advantage of residual income as a performance measure is that it considers both the minimum acceptable rate of return, invested assets, and the income from operations for each division. In doing so, residual income encourages division managers to maximize income from operations in excess of the minimum. This provides an incentive to accept any project that is expected to have a rate of return in excess of the minimum.

To illustrate, assume the following rates of return for the Northern Division of DataLink:

| | |
|---|---|
| Current rate of return on investment | 20% |
| Minimum acceptable rate of return on investment set by top management | 10% |
| Expected rate of return on investment for new project | 14% |

If the manager of the Northern Division is evaluated on new projects using only return on investment, the division manager might decide to reject the new project. This is because investing in the new project will decrease Northern's current rate of return of 20%. While this helps the division maintain its high ROI, it hurts the company as a whole because the expected rate of return of 14% exceeds DataLink's minimum acceptable rate of return of 10%.

In contrast, if the manager of the Northern Division is evaluated using residual income, the new project would probably be accepted because it will increase the Northern Division's residual income. In this way, residual income supports both divisional and overall company objectives.

**Example Exercise 24-5   Residual Income**

OBJ 4

The Wholesale Division of PeanutCo has income from operations of $87,000 and assets of $240,000. The minimum acceptable rate of return on assets is 12%. What is the residual income for the division?

**Follow My Example 24-5**

Income from operations . . . . . . . . . . . . . . . . . . . . . . . . . . . . . . . . . . . . . . . . . . . . . . . . . . .   $87,000
Minimum acceptable income from operations as a percent of assets ($240,000 × 12%) . . . . . . .   28,800
Residual income . . . . . . . . . . . . . . . . . . . . . . . . . . . . . . . . . . . . . . . . . . . . . . . . . . . . . . . . .   $58,200

Practice Exercises: PE 24-5A, PE 24-5B

## The Balanced Scorecard[2]

The **balanced scorecard** is a set of multiple performance measures for a company. In addition to financial performance, a balanced scorecard normally includes performance measures for customer service, innovation and learning, and internal processes, as shown in Exhibit 9.

**EXHIBIT 9**

**The Balanced Scorecard**

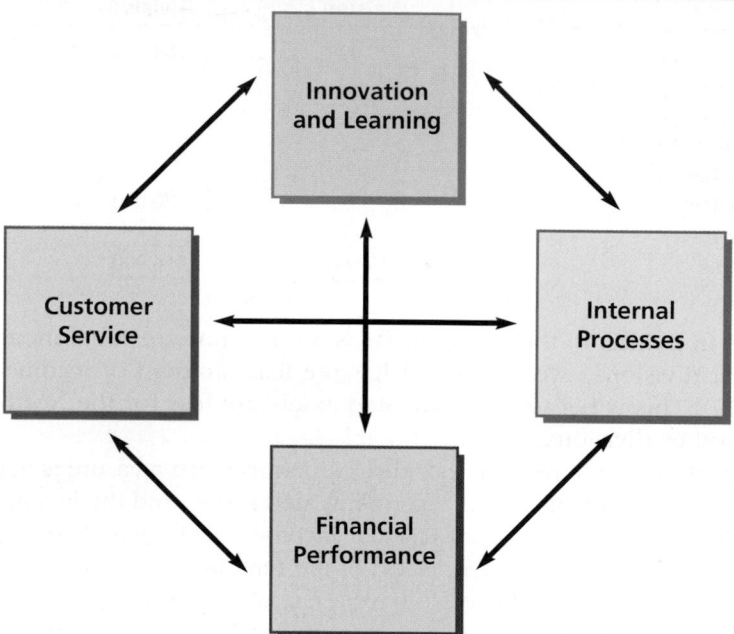

Performance measures for learning and innovation often revolve around a company's research and development efforts. For example, the number of new products developed during a year and the time it takes to bring new products to the market are performance measures for innovation. Performance measures for learning could include the number of employee training sessions and the number of employees who are cross-trained in several skills.

Performance measures for customer service include the number of customer complaints and the number of repeat customers. Customer surveys can also be used to gather measures of customer satisfaction with the company as compared to competitors.

Performance measures for internal processes include the length of time it takes to manufacture a product. The amount of scrap and waste is a measure of the efficiency

[2] The balanced scorecard was developed by R. S. Kaplan and D. P. Norton and explained in *The Balanced Scorecard: Translating Strategy into Action* (Cambridge: Harvard Business School Press, 1996).

of a company's manufacturing processes. The number of customer returns is a performance measure of both the manufacturing and sales ordering processes.

All companies will use financial performance measures. Some financial performance measures have been discussed earlier in this chapter and include income from operations, rate of return on investment, and residual income.

The balanced scorecard attempts to identify the underlying nonfinancial drivers, or causes, of financial performance related to innovation and learning, customer service, and internal processes. In this way, the financial performance may be improved. For example, customer satisfaction is often measured by the number of repeat customers. By increasing the number of repeat customers, sales and income from operations can be increased.

Some common performance measures used in the balanced scorecard approach are shown in Exhibit 10.

 **Hilton Hotels Corporation** uses a balanced scorecard to measure employee satisfaction, customer loyalty, and financial performance.

| Innovation and Learning |
| --- |
| • Number of new products |
| • Number of new patents |
| • Number of cross-trained employees |
| • Number of training hours |
| • Number of ethics violations |
| • Employee turnover |

| Customer Service |
| --- |
| • Number of repeat customers |
| • Customer brand recognition |
| • Delivery time to customer |
| • Customer satisfaction |
| • Number of sales returns |
| • Customer complaints |

| Internal Processes |
| --- |
| • Waste and scrap |
| • Time to manufacture products |
| • Number of defects |
| • Number of rejected sales orders |
| • Number of stockouts |
| • Labor utilization |

| Financial |
| --- |
| • Sales |
| • Income from operations |
| • Return on investment |
| • Profit margin and investment turnover |
| • Residual income |
| • Actual versus budgeted (standard) costs |

**EXHIBIT 10**

**Balanced Scorecard Performance Measures**

## Service ▸ Focus

### TURNING AROUND CHARLES SCHWAB

Customer service is a key component to any balanced scorecard, and it is a particularly critical component in service industries. Since 2003, **Bain & Company** consulting has helped companies improve customer service by focusing on a customer loyalty metric called the *Net Promoter Score*. This metric, when used as part of a balanced scorecard, evaluates customer service by assessing how likely a customer is to recommend the company to others.

**The Charles Schwab Corporation** is a full-service financial advisory firm that was founded in 1973. In 2004, the company was struggling. Although Schwab had been built on delivering exceptional customer service, the company had lost its way. When customers were surveyed, they gave Schwab a negative 35% Net Promoter Score, indicating that more customers wanted to see the company fail than would be willing to promote the company to others.

In response, Schwab enlisted Bain to help them improve the customer experience and customer loyalty. Bain helped Schwab develop and implement a Client Promoter System that focused on embedding the Client Promoter Score deep within the company's values and core strategy. As Schwab CEO Walt Bettinger describes, "If you serve clients in the way that you would like to be served, they are going to want to do more business with you." The results were significant. By 2008, the company's stock price had more than doubled, and in 2010, Schwab received a Net Promoter Score of 46%, the highest in its sector.

Source: "Schwab Earns Highest Customer Loyalty Ranking Among Brokerage & Investment Firms in Satmetrix Net Promoter's 2010 Industry Report," *BusinessWire*, March 25, 2010. "Seeing the world through the client's eyes," Bain & Co., http://www.netpromotersystem.com/videos/trailblazer-video/charles-schwab.aspx

**OBJ 5**

Describe and illustrate how the market price, negotiated price, and cost price approaches to transfer pricing may be used by decentralized segments of a business.

# Transfer Pricing

When divisions transfer products or render services to each other, a **transfer price** is used to charge for the products or services.[3] Because transfer prices will affect a division's financial performance, setting a transfer price is a sensitive matter for the managers of both the selling and buying divisions.

Three common approaches to setting transfer prices are as follows:

- Market price approach
- Negotiated price approach
- Cost approach

Transfer prices may be used for cost, profit, or investment centers. The objective of setting a transfer price is to motivate managers to behave in a manner that will increase the overall company income. As will be illustrated, however, transfer prices may be misused in such a way that overall company income suffers.

Transfer prices can be set as low as the variable cost per unit or as high as the market price. Often, transfer prices are negotiated at some point between variable cost per unit and market price. Exhibit 11 shows the possible range of transfer prices.

## EXHIBIT 11

**Commonly Used Transfer Prices**

To illustrate, Wilson Company, a packaged snack food company with no service departments, is used. Wilson has two operating divisions (Eastern and Western) that are organized as investment centers. Condensed income statements for Wilson, assuming no transfers between divisions, are shown in Exhibit 12.

## EXHIBIT 12

**Income Statements— No Transfers Between Divisions**

| | **Wilson Company**<br>**Income Statements**<br>**For the Year Ended December 31, 2016** | | |
| --- | --- | --- | --- |
| | **Eastern Division** | **Western Division** | **Total Company** |
| Sales: | | | |
| 50,000 units × $20 per unit . . . . . . . . . . . . . | $1,000,000 | | $1,000,000 |
| 20,000 units × $40 per unit . . . . . . . . . . . . . | | $800,000 | 800,000 |
| | | | $1,800,000 |
| Expenses: | | | |
| Variable: | | | |
| 50,000 units × $10 per unit . . . . . . . . . . . | $ 500,000 | | $ 500,000 |
| 20,000 units × $30* per unit . . . . . . . . . . | | $600,000 | 600,000 |
| Fixed . . . . . . . . . . . . . . . . . . . . . . . . . . . . . . . . | 300,000 | 100,000 | 400,000 |
| Total expenses . . . . . . . . . . . . . . . . . . . . . . | $ 800,000 | $700,000 | $1,500,000 |
| Income from operations . . . . . . . . . . . . . . . . . . | $ 200,000 | $100,000 | $ 300,000 |

*$20 of the $30 per unit represents materials costs, and the remaining $10 per unit represents other variable conversion expenses incurred within the Western Division.

---

[3] The discussion in this chapter highlights the essential concepts of transfer pricing. In-depth discussion of transfer pricing can be found in advanced texts.

# Market Price Approach

Using the **market price approach**, the transfer price is the price at which the product or service transferred could be sold to outside buyers. If an outside market exists for the product or service transferred, the current market price may be a proper transfer price.

Transfer Price = Market Price

To illustrate, assume that materials used by Wilson in producing snack food in the Western Division are currently purchased from an outside supplier at $20 per unit. The same materials are produced by the Eastern Division. The Eastern Division is operating at full capacity of 50,000 units and can sell all it produces to either the Western Division or to outside buyers.

A transfer price of $20 per unit (the market price) has no effect on the Eastern Division's income or total company income. The Eastern Division will earn revenues of $20 per unit on all its production and sales, regardless of who buys its product.

Likewise, the Western Division will pay $20 per unit for materials (the market price). Thus, the use of the market price as the transfer price has no effect on the Eastern Division's income or total company income.

In this situation, the use of the market price as the transfer price is proper. The condensed divisional income statements for Wilson would be the same as shown in Exhibit 12.

# Negotiated Price Approach

If unused or excess capacity exists in the supplying division (the Eastern Division), and the transfer price is equal to the market price, total company profit may not be maximized. This is because the manager of the Western Division will be indifferent toward purchasing materials from the Eastern Division or from outside suppliers. That is, in both cases the Western Division manager pays $20 per unit (the market price). As a result, the Western Division may purchase the materials from outside suppliers.

If, however, the Western Division purchases the materials from the Eastern Division, the difference between the market price of $20 and the variable costs of the Eastern Division of $10 per unit (from Exhibit 12) can cover fixed costs and contribute to overall company profits. Thus, the Western Division manager should be encouraged to purchase the materials from the Eastern Division.

The **negotiated price approach** allows the managers to agree (negotiate) among themselves on a transfer price. The only constraint is that the transfer price be less than the market price but greater than the supplying division's variable costs per unit, as follows:

Variable Costs per Unit < Transfer Price < Market Price

To illustrate, assume that instead of a capacity of 50,000 units, the Eastern Division's capacity is 70,000 units. In addition, assume that the Eastern Division can continue to sell only 50,000 units to outside buyers.

A transfer price less than $20 would encourage the manager of the Western Division to purchase from the Eastern Division. This is because the Western Division is currently purchasing its materials from outside suppliers at a cost of $20 per unit. Thus, its materials cost would decrease, and its income from operations would increase.

At the same time, a transfer price above the Eastern Division's variable costs per unit of $10 would encourage the manager of the Eastern Division to supply materials to the Western Division. In doing so, the Eastern Division's income from operations would also increase.

Exhibit 13 illustrates the divisional and company income statements, assuming that the Eastern and Western division managers agree to a transfer price of $15.

The Eastern Division increases its sales by $300,000 (20,000 units × $15 per unit) to $1,300,000. As a result, the Eastern Division's income from operations increases by $100,000 ($300,000 sales − $200,000 variable costs) to $300,000, as shown in Exhibit 13.

EXHIBIT 13

Income Statements—
Negotiated Transfer
Price

Dynamic
Exhibit

**Wilson Company**
**Income Statements**
**For the Year Ended December 31, 2016**

| | Eastern Division | Western Division | Total Company |
|---|---|---|---|
| Sales: | | | |
| 50,000 units × $20 per unit.............. | $1,000,000 | | $1,000,000 |
| 20,000 units × $15 per unit.............. | 300,000 | | 300,000 |
| 20,000 units × $40 per unit.............. | | $800,000 | 800,000 |
| | $1,300,000 | $800,000 | $2,100,000 |
| Expenses: | | | |
| Variable: | | | |
| 70,000 units × $10 per unit............ | $ 700,000 | | $ 700,000 |
| 20,000 units × $25* per unit........... | | $500,000 | 500,000 |
| Fixed ................................. | 300,000 | 100,000 | 400,000 |
| Total expenses ...................... | $1,000,000 | $600,000 | $1,600,000 |
| Income from operations.................. | $ 300,000 | $200,000 | $ 500,000 |

*$10 of the $25 represents variable conversion expenses incurred solely within the Western Division, and $15 per unit represents the transfer price per unit from the Eastern Division.

The increase of $100,000 in the Eastern Division's income can also be computed as follows:

Increase in Eastern (Supplying)
Division's Income from Operations = (Transfer Price – Variable Cost per Unit) × Units Transferred

= ($15 – $10) × 20,000 units = $100,000

The Western Division's materials cost decreases by $5 per unit ($20 – $15) for a total of $100,000 (20,000 units × $5 per unit). Thus, the Western Division's income from operations increases by $100,000 to $200,000, as shown in Exhibit 13.

The increase of $100,000 in the Western Division's income can also be computed as follows:

Increase in Western (Purchasing)
Division's Income from Operations = (Market Price – Transfer Price) × Units Transferred

= ($20 – $15) × 20,000 units = $100,000

Comparing Exhibits 12 and 13 shows that Wilson's income from operations increased by $200,000, computed as follows:

| | Income from Operations | | |
|---|---|---|---|
| | No Units Transferred (Exhibit 12) | 20,000 Units Transferred at $15 per Unit (Exhibit 13) | Increase (Decrease) |
| Eastern Division | $200,000 | $300,000 | $100,000 |
| Western Division | 100,000 | 200,000 | 100,000 |
| Wilson Company | $300,000 | $500,000 | $200,000 |

In the preceding illustration, any negotiated transfer price between $10 and $20 is acceptable, as shown in the following formula:

Variable Costs per Unit < Transfer Price < Market Price
$10 < Transfer Price < $20

Any transfer price within this range will increase the overall income from operations for Wilson by $200,000. However, the increases in the Eastern and Western divisions' income from operations will vary depending on the transfer price.

To illustrate, a transfer price of $16 would increase the Eastern Division's income from operations by $120,000, computed as follows:

$$\text{Increase in Eastern (Supplying) Division's Income from Operations} = (\text{Transfer Price} - \text{Variable Cost per Unit}) \times \text{Units Transferred}$$

$$= (\$16 - \$10) \times 20,000 \text{ units} = \$120,000$$

A transfer price of $16 would increase the Western Division's income from operations by $80,000, computed as follows:

$$\text{Increase in Western (Purchasing) Division's Income from Operations} = (\text{Market Price} - \text{Transfer Price}) \times \text{Units Transferred}$$

$$= (\$20 - \$16) \times 20,000 \text{ units} = \$80,000$$

With a transfer price of $16, Wilson Company's income from operations still increases by $200,000, which consists of the Eastern Division's increase of $120,000 plus the Western Division's increase of $80,000.

As shown, a negotiated price provides each division manager with an incentive to negotiate the transfer of materials. At the same time, the overall company's income from operations will also increase. However, the negotiated approach only applies when the supplying division has excess capacity. In other words, the supplying division cannot sell all its production to outside buyers at the market price.

## Example Exercise 24-6  Transfer Pricing

OBJ 5

The materials used by the Winston-Salem Division of Fox Company are currently purchased from outside suppliers at $30 per unit. These same materials are produced by Fox's Flagstaff Division. The Flagstaff Division can produce the materials needed by the Winston-Salem Division at a variable cost of $15 per unit. The division is currently producing 70,000 units and has capacity of 100,000 units. The two divisions have recently negotiated a transfer price of $22 per unit for 30,000 units. By how much will each division's income increase as a result of this transfer?

### Follow My Example 24-6

$$\text{Increase in Flagstaff (Supplying) Division's Income from Operations} = (\text{Transfer Price} - \text{Variable Cost per Unit}) \times \text{Units Transferred}$$

$$= (\$22 - \$15) \times 30,000 \text{ units} = \$210,000$$

$$\text{Increase in Winston-Salem (Purchasing) Division's Income from Operations} = (\text{Market Price} - \text{Transfer Price}) \times \text{Units Transferred}$$

$$= (\$30 - \$22) \times 30,000 \text{ units} = \$240,000$$

Practice Exercises: PE 24-6A, PE 24-6B

## Cost Price Approach

Under the **cost price approach**, cost is used to set transfer prices. A variety of costs may be used in this approach, including the following:

- Total product cost per unit
- Variable product cost per unit

If total product cost per unit is used, direct materials, direct labor, and factory overhead are included in the transfer price. If variable product cost per unit is used, the fixed factory overhead cost is excluded from the transfer price.

Actual costs or standard (budgeted) costs may be used in applying the cost price approach. If actual costs are used, inefficiencies of the producing (supplying) division are transferred to the purchasing division. Thus, there is little incentive for the producing (supplying) division to control costs. For this reason, most companies use standard costs in the cost price approach. In this way, differences between actual and standard costs remain with the producing (supplying) division for cost control purposes.

The cost price approach is most often used when the responsibility centers are organized as cost centers. When the responsibility centers are organized as profit or investment centers, the cost price approach is normally not used.

For example, using the cost price approach when the supplying division is organized as a profit center ignores the supplying division manager's responsibility for earning profits. In this case, using the cost price approach prevents the supplying division from reporting any profit (revenues – costs) on the units transferred. As a result, the division manager has little incentive to transfer units to another division, even though it may be in the best interests of the company.

## Integrity, Objectivity, and Ethics in Business

### THE ETHICS OF TRANSFER PRICES

Transfer prices allow large multinational companies to minimize taxes by shifting taxable income from countries with high tax rates to countries with low taxes. For example, a British company will pay U.S. taxes on income from its U.S. division, and British taxes on income from its British division. Because this company can set its own transfer price, it can minimize its overall tax bill by setting a high transfer price when transferring goods to the United States This increases cost of goods sold for the highly taxed U.S division and increases sales for the lesser taxed British division. The overall result is a lower tax bill for the multinational company as a whole. In recent years, government tax authorities like the Internal Revenue Service (IRS) have become concerned with tax avoidance through transfer price manipulation. In response, many countries now have guidelines for setting transfer prices that assure that transfer prices are not subject to manipulation for tax purposes.

Source: L. Eden, and L. M. Smith, "The Ethics of Transfer Pricing," unpublished working paper, Texas A&M University, 2011.

# At a Glance 24

**OBJ 1**

### Describe the advantages and disadvantages of decentralized operations.

**Key Points** In a centralized business, all major planning and operating decisions are made by top management. In a decentralized business, these responsibilities are delegated to unit managers. Decentralization may be more effective because operational decisions are made by the managers closest to the operations.

| Learning Outcomes | Example Exercises | Practice Exercises |
|---|---|---|
| • Describe the advantages of decentralization. | | |
| • Describe the disadvantages of decentralization. | | |
| • Describe the common types of responsibility centers and the role of responsibility accounting. | | |

**Prepare a responsibility accounting report for a cost center.**

**Key Points** Cost centers limit the responsibility and authority of managers to decisions related to the costs of their unit. The primary tools for planning and controlling are budgets and budget performance reports.

| Learning Outcomes | Example Exercises | Practice Exercises |
|---|---|---|
| • Describe cost centers. | | |
| • Describe the responsibility reporting for a cost center. | | |
| • Compute the costs over (under) budget for a cost center. | **EE24-1** | **PE24-1A, 24-1B** |

**Prepare responsibility accounting reports for a profit center.**

**Key Points** In a profit center, managers have the responsibility and authority to make decisions that affect both revenues and costs. Responsibility reports for a profit center usually show income from operations for the unit.

| Learning Outcomes | Example Exercises | Practice Exercises |
|---|---|---|
| • Describe profit centers. | | |
| • Determine how service department charges are allocated to profit centers. | **EE24-2** | **PE24-2A, 24-2B** |
| • Describe the responsibility reporting for a profit center. | | |
| • Compute income from operations for a profit center. | **EE24-3** | **PE24-3A, 24-3B** |

**Compute and interpret the rate of return on investment, the residual income, and the balanced scorecard for an investment center.**

**Key Points** In an investment center, the unit manager has the responsibility and authority to make decisions that affect the unit's revenues, expenses, and assets invested in the center. Three measures are commonly used to assess investment center performance: return on investment (ROI), residual income, and the balanced scorecard. These measures are often used to compare investment center performance.

| Learning Outcomes | Example Exercises | Practice Exercises |
|---|---|---|
| • Describe investment centers. | | |
| • Describe the responsibility reporting for an investment center. | | |
| • Compute the profit margin, investment turnover, and rate of return on investment (ROI). | **EE24-4** | **PE24-4A, 24-4B** |
| • Compute residual income. | **EE24-5** | **PE24-5A, 24-5B** |
| • Describe the balanced scorecard approach. | | |

**OBJ 5** Describe and illustrate how the market price, negotiated price, and cost price approaches to transfer pricing may be used by decentralized segments of a business.

**Key Points** When divisions within a company transfer products or provide services to each other, a transfer price is used to charge for the products or services. Transfer prices should be set so that the overall company income is increased when goods are transferred between divisions. One of three approaches is typically used to establish transfer prices: market price, negotiated price, or cost price.

| Learning Outcomes | Example Exercises | Practice Exercises |
|---|---|---|
| • Describe how companies determine the price used to transfer products or services between divisions. | | |
| • Determine transfer prices using the market price approach. | | |
| • Determine transfer prices using the negotiated price approach. | EE24-6 | PE24-6A, 24-6B |
| • Describe the cost price approach to determining transfer price. | | |

## Key Terms

balanced scorecard (1136)
controllable expenses (1128)
controllable revenues (1128)
cost center (1126)
cost price approach (1141)
DuPont formula (1132)

investment center (1131)
investment turnover (1132)
market price approach (1139)
negotiated price approach (1139)
profit center (1128)
profit margin (1132)

rate of return on investment (ROI) (1132)
residual income (1135)
responsibility accounting (1125)
service department charges (1128)
transfer price (1138)

## Illustrative Problem

Quinn Company has two divisions, Domestic and International. Invested assets and condensed income statement data for each division for the year ended December 31, 2016, are as follows:

| | Domestic Division | International Division |
|---|---|---|
| Revenues | $675,000 | $480,000 |
| Operating expenses | 450,000 | 372,400 |
| Service department charges | 90,000 | 50,000 |
| Invested assets | 600,000 | 384,000 |

### Instructions

1. Prepare condensed income statements for the past year for each division.

2. Using the DuPont formula, determine the profit margin, investment turnover, and rate of return on investment for each division.

3. If management's minimum acceptable rate of return is 10%, determine the residual income for each division.

### Solution

1.

**Quinn Company**
**Divisional Income Statements**
**For the Year Ended December 31, 2016**

| | Domestic Division | International Division |
|---|---|---|
| Revenues | $675,000 | $480,000 |
| Operating expenses | 450,000 | 372,400 |
| Income from operations before | | |
| service department charges | $225,000 | $107,600 |
| Service department charges | 90,000 | 50,000 |
| Income from operations | $135,000 | $ 57,600 |

2. Rate of Return on Investment = Profit Margin × Investment Turnover

$$\text{Rate of Return on Investment} = \frac{\text{Income from Operations}}{\text{Sales}} \times \frac{\text{Sales}}{\text{Invested Assets}}$$

$$\text{Domestic Division: ROI} = \frac{\$135,000}{\$675,000} \times \frac{\$675,000}{\$600,000}$$

$$= 20\% \times 1.125$$

$$= 22.5\%$$

$$\text{International Division: ROI} = \frac{\$57,600}{\$480,000} \times \frac{\$480,000}{\$384,000}$$

$$= 12\% \times 1.25$$

$$= 15\%$$

3. Domestic Division: $75,000 [$135,000 − (10% × $600,000)]
   International Division: $19,200 [$57,600 − (10% × $384,000)]

# Discussion Questions

1. Differentiate between centralized and decentralized operations.

2. Differentiate between a profit center and an investment center.

3. **Weyerhaeuser** developed a system that assigns service department expenses to user divisions on the basis of actual services consumed by the division. Here are a number of Weyerhaeuser's activities in its central Financial Services Department:
   - Payroll
   - Accounts payable
   - Accounts receivable
   - Database administration—report preparation
   For each activity, identify an activity base that could be used to charge user divisions for service.

4. What is the major shortcoming of using income from operations as a performance measure for investment centers?

5. In a decentralized company in which the divisions are organized as investment centers, how could a division be considered the least profitable even though it earned the largest amount of income from operations?

6. How does using the rate of return on investment facilitate comparability between divisions of decentralized companies?

7. Why would a firm use a balanced scorecard in evaluating divisional performance?

8. What is the objective of transfer pricing?

9. When is the negotiated price approach preferred over the market price approach in setting transfer prices?

10. When using the negotiated price approach to transfer pricing, within what range should the transfer price be established?

# Practice Exercises

SHOW
ME HOW

EE 24-1 *p. 1127*   **PE 24-1A   Budgetary performance for cost center**                    OBJ. 2

Caroline Company's costs were over budget by $319,000. The company is divided into West and East regions. The East Region's costs were under budget by $47,500. Determine the amount that the West Region's costs were over or under budget.

SHOW
ME HOW

EE 24-1 *p. 1127*   **PE 24-1B   Budgetary performance for cost center**                    OBJ. 2

Conley Company's costs were under budget by $198,000. The company is divided into North and South regions. The North Region's costs were over budget by $52,000. Determine the amount that the South Region's costs were over or under budget.

SHOW
ME HOW

EE 24-2 *p. 1130*   **PE 24-2A   Service department charges**                               OBJ. 3

The centralized employee travel department of Camtro Company has expenses of $528,000. The department has serviced a total of 6,000 travel reservations for the period. The Southeast Division has made 2,400 reservations during the period, and the Pacific Northwest Division has made 3,600 reservations. How much should each division be charged for travel services?

SHOW
ME HOW

EE 24-2 *p. 1130*   **PE 24-2B   Service department charges**                               OBJ. 3

The centralized computer technology department of Lee Company has expenses of $264,000. The department has provided a total of 2,500 hours of service for the period. The Retail Division has used 1,125 hours of computer technology service during the period, and the Commercial Division has used 1,375 hours of computer technology service. How much should each division be charged for computer technology department services?

SHOW
ME HOW

EE 24-3 *p. 1131*   **PE 24-3A   Income from operations for profit center**                 OBJ. 3

Using the data for Camtro Company from Practice Exercise 24-2A along with the following data, determine the divisional income from operations for the Northeast and Pacific divisions:

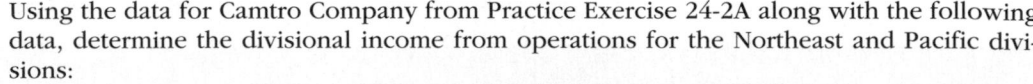

|  | Northeast Division | Pacific Division |
|---|---|---|
| Sales | $1,155,000 | $1,204,000 |
| Cost of goods sold | 590,800 | 658,000 |
| Selling expenses | 231,000 | 252,000 |

SHOW
ME HOW

EE 24-3 *p. 1131*   **PE 24-3B   Income from operations for profit center**                 OBJ. 3

Using the data for Lee Company from Practice Exercise 24-2B along with the following data, determine the divisional income from operations for the Division and the Commercial Division:

|  | Retail Division | Commercial Division |
|---|---|---|
| Sales | $945,000 | $966,000 |
| Cost of goods sold | 504,000 | 559,300 |
| Selling expenses | 156,800 | 175,000 |

EE 24-4 *p. 1134*   **PE 24-4A   Profit margin, investment turnover, and ROI**   **OBJ. 4**

Cash Company has income from operations of $112,500, invested assets of $750,000, and sales of $1,875,000. Use the DuPont formula to compute the rate of return on investment and show (a) the profit margin, (b) the investment turnover, and (c) the rate of return on investment.

EE 24-4 *p. 1134*   **PE 24-4B   Profit margin, investment turnover, and ROI**   **OBJ. 4**

Briggs Company has income from operations of $36,000, invested assets of $180,000, and sales of $720,000. Use the DuPont formula to compute the rate of return on investment and show (a) the profit margin, (b) the investment turnover, and (c) the rate of return on investment.

EE 24-5 *p. 1136*   **PE 24-5A   Residual income**   **OBJ. 4**

The Consumer Division of Hernandez Company has income from operations of $90,000 and assets of $450,000. The minimum acceptable rate of return on assets is 10%. What is the residual income for the division?

EE 24-5 *p. 1136*   **PE 24-5B   Residual income**   **OBJ. 4**

The Commercial Division of Herring Company has income from operations of $420,000 and assets of $910,000. The minimum acceptable rate of return on assets is 8%. What is the residual income for the division?

EE 24-6 *p. 1141*   **PE 24-6A   Transfer pricing**   **OBJ. 5**

The materials used by the North Division of Horton Company are currently purchased from outside suppliers at $60 per unit. These same materials are produced by Horton's South Division. The South Division can produce the materials needed by the North Division at a variable cost of $42 per unit. The division is currently producing 200,000 units and has capacity of 250,000 units. The two divisions have recently negotiated a transfer price of $52 per unit for 30,000 units. By how much will each division's income increase as a result of this transfer?

EE 24-6 *p. 1141*   **PE 24-6B   Transfer pricing**   **OBJ. 5**

The materials used by the Multinomah Division of Isbister Company are currently purchased from outside suppliers at $90 per unit. These same materials are produced by the Pembroke Division. The Pembroke Division can produce the materials needed by the Multinomah Division at a variable cost of $75 per unit. The division is currently producing 120,000 units and has capacity of 150,000 units. The two divisions have recently negotiated a transfer price of $82 per unit for 15,000 units. By how much will each division's income increase as a result of this transfer?

# Exercises

✔ a. (c) $3,540

**EX 24-1   Budget performance reports for cost centers**   **OBJ. 2**

Partially completed budget performance reports for Saskatoon Company, a manufacturer of light duty motors, follow:

**Saskatoon Company**
**Budget Performance Report—Vice President, Production**
**For the Month Ended June 30, 2016**

| Plant | Budget | Actual | Over Budget | Under Budget |
|---|---|---|---|---|
| Eastern Region | $936,000 | $933,750 | | $2,250 |
| Central Region | 669,600 | 666,000 | | 3,600 |
| Western Region | (g) | (h) | (i) | |
| | (j) | (k) | $   (l) | $5,850 |

*(Continued)*

**Saskatoon Company**
**Budget Performance Report—Manager, Western Region Plant**
**For the Month Ended June 30, 2016**

| Department | Budget | Actual | Over Budget | Under Budget |
|---|---|---|---|---|
| Chip Fabrication | (a) | (b) | (c) | |
| Electronic Assembly | $191,250 | $194,040 | $ 2,520 | |
| Final Assembly | 308,250 | 307,440 | | $810 |
| | (d) | (e) | $ (f) | $810 |

**Saskatoon Company**
**Budget Performance Report—Supervisor, Chip Fabrication**
**For the Month Ended June 30, 2016**

| Cost | Budget | Actual | Over Budget | Under Budget |
|---|---|---|---|---|
| Factory wages | $ 59,940 | $ 61,500 | $1,560 | |
| Materials | 156,600 | 155,520 | | $1,080 |
| Power and light | 8,640 | 10,260 | 1,620 | |
| Maintenance | 15,120 | 16,560 | 1,440 | |
| | $240,300 | $243,840 | $4,620 | $1,080 |

a. Complete the budget performance reports by determining the correct amounts for the lettered spaces.

b. ▬▬▬▶ Compose a memo to Robin Mooney, vice president of production for Saskatoon Company, explaining the performance of the production division for May.

---

**EX 24-2    Divisional income statements**                                            OBJ. 3

✔ Commercial
Division income from
operations, $179,890

The following data were summarized from the accounting records for Jersey Coast Construction Company for the year ended June 30, 2016:

| Cost of goods sold: | | Service department charges: | |
|---|---|---|---|
| Commercial Division | $912,250 | Commercial Division | $112,560 |
| Residential Division | 423,675 | Residential Division | 67,830 |
| Administrative expenses: | | Net sales: | |
| Commercial Division | $149,800 | Commercial Division | $1,354,500 |
| Residential Division | 128,625 | Residential Division | 743,780 |

Prepare divisional income statements for Jersey Coast Construction Company.

---

**EX 24-3    Service department charges and activity bases**                            OBJ. 3

For each of the following service departments, identify an activity base that could be used for charging the expense to the profit center:

a. Legal

b. Duplication services

c. Electronic data processing

d. Central purchasing

e. Telecommunications

f. Accounts receivable

**EX 24-4** **Activity bases for service department charges**

OBJ. 3

✔ c. 2

For each of the following service departments, select the activity base listed that is most appropriate for charging service expenses to responsible units:

| Service Department | Activity Base |
|---|---|
| a. Accounts Receivable | 1. Number of conference attendees |
| b. Central Purchasing | 2. Number of computers |
| c. Computer Support | 3. Number of employees trained |
| d. Conferences | 4. Number of cell phone minutes used |
| e. Employee Travel | 5. Number of purchase requisitions |
| f. Payroll Accounting | 6. Number of sales invoices |
| g. Telecommunications | 7. Number of payroll checks |
| h. Training | 8. Number of travel claims |

**EX 24-5** **Service department charges**

OBJ. 3

✔ b. Residential payroll, $33,400

SHOW
ME HOW

In divisional income statements prepared for LeFevre Company, the Payroll Department costs are charged back to user divisions on the basis of the number of payroll distributions, and the Purchasing Department costs are charged back on the basis of the number of purchase requisitions. The Payroll Department had expenses of $75,400, and the Purchasing Department had expenses of $42,000 for the year. The following annual data for Residential, Commercial, and Government Contract divisions were obtained from corporate records:

| | Residential | Commercial | Government Contract |
|---|---|---|---|
| Sales | $1,000,000 | $1,600,000 | $3,200,000 |
| Number of employees: | | | |
| Weekly payroll (52 weeks per year) | 300 | 150 | 200 |
| Monthly payroll | 75 | 160 | 90 |
| Number of purchase requisitions per year | 4,000 | 3,500 | 3,000 |

a. Determine the total amount of payroll checks and purchase requisitions processed per year by the company and each division.

b. Using the activity base information in (a), determine the annual amount of payroll and purchasing costs charged back to the Residential, Commercial, and Government Contract divisions from payroll and purchasing services.

c. ➤ Why does the Residential Division have a larger service department charge than the other two divisions, even though its sales are lower?

**EX 24-6** **Service department charges and activity bases**

OBJ. 3

✔ b. Help desk, $93,600

Middler Corporation, a manufacturer of electronics and communications systems, uses a service department charge system to charge profit centers with Computing and Communications Services (CCS) service department costs. The following table identifies an abbreviated list of service categories and activity bases used by the CCS department. The table also includes some assumed cost and activity base quantity information for each service for October.

| CCS Service Category | Activity Base | Budgeted Cost | Budgeted Activity Base Quantity |
|---|---|---|---|
| Help desk | Number of calls | $160,000 | 3,200 |
| Network center | Number of devices monitored | 735,000 | 9,800 |
| Electronic mail | Number of user accounts | 100,000 | 10,000 |
| Smart phone support | Number of smart phones issued | 124,600 | 8,900 |

One of the profit centers for Middler Corporation is the Communication Systems (COMM) sector. Assume the following information for the COMM sector:

- The sector has 5,200 employees, of whom 25% are office employees.
- All the office employees have been issued a smart phone, and 96% of them have a computer on the network.

(*Continued*)

- One hundred percent of the employees with a computer also have an e-mail account.
- The average number of help desk calls for October was 1.5 calls per individual with a computer.
- There are 600 additional printers, servers, and peripherals on the network beyond the personal computers.

a. Determine the service charge rate for the four CCS service categories for October.

b. Determine the charges to the COMM sector for the four CCS service categories for October.

---

**EX 24-7**  **Divisional income statements with service department charges**      **OBJ. 3**

✔ Commercial income from operations, $1,261,260

SHOW ME HOW

Yozamba Technology has two divisions, Consumer and Commercial, and two corporate service departments, Tech Support and Purchasing. The corporate expenses for the year ended December 31, 2016, are as follows:

| | |
|---|---:|
| Tech Support Department | $ 516,000 |
| Purchasing Department | 89,600 |
| Other corporate administrative expenses | 560,000 |
| Total corporate expense | $1,165,600 |

The other corporate administrative expenses include officers' salaries and other expenses required by the corporation. The Tech Support Department charges the divisions for services rendered, based on the number of computers in the department, and the Purchasing Department charges divisions for services, based on the number of purchase orders for each department. The usage of service by the two divisions is as follows:

| | Tech Support | Purchasing |
|---|---|---|
| Consumer Division | 375 computers | 1,960 purchase orders |
| Commercial Division | 225 | 3,640 |
| Total | 600 computers | 5,600 purchase orders |

The service department charges of the Tech Support Department and the Purchasing Department are considered controllable by the divisions. Corporate administrative expenses are not considered controllable by the divisions. The revenues, cost of goods sold, and operating expenses for the two divisions are as follows:

| | Consumer | Commercial |
|---|---|---|
| Revenues | $7,430,000 | $6,184,000 |
| Cost of goods sold | 4,123,000 | 3,125,000 |
| Operating expenses | 1,465,000 | 1,546,000 |

Prepare the divisional income statements for the two divisions.

---

**EX 24-8**  **Corrections to service department charges for a service company**      **OBJ. 3**

✔ b. Income from operations, Cargo Division, $84,400

Wild Sun Airlines Inc. has two divisions organized as profit centers, the Passenger Division and the Cargo Division. The following divisional income statements were prepared:

**Wild Sun Airlines Inc.**
**Divisional Income Statements**
**For the Year Ended December 31, 2016**

| | Passenger Division | | Cargo Division | |
|---|---|---|---|---|
| Revenues | | $3,025,000 | | $3,025,000 |
| Operating expenses | | 2,450,000 | | 2,736,000 |
| Income from operations before service department charges | | $ 575,000 | | $ 289,000 |
| Less service department charges: | | | | |
| Training | $125,000 | | $125,000 | |
| Flight scheduling | 108,000 | | 108,000 | |
| Reservations | 151,200 | 384,200 | 151,200 | 384,200 |
| Income from operations | | $ 190,800 | | $ (95,200) |

The service department charge rate for the service department costs was based on revenues. Because the revenues of the two divisions were the same, the service department charges to each division were also the same.

The following additional information is available:

|  | Passenger Division | Cargo Division | Total |
| --- | --- | --- | --- |
| Number of personnel trained | 350 | 150 | 500 |
| Number of flights | 800 | 1,200 | 2,000 |
| Number of reservations requested | 20,000 | 0 | 20,000 |

a. ━━━━ Does the income from operations for the two divisions accurately measure performance? Explain.

b. Correct the divisional income statements, using the activity bases provided in revising the service department charges.

---

### EX 24-9   Profit center responsibility reporting                                   OBJ. 3

✔ Income from operations, Summer Sports Division, $1,499,400

SHOW
ME HOW

XSport Sporting Goods Co. operates two divisions—the Winter Sports Division and the Summer Sports Division. The following income and expense accounts were provided from the trial balance as of December 31, 2016, the end of the fiscal year, after all adjustments, including those for inventories, were recorded and posted:

| | |
| --- | --- |
| Sales—Winter Sports Division.................................... | $10,500,000 |
| Sales—Summer Sports Division ................................... | 13,600,000 |
| Cost of Goods Sold—Winter Sports Division ...................... | 6,300,000 |
| Cost of Goods Sold—Summer Sports Division ...................... | 7,888,000 |
| Sales Expense—Winter Sports Division ........................... | 1,680,000 |
| Sales Expense—Summer Sports Division ........................... | 1,904,000 |
| Administrative Expense—Winter Sports Division ................... | 1,050,000 |
| Administrative Expense—Summer Sports Division................... | 1,210,400 |
| Advertising Expense ............................................ | 482,000 |
| Transportation Expense ......................................... | 240,000 |
| Accounts Receivable Collection Expense.......................... | 120,500 |
| Warehouse Expense.............................................. | 1,200,000 |

The bases to be used in allocating expenses, together with other essential information, are as follows:

a. Advertising expense—incurred at headquarters, charged back to divisions on the basis of usage: Winter Sports Division, $216,900; Summer Sports Division, $265,100.

b. Transportation expense—charged back to divisions at a charge rate of $8.00 per bill of lading: Winter Sports Division, 14,400 bills of lading; Summer Sports Division, 15,600 bills of lading.

c. Accounts receivable collection expense—incurred at headquarters, charged back to divisions at a charge rate of $5.00 per invoice. Winter Sports Division, 9,640 sales invoices; Summer Sports Division, 14,460 sales invoices.

d. Warehouse expense—charged back to divisions on the basis of floor space used in storing division products: Winter Sports Division, 94,000 square feet; Summer Sports Division, 106,000 square feet.

Prepare a divisional income statement with two column headings: Winter Sports Division and Summer Sports Division. Provide supporting calculations for service department charges.

**EX 24-10  Rate of return on investment**                                OBJ. 4

The income from operations and the amount of invested assets in each division of Magentic Zero Industries are as follows:

|  | Income from Operations | Invested Assets |
|---|---|---|
| Retail Division | $343,200 | $1,320,000 |
| Commercial Division | 320,000 | 1,600,000 |
| Internet Division | 176,000 | 800,000 |

a.  Compute the rate of return on investment for each division.

b.  Which division is the most profitable per dollar invested?

**EX 24-11  Residual income**                                            OBJ. 4

Based on the data in Exercise 24-10, assume that management has established a 10% minimum acceptable rate of return for invested assets.

a.  Determine the residual income for each division.

b.  Which division has the most residual income?

**EX 24-12  Determining missing items in rate of return computation**      OBJ. 4

One item is omitted from each of the following computations of the rate of return on investment:

| Rate of Return on Investment | = | Profit Margin | × | Investment Turnover |
|---|---|---|---|---|
| 13.2% | = | 6% | × | (a) |
| (b) | = | 10% | × | 1.80 |
| 10.5% | = | (c) | × | 1.50 |
| 15% | = | 5% | × | (d) |
| (e) | = | 12% | × | 1.10 |

Determine the missing items, identifying each by the appropriate letter.

**EX 24-13  Profit margin, investment turnover, and rate of return on investment**   OBJ. 4

The condensed income statement for the Consumer Products Division of Bantastic Industries Inc. is as follows (assuming no service department charges):

| | |
|---|---|
| Sales | $16,000,000 |
| Cost of goods sold | 11,660,000 |
| Gross profit | $ 4,340,000 |
| Administrative expenses | 2,100,000 |
| Income from operations | $ 2,240,000 |

The manager of the Consumer Products Division is considering ways to increase the rate of return on investment.

a.  Using the DuPont formula for rate of return on investment, determine the profit margin, investment turnover, and rate of return on investment of the Consumer Products Division, assuming that $8,000,000 of assets have been invested in the Consumer Products Division.

b.  If expenses could be reduced by $320,000 without decreasing sales, what would be the impact on the profit margin, investment turnover, and rate of return on investment for the Consumer Products Division?

**EX 24-14  Rate of return on investment**                               OBJ. 4

The Walt Disney Company has four profitable business segments, described as follows:

• **Media Networks:** The ABC television and radio network, Disney channel, ESPN, A&E, E!, and Disney.com

• **Parks and Resorts:** Walt Disney World Resort, Disneyland, Disney Cruise Line, and other resort properties

- **Studio Entertainment:** Walt Disney Pictures, Touchstone Pictures, Hollywood Pictures, Miramax Films, and Buena Vista Theatrical Productions
- **Consumer Products:** Character merchandising, Disney stores, books, and magazines

Disney recently reported sector income from operations, revenue, and invested assets (in millions) as follows:

|  | Income from Operations | Revenue | Invested Assets |
|---|---|---|---|
| Media Networks | $6,818 | $20,356 | $28,627 |
| Parks and Resorts | 2,220 | 14,087 | 22,056 |
| Studio Entertainment | 661 | 5,979 | 14,750 |
| Consumer Products | 1,112 | 3,811 | 7,506 |

a. Use the DuPont formula to determine the rate of return on investment for the four Disney sectors. Round whole percents to one decimal place and investment turnover to two decimal places.

b. ➤ How do the four sectors differ in their profit margin, investment turnover, and return on investment?

---

**EX 24-15 Determining missing items in rate of return and residual income computations**  OBJ. 4

✔ c. $46,250

Data for Uberto Company are presented in the following table of rates of return on investment and residual incomes:

| Invested Assets | Income from Operations | Rate of Return on Investment | Minimum Rate of Return | Minimum Acceptable Income from Operations | Residual Income |
|---|---|---|---|---|---|
| $925,000 | $185,000 | (a) | 15% | (b) | (c) |
| $775,000 | (d) | (e) | (f) | $93,000 | $23,250 |
| $450,000 | (g) | 18% | (h) | $58,500 | (i) |
| $610,000 | $97,600 | (j) | 12% | (k) | (l) |

Determine the missing items, identifying each item by the appropriate letter.

---

**EX 24-16 Determining missing items from computations**  OBJ. 4

✔ a. (e) $300,000

Data for the North, South, East, and West divisions of Free Bird Company are as follows:

|  | Sales | Income from Operations | Invested Assets | Rate of Return on Investment | Profit Margin | Investment Turnover |
|---|---|---|---|---|---|---|
| North | $860,000 | (a) | (h) | 17.5% | 7.0% | (c) |
| South | (d) | $51,300 | (e) | (f) | 4.5% | 3.8 |
| East | $1,020,000 | (g) | $680,000 | 15.0% | (h) | (i) |
| West | $1,120,000 | $89,600 | $560,000 | (j) | (k) | (l) |

a. Determine the missing items, identifying each by the letters (a) through (l). Round percents and investment turnover to one decimal place.

b. Determine the residual income for each division, assuming that the minimum acceptable rate of return established by management is 12%.

c. Which division is the most profitable in terms of (1) return on investment and (2) residual income?

---

**EX 24-17 Rate of return on investment, residual income for a service company**  OBJ. 4

Starwood Hotels & Resorts Worldwide provides lodging services around the world. The company is separated into two major divisions.

- **Hotel Ownership:** Hotels owned and operated by Starwood.
- **Vacation Ownership:** Resort properties developed, owned, and operated for timeshare vacation owners.

*(Continued)*

Financial information for each division, from a recent annual report, is as follows (in millions):

| | Hotel Ownership | Vacation Ownership |
|---|---|---|
| Revenues | $4,383 | $ 688 |
| Income from operations | 571 | 105 |
| Total assets | 6,440 | 2,139 |

a. Use the DuPont formula to determine the return on investment for each of the Starwood business divisions. Round whole percents to one decimal place and investment turnover to two decimal places.

b. Determine the residual income for each division, assuming a minimum acceptable income of 5% of total assets. Round minimal acceptable return to the nearest million dollars.

c. ➤ Interpret your results.

---

### EX 24-18 Balanced scorecard for a service company OBJ. 4

**American Express Company** is a major financial services company, noted for its American Express® card. Some of the performance measures used by the company in its balanced scorecard follow:

| | |
|---|---|
| Average card member spending | Number of Internet features |
| Cards in force | Number of merchant signings |
| Earnings growth | Number of new card launches |
| Hours of credit consultant training | Return on equity |
| Investment in information technology | Revenue growth |
| Number of card choices | |

For each measure, identify whether the measure best fits the innovation, customer, internal process, or financial dimension of the balanced scorecard.

---

### EX 24-19 Building a balanced scorecard OBJ. 4

Hit-n-Run Inc. owns and operates 10 food trucks (mobile kitchens) throughout metropolitan Los Angeles. Each food truck has a different food theme, such as Irish-Mexican fusion, traditional Mexican street food, Ethiopian cuisine, and Lebanese-Italian fusion. The company was founded three years ago by Juanita O'Brien when she opened a single food truck with a unique menu. As her business has grown, she has become concerned about her ability to manage and control the business. O'Brien describes how the company was built, its key success factors, and its recent growth.

"I built the company from the ground up. In the beginning it was just me. I drove the truck, set the menu, bought the ingredients, prepared the meals, served the meals, cleaned the kitchen, and maintained the equipment. I made unique meals from quality ingredients, and didn't serve anything that wasn't perfect. I changed my location daily, and notified customers of my location via twitter.

As my customer base grew, I hired employees to help me in the truck. Then one day I realized that I had a formula that could be expanded to multiple trucks. Before I knew it, I had 10 trucks and was hiring people to do everything that I used to do by myself. Now, I work with my team to build the menu, set daily locations for the trucks, and manage the operations of the business.

My business model is based on providing the highest quality street food and charging more for it than other trucks. You won't get the cheapest meal at one of my trucks, but you will get the best. The superior quality allows me to price my meals a little bit higher than the other trucks. My employees are critical to my success. I pay them a better wage than they could make on other food trucks, and I expect more from them. I rely on them to maintain the quality that I established when I opened my first truck.

Things are going great, but I'm feeling overwhelmed. So far, the growth in sales has led to a growth in profitability—but I'm getting nervous. If quality starts to fall off, my brand value erodes, and that could affect the prices that I charge for my meals and the success of my business."

Create balanced scorecard measures for Hit-n-Run Food Trucks. Identify whether these measures best fit the innovation, customer, internal process, or financial dimension of the balanced scorecard.

---

**EX 24-20    Decision on transfer pricing**                                OBJ. 5

✔ a. $3,000,000

Materials used by the Instrument Division of XPort Industries are currently purchased from outside suppliers at a cost of $210 per unit. However, the same materials are available from the Components Division. The Components Division has unused capacity and can produce the materials needed by the Instrument Division at a variable cost of $160 per unit.

a. If a transfer price of $180 per unit is established and 60,000 units of materials are transferred, with no reduction in the Components Division's current sales, how much would XPort Industries' total income from operations increase?

b. How much would the Instrument Division's income from operations increase?

c. How much would the Components Division's income from operations increase?

---

**EX 24-21    Decision on transfer pricing**                                OBJ. 5

✔ b. $1,200,000

Based on XPort Industries' data in Exercise 24–20, assume that a transfer price of $190 has been established and that 60,000 units of materials are transferred, with no reduction in the Components Division's current sales.

a. How much would XPort Industries' total income from operations increase?

b. How much would the Instrument Division's income from operations increase?

c. How much would the Components Division's income from operations increase?

d. ━━━━━▶ If the negotiated price approach is used, what would be the range of acceptable transfer prices and why?

---

# Problems: Series A

---

**PR 24-1A    Budget performance report for a cost center**                OBJ. 2

Valotic Tech Inc. sells electronics over the Internet. The Consumer Products Division is organized as a cost center. The budget for the Consumer Products Division for the month ended January 31, 2016, is as follows (in thousands):

| | |
|---|---:|
| Customer service salaries | $ 546,840 |
| Insurance and property taxes | 114,660 |
| Distribution salaries | 872,340 |
| Marketing salaries | 1,028,370 |
| Engineer salaries | 836,850 |
| Warehouse wages | 586,110 |
| Equipment depreciation | 183,792 |
| Total | $4,168,962 |

During January, the costs incurred in the Consumer Products Division were as follows:

| | |
|---|---:|
| Customer service salaries | $ 602,350 |
| Insurance and property taxes | 110,240 |
| Distribution salaries | 861,200 |
| Marketing salaries | 1,085,230 |
| Engineer salaries | 820,008 |
| Warehouse wages | 562,632 |
| Equipment depreciation | 183,610 |
| Total | $4,225,270 |

**Instructions**

1. Prepare a budget performance report for the director of the Consumer Products Division for the month of January.

2. For which costs might the director be expected to request supplemental reports?

**PR 24-2A** **Profit center responsibility reporting for a service company** OBJ. 3

Traxonia Railroad Inc. has three regional divisions organized as profit centers. The chief executive officer (CEO) evaluates divisional performance, using income from operations as a percent of revenues. The following quarterly income and expense accounts were provided from the trial balance as of December 31, 2016:

| | |
|---|---:|
| Revenues—East | $ 870,000 |
| Revenues—West | 1,032,000 |
| Revenues—Central | 1,872,000 |
| Operating Expenses—East | 563,300 |
| Operating Expenses—West | 618,240 |
| Operating Expenses—Central | 1,166,940 |
| Corporate Expenses—Shareholder Relations | 154,000 |
| Corporate Expenses—Customer Support | 400,000 |
| Corporate Expenses—Legal | 270,000 |
| General Corporate Officers' Salaries | 275,000 |

The company operates three service departments: Shareholder Relations, Customer Support, and Legal. The Shareholder Relations Department conducts a variety of services for shareholders of the company. The Customer Support Department is the company's point of contact for new service, complaints, and requests for repair. The department believes that the number of customer contacts is an activity base for this work. The Legal Department provides legal services for division management. The department believes that the number of hours billed is an activity base for this work. The following additional information has been gathered:

| | East | West | Central |
|---|---|---|---|
| Number of customer contacts | 5,000 | 6,000 | 9,000 |
| Number of hours billed | 1,350 | 2,160 | 1,890 |

**Instructions**

1. Prepare quarterly income statements showing income from operations for the three divisions. Use three column headings: East, West, and Central.

2. Identify the most successful division according to the profit margin.

3. ━━━► Provide a recommendation to the CEO for a better method for evaluating the performance of the divisions. In your recommendation, identify the major weakness of the present method.

**PR 24-3A** **Divisional income statements and rate of return on investment analysis** OBJ. 4

The Crunchy Granola Company is a diversified food company that specializes in all natural foods. The company has three operating divisions organized as investment centers. Condensed data taken from the records of the three divisions for the year ended June 30, 2016, are as follows:

| | Cereal Division | Snack Cake Division | Retail Bakeries Division |
|---|---|---|---|
| Sales | $25,000,000 | $8,000,000 | $9,750,000 |
| Cost of goods sold | 16,670,000 | 5,575,000 | 6,795,000 |
| Operating expenses | 7,330,000 | 1,945,000 | 2,272,500 |
| Invested assets | 10,000,000 | 4,000,000 | 6,500,000 |

The management of The Crunchy Granola Company is evaluating each division as a basis for planning a future expansion of operations.

**Instructions**

1. Prepare condensed divisional income statements for the three divisions, assuming that there were no service department charges.

2. Using the DuPont formula for rate of return on investment, compute the profit margin, investment turnover, and rate of return on investment for each division.

3. ━━━► If available funds permit the expansion of operations of only one division, which of the divisions would you recommend for expansion, based on parts (1) and (2)? Explain.

✔ 1. ROI, 16.8%

**PR 24-4A    Effect of proposals on divisional performance**    OBJ. 4

A condensed income statement for the Commercial Division of Maxell Manufacturing Inc. for the year ended December 31, 2016, is as follows:

| | |
|---|---:|
| Sales | $3,500,000 |
| Cost of goods sold | 2,480,000 |
| Gross profit | $1,020,000 |
| Operating expenses | 600,000 |
| Income from operations | $ 420,000 |
| Invested assets | $2,500,000 |

Assume that the Commercial Division received no charges from service departments. The president of Maxell Manufacturing has indicated that the division's rate of return on a $2,500,000 investment must be increased to at least 21% by the end of the next year if operations are to continue. The division manager is considering the following three proposals:

*Proposal 1:* Transfer equipment with a book value of $312,500 to other divisions at no gain or loss and lease similar equipment. The annual lease payments would exceed the amount of depreciation expense on the old equipment by $105,000. This increase in expense would be included as part of the cost of goods sold. Sales would remain unchanged.

*Proposal 2:* Purchase new and more efficient machining equipment and thereby reduce the cost of goods sold by $560,000 after considering the effects of depreciation expense on the new equipment. Sales would remain unchanged, and the old equipment, which has no remaining book value, would be scrapped at no gain or loss. The new equipment would increase invested assets by an additional $1,875,000 for the year.

*Proposal 3:* Reduce invested assets by discontinuing a product line. This action would eliminate sales of $595,000, reduce cost of goods sold by $406,700, and reduce operating expenses by $175,000. Assets of $1,338,000 would be transferred to other divisions at no gain or loss.

**Instructions**

1. Using the DuPont formula for rate of return on investment, determine the profit margin, investment turnover, and rate of return on investment for the Commercial Division for the past year.

2. Prepare condensed estimated income statements and compute the invested assets for each proposal.

3. Using the DuPont formula for rate of return on investment, determine the profit margin, investment turnover, and rate of return on investment for each proposal.

4. Which of the three proposals would meet the required 21% rate of return on investment?

5. If the Commercial Division were in an industry where the profit margin could not be increased, how much would the investment turnover have to increase to meet the president's required 21% rate of return on investment? Round to one decimal place.

**PR 24-5A    Divisional performance analysis and evaluation**    OBJ. 4

✔ 2. Business
Division ROI, 20.0%

SHOW
ME HOW

The vice president of operations of Pavone Company is evaluating the performance of two divisions organized as investment centers. Invested assets and condensed income statement data for the past year for each division are as follows:

| | Business Division | Consumer Division |
|---|---:|---:|
| Sales | $2,500,000 | $2,550,000 |
| Cost of goods sold | 1,320,000 | 1,350,000 |
| Operating expenses | 930,000 | 843,000 |
| Invested assets | 1,250,000 | 2,125,000 |

**Instructions**

1. Prepare condensed divisional income statements for the year ended December 31, 2016, assuming that there were no service department charges.

2. Using the DuPont formula for rate of return on investment, determine the profit margin, investment turnover, and rate of return on investment for each division.

3. If management desires a minimum acceptable rate of return of 17%, determine the residual income for each division.

4. ━━━━▶ Discuss the evaluation of the two divisions, using the performance measures determined in parts (1), (2), and (3).

✔ 3. Total income
from operations,
$1,759,680

### PR 24-6A Transfer pricing

OBJ. 5

Garcon Inc. manufactures electronic products, with two operating divisions, the Consumer and Commercial divisions. Condensed divisional income statements, which involve no intracompany transfers and which include a breakdown of expenses into variable and fixed components, are as follows:

**Garcon Inc.**
**Divisional Income Statements**
**For the Year Ended December 31, 2016**

|  | Consumer Division | Commercial Division | Total |
|---|---|---|---|
| Sales: |  |  |  |
| 14,400 units @ $144 per unit | $2,073,600 |  | $2,073,600 |
| 21,600 units @ $275 per unit |  | $5,940,000 | 5,940,000 |
|  | $2,073,600 | $5,940,000 | $8,013,600 |
| Expenses: |  |  |  |
| Variable: |  |  |  |
| 14,400 units @ $104 per unit | $1,497,600 |  | $1,497,600 |
| 21,600 units @ $193* per unit |  | $4,168,800 | 4,168,800 |
| Fixed | 200,000 | 520,000 | 720,000 |
| Total expenses | $1,697,600 | $4,688,800 | $6,386,400 |
| Income from operations | $ 376,000 | $1,251,200 | $1,627,200 |

*$150 of the $193 per unit represents materials costs, and the remaining $43 per unit represents other variable conversion expenses incurred within the Commercial Division.

The Consumer Division is presently producing 14,400 units out of a total capacity of 17,280 units. Materials used in producing the Commercial Division's product are currently purchased from outside suppliers at a price of $150 per unit. The Consumer Division is able to produce the materials used by the Commercial Division. Except for the possible transfer of materials between divisions, no changes are expected in sales and expenses.

### Instructions

1. ➤ Would the market price of $150 per unit be an appropriate transfer price for Garcon Inc.? Explain.

2. ➤ If the Commercial Division purchases 2,880 units from the Consumer Division, rather than externally, at a negotiated transfer price of $115 per unit, how much would the income from operations of each division and the total company income from operations increase?

3. Prepare condensed divisional income statements for Garcon Inc. based on the data in part (2).

4. ➤ If a transfer price of $126 per unit is negotiated, how much would the income from operations of each division and the total company income from operations increase?

5. a. ➤ What is the range of possible negotiated transfer prices that would be acceptable for Garcon Inc.?

   b. Assuming that the managers of the two divisions cannot agree on a transfer price, what price would you suggest as the transfer price?

## Problems: Series B

### PR 24-1B Budget performance report for a cost center

OBJ. 2

The Eastern District of Adelson Inc. is organized as a cost center. The budget for the Eastern District of Adelson Inc. for the month ended December 31, 2016, is as follows:

| | |
|---|---|
| Sales salaries | $ 819,840 |
| System administration salaries | 448,152 |
| Customer service salaries | 152,600 |
| Billing salaries | 98,760 |
| Maintenance | 271,104 |
| Depreciation of plant and equipment | 92,232 |
| Insurance and property taxes | 41,280 |
| Total | $1,923,968 |

During December, the costs incurred in the Eastern District were as follows:

| | |
|---|---|
| Sales salaries | $ 818,880 |
| System administration salaries | 447,720 |
| Customer service salaries | 183,120 |
| Billing salaries | 98,100 |
| Maintenance | 273,000 |
| Depreciation of plant and equipment | 92,232 |
| Insurance and property taxes | 41,400 |
| Total | $1,954,452 |

**Instructions**

1. Prepare a budget performance report for the manager of the Eastern District of Adelson for the month of December.

2. ➤ For which costs might the supervisor be expected to request supplemental reports?

---

**PR 24-2B    Profit center responsibility reporting for a service company** OBJ. 3

✔ 1. Income from operations, West Region, $820,800

SHOW
ME HOW

Thomas Railroad Company organizes its three divisions, the North (N), South (S), and West (W) regions, as profit centers. The chief executive officer (CEO) evaluates divisional performance, using income from operations as a percent of revenues. The following quarterly income and expense accounts were provided from the trial balance as of December 31, 2016:

| | |
|---|---|
| Revenues—N Region | $3,780,000 |
| Revenues—S Region | 5,673,000 |
| Revenues—W Region | 5,130,000 |
| Operating Expenses—N Region | 2,678,500 |
| Operating Expenses—S Region | 4,494,890 |
| Operating Expenses—W Region | 3,770,050 |
| Corporate Expenses—Dispatching | 182,000 |
| Corporate Expenses—Equipment Management | 1,200,000 |
| Corporate Expenses—Treasurer's | 734,000 |
| General Corporate Officers' Salaries | 1,380,000 |

The company operates three service departments: the Dispatching Department, the Equipment Management Department, and the Treasurer's Department. The Dispatching Department manages the scheduling and releasing of completed trains. The Equipment Management Department manages the railroad cars inventories. It makes sure the right freight cars are at the right place at the right time. The Treasurer's Department conducts a variety of services for the company as a whole. The following additional information has been gathered:

| | North | South | West |
|---|---|---|---|
| Number of scheduled trains | 650 | 1,105 | 845 |
| Number of railroad cars in inventory | 6,000 | 8,400 | 9,600 |

**Instructions**

1. Prepare quarterly income statements showing income from operations for the three regions. Use three column headings: North, South, and West.

2. Identify the most successful region according to the profit margin.

3. ➤ Provide a recommendation to the CEO for a better method for evaluating the performance of the regions. In your recommendation, identify the major weakness of the present method.

✔ 2. Mutual Fund
Division, ROI, 22.4%

### PR 24-3B  Divisional income statements and rate of return on investment analysis  OBJ. 4

E.F. Lynch Company is a diversified investment company with three operating divisions organized as investment centers. Condensed data taken from the records of the three divisions for the year ended June 30, 2016, are as follows:

|  | Mutual Fund Division | Electronic Brokerage Division | Investment Banking Division |
|---|---|---|---|
| Fee revenue | $4,140,000 | $3,360,000 | $4,560,000 |
| Operating expenses | 2,980,800 | 3,091,200 | 3,739,200 |
| Invested assets | 5,175,000 | 1,120,000 | 3,800,000 |

The management of E.F. Lynch Company is evaluating each division as a basis for planning a future expansion of operations.

**Instructions**

1. Prepare condensed divisional income statements for the three divisions, assuming that there were no service department charges.

2. Using the DuPont formula for rate of return on investment, compute the profit margin, investment turnover, and rate of return on investment for each division.

3. ▬▬▬▬▶ If available funds permit the expansion of operations of only one division, which of the divisions would you recommend for expansion, based on parts (1) and (2)? Explain.

---

✔ 3. Proposal 3 ROI,
16.0%

### PR 24-4B  Effect of proposals on divisional performance  OBJ. 4

A condensed income statement for the Electronics Division of Gihbli Industries Inc. for the year ended December 31, 2016, is as follows:

| | |
|---|---|
| Sales | $1,575,000 |
| Cost of goods sold | 891,000 |
| Gross profit | $ 684,000 |
| Operating expenses | 558,000 |
| Income from operations | $ 126,000 |
| Invested assets | $1,050,000 |

Assume that the Electronics Division received no charges from service departments.

The president of Gihbli Industries Inc. has indicated that the division's rate of return on a $1,050,000 investment must be increased to at least 20% by the end of the next year if operations are to continue. The division manager is considering the following three proposals:

*Proposal 1:* Transfer equipment with a book value of $300,000 to other divisions at no gain or loss and lease similar equipment. The annual lease payments would be less than the amount of depreciation expense on the old equipment by $31,400. This decrease in expense would be included as part of the cost of goods sold. Sales would remain unchanged.

*Proposal 2:* Reduce invested assets by discontinuing a product line. This action would eliminate sales of $180,000, reduce cost of goods sold by $119,550, and reduce operating expenses by $60,000. Assets of $112,500 would be transferred to other divisions at no gain or loss.

*Proposal 3:* Purchase new and more efficient machinery and thereby reduce the cost of goods sold by $189,000 after considering the effects of depreciation expense on the new equipment. Sales would remain unchanged, and the old machinery, which has no remaining book value, would be scrapped at no gain or loss. The new machinery would increase invested assets by $918,750 for the year.

**Instructions**

1. Using the DuPont formula for rate of return on investment, determine the profit margin, investment turnover, and rate of return on investment for the Electronics Division for the past year. Round investment turnover and the rate of return to one decimal place.

2. Prepare condensed estimated income statements and compute the invested assets for each proposal.

3. Using the DuPont formula for rate of return on investment, determine the profit margin, investment turnover, and rate of return on investment for each proposal. Round investment turnover and the rate of return to one decimal place.

4. Which of the three proposals would meet the required 20% rate of return on investment?

5. If the Electronics Division were in an industry where the profit margin could not be increased, how much would the investment turnover have to increase to meet the president's required 20% rate of return on investment? Round to one decimal place.

---

SHOW
ME HOW

✔ 2. Road Bike
Division ROI, 12.0%

### PR 24-5B   Divisional performance analysis and evaluation   OBJ. 4

The vice president of operations of Free Ride Bike Company is evaluating the performance of two divisions organized as investment centers. Invested assets and condensed income statement data for the past year for each division are as follows:

|  | Road Bike Division | Mountain Bike Division |
| --- | --- | --- |
| Sales | $1,728,000 | $1,760,000 |
| Cost of goods sold | 1,380,000 | 1,400,000 |
| Operating expenses | 175,200 | 236,800 |
| Invested assets | 1,440,000 | 800,000 |

### Instructions

1. Prepare condensed divisional income statements for the year ended December 31, 2016, assuming that there were no service department charges.

2. Using the DuPont formula for rate of return on investment, determine the profit margin, investment turnover, and rate of return on investment for each division.

3. If management's minimum acceptable rate of return is 10%, determine the residual income for each division.

4. ━━━▶ Discuss the evaluation of the two divisions, using the performance measures determined in parts (1), (2), and (3).

---

✔ 3. Navigational
Systems Division,
$179,410

### PR 24-6B   Transfer pricing   OBJ. 5

Exoplex Industries Inc. is a diversified aerospace company, including two operating divisions, Semiconductors and Navigational Systems divisions. Condensed divisional income statements, which involve no intracompany transfers and include a breakdown of expenses into variable and fixed components, are as follows:

**Exoplex Industries Inc.**
**Divisional Income Statements**
**For the Year Ended December 31, 2016**

|  | Semiconductors Division | Navigational Systems Division | Total |
| --- | --- | --- | --- |
| Sales: |  |  |  |
| 2,240 units @ $396 per unit | $887,040 |  | $ 887,040 |
| 3,675 units @ $590 per unit |  | $2,168,250 | 2,168,250 |
|  | $887,040 | $2,168,250 | $3,055,290 |
| Expenses: |  |  |  |
| Variable: |  |  |  |
| 2,240 units @ $232 per unit | $519,680 |  | $ 519,680 |
| 3,675 units @ $472* per unit |  | $1,734,600 | 1,734,600 |
| Fixed | 220,000 | 325,000 | 545,000 |
| Total expenses | $739,680 | $2,059,600 | $2,799,280 |
| Income from operations | $147,360 | $ 108,650 | $ 256,010 |

*$432 of the $472 per unit represents materials costs, and the remaining $40 per unit represents other variable conversion expenses incurred within the Navigational Systems Division.

The Semiconductors Division is presently producing 2,240 units out of a total capacity of 2,820 units. Materials used in producing the Navigational Systems Division's product are currently purchased from outside suppliers at a price of $432 per unit. The

*(Continued)*

Semiconductors Division is able to produce the components used by the Navigational Systems Division. Except for the possible transfer of materials between divisions, no changes are expected in sales and expenses.

**Instructions**

1. ━━━━▶ Would the market price of $432 per unit be an appropriate transfer price for Exoplex Industries Inc.? Explain.

2. ━━━━▶ If the Navigational Systems Division purchases 580 units from the Semiconductors Division, rather than externally, at a negotiated transfer price of $310 per unit, how much would the income from operations of each division and total company income from operations increase?

3. Prepare condensed divisional income statements for Exoplex Industries Inc. based on the data in part (2).

4. ━━━━▶ If a transfer price of $340 per unit is negotiated, how much would the income from operations of each division and total company income from operations increase?

5. a. ━━━━▶ What is the range of possible negotiated transfer prices that would be acceptable for Exoplex Industries Inc.?

   b. Assuming that the managers of the two divisions cannot agree on a transfer price, what price would you suggest as the transfer price?

# Cases & Projects

### CP 24-1   Ethics and professional conduct in business

Rambotix Company has two divisions, the Semiconductor Division and the X-ray Division. The X-ray Division may purchase semiconductors from the Semiconductor Division or from outside suppliers. The Semiconductor Division sells semiconductor products both internally and externally. The market price for semiconductors is $100 per 100 semiconductors. Dave Bryant is the controller of the X-ray Division, and Howard Hillman is the controller of the Semiconductor Division. The following conversation took place between Dave and Howard:

*Dave:* I hear you are having problems selling semiconductors out of your division. Maybe I can help.

*Howard:* You've got that right. We're producing and selling at about 90% of our capacity to outsiders. Last year we were selling 100% of capacity. Would it be possible for your division to pick up some of our excess capacity? After all, we are part of the same company.

*Dave:* What kind of price could you give me?

*Howard:* Well, you know as well as I that we are under strict profit responsibility in our divisions, so I would expect to get market price, $100 for 100 semiconductors.

*Dave:* I'm not so sure we can swing that. I was expecting a price break from a "sister" division.

*Howard:* Hey, I can only take this "sister" stuff so far. If I give you a price break, our profits will fall from last year's levels. I don't think I could explain that. I'm sorry, but I must remain firm—market price. After all, it's only fair—that's what you would have to pay from an external supplier.

*Dave:* Fair or not, I think we'll pass. Sorry we couldn't have helped.

━━━━▶ Was Dave behaving ethically by trying to force the Semiconductor Division into a price break? Comment on Howard's reactions.

### CP 24-2   Service department charges

The Customer Service Department of Door Industries Inc. asked the Publications Department to prepare a brochure for its training program. The Publications Department delivered the brochures and charged the Customer Service Department a rate that was 25% higher than could be obtained from an outside printing company. The policy of the company required the Customer Service Department to use the internal publications group for brochures. The Publications Department claimed that it had a drop in demand for its services during the fiscal year, so it had to charge higher prices in order to recover its payroll and fixed costs.

━━━━▶ Should the cost of the brochure be transferred to the Customer Service Department in order to hold the Customer Service Department head accountable for the cost of the brochure? What changes in policy would you recommend?

## CP 24-3 Evaluating divisional performance

The three divisions of Yummy Foods are Snack Goods, Cereal, and Frozen Foods. The divisions are structured as investment centers. The following responsibility reports were prepared for the three divisions for the prior year:

|  | Snack Goods | Cereal | Frozen Foods |
|---|---|---|---|
| Revenues | $2,200,000 | $2,520,000 | $2,100,000 |
| Operating expenses | 1,366,600 | 1,122,000 | 976,800 |
| Income from operations before service department charges | $ 833,400 | $1,398,000 | $1,123,200 |
| Service department charges: |  |  |  |
| Promotion | $ 300,000 | $ 600,000 | $ 468,000 |
| Legal | 137,400 | 243,600 | 235,200 |
| Total service department charges | $ 437,400 | $ 843,600 | $ 703,200 |
| Income from operations | $ 396,000 | $ 554,400 | $ 420,000 |
| Invested assets | $2,000,000 | $1,680,000 | $1,750,000 |

1. Which division is making the best use of invested assets and should be given priority for future capital investments?

2. ━━━━▶ Assuming that the minimum acceptable rate of return on new projects is 19%, would all investments that produce a return in excess of 19% be accepted by the divisions?

3. ━━━━▶ Can you identify opportunities for improving the company's financial performance?

## CP 24-4 Evaluating division performance over time

The Norsk Division of Gridiron Concepts Inc. has been experiencing revenue and profit growth during the years 2014–2016. The divisional income statements follow:

**Gridiron Concepts Inc.**
**Divisional Income Statements, Norsk Division**
**For the Years Ended December 31, 2014–2016**

|  | 2014 | 2015 | 2016 |
|---|---|---|---|
| Sales | $1,470,000 | $2,100,000 | $2,450,000 |
| Cost of goods sold | 1,064,000 | 1,498,000 | 1,680,000 |
| Gross profit | $ 406,000 | $ 602,000 | $ 770,000 |
| Operating expenses | 185,500 | 224,000 | 231,000 |
| Income from operations | $ 220,500 | $ 378,000 | $ 539,000 |

Assume that there are no charges from service departments. The vice president of the division, Tom Yang, is proud of his division's performance over the last three years. The president of Gridiron Concepts Inc., Anna Evans, is discussing the division's performance with Tom, as follows:

*Tom:* As you can see, we've had a successful three years in the Norsk Division.

*Anna:* I'm not too sure.

*Tom:* What do you mean? Look at our results. Our income from operations has more than doubled, while our profit margins are improving.

*Anna:* I am looking at your results. However, your income statements fail to include one very important piece of information, namely, the invested assets. You have been investing a great deal of assets into the division. You had $735,000 in invested assets in 2014, $1,500,000 in 2015, and $3,500,000 in 2016.

*Tom:* You are right. I've needed the assets in order to upgrade our technologies and expand our operations. The additional assets are one reason we have been able to grow and improve our profit margins. I don't see that this is a problem.

*Anna:* The problem is that we must maintain a 15% rate of return on invested assets.

(*Continued*)

1. Determine the profit margins for the Norsk Division for 2014–2016.

2. Compute the investment turnover for the Norsk Division for 2014–2016. Round to two decimal places.

3. Compute the rate of return on investment for the Norsk Division for 2014–2016.

4. ━━━━ Evaluate the division's performance over the 2014–2016 time period. Why was Anna concerned about the performance?

---

### CP 24-5 Evaluating division performance

Last Resort Industries Inc. is a privately held diversified company with five separate divisions organized as investment centers. A condensed income statement for the Specialty Products Division for the past year, assuming no service department charges, is as follows:

**Last Resort Industries Inc.—Specialty Products Division**
**Income Statement**
**For the Year Ended December 31, 2015**

| | |
|---|---|
| Sales | $32,400,000 |
| Cost of goods sold | 24,300,000 |
| Gross profit | $ 8,100,000 |
| Operating expenses | 3,240,000 |
| Income from operations | $ 4,860,000 |
| Invested assets | $27,000,000 |

The manager of the Specialty Products Division was recently presented with the opportunity to add an additional product line, which would require invested assets of $14,400,000. A projected income statement for the new product line is as follows:

**New Product Line**
**Projected Income Statement**
**For the Year Ended December 31, 2016**

| | |
|---|---|
| Sales | $12,960,000 |
| Cost of goods sold | 7,500,000 |
| Gross profit | $ 5,460,000 |
| Operating expenses | 3,127,200 |
| Income from operations | $ 2,332,800 |

The Specialty Products Division currently has $27,000,000 in invested assets, and Last Resort Industries Inc.'s overall rate of return on investment, including all divisions, is 10%. Each division manager is evaluated on the basis of divisional rate of return on investment. A bonus is paid, in $8,000 increments, for each whole percentage point that the division's rate of return on investment exceeds the company average.

The president is concerned that the manager of the Specialty Products Division rejected the addition of the new product line, even though all estimates indicated that the product line would be profitable and would increase overall company income. You have been asked to analyze the possible reasons why the Specialty Products Division manager rejected the new product line.

1. Determine the rate of return on investment for the Specialty Products Division for the past year.

2. Determine the Specialty Products Division manager's bonus for the past year.

3. Determine the estimated rate of return on investment for the new product line. Round whole percents to one decimal place and investment turnover to two decimal places.

4. ━━━━ Why might the manager of the Specialty Products Division decide to reject the new product line? Support your answer by determining the projected rate of return on investment for 2016, assuming that the new product line was launched in the Specialty Products Division, and 2016 actual operating results were similar to those of 2015.

5. ━━━━ Can you suggest an alternative performance measure for motivating division managers to accept new investment opportunities that would increase the overall company income and rate of return on investment?

PETER DASILVA/EPA/NEWSCOM

# Differential Analysis, Product Pricing, and Activity-Based Costing

## Facebook

Many of the decisions that you make depend on comparing the estimated costs of alternatives. The payoff from such comparisons is described in the following report from a University of Michigan study:

*Richard Nisbett and two colleagues quizzed Michigan faculty members and university seniors on such questions as how often they walk out on a bad movie, refuse to finish a bad meal, start over on a weak term paper, or abandon a research project that no longer looks promising. They believe that people who cut their losses this way are following sound economic rules: calculating the net benefits of alternative courses of action, writing off past costs that can't be recovered, and weighing the opportunity to use future time and effort more profitably elsewhere.*

*Among students, those who have learned to use cost-benefit analysis frequently are apt to have far better grades than their Scholastic Aptitude Test scores would have predicted. Again, the more economics courses the students have, the more likely they are to apply cost-benefit analysis outside the classroom.*

*Dr. Nisbett concedes that for many Americans, cost-benefit rules often appear to conflict with such traditional principles as "never give up" and "waste not, want not."*

Managers must also evaluate the costs and benefits of alternative actions. **Facebook**, the largest social networking site in the world, was co-founded by Mark Zuckerberg in 2004. Since then, it has grown to more than 1 billion users and made Zuckerberg a multibillionaire.

Facebook has plans to grow to well over 1 billion users worldwide. Such growth involves decisions about where to expand. For example, expanding the site to new languages and countries involves software programming, marketing, and computer hardware costs. The benefits include adding new users to Facebook.

Analysis of the benefits and costs might lead Facebook to expand in some languages before others. For example, such an analysis might lead Facebook to expand in Swedish before it expands in Tok Pisin (the language of Papua New Guinea).

In this chapter, differential analysis, which reports the effects of decisions on total revenues and costs, is discussed. Practical approaches to setting product prices are also described and illustrated. Finally, how production bottlenecks and activity-based costing influence pricing and other decisions is also discussed.

*Source:* Alan L. Otten, "Economic Perspective Produces Steady Yields," from People Patterns, *The Wall Street Journal*, March 31, 1992, p. B1.

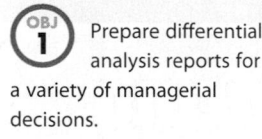
---

**OBJ 1**
Prepare differential analysis reports for a variety of managerial decisions.

# Differential Analysis

Managerial decision making involves choosing between alternative courses of action. Although the managerial decision-making process varies by the type of decision, it normally involves the following steps:

- Step 1. Identify the objective of the decision, which is normally maximizing income.
- Step 2. Identify alternative courses of action.
- Step 3. Gather information and perform a differential analysis.
- Step 4. Make a decision.
- Step 5. Review, analyze, and assess the results of the decision.

To illustrate, assume Bryant Restaurants Inc. is deciding whether to replace some of its customer seating (tables) with a salad bar. The differential analysis decision-making process is as follows.

---

**Step 1**  *Identify the objective of the decision.*
Bryant Restaurants' objective is to increase its income.

---

**Step 2**  *Identify alternative courses of action.*
The alternative courses of action are:

1. Use floor space for existing tables.
2. Replace the tables with a salad bar.

---

**Step 3**  *Gather information and perform a differential analysis.*
The following relevant data have been gathered:

| | Tables (Alternative 1) | Salad Bar (Alternative 2) |
|---|---|---|
| Revenues | $100,000 | $120,000 |
| Costs | 60,000 | 65,000 |
| Income (loss) | $ 40,000 | $ 55,000 |

The preceding information is used to perform differential analysis. **Differential analysis**, sometimes called *incremental analysis*, analyzes differential revenues and costs in order to determine the differential impact on income of two alternative courses of action.

**Differential revenue** is the amount of increase or decrease in revenue that is expected from a course of action compared to an alternative. **Differential cost** is the amount of increase or decrease in cost that is expected from a course of action as compared to an alternative. **Differential income (loss)** is the difference between the differential revenue and differential costs. Differential income indicates that a decision is expected to increase income, while a differential loss indicates the decision is expected to decrease income.

To illustrate, the differential analysis as of July 11 of the current year for Bryant Restaurants is shown in Exhibit 1.

**EXHIBIT 1**

**Differential Analysis—Bryant Restaurants**

**Differential Analysis**
**Tables (Alternative 1) or Salad Bar (Alternative 2)**
**July 11**

| | Tables (Alternative 1) | Salad Bar (Alternative 2) | Differential Effect on Income (Alternative 2) |
|---|---|---|---|
| Revenues.................. | $100,000 | $120,000 | $20,000 |
| Costs..................... | −60,000 | −65,000 | −5,000 |
| Income (loss).............. | $ 40,000 | $ 55,000 | $15,000 |

The differential analysis is prepared in three columns, where positive amounts indicate the effect is to increase income and negative amounts indicate the effect is to decrease income. The first column is the revenues, costs, and income for maintaining floor space for tables (Alternative 1). The second column is the revenues, costs, and income for using that floor space for a salad bar (Alternative 2). The third column is the difference between the revenue, costs, and income of one alternative over the other.

In Exhibit 1, the salad bar is being considered over retaining the existing tables. Thus, Column 3 in Exhibit 1 is expressed in terms of Alternative 2 (salad bar) over Alternative 1 (tables).

In Exhibit 1, the differential revenue of a salad bar over tables is $20,000 ($120,000 − $100,000). Because the increased revenue would increase income, it is entered as a positive $20,000 in the Differential Effect on Income column. The differential cost of a salad bar over tables is $5,000 ($65,000 − $60,000). Because the increased costs will decrease income, it is entered as a negative $5,000 in the Differential Effect on Income column.

The differential income (loss) of a salad bar over tables of $15,000 is determined by subtracting the differential costs from the differential revenues in the Differential Effect on Income column. Thus, installing a salad bar increases income by $15,000.

The preceding differential revenue, costs, and income can also be determined using the following formulas:

$$\text{Differential Revenue} = \text{Revenue (Alt. 2)} - \text{Revenue (Alt. 1)}$$
$$= \$120,000 - \$100,000 = \$20,000$$

$$\text{Differential Costs} = \text{Costs (Alt. 2)} - \text{Costs (Alt. 1)}$$
$$= -\$65,000 - (-\$60,000) = -\$5,000$$

$$\text{Differential Income (Loss)} = \text{Income (Alt. 2)} - \text{Income (Alt. 1)}$$
$$= \$55,000 - \$40,000 = \$15,000$$

*Step 4* **Make a decision.**

Based upon the differential analysis report shown in Exhibit 1, Bryant Restaurants should decide to replace some of its tables with a salad bar. Doing so will increase its income by $15,000.

*Step 5* **Review, analyze, and assess the results of the decision.**

Over time, Bryant Restaurants' decision should be reviewed based upon actual revenues and costs. If the actual revenues and costs differ significantly from those gathered in Step 3, another differential analysis might be necessary to verify that the correct decision was made.

In this chapter, differential analysis is illustrated for the following common decisions:

- Leasing or selling equipment
- Discontinuing an unprofitable segment
- Manufacturing or purchasing a needed part
- Replacing fixed assets
- Selling a product or processing further
- Accepting additional business at a special price

## Lease or Sell

Management may lease or sell a piece of equipment that is no longer needed. This may occur when a company changes its manufacturing process and can no longer use the equipment in the manufacturing process. In making a decision, differential analysis can be used.

To illustrate, assume that on June 22 of the current year, Marcus Company is considering leasing or disposing of the following equipment:

| | |
|---|---:|
| Cost of equipment | $200,000 |
| Less accumulated depreciation | 120,000 |
| Book value | $ 80,000 |
| Lease (Alternative 1): | |
| Total revenue for five-year lease | $160,000 |
| Total estimated repair, insurance, and property tax expenses during life of lease | 35,000 |
| Residual value at end of fifth year of lease | 0 |
| Sell (Alternative 2): | |
| Sales price | $100,000 |
| Commission on sales | 6% |

Exhibit 2 shows the differential analysis of whether to lease (Alternative 1) or sell (Alternative 2) the equipment.

| **EXHIBIT 2** | |
|---|---|

**Differential Analysis—Lease or Sell Equipment**

**Differential Analysis**
**Lease Equipment (Alternative 1) or Sell Equipment (Alternative 2)**
**June 22**

| | Lease Equipment (Alternative 1) | Sell Equipment (Alternative 2) | Differential Effect on Income (Alternative 2) |
|---|---:|---:|---:|
| Revenues............... | $160,000 | $100,000 | −$60,000 |
| Costs.................. | −35,000 | −6,000 | 29,000 |
| Income (loss)........... | $125,000 | $ 94,000 | −$31,000 |

If the equipment is sold, differential revenues will decrease by $60,000, differential costs will decrease by $29,000, and the differential effect on income is a decrease of $31,000. Thus, the decision should be to lease the equipment.

Exhibit 2 includes only the differential revenues and differential costs associated with the lease-or-sell decision. The $80,000 book value ($200,000 – $120,000) of the equipment is a *sunk cost* and is not considered in the differential analysis. **Sunk costs** are costs that have been incurred in the past, cannot be recouped, and are not relevant to future decisions. That is, the $80,000 is not affected regardless of which decision is made. For example, if the $80,000 were included in Exhibit 2, the costs for each alternative would both increase by $80,000, but the differential effect on income of –$31,000 would remain unchanged.

 Have you ever walked out on a bad movie? The cost of the ticket is a sunk cost and, thus, irrelevant to the decision to walk out early.

To simplify, the following factors were not considered in Exhibit 2:

- Differential revenue from investing funds
- Differential income tax

Differential revenue, such as interest revenue, could arise from investing the cash created by the two alternatives. Differential income tax could also arise from differences in income. These factors are discussed in Chapter 26.

---

## Example Exercise 25-1 Lease or Sell
**OBJ 1**

Casper Company owns office space with a cost of $100,000 and accumulated depreciation of $30,000 that can be sold for $150,000, less a 6% broker commission. Alternatively, the office space can be leased by Casper Company for 10 years for a total of $170,000, at the end of which there is no residual value. In addition, repair, insurance, and property tax that would be incurred by Casper Company on the rented office space would total $24,000 over the 10 years. Prepare a differential analysis on May 30, as to whether Casper Company should lease (Alternative 1) or sell (Alternative 2) the office space.

### Follow My Example 25-1

**Differential Analysis**
**Lease Office Space (Alternative 1) or Sell Office Space (Alternative 2)**
**May 30**

| | Lease Office Space (Alternative 1) | Sell Office Space (Alternative 2) | Differential Effect on Income (Alternative 2) |
|---|---|---|---|
| Revenues ............................. | $170,000 | $150,000 | –$20,000 |
| Costs ................................... | –24,000 | –9,000* | 15,000 |
| Income (loss)........................ | $146,000 | $141,000 | –$ 5,000 |

*$150,000 × 6%

Casper Company should lease the office space.

Practice Exercises: PE 25-1A, PE 25-1B

---

## Discontinue a Segment or Product

A product, department, branch, territory, or other segment of a business may be generating losses. As a result, management may consider discontinuing (eliminating) the product or segment. In such cases, it may be erroneously assumed that the total company income will increase by eliminating the operating loss.

Discontinuing the product or segment usually eliminates all of the product's or segment's variable costs. Such costs include direct materials, direct labor, variable factory overhead, and sales commissions. However, fixed costs such as depreciation, insurance, and property taxes may not be eliminated. Thus, it is possible for total company income to decrease rather than increase if the unprofitable product or segment is discontinued.

To illustrate, the income statement for Battle Creek Cereal Co. is shown in Exhibit 3. As shown in Exhibit 3, Bran Flakes incurred an operating loss of $11,000. Because Bran Flakes has incurred annual losses for several years, management is considering discontinuing it.

**EXHIBIT 3**

**Income (Loss) by Product**

| Battle Creek Cereal Co. Condensed Income Statement For the Year Ended August 31, 2016 | | | | |
|---|---|---|---|---|
| | **Corn Flakes** | **Toasted Oats** | **Bran Flakes** | **Total Company** |
| Sales..................................... | $500,000 | $400,000 | $100,000 | $1,000,000 |
| Cost of goods sold: | | | | |
|     Variable costs.......................... | $220,000 | $200,000 | $ 60,000 | $ 480,000 |
|     Fixed costs ........................... | 120,000 | 80,000 | 20,000 | 220,000 |
|         Total cost of goods sold............. | $340,000 | $280,000 | $ 80,000 | $ 700,000 |
| Gross profit............................. | $160,000 | $120,000 | $ 20,000 | $ 300,000 |
| Operating expenses: | | | | |
|     Variable expenses ..................... | $ 95,000 | $ 60,000 | $ 25,000 | $ 180,000 |
|     Fixed expenses........................ | 25,000 | 20,000 | 6,000 | 51,000 |
|         Total operating expenses ........... | $120,000 | $ 80,000 | $ 31,000 | $ 231,000 |
| Income (loss) from operations............. | $ 40,000 | $ 40,000 | $ (11,000) | $ 69,000 |

However, the differential analysis dated September 29, 2016, in Exhibit 4 indicates that discontinuing Bran Flakes (Alternative 2) actually decreases operating income by $15,000, even though it incurs a net loss of $11,000. This is because discontinuing Bran Flakes has no effect on fixed costs and expenses.

Exhibit 4 only considers the short-term (one-year) effects of discontinuing Bran Flakes. When discontinuing a product or segment, long-term effects should also be considered. For example, employee morale and productivity might suffer if employees have to be laid off or relocated.

**EXHIBIT 4**

**Differential Analysis—Continue or Discontinue Bran Flakes**

| Differential Analysis Continue Bran Flakes (Alternative 1) or Discontinue Bran Flakes (Alternative 2) September 29, 2016 | | | |
|---|---|---|---|
| | **Continue Bran Flakes (Alternative 1)** | **Discontinue Bran Flakes (Alternative 2)** | **Differential Effect on Income (Alternative 2)** |
| Revenues......................... | $100,000 | $ 0 | –$100,000 |
| Costs: | | | |
|     Variable........................ | –$ 85,000 | $ 0 | $ 85,000 |
|     Fixed ......................... | –26,000 | –26,000 | 0 |
|         Total costs..................... | –$111,000 | –$26,000 | $ 85,000 |
| Income (loss)..................... | –$ 11,000 | –$26,000 | –$ 15,000 |

**Example Exercise 25-2 Discontinue a Segment**

Product K has revenue of $65,000, variable cost of goods sold of $50,000, variable selling expenses of $12,000, and fixed costs of $25,000, creating a loss from operations of $22,000. Prepare a differential analysis dated February 22 to determine if Product K should be continued (Alternative 1) or discontinued (Alternative 2), assuming fixed costs are unaffected by the decision.

**Follow My Example 25-2**

**Differential Analysis**
**Continue K (Alternative 1) or Discontinue K (Alternative 2)**
**February 22**

|  | Continue Product K (Alternative 1) | Discontinue Product K (Alternative 2) | Differential Effect on Income (Alternative 2) |
|---|---|---|---|
| Revenues ..................................................... | $65,000 | $    0 | –$65,000 |
| Costs: |  |  |  |
|    Variable ................................................. | –$62,000* | $    0 | $62,000 |
|    Fixed...................................................... | –25,000 | –25,000 | 0 |
|    Total costs.............................................. | –$87,000 | –$25,000 | $62,000 |
| Income (loss)............................................... | –$22,000 | –$25,000 | –$ 3,000 |

*$50,000 + $12,000

Product K should be continued.

Practice Exercises: PE 25-2A, PE 25-2B

## Make or Buy

Companies often manufacture products made up of components that are assembled into a final product. For example, an automobile manufacturer assembles tires, radios, motors, interior seats, transmissions, and other parts into a finished automobile. In such cases, the manufacturer must decide whether to make a part or purchase it from a supplier.

Differential analysis can be used to decide whether to make or buy a part. The analysis is similar whether management is considering making a part that is currently being purchased or purchasing a part that is currently being made.

To illustrate, assume that an automobile manufacturer has been purchasing instrument panels for $240 a unit. The factory is currently operating at 80% of capacity, and no major increase in production is expected in the near future. The cost per unit of manufacturing an instrument panel internally is estimated on February 15 as follows:

| | |
|---|---|
| Direct materials | $ 80 |
| Direct labor | 80 |
| Variable factory overhead | 52 |
| Fixed factory overhead | 68 |
| Total cost per unit | $280 |

If the make price of $280 is simply compared with the buy price of $240, the decision is to buy the instrument panel. However, if unused capacity could be used in manufacturing the part, only the variable factory overhead costs would increase.

The differential analysis for this make (Alternative 1) or buy (Alternative 2) decision is shown in Exhibit 5. The fixed factory overhead cannot be eliminated by purchasing the panels. Thus, both alternatives include the fixed factory overhead. The differential analysis indicates there is a loss of $28 per unit from buying the instrument panels. Thus, the instrument panels should be manufactured.

**EXHIBIT 5**

**Differential Analysis—Make or Buy Instrument Panels**

| | Differential Analysis<br>Make Panels (Alternative 1) or Buy Panels (Alternative 2)<br>February 15 | | |
| --- | --- | --- | --- |
| | **Make Panels<br>(Alternative 1)** | **Buy Panels<br>(Alternative 2)** | **Differential Effect<br>on Income<br>(Alternative 2)** |
| Unit costs: | | | |
| Purchase price ......................... | $ 0 | –$240 | –$240 |
| Direct materials ........................ | –80 | 0 | 80 |
| Direct labor ............................ | –80 | 0 | 80 |
| Variable factory overhead ............. | –52 | 0 | 52 |
| Fixed factory overhead ................ | –68 | –68 | 0 |
| Income (loss).......................... | –$280 | –$308 | –$ 28 |

Other factors should also be considered in the analysis. For example, productive capacity used to make the instrument panel would not be available for other production. The decision may also affect the future business relationship with the instrument panel supplier. For example, if the supplier provides other parts, the company's decision to make instrument panels might jeopardize the timely delivery of other parts.

**Example Exercise 25-3  Make or Buy**

A company manufactures a subcomponent of an assembly for $80 per unit, including fixed costs of $25 per unit. A proposal is offered to purchase the subcomponent from an outside source for $60 per unit, plus $5 per unit freight. Prepare a differential analysis dated November 2, to determine whether the company should make (Alternative 1) or buy (Alternative 2) the subcomponent, assuming fixed costs are unaffected by the decision.

**Follow My Example 25-3**

| | Differential Analysis<br>Make Subcomponent (Alternative 1) or Buy Subcomponent (Alternative 2)<br>November 2 | | |
| --- | --- | --- | --- |
| | **Make Subcomponent<br>(Alternative 1)** | **Buy Subcomponent<br>(Alternative 2)** | **Differential Effect<br>on Income<br>(Alternative 2)** |
| Unit costs: | | | |
| Purchase price ..................................... | $ 0 | –$60 | –$60 |
| Freight .............................................. | 0 | –5 | –5 |
| Variable costs ($80 – $25) ..................... | –55 | 0 | 55 |
| Fixed factory overhead......................... | –25 | –25 | 0 |
| Income (loss) ...................................... | –$80 | –$90 | –$10 |

The company should make the subcomponent.

Practice Exercises: PE 25-3A, PE 25-3B

## Replace Equipment

The usefulness of a fixed asset may decrease before it is worn out. For example, old equipment may no longer be as efficient as new equipment.

Differential analysis can be used for decisions to replace fixed assets such as equipment and machinery. The analysis normally focuses on the costs of continuing to use the old equipment versus replacing the equipment. The book value of the old equipment is a sunk cost and, thus, is irrelevant.

To illustrate, assume that on November 28 of the current year, a business is considering replacing an old machine with a new machine:

| | |
|---|---|
| Old Machine | |
| Book value | $100,000 |
| Estimated annual variable manufacturing costs | 225,000 |
| Estimated selling price | 25,000 |
| Estimated remaining useful life | 5 years |
| New Machine | |
| Purchase price of new machine | $250,000 |
| Estimated annual variable manufacturing costs | 150,000 |
| Estimated residual value | 0 |
| Estimated useful life | 5 years |

The differential analysis for whether to continue with the old machine (Alternative 1) or replace the old machine with a new machine (Alternative 2) is shown in Exhibit 6.

**EXHIBIT 6**

**Differential Analysis—Continue with or Replace Old Equipment**

**Differential Analysis**
**Continue with Old Machine (Alternative 1) or Replace Old Machine (Alternative 2)**
**November 28**

| | Continue with Old Machine (Alternative 1) | Replace Old Machine (Alternative 2) | Differential Effect on Income (Alternative 2) |
|---|---|---|---|
| Revenues: | | | |
| Proceeds from sale of old machine......... | $         0 | $    25,000 | $  25,000 |
| Costs: | | | |
| Purchase price ........................... | $         0 | –$  250,000 | –$250,000 |
| Variable manufacturing costs (5 years) ..... | –1,125,000 | –750,000 | 375,000 |
| Total costs................................ | –$1,125,000 | –$1,000,000 | $125,000 |
| Income (loss) ............................. | –$1,125,000 | –$  975,000 | $150,000 |

As shown in Exhibit 6, there is five-year differential effect on income of $150,000 (or $30,000 per year) from replacing the machine. Thus, the decision should be to purchase the new machine and sell the old machine.

Other factors are often important in equipment replacement decisions. For example, differences between the remaining useful life of the old equipment and the estimated life of the new equipment could exist. In addition, the new equipment might improve the overall quality of the product and, thus, increase sales.

The time value of money and other uses for the cash needed to purchase the new equipment could also affect the decision to replace equipment.[1] The revenue that is forgone from an alternative use of an asset, such as cash, is called an **opportunity cost**. Although the opportunity cost is not recorded in the accounting records, it is useful in analyzing alternative courses of action.

---

[1] The time value of money in purchasing equipment (capital assets) is discussed in Chapter 26.

### Example Exercise 25-4 Replace Equipment

A machine with a book value of $32,000 has an estimated four-year life. A proposal is offered to sell the old machine for $10,000 and replace it with a new machine at a cost of $45,000. The new machine has a four-year life with no residual value. The new machine would reduce annual direct labor costs from $33,000 to $22,000. Prepare a differential analysis dated October 7 on whether to continue with the old machine (Alternative 1) or replace the old machine (Alternative 2).

### Follow My Example 25-4

**Differential Analysis**
**Continue with Old Machine (Alternative 1) or Replace Old Machine (Alternative 2)**
**October 7**

| | Continue with Old Machine (Alternative 1) | Replace Old Machine (Alternative 2) | Differential Effect on Income (Alternative 2) |
|---|---|---|---|
| Revenues: | | | |
| Proceeds from sale of old machine.................... | $        0 | $  10,000 | $10,000 |
| Costs: | | | |
| Purchase price ............................................... | $        0 | –$  45,000 | –$45,000 |
| Direct labor (4 years)....................................... | –132,000* | –88,000** | 44,000 |
| Total costs..................................................... | –$132,000 | –$133,000 | –$  1,000 |
| Total income (loss)............................................ | –$132,000 | –$123,000 | $  9,000 |

\*$33,000 × 4 years
\*\*$22,000 × 4 years

The old machine should be sold and replaced with the new machine.

Practice Exercises: PE 25-4A, PE 25-4B

## Process or Sell

During manufacturing, a product normally progresses through various stages or processes. In some cases, a product can be sold at an intermediate stage of production, or it can be processed further and then sold.

Differential analysis can be used to decide whether to sell a product at an intermediate stage or to process it further. In doing so, the differential revenues and costs from further processing are compared. The costs of producing the intermediate product do not change, regardless of whether the intermediate product is sold or processed further.

To illustrate, assume that a business produces kerosene as an intermediate product as follows:

| Kerosene: | |
|---|---|
| Batch size | 4,000 gallons |
| Cost of producing kerosene | $2,400 per batch |
| Selling price | $2.50 per gallon |

The kerosene can be processed further to yield gasoline as follows:

| Gasoline: | |
|---|---|
| Input batch size | 4,000 gallons |
| Less evaporation (20%) | 800 (4,000 × 20%) |
| Output batch size | 3,200 gallons |
| | |
| Cost of producing gasoline | $3,050 per batch |
| Selling price | $3.50 per gallon |

Exhibit 7 shows the differential analysis dated October 1 for whether to sell kerosene (Alternative 1) or process it further into gasoline (Alternative 2).

As shown in Exhibit 7, there is additional income of $550 per batch from further processing the kerosene into gasoline. Therefore, the decision should be to process the kerosene further into gasoline.

EXHIBIT 7

Differential
Analysis—Sell
Kerosene or Process
Further into Gasoline

**Differential Analysis**
**Sell Kerosene (Alternative 1) or Process Further into Gasoline (Alternative 2)**
**October 1**

| | Sell Kerosene (Alternative 1) | Process Further into Gasoline (Alternative 2) | Differential Effect on Income (Alternative 2) |
|---|---|---|---|
| Revenues........................... | $10,000* | $11,200** | $1,200 |
| Costs .............................. | –2,400 | –3,050 | –650 |
| Income (loss) ..................... | $ 7,600 | $ 8,150 | $ 550 |

*4,000 gallons × $2.50
**(4,000 gallons – 800 gallons) × $3.50

## Example Exercise 25-5  Process or Sell

Product T is produced for $2.50 per gallon. Product T can be sold without additional processing for $3.50 per gallon, or processed further into Product V at an additional total cost of $0.70 per gallon. Product V can be sold for $4.00 per gallon. Prepare a differential analysis dated April 8 on whether to sell Product T (Alternative 1) or process it further into Product V (Alternative 2).

### Follow My Example 25-5

**Differential Analysis**
**Sell Product T (Alternative 1) or Process Further into Product V (Alternative 2)**
**April 8**

| | Sell Product T (Alternative 1) | Process Further into Product V (Alternative 2) | Differential Effect on Income (Alternative 2) |
|---|---|---|---|
| Revenues, per unit....................................... | $3.50 | $4.00 | $0.50 |
| Costs, per unit............................................. | –2.50 | –3.20* | –0.70 |
| Income (loss), per unit................................. | $1.00 | $0.80 | –$0.20 |

*$2.50 + $0.70

The decision should be to sell Product T.

Practice Exercises: PE 25-5A, PE 25-5B

## Accept Business at a Special Price

A company may be offered the opportunity to sell its products at prices other than normal prices. For example, an exporter may offer to sell a company's products overseas at special discount prices.

Differential analysis can be used to decide whether to accept additional business at a special price. The differential revenue from accepting the additional business is compared to the differential costs of producing and delivering the product to the customer.

The differential costs of accepting additional business depend on whether the company is operating at less than capacity. If the company is operating at less than full capacity, then the additional production does not increase fixed manufacturing costs. However, selling and administrative expenses may change because of the additional business.

To illustrate, assume that B-Ball Inc. manufactures basketballs as follows:

| | |
|---|---|
| Monthly productive capacity | 12,500 basketballs |
| Current monthly sales | 10,000 basketballs |
| Normal (domestic) selling price | $30.00 per basketball |
| Manufacturing costs: | |
| Variable costs | $12.50 per basketball |
| Fixed costs | 7.50 |
| Total | $20.00 per basketball |

On March 10 of the current year, B-Ball Inc. received an offer from an exporter for 5,000 basketballs at $18 each. Production can be spread over three months without interfering with normal production or incurring overtime costs. Pricing policies in the domestic market will not be affected.

As shown in Exhibit 8, a differential analysis on whether to reject the order (Alternative 1) or accept the order (Alternative 2) shows that the special order should be accepted. The special business is accepted even though the sales price of $18 per unit is less than the manufacturing cost of $20 per unit because the fixed costs are not affected by the decision and are, thus, omitted from the analysis.

---

**EXHIBIT 8**

**Differential Analysis—Accept Business at a Special Price**

| Differential Analysis<br>Reject Order (Alternative 1) or Accept Order (Alternative 2)<br>March 10 | | | |
|---|---|---|---|
| | **Reject Order<br>(Alternative 1)** | **Accept Order<br>(Alternative 2)** | **Differential<br>Effect on Income<br>(Alternative 2)** |
| Revenues................................. | $0 | $90,000* | $90,000 |
| Costs: | | | |
| Variable manufacturing costs........... | 0 | −62,500** | −62,500 |
| Income (loss) ............................. | $0 | $27,500 | $27,500 |

  *5,000 units × $18
**5,000 units × $12.50 variable cost per unit

---

Proposals to sell products at special prices often require additional considerations. For example, special prices in one geographic area may result in price reductions in other areas, with the result that total company sales revenues decrease. Manufacturers must also conform to the Robinson-Patman Act, which prohibits price discrimination within the United States unless price differences can be justified by different costs.

## Business Connection

### 60% OFF!

Priceline.com Inc. was founded in the late 1990s and has become a successful survivor of the Internet revolution. Priceline offers deep discounts of up to 60% for travel services, such as hotels and travel. How does it work? For hotel services, Priceline has arrangements with hotels to provide deeply discounted rooms. These rooms are resold to customers on Priceline's Web site.

Why do hotels provide rooms at such a large discount? If the hotel has unused rooms, the variable cost of an incremental guest is low relative to the fixed cost of the room. Thus, during low occupancy times, any price greater than the variable cost of providing the room can add to the profitability of the hotel. Thus, hotels view Priceline as an additional source of profit from filling unused rooms during low demand periods.

## Example Exercise 25-6  Accept Business at Special Price

Product D is normally sold for $4.40 per unit. A special price of $3.60 is offered for the export market. The variable production cost is $3.00 per unit. An additional export tariff of 10% of revenue must be paid for all export products. Assume there is sufficient capacity for the special order. Prepare a differential analysis dated January 14 on whether to reject (Alternative 1) or accept (Alternative 2) the special order.

### Follow My Example 25-6

**Differential Analysis**
**Reject Order (Alternative 1) or Accept Order (Alternative 2)**
**January 14**

|  | Reject Order (Alternative 1) | Accept Order (Alternative 2) | Differential Effect on Income (Alternative 2) |
|---|---|---|---|
| Per unit: |  |  |  |
| Revenues ............................................................ | $0 | $3.60 | $3.60 |
| Costs: |  |  |  |
|    Variable manufacturing costs ............................ | $0 | –$3.00 | –$3.00 |
|    Export tariff ................................................ | 0 | –0.36* | –0.36 |
|    Total costs..................................................... | $0 | –$3.36 | –$3.36 |
| Income (loss) ...................................................... | $0 | $0.24 | $0.24 |

*$3.60 × 10%

The special order should be accepted.

Practice Exercises: PE 25-6A, PE 25-6B

# Setting Normal Product Selling Prices

**OBJ 2** Determine the selling price of a product, using the product cost concept.

The *normal* selling price is the target selling price to be achieved in the long term. The normal selling price must be set high enough to cover all costs and expenses (fixed and variable) and provide a reasonable profit. Otherwise, the business will not survive.

In contrast, in deciding whether to accept additional business at a special price, only differential costs are considered. Any price greater than the differential costs will increase profits in the short term. However, in the long term, products are sold at normal prices rather than special prices.

Managers can use one of two market methods to determine selling price:

• Demand-based concept
• Competition-based concept

The demand-based concept sets the price according to the demand for the product. If there is high demand for the product, then the price is set high. Likewise, if there is a low demand for the product, then the price is set low.

The competition-based concept sets the price according to the price offered by competitors. For example, if a competitor reduces the price, then management adjusts the price to meet the competition. The market-based pricing approaches are discussed in greater detail in marketing courses.

Managers can also use one of three cost-plus methods to determine the selling price:

• Product cost concept
• Total cost concept
• Variable cost concept

The product cost concept is illustrated in this section. The total cost and variable cost concepts are illustrated in the appendix to this chapter.

## Service ⬛ Focus

### REVENUE MANAGEMENT

Did you know that it is common to sit next to a person on a flight who paid much more for that seat than you did for yours (or vice versa)? While this may not seem fair, this practice is consistent with a type of differential analysis called revenue management. Revenue management strives to yield the maximum amount of profit from a perishable good. Examples of perishable goods in service include a seat on a flight, a hotel room for a given night, a ticket for a given event, or a cruise ship berth for a given voyage. The service is perishable because, once the date passes, the "product" expires.

Consider Delta Air Lines. Delta maximizes the profitability on a given flight by taking into account different customer behaviors and preferences. For example, a business person may pay a very high price for an airline ticket booked one day in advance to attend an emergency meeting. Next to her may be a college student on the same flight who booked two month's in advance at a very low price. The difference in behavior yields a different price. The airline sells early bookings at very favorable prices to fill out the flight. However, late emergency business bookings are priced high because the inventory of seats have diminished and, thus, have become valuable. However, if too many seats remain unoccupied very close to the flight time, the airline may release them at deep discounts to standby passengers to fill the flight. Thus, the flight is filled with different priced seats for different customers, all in attempt to fill the flight as profitably as possible.

## Product Cost Concept

Cost-plus methods determine the normal selling price by estimating a cost amount per unit and adding a markup, computed as follows:

$$\text{Normal Selling Price} = \text{Cost Amount per Unit} + \text{Markup}$$

Management determines the markup based on the desired profit for the product. The markup should be sufficient to earn the desired profit plus cover any costs and expenses that are not included in the cost amount.

As shown in Exhibit 9, under the **product cost concept**, only the costs of manufacturing the product, termed the *product costs,* are included in the cost amount per unit to which the markup is added. Estimated selling expenses, administrative expenses, and desired profit are included in the markup. The markup per unit is then computed and added to the product cost per unit to determine the normal selling price.

**EXHIBIT 9**

**Product Cost Concept**

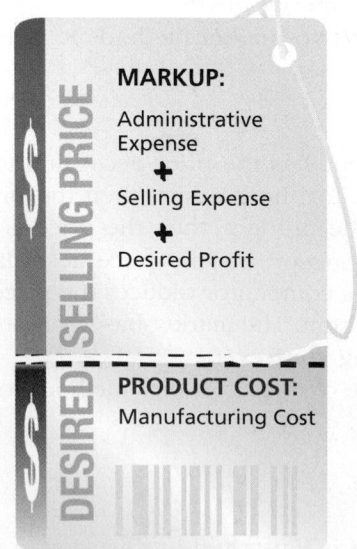

MARKUP:
Administrative Expense
+
Selling Expense
+
Desired Profit

PRODUCT COST:
Manufacturing Cost

The product cost concept is applied using the following steps:

- Step 1.   Estimate the total product costs as follows:

| | |
|---|---|
| Product costs: | |
| Direct materials | $XXX |
| Direct labor | XXX |
| Factory overhead | XXX |
| Total product cost | $XXX |

- Step 2.   Estimate the total selling and administrative expenses.
- Step 3.   Divide the total product cost by the number of units expected to be produced and sold to determine the total product cost per unit, computed as follows:

$$\text{Product Cost per Unit} = \frac{\text{Total Product Cost}}{\text{Estimated Units Produced and Sold}}$$

- Step 4.   Compute the markup percentage as follows:

$$\text{Markup Percentage} = \frac{\text{Desired Profit} + \text{Total Selling and Administrative Expenses}}{\text{Total Product Cost}}$$

The numerator of the markup percentage is the desired profit plus the total selling and administrative expenses. These expenses must be included in the markup percentage because they are not included in the cost amount to which the markup is added.

The desired profit is normally computed based on a rate of return on assets as follows:

$$\text{Desired Profit} = \text{Desired Rate of Return} \times \text{Total Assets}$$

- Step 5.   Determine the markup per unit by multiplying the markup percentage times the product cost per unit as follows:

$$\text{Markup per Unit} = \text{Markup Percentage} \times \text{Product Cost per Unit}$$

- Step 6.   Determine the normal selling price by adding the markup per unit to the product cost per unit as follows:

| | |
|---|---|
| Product cost per unit | $XXX |
| Markup per unit | XXX |
| Normal selling price per unit | $XXX |

To illustrate, assume the following data for 100,000 calculators that Digital Solutions Inc. expects to produce and sell during the current year:

| | |
|---|---|
| Manufacturing costs: | |
| Direct materials ($3.00 × 100,000) | $ 300,000 |
| Direct labor ($10.00 × 100,000) | 1,000,000 |
| Factory overhead | 200,000 |
| Total manufacturing costs | $1,500,000 |
| Selling and administrative expenses | 170,000 |
| Total cost | $1,670,000 |
| Total assets | $800,000 |
| Desired rate of return | 20% |

The normal selling price of $18.30 is determined under the product cost concept as follows:

- Step 1.   Total product cost: $1,500,000
- Step 2.   Total selling and administrative expenses: $170,000
- Step 3.   Total product cost per unit: $15.00

$$\text{Total Cost per Unit} = \frac{\text{Total Product Cost}}{\text{Estimated Units Produced and Sold}} = \frac{\$1,500,000}{100,000 \text{ units}} = \$15.00 \text{ per unit}$$

- Step 4.   Markup percentage: 22%

$$\text{Desired Profit} = \text{Desired Rate of Return} \times \text{Total Assets} = 20\% \times \$800,000 = \$160,000$$

$$\text{Markup Percentage} = \frac{\text{Desired Profit} + \text{Total Selling and Administrative Expenses}}{\text{Total Product Cost}}$$

$$= \frac{\$160,000 + \$170,000}{\$1,500,000} = \frac{\$330,000}{\$1,500,000} = 22\%$$

- Step 5.   Markup per unit: $3.30

$$\text{Markup per Unit} = \text{Markup Percentage} \times \text{Product Cost per Unit}$$
$$= 22\% \times \$15.00 = \$3.30 \text{ per unit}$$

- Step 6.   Normal selling price: $18.30

| | |
|---|---:|
| Total product cost per unit | $15.00 |
| Markup per unit | 3.30 |
| Normal selling price per unit | $18.30 |

Product cost estimates, rather than actual costs, may be used in computing the markup. Management should be careful, however, when using estimated or standard costs in applying the cost-plus approach. Specifically, estimates should be based on normal (attainable) operating levels and not theoretical (ideal) levels of performance. In product pricing, the use of estimates based on ideal operating performance could lead to setting product prices too low.

## Example Exercise 25-7  Product Cost Markup Percentage

Apex Corporation produces and sells Product Z at a total cost of $30 per unit, of which $20 is product cost and $10 is selling and administrative expenses. In addition, the total cost of $30 is made up of $18 variable cost and $12 fixed cost. The desired profit is $3 per unit. Determine the markup percentage on product cost.

## Follow My Example 25-7

Markup percentage on product cost: $\dfrac{\$3 + \$10}{\$20} = 65\%$

.................................................................................................................

Practice Exercises: PE 25-7A, PE 25-7B

# Integrity, Objectivity, and Ethics in Business

### PRICE FIXING

Federal law prevents companies competing in similar markets from sharing cost and price information, or what is commonly termed "price fixing." For example, the Federal Trade Commission (FTC) brought a suit against **U-Haul** for releasing company-wide memorandums to its managers telling them to encourage competitors to match U-Haul price increases. Commenting on the case, the chairman of the FTC stated, "It's a bedrock principle that you can't conspire with your competitors to fix prices, and shouldn't even try."

Source: Edward Wyatt, "U-Haul to Settle with Trade Agency in Case on Truck Rental Price-Fixing," *The New York Times*, June 10, 2010, p. B3.

## Target Costing

**Target costing** is a method of setting prices that combines market-based pricing with a cost-reduction emphasis. Under target costing, a future selling price is anticipated, using the demand-based or the competition-based concepts. The target cost is then determined by subtracting a desired profit from the expected selling price, computed as follows:

Target Cost = Expected Selling Price − Desired Profit

Target costing tries to reduce costs as shown in Exhibit 10. The bar at the left in Exhibit 10 shows the actual cost and profit that can be earned during the current period. The bar at the right shows that the market price is expected to decline in the future. The target cost is estimated as the difference between the expected market price and the desired profit.

The target cost is normally less than the current cost. Thus, managers must try to reduce costs from the design and manufacture of the product. The planned cost reduction is sometimes referred to as the cost drift. Costs can be reduced in a variety of ways such as the following:

- Simplifying the design
- Reducing the cost of direct materials
- Reducing the direct labor costs
- Eliminating waste

Target costing is especially useful in highly competitive markets such as the market for personal computers. Such markets require continual product cost reductions to remain competitive.

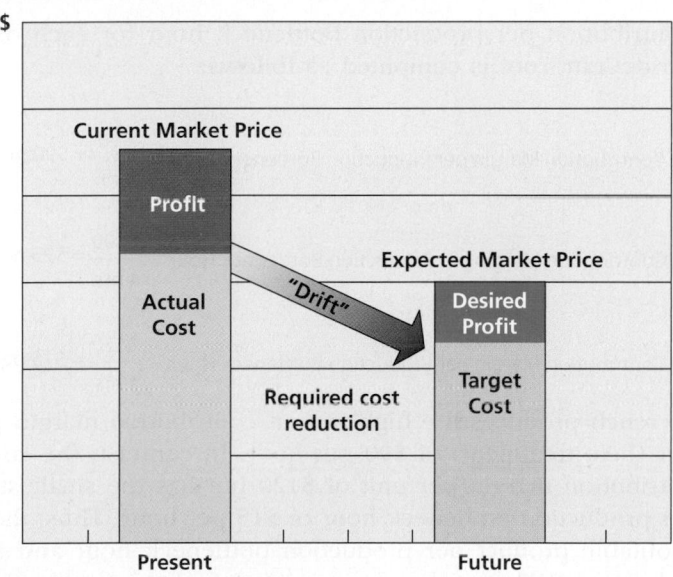

**EXHIBIT 10**

**Target Cost Concept**

# Production Bottlenecks

OBJ **3** Compute the relative profitability of products in bottleneck production processes.

A **production bottleneck** (or *constraint*) is a point in the manufacturing process where the demand for the company's product exceeds the ability to produce the product. The **theory of constraints (TOC)** is a manufacturing strategy that focuses on reducing the influence of bottlenecks on production processes.

When a company has a production bottleneck in its production process, it should attempt to maximize its profits, subject to the production bottleneck. In doing so, the unit contribution margin of each product per production bottleneck constraint is used.

To illustrate, assume that PrideCraft Tool Company makes three types of wrenches: small, medium, and large. All three products are processed through a heat treatment operation, which hardens the steel tools. PrideCraft Tool's heat treatment process is operating at full capacity and is a production bottleneck. The product unit contribution margin and the number of hours of heat treatment used by each type of wrench are as follows:

| | Small Wrench | Medium Wrench | Large Wrench |
|---|---|---|---|
| Unit selling price | $130 | $140 | $160 |
| Unit variable cost | 40 | 40 | 40 |
| Unit contribution margin | $ 90 | $100 | $120 |
| Heat treatment hours per unit | 1 hr. | 4 hrs. | 8 hrs. |

The large wrench appears to be the most profitable product because its unit contribution margin of $120 is the greatest. However, the unit contribution margin can be misleading in a production bottleneck operation.

In a production bottleneck operation, the best measure of profitability is the unit contribution margin per production bottleneck constraint. For PrideCraft Tool, the production bottleneck constraint is heat treatment process hours. Therefore, the unit contribution margin per bottleneck constraint is expressed as follows:

$$\text{Unit Contribution Margin per Production Bottleneck Hour} = \frac{\text{Unit Contribution Margin}}{\text{Heat Treatment Hours per Unit}}$$

The unit contribution per production bottleneck hour for each of the wrenches produced by PrideCraft Tool is computed as follows:

Small Wrenches

$$\text{Unit Contribution Margin per Production Bottleneck Hour} = \frac{\$90}{1 \text{ hr.}} = \$90 \text{ per hr.}$$

Medium Wrenches

$$\text{Unit Contribution Margin per Production Bottleneck Hour} = \frac{\$100}{4 \text{ hrs.}} = \$25 \text{ per hr.}$$

Large Wrenches

$$\text{Unit Contribution Margin per Production Bottleneck Hour} = \frac{\$120}{8 \text{ hrs.}} = \$15 \text{ per hr.}$$

The small wrench produces the highest unit contribution margin per production bottleneck hour (heat treatment) of $90 per hour. In contrast, the large wrench has the largest contribution margin per unit of $120 but has the smallest unit contribution margin per production bottleneck hour of $15 per hour. Thus, the small wrench is the most profitable product per production bottleneck hour and is the one that should be emphasized in the market.

**Example Exercise 25-8  Bottleneck Profit**  OBJ 3

Product A has a unit contribution margin of $15. Product B has a unit contribution margin of $20. Product A requires three furnace hours, while Product B requires five furnace hours. Determine the most profitable product, assuming the furnace is a constraint.

**Follow My Example 25-8**

| | Product A | Product B |
|---|---|---|
| Unit contribution margin......................................................................... | $15 | $20 |
| Furnace hours per unit.............................................................................. | ÷ 3 | ÷ 5 |
| Unit contribution margin per production bottleneck hour.......................... | $ 5 | $ 4 |

Product A is the most profitable in using bottleneck resources.

Practice Exercises: PE 25-8A, PE 25-8B

# Activity-Based Costing Method

**OBJ 4** Allocate product costs using activity-based costing.

Normal product prices can be computed from a markup on product cost, as illustrated earlier in this chapter. Product cost is the sum of direct material, direct labor, and factory overhead. In Chapter 19, factory overhead was allocated to products (jobs), using a predetermined factory overhead rate. This rate was computed as follows:

$$\text{Predetermined Factory Overhead Rate} = \frac{\text{Estimated Total Factory Overhead Costs}}{\text{Estimated Activity Base}}$$

The use of a single, predetermined factory overhead rate may, however, allocate factory overhead inaccurately. In such cases, normal product prices based on product cost markup may also be inaccurate. This may occur in manufacturing operations involving more than one product. In such cases, each product may use different types of factory overhead in different ways. Under such conditions, a single factory overhead rate will distort factory overhead allocation.

**Activity-based costing (ABC)** identifies and traces costs and expenses to activities and then to specific products. The ABC method is an alternative approach for allocating factory overhead when there are diverse products and processes. ABC uses multiple factory overhead rates based on activities. **Activities** are the types of work, or actions, involved in a manufacturing process or service activity. For example, assembly, inspection, and engineering design are activities.

## Estimated Activity Costs

ABC initially assigns estimated factory overhead costs to activities, resulting in estimated activity costs. To illustrate, assume that Ruiz Company produces snowmobiles and riding mowers. The overhead activities used in producing each product are as follows:

- *Fabrication,* which consists of cutting metal to shape the product. This activity is machine intensive.
- *Assembly,* which consists of manually assembling machined pieces into a final product. This activity is labor intensive.
- *Setup,* which consists of changing the characteristics of a machine to produce a different product. Each production run requires a **setup**.
- *Quality-control inspections,* which consist of inspecting the product for conformance to specifications. Inspection requires product tear-down and reassembly.
- *Engineering changes,* which consist of processing changes in design or process specifications for a product. The document that initiates changing a product or process is called an **engineering change order (ECO)**.

Ruiz Company's total estimated factory overhead of $1,600,000 is assigned to each activity as shown in Exhibit 11.

| Activity | Estimated Activity Cost |
|---|---|
| Fabrication | $ 530,000 |
| Assembly | 70,000 |
| Setup | 480,000 |
| Quality-control inspection | 312,000 |
| Engineering changes | 208,000 |
| Total estimated activity costs | $1,600,000 |

**EXHIBIT 11**

**Estimated Activity Costs**

## Activity Rates

The estimated activity costs are allocated to products using an **activity rate**. Activity rates are determined as follows:

$$\text{Activity Rate} = \frac{\text{Estimated Activity Cost}}{\text{Estimated Activity-Base Usage}}$$

The **activity base** is a measure of physical activity for each activity. For example, the activity base for the setup activity is the number of setups. The activity-base *usage* is the number of setups estimated to be used by the operations.

As shown in Exhibit 11, the estimated activity cost for setups is $480,000. Assume the activity-base usage for the setup activity is estimated to be 120 setups. The setup activity rate is $4,000 per setup, computed as follows:

$$\text{Setup Activity Rate} = \frac{\$480,000}{120 \text{ setups}} = \$4,000 \text{ per setup}$$

The estimated activity-base usage for each activity is shown in Exhibit 12.

---

**EXHIBIT 12**

**Ruiz Company Activity-Base Usage**

| Activity Base | Estimated Activity-Base Usage by Product | | Total Estimated Activity-Base Usage |
|---|---|---|---|
| | **Snowmobile** | **Riding Mower** | **Usage** |
| Number of fabrication direct labor hours | 8,000 dlh | 2,000 dlh | 10,000 dlh |
| Number of assembly direct labor hours | 2,000 dlh | 8,000 dlh | 10,000 dlh |
| Number of setups | 100 setups | 20 setups | 120 setups |
| Number of quality-control inspections | 100 insp. | 4 insp. | 104 insp. |
| Number of engineering change orders | 12 ECOs | 4 ECOs | 16 ECOs |

---

The activity rates for each activity are determined by dividing the estimated activity cost in Exhibit 11 by the total estimated activity-base usage for each activity in Exhibit 12. The activity rates for Ruiz Company are computed in Exhibit 13.

---

**EXHIBIT 13**

**Activity Rates—Ruiz Company**

| Activity | Estimated Activity Cost | ÷ | Estimated Activity-Base Usage | = | Activity Rate |
|---|---|---|---|---|---|
| Fabrication | $530,000 | ÷ | 10,000 direct labor hours | = | $53 per direct labor hour |
| Assembly | $ 70,000 | ÷ | 10,000 direct labor hours | = | $7 per direct labor hour |
| Setup | $480,000 | ÷ | 120 setups | = | $4,000 per setup |
| Quality-control inspection | $312,000 | ÷ | 104 inspections | = | $3,000 per inspection |
| Engineering changes | $208,000 | ÷ | 16 engineering changes | = | $13,000 per engineering change order |

---

## Overhead Allocation

The estimated activity costs are allocated to the snowmobiles and riding mowers by using the following equation for each product:

$$\text{Activity-Base Usage} \times \text{Activity Rate} = \text{Activity Cost}$$

The sum of these activity costs for each product is the total factory overhead cost for the product. This amount is divided by the total number of units produced to determine the factory overhead cost per unit. These computations are shown in Exhibit 14 for Ruiz Company.

**EXHIBIT 14**    **Activity-Based Product Cost Calculations**

| | A | B | C | D | E | F | G | H | I | J | K | L |
|---|---|---|---|---|---|---|---|---|---|---|---|---|
| 1 | | | | Snowmobile | | | | | | Riding Mower | | |
| 2 | | Activity- | | Activity | | Activity | | Activity- | | Activity | | Activity |
| 3 | Activity | Base Usage | × | Rate | = | Cost | | Base Usage | × | Rate | = | Cost |
| 4 | | | | | | | | | | | | |
| 5 | Fabrication | 8,000 dlh | | $53/dlh | | $ 424,000 | | 2,000 dlh | | $53/dlh | | $106,000 |
| 6 | Assembly | 2,000 dlh | | $7/dlh | | 14,000 | | 8,000 dlh | | $7/dlh | | 56,000 |
| 7 | Setup | 100 setups | | $4,000/setup | | 400,000 | | 20 setups | | $4,000/setup | | 80,000 |
| 8 | Quality-control | | | | | | | | | | | |
| 9 | inspections | 100 insp. | | $3,000/insp. | | 300,000 | | 4 insp. | | $3,000/insp. | | 12,000 |
| 10 | Engineering | | | | | | | | | | | |
| 11 | changes | 12 ECOs | | $13,000/ECO | | 156,000 | | 4 ECOs | | $13,000/ECO | | 52,000 |
| 12 | Total factory | | | | | | | | | | | |
| 13 | overhead cost | | | | | $1,294,000 | | | | | | $306,000 |
| 14 | Budgeted units | | | | | | | | | | | |
| 15 | of production | | | | | ÷ 1,000 | | | | | | ÷ 1,000 |
| 16 | Factory overhead | | | | | | | | | | | |
| 17 | cost per unit | | | | | $ 1,294 | | | | | | $ 306 |

The allocation of factory overhead using the ABC method for Ruiz Company is illustrated in Exhibit 15.

**EXHIBIT 15**    **Activity-Based Costing Method—Ruiz Company**

## Dangers of Product Cost Distortion

The allocation of factory overhead affects the accuracy of product costs. In turn, product costs are used for decisions such as establishing product price and determining whether to discontinue a product line.

Using an inappropriate factory overhead allocation method can lead to distorted product costs. To illustrate, assume that Ruiz Company used a single predetermined factory overhead rate to allocate factory overhead to the riding mower and snowmobile. Assume that total estimated factory overhead was allocated using direct labor hours. The single predetermined factory overhead rate for Ruiz is computed as follows:

$$\text{Predetermined Factory Overhead Rate} = \frac{\text{Estimated Total Factory Overhead Costs}}{\text{Estimated Activity Base}}$$

$$= \frac{\$1,600,000}{20,000 \text{ direct labor hours}}$$

$$= \$80 \text{ per direct labor hour}$$

Using this rate, riding mowers and snowmobiles are each allocated $800,000 of factory overhead ($80 per direct labor hour × 10,000 direct labor hours), or $800 per unit ($800,000 ÷ 1,000 units). Under the single predetermined factory overhead rate method, each product is allocated the same factory overhead. This is because riding mowers and snowmobiles consume the same amount of direct labor hours.

However, the snowmobiles and riding mowers do not consume setup, quality-control inspection, and engineering change activities in proportion to direct labor hours. For example, each snowmobile consumes more of these activities than does the riding mower, even though each product is budgeted for 10,000 direct labor hours.

As a result, under activity-based costing, factory overhead of $1,294 was allocated to each snowmobile and factory overhead of $306 was allocated to each riding mower (see Exhibit 14). Thus, a single predetermined factory overhead rate distorts the factory overhead allocation, and thus the product cost, of snowmobiles and riding mowers as follows:

|  | Factory Overhead per Unit | |
| --- | --- | --- |
|  | Single-Rate Method | ABC Method |
| Snowmobile | $800 | $1,294 |
| Riding mower | 800 | 306 |

As shown, activity-based costing better allocates factory overhead by recognizing differences in how each product uses factory overhead activities. As a result of more accurate product costs, management can make better decisions with respect to pricing, product discontinuance, and other strategic decisions.

## Example Exercise 25-9 Activity-Based Costing
**OBJ 4**

Thor Company has total estimated factory overhead for the year of $600,000, divided into four activities: fabrication, $300,000; assembly, $120,000; setup, $100,000; and materials handling, $80,000. Thor manufactures two products: snowboards and skis. The activity-base usage quantities for each product by each activity are as follows:

|  | Fabrication | Assembly | Setup | Materials Handling |
| --- | --- | --- | --- | --- |
| Snowboards | 5,000 dlh | 15,000 dlh | 30 setups | 50 moves |
| Skis | 15,000 | 5,000 | 220 | 350 |
|  | 20,000 dlh | 20,000 dlh | 250 setups | 400 moves |

Each product is budgeted for 5,000 units of production for the year. Determine (a) the activity rates for each activity and (b) the factory overhead cost per unit for each product, using activity-based costing.

## Follow My Example 25-9

a. Fabrication:     $300,000 ÷ 20,000 direct labor hours = $15 per dlh
   Assembly:      $120,000 ÷ 20,000 direct labor hours = $6 per dlh
   Setup:          $100,000 ÷ 250 setups = $400 per setup
   Materials handling:  $80,000 ÷ 400 moves = $200 per move

b.

| | A | B | C | D | E | F | G | H | I | J | K | L |
| --- | --- | --- | --- | --- | --- | --- | --- | --- | --- | --- | --- | --- |
| 1 | | | | Snowboards | | | | | | Skis | | |
| 2 | | Activity-Base | | Activity | | Activity | | Activity-Base | | Activity | | Activity |
| 3 | Activity | Usage | x | Rate | = | Cost | | Usage | x | Rate | = | Cost |
| 4 | | | | | | | | | | | | |
| 5 | Fabrication | 5,000 dlh | | $15/dlh | | $ 75,000 | | 15,000 dlh | | $15/dlh | | $ 225,000 |
| 6 | Assembly | 15,000 dlh | | $6/dlh | | 90,000 | | 5,000 dlh | | $6/dlh | | 30,000 |
| 7 | Setup | 30 setups | | $400/setup | | 12,000 | | 220 setups | | $400/setup | | 88,000 |
| 8 | Materials handling | 50 moves | | $200/move | | 10,000 | | 350 moves | | $200/move | | 70,000 |
| 9 | Total | | | | | $ 187,000 | | | | | | $ 413,000 |
| 10 | Budgeted units | | | | | ÷ 5,000 | | | | | | ÷ 5,000 |
| 11 | Factory overhead | | | | | | | | | | | |
| 12 | per unit | | | | | $ 37.40 | | | | | | $ 82.60 |

Practice Exercises: PE 25-9A, PE 25-9B

# A P P E N D I X

# Total and Variable Cost Concepts to Setting Normal Price

Recall from the chapter that cost-plus methods determine the normal selling price by estimating a cost amount per unit and adding a markup, as follows:

Normal Selling Price = Cost Amount per Unit + Markup

Management determines the markup based on the desired profit for the product. The markup should be sufficient to earn the desired profit plus cover any cost and expenses that are not included in the cost amount. The product cost concept was discussed in the chapter, and the total and variable cost concepts are discussed in this appendix.

## Total Cost Concept

As shown in Exhibit 16, under the **total cost concept**, manufacturing cost plus the selling and administrative expenses are included in the total cost per unit. The markup per unit is then computed and added to the total cost per unit to determine the normal selling price.

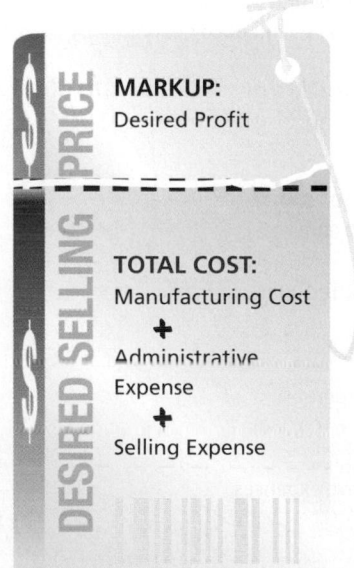

**EXHIBIT 16**

**Total Cost Concept**

The total cost concept is applied using the following steps:

- Step 1. Estimate the total manufacturing cost as follows:

| Manufacturing costs: | |
|---|---|
| Direct materials | $XXX |
| Direct labor | XXX |
| Factory overhead | XXX |
| Total manufacturing cost | $XXX |

- Step 2. Estimate the total selling and administrative expenses.
- Step 3. Estimate the total cost as follows:

| | |
|---|---|
| Total manufacturing costs | $XXX |
| Selling and administrative expenses | XXX |
| Total cost | $XXX |

- Step 4. Divide the total cost by the number of units expected to be produced and sold to determine the total cost per unit, as follows:

$$\text{Total Cost per Unit} = \frac{\text{Total Cost}}{\text{Estimated Units Produced and Sold}}$$

- Step 5. Compute the markup percentage as follows:

$$\text{Markup Percentage} = \frac{\text{Desired Profit}}{\text{Total Cost}}$$

The desired profit is normally computed based on a rate of return on assets as follows:

$$\text{Desired Profit} = \text{Desired Rate of Return} \times \text{Total Assets}$$

- Step 6. Determine the markup per unit by multiplying the markup percentage times the total cost per unit as follows:

$$\text{Markup per Unit} = \text{Markup Percentage} \times \text{Total Cost per Unit}$$

- Step 7. Determine the normal selling price by adding the markup per unit to the total cost per unit as follows:

| | |
|---|---|
| Total cost per unit | $XXX |
| Markup per unit | XXX |
| Normal selling price per unit | $XXX |

To illustrate, assume the following data for 100,000 calculators that Digital Solutions Inc. expects to produce and sell during 2016:

| | | |
|---|---|---|
| Manufacturing costs: | | |
| Direct materials ($3.00 × 100,000) | | $ 300,000 |
| Direct labor ($10.00 × 100,000) | | 1,000,000 |
| Factory overhead: | | |
| Variable costs ($1.50 × 100,000) | $150,000 | |
| Fixed costs | 50,000 | 200,000 |
| Total manufacturing cost | | $1,500,000 |
| | | |
| Selling and administrative expenses: | | |
| Variable expenses ($1.50 × 100,000) | $150,000 | |
| Fixed costs | 20,000 | |
| Total selling and administrative expenses | | 170,000 |
| Total cost | | $1,670,000 |
| Desired rate of return | | 20% |
| Total assets | | $ 800,000 |

Using the total cost concept, the normal selling price of $18.30 is determined as follows:

- Step 1. Total manufacturing cost: $1,500,000
- Step 2. Total selling and administrative expenses: $170,000
- Step 3. Total cost: $1,670,000
- Step 4. Total cost per unit: $16.70

$$\text{Total Cost per Unit} = \frac{\text{Total Cost}}{\text{Estimated Units Produced and Sold}} = \frac{\$1,670,000}{100,000 \text{ units}} = \$16.70 \text{ per unit}$$

- Step 5. Markup percentage: 9.6% (rounded)

Desired Profit = Desired Rate of Return × Total Assets = 20% × $800,000 = $160,000

$$\text{Markup Percentage} = \frac{\text{Desired Profit}}{\text{Total Cost}} = \frac{\$160,000}{\$1,670,000} = 9.6\% \text{ (rounded)}$$

- Step 6. Markup per unit: $1.60

Markup per Unit = Markup Percentage × Total Cost per Unit
= 9.6% × $16.70 = $1.60 per unit

- Step 7. Normal selling price: $18.30

| | |
|---|---|
| Total cost per unit | $16.70 |
| Markup per unit | 1.60 |
| Normal selling price per unit | $18.30 |

The ability of the selling price of $18.30 to generate the desired profit of $160,000 is illustrated by the income statement that follows:

**Digital Solutions Inc.**
**Income Statement**
**For the Year Ended December 31, 2016**

| | | |
|---|---|---|
| Sales (100,000 units × $18.30)...................................... | | $1,830,000 |
| Expenses: | | |
| Variable (100,000 units × $16.00) ,............................ | $1,600,000 | |
| Fixed ($50,000 + $20,000) ..................................... | 70,000 | 1,670,000 |
| Income from operations .......................................... | | $ 160,000 |

The total cost concept is often used by contractors who sell products to government agencies. This is because in many cases government contractors are required by law to be reimbursed for their products on a total-cost-plus-profit basis.

## Variable Cost Concept

As shown in Exhibit 17, under the **variable cost concept**, only variable costs are included in the cost amount per unit to which the markup is added. All variable

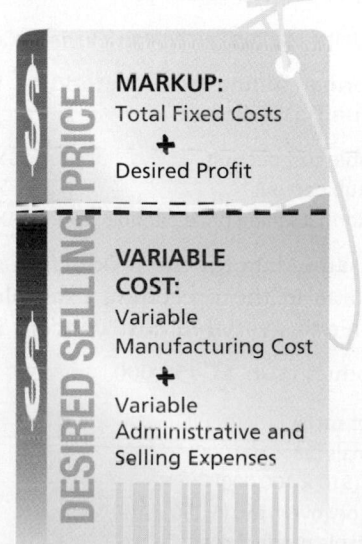

**EXHIBIT 17**

**Variable Cost Concept**

manufacturing costs, as well as variable selling and administrative expenses, are included in the cost amount. Fixed manufacturing costs, fixed selling and administrative expenses, and desired profit are included in the markup. The markup per unit is then added to the variable cost per unit to determine the normal selling price.

The variable cost concept is applied using the following steps:

- Step 1.  Estimate the total variable product cost as follows:

| Variable product costs: | |
| --- | --- |
| Direct materials | $XXX |
| Direct labor | XXX |
| Variable factory overhead | XXX |
| Total variable product cost | $XXX |

- Step 2.  Estimate the total variable selling and administrative expenses.
- Step 3.  Determine the total variable cost as follows:

| Total variable product cost | $XXX |
| --- | --- |
| Total variable selling and administrative expenses | XXX |
| Total variable cost | $XXX |

- Step 4.  Compute the variable cost per unit as follows:

$$\text{Variable Cost per Unit} = \frac{\text{Total Variable Cost}}{\text{Estimated Units Produced and Sold}}$$

- Step 5.  Compute the markup percentage as follows:

$$\text{Markup Percentage} = \frac{\text{Desired Profit} + \text{Total Fixed Costs and Expenses}}{\text{Total Variable Cost}}$$

The numerator of the markup percentage is the desired profit plus the total fixed costs (fixed factory overhead) and expenses (selling and administrative). These fixed costs and expenses must be included in the markup percentage because they are not included in the cost amount to which the markup is added.

As illustrated for the total and product cost concepts, the desired profit is normally computed based on a rate of return on assets as follows:

$$\text{Desired Profit} = \text{Desired Rate of Return} \times \text{Total Assets}$$

- Step 6.  Determine the markup per unit by multiplying the markup percentage times the variable cost per unit as follows:

$$\text{Markup per Unit} = \text{Markup Percentage} \times \text{Variable Cost per Unit}$$

- Step 7.  Determine the normal selling price by adding the markup per unit to the variable cost per unit as follows:

| Variable cost per unit | $XXX |
| --- | --- |
| Markup per unit | XXX |
| Normal selling price per unit | $XXX |

To illustrate, assume the same data for the production and sale of 100,000 calculators by Digital Solutions Inc. as in the preceding example. The normal selling price of $18.30 is determined under the variable cost concept as follows:

- Step 1.  Total variable product cost: $1,450,000

| Variable product costs: | |
| --- | --- |
| Direct materials ($3 × 100,000) | $ 300,000 |
| Direct labor ($10 × 100,000) | 1,000,000 |
| Variable factory overhead ($1.50 × 100,000) | 150,000 |
| Total variable product cost | $1,450,000 |

- Step 2. Total variable selling and administrative expenses: $150,000 ($1.50 × 100,000)
- Step 3. Total variable cost: $1,600,000 ($1,450,000 + $150,000)
- Step 4. Variable cost per unit: $16.00

$$\text{Variable Cost per Unit} = \frac{\text{Total Variable Cost}}{\text{Estimated Units Produced and Sold}} = \frac{\$1,600,000}{100,000 \text{ units}} = \$16 \text{ per unit}$$

- Step 5. Markup percentage: 14.4% (rounded)

$$\text{Desired Profit} = \text{Desired Rate of Return} \times \text{Total Assets} = 20\% \times \$800,000 = \$160,000$$

$$\text{Markup Percentage} = \frac{\text{Desired Profit} + \text{Total Fixed Costs and Expenses}}{\text{Total Variable Cost}}$$

$$= \frac{\$160,000 + \$50,000 + \$20,000}{\$1,600,000} = \frac{\$230,000}{\$1,600,000}$$

$$= 14.4\% \text{ (rounded)}$$

- Step 6. Markup per unit: $2.30

$$\text{Markup per Unit} = \text{Markup Percentage} \times \text{Variable Cost per Unit}$$
$$= 14.4\% \times \$16.00 = \$2.30 \text{ per unit}$$

- Step 7. Normal selling price: $18.30

| | |
|---|---:|
| Total variable cost per unit | $16.00 |
| Markup per unit | 2.30 |
| Normal selling price per unit | $18.30 |

# At a Glance 25

### OBJ 1

**Prepare differential analysis reports for a variety of managerial decisions.**

**Key Points** Differential analysis reports for various decisions are illustrated in the text. Each analysis focuses on the differential effects on income (loss) for alternative courses of action.

| Learning Outcomes | Example Exercises | Practice Exercises |
|---|---|---|
| • Prepare a lease or sell differential analysis. | EE25-1 | PE25-1A, 25-1B |
| • Prepare a discontinued segment differential analysis. | EE25-2 | PE25-2A, 25-2B |
| • Prepare a make-or-buy differential analysis. | EE25-3 | PE25-3A, 25-3B |
| • Prepare an equipment replacement differential analysis. | EE25-4 | PE25-4A, 25-4B |
| • Prepare a process-or-sell differential analysis | EE25-5 | PE25-5A, 25-5B |
| • Prepare an accept business at a special price differential analysis. | EE25-6 | PE25-6A, 25-6B |

**Determine the selling price of a product, using the product cost concept.**

**Key Points**   The three cost concepts commonly used in applying the cost-plus approach to product pricing are the product cost, total cost (appendix), and variable cost (appendix) concepts.
Target costing combines market-based methods with a cost-reduction emphasis.

| Learning Outcomes | Example Exercises | Practice Exercises |
|---|---|---|
| • Compute the markup percentage, using the product cost concept. | EE25-7 | PE25-7A, 25-7B |
| • Define and describe target costing. | | |

**Compute the relative profitability of products in bottleneck production processes.**

**Key Points**   The relative profitability of a product in a bottleneck production environment is determined by dividing the unit contribution margin by the bottleneck hours per unit.

| Learning Outcome | Example Exercises | Practice Exercises |
|---|---|---|
| • Compute the unit contribution margin per bottleneck hour. | EE25-8 | PE25-8A, 25-8B |

**Allocate product costs using activity-based costing.**

**Key Points**   Activity-based costing requires factory overhead to be assigned to activities. The estimated activity costs are allocated to products by multiplying activity rates by the activity-base usage quantity consumed for each product. Activity-based costing may provide more accurate allocation of factory overhead in complex product and manufacturing environments.

| Learning Outcomes | Example Exercises | Practice Exercises |
|---|---|---|
| • Compute activity rates. | EE25-8 | PE25-8A, 25-8B |
| • Allocate factory overhead costs to products using ABC. | EE25-9 | PE25-9A, 25-9B |

# Key Terms

activities (1183)
activity base (1184)
activity-based costing (ABC) (1183)
activity rate (1184)
differential analysis (1167)
differential cost (1167)
differential income (loss) (1167)

differential revenue (1167)
engineering change order (ECO) (1183)
opportunity cost (1173)
product cost concept (1178)
production bottleneck (1181)
setup (1183)

sunk cost (1169)
target costing (1180)
theory of constraints (TOC) (1181)
total cost concept (1187)
variable cost concept (1189)

# Illustrative Problem

Inez Company recently began production of a new product, a digital clock, which required the investment of $1,600,000 in assets. The costs of producing and selling 80,000 units of the digital clock are estimated as follows:

| Variable costs: | |
|---|---|
| Direct materials | $10.00 per unit |
| Direct labor | 6.00 |
| Factory overhead | 4.00 |
| Selling and administrative expenses | 5.00 |
| Total | $25.00 per unit |
| Fixed costs: | |
| Factory overhead | $800,000 |
| Selling and administrative expenses | 400,000 |

Inez Company is currently considering establishing a selling price for the digital clock. The president of Inez Company has decided to use the cost-plus approach to product pricing and has indicated that the digital clock must earn a 10% rate of return on invested assets.

## Instructions

1. Determine the amount of desired profit from the production and sale of the digital clock.

2. Assuming that the product cost concept is used, determine (a) the cost amount per unit, (b) the markup percentage, and (c) the selling price of the digital clock.

3. Under what conditions should Inez Company consider using activity-based costing rather than a single factory overhead allocation rate in allocating factory overhead to the digital clock?

4. Assume the market price for similar digital clocks was estimated at $38. Compute the reduction in manufacturing cost per unit needed to maintain the desired profit and existing selling and administrative expenses under target costing.

5. Assume that for the current year, the selling price of the digital clock was $42 per unit. To date, 60,000 units have been produced and sold, and analysis of the domestic market indicates that 15,000 additional units are expected to be sold during the remainder of the year. On August 7 Inez Company received an offer from Wong Inc. for 4,000 units of the digital clock at $28 each. Wong Inc. will market the units in Korea under its own brand name, and no selling and administrative expenses associated with the sale will be incurred by Inez Company. The additional business is not expected to affect the domestic sales of the digital clock, and the additional units could be produced during the current year, using existing capacity. Prepare a differential analysis dated August 7 to determine whether to reject (Alternative 1) or accept (Alternative 2) the special order from Wong.

## Solution

1. $160,000 ($1,600,000 × 10%)

2. a. Total manufacturing costs:

| Variable ($20 × 80,000 units) | $1,600,000 |
|---|---|
| Fixed factory overhead | 800,000 |
| Total | $2,400,000 |

Cost amount per unit: $2,400,000 ÷ 80,000 units = $30.00

b. Markup Percentage =

$$\frac{\text{Desired Profit} + \text{Total Selling and Administrative Expenses}}{\text{Total Product Cost}}$$

$$= \frac{\$160,000 + \$400,000 + (\$5 \times 80,000 \text{ units})}{\$2,400,000}$$

$$= \frac{\$160,000 + \$400,000 + \$400,000}{\$2,400,000}$$

$$= \frac{\$960,000}{\$2,400,000} = 40\%$$

c. 
| | |
|---|---:|
| Cost amount per unit | $30.00 |
| Markup ($30 × 40%) | 12.00 |
| Selling price | $42.00 |

3. Inez should consider using activity-based costing for factory overhead allocation when the product and manufacturing operations are complex. For example, if the digital clock was introduced as one among many different consumer digital products, then it is likely these products will consume factory activities in different ways. If this is combined with complex manufacturing and manufacturing support processes, then it is likely a single overhead allocation rate will lead to distorted factory overhead allocation. Specifically, the digital clock is a new product. Thus, it is likely that it will consume more factory overhead than existing stable and mature products. In this case, a single rate would result in the digital clock being undercosted compared to results using activity-based rates for factory overhead allocation.

4. 
| | |
|---|---:|
| Current selling price | $42 |
| Expected selling price | −38 |
| Required reduction in manufacturing cost to maintain same profit | $ 4 |

Revised revenue and cost figures:

| | Current | Desired |
|---|---:|---:|
| Selling price | $42 | $38 |
| Costs: | | |
| Variable selling and administrative expenses per unit | $ 5 | $ 5 |
| Fixed selling and administrative expenses per unit | | |
| ($400,000 ÷ 80,000 units) | 5 | 5 |
| Existing manufacturing cost per unit [part (2)] | 30 | |
| Target manufacturing cost per unit ($30 – $4) | | 26 |
| Total costs | $40 | $36 |
| Profit | $ 2 | $ 2 |

5.

**Differential Analysis—Wong Inc. Special Order**
**Reject Order (Alternative 1) or Accept Order (Alternative 2)**
**August 7**

| | Reject Order (Alternative 1) | Accept Order (Alternative 2) | Differential Effect on Income (Alternative 2) |
|---|---:|---:|---:|
| Revenues | $0 | $112,000* | $112,000 |
| Costs: | | | |
| Variable manufacturing costs | 0 | −80,000** | −80,000 |
| Income (loss) | $0 | $ 32,000 | $ 32,000 |

*4,000 units × $28 per unit
**4,000 units × $20 per unit

The proposal should be accepted.

# Discussion Questions

1. Explain the meaning of (a) differential revenue, (b) differential cost, and (c) differential income.

2. A company could sell a building for $250,000 or lease it for $2,500 per month. What would need to be considered in determining if the lease option would be preferred?

3. A chemical company has a commodity-grade and premium-grade product. Why might the company elect to process the commodity-grade product further to the premium-grade product?

4. A company accepts incremental business at a special price that exceeds the variable cost. What other issues must the company consider in deciding whether to accept the business?

5. A company fabricates a component at a cost of $6.00. A supplier offers to supply the same component for $5.50. Under what circumstances is it reasonable to purchase from the supplier?

6.  Many fast-food restaurant chains, such as McDonald's, will occasionally discontinue restaurants in their system. What are some financial considerations in deciding to eliminate a store?

7. In the long run, the normal selling price must be set high enough to cover what factors?

8. Although the cost-plus approach to product pricing may be used by management as a general guide line, what are some examples of other factors that managers should also consider in setting product prices?

9. How does the target cost concept differ from cost-plus approaches?

10. What is the appropriate measure of a product's value when a firm is operating under production bottlenecks?

11. Under what conditions might a company use activity-based costing to allocate factory overhead to products?

# Practice Exercises

EE 25-1 *p. 1169*

SHOW
ME HOW

**PE 25-1A   Lease or sell**    OBJ. 1

Claxon Company owns a machine with a cost of $305,000 and accumulated depreciation of $65,000 that can be sold for $262,000, less a 5% sales commission. Alternatively, the machine can be leased by Claxon Company for three years for a total of $272,000, at the end of which there is no residual value. In addition, the repair, insurance, and property tax expense that would be incurred by Claxon Company on the machine would total $21,600 over the three years. Prepare a differential analysis on January 12 as to whether Claxon Company should lease (Alternative 1) or sell (Alternative 2) the machine.

EE 25-1 *p. 1169*

SHOW
ME HOW

**PE 25-1B   Lease or sell**    OBJ. 1

Timberlake Company owns equipment with a cost of $165,000 and accumulated depreciation of $60,000 that can be sold for $82,000, less a 6% sales commission. Alternatively, the equipment can be leased by Timberlake Company for five years for a total of $84,600, at the end of which there is no residual value. In addition, the repair, insurance, and property tax expense that would be incurred by Timberlake Company on the equipment would total $7,950 over the five years. Prepare a differential analysis on March 23 as to whether Timberlake Company should lease (Alternative 1) or sell (Alternative 2) the equipment.

EE 25-2 *p. 1171*   **PE 25-2A   Discontinue a segment**                                 **OBJ. 1**

Product TS-20 has revenue of $102,000, variable cost of goods sold of $52,500, variable selling expenses of $21,500, and fixed costs of $35,000, creating a loss from operations of $7,000. Prepare a differential analysis as of September 12 to determine if Product TS-20 should be continued (Alternative 1) or discontinued (Alternative 2), assuming fixed costs are unaffected by the decision.

EE 25-2 *p. 1171*   **PE 25-2B   Discontinue a segment**                                 **OBJ. 1**

Product B has revenue of $39,500, variable cost of goods sold of $25,500, variable selling expenses of $16,500, and fixed costs of $15,000, creating a loss from operations of $17,500. Prepare a differential analysis as of May 9 to determine if Product B should be continued (Alternative 1) or discontinued (Alternative 2), assuming fixed costs are unaffected by the decision.

EE 25-3 *p. 1172*   **PE 25-3A   Make or buy**                                           **OBJ. 1**

A restaurant bakes its own bread for a cost of $165 per unit (100 loaves), including fixed costs of $43 per unit. A proposal is offered to purchase bread from an outside source for $110 per unit, plus $15 per unit for delivery. Prepare a differential analysis dated August 16 to determine whether the company should make (Alternative 1) or buy (Alternative 2) the bread, assuming fixed costs are unaffected by the decision.

EE 25-3 *p. 1172*   **PE 25-3B   Make or buy**                                           **OBJ. 1**

A company manufactures various sized plastic bottles for its medicinal product. The manufacturing cost for small bottles is $67 per unit (100 bottles), including fixed costs of $22 per unit. A proposal is offered to purchase small bottles from an outside source for $35 per unit, plus $5 per unit for freight. Prepare a differential analysis dated March 30 to determine whether the company should make (Alternative 1) or buy (Alternative 2) the bottles, assuming fixed costs are unaffected by the decision.

EE 25-4 *p. 1174*   **PE 25-4A   Replace equipment**                                     **OBJ. 1**

A machine with a book value of $126,000 has an estimated six-year life. A proposal is offered to sell the old machine for $84,000 and replace it with a new machine at a cost of $145,000. The new machine has a six-year life with no residual value. The new machine would reduce annual direct labor costs from $55,000 to $43,000. Prepare a differential analysis dated February 18 on whether to continue with the old machine (Alternative 1) or replace the old machine (Alternative 2).

EE 25-4 *p. 1174*   **PE 25-4B   Replace equipment**                                     **OBJ. 1**

A machine with a book value of $80,000 has an estimated five-year life. A proposal is offered to sell the old machine for $50,500 and replace it with a new machine at a cost of $75,000. The new machine has a five-year life with no residual value. The new machine would reduce annual direct labor costs from $11,200 to $7,400. Prepare a differential analysis dated April 11 on whether to continue with the old machine (Alternative 1) or replace the old machine (Alternative 2).

EE 25-5 *p. 1175*   **PE 25-5A   Process or sell**                                       **OBJ. 1**

Product T is produced for $5.90 per pound. Product T can be sold without additional processing for $7.10 per pound, or processed further into Product U at an additional cost of $0.74 per pound. Product U can be sold for $8.00 per pound. Prepare a differential analysis dated August 2 on whether to sell Product T (Alternative 1) or process further into Product U (Alternative 2).

EE 25-5 *p. 1175*

### PE 25-5B    Process or sell

OBJ. 1

Product D is produced for $24 per gallon. Product D can be sold without additional processing for $36 per gallon, or processed further into Product E at an additional cost of $9 per gallon. Product E can be sold for $43 per gallon. Prepare a differential analysis dated February 26 on whether to sell Product D (Alternative 1) or process further into Product E (Alternative 2).

EE 25-6 *p. 1177*

### PE 25-6A    Accept business at special price

OBJ. 1

Product R is normally sold for $52 per unit. A special price of $42 is offered for the export market. The variable production cost is $30 per unit. An additional export tariff of 30% of revenue must be paid for all export products. Assume there is sufficient capacity for the special order. Prepare a differential analysis dated October 23 on whether to reject (Alternative 1) or accept (Alternative 2) the special order.

EE 25-6 *p. 1177*

### PE 25-6B    Accept business at special price

OBJ. 1

Product A is normally sold for $9.60 per unit. A special price of $7.20 is offered for the export market. The variable production cost is $5.00 per unit. An additional export tariff of 15% of revenue must be paid for all export products. Assume there is sufficient capacity for the special order. Prepare a differential analysis dated March 16 on whether to reject (Alternative 1) or accept (Alternative 2) the special order.

EE 25-7 *p. 1180*

### PE 25-7A    Product cost markup percentage

OBJ. 2

Magna Lighting Inc. produces and sells lighting fixtures. An entry light has a total cost of $125 per unit, of which $80 is product cost and $45 is selling and administrative expenses. In addition, the total cost of $125 is made up of $90 variable cost and $35 fixed cost. The desired profit is $55 per unit. Determine the markup percentage on product cost.

EE 25-7 *p. 1180*

### PE 25-7B    Product cost markup percentage

OBJ. 2

Green Thumb Garden Tools Inc. produces and sells home and garden tools and equipment. A lawnmower has a total cost of $230 per unit, of which $160 is product cost and $70 is selling and administrative expenses. In addition, the total cost of $230 is made up of $120 variable cost and $110 fixed cost. The desired profit is $58 per unit. Determine the markup percentage on product cost.

EE 25-8 *p. 1182*

### PE 25-8A    Bottleneck profit

OBJ. 3

Product A has a unit contribution margin of $24. Product B has a unit contribution margin of $30. Product A requires four testing hours, while Product B requires six testing hours. Determine the most profitable product, assuming the testing is a bottleneck constraint.

EE 25-8 *p. 1182*

### PE 25-8B    Bottleneck profit

OBJ. 3

Product K has a unit contribution margin of $120. Product L has a unit contribution margin of $100. Product K requires five furnace hours, while Product L requires four furnace hours. Determine the most profitable product, assuming the furnace is a bottleneck constraint.

EE 25-9 *p. 1186*

### PE 25-9A    Activity-based costing

OBJ. 4

Mainline Marine Company has total estimated factory overhead for the year of $2,090,000, divided into four activities: fabrication, $750,000; assembly, $240,000; setup, $600,000; and inspection, $500,000. Mainline manufactures two types of boats: a speedboat and a bass boat. The activity-base usage quantities for each product by each activity are as follows:

|  | Fabrication | Assembly | Setup | Inspection |
|---|---|---|---|---|
| Speedboat | 1,200 dlh | 1,800 dlh | 60 setups | 600 inspections |
| Bass boat | 1,800 | 1,200 | 100 | 200 |
|  | 3,000 dlh | 3,000 dlh | 160 setups | 800 inspections |

Each product is budgeted for 200 units of production for the year. Determine (a) the activity rates for each activity and (b) the factory overhead cost per unit for each product, using activity-based costing.

EE 25-9 *p. 1186*

SHOW
ME HOW

### PE 25-9B Activity-based costing
OBJ. 4

Casual Cuts Inc. has total estimated factory overhead for the year of $225,000, divided into four activities: cutting, $90,000; sewing, $22,500; setup, $80,000; and inspection, $32,500. Casual Cuts manufactures two types of men's pants: jeans and khakis. The activity-base usage quantities for each product by each activity are as follows:

|  | Cutting | Sewing | Setup | Inspection |
|---|---|---|---|---|
| Jeans | 500 dlh | 1,000 dlh | 250 setups | 100 inspections |
| Khakis | 1,000 | 500 | 750 | 400 |
|  | 1,500 dlh | 1,500 dlh | 1,000 setups | 500 inspections |

Each product is budgeted for 10,000 units of production for the year. Determine (a) the activity rates for each activity and (b) the factory overhead cost per unit for each product, using activity-based costing.

## Exercises

### EX 25-1 Differential analysis for a lease or sell decision
OBJ. 1

✔ a. Differential revenue from selling, $5,000

SHOW
ME HOW

Eclipse Construction Company is considering selling excess machinery with a book value of $280,000 (original cost of $400,000 less accumulated depreciation of $120,000) for $221,000, less a 5% brokerage commission. Alternatively, the machinery can be leased for a total of $216,000 for five years, after which it is expected to have no residual value. During the period of the lease, Eclipse Construction Company's costs of repairs, insurance, and property tax expenses are expected to be $14,200.

a. Prepare a differential analysis, dated April 16 to determine whether Eclipse should lease (Alternative 1) or sell (Alternative 2) the machinery.

b. ━━━▶ On the basis of the data presented, would it be advisable to lease or sell the machinery? Explain.

### EX 25-2 Differential analysis for a lease or buy decision
OBJ. 1

SHOW
ME HOW

Carr Corporation is considering new equipment. The equipment can be purchased from an overseas supplier for $3,900. The freight and installation costs for the equipment are $515. If purchased, annual repairs and maintenance are estimated to be $410 per year over the four-year useful life of the equipment. Alternatively, Carr can lease the equipment from a domestic supplier for $1,750 per year for four years, with no additional costs. Prepare a differential analysis dated August 4 to determine whether Carr should lease (Alternative 1) or purchase (Alternative 2) the equipment. *Hint:* This is a "lease or *buy*" decision, which must be analyzed from the perspective of the equipment user, as opposed to the equipment owner.

### EX 25-3 Differential analysis for a discontinued product
OBJ. 1

✔ a. Differential revenues, –$390,000

A condensed income statement by product line for Celestial Beverage Inc. indicated the following for Star Cola for the past year:

| | |
|---|---|
| Sales | $390,000 |
| Cost of goods sold | 184,000 |
| Gross profit | $206,000 |
| Operating expenses | 255,000 |
| Loss from operations | $ (49,000) |

It is estimated that 20% of the cost of goods sold represents fixed factory overhead costs and that 30% of the operating expenses are fixed. Because Star Cola is only one of many products, the fixed costs will not be materially affected if the product is discontinued.

a. Prepare a differential analysis, dated January 21 to determine whether Star Cola should be continued (Alternative 1) or discontinued (Alternative 2).

b. ━━━━► Should Star Cola be retained? Explain.

---

### EX 25-4 Differential analysis for a discontinued product

OBJ. 1

✓ a. Alternative 1 loss, $2,200

The condensed product-line income statement for Dish N' Dat Company for the month of March is as follows:

**Dish N' Dat Company**
**Product-Line Income Statement**
**For the Month Ended March 31, 2016**

|  | Bowls | Plates | Cups |
|---|---|---|---|
| Sales | $71,000 | $105,700 | $31,300 |
| Cost of goods sold | 32,600 | 42,300 | 16,800 |
| Gross profit | $38,400 | $ 63,400 | $14,500 |
| Selling and administrative expenses | 27,400 | 42,800 | 16,700 |
| Income from operations | $11,000 | $ 20,600 | $ (2,200) |

Fixed costs are 15% of the cost of goods sold and 40% of the selling and administrative expenses. Dish N' Dat assumes that fixed costs would not be materially affected if the Cups line were discontinued.

a. Prepare a differential analysis dated March 31, 2016, to determine if Cups should be continued (Alternative 1) or discontinued (Alternative 2).

b. ━━━━► Should the Cups line be retained? Explain.

---

### EX 25-5 Segment analysis for a service company

OBJ. 1

**Internet Project**

Charles Schwab Corporation is one of the more innovative brokerage and financial service companies in the United States. The company recently provided information about its major business segments as follows (in millions):

|  | Investor Services | Institutional Services |
|---|---|---|
| Revenues | $3,228 | $1,583 |
| Income from operations | 865 | 514 |
| Depreciation | 148 | 48 |

a. ━━━━► How does a brokerage company like Schwab define the "Investor Services" and "Institutional Services" segments? Use the Internet to develop your answer.

b. Provide a specific example of a variable and fixed cost in the "Investor Services" segment.

c. Estimate the contribution margin for each segment, assuming depreciation represents the majority of fixed costs.

d. If Schwab decided to sell its "Institutional Services" accounts to another company, estimate how much operating income would decline.

---

### EX 25-6 Decision to discontinue a product

OBJ. 1

━━━━► On the basis of the following data, the general manager of Featherweight Shoes Inc. decided to discontinue Children's Shoes because it reduced income from operations by $17,000. What is the flaw in this decision, if it is assumed fixed costs would not be materially affected by the discontinuance?

*(Continued)*

**Featherweight Shoes Inc.**
**Product-Line Income Statement**
**For the Year Ended April 30, 2016**

| | Children's Shoes | Men's Shoes | Women's Shoes | Total |
|---|---|---|---|---|
| Sales | $235,000 | $300,000 | $500,000 | $1,035,000 |
| Costs of goods sold: | | | | |
|    Variable costs | $130,000 | $150,000 | $220,000 | $ 500,000 |
|    Fixed costs | 41,000 | 60,000 | 120,000 | 221,000 |
|    Total cost of goods sold | $171,000 | $210,000 | $340,000 | $ 721,000 |
| Gross profit | $ 64,000 | $ 90,000 | $160,000 | $ 314,000 |
| Selling and adminstrative expenses: | | | | |
|    Variable selling and admin. expenses | $ 46,000 | $ 45,000 | $ 95,000 | $ 186,000 |
|    Fixed selling and admin. expenses | 35,000 | 20,000 | 25,000 | 80,000 |
|    Total selling and admin. expenses | $ 81,000 | $ 65,000 | $120,000 | $ 266,000 |
| Income (loss) from operations | $ (17,000) | $ 25,000 | $ 40,000 | $ 48,000 |

---

**EX 25-7 Make-or-buy decision** **OBJ. 1**

✔ a. Differential loss from buying, $2.00 per case

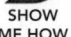

**SHOW ME HOW**

Jupiter Computer Company has been purchasing carrying cases for its portable computers at a purchase price of $70 per unit. The company, which is currently operating below full capacity, charges factory overhead to production at the rate of 40% of direct labor cost. The fully absorbed unit costs to produce comparable carrying cases are expected to be as follows:

| | |
|---|---|
| Direct materials | $45 |
| Direct labor | 20 |
| Factory overhead (40% of direct labor) | 8 |
| Total cost per unit | $73 |

If Jupiter Computer Company manufactures the carrying cases, fixed factory overhead costs will not increase and variable factory overhead costs associated with the cases are expected to be 15% of the direct labor costs.

a. Prepare a differential analysis, dated July 19 to determine whether the company should make (Alternative 1) or buy (Alternative 2) the carrying case.

b. ➤ On the basis of the data presented, would it be advisable to make the carrying cases or to continue buying them? Explain.

---

**EX 25-8 Make-or-buy decision for a service company** **OBJ. 1**

The Theater Arts Guild of Dallas (TAG-D) employs five people in its Publication Department. These people lay out pages for pamphlets, brochures, magazines, and other publications for the TAG-D productions. The pages are delivered to an outside company for printing. The company is considering an outside publication service for the layout work. The outside service is quoting a price of $13 per layout page. The budget for the Publication Department for the current year is as follows:

| | |
|---|---|
| Salaries | $224,000 |
| Benefits | 36,000 |
| Supplies | 21,000 |
| Office expenses | 39,000 |
| Office depreciation | 28,000 |
| Computer depreciation | 24,000 |
| Total | $372,000 |

The department expects to lay out 24,000 pages for the current year. The Publication Department office space and equipment would be used for future administrative needs, if the department's function were purchased from the outside.

a. Prepare a differential analysis dated February 22 to determine whether TAG-D should lay out pages internally (Alternative 1) or purchase layout services from the outside (Alternative 2).

b. ➤ On the basis of your analysis in part (a), should the page layout work be purchased from an outside company?

c. ➤ What additional considerations might factor into the decision making?

---

### EX 25-9 Machine replacement decision

OBJ. 1

SHOW
ME HOW

A company is considering replacing an old piece of machinery, which cost $600,000 and has $350,000 of accumulated depreciation to date, with a new machine that has a purchase price of $545,000. The old machine could be sold for $231,000. The annual variable production costs associated with the old machine are estimated to be $61,000 per year for eight years. The annual variable production costs for the new machine are estimated to be $19,000 per year for eight years.

a. Prepare a differential analysis dated September 13 to determine whether to continue with (Alternative 1) or replace (Alternative 2) the old machine.

b. What is the sunk cost in this situation?

---

### EX 25-10 Differential analysis for machine replacement

OBJ. 1

✔ a. Differential loss, $2,500

Kim Kwon Digital Components Company assembles circuit boards by using a manually operated machine to insert electronic components. The original cost of the machine is $60,000, the accumulated depreciation is $24,000, its remaining useful life is five years, and its residual value is negligible. On May 4 of the current year, a proposal was made to replace the present manufacturing procedure with a fully automatic machine that has a purchase price of $180,000. The automatic machine has an estimated useful life of five years and no significant residual value. For use in evaluating the proposal, the accountant accumulated the following annual data on present and proposed operations:

| | Present Operations | Proposed Operations |
|---|---|---|
| Sales | $205,000 | $205,000 |
| Direct materials | $ 72,000 | $ 72,000 |
| Direct labor | 51,000 | — |
| Power and maintenance | 5,000 | 18,000 |
| Taxes, insurance, etc. | 1,500 | 4,000 |
| Selling and administrative expenses | 45,000 | 45,000 |
| Total expenses | $174,500 | $139,000 |

a. Prepare a differential analysis dated May 4 to determine whether to continue with the old machine (Alternative 1) or replace the old machine (Alternative 2). Prepare the analysis over the useful life of the new machine.

b. Based only on the data presented, should the proposal be accepted?

c. ➤ What are some of the other factors that should be considered before a final decision is made?

---

### EX 25-11 Sell or process further

OBJ. 1

SHOW
ME HOW

Portland Lumber Company incurs a cost of $452 per hundred board feet (hbf) in processing certain "rough-cut" lumber, which it sells for $611 per hbf. An alternative is to produce a "finished cut" at a total processing cost of $559 per hbf, which can be sold for $748 per hbf. Prepare a differential analysis dated June 14 on whether to sell rough-cut lumber (Alternative 1) or process further into finished-cut lumber (Alternative 2).

---

### EX 25-12 Sell or process further

OBJ. 1

Rise N' Shine Coffee Company produces Columbian coffee in batches of 6,000 pounds. The standard quantity of materials required in the process is 6,000 pounds, which cost $5.50 per pound. Columbian coffee can be sold without further processing for $9.22 per pound. Columbian coffee can also be processed further to yield Decaf Columbian, which

*(Continued)*

can be sold for $11.88 per pound. The processing into Decaf Columbian requires additional processing costs of $10,230 per batch. The additional processing will also cause a 5% loss of product due to evaporation.

a. Prepare a differential analysis dated October 6 on whether to sell regular Columbian (Alternative 1) or process further into Decaf Columbian (Alternative 2).

b. ━━━▶ Should Rise N' Shine sell Columbian coffee or process further and sell Decaf Columbian?

c. Determine the price of Decaf Columbian that would cause neither an advantage nor a disadvantage for processing further and selling Decaf Columbian.

---

### EX 25-13 Decice on accepting additional business

**EX 25-13  Decision on accepting additional business** OBJ. 1

✔ a. Differential income, $54,000

Homestead Jeans Co. has an annual plant capacity of 65,000 units, and current production is 45,000 units. Monthly fixed costs are $54,000, and variable costs are $29 per unit. The present selling price is $42 per unit. On November 12 of the current year, the company received an offer from Dawkins Company for 18,000 units of the product at $32 each. Dawkins Company will market the units in a foreign country under its own brand name. The additional business is not expected to affect the domestic selling price or quantity of sales of Homestead Jeans Co.

a. Prepare a differential analysis dated November 12 on whether to reject (Alternative 1) or accept (Alternative 2) the Dawkins order.

b. ━━━▶ Briefly explain the reason why accepting this additional business will increase operating income.

c. What is the minimum price per unit that would produce a positive contribution margin?

---

**EX 25-14  Accepting business at a special price** OBJ. 1

Portable Power Company expects to operate at 80% of productive capacity during July. The total manufacturing costs for July for the production of 25,000 batteries are budgeted as follows:

| | |
|---|---|
| Direct materials | $162,500 |
| Direct labor | 70,000 |
| Variable factory overhead | 30,000 |
| Fixed factory overhead | 112,500 |
| Total manufacturing costs | $375,000 |

The company has an opportunity to submit a bid for 2,500 batteries to be delivered by July 31 to a government agency. If the contract is obtained, it is anticipated that the additional activity will not interfere with normal production during July or increase the selling or administrative expenses. What is the unit cost below which Portable Power Company should not go in bidding on the government contract?

---

**EX 25-15  Decision on accepting additional business** OBJ. 1

✔ a. Differential revenue, $2,320,000

SHOW
ME HOW

Brightstone Tire and Rubber Company has capacity to produce 170,000 tires. Brightstone presently produces and sells 130,000 tires for the North American market at a price of $175 per tire. Brightstone is evaluating a special order from a European automobile company, Euro Motors. Euro is offering to buy 20,000 tires for $116 per tire. Brightstone's accounting system indicates that the total cost per tire is as follows:

| | |
|---|---|
| Direct materials | $ 56 |
| Direct labor | 22 |
| Factory overhead (60% variable) | 25 |
| Selling and administrative expenses (45% variable) | 26 |
| Total | $129 |

Brightstone pays a selling commission equal to 5% of the selling price on North American orders, which is included in the variable portion of the selling and administrative expenses. However, this special order would not have a sales commission. If the order was accepted, the tires would be shipped overseas for an additional shipping cost of $7.50 per tire. In addition, Euro has made the order conditional on receiving European safety certification. Brightstone estimates that this certification would cost $165,000.

a. Prepare a differential analysis dated January 21 on whether to reject (Alternative 1) or accept (Alternative 2) the special order from Euro Motors.

b. What is the minimum price per unit that would be financially acceptable to Brightstone?

---

### EX 25-16  Accepting business at a special price for a service company

Cityscape Hotels has 200 rooms available in a major metropolitan city. The hotel is able to attract business customers during the weekdays, and leisure customers during the weekend. However, the leisure customers on weekends occupy fewer rooms than do business customers on weekdays. Thus, Cityscape plans to provide special weekend pricing to attract additional leisure customers. A hotel room is priced at $180 per room night. The cost of a hotel room night includes the following:

|  | Cost Per Room Night (at normal occupancy) |
|---|---|
| Housekeeping service | $ 23 |
| Utilities | 7 |
| Amenities | 3 |
| Hotel depreciation | 55 |
| Hotel staff (excluding housekeeping) | 42 |
| Total | $130 |

a. What is the contribution margin for a room night if only the hotel depreciation and hotel staff are assumed fixed for all occupancy levels?

b. ➤ What should be considered in setting a discount price for the weekends?

---

### EX 25-17  Product cost concept of product pricing                                OBJ. 2

✔ b. $40

**SHOW ME HOW**

La Femme Accessories Inc. produces women's handbags. The cost of producing 800 handbags is as follows:

| | |
|---|---|
| Direct materials | $18,000 |
| Direct labor | 8,500 |
| Factory overhead | 5,500 |
| Total manufacturing cost | $32,000 |

The selling and administrative expenses are $17,000. The management desires a profit equal to 22% of invested assets of $250,000.

a. Determine the amount of desired profit from the production and sale of 800 handbags.

b. Determine the product cost per unit for the production of 800 handbags.

c. Determine the product cost markup percentage for handbags.

d. Determine the selling price of handbags.

---

### EX 25-18  Product cost concept of product costing                                OBJ. 2

✔ d. $325

Smart Stream Inc. uses the product cost concept of applying the cost-plus approach to product pricing. The costs of producing and selling 10,000 cellular phones are as follows:

| Variable costs per unit: | | Fixed costs: | |
|---|---|---|---|
| Direct materials | $150 | Factory overhead | $350,000 |
| Direct labor | 25 | Selling and admin. exp. | 140,000 |
| Factory overhead | 40 | | |
| Selling and administrative expenses | 25 | | |
| Total | $240 | | |

*(Continued)*

Smart Stream desires a profit equal to a 30% rate of return on invested assets of $1,200,000.

a. Determine the amount of desired profit from the production and sale of 10,000 cellular phones.

b. Determine the product cost and the cost amount per unit for the production of 10,000 cellular phones.

c. Determine the product cost markup percentage for cellular phones.

d. Determine the selling price of cellular phones.

---

### EX 25-19   Target costing

**OBJ. 2**

**Toyota Motor Corporation** uses target costing. Assume that Toyota marketing personnel estimate that the competitive selling price for the Camry in the upcoming model year will need to be $27,000. Assume further that the Camry's total unit cost for the upcoming model year is estimated to be $22,500 and that Toyota requires a 20% profit margin on selling price (which is equivalent to a 25% markup on total cost).

a. What price will Toyota establish for the Camry for the upcoming model year?

b. ➤ What impact will target costing have on Toyota, given the assumed information?

---

### EX 25-20   Target costing

**OBJ. 2**

✔ b. $30

Instant Image Inc. manufactures color laser printers. Model J20 presently sells for $460 and has a product cost of $230, as follows:

| | |
|---|---|
| Direct materials | $175 |
| Direct labor | 40 |
| Factory overhead | 15 |
| Total | $230 |

It is estimated that the competitive selling price for color laser printers of this type will drop to $400 next year. Instant Image has established a target cost to maintain its historical markup percentage on product cost. Engineers have provided the following cost reduction ideas:

1. Purchase a plastic printer cover with snap-on assembly, rather than with screws. This will reduce the amount of direct labor by 15 minutes per unit.

2. Add an inspection step that will add six minutes per unit of direct labor but reduce the materials cost by $20 per unit.

3. Decrease the cycle time of the injection molding machine from four minutes to three minutes per part. Forty percent of the direct labor and 48% of the factory overhead are related to running injection molding machines.

The direct labor rate is $30 per hour.

a. Determine the target cost for Model J20, assuming that the historical markup on product cost and selling price is maintained.

b. Determine the required cost reduction.

c. Evaluate the three engineering improvements together to determine if the required cost reduction (drift) can be achieved.

---

### EX 25-21   Product decisions under bottlenecked operations

**OBJ. 3**

Mill Metals Inc. has three grades of metal product, Type 5, Type 10, and Type 20. Financial data for the three grades are as follows:

| | Type 5 | Type 10 | Type 20 |
|---|---|---|---|
| Revenues | $43,000 | $49,000 | $56,500 |
| Variable cost | $34,000 | $28,000 | $26,500 |
| Fixed cost | 8,000 | 8,000 | 8,000 |
| Total cost | $42,000 | $36,000 | $34,500 |
| Income from operations | $ 1,000 | $13,000 | $22,000 |
| Number of units | ÷ 5,000 | ÷ 5,000 | ÷ 5,000 |
| Income from operations per unit | $ 0.20 | $ 2.60 | $ 4.40 |

Mill's operations require all three grades to be melted in a furnace before being formed. The furnace runs 24 hours a day, 7 days a week, and is a production bottleneck. The furnace hours required per unit of each product are as follows:

| | |
|---|---|
| Type 5: | 6 hours |
| Type 10: | 6 hours |
| Type 20: | 12 hours |

The Marketing Department is considering a new marketing and sales campaign.

Which product should be emphasized in the marketing and sales campaign in order to maximize profitability?

---

### EX 25-22    Product decisions under bottlenecked operations

OBJ. 3

✔ a. Total income from operations, $269,000

Youngstown Glass Company manufactures three types of safety plate glass: large, medium, and small. All three products have high demand. Thus, Youngstown Glass is able to sell all the safety glass that it can make. The production process includes an autoclave operation, which is a pressurized heat treatment. The autoclave is a production bottleneck. Total fixed costs are $85,000 for the company as a whole. In addition, the following information is available about the three products:

| | Large | Medium | Small |
|---|---|---|---|
| Unit selling price | $184 | $160 | $100 |
| Unit variable cost | 130 | 120 | 76 |
| Unit contribution margin | $ 54 | $ 40 | $ 24 |
| Autoclave hours per unit | 3 | 2 | 1 |
| Total process hours per unit | 5 | 4 | 2 |
| Budgeted units of production | 3,000 | 3,000 | 3,000 |

a. Determine the contribution margin by glass type and the total company income from operations for the budgeted units of production.

b. Prepare an analysis showing which product is the most profitable per bottleneck hour.

---

### EX 25-23    Activity-based costing

OBJ. 4

✔ Activity cost per stationary bicycle, $92.40

CardioTrainer Equipment Company manufactures stationary bicycles and treadmills. The products are produced in the Fabrication and Assembly production departments. In addition to production activities, several other activities are required to produce the two products. These activities and their associated activity rates are as follows:

| Activity | Activity Rate |
|---|---|
| Fabrication | $22 per machine hour (mh) |
| Assembly | $12 per direct labor hour (dlh) |
| Setup | $40 per setup |
| Inspecting | $18 per inspection |
| Production scheduling | $8 per production order |
| Purchasing | $5 per purchase order |

The activity-base usage quantities and units produced for each product were as follows:

| | Stationary Bicycle | Treadmill |
|---|---|---|
| Machine hours | 1,680 | 1,070 |
| Direct labor hours | 243 | 131 |
| Setups | 45 | 20 |
| Inspections | 158 | 94 |
| Production orders | 60 | 32 |
| Purchase orders | 240 | 98 |
| Units produced | 500 | 350 |

Use the activity rate and usage information to compute the total activity costs and the activity costs per unit for each product.

✔ b. Custom, $90.65
per unit

## EX 25-24 Activity-based costing

OBJ. 4

Zeus Industries manufactures two types of electrical power units, custom and standard, which involve four factory overhead activities—production setup, procurement, quality control, and materials management. An activity analysis of the overhead revealed the following estimated activity costs and activity bases for these activities:

| Activity | Activity Cost | Activity Base |
|---|---|---|
| Production setup | $ 44,000 | Number of setups |
| Procurement | 13,500 | Number of purchase orders (PO) |
| Quality control | 97,500 | Number of inspections |
| Materials management | 84,000 | Number of components |
| Total | $239,000 | |

The activity-base usage quantities for each product are as follows:

| | Setups | Purchase Orders | Inspections | Components | Unit Volume |
|---|---|---|---|---|---|
| Custom | 290 | 760 | 1,200 | 500 | 2,000 |
| Standard | 110 | 140 | 300 | 200 | 2,000 |
| Total | 400 | 900 | 1,500 | 700 | 4,000 |

a. Determine an activity rate for each activity.

b. Assign activity costs to each product, and determine the unit activity cost, using the activity rates from part (a).

c. Assume that each product required one direct labor hour per unit. Determine the per-unit cost if factory overhead is allocated on the basis of direct labor hours.

d. ▬▬▶ Explain why the answers in parts (b) and (c) are different.

## EX 25-25 Activity rates and product costs using activity-based costing

OBJ. 4

✔ b. Dining room
lighting fixtures,
$71.60 per unit

BriteLite Inc. manufactures entry and dining room lighting fixtures. Five activities are used in manufacturing the fixtures. These activities and their associated activity costs and activity bases are as follows:

| Activity | Activity Costs (Budgeted) | Activity Base |
|---|---|---|
| Casting | $42,000 | Machine hours |
| Assembly | 13,500 | Direct labor hours |
| Inspecting | 5,800 | Number of inspections |
| Setup | 16,800 | Number of setups |
| Materials handling | 3,600 | Number of loads |

Corporate records were obtained to estimate the amount of activity to be used by the two products. The estimated activity-base usage quantities and units produced for each product and in total are provided in the following table:

| Activity Base | Entry | Dining | Total |
|---|---|---|---|
| Machine hours | 800 | 600 | 1,400 |
| Direct labor hours | 500 | 400 | 900 |
| Number of inspections | 140 | 150 | 290 |
| Number of setups | 80 | 60 | 140 |
| Number of loads | 50 | 40 | 90 |
| Units produced | 1,200 | 500 | 1,700 |

a. Determine the activity rate for each activity.

b. Use the activity rates in (a) to determine the total and per-unit activity costs associated with each product.

## Appendix
## EX 25-26 Total cost concept of product pricing

✔ b. 12.46%

Based on the data presented in Exercise 25-18, assume that Smart Stream Inc. uses the total cost concept of applying the cost-plus approach to product pricing.

a. Determine the total costs and the total cost amount per unit for the production and sale of 10,000 cellular phones.

b. Determine the total cost markup percentage (rounded to two decimal places) for cellular phones.

c. Determine the selling price of cellular phones. Round to the nearest dollar.

### Appendix
### EX 25-27   Variable cost concept of product pricing

✔ b. 35.42%

Based on the data presented in Exercise 25-18, assume that Smart Stream Inc. uses the variable cost concept of applying the cost-plus approach to product pricing.

a. Determine the variable costs and the variable cost amount per unit for the production and sale of 10,000 cellular phones.

b. Determine the variable cost markup percentage (rounded to two decimal places) for cellular phones.

c. Determine the selling price of cellular phones. Round to the nearest dollar.

# Problems: Series A

### PR 25-1A   Differential analysis involving opportunity costs                OBJ. 1

On October 1, White Way Stores Inc. is considering leasing a building and purchasing the necessary equipment to operate a retail store. Alternatively, the company could use the funds to invest in $180,000 of 6% U.S. Treasury bonds that mature in 16 years. The bonds could be purchased at face value. The following data have been assembled:

| | |
|---|---|
| Cost of store equipment | $180,000 |
| Life of store equipment | 16 years |
| Estimated residual value of store equipment | $15,000 |
| Yearly costs to operate the store, excluding depreciation of store equipment | $58,000 |
| Yearly expected revenues—years 1–8 | $85,000 |
| Yearly expected revenues—years 9–16 | $73,000 |

### Instructions

1. Prepare a differential analysis as of October 1 presenting the proposed operation of the store for the 16 years (Alternative 1) as compared with investing in U.S. Treasury bonds (Alternative 2).

2. Based on the results disclosed by the differential analysis, should the proposal be accepted?

3. If the proposal is accepted, what would be the total estimated income from operations of the store for the 16 years?

### PR 25-2A   Differential analysis for machine replacement proposal            OBJ. 1

Lexigraphic Printing Company is considering replacing a machine that has been used in its factory for four years. Relevant data associated with the operations of the old machine and the new machine, neither of which has any estimated residual value, are as follows:

| **Old Machine** | |
|---|---|
| Cost of machine, 10-year life | $89,000 |
| Annual depreciation (straight-line) | 8,900 |
| Annual manufacturing costs, excluding depreciation | 23,600 |
| Annual nonmanufacturing operating expenses | 6,100 |
| Annual revenue | 74,200 |
| Current estimated selling price of machine | 29,700 |

| **New Machine** | |
|---|---|
| Purchase price of machine, six-year life | $119,700 |
| Annual depreciation (straight-line) | 19,950 |
| Estimated annual manufacturing costs, excluding depreciation | 6,900 |

(*Continued*)

Annual nonmanufacturing operating expenses and revenue are not expected to be affected by purchase of the new machine.

**Instructions**

1. Prepare a differential analysis as of April 30 comparing operations using the present machine (Alternative 1) with operations using the new machine (Alternative 2). The analysis should indicate the total differential income that would result over the six-year period if the new machine is acquired.

2. ➤ List other factors that should be considered before a final decision is reached.

---

**PR 25-3A    Differential analysis for sales promotion proposal**                    **OBJ. 1**

✔ 1. Differential revenue, −$10,000

SHOW
ME HOW

Parisian Cosmetics Company is planning a one-month campaign for September to promote sales of one of its two cosmetics products. A total of $140,000 has been budgeted for advertising, contests, redeemable coupons, and other promotional activities. The following data have been assembled for their possible usefulness in deciding which of the products to select for the campaign:

|                              | Moisturizer | Perfume |
|------------------------------|:-----------:|:-------:|
| Unit selling price           | $55         | $60     |
| Unit production costs:        |             |         |
|    Direct materials         | $ 9         | $14     |
|    Direct labor             | 3           | 5       |
|    Variable factory overhead | 3          | 5       |
|    Fixed factory overhead    | 6          | 4       |
|    Total unit production costs | $21      | $28     |
| Unit variable selling expenses | 16        | 15      |
| Unit fixed selling expenses    | 12        | 6       |
|    Total unit costs           | $49      | $49     |
| Operating income per unit     | $ 6         | $11     |

No increase in facilities would be necessary to produce and sell the increased output. It is anticipated that 22,000 additional units of moisturizer or 20,000 additional units of perfume could be sold from the campaign without changing the unit selling price of either product.

**Instructions**

1. Prepare a differential analysis as of August 21 to determine whether to promote moisturizer (Alternative 1) or perfume (Alternative 2).

2. ➤ The sales manager had tentatively decided to promote perfume, estimating that operating income would be increased by $80,000 ($11 operating income per unit for 20,000 units, less promotion expenses of $140,000). The manager also believed that the selection of moisturizer would reduce operating income by $8,000 ($6 operating income per unit for 22,000 units, less promotion expenses of $140,000). State briefly your reasons for supporting or opposing the tentative decision.

---

**PR 25-4A    Differential analysis for further processing**                    **OBJ. 1**

✔ 1. Raw sugar income, $23,800

The management of Dominican Sugar Company is considering whether to process further raw sugar into refined sugar. Refined sugar can be sold for $2.20 per pound, and raw sugar can be sold without further processing for $1.40 per pound. Raw sugar is produced in batches of 42,000 pounds by processing 100,000 pounds of sugar cane, which costs $0.35 per pound of cane. Refined sugar will require additional processing costs of $0.50 per pound of raw sugar, and 1.25 pounds of raw sugar will produce 1 pound of refined sugar.

**Instructions**

1. Prepare a differential analysis as of March 24 to determine whether to sell raw sugar (Alternative 1) or process further into refined sugar (Alternative 2).

2. ➤ Briefly report your recommendations.

## Appendix

### PR 25-5A Product pricing using the cost-plus approach concepts; differential analysis for accepting additional business

OBJ. 1, 2

✔ 2. b. Markup percentage, 44%

Crystal Displays Inc. recently began production of a new product, flat panel displays, which required the investment of $1,500,000 in assets. The costs of producing and selling 5,000 units of flat panel displays are estimated as follows:

| Variable costs per unit: | | Fixed costs: | |
|---|---|---|---|
| Direct materials | $120 | Factory overhead | $250,000 |
| Direct labor | 30 | Selling and administrative expenses | 150,000 |
| Factory overhead | 50 | | |
| Selling and administrative expenses | 35 | | |
| Total | $235 | | |

Crystal Displays Inc. is currently considering establishing a selling price for flat panel displays. The president of Crystal Displays has decided to use the cost-plus approach to product pricing and has indicated that the displays must earn a 15% rate of return on invested assets.

### Instructions

1. Determine the amount of desired profit from the production and sale of flat panel displays.

2. Assuming that the product cost concept is used, determine (a) the cost amount per unit, (b) the markup percentage, and (c) the selling price of flat panel displays.

3. (*Appendix*) Assuming that the total cost concept is used, determine (a) the cost amount per unit, (b) the markup percentage (rounded to two decimal places), and (c) the selling price of flat panel displays (rounded to nearest whole dollar).

4. (*Appendix*) Assuming that the variable cost concept is used, determine (a) the cost amount per unit, (b) the markup percentage (rounded to two decimal places), and (c) the selling price of flat panel displays (rounded to nearest whole dollar).

5. ▬▬▬► Comment on any additional considerations that could influence establishing the selling price for flat panel displays.

6. Assume that as of August 1, 3,000 units of flat panel displays have been produced and sold during the current year. Analysis of the domestic market indicates that 2,000 additional units are expected to be sold during the remainder of the year at the normal product price determined under the product cost concept. On August 3, Crystal Displays Inc. received an offer from Maple Leaf Visual Inc. for 800 units of flat panel displays at $225 each. Maple Leaf Visual Inc. will market the units in Canada under its own brand name, and no variable selling and administrative expenses associated with the sale will be incurred by Crystal Displays Inc. The additional business is not expected to affect the domestic sales of flat panel displays, and the additional units could be produced using existing factory, selling, and administrative capacity.

    a. Prepare a differential analysis of the proposed sale to Maple Leaf Visual Inc.

    b. Based on the differential analysis in part (a), should the proposal be accepted?

### PR 25-6A Product pricing and profit analysis with bottleneck operations

OBJ. 3

✔ 1. High Grade, $10

Hercules Steel Company produces three grades of steel: high, good, and regular grade. Each of these products (grades) has high demand in the market, and Hercules is able to sell as much as it can produce of all three. The furnace operation is a bottleneck in the process and is running at 100% of capacity. Hercules wants to improve steel operation profitability. The variable conversion cost is $15 per process hour. The fixed cost is $200,000. In addition, the cost analyst was able to determine the following information about the three products:

| | High Grade | Good Grade | Regular Grade |
|---|---|---|---|
| Budgeted units produced | 5,000 | 5,000 | 5,000 |
| Total process hours per unit | 12 | 11 | 10 |
| Furnace hours per unit | 4 | 3 | 2.5 |
| Unit selling price | $280 | $270 | $250 |
| Direct materials cost per unit | $90 | $84 | $80 |

*(Continued)*

The furnace operation is part of the total process for each of these three products. Thus, for example, 4.0 of the 12.0 hours required to process High Grade steel are associated with the furnace.

**Instructions**

1. Determine the unit contribution margin for each product.

2. Provide an analysis to determine the relative product profitability, assuming that the furnace is a bottleneck.

---

### PR 25-7A  Activity-based costing                                    OBJ. 4

✔ 2. Brown sugar
total activity cost,
$138,550

Pure Cane Sugar Company manufactures three products (white sugar, brown sugar, and powdered sugar) in a continuous production process. Senior management has asked the controller to conduct an activity-based costing study. The controller identified the amount of factory overhead required by the critical activities of the organization as follows:

| Activity | Activity Costs |
| --- | --- |
| Production | $247,500 |
| Setup | 48,000 |
| Inspection | 12,500 |
| Shipping | 69,300 |
| Customer service | 27,600 |
| Total | $404,900 |

The activity bases identified for each activity are as follows:

| Activity | Activity Base |
| --- | --- |
| Production | Machine hours |
| Setup | Number of setups |
| Inspection | Number of inspections |
| Shipping | Number of customer orders |
| Customer service | Number of customer service requests |

The activity-base usage quantities and units produced for the three products were determined from corporate records and are as follows:

| | Machine Hours | Number of Setups | Number of Inspections | Number of Customer Orders | Number of Customer Service Requests | Units |
| --- | --- | --- | --- | --- | --- | --- |
| White sugar | 2,000 | 50 | 100 | 410 | 25 | 8,000 |
| Brown sugar | 1,250 | 70 | 160 | 1,100 | 200 | 5,000 |
| Powdered sugar | 1,250 | 80 | 240 | 800 | 120 | 5,000 |
| Total | 4,500 | 200 | 500 | 2,310 | 345 | 18,000 |

Each product requires 0.25 machine hour per unit.

**Instructions**

1. Determine the activity rate for each activity.
2. Determine the total and per-unit activity costs for all three products.
3. Why aren't the activity unit costs equal across all three products, since they require the same machine time per unit?

---

# Problems: Series B

---

### PR 25-1B  Differential analysis involving opportunity costs          OBJ. 1

On July 1, Coastal Distribution Company is considering leasing a building and buying the necessary equipment to operate a public warehouse. Alternatively, the company could use the funds to invest in $740,000 of 5% U.S. Treasury bonds that mature in

14 years. The bonds could be purchased at face value. The following data have been assembled:

| | |
|---|---|
| Cost of equipment | $740,000 |
| Life of equipment | 14 years |
| Estimated residual value of equipment | $75,000 |
| Yearly costs to operate the warehouse, excluding depreciation of equipment | $175,000 |
| Yearly expected revenues—years 1–7 | $280,000 |
| Yearly expected revenues—years 8–14 | $240,000 |

### Instructions

1. Prepare a differential analysis as of July 1 presenting the proposed operation of the warehouse for the 14 years (Alternative 1) as compared with investing in U.S. Treasury bonds (Alternative 2).

2. Based on the results disclosed by the differential analysis, should the proposal be accepted?

3. If the proposal is accepted, what is the total estimated income from operations of the warehouse for the 14 years?

---

**PR 25-2B    Differential analysis for machine replacement proposal**                OBJ. 1

Flint Tooling Company is considering replacing a machine that has been used in its factory for two years. Relevant data associated with the operations of the old machine and the new machine, neither of which has any estimated residual value, are as follows:

| **Old Machine** | |
|---|---|
| Cost of machine, eight-year life | $38,000 |
| Annual depreciation (straight-line) | 4,750 |
| Annual manufacturing costs, excluding depreciation | 12,400 |
| Annual nonmanufacturing operating expenses | 2,700 |
| Annual revenue | 32,400 |
| Current estimated selling price of the machine | 12,900 |

| **New Machine** | |
|---|---|
| Cost of machine, six-year life | $57,000 |
| Annual depreciation (straight-line) | 9,500 |
| Estimated annual manufacturing costs, exclusive of depreciation | 3,400 |

Annual nonmanufacturing operating expenses and revenue are not expected to be affected by purchase of the new machine.

### Instructions

1. Prepare a differential analysis as of November 8 comparing operations using the present machine (Alternative 1) with operations using the new machine (Alternative 2). The analysis should indicate the differential income that would result over the six-year period if the new machine is acquired.

2. ▬▬▬▶ List other factors that should be considered before a final decision is reached.

---

✔ 1. Differential revenue, $105,000

**PR 25-3B    Differential analysis for sales promotion proposal**                OBJ. 1

Sole Mates Inc. is planning a one-month campaign for July to promote sales of one of its two shoe products. A total of $100,000 has been budgeted for advertising, contests, redeemable coupons, and other promotional activities. The following data have been assembled for their possible usefulness in deciding which of the products to select for the campaign:

SHOW
ME HOW

*(Continued)*

| | Tennis Shoe | Walking Shoe |
|---|---|---|
| Unit selling price | $85 | $100 |
| Unit production costs: | | |
| Direct materials | $19 | $ 32 |
| Direct labor | 8 | 12 |
| Variable factory overhead | 7 | 5 |
| Fixed factory overhead | 16 | 11 |
| Total unit production costs | $50 | $ 60 |
| Unit variable selling expenses | 6 | 10 |
| Unit fixed selling expenses | 20 | 15 |
| Total unit costs | $76 | $ 85 |
| Operating income per unit | $ 9 | $ 15 |

No increase in facilities would be necessary to produce and sell the increased output. It is anticipated that 7,000 additional units of tennis shoes or 7,000 additional units of walking shoes could be sold without changing the unit selling price of either product.

### Instructions

1. Prepare a differential analysis as of June 19 to determine whether to promote tennis shoes (Alternative 1) or walking shoes (Alternative 2).

2. ➡ The sales manager had tentatively decided to promote walking shoes, estimating that operating income would be increased by $5,000 ($15 operating income per unit for 7,000 units, less promotion expenses of $100,000). The manager also believed that the selection of tennis shoes would reduce operating income by $37,000 ($9 operating income per unit for 7,000 units, less promotion expenses of $100,000). State briefly your reasons for supporting or opposing the tentative decision.

---

**PR 25-4B** **Differential analysis for further processing** **OBJ. 1**

✔ 1. Ingot income, $35,500

The management of International Aluminum Co. is considering whether to process aluminum ingot further into rolled aluminum. Rolled aluminum can be sold for $2,200 per ton, and ingot can be sold without further processing for $1,100 per ton. Ingot is produced in batches of 80 tons by smelting 500 tons of bauxite, which costs $105 per ton of bauxite. Rolled aluminum will require additional processing costs of $620 per ton of ingot, and 1.25 tons of ingot will produce 1 ton of rolled aluminum (due to trim losses).

### Instructions

1. Prepare a differential analysis as of February 5 to determine whether to sell aluminum ingot (Alternative 1) or process further into rolled aluminum (Alternative 2).

2. ➡ Briefly report your recommendations.

---

### Appendix

**PR 25-5B** **Product pricing using the cost-plus approach concepts;** **OBJ. 1, 2**
**differential analysis for accepting additional business**

✔ 2. b. Markup percentage, 30%

Night Glow Inc. recently began production of a new product, the halogen light, which required the investment of $600,000 in assets. The costs of producing and selling 10,000 halogen lights are estimated as follows:

| Variable costs per unit: | | Fixed costs: | |
|---|---|---|---|
| Direct materials | $32 | Factory overhead | $180,000 |
| Direct labor | 12 | Selling and administrative expenses | 80,000 |
| Factory overhead | 8 | | |
| Selling and administrative expenses | 7 | | |
| Total | $59 | | |

Night Glow Inc. is currently considering establishing a selling price for the halogen light. The president of Night Glow Inc. has decided to use the cost-plus approach to product pricing and has indicated that the halogen light must earn a 10% rate of return on invested assets.

**Instructions**

1. Determine the amount of desired profit from the production and sale of the halogen light.

2. Assuming that the product cost concept is used, determine (a) the cost amount per unit, (b) the markup percentage, and (c) the selling price of the halogen light.

3. (*Appendix*) Assuming that the total cost concept is used, determine (a) the cost amount per unit, (b) the markup percentage (rounded to two decimal places), and (c) the selling price of the halogen light (rounded to the nearest whole dollar).

4. (*Appendix*) Assuming that the variable cost concept is used, determine (a) the cost amount per unit, (b) the markup percentage (rounded to two decimal places), and (c) the selling price of the halogen light (rounded to nearest whole dollar).

5. ━━━▶ Comment on any additional considerations that could influence establishing the selling price for the halogen light.

6. Assume that as of September 1, 7,000 units of halogen light have been produced and sold during the current year. Analysis of the domestic market indicates that 3,000 additional units of the halogen light are expected to be sold during the remainder of the year at the normal product price determined under the product cost concept. On September 5, Night Glow Inc. received an offer from Tokyo Lighting Inc. for 1,600 units of the halogen light at $57 each. Tokyo Lighting Inc. will market the units in Japan under its own brand name, and no variable selling and administrative expenses associated with the sale will be incurred by Night Glow Inc. The additional business is not expected to affect the domestic sales of the halogen light, and the additional units could be produced using existing productive, selling, and administrative capacity.

   a. Prepare a differential analysis of the proposed sale to Tokyo Lighting Inc.

   b. Based on the differential analysis in part (a), should the proposal be accepted?

---

### PR 25-6B Product pricing and profit analysis with bottleneck operations OBJ. 3

✔ 1. Ethylene, $15

Wilmington Chemical Company produces three products: ethylene, butane, and ester. Each of these products has high demand in the market, and Wilmington Chemical is able to sell as much as it can produce of all three. The reaction operation is a bottleneck in the process and is running at 100% of capacity. Wilmington wants to improve chemical operation profitability. The variable conversion cost is $10 per process hour. The fixed cost is $400,000. In addition, the cost analyst was able to determine the following information about the three products:

|  | Ethylene | Butane | Ester |
|---|---|---|---|
| Budgeted units produced | 9,000 | 9,000 | 9,000 |
| Total process hours per unit | 4.0 | 4.0 | 3.0 |
| Reactor hours per unit | 1.5 | 1.0 | 0.5 |
| Unit selling price | $170 | $155 | $130 |
| Direct materials cost per unit | $115 | $88 | $85 |

The reaction operation is part of the total process for each of these three products. Thus, for example, 1.5 of the 4.0 hours required to process ethylene is associated with the reactor.

**Instructions**

1. Determine the unit contribution margin for each product.

2. Provide an analysis to determine the relative product profitabilities, assuming that the reactor is a bottleneck.

**PR 25-7B   Activity-based costing**                                              OBJ. 4

Southeastern Paper Company manufactures three products (computer paper, newsprint, and specialty paper) in a continuous production process. Senior management has asked the controller to conduct an activity-based costing study. The controller identified the amount of factory overhead required by the critical activities of the organization as follows:

| Activity | Activity Costs |
| --- | --- |
| Production | $220,000 |
| Setup | 117,000 |
| Moving | 21,000 |
| Shipping | 105,000 |
| Product engineering | 102,000 |
| Total | $565,000 |

The activity bases identified for each activity are as follows:

| Activity | Activity Base |
| --- | --- |
| Production | Machine hours |
| Setup | Number of setups |
| Moving | Number of moves |
| Shipping | Number of customer orders |
| Product engineering | Number of test runs |

The activity-base usage quantities and units produced for the three products were determined from corporate records and are as follows:

| | Machine Hours | Number of Setups | Number of Moves | Number of Customer Orders | Number of Test Runs | Units |
| --- | --- | --- | --- | --- | --- | --- |
| Computer paper | 400 | 80 | 230 | 310 | 50 | 1,000 |
| Newsprint | 500 | 30 | 70 | 140 | 15 | 1,250 |
| Specialty paper | 200 | 150 | 300 | 550 | 105 | 500 |
| Total | 1,100 | 260 | 600 | 1,000 | 170 | 2,750 |

Each product requires 0.4 machine hour per unit.

**Instructions**

1. Determine the activity rate for each activity.
2. Determine the total and per-unit activity cost for all three products.
3. Why aren't the activity unit costs equal across all three products, since they require the same machine time per unit?

## Cases & Projects

**CP 25-1   Ethics and professional conduct in business**

Aaron McKinney is a cost accountant for Majik Systems Inc. Martin Dodd, vice president of marketing, has asked Aaron to meet with representatives of Majik Systems' major competitor to discuss product cost data. Martin indicates that the sharing of these data will enable Majik Systems to determine a fair and equitable price for its products.

━━━━➤ Would it be ethical for Aaron to attend the meeting and share the relevant cost data?

**CP 25-2   Decision on accepting additional business**

A manager of Varden Sporting Goods Company is considering accepting an order from an overseas customer. This customer has requested an order for 20,000 dozen golf balls at a price of $22 per dozen. The variable cost to manufacture a dozen golf balls is $18 per dozen. The full cost is $25 per dozen. Varden has a normal selling price of $35 per dozen. Varden's plant has just enough excess capacity on the second shift to make the overseas order.

━━━━➤ What are some considerations in accepting or rejecting this order?

### CP 25-3    Accept business at a special price for a service company

If you are not familiar with Priceline.com Inc., go to its Web site. Assume that an individual "names a price" of $85 on Priceline.com for a room in Nashville, Tennessee, on August 22. Assume that August 22 is a Saturday, with low expected room demand in Nashville at a Marriott International, Inc., hotel, so there is excess room capacity. The fully allocated cost per room per day is assumed from hotel records as follows:

| | |
|---|---:|
| Housekeeping labor cost* | $ 38 |
| Hotel depreciation expense | 43 |
| Cost of room supplies (soap, paper, etc.) | 8 |
| Laundry labor and material cost* | 10 |
| Cost of desk staff | 6 |
| Utility cost (mostly air conditioning) | 5 |
| Total cost per room per day | $110 |

*Both housekeeping and laundry staff include many part-time
workers, so that the workload is variable to demand.

Should Marriott accept the customer bid for a night in Nashville on August 22 at a price of $85?

### CP 25-4    Cost-plus and target costing concepts

The following conversation took place between Juanita Jackson, vice president of marketing, and Les Miles, controller of Diamond Computer Company:

*Juanita:* I am really excited about our new computer coming out. I think it will be a real market success.

*Les:* I'm really glad you think so. I know that our success will be determined by our price. If our price is too high, our competitors will be the ones with the market success.

*Juanita:* Don't worry about it. We'll just mark our product cost up by 25%, and it will all work out. I know we'll make money at those markups. By the way, what does the estimated product cost look like?

*Les:* Well, there's the rub. The product cost looks as if it's going to come in at around $1,200. With a 25% markup, that will give us a selling price of $1,500.

*Juanita:* I see your concern. That's a little high. Our research indicates that computer prices are dropping and that this type of computer should be selling for around $1,250 when we release it to the market.

*Les:* I'm not sure what to do.

*Juanita:* Let me see if I can help. How much of the $1,200 is fixed cost?

*Les:* About $200.

*Juanita:* There you go. The fixed cost is sunk. We don't need to consider it in our pricing decision. If we reduce the product cost by $200, the new price with a 25% markup would be right at $1,250. Boy, I was really worried for a minute there. I knew something wasn't right.

a.    If you were Les, how would you respond to Juanita's solution to the pricing problem?

b.    How might target costing be used to help solve this pricing dilemma?

### CP 25-5    Pricing decisions and markup on variable costs

### Group Project

Many businesses are offering their products and services over the Internet. Some of these companies and their Internet addresses follow:

| Company Name | Internet Address (URL) | Product |
|---|---|---|
| Delta Air Lines | www.delta.com | Airline tickets |
| Amazon.com | www.amazon.com | Books |
| Dell Inc. | www.dell.com | Personal computers |

a.  In groups of three, assign each person in your group to one of the Internet sites listed. For each site, determine the following:

1.  A product (or service) description

2.  A product price

*(Continued)*

3. A list of costs that are required sell the product selected in part (1) as listed in the annual report on SEC Form 10-K

---

### CP 25-6 Identifying product cost distortion

Peachtree Beverage Company manufactures soft drinks. Information about two products is as follows:

| | Volume | Sales Price per Case | Gross Profit per Case |
|---|---|---|---|
| Jamaican Punch | 10,000 cases | $30 | $12 |
| King Kola | 800,000 cases | 30 | 12 |

It is known that both products have the same direct materials and direct labor costs per case. Peachtree Beverage allocates factory overhead to products by using a single plantwide factory overhead rate, based on direct labor cost. Additional information about the two products is as follows:

*Jamaican Punch:* Requires extensive process preparation and sterilization prior to processing. The ingredients are from Jamaica, requiring complex import controls. The formulation is complex, and it is thus difficult to maintain quality. Lastly, the product is produced in small production run sizes.

*King Kola:* Requires minor process preparation and sterilization prior to processing. The ingredients are acquired locally. The formulation is simple, and it is easy to maintain quality. Lastly, the product is produced in large production run sizes.

Explain the weakness in the per-case product profitability report in light of the additional data.

# Capital Investment Analysis

 ## Vail Resorts, Inc.

**W**hy are you paying tuition, studying this text, and spending time and money on a higher education? Most people believe that the money and time spent now will return them more earnings in the future. That is, the cost of higher education is an investment in your future earning ability. How would you know if this investment is worth it?

One method would be for you to compare the cost of a higher education against the estimated increase in your future earning power. The bigger the difference between your expected future earnings and the cost of your education, the better the investment. A business also evaluates its investments in fixed assets by comparing the initial cost of the investment to its future earnings and cash flows.

For example, **Vail Resorts, Inc.,** is one of the largest ski resort owner operators in the world. They are known for their Vail, Breckenridge, and Keystone ski resorts, among others. A ski resort requires significant investments in property and equipment. Thus, Vail routinely makes major investments in new or improved amenities, lodging, retail, lifts, snowmaking and grooming equipment, and technology infrastructure. These investments are evaluated by their ability to enhance cash flows.

In this chapter, the methods used to make investment decisions, which may involve thousands, millions, or even billions of dollars, are described and illustrated. The similarities and differences among the most commonly used methods of evaluating investment proposals, as well as the benefits of each method, are emphasized. Factors that can complicate the analysis are also discussed.

After studying this chapter, you should be able to:                                    *Example Exercises*

**OBJ 1**
Explain the nature and importance of capital investment analysis.
Nature of Capital Investment Analysis

**OBJ 2**
Evaluate capital investment proposals, using the average rate of return and cash payback methods.
Methods Not Using Present Values
    Average Rate of Return Method          **EE 26-1**
    Cash Payback Method          **EE 26-2**

**OBJ 3**
Evaluate capital investment proposals, using the net present value and internal rate of return methods.
Methods Using Present Values
    Present Value Concepts
    Net Present Value Method and Index          **EE 26-3**
    Net Present Value Method
    Present Value Index
    Internal Rate of Return Method          **EE 26-4**

**OBJ 4**
List and describe factors that complicate capital investment analysis.
Factors That Complicate Capital Investment Analysis
    Income Tax
    Unequal Proposal Lives          **EE 26-5**
    Lease Versus Capital Investment
    Uncertainty
    Changes in Price Levels
    Qualitative Considerations

**OBJ 5**
Diagram the capital rationing process.
Capital Rationing

**At a Glance 26**      Page 1235

---

**OBJ 1** Explain the nature and importance of capital investment analysis.

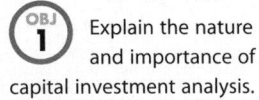

**The Walt Disney Company** and its partners will commit more than $4.4 billion to build Shanghai Disneyland, which is scheduled to open in 2016.

# Nature of Capital Investment Analysis

Companies use capital investment analysis to evaluate long-term investments. **Capital investment analysis** (or *capital budgeting*) is the process by which management plans, evaluates, and controls investments in fixed assets. Capital investments use funds and affect operations for many years and must earn a reasonable rate of return. Thus, capital investment decisions are some of the most important decisions that management makes.

Capital investment evaluation methods can be grouped into the following categories:

**Methods That Do Not Use Present Values**

- Average rate of return method
- Cash payback method

**Methods That Use Present Values**

- Net present value method
- Internal rate of return method

The two methods that use present values consider the time value of money. The **time value of money concept** recognizes that a dollar today is worth more than a dollar tomorrow because today's dollar can earn interest.

# Business  Connection

## BUSINESS USE OF INVESTMENT ANALYSIS METHODS

A survey of chief financial officers of large U.S. companies reported their use of the four investment methods as follows:

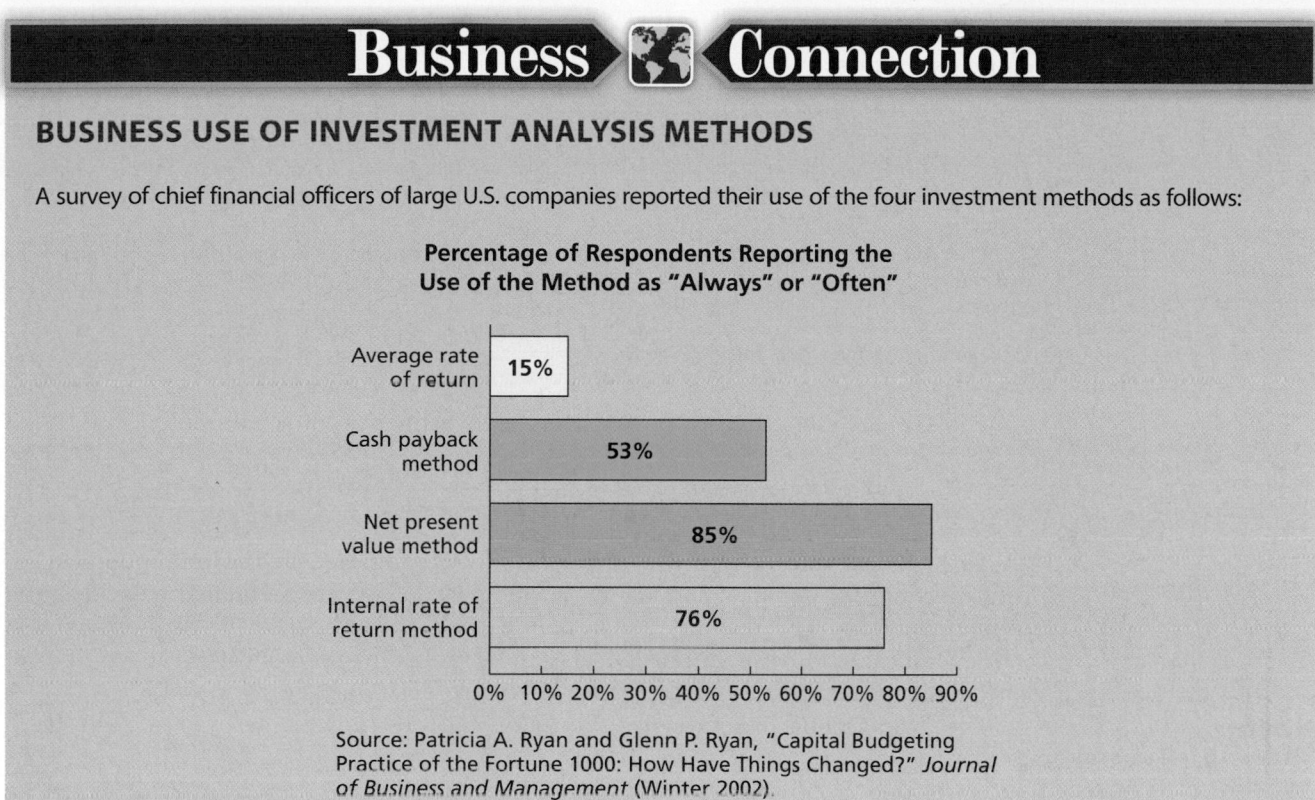

**Percentage of Respondents Reporting the Use of the Method as "Always" or "Often"**

| Method | Percentage |
|---|---|
| Average rate of return | 15% |
| Cash payback method | 53% |
| Net present value method | 85% |
| Internal rate of return method | 76% |

0% 10% 20% 30% 40% 50% 60% 70% 80% 90%

Source: Patricia A. Ryan and Glenn P. Ryan, "Capital Budgeting Practice of the Fortune 1000: How Have Things Changed?" *Journal of Business and Management* (Winter 2002).

# Methods Not Using Present Values

**OBJ 2** Evaluate capital investment proposals, using the average rate of return and cash payback methods.

The methods not using present values are often useful in evaluating capital investment proposals that have relatively short useful lives. In such cases, the timing of the cash flows (the time value of money) is less important.

Because the methods not using present values are easy to use, they are often used to screen proposals. Minimum standards for accepting proposals are set, and proposals not meeting these standards are dropped. If a proposal meets the minimum standards, it may be subject to further analysis using the present value methods.

## Average Rate of Return Method

The **average rate of return**, sometimes called the *accounting rate of return*, measures the average income as a percent of the average investment. The average rate of return is computed as follows:

$$\text{Average Rate of Return} = \frac{\text{Estimated Average Annual Income}}{\text{Average Investment}}$$

In the preceding equation, the numerator is the average of the annual income expected to be earned from the investment over its life, after deducting depreciation. The denominator is the average investment (book value) over the life of the investment. Assuming straight-line depreciation, the average investment is computed as follows:

$$\text{Average Investment} = \frac{\text{Initial Cost} + \text{Residual Value}}{2}$$

To illustrate, assume that management is evaluating the purchase of a new machine as follows:

| | |
|---|---|
| Cost of new machine | $500,000 |
| Residual value | 0 |
| Estimated total income from machine | 200,000 |
| Expected useful life | 4 years |

The average estimated annual income from the machine is $50,000 ($200,000 ÷ 4 years). The average investment is $250,000, computed as follows:

$$\text{Average Investment} = \frac{\text{Initial Cost} + \text{Residual Value}}{2} = \frac{\$500,000 + \$0}{2} = \$250,000$$

The average rate of return on the average investment is 20%, computed as follows:

$$\text{Average Rate of Return} = \frac{\text{Estimated Average Annual Income}}{\text{Average Investment}} = \frac{\$50,000}{\$250,000} = 20\%$$

The average rate of return of 20% should be compared to the minimum rate of return required by management. If the average rate of return equals or exceeds the minimum rate, the machine should be purchased or considered for further analysis.

Several capital investment proposals can be ranked by their average rates of return. The higher the average rate of return, the more desirable the proposal.

The average rate of return has the following three advantages:

**Note:**
The average rate of return method considers the amount of income earned over the life of a proposal.

- It is easy to compute.
- It includes the entire amount of income earned over the life of the proposal.
- It emphasizes accounting income, which is often used by investors and creditors in evaluating management performance.

The average rate of return has the following two disadvantages:

- It does not directly consider the expected cash flows from the proposal.
- It does not directly consider the timing of the expected cash flows.

---

**Example Exercise 26-1   Average Rate of Return**                    OBJ 2

Determine the average rate of return for a project that is estimated to yield total income of $273,600 over three years, has a cost of $690,000, and has a $70,000 residual value.

**Follow My Example 26-1**

| | |
|---|---|
| Estimated average annual income | $91,200 ($273,600 ÷ 3 years) |
| Average investment | $380,000 ($690,000 + $70,000) ÷ 2 |
| Average rate of return | 24% ($91,200 ÷ $380,000) |

Practice Exercises: PE 26-1A, PE 26-1B

---

## Cash Payback Method

A capital investment uses cash and must return cash in the future to be successful. The expected period of time between the date of an investment and the recovery in cash of the amount invested is the **cash payback period**.

When annual net cash inflows are equal, the cash payback period is computed as follows:

$$\text{Cash Payback Period} = \frac{\text{Initial Cost}}{\text{Annual Net Cash Inflow}}$$

To illustrate, assume that management is evaluating the purchase of the following new machine:

| | |
|---|---|
| Cost of new machine | $200,000 |
| Cash revenues from machine per year | 50,000 |
| Expenses of machine per year | 30,000 |
| Depreciation per year | 20,000 |

To simplify, the revenues and expenses other than depreciation are assumed to be in cash. Hence, the net cash inflow per year from use of the machine is as follows:

| | | |
|---|---|---|
| Net cash inflow per year: | | |
| Cash revenues from machine | | $50,000 |
| Less cash expenses of machine: | | |
| Expenses of machine | $30,000 | |
| Less depreciation | 20,000 | 10,000 |
| Net cash inflow per year | | $40,000 |

The time required for the net cash flow to equal the cost of the new machine is the payback period. Thus, the estimated cash payback period for the investment is five years, computed as follows:

$$\text{Cash Payback Period} = \frac{\text{Initial Cost}}{\text{Annual Net Cash Inflow}} = \frac{\$200,000}{\$40,000} = 5 \text{ years}$$

In the preceding illustration, the annual net cash inflows are equal ($40,000 per year). When the annual net cash inflows are not equal, the cash payback period is determined by adding the annual net cash inflows until the cumulative total equals the initial cost of the proposed investment.

To illustrate, assume that a proposed investment has an initial cost of $400,000. The annual and cumulative net cash inflows over the proposal's six-year life are as follows:

| Year | Net Cash Flow | Cumulative Net Cash Flow |
|---|---|---|
| 1 | $ 60,000 | $ 60,000 |
| 2 | 80,000 | 140,000 |
| 3 | 105,000 | 245,000 |
| 4 | 155,000 | 400,000 |
| 5 | 100,000 | 500,000 |
| 6 | 90,000 | 590,000 |

Cash Payback Period
Years

The cumulative net cash flow at the end of Year 4 equals the initial cost of the investment, $400,000. Thus, the payback period is four years.

If the initial cost of the proposed investment had been $450,000, the cash payback period would occur during Year 5. Because $100,000 of net cash flow is expected during Year 5, the additional $50,000 to increase the cumulative total to $450,000 occurs halfway through the year ($50,000 ÷ $100,000). Thus, the cash payback period would be 4½ years.[1]

A short cash payback period is desirable. This is because the sooner cash is recovered, the sooner it can be reinvested in other projects. In addition, there is less chance of losses from changing economic or business conditions. A short cash payback period is also desirable for quickly repaying any debt used to purchase the investment.

[1] Unless otherwise stated, net cash inflows are received uniformly throughout the year.

The cash payback method has the following two advantages:

- It is simple to use and understand.
- It analyzes cash flows.

The cash payback method has the following two disadvantages:

- It ignores cash flows occurring after the payback period.
- It does not use present value concepts in valuing cash flows occurring in different periods.

---

**Example Exercise 26-2   Cash Payback Period**   OBJ 2

A project has estimated annual net cash flows of $30,000. It is estimated to cost $105,000. Determine the cash payback period.

**Follow My Example 26-2**

3.5 years ($105,000 ÷ $30,000)

.......................................................................................................................................................

Practice Exercises: PE 26-2A, PE 26-2B

---

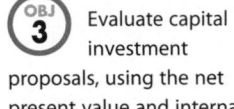

OBJ 3 Evaluate capital investment proposals, using the net present value and internal rate of return methods.

# Methods Using Present Values

An investment in fixed assets may be viewed as purchasing a series of net cash flows over a period of time. The timing of when the net cash flows will be received is important in determining the value of a proposed investment.

Present value methods use the amount and timing of the net cash flows in evaluating an investment. The two methods of evaluating capital investments using present values are as follows:

- Net present value method
- Internal rate of return method

## Present Value Concepts

Both the net present value and the internal rate of return methods use the following two **present value concepts**:

- Present value of an amount
- Present value of an annuity

**Present Value of an Amount** If you were given the choice, would you prefer to receive $1 now or $1 three years from now? You should prefer to receive $1 now, because you could invest the $1 and earn interest for three years. As a result, the amount you would have after three years would be greater than $1.

To illustrate, assume that you have $1 to invest as follows:

| | |
|---|---|
| Amount to be invested | $1 |
| Period to be invested | 3 years |
| Interest rate | 12% |

After one year, the $1 earns interest of $0.12 ($1 × 12%) and, thus, will grow to $1.12 ($1 × 1.12). In the second year, the $1.12 earns 12% interest of $0.134 ($1.12 × 12%) and, thus, will grow to $1.254 ($1.12 × 1.12) by the end of the second year. This process of interest earning interest is called *compounding*. By the end of the third year, your $1 investment will grow to $1.404 as shown in Exhibit 1.

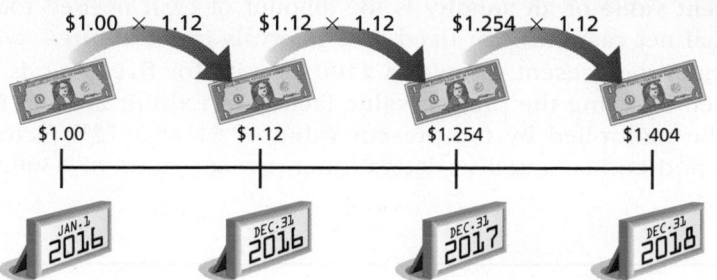

**EXHIBIT 1**

**Compound Amount of $1 for Three Periods at 12%**

On January 1, 2016, what is the present value of $1.404 to be received on December 31, 2018? This is a present value question. The answer can be determined with the aid of a present value of $1 table. For example, the partial table in Exhibit 2 indicates that the present value of $1 to be received in three years with earnings compounded at the rate of 12% per year is 0.712.[2]

| | Present Value of $1 at Compound Interest | | | | |
|---|---|---|---|---|---|
| Year | 6% | 10% | 12% | 15% | 20% |
| 1 | 0.943 | 0.909 | 0.893 | 0.870 | 0.833 |
| 2 | 0.890 | 0.826 | 0.797 | 0.756 | 0.694 |
| 3 | 0.840 | 0.751 | 0.712 | 0.658 | 0.579 |
| 4 | 0.792 | 0.683 | 0.636 | 0.572 | 0.482 |
| 5 | 0.747 | 0.621 | 0.567 | 0.497 | 0.402 |
| 6 | 0.705 | 0.564 | 0.507 | 0.432 | 0.335 |
| 7 | 0.665 | 0.513 | 0.452 | 0.376 | 0.279 |
| 8 | 0.627 | 0.467 | 0.404 | 0.327 | 0.233 |
| 9 | 0.592 | 0.424 | 0.361 | 0.284 | 0.194 |
| 10 | 0.558 | 0.386 | 0.322 | 0.247 | 0.162 |

**EXHIBIT 2**

**Partial Present Value of $1 Table**

Multiplying 0.712 by $1.404 yields $1 as follows:

| Present Value | | Amount to Be Received in 3 Years | | Present Value of $1 to Be Received in 3 Years (from Exhibit 2) |
|---|---|---|---|---|
| $1 | = | $1.404 | × | 0.712 |

That is, the present value of $1.404 to be received in three years using a compound interest rate of 12% is $1, as shown in Exhibit 3.

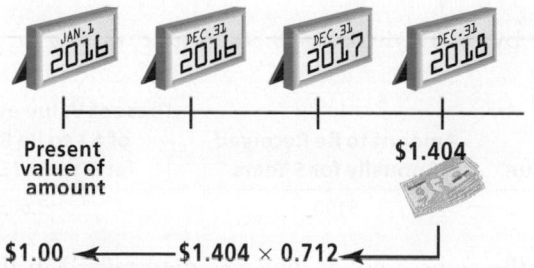

**EXHIBIT 3**

**Present Value of an Amount of $1.404**

$1.00 ←——— $1.404 × 0.712 ←———

**Present Value of an Annuity** An **annuity** is a series of equal net cash flows at fixed time intervals. Annuities are very common in business. Cash payments for monthly rent, salaries, and bond interest are all examples of annuities.

---

[2] The present value factors in the table are rounded to three decimal places. More complete tables of present values are in Appendix A.

The **present value of an annuity** is the amount of cash needed today to yield a series of equal net cash flows at fixed time intervals in the future.

To illustrate, the present value of a $100 annuity for five periods at 12% could be determined by using the present value factors in Exhibit 2. Each $100 net cash flow could be multiplied by the present value of $1 at a 12% factor for the appropriate period and summed to determine a present value of $360.50, as shown in Exhibit 4.

### EXHIBIT 4

**Present Value of a $100 Amount for Five Consecutive Periods**

Using a present value of an annuity table is a simpler approach. Exhibit 5 is a partial table of present value annuity factors.[3]

The present value factors in the table shown in Exhibit 5 are the sum of the present value of $1 factors in Exhibit 2 for the number of annuity periods. Thus, 3.605 in the annuity table (Exhibit 5) is the sum of the five present value of $1 factors at 12% from Exhibit 2, computed as follows:

|  | Present Value of $1 (Exhibit 2) |
| --- | --- |
| Present value of $1 for 1 year @12% | 0.893 |
| Present value of $1 for 2 years @12% | 0.797 |
| Present value of $1 for 3 years @12% | 0.712 |
| Present value of $1 for 4 years @12% | 0.636 |
| Present value of $1 for 5 years @12% | 0.567 |
| Present value of an annuity of $1 for 5 years (from Exhibit 5) | 3.605 |

Multiplying $100 by 3.605 yields $360.50 as follows:

| Present Value | | Amount to Be Received Annually for 5 Years | | Present Value of an Annuity of $1 to Be Received for 5 Years (Exhibit 5) |
| --- | --- | --- | --- | --- |
| $360.50 | = | $100 | × | 3.605 |

Thus, $360.50 is the same amount that was determined in the preceding illustration by five successive multiplications.

---

[3] The present value factors in the table are rounded to three decimal places. More complete tables of present values are in Appendix A.

**EXHIBIT 5**

**Partial Present Value of an Annuity Table**

| | Present Value of an Annuity of $1 at Compound Interest | | | | |
|---|---|---|---|---|---|
| Year | 6% | 10% | 12% | 15% | 20% |
| 1 | 0.943 | 0.909 | 0.893 | 0.870 | 0.833 |
| 2 | 1.833 | 1.736 | 1.690 | 1.626 | 1.528 |
| 3 | 2.673 | 2.487 | 2.402 | 2.283 | 2.106 |
| 4 | 3.465 | 3.170 | 3.037 | 2.855 | 2.589 |
| 5 | 4.212 | 3.791 | 3.605 | 3.353 | 2.991 |
| 6 | 4.917 | 4.355 | 4.111 | 3.785 | 3.326 |
| 7 | 5.582 | 4.868 | 4.564 | 4.160 | 3.605 |
| 8 | 6.210 | 5.335 | 4.968 | 4.487 | 3.837 |
| 9 | 6.802 | 5.759 | 5.328 | 4.772 | 4.031 |
| 10 | 7.360 | 6.145 | 5.650 | 5.019 | 4.192 |

# Net Present Value Method and Index

The net present value method and present value index are often used in combination, as we illustrate in this section.

## Net Present Value Method

The **net present value method** compares the amount to be invested with the present value of the net cash inflows. It is sometimes called the *discounted cash flow method*.

The interest rate (return) used in net present value analysis is the company's minimum desired rate of return. This rate, sometimes termed the *hurdle rate*, is based on such factors as the purpose of the investment and the cost of obtaining funds for the investment. If the present value of the cash inflows equals or exceeds the amount to be invested, the proposal is desirable.

To illustrate, assume the following data for a proposed investment in new equipment:

| | |
|---|---|
| Cost of new equipment | $200,000 |
| Expected useful life | 5 years |
| Minimum desired rate of return | 10% |
| Expected cash flows to be received each year: | |
| Year 1 | $ 70,000 |
| Year 2 | 60,000 |
| Year 3 | 50,000 |
| Year 4 | 40,000 |
| Year 5 | 40,000 |
| Total expected cash flows | $260,000 |

**Note:**
The net present value method compares an investment's initial cash outflow with the present value of its cash inflows.

The present value of the net cash flow for each year is computed by multiplying the net cash flow for the year by the present value factor of $1 for that year, as follows:

| Year | Present Value of $1 at 10% | × | Net Cash Flow | = | Present Value of Net Cash Flow |
|---|---|---|---|---|---|
| 1 | 0.909 | | $ 70,000 | | $ 63,630 |
| 2 | 0.826 | | 60,000 | | 49,560 |
| 3 | 0.751 | | 50,000 | | 37,550 |
| 4 | 0.683 | | 40,000 | | 27,320 |
| 5 | 0.621 | | 40,000 | | 24,840 |
| Total | | | $260,000 | | $202,900 |
| Less amount to be invested | | | | | 200,000 |
| Net present value | | | | | $ 2,900 |

The use of spreadsheet software such as Microsoft Excel can simplify present value computations.

The preceding computations are also graphically illustrated in Exhibit 6.

**EXHIBIT 6**

**Present Value of Equipment Cash Flows**

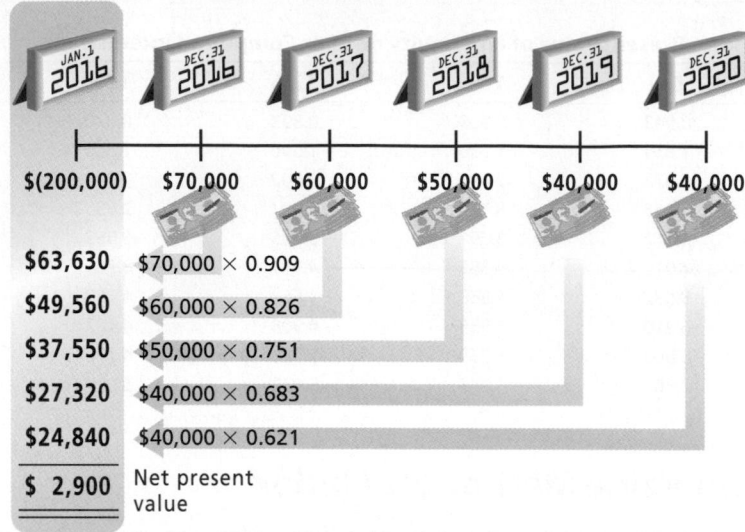

| | | | | | |
|---|---|---|---|---|---|
| $(200,000) | $70,000 | $60,000 | $50,000 | $40,000 | $40,000 |

$63,630    $70,000 × 0.909

$49,560    $60,000 × 0.826

$37,550    $50,000 × 0.751

$27,320    $40,000 × 0.683

$24,840    $40,000 × 0.621

$ 2,900    Net present value

The net present value of $2,900 indicates that the purchase of the new equipment is expected to recover the investment and provide more than the minimum rate of return of 10%. Thus, the purchase of the new equipment is desirable.

The net present value method has the following three advantages:

• It considers the cash flows of the investment.
• It considers the time value of money.
• It can rank projects with equal lives, using the present value index.

The net present value method has the following two disadvantages:

• It has more complex computations than methods that don't use present value.
• It assumes the cash flows can be reinvested at the minimum desired rate of return, which may not be valid.

## Present Value Index

When capital investment funds are limited and the proposals involve different investments, a ranking of the proposals can be prepared by using a present value index. The **present value index** is computed as follows:

$$\text{Present Value Index} = \frac{\text{Total Present Value of Net Cash Flow}}{\text{Amount to Be Invested}}$$

The present value index for the investment in the preceding illustration is 1.0145, computed as follows:

$$\text{Present Value Index} = \frac{\$202,900}{\$200,000} = 1.0145$$

Assume that a company is considering three proposals. The net present value and the present value index for each proposal are as follows:

| | Proposal A | Proposal B | Proposal C |
|---|---|---|---|
| Total present value of net cash flow | $107,000 | $86,400 | $86,400 |
| Less amount to be invested | 100,000 | 80,000 | 90,000 |
| Net present value | $ 7,000 | $ 6,400 | $ (3,600) |
| Present value index: | | | |
| Proposal A ($107,000 ÷ $100,000) | 1.07 | | |
| Proposal B ($86,400 ÷ $80,000) | | 1.08 | |
| Proposal C ($86,400 ÷ $90,000) | | | 0.96 |

A project will have a present value index greater than 1 when the net present value is positive. This is the case for Proposals A and B. When the net present value is negative, the present value index will be less than 1, as is the case for Proposal C.

Although Proposal A has the largest net present value, the present value indices indicate that it is not as desirable as Proposal B. That is, Proposal B returns $1.08 present value per dollar invested, whereas Proposal A returns only $1.07. Proposal B requires an investment of $80,000, compared to an investment of $100,000 for Proposal A. The possible use of the $20,000 difference between Proposals A and B investments should also be considered before making a final decision.

---

### Example Exercise 26-3  Net Present Value

OBJ 3

A project has estimated annual net cash flows of $50,000 for seven years and is estimated to cost $240,000. Assume a minimum acceptable rate of return of 12%. Using Exhibit 5, determine (a) the net present value of the project and (b) the present value index, rounded to two decimal places.

### Follow My Example 26-3

a. ($11,800)   [($50,000 × 4.564) − $240,000]
b. 0.95        ($228,200 ÷ $240,000)

Practice Exercises: PE 26-3A, PE 26-3B

---

## Internal Rate of Return Method

The **internal rate of return (IRR) method** uses present value concepts to compute the rate of return from a capital investment proposal based on its expected net cash flows. This method, sometimes called the *time-adjusted rate of return method*, starts with the proposal's net cash flows and works backward to estimate the proposal's expected rate of return.

To illustrate, assume that management is evaluating the following proposal to purchase new equipment:

| | |
|---|---|
| Cost of new equipment | $33,530 |
| Yearly expected cash flows to be received | $10,000 |
| Expected life | 5 years |
| Minimum desired rate of return | 12% |

The present value of the net cash flows, using the present value of an annuity table in Exhibit 5, is $2,520, as shown in Exhibit 7.

**EXHIBIT 7**

**Net Present Value Analysis at 12%**

| | |
|---|---|
| Annual net cash flow (at the end of each of five years) | $10,000 |
| Present value of an annuity of $1 at 12% for five years (Exhibit 5) | × 3.605 |
| Present value of annual net cash flows | $36,050 |
| Less amount to be invested | 33,530 |
| Net present value | $ 2,520 |

In Exhibit 7, the $36,050 present value of the cash inflows, based on a 12% rate of return, is greater than the $33,530 to be invested. Thus, the internal rate of return must be greater than 12%. Through trial and error, the rate of return equating the $33,530 cost of the investment with the present value of the net cash flows can be determined to be 15%, as shown in Exhibit 8.

**EXHIBIT 8**

**Present Value of an Annuity at the Internal Rate of Return Rate**

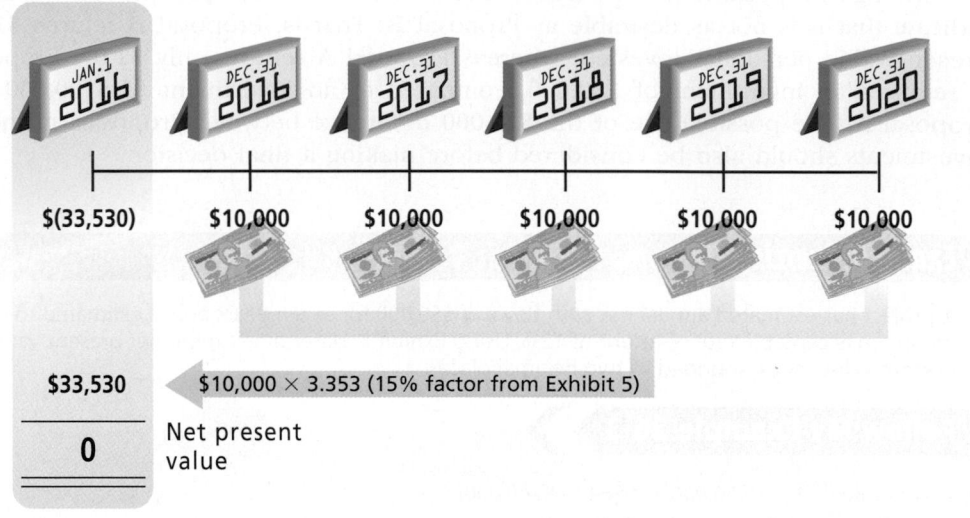

When equal annual net cash flows are expected from a proposal, as in the preceding example, the internal rate of return can be determined as follows:[4]

- Step 1. Determine a present value factor for an annuity of $1 as follows:

$$\text{Present Value Factor for an Annuity of \$1} = \frac{\text{Amount to Be Invested}}{\text{Equal Annual Net Cash Flows}}$$

- Step 2. Locate the present value factor determined in Step 1 in the present value of an annuity of $1 table (Exhibit 5) as follows:
    a. Locate the number of years of expected useful life of the investment in the Year column.
    b. Proceed horizontally across the table until you find the present value factor computed in Step 1.
- Step 3. Identify the internal rate of return by the heading of the column in which the present value factor in Step 2 is located.

To illustrate, assume that management is evaluating the following proposal to purchase new equipment:

| | |
|---|---|
| Cost of new equipment | $97,360 |
| Yearly expected cash flows to be received | $20,000 |
| Expected useful life | 7 years |

[4] To simplify, equal annual net cash flows are assumed. If the net cash flows are not equal, spreadsheet software can be used to determine the rate of return.

The present value factor for an annuity of $1 is 4.868, computed as follows:

$$\text{Present Value Factor for an Annuity of \$1} = \frac{\text{Amount to Be Invested}}{\text{Equal Annual Net Cash Flows}}$$

$$= \frac{\$97,360}{\$20,000} = 4.868$$

Using the partial present value of an annuity of $1 table shown in Exhibit 9 and a period of seven years, the factor 4.868 is related to 10%. Thus, the internal rate of return for this proposal is 10%.

---

| EXHIBIT 9 | **Steps to Determine the Internal Rate of Return** |
|---|---|

**Present Value of an Annuity of $1 at Compound Interest**

|  | Year | 6% | | Step 3<br>10% ◄ | 12% |
|---|---|---|---|---|---|
|  | 1 | 0.943 | | 0.909 | 0.893 |
|  | 2 | 1.833 | | 1.736 | 1.690 |
|  | 3 | 2.673 | | 2.487 | 2.402 |
|  | 4 | 3.465 | | 3.170 | 3.037 |
|  | 5 | 4.212 | | 3.791 | 3.605 |
|  | 6 | 4.917 | Step 2(b) | 4.355 | 4.111 |
| Step 2(a) | 7 | 5.582 | ──────► | 4.868 | 4.564 |
|  | 8 | 6.210 | | 5.335 | 4.968 |
|  | 9 | 6.802 | | 5.759 | 5.328 |
|  | 10 | 7.360 | | 6.145 | 5.650 |

**Step 1:** Determine present value factor for an annuity of $1 $= \dfrac{\$97,360}{\$20,000} = 4.868$

---

If the minimum acceptable rate of return is 10%, then the proposal is considered acceptable. Several proposals can be ranked by their internal rates of return. The proposal with the highest rate is the most desirable.

The internal rate of return method has the following three advantages:

- It considers the cash flows of the investment.
- It considers the time value of money.
- It ranks proposals based upon the cash flows over their complete useful life, even if the project lives are not the same.

The internal rate of return method has the following two disadvantages:

- It has complex computations, requiring a computer if the periodic cash flows are not equal.
- It assumes the cash received from a proposal can be reinvested at the internal rate of return, which may not be valid.

---

**°Example Exercise 26-4  Internal Rate of Return**                     OBJ 3

A project is estimated to cost $208,175 and provide annual net cash flows of $55,000 for six years. Determine the internal rate of return for this project, using Exhibit 5.

**Follow My Example 26-4**

15%  [($208,175 ÷ $55,000) − 3.785, the present value of an annuity factor for six periods at 15%, from Exhibit 5]

Practice Exercises: PE 26-4A, PE 26-4B

## Business Connection

### PANERA BREAD STORE RATE OF RETURN

Panera Bread owns, operates, and franchises bakery-cafes throughout the United States. A recent annual report to the Securities and Exchange Commission (SEC Form 10-K) allowed the following information to be determined about an average company-owned store:

| | |
|---|---|
| Operating profit | $ 470,000 |
| Depreciation | 96,000 |
| Investment book value | 1,000,000 |

Assume that the operating profit and depreciation will remain unchanged for the next 15 years. Assume operating profit plus depreciation approximates annual net cash flows and that the investment residual value will be zero. Lastly, assume the investment book value approximates the current investment required to open a store. The average rate of return and internal rate of return can then be estimated. The average rate of return on a company-owned store is:

$$\frac{\$470,000}{\$1,000,000 \div 2} = 94\%$$

The internal rate of return is calculated by first determining the present value of an annuity of $1:

$$\text{Present Value of an Annuity of } \$1 = \frac{\$1,000,000}{\$470,000 + \$96,000} = 1.77$$

For a period of three years, this factor implies an internal rate of return of more than 20% (from Exhibit 5). However, if we more realistically assumed these cash flows for 15 years, Panera's company-owned stores generate an estimated internal rate of return of approximately 57% (from a spreadsheet calculation). Clearly, both investment evaluation methods indicate a highly successful business.

Source: Panera Bread, *Form 10-K for the Fiscal Year Ended December 25, 2012.*

---

**OBJ 4** List and describe factors that complicate capital investment analysis.

# Factors That Complicate Capital Investment Analysis

Four widely used methods of evaluating capital investment proposals have been described and illustrated in this chapter. In practice, additional factors such as the following may impact capital investment decisions:

- Income tax
- Proposals with unequal lives
- Leasing versus purchasing
- Uncertainty
- Changes in price levels
- Qualitative factors

## Income Tax

The impact of income taxes on capital investment decisions can be material. For example, in determining depreciation for federal income tax purposes, useful lives that are much shorter than the actual useful lives are often used. Also, depreciation for tax purposes often differs from depreciation for financial statement purposes. As a result, the timing of the cash flows for income taxes can have a significant impact on capital investment analysis.[5]

## Unequal Proposal Lives

The prior capital investment illustrations assumed that the alternative proposals had the same useful lives. In practice, however, proposals often have different lives.

To illustrate, assume that a company is considering purchasing a new truck or a new computer network. The data for each proposal follows:

---

[5] The impact of taxes on capital investment analysis is covered in advanced accounting textbooks.

| | Truck | Computer Network |
|---|---|---|
| Cost | $100,000 | $100,000 |
| Minimum desired rate of return | 10% | 10% |
| Expected useful life | 8 years | 5 years |
| Yearly expected cash flows to be received: | | |
| Year 1.................................... | $ 30,000 | $ 30,000 |
| Year 2.................................... | 30,000 | 30,000 |
| Year 3.................................... | 25,000 | 30,000 |
| Year 4.................................... | 20,000 | 30,000 |
| Year 5.................................... | 15,000 | 35,000 |
| Year 6.................................... | 15,000 | 0 |
| Year 7.................................... | 10,000 | 0 |
| Year 8.................................... | 10,000 | 0 |
| Total .................................... | $155,000 | $155,000 |

The expected cash flows and net present value for each proposal are shown in Exhibit 10. Because of the unequal useful lives, however, the net present values in Exhibit 10 are not comparable.

---

**EXHIBIT 10**    **Net Present Value Analysis—Unequal Lives of Proposals**

| | A | B | C | D |
|---|---|---|---|---|
| 1 | | | Truck | |
| 2 | Year | Present | Net | Present |
| 3 | | Value of | Cash | Value of |
| 4 | | $1 at 10% | Flow | Net Cash Flow |
| 5 | 1 | 0.909 | $ 30,000 | $ 27,270 |
| 6 | 2 | 0.826 | 30,000 | 24,780 |
| 7 | 3 | 0.751 | 25,000 | 18,775 |
| 8 | 4 | 0.683 | 20,000 | 13,660 |
| 9 | 5 | 0.621 | 15,000 | 9,315 |
| 10 | 6 | 0.564 | 15,000 | 8,460 |
| 11 | 7 | 0.513 | 10,000 | 5,130 |
| 12 | 8 | 0.467 | 10,000 | 4,670 |
| 13 | Total | | $155,000 | $112,060 |
| 14 | | | | |
| 15 | Less amount to be invested | | | 100,000 |
| 16 | Net present value | | | $ 12,060 |

| | A | B | C | D |
|---|---|---|---|---|
| 1 | | | Computer Network | |
| 2 | Year | Present | Net | Present |
| 3 | | Value of | Cash | Value of |
| 4 | | $1 at 10% | Flow | Net Cash Flow |
| 5 | 1 | 0.909 | $ 30,000 | $ 27,270 |
| 6 | 2 | 0.826 | 30,000 | 24,780 |
| 7 | 3 | 0.751 | 30,000 | 22,530 |
| 8 | 4 | 0.683 | 30,000 | 20,490 |
| 9 | 5 | 0.621 | 35,000 | 21,735 |
| 10 | Total | | $155,000 | $116,805 |
| 11 | | | | |
| 12 | Less amount to be invested | | | 100,000 |
| 13 | Net present value | | | $ 16,805 |
| 14 | | | | |

**Cannot be compared (unequal lives)**

---

**EXHIBIT 11**

**Net Present Value Analysis—Equalized Lives of Proposals**

Truck Net Present Value Greater than Computer Network Net Present Value by $1,835

| | A | B | C | D |
|---|---|---|---|---|
| 1 | | Truck—Revised to 5-Year Life | | |
| 2 | Year | Present | Net | Present |
| 3 | | Value of | Cash | Value of |
| 4 | | $1 at 10% | Flow | Net Cash Flow |
| 5 | 1 | 0.909 | $ 30,000 | $ 27,270 |
| 6 | 2 | 0.826 | 30,000 | 24,780 |
| 7 | 3 | 0.751 | 25,000 | 18,775 |
| 8 | 4 | 0.683 | 20,000 | 13,660 |
| 9 | 5 | 0.621 | 15,000 | 9,315 |
| 10 | 5 (Residual | | | |
| 11 | value) | 0.621 | 40,000 | 24,840 |
| 12 | Total | | $160,000 | $118,640 |
| 13 | | | | |
| 14 | Less amount to be invested | | | 100,000 |
| 15 | Net present value | | | $ 18,640 |

**Compared (equal lives)**

To make the proposals comparable, the useful lives are adjusted to end at the same time. In this illustration, this is done by assuming that the truck will be sold at the end of five years. The selling price (residual value) of the truck at the end of five years is estimated and included in the cash inflows. Both proposals will then cover five years; thus, the net present value analyses will be comparable.

To illustrate, assume that the truck's estimated selling price (residual value) at the end of Year 5 is $40,000. Exhibit 11 shows the truck's revised present value analysis assuming a five-year life.

As shown in Exhibit 11, the net present value for the truck exceeds the net present value for the computer network by $1,835 ($18,640 – $16,805). Thus, the truck is the more attractive of the two proposals.

---

## Example Exercise 26-5   Net Present Value—Unequal Lives

Project 1 requires an original investment of $50,000. The project will yield cash flows of $12,000 per year for seven years. Project 2 has a calculated net present value of $8,900 over a five-year life. Project 1 could be sold at the end of five years for a price of $30,000. (a) Determine the net present value of Project 1 over a five-year life, with residual value, assuming a minimum rate of return of 12%. (b) Which project provides the greatest net present value?

### Follow My Example 26-5

a. Present value of $12,000 per year at 12% for 5 years    $43,260   [$12,000 × 3.605 (Exhibit 5, 12%, 5 years)]
   Present value of $30,000 at 12% at the end of 5 years    17,010   [$30,000 × 0.567 (Exhibit 2, 12%, 5 years)]
   Total present value of Project 1                        $60,270
   Total cost of Project 1                                  50,000
   Net present value of Project 1                          $10,270

b. Project 1—$10,270 is greater than the net present value of Project 2, $8,900.

Practice Exercises: PE 26-5A, PE 26-5B

---

## Lease Versus Capital Investment

Leasing fixed assets is common in many industries. For example, hospitals often lease medical equipment. Some advantages of leasing a fixed asset include the following:

- The company has use of the fixed asset without spending large amounts of cash to purchase the asset.
- The company eliminates the risk of owning an obsolete asset.
- The company may deduct the annual lease payments for income tax purposes.

A disadvantage of leasing a fixed asset is that it is normally more costly than purchasing the asset. This is because the lessor (owner of the asset) includes in the rental price not only the costs of owning the asset, but also a profit.

The methods of evaluating capital investment proposals illustrated in this chapter can also be used to decide whether to lease or purchase a fixed asset.

## Uncertainty

All capital investment analyses rely on factors that are uncertain. For example, estimates of revenues, expenses, and cash flows are uncertain. This is especially true for long-term capital investments. Errors in one or more of the estimates could lead to incorrect decisions. Methods that consider the impact of uncertainty on capital investment analysis are discussed in advanced accounting and finance textbooks.

## Service  Focus

### IF YOU BUILD IT, THEY WILL COME

A business model describes how an organization delivers products or services to make a profit. Many service companies use what is termed a *network business model*. A network business model connects people and businesses with each other or to a centralized service. Examples of network service businesses include telecommunication, transportation, power and natural gas distribution, cable, satellite, and internet companies.

Network businesses often require significant investment in physical assets in order to create the network. Often this is described as a *Field of Dreams strategy* (from the movie of that name) because the network can only generate revenue once it is largely built. For example, a cell phone company draws value from having many cell towers linking many callers together. A critical mass of cell towers must be pre-built in order to establish the business. This is risky. As a result, network business carefully evaluate capital investments prior to building networks.

## Changes in Price Levels

Price levels normally change as the economy improves or deteriorates. General price levels often increase in a rapidly growing economy, which is called **inflation**. During such periods, the rate of return on an investment should exceed the rising price level. If this is not the case, the cash returned on the investment will be less than expected.

Price levels may also change for foreign investments. This occurs as currency exchange rates change. **Currency exchange rates** are the rates at which currency in another country can be exchanged for U.S. dollars.

If the amount of local dollars that can be exchanged for one U.S. dollar increases, then the local currency is said to be weakening to the dollar. When a company has an investment in another country where the local currency is weakening, the return on the investment, as expressed in U.S. dollars, is adversely impacted. This is because the expected amount of local currency returned on the investment would purchase fewer U.S. dollars.[6]

## Qualitative Considerations

Some benefits of capital investments are qualitative in nature and cannot be estimated in dollar terms. However, if a company does not consider qualitative considerations, an acceptable investment proposal could be rejected.

Some examples of qualitative considerations that may influence capital investment analysis include the investment proposal's impact on the following:

- Product quality
- Manufacturing flexibility
- Employee morale
- Manufacturing productivity
- Market (strategic) opportunities

Many qualitative factors may be as important as, if not more important than, quantitative factors.

## Integrity, Objectivity, and Ethics in Business

### ASSUMPTION FUDGING

The results of any capital budgeting analysis depend on many subjective estimates, such as the cash flows, discount rate, time period, and total investment amount. The results of the analysis should be used to either support or reject a project. Capital budgeting should not be used to justify an assumed net present value. That is, the analyst should not work backwards, filling in assumed numbers that will produce the desired net present value. Such a reverse approach reduces the credibility of the entire process.

---

[6] Further discussion on accounting for foreign currency transactions is available on the companion Web site at www.cengagebrain.com.

Diagram the capital rationing process.

# Capital Rationing

**Capital rationing** is the process by which management allocates funds among competing capital investment proposals. In this process, management often uses a combination of the methods described in this chapter.

Exhibit 12 illustrates the capital rationing decision process. Alternative proposals are initially screened by establishing minimum standards, using the cash payback and the average rate of return methods. The proposals that survive this screening are further analyzed, using the net present value and internal rate of return methods.

---

**EXHIBIT 12** **Capital Rationing Decision Process**

Alternative capital investment proposals

Minimum cash payback and average rate of return standards met? — No → Rejected proposals

Yes

Proposals for further analysis

Net present value and internal rate of return standards met? — No → Rejected proposals

Yes

Proposals for further analysis

Rejected proposals ← Yes — Do qualitative considerations change the decision?

Do qualitative considerations change the decision? — No → Rejected proposals

No / Yes

Accepted proposals

Ranking of proposals

Funded proposals ← Yes — Capital funds available? — No → Unfunded proposals—Reconsider if funds subsequently become available

Qualitative factors related to each proposal should also be considered throughout the capital rationing process. For example, new equipment might improve the quality of the product and, thus, increase consumer satisfaction and sales.

At the end of the capital rationing process, accepted proposals are ranked and compared with the funds available. Proposals that are selected for funding are included in the capital expenditures budget. Unfunded proposals may be reconsidered if funds later become available.

# At a Glance 26

**OBJ 1**

### Explain the nature and importance of capital investment analysis.

**Key Points**   Capital investment analysis is the process by which management plans, evaluates, and controls investments involving fixed assets. Capital investment analysis is important to a business because such investments affect profitability for a long period of time.

| Learning Outcome | Example Exercises | Practice Exercises |
|---|---|---|
| • Describe the purpose of capital investment analysis. | | |

**OBJ 2**

### Evaluate capital investment proposals, using the average rate of return and cash payback methods.

**Key Points**   The average rate of return method measures the expected profitability of an investment in fixed assets. The expected period of time that will pass between the date of an investment and the complete recovery in cash (or equivalent) of the amount invested is the cash payback period.

| Learning Outcomes | Example Exercises | Practice Exercises |
|---|---|---|
| • Compute the average rate of return of a project. | EE26-1 | PE26-1A, 26-1B |
| • Compute the cash payback period of a project. | EE26-2 | PE26-2A, 26-2B |

**OBJ 3**

### Evaluate capital investment proposals, using the net present value and internal rate of return methods.

**Key Points**   The net present value method uses present values to compute the net present value of the cash flows expected from a proposal. The internal rate of return method uses present values to compute the rate of return from the net cash flows expected from capital investment proposals.

| Learning Outcomes | Example Exercises | Practice Exercises |
|---|---|---|
| • Compute the net present value of a project. | EE26-3 | PE26-3A, 26-3B |
| • Compute the internal rate of return of a project. | EE26-4 | PE26-4A, 26-4B |

**List and describe factors that complicate capital investment analysis.**

**Key Points** Factors that may complicate capital investment analysis include the impact of income tax, unequal lives of alternative proposals, leasing, uncertainty, changes in price levels, and qualitative considerations.

| Learning Outcomes | Example Exercises | Practice Exercises |
|---|---|---|
| • Describe the impact of income taxes in capital investment analysis. | | |
| • Evaluate projects with unequal lives. | **EE26-5** | **PE26-5A, 26-5B** |
| • Describe leasing versus capital investment. | | |
| • Describe uncertainty, changes in price levels, and qualitative considerations in capital investment analysis. | | |

**Diagram the capital rationing process.**

**Key Points** Capital rationing refers to the process by which management allocates available investment funds among competing capital investment proposals. A diagram of the capital rationing process appears in Exhibit 12.

| Learning Outcomes | Example Exercises | Practice Exercises |
|---|---|---|
| • Define *capital rationing*. | | |
| • Diagram the capital rationing process. | | |

# Key Terms

annuity (1223)
average rate of return (1219)
capital investment analysis (1218)
capital rationing (1234)
cash payback period (1220)

currency exchange rate (1233)
inflation (1233)
internal rate of return (IRR) method (1227)
net present value method (1225)

present value concept (1222)
present value index (1226)
present value of an annuity (1224)
time value of money concept (1218)

# Illustrative Problem

The capital investment committee of Hopewell Company is currently considering two investments. The estimated income from operations and net cash flows expected from each investment are as follows:

| | Truck | | Equipment | |
| --- | --- | --- | --- | --- |
| Year | Income from Operations | Net Cash Flow | Income from Operations | Net Cash Flow |
| 1 | $ 6,000 | $ 22,000 | $13,000 | $ 29,000 |
| 2 | 9,000 | 25,000 | 10,000 | 26,000 |
| 3 | 10,000 | 26,000 | 8,000 | 24,000 |
| 4 | 8,000 | 24,000 | 8,000 | 24,000 |
| 5 | 11,000 | 27,000 | 3,000 | 19,000 |
| | $44,000 | $124,000 | $42,000 | $122,000 |

Each investment requires $80,000. Straight-line depreciation will be used, and no residual value is expected. The committee has selected a rate of 15% for purposes of the net present value analysis.

## Instructions

1. Compute the following:

   a. The average rate of return for each investment.

   b. The net present value for each investment. Use the present value of $1 table appearing in this chapter (Exhibit 2).

2. Why is the net present value of the equipment greater than the truck, even though its average rate of return is less?

3. Prepare a summary for the capital investment committee, advising it on the relative merits of the two investments.

## Solution

1. a. Average rate of return for the truck:

$$\frac{\$44,000 \div 5}{(\$80,000 + \$0) \div 2} = 22\%$$

   Average rate of return for the equipment:

$$\frac{\$42,000 \div 5}{(\$80,000 + \$0) \div 2} = 21\%$$

   b. Net present value analysis:

| | | Net Cash Flow | | Present Value of Net Cash Flow | |
| --- | --- | --- | --- | --- | --- |
| Year | Present Value of $1 at 15% | Truck | Equipment | Truck | Equipment |
| 1 | 0.870 | $ 22,000 | $ 29,000 | $19,140 | $25,230 |
| 2 | 0.756 | 25,000 | 26,000 | 18,900 | 19,656 |
| 3 | 0.658 | 26,000 | 24,000 | 17,108 | 15,792 |
| 4 | 0.572 | 24,000 | 24,000 | 13,728 | 13,728 |
| 5 | 0.497 | 27,000 | 19,000 | 13,419 | 9,443 |
| Total | | $124,000 | $122,000 | $82,295 | $83,849 |
| Less amount to be invested | | | | 80,000 | 80,000 |
| Net present value | | | | $ 2,295 | $ 3,849 |

2. The equipment has a lower average rate of return than the truck because the equipment's total income from operations for the five years is $42,000, which is $2,000 less than the truck's. Even so, the net present value of the equipment is greater than that of the truck because the equipment has higher cash flows in the early years.

3. Both investments exceed the selected rate established for the net present value analysis. The truck has a higher average rate of return, but the equipment offers a larger net present value. Thus, if only one of the two investments can be accepted, the equipment would be the more attractive.

# Discussion Questions

1. What are the principal objections to the use of the average rate of return method in evaluating capital investment proposals?

2. Discuss the principal limitations of the cash payback method for evaluating capital investment proposals.

3. Why would the average rate of return differ from the internal rate of return on the same project?

4. Your boss has suggested that a one-year payback period is the same as a 100% average rate of return. Do you agree?

5. Why would the cash payback method understate the attractiveness of a project with a large residual value?

6. Why would the use of the cash payback period for analyzing the financial performance of theatrical releases from a motion picture production studio be supported over the net present value method?

7. A net present value analysis used to evaluate a proposed equipment acquisition indicated a $7,900 net present value. What is the meaning of the $7,900 as it relates to the desirability of the proposal?

8. Two projects have an identical net present value of $9,000. Are both projects equal in desirability?

9. What are the major disadvantages of the use of the net present value method of analyzing capital investment proposals?

10. What are the major disadvantages of the use of the internal rate of return method of analyzing capital investment proposals?

11. What are the major advantages of leasing a fixed asset rather than purchasing it?

12. Give an example of a qualitative factor that should be considered in a capital investment analysis related to acquiring automated factory equipment.

# Practice Exercises

EE 26-1 *p.1220*    **PE 26-1A    Average rate of return**                                                    OBJ. 2

Determine the average rate of return for a project that is estimated to yield total income of $170,000 over five years, has a cost of $320,000, and has a $20,000 residual value.

EE 26-1 *p.1220*    **PE 26-1B    Average rate of return**                                                    OBJ. 2

Determine the average rate of return for a project that is estimated to yield total income of $36,000 over three years, has a cost of $70,000, and has a $10,000 residual value.

EE 26-2 *p.1222* | **PE 26-2A**    **Cash payback period**           OBJ. 2

A project has estimated annual net cash flows of $118,600. It is estimated to cost $616,720. Determine the cash payback period. Round to one decimal place.

---

EE 26-2 *p.1222* | **PE 26-2B**    **Cash payback period**           OBJ. 2

A project has estimated annual net cash flows of $9,300. It is estimated to cost $41,850. Determine the cash payback period. Round to one decimal place.

---

EE 26-3 *p.1227* | **PE 26-3A**    **Net present value**           OBJ. 3

A project has estimated annual net cash flows of $6,800 for five years and is estimated to cost $23,125. Assume a minimum acceptable rate of return of 12%. Using Exhibit 5, determine (1) the net present value of the project and (2) the present value index, rounded to two decimal places.

---

EE 26-3 *p.1227* | **PE 26-3B**    **Net present value**           OBJ. 3

A project has estimated annual net cash flows of $96,200 for four years and is estimated to cost $315,500. Assume a minimum acceptable rate of return of 10%. Using Exhibit 5, determine (1) the net present value of the project and (2) the present value index, rounded to two decimal places.

---

EE 26-4 *p.1229* | **PE 26-4A**    **Internal rate of return**           OBJ. 3

A project is estimated to cost $104,328 and provide annual net cash flows of $21,000 for eight years. Determine the internal rate of return for this project, using Exhibit 5.

---

EE 26-4 *p.1229* | **PE 26-4B**    **Internal rate of return**           OBJ. 3

A project is estimated to cost $362,672 and provide annual net cash flows of $76,000 for nine years. Determine the internal rate of return for this project, using Exhibit 5.

---

EE 26-5 *p.1232* | **PE 26-5A**    **Net present value—unequal lives**           OBJ. 4

Project A requires an original investment of $32,600. The project will yield cash flows of $7,000 per year for nine years. Project B has a calculated net present value of $3,500 over a six-year life. Project A could be sold at the end of six years for a price of $15,000. (a) Determine the net present value of Project A over a six-year life, with residual value, assuming a minimum rate of return of 12%. (b) Which project provides the greatest net present value?

---

EE 26-5 *p.1232* | **PE 26-5B**    **Net present value—unequal lives**           OBJ. 4

Project 1 requires an original investment of $55,000. The project will yield cash flows of $15,000 per year for seven years. Project 2 has a calculated net present value of $5,000 over a four-year life. Project 1 could be sold at the end of four years for a price of $38,000. (a) Determine the net present value of Project 1 over a four-year life, with residual value, assuming a minimum rate of return of 20%. (b) Which project provides the greatest net present value?

# Exercises

**EX 26-1**    **Average rate of return**           OBJ. 2

✔ Testing equipment, 7%

The following data are accumulated by ChemLab Inc. in evaluating two competing capital investment proposals:

SHOW
ME HOW

|  | Testing Equipment | Vehicle |
|---|---|---|
| Amount of investment | $86,000 | $30,000 |
| Useful life | 6 years | 8 years |
| Estimated residual value | 0 | 0 |
| Estimated total income over the useful life | $18,060 | $12,000 |

Determine the expected average rate of return for each proposal.

### EX 26-2 Average rate of return—cost savings

OBJ. 2

Midwest Fabricators Inc. is considering an investment in equipment that will replace direct labor. The equipment has a cost of $132,000 with a $16,000 residual value and a 10-year life. The equipment will replace one employee who has an average wage of $34,000 per year. In addition, the equipment will have operating and energy costs of $5,380 per year.

Determine the average rate of return on the equipment, giving effect to straight-line depreciation on the investment.

### EX 26-3 Average rate of return—new product

OBJ. 2

✔ Average annual income, $405,000

SHOW ME HOW

Galactic Inc. is considering an investment in new equipment that will be used to manufacture a smartphone. The phone is expected to generate additional annual sales of 6,000 units at $250 per unit. The equipment has a cost of $850,000, residual value of $50,000, and an eight-year life. The equipment can only be used to manufacture the phone. The cost to manufacture the phone follows:

| Cost per unit: | |
|---|---|
| Direct labor | $ 15.00 |
| Direct materials | 134.00 |
| Factory overhead (including depreciation) | 33.50 |
| Total cost per unit | $182.50 |

Determine the average rate of return on the equipment.

### EX 26-4 Calculate cash flows

OBJ. 2

✔ Year 1: $(168,500)

SHOW ME HOW

Nature's Way Inc. is planning to invest in new manufacturing equipment to make a new garden tool. The new garden tool is expected to generate additional annual sales of 2,500 units at $60 each. The new manufacturing equipment will cost $227,000 and is expected to have a 10-year life and $17,000 residual value. Selling expenses related to the new product are expected to be 5% of sales revenue. The cost to manufacture the product includes the following on a per-unit basis:

| | |
|---|---|
| Direct labor | $ 8.00 |
| Direct materials | 22.00 |
| Fixed factory overhead—depreciation | 8.40 |
| Variable factory overhead | 3.60 |
| Total | $42.00 |

Determine the net cash flows for the first year of the project, Years 2–9, and for the last year of the project.

### EX 26-5 Cash payback period for a service company

OBJ. 2

✔ Location 1: 5 years

SHOW ME HOW

Fidelity Bancorp Inc. is evaluating two capital investment proposals for a drive-up ATM kiosk, each requiring an investment of $280,000 and each with an eight-year life and expected total net cash flows of $448,000. Location 1 is expected to provide equal annual net cash flows of $56,000, and Location 2 is expected to have the following unequal annual net cash flows:

| | | | | |
|---|---|---|---|---|
| Year 1 | $90,000 | | Year 5 | $42,000 |
| Year 2 | 70,000 | | Year 6 | 42,000 |
| Year 3 | 60,000 | | Year 7 | 42,000 |
| Year 4 | 60,000 | | Year 8 | 42,000 |

Determine the cash payback period for both location proposals.

### EX 26-6 Cash payback method
**OBJ. 2**

Lily Products Company is considering an investment in one of two new product lines. The investment required for either product line is $540,000. The net cash flows associated with each product are as follows:

| Year | Liquid Soap | Body Lotion |
|------|-------------|-------------|
| 1 | $170,000 | $ 90,000 |
| 2 | 150,000 | 90,000 |
| 3 | 120,000 | 90,000 |
| 4 | 100,000 | 90,000 |
| 5 | 70,000 | 90,000 |
| 6 | 40,000 | 90,000 |
| 7 | 40,000 | 90,000 |
| 8 | 30,000 | 90,000 |
| Total | $720,000 | $720,000 |

a. Recommend a product offering to Lily Products Company, based on the cash payback period for each product line.

b. ━━━━▶Why is one product line preferred over the other, even though they both have the same total net cash flows through eight periods?

### EX 26-7 Net present value method
**OBJ. 3**

✔ a. NPV, $4,238

The following data are accumulated by Dillon Company in evaluating the purchase of $39,600 of equipment, having a four-year useful life:

| | Net Income | Net Cash Flow |
|--------|------------|---------------|
| Year 1 | $ 4,100 | $14,000 |
| Year 2 | 8,100 | 18,000 |
| Year 3 | 7,100 | 17,000 |
| Year 4 | 2,100 | 12,000 |

SHOW
ME HOW

a. Assuming that the desired rate of return is 15%, determine the net present value for the proposal. Use the table of the present value of $1 appearing in Exhibit 2 of this chapter.

b. ━━━━▶Would management be likely to look with favor on the proposal? Explain.

### EX 26-8 Net present value method for a service company
**OBJ. 3**

✔ a. 2016, $13,000

AM Express Inc. is considering the purchase of an additional delivery vehicle for $55,000 on January 1, 2016. The truck is expected to have a five-year life with an expected residual value of $15,000 at the end of five years. The expected additional revenues from the added delivery capacity are anticipated to be $58,000 per year for each of the next five years. A driver will cost $42,000 in 2016, with an expected annual salary increase of $1,000 for each year thereafter. The annual operating costs for the truck are estimated to be $3,000 per year.

a. Determine the expected annual net cash flows from the delivery truck investment for 2016–2020.

b. Calculate the net present value of the investment, assuming that the minimum desired rate of return is 12%. Use the present value of $1 table appearing in Exhibit 2 of this chapter.

c. ━━━━▶Is the additional truck a good investment based on your analysis? Explain.

✔ a. $22 million

### EX 26-9 Net present value method—annuity for a service company
**OBJ. 3**

Winter Lake Hotels is considering the construction of a new hotel for $150 million. The expected life of the hotel is 30 years, with no residual value. The hotel is expected to earn revenues of $55 million per year. Total expenses, including depreciation, are expected to be $38 million per year. Winter Lake management has set a minimum acceptable rate of return of 14%.

SHOW
ME HOW

*(Continued)*

a. Determine the equal annual net cash flows from operating the hotel.

b. Calculate the net present value of the new hotel, using the present value of an annuity of $1 table found in Appendix A. Round to the nearest million dollars.

c. ■■■■■►Does your analysis support construction of the new hotel? Explain.

---

**EX 26-10   Net present value method—annuity**                    OBJ. 3

✔ a. $46,000

Briggs Excavation Company is planning an investment of $132,000 for a bulldozer. The bulldozer is expected to operate for 1,500 hours per year for five years. Customers will be charged $110 per hour for bulldozer work. The bulldozer operator costs $28 per hour in wages and benefits. The bulldozer is expected to require annual maintenance costing $8,000. The bulldozer uses fuel that is expected to cost $46 per hour of bulldozer operation.

a. Determine the equal annual net cash flows from operating the bulldozer.

b. Determine the net present value of the investment, assuming that the desired rate of return is 10%. Use the present value of an annuity of $1 table in the chapter (Exhibit 5). Round to the nearest dollar.

c. ■■■■■►Should Briggs invest in the bulldozer, based on this analysis? Explain.

d. Determine the number of operating hours such that the present value of cash flows equals the amount to be invested.

---

**EX 26-11   Net present value method for a service company**                    OBJ. 3

✔ a. $157,600,000

Carnival Corporation has recently placed into service some of the largest cruise ships in the world. One of these ships, the *Carnival Breeze*, can hold up to 3,600 passengers, and it can cost $750 million to build. Assume the following additional information:

• There will be 330 cruise days per year operated at a full capacity of 3,600 passengers.
• The variable expenses per passenger are estimated to be $140 per cruise day.
• The revenue per passenger is expected to be $340 per cruise day.
• The fixed expenses for running the ship, other than depreciation, are estimated to be $80,000,000 per year.
• The ship has a service life of 10 years, with a residual value of $140,000,000 at the end of 10 years.

a. Determine the annual net cash flow from operating the cruise ship.

b. Determine the net present value of this investment, assuming a 12% minimum rate of return. Use the present value tables provided in the chapter in determining your answer.

---

**EX 26-12   Present value index**                    OBJ. 3

✔ Ft. Collins, 0.98

Dip N' Dunk Doughnuts has computed the net present value for capital expenditure at two locations. Relevant data related to the computation are as follows:

|                                        | Ft. Collins | Boulder   |
|----------------------------------------|-------------|-----------|
| Total present value of net cash flow   | $607,600    | $624,000  |
| Less amount to be invested             | 620,000     | 600,000   |
| Net present value                      | $(12,400)   | $ 24,000  |

a. Determine the present value index for each proposal.

b. ■■■■■►Which location does your analysis support? Explain.

### EX 26-13 Net present value method and present value index OBJ. 3

✔ b. Packing
machine, 1.55

Diamond & Turf Inc. is considering an investment in one of two machines. The sewing machine will increase productivity from sewing 150 baseballs per hour to sewing 290 per hour. The contribution margin per unit is $0.32 per baseball. Assume that any increased production of baseballs can be sold. The second machine is an automatic packing machine for the golf ball line. The packing machine will reduce packing labor cost. The labor cost saved is equivalent to $21 per hour. The sewing machine will cost $260,000, have an eight-year life, and will operate for 1,800 hours per year. The packing machine will cost $85,000, have an eight-year life, and will operate for 1,400 hours per year. Diamond & Turf seeks a minimum rate of return of 15% on its investments.

a. Determine the net present value for the two machines. Use the present value of an annuity of $1 table in the chapter (Exhibit 5). Round to the nearest dollar.

b. Determine the present value index for the two machines. Round to two decimal places.

c. ▶ If Diamond & Turf has sufficient funds for only one of the machines and qualitative factors are equal between the two machines, in which machine should it invest? Explain.

### EX 26-14 Average rate of return, cash payback period, net present value OBJ. 2, 3
### method for a service company

✔ b. 5 years

**SHOW
ME HOW**

Bi-Coastal Railroad Inc. is considering acquiring equipment at a cost of $520,000. The equipment has an estimated life of eight years and no residual value. It is expected to provide yearly net cash flows of $104,000. The company's minimum desired rate of return for net present value analysis is 10%.

Compute the following:

a. The average rate of return, giving effect to straight-line depreciation on the investment.

b. The cash payback period.

c. The net present value. Use the present value of an annuity of $1 table appearing in this chapter (Exhibit 5). Round to the nearest dollar.

### EX 26-15 Cash payback period, net present value analysis, and qualitative OBJ. 2, 3, 4
### considerations

✔ a. 4 years

The plant manager of Shenzhen Electronics Company is considering the purchase of new automated assembly equipment. The new equipment will cost $1,400,000. The manager believes that the new investment will result in direct labor savings of $350,000 per year for 10 years.

a. What is the payback period on this project?

b. What is the net present value, assuming a 10% rate of return? Use the present value of an annuity of $1 table in Exhibit 5.

c. ▶ What else should the manager consider in the analysis?

### EX 26-16 Internal rate of return method OBJ. 3

✔ a. 3.785

**SHOW
ME HOW**

The internal rate of return method is used by Testerman Construction Co. in analyzing a capital expenditure proposal that involves an investment of $113,550 and annual net cash flows of $30,000 for each of the six years of its useful life.

a. Determine a present value factor for an annuity of $1, which can be used in determining the internal rate of return.

b. Using the factor determined in part (a) and the present value of an annuity of $1 table appearing in this chapter (Exhibit 5), determine the internal rate of return for the proposal.

**EX 26-17** **Internal rate of return method for a service company** OBJ. 3, 4

The Canyons Resort, a Utah ski resort, recently announced a $415 million expansion of lodging properties, lifts, and terrain. Assume that this investment is estimated to produce $99 million in equal annual cash flows for each of the first 10 years of the project life.

a. Determine the expected internal rate of return of this project for 10 years, using the present value of an annuity of $1 table found in Exhibit 5.

b. ➤What are some uncertainties that could reduce the internal rate of return of this project?

**EX 26-18** **Internal rate of return method—two projects** OBJ. 3

✔ a. Delivery truck, 15%

Munch N' Crunch Snack Company is considering two possible investments: a delivery truck or a bagging machine. The delivery truck would cost $43,056 and could be used to deliver an additional 95,000 bags of pretzels per year. Each bag of pretzels can be sold for a contribution margin of $0.45. The delivery truck operating expenses, excluding depreciation, are $1.35 per mile for 24,000 miles per year. The bagging machine would replace an old bagging machine, and its net investment cost would be $61,614. The new machine would require three fewer hours of direct labor per day. Direct labor is $18 per hour. There are 250 operating days in the year. Both the truck and the bagging machine are estimated to have seven-year lives. The minimum rate of return is 13%. However, Munch N' Crunch has funds to invest in only one of the projects.

a. Compute the internal rate of return for each investment. Use the present value of an annuity of $1 table appearing in this chapter (Exhibit 5).

b. ➤Provide a memo to management, with a recommendation.

**EX 26-19** **Net present value method and internal rate of return method for a service company** OBJ. 3

✔ a. ($12,845)

Buckeye Healthcare Corp. is proposing to spend $186,725 on an eight-year project that has estimated net cash flows of $35,000 for each of the eight years.

a. Compute the net present value, using a rate of return of 12%. Use the present value of an annuity of $1 table in the chapter (Exhibit 5).

b. ➤Based on the analysis prepared in part (a), is the rate of return (1) more than 12%, (2) 12%, or (3) less than 12%? Explain.

c. Determine the internal rate of return by computing a present value factor for an annuity of $1 and using the present value of an annuity of $1 table presented in the text (Exhibit 5).

**EX 26-20** **Identify error in capital investment analysis calculations** OBJ. 3

Artscape Inc. is considering the purchase of automated machinery that is expected to have a useful life of five years and no residual value. The average rate of return on the average investment has been computed to be 20%, and the cash payback period was computed to be 5.5 years.

➤Do you see any reason to question the validity of the data presented? Explain.

**EX 26-21** **Net present value—unequal lives** OBJ. 3, 4

✔ Net present value, Processing mill, $196,220

Bunker Hill Mining Company has two competing proposals: a processing mill and an electric shovel. Both pieces of equipment have an initial investment of $750,000. The net cash flows estimated for the two proposals are as follows:

| | Net Cash Flow | |
| --- | --- | --- |
| Year | Processing Mill | Electric Shovel |
| 1 | $310,000 | $330,000 |
| 2 | 260,000 | 325,000 |
| 3 | 260,000 | 325,000 |
| 4 | 260,000 | 320,000 |
| 5 | 180,000 | |
| 6 | 130,000 | |
| 7 | 120,000 | |
| 8 | 120,000 | |

The estimated residual value of the processing mill at the end of Year 4 is $280,000.

Determine which equipment should be favored, comparing the net present values of the two proposals and assuming a minimum rate of return of 15%. Use the present value tables presented in this chapter (Exhibits 2 and 5).

---

### EX 26-22    Net present value—unequal lives                                    OBJ. 3, 4

Daisy's Creamery Inc. is considering one of two investment options. Option 1 is a $75,000 investment in new blending equipment that is expected to produce equal annual cash flows of $19,000 for each of seven years. Option 2 is a $90,000 investment in a new computer system that is expected to produce equal annual cash flows of $27,000 for each of five years. The residual value of the blending equipment at the end of the fifth year is estimated to be $15,000. The computer system has no expected residual value at the end of the fifth year.

Assume there is sufficient capital to fund only one of the projects. Determine which project should be selected, comparing the (a) net present values and (b) present value indices of the two projects. Assume a minimum rate of return of 10%. Round the present value index to two decimal places. Use the present value tables presented in this chapter (Exhibits 2 and 5).

---

## Problems: Series A

---

### PR 26-1A    Average rate of return method, net present value method,      OBJ. 2, 3
### and analysis for a service company

✔ 1. a. 34%

SHOW
ME HOW

The capital investment committee of Touch of Eden Landscaping Company is considering two capital investments. The estimated income from operations and net cash flows from each investment are as follows:

|  | Front-End Loader | | Greenhouse Fixtures | |
|---|---|---|---|---|
| Year | Income from Operations | Net Cash Flow | Income from Operations | Net Cash Flow |
| 1 | $23,000 | $ 35,000 | $10,200 | $ 22,200 |
| 2 | 20,000 | 32,000 | 10,200 | 22,200 |
| 3 | 12,000 | 24,000 | 10,200 | 22,200 |
| 4 | (2,000) | 10,000 | 10,200 | 22,200 |
| 5 | (2,000) | 10,000 | 10,200 | 22,200 |
|  | $51,000 | $111,000 | $51,000 | $111,000 |

Each project requires an investment of $60,000. Straight-line depreciation will be used, and no residual value is expected. The committee has selected a rate of 12% for purposes of the net present value analysis.

### Instructions
1. Compute the following:

    a. The average rate of return for each investment. Round to one decimal place.

    b. The net present value for each investment. Use the present value of $1 table appearing in this chapter (Exhibit 2). Round present values to the nearest dollar.

2. ━━━▶Prepare a brief report for the capital investment committee, advising it on the relative merits of the two investments.

**PR 26-2A   Cash payback period, net present value method, and analysis**     OBJ. 2, 3

✔ 1. b. Plant expansion, $305,040

Elite Apparel Inc. is considering two investment projects. The estimated net cash flows from each project are as follows:

| Year | Plant Expansion | Retail Store Expansion |
|---|---|---|
| 1 | $ 450,000 | $ 500,000 |
| 2 | 450,000 | 400,000 |
| 3 | 340,000 | 350,000 |
| 4 | 280,000 | 250,000 |
| 5 | 180,000 | 200,000 |
| Total | $1,700,000 | $1,700,000 |

Each project requires an investment of $900,000. A rate of 15% has been selected for the net present value analysis.

**Instructions**

1. Compute the following for each product:

    a. Cash payback period.

    b. The net present value. Use the present value of $1 table appearing in this chapter (Exhibit 2).

2. ━━━►Prepare a brief report advising management on the relative merits of each project.

**PR 26-3A   Net present value method, present value index, and analysis**     OBJ. 3
**for a service company**

✔ 2. Computer Network, 1.20

Continental Railroad Company is evaluating three capital investment proposals by using the net present value method. Relevant data related to the proposals are summarized as follows:

| | Maintenance Equipment | Ramp Facilities | Computer Network |
|---|---|---|---|
| Amount to be invested | $8,000,000 | $20,000,000 | $9,000,000 |
| Annual net cash flows: | | | |
| Year 1 | 4,000,000 | 12,000,000 | 6,000,000 |
| Year 2 | 3,500,000 | 10,000,000 | 5,000,000 |
| Year 3 | 2,500,000 | 9,000,000 | 4,000,000 |

**Instructions**

1. Assuming that the desired rate of return is 20%, prepare a net present value analysis for each proposal. Use the present value of $1 table appearing in this chapter (Exhibit 2).

2. Determine a present value index for each proposal. Round to two decimal places.

3. ━━━►Which proposal offers the largest amount of present value per dollar of investment? Explain.

**PR 26-4A   Net present value method, internal rate of return method,**     OBJ. 3
**and analysis for a service company**

✔ 1. a. Wind turbines, $82,600

The management of Advanced Alternative Power Inc. is considering two capital investment projects. The estimated net cash flows from each project are as follows:

| Year | Wind Turbines | Biofuel Equipment |
|---|---|---|
| 1 | $280,000 | $300,000 |
| 2 | 280,000 | 300,000 |
| 3 | 280,000 | 300,000 |
| 4 | 280,000 | 300,000 |

The wind turbines require an investment of $887,600, while the biofuel equipment requires an investment of $911,100. No residual value is expected from either project.

**Instructions**

1. Compute the following for each project:

   a. The net present value. Use a rate of 6% and the present value of an annuity of $1 table appearing in this chapter (Exhibit 5).

   b. A present value index. Round to two decimal places.

2. Determine the internal rate of return for each project by (a) computing a present value factor for an annuity of $1 and (b) using the present value of an annuity of $1 table appearing in this chapter (Exhibit 5).

3. ━━━▶What advantage does the internal rate of return method have over the net present value method in comparing projects?

---

**PR 26-5A   Alternative capital investments**                      OBJ. 3, 4

✔ 1. Servers, $11,105

The investment committee of Sentry Insurance Co. is evaluating two projects, office expansion and upgrade to computer servers. The projects have different useful lives, but each requires an investment of $490,000. The estimated net cash flows from each project are as follows:

| | Net Cash Flows | |
| Year | Office Expansion | Servers |
| --- | --- | --- |
| 1 | $125,000 | $165,000 |
| 2 | 125,000 | 165,000 |
| 3 | 125,000 | 165,000 |
| 4 | 125,000 | 165,000 |
| 5 | 125,000 | |
| 6 | 125,000 | |

The committee has selected a rate of 12% for purposes of net present value analysis. It also estimates that the residual value at the end of each project's useful life is $0, but at the end of the fourth year, the office expansion's residual value would be $180,000.

**Instructions**

1. For each project, compute the net present value. Use the present value of an annuity of $1 table appearing in this chapter (Exhibit 5). (Ignore the unequal lives of the projects.)

2. For each project, compute the net present value, assuming that the office expansion is adjusted to a four-year life for purposes of analysis. Use the present value of $1 table appearing in this chapter (Exhibit 2).

3. ━━━▶Prepare a report to the investment committee, providing your advice on the relative merits of the two projects.

---

**PR 26-6A   Capital rationing decision for a service company involving**      OBJ. 2, 3, 5
**four proposals**

✔ 5. Proposal C, 1.57

Renaissance Capital Group is considering allocating a limited amount of capital investment funds among four proposals. The amount of proposed investment, estimated income from operations, and net cash flow for each proposal are as follows:

| | Investment | Year | Income from Operations | Net Cash Flow |
| --- | --- | --- | --- | --- |
| Proposal A: | $680,000 | 1 | $ 64,000 | $ 200,000 |
| | | 2 | 64,000 | 200,000 |
| | | 3 | 64,000 | 200,000 |
| | | 4 | 24,000 | 160,000 |
| | | 5 | 24,000 | 160,000 |
| | | | $240,000 | $ 920,000 |
| Proposal B: | $320,000 | 1 | $ 26,000 | $ 90,000 |
| | | 2 | 26,000 | 90,000 |
| | | 3 | 6,000 | 70,000 |
| | | 4 | 6,000 | 70,000 |
| | | 5 | (44,000) | 20,000 |
| | | | $ 20,000 | $340,000 |

*(Continued)*

| | | | | | |
|---|---|---|---|---|---|
| Proposal C: | $108,000 | 1 | $ 33,400 | $ 55,000 |
| | | 2 | 31,400 | 53,000 |
| | | 3 | 28,400 | 50,000 |
| | | 4 | 25,400 | 47,000 |
| | | 5 | 23,400 | 45,000 |
| | | | $142,000 | $ 250,000 |
| Proposal D: | $400,000 | 1 | $100,000 | $ 180,000 |
| | | 2 | 100,000 | 180,000 |
| | | 3 | 80,000 | 160,000 |
| | | 4 | 20,000 | 100,000 |
| | | 5 | 0 | 80,000 |
| | | | $300,000 | $700,000 |

The company's capital rationing policy requires a maximum cash payback period of three years. In addition, a minimum average rate of return of 12% is required on all projects. If the preceding standards are met, the net present value method and present value indexes are used to rank the remaining proposals.

## Instructions

1. Compute the cash payback period for each of the four proposals.

2. Giving effect to straight-line depreciation on the investments and assuming no estimated residual value, compute the average rate of return for each of the four proposals. Round to one decimal place.

3. Using the following format, summarize the results of your computations in parts (1) and (2). By placing the calculated amounts in the first two columns on the left and by placing a check mark in the appropriate column to the right, indicate which proposals should be accepted for further analysis and which should be rejected.

| Proposal | Cash Payback Period | Average Rate of Return | Accept for Further Analysis | Reject |
|---|---|---|---|---|
| A | | | | |
| B | | | | |
| C | | | | |
| D | | | | |

4. For the proposals accepted for further analysis in part (3), compute the net present value. Use a rate of 15% and the present value of $1 table appearing in this chapter (Exhibit 2).

5. Compute the present value index for each of the proposals in part (4). Round to two decimal places.

6. Rank the proposals from most attractive to least attractive, based on the present values of net cash flows computed in part (4).

7. Rank the proposals from most attractive to least attractive, based on the present value indexes computed in part (5).

8. ━━━▶Based on the analyses, comment on the relative attractiveness of the proposals ranked in parts (6) and (7).

# Problems: Series B

**PR 26-1B** **Average rate of return method, net present value method, and analysis for a service company**　　　OBJ. 2, 3

The capital investment committee of Ellis Transport and Storage Inc. is considering two investment projects. The estimated income from operations and net cash flows from each investment are as follows:

| Year | Warehouse | | Tracking Technology | |
| | Income from Operations | Net Cash Flow | Income from Operations | Net Cash Flow |
| --- | --- | --- | --- | --- |
| 1 | $ 61,400 | $135,000 | $ 34,400 | $108,000 |
| 2 | 51,400 | 125,000 | 34,400 | 108,000 |
| 3 | 36,400 | 110,000 | 34,400 | 108,000 |
| 4 | 26,400 | 100,000 | 34,400 | 108,000 |
| 5 | (3,600) | 70,000 | 34,400 | 108,000 |
| Total | $172,000 | $540,000 | $172,000 | $540,000 |

Each project requires an investment of $368,000. Straight-line depreciation will be used, and no residual value is expected. The committee has selected a rate of 15% for purposes of the net present value analysis.

**Instructions**

1. Compute the following:

   a. The average rate of return for each investment. Round to one decimal place.

   b. The net present value for each investment. Use the present value of $1 table appearing in this chapter (Exhibit 2). Round present values to the nearest dollar.

2. ■■■■■■► Prepare a brief report for the capital investment committee, advising it on the relative merits of the two projects.

---

**PR 26-2B   Cash payback period, net present value method, and analysis**          OBJ. 2, 3
**for a service company**

✔ 1. b. *Pro Gamer,*
$49,465

Social Circle Publications Inc. is considering two new magazine products. The estimated net cash flows from each product are as follows:

| Year | Sound Cellar | Pro Gamer |
| --- | --- | --- |
| 1 | $ 65,000 | $ 70,000 |
| 2 | 60,000 | 55,000 |
| 3 | 25,000 | 35,000 |
| 4 | 25,000 | 30,000 |
| 5 | 45,000 | 30,000 |
| Total | $220,000 | $220,000 |

Each product requires an investment of $125,000. A rate of 10% has been selected for the net present value analysis.

**Instructions**

1. Compute the following for each product:

   a. Cash payback period.

   b. The net present value. Use the present value of $1 table appearing in this chapter (Exhibit 2).

2. ■■■■■■► Prepare a brief report advising management on the relative merits of each of the two products.

---

**PR 26-3B   Net present value method, present value Index, and analysis**          OBJ. 3
**for a service company**

✔ 2. Branch office
expansion, 0.95

First United Bank Inc. is evaluating three capital investment projects by using the net present value method. Relevant data related to the projects are summarized as follows:

| | Branch Office Expansion | Computer System Upgrade | ATM Kiosk Expansion |
| --- | --- | --- | --- |
| Amount to be invested ........................... | $420,000 | $350,000 | $520,000 |
| Annual net cash flows: | | | |
| Year 1 ....................................... | 200,000 | 190,000 | 275,000 |
| Year 2 ....................................... | 160,000 | 180,000 | 250,000 |
| Year 3 ....................................... | 160,000 | 170,000 | 250,000 |

(*Continued*)

**Instructions**

1. Assuming that the desired rate of return is 15%, prepare a net present value analysis for each project. Use the present value of $1 table appearing in this chapter (Exhibit 2).

2. Determine a present value index for each project. Round to two decimal places.

3. ━━━Which project offers the largest amount of present value per dollar of investment? Explain.

---

**PR 26-4B   Net present value method, internal rate of return method, and analysis   OBJ. 3 for a service company**

✔ 1. a. *After Hours*
$100,800

The management of Style Networks Inc. is considering two TV show projects. The estimated net cash flows from each project are as follows:

| Year | After Hours | Sun Fun |
|------|-------------|---------|
| 1 | $320,000 | $290,000 |
| 2 | 320,000 | 290,000 |
| 3 | 320,000 | 290,000 |
| 4 | 320,000 | 290,000 |

*After Hours* requires an investment of $913,600, while *Sun Fun* requires an investment of $880,730. No residual value is expected from either project.

**Instructions**

1. Compute the following for each project:

   a. The net present value. Use a rate of 10% and the present value of an annuity of $1 table appearing in this chapter (Exhibit 5).

   b. A present value index. Round to two decimal places.

2. Determine the internal rate of return for each project by (a) computing a present value factor for an annuity of $1 and (b) using the present value of an annuity of $1 table appearing in this chapter (Exhibit 5).

3. ━━━What advantage does the internal rate of return method have over the net present value method in comparing projects?

---

**PR 26-5B   Alternative capital investments**   OBJ. 3, 4

✔ 1. Topeka,
$135,600

The investment committee of Auntie M's Restaurants Inc. is evaluating two restaurant sites. The sites have different useful lives, but each requires an investment of $900,000. The estimated net cash flows from each site are as follows:

| Year | Net Cash Flows | |
|------|---------|--------|
| | Wichita | Topeka |
| 1 | $310,000 | $400,000 |
| 2 | 310,000 | 400,000 |
| 3 | 310,000 | 400,000 |
| 4 | 310,000 | 400,000 |
| 5 | 310,000 | |
| 6 | 310,000 | |

The committee has selected a rate of 20% for purposes of net present value analysis. It also estimates that the residual value at the end of each restaurant's useful life is $0, but at the end of the fourth year, Wichita's residual value would be $500,000.

**Instructions**

1. For each site, compute the net present value. Use the present value of an annuity of $1 table appearing in this chapter (Exhibit 5). (Ignore the unequal lives of the projects.)

2. For each site, compute the net present value, assuming that Wichita is adjusted to a four-year life for purposes of analysis. Use the present value of $1 table appearing in this chapter (Exhibit 2).

3. ━━━Prepare a report to the investment committee, providing your advice on the relative merits of the two sites.

**PR 26-6B** **Capital rationing decision for a service company involving four proposals**

OBJ. 2, 3, 5

Clearcast Communications Inc. is considering allocating a limited amount of capital investment funds among four proposals. The amount of proposed investment, estimated income from operations, and net cash flow for each proposal are as follows:

| | Investment | Year | Income from Operations | Net Cash Flow |
|---|---|---|---|---|
| Proposal A: | $450,000 | 1 | $ 30,000 | $120,000 |
| | | 2 | 30,000 | 120,000 |
| | | 3 | 20,000 | 110,000 |
| | | 4 | 10,000 | 100,000 |
| | | 5 | (30,000) | 60,000 |
| | | | $ 60,000 | $510,000 |
| Proposal B: | $200,000 | 1 | $ 60,000 | $100,000 |
| | | 2 | 40,000 | 80,000 |
| | | 3 | 20,000 | 60,000 |
| | | 4 | (10,000) | 30,000 |
| | | 5 | (20,000) | 20,000 |
| | | | $ 90,000 | $290,000 |
| Proposal C: | $320,000 | 1 | $ 36,000 | $100,000 |
| | | 2 | 26,000 | 90,000 |
| | | 3 | 26,000 | 90,000 |
| | | 4 | 16,000 | 80,000 |
| | | 5 | 16,000 | 80,000 |
| | | | $120,000 | $440,000 |
| Proposal D: | $540,000 | 1 | $ 92,000 | $200,000 |
| | | 2 | 72,000 | 180,000 |
| | | 3 | 52,000 | 160,000 |
| | | 4 | 12,000 | 120,000 |
| | | 5 | (8,000) | 100,000 |
| | | | $220,000 | $760,000 |

The company's capital rationing policy requires a maximum cash payback period of three years. In addition, a minimum average rate of return of 12% is required on all projects. If the preceding standards are met, the net present value method and present value indexes are used to rank the remaining proposals.

**Instructions**

1. Compute the cash payback period for each of the four proposals.

2. Giving effect to straight-line depreciation on the investments and assuming no estimated residual value, compute the average rate of return for each of the four proposals. Round to one decimal place.

3. Using the following format, summarize the results of your computations in parts (1) and (2). By placing the calculated amounts in the first two columns on the left and by placing a check mark in the appropriate column to the right, indicate which proposals should be accepted for further analysis and which should be rejected.

| Proposal | Cash Payback Period | Average Rate of Return | Accept for Further Analysis | Reject |
|---|---|---|---|---|
| A | | | | |
| B | | | | |
| C | | | | |
| D | | | | |

4. For the proposals accepted for further analysis in part (3), compute the net present value. Use a rate of 12% and the present value of $1 table appearing in this chapter (Exhibit 2).

5. Compute the present value index for each of the proposals in part (4). Round to two decimal places.

*(Continued)*

6. Rank the proposals from most attractive to least attractive, based on the present values of net cash flows computed in part (4).

7. Rank the proposals from most attractive to least attractive, based on the present value indexes computed in part (5). Round to two decimal places.

8. Based on the analyses, comment on the relative attractiveness of the proposals ranked in parts (6) and (7).

# Cases & Projects

## CP 26-1   Ethics and professional conduct in business

Danielle Hastings was recently hired as a cost analyst by CareNet Medical Supplies Inc. One of Danielle's first assignments was to perform a net present value analysis for a new warehouse. Danielle performed the analysis and calculated a present value index of 0.75. The plant manager, Jerrod Moore, is very intent on purchasing the warehouse because he believes that more storage space is needed. Jerrod asks Danielle into his office and the following conversation takes place:

Jerrod: Danielle, you're new here, aren't you?

Danielle: Yes, I am.

Jerrod: Well, Danielle, I'm not at all pleased with the capital investment analysis that you performed on this new warehouse. I need that warehouse for my production. If I don't get it, where am I going to place our output?

Danielle: Well, we need to get product into our customers' hands.

Jerrod: I agree, and we need a warehouse to do that.

Danielle: My analysis does not support constructing a new warehouse. The numbers don't lie; the warehouse does not meet our investment return targets. In fact, it seems to me that purchasing a warehouse does not add much value to the business. We need to be producing product to satisfy customer orders, not to fill a warehouse.

Jerrod: The headquarters people will not allow me to build the warehouse if the numbers don't add up. You know as well as I that many assumptions go into your net present value analysis. Why don't you relax some of your assumptions so that the financial savings will offset the cost?

Danielle: I'm willing to discuss my assumptions with you. Maybe I overlooked something.

Jerrod: Good. Here's what I want you to do. I see in your analysis that you don't project greater sales as a result of the warehouse. It seems to me that if we can store more goods, then we will have more to sell. Thus, logically, a larger warehouse translates into more sales. If you incorporate this into your analysis, I think you'll see that the numbers will work out. Why don't you work it through and come back with a new analysis. I'm really counting on you on this one. Let's get off to a good start together and see if we can get this project accepted.

What is your advice to Danielle?

## CP 26-2   Personal investment analysis for a service company

A Masters of Accountancy degree at Central University costs $12,000 for an additional fifth year of education beyond the bachelor's degree. Assume that all tuition is paid at the beginning of the year. A student considering this investment must evaluate the present value of cash flows from possessing a graduate degree versus holding only the undergraduate degree. Assume that the average student with an undergraduate degree is expected to earn an annual salary of $50,000 per year (assumed to be paid at the end of the year) for 10 years. Assume that the average student with a graduate Masters of Accountancy degree is expected to earn an annual salary of $66,000 per year (assumed to be paid at the end of the year) for nine years after graduation. Assume a minimum rate of return of 10%.

1. Determine the net present value of cash flows from an undergraduate degree. Use the present value table provided in this chapter in Exhibit 5.

2. Determine the net present value of cash flows from a Masters of Accountancy degree, assuming no salary is earned during the graduate year of schooling.

3. ⬛⬛⬛➤What is the net advantage or disadvantage of pursuing a graduate degree under these assumptions?

### CP 26-3  Changing prices

Global Electronics Inc. invested $1,000,000 to build a plant in a foreign country. The labor and materials used in production are purchased locally. The plant expansion was estimated to produce an internal rate of return of 20% in U.S. dollar terms. Due to a currency crisis, the currency exchange rate between the local currency and the U.S. dollar doubled from two local units per U.S. dollar to four local units per U.S. dollar.

a. ▬▬▬▶Assume that the plant produced and sold product in the local economy. Explain what impact this change in the currency exchange rate would have on the project's internal rate of return.

b. ▬▬▬▶Assume that the plant produced product in the local economy but exported the product back to the United States for sale. Explain what impact the change in the currency exchange rate would have on the project's internal rate of return under this assumption.

### CP 26-4  Qualitative issues in investment analysis

The following are some selected quotes from senior executives:

*CEO, **Worthington Industries** (a high-technology steel company): "We try to find the best technology, stay ahead of the competition, and serve the customer.... We'll make any investment that will pay back quickly ... but if it is something that we really see as a must down the road, payback is not going to be that important."*

*Chairman of **Amgen Inc.** (a biotech company): "You cannot really run the numbers, do net present value calculations, because the uncertainties are really gigantic.... You decide on a project you want to run, and then you run the numbers [as a reality check on your assumptions]. Success in a business like this is much more dependent on tracking rather than on predicting, much more dependent on seeing results over time, tracking and adjusting and readjusting, much more dynamic, much more flexible."*

*Chief Financial Officer of **Merck & Co., Inc.** (a pharmaceutical company): "... at the individual product level—the development of a successful new product requires on the order of $230 million in R&D, spread over more than a decade—discounted cash flow style analysis does not become a factor until development is near the point of manufacturing scale-up effort. Prior to that point, given the uncertainties associated with new product development, it would be lunacy in our business to decide that we know exactly what's going to happen to a product once it gets out."*

▬▬▬▶Explain the role of capital investment analysis for these companies.

### CP 26-5  Net present value method for a service company

**Metro-Goldwyn-Mayer Studios Inc. (MGM)** is a major producer and distributor of theatrical and television filmed entertainment. Regarding theatrical films, MGM states, "Our feature films are exploited through a series of sequential domestic and international distribution channels, typically beginning with theatrical exhibition. Thereafter, feature films are first made available for home video (online downloads) generally six months after theatrical release; for pay television, one year after theatrical release; and for syndication, approximately three to five years after theatrical release."

Assume that MGM produces a film during early 2016 at a cost of $340 million and releases it halfway through the year. During the last half of 2016, the film earns revenues of $420 million at the box office. The film requires $90 million of advertising during the release. One year later, by the end of 2017, the film is expected to earn MGM net cash flows from online downloads of $60 million. By the end of 2018, the film is expected to earn MGM $20 million from pay TV; and by the end of 2019, the film is expected to earn $10 million from syndication.

a. Determine the net present value of the film as of the beginning of 2016 if the desired rate of return is 20%. To simplify present value calculations, assume all annual net cash flows occur at the end of each year. Use the table of the present value of $1 appearing in Exhibit 2 of this chapter. Round to the nearest whole million dollars.

b. ▬▬▬▶Under the assumptions provided here, is the film expected to be financially successful?

### CP 26-6 Capital investment analysis

**Group Project**

In one group, find a local business, such as a copy shop, that rents time on desktop computers for an hourly rate. Determine the hourly rate. In the other group, determine the price of a mid-range desktop computer at www.dell.com. Combine this information from the two groups and perform a capital budgeting analysis. Assume that one student will use the computer for 40 hours per semester for the next three years. Also assume that the minimum rate of return is 10%. Use the interest tables in Appendix A in performing your analysis. [*Hint:* Use the appropriate present value of an annuity of $1 factor for 5% compounded for six semiannual periods (periods = 6).]

Does your analysis support the student purchasing the computer?

# Appendices

# Appendix A

## Interest Tables

### Present Value of $1 at Compound Interest Due in *n* Periods

| Periods | 4.0% | 4.5% | 5% | 5.5% | 6% | 6.5% | 7% |
|---|---|---|---|---|---|---|---|
| 1 | 0.96154 | 0.95694 | 0.95238 | 0.94787 | 0.94340 | 0.93897 | 0.93458 |
| 2 | 0.92456 | 0.91573 | 0.90703 | 0.89845 | 0.89000 | 0.88166 | 0.87344 |
| 3 | 0.88900 | 0.87630 | 0.86384 | 0.85161 | 0.83962 | 0.82785 | 0.81630 |
| 4 | 0.85480 | 0.83856 | 0.82270 | 0.80722 | 0.79209 | 0.77732 | 0.76290 |
| 5 | 0.82193 | 0.80245 | 0.78353 | 0.76513 | 0.74726 | 0.72988 | 0.71299 |
| 6 | 0.79031 | 0.76790 | 0.74622 | 0.72525 | 0.70496 | 0.68533 | 0.66634 |
| 7 | 0.75992 | 0.73483 | 0.71068 | 0.68744 | 0.66506 | 0.64351 | 0.62275 |
| 8 | 0.73069 | 0.70319 | 0.67684 | 0.65160 | 0.62741 | 0.60423 | 0.58201 |
| 9 | 0.70259 | 0.67290 | 0.64461 | 0.61763 | 0.59190 | 0.56735 | 0.54393 |
| 10 | 0.67556 | 0.64393 | 0.61391 | 0.58543 | 0.55839 | 0.53273 | 0.50835 |
| 11 | 0.64958 | 0.61620 | 0.58468 | 0.55491 | 0.52679 | 0.50021 | 0.47509 |
| 12 | 0.62460 | 0.58966 | 0.55684 | 0.52598 | 0.49697 | 0.46968 | 0.44401 |
| 13 | 0.60057 | 0.56427 | 0.53032 | 0.49856 | 0.46884 | 0.44102 | 0.41496 |
| 14 | 0.57748 | 0.53997 | 0.50507 | 0.47257 | 0.44230 | 0.41410 | 0.38782 |
| 15 | 0.55526 | 0.51672 | 0.48102 | 0.44793 | 0.41727 | 0.38883 | 0.36245 |
| 16 | 0.53391 | 0.49447 | 0.45811 | 0.42458 | 0.39365 | 0.36510 | 0.33873 |
| 17 | 0.51337 | 0.47318 | 0.43630 | 0.40245 | 0.37136 | 0.34281 | 0.31657 |
| 18 | 0.49363 | 0.45280 | 0.41552 | 0.38147 | 0.35034 | 0.32189 | 0.29586 |
| 19 | 0.47464 | 0.43330 | 0.39573 | 0.36158 | 0.33051 | 0.30224 | 0.27651 |
| 20 | 0.45639 | 0.41464 | 0.37689 | 0.34273 | 0.31180 | 0.28380 | 0.25842 |
| 21 | 0.43883 | 0.39679 | 0.35894 | 0.32486 | 0.29416 | 0.26648 | 0.24151 |
| 22 | 0.42196 | 0.37970 | 0.34185 | 0.30793 | 0.27751 | 0.25021 | 0.22571 |
| 23 | 0.40573 | 0.36335 | 0.32557 | 0.29187 | 0.26180 | 0.23494 | 0.21095 |
| 24 | 0.39012 | 0.34770 | 0.31007 | 0.27666 | 0.24698 | 0.22060 | 0.19715 |
| 25 | 0.37512 | 0.33273 | 0.29530 | 0.26223 | 0.23300 | 0.20714 | 0.18425 |
| 26 | 0.36069 | 0.31840 | 0.28124 | 0.24856 | 0.21981 | 0.19450 | 0.17220 |
| 27 | 0.34682 | 0.30469 | 0.26785 | 0.23560 | 0.20737 | 0.18263 | 0.16093 |
| 28 | 0.33348 | 0.29157 | 0.25509 | 0.22332 | 0.19563 | 0.17148 | 0.15040 |
| 29 | 0.32065 | 0.27902 | 0.24295 | 0.21168 | 0.18456 | 0.16101 | 0.14056 |
| 30 | 0.30832 | 0.26700 | 0.23138 | 0.20064 | 0.17411 | 0.15119 | 0.13137 |
| 31 | 0.29646 | 0.25550 | 0.22036 | 0.19018 | 0.16425 | 0.14196 | 0.12277 |
| 32 | 0.28506 | 0.24450 | 0.20987 | 0.18027 | 0.15496 | 0.13329 | 0.11474 |
| 33 | 0.27409 | 0.23397 | 0.19987 | 0.17087 | 0.14619 | 0.12516 | 0.10723 |
| 34 | 0.26355 | 0.22390 | 0.19035 | 0.16196 | 0.13791 | 0.11752 | 0.10022 |
| 35 | 0.25342 | 0.21425 | 0.18129 | 0.15352 | 0.13011 | 0.11035 | 0.09366 |
| 40 | 0.20829 | 0.17193 | 0.14205 | 0.11746 | 0.09722 | 0.08054 | 0.06678 |
| 45 | 0.17120 | 0.13796 | 0.11130 | 0.08988 | 0.07265 | 0.05879 | 0.04761 |
| 50 | 0.14071 | 0.11071 | 0.08720 | 0.06877 | 0.05429 | 0.04291 | 0.03395 |

**Present Value of $1 at Compound Interest Due in *n* Periods**

| Periods | 8% | 9% | 10% | 11% | 12% | 13% | 14% |
|---|---|---|---|---|---|---|---|
| 1 | 0.92593 | 0.91743 | 0.90909 | 0.90090 | 0.89286 | 0.88496 | 0.87719 |
| 2 | 0.85734 | 0.84168 | 0.82645 | 0.81162 | 0.79719 | 0.78315 | 0.76947 |
| 3 | 0.79383 | 0.77218 | 0.75131 | 0.73119 | 0.71178 | 0.69305 | 0.67497 |
| 4 | 0.73503 | 0.70843 | 0.68301 | 0.65873 | 0.63552 | 0.61332 | 0.59208 |
| 5 | 0.68058 | 0.64993 | 0.62092 | 0.59345 | 0.56743 | 0.54276 | 0.51937 |
| 6 | 0.63017 | 0.59627 | 0.56447 | 0.53464 | 0.50663 | 0.48032 | 0.45559 |
| 7 | 0.58349 | 0.54703 | 0.51316 | 0.48166 | 0.45235 | 0.42506 | 0.39964 |
| 8 | 0.54027 | 0.50187 | 0.46651 | 0.43393 | 0.40388 | 0.37616 | 0.35056 |
| 9 | 0.50025 | 0.46043 | 0.42410 | 0.39092 | 0.36061 | 0.33288 | 0.30751 |
| 10 | 0.46319 | 0.42241 | 0.38554 | 0.35218 | 0.32197 | 0.29459 | 0.26974 |
| 11 | 0.42888 | 0.38753 | 0.35049 | 0.31728 | 0.28748 | 0.26070 | 0.23662 |
| 12 | 0.39711 | 0.35553 | 0.31863 | 0.28584 | 0.25668 | 0.23071 | 0.20756 |
| 13 | 0.36770 | 0.32618 | 0.28966 | 0.25751 | 0.22917 | 0.20416 | 0.18207 |
| 14 | 0.34046 | 0.29925 | 0.26333 | 0.23199 | 0.20462 | 0.18068 | 0.15971 |
| 15 | 0.31524 | 0.27454 | 0.23939 | 0.20900 | 0.18270 | 0.15989 | 0.14010 |
| 16 | 0.29189 | 0.25187 | 0.21763 | 0.18829 | 0.16312 | 0.14150 | 0.12289 |
| 17 | 0.27027 | 0.23107 | 0.19784 | 0.16963 | 0.14564 | 0.12522 | 0.10780 |
| 18 | 0.25025 | 0.21199 | 0.17986 | 0.15282 | 0.13004 | 0.11081 | 0.09456 |
| 19 | 0.23171 | 0.19449 | 0.16351 | 0.13768 | 0.11611 | 0.09806 | 0.08295 |
| 20 | 0.21455 | 0.17843 | 0.14864 | 0.12403 | 0.10367 | 0.08678 | 0.07270 |
| 21 | 0.19866 | 0.16370 | 0.13513 | 0.11174 | 0.09256 | 0.07680 | 0.06383 |
| 22 | 0.18394 | 0.15018 | 0.12285 | 0.10067 | 0.08264 | 0.06796 | 0.05599 |
| 23 | 0.17032 | 0.13778 | 0.11168 | 0.09069 | 0.07379 | 0.06014 | 0.04911 |
| 24 | 0.15770 | 0.12640 | 0.10153 | 0.08170 | 0.06588 | 0.05323 | 0.04308 |
| 25 | 0.14602 | 0.11597 | 0.09230 | 0.07361 | 0.05882 | 0.04710 | 0.03779 |
| 26 | 0.13520 | 0.10639 | 0.08391 | 0.06631 | 0.05252 | 0.04168 | 0.03315 |
| 27 | 0.12519 | 0.09761 | 0.07628 | 0.05974 | 0.04689 | 0.03689 | 0.02908 |
| 28 | 0.11591 | 0.08955 | 0.06934 | 0.05382 | 0.04187 | 0.03264 | 0.02551 |
| 29 | 0.10733 | 0.08215 | 0.06304 | 0.04849 | 0.03738 | 0.02889 | 0.02237 |
| 30 | 0.09938 | 0.07537 | 0.05731 | 0.04368 | 0.03338 | 0.02557 | 0.01963 |
| 31 | 0.09202 | 0.06915 | 0.05210 | 0.03935 | 0.02980 | 0.02262 | 0.01722 |
| 32 | 0.08520 | 0.06344 | 0.04736 | 0.03545 | 0.02661 | 0.02002 | 0.01510 |
| 33 | 0.07889 | 0.05820 | 0.04306 | 0.03194 | 0.02376 | 0.01772 | 0.01325 |
| 34 | 0.07305 | 0.05339 | 0.03914 | 0.02070 | 0.02121 | 0.01568 | 0.01162 |
| 35 | 0.06763 | 0.04899 | 0.03558 | 0.02592 | 0.01894 | 0.01388 | 0.01019 |
| 40 | 0.04603 | 0.03184 | 0.02209 | 0.01538 | 0.01075 | 0.00753 | 0.00529 |
| 45 | 0.03133 | 0.02069 | 0.01372 | 0.00913 | 0.00610 | 0.00409 | 0.00275 |
| 50 | 0.02132 | 0.01345 | 0.00852 | 0.00542 | 0.00346 | 0.00222 | 0.00143 |

**Present Value of Ordinary Annuity of $1 per Period**

| Periods | 4.0% | 4.5% | 5% | 5.5% | 6% | 6.5% | 7% |
|---|---|---|---|---|---|---|---|
| 1 | 0.96154 | 0.95694 | 0.95238 | 0.94787 | 0.94340 | 0.93897 | 0.93458 |
| 2 | 1.88609 | 1.87267 | 1.85941 | 1.84632 | 1.83339 | 1.82063 | 1.80802 |
| 3 | 2.77509 | 2.74896 | 2.72325 | 2.69793 | 2.67301 | 2.64848 | 2.62432 |
| 4 | 3.62990 | 3.58753 | 3.54595 | 3.50515 | 3.46511 | 3.42580 | 3.38721 |
| 5 | 4.45182 | 4.38998 | 4.32948 | 4.27028 | 4.21236 | 4.15568 | 4.10020 |
| 6 | 5.24214 | 5.15787 | 5.07569 | 4.99553 | 4.91732 | 4.84101 | 4.76654 |
| 7 | 6.00205 | 5.89270 | 5.78637 | 5.68297 | 5.58238 | 5.48452 | 5.38929 |
| 8 | 6.73274 | 6.59589 | 6.46321 | 6.33457 | 6.20979 | 6.08875 | 5.97130 |
| 9 | 7.43533 | 7.26879 | 7.10782 | 6.95220 | 6.80169 | 6.65610 | 6.51523 |
| 10 | 8.11090 | 7.91272 | 7.72173 | 7.53763 | 7.36009 | 7.18883 | 7.02358 |
| 11 | 8.76048 | 8.52892 | 8.30641 | 8.09254 | 7.88687 | 7.68904 | 7.49867 |
| 12 | 9.38507 | 9.11858 | 8.86325 | 8.61852 | 8.38384 | 8.15873 | 7.94269 |
| 13 | 9.98565 | 9.68285 | 9.39357 | 9.11708 | 8.85268 | 8.59974 | 8.35765 |
| 14 | 10.56312 | 10.22283 | 9.89864 | 9.58965 | 9.29498 | 9.01384 | 8.74547 |
| 15 | 11.11839 | 10.73955 | 10.37966 | 10.03758 | 9.71225 | 9.40267 | 9.10791 |
| 16 | 11.65230 | 11.23402 | 10.83777 | 10.46216 | 10.10590 | 9.76776 | 9.44665 |
| 17 | 12.16567 | 11.70719 | 11.27407 | 10.86461 | 10.47726 | 10.11058 | 9.76322 |
| 18 | 12.65930 | 12.15999 | 11.68959 | 11.24607 | 10.82760 | 10.43247 | 10.05909 |
| 19 | 13.13394 | 12.59329 | 12.08532 | 11.60765 | 11.15812 | 10.73471 | 10.33560 |
| 20 | 13.59033 | 13.00794 | 12.46221 | 11.95038 | 11.46992 | 11.01851 | 10.59401 |
| 21 | 14.02916 | 13.40472 | 12.82115 | 12.27524 | 11.76408 | 11.28498 | 10.83553 |
| 22 | 14.45112 | 13.78442 | 13.16300 | 12.58317 | 12.04158 | 11.53520 | 11.06124 |
| 23 | 14.85684 | 14.14777 | 13.48857 | 12.87504 | 12.30338 | 11.77014 | 11.27219 |
| 24 | 15.24696 | 14.49548 | 13.79864 | 13.15170 | 12.55036 | 11.99074 | 11.46933 |
| 25 | 15.62208 | 14.82821 | 14.09394 | 13.41393 | 12.78336 | 12.19788 | 11.65358 |
| 26 | 15.98277 | 15.14661 | 14.37519 | 13.66250 | 13.00317 | 12.39237 | 11.82578 |
| 27 | 16.32959 | 15.45130 | 14.64303 | 13.89810 | 13.21053 | 12.57500 | 11.98671 |
| 28 | 16.66306 | 15.74287 | 14.89813 | 14.12142 | 13.40616 | 12.74648 | 12.13711 |
| 29 | 16.98371 | 16.02189 | 15.14107 | 14.33310 | 13.59072 | 12.90749 | 12.27767 |
| 30 | 17.29203 | 16.28889 | 15.37245 | 14.53375 | 13.76483 | 13.05868 | 12.40904 |
| 31 | 17.58849 | 16.54439 | 15.59281 | 14.72393 | 13.92909 | 13.20063 | 12.53181 |
| 32 | 17.87355 | 16.78889 | 15.80268 | 14.90420 | 14.08404 | 13.33393 | 12.64656 |
| 33 | 18.14765 | 17.02286 | 16.00255 | 15.07507 | 14.23023 | 13.45909 | 12.75379 |
| 34 | 18.41120 | 17.24676 | 16.19290 | 15.23703 | 14.36814 | 13.57661 | 12.85401 |
| 35 | 18.66461 | 17.46101 | 16.37419 | 15.39055 | 14.49825 | 13.68696 | 12.94767 |
| 40 | 19.79277 | 18.40158 | 17.15909 | 16.04612 | 15.04630 | 14.14553 | 13.33171 |
| 45 | 20.72004 | 19.15635 | 17.77407 | 16.54773 | 15.45583 | 14.48023 | 13.60552 |
| 50 | 21.48218 | 19.76201 | 18.25593 | 16.93152 | 15.76186 | 14.72452 | 13.80075 |

**Present Value of Ordinary Annuity of $1 per Period**

| Periods | 8% | 9% | 10% | 11% | 12% | 13% | 14% |
|---|---|---|---|---|---|---|---|
| 1 | 0.92593 | 0.91743 | 0.90909 | 0.90090 | 0.89286 | 0.88496 | 0.87719 |
| 2 | 1.78326 | 1.75911 | 1.73554 | 1.71252 | 1.69005 | 1.66810 | 1.64666 |
| 3 | 2.57710 | 2.53129 | 2.48685 | 2.44371 | 2.40183 | 2.36115 | 2.32163 |
| 4 | 3.31213 | 3.23972 | 3.16987 | 3.10245 | 3.03735 | 2.97447 | 2.91371 |
| 5 | 3.99271 | 3.88965 | 3.79079 | 3.69590 | 3.60478 | 3.51723 | 3.43308 |
| 6 | 4.62288 | 4.48592 | 4.35526 | 4.23054 | 4.11141 | 3.99755 | 3.88867 |
| 7 | 5.20637 | 5.03295 | 4.86842 | 4.71220 | 4.56376 | 4.42261 | 4.28830 |
| 8 | 5.74664 | 5.53482 | 5.33493 | 5.14612 | 4.96764 | 4.79677 | 4.63886 |
| 9 | 6.24689 | 5.99525 | 5.75002 | 5.53705 | 5.32825 | 5.13166 | 4.94637 |
| 10 | 6.71008 | 6.41766 | 6.14457 | 5.88923 | 5.65022 | 5.42624 | 5.21612 |
| 11 | 7.13896 | 6.80519 | 6.49506 | 6.20652 | 5.93770 | 5.68694 | 5.45273 |
| 12 | 7.53608 | 7.16073 | 6.81369 | 6.49236 | 6.19437 | 5.91765 | 5.66029 |
| 13 | 7.90378 | 7.48690 | 7.10336 | 6.74987 | 6.42355 | 6.12181 | 5.84236 |
| 14 | 8.22424 | 7.78615 | 7.36669 | 6.96187 | 6.62817 | 6.30249 | 6.00207 |
| 15 | 8.55948 | 8.06069 | 7.60608 | 7.19087 | 6.81086 | 6.46238 | 6.14217 |
| 16 | 8.85137 | 8.31256 | 7.82371 | 7.37916 | 6.97399 | 6.60388 | 6.26506 |
| 17 | 9.12164 | 8.54363 | 8.02155 | 7.54879 | 7.11963 | 6.72909 | 6.37286 |
| 18 | 9.37189 | 8.75563 | 8.20141 | 7.70162 | 7.24967 | 6.83991 | 6.46742 |
| 19 | 9.60360 | 8.95011 | 8.36492 | 7.83929 | 7.36578 | 6.93797 | 6.55037 |
| 20 | 9.81815 | 9.12855 | 8.51356 | 7.96333 | 7.46944 | 7.02475 | 6.62313 |
| 21 | 10.01680 | 9.29224 | 8.64869 | 8.07507 | 7.56200 | 7.10155 | 6.68696 |
| 22 | 10.20074 | 9.44243 | 8.77154 | 8.17574 | 7.64465 | 7.16951 | 6.74294 |
| 23 | 10.37106 | 9.58021 | 8.88322 | 8.26643 | 7.71843 | 7.22966 | 6.79206 |
| 24 | 10.52876 | 9.70661 | 8.98474 | 8.34814 | 7.78432 | 7.28288 | 6.83514 |
| 25 | 10.67478 | 9.82258 | 9.07704 | 8.42174 | 7.84314 | 7.32998 | 6.87293 |
| 26 | 10.80998 | 9.92897 | 9.16095 | 8.48806 | 7.89566 | 7.37167 | 6.90608 |
| 27 | 10.93516 | 10.02658 | 9.23722 | 8.54780 | 7.94255 | 7.40856 | 6.93515 |
| 28 | 11.05108 | 10.11613 | 9.30657 | 8.60162 | 7.98442 | 7.44120 | 6.96066 |
| 29 | 11.15841 | 10.19828 | 9.36961 | 8.65011 | 8.02181 | 7.47009 | 6.98304 |
| 30 | 11.25778 | 10.27365 | 9.42691 | 8.69379 | 8.05518 | 7.49565 | 7.00266 |
| 31 | 11.34980 | 10.34280 | 9.47901 | 8.73315 | 8.08499 | 7.51828 | 7.01988 |
| 32 | 11.43500 | 10.40624 | 9.52638 | 8.76860 | 8.11159 | 7.53830 | 7.03498 |
| 33 | 11.51389 | 10.46444 | 9.56943 | 8.80054 | 8.13535 | 7.55602 | 7.04823 |
| 34 | 11.58693 | 10.51784 | 9.60857 | 8.82932 | 8.15656 | 7.57170 | 7.05985 |
| 35 | 11.65457 | 10.56682 | 9.64416 | 8.85524 | 8.17550 | 7.58557 | 7.07005 |
| 40 | 11.92461 | 10.75736 | 9.77905 | 8.95105 | 8.24378 | 7.63438 | 7.10504 |
| 45 | 12.10840 | 10.88120 | 9.86281 | 9.00791 | 8.28252 | 7.66086 | 7.12322 |
| 50 | 12.23348 | 10.96168 | 9.91481 | 9.04165 | 8.30450 | 7.67524 | 7.13266 |

# Appendix B

## Reversing Entries

Some of the adjusting entries recorded at the end of the accounting period affect transactions that occur in the next period. In such cases, a reversing entry may be used to simplify the recording of the next period's transactions.

To illustrate, an adjusting entry for accrued wages expense affects the first payment of wages in the next period. Without using a reversing entry, Wages Payable must be debited for the accrued wages at the end of the preceding period. In addition, Wages Expense must also be debited for only that portion of the payroll that is an expense of the current period.

Using a reversing entry, however, simplifies the analysis and recording of the first wages payment in the next period. As the term implies, a *reversing entry* is the exact opposite of the related adjusting entry. The amounts and accounts are the same as the adjusting entry, but the debits and credits are reversed.

Reversing entries are illustrated by using the accrued wages for **NetSolutions** presented in Chapter 3. These data are summarized in Exhibit 1.

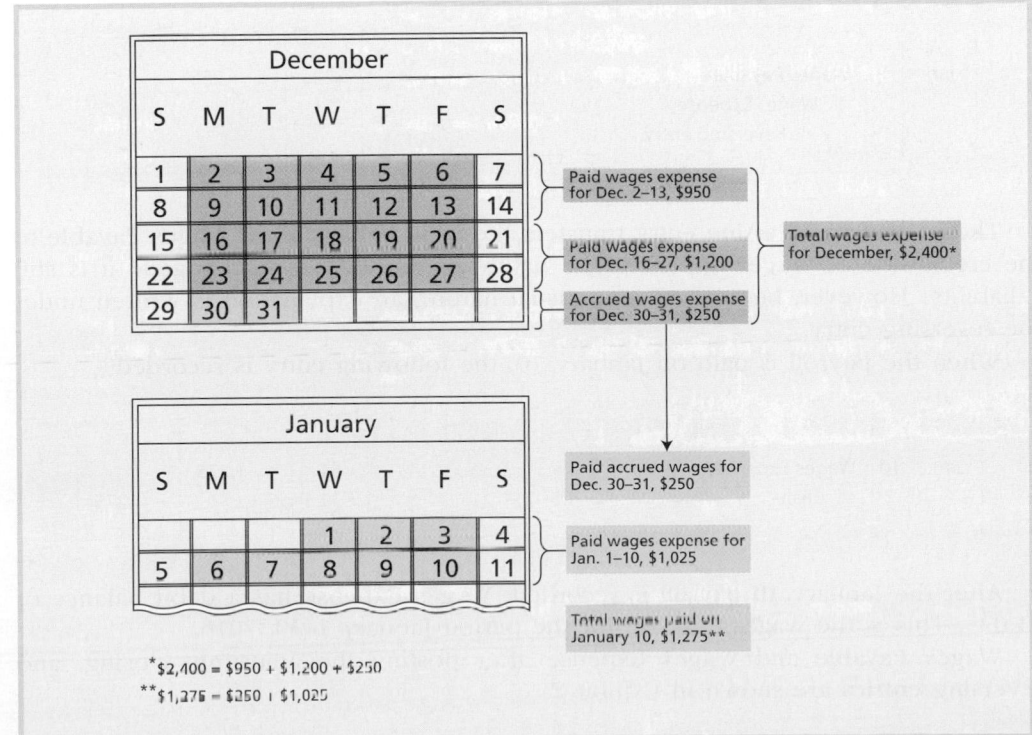

The adjusting entry for the accrued wages of December 30 and 31 is as follows:

| | 2015 | | | | | |
|---|---|---|---|---|---|---|
| | Dec. | 31 | Wages Expense | 51 | 250 | |
| | | | Wages Payable | 22 | | 250 |
| | | | Accrued wages. | | | |

After the adjusting entry is recorded, Wages Expense will have a debit balance of $4,525 ($4,275 + $250) and Wages Payable will have a credit balance of $250, as shown in Exhibit 2.

After the closing entries are recorded, Wages Expense will have a zero balance. However, because Wages Payable is a liability account, it is not closed. Thus, Wages Payable will have a credit balance of $250 as of January 1, 2016.

Without recording a reversing entry, the payment of the $1,275 payroll on January 10 would be recorded as follows:

| | 2016 | | | | | |
|---|---|---|---|---|---|---|
| | Jan. | 10 | Wages Payable | 22 | 250 | |
| | | | Wages Expense | 51 | 1,025 | |
| | | | Cash | 11 | | 1,275 |

To record the January 10 payroll correctly, Wages Payable must be debited for $250, as shown in the preceding entry. This means that the employee who records the January 10 payroll must refer to the December 31, 2015, adjusting entry or to the ledger to determine the amount to debit Wages Payable.

Because the January 10 payroll is not recorded in the normal manner, there is a greater chance that an error may occur. This chance of error is reduced by recording a reversing entry as of the first day of the next period. For example, the reversing entry for the accrued wages expense would be recorded on January 1, 2016, as follows:

| | 2016 | | | | | |
|---|---|---|---|---|---|---|
| | Jan. | 1 | Wages Payable | 22 | 250 | |
| | | | Wages Expense | 51 | | 250 |
| | | | Reversing entry. | | | |

The preceding reversing entry transfers the $250 liability from Wages Payable to the credit side of Wages Expense. The nature of the $250 is unchanged—it is still a liability. However, because of its unusual nature, an explanation is written under the reversing entry.

When the payroll is paid on January 10, the following entry is recorded:

| | | | | | | |
|---|---|---|---|---|---|---|
| | Jan. | 10 | Wages Expense | 51 | 1,275 | |
| | | | Cash | 11 | | 1,275 |

After the January 10 payroll is recorded, Wages Expense has a debit balance of $1,025. This is the wages expense for the period January 1–10, 2016.

Wages Payable and Wages Expense after posting the adjusting, closing, and reversing entries are shown in Exhibit 2.

**Account** *Wages Payable*　　　　　　　　　　　　　　　　　　　　　　*Account No. 22*

| Date | | Item | Post. Ref. | Debit | Credit | Balance Debit | Balance Credit |
|---|---|---|---|---|---|---|---|
| 2015 Dec. | 31 | Adjusting | 5 | | 250 | | 250 |
| 2016 Jan. | 1 | Reversing | 7 | 250 | | — | — |

**Account** *Wages Expense*　　　　　　　　　　　　　　　　　　　　　*Account No. 51*

| Date | | Item | Post. Ref. | Debit | Credit | Balance Debit | Balance Credit |
|---|---|---|---|---|---|---|---|
| 2015 Nov. | 30 | | 1 | 2,125 | | 2,125 | |
| Dec. | 13 | | 3 | 950 | | 3,075 | |
| | 27 | | 3 | 1,200 | | 4,275 | |
| | 31 | Adjusting | 5 | 250 | | 4,525 | |
| | 31 | Closing | 6 | | 4,525 | — | — |
| 2016 Jan. | 1 | Reversing | 7 | | 250 | | 250 |
| | 10 | | 7 | 1,275 | | 1,025 | |

**EXHIBIT 2**

**Wages Payable and Wages Expense Accounts**

In addition to accrued expenses (accrued liabilities), reversing entries are also used for accrued revenues (accrued assets). To illustrate, the reversing entry for NetSolutions' accrued fees earned as of December 31, 2015, is as follows:

| | | | | | |
|---|---|---|---|---|---|
| Jan. | 1 | Fees Earned | 41 | 500 | |
| | | Accounts Receivable | 12 | | 500 |
| | | Reversing entry. | | | |

The use of reversing entries is optional. However, in computerized accounting systems, data entry employees often input routine accounting entries. In such cases, reversing entries may be useful in avoiding errors.

# Exercises

### EX B-1　Adjusting and reversing entries

On the basis of the following data, (a) journalize the adjusting entries at December 31, the end of the current fiscal year, and (b) journalize the reversing entries on January 1, the first day of the following year:

1. Sales salaries are uniformly $11,750 for a five-day workweek, ending on Friday. The last payday of the year was Friday, December 26.
2. Accrued fees earned but not recorded at December 31, $51,300.

### EX B-2   Adjusting and reversing entries

On the basis of the following data, (a) journalize the adjusting entries at June 30, the end of the current fiscal year, and (b) journalize the reversing entries on July 1, the first day of the following year:

1. Wages are uniformly $66,000 for a five-day workweek, ending on Friday. The last payday of the year was Friday, June 27.

2. Accrued fees earned but not recorded at June 30, $25,000.

### EX B-3   Entries posted to the wages expense account

Portions of the wages expense account of a business follow:

| Account | Wages Expense | | | | | | Account No. 53 |
|---|---|---|---|---|---|---|---|
| | | | Post. | | | Balance | |
| Date | Item | | Ref. | Dr. | Cr. | Dr. | Cr. |
| 2015 | | | | | | | |
| Dec. 26 | (1) | | 125 | 15,400 | | 800,000 | |
| 31 | (2) | | 126 | 9,250 | | 809,250 | |
| 31 | (3) | | 127 | | 809,250 | — | — |
| 2016 | | | | | | | |
| Jan. 1 | (4) | | 128 | | 9,250 | | 9,250 |
| 2 | (5) | | 129 | 14,800 | | 5,550 | |

a. Indicate the nature of the entry (payment, adjusting, closing, reversing) from which each numbered posting was made.

b. Journalize the complete entry from which each numbered posting was made.

### EX B-4   Entries posted to the salaries expense account

Portions of the salaries expense account of a business follow:

| Account | Salaries Expense | | | | | | Account No. 62 |
|---|---|---|---|---|---|---|---|
| | | | Post. | | | Balance | |
| Date | Item | | Ref. | Dr. | Cr. | Dr. | Cr. |
| 2015 | | | | | | | |
| Dec. 27 | (1) | | 29 | 22,000 | | 1,200,000 | |
| 31 | (2) | | 30 | 13,200 | | 1,213,200 | |
| 31 | (3) | | 31 | | 1,213,200 | — | — |
| 2016 | | | | | | | |
| Jan. 1 | (4) | | 32 | | 13,200 | | 13,200 |
| 2 | (5) | | 33 | 24,000 | | 10,800 | |

a. Indicate the nature of the entry (payment, adjusting, closing, reversing) from which each numbered posting was made.

b. Journalize the complete entry from which each numbered posting was made.

**Nike Inc., Form 10-K**
**For the Fiscal Year Ended May 31, 2013**

# NIKE INC

# FORM 10-K
### (Annual Report)

# Filed 07/23/13 for the Period Ending 05/31/13

| | |
|---|---|
| Address | ONE BOWERMAN DR |
| | BEAVERTON, OR 97005-6453 |
| Telephone | 5036713173 |
| CIK | 0000320187 |
| Symbol | NKE |
| SIC Code | 3021 - Rubber and Plastics Footwear |
| Industry | Footwear |
| Sector | Consumer Cyclical |
| Fiscal Year | 05/31 |

## Management's Annual Report on Internal Control Over Financial Reporting

Management is responsible for establishing and maintaining adequate internal control over financial reporting, as such term is defined in Rule 13a-15(f) and Rule 15d-15(f) of the Securities Exchange Act of 1934, as amended. Internal control over financial reporting is a process designed to provide reasonable assurance regarding the reliability of financial reporting and the preparation of the financial statements for external purposes in accordance with generally accepted accounting principles in the United States of America. Internal control over financial reporting includes those policies and procedures that: (i) pertain to the maintenance of records that, in reasonable detail, accurately and fairly reflect the transactions and dispositions of assets of the Company; (ii) provide reasonable assurance that transactions are recorded as necessary to permit preparation of financial statements in accordance with generally accepted accounting principles, and that receipts and expenditures of the Company are being made only in accordance with authorizations of our management and directors; and (iii) provide reasonable assurance regarding prevention or timely detection of unauthorized acquisition, use or disposition of assets of the Company that could have a material effect on the financial statements.

While "reasonable assurance" is a high level of assurance, it does not mean absolute assurance. Because of its inherent limitations, internal control over financial reporting may not prevent or detect every misstatement and instance

of fraud. Controls are susceptible to manipulation, especially in instances of fraud caused by the collusion of two or more people, including our senior management. Also, projections of any evaluation of effectiveness to future periods are subject to the risk that controls may become inadequate because of changes in conditions, or that the degree of compliance with the policies or procedures may deteriorate.

Under the supervision and with the participation of our Chief Executive Officer and Chief Financial Officer, our management conducted an evaluation of the effectiveness of our internal control over financial reporting based upon the framework in *Internal Control — Integrated Framework* issued by the Committee of Sponsoring Organizations of the Treadway Commission (COSO). Based on the results of our evaluation, our management concluded that our internal control over financial reporting was effective as of May 31, 2013.

PricewaterhouseCoopers LLP, an independent registered public accounting firm, has audited (1) the consolidated financial statements and (2) the effectiveness of our internal control over financial reporting as of May 31, 2013, as stated in their report herein.

|  |  |
|---|---|
| **Mark G. Parker** | **Donald W. Blair** |
| *President and Chief Executive Officer* | *Chief Financial Officer* |

# Report of Independent Registered Public Accounting Firm

To the Board of Directors and Shareholders of NIKE, Inc.:

In our opinion, the consolidated financial statements listed in the index appearing under Item 15(a)(1) present fairly, in all material respects, the financial position of NIKE, Inc. and its subsidiaries at May 31, 2013 and 2012, and the results of their operations and their cash flows for each of the three years in the period ended May 31, 2013 in conformity with accounting principles generally accepted in the United States of America. In addition, in our opinion, the financial statement schedule listed in the appendix appearing under Item 15(a)(2) presents fairly, in all material respects, the information set forth therein when read in conjunction with the related consolidated financial statements. Also in our opinion, the Company maintained, in all material respects, effective internal control over financial reporting as of May 31, 2013, based on criteria established in *Internal Control — Integrated Framework* issued by the Committee of Sponsoring Organizations of the Treadway Commission (COSO). The Company's management is responsible for these financial statements and financial statement schedule, for maintaining effective internal control over financial reporting and for its assessment of the effectiveness of internal control over financial reporting, included in Management's Annual Report on Internal Control Over Financial Reporting appearing under Item 8. Our responsibility is to express opinions on these financial statements, on the financial statement schedule, and on the Company's internal control over financial reporting based on our integrated audits. We conducted our audits in accordance with the standards of the Public Company Accounting Oversight Board (United States). Those standards require that we plan and perform the audits to obtain reasonable assurance about whether the financial statements are free of material misstatement and whether effective internal control over financial reporting was maintained in all material respects. Our audits of the financial statements included examining, on a test basis, evidence supporting the amounts and disclosures in the financial statements, assessing the accounting principles used and significant estimates made by management, and evaluating the overall financial statement presentation. Our audit of internal control over financial reporting included obtaining an understanding of internal control over financial reporting, assessing the risk that a material weakness exists, and testing and evaluating the design and operating effectiveness of internal control based on the assessed risk. Our audits also included performing such other procedures as we considered necessary in the circumstances. We believe that our audits provide a reasonable basis for our opinions.

A company's internal control over financial reporting is a process designed to provide reasonable assurance regarding the reliability of financial reporting and the preparation of financial statements for external purposes in accordance with generally accepted accounting principles. A company's internal control over financial reporting includes those policies and procedures that (i) pertain to the maintenance of records that, in reasonable detail, accurately and fairly reflect the transactions and dispositions of the assets of the company; (ii) provide reasonable assurance that transactions are recorded as necessary to permit preparation of financial statements in accordance with generally accepted accounting principles, and that receipts and expenditures of the company are being made only in accordance with authorizations of management and directors of the company; and (iii) provide reasonable assurance regarding prevention or timely detection of unauthorized acquisition, use, or disposition of the company's assets that could have a material effect on the financial statements.

Because of its inherent limitations, internal control over financial reporting may not prevent or detect misstatements. Also, projections of any evaluation of effectiveness to future periods are subject to the risk that controls may become inadequate because of changes in conditions, or that the degree of compliance with the policies or procedures may deteriorate.

/S/ PRICEWATERHOUSECOOPERS LLP

Portland, Oregon July 23, 2013

## NIKE, Inc. Consolidated Statements Of Income

| | | Year Ended May 31, | |
|---|---|---|---|
| *(In millions, except per share data)* | **2013** | **2012** | **2011** |
| Income from continuing operations: | | | |
| Revenues | $ 25,313 | $ 23,331 | $ 20,117 |
| Cost of sales | 14,279 | 13,183 | 10,915 |
| Gross profit | 11,034 | 10,148 | 9,202 |
| Demand creation expense | 2,745 | 2,607 | 2,344 |
| Operating overhead expense | 5,035 | 4,458 | 4,017 |
| Total selling and administrative expense | 7,780 | 7,065 | 6,361 |
| Interest (income) expense, net (Notes 6, 7 and 8) | (3) | 4 | 4 |
| Other (income) expense, net (Note 17) | (15) | 54 | (25) |
| Income before income taxes | 3,272 | 3,025 | 2,862 |
| Income tax expense (Note 9) | 808 | 756 | 690 |
| **NET INCOME FROM CONTINUING OPERATIONS** | **2,464** | **2,269** | **2,172** |
| **NET INCOME (LOSS) FROM DISCONTINUED OPERATIONS** | **21** | **(46)** | **(39)** |
| **NET INCOME** | **$ 2,485** | **$ 2,223** | **$ 2,133** |
| | | | |
| Earnings per share from continuing operations: | | | |
| Basic earnings per common share (Notes 1 and 12) | $ 2.75 | $ 2.47 | $ 2.28 |
| Diluted earnings per common share (Notes 1 and 12) | $ 2.69 | $ 2.42 | $ 2.24 |
| | | | |
| Earnings per share from discontinued operations: | | | |
| Basic earnings per common share (Notes 1 and 12) | $ 0.02 | $ (0.05) | $ (0.04) |
| Diluted earnings per common share (Notes 1 and 12) | $ 0.02 | $ (0.05) | $ (0.04) |
| | | | |
| Dividends declared per common share | $ 0.81 | $ 0.70 | $ 0.60 |

*The accompanying notes to consolidated financial statements are an integral part of this statement.*

## NIKE, Inc. Consolidated Statements of Comprehensive Income

| (In millions) | Year Ended May 31, | | | | | |
|---|---|---|---|---|---|---|
| | | 2013 | | 2012 | | 2011 |
| Net income | $ | 2,485 | $ | 2,223 | $ | 2,133 |
| Other comprehensive income (loss), net of tax: | | | | | | |
|   Foreign currency translation and other[1] | | 30 | | (295) | | 263 |
|   Net gain (loss) on cash flow hedges[2] | | 117 | | 255 | | (242) |
|   Net gain (loss) on net investment hedges[3] | | — | | 45 | | (57) |
|   Reclassification to net income of previously deferred (gains) losses related to hedge derivative instruments[4] | | (105) | | 49 | | (84) |
|   Release of cumulative translation loss related to Umbro[5] (Notes 14 and 15) | | 83 | | — | | — |
| Total other comprehensive income, net of tax | | 125 | | 54 | | (120) |
| **TOTAL COMPREHENSIVE INCOME** | $ | **2,610** | $ | **2,277** | $ | **2,013** |

(1)  Net of tax (expense) benefit of $(12) million, $0 million, and $(121) million, respectively.

(2)  Net of tax (expense) benefit of $(22) million, $(8) million, and $66 million, respectively.

(3)  Net of tax benefit of $0 million, $0 million, and $28 million, respectively.

(4)  Net of tax (benefit) expense of $0 million, $(14) million, and $24 million, respectively.

(5)  Net of tax (benefit) of $(47) million, $0 million, and $0 million, respectively.

*The accompanying notes to consolidated financial statements are an integral part of this statement.*

## NIKE, Inc. Consolidated Balance Sheets

| | May 31, | |
|---|---|---|
| *(In millions)* | 2013 | 2012 |
| **ASSETS** | | |
| Current assets: | $    3,337 | |
| Cash and equivalents | | $    2,317 |
| Short-term investments (Note 6) | 2,628 | 1,440 |
| Accounts receivable, net (Note 1) | 3,117 | 3,132 |
| Inventories (Notes 1 and 2) | 3,434 | 3,222 |
| Deferred income taxes (Note 9) | 308 | 262 |
| Prepaid expenses and other current assets (Notes 6 and 17) | 802 | 857 |
| Assets of discontinued operations (Note 15) | — | 615 |
| Total current assets | 13,626 | 11,845 |
| Property, plant and equipment, net (Note 3) | 2,452 | 2,209 |
| Identifiable intangible assets, net (Note 4) | 382 | 370 |
| Goodwill (Note 4) | 131 | 131 |
| Deferred income taxes and other assets (Notes 6, 9 and 17) | 993 | 910 |
| **TOTAL ASSETS** | $    17,584 | $    15,465 |
| **LIABILITIES AND SHAREHOLDERS' EQUITY** | | |
| Current liabilities: | | |
| Current portion of long-term debt (Note 8) | $    57 | $    49 |
| Notes payable (Note 7) | 121 | 108 |
| Accounts payable (Note 7) | 1,646 | 1,549 |
| Accrued liabilities (Notes 5, 6 and 17) | 1,986 | 1,941 |
| Income taxes payable (Note 9) | 98 | 65 |
| Liabilities of discontinued operations (Note 15) | 18 | 170 |
| Total current liabilities | 3,926 | 3,882 |
| Long-term debt (Note 8) | 1,210 | 228 |
| Deferred income taxes and other liabilities (Notes 6, 9 and 17) | 1,292 | 974 |
| Commitments and contingencies (Note 16) | — | — |
| Redeemable Preferred Stock (Note 10) | — | — |
| Shareholders' equity: | | |
| Common stock at stated value (Note 11): | | |
| Class A convertible — 178 and 180 shares outstanding | — | — |
| Class B — 716 and 736 shares outstanding | 3 | 3 |
| Capital in excess of stated value | 5,184 | 4,641 |
| Accumulated other comprehensive income (Note 14) | 274 | 149 |
| Retained earnings | 5,695 | 5,588 |
| Total shareholders' equity | 11,156 | 10,381 |
| **TOTAL LIABILITIES AND SHAREHOLDERS' EQUITY** | $    17,584 | $    15,465 |

*The accompanying notes to consolidated financial statements are an integral part of this statement.*

# NIKE, Inc. Consolidated Statements of Cash Flows

| | Year Ended May 31, | | |
| --- | --- | --- | --- |
| (In millions) | 2013 | 2012 | 2011 |
| **Cash provided by operations:** | | | |
| Net income | $ 2,485 | $ 2,223 | $ 2,133 |
| Income charges (credits) not affecting cash: | | | |
| Depreciation | 438 | 373 | 335 |
| Deferred income taxes | 21 | (60) | (76) |
| Stock-based compensation (Note 11) | 174 | 130 | 105 |
| Amortization and other | 75 | 32 | 23 |
| Net gain on divestitures | (124) | — | — |
| Changes in certain working capital components and other assets and liabilities: | | | |
| Decrease (increase) in accounts receivable | 142 | (323) | (273) |
| (Increase) in inventories | (197) | (805) | (551) |
| (Increase) in prepaid expenses and other current assets | (28) | (141) | (35) |
| Increase in accounts payable, accrued liabilities and income taxes payable | 41 | 470 | 151 |
| Cash provided by operations | 3,027 | 1,899 | 1,812 |
| **Cash (used) provided by investing activities:** | | | |
| Purchases of short-term investments | (3,702) | (2,705) | (7,616) |
| Maturities of short-term investments | 1,501 | 2,585 | 4,313 |
| Sales of short-term investments | 998 | 1,244 | 2,766 |
| Additions to property, plant and equipment | (636) | (597) | (432) |
| Disposals of property, plant and equipment | 14 | 2 | 1 |
| Proceeds from divestitures | 786 | — | — |
| Increase in other assets, net of other liabilities | (28) | (37) | (30) |
| Settlement of net investment hedges | — | 22 | (23) |
| Cash (used) provided by investing activities | (1,067) | 514 | (1,021) |
| **Cash used by financing activities:** | | | |
| Net proceeds from long-term debt issuance | 986 | — | — |
| Long-term debt payments, including current portion | (49) | (203) | (8) |
| Increase (decrease) in notes payable | 15 | (65) | 41 |
| Proceeds from exercise of stock options and other stock issuances | 313 | 468 | 345 |
| Excess tax benefits from share-based payment arrangements | 72 | 115 | 64 |
| Repurchase of common stock | (1,674) | (1,814) | (1,859) |
| Dividends — common and preferred | (703) | (619) | (555) |
| Cash used by financing activities | (1,040) | (2,118) | (1,972) |
| Effect of exchange rate changes | 100 | 67 | 57 |
| Net increase (decrease) in cash and equivalents | 1,020 | 362 | (1,124) |
| Cash and equivalents, beginning of year | 2,317 | 1,955 | 3,079 |
| **CASH AND EQUIVALENTS, END OF YEAR** | $ 3,337 | $ 2,317 | $ 1,955 |
| **Supplemental disclosure of cash flow information:** | | | |
| Cash paid during the year for: | | | |
| Interest, net of capitalized interest | $ 20 | $ 29 | $ 32 |
| Income taxes | 702 | 638 | 736 |
| Dividends declared and not paid | 188 | 165 | 145 |

*The accompanying notes to consolidated financial statements are an integral part of this statement.*

## NIKE, Inc. Consolidated Statements of Shareholders' Equity

| (In millions, except per share data) | Common Stock | | | | Capital in Excess of Stated Value | Accumulated Other Comprehensive Income | Retained Earnings | Total |
|---|---|---|---|---|---|---|---|---|
| | Class A | | Class B | | | | | |
| | Shares | Amount | Shares | Amount | | | | |
| **Balance at May 31, 2010** | 180 | $ — | 788 | $ 3 | $ 3,441 | $ 215 | $ 6,095 | $ 9,754 |
| Stock options exercised | | | 14 | | 368 | | | 368 |
| Repurchase of Class B Common Stock | | | (48) | | (14) | | (1,857) | (1,871) |
| Dividends on Common stock ($0.60 per share) | | | | | | | (569) | (569) |
| Issuance of shares to employees | | | 2 | | 49 | | | 49 |
| Stock-based compensation (Note 11) | | | | | 105 | | | 105 |
| Forfeiture of shares from employees | | | — | | (5) | | (1) | (6) |
| Net income | | | | | | | 2,133 | 2,133 |
| Other Comprehensive Income | | | | | | (120) | | (120) |
| **Balance at May 31, 2011** | 180 | $ — | 756 | $ 3 | $ 3,944 | $ 95 | $ 5,801 | $ 9,843 |
| Stock options exercised | | | 18 | | 528 | | | 528 |
| Repurchase of Class B Common Stock | | | (40) | | (12) | | (1,793) | (1,805) |
| Dividends on Common stock ($0.70 per share) | | | | | | | (639) | (639) |
| Issuance of shares to employees | | | 2 | | 57 | | | 57 |
| Stock-based compensation (Note 11) | | | | | 130 | | | 130 |
| Forfeiture of shares from employees | | | — | | (6) | | (4) | (10) |
| Net income | | | | | | | 2,223 | 2,223 |
| Other comprehensive income | | | | | | 54 | | 54 |
| **Balance at May 31, 2012** | 180 | $ — | 736 | $ 3 | $ 4,641 | $ 149 | $ 5,588 | $ 10,381 |
| Stock options exercised | | | 10 | | 322 | | | 322 |
| Conversion to Class B Common Stock | (2) | | 2 | | | | | — |
| Repurchase of Class B Common Stock | | | (34) | | (10) | | (1,647) | (1,657) |
| Dividends on Common stock ($0.81 per share) | | | | | | | (727) | (727) |
| Issuance of shares to employees | | | 2 | | 65 | | | 65 |
| Stock-based compensation (Note 11) | | | | | 174 | | | 174 |
| Forfeiture of shares from employees | | | — | | (8) | | (4) | (12) |
| Net income | | | | | | | 2,485 | 2,485 |
| Other comprehensive income | | | | | | 125 | | 125 |
| **Balance at May 31, 2013** | 178 | $ — | 716 | $ 3 | $ 5,184 | $ 274 | $ 5,695 | $ 11,156 |

*The accompanying notes to consolidated financial statements are an integral part of this statement.*

# NOTE 1 — Summary of Significant Accounting Policies

### Description of Business

NIKE, Inc. is a worldwide leader in the design, development and worldwide marketing and selling of athletic footwear, apparel, equipment, accessories and services. Wholly-owned NIKE, Inc. subsidiaries include Converse Inc., which designs, markets and distributes casual footwear, apparel and accessories and Hurley International LLC, which designs, markets and distributes action sports and youth lifestyle footwear, apparel and accessories.

### Basis of Consolidation

The consolidated financial statements include the accounts of NIKE, Inc. and its subsidiaries (the "Company"). All significant intercompany transactions and balances have been eliminated.

The Company completed the sale of Cole Haan during the third quarter ended February 28, 2013 and completed the sale of Umbro during the second quarter ended November 30, 2012. As a result, the Company reports the operating results of Cole Haan and Umbro in the net income (loss) from discontinued operations line in the consolidated statements of income for all periods presented. In addition, the assets and liabilities associated with these businesses are reported as assets of discontinued operations and liabilities of discontinued operations, as appropriate, in the consolidated balance sheets (refer to Note 15 — Discontinued Operations). Unless otherwise indicated, the disclosures accompanying the consolidated financial statements reflect the Company's continuing operations.

On November 15, 2012, the Company announced a two-for-one split of both NIKE Class A and Class B Common shares. The stock split was a 100 percent stock dividend payable on December 24, 2012 to shareholders of record at the close of business December 10, 2012. Common stock began trading at the split-adjusted price on December 26, 2012. All share numbers and per share amounts presented reflect the stock split.

### Recognition of Revenues

Wholesale revenues are recognized when title and the risks and rewards of ownership have passed to the customer, based on the terms of sale. This occurs upon shipment or upon receipt by the customer depending on the country of the sale and the agreement with the customer. Retail store revenues are recorded at the time of sale. Provisions for post-invoice sales discounts, returns and miscellaneous claims from customers are estimated and recorded as a reduction to revenue at the time of sale. Post-invoice sales discounts consist of contractual programs with certain customers or discretionary discounts that are expected to be granted to certain customers at a later date. Estimates of discretionary discounts, returns and claims are based on historical rates, specific identification of outstanding claims and outstanding returns not yet received from customers, and estimated discounts, returns and claims expected but not yet finalized with customers. As of May 31, 2013 and 2012, the Company's reserve balances for post-invoice sales discounts, returns and miscellaneous claims were $531 million and $455 million, respectively.

### Cost of Sales

Cost of sales consists primarily of inventory costs, as well as warehousing costs (including the cost of warehouse labor), third party royalties, certain foreign currency hedge gains and losses, and research, design and development costs.

### Shipping and Handling Costs

Shipping and handling costs are expensed as incurred and included in cost of sales.

### Operating Overhead Expense

Operating overhead expense consists primarily of payroll and benefit related costs, rent, depreciation and amortization, professional services, and meetings and travel.

### Demand Creation Expense

Demand creation expense consists of advertising and promotion costs, including costs of endorsement contracts, television, digital and print advertising, brand events, and retail brand presentation. Advertising production costs are expensed the first time an advertisement is run. Advertising placement costs are expensed in the month the advertising appears, while costs related to brand events are expensed when the event occurs. Costs related to retail brand presentation are expensed when the presentation is completed and delivered.

A significant amount of the Company's promotional expenses result from payments under endorsement contracts. Accounting for endorsement payments is based upon specific contract provisions. Generally, endorsement payments are expensed on a straight-line basis over the term of the contract after giving recognition to periodic performance compliance provisions of the contracts. Prepayments made under contracts are included in prepaid expenses or other assets depending on the period to which the prepayment applies.

Some of the contracts provide for contingent payments to endorsers based upon specific achievements in their sports (e.g., winning a championship). The Company records selling and administrative expense for these amounts when the endorser achieves the specific goal.

Some of the contracts provide for payments based upon endorsers maintaining a level of performance in their sport over an extended period of time (e.g., maintaining a top ranking in a sport for a year). These amounts are recorded in selling and administrative expense when the Company determines that it is probable that the specified level of performance will be maintained throughout the period. In these instances, to the extent that actual payments to the endorser differ from our estimate due to changes in the endorser's athletic performance, increased or decreased selling and administrative expense may be recorded in a future period.

Some of the contracts provide for royalty payments to endorsers based upon a predetermined percentage of sales of particular products. The Company expenses these payments in cost of sales as the related sales occur. In certain contracts, the Company offers minimum guaranteed royalty payments. For contractual obligations for which the Company estimates it will not meet the minimum guaranteed amount of royalty fees through sales of product, the Company records the amount of the guaranteed payment in excess of that earned through sales of product in selling and administrative expense uniformly over the remaining guarantee period.

Through cooperative advertising programs, the Company reimburses retail customers for certain costs of advertising the Company's products. The Company records these costs in selling and administrative expense at the point in time when it is obligated to its customers for the costs, which is when the related revenues are recognized. This obligation may arise prior to the related advertisement being run.

Total advertising and promotion expenses were $2,745 million, $2,607 million, and $2,344 million for the years ended May 31, 2013, 2012 and 2011, respectively. Prepaid advertising and promotion expenses recorded in prepaid expenses and other current assets totaled $386 million and $281 million at May 31, 2013 and 2012, respectively.

## Cash and Equivalents

Cash and equivalents represent cash and short-term, highly liquid investments, including commercial paper, U.S. treasury, U.S. agency, and corporate debt securities with maturities of three months or less at date of purchase.

## Short-Term Investments

Short-term investments consist of highly liquid investments, including commercial paper, U.S. treasury, U.S. agency, and corporate debt securities, with maturities over three months from the date of purchase. Debt securities that the Company has the ability and positive intent to hold to maturity are carried at amortized cost. At May 31, 2013 and 2012, the Company did not hold any short-term investments that were classified as trading or held-to- maturity.

At May 31, 2013 and 2012, short-term investments consisted of available- for-sale securities. Available-for-sale securities are recorded at fair value with unrealized gains and losses reported, net of tax, in other comprehensive income, unless unrealized losses are determined to be other than temporary. Realized gains and losses on the sale of securities are determined by specific identification. The Company considers all available-for-sale securities, including those with maturity dates beyond 12 months, as available to support current operational liquidity needs and therefore classifies all securities with maturity dates beyond three months at the date of purchase as current assets within short-term investments on the consolidated balance sheets.

Refer to Note 6 — Fair Value Measurements for more information on the Company's short-term investments.

## Allowance for Uncollectible Accounts Receivable

Accounts receivable consists primarily of amounts receivable from customers. The Company makes ongoing estimates relating to the collectability of its accounts receivable and maintains an allowance for estimated losses resulting from the inability of its customers to make required payments. In determining the amount of the allowance, the Company considers historical levels of credit losses and makes judgments about the creditworthiness of significant customers based on ongoing credit evaluations. Accounts receivable with anticipated collection dates greater than 12 months from the balance sheet date and related allowances are considered non-current and recorded in other assets. The allowance for uncollectible accounts receivable was $104 million and $91 million at May 31, 2013 and 2012, respectively, of which $54 million and $45 million, respectively, was classified as long-term and recorded in other assets.

## Inventory Valuation

Inventories are stated at lower of cost or market and valued primarily on an average cost basis. Inventory costs primarily consist of product cost from our suppliers, as well as freight, import duties, taxes, insurance and logistics and other handling fees.

## Property, Plant and Equipment and Depreciation

Property, plant and equipment are recorded at cost. Depreciation for financial reporting purposes is determined on a straight-line basis for buildings and leasehold improvements over 2 to 40 years and for machinery and equipment over 2 to 15 years.

Depreciation and amortization of assets used in manufacturing, warehousing and product distribution are recorded in cost of sales. Depreciation and amortization of other assets are recorded in selling and administrative expense.

## Software Development Costs

*Internal Use Software.* Expenditures for major software purchases and software developed for internal use are capitalized and amortized over a 2 to 10 year period on a straight-line basis. The Company's policy provides for the capitalization of external direct costs of materials and services associated with developing or obtaining internal use computer software. In addition, the Company also capitalizes certain payroll and payroll-related costs for employees who are directly associated with internal use computer software projects. The amount of capitalizable payroll costs with respect to these employees is limited to the time directly spent on such projects. Costs associated with preliminary project stage activities, training, maintenance and all other post-implementation stage activities are expensed as incurred.

*Computer Software to be Sold, Leased or Otherwise Marketed.* Development costs of computer software to be sold, leased, or otherwise marketed as an integral part of a product are subject to capitalization beginning when a product's technological feasibility has been established and ending when a product is available for general release to customers. In most instances, the Company's products are released soon after technological feasibility has been established. Therefore, costs incurred subsequent to achievement of technological feasibility are usually not significant, and generally most software development costs have been expensed as incurred.

## Impairment of Long-Lived Assets

The Company reviews the carrying value of long-lived assets or asset groups to be used in operations whenever events or changes in circumstances indicate that the carrying amount of the assets might not be recoverable. Factors that would necessitate an impairment assessment include a significant adverse change in the extent or manner in which an asset is used, a significant adverse change in legal factors or the business climate that could affect the value of the asset, or a significant decline in the observable market value of an asset, among others. If such facts indicate a potential impairment, the Company would assess the recoverability of an asset group by determining if the carrying value of the asset group exceeds the sum of the projected undiscounted cash flows expected to result from the use and eventual disposition of the assets over the remaining economic life of the primary asset in the asset group. If the recoverability test indicates that the carrying value of the asset group is not recoverable, the Company will estimate the fair value of the asset group using appropriate valuation methodologies, which would typically include an estimate of discounted cash flows. Any impairment would be measured as the difference between the asset group's carrying amount and its estimated fair value.

## Identifiable Intangible Assets and Goodwill

The Company performs annual impairment tests on goodwill and intangible assets with indefinite lives in the fourth quarter of each fiscal year, or when events occur or circumstances change that would, more likely than not, reduce the fair value of a reporting unit or an intangible asset with an indefinite life below its carrying value. Events or changes in circumstances that may trigger interim impairment reviews include significant changes in business climate, operating results, planned investments in the reporting unit, planned divestitures or an expectation that the carrying amount may not be recoverable, among other factors. The Company may first assess qualitative factors to determine whether it is more likely than not that the fair value of a reporting unit is less than its carrying amount. If, after assessing the totality of events and circumstances, the Company determines that it is more likely than not that the fair value of the reporting unit is greater than its carrying amount, the two-step impairment test is unnecessary. The two-step impairment test first requires the Company to estimate the fair value of its reporting units. If the carrying value of a reporting unit exceeds its fair value, the goodwill of that reporting unit is potentially impaired and the Company proceeds to step two of the impairment analysis. In step two of the analysis, the Company measures and records an impairment loss equal to the excess of the carrying value of the reporting unit's goodwill over its implied fair value, if any.

The Company generally bases its measurement of the fair value of a reporting unit on a blended analysis of the present value of future discounted cash flows and the market valuation approach. The discounted cash flows model indicates the fair value of the reporting unit based on the present value of the cash flows that the Company expects the reporting unit to generate in the future. The Company's significant estimates in the discounted cash flows model include: its weighted average cost of capital; long-term rate of growth and profitability of the reporting unit's business; and working capital effects. The market valuation approach indicates the fair value of the business based on a comparison of the reporting unit to comparable publicly traded companies in similar lines of business. Significant estimates in the market valuation approach model include identifying similar companies with comparable business factors such as size, growth, profitability, risk and return on investment, and assessing comparable revenue and operating income multiples in estimating the fair value of the reporting unit.

Indefinite-lived intangible assets primarily consist of acquired trade names and trademarks. The Company may first perform a qualitative assessment to determine whether it is more likely than not that an indefinite-lived intangible asset is impaired. If, after assessing the totality of events and circumstances, the Company determines that it is more likely than not that the indefinite-lived intangible asset is not impaired, no quantitative fair value measurement is necessary. If a quantitative fair value measurement calculation is required for these intangible assets, the Company utilizes the relief-from-royalty method. This method assumes that trade names and trademarks have value to the extent that their owner is relieved of the obligation to pay royalties for the benefits received from them. This method requires the Company to estimate the future revenue for the related brands, the appropriate royalty rate and the weighted average cost of capital.

## Operating Leases

The Company leases retail store space, certain distribution and warehouse facilities, office space, and other non-real estate assets under operating leases. Operating lease agreements may contain rent escalation clauses, rent holidays or certain landlord incentives, including tenant improvement allowances. Rent expense for non-cancelable operating leases with scheduled rent increases or landlord incentives are recognized on a straight-line basis over the lease term, beginning with the effective lease commencement date, which is generally the date in which the Company takes possession of or controls the physical use of the property. Certain leases also provide for contingent rents, which are determined as a percentage of sales in excess of specified levels. A contingent rent liability is recognized together with the corresponding rent expense when specified levels have been achieved or when the Company determines that achieving the specified levels during the period is probable.

## Fair Value Measurements

The Company measures certain financial assets and liabilities at fair value on a recurring basis, including derivatives and available-for-sale securities. Fair value is the price the Company would receive to sell an asset or pay to transfer a liability in an orderly transaction with a market participant at the measurement date. The Company uses a three-level hierarchy established by the Financial Accounting Standards Board ("FASB") that prioritizes fair value measurements based on the types of inputs used for the various valuation techniques (market approach, income approach, and cost approach).

The levels of hierarchy are described below:

- Level 1: Observable inputs such as quoted prices in active markets for identical assets or liabilities.

- Level 2: Inputs other than quoted prices that are observable for the asset or liability, either directly or indirectly; these include quoted prices for similar assets or liabilities in active markets and quoted prices for identical or similar assets or liabilities in markets that are not active.

- Level 3: Unobservable inputs for which there is little or no market data available, which require the reporting entity to develop its own assumptions.

The Company's assessment of the significance of a particular input to the fair value measurement in its entirety requires judgment and considers factors specific to the asset or liability. Financial assets and liabilities are classified in their entirety based on the most conservative level of input that is significant to the fair value measurement.

Pricing vendors are utilized for certain Level 1 and Level 2 investments. These vendors either provide a quoted market price in an active market or use observable inputs without applying significant adjustments in their pricing. Observable inputs include broker quotes, interest rates and yield curves observable at commonly quoted intervals, volatilities and credit risks. The Company's fair value processes include controls that are designed to ensure appropriate fair values are recorded. These controls include an analysis of period-over-period fluctuations and comparison to another independent pricing vendor.

Refer to Note 6 — Fair Value Measurements for additional information.

## Foreign Currency Translation and Foreign Currency Transactions

Adjustments resulting from translating foreign functional currency financial statements into U.S. Dollars are included in the foreign currency translation adjustment, a component of accumulated other comprehensive income in shareholders' equity.

The Company's global subsidiaries have various assets and liabilities, primarily receivables and payables, which are denominated in currencies other than their functional currency. These balance sheet items are subject to remeasurement, the impact of which is recorded in other (income) expense, net, within the consolidated statements of income.

## Accounting for Derivatives and Hedging Activities

The Company uses derivative financial instruments to reduce its exposure to changes in foreign currency exchange rates and interest rates. All derivatives are recorded at fair value on the balance sheet and changes in the fair value of derivative financial instruments are either recognized in other comprehensive income (a component of shareholders' equity), debt or net income depending on the nature of the underlying exposure, whether the derivative is formally designated as a hedge, and, if designated, the extent to which the hedge is effective. The Company classifies the cash flows at settlement from derivatives in the same category as the cash flows from the related hedged items. For undesignated hedges and designated cash flow hedges, this is within the cash provided by operations component of the consolidated statements of cash flows. For designated net investment hedges, this is generally within the cash provided or used by investing activities component of the cash flow statement. As our fair value hedges are receive-fixed, pay- variable interest rate swaps, the cash flows associated with these derivative instruments are periodic interest payments while the swaps are outstanding. These cash flows are reflected within the cash provided by operations component of the cash flow statement.

Refer to Note 17 — Risk Management and Derivatives for more information on the Company's risk management program and derivatives.

## Stock-Based Compensation

The Company estimates the fair value of options and stock appreciation rights granted under the NIKE, Inc. 1990 Stock Incentive Plan (the "1990 Plan") and employees' purchase rights under the Employee Stock Purchase Plans ("ESPPs") using the Black-Scholes option pricing model. The Company recognizes this fair value, net of estimated forfeitures, as selling and administrative expense in the consolidated statements of income over the vesting period using the straight-line method.

Refer to Note 11 — Common Stock and Stock-Based Compensation for more information on the Company's stock programs.

## Income Taxes

The Company accounts for income taxes using the asset and liability method. This approach requires the recognition of deferred tax assets and liabilities for the expected future tax consequences of temporary differences between the carrying amounts and the tax basis of assets and liabilities. The Company records a valuation allowance to reduce deferred tax assets to the amount management believes is more likely than not to be realized. United States income taxes are provided currently on financial statement earnings of non-U.S. subsidiaries that are expected to be repatriated. The Company determines annually the amount of undistributed non-U.S. earnings to invest indefinitely in its non-U.S. operations.

The Company recognizes a tax benefit from uncertain tax positions in the financial statements only when it is more likely than not that the position will be sustained upon examination by relevant tax authorities. The Company recognizes interest and penalties related to income tax matters in income tax expense.

Refer to Note 9 — Income Taxes for further discussion.

## Earnings Per Share

Basic earnings per common share is calculated by dividing net income by the weighted average number of common shares outstanding during the year. Diluted earnings per common share is calculated by adjusting weighted average outstanding shares, assuming conversion of all potentially dilutive stock options and awards.

Refer to Note 12 — Earnings Per Share for further discussion.

## Management Estimates

The preparation of financial statements in conformity with generally accepted accounting principles requires management to make estimates, including estimates relating to assumptions that affect the reported amounts of assets and liabilities and disclosure of contingent assets and liabilities at the date of financial statements and the reported amounts of revenues and expenses during the reporting period. Actual results could differ from these estimates.

## Recently Adopted Accounting Standards

In July 2012, the FASB issued an accounting standards update intended to simplify how an entity tests indefinite-lived intangible assets other than goodwill for impairment by providing entities with an option to perform a qualitative assessment to determine whether further impairment testing is necessary. This accounting standard update will be effective for the Company beginning June 1, 2013, and early adoption is permitted. The Company early adopted this standard and the adoption did not have a material impact on its consolidated financial position or results of operations.

In September 2011, the FASB issued updated guidance on the periodic testing of goodwill for impairment. This guidance will allow companies to assess qualitative factors to determine if it is more-likely-than-not that goodwill might be impaired and whether it is necessary to perform the two-step goodwill impairment test required under current accounting standards. This new guidance was effective for the Company beginning June 1, 2012 and the adoption did not have a material effect on its consolidated financial position or results of operations.

In June 2011, the FASB issued guidance on the presentation of comprehensive income. This new guidance eliminates the current option to report other comprehensive income and its components in the statement of shareholders' equity. Companies are now required to present the components of net income and other comprehensive income in either one continuous statement, referred to as the statement of comprehensive income, or in two separate, but consecutive statements. This requirement was effective for the Company beginning June 1, 2012. As this guidance only amended the presentation of the components of comprehensive income, the adoption did not have an impact on the Company's consolidated financial position or results of operations. Further, this guidance required companies to present reclassification adjustments out of accumulated other comprehensive income by component in both the statement in which net income is presented and the statement in which other comprehensive income is presented. This requirement will be effective for the Company beginning June 1, 2013. As this guidance only amends the presentation of the components of comprehensive income, the Company does not anticipate the adoption will have an impact on the Company's consolidated financial position or results of operations.

## Recently Issued Accounting Standards

In December 2011, the FASB issued guidance enhancing disclosure requirements surrounding the nature of an entity's right to offset and related arrangements associated with its financial instruments and derivative instruments. This new guidance requires companies to disclose both gross and net information about instruments and transactions eligible for offset in the statement of financial position and instruments and transactions subject to master netting arrangements. This new guidance is effective for the Company beginning June 1, 2013. As this guidance only requires expanded disclosures, the Company does not anticipate the adoption will have an impact on its consolidated financial position or results of operations.

## NOTE 2 — Inventories

Inventory balances of $3,434 million and $3,222 million at May 31, 2013 and 2012, respectively, were substantially all finished goods.

## NOTE 3 — Property, Plant and Equipment

Property, plant and equipment included the following:

| | As of May 31, | |
| | 2013 | 2012 |
|---|---|---|
| (In millions) | | |
| Land | $ 268 | $ 252 |
| Buildings | 1,174 | 1,158 |
| Machinery, equipment and internal-use software | 2,985 | 2,654 |
| Leasehold improvements | 945 | 883 |
| Construction in process | 128 | 110 |
| Total property, plant and equipment, gross | 5,500 | 5,057 |
| Less accumulated depreciation | 3,048 | 2,848 |
| **TOTAL PROPERTY, PLANT AND EQUIPMENT, NET** | **$ 2,452** | **$ 2,209** |

Capitalized interest was not material for the years ended May 31, 2013, 2012, and 2011. The Company had $81 million in capital lease obligations as of May 31, 2013 included in machinery, equipment, and internal-use software; there were no capital lease obligations as of May 31, 2012.

## NOTE 4 — Identifiable Intangible Assets and Goodwill

The following table summarizes the Company's identifiable intangible asset balances as of May 31, 2013 and 2012:

| | As of May 31, 2013 | | | As of May 31, 2012 | | |
| (In millions) | Gross Carrying Amount | Accumulated Amortization | Net Carrying Amount | Gross Carrying Amount | Accumulated Amortization | Net Carrying Amount |
|---|---|---|---|---|---|---|
| Amortized intangible assets: | | | | | | |
| Patents | $ 119 | $ (35) | $ 84 | $ 99 | $ (29) | $ 70 |
| Trademarks | 43 | (32) | 11 | 40 | (26) | 14 |
| Other | 20 | (16) | 4 | 19 | (16) | 3 |
| **TOTAL** | **$ 182** | **$ (83)** | **$ 99** | **$ 158** | **$ (71)** | **$ 87** |
| Unamortized intangible assets — Trademarks | | | 283 | | | 283 |
| **IDENTIFIABLE INTANGIBLE ASSETS, NET** | | | **$ 382** | | | **$ 370** |

Amortization expense, which is included in selling and administrative expense, was $14 million, $14 million, and $13 million for the years ended May 31, 2013, 2012, and 2011, respectively. The estimated amortization expense for intangible assets subject to amortization for each of the years ending May 31, 2014 through May 31, 2018 are as follows: 2014: $13 million; 2015: $9 million; 2016: $9 million; 2017: $7 million; 2018: $6 million.

Goodwill was $131 million at May 31, 2013 and May 31, 2012, respectively, and is included in the Company's "Other" category for segment reporting purposes. There were no accumulated impairment balances for goodwill as of either period end.

## NOTE 5 — Accrued Liabilities

Accrued liabilities included the following:

| (In millions) | As of May 31, 2013 | As of May 31, 2012 |
|---|---|---|
| Compensation and benefits, excluding taxes | $ 713 | $ 691 |
| Endorsement compensation | 264 | 288 |
| Taxes other than income taxes | 192 | 169 |
| Dividends payable | 188 | 165 |
| Import and logistics costs | 111 | 133 |
| Advertising and marketing | 77 | 94 |
| Fair value of derivatives | 34 | 55 |
| Other[1] | 407 | 346 |
| **TOTAL ACCRUED LIABILITIES** | $ **1,986** | $ **1,941** |

*(1)   Other consists of various accrued expenses with no individual item accounting for more than 5% of the balance at May 31, 2013 and 2012.*

## NOTE 6 — Fair Value Measurements

The following table presents information about the Company's financial assets and liabilities measured at fair value on a recurring basis as of May 31, 2013 and   2012, and indicates the fair value hierarchy of the valuation techniques utilized by the Company to determine such fair value. Refer to Note 1 – Summary of   Significant Accounting Policies for additional detail regarding the Company's fair value measurement methodology.

| (In millions) | Fair Value Measurements Using Level 1 | Level 2 | Level 3 | Assets/Liabilities at Fair Value | Balance Sheet Classification |
|---|---|---|---|---|---|
| **ASSETS** | | | | | |
| Derivatives: | | | | | |
| Foreign exchange forwards and options | $   — | $   278 | $   — | $   278 | Other current assets and other long-term assets |
| Interest rate swap contracts | — | 11 | — | 11 | Other current assets and other long-term assets |
| Total derivatives | — | 289 | — | 289 | |
| Available-for-sale securities: | | | | | |
| U.S. Treasury securities | 425 | — | — | 425 | Cash and equivalents |
| U.S. Agency securities | — | 20 | — | 20 | Cash and equivalents |
| Commercial paper and bonds | — | 1,035 | — | 1,035 | Cash and equivalents |
| Money market funds | — | 836 | — | 836 | Cash and equivalents |
| U.S. Treasury securities | 1,583 | — | — | 1,583 | Short-term investments |
| U.S. Agency securities | — | 401 | — | 401 | Short-term investments |
| Commercial paper and bonds | — | 644 | — | 644 | Short-term investments |
| Non-marketable preferred stock | — | — | 5 | 5 | Other long-term assets |
| Total available-for-sale securities | 2,008 | 2,936 | 5 | 4,949 | |
| **TOTAL ASSETS** | $ **2,008** | $ **3,225** | $   **5** | $   **5,238** | |
| **LIABILITIES** | | | | | |
| Derivatives: | | | | | |
| Foreign exchange forwards and options | $   — | $   34 | $   — | $   34 | Accrued liabilities and other long-term liabilities |
| **TOTAL LIABILITIES** | $   **—** | $   **34** | $   **—** | $   **34** | |

As of May 31, 2013

|  |  |  |  |  |  |  |
|---|---|---|---|---|---|---|
|  | | **As of May 31, 2012** | | | | |
|  | **Fair Value Measurements Using** | | | **Assets / Liabilities at** | | |
| *(In millions)* | **Level 1** | **Level 2** | **Level 3** | **Fair Value** | | **Balance Sheet Classification** |
| **ASSETS** | | | | | | |
| Derivatives: | | | | | | |
| Foreign exchange forwards and options | $ — | $ 265 | $ — | $ 265 | | Other current assets and other long-term assets |
| Embedded derivatives | — | 1 | — | 1 | | Other current assets |
| Interest rate swap contracts | — | 15 | — | 15 | | Other current assets and other long-term assets |
| Total derivatives | — | 281 | — | 281 | | |
| Available-for-sale securities: | | | | | | |
| U.S. Treasury securities | 226 | — | — | 226 | | Cash and equivalents |
| U.S. Agency securities | — | 254 | — | 254 | | Cash and equivalents |
| Commercial paper and bonds | — | 159 | — | 159 | | Cash and equivalents |
| Money market funds | — | 770 | — | 770 | | Cash and equivalents |
| U.S. Treasury securities | 927 | — | — | 927 | | Short-term investments |
| U.S. Agency securities | — | 230 | — | 230 | | Short-term investments |
| Commercial paper and bonds | — | 283 | — | 283 | | Short-term investments |
| Non-marketable preferred stock | — | — | 3 | 3 | | Other long-term assets |
| Total available-for-sale securities | 1,153 | 1,696 | 3 | 2,852 | | |
| **TOTAL ASSETS** | **$ 1,153** | **$ 1,977** | **$ 3** | **$ 3,133** | | |
| **LIABILITIES** | | | | | | |
| Derivatives: | | | | | | |
| Foreign exchange forwards and options | $ — | $ 55 | $ — | $ 55 | | Accrued liabilities and other long-term liabilities |
| **TOTAL LIABILITIES** | **$ —** | **$ 55** | **$ —** | **$ 55** | | |

Derivative financial instruments include foreign exchange forwards and options, embedded derivatives and interest rate swap contracts. The fair value of derivative contracts is determined using observable market inputs such as the daily market foreign currency rates, forward pricing curves, currency volatilities, currency correlations and interest rates, and considers nonperformance risk of the Company and that of its counterparties. Adjustments relating to these nonperformance risks were not material at May 31, 2013 or 2012. Refer to Note 17 — Risk Management and Derivatives for additional detail.

Available-for-sale securities comprise investments in U.S. Treasury and Agency securities, money market funds, corporate commercial paper and bonds. These securities are valued using market prices on both active markets (Level 1) and less active markets (Level 2). Pricing vendors are utilized for certain Level 1 or Level 2 investments. These vendors either provide a quoted market price in an active market or use observable inputs without applying significant adjustments in their pricing. Observable inputs include broker quotes, interest rates and yield curves observable at commonly quoted intervals, volatilities and credit risks. The carrying amounts reflected in the consolidated balance sheets for short-term investments and cash and equivalents approximate fair value.

The Company's Level 3 assets comprise investments in certain non- marketable preferred stock. These investments are valued using internally developed models with unobservable inputs. These Level 3 investments are an immaterial portion of our portfolio. Changes in Level 3 investment assets were immaterial during the years ended May 31, 2013 and 2012.

No transfers among the levels within the fair value hierarchy occurred during the years ended May 31, 2013 or 2012.

As of May 31, 2013 and 2012, the Company had no assets or liabilities that were required to be measured at fair value on a non-recurring basis.

## Short-Term Investments

As of May 31, 2013 and 2012, short-term investments consisted of available- for-sale securities. As of May 31, 2013, the Company held $2,229 million of available-for-sale securities with maturity dates within one year from the purchase date and $399 million with maturity dates over one year and less than five years from the purchase date within short-term investments. As of May 31, 2012, the Company held $1,129 million of available for-sale securities with maturity dates within one year from purchase date and $311 million with maturity dates over one year and less than five years from purchase date within short-term investments.

Short-term investments classified as available-for-sale consist of the following at fair value:

| | As of May 31, | |
|---|---|---|
| *(In millions)* | **2013** | **2012** |
| Available-for-sale investments: | | |
| U.S. treasury and agencies | $ 1,984 | $ 1,157 |
| Commercial paper and bonds | 644 | 283 |
| **TOTAL ACCRUED LIABILITIES** | **$ 2,628** | **$ 1,440** |

Included in interest (income) expense, net was interest income related to cash and equivalents and short-term investments of $26 million, $27 million, and $28 million for the years ended May 31, 2013, 2012, and 2011, respectively.

For fair value information regarding notes payable and long-term debt, refer to Note 7 — Short-Term Borrowings and Credit Lines and Note 8 — Long-Term Debt.

## NOTE 7 — Short-Term Borrowings and Credit Lines

Notes payable and interest-bearing accounts payable to Sojitz Corporation of America ("Sojitz America") as of May 31, 2013 and 2012, are summarized below:

| | As of May 31, | | | |
|---|---|---|---|---|
| | 2013 | | 2012 | |
| *(In millions)* | **Borrowings** | **Interest Rate** | **Borrowings** | **Interest Rate** |
| *Notes payable:* | | | | |
| U.S. operations | $ 20 | 0.00%[1] | $ 30 | 5.50%[1] |
| Non-U.S. operations | 101 | 4.77%[1] | 78 | 9.46%[1] |
| **TOTAL NOTES PAYABLE** | **$ 121** | | **$ 108** | |
| *Interest-Bearing Accounts Payable:* | | | | |
| Sojitz America | $ 55 | 0.99% | $ 75 | 1.10% |

*(1)  Weighted average interest rate includes non-interest bearing overdrafts.*

The carrying amounts reflected in the consolidated balance sheets for notes payable approximate fair value.

The Company purchases through Sojitz America certain athletic footwear, apparel and equipment it acquires from non-U.S. suppliers. These purchases are for the Company's operations outside of the United States, Europe and Japan. Accounts payable to Sojitz America are generally due up to 60 days after shipment of goods from the foreign port. The interest rate on such accounts payable is the 60-day London Interbank Offered Rate ("LIBOR") as of the beginning of the month of the invoice date, plus 0.75%.

As of May 31, 2013 and 2012, the Company had no amounts outstanding under its commercial paper program.

In November 2011, the Company entered into a committed credit facility agreement with a syndicate of banks which provides for up to $1 billion of borrowings pursuant to a revolving credit facility with the option to increase borrowings to $1.5 billion with lender approval. The facility matures on November 1, 2016, with a one-year extension option prior to both the second and third anniversary of the closing date, provided that extensions shall not extend beyond November 1, 2018. Based on the Company's current long- term senior unsecured debt ratings of A+ and A1 from Standard and Poor's Corporation and Moody's Investor Services, respectively, the interest rate charged on any outstanding borrowings would be the prevailing LIBOR plus 0.56%. The facility fee is 0.065% of the total commitment. Under this committed credit facility, the Company must maintain, among other things, certain minimum specified financial ratios with which the Company was in compliance at May 31, 2013. No amounts were outstanding under this facility as of May 31, 2013 or 2012.

## NOTE 8 — Long-Term Debt

Long-term debt, net of unamortized premiums and discounts and swap fair value adjustments, comprises the following:

| Scheduled Maturity (Dollars in millions) | Original Principal | | Interest Rate | Interest Payments | Book Value Outstanding As of May 31, | |
|---|---|---|---|---|---|---|
| | | | | | 2013 | 2012 |
| Corporate Bond Payables:[4] | | | | | | |
| July 23, 2012[1] | $ | 25 | 5.66% | Semi-Annually | $ — | $ 25 |
| August 7, 2012[1] | $ | 15 | 5.40% | Semi-Annually | — | 15 |
| October 1, 2013 | $ | 50 | 4.70% | Semi-Annually | 50 | 50 |
| October 15, 2015[1] | $ | 100 | 5.15% | Semi-Annually | 111 | 115 |
| May 1, 2023[5] | $ | 500 | 2.25% | Semi-Annually | 499 | — |
| May 1, 2043[5] | $ | 500 | 3.63% | Semi-Annually | 499 | — |
| Promissory Notes:[2] | | | | | | |
| April 1, 2017 | $ | 40 | 6.20% | Monthly | 40 | — |
| January 1, 2018 | $ | 19 | 6.79% | Monthly | 19 | — |
| Japanese Yen Notes: | | | | | 34 | |
| August 20, 2001 through November 20, 2020[3] | ¥ | 9,000 | 2.60% | Quarterly | | 50 |
| August 20, 2001 through November 20, 2020[3] | ¥ | 4,000 | 2.00% | Quarterly | 15 | 22 |
| Total | | | | | 1,267 | 277 |
| Less current maturities | | | | | 57 | 49 |
| **TOTAL LONG-TERM DEBT** | | | | | $ **1,210** | $ **228** |

(1) The Company has entered into interest rate swap agreements whereby the Company receives fixed interest payments at the same rate as the note and pays variable interest payments based on the six-month LIBOR plus a spread. The swaps have the same notional amount and maturity date as the corresponding note. At May 31, 2013, the interest rates payable on these swap agreements ranged from approximately 0.3% to 0.4%.

(2) The Company assumed a total of $59 million in bonds payable on May 30, 2013 as part of its agreement to purchase certain Corporate properties, which was treated as a non-cash financing transaction. The property serves as collateral for the debt. The purchase of these properties was accounted for as a business combination where the total consideration of $85 million was allocated to the land and buildings acquired; no other tangible or intangible assets or liabilities resulted from the purchase. The bonds mature in 2017 and 2018 and the Company does not have the ability to re-negotiate the terms of the debt agreements and would incur significant financial penalties if the notes are paid off prior to maturity.

(3) NIKE Logistics YK assumed a total of ¥13.0 billion in loans as part of its agreement to purchase a distribution center in Japan, which serves as collateral for the loans. These loans mature in equal quarterly installments during the period August 20, 2001 through November 20, 2020.

(4) Senior unsecured obligations rank equally with our other unsecured and unsubordinated indebtedness.

(5) The bonds carry a make whole call provision and are redeemable at any time prior to maturity. The bonds also feature a par call provision payable 3 months and 6 months prior to the scheduled maturity date for the bonds maturing on May 1, 2023 and May 1, 2043, respectively.

The scheduled maturity of long-term debt in each of the years ending May 31,  2014 through 2018 are $57 million, $7 million, $108 million, $45 million and $25 million, respectively, at face value.

The fair value of the Company's long-term debt, including the current portion,  was approximately $1,219 million at May 31, 2013 and $283 million at May 31, 2012. The fair value of long-term debt is estimated based upon  quoted prices of similar instruments (level 2).

## NOTE 9 — Income Taxes

Income before income taxes is as follows:

| (In millions) | Year Ended May 31, | | |
|---|---|---|---|
| | 2013 | 2012 | 2011 |
| Income before income taxes: | | | |
| United States | $ 1,240 | $ 804 | $ 1,040 |
| Foreign | 2,032 | 2,221 | 1,822 |
| **TOTAL INCOME BEFORE INCOME TAXES** | $ 3,272 | $ 3,025 | $ 2,862 |

The provision for income taxes is as follows:

| (In millions) | Year Ended May 31, | | |
| --- | --- | --- | --- |
| | 2013 | 2012 | 2011 |
| Current: | | | |
| United States | | | |
| Federal | $ 434 | $ 289 | $ 298 |
| State | 69 | 51 | 57 |
| Foreign | 398 | 488 | 435 |
| Total | 901 | 828 | 790 |
| Deferred: | | | |
| United States | | | |
| Federal | 1 | (48) | (62) |
| State | (4) | 5 | — |
| Foreign | (90) | (29) | (38) |
| Total | (93) | (72) | (100) |
| **TOTAL INCOME TAX EXPENSE** | $ 808 | $ 756 | $ 690 |

A reconciliation from the U.S. statutory federal income tax rate to the effective income tax rate is as follows:

| | Year Ended May 31, | | |
| --- | --- | --- | --- |
| | 2013 | 2012 | 2011 |
| Federal income tax rate | 35.0% | 35.0% | 35.0% |
| State taxes, net of federal benefit | 1.4% | 1.3% | 1.3% |
| Foreign earnings | -11.8% | -11.9% | -11.4% |
| Other, net | 0.1% | 0.6% | -0.8% |
| **EFFECTIVE INCOME TAX RATE** | **24.7%** | **25.0%** | **24.1%** |

The effective tax rate from continuing operations for the year ended May 31, 2013 was 30 basis points lower than the effective tax rate from continuing operations for the year ended May 31, 2012 primarily due to tax benefits received from the intercompany sale of intellectual property rights outside of the U.S., the retroactive reinstatement of the research and development credit and the intra-period allocation of tax expense between continuing operations, discontinued operations, and other comprehensive income. The decrease in the effective tax rate was partially offset by a higher effective tax rate on operations as a result of an increase in earnings in higher tax jurisdictions. The effective tax rate from continuing operations for the year ended May 31, 2012 was 90 basis points higher than the effective tax rate from continuing operations for the year ended May 31, 2011 primarily due to the changes in uncertain tax positions partially offset by a reduction in the effective rate related to a decrease in earnings in higher tax jurisdictions.

Deferred tax assets and (liabilities) comprise the following:

| | As of May 31, | |
|---|---|---|
| (In millions) | 2013 | 2012 |
| **Deferred tax assets:** | | |
| Allowance for doubtful accounts | $ 20 | $ 17 |
| Inventories | 40 | 37 |
| Sales return reserves | 101 | 84 |
| Deferred compensation | 197 | 186 |
| Stock-based compensation | 140 | 126 |
| Reserves and accrued liabilities | 66 | 66 |
| Foreign loss carry-forwards | 19 | 35 |
| Foreign tax credit carry-forwards | 106 | 216 |
| Undistributed earnings of foreign subsidiaries | 162 | 82 |
| Other | 47 | 62 |
| Total deferred tax assets | 898 | 911 |
| Valuation allowance | (5) | (27) |
| Total deferred tax assets after valuation allowance | 893 | 884 |
| **Deferred tax liabilities:** | | |
| Property, plant and equipment | (241) | (191) |
| Intangibles | (96) | (98) |
| Other | (20) | (22) |
| Total deferred tax liability | (357) | (311) |
| **NET DEFERRED TAX ASSET** | $ 536 | $ 573 |

The following is a reconciliation of the changes in the gross balance of unrecognized tax benefits:

| | As of May 31, | | |
|---|---|---|---|
| (In millions) | 2013 | 2012 | 2011 |
| Unrecognized tax benefits, as of the beginning of the period | $ 285 | $ 212 | $ 282 |
| Gross increases related to prior period tax positions | 77 | 48 | 13 |
| Gross decreases related to prior period tax positions | (3) | (25) | (98) |
| Gross increases related to current period tax positions | 130 | 91 | 59 |
| Gross decreases related to current period tax positions | (9) | (1) | (6) |
| Settlements | — | (20) | (43) |
| Lapse of statute of limitations | (21) | (9) | (8) |
| Changes due to currency translation | (12) | (11) | 13 |
| **UNRECOGNIZED TAX BENEFITS, AS OF THE END OF THE PERIOD** | $ 447 | $ 285 | $ 212 |

As of May 31, 2013, the total gross unrecognized tax benefits, excluding related interest and penalties, were $447 million, $281 million of which would affect the Company's effective tax rate if recognized in future periods.

The Company recognizes interest and penalties related to income tax matters in income tax expense. The liability for payment of interest and penalties increased $4 million, $17 million, and $10 million during the years ended May 31, 2013, 2012, and 2011, respectively. As of May 31, 2013 and 2012, accrued interest and penalties related to uncertain tax positions was $112 million and $108 million, respectively (excluding federal benefit).

The Company is subject to taxation primarily in the U.S., China, the Netherlands, and Brazil, as well as various state and other foreign jurisdictions. The Company has concluded substantially all U.S. federal income tax matters through fiscal 2010. The Company is currently under audit by the Internal Revenue Service for the 2011 through 2013 tax years. Many issues are at an advanced stage in the examination process, the most significant of which includes the negotiation of a U.S. Unilateral Advanced Pricing Agreement that covers intercompany transfer pricing issues for fiscal years May 31, 2011 through May 31, 2015. In addition, the Company is in appeals regarding the validation of foreign tax credits taken. The Company's major foreign jurisdictions, China, the Netherlands and Brazil, have concluded substantially all income tax matters through calendar 2005, fiscal 2007 and calendar 2006, respectively. Although the timing of resolution of audits is not certain, the Company evaluates all domestic and foreign audit issues in the aggregate, along with the expiration of applicable statutes of limitations, and estimates that it is reasonably possible the total gross unrecognized tax benefits could decrease by up to $86 million within the next 12 months.

We provide for United States income taxes on the undistributed earnings of foreign subsidiaries unless they are considered indefinitely reinvested outside the United States. At May 31, 2013, the indefinitely reinvested earnings in foreign subsidiaries upon which United States income taxes have not been provided was approximately $6.7 billion. If these undistributed earnings were repatriated to the United States, or if the shares of the relevant foreign subsidiaries were sold or otherwise transferred, they would generate foreign tax credits that would reduce the federal tax liability associated with the foreign dividend or the otherwise taxable transaction. Assuming a full utilization of the foreign tax credits, the potential net deferred tax liability associated with these temporary differences of undistributed earnings would be approximately $2.2 billion at May 31, 2013.

A portion of the Company's foreign operations are benefiting from a tax holiday, which will phase out in 2019. This tax holiday may be extended when certain conditions are met or may be terminated early if certain conditions are not met. The impact of this tax holiday decreased foreign taxes by $108 million, $117 million, and $36 million for the fiscal years ended May 31, 2013, 2012, and 2011, respectively. The benefit of the tax holiday on net income per share (diluted) was $0.12, $0.12, and $0.04 for the fiscal years ended May 31, 2013, 2012, and 2011, respectively.

Deferred tax assets at May 31, 2013 and 2012 were reduced by a valuation allowance relating to tax benefits of certain subsidiaries with operating losses. The net change in the valuation allowance was a decrease of $22 million, an increase of $23 million, and a decrease of $1 million for the years ended May 31, 2013, 2012, and 2011, respectively.

The Company does not anticipate that any foreign tax credit carry-forwards will expire unutilized.

The Company has available domestic and foreign loss carry-forwards of $58 million at May 31, 2013. Such losses will expire as follows:

| | | | | | Year Ending May 31, | | |
|---|---|---|---|---|---|---|---|
| (In millions) | 2014 | 2015 | 2016 | 2017 | 2018-2032 | Indefinite | Total |
| Net Operating Losses  $ | — | — | 2 | — | 52 | 4  $ | 58 |

During the years ended May 31, 2013, 2012, and 2011, income tax benefits attributable to employee stock-based compensation transactions of $76 million, $120 million, and $68 million, respectively, were allocated to shareholders' equity.

## NOTE 10 — Redeemable Preferred Stock

Sojitz America is the sole owner of the Company's authorized Redeemable Preferred Stock, $1 par value, which is redeemable at the option of Sojitz America or the Company at par value aggregating $0.3 million. A cumulative dividend of $0.10 per share is payable annually on May 31 and no dividends may be declared or paid on the common stock of the Company unless dividends on the Redeemable Preferred Stock have been declared and paid in full. There have been no changes in the Redeemable Preferred Stock in the three years ended May 31, 2013, 2012, and 2011. As the holder of the Redeemable Preferred Stock, Sojitz America does not have general voting rights but does have the right to vote as a separate class on the sale of all or substantially all of the assets of the Company and its subsidiaries, on merger, consolidation, liquidation or dissolution of the Company or on the sale or assignment of the NIKE trademark for athletic footwear sold in the United States. The Redeemable Preferred Stock has been fully issued to Sojitz America and is not blank check preferred stock. The Company's articles of incorporation do not permit the issuance of additional preferred stock.

## NOTE 11 — Common Stock and Stock-Based Compensation

The authorized number of shares of Class A Common Stock, no par value, and Class B Common Stock, no par value, are 200 million and 1,200 million, respectively. Each share of Class A Common Stock is convertible into one share of Class B Common Stock. Voting rights of Class B Common Stock are limited in certain circumstances with respect to the election of directors. There are no differences in the dividend and liquidation preferences or participation rights of the Class A and Class B common shareholders.

In 1990, the Board of Directors adopted, and the shareholders approved, the NIKE, Inc. 1990 Stock Incentive Plan (the "1990 Plan"). The 1990 Plan provides for the issuance of up to 326 million previously unissued shares of Class B Common Stock in connection with stock options and other awards granted under the plan. The 1990 Plan authorizes the grant of non-statutory stock options, incentive stock options, stock appreciation rights, restricted stock, restricted stock units, and performance-based awards. The exercise price for stock options and stock appreciation rights may not be less than the fair market value of the underlying shares on the date of grant. A committee of the Board of Directors administers the 1990 Plan. The committee has the authority to determine the employees to whom awards will be made, the amount of the awards, and the other terms and conditions of the awards. Substantially all stock option grants outstanding under the 1990 Plan were granted in the first quarter of each fiscal year, vest ratably over four years, and expire 10 years from the date of grant.

The following table summarizes the Company's total stock-based compensation expense recognized in selling and administrative expense:

| | Year Ended May 31, | | |
|---|---|---|---|
| (In millions) | 2013 | 2012 | 2011 |
| Stock options [1] | $    123 | $    96 | $    77 |
| ESPPs | 19 | 16 | 14 |
| Restricted stock | 32 | 18 | 14 |
| **TOTAL STOCK-BASED COMPENSATION EXPENSE** | $    174 | $    130 | $    105 |

(1) Expense for stock options includes the expense associated with stock appreciation rights. Accelerated stock option expense is recorded for employees eligible for accelerated stock option vesting upon retirement. Accelerated stock option expense for years ended May 31, 2013, 2012, and 2011 was $22 million, $17 million, and $12 million, respectively.

As of May 31, 2013, the Company had $199 million of unrecognized compensation costs from stock options, net of estimated forfeitures, to be recognized as selling and administrative expense over a weighted average period of 2.3 years.

The weighted average fair value per share of the options granted during the years ended May 31, 2013, 2012, and 2011, as computed using the Black-Scholes   pricing model, was $12.71, $11.08, and $8.84, respectively. The weighted average assumptions used to estimate these fair values are as follows:

| | Year Ended May 31, | | |
| --- | --- | --- | --- |
| | 2013 | 2012 | 2011 |
| Dividend yield | 1.5% | 1.4% | 1.6% |
| Expected volatility | 35.0% | 29.5% | 31.5% |
| Weighted average expected life (in years) | 5.3 | 5.0 | 5.0 |
| Risk-free interest rate | 0.6% | 1.4% | 1.7% |

The Company estimates the expected volatility based on the implied volatility  in market traded options on the Company's common stock with a term greater than one year, along with other factors. The weighted average expected life of options is based on an analysis of historical and expected future exercise patterns. The interest rate is based on the U.S. Treasury (constant maturity) risk-free rate in effect at the date of grant for periods  corresponding with the expected term of the options.

The following summarizes the stock option transactions under the plan discussed above:

| | Shares[1] | | Weighted Average Option Price |
| --- | --- | --- | --- |
| | (In millions) | | |
| Options outstanding May 31, 2010 | 72.2 | $ | 23.30 |
| Exercised | (14.0) | | 21.35 |
| Forfeited | (1.3) | | 29.03 |
| Granted | 12.7 | | 34.60 |
| Options outstanding May 31, 2011 | 69.6 | $ | 25.65 |
| Exercised | (18.0) | | 22.81 |
| Forfeited | (1.0) | | 35.61 |
| Granted | 13.7 | | 45.87 |
| Options outstanding May 31, 2012 | 64.3 | $ | 30.59 |
| Exercised | (9.9) | | 24.70 |
| Forfeited | (1.3) | | 40.14 |
| Granted | 14.6 | | 46.55 |
| Options outstanding May 31, 2013 | 67.7 | $ | 34.72 |
| Options exercisable at May 31, | | | |
| 2011 | 40.1 | $ | 22.03 |
| 2012 | 33.9 | | 24.38 |
| 2013 | 35.9 | | 27.70 |

(1)  Includes stock appreciation rights transactions.

The weighted average contractual life remaining for options outstanding and  options exercisable at May 31, 2013 was 6.3 years and 4.7 years, respectively. The aggregate intrinsic value for options outstanding and  exercisable at May 31, 2013 was $1,823 million and $1,218 million, respectively. The aggregate intrinsic value was the amount by which the market value of the underlying stock exceeded the exercise price of the options. The total intrinsic value of the options exercised during the years  ended May 31, 2013, 2012, and 2011 was $293 million, $453 million, and $267 million, respectively.

In addition to the 1990 Plan, the Company gives employees the right to  purchase shares at a discount to the market price under employee stock purchase plans ("ESPPs"). Employees are eligible to  participate through payroll deductions of up to 10% of their compensation. At the end of each six-  month offering period, shares are purchased by the participants at 85% of the  lower of the fair market value at the beginning or the end of the offering period. Employees purchased 1.6 million, 1.7 million, and 1.6 million shares during  each of the three years ended May 31, 2013, 2012 and 2011, respectively.

From time to time, the Company grants restricted stock units and restricted stock to key employees under the 1990 Plan. The number of shares underlying such awards granted to employees during the years ended May 31, 2013, 2012, and 2011 were 1.6 million, 0.7 million, and 0.4 million with weighted average values per share of $46.86, $49.49, and $35.11, respectively. Recipients of restricted stock are entitled to cash dividends and to vote their respective shares throughout the period of restriction. Recipients of restricted stock units are entitled to dividend equivalent cash payments upon vesting. The value of all grants of restricted stock and restricted stock units was established by the market price on the date of grant. During the years ended May 31, 2013, 2012, and 2011, the aggregate fair value of restricted stock and restricted stock units vested was $25 million, $22 million, and $15 million, respectively, determined as of the date of vesting.

## NOTE 12 — Earnings Per Share

The following is a reconciliation from basic earnings per share to diluted earnings per share. Options to purchase an additional 0.1 million, 0.2 million, and 0.3 million shares of common stock were outstanding at May 31, 2013, 2012, and 2011 respectively, but were not included in the computation of diluted earnings per share because the options were anti-dilutive.

| (In millions, except per share data) | | Year Ended May 31, | | | | |
|---|---|---|---|---|---|---|
| | | 2013 | | 2012 | | 2011 |
| Determination of shares: | | | | | | |
| Weighted average common shares outstanding | | 897.3 | | 920.0 | | 951.1 |
| Assumed conversion of dilutive stock options and awards | | 19.1 | | 19.6 | | 20.2 |
| **DILUTED WEIGHTED AVERAGE COMMON SHARES OUTSTANDING** | | **916.4** | | **939.6** | | **971.3** |
| | | | | | | |
| Earnings per share from continuing operations: | | | | | | |
| Basic earnings per common share | $ | 2.75 | $ | 2.47 | $ | 2.28 |
| Diluted earnings per common share | $ | 2.69 | $ | 2.42 | $ | 2.24 |
| | | | | | | |
| Earnings per share from discontinued operations: | | | | | | |
| Basic earnings per common share | $ | 0.02 | $ | (0.05) | $ | (0.04) |
| Diluted earnings per common share | $ | 0.02 | $ | (0.05) | $ | (0.04) |
| | | | | | | |
| Basic earnings per common share for NIKE, Inc. | $ | 2.77 | $ | 2.42 | $ | 2.24 |
| Diluted earnings per common share for NIKE, Inc. | $ | 2.71 | $ | 2.37 | $ | 2.20 |

# NOTE 13 — Benefit Plans

The Company has a profit sharing plan available to most U.S.-based employees. The terms of the plan call for annual contributions by the Company as determined by the Board of Directors. A subsidiary of the Company also had a profit sharing plan available to its U.S.-based employees prior to fiscal 2012. The terms of the plan called for annual contributions as determined by the subsidiary's executive management. Contributions of $47 million, $40 million, and $39 million were made to the plans and are included in selling and administrative expense for the years ended May 31, 2013, 2012, and 2011, respectively. The Company has various 401(k) employee savings plans available to U.S.-based employees. The Company matches a portion of employee contributions. Company contributions to the savings plans were $46 million, $42 million, and $38 million for the years ended May 31, 2013, 2012, and 2011, respectively, and are included in selling and administrative expense.

The Company also has a Long-Term Incentive Plan ("LTIP") that was adopted by the Board of Directors and approved by shareholders in September 1997 and later amended in fiscal 2007. The Company recognized $50 million, $51 million, and $31 million of selling and administrative expense related to cash awards under the LTIP during the years ended May 31, 2013, 2012, and 2011, respectively.

The Company has pension plans in various countries worldwide. The pension plans are only available to local employees and are generally government mandated. The liability related to the unfunded pension liabilities of the plans was $104 million and $113 million at May 31, 2013 and May 31, 2012, respectively, which was primarily classified as long-term in other liabilities.

# NOTE 14 — Accumulated Other Comprehensive Income

The components of accumulated other comprehensive income, net of tax, are as follows:

| (In millions) | | May 31 | | |
|---|---|---|---|---|
| | | 2013 | | 2012 |
| Cumulative translation adjustment and other | $ | (14) | $ | (127) |
| Net deferred gain on cash flow hedge derivatives | | 193 | | 181 |
| Net deferred gain on net investment hedge derivatives | | 95 | | 95 |
| **ACCUMULATED OTHER COMPREHENSIVE INCOME** | $ | **274** | $ | **149** |

Refer to Note 17 — Risk Management and Derivatives for more information on the Company's risk management program and derivatives.

# NOTE 15 — Discontinued Operations

The Company continually evaluates its existing portfolio of businesses to ensure resources are invested in those businesses that are accretive to the NIKE Brand and represent the largest growth potential and highest returns. During the year, the Company divested of Umbro and Cole Haan, allowing it to focus its resources on driving growth in the NIKE, Jordan, Converse and Hurley brands.

On February 1, 2013, the Company completed the sale of Cole Haan to Apax Partners for an agreed upon purchase price of $570 million and received at closing $561 million, net of $9 million of purchase price adjustments. The transaction resulted in a gain on sale of $231 million, net of $137 million in tax expense; this gain is included in the net income (loss) from discontinued operations line item on the consolidated statements of income. There were no adjustments to these recorded amounts as of May 31, 2013. Beginning November 30, 2012, the Company classified the Cole Haan disposal group as held-for-sale and presented the results of Cole Haan's operations in the net income (loss) from discontinued operations line item on the consolidated statements of income. From this date until the sale, the assets and liabilities of Cole Haan were recorded in the assets of discontinued operations and liabilities of discontinued operations line items on the consolidated balance sheets, respectively. Previously, these amounts were reported in the Company's segment presentation as "Other Businesses."

Under the sale agreement, the Company agreed to provide certain transition  services to Cole Haan for an expected period of 3 to 9 months from the date of sale. The Company will also license NIKE proprietary Air and Lunar technologies to Cole Haan for a transition period. The continuing cash flows related to these items are not expected to be significant to Cole Haan and the  Company will have no significant continuing involvement with Cole Haan  beyond the transition services. Additionally, preexisting guarantees of certain Cole Haan lease payments remain in place after the sale; the maximum  exposure under the guarantees is $44 million at May 31, 2013. The fair value of the guarantees is not material.

On November 30, 2012, the Company completed the sale of certain assets of  Umbro to Iconix Brand Group ("Iconix") for $225 million. The Umbro disposal  group was  classified as held-for-sale as of November 30, 2012 and the  results of Umbro's operations are presented in the net income (loss) from  discontinued operations line item on the consolidated statements of income.  The remaining liabilities of Umbro are recorded in the liabilities of discontinued  operations line items on the consolidated balance sheets. Previously, these  amounts were reported in the Company's segment presentation as "Other  Businesses." Upon meeting the held-for-sale criteria, the Company recorded  a loss of $107 million, net of tax, on the sale of Umbro and the loss is included  in the  net income (loss) from  discontinued operations line item on the consolidated statements of income. The loss on sale was calculated as the  net sales  price less Umbro assets of $248 million, including intangibles, goodwill, and fixed assets, other miscellaneous charges of $22 million, and the  release of the associated cumulative translation adjustment of $129 million. The tax benefit on the loss was $67 million. There were no  adjustments to these recorded amounts as of May 31, 2013.

Under the sale agreement, the Company provided transition services to Iconix  while certain markets were transitioned to Iconix-designated licensees. These  transition services are complete and the Company has wound down the  remaining operations of Umbro.

For the year ended May 31, 2013, net income (loss) from discontinued  operations included, for both businesses, the net gain or loss on sale, net  operating losses, tax expenses, and approximately $20 million in wind down  costs.

Summarized results of the Company's discontinued operations are as follows:

| | | | Year Ended May 31, | | |
|---|---|---|---|---|---|
| (In millions) | | 2013 | | 2012 | 2011 |
| Revenues | $ | 523 | $ | 796  $ | 746 |
| Income (loss) before income taxes | | 108 | | (43) | (18) |
| Income tax expense (benefit) | | 87 | | 3 | 21 |
| **Net income (loss) from discontinued operations** | $ | 21 | $ | (46)  $ | (39) |

As of May 31, 2013 and 2012, the aggregate components of assets and liabilities classified as discontinued operations and included in current assets and current  liabilities consisted of the following:

| | | | As of May 31, | |
|---|---|---|---|---|
| (In millions) | | 2013 | | 2012 |
| Accounts Receivable, net | $ | — | $ | 148 |
| Inventories | | — | | 128 |
| Deferred income taxes and other assets | | — | | 35 |
| Property, plant and equipment, net | | — | | 70 |
| Identifiable intangible assets, net | | — | | 234 |
| **TOTAL  ASSETS** | $ | — | $ | 615 |
| Accounts payable | $ | 1 | $ | 42 |
| Accrued liabilities | | 17 | | 112 |
| Deferred income taxes and other liabilities | | — | | 16 |
| **TOTAL LIABILITIES** | $ | 18 | $ | 170 |

## NOTE 16 — Commitments and Contingencies

The Company leases space for certain of its offices, warehouses and retail  stores under leases expiring from 1 to 21 years after May 31, 2013. Rent  expense was $482 million, $431 million, and $386 million for the years ended  May 31, 2013, 2012 and 2011, respectively. Amounts of minimum future  annual rental commitments under non-cancelable operating leases in each of  the five years ending May 31, 2014 through 2018 are $403 million, $340  million, $304 million, $272 million, $225 million, respectively, and $816 million  in later years. Amounts of minimum future annual commitments under non-  cancelable capital leases in each of the four years ending May 31, 2014  through 2017 are $23 million, $28 million, $21 million, and $9 million,  respectively; the Company has no capital lease obligations beyond the year  ending May 31, 2017.

As of May 31, 2013 and 2012, the Company had letters of credit outstanding  totaling $149 million and $137 million, respectively. These letters of credit  were generally issued for the purchase of inventory and guarantees of the  Company's performance under certain self-insurance and other programs.

In connection with various contracts and agreements, the Company provides  routine indemnifications relating to the enforceability of intellectual property  rights, coverage for legal issues that arise and other items where the  Company is acting as the guarantor. Currently, the Company has several  such agreements in place. However, based on the Company's historical  experience and the estimated probability of future loss, the Company has  determined that the fair value of such indemnifications is not material to the  Company's financial position or results of operations.

In the ordinary course of its business, the Company is involved in various legal  proceedings involving contractual and employment relationships, product liability claims, trademark rights, and a variety of other matters. While the  Company cannot predict the outcome of its pending legal matters with certainty, the Company does not believe any currently identified claim, proceeding or litigation, either individually or in aggregate, will have a material impact on the Company's results of operations, financial position or cash flows.

## NOTE 17 — Risk Management and Derivatives

The Company is exposed to global market risks, including the effect of changes in foreign currency exchange rates and interest rates, and uses derivatives to manage financial exposures that occur in the normal course of business. The Company does not hold or issue derivatives for trading or speculative purposes.

The Company may elect to designate certain derivatives as hedging instruments under the accounting standards for derivatives and hedging. The Company formally documents all relationships between designated hedging instruments and hedged items as well as its risk management objective and strategy for undertaking hedge transactions. This process includes linking all derivatives designated as hedges to either recognized assets or liabilities or forecasted transactions.

The majority of derivatives outstanding as of May 31, 2013 are designated as cash flow or fair value hedges. All derivatives are recognized on the balance sheet at fair value and classified based on the instrument's maturity date. The total notional amount of outstanding derivatives as of May 31, 2013 was approximately $9 billion, which primarily comprises cash flow hedges for Euro/U.S. Dollar, British Pound/Euro, and Japanese Yen/U.S. Dollar currency pairs. As of May 31, 2013, there were outstanding currency forward contracts with maturities up to 24 months.

The following table presents the fair values of derivative instruments included within the consolidated balance sheets as of May 31, 2013 and 2012:

| (In millions) | Asset Derivatives Balance Sheet Location | 2013 | 2012 | Liability Derivatives Balance Sheet Location | 2013 | 2012 |
|---|---|---|---|---|---|---|
| Derivatives formally designated as hedging instruments: | | | | | | |
| Foreign exchange forwards and options | Prepaid expenses and other current assets | $ 141 | $ 203 | Accrued liabilities | $ 12 | $ 35 |
| Foreign exchange forwards and options | Deferred income taxes and other long-term assets | 79 | 7 | Deferred income taxes and other long-term liabilities | — | — |
| Interest rate swap contracts | Deferred income taxes and other long-term assets | 11 | 15 | Deferred income taxes and other long-term liabilities | — | — |
| Total derivatives formally designated as hedging instruments | | $ 231 | $ 225 | | $ 12 | $ 35 |
| Derivatives not designated as hedging instruments: | | | | | | |
| Foreign exchange forwards and options | Prepaid expenses and other current assets | $ 58 | $ 55 | Accrued liabilities | $ 22 | $ 20 |
| Embedded derivatives | Prepaid expenses and other current assets | — | 1 | Accrued liabilities | — | — |
| Total derivatives not designated as hedging instruments | | 58 | 56 | | 22 | 20 |
| **TOTAL DERIVATIVES** | | **$ 289** | **$ 281** | | **$ 34** | **$ 55** |

The following tables present the amounts affecting the consolidated statements of income for years ended May 31, 2013, 2012 and 2011:

| (In millions) | Amount of Gain (Loss) Recognized in Other Comprehensive Income on Derivatives[1] Year Ended May 31, 2013 | 2012 | 2013 | Amount of Gain (Loss) Reclassified From Accumulated Other Comprehensive Income into Income[1] Location of Gain (Loss) Reclassified From Accumulated Other Comprehensive Income Into Income[1] | Year Ended May 31, 2013 | 2012 | 2013 |
|---|---|---|---|---|---|---|---|
| Derivatives designated as cash flow hedges: | | | | | | | |
| Foreign exchange forwards and options | $ 42 | $ (29) | $ (87) | Revenue | $ (19) | $ 5 | $ (30) |
| Foreign exchange forwards and options | 67 | 253 | (152) | Cost of sales | 113 | (57) | 103 |
| Foreign exchange forwards and options | (3) | 3 | (4) | Selling and administrative expense | 2 | (2) | 1 |
| Foreign exchange forwards and options | 33 | 36 | (65) | Other (income) expense, net | 9 | (9) | 34 |
| Total designated cash flow hedges | $ 139 | $ 263 | $ (308) | | $ 105 | $ (63) | $ 108 |
| Derivatives designated as net investment hedges: | | | | | | | |
| Foreign exchange forwards and options | $ — | $ 45 | $ (85) | Other (income) expense, net | $ — | $ — | $ — |

(1) For the years ended May 31, 2013, 2012, and 2011, the amounts recorded in other (income) expense, net as a result of hedge ineffectiveness and the discontinuance of cash flow hedges because the forecasted transactions were no longer probable of occurring were immaterial.

| (In millions) | Amount of Gain (Loss) Recognized in Income on Derivatives | | | Location of Gain (Loss) Recognized in Income on Derivatives |
| | Year Ended May 31, | | | |
| | 2013 | 2012 | 2011 | |
|---|---|---|---|---|
| Derivatives designated as fair value hedges: | | | | |
| Interest rate swaps[1] | $    5 | $    6 | $    6 | Interest (income) expense, net |
| Derivatives not designated as hedging instruments: | | | | |
| Foreign exchange forwards and options | 51 | 64 | (30) | Other (income) expense, net |
| Embedded derivatives | $    (4) | $    1 | $    — | Other (income) expense, net |

(1) All interest rate swap agreements meet the shortcut method requirements under the accounting standards for derivatives and hedging. Accordingly, changes in the fair values of the interest rate swap agreements are considered to exactly offset changes in the fair value of the underlying long-term debt. Refer to "Fair Value Hedges" in this note for additional detail.

Refer to Note 5 — Accrued Liabilities for derivative instruments recorded in accrued liabilities, Note 6 — Fair Value Measurements for a description of how the above financial instruments are valued, Note 14 — Accumulated Other Comprehensive Income and the consolidated statements of shareholders' equity for additional information on changes in other comprehensive income for the years ended May 31, 2013, 2012 and 2011.

## Cash Flow Hedges

The purpose of the Company's foreign currency hedging activities is to protect the Company from the risk that the eventual cash flows resulting from transactions in foreign currencies will be adversely affected by changes in exchange rates. Foreign currency exposures that the Company may elect to hedge in this manner include product cost exposures, non-functional currency denominated external and intercompany revenues, selling and administrative expenses, investments in U.S. Dollar-denominated available- for-sale debt securities and certain other intercompany transactions.

Product cost exposures are primarily generated through non-functional currency denominated product purchases and the foreign currency adjustment program described below. NIKE entities primarily purchase products in two ways: (1) Certain NIKE entities purchase product from the NIKE Trading Company ("NTC"), a wholly-owned sourcing hub that buys NIKE branded products from third party factories, predominantly in U.S. Dollars. The NTC, whose functional currency is the U.S. Dollar, then sells the products to NIKE entities in their respective functional currencies. When the NTC sells to a NIKE entity with a different functional currency, the result is a foreign currency exposure for the NTC; (2) Other NIKE entities purchase product directly from third party factories in U.S. Dollars. These purchases generate a foreign currency exposure for those NIKE entities with a functional currency other than the U.S. Dollar.

In January 2012, the Company implemented a foreign currency adjustment program with certain factories. The program is designed to more effectively manage foreign currency risk by assuming certain of the factories' foreign currency exposures, some of which are natural offsets to our existing foreign currency exposures. Under this program, the Company's payments to these factories are adjusted for rate fluctuations in the basket of currencies ("factory currency exposure index") in which the labor, materials and overhead costs incurred by the factories in the production of NIKE branded products ("factory input costs") are denominated. For the portion of the indices denominated in the local or functional currency of the factory, the Company may elect to place formally designated cash flow hedges. For all currencies within the indices, excluding the U.S. Dollar and the local or functional currency of the factory, an embedded derivative contract is created upon the factory's acceptance of NIKE's purchase order. Embedded derivative contracts are separated from the related purchase order and their accounting treatment is described further below.

The Company's policy permits the utilization of derivatives to reduce its foreign currency exposures where internal netting or other strategies cannot be effectively employed. Hedged transactions are denominated primarily in Euros, British Pounds and Japanese Yen. The Company may enter into hedge contracts typically starting up to 12 to 18 months in advance of the forecasted transaction and may place incremental hedges for up to 100% of the exposure by the time the forecasted transaction occurs.

All changes in fair value of derivatives designated as cash flow hedges, excluding any ineffective portion, are recorded in other comprehensive income until net income is affected by the variability of cash flows of the hedged transaction. In most cases, amounts recorded in other comprehensive income will be released to net income some time after the maturity of the related derivative. Effective hedge results are classified within the consolidated statements of income in the same manner as the underlying exposure, with the results of hedges of non-functional currency denominated revenues and product cost exposures, excluding embedded derivatives as described below, recorded in revenues or cost of sales, when the underlying hedged transaction affects consolidated net income. Results of hedges of selling and administrative expense are recorded together with those costs when the related expense is recorded. Results of hedges of anticipated purchases and sales of U.S. Dollar-denominated available-for-sale securities are recorded in other (income) expense, net when the securities are sold. Results of hedges of certain anticipated intercompany transactions are recorded in other (income) expense, net when the transaction occurs. The Company classifies the cash flows at settlement from these designated cash flow hedge derivatives in the same category as the cash flows from the related hedged items, generally within the cash provided by operations component of the cash flow statement.

Premiums paid on options are initially recorded as deferred charges. The Company assesses the effectiveness of options based on the total cash flows method and records total changes in the options' fair value to other comprehensive income to the degree they are effective.

The Company formally assesses, both at a hedge's inception and on an ongoing basis, whether the derivatives that are used in the hedging transaction have been highly effective in offsetting changes in the cash flows of hedged items and whether those derivatives may be expected to remain highly effective in future periods. Effectiveness for cash flow hedges is assessed based on forward rates. Ineffectiveness was not material for the years ended May 31, 2013, 2012 and 2011.

The Company discontinues hedge accounting prospectively when (1) it determines that the derivative is no longer highly effective in offsetting changes in the cash flows of a hedged item (including hedged items such as firm commitments or forecasted transactions); (2) the derivative expires or is sold, terminated, or exercised; (3) it is no longer probable that the forecasted transaction will occur; or (4) management determines that designating the derivative as a hedging instrument is no longer appropriate.

When the Company discontinues hedge accounting because it is no longer probable that the forecasted transaction will occur in the originally expected period, but is expected to occur within an additional two-month period of time thereafter, the gain or loss on the derivative remains in accumulated other comprehensive income and is reclassified to net income when the forecasted transaction affects consolidated net income. However, if it is probable that a forecasted transaction will not occur by the end of the originally specified time period or within an additional two-month period of time thereafter, the gains and losses that were accumulated in other comprehensive income will be recognized immediately in other (income) expense, net. In all situations in which hedge accounting is discontinued and the derivative remains outstanding, the Company will carry the derivative at its fair value on the balance sheet, recognizing future changes in the fair value in other (income) expense, net. For the years ended May 31, 2013, 2012 and 2011, the amounts recorded in other (income) expense, net as a result of the discontinuance of cash flow hedging because the forecasted transaction was no longer probable of occurring were immaterial.

As of May 31, 2013, $132 million of deferred net gains (net of tax) on both outstanding and matured derivatives accumulated in other comprehensive income are expected to be reclassified to net income during the next 12 months concurrent with the underlying hedged transactions also being recorded in net income. Actual amounts ultimately reclassified to net income are dependent on the exchange rates in effect when derivative contracts that are currently outstanding mature. As of May 31, 2013, the maximum term over which the Company is hedging exposures to the variability of cash flows for its forecasted transactions is 24 months.

## Fair Value Hedges

The Company is also exposed to the risk of changes in the fair value of certain fixed-rate debt attributable to changes in interest rates. Derivatives currently used by the Company to hedge this risk are receive-fixed, pay-variable interest rate swaps. As of May 31, 2013, all interest rate swap agreements are designated as fair value hedges of the related long-term debt and meet the shortcut method requirements under the accounting standards for derivatives and hedging. Accordingly, changes in the fair values of the interest rate swap agreements are considered to exactly offset changes in the fair value of the underlying long-term debt. The cash flows associated with the Company's fair value hedges are periodic interest payments while the swaps are outstanding, which are reflected within the cash provided by operations component of the cash flow statement. The Company recorded no ineffectiveness from its interest rate swaps designated as fair value hedges for the years ended May 31, 2013, 2012, or 2011.

## Net Investment Hedges

The Company has hedged and may, in the future, hedge the risk of variability in foreign-currency-denominated net investments in wholly-owned international operations. All changes in fair value of the derivatives designated as net investment hedges, except ineffective portions, are reported in the cumulative translation adjustment component of other comprehensive income along with the foreign currency translation adjustments on those investments. The Company classifies the cash flows at settlement of its net investment hedges within the cash provided or used by investing component of the cash flow statement. The Company assesses hedge effectiveness based on changes in forward rates. The Company recorded no ineffectiveness from its net investment hedges for the years ended May 31, 2013, 2012, or 2011.

## Embedded Derivatives

As part of the foreign currency adjustment program described above, currencies within the factory currency exposure indices that are neither the Dollar nor the local or functional currency of the factory, an embedded derivative contract is created upon the factory's acceptance of NIKE's purchase order. Embedded derivative contracts are treated as foreign currency forward contracts that are bifurcated from the related purchase order and recorded at fair value as a derivative asset or liability on the balance sheet with their corresponding change in fair value recognized in other (income) expense, net from the date a purchase order is accepted by a factory through the date the purchase price is no longer subject to foreign currency fluctuations. At May 31, 2013, the notional amount of embedded derivatives was approximately $136 million.

## Undesignated Derivative Instruments

The Company may elect to enter into foreign exchange forwards to mitigate the change in fair value of specific assets and liabilities on the balance sheet and/or the embedded derivative contracts explained above. These forwards are not designated as hedging instruments under the accounting standards for derivatives and hedging. Accordingly, these undesignated instruments are recorded at fair value as a derivative asset or liability on the balance sheet with their corresponding change in fair value recognized in other (income) expense, net, together with the re-measurement gain or loss from the hedged balance sheet position or embedded derivative contract. The Company classifies the cash flows at settlement from undesignated instruments in the same category as the cash flows from the related hedged items, generally within the cash provided by operations component of the cash flow statement.

## Credit Risk

The Company is exposed to credit-related losses in the event of non-performance by counterparties to hedging instruments. The counterparties to all derivative transactions are major financial institutions with investment grade credit ratings. However, this does not eliminate the Company's exposure to credit risk with these institutions. This credit risk is limited to the unrealized gains in such contracts should any of these counterparties fail to perform as contracted. To manage this risk, the Company has established strict counterparty credit guidelines that are continually monitored.

The Company's derivative contracts contain credit risk related contingent features designed to protect against significant deterioration in counterparties' creditworthiness and their ultimate ability to settle outstanding derivative contracts in the normal course of business. The Company's bilateral credit related contingent features generally require the owing entity, either the Company or the derivative counterparty, to post collateral for the portion of the fair value in excess of $50 million should the fair value of outstanding derivatives per counterparty be greater than $50 million. Additionally, a certain level of decline in credit rating of either the Company or the counterparty could also trigger collateral requirements. As of May 31, 2013, the Company was in compliance with all credit risk related contingent features and the fair value of its derivative instruments with credit risk related contingent features in a net liability position was insignificant. Accordingly, the Company was not required to post any collateral as a result of these contingent features. Further, as of May 31, 2013 those counterparties which were required to post collateral complied with such requirements. Given the considerations described above, the Company considers the impact of the risk of counterparty default to be immaterial.

## NOTE 18 — Operating Segments and Related Information

*Operating Segments.* The Company's operating segments are evidence of the structure of the Company's internal organization. The major segments are defined by geographic regions for operations participating in NIKE Brand sales activity excluding NIKE Golf. Each NIKE Brand geographic segment operates predominantly in one industry: the design, development, marketing and selling of athletic footwear, apparel, and equipment. The Company's reportable operating segments for the NIKE Brand are: North America, Western Europe, Central & Eastern Europe, Greater China, Japan, and Emerging Markets. The Company's NIKE Brand Direct to Consumer operations are managed within each geographic segment.

The Company's "Other" category is broken into two components for presentation purposes to align with the way management views the Company. The "Global Brand Divisions" category primarily represents NIKE Brand licensing businesses that are not part of a geographic operating segment, demand creation and operating overhead expenses that are centrally managed for the NIKE Brand, and costs associated with product development and supply chain operations. The "Other Businesses" category consists of the activities of Converse Inc., Hurley International LLC, and NIKE Golf. Activities represented in the "Other" category are considered immaterial for individual disclosure.

Corporate consists largely of unallocated general and administrative expenses, including expenses associated with centrally managed departments, depreciation and amortization related to the Company's headquarters, unallocated insurance and benefit programs, including stock- based compensation, certain foreign currency gains and losses, including certain hedge gains and losses, certain corporate eliminations and other items.

The primary financial measure used by the Company to evaluate performance of individual operating segments is earnings before interest and taxes (commonly referred to as "EBIT"), which represents net income before interest (income) expense, net and income taxes in the consolidated statements of income. Reconciling items for EBIT represent corporate expense items that are not allocated to the operating segments for management reporting.

As part of our centrally managed foreign exchange risk management program, standard foreign currency rates are assigned twice per year to each NIKE Brand entity in our geographic operating segments and certain Other Businesses. These rates are set approximately nine months in advance of the future selling season based on average market spot rates in the calendar month preceding the date they are established. Inventories and cost of sales for geographic operating segments and certain Other Businesses reflect use of these standard rates to record non-functional currency product purchases in the entity's functional currency. Differences between assigned standard foreign currency rates and actual market rates are included in Corporate, together with foreign currency hedge gains and losses generated from our centrally managed foreign exchange risk management program and other conversion gains and losses.

Accounts receivable, inventories and property, plant and equipment for operating segments are regularly reviewed by management and are therefore provided below. Additions to long-lived assets as presented in the following table represent capital expenditures.

Certain prior year amounts have been reclassified to conform to fiscal 2013 presentation.

66

| | Year Ended May 31, | | |
|---|---|---|---|
| *(In millions)* | 2013 | 2012 | 2011 |
| **REVENUE** | | | |
| North America | $ 10,387 | $ 8,839 $ | 7,579 |
| Western Europe | 4,128 | 4,144 | 3,868 |
| Central & Eastern Europe | 1,287 | 1,200 | 1,040 |
| Greater China | 2,453 | 2,539 | 2,060 |
| Japan | 791 | 835 | 773 |
| Emerging Markets | 3,718 | 3,411 | 2,737 |
| Global Brand Divisions | 117 | 111 | 96 |
| Total NIKE Brand | 22,881 | 21,079 | 18,153 |
| Other Businesses | 2,500 | 2,298 | 2,041 |
| Corporate | (68) | (46) | (77) |
| **TOTAL NIKE CONSOLIDATED REVENUES** | $ 25,313 | $ 23,331 $ | 20,117 |
| **EARNINGS BEFORE INTEREST AND TAXES** | | | |
| North America | $ 2,534 | $ 2,030 $ | 1,736 |
| Western Europe | 640 | 597 | 730 |
| Central & Eastern Europe | 259 | 234 | 244 |
| Greater China | 809 | 911 | 777 |
| Japan | 133 | 136 | 114 |
| Emerging Markets | 1,011 | 853 | 688 |
| Global Brand Divisions | (1,396) | (1,200) | (971) |
| Total NIKE Brand | 3,990 | 3,561 | 3,318 |
| Other Businesses | 456 | 385 | 353 |
| Corporate | (1,177) | (917) | (805) |
| Total NIKE Consolidated Earnings Before Interest and Taxes | 3,269 | 3,029 | 2,866 |
| Interest (income) expense, net | (3) | 4 | 4 |
| **TOTAL NIKE CONSOLIDATED EARNINGS BEFORE TAXES** | $ 3,272 | $ 3,025 $ | 2,862 |
| **ADDITIONS TO LONG-LIVED ASSETS** | | | |
| North America | $ 201 | $ 131 $ | 79 |
| Western Europe | 74 | 93 | 75 |
| Central & Eastern Europe | 22 | 20 | 5 |
| Greater China | 52 | 38 | 43 |
| Japan | 6 | 14 | 9 |
| Emerging Markets | 49 | 27 | 21 |
| Global Brand Divisions | 216 | 131 | 44 |
| Total NIKE Brand | 620 | 454 | 276 |
| Other Businesses | 29 | 24 | 27 |
| Corporate | 131 | 109 | 118 |
| **TOTAL ADDITIONS TO LONG-LIVED ASSETS** | $ 780 | $ 587 $ | 421 |
| **DEPRECIATION** | | | |
| North America | $ 85 | $ 78 $ | 70 |
| Western Europe | 68 | 62 | 52 |
| Central & Eastern Europe | 9 | 6 | 4 |
| Greater China | 34 | 25 | 19 |
| Japan | 21 | 23 | 22 |
| Emerging Markets | 20 | 15 | 14 |
| Global Brand Divisions | 83 | 53 | 39 |
| Total NIKE Brand | 320 | 262 | 220 |
| Other Businesses | 24 | 25 | 24 |
| Corporate | 74 | 66 | 71 |
| **TOTAL DEPRECIATION** | $ 418 | $ 353 $ | 315 |

| (In millions) | As of May 31, 2013 | As of May 31, 2012 |
|---|---|---|
| **ACCOUNTS RECEIVABLE, NET** | | |
| North America | $ 1,214 | $ 1,149 |
| Western Europe | 356 | 420 |
| Central & Eastern Europe | 301 | 261 |
| Greater China | 52 | 221 |
| Japan | 133 | 152 |
| Emerging Markets | 546 | 476 |
| Global Brand Divisions | 28 | 30 |
| Total NIKE Brand | 2,630 | 2,709 |
| Other Businesses | 436 | 401 |
| Corporate | 51 | 22 |
| **TOTAL ACCOUNTS RECEIVABLE, NET** | $ 3,117 | $ 3,132 |
| **INVENTORIES** | | |
| North America | $ 1,435 | $ 1,272 |
| Western Europe | 539 | 488 |
| Central & Eastern Europe | 207 | 180 |
| Greater China | 204 | 217 |
| Japan | 60 | 83 |
| Emerging Markets | 555 | 521 |
| Global Brand Divisions | 32 | 35 |
| Total NIKE Brand | 3,032 | 2,796 |
| Other Businesses | 400 | 384 |
| Corporate | 2 | 42 |
| **TOTAL INVENTORIES** | $ 3,434 | $ 3,222 |
| **PROPERTY, PLANT AND EQUIPMENT, NET** | | |
| North America | $ 406 | $ 378 |
| Western Europe | 326 | 314 |
| Central & Eastern Europe | 44 | 30 |
| Greater China | 213 | 191 |
| Japan | 269 | 359 |
| Emerging Markets | 89 | 59 |
| Global Brand Divisions | 353 | 205 |
| Total NIKE Brand | 1,700 | 1,536 |
| Other Businesses | 77 | 76 |
| Corporate | 675 | 597 |
| **TOTAL PROPERTY, PLANT AND EQUIPMENT, NET** | $ 2,452 | $ 2,209 |

*Revenues by Major Product Lines.* Revenues to external customers for NIKE Brand products are attributable to sales of footwear, apparel and equipment. Other   revenues to external customers primarily include external sales by Converse, Hurley, and NIKE Golf.

| (In millions) | Year Ended May 31, 2013 | Year Ended May 31, 2012 | Year Ended May 31, 2011 |
|---|---|---|---|
| Footwear | $ 14,539 | $ 13,428 | $ 11,519 |
| Apparel | 6,820 | 6,336 | 5,516 |
| Equipment | 1,405 | 1,204 | 1,022 |
| Other | 2,549 | 2,363 | 2,060 |
| **TOTAL NIKE CONSOLIDATED REVENUES** | $ 25,313 | $ 23,331 | $ 20,117 |

# International Financial Reporting Standards (IFRS)

**◀IFRS▮▮▮**

## The Need for Global Accounting Standards

As discussed in Chapter 1, the Financial Accounting Standards Board (FASB) establishes generally accepted accounting principles (GAAP) for public companies in the United States. Of course, there is a world beyond the borders of the United States. In recent years, the removal of trade barriers and the growth in cross-border equity and debt issuances have led to a dramatic increase in international commerce. As a result, often companies are reporting financial results to users outside of the United States.

Historically, accounting standards have varied considerably across countries. These variances have been driven by cultural, legal, and political differences and resulted in financial statements that were not easily comparable and difficult to interpret. These differences caused problems for companies in Europe and Asia, where local economies have become increasingly tied to international commerce.

During the last decade, however, a common set of International Financial Reporting Standards (IFRS) has emerged to reduce cross-country differences in accounting standards, primarily in countries outside of North America. While much of the world has migrated to IFRS, the United States has not. Because of the size of the United States and its significant role in world commerce, U.S. GAAP still has a global impact. As a result, there are currently two major accounting standard-setting efforts in the world, U.S. GAAP and IFRS. These two sets of accounting standards add cost and complexity for companies doing business and obtaining financing internationally.

## Overview of IFRS

International Financial Reporting Standards have emerged during the last 10 years to meet the financial reporting needs of an increasingly global business environment.

**What Is IFRS?** International Financial Reporting Standards are a set of global accounting standards developed by an international standard-setting body called the International Accounting Standards Board (IASB). Like the Financial Accounting Standards Board, the IASB is an independent entity that establishes accounting rules. Unlike the FASB, the IASB does not establish accounting rules for any specific country. Rather, it develops accounting rules that can be used by a variety of countries, with the goal of developing a single set of global accounting standards.

**Who Uses IFRS?** IFRS applies to companies that issue publicly traded debt or equity securities, called **public companies**, in countries that have adopted IFRS as their accounting standards. Since 2005, all 28 countries in the European Union (EU) have been required to prepare financial statements using IFRS. In addition, more than 100 other countries have adopted IFRS for public companies (see Exhibit 1). In other major economies, Japan is considering mandatory adoption by 2016, India allows limited use of IFRS, and China is converging its standards with IFRS over time. In addition, the G20 (Group of 20) leadership has called for uniform global accounting standards.

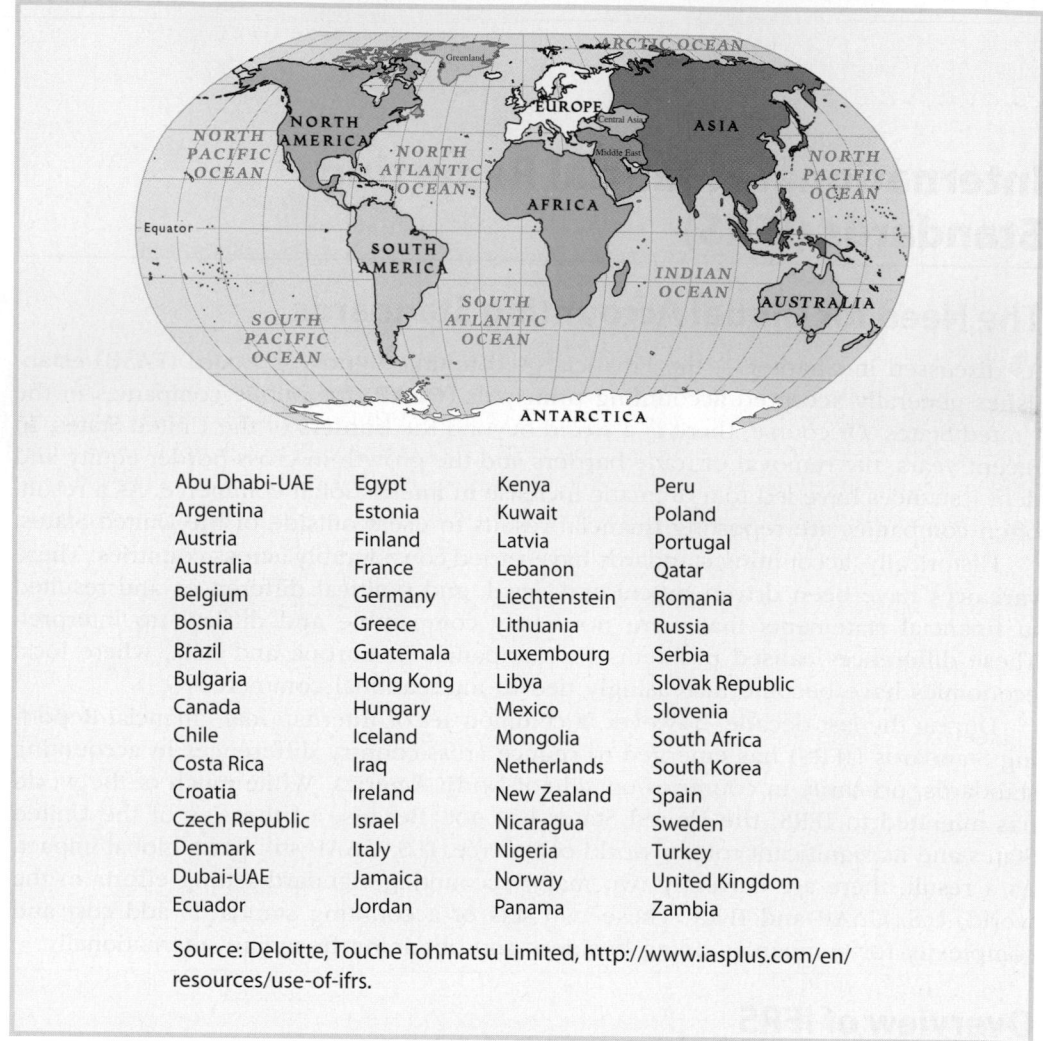

**EXHIBIT 1**

**IFRS Adopters**

| | | | |
|---|---|---|---|
| Abu Dhabi-UAE | Egypt | Kenya | Peru |
| Argentina | Estonia | Kuwait | Poland |
| Austria | Finland | Latvia | Portugal |
| Australia | France | Lebanon | Qatar |
| Belgium | Germany | Liechtenstein | Romania |
| Bosnia | Greece | Lithuania | Russia |
| Brazil | Guatemala | Luxembourg | Serbia |
| Bulgaria | Hong Kong | Libya | Slovak Republic |
| Canada | Hungary | Mexico | Slovenia |
| Chile | Iceland | Mongolia | South Africa |
| Costa Rica | Iraq | Netherlands | South Korea |
| Croatia | Ireland | New Zealand | Spain |
| Czech Republic | Israel | Nicaragua | Sweden |
| Denmark | Italy | Nigeria | Turkey |
| Dubai-UAE | Jamaica | Norway | United Kingdom |
| Ecuador | Jordan | Panama | Zambia |

Source: Deloitte, Touche Tohmatsu Limited, http://www.iasplus.com/en/resources/use-of-ifrs.

## U.S. GAAP and IFRS: The Road Forward

The United States has not formally adopted IFRS for U.S. companies. The wide acceptance being gained by IFRS around the world, however, has placed considerable pressure on the United States to align U.S. GAAP with IFRS. There are two possible paths that the United States could take to achieve this: (1) adoption of IFRS by the U.S. Securities and Exchange Commission or (2) convergence of U.S. GAAP and IFRS. These two options are briefly discussed in this section.

**Adoption of IFRS by the SEC** The U.S. Securities and Exchange Commission (SEC) is the U.S. governmental agency that has authority over the accounting and financial disclosures for U.S. public companies. Only the SEC has the authority to adopt IFRS for U.S. public companies. After considerable deliberation over a period of nearly five years, the SEC published a Final Report on the issues surrounding IFRS adoption.[1] Notably, this report did not include a final policy decision or recommendation in favor of U.S. public companies adopting IFRS. Indeed, since this report, the SEC has distanced itself from the adoption position, and it is now acknowledged as unsupported. This leaves what remains of the convergence pathway.

**Convergence of U.S. GAAP and IFRS** Convergence involves aligning IFRS and U.S. GAAP one topic at a time, by slowly merging IFRS and U.S. GAAP into two broadly uniform sets of accounting standards. To this end, the FASB and IASB have agreed to work together on a select number of difficult and high-profile accounting issues. These issues frame a large portion of the disagreement between the two sets of standards and, if accomplished, will significantly reduce the differences between U.S. GAAP and IFRS. The projects selected for the convergence effort represent some of the more technical topics in accounting and are covered in intermediate and advanced accounting courses. As of 2013, there remain a small number of topics as part of the formal convergence effort between the FASB and IASB. Once these topics have been completed, the formal joint convergence effort will end. It is unclear how convergence between the two boards will proceed after these topics are converged.

One of the major limitations of convergence is that both the FASB and IASB continue to operate as the accounting standard-setting bodies for their respective jurisdictions. As such, convergence would not result in a single set of global accounting standards. Only those standards that go through the joint FASB–IASB standard-setting process would be released as uniform. Standards that do not go through a joint standard-setting process may create inconsistencies between U.S. GAAP and IFRS. Thus, convergence does not guarantee complete uniformity between U.S. GAAP and IFRS. Thus, there will remain differences in U.S. GAAP and IFRS in the foreseeable future. Understanding these differences are important because of increased globalization of business.

## Differences Between U.S. GAAP and IFRS

U.S. GAAP and IFRS differ both in their approach to standard setting, as well as their financial statement presentation and recording of transactions.

**Rules-Based Versus Principles Approach to Standard Setting** U.S. GAAP is considered to be a "rules-based" approach to accounting standard setting. The accounting standards provide detailed and specific rules on the accounting for business transactions. There are few exceptions or varying interpretations of the accounting for a business event. This structure is consistent with the U.S. legal and regulatory system, reflecting the social and economic values of the United States.

In contrast, IFRS is designed to meet the needs of many countries. Differences in legal, political, and economic systems create different needs for and uses of financial information in different countries. For example, Germany needs a financial reporting system that reflects the central role of banks in its financial system, while the Netherlands needs a financial reporting system that reflects the significant role of outside equity in its financial system.

To accommodate economic, legal, and social diversity, IFRS must be broad enough to capture these differences while still presenting comparable financial statements. Under IFRS, there is greater opportunity for different interpretations of the accounting treatment of a business event across different business entities. To support this, IFRS often has more extensive disclosures that support alternative assumptions. Thus, IFRS provides more latitude for professional judgment than typically found in comparable U.S. GAAP. Many countries find this feature attractive in reducing regulatory costs associated with using and auditing financial reports. This "principles-based" approach presents one of the most significant challenges to adopting IFRS in the United States.

[1] Work Plan for the Consideration of Incorporating International Financial Accounting Standards into the Financial Reporting System for U.S. Issuers: Final Staff Report, U.S. Securities Exchange Commission, July 13, 2012.

**Technical Differences Between IFRS and U.S. GAAP** Although U.S. GAAP is similar to IFRS, differences arise in the presentation format, balance sheet valuations, and technical accounting procedures. The Mornin' Joe International financial statements presented after Chapter 15 highlight the financial statement format, presentation, and recording differences between U.S. GAAP and IFRS. In addition, the International Connection boxes in Chapters 1, 4, 7, 10, 13, and 16 discuss some of the significant differences between U.S. GAAP and IFRS. A more comprehensive summary of the key differences between U.S. GAAP and IFRS that are relevant to an introductory accounting course is provided in Exhibit 2.

## Discussion Questions

1. Briefly discuss why global accounting standards are needed in today's business environment.

2. What are International Financial Reporting Standards? Who uses these accounting standards?

3. What body is responsible for setting International Financial Reporting Standards?

4. Briefly discuss the differences between (a) adoption of IFRS by the U.S. Securities and Exchange Commission and (b) convergence of U.S. GAAP with IFRS.

5. Briefly discuss the difference between (a) a "rules-based" approach to accounting standard setting and (b) a "principles-based" approach to accounting standard setting.

6. How is property, plant, and equipment measured on the balance sheet under IFRS? How does this differ from the way property, plant, and equipment is measured on the balance sheet under U.S. GAAP?

7. What inventory costing methods are allowed under IFRS? How does this differ from the treatment under U.S. GAAP?

| EXHIBIT 2 | Comparison of Accounting for Selected Items Under U.S. GAAP and IFRS | | |
| --- | --- | --- | --- |
| | **U.S. GAAP** | **IFRS** | **Text Reference** |
| **General:** | | | |
| Financial statement titles | Balance Sheet | Statement of Financial Position | |
| | Statement of Stockholders' Equity | Statement of Changes in Equity | General |
| | Statement of Cash Flows | Statement of Cash Flows | General |
| Financial periods presented | Public companies must present two years of comparative information for income statement, statement of stockholders' equity, and statement of cash flows | One year of comparative information must be presented | General |
| Conceptual basis for standard setting | "Rules-based" approach | "Principles-based" approach | General |
| Internal control requirements | Sarbanes-Oxley Act (SOX) Section 404 | | Ch 8; LO 1 |
| **Balance Sheet:** | ***Balance Sheet*** | ***Statement of Financial Position*** | |
| Terminology differences | "Payable" | "Provision" | Ch 11 |
| | "Stockholders' Equity" | "Capital and Reserves" | Ch 13 |
| | "Net Income (Loss)" | "Profit or (Loss)" | General |
| Inventory—LIFO | LIFO allowed | LIFO prohibited | Ch 7; LO 3, 4, 5 |
| Inventory—valuation | Market is defined as "replacement value" | Market is defined as "fair value" | Ch 7; LO 6 |
| | Reversal of lower-of-cost-or-market write-downs not allowed | Reversal of write-downs allowed | Ch 7; LO 6 |
| Long-lived assets | May NOT be revalued to fair value | May be revalued to fair value on a regular basis | Ch 10; LO 1 |

*(Continued)*

**EXHIBIT 2**    **Comparison of Accounting for Selected Items Under U.S. GAAP and IFRS (Continued)**

| | U.S. GAAP | IFRS | Text Reference |
|---|---|---|---|
| Land held for investment | Treated as held for use or sale, and recorded at historical cost | May be accounted for on a historical cost basis or on a fair value basis with changes in fair value recognized through profit and loss | Ch 10; LO 1 |
| Property, plant, & equipment—valuation | Historical cost | May select between historical cost or revalued amount (a form of fair value) | Ch 10; LO 1 |
| | If impaired, impairment loss may NOT be reversed in future periods | If impaired, impairment loss may be reversed in future periods | |
| Cost of major overhaul (Capital and revenue expenditures) | Different treatment for ordinary repairs and maintenance, asset improvement, extraordinary repairs | Typically included as part of the cost of the asset or asset component if future economic benefit is probable and can be reliably measured | Ch 10; LO 1 |
| Intangible assets—valuation | Acquisition cost, unless impaired | Fair value permitted if the intangible asset trades in an active market | Ch 10; LO 5 |
| Intangible assets—impairment loss reversal | Prohibited | Prohibited for goodwill but allowed for other intangible assets | Ch 10; LO 5 |
| Deferred tax liability | The amount due within one year classified as current | Always noncurrent | Appendix D |
| **Income Statement:** | **Income Statement** | **Statement of Comprehensive Income** | |
| Revenue recognition | Detailed guidance depending on the transaction | Broad guidance | Ch 3; LO 1 |
| Classification of expenses on income statement | Public companies must present expenses on the income statement by function (e.g., cost of goods sold, selling, administrative) | Expenses may be presented based either by function (e.g., cost of goods sold, selling) or by the nature of expense (e.g., wages expense, interest expense) | Ch 6; LO 1 |
| Research and development costs | Expensed as incurred | Research costs expensed | Ch 10; LO 5 |
| | | Development costs capitalized once technical and economic feasibility attained | |
| Extraordinary items | Allowed for items that are both unusual in nature and infrequent in occurrence | Prohibited | Ch 17; Appendix D |

*(Continued)*

| EXHIBIT 2 | Comparison of Accounting for Selected Items Under U.S. GAAP and IFRS *(Concluded)* | | |
|---|---|---|---|
| | **U.S. GAAP** | **IFRS** | **Text Reference** |
| **Statement of Cash Flows:** | *Statement of Cash Flows* | *Statement of Cash Flows* | |
| Classification of interest paid or received | Treated as an operating activity | Interest paid may be treated as either an operating or a financing activity; interest received may be treated as an operating or investing activity | Ch 16; LO 3 |
| Classification of dividend paid or received | Dividend paid treated as a financing activity, dividend received treated as an operating activity | Dividend paid may be treated as either an operating or a financing activity; dividend received may be treated as an operating or investing activity | Ch 16; LO 3 |

# Revenue Recognition

Companies recognize revenue when services have been performed or products have been delivered to customers. For example, when McDonald's sells a hamburger, the revenue is earned when the hamburger is delivered to the customer. In this example, revenue recognition is simple because the hamburger is delivered and cash is received at a single point in time.

Revenue recognition is more complex, however, when a transaction includes several items that are sold together, items that are delivered over time, or items whose prices depend upon future events. To address these more complex transactions, the Financial Accounting Standards Board (FASB) issued a new accounting standard in May 2014.[1] The new Standard uses a five-step method for determining when revenue should be recognized. The five steps are as follows:

- Step 1. *Identify the contract with the customer.* The new Standard treats every revenue transaction as a contract. A contract is an agreement by the seller to provide a good or service in exchange for payment from the buyer. A contract may be verbal and implicit, such as the purchase of a McDonald's hamburger, or written and explicit, such as a cell phone contract.

- Step 2. *Identify the separate performance obligations in the contract.* Every contract requires the seller and buyer to perform. For example, when you purchase a McDonald's hamburger, you (the buyer) perform by paying and McDonald's (the seller) performs by delivering a hamburger. When you purchase a cell phone from Verizon, the transaction is more complex. You perform by paying cash or charging your credit card and signing a written contract. Verizon performs by delivering you the phone and promising to provide you cellular service in the future. In this case, Verizon has two performance obligations: (1) to provide the phone and (2) to provide cellular service in the future.

- Step 3. *Determine the transaction price.* The transaction price is the amount the seller is entitled to receive in exchange for the goods and services they have provided. In the case of the McDonald's hamburger, the transaction price is the amount paid for the hamburger. In the case of Verizon, the transaction price must be estimated for the phone (the first performance obligation) and cellular service (the second performance obligation).

- Step 4. *Allocate the transaction price to the separate performance obligations.* Since the sale of a McDonald's hamburger involves the sale of a single item that is immediately delivered, the entire transaction price is allocated to the hamburger. In more complex transactions, such as a Verizon cellular service contract, the revenue received from the customer must be allocated among the performance obligations. This allocation is often based on the stand-alone (separate) price of each good or service. For example, Verizon should allocate the revenue from the customer between the phone

[1] Accounting Standards Update, *Revenue from Contracts with Customers (Topic 606)*, Financial Accounting Standards Board, May 2014, Norwalk, CT.

(first performance obligation) and the commitment to provide cellular service (second performance obligation).

- Step 5. *Recognize revenue when each separate performance obligation is satisfied.* The seller should recognize (record) revenue as each performance obligation is satisfied. In the case of McDonald's, the performance obligation is satisfied when the clerk delivers the hamburger to the customer. At this point, the control of the hamburger has passed to the customer. In the case of Verizon, it satisfies its first performance obligation when it delivers you the phone. Verizon satisfies its second performance obligation over time by providing you cellular service. Thus, Verizon should record some revenue at the time you sign the contract and receive your phone and some revenue as you are provided cellular service.

To illustrate, assume that on March 1, 2016, Chandler Evans upgrades (replaces) his cell phone with Star Cellular at no cost by signing a two-year agreement. The new agreement cannot be cancelled and requires a payment of $90 per month. The cell phone selected by Evans cost Star Cellular $250.

The five-step method would be applied by Star Cellular as follows:

- Step 1. *Identify the contract with the customer.* The contract with Chandler Evans is the two-year cellular service agreement that includes delivery of a new cell phone.

- Step 2. *Identify the separate performance obligations in the contract.* Star Cellular has two separate performance obligations to Evans under the contract. First, Star Cellular must deliver a new cell phone at the time that Evans signs the service agreement. Second, Star Cellular must provide Evans cell service for two years.

- Step 3. *Determine the transaction price.* The transaction price is the total amount Star Cellular will receive over the contract period. In this case, Star Cellular will receive $2,160 ($90 × 24 months) over the contract period.[2]

- Step 4. *Allocate the transaction price to the separate performance obligations.* Assume that Star Cellular sells the cell phone and cell service separately at the following prices:

| | |
|---|---|
| Cell phone | $ 600 |
| Cell service for two years | 3,000 |
| Total price if sold separately | $3,600 |

The transaction price is allocated to each performance obligation based upon what each obligation would sell for separately as a stand-alone product. To illustrate, the cell phone is allocated $360 of the transaction price of $2,160, computed as follows:

$$\text{Cell Phone} = \text{Contract Price} \times \frac{\text{Price of Cell Phone Sold Separately}}{\text{Total Price of Cell Phone and Cell Service Sold Separately}}$$

$$\text{Cell Phone} = \$2,160 \times \frac{\$600}{\$3,600} = \$360$$

The cell service is allocated $1,800 of the transaction price of $2,160, computed as follows:

$$\text{Cell Service} = \text{Contract Price} \times \frac{\text{Price of Cell Service Sold Separately}}{\text{Total Price of Cell Phone and Cell Service Sold Separate}}$$

$$\text{Cell Service} = \$2,160 \times \frac{\$3,000}{\$3,600} = \$1,800$$

---

[2] An interest component may need to be considered in long-term contracts. To simplify, we ignore interest.

- Step 5. *Recognize revenue when each separate performance obligation is satisfied.* The $360 of revenue from the cell phone is recognized when the customer signs the service agreement and receives the phone. At this point, the first performance obligation has been satisfied by Star Cellular and the control of the phone has passed to the customer. The journal entry to record cell phone revenue on March 1, 2016, is as follows:

| 2016 | | | | | |
|------|---|--------------------------------------------|-----|-----|
| Mar. | 1 | Accounts Receivable—Chandler Evans | 360 | |
| | | Sales | | 360 |
| | | Cost of Merchandise Sold | 250 | |
| | | Merchandise Inventory | | 250 |

The $1,800 of cell service revenue is recognized as the performance obligation is satisfied over the two-year term of the contract. For example, $75 ($1,800 ÷ 24 months) of service revenue would be recorded each month. The journal entry to record the service revenue for March is as follows:

| 2016 | | | | | |
|------|----|--------------------------------------------|----|----|
| Mar. | 31 | Cash | 90 | |
| | | Accounts Receivable ($360 ÷ 24 months) | | 15 |
| | | Cell Service Revenue ($1,800 ÷ 24 months) | | 75 |

The preceding journal entries illustrate how over the life of the two-year contract the total revenue from the contract of $2,160 is divided between the sale of the cell phone ($360 of revenue) and providing of cell service ($1,800 of revenue). In addition, the journal entries illustrate when revenue from the phone and service is recorded.

Exhibit 1 summarizes the division of revenue and its recording over the two-year contract.

---

**EXHIBIT 1**     **Recording Revenue over Two-Year Contract**

---

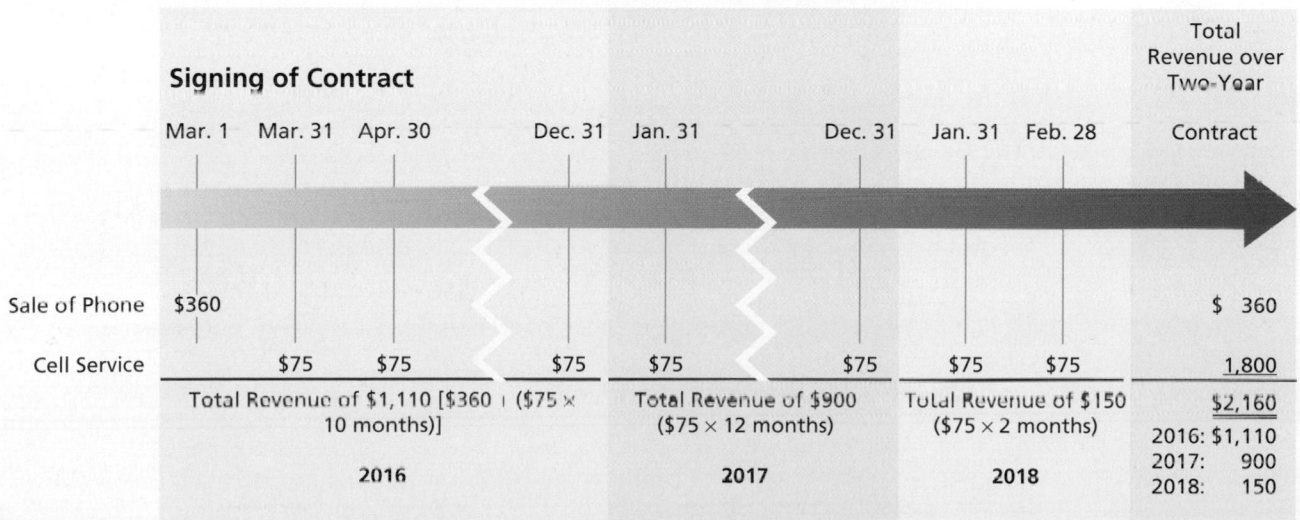

# Glossary

## A

**absorption costing** The reporting of the costs of manufactured products, normally direct materials, direct labor, and factory overhead, as product costs. (Ch. 21)

**accelerated depreciation method** A depreciation method that provides for a higher depreciation amount in the first year of the asset's use, followed by a gradually declining amount of depreciation. (Ch. 10)

**account** An accounting form that is used to record the increases and decreases in each financial statement item. (Ch. 2)

**account form** The form of balance sheet that resembles the basic format of the accounting equation, with assets on the left side and Liabilities and Owner's Equity sections on the right side. (Chs. 1, 6)

**account payable** The liability created by a purchase on account. (Ch. 1)

**account receivable** A claim against the customer created by selling merchandise or services on credit. (Chs. 1, 2, 9)

**accounting** An information system that provides reports to stakeholders about the economic activities and condition of a business. (Ch. 1)

**accounting cycle** The process that begins with analyzing and journalizing transactions and ends with the post-closing trial balance. (Ch. 4)

**accounting equation** Assets = Liabilities + Owner's Equity. (Ch. 1)

**accounting period concept** The accounting concept that assumes that the economic life of the business can be divided into time periods. (Ch. 3)

**accounting system** The methods and procedures used by a business to collect, classify, summarize, and report financial data for use by management and external users. (Ch. 5)

**accounts payable subsidiary ledger** The subsidiary ledger containing the individual accounts with suppliers (creditors). (Ch. 5)

**accounts receivable analysis** A company's ability to collect its accounts receivable. (Ch. 17)

**accounts receivable subsidiary ledger** The subsidiary ledger containing the individual accounts with customers. (Ch. 5)

**accounts receivable turnover** The relationship between net sales and accounts receivable, computed by dividing the net sales by the average net accounts receivable; measures how frequently during the year the accounts receivable are being converted to cash. (Chs. 9, 17)

**accrual basis of accounting** Under this basis of accounting, revenues and expenses are reported in the income statement in the period in which they are earned or incurred. (Ch. 3)

**accrued expenses** Expenses that have been incurred but not recorded in the accounts. (Ch. 3)

**accrued revenues** Revenues that have been earned but not recorded in the accounts. (Ch. 3)

**Accumulated Depreciation** The contra asset account credited when recording the depreciation of a fixed asset. (Ch. 3)

**accumulated other comprehensive income** The cumulative effects of other comprehensive income items reported separately in the Stockholders' Equity section of the balance sheet. (Ch. 15)

**activities** The types of work, or actions, involved in a manufacturing process or service activity. (Ch. 25)

**activity base (driver)** A measure of activity that is related to changes in cost. Used in analyzing and classifying cost behavior. Activity bases are also used in the denominator in calculating the predetermined factory overhead rate to assign overhead costs to cost objects. (Chs. 19, 21, 25)

**activity rate** The estimated activity cost divided by estimated activity-base usage. (Ch. 25)

**activity-based costing (ABC)** A cost allocation method that identifies activities causing the incurrence of costs and allocates these costs to products (or other cost objects), based on activity drivers (bases). (Chs. 19, 25)

**adjusted trial balance** The trial balance prepared after all the adjusting entries have been posted. (Ch. 3)

**adjusting entries** The journal entries that bring the accounts up to date at the end of the accounting period. (Ch. 3)

**adjusting process** An analysis and updating of the accounts when financial statements are prepared. (Ch. 3)

**administrative expenses (general expenses)** Expenses incurred in the administration or general operations of the business. (Ch. 6)

**aging the receivables** The process of analyzing the accounts receivable and classifying them according to various age groupings, with the due date being the base point for determining age. (Ch. 9)

**Allowance for Doubtful Accounts** The contra asset account for accounts receivable. (Ch. 9)

**allowance method** The method of accounting for uncollectible accounts that provides an expense for uncollectible receivables in advance of their write-off. (Ch. 9)

**amortization** The periodic transfer of the cost of an intangible asset to expense. (Chs. 10, 14)

**annuity** A series of equal cash flows at fixed intervals. (Chs. 14, 26)

**assets** The resources owned by a business. (Chs. 1, 2)

**available-for-sale securities** Securities that management expects to sell in the future but which are not actively traded for profit. (Ch. 15)

**average rate of return** A method of evaluating capital investment proposals that focuses on the expected profitability of the investment. (Ch. 26)

# B

**bad debt expense** The operating expense incurred because of the failure to collect receivables. (Ch. 9)

**balance of the account** The amount of the difference between the debits and the credits that have been entered into an account. (Ch. 2)

**balance sheet** A list of the assets, liabilities, and owner's equity as of a specific date, usually at the close of the last day of a month or a year. (Ch. 1)

**balanced scorecard** A performance evaluation approach that incorporates multiple performance dimensions by combining financial and nonfinancial measures. (Ch. 24)

**bank reconciliation** The analysis that details the items responsible for the difference between the cash balance reported in the bank statement and the balance of the cash account in the ledger. (Ch. 8)

**bank statement** A summary of all transactions mailed to the depositor or made available online by the bank each month. (Ch. 8)

**bond** A form of an interest-bearing note used by corporations to borrow on a long-term basis. (Ch. 14)

**bond indenture** The contract between a corporation issuing bonds and the bondholders. (Ch. 14)

**book value** The cost of a fixed asset minus accumulated depreciation on the asset. (Ch. 10)

**book value of the asset (or net book value)** The difference between the cost of a fixed asset and its accumulated depreciation. (Ch. 3)

**boot** The amount a buyer owes a seller when a fixed asset is traded in on a similar asset. (Ch. 10)

**break-even point** The level of business operations at which revenues and expired costs are equal. (Ch. 21)

**budget** An accounting device used to plan and control resources of operational departments and divisions. (Ch. 22)

**budget performance report** A report comparing actual results with budget figures. (Ch. 23)

**budgetary slack** Excess resources set within a budget to provide for uncertain events. (Ch. 22)

**budgeted variable factory overhead** The standard variable overhead for the actual units produced. (Ch. 23)

**business** An organization in which basic resources (inputs), such as materials and labor, are assembled and processed to provide goods or services (outputs) to customers. (Ch. 1)

**business combination** A business making an investment in another business by acquiring a controlling share, often greater than 50%, of the outstanding voting stock of another corporation by paying cash or exchanging stock. (Ch. 15)

**business entity concept** A concept of accounting that limits the economic data in the accounting system to data related directly to the activities of the business. (Ch. 1)

**business transaction** An economic event or condition that directly changes an entity's financial condition or directly affects its results of operations. (Ch. 1)

# C

**capital account** An account used for a proprietorship that represents the owner's equity. (Ch. 2)

**capital expenditures** The costs of acquiring fixed assets, adding to a fixed asset, improving a fixed asset, or extending a fixed asset's useful life. (Ch. 10)

**capital expenditures budget** The budget summarizing future plans for acquiring plant facilities and equipment. (Ch. 22)

**capital investment analysis** The process by which management plans, evaluates, and controls long-term capital investments involving property, plant, and equipment. (Ch. 26)

**capital lease** A lease that includes one or more provisions that result in treating the leased assets as purchased assets in the accounts. (Ch. 10)

**capital rationing** The process by which management plans, evaluates, and controls long-term capital investments involving fixed assets. (Ch. 26)

**carrying amount** The balance of the bonds payable account (face amount of the bonds) less any unamortized discount or plus any unamortized premium. (Ch. 14)

**cash** Coins, currency (paper money), checks, money orders, and money on deposit that is available for unrestricted withdrawal from banks and other financial institutions. (Ch. 8)

**cash basis of accounting** Under this basis of accounting, revenues and expenses are reported in the income statement in the period in which cash is received or paid. (Ch. 3)

**cash budget** A budget of estimated cash receipts and payments. (Ch. 22)

**cash dividend** A cash distribution of earnings by a corporation to its shareholders. (Ch. 13)

**cash equivalents** Highly liquid investments that are usually reported with cash on the balance sheet. (Ch. 8)

**cash flow per share** Normally computed as cash flow from operations per share. (Ch. 16)

**cash flows from financing activities** The section of the statement of cash flows that reports cash flows from transactions affecting the equity and debt of the business. (Ch. 16)

**cash flows from investing activities** The section of the statement of cash flows that reports cash flows from transactions affecting investments in noncurrent assets. (Ch. 16)

**cash flows from operating activities** The section of the statement of cash flows that reports the cash transactions affecting the determination of net income. (Ch. 16)

**cash payback period** The expected period of time that will elapse between the date of a capital expenditure and the complete recovery in cash (or equivalent) of the amount invested. (Ch. 26)

**cash payments journal** The special journal in which all cash payments are recorded. (Ch. 5)

**cash receipts journal** The special journal in which all cash receipts are recorded. (Ch. 5)

**cash short and over account** An account which has recorded errors in cash sales or errors in making change causing the amount of actual cash on hand to differ from the beginning amount of cash plus the cash sales for the day. (Ch. 8)

**Certified Public Accountant (CPA)** Public accountants who have met a state's education, experience, and examination requirements. (Ch. 1)

**chart of accounts** A list of the accounts in the ledger. (Ch. 2)

**clearing account** Another name for the income summary account because it has the effect of clearing the revenue and expense accounts of their balances. (Ch. 4)

**closing entries** The entries that transfer the balances of the revenue, expense, and drawing accounts to the owner's capital account. (Ch. 4)

**closing process** The transfer process of converting temporary account balances to zero by transferring the revenue and expense account balances to Income Summary, transferring the income summary account balance to the owner's capital account, and transferring the owner's drawing account to the owner's capital account. (Ch. 4)

**closing the books** The process of transferring temporary accounts balances to permanent accounts at the end of the accounting period. (Ch. 4)

**common stock** The stock outstanding when a corporation has issued only one class of stock. (Ch. 13)

**common-sized statement** A financial statement in which all items are expressed only in relative terms. (Ch. 17)

**compensating balance** A requirement by some banks requiring depositors to maintain minimum cash balances in their bank accounts. (Ch. 8)

**comprehensive income** All changes in stockholders' equity during a period, except those resulting from dividends and stockholders' investments. (Ch. 15)

**consigned inventory** Merchandise that is shipped by manufacturers to retailers who act as the manufacturer's selling agent. (Ch. 7)

**consignee** The name for the retailer in a consigned inventory arrangement. (Ch. 7)

**consignor** The name for the manufacturer in a consigned inventory arrangement. (Ch. 7)

**consolidated financial statements** Financial statements resulting from combining parent and subsidiary statements. (Ch. 15)

**contingent liabilities** Liabilities that may arise from past transactions if certain events occur in the future. (Ch. 11)

**continuous budgeting** A method of budgeting that provides for maintaining a 12-month projection into the future. (Ch. 22)

**continuous process improvement** A management approach that is part of the overall total quality management philosophy. The approach requires all employees to constantly improve processes of which they are a part or for which they have managerial responsibility. (Ch. 18)

**contra accounts (or contra asset accounts)** An account offset against another account. (Ch. 3)

**contract rate** The periodic interest to be paid on the bonds that is identified in the bond indenture; expressed as a percentage of the face amount of the bond. (Ch. 14)

**contribution margin** Sales less variable costs and variable selling and administrative expenses. (Ch. 21)

**contribution margin ratio** The percentage of each sales dollar that is available to cover the fixed costs and provide an operating income. (Ch. 21)

**control environment** The overall attitude of management and employees about the importance of controls. (Ch. 8)

**controllable expenses** Costs that can be influenced by the decisions of a manager. (Ch. 24)

**controllable revenues** Revenues earned by the profit center. (Ch. 24)

**controllable variance** The difference between the actual amount of variable factory overhead cost incurred and the amount of variable factory overhead budgeted for the standard product. (Ch. 23)

**controller** The chief management accountant of a division or other segment of a business. (Ch. 18)

**controlling** A phase in the management process that consists of monitoring the operating results of implemented plans and comparing the actual results with the expected results. (Ch. 18)

**controlling account** The account in the general ledger that summarizes the balances of the accounts in a subsidiary ledger. (Ch. 5)

**conversion costs** The combination of direct labor and factory overhead costs. (Ch. 18)

**copyright** An exclusive right to publish and sell a literary, artistic, or musical composition. (Ch. 10)

**corporation** A business organized under state or federal statutes as a separate legal entity. (Ch. 1)

**correcting journal entry** An entry that is prepared when an error has already been journalized and posted. (Ch. 2)

**cost** A payment of cash (or a commitment to pay cash in the future) for the purpose of generating revenues. (Ch. 18)

**cost accounting systems** Systems that measure, record, and report product costs. (Ch. 19)

**cost allocation** The process of assigning indirect cost to a cost object, such as a job. (Ch. 19)

**cost behavior** The manner in which a cost changes in relation to its activity base (driver). (Ch. 21)

**cost center** A decentralized unit in which the department or division manager has responsibility for the control of costs incurred and the authority to make decisions that affect these costs. (Ch. 24)

**cost concept** A concept of accounting that determines the amount initially entered into the accounting records for purchases. (Ch. 1)

**cost method** A method of accounting for equity investments representing less than 20% of the outstanding shares of the investee. The purchase is at original cost, and any gains or losses upon sale are recognized by the difference between the sale proceeds and the original cost. (Ch. 15)

**cost object** The object or segment of operations to which costs are related for management's use, such as a product or department. (Ch. 18)

**cost of finished goods available for sale** The beginning finished goods inventory added to the cost of goods manufactured during the period. (Ch. 18)

**cost of goods manufactured** The total cost of making and finishing a product. (Ch. 18)

**cost of goods sold** The cost of finished goods available for sale minus the ending finished goods inventory. (Ch. 18)

**cost of goods sold budget** A budget of the estimated direct materials, direct labor, and factory overhead consumed by sold products. (Ch. 22)

**cost of merchandise sold** The cost that is reported as an expense when merchandise is sold. (Chs. 6, 18)

**cost of production report** A report prepared periodically by a processing department, summarizing (1) the units for which the department is accountable and the disposition of those units and (2) the costs incurred by the department and the allocation of those costs between completed and incomplete production. (Ch. 20)

**cost per equivalent unit** The rate used to allocate costs between completed and partially completed production. (Ch. 20)

**cost price approach** An approach to transfer pricing that uses cost as the basis for setting the transfer price. (Ch. 24)

**cost variance** The difference between actual cost and the flexible budget at actual volumes. (Ch. 23)

**cost-volume-profit analysis** The systematic examination of the relationships among selling prices, volume of sales and production, costs, expenses, and profits. (Ch. 21)

**cost-volume-profit chart** A chart used to assist management in understanding the relationships among costs, expenses, sales, and operating profit or loss. (Ch. 21)

**credit** Amount entered on the right side of an account. (Ch. 2)

**credit memorandum (credit memo)** A form used by a seller to inform the buyer of the amount the seller proposes to credit to the account receivable due from the buyer. (Ch. 6)

**credit period** The amount of time the buyer is allowed in which to pay the seller. (Ch. 6)

**credit terms** Terms for payment on account by the buyer to the seller. (Ch. 6)

**cumulative preferred stock** Stock that has a right to receive regular dividends that were not declared (paid) in prior years. (Ch. 13)

**currency exchange rate** The rate at which currency in another country can be exchanged for local currency. (Ch. 26)

**current assets** Cash and other assets that are expected to be converted to cash or sold or used up, usually within one year or less, through the normal operations of the business. (Ch. 4)

**current liabilities** Liabilities that will be due within a short time (usually one year or less) and that are to be paid out of current assets. (Ch. 4)

**current position analysis** A company's ability to pay its current liabilities. (Chs. 11, 17)

**current ratio** A financial ratio that is computed by dividing current assets by current liabilities. (Chs. 4, 17)

**currently attainable standards** Standards that represent levels of operation that can be attained with reasonable effort. (Ch. 23)

# D

**debit** Amount entered on the left side of an account. (Ch. 2)

**debit memorandum (debit memo)** A form used by a buyer to inform the seller of the amount the buyer proposes to debit to the account payable due the seller. (Ch. 6)

**debt securities** Notes and bond investments that provide interest revenue over a fixed maturity. (Ch. 15)

**decision making** A component inherent in the other management processes of planning, directing, controlling, and improving. (Ch. 18)

**deficiency** The debit balance in the owner's equity account of a partner. (Ch. 12)

**deficit** A debit balance in the retained earnings account. (Ch. 13)

**defined benefit plan** A pension plan that promises employees a fixed annual pension benefit at retirement, based on years of service and compensation levels. (Ch. 11)

**defined contribution plan** A pension plan that requires a fixed amount of money to be invested on the employee's behalf during the employee's working years. (Ch. 11)

**depletion** The process of transferring the cost of natural resources to an expense account. (Ch. 10)

**depreciate** To lose usefulness as all fixed assets except land do. (Ch. 3)

**depreciation** The systematic periodic transfer of the cost of a fixed asset to an expense account during its expected useful life. (Chs. 3, 10)

**depreciation expense** The portion of the cost of a fixed asset that is recorded as an expense each year of its useful life. (Ch. 3)

**differential analysis** The area of accounting concerned with the effect of alternative courses of action on revenues and costs. (Ch. 25)

**differential cost** The amount of increase or decrease in cost expected from a particular course of action compared with an alternative. (Ch. 25)

**differential income (loss)** The difference between the differential revenue and the differential costs. (Ch. 25)

**differential revenue** The amount of increase or decrease in revenue expected from a particular course of action as compared with an alternative. (Ch. 25)

**direct costs** Costs that can be traced directly to a cost object. (Ch. 18)

**direct labor cost** The wages of factory workers who are directly involved in converting materials into a finished product. (Ch. 18)

**direct labor cost budget** Budget that estimates direct labor hours and related costs needed to support budgeted production. (Ch. 22)

**direct labor rate variance** The cost associated with the difference between the standard rate and the actual rate paid for direct labor used in producing a commodity. (Ch. 23)

**direct labor time variance** The cost associated with the difference between the standard hours and the actual hours of direct labor spent producing a commodity. (Ch. 23)

**direct materials cost** The cost of materials that are an integral part of the finished product. (Ch. 18)

**direct materials price variance** The cost associated with the difference between the standard price and the actual price of direct materials used in producing a commodity. (Ch. 23)

**direct materials purchases budget** A budget that uses the production budget as a starting point to budget materials purchases. (Ch. 22)

**direct materials quantity variance** The cost associated with the difference between the standard quantity and the actual quantity of direct materials used in producing a commodity. (Ch. 23)

**direct method** A method of reporting the cash flows from operating activities as the difference between the operating cash receipts and the operating cash payments. (Ch. 16)

**direct write-off method** The method of accounting for uncollectible accounts that recognizes the expense only when accounts are judged to be worthless. (Ch. 9)

**directing** The process by which managers, given their assigned level of responsibilities, run day-to-day operations. (Ch. 18)

**discount** The interest deducted from the maturity value of a note or the excess of the face amount of bonds over their issue price. (Chs. 13, 14)

**dishonored note receivable** A note that the maker fails to pay on the due date. (Ch. 9)

**dividend yield** A ratio, computed by dividing the annual dividends paid per share of common stock by the market price per share at a specific date, that indicates the rate of return to stockholders in terms of cash dividend distributions. (Chs. 15, 17)

**dividends** Distribution of a corporation's earnings to stockholders. (Ch. 13)

**dividends per share** Measures the extent to which earnings are being distributed to common shareholders. (Ch. 17)

**double-declining-balance method** A method of depreciation that provides periodic depreciation expense based on the declining book value of a fixed asset over its estimated life. (Ch. 10)

**double-entry accounting system** A system of accounting for recording transactions, based on recording increases and decreases in accounts so that debits equal credits. (Ch. 2)

**drawing** The account used to record amounts withdrawn by an owner of a proprietorship. (Ch. 2)

**DuPont formula** An expanded expression of return on investment determined by multiplying the profit margin by the investment turnover. (Ch. 24)

# E

**earnings** The amount by which revenues exceed expenses. (Ch. 1)

**earnings per common share (EPS)** Net income per share of common stock outstanding during a period. (Chs. 13, 14)

**earnings per share (EPS) on common stock** The profitability ratio of net income available to common shareholders to the number of common shares outstanding. (Ch. 17)

**e-commerce** The use of the Internet for performing business transactions. (Ch. 5)

**effective interest rate method** The method of amortizing discounts and premiums that provides for a constant rate of interest on the carrying amount of the bonds at the beginning of each period; often called simply the "interest method." (Ch. 14)

**effective rate of interest** The market rate of interest at the time bonds are issued. (Ch. 14)

**electronic funds transfer (EFT)** A system in which computers rather than paper (money, checks, etc.) are used to effect cash transactions. (Ch. 8)

**elements of internal control** The control environment, risk assessment, control activities, information and communication, and monitoring. (Ch. 8)

**employee fraud** The intentional act of deceiving an employer for personal gain. (Ch. 8)

**employee's earnings record** A detailed record of each employee's earnings. (Ch. 11)

**engineering change order (ECO)** The document that initiates changing a product or process. (Ch. 25)

**equity method** A method of accounting for an investment in common stock by which the investment account is adjusted for the investor's share of periodic net income and cash dividends of the investee. (Ch. 15)

**equity securities** The common and preferred stock of a firm. (Ch. 15)

**equivalent units of production** The number of production units that could have been completed within a given accounting period, given the resources consumed. (Ch. 20)

**ethics** Moral principles that guide the conduct of individuals. (Ch. 1)

**expenses** Assets used up or services consumed in the process of generating revenues. (Chs. 1, 2)

**extraordinary item** An event or a transaction that is both (1) unusual in nature and (2) infrequent in occurrence. (Ch. 17)

# F

**face amount** An amount at which bonds sell if the market rate equals the contract rate. (Ch. 14)

**factory burden** Another term for manufacturing overhead or factory overhead. (Ch. 18)

**factory overhead cost** All of the costs of producing a product except for direct materials and direct labor. (Ch. 18)

**factory overhead cost budget** Budget that estimates the cost for each item of factory overhead needed to support budgeted production. (Ch. 22)

**factory overhead cost variance report** Reports budgeted and actual costs for variable and fixed factory overhead along with the related controllable and volume variances. (Ch. 23)

**fair value** The price that would be received for selling an asset or paying off a liability, often the market price for an equity or debt security. (Ch. 15)

**favorable cost variance** A variance that occurs when the actual cost is less than standard cost. (Ch. 23)

**feedback** Measures provided to operational employees or managers on the performance of subunits of the organization. These measures are used by employees to adjust a process or a behavior to achieve goals. See management by exception. (Ch. 18)

**fees earned** Revenue from providing services. (Ch. 1)

**FICA tax** Federal Insurance Contributions Act tax used to finance federal programs for old-age and disability benefits (social security) and health insurance for the aged (Medicare). (Ch. 11)

**financial accounting** The branch of accounting that is concerned with recording transactions using generally accepted accounting principles (GAAP) for a business or other economic unit and with a periodic preparation of various statements from such records. (Chs. 1, 18)

**Financial Accounting Standards Board (FASB)** The authoritative body that has the primary responsibility for developing accounting principles. (Ch. 1)

**financial statements** Financial reports that summarize the effects of events on a business. (Ch. 1)

**finished goods inventory** The direct materials costs, direct labor costs, and factory overhead costs of finished products that have not been sold. (Ch. 18)

**finished goods ledger** The subsidiary ledger that contains the individual accounts for each kind of commodity or product produced. (Ch. 19)

**first-in, first-out (FIFO) inventory cost flow method** The method of inventory costing based on the assumption that the costs of merchandise sold should be charged against revenue in the order in which the costs were incurred. (Chs. 7, 20)

**fiscal year** The annual accounting period adopted by a business. (Ch. 4)

**fixed asset turnover ratio** The number of dollars of sales that are generated from each dollar of average fixed assets during the year, computed by dividing the net sales by the average net fixed assets. (Ch. 10)

**fixed assets (or plant assets)** Long-term or relatively permanent tangible assets such as equipment, machinery, and buildings that are used in the normal business operations and that depreciate over time. (Chs. 3, 4, 10)

**fixed costs** Costs that tend to remain the same in amount, regardless of variations in the level of activity. (Ch. 21)

**flexible budget** A budget that adjusts for varying rates of activity. (Ch. 22)

**FOB (free on board) destination** Freight terms in which the seller pays the transportation costs from the shipping point to the final destination. (Ch. 6)

**FOB (free on board) shipping point** Freight terms in which the buyer pays the transportation costs from the shipping point to the final destination. (Ch. 6)

**free cash flow** The amount of operating cash flow remaining after replacing current productive capacity and maintaining current dividends. (Ch. 16)

**fringe benefits** Benefits provided to employees in addition to wages and salaries. (Ch. 11)

**future value** The value of an asset or cash at a specified date in the future that is equivalent in value to a specified sum today. (Ch. 14)

# G

**general journal** The two-column form used for entries that do not "fit" in any of the special journals. (Ch. 5)

**general ledger** The primary ledger, when used in conjunction with subsidiary ledgers, that contains all of the balance sheet and income statement accounts. (Ch. 5)

**general-purpose financial statements** A type of financial accounting report that is distributed to external users. The term "general purpose" refers to the wide range of decision-making needs that the reports are designed to serve. (Ch. 1)

**generally accepted accounting principles (GAAP)** Generally accepted guidelines for the preparation of financial statements. (Ch. 1)

**goal conflict** A condition that occurs when individual objectives conflict with organizational objectives. (Ch. 22)

**goodwill** An intangible asset that is created from such favorable factors as location, product quality, reputation, and managerial skill. (Ch. 10)

**gross pay** The total earnings of an employee for a payroll period. (Ch. 11)

**gross profit** Sales minus the cost of merchandise sold. (Ch. 6)

**gross profit method** A method of estimating inventory cost that is based on the relationship of gross profit to sales. (Ch. 7)

## H

**held-to-maturity securities** Investments in bonds or other debt securities that management intends to hold to their maturity. (Ch. 15)

**high-low method** A technique that uses the highest and lowest total costs as a basis for estimating the variable cost per unit and the fixed cost component of a mixed cost. (Ch. 21)

**horizontal analysis** Financial analysis that compares an item in a current statement with the same item in prior statements. (Chs. 2, 17)

## I

**ideal standards** Standards that can be achieved only under perfect operating conditions, such as no idle time, no machine breakdowns, and no materials spoilage; also called theoretical standards. (Ch. 23)

**in arrears** Cumulative preferred stock dividends that have not been paid in prior years are said to be in arrears. (Ch. 13)

**income from operations (operating income)** Revenues less operating expenses and service department charges for a profit or an investment center. (Ch. 6)

**income statement** A summary of the revenue and expenses for a specific period of time, such as a month or a year. (Ch. 1)

**Income Summary** An account to which the revenue and expense account balances are transferred at the end of a period. (Ch. 4)

**indirect costs** Costs that cannot be traced directly to a cost object. (Ch. 18)

**indirect method** A method of reporting the cash flows from operating activities as the net income from operations adjusted for all deferrals of past cash receipts and payments and all accruals of expected future cash receipts and payments. (Ch. 16)

**inflation** A period when prices in general are rising and the purchasing power of money is declining. (Ch. 26)

**installment note** A debt that requires the borrower to make equal periodic payments to the lender for the term of the note. (Ch. 14)

**intangible assets** Long-term assets that are useful in the operations of a business, are not held for sale, and are without physical qualities. (Ch. 10)

**interest revenue** Money received for interest. (Ch. 1)

**internal controls** The policies and procedures used to safeguard assets, ensure accurate business information, and ensure compliance with laws and regulations. (Chs. 5, 8)

**internal rate of return (IRR) method** A method of analysis of proposed capital investments that uses present value concepts to compute the rate of return from the net cash flows expected from the investment. (Ch. 26)

**International Accounting Standards Board (IASB)** An organization that issues International Financial Reporting Standards for many countries outside the United States. (Ch. 1)

**inventory analysis** A company's ability to manage its inventory effectively. (Ch. 17)

**inventory shrinkage (inventory shortage)** The amount by which the merchandise for sale, as indicated by the balance of the merchandise inventory account, is larger than the total amount of merchandise counted during the physical inventory. (Ch. 6)

**inventory turnover** The relationship between the volume of goods sold and inventory, computed by dividing the cost of goods sold by the average inventory. (Chs. 7, 17)

**investee** The company whose stock is purchased by the investor. (Ch. 15)

**investment center** A decentralized unit in which the manager has the responsibility and authority to make decisions that affect not only costs and revenues but also the fixed assets available to the center. (Ch. 24)

**investment turnover** A component of the rate of return on investment, computed as the ratio of sales to invested assets. (Ch. 24)

**investments** The balance sheet caption used to report long-term investments in stocks not intended as a source of cash in the normal operations of the business. (Ch. 15)

**investor** The company investing in another company's stock. (Ch. 15)

**invoice** The bill that the seller sends to the buyer. (Chs. 5, 6)

## J

**job cost sheet** An account in the work in process subsidiary ledger in which the costs charged to a particular job order are recorded. (Ch. 19)

**job order cost system** A type of cost accounting system that provides for a separate record of the cost of each particular quantity of product that passes through the factory. (Ch. 19)

**journal** The initial record in which the effects of a transaction are recorded. (Ch. 2)

**journal entry** The form of recording a transaction in a journal. (Ch. 2)

**journalizing** The process of recording a transaction in the journal. (Ch. 2)

**just-in-time (JIT) processing** A processing approach that focuses on eliminating time, cost, and poor quality within manufacturing and nonmanufacturing processes. (Ch. 20)

# L

**last-in, first-out (LIFO) inventory cost flow method** A method of inventory costing based on the assumption that the most recent merchandise inventory costs should be charged against revenue. (Ch. 7)

**ledger** A group of accounts for a business. (Ch. 2)

**leverage** Using debt to increase the return on an investment. (Ch. 17)

**liabilities** The rights of creditors that represent debts of the business. (Chs. 1, 2)

**limited liability company (LLC)** A business form consisting of one or more persons or entities filing an operating agreement with a state to conduct business with limited liability to the owners, yet treated as a partnership for tax purposes. (Chs. 1, 12)

**line department** A unit that is directly involved in the basic objectives of an organization. (Ch. 18)

**liquidation** The winding-up process when a partnership goes out of business. (Ch. 12)

**liquidity** The ability to convert assets into cash. (Chs. 4, 17)

**long-term liabilities** Liabilities that usually will not be due for more than one year. (Ch. 4)

**lower-of-cost-or-market (LCM) method** A method of valuing inventory that reports the inventory at the lower of its cost or current market value (replacement cost). (Ch. 7)

# M

**management (or managerial) accounting** The branch of accounting that uses both historical and estimated data in providing information that management uses in conducting daily operations, in planning future operations, and in developing overall business strategies. (Chs. 1, 18)

**management by exception** The philosophy of managing which involves monitoring the operating results of implemented plans and comparing the expected results with the actual results. This feedback allows management to isolate significant variations for further investigation and possible remedial action. (Ch. 18)

**management process** The five basic management functions of (1) planning, (2) directing, (3) controlling, (4) improving, and (5) decision making. (Ch. 18)

**Management's Discussion and Analysis (MD&A)** An annual report disclosure that provides management's analysis of the results of operations and financial condition. (Ch. 17)

**manufacturing business** A type of business that changes basic inputs into products that are sold to individual customers. (Ch. 1)

**manufacturing cells** A grouping of processes where employees are cross-trained to perform more than one function. (Ch. 20)

**manufacturing overhead** Costs, other than direct materials and direct labor costs, that are incurred in the manufacturing process. (Ch. 18)

**margin of safety** Indicates the possible decrease in sales that may occur before an operating loss results. (Ch. 21)

**market price approach** An approach to transfer pricing that uses the price at which the product or service transferred could be sold to outside buyers as the transfer price. (Ch. 24)

**market rate of interest** The rate determined from sales and purchases of similar bonds. (Ch. 14)

**master budget** The comprehensive budget plan linking all the individual budgets related to sales, cost of goods sold, operating expenses, projects, capital expenditures, and cash. (Ch. 22)

**matching concept (or matching principle)** A concept of accounting in which expenses are matched with the revenue generated during a period by those expenses. (Chs. 1, 3)

**materials inventory** The cost of materials that have not yet entered into the manufacturing process. (Ch. 18)

**materials ledger** The subsidiary ledger containing the individual accounts for each type of material. (Ch. 19)

**materials requisition** The form or electronic transmission used by a manufacturing department to authorize materials issuances from the storeroom. (Ch. 19)

**maturity value** The amount that is due at the maturity or due date of a note. (Ch. 9)

**merchandise available for sale** The cost of merchandise available for sale to customers calculated by adding the beginning merchandise inventory to net purchases. (Ch. 18)

**merchandise inventory** Merchandise on hand (not sold) at the end of an accounting period. (Ch. 6)

**merchandising business** A type of business that purchases products from other businesses and sells them to customers. (Ch. 1)

**mixed costs** Costs with both variable and fixed characteristics, sometimes called semivariable or semi-fixed costs. (Ch. 21)

**mortgage notes** An installment note that may be secured by a pledge of the borrower's assets. (Ch. 14)

**multiple-step income statement** A form of income statement that contains several sections, subsections, and subtotals. (Ch. 6)

# N

**natural business year** A fiscal year that ends when business activities have reached the lowest point in an annual operating cycle. (Ch. 4)

**negotiated price approach** An approach to transfer pricing that allows managers of decentralized units to agree (negotiate) among themselves as to the transfer price. (Ch. 24)

**net income or net profit** The amount by which revenues exceed expenses. (Ch. 1)

**net loss** The amount by which expenses exceed revenues. (Ch. 1)

**net pay** Gross pay less payroll deductions; the amount the employer is obligated to pay the employee. (Ch. 11)

**net present value method** A method of analysis of proposed capital investments that focuses on the present value of the cash flows expected from the investments. (Ch. 26)

**net realizable value** The estimated selling price of an item of inventory less any direct costs of disposal, such as sales commissions. (Chs. 7, 9)

**net sales** Revenue received for merchandise sold to customers less any sales returns and allowances and sales discounts. (Ch. 6)

**nonfinancial performance measure** A performance measure expressed in units rather than dollars. (Ch. 23)

**normal balance of an account** The normal balance of an account can be either a debit or a credit depending on whether increases in the account are recorded as debits or credits. (Ch. 2)

**notes receivable** A customer's written promise to pay an amount and possibly interest at an agreed-upon rate. (Chs. 4, 9)

**number of days' sales in inventory** The relationship between the volume of sales and inventory, computed by dividing the inventory at the end of the year by the average daily cost of goods sold. (Chs. 7, 17)

**number of days' sales in receivables** The relationship between sales and accounts receivable, computed by dividing the net accounts receivable at the end of the year by the average daily sales. (Chs. 9, 17)

**number of times interest charges are earned** A ratio that measures creditor margin of safety for interest payments, calculated as income before interest and taxes divided by interest expense. (Chs. 14, 17)

**O**

**objectives (goals)** Developed in the planning stage, these reflect the direction and desired outcomes of certain courses of action. (Ch. 18)

**objectivity concept** A concept of accounting that requires accounting records and the data reported in financial statements to be based on objective evidence. (Ch. 1)

**operating cycle** The process by which a company spends cash, generates revenues, and receives cash either at the time the revenues are generated or later by collecting an accounts receivable. (Ch. 6)

**operating lease** A lease that does not meet the criteria for capital leases and thus is accounted for as an operating expense. (Ch. 10)

**operating leverage** A measure of the relative mix of a business's variable costs and fixed costs, computed as contribution margin divided by operating income. (Ch. 21)

**operational planning** The development of short-term plans to achieve goals identified in a business's strategic plan. Sometimes called tactical planning. (Ch. 18)

**opportunity cost** The amount of income forgone from an alternative to a proposed use of cash or its equivalent. (Ch. 25)

**other comprehensive income** Specified items that are reported separately from net income, including foreign currency items, pension liability adjustments, and unrealized gains and losses on investments. (Ch. 15)

**other expense** Expenses that cannot be traced directly to operations. (Ch. 6)

**other income** Revenue from sources other than the primary operating activity of a business. (Ch. 6)

**outstanding stock** The stock in the hands of stockholders. (Ch. 13)

**overapplied factory overhead** The amount of factory overhead applied in excess of the actual factory overhead costs incurred for production during a period. (Ch. 19)

**owner's equity** The owner's right to the assets of the business. (Chs. 1, 2)

**P**

**paid-in capital** Capital contributed to a corporation by the stockholders and others. (Ch. 13)

**par** The monetary amount printed on a stock certificate. (Ch. 12)

**par value** A dollar amount assigned to each share of stock. (Ch. 13)

**parent company** The corporation owning all or a majority of the voting stock of the other corporation. (Ch. 15)

**partnership** An unincorporated business form consisting of two or more persons conducting business as co-owners for profit. (Chs. 1, 12)

**partnership agreement** The formal written contract creating a partnership. (Ch. 12)

**patents** Exclusive rights to produce and sell goods with one or more unique features. (Ch. 10)

**payroll** The total amount paid to employees for a certain period. (Ch. 11)

**payroll register** A multicolumn report used to assemble and summarize payroll data at the end of each payroll period. (Ch. 11)

**pension** A cash payment to retired employees. (Ch. 11)

**period costs** Those costs that are used up in generating revenue during the current period and that are not involved in manufacturing a product, such as selling, general, and administrative expenses. (Ch. 18)

**periodic inventory system** The inventory system in which the inventory records do not show the amount available for sale or sold during the period. (Ch. 6)

**perpetual inventory system** The inventory system in which each purchase and sale of merchandise is recorded in an inventory account. (Ch. 6)

**petty cash fund** A special cash fund to pay relatively small amounts. (Ch. 8)

**physical inventory** A detailed listing of merchandise on hand. (Chs. 6, 7)

**planning** A phase of the management process whereby objectives are outlined and courses of action determined. (Ch. 18)

**posting** The process of transferring the debits and credits from the journal entries to the accounts. (Ch. 2)

**predetermined factory overhead rate** The rate used to apply factory overhead costs to the goods manufactured. The rate is determined by dividing the budgeted overhead cost by the estimated activity usage at the beginning of the fiscal period. (Ch. 19)

**preferred stock** A class of stock with preferential rights over common stock. (Ch. 13)

**premium** The excess of the issue price of a stock over its par value or the excess of the issue price of bonds over their face amount. (Chs. 13, 14)

**prepaid expenses** Items such as supplies that will be used in the business in the future. (Chs. 1, 3)

**present value concept** Cash to be received (or paid) in the future is not the equivalent of the same amount of money received at an earlier date. (Chs. 14, 26)

**present value index** An index computed by dividing the total present value of the net cash flow to be received from a proposed capital investment by the amount to be invested. (Ch. 26)

**present value of an annuity** The sum of the present values of a series of equal cash flows to be received at fixed intervals. (Chs. 14, 26)

**price-earnings (P/E) ratio** The ratio of the market price per share of common stock, at a specific date, to the annual earnings per share. (Ch. 17)

**prime costs** The combination of direct materials and direct labor costs. (Ch. 18)

**prior period adjustments** Corrections of material errors related to a prior period or periods, excluded from the determination of net income. (Ch. 13)

**private accounting** The field of accounting whereby accountants are employed by a business firm or a not-for-profit organization. (Ch. 1)

**process** A sequence of activities linked together for performing a particular task. (Ch. 23)

**process cost system** A type of cost system that accumulates costs for each of the various departments within a manufacturing facility. (Chs. 19, 20)

**process manufacturer** A manufacturer that uses large machines to process a continuous flow of raw materials through various stages of completion into a finished state. (Ch. 20)

**product cost concept** A concept used in applying the cost-plus approach to product pricing in which only the costs of manufacturing the product, termed the product cost, are included in the cost amount to which the markup is added. (Ch. 25)

**product costs** The three components of manufacturing cost: direct materials, direct labor, and factory overhead costs. (Ch. 18)

**production bottleneck** A condition that occurs when product demand exceeds production capacity. (Ch. 25)

**production budget** A budget of estimated unit production. (Ch. 22)

**profit** The difference between the amounts received from customers for goods or services provided and the amounts paid for the inputs used to provide the goods or services. (Ch. 1)

**profit center** A decentralized unit in which the manager has the responsibility and the authority to make decisions that affect both costs and revenues (and thus profits). (Ch. 24)

**profit margin** A component of the rate of return on investment, computed as the ratio of income from operations to sales. (Ch. 24)

**profit-volume chart** A chart used to assist management in understanding the relationship between profit and volume. (Ch. 21)

**profitability** The ability of a firm to earn income. (Ch. 17)

**proprietorship** A business owned by one individual. (Ch. 1)

**public accounting** The field of accounting where accountants and their staff provide services on a fee basis. (Ch. 1)

**public companies** Companies that issue publicly traded debt or equity securities. (App. D)

**Public Company Accounting Oversight Board (PCAOB)** A new oversight body for the accounting profession that was established by the Sarbanes-Oxley Act. (Ch. 1)

**purchase order** The purchase order authorizes the purchase of the inventory from an approved vendor. (Ch. 7)

**purchases discounts** Discounts taken by the buyer for early payment of an invoice. (Ch. 6)

**purchases journal** The journal in which all items purchased on account are recorded. (Ch. 5)

**purchases returns and allowances** From the buyer's perspective, returned merchandise or an adjustment for defective merchandise. (Ch. 6)

## Q

**quick assets** Cash and other current assets that can be quickly converted to cash, such as marketable securities and receivables. (Chs. 11, 17)

**quick ratio** A financial ratio that measures the ability to pay current liabilities with quick assets (cash, marketable securities, accounts receivable). (Chs. 11, 17)

## R

**rate earned on common stockholders' equity** A measure of profitability computed by dividing net income, reduced by preferred dividend requirements, by common stockholders' equity. (Ch. 17)

**rate earned on stockholders' equity** A measure of profitability computed by dividing net income by total stockholders' equity. (Ch. 17)

**rate earned on total assets** A measure of the profitability of assets, without regard to the equity of creditors and stockholders in the assets. (Ch. 17)

**rate of return on investment (ROI)** A measure of managerial efficiency in the use of investments in assets, computed as income from operations divided by invested assets. (Ch. 24)

**ratio of cash to monthly cash expenses** Ratio that helps assess how long a company can continue to operate without additional financing or generating positive cash flows from operations. (Ch. 8)

**ratio of fixed assets to long-term liabilities** A leverage ratio that measures the margin of safety of long-term creditors, calculated as the net fixed assets divided by the long-term liabilities. (Ch. 17)

**ratio of liabilities to owner's (stockholders') equity** A comprehensive leverage ratio that measures the relationship of the claims of creditors to stockholders' equity. (Chs. 1, 17)

**ratio of net sales to assets** Ratio that measures how effectively a company uses its assets, computed as net sales divided by average total assets. (Chs. 6, 17)

**real (permanent) accounts** Term for balance sheet accounts because they are relatively permanent and carried forward from year to year. (Ch. 4)

**realization** The sale of assets when a partnership is being liquidated. (Ch. 12)

**receivables** All money claims against other entities, including people, business firms, and other organizations. (Ch. 9)

**receiving report** The form or electronic transmission used by the receiving personnel to indicate that materials have been received and inspected. (Chs. 7, 19)

**relevant range** The range of activity over which changes in cost are of interest to management. (Ch. 21)

**rent revenue** Money received for rent. (Ch. 1)

**report form** The form of balance sheet with the Liabilities and Owner's Equity sections presented below the Assets section. (Ch. 6)

**residual income** The excess of divisional income from operations over a "minimum" acceptable income from operations. (Ch. 24)

**residual value** The estimated value of a fixed asset at the end of its useful life. (Ch. 10)

**responsibility accounting** The process of measuring and reporting operating data by areas of responsibility. (Ch. 24)

**responsibility center** An organizational unit for which a manager is assigned responsibility over costs, revenues, or assets. (Ch. 22)

**restrictions** Amounts of retained earnings that have been limited for use as dividends. (Ch. 13)

**retail inventory method** A method of estimating inventory cost that is based on the relationship of gross profit to sales. (Ch. 7)

**retained earnings** Net income retained in a corporation. (Ch. 13)

**retained earnings statement** A summary of the changes in the retained earnings in a corporation for a specific period of time, such as a month or a year. (Ch. 13)

**revenue expenditures** Costs that benefit only the current period or costs incurred for normal maintenance and repairs of fixed assets. (Ch. 10)

**revenue journal** The journal in which all sales and services on account are recorded. (Ch. 5)

**revenue per employee** A measure of the efficiency of the business in generating revenues, which is computed as revenue divided by number of employees. (Ch. 12)

**revenue recognition concept** The concept that supports recording revenues when services have been performed or products delivered to customers. (Ch. 3)

**revenues** Increases in assets from performing services or delivering products to customers. (Chs. 1, 2)

**rules of debit and credit** In the double-entry accounting system, specific rules for recording debits and credits based on the type of account. (Ch. 2)

# S

**sales** The total amount charged customers for merchandise sold, including cash sales and sales on account. (Chs. 1, 6)

**sales budget** One of the major elements of the income statement budget that indicates the quantity of estimated sales and the expected unit selling price. (Ch. 22)

**sales discounts** From the seller's perspective, discounts that a seller may offer the buyer for early payment. (Ch. 6)

**sales mix** The relative distribution of sales among the various products available for sale. (Ch. 21)

**sales returns and allowances** From the seller's perspective, returned merchandise or an adjustment for defective merchandise. (Ch. 6)

**Sarbanes-Oxley Act (SOX)** An act passed by Congress to restore public confidence and trust in the financial statements of companies. (Chs. 1, 8)

**Securities and Exchange Commission (SEC)** An agency of the U.S. government that has authority over the accounting and financial disclosures for companies whose shares of ownership (stock) are traded and sold to the public. (Ch. 1)

**selling expenses** Expenses that are incurred directly in the selling of merchandise. (Ch. 6)

**service business** A business providing services rather than products to customers. (Ch. 1)

**service department charges** The costs of services provided by an internal service department and transferred to a responsibility center. (Ch. 24)

**setup** An overhead activity that consists of changing tooling in machines in preparation for making a new product. (Ch. 25)

**single-step income statement** A form of income statement in which the total of all expenses is deducted from the total of all revenues. (Ch. 6)

**slide** An error in which the entire number is moved one or more spaces to the right or the left, such as writing $542.00 as $54.20 or $5,420.00. (Ch. 2)

**solvency** The ability of a firm to pay its debts as they come due. (Chs. 4, 17)

**special journals** Journals designed to be used for recording a single type of transaction. (Ch. 5)

**special-purpose funds** Cash funds used for a special business need. (Ch. 8)

**specific identification inventory cost flow method** Inventory method in which the unit sold is identified with a specific purchase. (Ch. 7)

**staff department** A unit that provides services, assistance, and advice to the departments with line or other staff responsibilities. (Ch. 18)

**standard cost** A detailed estimate of what a product should cost. (Ch. 23)

**standard cost systems** Accounting systems that use standards for each element of manufacturing cost entering into the finished product. (Ch. 23)

**standards** Performance goals, often relating to how much a product should cost. (Ch. 23)

**statement of cash flows** A summary of the cash receipts and cash payments for a specific period of time, such as a month or a year. (Chs. 1, 16)

**statement of cost of goods manufactured** The income statement of manufacturing companies. (Ch. 18)

**statement of members' equity** A summary of the changes in each member's equity in a limited liability corporation that have occurred during a specific period of time. (Ch. 12)

**statement of owner's equity** A summary of the changes in owner's equity that have occurred during a specific period of time, such as a month or a year. (Ch. 1)

**statement of partnership equity** A summary of the changes in each partner's capital in a partnership that have occurred during a specific period of time. (Ch. 12)

**statement of partnership liquidation** A summary of the liquidation process whereby cash is distributed to the partners based on the balances in their capital accounts. (Ch. 12)

**statement of stockholders' equity** A summary of the changes in the stockholders' equity in a corporation that have occurred during a specific period of time. (Ch. 13)

**static budget** A budget that does not adjust to changes in activity levels. (Ch. 22)

**stock** Shares of ownership of a corporation. (Ch. 13)

**stock dividend** A distribution of shares of stock to its stockholders. (Ch. 13)

**stock split** A reduction in the par or stated value of a common stock and the issuance of a proportionate number of additional shares. (Ch. 13)

**stockholders** The owners of a corporation. (Ch. 13)

**stockholders' equity** The owners' equity in a corporation. (Ch. 13)

**straight-line method** A method of depreciation that provides for equal periodic depreciation expense over the estimated life of a fixed asset. (Ch. 10)

**strategic planning** The development of a long-range course of action to achieve business goals. (Ch. 18)

**strategies** The means by which business goals and objectives will be achieved. (Ch. 18)

**subsidiary company** The corporation that is controlled by a parent company. (Ch. 15)

**subsidiary inventory ledger** The subsidiary ledger containing individual accounts for items of inventory. (Ch. 7)

**subsidiary ledger** A ledger containing individual accounts with a common characteristic. (Ch. 5)

**sunk cost** A cost that is not affected by subsequent decisions. (Ch. 25)

# T

**T account** The simplest form of an account. (Ch. 2)

**target costing** The target cost is determined by subtracting a desired profit from a market method determined price. The resulting target cost is used to motivate cost improvements in design and manufacture. (Ch. 25)

**temporary (nominal) accounts** Accounts that report amounts for only one period. (Ch. 4)

**theory of constraints (TOC)** A manufacturing strategy that attempts to remove the influence of bottlenecks (constraints) on a process. (Ch. 25)

**time tickets** The form on which the amount of time spent by each employee and the labor cost incurred for each individual job, or for factory overhead, are recorded. (Ch. 19)

**time value of money concept** The concept that an amount of money invested today will earn income. (Ch. 26)

**total cost concept** A concept used in applying the cost-plus approach to product pricing in which all the costs of manufacturing the product plus the selling and administrative expenses are included in the cost amount to which the markup is added. (Ch. 25)

**total manufacturing cost variance** The difference between total standard costs and total actual costs for units produced. (Ch. 23)

**trade discounts** Discounts from the list prices in published catalogs or special discounts offered to certain classes of buyers. (Ch. 6)

**trade-in allowance** The amount a seller allows a buyer for a fixed asset that is traded in for a similar asset. (Ch. 10)

**trademark** A name, term, or symbol used to identify a business and its products. (Ch. 10)

**trading securities** Securities that management intends to actively trade for profit. (Ch. 15)

**transfer price** The price charged one decentralized unit by another for the goods or services provided. (Ch. 24)

**transposition** An error in which the order of the digits is changed, such as writing $542 as $452 or $524. (Ch. 2)

**treasury stock** Stock that a corporation has once issued and then reacquires. (Ch. 13)

**trial balance** A summary listing of the titles and balances of accounts in the ledger. (Ch. 2)

# u

**unadjusted trial balance** A summary listing of the titles and balances of accounts in the ledger prior to the posting of adjusting entries. (Ch. 2)

**underapplied factory overhead** The amount of actual factory overhead in excess of the factory overhead applied to production during a period. (Ch. 19)

**unearned revenue** The liability created by receiving revenue in advance. (Chs. 2, 3)

**unfavorable cost variance** A variance that occurs when the actual cost exceeds the standard cost. (Ch. 23)

**unit contribution margin** The dollars available from each unit of sales to cover fixed costs and provide operating profits. (Ch. 21)

**unit of measure concept** A concept of accounting requiring that economic data be recorded in dollars. (Ch. 1)

**units-of-output method** A method of depreciation that provides for depreciation expense based on the expected productive capacity of a fixed asset. (Ch. 10)

**unrealized gain or loss** Changes in the fair value of equity or debt securities for a period. (Ch. 15)

# v

**variable cost concept** A concept used in applying the cost-plus approach to product pricing in which only the variable costs are included in the cost amount to which the markup is added. (Ch. 25)

**variable costing** The concept that considers the cost of products manufactured to be composed only of those manufacturing costs that increase or decrease as the volume of production rises or falls (direct materials, direct labor, and variable factory overhead). (Ch. 21)

**variable costs** Costs that vary in total dollar amount as the level of activity changes. (Ch. 21)

**vertical analysis** An analysis that compares each item in a current statement with a total amount within the same statement. (Chs. 3, 17)

**volume variance** The difference between the budgeted fixed overhead at 100% of normal capacity and the standard fixed overhead for the actual production achieved during the period. (Ch. 23)

**voucher** A special form for recording relevant data about a liability and the details of its payment. (Ch. 8)

**voucher system** A set of procedures for authorizing and recording liabilities and cash payments. (Ch. 8)

# w

**weighted average inventory cost flow method** A method of inventory costing in which the cost of the units sold and in ending inventory is a weighted average of the purchase costs. (Ch. 7)

**whole units** The number of units in production during a period, whether completed or not. (Ch. 20)

**work in process inventory** The direct materials costs, the direct labor costs, and the applied factory overhead costs that have entered into the manufacturing process but are associated with products that have not been finished. (Ch. 18)

**working capital** The excess of the current assets of a business over its current liabilities. (Chs. 4, 17)

# y

**yield** A measure of materials usage efficiency. (Ch. 20)

# z

**zero-based budgeting** A concept of budgeting that requires all levels of management to start from zero and estimate budget data as if there had been no previous activities in their units. (Ch. 22)

# Index

# The Basics

## Accounting Equation:

Assets = Liabilities + Owner's Equity

## T Account:

| Account Title | |
|---|---|
| Left side | Right side |
| debit | credit |

## Rules of Debit and Credit:

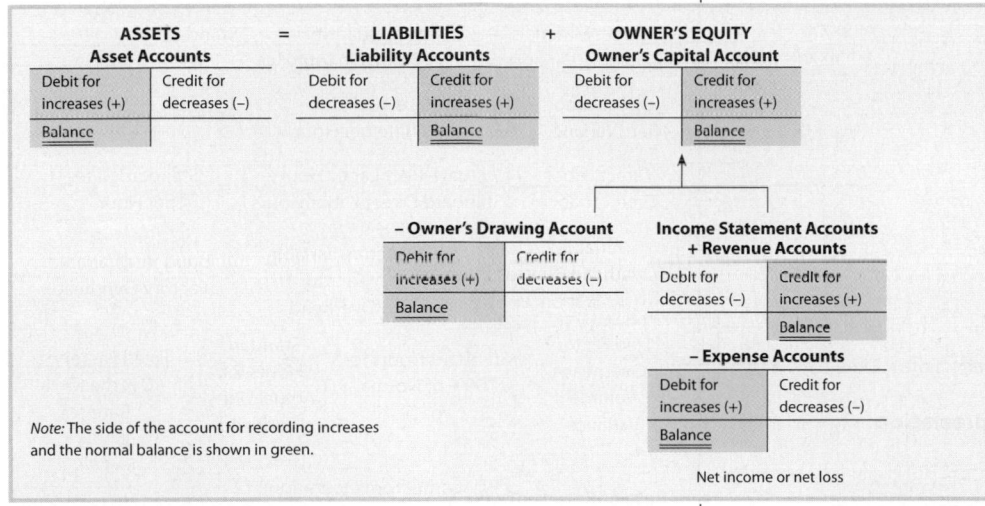

*Note:* The side of the account for recording increases and the normal balance is shown in green.

## Accounting Cycle:

1. Transactions are analyzed and recorded in the journal.
2. Transactions are posted to the ledger.
3. An unadjusted trial balance is prepared.
4. Adjustment data are assembled and analyzed.
5. An optional end-of-period spreadsheet is prepared.
6. Adjusting entries are journalized and posted to the ledger.
7. An adjusted trial balance is prepared.
8. Financial statements are prepared.
9. Closing entries are journalized and posted to the ledger.
10. A post-closing trial balance is prepared.

## Types of Adjusting Entries:

- Prepaid expense (deferred expense)
- Unearned revenue (deferred revenue)
- Accrued revenue (accrued asset)
- Accrued expense (accrued liability)
- Depreciation expense

Each entry will always affect both a balance sheet account and an income statement account.

## Closing Entries:

1. Revenue account balances are transferred to an account called Income Summary.
2. Expense account balances are transferred to an account called Income Summary.
3. The balance of Income Summary (net income or net loss) is transferred to the owner's capital account.
4. The balance of the owner's drawing account is transferred to the owner's capital account.

## Analyzing and Journalizing Transactions

1. Carefully read the description of the transaction to determine whether an asset, a liability, an owner's equity, a revenue, an expense, or a drawing account is affected.
2. For each account affected by the transaction, determine whether the account increases or decreases.
3. Determine whether each increase or decrease should be recorded as a debit or a credit, following the rules of debit and credit.
4. Record the transaction using a journal entry.
5. Periodically post journal entries to the accounts in the ledger.
6. Prepare an unadjusted trial balance at the end of the period.

## Financial Statements:

- **Income statement:** A summary of the revenue and expenses of a business entity for a specific period of time, such as a month or a year.
- **Statement of owner's equity:** A summary of the changes in the owner's equity of a business entity that have occurred during a specific period of time, such as a month or a year.
- **Balance sheet:** A list of the assets, liabilities, and owner's equity of a business entity as of a specific date, usually at the close of the last day of a month or a year.
- **Statement of Cash Flows:** A summary of the cash receipts and cash payments of a business entity for a specific period of time, such as a month or a year.

## Special Journals:

Providing services
on account → recorded in → Revenue journal

Receipt of cash from
any source → recorded in → Cash receipts journal

Purchase of items
on account → recorded in → Purchases journal

Payments of cash for
any purpose → recorded in → Cash payments journal

## Shipping Terms:

| | FOB Shipping Point | FOB Destination |
|---|---|---|
| Ownership (title) passes to buyer when merchandise is................. | delivered to freight carrier | delivered to buyer |
| Freight costs are paid by........................ | buyer | seller |

## Format for Bank Reconciliation:

| | | | |
|---|---|---|---|
| Cash balance according to bank statement | | | $XXX |
| Add: | Additions by company not on bank statement | $XXX | |
| | Bank errors | XXX | XXX |
| | | | $XXX |
| Deduct: | Deductions by company not on bank statement | $XXX | |
| | Bank errors | XXX | XXX |
| Adjusted balance | | | $XXX |
| | | | |
| Cash balance according to company's records | | | $XXX |
| Add: | Additions by bank not recorded by company | $XXX | |
| | Company errors | XXX | XXX |
| | | | $XXX |
| Deduct: | Deductions by bank not recorded by company | $XXX | |
| | Company errors | XXX | XXX |
| Adjusted balance | | | $XXX |

## Inventory Costing Methods:

- First-in, First-out (FIFO)
- Last-in, First-out (LIFO)
- Average Cost

## Interest Computations:

$$\text{Interest} = \text{Face Amount (or Principal)} \times \text{Rate} \times \text{Time}$$

## Methods of Determining Annual Depreciation:

**Straight-Line:** $\dfrac{\text{Cost} - \text{Estimated Residual Value}}{\text{Estimated Life}}$

**Double-Declining-Balance:** Rate* × Book Value at Beginning of Period

*Rate is commonly twice the straight-line rate (1 ÷ Estimated Life).

## Adjustments to Net Income (Loss) Using the Indirect Method:

| | Increase (Decrease) |
|---|---|
| Net income (loss) | $ XXX |
| Adjustments to reconcile net income to net cash flow from operating activities: | |
| Depreciation of fixed assets | XXX |
| Amortization of intangible assets | XXX |
| Losses on disposal of assets | XXX |
| Gains on disposal of assets | (XXX) |
| Changes in current operating assets and liabilities: | |
| Increases in noncash current operating assets | (XXX) |
| Decreases in noncash current operating assets | XXX |
| Increases in current operating liabilities | XXX |
| Decreases in current operating liabilities | (XXX) |
| Net cash flow from operating activities | $ XXX |
| | or |
| | $(XXX) |

**Contribution Margin Ratio** $= \dfrac{\text{Sales} - \text{Variable Costs}}{\text{Sales}}$

---

**Break-Even Sales (Units)** $= \dfrac{\text{Fixed Costs}}{\text{Unit Contribution Margin}}$

**Sales (Units)** $= \dfrac{\text{Fixed Costs} + \text{Target Profit}}{\text{Unit Contribution Margin}}$

**Margin of Safety** $= \dfrac{\text{Sales} - \text{Sales at Break-Even Point}}{\text{Sales}}$

**Operating Leverage** $= \dfrac{\text{Contribution Margin}}{\text{Income from Operations}}$

## Variances:

$$\text{Direct Materials Price Variance} = \left( \begin{array}{c} \text{Actual Price} - \\ \text{Standard Price} \end{array} \right) \times \text{Actual Quantity}$$

$$\text{Direct Materials Quantity Variance} = \left( \begin{array}{c} \text{Actual Quantity} - \\ \text{Standard Quantity} \end{array} \right) \times \begin{array}{c} \text{Standard} \\ \text{Price} \end{array}$$

$$\text{Direct Labor Rate Variance} = \left( \begin{array}{c} \text{Actual Rate per Hour} - \\ \text{Standard Rate per Hour} \end{array} \right) \times \text{Actual Hours}$$

$$\text{Direct Labor Time Variance} = \left( \begin{array}{c} \text{Actual Direct Labor Hours} - \\ \text{Standard Direct Labor Hours} \end{array} \right) \times \begin{array}{c} \text{Standard Rate} \\ \text{per Hour} \end{array}$$

$$\begin{array}{c} \text{Variable Factory} \\ \text{Overhead Controllable} \\ \text{Variance} \end{array} = \begin{array}{c} \text{Actual Variable} \\ \text{Factory} \\ \text{Overhead} \end{array} - \begin{array}{c} \text{Budgeted Variable} \\ \text{Factory Overhead} \end{array}$$

$$\begin{array}{c} \text{Fixed Factory} \\ \text{Overhead} \\ \text{Volume} \\ \text{Variance} \end{array} = \left( \begin{array}{c} \text{Standard Hours for} \\ \text{100\% of Normal} \\ \text{Capacity} \end{array} - \begin{array}{c} \text{Standard} \\ \text{Hours for} \\ \text{Actual Units} \\ \text{Produced} \end{array} \right) \times \begin{array}{c} \text{Fixed Factory} \\ \text{Overhead} \\ \text{Rate} \end{array}$$

**Rate of Return on Investment (ROI)** $= \dfrac{\text{Income from Operations}}{\text{Invested Assets}}$

Alternative ROI Computation:

$$\text{ROI} = \dfrac{\text{Income from Operations}}{\text{Sales}} \times \dfrac{\text{Sales}}{\text{Invested Assets}}$$

## Capital Investment Analysis Methods:

Methods That Ignore Present Values:

- Average Rate of Return Method
- Cash Payback Method

Methods That Use Present Values:

- Net Present Value Method
- Internal Rate of Return Method

**Average Rate of Return** $= \dfrac{\text{Estimated Average Annual Income}}{\text{Average Investment}}$

**Present Value Index** $= \dfrac{\text{Total Present Value of Net Cash Flow}}{\text{Amount to Be Invested}}$

**Present Value Factor for an Annuity of $1** $= \dfrac{\text{Amount to Be Invested}}{\text{Equal Annual Net Cash Flows}}$

# Abbreviations and Acronyms Commonly Used in Business and Accounting

| | |
|---|---|
| AAA | American Accounting Association |
| ABC | Activity-based costing |
| AICPA | American Institute of Certified Public Accountants |
| B2B | Business-to-business |
| B2C | Business-to-consumer |
| CFO | Chief Financial Officer |
| CMA | Certified Management Accountant |
| COGM | Cost of goods manufactured |
| COGS | Cost of goods sold |
| CPA | Certified Public Accountant |
| Cr. | Credit |
| CVP | Cost-volume-profit |
| Dr. | Debit |
| EFT | Electronic funds transfer |
| EPS | Earnings per share |
| ERP | Enterprise resource planning |
| FASB | Financial Accounting Standards Board |
| FICA tax | Federal Insurance Contributions Act tax |
| FIFO | First-in, first-out |
| FOB | Free on board |
| FUTA | Federal unemployment compensation tax |
| GAAP | Generally accepted accounting principles |
| IASB | International Accounting Standards Board |
| IFRS | International Financial Reporting Standards |
| IMA | Institute of Management Accountants |
| IRC | Internal Revenue Code |
| IRR | Internal rate of return |
| IRS | Internal Revenue Service |
| JIT | Just-in-time |
| LIFO | Last-in, first-out |
| LCM | Lower of cost or market |
| MACRS | Modified Accelerated Cost Recovery System |
| MD&A | Management's Discussion and Analysis |
| n/30 | Net 30 |
| n/eom | Net, end-of-month |
| NPV | Net present value |
| NSF | Not sufficient funds |
| P/E Ratio | Price-earnings ratio |
| POS | Point of sale |
| ROI | Return on investment |
| R&D | Research and development |
| SCM | Supply chain management |
| SEC | Securities and Exchange Commission |
| SOX | Sarbanes-Oxley Act |
| TQC | Total quality control |
| W-4 | Employee's Withholding Allowance Certificate |
| WIP | Work in process |

# Classification of Accounts

| Account Title | Account Classification | Normal Balance | Financial Statement |
|---|---|---|---|
| Accounts Payable | Current liability | Credit | Balance sheet |
| Accounts Receivable | Current asset | Debit | Balance sheet |
| Accumulated Depletion | Contra fixed asset | Credit | Balance sheet |
| Accumulated Depreciation | Contra fixed asset | Credit | Balance sheet |
| Advertising Expense | Operating expense | Debit | Income statement |
| Allowance for Doubtful Accounts | Contra current asset | Credit | Balance sheet |
| Amortization Expense | Operating expense | Debit | Income statement |
| Bonds Payable | Long-term liability | Credit | Balance sheet |
| Building | Fixed asset | Debit | Balance sheet |
| _____ Capital | Owner's equity | Credit | Statement of owner's equity/ Balance sheet |
| Cash | Current asset | Debit | Balance sheet |
| Cash Dividends | Stockholders' equity | Debit | Retained earnings statement |
| Cash Dividends Payable | Current liability | Credit | Balance sheet |
| Common Stock | Stockholders' equity | Credit | Balance sheet |
| Cost of Merchandise (Goods) Sold | Cost of merchandise (goods) sold | Debit | Income statement |
| Customer Refunds Payable | Current liability | Credit | Balance sheet |
| Delivery Expense | Operating expense | Debit | Income statement |
| Depletion Expense | Operating expense | Debit | Income statement |
| Discount on Bonds Payable | Long-term liability | Debit | Balance sheet |
| Dividend Revenue | Other income | Credit | Income statement |
| Dividends | Stockholders' equity | Debit | Retained earnings statement |
| _____ Drawing | Owner's equity | Debit | Statement of owner's equity |
| Employees Federal Income Tax Payable | Current liability | Credit | Balance sheet |
| Equipment | Fixed asset | Debit | Balance sheet |
| Estimated Returns Inventory | Current asset | Debit | Balance sheet |
| Factory Overhead (Overapplied) | Deferred credit | Credit | Balance sheet (interim) |
| Factory Overhead (Underapplied) | Deferred debit | Debit | Balance sheet (interim) |
| Federal Income Tax Payable | Current liability | Credit | Balance sheet |
| Federal Unemployment Tax Payable | Current liability | Credit | Balance sheet |
| Finished Goods | Current asset | Debit | Balance sheet |
| Freight In | Cost of merchandise sold | Debit | Income statement |
| Freight Out | Operating expense | Debit | Income statement |
| Gain on Disposal of Fixed Assets | Other income | Credit | Income statement |
| Gain on Redemption of Bonds | Other income | Credit | Income statement |
| Gain on Sale of Investments | Other income | Credit | Income statement |
| Goodwill | Intangible asset | Debit | Balance sheet |
| Income Tax Expense | Income tax | Debit | Income statement |
| Income Tax Payable | Current liability | Credit | Balance sheet |
| Insurance Expense | Operating expense | Debit | Income statement |
| Interest Expense | Other expense | Debit | Income statement |
| Interest Receivable | Current asset | Debit | Balance sheet |
| Interest Revenue | Other income | Credit | Income statement |
| Investment in Bonds | Investment | Debit | Balance sheet |
| Investment in Stocks | Investment | Debit | Balance sheet |
| Investment in Subsidiary | Investment | Debit | Balance sheet |
| Land | Fixed asset | Debit | Balance sheet |
| Loss on Disposal of Fixed Assets | Other expense | Debit | Income statement |
| Loss on Redemption of Bonds | Other expense | Debit | Income statement |

| Account Title | Account Classification | Normal Balance | Financial Statement |
|---|---|---|---|
| Loss on Sale of Investments | Other expense | Debit | Income statement |
| Marketable Securities | Current asset | Debit | Balance sheet |
| Materials | Current asset | Debit | Balance sheet |
| Medicare Tax Payable | Current liability | Credit | Balance sheet |
| Merchandise Inventory | Current asset/Cost of merchandise sold | Debit | Balance sheet/Income statement |
| Net Sales | Revenue from sales | Credit | Income statement |
| Notes Payable | Current liability/Long-term liability | Credit | Balance sheet |
| Notes Receivable | Current asset/Investment | Debit | Balance sheet |
| Patents | Intangible asset | Debit | Balance sheet |
| Paid-In Capital from Sale of Treasury Stock | Stockholders' equity | Credit | Balance sheet |
| Paid-In Capital in Excess of Par (Stated Value) | Stockholders' equity | Credit | Balance sheet |
| Payroll Tax Expense | Operating expense | Debit | Income statement |
| Pension Expense | Operating expense | Debit | Income statement |
| Petty Cash | Current asset | Debit | Balance sheet |
| Preferred Stock | Stockholders' equity | Credit | Balance sheet |
| Premium on Bonds Payable | Long-term liability | Credit | Balance sheet |
| Prepaid Insurance | Current asset | Debit | Balance sheet |
| Prepaid Rent | Current asset | Debit | Balance sheet |
| Purchases | Cost of merchandise sold | Debit | Income statement |
| Purchases Discounts | Cost of merchandise sold | Credit | Income statement |
| Purchases Returns and Allowances | Cost of merchandise sold | Credit | Income statement |
| Rent Expense | Operating expense | Debit | Income statement |
| Rent Revenue | Other income | Credit | Income statement |
| Retained Earnings | Stockholders' equity | Credit | Balance sheet/Retained earnings statement |
| Salaries Expense | Operating expense | Debit | Income statement |
| Salaries Payable | Current liability | Credit | Balance sheet |
| Sales Tax Payable | Current liability | Credit | Balance sheet |
| Social Security Tax Payable | Current liability | Credit | Balance sheet |
| State Unemployment Tax Payable | Current liability | Credit | Balance sheet |
| Stock Dividends | Stockholders' equity | Debit | Retained earnings statement |
| Stock Dividends Distributable | Stockholders' equity | Credit | Balance sheet |
| Supplies | Current asset | Debit | Balance sheet |
| Supplies Expense | Operating expense | Debit | Income statement |
| Treasury Stock | Stockholders' equity | Debit | Balance sheet |
| Uncollectible Accounts Expense | Operating expense | Debit | Income statement |
| Unearned Rent | Current liability | Credit | Balance sheet |
| Utilities Expense | Operating expense | Debit | Income statement |
| Vacation Pay Expense | Operating expense | Debit | Income statement |
| Vacation Pay Payable | Current liability/Long-term liability | Credit | Balance sheet |
| Work in Process | Current asset | Debit | Balance sheet |

# Abbreviations and Acronyms Commonly Used in Business and Accounting

| | |
|---|---|
| AAA | American Accounting Association |
| ABC | Activity-based costing |
| AICPA | American Institute of Certified Public Accountants |
| B2B | Business-to-business |
| B2C | Business-to-consumer |
| CFO | Chief Financial Officer |
| CMA | Certified Management Accountant |
| COGM | Cost of goods manufactured |
| COGS | Cost of goods sold |
| CPA | Certified Public Accountant |
| Cr. | Credit |
| CVP | Cost-volume-profit |
| Dr. | Debit |
| EFT | Electronic funds transfer |
| EPS | Earnings per share |
| ERP | Enterprise resource planning |
| FASB | Financial Accounting Standards Board |
| FICA tax | Federal Insurance Contributions Act tax |
| FIFO | First-in, first-out |
| FOB | Free on board |
| FUTA | Federal unemployment compensation tax |
| GAAP | Generally accepted accounting principles |
| IASB | International Accounting Standards Board |
| IFRS | International Financial Reporting Standards |
| IMA | Institute of Management Accountants |
| IRC | Internal Revenue Code |
| IRR | Internal rate of return |
| IRS | Internal Revenue Service |
| JIT | Just-in-time |
| LIFO | Last-in, first-out |
| LCM | Lower of cost or market |
| MACRS | Modified Accelerated Cost Recovery System |
| MD&A | Management's Discussion and Analysis |
| n/30 | Net 30 |
| n/eom | Net, end-of-month |
| NPV | Net present value |
| NSF | Not sufficient funds |
| P/E Ratio | Price-earnings ratio |
| POS | Point of sale |
| ROI | Return on investment |
| R&D | Research and development |
| SCM | Supply chain management |
| SEC | Securities and Exchange Commission |
| SOX | Sarbanes-Oxley Act |
| TQC | Total quality control |
| W-4 | Employee's Withholding Allowance Certificate |
| WIP | Work in process |

# Classification of Accounts

| Account Title | Account Classification | Normal Balance | Financial Statement |
|---|---|---|---|
| Accounts Payable | Current liability | Credit | Balance sheet |
| Accounts Receivable | Current asset | Debit | Balance sheet |
| Accumulated Depletion | Contra fixed asset | Credit | Balance sheet |
| Accumulated Depreciation | Contra fixed asset | Credit | Balance sheet |
| Advertising Expense | Operating expense | Debit | Income statement |
| Allowance for Doubtful Accounts | Contra current asset | Credit | Balance sheet |
| Amortization Expense | Operating expense | Debit | Income statement |
| Bonds Payable | Long-term liability | Credit | Balance sheet |
| Building | Fixed asset | Debit | Balance sheet |
| _____ Capital | Owner's equity | Credit | Statement of owner's equity/ Balance sheet |
| Cash | Current asset | Debit | Balance sheet |
| Cash Dividends | Stockholders' equity | Debit | Retained earnings statement |
| Cash Dividends Payable | Current liability | Credit | Balance sheet |
| Common Stock | Stockholders' equity | Credit | Balance sheet |
| Cost of Merchandise (Goods) Sold | Cost of merchandise (goods) sold | Debit | Income statement |
| Customer Refunds Payable | Current liability | Credit | Balance sheet |
| Delivery Expense | Operating expense | Debit | Income statement |
| Depletion Expense | Operating expense | Debit | Income statement |
| Discount on Bonds Payable | Long-term liability | Debit | Balance sheet |
| Dividend Revenue | Other income | Credit | Income statement |
| Dividends | Stockholders' equity | Debit | Retained earnings statement |
| _____ Drawing | Owner's equity | Debit | Statement of owner's equity |
| Employees Federal Income Tax Payable | Current liability | Credit | Balance sheet |
| Equipment | Fixed asset | Debit | Balance sheet |
| Estimated Returns Inventory | Current asset | Debit | Balance sheet |
| Factory Overhead (Overapplied) | Deferred credit | Credit | Balance sheet (interim) |
| Factory Overhead (Underapplied) | Deferred debit | Debit | Balance sheet (interim) |
| Federal Income Tax Payable | Current liability | Credit | Balance sheet |
| Federal Unemployment Tax Payable | Current liability | Credit | Balance sheet |
| Finished Goods | Current asset | Debit | Balance sheet |
| Freight In | Cost of merchandise sold | Debit | Income statement |
| Freight Out | Operating expense | Debit | Income statement |
| Gain on Disposal of Fixed Assets | Other income | Credit | Income statement |
| Gain on Redemption of Bonds | Other income | Credit | Income statement |
| Gain on Sale of Investments | Other income | Credit | Income statement |
| Goodwill | Intangible asset | Debit | Balance sheet |
| Income Tax Expense | Income tax | Debit | Income statement |
| Income Tax Payable | Current liability | Credit | Balance sheet |
| Insurance Expense | Operating expense | Debit | Income statement |
| Interest Expense | Other expense | Debit | Income statement |
| Interest Receivable | Current asset | Debit | Balance sheet |
| Interest Revenue | Other income | Credit | Income statement |
| Investment in Bonds | Investment | Debit | Balance sheet |
| Investment in Stocks | Investment | Debit | Balance sheet |
| Investment in Subsidiary | Investment | Debit | Balance sheet |
| Land | Fixed asset | Debit | Balance sheet |
| Loss on Disposal of Fixed Assets | Other expense | Debit | Income statement |
| Loss on Redemption of Bonds | Other expense | Debit | Income statement |